ISBN 0-406-91274-2

Immigration Law and Practice in the United Kingdom

Fifth edition

General Editors

Ian A Macdonald QC

Frances Webber

of 2 Garden Court Chambers, Middle Temple

Contributors

Nadine Finch

Laurie Fransman QC

Stephanie Harrison

David Jones

Patrick Lewis

Sonali Naik

Julia Onslow-Cole

Melanie Plimmer

Rick Scannell

Duran Seddon

Philip Trott

Amanda Weston

Butterworths

A Member of the LexisNexis Group

Members of the LexisNexis Group worldwide

United Kingdom	Butterworths Tolley, a Division of Reed Elsevier (UK) Ltd, Halsbury House, 35 Chancery Lane, LONDON, WC2A 1EL, and 4 Hill Street, EDINBURGH EH2 3JZ
Argentina	Abeledo Perrot, Jurisprudencia Argentina and Depalma, BUENOS AIRES
Australia	Butterworths, a Division of Reed International Books Australia Pty Ltd, CHATSWOOD, New South Wales
Austria	ARD Betriebsdienst and Verlag Orac, VIENNA
Canada	Butterworths Canada Ltd, MARKHAM, Ontario
Chile	Publitecsa and Conosur Ltda, SANTIAGO DE CHILE
Czech Republic	Orac sro, PRAGUE
France	Editions du Juris-Classeur SA, PARIS
Hong Kong	Butterworths Asia (Hong Kong), HONG KONG
Hungary	Hvg Orac, BUDAPEST
India	Butterworths India, NEW DELHI
Ireland	Butterworths (Ireland) Ltd, DUBLIN
Italy	Giuffré, MILAN
Malaysia	Malayan Law Journal Sdn Bhd, KUALA LUMPUR
New Zealand	Butterworths of New Zealand, WELLINGTON
Poland	Wydawnictwa Prawnicze PWN, WARSAW
Singapore	Butterworths Asia, SINGAPORE
South Africa	Butterworths Publishers (Pty) Ltd, DURBAN
Switzerland	Stämpfli Verlag AG, BERNE
USA	LexisNexis, DAYTON, Ohio

© Reed Elsevier (UK) Ltd 2001

First edition	1983
Second edition	1987
Third edition	1991
Fourth edition	1995
Fifth edition	2001
Reprinted	2002

A CIP Catalogue record for this book is available from the British Library.

ISBN 0 406 91274 2

Typeset by Doyle & Co, Colchester
Printed by and bound in Great Britain by The Bath Press, Bath

Visit Butterworths LexisNexis direct at www.butterworths.com

Preface

In the last edition we sought to state the law as at 1 April 1995 and we then updated with a supplement up to 31 March 1997.

Since then there have been the most momentous changes in immigration and asylum law, both as regards legislation and in the development of case law, so much so that using the old edition of *Macdonald* has become more of a liability than a benefit. For this edition the book has been overhauled; much of it has been rewritten and there is an entirely new chapter dealing with welfare provision including asylum support.

A new government took office in 1997. Its first step was to fulfil an election pledge to abolish the primary purpose rule, under which parties to a marriage had to prove that it was *not* entered into *primarily* to obtain admission to the UK. This was abolished by HC26, para 1 with effect from 5 June 1997.

The second step was to make available much (although not all) of what had previously been the secret departmental instructions to immigration and entry clearance officers on immigration and asylum. These are now available in many libraries and on the internet. This edition is the first in which we have been able to describe the law and practice with access to these instructions.

Then came the Special Immigration Appeals Commission Act 1997, which set up the Special Immigration Appeals Commission and an entirely discrete system of appeals for cases involving national security. The new appeals system was prompted by the criticisms of the European Court of Human Rights in the landmark case of *Chahal v UK*.[1]

The enactment of the 1997 Act illustrates what is becoming an increasingly important feature of immigration and asylum law. Individual nation states no longer have a completely free hand to enact immigration or asylum laws or to pursue measures in this field to suit the needs or whims of narrowly based, narrow-minded, or narrowly nationalistic and xenophobic electorates. These choices are still available, especially in those areas of policy aimed at reducing the social costs of asylum. But increasingly the content of laws and of policies has to be measured against international human rights standards and the framework of international and regional institutions and policies.

The new government took a proactive and far-reaching stance in this regard by enacting the Human Rights Act 1998, thereby bringing within the jurisdiction of all UK courts and tribunals the rights and freedoms contained in the European Convention on Human Rights (ECHR). The ECHR has always been a tool of

---

1   (1996) 23 EHRR 413, ECtHR.

immigration lawyers, and in this edition we try to evaluate its likely impact on immigration and asylum law now that the Human Rights Act is in force.

A new chapter in UK immigration law came into being when the UK joined the European Common Market on 1 January 1973 – the same day that the Immigration Act 1971 came into force. Immigration law was affected by the free movement rights given to citizens of all other member states and later extended to all EEA citizens. A system based on entitlement operated alongside a domestic system based on permission and discretion.

Since the UK's adherence in 1973, the Common Market, enlarged by the addition of other countries, has become the European Economic Community and now the European Union, with a common European citizenship and a common currency. Alongside these changes, the Maastricht Treaty of 1993 created a new framework for inter-governmental co-operation on immigration, asylum, and common visas. Agreements, joint positions and resolutions were hammered out on a wide range of immigration and asylum topics. The so-called Schengen Group of countries, which did not include the UK or Ireland, reached separate agreements aimed at abolishing internal frontiers. During this period common developments within the European Union on immigration and asylum were a matter of inter-governmental co-operation. Now the Amsterdam Treaty, which came into force on 1 May 1999, has brought all these subjects and the so-called 'Schengen *acquis*' into the jurisdiction of the European Community.

Under Title IV of the Amsterdam Treaty, the European Council is mandated to put forward new laws on all these topics. At this stage we do not know the exact shape of these proposals, but what seems certain is that existing and any new member states will in future have to deal with their own domestic immigration and asylum laws and practices within a framework of European standards enforceable by the institutions of the European Union. That, however, will be for a new edition of *Macdonald*, not this one. However, we do set out the constitutional arrangements for the new legislative framework within the European Community (EC) Treaty.

On the domestic front, we have had to grapple with the very many changes brought about by the Immigration and Asylum Act 1999. The new Act deals with many things, from regulating immigration advisers and imposing duties on marriage registrars, to overhauling immigration appeals. It changes the structure of immigration control, by allowing leave to enter to be granted or refused extra-territorially. It also virtually completes the project, started in the late 1970s, of tying access to social and welfare benefits firmly to immigration status, finally burying the welfare-state notion of provision based on need, and introduces a workhouse-type system of support for asylum seekers.

The courts have played an important and valuable role in this field, in restraining the executive and mitigating some of the harshness of the legislation. In *R v Secretary of State for Social Security, ex p JCWI*[2] the Court of Appeal held that the rule removing asylum seekers' entitlement to safety-net benefits was *ultra vires*; in *R v Hammersmith and Fulham London Borough Council, ex p M*[3] they found that local authorities were obliged to provide for destitute asylum seekers; and illegal entrants were held to be included among those to

---

2   [1997[1 WLR 275, [1996] 4 All ER 385.
3   [1997] 1 CCL Rep 69, QBD, affirmed by the Court of Appeal at (1997) 30 HLR 10, CA.

whom basic duties were owed in *R v Wandsworth London Borough Council, ex p O*.[4] We look forward to the courts giving early consideration to the compatibility of the voucher and dispersal scheme with the rights protected by the ECHR.

The 1999 Act also strengthens the visa and carrier sanctions regime, completing the equation of asylum seekers with illegal entrants. Civil and criminal sanctions are now routinely used against carriers who bring either of these categories to the UK. They are equally liable whether they are conveying the persecuted or the merely desperate. With all the visa and other obstacles on travel, it is now impossible for those fleeing persecution to travel legally to a safe haven. They either enter by deception as to the real purpose of their visit, on false documents, or they must come in clandestinely. There is no other way. The battery of controls erected by governments of every hue have spawned and created a new and unlawful travel industry, ever anxious for new and extremely profitable business, to which genuine refugees, as well as others, must of necessity have recourse. We wonder whether greater use might be made in this context of duress of circumstances or the defence of necessity. At least the unlawful use of criminal sanctions against asylum seekers entering the UK on false documents was brought to an end by the Divisional Court in 1999 in the case of *Adimi*.[5]

The UK courts have contributed to international jurisprudence on the Refugee Convention. The case of *Shah and Islam*[6] provided a coherent basis for the development of claims based on membership of a particular social group, and flung open the Convention to claims based on sex and gender. In *Adan and Aitseguer*[7] the Lords recognised (as they had in the earlier *Adan*[8] case) that failure of state protection, not state persecution, was at the heart of the Convention. In terms of procedure, the importance of access to the Tribunal was underlined in *Asifa Saleem*,[9] there has been welcome recognition in cases such as *Karanakaran*[10] and *Ejon*[11] of the difficulties faced by asylum claimants, both physical and psychological, in providing evidence in support of their claims, and we hope that the mechanistic 'discrepancy-counting' approach to asylum claimants' credibility, too frequently observed in the Home Office and occasionally in the appellate authority, is well and truly on its way out. Since the last edition, the courts and appellate authorities have been devising means to overcome what we and others called the culture of disbelief.

Refugee protection in the UK is threatened now by the political imperative of speedy decision-making, leading to a huge growth in so-called 'non-compliance refusals' – refusal of asylum without consideration of the claim, for failure to

---

4 [2000] 4 All ER 590.
5 *R v Uxbridge Magistrates Court, ex p Adimi, R v Secretary of State for the Home Department, ex p Sorani and Kaziu* [1999] INLR 490.
6 *R v IAT and Secretary of State for the Home Department, ex p Shah; Islam v Secretary of State for the Home Department* [1999] 2 WLR 1015, [1999] INLR 144, HL.
7 *R v Secretary of State for the Home Department, ex p Adan; R v Secretary of State for the Home Department, ex p Aitseguer* [2001] INLR 44, HL.
8 *Adan v Secretary of State for the Home Department* [1998] Imm AR 338, [1998] INLR 325, HL.
9 *R v Secretary of State for the Home Department, ex p Asifa Saleem* [2000] INLR 413, CA.
10 *Karanakaran v Secretary of State for the Home Department* [2000] Imm AR 271, [2000] INLR 122, CA.
11 *R v Secretary of State for the Home Department, ex p Ejon* [1998] INLR 195, QBD.

complete (in full and in English) and return the lengthy and detailed statement of evidence form within 14 days – and to substantive refusals which are often ill-considered, sometimes contain misleading information and are occasionally insulting (such as the infamous 'your account is a pile of pants' decision letter). Bad decisions in this field cause enormous anxiety and suffering (occasionally leading to suicide) and are expensive, overloading the appellate system. The other threat to refugee protection is the recent banning of 21 organisations and of all manifestations of support for them by Order under the Terrorism Act 2000. Asylum claimants whose claims are based on support for the modern-day equivalents of the ANC run the risk of arrest if they admit their allegiance or support, and of refusal and return to the country of persecution if they don't.

Understanding and describing the new Act is not made any easier by the plethora of Orders, Regulations, Rules, and Codes of Practice made under it. Even as this edition of the book goes to press, a new consolidating set of Immigration Rules is pending. Then there is the whole body of departmental instructions – the IDI and API. The materials are voluminous. At the same time practitioners are being bombarded by new case law from at least four major sources of jurisprudence: decisions of UK courts and tribunals; decisions of the European Court of Human Rights; decisions of the European Court of Justice; and decisions of courts throughout the world on the Refugee Convention.

Fortunately, access to the subordinate legislation and the new rules is easily obtainable on the internet. The reporting of court and tribunal decisions has been speeded up and greatly improved since the last edition, particularly with the publication since 1997 of the Immigration and Nationality Law Reports (INLR) and by a variety of Human Rights Reports. New decisions are becoming increasingly available on the internet, which is now an indispensable tool of all immigration practitioners.

Notwithstanding the broad range now covered by immigration law and practice and the enormous number of changes which are continually taking place, we think it important to keep *Macdonald* as a single volume book, which can be carried relatively easily from office to courtroom, and which contains within it our description of the law and practice plus the necessary texts of statutes, statutory instruments and rules together with the main European texts.

Nick Blake QC co-edited the last two editions, in which all the chapters (from first draft to last) were written by just two people. This time Nick is no longer involved, but the book still contains much that is his, and we take this opportunity to pay great tribute to him and his contribution. It was a long and fruitful friendship and partnership.

For this edition a whole team of people have co-operated in preparing the text – colleagues from 2 Garden Court Chambers in London and Garden Court North in Manchester and Julia Onslow-Cole, Partner, CMS Cameron McKenna, and Philip Trott, Partner, Bates, Wells & Braithwaite, two very experienced solicitors in commercial immigration practice. But the responsibility for what now appears, both in terms of style and content, is ours. It has been an exacting and hopefully fruitful task.

In addition to the named contributors, we would like to thank:

Peter Morris
Steve Peers
Elspeth Guild
Glen Hodgetts

Susan Rowlands and others at ILPA
Stephen Knafler of the housing team in chambers
Simon Cox
Nathalia Berkowitz
Attorney-General's Office and Ministry of Justice of the Republic of Ireland
Yvonne Dixon who prepared the index
Jeanette Fryer who helped with some of the typing -
and the clerks at 2 Garden Court and Garden Court North.

We are painfully conscious of the speed of change – at proof stage, we learn, for example, that the Department for Education and Employment, referred to throughout Chapter 10, has gone, and that the Home Office has taken over responsibility for work permits! But we have sought to state the law as at 20 May 2001.

2 Garden Court   Ian Macdonald QC
Temple   Frances Webber
London
EC4Y 9BL
June 2001

Contents

Contents

Contents

Contents

International materials

APPENDIX 2
Useful addresses, telephone numbers and websites   1691

Contributors

General editors

Ian A Macdonald QC
Frances Webber
of 2 Garden Court Chambers, Middle Temple

Contributors

Nadine Finch
Laurie Fransman QC
Stephanie Harrison
David Jones
Patrick Lewis
Sonali Naik
Rick Scannell
Duran Seddon
of 2 Garden Court Chambers, Middle Temple
Melanie Plimmer
Amanda Weston
of 2 Garden Court North Chambers, Manchester
Julia Onslow-Cole
Partner, CMS Cameran McKenna
Philip Trott
Partner, Bates, Wells & Braithwaite

Table of statutes

References to *Statutes* are to Halsbury's Statutes of England showing the volume and page at which the annotated text of the Act will be found. References to appendices are to page number and are in **bold** type.

Table of statutory instruments

References to appendices are to page number and are in **bold** type.

Table of immigration rules

References to appendices are to page number and are in **bold** type.

Table of conventions and agreements

References to appendices are to page number and are in **bold** type.

Table of conventions and agreements

Table of EC legislation

References to appendices are to page number and are in **bold** type.

Table of cases

E

G

H

PARA

I

L

PARA

O

S

Table of cases

X

Decisions of the European Court of Justice are listed below numerically. These decisions are also included in the preceding alphabetical list.

PARA

Chapter 1

INTRODUCING IMMIGRATION LAW

INTRODUCTION

1.1 The cornerstone of UK immigration law is still the Immigration Act 1971, which came into force on 1 January 1973, and the Immigration Rules made under it. However, the 1971 Act has been significantly amended by the British Nationality Act 1981, the Immigration (Carriers' Liability) Act 1987, the Immigration Act 1988, the Asylum and Immigration Appeals Act 1993, the Asylum and Immigration Act 1996, the Special Immigration Appeals Commission Act 1997 and the Immigration and Asylum Act 1999. Only the Immigration (Carriers' Liability) Act 1987 has been repealed in full by later Acts, but its provisions have been re-enacted and enlarged by the 1999 Act. Some consolidation has been done, for example, over appeals, but seven separate statutes still have to be consulted. In addition, the 1971 Act provisions have been modified as regards entry through the Channel Tunnel by the Channel Tunnel (International Arrangements) Order 1993.[1] As well as the Immigration Rules made under the 1971 Act, which have been made and amended, recast and consolidated on many occasions, there is a large body of statutory instruments, most made under provisions of the 1999 Act which, despite its size, often does no more than sketch a field within which the regulations operate. There are Codes of Practice under the 1996 and 1999 Acts, setting out how employers can avoid racial discrimination and how lorry drivers, coach operators and others can avoid carriers' liability. Specialist adjudicators, an Immigration Appeal Tribunal, created before the 1971 Act, and a Special Immigration Appeals Commission for national security cases hear immigration appeals, which are subject to their own procedure rules and practice directions. The status of the Immigration Appeal Tribunal has recently been enhanced considerably by the appointment of a High Court judge as President. The Special Immigration Appeals Commission also boasts a presiding High Court judge. A vast body of case law has come into being, both from the Tribunal and the High Court, and is reported in two different sets of specialist reports.

1   SI 1993/1813.

1.2   At the same time, British immigration law is becoming more integrated with European law. The free movement provisions of EC law are reflected in domestic law, in the Immigration Act 1988 and the Immigration (European Economic Area) Regulations 2000[1] (replacing the European Economic Area Order 1994),[2] and practitioners are becoming ever more familiar with the small print of Association Agreements, and applying EC criteria in deportation and expulsion cases. The Dublin Convention criteria govern the responsibility of the UK government vis-à-vis its European counterparts in dealing with asylum claims, while the Amsterdam Treaty offers the possibility of a wholly integrated European immigration and asylum law, procedural and substantive, although the UK government has negotiated an 'opt out, opt in' position which makes the future hard to predict in this area.

1   SI 2000/2326.
2   SI 1994/1895.

1.3   Refugee law is part of international humanitarian law, rather than of immigration law, and it is only the exclusionary policies of the UK and other western governments which have linked it inexorably with immigration law. The appellate authorities and the courts have become very familiar with the refugee definition in the UN Convention Relating to the Status of Refugees (Geneva, 1951) and its Protocol of 1967 (referred to collectively as the 'Refugee Convention'). Nor did practitioners in the field wait until the coming into force of the Human Rights Act 1998 in October 2000 to urge compliance with the 1950 European Convention on Human Rights (ECHR) – although now at least these demands must be heard. Cases in the field have contributed to the development of administrative accountability and to the broadening and deepening of fundamental human rights. Immigration law has developed from small beginnings into an important and valuable branch of law.

A BRIEF HISTORY OF IMMIGRATION LAW

Aliens

1.4   Aliens – those owing no allegiance to the British crown – have long been subject to laws regulating the conditions under which they could come to and remain in Britain.[1] The first of the modern laws was the Aliens Act 1905, passed in response to the Jewish immigration to Britain between 1880 and 1905 and the anti-Jewish campaign which accompanied it.[2] This Act forbade aliens to land except at authorised ports and gave immigration officers power to refuse leave to land to 'undesirable aliens'. Exceptions were made for those seeking asylum from religious or political persecution. Drastic powers for deportation of immigrants who became destitute were provided. The Act's main innovations were (i) the creation of an immigration inspectorate, consisting of immigration officers to oversee immigration control,[3] and (ii) the right of appeal to an Immigration Appeal Board, set up in every major port.

1   See eg Holdsworth *History of English Law* Vol 9 (1944) p 90ff; Richard Plender *International Migration Law* (2nd edn, 1988) p 64ff.
2   See Paul Foot *Immigration and Race in British Politics* (1965); Ann Dummett and Andrew Nicol *Subjects, Citizens, Aliens and Others* (1990). The Aliens Act 1905 was described by Professor Dicey as one of the greatest inroads on individual liberty: A V Dicey *Lectures on the Relations Between Law and Public Opinion* (1905) p 298.
3   See *R v Secretary of State for the Home Department, ex p Alexander and Oladehinde* [1991] 1 AC 254, [1990] 3 All ER 393, HL.

1.5   The powers under the Aliens Act 1905 were extended on the outbreak of war in 1914. The Aliens Restriction Act 1914 enabled the King in Council to make Orders to prohibit or restrict the landing or embarkation of aliens; to deport them; to require them to live in specified areas; to make them comply with any provisions as to registration; to prohibit or require them to change their abode; or to restrict their travel. Almost immediately after the passage of the 1914 Act, severe Restriction Orders were brought into force.[1] The 1914 Act was introduced as a temporary measure during wartime, but at the end of the war it was extended for one year by the Aliens Restriction (Amendment) Act 1919 and the 1905 Act (including the short-lived right of appeal) was repealed. The 1914 and 1919 Acts were thereafter renewed each year by the Expiring Laws Continuance Acts. On the passage of the 1919 Act a new Aliens Order was made.[2] That Order continued in force, with numerous amendments, until 1953 when it was replaced by the Aliens Order 1953.[3] This, with a few amendments, governed the position of aliens until its repeal by the Immigration Act 1971. (An alien meant a person who was not a British subject, a British Protected Person or a citizen of the Republic of Ireland.)[4] Under the 1953 Aliens Order, aliens who came to the UK to work had to obtain a work permit, issued by what is now the Department for Education and Employment.[5] The issue of permits by the Department took into account the local labour situation.[6] Aliens admitted to work were usually given a work permit valid for 12 months; this was extended each year and after four years the restrictions usually were removed. This work permit scheme was later extended to Commonwealth citizens as well as aliens by the 1971 Act and remains broadly the same today.

1   Aliens Restriction (Consolidation) Order 1914, SR & O 1914/1374. Also Aliens Restriction (Belgian Refugees) Order 1914, SR & O 1914/1478. Perhaps the greatest innovation was the need for aliens to register with the police. This enabled a massive war-time round-up of all Germans between the ages of 17 and 55: see Dummett and Nicol **1.4** fn 2 above, p 107; P and L Gillman *Collar The Lot* (1980).
2   Aliens Order 1920, SR & O 1920/448.
3   SI 1953/1671.
4   British Nationality Act 1948, s 32; Status of Aliens Act 1914, s 27.
5   See Aliens Order 1953, SI 1953/1671, arts 4 and 22.
6   More particularly see Bob Hepple *Race, Jobs and the Law in Britain* (2nd edn, 1970) pp 51–52 (policy on issue of permits), p 281 (specialist department issuing work permits), p 292 (agreement with Italian government for bulk recruitment).

British subjects

Right of abode at common law

1.6   The position of British subjects stood in direct contrast to that of aliens.[1] At common law all British subjects had a right of abode in the UK. Prior to 1962 they enjoyed this right whether they lived in the UK or elsewhere, and whether or not they were citizens of the United Kingdom and Colonies (CUKCs). Under the British Nationality Act 1948 British subjects were also known as 'Commonwealth citizens' and the two terms were interchangeable until 1983.[2] British Protected Persons were not British subjects and, therefore, had no right of abode.[3] In *DPP v Bhagwan*[4] Lord Diplock referred to this right of abode:

> 'Prior to the passing of the Commonwealth Immigrants Act 1962, the Respondent as a British Subject had the right at common law to enter the United Kingdom without let or hindrance when and where he pleased and to remain here as long as he liked. That right he still retained in 1967 save insofar as it was restricted or qualified by the provisions of the Act.'[5]

1   See *Calvin's Case* (1608) 2 State Tr 559; *Musgrove v Chun Teeong Toy* [1891] AC 272; *A-G for Canada v Cain*; *A-G for Canada v Gilhula* [1906] AC 542.
2   British Nationality Act 1948, s 1(2); British Nationality Act 1981, s 51.
3   British Nationality Act 1948, s 1(3); *R v Secretary of State for the Home Department, ex p Thakrar* [1974] QB 684, [1974] 2 All ER 261, CA; *R v Chief Immigration Officer, Gatwick Airport, ex p Singh* [1987] Imm AR 346, QBD.
4   [1972] AC 60, [1970] 3 All ER 97, HL.
5   [1970] 3 All ER 97 at 99.

1.7 Commonwealth citizens were first made subject to immigration control in the UK by the Commonwealth Immigrants Act 1962. This Act was brought into force mainly as a result of a campaign against black Commonwealth citizens already here. The Act made a distinction between CUKCs and citizens of independent Commonwealth countries, and based control upon the kind of passport held by the would-be immigrant. All Commonwealth citizens became subject to immigration control except the following:

(a)   persons born in the UK;
(b)   holders of UK passports issued by the UK government as opposed to those issued on behalf of the government of a Crown colony or of some other part of the Commonwealth;[1]
(c)   other persons included in the passport of one of the persons excluded from immigration control under (a) or (b) above.

1   Commonwealth Immigrants Act 1962, s 1(2) and (3); *R v Secretary of State for the Home Department, ex p Bhurosah* [1968] 1 QB 266, [1967] 3 All ER 831, CA. Other exemptions from control were given to diplomats (s 17(1)); certain members of Commonwealth armed forces (s 17(2)); persons exempted by the Secretary of State for the Home Department (Commonwealth Immigrants (Control of Immigration) Exemption Order 1965, SI 1965/153); and persons who landed in the UK and spent 28 days without submitting to examination by immigration officers (Commonwealth Immigrants Act 1962, Sch 1, para 1(2), as amended by Commonwealth Immigrants Act 1968, s 4; and see *R v Governor of Brixton Prison, ex p Ahsan* [1969] 2 QB 222, [1969] 2 All ER 347).

1.8 In short, CUKCs were exempted from control, except those who were born in Crown Colonies and obtained their passports there. CUKCs who were born in independent Commonwealth countries and who retained that status after independence were exempted from control provided they had a UK passport. A passport issued by the High Commissioner would normally qualify. This category of CUKC comprised, among others, large sections of the Asian community in Kenya, who expressly had been given the option of UK citizenship by the Kenya Independence Act 1963 on exactly the same basis as the European settlers. Similar provisions had been made when Uganda became independent. Under the Commonwealth Immigrants Act 1962 all of these persons were entitled to come to Britain as of right, and many did so, because of the policy of Kenyanisation adopted by the Kenyan government and a similar policy of preference to their own citizens adopted by other East African countries.[1]

1 On 'The Legal Basis for the Asian Exodus from Kenya' see Alan H Smith in *Law Guardian* (November 1970). It should also be noted that Asians who opted for Kenyan citizenship rather than UK citizenship after independence were unaffected. Those who opted for UK citizenship, however, clearly did so because they assumed (rightly at the time) that it offered greater security. See further Plender *International Migration Law* (2nd edn, 1988) pp 88–93 and 156.

1.9 The Commonwealth Immigrants Act 1968 sought to change all this. Its aim was to bring the East African Asians under immigration control;[1] its method was to divide holders of UK passports into two separate categories, those who could enter Britain without restriction and those who could not. A CUKC, who was the holder of a UK passport issued by the UK government, was now subject to immigration control unless he or she, or at least one parent or grandparent, was born, adopted, naturalised or registered as a CUKC in the UK. Ancestral connection to the UK became the key factor in determining which CUKCs were subject to immigration control. The intention was to keep out East African Asians and it was not difficult to see that the mechanism for doing this was the section defining the necessary ancestral connection. The immediate precedent was to be found in the British Nationality Act 1964, the main aim of which had been to preserve the right to resume UK citizenship to white settlers in Africa who were then under pressure to assume the citizenship of newly-independent African countries. It is a formula which enables politicians and officials to proclaim that there is nothing racist about such laws. In 1971 the requirement of an ancestral connection was further refined by the enactment of the 'patrial' section in the Immigration Act 1971. When British nationality was reformed by the British Nationality Act 1981, 'patriality' was replaced by an extended definition of 'British citizenship', which we look at in chapter 2 below.

1 See in particular *East African Asians v United Kingdom* (1973) 3 EHRR 76, paras 76, 83–84, 96.

1.10 By the time of the Commonwealth Immigrants Act 1968, the UK had already granted individuals the right to petition the EComHR over alleged breaches of their human rights, a right whose first exercise was by Commonwealth immigrants, with mixed success.[1] But it was the Asian CUKCs excluded from their country of nationality by the 1968 Act who really began the trend of using the ECHR to seek redress for immigration grievances. Their common law right to enter the UK freely was replaced by a discretionary scheme of special vouchers. Many also lost the right to remain and work in the countries where they were living. Some became destitute. But when they tried to enter Britain they found themselves being shuttlecocked in and out, or being kept in prison.[2] The International Commission of Jurists criticised the 1968 Act at the time of its passing as a violation of international law.[3] In *East African Asians v United Kingdom*[4] complaints by 25 applicants, that their human rights had been infringed by the operation of the 1968 Act, were upheld, and in particular the Commission found as a fact that, notwithstanding the neutrality of the language of the statute, it had racial motives and covered a racial group, and that the racial discrimination in its operation constituted degrading treatment.[5] The voucher system is still in operation and we explain its terms at **8.85**ff below. The huge opposition to the 1962 and 1968 Acts, and the real sense of grievance within the immigrant communities, may have been among the factors leading to the setting up of the Committee on Immigration Appeals, whose report led to the Immigration Appeals Act 1969. The 1969 Act instituted the two-tier system of appeal which contains the key characteristics of the present-day immigration appellate system. It gave appeal rights only to Commonwealth citizens, but these were extended to aliens by the Immigration Act 1971.

1   *Mohammed Alam v UK* (2991/66); *Harbajan Singh v UK* (2992/66) (1967) The Times, 12 October.
2   'Return to Sender, Report on Shuttlecocks' (September 1970) JCWI p 1.
3   Bulletin No 34, pp 36–37.
4   (1973) 3 EHRR 76.
5   (1973) 3 EHRR 76, at paras 197, 202 and 207.

1.11   The Immigration Act 1971 repealed all previous legislation, with minor exceptions, and spelled the end of large-scale primary immigration for settlement from the 'new Commonwealth'. The benefits of the right of abode had shrunk to a small, exclusive, largely white group of 'patrials', defined by their connection to the UK through their ancestry. On the same day that the 1971 Act came into force, 1 January 1973, the Treaty of Rome provisions came into force in the UK, giving rights of free movement for work and establishment in business or self-employment to all citizens of the EEC's member states.[1] The extension of the work permit scheme to Commonwealth citizens completed the shift in focus from the Commonwealth to Europe, and from immigration for settlement to time-limited, guest-worker migration.[2] The 1971 Act virtually assimilated Commonwealth citizens with aliens, although the former had some residual benefits: some were eligible for the right of abode (which aliens could never have, except on naturalisation), or for exemption from deportation on fulfilling certain residence requirements; and there was a standstill clause preventing the rules on settlement from becoming more restrictive than those enjoyed before 1973 (which operated mainly to exclude Commonwealth citizens seeking family reunion from having to comply with maintenance and accommodation requirements). The standstill clause was repealed in 1988. Commonwealth citizens, in addition, have never had to register with the police.

1   At that time France, Germany, Belgium, Netherlands, Luxembourg, Ireland and Italy.
2   See Sivanandan *Race, Class and the State* (1976) Institute of Race Relations.

1.12   The concept of patriality was introduced to entrench the division between persons with the right of abode and those who needed leave to enter. All aliens were non-patrial, as were some Commonwealth citizens and some UK citizens. Thus the harmony between nationality and free movement was destroyed between 1962 and 1971. The British Nationality Act of 1981 attempted to re-align nationality with immigration rights, and in doing so created further confusion and anger. The 1981 Act created out of the former UK and Colonies citizenship several different types of British nationality, only the first of which, British citizenship, carried the right of abode. The other 'citizens', British Dependent Territories citizens, British Overseas citizens, British subjects without citizenship, and British Nationals Overseas, remained subject to immigration control. Only the return of Hong Kong to Chinese control in 1997, and the resulting dramatic reduction in the numbers of British Dependent Territories citizens and British Nationals (Overseas) with no other citizenship, has enabled the government to offer the few remaining British Dependent Territories citizens and British Nationals (Overseas) British citizenship.[1] No such offer is on the table or likely to be for the other main category of former CUKCs given lesser citizenship status by the 1981 Act, the British Overseas citizens, a category with no right of entry anywhere. They, together with British Protected Persons and British subjects without citizenship, must queue and establish eligibility for the special voucher scheme set up in 1968 (see chapter 8 below) or comply with the requirements of the ordinary Immigration Rules.

1   British Nationality (Hong Kong) Act 1997; White Paper *Partnership for Progress and Prosperity* (1999).

1.13   The politics of immigration and race continued to play a decisive role in developing the law in the 1970s and 1980s. Rules on family settlement became tighter and ever more strictly applied, with virginity tests for brides from the Indian sub-continent causing a furore in the late 1970s[1] and the primary purpose rule[2] keeping husbands out throughout the 1980s and 1990s. The 'standstill' clause preventing the application of harsher rules to Commonwealth settlement was repealed in 1988,[3] and appeal rights on deportation were curtailed for those who had been in the UK for less than seven years.[4] By the mid-1980s the first visa controls had been imposed on Commonwealth citizens,[5] and these were swiftly followed by the first carriers' liability measure, the Immigration (Carriers' Liability) Act 1987, pushed through in response to the arrival of visa-less Tamils fleeing Sri Lanka.

1   See Yellowlees report on medical examination of immigrants, 15 December 1980.
2   HC 394, para 50 (1980); the burden of proof shifted to the couple to prove that the primary purpose was not settlement in HC 66, para 54 (1982).
3   Immigration Act 1988, s 1.
4   Immigration Act 1988, s 5.
5   India, Sri Lanka, Bangladesh, Ghana, Nigeria.

1.14   The introduction of visa controls on Commonwealth citizens, and of carrier sanctions, were the first domestic manifestation of a pan-European policy to deal with the increasing numbers of asylum seekers arriving in Europe, and it is asylum which has become the big issue in the past decade. Britain and most European countries had signed up to the 1951 Refugee Convention and its 1967 Protocol. But when Britain and Europe sought unskilled migrant labour to rebuild their ravaged infrastructure and economy, their governments neither knew nor cared what the migrants' motives were. Many who came from Africa and Asia would have been eligible for refugee status under the Convention, but so long as migration was possible, the last resort of asylum, with its connotations of exile, was unnecessary. The closing of all avenues of migration (save for the highly educated or talented, through the work permit scheme, and the wealthy, through the business and independent means categories) left no alternative but asylum for those forced to leave their own country to seek refuge in a country still believed by many to be the home of human rights. Developments in immigration law in the past decade reflect the battle between the exclusionary imperatives of European immigration policy to the poor countries of the world, on the one hand, and the humanitarian imperatives of international humanitarian law on the other. Visa controls and carrier sanctions were thus calculated to stop refugees and others arriving in Europe. Non-British and non-EU travellers from 'refugee-producing' countries required visas and could not get them.[1] Airlines would not sell tickets to those without visas. Thus the trade in false passports and documents began, and the trafficking trade, with which many of the laws of the 1990s deal.

1   A person is not a 'refugee' under the 1951 Refugee Convention unless he or she is outside his or her own country, and so it is impossible to obtain a 'refugee visa'.

1.15   The Immigration Act 1971 did not deal with asylum, and rules made under it merely recorded that full account was to be taken of the UK's obligations under the 1951 Refugee Convention when a person seeking to enter or being removed claimed asylum or indicated a fear of persecution. This changed with the Asylum and Immigration Appeals Act 1993, which, with new Immigration Rules introduced in 1994 and asylum procedure rules, made up a statutory scheme for asylum determination and appeals. The scheme gave effect to the developing inter-governmental initiatives in the EEC, in particular the Dublin Convention 1990[1] and the London Resolutions 1992[2] which indicated a common approach to asylum seekers who had travelled through 'safe third countries', or whose claims were otherwise believed to be manifestly ill-founded. On the one hand, the 1993 Act gave in-country appeal rights to all asylum seekers, including those who had travelled through a 'safe' third country, although appeals in such cases were subject to an accelerated procedure. On the other hand, the 1993 Act began the process of placing asylum seekers in a class apart, subjecting them to mass fingerprinting and to separate and inferior provision in the fields of housing and social security. The 1993 Act also removed appeal rights from visitors and other groups defined by the purpose or length of their proposed stay, or by their lack of appropriate documents or other qualifying conditions. It also replaced the right to seek judicial review of Immigration Appeal Tribunal final determinations by an appeal to the Court of Appeal, restricting the breadth of appeals.

1   Convention determining the State responsible for examining applications for asylum lodged in one of the Member States of the European Communities, Dublin, 15 June 1990.
2   Resolution on a harmonised approach to questions concerning host third countries (SN 4823/92 WGI 1283 AS 147); Resolution on manifestly unfounded applications for asylum (SN 4822/92 WGI 1282 ASIM 146), adopted 30 November 1992 and 1 December 1992 by immigration ministers of the EU states; in *Key texts on Justice and Home Affairs in the EU* Vol 1 (1976–1993) (1997) Statewatch Publications.

1.16   The Asylum and Immigration Act 1996 reduced the rights of immigrants and asylum seekers, without any compensatory improvements. Accelerated appeal procedures were extended from third-country cases to whole new categories of asylum seekers.[1] The 1996 Act responded to widespread concern among adjudicators about the admissibility procedures of several European countries, particularly Italy, France and Belgium, by abolishing the suspensive appeal in the case of removal of asylum seekers to an EU destination. This led to a series of judicial review challenges which established that if the concern as to the third country was about its *application of the Convention* (eg its admissibility procedures) the Secretary of State's view of the matter would prevail unless *Wednesbury* unreasonable;[2] but if the third country's *interpretation of the Convention* did not correspond to its international meaning (eg if it did not accept those whose fear of persecution emanated from non-state agents of persecution), then the Secretary of State could not lawfully return affected asylum seekers there.[3] The 1996 Act also introduced employer sanctions to ensure that those subject to prohibitions on taking employment did not work. But the other, more shocking, change was the wholesale removal from entitlement to basic subsistence benefits of virtually everyone subject to immigration control except for port asylum claimants. Regulations to this effect were introduced in February 1996,[4] but were declared *ultra vires* in their application to asylum seekers in July 1996, because they 'necessarily contemplate for some a life so destitute that ... no civilised nation can tolerate it ... Something so uncompromisingly draconian can only be achieved by primary legislation'.[5] The government duly obliged, enacting the condemned regulation as section 11 of the 1996 Act.

1 The 'white list' of so-called safe countries under the Asylum (Designated Countries of Destination and Designated Safe Third Countries) Order 1996, SI 1996/2671, included Pakistan, from which women, Ahmadis, Christians and political activists have been found to be refugees. See *Iftikhar Ahmed v Secretary of State for the Home Department* [2000] INLR 1 (Ahmadis); *Islam v Secretary of State for the Home Department; R v Immigration Appeal Tribunal and Secretary of State for the Home Department, ex p Shah* [1999] 2 AC 629; [1999] INLR 144 (HL) (women). The designation of Pakistan was held unlawful in *R (Javed Ali) v Secretary of State for the Home Department* 17 May 2001, CA.
2 *Canbolat v Secretary of State for the Home Department* [1997] Imm AR 442; *R v Secretary of State for the Home Department, ex p Kerrouche* [1997] Imm AR 610; *R v Secretary of State for the Home Department, ex p Iyadurai* [1998] Imm AR 470; see chapter 12 below.
3 *R v Secretary of State for the Home Department, ex p Lul Omar Adan, Sittampalan Subaskaran and Hamid Aitseguer* [1999] Imm AR 521, [1999] INLR 362, CA; [2001] INLR 44, HL.
4 Social Security (Persons from Abroad) Miscellaneous Amendments Regulations 1996, SI 1996/30.
5 *R v Secretary of State for Social Security, ex p JCWI* [1997] 1 WLR 275, per Simon Brown LJ.

1.17 In the same year, the lack of due process afforded to those liable to removal on national security grounds came in for condemnation by the ECHR in *Chahal v UK*.[1] The extra-statutory advisory panel, whose recommendation did not bind the Secretary of State, and before which there was a right to appear but not to know the basis for removal, was not a 'court', and did not provide an effective remedy for possible breaches of Article 3 of the ECHR involved in the removal of such persons. The judgment led to the setting up of the Special Immigration Appeals Commission by the Special Immigration Appeals Commission Act 1997, which provides a parallel appeal system for 'national security' cases aiming both to safeguard the rights of the subject and to pay due regard to security concerns. Both appeals heard by the Commission were successful at first instance, although one was overturned on appeal and is, at the time of writing, awaiting final decision in the House of Lords.[2]

1 (1996) 23 EHRR 413.
2 *Rehman (Shafiq Ur) v Secretary of State for the Home Department* [1999] INLR 517, SIAC; on appeal [2000] INLR 531, CA.

1.18 The latest Acts are the Immigration and Asylum Act 1999, not all of which is in force, and the Race Relations (Amendment) Act 2000, which extended the provisions of the Race Relations Act 1976 to immigration control, on a very limited basis.

OUTLINE OF CURRENT IMMIGRATION AND ASYLUM LAW

The Immigration Act 1971

1.19 The Immigration Act 1971 contains the structure of immigration law, making provision for the right of abode,[1] for leave to enter and remain for those who do not have the right of abode,[2] and for the removal of those who have no right to remain or whose conduct is seen to merit removal.[3] It delineates responsibility for immigration control: immigration officers at the port, dealing with leave to enter and with illegal entrants; the Secretary of State for the Home Department dealing with leave to remain and enforcement against overstayers.[4] It creates myriad offences to do with avoiding or obstructing or helping others to avoid or obstruct immigration controls,[5] as well as the unique offence of helping people to obtain the fundamental human right of claiming asylum.[6] The 1971 Act contains the basic rule-making power enabling the Secretary of State to make detailed rules as to eligibility for entry and stay for persons coming for employment, for visits or for family reunion.[7] Schedule 2 to the Act sets out immigration officers' powers of examination, detention and removal, while Schedule 3 sets out parallel powers of the Secretary of State in relation to deportation.

1 Immigration Act 1971, s 2.
2 Immigration Act 1971, s 3.
3 Immigration Act 1971, ss 3(5), 3(6), 5, 6.
4 Immigration Act 1971, s 4.
5 Immigration Act 1971, s 24–27.
6 Immigration Act 1971, s 25(1)(b). Gain is an essential ingredient of the offence: see chapter 14 below.
7 Immigration Act 1971, s 1(4).

1.20 New sections 3A and 3B of the Immigration Act 1971, inserted by the Immigration and Asylum Act 1999, allow the Secretary of State to change the structure of control. The Immigration (Leave to Enter and Remain) Order 2000[1] made under these sections, provides that leave to enter may be granted and refused, curtailed and varied abroad, and that in various circumstances defined in the Order, it does not lapse, as before, when the holder leaves the UK. The changes make control more flexible, allowing frequent travellers to continue travelling while applying to extend their stay, and removing for the most part the dual-control of entry clearance followed by lengthy port procedures. A more profound effect of the changes is the possibility it creates for asylum to be granted – or refused – abroad, something the Home Secretary has canvassed both as a means of legalising refugees' travel to the UK (which would of course be welcome) and, more controversially, to reduce numbers by applying a quota, which could have an adverse impact on the right of asylum.[2]

1 SI 2000/1161.
2 Jack Straw 'An effective protection regime for the twenty-first century', speech to IPPR, 6 February 2001.

The Immigration and Asylum Act 1999

1.21 The Immigration and Asylum Act 1999, which applies throughout the UK, received the Royal Assent on 11 November 1999. Section 170 sets out which sections came into force on that day, and other provisions have come into force piecemeal since then (with the exception of the bail provisions, still not in force). Much of the meat of the new legislation is not in the text of the Act itself but is to be found in the plethora of Orders and Regulations to which it has given birth. Then there are the many consultation papers and Home Office guidance to explain the meaning and purpose of the new provisions. Steering a clear course through the vast amount of paper is not easy. One of the tasks of this work is to incorporate the new with the old and give a coherent account of where law and practice stand. As its title indicates, the Act not only changes the asylum regime, but also makes numerous and diverse changes in the broader field of immigration control.

1.22   Part I of the Immigration and Asylum Act 1999 contains a random grouping of disparate measures, many amending parts of the Immigration Act 1971. They should be read in conjunction with the changes made in other Parts of the Act:

(i)   *Leave and fees.* These include the new provisions about leave to enter or remain described above,[1] and a power to charge fees on applications for leave[2] and for travel documents.[3]

(ii)   *Financial bonds.* Sections 16 and 17 provide for financial bonds or security to be taken by the government as a condition of the grant of entry clearance and extensions of leave, but the government has indicated that it is not going ahead with the scheme, at least for the time being.

(iii)   *Information and control facilities.* There are various administrative measures for obtaining passenger and criminal intelligence information,[4] for monitoring refusals of entry clearance,[5] and for the provision of immigration control facilities at ports of entry.[6] In committee the Government stated that that the supply of information to the Home Office would be subject to the requirements of the data protection laws and the Human Rights Act 1998 (protection of privacy).

(iv)   *Bail hostels.* Section 4 deals with the provision of alternative accommodation for those temporarily admitted or released from detention and is clearly intended to reduce the need to detain people who have no address to go to. The provision is a general one, but links in with the very detailed provision, referred to below, of support for asylum seekers (Part VI).

(v)   *Safety of third country removals.* Sections 11 to 15 deal with the removal of asylum seekers to so-called safe third countries. In particular, section 11 deems EU member states safe when asylum seekers are removed under the Dublin Convention, in an attempt to prevent the courts from quashing such removals.

(vi)   *Overstayers.* One of the most significant and controversial changes is the placing of overstayers and others who breach conditions on the same footing as illegal entrants subject to summary removal, with a consequent loss of appeal rights against deportation.[7] Section 9 provided a transitional period[8] during which overstayers could seek to regularise their position and thereby retain their right of appeal against deportation. Those whose deportation is conducive to the public good and family members of deportees can still be deported and will have an appeal against deportation as before.[9]

(vii)   *Criminal offences.* Sections 28 to 30 amend the Immigration Act 1971 to strengthen and extend the criminal offences contained in it, especially deception. Section 31 is a response to the Divisional Court decision in *Ex p Adimi*[10] which held that the prosecution of asylum seekers for travelling with false documents is a breach of Article 31 of the 1951 Refugee Convention. The new section gives a statutory defence using Article 31, but in more limited circumstances than those set out in the judgments in *Adimi*.

(viii) *Miscellaneous*. Section 8 provides for compulsory exclusion from the UK of persons condemned by a UN Security Council or EU Council resolution. Section 22 provides for a Code of Practice so that employers do not commit race discrimination if they avoid employing persons not allowed to work by immigration control. New duties are placed on registrars to report suspected 'sham' marriages to the Home Office,[11] a power which goes hand-in-hand with a new regime governing the celebration of all marriages, not just those with an immigration slant, contained in Part IX.[12]

1 Immigration and Asylum Act 1999, ss 1 and 2; see **1.19** above.
2 Immigration and Asylum Act 1999, s 5.
3 Immigration and Asylum Act 1999, s 7.
4 Immigration and Asylum Act 1999, s 18–20.
5 Immigration and Asylum Act 1999, s 23.
6 Immigration and Asylum Act 1999, s 25–26.
7 Immigration and Asylum Act 1999, s 10 and Sch 14, para 44.
8 From 1 February to 1 October 2000; see Immigration (Regularisation Period for Overstayers) Regulations 2000, SI 2000/265.
9 Immigration and Asylum Act 1999, s 63 and Sch 14, para 44.
10 *R v Uxbridge Magistrates' Court, ex p Adimi* [1999] 4 All ER 520, [1999] INLR 490, DC. See further chapter 14 below; Jill Francis 'Section 31 of the Immigration and Asylum Act – Defences based on Article 31(1) of the Refugee Convention' (2000) INLP 81.
11 Immigration and Asylum Act 1999, s 24.
12 Immigration and Asylum Act 1999, ss 160–163 and Sch 14, paras 1–32.

1.23   The extension of criminal sanctions in Part I of the Immigration and Asylum Act 1999 is matched by the extension of the powers of immigration officers in Part VII, including greatly increased fingerprinting powers[1] and the power to use force,[2] which enable immigration officers to act as fully fledged immigration police. There are further punitive powers in Part II dealing with carriers' liability. The Immigration (Carriers' Liability) Act 1987 is repealed, but its provisions are re-enacted and extended. Civil penalties for failure to fulfil the extensive duties to check and control passengers are re-imposed. A new civil penalty is imposed on those responsible for the transport of clandestine entrants to the UK, with a focus on road hauliers.[3] These are dealt with in chapter 14 below.

1   Immigration and Asylum Act 1999, s 141ff.
2   Immigration and Asylum Act 1999, s 146.
3   Immigration and Asylum Act 1999, ss 32–43 and Sch 1. See also the Carriers' Liability (Clandestine Entrants) (Code of Practice) Order 2000, SI 2000/684; Carriers' Liability (Clandestine Entrants and Sale of Transporters) Regulations 2000, SI 2000/685.

1.24   Bail and detention are dealt with in Parts III and VIII of the Immigration and Asylum Act 1999. Part III, not yet in force, makes long overdue reform of the bail provisions for immigrants and asylum seekers, and provides a presumption of bail and the possibility of two routine bail hearings within ten and 38 days after detention. Part VIII provides for the regulation of detention centres and their staff for the first time.[1]

1   See also Immigration and Asylum Act 1999, Schs 11 and 12, and the Detention Centre Rules 2001, SI 2001/238.

1.25   Part IV and Schedule 4 of the Immigration and Asylum Act 1999 contains a wholesale revision and consolidation of appeal rights. Among the changes are the appellate authorities' new jurisdiction to deal with breaches of the ECHR in accordance with the Human Rights Act 1998[1] and the much publicised 'one stop appeal'.[2] In the revamp of appeal rights, the whole of Part II of the Immigration Act 1971 has been replaced by sections 58 to 68 of the 1999 Act. Visit appeals, removed in 1993, are back, but only for family visits – some 17,000 per annum are expected, but fees are charged for appealing against the refusal of a family visit,[3] a matter which has caused considerable disquiet.[4] The new appeal provisions are explained in chapter 18 below.

1   Immigration and Asylum Act 1999, s 65.
2   Immigration and Asylum Act 1999, ss 74–77. See also the Immigration and Asylum Appeals (One-Stop Procedure) Regulations 2000, SI 2000/2244.
3   Immigration and Asylum Act 1999, s 60(6); see the Immigration Appeals (Family Visitor) (No 2) Regulations 2000, SI 2000/2446, as amended by the Immigration Appeals (Family Visitor) (Amendment) Regulations 2001, SI 2001/52. The fees are £125 for oral hearings and £50 for paper hearings.
4   See 'MP Joins Attack on Visa Appeal Fee Plan' *Guardian*, 29 August, 2000.

1.26 Part V of the Immigration and Asylum Act 1999 provides a long-promised scheme for the registration and supervision of those advising on immigration and asylum matters who have no professional qualification as solicitors or barristers. The new provisions make it a criminal offence for unregistered advisers to provide advice. Although members of the legal professions are exempt, there are powers to bring them into the scheme at a later date. An Immigration Services Commissioner and an Immigration Services Tribunal will oversee registration and disciplinary measures. The Commissioner will also have powers in relation to discipline by professional bodies.[1]

1   Immigration and Asylum Act 1999, ss 82–93; Schs 5–7.

1.27 Some of the most far-reaching changes in the Immigration and Asylum Act 1999 are those dealing with support for asylum seekers, contained in Part VI and given meat by the Asylum Support Regulations.[1] Persons subject to immigration control, as defined in this Part, are removed from social security benefits and related provisions. Instead, asylum seekers are to receive their support from a regulation-based and Home Office-run system, which is intended to replace benefits and support under the National Assistance Act 1948 and the Children Act 1989. Access to this voucher-based system of support is to be controlled by a test of destitution. Part VI also provides the framework for the involuntary dispersal of asylum seekers throughout the UK. To make this dreadful scheme more palatable, the Act sets up a whole new set of appeals to Asylum Support Adjudicators against refusal of support.[2] The new provisions are described fully in chapter 13 below.

1   SI 2000/704; see also Asylum Support (Interim Provision) Regulations 1999, SI 1999/3056.
2   See Immigration and Asylum Act 1999, Schs 8–10. Schedule 9, which came into force in December 1999, provided an interim support scheme which is similar in outline but which is run by local authorities. It runs in parallel with the Home Office scheme until it is phased out, expected in about 2002.

The Race Relations (Amendment) Act 2000

1.28 The Race Relations (Amendment) Act 2000 makes general provision extending the scope of the Race Relations Act 1976 in relation to public authorities, outlawing race discrimination in functions not previously covered. The new section 19B makes it unlawful for a public authority to do any act which constitutes discrimination. This covers all public authorities carrying out immigration and nationality functions, such as the Home Office, Foreign Office, Department for Education and Employment, and local authorities involved in providing for asylum seekers. However, the ambit of the new power is severely curtailed. A minister of the Crown and immigration officials[1] are never allowed to discriminate on grounds of *race* or *colour*[2] in immigration, asylum and nationality matters,[3] but have been given *carte blanche* to do so on grounds of *nationality* or *ethnic or national origins*. Kurds or Afghans may therefore be given a harder time by immigration officers simply because of who they are.[4] This new licence has been rightly criticised by some commentators.[5] No similar amendment has been made to the Sex Discrimination Act 1975, and it therefore continues to be of no relevance to immigration and nationality decisions.[6] Where the immigration service is involved in the investigation and prosecution of offences in Part III of the Immigration Act 1971, they are in the same position under the Race Relations Act 1976 as the police.[7]

1   Race Relations Act 1976, s 19D(2), as amended by Race Relations (Amendment) Act 2000.
2   Race Relations Act 1976, s 19D(1).
3   Race Relations Act 1976, s 19D(3). Section 19D(4) defines these as functions exercisable by virtue of the Immigration Acts, the British Nationality Act 1981 and the other statutes mentioned in the 1976 Act, s 19D(5).
4   See the Race Relations (Immigration and Asylum) Authorisation, in IDI Mar/01, Ch 1 s 11, Annex EE.
5   Ann Dummett 'The immigration exceptions in the Race Relation (Amendent) Act 2000', ILPA, 2001.
6   *Re Amin* [1983] 2 AC 818, HL.
7   Race Relations Act 1976, s 19D(5)(a).

1.29   Section 71 of the Race Relations Act 1976 is replaced by a new section[1] imposing a duty on public authorities to have due regard to the need to eliminate unlawful discrimination and to promote equality of opportunity and good relations between persons of different racial groups. Public authorities such as the Home Office, which carry out immigration and nationality functions, are subject to these duties insofar as they require the promotion of equality of opportunity between persons of different racial groups.[2]

1   Race Relations Act 1976, s 71, as amended by Race Relations (Amendment) Act 2000, s 2.
2   Race Relations Act 1976, s 71A(1).

1.30   Where complaints of race discrimination are made relating to immigration decisions,[1] they should be brought before the immigration appellate authorities in the same way as an appeal on human rights grounds, rather than in the county court.[2] An immigration appeal may be allowed solely on the ground that there has been unlawful discrimination, and the adjudicator, Immigration Appeal Tribunal or Special Immigration Appeals Commission can then refer the case to the county court for assessment of a claim for damages.[3] A county court cannot question an immigration decision.[4] Finally, section 65 of the Immigration and Asylum Act 1999 is amended to include a race relations claim.[5]

1   Race Relations Act 1976, s 57A(2), inserted by Race Relations (Amendment) Act 2000, s 6.
2   Race Relations Act 1976, s 57A(1).

3 Race Relations Act 1976, s 57A(3).
4 Race Relations Act 1976, s 57A(4).
5 Immigration and Asylum Act 1999, s 65, as amended by Race Relations (Amendment) Act 2000, s 6(3) and (4).

UK and EU law

1.31 The free movement provisions of the EC Treaty are reflected in section 7 of the Immigration Act 1988 and in the Immigration (European Economic Area) Regulations 2000.[1] The integration of domestic law with EU law on free movement, immigration and asylum proceeds in fits and starts. It was hoped that Articles 17 EC (ex Article 8) and 18 EC (ex Article 8a) would confer real citizenship rights on citizens of the EU, and particularly that the right of free movement would be an attribute of citizenship rather than ancillary to economic activity within the Community. That hope has not been realised, and free movement remains a partial right, not available independently of the status of worker, student or self-employed person exercising rights of establishment, or as against the national authorities of citizens' own states.[2] But the ECJ at least rejected the fiction of temporary admission in *Yiadom*,[3] in holding that the safeguards against expulsion of those enjoying Treaty rights apply equally to those physically in the country for a period of time pending a decision on admission. Attempts to strengthen the human rights foundation of EC law have met with scant success. In *Manjit Kaur*[4] the ECJ refused to get embroiled in the argument about the extent to which fundamental human rights contained in Protocols of the ECHR not signed by all member states form part of the *corpus* of human rights on which the Community is founded.

1 SI 2000/2326, as amended by the Immigration (European Economic Area) (Amendment) Regulations 2001, SI 2001/865.
2 Except on return from the exercise of EC Treaty rights elsewhere in the EEA, as in Case C-370/90: *R v Immigration Appeal Tribunal and Surinder Singh, ex p Secretary of State for the Home Department* [1992] 3 All ER 798, [1992] Imm AR 565, ECJ.
3 *R v Secretary of State for the Home Department, ex p Nana Yiadom* C-357/98 [2001] All ER (EC) 267, ECJ.
4 *R v Secretary of State for the Home Department, ex p Manjit Kaur*, 7 March 2001, ECJ.

1.32 The institutional framework of the EU has been modified by the Treaty of Amsterdam, which incorporates into the framework of the EU the two Schengen agreements made in 1985 and 1990 and various measures taken to implement them (collectively known as the Schengen *acquis*). These, together with Articles 14 and 61 to 63 of the consolidated EC Treaty, lay the foundations for a common European immigration and asylum policy, including control of external frontiers, common visa policy, expulsion measures, harmonised family reunion measures and common asylum criteria and procedures. Because the UK was not prepared to lift immigration controls at internal frontiers, the UK and Ireland have been allowed to opt out of the Schengen *acquis* and Articles 61 to 63, with a choice to opt in to any measure, subject to the procedures agreed. There are Commission and Council proposals for directives in some areas covered by these Articles, notably minimum asylum procedures and family reunion, but no final directives. This is, however, an area which will become increasingly important. Chapter 7 below deals with EU law.

UK refugee law

1.33 Substantive refugee law is governed by the 1951 Convention relating to the Status of Refugees and its 1967 Protocol, known collectively as the Refugee Convention. Section 2 of the Asylum and Immigration Appeals Act 1993, still in force, gives primacy to the Convention over any UK Immigration Rules, and the Convention is effectively incorporated into domestic law.[1] Apart from the safe third country issue referred to at **1.15–1.16** above, the most litigated matters in UK refugee law concern the definition of 'refugee' in Article 1A(2) of the Convention. Recent case law establishes that a person in fear of persecution from non-state agents may be a refugee if his or her state is unable to provide a sufficiency of protection;[2] that the protection may be provided by a body to which the powers of the state have been transferred;[3] that the fear may be based on unreasonable activities[4] or even ones performed in bad faith;[5] but that the ordinary risks inherent in civil war do not found a refugee claim;[6] that the fundamental purpose of the Convention is counteracting discrimination and persecution based on gender or other immutable characteristic founds refugee status;[7] that where persecution is localised, a person may be a refugee if internal relocation would be unduly harsh;[8] and that in assessing a claim, all the available evidence must be weighed for what it is worth[9] and that the focus of the inquiry is on the future risk of persecution.[10] Chapter 12 below gives a comprehensive exposition of current UK asylum law.

1 *R v Secretary of State for the Home Department, ex p Sivakumaran* [1988] AC 958; *R v Uxbridge Magistrates' Court, ex p Adimi* [1999] INLR 490.
2 *Horvath v Secretary of State for the Home Department* [2000] INLR 239, HL.
3 *R oa Vallaj v Immigration Appeal Tribunal* (CO 2738/2000) 21 December 2000, QBD.
4 *Iftikhar Ahmed v Secretary of State for the Home Department* [2000] INLR 1.
5 *Danian v Secretary of State for the Home Department* [2000] Imm AR 96, CA.
6 *Adan v Secretary of State for the Home Department* [1999] 1 AC 293, HL.
7 *R v Immigration Appeal Tribunal and Secretary of State for the Home Department, ex p Shah, Islam v Immigration Appeal Tribunal* [1999] 2 AC 629, HL.
8 *R v Secretary of State for the Home Department, ex p Robinson* [1998] QB 929, CA.
9 *Karanakaran v Secretary of State for the Home Department* [2000] 3 All ER 449, [2000] INLR 122, [2000] Imm AR 271, CA.
10 *Karanakaran* above; *R v Secretary of State for the Home Department, ex p Ravichandran* [1996] Imm AR 97, CA.

UK immigration-related human rights law

1.34 It is well established that immigration decisions such as exclusion and expulsion engage obligations under international human rights law.[1] Now, for the first time, the human rights guaranteed by the ECHR are enforceable in all UK courts and tribunals as a result of the coming into force of the Human Rights Act 1998 – in England and Wales as from 2 October 2000; in Scotland as from this date, except where it affected devolution, when the date is 1999. It is no longer necessary to go to Strasbourg to get redress, although Strasbourg is still available if earlier attempts in the domestic courts are unsuccessful. Decisions relating to entry to or stay in the UK which are said to interfere with fundamental human rights are appealable, by virtue of section 65 of the Immigration and Asylum Act 1999, to the appellate authority. The Home Office and the UK courts have accepted that removal to circumstances in which life expectancy is significantly reduced by lack of medical treatment, or to extreme poverty and destitution, may be in breach of Article 3 of the ECHR (prohibition of torture or inhuman or degrading treatment).[2] Amendments to the rules dealing with the admission of new groups such as unmarried partners,[3] improved rules on admission for contact with UK-based children,[4] and policies on long residence and family ties in the context of removal are designed to give effect to family and private life rights in Article 8 of the Convention. Article 8 has also affected the maintenance and accommodation rules for family reunion[5] and their interpretation.[6] Chapter 8 below looks in detail at the UK's human rights obligations and their implementation.

1   *Abdulaziz, Cabales and Balkandali v UK* (1985) 7 EHRR 471; *Soering v UK* (1989) 11 EHRR 439.
2   *R v Secretary of State for the Home Department, ex p Kebbeh* (CO 1269/1998) 30 April 1998; *R v Secretary of State for the Home Department, ex p M* [1999] Imm AR 548, QBD; Home Office policy on exceptional leave, Asylum Policy Instructions, Ch 5, s 1, reproduced in *Butterworths Immigration Law Service*, **2B**[22]. See **12.179** below.
3   HC 395, paras 295A–M, as amended by Cm 4851, 2 October 2000.
4   HC 395, paras 248A–F.
5   See HC 395, para 6A, inserted by Cm 4851.
6   *R v Secretary of State for the Home Department, ex p Arman Ali* [2000] INLR 89, QBD.

SOURCES OF IMMIGRATION LAW AND PRACTICE

Immigration statutes and the orders and regulations made under them

1.35   The main sources of immigration and asylum law are the Immigration Act 1971 and the amending statutes described in the previous sections.[1] The 1971 Act contains the rule-making power, and it and the other legislation provide for implementing Orders and Regulations, usually to be made by statutory instrument, sometimes by Order in Council. The Immigration and Asylum Act 1999 is the worst offender. On a rough count there are 12 instances of powers to make Orders by statutory instrument; 26 for regulations; seven for rules; seven codes of practice will apply; two sets of directions; one Order in Council; and one set of arrangements. Not all these powers have been or will be used, but the list of Orders and Regulations, covering a very wide span, is formidable. All are subject to change. Increasingly, it is going to be necessary for readers to consult an immigration encyclopaedia or the internet to check the up-to-date position.[2] The key rules are still *The Statement of Immigration Rules*, made under the 1971 Act and usually published as a House of Commons paper (currently HC 395), setting out the criteria for entry and stay in the various immigration categories. A new consolidated set of Immigration Rules is expected very soon. Then come the rules of procedure for immigration and asylum appeals[3] and the regulations for the service of notices in connection with appeals.[4] The validity of these subordinate rules and regulations may be challenged. One provision of an Immigration Rule has been held so unreasonable as to be invalid,[5] as has one procedure rule,[6] as well as the social security regulation denying benefits to in-country and rejected asylum seekers,[7] and other delegated legislation has been subject to several challenges, of which only one was conceded.[8] The Human Rights Act 1998 offers further scope for challenge on the basis that the rule or regulation in question infringes ECHR rights and is not required to do so by the primary legislation.[9] If the primary legislation requires the infringement, the immigration appellate authorities can do nothing, but the High Court can make a declaration of incompatibility.[10]

1 There is very little left of the Asylum and Immigration Appeals Act 1993 and the Asylum and Immigration Act 1996. The primacy of the 1951 Refugee Convention survives (1993 Act, s 2); as does bail pending an appeal to the Tribunal (s 9A); of the 1996 Act, the amendments to the Immigration Act 1971 by way of new offences and increased penalties, increased immigration officer powers and provisions for bail continue to apply (ss 4–6 and Sch 2) as do employer sanctions (s 8).
2 Useful websites are set out in Appendix 2.
3 Immigration and Asylum Appeals (Procedure) Rules 2000, SI 2000/2333.
4 Immigration and Asylum Appeals (Notices) Regulations 2000, SI 2000/2246, as amended by the Immigration and Asylum Appeals (Notices) (Amendment) Regulations 2001, SI 2001/868.
5 *R v Immigration Appeal Tribunal, ex p Manshoora Begum* [1986] Imm AR 385, QBD.
6 *R v Secretary of State for the Home Department, ex p Asifa Saleem* [2000] INLR 413.
7 *R v Secretary of State for Social Security, ex p JCWI* [1997] 1 WLR 275.
8 See eg *R v Immigration Appeal Tribunal, ex p Mehmet* [1977] 2 All ER 602, [1977] Imm AR 56, QBD; *R v Immigration Appeal Tribunal and Secretary of State for the Home Department, ex p Jones* [1986] Imm AR 496, QBD; affd *sub nom R v Immigration Appeal Tribunal, ex p Jones* [1988] 2 All ER 65, [1988] 1 WLR 477, CA; *Singh v Secretary of State for the Home Department* [1992] 4 All ER 673, [1992] 1 WLR 1052, HL (Sc). However, note that aspects of the Immigration (Restricted Right of Appeal against Deportation) (Exemption) (No 2) Order 1988, SI 1988/1203 were recognised as invalid by the Home Office.
9 Human Rights Act 1998, s 6(1) and (2).
10 Human Rights Act 1998, s 4(4). See chapter 8 below.

The prerogative

1.36 The prerogative powers of the Secretary of State for the Home Department are another source of immigration law, although in practice their importance is now diminished virtually to vanishing point. Although section 33(5) of the Immigration Act 1971 states that the Act 'shall not be taken to supersede or impair any power exercisable by Her Majesty in relation to aliens by virtue of her prerogative', in practice immigration control involves an almost exclusive exercise of statutory powers. The prerogative powers on immigration control never applied and cannot apply to Commonwealth citizens,[1] but aliens were always governed by prerogative powers of the Crown which continued alongside the statutory code, both in war and in peacetime.[2] The whole area of leave to enter and deportation is now, however, fully and comprehensively covered by the Immigration Act 1971 and the subsequent legislation. Despite the terms of section 33(5) of the 1971 Act, the doctrine of abeyance means that the statutory provisions take preference, so long as the statute is in force.[3] The prerogative power is not impaired or superseded, merely put in abeyance.[4] Its current operation is, therefore, confined to areas where the Immigration Acts do not operate, for example, (i) in dealing with diplomats who are exempted from immigration control by section 8(3), which expressly states that the 'provisions of this Act . . . shall not apply . . .';[5] (ii) in conferring a benefit for which no statutory provision is made.

1 See *DPP v Bhagwan* [1972] AC 60, [1970] 3 All ER 97; *R v Immigration Appeal Tribunal, ex p Secretary of State for the Home Department* [1990] 3 All ER 652, [1990] 1 WLR 1126.
2 See the previous edition of this work, **1.21**ff for details.
3 *A-G v de Keyser's Royal Hotel Ltd* [1920] AC 508 at 539–540, HL, per Lord Atkinson; *R v Secretary of State for the Home Department, ex p Northumbria Police Authority* [1989] QB 26, [1988] 1 All ER 556, CA.
4 *R v Immigration Appeal Tribunal, ex p Secretary of State for the Home Department* [1990] 3 All ER 652 at 657 and 661, [1990] 1 WLR 1126 at 1133 and 1136, CA.

5   See *R v Secretary of State for the Home Department, ex p Bagga* [1991] 1 QB 485,
    1 All ER 777.

1.37   Where the Secretary of State overrules an immigration officer, grants
someone exceptional leave to remain when the Immigration Rules say he or she
should go, or adopts a policy that people of a particular class or nationality
should get exceptional leave, or grants a general amnesty, the source of the
discretion – prerogative or statute – has caused some difficulty. Our view is
that it derives from the Secretary of State's and the immigration officers' statutory
powers, and, in particular, from the discretion under section 4(1) of the
Immigration Act 1971, which is a very broad discretion, not made subject to
the Immigration Rules. The Secretary of State can, therefore, waive a requirement
of the Rules in an individual case as a matter of statutory discretion. But there
are dicta in two cases which suggest that the power to treat an immigrant more
favourably than the Rules dictate derives from prerogative rather than statute.[1]
This may apply to aliens where there is a prerogative power in abeyance, but it
cannot be right so far as Commonwealth citizens are concerned, because the
1971 Act has only retained the prerogative power over aliens.[2] It is difficult to
identify any other prerogative power to which the judges could be referring,
unless it is the Crown's prerogative as 'fountain of justice.'[3] In *Ahmed and
Patel*[4] the parties were agreed that the Secretary of State was using prerogative
powers in the formulation and application of extra-statutory policies such as
those on long residence or marriage and children in relation to removal. But
the court held that a Treaty entered into by the executive, such as the ECHR or
the UN Convention on the Rights of the Child, could have no greater effect in
relation to the exercise of a discretion under the prerogative than in the case of
a statutory discretion.

1   *R v Secretary of State for the Home Department, ex p Kaur* [1987] Imm AR 278, DC;
    R v Secretary of State for the Home Department, ex p Ounejma [1989] Imm AR 75. In
    R v Secretary of State for the Home Department, ex p Northumbria Police Authority
    Purchas LJ approved of this kind of residual use of the prerogative power, stating that:
        'where the executive action is directed towards the benefit or protection of the individual,
        it is unlikely that its use will attract the intervention of the courts . . . Before the courts
        will hold that such executive action is contrary to legislation, express and unequivocal
        terms must be found in the statute which deprive the individual from receiving the
        benefit or protection intended by the exercise of the Prerogative power'.
2   Commonwealth citizens had a common law right to come and go without let or hindrance:
    DPP v Bhagwan [1972] AC 60 at 80; *R v Immigration Appeal Tribunal, ex p Secretary of
    State for the Home Department* [1990] 3 All ER 652 at 657 and 661, [1991] 1 WLR 1126
    at 1133 and 1136, CA.
3   See Chitty *Treatise on the Law of the Prerogative of the Crown* (1820) chapter 7;
    R v Secretary of State for the Home Department, ex p Northumbria Police Authority
    [1988] 1 All ER 556 at 563, CA.
4   *R v Secretary of State for the Home Department, ex p Ahmed and Patel* [1998] INLR 570.

1.38   The prerogative powers in relation to national security affected
immigration law adversely until very recently, overriding normally applicable
Immigration Rules[1] or the obligations under the 1951 Refugee Convention.[2]
The courts retained no more than a nominal power to quash the decision on
normal judicial review grounds.[3] But this has all changed now owing (i) to the
Chahal case,[4] where the European Court held that the applicant's rights not to
be subjected to torture, inhuman and degrading treatment (under Article 3 of
the ECHR) overrode any interests of national security; and (ii) the enactment of
the Special Immigration Appeals Commission Act 1997, passed as a direct

response to the European Court in *Chahal,* which set up the Special Immigration Appeals Commission to hear appeals involving national security. We deal with these in later chapters.

1   *R v Secretary of State for the Home Department, ex p Hosenball* [1977] 3 All ER 452, [1977] 1 WLR 766, CA; *NSH v Secretary of State for the Home Department* [1988] Imm AR 389, CA; *R v Secretary of State for the Home Department, ex p Chahal* [1994] Imm AR 107, CA.

2   Although the Secretary of State was under an obligation to asylum seekers lawfully in the UK to balance their interests under the 1951 Refugee Convention against the interests of national security: see *NSH v Secretary of State for the Home Department* above; *Ex p Chahal* above.

3   See *The Zamora* [1916] 2 AC 77, PC; the speech of Lord Atkin in *Liversidge v Anderson* [1942] AC 206, [1941] 3 All ER 338, HL; *Council of Civil Service Unions v Minister for the Civil Service* [1985] AC 374 at 420–423, HL, per Lord Roskill; *Hussain v Secretary of State for the Home Department* [1993] Imm AR 353, CA; *Ex p Hosenball* above; *NSH v Secretary of State for the Home Department* above; *Chahal* above.

4   *Chahal v United Kingdom* (1996) 23 EHRR 413, ECtHR.

Decisions of the Tribunal and courts

1.39   The most voluminous source of immigration and asylum law is the case law of the higher courts and the Immigration Appeal Tribunal on the meaning, effect, and application of the primary and subordinate legislation, the Immigration Rules and Home Office policies outside the Rules. Decisions of the Immigration Appeal Tribunal are not strictly binding, but the President, Mr Justice Collins, has recently instituted a system of key decisions (starred cases) which are to be followed in subsequent cases, in order to end the previously common situation where there were conflicting decisions by different Tribunals.[1] Unreported decisions of the Tribunal are referred to by their bracket number and are available in the Supreme Court and Law Society Libraries and, in electronic form, through the Electronic Immigration Network.[2] Administrative Court, Court of Appeal and House of Lords decisions, if not reported, are similarly available in the Libraries, in summary form in the digests and on the Electronic Immigration Network, and as full transcripts in electronic form.[3] With two competing sets of specialist immigration law reports, two digests of unreported Tribunal decisions and the EIN, more decisions of importance are now reported or otherwise available to practitioners. In this situation we have included more unreported cases than in previous editions. In addition to the reports of decisions of domestic courts, there is a growing body of European decisions from both Luxembourg[4] and Strasbourg.[5] We refer to these in the sections below.

1   Adjudicators should regard themselves as bound by starred decisions of the IAT, and the IAT should itself follow an earlier starred decision unless it is satisfied that the decision is clearly wrong: *Sepet and Bulbul v Secretary of State for the Home Department* C/2777 and C/2000/2794, 11 May 2001, CA, per Laws LJ, para 99.

2   The Electronic Immigration Network website is at www.ein.org and its public resources homepage is an excellent gateway into most websites which immigration practitioners would need. The Tribunal decisions are available by subscription.

3   Through the website of the Court Service, www.courtservice.gov.uk, and that of shorthand writers Smith Bernal, at www.casetrack.com. House of Lords decisions are available on the House of Lords website, at www.parliament.the-stationery-office.co.uk.

3   ECJ judgments and Opinions are available on the Internet at www.curia.eu.int.

4   ECtHR judgments are available at www.echr.coe.int.

The Immigration Rules

1.40 These are made by the Secretary of State for the Home Department in accordance with sections 1(4) and (5) and 3(2) of the Immigration Act 1971. Statements of the Rules must be laid before Parliament and they then take effect, unless either House votes against them. The same procedure applies to changes in the Rules. There are few statutory or other restrictions on the rule-making power.[1] Section 1(4) of the 1971 Act provides that the Rules must include provisions for the admission of persons coming for employment and study, and as visitors or dependants. There is no similar requirement for 'after entry' rules. The general rule-making power is contained in section 3(2) of the 1971 Act and it expressly provides that in framing the Rules there is no need to have uniform provisions as regards admission of persons for employment, study or as visitors of dependants and account may be taken of citizenship or nationality. It is not subject to the provisions of the Human Rights Act 1998 which make it unlawful for public authorities to act in a way which is incompatible with a right protected by the ECHR,[2] or the provisions of the Race Relations Act 1976 prohibiting racial discrimination by public authorities,[3] thus preserving parliamentary sovereignty. But a rule which infringes basic rights such as the right of access to a tribunal, which is not expressly or by necessary implication authorised by an Act of Parliament, is *ultra vires*.[4]

1 The Asylum and Immigration Appeals Act 1993, s 2 provides that nothing in the Immigration Rules shall lay down any practice which would be contrary to the 1951 Refugee Convention. Before its repeal by Immigration Act 1988, s 1, s 1(5) of the 1971 Act imposed mandatory and negative obligations on the rule-making power of the Secretary of State for the Home Department, by providing that the Rules should be so framed that Commonwealth citizens settled in the UK on 1 January 1973, and their wives and children, were no less free to come into and go from the UK than if the 1971 Act had not been passed. In *R v Immigration Appeal Tribunal, ex p Haque, Rahman and Ruhul* [1987] Imm AR 587 the Court of Appeal held that an Immigration Rule infringing the mandatory and negative obligations contained in s 1(5) was *ultra vires* and void, but that could not lead to a resurrection of any of the pre-1973 rules. For standstill clauses in EC law, see 7.157 below.
2 Human Rights Act 1998, s 6.
3 Race Relations Act 1976, s 19, as amended by Race Relations (Amendment) Act 2000.
4 *R v Secretary of State for the Home Department, ex p Saleem (Asifa)* [2000] INLR 413.

1.41 The rule-making power is a statutory one and the Immigration Rules must conform to the statutory parameters; they cannot require officials to do what the statute does not allow. The Rules might be challenged as *ultra vires* if they impose an unlawful fetter on the discretion of the immigration official or unlawfully delegate a discretionary power. Such challenges have been made unsuccessfully in relation to rules which provide for mandatory refusal of leave for those arriving in the UK without a proper visa or entry clearance.[1] The *vires* of an Immigration Rule may also be challenged on the basis that it is unreasonable, in the sense of being impartial or unequal in its operation as between classes; manifestly unjust; made in bad faith; or involving such oppressive or gratuitous interference with the rights of those affected by them as could find no justification in the minds of reasonable persons.[2] In *R v Immigration Appeal Tribunal, ex p Manshoora Begum* a provision in one of the family rules was struck down on this ground.

1 *R v Secretary of State for the Home Department, ex p Kaur (Rajinder)* [1987] Imm AR 278, DC; *R v Secretary of State for the Home Department, ex p Hassan* [1989] Imm AR 75, DC.

2 Per Lord Russell CJ in *Kruse v Johnson* [1898] 2 QB 91. Applied in *R v Immigration Appeal Tribunal, ex p Begum (Manshoora)* [1986] Imm AR 385, QBD. In *R v Immigration Appeal Tribunal, ex p Begum (Hasna)* [1995] Imm AR 249, QBD the court held that HC 251, para 3, dealing with polygamous marriages, was not *ultra vires*.

1.42 Where changes are made to the Immigration Rules, it is sometimes difficult to establish whether the old or new Rules apply. Generally, the Rules which are in operation at the time of the immigration authorities' decision rather than those operating at the date of application are the applicable Rules,[1] but the current Rules make savings for applications made before 1 October 1994. New editions of the Rules often contain transitional provisions which may give rise to problems of interpretation.[2]

1 See HC 395, para 4; *R v Immigration Appeal Tribunal, ex p Nathwani* [1979–80] Imm AR 9, QBD.
2 For reported decisions on transitional provisions see *Shamseddin* [1981] Imm AR 66; *Kamry* [1981] Imm AR 118; *Pope* [1987] Imm AR 10; *Minah Begum* [1990] Imm AR 38; *Pardeepan* [2000] INLR 447. Recent unreported decisions include *Wilby* (18380); *Sukhdev Singh* (17798); *Gremesty* (01 TH 00096).

1.43 There has been considerable debate about the legal status of the Immigration Rules – whether they are rules of law or not. In *Pearson v Immigration Appeal Tribunal*[1] the Court of Appeal stated that although the Rules are not delegated legislation or rules of law, but rules of practice laid down for the guidance of those entrusted with the administration of the Act, they had the force of law for adjudicators hearing immigration appeals.[2] This is made clear by paragraph 21 of Schedule 4 to the Immigration and Asylum Act 1999, which provides that an adjudicator 'shall allow an appeal if he [or she] considers that the decision or action appealed against was not in accordance with . . . any immigration rules applicable to the case'. The same applies to the Immigration Appeal Tribunal.[3] It is, therefore, clear that the rules are far more a source of law than, for example, the Code of Practice under section 8 of the Asylum and Immigration Act 1996, which is a relevant consideration in deciding whether an employer has discriminated unlawfully in hiring or refusing to hire someone. The Rules have more immediate and binding effect, as any cursory reading of the reported decisions of the Immigration Appeal Tribunal makes clear. The appellate authorities are always concerned to see whether immigration officials have followed the Immigration Rules applicable to the case. If they have failed to do so, the appeal must be allowed.[4] If the Rule gives the immigration official a discretion, the adjudicator or Tribunal can review the exercise of that discretion and decide that it ought to have been exercised differently.[5] If, however, the wording of the Rule is in mandatory terms and the immigration officer has followed it, the prevailing view is that there is no exercise of discretion by the immigration officer to review on the merits and so there is no room for any decision under paragraph 21(1)(b) of Schedule 4 to the 1999 Act[6] (save on human rights grounds). As immigration law becomes more sophisticated, the Immigration Rules tend to be drafted in a more comprehensive form.[7] The current Rules make it mandatory to refuse entry clearance, leave to enter, or a variation for a purpose not covered by the Rules,[8] putting at risk all those whose immigration status is and remains regulated outside the Rules, such as the domestic servants of the rich, and asylum seekers granted exceptional leave.

1 [1978] Imm AR 212.

2   See further *R v Secretary of State for the Home Department, ex p Hosenball* [1977] 3 All ER 452, [1977] 1 WLR 766, CA.
3   Immigration and Asylum Act 1999, Sch 4, para 22.
4   Immigration and Asylum Act 1999, Sch 4, para 21(1)(a).
5   Immigration and Asylum Act 1999, Sch 4, para 21(1)(b).
6   See eg *Kausar* [1998] INLR 141; *Botan* (18175); **18.77** below.
7   For a discussion of the appellate jurisdiction under the old rules, see the previous edition at **2.51**.
8   HC 395, paras 320(1) and 322(1). See also *Somasundaram* [1990] Imm AR 16.

1.44   The Immigration Rules also play a very important role in judicial review where the decisions of immigration officers and the appellate authorities are challenged in the Administrative Court. In this context, the Rules are not rules of law, because they are not made by statutory instrument but are described in the Immigration Act 1971 as rules of practice to be followed in the administration of the Act for regulating entry to and stay in the UK. This characterisation of the rules has a number of consequences:

(i)   the language of the Rules is that of the administrator rather than that of the parliamentary draftsman. Often, they are no more than descriptive. They are, therefore, to be given a purposive rather than a strict construction unless, the words used are wholly unambiguous;[1]

(ii)   the power to make any decision on entry, stay or deportation comes from the 1971 Act, not the Rules, and is unfettered.[2] In particular, it is not made subject to the Immigration Rules;[3]

(iii)   the existence of a residuary discretion outside the Rules means that the Secretary of State can make some Rules mandatory without risk of unlawfully fettering his or her discretion, because in each case, he or she can decide whether to depart from the Rules.[4] It is probably also why an immigration officer who gives leave mistakenly is not acting outside his or her authority;[5]

(iv)   the Rules are not binding on the Administrative Court in the way that statutes are. Indeed, as we have seen,[6] in exceptional cases, the court may strike out a Rule as being wholly or in part invalid for unreasonableness or unnecessary infringement of human rights.[7] In most cases however, the court is concerned with the interpretation, rather than the *vires* of the Rules.

1   *Alexander v Immigration Appeal Tribunal* [1982] 2 All ER 766, [1982] 1 WLR 1076, HL; *Singh v Immigration Appeal Tribunal* [1986] 2 All ER 721, [1986] Imm AR 352, HL; *R v Immigration Appeal Tribunal, ex p Rahman* [1987] Imm AR 313, CA; *Gurdev Singh v Immigration Appeal Tribunal* [1988] Imm AR 510, CA; *R v Immigration Appeal Tribunal, ex p Manshoora Begum* [1986] Imm AR 385, QBD; *R v Immigration Appeal Tribunal, ex p Zanib Bibi* [1987] Imm AR 392, QBD; *Entry Clearance Officer, Bombay v De Noronha* [1995] Imm AR 341, CA; *R v Secretary of State for the Home Department, ex p Arman Ali* [2000] INLR 89.
2   Immigration Act 1971, s 4(1).
3   See **1.32**ff above for a discussion on the source of the residuary discretion.
4   See *Pearson v Immigration Appeal Tribunal* [1978] Imm AR 212, CA; per Banks LJ in *R v Port of London Authority, ex p Kynoch Ltd* [1919] 1 KB 176 at 184, CA; *British Oxygen Co Ltd v Minister of Technology* [1971] AC 610, [1970] 3 All ER 165, HL. A good example of a fettering of discretion is *R v LCC, ex p Corrie* [1918] 1 KB 68 – a decision of the London County Council to refuse all further permits, without exception, to distribute literature in London public parks. In considering the exercise of the discretion outside the Immigration Rules, the Secretary of State is entitled to act so as to ensure that generally speaking the Rules are followed, to ensure fairness between applicants: *R v Secretary of State for the Home Department, ex p Ahmed* [1995] Imm AR 210, CS.

5   See *R v Secretary of State for the Home Department, ex p Ram* [1979] 1 All ER 687, [1979] 1 WLR 148.
6   See **1.37** above.
7   *R v Immigration Appeal Tribunal, ex p Manshoora Begum* [1986] Imm AR 385; *R v Secretary of State for the Home Department, ex p Dhahan* [1988] Imm AR 257, QBD; *R v Secretary of State for the Home Department, ex p Saleem (Asifa)* [2000] INLR 413, CA.

Administrative practice and discretion outside the Immigration Rules

1.45   Unfortunately, the Immigration Rules are not a comprehensive code of all the practices regulating entry into the UK. There are great gaps, some of which are covered by well-known practices, which in some cases have an almost equivalent status to the Rules but for reasons best known to the Home Office are not incorporated into them. For example, the policy to grant refugees indefinite leave to remain immediately is not mentioned in the Rules,[1] although family reunion for refugees has now been incorporated.[2] Secondly, the Secretary of State or immigration official is frequently asked to sanction a waiver of part of a Rule, or a departure from the Rule, based on the particular personal circumstances of the applicant, usually of a compassionate nature. Alternatively, the departure may be of such general application that it has become something of a practice or general concession, at least for the time being. For example, those given exceptional leave to remain used to have to wait for seven years before getting indefinite leave to remain. Now they need to have spent an aggregate of four years in the UK.[3] Most of these policies are now being collected and put into the Immigration Directorate Instructions (IDI) and Asylum Policy Instructions (API), published by the Home Office since 1998 as part of its commitment to greater transparency or openness. These instructions are an invaluable guide, not just to policies outside the Rules but also to latest practice in the interpretation of the Rules. They are available on the internet, in most law libraries and in a number of organisations, including the Immigration Law Practitioners' Association.[4] We refer to relevant IDI and API throughout this work.

1   See 'New measures for dealing with asylum claims', Asylum and Appeals Policy Directorate letter, April 1999, in *Butterworths Immigration Law Service*, 2B, 27 [14].
2   HC 395, paras 352A–F, as amended by Cm 4851.
3   See 'New measures' fn 1 above. A collection of these practices and policies is contained in *Butterworths Immigration Law Service*.
4   IDI and API (formerly Asylum Directorate Instructions, ADI) were made available to the public under the government's *Code of Practice on Access to Government Information*. They are available at www.homeoffice.gov.uk/ind/idi. The Department for Education and Employment, which is responsible for work permits, publishes similar guidance on its website, www.dfee.gov.uk/ols.

1.46   Although some of these general practices or concessions are of a temporary nature, designed to deal with political upheaval in a particular country, we refer to all of them as established practices or concessions because they are sufficiently detailed, well known and consistently applied. A failure to take such a practice or policy into account, or a misinterpretation or misapplication, might well open the decision to a successful challenge, either on appeal on the basis that the decision is not in accordance with the law,[1] or on judicial review on the basis that it is unreasonable or unfair.[2] The existence of the policy may give rise to a legitimate expectation that it will be invoked in the applicant's favour.[3] If the policy is unpublished no legitimate expectation arises, but it would be unreasonable for the Secretary of State to apply the policy inconsistently or unfairly as between one person and another.[4]

1 *Abdi v Secretary of State for the Home Department* [1996] Imm AR 148, CA; *Hersi v Secretary of State for the Home Department* [1996] Imm AR 569 at 580, CA, per Otton LJ.
2 *A-G of Hong Kong v Ng Yuen Shiu* [1983] 2 AC 629, [1983] 2 All ER 346, PC; *R v Secretary of State for the Home Department, ex p Khan* [1985] 1 All ER 40, [1984] 1 WLR 1337, CA; *R v Immigration Appeal Tribunal, ex p Bastiampillai* [1983] 2 All ER 844, [1983] Imm AR 1; *Asif Mahmood Khan v Immigration Appeal Tribunal* [1984] Imm AR 68, CA.
3 *Gyeabour* [1989] Imm AR 94. Recent cases involving Home Office policies include *R v Secretary of State for the Home Department, ex p Ahmed and Patel* [1999] Imm AR 22, CA (marriage and deportation); *R v Secretary of State for the Home Department, ex p Najem* [1999] Imm AR 107, QBD (travel documents; grounds for grant of exceptional leave to remain); *Warsame v Entry Clearance Officer, Nairobi* [2000] Imm AR 155, CA (Somali family reunion); *R v Secretary of State for the Home Department, ex p Tarlok Singh* [2000] Imm AR 508, QBD (children and deportation).
4 *R v Secretary of State for the Home Department, ex p Amankwah* [1994] Imm AR 240, QBD (policy on marriage and deportation DP2/93); see also *R v Secretary of State for the Home Department, ex p Ozminnos* [1994] Imm AR 287, QBD.

European Community law

1.47 On the same day that the Immigration Act 1971 came into effect, the UK's membership of the EC also took effect. Joining the Common Market, as it was then known, has meant that the development of domestic immigration law has gone hand in hand with that of EC law on free movement rights.[1] The Immigration Acts are not the last word; their provisions must yield to EC law, when it is applicable.[2] Where national courts have to interpret domestic law in a field governed by EC law, the courts must interpret that law in the light of the wording and purpose of EC law, so far as it is possible for them to do so.[3] The 'so far as possible' principle of interpretation contained in *Marleasing* has now been incorporated into the Human Rights Act 1998[4] in order to minimise conflict between domestic law and the ECHR.[5] It is now a requirement of European law that the rights guaranteed by the ECHR are respected as general principles of EC law.[6] This means that in imposing limitations on the right of free movement of EU nationals (such as deportation), member states must respect any relevant provision of the ECHR.[7] By this process, parts of the ECHR which are not included in the list of substantive rights set out in the Human Rights Act 1998 because they are unratified, such as the fourth Protocol, may also find their way into UK domestic law, as part of the *corpus* of law to be taken into account in construing EC law.[8] Reports of decisions of the ECJ are published on the internet[9] and in the European Court Reports (ECR),[10] and in the commercially published Common Market Law Reports and European All ERs. A useful summary of ECJ judgments and opinions of the Advocate General is published and distributed from Luxembourg each month.

1 See **1.31–1.32** above; chapter 7 below.
2 See European Communities Act 1972, s 2; Treaty Establishing the European Community (consolidated version of Treaty of Rome), art 10 (ex art 5); *R v Secretary of State for Employment, ex p Equal Opportunities Commission* [1995] 1 AC 1, HL.
3 *Marleasing SA v La Comercial Internacional de Alimentacion SA* [1990] ECR I-4135, ECJ; applied by the HL in *Litster v Forth Dry Dock and Engineering Co Ltd* [1990] 1 AC 546.

4 Human Rights Act 1998, s 3(1).
5 See **1.48** below.
6 Treaty on European Union, art 6 (ex art F); *Elliniki Radiophonia Tileorassi AE v Pliroforissos and Kouvelas* [1991] ECR I-2925, ECJ.
7 *B v Secretary of State for the Home Department* [2000] INLR 361, [2000] Imm AR 478, CA.
8 This argument was not, however, addressed by the ECJ in *R v Secretary of State for the Home Department, ex p Manjit Kaur* (CO 0985/1998) 7 March 2001.
9 At www.curia.eu.int.
10 The official reports published by the ECJ registry.

The European Convention of Human Rights

1.48 The ECHR and its case law, consisting mainly of judgments of the ECtHR in Strasbourg and (previously) opinions of the EComHR,[1] has long been a necessary part of the immigration lawyer's briefcase and we have dealt with its very considerable impact on immigration law in all of the previous editions of this work. Unlike EC law, ECHR law does not have primacy over UK domestic legislation, unless it is applied as part of the *corpus* of EC law.[2] However, all domestic courts and tribunals must 'so far as it is possible' read and give effect to primary and subordinate legislation in a way which is compatible with Convention rights.[3] If this is not possible, Convention rights will have to yield to the UK provisions in the time-honoured way, and only a higher court (not the appellate authority) can then declare the law to be incompatible with the Convention rights. By section 2 of the Human Rights Act 1998 a court or tribunal determining a question which has arisen in connection with a Convention right must take into account the case law of the ECtHR, the opinions and decisions of the EComHR, and decisions of the Committee of Ministers. This whole body of law must, therefore, become an essential part of the immigration lawyer's repertoire. The case law is to be found on the court's website, which also gives access to press releases of forthcoming cases and summaries of recent decisions;[4] in the printed decisions of the ECtHR or the EComHR (the Series A reports); the case law summaries published by the court; and the commercially published Human Rights Law Digest (for decisions of the Committee of Ministers up to 1998), the European Human Rights Reports and the European Human Rights Law Review.

1 Abolished by Protocol 11 of the ECHR as from 1 November 1998.
2 See **1.47** above.
3 Human Rights Act 1998, s 3 (1).
4 At www.echr.coe.int.

The Convention Relating to the Status of Refugees

1.49 The Convention Relating to the Status of Refugees (Geneva, 1951) and its 1967 Protocol (collectively the Refugee Convention) and the very considerable body of UK and foreign case law are key sources of asylum law, to be read with the provisions of the UK statutes and rules which give effect to the Convention in this country.[1] The Convention is a primary source of asylum law and its provisions are now construed routinely by the courts. In doing so, the courts use a number of UNHCR materials as aids to interpretation, in particular the UNHCR *Handbook*[2] and Executive Committee (ExCom) recommendations and conclusions. These may also be relevant to the exercise of a broad discretion, even though they are not themselves the source of obligations and duties.[3] Although the Convention is an international instrument, there is no supra-national court which can provide an international interpretation of its provisions. Inevitably, therefore, any examination of a particular provision by the courts will involve looking at a wide range of case law from different countries. Some familiarity with the leading case law of countries such as Canada, the US, New Zealand and Australia has been, and no doubt will continue to be, essential for those practicing in this field. Much of this case law is available on the internet, through the Electronic Immigration Network or law libraries' websites.[4]

1   Asylum and Immigration Appeals Act 1993, s 2; see **1.33** above.
2   UNHCR *Handbook on Procedures and Criteria for Determining Refugee Status* (1979), 'the *Handbook*'.
3   See **12.12** below.
4   The Electronic Immigration Network website is at www.ein.org.

International treaties and obligations

1.50   Until the last decade, international instruments other than the Refugee Convention and the ECHR have played a rather background role in immigration and asylum, because they were not part of domestic law and their role as sources of immigration law was either very obscure or barely counted. For example, there are a number of Conventions which have led to the adoption of particular provisions in the Immigration Rules, such as the rule providing for settlement after four years in employment, which derives from the International Labour Organisation Convention regarding Migration for Employment, or the long residence concession, which derives from the European Convention on Establishment. With the incorporation of the ECHR into British law, UK courts and tribunals are expected to develop their own human rights jurisprudence. A number of other human rights instruments and the case law built round them is both relevant and helpful. These have already played a role in the development of Strasbourg jurisprudence. They are recognised as important aids to construction in the Convention itself. Article 53 provides that nothing in the Convention shall be construed as limiting or derogating from any of the human rights and fundamental freedoms under any other agreement to which any High Contracting Party is a party. These include the International Covenant on Civil and Political Rights and decisions of the UN Human Rights Committee set up to receive complaints under this Covenant; the Convention on the Rights of the Child; the Convention for the Elimination of all Forms of Racial Discrimination; the Convention on the Elimination of all Forms of Discrimination Against Women; the UN Convention Against Torture and Other Cruel, Inhuman and Degrading Treatment; the European Convention for the Prevention of Torture and Inhuman and Degrading Treatment or Punishment; and the UN Body of Principles on All Forms of Detention (1988). Texts of these and a whole host of other important international documents can be found in Plender's *Basic Documents on International Migration Law*[1] and on websites such as that of the UN. The *Commonwealth Human Rights Digest* is another source of information.

1   2nd edn, (1999) Nijhoff.

THE PERSONNEL OF IMMIGRATION CONTROL

1.51 Control of immigration and asylum, as we have just seen, is administered within the framework of the Immigration Act 1971 and subsequent primary and subordinate legislation, EC law, the 1951 Refugee Convention, the ECHR and, of course, the Immigration Rules. All this has created a lot of officials and has placed onerous responsibilities and duties on airlines and other carriers, road hauliers, employers, local authorities, marriage registrars and others. It has generated a whole industry of advisers, some more caring, scrupulous and competent than others. The purpose of the remainder of this chapter is to describe the key elements of the administration of immigration control, by looking at the principal personnel and the main sources and limits of their power. At one level it is all about the Home Office, immigration officers, airlines and immigration advisers. But at another level it is about power, legality, and the particular tools of trade of a very large and powerful administrative organisation and the attempt to involve and regulate those involved in asylum or immigration for commercial reasons.

The Home Office and Secretary of State for the Home Department

1.52 The Home Office is responsible for immigration control. The Secretary of State for the Home Department is the minister in charge. But the statutes make no express reference to either. The Immigration Act 1971 refers only to the Secretary of State. Under Schedule 1 to the Interpretation Act 1978 it is provided that in every Act the expression 'Secretary of State' shall mean 'one of Her Majesty's principal Secretaries of State for time being'. In practice, it is the Secretary of State for the Home Department (the Home Secretary) who is in overall control and has the last word.[1] In Scotland it might be thought that the powers would be exercisable by the Secretary of State for Scotland, but it has been held that this is not so, and the Home Secretary in London can validly order someone who is within the Scottish jurisdiction to be deported,[2] or in some cases, admitted.[3] The administration of immigration control is not, however, entirely run by the Home Secretary. For example, entry clearance officers in overseas posts are usually attached to the Foreign and Commonwealth Office,[4] and approval of work permits is the responsibility of the Secretary of State for Education and Employment. The Lord Chancellor is responsible for appointing adjudicators and members of the Immigration Appeal Tribunal[5] and making rules of procedure for appeals.[6]

1   *Pearson v Immigration Appeal Tribunal* [1978] Imm AR 212, CA.
2   *Agee v Murray* (23 February 1977, unreported), CS, per Lord Kincraig.
3   In 2000 the Home Secretary ordered the admission of boxer Mike Tyson, who had a conviction for rape, a decision upheld in *R v Secretary of State for the Home Department, ex p Bindel* [2001] Imm AR 1, QBD.
4   The Home office and Foreign Office have formed a Joint Entry Clearance Unit which will be responsible for coordination of entry clearance policy and practice.
5   Immigration and Asylum Act 1999, s 57 and Schs 2, 3.
6   Immigration and Asylum Act 1999, Sch 4, para 3.

1.53 Within the Home Office there is a clear division of responsibility between the Secretary of State and immigration officers. Under section 4(1) of the Immigration Act 1971, immigration officers are responsible for giving leave to enter and the Secretary of State for giving leave to remain or varying leave.

The Secretary of State also has responsibility for making the Immigration Rules and laying them before Parliament,[1] and for making various Orders, rules and regulations under the 1971 Act and the Immigration and Asylum Act 1999. The various tasks of the Secretary of State are normally carried out by responsible departmental officials operating within normal *Carltona* principles,[2] but certain decisions such as the exclusion of persons on grounds of national security must be taken by the Secretary of State in person.[3] The signing of deportation orders is normally done by the Secretary of State in person, reflecting the significance of his or her decision.[4] In *R v Secretary of State for the Home Department, ex p Oladehinde*[5] the House of Lords held that although immigration officers had independent statutory powers, they were members of the Home Office and accordingly the Secretary of State could devolve decisions to deport to them.

1 Immigration Act 1971, s 3(2).
2 *Carltona Ltd v Works Comr* [1943] 2 All ER 560, CA.
3 Immigration and Asylum Act 1999, ss 60(9), 62(4), 64(2).
4 Earlier rules reflected this: HC 251, para 175, but not the current Immigration Rules. See per Woolf LJ in *R v Secretary of State for the Home Department, ex p Alexander and Oladehinde* [1990] 2 WLR 1195 at 1202, DC; further *Re Amanullah Khan* [1986] Imm AR 485, QBD.
5 [1991] 1 AC 254, [1990] 3 All ER 393, HL.

1.54 The Secretary of State for the Home Department is expected to carry out his or her functions in accordance with the established principles of administrative law and not to do anything which breaches any person's human rights.[1] As a public authority he or she must not discriminate unlawfully on racial grounds, although discrimination on grounds of nationality or ethnic or national origin in certain areas is permissible.[2] He or she must keep within the limits of the statutory powers, under which decisions are taken, and must exercise prerogative powers fairly (see **6.60** below). In situations covered by the Immigration Rules, the Secretary of State must act in accordance with them, unless it be to make a decision more favourable to an immigrant (see **1.44** above). The Secretary of State is now fully susceptible to control by the courts and may be restrained by interim or final injunctions and is guilty of contempt of court if he or she breaches an injunction or undertaking given to the court.[3]

1 Human Rights Act 1998, s 6.
2 Race Relations Act 1976, ss 19B, 19D, as amended by Race Relations (Amendment) Act 2000.
3 *Re M* [1994] 1 AC 377, [1993] 3 All ER 537, HL.

Immigration officers

1.55 Immigration officers are part of the immigration service, which consists of immigration officers, chief immigration officers and immigration inspectors, all of whom are appointed by the Secretary of State under the Immigration Act 1971.[1] They have their own statutory functions as immigration officers, but they are also civil servants[2] and can, therefore, be asked to make decisions to deport on behalf of the Secretary of State.[3] Their main functions are to examine those who arrive in this country and to grant, refuse, suspend or cancel leave to enter.[4] They also have important policing functions under Schedules 2 and 3 to the 1971 Act and under Part VII of the Immigration and Asylum Act 1999. It is a criminal offence to obstruct immigration officers in carrying out their functions under the 1971 Act.[5]

1   Immigration Act 1971, Sch 2, para 1(2).
2   See per Woolf LJ in *R v Secretary of State for the Home Department, ex p Oladehinde and Alexander* [1990] 2 WLR 1195 at 1203.
3   *R v Secretary of State for the Home Department, ex p Oladehinde* [1991] 1 AC 254, [1990] 3 All ER 393, HL.
4   Immigration Act 1971, Sch 2, paras 2–6, as amended by Immigration (Leave to Enter and Remain) Order 2000, SI 2000/1161. In doing so they are entitled to mark passports: *R v Secretary of State for the Home Department, ex p Raju* [1986] Imm AR 348, QBD.
5   Immigration Act 1971, s 26(1)(g). For other criminal offences see chapter 14 below.

1.56   In exercising their statutory functions immigration officers must act in accordance with the law, the Immigration Rules, and any instructions given to them by the Secretary of State for the Home Department, provided these are not inconsistent with the Immigration Rules,[1] and they must not do anything which breaches a person's human rights[2] or constitutes unlawful racial discrimination.[3] The need to act in accordance with the law and the Immigration Rules is consistent with the general principles of administrative law and includes the duty to act fairly, which we look at in more detail below. But it also derives quite specifically from paragraph 21 of Schedule 4 to the Immigration and Asylum Act 1999.[4] This requires an adjudicator to allow an appeal if the decision is not in accordance with the law or the Immigration Rules applicable to the case. Uncertainty still hangs over the extent of an adjudicator's jurisdiction in respect of a decision which is *Wednesbury* unreasonable, taken in bad faith or unfairly (see chapter 18 below), but this does not affect the clear restraints placed upon the immigration officer's powers and the manner in which they must be exercised. It appears that immigration officers share the Secretary of State's discretion to depart from the Rules in a manner favourable to the immigrant,[5] an issue the court left open in *Ex p Ounejma*.[6]

1   Immigration Act 1971, Sch 2, para 1(3).
2   Human Rights Act 1998, s 6.
3   Race Relations Act 1976, s 19B, as amended by Race Relations (Amendment) Act 2000; but immigration officers may discriminate on grounds of nationality or ethnic or national origins: s 19D.
4   Previously Immigration Act 1971, s 19(1)(a)(i).
5   See **1.37** and **1.44** above.
6   [1989] Imm AR 75.

1.57   In *Ex p Safira Begum*[1] the Divisional Court said there was no obligation on immigration officers to make any inquiries on their own initiative in an attempt to assist would-be entrants; they could merely stand at their bench and wait for intending entrants to say what they had to say. This may be an overstatement of the immigration officer's position. In their dealings with immigrants they must act honestly and fairly.[2] This means that in all cases the would-be entrant should be given a real opportunity of satisfying the immigration officer that he or she should be admitted,[3] and where immigration officers' suspicions are aroused they must make them known to the immigrant and give him or her a chance to explain.[4] An immigration officer who makes insufficient inquiries may be failing to act reasonably. Thus in one case, a simple inquiry of the Home Office would have revealed a Home Office report that a woman passenger's marriage was genuine.[5] In *Ex p Mughal* the Court of Appeal emphasised that immigration officers were administrative officers engaged in administrative inquiries and that the rules of natural justice must not be stretched too far.[6] So when immigration officers obtained further information which confirmed their suspicions there was no need to tell immigrants of this or give them a further opportunity to explain. In *Ex p Ajekukor,* where a passenger was found to have a forged stamp in her passport and could give no explanation, the immigration officer was held to be under no duty to make further inquiries and a failure to do so was not a breach of the rules of natural justice.[7] But in *Ex p Moon* the Divisional Court held that it was unfair not to give a visa applicant an opportunity to deal with objections to his admission.[8] This later decision brings the position of immigration officers vis-à-vis the duty of fairness closer to that of departmental officers making decisions on asylum[9] or naturalisation applications.[10] In carrying out investigations, arrests, searches and other policing functions immigration officers are subject to modified Police and Criminal Evidence Act 1984 (PACE) Codes of Practice.[11]

1   *R v Secretary of State for the Home Department, ex p Begum (Safira)* (1976) Times, 27 May, QBD.
2   *Re HK (infant)* [1967] 2 QB 617 at 630, per Lord Parker CJ; *Re Mohamed Arif (an infant)* [1968] Ch 643, [1968] 2 All ER 145, CA; *R v Chief Immigration Officer, Lympne Airport, ex p Amrik Singh* [1969] 1 QB 333, [1968] 3 All ER 163; *R v Secretary of State for the Home Department, ex p Mughal* [1974] QB 313, CA.
3   *Ex p Mughal* above, at 331, per Scarman LJ.
4   *Ex p Mughal* above at 325, per Lord Denning MR.
5   *R v Secretary of State for the Home Department, ex p Ramnial* [1983] LS Gaz R 30, DC.
6   *Ex p Mughal* above. See further *Kumar v Entry Clearance Officer, New Delhi* [1985] Imm AR 242 (entry clearance officers exercising administrative, not judicial function, when carrying out interviews).
7   *R v Immigration Officer, ex p Ajekukor* [1982] Imm AR 3, DC.
8   *R v Secretary of State for the Home Department, ex p Moon* (1995) Times, 8 December.
9   *Thirakumar v Secretary of State for the Home Department* [1989] Imm AR 402, CA.
10 *R v Secretary of State for the Home Department, ex p Fayed* [1997] 1 All ER 228, CA.
11 See chapter 14 below.

Police

1.58   Although immigration officers will take over much of the policing of immigration control with the powers given to them under Part VII of the Immigration and Asylum Act 1999, the police retain a considerable role. They are responsible for the registration of foreign nationals[1] and for the enforcement of those parts of the criminal law, including immigration offences, which involve immigration. Like immigration officers, they have powers under the Immigration Act 1971 to arrest suspected overstayers, illegal entrants and absconders for the purposes of administrative detention,[2] as well as immigration offenders.[3] They can arrest illegal entrants and others, and can obtain warrants for the search and arrest of such persons.[4] In addition to these powers, the police are also used for the service of documents such as decisions to deport, and have been used in the collection of information about the home circumstances of sponsors wishing to bring relatives and family into this country. Immigration law makes a distinction between police acting in the execution of the Immigration Acts (ie performing an administrative function given to them under the Acts) and police exercising common law powers to investigate crime.[5]

1   Immigration Act 1971, s 4(3); Immigration (Registration with Police) Regulations 1972, SI 1972/1758 (amended on many occasions only in respect of the fee for issue of a certificate of registration).
2   Immigration Act 1971, Sch 2, para 17.
3   Immigration Act 1971, s 28A(1), as amended by Immigration and Asylum Act 1999 (arrest without warrant for certain immigration offences).

4   Immigration Act 1971, s 28B.
5   *R v Clarke* [1985] AC 1037, [1985] 2 All ER 777, HL.

Entry clearance officers

1.59   The citizens of approximately one hundred countries now need visas even for a visit to the UK, and visas or entry clearance are also required for citizens of every non-EEA country who wish to come to the UK for work, business or family reunion. Visas and entry clearances are granted by entry clearance officers and visa officers, who work under the aegis of the Foreign Office, rather than the Home Office.[1] A Joint Entry Clearance Unit was set up in 1999 to ensure proper co-ordination between entry clearance officers and the Home Office. It is a joint Home Office and Foreign and Commonwealth Office initiative to manage and staff entry clearance posts abroad and monitor their performance.[2] 'Entry clearance' is defined in the Immigration Acts[3] and in many cases there is an appeal against the refusal.[4] Yet entry clearance officers are not mentioned, as such, in the Acts, which is surprising in view of the vitally important role they play in granting entry clearances which operate as leave to enter,[5] and in determining in the country of origin whether someone is eligible for admission to the UK.[6] They may also issue certificates of entitlement for British citizens and other persons having the right of abode, and travel documents for refugees or stateless persons living in the UK. The same rules of fairness apply to entry clearance officers as apply to immigration officers[7] and likewise they are not to act in breach of a person's human rights.[8]

1   See *R v Secretary of State for the Home Department, ex p Phansopkar* [1976] QB 606, [1975] 3 All ER 497, CA. In many cases entry clearance officers refer applications back to London for decision. In some cases this is mandatory; in others optional.
2   The Foreign and Commonwealth Office website, www.fco.gov.uk, provides access to entry clearance posts, up-to-date information on fees and e-mail addresses of posts. The Joint Entry Clearance Unit is at 89 Albert Embankment, London SE1 7TP, tel 020 7238 3000, e-mail visas.foruk@jecu.mail.fco.gov.uk.
3   Immigration Act 1971, s 33(1); Immigration and Asylum Act 1999, s 167(2).
4   Immigration and Asylum Act 1999, s 59(2).
5   Immigration Act 1971, s 3A, inserted by Immigration and Asylum Act 1999, s 1; Immigration (Leave to Enter and Remain) Order 2000, SI 2000/1161, arts 2–4.
6   See *R v Secretary of State for the Home Department, ex p Ounejma* [1989] Imm AR 75, DC for the suggestion that they may be creatures of the prerogative.
7   *Kumar* [1985] Imm AR 242; *R v Secretary of State for the Home Department, ex p Moon* (1995) Times, 8 December, QBD.
8   Human Rights Act 1998, s 6. The provisions of ss 19B and 19D of the Race Relations Act 1976, as amended by the Race Relations (Amendment) Act 2000 also apply.

Airlines and other carriers

1.60   Airlines and other carriers which bring passengers to the UK have responsibilities for checking passengers' passports and visas and now perform public law duties and have public law powers in respect of immigration control beyond any rights and liabilities arising from the contract of carriage.[1] The Immigration Act 1971 and the Immigration and Asylum Act 1999 make special provision for them. First, they are generally expected to call or, in the case of trains, stop only at specified ports of entry or terminal control points.[2] There they are under a duty to co-operate with the immigration authorities in ensuring that passengers embark and disembark in designated controlled areas and observe the conditions and restrictions which apply.[3] During the journey they must supply passengers with landing or embarkation cards as required.[4] The captain of a ship or aircraft and the manager of a train arriving in the UK is required to stop passengers disembarking, except in accordance with the arrangements made for their examination by immigration officers,[5] and is required to furnish immigration officers with lists of passengers and crew members,[6] and with arrival times of ships, trains or aircraft expected to carry non-EEA nationals,[7] as required.

1   See generally 5 *Halsbury's Laws* (4th edn) para 301ff; Carriage by Air Act 1961.
2   Immigration Act 1971, Sch 2, para 26(1), modified in relation to Channel Tunnel trains by the Channel Tunnel (International Arrangements) Order 1993, SI 1993/1813, Sch 4 para 1(11)(r).
3   Immigration Act 1971, Sch 2, para 26(2), as modified for the Channel Tunnel by SI 1993/1813.
4   Immigration Act 1971, Sch 2, para 5, modified in relation to Channel Tunnel trains by SI 1993/1813, para 1(11)(g); Immigration (Landing and Embarkation Cards) Order 1972, SI 1972/1666, as amended by SI 1975/65.
5   Immigration Act 1971, Sch 2, para 27(1), modified in relation to Channel Tunnel trains by SI 1993/1813, para 1(11)(r).
6   Immigration Act 1971, paras 27(2) and 27B, inserted by Immigration and Asylum Act 1999, s 18, modified in relation to Channel Tunnel trains by SI 2000/913; Immigration (Particulars of Passengers and Crew) Order 1972, SI 1972/1667, as amended; Immigration (Passenger Information) Order 2000, SI 2000/912.
7   Immigration Act 1971, para 27C, inserted by Immigration and Asylum Act 1999, s 19, modified in relation to Channel Tunnel trains by SI 2000/913.

1.61   Carriers or their agents may be required to remove or make arrangements for the removal from the UK of any passengers who are refused leave to enter or are illegal entrants.[1] Normally the cost of removal will fall on the carrier, but in the case of passengers refused admission there is a two-month time limit for the giving of directions for their removal, after which the cost of removal falls on the Secretary of State for the Home Department.[2] Carriers are also liable to pay up to 14 days' detention costs for those refused leave to enter, illegal entrants and certain crew members who overstay their shore leave.[3] The costs of detaining illegal entrants by deception is not payable, however, unless their leave was cancelled within 24 hours of the conclusion of their examination.[4] In the case of deportees, the owners or agents of any ship, train or aircraft or the captain are required to comply with the directions given by the Secretary of State for the removal of the person from the UK.[5] The captain of a ship or aircraft, or a train manager, may also be required to prevent the escape of a person placed on board pending removal from the UK and has power to detain such person in custody for this purpose.[6] Breaches of their respective duties under the Immigration Act 1971 by either the owners, their agents or the captain or manager may make them liable to criminal penalties under section 27 of the 1971 Act.[7] If passengers arrive in the UK without proper documentation, the carrier may, in addition to the cost of removal and detention, be liable for a £2,000 penalty.[8] Carriers' liability is treated in detail in chapter 14 below.

1   Immigration Act 1971, Sch 2, paras 8–9, modified in relation to Channel Tunnel trains by SI 1993/1813, Sch 4, para 1(11)(h)–(l); see also *R v Immigration Officer, ex p Shah* [1982] 2 All ER 264, [1982] 1 WLR 544; *Parshotam Singh v Secretary of State for the Home Department* [1989] Imm AR 469, CA.
2   Immigration Act 1971, Sch 2, paras 8(2) and 10(3).
3   Immigration Act 1971, Sch 2, paras 19(1) and 20(1), as amended by Asylum and Immigration Act 1996, Sch 2, paras 8, 9, modified in relation to Channel Tunnel trains by SI 1993/1813, Sch 4, para 1(11)(q).

4   Immigration Act 1971, Sch 2, para 20(1A), inserted by Asylum and Immigration Act 1996, Sch 2, para 9(2).
5   Immigration Act 1971, Sch 3, para 1(1) and (2), modified in relation to Channel Tunnel trains by SI 1993/1813, Sch 4, para 1(12).
6   Immigration Act 1971, Sch 2, para 16(4) and Sch 3, para 1(3), modified in relation to Channel Tunnel trains by SI 1993/1813, Sch 4, para 1(11)(p), 1(12).
7   Modified in relation to Channel Tunnel trains by SI 1993/1813, Sch 4, para 1(9).
8   Immigration and Asylum Act 1999, s 40(2).

Marriage registrars

1.62   Section 24 of the Immigration and Asylum Act 1999 imposes a duty on registrars to whom notice of marriage has been given, and those who have attested a declaration accompanying the notice, to report to the Secretary of State for the Home Department any suspicion on reasonable grounds that the marriage is, or will be, a sham marriage. A 'sham marriage' is defined as one involving a non-EEA national, entered into for the purpose of avoiding the effect of a provision of UK immigration law or the Immigration Rules.[1] This definition is considered at **11.46** below. The registrars must report their suspicions without delay. They are given powers to require specified evidence from persons giving notice of marriage to them.[2]

1   Immigration and Asylum Act 1999, s 24(5).
2   Marriage Act 1949, ss 28A and equivalent in Ireland, inserted by Immigration and Asylum Act 1999, s 162.

Immigration advisers

Unqualified practitioners

1.63   The Immigration and Asylum Act 1999 makes provision for the regulation of immigration advisers and service providers. This follows widespread public concern at the incompetent and sometimes unscrupulous advisers who have been active in this field, taking advantage of the vulnerability and lack of proficiency in the English language of their clients. The scheme focuses on non-legally qualified advisers, but there is scope for control of professionally qualified practitioners, should the professional bodies fail. It is now unlawful for any person to provide immigration advice or services[1] unless he or she is (i) registered by the Immigration Services Commissioner or by an equivalent body in the EEA; (ii) authorised to practice by a designated professional body in the UK or the EEA; (iii) a Crown officer or employee of a government department acting in that capacity; (iv) exempt under the terms of the 1999 Act; or (v) works for or under the supervision of any of the above.[2] Voluntary bodies such as immigration aid units, and publicly funded bodies like CABx or the Refugee Legal Centre are exempt, but have to comply with the requirements of the scheme. The Commissioner has developed a Code of Standards and Guidance on Competences detailing the regulatory requirements for organisations seeking exemption.[3] Advisers charging for their services must register with the Commissioner, and will need to show that they are capable of complying with the Commissioner's Rules and Codes of Standards.[4] The fee for registration is £1,800 for a sole adviser and increases to £6,000 for a firm with 20 or more advisers.[5] All advisers applying for exemption or registration must complete a statement of competence.[6] Those authorised to practice by a designated professional body whose members are regulated by that body (eg the Bar Council or the Law Society)[7] do not need to apply for exemption or registration, and nor does anyone working under the supervision of such a person. Contravention of the prohibition on unqualified advice or services is an offence,[8] which we deal with in chapter 14 below.

1   As defined in Immigration and Asylum Act 1999, s 82.
2   Immigration and Asylum Act 1999, s 84.
3   Under the Immigration and Asylum Act 1999, Sch 5, para 3.
4   Immigration and Asylum Act 1999, Sch 5, paras 1–3.
5   Immigration Services Commissioner (Registration Fee) Order 2000, SI 2000/2735, arts 3, 4.
6   Letter from Office of Immigration Services Commissioner to ILPA, 30 January 2001.
7   Immigration and Asylum Act 1999, s 86.
8   Immigration and Asylum Act 1999, s 91.

1.64   The scheme covers the whole spectrum of immigration, nationality and asylum work in connection with the UK and the EEA, including appeals and judicial review. Criminal proceedings are not covered by the regulation,[1] but advice on unlawful entry is, and also bail applications in the context of immigration detention.[2] Advisers may have a full registration or one limiting them to one field, for example work permits, or to a specified category of client, for example Iraqi Kurds.[3] The regulation and registration of immigration advisers is the responsibility of the Immigration Services Commissioner.[4] An Immigration Services Tribunal, an independent body, with its own rules of procedure,[5] will hear disciplinary charges laid by the Commissioner and deal with appeals from the Commissioner's decisions, such as a refusal to register or to continue the registration of an adviser.[6] The Commissioner has a wide range of powers and responsibilities. First, he or she has a general duty to promote good practice, and will be concerned with the competence and scruples of advisers.[7] Secondly, he or she is in charge of the registration and exemption schemes and must keep and maintain registers of qualified advisers.[8] Thirdly, he or she may make rules to regulate the professional practice, conduct and discipline of immigration advisers,[9] and may prepare a Code of Standards for all immigration advisers, except members of the professional bodies.[10] The Commissioner must also establish a complaints system for the public.[11]

1   Immigration and Asylum Act 1999, s 82(1) under the definition of 'immigration advice'.
2   Immigration and Asylum Act 1999, s 82(1) under the definition of 'relevant matters'.
3   Immigration and Asylum Act 1999, Sch 6, para 2.
4   Immigration and Asylum Act 1999, s 83(1) and (2) and Sch 5, Pt II. The first Commissioner, John Scampion, was appointed in May 2000, and the prohibition on unregulated advice was due to come into force in April 2001.
5   Immigration and Asylum Act 1999, s 87(1) and Sch 7; Immigration Services Tribunal Rules 2000, SI 2000/2739.
6   Immigration and Asylum Act 1999, s 87(3) and (4).
7   Immigration and Asylum Act 1999, s 83(3) and (5).
8   Immigration and Asylum Act 1999, s 85 and Sch 6.
9   Immigration and Asylum Act 1999, Sch 5, paras 1 and 2. See **1.63** above.
10 Immigration and Asylum Act 1999, Sch 5, paras 3 and 4. The Commissioner has prepared two such Codes, one for those who are to register and the other for exempt organisations: see **1.63** above.
11 Immigration and Asylum Act 1999, Sch 5, paras 5–10.

Professionally qualified practitioners

1.65   Concern has also been voiced about members of the legal profession, both by the Lord Chancellor and the Legal Aid Board, the predecessor to the Legal Services Commission. In 1998 the Lord Chancellor's Advisory Committee on Legal Education and Conduct reported that immigration law was an area where solicitors and barristers lack both knowledge and expertise, involving as it did many non-traditional sources such as the quantity of administrative guidance, with some of which many practitioners were unfamiliar.[1] The Legal Aid Board went further, complaining of a significant increase in poor quality, ill-supervised and sometimes unnecessary work.[2] To meet the criticisms, there have been several reforms, including franchising and immigration contracts, which involve solicitors demonstrating compliance with key quality criteria; and the Law Society's setting up of a specialist panel of immigration practitioners who meet fairly rigorous criteria of competence and proper case management. So far as the Bar is concerned, the Bar Council has set up an accreditation scheme for barristers in the immigration, nationality and asylum fields.

1   Advisory Committee on Legal Education and Conduct, *Improving the quality of immigration advice and representation: A report* (July 1998).
2   Legal Aid Board (now Legal Services Commission) *Access to quality services in the immigration category* (May 1999).

Chapter 2

RIGHT OF ABODE AND CITIZENSHIP

INTRODUCTION

2.1 British citizenship now largely determines who obtains the right of abode in UK domestic law and who obtains the right of free movement and residence as a European citizen. However, the meaning of British citizen for the purpose of the right of abode and freedom from immigration control in the UK domestic context is different from the meaning of UK nationals for the purpose of free movement and residence under EC law. In this chapter we explain the link between British citizenship and the right of abode. The meaning of UK nationals in the EU is explained in chapter 7.

THE RIGHT OF ABODE

2.2 When British nationality was reorganised in 1948, possession of British citizenship gave an automatic right of abode to all British nationals, not just Citizens of the UK and Colonies (CUKCs). It was a common law concept. After Commonwealth immigration control was introduced in 1962, the right of abode became a status of enormous importance. Between 1962 and 1973, when the Immigration Act 1971 came into force, it remained a common law concept, subject to such derogations as were required by clear provisions of the Commonwealth Immigrants Act 1962.[1] After 1973 it took on a statutory form, and became quite separate from the broad concept of British nationality and the status of Commonwealth citizen which went with it. But the definition of persons who had a right of abode was still linked to one or more of the categories

37

of British subject. It is therefore necessary to look at the outlines of British nationality law.

1   *DPP v Bhagwan* [1972] AC 60.

2.3 Under the Immigration Act 1971, section 1(1) it is provided that all those who are expressed to have the right of abode in the UK shall be free to live in, and to come and go into and from, the UK without let or hindrance except such as may be required by the Act to enable their right to be established or as may be otherwise lawfully imposed on any person. For example, they may be asked to produce their passports on entry,[1] and they may be refused entry if they do not have the requisite passport or certificate to prove their entitlement. Under section 3(9) of the 1971 Act they must have either:

(a)   a UK passport describing them as a British citizen or as a CUKC having the right of abode; or

(b)   a certificate of entitlement certifying that they have such a right.[2]

There are two groups of people who have a right of abode:

(1)   British citizens;[3] and

(2)   Commonwealth citizens who for the purpose of the Immigration Act 1971 are treated as British citizens.

By virtue of the right of abode, all these people are free from immigration control and cannot be deported.[4] The possession of British citizenship confers a status on the holder, and normally it can only be acquired by a strict application of nationality law or the exercise of a discretion under it by a minister or governor. This means that there is normally no room for the grant of citizenship by a representation from an immigration official or member of the staff at a High Commission or consulate that a person is entitled to it, unless possibly that person is acting on behalf of a minister or governor who has authority to grant citizenship.[5]

1   Immigration Act 1971, s 1(1) and Sch 2, paras 2 and 3.
2   A 'Confirmation of Right of Abode' document was issued between 1 January 1983 and 1 August 1988 to those entitled to the right of abode under s 2(1)(a) and (b) of the Immigration Act 1971 as originally in force. Although it is no longer issued it remains valid with the validity of the passport to which it is attached. If someone with a Confirmation of Right of Abode obtains a new passport he or she will be issued with a certificate of entitlement: IDI Nov/00, Ch 1, s 1, Annex A, para 5.1.
3   These include dual nationals, who may be travelling on the passport of another country.
4   Immigration Act 1971, ss 2, 3(1) and (6).
5   *Christodoulidou* [1985] Imm AR 179; *Gowa v A-G* (1984) 129 Sol Jo 131,CA, upheld in HL on different grounds: [1985] 1 WLR 1003.

2.4 The right of abode must be distinguished from: (1) rights of free movement within the common travel area comprising the UK, Channel Islands, Isle of Man and the Republic of Ireland; (2) exemptions from immigration control conferred on diplomats and others; (3) EC rights of free movement and residence; and (4) settlement or indefinite leave to remain granted to persons who are subject to immigration control and do not have the right of abode. The distinctions are to some extent technical and artificial, but behind them lies the difference between different degrees of immigration control and coming or going without let or hindrance.

2.5 What has to be understood is that essentially the right of abode stems from citizenship and is an automatic benefit of it, whereas the other rights (common travel, free movement, exemption, settlement) flow from separate quite specific provisions of the Immigration Act 1971. Only EC law is comparable. Since 1993 the right of free movement and residence within Europe is for the first time tied to citizenship, and a fledgling European right of abode is discernible. Who benefits from the right of abode under UK law cannot be understood until we have dealt with the main provisions of citizenship and nationality law.

Right of Abode and the ECHR

2.6 Protocol 4 of the ECHR contains provisions which give the nationals of signatory states rights which are akin to the right of abode in UK domestic law. First, it provides that no-one shall be deprived of the right to enter the territory of the state of which he or she is a national.[1] Secondly, no-one shall be expelled, by means of a collective or individual measure, from the territory of the state of which he or she is a national.[2] Thirdly, once lawfully in the country, everyone (not just nationals) has a right to move freely throughout the territory, to choose a residence and to leave the country,[3] subject to such restrictions as are in accordance with the law and are necessary in a democratic society in the interests of national security or public safety, for the maintenance of public order, the prevention of crime, the protection of health and morals or for the protection of the rights and freedoms of others.[4] However, as we shall see, the right of abode in UK domestic law is not conferred on all British nationals and so there are important groups of British nationals, who do not enjoy its benefits. Protocol 4 would give them a broadly equivalent right, which is the principal reason why it has not been ratified so far by the British government.[5] Notwithstanding this, the principles of the Protocol may still have consequences for UK immigration law. First, the wording of Article 3(2) 'no-one shall *be deprived of* the right to enter . . .' (our emphasis) is posited on the existence of a right of entry of nationals.[6] This reflects the position in international human rights law, under which there is a duty on a state to admit its own nationals.[7] This right has in fact been relied on by the British government in arguing (unsuccessfully) against the application of EC law to the return to the UK of a British national who has gone to another member state of the EU in the exercise of her free movement rights.[8] Secondly, notwithstanding the non-ratification of Protocol 4 by the UK, the ECHR and all the human rights contained in it (including the Protocols) are part of the *corpus* and general principles of EC law,[9] and may therefore be used in the construction of EC law. In the referred application of *Manjit Kaur* it was argued that Article 3(2) of Protocol 4 could and should be used as an aid to the construction of Article 8 of EC Treaty (now after amendment Article 17 EC), so as to entitle a British Overseas citizen to enter and remain in the UK. This question was not dealt with in the judgment of the court.[10]

1   ECHR, Protocol 4, Art 3(2).
2   ECHR, Protocol 4, Art 3(1).
3   ECHR, Protocol 4, Art 2(1) and (2).
4   ECHR, Protocol 4, Art 2(3).
5   See Laurie Fransman 'Human Rights and British Nationality' in Butterworth's *A Guide to the Human Rights Act 1998* (1999) pp 134ff.
6   See *East African Asians v UK* (1973) 3 EHRR 76, para 242, per Professor JES Fawcett.
7   See eg the UN International Covenant on Civil and Political Rights, 1966 art 12(4) which provides that no one shall be arbitrarily deprived of the right to enter his own country. For

texts see Brownlie *Basic Documents on Human Rights* (3rd edn, 1992) Clarendon pp 125 and 144. See further Universal Declaration of Human Rights, Art 13(2), Brownlie p 24; Fransman fn 5 above, para 3.1.
8 *Surinder Singh* [1992] Imm AR 565, ECJ, at 22, quoted in Fransman above.
9 EU Treaty, art 6 (ex art F.1); *Elliniki Radiophonia Tiléorassi AE v Pliroforissis and Kouvelas* [1994] ECR I-2951 ECJ; *B v Secretary of State for the Home Department* [2000] Imm AR 478, paras 13–14.
10 Case C-192/99: *R v Secretary of State for the Home Department, ex p Manjit Kaur* [2001] All ER (EC) 250, ECJ.

2.7 Other possible areas in which the ECHR may be engaged in is in respect of the refusal to grant discretionary registration or to naturalise someone as a British citizen where, on the face of it, the Secretary of State for the Home Department is not required to give reasons and there is no right of appeal.[1] We deal with this at **2.60** below.

1 British Nationality Act 1981, s 44(2).

Restrictions on the right of abode

2.8 The statutory definition of the right of abode refers to 'let or hindrance' which may be lawfully imposed on any person. The extent of this exception is unclear and untested, but is thought to refer to five restrictions:

(i)   lawful imprisonment and other restrictions (eg bail conditions restricting residence) imposed by criminal courts in the exercise of their normal jurisdiction;[1]

(ii) lawful detention and other restrictions imposed under other statutory powers, for example, under the Mental Health Act 1983;

(iii) restrictions lawfully imposed on the movement of children by an order of a court in matrimonial, wardship and Children Act 1989 proceedings;[2]

(iv) restraints imposed by the issue of a writ '*ne exeat regno*', restraining the subject from leaving the kingdom, now largely superseded by injunction;[3]

(v)   restrictions, other than normal bail conditions, requiring surrender of a passport and a ban on foreign travel. This concerns measures taken, for example to deal with football hooliganism.

1 See *R v Saunders*: Case 175/78 [1979] 2 All ER 267 at 275, ECJ where a similar exemption with regard to EC free movement provisions is discussed. Any loss of liberty must also be justifiable under ECHR, art 5.
2 See *Re Mohamed Arif (an infant)* [1968] Ch 643, [1968] 2 All ER 145, CA.
3 For discussion of the writ '*Ne exeat regno*' see the previous edition of this work at 6.6.

2.9 An example of lawful restrictions which may be imposed on the right of abode is contained in the Football Spectators Act 1989. Under this Act a person who has been convicted of a football related offence may be required to report to a police station on the occasion of a football match. The Football Offences and Disorder Act 1999 allowed for the granting of international banning orders by imposing a requirement to report to a police station when England or Wales or a League club was playing abroad or a non-League club was playing in a UEFA competition. The Football Disorder Act 2000 goes considerably further. There is no longer a requirement for a person to have been convicted before a banning order is imposed. It also enacts that everyone subject to a banning order must surrender their passport, unless there are 'exceptional circumstances'. Banning orders can now be made on a complaint 'where there are reasonable grounds for believing that a banning order would help prevent violence or disorder at or in connection with certain association football matches'. The police have power to prevent people from leaving the country where there are grounds for believing that the person has previously caused or contributed to any violence or disorder, or if the person's behaviour suggests that inquiries should be made to check whether or not there is evidence to that effect.[1]

1   Both the Football Offences and Disorder Act 1999 and the Football Disorder Act 2000 consist entirely of amendments to the Football Spectators Act 1989. The 1999 Act changes have now been entirely superseded by the 2000 Act, which inserted new ss 14A-H into the 1989 Act. These are printed and commented upon in Archbold *Criminal Pleading Evidence and Practice* (2001) Sweet & Maxwell, paras 5–538ff.

The right of abode 1973 to 1983

2.10   Prior to 1 January 1983 the statutory right of abode depended on whether or not a person was 'patrial' as defined in the Immigration Act 1971, section 2. Since that date (when the British Nationality Act 1981 came into force) it depends on the definition of 'British citizen' set out in the new section 2. Under pre-1983 law, patriality was conferred on certain citizens of the UK and Colonies (CUKCs) and certain other Commonwealth citizens. The British Nationality Act 1981 redefined citizenship and divided up former CUKCs into three new categories of citizenship and, as a result, changed the definition of those who have the right of abode. Under the Immigration Act 1971, before amendment, the following (broadly speaking) were patrials:

(i)   CUKCs by birth, adoption, naturalisation or registration in the UK;[1]
(ii)   CUKCs with similar connections to the UK through a parent or grandparent;[2]
(iii)   CUKCs who had been ordinarily resident in the UK for five years;[3]
(iv)   Commonwealth citizens with a parent born in the UK;[4]
(v)   Commonwealth women who become patrial through marriage.[5]

1   Immigration Act 1971, old s 2(1)(a).
2   Immigration Act 1971, old s 2(1)(b).
3   Immigration Act 1971, old s 2(1)(c).
4   Immigration Act 1971, old s 2(1)(d).
5   Immigration Act 1971, old s 2(2).

RIGHT OF ABODE AFTER BRITISH NATIONALITY ACT 1981

2.11   Under the new provisions of the British Nationality Act 1981 the old category of 'patrials' was swept away. The old section 2 was entirely replaced by a new section 2.[1] Those who have the right of abode are defined in terms of British citizenship. But this has been given a special extended meaning for the purpose of the Immigration Act 1971. 'British citizens' has one meaning for nationality purposes (getting a passport and EU citizenship) and a somewhat different meaning in the amended section 2 of the 1971 Act, which preserves the right of abode for those Commonwealth citizens who were not CUKCs but had the status of 'patrial'. They are classed as 'British citizens' for immigration control purposes under the amended section 2. They consist mainly of those who were previously patrial under the old section 2(1)(d) of the Immigration Act 1971 because one of their parents was born in the UK.

1   British Nationality Act 1981, s 39.

2.12 Those who have the right of abode under the post-1983 definition of British citizenship are:

(i)   British citizens. These will include all the old CUKCs who prior to commencement were 'patrials', ie CUKCs born, adopted, registered or naturalised in the UK, those with the necessary ancestral connections with the UK, and those who were ordinarily resident here for five years free of immigration restrictions;

(ii)   Commonwealth citizens who immediately before commencement had the right of abode by virtue of having a parent who was born in the UK under the old section 2(1)(d) of the Immigration Act 1971; and

(iii)   Commonwealth women who immediately before commencement had a right of abode by virtue of their marriage to a patrial under the old section 2(2) of the 1971 Act.

Since only CUKCs who became British citizens obtained an automatic right of abode under the British Nationality Act 1981, this meant that resident CUKCs who were free from immigration conditions and who would previously have expected to become patrial after five years ordinary residence in the UK[1] lost out. If they merely became British Dependent Territories citizens or British Overseas citizens, they lost the chance to acquire the right of abode after five years' ordinary residence. Instead, they have to take up their entitlement to register under section 4 of the British Nationality Act 1981. This applies to any British Dependent Territories citizens, British National (Overseas) citizens, British Overseas citizens, British subjects under the Act, and British Protected Persons who have spent the last five years in the UK (without absence for more than 450 days during the whole period and 90 days in the final 12 months), have had indefinite leave for at least the last 12 months and have not been in breach of the immigration laws during the five-year period.[2] This way of acquiring the right of abode will be available to all those categories of British nationals (not British citizens) and British Protected Persons, who are freely admitted under paragraphs 16 and 17 of HC 395, and to British Overseas citizens who qualify for entry under the voucher system,[3] once they have completed the necessary period of stay in the UK and satisfy the other requirements of section 4. However, British Dependent Territories citizens from Gibraltar and the Falkland Islands were granted privileged access to British citizenship,[4] and it is proposed to extend British citizenship to the remaining British Dependent Territories citizens. In the White Paper *Partnership for Progress and Prosperity – Britain and the Overseas Territories*[5] the government states: 'We have decided that British citizenship – and so the right of abode – should be offered to those BDTCs who do not already enjoy it and who want to take it up.'[6]

1   Immigration Act 1971, s 2(1)(c), before amendment.
2   See British Nationality Act 1981, s 4.
3   HC 395, paras 249–250.
4   British Nationality Act 1981, s 5 (Gibraltar); British Nationality (Falkland Islands) Act 1983 (Falkland Islands).
5   Cm 4264, March 1999.
6   Cm 4264, para 3.7.

2.13 The second main change made by the British Nationality Act 1981 was that Commonwealth women no longer automatically obtained a right of abode by marriage to British men. Since 1 January 1983 they can only acquire a right of abode if they are naturalised as British citizens under section 6 of the 1981 Act. The effect of this change was that many wives who were previously entitled to join their husband in the UK without let or hindrance[1] have had to join the queue of wives and obtain entry clearance.[2] However, those who previously had the right of abode did not lose it. But they will need to have the requisite UK passport or a certificate of entitlement before travelling to the UK.[3] The third main change is that Commonwealth citizens born after commencement of the 1981 Act will not obtain a right of abode by virtue of having a parent born in the UK, as used to happen under the old section 2(1)(d) of the Immigration Act 1971, as originally in force. Commonwealth citizens born after commencement of the 1981 Act will only obtain a right of abode if they acquire British citizenship by descent. Under section 2(1) of the 1981 Act, this can now be inherited from either the mother or the father (or the mother alone in the case of illegitimate children).[4] In practice the change will make no difference, because the widening of the rules under which a person may have citizenship by descent creates a right exactly similar to that contained in the old section 2(1)(d) of the 1971 Act. Fourthly, it should be noted that Commonwealth citizens born before 1 January 1983 (the commencement date of the 1981 Act) who were patrial do not lose this status, provided they have not ceased to be Commonwealth citizens in the meanwhile.[5] Commonwealth citizens who were not patrial were able to register as CUKCs after five years' ordinary residence under section 5A(1) of the British Nationality Act 1948, and these persons were able to register as a British citizen under this entitlement until 1988.[6]

1   See *R v Secretary of State for the Home Department, ex p Phansopkar* [1976] QB 606, [1975] 3 All ER 497, CA.
2   See *Brahmbhatt v Chief Immigration Officer, Heathrow* [1984] Imm AR 202, CA. See also *R v Secretary of State for the Home Department, ex p Ali* (1987) Times, 17 January, QBD; *R v Secretary of State for the Home Department, ex p Kaur* [1987] Imm AR 278, QBD.
3   Immigration Act 1971, s 3(9) as amended, and s 33, as amended.
4   British Nationality Act 1948, s 50(9), although see **2.37** below for discretionary policy.
5   Immigration Act 1971, s 2(1)(b), as amended.
6   British Nationality Act 1981, s 7(1).

2.14 Being a patrial meant having a claim to a right which could only be rejected if it was ill-founded in fact or in law.[1] Claiming patriality was one thing. Proving it was another. The same is now true of British citizenship. Under section 3(8) of the Immigration Act 1971 it is provided that when any question arises under the Immigration Acts whether or not a person is a British citizen, it lies on the person asserting the claim to prove it. This will arise when people apply for a passport on a certificate of entitlement or pass through immigration control in the course of their travel. Section 3(9) makes provision for the means of proof for someone seeking to enter the UK and claiming a right of abode. Proof is provided by the production of a UK passport describing the person as a British citizen or as a CUKC having the right of abode, or of a certificate of entitlement. The reference to a UK passport means a full passport, not a British visitor's passport, which is insufficient.[2] The passport must be a current one.[3]

1   *R v Secretary of State for the Home Department, ex p Phansopkar* [1976] QB 606, [1975] 3 All ER 497, CA.
2   *Minta v Secretary of State for the Home Department* [1992] Imm AR 380, CA.
3   Immigration Act 1971, s 33(1); see *Akewushola v Immigration Officer* [1999] INLR 433, CA. For the effect of production of the required passport see **2.55** below.

2.15 In most cases proving a right of abode is not a problem and involves collecting the necessary birth, marriage or death certificates and applying for a passport or a certificate of entitlement. The problem areas arise where:

(i) persons cannot prove an essential ingredient of the claim to British citizenship, such as their place of birth, their parent's nationality at the relevant time, or that a birth certificate relates to them;

(ii) the Home Office or immigration officer disputes the validity of an existing full UK passport or certificate of entitlement.

In the first situation the burden remains throughout on the applicant.[1] In the second case the burden of proving any alleged fraud or deception will be on the Home Office or immigration officer, and since the allegation involves fraud or deception, proof will need to be by a preponderance of probability.[2]

1 *Re Bamgbose* [1990] Imm AR 135, CA; *Mokuolo v Secretary of State for the Home Department* [1989] Imm AR 51, CA.
2 *R v Secretary of State for the Home Department, ex p Obi* [1997] Imm AR 420; *Khawaja v Secretary of State for the Home Department* [1984] AC 74, [1983] 1 All ER 765, HL. See 2.55 below.

2.16 Although the right of abode has become a concept distinct from that of British nationality, the definition is still linked to one or more of the categories of British nationality. It is therefore necessary to look at the outlines of British nationality law.[1]

1 We do so only to identify the right of abode. Anyone wishing to deal with the wider issues of nationality should consult Fransman's *British Nationality Law*, (2nd edn, 1998) Butterworths.

SOME GENERAL PRINCIPLES OF BRITISH NATIONALITY LAW

2.17 Before the 1948 Act, the status of British subject belonged to all those who owed allegiance to the Crown in whichever Crown territory they were born. A subsidiary category was the status of British Protected Person, that is to say people who had placed themselves under the protection of the British Crown without becoming the subject of the Sovereign. Unlike British subjects, their position was regulated by prerogative rather than common law. With the break up of the British empire and the creation of separate citizenships in the self-governing dominions, it was thought necessary to devise citizenship laws which were appropriate to a number of self-governing units within a unified Commonwealth. The principle of separate citizenships for each of the self-governing units was expressly recognised, but at the same time the universal status of 'British subject' or 'Commonwealth citizen' was retained. For our purposes, the point about having the status of British subject or Commonwealth citizen (the two terms then had the same meaning)[1] was that it gave an unqualified common law right of abode to such persons in the UK.[2] Aliens alone were subject to immigration control.

1 British Nationality Act 1948, s 1(2). See now British Nationality Act 1981, s 37.
2 *DPP v Bhagwan* [1972] AC 60, [1970] 3 All ER 97, HL.

2.18 Although entry to the UK for British subjects was unrestricted, this did not mean that the same thing applied to independent Commonwealth countries or to colonial territories. The opposite was the case, and had been so for many years. In fact the mechanisms of immigration control introduced for the UK in 1962 had been tried and tested many years earlier in the dominion territories in attempts to keep out Chinese, Japanese and Indian migrants.[1] But in 1948 the status of British subject or Commonwealth citizen gave an unrestricted right of entry to the UK. When immigration controls were later imposed by the Commonwealth Immigrants Act 1962 and its amending Act of 1968,[2] the method used was to make subdivisions within the three main categories of Commonwealth citizen:

- CUKCs
- citizens of independent Commonwealth countries
- British subjects without citizenship.

Initially, under the 1962 Act the dividing line between a continuing right of abode and being subject to immigration control depended on the place of issue of the person's British passport. Under the 1968 Act, the need for an ancestral connection to the UK was introduced. By the time of the Immigration Act 1971, ancestral connection to the UK was the principal distinction between 'patrials' and 'non-patrials'. Patrials had a right of abode; non-patrials were subject to control. Possession of British nationality no longer qualified British subjects for a right of abode in their country of nationality. The British Nationality Act 1981 formally reconnects the right of abode to British citizenship; but it only does so by creating a hierarchy of different British nationalities. British citizens are in the premier league and get all the benefits of free movement, but other categories of British nationals still exist and languish in the lower leagues, all of which hold out some slim hopes of promotion and are all subject to immigration control.[3]

1   See the third edition of this work, pp 12–15.
2   Commonwealth Immigrants Act 1968.
3   For the promise of British citizenship to former CUKCs who became BDTCs see **2.12** above.

2.19 Throughout the period from 1948 to 1971 all classes of British subject were to be distinguished from: (i) Irish citizens; (ii) aliens, ie all foreigners other than Irish citizens, and (iii) British Protected Persons. So far as aliens and British Protected Persons are concerned, they never became 'patrial' under the Immigration Act 1971 unless they had dual nationality[1] or acquired the status of CUKC through marriage or naturalisation. Some Irish citizens were Commonwealth citizens and could therefore be patrial, though this was really an unimportant category because Ireland was part of the common travel area and later a member state of the EEC. The right of abode of an Irish citizen, therefore, usually only arose when there was an issue of deportation.

1   The status of British Protected Person was not inconsistent with that of CUKC and so a person could be both CUKC and British Protected Person – a sort of domestic dual nationality: *Motala v A-G* [1992] 1 AC 281, [1992] Imm AR 112, HL, overruling CA [1991] 2 All ER 312 at 315.

Dual nationality

2.20 Some countries forbid their citizens to have dual nationality, but this is not the case in the UK. So the fact that a person has another nationality, and travels under another country's passport, does not mean that he or she is not a CUKC or, under the British Nationality Act 1981, a British citizen. For example, there are large numbers of persons living in Malaysia and Singapore who are citizens of those countries and British Overseas citizens at the same time. Indeed, the 1981 Act quite clearly confers dual nationality on possibly quite large numbers of persons. For example, as we shall see, CUKCs who were patrial through five years' residence in the UK became British citizens on commencement, but may have become, by virtue of their connection to a dependent territory, British Dependent Territories citizens as well or, in other cases, British Overseas citizens.[1] Under the pre-1983 patriality provisions of the Immigration Act 1971, one category of patrial citizens was Commonwealth citizens with a parent born in the UK.[2] This provision was intended for holders of Australian, New Zealand, and other 'old' Commonwealth passports, but in fact if their fathers were born in the UK they had dual nationality – Australian or New Zealand by birth and CUKC by descent through their father. Under the 1981 Act, British citizenship can descend through the mother as well as the father and this will create large numbers of Commonwealth citizens who have dual nationality.

1   This sort of domestic double nationality was expressly approved of by the House of Lords in *Motala v A-G* [1992] 1 AC 281, [1992] Imm AR 112, HL; see further *Patel v Secretary of State for the Home Department* [1993] Imm AR 509, CA. In both these cases it was held that a British Protected person could simultaneously be a CUKC.
2   Immigration Act 1971, s 2(1)(d).

CITIZENSHIP UNDER BRITISH NATIONALITY ACT 1948

2.21 In order to understand the concept and status of 'British citizen', which is the term used in the Immigration Act 1971, as amended by the British Nationality Act 1981, to separate those who have a right of abode from those who are subject to immigration control, it is necessary to go back to the three main classifications of British national used in the British Nationality Act 1948. But beware! In this part of this chapter we set out what is at best a very brief summary. For fuller treatment it is essential to refer to a specialist textbook on British nationality law.[1]

1   Fransman *British Nationality Law* (Butterworths, 2nd edn, 1998) which contains a full account and texts of the relevant provisions of every Commonwealth country as well as the UK.

Citizens of Commonwealth countries

2.22 Each independent Commonwealth country has its own citizenship laws which determine who are citizens of that country. Once a country achieves political independence with its own constitution and laws, the determination of its citizenship is no longer a matter for UK law[1] or the UK Parliament. All UK law determines is that for the purposes of UK law citizens of independent Commonwealth countries are Commonwealth citizens. Nothing more. To find out whether someone is or becomes a citizen of an independent Commonwealth country it is always necessary to look at that country's own citizenship laws. Depending upon the answer to that question, UK nationality law may have something to say about that person's status, for example, whether they remain British citizens or not.

1   See *Oppenheimer v Cattermole* [1976] AC 249, [1975] 1 All ER 538, HL. Although the question of whether a person is a citizen of a Commonwealth country is under English private international law a matter for the law of that country, one English court has determined that question as one of purely domestic English law when it affects a claim to British citizenship, even though it reached a conclusion different from that of the governing authorities of the country concerned: *Bibi v Secretary of State for the Home Department* [1987] Imm AR 340, CA.

2.23   The difficulties do not arise so much with regard to persons born in a Commonwealth country after independence,[1] but with those born before independence and living there or in the UK at the time of independence. CUKCs who acquired their citizenship through connection with a colony may have lost that citizenship when the colony became independent. This often happened through the operation of statute, without the person realising it. A person from Grenada or St Lucia might have been patrial one day and have ceased to be so on the next day following independence. In all cases where there is a history of this kind it is necessary to examine the particular statute that granted independence and the new citizenship laws of the newly independent country, in order to find out who lost and who retained their status as a CUKC.[2] On decolonisation the usual provision was that any persons who acquired citizenship of the new Commonwealth country lost their former citizenship of the UK and colonies, unless they had a parent or grandparent who was born in the UK or in a country which remained a colony at that time. But the formulations differed from country to country. In order to discover whether a person acquired citizenship of the new country, it is always necessary to examine the constitution or citizenship laws of the new country. In East Africa, some CUKCs were specifically permitted to retain their UK citizenship.[3] At the time of decolonisation, these CUKCs were free from immigration control, although they continued to live in East Africa. In 1968, however, they became subject to immigration control under the Commonwealth Immigrants Act 1968. So when living in East Africa was made difficult or they were expelled, they had nowhere to go. This is the source of what was referred to as the 'problem' of the East African Asians.[4]

1   Although there is always a question of whether such persons are British citizens or some other citizen by descent.
2   See Fransman *British Nationality Law* (Butterworths, 2nd edn, 1998) where all the independence statutes and Commonwealth citizenship laws are gathered.
3   For the position in Kenya see *AA Mohammed* [1979–80] Imm AR 103.
4   See *East African Asians v UK* (1973) 3 EHRR 76.

Citizens of the UK and Colonies (CUKCs)

Birth

2.24   Under the British Nationality Act 1948 a person born in the UK and Colonies after commencement (1 January 1949) became a CUKC by birth, unless the person's father was a foreign diplomat or an enemy alien and the birth occurred in enemy-occupied territory.[1] Thus those born in the Channel Islands of a German father during the 1939–45 war would not be CUKCs; similarly, babies fathered by Argentinian nationals and born in the Falkland Islands during the Argentinian occupation. But these cases are very much the exception.

1   British Nationality Act 1948, s 14.

Adoption

2.25 Adopted children could also acquire citizenship. In England and Wales the Adoption Acts of 1949 and 1976 and in Scotland the Adoption (Scotland) Act 1978 provided that a child adopted in the UK by a CUKC became a CUKC, if not already one, from the date of the adoption order. In the case of a joint adoption, where the adopting parents had different nationalities, the child only became a CUKC if that was the male adopter's nationality. An adoption outside the UK did not, and still does not, confer the British nationality of the adoptive parent.[1]

1   *R v Secretary of State for the Home Department, ex p Brassey and Brassey* [1989] FCR 423, [1989] Imm AR 258, DC.

Descent

2.26 Citizenship by birth in the UK or colonies was the most common method of acquiring the status of CUKC. This was citizenship by *jus soli* (country of birth). But English law also recognises the *jus sanguinis* (citizenship by descent).[1] Persons born outside British territory could therefore be CUKCs by descent if their father was such a citizen[2] at the time of the person's birth.[3] This applied in general to persons born before and after 1948.[4] However, for persons born since 1948 the right to become a CUKC by descent was limited where the person's father himself acquired this citizenship by descent.[5]

1   See British Nationality Bill 1948 (Cm 7326) p 9.
2   British Nationality Act 1948, s 5(1).
3   *R v Immigration Appeal Tribunal, ex p Uddin* [1989] Imm AR 391, QBD.
4   British Nationality Act 1948, s 12(2).
5   For exceptions, such as registration at a British consulate, see British Nationality Act 1948, s 5(1)(a)–(d) and (2).

2.27 Citizenship by descent could only be acquired through the father under the British Nationality Act 1948, never through the mother, and never if the child was born illegitimate. An illegitimate child was not considered to be the child of its father for nationality purposes unless legitimated by the subsequent marriage of its parents.[1] A legitimate child born after the death of his or her father would acquire the status of the father at the time of the father's death.[2]

1   British Nationality Act 1948, ss 32(2) and 23.
2   British Nationality Act 1948, s 24.

Registration

2.28 An important method of acquiring the status of CUKC after 1948 was by registration. In some cases it was a right; in others it was within the Secretary of State's discretion. Registration was only open to Commonwealth citizens, citizens of the Republic of Ireland, their children, and to women, alien or Commonwealth, who married CUKCs. Registration could be completed in the UK or outside. In the UK it was done by the Secretary of State, in the Colonies usually by the Governor and in Commonwealth countries by the British High Commissioner.[1] With the coming into force of successive Immigration Acts between 1962 and 1973 the right of Commonwealth citizens to register was much changed from the originally enacted position in 1948.[2] For women married to CUKCs the right was almost an absolute one, unless they had gained the right to registration by fraudulent or other criminal means.[3]

1 British Nationality Act 1948, s 8.
2 See previous edition **6.21–6.23.**
3 British Nationality Act 1948, s6 and see *R v Secretary of State for the Home Department, ex p Puttick* [1981] QB 767, [1981] 1 All ER 776.

Naturalisation

2.29 Naturalisation was the mechanism under the British Nationality Act 1948 by which aliens and British Protected Persons could become CUKCs, although the residence requirements differed.[1] The grant was a matter of discretion. Decisions were unappealable and section 26 of the 1948 Act provided that no reasons need be given and the decision was not reviewable in any court. The same ouster clause was inserted in the British Nationality Act 1981,[2] which we examine at **2.51** below.

1 British Nationality Act 1948, s 10 and Sch 2 as amended by Commonwealth Immigrants Act 1962, s 20(2).
2 British Nationality Act 1981, s 44(2).

Loss of citizenship of the UK and Colonies

2.30 The status of CUKC, as we have seen, could be acquired in a number of ways. It could also be lost. This happened in three ways. The first was the most common:

(i)   CUKCs connected with a Crown colony could lose their citizenship when the colony became independent;[1]

(ii)   Persons having dual nationality or acquiring a new nationality could lose their UK citizenship by making a declaration of renunciation;[2]

(iii)   CUKCs could be deprived of their UK citizenship by the Secretary of State for the Home Department if they had acquired it by registration or naturalisation.[3]

1 See *Motala v A-G* [1992] 1 AC 281, [1992] Imm AR 112, HL; *Patel v Secretary of State for the Home Department* [1993] Imm AR 508, CA; *R v Secretary of State for Foreign and Commonwealth Affairs Department, ex p Shah* [1993] Imm AR 261, QBD; *Patel* [1988] Imm AR 521, Immigration Appeal Tribunal; *Liew* [1989] Imm AR 62, Immigration Appeal Tribunal.
2 British Nationality Act 1948, s 19.
3 British Nationality Act 1948, s 20, which conferred a right to a hearing before an independent tribunal. A naturalisation or registration could be of no effect and s 20 would not come into play if the applicant could not prove that he was the person named in the certificate: *R v Secretary of State for the Home Department, ex p Parvaz Akhtar* [1981] QB 46, [1980] 2 All ER 735.

Resumption of citizenship

2.31 Resumption of citizenship following renunciation was governed by section 1(1) of the British Nationality Act 1964. A person who was obliged to renounce their CUKC status in order to avoid being deprived of another citizenship (a circumstance which arose when a number of Commonwealth countries became independent) and had a qualifying connection with the UK and colonies or a protectorate or protected state or, if a woman, had been married to such a person, was able to apply for registration.

British subject without citizenship

2.32 The British Nationality Acts 1948 and 1965 created a number of residual categories of British subject. These were people who were neither citizens of independent Commonwealth countries nor CUKCs.[1] They were:

(a)   British subjects without citizenship, who consisted of:
  (i)   persons who were regarded by the British Nationality Act 1948 as potential citizens of an independent Commonwealth country, but who did not become citizens of that country when they passed citizenship laws;[2] and
  (ii)   persons who are declared to be British subjects without citizenship. They are persons who before 1 January 1949 ceased, on the loss of British nationality by a parent, to be a British subject and, but for this, would have become British subjects without citizenship;[3]
(b)   married women who registered as British subjects under the 1965 Act.[4] These are alien women who married a man who was within one or other of the residual categories of British subject;
(c)   Irish citizens born before 1949 who were also British subjects and remained such if they wrote to the Home Secretary and claimed to remain such.[5]

The British Nationality Act 1981 continues these categories of citizenship and refers to them as British subjects under the Act.[6] Under both the 1948 and 1981 Acts, they are Commonwealth citizens.[7] Clearly they are a diminishing group, who now lose their British subject status if they acquire any other citizenship or nationality in whatever circumstances.[8]

1   See Ann Dummett *Citizenship and Nationality* (1976) Runnymede Trust, p 23.
2   British Nationality Act 1948, s 13. Such persons did not become CUKCs under s 13(2) of the 1948 Act as might have been supposed because of the definition of citizenship law in s 32(8) of that Act.
3   British Nationality Act 1948, s 16.
4   British Nationality Act 1965, s 1.
5   British Nationality Act 1948, s 2.
6   British Nationality Act 1981, ss 30 and 31.
7   British Nationality Act 1948, s 1(2) and British Nationality Act 1981, s 37(1)(a).
8   British Nationality Act 1981, s 35

BRITISH NATIONALITY ACT 1981

2.33 The British Nationality Act 1981 recast British citizenship and replaced the existing definition of patriality by an entirely new section 2 of the Immigration Act 1971. This defined the right of abode in terms of the new categories of citizenship. The right of abode and British citizenship are to be more or less equated. To understand who gets the right of abode it is therefore necessary to know what became of CUKCs and who become British citizens. The 1981 Act divided CUKCs into three new citizenships:[1]

- British citizens
- British Dependent Territories citizens
- British Overseas citizens.

The Hong Kong (British Nationality) Order 1986[2] added another citizenship: that of British National (Overseas). Other categories of Commonwealth citizens are virtually unaltered. Irish citizens who are British subjects and British subjects without citizenship are referred to as British subjects under the Act. The overall category of 'Commonwealth citizen' is retained. So under the 1981 Act Commonwealth citizens comprise:[3]

- British citizens
- British Dependent Territory citizens
- British Overseas citizens
- British subjects under the Act
- Citizens of independent Commonwealth countries.

1 British Nationality Act 1981, s 51(3).
2 SI 1986/948, in force 1 July 1987.
3 British Nationality Act 1981, ss 37, 51.

2.34 British Protected Persons are not Commonwealth citizens,[1] but are also excluded from the definition of aliens.[2] Traditionally they were excluded from being classed as British nationals in domestic law[3] or being treated as UK nationals under ECHR law,[4] but they are equated with British Dependent Territories citizens, British Overseas citizens, and British subjects under the 1981 Act as having a right to register as BCs after five years' residence in the UK,[5] and are increasingly being included in modern legislation in the list of UK nationals.[6]

1 British Nationality Act 1981, s 38.
2 British Nationality Act 1981, s 50(1).
3 *R v Secretary of State for the Home Department, ex p Thakrar* [1974] QB 684, [1974] 2 All ER 261, CA.
4 *East African Asians v UK* (1973) 3 EHRR 76.
5 British Nationality Act 1981, s 4.
6 See L Fransman 'A Right to British Nationality' in Butterworth's *A Guide to the Human Rights Act 1998* (1999) p 131 where he cites definitions of UK nationals in Antarctic Act 1994, Chemical Weapons Act 1996, s 3(4) and Outer Space Act 1996.

British citizenship on commencement of the 1981 Act

CUKCs

2.35 With two exceptions, a person who immediately before commencement of the British Nationality Act 1981 was a CUKC and had the right of abode under the Immigration Act 1971 became a British citizen upon commencement.[1] The two exceptions are:

(i)   an illegitimate and formerly stateless person who became a CUKC by registration under the British Nationality (No 2) Act 1964;[2]
(ii)   a British subject who became a CUKC by registration outside the UK by reason of an ancestral connection with the UK.[3]

1   British Nationality Act 1981, s 11(1).
2   British Nationality Act 1981, s 11(2). Such a person is likely to have become a British Dependent Territories citizen (1981 Act, s 23(1)) or a British Overseas citizen (1981 Act, s 26). If the person is already resident in the UK but has not completed five years' residence, he or she will have a right to register as a British citizen on completion of the five years under s 4 of the 1981 Act.
3   British Nationality Act 1981, s 11(3). Such a person may in fact have qualified for a right of abode by another route, eg by completing five years' ordinary residence in the UK prior to 1983, and thus qualifying as patrials under the old s 2(1)(c) of the Immigration Act 1971. If they did not qualify under the pre-1983 regime and are resident in the UK, they qualify to register as British citizens on completion of five years' residence under s 4 of the 1981 Act.

Falkland Islanders

2.36 Persons from the Falkland Islands who would normally have become British Dependent Territories citizens on commencement in fact became British citizens, if immediately before commencement:

(i)   they were CUKCs born, naturalised or registered in the Falkland Islands; or
(ii)   one of their parents was such a CUKC or would have been but for their death; or
(iii)   in the case of a woman she was at any time married to a man who benefits from provisions (i) or (ii) above.[1]

1   British Nationality (Falkland Islands) Act 1983, s 1(1).

Acquiring British citizenship after commencement

Birth in the UK

2.37 The British Nationality Act 1981 abolished citizenship by birth in the UK, pure and simple. Children born in the UK or islands after commencement will only become British citizens if one of their parents is a British citizen or is settled in the UK.[1] A child may trace entitlement through either parent, provided that the child is legitimate or has been legitimised by the subsequent marriage of its parents. An illegitimate child can only trace entitlement through its mother.[2] The Secretary of State for the Home Department may use his or her discretion under section 3(1) of the 1981 Act to register as a British citizen the illegitimate child of a British father, but a refusal to do so is neither a breach of Article 8 of the ECHR or of Article 8 read with Article 14.[3] Since March 2000, the Immigration Nationality Directorate policy is to register the illegitimate child of a British citizen father where: (a) there are no doubts about paternity; (b) no reasonable objections from either parent or those with parental responsibility, and (c) there are no good character objections, bearing in mind the age of the child.[4]

1   British Nationality Act 1981, s 1. The Immigration Rules for children born in the UK who are not British citizens are at HC 395, paras 304–309.
2   British Nationality Act 1981, s 50(9). The Family Law Reform Act 1987 abolishes the distinction for legislation passed subsequent to that Act, unless the contrary intent is expressed. It has not altered immigration and nationality law. For the purposes of English law, a child is not necessarily illegitimate if its parents' marriage is subsequently shown to be void. Under the Legitimacy Act 1976, s 1 (which applies to a child of a void marriage whenever born), such a child is treated as legitimate if at the time of the act of intercourse resulting in the birth, or at the time of the celebration of the marriage, if later, either

parent reasonably believed that the marriage was valid. The provision only applies, however, where the father of the child is domiciled in England and Wales at the time of the birth, or, if he died before the birth, was so domiciled immediately before his death. Many other countries, however, have similar provisions and it may be necessary to look at these in cases where the legitimacy of a child is in question.

3 *R (Montana) v Secretary of State for the Home Department* [2001] 1 WLR 552, CA.
4 Letter from Immigration Nationality Directorate to Bindman & Partners, 31 March 2000.

2.38 Section 47 of the British Nationality Act 1981 provides that a person born out of wedlock is to be treated as having been born legitimate for nationality purposes, if that person was legitimated by the subsequent marriage of his or her parents. Section 47(2) provides that the appropriate national law to determine whether a subsequent marriage legitimated the child shall be the domiciliary law of the father at the time of the marriage. A child will only be legitimated by the subsequent marriage of the parents under the Act if the appropriate law provides that the marriage operated immediately or subsequently to legitimise the child, and not otherwise.

2.39 A child may trace entitlement to British citizenship through a parent who died before his or her birth. Under the British Nationality Act 1981 the definition of 'parent' includes the parent of a child born posthumously. The status of the mother or father shall be the status of the parent in question at the time of that parent's death.[1]

1 British Nationality Act 1981, s 48.

2.40 Where a child wishes to trace entitlement through its parent, it is the status of the parent at the time of the birth, or in the case of posthumous children, at the time of the death, which counts. If the parent becomes a British citizen by registration or naturalisation after the birth of the child, the child does not automatically become a British citizen by birth but is entitled to be registered as such on making an application under section 1(3) of the British Nationality Act 1981.

2.41 The alternative to having a parent who is a British citizen is to have a parent who at the time of the child's birth is settled in the UK. Under section 50(2) of the British Nationality Act 1981 a person is settled for the purposes of the Act if he or she is 'ordinarily resident in the United Kingdom . . . without being subject under the immigration laws to any restriction on the period for which he may remain'.[1] Section 50(3) of the 1981 Act excludes from this definition people who are in the UK as diplomats, international functionaries or as members of Commonwealth or visiting armed forces and are exempt from immigration control.[2] In some cases persons who have been entitled to a diplomatic exemption may be able to bestow British citizenship on their children born in the UK if they were settled in the UK before they took up their diplomatic posts.[3]

1 Freedom from immigration restrictions and conditions is the first requirement of settlement. Ordinary residence is the second requirement. This is discussed in detail at **4.15–4.19** below. Section 50(5) of the British Nationality Act 1981 provides that a person is not to be treated as ordinarily resident in the UK when he or she is in the UK in breach of the immigration laws. The 'immigration laws' are defined by section 50(1) of the 1981 Act in relation to the UK as meaning the Immigration Act 1971 and 'any law for purposes similar to that Act which is for the time being or has at any time been in force in any part of the UK'.
2 See Immigration Act 1971, s 8(3) and (4)(b) and (c).
3 British Nationality Act 1981, s 50(4).

2.42 From this short account it can be seen that disputes about whether a child's parents are 'settled' in the UK at the time of the birth are among the most contentious issues arising under the British Nationality Act 1981. This is particularly so where EEA nationals are involved.[1] The government recognised that doubts about parents' immigration status might arise many years after the birth of the child, and so modified the effect of the rule by providing for citizenship by registration for children born in the UK whose parents could not meet the settlement requirement.

1   See Fransman, *British Nationality Law* (Butterworths, 2nd edn, 1998) para 11.2.

2.43 Section 1(4) of the British Nationality Act 1981 provides that a person born in the UK who has not been out of the country for more than 90 days in each of the first ten years of his or her life may register as a British citizen at any time. The immigration status of the person is irrelevant, and his or her residence may have been lawful or unlawful.[1] It is also provided that where a child's parents become settled after the birth of the child, that child gets an automatic right to be registered as a UK citizen under section 1(3) of the 1981 Act. Limited provision is also made for people born in the UK who would otherwise be stateless. In some cases they automatically become British citizens and in other cases they may register.[2]

1   Letter from Immigration and Nationality Directorate to Afrira & Partners 3 August 1999.
2   British Nationality Act 1981, s 36 and Sch 2, paras 1 and 3.

Abandoned infants

2.44 Where a newborn infant is found abandoned in the UK, section 1(2) of the British Nationality Act 1981 provides that the qualifying conditions for citizenship in section 1(1) are deemed to apply to that child unless the contrary is shown. There is no definition of 'newborn' in the Act and this must be construed as a matter of fact by the Secretary of State and possibly the courts.[1] Children who have been found abandoned but are patently not newborn may be registered under section 3(1) at the minister's discretion.

1   Of course, the precise age of the child is unlikely to be known by the very circumstances of abandonment. In the committee stages of the British Nationality Bill the minister suggested that a child of about 12 months might be considered to be newborn in certain circumstances; it would be the minister's intention to give the phrase a generous interpretation: HC Official Report (5th series) col 212, 26 February 1981, 6th sitting.

Adoption

2.45 A child adopted under an adoption order made in the UK will become a British citizen if the adopter is a British citizen or, in the case of a joint adoption, if one of the adopters is a British citizen.[1] An adoption order made in a foreign court in favour of adopters who are British citizens will not give the adopted child citizenship automatically. An adopted child who is resident in the UK may be able to obtain citizenship by registration or naturalisation.[2]

1   British Nationality Act 1981, s 1(5) and (6). See Adoption Act 1976; Adoption (Scotland) Act 1978; Adoption (Northern Ireland) Order 1987. The courts are aware of the immigration consequences of adoption and regard it as a relevant factor and have now held that if the

benefits from the acquisition of British nationality occur during childhood, they are benefits to which first consideration should be given under s 6 of the Adoption Act 1976: *Re B (Adoption Order: Nationality)* [1999] INLR 125, HL. For the provisions of the Immigration Rules dealing with the admission of adopted children to join their parents in this country see chapter 11 below and Claudia Mortimore *Immigration and Adoption* (1994) Trentham Books.

2   British Nationality Act 1981, ss 4, 5 or 6. The possibilities depend on parents' status, residence in the UK and so forth.

Birth and adoption in the Falkland Islands

2.46 A person born in the Falkland Islands after commencement becomes a British citizen by birth, provided that his or her mother or father was born or settled in the Falkland Islands at the time of the birth.[1] Abandoned babies are deemed to have been so born unless the contrary is shown and will therefore be British citizens.[2] Similarly, adoption in the Falkland Islands by a British citizen confers full British citizenship.[3]

1   British Nationality (Falkland Islands) Act 1983, s 1(2).
2   British Nationality (Falkland Islands) Act 1983, s 1(3).
3   British Nationality (Falkland Islands) Act 1983, s 1(4).

Descent

2.47 Where a child is born outside the UK, the British Nationality Act 1981 provides for automatic transmission of citizenship from parent to child for just one generation, but provides exceptions for those working abroad in government or designated service. Descent may now be traced through the mother as well as the father. In more detail, the Act provides that persons born overseas after commencement automatically become British citizens from birth if their mother or father was a British citizen otherwise than by descent at the time of their birth.[1] Parents who are British citizens by descent cannot normally transmit their citizenship to children born overseas, unless at the time of the child's birth they are in Crown or similar service outside the UK or are working for a Community institution within the EC.[2] The 'one generation' restriction may produce some harsh results and so citizenship by descent is complemented by a scheme of registration to alleviate its deficiencies.[3]

1   British Nationality Act 1981, s 2(1)(a). Citizenship by descent is defined in the 1981 Act, s 14. See further British Nationality (Hong Kong) Act 1997, s 2.
2   British Nationality Act 1981, s 2(1)(b) and (4).
3   British Nationality Act 1981, s 3(2)–(6). In *R (Ullah) v Secretary of State for the Home Department* (10 May 2001, unreported), CA the CA held that a British citizen by descent cannot naturalise.

Registration

2.48 Under the British Nationality Act 1981 previous entitlements to register as CUKCs were swept away either immediately the Act came into force or after a transitional period and are generally replaced by naturalisation, except for minors[1] and for residual classes of British nationals and British Protected persons settled in the UK who wish to upgrade to British citizens.[2] In both cases registration is discretionary.[3] Other groups (from dependent territories or former colonies) have an entitlement to register. They are:

(i)   British Dependent Territories citizens from Gibraltar;[4]
(ii)   Falkland Islanders;[5]
(iii)   'Selected key people' from Hong Kong who were registered as British citizens under the selection scheme made by Order in Council under the British Nationality (Hong Kong) Act 1990 (this category is now closed);[6]
(iv)   Hong Kong ethnic minorities who, prior to the return of the colony to the sovereignty of China on 4 February 1997, had been a Hong Kong British Dependent Territories citizen, British Overseas citizen, British subject, or a British Protected person, and but for that British status would have become stateless after handover, if they were ordinarily resident in Hong Kong immediately before that date.[7]

The White Paper on nationality[8] proposes that all other British Dependent Territories citizens will have access to British citizenship.[9]

1   British Nationality Act 1981, s 3(1).
2   British Nationality Act 1981, s 4.
3   For discretionary registration of illegitimate children born to British fathers see **2.37** above.
4   British Nationality Act 1981, s 5.
5   British Nationality (Falkland Islands) Act 1983.
6   See previous edition **6.86–6.89**.
7   Many Hong Kong British Dependent Territories citizens registered as British Nationals (Overseas) in order to have an appropriate British status and travel document, which would survive the handover of sovereignty to China in 1997: see Hong Kong (British Nationality) Order 1986, SI 1986/948, art 4 and previous edition **6.84–6.85**. About 3.4 million registered as British Nationals (Overseas), but, save for about 8,000 to 10,000, these were ethnic Chinese and would have acquired Chinese nationality on handover: see Fransman *British Nationality Law* (Butterworths, 2nd edn, 1998) p 585.
8   *Partnership for Progress and Prosperity – Britain and the Overseas Territories* (Cm 4264, March 1999).
9   See **2.12** above.

Naturalisation

2.49 An application for naturalisation can be made under section 6(1) of the British Nationality Act 1981 or, in the case of persons (men or women) married to British citizens, under section 6(2). There is a residence qualification, which is different in each case. In the non-marriage cases the applicant must have been in the UK for five years without any absences in excess of 450 days.[1] In the case of spouses the period of required residence is three years with no absence in excess of 270 days.[2] During either residence period, the applicant must not have been in breach of the immigration laws.[3] In addition to the requirement of a fixed period of residence in the UK, the applicant must also have attained settled status under the 1981 Act. Essentially this means being ordinarily resident in the UK and free from any restriction under the immigration laws on the period for which the person may remain.[4] It was the normal practice of the government to treat as settled in the UK, for these purposes, any person resident in the UK in exercise of a right conferred by the EC Treaty, as extended by the European Economic Area Agreement 1992.[5] This was on the basis that they were free from restrictions on the length of their stay in the UK. Regulation 8 of the Immigration (European Economic Area) Regulations 2000[6] now contains a more limited definition of EEA nationals who are to be regarded as free from a time restriction on their stay. Anyone within the groups set out in regulation 8 will, therefore, be 'settled' if they are ordinarily resident in the UK. Other EEA nationals, such as workers and the self-employed, will have to wait four years, until they qualify for permission to remain indefinitely under paragraph 255 of HC 395, as amended.

1   British Nationality Act 1981, Sch 1, para 1(2)(a).
2   British Nationality Act 1981, Sch 1, para 3.
3   British Nationality Act 1981, Sch 1, paras 1(2)(d) and 3(d).
4   British Nationality Act 1981, s 50(2) but subject to the special cases dealt with under s 50(3) and (4). See Fransman 2.48 fn 7, para 11.2. See now the Immigration (European Economic Area) Regulations 2000, SI 2000/2326, Reg 8, and HC 395, para 255, as amended.
5   Notwithstanding the Tribunal decision in *Gal* (10620), the UK Passport Agency continued to accept EC nationals exercising EC Treaty rights as 'settled': see Fransman, para 11.2.1.8, and Immigration and Nationality Directorate letter to Walthamstow CAB, 6 December 1999. Prospective applicants were advised to apply for indefinite leave to remain under the Immigration Rules as a precautionary measure.
6   SI 2000/2326.

2.50   There are other differences between the naturalisation of spouses and non-spouses. A spouse can apply immediately after receiving indefinite leave, but others must normally wait 12 months before applying.[1] In the case of EEA nationals there will be no need for them to wait 12 months if they have obtained indefinite permission to remain or are to be treated otherwise as subject to no time restriction under the Immigration (European Economic Area) Regulations 2000[2], and fulfil all the other conditions of the British Nationality Act 1981.[3] In non-marriage cases the applicant must normally have sufficient knowledge of the English, Welsh or Scottish Gaelic language and intend, if naturalised, to live principally in the UK or work in Crown or similar service, or for a UK-established company.[4] Spouses do not have to comply with a language test or show an intention to make the UK their home. But in both cases the applicants have to show that they are of good character.[5] A criminal record is taken into account, but is not fatal. Someone with a life sentence can qualify, if he or she was released at least 20 years ago, has been above suspicion ever since, has no further convictions, and has made sustained attempts to contribute to society since release.[6] Illegal employment of an overseas domestic worker is unlikely to count against the employer, if the worker's position was later regularised under the domestic workers' concession.[7]

1   British Nationality Act 1981, Sch 1, para 1(2)(c).
2   SI 2000/2326.
3   Letter from Immigration and Nationality Directorate to Cameron McKenna, 5 October 1998.
4   British Nationality Act 1981, Sch 1, para 1(1). For the meaning of UK-established company see *R v Secretary of State for the Home Department, ex p Mehta* [1992] Imm AR 512. Normally the IND expects evidence that employment will continue for five years as a reasonable minimum alternative to an intention to make a permanent home in the UK: IND letter to Cameron McKenna, 4 September 1998. An employee of a multinational company seconded to an associate non-UK registered company (parent or subsidiary) would be expected to have a contract of employment with the UK-established company or will be regarded as one of its own career staff: IND letter to Cameron McKenna, 24 August 1998.
5   Some indication of how this test is presently interpreted was given by the minister during the committee stage of the Bill: HC Official Report (5th series) col 692, 19 March 1981. He said:
    'A person with a serious criminal record cannot be regarded as a person of good character. Equally it is normal to refuse applicants with few or no convictions who are

strongly suspected of being engaged in crime or are known associates of serious criminals. Sexual morality, however, is not normally taken into account, nor are, for instance, homosexual activities within the law. Scandalous sexual behaviour might, however, when combined with other personal characteristics, be a factor in a very few cases. Applicants are expected to meet their financial responsibilities. Financial irresponsibility, serious insolvency or bankruptcy, invariably leads to refusal. But mere financial incompetence is not necessarily a bar, and neither is unemployment or receipt of Social Security benefits. Where a person is in debt but is making efforts to repay what he owes, it is usual to postpone a decision on his application for a year or two to give him time to put matters right. Commercial malpractices are taken seriously. They are usually calculated and sustained acts which reflect adversely on the applicant's general character. Defects of temperament on their own are not normally held to bar an applicant on grounds of character. Heavy drinking, gambling or a disinclination to work are not in themselves sufficient to warrant refusal. There comes a point in very few cases, however, where failings of this type become so pronounced, or notorious in the locality, that it would be unwise to grant naturalisation. Honesty and integrity are essential elements in any definition of good character, and it follows, therefore, that applicants are required to be frank with the Home Office in the statements made on their application forms, which have to be declared before a Magistrate or Commissioner for Oaths. They must also tell the truth to the interviewing officer. False statements made to improve an applicant's chances of naturalisation obviously throw doubt on his fitness.'

For further details of the considerations taken into account in assessing character see Fransman *British Nationality Law* (2nd edn, 1998).

6 Immigration and Nationality Directorate letter to Bindman & Partners, 23 September 1998.

7 Immigration and Nationality Directorate letter to Cameron McKenna, 19 October 1999.

Challenging registration and naturalisation decisions

2.51 In some registrations and in all naturalisations, the award of British citizenship is discretionary.[1] There are no published rules or guidelines on the way in which that discretion should be exercised. There is no appeal to an adjudicator or Immigration Appeal Tribunal and section 44(2) of the British Nationality Act 1981 provides that, first, the Secretary of State for the Home Department need give no reason for the grant or refusal of any application, on which the decision is at his or her discretion; secondly, the decision on such applications is not to be subject to 'appeal to or review in' any court. The effect is to rule out any challenge to the exercise of the discretion on the normal *Wednesbury* grounds for bringing judicial review, but it does not rule out challenges to the legality[2] or fairness of the decision.[3] In *Ex p Mehta*[4] the Secretary of State set out in a letter the reasons why he had refused to grant naturalisation. In perusing his reasons, it became clear that he had taken a very restricted view of the meaning of a company 'established in the United Kingdom'. The court held that he had misdirected himself in law and that section 44(2) did not oust the court's jurisdiction to say so. In *Ex p Fayed*,[5] the Court of Appeal held that although the Secretary of State is not required to give reasons by virtue of section 44(2) of the 1981 Act, he was under a duty to act fairly, and this meant that during the process of reaching a decision he was required to give the applicant sufficient information about the subject matter of his concerns to enable the applicant to make representations. If doing so would involve disclosing matters not in the public interest, the Secretary of State should indicate that this was the position. The case is, therefore, not so much about reasons after the decision is reached, as about letting the applicant know of Home Office concerns prior to the decision being made. Since *Ex p Fayed*, the Secretary of State has confirmed that in future reasons for refusal will be given.[6]

1 The Secretary of State is authorised to discriminate on grounds of nationality, ethics or nationl origin: see Race Relations Act 1976, s 19D(1) as amended; IDI Mar/01 Ch 1 s 11 Annex B.
2 See *Anisminic Ltd v Foreign Compensation Commission* [1969] 2 AC 147 at 171B–D, HL; *A-G v Ryan* [1980] AC 718, PC; *South East Asia Fire Bricks Sdn Bhd v Non-Metallic Mineral Products Manufacturing Employees Union* [1981] AC 363, [1980] 2 All ER 689, PC; *Re Racal Communications Ltd* [1981] AC 374, [1980] 2 All ER 634, HL; *Gowa v A-G* [1985] 1 WLR 1003, HL.
3 *A-G v Ryan* above; *R v Secretary of State for the Home Department, ex p Fayed* [1997] 1 All ER 228, CA.
4 *R v Secretary of State for the Home Department, ex p Mehta* [1992] Imm AR 512, QBD.
5 [1997] 1 All ER 228.
6 HC Official Report (6th series) written answers col 564, 22 December 1997.

Loss of British citizenship

2.52 Under the scheme of the British Nationality Act 1981 those connected with a colony (dependent territory) become British Dependent Territories citizens, not British citizens.[1] So the loss of British citizenship by the process of decolonisation will not occur unless this process happens within the UK, for example, by the granting of self-determination to Scotland and Wales. The two means of losing British citizenship are:

(i) those with dual nationality or about to acquire another nationality can renounce their British citizenship by a declaration of renunciation;[2]
(ii) the Secretary of State for the Home Department can make an order depriving someone of British citizenship, but this only applies to those who have acquired it by registration or naturalisation.[3]

There are two main grounds upon which a British citizen may be deprived of citizenship under the 1981 Act:

(a) where registration or naturalisation has been obtained by fraud, false representation or concealment of material facts;[4]
(b) in cases of disloyalty, or imprisonment of those who were naturalised before the 1981 Act came into force and those who have been registered or naturalised after it came into force.[5] Imprisonment is only a ground for deprivation if it is a sentence over 12 months imposed within five years of the date of registration or naturalisation.

In all cases of deprivation there is a right of inquiry before a specially-appointed committee of inquiry.[6]

1 British Nationality Act 1981, s 25.
2 British Nationality Act 1981, s 12.
3 British Nationality Act 1981, s 40.
4 British Nationality Act 1981, s 40(1), (2) and (5)(a).
5 British Nationality Act 1981, s 40(3), (4) and (5).
6 British Nationality Act 1981, s 40(6)–(9). See British Citizenship (Deprivation) Rules 1982, SI 1982/988. There are similar provisions for the deprivation of British Dependent Territories citizenship in s 40 and British Dependent Territories Citizenship (Deprivation) Rules 1982, SI 1982/989.

2.53 Deprivation requires a positive act by the Secretary of State for the Home Department and is to be distinguished from those cases where the Secretary of State can treat the registration or naturalisation as of no effect. In

Ex p Mahmood[1] the applicant had obtained entry into the UK and subsequently registration as a CUKC by assuming the identity of a dead man. The Court of Appeal held that he had never become a CUKC. In *Ex p Akhtar*[2] the applicant had obtained his registration as a CUKC on the basis that he was the son of WA, but WA later denounced him and said he was not his son. On his return to the UK he had no passport and was refused entry on the basis that his registration as a CUKC was a nullity. His case went to the Court of Appeal who held that, since the applicant could not prove that he was the son of WA as claimed in the certificate of registration or that he was the person named in the certificate, he could not rely on it. The court preferred to rest their decision on an absence of proof, rather than on a distinction between void and voidable registrations.[3] In *Ex p Ejaz*[4] the applicant was naturalised as a British citizen on the basis of her marriage, but it later turned out that her husband had never become a British citizen. The Secretary of State claimed that her naturalisation was a nullity on the ground that the Secretary of State has no power to grant naturalisation where the husband is not in fact a British citizen. The Court of Appeal rejected that argument and held that she became a British citizen as from the date on which her certificate of naturalisation was granted[5] and remained such unless and until the Secretary of State invoked the deprivation machinery under section 40 of the British Nationality Act 1981.

1   *R v Secretary of State for the Home Department, ex p Mahmood* [1981] QB 58n, [1980] 3 WLR 312n, CA.
2   *R v Secretary of State for the Home Department, ex p Parvaz Akhtar* [1981] QB 46, [1980] 2 All ER 735, CA.
3   Per Megaw LJ.
4   *R v Secretary of State for the Home Department, ex p Ejaz* [1994] QB 496, [1994] 2 All ER 436, CA.
5   British Nationality Act 1981, s 42(5). In cases of registration the same rule applies; so the date of registration and not the date of application determines when citizenship is granted: *R v Secretary of State for the Home Department, ex p Amina Bibi* [1995] Imm AR 185, QBD.

2.54 The upshot of these cases is not easy to fathom. There is difficulty in identifying their true rationale. Does it mean that where the identity of the person is in issue, the Secretary of State for the Home Department can treat the registration or naturalisation as of no effect, but in all other cases the deprivation machinery must be invoked? Or does it turn on who has the burden of proving nationality or lack of it? The difficulty with the *Parvez Akhtar* cases is in locating the proper burden and standard of proof. *Akhtar* was a refusal of entry case and the court relied on section 3(8) of the Immigration Act 1971, which put the burden of proving the claim to patriality and citizenship on the applicant; but it also held that the immigration officer had reasonable grounds for rejecting the applicant's claim to be a CUKC – which was the pre-*Khawaja* formulation of the burden of proof in entry by deception cases. In other cases of disputed citizenship, where the applicant has had neither the requisite British passport nor a certificate of entitlement, section 3(8) of the 1971 Act has been crucial.[1] In such cases the court has expressly rejected the argument that once the applicant's British visitor's passport or birth certificate is produced, this is *prima facie* proof of citizenship and the burden shifts to the immigration authorities to prove the contrary. In both *Minta*[2] and *Bamgbose*[3] the Court of Appeal held that *Khawaja v Secretary of State for the Home Department*[4] has no bearing on the question of British citizenship which is expressly dealt with by section 3(8).

1   *Minta v Secretary of State for the Home Department* [1992] Imm AR 380, CA; *Re Bamgbose*
    [1990] Imm AR 135, CA; *Mokuolo v Secretary of State for the Home Department* [1989]
    Imm AR 51, CA.
2   [1992] Imm AR 380, CA.
3   [1990] Imm AR 135, CA.
4   [1984] AC 74, [1983] 1 All ER 765, HL.

2.55 But what about the cases where applicants meet the requirements of
section 3(9) of the Immigration Act 1971 by producing either a UK passport
describing them as British citizens or a certificate of entitlement certifying them
as such? In *Ex p Obi*[1] Sedley J held that the production of a genuine UK passport,
issued to the applicant and describing him as a British citizen, discharges the
burden of proof and there was no need for further proof, even though the Secretary
of State for the Home Department called into question the applicant's identity.
This, however, does not stop the Home Office trying to rebut the presumption
of citizenship created by the passport by trying to prove that it was obtained by
fraud. At that point *Khawaja* will have a bearing. The burden of proving that
citizenship or a certificate of entitlement was obtained by fraud will be on the
Home Office and must be proved to a high degree of probability.[2]

1   *R v Secretary of State for the Home Department, ex p Obi* [1997] Imm AR 420, QBD.
2   See *Minta*, above; *R v Secretary of State for the Home Department, ex p Rouse and
    Shrimpton* (13 November 1985, unreported), QBD.

2.56 It is now possible to be clearer about the burden and standard of proof. In
Khawaja and the section 3(9) cases the applicant has to prove an initial entitlement
before the burden shifts to the Secretary of State for the Home Department. In
Khawaja-type cases it is a leave stamp in the passport;[1] in the section 3(9) cases
the passport or certificate of entitlement. In *Ejaz*[2] the deprivation machinery was
set off by the production of the naturalisation certificate. Thereafter the burden of
negativing the leave stamp, the passport, certificate of entitlement or the
naturalisation or registration certificate is on the Secretary of State. Proof is on a
preponderance of probability as set out in *Khawaja*.[3]

1   *Khawaja v Secretary of State for the Home Department* [1984] AC 74 at 114, per Lord
    Scarman and 122–125, per Lord Bridge.
2   *R v Secretary of State for the Home Department, ex p Ejaz* [1994] QB 496, [1994]
    2 All ER 436, CA.
3   *Khawaja v Secretary of State for the Home Department* [1984] AC 74 at 112–114, per
    Lord Scarman.

Resumption of citizenship

2.57 Where a person had acquired the right to resume citizenship under the
British Nationality Act 1964, the transitional provisions of the British Nationality
Act 1981 gave a right to register as a British citizen, provided that the person
had what was known as 'an appropriate qualifying connection' with the UK.[1] A
person who makes a declaration of renunciation after the 1981 Act came into
force is entitled to resume citizenship only if the renunciation of British citizenship
was necessary in order to retain or acquire some other citizenship or nationality.
This resumption is achieved by an application to the Secretary of State for the
Home Department for registration by a person of full capacity. In addition to
the right to resume under section 13(1) of the 1981 Act, there is also a general
discretion to allow resumption under section 13(3).

1   British Nationality Act 1981, s 10. The meaning of 'an appropriate qualifying connection' was considered in *R v Secretary of State for the Home Department, ex p Patel and Wahid* [1991] Imm AR 25, QBD.

APPEALS

2.58   No appeal lies against the refusal of the Secretary of State for the Home Department to register or naturalise a person as a British citizen. The only remedy is, therefore, by way of judicial review. But in disputed claims to citizenship and right of abode an appeal to an adjudicator is possible. First, there are entrants who are told that they require leave to enter. They have a right of appeal to an adjudicator against that decision,[1] but only if they hold a current UK passport describing them as a British citizen or a CUKC having a right of abode in the UK or a certificate of entitlement.[2] Such an appeal will be limited to dealing with such issues as whether the passport is a forgery or the person seeking to enter is the same as the person described in the passport, and does not entitle an appellant to prove his or her right of abode by any admissible means.[3]

1   Immigration and Asylum Act 1999, s 59(1).
2   Immigration and Asylum Act 1999, s 60(1).
3   *Akewushola v Immigration Officer, Heathrow* [1999] INLR 433, CA.

2.59   Secondly, a right of appeal is available to those who have applied for a certificate of entitlement and have been refused.[1] The appellant may be abroad or in the UK at the time of the hearing. In the past, the appellate authority has treated passport refusals and disputed claims to a right of abode as constituting certificate of entitlement appeals under section 13(2) of the Immigration Act 1971, even though no formal request for a certificate has been made.[2] The wording of section 59(2) of the Immigration and Asylum Act 1999 is no different – both require there to be an application duly made; it is, therefore, advisable to apply for a certificate of entitlement in all cases of doubt or dispute over citizenship or entitlement to a right of abode.

1   Immigration and Asylum Act 1999, s 59(2).
2   See *Antoniades* [1993] Imm AR 57; *Menon* [1993] Imm AR 577.

2.60   Thirdly, the question arises whether someone who has been refused British nationality has a human rights appeal under section 65 of the Immigration and Asylum Act 1999. This is unlikely. Although everyone has a right to a nationality under international law,[1] this does not mean any person can demand British nationality.[2] Further, although under section 44(2) of the British Nationality Act 1981, the Secretary of State for the Home Department is not required to assign any reason for the grant or refusal of naturalisation or a discretionary registration, in practice he or she will increasingly do so. This arises from a number of recent developments. First, in *Fayed*[3] the Court of Appeal held that in certain cases the Secretary of State was under a duty to give the applicant notice of his or her areas of concern.[4] Secondly, the European Convention on Nationality 1997, which requires all decisions to be reasoned, has prompted the Secretary of State to announce that henceforth reasons will be given.[5] So in future an absence of reasons is unlikely to be a cause for complaint. The second question is whether the absence of an appeal right can engage the Convention.

It is difficult, at present, to see how this might happen. The first difficulty is to find a way in which Article 6(1) is engaged at all, given the current Strasbourg jurisprudence on the meaning of 'civil' rights (see **8.51** below). If Article 6 is not engaged, it is difficult to see how the absence of an appeal right can be linked to any of the provisions of the Convention or give rise to a section 65 appeal.

1 See Universal Declaration of Human Rights 1948, art 15; International Covenant on Civil and Political Rights 1966, art 24(3); European Convention on Nationality 1997, art 4a.
2 See *R (Montana) v Secretary of State for the Home Department* [2001] 1 WLR 552, CA (arts 8 and 14). See also Laurie Fransman 'The Human Rights Act and British Nationality' in Butterworths *A Guide to the Human Rights Act 1998* (1999) p 129.
3 [1997] 1 All ER 228.
4 See 2.51 above.
5 Hansard HC Official Report (6th series) written answers col 564, 22 December 1997; see Fransman 2.21 fn 1, p 134.

THE RIGHT TO A BRITISH PASSPORT

A Prerogative Power

2.61 Travellers may be refused a British passport because their citizenship is not recognised. We have dealt with the remedies for this situation in the last section. But passports may also be withheld from British citizens for a variety of reasons, and this will obviously affect their ability to travel and, therefore, to enjoy the benefits of their statutory right of abode. The power to issue passports is not statutory but is derived from the prerogative.[1] Passports are issued by the UK Passport Agency which is an executive agency of the Home Office, referred to as the Passport Office. Overseas they are issued by British consulates, British High Commissions and British dependent territory authorities. A passport is not an entry clearance document for the purposes of an appeal under section 59(2) of the Immigration and Asylum Act 1999. Thus where a person succeeds in proving a disputed relationship and by reason of that relationship is a British citizen by descent, the appellate authority cannot require the entry clearance officer to issue a passport, only a certificate of entitlement.[2] On the other hand, for the purposes of entry a passport is proof that the holder has a right of abode.[3] It is, therefore, a very valuable and essential document. Yet, so far no court or tribunal has been willing to sanction the existence of any implied duty to order the issue of a passport.

1 Wade and Forsyth do not regard this as a true prerogative power for the highly questionable reason that the grant or cancellation of a passport involves no direct legal consequences; see *Administrative Law* (7th edn, 1994) Clarendon pp 249 and 383. This may be based on an early judicial view of a passport as a document merely to be used for purposes of consular protection: see *R v Brailsford* [1905] 2 KB 730 at 745. In *R v Secretary of State for Foreign and Commonwealth Affairs, ex p Everett* [1989] QB 811, [1989] 1 All ER 655, CA O'Connor LJ said it was a prerogative power.
2 *Khatoori Kassun* (4272).
3 Immigration Act 1971, s 3(9). See *R v Secretary of State for the Home Department, ex p Obi* [1997] Imm AR 420, QBD.

2.62 It was stated in the House of Lords in 1958: 'No British subject has a legal right to a passport. The grant of a UK passport is a royal prerogative exercised through Her Majesty's ministers and in particular the Foreign Secretary.'[1] Details of how the prerogative was usually exercised were given to the House. These reasons were amplified in 1974 and 1981.[2] There are five reasons for refusal or withdrawal of a passport. These are:

(a)   minors being taken out of the jurisdiction illegally, or contrary to the wishes of a parent or other person awarded parental rights;

(b)   applicants wishing to leave the country where there is good evidence to believe that they wish to avoid prosecution;

(c)   applicants whose conduct is so demonstrably undesirable that continued enjoyment of passport facilities is contrary to the public interest;[3]

(d)   persons repatriated at the public expense who have not refunded the cost of their repatriation;[4]

(e)   persons for whose arrest a warrant has been issued in the UK[5] or who are wanted for serious crime in the UK.[6]

1   209 HL Official Report (5th series) col 860 (PQ). See David W Williams 'Without Let or Hindrance' [1973] NLJ 605; JUSTICE *Going abroad*.

2   See 881 HC Official Report (5th series) written answers col 265, 15 November 1974; 416 HL Official Report (5th series) written answers col 558, 22 January 1981.

3   Only about 20 people were denied passports on political grounds between 1945 and 1968. Then there were the exceptional cases during the Rhodesian rebellion; see 764 HC Official Report (5th series) col 1107, 14 May 1968.

4   This was said to occur only once or twice a year and the practice was confirmed in 792 HC Official Report (5th series) col 232. In 1968 it was stated in a parliamentary question that 2,400 passports had been impounded since 1951 (764 HC Official Report (5th series) col 183); a later debate in the House of Commons revealed that the overwhelming majority of these 2,400 refusals or withdrawals were people who had run out of money on holiday and handed in their passports to get their fares home paid: 764 HC Official Report (5th series) col 1107, 14 May 1968; see further David W Williams 'Without Let or Hindrance' [1973] NLJ 605.

5   *R v Secretary of State for Foreign and Commonwealth Affairs, ex p Everett* [1989] QB 811, [1989] 1 All ER 655, CA.

6   It is not clear how far (b) and (e) overlap.

Challenging refusals

2.63 Since it is now possible to challenge decisions taken under the prerogative on judicial review,[1] it is also possible to challenge a refusal to issue a passport. In *Ex p Everett*,[2] the Court of Appeal held that the Secretary of State for Foreign and Commonwealth Affairs was entitled to refuse a passport, but had to give reasons for doing so. Where the refusal was because of an outstanding arrest warrant, the applicant should be told when and where the warrant was issued and what for. When notifying the applicant he or she should be told to tell the Secretary of State of any exceptional grounds for issuing a passport, for example, when the applicant was ill in a foreign country. *Everett* focuses on the need to give reasons after the decision is made, but there may now also be cases where it will be necessary as a matter of fairness for the passport office to indicate areas of concern to applicants *before* the decision in sufficient detail to enable them to make representations.[3]

1   *Council of Civil Service Unions v Minister for the Civil Service* [1984] 3 All ER 935 at 948, 951 and 956, HL. See further *R v Secretary of State for the Home Department, ex p Bentley* [1994] QB 349, [1993] 4 All ER 442 (challenge to the prerogative of mercy).

2   *R v Secretary of State for Foreign and Commonwealth Affairs, ex p Everett* [1989] QB 811, [1989] 1 All ER 655, CA.

3   *R v Secretary of State for the Home Department, ex p Fayed* [1997] 1 All ER 228, CA.

A new approach

2.64 Today an unfettered prerogative power to refuse a passport is probably a thing of the past. First, a passport is not just a document to be used for the individual's protection as a British subject.[1] It may also be needed to give effect to the statutory right under section 1 of the Immigration Act 1971 to leave or enter the UK. Under EC law there is an obligation to allow British nationals to leave the country in pursuit of their free movement rights (see chapter 7 below). In our view neither this right nor the right to reside in another EC country in pursuit of free movement rights can be impeded by the refusal of the passport or other suitable identity document, except on public policy grounds within the terms of EC Council Directive 64/221.

1   Per Lord Alverstone in *R v Brailsford* [1905] 2 KB 730 at 745.

2.65 The question is whether a passport can be withheld for travel outside the EC. We have already referred to Articles 2(2) and 3(2) of the Fourth Protocol of the ECHR at **2.6** above.[1] However, there is a much older common law right of a British subject to come and go without let or hindrance referred to in *DPP v Bhagwan*.[2] This echoes Blackstone's view that an Englishman had a right at common law to leave the realm, subject only to the restraints of the writ *ne exeat regno*.[3] The right is now a statutory right set out in section 1 (1) of the Immigration Act 1971. However, without a passport it is largely useless. Does this mean that there is now a concomitant right to a passport, which can only be withheld in the limited circumstances to which section 1(1) relates?[4] Or are the restraints set out in the parliamentary answers referred to in **2.62** above ones which can be lawfully imposed? *Everett* was argued on the basis that such restraints were not to be questioned and the only issue dealt with in that case was unfairness. The question must be open to argument in a future case. In France the Cour de Cassation has held that there is a right to leave France and that refusal of a passport is a restriction of that right.[5] Will Britain follow suit? Cases are awaited.

1   Identical provisions on the right to leave are contained in art 12(2) and (3) of the UN International Covenant on Civil and Political Rights 1966. Britain is a party to this and the optional protocol, giving individuals a right to complain to the Human Rights Committee. The Covenant may give a right of complaint but it has not been incorporated into UK municipal law and it is, therefore, thought unlikely that it could found a judicial review challenge on any refusal or withdrawal of a passport. For text see Brownlie *Basic Documents on Human Rights* (3rd edn, 1992) Clarendon, pp 125 and 144.
2   [1972] AC 60, [1970] 3 All ER 97.
3   See **2.8** above.
4   See **2.8** above.
5   Roger Errera 'Recent decisions of the French Conseil D'Etat' [1986] PL 637; and [1987] PL 464.

Chapter 3

CONTROL OF ENTRY

INTRODUCTION

3.1 Until the changes brought about by the Immigration and Asylum Act 1999, control on entry was exercised geographically and by particular personnel. Pre-entry control meant visas and entry clearance, always obtained abroad from entry clearance officers or visa officers. On-entry control meant the grant or refusal of leave to enter, always exercised at the port by immigration officers. Post-entry control, meaning the grant or variation of leave to remain (disregarding enforcement), was always exercised in the UK by the Secretary of State for the Home Department. The 1999 Act changes have removed the geographical and to some extent the personnel nexus and eroded the boundaries between the forms of control. Now, entry clearance may operate as leave to enter. Leave to enter may be granted (or refused) before the traveller embarks for the UK or during the journey. Leave does not normally lapse when the holder leaves the UK, but may be cancelled while the holder is abroad. An immigration officer at the port may grant, refuse, suspend or cancel leave to enter and may vary leave to remain on behalf of the Secretary of State. Leave may be varied by the Secretary of State while the holder is abroad. While some aspects of the changes are clearly beneficial, for example the provision for non-lapsing leave, there are dangers in going too far in making immigration control extra-territorial. It is more difficult to monitor examinations and control procedures conducted abroad to ensure their fairness and their compatibility with fundamental rights. We comment elsewhere on the destructive effect that the carrier sanctions and airline liaison officer schemes have on those fleeing persecution or other ill-treatment, and on the protection duties of the UK. The Secretary of State's proposals to remove asylum determination from public scrutiny by having it all done overseas[1] is, in this connection, a worrying development, and could give rise to further serious but largely unnoticed breaches of international obligations.

1   See Jack Straw, 'An effective protection regime for the twenty-first century', speech to IPPR, 6 February 2001.

3.2 Other changes allow the Secretary of State for the Home Department to make use of new technologies in controlling immigration: leave to enter may now be granted by e-mail or telephone as well as by a stamp in the passport. These changed procedures need careful monitoring to ensure that injustice does not result from haste or lack of care in considering applications. However, the procedure at the port is likely to be speeded up considerably for those deemed 'low risk passengers'.[1] The changes overall should at least put an end to some of the more arcane legal arguments about the effect of illegible stamps and the circumstances in which deemed leave was granted. Anyone wanting a comprehensive account of the law in these areas should refer to the previous edition of this work at 3.47-3.60.

1   See 'Background Information' issued by the Immigration and Nationality Directorate pursuant to the *Statement of Changes to the Immigration Rules* 28 July 2000 (HC 704) and available on the IND website. Some concern has been expressed as to the criteria which immigration officers propose to apply in their assessment of those passengers deemed 'high risk' and therefore liable to detailed inquiry on arrival, notwithstanding possession of entry clearance which is to be treated as leave to enter, particularly in the light of s 19D of the Race Relations Act 1976 as amended by the Race Relations (Amendment) Act 2000, and the Race Relations (Immigration and Asylum) Authorisation 2001, which permit discrimination on grounds of ethnic or national origin in the operation of controls under specified circumstances.

LEAVE TO ENTER

3.3   Leave to enter is the cornerstone of UK immigration law. No one may enter the UK without leave except:

(i)   British citizens and Commonwealth citizens who have the right of abode;[1]
(ii)   persons arriving from Ireland or another part of the common travel area, in circumstances where leave is not required;[2]
(iii)   persons exempt from control, such as diplomats, crew members and others;[3]
(iv)   persons exempt from the requirement of leave under the Immigration (European Economic Area) Regulations 2000;[4]
(v)   prisoners being brought to the UK to give evidence in drug trafficking cases.[5]

Unfortunately, the description in the Immigration Rules of those requiring leave to enter continues to be inadequate, misleading and wrong,[6] although the IDI fortunately give more accurate guidance.

1   Immigration Act 1971, ss 3(1), 2(1)(b), 2(2). See chapter 2 above.
2   Immigration Act 1971, s 9; Immigration (Control of Entry through Republic of Ireland) Order 1972, SI 1972/1610 as amended. See chapter 6 below.
3   Immigration Act 1971, s 8. See chapter 6 below.
4   SI 2000/2326, regs 12 and 14.
5   Criminal Justice (International Co-operation) Act 1990, s 6.
6   HC 395, para 7.

3.4 Leave to enter used only to be granted or refused on arrival in the UK. Arrival and entry are two distinct concepts in immigration law. Section 11 of the Immigration Act 1971 defines the point at which someone who arrives in this country is treated as having entered. First, it provides that persons arriving by ship or aircraft are not deemed to 'enter' unless and until they disembark.[1] Secondly, on disembarkation they are still deemed not to have entered so long as they remain in any part of the port which has been approved for use for immigration control. They only enter once they pass through immigration control. Thirdly, they will still not be treated as having entered if they are detained by immigration officers pending examination or removal or are temporarily admitted or released while liable to such detention.[2] This is of practical importance given the increasing use and length of temporary admission, and means that a person on temporary admission may be physically in the UK for years, marry and have children, but will still require leave to enter.

1 Immigration Act 1971, s 11(1). For those coming by train through the Channel Tunnel, they 'enter' the UK when they leave a designated control area or stay on a through train after it has ceased to be in a control area: Immigration Act 1971, s 11(1), as modified by Channel Tunnel (International Arrangements) Order 1993, SI 1993/1813, Sch 4, para 1(5).
2 Immigration Act 1971, s 4(1).

3.5 Now, however, leave to enter will be granted and refused in the country of departure in most cases. The Immigration (Leave to Enter and Remain) Order 2000[1] provides that leave to enter may be given or refused before the person leaves for or arrives in the UK.[2] In most cases, entry clearance will operate as advance leave to enter. The power to give or refuse leave to enter was previously to be exercised only by immigration officers but Orders under section 3A of the Immigration Act 1971 may provide that it be exercised by the Secretary of State (and his or her officers).[3] However, immigration officers and the Secretary of State are authorised to refuse advance leave to enter by reason of a person's nationality, if justified by statistical evidence showing a trend of breach of immigration laws by persons of that nationality, or intelligence suggests that they might.[4]

1 SI 2000/1161.
2 SI 2000/1161, art 7, made under Immigration Act 1971 s 3A inserted by Immigration and Asylum Act 1999, s 1.
3 This has not been exercised in the Immigration (Leave to Enter and Remain) Order 2000, which does, however, provide that the Secretary of State may vary leave while the holder is abroad (art 13(6)), or cancel leave to remain in similar circumstances (art 13(7)).
4 Race Relations (Immigration and Asylum) Authorisation 2001, para 4(2)(a), 6, published in IDI Mar/01, Ch 1, s 11, Annex B.

3.6 Leave to enter may be granted for a limited or indefinite period.[1] If limited leave is given, it may be subject to conditions[2] restricting employment or occupation in the UK; requiring the holder to maintain and accommodate himself or herself and any dependants without recourse to public funds; or requiring him or her to register with the police.[3] Conditions may be imposed by reason of the foreigner's nationality.[4] Indefinite leave to enter (or remain) may not be made subject to any conditions.

1 Immigration Act 1971, s 3(1)(b): leave may be limited in time (eg six months) or to a period of employment: see *R v Immigration Appeal Tribunal, ex p Coomasaru* [1983] 1 All ER 208, [1983] 1 WLR 14, CA.
2 The immigration officer may require a person arriving in the UK and granted leave to enter to submit to a medical examination after entry, under the Immigration Act 1971,

Sch 2, para 7, but this is not a condition of leave under the 1971 Act. See IDI Nov/00, Ch 1, s 8, para 2.11.
3 Immigration Act 1971, s 3(1)(c).
4 Race Relations (Immigration and Asylum) Authorisation 2001, para 3(e). The power is exercisable on statistical evidence or intelligence information indicating a tendency to breach the controls by persons of that nationality: para 6.

ENTRY CLEARANCE

3.7 As we indicated above, everyone seeking leave to enter for other than temporary purposes, and all visa nationals, will have had to obtain an entry clearance, which will, in most cases, operate as advance leave to enter.[1] Entry clearances under the Immigration Act 1971 consist of visas for visa nationals[2] and entry certificates for non-visa nationals.[3] An entry clearance may be for a single journey or for multiple visits. A multiple entry visa is available for frequent visitors and is usually valid for a period of two years, although it may have a five-year validity. It may be for simple visits or for business trips. When entry clearance is granted it will usually take the form of a stamp in the passport. Whether or not this is the case, it will usually be endorsed with a period within which it must be used. Previously, an entry clearance which was not a multiple entry visa was only valid for one visit and was not re-usable for further visits within the same period.[4] The Immigration (Leave to Enter and Remain) Order 2000 provides that a visit visa which has effect as leave to enter is good for multiple entries within the period of its validity.[5] When the holder of an entry clearance arrives in the UK, admission is not automatic and entry to the UK may still be refused.

1 HC 395, para 25A; Immigration (Leave to Enter and Remain) Order 2000, SI 2000/1161, arts 2-4.
2 See **3.8** below.
3 HC 395, para 25. The statutory definition in Immigration Act 1971, s 33(1) includes other documents but excludes a work permit.
4 *Andronicou* [1974] Imm AR 87, Immigration Appeal Tribunal.
5 SI 2000/1161, art 4.

Who needs entry clearance

3.8 Visa nationals normally require an entry clearance whatever the purpose of their travel to the UK and will be refused entry if they do not have one.[1] The list of visa countries is set out in Appendix 1 to the current Immigration Rules. It includes stateless persons and persons who hold non-national documents. This list is frequently amended and care should be taken to ensure that a particular country has not been added to the list or removed from it. The exceptions are:

(i)   no visa is required for returning residents (those with indefinite leave who return within two years of departure from the UK);[2]

(ii)   no visa is required for those seeking to re-enter during the period of their original leave, unless it was for a period of six months or less, or was granted by statute;[3]

(iii)   no visa is required for visitors who obtained a visit visa and are re-entering the UK within the period of validity of their original visa;[4]

(iv)   refugees resident in or nationals of countries which are signatories to the Council of Europe Agreement on the Abolition of Visas for Refugees

1959[5] do not need a visa provided that entry is as a visitor for three months or less;[6]

(v)   schoolchildren living in other EU states travelling in school groups do not need visas if the group is accompanied by a teacher and their names are included on the official form to be obtained by the school;[7]

(vi)   foreign seamen settled in the UK who signed on in the UK who are discharging from a vessel or arriving as passengers having signed off abroad, foreign seamen arriving in the UK as crew members for discharge or for temporary shore leave, or those with a seafarer's identity document who come to join a ship in the UK, and aircrew who are to leave within seven days, may be admitted without visas.[8]

If visa nationals arrive in the UK from Ireland and have no visa for the UK, they must obtain leave to enter.[9] Note that visa nationals will require a visa if they intend to enter the UK on a stopover to another destination. This is not the same as a transit visa, which nationals of particular countries designated under the Transit Visa Order 1993[10] must obtain when passing through the UK to another country without entering.[11] The latest list of countries for whose nationals transit visas are required is set out in the Immigration (Transit Visa) Amendment Order 2000,[12] made under section 41 of the Immigration and Asylum Act 1999.[13] The list reads like a roll call of refugee-producing countries.

1   HC 395, para 24. The imposition of visa requirements on Commonwealth citizens under the Immigration Rule is not *ultra vires*: *R v Secretary of State for the Home Department, ex p Suresh Kumar* [1986] Imm AR 420, QBD. The discrimination inherent in the concept of visa nationals, and in the differential treatment of applicants according to nationality, is made lawful in domestic law by s 19D of the Race Relations Act 1976 (inserted by the Race Relations (Amendment) Act 2000).
2   HC 395, as amended, Appendix 1 para 2(a).
3   HC 395, as amended, Appendix 1, para 2(b). See also SI 2000/1161, art 13(2)-(4): for such persons, their original leave now does not lapse when they leave the UK.
4   SI 2000/1161, art 4.
5   These countries are Belgium, Denmark, Finland, France, Germany, Iceland, Ireland, Italy, Liechtenstein, Luxembourg, Malta, Netherlands, Norway, Portugal, Spain, Sweden, Switzerland.
6   HC 395, as amended, Appendix 1, para 2(c).
7   IDI Nov/00, Ch 1, Annex U, para 5, referring to an EU Council Agreement to waive visa requirements. This is a concession only, not incorporated into the rules.
8   See IDI Nov/00, Ch 1, Annex U, paras 8, 9; chapter 6 below.
9   Immigration (Control of Entry through Republic of Ireland) Order 1972, SI 1972/1610, art 3. See also *Mohan v Secretary of State for the Home Department* [1989] Imm AR 436. If they have gone from Ireland to one of the Islands without the appropriate visa, they require leave. If they fail to get it and proceed to the UK, they will be illegal entrants.
10 Immigration (Transit Visa) Order 1993, SI 1993/1678, as amended by SI 1998/55; SI 1998/1014; SI 2000/1381.
11 Immigration and Asylum Act 1999, s 41(2).
12 SI 2000/1381.
13 A re-enactment of the Immigration (Carriers' Liability) Act 1987, s 1A.

3.9 Article 62 (formerly Article 73) of the Consolidated EC Treaty provides for common lists of third countries whose nationals must possess a visa and for those who need not, for common rules on the issue of short-stay visas and for uniform formats. This Article is optional so far as the UK and Ireland are concerned.[1] However, an EC Regulation, which determines the third countries whose nationals must be in possession of a visa when crossing the external borders of the member states, is binding.[2]

1   See Protocol No 4 (1997) on the position of the UK and Ireland, providing that the UK and Ireland are not bound by any provision of Title IV (measures on immigration and asylum) but may opt in by giving notice. See chapter 7.
2   Council Regulation (EC) 574/99.

3.10 Non-visa nationals have no need for an entry clearance if they come for a visit, to study or for certain other temporary purposes, or are returning residents or are born in the UK. Entry clearance is necessary for all other purposes.[1] The fact that entry clearance is made mandatory for almost all purposes in the Immigration Rules is not unlawful. The courts have held that it is not *ultra vires* the Secretary of State's rule-making power, either as being an unlawful delegation of power to entry clearance officers or as a fetter on the discretionary powers of immigration officers to give or refuse leave to enter under section 4(1) of the Immigration Act 1971.[2] The immigration officers' discretion is retained in the new dispensation, where entry clearance operates as leave to enter, through their power to cancel leave.[3]

1   Entry clearance requirements are set out for entry in all immigration categories as they are dealt with: see chapters 9-11 below.
2   See *R v Secretary of State for the Home Department, ex p Rofathullah* [1989] QB 219, [1988] Imm AR 514, CA; *R v Secretary of State for the Home Department, ex p Ounejma* [1989] Imm AR 75, DC. See further *R v Secretary of State for the Home Department, ex p Kaur* [1987] Imm AR 278, DC, a challenge to the *vires* of rules made under the Commonwealth Immigrants Act 1962.
3   Under Immigration Act 1971, Sch 2, para 2A, inserted by Immigration and Asylum Act 1999, Sch 14, para 57.

Making an application for entry clearance

3.11 Applications for entry clearance are to be considered in accordance with the provisions of the Immigration Rule relating to the grant or refusal of leave to enter, and the term 'entry clearance officer' may be substituted for the term 'immigration officer' where this is appropriate.[1] To qualify for the grant of an entry clearance as a visitor, family member, business person or whatever, the person must fulfil the requirements of the particular Immigration Rule which deals with that particular type of entrant. But qualifying in this way may not be enough. Entry clearance may still be refused on a number of general grounds which apply across the board. These are described at **3.23**ff below.

1   HC 395, para 26.

Where to apply

3.12 First, all applicants must be outside the UK and Islands at the time of application.[1] Secondly, the application has to be made to the British Embassy or High Commission, a British Consular post or special authorised person outside the UK and Islands.[2] A list of designated posts is published by the Foreign and Commonwealth Office.[3] A distinction is made between visit entry clearances and others. Visitors can apply to any post designated by the Secretary of State to accept applications for visit visas from that category of applicants. They do not need to be in the country where they live. All other visa applications have to be made in the country where the applicant 'is living', unless there is no designated post in that country able to receive applications for that purpose from that category of applicants. Then the visa can be applied for and obtained elsewhere.[4] No definition of what is meant by 'living' is given, and this leads to widely divergent practices at British overseas posts. Some, it seems, will take applications from anyone with an address, however temporary, in the country concerned; others require the person to have a more permanent residence status. In view of these divergent practices, it is unsafe to take any view based on the language of the Immigration Rules. In particular cases, it may be necessary for advisers to contact the Embassy or Consulate to ascertain the prevailing practice. The advent of the Joint Entry Clearance Unit (JECU), combining officials from the Foreign and Commonwealth and the Home Office (see 3.84 below) should provide a measure of clarification and harmonisation of criteria and practice between posts.

1   HC 395, para 28.
2   HC 395, para 29.
3   It is available on the Foreign and Commonwealth Office website, whose address is www.fco.gov.uk.
4   For example, since 1991 Somalis have applied for entry clearance to posts at Addis Ababa and Nairobi. Under the Somali Family Reunion policy which operated until 1994, UK sponsors obtained indications from the Home Office on the likely outcome of visa applications which were then formally made at the post: see *Secretary of State for the Home Department v Dahir and Abdi* [1995] Imm AR 570, CA. Until 1 November 1999 a concession allowed Vietnamese refugees in the UK to apply direct to the Home Office by letter for their relatives in Vietnam to join them: API Aug/00, Ch 6, s 2.

3.13 Fees are charged for the issue of visas and entry clearances.[1] Previously this applied only to aliens, but from 1 January 1985 Commonwealth citizens have also been charged. Visa fees are not payable where the sponsor in the UK has been recognised as a refugee and the applicants are coming as his or her dependants.[2] There is a reduced fee for dependants of those on exceptional leave.[3] There is power to waive the fee in other circumstances.[4] An application for entry clearance is not made until any fees have been paid.[5] The level of fees charged for family settlement may be prohibitive in some cases, for example, where a spouse and a number of dependent children seek entry, and could constitute a disproportionate obstacle to the right to respect for family life. Refusal by an entry clearance officer to process an application in such circumstances could, we suggest, be challenged by way of judicial review, or appealed under section 65 of the Immigration and Asylum Act 1999.[6]

1   The Consular Fees (No 2) Order 1999, SI 1999/3132 sets out the current fees, which range from £33 for a single entry visit or student visa to £240 for a settlement visa for a spouse, fiancé(e) or child. Current fees are also displayed on the Foreign and Commonwealth Office website; see 3.12 fn 3.
2   *Abdi* (11000); *Ibrahim* (9347). The rules on refugee family reunion are silent on this, as are the IDI, but the Joint Entry Clearance Unit has confirmed this.
3   The Joint Entry Clearance Unit has stated that the visa fee for immediate family members of people with exceptional leave to remain is £50.00.
4   Fees will be waived in compelling compassionate circumstances.
5   HC 395, para 30, reversing *Ross* [1992] Imm AR 493, Immigration Appeal Tribunal.
6   The decision relates to entitlement to enter, and is made under the Immigration Rules, para 30.

The application

3.14 The date when an application for entry clearance is made is important because, although the key date for judging whether someone is eligible for a visa or entry certificate is usually the date of the decision rather than the date of the application,[1] the date of the application may count in certain cases.[2] For example, in the case of a child wishing to join parents who are settled in the UK, eligibility will depend upon the age of the applicant at the time when the application for entry clearance is made, and an application may not be refused solely on account of an applicant becoming over-age between the date of the application and the date of the decision on it.[3] The rules for entry clearance applications, unlike those for variations of leave from persons already in the UK, do not prescribe the use of particular forms, so that although the overseas posts all have stocks of standard forms (and the forms are available for downloading from the Foreign and Commonwealth Office website) their use is not mandatory. Before HC 395 the case law had established that an application for entry clearance did not require any particular formality, merely a request 'in quite unambiguous terms for an entry certificate to be issued to a particular person'.[4] The issue was one of fact to be determined in the light of all the circumstances.[5] The Court of Appeal has held, however, that an inquiry by relatives in the UK as to the likely outcome of an application for entry clearance and a reply from the Home Office did not amount to an application.[6] The Rules attempt to overcome the uncertainties of the case law by saying that an application is not made until the fees are paid.[7]

1 HC 395, para 27.
2 In *R v Immigration Appeal Tribunal, ex p Bibi and Purvez* [1986] Imm AR 61, DC the date of application was used to determine whether the Pakistani wife and children of a Commonwealth citizen settled in the UK on 1 January 1973 should be treated as Commonwealth citizens or aliens. The date of application is often the important date in transitional provisions for new rules and policies.
3 HC 395, para 27. For some unexplained reason, children of students, work permit holders, businessmen, etc do not benefit from the concession in para 27, although refusal of admission in these categories on the ground that the child has become over-age by the date of decision may be irrational and unfair, and may also engage art 8 of the ECHR.
4 *Brown v Entry Clearance Officer, Kingston* [1976] Imm AR 119; *Prajapati v Immigration Appeal Tribunal* [1982] Imm AR 56, CA; *Malik v Secretary of State for the Home Department* [1982] Imm AR 183. See further *R v Immigration Appeal Tribunal, ex p Kobir* [1986] Imm AR 311, QBD.
5 See further *Hussain* (2347), where there was no application form but the entry clearance officer received (1) declarations containing the name and address of the appellant and his fiancée who sought admission (2) confirmation that the fiancée was sponsoring the appellant and (3) her date of birth. The application was held to be good. In *Mann* (2435) there was a letter to the High Commission from the appellant stating his intention to marry, naming and giving the address of his fiancée and asking for forms for proceeding to the UK. This was held to be sufficient for an application.
6 *Secretary of State for the Home Department v Dahir and Abdi* [1995] Imm AR 570. See **3.11** fn 4 above.
7 HC 395, para 30.

3.15 But the Immigration Rules highlight another problem relating to visa applications. Under section 59(2) of the Immigration and Asylum Act 1999, a right of appeal is given to a person who, 'on an application duly made', is refused an entry clearance. This raises the question of when an application is 'duly made'.[1] If it is made at the wrong post, or where the applicant is not living, or the fee is not paid, and if the entry clearance officer refuses to consider the application for one of these reasons, there will be no decision, no refusal and, therefore, no appeal.[2] Nor will the applicant be able to mount any challenge on judicial review because the official is merely carrying out the policy laid down by the Secretary of State.[3] But the entry clearance officer must also have a measure of discretion and if he or she decides to consider the application notwithstanding a failure to comply with the geographical, financial or other procedural requirements of the Rules, there must be a strong presumption that the application is duly made, and the entry clearance officer would be estopped from denying it is so.

1   See *Abdi* (11000) for a discussion of when an application is duly made. The CA (*Dahir and Abdi* above) did not go over this ground again.
2   This is subject to the comments made about fee levels at **3.12** above; it may be that an unreasonable refusal to entertain an application where an applicant is not living (because of insuperable difficulties in compliance) would similarly be challengeable if fundamental human rights were at issue. See chapter 8 below.
3   See previous fn.

3.16 Once an application for entry clearance is duly made, it must be considered by the visa or entry clearance officer. Sponsorship and other documentation must be in place.[1] Often there will be an interview. In spouse and family cases it is a central feature of the application. Like immigration officers, entry clearance officers have a duty to be fair. Like immigration officers, they are under a duty not to act in a way which breaches a person's fundamental human rights,[2] nor in a way which discriminates on grounds of race or colour.[3] In the interview the entry clearance officer should check that the person being interviewed is well and understands the questions. Unfair questions should not be put. Leading questions do not particularly advance the case against an applicant or assist the interview, but entry clearance officers are carrying out administrative, not judicial, functions and there is, therefore, nothing improper in asking such questions.[4] An entry clearance officer should afford an applicant an opportunity to address any adverse evidence or conclusions which will affect his or her decision.[5] The conduct of interviews will now also be subject to the scrutiny of the Independent Race Monitor.[6] Complaints are now to be directed to the Joint Entry Clearance Unit.[7]

1   The Foreign and Commonwealth Office website contains all the relevant leaflets which give guidance as to documentation required: www.fco.gov.uk.
2   Human Rights Act 1998, s 6(1).
3   Race Relations Act 1976, s 19B, inserted by Race Relations (Amendment) Act 2000, s 1. However, s 19D allows discrimination on grounds of nationality, ethnic or national origin in the performance of immigration functions, making the amendment of little value. See Dummett, *The immigration exemptions in the Race Relations (Amendment) Act 2000*, ILPA, April 2001.
4   *Kumar* [1985] Imm AR 242.
5   *R v Secretary of State for the Home Department, ex p Moon* [1997] INLR 165; see also *Secretary of State for the Home Department v Thirukumar* [1989] Imm AR 270, QBD, 402, CA (on entry); *R v Secretary of State for the Home Department, ex p Fayed* [1997] 1 All ER 228, CA.
6   Race Relations Act 1976, s 19E, inserted by Race Relations Amendment Act 2000, s 1.
7   Joint Entry Clearance Unit, Visa Correspondence Unit, Desk Officer for (name of post where application made), 89 Albert Embankment, London SE1 7TP. Fax: 020 7238 3759/3761.

3.17 Although entry clearance officers are applying the Immigration Rules, this is not a mechanical exercise of applying rules to the facts of applications as presented to them. They are entitled to and do carry out their own investigations,[1] sometimes making village visits.[2] Sometimes these will prove the existence of a relationship previously in doubt, but they may also prove that an applicant is disqualified in some other way, for example, because a child seeking entry to join a parent has married. Usually entry clearance officers are not precluded from acting on the results of their investigations.[3] Applications may also be referred back to the Home Office for inquiries to be made in the UK, for guidance to be given in a complicated case or because of a special policy.

1 *R v Immigration Appeal Tribunal, ex p Hoque and Singh* [1988] Imm AR 216, CA.
2 See eg IDI Dec/00, Ch 8, Annex X which deals with village visits in dependent relatives' applications.
3 *R v Immigration Appeal Tribunal, ex p Kobir* [1986] Imm AR 311, QBD. But they should not act on anonymous denunciations or statements made by persons who are not prepared for the applicant to be aware of their evidence.

3.18 In the past, applications by spouses have caused problems if applicants were unsure how long they intended to remain in the UK after marriage. At one time the Tribunal said that the onus was on applicants to define their position and bring themselves within one or another Immigration Rule[1] but this approach has since been held to be a misapplication of the Rules.[2] Applicants do have to make clear the factual foundation of what they want, but applications are not formal documents and there is certainly no need for an applicant to specify any applicable Immigration Rule. That, it is thought, is the task of the entry clearance officer, who, like an immigration officer, must consider all relevant rules without having to conduct a roving expedition through all conceivably relevant rules.[3]

1 *Hussain* [1989] Imm AR 46.
2 *R v Immigration Appeal Tribunal, ex p Rafique* [1990] Imm AR 235, QBD.
3 *Ali v Secretary of State for the Home Department* [1988] Imm AR 274, CA. See now IDI Dec/00, Ch 8, Annex K, 'Visits for marriage', which allows for uncertainty in an applicant.

3.19 Where there has already been a successful application but the entry clearance was for some reason not used, and the applicant has had to re-apply, the previous application is strong evidence in favour of the applicant.[1] Where an applicant has successfully appealed against the refusal of entry clearance, it is wholly improper for an attempt to be made to circumvent the adjudicator's decision by pursuing fresh inquiries with a view to denying entry on a different basis, but in such cases entry clearance officers are entitled to ask questions in order to see if there has been a change of circumstances or there has been fraud or deception.[2] All this means that there may be considerable delay before applications are decided. The queues in India, Pakistan and Bangladesh are notorious and result in inordinate delay in some cases.[3] The existence of delay, however, does not invalidate the need for entry clearance,[4] although in a particular case it might give rise to a challenge on the ground of unfairness, and failure to take a decision after a reasonable period of time may be challenged by an application for a mandatory order.

1 *Bi (Channo)* [1978] Imm AR 182; *Begum (Sarwar)* [1986] Imm AR 192.
2 *R v Secretary of State for the Home Department, ex p Yousuf* [1989] Imm AR 554, QBD.
3 Since August 1985 there have been four queues: (i) right of abode applicants, dependants over 70, and special compassionate cases; (ii) spouses and children under 18; (iii) fiancé(e)s and other applicants for settlement; and (iv) re-applicants. Waiting times at the end of the first half of 2000 in Dhaka broadly showed three-and-a-half months for the first queue; seven months for the second; three-and-a-half months for the third; and nine to eleven months for the fourth. Bombay and Delhi were better (averaging about one-and-a-half and three months respectively: *Control of Immigration Statistics* (first half 2000), available via the Home Office website at www.homeoffice.gov.uk). However, these times do not take into account the further delay between interview and decision.
4 *R v Secretary of State for the Home Department, ex p Rofathullah* [1989] QB 219, [1988] Imm AR 514, CA.

Revocation of entry clearance

3.20 After an entry clearance has been issued, an entry clearance officer or immigration officer may revoke it[1] if satisfied that:

(i)   whether or not to the holder's knowledge false representations were employed or material facts were not disclosed, either in writing or orally, for the purpose of obtaining the entry clearance; or

(ii)   a change of circumstances since the issue of the entry clearance has removed the basis for admission to the UK, except where the change of circumstances amounts solely to a child coming for settlement becoming over-age since the issue of the entry clearance; or

(iii)   the holder's exclusion from the UK would be conducive to the public good.

These rules enable revocation of entry clearance before arrival in the UK, and are similar to (although not as extensive as) immigration officers' powers to refuse leave to enter to an entry clearance holder (where the entry clearance does not operate as leave to enter). The immigration officer may also cancel an entry clearance which operates as leave to enter. The criteria for cancellation are stricter. For detailed consideration of these grounds see **3.44-3.47** below.

1   HC 395, para 30A, added by HC 329 from 3 June 1996.

ENTRY CLEARANCE AS LEAVE TO ENTER

3.21   Section 3A of the Immigration Act 1971 (inserted by section 1 of the Immigration and Asylum Act 1999) creates 'greater flexibility in the way permission to enter the UK may be granted'[1] by empowering the Secretary of State to make Orders which (*inter alia*) allow entry clearance to have effect as leave to enter the UK, thereby reducing the role of immigration officers at the port of entry. As with much of the 1999 Act, the substance of the new provision is contained in the subordinate legislation, in this case the Immigration (Leave to Enter and Remain) Order 2000.[2] Under this Order, entry clearance will have effect as leave to enter provided it specifies the purpose for which the holder wishes to enter the UK[3] and is endorsed with the conditions to which it is subject,[4] or a statement that it is to have effect as indefinite leave to enter the UK.[5] Visit visas are to have effect as leave to enter on an unlimited number of occasions during their period of validity.[6] Leave to enter as a visitor will be for a period of six months where six months or more remain of the visa's period of validity and, where less than six months remain, for the remaining period.[7] Entry clearances for purposes other than visit(s) are to have effect as leave to enter the UK on one occasion only during the period of their validity,[8] whether that leave to enter is for an indefinite period[9] or endorsed with conditions.[10]

1   Explanatory notes to the Immigration and Asylum Act 1999, para 7.
2   SI 2000/1161.
3   SI 2000/1161, art 3(2).
4   SI 2000/1161, art 3(2)(a).
5   SI 2000/1161, art 3(2)(b). For power to refuse on the basis of nationality, see **3.5** above.
6   SI 2000/1161, art 4(1). 'Period of validity' is defined in art 4 as 'the period beginning on the day which the entry clearance becomes effective and ending on the day on which it expires'. Most visit visas only run for six months, but can run for up to five years for frequent travellers.
7   SI 2000/1161, art 4(2).
8   This is because leave to enter (except as a visitor) normally does not lapse on leaving the UK, so the same leave to enter can be used repeatedly: see **4.4** below.
9   SI 2000/1161, art 4(3)(a).

10 SI 2000/1161, art 4(3)(b). The conditions which can be imposed will be those which can be imposed on leave to enter under Immigration Act 1971, s 3(1)(c), ie restricting employment, precluding recourse to public funds and requiring registration with police.

3.22 Entry clearance does not operate as leave to enter if it does not specify its purpose, or if the holder arrives in the UK before it becomes effective,[1] or seeks entry for a different purpose.[2] In the latter two cases, the immigration officer at the port may cancel the entry clearance.[3] Where entry clearance operates as leave to enter, the immigration officer may examine the holder at the port to decide whether the leave to enter should be cancelled. We deal with cancellation of leave and port examinations below. In practice, it is hard to think of cases where entry clearance will not stand as leave to enter but will remain valid. If there is such a case,[4] when the holder seeks leave to enter it may be refused on the same grounds as those on which the entry clearance officer may revoke entry clearance, set out at **3.17** above. These are that false representations were made or material facts not disclosed for the purpose of obtaining entry clearance, or that there has been a relevant change in circumstances, or that exclusion is conducive to the public good. These grounds are considered in detail below, together with the additional grounds on which leave to enter may be refused, or cancelled, where entry clearance operated as leave to enter.

1 Immigration (Leave to Enter and Remain) Order 2000, SI 2000/1161, art 6(2)(a); HC 395, para 30C.
2 SI 2000/1161, art 6(2)(b); HC 395, para 30C.
3 SI 2000/1161, art 6(2), HC 395, para 30C. Cancellation of the entry clearance is not the same as cancellation of leave to enter. Cancellation of leave under Immigration Act 1971, Sch 2, para 2A(8) attracts the right of appeal as if it were refusal of leave to a holder of a current entry clearance. It may be that cancellation of entry clearance removes the right of appeal. For appeal rights see **3.74** below.
4 This scenario is envisaged in SI 2000/1161, art 6(3).

GENERAL GROUNDS FOR REFUSING ENTRY CLEARANCE OR LEAVE TO ENTER

3.23 An application for leave to enter, or for entry clearance, will be determined according to the detailed Immigration Rules dealing with the particular purpose for which the applicant wishes to come to the UK - visit, study, business, family reunion and so forth. The Rules also contain two additional lists – one where leave to enter or entry clearance 'is to be refused' and one where it 'should normally be refused'. They do not apply in cases where a person who already has entry clearance seeks leave to enter, where the grounds for refusing leave to enter are much more restricted. These are set out at **3.44-3.47** below. Leave to enter or entry clearance is to be refused under HC 395, paragraph 320 in the following cases:[1]

(1) entry is being sought for a purpose not covered by the Rules;
(2) the person seeking entry is currently the subject of a deportation order;
(3) failure to produce a valid national passport or other document satisfactorily establishing identity and nationality;
(4) failure to show that he or she is acceptable to the immigration authorities in another part of the common travel area to which the applicant wishes to travel;
(5) failure to produce entry clearance, if one was required;

(6)   the Secretary of State has personally directed that exclusion is conducive to the public good;

(7)   refusal on medical grounds (unless the person is settled in the UK or there are strong compassionate circumstances).

Grounds on which entry clearance should normally be refused are as follows:

(8)   failure by a person arriving in the UK to provide information to the immigration officer;

(8A) failure, by a person outside the UK, to provide information, documents or medical reports required to the immigration officer;

(9)   failure by a returning resident to meet the requirements of paragraph 18 of the Rules;

(10) production of a passport which is from an unrecognised territory or which is otherwise unacceptable;

(11) failure to observe the time limit or conditions attached to a past leave;

(12) obtaining a previous leave by deception;

(13) restricted returnability of a person other than those eligible for admission for settlement or a spouse eligible for admission under paragraph 282;

(14) refusal by a sponsor to give an undertaking in writing to be responsible for the applicant's maintenance and accommodation for the period of any leave granted;

(15) the making of false representations or the failure to disclose any material fact for the purpose of obtaining a work permit;

(16) failure, in the case of an unaccompanied child under the age of 18 years other than an asylum seeker, to provide written consent to the application from his parent(s) or legal guardian;

(17) save in relation to a person settled in the United Kingdom, refusal to undergo a medical examination;

(18) save where admission would be justified for strong compassionate reasons, conviction in any country of a serious criminal offence;

(19) exclusion is conducive to the public good in the light of the person's character, conduct or associations.

1   This Rule must be read with HC 395, para 26, which allows the word 'entry clearance officer' to be used for 'immigration officer' where appropriate, and para 39 which gives entry clearance officers the same discretion in relation to medical examinations as immigration officers.

The mandatory grounds

3.24 Leave to enter or entry clearance is to be refused if admission is sought for a purpose not covered by the Immigration Rules.[1] The Rules are drafted so narrowly that large numbers of people and purposes are omitted. Until recently, no provision was made in the Rules for the admission of unmarried partners. There is still no provision in the Rules for the admission of certain relatives, such as step-children or step-parents where the natural parent is still alive. Nor is there provision for the admission of the family members of those in the UK with exceptional leave to remain. Earlier rules were silent on these categories, but since 1994 the Rules have provided for mandatory refusal. This does not prevent immigration officers exercising discretion to admit them outside the Rules,[2] but it does restrict appeal rights to an examination of the lawfulness, rather than the merits, of the decision,[3] unless human rights are engaged.[4]

1   HC 395, para 320(1).
2   *Kuku v Secretary of State for the Home Department* [1990] Imm AR 27, CA; *Adac-Bosompra* [1992] Imm AR 579, Immigration Appeal Tribunal. See IDI Dec/00, Ch 9, s 2; immigration officers should consider eligibility under any concession as well as under the Rules.
3   See **18.76** below.
4   See chapter 8 below.

3.25 Other mandatory grounds are self-explanatory. A person who is the subject of a current deportation order must be refused leave to enter or entry clearance[1] since the deportation order prohibits entry to the UK.[2] A deportation order is not invalidated by leave to enter granted in error. However, if the deportation followed a conviction which is spent, refusal is not automatic.[3] A person who is subject to an Irish deportation order is not to be refused for that reason alone.[4] Passengers who do not satisfy the entry clearance officer or immigration officer of their identity or nationality are to be refused,[5] unless there are strong compassionate or other reasons for granting leave.[6] When they seek leave to enter, whether they are in the UK or abroad, they must submit to examination and to produce valid documents establishing identity and nationality.[7] Those who are travelling to another part of the common travel area but are not acceptable to the authorities there must be refused entry to the UK.[8] Those seeking leave to enter (whether in the UK or abroad) who are required to hold entry clearance but do not have one, are to be refused.[9] The Secretary of State for the Home Department may give a personal direction not to grant leave to enter or entry clearance on the ground that exclusion is conducive to the public good.[10] That ground is considered further below, as are medical grounds for exclusion (**3.30-3.33**).

1   HC 395, para 320(2).
2   Immigration Act 1971, s 5(1).
3   IDI Dec/00, Ch 9, s 2, para 3.3.
4   IDI Dec/00, Ch 9, s 2, para 3.3.
5   HC 395, para 320(3).
6   IDI Dec/00, Ch 9, s 2, para 4, revealing a discretion even in 'mandatory refusal' cases.
7   Immigration Act 1971, Sch 2, para 4 (persons arriving in the UK); Immigration (Leave to Enter and Remain) Order 2000, SI 2000/1161, art 7(2), (4) (persons seeking leave to enter abroad).
8   HC 395, para 320(4).
9   HC 395, para 320(5).
10 HC 395, para 320(6).

The discretionary grounds

3.26 The discretionary grounds, which allow but do not require leave to enter or entry clearance to be refused, are wide-ranging, and many are self-explanatory. We examine some of them in detail below.

Unacceptable passport

3.27 The immigration officer may refuse entry to persons using passports issued by governments of entities not recognised by the UK government.[1] Currently these are the Turkish Republic of Northern Cyprus (TRNC), Republic of China (Taiwan) and Palestine. However, the IDIs state that Turkish Republic of Northern Cyprus passport holders should not be refused entry under this paragraph, although their passports should not be endorsed. Taiwanese passports may be stamped notwithstanding non-recognition. Palestinian Authority travel documents are acceptable for travel to the UK and may be endorsed, although the IDIs hasten to add that 'this does not imply recognition of a separate State of Palestine'.[2]

1 HC 395, para 320(10).
2 IDI Dec/00, Ch 9, s 2, para 12.4.

Restricted returnability

3.28 Passengers who do not satisfy the immigration officer that they would be admitted to another country after a stay in the UK may be refused leave to enter,[1] but this Rule does not apply to persons who are eligible for admission for settlement or to a spouse who is admitted for an initial 12-month period with a view to settlement. It does, however, apply to unmarried partners given an initial period of up to two years[2] and to children given an initial 12 months, and is not disapplied just because the passenger holds an entry clearance.[3] Where a person's returnability to another country is restricted, leave to enter may nevertheless be given, subject to severe limits on the length of stay.[4]

1 HC 395, para 320(13).
2 HC 395, para 295B.
3 See *R v Secretary of State for the Home Department, ex p Sadiq* [1990] Imm AR 364, QBD.
4 See HC 395, paras 21-23.

Previous breaches of immigration law

3.29 Previous breaches of immigration control form separate grounds for refusal. Overstaying or breach of conditions on a previous stay, such as working or recourse to public funds, can give grounds for refusing leave to enter or entry clearance,[1] but should not do so unless the breach was reasonably serious.[2] Obtaining a previous leave to enter or remain by deception also grounds refusal of leave to enter or of entry clearance.[3] A person who has a work permit may be refused leave to enter if, whether or not to his or her knowledge, false representations were employed or material facts not disclosed, for the purpose of obtaining it.[4]

1 HC 395, para 320(11). See *Marquez* [1992] Imm AR 352, which mirrors *R v Secretary of State for the Home Department, ex p Sadiq* [1990] Imm AR 364, QBD (student working in breach of conditions on earlier stay). Emergency recourse to public funds should not ground refusal; see next fn.
2 See **4.25** and **4.26** below. If the breach is not serious enough to warrant refusal of variation of leave, it should not ground refusal of leave to enter or entry clearance.
3 HC 395, para 320(12). The deception does not need to be that of the applicant, under this Rule, so a person brought in illegally as a child could be penalised years later when seeking to enter as an adult. In these circumstances refusal on this basis could be held unfair or irrational.
4 HC 395, para 320(15). This Rule parallels the Rule allowing immigration officers to refuse leave to enter to those with entry clearance: see **3.44ff** below.

Medical grounds

3.30 Entry clearance officers abroad have no power to refer intending travellers for medical examination but do have power to require a medical report, and leave to enter may be refused if such a report is not produced.[1] Immigration officers at the port may refer anyone seeking leave to enter on arrival in the UK, and anyone arriving with advance leave, to a medical officer for medical examination.[2] The Immigration Rules state that a passenger who intends to stay in the UK for more than six months should normally be referred to the medical inspector for examination.[3] Passengers mentioning health or medical treatment as a reason for their visit, or who appear not to be in good mental or physical health, should also be referred to the medical inspector.[4] Immigration officers have a discretion, which should be exercised sparingly, to refer for examination in any other case.[5] Doctors should be used only to determine whether there are medical reasons for refusing admission or making admission subject to a requirement that the person has further examination or treatment. It is quite wrong to use doctors for other purposes in the administration of immigration control.[6] Refusal to undergo a medical examination is a ground for refusal of leave to enter except where the person is a returning resident.[7]

1　Immigration (Leave to Enter and Remain) Order 2000, SI 2000/1161, art 7(3) and (4).
2　Immigration Act 1971, Sch 2, para 2; 2A(4). See **3.63** below.
3　HC 395, para 36.
4　HC 395, para 39.
5　The IDI Nov/00, Ch 1, s 8 suggest that a person who is 'obviously unwell or [who] appears bodily dirty' could be referred.
6　In 1979, after the 'virginity testing' scandal, the Secretary of State gave instructions that medical inspectors should not be asked to examine passengers to establish whether they have borne children or have had sexual relations. In 1982 the Secretary of State gave further instructions that medical inspectors should not be asked to X-ray persons for the purpose of assessing their age. The IDI stress that it is essential that these instructions be strictly observed. A woman should not be referred for confirmation of a suspected pregnancy unless there is strong evidence that the purpose of her visit is to take advantage of NHS facilities: IDI Nov/00, ch 1, s 8, para 2.6. But seeking to take such advantage is not a ground for refusal of entry. So what is the point of referral?
7　HC 395, para 320(17).

3.31 Where the medical inspector at the port advises that for medical reasons it is undesirable to admit someone, the immigration officer must refuse leave to enter unless the person is settled here or there are 'strong compassionate reasons justifying admission.'[1] According to the IDI, the medical inspector would normally certify that it is undesirable to admit a passenger who is found or suspected to be suffering from pulmonary tuberculosis, venereal disease, leprosy or trachoma, or if the passenger is heavily infested with lice, is bodily dirty or is suffering from scabies.[2] The IDI indicate that medical inspectors may also issue a certificate if the nature of the person's condition would interfere with his or her ability to comply with the no recourse to public funds requirements.[3] However, medical inspectors should only certify that it is undesirable to admit a passenger to the UK when satisfied that his or her condition represents a significant risk to public health.[4] This suggests that a medical certificate of undesirability based on economic rather than public health criteria would be unlawful, although an immigration officer would be entitled to refuse the passenger leave to enter or entry clearance on 'recourse to public funds' grounds. A passenger who is diagnosed as suffering from AIDS or HIV infection should not be refused on public health grounds alone.[5] The IDI state that immigration officers are entitled to take into account the cost of any treatment which may be required. Since NHS treatment does not count as 'public funds', leave could not be refused on the ground that the passenger is likely to seek such treatment, and the immigration officer would therefore have to justify refusal of leave or entry clearance to an AIDS or HIV sufferer on other grounds. The policy on admission of AIDs and HIV-infected passengers is less generous than the after-entry policy,[6] but where an AIDs or HIV sufferer has been in the UK for a considerable period in circumstances where the UK may be said to have assumed responsibility (by eg starting treatment which it would be dangerous to stop), then even where the passenger has been on temporary admission throughout, refusal by reference to the on-entry policy may be unlawful and in breach of Article 3 of the ECHR.[7]

1 HC 395, para 320(7).
2 IDI Nov/00, Ch 1, s 8, para 2.1.
3 IDI Nov/00, Ch 1, s 8, para 2.1; see also HC 395 para 37.
4 IDI Nov/00, Ch 1, s 8, para 2.2.
5 IDI Nov/00, Ch 1, s 8, para 2.5.
6 See IDI Nov/00, Ch 1, s 8, para 3.3; *Davoren v Secretary of State for the Home Department* [1996] Imm AR 307.
7 *D v UK* (1997) 24 EHRR 423.

3.32 The Rule appears to give medical inspectors enormous powers, as refusal is based (a) on the medical inspector's diagnosis and (b) on his or her views on the desirability of admission, and the wording of the Rule is that immigration officers can only overrule the medical inspector if 'strong compassionate grounds' warrant admission. The Tribunal in *Al-Tuwaidji* took the view that refusal was mandatory even if independent medical evidence puts into question the diagnosis or advice of the medical inspector. It held that a medical inspector's diagnosis of schizophrenia could not be challenged on appeal, and that in the absence of compassionate circumstances leave should be refused.[1] We suggest that this decision cannot stand today, since it embodies fundamental unfairness,[2] as well as involving unlawful delegation of power from immigration officers to medical inspectors which is not warranted by the terms of the Immigration Act 1971. A better view of HC 395, paragraph 320(7) would be to treat the medical advice as a factor to be taken into account by immigration officers in the exercise of their own discretion, enabling them to take into account alternative medical diagnosis and opinions as well as the advice of the medical inspector.[3]

1 [1974], Imm AR 34. Followed in *Mohazeb* [1990] Imm AR 555.
2 See Chapter 8 below.
3 See *Pearson v Immigration Appeal Tribunal* [1978] Imm AR 212, CA; *R v Secretary of State for the Home Department, ex p Ounejma* [1989] Imm AR 75, QBD where a similar argument as regards mandatory entry clearance was rejected. See further *R v Secretary of State for the Home Department, ex p Rofathullah* [1989] QB 219, [1988] Imm AR 514, CA. This is also the view of the Home Office: see IDI Dec/00, Ch 9, s 2, para 8.1.

3.33 The Tribunal has in the past mitigated the effect of the mandatory refusal by a liberal interpretation of strong compassionate circumstances warranting admission.[1] The fact that a patient has undergone a cure would itself be a compassionate circumstance.[2]

1 See *Sacha* [1973] Imm AR 5.
2 See *Parvez* [1979–80] Imm AR 84, and *Bhatti* [1979–80] Imm AR 86n.

Criminal record

3.34 Certain persons who have committed a criminal offence are to be refused leave to enter or entry clearance unless the entry clearance officer or immigration officer considers admission to be justified on strong compassionate grounds.[1] The Rule applies to spouses or children under 18 coming for settlement, but in those cases there are more likely to be strong compassionate reasons.[2] Offences which count are those which, if committed in the UK, are punishable with imprisonment for a term of 12 months or more or, if committed outside the UK, would be so punishable if the conduct constituting the offence had occurred in the UK. Where the fact of conviction is disputed the burden is on the immigration officer.[3] It is unclear whether a 'conviction' can be disregarded if it was obtained without due process or *in absentia*, but the entry clearance officer or immigration officer may in such circumstances exercise discretion to grant leave or entry clearance.[4] Spent convictions must be disregarded.[5]

1 HC 395, para 320(18).
2 But see *Vasiljevic* [1975] Imm AR 100.
3 *Hashim* (6421) Immigration Appeal Tribunal, unreported.
4 *Hashim* (6421) Immigration Appeal Tribunal, unreported.
5 See IDI Dec/00, Ch 9, s 2, para 20.1.

3.35 In decisions under the old rules, the Tribunal held that admission would only be allowed if there are 'strong compassionate circumstances'.[1] 'Strong compassionate circumstances' are not further defined or qualified in the Immigration Rules and ought to be given their ordinary meaning. Thus in *Liberto*[2] it was held that strong compassionate circumstances did not include the need personally to be present in order to prosecute civil proceedings in the English courts. In another case it was held that there were strong compassionate grounds where the appellant had been convicted for possession of a small amount of cannabis, but had a wife and children born in the UK who, for family reasons, did not want to leave and who had had previous visits without incident or complaint.[3] What constitutes compassionate circumstances is largely a question of fact in each case. The seriousness of the offence and the immigrant's propensity to re-offend will be relevant.[4] In *Palacio*[5] the applicant, who had a conviction for fraud, wished to visit this country for one week in order to see his fiancée and two of his children by a former marriage. He was refused entry and this was upheld by the Tribunal, ruling that the circumstances were not 'of a totally exceptional and compelling nature' so as to justify admission.[6] The Divisional Court said the Tribunal was wrong to redefine 'strong compassionate circumstances', but did not reverse the decision, suggesting instead that the appellant make a fresh application.

1 *Vasiljevic* [1975] Imm AR 100; *Sanchez* (4731) following *R v Secretary of State for the Home Department, ex p Guediche* (18 December 1985, unreported), DC.
2 [1975] Imm AR 61. However, the quality of aims requirements of Art 6 ECHR might dictate a different conclusion today; see *R v Immigration officer, ex p John Quaguah* [2000] INLR 196, QBD.
3 *Bailey* (3670).
4 *Langridge* [1972] Imm AR 38.
5 *R v Immigration Appeal Tribunal, ex p Palacio* [1979–80] Imm AR 178.
6 A test formulated by the Tribunal in *Awadallah* [1978] Imm AR 5.

3.36 However, the Rule is not mandatory in terms but discretionary, and it is not necessary for there to be strong compassionate circumstances in order for discretion to be exercised in the applicant's favour. The fact that there is a residual discretion under which a person to whom the paragraph applies may be given leave to enter the UK was emphasised by Sullivan J in the Mike Tyson case,[1] in which Justice for Women challenged the Secretary of State for the Home Department's instruction to admit the heavyweight boxer, who had been sentenced to six years' imprisonment in the US for rape. He pointed out that it may be considered that it is in the public interest that that person be permitted to come to the UK, given some learning, entertainment or economic value that he can bring to this country. Whether those advantages are such as to justify an exception being made to the normal rule is a matter, in normal cases, for the immigration officer to decide. But he expressly upheld the general discretion to admit in the absence of strong compassionate circumstances – a discretion belonging both to the immigration officer and to the Secretary of State.

1   *R v Secretary of State for the Home Department, ex p Bindel* [2001] Imm AR 1, QBD.

3.37   The criteria for exclusion under HC 395, paragraph 320(18) remain distressingly vague. Those entitled to rely on EC law are much better off, since exclusion must be much more rigorously justified.[1] Care must also be taken to ensure that the right to family life is not interfered with in a manner contrary to Article 8 of the ECHR by taking disproportionate measures which are not necessary in a democratic society (see chapter 8 below). No one claiming asylum can be refused leave to enter on the basis of this or any other general Immigration Rule; the Convention criteria for exclusion must be applied.[2] Similarly, no one claiming a fear of treatment contrary to Article 3 of the ECHR may be refused leave to enter by virtue of this Rule, or any other.[3]

1   See C-348/96 *Donatella Calfa* [1999] INLR 333, ECJ. See chapter 7 below.
2   See chapter 12 below.
3   See chapter 8 below.

Exclusion for the public good

3.38   The Immigration Rules provide for refusal of leave to enter or of entry clearance, or cancellation of advance leave on arrival, on 'conducive to the public good' grounds in two distinct situations. Refusal is mandatory, where the Secretary of State for the Home Department personally has so directed.[1] But even where there is no such direction, leave should normally be refused,[2] or is to be cancelled,[3] where the immigration officer has information which makes it seem right to refuse leave to enter, for example, in the light of the passenger's character, conduct or associations. Refusal on 'conducive grounds' may thus result from a prior ban imposed by the Secretary of State or from an on-the-spot decision by an immigration officer. An example of a prior blanket ban was that imposed on Scientologists in 1968 on the grounds that Scientology was 'socially harmful' and a 'serious danger to … health'.[4] This ban was only lifted in 1980.[5] The Secretary of State has imposed bans on notorious racists such as Ku Klux Klan imperial wizard Bill Wilkinson,[6] and on US Nation of Islam leader Louis Farrakhan. An example of an on-the-spot refusal is the case where a man is given leave to enter by the immigration officer and passes through to Customs, where drugs are discovered in his baggage and he is refused leave on 'conducive' grounds.[7]

1   HC 395, paras 320(6) and 321A(4).

2   HC 395, para 320(19).
3   HC 395, para 321A(5).
4   769 HC Official Report (5th series) written answers col 189.
5   988 HC Official Report (5th series) written answers col 578. See further Case No 41/74: *Van Duyn v Home Office (No 2)* [1975] Ch 358, [1974] ECR 1337, ECJ.
6   (1978) Guardian, 17 February.
7   *Villone* [1979–80] Imm AR 23. Other examples might be where someone has no criminal record but is suspected to be involved in organised crime (for someone refused entry on these grounds and because of their criminal record see *R v Immigration Appeal Tribunal, ex p Palacio* [1979–80] Imm AR 178).

3.39 In determining whether a person should be refused admission on 'public good' grounds, the discretion is wide, but the reasons are not to be trivial or light.[1] This, however, has not prevented refusals for possession of trivial amounts of cannabis,[2] or preventing the entry of someone who has been tried and acquitted of a charge of illegal importation of drugs, just because the immigration officer took a different view from the jury.[3] Nor has it prevented the Tribunal suggesting that there is a general rule that it is conducive to the public good to refuse admission to anyone attempting to import opium.[4] The upshot is that in drug smuggling cases, the offender or suspect is unlikely to obtain admission and the Immigration Rules will be administered without regard to any of the principles governing deportation recommendations by a criminal court or decisions to deport by the Home Office. In deception cases, however, there is likely to be a greater cross-reference to the deportation decisions, particularly since the House of Lords held in *R v Immigration Appeal Tribunal, ex p Patel*[5] that past dishonest deception was covered by the power to deem deportation conducive to the public good.[6] Refusal of entry on conducive grounds based on serious deception, past or present, is unlikely to be struck down as unreasonable on a judicial review challenge.[7]

1   *Scheele* [1976] Imm AR 1.
2   *Villone* as above. Now, however, IDI Dec/00, Ch 9, s 2, para 21.2 indicate a different attitude. Dealing with those caught at the airport in possession of drugs, they say that if the quantity is small and the passenger has enough money to pay the fine and cover his or her proposed stay in the UK, he or she should be admitted. Refusal of leave should only follow if there is good reason to believe that the drugs are intended for sale, or if the passenger is an addict or regular user: IDI Dec/00, Ch 9, s 2, para 21.2.
3   *Nkiti v Immigration Officer, Gatwick* [1989] Imm AR 585, CA. Now, however, the immigration officer must be satisfied 'beyond reasonable doubt' before refusing on the basis that a passenger is a trafficker in pornography, although seizure of material by Customs would constitute *prima facie* grounds for refusal.
4   *Khazrai* [1981] Imm AR 9.
5   [1988] AC 910, [1988] 2 All ER 378.
6   Immigration Act 1971, s 3(5)(a).
7   See *R v Secretary of State for the Home Department, ex p Kwapong* [1993] Imm AR 569 (Nigerian with indefinite residence facilitates an illegal entry by bringing with him a child travelling on a false passport); *R v Secretary of State for the Home Department, ex p Sanyaolu* [1993] Imm AR 505 (applicant had obtained his previous leave by saying he was supported by an uncle, when in fact he was working in breach of conditions).

3.40 Before the adjudicator and Tribunal the test is not so stringent. They are dealing with an appeal on the merits and are able to assess the exercise of discretion by the immigration officer. This means that Tribunal decisions can often throw greater light on the proper exercise by immigration officers of their discretion. In *Olufosoye*[1] the Tribunal gave guidance on public good refusals, where the holder of a multiple entry visit visa had worked in breach of her leave conditions on a first visit, and was refused entry when she returned to the

UK. First, the Tribunal held that where the immigration authorities contended that exclusion was conducive to the public good, whether on a decision to deport or a refusal of leave to enter, it was for them to satisfy the appellate authority that the decision was justified. In so far as the justification consists of deception or other criminal conduct, the standard of proof will be at the higher end of the spectrum of balance of probability. Secondly, in the light of the provisions of HC 395, paragraph 320(11) and (12), it was necessary to prove grounds other than those set out in those paragraphs to justify exclusion as conducive to the public good. The general reasons for refusing the grant of an entry clearance, such as breach of the time limit or conditions of a previous leave, are a different set of criteria from exclusion on conducive grounds, and paragraph 320(19) should not be used as a back door so as to import into paragraph 321 extra grounds for refusing leave to the holder of an entry clearance. Thirdly, the fact that particular conduct would not provide the basis for a decision to deport on conducive grounds was relevant in considering whether the same conduct should lead to a refusal of leave to enter on 'conducive grounds'.[2] Where a decision on conducive grounds is based on conduct which has been the subject of previous investigation or adjudication, the immigration officer should not normally depart from the results of that inquiry.[3]

1   [1992] Imm AR 141.
2   See also *Miyoba* (2984).
3   See *Ali v Secretary of State for the Home Department* [1984] 1 All ER 1009, [1984] 1 WLR 663, CA; see also (in another context) *R v Secretary of State for the Home Department, ex p Danaie* [1998] Imm AR 84.

3.41   Refusal on conducive grounds will normally be made in the light of the passenger's character, conduct or associations, but it need not be confined to reasons of this kind. This was made clear by the Divisional Court in *Ajaib Singh*.[1] There a man had obtained an entry certificate to come to the UK for marriage. At the time, however, his bride-to-be was only 14½ years old. This had been overlooked by the entry clearance officer, although fully disclosed, but was spotted by the immigration officer on his arrival and leave to enter was refused. If the reason had been merely to correct an executive or administrative error by the entry clearance officer, the Divisional Court suggested that refusal would be wrong. But more was involved. The discretion to refuse on public good grounds was deliberately left in wide terms so that an immigration officer could exercise a wide discretion. The public good rule has thus been invoked to exclude a man who obtained his prior residence status by a marriage of convenience.[2]

1   *R v Immigration Appeal Tribunal, ex p Ajaib Singh* [1978] Imm AR 59. This situation is now covered by HC 395, para 277.
2   *Osama v Immigration Officer, London (Gatwick) Airport* [1978] Imm AR 8. See also *R v Immigration Appeal Tribunal, ex p Cheema* [1982] Imm AR 124, CA.

EC joint list of persons to be refused entry

3.42   The Schengen Information System, set up under the Schengen Agreements of 1985 and 1990, is a system for the exchange of information concerning persons who for one reason or another – commission of criminal offences, immigration irregularities, football hooliganism, suspected involvement with banned organisations – are considered undesirable for entry into member states. The UK has opted out of the Schengen *acquis* which now forms part of the 'framework' of the EU,[1] but has indicated its intention to be part of the Schengen Information System. It is probable that persons whose names come up on the computer from other member states are in fact refused on conducive grounds by an operational practice of co-operation which is not fully transparent.

1   Protocol 2 to the Consolidated EC Treaty incorporates the Schengen *acquis* into the framework of the EU, but acknowledges that the UK and Ireland are not parties to the Agreements, although they should be allowed to opt in to some parts. See **7.21** and **7.22** below.

Excluded persons under international obligations

3.43   Section 8B of the Immigration Act 1971 (inserted by section 8 of the Immigration and Asylum Act 1999) provides for mandatory refusal or cancellation of leave to enter of 'excluded persons', defined as persons named or described by UN Resolution or EU Council instrument in designated Orders under the 1971 Act.[1] Such persons are also to be stripped of diplomatic exemption.[2] The Immigration (Designation of Travel Bans) Order 2000[3] provides that persons named by, or under, or described by a designated instrument (as set out in the Schedule) need not be excluded from the UK if admitting them would not be contrary to the obligations in the designated instruments listed in Article 2 of the Order; or if their exclusion breached the UK's obligations under the ECHR or the Geneva Convention. The designated list is now contained in the Schedule to the Immigration (Designation of Travel Bans) (Amendment) Order 2000.[4] Clearly, these provisions are designed to exclude war criminals and persons of that ilk, rather than football hooligans. However, they may well be used to exclude members and supporters of organisations perceived as terrorist under the very wide new definitions on the domestic and European plane, and the designation orders should therefore be monitored with care.

1   Immigration Act 1971, as amended, s 8B(4).
2   Immigration Act 1971, s 8B(3).
3   SI 2000/2724, in force 10 October 2000.
4   SI 2000/3338, in force 21 December 2000. It refers to UN Security Council and EU Council resolutions in relation to Angola, Burma, Sierra Leone and the Federal Republic of Yugoslavia.

False representation to obtain entry clearance

3.44   Entry clearance may be revoked,[1] or leave to enter refused,[2] if the entry clearance officer or immigration officer is satisfied that false representations were used to obtain entry clearance, whether or not to the holder's knowledge. If the entry clearance operated as leave to enter, however, that leave may only be cancelled if the false representations were made by the applicant.[3] The representations may be written or oral. It is incumbent on the officer to prove the case to the requisite standard, ie prove a representation, its falsity and the fact that it was made for the purpose of gaining entry clearance.[4] The Court of Appeal has ruled that a false representation is simply a representation that is inaccurate, and does not necessarily connote fraud.[5] Where fraud is alleged the standard of proof will have to be higher. A representation will not be false if it is only a statement of the existence of facts on a certain day, and not a continuing representation of future matters. Does the false representation have to be material in the sense of decisive of the application? In *Sukhjinder Kaur*,[6] a woman coming to join her husband for settlement in the UK failed to mention to the entry clearance officer that he was in prison on remand for homicide. The Court of Appeal upheld the immigration officer's refusal of leave to enter, following its earlier decision in *Akhtar*,[7] and holding that the false representation does not need to have been determinative in the sense that the entry clearance officer would have been bound to refuse entry clearance if he or she had known the true facts.[8] All that is required is that the immigration officer should be satisfied that false representations were employed for the purposes of obtaining the clearance. The court also held that the false representations did not need to be material to the decision.[9]

1   HC 395, para 30A(i).
2   HC 395, para 321(i).
3   HC 395, para 321A(2).
4   The standard required will be particularly high where the entry clearance has been issued following a successful appeal to an adjudicator where the starting point is a binding decision in favour of the appellant: *R v Secretary of State for the Home Department, ex p Miah* [1983] Imm AR 91, DC; *Ali v Secretary of State for the Home Department* [1984] 1 All ER 1009, [1984] 1 WLR 663, CA. See also *R v Secretary of State for the Home Department, ex p Danaie* [1998] Imm AR 84, CA.
5   *Akhtar v Immigration Appeal Tribunal* [1991] Imm AR 326, CA.
6   *Sukhjinder Kaur v Secretary of State for the Home Department* [1998] Imm AR 1, CA.
7   *Akhtar v Immigration Appeal Tribunal* above.
8   This was the old test in the illegal entry cases on false representation to secure entry: see *R v Secretary of State for the Home Department, ex p Jayakody* [1982] 1 All ER 461, Imm AR 205, CA; *R v Secretary of State for the Home Department, ex p Ming* [1994] Imm AR 216, QBD.
9   *Sukhjinder Kaur* above. In *Akhtar* the CA left this question open; in *Eusebio* (4739) the Tribunal had held that false representations had to be material.

Non-disclosure of material facts

3.45 The second main ground for revoking an entry clearance or refusing leave to enter on an entry clearance which is ineffective as leave to enter is where the immigration officer is satisfied that material facts were not disclosed for the purpose of obtaining entry clearance. Here, the critical question is the meaning of 'material'. In *Sukhjinder Kaur*[1] the Court of Appeal again adopted a different approach from that taken in the illegal entry cases, holding that 'material' did not mean 'decisive', as the court had previously held in *Jayakody*,[2] but it was only necessary that the facts not disclosed would be likely to have influenced the decision. All that immigration officers need show is that passengers have failed to disclose facts which they knew or ought to have known would be relevant in considering whether to grant the visa. However, in practice the scope of relevant questions is usually determined by those posed in the application form and any oral questions. In determining whether facts are 'material', the critical question is the effect they would have had on the application actually made. Where the entry clearance operated as leave to enter, it can only be cancelled on this ground if the failure was that of the applicant, not if a third party was responsible.[3] An immigrant who has obtained an entry clearance on an inaccurate basis cannot replace the actual application with a wholly different application on arrival and argue that since he or she might have been admitted on this new application the previous non-disclosures are immaterial.[4] As we have seen, an immigration officer may cancel an entry clearance if the holder seeks leave to enter for a different purpose.[5]

1   [1998] Imm AR 1, CA. See also *Marquez* [1992] Imm AR 354.
2   *R v Secretary of State for the Home Department, ex p Jayakody* [1982] 1 All ER 461, [1981] Imm AR 205, CA; see also *R v Secretary of State for the Home Department, ex p Ming* [1994] Imm AR 216, QBD.
3   HC 395, para 321A(2).
4   *Bugdaycay v Secretary of State for the Home Department* [1987] AC 514 at 525, HL.
5   Immigration (Leave to Enter and Remain) Order, SI 2000/1161, art 6(2); HC 395, para 30C.

Change of circumstances since issue

3.46 The entry clearance officer or immigration officer may revoke entry clearance[1] or refuse leave to enter, or cancel it if the entry clearance operated as leave to enter, if a change of circumstances since the issue of entry clearance has removed the basis of the holder's claim to admission.[2] This does not include children coming to join parents settled in the UK who become over-age between the issue of entry clearance and travelling to the UK.[3] The change of circumstances must be sufficient to remove the basis of the holder's claim to admission, so only decisive changes will suffice, such as marriage by a child seeking entry as a dependant of his or her parents.[4] Other changes may often be a matter of degree and will depend on the facts.[5] Marriage by a dependent child is perhaps the most frequent decisive change, but there has to be a valid marriage and the burden of proving that is on the immigration officer. Where a decision on entry has been delayed and the entrant has been on temporary admission, the change of circumstances may arise after arrival in the UK. Thus, where an Iranian was a genuine visitor on arrival but decided to remain as a businessman prior to the decision to grant or refuse entry, this was a change of circumstances.[6] Decisions on this provision are sometimes very harsh, as in cases where the sponsor or the accompanying parent dies between the date of issue of the entry clearance and arrival in the UK.[7]

1   HC 395, para 30A(ii).
2   HC 395, paras 321(ii) and 321A(1).
3   This concession does not apply to children joining parents who are not settled: see **3.14** fn 3 above.
4   The burden of proof is on the immigration officer. See *R v Immigration Appeal Tribunal, ex p Suily Begum* [1990] Imm AR 226, QBD.
5   *Salmak* [1991] Imm AR 191, Immigration Appeal Tribunal; *Olufosoye* [1992] Imm AR 141, Immigration Appeal Tribunal.
6   *Teflisi* (3522) unreported.
7   See *Arshad* [1977] Imm AR 19; *R v Secretary of State for the Home Department, ex p Angur Begum* [1989] Imm AR 302, QBD.

Additional grounds for refusal or cancellation of leave to enter

3.47 Apart from the three general grounds on which entry clearance may be revoked or leave to enter refused or cancelled (false representations, non-disclosure of material facts and change of circumstances), there are additional grounds which do not entitle the entry clearance officer to revoke entry clearance but which entitle him or her, or an immigration officer on arrival, to refuse or cancel leave to enter.[1] Leave to enter may be refused to an entry clearance holder (but not cancelled if it operates as leave to enter) if the passenger cannot satisfy the immigration officer that he or she would be admitted to another country after staying in the UK.[2] Leave may be refused or cancelled on medical grounds;[3] at the personal direction of the Secretary of State for the Home Department on grounds of public good; or on general grounds that entry would not be conducive to the public good, such that it seems right to cancel leave. In addition, a holder of an entry clearance may be refused leave to enter on the ground of restricted returnability (but may not have advance leave to enter cancelled on this ground).

1   Immigration (Leave to Enter and Remain) Order 2000, SI 2000/1161, art 13(7); Immigration Act 1971, Sch 2, para 2A; HC 395, paras 321, 321A.
2   HC 395, para 321(iii); see *R v Secretary of State for the Home Department, ex p Sadiq* [1990] Imm AR 364.
3   See 3.30–3.33 above.

Re-determining admissibility

3.48   Where the validity of a visa or an entry certificate has been effectively undermined by false representations, a failure to disclose material facts or by a change of circumstance, the reality is that in most cases a refusal or cancellation of leave will be the inevitable consequence. But there will always be a residue of cases where this is not necessarily so. The Court of Appeal decision in *Akhtar*[1] leaves undecided the consequences of a finding by the immigration officer that false representations were employed in obtaining entry clearance. Can immigration officers re-determine admissibility in any case, or must they refuse or cancel leave to enter and treat the entry clearance as ineffective in all cases? The wording of the rule relating to cancellation of advance leave (whether or not granted by entry clearance) is mandatory: leave to enter or remain which is in force 'is to be cancelled' on these grounds.[2] The consequence of cancellation of advance leave to enter is that the entry clearance ceases to have effect.[3] This contrasts with the language of the earlier rule relating to refusal of leave to enter of those holding entry clearance, which is on its face discretionary, but which was held to be mandatory in effect. The arcane debate on the extent to which entry clearance remains 'current' for the purposes of appeals[4] is, we suggest, made redundant by the new provisions in Schedule 2 to the Immigration Act 1971,[5] which provide that if advance leave to enter is cancelled, there is a right of appeal as if the person concerned was refused leave to enter at a time when he or she had a current entry clearance.

1   [1991] Imm AR 326, CA.
2   HC 395, para 321A.
3   Immigration (Leave to Enter and Remain) Order 2000, SI 2000/1161, art 6(1).
4   See last edition, 3.21–3.23.
5   Immigration Act 1971, Sch 2, para 2A(8).

PRE-ARRIVAL IMMIGRATION CHECKS

3.49   The theme of this chapter is the drive to move as much of the detailed scrutiny of passengers' eligibility for entry out of UK ports, a process which started with the system of visas and entry clearance,[1] and was continued by section 8 of the Immigration Act 1988, which envisaged a voluntary examination of passengers by immigration officers prior to their arrival in the UK, leading to the grant of leave.[2] The system of pre-arrival checks envisaged by section 8 of the 1988 Act has been made compulsory and widely expanded by section 3A of the Immigration Act 1971 and the Immigration (Leave to Enter and Remain) Order 2000,[3] as we have seen, so that leave to enter granted (or refused) before embarkation for the UK may well become the norm. The new system requires that entry clearance officers abroad have similar powers of examination as those available to immigration officers on arrival. We look at the powers of examination before and on arrival in the UK below.

1 In this chapter we do not deal with the enforcement of that system through carrier sanctions, for which see chapter 14 below.
2 Repealed by Immigration and Asylum Act 1999, Sch 14, para 35.
3 SI 2000/1661.

3.50 Before turning to those powers, however, we should mention the other way in which immigration controls have been made extra-territorial: through the provisions relating to the Channel Tunnel. What these provisions do is to make a swathe of French and Belgian territory, and trains travelling through it, effectively part of the UK for immigration purposes.

The Channel Tunnel

3.51 The Channel Tunnel Act 1987, passed to implement the Canterbury Treaty of 12 February 1986, included provision for the construction and operation of the Channel Tunnel; for the incorporation of the British part of the tunnel system into England and the district of Kent and for English law to apply accordingly;[1] for the application and enforcement of law in relation to it and otherwise for the regulation of the tunnel system and matters connected with it. The principal order made under the Act is the Channel Tunnel (International Arrangements) Order 1993,[2] which came into force on 2 August 1993, initially covering arrangements with France, but amended by the Channel Tunnel (Miscellaneous Provisions) Order 1994[3] so as to cover both France and Belgium.

1 Channel Tunnel Act 1987, s 10.
2 SI 1993/1813, as amended by the Channel Tunnel (Security) Order 1994, SI 1994/570, the Channel Tunnel (International Arrangements) (Amendment) Order 1996, SI 1996/2283, the Channel Tunnel (International Arrangements) (Amendment) Order 2000, SI 2000/913 and the Channel Tunnel (International Arrangements) (Amendment No 2) Order 2000, SI 2000/1775.
3 SI 1994/1405.

3.52 The Channel Tunnel (International Arrangements) Order 1993[1] incorporates into UK law[2] the terms of the agreement between France and the UK for the running of the tunnel system, referred to as the 'International Articles'. The Order and its 1994 counterpart[3] enable UK immigration officers to operate on French and Belgian territory and vice versa and allow immigration controls to be carried out on the trains running between London, Paris and Lille,[4] and Brussels. The Orders extend the powers of immigration officers under the Immigration Act 1971 to carry out immigration control within a 'control zone' within French and Belgian territory.[5] A 'control zone' means that part of French or Belgian territory within which immigration officers (and now also the Secretary of State for the Home Department)[6] are empowered to effect immigration and other controls.[7] The provisions of the Immigration Act 1971 are modified in relation to those entering and leaving through the tunnel system, so as to include leaving a control zone in the definition of entry,[8] and to allow examination, and the grant, refusal or cancellation of leave, to take place in control zones as if they were at the port of entry in the UK.[9]

1 SI 1993/1813, as amended by the Channel Tunnel (Security) Order 1994, SI 1994/570, the Channel Tunnel (International Arrangements) (Amendment) Order 1996, SI 1996/2283, the Channel Tunnel (International Arrangements) (Amendment) Order 2000, SI 2000/913 and the Channel Tunnel (International Arrangements) (Amendment No 2) Order 2000, SI 2000/1775.
2 SI 1993/1813, art 3(1).
3 Channel Tunnel (Miscellaneous Provisions) Order 1994, SI 1994/1405.
4 SI 1993/1813, art 7.
5 Articles 5, 8, 9 and 10 contained in Sch 2 to SI 1993/1813; art 4(1) of the Channel Tunnel (Miscellaneous Provisions) Order 1994, SI 1994/1405.
6 Immigration Act 1971, s 3A(7) and (8), as inserted by Immigration and Asylum Act 1999, s 1.
7 See art 1(2)(g) of the International Articles in Sch 2 to SI 1993/1813.
8 Immigration Act 1971, s 11, as amended by SI 1993/1813.
9 SI 1993/1813, Sch 4, para 1(11)(d), as amended by SI 1994/1405; SI 2000/1775, art 4.

Examination abroad for the grant of leave

3.53 As we have seen above, an immigration officer, whether or not in the UK, may give or refuse a person leave to enter the UK at any time before that person's departure for the UK, or in the course of their journey.[1] To determine whether or not to give leave to enter, and if so for what period and subject to what conditions, the immigration officer may seek the information and documents that he or she would be entitled to obtain in an examination at the port.[2] Since the immigration officer examining someone abroad cannot refer the applicant to the port medical inspector, an up-to-date medical report can be requested instead.[3] Failure to provide the information, documents or medical report is a ground for refusal of leave.[4] The immigration officer or Secretary of State is authorised to use the power of examination in a discriminatory way against persons of a particular nationality if justified by statistical or intelligence information indicating that persons of that nationality have breached or will attempt to breach immigration laws.[5]

1 Immigration (Leave to Enter and Remain) Order, SI 2000/1161, art 7(1).
2 SI 2000/1161, art 7(2).
3 SI 2000/1161, art 7(3).
4 SI 2000/1161, art 7(4). Presumably it is a discretionary ground.
5 Race Relations (Immigration and Asylum) Authorisation 2001, para 4(2)(b), 6, in IDI Mar/01, Ch 1, s 11, Annex B.

EXAMINATION AT THE PORT OF ENTRY[1]

Who is examined

3.54 All passengers arriving at a port of entry in the UK are required to submit to examination by immigration officers. This applies to British citizens,[2] other citizens of the EU,[3] and other people who do not require leave to enter. In order to retain these frontier controls, which run counter to the establishment in the EC of a single market without internal frontiers,[4] the UK has negotiated a special protocol to the Consolidated Treaty of the EC.[5] In order to find out who is eligible and if so on what conditions they should be given leave to enter, immigration officers are given power under the Immigration Act 1971 to examine all those who have arrived in the UK by ship, aircraft or train, even if they are merely in transit and do not wish to enter the UK.[6] The purpose of doing so is to establish:

(i)   whether any of them are British citizens (or Commonwealth citizens with a right of abode); and

(ii)   if subject to control, whether they can or cannot enter without leave; and

(iii) if they may not, whether they have been given leave which is still in force;

(iv) if not, whether they should be given leave and for what period and on what conditions (if any); or

(v)   should be refused it.

In respect of passengers arriving with leave to enter which is in force but was given before their arrival, the immigration officer's examination is to establish:

(i)   whether there has been such a change in the circumstances of the case that it should be cancelled;

(ii)   whether the leave was obtained as a result of false information given by the passenger or his or her failure to disclose material facts;

(iii) whether there are medical grounds on which leave should be cancelled;[7]

(iv) whether it would be conducive to the public good for the leave to be cancelled.[8]

It is a criminal offence to refuse to submit to this examination.[9] Normally, examination of holders of UK passports describing the holder as a British citizen or as a citizen of the UK and Colonies having the right of abode in the UK, will be cursory. Similarly those with EEA passports (who do not require leave to enter) will normally be waved through.[10] Passengers who have certificates of entitlement, and those who have continuing leave to enter or remain will normally have a fairly cursory examination. Ministerial authorisation under the Race Relations Act[11] enables the immigration officer to subject passengers to a more rigorous examination, require them to submit to further examination, examine and detain their documents, search them, detain them and impose conditions on temporary admission by reason of their nationality, if there is statistical evidence showing a trend of breach of the immigration laws by persons of that nationality, or intelligence suggesting that a significant number of persons of that nationality have breached or will breach the immigration laws. The Act itself permits discrimination on grounds of ethnic origin.[12] Tamils, Kurds, Pontic Greeks, Roma, Somalis, Albanians, Afghans and ethnic Chinese presenting Malaysian or Japanese travel documents are currently targeted.[13]

1 The term includes areas and trains in France and Belgium defined as control zones under the Channel Tunnel (International Arrangements) Order 1993, SI 1993/1813, as amended. See **3.51-3.52** above.

2 Immigration Act 1971, ss 1(1), 3(9).

3 Immigration (European Economic Area) Regulations 2000, SI 2000/2326, reg 24.

4 See art 14 EC (formerly art 7a).

5 See Protocol on the application of certain aspects of art 14 of the Treaty establishing the European Community to the UK and to Ireland.

6 Immigration Act 1971, Sch 2, para 2(1); *R v Secretary of State for the Home Department, ex p Connhye* [1987] Imm AR 478, QBD.

7 Immigration Act 1971, Sch 2, para 2A(2).

8 Immigration Act 1971, Sch 2, para 2A(3).

9 Immigration Act 1971, s 26(1)(a).

10 The 'Bangemann wave' was the historic compromise between the UK government's demand to retain immigration controls at internal frontiers and the other EU governments' demand that they be removed. In practice EEA nationals' passports are examined as cursorily as those of British citizens.

11 Race Relations (Immigration and Asylum) Authorisation 2001, in IDI Mar/01, Ch 1, s 11, Annex EE.
12 Race Relations Act 1976, s 19D, inserted by Race Relations (Amendment) Act 2000.
13 Written Answer 1 May 2001, col 636W, HC.

3.55 Apart from refugees and passengers relying on provisions of the ECHR, all other travellers to the UK must be in possession of some kind of documentation to obtain entry under the Immigration Act 1971 and the Immigration Rules.[1] The main kinds of document needed on arrival at a port of entry are:

- passport or recognised travel document;
- identity card;
- medical certificate;
- certificate of entitlement;
- visa;
- entry certificate;
- work permit; and
- landing card.

A valid national passport or other document 'satisfactorily' establishing identity and nationality must be produced by every passenger arriving at a port of entry if demanded by an immigration officer.[2] However, inability to produce such a document does not make the passenger an illegal entrant.[3] Section 141 of the Immigration and Asylum Act 1999 contains power to fingerprint passengers who fail on request to produce a valid passport or other identification,[4] unless they have a reasonable excuse.[5] EC nationals can travel with valid national identity cards instead of passports.[6] If a person has a passport or travel document from a country which either is not recognised as a state by the UK, or is not dealt with as a government by the UK, or does not accept valid UK passports for its own immigration control, or does not comply with international passport practice, the person should normally be refused leave to enter on that ground alone.[7]

1 Those with the right of abode are entitled to come and go without let or hindrance except such as may be required under the Act to enable their right to be established: Immigration Act 1971, s 1(1). If their right of abode is disputed, they must prove it by means of a passport or a certificate of entitlement: s 3(9); HC 395, paras 12, 13.
2 Immigration Act 1971, Sch 2, para 4(2)(a); HC 395, para 11.
3 *R v Naillie* [1993] AC 674; [1993] 2 All ER 782, HL.
4 Immigration and Asylum Act 1999, s 141(7), exercisable by immigration officers, police and prison officers: s 141(5).
5 Immigration and Asylum Act 1999, s 141(10).
6 Immigration (European Economic Area) Regulations 2000, SI 2000/2326, reg 12.
7 HC 395, para 320(10). See **3.27** above; note the concessions and the fact that leave may not be cancelled on this ground.

3.56 Passengers in transit to another country outside the common travel area will not normally be given any detailed examination once it is established that they are in transit, have the means and intention of proceeding at once to another country, are assured of entry there and intend to leave the UK within 48 hours.[1] Leave to enter may be given for 48 hours, no more.[2] Transit passengers, however, can be stopped and detained and removed to a different destination.[3] Leave to enter will be refused if an immigration officer is not satisfied about the passenger's intentions, means, or that he or she will be admitted to the country of destination.[4]

1 HC 395, para 47.

2   HC 395, paras 48 and 50.
3   HC 395, para 49; Immigration Act 1971, Sch 2, paras 8 and 16. See the case of *Ex p Williams* [1970] Crim LR 102, a black civil rights leader, who was detained in transit while on his way back from China to the US.
4   HC 395, para 49; see *R v Secretary of State for the Home Department, ex p Connhye* [1987] Imm AR 478; affd (1988) Independent, 20 April, CA, where it was held proper for an immigration officer to examine the financial means of a transit passenger.

3.57 In order to assist immigration officers in their task, a duty is cast on all persons who are examined by immigration officers (either on arrival or departure) to answer any questions put to them, say what documents they may be carrying and to produce their passport or other identity document.[1] These may be retained by the immigration officer until either leave to enter is granted or, if it is refused, until the passenger is about to be removed following refusal of leave.[2] Landing cards are also required for all passengers over 16 who are not British citizens, except on journeys within the common travel area.[3] Although there is no obligation on an entrant to volunteer information and a person will not be an illegal entrant if they accidentally and without intention to mislead offer incorrect information, deception is likely to be inferred where an entrant is deliberately silent about a change of intention.[4]

1   Immigration Act 1971, Sch 2, para 4.
2   Immigration Act 1971, Sch 2, para 4(2A). The IDI state that once a passenger has been refused leave to enter, the passport should not be returned before removal unless there is a valid reason (eg to obtain a foreign visa or have it revalidated). The chief immigration officer must be satisfied that there is no risk of the passenger absconding or defacing the passport to frustrate removal: IDI Dec/00, Ch 9, s 6, para 6.
3   Immigration Act 1971, Sch 2, para 5; Immigration (Landing and Embarkation Cards) Order 1975, SI 1975/65, art 4. They are supplied by the carriers: art 4(2).
4   *R v Secretary of State for the Home Department , ex p Awan* [1996] Imm AR 354, QBD.

3.58 In carrying out their examination, immigration officers can search the person, baggage or vehicle of an entrant, and any ship, aircraft or vehicle on which he or she arrived, for any documents that they wish to see.[1] They may retain any documents produced or found in a search, for a maximum of seven days, unless they need them for an appeal or for a criminal prosecution, in which case they may keep them for as long as they are needed. There are limits on the documents they may take. Like police powers of search and seizure, where, broadly speaking, only documents which are relevant to some crime may be seized,[2] only documents relevant to the discharge of immigration control may be taken by immigration officers.[3] According to the Home Office, immigration officers may, in appropriate cases, make photocopies of documents belonging to those seeking entry to the UK.[4] The main use of these powers is to discover whether an entrant possesses documents which might show that the real purpose of coming to the UK is something other than that stated. A number of refusals have resulted from such searches.[5]

1   Immigration Act 1971, Sch 2, para 4(3).
2   See *Chic Fashions (West Wales) Ltd v Jones* [1968] 2 QB 299, [1968] 1 All ER 229, CA; *Ghani v Jones* [1970] 1 QB 693, [1969] 3 All ER 1700, CA.
3   For detailed powers of search and seizure see chapter 14 below.
4   See IDI Dec/00, Ch 9, s 6. The photocopying of documents relating to an international conference organised by the South West Africa Peoples Organisation in 1971 was surely not an appropriate case (Guardian, 26 December 1971).
5   See *Baldacchino* [1972] Imm AR 14 at 15, where the search of the immigrant's baggage was crucial. In *R v Secretary of State for the Home Department, ex p Hindjou* [1989] Imm AR 24, QBD, the immigration officer drew unreasonable inferences from letters found in the passenger's luggage, and the refusal of leave to enter was quashed.

3.59 It is a criminal offence to give false information or documents to an immigration officer,[1] or not to give information which is required or to refuse to hand over documents, unless there is a reasonable excuse.[2] There is no duty to volunteer unsolicited information, although silence accompanied by conduct can in some circumstances amount to a false representation.[3] Fingerprints may be taken from asylum seekers, illegal entrants, overstayers and other defined groups, and their dependants.[4]

1 Immigration Act 1971, s 26(1)(c).
2 Immigration Act 1971, s 26(1)(b). See **14.44** below.
3 See *Khawaja v Secretary of State for the Home Department* [1984] AC 74, [1983] 1 All ER 765, HL. There is no commensurate duty to attend for interview with an entry clearance officer or to provide documents, but failure to do so may result in an adverse inference being drawn (*R v Immigration Appeal Tribunal, ex p Hubbard* [1985] Imm AR 110, QBD) or even in the entry clearance officer deeming the application to have been withdrawn.
4 Asylum and Immigration Appeals Act 1993, s 3, Immigration and Asylum Act 1999, s 141. See **14.44** below.

Passenger information

3.60 The immigration officer may come to this examination holding information about the passengers. Carriers bringing passengers to the UK (whether owners or agents of ships or aircraft or the operators of the Channel Tunnel through trains) must on request supply information about the passengers to the immigration officer.[1] The information to be supplied by shipping companies and airlines includes not just name and nationality, as previously, but also gender, date of birth, type of travel document held and expiry date, ticket number, date and place of issue, how it was paid for, the passenger's itinerary, the names of all other passengers appearing together on one reservation, and (if the passenger is in a vehicle) its registration number.[2]

1 Immigration Act 1971, Sch 2, para 27, modified in relation to the Channel Tunnel by SI 1993/1813, Sch 4, para 1(11)(r), allows the Secretary of State for the Home Department to make Orders requiring the provision of passenger lists giving names and nationality of passengers and crew. Paragraph 27B requires carriers to provide passenger information. Paragraph 27C requires them to notify the Secretary of State of the arrival of any ship or aircraft expected to carry non-EEA nationals.
2 Immigration (Passenger Information) Order 2000, SI 2000/912.

3.61 The very extensive powers of examination described above are inappropriate for citizens of the EU and others exercising their rights under EC law. Even if they are making a journey from outside the EU, they do not require leave to enter and extensive examination is unnecessary.[1] For the immigration officer's power to discriminate on grounds of nationality, ethnic or national origin in carrying out the examination see **3.54** above.

1 See Council Directive (EEC) 360/68, arts 2(1) and 3(1); and Council Directive (EEC) 148/73, art 3(1)(2); below chapter 7.

3.62 An immigration officer may want to ask further questions or obtain further information before deciding whether or not to admit a passenger. This most frequently happens with asylum seekers, since immigration officers themselves cannot deal with such an application at the port, but it often happens with visitors and other passengers too. In that case, he or she may require the passenger to submit to further examination.[1] The passenger may be arriving with or without advance leave. The requirement to submit to further examination must be in writing.[2] In the case of a passenger with advance leave, the immigration officer may suspend the leave to enter during the examination or pending further examination.[3] The request to submit to further examination does not prevent a transit passenger or a member of a crew from leaving on his or her intended ship, aircraft or train.[4] Passengers arriving without leave, or those whose leave has been suspended, may be detained under the immigration officer's authority pending the examination or further examination and pending a decision to give, refuse or cancel leave to enter.[5] In deciding whether to detain a passenger pending examination or further examination, the immigration officer is entitled to discriminate on nationality grounds if justified by statistical or intelligence information.[6] The power of detention is usually enforced without any need to arrest, but a backup power of arrest is available.[7] In such cases the passenger may be released on temporary admission instead of being detained.[8] Detainees awaiting further examination may be eligible for bail.[9] During interviews a passenger may be represented by a friend or lawyer, but there is no right to have a representative present at the interview. This is a matter for the immigration officer, who must, however, exercise the discretion properly.[10] Where a person who has been released on temporary admission pending a decision fails to report to an immigration officer for further examination as required, the immigration officer may direct that the person's examination is concluded and refuse or cancel leave to enter forthwith.[11]

1 Immigration Act 1971, Sch 2, paras 2(3), 2A(5).
2 Immigration Act 1971, Sch 2, paras 2(3), 2A(5) and 2A(10).
3 Immigration Act 1971, Sch 2, para 2A(7). The suspension of leave must also be in writing: para 2A(10).
4 Immigration Act 1971, Sch 2, para 2(3), 2A(6), SI 1993/1813, Sch 4, para 1(11)(e), (ea), inserted by SI 2000/1775.
5 Immigration Act 1971, Sch 2, para 16(1), (1A).
6 Race Relations (Immigration and Asylum) Authorisation 2001, para 3(c) and 6, published in IDI Mar/01, Ch 1, s 1, Annex EE.
7 Immigration Act 1971, Sch 2, para 17. See chapter 17 below.
8 Immigration Act 1971, Sch 2, para 21.
9 Immigration Act 1971, Sch 2, para 22. Immigration and Asylum Act 1999, s 44, when in force, provides for automatic bail hearings for those detained under the Schedule. See further chapter 17 below.
10 *R v Secretary of State for the Home Department, ex p Lawson* [1994] Imm AR 58, QBD. For asylum interviews see **12.84** below.
11 Immigration Act 1971, Sch 2, para 21(3), (4).

Medical examination

3.63 Anyone seeking to enter the UK may be examined by a medical inspector.[1] The power to require further examination applies to medical examinations as well as others.[2] This is dealt with at **3.30-3.32** above. If the immigration officer decides to grant leave to enter (or, in the case of advance leave, not to cancel it), but that (on the advice of a medical inspector or other qualified practitioner) a further medical test or examination may be required in the interests of public health, the passenger may be given notice in writing requiring him or her to report to a medical officer for any further tests or examination that person deems necessary.[3] This requirement is not, however, a condition of leave under section 3(1)(c) of the Immigration Act 1971, so failure to comply cannot found a prosecution, a decision to remove, or to curtail or refuse to extend leave, as a breach of conditions (although it might found a decision to deport, or to refuse to extend leave on public good grounds, in extreme cases).

1   Immigration Act 1971, Sch 2, paras 2(2), 2A(4).
2   Immigration Act 1971, Sch 2, paras 2(3), 2A(5).
3   Immigration Act 1971, Sch 2, para 7.

3.64 As indicated above, the examination powers extend to control zones in France and Belgium under the modifications to the Immigration Act 1971 made by the Channel Tunnel international arrangements.[1] Immigration officers also have power to board any ship, aircraft or Channel Tunnel train to carry out their examination on board.[2] These powers have been used, sometimes with unfortunate consequences, where large numbers of asylum seekers are expected to arrive from a particular refugee hot spot, such as Turkey or Sri Lanka.[3] Treating passengers in haste in this way has led to asylum claims being ignored. Secondly, because of the pressure on airlines and the threat of penalties under the carriers' liability provisions in Part II of the Immigration and Asylum Act 1999,[4] there may be a temptation for airlines and ferry captains to prevent a passenger landing and to call in immigration officials to conduct an on-the-spot examination. In both such cases there is a grave risk of the examination being carried out in an unfair manner, and because abuses can be carried out unseen, and the victim may be quietly removed, the power is a dangerous one.[5] It seems to us that the cases where an 'on board' examination is justified must be very few and far between.

1   See **3.51–3.52** above.
2   Immigration Act 1971, Sch 2, para 1(4), as modified in relation to the Channel Tunnel by SI 1993/1813, Sch 4, para 1(11)(a).
3   See Alison Stanley 'The Legal Status of International Zones, the British experience' [1992] 6 Immigration & Nationality Law & Practice at 126.
4   Re-enacting the Immigration (Carriers' Liability) Act 1987. See chapter 14 below.
5   These concerns are accentuated by the provisions authorising discrimination on grounds of nationality, ethnic or national origin in s 19D of the Race Relations Act 1976 (inserted by Race Relations (Amendment) Act 2000) and the specific authorisation of nationality-based discrimination in pre- and on-entry controls discussed at **3.4** and **3.54** above.

Examination, decision and the 24-hour rule

3.65 Passengers with advance leave to enter (by means of entry clearance or otherwise) whose leave is not to be suspended or cancelled will emerge from the examination by the immigration officer with no further passport stamp or notice, just as British citizens do. Other passengers need notice of a decision. Previously, where leave was granted, written notice had to be given to the person affected and this was usually done by a stamp in the passport.[1] The Immigration and Asylum Act 1999 gave the Secretary of State the power to add to the ways in which leave may be given, refused or varied. Leave to enter need no longer be granted or refused in writing, but may be given by fax and e-mail,[2] and in the case of visitors, may be given orally, including by telecommunication.[3] Leave to enter may also be given or refused by a notice to a responsible third party,[4] who might include the person appearing to be in charge of a group of people arriving together, a tour operator, a carrier, a control port manager or a British Embassy or consulate official.[5] The notice does not need to name the individuals covered by it, but can describe them by reference to a group.[6] However, if leave is refused orally or to a responsible third party, a notice in writing must be given as soon as practicable, confirming the refusal and giving the reasons.[7] If the refusal attracts a right of appeal under Part IV of the 1999 Act, notice must be given under the Immigration and Asylum Appeals (Notices) Regulations 2000,[8] and notice under the Notices Regulations is good notice under the Immigration (Leave to Enter and Remain) Order 2000.[9] A notice which is irregular in that it fails to tell of rights of appeal or gives incorrect information is still a good notice under the 1999 Act and its defects can be corrected.[10] Notice need not be signed.[11] If leave to enter is to be granted, this can be done by the immigration officer who carries out the initial examination. But if leave is to be refused, or advance leave cancelled, immigration officers cannot take the decision on their own but must obtain the authority of a chief immigration officer or an immigration inspector in all cases.[12]

1 Immigration Act 1971, s 4(1). In granting or refusing leave immigration officers are entitled to mark the passport: *R v Secretary of State for the Home Department, ex p Raju* [1986] Imm AR 348, QBD.
2 Immigration (Leave to Enter and Remain) Order 2000, SI 2000/1161, art 8(1), (2).
3 SI 2000/1161, art 8(3). The immigration officer may decline to use these methods on the basis of the passenger's nationality: Race Relations (Immigration and Asylum) Authorisation 2001, para 3(d).
4 SI 2000/1161, art 9(1).
5 SI 2000/1161, art 1(3).
6 SI 2000/1161, art 9(2).
7 SI 2000/1161, art 10(1). In the case of someone who is illiterate or unable to understand the notice, it may be sent to a representative if there is one: *R v Chief Immigration Officer of Manchester Airport, ex p Insah Begum* [1972] 1 All ER 6; affd [1973] 1 All ER 594, [1973] 1 WLR 141, CA.
8 SI 2000/2246, regs 4 and 5. On the immigration officer's power to change the reasons for refusal, see *Dagdalen v Secretary of State for the Home Department* [1988] Imm AR 425, CA. This will usually be regarded as a refinement of the notice and will not require a new notice: *Hettierarachchi v Secretary of State for the Home Department* [1991] Imm AR 499, CA; see further *Rajendran* [1989] Imm AR 512, Immigration Appeal Tribunal.
9 SI 2000/1161, art 10(2).
10 *Labiche v Secretary of State for the Home Department* [1991] Imm AR 263, CA; *R v Secretary of State for the Home Department, ex p Lateef* [1991] Imm AR 334, QBD. See further *R v Secretary of State for the Home Department, ex p Abeywickrema* [1991] Imm AR 535, QBD.
11 *R v Secretary of State for the Home Department, ex p Kondo* [1992] Imm AR 326, QBD.
12 HC 395, para 10.

3.66 After completing the examination of a person arriving in the UK without advance leave and wishing to enter in a capacity attracting limited leave, the immigration authorities normally have 24 hours in which to give their decision, failing which the passenger is deemed to have been given six months' leave to enter with a condition prohibiting employment.[1] This provision, known as the '24-hour rule', used to be of considerable importance before 1988, when failure to give proper notice resulted in the deemed grant of indefinite leave. The courts held that an illegible passport stamp was not good notice, since it did not notify the entrant of the terms of the leave, and so passengers whose passports had been stamped illegibly on entry obtained indefinite leave. In 1988 the paragraph was amended to grant a deemed leave of only six months, meaning that only those who should not have been granted leave at all, or transit passengers who would not have expected as much as six months' leave, gained from it. The effect of the 24-hour rule has been further eroded by Article 12 of the Immigration (Leave to Enter and Remain) Order 2000,[2] which deals with the situation where an examination has begun but has been adjourned for further inquiries, or the applicant has been required to submit to further examination, after which the immigration officer considers that the applicant does not need to be re-interviewed. In such a situation, any notice which is subsequently given in conformity with the requirements of the Order is deemed to comply with the requirement to give notice within 24 hours. This provision does away with much of the old case law dealing with when an examination comes to an end and the 24-hour time limit begins to run.[3] In addition, the Immigration Act 1971 provides that if a passenger who is on temporary admission pending further examination fails to report to an immigration officer as required, his or her examination may be treated as concluded and there is no need for notice to comply with the 24-hour rule.[4]

1   Immigration Act 1971, Sch 2, para 6(1), as amended.
2   SI 2000/1161, art 12.
3   See the previous edition of this work, at **3.37-3.40**.
4   Immigration Act 1971, Sch 2, para 21(3), (4).

What is an examination?

3.67 The problem remains, however, as to whether any 'examination' at all has taken place. Not everyone passing through immigration control comes face to face with an immigration officer. Not everyone is interrogated. For example, babes in arms, persons on excursions or named in a collective passport may never be spoken to by an immigration officer on their way through immigration control. These situations are now dealt with by the provision that leave, and notice of it, may be given collectively, to the responsible third party in charge of the party.[1] Examination of all passengers is not mandatory, but permissive;[2] the important thing is that leave is granted to all those who need it. The responsible third party includes anyone who appears to be in charge of a group travelling together,[3] and a family is of course a group *par excellence*. This provision would avoid the result in *Ex p Ghazalgoo*,[4] where a 16-year-old Iranian boy was included on his father's passport. They arrived together at immigration control, but only the father was asked questions. The passport was stamped for the father only and the boy was completely ignored. The court held that there had been no examination of the boy, no leave given to him, and he was an illegal entrant – an absurdly harsh decision.

1   Immigration Act 1971, Sch 2, para 6(4); SI 2000/1161, art 9; see **3.65** fn 4 above.
2   *R v Secretary of State for the Home Department, ex p Kumar* [1990] Imm AR 265, QBD.
3   SI 2000/1161, art 1(3).
4   [1987] Imm AR 448.

Leave given by mistake

3.68 Immigration officers are fallible and do make mistakes. Sometimes they stamp a passport with indefinite leave to enter. This is what happened in *Ex p Ram*.[1] A mistake had been made, and the applicant was given indefinite leave. The Divisional Court held that the immigration officer had been acting within his powers under section 4 of the Immigration Act 1971; it could not be said in the absence of any fraud or dishonesty on the part of the applicant that he had no authority to act as he did. And so an immigrant, given a leave by mistake, is allowed to keep it. We suggest that the same doctrine applies to a leave granted abroad, since the mistaken grant of leave is not one of the grounds for cancellation of leave when a passenger arrives at the port.[2]

1   *R v Secretary of State for the Home Department, ex p Ram* [1979] 1 All ER 687, [1979] 1 WLR 148.
2   See **3.44-3.47** above.

Illegible stamps

3.69 The doctrine of grant of deemed leave by an illegible stamp in a passport is now, we suggest, for all practical purposes a dead letter. When the grant of leave to enter had to be by notice in writing to the person affected, an illegible stamp was held not to be an effective notice and so, under the provisions of Schedule 2, paragraph 6 to the Immigration Act 1971, indefinite leave, later amended to a six months' leave, with a prohibition on employment, was deemed to have been granted.[1] But now that leave to enter may be granted in other ways, a passenger may have other evidence of the grant of leave, and it will only be in those cases where there is no other evidence of leave having been granted that the defective stamp will need to be relied on. It is only transit passengers who might benefit from the deemed leave to obtain something more than they would otherwise have been entitled to; in *Low*[2] the Tribunal held that if transit leave is all that is intended, the leave stamp must make that clear; otherwise a visitor leave will be granted (with a right to apply for an extension and to appeal).

1   Immigration Act 1971, Sch 2, para 6 provides that leave must be granted or refused 24 hours after the end of the immigration officer's examination; if not, leave of six months is deemed given. An ineffective notice did not operate to grant leave, thus engaging para 6. See *R v Secretary of State for the Home Department, ex p Tolba* [1988] Imm AR 78, QBD; *R v Secretary of State for the Home Department, ex p Katoorah* [1996] Imm AR 595, CA; *Minton v Secretary of State for the Home Department* [1990] Imm AR 199, CA.
2   [1995] Imm AR 435.

No stamp given

3.70 A doctrine which deserves to fall by the wayside is that of illegal entry by the immigration officer's failure to stamp a passport. The demise of this pernicious and unfair doctrine is long overdue. It arose because a person who requires leave to enter and enters the UK without obtaining such leave is in breach of section 3(1) of the Immigration Act 1971 and is an illegal entrant.[1] When the only way that leave could be granted was by a stamp in the entrant's passport, the lack of such a stamp was held to mean that no leave had been granted. The lack of stamp could have been the fault of the immigration officer, who mistakenly believed that the person had a right of abode or was exempt from immigration control. The doctrine originated in *Rehal*,[2] where the applicant was a British Overseas citizen but the immigration officer who examined him, thinking he was a British citizen, waved him through without stamping his passport. It had been thought that where a mistake of this kind was made, the immigrant always obtained the benefit of a deemed leave to enter,[3] but the

Court of Appeal rejected this view, holding that this was limited to cases where the immigration officer intended either to grant or refuse leave and had no application to any other case.[4] In this way innocent travellers became stigmatised as illegal entrants and liable to removal through immigration officers' mistakes. The only remedy was to seek leave to remain from the Secretary of State for the Home Department,[5] and to challenge refusal, or the exercise of discretion to remove as an illegal entrant, as irrational, as failing to take into account a legitimate expectation of admission to the UK, created by the error of the immigration officer without any inaccurate representation on behalf of the immigrant.

1 Immigration Act 1971, ss 3(1), 33(1).
2 *Rehal v Secretary of State for the Home Department* [1989] Imm AR 576, CA.
3 By virtue of Immigration Act 1971, Sch 2, para 6; see **3.69**.
4 The argument that the immigrant in this situation benefited from deemed leave had been accepted in *Amoako* (4679) and consensually in *R v Secretary of State for the Home Department, ex p Malik* (2 October 1987, unreported), QBD, with the sensible result that innocent persons did not become illegal entrants.
5 See chapter 4 below.

3.71 Now that leave to enter does not have to be in writing in all cases, but can be by fax, e-mail, telephone or oral, the lack of a passport stamp no longer leads to the inference that the passenger entered without leave. He or she may have been granted leave orally or benefited from a collective grant of leave to a responsible person.[1] However, the person in the situation of Mr Rehal would be no better off, if unable to prove that leave had been granted or intended in one of these ways.[2]

1 See **3.65** above.
2 The burden of proof that leave has been granted in one of these ways is on the entrant: Immigration (Leave to Enter and Remain) Order 2000, SI 2000/1161, art 11.

Date stamp only

3.72 Where the passport is stamped with a rectangular date stamp and nothing more, the effect of the stamp seems to depend on the factual situation; if there are indications in the factual matrix suggestive of indefinite leave to enter, following *Ex p Badaike*,[1] the rectangular stamp in the passport would amount to a written notice of indefinite leave to enter, and would be an effective leave unless the Secretary of State could prove otherwise (for example, if the immigration officer was misled by the applicant). In *Bagga*[2] the Court of Appeal held that such a stamp did not confer indefinite leave to enter if it was placed in the passport by an immigration officer in the belief that the holder was exempt from immigration control, so that, following *Rehal*,[3] there was no room for the operation of paragraph 6(1) of Schedule 2 to the Immigration Act 1971. This would have the same effect as no stamp at all, that is, it would mean that the person had been granted no leave and was therefore an illegal entrant.[4] The problem starts with *Rehal*, and the court's interpretation of the examination powers of immigration officers, in particular paragraphs 2(1) and 6(1) of Schedule 2 to the 1971 Act. The Court interpreted the words 'where a person examined by an immigration officer . . . *is to be given* a limited leave etc' as referring to the immigration officer's *intentions* after conducting the examination. This subjective approach means that paragraph 6(1) deals with delays only, but not mistakes. In *Rehal* the court rejected an objective interpretation of the words 'is to be given'. In other words, if, on a proper examination, a person does not have a right of abode, then he or she is a person who 'is to be given' leave. At a stroke, all the present injustices would go. Instead of mistakes turning innocent people into illegal entrants, they would get an automatic six months' leave and an opportunity of resolving the position with the Home Office.

1   *R v Secretary of State for Home Affairs, ex p Badaike* (1977) Times, 4 May, DC.
2   *R v Secretary of State for the Home Department, ex p Bagga* [1991] 1 QB 485, [1990] Imm AR 413, CA.
3   *Rehal v Secretary of State for the Home Department* [1989] Imm AR 576, CA.
4   See **3.71**.

3.73 A person who has been granted leave to enter on arrival may have his or her leave cancelled up to 24 hours after the conclusion of the immigration officer's examination.[1] This happens most frequently when someone is given leave to enter by immigration control and then passes through to customs, who discover large quantities of drugs in his or her baggage.[2] In the same way, a person refused leave to enter at the port may have that refusal cancelled; in this case the 24-hour time limit does not apply, but if indefinite or limited leave is not granted at the same time that the original refusal of leave is cancelled, then six months' leave is deemed granted.[3]

1   Immigration Act 1971, Sch 2, para 6(2), as amended.
2   See eg *Villone* [1979–80] Imm AR 23.
3   Immigration Act 1971, Sch 2, para 6(3), as amended.

RIGHTS OF APPEAL

3.74 A refusal of an entry clearance or a refusal of leave to enter on arrival gives rise to a right of appeal to an adjudicator only where detailed conditions relating to age, possession of relevant documents and category of entrant are met. Visitors (except for family visitors), short-term students and long-term students who have not yet been accepted on a course and their dependants, have no right of appeal against refusal of entry clearance,[1] and no one who needs leave to enter has a right of appeal against refusal unless they arrived with a current entry clearance (or work permit).[2] Passengers in possession of entry clearance which operates as leave to enter, whose leave is cancelled on arrival, are treated as passengers with entry clearance refused leave to enter.[3] Someone seeking leave in one capacity and refused may have rights of appeal on grounds raised subsequently to the refusal, under the one-stop, asylum and human rights provisions of the Immigration and Asylum Act 1999. All of these rights of appeal are dealt with in detail in chapter 18 below.

1   Immigration and Asylum Act 1999, s 60(4), (5). There is provision in the Immigration and Asylum Act 1999, s 23 for the monitoring of refusals of entry clearance where there is no right of appeal. The reports of the independent monitor are available on the Foreign and Commonwealth Office website at www.fco.gov.uk. They tend to recommend general procedural improvements, but do not deal with the merits of any individual case.
2   Immigration and Asylum Act 1999, s 60(3).
3   Immigration Act 1971, Sch 2, para 2A(9).

Chapter 4

CONTROL AFTER ENTRY

EXTENDING AND VARYING LEAVE

4.1 Immigration control does not end at the port of entry, but continues after entry. In this chapter we are not concerned with formal qualifications needed by students, businessmen and so forth, who are seeking extensions of leave. Nor are we concerned with appeals or post-entry control exercised through the enforcement of the criminal law and deportation, or removal of persons unlawfully in the UK. These are all dealt with in later chapters. Here we are only concerned with the general framework of post-entry control; the powers of the Secretary of State for the Home Department and civil servants to extend, refuse to extend, or curtail leave to enter or remain in the UK; requirements to register with the police, and for hotels to keep registers of guests. Traditionally, control after entry has been much less regulated in the UK than control on arrival. This process has been changing with the increasing integration of the UK into the EU, although progress towards the abolition of controls on all journeys to the UK which start within the EU has been stalled with the UK government's refusal to sign up to the Schengen *acquis* now integrated into the framework of the EU, which requires the lifting of such controls. At present there are elements of the worst of both worlds, with an increase in intrusive after-entry control, including vastly increased police and immigration officers' powers, the criminalisation of employers and tying access to social welfare and housing to immigration status, added to the pre-existing strict perimeter control.

Meaning of entry

4.2 Under the Immigration Act 1971 a very clear division of responsibility was made between control on entry and control after entry. Under section 4(1) of the Act, immigration officers are given power to grant or refuse leave to enter and carry out examinations, as we have seen. But once someone has entered the UK, the power to give leave to remain or vary any leave is to be exercised by the Secretary of State for the Home Department.[1] We discussed in the previous chapter the point at which someone who arrives in this country is treated as having entered.[2] Leave to remain, as opposed to leave to enter, can only be granted by the Secretary of State and his or her civil servants.[3] Although leave to remain may now be granted by variation outside the UK under the provisions of the Immigration (Leave to Enter and Remain) Order 2000,[4] it is still the Secretary of State who grants it. In the one situation where the immigration officer may grant a variation of leave to remain at the port, he or she does so on behalf of the Secretary of State.[5] The rigid categorisation of functions is, however, breaking down as a result of the Immigration (Leave to Enter and Remain) Order 2000 and the Immigration and Asylum Act 1999 provisions. The Secretary of State now has the power to prescribe circumstances in which he or she may grant leave to enter,[6] and although no order has yet been made, when it is, the Secretary of State's officers will be able to exercise all the examination and removal powers currently exercised exclusively by immigration officers.[7]

1   Immigration Act 1971, s 4(1).
2   See **3.4** above.
3   This very clear distinction was thrown into confusion by the Divisional Court in *Singh v Hammond* [1987] 1 All ER 829, [1987] 1 WLR 283—a case which has not been followed and was confined to its particular facts. The distinction was crucial in *R v Naillie* [1993] AC 674, HL.
4   SI 2000/1161, art 13(6); HC 395, para 33A, inserted by HC 704.
5   HC 395, para 31A, inserted by HC 704.
6   Immigration Act 1971, s 3A(7), inserted by Immigration and Asylum Act 1999, s 1.
7   Immigration Act 1971, s 3A(8).

Leave to remain

4.3   Leave to remain is a generic term applying to leave granted to anyone who has entered the UK, whether or not with leave. Further leave granted to someone who already has leave is sometimes known as a variation of leave, whereas those who have no leave have nothing to vary. Those who are in the UK with no leave and who might seek leave to remain[1] include:

(i)   former Commonwealth citizens (mainly CUKCs and British citizens) and Irish citizens who had a right of abode[2] or the benefit of uncontrolled travel under the common travel area,[3] but have lost it by renouncing or losing their nationality;

(ii)   former citizens of the EEA[4] who cease to be citizens of an EEA state and have not been given leave to enter or remain in the UK;

(iii)   members of the crew of a ship or aircraft who have entered without leave,[5] but wish to remain in the UK;

(iv)   diplomats and others exempted under section 8(2) and (3) of the Immigration Act 1971, who are treated as having been given 90 days' leave to remain when they cease to be exempt, and wish to remain longer in the UK;[6]

(v)   illegal[7] entrants who seek to be allowed to stay.

As with leave to enter, leave to remain may be of limited or indefinite duration, and, if limited, may be subject to conditions[8] (see **3.6**). The only difference is that since leave to remain is granted under different powers from the immigration officers' examination powers under Schedule 2, no condition of submitting to a medical test or examination[9] may be imposed. Since 1996 the Secretary of State has had power to impose a condition requiring the person to maintain him or herself without recourse to public funds.[10] Failure to comply renders a person liable to removal under section 10 of the Immigration and Asylum Act 1999, as well as to potential prosecution under section 24(1)(b) of the Immigration Act 1971.

1 Immigration Act 1971, s 3(1)(b).
2 Immigration Act 1971, s 1(1).
3 Immigration Act 1971, s 1(3); Immigration (Control of Entry through the Republic of Ireland) Order 1972, SI 1972/1610, as amended.
4 Immigration Act 1988, s 7(1) and Immigration (European Economic Area) Regulations 2000, SI 2000/2326.
5 Immigration Act 1971, s 8(1).
6 Immigration Act 1971, s 8A(2), inserted by Immigration and Asylum Act 1999, s 6.
7 Immigration Act 1971, s 33(1).
8 Immigration Act 1971, s 3(1)(c) and 3B(2)(b), inserted by Immigration and Asylum Act 1999, s 2.
9 See Immigration Act 1971, Sch 2, para 7.
10 Immigration Act 1971, s 3(1)(c)(ii), inserted by Asylum and Immigration Act 1996, Sch 2, para 1. For the definition of 'public funds' see HC 395, para 6.

Effect of leaving the UK on leave to remain

4.4   Until the amendments brought about by the Immigration and Asylum Act 1999, a person's leave to enter or remain in the UK lapsed on his or her leaving the common travel area. This meant that many persons with limited leave (as students, for example) who left the UK for a short holiday were refused leave to enter on their return, even if it was the middle of term or they had exams to sit. To add insult to injury, they were told that they could not stay in the UK to appeal against the refusal of leave to enter (unless they had obtained a visa to return to the UK, which, after a short holiday in mid-course, was unheard of). Nor would the High Court listen to judicial review applications, citing as the 'alternative remedy' of appeal, the right to appeal from abroad which prejudiced appellants by excluding them from being present at the appeal. The provisions of the Immigration (Leave to Enter and Remain) Order 2000[1], made under sections 3A and 3B of the Immigration Act 1971 which were added by the 1999 Act,[2] should put an end to this injustice. Leave to enter or remain does not lapse when the holder goes abroad, if it was conferred by an entry clearance (other than a visit visa) or by an immigration officer or the Secretary of State for more than six months.[3] The only exception is where leave has been varied by the Secretary of State and, following the variation, there is less than six months left.[4] Students, and everyone who had entry clearance which operated as leave to enter, except for visitors, can leave the country during the period of their leave without worrying that they will be excluded on return. So can those granted leave as students by an immigration officer on arrival, or those granted leave by the Secretary of State after arrival. Leave only lapses if they remain outside the UK for more than two years, if it has not expired by then.[5]

1   SI 2000/1161.
2   Immigration and Asylum Act 1999, ss 1 and 2.
3   Immigration (Leave to Enter and Remain) Order 2000, SI 2000/1161, art 13(2).
4   SI 2000/1161, art 13(3).
5   SI 2000/1161, art 13(4).

Variation of leave to enter or remain

4.5 As we have seen, leave to enter or remain may be either for a limited or an indefinite period.[1] Indefinite leave cannot be varied or curtailed, although in some circumstances it may lapse.[2] A person in the UK with limited leave may have that leave varied, whether by restricting, enlarging or removing the limit on its duration, or by adding, varying or revoking conditions.[3] But if the limit on its duration is removed, any conditions attached to the leave shall cease to apply. In other words, when someone is given settlement, with indefinite leave, any conditions restricting or prohibiting employment or recourse to public funds, and any requirements to register with the police, cease to have effect.

1   Immigration Act 1971, s 3(1)(b).
2   If the holder remains out of the UK for two years: Immigration (Leave to Enter and Remain) Order 2000, SI 2000/1161, art 13(4)(a).
3   Immigration Act 1971, s 3(3).

Applying for variation of leave

4.6 Applications for variation of leave or for all time limits to be removed should always be made before the expiry of the existing leave. This is important for three reasons:

(i)   the application may otherwise be dismissed on the grounds of breach of the Acts;[1]
(ii)   otherwise the right of appeal is lost;[2] and
(iii)   there is a risk of being removed for overstaying.[3]

Except for applications to remain for asylum or on human rights grounds, and applications to remain for which a work permit is required, all applications for leave to remain or for a variation of leave by non-EEA nationals are by compulsory application forms.[4] The Immigration Rules require the prescribed form[5] to be completed in the manner required by the form and be accompanied by the documents and photographs specified in the form. An application made in any other way is not valid, according to the rule. Prior to the rule change, an 'application' had been held to mean a request in unambiguous terms to a person in authority to grant a specified immigration status, no matter what form the request took.[6] In *ex p ILPA*[7] Collins J held that the statutory power under section 3(2) of the Immigration Act 1971 to make rules to regulate the practice under the Act was broad enough to allow the Secretary of State to redefine how an application should be made.

1   Immigration and Asylum Act 1999, s 10; HC 395, para 322(3).
2   Section 61 of the Immigration and Asylum Act 1999, like the Immigration Act 1971, s 14, requires extant leave in order to appeal against refusal to extend it. See **4.13** below.
3   Immigration and Asylum Act 1999, s 10.

4   HC 395, para 32, as amended by HC 329, effective from 3 June 1996.
5   The forms are FLR(M) (leave to remain for marriage), FLR(S) (students), FLR(O) (temporary and permit-free work, dependent relatives and other categories), SET(M) (settlement for spouse), SET(F) (settlement for family members), SET(O) (settlement for work and other categories), BUS (business, investor and innovator), ELR (exceptional leave to remain). In addition there is a form EEC for EEA nationals, but this is not mandatory.
6   *Brown* [1976] Imm AR 119; *Prajapati v Immigration Appeal Tribunal* [1982] Imm AR 56, CA at 60; *Soyemi* [1990] Imm AR 564, Immigration Appeal Tribunal.
7   *R v Secretary of State for the Home Department, ex p ILPA* [1997] Imm AR 189, followed by the Tribunal in *Derouiche* [1998] INLR 286

4.7   Rejection of an invalid application is not treated as a refusal of leave. This can have very serious consequences. The effect of the rejection of an application as invalid is that no application has been made. If the application is resubmitted after leave expires and is rejected, the right of appeal is lost.[1] The decision on whether an application is valid is made by the Initial Consideration Unit or for those attending in person, the Public Caller Unit as appropriate. The forms and accompanying documents are checked for compliance, and the merits of the application are disregarded at that stage. Invalid applications are returned to applicants or their advisers, endorsed with the defects which need remedying, or enclosing appropriate forms if the application was incorrectly made by letter. The aim is to check and determine validity of all applications within 24 hours.

1   See **4.15** below

4.8   Clearly, it is vitally important that the application is validly made to the satisfaction of the Initial Consideration Unit or Public Caller Unit. A checklist of good practice to ensure this might include the following:

(i)   the correct form for the application must be used. In *Sithole*,[1] an application made on the wrong form was held to be invalid, and since no valid application was made in time, there was no right of appeal against refusal;

(ii)   if the application is phrased in the alternative, more than one of the forms may be appropriate. Applicants should not be afraid to use more than one form;

(iii)   the form should be completed and an answer given to every applicable question;

(iv)   alteration of the form will automatically make the application invalid, so qualifications and explanations should be made in covering letters;

(v)   covering letters may also be used to complement answers, but the form should still be properly completed and should not merely state 'see covering letter';

(vi)   the original of every document requested should be provided or, if it is not available or only a photocopy is available, a clear explanation should be given as to why the original cannot accompany the form;

(vii)   the application should be made well before the current leave expires in order to avoid becoming out of time if the first attempt at the application is rejected as invalid;

(viii) if an application is returned as invalid, any arguments to the contrary should be submitted in writing to the Initial Consideration Unit together with the application as amended in the manner indicated.

If the application is finally made to the satisfaction of the Initial Consideration Unit before the applicant's current leave expires, the initial rejection of the application will have caused no prejudice. If the revised application is out of time but is successful, the applicant may have suffered a short period in which he or she is regarded as having overstayed leave. This might be of significant disadvantage in the future and the Home Office ought to be asked to confirm that no prejudice will result. Home Office policy is to count short delays in submitting applications as lawful residence (for the purpose of the long residence concession) provided the application is successful.[2] But if the application as revised is out of time *and* refused, significant and difficult questions of law may arise. To safeguard the applicant's position, a notice of appeal to the appellate authorities should be lodged, stating clearly that a preliminary issue arises as to whether the rejection of the initial application was valid or whether it should have been considered as a valid application.[3] The issue for the appellate authority would be whether the application was valid or should have been treated as valid. In *Derouiche*,[4] the Tribunal found that the wording of the form FLR(S) was misleading and imprecise and that, since it had to be used by applicants who may not speak or understand English, rejection of an application for a minor non-compliance was unfair and unjust. The Court of Appeal was concerned in *Ravichandran and Jeyeanthan*[5] with the failure by the Secretary of State to complete a statement of truth when appealing to the Immigration Appeal Tribunal, as required by the Procedure Rules. However, the principles it outlines have wider application. The first question is whether there has been substantial compliance with the procedural requirements, even if there has not been strict compliance. The second is whether the non-compliance is capable of being waived, and if so, whether it has been. That will not arise in this situation, which is predicated on the Secretary of State's refusal to waive the non-compliance. The third is what are the consequences of non-compliance.[6] The draconian consequences of non-compliance[7] are such that the appellate authority should, we suggest, lean in favour of a generous approach and find substantial compliance whenever reasonably possible.

1   *Sithole (Hettie) (00 TH 1969)* 7 August 2000, Immigration Appeal Tribunal (Collins J).
2   IDI Dec/00, Ch 18, para 3.
3   Immigration and Asylum Appeals (Procedure) Rules 2000, SI 2000/2333, r 12. The respondent would be alleging that the appellant was not entitled to appeal by reason of s 61 of the Immigration and Asylum Act 1999 in that he or she did not have current leave when the application was refused: r 12(1)(a)(i).
4   *Derouiche* [1998] INLR 286.
5   *Ravichandran v Secretary of State for the Home Department, Secretary of State for the Home Department v Jeyeanthan* [2000] Imm AR 10.
6   *Ravichandran* above, per Woolf MR at 17.
7   *Ravichandran* above, at 13.

4.9   Applications can be sent through the post or can be made by a personal visit to the Home Office. Applications in the work permit and business categories may be made by e-mail.[1] Where an application is sent by post, the practice has been for the Home Office to treat an application as having been made on the date of the sending by post rather than of its receipt, and the Tribunal case of *Lubetkin*,[2] the authority for this proposition, is still good law and has not been overruled. However, to safeguard their position, applicants should take care to ensure that the application is *received* by the Home Office before the expiry of leave.[3] Recorded delivery is better than the ordinary post because of the presumption of delivery incorporated by section 7 of the Interpretation Act 1978.

1   For details see Department for Education and Employment and Nationality Directorate websites (www.dfee.gov.uk and   www.ind.homeoffice.gov.uk.)
2   *Lubetkin* [1979–80] Imm AR 162.
3   The date of receipt rather than the date of sending is the relevant date for the purpose of appeals to the appellate authority: see *R v Immigration Appeal Tribunal, ex p Secretary of State for the Home Department* [1990] Imm AR 166, DC; *R v Immigration Appeal Tribunal, ex p Rocha* [1982] Imm AR 12, QBD; *Petrou* [1978] Imm AR 87, Immigration Appeal Tribunal, and the provisions as to calculation of time in Immigration and Asylum Appeals (Procedure) Rules 2000, SI 2000/2333, r 48.

4.10   The date of application is important for two reasons. First, as indicated above, it is essential to apply before the current leave expires if the person is to have a right of appeal under section 61 of the Immigration and Asylum Act 1999 (see **4.15** below). Secondly, the date of the application may be important where the applicant is a child who becomes over-age before the date of the decision. Thirdly, the date of the application is important if there have been rule changes, since in a number of the transitional provisions in the Immigration Rules, the date of the application is crucial to which set of rules apply.[1]

1   See eg HC 395, para 4.

Withdrawal and lapsing of applications

4.11   Normally when an application is duly made, it must be considered by the Home Office, although there is no particular order in which applications must be considered.[1] There is no power to cancel an application unilaterally.[2] But if a further application is made before the first has been determined, the Secretary of State may be entitled to treat the earlier one as lapsed and superseded by the second one.[3] Section 3C of the Immigration Act 1971 expressly provides that an application may be varied. Whether a second application is treated as varying or superseding the first may depend on whether the two applications are inconsistent. For example, an application for leave to remain as a spouse would be inconsistent with an earlier application for further leave as a visitor, since it negatives the intention to leave required by the visitor rules, but an application to remain as a student should, we suggest, be treated as a variation of the original application, and each limb of the amended application should be considered.

1   *R v Secretary of State for the Home Department, ex p Khasawneh* [1995] Imm AR 315, QBD, where the division of applications into queues and the prioritisation of newer applications under the Asylum and Immigration Appeals Act 1993 was held lawful.
2   *Dungarwalla* [1989] Imm AR 476.
3   *R v Immigration Appeal Tribunal, ex p Majid* [1988] Imm AR 315, QBD.

Leaving the UK = withdrawal of application?

4.12   Then there is the case where the person makes an application and then goes abroad before the application is determined. Does the application lapse? The lapsing of an application for variation of leave is an important matter, because it may affect whether there is a subsequent right of appeal. The

Immigration Rules say that when passengers ask for the return of their passports for the purpose of travel outside the common travel area, their applications for variation of leave lapse, as soon as the passport is returned, provided the original application is being considered and has not yet been decided.[1] This rule has not been deleted, and appears to be inconsistent with the provisions of the Immigration (Leave to Enter and Remain) Order 2000[2] and has arguably been superseded by these. It has led to inconvenience, hardship and injustice. First, there are many people who need to travel frequently on business or for family reasons, but still need to have their application for a variation of leave dealt with and have no wish to abandon it. A 1994 concession for work permit holders who travelled while their application was pending assumed that the application remained live while they were abroad.[3] Secondly, the rule may catch people who ask for their passport back, then change their minds and do not travel. Furthermore, as drafted, the rule leaves untouched the position of people who (i) merely lodge a photocopy of their passport with the Home Office, keeping the original until such time as the decision is about to be made, or (ii) have more than one passport and can, therefore, travel without having to request the return of the passport which has been lodged with the Home Office. In *R v Immigration Appeal Tribunal, ex p Gopal*,[4] Forbes J held that an application does not lapse if the circumstances show that the Home Office were prepared to treat it as continuing so long as the applicant returns to the UK. This test perhaps placed too much emphasis on the intentions of the Home Office and too little upon the intention of the applicant. The underlying rationale of paragraph 34 of HC 395, and the key to its proper interpretation, lies in the fact that prior to the Immigration and Asylum Act 1999 amendments, when someone left the common travel area, his or her leave lapsed. There was, therefore, nothing for the application to vary to attach to. If this is the correct rationale there are two consequences. First, although the rule is expressed in terms of a request for the return of the passport, in fact the key event on which it bites is travel outside the common travel area. So collecting a passport and then cancelling the trip abroad would not result in the application lapsing. Secondly, where travelling outside the common travel area does not result in the leave lapsing, as will be the case under the Immigration (Leave to Enter and Remain) Order 2000, then the application to vary that leave does not lapse either. There is therefore no inconsistency between the rules and the 1999 Act changes.

1   HC 395, para 34.
2   SI 2000/1161, art 13(6); see below.
3   See statement on work permit holders who travel while a work permit application is pending: *Butterworths Immigration Law Service*, D[107], p 851]. A similar concession applies to business people.
4   (1983) Times, 5 March, DC.

4.13   The whole position on lapsing of leave has changed with the insertion of section 3B and 3C into the Immigration Act 1971 and by Article 13 of the Immigration (Leave to Enter and Remain) Order 2000.[1] Article 13(6) provides that where the leave remains in force while the holder is outside the UK, the Secretary of State for the Home Department may vary leave.[2] What this seems to mean is that:

(i)   people who entered the UK with entry clearance (for example, as a spouse or as a business person) may go abroad and their leave remains in force.[3] An application for variation can be made before departure and dealt with by the Home Office in their absence;

(ii)   people who were granted leave to enter or remain for over six months may similarly go abroad and their leave remains in force.[4] They could be students who are non-visa nationals, people granted exceptional leave to enter or remain or people granted leave in one of the immigration categories requiring entry clearance, where the entry clearance requirement was waived. Their application for variation can be dealt with by the Home Office in their absence;

(iii)   however, the Immigration (Leave to Enter and Remain) Order 2000 seems to provide that only the first variation of leave can take place while the applicant is abroad. Leave granted by variation, which has less than six months left to run when the holder goes abroad, lapses when the holder leaves the common travel area.[5] An application for an extension will always be made when current leave has less than six months to run, so a person whose leave has already been varied once and who seeks a further variation cannot have the variation dealt with under Article 13(6) while he or she is abroad.

1   SI 2000/1161.
2   SI 2000/1161, art 13(6).
3   SI 2000/1161, art 13(2)(a).
4   SI 2000/1161, art 13(2)(b).
5   SI 2000/1161, art 13(3).

4.14 The Secretary of State may vary leave as above where the holder is outside the UK, including any conditions to which it is subject, in such form and manner as permitted by the Immigration Act 1971 or the Immigration (Leave to Enter and Remain) Order 2000[1] for the giving of leave to enter. Leave may, as we have seen, be varied by restricting it as well as enlarging it, but the Immigration Rules clearly envisage applications for variation being made while the person is outside the UK, although the Secretary of State is not obliged to consider such applications.[2] What this means is that someone whose leave to remain is due to expire while they are abroad can apply to a British Consulate or High Commission to extend leave. In order to consider whether to vary leave, the Secretary of State (by his or her officers) has powers to seek the information and documents that an immigration officer would be entitled to seek in an examination on arrival.[3] A passenger arriving at a UK port (or a control zone) with leave may seek to vary it, and the immigration officer may (acting on behalf of the Secretary of State) vary such leave at the port, although he or she is not obliged to consider the application.[4] If the immigration officer declines to consider the variation application, the passenger is advised to apply to the Home Office.[5] Neither applications for variation made abroad nor those made at the port need be made on the forms prescribed for all other variation applications.[6]

1   SI 2000/1161.
2   HC 395, para 33A, inserted by HC 704.
3   HC 395, Art 13(8). For immigration officers' powers of examination see 3.53 above.
4   HC 395, para 31A, inserted by HC 704.
5   HC 395, para 31A, inserted by HC 704.
6   HC 395, para 32.

Variation of leave by statute

4.15 The time taken to consider applications for leave varies. Some may take a long time, involving lengthy investigations and, possibly, an interview with the applicant and his or her spouse. Others are quite routine and can be dealt with in a straightforward manner without fuss or difficulty. Yet these variations in time can have a serious adverse impact on the subsequent appeal rights of unsuccessful applicants. Under section 61 of the Immigration and Asylum Act 1999 there is, in general, a right of appeal against a variation or refusal to vary leave whose result is to require the applicant to leave the UK within 28 days.[1] The wording of the appeal provisions of the 1999 Act, following the Immigration Act 1971, provides that a person may appeal against refusal to vary any limited leave 'which he has'.[2] The old case of *Suthendran*[3] held that the use of the present tense in the appeal provision meant that a person refused further leave to remain has no right of appeal unless he or she has current leave at the time the notice of appeal is lodged. That meant that the Home Office could prevent people appealing by delaying decisions on their applications until after their leave had expired. This obvious injustice was remedied, not by amending the statutory words, but by making provision for leave to continue by law if an application to extend it was submitted before it expired.[4] This is now achieved by section 3C of the 1971 Act,[5] which provides that if a person who has limited leave applies to the Secretary of State *before his leave expires* for it to be varied, and when it expires no decision has been taken, the leave is to be treated as continuing until the end of the period provided under procedure rules for appealing. Then, once the appeal has been lodged and while it is pending,[6] Schedule 4 of the 1999 Act makes provision for statutory leave to continue, complete with the conditions as attached to the original leave.[7] The variation applied for does not take effect while the appeal is pending.[8] However, the original leave is only extended in this way if the application to vary is made to the Secretary of State before the expiry of the original leave.[9] The purpose of extending leave in this way is to preserve the right of appeal under section 61 of the 1999 Act and to ensure that people who make valid in-time applications are not prejudiced by routine Home Office delays. So if leave has been extended under this provision, and during this extension a further application for a variation of leave is made by the applicant, there will be no further extensions, and consequently no further right of appeal.[10]

1   Immigration and Asylum Act 1999, s 61. The right of appeal has been severely restricted; Immigration Act 1971 permitted appeals against any variation or refusal to vary, including refusal to remove conditions. See chapter 18 below.
2   Immigration and Asylum Act 1999, s 61. Section 14(1) of the Immigration Act 1971 provided that a person 'who has' a limited leave may appeal against a refusal to vary it.
3   *Suthendran v Immigration Appeal Tribunal* [1977] AC 359, [1977] Imm AR 44, HL.
4   The Immigration (Variation of Leave) Order 1976, SI 1976/1572 provided for an extension of leave until the expiration of 28 days after the Secretary of State's decision: art 3(1). This enabled an appeal to be lodged during the extended leave.
5   Inserted by Immigration and Asylum Act 1999, s 3. See chapter 18 for the effect of this change.
6   An appeal is pending until it is finally determined, withdrawn or abandoned, and is not finally determined if a further appeal can be brought, but an appeal is treated as abandoned if the appellant leaves the UK or if a deportation order is made against him or her: Immigration and Asylum Act 1999, s 58(5)-(10).
7   Immigration and Asylum Act 1999, Sch 4, para 17. This marks a change from the position under the Immigration Act 1971, s 14, which merely provided that the appellant was 'not required to leave the UK' pending the appeal. These words were held not to constitute leave in *R v Immigration Appeal Tribunal, ex p Subramaniam* [1977] QB 190, [1976] Imm AR 155, CA, but merely a stay. See also *Idrish* [1985] Imm AR 155 at 167.
8   Immigration and Asylum Act 1999, Sch 4, para 16.

9 An application sent on the working day after leave expired is not in time: *R v Secretary of State for the Home Department, ex p Jecka* [1997] Imm AR 342.
10 Immigration Act 1971, s 3C(2). See further *Moussavi* [1986] Imm AR 39. But see **4.10** above.

4.16 Extensions of leave under section 3C of the Immigration Act 1971 and Schedule 4 of the Immigration and Asylum Act 1999 are examples of automatic grant or extension of leave by statute. Another example is persons formerly entitled to diplomatic or other exemption from immigration control by virtue of sections 8(2) and 8(3) of the 1971 Act.[1] When their exemption ended (because they left their post, for example), the position under the pre-1999 Act law was that they were in the UK without leave. Now, by virtue of section 8A of the 1971 Act,[2] they have 90 days' leave to remain when their exemption ends, unless they already had a shorter leave, in which case that leave operates.[3] In addition, the Secretary of State has powers under sections 3B and 4(1) to make orders by statutory instrument for general variations of leave and the conditions attached to it, in respect of any class of persons. The only Order made so far was one made during the Gulf War in 1991, which required all Iraqi nationals with limited leave to register with the police.[4]

1 See chapter 6 below.
2 Inserted by Immigration and Asylum Act 1999, s 7.
3 Immigration Act 1971, ss 8(2) and (3), and 8A, as amended by the 1999 Act, ss 6 and 7: s 8A(2)(b).
4 Immigration (Variation of Leave) Order 1991, SI 1991/77.

4.17 Apart from these statutory extensions of leave, all other extensions are granted or refused by the Home Office dealing with each case on an individual basis. Section 4(1) of the Immigration Act 1971, which requires the Secretary of State to exercise the power to give leave to remain or to vary any leave by notice in writing given to the person affected, is modified by section 3B, inserted by the Immigration and Asylum Act 1999, allowing the Secretary of State by Order to make provision for changes in the form or manner in which leave may be given, refused or varied.[1] No such changes have yet been made, although the Immigration (Leave to Enter and Remain) Order 2000[2] now permits the grant or refusal of leave to *enter* otherwise than by notice in writing.[3] It is likely that leave will soon be varied or refused by e-mail. But for now, where leave is varied, this is usually effected either by an entry in the passport, travel document or registration certificate, which serves as the section 4(1) notice. Sometimes there is only a letter, and sometimes a combination of letter and stamp in the passport. However, in *Robina Rafiq*[4] the Court of Appeal held that in the light of the requirement of notice, communication was essential to a decision. Hence where, in response to an application for indefinite leave to remain, an indefinite leave stamp had been endorsed in a passport which had not been returned to the holder, the Secretary of State could cancel the stamp and refuse the application.[5] If a notice letter indicates that leave is varied for a limited period, but omits to say what that period is, it does not constitute written notice under section 4(1) of the 1971 Act and, in consequence, the Secretary of State has not exercised his or her power to vary leave. What then is the position? In *Ah-Time*[6] the Tribunal pointed out that for variation of leave there is no equivalent to paragraph 6(1) of Schedule 2 (which deems a six-month grant of leave to enter in the absence of proper notice of the decision), and so no deemed leave takes effect. Instead, by virtue of what is now section 3C of the 1971 Act, the applicant's original leave would continue to operate until the Secretary of State corrected the mistake or reached a fresh decision. Where the notice granting leave is ambiguous over the date from which the leave is to run, this ambiguity should be construed in favour of the immigrant.[7]

1   Immigration Act 1971, s 3B(1), (2)(a), inserted by Immigration and Asylum Act 1999, s 2.
2   SI 2000/1161.
3   SI 2000/1161, art 8, made under Immigration Act 1971, s 3A, inserted by Immigration and Asylum Act 1999, s 1. See chapter 2 above.
4   *Robina Rafiq v Secretary of State* [1998] INLR 349.
5   The requirement for communication cuts both ways. In *R v Secretary of State for the Home Department, ex p Popatia; R v Secretary of State for the Home Department, ex p Chew* [2001] Imm AR 46, Sullivan J held that a deportation order which never actually came to the notice of its subject did not 'stop the clock' for the purpose of the long residence concession.
6   *Ah-Time* [1989] Imm AR 340, Immigration Appeal Tribunal. If the purported grant of leave is sent out in response to an out-of-time application, it might amount to an 'authorisation' by the Secretary of State to remain in the UK: see *Idrish* [1985] Imm AR 155 at 168, Immigration Appeal Tribunal.
7   *Behrooz* [1991] Imm AR 82, Immigration Appeal Tribunal.

4.18   At present, as indicated above, under section 4(1) of the Immigration Act 1971 a proper exercise of the Secretary of State's power depends upon written notice being given to the unsuccessful applicant. The Secretary of State must in any event give written notice to the 'requisite person' of any decision which is appealable, under the Immigration and Asylum Appeal (Notices) Regulations 2000 made under Schedule 4 to the Immigration and Asylum Act 1999.[1] The notice must set out the reasons for refusal, and give details of any right of appeal and how to exercise it.[2] Thus there is a double requirement to give notice: (i) in all cases under section 4(1) and (ii) in cases where there is a right of appeal, under the Notices Regulations. The two requirements are married by regulation 6 of the Notices Regulations, which provides that the notice can be the same one for both purposes, provided that it contains all the necessary information. It also provides that the notice is deemed to have been received on the second day after posting by first-class post.[3] In addition, in all cases where leave is refused or ended so that the applicant may be required to leave the UK within 28 days, and the decision attracts a right of appeal, section 74 of the 1999 Act requires the Secretary of State to serve a notice on the applicant and on all relevant family members, requiring them to state any additional grounds they may have for wishing to stay in the UK.[4] In response to such a statement, leave to remain may be granted or, if refused, a supplementary refusal notice is served.[5]

1   Immigration and Asylum Act 1999, Sch 4, para 1(1)(a); Immigration and Asylum Appeals (Notices) Regulations 2000, SI 2000/2246, reg 4(1). No notice is required by reason only of the fact that the decision could be appealed if the person alleged that the Secretary of State for the Home Department had acted in breach of his or her human rights or racially discriminated in taking it, but if such an allegation is made, notice must be given: SI 2000/2246, reg 4(4).
2   SI 2000/2246, reg 5; see chapter 18 below.
3   By applying the provisions of Immigration and Asylum Act 1999, Sch 4, para 2: SI 2000/2246, reg 6(2). Notices sent abroad are deemed received 28 days after posting: SI 2000/2246, reg 8, inserted by SI 2001/868, reg 2.
4   Immigration and Asylum Act 1999, s 74(2) and (4).
5   See the Immigration and Asylum Appeals (One-Stop Procedure) Regulations 2000, SI 2000/2244 and chapter 18 below.

What constitutes an extension of leave?

4.19 In complicated cases considerable correspondence may pass between the applicant and the Home Office. Sometimes Home Office letters give the indication that an existing leave has been extended, when in fact, this was not the intention of the Home Office. Thus in *R v Immigration Appeal Tribunal, ex p Venna Ahluwalia*[1] the applicant had received a letter from the Home Office in reply to her application for variation of her leave to remain, which stated: 'Meanwhile this acknowledgment may be regarded as authority for the holder to remain in the UK pending a decision on any application made for an extension of stay'. This was held to be leave. In contrast, the recitation of the statutory protection provided by section 14 of the Immigration Act 1971, 'the appellant will not be required to leave the UK while the appeal is pending', was held not to constitute leave in *R v Immigration Appeal Tribunal, ex p Subramaniam.*[2] Matters have been considerably clarified by the enactment of statutory leave pending appeal in the Immigration and Asylum Act 1999.[3]

1 [1979–80] Imm AR 1. See further *Secretary of State for the Home Department v Enorzah* [1975] Imm AR 10.
2 [1977] QB 190, [1976] Imm AR 155, CA. See **4.15** fn 7 above.
3 Immigration and Asylum Act 1999, Sch 4, para 17; see **4.15** above.

'Packing-up time'

4.20 Where an application has been refused and the applicant has been allowed a short period to organise his or her affairs, pack up and leave, the view of Lord Russell in *Suthendran v Immigration Appeal Tribunal*[1] was that such 'packing up time' constituted a fresh grant of leave.[2] However this view is, we believe, no longer tenable, at least where the Secretary of State makes it clear that the intention is not to grant further leave but merely to assure an applicant that no action will be taken to enforce departure pending the taking of an exam, the selling of a house or the birth of a child.[3]

1 [1977] AC 359 at 372, HL.
2 He repeated his view in *Halil v Davidson* [1979–80] Imm AR 164, HL.
3 See *R v Immigration Appeal Tribunal, ex p Bhanji* [1977] Imm AR 89, CA; *Theori* [1979–80] Imm AR 126, Immigration Appeal Tribunal; *R v Secretary of State for the Home Department, ex p Smith* [1996] Imm AR 331.

Cancellation of leave to remain

4.21 The new measures made under section 3B of the Immigration Act 1971[1] introduce cancellation of leave to enter or remain. Cancellation of advance leave to enter on arrival is not too unfamiliar, since it is similar to the power to refuse entry to someone holding an entry clearance.[2] But cancellation of leave to remain is unfamiliar. Article 13(7) of the Immigration (Leave to Enter and Remain) Order 2000[3] provides that non-lapsing leave may be cancelled while its holder is outside the UK.[4] The powers to seek information and documents are those of the immigration officer in conducting an examination at the port, with the additional power of calling for a medical report (since there is no power to refer the person abroad to a medical inspector) and failure to provide the requested information, documentation or report is itself a ground for cancellation of leave.[5] The Immigration Rules state that an immigration officer at the port may cancel leave to remain,[6] although in fact this may not be correct, since Schedule 2 to the 1971 Act gives immigration officers at the port powers to cancel leave to enter, but there is no mention of cancellation of leave to remain.[7] Cancellation of leave to enter which is in force is dealt with in chapter 3 above. It attracts an in-country right of appeal as if the passenger was refused entry at the port while holding a current entry clearance.[8] Regrettably, there is little flesh on the bones and it is too early to tell how the provisions will operate in practice.

1   Inserted by Immigration and Asylum Act 1999, s 2.
2   See chapter 3.
3   SI 2000/1161.
4   SI 2000/1161, art 13(7).
5   SI 2000/1161, arts 13(8), (9).
6   HC 395, para 10B, inserted by HC 704.
7   Immigration Act 1971, as amended, Sch 2, para 2A(1).
8   Immigration Act 1971, as amended, para 2A(8).

SOME GENERAL CONSIDERATIONS

Formal requirements of rules

4.22   In determining whether to vary leave, refuse to vary it or curtail it, the Secretary of State has to consider not only the formal requirements of the Immigration Rules regarding visitors, students, and so forth, but also certain general rules. Where someone is granted exceptional leave outside the Rules, the Secretary of State is entitled to apply the Rules when a variation of leave is sought, provided that the wording of the rule fits the applicant's case.[1] Similarly, in dealing with the formal requirements of the Rules, the Secretary of State has a general discretion to vary leave outside the Rules, and can for example extend leave for someone whose case falls partly within one category and partly in another ('cross-fertilisation'), but if he or she declines to do so the appellate authority cannot 'bend' the Rules itself.[2] In *R v Immigration Appeal Tribunal, ex p Martin*,[3] decided under earlier rules, an Australian woman only had sufficient means to maintain herself if she combined her earnings as a self-employed seamstress with a private income received from her father, but neither source was sufficient by itself. The adjudicator held that she could qualify as a person who 'set up in business' and that her private income could be taken into account, albeit that it was not large enough for her to qualify as a person of independent means. The Tribunal's reversal of this decision was upheld by the Divisional Court, which held that an applicant for an extension of leave must clearly bring herself within one or other of the categories in the Immigration Rules.[4]

1   *Mamon v Immigration Appeal Tribunal* [1988] Imm AR 364, CA.
2   'Bending' the Rules is not the same as giving them a construction which accords with their general humanitarian purpose: *R v Immigration Appeal Tribunal, ex p Swaran Singh* [1987] Imm AR 563, CA; or with the ECHR: *R v Secretary of State for the Home Department, ex p Arman Ali* [2000] INLR 89.
3   [1972] Imm AR 275.
4   See further *R v Immigration Appeal Tribunal, ex p Aisha Khatoon Ali* [1979–80] Imm AR 195, qualified by *R v Immigration Appeal Tribunal, ex p Coomasaru* [1983] 1 All ER 208, [1983] 1 WLR 14, CA.

4.23   Just as cross-fertilisation of the different categories is allowed to the Secretary of State but not to the appellate authorities on appeal, so too it has been held that adjudicators cannot construe the Immigration Rules so as to extend the categories of dependent relatives eligible for entry under the rules on family reunion.[1] However, as public authorities, the appellate authorities must act compatibly with the ECHR[2] and must construe the Rules purposively to give effect to the rights protected by the Convention, which might involve reading words in where necessary.[3]

1   *Nisa v Secretary of State for the Home Department* [1979–80] Imm AR 20. But see *Arman Ali* [2000] INLR 89.
2   Human Rights Act 1998, s 6; see chapter 8 below.
3   Human Rights Act 1998, s 3.

The 'no switching' rule

4.24   Prior to 1980, persons in the UK as visitors, students and other temporary entrants could obtain extensions of leave to set up in business[1] or become persons of independent means. Since March 1980 the clearly stated policy is against such changes being allowed. The current Immigration Rules prevent switching categories, with very few exceptions. For example, visa nationals in the UK as visitors cannot become students.[2] Students may be granted extensions of stay for Department of Employment-approved training,[3] or for post-graduate medical or dental training,[4] but neither they nor visitors may remain (under the Rules) for work permit or permit-free employment[5] or to set up in business.[6] Visitors and students cannot remain as au pairs or working holidaymakers.[7] However, men or women admitted in a temporary capacity can stay on if they qualify under the unmarried partners or marriage rules,[8] and people visiting family members settled in the UK may apply to remain with them permanently.[9]

1   Visitors could set up in business, but the wording of HCs 80 and 82 may have excluded students.
2   HC 395, para 60(i).
3   HC 395, para 119(i).
4   HC 395, para 73.
5   A concession operates to allow switching into shortage occupations in exceptional circumstances: see chapter 10 below.
6   However, Turkish nationals admitted as visitors may be able to remain to set up in business under the 'standstill' provisions of the EC-Turkey Association Agreement and its additional protocol: *R v Secretary of State for the Home Department, ex p Savas* [2000] INLR 398, ECJ.
7   HC 395, paras 92(i), 98(i).
8   HC 395, paras 295D, 284.
9   HC 395, paras 298(ii)(a) and 299; 317 and 318.

General grounds for refusing variations and curtailing leave

4.25   Prior to 1994, an application for leave to remain for a purpose not covered by the Immigration Rules, if refused, attracted a right of appeal on its merits.[1] The loophole was closed by the 1994 Rules,[2] which provided that (1) a variation of leave 'is to be refused' if leave is being sought for a purpose not covered by the Rules. The Secretary of State may of course still allow such an application outside the Rules, but a refusal is not appealable on the merits.[3] In addition to this general ground on which an extension of leave must be refused under the Rules, there are further grounds on which such an application 'should normally' be refused.[4] These are:

(2) the making of false representations or the failure to disclose any material fact for the purpose of obtaining leave to enter or a previous variation of leave;

(3) failure to comply with any conditions of leave;

(4) failure by the person concerned to maintain or accommodate himself and any dependants without recourse to public funds;

(5) the undesirability of permitting the person concerned to remain in the light of his or her character, conduct or associations or because of a threat to national security;

(6) refusal by a sponsor to give an undertaking in writing to be responsible for maintenance and accommodation or failure to honour such an undertaking;

(7) failure by the applicant to honour any declaration or undertaking given orally or in writing as to the intended duration and/or purpose of his or her stay;

(8) failure, except by those who qualify for settlement or who are married to someone settled in the UK, to satisfy the Secretary of State that he or she will be returnable to another country if allowed to remain in the UK for a further period;

(9) failure to produce within a reasonable time documents or other evidence required by the Secretary of State to establish a claim to remain under the Rules;[5]

(10) failure, without providing a reasonable explanation, to attend for interview;

(11) failure in the case of a child (other than an asylum seeker) making an application to remain other than in conjunction with his or her parents, to produce written consent to the application from a parent or legal guardian to the Secretary of State, if required to do so.

Rule 323 provides that a person's leave to enter or remain may be curtailed on any of the grounds set out in paragraphs (2)–(5) above or if the person ceases to meet the requirements of the Rules under which leave to enter or remain was granted.

1 Since there was no applicable rule, there was no application to depart from the Immigration Rules, and so the appellate authority was not precluded from exercising its own discretion: see eg *Livingstone* (10964); *Lizarzaburu* (10848); *Rahman (Jinnah)* [1989] Imm AR 325.
2 HC 395, para 322(1).
3 See chapter 18.
4 HC 395, para 322(2)-(11). We retain the numbering of the sub-paragraphs here.
5 See *R v Secretary of State for the Home Department, ex p Animashaun* [1990] Imm AR 70, QBD. It is the asylum equivalent of this rule, HC 394, para 340, combined with absurdly short compliance times, which has led to over a third of asylum claims being rejected on non-compliance grounds at times, and to widespread anger at the cynical abuse of the procedure by the Secretary of State to inflate refusal figures for political purposes.

4.26 The general considerations expressly apply to curtailment of leave as well as refusal to vary. Curtailment of leave is rather more drastic than a refusal to vary it, and it will normally only be used in exceptional circumstances.[1] It will not be used if less than six months' leave remains.[2] There is only one situation where curtailment is the norm, and that is where a person who is in the UK in a temporary capacity, such as student or au pair, applies for asylum which is refused.[3] If the person is not granted exceptional leave to remain, and was warned of his or her liability to curtailment,[4] and does not qualify for leave under any other provision of the Immigration Rules, leave will be curtailed on the basis that the applicant ceases to meet the requirements of the Immigration Rules (ie, the requirement that they intend to leave the UK at the end of their stay).[5] Exceptions are persons under 18 or over 65; those married to British citizens or to EEA nationals exercising Treaty rights; holders of leave in a category leading to settlement (work or business); or passengers who are terminally ill or so ill that removal would seriously endanger their life.[6] So far as refusal to vary leave is concerned, the long list of specific reasons suggests that a person who satisfies the formal qualifications of the particular rule, as a student or employee for example, and does not fall foul of one of the listed general considerations, would be entitled to a variation. Many of the features of the general grounds for refusing extensions are to be found in the general grounds for refusing leave to enter set out in chapter 3[7] and little further explanation is needed. Other general grounds are self-evident and no further explanation is given. Our further comments are set out in the paragraphs which follow.

1   The IDI on maintenance and accommodation for spouses suggest that curtailment would only be appropriate where someone has persistent recourse to public funds shortly after marriage and the situation is unlikely to change: IDI Dec/00, Ch 8, Annex H.
2   See API, Pt 1, Ch 5.3.
3   API, Pt 1, Ch 5.3.
4   The API, Pt 1, Ch 5.3 state that a curtailment warning is given during the asylum interview to the principal applicant where he or she has six months or more substantive leave remaining, or if it is not given then, it may be issued in writing. It warns the applicant of his or her liability to have leave curtailed if the asylum claim is refused.
5   API, Pt 1, Ch 5.3, para 4.1.
6   API, Pt 1, Ch 5.3, para 4.2.
7   At **3.23** above.

False representations and non-disclosure

4.27   False representations must have been made or material facts not disclosed in order to obtain leave to enter or a previous variation of leave.[1] An innocent failure will not be enough. Although the Court of Appeal has held that a false representation is simply a representation which is inaccurate, and does not necessarily connote fraud,[2] it is still incumbent on the Home Office to prove the case to the requisite standard; ie prove a representation, its falsity and the fact that it was made for the purpose of obtaining leave or an earlier variation. Where fraud is alleged, the standard of proof will have to be higher.[3] Where non-disclosure is relied on, the applicant should not be punished for a failure to realise that facts not disclosed were material.[4] Otherwise, one effect of the Rule will be to rectify mistakes by immigration officials in granting earlier leave, at the expense of the innocent applicant. See further **3.44-3.45** above.

1   HC 395, para 322(2). Note that, by virtue of s 24A(1)(a) of the Immigration Act 1971 (inserted by Immigration and Asylum Act 1999, s 28) it is a criminal offence to obtain leave to remain by means which include deception.
2   *Akhtar v Immigration Appeal Tribunal* [1991] Imm AR 326, CA. See **3.44** above.
3   *Khawaja v Secretary of State for the Home Department* [1984] AC 74, [1983] Imm AR 139, HL.
4   On what is meant by 'material' see **3.45** above, **16.33** below.

Failure to comply with conditions attached to stay

4.28 A failure to comply with conditions attached to stay[1] will lead to refusal of further leave only where a person has shown by his or her conduct that he or she has deliberately and consistently breached conditions of stay. It is not intended that the paragraph should be used indiscriminately where, for example, a person has overstayed leave unintentionally or an application was submitted a few days late.[2] The fact that a past breach has been overlooked, in the sense that further leave has been granted despite it, does not mean that it has been condoned in the sense of full forgiveness. Thus, where a student had overstayed once but had been given an extension, and had then overstayed a second time, it did not mean that the first overstay could not subsequently be used to ground a refusal.[3] However, in all cases, the decision must be personal to the applicant and it would still be wrong to refuse a variation solely to deter others from overstaying or breaching their conditions.[4]

1   HC 395, para 322(3).
2   IDI Ch 9, s 4.
3   *Secretary of State for the Home Department v Sidique* [1976] Imm AR 69.
4   *Lee v Secretary of State for the Home Department* [1975] Imm AR 75.

Recourse to public funds

4.29 If leave was subject to a condition of no recourse to public funds (which would be stamped in the passport), the previous paragraph could be used to refuse further leave. If no such formal condition was imposed, this paragraph could be relied on to refuse applicants who have failed to maintain and accommodate themselves and any dependants without recourse to public funds.[1] 'Public funds' covers housing under Part II or III of the Housing Act 1985 and the equivalent enactments in Scotland and Northern Ireland, attendance allowance, severe disablement allowance, invalid care allowance and disability allowance under Part III, income support, family credit, council tax benefit, disability working allowance and housing benefit under Part VII and child benefit under Part IX of the Social Security Contribution and Benefits Act 1992, the equivalent benefits in Northern Ireland, and income-based jobseeker's allowance under the Jobseekers Act 1995.[2] The definition is often amended and should be checked in the current version of the Immigration Rules. An applicant is not treated as having recourse to public funds by relying on funds provided to the sponsor in his or her own right, provided that the applicant's presence in the UK has not resulted in increased entitlement for the sponsor.[3] In the context of settlement for spouses, if a person has, through no fault of his or her own, had to have strictly temporary assistance from public funds, he or she should not be refused settlement in reliance on this paragraph.[4]

1   HC 395, para 322(4).
2   HC 395, para 6.
3   HC 395, para 6A.
4   IDI Dec/00, Ch 8, Annex H, para 8.

Character, conduct or associations

4.30 Curtailment or refusal is in order if it is undesirable to permit the applicant to remain in the UK in the light of his or her character, conduct or associations.[1]

These are wide-ranging words which give the Secretary of State a discretion in the light of an applicant's criminal record, or other bad behaviour or associations. Curtailment is unlikely since the Secretary of State can simply use deportation powers.

1   HC 395, para 322(5).

Breach of undertakings

4.31   An application for variation of leave may be refused if the person has failed to honour any declaration or undertaking given orally or in writing as to the intended duration and/or purpose of that person's stay.[1] The situation arises most often when a family visitor decides to apply for leave to remain in the UK with the sponsoring family member, having said on arrival or at entry clearance interview that he or she would return home at the end of the visit. A 'declaration' must, we suggest, be something more definite than a mere statement of intention, but exactly what will amount to a 'declaration' or how cogent the evidence must be to prove a 'declaration' is still unclear. So far as 'undertakings' are concerned, Tribunal authorities under earlier rules held that the only undertakings which count are those which amount to false representations. In other words, a genuine change of circumstances since the 'undertaking' will not prevent an extension of leave.[2] This appears to be the way the Rule is interpreted by the Home Office in the IDI, which state that where there is good reason for the applicant's change of mind, such as unforeseen circumstances, leave may be granted; only where there does not appear to be a good reason, and particularly where there is reason to doubt the applicant's future intentions, should leave be refused.[3] The Tribunal authority suggesting otherwise is, we suggest, not to be followed.[4]

1   HC 395, para 322(7).
2   *Ridha* (3060), unreported; *Perera* (3063), unreported.
3   IDI Dec/00, Ch 9, s 4, para 8.
4   *Amoah* (4943), which held that the Secretary of State was entitled to refuse an extension on the basis of failure to honour undertakings even if these had been given in the utmost good faith.

4.32   The current Immigration Rules provide that they do not generally apply to EEA nationals.[1] Curtailment or refusal to renew residence permits or other leave granted to EEA nationals who benefit from the free movement provisions must all be justifiable by reference to EC law and, in particular, to the public policy provisions (see chapter 7 below).

1   HC 395, para 5.

REGISTRATION WITH THE POLICE

4.33   Under the Immigration Act 1971 the government has power to make any group of immigrants register with the police. The present policy is to limit this to aliens, but this can be changed at any time, subject to annulment in Parliament.[1] The current regulations are the Immigration (Registration with Police) Regulations 1972.[2] They apply only to aliens who have a limited leave to enter or remain in the UK which is for the time being subject to a condition requiring registration with the police.[3]

1   Immigration Act 1971, s 4(3). Possibly it was for fear of reprisals that the Police Federation opposed the registration with police of Commonwealth citizens under the 1971 Act. It cannot have been because of the administrative burden, because only 15 new personnel would have been required: see 813 HC Official Report (5th series) col 51.
2   SI 1972/1758, amended on many occasions in respect of the fee for issue of a certificate of registration. The fee for registration now stands at £34. See the Immigration (Registration with Police) (Amendment) Regulations 1995, SI 1995/2928.
3   SI 1972/1758, Reg 3.

4.34   The current Immigration Rules[1] provide that a condition requiring registration will normally be imposed on any relevant foreign national[2] aged 16 or over who is given limited leave to enter:

(i)   for employment for longer than six months, unless he or she has been admitted for permit-free employment as a seasonal worker, a minister of religion, or a private servant in a diplomatic household; or
(ii)   for longer than six months as a student, au pair, business or self-employed person, investor or person of independent means or creative artist; or
(iii)   the spouse or child of someone who is required to register with the police.

Exceptionally, a requirement to register with the police may be imposed in any other case in order to ensure that a foreign national complies with the terms of his or her leave.[3] Where a condition requiring registration was not imposed on arrival, it should normally be imposed where an extension of stay is granted and the effect of the extension is to put the person in one of the above categories. This condition cannot be imposed on children under 16, ministers of religion, diplomats' private servants, spouses of persons settled in the UK or those granted asylum.[4]

1   HC 395, paras 325 and 326, as amended by Cm 3953 from 11 May 1998.
2   Foreign nationals are synonymous with aliens, ie, they are non-Commonwealth citizens. Relevant foreign nationals for registration purposes are defined in HC 395, para 324 and Appendix 2.
3   HC 395, para 325 (2).
4   HC 395, para 326.

4.35   Registration involves going to the local police station within seven days of the requirement to register[1] and giving detailed particulars, including name, address, marital status, details of employment or occupation, including employer's name and address, a photograph, and paying the registration fee. While the person is required to register, changes of address must be notified to the police within seven days, and changes in marital status, nationality and employment or occupation within eight days of the change.[2] In return the foreign national receives from the police a certificate of registration. The requirement to register continues in the case of all relevant foreign nationals until they are granted indefinite leave to remain. EEA nationals and their non-EEA family members are not required to register, since such a condition is contrary to free movement rights under EC law.[3]

1   SI 1972/1758, reg 5.
2   SI 1972/1758, reg 7 (changes of residence or address) and 8 (other changes).
3   See chapter 7 below.

4.36   Someone who, without reasonable excuse, fails to comply with any of the registration requirements, ie fails to register or fails to notify a change of particulars, commits a criminal offence under section 26(1)(f) of the Immigration Act 1971. This is a summary offence with a six-month time limit. It is continuous up to the time when limited leave expires, but once the period of leave has expired, the registration regulations cease to apply, although offences against the regulation committed prior to the date of expiry of leave might still be prosecuted within the six-month time limit.[1]

1 *R v Naik* (1978) Times, 26 July, CA.

HOTEL REGISTERS

4.37 The Immigration Act 1971 contains power to make regulations requiring hotels and guest houses to keep records of persons staying there,[1] and under the Immigration (Hotel Records) Order 1972, hotels and other premises where lodging or sleeping accommodation is provided for reward must normally keep registers.[2] All visitors over the age of 16 who stay there must on arrival inform the keeper of the premises of their full name and nationality. That applies to everyone. Aliens (non-Commonwealth citizens) must also give passport details and inform the hotel of their next address.[3] The keeper of the premises must record this information and keep it available for inspection for at least 12 months.[4] It is not clear how effective or how necessary is the maintenance of hotel registers.

1 Immigration Act 1971, s 4(4).
2 SI 1972/1689.
3 SI 1972/1689, Art 3.
4 SI 1972/1689, Art 5.

CONTROL OF DEPARTURE

4.38 UK immigration law does not expressly recognise a right of departure from the UK, though one might be tempted to think that it does, because of the grandiloquent opening to the Immigration Act 1971:

> 'all those who are in this Act expressed to have the right of abode in the United Kingdom shall be free to live in, and to come and go into and from the United Kingdom without let or hindrance ...'[1]

This, however, is subject to two limitations affecting the right to depart. First, the right to go without let or hindrance is subject to such limits as may be 'lawfully imposed' on any person.[2] Secondly, the right to depart depends upon the person being able to acquire a passport.[3] Although the position in UK law is somewhat obscure, under EC law there is a clearly defined right to depart.[4] British citizens wishing to exercise their right to depart for a Community purpose can invoke these provisions of EC law if they are refused a passport or other travel document valid in the territories of other EC countries. For a full discussion, see **2.42–2.44** above.

1 Immigration Act 1971, s 1(1).
2 Immigration Act 1971, s 1(1). See **2.6** above.
3 The refusal of a passport is now subject to judicial review: *R v Secretary of State for Foreign and Commonwealth Affairs, ex p Everett* [1989] QB 811, [1989] Imm AR 155, CA. See **2.41** above.
4 See chapter 7 below.

Right to depart – immigration officers' powers

4.39 An immigration officer may examine someone seeking to leave the UK for the purpose of determining whether he or she has the right of abode and, if not, in order to establish his or her identity.[1] For the purpose of this examination, the immigration officer can require the person wishing to leave the UK to produce either a valid passport with photograph or some other document which satisfactorily establishes the person's identity and nationality or citizenship.[2] Immigration officers may also require the provision of other documents and may carry out searches, as on entry.[3] But there is no express power to detain or require a person to submit to further examination, and there is certainly, except in the limited situation referred to below, no power to prevent the person's departure for any immigration reason. Clearly there is power to arrest and detain under other powers, for example if there is a warrant for the arrest of the person in connection with a criminal offence.[4] But immigration powers of detention do not apply to persons leaving the UK.

1 Immigration Act 1971, Sch 2, para 3(1).
2 Immigration Act 1971, Sch 2, para 4.
3 Immigration Act 1971, Sch 2, para 4.
4 For immigration officers' powers of arrest for immigration offences see Immigration Act 1971, ss 28Aff; see chapter 14.

Emergency and safety powers

4.40 Under section 3(7) of the Immigration Act 1971 power is given to make provision for prohibiting nationals or citizens of a particular country from leaving the UK, or from doing so other than at a port of exit or for imposing conditions or restrictions on them when they wish to leave. Such an order can only be made where it appears to Her Majesty proper to do so by reason of restrictions or conditions imposed on British citizens when they want to leave a particular country or territory. Provision may also be made by Order in Council to prohibit all those who do not have the right of abode in the UK from leaving on a ship or aircraft specified or indicated in the prohibition in the interests of safety.[1] Where such an order is in force, an immigration officer has additional powers of examining persons who are leaving or seeking to leave the UK to determine:

(a)   whether any of the provisions of the order apply to them; and
(b)   whether, if so, any power conferred by the order should be exercised in relation to them and in what way.[2]

No such order has been made or is in force since the Immigration Act 1971 came into force.

1 Immigration Act 1971, s 3(7).
2 Immigration Act 1971, Sch 2, para 3(2).

Chapter 5

SETTLEMENT AND RETURN

5.1   Settlement
5.19   Return to the UK

SETTLEMENT

Definition

5.1   A person with the right of abode does not need to qualify for admission to the UK under the Immigration Act 1971 or the Immigration Rules. The concept of a 'right of abode' is to be distinguished from the concept of 'settlement' or the right to permanent residence. The right to permanent residence, or settled status, does not confer freedom from immigration control. Being 'settled' means being ordinarily resident without being subject under the immigration laws to any restriction on the period of stay.[1] Ordinary residence and being free from restrictions on the length of permitted stay under the Immigration Rules are the two key elements. The word 'settled', therefore, covers persons with a right of abode and those with indefinite leave to enter or remain, provided each is ordinarily resident in the UK. Settled status is defined by the Immigration Rules to mean that the person concerned is free from any restriction on the period of stay (excluding those exempt from control under section 8), and is ordinarily resident in the UK without having entered or remained in breach of immigration laws or, having entered or remained unlawfully, has subsequently entered lawfully or has been granted leave to remain and is so resident.[2] It has also been held in the context of family reunion that a person coming for 'settlement' to the UK must intend to become ordinarily resident.[3]

1   Immigration Act 1971, s 33(2A), as amended by British Nationality Act 1981, s 39(6) and Sch 4, para 7. See also British Nationality Act 1981, s 50(2)–(4), where a more comprehensive definition (necessary for the purpose of nationality law) is given: **5.4** below. For EEA nationals reg 8 of the Immigration (European Economic Area) Regulations 2000, SI 2000/2326 defines those who are to be treated as not subject to any restriction on their period of stay.
2   HC 395, para 6.
3   *Rashida Biba v Immigration Appeal Tribunal* [1988] Imm AR 298, CA.

5.2 Whether a person is free from immigration restrictions on their length of stay is not normally difficult to determine. Thus, a person with a six-month or 12-month leave cannot be regarded as 'settled'. The Immigration Act 1971 distinguishes between a limited leave and indefinite leave,[1] and normally the person must have been granted one or other of them, there being no half-way house between the grant of leave and entry without leave.[2] The position is different for EEA nationals and their families, who may have entered under EEA free movement rights and not have been granted indefinite leave to remain under UK domestic Immigration Rules. Their position is now regulated by regulation 8 of the Immigration (European Economic Area) Regulations 2000, under which the general rule is that freedom from restrictions on length of stay only occurs if indefinite permission is granted or in other specified circumstances.[3]

1   Immigration Act 1971, s 3(1).
2   *Mokuolo v Secretary of State for the Home Department* [1989] Imm AR 51, CA.
3   Immigration (European Economic Area) Regulations 2000, SI 2000/2326, reg 8.

5.3 Indefinite leave to enter or remain is usually indicated in one of two ways: either by a stamp in the passport endorsed by the immigration officer on entry or by the Immigration and Nationality Directorate after entry; or by an indication on an entry certificate, which is now treated as a leave to enter.[1] A stamp in a passport indicating leave to enter or remain for an indefinite period is clearly an express grant of indefinite leave. An alternative expression employed by the Home Office is 'there is at present no time restriction on the leave to remain'. This is a somewhat curious form of wording since there is no power to impose a limitation on an indefinite leave, and it must, therefore, be treated as a form of permission for those who have entered and remained, for example, under EEA free movement rights, without requiring leave to enter or remain. Greater difficulties arise where all that has been used is a rectangular stamp with a date but no clear words indicating any sort of leave, limited or unlimited. In the case of returning residents, such a stamp would be enough to constitute indefinite leave to enter, but in other cases, this is unlikely. The Court of Appeal has held that in the circumstances of the particular case such a stamp was not the grant of a leave to enter at all, but merely a record of the person's passage through immigration control.[2] In *Ex p Coomasaru*[3] the court held that a date stamp accompanied by the words 'employed with the Sri Lanka HC' was a grant of leave limited to the duration of such employment. Whether such a stamp confers limited leave or no leave at all, the upshot is that the applicant cannot be regarded as 'settled' in the UK. Illegible stamps in passports (which once gave rise to indefinite leave to enter) are deemed to grant six months' leave with a condition prohibiting employment.[4] Settlement can only occur where there is no time limit on stay.

1   Under arts 2–4 of the Immigration (Leave to Enter and Remain) Order 2000, SI 2000/1161 a visa or other entry clearance may have effect as indefinite leave to enter if (a) it specifies the purpose of entry and (b) states it is to have effect as indefinite leave to enter (arts 3(3)(b) and 4(3)(a)). See generally chapter 3 above.
2   *R v Secretary of State for the Home Department, ex p Bagga* [1991] 1 QB 485, [1990] Imm AR 413, CA: see **2.50** above.
3   *R v Immigration Appeal Tribunal, ex p Coomasaru* [1983] 1 All ER 208, [1982] Imm AR 77, CA.
4   Since an illegible stamp is not an effective 'notice giving or refusing leave' as required by Immigration Act 1971, s 4(1); Sch 2, para 6(1), as amended, applies.

5.4 A similar definition of settlement applies for the purposes of the British Nationality Act 1981, except that for nationality purposes residents in the Channel Islands or Isle of Man, as well as in the UK, are included.[1] Persons who are subject to exemptions from immigration control, such as diplomats, consuls, members of visiting forces and so forth, are not normally regarded as 'settled' during any period when they are entitled to exemption.[2] Limited exceptions apply to enable the children of an 'exempted' parent to obtain British citizenship by birth in the UK under section 1 of the British Nationality Act 1981.[3]

1   British Nationality Act 1981, s 50(1), (2).
2   Immigration Act 1971, s 8(5). See also British Nationality Act 1981, s 50(3).
3   Immigration Act 1971, s 8(5A), as amended; British Nationality Act 1981, s 50(4).

Consequences of being settled

5.5 Settlement brings many advantages. Persons subject to immigration control who are 'settled' have in general a right to permanent residence in the UK, provided they continue living here, but they are liable to deportation, unless they have an exemption,[1] and may be deported if they commit serious crimes or their presence is no longer conducive to the public good for this or some other reason.[2]

1   Immigration Act 1971, s 7.
2   Immigration Act, s 3(5)(a) and (6).

5.6 Other important consequences of being 'settled' are that persons who were previously tied to doing a particular job can change employment without permission;[1] persons here on independent means can take up employment or go into business if they choose; and all can take the full benefits of the welfare state (unless they are sponsored immigrants in the UK for less than five years and their sponsor is still alive).[2] Another important practical consequence is that the 'settled' person is in a position to call for members of their family and other dependants to join them in the UK, provided the necessary accommodation is available and there will be no additional recourse to public funds as a result.[3] There is a wider range of options for family reunion for those settled in the UK than for those with only a limited leave.[4] Foreign nationals who previously were required to register with the police no longer need to do so on being granted settlement.[5] Having the right to settle leads to eligibility for naturalisation or registration as a British citizen.[6] Settlement enables a parent to qualify his or her child for British citizenship, if the child is born in the UK,[7] although this is not a precondition of registration or naturalisation.[8]

1   Under Immigration Act 1971, s 3(1) restrictions on employment can only be imposed on a person with limited leave.
2   Immigration and Asylum Act 1999, ss 115(9)(c), 116, 117; Social Security (Immigration and Asylum) Consequential Amendments Regulations 2000, SI 2000/636, Sch, para 1. See chapter 13.
3   HC 395, paras 6A, inserted by Cm 4851, and 317(iv).
4   Compare eg HC 395, paras 194–199 with para 298.
5   HC 395, paras 325–326.
6   British Nationality Act 1981, ss 4 and 6.
7   British Nationality Act 1981, ss 1(1) and 50(4).
8   British Nationality Act 1981, ss 4, 6 and Sch 1.

Settlement under the Immigration Rules

5.7   Under the Immigration Rules certain categories of immigration status never lead to settlement, for example, visitor,[1] student,[2] working holiday,[3] au pair,[4] work training,[5] seasonal workers at agricultural camps[6] and teachers and language assistants on approved exchange schemes.[7] In all these cases the person is expected to leave at the end of the allotted period and they cannot generally switch into a category which qualifies for settlement.[8] But in other categories settlement is given straightaway or the persons are admitted on a temporary basis with a view to eventual settlement. Thus spouses are given a 12-month trial period before qualifying for settlement.[9] So too are any children who come with them.[10] Otherwise, children and other dependent relatives obtain immediate settlement on arrival.[11] Children born in the UK who are not British citizens may also qualify for immediate settlement if one of their parents qualifies for it, or acquires a right of abode or the child goes into local authority care.[12] Bereaved spouses of settled persons who died during the initial 12-month probationary period qualify for settlement,[13] as do non-custodial parents exercising access rights to children resident in the UK (for whom the qualifying period is also 12 months),[14] and unmarried partners, whether of the same or opposite sex, although the qualifying period for settlement in this case is two years.[15]

1 HC 395, para 44.
2 HC 395, paras 60 and 67.
3 HC 395, para 98.
4 HC 395, para 92.
5 HC 395, para 119.
6 HC 395, para 107.
7 HC 395, para 113.
8 See fnn 1–7 above.
9 HC 395, para 282. Not all of this time need be spent in the UK: *Qureshi* (18312), [1999] 5 ILD 4 at 23; IDI Dec/00, Ch 8, s 1.
10 HC 395, para 302.
11 HC 395, paras 299, 308 and 317.
12 HC 395, paras 305–308.
13 HC 395, para 287(b), inserted by Cm 4851, para 30.
14 HC 395, para 248D, inserted by Cm 4851, para 22.
15 HC 395, para 295G, inserted by Cm 4851, para 32. Bereaved unmarried partners qualify under HC 395, paras 295M-O.

5.8   Apart from family reunion the other categories who may qualify for eventual settlement are work permit holders,[1] those in permit-free employment,[2] business and self-employed persons,[3] writers, composers and artists,[4] investors and retired persons of independent means[5] and Commonwealth citizens with grandparents born in the UK who wish to take or seek employment in the UK.[6] Under the Immigration Rules, these last groups of people qualify for settlement if they have 'spent a continuous period of four years in the UK in this capacity'.[7] The Rules require continuity of residence in the UK for four years while in a particular capacity. A person whose continuity of residence in the UK has been broken would only qualify for an extension of stay in the same capacity and not for settlement. The general practice is to disregard absences of three months in any one year, and, exceptionally, longer periods.[8] While the legal effect of settlement is to allow people to change jobs or business, its grant is dependent in many cases on the prospect of being able to continue in the existing capacity. In employment cases, continuation with the present employer is an express requirement and the employer must give a certificate to this effect.[9] In business cases, evidence of the continuing viability of the business and the applicant's involvement with it is required.[10]

1   HC 395, para 134.
2   HC 395, paras 142, 150, 158, 167, 176 and 184.
3   HC 395, paras 209 and 222.
4   HC 395, para 238.
5   HC 395, paras 230 and 269.
6   HC 395, para 192.
7   This phrase recurs in each of the 13 settlement rules just referred to, viz paras 134, 142, 150, 158, 167, 176, 184, 192, 209, 222, 230, 238 and 269. For a discussion of its meaning see **10.90** below.
8   In *Shahbakhti* (16978) 1999 5 ILD 1 at 30, twenty months' absence in four years was too long for a work permit holder.
9   HC 395, para 134.
10 HC 395, para 209.

5.9   Although the grant of settlement after four years in a particular capacity depends upon the exercise of discretion by the Home Office, settlement is normally given as a matter of course where the requirements of the Immigration Rules are satisfied, and before refusing settlement the Secretary of State must remain unsatisfied about one or more of these requirements unless a general ground for refusing indefinite leave is relied on, such as breach of a condition or undertaking or bad character.[1] But while under earlier rules a failure to fulfil one of the requirements of the rules during the four-year period could be overlooked,[2] it leads to mandatory refusal under the current Rules. In such a situation, settlement may only be given as a concession outside the Rules, an exercise of discretion which cannot be reviewed as to its merits on appeal.

1   The general grounds for refusing variation of leave are set out at HC 395, para 322. The Secretary of State is entitled to delay a decision on an application for indefinite leave to remain, despite the existence of compassionate circumstances, to await the outcome of a police investigation: *R v Secretary of State for the Home Department, ex p Hina Memon* [1999] Imm AR 85.
2   *Fanous v Secretary of State for the Home Department* [1993] Imm AR 200, Immigration Appeal Tribunal.

5.10   In addition to these Rules, special provision is made for the removal of the time limit on the stay of EEA nationals and their families.[1] The basis of these provisions is dealt with in chapter 7 below.

1   HC 395, paras 255–257.

Settlement outside the Immigration Rules

5.11   Discretionary settlement outside the Immigration Rules may also be given to a variety of people. First, there are refugees and asylum seekers who were granted exceptional leave to enter or remain. The current practice, introduced in 1998, is to give refugees settlement immediately and those granted exceptional leave after four.[1] Settlement may also be given outside the Rules to persons who have lived in the UK for a continuous period of ten years, if here lawfully, and 14 years if any part of that time has been unlawful (**15.49–15.52** below).[2] British Overseas citizens who have been in the UK with limited leave for seven years may be granted settlement.[3] Another policy which envisages the grant of settled status outside the Rules is the domestic violence concession (benefiting spouses who faced domestic violence within the probationary year following admission).[4] Other policies (allowing for the grant of settlement to unmarried partners and to bereaved spouses and bereaved unmarried partners) were brought within the framework of the Immigration Rules in October 2000.[5] In addition, persons benefiting from the Secretary of State's policies precluding enforcement action against overstayers and illegal entrants on family life grounds may be eligible for a discretionary grant of settlement.[6] The same may also result from the application of ECHR, Article 8.[7]

1　The White Paper of July 1998, *Fairer, Faster and Firmer – A Modern Approach to Immigration and Asylum*, announced the reduction in the qualifying period for settlement from the previous four years for refugees and seven years for those with exceptional leave to remain. A table setting out the transitional arrangements for settlement for those with limited leave under the earlier system is to be found in *Butterworths Immigration Law Service*, **2B** [28].
2　Commonly referred to as the 'ten year rule' and '14 year rule' although they are both in fact concessions contained (now) within IDI Dec/00, Ch 18.
3　See letter from the Home Office to JCWI referred to in *R v Secretary of State for the Home Department, ex p Patel* [1993] Imm AR 257, QBD and 392, CA.
4　See *Butterworths Immigration Law Service*, D[189]. The original concession included bereaved spouses, but this is now dealt with by the Immigration Rules, see fn 5 below.
5　By Cm 4851, inserting new provisions 287(b) (bereaved spouses), 295G (unmarried partners) and 295M (bereaved unmarried partners) into the Immigration Rules, HC 395.
6　See DP3/96 (previously DP2/93, replaced on 16 March 1996), DP4/96 dealing with divorced or separated parents, and DP5/96 dealing with families with children resident in the UK for seven years (reduced from ten years by a ministerial statement of 24 February 1999 (For these policies see *Butterworths Immigration Law Service*, D[61B], D[67], D[83], D[87], D[188]).
7　*R v Secretary of State for the Home Department, ex p Isiko* [2001] 1 FLR 633, CA.

Settlement on the coming into force of the Immigration Act 1971

5.12 So far we have dealt with those who are granted indefinite leave to enter or remain in the exercise of the discretion of an immigration officer or the Home Office. There is a further category of persons who were granted indefinite leave by statute. These are all persons who were either settled in the UK before the coming into force of the Immigration Act 1971 on 1 January 1973 or were given unconditional admission or leave to land under the earlier immigration laws. Section 1(2) of the 1971 Act provides that indefinite leave to enter or remain shall be treated as having been given under the 1971 Act to those in the UK at its coming into force, if they were then settled there and not exempt from immigration control. The benefit of section 1(2) only applies to those physically present in the UK on 1 January 1973. Where the protection of that section is claimed, the burden is on the immigrant to show that he or she was settled.[1]

1　*R v Secretary of State for the Home Department, ex p Mughal* [1974] QB 313, [1973] 3 All ER 796, CA.

5.13 If such persons had not yet become ordinarily resident by 1 January 1973, or they were absent from the UK on that date, they may still rely upon the provisions of section 34(2) and (3). Section 34(2) provides that leave to land by virtue of earlier legislation is to be treated as leave to enter under the Immigration Act 1971. Section 34(3) provides that a person treated as having leave to enter is to be treated as having indefinite leave if that person was not, on 1 January 1973, subject to a condition limiting his or her stay in the UK. These provisions cannot, however, benefit persons who were illegal entrants.[1]

1 *Azam v Secretary of State for the Home Department* [1974] AC 18, [1973] 2 All ER 765, HL; *R v Secretary of State for the Home Department, ex p Razak* [1986] Imm AR 44, DC; affd (25 March 1986, unreported), CA; *R v Secretary of State for the Home Department, ex p Miah* [1990] 2 All ER 523, [1989] Imm AR 559, CA; *R v Secretary of State for the Home Department, ex p Khan* [1990] 2 All ER 531, [1990] Imm AR 327, CA.

Ordinarily resident

5.14 The term 'ordinarily resident' is used in a number of different statutes,[1] including the Immigration Act 1971 and the British Nationality Acts 1948 and 1981. The term is also used as a criterion of eligibility for educational and other social services provided by central and local government.[2] A trend towards defining ordinary residence in terms of immigration status in the context of education was rejected in *Shah v Barnet London Borough Council*,[3] where the House of Lords held that an overseas student habitually and normally resident in the UK for study, apart from temporary or occasional absences of long or short duration, was 'ordinarily resident' in the natural and ordinary meaning of those words used in the Education Acts and implementing regulations. Lord Scarman, who gave the leading speech, unhesitatingly subscribed to the view that 'ordinarily resident' referred to persons' abode in a particular place or country which they had adopted voluntarily and for settled purposes as part of the regular order of their life for the time being, whether of short or long duration. The purpose might be one or several, specific or general, and did not require that the person intended to stay indefinitely; indeed, the person's purpose might be for a limited period. Education, business or profession, employment, health, family, or merely love of the place sprang to mind as common reasons for a choice of regular abode. All that was necessary was that the purpose of living where one did had a sufficient degree of continuity to be properly described as settled. It was wrong to attach any decisive importance to the immigration status of the persons claiming to be ordinarily resident, except in the case of a person whose presence was unlawful.[4] Further, the notion that ordinary residence required a permanent or indefinitely enduring purpose derived from a confusion of ordinary residence with domicile. The 'real home' test did not apply to determining ordinary residence.[5]

1 See eg Military Service Act 1916, s 1; National Service Act 1948, s 34(4).
2 But increasingly immigration status rather than 'ordinary residence' defines eligibility for housing, social services and social security (as well as employment): see chapter 13 below.
3 [1983] 2 AC 309, [1983] 1 All ER 226.
4 See *R v Secretary of State for the Home Department, ex p Margueritte* [1983] QB 180, [1982] 3 All ER 909, CA; *Immigration Appeal Tribunal v Chelliah* [1985] Imm AR 192, CA.
5 See *Stransky v Stransky* [1954] P 428, [1954] 2 All ER 536.

5.15 Thus ordinary residence is to be distinguished from the more traditional concept of domicile, which is used in private international law. Ordinary residence may be acquired without any intention permanently to reside in the country, whereas an intention permanently to remain is essential to the acquisition of a new domicile.[1] Thus persons who come to the UK for a visit and remain for reasons beyond their control may be ordinarily resident though they cannot acquire a domicile of choice because of absence of any necessary intention.[2] At common law, persons may be ordinarily resident although they are liable to removal or deportation under the immigration laws,[3] but it is not clear whether they may be ordinarily resident if their residence in the UK is not voluntary because, for example, they are in prison or a psychiatric institution.[4] A person may be ordinarily resident in two places at one time.[5] It is also clear that ordinary residence is not lost through temporary absences abroad,[6] though clearly this is always a matter of degree. In *R v Hussain*[7] an absence abroad for a period of 20 months was held to break the period of ordinary residence for the purposes of exemption from deportation under the Commonwealth Immigrants Act 1962. On the other hand, in *R v Edgehill*[8] a sentence of less than six months' imprisonment imposed by a foreign court did not prevent a defendant from having been 'ordinarily' and 'continuously' resident here for five years so as to exempt him from deportation under the 1962 Act. In *R v Immigration Appeal Tribunal, ex p Siggins*,[9] a nine-month absence in the US was insufficient to break the period of ordinary residence. In each case the test to apply is whether the applicant intends to return to the UK so that the break in residence is a mere temporary one. Where the applicant intends to reside in a new country for the foreseeable future, ordinary residence in the UK will end.[10]

1 See *Hopkins v Hopkins* [1951] P 116 at 121–122 and *Stransky v Stransky* [1954] P 428 at 437. For a fuller discussion of domicile see chapter 11.
2 *Re Mackenzie* [1941] Ch 69, [1940] 4 All ER 310; and cf *Re Bright, ex p Bright* (1903) 51 WR 342, CA; *R v Denman, ex p Staal* (1917) 86 LJKB 1328; *Pittar v Richardson* (1917) 87 LJKB 59.
3 *Boldrini v Boldrini and Martini* [1932] P 9, CA; *May v May and Lehmann* [1943] 2 All ER 146; *Cruh v Cruh* [1945] 2 All ER 545.
4 See *IRC v Lysaght* [1928] AC 234, per Viscount Sumner at 243; contrast *Re Mackenzie* [1941] Ch 69, per Morton J at 77.
5 *Re Norris, ex p Reynolds* (1888) 4 TLR 452, CA (bankrupt ordinarily resident in Brussels and London); see further *Fox v Stirk and Bristol Electoral Registration Officer* [1970] 2 QB 463, [1970] 3 All ER 7, CA, per Lord Denning MR at 475 (a person may have two residences).
6 See *Hopkins v Hopkins* [1951] P 116, [1950] 2 All ER 1035; *Stransky v Stransky* [1954] P 428, [1954] 2 All ER 536; *Lewis v Lewis* [1956] 1 All ER 375, [1956] 1 WLR 200; *R v Immigration Appeal Tribunal, ex p Siggins* [1985] Imm AR 14, QBD; *Secretary of State for the Home Department v Haria* [1986] Imm AR 165.
7 *R v Hussain* (1971) 56 Cr App Rep 165, CA.
8 [1963] 1 QB 593, [1963] 1 All ER 181, CCA.
9 [1985] Imm AR 14, above.
10 *R v Immigration Appeal Tribunal, ex p NG* [1986] Imm AR 23, QBD; *Ex p Siggins* above.

5.16 The ordinary residence of children may cause problems. In *Re P (GE) (an infant)*[1] it was held that the ordinary residence of children too young to decide for themselves where to live was the home of their parents, even while they were away at boarding school. They did not lose that status by temporary absence abroad or by being kidnapped by one of the parents without consent of the other. In an Australian case[2] it was held that though a child spent more time at boarding school than at her parents' home, she was nevertheless ordinarily resident with her father because this had been her permanent home at all times and the time spent at school was for the special purpose of education. This is in contrast to the position of adult students, for whom study may be a 'settled purpose' which establishes ordinary residence: see *Shah v Barnet* above.

1 [1965] Ch 568, [1964] 3 All ER 977, CA.
2 *Clark v Insurance Office of Australia Ltd* [1965] 1 Lloyd's Rep 308, SC of Victoria.

Residence in breach of the immigration laws

5.17 For the purposes of immigration and nationality law, ordinary residence contains statutory requirements over and above those in the common law. The Immigration Act 1971 and British Nationality Act 1981 both deal with the question whether a person can be ordinarily resident while in breach of the immigration laws. For purposes of exemption from deportation, once ordinarily resident, a person does not cease to be so while in breach of the immigration laws.[1] But for other Immigration Act purposes, it is expressly provided that a person cannot be ordinarily resident at a time when he or she is in breach of the immigration laws.[2] A similar qualification is made under the British Nationality Act 1981: a person is not to be treated as ordinarily resident for the purposes of that Act when he or she is in the UK in breach of the immigration laws.[3] Under the British Nationality Act 1948 no such qualification was made, but in *Ex p Margueritte* the Court of Appeal held that lawful presence was imported into the meaning of ordinary residence under that Act.[4]

1   Immigration Act 1971, s 7(2).
2   Immigration Act, s 33(2).
3   British Nationality Act 1981, s 50(5).
4   *R v Secretary of State for the Home Department, ex p Margueritte* [1983] QB 180, [1982] 3 All ER 909, CA, distinguishing *Azam v Secretary of State for the Home Department* [1974] AC 18, [1973] 2 All ER 765, HL where in a number of their Lordships' speeches it was assumed that a person could be ordinarily resident although an illegal entrant.

5.18 In *Shah v Barnet London Borough Council*,[1] the House of Lords, going further than the statutes required, held that unlawful residence could never be relied on by the resident as establishing ordinary residence.[2] We suggest that there are four situations where someone will be held not to be ordinarily resident on account of breaches of the immigration laws: (1) where the person is in breach of a deportation order;[3] (2) where a person who requires leave to enter enters without leave,[4] even if the person has acted quite innocently;[5] (3) where leave to enter or remain has been obtained by a material deception;[6] and (4) where the person has overstayed the time limited by a leave to enter, even if this is done innocently through ignorance or oversight.[7]

1   [1983] 2 AC 309 at 343.
2   Although such residence could be relied on by the Crown for tax purposes: [1983] 2 AC 309 at 343.
3   Immigration Act 1971, s 33(1).
4   See *Azam v Secretary of State for the Home Department* above.
5   *R v Governor of Ashford Remand Centre, ex p Bouzagou* [1983] Imm AR 69, CA; *Rehal v Secretary of State for the Home Department* [1989] Imm AR 576, CA.
6   See chapter 16 below.
7   *Immigration Appeal Tribunal v Chelliah* [1985] Imm AR 192, CA; *Sui-Ling Lui* [1986] Imm AR 287

RETURN TO THE UK

5.19 Under section 3(4) of the Immigration Act 1971, all leave, including indefinite leave,[1] lapses on leaving the common travel area,[2] unless the holder returns in circumstances in which leave to enter is not required, in which case the previous leave, and the conditions attached to it, continue to apply. The section applies equally to visa nationals and those not requiring visas by virtue of their nationality.[3] Prior to the passage of the Immigration and Asylum Act 1999[4] and the making of the Immigration (Leave to Enter and Remain) Order 2000[5] under it, the exemption from obtaining leave on return applied only to very limited classes of people, such as certain government officials and Commonwealth citizens on day trips to the continent.[6] The automatic lapsing of leave for everyone else gave rise to absurdity and injustice, as students midway through degree courses found themselves barred from re-entering the UK after a mid-term break in Paris, and long-settled immigrants on contracts abroad lost their right of permanent residence when they returned for short visits, because they did not utter the magic words 'returning to resume settlement'. Section 3(4) still remains the general rule, but the 1999 Act and the Immigration (Leave to Enter and Remain) Order[7] provisions have enormously eroded its scope. Leave does not lapse on leaving the common travel area, if it was conferred by means of an entry clearance[8] (other than a visit visa). Nor does leave to enter or remain granted in the ordinary way, if it was for more than six months.[9] We examine below how these new provisions work.

1 *Ghassemian v Home Office* [1989] Imm AR 42, CA.
2 See chapter 6 below.
3 *Re Wijesundera* [1989] Imm AR 291, CA; *Kuku v Secretary of State for the Home Department* [1990] Imm AR 27, CA.
4 Immigration and Asylum Act 1999, ss 1 and 2, inserting new ss 3A and 3B into the Immigration Act 1971.
5 SI 2000/1161.
6 Immigration Act 1971, s 8(2); Immigration (Exemption from Control) Order 1972, SI 1972/1613, as amended: see **6.53–6.54** below.
7 SI 2000/1161.
8 For discussion of entry clearance as leave to enter see chapter 3 above.
9 SI 2000/1161, art 13(2).

Travellers on temporary leave

5.20 The effect of the Immigration (Leave to Enter and Remain) Order 2000[1] provisions is that leave to enter and remain given for a period of more than six months will remain in force so as to enable students, au pairs, working holidaymakers and others on temporary leave to go abroad and return on the same leave and subject to the same conditions. Only visitors,[2] those admitted or allowed to remain for six months or less,[3] and those whose leave to remain (granted by the Secretary of State) is due to expire within six months[4] will find that their leave lapses on departure. But even those with visit visas gain protection from the Order. Article 4 provides that during the period of validity of a visit visa, it has the effect of leave to enter on an unlimited number of occasions.[5] On each occasion that the holder arrives in the UK, he or she is to be treated as having been granted before arrival leave to enter for six months, beginning on the date of arrival, if six months or more remain of the visa's period of validity, and for the visa's remaining period of validity if it has less than six months to run.[6] Thus visa nationals who leave the UK during the period of leave do not need to obtain a further visa to re-enter.

1 SI 2000/1161.
2 SI 2000/1161, art 13(2)(a). The visit visa might be a five-year multiple entry one, but visit leave always lapses on departure. See below.
3 SI 2000/1161, art 13(2)(b).
4 SI 2000/1161, art 13(3).

5 SI 2000/1161, art 4(1).
6 SI 2000/1161, art 4(2). Although a visit leave may not exceed six months under the Immigration Rules (HC 395, paras 42 and 52), a visit visa may well have a much longer validity, eg multiple visit visas are usually valid for a period of two years.

5.21 The purpose and likely effect of the provisions is to obviate the need for repeated scrutiny on each return to the UK of those whose application for entry to or stay in the UK has previously been approved by an immigration officer or a Home Office civil servant. Such persons may still be examined at the port on re-entry, but they do not have to establish a case for re-entry, as was the case under the old law.[1] The object of the immigration officer's examination on re-entry is to establish whether leave previously granted is still in force,[2] and if so, whether there has been a change of circumstances such that it should be cancelled;[3] whether it was obtained by false information given by the passenger or by his or her failure to disclose material facts;[4] whether there are medical grounds for the cancellation of leave;[5] or whether cancellation is conducive to the public good.[6] The passenger may be required to submit to further examination,[7] or to be examined by a medical inspector,[8] and the leave may be suspended pending further inquiries.[9] In this event the ordinary powers of detention and temporary admission apply.[10] If leave is cancelled,[11] the passenger has an in-country right of appeal against cancellation.[12] It is noteworthy that for the purposes of cancellation of leave any false information or failure to disclose material facts must be attributable to the passenger and not to any third party, in contrast to the provisions of the previous law.[13]

1 See *Secretary of State for the Home Department v Patel* [1992] Imm AR 486, CA.
2 Ie because it has not lapsed by virtue of art 13 of the Immigration (Leave to Enter and Remain) Order 2000, SI 2000/1161 or because, as a visit leave, it is deemed to have been granted afresh abroad under art 4. Immigration Act 1971 Sch 2, para 2(1)(c)(i), substituted by Immigration and Asylum Act 1999, Sch 14, para 56.
3 Immigration Act 1971, Sch 2, para 2A(2)(a).
4 Immigration Act 1971, Sch 2, para 2A(2)(b).
5 Immigration Act 1971, Sch 2, para 2A(2)(c).
6 Immigration Act 1971, Sch 2, para 2A(3).
7 Immigration Act 1971, Sch 2, para 2A(5).
8 Immigration Act 1971, Sch 2, para 2A(4)
9 Immigration Act 1971, Sch 2, para 2A(7).
10 Immigration Act 1971, Sch 2, para 16(1A), 21.
11 Immigration Act 1971, Sch 2, para 2A(8).
12 Immigration Act 1971, Sch 2, para 2A(9).
13 Immigration Act 1971, Sch 2, para 2A(2)(b).

5.22 The Immigration (Leave to Enter and Remain)Order 2000[1] also provides that leave to enter or remain may be varied (or cancelled) while the holder is abroad.[2] For that purpose, immigration officers (or Home Office officials) may seek information and documents which they would be entitled to obtain in an ordinary immigration examination under Schedule 2 of the Immigration Act 1971,[3] and may require the holder of the leave to supply an up to date medical report.[4] Failure to provide the information, documents or report requested is a ground for cancellation of leave.[5] These provisions enable a person whose continuing leave expires while he or she is abroad, or who wishes to change the basis of leave (say, from student to trainee or spouse) to apply for an extension or variation while abroad. They also enable leave to be cancelled while the holder is abroad if, for example, it was discovered that the passenger had used deception to obtain the leave or if terrorist activities became known such that cancellation of leave would be conducive to the public good. However there is as yet no provision for appeals against a refusal to vary leave abroad (because of the limitation on the variation appeal under section 61 of the Immigration and Asylum Act 1999 to cases where, as a result of the adverse decision, the person is required to leave the UK within 28 days), or against cancellation of leave if this takes place abroad. Furthermore, if leave carries on while the holder is abroad, and an extension can be applied for while abroad, it seems logical that an application to vary leave should also continue until it is determined, and not lapse, as at present, if the applicant goes abroad before it is determined.[6]

1   SI 2000/1161.
2   SI 2000/1161, art 13(6), (7).
3   SI 2000/1161, art 13(8).
4   SI 2000/1161, art 13(8).
5   SI 2000/1161, art 13(9).
6   See **4.12** above.

5.23   The provisions of the Immigration (Leave to Enter and Remain) Order 2000[1] abolish the need for visas on return to the UK within the period of leave (or to resume residence pursuant to indefinite leave, as to which see below). At a stroke the body of law which was developed over the years to mitigate the harshness of the unmodified section 3(4), on the effect of the section 3(3)(b) stamp and the grant of earlier leave and whether these were capable of giving rise to a legitimate expectation of re-entry, becomes redundant.[2] The only categories of passenger who do not benefit from the Order are non-visa nationals granted leave to enter as visitors at the port (who thus do not have visit visas), passengers granted six months leave or less in a non-visit capacity, and those granted leave to remain by the Secretary of State which is due to expire in less than six months. These persons' leave lapses on their departure from the common travel area and does not take effect as a new pre-arrival leave to enter under Article 4. Additionally leave lapses if, during the period of leave, the holder remains outside the UK for longer than two years.[3] Although section 3(3)(b) of the Immigration Act 1971 is not repealed, its scope is now limited to these residual categories. Unlike the old section 3(3)(b) stamp, the cancellation of continuing leave on re-entry gives rise to a right of appeal before removal. This applies equally to family visitors with visas who re-enter during the validity of the visa.

1   SI 2000/1161.
2   See the previous edition of this work **5.22–5.26**.
3   SI 2000/1161, art 13(4)(a).

Returning residents

5.24   A variety of returning resident rights are catered for by the Immigration Rules. The two main categories are those who can return freely however long they have been away and those who should return within two years. Once British nationals without the right of abode, such as British Overseas citizens, have been given indefinite leave to enter or remain, they may be in a better position to return to the UK than other returning residents. The Rules reflect the piecemeal history of the imposition of immigration control on British nationals and the quirks of policy and practice in the past.

Holders of UK passports issued in the UK or Ireland

5.25   Paragraph 16 of HC 395 provides that British Dependent Territories citizens, British Nationals (Overseas), British Overseas citizens, British Protected persons, or British Subjects under the British Nationality Act 1981, who can produce a passport issued in the UK and Islands or the Republic of Ireland before 1 January 1973, should be admitted freely unless the passport has been endorsed to show that they were subject to immigration control.[1] This Rule reflects the rights of residual categories of former nationals of the UK and protected persons who were not subject to control prior to the coming into force of the Immigration Act 1971 but who did not become patrial under that Act or British citizens under the 1981 Act. The Rule seems to require the actual production of the historic passport that gives rise to the right, but if a replacement passport has been endorsed with the right of re-admission, the passport holder should be entitled to rely on that, even if the historic document has been lost; the endorsement in a current passport would give rise to legitimate expectations of admission unless a person's nationality has changed.[2] It may, however, be necessary to produce the historic passport or its replacement to obtain the endorsement in any subsequent passport. A further question arises where the historic passport was issued to a parent but is endorsed with details of a dependent child during its currency; can the child obtain admission years later in reliance on such a document? This remains unclear.

1   See IDI, Ch 1, s 3, Annex M.
2   See *Liew v Secretary of State for the Home Department* [1989] Imm AR 62. See further *Lee* (21753) Immigration Appeal Tribunal, 2000 6 ILD 1 at 36.

5.26   British Overseas citizens who hold a UK passport, wherever issued, and can satisfy the immigration officer that they have been given indefinite leave to enter the UK since 1 March 1968, should be given indefinite leave to enter.[1] There is thus no obligation to comply with the two year rule, and the presence of any intervening limited leave will not prevent such re-admission. Previous versions of this Rule referred to British Overseas citizens 'who have previously been admitted for settlement'. This was held only to cover those who had been admitted at a time when they were subject to immigration control.[2] It would appear that British Protected Person voucher holders who are admitted for settlement will have to comply with the two year rule in respect of absences abroad.

1   HC 395, para 17. See IDI, Ch 1, s 3, Annex M.
2   *R v Secretary of State for the Home Department, ex p Himalyaishwar* (1984) Times, 21 February, QBD.

Refugees

5.27   Persons recognised as refugees and issued with a Convention travel document must be re-admitted at any time during the validity of the document.[1] They need not comply with the two year rule

1   1951 Convention relating to the status of refugees, (Geneva, 1951) Sch, para 13(1).

Return within two years

5.28   The system of non-lapsing leave described in paras **5.20–5.24** above applies equally to those with indefinite leave to remain, provided that they have not stayed outside the UK for a continuous period of more than two years.[1] The change is of great benefit to settled residents who return to the UK within two years. In the past, because leave lapsed every time they went abroad, every time they returned to the UK they had to apply for leave to enter anew. Workers on a contract abroad coming to the UK for a short visit found themselves losing their returning resident status by having their passport stamped with visit leave. Now, leave continues and will be suspended or cancelled only for good reason.[2]

1   Immigration (Leave to Enter and Remain) Order 2000, SI 2000/1161, art 13(4)(a).
2   See **5.21** above.

5.29   Under the Immigration Rules,[1] which have not yet been superseded, returning residents must satisfy the immigration officer that they had indefinite leave to enter or remain in the UK when they *last* left, they have not been away longer than two years, they did not receive public assistance towards the cost of leaving, and they *now seek admission for the purpose of settlement*.[2] Under the Immigration (Leave to Enter and Remain) Order 2000[3] a passenger with continuing leave who does not intend to resume ordinary residence may have leave cancelled,[4] but the Home Office has accepted that where there is some continuity of connections or residence, a short return visit should not lead to the cancellation of indefinite leave. The IDI state that

> 'a person returning temporarily to the United Kingdom is not necessarily a visitor. Many people who have their home in the United Kingdom may spend substantial periods overseas on short term business contracts or for studies and return to the United Kingdom for only a short period during holidays. This will not disqualify a person from readmission as a returning resident provided he is normally resident in the United Kingdom, at the time of admission he considers himself to be domiciled in the United Kingdom, and he has not been away from the United Kingdom for more than two years and he intends to return to the United Kingdom for settlement in the future on completion of his employment, business or studies etc.'[5]

Cancellation attracts an in-country appeal as a refusal of leave to enter,[6] but cancellation and the imposition of limited leave instead does not,[7] since leave to enter has been granted, albeit in a different capacity. If there is no right of appeal in this situation, judicial review would be available to challenge the decision.[8] But the big difference from the previous law is that in the past, the onus was on the returning resident to obtain a fresh leave by satisfying the immigration officer that he or she fulfilled the criteria; the immigration officer had no obligation to offer admission for settlement if the passenger did not ask for it.[9] When the passenger was granted limited leave instead of indefinite leave on return, Home Office policy was to grant returning resident status on an after-entry application if the applicant always wanted to be and could have been treated as a returning resident when he or she last entered the UK, but was misunderstood or was refused indefinite leave on entry.[10] It did not apply to those who were unaware that they could have sought entry as a returning resident.[11] Now, the onus is on the immigration officer to justify cancelling leave by reference to a change in circumstances. In the vast majority of cases little examination should be necessary. Returning residents may have their leave cancelled if on inquiry it is discovered that the original leave to enter was secured by their deception.[12] The requirement that returning residents had indefinite leave to remain in the UK when they last left used to pose a problem for passengers whose passport had been stamped with visit leave on their last return to the UK and, in haste or inadvertence, they had failed to remedy the situation before leaving the UK. A person who has lost indefinite leave in this way cannot benefit from the discretion in paragraph 19 of HC 395 to grant fresh leave as a returning resident.[13] With the change in the law, however, this scenario is now very unlikely; only those whose indefinite leave has been cancelled and replaced by visit leave will be affected, a process which will have involved full inquiry into the passenger's intentions.

1 HC 395, para 18. By para 19A, added by Cm 4851, spouses accompanying members of HM Forces, of British diplomats and of comparable UK-based staff members of the British Council who are serving overseas are exempt from the two year rule and from the rule preventing travel at public expense (sub-paras (ii) and (iii)).

2 In *Cawte* (HX 00639) the Tribunal held, following *Ex p Coomasaru* [1983] 1 All ER 208, that an appellant could qualify as a returning resident if she intended to return as such, even if she did not tell the immigration officer on arrival. See fn 5 below. See also *Ali Yazidi* (16387) 16 April 1998, Immigration Appeal Tribunal.

3 SI 2000/1161.

4 The IDI, Ch 1, s 3, para 2.2, state that a person who is returning only for a limited period (eg as a visitor) simply so as to show a period of residence here within two years of departure, should not be re-admitted. But see below.

5 IDI, Ch 1, s 3, para 2.2. See also *R v Secretary of State for the Home Department, ex p Chugtai* [1995] Imm AR 559 where Collins J accepted that a person may retain ordinary residence although working outside the UK for a substantial or indefinite period. However, in *Nejad* (18309) 15 July 1999 the Tribunal dismissed an appeal by someone who returned to the UK for a short visit during studies in Iran but informed the immigration officer on arrival that he intended to return to the UK after finishing the studies.

6 Immigration Act 1971, Sch 2, para 2A(9).

7 *Ishaq v Secretary of State for the Home Department* [1996] Imm AR 80, decided under the previous law but still good, unless the decision can be said to breach the passenger's human rights and thus gives rise to a human rights appeal under Immigration and Asylum Act 1999, s 65.

8 Permission was granted in *R v Secretary of State for the Home Department, ex p Pearson* (CO 1397/1998) and a grant of leave to enter as a visitor quashed by consent and indefinite leave reinstated.

9 *R v Secretary of State for the Home Department, ex p Tolba* [1988] Imm AR 78, QBD. See also *R v Immigration Appeal Tribunal, ex p Coomasaru* [1983] 1 All ER 208, [1982] Imm AR 77, CA where the court held that if this had been the intention of the passenger he was entitled to returning resident status. Sharp practice in obtaining a visa may deprive an applicant of this advantage: *Nazari* 2000 6 ILD 1 at 36.

10 IDI, Ch 1, s 3, Annex L.

11 IDI, Ch 1, s 3, Annex L. Discretion will be exercised to grant indefinite leave to remain outside the rules in 'wholly exceptional cases', such as where the applicant has lived in the UK for most of his or her life.

12 Immigration Act 1971, Sch 2, para 2A(2)(b); see *Sattar v Secretary of State for the Home Department* [1988] Imm AR 190, CA; *Ali v Secretary of State for the Home Department* [1988] Imm AR 274, CA; *R v Secretary of State for the Home Department, ex p Musk* (CO 3956/1996) 26 March 1996, QBD. However, the dicta on the standard of proof may not apply to this situation, since leave is not being merely refused, but cancelled.

13 *ECO Bombay v de Noronha* [1995] Imm AR 341, CA. See *Macdalla* (L00010) 2000 4 ILD No 4, p 33.

Return after two years

5.30 The leave of persons who have been away from the UK longer than two years lapses.[1] Such former residents may nevertheless be admitted for further settlement at the discretion of the immigration authorities under the provisions of HC 395, paragraph 19.[2] One example given is persons who have lived here for most of their lives.³ But it is only an example, and a combination of a shorter period of residence and family or other ties may be sufficient.⁴ Ties in the UK constituting family life or private life for the purposes of Article 8 of the ECHR would clearly be highly relevant to the exercise of discretion under the paragraph.⁵ In *Buckle*⁶ the Tribunal said the question was whether the facts point to an intentional break of residence or not; children are in a special position, as it is less easy for them to make an intentional break.

1 Immigration (Leave to Enter and Remain) Order 2000, SI 2000/1161, art 13(4).
2 Spouses accompanying British soldiers, diplomats or other comparable staff members of the British Council on tours overseas are not obliged to return to the UK within two years: HC 395, para 19A, inserted by Cm 4851.
3 HC 395, para 19. The phrase 'most of his life' does not mean 'most of his adult life': *Peart* [1979–80] Imm AR 41.
4 *Costa* [1974] Imm AR 69.
5 See eg *Forou* (00 TH 01101) 28 April 2000, Immigration Appeal Tribunal.
6 (15012) Immigration Appeal Tribunal, 8 May 1997, 1999 5 ILD No 1, p 29. See also *Gomez (Joffrey)* (00 TH 02294) 5 October 2000, where parental obstruction of a young adult's attempts to return to the UK from Ecuador constituted grounds for the exercise of discretion to admit him.

5.31 The purpose of this discretionary Rule is to avoid injustice or undue hardship which might arise from an inflexible application of the two year rule and 'the discretion must be exercised in a manner to give effect to this purpose.' In *Armat Ali*¹it was suggested that the guidelines, set out in *Costa's* case,² that the person 'must show strong connections with this country by a combination of length of residence and family or other ties' were applicable when the applicant for re-entry had voluntarily stayed away for more than two years, but not where the absence was involuntary. In *Ex p Ademuyiwa*³ Farquharson J did not dissent from the *Armat Ali* interpretation where the applicant had originally left because of family illness but had remained to engage in business. In considering whether to admit such a person as a returning resident, he said, the immigration officer or the minister has to review a number of matters, such as: (i) the length of the original residence of the applicant; (ii) the time the applicant has been outside the UK; (iii) the reason for the delay which has extended the applicant's absence beyond two years - was it at the applicant's own wish or through no fault of the applicant?; (iv) what is the purpose and intent of the applicant in returning at the particular time?; (v) what is the nature of the family ties? - how close are they and to what extent has the applicant maintained them while absent from the UK?; (vi) whether the applicant has a home in this country and if admitted to the UK, is it his or her intention to remain and live in that home? The IDI adopt the criteria in *Armat Ali* in giving guidance on when those remaining abroad over two years may be re-admitted. In addition, the instructions set out other more specific circumstances which might apply in favour of an individual as: travel and service abroad with a particular employer prior to returning with him or her; service abroad for the UK government, as an employee of a quasi/government body, a British company or a UN organisation; employment abroad in the public service of a friendly country by a person who could not reasonably be expected to settle in that country permanently; a prolonged period of study abroad by a person who wished to rejoin their family here at the end of their studies; prolonged medical treatment abroad of a kind not available here; and whether the person contacted a post abroad within two years to express their future intention to return to the UK.⁴

1   *Ali* [1981] Imm AR 51.
2   [1974] Imm AR 69 at 74.
3   *R v Secretary of State for the Home Department, ex p Ademuyiwa* [1986] Imm AR 1,
       followed by the Tribunal in *Agyen-Frempong* [1986] Imm AR 108 (upheld by CA at
       [1988] Imm AR 262).
4   IDI, Ch 1, Annex K, para 2.1.

5.32   In cases where the absence has been prolonged beyond the two years
through no fault of the applicant, Tribunal decisions have tended to be favourable
to the applicant. Examples are where a passport had to be surrendered because
of legal proceedings abroad, and delay caused by illness,[1] accident or civil
disturbance.[2] On the other hand, the longer the period which an applicant has
remained out of the UK the more difficult it will be to qualify for admission
under Immigration Rule, para 19.[3]

1   *Khokhar v Visa Officer, Islamabad* [1981] Imm AR 56n.
2   *Gokulsing* (1632) (1978, unreported). See also *Gomez (Joffrey)* (00 TH 02294) (parental
       obstruction).
3   *R v Secretary of State for the Home Department, ex p Ademuyiwa* [1986] Imm AR 1, DC;
       Agyen-Frempong [1986] Imm AR 108; *R v Immigration Appeal Tribunal, ex p Saffiullah*
       [1986] Imm AR 424, DC. An appellant who had been out of the country for six years and
       acquired citizenship of another country on marriage succeeded in *Cawte* (HX00639)
       8 February 2000; another away for nearly seven years succeeded because of his four
       children in the UK (*Forou* (00 TH 01101)).

5.33   Refusal of leave to enter to a returning resident away for over two years
will not attract an in-country right of appeal in the absence of entry clearance
(unless human rights issues are raised),[1] but would be challengeable by judicial
review.[2] However, an appeal, albeit outside the country, is often preferable
because of the power of the appellate authority to reverse decisions to refuse
entry on the merits in what are often finely balanced cases.[3] Refusal of entry
clearance as a returning resident whose leave has lapsed would attract a right
of appeal.[4]

1   Immigration and Asylum Act 1999, s 60(3).
2   The principle that judicial review may not be sought where there is a statutory right of
       appeal, even when this is less convenient (*Swati* [1986] Imm AR 88) has never been held
       to apply to returning residents, even those who have remained out of the country for over
       two years.
3   See comments of Carnwath J in *R v Secretary of State for the Home Department, ex p Musk*
       (CO 3956/1996) 26 March 1996.
4   Immigration and Asylum Act 1999, s 59(2).

Chapter 6

COMMON TRAVEL AREA, CREW MEMBERS AND EXEMPTED GROUPS

INTRODUCTION

6.1 This chapter deals with a number of special cases under UK immigration law. First, there are Irish citizens who, because of the common travel area, can come and go more or less as they like, but who are still subject to exclusion and deportation and removal. Then there are the inhabitants of the Channel Islands and the Isle of Man, who nominally have their own immigration control, but whose laws are, in fact, closely integrated with those of the mainland. Like Irish citizens, they too are part of the common travel area. Then there are such anomalous groups as seamen and air and train crews, diplomats and military personnel. This chapter is about these groups.

COMMON TRAVEL AREA

6.2   The common travel area predates the development in Europe of free movement rights in the original Common Market and now in the EU. The Single European Act of 1987 envisaged within the EU an internal market 'without internal frontiers'. Although this is not yet fully effective, the adoption into Community law of the Schengen *acquis* by the Treaty of Amsterdam in 1997[1] has brought an EU without internal frontiers even closer, at least for those countries within the EU who have fully signed up. This does not include Ireland and the UK, whose governments have, so far, opted out of this part of the Schengen *acquis*. That is one reason for the continued importance of the common travel area. But it does not just embrace Ireland and the UK. The Channel

Islands, Guernsey and Jersey, and the Isle of Man, referred to hereafter as the Islands, are involved as well. Since they are not fully integrated into the EC, the common travel area provides an important ongoing link with the UK, which preserves their special constitutional position, but at the same time operates on the basis of very close harmony between the immigration laws of mainland and Islands.

1   See chapter 7 below.

6.3   Until the Immigration Act 1971, the common travel area was a purely administrative arrangement allowing free travel between Northern Ireland and the Republic of Ireland, between Britain and Ireland, and between these places and the Isle of Man and the Channel Islands. Since 1971 the common travel area has been given full statutory recognition, but this has also meant it has become hedged around by quite complicated rules, as we shall see. It is these rules which are affected by EC law. Also, because of the situation in Northern Ireland, a continuing surveillance over travel between Ireland and the UK has long been in operation which, in practice, has meant a quite rigorous system of covert port and border controls.

6.4   The first principle of the common travel area is that local journeys within it are exempt from control, but journeys which start from or extend outside it are not. Thus section 1(3) of the Immigration Act 1971 provides that, subject to exceptions, arrivals and departures on local journeys 'shall not be subject to control under this Act,[1] nor shall a person be required leave to enter the UK on so arriving'. A local journey is one which begins and ends in the common travel area and is not made by a ship or aircraft which:

(i)   arrives in the UK, but began its voyage from a place outside the common travel area or has called at such a place during its voyage; or

(ii)   leaves the UK, but is due to end its voyage at a place outside the common travel area or to call at such a place in the course of its voyage.[2]

The common travel area consists of the UK, the Republic of Ireland, the Channel Islands and the Isle of Man.[3] The Immigration Rules state that a person who has been examined for the purpose of immigration control at the point at which he or she entered the area does not normally require leave to enter any other part of it.[4] However, there are exceptions,[5] and provision is also made to change the boundaries of the common travel area if the immigration laws of the Islands get out of line with the UK, or for specified purposes in Ireland.[6]

1   'Control under this Act' refers to the control on entry envisaged by ss 3 and 4 of the Immigration Act 1971, and since 30 July 2000 by the Immigration (Leave to Enter and Remain) Order 2000, SI 2000/1161, and to the examination provisions in Immigration Act 1971, Sch 2, paras 2–7. We refer to it loosely in the text as passport or frontier control, which is to be contrasted with immigration control, to which all non-British citizens are subject irrespective of their right to cross a border without submitting to any passport control or obtaining leave to enter.
2   Immigration Act 1971, s 11(4).
3   Immigration Act 1971, ss 1(3), 11(4) and 33(1).
4   HC 395, para 15.
5   Immigration Act 1971, s 9(4), Sch 4, para 4 and Immigration (Control of Entry Through the Republic of Ireland) Order 1972, SI 1972/1610, as amended, art 3(2).
6   Immigration Act 1971, s 9(5) and (6).

6.5   The Immigration Act 1971 clearly intended to retain the notion of a travel area which is free from frontier immigration control. On the other hand, the government did not want the common travel area to become a loophole in an otherwise strict immigration control.[1] A compromise is therefore struck between a frontier-free area and the exceptions. The existence of the common travel area means that:

(i)   all British and Irish citizens are free to travel between Ireland, the UK and the Islands without any passport control. This does not mean that there is no immigration control. That still exists, in that Irish citizens may still be subject to exclusion or to deportation on public policy grounds, and can then be refused entry. We deal with this at **6.23** below;

(ii)   third-country nationals who have settled status in any of the territories of the common travel area are free to travel to another part of the common travel area and to take up employment or occupation and residence there;

(iii) people with limited leave to enter or remain in one part of the common travel area are free to travel to any other part and to remain there for the remainder of their leave. As between Ireland and the UK, they can probably also work without the need for a work permit,[2] but not as between the Islands and the UK.[3]

1   See *Qureshi v Harrington* [1970] 1 All ER 262, [1970] 1 WLR 138 (a decision under the Commonwealth Immigrants Act 1962).
2   See **10.38** below.
3   See **6.8** below.

6.6   As the original measures on the common travel area have been amended to plug possible loopholes, its provisions have become quite detailed. In practice they operate by a sort of remote control, especially those governing travel between the Republic of Ireland and the UK. Elsewhere in UK immigration law, the general rule is that every immigrant who has a time limit or conditions imposed on his or her stay should be personally notified of the fact.[1] Usually this is done, on leave to enter being granted, by a stamp in the passport. In the case of the Islands, leave granted there is automatically deemed to be leave of the same duration as that given in the UK.[2] In the case of Ireland, a time limit and conditions may be imposed by statutory instrument and the traveller may be quite unaware of them.[3] In other cases the special provisions applying to the common travel area by section 1(3) of the Immigration Act 1971 are excluded altogether and the traveller must obtain leave to enter, failing which he or she will be an illegal entrant.

1   Immigration Act 1971, s 4(1) and Sch 2, para 6. See *Minton v Secretary of State for the Home Department* [1990] Imm AR 199, CA, **3.65** above.
2   See **6.8** below.
3   See **6.22** below.

6.7   Section 1(3) of the Immigration Act 1971 does not affect the operation of a deportation order.[1] This means that where an Irish citizen has been deported from the UK, he or she can be refused leave to enter. The exercise of this power must, however, be in accordance with the EC public policy directive (see chapter 7 below). Secondly, the existence of the common travel area does not prevent the Secretary of State from banning non-British citizens from the UK for reasons of national security.[2] Although this power is mainly targeted on Irish citizens, it prevents anyone else who is subject to such a ban from entering the UK through Ireland or the Islands. Thirdly, leave may be refused where a person has been refused leave to enter the UK at any time in the past and has not subsequently been granted leave. This, however, may not be as wide a power as it first appears. First, if someone has been given leave in one of the Islands, that counts as a leave in the UK, if it is still current.[3] Secondly, if someone has been given an advance leave under the Immigration (Leave to Enter and Remain) Order 2000,[4] that will override this exception to section 1(3) of the 1971 Act. Thirdly, EEA nationals exercising their free movement rights do not require leave to enter, and these rights override the provisions relating to the common travel area.[5]

1   Immigration Act 1971, s 9(4).
2   Immigration Act 1971, s 9(4). See further **6.23** below.
3   Immigration Act 1971, Sch 4, para 4. See **6.8** below.
4   SI 2000/1161, in force since 30 July 2000.
5   The Immigration Act 1988, s 7(1) and Immigration (European Economic Area) Regulations 2000, SI 2000/2326 give effect in domestic UK law to EC law, in *R v Pieck* [1981] QB 571, ECJ. Though reg 12 of SI 2000/2326 is premised on the EEA national entering through a recognised control point, reg 14 makes it clear that the right to remain in the UK derives directly from EC law without any need for a leave under domestic law. The right to enter under EC law is, of course, subject to public policy considerations: see *R v Secretary of State for the Home Department, ex p Shingara* [1999] Imm AR 257.

Immigration laws in the Islands

6.8   The Channel Islands and the Isle of Man have nominally separate immigration laws from the UK. In practice the Immigration Acts of 1971 and 1988 extend to the Islands, with modifications, and although the Islands have their own Immigration Rules (called Directions in Jersey), they closely follow the UK ones.[1] Following the enactment of the Immigration and Asylum Act 1999, further changes will be needed to update the Islands' laws and keep them in step. No doubt this will be done in due course. Meanwhile the following measures still apply:

(i)   Orders in Council have been enacted to extend the provisions of the UK Acts with any necessary changes to each of the Islands. In the case of Guernsey, the Order is the only effective immigration law, but in the case of Jersey the 1937 Loi sur les Etrangers still operates in addition to the extended Immigration Act, and in the Isle of Man employment is controlled by the Control of Employment Act 1975, as amended;

(ii)   machinery is laid down in the Orders and in Schedule 4 to the Immigration Act 1971 for decisions taken in the Islands to apply in the UK and vice versa.

Schedule 4 of the 1971 Act, as amended by the Immigration and Asylum Act 1999 provides *inter alia*:

(a)   Any leave to enter or remain and time limit or conditions attached to it by the immigration authorities in the Isle of Man, Jersey or Guernsey will still apply to a person who subsequently arrives in the UK from one of the islands before the expiry of any time limit;[2]

(b)   In the case of limited leave, applications can then be made to the Home Office for further extensions or the revocation of conditions as if the leave and conditions had originated under UK immigration law. If an extension of leave is refused, the normal rights of appeal under UK law apply;[3]

(c)   A deportation order or its equivalent made in one of the Islands operates in the UK, where it has the same effect as a deportation order made in the UK, except where the person is a British citizen, EEA national, member of the family of an EEA national, or the member of the family of a British citizen who is neither a British citizen or EEA national.[4] Except in the case of British citizens (who cannot be deported from the UK),[5] the Secretary of State can decide to enforce an Island deportation against one of these people,[6] but must bear in mind the public order provisions of EC law. These categories of Island deportees can appeal against an adverse decision under section 80 of the 1999 Act.[7] From October 2000 the Secretary of State can no longer revoke an Island deportation order which is operating in the UK.[8] It is not unlawful for a deportee to enter the UK in transit to a place outside the UK;[9]

(d)   There are integrated removal powers after a refusal of leave. Anyone refused leave to enter one of the Islands is treated as if they had been refused leave to enter the UK.[10] The Island authorities can arrange for the UK authorities to remove that person;

(e)   There are also integrated removal powers for illegal entrants. Paragraph 4 provides that notwithstanding the principle of travel without leave 'it shall not be lawful for a person who is not a British citizen to enter the UK from any of the Islands where his presence was unlawful under the immigration laws of the Island, unless he is given leave to enter'. So, if someone with leave to enter the UK goes to one of the Islands, and his or her leave then expires, that person's return to the UK, without getting further leave, makes that person an illegal entrant. The same applies to persons who overstay leave given to them in one of the Islands and then travel to the UK.[11]

Immigration officers in the Islands act in liaison with the Immigration service in the UK.[12]

 1 IDI, Ch 1, s 2, Annex H.
 2 Immigration Act 1971, Sch 4, para 1(1) and (2). *Teixeira* [1989] Imm AR 432.
 3 Immigration Act 1971, Sch 4, para 1(3).
 4 Immigration Act 1971, Sch 4, para 3(1) and (2), as amended.
 5 Immigration Act 1971, s 3(5), (6).
 6 Immigration Act 1971, Sch 4, para 3(4), as amended
 7 Immigration Act 1971, Sch 4, para 3(6), as amended.
 8 Immigration Act 1971, Sch 4, para 3(3), as amended.
 9 Immigration Act 1971, Sch 4, para 3(5), as amended.
10 Immigration Act 1971, Sch 4, para 1(1).
11 Immigration Act 1971, Sch 4, para 1(1).
12 IDI, Ch 1, s 2, Annex H.

6.9   In the Islands the same integration of their laws with those of the UK and other Islands is achieved by the provisions in the various Orders in Council which extend and adapt Schedule 4 to the particular Island. So leave given in the UK continues to operate when someone travels to one of the Islands; UK deportation orders have effect there; and the island authorities can deal with UK or other Island overstayers and illegal entrants.

6.10   This integration nevertheless leaves some areas of autonomy to each of the Islands. Though the content of each Island's immigration law is almost identical to the mainland Immigration Acts of 1971 and 1988, each administers its own controls and therefore retains a large measure of discretion over whom to admit or refuse. This is particularly important in the area of employment, where each Island retains full control over the granting of work permits and is therefore able to fit immigration control into any existing employment restrictions. Apart from the retention of administrative control over immigration, perhaps the most important difference between the laws operating in the Islands and in mainland UK is the continuing absence of any appeal machinery in the Channel Islands. Only the Order in Council for the Isle of Man extends the rights of appeal set out in Part II of the 1971 Act. For the time being this too may pose a problem, since the Immigration and Asylum Act 1999 has repealed Part II and put in place an entirely new appeal regime. We look at this in the next paragraph.

Isle of Man

6.11   The provisions of the UK Immigration Acts are extended here by the Immigration (Isle of Man) Orders 1991 and 1997.[1] The appointment of immigration officers and the administration of control is under the Lieutenant-Governor. Changes in the Immigration Rules must be laid by Tynwald. Under the 1997 Order, the rights of appeal operating under Part II of the Immigration Act 1971 are applied with suitable modifications to the Isle of Man, the High Bailiff and Deputy High Bailiff acting as adjudicators.[2] Part II has now been repealed by the Immigration and Asylum Act 1999 and replaced by new appeal provisions (chapter 18 below). However, it is thought that the existing incorporated appeal system still stands until a further updating Order is made, although this is not entirely certain.

1   SI 1991/2630 and SI 1997/275.
2   SI 1997/275, Sch, para 1.

6.12   Apart from immigration controls applying to non-British citizens under the extended Immigration Act 1971, there is also strict control over the employment in the Isle of Man of anyone who is not an 'Isle of Man worker' as defined by the Control of Employment Act 1975, as amended in 1983. This status is acquired by birth or long residence in the Isle, or descent from or marriage to an Islander. Subject to exceptions, anyone who is not an 'Isle of Man worker' needs a work permit from the Isle of Man Board of Social Security. EC law rights of free movement are excluded.[1]

1   See *Department of Health and Social Security v Barr* [1991] 3 CMLR 325, ECJ, for an examination of these provisions applying to a British citizen seeking employment in the Isle of Man.

6.13   In the Isle of Man, entry from the Republic of Ireland is subject to similar restraints to those operating under UK law. The same categories of person who require leave to enter the UK from Ireland require leave to enter the Isle of Man from there.[1] Secondly, an automatic time limit and condition prohibiting employment is imposed on non-British or Irish citizens arriving in the Isle of

Man from Ireland, who entered the Republic from a place outside the common travel area; or who left the Isle of Man while having a limited leave to be there and this leave has since expired.

1 See **6.24** below.

Guernsey

6.14 The UK Immigration Acts are extended here by the Immigration (Guernsey) Order 1993.[1] Control under it is exercised by immigration officers, who have power to give or refuse leave to enter, the Lieutenant-Governor, who has power to vary the length of any leave, and the Board of Administration, which deals with restrictions and prohibitions on employment and registration with the police as well as making the Immigration Rules. These have to be laid before the States of Guernsey. The power to make subordinate Orders under the extended Act is divided between the States and the Lieutenant-Governor.

1 SI 1993/1796.

6.15 Special provision is made for entry into Guernsey from the Republic of Ireland. The restraints are almost identical to those operating under UK law. Leave to enter Guernsey from Ireland is required for the same category of persons as require leave to enter the UK from there,[1] and similar restrictions are placed on persons arriving in Guernsey from Ireland (1) who entered Ireland from a place outside the common travel area or (2) who left Guernsey having a limited leave to be there and this leave has since expired.

1 See **6.24** below.

Jersey

6.16 The UK Immigration Acts are extended to the Bailiwick of Jersey by the Immigration (Jersey) Order 1993.[1] This is not the Island's only legislation governing the admission and control of non-British citizens. In addition there is the 1937 Loi sur les Etrangers. The administration of control is divided between the States of Jersey Defence Committee, which deals with the regulation of employment and registration with the police, and the Lieutenant-Governor who has overall direction and authority.

1 SI 1993/1797.

6.17 The extended UK Acts apply to all non-British citizens, alien and Commonwealth, but the 1937 Loi only applies to aliens. Under it no aliens can take jobs in the Island without a work permit, whatever their status on the mainland.[1] They may need a guarantor as a condition of getting a permit[2] and if, within a year of arrival, they become chargeable to the public of the Island they may be removed,[3] with the guarantor, no doubt, having to foot the bill for removal. A register of aliens is kept and it is the duty of aliens over the age of 15 who reside in the Island for over three months to register.[4] In addition to the deportation powers given under the extended Immigration Act, the 1937 Loi expressly retains the powers of 'banishment and of repatriation possessed by the Royal Court of Jersey'.[5] The same provision is made for entry into Jersey from the Republic of Ireland, as applies in the case of Guernsey and the Isle of Man: see **6.13** and **6.15** above.

1   1937 Loi sur les Etrangers, art 4.
2   1937 Loi sur les Etrangers, art 5.
3   1937 Loi sur les Etrangers, art 8.
4   1937 Loi sur les Etrangers, arts 12(1) and 15.
5   1937 Loi sur les Etrangers, art 24.

The Islands and the EC

6.18   The Channel Islands and the Isle of Man enjoy a special relationship with the EC, as opposed to full membership.[1] But the extent of it is unclear. The Islands are within the definition of the UK for the purpose of British nationality law,[2] and so connection to the Islands as opposed to mainland UK makes not the slightest bit of difference to the acquisition or possession of full British citizenship. Furthermore, Islanders are included in the declaration by the UK government on the meaning of a British national for the purposes of the European Treaties (see **7.29** below). On the other hand, when Britain joined the Common Market, Channel Islanders and Manxmen were expressly excluded from the free movement provisions of the EEC Treaty by Protocol 3 of the Treaty of Accession of the UK to the Common Market (as it was then known).[3] Under Article 6 of the Protocol, the following definition is given of a Channel Islander and a Manxman:

> 'In this Protocol, Channel Islander or Manxman shall mean any citizen of the United Kingdom and Colonies[4] who holds that citizenship by virtue of the fact that he, a parent or grandparent was born, adopted, naturalised or registered in the island in question; but such a person shall not for this purpose be regarded as a Channel Islander or Manxman if he, a parent or a grandparent was born, adopted, naturalised or registered in the United Kingdom. Nor shall he be so regarded if he has at any time been ordinarily resident in the UK for five years.'

On the basis of this definition, Islanders, although EU citizens, enjoy no free movement rights, unless they have been ordinarily resident in the UK at any time for a period of five years. In practice this provision is either a dead letter or virtually unenforceable. A passport shows place of birth, but does not show places of residence during a person's lifetime, and says nothing about the place of birth of parents or grandparents. The real effect of the Protocol is that it prevents free movement rights into the Islands and thus protects the residence and employment restrictions operating there. This is, we think, the clear effect of Article 3 to the Protocol read with Article 4, as interpreted by the European Court of Justice. Article 4 requires the Islands to apply 'the same treatment to all natural and legal persons of the Community'. This means that they must treat the nationals of other member states in the same way as they treat British nationals, who have visiting rights by virtue of the common travel area but are subject to restrictions on residence and employment. These restrictions will thus also apply to those from the EEA. The principle of non-discrimination could not, therefore, give employment rights to EEA nationals in the Isle of Man.[5]

1   Article 227(5) of EC Treaty (now, after amendment, art 299(6)(c)) and Protocol No 3 to Treaty of Accession.
2   British Nationality Act 1981, s 50(1). They were also part of the UK for the purpose of the 1948 Act: British Nationality Act 1948, s 3(1).
3   Article 2 of Protocol No 3 to Treaty of Accession. See further chapter 7 below.
4   For the meaning of 'citizen of the UK and Colonies' see now British Nationality Act 1981, s 51(3)(a), which provides that after 1 January 1983 it means a British citizen, a British Dependent Territories citizen or a British Overseas citizen.
5   *Department of Health and Social Security v Barr* [1991] 3 CMLR 325, ECJ, where the Court warned that the exclusion could not be permitted to operate in a discriminatory manner as between those excluded from the right.

Immigration law in the Republic of Ireland

6.19 In order to complete the picture of immigration control within the common travel area, it is necessary to consider briefly the immigration laws operating in the Republic of Ireland. The enabling statute is the Aliens Act 1935. The Aliens Order 1946[1] is the principal order made under it, and this has been amended at various times.[2] Under the Act and Orders the system of control to some extent parallels that of the UK, but is not nearly so complicated. 'Aliens' are all those who are not citizens of Saorstat Eireann[3] or British citizens.[4] Secondly, it is made clear that the system of control set out in these Orders does not affect the operation of the free movement provisions of the EC, of which the Republic is a member.[5]

1   SR & O 1946/380.
2   See Aliens (Amendment) Order 1975, SI 1975/128; Aliens (Amendment) (No 3) Order 1997, SI 1997/277; Aliens (Amendment) Order 1999, SI 1999/17; Aliens (Exemption) Order 1999, SI 1999/97. There are frequent minor amending Orders, mainly adjusting visa requirements.
3   Aliens Act 1935, s 2; SI 1999/17; 1999/97.
4   Aliens (Amendment) (No 2) Order 1999, SI 1999/24.
5   SI 1975/128, art 8.

6.20 As in UK law, the controls distinguish between those who arrive from another part of the common travel area and those who come from outside. Those who come from outside must present themselves to an immigration officer for leave to land.[1] Immigration officers have wide discretion to refuse leave.[2] One ground for refusal is that the alien 'intends to travel (whether immediately or not) to Great Britain or Northern Ireland and the officer is satisfied that the alien would not qualify for admission to Great Britain or Northern Ireland if he arrived there from a place other than the State . . . '.[3] In other words in deciding whether to admit an alien into the Republic, Irish immigration officers can take into account the UK Immigration Rules, and refuse admission to someone who they consider would not qualify under them.

1   Aliens Order 1946, SR & O 1946/380, art 5(1), as amended by Aliens (Amendment) Order 1975, SI 1975/128, art 3 and Aliens (Amendment) (No 2) Order 1999, SI 1999/24.
2   SR & O 1946/380, art 5(2), as amended.
3   SR & O 1946/380, art 5(2)(j), as amended. This matches the reciprocal rule in the UK Immigration Rules: HC 395, para 320(13).

6.21 Aliens entering the Republic of Ireland through the common travel area, that is from Great Britain, the Channel Islands or Northern Ireland, were until 1997 not required to submit to examination by immigration officers on arrival.

Now, they may be examined by immigration officers in the same way as those arriving from elsewhere, and may be refused leave to land on the same grounds.[1] If they are not so examined, they are automatically subject to time limits on their stay. In the case of workers and those wishing to establish themselves in business, the time limit is one month and in the case of everyone else, three months. They must obtain extensions from the Minister of Justice.[2] Anyone in contravention commits an offence[3] and can be arrested without warrant[4] and eventually deported.[5]

1 Aliens (Amendment) (No 3) Order 1997, SI 1997/277.
2 Aliens Order 1946, SR & O 1946/380, art 5(7)(d) and (e), as amended by Aliens Order 1975, SI 1975/128, art 3.
3 Aliens Act 1935, s 6.
4 SR & O 1946/380, art 17.
5 SR & O 1946/380, art 13. Deportation is always tested by the 'public good'.

Arriving in the UK through Ireland

6.22 Despite the existence of the common travel area, a number of restrictions are placed on non-British citizens who travel to the UK from the Republic of Ireland. These are all exceptions to the principle of travel without leave set out in section 1(3) of the Immigration Act 1971. In most of the cases set out below the exceptions apply only to those who arrive in the UK from Ireland. Some people may already have been refused leave in the UK, and if they enter the UK without a fresh leave, clearly they are illegal entrants and can be removed. Others require leave, and if they do not obtain it they too become illegal entrants and can be removed.[1] Others are made subject to an automatic condition limiting the length of their stay in the UK and prohibiting employment. Usually the time limit is three months. If such people stay in the UK longer than this, they become overstayers and liable to summary removal.[2] These restrictions are intended to stop the free movement of Irish citizens to the UK if they are regarded as security risks or are under a deportation order, but otherwise they are intended to prevent the common travel area creating loopholes in immigration control. No doubt these restrictions stop loopholes, but they also lay serious traps for the unwary and innocent, who find themselves subject to restrictions and conditions, which no one has told them about. In many cases the result is that they are arrested, held in custody, and removed or deported from the UK.[3] We now look at each group of restrictions in turn.

1 See *R v Governor of Ashford Remand Centre, ex p Bouzagou* [1983] Imm AR 69, CA.
2 Immigration and Asylum Act 1999, s 10. Prior to 2 October 2000, overstayers were subject to deportation under the Immigration Act 1971, s 3(5)(a) which applied to automatic restrictions imposed on travel from Ireland by virtue of s 9(3): see *Kaya* [1991] Imm AR 572.
3 *Bouzagou* above.

Refusing leave on grounds of national security

6.23 As we have seen, any non-British citizen, including Irish citizens, can be barred from entry to the UK, if the Secretary of State directs that there are national security reasons for their exclusion, and this applies whether the person is travelling from Ireland or one of the Islands.[1] In the case of travel from Ireland the power is more extensive. The Secretary of State can bar entry by giving a direction that their exclusion is conducive to the public good without any mention of the interests of national security.[2] Anyone who enters in defiance of such a direction is an illegal entrant and can be removed.¹ However, the power can only be exercised against Irish and other EEA nationals in a manner consistent with the scope and procedural requirements of the public policy derogation under EC law (see chapter 7).

1 Immigration Act 1971, s 9(4)(a).
2 The Immigration (Control of Entry through Republic of Ireland) Order 1972, SI 1972/1610, as amended, art 3(1)(b)(iv).

Where leave to enter UK is required

6.24 Leave to enter the UK is required in the following cases:¹

(1) *previous refusal of entry.* We have already noted this power and its limitations in the light of EC law at **6.7**;

(2) *transit passengers.* Passengers (by ship or aircraft) from outside the common travel area who have merely stopped in transit in the Republic of Ireland without being given leave to land there require leave;²

(3) *visa nationals,* who have no valid visa to enter the UK, require leave;³

(4) *illegal immigrants in Ireland.* Those who have entered the Republic unlawfully from outside the common travel area require leave;

(5) *illegal entrants and overstayers.* Those who are illegal entrants or overstayers in the UK or any of the Islands who have gone to Ireland, and have not subsequently obtained leave to enter the UK or any of the Islands, require leave if they try to return to the UK. This does not apply to someone who is exempt from UK immigration control and travels to Ireland after the exemption comes to an end;⁴

(6) *deportation orders and removal directions.* The existence of the common travel area does not affect the operation of a deportation order.⁵ Irish citizens may be able to travel freely between the Republic and the UK, but not if they are the subject of a deportation order made in the UK. Prior to 2 October 2000 this was the way in which overstayers and those in breach of conditions were dealt with, but now they can only be given removal directions under section 10 of the Immigration and Asylum Act 1999, which merely invalidate an existing UK leave.⁶ They would now be caught under sub-paragraph 5 above.

1 Immigration Act 1971, s 9(4)(b), and the Immigration (Control of Entry through Republic of Ireland) Order, SI 1972/1610, art 3.
2 Under the transit visa schedule for Ireland, amended on 8 October 1996, aliens arriving in Ireland from outside the common travel area will not be given leave to land, unless they have a valid transit visa, if they are nationals of Afghanistan, Albania, Bulgaria, Cuba, Ethiopia, Eritrea, Ghana, Iran, Iraq, Lebanon, Moldova, Nigeria, Romania, Somalia, Sri Lanka, Federal Republic of Yugoslavia or former Zaire.
3 SI 1972/1610, art 3(1)(b)(i).
4 *R v Secretary of State for the Home Department, ex p Wuan* [1989] Imm AR 501, QBD.
5 Immigration Act 1971, s 9(4).
6 Immigration and Asylum Act 1999, s 10(8).

Automatic time limit and conditions prohibiting employment

6.25 Then there are those who do not require leave to enter, but are liable to the imposition of automatic time limits on their stay in the UK and conditions prohibiting their taking employment. Obviously, they must apply for leave to remain before their time limit runs out if they wish to stay on. A refusal to vary the time limit attracts a right of appeal under section 61 of the Immigration and Asylum Act 1999.[1] This group consists of persons who (i) are neither British nor Irish citizens, (ii) have not obtained an advance leave to enter the UK under the Immigration (Leave to Enter and Remain) Order 2000[2] and (iii) have not been excluded from the benefits of the common travel area for any of the reasons set out in **6.23** or **6.24** above.[3] Automatic restrictions on length of stay and conditions apply to persons in this group:

(a)   who entered the Republic of Ireland from a place outside the common travel area. They are subject to an automatic time limit on their stay (three months normally, but one month if they have a 'short-visit' visa), and, unless they are EC nationals, a condition prohibiting them from engaging in any occupation for reward or any employment.[4] If they have a 'short-stay' visa and are over 16, they must also register with the police;[5]

(b)   who left the UK for Ireland while having a limited leave to be in the UK and this leave has since expired.[6] On their return to the UK from Ireland they become subject to an automatic limit on their stay of seven days[7] and, unless they are EC nationals, to a condition prohibiting them from engaging in any occupation for reward or any employment.[8] If they have a 'short-visit' visa and are over 16, they must also register with the police.[9]

There are a number of difficulties and objections to these provisions. First, they take no account of the length of time between arrival in Ireland and departure for the UK. There is a world of difference between a person who arrives in Dublin, works there for five years and then travels to the UK and someone who only stays there for three days. The restrictions imposed under UK law on travel from the Republic of Ireland do not, however, take this distinction into account. Secondly, there is the trap to the unwary, already referred to in **6.22**. Time limits and conditions are imposed without the people either being told or being in a position to find out. Yet the full rigours of removal may apply to them if they overstay.[10] It should be noted that those who go to Ireland and return to the UK within the period of their limited leave remain by virtue of that leave, which does not lapse.[11]

1   See Ch 18. There is no longer an appeal against conditions, or against the grant of a shorter leave than that requested: Immigration and Asylum Act 1999, s 61.
2   SI 2000/1161.
3   Immigration (Control of Entry through the Republic of Ireland) Order 1972, SI 1972/1610, art 4(2), as amended by SI 2000/1776.
4   SI 1972/1610, art 4, as amended in 1985 and 1990, contains a very outdated exemption from the employment prohibition for EC nationals other than those of Portugal or Spain, who at that time enjoyed the right of establishment, but not yet the rights of worker movement. There is also an exemption from the condition prohibiting engagement in an occupation, but it is confined to EC nationals and does not extend to all EEA nationals: SI 1972/1610, art 4(4)(b) and (c). These deficiencies do not particularly matter, because the provisions of EC law cover the situation quite adequately: see chapter 7 below.
5   SI 1972/1610, art 4(6).
6   SI 1972/1610, art 4(1)(b).
7   SI 1972/1610, art 4(7).
8   SI 1972/1610, art 4(4) (b) and (c), as amended: see fn 3 above.
9   SI 1972/1610, art 4(6).
10 Immigration and Asylum Act 1999 s 10 (removal, previously dealt with by deportation under Immigration Act 1971 ss 9(3) and 3(5)(a); *Kaya* [1991] Imm AR 572).

11 Immigration Act 1971, s 3(4). Under the Immigration (Leave to Enter and Remain) Order 2000, SI 2000/1161 there is also now provision for leave not to lapse when persons leave the common travel area: see chapter 4 above.

Effect of EC law on Irish travel

6.26 The control on entry provisions of the common travel area outlined above have to be read in conjunction with free movement and residence rights under EC law. It is not just Irish citizens who are affected, but all EEA nationals and members of their families. Where EC law is engaged there is a right to enter without any need for leave under UK domestic law.[1] This right prevails over the common travel area provisions covering travel from Ireland to the UK where there is a conflict. Similarly, where there are conditions imposed prohibiting employment or occupation for gain, they must yield to the requirements of EC law, not in the terms set out in the Control of Entry Order, SI 1972/1610 but on the terms of current EC law.[2]

1 See **6.7** fn 5 above
2 See **6.25** fn 3 above.

Entering UK en route to another part of common travel area

6.27 Where passengers arrive in the UK intending to travel on to the Republic of Ireland or one of the Islands, special rules apply. The objective of the common travel area, according to the IDI, is that all territories should be treated as a single unit for the purpose of travel within the common travel area. So an immigration officer should not give leave to enter to anyone proceeding to one of the other territories for any purpose, unless that person qualifies to enter the UK for a similar purpose.[1] As an attempt at a rationale of current policy in this area, this statement is more misleading than helpful. A woman coming to marry in Ireland clearly does not qualify to enter the UK for that purpose, because the man she intends to marry is not in the UK. Likewise, the holder of a work permit destined for the Isle of Man does not qualify to enter the UK for that purpose, because there is no job and no work permit issued in the UK. Better guidance is contained in the examples of current practice, given in the IDI.

1 IDI, Ch 1, s 2, annex H.

6.28 Foreign nationals (as defined by Irish law) who wish to travel to Ireland, may require a visa to enter the Republic. If they have no visa, the person will not be refused entry to the UK until the UK immigration service has contacted the Irish Department of Justice in Dublin and has established that the person is not acceptable to the immigration authorities there.[1] If the passenger qualifies for indefinite leave to enter the UK, that is the leave he or she should be given.[2] Workers arriving in the UK en route to Ireland in possession of an Irish labour permit, or an official confirmation that one is available, should be given one month's leave to enter the UK.[3] Seamen coming to join ship in Ireland or students going there to study should also be given one month's leave to enter the UK.[4]

1 IDI, Ch 1, s 2, para 2.1

2   IDI, Ch 1, s 2, para 2.2.
3   IDI, Ch 1, s 2, para 2.3.
4   IDI, Ch 1, s 2, para 2.4

6.29   Similar rules apply to those passing through the UK en route to the Channel Islands or the Isle of Man. Visa nationals without visas will normally be refused leave to enter.[1] Work permit holders going to the Channel Islands are given one month;[2] those going to the Isle of Man are given leave to enter for the period of validity of the work permit.[3] Passengers subject to control who have indefinite leave in one of the Islands are dealt with as if they are returning residents to the UK,[4] and will be given indefinite leave to enter.[5] Those returning to one of the Islands with an extant leave are to be given leave to enter for the period remaining on that leave.[6] Other persons are dealt with as if seeking to enter the UK.[7]

1   IDI, Ch 1, s 2, paras 3.1 and 4.1.
2   IDI, Ch 1, s 2, para 3.2.
3   IDI, Ch 1, s 2, para 4.2.
4   HC 395, paras 18 and 19.
5   IDI, Ch 1, s 2, paras 3.3 and 4.3.
6   IDI, Ch 1, s 2, paras 3.4 and 4.4.
7   IDI, Ch 1, s 2, paras 3.5 and 4.5.

6.30   Leave to enter the UK should not be refused on general grounds, according to the IDI, unless the immigration officer has reason to believe that any passenger arriving in the UK en route to another part of the common travel area would not be acceptable there.[1] Before any refusal, the immigration officer is expected to contact the appropriate immigration authority in the Republic of Ireland or the Islands. Leave may also be refused if the immigration officer believes that the passenger's real intentions are to use his or her documentation to remain in the UK.[2]

1   IDI, Ch 1, s 2, para 5.
2   See IDI, Ch 1, s 2, para 5.1.

Irish citizens and terrorism laws

6.31   The existence of the common travel area does not mean that Irish citizens are totally exempt from UK immigration control. Citizens of the Republic, unless they also have British citizenship, are subject to immigration control. Though they can normally come to the UK without needing leave to enter, they may, as we have seen, be refused entry as security risks; they may be deported, and cannot then return without leave or until the deportation order is revoked; they may also be refused admission to the UK on EC public policy grounds.[1] Before the peace process in Northern Ireland these were important powers, but could only be used against Irish citizens and did not deal with movement and travel between Northern Ireland and mainland UK. This was dealt with through extensive powers of exclusion or banishment, in order to prevent acts of terrorism, contained in the Prevention of Terrorism (Temporary Provisions) Act 1989. Under this Act the Secretary of State for the Home Department could make an exclusion order against anyone he or she was satisfied was involved in terrorism, including British citizens, who could be restricted to living either in Northern Ireland or in Great Britain (England, Scotland or Wales).[2] The Act also contained draconian powers of arrest and detention, which gave rise to considerable case law.[3]

1 Council Directive (EEC) 64/221. See chapter 7 below.
2 Prevention of Terrorism (Temporary Provisions) Act 1989, ss 5(1), 6(1), 7(1).
3 Prevention of Terrorism (Temporary Provisions) Act 1989, s 14. See the Northern Ireland
   High Court in *Hanna v Chief Constable of the Royal Ulster Constabulary* [1986] 13 NIJB 71
   (Carswell J); *Brogan v United Kingdom* (1988) 11 EHRR 117, where the ECHR held that
   four people who had been arrested and detained for periods of at least four days and six
   hours under the Prevention of Terrorism Act 1984 had been detained in violation of art 5(3)
   and (5) of the ECHR; *Brannigan and McBride v UK* (1993) 17 EHRR 539, ECtHR, where
   the ECtHR upheld the UK government's later derogation from its Convention obligations.
   As regards the validity of exclusion orders under EC law, see the references in *Ex p Gallagher*
   [1996] 1 CMLR 557, ECJ; and *Ex p Adams* [1995] All ER (EC) 177, DC, a reference
   subsequently withdrawn by CA after revocation of the exclusion order.

6.32 The peace process in Northern Ireland has made the exclusion powers in
the 1989 Act redundant and the whole Act has in fact been repealed by the
Terrorism Act 2000.[1] Although various special powers are still retained for
Northern Ireland, the Secretary of State can no longer make exclusion orders
banning suspected terrorists from travel between Northern Ireland, Great Britain
and the Republic. The Terrorism Act 2000[2] re-enacts provisions similar to those
in the 1989 Act dealing with port and border controls on travel to and from
Northern Ireland, using police, immigration and customs officers,[3] who have
extensive powers of examination and search of vehicles, aircraft and ships in
order to identify people concerned in the commission, preparation or instigation
of acts of terrorism.[4]

1 Terrorism Act 2000, Sch 16.
2 In force February 2001.
3 Terrorism Act 2000, s 53 and Sch 7.
4 Terrorism Act 2000, s 40(1)(b). Terrorism is given a very wide definition in s 1 of the Act,
   which may conflict with international law definitions, particularly as regards 'action'
   outside the UK: see s 4(4)(a).

CONTROL OF SHIP, AIRCRAFT AND TRAIN CREWS

6.33 Members of the crews of ships, aircraft and Channel Tunnel trains are in
fact subject to more rigorous control than other groups of travellers. Their
admission, unless they are resident in the UK or qualify in some other capacity, is
always temporary – usually dependent on the turn-around time of their ship,
aircraft or train – and they are liable to instant removal without time limit or any
effective right of appeal if they overstay. But, because they are usually given
temporary admission until the next departure of their ship, aircraft or train and
do not normally need to obtain the express leave of an immigration officer on
arrival, they are an exempt category,[1] and so are dealt with in this chapter.

1 The exemptions arise from the application under UK immigration law of international
   standards and practices which have been adopted in order to expedite international
   travel and to prevent unnecessary delays owing to immigration procedures. Under the
   1958 Seafarers' National Identity Documents Convention parties to the Convention are
   obliged to admit the holder of a seaman's card for temporary shore leave to enable him
   to join a ship or to transfer to another. Under the International Labour Organisation
   Convention No 108 seamen with a Convention document do not require a visa when
   they are travelling as a crew member to or through countries which have ratified the
   Convention. A list of countries which have ratified is contained in IDI Dec/00, Ch 16,
   Annex A. For a fuller account, see Goodwin-Gill *International Law and the Movement
   of Persons between States* (1978), pp 156-159; Turack *The Passport in International
   Law*, chapters 14 and 15.

Meaning of crew member

6.34   Normally there is no difficulty in telling who is a member of the crew of a ship, aircraft or train[1] and who is not. Under section 33(1) of the Immigration Act 1971 the crew means all persons 'actually employed in the working or service' of the ship, aircraft or through train or shuttle train, including the captain or train manager.[2] But in one case the tribunal had to decide whether the wives of two ship's officers were members of the crew. In the ship's articles they were listed as stewardesses, but they were not actually engaged in any duties on board ship and only received pay at a nominal rate. They were East Germans and would normally require a visa. They had none. The immigration officer refused to treat them as crew members or let them enter, and the Immigration Appeal Tribunal agreed with him. In the definition of 'crew' the words 'actually employed' were intended to differentiate between persons who are necessary to the working and service of the ship and others, like these wives, who are supernumerary and carry out no duties.[3]

1   'Aircraft' is defined to include hovercraft: Immigration Act 1971, s 33(1).
2   Immigration Act 1971, s 33(1), modified in relation to trains by the Channel Tunnel (International Arrangements) Order 1993, SI 1993/1813, Sch 4, para 1(10). Crew members on ships can include croupiers, waiters, hairdressers, painters and repairmen, but not supernumeraries or stowaways: see IDI, Ch 16, s 1, para 3.
3   *Diestel* [1979] Imm AR 51. See CA definition of 'operational staff' of airlines in *Attivor v Secretary of State for the Home Department* [1988] Imm AR 109, CA.

Automatic shore leave or break between flights or trains

6.35   Under section 8(1) of the Immigration Act 1971 no leave to enter is normally needed for crew members of a ship who are contracted to leave the UK on the same ship, or air or train crew between flights or trains. Ships' crews are given until their ship departs; air and train crews do not necessarily go out on the same plane or train that they came in on, and are, therefore, in effect given seven days. But if there is a delay in the departure of a particular aircraft, they are entitled to remain until their plane leaves.[1] This leave-free entry does not operate in the case of crew members who are subject to deportation orders, who were refused leave on their last visit or who are required to submit to examination by an immigration officer.[2] Air crews whose breaks between flights exceed seven days may also be exempt from the need to obtain leave to enter if they had a limited leave before their last flight and they returned to the UK within the period of that leave.[3] If that happens, the limited leave does not lapse but continues to have effect as before.[4]

1   Immigration Act 1971, s 8(1), modified in relation to train crews by Channel Tunnel (International Arrangements) Order 1993, SI 1993/1813, Sch 4, para 1(4). For the government's explanation of this provision see 817 HC Official Report, cols 1006–1007.
2   Immigration Act 1971, s 8(1)(a), (b), and (c).
3   Immigration (Exemption from Control) Order 1972, SI 1972/1613, art 5(1)(e).
4   Immigration Act 1971, s 3(4).

Leave to enter for shore leave or longer breaks

6.36   Crew members of ships or aircraft who wish to enter the UK for longer periods will normally be required to obtain leave, as will deportees, those refused entry on a previous visit[1] and anyone required to submit to examination by an immigration officer, who may decide to examine any or all crew members.[2] Notice granting leave will usually require them to leave on a ship or aircraft specified or indicated in the notice,[3] or within a specified period in accordance with the arrangements to be made for their return home.[4] But where leave is given to enable crew-members to get hospital treatment, they are allowed to stay until completion of the treatment and will then be required to leave the UK in accordance with the arrangements made for their return home.[5] These provisions do not apply to train crews.

1   Immigration Act 1971, s 8(1).
2   Immigration Act 1971, Sch 2, para 2(1). This will usually happen because the vessel or certain crew members have been identified as problems: IDI Dec/00, Ch 16, s 1, para 1. The requirements for leave to enter for temporary shore leave are set out in IDI Dec/00, Ch 16, s 1, paras 5.1 and 5.2.
3   Immigration Act 1971, Sch 2, para 13(1)(a).
4   Immigration Act 1971, Sch 2, para 13(1)(c). There is a concession outside the Immigration Rules allowing for air crew of certain airlines to be based in the UK; they may be granted leave for up to 12 months at a time for this purpose and may be joined by family members. See IDI Dec/00, Ch 16, Annex E.
5   Immigration Act 1971, Sch 2, para 13(1)(b).

Coming to join a ship or aircraft

6.37   Crew members coming to the UK to join a ship or aircraft require leave. They should have an entry clearance, but do not need a work permit[1] unless the ship they are joining operates wholly or largely within British waters.[2] These provisions do not apply to train crews.

1   Immigration Act 1971, Sch 2, para 12(1). See further HC 395, para 324 (there is no equivalent on-entry rule); *Ekinci* [1989] Imm AR 346.
2   From 1 January 2001 all non-EEA seafarers working on ships engaged in scheduled domestic freight services must have a valid work permit. The work permit requirements will then be extended to other types of ship which operate solely or mainly in British waters. IDI Dec/00, Ch 16, Annex B, para 4.

Discharged seamen

6.38   Where seamen are discharged from their ship on its arrival in the UK, they do not qualify for automatic shore leave and will require leave to enter. If the immigration officer is satisfied that they have the proper documents, do not intend to take employment, intend to leave the UK, have made satisfactory arrangements for their onward travel and there are no general grounds for refusal, leave to enter will normally be given for a limited period pending departure.[1] If they require hospital treatment, the owners or agents must be willing to meet all the costs involved and to arrange for repatriation at the end of the treatment.[2] Discharged seamen may also be given leave to enter as visitors in a suitable case.[3] Visa requirements are waived.[4] Certain seamen who are discharged from their ship on their arrival in the UK are exempt from the need to obtain leave. These are Commonwealth citizens who hold a British seaman's card and Irish citizens if (in either case) they were engaged as crew members of a ship in a place within the common travel area.[5] The assumption behind this exemption is that seamen within this group are based in the UK or Ireland, and will be seeking their next engagement within the common travel area.

1   IDI Dec/00, Ch16, s 1, para 5.4.
2   IDI Dec/00, Ch 16, s 1, paras 5.4(c) and 5.6.
3   IDI Dec/00, Ch 16, s 1, para 5.12.
4   IDI Dec/00, Ch 16, s 1, para 5.5.
5   Immigration (Exemption from Control) Order 1972, SI 1972/1613, art 5(1)(d).

Arrest, detention and removal of crew members

6.39   In each of these cases the temporary nature of the crew members' stay is emphasised and reinforced by the powers given to the immigration service to deal with those who do not comply. Under Schedule 2 to the Immigration Act 1971, crew members who remain beyond the time allowed by section 8(1) or by any express leave can be arrested, detained and summarily removed from the UK.[1] Jumping ship is put on a par with illegal immigration or overstaying. In fact the powers may be more severe. Crew members can be arrested, detained and removed not only if they have actually failed to comply, but also if they are 'reasonably suspected' by an immigration officer of intending to do so. There is no in-country right of appeal unless the facts give rise to a human rights appeal, and except in such a case, the only remedy against such drastic action is an application for *habeas corpus* or judicial review. There is no time limit on the exercise of the powers of removal. Someone who jumped ship ten years ago is as liable to removal, it seems, as someone who did so last week. Train crews are liable to removal if they fail to return to their train or remain beyond the time allowed by their exemption under section 8(1).[2]

1   Immigration Act 1971, Sch 2, paras 12(2) and 13(2).
2   Immigration Act 1971, Sch 2, para 13(2), modified by the Channel Tunnel (International Arrangements) Order 1993, SI 1993/1813, Sch 4, para 1(11)(n).

Shipwrecked seamen

6.40   Where a ship is wrecked, shipwrecked seamen should normally be given leave to enter.[1] They will usually be cared for by a local shipping agent, the Shipwrecked Mariners Society or the Mission of Seamen. Seamen for this purpose include non-professional seamen.[2]

1   IDI Dec/00, Ch 16, s 1, Annex B, para 8.
2   IDI Dec/00, Ch 16, s 1, Annex B, para 8.

GROUPS COVERED BY EXEMPTION ORDER

Consular officers and employees

6.41   Consular officers are appointed by their governments to live in a foreign port or city, chiefly as a representative of their country's commercial interests. They differ from diplomats, who are dealt with at **6.44**ff below. There is also a distinction between full and partial exemption. Full exemption means not only freedom to enter and leave the country freely but also freedom from deportation. Partial exemption means officials are exempt from all control except deportation. Where consular Conventions have been concluded between the UK and another state,[1] full exemption from immigration control is given to any consular officer or employee[2] in the service of that state, and to any member of the family of such a person who forms part of his or her household.[3] Consular employees only get the exemption if they are in the full-time service of the state concerned and are not engaged in the UK in any private occupation for gain.[4]

1 The list of states with which the UK has concluded such Conventions is set out in IDI Dec/00, Ch 14, s 1.
2 For definitions see Consular Relations Act 1968, Sch 1, art 1(d), (e).
3 Immigration (Exemption from Control) Order 1972, SI 1972/1613, as amended, art 3(1).
4 SI 1972/1613, art 3(2).

6.42 Exemption from all immigration control except deportation[1] is given under the Immigration (Exemption from Control) Order 1972[2] to the following:

(i) members of foreign governments on official business, representatives of foreign governments attending certain conferences, and consular officers and employees of states who have not signed a consular convention with the UK;[3]

(ii) senior officials from international organisations like the International Monetary Fund, International Bank for Reconstruction and Development, International Finance Corporation, International Development Association, the Hong Kong Economic and Trade Office, the Independent International Commission on Decommissioning and the North Atlantic Salmon Conservation Organisation;[4]

(iii) persons connected with international organisations or international tribunals who attend certain conferences in the UK;[5]

(iv) representatives of Commonwealth countries attending conferences[6] or performing consular functions;[7]

(v) officials of the Commonwealth Secretariat who are entitled to limited immunities under Schedule 6 of the Commonwealth Secretariat Act 1966, but not to full diplomatic immunity.[8]

In each of these cases the exemption also applies to any member of the family forming a part of the exempted person's household.[9]

1 Under Immigration Act 1971, s 3(5)(a) and (b).
2 SI 1972/1613.
3 SI 1972/1613, art 4(a), (h), (i).
4 SI 1972/1613, art 4(b), (c), (d), (k), (l), (m).
5 SI 1972/1613, art 4(g). The IDI have a full list of organisations whose delegates would be exempt: IDI Dec/00, Ch 14, Annex B.
6 SI 1972/1613, art 4(e).
7 SI 1972/1613, art 4(f).
8 SI 1972/1613, art 4(j).
9 SI 1972/1613, art 4(n). Family members for these purposes include dependent offspring over 18 who are still in full-time education, dependent relatives forming part of the household abroad and other close relatives with no one else to look after them: IDI Dec/00, Ch 14, s 1. For the position of unmarried and same-sex partners of consular officials see IDI Dec/00, Ch 14, s 1. There is an issue as to whether family members benefit if the relevant person is a British citizen. The Home Office argues that art 4 of the Immigration

(Exemption from Control) Order 1972, SI 1972/1613 provides exemption from any provisions of the Immigration Act 1971 relating to those who are not British citizens and that British citizens are not exempt. The alternative view is that a British citizen can be both exempt and have a right of abode; and where Parliament wants to limit exemption to non-British citizens it uses the formula in art 5 of the 1972 Order: 'the following persons who are not British citizens are exempt . . .'

Other exempted groups

6.43 Under the Immigration (Exemption from Control) Order 1972[1], made under section 8(2) of the Immigration Act 1971, the following classes of persons, not already referred to, who are not British citizens, have a limited exemption from the requirement under section 3(1)(a) of the 1971 Act to obtain leave to enter:[2]

(i)   any Commonwealth citizen included in a collective passport issued in the UK or Islands;[3]

(ii)   any Irish or Commonwealth citizens returning from an excursion to France, Belgium or the Netherlands who hold a valid identity document issued for such excursions;[4]

(iii)   certain holders of a British seaman's card and certain members of the crew of an aircraft.[5]

These exemptions do not apply to any person against whom there is a deportation order in force, or who has previously entered the UK unlawfully and has not subsequently been given leave to enter or remain.[6] For these purposes Commonwealth citizens include British Protected persons.[7]

1   SI 1972/1613.
2   Former CUKCs (British Dependent Territories and British Overseas citizens) holding a British visitor's passport are expressed to be exempt under Article 5(1)(a) of SI 1972/1613, but British visitor's passports have now been abolished, so this exemption has been omitted from the main text.
3   SI 1972/1613, art 5(1)(b).
4   SI 1972/1613, art 5(1)(c).
5   SI 1972/1613, art 5(1)(d) and (e). See **6.34** above.
6   SI 1972/1613, art 5(2).
7   SI 1972/1613, art 5(3).

DIPLOMATIC EXEMPTION

6.44 Representatives of foreign governments and of international organisations, such as the UN, and their families are exempt from control under either the Immigration (Exemption from Control) Order 1972[1] made under section 8(2) of the Immigration Act 1971 or under section 8(3). In some cases full exemption is given, and in others officials are exempt from all control except deportation. Consular exemption, described at **6.41-6.42** above, is sometimes full exemption, meaning freedom to enter and leave the UK and freedom from deportation during the period of exemption, and sometimes partial, meaning that deportation is still possible. Diplomatic exemption, which we now consider, is always full exemption.

1   SI 1972/1613.

Diplomats and their staff

6.45 Diplomatic staff carry on the diplomatic relations of the state they represent in the country to which they have been appointed. Members of diplomatic missions and members of their families who form part of their household are fully exempt under section 8(3) of the Immigration Act 1971. The Diplomatic Privileges Act 1964 divides those members of diplomatic missions entitled to diplomatic immunity into three categories:

(i)   diplomatic agents, who are heads of the mission and members of their diplomatic staff;
(ii)   members of the administrative and technical staff, consisting of clerical staff, translators, coding clerks, press representatives, etc; and
(iii)   members of the service staff, who are chauffeurs, cooks, cleaners, etc.[1]

Each of these categories is entitled to differing degrees of immunity from civil and criminal proceedings, but all are exempt from immigration control under section 8(3) of the 1971 Act, except staff recruited in this country. Section 8(3A), as amended by the Immigration and Asylum Act 1999, provides that members of a mission, other than diplomatic agents, are only exempt if (a) they were resident outside the UK, and were not in the UK, when they were offered their post, and (b) they have not ceased to be a member of the mission after having taken up the post.[2]

1   See Diplomatic Privileges Act 1964, Sch 1, para 1.
2   The original s 8(3A) of the Immigration Act 1971 was inserted by Immigration Act 1988, s 4. It ensured that foreign nationals in the UK, who took up posts in diplomatic missions, other than as diplomatic agents, were not exempt from immigration control. But there was a lacuna in the law. If these locally recruited people left the UK and then returned while still in post, the original s 8(3A) operated to free them from immigration control on their return. By the Immigration and Asylum Act 1999 amendment, the new s 8(3A) closes this loophole, but at the same time ensures that they do not remain subject to immigration control for ever. A person who has held such a post in the past, but has subsequently left it, and has then been appointed from abroad, will enjoy full diplomatic exemption.

6.46 The distinction between service staff who are exempt from control and other employees of a mission is sometimes difficult to make. In practice the distinguishing feature appears to be whether or not they are liable to pay UK tax. Under Article 37(3) of the Vienna Convention, members of the service staff of the mission are exempt from local taxes. Thus in *Kandiah*[1] the Tribunal held that a messenger working for a mission was not exempt from immigration control where it was a condition of his employment that he paid local taxes.[2] Equally, it is doubtful if a housekeeper in the household of the deputy head of mission would be exempt from control, even if he or she has his or her contract with the government concerned.[3] The service staff of the mission is not the same as the service staff of one of its members. The Tribunal, however, seemed to take a different view in the case of *Florentine*.[4] The private servants of heads of state have total exemption unless the Secretary of State otherwise directs.[5]

1   (2699) unreported.
2   See *Pintucan* (16451) (1999) ILD No 1, p 27.
3   The test of exemption is not the mere fact of being employed at a diplomatic mission. IDI Dec/00, Ch 14, Annex A distinguishes between a servant of the head of the mission paid by the country, and one paid by the head of mission, the latter being a private servant in a diplomatic household requiring leave to enter under HC 395, para 152ff.

4   (4811) unreported.
5   IDI Dec/00, Ch 14, s 1.

UN officials

6.47 Persons entitled to like immunity from jurisdiction as is conferred by the Diplomatic Privileges Act 1964 on 'diplomatic agents' are fully exempt from immigration control.[1] Like immunities are conferred on high officers of a number of foreign organisations, such as the UN, by Orders in Council made under the International Organisations (Immunities and Privileges) Act 1950, as continued by the International Organisations Act 1968, section 12(5), and on senior officers of the Commonwealth Secretariat under the Commonwealth Secretariat Act 1966. The range of employees covered and whether the exemption extends to any member of the person's family forming part of his or her household depends upon the terms of the agreement reached with each organisation.[2]

1   Immigration Act 1971, s 8(3).
2   The family has exemption because they obtain like immunity under the relevant agreement, not because of any express mention of a family in Immigration Act 1971, s 8(3).

Members of the diplomat's family

6.48 In all the immunities granted to diplomats and international functionaries, the exemption extends to members of their family who form part of their household.[1] This can be a difficult issue. In *Gupta*[2] the question in issue was whether the widowed sister of an Indian diplomat qualified. She claimed she was entitled to remain here as a member of her brother's family who formed part of his household within the meaning of section 8(3) of the Immigration Act 1971. The High Court held that she was exempt from control. The IDI now give some guidance, giving the term a more generous interpretation than that used for persons subject to immigration control and having more in common with the EC definition.[3] It extends to children over 18 who are still in full-time education; dependent relatives forming part of the household abroad; and other close relatives with no one else to look after them.[4] Unmarried partners are not exempt from control, but may seek leave to enter under the Immigration Rules.[5]

1   See eg Immigration Act 1971, s 8(3); Immigration (Exemption from Control) Order 1972, SI 1972/1613, art 3(1)(c) and 4(l).
2   [1979] Imm AR 52. See *Florentine* [1987] Imm AR 1.
3   In Council Regulation (EEC) 1612/68, art 10.
4   IDI Dec/00, Ch 14, s 1.
5   IDI Dec/00, Ch 14, s 1, para 9.

CEASING TO HAVE DIPLOMATIC AND OTHER EXEMPTION

6.49 When diplomats and others exempted under section 8(2) and (3) of the Immigration Act 1971 cease to be exempt and, as a result, require leave to remain, they are treated as if they had been given leave for a period of 90 days, beginning on the day exemption ceases.[1] If, however, the person already has a leave which expires before the end of the 90-day period, his or her leave is treated as expiring at the end of the shorter period.[2] This provision, together with the new section 8(3A), which came into force on 1 March 2000,[3] disposes of many of the practical problems of diplomatic exemption referred to in the previous editions of this work.[4] The position now is:

(i) if clearly indicated indefinite leave was given on arrival in the UK and before taking up the diplomatic post, this will remain unaffected by the exemption. Since under section 8(3) 'the provisions of this Act . . . shall not apply . . . so long as' the person remains exempt, such leave will not lapse due to trips overseas,[5] and it cannot be curtailed, like a limited leave, by the Home Office.[6] The former diplomat will be free to remain;

(ii) a mere rectangular stamp in a passport with a date but no words indicating any sort of leave does not operate as the grant of indefinite leave.[7] Further, a grant of indefinite leave on arrival in the UK is unlikely, since it is now the law that those who come from overseas to take up a diplomatic post become members of the mission on arrival in the UK, and not when they actually take up the appointment or when the appointment is officially notified to the UK government;[8]

(iii) persons with prior limited leave are dealt with by sections 8(5) and 8A(3)(b) of the 1971 Act. If they wish to remain longer they need to apply before the end of the period of their leave in the normal way;

(iv) there is uncertainty as to the effect of an express grant of leave (indefinite or limited) given to somebody who is exempt from control as a diplomat.[9]

1 Immigration Act 1971, s 8A(2), inserted by the Immigration and Asylum Act 1999, s 6.
2 Immigration Act 1971, s 8A(3).
3 SI 2000/168.
4 4th edition **7.46ff**.
5 As would have been the case under Immigration Act 1971, s 3(4); the provisions of the Immigration (Leave to Enter and Remain) Order 2000, SI 2000/1161 would now in any event prevent the lapsing of indefinite leave.
6 Immigration Act 1971, s 3(3).
7 *Secretary of State for the Home Department v Bagga* [1990] Imm AR 413, CA.
8 *Bagga* above, overruling *R v Governor of Pentonville Prison, ex p Teja* [1971] 2 QB 274, [1971] 2 All ER 11; *R v Lambeth Justices, ex p Yusufu* [1985] Crim LR 510; *Re Osman (No 2)* (21 December 1988, unreported), DC; and *Rahi* [1987] Imm AR 293 on the issue that immunity depends on notification and acceptance.
9 One argument is that such leave is ineffective as contrary to section 8(3) of the Immigration Act 1971. The opposing argument is that exemption from the requirement to obtain leave does not preclude reliance being placed subsequently on such a leave when the person ceases to be exempt. In practice the Home Office recognises that there has been a pledge of public faith by immigration officials and the grant of leave is usually honoured: IDI Dec/00, Ch 14, s 1, para 8.5. This does not apply if the leave was limited and expires within three months of the exemption ending: IDI Dec/00, Ch 14, s 1.

MILITARY PERSONNEL

6.50 Section 8 of the Immigration Act 1971 also gives a limited exemption to members of the home forces subject to service law, to members of Commonwealth forces training with the home forces and to members of a visiting force, such as US servicemen, posted in the UK.[1] The exemption is limited since it exempts from control on and after entry, but not from deportation.

1 Immigration Act 1971, s 8(4) and (6). See *R v Secretary of State for the Home Department, ex p Wuan* [1989] Imm AR 501, QBD.

CHILDREN BORN IN THE UK

6.51 The British Nationality Act 1981 made provision[1] for the Secretary of State for the Home Department to exempt by Order from immigration control any person or class of person regarded as settled in the UK for the purposes of section 1 of the 1981 Act. This will apply to children born in the UK after 1983, but who do not acquire British citizenship by birth. No such Order has yet been made.

1 By inserting a new s 8(5)(a) into the Immigration Act 1971.

Chapter 7

EUROPEAN COMMUNITY LAW AND RELATED OBLIGATIONS

INTRODUCTION

7.1 This chapter is concerned with the impact on immigration law of rights of freedom of movement and associated provisions afforded under the Treaty of Rome 1959 (the EEC Treaty), as amended by the Single European Act 1987, the Treaty on European Union 1993 (the Maastricht Treaty), and the Treaty of Amsterdam 1997. The UK became a member of the European Communities with effect from 1 January 1973.[1] Since this date the Treaty, and directives and regulations made under it, are binding in the UK by virtue of the European Communities Act 1972.[2] So also are decisions and interpretations on these provisions by the European Court of Justice (ECJ).[3] Contrary to the general policy of the Immigration Act 1971, whose clear purpose is to restrict the right of individuals to enter or remain in the UK, the main characteristic of these freedom of movement provisions is that they grant rights directly to individuals and restrict the powers of the national authority. Interpretation of the Community texts by the ECJ tends, therefore, to favour the individual rather than the member state. This is in sharp contrast to the interpretation of domestic immigration law, which tends to give fuller recognition to the extensive discretionary power of the immigration authorities at the expense of the individual. From its inception, the freedom of movement of persons was characterised as one of the European Economic Community's (EEC's) principal foundations, along with freedom of movement for goods, services and capital.[4]

1 European Communities Act 1972.
2 European Communities Act 1972, s 2.
3 European Communities Act 1972, s 3; see *EC Commission v Luxembourg* [1997] ECR 1-3207, [1996] 3 CMLR 981; *Orfinger v Belgium* [2000] 1 CMLR 612, ECJ.
4 See Case 167/73 *EC Commission v France* [1974] ECR 359, [1974] 2 CMLR 216, ECJ; Preamble to Council Regulation (EEC) 1612/68.

7.2 Since 1 November 1993 and the amendments made at Maastricht by the Treaty on European Union (TEU) the EEC is now known as the European Community (EC). This suggests that the Community is concerned with political and social rights as well as purely economic ones. From this date the member states of the EC have formed the European Union (EU) which includes, but is a different body from, the EC.[1] A national of a member state is now, by virtue of that nationality, also a citizen of the EU.[2] The free movement rights of EU citizens and members of their families remain the core of Community law as it affects immigration, but the Treaty on European Union also provided a structure for inter-governmental co-operation on asylum and immigration of third-country nationals in what became known as the third pillar of the EU. On 2 October 1997 member states signed the Treaty of Amsterdam with a view to improving the efficiency, democracy and transparency of the EU, and to prepare it for the next enlargement of membership.[3] The central change has been the integration into the framework of the EU of the Schengen *acquis*[4] and a new Title IV of the EC Treaty, containing the power to make new Community law on immigration and asylum, matters which had previously been dealt with on an inter-governmental basis under the Justice and Home affairs provisions of the Treaty on European Union (the 'third pillar'). As a result of Amsterdam, the EC Treaty has been extensively amended and renumbered (see **7.14** below).[5]

1 Selected articles of the EC and EU Treaties are set out in the Appendix. For the full texts see *Butterworths Immigration Law Service*, F[31], [201]. The Treaty on European Union was adopted in the UK by the European Communities (Amendment) Act 1993, which received the Royal Assent in July 1993. Implementation was delayed until the House of Commons voted on the UK's opt out of the Protocol on Social Policy. A challenge was also made to the power of the Secretary of State for Foreign Affairs to conclude the Treaty (*R v Secretary of State for Foreign and Commonwealth Affairs, ex p Rees-Mogg* [1994] QB 552, [1993] 3 CMLR 101). The Treaty on European Union had also to receive approval from the German and French Constitutional courts (see [1994] 1 CMLR 57).
2 Article 17 EC (ex art 8).
3 See Kay Hailbronner 'The Treaty of Amsterdam and Migration Law' 1999 EJM&L 9.
4 The Schengen *acquis* derived from agreement on the gradual abolition of checks at common borders signed by other EC member states on 14 June 1985 and 19 June 1990. See 7.15ff below.
5 For the renumbered texts, see *Butterworths Immigration Law Service*, F[31]; British Management Data Foundation *Treaty of Amsterdam in Perspective* (2nd edn, 1998).

7.3 The member states of the EU are Austria, Belgium, Denmark, Finland, France, Germany, Greece, Holland, Ireland, Italy, Luxembourg, Portugal, Spain, Sweden and the UK. Other countries that have submitted applications to join the EU include Bulgaria, Cyprus, the Czech and Slovak Republics, Hungary, Turkey and Poland. The EC Treaty gives powers to the EEC and the member states to enter association agreements with other states.[1] These are binding in Community law. The exercise of these powers has led to various association agreements, of which the most significant for immigration lawyers are the Ankara Agreement 1963, the EC Agreements with North African states, the more recent agreements with Eastern European states, and the 1999 Agreement with Switzerland.

1   Article 310 EC (ex Art 238 of the EEC Treaty, as amended by the Single European Act 1987).

7.4 A completely new entity, the European Economic Area (EEA) has been created by an agreement made with the former European Free Trade Association countries under the EC Treaty, giving the same free movement rights within the area to both EU nationals and to nationals of Norway, Iceland and Liechtenstein.[1] It has an advanced institutional structure, including a distinct Court and Surveillance Authority. Switzerland originally intended to become a member of the EEA, but the agreement was rejected in a Swiss referendum and so Switzerland remains outside.[2] However, in June 1999 the EC and Switzerland entered into an agreement intended to extend full free movement rights between the community and Switzerland, when it eventually comes into force.[3] The Agreement on the European Economic Area 1992 has the force of law in the UK by virtue of the European Economic Area Act 1993, which amends the European Communities Act 1972. The freedom of movement rights under the 1992 Agreement were implemented in UK law as from 20 July 1994 by the European Economic Area Order in Council 1994.[4] This has now been replaced since 2 October 2000 by the Immigration (European Economic Area) Regulations 2000.[5] In the 2000 Regulations a national of a state that is party to the EEA Agreement is called a 'qualified person' irrespective of whether or not he or she is a national of the EU. In this chapter, in considering free movement rights we will refer to EEA nationals rather than EC or EU nationals, unless separate consideration is required for the latter. The rights accruing under association agreements will be considered separately in **7.145ff**.

1   See European Economic Area Act 1993, applying the Agreement on the European Economic Area signed at Oporto on 2 May 1992, as adjusted by the Protocol signed at Brussels on 17 March 1993 OJ L86 20.4.1995. The implementation of the Agreement was delayed until the ECJ was satisfied that the joint committee established to monitor the Agreement did not impinge on the court's jurisdiction; see ECJ Opinion 1/92 given on 10 April 1992. For the rules of the joint committee and the EEA Court see [1994] 1 CMLR 84.
2   See S Peers 'The EC-Switzerland Agreement on Free Movement of Persons: Overview and Analysis' 2000 EJM&L 127.
3   COM (1999) 229, 4 May 1999. See Peers above.
4   SI 1994/1895.
5   SI 2000/2326.

THE SOURCES AND INSTITUTIONS OF EC LAW

7.5 The EEC Treaty, by which the Common Market was first established In 1959, remains the fundamental source of the constitution of the EC, and distributes functions between the Council, the European Commission, the ECJ and the European Parliament.[1] The Council and the Commission are given the task of making regulations, issuing directives, taking decisions, making recommendations or delivering opinions in accordance with the provisions of the Treaty.[2] The ECJ has the task of interpretation of the Treaty and the acts of Community institutions.[3] Community law consists of the totality of legally enforceable obligations; a wider concept is the *acquis communitaire* which includes the actions and opinions of Community institutions. The *acquis communitaire* is to be respected and built upon by the EU.[4]

1 See Pt V, Title 1, arts 189-267 EC (ex arts 137-198). A full description of the workings of Community law and its institutions is beyond the scope of this work. The reader is referred to Vaughan *Law of the European Communities* (Butterworths); Wyatt and Dashwood *European Union Law*, 4th edn, 2000, Sweet & Maxwell; Craig and De Burca, eds *The Evolution of EU Law* 1999, OUP; Craig and De Burca, *EU Law* 2nd edn, 1998, OUP; Lasok *Law and Institution of the European Union* 7th edn, 2001, Butterworths.
2 Article 249 EC (ex art 189). As well as initiating Community legislation the Commission has the task of ensuring that member states comply with their obligations under Community law and can bring proceedings before the ECJ if they have failed to do so, despite the issue of a Commission opinion: see art 226 EC (ex art 169).
3 Article 234 EC (ex art 177).
4 Article 3 EU (ex art C).

7.6 In its original form the EEC Treaty provided in general terms for the progressive reduction of all the barriers preventing the free movement of nationals of member countries from one EEC country to another.[1] Free movement rights were specifically provided for in connection with economic activities. The key articles are Articles 39 and 40 EC (ex Articles 48 and 49) which deal with the free movement of workers, Articles 43 EC (ex Article 52) *et seq*, which deal with the right of establishment, including the right to engage in and carry on self-employed occupations, and Articles 48 EC (ex Article 58) *et seq*, which deal with the provision of services in another member state.[2] The Treaty set out the general principles and provided for transitional stages before full implementation. All these stages have long since been completed.

1 Article 3(c) EEC.
2 The text of these articles is set out in the Appendix.

7.7 Effect was given to these Articles by Community legislation in the form of directives and regulations. But whereas Article 39 EC (ex Article 48) refers to workers or workers of member states, Council Regulation (EEC) 1612/68 refers to workers who are nationals of member states. From the conclusion of the transitional periods for establishing free movement for workers in 1972, there has been a debate as to whether Community competence in respect of 'workers of member states' extends to a broader class than merely workers who are nationals of such states.[1] Following the Amsterdam Treaty, new Community law may now be adopted under Title IV EC on the position of third-country nationals lawfully resident in the EU.

1 See Elspeth Guild 'Discretion, Competence and Migration in the European Union' [1999] EJM&L 61 at 72-77; R Plender 'Competence, European Community Law and Nationals of Non-Member States' [1990] 39 ICLQ 599; T Hoogenboom 'The Position of those who are not Nationals of the Community Member States' in Cassese, Clapham, Weiler (eds) *Human Rights in the European Community. Methods of Protection* (1991); P Stangos 'Les Ressortissants d'etats Tiers au sein de L'ordre Juridique Communautaire, Cahiers des Communautés Européenes vis-à-vis des Ressortissants de Pays Tiers' in Den Boer (ed) *The Implementation of Schengen: First Widening, now Deepening* (1997).

7.8 The Single European Act 1987, which came into force on 1 July 1987, carried the process further and required the Community to adopt measures with the aim of progressively establishing the internal market over a period expiring on 31 December 1992. According to what is now Article 14 of the EC Treaty, the internal market comprises an area 'without internal frontiers in which the free movement of goods, persons, services and capital is ensured in accordance with the provisions of this Treaty'.[1] Shortly before this happened, Germany, France and the three Benelux countries entered into the first Schengen Agreement in 1985, aimed at reducing frontier control between their countries. The Agreement was supplemented by the Schengen Convention of 1990, which came into force in 1995. Schengen marks an important stage in the recent development of EC and EU law and we shall come back to it in more detail at **7.15** below.

1 Article 14 EC (ex art 7a).

7.9 The next stage was the Maastricht Treaty or the Treaty on European Union (TEU), which came into force on 1 November 1993. It contained important amendments to the EEC Treaty (the old Treaty of Rome), which now became the EC Treaty. These amendments included the creation of a European citizenship[1] with concomitant rights, of which the most controversial is the right to move and reside freely in the territory of the member states 'subject to the limitations and conditions laid down in this Treaty and by the measures adopted to give it effect'.[2]

1 Article 17 EC (ex art 8).
2 Article 18 EC (ex art 8a).

The EC and the EU

7.10 The Treaty on European Union did not merely amend the EEC Treaty and change the EEC to EC. It also created the European Union (the EU), which has been described as a temple supported by three pillars. These are: the European Community (based on the old EEC Treaty, as amended), co-operation on a common foreign and security policy (Title V) and co-operation in the fields of justice and home affairs (Title VI). Linking the three aspects of the EU is the European Council—the lintel over the columns, to pursue the architectural metaphor.[1] Under Title VI (the third pillar) a new dimension was added to European immigration law. Article K.1 stated:

> 'for the purposes of achieving the objectives of the Union, in particular the free movement of persons, and without prejudice to the powers of the European Community, Member States shall regard the following areas as matters of common interest:
> 1. asylum policy;
> 2. rules governing the crossing by persons of external borders of the Member States and the exercise of control thereon;
> 3. immigration policy and policy regarding nationals of third countries.'

1 Treaty on European Union, Title 1, arts C, D, E and F (now, after amendments, arts 3, 4, 5 and 6 EU).

The Treaty of Amsterdam

7.11 The Treaty of Amsterdam entered into force on 1 May 1999. Under it the EC acquired jurisdiction to deal with wider questions of immigration and asylum, bringing the possibility of much great impact than ever before on the substance of UK immigration law. At the moment the Treaty has created the framework for future action and legislation, but no actual directives or regulations, other than in draft. The main changes effected by the Amsterdam Treaty have been (i) to integrate the Schengen *acquis* into the framework of the EU and (ii) moving immigration, asylum and civil cooperation from the third pillar of the union into the first pillar (EC) under the new Title IV EC, whilst leaving police, criminal and customs co-operation in the third pillar (Title VI EU).

7.12 Following Maastricht we can now distinguish EC law, the law of the Community, including free movement law, and EU law, the law of the Union, which comprises EC law (the law of the first pillar) and all the inter-governmental co-operation, falling within EU Justice and Home Affairs or the third pillar of the Union. The processes and results of this co-operation have been charted in detail in Peers' *EU Justice and Home Affairs Law*,[1] which we have used extensively in the preparation of this chapter. As we shall see, the consequence of the Amsterdam Treaty, in moving immigration and asylum from the third pillar into the first pillar, is that these topics have now become part of EC law within the competence of the EC institutions (the Council, Commission and ECJ). The same thing has happened with the whole Schengen regime (the Schengen *acquis)* which previously was completely outside the EU. This whole process is often referred to as the 'communitarising' of the third pillar and Schengen powers - a mind-blocking word we would prefer to avoid.

1   2000, Pearson Education.

7.13 Some parts of the Schengen *acquis*, as we shall see, have been allocated to the EC and others go to the third pillar of the EU under Title VI. As regards immigration and asylum and those parts of Schengen allocated to Title IV of the EC Treaty, the transferred items are subject to a special regime for a five-year period, and the Council is given this relatively short period in which to adopt new Community laws under this Title. So far as the EC Treaty is concerned, there have been considerable amendments and the whole Treaty has been renumbered. There has also been considerable rewriting of the Treaty on European Union and Articles have been given numbers where previously they had letters, but there have also been some substantial changes. Article 1 EU now also provides that decisions are to be taken 'as openly as possible' to the citizen. Article 2 EU now includes a far more detailed objective than merely 'to develop close cooperation on justice and home affairs'. Now the objective is 'to maintain and develop the Union as an area of freedom, security and justice, in which the free movement of persons is assured in conjunction with appropriate measures with respect to external border controls, asylum, immigration and the prevention and combating of crime'. Article 6(1) EU now provides that 'the Union is founded on principles of liberty, democracy, respect for human rights and fundamental freedoms, and the rule of law'. A new Article 7 EU sets out a procedure by which a member state judged to be in 'serious and persistent breach' of these principles might have certain of its EU and EC Treaty rights suspended.[1]

1   Peers **7.12** above, p 12.

Referring to renumbered Articles of the Treaties

7.14 The renumbering of the Treaties is part of a process to simplify and update. Some Articles and paragraphs which have lapsed and are no longer relevant have been removed. Owing to the potential confusion over renumbering, the

ECJ has decided that in identifying the Articles in the various Treaties, the following designations will be used:

(1)   Treaty on European Union – EU;
(2)   Treaty establishing the European Community – EC;
(3)   Euratom Treaty – EA;
(4)   European Coal and Steel Community – CS.

These designations will appear after the Article number, eg Article 23 EC. In addition the court will refer to Articles as they stood before the Amsterdam changes as follows:

(1)   where the Article number but not the text has changed: 'Article 23 EC (ex Article 9)';

(2)   where the text and Article number have changed: 'Article 9 of the EC Treaty (now, after amendment, Article 23 EC)'.

The Schengen Agreements

7.15 The original Schengen Agreement of 14 June 1985[1] had two objectives:

(i)   to reduce common frontier controls by instituting 'a simple visual check on private vehicles crossing the common frontier at a reduced speed without requiring the vehicle to stop';[2]

(ii)   to abolish internal controls on all persons, whatever their origins.

The Schengen Convention of 19 June 1990, which came into force on 26 March 1995, aimed to create a zone with only one external border and free movement within it. In order to achieve this, the 1990 Convention established common conditions of entry,[3] including a common visa[4] for non-EU nationals wishing to cross the external borders of the Schengen states.[5] Common visas can be issued for any period not exceeding three months.[6] Non-EU nationals admitted with such a visa, non-EU nationals who do not require a visa and those who are resident in one of the Schengen states may move freely within those territories for a period up to three months, depending on the period of their visa.[7] However, the Schengen Agreements give no right of residence to third-country nationals within any of the Schengen territories. Only short temporary stays outside the state of residence are permitted. A third-country national illegally resident within a Schengen state can be expelled from the whole of the Schengen area.[8] Such an individual can be expelled to his or her country of origin or to a third country that has signed an agreement on the readmission of clandestine immigrants with the Schengen states. For example, such an agreement was signed with Poland on 29 March 1991, obliging Poland to readmit persons who are illegally in the Schengen zone, regardless of nationality, who entered by crossing the Schengen-Polish border.[9] In order to combat illegal immigration, carriers will have to check whether passengers have adequate documentation when they enter the Schengen area and are liable to penalties if they are negligent in these checks.[10] There are also sanctions for assisting illegal entry.[11]

1   See *Butterworths Immigration Law Service*, F[6551].
2   Schengen Agreement 1985, art 2.
3   Schengen Convention 1990, art 9.
4   Schengen Convention 1990, art 10.

5 Airports are now considered to be external borders for flights to or from third countries and internal borders for flights between Schengen states. The same applies to seaports. See *Butterworths Immigration Law Service*, F[6508].
6 Schengen Convention 1990, art 11.
7 Schengen Convention 1990, arts 19, 20 and 21.
8 Schengen Convention 1990, arts 23(3)-(5).
9 *Butterworths Immigration Law Service*, F[6507].
10 Schengen Convention 1990, art 26(2).
11 Schengen Convention 1990, art 27(1).

7.16 The Schengen Agreements were seen as a forerunner to the implementation of Article 7A of the EC Treaty (now Article 14 EC), providing for the abolition of internal borders between participating states.[1] To this we now turn.

1 Elspeth Guild 'Discretion, Competence and Migration in the European Union' [1999] EJML 61 at 82; D O'Keefe 'Free Movement of Persons and the Single Market' (1992) Eur Law Review 17 at 3-13.

Abolition of internal borders

7.17 The abolition of internal border controls is at the heart of the European integration project, at least as far as the Schengen members of the EU are concerned. The dispute over internal border control began with the insertion of Article 8a (later Article 7a and now Article 14 EC) into the EEC Treaty by the Single European Act 1987, agreed in late 1985 and coming into force in 1987. It requires the EC 'To adopt measures with the aim of progressively establishing the internal market over a period expiring on 31 December 1992 . . .' The internal market means 'an area without internal frontiers in which the free movement of goods, persons, services and capital is ensured in accordance with the provisions of this Treaty'.[1] The UK government took the view that only some persons were covered by the internal market principle and that it was, therefore, necessary to check everyone at the border to see who was an EC national and who was not.[2] Other governments said it meant the abolition of all checks. If it meant that, then it made no sense to maintain completely distinct policies over visas, external borders, immigration of third-country nationals and asylum.[3] But at that time the EC lacked competence to deal with these questions under the existing Treaty provisions.[4]

1 Article 7a was not of direct effect and did not of itself create any legal rights: see *R v Secretary of State for the Home Department, ex p Flynn* [1995] 3 CMLR 397, QBD.
2 Peers 7.12 above, p 64.
3 Peers above, p 64.
4 The Commission tried but failed in its attempt to use art 100 EC for a directive on illegal immigration and employment law: see Peers above, p 65.

7.18 This lack of competence is now remedied by the Amsterdam Treaty, with its integration of the Schengen *acquis* into the framework of the EU and the new Title IV, which enables the Community to introduce measures in respect of the movement and residence of third country nationals. The underlying principle remains the completion of the internal market and the abolition of intra-Community borders,[1] even although Title IV gives a 'flanking' Community competence to regulate immigration and asylum, but without any clearly defined goals or objectives, other than the establishment of an area of freedom, security and justice.[2] We deal first with the Schengen *acquis* and then with Title IV.

1   Elspeth Guild 'Discretion, Competence and Migration in the European Union' [1999] EJM&L 61 at 84.
2   Article 61(a) EC.

Schengen acquis

7.19 The Schengen a*cquis* consist of the Schengen Agreement of 14 June 1985, the Schengen Convention 1990, the accession protocols and agreements creating new members of Schengen, and the decisions and declarations adopted by the Schengen Executive Committee, as well as the acts adopted for its implementation.[1] Protocol 2 which is annexed to the Treaty on European Union and EC Treaty, applies the Schengen *acquis* to the 13 participating member states,[2] and brings the provisions of the Schengen *acquis* into the framework of the EU, the idea being that these provisions will be split up and allocated to the relevant part of the EU and EC Treaties, while at the same time preserving a special 'pick and choose' position for the UK and Ireland,[3] and an associate participation for two non-EU states, Norway and Iceland .[4]

1   Annexe to Protocol 2 to TEU and TEC; see *Butterworths Immigration Law Service*, F[62]–[76].
2   The participating member states are Austria, Belgium, Denmark, France, Finland, Germany, Greece, Italy, Luxembourg, Netherlands, Portugal, Spain and Sweden.
3   Now an 'opt out' with the right to opt in; see Peers **7.12** above, p 56; **7.27**ff below.
4   Protocol 2, art 6. The Council concluded an agreement with Norway and Iceland in 1999 (OJ 1999 L 176/35) setting out procedures for their 'association' with existing Schengen *acquis* and measures building on it, and together with Ireland and the UK made a separate agreement with Norway and Iceland on the one hand and the UK and Ireland on the other to the extent that the UK and Ireland opted in to the Schengen *acquis*: see Peers above, p 57.

7.20 In May 1999 the Council agreed on the allocation of all the Schengen *acquis* with the exception of the Schengen Information Services (SIS), which is used by police and customs to prevent crime and by the immigration authorities to control entry and is, therefore, difficult to place in either the Treaty on European Union or the EC Treaty.[1] In dealing with the allocation it was decided that not all the *acquis* would be allocated.[2] For example, the asylum provisions of Schengen had been overtaken by the ratification of the Dublin Convention and did not, therefore, need to be allocated.[3] After allocation, measures building upon the *acquis* will become regular parts of EC or EU law with no special rules applying, or as Peers puts it: 'Conceptually, this is the legal equivalent of breaking a large lump of sugar into two separate lumps, and then dissolving these lumps into two separate cups of tea.'[4] In the immigration field, the Schengen *acquis* thus form a further basis for community legislation on border controls and the position of third-country nationals within the EC.

1   Decision of May 1999 (OJ 1999 L 176/17). Peers **7.12** above. P 59. As a result of the failure to allocate the Schengen Information Services provisions the 'default' position operates and they are to be regarded as third pillar Acts based on Title VI of the Treaty on European Union: see Protocol 2, art 2.1.
2   Peers above, p 57.
3   Peers above, p 57.
4   Peers above, p 57.

EC Title IV

7.21 The implementation of Title IV is to be carried out by the Council on a five-year programme.[1] It must act unanimously.[2] During this time it must adopt measures in a number of fields, including immigration and asylum. Within this area the Council must adopt:

(a)   measures to complete the establishment of the internal market under Article 14 EC and to put in place directly related 'flanking' measures on external border controls, asylum and immigration, and measures to prevent and combat crime;[3]

(b)   other measures in the fields of asylum, immigration and safeguarding the rights of third-country nationals;[4]

(c)   measures in the field of judicial co-operation in civil matters as provided by Article 65;

(d)   measures to strengthen and encourage administrative co-operation, as set out in Article 66;

(e)   measures in the field of police and judicial co-operation in criminal matters.

The measures referred to in (c) to (e) are not immigration or asylum matters and we say no more about them.

1   Article 61(a) EC. For the exceptions see **7.25** below. To date there have been over 15 proposals for community legislation under Title IV.
2   Article 67 EC. For the exceptions see **7.23** below.
3   Article 61(a) EC.
4   Article 61(b) EC.

7.22   Article 62 EC provides that the Council shall adopt within five years:

(1)   measures with a view to ensuring, in compliance with Article 14, the absence of any controls on persons, whether citizens of the Union or nationals of third countries, when crossing internal borders;

(2)   measures on the crossing of the external borders of the member states which shall establish:

    (a)   standards and procedures to be followed by member states in carrying out checks on persons at such borders;

    (b)   rules on visas for intended stays of no more than three months, including:

        (i)   the list of third countries whose nationals must be in possession of visas when crossing the external borders and those whose nationals are exempt from that requirement;

        (ii)   the procedures and conditions for issuing visas by member states;

        (iii)   a uniform format for visas;

        (iv)   rules on a uniform visa;

(3)   measures setting out the conditions under which nationals of third countries shall have the freedom to travel within the territory of the member states during a period of no more than three months.

This Article complements Article 14 EC (ex Article 7a) and provides the legal base for the measures which the Community will need to take in order to achieve the goal of abolishing internal borders. But its provisions also match closely the bulk of Articles 2 to 27 of the Schengen Convention 1990, and it is no surprise that the bulk of these provisions have in fact been allocated by the Council, when it allocated the Schengen *acquis,* to parts of Article 62.[1] If Article 14 still has any independent legal effect separate from Title IV, it will be open to all national courts and tribunals in all member states to refer questions to the ECJ for interpretation. In respect of Article 62 the jurisdiction of the ECJ is much more limited, as we shall see.[2]

1   Final decision on allocation of Schengen *acquis* OJ 1999 L 176/17. A few of the provisions on legal and illegal migration were allocated to Article 63(3) EC.
2   **7.39** below.

7.23   Article 62 (2) (b) (i) and (ii) EC, which deal with common visas, re-enact ex-Article 100C, which was repealed by the Amsterdam Treaty. This was one of the areas which was under Community competence after the Treaty on European Union and was subject to two binding regulations: Council Regulation (EC) 1683/95 on a uniform visa format and Council Regulation (EC) 539/01 on the list of third-country nationals who need visas to enter the EC.[1] Both are binding on all EU member states, including the UK and Ireland. So far as relevant they are printed in the Appendix. Ex-Article 100C was limited, as is Article 62(2)(b)(i), to visas 'when crossing the external borders'. In 1998 the ECJ held that the Article was not drafted widely enough to enable joint measures on the airside transit visa (ATV).[2] According to a Commission working paper, Article 62 may not be wide enough to accommodate a proposed regulation on the same subject,[3] because the relevant subsections are taken from ex-Article 100C. In framing new measures under Article 62, the Council may act on a qualified majority on a proposal from the Commission and after consultation with the European Parliament.[4] This contrasts with the position on the rest of Title IV, which requires Council unanimity.[5]

1   Council Regulation (EC) 574/99 is replaced by Council Regulation (EC) 539/01 of 15 March 2001.
2   Case C-170/96 *EU Commission v EU Council* [1998] 2 CMLR 1092.
3   Commission Staff Working Paper on Visa Policy, 16 July 1999, SEC (1999) 1213, para 6. Initiative of Finland with a view to adoption of Council Regulation on airport transit arrangements 10867/99 DGH1.
4   Article 67(3) EC.
5   Article 67(1) EC.

7.24   As regards asylum, Article 63 EC requires the Council to adopt within five years:

(1)   Measures of asylum in accordance with the Refugee Convention of 1951 and the Protocol of 1967 and other relevant treaties, within the following areas:
   (a)   criteria and mechanisms for determining which member state is responsible for considering an asylum application submitted by a third country national in one of the member states;
   (b)   minimum standards on the reception of asylum seekers in member states;
   (c)   minimum standards with respect to the qualification of nationals of third countries as refugees;
   (d)   minimum standards on procedures in member states for granting or withdrawing refugee status.
(2)   Measures on refugees and displaced persons within the following areas:
   (a)   minimum standards for giving temporary protection to displaced persons from third countries who cannot return to their country of origin and for persons who otherwise need international protection;

(b)   promoting a balance of effort between member states in receiving and bearing the consequences of receiving refugees and displaced persons.

These provisions have been drafted with many of the pre-existing EU asylum measures in mind. Article 63(1)(a) EC refers to the Dublin Convention;[1] Article 63(1)(b) EC to the aborted Joint Position; 63 (1) (c) EC to the 1996 Joint Position and so forth.[2] The only part of Article 63 EC which is not matched by previous efforts under the EU is Article 63(2)(a) EC which clearly refers to subsidiary protection. A number of the paragraphs refer to the adoption of minimum standards, and it is clear that the Council will not be aiming for complete harmonisation of national law in this area.[3] In line with this, the Council has produced a proposed directive entitled 'Minimum standards on procedures in member states for granting and withdrawing refugee status'.[4] Then there is Protocol 6, which deals with asylum for EC nationals, and, although drafted in general terms, it is designed to prevent Belgium considering asylum claims by Basque nationalists whom Spain wishes to try for terrorist offences.[5]

1   Text at *Butterworths Immigration Law Service*, 2D[81]. The Dublin Convention entered into force on 1 October 1997, Austria and Spain joining on 1 December 1997 and Finland on 1 January 1998.
2   See Peers **7.12** above, p 127.
3   Peers above, p 127.
4   21 September 2000.
5   Peers **7.12** above, p 129.

7.25 Title IV does not provide for Community powers over every aspect of immigration policy and the precise scope is still a matter for debate.[1] Legal and illegal migration is now addressed in Articles 63(3) and (4) of the EC Treaty. Article 63(3) enables the Council to adopt measures on immigration policy within the following areas:

(a)   conditions of entry and residence, and standards on procedures for the issue by member states of long term visas and residence permits, including those for the purpose of family reunion;
(b)   illegal immigration and illegal residence, including repatriation of illegal residents.

The five-year deadline does not apply to the burden sharing provision in Article 63(2)(b) or to Article 63(3)(a) and (4).[2]

1   See Hailbronner 'European Immigration and Asylum Law after the Amsterdam Treaty' (1998) 35 CMLR 1047; 'Treaty of Amsterdam and Migration Law' (1999) EHML 12; Monat 'Justice and Home Affairs in the Treaty of Amsterdam' (1998) 23 ELR EV 320; Peers **7.12** above, pp 100-101.
2   Article 63 EC.

7.26 In dealing with the new powers, it should also be noted that all the pre-Amsterdam EC law competences on migration still apply, including the working conditions of third country nationals after the integration of the Agreement on Social Policy into the main EC Treaty under Article 137(3) EC. In *El-Yassini* the ECJ ruled that, in some circumstances, immigration status falls within the concept of 'working conditions'.[1] Lastly it should be noted that Article 64 EC substantially re-enacts the 'national safeguard' clauses contained in ex Article 100C(2) and (5). These are no longer confined to safeguards on visas, but cover the whole Title IV package, providing for Council measures to meet a 'sudden inflow' to any particular member state of third country nationals[2] and to make clear that Title IV does not affect member states' responsibility for the maintenance of law and order and safeguarding its own internal security.[3]

1 Case C-416/96 *El-Yassini* [1999] ECR I-1209.
2 Article 62(2) EC.
3 Article 64(1) EC.

UK and Ireland

7.27 Notwithstanding the integration of the Schengen *acquis* into the framework of the EU and all the new EC provisions in Title IV enabling the Community to issue regulations and directives on immigration, asylum and the common visa, the UK and Ireland have opted out for the time being and decided not to surrender sovereignty over immigration and asylum policy, but to keep their own systems of immigration control. This is done in a number of ways. First, Protocol 2, which integrates the Schengen *acquis* into the framework of the EU, gives the UK and Ireland an extraordinary 'opt out, opt in' position. The Protocol recognises that neither country is a party to the Schengen Agreements and that they should, therefore, be allowed 'to accept some or all of the provisions thereof'. So Article 4 provides that the UK and Ireland may at any time request to take part in some or all of its provisions. The Council must then make a unanimous decision on the request.[1] The two countries may also be allowed to take part in proposals and initiatives to build upon the Schengen *acquis*.[2]

1 Protocol 2, art 4.
2 Protocol 2, art 5. So far the UK has indicated that it wishes to take part in the criminal and policing rules of the Schengen *acquis*, except for cross-border pursuits, with related Schengen Information Services access, plus arts 26 (carriers' liability) and 27 (illegal immigration), but not in any of the other immigration or asylum matters. This was agreed by the EC Council on 2 December 1999, except for the territorial scope and partial access to Schengen Information Systems.

7.28 Secondly, Protocol 3, which is annexed to both Treaties, specifically exempts the UK[1] and Ireland[2] from any EC laws or measures requiring the abolition of border controls and allows them to exercise frontier control over persons seeking to enter.[3] It further entitles the UK and Ireland to maintain the common travel area and to check individuals coming from other member states, no matter what the Treaties say or what measures other member states may take.[4] It allows other member states to have reciprocal control on persons seeking to enter their territory from Ireland or the UK.[5]

1 Protocol 3, art 1.
2 Protocol 3, art 2. The exemption of Ireland is conditional on the continuance of the common travel area.
3 Protocol 3, art 1.
4 Protocol 3, art 2.
5 Protocol 3, art 3.

7.29 The third exempting measure is Protocol 4, which deals with the position of the UK and Ireland as regards new Title IV of the EC Treaty. It provides that the UK and Ireland are to take no part in the adoption of the new Community legislation under Title IV on immigration, asylum or visas,[1] unless either or both have notified the President of the Council that they wish to do so.[2] Neither country is bound by any of the provisions of Title IV of the Treaty establishing the EC, any measure adopted pursuant to that Title, or provision of any international agreement concluded by the Community pursuant to it, or any decision of the ECJ interpreting any such provision or measure.[3] They only become bound if they notify the Council and Commission that they wish to accept an immigration or asylum measure already adopted by the Council.[4] They can do so at any time. The Commission then has three months in which to give an opinion to the Council and a further month in which to make a decision whether to accept the British or Irish request and to make any necessary arrangements.[5] In March 1999 the UK government indicated that in principle it would opt into all civil co-operation and asylum measures, along with many immigration and external border control ones.[6] In a similar vein, Ireland has stated that it will opt into Title IV measures 'to the maximum extent compatible with the maintenance of its common travel area with the United Kingdom'.[7] Where the UK or Ireland is bound by any measure, the relevant provisions of the EC Treaty, including those relating to the ECJ, shall apply to that country in respect of that measure.[8] If Ireland wishes to opt out of Protocol 4 and be bound by Title IV, it can do so by a simple written notification to the President of the Council.[9] A separate Protocol exempts Denmark in much the same way as the UK and Ireland, except that it is not exempted from measures relating to a common entry visa.[10] Because it is already one of the Schengen countries, special provision is made for Denmark with regard to proposals or initiatives to build on the Schengen *acquis* by adopting new Community legislation under Title IV.[11]

1 Protocol 4, art 1.
2 Protocol 4, art 3.
3 Protocol 4, art 2.
4 Protocol 4, art 4.
5 Article 11 (3) EC, as adapted by Protocol 3, art 4.
6 Peers **12.1** above, p 55.
7 Unilateral Declaration 4 to Amsterdam Treaty; see *Butterworths Immigration Law Service*, at F[281].
8 Protocol 4, art 6.
9 Protocol 4, art 8.
10 Protocol 5, art 4.
11 Protocol 5, art 5.

THE APPLICATION OF EC FREE MOVEMENT LAW

7.30 There are three principal ways in which effect is given to EC law in the domestic legal systems of member states: (i) the enactment of national measures to give effect to Community obligations; (ii) the duty of national courts to interpret general legislation to conform with Community obligations; and (iii) finally, the doctrine of direct effect, where aggrieved individuals can rely on the Community duty as directly applicable, although not specifically so enacted. There is an inter-relationship between the three. In the area of free movement, for example, we find effect being given to EC law by section 7 of the Immigration Act 1988, by the Immigration Rules, and by the Immigration (European Economic Area) Regulations 2000.[1] At the same time, measures of EC law are directly applicable, in ways we explore below. Thirdly, UK courts are bound by Community jurisprudence to interpret all measures within the field of Community competence in accordance with the principles and policy of the Community obligation giving rise to these measures. This has been described as the 'teleological' principle of construction, frequently at odds with the common law concept of strict statutory construction.[2] Courts must interpret all statutes and inferior measures, whether passed before or after the obligation arose, so that they accord with the requirements of Community law, if it is possible to do so without distortion.[3] This principle of construction has now been adopted for UK courts dealing with human rights by section 3 of the Human Rights Act 1998.[4]

1 SI 2000/2326.
2 See Lord Denning in *James Buchanan & Co Ltd v Babco Forwarding and Shipping (UK) Ltd* [1977] 1 All ER 518 at 522, CA; *Freight Transport Association Ltd v London Borough Transport Committee* [1991] 3 All ER 915, [1991] 1 WLR 828, HL; *R v Secretary of State for the Home Department, ex p Adams* [1995] All ER (EC) 177, DC.
3 *Duke v GEC Reliance Ltd* [1988] AC 618, [1988] 1 All ER 626, HL; Case C-106/89 *Marleasing SA v La Comercial Internacional de Alimentacion SA* [1990] ECR I-4135, [1992] 1 CMLR 305, ECJ.
4 It has been described as a 'new canon of interpretation' and 'a strong adjuration' by Lord Cooke in *R v DPP, ex p Kebeline* [1999] 4 All ER 801, at 837.

National measures

7.31 In the UK, the duty of giving effect to EC Treaty rights is achieved by the European Communities Act 1972. The Act has been extensively amended as the Community has developed from Common Market to European Union. The latest amendments are by the European Communities (Amendment) Act 1998, which makes provision as a consequence of the Treaty of Amsterdam. The key sections of the 1972 Act, as amended, are set out in the Appendix. We do not print those parts of the amending Acts of 1993 or 1998 which stand alone, because they do not relate to free movement of persons.[1] The European Economic Area Act 1993[2] was passed to make provision in respect of the EEA following the Agreement on the European Economic Area of 2 May 1992 and Protocol of 17 March 1993. The 1992 Agreement is a Community Treaty and has direct effect by virtue of the 1972 Act.[3] Section 2 of the European Economic Area Act 1993 makes provision for a consistent application of EC law to the whole of the EEA, and section 3 ensures that implementing Orders in Council, passed under the powers set out in the 1972 Act, apply to the EEA.

1 See 17 *Halsbury's Statutes* (4th edn) for the full text of all relevant statutes.
2 17.
3 See European Communities Act 1972, ss 1 and 2.

7.32 By section 2 of the European Communities Act 1972, provision is made for regulations and directives of the EEC to have effect in the UK. This means that Community legislation is directly applicable in accordance with the principles discussed at **7.34-7.36** below. It creates rights which British courts must protect. The UK government initially sought to implement the free movement directives by provisions in the Immigration Rules relating to EC nationals. But this was woefully inadequate; it left in place the statutory regime of requiring EC nationals to obtain leave to enter, which was a breach of Community law.[1] The right to enter for a Community purpose flows directly from EC law rather than from permission given by an official. Thus a residence permit issued under Community law is only evidence of this right and not the source of it.[2] Visas and other formalities not envisaged by Community law cannot be required; under EC law the only formal requirement at the frontier is production of a passport or national identity document.[3] This fundamental principle of EC law was eventually given effect in UK statute law by section 7 of the Immigration Act 1988, which expressly absolved EC nationals from the need to obtain leave when exercising enforceable Community law rights,[4] and enabled the Secretary of State for the Home Department to make provision for a limited period of automatic leave to be given to EC nationals who do not benefit from an EC free movement right. Section 7 was not brought into force until the Immigration (European Economic Area) Order 1994 took effect on 20 July 1994.[5] Now the main implementing measure is the Immigration (European Economic Area) Regulations 2000,[6] which came into effect on 2 October 2000.

1 See especially Case C-157/79 *R v Pieck* [1981] QB 571, [1981] 3 All ER 46, ECJ; Case 321/87 *Commission v Belgium* [1989] ECR 997, [1990] 2 CMLR 492, ECJ.
2 *R v Pieck* above; *Commission v Belgium* above; Case C-59/85 *Netherlands v Reed* [1986] ECR 1283, [1987] 2 CMLR 448; Case C-357/89 *Raulin v Minister van Onderwijs en Wetenschappen* [1992] ECR I-1027, [1994] 1 CMLR 227, ECJ.
3 See Council Directive (EEC) 68/360, art 3; Immigration (European Economic Area) Order 1994, SI 1994/1895, art 12.
4 See Immigration Act 1988, s 12(3) and (4) and the Immigration Act 1988 (Commencement No 1) Order 1988, SI 1988/1133.
5 SI 1994/1923.
6 SI 2000/2326, as amended by the Amendment Regulations SI 2001/865.

Direct effect

7.33 The doctrine of direct effect began as a way of bringing into effect provisions of the common market Treaties, even though member states were dragging their feet over completion of timetables set out in the Treaties. Once the timetable for implementation has expired, the doctrine allows aggrieved individuals or institutions to seek direct implementation of a Community measure against the state or its emanations if the obligation is sufficiently precise to be capable of direct enforcement.[1] This is the so-called vertical effect, as opposed to the horizontal effect, which applies when one private citizen or corporation sues another.[2] Plainly, individuals who have free movement rights under Community law which the UK has failed to implement may invoke the direct applicability of the measure, and thus come within its 'vertical effect'. Recent decisions in the national courts suggest that direct effect may be relied on by organisations such as the Equal Opportunities Commission, as well as individuals aggrieved by particular decisions.[3]

1 Case 26/62 *Algemene Transport-en Expeditie Onderneming van Gend & Loos NV v Nederlandse administratie der belastingen* [1963] ECR 1, [1963] CMLR 105, ECJ; Case 104/81 *Hauptzollamt Mainz v C A Kupferberg & Cie KG* [1982] ECR 3641, [1983] 1 CMLR 1, ECJ; Case 152/84 *Marshall v Southampton and South West Hampshire Area Health Authority* [1986] ECR 723, [1986] 1 CMLR 688, ECJ; Case C-188/89 *Foster v British Gas* [1991] 2 AC 306, [1991] 2 All ER 705, HL; *Webb v EMO Air Cargo (UK) Ltd* [1992] 4 All ER 929, [1993] 1 WLR 49, HL; Case C-127/92 *Enderby v Frenchay Health Authority* [1994] 1 All ER 495, [1994] 1 CMLR 8, ECJ. Article 39 (ex Art 48) EC may also have horizontal effect: see Case 36/74 *Walrave* [1974] ECR 1405.

2 See *Angonese Cassa di Risparmio di Bolzano SpA* Case C-281/98 [2000] All ER (EC) 577, where the ECJ stated at para 36 that the prohibition of discrimination in art 39 EC (ex art 48) applies to private persons as well as public bodies; see also Case 36/74 *Walrave and Koch v Association Union Cycliste Int* [1974] ECR 1405, para 16 (rules made by private persons or bodies aimed at regulating gainful employment in a collective manner); *Bosman* [1995] ECR I-4821, at paras 84 and 87 (agreements or acts concluded by private persons or bodies which determine the terms on which professional sportsmen can engage in professional sport); Joined Cases C-51/96 and C-191/97 *Deliège* and *Lehtonen* 11 April 2000 (judo and basketball rules); *Wilander v Tobin* [1997] 2 CMLR 346, CA (rules of Tennis Federation regarding drugs).

3 *R v Secretary of State for Employment, ex p Equal Opportunities Commission* [1995] 1 AC 1, [1994] 1 All ER 910, HL. The decisions on *locus standi* in judicial review have also established that representative organisations with a proven interest in the subject-matter of the decision may be able to challenge decisions on grounds of Community law: *R v Inspectorate of Pollution, ex p Greenpeace* [1994] 4 All ER 321, [1994] 1 WLR 570, CA; *R v Secretary of State for the Environment, ex p Friends of the Earth Ltd* [1994] 2 CMLR 760. It is possible that an organisation such as the Joint Council for the Welfare of Immigrants or ILPA could seek judicial review of Immigration Rules that were not in accordance with Community law.

Direct effect of Treaty obligations

7.34 Articles 39, 43 and 50 EC (ex Articles 48, 52 and 60) are now directly applicable.[1] The free movement provisions contained within them are subject to important qualifications which give member states an element of discretion in enforcement, on grounds of public policy, public security or public health. However, the ECJ has ruled that this is no bar to the direct effectiveness of these provisions.[2] There is a distinction between obligations which are sufficiently precise to be binding and those which have the character of a general programme or aspiration. The existence of direct effect turns on the context of the Article in question, so similar words in different measures may result in different interpretations as to direct effect. Thus the provisions for free movement in the EC/Turkish Association Agreement were held not to be capable of direct effect notwithstanding the expiry of the transitional period, whereas the specific decisions of the Association Council established under that Agreement could be if they produced clear and precise obligations not subject to the adoption of any subsequent measure.[3] In *Savas*[4] the court held that a standstill provision in Article 41(1) of the Additional Protocol to the Turkish Agreement was of direct effect, which means that the UK has to apply the 1973 business rules to Turkish business people seeking to establish themselves in the UK. In *El-Yassini*[5] an anti-discrimination clause, art 40 of the EC Moroccan Cooperation Agreement, was held to be of direct effect. The ECJ has held that a provision in an agreement with non-member states is directly effective when, regard being had to its wording and the purpose and nature of the agreement, the provision contains a precise and clear obligation which is not subject in its implementation or effects to the adoption of any subsequent measure.[6] In *Gloszczuk*[7] the ECJ held that Article 44 of the Polish Association Agreement gives a directly effective right of establishment in an EU member state, in that case the UK. Attempts have been made to argue that Articles 14 EC (ex Article 7a) (removal of internal borders) and 18 EC (ex Article 8a) (right of EU citizen to move and reside freely within the territory of member states) are also of direct effect, but so far unsuccessfully. Article 14 has been very much overshadowed by the integration of the Schengen *acquis* into the framework of the EU and of the transfer of the border control and visa provisions of the third pillar (Title VI EU) into Title IV

EC.[8] Article 18 may be different. The English courts have said it is not of direct effect.[9] This view is unsustainable in the light of subsequent developments in EC law, and is contradicted by the emerging opinions of the ECJ's Advocates General[10] and by commentators.[11]

1 Case 2/74 *Reyners v Belgium* [1974] ECR 631, [1974] 2 CMLR 305, ECJ; Case 33/74 *Van Binsbergen v Bestuur van de Bedrijfsvereniging voor de Metaalnijverheid* [1974] ECR 1299, [1975] 1 CMLR 298, ECJ. If a provision of national law is incompatible with a directly applicable provision of the EEC Treaty and is retained unchanged, this in itself constitutes an infringement of the Treaty: Case 168/85 *Commission v Italy* [1986] ECR 2945, [1988] 1 CMLR 580, ECJ; Case 147/86 *Commission v Greece* [1988] ECR 1637, [1989] 2 CMLR 845, ECJ. For the superior position of EC law in the UK see Case C-213/89 *R v Secretary of State for Transport, ex p Factortame (No 2)* [1991] 1 AC 603, [1990] ECR I-2433, ECJ and *(No 3)* [1992] QB 680, [1991] ECR I-3905, ECJ.
2 Case 41/74 *Van Duyn v Home Office (No 2)* [1974] ECR 1337, [1975] 1 CMLR 1, ECJ. See further on direct applicability of arts 59 and 60 EC Case 33/74 *Van Binsbergen v Bestuur van de Bedrijfsvereniging voor de Metaalnijverheid* [1974] ECR 1299, [1975] 1 CMLR 298, ECJ.
3 Case 12/86 *Demirel v Stadt Schwäbisch Gmünd* [1987] ECR 3719, [1989] 1 CMLR 421, ECJ; Case C-192/89 *Sevince v Staatsecretaris van Justitie* [1990] ECR I-3461, [1992] 2 CMLR 57, ECJ; *R v Secretary of State for the Home Department, ex p Narin* [1990] 2 CMLR 233, CA; Case C-237/91 *Kus v Landeshauptstadt Wiesbaden* [1992] ECR I-6781, [1993] 2 CMLR 887, ECJ. See also Case C-312/91 *Metalsa Srl v Public Prosecutor (Italy)* [1994] 2 CMLR 121, ECJ where the court gave a different interpretation to a provision of the Austria/EC Agreement identical to the EEC Treaty.
4 *R v Secretary of State for the Home Department, ex p Savas* Case C-37/98 [2000] 1 WLR 1828; see 7.157 below.
5 *El-Yassini v Secretary of State for the Home Department* Case C-416/96 [1999] ECR I-1209, ECJ.
6 Case C-432/92 *R v MAFF, ex p Anastasiou (Pissouri) Limited* [1995] 1 CMLR 569, ECJ (Original Protocol to EEC Cyprus Association Agreement held to be of direct effect).
7 Case C-63/99 *R v Secretary of State for the Home Department, ex p Glosczuk*, 14 September 2000 (A-G's opinion).
8 Case C-378/97 *Wijenbeek* (1999) Times, 12 October, ECJ; *R v Secretary of State for the Home Department, ex p Rizrani* [1995] Imm AR 396, QBD (CA unreported); *R v Secretary of State for the Home Department, ex p Flynn* [1995] 3 CMLR 397, QBD.
9 *Phull v Secretary of State for the Home Department* [1996] Imm AR 72, CA: *R v Secretary of State for the Home Department, ex p Vitale* [1996] All ER (EC) 461, CA.
10 Case C-85/96 *Sala v Freistaat Bayern* [1998] ECR I-2691, ECJ: Case C-378/97 *Wijsenbeek* (1999) Times, 12 October, ECJ; Case C-274/96 *Bickel and Franz* [1998] ECR I-7637, A-G's opinion, paras 22–25, ECJ at para 15.
11 Martin and Guild *Free Movement of Persons in the European Union* (1996). See 7.56 below.

Direct effect of regulations and directives

7.35 The position with regulations and directives is simpler. Under Article 249 EC (ex Article 189), regulations are 'binding in their entirety and take direct effect in each member state', and directives are 'binding as to the result to be achieved'. As regards regulations, this means that they are to be treated as law, and national courts must take judicial notice of them in their entirety. Depending on their proper interpretation, specific provisions may bestow on individuals rights as against other individuals or a member state.[1] Although there is no mention of directives having direct effect, a series of court decisions has in effect put them on exactly the same footing as regulations. In Case 41/74 *Van Duyn v Home Office (No 2)*[2] the ECJ stated that a directive which itself imposed substantive obligations could be directly effective. Otherwise the 'useful effect' of the directive would be weakened. What this means in practice is that Community rules are to be enforced by national courts and take precedence over the provisions of national law. This was stated quite clearly by the ECJ in *Rutili v Minister for the Interior*,[3] where the court referred to some of the free movement provisions contained in directives and said:

> 'The effect of all these provisions, without exception, is to impose duties on member states, and it is, accordingly, for the courts to give the rules of the Community Law which may be pleaded before them precedence over the provisions of national law.' (paragraph 16.)

1 Case 43/71 *Politi v Italian Ministry of Finance* [1971] ECR 1039, para 9; Case 93/71 *Leonesio v Italian Ministry of Agriculture and Forestry* [1972] ECR 287 at 300. See Wyatt and Dashwood 7.5 fn 1, pp 84-88.
2 [1974] ECR 1337, [1975] 1 CMLR 1, ECJ.
3 Case 36/75 [1975] ECR 1219, [1976] 1 CMLR 140, ECJ. The superiority of Community law to municipal law, both common law and statutory, was exemplified most clearly in *R v Secretary of State for Transport, ex p Factortame (No 2)* [1991] 1 AC 603, [1991] 1 All ER 70, HL. See further Case C-473/93 *EC Commission v Luxembourg* [1997] ECR I-3207, [1996] 3 CMLR 981, para 37; *Orfinger v Belgium* [2000] 1 CMLR 612, paras 8-10, Belgian Conseil d'Etat.

7.36 In *Re Watson and Belmann*[1] the court spelt out what was meant by the binding effect of both the Treaty provisions on free movement and the implementing regulations and directives:

> 'Article 48 of the Treaty and the measures adopted by the Community in application thereof implement a fundamental principle of the Treaty, confer on persons whom they concern individual rights which the national courts must protect and take precedence over any national rule which might conflict with them.'

1 Case 118/75 [1976] ECR 1185, [1976] 2 CMLR 552, ECJ.

The European Court of Justice

7.37 Where a member state fails to fulfil an obligation under the EC Treaty, it may be taken to task by the Commission[1] or another member state[2] before the ECJ. Without going into detail on the available sanctions, one remedy which the ECJ has endorsed is that damages can be awarded to aggrieved individuals, where a member state fails to implement a directive.[3] Public law bodies may also be liable for damages, instead of or in addition to central government.[4]

1 Article 222 EC (ex Art 169).
2 Article 227 EC (ex Art 170).
3 Case C-6, 9/90 *Francovich and Bonifaci v Italy* [1991] ECR I-5357, [1993] 2 CMLR 66, superseding the dicta to the contrary in *Bourgoin SA v MAFF* [1986] QB 716, [1985] 3 All ER 585. See also Case C-334/92 *Wagner Miret v Fondo de Garantía Salarial* [1993] ECR I-6911; *R v HM Treasury v British Telecommunications* Case C-392/93 [1996] All ER (EC) 411, [1996] 2 CMLR 217, ECJ; C-46 and 48/93 *Brasserie du Pêcheur v Germany, Factortame v UK* [1996] QB 404, [1996] 1 CMLR 889, ECJ, Case C-594 *R v MAFF, ex p Hedley Lomas* [1997] QB 139, [1996] ECR I-2553, ECJ; Case C-178-190/94 [1997] QB 259, [1996] All ER (EC) 917, ECJ; cf *ex p Gallagher (No 2)* [1996] 2 CMLR 951, CA (damages refused, because no causal link between the violation and exclusion of the EU national).
4 Case C-424/97 *Haim v Kassenzahnarztliche Vereinigong Nordrhein*, 4 July 2000, ECJ.

7.38 The clear effect of the EC Treaty and the ECJ decisions is that national courts must apply Community law. Where doubtful points about the effect of Community law arise, they can be settled by a reference of the point to the ECJ under Article 234 EC (ex Article 177).[1] A reference can be made by any court or independent tribunal, if it considers that a decision on the question is necessary to enable it to give judgment. In the UK, magistrates' courts, adjudicators and the Immigration Appeal Tribunal have made references,[2] and clearly have a discretion to do so.[3] If a reference is made by the High Court, English legal service funding will usually be available to cover the reference proceedings. On a reference by an adjudicator or the Immigration Appeal Tribunal, it is open to the ECJ to grant legal service funding if the case is not covered by controlled legal help or representation.[4] The decision whether to make a reference to the ECJ where a Community law point requires determination is discretionary, save in courts against whose decisions there is no judicial remedy under national law.[5] Where a reference is inevitable it should be made as soon as possible to avoid extra delay.[6] The criteria for a reference by a national court, other than a final Court of Appeal, have been set out by the Master of the Rolls in *R v International Stock Exchange of the United Kingdom and the Republic of Ireland Ltd, ex p Else*:[7]

> 'If the facts have been found and the Community law issue is critical to the court's final decision, the appropriate course is ordinarily to refer the issue to the Court of Justice itself unless the national court can with complete confidence resolve the issue itself. In considering whether it can with complete confidence resolve the issue itself, the national court must be fully mindful of the differences between national and Community legislation, of the pitfalls which face a national court venturing into what may be an unfamiliar field, of the need for uniform interpretation throughout the Community and of the great advantages enjoyed by the Court of Justice in construing Community instruments. If the national court has any real doubt it should refer.'

1   See CPR Schedule 1, RSC Ord 114 for the procedure for a reference in the High Court. A reference need not be made if the question is *acte claire* or the issues can be disposed of without determining the point of Community law: *R v Plymouth Justices, ex p Rogers* [1982] QB 863, [1982] 2 All ER 175, QBD; *Polydor Ltd and RSO Records Inc v Harlequin Record Shops and Simons Records* [1980] 2 CMLR 413, CA; *R v Henn and Darby* [1980] AC 850, [1980] 2 All ER 166, HL; *HP Bulmer Ltd v J Bollinger SA* [1974] Ch 401, [1974] 2 All ER 1226, CA; Case 166/73 *Rheinmühlen Düsseldorf v Einfuhrñund Vorratsstelle für Getreide und Futtermittel* [1974] ECR 33, [1974] 1 CMLR 523, ECJ. Even if the meaning of an instrument seems clear to the national court, it may still make a reference, if it considers it appropriate to do so by reason of the importance of the issue raised or otherwise: *CILFIT Srl v Ministry of Health* [1982] ECR 3415.

2   Case 30/77 *R v Bouchereau* [1978] QB 732, [1977] ECR 1999, ECJ (magistrates court); Case C-356/98 *Kaba v Secretary of State for the Home Department* [2000] All ER (EC) 537, ECJ (adjudicator); Case C-416/96 *El-Yassini v Secretary of State for the Home Department* [1999] ECR I-1209 (adjudicator); *Baumbast* (21263) IAT; Case C-60/00 *Carpender*, IAT.

3   *R v Immigration Appeal Tribunal, ex p Antonissen* [1992] Imm AR 196; *El-Yassini* above; Case C-195/98 *Osterreichischer Gewerkschaftsbund v Republik Osterreich*, 30 November 2000, ECJ.

4   Dine, Douglas-Good and Derscard, *Procedure in the European Court* (1991) p 55.

5   Article 234 EC (ex Art 177). Usually in the UK this is the House of Lords, the Privy Council in devolution cases, and the High Court of Justiciary in Scottish criminal cases, from which there is no right of appeal to the HL: *McIntosh v Lord Advocate* (1876) 2 App Cas 41.

6   *R v Pharmaceutical Society of Great Britain and Secretary of State for Social Services, ex p Association of Pharmaceutical Importers* [1987] 3 CMLR 951, CA.

7   [1993] QB 534 at 545. For the principles on which interim relief may be granted restraining the implementation of a national law pending a reference see *R v HM Treasury, ex p British Telecom plc* [1994] 1 CMLR 621.

7.39 Modifications have been made to the powers of the ECJ as a result of the Treaty of Amsterdam. Article 234 EC (ex Article 177) remains so far as the free movement provisions in Part III of the EC Treaty are concerned and all courts may make references. But when it comes to visas, immigration and asylum under

Title IV of the EC Treaty, the powers of national courts to make references are more limited. Under Article 68(1) EC only a court from which 'there is no judicial remedy under national law' can make a reference, and it must do so if a decision of the ECJ on the question is necessary to enable that court to give judgment. Requests can also be made by the Council, Commission or a member state for a ruling on the interpretation of Title IV or of acts of the institutions of the Community based on it.[1] But where the EC has adopted measures requiring the abolition of internal border controls under Article 62(1) EC the ECJ has no jurisdiction to rule.[2] As regards the remaining third pillar in the EU Treaty (Title VI), the ECJ has a mandatory jurisdiction over dispute settlement, but its role still falls short of its role under the first pillar.[3] But the Treaty of Amsterdam has now formally granted the ECJ power to interpret the human rights clause contained in Article 6(2) EU (formerly art F(2)), a power which it did not previously possess. Article 45 EU now allows the ECJ jurisdiction over Article 6(2) EU with regard to actions of the institutions, insofar as the court has jurisdiction under the Treaties establishing the European Communities and under the Treaty on European Union. No doubt this is a purely formal amendment (see **7.40** below), but it still has symbolic importance. As regards the Schengen *acquis*, the ECJ has the powers it otherwise has under the relevant applicable provisions of the Treaties once the Council has determined the legal basis for each of the provisions or decisions which constitute the Schengen *acquis*, except that it has no jurisdiction on measures or decisions relating to the maintenance of law and order or the safeguarding of internal security.[4]

1   Article 68 (3) EC.
2   Article 68 (2) EC.
3   See Peers **7.12** above, pp 46-48.
4   Protocol 2, art 2.1.

European Court of Justice and human rights

7.40 The European Community is under an obligation, contained in Article 6(2) EU, to respect fundamental rights as guaranteed by the ECHR as general principles of Community law. The Treaty of Amsterdam has now brought Article 6(2) directly within the jurisdiction of the ECJ. This is a formal rather than a substantive change.[1] Though it means that the court can interpret and apply the different rights and freedoms contained in the ECHR, the court is not bound to follow Strasbourg case law or to have regard to it, and has not always done so.[2] ECJ decisions cannot be challenged before the Strasbourg court, since Article 34 of the ECHR only allows complaints against one of the High Contracting Parties and not against the EU or Community.[3] Individual recourse to the ECJ is very limited,[4] and offers no realistic possibility of challenge to the provisions of EC law or the implementation of any measure, which is in breach of the ECHR. The ECHR has made it clear that anyone wishing to go to Strasbourg on an EC law issue will face formidable hurdles. First, in *Matthews v UK*[5] the court has stated that acts of the EC as such cannot be challenged before the court, because the Community is not a contracting party. However, the court went on to rule that in certain circumstances an individual could bring complaints against a member state for a failure to secure Convention rights for that individual as regards the implementation of EC law. *Matthews* dealt with the responsibility of contracting states as regards the provisions of the EC Treaties. The court reasoned that if the provision of a Treaty could not be challenged before the

ECJ, then the only available recourse would be before the court in Strasbourg. Normally, no such obstacle would apply in the case of directives or regulations. Can a member state be taken to task for failing to apply these? In *Cantoni v France*[6] the court suggests that there is a similar responsibility on member states to secure human rights as regards EC Council Directives, as in the case of Treaties. If the rationale for interference is not based on the fact that the ECJ has no jurisdiction, then there is no reason why Strasbourg competence should not extend to regulations and Council Directives as well. At least one commentator has remarked that while the ECJ has been criticised for overlooking relevant Strasbourg case law, the court in Strasbourg is capable of being equally at sea with EC law. Unlike UK courts fulfilling their new jurisdiction under the Human Rights Act 1998, there is no obligation on either of the European courts to have regard to the relevant case law of the other.[7]

1   The ECJ was already applying ECHR law: see the ERT case: *Elliniki Radiophonia Tileorassi AE v Pliroforissis and Kouvelas* Case C-260/89 [1994] 4 CMLR 540, ECJ.
2   Case 374/87 *Orkem v Commission* [1989] ECR 3283, ECJ. See Lord Hope 'Human Rights – where are we now?' [2000] EHRLR 439, where he discusses other cases of divergence.
3   See further *Matthews v UK* (1999) 28 EHRR 361.
4   Article 230 EC (ex Art 173).
5   *Matthews* above (case concerned voting rights in Gibraltar under art 3 of Protocol 1 of the ECHR).
6   *Cantoni v France* Appn 17862/91, 15 November 1996.
7   ILPA European Update (October 1999) p 8.

SCOPE OF FREE MOVEMENT RIGHTS

Territorial, personal and material scope

7.41 Entitlement to free movement rights depends on the *personal* and *territorial* scope of the EC and EEA Treaties. Thus art 47 of Council Regulation (EEC) 1612/68, the main regulation dealing with the free movement of workers and their families, applies the regulation to the territories of member states and to their nationals. If someone is within the *territorial* and *personal* scope of the Community provisions, questions then arise regarding rights of entry and residence of workers and their families or persons seeking to establish themselves, or questions whether and to what extent member states can discriminate on grounds of nationality or have conditions or requirements which hinder free movement. Rules regarding these questions fall within the *material* scope of Community law. We shall be mainly concerned with the personal and material scope of the Treaties, but the territorial scope assumes importance with regard to Overseas Countries and Territories, such as the Cayman Islands and places such as the Channel Islands, Isle of Man and Gibraltar.

Territorial scope

7.42 Article 299(1) EC (ex Article 227(1) applies the EC Treaty to the territories of each of the member states.[1] Article 299 (2) EC provides that it applies to the French Overseas Departments, the Azores, Madeira and the Canary Islands,[2] but the Council may adopt specific measures aimed at laying down the conditions of application of the Treaty to these regions, including common policies. When Spain joined the Community, Article 25 of the Treaty of Accession applied free movement rights to the Canary Islands, Ceuta and Melilla without derogation, but Andorra is outside Community territory.

1   The territorial scope of Community law is established by art 299 EC, but it should be noted that the territory which applies for free movement rights is not the same as the territory for customs' purposes: See Martin and Guild 7.34 above, p 48.
2   The Treaty of Amsterdam amends art 299 (2) EC and simplifies the position. In Case 148/77 *Hansen* [1979] 1 CMLR 604, the ECJ held that the provisions of the Treaty and derived rights apply automatically to the French overseas territories from 1 January 1960, inasmuch as they are an integral part of the French Republic, but that it always remains possible subsequently for specific measures to be adopted in order to meet the needs of those territories. This view was upheld in Case C-163/90 *Legros* [1992] ECR I-4625, ECJ. In 1964, Council Decision 64/350 applied the Treaty provisions regarding the right of establishment to these territories. In 1968, Decision 68/359 did the same for workers. In the light of *Hansen* and *Legros* and the latest amendment to former Article 227, these decisions seem unnecessary: see further Martin and Guild above, pp 182-183 on the position prior to the Treaty of Amsterdam.

7.43 Special arrangements for association with a number of countries and territories, which have special relations with Denmark, France, the Netherlands and the UK, are contained in Articles 182 to 187 EC (ex Articles 131 to 136a). They are, therefore, within the territorial scope of the EC Treaty for some purposes, although not generally for freedom of movement.[1] The countries and territories are Greenland, British Indian Ocean Territory, British Antarctic Territory, French Southern and Antarctic Territories, Pitcairn, British Virgin Islands, Bermuda, Cayman Islands and the Falkland Islands.[2] Apart from this list, no other countries or territories having a special relationship with the UK are included.[3] However, the Treaty applies to those European territories for whose external relations a member state is responsible.[4] This provision covers Gibraltar, and British Dependent Territories citizens with a Gibraltarian connection are included in the definition of a UK national for the purposes of the Treaty. But it does not cover the Sovereign Base Areas of the UK in Cyprus, nor the Faroe Islands.[5] It applies to the Channel Islands and the Isle of Man 'only to the extent necessary to ensure the implementation of the arrangements for those Islands' as set out in Protocol 3 to the Treaty of Accession of the UK to the EC. We have already dealt with the special position of the Islands in **6.8** above. In Italy, the Republic of San Marino is part of the customs territory of the EU, but is a state independent of Italy and for whose external relations Italy is not responsible, and is, therefore, outside the territorial scope of the EU. The same applies to the Vatican for the same reasons.[6] Lastly, the EC Treaty applies to the Åland Islands (Finland) in accordance with the arrangements set out in Protocol 2 to the Treaty of Accession for Austria, Finland and Sweden.[7]

1   Article 299 (3) EC (ex art 227 (3)).
2   Annex II to EC Treaty. Greenland was defined as an Overseas Country from 1 February 1985 by a Treaty amendment of 13 March 1984 (OJ L89 1.2.85 p 1); see Martin and Guild 7.34 fn 11 above, p 48, and is the subject of specific provisions detailed in Protocol 15 to the EC Treaty.
3   Article 299 (3) EC (ex art 227 (3)).
4   Article 299 (4) EC (ex art 227 (4)).
5   Article 299 (6) EC (ex art 227 (5)).
6   Martin and Guild 7.34 fn 11 above, p 48.
7   Article 299 (5) EC; OJ L75 4.4.95 p 18.

7.44 The geographical application of the EC Treaty is defined in Article 299 EC (ex Article 227), as we have seen, but that Article does not preclude

Community rules from having effects outside the territories of the Community.[1]
The European case law has consistently held that EC law may apply to
professional activities pursued outside Community territory, so long as the
employment relationship retains a sufficiently close link with the Community.
The starting premise is that in an employment relationship between a Community
undertaking and a national of another member state, the rules on freedom of
movement for workers (particularly those prohibiting discrimination on grounds
of nationality) are in principle applicable. The case law makes it clear that
their application in principle is not affected by the fact that the work is carried
out abroad, whether temporarily and occasionally,[2] or permanently and
exclusively.[3] The criterion for applying these rules to an employment relationship
existing abroad is the existence of a 'sufficiently close link with the Community'.
In *Boukhalfa*[4] the Advocate General's opinion was that it was a matter for the
national court to determine whether such a link actually exists. This, however,
was not endorsed by the ECJ, which concluded that a Belgian woman working
in the German embassy in Algeria, who was paid less than her German
colleagues, was sufficiently linked to German law as to come within the
Community provisions on discrimination. In determining the existence of the
link, the ECJ or national court will look at a number of factors, such as whether
the employment relationship was entered into by a EU national and an
undertaking of another member state, whether recruitment took place in a
member state, whether the Community worker was established in a member
state at the time of the recruitment, where the employer is established, whether
the contract of employment is governed by the law of a member state and so
forth.

1 Case C-214/94 *Boukhalfa v Germany* [1996] 3 CMLR 22, para 14.
2 Case 36/74 *Walrave & Koch* [1974] ECR 1405, ECJ; Case 237/83 *Prodest* [1984] ECR 3153, para 6.
3 Case 9/88 *Lopes Veiga* [1989] ECR 2989, [1991] 1 CMLR 217, para 15; Case C-60/93 *Aldewereld* [1994] ECR I-2991, para 14.
4 *Boukhalfa* above.

7.45 The Immigration (European Economic Area) Regulations 2000[1] do not
address the question of the territorial scope of the EC Treaty, but deal with
'qualified persons' purely in terms of the personal scope of the Treaties.
Regulations 12 and 14 give effect in UK domestic law to the right of admission
and right of residence of 'qualified persons' as regards the UK. The Channel
Islands and Isle of Man are within Community territory for customs purposes,[2]
but not for free movement and the provision of services. The 2000 Regulations
do not address the position of EEA nationals arriving in the UK under free
movement rights and moving on to one or other of the Islands. That is dealt
with under a different regime, as we have seen in chapter 6 above. Under the
various Orders in Council dealing with the Islands it is provided that EEA
nationals, who are entitled to enter and remain in the UK by virtue of an
enforceable Community right, do not need leave to enter or remain in that
particular Island.[3]

1 SI 2000/2326.
2 EC Treaty, Protocol 3, art 1.
3 Immigration Act 1988, s 7, as amended by Immigration (Isle of Man) Order 1991,
SI 1991/2630, Sch 1, Pt IV, para 2; Immigration (Guernsey) Order 1993, SI 1993/1796,
Sch 1, Pt III, para 2; Immigration (Jersey) Order 1993, SI 1993/1797, Sch 1, Pt III,
para 2.

PERSONAL SCOPE (1) NATIONALS

EU and EEA nationals

7.46 Although Article 39 EC (ex Article 48) refers only to 'workers' and does not contain any words limiting its application to nationals of a member state, the ECJ and the subsidiary regulations and directives have all made it clear that this provision may only be relied on by nationals of member states.[1] Articles 43 EC (ex Article 52) (right of establishment) and 49 EC (ex Article 59) (provision of services) are expressly limited to nationals of member states. To come within the personal scope of EC free movement rights someone must, therefore, be a national of an EU member state, which now qualifies them as an EU citizen under Article 17 EC (ex Article 8). Because the EEA Treaty extends EC free movement rights to all EEA nationals, being a national of an EEA state can properly be described as the main requirement to come within the personal scope of free movement rights. In this context, EEA nationals include UK nationals. However, as regards admission to the UK, a narrower definition of 'EEA nationals' applies. EEA nationals are nationals of all EEA states other than the UK, which were contracting parties to the Agreement on the European Economic Area of 2 May 1992 and its Brussels Protocol of 17 March 1993.[2] In due course the group will include Swiss nationals under the provisions of the EC/Switzerland Agreement of 1999.[3]

1   Council Regulation (EEC) 1612/68, arts 1 and 2; Council Directive (EEC) 68/360, art 1; Case 238/83 *Meade* [1984] ECR 2631; see Martin and Guild **7.34** fn 11 above, p 95.
2   Immigration (European Economic Area) Regulations 2000, SI 2000/2326, reg 2(1). The list of countries is set out at **7.3** above
3   See **7.3** above

7.47 This group broadly corresponds with those who are within the definition of a 'qualified person' in the UK's Immigration (European Economic Area) Regulations 2000[1], which give effect to obligations under the EC Treaty and the Agreement on the European Economic Area 1992. A 'qualified person' is any national of an EEA member state other than the UK, who is in the UK as a worker, self-employed person, provider of services, recipient of services, self-sufficient person, retired person, student, or a person who has ceased activity. Dependants and members of an EEA member's household are not qualified persons, but family members may be, in a very limited group of cases, where the qualified person has died.[2] We shall look at each of these categories in turn. In reading the 2000 Regulations, it is important to note their limitations. First, they are a national measure intended to give effect to Community law as regards entry into and stay in the UK. This is made clear by regulations 12 to 14. They do not, therefore, deal with the free movement rights of UK nationals, who wish to exercise their rights on the territories of other member states. 'Qualified persons' do not, therefore, include any UK nationals, unless they are dual nationals having the nationality of one of the other member states. Similarly, apart from the *Surinder Singh* situation, which is expressly dealt with by Regulation 11 (see **7.52**) they do not acknowledge that UK nationals who have exercised one or more of their Community rights in another member state may be covered by Community law on their return to the UK,[3] and may, for example, be 'workers'[4] entitled to the benefit of EC rules on non-discrimination and access to social security and welfare benefits. Thirdly, where they conflict with EC law, Community law prevails.

1 SI 2000/2326.
2 SI 2000/2326, reg 5(1)(h) and (4).
3 Case C-19/92 *Kraus* [1993] ECR I-1663 (obtaining qualifications recognised by EC law);
   Case C-370/90 *Singh* [1992] ECR I-4265, [1992] 3 All ER 798 (working on the territory
   of another member state).
4 All Community nationals, whatever their place of residence or nationality, who have
   exercised a free movement right and have worked in another member state come within
   art 48 EC and are to be classed as 'workers': see Case C-419/92 *Scholz* [1994] ECR I-505,
   [1994] 1 CMLR 873, ECJ; Case C-443/93 *Vougioukas* [1995] ECR I-4033.

7.48 Only nationals of a state party to the EEA Agreement can take direct
advantage of free movement rights. But there are circumstances, such as
membership of the family or household of an EEA national, that bring collateral
rights of free movement to non-nationals.[1] Nationality is the principal connecting
factor so far as natural persons are concerned, but it is inappropriate for
companies. Article 48 EC (ex Article 58) therefore provides that a company or
firm which has its registered office, central administration or principal place of
business within the Community will be treated in the same way as a natural
person who is a Community national. Companies so defined have the right of
establishment in the territory of another member state.[2] In some cases residence
in Community territory is required, in addition to nationality. Thus a period of
residence in the UK is necessary before British citizens from the Channel Islands
and Isle of Man can benefit from the free movement provisions.[3] Similarly,
nationals of Denmark who are resident in the Faroe Islands are outside the
personal scope of the EC Treaty.[4]

1 See **7.53** and **7.79ff** below.
2 Article 48 EC (ex art 58).
3 See **6.18** above.
4 Article 4 of Protocol 2 to Danish Act of Accession; see also Art 299(6)(a) EC (ex art 227).

7.49 Whether someone is or is not a national of a member state depends on
each state's municipal law.[1] The criteria for obtaining nationality vary from
state to state. In theory each state can unilaterally expand or reduce the scope
of the free movement provisions by changing its nationality law. Thus those
born in the UK after 1 January 1983 will not automatically acquire the free
movement rights they would have done following birth in the UK in the ten
years prior to that date.[2] Equally, it has been possible for member states on
joining the EC to create for EC purposes special definitions of nationality which
derive from, but are different to, the normal definition of nationality in that
state's municipal law. The issue has not yet presented real problems, except for
Germany[3] and the UK. In the UK the problem arises because British nationality
is subdivided into a number of different citizenships which carry different
immigration rights.

1 See *Oppenheimer v Cattermole* [1976] AC 249, [1975] 1 All ER 538, HL; *Stoeck v Public
   Trustee* [1921] 2 Ch 67; *(Mahaboob) Bibi v Secretary of State for the Home Department*
   [1987] Imm AR 340, CA. This also accords with the rule of public international law that
   in general each state may determine who are its nationals: see R Plender *International
   Migration Law* (2nd edn, 1988) p 39ff.
2 British Nationality Act 1981, s 1.
3 The German definition of citizenship according to its Constitution prevailed for EC
   purposes, and this extended German nationality not only to East German nationals but
   also a wider range of persons of German extraction, thus bringing them within the
   personal scope of free movement rights. German reunification has caused the problem to
   vanish.

UK nationals for EC purposes

7.50 At the time of signing the Treaty of Accession to the EEC, the British government made a declaration on the meaning of a UK national for the purposes of the Treaties.[1] Since then the government has made a new declaration, which took effect on 1 January 1983, when the British Nationality Act 1981 came into force.[2] So far as the UK is concerned, the term 'national' or 'nationals' in any Community document now means:

(a)   British citizens;
(b)   British subjects with the right of abode in the UK;
(c)   British Dependent Territories citizens who acquire that citizenship from a connection with Gibraltar.

Two features of the declaration should be noted. First, it excludes those citizens of a Commonwealth country who have obtained the right of abode in the UK, but not British citizenship.[3] Secondly, it includes Gibraltarians, who can move to any other country of the EU but might otherwise be denied entry to the UK under UK immigration law. This can be overcome if they register as British citizens under the British Nationality Act 1981.[4] Just as Gibraltarians can move to other member states, nationals of those states can move to Gibraltar, to whose territory freedom of movement is extended in accordance with Article 299(4) EC (ex Article 227(4)). The validity of the UK Declaration has recently been upheld by the ECJ in *R v Secretary of State for the Home Department, ex p Manjit Kaur*.[5]

1   (1972) (Cm 4862) p 118. Under this declaration a UK national was a CUKC or a British subject without citizenship, having in either case the right of abode, or a CUKC by connection with Gibraltar.
2   28 January 1983, (1983) OJ C 23, p 1, (1983) (Cmnd 9062). There may be some doubt as to the legal authority for this new declaration. It is a unilateral declaration not a treaty document. It is made without any statutory authority or parliamentary approval. It is not the judgment of a competent court.
3   Immigration Act 1971, s 2(1)(b).
4   British Nationality Act 1981, s 5.
5   Case C-192/99 [2001] All ER (EC) 250.

7.51 Some people may have the nationality of more than one member state. Dual nationality does not hinder the enjoyment of fundamental freedoms under Community law where this applies. This will be the case where the person is both a national of a member state and of a third state or is a national of two member states at the same time. In *Micheletti* the ECJ held that a member state may not restrict the effects of the grant of nationality of another member state by imposing conditions (such as a habitual residence requirement on the territory of the member state in question) for recognition of that nationality with a view to the exercise of one of the Treaty's fundamental freedoms. Effectively the member state is precluded from treating a person who is both an EU national and a national of a non-member state as if he or she were not such an EU national.[1] In the UK this issue has arisen most frequently with respect to Irish nationals. Thus in *Ex p Aradi*[2] a dual Irish and British citizen had never been out of the UK in her whole life. Her possession of dual nationality was held, therefore, not to bring into play the more beneficial provisions of EEC law on family reunion in what would otherwise be a purely internal British situation. It is doubtful whether this decision would be followed today[3] in the light of developments in EC law, including the enactment of Article 18 EC (ex Article 8a).[4] In the case of *Brown v Secretary of State for Scotland*[5] the possession of British nationality did not prevent a young Frenchman from invoking Community law provisions regarding his engineering course at a British university, to which he was admitted after completing his baccalauréat in France. The fact that people may not need to rely on their EC nationality to gain admission does not mean that rights incidental to such a claim are ineffective.[6] Where an applicant claims that he or she is a citizen of a particular member state, the burden of proof is on the applicant and no different principle is imported because of the implications of Community law.[7]

1 Case C-369/90 *Micheletti v Delegacion del Gobierno en Cantabria* [1992] ECR I-4239; see also Jauler Carrescosa in (1994) 8 INLP 1.
2 *R v Immigration Appeal Tribunal, ex p Aradi* [1987] Imm AR 359, QBD.
3 This was one of the issues in the case of *R v Secretary of State for the Home Department, ex p Adams* [1995] All ER (EC) 177; Case C-235/87 *Matteucci* [1989] 1 CMLR 357, ECJ (child of worker born in host country who has always lived there is worker, when he or she takes employment there).
4 Article 18 EC directly links free movement rights and residence to being a national of a member state, thus adding real value to the existing provisions of the Treaty: see Martin and Guild 7.34 fn 11 above, p 98.
5 Case 197/86 *Brown v Secretary of State for Scotland* [1988] ECR 3205, [1988] 3 CMLR 403, ECJ; see also Case 292/86 *Gullung v Conseil de l'Ordre des Avocats etc* [1990] 1 QB 234, [1988] ECR 111, ECJ. The Home Office has made clear in correspondence that Irish nationals can 'elect' to be treated under EC law in a letter dated July 1994. Even the concept of election is inappropriate, if, as we suggest, a dual national can rely on the best of both rights: see text.
6 Cases C-389 and 390/87 *Echternach v Minister van Onderwijs en Wetenschappen* [1989] ECR 723, [1990] 2 CMLR 305, ECJ; Case C-370/90 *R v Immigration Appeal Tribunal and Surinder Singh, ex p Secretary of State for the Home Department* [1992] 3 All ER 798, [1992] Imm AR 565, ECJ.
7 *Surinder Singh* above.

7.52 Before the inclusion of Article 18 EC (ex Article 8a) in the amended EC Treaty, the ECJ dealt with an important question as to whether EU nationals can be said to be exercising EC rights when entering the territory of their own state.[1] The court held that where a British citizen had exercised Community rights in another part of the EU or the EEA and returned to the UK with non-national family members, he or she was exercising Community as well as national rights of entry, and the family members could not be treated less favourably than required by Community law.[2] The Immigration (European Economic Area) Regulations 2000[3] now expressly deal with this situation in regulation 11, which seeks to implement the ECJ judgment, by extending Community rights (in certain circumstances) to family members of a UK national. The circumstances include a need to prove (by whom is not clear) that the UK national did not leave the UK 'in order to enable his family member to acquire rights under these regulations and thereby evade the application of UK immigration law'. In our view, this requirement is doubly misconceived. First, rights are acquired under EC law, not under the regulations. Secondly, free movement rights arise from being an EU citizen and a worker or self-employed person, and do not depend on intention.[4] The sooner this vindictive little condition is withdrawn the better!

1 For the cases where the ECJ has held Community law to be inapplicable because of a wholly internal situation see **7.54** below.

2   Case C-370/90 *R v Immigration Appeal Tribunal and Surinder Singh, ex p Secretary of State for the Home Department* [1992] 3 All ER 798, [1992] Imm AR 565, ECJ.
3   SI 2000/2326.
4   See Case 23/93 *TVIO* [1994] ECR I-4795, [1995] 3 CMLR 284, ECJ, see **7.55** below.

Non-nationals

7.53 Non-nationals are normally outside the personal scope of the Treaty provisions. But, as always, there are exceptions. These are:

(1)   family members of qualified persons;[1]
(2)   directors and staff of a company constituted in one member state and carrying out services in another. A company providing services in another member state may travel with the whole of its staff for the duration of the work undertaken.[2] See **7.67-7.68** below;
(3)   stateless persons and refugees recognised in one member state, who have been admitted to the territory of another, are entitled to carry with them accrued social security rights in the same way as EC nationals.[3] As regards free movement rights, the Council declared in 1964 that refugees moving from one member state to another to seek employment should receive 'the most favourable treatment possible', and their entry 'must be given especially favourable consideration'. This declaration has no direct effect and does not bring refugees within the personal scope of the EC, but it is the strongest possible invitation to member states to take the declaration into account when considering the grant of leave to enter.[4]

Once the Council puts into effect the measures on immigration and asylum under Title IV of the EC Treaty, there will inevitably be a widening of the personal scope of the EC Treaty, but it will apply to Title IV immigration and asylum provisions and not to free movement rights.

1   Case 131/85 *Gül v Regierungspräsident Düsseldorf* [1986] ECR 1573, [1987] 1 CMLR 501, ECJ. But the Community national member of the family must have exercised free movement rights. Community law has no application to a wholly internal situation: see **7.54** below.
2   Case C-113/89 *Rush Portuguesa Lda v ONI* [1990] ECR I-1417, [1991] 2 CMLR 818; see also the important decision of the ECJ in Case C-43/93 *Van Der Elst v OMI* [1994] ECR I-3803 where a Moroccan worker lawfully resident in Belgium was held entitled to work for a Belgian company undertaking a project in France.
3   Council Regulation (EEC) 1408/71 which deals with social security benefits for migrant workers.
4   See further Martin and Guild **7.34** fn 11 above, chapter 21. It is arguable that the Home Office must have regard to the words quoted in deciding whether to admit Convention refugees recognised in another member state: *R v Secretary of State, ex p Obomalayat* (16 August 1978, unreported), QBD cited in *Vaughan* **7.5** fn 1 above, para 15.363. See further **12.101** below.

Internal situations

7.54 Article 39 EC (ex Article 48) only applies to situations within the scope of Community law, namely the free movement of workers, and envisages someone moving from one member state to another to seek or take up employment. Those who have never exercised a free movement right within the Community do not come within Article 39 and cannot be classified as 'workers'. In

R v Saunders[1] it was held that the free movement provisions of the EC Treaty cannot apply to situations which are wholly internal to a member state. In *Morson and Jhanjan*[2] this was interpreted to mean that where workers have never exercised a right to free movement within the Community there is no EC link, and the member state in question cannot be prevented by EC law from refusing entry or stay to the non-EC parents or spouse of a local national. The purely internal situation does not just apply to Article 39 and workers. The provisions on freedom of establishment do not apply to obstacles which affect nationals of member states on their own territory without any connecting factor to a situation covered by EC law. In the same way Article 49 EC (ex Article 59) cannot be applied to activities which are confined in all respects within a single member state. Thus a company operating in one member state with its head office there does not come within Community law by simply extending its activities in that country.[3]

1 Case 175/78 [1980] QB 72, [1979] ECR 1129, ECJ; Case C-206/91 *Poirrez* [1992] ECR I-6685, ECJ.
2 Case 35, 36/82 *Morson and Jhanjan v Netherlands* [1982] ECR 3723, [1983] 2 CMLR 221, ECJ; Cases C-297/88 and 197/89 *Dzodzi* [1990] ECR I-3763. A hypothetical possibility of professional activity in another member state is not enough: Case 180/83 *Moser* [1984] ECR 2539, ECJ, nor is a mere intention to become an EEC worker without any practical steps being taken sufficient: *Bouanimba* [1986] Imm AR 343, IAT. In Case 44/84 *Hurd v Jones* [1986] QB 892, [1986] 2 CMLR 1, ECJ the same principles were applied to a UK national employed at the European Community School. He was the only teacher not granted a tax exemption by the UK government, but the court held that he could not invoke the non-discrimination provisions of what was then art 7 of the Treaty against the UK government because he had never exercised his free movement right and was not, therefore, within the protection of Art 48. See further *R v Immigration Appeal Tribunal, ex p Aradi* [1987] Imm AR 359, QBD; *Tombofa v Secretary of State for the Home Department* [1988] Imm AR 400, CA. Case 147/87 *Zaoui v CRAM de l'Ile de France* [1987] ECR 5511, [1989] 2 CMLR 646, ECJ. Other examples where the ECJ has held a situation to be wholly internal are Case C-60/91 *Re Morais* [1992] ECR I-2085, [1992] 2 CMLR 533, ECJ (prosecution of a driving instructor); Case C-147/91 *Ministerio Fiscal v Ferrer Laderer* [1992] 3 CMLR 273, ECJ (prosecution of an estate agent); Case C-332/90 *Steen v Deutsche Bundespost* [1992] ECR I-341, [1992] 2 CMLR 406 (recruitment of a German national to the post office); Case C-153/91 *Petit v ONP* [1992] ECR I-4973, [1993] 1 CMLR 476 (adopted child not exercising community rights).
3 Case C-134/94 *Esso* [1995] ECR I-4223.

7.55 On the other hand, where there is a sufficient link to a situation envisaged by EC law, the matter is no longer purely internal and EC law can be invoked. Some examples might be a travel agent with offices in London and Brussels, or a restaurant owner with a restaurant in Dublin and Paris. So where a broadcasting body establishes itself in another member state in order to avoid the legislation applicable in the receiving state to domestic broadcasters, its broadcasts were regarded as services within the meaning of Article 49, irrespective of its motive for relocating.[1] Where a national of a member state has entered into a contract of employment with an employee in another member state with a view to exercising gainful employment, the situation cannot be called a purely internal one, even if the offer of employment is never taken up. This is what happened in the case of *Bosman*,[2] a Belgian footballer who was prevented by the Belgian FA's transfer rules from moving to a French club. The ECJ held that this was not an internal situation. Where a worker has exercised the right of free movement within the Community by taking employment in another member state, he or she is entitled to rely upon

Community law on returning to his or her own state. The decision of the ECJ in *Surinder Singh*[3] upheld the conclusion of the Immigration Appeal Tribunal, that where there has been a genuine exercise of Community rights, the returning national and the non-national spouse or relative are entitled to any more favourable treatment provided by Community law, despite the fact that there is also a right of entry under national law. This case was followed in *Kraus v Land Baden-Württemberg*,[4] where a German national wished to use a university title received following study in the UK on return to his native Germany. See **7.52** above.

1   Case C-23/93 *TV10* [1994] ECR I-4795, [1995] 3 CMLR 284, ECJ.
2   Case C-415/93 *URBSFA v Bosman* [1995] ECR I-4921, [1996] 1 CMLR 645, paras 88-91, ECJ.
3   Case C-370/90 *R v Immigration Appeal Tribunal and Surinder Singh, ex p Secretary of State for the Home Department* [1992] ECR I-4265, ECJ, [1992] Imm AR 565.
4   Case C-19/92 [1993] ECR I-1663.

7.56 Prior to 1993, the sole fact of moving residence from one member state to another did not constitute a sufficient connecting factor, as the ECJ held in *Werner*.[1] This case pre-dates the introduction of Article 18 EC (ex Article 8a) which for the first time confers directly on every citizen of the EU the right to move and reside freely within the territory of the member states. However, the right is not unconditional, but is made subject to the limitations and conditions laid down in the Treaty and by measures adopted to give it effect. We have already referred to the Court of Appeal's view of the direct effect of this Article in *Ex p Phull*,[2] where that court also held that Article 18 did not abolish the previous case law on purely internal effect and give a right to remain in one's *own member state* without ever having exercised free movement rights elsewhere. But that still leaves open the question whether the reasoning of the ECJ in *Werner* is still applicable. Under *Werner* the fact of residence in *another member state* embodied no Community right, such as would be derived from obtaining a professional qualification[3] or exercising some economic activity.[4] Martin and Guild think something of that kind is still required.[5] We are not so sure. The Community right to which the *Werner* situation is now linked is the right of residence under Article 18. In *Naseer Ahmed* Buxton LJ thought the change wrought by Article 18 was plain:[6]

> 'Once a person is a national of any member state he has the right to reside within any other member state that is a member of the Union on the same terms as nationals of that receiving state, without having additionally to establish that he is in the receiving state for one of the reasons to which the Community interest was formerly limited, most obviously the free movement of workers.'

This may be too sweeping a view, but if it is right, the situation is no longer internal, but there is a connecting factor and Community law applies.

1   Case C-112/91 [1993] ECR I-429.
2   [1996] Imm AR 72, CA; followed in *Naseer Ahmed v Secretary of State for the Home Department* [2000] Imm AR 370, CA (renewed application for leave). See **7.34** above.
3   Case C-19/92 *Kraus v Land Baden-Württemberg* [1993] ECR I-1663, ECJ.
4   Case C-15/90 *Middleburgh v Chief Adjudication Officer* [1991] ECR I-4655, ECJ; Case C-152/94 *Van Buynder v Openbaar Ministerie* [1995] ECR I-3981.
5   Martin and Guild 7.34 fn 11 above.
6   [2000] Imm AR 370 at 377, CA.

PERSONAL SCOPE (2) WORKERS

7.57 A national of an EEA member state only comes within the personal scope of Article 39 EC if he or she is a worker. Regulation 3(1) of the Immigration (European Economic Area) Regulations 2000 defines a 'worker' as a worker within the meaning of Article 39 of the EC Treaty.[1] It thus relies entirely on the interpretation given to this term by Community law. Although Article 39 refers to 'freedom of movement for workers', 'workers of the member states' and 'workers of other member states' and Article 50 EC envisages a programme to encourage the exchange of 'young workers', the Treaty does not define the term 'worker'. However, at an early stage of the EEC it was established by the ECJ[2] that the term must have a Community meaning rather than definitions given by laws of individual member states.[3] Under the EC Treaty, rights of 'workers' are distinguished from those relating to 'establishment' and 'services', and this suggests that a worker is a person employed, actually or potentially, under a contract of employment and is not a self-employed person, who would be eligible to benefit from freedom of establishment (Article 52) and freedom to provide services (Article 59).[4]

1 Immigration (European Economic Area) Regulations 2000, reg 3(1)(a).
2 Case 75/63 *Hoekstra (née Unger) v Bestuur der Bedrijfsvereniging voor Detailhandel en Ambachten* [1964] ECR 177 at 184, ECJ.
3 Case 17/76 *Brack v Insurance Officer* [1976] ECR 1429 at 1448, ECJ; Case 53/81 *Levin v Secretary of State for Justice* [1982] ECR 1035 at 1049, ECJ.
4 See C Maestripieri *La Libre Circulation Des Personnes et des Services dans la CEE* (1972) p 46. Sometimes it is difficult to distinguish a worker from the self-employed or a service provider. See Case C-106/91 *Ramrath* [1992] 3 CMLR 173; Case C-202/90 *Ayuntamiento de Sevilla* [1994] 1 CMLR 424, ECJ; Case C-3/87 *Agegate* [1990] 2 QB 151, [1990] 1 CMLR 366, ECJ.

7.58 Early decisions of national courts and tribunals gave a narrow and restrictive definition to 'workers' and suggested that the term excluded casual, intermittent and part-time employment.[1] The ECJ, however, has made it clear that, since the terms 'worker' and 'activity as an employed person' define the spheres of application of one of the fundamental freedoms guaranteed by the Treaty, they may not be interpreted restrictively.[2] In *Levin*[3] a woman with a part-time job as a hotel chambermaid was a worker. The court held that an income less than the minimum required for subsistence is enough, provided only that the person pursues an activity as an employed person which is effective and genuine, and it does not matter what the motive was for taking it. Thus, contrary to what regulation 11(2)(b) of the Immigration (European Economic Area) Regulations 2000[4] says, an EEA national wife may take part-time employment for the purpose of giving her non-EEA national husband rights under Community law. In *Lawrie-Blum v Land Baden-Württemberg*[5] the ECJ stated that the essential characteristic of the employment relationship is the fact that during a given time one person provides services for and under the direction of another in return for remuneration. This applies to trainees and apprentices if they do work for an employer for pay, however low, even though they are under supervision and the work is preparation for a qualifying exam or to qualify the employee for work elsewhere.[6] Remuneration appears to be the key. However, payment need not be enough to live on or it may be in kind, rather than a formal wage. In *Kempf v Staatssecretaris van Justitie*[7] the court went further. A person may still be a worker even if the pay is so low that he or she needs to supplement it with unemployment benefit or has to apply for sickness benefit during a period of illness, provided that the effectiveness and genuineness of the activities as an employed person are established. In *Steymann v Staatssecretaris van Justitie*[8] a German plumber went to Holland and joined a religious community, which secured its economic independence by commercial activities, such as the operation of a bar, discotheque and launderette. The claimant worked for them and in return was provided with his material needs, including pocket money. The court held that where commercial activity was an inherent part of membership of the community, the upkeep of the member of the community could be regarded as an indirect countervailing charge for their work, even though it was not a formal wage. Provided the work is genuine and effective (which is a question for the national courts) and not purely marginal and incidental, it can be considered an economic activity. The purpose of the work is irrelevant, whether it be of a non-commercial nature, such as state education, or part of the public service.[9] Playing sport is not usually regarded as an economic activity, but it is in the case of professional or semi-professional sports players, who thereby become workers.[10] The employer need not be an undertaking; all that is required is the existence of or the intention to create an employment relationship.[11]

1 *Re Expulsion of an Italian National* [1965] CMLR 285; *R v Secchi* [1975] 1 CMLR 383 at 393; *City of Wiesbaden v Barulli* [1968] 9 CMLR 239; *Nijssen v Immigration Officer, London (Heathrow) Airport and Immigration Officer, Sheerness* [1978] Imm AR 226.
2 Case 53/81 *Levin v Secretary of State for Justice* [1982] ECR 1035 at 1052, ECJ; but see Case C-171/91 *Tsiotras v Landeshauptstadt Stuttgart* [1993] ECR I-2925, ECJ.
3 See *Levin* above.
4 SI 2000/2326.
5 Case 66/85 [1986] ECR 2121, [1987] 3 CMLR 389. Followed in respect of Turkish 'workers' in Case C-36/96 *Günaydin v Freistaat Bayern* [1997] ECR I-5143. Employment from 10 up to 18 hours a week has been acceptable in *Kempf* fn 7 below; Case C-171/88, *Rinner-Kühn* [1993] 2 CMLR 932; Case C-102/88; *Ruzius-Wilbrink* [1991] 2 CMLR 202, ECJ; Case C-444/93 *Megner* [1996] All ER (EC) 212, [1996] IRLR 236, ECJ. Low productivity does not prevent a person from being a worker: Case 344/87 *Bettray* [1989] ECR 1621, [1991] 1 CMLR 459, ECJ.
6 *Gunaydin* above; Case C-27/91 *Lemanoir* [1991] ECR I-5531, ECJ (trainee employed over the summer months in a hotel school).
7 Case 139/85 [1986] ECR 1741, [1987] 1 CMLR 764, ECJ; see also *Berney* (5743), an unreported Immigration Appeal Tribunal case to the effect that casual employment for cash makes a person a 'worker'.
8 Case 196/87 [1988] ECR 6159, [1989] 1 CMLR 449, ECJ.
9 Work which merely constitutes a means of rehabilitation or re-integration of a person into the workforce may not be regarded as effective and genuine: *Bettray* above.
10 Case C-415/93 *URBSFA v Bosman* [1996] 1 CMLR 645, ECJ; Case 36/74 *Walrave and Koch v Association Union Cycliste Internationale* [1974] ECR 1405, [1974] 1 CMLR 320, ECJ; Case 13/76 *Donà v Mantero* [1976] ECR 1333 at 1340, ECJ.
11 *Bosman* above, para 74.

7.59 The term 'worker' does not cover only actual workers, but also job seekers,[1] those between jobs,[2] workers undergoing vocational training in their own field or in some cases retraining in a different field,[3] the involuntarily unemployed, and sick,[4] injured and retired workers. In the case of *Bernini*[5] an Italian national who had undergone occupational training in the Netherlands retained the status of worker when undergoing full-time study in Italy where there was a link between the previous occupational activity and the studies in question. The amount of time given to job seekers to find work is not fixed. The effectiveness of Article 39 EC is secured if they have a reasonable time in which to do so. Member states may allow them to remain for a reasonable period, but cannot require them to leave at the end of that period, if the person concerned produces evidence that he or she is continuing to seek employment and has genuine chances of being engaged.[6] Workers who have not yet found employment may not be entitled to the fuller rights available to those who have found employment. In particular the right to enjoy the same social and tax advantages may not accrue until employment is found.[7] The Immigration (European Economic Area) Regulations 2000 do not expressly deal with the time allowed to find work, but they do deal with those who cease to be qualified. They state that a worker does not cease to be a qualified person solely because (a) he or she is temporarily incapable of work as a result of illness or accident or (b) is involuntarily unemployed, if that fact is duly recorded by the relevant employment office.[8]

1   Case C-292/89 *R v Immigration Appeal Tribunal, ex p Antonissen* [1991] ECR I-745, [1991] 2 CMLR 373, para 10.
2   Case 75/63 *Hoekstra (née Unger) v Bestuur der Bedrijfsvereniging voor Detailhandel en Ambachten* [1964] ECR 177 at 184, ECJ.
3   Case 39/86 *Lair v Hanover University* [1988] ECR 3161, [1989] 3 CMLR 545, ECJ, as qualified by Case 197/86 *Brown v Secretary of State for Scotland* [1988] ECR 3205, [1988] 3 CMLR 403, ECJ.
4   *Lair* above. See also *Giangregorio v Secretary of State for the Home Department* [1983] 3 CMLR 472, [1983] Imm AR 104, IAT; *Monteil v Secretary of State for the Home Department* [1983] Imm AR 149, [1984] 1 CMLR 264, IAT. Case C-302/90 *Caisse Auxiliaire díAssurance Maladie-Invaliditié v Faux* [1991] ECR I-4875. A former employee in receipt of invalidity benefit remains a worker, unless the contrary is proved: *Hurley* (12936).
5   Case C-3/90 *Bernini v Minister van Onderwijs en Wetenschappen* [1992] ECR I-1071. For another case on the interrelation of studies and work see Case C-357/89 *Raulin v Minister van Onderwijs en Wetenschappen* [1992] ECR I-1027, [1994] 1 CMLR 227, ECJ.
6   See *EC Commission v Belgium* Case C-344/95 [1997] 2 CMLR 187, ECJ; Case C-292/89 *R v Immigration Appeal Tribunal, ex p Antonissen* [1991] ECR I-745, [1991] 2 CMLR 373.
7   See Council Regulation (EEC) 1612/68, art 7. The directive makes a distinction between work seekers and those who have found employment, although they may be workers for the purpose of art 39.
8   Immigration (European Economic Area) Regulations 2000, SI 2000/2326, reg 5(2).

Employment in the public service

7.60 Article 39(4) EC (ex Article 48(4)) takes account of the legitimate interest of each member state in the protection of its national interest by restricting employment in the public service to its own nationals.[1] But, since the exercise of this power is a derogation from the fundamental principle that workers in the Community should enjoy freedom of movement without discrimination on nationality grounds, it must be construed in such a way as to limit its scope to what is strictly necessary for safeguarding the interests which that provision allows them to protect.[2] According to the established case law, the derogation must be restricted to activities which in themselves are directly and specifically connected with the exercise of official authority.[3] The test is not the status of the civil servant, but whether the employee is responsible for exercising powers conferred by public law or for safeguarding the general interests of the state. There has to be direct and specific participation in the exercise of official authority. The exemption presupposes the existence of a special relationship to the state and the posts excluded are limited to those which, on account of the tasks and responsibilities attaching to them, are likely to have the characteristics of special administrative activities in these areas.[4] Rather surprisingly, the post of head, technical office supervisor, principal supervisor, work supervisor, stock controller, municipal night watchman and municipal architect in Belgium have been held to fall within the meaning of public service.[5] On the other hand trainee locomotive drivers, loaders, plate-layers, shunters and signallers with the Belgian National Railway, and unskilled workers with a local Belgian railway company, as well as hospital nurses, children's nurses, plumbers, carpenters, electricians and garden hands with the City of Brussels and the Commune of Auderghem have been held to be outside the category.[6] A nurse and trainee teacher, though having the status of civil servant, have also been held outside the exemption.[7] Court officials may be outside the exemption, but not judges.[8] In the case of research scientists, only those with duties of management or advising the state on scientific and technical questions would qualify.[9]

1   Case C-443/93 *Vougioukas* [1995] ECR I-4033, ECJ.
2   Case C-147/86 *Commission v Greece* [1989] 2 CMLR 845, para 7, ECJ; Case C-114/97 *Commission v Spain* [1999] 2 CMLR 701, para 34, ECJ.
3   *Commission v Spain* above, para 35; Case 2/74 *Reyners* [1974] 2 CMLR 305, para 45, ECJ; Case C-42/92 *Thijssen* [1993] ECR I-4047, para 8, ECJ.
4   Case C-42/92 *Thijssen v Controldienst voor de Verzeringen* [1993] ECR I-4047, ECJ (insurance commissioners in Belgium not covered by exemption); Case C-4/91 *Bleis v Ministère de l'Education Nationale* [1991] ECR I-5627, [1994] 1 CMLR 793, ECJ (school teachers not exempt); Case C-213/90 *ASTI (Association de Soutien aux Travailleurs Immigrés) v Chambre des Employés Privés* [1991] ECR I-3507, [1993] 3 CMLR 621, ECJ (guilds with policy advisory function not exempt).
5   Case 149/79 *Commission v Belgium (No 2)* [1982] ECR 1845 at 1851, ECJ.
6   *Commission v Belgium* above, at 1852; see also [1980] ECR 3881 at 3898, ECJ.
7   Case 66/85 *Lawrie-Blum v Land Baden-Württemberg* [1986] ECR 2121, [1987] 3 CMLR 389, at para 28, ECJ (trainee teachers); Case 307/84 *Commission v France* [1986] ECR 1725, [1987] 3 CMLR 555, ECJ (nurses in public hospital). Case C-4/91 *Bleis v Ministere de l'Education Nationale* [1991] ECR I-5627, [1994] 1 CMLR 793, para 7, ECJ (secondary school teachers). Case C-259/91 *Allue* [1993] ECR I-4309, ECJ (university teachers); *Commission v Luxembourg* Case C-473/93 [1997] ECR I-3207, at para 33-34 (primary school teachers).
8   Case 2/74 *Reyners v Belgium* [1974] ECR 631 at 655, ECJ. But for insurance commissioners see Case C-42/92 *Thijssen v Controldienst voor de Verzekeringen* [1993] ECR I-4047, ECJ.
9   *Lawrie-Blum*, above; Case 225/85 *Commission v Italy* [1987] ECR 2625, [1988] 3 CMLR 635, ECJ.

7.61 The interests which the public service exception allows member states to protect are satisfied by the opportunity of restricting admission of foreign nationals to certain activities in the public service. But Article 39(4) EC goes no further than this, and cannot be used to justify discrimination as regards pay or other terms and conditions of employment against non-national workers once they have been admitted to the public service.[1] However, Article 39(4) may allow the exclusion of nationals of other member states from the benefit of certain promotions or transfers within the public service, if these involve performing functions required to safeguard the general interests of the state.[2]

1   Case 152/73 *Sotgiu* [1974] ECR 153, ECJ; Case 225/85 *Commission v Italy* [1988] 3 CMLR 635, ECJ; Case 390/87 *Echternach* [1990] 2 CMLR 305, ECJ; Case 33/88 *Allué* [1991] 1 CMLR 283, ECJ.
2   See further Martin and Guild 7.34 fn 11 above, pp 44–47.

Workers benefiting from other provisions of Community law

7.62 The Euratom Treaty 1973 and the European Coal and Steel Community Treaty 1979 (ECSC Treaty) make independent provisions governing the free movement of workers in the coal and steel industry and in the field of nuclear energy.[1] These separate provisions are preserved by the principle that the EC Treaty should not affect the ECSC Treaty or derogate from the Euratom Treaty.[2] However EC legislation will still apply to such workers in so far as their legal position is not governed by the other treaties.[3]

1   ECSC Treaty, art 69(1); Euratom Treaty, art 96.
2   Article 305 EC (ex art 232).
3   Vaughan 7.5 fn 1 above, para 15.44; Council Regulation (EEC) 1612/68, Art 42(1); Council Directive (EEC) 68/360, Art 11(2).

PERSONAL SCOPE (3) ESTABLISHMENT

7.63   Free movement rights apply to nationals of member states and thereby to all EEA nationals who wish to establish themselves in another member state or EEA country in business or as a self-employed person.[1] They apply to natural persons and to companies. The main provision is contained in Article 52 EC (now after amendment Article 43 EC). Article 43(1) now 'prohibits' restrictions on the freedom of establishment by nationals of a member state in the territory of another member state, including the setting up of agencies, branches or subsidiaries. Article 43(2) states that the freedom of establishment includes the right to take up and pursue activities as a self-employed person as well as the right to set up and manage undertakings. These measures are implemented by Council Directive (EEC) 73/148, Article 1 of which provides that freedom of movement rights extend to those who wish to establish themselves in a member state. So, just as job seekers can benefit from free movement rights under Article 39, so also can those seeking opportunities for self-employment. This is mirrored in the Immigration (European Economic Area) Regulations 2000[2]. Regulation 5(1)(b) includes among 'a qualified person' an EEA national who is in the UK as 'a self-employed person'. 'Self-employed person' is then defined in regulation 3(1)(b) as someone who 'establishes himself in order to pursue activity as a self-employed person in accordance with Article 43 of the EC Treaty or who seeks to do so'. Although the right of establishment extends to companies, we are only dealing with the effect on people.

1   The expression 'self-employed' is defined in Case 300/84 *Van Roosmalen* [1986] ECR 3097, [1988] 3 CMLR 471, ECJ. For the position of families see **7.79**ff below.
2   SI 2000/2326.

7.64   Although Article 43 EC (ex Article 52) confers a direct right of establishment free of restrictions based on nationality and non-discriminatory obstacles, it will only be a complete right when each member state recognises training and educational and professional qualifications, obtained or recognised in other member states, as equivalent to its own. There is a whole body of EC law dealing with the harmonisation of professional qualifications, their standardisation and mutual recognition which is outside the scope of the present work.[1]

1   See, for example, Council Directives (EEC) 75/362 and 75/363 relating to the free movement of doctors. Free movement is limited to those doctors who are EEA nationals and who hold basic medical qualifications gained within the EEA. This excludes doctors of Asian origin who qualified outside the EEA. See Council Directive (EEC) 92/51 of 18 June 1992 (OJ L209 24.7.92 p 25) on a general system for recognition of professional education and training; Council resolution concerning nationals of members states who hold a diploma awarded in a third country (OJ C187 24.7.92 p 1); Case C-309/90 *Commission v Greece* [1991] ECR I-5311, ECJ (architects' qualifications); Case C-313/89 *Commission v Spain*

[1991] ECR I-5231, ECJ (midwives); Case C-351/90 *Commission v Luxembourg* [1992] 3 CMLR 124, ECJ (medical, dental and veterinary practitioners); Case C-377/90 *Commission v Belgium* [1992] ECR I-1229, ECJ (waterway transporters); Case C-166/91 *Bauer v Conseil National de l'Ordre des Architectes* [1993] 1 CMLR 141, ECJ; Case C-106/91 *Ramrath v Ministre de la Justice* [1992] 3 CMLR 173, ECJ (restrictions on practice as auditors); Case C-61/89 *Re Bouchoucha* [1990] ECR I-3551, [1992] 1 CMLR 1033, ECJ (non-recognition of osteopathy qualification gained in the UK); Case C-294/89 *Commission v France* [1991] ECR I-3591, [1993] 3 CMLR 569, ECJ (restriction of rule that local lawyer must be retained when non-national lawyers exercising Treaty rights).

7.65 Under Article 45 EC (ex Article 55) member states are allowed to exclude from the equal treatment rule certain official activities, if they are activities which in the member state are connected, even occasionally, with the exercise of official authority.[1] It is for each member state to decide what constitutes official authority, but since the exception derogates from the fundamental rule of freedom of establishment, its scope is limited to what is strictly necessary in order to safeguard the interests which it allows the member state to protect.[2] Setting up a supplementary school, a language school, a music school or a vocational training centre, or giving private tuition from home do not fall within the Article 45 exception.[3] The profession of 'notary' belongs within the exception,[4] but not that of lawyer.[5]

1　Article 45 EC (ex art 55). See **7.60** above, regarding employment in the public service.
2　Case 147/86 *Commission v Greece* [1988] ECR 1637, [1989] 2 CMLR 845, ECJ. See also **7.60** above with respect to excluded categories of workers.
3　*Commission v Greece* above.
4　Martin and Guild **7.34** fn 11 above, p 67.
5　Case 2/74 *Reyners* [1974] ECR 631, [1974] 2 CMLR 305, ECJ. Other activities which have been excluded from the exception are: a lottery concessionaire and activities relating to the design, programming and operation of data systems for the public service (Case C-272/91 *Commission v Italy 'Public supply contract 3 – loto'* [1994] ECR I-1409 [1995] 2 CMLR 673, ECJ); activities of traffic accident experts (Case C-306/89 *Commission v Greece* [1991] ECR I-5863, [1994] 1 CMLR 803, ECJ); and the post of Approved Insurance Commissioner (Case C-42/92 *Thijssen* [1993] ECR I-4047, ECJ).

PERSONAL SCOPE (4) PROVISION AND RECEIPT OF SERVICES

Providing services

7.66 Akin to the right of establishment is the right given by the EC Treaty to provide services in another member country. The idea is that persons established in one country, for example, doctors, plumbers, tailors, etc, should be able to provide their services in other member countries. Article 49 EC (ex Article 59) prohibits restrictions on this right. Article 50 EC (ex Article 60) provides that the person providing a service may, in order to do so, temporarily pursue his activity in the state where the service is provided. The right to provide services includes the right to travel to the other country and to remain there long enough to perform them.[1] The right applies to companies as well as persons[2] but there are four conditions. First, the service provider, who is a natural person, must be a national of a member state (an EEA national in our wider context). Secondly, he or she must be 'established' in a member state.[3] Thirdly, the services must normally be provided for remuneration, thereby excluding free state education or health services.[4] Fourthly, the right only arises if the provider of the services is established in country A and wishes to travel to country B. Visits to country

B are clearly envisaged as temporary. If anything more permanent is intended, the provisions relating to establishment or workers will apply.[5]

1   Council Directive (EEC) 73/148, art 1(1)(a).
2   Articles 48 EC (ex art 58) and 55 EC (ex art 66).
3   An employed person, whether in his or her own state or in another, may benefit from art 49 EC as someone 'established': see Case C-106/91 *Ramrath* [1992] ECR I-3351, [1992] 3 CMLR 173, ECJ; Case 143/87 *Stanton* [1988] ECR 3877, [1989] 3 CMLR 761, ECJ.
4   Case 263/86 *Humbel* [1988] ECR 5365, [1989] 1 CMLR 393, ECJ. Taking part in sporting events may involve engaging in economic activity, and therefore be the provision of services, even though those taking part are amateur athletes or players: Cases C-51 and 191/97 *Deliège v Ligne Francophone de Judo* 11 April 2000, ECJ.
5   Case 196/87 *Steymann v Staatssecretaris Van Justitie* [1988] ECR 6159, [1989] 1 CMLR 449, ECJ. See further Case 220/83 *Commission v France* [1986] ECR 3663, [1987] 2 CMLR 113, ECJ (co-insurance services); Case C-113/89 *Rush Portuguesa Lda v ONI* [1990] ECR I-1417, [1991] 2 CMLR 818, ECJ.

7.67   The right to provide services is a kind of mini-right of establishment. It allows such persons to leave their own country,[1] to enter the territory of another member state[2] and gives a right of residence 'of equal duration with the period during which the services are provided'.[3] For visits of less than three months, no formalities other than having an identity card or passport are needed, but if the visit exceeds three months the person becomes entitled to be issued with what is referred to in the directive as a 'right of abode as proof of the right of residence'.[4] Family members are included in the free movement rights on the same basis as workers.[5] The restriction of rights in the case of the exercise of official authority are the same as for business people.[6]

1   Council Directive (EEC) 73/148, art 2.
2   Council Directive (EEC) 73/148, art 3.
3   Council Directive (EEC) 73/148, art 4(2).
4   Council Directive (EEC) 73/148, art 4.
5   See **7.79** below.
6   See **7.65** above.

7.68   Where companies carry out contracts in another member state, they will usually bring with them a mixture of employees. Some will be nationals of member states (or EEA nationals). They will often qualify as 'workers' and be covered by Article 39 EC. But in other cases posted personnel may properly be considered as falling within the scope of Article 49 EC rather than Article 39, although it may be difficult to determine which.[1] In either case, the concern (especially in the building trade) is whether the posted workers are being subjected to an exploitative regime. Although normally national legislation in the receiving state is unable to restrict the provision of services, the public interest relating to the social protection of workers may constitute an overriding requirement, justifying such a restriction, if there is insufficient protection in the state where the service provider is established.[2] However, other posted personnel may be third country nationals, whom the service-providing company wishes to bring with it. Here we have one of the most significant developments with regard to the provision of services by companies. In the *Rush Portuguesa* case[3] it was held that a company established in the EC has the right to transfer its non-EC national labour force to another member state for the duration of the project. It is unnecessary to obtain work permits for the posted non-EC national employees and a failure to do so cannot make the employer liable to penal sanctions, as happened in the *Vander Elst* case,[4] where the posted worker was a Moroccan who was settled in Belgium and posted to France.

However, there is nothing in Article 49 or the case law to prevent the employer recruiting his or her labour force from nationals of a third country, who habitually work in that third country, for example in a subsidiary of the main undertaking.

1   Case C-106/91 *Ramrath v Luxembourg* [1992] ECR 1-3351, ECJ.
2   Case C-272/94 *Guiot* [1996] ECR I-1905, ECJ.
3   Case C-113/89 *Rush Portuguesa Lda v ONI* [1990] ECR I-1417, [1991] 2 CMLR 818, ECJ.
4   Case C-43/93 *Raymond Vander Elst v OMI* [1994] ECR I-3803, ECJ.

7.69 Posted staff may be subjected to the requirements of the host country's labour law or collective bargaining agreements regarding a minimum wage, but not to other measures of social protection for workers or to host country requirements to keep staff records. These cannot be regarded as overriding requirements which would justify putting such obstacles in the way of free movement.[1] Where the requirements of the host state create obstacles to free movement rights, a breach of Article 39 EC may occur without any need to consider whether there has been indirect discrimination on nationality grounds under Article 39(2) EC.[2]

1   Case C-369/96 *Arblade* [1999] ECR I-8453.
2   Case C-18/95 *Terhoeve* [1999] ECR I-345.

Receiving services

7.70 Where the provisions dealing with services broke new ground was in the implementing provisions. Article 1(1)(b) of Council Directive (EEC) 73/148 provides that *recipients* of services, not just providers, are entitled to enter the territory of another member state to receive services. The far-reaching nature of these provisions was established in the landmark decision in *Luisi and Carbone.*[1] There the ECJ held that the freedom to provide services includes the freedom, for the recipients of the services, to go to another member state in order to receive a service there, and that tourists, persons receiving medical treatment and persons travelling for the purpose of education and business are to be regarded as recipients of services. This decision was followed by *Cowan v Trésor Public*[2] where it was held that a British tourist to Paris was exercising rights to seek services, and therefore could not be excluded from compensation for criminal injuries on the grounds of nationality.

1   Joined Cases 286/82 and 26/83 *Luisi and Carbone v Ministero del Tesoro* [1984] ECR 377, [1985] 3 CMLR 52, ECJ. To qualify as a person who can be said to be in receipt of services under the free movement rights, there needs to be something more substantial than listening to Radio Luxembourg (see *R v Secretary of State for the Home Department, ex p Tombofa* [1988] 2 CMLR 609, [1988] Imm AR 400, CA), or pursuing a court case in the Family Division of the High Court in the UK (see *Liem* (5983), IAT, unreported). Normally there will have to be a crossing of the frontiers of one EC state to another to bring Art 49 into play. See further *Tisseyre* (6052), IAT, unreported, where the visit was to a friend and the only services used would be those needed to travel there; held not sufficient to bring into play art 49 EC.
2   Case 186/87 *Cowan v Trésor Public* [1989] ECR 195, [1990] 2 CMLR 613, ECJ.

7.71 In *Belgium v Humbel*[1] the court restricted the principle, so far as students are concerned, to services 'normally provided for remuneration'. These will include services of an industrial and commercial character as well as the activities of craftsmen and professionals, but not courses of study provided within the framework of the national education system, even where pupils of parents have to pay fees or make other financial contributions. Students at state institutions may not benefit, but it is thought that genuine students at private educational establishments and tourists both benefit, as well as their spouses.[2] Vocational students in state education now qualify for residence during their studies under Council Directive (EEC) 93/96, which we consider at **7.74** below.

1   Case 263/86 [1988] ECR 5365, [1989] 1 CMLR 393, ECJ. For confirmation that fee-paying students are receiving services, see Case C-109/92 *Wirth v Landefhauptstadt Hannover* [1993] ECR I-6447, ECJ.
2   See Case C-357/89 *Raulin* [1992] ECR I-1027.

7.72   The nationality of the provider of services is crucial for the application of Articles 49 and 50 EC rights, but in *Svensson* the ECJ held that nationality was irrelevant so far as concerned the recipient of services.[1] Does this mean that a recipient of services, who happens to be a third country national, may move within the Community in order to enable the provider of a service effectively to provide that service? Does the application of Article 49 to third country nationals, as recipients of services, allow them to travel freely to another member state, if that is an essential element of the provision of the services? It is much more likely that the proposition only holds good when considering the free movement rights of the provider of services, but not *vice versa*.

1   Case C-484/93 [1995] ECR I-3955.

PERSONAL SCOPE (5) STUDENTS, THE SELF-SUFFICIENT AND THE RETIRED

Students

7.73   We have already seen that fee-paying students will qualify for admission to another member state as a recipient of services.[1] Dependants of EC workers or the self-employed will also have rights of access to general and vocational education and consequential rights to remain under the directive dealing with family members.[2] Vocational training referred to in Article 150 EC (ex Article 127) has long been an indispensable element in the Community, to be available to nationals of member states without discrimination.[3] But it does not, as such, give a right of entry or general residence.[4] In order to give effect to free movement in the single market, it was considered necessary to make some provision for those who do not enjoy rights under other parts of Community law.

1   See **7.71** above. For a general summary of the position of EEA students see **9.30** fn 1 below.
2   Council Regulation (EEC) 1612/68, art 12.
3   Case 293/83 *Gravier v City of Liège* [1985] ECR 593, ECJ; *Humbel* [1988] ECR 5365; *Blaizot* [1988] ECR 379; Case 42/87 *Commission v Belgium 'Access to vocational training'* [1988] ECR 5445; Case C-47/93 *Commission v Belgium 'Access to university'* [1994] ECR I-1593.
4   The right of residence implied by the non-discrimination requirement is limited to the purpose and duration of the studies: Case C-357/89 *Raulin v Minister von Ordernijs* [1992] ECR I-1027.

7.74   Council Directive (EEC) 93/96 provides for a right of residence during the duration of a course of studies at a recognised educational establishment, if the principal purpose of the enrolment is to follow a vocational training course.[1] The ambit of the Directive is quite limited, and students are likely to be better off relying on other provisions of Community law if they can. First, there is no right to any maintenance grant.[2] Secondly, students must be covered by sickness insurance in respect of all risks in the member state.[3] Thirdly, they must show that they have 'sufficient resources to avoid becoming a burden on the social assistance system of the host member state during their period of residence'.[4] Vocational training is given a broad definition and is likely to include any courses beyond primary education which are linked to preparation for a career or professional qualifications.[5]

1   Council Directive (EEC) 93/96, art 1(1).
2   Council Directive (EEC) 93/96, art 3.
3   Council Directive (EEC) 93/96, art 1.
4   Council Directive (EEC) 93/936, art 1.
5   Case C-295/90 *Parliament v Council* [1992] ECR I-4193, [1992] 3 CMLR 281, ECJ; *Gravier* above; *Humbel* above.

7.75 Students qualifying under the Council Directive (EEC) 93/936 can be joined by a spouse and dependent children but do not enjoy the rather more generous family provisions for the self-sufficient and retired. Family members joining a student can take employment irrespective of their nationality.[1]

1   Council Directive (EEC) 93/936, arts 1(1) and 2(2).

The self-sufficient

7.76 Nationals of member states who do not work but have sufficient resources to avoid becoming a burden on the social assistance system of the host member state are entitled to a right of residence unless they qualify under some other provision of Community law, provided that they and their families are covered in respect of all risks by sickness insurance during the period of residence.[1]

1   Council Directive (EEC) 90/364, art 1(1).

7.77 The family members who can join the self-sufficient are a spouse and any dependent descendants of that person, or the spouse and any of their dependent relatives in the ascending line (ie parents and grandparents).[1] The spouse and dependent children are entitled to take employment or self-employment irrespective of whether they are nationals of a member state.[2]

1   Council Directive (EEC) 90/364, art 1(2).
2   Council Directive (EEC) 90/364, art 2(2).

The retired

7.78 Workers and the self-employed who reach pensionable age or are invalided out of work or incapacitated in the host country are entitled to remain in permanent residence under the provisions of Council Directive 90/365 (EEC) which also applies to those who wish to move to another member state after retirement without having previously exercised economic activity there. To qualify for this right a retired person must be in receipt of an invalidity or early retirement pension, or old age benefits or a pension in respect of an industrial accident or disease. The funds so received must be sufficient to avoid the person and any family members becoming a burden on the social security system of the host member state during the period of residence.[1] The person and accompanying family members must be covered by sickness insurance in respect of all risks. The family reunion rights are the same as for self-sufficient persons.[2]

1   Council Directive (EEC) 90/365, art 1(1).
2   Council Directive (EEC) 90/365, art 1(2).

MEMBERS OF THE FAMILY

7.79 In addition to workers, the self-employed, students and those providing or receiving services, the right of free movement is also given to the spouse and other family members of such persons. This is principally done through Part I, Title III of Council Regulation (EEC) 1612/68, and Council Directives (EEC) 68/360 and 73/148, all of which are printed in the Appendix.[1] Although the exercise of family rights depends on the exercise of Community rights by the principal, in content they are virtually the same as the principal's right to enter, reside in and remain in another EEA country.[2] They are given irrespective of the sex or nationality of the family members. Thus the Pakistani or American husband of a woman who is an EU national is entitled to accompany his wife when she exercises her right to set up in business, to seek work or to receive or provide services. The provisions in Community law relating to family members are designed to give effect to the free movement rights of the EU national, and are based upon the notion that obstacles to workers being joined by their families and integrated into the host state are obstacles to free movement within the EU.[3] The ECJ has stressed that the integration of EEA nationals and their family members into the host state is a fundamental objective required to ensure that workers and their families resident in a host state enjoy no disadvantage with respect to those who are nationals of the host state.[4] In Case C-308/89 *Di Leo v Land Berlin*[5] (a case involving the right to education for children of EU workers) the court stated:

'... the aim of Regulation 1612/68, namely freedom of movement for workers, requires for such freedom to be guaranteed in compliance with the principles of liberty and dignity, the best possible conditions for the integration of the Community worker's family in the society of the host country.'

1   Article 10 of Council Regulation (EEC) 1612/68 is incorporated into Council Regulation (EEC) 1251/70 and Directive 72/194; art 1 of Council Directive (EEC) 73/148 is incorporated by Council Directive (EEC) 75/34. Council Directives (EEC) 90/364, 90/365 and 90/366 have their own definitions of family members.
2   Case 131/85 *Gül v Regierungspräsident Düsseldorf* [1986] ECR 1573, [1987] 1 CMLR 501, ECJ.
3   The recital of the third Preamble to Council Regulation (EEC) 1612/68 recognises that 'freedom of movement constitutes a fundamental right of workers and their families' and the fifth recital affirms that in order for the right to be exercised with freedom and dignity 'equality of treatment shall be secured in fact and in law'.
4   Case 249/86 *Commission v Germany* [1989] ECR 1263, paras 11-12; [1990] 3 CMLR 540; see also Case 267/83 *Diatta v Land Berlin* [1985] ECR 567, [1986] 2 CMLR 164, paras 14-18 and 20, ECJ. In the context of Association Agreements see Case C-351/95 *Kadiman v Freistaat Bayern* [1997] ECR I-2133, para 30.
5   [1990] ECR I-4185, para 13.

7.80 The Immigration (European Economic Area) Regulations 2000[1] replace, refine and extend the 1994 definition of 'family member', which was limited to a spouse, descendants of EEA nationals or their spouse who are under 21 years of age or dependent, and dependent relatives in the ascending line.[2] This definition met the requirements of Article 10(1) of Council Regulation (EEC) 1612/68 but did not give effect to the broader obligation in Article 10(2) to facilitate the admission of family members, not coming within the above list, if they are dependent on the person with the primary right or were living under their roof in the country from which they have come.[3] The 2000 Regulations are more comprehensive and attempt to give effect to the broad scope of family rights provided under Community law. Under regulation 6 of the 2000 Regulations, the range of family members who are entitled to join the EEA national depends on the primary right exercised by the EEA national, so that:

(1)   *students* – can be joined by spouse and dependent children;[4]
(2)   *other cases (including workers, the self-sufficient and retired)* – can be joined by spouse, descendants of either spouse under 21 or dependent; dependent relatives in the ascending line of either spouse.[5]

So the categories of persons who may benefit are:

•   spouse;
•   children under 21 or dependent on their parents;
•   dependent grandchildren;
•   non-dependent grandchildren under 21 (in the case of workers only);
•   dependent relatives in the ascending line (eg parents, grandparents).

1   SI 2000/2326.
2   Immigration (European Economic Area) Order 1994, SI 1994/1895, art 2.
3   Council Regulation (EEC) 1612/68, art 10(2)
4   SI 2000/2326, reg 6(2).
5   SI 2000/2326, reg 6(4). Regulation 6(3) has been deleted by SI 2001/865.

Spouse

7.81 Currently, a spouse means a person who is formally contracted in a legal marriage.[1] The Immigration (European Economic Area) Regulations 2000 do not give any definition, except to exclude 'a party to a marriage of convenience'.[2] This is a controversial limitation the effect of which has never been authoritatively decided.[3] The EC Regulation and Directives refer simply to 'spouse'. Community law does not permit an examination into how the couple met or why they married. The right of residence must be acknowledged by the host state on production of the documents identified by Community legislation.[4] Thus there has never been any equivalent notion of a 'primary purpose' test in Community law.[5] The Home Office view is that such a marriage is outside the protection of Community law and does not give rise to rights; hence the definition of 'spouse' in the Immigration (European Economic Area) Order 1994 and now the Immigration (European Economic Area) Regulations 2000.[6] The Tribunal has also taken the same line,[7] concluding that a marriage of convenience which does not involve cohabitation or family life at all is unlikely to be relevant to the purposes of the legislation. The furthest the ECJ has gone in this regard is to note that fraudulent conduct or use of Community law to evade national provisions is not permitted.[8] The reference to fraudulent conduct suggests that, to derogate from the directives and regulation on family reunion, it will be necessary to rely on grounds of public policy, public security or public health, as interpreted in Community law.[9]

1 Case 59/85 *Netherlands v Reed* [1986] ECR 1283; Compare Case T-65/92 *Arauxo-Dumay* [1993] ECR II-597. See *R v Secretary of State for the Home Department, ex p Lopez* [1997] Imm AR 11, QBD.
2 SI 2000/2326, reg 2(1). See **11.45** below.
3 A Council Resolution on marriages of convenience makes a broad statement of policy against such arrangements and a commitment by member states to combat their use to obtain admission and residence, but is expressly stated to be 'without prejudice to Community law'.
4 The member state may only require from the spouse the document on which he or she entered the territory and a document issued by a competent authority proving the relationship. See eg Council Directive (EEC) 68/360, art 4(3).
5 See below; however, EU policy on third-country nationals suggests that governments are attracted to some such test as propounded by the UK: see London Resolution of European Council, December 1992.
6 SI 2000/2326, reg 2(1), Immigration (European Economic Area) Order 1994, SI 1994/1923, art 2(2). The minister introducing the 1994 Order in Parliament recognised that 'EC law does not enable us to apply all the provisions of the immigration rules, such as the primary purpose test, in EEA marriage cases, but we do not accept that a party to a marriage of convenience has any right to benefit from EC law relating to the admission and residence of family members. We intend to maintain a strong line against bogus marriages and we will ensure that non-EEA nationals are not able to use marriages of convenience as a way of obtaining residence in the United Kingdom'. (HC Official Report (6th series) col 68, 9 May 1994).
7 *Yee-Kee Kwong* (10661); *Kam Yu Lau* (10859), applied in *Desmond* (15063), *Yuen* (18283) 16 June 1998, IAT.
8 Case C-370/90 *R v Immigration Appeal Tribunal and Surinder Singh, ex p Secretary of State for the Home Department* [1992] Imm AR 565 at 569-570; [1992] ECR I-4265, ECJ.
9 Council Directives (EEC) 64/221 and 73/148, art 8. In the case of *R v Immigration Appeal Tribunal, ex p Cheema and Ullah* [1982] Imm AR 124 the CA held that it was in the public interest to deport those who had gained admission by marriages of convenience, and thereby undermined a fundamental institution of society. At first instance Woolf J had interpreted the power to deport under s 3(5)(b) of the Immigration Act 1971 by reference to the EC concept of public policy under Council Directive (EEC) 64/221 and held that deportation on such grounds was permissible. See **7.109** below.

7.82 These issues were to be litigated in the case of *Ex p Naseem Clinton*,[1] where permission was granted to challenge the expulsion of a spouse of a Community national whose marriage was alleged to be one of convenience. One of the grounds of challenge was that the Immigration (European Economic Area) Order 1994[2] violated Community law in excluding such spouses from the definition of family member, and that expulsion was only possible if the Secretary of State for the Home Department could establish a public policy derogation.[3] However, the case was conceded and the claimant was granted indefinite leave to enter in the light of the affidavit evidence suggesting that the marriage was not one of convenience.[4] In *Chang*,[5] a starred Tribunal held that Article 4(3) of Council Directive (EEC) 68/360 did not preclude fuller investigation of a relationship which came into existence after the applicant last entered the UK, and that Community law did not prevent the UK from regulating marriage. On the facts, the appellant's marriage was one of convenience, and he was not a family member of an EU national.

1 (CO 3111/94) 27 October 1994, Turner J.
2 SI 1994/1895.
3 Likewise, leave to appeal to the Court of Appeal was granted in *Kwong* (10661) on the central issue of whether the nature of the marriage or a public policy derogation determined the status of the spouse, but the appeal was withdrawn.
4 This contrasts with the refusal of permission in *R v Immigration Appeal Tribunal, ex p Cheung* [1995] Imm AR 104 where Popplewell J assumed without deciding that the Tribunal in *Lau* was correct, and determined the application on a *Wednesbury* basis, concluding that there was material upon which a reasonable Secretary of State for the Home Department could conclude that the marriage was one of convenience.
5 *Chang* (01 TH00100) 24 April 2001, IAT.

7.83 In our opinion, it is inappropriate for national legislation to qualify Community rights by giving a restrictive definition of spouse when there is no definition of 'marriage of convenience' in the directives or regulations, when opinions differ as to the meaning of this phrase and when the proper approach must be through the public policy derogation. In correspondence arising from the parliamentary debate in respect of the Immigration (European Economic Area) Order 1994,[1] the minister offered the following definition:

> 'A marriage of convenience is regarded as a sham marriage which is entered into solely for immigration purposes where the partners have no intention of living with the other as man and wife in a settled and genuine relationship.'[2]

This is a high test and may be at odds with Community law, which does not require a couple to live under the same roof, so that a genuine relationship as man and wife can exist irrespective of cohabitation.[3] Furthermore, evidence of some disqualifying aspect to the marriage may be hard to find. There is no power of compulsory interview for any alien (EEA citizen or not) *after* entry to the UK. Detailed and intrusive questioning as to the couple's motives is inconsistent with the swift and summary procedure for obtaining confirmation of the rights of admission under EC law. It may be that if a member state's authorities can demonstrate that a marriage to an EEA national possesses all the disqualifying characteristics, then a residence permit can be refused or expulsion initiated in the absence of other grounds to remain. The burden of proof is firmly on the state, and since under the Immigration (European Economic Area) Regulations 2000[4] admission under EC law depends on the definition of 'spouse', and is, therefore, a matter of jurisdiction, proof that a marriage is one of convenience should be treated as a 'precedent fact'. The issue has not been resolved in the Administrative Court.[5] If public policy permits member states to take measures to deny residence to those *prima facie* entitled to it, the derogation must be strictly construed, and the exercise of such power should not be used to apply some version of the discredited primary purpose rule, with its concomitant paraphernalia of delay, humiliating investigation, separation and suffering.

1   SI 1994/1895.
2   Lord Annaly to Lord McIntosh, 24 May 1994. This test is stricter than the definition under the previous Immigration Rules (see *R v Immigration Appeal Tribunal, ex p Mahmud Khan* [1983] QB 790, [1982] Imm AR 134).
3   See Case 267/83 *Diatta v Land Berlin* [1986] 2 CMLR 164, ECJ.
4   SI 2000/2326.
5   See 7.82 above.

7.84 In *Reed v Netherlands*[1] the ECJ ruled that cohabiting but unmarried heterosexual couples could not be included in the definition of spouse. The court acknowledged the need to give a purposive approach to Community legislation, but decided that it could not yet give such a broad interpretation, in the absence of evidence of a clear consensus within the member states of the Community, to treat common law relationships on the same basis as marriage.[2] In *Reed* it was not argued that an unmarried partner may qualify under the broader provisions of Article 10(2) of Council Regulation (EEC) 1612/68, which refers to 'any other family member'. Instead, the court ruled that since the Netherlands allowed cohabiting partners of Dutch nationals to obtain residence in the country on the basis of the relationship, it violated the principles of non-discrimination to refuse to extend the same benefit to the unmarried partners of

EU nationals. The presence of such a partner was recognised as a 'social advantage' for the purposes of the non-discrimination provision of Article 7 of regulation 1612/68.[3] The non-discrimination principle can found a right of residence.[4] The extent to which non-married partnerships have become a recognised fact of life since *Reed* is reflected in the European Commission proposal of June 1998 to amend Article 10(1) of regulation 1612/68 to include the following:

- a spouse *or any person with similar status* under the system of the host country and their descendants;
- relatives in the ascending line of the worker or the spouse *or any person with similar status* under the system of the host country;
- any other members of the family in the country of origin who are dependent on or living under the roof of the worker or the spouse or person with *a similar status* under the system of the host country.

1   Case 59/85 *Netherlands v Reed* [1986] ECR 1283, [1987] 2 CMLR 448, ECJ.
2   A decade-and-a-half later this conclusion should perhaps be revisited, given the social developments and increased recognition afforded to cohabiting relationships within the Union.
3   Article 7 of Council Regulation (EEC) 1612/68 prohibits discrimination on the grounds of nationality in respect of the conditions of employment and work (arts 7(1) and (4)), and provides for equality of treatment in respect of social and tax advantages (art 7(2)), and in the conditions for access to training in vocational schools and retraining centres (art 7(3)).
4   See Case C-237/91 *Kus v Landeshauptstadt Wiesbaden* [1992] ECR I-6781, para 28, where the ECJ recognised, in the context of the Turkish Association Agreement, that the right of residence must necessarily be implied to give effect to the non-discrimination provisions.

7.85 It has been observed[1] that although the Commission proposals recognise the need to update the categories of family members in the light of contemporary social developments, they would not so much extend Community law as currently drafted, as codify existing practice, achieved through the non-discrimination provisions recognised in the *Reed* decision. They do, however, lend force to the view of the Commission that it is necessary to 'allow family reunification in a way which is consistent with today's demographic and sociological patterns within the European Union'.[2]

1   Adams and Rollason 'New rights for family members – a proposal from the European Commission' [1999] 13 INLP 47.
2   It remains open to the court to extend the legal definition of spouse to reflect changes in social norms since 1968 and since the judgment in *Reed* in 1986; compare Case T-43/90 *Diaz Garcia v European Parliament* [1992] ECR II-2619 ('legal responsibility to maintain' in staff regulations does not apply to cohabitee).

7.86 The extent to which family rights depend on the parties living together in the same household was decided by the ECJ in *Diatta*.[1] The case concerned worker rights and in particular the provisions of Articles 10 and 11 of Council Regulation (EEC) 1612/68, but the reasoning is also applicable to family rights under Council Directive (EEC) 73/148 dealing with establishment and services, where the wording is less restrictive than that of Article 10 of regulation 1612/68.[2] Mrs Diatta married a French national living and working in Berlin. She had been working continuously in Berlin since February 1978. After living with him for some time, she left her husband in August 1978 with the intention of obtaining a divorce and had since then been living separately. The court held that Article 10 of the regulation could not be interpreted restrictively; the provision that members of the families of migrant workers had the right to install themselves with the worker did not mean that they had to live permanently with the worker. A requirement that the family must live permanently under the same roof cannot be implied. The only requirement was that accommodation which the worker has available must be such as may be considered normal for the purpose of accommodating his or her family. The court also made it clear that Article 11 of the regulation gave family members the right to take up any activity as an employed person throughout the territory of the member state concerned, even if the activity was pursued at a place far removed from the residence of the migrant worker. In the course of argument, the European Commission had contended that the rights of family members continued even though the family relationship was severed. The court's only response was to state that marital relationships cannot be regarded as dissolved, provided they have not been terminated by a competent authority. The effect was that even though Mrs Diatta was separated and intended to divorce, she was still protected at least until actually she was divorced.[3]

1 Case 267/83 *Diatta v Land Berlin* [1986] 2 CMLR 164, ECJ.
2 Council Directive (EEC) 73/148, art 1 makes no reference to spouses installing themselves with the worker, nor does it require accommodation to be available.
3 See also the Tribunal case of *Buyuuyilmaz* (11769), IAT.

7.87 The spouse's right of residence is generally dependent on that of the principal. Thus where the worker leaves the territory permanently, adjectival rights will generally cease. In the case of *Sandhu*[1] the couple separated and the applicant's EEC spouse had gone back to Germany. The Court of Appeal in England held that the applicant was no longer within EEC protection and his residence in the UK could, therefore, be curtailed. The House of Lords dismissed an appeal, concluding that the decision in *Diatta* rendered the question *acte claire*.[2] In *Botta*[3] a deportation order was made against the EEC wife of a non-EEC alien, and the English court held that he lost his EEC right of residence as from that moment. The position can now be summarised as follows: A non-EEA spouse in the UK loses the benefit of EC law if (a) the parties divorce, but not if they separate and remain in the UK; (b) they separate and the EEA spouse leaves the UK to live permanently in another country; or (c) the EEA national is deported. In the case of *Baumbast*,[4] referred by the Immigration Appeal Tribunal, the ECJ are to consider the rights of a non-national spouse to continue to reside in the UK when her German husband is no longer employed in the UK or in any part of the EEA, but retains his place of residence in the UK, where he has established a home with his wife and minor children, who are in full-time education. One of the contentions of the claimant is that the spouse and children's right of residence survives the ceasing of economic activity in the UK and the temporary departure of the husband and father. Whilst the submission calls for a purposive and creative approach to Community law, increasingly it is one which may be required. If integration into the host state of family members, particularly children, is to be meaningful, it may mean that some changes in circumstances following installation should not deprive family members of continuing rights of residence, providing that a Community nexus exists between the EEA national and his family.

1 *R v Secretary of State for the Home Department, ex p Sandhu* [1983] 3 CMLR 131, CA.
2 (1985) Times, 10 May.
3 *R v Secretary of State for the Home Department, ex p Botta* [1987] 2 CMLR 189, QBD.
4 *Baumbast* (21263), IAT, linked with *R* (21326), IAT. Reference under Article 177 in January 1999; hearing in the ECJ in February 2001; Advocate General's opinion to be delivered in June 2001.

7.88 Special provision is made in the case of the death of the person with the primary right. If the principal dies during his or her working life and before acquiring the right to remain under national or Community law, the members of the family can remain permanently if any one of the following conditions is fulfilled:

(i)   the deceased resided continuously in the host country for the two years before death; or

(ii)   he or she died from an accident at work or an occupational disease; or

(iii)   the surviving spouse was a national of the host state, but lost that nationality on marriage to the deceased.[1]

1   Council Regulation (EEC) 1251/70 and Directive (EEC) 75/34, art 3(2).

Descendants: children

7.89 There is no definition of descendants in the Immigration (European Economic Area) Regulations 2000,[1] nor is there any authoritative case law. The notion of descendant is wider than children. It plainly covers all blood children, legitimate or not, and whose parents are divorced or not, as well as grandchildren, great-grandchildren and so forth. The purposive approach to interpretation of Treaty rights would strongly suggest that it would include step-children and adopted children, including children in *de facto* adoptions where there was clear evidence of the assumption of parental responsibility and dependency.[2] In any event the scope should not be less favourable than that provided in domestic law[3]and practice, in order to keep within the non-discrimination provisions. Further children, who are not descendants but who are part of the EEA worker's household, may qualify under Article 10(2) of regulation 1612/68 as any other member of the family (see below).

1   SI 2000/2326.
2   See Hartley *EEC Immigration law*, 1978, North Holland, p 132; Vaughan *Law of European Communities*, 1986, Butterworths, para 15.16, 15.11. In interpreting Community law the ECJ will have regard to the obligations of the contracting states under the ECHR: Case C-260/89 *Elliniki Radiophonia Tileorassi AE v Pliroforissis* (*ERT*) [1991] ECR I-2925; and the opinion of Advocate General Jacobs in Case C-168/91 *Konstantinidis v Stadt Altensteig Standesamt* [1993] ECR I-1191.
3   See Immigration Rules, HC 395, rule 6 where the definition of 'parent' would mean the inclusion of certain step-children, children born out of marriage and certain adoptive children.

7.90 Children of migrant workers, therefore, have rights of residence derived from their EEA national parent under Article 10(1) of Council Regulation (EEC) 1612/68. They also have a right under Article 12 to be admitted to the host state's general educational and other training and vocational courses under the same conditions as nationals of the host state.[1] The member states also have an obligation 'to encourage all efforts to enable such children to attend these courses under the best possible conditions'.[2] Interpretation of Article 12 by the ECJ means that children of migrant workers may retain rights of their own under Community law, notwithstanding the departure of their EEA national parent, where they have entered the educational system of the host state at a time when the parent was exercising Treaty rights. In the case of *Echternach and Moritz*[3] a student had entered the general educational system of a host state while his father was working there. The employment of the father in that state ceased and the family left the territory. The student discovered that there were difficulties in proceeding to further education in the country of origin in the light of the qualifications received in the host state. He therefore returned there and entered further education. The court held that he was entitled to a grant under Article 12 of regulation 1612/68 notwithstanding the departure of the father. The Article 12 right is not, however, freestanding, and the position is different if the child was not installed with his or her parents pursuant to the exercise of their free movement rights.[4]

1 Council Regulation (EEC) 1612/68, art 12 covers general measures intended to facilitate educational attendance and not just rules of admission: Case 9/74 *Casagrande v Landeshauptstadt München* [1974] ECR 773, [1974] 2 CMLR 423, ECJ; Case 68/74 *Alamio v Préfet du Rhône* Case [1975] ECR 109, [1975] 1 CMLR 262, ECJ Case C-389, 390/87 *Echternach* fn 3 below; Case C-308/89 *Di Leo* [1990] ECR I-4185. This, coupled with art 7(2) non-discrimination, has resulted in broad application of this measure to ensure state assistance for educational purposes, especially the funding of grants: *Commission v Belgium* [1988] ECR 5445, including for non-dependent children over the age of 21 as in Case C-7/92 *Lubor Gaal* [1995] ECR I-1031, ECJ.
2 Council Regulation (EEC) 1612/68, art 12. Case 42/87 *Re Higher Education Funding: Commission v Belgium* [1989] 1 CMLR 457, ECJ. These rights continue after the child is 21 and/or no longer dependent.
3 Case C-389, 390/87 *Echternach and Moritz v Minister van Onderwijs* [1989] ECR 723, [1990] 2 CMLR 305, ECJ.
4 Thus, a child of a migrant worker was not entitled to an educational grant, although residing in a host member state where his parents had exercised Community rights before the child's birth: *Brown* [1988] 3205; Case C-7/92 *Gaal* [1995] ECR I-1031.

7.91 In the case of *Gal*[1] the Immigration Appeal Tribunal followed *Echternach and Moritz*[2] in holding that children who had entered primary school before the departure of their father had a right to continue their education, notwithstanding the permanent departure of the EEA worker. The right to admission to the educational system implies a right to remain in the UK for this purpose.[3] However, the Tribunal held that the Israeli mother of the children was not entitled to remain to look after the children to give effect to their rights. Appeals by both parties to the Court of Appeal were withdrawn following a compromise on the mother's status. Both parties had been in agreement that a reference to the ECJ was necessary to resolve the issues as to the position of the children and the mother. The point has, however, come before the Tribunal again in the joined cases of *Baumbast and R*,[4] in which a reference was made asking whether a right of residence was available to the non-national mothers and primary carers of such children, to give practical effect to the right to equal access to and conditions of education, and in furtherance of the obligation to encourage the 'best possible conditions' for their educational attendance. In both cases the Home Office accepted that the children had a right to reside in the UK. The area of dispute is about the rights of the mothers, whose Community law nexus is affected in *Baumbast* by the departure of the EEA national father to work outside the EEA, and in *R* as a result of divorce, where joint arrangements continue for the care of the children. In the *R* case, emphasis is placed on the right to family life guaranteed by Article 8 of the ECHR, since the effect of refusing a right of residence to the non-EEA mother would be the departure of the children and an interference with the regular and frequent contact enjoyed by the father. It has been stated by the court on several occasions that Council Regulation (EEC) 1612/68 should be interpreted consistently with the rights under Article 8 of the ECHR,[5] and that measures incompatible with the observance of human rights would not be acceptable under Community law.[6] The extent to which this approach will determine the outcome of the *Baumbast and R* case is awaited.

1   *Gal* (10620) INLP vol 8(2) 1994 p 69.
2   Case C-389, 390/87 *Echternach and Moritz v Minister van Onderwijs* [1990] 2 CMLR 305, ECJ.
3   For another instance of such an implication see Case C-237/91 *Kus v Landshasplstadt Wiesbaden* [1993] 2 CMLR 887, ECJ where a right to a renewal of a work permit for a Turkish national imported a right to renewal of a residence permit.
4   (21263), (21326), IAT.
5   Case 4/73 *Nold v Commission* [1974] ECR 491, para 13.
6   Case C-260/89 *Elliniki Radiophonia Tileorassi AE v Pliroforissis* (ERT) [1991] ECR I-2925. See for further examples Case 44/79 *Hauer v Rheinland Pflaz* [1979] ECR 3727, para 17; Case 63/83 *R v Kirk* [1984] ECR 2689, para 22; Case C-404/92P *X v Commission* [1994] ECR I-4737, para 17; Case C-415/93 *URBSFA v Bosman* [1995] ECR I-4921, para 79; Case C-199/92P *Hüls v Commission* [1999] ECR I-1000, paras 149-150; Case C-235/92P *Montecatini v Commission* [1999] ECR I-4539, para 37.

7.92 A child is entitled to the rights set out in Council Regulation (EEC) 1612/68 if he or she is under 21 years of age or is dependent on the worker. Accordingly, a handicapped child who is prevented from acquiring the status of a worker because of the handicap and qualifies during minority for benefits for the handicapped, remains entitled to equality of treatment even after attaining the age of 21.[1]

1   Case 7/75 *F v Belgium* [1975] ECR 679, [1975] 2 CMLR 442, ECJ. See also Case C-7/92 *Lubor Gaal* [1995] ECR I-1031, [1995] 3 CMLR 17.

7.93 When a child of a worker or self-employed person who is also an EEA national takes up employment, he or she can rely on the provisions of the Treaty and Council Regulation (EEC) 1612/68 even if he or she was born in the host member state and/or has never exercised free movement rights.1

1   Case 235/87 *Matteucci* [1988] ECR 5589; see also by way of illustration Case C-243/91 *Taghavi Iannino v Belgium* [1992] ECR I-4401.

Relatives in the ascending line

7.94 The notion of relatives in the ascending line covers not only the father and mother of the worker and his or her spouse, but also grandparents and great-grandparents and, on the basis of the above analysis, step-parents and adoptive parents.

Other family members

7.95 Regulation 10 of the Immigration (European Economic Area) Regulations 2000[1] attempts to give effect to the provisions of regulation 10(2) of Council Regulation (EEC) 1612/68.[2] It applies to dependants and members of the household of EEA nationals who are workers or self-employed.[3] Family permits, residence permits or residence documents (as the case may be)[4] can be issued to relatives of EEA nationals or their spouses[5] if they:

(a)   are dependent on the EEA national or his or her spouse;
(b)   are living as part of the EEA national's household outside the UK; or
(c)   were living as part of the EEA national's household before the EEA national came to the UK.[6]

1   SI 2000/2326.

2   Article 10(2) of Council Regulation (EEC) 1612/68 creates an obligation to 'facilitate the admission of any member of the family not coming within paragraph 1 if dependent upon the worker . . . or living under the same roof in the country whence he comes'.
3   SI 2000/2326, reg 10(5).
4   SI 2000/2326, reg 10(1).
5   The 'relative' requirement was added by the Immigration (European Economic Area) (Amendment) Regulations 2001, SI 2001/865, in force 2 April 2001.
6   SI 2000/2326, reg 10(4).

7.96 The concept of 'relative' is not defined in the Immigration (European Economic Area) Regulations 2000[1] and is not found in Community law. It will need to be interpreted consistently and purposively in line with the broad scope of 'member of the family' in Article 10(2) of Council Regulation (EEC) 1612/68. Whilst persons such as aunts, uncles, brothers, sisters or cousins will fall within regulation 10 of the 2000 Regulations, Community law requires a purposive approach to the definition of 'member of the family' which gives practical effect to the central principles of free movement and integration in the host state. The definition goes beyond formal legal relationships and is not restricted to marriage or blood/biological relationships.[2] Where *de facto* relationships such as cohabitation or adoption are concerned, it ought properly to be a question of evidence as to the duration, nature and stability of the relationship which determines whether it has the characteristics of family, and not some biological hurdle that can never be crossed. Unmarried partners are clearly an important category, and there is no decided authority on the issue of heterosexual relationships, although the Turkish Association Agreement case of *Safet Eyup*[3] is the closest the court has yet come to considering this point. An argument was advanced on behalf of Mrs Eyup that 'the family of a migrant worker includes a cohabitee'. Advocate General La Pergola gave his opinion in favour of this construction, placing considerable reliance on Article 8 of the ECHR[4] and concluding that 'members of the family' includes 'the extra-marital cohabitee provided there is a serious and stable family bond between the two people . . .'.[5] Mr and Mrs Eyup had lived together for a continuous period of 13 years during which time they had divorced and later remarried, and had had several children together, some born while they were divorced. The ECJ ruled in the Eyups' favour, but on different grounds, and was silent as to the approach of the Advocate General on the construction of family.

1   SI 2000/2326.
2   It is perfectly conceivable and consistent with the broad and purposive approach to envisage a person, such as a nanny who has been in long service in the household, as being a member of the family without distorting the concept and in order to give effect to the primary right of free movement.
3   Case C-65/98 *Safet Eyüp v Landesgeschaftsstelle des Arbeitsmarktservice Vorarlberg* 22 June 2000. See further **7.152** fn 2.
4   Opinion delivered 18 November 1999, paras 24-25.
5   Opinion above, Conclusion, para 39(1).

7.97 As far as same-sex couples are concerned, the Administrative Court in *R v Secretary of State for the Home Department, ex p McCollum*[1] refused to construe membership of the family so as to include a long-standing and stable same-sex relationship. The court declined to follow the approach and the definition of family member as including a same-sex partnership, which the House of Lords applied to the Rent Acts in *Fitzpatrick v Sterling Housing Trust*.[2] Nor did the court place reliance on the fact that it is the practice of the Home Office to treat cohabiting relationships, including those between same-sex partners, as akin to marriage.[3]

1   CO 589/99, 24 January 2001, CA.
2   [2001] 1 AC 27. The House of Lords adopted the following as the hallmarks of what were described as '*de facto* relationships capable of creating membership of the . . . family', namely: 'there should be a degree of mutual interdependence, of the sharing of lives, of caring and love, of commitment and support.'
3   An appeal to the CA was withdrawn on the Home Office indicating its willingness to issue a residence permit, so the question of principle was not decided.

7.98 Regulation 10(1) of the Immigration (European Economic Area) Regulations 2000[1] gives a broad discretion to the decision maker to issue a residence permit to persons falling within regulation 10(4) 'if in all the circumstances it appears . . . appropriate to do so'. There is no equivalent provision in the Immigration Rules and it is likely that if such indeterminate grounds were used to refuse a residence permit to a member of the family who satisfied the substantive conditions of the 2000 Regulations, the refusal would be impermissible in Community law, either as a failure to facilitate admission or as a discriminatory measure.

1   SI 2000/2326.

Dependency

7.99 If regulation 10(4) of the Immigration (European Economic Area) Regulations 2000[1] is to be read consistently with the Community law provision in regulation 10(2) of Council Regulation (EEC) 1612/68, then regulation 10(4)(a) of the 2000 Regulations must be disjunctive, ie in the alternative to 10(4)(b) and 10(4)(c) of the 2000 Regulations. Otherwise it is incompatible with regulation 10(2) of 1612/68, which speaks of the family member being 'dependent . . . *or* living under his roof . . .' (our emphasis). Dependency in Community law is a factual question only. There is no need to establish the reason for the dependency nor that it be a dependency of necessity (in contrast to the domestic Immigration Rules). A person may be dependent even if able to take up employment in his or her own right.[2] The fact that the family member applies for or receives social assistance does not mean that he or she is no longer dependent. To hold otherwise would deny equality of treatment between nationals.[3] Furthermore, dependency need not have arisen before admission to the UK.[4] The contrary was held in a refusal of permission for judicial review in the case of *R v Secretary of State for the Home Department, ex p Yenin*[5] but *Lebon* was not cited, nor a Tribunal case of *Mustafa*[6] which had considered the point in detail and concluded that dependency need not arise prior to admission.

1   SI 2000/2326.
2   Case 316/85 *Lebon v Centre Public d'Aide Sociale* [1987] ECR 2811.
3   In *Lebon* above the assistance was the Belgian 'minimex' and in Case 256/86 *Frascogna v Caisse des dépôts et Consignations* [1987] ECR 3431 at para 7 an old-age allowance.
4   *Lebon* above.
5   [1995] Imm AR 93.
6   (11495), IAT.

7.100 It would therefore seem that an opportunity has been missed to provide a comprehensive and clear domestic code giving effect to the full ambit of Article 10 of Council Regulation (EEC) 1612/68. This means that litigation on the scope of Community law rights for family members of workers will continue, and direct reliance on the Community regulations and questions of compatibility of domestic law will continue to arise.

MATERIAL SCOPE (1) FREE MOVEMENT RIGHTS

Abolishing discrimination and other obstacles to free movement

7.101 Our principal concern is with the rules relating to entry into and stay in the UK arising from EC rules on free movement. But a large part of free movement law is concerned with the removal of restrictions and obstacles, which put the incomer at a disadvantage as against nationals of the receiving member state, or simply act as an unjustifiable obstacle to free movement. No account of free movement rights would be complete without some mention of two of the key elements in the material scope of free movement rights, but this is a vast subject with an extensive case law and within the scope of this work we can only highlight the main outlines:

(i)   the abolition of any discrimination based on nationality; and
(ii)   the abolition of non-discriminatory obstacles.

Non-discrimination

7.102 The principle of non-discrimination is one of the fundamental principles of Community law. Article 12 EC (ex Article 6) provides:

> 'Within the scope of application of this treaty and without prejudice to special provisions therein any discrimination on the grounds of nationality shall be prohibited.'

The Article, although renumbered, is in that part of the EC Treaty entitled 'Principles' and constitutes the foundation stone upon which the Treaty rests, its fundamental base.[1] It is the express statement of the general principle of equality and is the source of specific provisions elsewhere in the Treaty prohibiting discrimination in different Treaty fields. It applies independently only to situations governed by Community law, where the Treaty contains no specific prohibition of discrimination. In practice the only direct beneficiaries of Article 12 have been students.[2] All the other areas of free movement contain their own express prohibitions. Article 39(2) EC (ex Article 48(2)) outlaws discrimination based on nationality between workers of member states as regards employment, remuneration, and other conditions of work and employment. Article 7(1) of Council Regulation (EEC) 1612/68 provides for non-discrimination on the grounds of nationality in the field of employment and vocational training,[3] and Article 9 relates to the field of housing.[4] Article 7(2) provides that an EU worker in the territory of a host member state must enjoy the same 'social and tax advantages' as nationals of the host state. Thus even where there are no Community law rights to a social security benefit, it may be unlawful to provide it to own nationals but not to other EEA nationals.[5] Similarly, the court has interpreted social advantage very broadly. Thus a national provision allowing those who are nationals or permanently settled to be joined by their common law partners has to be extended to EEA workers in the host state.[6] Anti-discrimination provisions are also contained in Articles 43 EC (ex Article 52) (right of establishment) and 54 (ex Article 65) (services). These provisions are extensive in their application and the ECJ's case law is extensive.[7] It covers direct discrimination, where less favourable treatment is given to one set of nationals,[8] and indirect discrimination, where one set of nationals can fulfil more easily conditions applicable to everyone.[9] For the purposes of immigration law the aggregate effect of these various non-discrimination provisions is much wider than the protection of wages and other conditions of employment referred to in Article 39(2) (ex Art 48(2)) or the housing, education and trade union rights dealt with by regulation 1612/68. They are fundamental to the enjoyment of free movement rights. Advocate General Jacobs expressed it thus in his opinion in the case of *Collins*:[10]

> 'The nationals of each member state are entitled to live, work, and do business in other member states on the same terms as the local population. They must not simply be tolerated as aliens, but welcomed by the authorities of the host state as Community nationals who are entitled, within the scope of application of the Treaty "to all the privileges and advantages enjoyed by the nationals of the host state". No other aspect of Community law touches the individual more directly or does more to foster the sense of common identity and shared destiny without which "the ever-closer union among the peoples of Europe" proclaimed by the preamble to the Treaty would be an empty slogan.'

1   Martin and Guild **7.34** fn 11 above, p 14.
2   See **7.73** above. As regards the Turkish Association Agreement, see *Sürül* Case C-262/96 [1999] ECR I-2685; **7.155** below.
3   Case 293/83 *Gravier v City of Liège* [1985] ECR 593, [1985] 3 CMLR 1, ECJ; Case 235/87 *Matteucci v Communaute Française de Belgique* [1989] 1 CMLR 357, ECJ; Case 24/86 *Blaizot v University of Liège* [1988] ECR 379, [1989] 1 CMLR 57, ECJ; Case 263/86 *Belgium v Humbel* [1989] 1 CMLR 393, ECJ; Case 42/87 *Re Higher Education Funding: EC Commission v Belgium* [1989] 1 CMLR 457, ECJ; Case 197/86 *Brown v Secretary of State for Scotland* [1988] 3 CMLR 403, ECJ; Case 261/83 *Castelli v ONPTS* [1987] 1 CMLR 465, ECJ; Case 39/86 *Lair v University of Hanover* [1989] 3 CMLR 545, ECJ.
4   Case 63/86 *Re Housing Aid: EC Commission v Italy* [1989] 2 CMLR 601, ECJ.
5   Under art 42 EC (ex art 51) the Council was required to set up a system to enable workers to overcome obstacles with which they might be confronted in national social security rules. It did so by the enactment of Council Regulations (EEC) 1408/71 and 574/72. A notable application of the principle of non-discrimination in social security is Case C-18/90 *Office National de l'Emploi v Kziber* [1991] ECR I-199, ECJ a decision on the Morocco Association agreement. *Kziber* has been followed by the ECJ in Case C-58/93 *Yoursfi v Belgium* [1994] ECR I-1353, ECJ despite attempts by member states to persuade the court to overturn it.
6   Case 59/85 *Netherlands v Reed* [1987] 2 CMLR 448, ECJ.
7   See in particular Case 2/74 *Reyners v Belgium* [1974] ECR 631, [1974] 2 CMLR 305, ECJ; Case 33/74 *Van Binsbergen v Bestuur* [1974] ECR 1299, [1975] 1 CMLR 298, ECJ; Case 36/74 *Walrave and Koch v Association Union Cycliste Internationale* [1974] ECR 1405, [1975] 1 CMLR 320, ECJ; Case 11/77 *Patrick v Ministre des Affaires Culturelles* [1977] ECR 1199, [1977] 2 CMLR 523, ECJ; Case 136/78 *Ministère Public v Auer* [1979] ECR 437, [1979] 2 CMLR 373, ECJ; Case 107/83 *Ordre des Avocats v Klopp* [1985] QB 711, [1985] 1 CMLR 99, ECJ; Case 222/86 *Union Nationale des Entralneurs v Heylens* [1989] 1 CMLR 901, ECJ. Case C-179/90 *Merci Convenzionali Porto di Genova Spa v Siderurgica Gabriella SpA* [1991] ECR I-5889, ECJ; Case C-360/89 *EC Commission v Italy* [1992] ECR I-3401, ECJ; Case C-419/92 *Scholz v Opera Universitaria di Cagliari* [1994] ECR I-505.
8   See *R v Trinity House Pilotage Committee, ex p Jensen and Leu* [1985] 2 CMLR 413, QBD; *R v Inner London Education Authority, ex p Hinde* [1985] 1 CMLR 716, QBD; Case C-293/83 *Gravier v City of Liege* [1985] 3 CMLR 1, ECJ.
9   Case 152/73 *Sotgiu v Deutsche Bundespost* [1974] ECR 153, ECJ; Case 1/78 *Kenny v National Insurance Comr* [1978] ECR 1489, [1978] 3 CMLR 651, ECJ; Case 182/83 *Robert Fearon & Co v Irish Land Commission* [1985] 2 CMLR 228, ECJ; Case 41/84 *Pietro Pinna v Caisse D'Allocations Familiales de la Savoie* 1 [1988] 1 CMLR 350; Case 33/88 *Allue v Università degli Studi Venezia* [1989] ECR 1591, [1991] 1 CMLR 283; ECJ; Case C-175/88 *Biehl v Luxembourg* [1990] ECR I-1779, [1990] 3 CMLR 143; Case C-204/90 *Bachmann v Belgium* [1992] ECR I-249, [1993] 1 CMLR 785, ECJ.
10   Case C-92/92 *Phil Collins v IMTRAT Handelsgesellschaft mbH* [1993] 3 CMLR 773 at 785.

7.103 The material scope of any free movement right is usually to be determined by the yardstick of what the local nationals can do. All EEA nationals must be put on the same footing as nationals of the host state. Thus in *Watson and Belman*[1] it was held that although penalties could be imposed for illegally entering or remaining in a country, they must be comparable to penalties attaching to local nationals for breaches of provisions of equal importance and should not be so disproportionate that they become an obstacle to free movement.[2] Clearly the comparison between the position of own nationals and those of another member state is not an exact one in this kind of situation, and this is always likely to be the case as regards rights of entry or stay. Normally the court does not draw such a distinction when dealing with the grant of a social advantage. Thus in *Sala*[3] the principle of equal treatment precluded the member state from requiring a national of another member state to be in possession of a residence permit in order to be granted a social advantage when no such requirement was imposed on its own nationals.[4] However, exceptions to the principle of discrimination have been acknowledged by the court many times on the basis of 'objective discrimination', which arises from the simple fact that certain requirements are necessary for non-nationals or non-residents which would not apply to own nationals, such as the requirement to hold their national driving licence;[5] to notify the appropriate authorities of the person's presence on the territory;[6] or to have a passport or identity document.[7] In *Kaba*[8] the distinction was made and it was said that the UK could rely on 'any objective difference' between the position of its own nationals and those of another member state so far as the obtaining of settlement was concerned. The distinction between *Kaba* and a case like *Sala* is that in *Kaba* the claimed 'social advantage' was indefinite leave. This was something which no own national either needed to or could acquire. If on the other hand the claimed 'social advantage' was some social security benefit or a family allowance, it could be acquired by own nationals, and like could be compared with like. It should also be noted that the public policy exceptions, allowing exclusion or expulsion on public policy grounds, can by definition only apply to other nationals and not to own nationals, but this does not constitute discrimination.[9]

1   Case 118/75 *Re Watson and Belmann* [1976] ECR 1185, [1976] 2 CMLR 552, ECJ. See Case 8/77 *Sagulo* [1977] ECR 1495, [1977] 2 CMLR 585, ECJ and Case 157/79 *R v Pieck* [1981] QB 571, [1981] 3 All ER 46, ECJ at paras 12 and 13, where the need to bring the position of workers of other member states into line with that of local nationals is referred to.
2   See further Case 321/87 *Re Belgium Passport Control: Commission v Belgium* [1990] 2 CMLR 492, ECJ.
3   Case C-85/96 *Sala v Freistaat Bayern* [1998] ECR I-2691, ECJ.
4   See further Case C-262/96 *Sürül* [1999] ECR I-2685, ECJ.
5   Case 16/78 *Choquet v Germany* [1978] ECR 2293.
6   Case 118/75 *Watson and Belmann* [1976] ECR 1185, [1976] 2 CMLR 552, ECJ.
7   Case 8/77 *Re Sagulo, Brenca and Bakhouche* [1977] ECR 1495, [1977] 2 CMLR 585, ECJ.
8   Case C-356/98 [2000] All ER (EC) 537, ECJ.
9   Case 41/74 *Van Duyn v Home Office* [1975] Ch 358, [1975] 3 All ER 190, ECJ; Joined Cases C-65/95 and 111/95 *Shingara and Radiom* [1997] 3 CMLR 703, ECJ.

7.104 Although the wording of Articles 39(2), 43 and 54 EC suggests that the principle of equal treatment applies without exception, the ECJ now accepts that in cases of indirect discrimination, where a measure applies to everyone irrespective of nationality, the discrimination may be justified if based on objective considerations independent of the nationality of the workers concerned, and they are proper to the legitimate aim pursued by the national law and not disproportionate.[1]

1   Case C-237/94 *O'Flynn* [1996] ECR I-2617. In another line of cases, the test for justification of indirect discrimination is imperative reasons relating to the public interest: Case 33/88 *Allué v Università degli Studi Venezia* [1989] ECR 1591, ECJ; Case C-175/88 *Biehl v Luxemburg* [1990] ECR I-1779, ECJ; Case C-204/90 *Bachmann v Belgium* [1992] ECR I-249; Case C-398/92 *Mund and Fester v Hatrex Insuratiaal Transport* [1994] ECR I-467, ECJ; Case C-80/94 *Wielockx v Netherlands* [1995] ECR I-2493, ECJ.

Non-discriminatory obstacles

7.105 This development in the case law is closely connected to a further development – that of non-discriminatory obstacles to free movement, which gained particular prominence in the *Bosman* case, concerning the effect of football transfer fees on free movement. The concept was borrowed from earlier case law on the freedom of movement of goods, which held that Article 28 EC (ex Article 30) prohibited not only discriminatory measures in relation to the movement of goods, but also unjustifiable non-discriminatory obstacles.[1] In *Kraus*[2] the ECJ held that Articles 48 and 52 (now Articles 39 and 43 EC) did not permit any national measure relating to the conditions for use of a postgraduate university degree acquired in another member state, which, even though applied without discrimination on the basis of nationality, was capable of hindering or making less attractive the exercise of fundamental freedoms contained in the Treaty by Community nationals, including nationals of the member state which had taken the measure. This rather startling innovation was later confirmed and clarified by the court in *Bosman* and *Gebhard*. In *Bosman*[3] the court held that provisions which preclude or deter nationals of a member state from leaving their country of origin in order to exercise their right of free movement constitute an obstacle to that freedom, even if they apply without regard to the nationality of workers. In *Gebhard*[4] the court held that where national measures are liable to hinder or make less attractive the exercise of fundamental freedoms guaranteed by the Treaty, they must fulfil four conditions: (i) they must be applied in a non-discriminatory manner; (ii) they must be justified by imperative requirements of the general interest; (iii) they must be suitable for securing the attainment of the objective which they pursue; and (iv) they must not go beyond what is necessary in order to attain it. Here the court was repeating the reasoning already handed down in an earlier decision on the application of Article 59 EC (now Article 49).[5] More recently, the ECJ has confirmed that where obstacles to free movement rights have been identified there is no need to consider whether there is indirect discrimination on grounds of nationality.[6]

1   Case 8/74 *Dassonville* [1974] ECR 837, ECJ; later limited in Case C-267/91 *Keck* [1993] ECR I-6097.
2   Case C-19/92 *Kraus* [1993] ECR I-1663, ECJ.
3   Case C-415/93 *Bosman* [1996] All ER (EC) 97, [1995] ECR I-4921, ECJ.
4   Case C-55/94 *Gebhard* [1995] ECR I-4165, ECJ.
5   Case C-288/89 *Gouda v Commissariat voor de Media* [1991] ECR I-4007, ECJ.
6   Case C-18/95 *Terhoeve* [1999] ECR I-345, ECJ; Case C-337/97 CPM Meeusen [1999] ECR I-3289, ECJ.

Reverse discrimination

7.106 Non-discrimination is important for the protection of other EEA nationals coming to the UK and of UK nationals going to other EEA countries. But can it assist UK nationals who suffer discrimination at the hands of the UK government?

This practice is referred to as 'reverse discrimination'.[1] There is clear reverse discrimination by the UK government in the field of family rights. Other EEA nationals in the UK have few problems in being joined by members of their families. British citizens, on the other hand, have a host of obstacles to overcome: maintenance and accommodation, sole responsibility, exceptional compassionate circumstances are a few of them. There is no doubt that the non-discrimination provisions can apply to member states in respect of their own nationals in certain circumstances. This was first recognised in *Knoors*[2] where a Dutch plumber who had practised his trade in Belgium for seven years was refused a permit to practise by the Dutch government on his return to Holland. He claimed that this was contrary to EC law. The ECJ stated that the wording of Article 43 EC (ex Article52), which refers to 'nationals of one member state in the territory of another', did not exclude 'own' nationals from the benefit of EC law or from the application of non-discrimination provisions. An 'own' national could qualify where, by lawful residence on the territory of another member state, his or her situation has become assimilated to that of any other persons enjoying the rights and liberties guaranteed by the Treaty. A state cannot discriminate against its own nationals who are within the protection of one or other provision of EC law. The principle is now widely accepted[3] and extends to non-discriminatory measures adopted by the home state, which are obstacles to a home national's free movement.[4] The problem in these cases is not 'reverse discrimination' but establishing a link to a provision of Community law, which removes the case from a wholly internal situation.[5]

1 See D Pickup 'Reverse Discrimination and Freedom of Movement for Workers' (1986) 23 CML Rev 135.
2 Case 115/78 *Knoors v Secretary of State for Economic Affairs* [1979] ECR 399, [1979] 2 CMLR 357, ECJ, at para 24. In Case 1/78 *Kenny v National Insurance Comr* [1978] ECR 1489, [1978] 3 CMLR 651, ECJ the court held that discrimination by a member state against its own nationals, as much as discrimination by a member state against nationals of another member state, was forbidden. In Case 136/78 *Ministère Public v Auer* [1979] ECR 437, [1979] 2 CMLR 373, ECJ the court indicated at para 28 that EEC nationals were protected against their own state, provided that the other conditions for the application of the rule on which they rely are fulfilled. See further Case 292/86 *Gullung v Conseil de l'Ordre des Avocats* [1990] 1 QB 234, [1988] 2 CMLR 57, ECJ.
3 *Bosman* [1996] All ER (EC) 97 above; Case C-379/92 *Peralta* [1994] ECR I-3453, ECJ.
4 7.105 fn 6, above.
5 See *Phull v Secretary of State for the Home Department* [1996] Imm AR 72, CA.

7.107 Where there is a link to some provision of EC law and where reverse discrimination applies, the advantage which own nationals can take of it is nevertheless restricted in the circumstances of the criminal law. The ECJ in *Saunders* noted:[1]

'Although the rights conferred upon workers by Article 48 may lead the member state to amend their legislation, where necessary, even with respect to their own nationals, this provision does not however aim to restrict the power of the member states to lay down restrictions, within their own territory, on the freedom of movement of all persons subject to their jurisdiction in implementation of domestic criminal law.'

Putting someone in prison after conviction and sentence in the criminal courts is undoubtedly a restriction on that person's freedom of movement, but is not in any way intended to be restricted by any of the free movement provisions. The English High Court extended this rule to extradition procedures and the handover procedure under the Visiting Forces Act 1952.[2] The rationale was explained by Robert Goff LJ in *Ex p Healy*.[3] Using the purposive construction of Article 48 EEC (now Article 39) by the ECJ in *Saunders* he stated that Article 48 did not aim to restrict the power of member states to lay down restrictions within their own territories on the freedom of movement of all persons subject to their jurisdiction in the implementation of extradition procedure or the handover procedure under the Visiting Forces Acts.

1   Case 175/78 *R v Saunders* [1979] ECR 1129, [1980] QB 72, ECJ (application of restrictions of domestic criminal law to own national); Case 180/83 *Moser v Land Baden-Würtemberg* [1984] 3 CMLR 720, ECJ (denial to own national of access to further education); Case 298/84 *Iorio v Azienda Autonoma delle Ferrovie dello Stato* [1986] 2 CMLR 665, ECJ (dispute by own national with state railway over limited access to trains); Joined Cases 35 and 36/82 *Morson and Jhanjan v Netherlands* [1982] ECR 3723, [1983] 2 CMLR 221, ECJ (own nationals who have never worked outside home country); Case 44/84 *Hurd v Jones, Inspector of Taxes* [1986] QB 892, [1986] 2 CMLR 1, ECJ; Case C-104/91 *Colegio Oficial de Agentes de la Propriedad Inmobiliaria v Aguirre Borrell Newman* [1992] ECR I-3003 and Joined Cases C-330/90 and 331/90 *Ministerio Fiscal v A Lopez Brea and C H Palacios* [1992] 2 CMLR 397, ECJ (proceedings against Spanish estate agents).
2   *R v Governor of Pentonville Prison, ex p Budlong* [1980] 1 All ER 701; *Re Budlong and Kember* [1980] 2 CMLR 125, DC; *Re Virdee* [1980] 1 CMLR 709, QBD.
3   *R v Governor of Pentonville Prison, ex p Healy* [1984] 3 CMLR 575, DC.

MATERIAL SCOPE (2) RIGHT TO LEAVE, ENTER AND RESIDE

Right to leave own country

7.108   In EC law the right to depart is expressly given to workers and the self-employed and those providing or receiving services. Article 2(1) of Council Directives (EEC) 68/360 (workers) and 73/148 (self-employed) requires member states to grant workers the right to leave their territory. What this means is that member states must be prepared to let any EC workers leave their territory on production of a valid identity card or passport, and in the case of their own nationals to issue to them and renew their identity cards and passports, which should state the holder's nationality.[1] A passport must be valid at least for all member states and for countries through which the holder must pass when travelling between member states (for example Switzerland and Austria in the case of travel from Italy to Germany or vice versa).[2] Where a passport is the only document on which the holder can lawfully leave the country, its period of validity should be not less than five years.[3] Member states cannot demand any exit visas or equivalent document.[4] Where a country has issued an identity card or passport it must allow the holder to re-enter its territory without any formality, even if the document is no longer valid or the nationality of the holder is in dispute.[5] Thus the right to leave your country is matched by a right under EC law to re-enter it.

1   Council Directives (EEC) 68/360 and 73/148, art 2(1).
2   Council Directives (EEC) 68/360 and 73/148, art 2(2).
3   Council Directives (EEC) 68/360 and 73/148, art 2(3).
4   Council Directives (EEC) 68/360 and 73/148, art 2(4).
5   Council Directive (EEC) 64/221, art 3(4).

Right to enter

7.109   Article 39 (ex Article 48) of the EC Treaty clearly gives a right to enter to workers who have definite jobs to go to. Article 1 of Council Regulation

(EEC) 1612/68 refers to the right to take up activity as an employed person and the right to take up available employment in the territory of another member state on the same priority as the nationals of that state. The case law has made it clear that the right includes the right to enter to find available employment and to respond to offers of employment.[1] A similar right to enter is given to business people, the self-employed, and providers and recipients of services, and those covered by the June 1990 directives: students, the self-sufficient and the retired. All these are referred to by the Immigration (European Economic Area) Regulations 2000 as 'qualified persons'.[2] Under EC law the right involves both entry and internal free movement,[3] and is exercisable by EEA nationals 'simply on production of a valid identity card or passport'.[4] No prior leave to enter or permission is required, because the right to enter flows directly from EC law.[5] This entitlement is given effect in UK law by section 7 of the Immigration Act 1988 and by the 2000 Regulations, which provide that admission must be granted to EEA nationals if they produce on arrival a valid passport or national identity card issued by another EEA state.[6] In addition to a passport or identity document, family members who are not EEA nationals need 'an EEA family permit' or residence document if they are either visa nationals or coming to install themselves with the qualified person.[7] In all other cases, a document proving that he or she is a family member of the qualified person will be enough.[8] Family permits are issued by entry clearance officers free of charge to family members of EEA nationals who are already qualified persons or will be so on arrival in the UK.[9] The Immigration Rules provide that an EEA permit can be refused if the entry clearance officer is not satisfied that the applicant is a family member of a qualified person and not a person subject to exclusion on grounds of public policy, public security or public health.[10] The 2000 Regulations incorporate the power of examination under Schedule 2 to the Immigration Act 1971 for family members of EEA nationals and those who might fall to be excluded from the UK on public policy grounds.[11]

1 See **7.57** above.
2 SI 2000/2326, reg 5.
3 Case 36/75 *Rutili* [1975] ECR 1219, [1976] 1 CMLR 140.
4 Council Directive (EEC) 68/360, art 3(1) and 73/148, art 3(1).
5 Case 157/79 *R v Pieck* [1981] QB 571, [1981] 3 All ER 46, ECJ; Case 321/87 *EC Commission v Belgium* [1990] 2 CMLR 492.
6 SI 2000/2326, reg 12(1).
7 SI 2000/2326, reg 12(2).
8 SI 2000/2326, reg 13.
9 SI 2000/2326, reg 13.
10 HC 395, para 259.
11 SI 2000/2326, reg 24. A person who has been deported on public policy grounds can be refused re-admission under Community law rather than treated as an illegal entrant under national law: *R v Secretary of State for the Home Department, ex p Shingara and Radiom* (3 February 1995, unreported), QBD citing Case 115/89 *Adoui* [1982] ECR 1665 at 1709.

Right of residence

7.110 After admission to the territory of a member state, Community law enables qualified persons to obtain a residence permit as confirmation of their right of residence.[1] It is important to note that the residence permit is not the source of rights or a permission to remain, and a qualified person does not lose rights through the absence of a residence permit.[2] Non-national family members are given a residence document which must be of equivalent validity.[3] In the UK the Immigration (European Economic Area) Regulations 2000[4] bring together the rights to a residence permit under the various EC Directives. It is granted to EEA nationals upon production of the document on which the person entered the territory and proof that they are a qualified person.[5] In the case of workers such proof need not be more than confirmation of employment from an employer.[6] There is no requirement to give a residence permit to workers who are temporary workers engaged for under three months,[7] frontier workers who return to their residence in another member state at least once a week,[8] or seasonal workers whose contracts have been approved by the Department for Education and Employment.[9] Persons providing or receiving services for no more than three months may be refused a residence permit.[10] Family members of a qualified person receive a 'residence permit' if they too are EEA nationals, and a 'residence document' (which will usually be in the form of a stamp in the passport),[11] if they are not.[12] They need to have their identity document or passport and a 'family permit' if that was required for admission, or other proof that they are a family member of the qualified person.[13] Member states may derogate from the duty to issue a residence permit on grounds of public policy, public security or public health.[14] Under Article 5 of Council Directive (EEC) 64/221, a decision to grant or refuse a first residence permit is to be taken as soon as possible and not later than six months from the date of application. During this period the applicant is allowed to remain temporarily in the country concerned.

1   Member states are required to grant workers the right of residence under Council Directive (EEC) 68/360, art 4(4), and the right of permanent residence to those who are established or wish to be established or provide or receive services under Council Directive (EEC) 73/148, Art 4. Little turns on the distinction, which is not reflected in the Immigration (European Economic Area) Regulations 2000, SI 2000/2326. In the case of workers, the residence permit must include the wording set out in the Annex to Directive 68/360, which is as follows: 'this permit is issued pursuant to regulation (EEC) number 1612/68 of the Council of the European Communities of 15 October 1968 and to the measures taken in implementation of the Council Directive of 15 October 1968.'
2   Case 48/75 *Royer* [1976] ECR 497, [1976] 2 CMLR 619; Case 8/77 *Sagulo* [1977] ECR 1495, [1977] 2 CMLR 585; *R v Pieck* [1981] QB 571; Case 59/85 *Netherlands v Reed* [1986] ECR 1283, [1987] 2 CMLR 448.
3   Council Directives (EEC) 68/360, art 4(4) and 73/148, art 4(3). The Immigration Appeal Tribunal held in *Layne* [1987] Imm AR 243 that the rights attached to the non-national document must be the same. Under para 255 of HC 395 holders of both residence permits and documents can apply for indefinite permission to remain under the Immigration Rules.
4   SI 2000/2326.
5   SI 2000/2326, reg 15(1).
6   SI 2000/2326, reg 15(3).
7   SI 2000/2326, reg 16(1)(a), Council Directive (EEC) 68/360, art 8(1)(a).
8   SI 2000/2326, reg 16(1)(b), Council Directive (EEC) 68/360, art 8(1)(b). Special rules are also made for EC nationals who are non-nationals of country A who wish to work in country B while retaining their residence in country A. If they have been workers or self-employed in country A for three years, they can go on living there, and work in country B provided they return home (country A) 'as a rule, each day or at least once a week'. They become entitled to permanent residence in country A under Council Directive (EEC) 75/34 (self-employed) or Council Regulation (EEC) 1251/70 (workers).
9   SI 2000/2326, reg 16(1)(c), Council Directive (EEC) 68/360, art 8(1)(c).
10 SI 2000/2326, reg 16(1)(d).
11 SI 2000/2326, reg 17(2).
12 SI 2000/2326, reg 15(2).
13 SI 2000/2326, reg 15(2).

14 Council Directive (EEC) 68/360, art 10 and 73/148, art 8, and there are equivalent provisions in the June 1990 Directives. SI 2000/2326, reg 22(1).

Duration of first residence permit

7.111 The first residence permit must normally be valid for at least five years and be renewable,[1] but a lesser period is permitted:[2]

(i)   if the employment is for between three and 12 months, for the duration of the employment;

(ii)   if seasonal employment is for more than three months, for the duration of the employment;

(iii)   in the case of provision or receipt of services, for the period of such provision;

(iv)   in the case of students, for the duration of the studies, or for 12 months in the first instance in the case of studies exceeding 12 months;

(v)   in the case of a retired or self-sufficient person, two years in the first instance, followed by revalidation.

The validity of a residence permit is not affected by absence from the UK for periods of up to six months or absence on military service.[3]

1   Immigration (European Economic Area) Regulations 2000, SI 2000/2326, regs 18 and 19, applying the requirements of the Council Directives (EEC) 68/360, 73/148, 90/364, 90/365 and 93/96; Directives 90/364 and 365 for the self-sufficient and retired. Article 2 states the residence permit may be limited to five years on a renewable basis but member states may where they deem it necessary require revalidation of the permit at the end of the first two years of residence.
2   SI 2000/2326, reg 18.
3   SI 2000/2326, reg 18(7).

Renewal of residence permit

7.112 Residence permits are renewable on the basis that the person remains a qualified person or the family member of such a person.[1] Family membership continues as long as the parties are not finally divorced and the qualified person has not permanently abandoned residence in the UK. Cohabitation under the same roof is not necessary.[2] A worker remains qualified despite periods of sickness or unemployment. Council Directive (EEC) 68/360, Article 7(2) provides that when a worker's residence permit is first renewed, the period of residence may be restricted (but to no less than 12 months) where the worker has been involuntarily unemployed in the member state for more than 12 consecutive months.[3] The implication of such a provision is that no such restriction on a worker's residence can be imposed where the residence permit is renewed for a second or subsequent time; and it also suggests that no grounds other than 'voluntary' unemployment, or public policy, public security or public health (see Article 10 of Council Directive (EEC) 68/360) can justify restricting the period of residence even on a first renewal. This is certainly the view of the Immigration Appeal Tribunal, which has allowed a number of appeals against government attempts to curtail the residence of EEA citizens because they have become a charge on public funds.[4] Persons who have been involuntarily unemployed for more than 12 consecutive months will not have completed four years' employment by the end of their first full-length residence permit, and will not qualify for permanent residence in national law after four years' residence with a permit.[5] For those covered by Council Directive (EEC) 73/148 who remain established for business purposes in the UK, renewal of a residence permit is automatic and residence is described in Article 4(1) as 'permanent'. Regulation 19 of the Immigration (European Economic Area) Regulations 2000[6] provides for renewal of a residence permit on application, subject to the Secretary of State's powers under regulation 22 of the 2000 Regulations to revoke or refuse to renew a residence permit or document:

(i)   where the revocation or refusal is justified on grounds of public policy, public security or public health; or

(ii)   the person to whom the residence permit or residence document was issued has ceased to be a qualified person, or is not, or has ceased to be, the family member of a qualified person.

Students with a 12-month first residence permit may have the renewed permit limited to periods of one year, as may workers who have been involuntarily unemployed in the UK for more than one year.[7]

1   Immigration (European Economic Area) Regulations 2000, SI 2000/2326, reg 22(2).
2   See *Diatta v Land Berlin* and the discussion of family membership at **7.86** above.
3   For 'voluntary' unemployment, see below. The 2000 Regulations reflect this provision in SI 2000/2326, reg 19(2).
4   See *Giangregorio* [1983] Imm AR 104, [1983] 3 CMLR 472, IAT; *Monteil* [1983] Imm AR 149, [1984] 1 CMLR 264, IAT; *Lubbersen* [1984] Imm AR 56, [1984] 3 CMLR 77, IAT.
5   HC 375, para 255; see **7.114** below.
6   SI 2000/2326.
7   SI 2000/2326, reg 19(2) and (3).

Public funds and voluntary unemployment

7.113 A detailed analysis of when an EEA national is entitled to claim public funds under the social security system of the UK is beyond the scope of the present work,[1] although many of the ECJ cases on free movement turn on this issue. Here we are concerned solely with the question of what effect recourse to public funds has on an EEA national's right to remain. The EC Directives distinguish between recourse to such funds prior to the issue of a first residence permit and thereafter. The ECJ decision in *Antonissen* has provided some guidance as to when a person retains Community law rights as a worker after admission to the territory of the host state but before a residence permit is issued, and may be summarised as follows:

(i)   a reasonable period (which may be six months) is *prima facie* sufficient for a person seeking employment to have obtained it. During that period a person will remain a worker, and cannot be discriminated against on social security grounds compared with UK nationals;

(ii)   thereafter a person who claims to be considered as a worker will have to produce evidence of attempts to seek employment in order to meet the Community definition of worker and thus remain a qualified person;

(iii)   if employment is obtained a residence permit cannot be refused solely on the ground of recourse to public funds.[2]

Regulation 5(2) of the Immigration (European Economic Area) Regulations 2000[3] provides that a worker does not cease to be a qualified person on the ground of unemployment if he or she is temporarily incapable of work as a result of illness or accident or is involuntarily unemployed and that fact is duly recorded by the relevant employment office. Thus whilst a worker is registered as seeking employment, he or she will not be considered as voluntarily unemployed. Community law envisages that evidence other than registration for work with the employment office will demonstrate that the person is still actively seeking work and remains a qualified person.[4] Where the worker is employed and relies on public funds to supplement his or her income, there is no incompatibility with the free movement provisions relating to workers, as has been held by the ECJ in *Kempf*.[5] The same must apply to those relying on the right of establishment. A former worker may also qualify under some other provision of Community law, but, apart from those permanently disabled by industrial accident, permanent reliance on the social security system of a host state is likely to become incompatible with the provisions of free movement. If someone leaves a job in order to obtain a better one or to enter further education or training, this is not voluntary unemployment which might lead to a curtailment of residence. In *Hoekstra-Unger*[6] the ECJ held that someone who had left one job and was capable of taking another one was still a 'worker entitled to the protection of the free movement provisions'. The case concerned a woman who became pregnant and left her employment. This certainly suggests that a person who is claiming unemployment or social security benefit and is actively seeking another job is still covered by the provisions of Article 39 EC, since it provides that a worker is someone who is seeking employment in the territory of another member state. Someone who gives up their current job to return to study or training in order to obtain better qualifications does not necessarily lose their status of 'worker', as the ECJ has held in *Lair*.[7] In such circumstances claiming unemployment or social security benefits or seeking an education grant can be done without risk of penalty.

1   Chapter 13 below contains an outline, including the concept of 'habitual residence'.
2   See also Case 53/81 *Levin* [1982] ECR 1035, [1982] 2 CMLR 454, ECJ and Case 139/85 *Kempf* [1987] 1 CMLR 764, ECJ.
3   SI 2000/2326.
4   *Antonissen* above.
5   Case 139/85 [1987] 1 CMLR 764, ECJ.
6   Case 75/63 *Hoekstra-Unger* [1964] ECR 177.
7   Case 39/86 *Lair v University of Hanover* [1989] 3 CMLR 545; Case C-357/89 *Raulin* [1994] 1 CMLR 227, ECJ.

Permanent residence in the UK

7.114 The entitlement to a residence permit discussed above presupposes that the person concerned fulfils the criteria of a qualified person or family member at the time of issue or renewal. Thus, a person who is established in business and has a right to a permanent residence may lose that right if he or she ceases to carry on business. There is a difference between the right of permanent residence under Community law and the grant of indefinite or permanent leave to remain under UK domestic immigration law. It is not clear whether and in what circumstances permanent residence can be revoked or curtailed under EC law other than for public policy reasons, nor exactly at which point a temporary or conditional right of residence turns into a permanent one.[1] The position under UK domestic law, on the other hand, is clear, and domestic law has also made provision for Community rights of residence to take effect as permanent permission under domestic law.[2] This, it seems, is the only permissible meeting point for the two systems; for the English Court of Appeal has made it very clear that the two systems of law are distinct and no reliance can be placed on an amalgam of the two.[3] So indefinite leave has to be pursued down the domestic route without tacking on helpful bits of EC law. Furthermore, the ECJ has held in *Kaba*[4] that even though the spouse of a UK national can achieve indefinite leave to remain in 12 months, the fact that it takes four years to achieve the same thing for the spouse of another EEA national is not a breach of the EC's rules against discrimination on nationality grounds. In this situation of uncertainty, the only sure path is to rely on the grant of permanent permission or indefinite leave given to EEA nationals under the Immigration Rules. The right to remain permanently under domestic law for those who have entered and remained under Community law is conveniently summarised in paragraphs 255 to 257 of the UK Immigration Rules (HC 395).

1 For nationality purposes, the Immigration (European Economic Area) Regulations 2000, SI 2000/2326 treat a very small group of EEA qualified persons as not being subject to restrictions on the period for which they may remain: reg 8(1) and (2). Significantly, workers and the self-employed are outside the group. In Case C-356/98 *Kaba* [2000] All ER (EC) 537 the ECJ stated that EC migrant workers' rights of residence are not unconditional, but did not say why (para 30).
2 HC 395, paras 255-257.
3 *Secretary of State for the Home Department v Sahota; Zeghraba v Secretary of State for the Home Department* [1997] Imm AR 429, CA; *Boukssid v Secretary of State for the Home Department* [1998] INLR 275, CA.
4 Case C-356/98 [2000] All ER (EC) 537, ECJ.

7.115 Paragraph 256 of the Immigration Rules permits self-employed EEA nationals who have ceased economic activity in the UK, and their family members, to remain in the UK indefinitely. The term 'ceased economic activity' is itself defined by regulation 4(2) of the Immigration (European Economic Area) Regulations 2000[1] and means:

(i) a person who has reached the state retirement age when he or she terminates activity, after having been self-employed in the UK for 12 months, and who has resided in the UK for more than three years;[2]

(ii) a person who has resided in the UK for more than two years and has terminated that activity as a result of permanent incapacity to work;[3]

(iii) a person who has resided in the UK and pursued self-employment but has terminated the activity as a result of permanent incapacity to work owing to an accident at work or occupational illness entitling the person to a state pension;[4]

(iv) a person who has been continuously resident and active in a self-employed capacity in the UK for three years, and is also active in a self-employed capacity in the territory of another member state but returns to his or her residence in the UK at least once a week.[5]

Spouses of UK nationals do not have to satisfy length of residence conditions in the first two categories, nor the self-employment condition in the first (retirement).[6] Family members of self-employed persons who die can also obtain permission to remain indefinitely if the qualified person resided in the UK during their working life continuously for more than two years or their death resulted from an accident at work or occupational disease.[7]

1   SI 2000/2326.
2   SI 2000/2326, reg 4(1)(a).
3   SI 2000/2326, reg 4(1)(b).
4   SI 2000/2326, reg 4(1)(c).
5   SI 2000/2326, reg 4(1)(d).
6   SI 2000/2326, reg 4(2).
7   HC 395, para 257(v) applying Council Directive (EEC) 75/34 EEC, art 3(2).

7.116 Workers and their families qualify for permanent residence if:

(i)   they are permanently incapacitated for work, due to an accident at work, an occupational disease entitling the person to a state disability pension, or from any other cause, after two years continuous residence in the UK;[1] or

(ii)   they have been continuously resident in the UK for three years, have been in employment in the UK or any other EEA state for the preceding 12 months, and have reached the state retirement age.[2]

Family members of workers who die can also obtain permission to remain indefinitely if the qualified person had resided in the UK during their working life continuously for more than two years or their death resulted from an accident at work or occupational disease.[3]

1   HC 395, para 257(ii)-(iii), applying Council Regulation (EEC) 1251/70, art 2.
2   HC 395, para 257(i), applying Council Regulation (EEC) 1251/70, art 2.
3   HC 395, para 257(v), applying Council Regulation (EEC) 1251/70, art 3.

7.117 These provisions of the UK Immigration Rules reflect the EC Directives, and the regulations also refer to the fact that workers and self-employed persons can choose to retire irrespective of the period of qualifying residence in the host country if they are married to a spouse who is or was a national of that country.[1] Such persons would almost certainly qualify for settlement under UK immigration law in any event. Continuity of residence, where it is required, is not affected by temporary absences of up to three months per year, nor by longer absences due to compliance with the obligations of military service.[2] Periods of involuntary unemployment or absences due to illness or accident count as periods of employment for these purposes.[3] No formalities are needed in order to exercise the right to remain.[4] Those exercising the right to remain after retirement are entitled to a residence permit, which, like all EC residence permits, must be valid throughout the territory of the member state issuing it, last for at least five years and be renewable automatically.[5]

1   Immigration (European Economic Area) Regulations 2000, SI 2000/2326, reg 4(2)(a), reflecting Council Directive (EEC) 75/34, art 3(2) and regulation (EEC) 1251/70, art 3(2).
2   SI 2000/2326, reg 4(4)(a) (for self-employed persons), reflecting Council Directive (EEC) 75/34 and regulation (EEC) 1251/70, art 4(1).
3   SI 2000/2326, reg 4(4)(b) (for self-employed persons), reflecting Council Directive (EEC) 75/34 and regulation (EEC) 1251/70, art 4(2).
4   Council Directive (EEC) 75/34 and regulation (EEC) 1251/70, art 5(2).
5   Council Directive (EEC) 75/34 and regulation (EEC) 1251/70, art 6.

7.118 In addition to reflecting Community rights, the Immigration Rules also provide that indefinite permission to remain may be granted to the holder of a residence permit or document valid for five years, who has remained for four years in accordance with the Immigration (European Economic Area) Order 1994[1] or the Immigration (European Economic Area) Regulations 2000[2] and continues so to do.[3] Permanent residence of this kind given under national law entitles the recipient to remain irrespective of their subsequent economic activity or later recourse to public funds. Although the Rules avoid the use of the word 'indefinite leave to remain', given that these nationals do not require leave to enter, the holder of this endorsement will be in a similar position in practice to someone who has an indefinite leave stamp.[4] The endorsement will also certainly remove any doubt about the eligibility of the EEA national to naturalise as a British citizen.[5] All attempts to cut short the waiting period using EC law have so far failed.[6]

1   SI 1994/1895.
2   SI 2000/2326.
3   HC 395, para 255.
4   This status does not lapse after a visit abroad: see Immigration Act 1971, s 3(4).
5   See **7.114** fn 1 above for discussion of whether there is any restriction on the period for which such nationals may stay.
6   *Sahota; Boukssid; Kaba* at **7.114** above, fnn 3 and 4.

Appeals against adverse decisions of UK immigration authorities

7.119 EEA nationals or family members who are excluded from the UK, refused a residence permit or residence document, or whose permit or document is withdrawn, may appeal against the refusal under appeal rights contained in Part VII of the Immigration (European Economic Area) Regulations 2000.[1] We deal with all the appeals affecting EEA nationals in chapter 18 below.

1   SI 2000/2326.

TERMINATION OF THE RIGHT TO RESIDE: CESSATION OF ENTITLEMENT AND EXCLUSION

Cessation and public policy

7.120 We have seen in the previous section that Community rights granted to the economically active continue whilst that activity is being exercised, with exceptions for retirement and permanent disability. What happens if it stops? An able-bodied EEA national below the age of retirement might cease to be economically active. The question then arises of whether a right to remain ceases to exist or can be terminated by non-renewal of a residence permit, and whether there is a power of expulsion which can then be exercised. In practice, the issue is unlikely to arise except in the case of an EEA national who is looking to long-term reliance on social security and public funds without any prospect of exercising any economic activity provided for by Community law. An EEA national who is self-supporting has a good chance of qualifying under one or other of the directives discussed above.[1]

1   See **7.73-7.78** above. It is only recourse to income support that leads to cesser of qualification.

7.121 In *Antonissen*[1] an EC national who had not worked in the UK had committed drugs offences during the course of his stay, and the question was whether he could rely on Community rights in the deportation appeal. He was held not to be a worker, and therefore had no rights in EC law. There are several early Immigration Appeal Tribunal decisions upholding refusals of admission to EC nationals on the grounds that they had not been working on previous visits to the UK and were not seeking to enter under one of the directives 68/360 or 73/148. Some of these cases must be regarded as unsound in the light of the later ECJ case law defining a 'worker' as someone genuinely seeking work.

1   Case C-292/89 [1991] ECR I-745, (1991) 2 CMLR 373, ECJ. It may be that the ruling in *Antonissen* is restricted to the case where an EU national has never obtained employment at all, and different considerations apply as to cesser of qualification after a number of years employment in the host state. See also *Monteil v Secretary of State for the Home Department* [1983] Imm AR 149, [1984] 1 CMLR 264, IAT; *Lubbersen v Secretary of State for the Home Department* [1984] Imm AR 56, [1984] 3 CMLR 77, IAT.

7.122 The UK stance on the possibility of removal of EEA nationals who cease to qualify has changed since the time of the Immigration (European Economic Area) Order 1994.[1] Then, the government considered that *either* ceasing to qualify *or* public policy was a ground for removal from the UK. This was made clear by Article 15(2) of the 1994 Order. Now, under the Immigration (European Economic Area) Regulations 2000,[2] ceasing to qualify is merely a ground for revoking or refusing to renew a residence permit or document.[3] The consequences of such action are left unstated, and rightly so. It is still uncertain whether an attempt to exclude an EEA national purely on the grounds of ceasing to qualify would be successful without any other aspect of conduct that brings public policy into play. Ceasing to qualify is not like overstaying leave - a clear breach of the conditions of leave which is met with the sanction of removal. They are conceptually quite different. A major difficulty facing the Home Office, which has the burden of proof,[4] would be to identify the moment when a person ceased to qualify. A person may remain a worker even when not actually in work or seeking work, for example, if employment is interrupted by pregnancy, illness or vocational training.[5] Further, there is the question of enforcement. Removal following a refusal of a residence permit can only be enforced by a decision to deport.[6] Deportation in UK law is not merely a measure to ensure removal, but also prevents re-entry during the currency of the Order.[7] It must be doubtful whether a mere failure to seek to carry on an economic activity would enable a member state to exclude an EEA national and prevent admission in the future, even for EC activities such as the receipt of services.[8]

1   SI 1994/1895.
2   SI 2000/2316.
3   SI 2000/2316, reg 22(2).
4   See observations of Immigration Appeal Tribunal in *Giangregorio* [1983] Imm AR 104, [1983] 2 CMLR 472, IAT; decision of ECJ in *Antonissen* (1991) 2 CMLR 373.
5   See **7.113** above.
6   Because EEA nationals do not require leave to enter, they do not become overstayers and cannot be removed under the Immigration and Asylum Act 1999, s 10.
7   Immigration Act 1971, s 5: see chapter 15 below.
8   A person who has ceased to be a worker may seek to enter as a provider or recipient of services, or indeed to cross internal frontiers as a citizen of the EU. There has been concern to stop income support but no attempt has been made to deport such persons. See *R v Secretary of State for the Home Department, ex p Vitale* [1996] All ER (EC) 461, CA.

7.123   The implications of Article 18 EC (ex Article 8a) of the EEC Treaty, as amended by the Treaty on European Union, also fall to be considered. The UK avoids these questions in the Immigration (European Economic Area) Regulations 2000[1] by elision of the rights of EU nationals and the rights of other EEA nationals under the EEA agreement. But EU nationals have the right to move and reside freely within the territory of member states, 'subject to the limitations and conditions laid down in this Treaty and the measures adopted to give it effect'.[2] Expulsion of an EU national on the ground that he or she is no longer a qualified person within the meaning of the 2000 Regulations would materially affect the right of residence. The limitations referred to in Article 18 are unclear, but most likely mean the public policy provisions which we shall consider in the next section. It is unclear whether the reference to 'conditions' is also a reference to these provisions as developed in the directives and case law. It would be highly contentious to assert that an EU national who qualified for admission to the territory of another member state failed to meet the conditions of the EC Treaty when no longer exercising a specific economic activity. None of the other provisions of the Treaty qualifies or limits a broad construction of Article 18 or provides that a person who falls outside of the definition of worker, self-employed and the like can be expelled. If Articles 39 to 50 EC (ex Articles 48 to 60) were exhaustive of the rights of entry and free movement, then there would be no room for the 1990 and 1993 Directives giving free movement rights to the self-sufficient, the retired and students.[3]

1   SI 2000/2326.
2   See *Ex p Vitale* [1995] NLJR 631.
3   See 7.73–7.78 above.

7.124   We suggest that the principle of proportionality, as developed in Community law,[1] makes it unlikely that the ECJ would countenance the use of the power of deportation against an EEA national for ceasing to qualify under the directives, in the absence of public policy grounds for the expulsion. In our view some element of public policy, public security or public health beyond mere cesser of qualification is needed.

1   See Case 222/84 *Johnston v Chief Constable of the Royal Ulster Constabulary* [1986] ECR 1651, ECJ.

Public policy

7.125   The free movement provisions of the EC Treaty are all subject to what EC law calls 'the public policy proviso', although public policy is but one limb. For workers, Article 39(3) EC (ex Article 48(3)) says that the free movement provisions, but not the provisions for the abolition of discrimination based on nationality, shall be 'subject to limitations justified on grounds of public policy, public security or public health'. So far as concerns the right of establishment, Article 46(1) EC (ex Article 56(1)) says:

> 'the provisions of this Chapter and measures taken in pursuance thereof shall not prejudice the applicability of provisions laid down by law, regulation or administrative action providing for special treatment for foreign nationals on grounds of public policy, public security or public health.'

So far as services are concerned, Article 55 EC (ex Article 66) of the Consolidated Treaty of Rome provides that the provisions of Articles 45-48 EC (ex Article 55–58) apply also to the matters covered in the chapter concerning services. This means that the provisions of Article 46(1) EC apply to the provision of services as well as to the right of establishment. Although the wording of the public policy proviso is slightly different as between workers and those relying on the right of establishment, the ECJ has made it clear that in practice there should be no difference.[1] The rights of free movement of the self-sufficient, the retired and vocational students are also subject to the public policy proviso.[2]

1   Case 48/75 *Royer* [1976] ECR 497, [1976] 2 CMLR 619.
2   See Council Directives (EEC) 90/364, 90/365 and 93/96 relating to residence rights of self-sufficient and retired persons and students respectively.

Implementation of the public policy proviso

7.126   The public policy proviso is implemented by Council Directive (EEC) 64/221 of 25 February 1964. This applies to nationals of a member state who are workers, self-employed persons or providers or recipients of services, and their families. Its provisions are also expressly made to cover those who have ceased to be economically active as a result of retirement or incapacity, to the economically self-sufficient, and to students.[1] The Directive applies to all measures on grounds of public policy, public security or public health concerning entry into, the issue or renewal of residence permits in and expulsion from an EU country.[2] In the UK the provisions of the Directive are reflected in the Immigration (European Economic Area) Regulations 2000,[3] regulation 21(1), dealing with exclusion from the UK; regulation 21(3)(b), dealing with removal; regulation 22(1), dealing with refusal to issue a residence permit or document; regulation 22(2)(a), dealing with revocation of or refusal to renew a residence permit or document; and regulation 22(4)(a), dealing with an immigration officer's power to revoke an EEA family permit on arrival in the UK. They apply to all EEA nationals and their families, and to persons exercising rights under Association Agreements.[4] A member state cannot invoke the public policy proviso to serve economic ends, such as protecting the employment prospects of its own nationals as against other EEA nationals.[5] The Directive also makes it clear that the expiry of the travel documents or passports, which EEA nationals had on arrival, is not a good reason for their expulsion from the country, and that despite their expiry such nationals are free to travel back to their own country.[6] It also imposes important substantive[7] and procedural limits on the operation of the public policy proviso.[8]

1   See Council Directive (EEC) 72/194, art 1, applying Council Directive (EEC) 64/221 to retired workers; Council Directives (EEC) 90/364 and 90/365, art 2, applying it to self-sufficient and retired persons; and Council Directive (EEC) 93/96, art 2, applying it to students. A useful account of Directive 64/221 is given in the Commission Communication to the Council and the European Parliament, August 1999.
2   Council Directive (EEC) 64/221, art 2(1).
3   SI 2000/2326, as amended by the Immigration (European Economic Area) (Amendment) Regulations 2001, SI 2001/865.
4   By Article 14 of Commission Decision (ECSC) 1/80 under the Ankara Agreement: see C-340/97 *Nazli v Stadt Nürnberg* [2000] ECR I-957, para 63.
5   Council Directive (EEC) 64/221, art 2; SI 2000/2326, reg 23(a).
6   Council Directive (EEC) 64/221, art 3(3) and (4).
7   Council Directive (EEC) 64/221, art 3(1): see below.
8   Council Directive (EEC) 64/221, arts 8 and 9.

7.127 In a series of important early decisions, the ECJ made it clear that (in contrast to the position in UK immigration law) the principle of free movement within the EEA is far more important than any exceptions to it. First, it stipulated that in any case in which a member state is relying on the public policy proviso, it has to show that the measure in question is justified on the basis of some objective which forms part of public policy, public security or public health.[1] Secondly, the ECJ has repeatedly held that free movement is a fundamental general principle and that the public policy proviso is an exception which, like all derogations from a fundamental principle of the EC Treaty, should be construed restrictively.[2] Thirdly, the court has repeatedly emphasised that exclusion or expulsion on the ground of public policy should not occur unless the person's 'presence or conduct constitutes a genuine and sufficiently serious threat to public policy'.[3] So the person's presence must not only be a genuine threat to the public policy objective, but also a sufficiently serious one.

1   Case 48/75 *Royer* [1976] ECR 497, [1976] 2 CMLR 619, ECJ.
2   Case 41/74 *Van Duyn v Home Office* [1974] ECR 1337; Case 67/74 *Bonsignore v Stadt Köln* [1975] ECR 297; Case 36/75 *Rutili* [1975] ECR 1219, [1976] 1 CMLR 140, ECJ; Case 139/85 *Kempf v Staatssecretaris van Justitie* [1986] ECR 1741; Case C-348/96 *Calfa* [1999] ECR I-11; Case C-340/97 *Nazli v Stadt Nürnberg* [2000] ECR I-957.
3   Case 30/77 *R v Bouchereau* [1977] ECR 1999; *Bonsignore, Calfa, Nazli* above.

7.128 Article 3(1) of Council Directive (EEC) 64/221 provides that measures taken on the grounds of public policy or public security should be based exclusively on the personal conduct of the individual concerned. What is meant by this was explained in two early cases before the ECJ. In *Van Duyn v Home Office (No 2)*[1] a member of the Church of Scientology challenged her refusal of entry to Britain under the general ban on scientologists, and her case was referred to the ECJ. The court explored the term 'personal conduct' and concluded that, while a person's past association does not in general suffice, present association 'which reflects participation in the activities of the body or organisation and identification with its aims and designs' may be considered a voluntary act of the person concerned and thus part of his or her personal conduct. Being a member of the Church of Scientology was personal conduct by which the UK government could justify her exclusion from the UK on the ground that her presence was not conducive to the public good. But if the ban or expulsion is for reasons that go much wider than the personal conduct of the person concerned, this may not be allowed. In *Bonsignore*[2] an Italian worker resident in Cologne purchased a Beretta gun from an unidentified source, and while manipulating the gun he accidentally killed his younger brother. He was found guilty by a German court of illegal possession of firearms and causing death by negligence. The German authorities wanted to deport him, but clearly the only reason for doing this was as a general deterrent and not because Bonsignore was likely to commit similar offences again. The ECJ held that Article 3(1) of the Directive made it clear that EEC nationals could not be subjected to decisions made on grounds extraneous to their personal and individual cases. Read together with Article 3(2) it barred member states from expelling EEC nationals in order to deter other aliens from committing identical or similar offences, that is to say for 'general preventive' or 'deterrent' reasons. This reasoning has been upheld in subsequent cases so as to prevent the automatic expulsion of persons committing drugs offences in particular.[3]

1   Case 41/74 [1974] ECR 1337, [1975] Ch 358.
2   Case 67/74 [1975] ECR 297, [1975] 1 CMLR 472.

3   Case C-348/96 *Calfa* [1999] ECR I-11; Case C-340/97 *Nazli v Stadt Nürnberg* [2000] ECR I-957, ECJ.

7.129   Article 3(2) of Council Directive (EEC) 64/221, on which the court relied in *Bonsignore*, provides that previous criminal convictions shall not in themselves constitute grounds for the taking of measures on the grounds of public policy or public security. The *Bonsignore* case makes it clear that exclusion or deportation of an EEA national cannot be justified on the grounds of general deterrence. The Article also means that a country's authorities cannot apply a blanket rule excluding from their territory anyone with a criminal record, and certainly renders inapplicable to EEA nationals immigration rules preventing the entry of persons convicted of an extraditable offence unless there are 'strong compassionate reasons'.[1]

1   See HC 395, r 320(18).

7.130   In *Bonsignore* the court further held that public policy measures should only be applied if there is a likelihood that the offender will commit further offences or in some other way infringe public security or policy. In *R v Bouchereau*,[1] a case concerning a French national who pleaded guilty to drug offences before an English court which wished to recommend him for deportation, the ECJ described the public policy limitation as follows:

> 'In so far as it may justify certain restrictions on the free movement of persons subject to Community law, recourse by a national authority to the concept of public policy presupposes, in any event, the existence, in addition to the perturbation of the social order which any infringement of the law involves, of a genuine and sufficiently serious threat to the requirements of public policy affecting one of the fundamental interests of society.'

The court held that a criminal conviction can be taken into account only in so far as the circumstances which gave rise to the conviction are evidence of personal conduct:

> 'constituting a present threat to the requirements of public policy. . . . Although, in general, a finding that such threat exists implies the existence in the individual concerned of a propensity to act in the same way in the future, it is possible that past conduct alone may constitute such a threat to the requirements of public policy.'

1   Case 30/77 *R v Bouchereau* [1978] QB 732, [1977] ECR 1999, ECJ.

7.131   There was uncertainty in the UK case law applying these principles as to whether a propensity to re-offend was required and in what circumstances it might not be required. In considering a recommendation for deportation of a convicted rapist, the Court of Appeal in *R v Secretary of State for the Home Department, ex p Santillo*[1] considered that future risk posed by the possibility of re-offending was required as a matter of Community law and common sense. In *R v Secretary of State for the Home Department, ex p Al-Sabah*[2] the Court of Appeal doubted these remarks, regarding them as inconsistent with *Bouchereau*. In *Marchon*[3] a Portuguese doctor who had been convicted of importing 4.5 kilos of heroin and sentenced to 14 years' imprisonment was held not to need any propensity to re-offend in order to merit deportation on public good grounds. The court regarded this conduct by a doctor as particularly disgraceful, and indicative of a disregard for the basic or fundamental moral tenets of society.

1   [1981] QB 778, CA.
2   [1992] Imm AR 223, CA.
3   *Marchon* [1993] Imm AR 384, CA.

7.132 The confusion has, we believe, been cleared up by more recent ECJ cases such as *Nazli v Stadt Nürnberg*,[1] involving a Turkish worker exercising rights under the Ankara Agreement and Commission Decision (ECSC) 1/80 under it in Germany. Mr Nazli had been convicted of a drugs-related offence in circumstances indicating no propensity to re-offend, but German aliens' law provided for mandatory expulsion after conviction of drugs offences.[2] The court held that a person enjoying Treaty rights and rights analogous to them under the Association Agreement could not be expelled 'as a deterrent to other aliens without the personal conduct of the person concerned giving reason to consider that he will commit other serious offences prejudicial to the requirements of public policy in the host member state'.[3] Earlier in its judgment the court referred to the requirement that the expulsion measure 'is justified because . . . personal conduct indicates a risk of new and serious prejudice to the requirements of public policy'. This means that in every case the personal conduct of the person involved, and in particular the indications of future risk of threats to public policy, must be assessed. Criminal convictions even for the most heinous crimes will, we suggest, never be enough by themselves.

1   Case C-340/97 [2000] ECR I-957, ECJ.
2   See also Case C-348/96 *Re Donatella Calfa* [1999] 2 CMLR 1138, ECJ, a case involving a tourist expelled for life under Greek law for possession of drugs.
3   *Nazli* fn 1 above, para 64.

Proportionality

7.133 Measures taken by member states in respect of nationals of other member states must be reasonable and not disproportionate to the gravity of their conduct.[1] As the Court of Appeal observed in *International Traders' Ferry*,[2] proportionality 'requires the court to judge the necessity of the action taken as well as whether it was within the range of courses of action that could reasonably be followed', and it may be a more exacting test than a *Wednesbury* formulation.[3] In *B v Secretary of State for the Home Department*[4] Simon Brown LJ pointed out that even if the deportation of an EC national could be justified by the existence of 'a genuine and sufficiently serious threat to the requirements of public policy affecting one of the fundamental interests of society',[5] the requirement of proportionality was held to mean that deportation 'must be both appropriate and necessary for the attainment of the public policy objective sought—the containment of the threat—and also must not impose an excessive burden on the individual, the deportee'. In that case, which pre-dated the coming into force of the Human Rights Act 1998, the Court of Appeal considered the proportionality of a proposed deportation of an EU national convicted of persistent sexual abuse of his daughter on public good grounds, both through the free movement provisions of the EC Treaty and also through the constitutional requirement to respect fundamental rights as guaranteed by the ECHR, enshrined in Article 6 of the consolidated Treaty on European Union (formerly Article F), which gave statutory force to the case law of the ECJ.[6] It held that although the Tribunal was entitled to find the existence of a relevant threat to the requirements of public policy arising both from the intrinsic seriousness of the appellant's offending and from a propensity to re-offend, the remaining and determinative issue was that of proportionality, which was a matter of law. In the circumstances of the case, given the appellant's extremely long residence in the UK, the court held deportation a disproportionate response.

1   *R v Bouchereau* [1978] QB 732 at 743, per Advocate General Warner.
2   *R v Chief Constable of Sussex, ex p ITF Ltd* [1997] 2 CMLR 164, CA. The House of Lords upheld the CA's decision that the Chief Constable's refusal to police the port more than twice a week, meaning that export of live animals was restricted on other days because of demonstrators, was a proportionate measure to maintain public order, although it had a restrictive effect on exports, and was therefore justified under Article 36 EC (now art 30): [1999] 1 All ER 130.
3   In *Wilander v Tobin* [1997] 2 CMLR 346 the Court of Appeal, holding that mandatory drug testing of sporting competitors was justified by compelling reasons of public interest, observed that proportionality was close to concepts of reasonableness and natural justice, and that the combination of safeguards such as the review body, the appeal committee and the courts made the measure proportionate (assuming without deciding that it restricted art 39 EC free movement rights).
4   [2000] Imm AR 478.
5   *R v Bouchereau* [1978] QB 732 at 760.
6   Case 260/89 *Elliniki Radiophonia Tileorassi AE v Pliroforissis and Kouvelas* [1991] ECR I-2925.

7.134 Although the application of the proviso depends on the personal conduct of the person involved, the ECJ has held that the activities in question need not be illegal for public policy to be invoked; the activities of scientologists which led to the blanket ban on their immigration to the UK in *Van Duyn* are sufficient. The decision in *Van Duyn*[1] indicates that a ban on the immigration of foreign nationals for public policy reasons is not invalidated merely because no such ban has been imposed on its own nationals. Under international law it is not normally possible for a country to ban its own nationals. The decision makes it clear that the application of the public policy proviso to EC immigration law inevitably involves some discrimination against foreign nationals. However, it is doubtful to what extent a host state can take measures on public policy grounds that it cannot take against own nationals. *Rutili v Minister for the Interior*[2] concerned an Italian national who had spent most of his life in Alsace-Lorraine. He was a political activist who had been involved in the 'events' of May 1968 in France, but had never been convicted of any offence. The French Ministry of the Interior made an order banning him from Alsace-Lorraine. The ECJ ruled, amongst other things, that the public policy proviso does not apply to the right to move freely within the territory of a particular member state, and so a partial residence prohibition, restraining a migrant from working in one part of the territory of a member state could only be applied in those circumstances when such a limitation would be justified under national law in the case of a national.

1   [1975] Ch 358, [1974] ECR 1337.
2   [1975] ECR 1219, [1976] 1 CMLR 140, ECJ.

7.135 Further in *Adoui and Cornuaille*[1] the court considered the applicability of expulsion on grounds relating to prostitution, which was not specifically prohibited by Belgian law. The court noted:

'Although Community law does not impose upon the member states a uniform scale of values as regards the assessment of conduct which may be considered as contrary to public policy, it should nevertheless be stated that conduct may not be considered as being of a sufficiently serious nature to justify restrictions on the admission of nationals of another member state in a case where the former member state does not adopt, with respect to the same conduct on the part of its own nationals, repressive measures or other genuine and effective measures intended to combat such conduct.'

Applying this dictum to the Church of Scientology case, it would appear that unless the UK is prepared to take repressive measures on the grounds of adherence to Scientology against all, including own nationals, it is not entitled to refuse admission to EEA nationals on this ground alone.

1   Case 115/81 [1982] ECR 1665, [1982] 3 CMLR 631.

Public health

7.136 Article 4 of Council Directive (EEC) 64/221 provides that the only diseases or disabilities justifying refusal of entry into a territory or refusal to issue a first residence permit are those listed in the Annexe. These are infectious or contagious diseases requiring quarantine, active tuberculosis, syphilis, and other infectious or contagious diseases if they are the subject of provisions for the protection of nationals of the host country. Drug addiction and profound mental disturbance are listed as diseases and disabilities which might threaten public policy or public security. Article 4(2) makes it clear that a disease or disability occurring after a residence permit has been issued for the first time does not justify a refusal to renew the permit or to order the expulsion of the person from the country. Article 4(3) states that EC countries may not introduce new provisions or practices which are more restrictive than those in force at the date of the Directive. In the UK these provisions are reflected in regulation 23(d) and (e) and Schedule 1 to the Immigration (European Economic Area) Regulations 2000.[1]

1   SI 2000/2326.

Procedural safeguards

7.137 In addition to the substantive limitations on the power of member states to apply the public policy proviso, Council Directive (EEC) 64/221 also includes important procedural safeguards, namely the right to be given reasons when a decision is made on public policy grounds and the right to some form of judicial review.

Reasons

7.138 Article 7 of Council Directive (EEC) 64/221 gives the persons concerned the right to be notified of any decision to refuse the issue or renewal of a residence permit or to expel them from the territory. The notice should also state the period allowed for leaving the territory and, except in cases of urgency, this period should be not less than 15 days if the person has not yet been granted a residence permit and not less than one month in all other cases. Article 6 of the Directive provides that where any decision is taken on grounds of public policy, public security or public health, that person shall be informed of the ground, unless this is contrary to the interests of the security of the state involved.[1] In the

Rutili case[2] the ECJ stated that this provision meant giving the immigrant 'a precise and comprehensive statement of the grounds for the decision' to enable him or her to take effective steps to prepare a defence.

1   See Immigration (European Economic Area) Regulations 2000, SI 2000/2326, reg 23(f).
2   Case 36/75 *Rutili* [1975] ECR 1219, [1976] 1 CMLR 140, ECJ.

Review and appeal

7.139 Article 8 of Council Directive (EEC) 64/221 requires member states to provide for persons relying on EC rights the same legal remedies in respect of decisions concerning entry, or refusing the issue or renewal of a residence permit, or ordering expulsion from the territory, as are available to nationals of the state concerned in respect of acts of the administration. In *Shingara and Radiom* the ECJ held that this does not mean that EEA nationals refused entry should be given the same rights of appeal as British citizens whose claim is disputed,[1] since nationals of the member state have a right of entry which is not comparable with the situation of a national of another member state whose exclusion might be justified on public policy or national security grounds.[2] Article 9 of the Directive grants further rights to those refused a renewal of their residence permit or ordered to be expelled. Where there is no appeal, or where the appeal goes only to the legal validity of the decision and not to the merits, or is not suspensive, they are entitled to the opinion of a competent authority which is different from the one which makes the decision[3] so as to enable an exhaustive examination of all the facts and circumstances, including the expediency of the proposed measure, to be carried out before the decision is finally taken.[4] In *R v Secretary of State for the Home Department, ex p Santillo*[5] the court held that a recommendation for deportation by a criminal court could constitute such an opinion. Although Article 9 imposed obligations on member states which may be relied on by individuals, it left a margin of discretion to the state to define the 'competent authority'. It needed to be independent of the administrative body which made the decision, and the person affected by the decision must enjoy the right of representation and defence before it.[6]

1   Under Immigration and Asylum Act 1999, s 59.
2   Joined Cases C-111/95 and C-65/95 *R v Secretary of State for the Home Department, ex p Shingara and Radiom* [1997] 3 CMLR 703, ECJ.
3   A decision to refuse the first issue of a residence permit, or to expel someone before issue of the permit, may on request be referred to an independent competent authority under Council Directive 64/221, art 9(2), in cases where there is no effective or suspensive appeal: *Shingara and Radiom* above.
4   *Santillo* fn 5 below; Case 115/81 *Adoui and Cornuaille* [1982] ECR 1665; Case C-175/94 *R v Secretary of State for the Home Department, ex p Gallagher* [1995] ECR I-4253.
5   [1980] ECR 1585, [1980] 2 CMLR 308, ECJ.
6   See also *Adoui and Cornuaille* above.

7.140 In *Gallagher*[1] the ECJ held that Article 9 of Council Directive (EEC) 64/221 did not preclude the authority which made the order from appointing the competent authority, provided the latter performed its duties independently and without being subject to the body making the decision. The court also confirmed that in cases under Article 9(1) where there is no effective appeal, the opinion of the competent authority as to deportation must be obtained before the decision to expel.[2] This is the case in recommendations for deportation under section 3(6) of the Immigration Act 1971, where the criminal court recommending deportation has been held to be a competent authority.[3] In cases where there is an appeal before the appellate authority, the decision precedes the appeal, but no order is made unless the decision is upheld on appeal. regulation 29 of the Immigration (European Economic Area) Regulations[4] provides appeal rights for EEA nationals reflecting those of non-EEA nationals.

1   [1996] 1 CMLR 557.
2   Case 175/94 *Gallagher* [1996] 1 CMLR 557, ECJ.
3   *R v Secretary of State for the Home Department, ex p Dannenberg* [1984] QB 766.
4   SI 2000/2326.

7.141 In *Yiadom*[1] the ECJ held that the safeguards of Article 9 of Council Directive (EEC) 64/221 did not apply to persons excluded from the territory, ie refused leave to enter. In that case, the applicant had been on temporary admission under paragraph 21 of Schedule 2 to the Immigration Act 1971 for seven months awaiting a decision on leave to enter. The court condemned the fiction of temporary admission and said that for EC purposes, a decision to remove an EU national pursuant to a refusal of leave to enter after such a protracted period on temporary admission was in fact an expulsion decision, and attracted the appropriate safeguards of Article 9. The lack of in-country appeal rights in cases of refusal of leave to enter has been the subject of domestic legal challenge[2] on the ground of disproportionate interference with freedom of movement and with the right to a fair trial and equality of arms.[3] In *Shingara* the court held that, since the prohibition of entry derogated from a fundamental principle and could not therefore be of indefinite duration, Community nationals were entitled to have their situation re-examined if they thought the circumstances justifying their refusal of entry no longer existed.[4] The new decision may be the subject of an appeal on the basis of Article 8 and, where appropriate, Article 9 of the Directive.[5]

1   Case C-357/98 *R v Secretary of State for the Home Department, ex p Yiadom* [2001] All ER (EC) 267, ECJ.
2   In *Darwiche* (CO 413/1998) April 2000 an application for judicial review which challenged the lack of suspensive appeal against on-entry refusal of an EEA national with permanent residence was settled by consent after the grant of permission.
3   In *Loutchansky*, however, the applicant, who was subject to an exclusion order on the personal direction of the Secretary of State for the Home Department, and had a pending Special Immigration Appeals Commission appeal, wished to enter the UK to pursue legal proceedings. On refusal of leave to enter he took proceedings alleging breach of Article 6 equality of arms, and the matter was settled by the Home Office issuing him with a multiple-entry 'laissez-passer' enabling him to come and go to and from the UK, and granting him temporary admission on arrival, although the exclusion order remained in place.
4   *Shingara and Radiom* 7.139 fn 2 above, para 40.
5   *Shingara and Radiom* above, para 42.

Recommendation for deportation

7.142 In *Santillo*[1] an EC national had been sentenced to a long prison sentence for rape and the Secretary of State for the Home Department signed an order at the beginning of the sentence pursuant to a recommendation for deportation made by the sentencing court. The ECJ accepted that, since the criminal courts in the UK were independent of the administration and the person concerned had a right to be represented and to exercise his or her rights of defence before such courts, a recommendation for deportation by a criminal court at the time of conviction could constitute an 'opinion' under Article 9 of Council Directive (EEC) 64/221. But, it added, the criminal court must take account in particular of the provisions of Article 3 of the Directive inasmuch as the mere existence of criminal convictions cannot automatically constitute grounds for deportation. The ECJ was concerned at the time lapse between the making of a recommendation and its implementation by the Secretary of State. A long prison sentence may have intervened. The court stated that the opinion of the competent authority must be sufficiently proximate in time to the decision ordering expulsion to ensure that there are no new factors to be taken into consideration, and that both the administration and the person concerned are in a position in the normal case to take cognisance of the reasons which led the competent authority to make its recommendation. A lapse of time amounting to several years between the recommendation and the decision to deport is liable to deprive the recommendation of its function as an opinion within the meaning of Article 9. It is essential that the social danger resulting from a foreign national's presence be assessed at the very time when the deportation decision is made against him or her, as the facts to be taken into account, particularly those concerning his or her conduct, are likely to change in the course of time. When the case returned to the Court of Appeal[2] it held that a lapse of four-and-a-half years was not, in the particular circumstances, sufficient to deprive the recommendation of its function as an 'opinion'. In *R v Secretary of State for the Home Department, ex p Dannenberg*[3] the Court of Appeal held that, where a criminal court's recommendation to deport constitutes the opinion of the competent authority for the purposes of Article 9, it must be reasoned to such a degree as to enable the deporting agency to monitor its lawfulness and the alien to decide whether to challenge it. This meant that magistrates had to give reasons for a decision to recommend deportation of an EC national, even though they do not normally give reasons when imposing a sentence.

1   [1980] ECR 1585.
2   [1981] QB 778, [1981] 2 All ER 897.
3   [1984] QB 766.

Appeal to the appellate authority

7.143 In expulsion cases, the Secretary of State's policy is not to rely on a recommendation for deportation in the case of EEA nationals, but to institute deportation proceedings so as to ensure that the person concerned has an appeal.[1] Further, there are cases of proposed deportation on grounds conducive to the public good that do not involve criminal conduct. Expulsion on grounds of public policy, public security or public health equates with deportation on public good grounds in domestic law. All EEA deportations except for those involving national security will thus come before the appellate authority. In *Marchon* the Court of Appeal held that the failure of the criminal court to make a recommendation was irrelevant to the appellate authority's consideration of public policy.[2] But if a criminal court has considered a recommendation and decides that the criminality involved does not merit one, it is difficult to see how such comments are irrelevant, especially as this is the expression of an opinion as required by the Council Directive (EEC) 64/221. Even if the opinion is not binding on the competent authority, regard must be had to it.[3] The appellate authority must consider the question of public good, in the light of the Community rules discussed above: thus the mere existence of the conviction is insufficient, and sufficient reasons must be given to justify the deportation of a qualified person on grounds of public policy.

1   IDI Nov/00, Ch 13, s 1, para 2.8.
2   *R v Secretary of State for the Home Department, ex p Marchon* [1993] Imm AR 384, CA.
3   See *Dannenberg* [1984] QB 766 at 775F–H.

National security cases

7.144 Where a decision to exclude, or to refuse a residence permit or expel an EEA national is the personal decision of the Secretary of State for the Home Department for political or diplomatic reasons, or is based on national security grounds, regulations 27 and 31 of the Immigration (European Economic Area) Regulations 2000[1] apply and the appeal is to the Special Immigration Appeals Commission instead of the appellate authority. In national security cases there is a derogation from the duty of giving reasons.[2] The Special Immigration Appeals Commission procedure would undoubtedly be deemed compliant with the reduced duty, given the procedural safeguard of the special advocate who sees all the national security evidence not available to the appellant and represents the appellant's interests in relation to that evidence.

1   SI 2000/2326.
2   Council Directive (EEC) 64/221, art 6; SI 2000/2326, reg 23(f).

RIGHTS UNDER ASSOCIATION AGREEMENTS

7.145 The EC Treaty provides, under Article 310 EC (ex Article 238), that the Community may conclude with a third state, a union of states or an international organisation, an agreement establishing an association, involving reciprocal rights and obligations, common actions and special procedures. Article 300 EC (ex Article 228) provides that such agreements shall be negotiated by the Commission, and concluded by the Council, after consulting the European Parliament where required. Agreements concluded under these conditions shall be binding on the institutions of the Community and on member states.[1] A number of these agreements have implications for immigration rights of nationals of third countries with whom such agreements have been concluded. Agreements entered into by both the EC and member states and a third country are mixed agreements, but do not for that reason cease to be enforceable in Community law.[2]

1   Article 300(2) EC (ex art 228(2)).
2   Case 12/86 *Demirel v Stadt Schwäbisch Gmünd* [1987] ECR 3719, [1989] 1 CMLR 421, ECJ.

Turkish Association Agreement

7.146 On 12 September 1963 at Ankara the EC signed the Turkey EEC Association Agreement, which was supplemented on 23 November 1970 by the

Brussels Protocol.[1] These Agreements aimed to establish free movement provisions between Turkey and the EC within 22 years, and this itself was intended as a step towards full Turkish membership of the EC. These aspirations have never been achieved by implementing measures, and full Turkish membership has been a somewhat distant prospect as a result of strained political relations arising from the 1980 military coup in Turkey and the subsequent war. However, the Agreement provided for a Council of Association on which the various parties are represented.[2] By Article 36 of the 1970 Protocol, the Council of Association is given the power to decide on the rules necessary to implement the progressive stages for the free movement of workers within the 20-year period.[3] The Association Council adopted three decisions: Decisions 2/76 of 20 December 1976, 1/80 of 19 September 1980 and 3/80 of the same date,[4] which for long were unpublished but have become important for Turkish nationals already resident in the EU by reason of a series of decisions of the ECJ starting with the decisions in *Sevince*[5] and *Kus*.[6]

1   A full description of the Association Agreement is not possible within the confines of this volume, but the reader is referred to N Rogers *A Practitioner's Guide to the Turkey-EC Association Agreement* published by ILPA (2000, Kluwer); Martin and Guild *Free movement of persons in the European Union*, (1996).
2   *Ankara Agreement* 1963, art 6, OJ C113/2 24.12.1963.
3   Additional Protocol signed at Brussels, 23 November 1970, art 36, OJ C/113/2 24.12.1973. There is also a power to make recommendations in art 38, but it is the rules which are binding.
4   The decisions are not published in the OJ, but are set out in full in the ILPA guide.
5   Case C-192/89 *Sevince v Staatsecretaris van Justitie* [1992] 2 CMLR 57.
6   Case C-237/91 *Kazim Kus v Landeshaupstadt Wiesbaden* [1993] 2 CMLR 887, ECJ. Followed in *Eroglu v Land Baden-Württemberg*: Case C-355/93 [1994] ECR I-5113, ECJ.

7.147 The decisions of the ECJ in *Demirel*[1] and *Sevince*[2] held that the programme for free movement of persons between Turkey and the EC by the end of 1985 was not itself of direct effect and therefore gave no rights to Turkish nationals to enter the territory of the EC, even though the Turkey-EC Association Agreement was potentially capable of giving rise to individual rights, if the rules on direct effect were met.[3] However, in *Sevince* the court held that some decisions of the Association Council were sufficiently clear and precise as to be capable of direct effect, although the decision in question was of no assistance to the particular applicant in that case because he was not legally employed. It was only in *Kus*[4] that a Turkish worker succeeded in using an Association Council decision to obtain a fresh work and residence permit in reliance on Community law. The crucial provision relied on in *Kus* is Article 6 of Decision 1/80. This provides:

'1. Subject to Article 7 on free access to employment for members of his family, a Turkish worker duly registered as belonging to the labour force of a member state:
   – shall be entitled in that member state, after one year's legal employment, to the renewal of his permit to work for the same employer, if a job is available;
   – shall be entitled in that member state, after three years of legal employment and subject to the priority to be given to workers of member states of the Community, to respond to another offer of employment, with an employer of his choice, made under normal conditions and registered with the employment services of that State for the same occupation;
   – shall enjoy free access in that member state to any paid employment of his choice, after four years of legal employment.'[5]

1 [1987] ECR 3719, [1989] 1 CMLR 421, ECJ.
2 Case C-192/89 *Sevince v Staatsecretaris van Justitie* [1992] 2 CMLR 57.
3 Following *Demirel* the Court of Appeal in the UK held that art 12 of the Ankara Agreement of 12 September 1963 gave no free movement rights to Turkish nationals: *R v Secretary of State for the Home Department, ex p Narin* [1990] 2 CMLR 233, CA.
4 [1993] 2 CMLR 887.
5 Decision 1/80, art 6.

7.148 This right only applies after Turkish nationals have entered a member state and taken up lawful employment there. It does not grant a right to enter or obtain a work permit, and it does not allow a Turkish worker to move from one member state to another, so it is different from the rights of EEA nationals to seek and obtain work. It is not a free movement right, but gives Turkish workers a progressive series of rights over a four-year period, leading to their eventual integration into the host state's workforce. In setting out the considerable ambit and scope of these rights, the ECJ considers that Article 6 of Decision 1/80 forms part and thus constitutes a further stage in securing freedom of movement of workers on the basis of Articles 39 to 41 EC, and so says it is essential to extend so far as possible the principles in the EC Articles to Turkish workers.[1] This is consistent with Article 12 of the Ankara Agreement, which states:

> 'The contracting parties agree to be guided by Articles 48, 49 and 50 [now Articles 39-41] of the Treaty establishing the Community for the purposes of progressively securing freedom of movement for workers between them.'

Thus 'worker' is given the same meaning as under Article 39 EC.[2] Administrative documents are declaratory and evidential, rather than conditions of entitlement, in the case of Turkish workers, as is the case with residence permits under Article 39.[3] The public policy derogation is interpreted in the same way as under Council Directive (EEC) 64/221.[4] The position of the children of Turkish workers compares with those of workers under the main EC Treaty.[5]

1 Case C-98/96 *Ertanir* [1997] ECR I-5179, para 21; Case C-434/93 *Bozkurt* [1995] ECR I-1475, paras 14, 19 and 20; Case C-171/95 *Tetik* [1997] ECR I-329, para 20.
2 Case C-36/96 *Günaydin* [1997] ECR I-5143, ECJ; *Ertanir* above; Case C-1/97 *Birden* [1998] ECR I-7747, ECJ.
3 *Bozkurt* above; Case C-329/97 *Ergat v Stadt Ulm* 16 March 2000, ECJ. Cf Case 48/75 *Royer* [1976] ECR 497.
4 Case C-340/97 *Nazli v Stadt Nürnberg* [2000] ECR I-957, ECJ; *Ergat* above, ECJ.
5 Case C-210/97 *Akman* [1998] ECR I-7519, ECJ.

7.149 In a series of cases on the application of Article 6 of Decision 1/80, the ECJ has established the following guidelines for Turkish nationals:

(1) he or she has to be a worker and not self-employed, that is, someone bound by an employment relationship covering a genuine and effective economic activity pursued for the benefit of and under the direction of another for remuneration.[1] It makes no difference to the definition that employment is for the sole purpose of preparing the employee to work elsewhere,[2] or is specific work for a specific employer for a limited period.[3] A person may qualify as a worker even although the job is a temporary one to enable recipients of social assistance to integrate into working life and takes place at a cultural centre funded by public money and not in competition with undertakings in the general labour market;[4]

(2) he or she has to be duly registered as belonging to the labour force of a member state. This means either being in employment which is located within the territory of a member state or which retains a sufficiently close link with it, as in the case of an international lorry-driver who has sufficient links with one member state.[5] To establish a close link with a particular member state, it will be necessary to take into account the place where the worker was hired, the territory on which or from which employment is pursued, and the applicable national legislation in the field of employment and social security.[6] A worker will be treated as duly registered if he or she is employed on the same conditions of work and pay as those claimed by workers who pursue identical or similar activities,[7] and complies with the requirements laid down by the rules and regulations in the member state concerned;[8]

(3) he or she has to be in legal employment. This means having a stable and secure position in the labour force and an undisputed right of residence.[9] Legal employment is a concept of Community law, which must be defined objectively and uniformly in the light of the spirit and purpose of Article 6 of Decision 1/80.[10] Accordingly, it does not matter that the worker may have been aware of the restrictions imposed by the host state.[11] Employment of less than 12 months does not have sufficient stability to qualify,[12] but the fact that employment contracts are temporary is of no relevance.[13] The immigration status of the Turkish worker is of relevance to the issue of a stable and secure position. Where a worker has obtained his or her residence permit in fraudulent circumstances, he or she will not qualify,[14] nor does one who is resident on a provisional basis awaiting the grant of a residence permit,[15] or someone who is authorised to work while he or she appeals against a decision refusing a right of residence.[16]

1 Case C-36/96 *Günaydin v Freistaat Bayern* [1997] ECR I-5143, ECJ; Case C-1/97 *Birden* [1998] ECR I-7747, ECJ,
2 *Günaydin* above.
3 Case C-98/96 *Ertanir* [1997] ECR I-5179, ECJ.
4 *Birden* above. Case C-188/00 *Kurz* (not yet decided) asks whether part-time work by a student is within Art 6 of Decision 1/80.
5 Case C-434/95 *Bozkurt* [1995] ECR I-1475, ECJ.
6 *Bozkurt* above.
7 *Günaydin* above.
8 *Birden* above.
9 Case C-192/89 *Sevince* [1990] ECR I-3461, para 30; Case C-237/91 *Kus* [1992] ECR I-6781, para 12; *Bozkurt* above, para 26; Case C-285/95 *Kol* [1997] ECR I-3069, para 21.
10 *Ertanir* above.
11 *Ertanir* above.
12 Case C-306/95 *Eker* [1997] ECR I-2697.
13 *Ertanir* above.
14 *Kol* above.
15 *Kus* above, para 21.
16 *Sevince* above, para 31.

7.150 Under the first indent of Article 6 of Decision 1/80, workers have to work continuously for the same employer. If they change employers during the first year, they cannot benefit.[1] Similarly, to qualify under the second indent of Article 6, a worker must continue working for the same employer.[2] It is only at the end of three years' continuous employment that a Turkish worker is entitled to accept offers of work from a different employer, but even then must remain in the same occupation as before, and the new employer must respect the right of priority of Community nationals. At the end of four years' employment, the worker can then choose any job in any occupation with any employer. Workers in this position may then voluntarily terminate their existing employment to look for new work on the same conditions as Community work seekers. They must remain duly registered as belonging to the labour force, and this may mean registering with the local employment office as a person seeking employment.[3]

1   Case C-306/95 *Eker* [1997] ECR I-2697.
2   Case C-355/93 *Eroglu* [1994] ECR I-5113.
3   Case C-171/95 *Tetik* [1997] ECR I-329.

7.151 Article 6(2) of Decision 1/80 deals with continuity of employment. Annual holidays and absences for reasons of maternity or accident at work, or short periods of sickness, are treated as periods of legal employment. Periods of involuntary unemployment, duly certified by the relevant authorities, and long absences on account of sickness, are not treated as periods of legal employment, but do not break continuity. Article 6(2) of the Decision states that they shall not affect rights acquired as the result of the preceding period of employment. The ECJ has held that short interruptions between the expiry of a residence permit and the obtaining of a new one do not affect the Turkish worker's rights.[1] In *Nazli*[2] a lengthy period in prison on remand did not destroy the worker's right of access to employment, and the ECJ held that he continued to have his rights provided he found a job again within a reasonable period after his release. In that case and in *Tetik*,[3] the court has recognised that once Turkish workers are free to change their jobs under Article 6, they should have a reasonable period to seek new employment in the same way as Community nationals.[4]

1   Case C-98/96 *Ertanir* [1997] ECR I-5179, ECJ.
2   Case C-340/97 [2000] ECR I-957, ECJ.
3   Case C-171/95 [1997] ECR I-329, ECJ.
4   See Case C-292/89 *Antonissen* [1991] ECR I-745, [1991] 2 CMLR 373.

Family members

7.152 Article 7 of Decision 1/80 deals with the employment rights of family members of Turkish workers, and has been held to be directly effective.[1] Under Article 7, two distinct rights are given to family members of Turkish workers. First, members of the family of a Turkish worker who is duly registered as belonging to the labour force of a member state are entitled after a time to take up job offers, if they 'have been authorised to join' him or her.[2] Secondly, children of Turkish workers who have completed a course of vocational training in the host country have a right to take any job once one of their parents has been in legal employment for a certain period. We look at each of these entitlements in more detail.

1   Case C-329/97 *Kadiman* [1997] ECR I-2133.
2   For the definition of 'family' see **7.95**. In *Eyup* Case C-69/98, 22 June 2000, the ECJ declined to hold that a cohabitee could be a member of the family, but held that a Turkish couple who had married, then divorced and later re-married, but who had always lived together, had 'constantly maintained a common legal residence' within the meaning of Art 7(1) of Decision 1/80.

7.153 First, the right of family members only arises if they have been authorised by the host state to join the primary worker. If they have entered for some other purpose it does not arise. Secondly, there needs to be a period of cohabitation. In

Kadiman[1] the ECJ held that the words in the first paragraph of Article 7(1) of Decision 1/80, 'authorised to join him', cannot be interpreted as merely requiring the host member state to have authorised a family member to enter its territory to join a Turkish worker, without at the same time requiring the person concerned to reside there continually with the migrant worker until he or she is entitled to enter the labour market. In other words, there has to be a specified period of cohabitation in a household with the primary worker before any employment rights accrue. This rather strict condition is at odds with the rather more lax rules for family members under Council Regulation (EEC) 1612/68, and was prompted by fears of the rules being manipulated by sham marriages. Conscious of the harshness of its interpretation, the court stated that allowances can be made if the person's job or training takes him or her away from home. It is for the national court to determine whether the circumstances justify living apart. It remains to be seen whether domestic violence would constitute such a circumstance. Apart from the hurdle of an initial period of cohabitation, family members are entitled to respond to any offers of employment, subject to the priority to be given to workers of member states, once they have been legally resident for at least three years. After five years they are free to take any job, without any need to give priority to Community workers. At that point they have independent rights of residence, even if they no longer live with the family member they had been authorised to join.[2] During the periods of legal residence absences for reasonable periods and for legitimate reasons, such as holidays, do not break continuity.[3]

1 *Kadiman* 7.152 fn 1 above, paras 37–42.
2 Case C-329/97 *Ergat v Stadt Ulm*, 16 March 2000, ECJ.
3 *Kadiman* above, paras 37–42.

7.154 Under the second paragraph of Article 7 of Decision 1/80, children of Turkish workers who have completed a course of vocational training in the host state are free to take any job, irrespective of the time they have spent there, provided that one of their parents has been legally employed in the member state concerned for at least three years. In *Eroglu*[1] the court held that the second paragraph of Article 7 gives a Turkish national who satisfies the conditions a right to respond to any offer of employment and to rely on the right in order to obtain a new work permit; secondly that the right necessarily implies a recognition of a right of residence, giving the person an opportunity to look for job opportunities; and thirdly, that the right is not subject to any conditions concerning the ground on which the right to enter and stay was granted. So it was immaterial that the person was given leave to enter the host state as a student and not as a family member.

1 Case C-355/93 *Eroglu* [1994] ECR I-5113, ECJ.

7.155 Decisions made under the Turkey Association Agreement also deal with discrimination on grounds of nationality, in relation to education of the children of Turkish workers and as regards social security. Under Article 9 of Decision 1/80, such children are entitled to education on the same footing as own nationals. This accords with the rights such children would have under Article 2 of Protocol 1 of the ECHR, read with Article 14. In *Sürül*[1] the ECJ held that Article 9 of the Decision was of direct effect. The case dealt with Article 3 of Decision 3/80, under which the applicant claimed family allowance in Germany. She was refused on the basis that, although she was lawfully resident, she had only a limited stay. The court held that this was discriminatory, since a member state cannot impose on Turkish nationals more or stricter controls than those imposed on own nationals, for whom the only requirement was domicile or habitual residence.

1 Case C -262/96 [1999] ECR I-2685, ECJ. See further joined cases C-102 and 211/98, *Kocak and Ramazan*, 14 March 2000, ECJ.

7.156 The provisions of Decision 1/80 are subject to limitations based on public policy, public security or public health.[1] Turkish nationals who benefit from the provisions will therefore face deportation on the same basis as EEA nationals.[2] In *Nazli*[3] the ECJ held that the same principles applied as in public policy cases under Article 39(3) EC.[4] So a Turkish worker could not be expelled as a deterrent to others without his or her personal conduct giving reason to believe that he or she would commit other serious offences prejudicial to the requirements of public policy in the host member state. The same applies to family members.[5]

1 Decision 1/80, art 14(1).
2 See discussion at **7.125**ff above.
3 Case C-340/97 *Nazli v Stadt Nürnberg* [2000] ECR I-957, ECJ.
4 See *R v Bouchereau* [1978] QB 732.
5 See Case C-329/97 *Ergat v Stadt Ulm*, 16 March 2000, ECJ.

7.157 As regards establishment, Article 13 of the Ankara Agreement states that the parties agree to be guided by Articles 52 to 56 EC (now 42 to 46) for the purpose of abolishing restrictions on the freedom of establishment between them. Article 14 made similar provision for services. Article 41 EC is a standstill provision, which requires the Parties to refrain from introducing between themselves any new restrictions on the freedom of establishment and the freedom to provide services.[1] In *Savas*[2] a Turkish couple who had overstayed their leave in the UK set up a very successful business and wished to regularise their position. The UK authorities wished to deport them. The case was referred to the ECJ, which ruled that Articles 13 and 41(2) did not have direct effect, but that the standstill clause in Article 41(1) prohibited the introduction of new national restrictions. It was for the national court to determine if the rules applied were less favourable than before the time that the Additional Protocol came into force. However, the clause is not in itself capable of conferring upon a Turkish national the benefit of the right of establishment or of residence which goes with it. The upshot of this is that so far as the UK is concerned the 1973 business rules (HC 510) will apply to Turkish nationals. These are very much less onerous than the current rules and contain no minimum capital requirement or a need to create new jobs.

1 For the UK this means no new restrictions after 1 January 1973, the date of the UK's adherence to the EEC.
2 Case C-37/98 [2000] INLR 398, ECJ.

The Maghreb Cooperation Agreements

7.158 The EC has entered into Cooperation Agreements with Morocco, Tunisia and Algeria[1] (the Maghreb Agreements) (they are all in similar terms, so references hereafter are to the Morocco Agreement). In the case of Tunisia and Morocco these have been supplemented by Euro-Mediterranean Agreements.[2] Despite this, there have been no specific free movement rights granted to Maghreb workers. But there are provisions prohibiting discrimination in the field of employment and social security. In the case of *Office National de l'Emploi v Kziber*[3] the ECJ held that an article of the Morocco Agreement prohibiting discrimination in the field of social security had direct effect. Following *Kziber* the ECJ held in *El-Yassini*[4] that Article 40 of the Morocco Cooperation Agreement was of direct effect. The case concerned a Moroccan who married a British citizen and was given 12 months leave to enter the UK. He obtained a job. Before he qualified for indefinite leave to remain the marriage broke down. He argued that refusing to extend his leave to remain amounted to discrimination as regards his working conditions contrary to Article 40 EC. This provides that as regards working conditions and remuneration there should be no discrimination as against nationals of the member state where the Moroccan workers are employed. The court rejected this argument. 'Working conditions' did not cover the conditions of residence and Article 40 EC did not give any further right of residence.

1 See OJ 1978 L 264, 27 September, and Council Regulation (EEC) 2211/78 26 September 1978 annexing the Morocco Agreement which provides that the regulation shall be binding in its entirety and directly applicable. The Tunisian and Algerian Agreements are set out in the ensuing pages of the Official Journal.

2 See OJ 1998 L 97/2 (Tunisia); OJ 2000 L 70/2 (Morocco); see also Euro-Mediterranean Agreement with Israel OJ 2000 L 147/3. The Tunisian Agreement is also set out in *Butterworths Immigration Law Service*, F[5761].

3 Case C-18/90 *Kziber* [1991] ECR I-199, ECJ; the decision was followed in Case C-58/93 *Yousfi v Belgium* [1994] ECR I-1353, ECJ and *Krid* (1995) unreported.

4 Case C-416/96 *El-Yassini v Secretary of State for the Home Department* [1999] ECR I-1209, [1999] All ER (EC) 193, ECJ.

Lomé Convention with African, Caribbean and Pacific countries

7.159 The EC has also entered the Lomé Agreements with African, Caribbean and Pacific (ACP) countries, but ACP nationals who are workers in the EU have obtained little benefit by way of free movement provisions from these Conventions.[1] In the case of *Poirrez*[2] neither the non-discrimination provisions of the EC Treaty nor the ACP-EEC Convention assisted a claim to benefit by an Ivory Coast national who was the adopted child of a French worker who had never exercised Community rights. In the earlier decision of *Ratzanatsimba*[3] the non-discrimination provision of the 1975 Lomé Convention did not prohibit different treatment between EC and ACP nationals, or even between different ACP nationals with respect to training as a pupil barrister.[4]

1 The new Lomé Convention, agreed in February 2000, contains draconian rules on the repatriation of people illegally in the EU: see Statewatch vol 10 no 2, March-May 2000.

2 Case C-206/91 *Ettien Poirrez v CAF de la Seine Saint Denis* [1992] ECR I-6685, ECJ.

3 Case 65/77 *Jean Ratzanatsimba* [1978] 1 CMLR 246. Article 62 of the 1975 Lomé Convention provided:
   'As regards arrangements that may be applied in matters of establishment and provisions of services, the . . . member states shall treat nationals and companies or firms of the . . . ACP States respectively on a non-discriminatory basis. However if, for a given activity, a . . . state is unable to provide such treatment, the (other) state shall not be bound to accord such treatment for this activity.'

4 This tentative non-discrimination clause may have resulted in the conclusion that discrimination was not prohibited.

Central and Eastern European Agreements

7.160 The EC and the member states have also entered into association agreements with Hungary, Poland,[1] Romania, Bulgaria, Slovenia, the Czech and Slovak Republics, Estonia, Latvia and Lithuania.[2] The first agreements were signed in December 1991 but only came into force in January 1994.[3] The last was signed in 1999. All are in similar terms, save that Hungarians will have to establish a UK-registered company to benefit, but reference will be made here to the Poland Agreement. There are provisions for non-discrimination in working conditions similar to the Morocco Agreement discussed above,[4] and for an Association Council to co-ordinate social security measures for nationals of association agreement states in the EC and vice versa.

1   The texts of the Polish and Hungarian agreements are published in *Butterworths Immigration Law Service*, F[5401] (Poland) and F[5601] (Hungary) respectively.
2   The agreements for Lithuania, Latvia and Estonia came into force on 1 February 1997, but only *companies* could take advantage until 1 January 2000, when they applied to the *self-employed*: IND letter 23.6.99.
3   Agreements similar to the Polish Agreement have come into force on 1 February 1995 for the Czech and Slovak Republics, Bulgaria and Romania: OJ L/357 L/358, L360/4 (31 December 1994).
4   Article 37(1) of the Poland agreement.

7.161   It is the measures to promote freedom of establishment and the supply of services that give rise to immigration law issues. Article 44(3) of the Poland Agreement[1] provides that:

> 'Each member state shall grant from entry into force of this Agreement, a treatment no less favourable than that accorded to its own companies and nationals for the establishment of Polish companies and nationals . . . and shall grant in the operation of Polish companies and nationals established in its territory a treatment no less favourable than that accorded to its own companies and nationals.'

Establishment includes the right to take up and pursue economic activities as self-employed persons and to set up and manage undertakings, in particular companies, which they effectively control; but self-employment shall not extend to seeking or taking employment in the labour market, nor does it confer a right of access to the labour market of another party.[2] A relevant company is defined by its place of registration, but if the enterprise has only its registered office in the territory of the Community or Poland, its operations must possess a real and continuous link with the economy of one of the member states or Poland respectively.[3]

1   Article 44(3) of the Poland Agreement.
2   Article 44 (4) of the Poland Agreement; art 44(5) of the Hungary Agreement limits the right to set up companies.
3   Article 48 of the Poland Agreement.

7.162   The UK has recognised that these provisions are of direct effect and has sought to give effect to them in paragraphs 211 to 223 of HC 395, which make special rules for those Polish, Romanian, Bulgarian, Slovenian, Czech, Slovak, Estonian, Latvian, Lithuanian and Hungarian nationals who seek to come to the UK to establish themselves in a business. 'Business' means an enterprise as a sole trader, a partnership or a company registered in the UK.[1] The substantive requirements for admission are that the person is investing sufficient money under his or her control in the business to establish him or herself in the UK.[2] The share of the profits of the business must provide a sufficient income to maintain and accommodate the person and any dependants without recourse to employment outside the business or to public funds, and there must be sufficient funds for this purpose until the business becomes profitable.[3] Those establishing themselves in a company must have a controlling interest in it and be actively involved in the promotion and management of the company. The company must be registered in the UK and be trading or providing services here.[4] Self-employed Association Agreement nationals must be actively trading and own the assets of the business solely or jointly with any partners, and in the case of partnership their role must not amount to disguised employment.[5] Those taking over an existing business must provide audited accounts.[6] An entry clearance is necessary for admission.[7] Entry is given for 12 months,[8] which is renewable,[9] and settlement may be given after four years.[10]

1 HC 395, para 211. But Hungarians are limited to setting up companies under r 213.
2 HC 395, para 212(ii).
3 HC 395, para 212(ii) and (iv).
4 HC 395, para 213.
5 HC 395, para 214. Hungarians are excluded from this provision.
6 HC 395, para 213(vi), r 214(v).
7 HC 395, paras 215 and 216. It is doubtful whether this requirement conforms with Community law.
8 HC 395, para 215.
9 HC 395, para 220.
10 HC 395, para 222.

7.163 These provisions reflect the old 1973 business rules and certainly do not require a minimum investment, profit margins or the creation of new employment.[1] In so far as they set minimum standards for establishing a genuine enterprise within the terms of the Association Agreement, there is little to quarrel about. However, the practice suggests that the Home Office administration of the rules is so rooted in the rules and the very wide discretion devolved to national rules and regulations by the Agreements[2] that it is increasingly out of keeping with the intention and spirit of the Agreements and the principles of non-discrimination under EC law.[3] In fact, it is difficult to comment sensibly at present on the extent to which the national conception of the way things should be done is out of kilter with EC law and a Community right of establishment, because so many of those questions are before the ECJ awaiting judgment.[4] We do know that the key provisions of the Agreements on the right of establishment are of direct effect,[5] but the major questions still await answers.[6] (i) Is there need for prior permission before entry, even where there is no general visa requirement for those coming from the country in question? (ii) Do visa requirements 'nullify or impair' the specific provisions of the Association Agreements and is it disproportionate to require an applicant to return home and apply for a visa? (iii) Does the right of establishment confer an implied right of residence? (iv) Does the right of establishment correspond with the same right under the EC Treaty? (v) Is any assistance to be drawn from the Turkish cases? (vi) Does illegal entry or illegal presence nullify the right? (vii) How effective and/or genuine must the self-employed activity be? (viii) Must the applicant show that the business is viable? Community law principles of non-discrimination might suggest that failure to adhere to national rules may be irrelevant if the basic enterprise is within the contemplation of the Association Agreement.

1 See HC 80, para 21 and note comment on Turkish Agreement at **7.154** above.
2 See art 58 of Polish Agreement.
3 See the trenchant and very relevant criticism in Gulat and Flyn 'Whatever happened to the European Agreements?' (2000) 14 INLP 89.
4 *R v Secretary of State for the Home Department, ex p Kondova* (CO 3242/1996); *R v Secretary of State for the Home Department, ex p Barkoci* (CO 966/1998); *R v Secretary of State for the Home Department, ex p Malik* (CO 967/1998); Case C-268/99 *Jany v Staatssecretaris van Justitie* (A-G's opinion delivered 8 May 2001).
5 Case C-63/99 *R v Secretary of State for the Home Department, ex p Gloszcuk* 14 September 2000.
6 See comments of Immigration Appeal Tribunal in deferring any decision in *Koprinkor, Petlova and Ganeva* (01/771/00091).

7.164 The Agreements require the parties to permit the temporary admission of natural persons who provide services[1] or are employed by a service provider as key personnel. They can enter to negotiate the provision of services, but not to make direct sales to the public or to supply services themselves.[2] Such provisions are well accommodated within the business visitor rules, but in any judicial review proceedings to challenge a refusal of admission to any Association Agreement national business person, reference should be made to the Community law obligations and not just the UK Immigration Rules. A belief by an immigration officer that a person may stay longer than the period asked for should not prevent temporary admission to carry out activities covered by the Agreement.

1 In *Jany* above, Advocate General Leger held that self-employed prostitutes engage in economic activity which is covered by the Agreements, although member states were free to impose restrictions on prostitution, provided they were non-discriminatory, for the protection of public order.
2 Poland Agreement, art 55(2).

HUMAN RIGHTS LAW

INTRODUCTION

8.1 Of the numerous international human rights instruments to which the UK is a party,[1] the European Convention of Human Rights (ECHR)[2] had already become the most significant and most frequently cited source of rights outside the common law well before 2 October 2000, when the Human Rights Act 1998 brought its provisions within the reach of the domestic courts. Since the coming into force of the 1998 Act, the ECHR has taken its place at the heart of UK human rights law. This chapter will look at the Convention, at how the 1998 Act incorporates it, and at some of the incorporated rights as they affect immigration law. It will also briefly look at obligations outside the incorporated rights, both under the ECHR and outside it.

1   Of which the most important are the UN Universal Declaration of Human Rights 1948 (UDHR), the UN International Covenant on Civil and Political Rights 1966 (ICCPR), the UN Convention Against Torture 1984 (UNCAT), the UN Convention on the Rights of the Child 1989(COROC), the Convention on the Elimination of all forms of Discrimination against Women (CEDAW) and the European Convention against Torture and Inhuman and Degrading Treatment 1984.
2   To give it its full title, the European Convention for the Protection of Human Rights and Fundamental Freedoms, Rome, 4 November 1950.

HISTORY OF THE ECHR

8.2 The ECHR was produced by the Council of Europe, an inter-governmental body formed in 1949 by ten member states[1] to foster European unity and reduce the risk of future wars. The Charter of the Council of Europe required member states to subscribe to the rule of law and to afford human rights and fundamental freedoms to all within their jurisdiction.[2] The Convention was one of the Council's earliest projects. Its two principal objectives were to maintain and further realise human rights and fundamental freedoms, and to foster effective political democracy.[3] It was designed to 'secure the universal and effective recognition and observance' of the rights set out in the Universal Declaration of Human Rights 1948, by making contracting states responsible under public international law for ensuring that their laws and practices gave effect to such rights and creating mechanisms of enforcement if they did not. Article 19 of the Convention set up the Commission and the Court. Article 25 provided that contracting states could recognise individuals' right to petition the Commission and Article 46 provided that they could accept the compulsory jurisdiction of the Court. Article 13 required states to provide an effective remedy in their domestic courts for violation of the rights in the Convention.

1   Belgium, Denmark, France, Ireland, Italy, Luxembourg, Netherlands, Norway, Sweden and the UK. As of the end of 2000 there were 41 member states: Albania, Andorra, Austria, Belgium, Bulgaria, Croatia, Cyprus, Czech Republic, Denmark, Estonia, Finland, France, Georgia, Germany, Greece, Hungary, Iceland, Ireland, Italy, Latvia, Liechtenstein, Lithuania, Luxembourg, Malta, Moldova, Netherlands, Norway, Poland, Portugal, Romania, Russian Federation, San Marino, Slovakia, Slovenia, Spain, Sweden, Switzerland, former Yugoslav Republic of Macedonia, Turkey, Ukraine and the UK.
2   Statute of the Council of Europe 1949 (Cmd 7778).
3   See judgment of Lord Steyn in *Brown v Stott (Procurator Fiscal, Dunfermline)* [2001] 2 All ER 97, PC.

8.3   The right of individual petition and the compulsory jurisdiction of the court are the mechanisms behind the success of the ECHR as a living and well-used instrument. When the Convention first came into operation in 1953, the Commission could only receive inter-state applications under Article 24, and the Court was not operative. Individual petitions under Article 25 were allowed in 1955, and only in 1958 did the Court achieve competence. The UK did not recognise the right, or submit to the compulsory jurisdiction of the Court, until 1966,[1] citing the superiority of British law, concern that a 'flood of fatuous or insincere applications would roll in', causing extra work and adverse publicity,[2] and arguing that 'the State, not the individual, is the proper subject of international law'.[3] The real reason for the delay was Britain's colonial situation— in the course of fighting against the liberation warriors of the colonies, the UK had issued ten derogations from Article 5 (the right to liberty and security of person) from 1953 to May 1960.[4] Once the right of individual petition was recognised in the UK, it was frequently used to challenge immigration control measures. The very first British case where the individual right of petition was exercised was an immigration case.[5] The UK renewed the right of petition and its submission to the compulsory jurisdiction every five years. Since November 1998,[6] contracting states have been obliged to recognise the right of individual petition and to submit to the compulsory jurisdiction of the court. Thus the Convention has 'evolved into a European bill of rights, with the European Court of Human Rights having a role akin to that of a constitutional court in a federal legal system'.[7]

1   For the full text of the letters from the UK government see (1966) 15 ICLQ 539.
2   HC Official Report (5th Series) 23 May 1960, col 174.
3   HC Official Report (5th Series) 23 May 1960, col 180.

4   HC Official Report (5th Series) 23 May 1960, col 174 and 182: 'Among emerging communities political agitators thrive, and one may well imagine the use which political agitators would make of the right of individual petition.' See further Ian Macdonald *A Guide to the Human Rights Act 1998* 1999 *Butterworths Immigration Law Service* Special Bulletin.
5   Application 2991/66, *Alam v UK* (1967) *Times*, 12 October, relating to the refusal to allow a 12-year-old boy to join his father in the UK. It led to a friendly settlement.
6   With the coming into force of ECHR, Protocol 11: see below.
7   Harris, O'Boyle and Warbrick *Law of the European Convention on Human Rights* (1995) Butterworths, p 2.

ECHR PRINCIPLES

8.4 The ECHR is based on the obligation of contracting states to give effect to the core values of a democratic society: pluralism, openness and broadmindedness,[1] the rule of law,[2] freedom of expression,[3] and is designed to maintain and promote those values.[4] It is a living instrument which must be interpreted in the light of present-day conditions.[5] In *Selmouni v France*[6] the court observed that:

> 'certain acts which were classified in the past as "inhuman and degrading treatment" as opposed to "torture" could be classified differently in future ... the increasingly high standard being required in the area of the protection of human rights and fundamental liberties correspondingly and inevitably requires greater firmness in assessing breaches of the fundamental values of democratic societies.'

The 'living instrument' or dynamic approach to Convention rights applies with force to areas affected by rapidly changing views of private morality,[7] and in particular to the rights of sexual minorities in the context of protection of private life.[8] It also applies to rights to fair trial, as the requirements of fairness have evolved considerably in the court's case law.[9] We shall consider later the relevance of Article 6 'fair trial' requirements to immigration and asylum cases.[10]

1   *Handyside v UK* (1976) 1 EHRR 737, para 49.
2   See Preamble; *Golder v UK* (1975) 1 EHRR 524, para 34; *Klass v Germany* (1978) 2 EHRR 214, para 55.
3   *Handyside v UK* above.
4   Preamble; *Kjeldsen v Denmark* (1976) 1 EHRR 711, para 53.
5   *Tyrer v UK* (1978) 2 EHRR 1, para 31; *Marckx v Belgium* (1979) 2 EHRR 330; *Loizidou v Turkey* (1995) 20 EHRR 99, at para 71. This means that the content and scope of rights might be deepened and broadened over time, see eg *Sutherland v UK* [1998] EHRLR 117, but not that entirely new rights are created: *Johnston v Ireland* (1986) 9 EHRR 203; *Feldbrugge v Netherlands* (1986) 8 EHRR 425.
6   (1999) 29 EHRR 403.
7   *Marckx v Belgium* (1979) 2 EHRR 330.
8   *Dudgeon v UK* (1981) 4 EHRR 149; *Smith and Grady v UK* (1999) 29 EHRR 493, para 97.
9   See *Borgers v Belgium* (1991) 15 EHRR 92, para 24.
10 See **8.51** below.

8.5 The concept of state responsibility for the protection of fundamental rights is at the heart of the ECHR. States have negative and positive obligations under the Convention: not to interfere with core human rights, and to protect those within their jurisdiction from violations.[1] A positive obligation may also require action to give effect to rights, such as the provision of legal aid to enable access to a court to be effective.[2] The positive obligation to protect against killing and torture extends to an effective investigation when individuals have been killed (whether by state agents or private individuals) or when they allege torture.[3] In accordance with the ideas expressed in the Preamble and Article 1, the Convention is intended to guarantee rights that are practical and effective, not theoretical and illusory.[4] Thus, rights must not be subject to conditions for their exercise which render them useless.[5]

1   By, for example, not sending someone to a country where their human rights will be violated: *Soering v UK* (1989) 11 EHRR 439, or by preventing a death which was eminently foreseeable: *Osman v UK* (1998) 29 EHRR 245, para 115. See also *A v UK* (1998) 27 EHRR 611 (prevention of assaults on children by appropriate criminal penalties); *Platform Ärzte fur das Leben v Austria* (1988) 13 EHRR 204, para 32 (dealing with threats of violence by opponents on demonstrations to ensure freedom of assembly).
2   *Airey v Ireland* (1979) 2 EHRR 305, para 24. See also *Marckx v Belgium* (1979) 2 EHRR 330: 'Fulfilment of a duty under the Convention on occasion necessitates some positive action on the part of the State; in such circumstances the State cannot simply remain passive.'
3   *Kaya v Turkey* (1998) 28 EHRR 1; *Gülec v Turkey* (1998) 28 EHRR 131, para 78; *Mahmut Kaya v Turkey* (28 March 2000, unreported), ECtHR, para 106-107.
4   *Airey* above; *Golder v UK* (1975) 1 EHRR 524, paras 28-36.
5   *Winterwerp v Netherlands* (1979) 2 EHRR 387, para 60; *Artico v Italy* (1980) 3 EHRR 1, para 33; *Ashingdane v UK* (1985) 7 EHRR 528, para 57.

8.6 The ECHR allows the state a margin of appreciation in deciding how best to give effect to the rights enshrined in it pursuant to its obligations under Article 1 and Article 13 (provision of effective remedies for violation of the rights).[1] The margin of appreciation has been defined as the degree of latitude accorded to the national authorities and courts in recognition of the fact that 'by reason of their direct and continuous contact with the vital forces of their countries, the national authorities are in principle better placed than an international court to evaluate local needs and conditions'.[2] By conceding a margin of appreciation to each national system, the ECtHR has recognised that the Convention does not need to be applied uniformly by all states, but may vary in its application according to local needs and conditions.[3] The margin applies in relation to justification for derogation[4] from or interference with a Convention right,[5] the scope of positive obligations[6] and in assessing what constitutes objective and reasonable justification for discrimination under Article 14.[7] It reflects the principle of subsidiarity.[8] But the Court must give the final ruling on whether a restriction is reconcilable with protected rights, and its supervision is not limited merely to ascertaining whether a state exercised its discretion reasonably, carefully and in good faith.[9] The limits of the 'margin of appreciation' vary according to the importance of the rights at stake, the purpose pursued by the state and the degree to which practice varies across contracting states. The limits are wider in cases involving national security,[10] planning policy,[11] tax,[12] social and economic policy, and narrower in the fields of criminal law, free speech and private morality.[13] The technique is not available to the national courts, when they are considering Convention issues arising in their own countries.[14] However, as Lord Hope pointed out in *Kebilene*, something akin to the margin of appreciation may operate in some circumstances in the domestic jurisdiction, because the alleged breach of the Convention may involve an area of judgment within which the judiciary will defer to the considered opinion of the minister or departmental official.[15] We shall come back to this at **8.29** below.

1   'The State has a choice of various means, but a law that fails to satisfy the requirement [protection of family life] violates Article 8': *Marckx v Belgium* above, para 31.
2   *Handyside v UK* (1976) 1 EHRR 737, paras 48-49; *Buckley v UK* (1996) 23 EHRR 101, paras 74-75.
3   *R v DPP, ex p Kebilene* [1999] 4 All ER 801 at 844B, per Lord Hope.
4   Ie, in deciding whether a 'public emergency threatens the life of the nation' under Art 15: *Ireland v UK* (1978) 2 EHRR 25, para 207.

5 *Handyside* above fn 2.
6 *Abdulaziz, Cabales and Balkandali v UK* (1985) 7 EHRR 471, para 67; *Osman v UK* [1999] 1 FLR 193.
7 *Rasmussen v Denmark* (1984) 7 EHRR 371, para 40.
8 Clayton and Tomlinson *The Law of Human Rights* (2000) OUP; R Ryssdall, 'The coming of age of the European Convention on Human Rights' [1996] EHRLR 18–27. See further Lord Mackenzie-Stuart 'Subsidiarity – a busted flush?' in Curtin and O'Keefe *Constitutional adjudication in European Community law and national law*, 1992, Butterworths.
9 *Sunday Times v UK* (1979) 2 EHRR 245, para 59.
10 The concept was developed initially to ensure freedom of action for national governments in derogating from the ECHR under art 15: *Lawless v Ireland* 332/57, A61.501, 48-49, Commission. See also *Brannigan and McBride v UK* (1993) 17 EHRR 539.
11 *Buckley v UK* (1996) 23 EHRR 101, para 129.
12 *Gasus-Dosier-und Fördertechnik GmbH v Netherlands* (1995) 20 EHRR 403.
13 *Smith and Grady v UK* (1999) 29 EHRR 493.
14 *R v Stratford Justices, ex p Imbert* (1999) 2 Cr App Rep 276 at 286, per Buxton LJ; *R v Secretary of State for the Home Department, ex p Amjad Mahmood* [2001] 1 WLR 840 at para 31, per Laws LJ.
15 *Amjad Mahmood* above at para 33 *R (Daly) v Secretary of State for the Home Department* [2001] UKHL 26, [2001] 2 WLR 1622. See also Lester and Pannick *Human Rights Law and Practice* (Butterworths, 1999) para 3.21; Tomlinson, fn 8 above, paras 6.32, 6.37, 6.82ff; Singh, Hunt and Demetriou 'Is there a role for the "Margin of Appreciation" in national law after the Human Rights Act?' [1999] 1 EHRLR 15–22.

8.7 The margin of appreciation involves a recognition by the ECtHR that the ECHR need not be applied uniformly by all states, but may vary according to local needs and conditions (see **8.6** above). But this is limited in practice by another strand of the Strasbourg jurisprudence, namely the principle that terms such as 'civil rights and obligations',[1] 'criminal charges',[2] 'penalty',[3] 'property', 'law' 'association'[4] have an autonomous meaning under the Convention[5] and cannot be redefined by states so as to avoid their obligations.[6]

1 *König v Germany* (1978) 2 EHRR 170, para 95. See **8.45** below.
2 *Engel v Netherlands* (1976) 1 EHRR 647, para 82; *Deweer v Belgium* (1980) 2 EHRR 439, para 46.
3 *Welch v UK* (1995) 20 EHRR 247, para 27; *Lauko v Slovakia* [1999] EHRLR 105.
4 *Chassagnou v France* (1999) 7 BHRC 151, 29 EHRR 615, para 100.
5 *Adolf v Austria* (1982) 4 EHRR 313, para 30.
6 This rationalisation of the concept was given in *Chassagnou* fn 4 above.

8.8 There are three kinds of rights protected under the ECHR:

(i)   Absolute rights, which apply without qualification and from which states may not derogate even in time of war or public emergency threatening the life of the nation.[1] These are the right to life,[2] the abolition of the death penalty except in time of war,[3] the right not to be subjected to torture or to inhuman or degrading treatment or punishment,[4] the right not to be held in slavery or servitude,[5] freedom of conscience[6] and the right not to be punished by retrospective laws.[7]

(ii)   Rights which are written in unqualified terms but which in practice are qualified and limited. They include rights to liberty and security[8] and to fair[9] and open trial,[10] of appeal in criminal matters,[11] to compensation for wrongful conviction,[12] not to be tried or punished twice[13] and the right to education.[14]

(iii)   qualified rights, which may be limited in strictly defined circumstances, and must thus be balanced against, and if necessary may give way to, other public interests. They include rights to family life,[15] to freedom to manifest religion or beliefs,[16] expression,[17] assembly and association,[18] to protection of property,[19] to freedom of movement,[20] the right of aliens to procedural safeguards relating to expulsion,[21] to equality between spouses[22] and the right to enjoy Convention rights and freedoms without discrimination.[23]

1 By art 15(1).
2 Article 2. But death may be inflicted in self-defence, to effect a lawful arrest or to prevent the escape of a lawfully detained person, or in quelling a riot, if it results from the use of force which is no more than absolutely necessary: see *McCann, Farrell and Savage v UK* (1995) 21 EHRR 97; *Ogur v Turkey* (Application No 21594/93), 20 May 1999, para 78.
3 Protocol 6.
4 Article 3. See *Chahal v UK* (1996) 23 EHRR 413, para 79.
5 Article 4(1).
6 Article 9. Contrast freedom to manifest belief, which is qualified.
7 Article 7.
8 Article 5, which spells out situations where detention is lawful, and is derogable under art 15, but only a narrow interpretation of the exceptions is consistent with the aim and purpose of the provision, which is to ensure that no-one is arbitrarily deprived of his or her liberty: *Quinn v France* (1995) 21 EHRR 529; see 8.48 below. Article 1 of Protocol 4 (not ratified by the UK) prohibits imprisonment for debt.
9 The right to a fair trial is absolute, but the subsidiary rights contained it (eg the presumption of innocence) are not: *Brown v Stott (Procurator Fiscal, Dunfermline)* [2001] 2 All ER 97, PC.
10 Article 6, which provides for less than open justice when circumstances require and is derogable under art 15.
11 Protocol 7, art 2.
12 Protocol 7, art 3.
13 Protocol 7, art 4.
14 Protocol 1, art 2.
15 Article 8.
16 Article 9.
17 Article 10.
18 Article 11.
19 Protocol 1, art 1(2).
20 Protocol 4, art 2(3). This has not yet been ratified by the UK government.
21 Protocol 7, art 1(2). This has not yet been ratified by the UK government.
22 Protocol 7, art 5. This has not yet been ratified by the UK government.
23 Article 14.

8.9 The right to respect for private and family life, home and correspondence, which is protected by ECHR, Article 8, permits interference which is in accordance with the law, and is necessary in a democratic society in the interests of national security, public safety, the economic well-being of the country, for the prevention of disorder or crime, for the protection of health or morals, or for the protection of the rights and freedoms of others.[1] Other qualified rights permit interference in similar, though not identical, terms. These interests are the legitimate aims which might justify interference with the protected rights. They are exhaustive, not illustrative,[2] and are to be construed strictly.[3] In *Miailhe v France*[4] the ECtHR stated that the exceptions in Article 8(2) are to be interpreted narrowly and the need for them in a given case must be convincingly established. The permitted restrictions must not be applied for any collateral purpose.[5]

1 Article 8(2).
2 *De Wilde, Ooms and Versyp v Belgium* (1971) 1 EHRR 373; *Golder v UK* (1975) 1 EHRR 524, para 44.
3 *Sunday Times v UK* (1979) 2 EHRR 245; *Smith and Grady v UK* (1999) 29 EHRR 493 ('pandering to the prejudices of members of the population is not a legitimate aim').
4 (1993) 16 EHRR 332, para 38; see also *Funke v France* (1993) 16 EHRR 297, para 55; *Klass v Germany* (1978) 2 EHRR 214; *Lustig-Prean and Beckett v UK* (1999) 29 EHRR 548

(need for particularly serious reasons where restrictions concern a most intimate part of individuals' private life).
5 Article 18.

8.10 Once it is established that the interference has a legitimate aim as defined within the relevant Article of the ECHR, assessing permissible interference with or restriction of qualified rights requires consideration of legality and proportionality. Legality, or the requirement that interference with rights is 'in accordance with the law' or 'prescribed by law', means not just that the interference is allowed by domestic law[1] but that the law itself is sufficiently accessible[2] and precise[3] to enable the citizen to regulate his or her conduct.[4] To conform with the requirements of accessibility and precision, a law conferring discretion must indicate its scope and set out the way discretion is to be exercised.[5]

1 Including subordinate legislation: *Barthold v Germany* (1985) 7 EHRR 383.
2 Home Office internal policy guidelines are not 'accessible' unless they are published: *Malone v UK* (1984) 7 EHRR 14.
3 *Amuur v France* (1996) 22 EHRR 533, para 50; *Camenzind v Switzerland* (1999) 28 EHRR 458, para 45; *Hashman and Harrup v UK* [2000] Crim LR 185 (bind over to 'be of good behaviour' not sufficiently precise).
4 *Sunday Times v UK* (1979) 2 EHRR 245, para 49. Unwritten law may fulfil these criteria: para 47.
5 *Silver v UK* (1983) 5 EHRR 347. See also *Huvig v France* (1990) 12 EHRR 528 (what is required is detailed rules setting out when intrusive measures may be carried out); *Leander v Sweden* (1987) 9 EHRR 433.

8.11 The balance between the protection of individual rights and the interests of the wider community is at the heart of the ECHR,[1] and the balance is achieved when interference with the individual's rights is strictly proportionate to the legitimate aim pursued in restricting it.[2] As Sedley LJ put it succinctly in *B*:[3]

'A measure which interferes with a human right must not only be authorised by law but must correspond to a pressing social need and go no further than is strictly necessary in a pluralistic society to achieve its permitted purpose; or, more shortly, must be appropriate and necessary to its legitimate aim.'[4]

The requirement that a restriction on a fundamental right be 'necessary' is strict; 'necessary' is not so flexible a term as 'useful' or 'desirable',[5] and the phrase 'necessary in a democratic society' refers to a pluralistic, tolerant and broadminded society.[6] In *Sunday Times v UK (No 2)*[7] the ECtHR stated:

'The Court's task, in exercising its supervisory jurisdiction, is not to take the place of the competent national authorities but rather to review under Article 10 the decision they delivered pursuant to their powers of appreciation. This does not mean that the supervision is limited to ascertaining whether the respondent exercised its jurisdiction reasonably and carefully and in good faith; what the Court has to do is to look at the interference complained of in the light of the case as a whole and determine whether it was "proportionate to the legitimate aim pursued" and whether the reasons adduced by the national authorities to justify it are "relevant and sufficient".'

1 *Sporrong and Lönnroth v Sweden* (1982) 5 EHRR 35, para 52.
2 *Handyside v UK* (1976) 1 EHRR 737, para 49. For the principle of proportionality see Clayton and Tomlinson 8.6 fn 8, para 6.40ff; Lester and Pannick *Human Rights Law and Practice* (1999) Butterworths, para 3.10; Grosz, Beatson and Duffy *Human Rights* (2000) Sweet & Maxwell, pp112-114; Starmer *European Human Rights Law* (1999) LAG, pp 169-180; Wadham and Mountfield (1999) Blackstone *The Human Rights Act 1998*, pp13-16. De Smith, Woolf and Jowell *Judicial Review of Administrative Action* (5th edn, 1995) Sweet & Maxwell, pp 593-606.

3   *B v Secretary of State for the Home Department* [2000] Imm AR 478.
4   Para 17. It was accepted by both parties that the test of proportionality under the ECHR was the same as that in EU law: Para 7. See chapter 7 above.
5   *Chassagnou v France* (1999) 7 BHRC 151.
6   *Handyside* fn 2 above; *Dudgeon v UK* (1981) 4 EHRR 149 (criminalisation of homosexual acts disproportionate to aim of protection of morals).
7   (1991) 14 EHRR 229, para 50. See further *Hertel v Switzerland* (1998) 28 EHRR 534, para 46; *Grigoriades v Greece* (1997) 27 EHRR 464, para 44.

8.12   Factors relevant to assessing the proportionality of a restriction have been held to include the extent of the interference[1] and whether there was a less restrictive alternative;[2] and whether there are fair procedures[3] and safeguards against abuse.[4] The absence of relevant and sufficient reasons for the restriction[5] is likely to result in a finding that the restriction was not necessary or was disproportionate. The principle of proportionality is not limited to the rights in respect of which interference is expressly defined,[6] but also applies, for example, to Article 6 rights, to the prohibition of discrimination in the enjoyment of ECHR rights under Article 14[7] and to the scope of positive obligations under the Convention.[8]

1   Restrictions which impair the 'very essence' of the right in question will be disproportionate: *F v Switzerland* (1987) 10 EHRR 411, para 40; *Rees v UK* (1986) 9 EHRR 56, para 50.
2   *Informationsverein Lentia v Austria* (1993) 17 EHRR 93, para 40; *Campbell v UK* (1992) 15 EHRR 137.
3   *W v UK* (1987) 10 EHRR 29, para 62; *Buckley v UK* (1996) 23 EHRR 101, para 76.
4   *Klass v Germany* (1978) 2 EHRR 214, paras 55, 59; *Camenzind v Switzerland* (1997) 28 EHRR 458, para 45.
5   *Observer and Guardian v UK* (1991) 14 EHRR 153, para 59; *Vogt v Germany* (1996) 21 EHRR 205, para 52.
6   Thus the right of access to a court may be limited, but limitation will not be compatible with ECHR, art 6(1) unless it pursues a legitimate aim and there is a reasonable relationship of proportionality between the means employed and the aim sought to be achieved: *Ashingdane v UK* (1985) 7 EHRR 528, para 57.
7   'Very weighty reasons would have to be advanced before a difference in treatment on grounds of sex could be considered compatible with the Convention': *Abdulaziz, Cabales and Balkandali v UK* (1985) 7 EHRR 471, para 78. See **8.68** below.
8   See *Powell and Rayner v UK* (1990) 12 EHRR 355.

THE UK AND THE ECHR

8.13   As noted above,[1] the UK government's approach to the ECHR was always ambivalent; on the one hand, it took part in the drafting, and in 1953 accepted that the Convention applied to 42 overseas territories,[2] while on the other, it feared a stream of cases from those same territories if it recognised the right of individual petition. In fact, it was an inter-state case, *Ireland v UK*,[3] which exposed the practices of hooding, wall-standing, exposure to white noise, deprivation of sleep, food and drink inflicted on Republican internees in Northern Ireland, which the ECHR condemned as inhuman and degrading treatment. A clutch of individual petitions from colonial citizens, in the *East African Asians* case,[4] resulted in a finding by the Commission of rank racial discrimination in the Commonwealth Immigrants' Act 1968, which excluded UK and Colonies citizens from the UK on grounds of race.[5] The fact that individual immigrants were invoking the right of individual petition as soon as it became available[6] contributed to the introduction in 1969 of the immigration appellate system.[7]

1   See **8.3** above. For a fuller description, see the first edition of this work.

2   Declaration of Her Majesty's Government of 23 October 1953, Cmd 9045. See HC Official
    Report (5th Series) 23 May 1960, cols 174-181; HC Official Report (5th Series) 19 May
    1960 written answers cols 133-134. An irony of the colonial situation was the willingness
    of the UK government to see guarantees of fundamental rights inserted into the constitutions
    of the newly independent ex-colonies: see De Smith *Constitutions of the Commonwealth*
    chapter 5, above.
3   (1978) 2 EHRR 25.
4   (1973) 3 EHRR 76.
5   'Publicly to single out a group of persons for differential treatment on the basis of race
    might in certain circumstances constitute a special form of affront to human dignity, and
    . . . might be capable of constituting degrading treatment when differential treatment on
    some other ground would raise no such question': (1973) 3 EHRR 76, para 207.
6   The first cases were *Alam v UK* 2991/66 and *Harbahjan Singh v UK* 2992/96, reported at
    (1967) Times, 12 October. See **8.3** fn 5 above.
7   See chapter 18 below.

8.14 Judicial opinion in the UK was divided on the desirability of incorporation,[1]
as it was on the relevance of the unincorporated ECHR to the interpretation of
statute and administrative powers. The presumption that Parliament did not
intend to enact laws that were contrary to the UK's international obligations[2]
led to a difference between the school of judicial thought which believed that
wherever possible a statute should be construed in conformity with those
obligations (the *Garland*[3] view), and the restrictive school, which held that
regard should be had to the Convention only in the construction of ambiguous
statutes (the *Brind*[4] view).[5] The *Brind* view prevailed, meaning that the Secretary
of State was not obliged to have regard to the Convention when framing rules
or directives under primary legislation. Where a statutory administrative power
was enacted in general terms, the holder did not need to consult or have regard
to the Convention in reaching decisions, since the power was 'unambiguous'.[6]
To hold otherwise, the House of Lords ruled, would be to incorporate the
Convention through the back door, usurping Parliament's function.[7]

1   See the previous edition of this work, **13.102** fn 2. For a full description of the attitude of the
    courts see Murray Hunt *Using human rights law in the English courts* (1997) Hart Publishing.
2   See *Salomon v Customs and Excise Comrs* [1967] 2 QB 116, per Diplock LJ; *Waddington
    v Miah* [1974] 2 All ER 377 where the House of Lords decided, having regard to art 7 of
    the ECHR (no retrospective criminality), that the penal provisions of the Immigration Act
    1971 were not retrospective.
3   *Garland v British Rail Engineering* [1983] 2 AC 751 at 771, per Lord Diplock (this was,
    however, a case involving EC law).
4   *R v Secretary of State for the Home Department, ex p Brind* [1991] 1 AC 696 at 748.
5   In *Pan American World Airways Inc v Department of Trade* [1976] 1 Lloyd's Rep 257
    Scarman LJ said that an international Convention should be consulted in three situations:
    where Parliament expressly or implicitly requires it; when two courses are reasonably
    open, only one of which would lead to a result consistent with obligations under the
    Convention; and where statutory words have to be construed or a legal principle formulated
    in an area of law where the government has accepted international obligations, as part of
    the full context or background.
6   The Court of Appeal had previously held in *Chundawadra v Immigration Appeal Tribunal*
    [1988] Imm AR 161 that immigration officers did not have to have regard to the ECHR
    in deciding whether to grant leave to enter, following Lord Denning's recantation in
    Salamat Bibi [1976] 3 All ER 843, [1976] 1 WLR 979, CA of remarks in *R v Secretary of
    State for the Home Department, ex p Bhajan Singh* [1976] QB 198 to the effect that
    immigration officers ought to bear in mind the principles stated in the Convention.
7   But in *R v Secretary of State for the Home Department, ex p Thompson and Venables*
    [1998] AC 407, the House of Lords held, in relation to the UN Convention on the Rights
    of the Child, that 'it is legitimate . . . to assume that Parliament has not maintained on the
    statute book a power capable of being exercised in a manner inconsistent with the treaty
    obligations of this country' (per Lord Browne-Wilkinson at 499).

8.15 Prior to incorporation, however, the ECHR played a large part in developing the common law and, through it, the principles of judicial review of administrative discretion.[1] In *Brind* the House of Lords recognised that principles of protection of fundamental rights were relevant in deciding whether restrictions on them were reasonable.[2] In *McQuillan*[3] Sedley J observed that:

'Once it is accepted that the standards articulated in the European Convention are standards which both march with those of the common law and inform the jurisprudence of the European Union, it becomes unreal and potentially unjust to continue to develop English public law without reference to them.'[4]

In *Smith*[5] Bingham MR moved towards a proportionality review:

'The court may not interfere with the exercise of an administrative discretion on substantive grounds save where the court is satisfied . . . that it is beyond the range of responses open to a reasonable decision-maker. But in judging whether the decision-maker has exceeded this margin of appreciation the human rights context is important. The more substantial the interference with human rights, the more the court will require by way of justification before it is satisfied that the decision is reasonable in the sense outlined above.'[6]

This was further developed in the *Lord Saville*[7] case:

'[W]hen a fundamental right such as the right to life is engaged, the options available to the reasonable decision-maker are curtailed . . . it is unreasonable to reach a decision which contravenes or could contravene human rights unless there are sufficiently significant countervailing considerations. In other words it is not open to the decision-maker to risk interfering with fundamental rights in the absence of compelling justification. Even the broadest discretion is constrained by the need for there to be countervailing circumstances justifying interference with human rights.'[8]

In each of these cases, ECHR principles were put to work to develop the common law, in recognising a varying intensity of review depending on the nature of the rights affected—building on the dictum of Lord Bridge in *Bugdaycay*[9] a decade earlier. A similar approach was taken in *Saleem*[10] where the Court of Appeal held, quashing a procedure rule deeming service of an adjudicator's determination to have been effected regardless of whether it had in fact been received, that the right of access to a tribunal is a fundamental right.

1   Initially in the field of press freedom: *A-G v Guardian Newspapers* [1987] 1 WLR 1248, *(No 2)* [1990] 1 AC 109 (the 'Spycatcher' litigation); *Derbyshire County Council v Times Newspapers* [1992] QB 770 at 810, CA. The House of Lords upheld the court's conclusion that local authorities could not restrict freedom of speech by suing for libel, without reference to the ECHR: [1993] AC 534 at 550-553.
2   Lord Templeman used the language of proportionality in saying that a *Wednesbury* challenge to interference with human rights was no longer appropriate, and that 'the courts cannot escape from asking themselves whether a reasonable Secretary of State, on the material before him, could reasonably conclude that the interference . . . was justifiable. In terms of the Convention . . . the interference with freedom of expression must be necessary and proportionate to the damage which the restriction is designed to prevent': [1991] 1 AC 696 at 751.
3   *R v Secretary of State for the Home Department, ex p McQuillan* [1995] 4 All ER 400. He drew on the article by Sir John Laws 'Is the High Court the Guardian of Fundamental Human Rights?' in (1993) PL 59.
4   This approach was reflected in Simon Brown LJ's judgment in *R v Secretary of State for Social Security, ex p JCWI* [1997] 1 WLR 275 at 292: 'So basic are the human rights here

at issue that it cannot be necessary to resort to the ECHR to take note of their violation.' He gave effect to the rights (not to be left wholly destitute as the price of pursuing an asylum claim) by declaring unlawful regulations which had that effect.

5 *R v Ministry of Defence, ex p Smith* [1996] QB 517 (the 'gays in the military' case). The CA went on to decry the unavailability of a proper proportionality test for policy in the domestic court, however, which enabled the ECtHR to hold that judicial review of the ban was an ineffective remedy for the breach of art 8 of the ECHR: *Smith and Grady v UK* (1999) 29 EHRR 493.

6 *Smith* above at 554.

7 *R v Lord Saville, ex p A* [1999] 4 All ER 860 (on anonymity for soldiers testifying to the Saville Inquiry on Bloody Sunday).

8 Para 37.

9 The most fundamental right is the individual's right to life, and when an administrative decision under challenge is said to be one which may put the applicant's life at risk, the basis of the decision must surely call for the most anxious scrutiny: *Bugdaycay v Secretary of State for the Home Department* [1987] AC 514, HL.

10 *Asifa Saleem v Secretary of State for the Home Department* [2000] INLR 413, upholding Hooper J at [1999] INLR 621; see **18.1**.

8.16 Another approach to the problem of giving effect to unincorporated rights was taken by the court in *Ahmed and Patel*,[1] where Lord Woolf MR accepted that the entering into a Treaty could give rise to a legitimate expectation that the Secretary of State would act in accordance with the Treaty obligations, and an applicant would be entitled to relief if the Secretary of State without reason acted inconsistently with those obligations.[2] He endorsed the judgment of the High Court of Australia in *Teoh*[3] to that effect. This approach was followed by the Divisional Court in *Adimi*[4] in respect of obligations under the Refugee Convention 1951 not expressly incorporated into UK law by the Asylum and Immigration Appeals Act 1993.

1 *R v Secretary of State for the Home Department, ex p Ahmed and Patel* [1998] INLR 570, CA.

2 At 583G. The Treaty in question was, however, not the ECHR but the UN Convention on the Rights of the Child 1989, which contains express reservations relating to immigration control in respect of the principle that the welfare of the child should be the paramount consideration in court proceedings.

3 *Minister for Immigration and Ethnic Affairs v Teoh* (1995) 183 CLR 273.

4 *R v Uxbridge Magistrates Court, ex p Adimi* [1999] INLR 490.

8.17 In a number of areas of immigration law, the Secretary of State developed policies purporting to reflect ECHR principles prior to incorporation. Thus, internal instructions which emerged[1] in 1993, on when to proceed with enforcement action against overstayers and illegal entrants with ties of marriage or children in the UK, were explicitly based on Article 8 considerations.[2] Although these guidelines used the language, not of Article 8, but of the Immigration Rules on deportation (public interest balanced against compassionate circumstances), they were held expressly by the Court of Appeal to be compatible with the Convention.[3] However, the debate in the courts at that time always took place within a strictly *Wednesbury* framework.[4] But in *Zighem*[5] it was held that where the Secretary of State purported to have regard to the Convention, he had to show that he had applied the two-part test in Article 8, and the decision did not show that he had done so.[6]

1 The emergence of the guidelines—important policies which were hitherto unpublished and as such probably breached the ECHR requirements of transparent, precise and predictable law—indeed were the antithesis of it (see **8.10** above)—contributed to concern among practitioners and members of the judiciary at the secretive and unaccountable exercise of Home Office extra-statutory discretion in the field of immigration. See the previous

edition of this work, **13.116**. From 1998, Immigration Directorate and Asylum Directorate (now Policy) instructions (IDI and ADI, now API) have been publicly available, both on the internet and in paper form at specific sites, although 'sensitive' sections are not disclosed.

2   DP2/93, subsequently published in *Butterworths Immigration Law Service*, D[xi]. DP3/96 and its companions DP4/95 and 5/96 which replaced it, removed the references to ECHR. See Ch 11.

3   *Gangadeen v Secretary of State for the Home Department* [1998] Imm AR 106, CA.

4   *R v Secretary of State for the Home Department, ex p Amankwah* [1994] Imm AR 240; *R v Secretary of State for the Home Department, ex p Sujon Miah* (6 December 1994, unreported), QBD. In *R v Secretary of State for the Home Department, ex p Ajayi* (12 May 1994, unreported) Laws J assumed without deciding that the policy required the Secretary of State to make good a legitimate expectation that the ECHR would be regarded in decisions under the policy.

5   *R v Secretary of State for the Home Department, ex p Zighem* [1996] Imm AR 194.

6   See also *R v Secretary of State for the Home Department, ex p Launder (No 2)* [1998] QB 994 [1997] 3 All ER 961, [1997] 1 WLR 839, HL; *R v Secretary of State for the Home Department, ex p Arman Ali* [2000] INLR 89, QBD.

8.18   These various ways in which the courts may have regard to international obligations are of course still highly relevant. The UK has, after all, international obligations respecting human rights, even fundamental human rights, which are not contained in the ECHR, of which the most important are rights to work, to shelter, to subsistence[1] and to health care.[2] So, while it may well be possible on the one hand to enlarge the scope of some of the rights protected by the ECHR in the domestic courts, by approaching them through the medium of the common law,[3] through the construction rule contained in Article 53 of the ECHR, and by use of Commonwealth jurisprudence,[4] on the other hand it will always be necessary to persuade the courts to have regard to other international obligations which past and present governments have seen fit to sign up to without incorporating them into domestic law.

1   It may be that the right to subsistence would be considered an aspect of the right to life (art 2) or the right not to be subjected to inhuman treatment (art 3). See Simon Brown LJ in *R v Secretary of State for Social Security, ex p JCWI* [1997] 1 WLR 275 at 292.

2   All these rights are contained in the UN's companion to the ICCPR, the International Covenant on Economic, Social and Cultural Rights 1966 (ICESCR), but unlike the ICCPR's optional right of individual petition to the Human Rights Committee, the ICESCR has no enforcement mechanism at the suit of individuals, although states are monitored and have reporting obligations.

3   In accordance with the injunctions of Lord Lester of Herne Hill QC. See per Lord Steyn in *R v Secretary of State for the Home Department, ex p Thompson and Venables* [1998] AC 407.

4   The Indian Supreme Court held in *Tellis v Bombay Corpn* [1987] LRC (Const) 351 that the right to life comprehended the right to livelihood, so that the interference with the livelihood of a pavement salesman had to be justified by reference to human rights standards.

8.19   Prior to the incorporation of the ECHR into British domestic law, it was possible to have full regard to its provisions in the domestic courts in cases involving EC law.[1] Article 6(2) of the revised Treaty on European Union (formerly Article F(2)) requires the Union to 'respect fundamental rights as guaranteed by the ECHR and as they result from the constitutional conditions common to the member states, as general principles of Community law'. This means that, although the EU cannot be a party to the ECHR, because it is a supra-national institution,[2] its standards have become part of EC law.[3] So all EC law on immigration and asylum under Articles 61–64 of the revised Treaty of the European Communities, and any national law based on it, will need to be compatible with the Convention.[4] The EU's judicial institutions must have regard to the Convention in interpreting and formulating the requirements of EC law.[5] Thus, even rights contained in Protocols to which the UK is not a party, such as the right of nationals to enter their country, are, in our view, part of the *corpus* of law to be taken into account in construing the Treaty.[6]

1 See *Elliniki Radiophonia Tileorassi AE v Pliroforissis and Kouvelas* [1991] ECR I-2925, [1994] 4 CMLR 540, ECJ, the rationale of which is now contained in art 6(2) EU (formerly art F(2); see further *B v Secretary of State for the Home Department* [2000] Imm AR 478, CA.
2 *Re the Accession of the Community to the ECHR* (Opinion 2/94) [1996] 2 CMLR 265, ECJ.
3 Case 29/69 *Stauder v City of Ulm* [1969] ECR 419; Case 11/70 *Internationale Handelsgesellschaft mbH v Einfuhr und Vorratstelle für Getreide und Futtermittel* [1970] ECR 1125; Case 4/73 *Nold v EC Commission* [1974] ECR 491.
4 In *Elliniki Radiophonia* above (the ERT case), the Court of Justice held that, when considering national legislation falling within the field of application of EC law, it 'must provide the national court with all the elements of interpretation which are necessary in order to enable it to assess the compatibility of that legislation with the fundamental rights as laid down in particular in the European Convention on Human Rights, the observance of which the Court ensures'.
5 The ERT case, fn 1 above.
6 *R v Immigration Appeal Tribunal and Surinder Singh, ex p Secretary of State for the Home Department* [1992] Imm AR 565, (ECJ) para 22. In *R v Secretary of State for the Home Department, ex p Manjit Kaur* (14 April 1999, unreported), a British Overseas citizen claimed to be an EU citizen under art 17 EC (formerly art 8) on the basis, *inter alia*, that the Treaty reference to 'nationals' of a member state should not be construed in a manner which is incompatible with the fundamental rights of the applicant. A reference was made to the European Court of Justice, whose ruling however sidestepped the argument: Case C-192/99 [2001] All ER (EC) 250.

8.20 In *Rutili v Ministry of Interior*[1] the Court of Justice held that the ECHR provisions applied to measures taken by member states in derogation of free movement rights. Thus an order banning free movement in a part of France could infringe the ECHR, Article 11 right of freedom of association, holding out the possibility that a removal or refusal of entry involving EC free movement rights could be challenged on the basis that it infringes a Convention right such as family life.[2] This possibility was realised in the domestic context in *B*,[3] in which the Court of Appeal used the EU route to apply proportionality principles to a decision to deport which was said to infringe the applicant's combined rights of free movement and family life.[4]

1 Case 36/75 [1975] ECR 1219. See also Case 98/79 *Pecastaing v Belgium* [1980] ECR 691; Case 222/84 *Johnston v RUC* [1986] ECR 1651; C-297/88, C-197/89 *Dzodzi v Belgium* [1990] ECR I-3763; C-159/90 *Society for the Protection of Unborn Children v Grogan* [1991] ECR I-4685.
2 See also the opinion of Advocate General Jacobs in C-168/91 *Konstantinidis* [1993] 3 CMLR 401. In *R v Secretary of State for the Home Department, ex p Adams* [1995] All ER (EC) 177, and *R v Secretary of State for the Home Department, ex p McQuillan* [1995] 4 All ER 400, exclusion orders under the Prevention of Terrorism (Temporary Provisions) Act 1989 were challenged as derogating from EC free movement rights (both applicants were EU nationals prevented from travelling to Britain from Northern Ireland) in a manner which violated fundamental rights under the ECHR—free speech in Adams' case (he was prevented from addressing a meeting in the House of Commons), while in McQuillan's it was rights to life and freedom from inhuman treatment, since in Northern Ireland he had been subject to several assassination attempts. The court made a reference to the European Court of Justice in Adams' case and stayed the EU point in *McQuillan* pending the result of the *Adams* reference. The IRA ceasefire of September 1994 and the lifting of the relevant exclusion orders supervened and the point did not reach the ECJ.
3 *B v Secretary of State for the Home Department* [2000] Imm AR 478.

4   See also *R v Secretary of State for Employment, ex p Equal Opportunities Commission* [1995] 1 AC 1, HL.

THE HUMAN RIGHTS ACT 1998

8.21   The Human Rights Act 1998 does not incorporate the ECHR, but has as its purpose to 'make more directly accessible the rights which British people already enjoy under the Convention'[1] by providing access to those rights through the domestic courts. The two principal mechanisms for giving effect to Convention rights are the interpretative obligation[2]—to interpret all legislation compatibly with the Convention whenever possible—and the obligation imposed on all public authorities, including courts, to act compatibly with Convention rights.[3] With these two mechanisms, it is intended that domestic law becomes compatible with the Convention, so that 'disappointed litigants [do not] leave our courts believing that there exists elsewhere a superior form of justice which our courts are not allowed to administer'.[4] In the words of Lord Hope in *Kebeline:*[5] '. . . incorporation of the . . . Convention . . . into our domestic law will subject the entire legal system to a fundamental process of review and, where necessary, reform by the judiciary'. This is to be done without offending against the sovereignty of Parliament, which is not a public authority[6] and so is exempt from the obligation to act compatibly with the Convention (although there is a clear expectation that it will do so). The interpretative obligation does not affect the validity of primary legislation which is incompatible with the Convention, nor does a declaration of incompatibility[7] affect its validity or oblige Parliament to remedy the incompatibility. The remedy is available but not compulsory. New legislation may be incompatible with the Convention, so long as it declares itself so;[8] and public authorities are not required to act compatibly with the Convention if primary legislation prevents them from doing so. These features of the 1998 Act, designed to reassure those sceptics who feared a shift in the constitutional balance in favour of the judiciary, sets it apart from most Bills of Rights and constitutions, which allow courts to strike down incompatible legislation, and from EC law, which takes precedence over incompatible national law.[9]

1   *Rights Brought Home* (Cm 3782, 1997) para 1.19. Sedley LJ's phrase is 'patriating' the ECHR rights: see The Hamlyn Lectures *Freedom, Law and Justice* (1999).
2   Section 3.
3   Section 6.
4   Lord Bingham, 582 HL Official Report (5th series) col 1246, 3 November 1997.
5   *R v DPP, ex p Kebeline* [1999] 4 All ER 801, 838.
6   Section 6(3).
7   Under s 4 of the Human Rights Act 1998.
8   By s 19.
9   *R v Secretary of State for Transport, ex p Factortame (No 2)* [1991] 1 AC 603, HL.

8.22   The rights protected under the Human Rights Act 1998 are the substantive ECHR rights set out in Articles 2–12 and 14, Articles 1–3 of Protocol 1, and Articles 1 and 2 of Protocol 6, all as read with Articles 16–18.[1] Article 1 of the Convention, the obligation to secure the Convention rights and freedoms to everyone within the jurisdiction, is effected by the 1998 Act itself. The same reason is given for the omission of Article 13 (the right to an effective remedy for violations of the Convention),[2] and clearly courts' and tribunals' powers should be construed with Article 13 in mind.[3] The rights protected have effect subject to designated derogations and reservations.[4] The UK currently derogates from Article 5(3) (the right of a detained person to be brought before a court),[5] and has a reservation in respect of Article 2 of Protocol 1 (education in conformity with parental convictions).[6] The 1998 Act contains provisions for monitoring derogations and reservations to ensure they are not retained after the need for them has gone.[7] Derogations are to have a life of five years,[8] unless extended by Order.[9] Reservations are to be reviewed after five years and the minister must report to Parliament on the review.[10] There is scope for amendment of the Act by Order[11] to bring within the Act further rights in Protocols to be ratified, or signed with a view to ratification, in the future.[12]

1 Human Rights Act 1998, s 1(1).
2 Lord Irvine, 583 HL Official Report (5th series) col 475, 18 November 1997.
3 583 HL Official Report (5th series) col 479, 18 November 1997.
4 Human Rights Act 1998, s 1(2).
5 On the now somewhat extraordinary basis that there is a public emergency threatening the life of the nation: ECHR, art 15(1). See Human Rights Act 1998, s 14 and Sch 3, Pt I.
6 See Human Rights Act 1998, s 15 and Sch 3, Pt II.
7 Human Rights Act 1998, ss 16 and 17.
8 The current derogation is to last for five years from the coming into force of s 1(2) of the Human Rights Act 1998.
9 Human Rights Act 1998, s 16(2); the power to make orders under this section is exercisable by statutory instrument subject to affirmative resolution: s 20(4).
10 Human Rights Act 1998, s 17.
11 Human Rights Act 1998, s 1(4). Orders under this section are also subject to the affirmative resolution procedure under s 20(4).
12 ECHR, Protocol 4 (rights of nationals and aliens in respect of entry, movement within the territory and expulsion) was signed in 1963, but never ratified because of concerns about the scope of the obligation giving the right of entry to own nationals. The government has no present intention to ratify it, according to Lord Williams of Mostyn, Parliamentary Under-Secretary at the Home Office, during the Committee stage in the House of Lords (583 HL Official Report (5th series) col 504, 18 November 1997). Protocol 7 gives aliens procedural rights on expulsion and deals with double jeopardy, appeal rights and compensation in criminal cases, and with spousal equality in marriage. The government intends to sign and ratify it in due course.

8.23 The interpretative obligations are set out in sections 2 and 3 of the Human Rights Act 1998. Section 2 requires a court or tribunal determining questions in connection with ECHR rights to take into account the jurisprudence of the ECtHR[1] (and of the Commission before its demise,[2] and of the Committee of Ministers)[3] whenever it was made or given.[4] Rules under section 2(2) will indicate how evidence of the relevant jurisprudence is to be given. In practice, Court judgments, Commission opinions and admissibility decisions (of the Commission and now of the Court) will be the most useful and used jurisprudence. The jurisprudence which must be taken into account is not limited to that on the incorporated Articles; the Lord Chancellor confirmed during the passage of the Act that courts could have regard to jurisprudence on Article 13 of the ECHR, which may be of considerable significance for issues such as the intensity of review required by the court.[5]

1 Including not only judgments (arts 29, 42, 44), but also decisions (on admissibility under arts 29 and 35, striking out under art 37, friendly settlement under art 39, and on just satisfaction under art 41), declarations (of admissibility, arts 28 and 45), and advisory opinions under art 47: s 2(1)(a). In fact, the Court has never given an advisory opinion, the scope of which is in any event severely limited: see Grosz, Beatson and Duffy *Human Rights: the 1998 Act and the European Convention* (Sweet & Maxwell, 2000) para 2–18.
2 Human Rights Act 1998, s 2(1)(b), (c) and 21(2). Before the coming into force of Protocol 11, the Commission made the decision on admissibility under arts 26 and 27 of the (unamended)

ECHR, and if the application was declared admissible, would (unless a friendly settlement was reached) prepare a Report stating its opinion on whether the facts found disclosed a breach of the Convention, under art 31. Decisions and opinions of the Commission under the transitional provisions of Protocol 11 are included: s 21(4).

3   Human Rights Act 1998, s 2(1)(d). The Committee of Ministers, comprising political representatives of the Council of Europe's member states, took unreasoned decisions on the merits in secret under art 32 of the unamended ECHR, and supervised the implementation of judgments under art 54. The former function has been removed with Protocol 11 and the only reports which will emanate from it under art 46 will be on implementation of judgments. As Grosz *et al* remark (**2.17**), the nature of their past proceedings means little juridical significance can attach to their pronouncements.

4   Ie before or after the coming into force either of Protocol 11 or of the Human Rights Act 1998.

5   In particular, the observations of the Court in *Chahal v UK* (1996) 23 EHRR 413, paras 153–154; *Smith and Grady v UK* (1999) 29 EHRR 493, para 136; *Lustig-Prean and Beckett v UK* (1999) 29 EHRR 548.

8.24 The obligation under section 2 of the Human Rights Act 1998 holds the balance between bringing ECHR rights into UK law and retaining a national common law approach, by merely requiring that the courts take Strasbourg jurisprudence into account rather than making that case law binding. So UK courts are free to develop their own human rights jurisprudence, mindful always that an aggrieved person still has the right to go to the European Court in Strasbourg, once local remedies have been exhausted.[1] So, although the Strasbourg case law is not binding, it is likely to be highly persuasive. At the same time it has to be remembered that, since the Convention is a living instrument, to be interpreted purposively[2] and dynamically in the light of current conditions,[3] the ECtHR is not itself bound by its own previous case law.[4] A further factor in having regard to Strasbourg case law is that UK courts may need to discount the effect of the European Court's application of the 'margin of appreciation', which is applicable only on the international plane, as an aspect of the subsidiarity principle, and not in domestic law.[5] In deciding on the scope and content of the rights protected by the Convention, it will often be fruitful and necessary to refer to Privy Council cases and to the jurisprudence of Commonwealth countries, with which the UK shares a legal tradition.[6]

1   *Rights brought home*, para 2.5, Home Secretary Jack Straw at 306 HC Official Report (6th series) col 769, 16 February 1998. 'Our courts must be free to develop human rights jurisprudence . . . and to move out in new directions': Lord Chancellor, 583 HL Official Report (5th series) col 783, 24 November 1997. The Lord Chancellor also said that 'it is possible that [our courts] might give a successful lead to Strasbourg': 583 HL Official Report (5th series) col 514, 18 November 1997.

2   Ie by looking at the objectives of the ECHR and particularly its aim to give full and practical effect to human rights: *Golder v UK* (1975) 1 EHRR 524; *Artico v Italy* (1980) 3 EHRR 1.

3   See **8.4** above. For similar 'dynamic interpretation' in the UK courts see eg *Fitzpatrick v Sterling Housing Association* [1999] 4 All ER 705, [2000] 1 FLR 271, HL.

4   Although for legal certainty and the orderly development of the case law it usually follows its own precedents: *Sheffield and Horsham v UK* (1998) 27 EHRR 163.

5   See **8.6** above. For discussion of the domestic equivalent, the 'area of discretion' or intensity of review see **8.30** below.

6   The citation of Commonwealth authority has already become common in human rights cases; see eg *R v Secretary of State for the Home Department, ex p Ahmed and Patel* [1998] INLR 570, approving the Australian case of *Minister for Immigration and Ethnic Affairs v Teoh* (1995) 183 CLR 273.

8.25 The second and revolutionary interpretative obligation requires all legislation—primary and subordinate, past and future—to be read and given effect so far as possible in a way which is compatible with ECHR rights.[1] This interpretative formula is borrowed from EC law,[2] but is a fundamental break with normal principles of statutory interpretation: the 'true meaning',[3] the 'plain meaning of the words',[4] the 'intention of the legislature',[5] and it is by this means that domestic law will in time conform to the basic human rights norms expressed in the Convention.[6] The courts are expected to 'strive to find an interpretation of legislation which is consistent with Convention rights so far as the language of the legislation allows, and only in the last resort to conclude that the legislation is simply incompatible with them'.[7] This does not depend on statutory ambiguity, as the House of Lords said it did in *Brind*.[8] In seeking a meaning which will prevent incompatibility, the courts will not be bound by previous interpretations,[9] and will become accustomed to 'reading in' safeguards by way of provisos to apparently absolute restrictions[10]—for example, the statutory bar on appeals under section 72(3) of the Immigration and Asylum Act 1999 for non-compliance with procedural requirements[11] may now need to be read subject to a 'reasonable excuse' proviso and a '*de minimis*' proviso in order to ensure compatibility with ECHR, Article 6 fair trial rights[12] and even more crucially, to protect appellants from removals which could engage Article 3 or Article 8 rights. They will also learn to 'read down' provisions which are on their face incompatible with Convention rights,[13] by limiting the scope and effect of the words to enable compatibility.[14]

1 Human Rights Act 1998, s 3(1)(a). It does not affect the validity and continuing operation or enforcement of incompatible legislation, however—another balancing mechanism with parliamentary sovereignty: s 3(1)(b) and (c).
2 *Marleasing SA v La Comercial Internacional de Alimentacion SA*, C-106/89 [1992] 1 CMLR 305, ECJ.
3 In practice this will mean 'a rebuttable presumption in favour of an interpretation consistent with Convention rights': Lord Steyn 'Incorporation and Devolution—A few reflections on the changing scene' [1998] EHRLR 153. A ministerial statement of compatibility under s 19 of the Human Rights Act 1998 (see **8.32** below) will support such a presumption.
4 Bennion *Statutory Interpretation* (3rd edn, 1997) Butterworths, pp 423ff.
5 Bennion above, pp 740ff.
6 *R v DPP, ex p Kebilene* [1999] 4 All ER 801 at 838.
7 583 HL Official Report (5th series) col 535, 18 November 1997.
8 *R v Secretary of State for the Home Department, ex p Brind* [1991] 1 AC 696; see **8.13**, above.
9 Starmer *European Human Rights Law*, **8.11** fn 2 above, p 16.
10 As the House of Lords did in *Litster v Forth Dry Dock and Forth Estuary Engineering* [1990] 1 AC 546, to ensure compatibility with an EU obligation.
11 See **8.74** and **18.16** below.
12 As to the applicability of art 6 to immigration and asylum cases see **8.51** below. However, access to justice now has the status in UK domestic law of a constitutional right: see *R v Secretary of State for the Home Department, ex p Leech (No 2)* [1994] QB 198; *R v Lord Chancellor, ex p Witham* [1998] QB 575. In the immigration context see *Asifa Saleem v Secretary of State for the Home Department* [2000] INLR 413, upholding Hooper J at [1999] INLR 621. *R v Secretary of State for the Home Department, ex p Simms and O'Brien* [1999] 3 WLR 328 at 340, per Lord Steyn, 341, per Lord Hoffmann.
13 See *R v Secretary of State for the Home Department, ex p Pierson* [1998] AC 539 at 573-575, per Lord Browne-Wilkinson, 587-590, per Lord Steyn.
14 See eg *R v DPP, ex p Kebilene*, HL above, where some of the speeches acknowledged the possibility that a statutory provision reversing the burden of proof in a criminal case (and thus potentially offending against the presumption of innocence in art 6(2)) could be read as imposing an evidential but not a legal burden on the defendant, rendering it compatible.

8.26 The interpretative obligation also applies to subordinate legislation.[1] If it is impossible to interpret a provision in subordinate legislation in a way which is compatible with ECHR rights, and there is nothing in the parent Act requiring this incompatibility,[2] the offending provision may be disapplied or struck down as *ultra vires* the parent Act.[3]

1   In *R v Secretary of State for the Home Department, ex p Arman Ali* [2000] INLR 89, Collins J interpreted the rules relating to recourse to public funds so as to give effect to ECHR, art 8 obligations.
2   For example, if the rules are made in exercise of a general rule-making power such as that under Immigration Act 1971, s 3(2).
3   The important question in the immigration context is: by whom? In *Pardeepan* [2000] INLR 447 and Koprinov (01 TH 00095) Collins J said the Tribunal had no such power, but another division of the Tribunal has claimed the power. See **18.66** below. In any event, the appellate authority is accustomed to setting aside a decision of the Secretary of State which is in accordance with the Immigration Rules but 'not in accordance with the law' (Sch 4, para 21(1)(a)(i) of the Immigration and Asylum Act 1999, formerly s 19(1)(a)(i) of the Immigration Act 1971). 'The law' will of course now include the ECHR.

8.27   If incompatibility of primary legislation cannot be remedied by the new method of construction, or subordinate legislation cannot be read compatibly because the parent Act prevents this, the only remedy is a declaration of incompatibility.[1] A declaration of incompatibility may be made only by the higher courts, ie the High Court, the Court of Appeal, the Privy Council and the House of Lords, and in Scotland the High Court of Judiciary (except when it sits as a trial court) and the Court of Session.[2] It is a discretionary remedy; the court may decide to leave the incompatibility (although it is hard to reconcile this with its own duty as a public authority to act compatibly with the ECHR, under section 6).[3] If a court is considering making a declaration, the Crown is entitled to notice[4] and to be joined as a party.[5] In another example of the balancing of judicial guardianship of fundamental rights with parliamentary sovereignty, a declaration of incompatibility does not affect the continuing validity, operation and enforcement of the incompatible legislation, nor does it bind the parties.[6] If a minister insisted on a remedy (such as removal) which was dependent on legislation which has been held incompatible with the Convention, however, it is likely that the court would grant a stay pending parliamentary consideration of a remedial amendment. The declaration empowers, but does not oblige Parliament to remedy the incompatibility,[7] and if Parliament does not do so the victim will be able to apply to the ECtHR as before.

1   Human Rights Act 1998, s 4(1)-(4).
2   Human Rights Act 1998, s 4(5).
3   Human Rights Act 1998, s 6(3)(a); see **8.28** below.
4   Human Rights Act 1998, s 5(1).
5   Human Rights Act 1998, s 5(2). The court may be sympathetic to public interest organisations applying to be joined as interveners: see **8.34** below.
6   Human Rights Act 1998, s 4(6). The purpose of the declaration is to put Parliament under pressure to remedy the incompatibility: Lord Chancellor, 583 HL Official Report (5th series) col 546, 18 November 1997. Since the offending legislation continues in force, there can be no award of damages when a declaration is made: *Re K (a child)* [2001] 2 ll ER 719, CA, para 128–130, although costs should be awarded.
7   Parliament is not a 'public authority' for the purposes of the Human Rights Act 1998: s 6(3) (except for the judicial committee of the House of Lords: s 6(4)), and has no obligation to act compatibly with the ECHR, save under international law. Detailed description of the mechanism for remedying statutory incompatibility is beyond the scope of this work. In essence, the offending legislation may simply be amended when there is parliamentary time, or in cases where the minister considers there are compelling reasons not to wait, he or she may amend the legislation by an order under s 10, known as a

remedial order. Schedule 2 of the 1998 Act contains the fairly complex procedural requirements for a valid remedial order.

8.28 The interpretative obligation is one of the two mechanisms to bring the ECHR into UK law. The other is the obligation on public authorities to act compatibly with the Convention. Section 6 of the Human Rights Act 1998 makes it unlawful for a public authority to act in a way incompatible with a Convention right,[1] unless the authority could not have acted differently because of a provision of primary legislation,[2] or because it was acting to enforce or give effect to such an (incompatible) provision.[3] An act includes a failure to act.[4] A public authority includes a court or tribunal[5] but not Parliament (except the House of Lords in its judicial capacity),[6] and also includes a person[7] some of whose functions are of a public nature.[8] The jurisprudence relating to judicial review will be relevant in determining who is a 'public authority',[9] as will be the Strasbourg jurisprudence on bodies which engage the responsibility of the state for the purposes of the Convention.[10] Purely public authorities such as immigration officers must always act compatibly; private companies which have private and public functions must do so only in relation to their public functions.[11] Thus, while British Airways is selling tickets to members of the public (a commercial operation) it has no obligation to act compatibly;[12] but while it is transporting deportees our view is that it does. Difficult questions arise when its staff refuse to allow an inadequately documented asylum seeker to board an aircraft, as to whether this is a commercial or a public law decision and whether British Airways is a public authority in performing this function.[13]

1 Human Rights Act 1998, s 6(1).
2 Human Rights Act 1998, s 6(2)(a). The provision of primary legislation must of course be read compatibly if possible, and if this is possible, or if the legislation does not compel the authority to act in the way it has, the authority cannot rely on this exception. See *Hampson v Department of Education and Science* [1990] IRLR 302, and see discussion in Grosz, Beatson and Duffy, **8.11** fn 2 above, paras 4.21ff.
3 Human Rights Act 1998, s 6(2)(b).
4 Human Rights Act 1998, s 6(6). This accords with Strasbourg jurisprudence on positive obligations: see **8.5** above.
5 Human Rights Act 1998, s 6(3)(a).
6 Human Rights Act 1998, s 6(3), (4).
7 This includes legal persons, ie companies such as Group 4 and British Airways, but probably not unincorporated associations.
8 Human Rights Act 1998, s 6(3)(b).
9 A body is 'public' if (for example) the source of its power is statutory or prerogative or it is institutionally or structurally controlled by government, whether the power it exercises is 'governmental in nature' and would be exercised by government if not by the body concerned: *R v Take-Over Panel, ex p Datafin* [1987] QB 815.
10 For a useful discussion on the scope of 'public authorities' and 'public functions' see Grosz, Beatson and Duffy **8.11** fn 2 above, paras 4.02–4.15.
11 Human Rights Act 1998, s 6(5). The Lord Chancellor accepted that a private security company would be exercising public functions in its management of a contracted-out prison: 583 HL Official Report (5th series) col 811, 24 November 1997.
12 *Griffiths v Smith* [1941] AC 170, 205.
13 See *R v Secretary of State for the Home Department, ex p Hoverspeed* [1999] INLR 591. Even if this was held to be a public function, it would argue that it is giving effect to provisions of primary legislation, ie the carriers' liability provisions of s 40 of the Immigration and Asylum Act 1999, and is therefore not obliged to act compatibly with the ECHR: Human Rights Act 1998, s 6(2)(b).

8.29 The requirement that courts and tribunals act compatibly with the ECHR embraces both judicial and procedural or administrative functions of the court.

Despite the jurisprudence of the ECtHR indicating that immigration and asylum matters do not relate to 'civil rights and obligations' and so are not within the province of ECHR, Article 6 fair trial rights,[1] the legislation on immigration and asylum appeals[2] and the procedure rules[3] which came into force on 2 October 2000 are clearly intended to reflect Article 6 requirements of due process, openness and fairness.[4] In cases involving human rights, the appellate authorities and the courts thus have a dual function: to review the decision of an immigration officer or the Secretary of State for the Home Department, or of a lower court or tribunal, for compatibility with the Convention, and to act compatibly with the Convention themselves. In the performance of this dual function, the courts are bound to determine for themselves whether the act the appellant complains of is unlawful. This involves determining:

(a)   whether there is a Convention right in play;

(b)   whether any exceptions are permitted in respect of that right under the Convention or whether any reservation or derogation applies;

(c)   if so, whether the exception is provided for by the domestic law (ie the Immigration Acts or the Rules);

(d)   in the case of a qualified right, whether the government has a legitimate aim in applying the exception;

(e)   in such a case, whether the application of the exception is necessary to achieve the legitimate aim, ie is proportionate to it.

1   See **8.51** below.
2   Immigration and Asylum Act 1999, Pt IV and Schs 2-4.
3   Immigration and Asylum Appeals (Procedure) Rules 2000, SI 2000/2333.
4   The language of SI 2000/2333, r 40, setting out exceptions to the norm of public hearings, mirrors the language of ECHR, art 6(1), for example. See **18.158** below.

8.30 There has been intense debate as to the existence and scope of the 'discretionary area of judgment' to be afforded to ministers and lower courts by the court reviewing the decision for compatibility with the ECHR.[1] It is thought that this will have no application in appeals before the Immigration Appellate Authority, which has an original jurisdiction over both law and facts,[2] and can and should decide for itself both issues of fact[3] (for example, the extent of a family's ties in the UK and in the country of origin), interference (whether the family can relocate abroad, and so whether removing a spouse for overstaying constitutes an interference with family life within Article 8(1) of ECHR), and law (for example, if the family cannot reconstitute itself abroad, whether the interference with family life caused by the spouse's removal can be justified under Article 8(2) of the Convention). The difficulties arise in the higher courts, on judicial review and on an appeal on law from the Immigration Appeal Tribunal to the Court of Appeal, where the function of the court is confined to issues of law. In *Ex p Kebilene*[4] Lord Hope dealt first with the place of the margin of appreciation in domestic law (see **8.9** above) and then turned his attention to the 'discretionary area of judgment':

'In this area difficult choices may have to be made by the executive or the legislature between the rights of the individual and the needs of society. In some circumstances it will be appropriate for the Court to recognise that there is an area of judgment within which the judiciary will defer, on democratic grounds, to the considered opinion of the elected body or person whose act or decision is said to be incompatible with the Convention . . . It will be easier for such an area of judgment to be recognised where the Convention itself requires a balance to be struck, much less so where the right is stated in terms which are unqualified. It will be easier for it to be recognised where the issues involve questions of social or economic policy, much less so where the rights are of high constitutional importance or are of a kind where the Courts are especially well placed to assess the need for protection . . .'

The principle, as set out in the above passage, is clear and straightforward. The difficulty is in recognising the circumstances in which deference is called for and the extent to which such deference need be given. In Lord Hope's formulation, it is posed as a constitutional question, marking out the boundaries between the considered opinions of the elected body and those of the judiciary. But deference does not always rest on this distinction.[5] It may be because of the particular knowledge and expertise of the decision maker,[6] or of a lower tribunal with specialist knowledge of the subject matter.[7] Thus in *R v Chief Constable of Sussex, ex p ITF*,[8] which involved the deployment of scarce police resources, the court deferred to the considered opinion of the chief constable. In *Ex p Turgut*,[9] a case involving an evaluation of likely mistreatment of the appellant on his return to Turkey, the court concluded that 'what has been called the "discretionary area of judgment". . . is a decidedly narrow one'.[10]

1 See Lester and Pannick *Human Rights Law and Practice* (1999) **8.11** fn 2 above, p 74, para 3.21.
2 Immigration and Asylum Act 1999, Sch 4, para 21(2). See chapter 18 below.
3 See *R v Secretary of State for the Home Department, ex p Husbadak* [1982] Imm AR 8, QBD.
4 *R v DPP, ex p Kebilene* [1999] 3 WLR 972, per Lord Hope at 993-994, and see *Brown v Stott* [2001] 2 All ER 97, PC.
5 Singh, Hunt and Demetriou suggest in 'Is there a role for the "Margin of Appreciation" in National Law after the Human Rights Act?' [1999] 1 EHRLR 15-22, that the proper level of deference will vary according to the importance of the right at stake, the seriousness of the interference with it, the relative specialist knowledge or experience of the body under review on the one hand and the court on the other, whether the body under review is elected or otherwise accountable, whether the aim of the measure under review is to promote other human rights (including social and economic ones) whether the applicants are likely to be particularly vulnerable or unpopular (eg minorities requiring heightened vigilance) and whether the context is one in which there are fairly constant standards throughout democratic societies or whether no discernible standards have yet emerged. See also Clayton and Tomlinson, **8.6** fn 8, p 253.
6 *R v Chief Constable of Sussex, ex p ITF* [1999] 2 AC 417, HL.
7 *B v Secretary of State for the Home Department* [2000] Imm AR 478, paras 24-27, per Sedley LJ.
8 [1999] 2 AC 418, HL.
9 *R v Secretary of State for the Home Department, ex p Turgut* [2000] Imm AR 306, CA.
10 This passage was cited in the ECtHR in *Hilal v UK* (Application no 45276/99), 6 March 2001, in support of the court's conclusion that judicial review was an effective remedy for the purposes of art 13 in cases raising asylum or art 3 issues.

8.31 In the *ITF* case in the Court of Appeal, the court recognised that there was a difference between a proportionality test and traditional *Wednesbury* irrationality, but said that where the court needed to defer, the difference between the two tests became paper thin.[1] An echo of this can be found in the Strasbourg jurisprudence in cases where a very large margin of appreciation is to be accorded to the state, particularly in matters dealing with town planning and compulsory purchase orders and the protection of property rights which come within ECHR, Protocol 1, Article 1.[2] But the 'fair balance' test used for these purposes should not be employed to justify the continuation in the English domestic court of a

Wednesbury test in areas where European case law lays down a test of proportionality. Time and time again the ECtHR has made clear that, in determining whether a breach of the ECHR can be justified under Articles 8(2) or 10(2), the court's supervision goes beyond ascertaining whether the respondent state has exercised its discretion reasonably, carefully or in good faith, and requires it to determine whether it was 'proportionate to the legitimate aim pursued' and whether the reasons adduced by the national authorities to justify it are 'relevant and sufficient'.[3] The European Court decision in *Smith and Grady v UK*[4] makes it clear, in our view, that there is a marked difference in the UK legal zone between life before October 2000 and life after this date. In deciding whether the test put forward by the Master of the Rolls in *Ex p Smith*[5] provided an adequate remedy under Article 13 of the Convention, the European Court stated that:

> '. . . the threshold . . . was placed so high that it effectively excluded any consideration by the domestic court of the question of whether the interference with the applicant's rights answered a pressing social need or was proportionate to the national security and public order aims pursued, principles which lie at the heart of the court's analysis of complaints under Article 8 of the Convention.'[6]

In *B*,[7] an appeal from the Immigration Appeal Tribunal's upholding of a decision to deport an EU national who had been convicted of a serious criminal offence, Simon Brown LJ stated at para 47:

> 'It was common ground before us that proportionality involves a question of law and that, on a statutory appeal of this nature, the court is required to form its view on whether the test is satisfied, although, of course in doing so it will give such deference to a Tribunal's decision as appropriately recognises their advantage in having heard the evidence . . . it would not be proper for us to say that we disagree with the Tribunal's decision on proportionality but that since there is clearly room for two views and their view cannot be stigmatised as irrational, we cannot interfere.'

In *Ex p Mahmood*[8] and *Ex p Isiko*[9] the Court of Appeal took a different view of the proper approach to proportionality in immigration cases involving ECHR Article 8. In *Daly*[10] the House of Lords affirmed that there is no place for a *Wednesbury* test in human rights law; the court must review for proportionality.

1 [1997] 2 All ER 65 at 79, per Kennedy LJ.
2 *Sporrong v Sweden* (1982) 5 EHRR 35.
3 *Sunday Times v UK (N o 2)* (1991) 14 EHRR 229; *Hertel v Switzerland* (1998) 28 EHRR 534.
4 (1999) 29 EHRR 493.
5 *R v Ministry of Defence, ex p Smith* [1996] QB 517.
6 *Smith and Grady v UK* **8.4** fn 8 above, para 138.
7 *B v Secretary of State for the Home Department* [2000] Imm AR 478.
8 *R v Secretary of State for the Home Department, ex p Amjad Mahmood* [2001] 1 WLR 840.
9 *R v Secretary of State for the Home Department, ex p Isiko* [2001] INLR 109, CA.
10 *R (Daly) v Secretary of State for the Home Department* [2001] UKHL 26.

8.32 In accordance with the constitutional balance of the Human Rights Act 1998, Parliament is excluded from the definition of a public authority for the purposes of compliance with the ECHR, as noted above, as is any person exercising functions in connection with proceedings in Parliament.[1] A failure to introduce or propose legislation or to make any primary legislation or remedial order is not 'an act' which can be challenged in the courts.[2] The one obligation imposed on ministers is that of stating, before second reading of any Bill, whether in his or her view the Bill's provisions are compatible with the Convention rights (a 'statement of compatibility') or not. The purpose of this is twofold: to ensure that ministers and Parliament address compatibility with the Convention when legislation is debated (which itself makes the legislation more likely to be compatible), and to create a presumption that, since compatibility was intended, there is a strong presumption that it is so compatible, in the face of apparently incompatible provisions.[3]

1   Human Rights Act 1998, s 6(3).
2   Human Rights Act 1998, s 6(6).
3   For example, the fact that the minister declared the Immigration and Asylum Act 1999 to be compatible with ECHR rights makes it possible to read the restrictions on appeal rights in s 72(3) subject to safeguards ensuring that appeal rights are not denied for minimal procedural irregularity, which would contravene art 6 rights of access to a tribunal.

8.33 A victim of an unlawful act may bring proceedings for a breach or proposed breach of an ECHR right under section 7(1) of the Human Rights Act 1998 in an appropriate court or tribunal,[1] or may rely on the Convention right in any legal proceedings.[2] The intention behind the sub-section appears to be to ensure that Convention rights may be relied on in any legal proceedings, whether brought by the public authority or not, and whether the public authority is a party or not.[3] Section 7(11) gives the minister power to enlarge the jurisdiction of the tribunal hearing a human rights case, both as regards the grounds on which it may allow an appeal and as to the remedies it may afford. The provision was a response to concerns of immigration practitioners that the scope of asylum appeals under the Asylum and Immigration Appeals Act 1993 did not encompass non-refugee Convention claims which engaged ECHR, Article 3, which precluded persons fearing torture for a non-Convention reason[4] and those excluded from the Refugee Convention by their behaviour,[5] leading to a protection gap. The gap was plugged by the human rights appeal in section 65 of the Immigration and Asylum Act 1999. The power to allow the tribunal to grant further remedies could be used to remove the doubts as to the appellate authorities' jurisdiction to set aside incompatible secondary legislation (such as immigration rules which breach Article 8 of the ECHR).

1   Section 7(1)(a).
2   Section 7(1)(b). 'Legal proceedings' for the purposes of this sub-section includes proceedings brought by the authority or at its instigation (the most obvious example being a criminal case) and an appeal against the decision of a court or tribunal: s 7(6). It must also include an appeal against the decision of the public authority, eg an immigration appeal.
3   Where the proceedings were brought by or at the instigation of a public authority, ECHR rights may be relied on even if the unlawful act complained of happened before the Human Rights Act 1998 came into force: s 22(4). But an administrative decision to refuse entry or to remove for overstaying cannot be categorised as a 'proceeding', much less a 'legal proceeding', and so a decision to refuse entry before the Act came into force on 2 October 2000 could not be impugned after that date on Convention grounds under the Act. A decision to remove is however different, since it relates to a proposed action. The Act envisages challenges to proposed acts as well as past acts, and in *R v Secretary of State for the Home Department, ex p Amjad Mahmood* [2001] 1 WLR 840 the Court of Appeal considered an argument that the Human Rights Act 1998 applied to a pre-October 2000 decision to remove because in substance the challenge was to its future implementation. Its rejection of the argument on the basis that it was no part of its function to give 'advisory opinions' was, we suggest, wrong and failed to have regard to the approach of the ECtHR in *Chahal v UK* (1996) 23 EHRR 413 and in ECHR art 8 cases such as *Nasri v France* (1995) 21 EHRR 458.

4   Such as the appellants in *Quijano v Secretary of State for the Home Department* [1997]
    Imm AR 227 (a Colombian in fear of the drug cartels) and *Ouanes v Secretary of State for
    the Home Department* [1998] Imm AR 76 (an Algerian midwife).
5   Such as the appellant in *T v Secretary of State for the Home Department* [1996]
    Imm AR 443, HL.

8.34 Only a 'victim' of an unlawful act or proposed act may bring proceedings
or rely on ECHR rights under section 7 of the Human Rights Act 1998,[1] and
'victim' is to have the same meaning as in the Strasbourg jurisprudence on
Article 34 of the ECHR.[2] Article 34 allows applications from 'any person, non-
governmental organisation or group of individuals claiming to be the victim of
a violation'. This provision presents little difficulty in statutory appeals. In the
vast majority of cases it is the appellant's own Convention rights which will be
at issue, under Article 3[3] or Article 8 of the ECHR. In Article 8 cases where the
rights of other family members are engaged, appellants will still be 'victims' of
an action which removes them from or prevents them joining family members
whose own Article 8 rights to family life are thereby violated.[4] However, the
definition of victim is considerably narrower than the 'sufficient interest' test
for standing to bring judicial review proceedings, allowing only those persons
or bodies whose rights are affected or are likely to be affected,[5] and not public
interest organisations, to challenge decisions, policy or legislation on Convention
grounds. This precludes an organisation such as the Joint Council for the Welfare
of Immigrants from challenging rules or policy as contrary to the Convention,
although it could still launch a challenge on common law principles.[6] The
action or decision complained of does not need to have caused prejudice to the
person claiming victim status,[7] which means that an organisation of asylum
seekers (rather than one assisting them) could bring a challenge to the lack of
independence of the asylum support appeal system,[8] whether or not they were
seeking to appeal a National Asylum Support Service (NASS) decision, since
the structure of an appeal system to which they might need recourse violates
Article 6(1) of the ECHR. There has however been considerable concern about
the narrowness of the 'victim' test in relation to the use of judicial review to raise
issues of general importance involving Convention rights.[9] To some extent this
concern will be allayed by the increasing acceptance of intervention by third
parties, in particular by public interest organisations, both in Strasbourg[10] and in
the UK courts.[11] The need to wait or search for a 'victim' in order to remedy an
incompatibility affecting thousands is clearly unsatisfactory, however, and there
seems no good reason for the restrictive approach to survive in UK jurisprudence.

1   Section 7(1).
2   Section 7(7).
3   Clearly an applicant faced with an imminent act such as a deportation which might
    expose him or her to a breach of an ECHR right is a 'victim': *Soering v UK* (1989)
    11 EHRR 439.
4   It is clear that an applicant may claim to be a 'victim' as a close relative of an affected
    person: *McCann v UK* (1995) 21 EHRR 97. See Harris, O'Boyle and Warbrick, 8.3 fn 7,
    p 637. In art 8 cases on family life, in the Strasbourg jurisprudence, all members of a
    family are victims.
5   *Klass v Germany* (1978) 2 EHRR 214; *Marckx v Belgium* (1979) 2 EHRR 330. In *Open
    Door Counselling and Dublin Well Women v Ireland* (1992) 15 EHRR 244, all women of
    child-bearing age were held victims of an injunction granted by a domestic court preventing
    dissemination of information about abortion facilities abroad.
6   See *R v Secretary of State for Social Security, ex p JCWI* [1997] 1 WLR 275.
7   *Lüdi v Switzerland* (1992) 15 EHRR 173, para 34. See also *Open Door Counselling* fn 5
    above.

8 Section 102 and Sch 10 of the Immigration and Asylum Act 1999.
9 See Lord Lester, 583 HL Official Report (5th series) cols 823–837, 24 November 1997; Lord Slynn and Lord Lester, vol 585, cols 805–812, 5 February 1998.
10 See for example *HLR v France* (1997) 26 EHRR 29.
11 For example, Amnesty International, the Medical Foundation, Redress, Human Rights Watch and organisations of relatives of the 'disappeared' were allowed to intervene, either orally or by written submissions, in *R v Bow Street Metropolitan Stipendiary Magistrate, ex p Pinochet Ugarte* [1998] 4 All ER 897; *(No 2)* [1999] 1 All ER 577. UNHCR intervened in *R v Secretary of State for the Home Department, ex p Sivakumaran* [1988] AC 958 and in *R v Immigration Appeal Tribunal, ex p Shah; Islam v Immigration Appeal Tribunal* [1999] 2 AC 629. See Lord Woolf's endorsement of the Justice/Public Law Project report on public interest interventions in *R v Chief Constable of North Wales Police, ex p AB* [1998] 3 WLR 57 at 66.

8.35 Victim status is lost once the breach has been effectively remedied. But the grant of a temporary or provisional status to someone who claims that removal would violate an ECHR right does not bring victim status to an end so as to preclude recourse to a court.[1]

1 *Ahmed v Austria* (1996) 24 EHRR 278.

8.36 The court or tribunal making a finding that an act or proposed act breaches the ECHR is empowered by section 8 of the Human Rights Act 1998 to grant a relief or remedy or make an order within its powers which it considers just and appropriate. The section does not allow the appellate authority to grant a remedy it has no statutory power to grant, such as damages, although in appropriate cases it may recommend the award of an *ex gratia* payment of compensation for violation of Convention rights.[1] As noted below, the Immigration Appeal Tribunal is divided on whether the appellate authority is empowered to strike down an immigration rule (substantive or procedural) for incompatibility with Convention rights,[2] and this issue awaits clarification by the higher courts. It is unlikely that the appellate authority has the power to quash an incompatible rule or to direct the Secretary of State for the Home Department to modify or replace such a rule. This would seem to trespass on the High Court's role. But what seems uncontroversial from the wording of the section and of section 6 is that it must be able to *disregard* an immigration rule which is incompatible with Convention rights. It must allow an appeal if a decision is not in accordance with the law, even if the decision is in accordance with the Rules,[3] and may issue directions to give effect to its determination. Consistently with the appellate authority's own duty as a public authority which can only act incompatibly with the Convention if required to do so by primary legislation,[4] it must therefore be able to issue directions for the issue of entry clearance or for the grant of leave to remain even if the refusal appealed against is in accordance with the rules.

1 On issue of damages uder the HRA 1998 see Law Commision Paper No 266 of October 2000.
2 See **8.76** and **18.42** below.
3 See Immigration and Asylum Act 1999, Sch 4, para 21.
4 Human Rights Act 1998, s 6(3).

8.37 Section 11 of the Human Rights Act 1998 ensures that reliance on ECHR rights does not restrict any other rights or freedoms conferred in law. This is the section which allows reliance on unincorporated rights from other Conventions which have been ratified by the UK, by the 'legitimate expectation' route mapped out in *Ahmed and Patel*,[1] and on rights identified and recognised by the common law,[2] and adverted to in Article 53 of the ECHR.

1 See **8.16** above.
2 Such as the 'law of common humanity' which prevents foreigners from starving, *R v Inhabitants of Eastbourne* (1803) 4 East 103 cited by Simon Brown LJ in *R v Secretary of State for Social Security, ex p JCWI* [1997] 1 WLR 275.

THE ECHR RIGHTS

8.38 The main ECHR rights of relevance in immigration law are: the right to life (Article 2) and the prohibition of the death penalty (Protocol 6, Article 1); the prohibition of torture and inhuman or degrading treatment or punishment (Article 3); the prohibition of slavery and forced labour (Article 4); the right to liberty and security (Article 5); fair trial rights (Article 6); rights to the protection of private and family life (Article 8) and the prohibition of discrimination in the enjoyment of these rights (Article 14). Other rights of some relevance, particularly in asylum appeals, are freedom of conscience, expression and assembly (Articles 9–11). The right to marry and found a family (Article 12) is of less relevance than might be supposed. For reasons of space we refer here only to the main Articles of relevance to immigration and asylum law.[1]

1 For full coverage of the ECHR see Clayton and Tomlinson *The Law of Human Rights* (2000) OUP; Grosz, Beatson and Duffy, *Human Rights: the 1998 Act and the European Convention* (2000) Sweet & Maxwell; Lester and Pannick *Human Rights Law and Practice* (1999) Butterworths; Starmer *European Human Rights Law* (1999) LAG.

Right to life

8.39 Article 2 of the ECHR states that:

'1 Everyone's right to life shall be protected by law. No one shall be deprived of his life intentionally save in the execution of a sentence of a court following his conviction of a crime for which this penalty is provided by law.
2 Deprivation of life shall not be regarded as inflicted in contravention of this article when it results from the use of force which is no more than absolutely necessary:
(a) in defence of any person from unlawful violence;
(b) in order to effect a lawful arrest or to prevent the escape of a person lawfully detained;
(c) in action lawfully taken for the purpose of quelling a riot or insurrection.'

Article 1 of the Sixth Protocol states that:

'The death penalty shall be abolished. No one shall be condemned to such penalty or executed.' (The protocol provides that the death penalty may be used in time of war.)

The obligation under Article 2 is a negative obligation not to take life except in clearly defined circumstances, and a positive obligation of protection of life. The obligation:

'extends beyond its primary duty to secure the right to life by putting in place effective criminal law provisions to deter the commission of offences against the person backed up by law-enforcement machinery for the prevention, suppression and sanctioning of breaches of such provisions . . . Article 2 may well also imply in certain well-defined circumstances a positive obligation on the authorities to take preventive operational measures to protect an individual whose life is at risk from the criminal acts of another individual.'[1]

The obligation extends to effective investigation where individuals have been killed as a result of the use of force, in particular to 'secure the accountability of agents of the state for their use of lethal force'.[2] The use of lethal force by agents of the state must be 'absolutely necessary', which is a 'stricter and more compelling test of necessity than that normally applicable when determining whether State action is "necessary in a democratic society" under paragraph 2 of Articles 6 to 12'.[3] On the other hand, Article 2 does not extend to an obligation to protect the life of a serving soldier, whose life is by definition a hazardous one.[4]

1   *Osman v UK* [1999] Fam Law 86, para 115.
2   *Kaya v Turkey* (1998) 28 EHRR 1; *Güleç v Turkey* (1998) 28 EHRR 121.
3   *Ogur v Turkey* App no 21594/93, 20 May 1999. See also *McCann, Farrell and Savage v UK* (1995) 21 EHRR 97.
4   See *R v Secretary of State for the Home Department, ex p Fadli* [2001] 02 LS Gaz R 40, CA para 18 (an asylum case).

8.40   The prohibition on the death penalty in time of peace under Protocol 6 of the ECHR, ratified by the UK only in January 1999, supersedes the first sentence of Article 2. In the immigration context, it means that no one may be returned to a state where he or she is likely to be subject to the death penalty.[1] Article 2 may be cited whenever there is a risk of extra-judicial or judicial killing by agents of the state, or where there is a risk of fatal violence from others, against which the state cannot offer the requisite standard of protection.[2]

1   *Cruz Varas v Sweden* (1991) 14 EHRR 1.
2   *Osman v UK* above.

Exposure to torture or inhuman or degrading treatment or punishment

8.41   Article 3 of the ECHR states that:

'No one shall be subjected to torture or to inhuman or degrading treatment or punishment.'

In international law[1] 'torture' comprises three elements: severe pain or suffering, physical or mental; intentionally inflicted for purposes such as obtaining information or a confession or for punishment, for intimidation or coercion or from discrimination; inflicted by or at the instigation of, or with the consent or acquiescence of, a public authority or person acting in an official capacity.[2] Torture is, however, not defined in the ECHR, although the UN Convention Against Torture definition was cited in *Selmouni*[3] to contrast it with inhuman or degrading treatment. It implies deliberately inflicted suffering of particular intensity and cruelty,[4] but because the Convention is a living instrument, acts which were previously classified as inhuman treatment could be classified as torture in the future, as standards in the protection of human rights and fundamental liberties rise.[5] Rape has been recognised as torture,[6] and rape of a detainee by a state official is a specially grave and abhorrent form of ill-treatment because of the vulnerability and weakened resistance of the victim.[7] Inhuman treatment requires less serious suffering than torture, although the threshold is still high, and it need not be deliberately inflicted.[8] What constitutes inhuman treatment will depend on the characteristics of the individual such as their age, sex and state of health.[9] A threat of torture, if sufficiently real and immediate, may give rise to such mental suffering as to constitute inhuman treatment.[10] Conditions of detention may constitute inhuman treatment,[11] as may the agony of waiting on death row.[12] An excessively long sentence may also give rise to a finding of inhuman treatment or punishment.[13]

1   Article 1, UN Convention against Torture and other Cruel, Inhuman or Degrading Treatment or Punishment 1984.
2   In the absence of central government, armed factions (eg in Somalia) could be 'public officials': *Elmi v Australia* [1999] INLR 341 (UN Committee Against Torture).
3   *Selmouni v France* (1999) 29 EHRR 403.
4   *Ireland v UK* (1978) 2 EHRR 25 where the 'five techniques' of hooding, wall standing, subjection to noise, sleep deprivation and deprivation of food and drink were held not to occasion suffering of the particular intensity and cruelty implied by the word 'torture', although they constituted inhuman or degrading treatment.
5   *Selmouni v France* above, para 97.
6   *Aydin v Turkey* (1997) 3 BHRC 300, 25 EHRR 251. In refugee law there has been a regrettable tendency to focus on the motivation of the perpetrator rather than the seriousness of the harm caused to the victim: see eg *R v Special Adjudicator, ex p Okonkwo* [1998] Imm AR 502. The incorporation of ECHR, art 3 should remedy this.
7   *Aydin v Turkey* para 83. See also the International War Crimes Tribunal for the former Yugoslavia judgment in *Furundzija*, IT-95-17/1-T, 10 December 1998.
8   The techniques in *Ireland v UK*, fn 4 above, were held to constitute inhuman treatment since, without causing bodily injury, they caused intense physical and mental suffering and led to psychiatric disturbances during interrogation. In *Tomasi v France* (1992) 15 EHRR 1 a 40-hour interrogation including slapping, kicking, punching, being threatened with a firearm and made to stand for long periods handcuffed or naked was held to constitute inhuman and degrading treatment.
9   *Tyrer v UK* (1978) 2 EHRR 1; *Campbell and Cosans v UK* (1982) 4 EHRR 293, paras 28–30; *Soering v UK* (1989) 11 EHRR 439, para 100. In *Selçuk and Asker v Turkey* (1998) 26 EHRR 477 the destruction of the homes and property of two elderly residents of a Turkish village by security forces, 'carried out contemptuously and without respect for the feelings' of the applicants, was held to constitute inhuman treatment.
10 *Campbell and Cosans v UK* (1982) 4 EHRR 293.
11 The *Greek case* (1969) 12 YB 186; *Cyprus v Turkey* (1984) 4 EHRR 482; *Loukanov v Bulgaria* (1995) 19 EHRR CD 65. But most complaints in relation to prison conditions have failed. Solitary confinement is not itself inhuman treatment but is capable of being so depending on the particular conditions, the duration and stringency of the measure, its objective and its effects. Complete sensory and social isolation may be so by virtue of its effect of breaking down the personality: *Ensslin, Baader and Raspe v Germany* (1978) 14 DR 64.
12 *Soering v UK* (1989) 11 EHRR 439, applied in *Kurt v Turkey* (1998) 27 EHRR 373 to waiting for news of the 'disappeared'.
13 *Weeks v UK* (1988)10 EHRR 293, para 47; *Hussain v UK* (1996) 22 EHRR 1, para 53. But it is not enough that the sentence is more severe than might apply in other European states: *C v Germany* 46 DR 179.

8.42 Degrading treatment is treatment which is grossly humiliating, arousing feelings of 'anguish and inferiority capable of humiliating and debasing' the victim.[1] Corporal punishment has been held to constitute degrading punishment.[2] Race discrimination is capable of constituting degrading treatment, as 'publicly to single out a group of persons for differential treatment on the basis of race might . . . constitute a special form of affront to human dignity'.[3]

1   *Ireland v UK* (1978) 2 EHRR 25. See *Hurtado v Switzerland* (1994) Series A, 280A where the Commission found degrading treatment where a detainee was not permitted to change his clothes after he had soiled his trousers, and *Gurdogan v Turkey* (1986) 76 DR 9 (smearing excrement on the mouths of Kurdish villagers).

2   In *Tyrer v UK* (1978) 2 EHRR 1 (judicial birching of a 15-year-old which was 'institutionalised violence' on someone 'in the power of the authorities'). But cf *Costello-Roberts v UK* (1993) 19 EHRR 112 where smacking the bottom of a 7-year-old boy in a private school was held not to reach the minimum necessary level of severity. In *A v UK* (1998) 27 EHRR 611, however, a parent's beating of his 9-year-old stepson, leaving bruising, was held sufficiently serious.

3   *East African Asians v UK* (1973) 3 EHRR 76, Commission. The Commission in this case said treatment is degrading if 'it lowers [a person] in rank, position, reputation or character, whether in his own eyes or in the eyes of other people', and reaches a certain level of severity. The applicants in that case were being deprived of their livelihood and being left destitute in Africa, and were reduced to the status of second-class citizens by the UK government, which denied them admission to their country of nationality. In *X and Y v UK* App 5302/71, 44 CD 29, Kenyan Asians had gone to India where they were established and had strong family links. Their application was declared inadmissible, since 'unlike their fellow citizens in East Africa they had work and a place to live'. See also *Lalljee v UK* (1985) 8 EHRR 84 where a quota system for immigration was held not to be degrading.

8.43   The landmark case of *Soering*[1] established that extradition to a country where there is a real risk of treatment contrary to Article 3 of the ECHR engages the UK's responsibility under Article 3. The principle has since been extended to expulsion of rejected asylum seekers,[2] deportation on national security grounds[3] and other removals. In *Vilvarajah*[4] the court held that the expelling state's responsibility was engaged:

'where substantial grounds have been shown for believing that the person concerned faces a real risk of being subjected to torture or inhuman or degrading treatment or punishment in the country to which he is returned.'[5]

1   *Soering v UK* (1989) 11 EHRR 439 where the applicant was awaiting extradition to the US, where he faced the prospect of waiting on death row for many years. The court upheld the principle that the sending state was responsible for 'all and any foreseeable consequences of extradition suffered outside their jurisdiction'.

2   In *Cruz Varas v Sweden* (1991) 14 EHRR 1 the court held that the test in *Soering* applied *a fortiori* to expulsions of aliens. See also *Hilal v UK* (Application no 45276/99) 6 March 2001, ECtHR: rejection of claim of Tanzanian and decision to remove him breached art 3. The court conducted a fact-finding exercise to reach this conclusion, differing from the Secretary of State, the adjudicator and the domestic courts.

3   *Chahal v UK* (1996) 23 EHRR 413. See also, in the domestic court, *R v Secretary of State for the Home Department, ex p McQuillan* [1995] 4 All ER 400 (exclusion under the Prevention of Terrorism (Temporary Provisions) Act 1989).

4   *Vilvarajah v UK* (1991) 14 EHRR 248.

5   See also *Matumbo v Switzerland* (1994) 15 HRLJ 164, a case on the UN Convention Against Torture. But in *Vijayanathan v France* (1992) 15 EHRR 62 it was held that applicants could not claim a violation of art 3 of the ECHR on rejection of their asylum claims where no expulsion measure had been taken.

8.44   The right not to be tortured or subjected to inhuman or degrading treatment contrary to Article 3 of the ECHR is an unqualified right and can never be balanced or give way to competing considerations as most of the other fundamental rights may. It:

'enshrines one of the fundamental values of democratic societies, prohibits in absolute terms torture or inhuman or degrading treatment or punishment, irrespective of the victim's conduct. Unlike most of the substantive clauses of the Convention . . . it makes no provision for exceptions and no derogation from it is permissible even in the event of a public emergency threatening the life of the nation . . . the activities of the individual in question, however undesirable or dangerous, cannot be a material consideration.'[1]

Owing to the absolute nature of the right, the court has accepted that Article 3 of the ECHR may also apply where the danger emanates from persons or groups who are not public officials, where the risk is real and the authorities of the receiving state are unable to obviate it by providing appropriate protection.[2] The standard of protection required by the receiving state to exclude responsibility by the UK must be such as to remove the real risk of ill-treatment.[3] The source of the harm need not be human agency at all, but the effects of terminal illness, or severe mental illness,[4] unmitigated by adequate medical provision or carers in the receiving state.[5] Exposure to conditions of severe destitution violates Article 3.[6]

1   *Chahal v UK* (1996) 23 EHRR 413. See also *Ahmed v Austria* (1996) 24 EHRR 278, para 41.
2   *HLR v France* (1997) 26 EHRR 29 (fear of death at the hands of the Colombian drug mafia). See also *Ahmed v Austria* above and *Ould Barar v Sweden* (1999) 28 EHRR CD 213 (fear of punishment by slave master).
3   There is a conceptual difference between protection under the Refugee Convention 1951, whose rationale and prerequisite is the failure of protection by the individual's own state (see *Horvath v Secretary of State for the Home Department* [2000] INLR 239, HL) and the common responsibility for the observance of human rights underlying the ECHR (see the Preamble) which makes the *Horvath* test inappropriate in the ECHR context.
4   In *Bensaid v UK*, 44599/98, 6 February 2001, the claim of an Algerian schizophrenic against return to Algeria failed on its facts because of the availability of treatment.
5   *D v UK* (1997) 24 EHRR 423; *BB v France*, 30930/96, 9 March 1998, Commission. The principle has been applied in the domestic courts in *R v Secretary of State for the Home Department, ex p M* [1999] Imm AR 548, QBD; *R v Secretary of State for the Home Department, ex p Kebbeh* (30 April 1998, unreported), QBD; and in relation to a likely psychiatric relapse because of unavailability of treatment save at exorbitant cost see *R (Njai) v Secretary of State for the Home Department* (CO 3391/1999), 1 December 2000, QBD.
6   In *Fadele v UK* App 13078/87 (1990) HRCD Vol 1(1) 15, the Commission held admissible under art 3 of the ECHR (as well as art 8) the refusal of admission to the UK of a Nigerian father with a bad immigration history after the mother of the UK-based children was killed, leading to the children having to live in Nigeria in poor conditions which jeopardised their health and education. A friendly settlement ensued. See also the domestic cases of *R v Secretary of State for the Home Department, ex p Kebbeh* (30 April 1998, unreported), QBD; *R v Secretary of State for Social Security, ex p JCWI* [1997] 1 WLR 275.

8.45 Article 3 of the ECHR is thus considerably broader in its application than the Refugee Convention. There are no exclusions from Article 3 protection on national security or criminality grounds;[1] there is no need to show that the harm feared is for reasons of the applicant's race, religion, nationality, membership of a particular social group or political opinion;[2] the harm feared need not have the character of 'persecution'[3] or even be attributable to aggressive action.[4] In *Chahal* the ECtHR said that given the irreversible nature of the harm that might occur if the risk of ill-treatment materialised and the importance the Court attaches to Article 3, the notion of an effective remedy under Article 13 required independent scrutiny of the claim that there exist substantial grounds for fearing a real risk of treatment contrary to Article 3.[5] Article 3 is the only Article expressly referred to in the Immigration and Asylum Act 1999,[6] but this does not mean that it is the only Article which needs to be considered by the Immigration and Nationality Directorate or the appellate authorities.

1   *Chahal v UK* (1996) 23 EHRR, 413; cf *T v Immigration Officer* [1996] AC 742, HL.
2   The 'Convention grounds' of art 1A(2) of the Refugee Convention 1951: see *Quijano v Secretary of State for the Home Department* [1997] Imm AR 227; *Ouanes v Secretary of State for the Home Department* [1998] INLR 230, CA; *Danaie v Secretary of State for the Home Department* [1998] Imm AR 84.

3   *Adan v Secretary of State for the Home Department* [1998] INLR 325 (widespread clan-based killing); *Kagema v Secretary of State for the Home Department* [1997] Imm AR 137 (repeated forcible displacement and associated ill-treatment); *Faraj v Secretary of State for the Home Department* [1999] INLR 451 (peacekeeping).
4   *D v UK* (1997) 24 EHRR 423.
5   *Chahal v UK* (1996) 23 EHRR 413, para 151.
6   Immigration and Asylum Act 1999, ss 77(3)(b) (post-decision evidence on appeals), 94 (asylum support).

8.46 Although Article 3 of the ECHR will mainly be engaged in relation to proposed removal, it may have application in relation to conditions in which asylum seekers are detained,[1] the manner of their support or the deprivation of all support in the UK.[2] There is certainly evidence that the voucher system is found by those forced to use it to be degrading and humiliating in practice.[3]

1   *Cyprus v Turkey* (1984) 4 EHRR 482, 541; *CG v Austria* (1994) 18 EHRR CD 51; *Dongoz v Greece* (40907/98) 6 March 2001 (conditions of detention of alien held pending expulsion). However the threshold is high: see *Zhu v UK*, 36790/97, 12 September 2000 (18-month detention with racist abuse and intimidation from other prisoners: not severe enough to give rise to arguable breach of ECHR art 3: manifestly unfounded.)
2   See the destitution cases **8.44** above fn 6. One issue might be whether the harm was self-inflicted: *McFeeley v UK* (1980) 20 DR 44.
3   See eg the evidence from the African-Caribbean and Refugee Support Project and of Hackney Churches Refugee Network, presented to the House of Commons Special Standing Committee during the passage of the Immigration and Asylum Act 1999.

Slavery and forced labour

8.47 Article 4 of the ECHR states that:

'1   No one shall be held in slavery or servitude.
2   No one shall be required to perform forced or compulsory labour.
For the purposes of this article the term "forced or compulsory labour" shall not include:
(a) any work required to be done in the ordinary course of detention imposed according to the provisions of Article 5 of this Convention or during conditional release from such detention;
(b) any service of a military character or, in the case of conscientious objectors in countries where they are recognised, service exacted instead of compulsory military service;
(c) any service exacted in case of an emergency or calamity threatening the life or well-being of the community;
(d) any work or service which forms part of normal civic obligations.'

Article 4(1) absolutely prohibits slavery and servitude. The prohibition, like that in Article 3, is unqualified. There has been only one reported case on Article 4 in relation to expulsion to slavery, which was lost on its facts.[1] There is, however, potential for its use where expulsion could give rise to enslavement by gangs trafficking in women or children for prostitution purposes, although this scenario is likely to engage Article 3 in any event. Article 4(2) expressly permits military service forced labour in lieu in those countries which recognise a right to conscientious objection. Article 4(2) is a sanction for forced labour in limited terms, but it is not a denial of a right of conscientious objection. Indeed it has been held that punishment for refusal to perform military service which is motivated by religious beliefs may breach Article 9 (freedom of conscience and religion).[2] Article 9 may not be enough on its own to lay the foundations for a general right of conscientious objection, but it is consistent with an emerging rule of customary international law to that effect.[3]

1   *Ould Barar v Sweden* (1999) 28 EHRR CD 213 (fear of punishment by slave master).
2   *Thlimmenos v Greece*, 34369/97, 6 April 2000.
3   See Asbjørn Eide and Chama Mubanga-Chipoya 'Conscientious Objection to Military Service' UN document E/CN/4/Sub/2/1983/30/Rev.1; Commission on Human Rights Resolution 1998/77, 22 April 1998: 'Conscientious Objection to Military Service', recalled in Resolution 2000/34, 20 April 2000. In the domestic sphere see *Zaitz v Secretary of State for the Home Department* [2000] INLR 346, CA; *Foughali* (00 TH 01513), IAT. However, in *Sepet and Bulbul v Secretary of State for the Home Department* [2001] EWCA Civ 681, the CA, by a majority, held that such a right had not yet been established.

Detention

8.48   Article 5 of the ECHR states that:

'1   Everyone has the right to liberty and security of person. No one shall be deprived of his liberty save in the following cases and in accordance with a procedure prescribed by law:
  (a) the lawful detention of a person after conviction by a competent court;
  (b) the lawful arrest or detention of a person for non-compliance with the lawful order of a court or in order to secure the fulfilment of any obligation prescribed by law;
  (c) the lawful arrest or detention of a person effected for the purpose of bringing him before the competent legal authority on reasonable suspicion of having committed an offence or when it is reasonably considered necessary to prevent his committing an offence or fleeing after having done so;
  (d) the detention of a minor by lawful order for the purpose of educational supervision or his lawful detention for the purpose of bringing him before the competent legal authority;
  (e) the lawful detention of persons for the prevention of the spreading of infectious diseases, of persons of unsound mind, alcoholics or drug addicts or vagrants;
  (f) the lawful arrest or detention of a person to prevent his effecting an unauthorised entry into the country or of a person against whom action is being taken with a view to deportation or extradition.
2   Everyone who is arrested shall be informed promptly, in a language which he understands, of the reasons for his arrest and of any charge against him.
3   Everyone arrested or detained in accordance with the provisions of paragraph 1.c of this article shall be brought promptly before a judge or other officer authorised by law to exercise judicial power and shall be entitled to trial within a reasonable time or to release pending trial. Release may be conditioned by guarantees to appear for trial.
4   Everyone who is deprived of his liberty by arrest or detention shall be entitled to take proceedings by which the lawfulness of his detention shall be decided speedily by a court and his release ordered if the detention is not lawful.
5   Everyone who has been the victim of arrest or detention in contravention of the provisions of this article shall have an enforceable right to compensation.

Article 5 of the ECHR, the right to liberty and security of person, is designed to protect against arbitrary detention.[1] Deprivation of liberty must be in accordance with a procedure prescribed by law and, in the immigration context, is lawful only to prevent the person effecting an unauthorised entry into the country, or with a view to removal.[2] Restrictions on freedom of movement such as residence conditions imposed on temporary admission[3] probably do not involve sufficient deprivation of liberty to amount to detention,[4] although other Convention rights might be engaged.[5] In *Amuur*[6] the French government argued that asylum seekers held at the 'international zone' of the airport were not detained because they could 'at any time have removed themselves from the sphere of application of the measure'. The argument was rejected by the ECtHR, both on the ground that the 'international zone' was a fiction and was French territory, and that an asylum seeker's decision to remain on the territory to make a claim could not be construed as voluntary detention.[7] The case is also important for the principle that detention 'in accordance with the law' means more than simply the existence of a domestic law, but imports considerations of accessibility and precision[8] requiring clear criteria for detention, as opposed to an untrammelled executive discretion.[9]

1 *Winterwerp v Netherlands* (1979) 2 EHRR 387, paras 37-39. The list of exceptions to the right to liberty secured in ECHR, art 5(1) is an exhaustive one and only a narrow interpretation of those exceptions is consistent with the aim and purpose of that provision, namely to ensure that no one is arbitrarily deprived of his or her liberty: *Quinn v France* (1995) 21 EHRR 529, para 42.
2 Article 5(1)(f).
3 Under Immigration Act 1971, Sch 2, para 21(2)-(2B), under which regulations may prohibit unauthorised absence from designated accommodation.
4 In *Guzzardi v Italy* (1980) 3 EHRR 333 compulsory residence of a suspect on a small island under strict police supervision was a deprivation of liberty engaging art 5, while restriction on a larger island subject to a less strict regime was not.
5 Notably art 8, because of restrictions on private life and home resulting from the restrictions.
6 *Amuur v France* (1996) 22 EHRR 533.
7 *Amuur v France* (1996) 22 EHRR 533, paras 43, 46, 52.
8 *Zamir v UK* (1983) 40 DR 42, paras 90-91; *Steel v UK* (1999) 28 EHRR 603.
9 *Amuur v France*, para 50. Criteria for detention were contained in extra-statutory guidance dated 3 December 1991 and 20 September 1994 (published in *Butterworths Immigration Law Service*, D[971]. There are now statutory criteria for withholding bail (not quite the same thing) contained in Immigration and Asylum Act 1999, s 46(2).

8.49 Detention must, in accordance with ECHR principles, be necessary and proportionate to the legitimate aim.[1] Thus, to prevent unauthorised entry, a short period of restriction of liberty at the port would be permissible satisfactorily to establish identity, nationality and purpose of entry, such as domestic law provides in Schedule 2 to the Immigration Act 1971.[2] Automatic detention of those arriving without identity documents or visas would not be justified, however,[3] nor would longer detention of asylum seekers pending a decision on their claim, unless there were extremely strong grounds for believing the detainee would otherwise go to ground (effecting an unauthorised entry). The conditions for lawful detention pending removal under Article 5(1)(f) of the ECHR are the same as in the common law: detention will only be lawful if measures to effect removal are being pursued with due diligence and removal can be effected within a reasonable time, otherwise detention ceases to be 'pending removal'.[4] The domestic courts have, however, held detention 'pending removal' lawful despite a supervening asylum claim precluding immediate removal,[5] a decision which should, we suggest, be limited to apparently abusive asylum claims.

1 *A v Australia* (1997) 4 BHRC 210 UN Human Rights Committee, Communication No 560/1993, 3 April 1997 *Butterworths Immigration Law Service*, 3D[634], on art 9 of the International Convention on Civil and Political Rights, an equivalent right to liberty.

2   Immigration Act 1971, Sch 2, para 16(1) and (1A), authorising detention of arriving passengers pending examination and a decision to grant or refuse entry or to cancel leave to enter obtained abroad, and para 16(2), authorising detention on reasonable suspicion that the person is an illegal entrant, an absconded seaman or aircrew member, or a person to be refused leave to enter.
3   Since arrival without documents is not evidence of intention to effect an unauthorised entry: *R v Naillie* [1993] AC 674.
4   *R v Governor of Durham Prison, ex p Hardial Singh* [1984] 1 WLR 704; *Tan Le Lam v Tai A Chau Detention Centre* [1997] AC 97. Lengthy detention pending deportation was held unlawful in the absence of a threat to public order in *Dongoz v Greece* (40907/98) 6 March 2001, ECtHR.
5   *R v Secretary of State for the Home Department, ex p Khan* [1995] Imm AR 348, CA; *Re Samateh* [1996] Imm AR 1.

8.50 Detention must be adequately reasoned[1] and subject to prompt and regular review by a court[2] to comply with the procedural requirements of ECHR, Article 5(2) and 5(4).[3] Detainees are entitled to legal advice and assistance for the fundamental right of review by a court to be effective.[4] The court must be able to determine the legality of the detention, not merely according to the statutory provisions but also the requirements of human rights law.[5] There must be an enforceable right to compensation for detention which does not comply with Article 5 requirements.[6]

1   *X v UK* (1981) 4 EHRR 188, para 66.
2   *Amuur v France* (1996) 22 EHRR 533, para 43. In *Chahal v UK* (1996) 23 EHRR 413 the ECtHR found a violation of ECHR, art 5(4) because there was no court which could properly review the detention and the national security grounds for it. The decision led to the creation of the Special Immigration Appeals Commission; see **18.186** below.
3   Immigration and Asylum Act 1999, Pr III, not yet in force, provides for automatic references to a court by the eighth and 36th days following detention, and the court must hear the referred applications by the tenth and 38th days of detention (s 44). Seven-day detention before access to a court equates immigration detainees with suspected terrorists under anti-terrorism legislation, as pointed out by Nicholas Blake QC in 'The International Principles Governing Detention of Asylum Seekers' in Blake and Fransman (eds) *A Guide to the Human Rights Act 1998* (1999) Butterworths.
4   *Golder v UK* (1975) 1 EHRR 524; *Airey v Ireland* (1979) 2 EHRR 305; *Megyeri v Germany* (1992) 15 EHRR 584, para 27. See also *A v Australia* (1997) 4 BHRC 210, **8.49** fn 1. Legal aid was always available for *habeas corpus* and judicial review applications (subject to means) and since January 2000 has been available for bail applications under the Immigration Act 1971 and (when in force) Pt III of the Immigration and Asylum Act 1999.
5   *Amuur v France* above, paras 50 and 53. *Habeas corpus* was not an adequate remedy for asylum seekers detained under the Immigration Act 1971, Sch 2, para 16 prior to the coming into force of the Human Rights Act 1998, because it was concerned merely with the lawfulness of detention under domestic law: *X v UK* (1981) 4 EHRR 188, paras 58–61. A court on a *habeas corpus* application is now required to apply ECHR requirements of legality—including proportionality and necessity—to ensure that the decision to detain was compatible with ECHR, art 5 rights.
6   ECHR, art 5(5); see *W v Home Office* [1997] Imm AR 302. Adjudicators have no powers to award damages, but the High Court will be able to do so on an application for judicial review of detention.

Fair trial

8.51 Article 6 of the ECHR states (so far as relevant) that:

'1. In the determination of his civil rights and obligations or of any criminal charge against him, everyone is entitled to a fair and public hearing within a reasonable time by an independent and impartial tribunal established by law. Judgment shall be pronounced publicly but the press and public may be excluded from all or part of the trial in the interests of morals, public order or national security in a democratic society, where the interests of juveniles or the protection of the private life of the parties so require, or the extent strictly necessary in the opinion of the court in special circumstances where publicity would prejudice the interests of justice.'[1]

The right to fair administration of justice holds a central place in a democratic society[2] and Article 6 of the ECHR is the most frequently invoked provision of the Convention. Article 6 guarantees rights to a fair and public hearing within a reasonable time by an independent and impartial tribunal established by law in the determination of civil rights and obligations or of criminal charges.[3] In the ECHR jurisprudence, the right to a fair trial guaranteed by Article 6 has been held not to apply to decisions about the entry and residence of aliens,[4] since 'civil rights' is an autonomous concept equated by and large with private law rights as opposed to administrative discretions.[5] Substantive Convention rights such as the right to liberty[6] and family life rights[7] are 'civil rights', even if they involve the exercise of discretion, so that bail hearings and hearings relating to contact with children attract Article 6 guarantees of equality of arms.[8] The common law also recognises the rights guaranteed by Article 6 as applicable to cases before the immigration appellate authorities,[9] and clearly this is an area where the common law can influence the development of domestic Article 6 jurisprudence.

1   Article 6 (2) and (3) of the ECHR relate only to criminal trials and have not been reproduced here.
2   *Delcourt v Belgium* (1970) 1 EHRR 355, para 26.
3   Article 6(1). Article 6 has been held to apply to extradition proceedings: *R v Secretary of State for the Home Department, ex p Johnson* [1999] QB 1174, QBD.
4   *Agee v UK* (1976) 7 DR 164; *P v UK* (1987), App 13162/87, 54 D&R 211; *Alam Khan v UK* 19 Yb 478; *Uppal v UK* (1980) 3 EHRR 391; *Maaouia v France*, 39652/98, 5 October 2000; *Ilic v Croatia*, 42389/98, 19 September 2000. Arguably, the status of refugee is a civil right, although the IAT has held in the starred case of *MNM* (00 TH 02423*) 1 November 2000, that Article 6 does not apply to asylum appeals.
5   *König v Germany* (1978) 2 EHRR 170. However, in the domestic courts, planning appeals (which clearly relate to administrative discretion) have been held to attract the protection of art 6: *R v Secretary of State for the Environment, Transport and the Regions, ex p Alconbury Developments*, 13 December 2000, QBD. Rights to social security and social assistance have been recognised as 'civil rights' attracting art 6 protection: *Feldbrugge v Netherlands* (1986) 8 EHRR 425; *Salesi v Italy* (1993) 26 EHRR 187; *Schüler-Zgraggen v Switzerland* (1993) 16 EHRR 405.
6   *Aerts v Belgium* (1998) 5 BHRC 382, 29 EHRR 50.
7   *W v UK* (1987) 10 EHRR 29.
8   *Toth v Austria* (1991) 14 EHRR 551, para 84; *Lamy v Belgium* (1989) 11 EHRR 529, para 29.
9   See *Saleem v Secretary of State for the Home Department* [2000] INLR 413.

8.52   The ECHR, Article 6(1) requirement of independence of the immigration appellate authorities is secured by their appointment by the Lord Chancellor's Department instead of, as before 1987, the Home Office. There remains an issue as to the lack of independence of the asylum support adjudicators appointed by the Secretary of State for the Home Department to hear appeals against decisions to refuse or terminate support by his or her own National Asylum Support Service.[1] It has been held that the requirement of impartiality has not been automatically breached when a tribunal has previously been involved in the case at a pre-trial stage,[2] but the presence on the Tribunal of a chair whose refusal of permission to appeal was successfully challenged on judicial review might give rise to concerns under Article 6(1).[3] The ethnicity or rationality of an adjudicator is not on its own a sound basis for a complaint of partiality.[4]The openness of the hearings is dealt with in procedure rules whose exceptions mirror those set out in Article 6(1).[5]

1   See by analogy *Bryan v UK* (1995) 21 EHRR 342, para 38 (planning inspector in quasi-judicial role appointed by Secretary of State not independent). Cf EU case law: *Adouai and Cornuaille v Belgium* [1982] ECR 1665; *R v Secretary of State for the Home Department, ex p Gallagher* [1994] 3 CMLR 295 (on EC Directive 64/221, art 9).
2   *Bulut v Austria* (1996) 24 EHRR 84, para 33.
3   The Court of Appeal held in *Mwakulna v Secretary of State for the Home Department* (98/7306/4, 4 March 1999) that this gave rise to no problem, although the Tribunal held in *Huang* (14058) that it would be inappropriate for a member who had made adverse credibility findings to hear the appeal.
4   *R (Krishnarajah) v IAT* [2001] EWHC Admin 351 (Tamil asylum seeker's complaint that adjudicator's Sinhalese ethnicity gave rise to danger of bias rejected).
5   Immigration and Asylum (Procedure) Rules 2000, SI 2000/2333, r 40: see **18.158** below.

8.53 Since the rule of law, included in the Preamble to the ECHR, is scarcely conceivable without access to the court, the right to a fair hearing presupposes access to a court.[1] This right is fundamental and cannot be blocked by unnecessary procedural obstacles.[2] Thus restrictions on appeals because of non-compliance with minor procedural requirements[3] would arguably contravene Article 6, particularly if the subject-matter of the appeal is a Convention right such as family life or the right not to be exposed to treatment contrary to Article 3 by removal. The right of access to a court implies the right to legal assistance when this is compulsory or if it is made necessary by reason of the complexity of the procedure or of the case.[4] In such circumstances, if the applicant cannot pay for legal aid, denial of it can amount to a breach of the right of access to a court.[5] There must be access to a court of 'full jurisdiction' for compliance with Article 6(1),[6] but an appellate body does not have to be able to remake findings of fact for it to be a court of 'full jurisdiction', so long as it can review the decision-maker's factual findings.[7] Delays in appeals to the asylum support adjudicators could violate the right to have a hearing within a reasonable time, because of the potentially irremediable hardship and injustice to which appellants are subjected by denial of all support.[8] In recognition of the need for speed, they are the only appeals in respect of which strict time limits are prescribed.

1   *Golder v UK* (1975) 1 EHRR 524, paras 34-36.
2   *Aït-Mohoub v France* (1998) 30 EHRR 382 (security for costs); *R v Lord Chancellor, ex p Witham* [1998] QB 575 (court fees); *Tinnelly and McElduff v UK* (1998) 27 EHRR 249 (public interest immunity certificates).
3   Under Immigration and Asylum Act 1999, s 72(3) and the Immigration and Asylum (Procedure) Rules 2000, SI 2000/2333, r 33, which allows appeals to be disposed of without consideration of the merits for procedural non-compliance.
4   *Airey v Ireland* (1979) 2 EHRR 305 para 26.
5   *Aerts v Belgium* (1998) 29 EHRR 50, para 60, where the ECtHR held that the refusal of legal aid by the Legal Aid Board on the ground that the case did not appear well-founded impaired the applicant's right of access to a court. Legal aid was made available for all UK immigration appeals (subject to means and merits tests) from 1 January 2000.
6   *Le Compte, Van Leuven and De Meyer v Belgium* (1981) 4 EHRR 1, para 51.
7   See *Kaplan v UK* (1980) 4 EHRR 64, para 158; *Bryan v UK* (1995) 21 EHRR 342, para 44, and see discussion in Grosz, Beatson and Duffy, **8.11** fn 2, paras 5.32ff. In most cases judicial review is likely to satisfy 'fair trial' requirements.
8   *Zimmerman v Switzerland* (1983) 6 EHRR 17; *Guincho v Portugal* (1984) 7 EHRR 223.

8.54 The right to a fair hearing under Article 6 of the ECHR and under the common law embraces the principle of equality of arms, which affords parties a reasonable opportunity of presenting their case to the court under conditions which do not place them at a substantial disadvantage vis-à-vis their opponents.[1] So far as it is relevant in the immigration context, the principle requires adequate reasons for an administrative decision which may be the subject of an appeal,[2] and disclosure of all relevant evidence in the possession of the authorities.[3] In *Quaquah* deportation which would severely hamper a claimant in the preparation of his civil action against the Home Office for malicious prosecution was held to violate the principle of equality of arms.[4]

1 *Kaufman v Belgium* (1986) 50 DR 98; *Delcourt v Belgium* (1970) 1 EHRR 355; *Neumeister v Austria* (1968) 1 EHRR 91.
2 *X v UK* (1981) 4 EHRR 188, para 66.
3 *Lamy v Belgium* (1989) 11 EHRR 529, para 29; *McMichael v UK* (1995) 20 EHRR 205, para 82.
4 *R v an Immigration Officer, ex p John Quaquah* [2000] INLR 196.

8.55 In *Soering*[1] the European Court acknowledged that an expulsion could engage ECHR, Article 6 in circumstances where the fugitive has suffered or risks suffering a flagrant denial of a fair trial in the receiving country.[2]

1 *Soering v UK* (1989) 11 EHRR 439.
2 *Soering v UK* (1989) 11 EHRR 439, para 113.

Family and private life

8.56 Article 8 of the ECHR states that:

'1. Everyone has the right to respect for his private and family life, his home and his correspondence.
2. There shall be no interference by a public authority with the exercise of this right except such as is in accordance with the law and is necessary in a democratic society in the interests of national security, public safety or the economic well-being of the country, for the prevention of disorder or crime, for the protection of health or morals, or for the protection of the rights and freedoms of others.'

Article 8(1) protects the right to respect for four separate rights: to family life, private life, home and correspondence. Only the first two are important for most immigration purposes, although the other two may be relevant on occasion.[1] Article 8 rights will most often be engaged by decisions to refuse entry or to remove or deport someone with relevant ties to the UK, although they may be engaged in other contexts such as detention and asylum support. Article 8(2) qualifies those rights as set out above.

1 In particular the rights to respect for home and correspondence would be engaged by the search and seizure provisions of Immigration Act 1971, as amended by Pt VII of the Immigration and Asylum Act 1999: see **8.65** below.

8.57 A lawful and genuine marriage will be enough to constitute family life between two people,[1] even if the couple are not cohabiting,[2] but a sham marriage will not give rise to family life.[3] A formally invalid marriage believed valid by the parties gives rise to family life.[4] A child born of an existing marital union will usually become part of the family from birth and will only cease to be so in exceptional circumstances.[5] The presumption in favour of family life between parent and child operates between a child and its natural father, provided he continues to have contact with the child.[6] Family ties may be established through adoption and fostering as well as through biological connections.[7] Although the most important 'family' relationships are those between husband and wife and parent and child, relationships between siblings, between grandparents and grandchildren,[8] and uncle and nephew[9] are all potentially within the scope of 'family life',[10] depending on the strength of the emotional ties. But the Commission has held that Article 8 of the ECHR was not engaged by the deportation of a woman with her children from a country where her parents and sisters lived, on the ground that she and her children formed an independent family unit, so that the relationship with the extended family did not constitute family life.[11] Generally, relationships between adult siblings or adult children and their parents will not fall within the scope of Article 8,[12] but in each case it is a question of fact whether there exist ties strong enough to constitute family life within the meaning of the Article. Whether a relationship amounts to 'family life' depends on substance as much as form;[13] so informal heterosexual relationships of sufficient substance and stability have been classified as 'family life,'[14] although stable homosexual relationships have not.[15] The existence of family life is to be assessed at the time when the decision constituting an alleged interference is made, so that no account will be taken of the establishment of family life between the making of a decision to remove someone and its intended implementation.[16]

1 *Abdulaziz, Cabales and Balkandali v UK* (1985) 7 EHRR 471, para 62.
2 *Abdulaziz* above; *Wakefield v UK* (1990) 66 DR 251. Cohabitation is not a *sine qua non* of family life: *Kroon v Netherlands* (1994) 19 EHRR 263; *Berrehab v Netherlands* (1988) 11 EHRR 322, para 21; *Boughanemi v France* (1996) 22 EHRR 228; but will be relevant in deciding whether interference is proportionate: *Söderbäck v Sweden* (1998) 29 EHRR 95.
3 However the definition of a 'sham' marriage in Immigration and Asylum Act 1999, s 24(5) is almost certainly too wide, since many of the marriages caught within it are based on genuine relationships which would in any event attract ECHR, art 8 protection. See **11.45**ff below.
4 *A and A v Netherlands* (1992) 72 DR 118. In *R v Secretary of State for the Home Department, ex p Glowacka* (26 June 1997, unreported), QBD, the Home Office agreed to treat the parties to an invalid Roma marriage as if they were validly married for the purposes of refugee family reunion following the grant of permission for judicial review. In relation to polygamous marriages, the ECtHR has held it legitimate on public policy grounds to prevent two wives living together with their husband: *Bibi v UK* App 19628/92.
5 *Berrehab v Netherlands* fn 2 above, para 21; *Ciliz v Netherlands*, [2000] 2 FLR 469, paras 33, 44.
6 Even if at the time of the birth the relationship between the parents had ended: *Keegan v Ireland* (1994) 18 EHRR 342. The presumption may be defeated in the face of a total lack of interest or contact by the father.
7 *X v France* (1992) 31 DR 241. Rules restricting the admission of adopted children (HC 395, paras 310, 311, 314 and 315), requiring adoption to be based on the inability of the birth parents to care for the child and cessation of all ties with the child's birth parents are likely to be the subject of early litigation under art 8.
8 *Marckx v Belgium* (1979) 2 EHRR 330, para 45.
9 *Boyle v UK* (1995) 19 EHRR 179, Commission. The boy's father had died and the uncle stayed frequently.
10 *Moustaquim v Belgium* (1991) 13 EHRR 802; *X v Germany* (1978) 9 YB 449. Immigration Rules providing for the admission of only certain categories of 'distressed relatives' will need to be read so as to include other categories, not mentioned, to avoid offending against art 8.
11 *A and family v Sweden* (1994) 18 EHRR CD 209. See also *Papayianni v UK* [1974] Imm AR 7, No 5269/71, 39 CD 104; cf *Uppal v UK* 8244/78 (1979) 3 EHRR 391, a case where family life between children, parents, grandparents and married sisters forming a large and close family unit was argued, held admissible and subject of a friendly settlement.

12 *Advic v UK* (1995) 20 EHRR CD 125.

13 *Marckx* above, para 31.

14 *Johnston v Ireland* (1986) 9 EHRR 203; *Marckx v Belgium* above.

15 *X v UK* (1983) 32 DR 220; *S v UK* (1986) 47 D&R 274, para 2; *Kerkhoven v Netherlands* (19 May 1992) (relationship between a woman and the child of her long-term, same-sex partner not 'family life'). The same view was upheld in the European Court of Justice in *Grant v South West Trains* [1998] ECR I-621. But in *X, Y and Z v UK* (1997) 24 EHRR 143, the relationship between a transexual, her female partner and their child was '*de facto*' family life. And in the UK a stable same-sex partner has been held to be 'part of the family' for the purposes of succession to a tenancy: *Fitzpatrick v Sterling Housing Association* [1998] Ch 304, CA; revsd [2000] 1 FLR 271, [1999] 4 All ER 705, HL. This is another area where the common law can fertilise ECHR jurisprudence in the UK courts.

16 *Boucheikia v France* (1997) 25 EHRR 886. In this it differs from art 3, where the risk is assessed at the time of the court's consideration of the case: *Chahal v UK* (1996) 23 EHRR 413.

8.58 Not every exclusion or removal from the country of residence of the applicant's family constitutes an 'interference' with the right to respect for family life. Article 8 of the ECHR does not expressly deal with immigration. Indeed, the right of a foreigner to enter or remain in a country is not as such guaranteed by the ECHR, but immigration controls have to be exercised consistently with the obligations under the Convention. The right to family life is, therefore, to be seen in the context of the right of states to control the entry of non-nationals onto their territory, and Article 8 does not oblige states to respect the choice by married couples of their matrimonial residence or to accept the non-national spouse for settlement in the country.[1] The same applies to members of a family other than spouses.[2] Whether removal or exclusion of a family member will amount to interference with family life depends on whether there are obstacles to family life being conducted elsewhere.[3] Where a couple marry knowing that one of them has immigration difficulties, there will need to be other factors to overcome the expectation that they should live in the other country. If enforcement action has already begun, and there are no other factors present, the European Court has said that there will only be an interference in the most exceptional circumstances. In reading the case law here, it is, in our view, important to recognise that the discussion of where the 'family' can reasonably be expected to reside is conducted in relation to whether or not there has been an interference with Article 8(1) rights. It is only if such interference is established that the Court or Tribunal needs to move on to the question of justification under Article 8(2).

1 *Abdulaziz* above, para 68.

2 *PP v UK* (1996) 21 EHRR CD 81.

3 *Abdulaziz* above. The paradigm case is where a non-national father seeks to remain to see his child who is to remain in the country with the mother, who is a national. The father's removal inevitably interferes with his family life with his child, although the Home Office sometimes seeks to argue, wrongly, that family life between parent and child has broken down as a result of the parents' separation. See *Berrehab v Netherlands* (1988) 11 EHRR 322.

8.59 As well as legal obstacles and exceptional difficulties,[1] relevant factors in deciding whether family life can be expected to take place in another country might include past residence, ability to adapt to living abroad, links between the family members and the proposed country of destination, the existence of relationships with other family members there, language difficulties, cultural, religious and social practices, the prospect of joint residence in the respondent state at the time the family was founded,[2] compelling reasons of health, employment or family commitments[3] preventing the family from living together abroad[4] and the economic consequences of removal.[5] Where removal of a parent will result in what has been called 'constructive deportation' of a child with residence rights,[6] such rights of residence are relevant but not decisive, other factors being the age and adaptability of the child[7] and the hardship to which he or she might be subjected.[8]

1 *Salah Abdadou (Petitioner)* 1998 SC 504, CS: *Butterworths Immigration Law Service*, 3D[91].
2 In *Abdulaziz* and in *Poku v UK* (1996) 22 EHRR CD 94 the knowledge of the settled spouse of the precariousness of the non-national spouse's immigration situation when family life was entered into has been held relevant to the question of interference with it.
3 In *Gul v Switzerland* (1996) 22 EHRR 93 the ECtHR found no obstacle to family life in Turkey for a family comprising a couple with humanitarian leave to remain in Switzerland (one of whom required medical treatment which was only available there), their daughter who was in care in Switzerland, and their six-year-old son in Turkey. It upheld the refusal of entry to the son on the basis that it had not been established that the family could not continue family life in Turkey, since the couple had visited their son there and it had not been established that there was no medical treatment available there for the mother. The relationship with the daughter seems to have been overlooked by the court in a very harsh decision.
4 *X and Y v UK* App 5445, 5446/72, 1973.
5 The fact that a spouse, particularly the national of the expelling state, would have to give up a career is relevant in looking at obstacles to setting up family life elsewhere: *Adegbie v Austria* (1997) 90 DR 31, CD.
6 See Nuala Mole 'Constructive Deportation' (1995) EHRLR Launch Issue at 63.
7 *Sorabjee v UK* App 239938/93, 1995; *PP v UK* (1996) 21 EHRR CD 81; *Jaramillo v UK* App 24865/94, 1995.
8 The poor living conditions and lack of educational opportunities for British-born children in Nigeria were relevant in *Fadele v UK* App 13078/87 (1990) HRCD Vol 1(1) 15.

8.60 If it is established that the immigration measure will interfere with respect for family life, it is for the state to demonstrate that the interference is in accordance with the law (in both its meanings),[1] corresponds to a pressing social need and is proportionate to the legitimate aim pursued. The economic well-being of the country, frequently cited as the legitimate aim pursued by immigration control generally, is unlikely to justify an interference on its own,[2] but the prevention of disorder or crime[3] and the protection of the rights and freedoms of others are also legitimate aims justifying the removal of illegal immigrants and the deportation of those convicted of serious or repeated criminal offences.[4] While the aim of the removal or exclusion may be legitimate, the action itself may be a disproportionate response, ie not necessary in a democratic society or not answering a pressing social need. In each case the factors in favour of the individual and of the wider community must be balanced.[5] In *Berrehab*[6] the ECtHR held that expulsion of a divorced father would constitute an interference with the relationship with his young daughter, whom he saw regularly, and that the interference was not necessary or proportionate on economic or public order grounds, taking into account the strength of the relationship, the fact that it began when the father was lawfully resident in the country and that it could not be continued by visits to Morocco.

1 See discussion at **8.10** above.
2 *Berrehab v Netherlands* (1988) 11 EHRR 322, para 29.
3 To be understood in a general, not a literal and specific sense: the state does not need to show that the person it is proposed to exclude or remove is likely to cause riots or has a propensity to commit crimes in order to rely on prevention of disorder or crime as legitimate aims. But the state must produce evidence showing the link between the measure proposed and the prevention of disorder or crime.

4   *Moustaquim v Belgium* (1991) 13 EHRR 802; *Beldjoudi v France* (1992) 14 EHRR 801;
    Boughanemi v France (1996) 22 EHRR 228; *Bouchelikia v France* (1997) 25 EHRR 886.
5   *Sporring and Lönroth v Sweden* (1982) 5 EHRR 35, para 69; *Cossey v UK* (1990) 13
    EHRR 622. In the domestic context, see Laws LJ in *Amjad Mahmood* [2001] 1 WLR 840.
6   *Berrehab v Netherlands* (1989) 11 EHRR 322. See also *Ciliz v Netherlands* [2000] 2 FLR 469.

8.61 Immigration Rules providing for access visits to UK-based children by parents living abroad were relied on by the Home Office to justify enforcement action against non-custodial parents, who argued that their removal would interfere with family life rights. These Rules were amended in October 2000 to make them more ECHR-compatible.[1] Instead of mere visits, the right of access may now lead to settlement after 12 months.[2] In addition, the replacement of deportation action (carrying with it a prohibition on re-entry normally not lifted for at least three years) by administrative removal (carrying no such prohibition on re-entry) for overstayers makes it much easier than in the past for the Home Office to insist that non-custodial parents in breach of immigration control return home and apply from there for a visa for re-entry under the parental contact rules.

1   HC 395, as amended, paras 246-248F.
2   HC 395, as amended, para 248D.

8.62 Deportation following conviction for criminal offences of young men who have lived for most of their life in Europe and have few if any remaining ties, linguistic or social, with their country of origin has been held disproportionate to the legitimate aim in a number of ECtHR cases.[1] In *Lamguindaz*,[2] a case involving the proposed deportation on conducive grounds of a Moroccan youth who had lived in the UK since the age of seven, Judge Schermers, in his concurring opinion, said:

'Even independent of human rights considerations I doubt whether modern international law permits a state which has educated children of admitted aliens to expel these children when they become a burden. Shifting this burden to the state of origin of the parents is no longer so clearly acceptable under modern international law.'[3]

In *Beldjoudi*[4] Judge Martens, in his concurring opinion, said that 'mere nationality' should not constitute an:

'objective and reasonable justification for the existence of a difference as regards the admissibility of expelling someone from what may be called "his own country"... An increasing number of member States of the Council of Europe accept the principle that such "integrated aliens" should be no more liable to expulsion than nationals, an exception being justified if at all, only in very exceptional circumstances.'

1   *Moustaquim, Beldjoudi* above; *Lamguindaz v UK* (1993) 17 EHRR 213; *Nasri v France*
    (1995) 21 EHRR 458.
2   *Lamguindaz v UK* (1993) 17 EHRR 213.
3   The government has accepted, in the amended policy DP5/96 (published in *Butterworths
    Immigration Law Service*, **D[651]**) relating to the removal of children, that children who
    have lived in the UK for seven years cannot be expected to adapt to life abroad.
4   *Beldjoudi v France* (1992) 14 EHRR 801.

8.63 There is clearly an emerging view in the jurisprudence of the European Court that it is wrong to review deportations or removals, especially of 'integrated aliens', in the context of protection of family life, without also considering the obligation of states to give protection to private life. Thus in his partly dissenting opinion in *Nasri*[1] Judge Marcuillo emphasised that:

> 'deportation from a country in which a person has lived from birth or from childhood constitutes an interference with his private and personal sphere where it entails . . . the separation of the person concerned from his essential social environment, his emotional and social circle, and his family.'

In the same case Judge Wildhaber called the family life approach

> 'somewhat artificial, because the element of respect for his private life is missing. In such cases it would be more realistic to look at the whole social fabric which is important to the applicant, and the family is only part of the entire context, albeit an essential one.'[2]

In his concurring opinion in *Beldjoudi*,[3] Judge Martens also suggested that it was preferable to look at the sum of the ties a person had with his or her country of residence under the rubric of private, rather than family, life.[4]

1   *Nasri v France* (1995) 21 EHRR 458.
2   *C v Belgium.* See further *Bouchelikia v France* (1997) 25 EHRR 886; *El Boujaïdi v France* (1997) 30 EHRR 223; *Boujlifa v France* (1997) 30 EHRR 419, para 36. We are grateful for these case law leads to P van Dijk 'Protection of Integrated Aliens Against Expulsion under ECHR' [1999] 1 EJML 293. Looking at ECHR, art 8 rights in this more integrated way also means that it is less relevant to focus on the precise meaning of 'family life': Van Dijk at 300-301.
3   *Beldjoudi v France* (1992) 14 EHRR 801.
4   This was acknowledged in the domestic context in the case of *R v Immigration Officer, ex p James* (CO 2187/1999) where the Home Office accepted 16 years' residence, a close circle of friends, home and employment in the UK as engaging private life considerations.

8.64 The right to respect for private life is linked with personal autonomy, physical and psychological integrity, and the guarantee afforded by Article 8 of the ECHR is primarily intended to ensure the development, without outside interference, of the personality of each individual in his or her relations with other human beings.[1] Thus, enforcement action against carers who enable disabled or ill friends or relatives to live an independent and dignified life at home may constitute a disproportionate interference in the private life rights of the person cared for.[2] Same-sex relationships are an aspect of private life protected by Article 8.[3] Although as yet there has been no ECtHR case in which interference with a homosexual relationship by removal or exclusion of a partner has been held to violate the right of respect to private life, now that such relationships are recognised under the UK Immigration Rules as conferring rights of residence in domestic law on a par with cohabiting heterosexual couples,[4] there can no longer be any justification for a differential approach to interference with these relationships in the domestic courts. In a different context, the stigma, control, isolation and social marginalisation to which the system of cashless support and no-choice accommodation subjects asylum seekers may raise issues relating to the right of respect for private life under Article 8.[5]

1   *Botta v Italy* (1998) 26 EHRR 241, para 32; *Niemietz v Germany* (1992) 16 EHRR 87, para 29.
2   The invaluable role of carers is recognised in the government White Paper *Caring for People* (Cmd 849) and policy guidance *Community Care in the next decade and beyond.* The Home Office policy on carers, BDI 2/95, is heavily restricted in time. The importance

of care provided by friends or relatives was held to outweigh immigration control considerations in *R v Secretary of State for the Home Department, ex p Zakrocki* [1996] COD 304. See also *R v Secretary of State for the Home Department, ex p Green*, 29 October 1996, QBD, 31 January 1997, CA.

3 *Dudgeon v UK* (1981) 3 EHRR 40, paras 96-97; *Modinos v Cyprus* (1993) 16 EHRR 485; *Sutherland v UK* [1998] EHRLR 117; *Smith and Grady v UK* (1999) 29 EHRR 493.
4 HC 395, as amended by Cm 4851, paras 295A and D.
5 The legislation *requires* no account to be taken of the applicant's preference as regards location—although preference can be a reflection of real need.

8.65 The rights to respect for private life, home and correspondence are engaged by searches of premises,[1] which must be a proportionate measure in all the circumstances,[2] justified by relevant and sufficient reasons and accompanied by adequate and effective safeguards.[3] The ECtHR has given a broad interpretation to 'home', requiring no legal right of occupation but constituting a haven against intervention by public authorities.[4] A summary eviction of asylum seekers from the only accommodation they have following rejection of an asylum appeal may constitute unjustifiable interference with the right to respect for 'home' if they have been in occupation for a reasonable period and may need to remain in the country (to seek judicial review, or for medical or other special reasons). The right to respect for home may be engaged by a refusal of readmission after a long absence, where the applicant has no other home.[5]

1 *Funke v France* (1993) 16 EHRR 297; *Miailhe v France* (1993) 16 EHRR 332; *Niemietz v Germany* (1993) 16 EHRR 97; *Chappell v UK* (1989) 12 EHRR 1.
2 *McLeod v UK* (1998) 27 EHRR 493.
3 *Camenzind v Switzerland* (1997) 28 EHRR 458, para 45.
4 *Wiggins v UK* (1978) 13 DR 40; *Buckley v UK* (1996) 23 EHRR 101.
5 *Gillow v UK* (1986) 11 EHRR 335 where refusal of a resident's licence to live in a house in Guernsey built by the applicant after 18 years' absence was held to breach ECHR, art 8.

Freedom of thought, conscience and religion

8.66 Article 9 of the ECHR provides that:

'1 Everyone has the right to freedom of thought, conscience and religion; this right includes freedom to change his religion or belief and freedom, either alone or in community with others and in public or private, to manifest his religion or belief, in worship, teaching, practice and observance.
2 Freedom to manifest one's religion or beliefs shall be subject only to such limitations as are prescribed by law and are necessary in a democratic society in the interests of public safety, for the protection of public order, health or morals, or for the protection of the rights and freedoms of others.

The right in paragraph 1 includes the absolute and non-derogable right to freedom of thought, conscience and religion, reflecting the ECtHR's general understanding that it is 'one of the foundations of a "democratic society"'.[1] In the context of immigration its main relevance is in relation to conscientious objection to military service, in conjunction with ECHR, Article 4, which leaves open the possibility that failure to take account of the individual's beliefs may violate his or her human rights.[2] There is growing support in international human rights law for the proposition that there is a human right of conscientious objection to military service, although no international human rights instrument as yet expressly recognises such a right.[3] In 1973, the Commission found that

Article 9, as qualified by Article 4(3)(b), 'does not impose on a state the obligation to recognise conscientious objectors and . . . does not prevent a state . . . from punishing those who refuse to do military service'.[4] But this case law is now thought to be out of date. All countries in the Council of Europe, except three, now recognise such a right in their domestic law. Such recognition is required before new members are admitted to the Council, and in *Thlimmenos v Greece*[5] the Commission members accepted (without deciding) that punishment for refusal to perform military service which is motivated by religious beliefs may breach Article 9 (freedom of conscience and religion).[6] By 1979, the UNHCR's position was that 'it would be open to contracting states to grant refugee status to persons who object to performing military service for genuine reasons of conscience'.[7] In *Sepet and Bulbul*[8] the CA held that the right to conscientious objection was not so established that denial of it constituted persecution for the purposes of the Refugee Convention. The Court acknowledged that Article 9 might in future lay the foundations for a general right of conscientious objection.

1   *Kokkinakis v Greece* (1993) 17 EHRR 397, para 31. Freedom to *manifest* religion or beliefs is however qualified.
2   See Goodwin-Gill, Guy, report in *Sepet and Bulbul*, para 48.
3   See Asbjørn Eide and Chama Mubanga-Chipoya 'Conscientious Objection to Military Service,' UN document E/CN/4/Sub/2/1983/30/Rev.1; Commission on Human Rights Resolution 1998/77, 22 April 1998: 'Conscientious Objection to Military Service', recalled in Resolution 2000/34, 20 April 2000. See also judgment of Wallis LJ in *Sepet and Bulbul* [2001] EWCA Civ 681, and *Foughali* (00 TH 01513), IAT.
4   *X v Austria* (1973) 43 CD 161.
5   App 34369/97, 4 December 1998, Commission; 6 April 2000, Court.
6   *Thlimmenos v Greece*, Commission opinion above at para 44-45. The Court based its judgment on ECHR, art 14, and did not deal with this aspect of the case.
7   *Handbook*, para 173.
8   *Sepet and Bulbul v Secretary of State for the Home Department* [2001] EWCA Civ 681.

The right to marry and found a family

8.67   Article 12 of the ECHR provides that:

'Men and women of marriageable age have the right to marry and found a family according to the national laws governing the exercise of his right.'

The right to marry and found a family is one right, not two, and it applies only to persons of opposite biological sex.[1] Separation of fiancés by immigration measures could breach Article 12, but has usually been litigated under Article 8. The refusal of a marriage registrar to marry a couple could engage Article 12,[2] although since the Commission has held that the same qualifications should be read into Article 12 as appear in Article 8(2),[3] there would only be an interference with the right if the couple were unable to marry elsewhere. Arrest of an illegal entrant immediately before his or her marriage could found an Article 12 claim if it had the effect of preventing or substantially delaying it.[4]

1   *Rees v UK* (1986) 9 EHRR 56, para 49; *Cossey v UK* (1990) 13 EHRR 622 para 43.
2   But registrars are merely giving effect to primary legislation, Immigration and Asylum Act 1999 s 24(5) and so would not be liable under the Human Rights Act 1998. For discrimination in pre-marriage checks see *Tejani v Superintendent Registrar for the District of Peterborough* [1986] IRLR 502, CA. ECHR, art 12 should be read with art 14.

3   App 8166/78, 13 DR 241; App 7175, 6 DR 136.
4   *Shahara and Rinea v Netherlands* App 10915/85, held inadmissible because the marriage was only deferred for nine days.

Non-discrimination

8.68 Article 14 of the ECHR prevents discrimination in the enjoyment of the Convention rights on grounds of sex, race, colour, language, religion, political or other opinion, national or social origin, association with a national minority, property, birth or other status. The Article does not create a free-standing right not to be discriminated against,[1] but one linked to enjoyment of Convention rights.[2] It is not necessary to show a breach of a substantive right, however, to establish a breach of Article 14.[3] The questions which arise in relation to a claim engaging Article 14 are similar to those arising in respect of qualified substantive rights: has there been a difference in treatment in an area within the ambit of the Convention; if so was it on a ground such as sex, race, etc;[4] did the differential treatment have a legitimate aim, and an objective or reasonable justification, ie was there a reasonable relationship of proportionality between the means employed and the aim sought to be realised?[5] Certain forms of discrimination, such as that based on race,[6] sex[7] or legitimacy,[8] are identified as particularly serious. They are marked by a consensus in the member states to eliminate such forms of discrimination, backed by international instruments,[9] and in such cases a heavier burden is placed upon the state to justify the difference in treatment.[10] An unjustifiable difference in treatment in the operation of the Immigration Rules regarding admission of spouses on grounds of gender was held to constitute a breach of the anti-discrimination provision of ECHR, Article 14 in conjunction with Article 8 in *Abdulaziz*.[11] However, in the same case the ECtHR rejected the argument that the Rules also discriminated on grounds of race, an argument which relied on the disproportionate impact the Rules had on immigrants from the Indian sub-continent as constituting indirect discrimination. The broad margin of appreciation which the court gave there to the domestic authorities meant it could not establish any ulterior discriminatory purpose behind government policy. This approach can of course be avoided by looking at the discriminatory effect of policy rather than seeking a discriminatory purpose, the approach of the European Court of Justice and of the UK courts under the Equal Treatment Directive[12] and the Sex Discrimination and Race Relations Acts.[13] Since *Abdulaziz* there has been no definitive rejection or acceptance of indirect discrimination as founding an Article 14 claim. The question is still open. The adoption provisions of the Immigration Rules[14] would be among the first candidates for litigation based on Article 14 with Article 8 on the basis of indirect discrimination on grounds of race, in that they effectively preclude the admission of children adopted by Indian subcontinent families.[15]

1   Such a free-standing right is created by ECHR, Protocol 12, adopted by the Committee of Ministers in June 2000 and opened for signature in November 2000. It will enter into force once ratified by ten EC states.
2   The Secretary of State's refusal to register as a British citizen an illegitimate child of a British father was held not to violate ECHR, art 14 together with art 8 in *R (Montana) v Secretary of State for the Home Department* [2001] 1 WLR 552, CA.
3   *Inze v Austria* (1987) 10 EHRR 394.
4   The prohibited grounds set out in art 14 are illustrative, not exhaustive.

5 *Belgian Linguistics Case (No 2)* (1968) 1 EHRR 252; *Marckx v Belgium* (1979) 2 EHRR 330; *Rasmussen v Denmark* (1984) 7 EHRR 371; *Abdulaziz, Cabales and Balkandali v UK* (1985) 7 EHRR 471.
6 *East African Asians' case* (1973) 3 EHRR 76.
7 *Abdulaziz* above.
8 *Marckx* fn 3 above.
9 Convention for the Elimination of All forms of Discrimination Against Women 1978 (CEDAW); Convention for the Elimination of all forms of Racial Discrimination (CERD).
10 *Abdulaziz* above.
11 *Abdulaziz* above, where the Court rejected the government's attempt to justify on economic grounds and grounds of 'public tranquillity' the rules which made it more difficult for foreign husbands to join wives in the UK than vice versa.
12 ETD 76/207.
13 Sex Discrimination Act 1975; Race Relations Act 1976. See the House of Lords' application of the proportionality test to a situation of indirect discrimination in *R v Secretary of State for Employment and Education, ex p Equal Opportunities Commission* [1995] 1 AC 1.
14 HC 395, paras 310-315.
15 See *Pawandeep Singh v Secretary of State for the Home Department*, 2 December 1999, CA, currently the subject of an application to the ECtHR.

8.69 In *Arman Ali*[1] Collins J held that the Immigration Rules requiring spouses to support and accommodate themselves and their dependants without recourse to public funds as a prerequisite of admission must be read so as to include the possibility that they could be maintained indefinitely by third parties or by their nominal dependants, so as to ensure compatibility with ECHR, Article 8 rights. Otherwise the Rule could discriminate on grounds of disability or age against couples too old or ill to work but with family support. If indirect discrimination is admitted into the purview of Article 14 in the domestic courts, the impact of the 'no recourse to public funds' rules on women, disabled and non-whites will have to be looked at for compatibility with Article 14 in conjunction with Article 8. Discrimination against homosexuals in an immigration context has, however, been accepted as legitimate by the ECtHR, which has held in a number of cases that national provisions which treat married couples and heterosexuals more favourably on public policy grounds relating to the promotion of families do not breach Article 14.[2] Given the fact that the Convention is a 'living instrument', however, which must adapt in tune with the times, this approach may not survive long.[3]

1   *R v Secretary of State for the Home Department, ex p Arman Ali* [2000] INLR 89.
2   *S v UK* (1986) 47 DR 274, para 7; *B v UK* (1990) 64 DR 278, para 2.
3   See ECtHR's observations in *Smith and Grady v UK* (1999) 29 EHRR 493.

Effective remedy

8.70 Article 13 of the ECHR provides that:

> 'Everyone whose rights and freedoms as set forth in this Convention are violated shall have an effective remedy before the national authority notwithstanding that the violation has been committed by persons acting in an official capacity.'

Article 13 requires a remedy at national level to enforce the substance of Convention rights and freedoms in whatever form they have to be secured in the domestic legal order.[1] It does not stand alone, but has to be considered in conjunction with other Convention rights. Article 13 is not among the Convention rights listed in the Human Rights Act 1998, because the Lord Chancellor believes that section 8 of the Act meets the UK's obligations under Article 13.[2] The human rights appeal, in the appellate authority and in the Special Immigration Appeals Commission, certainly provides the necessary procedural safeguards to constitute an effective remedy. The remedy must consider the substance of an arguable complaint under the Convention, and grant appropriate relief. It must be effective in practice and in law, and its exercise must not be unjustifiably hindered by the acts or omissions of the respondent state authorities.[3] Judicial review has been held to constitute an effective remedy in expulsion cases raising Article 3 issues in *Soering v UK*,[4] and subsequent cases, on the basis that the courts could effectively control the legality of executive discretion on substantive and procedural grounds and quash decisions.[5] In *Chahal v UK*[6] the court found the scope of review, and so the effectiveness of the remedy, restricted because of the national security element. That has now been remedied by the Special Immigration Appeals Commission mechanism.[7] However, in *Smith and Grady v UK*[8] it was held that judicial review was ineffective to deal with the requirements of Article 8(2) in a case in which homosexuals were banned from the armed forces. The ECtHR held that the domestic court placed the threshold of irrationality 'so high that it effectively excluded any consideration by the domestic courts of the question whether the interference with the applicants' rights answered a pressing social need or was proportionate to the national security and public order aims pursued'.[9] In *Daly*[10] the House of Lords affirmed that, although the intensity of review varies according to the subject matter, the domestic courts must now review decisions for proportionality.

1 *Boyle and Rice v UK* (1988) 10 EHRR 425, para 52.
2 HL Official Report (5th series) cols 476–477, 18 November 1997.
3 *Aksoy v Turkey* (1996) 23 EHRR 553; *Aydin v Turkey* (1997) 25 EHRR 251.
4 (1989) 11 EHRR 439; *Vilvarajah v UK* (1991) 14 EHRR 248; *Hilal v UK*, App 45276/99, 6 March 2001.
5 *Hilal v UK* above, paras 77-78.
6 (1996) 23 EHRR 413.
7 Special Immigration Appeals Commission Act 1997; see chapter 18.
8 (1999) 29 EHRR 493.
9 (1999) 29 EHRR 493, paras 136-139.
10 *R (Daly) v Secretary of State for the Home Department* [2001] UKHL 26, disapproving the *Wednesbury* approach of Phillips MR in *R v Secretary of State for the Home Department, ex p Mahmood* [2001] 1 WLR 840. The case of *R v Secretary of State for the Home Department, ex p Isiko* [2001] INLR 175, CA must now be read in the light of *Daly*. See 8.30-8.31 above.

HUMAN RIGHTS APPEALS

8.71 Sections 6 and 7 of the Human Rights Act 1998 are given effect so far as statutory immigration appeals are concerned by section 65 of the Immigration and Asylum Act 1999. A person who alleges that the Secretary of State, an immigration officer or an entry clearance officer has 'in taking any decision . . . relating to the appellant's entitlement to enter or remain in the UK' acted in breach of his or her human rights or racially discriminated against him or her in breach of section 19B of the Race Relations Act 1976[1] may appeal to an adjudicator or (if appropriate) to the Special Immigration Appeals Commission.[2] For the purposes of the appeal, an immigration authority acts in breach of a person's human rights if he or she acts or fails to act in relation to that person in a way which is made unlawful under section 6(1) of the Human Rights Act 1998.[3] The human rights ground may be the subject of a free-standing appeal (as, for example, where there is no other right of appeal, as in a case of refusal of leave to enter where the person has no entry clearance)[4] or it may form an additional ground of an immigration appeal.[5] In either case, the adjudicator or the Immigration Appeal Tribunal have jurisdiction to consider the question and to allow an appeal on that ground.[6] The inclusion of entry clearance officers in section 65 of the 1999 Act makes it clear that the human rights jurisdiction extends to appeals against the refusal of entry clearance.[7] The section does not include decisions of airline liaison officers (civil servants) or airline officials (persons carrying out public functions, and so public authorities for the purposes of the 1998 Act),[8] but decisions of an immigration officer or entry clearance adopting or relying on them would be appealable.

1   Immigration and Asylum Act 1999, s 65, as amended by Race Relations (Amendment) Act 2000, s 6(4) and Sch 2, para 32.
2   Immigration and Asylum Act 1999, s 65(1), (6); and see s 2A of the Special Immigration Appeals Commission Act 1997, inserted by Immigration and Asylum Act 1999, Sch 14, para 121.
3   Immigration and Asylum Act 1999, s 65(2)(b).
4   Immigration and Asylum Act 1999, s 65(1).
5   Immigration and Asylum act 1999, s 65(3).
6   Immigration and Asylum Act 1999, s 65(4), (5).
7   Immigration and Asylum Act 1999, s 65(7).
8   Human Rights Act 1998, s 6(3)(b).

8.72 The wording of section 65 of the Immigration and Asylum Act 1999 leaves open a number of questions which may need to be resolved by litigation. First, the appellate authority's jurisdiction is limited to actual decisions relating to a person's entitlement to enter or remain or to acts or omissions in the course of reaching such decisions. Pure delay may, therefore, be appealable on the basis that it is a delay in 'taking' a 'decision'. This makes more sense than construing the words 'taking any decision' in section 65(1) as referring only to a decision which has been taken. Secondly, although section 65(1) refers to a person's 'entitlement' to enter or remain, it is thought that this must refer to (i) entitlements which flow from a decision granting leave to enter or remain or an entry clearance; (ii) entitlements which derive from law, such as EC free movement rights, without the need for a discretionary decision by an immigration official granting leave; and (iii) decisions refusing or cancelling entitlements to enter or remain, such as removal directions and deportation decisions. Thirdly, it is arguable that acts or omissions 'in taking any decision' include searches of premises and removal of property in immigration swoops, as well as decisions to detain, impose bail conditions or exact sureties, in sums which the detainee cannot meet, since these are all steps on the way to taking a relevant immigration decision. But asylum support decisions, living conditions and treatment in detention centres would not, since they are collateral matters. To be within section 65 such acts or omissions must be shown to relate to, or be a step in the process of, 'taking' such a decision.

8.73 Section 65 of the Immigration and Asylum Act 1999 contains two principles, not one: first, that appellants should have a human rights appeal before the immigration appellate authorities;[1] and secondly, that those authorities should be able to allow an appeal if there has been a breach of the appellant's human rights,[2] as set out in section 65(2)(b). The basis for allowing the appeal under section 65(5) is confined to section 65, and must be seen as a separate and additional basis to that contained in paragraph 21 of Schedule 4, which applies to all appeals under Part IV of the 1999 Act (including section 65). So on section 65 appeals the appellate authority can also allow an appeal on the grounds that the decision or action against which the appeal is brought is not in accordance with the law, with the Immigration Rules, or that a discretion exercised under the Rules should have been exercised differently. In addition, the appellate authority may review the facts, as in all other Part IV appeals. Clearly, the appellate authority has a very broad jurisdiction, giving it very wide power to revisit and review very closely the decision or action in question.

1   Immigration and Asylum Act 1999, s 65(4).
2   Immigration and Asylum Act 1999, s 65(5).

8.74 The Immigration and Asylum Act 1999 allows the Secretary of State to curtail the ambit of the section 65 appeal by issuing different certificates,[1] which we describe in chapter 18.[2] Where the jurisdiction or further jurisdiction under section 65 is curtailed in this way, the only means of challenge will be by way of judicial review. Most human rights appeals will be against refusal of leave to enter or a removal decision relating to an illegal entrant or overstayer, on quasi-asylum grounds (ie that removal would expose the appellant to a real risk of torture or inhuman or degrading treatment)[3] or on family life grounds (ie, that refusal or removal would constitute disproportionate interfere with respect for the appellant's family or private life).[4] Since the special jurisdiction under section 65 requires consideration of whether the *appellant's* human rights have been breached, the rights of a UK sponsor or child, for example to respect for family life with the appellant, could not be the subject of an appeal in their own right. But the rights of third parties would have to be considered in the appellant's section 65 appeal, and a decision which violated them would not be 'in accordance with the law'.[5]

1   See Immigration and Asylum Act 1999, ss 72 and 73.
2   See **18.20** for certificates under Immigration and Asylum Act 1999, s 72(2) that allegation of breach of human rights is manifestly unfounded; **18.112** for certificates under s 73.
3   ECHR, art 3.
4   ECHR, art 8.
5   Immigration and Asylum Act 1999, Sch 4, para 21.

8.75 In a section 65 appeal (whether free-standing or as one of a number of grounds of appeal) the process which appellate authorities need to go through to ensure that a decision is 'in accordance with the law' is of a different order from that in the customary appeal. When a decision is in accordance with the Immigration Rules (as to which see below), it will no longer be sufficient to 'ascertain that the decision-maker has adverted to a policy, correctly appreciated relevant facts, and considered whether to exercise discretion in the appellant's favour'.[1] In addition to the matters referred to at **8.29** above, it should be noted that the section 65 appeal broadens the scope of the adjudicator's jurisdiction in two ways. First, the adjudicator will be required to scrutinise the exercise of discretion outside, as well as inside, the Rules, to determine, if appropriate, whether the decision constitutes an unnecessary or disproportionate restriction on a qualified right (eg expulsion putting an end to regular contact with a child, in breach of Article 8 of the ECHR),[2] or violates an absolute one (eg expulsion to a real risk of acute physical or mental suffering).[3]

1   The Tribunal's view of its task in *Kausar v Entry Clearance Officer* [1998] INLR 141.
2   *Berrehab v Netherlands* (1988) 11 EHRR 322.
3   *D v UK* (1997) 24 EHRR 423; see cases cited at **8.42** fn 5 above. A starred Tribunal in
    Kacai (CC/23044/2000) has held that the standard of proof in Art 3 cases is the same as
    in asylum appeals.

8.76 Secondly, the appellate authorities must interpret both primary and subordinate legislation so as to give effect to ECHR rights wherever possible.[1] This may mean reading words in to rules or statutes: for example, could the absolute denial of appeal rights for non-compliance in section 72(3) of the Immigration and Asylum Act 1999 be qualified by reading in 'without reasonable excuse' or 'which is not a minimal failure' so as to achieve compatibility with ECHR, Article 6 principles of access to a court?[2] If it is impossible to read Immigration Rules or other subordinate legislation so as to give effect to Convention rights, the adjudicator will be empowered, even required, to disapply them if their application leads to a decision in breach of human rights. For example, the requirement of the Immigration Rules that certain dependent relatives be 'living alone in the most exceptional compassionate circumstances' before being able to join a sponsoring relative in the UK[3] might amount to a disproportionate obstacle to the enjoyment of family life contrary to Article 8 of the ECHR, particularly where comparison is made with family reunion rights of EEA nationals,[4] which might engage ECHR, Article 14 in conjunction with Article 8. Whether the appellate authority has the power to strike down immigration rules as *ultra vires* or in breach of the Convention (as opposed to simply not applying them in a particular case) is doubtful; its powers under the Human Rights Act 1998 are confined to granting 'such relief or remedy . . . within its powers as it considers just and appropriate'.[5] The appellate authority may not disapply primary legislation which cannot be read compatibly with Convention rights, nor subordinate legislation made as an inevitable result of primary legislation.[6] Nor may it declare such legislation incompatible with Convention rights. It must leave such a declaration of incompatibility to the higher courts, which must in turn leave the decision to remove the offending legislation to Parliament.[7]

1   See **8.25** above.
2   See *Golder v UK* (1975) 1 EHRR 524.
3   HC 395, para 317.
4   See the considerably more generous family reunion provisions of Council Regulation
    (EEC) 1612/68, art 10 and the Immigration (European Economic Area) Regulations
    2000, SI 2000/2326.
5   Human Rights Act 1998, s 8(1). In *Koprinov* (01 TH 00091) the Tribunal held it had no
    jurisdiction to strike down rules, see **18.66** below.
6   Human Rights Act 1998, s 6(2).
7   Human Rights Act 1998, s 4.

8.77 An issue that arose immediately after the entry into force of the Human Rights Act 1998 was the extent to which, if at all, the appellate authority had human rights jurisdiction in respect of decisions taken before 2 October 2000. The clear words of the transitional provisions to the Immigration and Asylum Act 1999 stated that no appeal lies against 'events' which took place before that date, and an 'event' is a decision, a notice, directions or a certificate.[1] The Tribunal declined to deal with the *vires* of the Order containing the provisions, and held that it had no jurisdiction to decide whether a pre-October 2000 decision to remove violated the Human Rights Convention.[2] The Home Office said that a post-October removal based on a pre-October decision was a separate decision which would be the subject of separate consideration by the Secretary of State and which could be the subject of a later section 65 appeal.

1 The Immigration and Asylum Act 1999 (Commencement No 6, Transitional and Consequential Provisions) Order 2000, SI 2000/2444, arts 3(1), 4(2).
2 *Pardeepan* [2000] INLR 447.

GOING TO EUROPE

8.78 For those cases where the applicant cannot obtain an effective remedy from the appellate authorities or the courts in the UK, there remains the possibility of applying to the ECtHR. A detailed exposition of the procedures of the court is beyond the scope of this work, but a brief summary follows.[1] The court became full-time and took over the functions of the Commission in November 1998, with the coming into force of Protocol 11 of the ECHR in an attempt to streamline the procedure and reduce the huge delay in getting a case heard in Strasbourg.[2] With the abolition of the Commission, the court decides on admissibility of applications itself.[3] It is organised into committees of three judges and chambers of seven judges, and a Grand Chamber of seventeen judges.[4] Committees may declare applications inadmissible by unanimous decision,[5] and if not, a chamber decides on admissibility and merits.[6] Cases concerning serious questions affecting the interpretation of the Convention or Protocols may go to the Grand Chamber, unless one of the parties objects.[7] The role of the Committee of Ministers has been reduced to supervising the execution of judgments.[8]

1 The reader is referred to Starmer *European Human Rights Law* (1999) LAG for a clear and concise summary of procedures.
2 Unfortunately the backlog had in fact increased from about 5,000 cases in 1996 to over 15,000 at 1 September 2000.
3 In the first nine months of 2000, only 650 out of 4,000 applications were declared admissible.
4 ECHR, art 27.
5 ECHR, art 28.
6 ECHR, art 29.
7 ECHR, art 30.
8 ECHR, art 46(2).

Procedure

8.79 An application should be made on the application form provided by the Registry.[1] The application must contain (in addition to the applicant's personal details and a clear and concise statement of the facts and relevant domestic law) the ECHR provisions relied on, the object of the application, details of domestic remedies pursued and any judgments or decisions obtained. If it does not, it may not be registered.[2] A judge rapporteur is then appointed to examine the application, request further information, decide whether to refer the case to a committee or to a chamber and prepare a report to that body.[3] A chamber has the power to request or take evidence.[4] In cases which are not obviously inadmissible, the respondent government is usually asked to submit observations on an application.[5] There may be an oral hearing on admissibility.[6] If an application is declared admissible, the chamber may attempt a friendly settlement[7] while pursuing the merits of the case. A hearing on the merits may be requested if there was no hearing at admissibility stage, otherwise it is at the chamber's discretion.[8] The President of the Chamber may grant leave for third-party interventions, either in writing or, in exceptional cases, orally.[9]

1 Rules of the European Court of Human Rights, r 47(1). There is provision for urgent applications to be made otherwise: rr 47(i) and 47(5).
2 Rules of the European Court of Human Rights, r 47(4).
3 Rules of the European Court of Human Rights, r 49.
4 Rules of the European Court of Human Rights, r 42. The power has been frequently used in recent years in respect of applications under ECHR, arts 2 and 3 from Turkey, where the government disputes the facts. See eg *Akdivar v Turkey* (1996) 23 EHRR 143.
5 Rules of the European Court of Human Rights, r 54(3).
6 Rules of the European Court of Human Rights, r 54(4).
7 Rules of the European Court of Human Rights, r 62.
8 Rules of the European Court of Human Rights, r 59.
9 Rules of the European Court of Human Rights, r 61.

Interim measures

8.80 The Court has no power to grant an injunction against the respondent state, but if the applicant is about to be expelled or deported, the application may contain a request for an interim measure under Rule 39 of the Court's procedure rules, which provides that the Chamber or, where appropriate, its President may 'indicate to the parties any interim measure which it considers should be adopted in the interests of the parties or of the proper conduct of the proceedings before it'. This would include a request not to proceed with a removal. The power to make a Rule 39 request is used very sparingly, and is not always complied with by the respondent state.[1]

1 See eg *Cruz Varas v Sweden* (1991) 14 EHRR 1.

Admissibility

8.81 An application will be declared inadmissible if it fails to comply with the requirements of Article 35 of the ECHR. The Rules set out there are:

(i)   the six-month rule: the application must be communicated within six months of the last domestic decision.[1] This is strict and cannot be waived. The time limit may not be relevant in the case of complaints of continuing breaches, although these are strictly interpreted;[2]

(ii)   exhaustion of domestic remedies: the application will be inadmissible if available remedies were not pursued,[3] whether this was because of an adviser's failure or for other reason, unless the failure was due to the respondent state's obstruction.[4] But this rule only requires potentially effective remedies to be exhausted; where a binding authority meant certain failure, a domestic remedy need not be pursued. But a remedy may be effective even if success is not guaranteed;[5]

(iii)   manifestly ill-founded applications, ie those disclosing no *prima facie* breach of a Convention right, or where the complaint is unsubstantiated or the applicant has ceased to be a victim,[6] and applications considered an abuse of the right of application,[7] will be rejected as inadmissible;

(iv)   Anonymous complaints are inadmissible.[8] An applicant must disclose his or her identity when applying, although there is provision for non-disclosure of identity to the public;

(v) Repetitive applications are inadmissible, although if the complaint is based on new factual information it will not be disqualified;[9]

(vi) Applications which are incompatible with the Convention are inadmissible. A claim is incompatible if it falls outside the terms of the Convention, either in terms of time (eg a claim based on a Protocol not ratified by the respondent state at the time) or place (ie there is no territorial link with the respondent state), or because it covers matters not within the terms of the Convention at all, such as a right to work in a particular occupation,[10] or matters covered by a derogation.[11]

1 ECHR, art 35(1).
2 Application 9852 *UK and Ireland* (1985) 8 EHRR 49.
3 ECHR, art 35(1).
4 See eg *Hilton v UK* (1976) 4 DR 177.
5 See *Soering v UK* (1989) 11 EHRR 439. On non-exhaustion of effective remedies see Starmer, *European Human Rights Law* (1999) LAG, p 706ff.
6 Eg by accepting damages in settlement of a civil claim: see *Hay v UK*, App 41894/98, 17 October 2000.
7 Eg with no legal foundation, to make a political or other point.
8 ECHR, art 35(2)(a).
9 ECHR, art 35(2)(b).
10 *X v Germany* 6742/74, (1975) 3 DR 98.
11 *Brannigan and McBride v UK* (1993) 17 EHRR 539.

OTHER INTERNATIONAL OBLIGATIONS

8.82 Many of the obligations under the ECHR are also provided for in the International Covenant on Civil and Political Rights (ICCPR), ratified by the UK in 1976.[1] But the Covenant contains rights not in the ECHR, or contained in Protocols which the UK has not signed, such as the right to enter a person's own country.[2] However, as the UN Human Rights Committee commented in 1995, the UK's legal system does not fully ensure effective remedies. The impediments to full implementation identified by the Committee include the UK's failure to incorporate the Covenant, its failure to accede to the first Optional Protocol (providing a right of individual petition to the Committee),[3] and the absence of a constitutional Bill of Rights.[4] It remains to be seen how far incorporation of the ECHR into UK law will remedy the defects identified. Following the decisions in *Ahmed and Patel*[5] and *Adimi*[6] it might have been possible to argue that the UK's ratification of the Covenant gave rise to a legitimate expectation that the rights contained in it would be respected. But the UK has made a general reservation from the Covenant rights concerning immigration and nationality, and has consistently refused to withdraw it, a position which the Human Rights Committee 'regrets' in its latest observations.[7] The UK has made similar reservations from the UN Convention on the Rights of the Child, a reservation which the Committee monitoring compliance suggests 'does not appear to be compatible with the principles and provisions of the Convention'.[8] These remarks fall short of express condemnation, and so the rights contained in these international instruments cannot be directly invoked to call into question UK immigration and nationality laws and practices.[9] The ICCPR however remains an important source of principles of international human rights law.

1   The text of this, as of other UN Conventions, is available on the UN website at www.unhchr.ch/intlinst.htm. See also Harris and Joseph *The International Covenant on Civil and Political Rights and United Kingdom Law* (1995).
2   International Covenant on Civil and Political Rights, art 12(4), reflecting Protocol 4, art 3(2) of ECHR, not signed by the UK.
3   In April 2000 the government stated it had no present plans to grant new rights of petition under any UN human rights treaty: 612 HL Official Report (5th series), 12 April 2000, WA 49.
4   See the UN Human Rights Committee report, CCPR/C/79/Add.55, paras 408-435 of 3 October 1995, which also expressed concern at the treatment of illegal entrants, asylum seekers and those to be deported, in particular their lengthy incarceration and incidences of the use of excessive force in the execution of deportation orders, and at the privatisation of state activities involving the use of force and detention.
5   *R v Secretary of State for the Home Department, ex p Ahmed and Patel* [1998] INLR 570, CA.
6   *R v Uxbridge Magistrates' Court, ex p Adimi* [1999] INLR 490, QBD.
7   UN Human Rights Committee Report above.
8   CRC/C/15/Add.34, 15 February 1995.
9   See Nuala Mole 'Constructive Deportation and the European Convention' (1995) EHRLR Launch Issue 63 at 65 for an important discussion of the legality of the UK's immigration reservations to international instruments.

BRITISH NATIONALS WITHOUT THE RIGHT OF ABODE

8.83 The traditional view in international law, that the state's obligation to admit its own nationals applies only as between states and is not an obligation to the nationals, was invoked during the passage of the Commonwealth Immigrants Act 1968.[1] That Act, passed to prevent UK citizens of Asian descent who were threatened with expulsion from Kenya from coming to Britain, removed the previous common law right of certain UK citizens without ancestral connections with the UK to enter the country. A less restrictive interpretation of international law acknowledges that the state's duty to admit its own nationals is the corollary of the individual's right to enter the territory of his or her own state, deriving from the Universal Declaration on Human Rights, international instruments such as the International Covenant on Civil and Political Rights, and the general principles of customary international law.[2] The judgment of Orr LJ in *R v Secretary of State for the Home Department ex p Thakrar*[3] indicates the extent to which municipal law recognises this duty, to the effect that it is limited to cases of expulsion from the country of residence where the applicant has nowhere else to go. Successive UK governments, despite failing to give full acknowledgement or effect to the duty towards individuals, have made arrangements whereby most categories of British nationals—at least those with no other nationality—may be admitted to the UK somehow or another. To these arrangements we now turn.

1   See Plender *International Migration Law* (2nd edn, 1988), pp 133ff for the debate.
2   Universal Declaration on Human Rights, art 13(2); International Covenant on Civil and Political Rights, art 12(4); International Covenant on the Elimination of all forms of Racial Discrimination, art 5(d)(ii); ECHR, Protocol 4, art 3(2); see also UN Human Rights Committee General Comments No 27 on Free Movement, 1999.
3   [1974] QB 684, CA.

8.84 Of the residuary categories of British national created by the British Nationality Act 1981, British Dependent Territories citizens (BDTCs), in effect the citizens of the UK's remaining colonies or 'overseas territories', are to be offered British citizenship, and so the right of abode in the UK, if they want it.[1]

British Nationals (Overseas) in Hong Kong who are effectively stateless are entitled to register as British citizens under the British Nationality (Hong Kong) Act 1997. That leaves British Overseas citizens (BOCs), British Protected Persons (who are not nationals in municipal law, but are issued with British passports and are considered to be British nationals in international law) and British subjects without citizenship (former UK and Colonies citizens who were expected to obtain citizenship of an independent Commonwealth country but never did). These groups of British nationals are not to be given British citizenship, but may be admissible under the special voucher scheme.

1   See White Paper *Partnership for Progress and Prosperity—Britain and the Overseas Territories* (Cm 4264, March 1999). BDTCs from the British Indian Ocean Territory or the Sovereign Base Area in Cyprus are to be excluded: see Fransman 'The Human Rights Act and British Nationality' in *A Guide to the Human Rights Act* (1999) Butterworths 129 at 136.

Special voucher scheme

8.85   The special voucher scheme was introduced in 1968 with the passage of the Commonwealth Immigrants Act 1968. The annual allocation of 1,500 'special quota' vouchers was increased to 3,000 in 1971 and 5,000 in 1975, at which figure it has stayed. The allocation comprises separate quotas for Kenya, Tanzania, Zambia, India and other countries.[1] The scheme remained in more or less the same form after the British Nationality Act 1981 relegated the UK and Colonies citizens eligible for entry under it to British Overseas citizens, and it also benefits British Protected Persons and British Subjects without citizenship. The scheme is outside the Immigration Rules, but detailed guidance is contained in the IDI. British Overseas citizens, British Protected Persons and British Subjects without citizenship resident in an East African country with its own quota are eligible, as are British Overseas citizens, British Protected Persons and British Subjects without citizenship resident in India who have an East African connection.[2] British Overseas citizens, British Protected Persons and British Subjects without citizenship resident in the rest of the world who have an East African connection are eligible only if they are under pressure to leave.[3] Applicants must hold no other citizenship, and so dual nationals are ineligible (including those who renounce a second citizenship voluntarily),[4] but those who are deprived of a second citizenship as a consequence of asserting a claim to British nationality are eligible.[5] They must also have nowhere else to go,[6] and intend to settle in the UK.[7]

1   IDI Dec/00, Ch 7, Annex C, para 2.
2   An East African connection means British nationality acquired by birth or registration in Kenya, Uganda, Zambia, Malawi or the People's Democratic Republic of Yemen, or by birth to someone with such a connection, or a period of settlement (current or past) in any of the countries listed: IDI Dec/00, Ch 7, Annex C, para 3.3.
3   IDI Dec/00, Ch 7, Annex C, para 3. Pressure to leave is assumed in categories (i) and (ii). Those in category (iii) must have no unqualified right of entry to any other country and be about to be deported, or have an expired or cancelled residence permit with no possibility of obtaining a further permit, or must have a standard of living substantially below that of the country of residence as a direct result of restriction on trade, residence or employment applied to non-citizens generally or to UK passport holders in particular: para 3.4.
4   IDI Dec/00, Ch 7, Annex C, para 3.6.
5   This will apply to those who lose Kenyan nationality at age 23 for failure to renounce UK citizenship; those who lose Tanzanian nationality for the same reason at 19; and those who notify the South Yemen authorities at 18 that they wish to remain British: Addendum to IDI Dec/00, Ch 7, Annex C, para 3.6.

6   Anyone with an unqualified right of entry elsewhere is ineligible, but an applicant who merely has the option of going to a third country (eg to India) is eligible: IDI Dec/00, Ch 7, Annex C, para 3.6. Those who were eligible for special vouchers in Kenya but preferred to go to India are guaranteed later entry to the UK: para 8.6; as are those who were expelled from Uganda and accepted by India on a temporary basis: para 8.7.

7   IDI Dec/00, Ch 7, Annex C, para 3.7.

8.86 Special vouchers are normally only issued to heads of household. The scheme here is frankly discriminatory. Men aged over 18 are heads of household, while women over 18 only qualify if they are single, widowed, divorced, or married to a man who is 'incapable of fulfilling the role of head of household for medical reasons'.[1] In *Amin*[2] the House of Lords held that this blatant sex discrimination in the operation of the scheme was outside the scope of the Sex Discrimination Act 1975 and consequently was not unlawful discrimination. The Race Relations Act 1976 now applies in this area, but not the 1975 Act.[3] Similar difficulties could attend a challenge reliant on Article 14 of the ECHR, since discrimination is only contrary to Article 14 if it is in the enjoyment of a Convention right, and Article 3 of Protocol 4 (the right to enter the country of nationality) is not a Convention right so far as the UK is concerned. Unmarried and unemployed dependent children between the ages of 18 and 25 are eligible for vouchers in their own right if their parents have not applied for vouchers and they intend to go to the UK for settlement without their parents. An engaged woman should be treated as single but if she marries between receipt of the voucher and travelling to the UK, she loses her entitlement.[4]

1   IDI Dec/00, Ch 7, Annex C, para 3.5. Examples of such medical reasons are advanced Parkinson's disease or severe mental handicap.

2   *Re Amin* [1983] 2 AC 818, [1983] 2 All ER 864, HL.

3   See s 19Bff of the Race Relations Act 1976, inserted by the Race Relations (Amendment) Act 2000.

4   IDI Dec/00, Ch 7, Annex C, para 3.5.

8.87 Where the head of household is issued with a special voucher, entry clearance may at the same time be issued to eligible dependants of whatever nationality. Wives (sic) of heads of household qualify as dependants. Dependent children, who are under 25 when their parent receives a voucher, qualify for entry clearance, as do married and employed UK passport-holder sons and employed but unmarried daughters under 25, provided they were listed as dependants in their parents' application and would qualify in their own right. The maintenance and accommodation requirements in the Immigration Rules do not apply to special voucher applicants and the IDI say they 'should not be applied vigorously' to dependants, although entry clearance should not be granted if it is obvious that the family will need to have immediate recourse to public funds.[1] British Overseas citizens over 65 and widows with children settled in the UK who are able and willing to support them qualify.[2]

1   IDI Dec/00, Ch 3, Annex C, para 8.1.

2   IDI Dec/00, Ch 3, Annex C, para 3.7.

No right of appeal

8.88 In *Amin*[1] the House of Lords held that there was no appeal against refusal of a special voucher. The rationale was that, since the criteria for grant were not published in the Immigration Rules (or at all), a special voucher is neither an entry clearance nor evidence of a person's eligibility under the rules for the purpose of section 33(1) of the Immigration Act 1971 and for the right of appeal under section 13 (now section 59 of the Immigration and Asylum Act 1999). Now that the IDI are published, possession of a special voucher is clearly evidence of eligibility for entry, but not for eligibility *under the Rules*. In appropriate cases refusal will attract a human rights appeal under section 65 of the 1999 Act. Otherwise, the only remedy for refusal is judicial review. An unreasoned refusal or one which ignored or misapplied the published criteria would be reviewable. Refusal of entry clearance for dependants is appealable.[2]

1   *Re Amin* [1983] 2 AC 818, [1983] 2 All ER 864, HL.
2   Because it is entry clearance which is refused: HC 395, paras 252-254.

8.89 Apart from the special voucher provisions, and the exemption from the two-year requirement for returning residents for settled British nationals without the right of abode,[1] the other provisions of the Immigration Rules apply equally as to other Commonwealth citizens. However, it is recognised that once such a British national has entered the UK there may be significant obstacles to removal. In the past, a British Overseas citizen with no other nationality who was in the UK used not to find it too difficult to obtain indefinite leave to remain if he or she was unwilling to comply with immigration formalities to obtain admission to another country. However, policy hardened and the Home Office began to remove such persons wherever it was possible to do so under the removal powers,[2] or, where they appeared irremovable, to refuse leave to remain, allowing them to remain in an immigration limbo.[3] In *Pushpaben Kiritai Patel*[4] the Court of Appeal held that there is jurisdiction to remove those people who appear to be admissible to another state provided they completed the formalities; a refusal to co-operate in immigration formalities to secure entry elsewhere did not require the Secretary of State to abandon enforcement action. However, if another country rejects British Overseas citizens at the border, the international principles referred to above and the fact that it may be inhuman and degrading treatment to persist with unenforceable removals may well give rise to a duty to admit the national to the UK.

1   See **5.26** above.
2   Immigration Act 1971, Sch 2, para 8(1)(c). See **16.62** below.
3   In certain circumstances such an unrecognised status, which gives rise to no rights to work or to receipt of any social benefits whatever, may engage art 3 or 8 of the ECHR. See **8.46** and **8.64** above.
4   [1993] Imm AR 392.

STATELESSNESS

8.90 Persons born in the UK who would otherwise be stateless are eligible for British citizenship in accordance with provisions to reduce statelessness under the British Nationality Act 1981, pursuant to the UK's obligations under the 1961 Convention on the Reduction of Statelessness. The Convention was ratified by the UK in 1966 and came into force in 1967.[1] Stateless persons are not refugees under the 1951 Refugee Convention simply by virtue of being stateless,[2] but they may be refugees if they are fleeing persecution in their country of habitual residence.[3] Deprivation of the benefits of citizenship may itself constitute persecution.[4]

1   For text see fn 1.
2   *Revenko v Secretary of State for the Home Department* [2000] INLR 646, CA.
3   See below **12.36**.
4   *Lazarevic v Secretary of State for the Home Department* [1997] Imm AR 251, CA.

8.91 The 1954 Convention on the Status of Stateless Persons was ratified by the UK in 1959.[1] It contains provisions very similar to those in the 1951 Convention on the Status of Refugees, and affords similar rights to stateless persons with regard to employment, education and welfare. Articles 27 and 28, common to both Conventions, provide for the issue of identity and travel documents. Article 31 of the 1954 Convention provides that contracting states shall not expel stateless persons lawfully in their territory except on national security or public order grounds, and in such cases requires procedural safeguards. Overstaying was held to justify expulsion on public order grounds in *Kelzani*.[2] However, where no other country will receive a stateless person, there is no defiance of immigration control and no strong public order grounds for removal (apart from the actual impossibility of removal).

1   Cmnd 1098, 1960. The text is to be found on the UN website, at www.unhchr.ch/intlinst.htm, or in Plender *Documents on International Migration Law* (2nd revised edition, 1999) Nijhoff.
2   [1978] Imm AR 193, IAT.

VISITS, STUDY AND TEMPORARY PURPOSES

INTRODUCTION

9.1 In this chapter we deal with the formal requirements of the Immigration Rules relating to visits, study, and admission for other temporary purposes. It should be noted, however, that compliance with these Rules may not be sufficient to gain entry and the general requirements for refusal of entry may apply. Passengers who qualify formally for admission may be refused entry because of their restricted returnability, their past immigration or criminal record, for medical reasons or for the other general reasons already referred to.[1] Similarly, extensions of leave may be refused on any of the general grounds contained in the Immigration Rules, even though the formal requirements for an extension are satisfied.[2] In addition, section 8B of the Immigration Act 1971[3] provides for the mandatory exclusion of 'excluded persons' named or described in a designated UN Security Council Resolution or an instrument of the EU Council as war criminals.[4]

1   HC 395, para 320. Grounds (1) to (7) specify circumstances in which entry clearance or leave to enter *is* to be refused and (8) to (19) where it *should normally* be refused. It was with reference to sub-para (18) that a group representing women victims of violence sought judicial review of the admission of boxer Mike Tyson in 2000, on what the Secretary of State for the Home Department submitted were the 'exceptional circumstances' of not wishing to disappoint third parties, ie businessmen and ticket holders: *R v Secretary of State for the Home Department, ex p Bindel* [2001] Imm AR 1, Sullivan J. The wide scope of such circumstances employed by the Secretary of State in this case may of benefit to other less famous applicants. See **3.23**ff above
2   HC 395, para 322(1) where leave *is to* be refused, and (2) to (11) where leave *should normally* be refused. See **4.25**ff above.
3   Inserted by Immigration and Asylum Act 1999, s 8.
4   The Immigration (Designation of Travel Bans) Order 2000, SI 2000/2724, made under Immigration and Asylum Act 1999, s 8B, designates two UN Security Council resolutions, relating to Angola and Sierra Leone, and eight EU Council instruments, relating to Angola, Burma, Burundi, the Federal Republic of Yugoslavia and Sierra Leone. See **3.43** above.

9.2 All visa nationals require a visa. Entry clearance is not essential for non-visa nationals coming for purposes considered in this chapter, unless they are coming as working holidaymakers.[1] However, prior entry clearance, although not compulsory, may be desirable in the case of au pairs[2] and students from non-visa countries, to ensure that they do not waste the cost of travel, and in the case of students, that they do not waste an academic year by a refusal at the port of entry. Entry clearance operates as a grant of leave to enter.[3] Refusal of entry clearance attracts no right of appeal in the case of short-term and prospective students and non-family visitors. The Asylum and Immigration Appeals Act 1993 abolished rights of appeal against refusal of entry clearance for all visitors, short-term and prospective students. The Immigration and Asylum Act 1999 re-introduced appeal rights for family visitors and also provides rights of appeal on human rights grounds where appropriate. The effect of the 1993 removal of appeal rights has been a dearth of recent tribunal authority in relation to visitors, and almost the only challenges in recent years in visitor cases have been by way of judicial review.

1   HC 395, para 95(x).
2   HC 395, para 90 (which offers this express advice to proposed au pairs).
3   Immigration (Leave to Enter and Remain) Order 2000, SI 2000/1161, art 2.

VISITORS

9.3 People may visit this country for a variety of reasons - as tourists, to see relatives or friends, to transact business, to take part in a conference or in some sporting competition or to seek medical treatment. A visit is any temporary stay in the UK for a purpose which does not place the person in a different category of the Immigration Rules.[1] It is perfectly proper for a person to seek entry as a visitor in order to give evidence at his or her own appeal,[2] to take over domestic responsibilities for a short while for genuine family reasons,[3] to look after a child temporarily,[4] to visit a spouse who is a student[5] or a working holidaymaker,[6] or indeed for the purpose of marriage, although the applicant would have to be able to satisfy the immigration officer that he or she intended to leave the UK after the period of the visit. Entry under the domestic servant concession, however, is not for the purposes of a visit.[7]

1   *Xu (Yi Fan)* [1993] Imm AR 519; *Kelada* [1991] Imm AR 400.
2   *Patel (Chhaganbai)* [1991] Imm AR 97; *Patel Aiyub* [1991] Imm AR 273. In *Gaud* (16386) 1999 2 IAS No 6, the Tribunal held that visitor was the correct category for someone in the UK awaiting trial for a criminal offence. See also IDI Nov/00, Ch 2, s 1, Annex B, para 2.
3   *Kaur (Manjit)* (8713) unreported. See also IDI Nov/00, Ch 2, s 1, Annex B, para 5.
4   *Magalso* [1993] Imm AR 293; IDI Nov/00, Ch 2, s 1, Annex B, para 5.
5   *Xu (Yi Fan)* [1993] Imm AR 519.
6   *Deen* (9563) unreported; referred to in [1993] INLP 73.
7   *Mendoza* [1992] Imm AR 122.

9.4 The IDI refer to a number of 'special classes of visitor',[1] such as academic visitors,[2] persons coming to the UK for job interviews[3] and to apply for visas for settlement in third countries,[4] volunteers on archaeological excavations,[5] temporary childminders for close relatives (as long as they do not enter into an employment relationship),[6] carers of sick relatives (who may be admitted for a period of up to three months initially),[7] doctors coming for Professional and Linguistic Assessment

Board (PLAB) tests,[8] amateur entertainers and sportspersons.[9] Professional sportspersons and entertainers may be admitted as visitors, though this is described as entry under a permit-free concession outside the Immigration Rules which would otherwise fall foul of the no employment provision of the visit rules.[10] There are a number of similar categories where admission may be given, such as British Universities North America Club (BUNAC) students,[11] unpaid volunteers for certain charitable organisations and registered charities.[12] Parents accompanying children under 12 at school in the UK have now been brought within the rules.[13] Previously this was a concession outside the rules for mothers only.

1   IDI Nov/00, Ch 2, s 1, Annex B.
2   IDI Nov/00, Ch 2, s 1, Annex B, para 1.
3   IDI Nov/00, Ch 2, s 1, Annex B, para 12.
4   IDI Nov/00, Ch 2, s 1, Annex B, para 12.
5   IDI Nov/00, Ch 2, s 1, Annex B, para 3.
6   IDI Nov/00, Ch 2, s 1, Annex B, para 6.
7   IDI Nov/00, Ch 2, s 1, Annex B, para 5; see also Ch 17, s 2.
8   IDI Nov/00, Ch 2, s 1, Annex B, para 8.
9   IDI Nov/00, Ch 2, s 1, Annex B, para 9.1.
10 IDI Nov/00, Ch 17, s 9: see chapter 10 below.
11 IDI Nov/00, Ch 17, s 9, Annex C. See also Race Relations (Immigration and Asylum) Authorisation 2001, IDI Mar/01, Ch 1, s 11, Annex EE paras 8, and **9.56** below.
12 IDI Nov/00, Ch 17, s 9, Annex C.
13 HC395, para 56A-C, inserted by Cm 4851 on 2 October 2000.

9.5 Save for visitors in transit and medical visitors, the same considerations apply whatever the purpose of the visit, although the purpose may influence the decision whether or not to admit. Independent tourists are likely to receive less attention from immigration officers than persons coming to visit relatives and friends who have themselves come from overseas and settled in the country. Another factor influencing the immigration officer's assessment of whether a person is a genuine visitor or not is the country from which a visitor comes and the general standard of living there, although this is not officially acknowledged.[1] From the immigration statistics it is possible to calculate the ratio of admissions to refusals for nationals of different countries.[2] They invariably show a much higher refusal rate from countries such as Ghana or Nigeria, Pakistan, Bangladesh (whose nationals all require visas) and Jamaica[3] compared with the US, Canada, Australia or New Zealand (whose nationals do not).[4]

1   See para **9.10** below.
2   See eg *Control of Immigration Statistics* – UK, published annually by HMSO, which continues to show huge disparities in the proportion of passengers from rich and poor countries refused entry.
3   The refusal rate for Jamaican nationals has drastically increased from 1 in 650 in 1984 to 1 in 67 in 1991 to 1 in 23 in 1999. This compares with a 1 in 2,014 refusal rate for US nationals in 1991, falling to 1 in 4,390 in 1999: *Control of Immigration Statistics*: UK (Cm 4876, October 2000) Table 3.2. See further Target Caribbean: *The rise in visitor refusals from the Caribbean* (JCWI, 1990); S Leigh *An Analysis of Racial Discrimination in Law and Practice of Immigration Control*; also CRE 'Immigration Control Procedures; Report of a Formal Investigation' (1985) p 78. Such statistical analysis may be of use in ECHR, art 14 discrimination cases brought under the Human Rights Act 1998. Discrimination on the basis of nationality and ethnic origin is expressly authorised by the Race Relations Act 1976, s 19D inserted by the Race Relations (Amendment) Act 2000, and by the ministerial authorisation set out in IDI Mar/01, Ch 1, s 11, Annex EE. See **3.54** above.
4   The position may in fact be worse than is suggested by the statistics, because of the practice of telling applicants for entry clearance that they should withdraw their application, because the entry clearance officer is minded to refuse.

9.6 The high refusal rates from West Africa and the Indian subcontinent were institutionalised by the late 1980s by making citizens of Bangladesh, Ghana, India, Nigeria, Pakistan, Sri Lanka, Uganda and Zaire visa nationals,[1] meaning that these citizens now have to obtain a prior entry clearance even if they only wish to come for a visit, although they are Commonwealth countries with allegiance to the Crown, whose nationals are not aliens, nor 'foreign nationals' for the purpose of registration with the police.[2] The list of countries whose nationals require a visa now includes most of the newer refugee producing countries including Colombia, Ecuador, the Federal Republic of Yugoslavia and most eastern European countries and countries of the former Soviet Union. Visas must be imposed on nationals of countries listed in the European common visa list.[3]

1   HC 395, Appendix 1. The imposition of a visa requirement on Commonwealth citizens is not *ultra vires*: *R v Secretary of State for the Home Department, ex p Suresh Kumar* [1986] Imm AR 420, QBD.
2   HC 395, paras 324A-326.
3   Council Regulation (EC) 574/799 of 12 March 1999, Annex, printed in *Butterworths Immigration Law Service*, F[1971]. See chapter 7 above.

Rules on admission

9.7 The rules relating to the admission of visitors are contained in HC 395, paragraphs 40–46. The IDI give further guidance.[1] Under paragraph 41 passengers seeking entry as visitors must satisfy the immigration authority that:

(i)   they are genuinely seeking entry for a limited period as stated by them, not exceeding six months; and
(ii)   they intend to leave the UK at the end of the period of the visit; and
(iii)   they do not intend to take employment in the UK; and
(iv)   they do not intend to produce goods or provide services within the UK, including the selling of goods or services direct to members of the public; and
(v)   they do not intend to study at a maintained school; and
(vi)   they will maintain and accommodate themselves and any dependants adequately out of resources available to them without recourse to public funds or taking employment, or will, with any dependants, be maintained and accommodated adequately by relatives or friends; and
(vii)   they can meet the cost of the return or onward journey.

Leave to enter is discretionary and will not be given for a period exceeding six months[2] and will be subject to a condition prohibiting employment. The immigration officer must be satisfied that each of the requirements of paragraph 41 is met;[3] otherwise, leave will be refused.

1   IDI Nov/00, Ch 2, s 1.
2   HC 395, para 42, but academic visitors, volunteers on archaeological digs and other 'special' categories may be granted 12 months: IDI Ch 2, Annex B.
3   HC 395, para 42.
4   HC 395, para 43.

Specifying the length of stay

9.8 The first thing someone wishing to visit Britain must do is to specify the length of the proposed visit. Under the current Immigration Rules it must not exceed six months. Though six months is understood to be the norm, the Rules give no guidance and the exact time given is a matter within the immigration officer's discretion.[1] The courts have said that it is the job of immigration officers to consider what period would be suitable given the visitor's financial and other circumstances.[2] Persons who are extremely vague about their length of stay may fail to satisfy the immigration authorities that they could support themselves without working for the period of visit as stated by them,[3] or the length of the proposed visit may be too vague.[4] On the other hand, where, in the nature of the visit, it is not possible to give an exact date for leaving, leave should still be given if the visit is for an ascertainable period of less than six months and the visitors can show that they would leave when the purpose of the visit had been achieved.[5] The Rules make no reference to a visitor who leaves the UK before the expiry of six months but then returns for another substantial period shortly thereafter. In *Powell*[6] it was held that as long as the appellant was a genuine visitor who intended to leave the country within the period stated by her, the immigration officer should not have been concerned with the number of visits that had been made. The IDI point out that there is no restriction on the number of visits a person may make to the UK nor any requirement that a specified time must elapse between successive visits, and the fact that a person has made a series of visits with only brief intervals between them would not, in the absence of any other relevant factors, constitute a sufficient ground for refusal.[7] But a visitor should not normally spend more than six out of any 12 months in this country.[8] A multiple visit visa (for example, of two or five years' duration) can be used on an unlimited number of occasions and operates as leave to enter on each occasion the holder enters the UK, usually for a period of six months.[9] A change of circumstances after a visitor's visa was issued is not necessarily a ground for cancellation, if the passenger was seeking a limited period of stay.[10]

1 HC 395, paras 42 and 44. Three months is the norm for the common European visa, but so far there has been no attempt to harmonise downwards on this.
2 *R v Secretary of State for Home Affairs, ex p Harniak Singh* [1969] 1 WLR 835; *Khan* (18 April 1969, unreported), CA, referred to in *Schönenburger* [1975] Imm AR 7 at 9.
3 *Schönenburger* [1975] Imm AR 7.
4 *Hashim* [1982] Imm AR 113 – a vague period of medical treatment.
5 *R v Secretary of State for the Home Department, ex p Arjumand* [1983] Imm AR 123, QBD (a period depended on father's health and winding up of his business); *Patel (Aiyub)* [1991] Imm AR 273 (entry clearance sought for visit to give evidence at entry clearance appeal, no date for the appeal having been fixed).
6 (3129) unreported.
7 IDI Ch 2, Annex A, para 4.
8 IDI, Ch 2, Annex A, para 4.
9 Immigration (Leave to Enter and Remain) Order 2000, SI 2000/1161, art 4. See further **9.20** below. The background notes to the July 2000 Changes in Immigration Rules refer to long-term visit visas with a validity of up to five years. An ordinary visit visa of six months' validity also operates as leave to enter if the holder leaves the UK and returns within the period of its validity.
10 *Corte* (12708) (1996) 10 INLP.

Genuine visit

9.9 Before granting admission the immigration authority has to be satisfied that the applicant is genuinely seeking entry for the period of the visit as stated by him or her and does not intend to overstay or take employment. If the immigration authority is satisfied that the applicant will leave, but not within the period stated, this does not necessarily mean it is not a genuine visit.[1] For reasons we have discussed, the exact length of stay may be difficult to ascertain, and it is quite wrong for the immigration officer to refuse leave, merely because he or she thinks the passenger may seek an extension of stay.[2] Most disputed cases, however, are concerned with visitors who, according to the immigration authorities, intend to stay on at the end of their leave. In considering these cases the person's incentives to stay or leave are clearly of great importance. In one case the evidence was that a widower, whose two sons lived in England, had money of his own and property in India and could not live in a cold climate because of his rheumatoid arthritis. This showed a clear incentive to leave at the end of the stated period of visit and persuaded a tribunal to reverse earlier decisions to refuse entry.[3] Employment to return to in another country may well be a material consideration, and evidence confirmatory of such employment and a period of leave is frequently helpful.[4] But loss of such employment between issue of entry clearance and arrival here might amount to a change of circumstances that enables the immigration officer to go behind the entry clearance and cancel the deemed leave to enter.[5]

1   *Malek* [1979–80] Imm AR 111.
2   *Ex p Arjumand* [1983] Imm AR 123, QBD.
3   *Singh (Bhagat)* [1978] Imm AR 134.
4   *Huda* [1976] Imm AR 109; see also *Ashraf* [1979–80] Imm AR 45.
5   *Leslie* (1352) unreported.

9.10   Other factors which may be taken into account in deciding whether a person genuinely seeks entry as a visitor include the family's immigration history,[1] the length and purpose of the visit and their means and position in their own country.[2] Previous immigration history and evidence of a pattern of family migration, both here and abroad, may be taken into account. The IDI state that a visitor's proposed purpose in coming to the UK must bear some reasonable relationship to his or her financial means and his or her family, social and economic background.[3] Sometimes the Tribunal is not clear about what is or is not a relevant factor. For example, whether possession of a UK passport is relevant or not is the subject of contradictory decisions. In *Mohamed Din*[4] the fact that the applicant was a non-patrial UK passport holder, and therefore unlikely to be removed from the UK if he overstayed, was held not of itself to be a relevant consideration when determining whether the applicant intended more than a visit, unless there were indications of bad faith. His appeal was allowed. But in *Patel*[5] a differently constituted Tribunal held that the possession of a UK passport was a matter which the immigration authority must take into account, and this together with other factors, meant that the applicant had been properly refused a visit.

1   *R v Secretary of State for the Home Department, ex p Kurumoorthy* [1998] Imm AR 401.
2   Persons of means and position in their own country might well be accepted as genuine visitors even if their declared intention was 'only to visit the maze at Hampton Court', but where it was proposed that a considerable sum of money should be expended by a family with limited resources, the immigration authorities were entitled to consider carefully the reasons for the expenditure: *Manmohan Singh* [1975] Imm AR 118, Immigration Appeal Tribunal.
3   IDI Ch 2, s 1, Annex A, para 1.
4   [1978] Imm AR 56.
5   [1978] Imm AR 154.

9.11 In considering an applicant's intentions, a distinction has to be drawn between a wish and an intention. The distinction was drawn in another context in *Masood* *v Immigration Appeal Tribunal*,[1] where Glidewell LJ said that a wish is not an intention, unless there is some reasonable prospect of its being fulfilled. The previous expression of a wish to settle or study in the UK is not necessarily prejudicial to a subsequent application for a visit.[2] Otherwise, someone who discloses an earlier wish to settle could never subsequently qualify as a *bona fide* visitor.[3] On the other hand, the distinction between a wish and an intention will disappear if, taking that and the other circumstances of the case into consideration, there is a strong inference of an intention not just to visit but to stay for study or work.[4] By way of an exception, Home Office policy allows overseas doctors who come to the UK for the Professional and Linguistic Assessment Board (PLAB) test to remain for postgraduate training in the UK if they are successful.[5] A person coming to look after children and learn English may qualify as a visitor, although the application may look like an 'au pair' application, so long as the intention is to leave at the end of the visit and what is sought is not employment,[6] but if the purpose is quite different from a visit, for example, to claim asylum, seeking entry as a visitor will make the person an illegal entrant.[7]

1 [1992] Imm AR 69, CA at 78. See also *R v Immigration Appeal Tribunal, ex p Shaikh* [1981] 3 All ER 29, [1981] 1 WLR 1107, QBD.
2 *Patel v Immigration Appeal Tribunal* [1983] Imm AR 76, CA, per Dillon LJ at 80, CA; *Ex p Arjumand*, above.
3 *Lai* [1974] Imm AR 98; *El Atrash* (3209) and *Ghailane* (3648) where the appellant had made an application in the alternative either for settlement to join his wife and children or to visit them; see also *Karachiwalla* (4726) where the appellant was held to be a genuine visitor despite a wish to settle in the UK with her family.
4 *R v Secretary of State for the Home Department, ex p Brakwah* [1989] Imm AR 366, DC; see further *Adesina v Secretary of State for the Home Department* [1988] Imm AR 442, CA (both illegal entry cases): see **9.43–9.44** below. But a genuine visitor may study during the visit: *R v Secretary of State for the Home Department, ex p Montezano* (CO 1000/2000) 9 November 2000, QBD.
5 IDI, Ch 2, Annex B, para 8.
6 *Gusakov* (11672).
7 *Re Musisi* [1987] AC 514; *Rasmish Al-Zahrany v Secretary of State for the Home Department* [1995] Imm AR 510, CA. See also *R (Montezano) v Secretary of State for the Home Department* [2001] EWHC Admin 285, where the AC held that, where an entrant's answers to the IO admit two possible bases for entry (visit or study) the IO does not act reasonably or lawfully if he or she considers only one of the activities.

9.12 It is always the applicant's intentions which count rather than those of the sponsoring relative or friend in this country.[1] It is the intention on the present visit that is critical rather than any previous deception.[2] The fact that the sponsor is likely to ensure the applicant's departure is a relevant factor to be taken into account, since it tends to show an intention to depart.[3] But immigration officers are warned that it is not possible to enforce guarantees by sponsors that a passenger will abide by conditions of stay or leave the UK at the end of a specific period, and no such written guarantee or undertaking should be either sought or accepted.[4]

1 *Ragavan* (3418) and cases cited therein.
2 *Chaudhury* (3157).
3 *Kumar* [1978] Imm AR 185; *Chaudhury* (3157).
4 IDI, Ch 2, s 1, para 4.2.

Maintenance and accommodation

9.13 The ability of visitors to maintain and accommodate themselves using resources available to them without taking employment or becoming a charge on public funds is always an important factor.[1] Obviously, ordinary tourists will need to have their own funds. In the case of persons staying with relatives or friends, it does not matter whether they maintain themselves or are maintained by their relatives. The Immigration Rules now allow indirect reliance on public funds provided to the sponsor, so long as the passenger's presence does not result in entitlement to an increased amount.[2] But notwithstanding this relaxation, the provisions regarding visitors make it much more difficult for poor people to be allowed to visit this country than the well-off. As well as being less likely to be accepted as genuine visitors, they have a much greater chance of being rejected on maintenance and accommodation grounds, even though, as 'persons from abroad' for the purposes of social security and homelessness legislation, they are ineligible to claim any assistance.[3] It would appear that immigration officers are more concerned with the possibility of visitors working in the UK without permission than claiming benefit; in this connection the severe strictures against taking employment are in stark contrast with the specific provision allowing Commonwealth citizens entry on working holidays.[4] Formerly, tribunals were apt to pay no attention to 'undertakings' by sponsors that the visitor would not have recourse to means-tested benefits,[5] but since 1994 the Immigration Rules have provided that a sponsor may be asked to give an undertaking in writing to be responsible for the visitor's maintenance and accommodation for the period of any leave granted, including any further variation.[6] The Department of Social Security may seek to recover from the person giving such an undertaking any income support paid under the social security legislation to meet the needs of the person in respect of whom the undertaking has been given.[7]

1   HC 395, para 41(vi).
2   HC 395, para 6A, inserted by Cm 4851.
3   See eg Income Support (General) Regulations 1987, SI 1987/1967, reg 21(3)(a), Sch 7; Housing Benefit (General) Regulations 1987, SI 1987/1971, reg 7A; Asylum and Immigration Act 1996, s 11; Immigration and Asylum Act 1999, s 115; Social Security (Immigration and Asylum) (Consequential Amendments) Regulations 2000, SI 2000/636; see chapter 13 below.
4   HC 395, paras 95–100.
5   *Devi* [1976] Imm AR 171; cf *Rafaqat* (9445).
6   HC 395, para 35.
7   Social Security Administration Act 1992, s 78(6)(c) (England and Wales), Social Security Administration (Northern Ireland) Act 1992 (for Northern Ireland, where the collecting agency is the Department of Health and Social Services).

Visits for family reasons

9.14 Under early Immigration Rules, visits for family purposes for quite long periods at a time were allowed.[1] In *Hamilton v Entry Clearance Officer, Kingston, Jamaica*[2] a three-year visit by a mother, while her daughter did a teachers' training course, was allowed. Family visits to be with older children have long been impossible, because of the six-month time limit,[3] but there is now specific provision in the Rules for the parents of young children (under 12) at independent fee-paying schools, who have their main home outside the UK, to be given leave to remain for 12 months at a time.[4] Thus the parent who wishes to remain continuously in the UK with a child during his or her primary education may do so.

1   See Cmnd 4298 (pre-1973 Rules), para 12; *Afoakwah* [1972] Imm AR 17.
2   [1974] Imm AR 43. See *Nourai* [1978] Imm AR 200; *Obeyesekere* [1976] Imm AR 16.

3   *Kelada* [1991] Imm AR 400.
4   Paragraph 56A-C of HC 395, inserted by Cm 4851. The Rule requires satisfactory evidence of adequate and reliable funds for maintaining a second home in the UK and compliance with all the visitor requirements save the six-month time limit.

9.15   The Immigration Rules offer no other route for the admission and stay of carers, either of children or of sick relatives or friends, but visitors may obviously perform these functions,[1] so long as they are not paid for them.[2] The IDI state that visitors may act as temporary child-minders for close relatives where neither parent is able to supervise the daytime care of the child, provided it is not simply an arrangement to enable both parents to take paid employment or to study, and the visitor will not receive a salary (as opposed to board, accommodation and pocket money) and intends to remain in the UK for no longer than six months. Neither parent must be in a category leading to settlement.[3]

1   For the position of visitors seeking leave to remain to care for a sick relative or a friend suffering from a terminal illness, see IDI Ch 17, s 2; see 'Extensions of stay as a visitor' **9.19** below.
2   See *Goodluck* (4244) (undertaking child-minding duties for a young mother and her baby for payment was employment, not just a visit); *Tan (Swee Hong)* (5212) (looking after a sister's baby for payment was employment).
3   IDI, Ch 2, s 1, Annex B, para 6.

Business visits

9.16   Passengers do not qualify as visitors if they intend to take employment or to produce goods or provide services in the UK, including selling goods and services direct to the public.[1] They are normally prohibited from taking employment by a condition stamped in their passport,[2] and sometimes the stamp also prohibits them from entering any business or profession, although there is no provision for this condition in the Acts or the immigration rules. However, neither prohibition prevents business visitors from transacting business during their visit. Under the Immigration Rules a visitor includes a person living and working outside the UK who comes to transact business, including attending meetings and briefings, fact finding, negotiating or making contracts with UK businesses to buy or sell goods or services.[3] The 'list of typical business visitors' in the current IDI[4] also includes those coming to purchase trade goods and those coming for training in techniques and work practices used in the UK, provided that the training is confined to observation, familiarisation and classroom instruction. Others accepted as business visitors under the instructions as a matter of administrative policy, although strictly falling outside the visitor provisions, include:

- those delivering goods and passengers from abroad, such as lorry drivers and coach drivers, provided they are genuinely working an international route;[5]
- tour group couriers who are contracted to a firm outside the UK, who seek entry to accompany a tour group and intend to leave with that group;
- those coming as speakers at a 'one-off', non-commercial conference;
- advisers, consultants, trainers, trouble-shooters, etc who are employed abroad (directly or under contract) by the same company or group of companies to which the client firm in the UK belongs. Their involvement

must not extend to actual project management or to providing advice or consultancy services direct to clients of the UK company. Training should be for a specific 'one-off' purpose (eg in the use of products manufactured overseas, or specific to the operation of the group of companies of which the UK firm is a member), should not go beyond classroom instruction and should not otherwise be readily available here;

- representatives of computer software companies coming to install, debug or enhance their products. They may also be admitted as visitors to be briefed as to the requirements of a UK customer but may not use their expertise to make a detailed assessment of a potential customer's requirements, which is regarded as consultancy work for which a work permit is required;
- representatives of foreign manufacturers coming to service or repair their company's products within the guarantee period;
- representatives of foreign machine manufacturers coming to erect and install machinery too heavy to be delivered in one piece, as part of the contract of purchase and supply;
- monteurs—workers coming for up to six months to erect, dismantle, install, service, repair or advise on the development of foreign-made machinery.

In addition, permission may be given to allow a visitor entry for purposes which arguably involve provision of a service such as giving professional advice or taking instructions, where the visit is short (for a day or so), is 'one-off' and without significant implications for the resident workforce.[6]

1   HC 395, para 41(iii), (iv).
2   HC 395, para 42.
3   HC 395, para 40.
4   IDI Nov/00, Ch 2, s 1, Annex B.
5   The majority of long-distance lorry-drivers come from the EEA in any event, or are employed by an EEA-established company; in either case they are covered by the EC free movement provision: *Rush Portuguesa Lda v Office National d'Immigration* [1990] ECR I-1417; see chapter 7 below.
6   IDI Nov/00, Ch 2, s 1, Annex B, para 4.

9.17 Most of the above guidance deals with the distinction between employment and a visit and leaves untouched the distinction between transacting business and establishing a business, which determines whether a passenger should be admitted as a business visitor or should be required to return home and obtain a visa for the purpose of setting up a business.[1] In one tribunal case it was held that forming a company, setting up an office and training a partner went too far.[2] Essentially it will be a question of fact in each case.

1   HC 395, paras 200–205; see chapter 10 below. Visitors from Europe Agreement countries may set up in business after entry as visitors, however: see **9.25** below.
2   *Hossain (Sardar)* [1990] Imm AR 520. In *Ayoola* [1992] Imm AR 170, CA it was held that becoming a director of a UK-incorporated company went beyond transacting business.

Time limits and other conditions on stay

9.18 The immigration authority will always impose a time limit on the period of the visitor's stay and of any dependants. A period of six months will normally be appropriate[1] unless there are particular circumstances, such as restricted returnability, or if the passenger is booked out on a particular charter flight, or the visitor's case ought to be subject to early review by the Home Office.[2] Visitors are normally prohibited from taking employment.[3] Visitors from the Commonwealth never have to register with the police, and foreign nationals[4] may only be required to do so in exceptional cases.[5]

1 HC 395, para 42.
2 *Thabet* [1977] Imm AR 75.
3 HC 395, para 40.
4 See Appendix 2 to the Immigration Rules HC 395, added by Cm 3953, May 1998.
5 HC 395, para 325(iv).

Extension of stay as a visitor

9.19 Six months is the maximum permitted leave which may be granted to a visitor.[1] A visitor who has been given less than six months on entry may, however, extend his or her visit up to the six-month period.[2] To obtain an extension a visitor must continue to meet the requirements for a visit, in particular the maintenance and accommodation provisions and the ability to meet the cost of the return or onward journey. If these requirements continue to be met an extension may be granted,[3] but otherwise refusal is mandatory.[4] Where a visitor had leave for less than six months and seeks an extension which, if granted, would take him or her over the maximum, the Secretary of State should not refuse an extension outright but should consider granting leave up to the six month limit, and if this is refused there is a right of appeal.[5] Those caring for sick or disabled relatives may obtain extensions of stay under the carers' concession, which provides for the grant of three months' leave to remain in the first instance, and further leave of 12 months at a time if medical and social services evidence warrants it.[6]

1 HC 395, para 44. However, 12 months' leave may have been given to special categories such as academic visitors, including postgraduate researchers sponsored by particular bodies, privately funded researchers, visiting lecturers, etc (IDI Nov/00, Ch 2, s 1, Annex B, para 1), and volunteers on archaeological excavations (IDI Nov/00, Ch 2, s 1, Annex B, para 3).
2 HC 395, para 44(ii).
3 HC 395, para 45.
4 HC 395, para 46. But see fn 1 above. Persons in these categories may obtain extensions taking them over the six months' limit, and sometimes over the 12 months, outside the Rules.
5 *Wong* [1995] Imm AR 451.
6 For details see IDI Dec/00, Ch 17, s 2 ('Employment outside the rules'). See also *R v Secretary of State for the Home Department, ex p Zakrocki* [1996] COD 304.

Departure and return

9.20 A visit visa operates as leave to enter on each occasion on which the holder enters the UK during the period of its validity. The holder will be treated as having been granted six months' leave to enter beginning on the date of arrival where six months or more remain of the period of validity, and the period left if less than six months.[1] To operate as leave to enter, the entry clearance must be endorsed with any conditions to which it is subject.[2]

1 Immigration (Leave to Enter and Remain) Order 2000, SI 2000/1161, art 4(1), (2).
2 SI 2000/1161, art 3(3)(a).

Visitors in transit

9.21 Special requirements apply to visitors who arrive in the UK in transit to another country. First, they must be in transit to a country outside the common travel area; secondly, they must have both the means and the intention of proceeding there at once; thirdly, they must be assured of entry there; and fourthly, they must intend and be able to leave the UK within 48 hours.[1] Passengers meeting these conditions will be given a leave not exceeding 48 hours with a prohibition on employment.[2] Otherwise leave is to be refused.[3] Forty-eight hours is the maximum permitted leave and any application for an extension beyond this period is to be refused.[4] Where a woman on a tour party was given 48 hours by an immigration officer who wished to treat her as a transit passenger, but did not make this clear in the leave stamp, the Tribunal held that she was to be treated as an ordinary visitor with a right to apply for an extension and, if necessary, to appeal against a refusal.[5]

1   HC 395, para 47.
2   HC 395, para 48.
3   HC 395, para 49.
4   HC 395, para 50.
5   *Low* [1995] Imm AR 435.

Medical treatment

9.22 Under the Immigration Rules visitors may be admitted for private medical treatment at their own expense, provided that they meet the ordinary requirements of the visitor rule (no work or provision of services, no study at a maintained school, maintenance and accommodation and ability to meet the costs of the return or onward journey).[1] In the case of a passenger suffering from a communicable disease, the medical inspector must be satisfied that there is no danger to public health.[2] If required to do so, the passenger must be able to show that any proposed course of treatment is of finite duration and that he or she intends to leave the UK at the end of it,[3] but the passenger is not required to be precise about the length of it.[4] Before being admitted for medical treatment a passenger may be required to produce evidence of his or her medical condition, of the arrangements for consultation and treatment, the estimated costs, the likely duration and the availability of sufficient funds in the UK to meet the cost, and may be required to give an undertaking to this effect.[5] The IDI state that the treatment may be from a GP or alternative medical practitioner, but that leave granted for such treatment will not be extended beyond six months.[6] The reference in the Rules to consultation or treatment 'at his own expense' does not mean that the visitor must necessarily pay personally.[7] Nor is the availability of treatment in the passenger's own country a ground for refusing admission.[8] Where leave is granted it will normally be for a period not exceeding six months, subject to a condition prohibiting employment.[9] If the passenger cannot meet all the requirements of the Rules, leave is to be refused.[10]

1   HC 395, para 51(i), referring to para 41(iii)-(vii).
2   HC 395, para 51(ii).
3   HC 395, para 51(iii) and (iv).
4   See *Foon* [1983] Imm AR 29 and *Onofriou* (2704).
5   HC 395 para 51(v).
6   IDI Nov/00, Ch 2, s 3, Annex F, para 6.

7 See *Foon* [1983] Imm AR 29.
8 *Mohan* [1973] Imm AR 9.
9 HC 395, para 52.
10 HC 395, para 53.

9.23 An extension of stay for a medical visit can only be granted if the requirements for entry continue to be met.[1] In addition, evidence must be produced from a registered medical practitioner, who holds an NHS consultant post, of satisfactory arrangements for private medical consultation or treatment and its likely duration; and, where treatment has already begun, its progress.[2] Patients must also be able to show that they have met any costs and expenses incurred in relation to their treatment in the UK out of the resources available to them,[3] and that they have sufficient funds available in the UK to meet further likely costs and intend to do so.[4] If sufficient evidence of these matters is produced, an extension of stay will normally be given.[5] If there is reason to believe the treatment will be at public expense or that the applicant does not intend to leave the UK at the end of the treatment,[6] or if insufficient evidence of the other matters is available, leave will be refused.[7]

1 HC 395, para 54(i).
2 HC 395, para 54(ii). The IDI indicate that it is reasonable for Home Office caseworkers to scrutinise carefully the likely duration and success of, for example, fertility treatment which could have been going on for some years without success. It would be acceptable (with the applicant's consent) to approach the consultant direct to ask about the likelihood of eventual success of the treatment (IDI Nov/00, Ch 2, s 3, Annex F, para 2).
3 HC 395, para 54(iii).
4 HC 395, para 54(iv).
5 HC 395, para 55(vi).
6 See *Foon* [1983] Imm AR 29 and *Onofriou* (2704).
7 HC 395, para 56.

NHS treatment

9.24 The Immigration Rules do not provide for persons to be granted leave for the sole purpose of receiving free treatment under the NHS, and normally entry clearance or leave to enter for this purpose will be refused.[1] There are exceptional arrangements for the admission of a handful of people each year from countries with which the UK has reciprocal arrangements.[2] Additionally, applications for leave to remain to complete a course of NHS treatment which has already begun will not be refused if it would clearly be unreasonable to require the applicant to leave the UK (eg because he or she was in hospital following an accident).[3]

1 IDI Nov/00, Ch 2, s 3, Annex F.
2 IDI Nov/00, Ch 2, s 3, Annex F; see also **13.169** below.
3 IDI Nov/00, Ch 2, s 3, Annex F.

Visitors—switching categories

9.25 Visitors who wish to remain in the UK in order to do something else have quite limited options. They can no longer switch to other temporary categories such as trainee,[1] au pair[2] or working holidaymaker;[3] switching to student status is also difficult. Visitors may only become students or student nurses if they do not come from one of the visa countries listed in Appendix 1 to the Immigration

Rules.[4] If they do, they should obtain a prospective student visa before leaving home. A non-visa national who obtains entry as a visitor while harbouring an intention to study risks summary removal as an illegal entrant.[5] Under the current Rules it is not possible for visitors to remain for employment,[6] as investors,[7] retired persons of independent means,[8] writers, composers, artists[9] or in business,[10] unless they are able to establish themselves in business under the relevant EC Association Agreements, which currently apply to Bulgarian, Czech, Estonian, Hungarian, Latvian, Lithuanian, Polish, Romanian, Slovakian and Slovenian nationals.[11] These nationals may establish themselves in business or self-employment without having to fulfil the stringent financial requirements and without having obtained entry clearance in that capacity.[12]

1 HC 395, para 119(ii).
2 HC 395, para 92(i).
3 HC 395, para 98(i).
4 HC 395, paras 60(i) (students), 67(ii) (student nurses). Under the earlier Immigration Rules such a switch was possible despite some judicial hesitation: see *Jalloh* [1988] Imm AR 544. A visa national who comes in as a visitor cannot switch to student status and refusal of an extension is mandatory (*Okello v Secretary of State for the Home Department* [1995] Imm AR 269, CA).
5 See *Adesina v Secretary of State for the Home Department* [1988] Imm AR 442, CA; *Re Olusanya* [1988] Imm AR 117, DC; *R v Secretary of State for the Home Department, ex p Brakwah* [1989] Imm AR 366, QBD.
6 HC 395, paras 131(i) (work permit holders), 139(i), 147(i), 155(i), 164(i), 173(i), 181(i) (categories of permit-free employment).
7 HC 395, para 227(i).
8 HC 395, para 266(i).
9 HC 395, para 235(i).
10 HC 395, para 206(i).
11 HC 395, paras 211-223 as amended by Cm 4851.
12 HC 395, paras 211-223 as amended. We consider that Turkish nationals are in the same position and should be included in the Rules, by virtue of the 'standstill' provisions of the EC-Turkey Association Agreement. See *R v Secretary of State for the Home Department, ex p Savas* [2000] INLR 398, ECJ, and see chapter 7 above.

9.26   There are further exceptions to the no-switching rule. Commonwealth citizens with a UK-born grandparent may stay to seek and take employment;[1] close relatives of persons settled in the UK may apply to remain with them;[2] and a visitor may apply for leave to remain as the spouse or unmarried partner of someone in the UK.[3] Persons with visit leave may also apply for asylum[4] or for exceptional leave on human rights grounds.[5] Visitors who came to visit their close relatives in the UK may apply for indefinite leave, but clearly they must satisfy all the requirements regarding the admission of relatives for settlement. Because of the possibility of switching and the relative ease that a parent or parents over 65 have in meeting the requirements of the Immigration Rules, there is a danger of their being refused visit visas on suspicion that they may apply to switch. Those who do not wish to settle in the UK, or cannot be persuaded to by their family members in the UK, may thus suffer from pre-emptive action against application of this rule. Normally those seeking leave to remain in another capacity should have genuinely changed their mind since entry; otherwise there is a risk of the application being refused under the general considerations[6] or, worse still, of treatment as an illegal entrant.[7]

1 HC 395, para 189.
2 HC 395, paras 298(ii) (children generally), 306 (children born in UK), 311(ii) (adopted children), and 317(vi), 318 (parents, grandparents and dependent relatives).

3 HC 395, paras 284(i), 295D(i), inserted by Cm 4851.
4 See chapter 12 below.
5 See chapter 8 above.
6 Eg under HC 395, para 322.
7 *Re Musisi* [1987] AC 514.

Appeals by visitors

9.27 Visitors refused leave to enter have no right of appeal unless they held a current entry clearance at the time of refusal,[1] and may not appeal against refusal of entry clearance unless they are family visitors.[2] In addition, they have no right of appeal if they are seeking entry for a period in excess of the Immigration Rules.[3] Visa holders may exercise their right of appeal without leaving the country.[4] If they sought entry through the Channel Tunnel, they may be brought through the tunnel after giving notice of appeal to enable them to pursue their appeal.[5] Visitors refused an extension may appeal to an adjudicator, provided the variation asked for would not result in the duration of their leave exceeding six months (in the case of a non-medical visit).[6] There is no right of appeal against refusal of an extension if the visitor's leave has already exceeded the period permitted by the Immigration Rules,[7] even if the Secretary of State has a policy providing for extension beyond the usual maximum under the rules.[8] Refusal or cancellation of leave on conducive grounds by the Secretary of State attracts rights of appeal as above, but to the Special Immigration Appeals Commission rather than to the appellate authority.[9]

1 Immigration and Asylum Act 1999, s 59(1)(b), 60(4)(a), (5)(b).
2 Immigration and Asylum Act 1999, s 60(5)(a); see below.
3 Immigration and Asylum Act 1999, s 60(7)(c).
4 Immigration and Asylum Act 1999, s 60(3), HC 395, para 355.
5 HC 395, para 355.
6 Immigration and Asylum Act 1999, ss 61, 62(1)(c); HC 395, para 44.
7 *R v Immigration Appeal Tribunal, ex p Sam* [1996] Imm AR 272.
8 This is because there is a distinction between policy and rules, and leave exceeding the maximum permitted under the rules deprives the appellate authority of jurisdiction to hear an appeal. Considerations of whether the decision is 'in accordance with the law' under Immigration and Asylum Act 1999, Sch 4, para 21 do not therefore arise.
9 Immigration and Asylum Act 1999, ss 60(9), 62(3), (4); Special Immigration Appeals Commission Act 1997, s 2(1).

9.28 The Immigration and Asylum Act 1999 introduced a right of appeal for 'family visitors' against the refusal of an entry clearance.[1] A 'family visitor' is a person who applies for entry clearance to visit a spouse, father, mother son, daughter, grandfather, grandmother grandson, granddaughter, brother, sister, uncle, aunt, nephew, niece or first cousin, the father, mother, brother or sister of his or her spouse, the spouse of his or her son or daughter, his or her step-father, stepmother, stepson, stepbrother or stepsister, or unmarried partner with whom he or she has lived for two of the last three years.[2] It is not clear whether this covers adoptive relationships. The list could be amenable to challenge if it excludes from appeal rights others who enjoy close relationships with UK-based family members.[3] The right of appeal attaches only to refusal of entry clearance, not to the refusal of leave to enter in this capacity. Thus application for entry clearance is essential to obtain appeal rights. There is a fee payable in order to exercise this right of appeal, refundable only if the appeal is successful,[4] and varying according to whether an oral hearing[5] or an appeal on the papers[6] is sought. The fee must be paid by the appellant in local currency before an appeal will be entertained.[7]

1   Immigration and Asylum Act 1999, s 60(5).
2   Immigration Appeals (Family Visitor) (No 2) Regulations 2000, SI 2000/2446, reg 2(2).
3   See chapter 11 below.
4   SI 2000/2446, reg 3(3).
5   Currently £125 (SI 2000/2446, reg 3(1)(a), as amended by the Immigration Appeals (Family Visitor) (Amendment) Regulations 2001, SI 2001/52 from 12 January 2001).
6   Currently £50 (SI 2000/2446, reg 3(1)(b), as amended).
7   SI 2000/2446, para 3(2).

9.29   Visitors who have no right of appeal against refusal of entry clearance or refusal of leave to enter or remain may apply for judicial review if they can show unfairness or an error of law by the immigration officer,[1] but those with a right of appeal should exercise it rather than seek judicial review.[2] Judicial review of refusal of leave to enter as a visitor may be pursued after an applicant has left the UK,[3] but may by then be academic.

1   *R v Secretary of State for the Home Department, ex p Arjumand* [1983] Imm AR 123, QBD.
2   *R v Secretary of State for the Home Department, ex p Swati* [1986] 1 All ER 717, [1986] Imm AR 88, CA. This is so even if the appeal can only be exercised after departure.
3   In *Kekana* [1998] Imm AR 136 Potts J held that it was academic to pursue such an action where the applicant had already left the UK; in *R v Secretary of State for the Home Department, ex p Honegan*, 10 April 1995, Tucker J held that it was not, and an application to set aside leave in *R v Secretary of State for the Home Department, ex p Dombaj* (CO 3150/1997) was dismissed by Owen J on 25 March 1998 (reported in *Legal Action* November 1998; the immigration officer's decision was quashed on 1 December 1998).

STUDENTS

9.30   The admission of students is dealt with in HC 395, paragraphs 57–87. These rules are separate from the educational rights given to EEA nationals and their families under EC law, which are touched on briefly in Chapter 7.[1] The main point about overseas students is that they must be full-time, able to pay for their course and living expenses, and intend to return home when their studies are complete.[2] The student rules cover ordinary students, student nurses,[3] postgraduate doctors and dentists, prospective students and their spouses and children. Except in areas of nursing which are in short supply,[4] student nurses are not allowed to switch to work permit employment once they have qualified. Entry as a student requires acceptance for a course of study. Those whose plans are not so advanced or definite may, however, come as prospective students provided their intentions of studying are genuine and realistic.[5] The student rules, as we shall see, are fairly complicated, and, although non-visa nationals do not require entry clearance, it is usually advisable, in order to avoid unnecessary difficulties at the airport and the possible waste of an academic year. Visa nationals require entry clearance whether they are coming as actual or prospective students. If they arrive without a visa, refusal of entry is mandatory.[6]

1   Once he or she has been in employment, an EEA migrant has a right to vocational training on the same conditions as UK nationals: Art 7(2) and (3) of Regulation 1612/68. Vocational training is given a wide definition: see Case 293/83 *Gravier v City of Liège* [1985] ECR 593, ECJ and Case 24/86 *Blaizot v Université de Liège* [1988] ECR 379, ECJ. EEA workers retain the right of residence as a worker, if they give up their job and undertake a course of study

which is linked to their employment: Case 39/86 *Lair v Universität Hanover* [1988] ECR 3161, para 39. Spouses (of whatever nationality) have the same educational opportunities as the migrant workers, but their children have access to general education and can remain in the member state, even if their parents have returned home: Cases 389 and 390/87 *Echternach and Moritz* [1989] ECR 723, ECJ. The principle of equality of access means students from EEA countries cannot be charged higher fees: Case 152/82 *Forcheri v Belgium* [1983] ECR 2323, ECJ.
2   HC 395, para 57. See below for details.
3   HC 395, para 65ff confirms the position reflected in early Tribunal determinations that student nurses are classed as students and not as trainees: *Oh* [1972] Imm AR 236; *Kulatilake* [1992] Imm AR 257.
4   IDI Nov/00, Ch 3, Annex F, para 3.2.
5   HC 395, para 82(i).
6   HC 395, para 320(5).

Ordinary students

9.31 The requirements to be met by an ordinary student are contained in paragraph 57 of HC 395. There are six main requirements, which we explain more fully below. First, students must have been accepted on a course of study at a university or similar institution, a private college or a fee-paying school outside the maintained sector. Secondly, the studies must be full-time and not consist of a collection of part-time courses at a number of educational establishments. Thirdly, children under 16 must be in full-time schooling meeting Education Acts requirements. Fourthly, students must intend to leave at the end of their course of study. Fifthly, they must not intend to engage in business or to take work other than approved part-time or vacation jobs. Sixthly, they must be able to meet all their costs without having to work or have recourse to public funds. A student who meets all these requirements will be given leave to enter for an appropriate period, depending on the length of the student's course of study and means, and with a condition restricting his or her freedom to take employment.[1] Unless each of the requirements of the rules is met, leave to enter as a student is to be refused.[2]

1   HC 395, para 58.
2   HC 395, para 57.

Prospective students

9.32 Students who are not yet enrolled on a course can obtain entry clearance and admission as prospective students.[1] To obtain leave in this capacity, prospective students must be able to satisfy the immigration authorities that: (i) they have genuine and realistic intentions of studying in the UK[2] within six months of their date of entry; (ii) they intend to leave the UK on completion of their studies or on the expiry of their leave to enter if they do not qualify for further stay as an ordinary student or a student nurse; and (iii) they can, without working and without recourse to public funds, meet the costs of their intended course and of their own maintenance and accommodation and that of any dependants while making arrangements to study and during the course. They may then be admitted for a period not exceeding six months with a condition prohibiting employment.[3] Unless each of the three requirements is met, the prospective student's application will be refused.[4] If less than six months' leave is given, prospective students can obtain an extension to give them more time to find a college or school place, but six months is the maximum leave in this category and they cannot extend it beyond this time.[5] At all times the prospective student must show 'genuine and realistic intentions' of studying, a phrase to which we shall return below.

1   HC 395, para 82.
2   On a course of study meeting the requirements of student or student nurse admission: HC 395, para 82.
3   HC 395, para 83.
4   HC 395, para 84.
5   HC 395, paras 85–87.

Student nurses

9.33   For the purpose of the Immigration Rules the term 'student nurse' means a person accepted for training as a student nurse or midwife leading to a registered nursing qualification; or an overseas nurse or midwife who has been accepted on an adaptation course leading to registration as a nurse within the UK Central Council for Nursing, Midwifery and Health Visiting.[1] To qualify for entry student nurses must fulfil seven requirements.[2] First, they must come within the above definition of a student nurse. Secondly, they must have been accepted on a course of study in a recognised nursing educational establishment offering a recognised nursing training. Thirdly, acceptance must not have been obtained by misrepresentation. Fourthly, they must be able and intend to follow the course. Fifthly, they must not intend to engage in business or take employment except in connection with the training course. As a concession outside the Rules, however, before they start the course, student nurses and midwives may work at the hospitals where they are to be trained, for a maximum of eight weeks.[3] Sixthly, they must intend to leave the UK at the end of the course. Nurses may not switch into employment, although a switching application may be exceptionally recommended for approval by the Department for Education and Employment if it is in a shortage area of nursing.[4] Seventhly, they must have sufficient funds to meet all their accommodation and maintenance expenses without engaging in business or taking employment (except in connection with the training course) or having recourse to public funds. Project 2000 students[5] and direct-entry midwifery students receive non-means tested bursaries instead of a salary. Other student nurses and midwives enter into contracts with district health authorities, although treated as students. Because student nurses will be in receipt of either a salary or a bursary, evidence of funds is not normally required.[6] If one or more of these requirements cannot be met, the application to come as a student nurse will be refused.[7] When leave to enter is given this is usually for the duration of the training course with a restriction on the freedom to take employment.[8]

1   HC 395, para 63. The IDI Nov/00, Ch 3, Annex G gives details of nursing courses and qualifications.
2   HC 395, para 64.
3   IDI Nov/00, Ch 3, Annex F, para 1.
4   IDI Nov/00, Ch 3, Annex F, para 3.2.
5   The majority of nurses are now trained under this scheme, in which they are attached to colleges and when on clinical placements are supernumerary to ward staff. They undergo 18 months foundation training and 18 months specialist training to achieve registered nurse (RN) status. See IDI Nov/00, Ch 3, Annex G, para 2.1.
6   IDI Nov/00, Ch 3, Annex G, para 3.
7   HC 395, para 66.
8   HC 395, para 65.

Postgraduate doctors and dentists

9.34 To become a fully registered doctor in the UK, a medical student must not only pass the necessary exams[1] but also have worked as a house officer for 12 months.[2] There is no similar requirement for dentists,[3] but graduate doctors and dentists may both wish to spend time training for further qualifications at basic or higher specialist level. Although both these situations are clearly in the nature of employment training, the Immigration Rules make provision for them under the student rules. There are two situations where a postgraduate doctor or a dentist may qualify for a period of training under the student rules. First there is the graduate from a medical school,[4] eligible for provisional or limited registration with the General Medical Council, who intends to undertake pre-registration house officer employment for up to 12 months, as required for full registration.[5] He or she must not have spent more than 12 months in aggregate in such employment.[6] Secondly, there is the doctor or dentist, eligible for full or limited registration with the General Medical Council or the General Dental Council, who intends to undertake postgraduate training in a hospital, the community health services, or both.[7] In both cases the graduate doctor or dentist must intend to leave the UK on completion of the training period.[8] In addition they must be able to maintain and accommodate themselves and any dependants without recourse to public funds.[9] Doctors sponsored for postgraduate training under the Overseas Doctors' Training Scheme[10] or by the British Council, the World Health Organization or the Commonwealth Scholarship Foundation should be admitted without further inquiry.[11] Where the graduate doctor or dentist meets the requirements of the Immigration Rules leave will be granted for a period not exceeding 12 months (for pre-registration house officer employment)[12] or three years (for post-graduate training in hospital or community health services or both).[13] Unless each of the requirements is met the application will fail.[14] An extension of leave may be granted both to house officers and to those undergoing postgraduate training in a hospital or community health services.[15] In the latter (post-registration) category, an extension of leave is contingent on evidence of satisfactory progress, including the passing of any relevant examinations.[16] In the case of a pre-registration house officer, 12 months is the maximum time to be spent in such employment and no extension in this category beyond that period will be given.[17] In the case of postgraduate medical and dental hospital or community health service training, three years is the maximum period which will be given and no more than four years in aggregate may be spent in senior house officer basic specialist training, or equivalent.[18] Those engaged in higher specialist training (specialist registrar or equivalent grades) may be granted extensions of up to three years at a time without any maximum limit.[19] Extensions are only given where the doctor or dentist intends to leave the UK on completion of the training period.[20] Moves to full employment are not contemplated by the Rules, but may be granted exceptionally outside the Rules.

1 This means obtaining a primary UK qualification (the equivalent of a degree): Medical Act 1983, ss 4(3), 55, 56 and Sch 6, para 22, and passing the qualifying examination: s 4(2). See further 30 *Halsbury's Laws* (4th edn) para 85ff.

2 The requirements are that the doctor must have been engaged for a period prescribed by regulations in employment in a resident medical capacity in one or more approved hospitals or approved institutions and have obtained an appropriate certificate from his or her examining body. Employment in a resident medical capacity means employment in the practice of any branch of medicine prescribed for the purposes of the Medical Act 1983, s 10, where the person employed is resident in the hospital or institution where he or she is employed or

conveniently near to it and is by the terms of his or her employment required to be so resident: Medical Act 1983, s 11(3). The Medical Act 1950 (Period of Employment as House Officers) Regulations Approval Order in Council 1952, SI 1952/2050 prescribes a period of 12 months. These regulations have effect as if made under the Medical Act, 1983, ss 10 and 11.

3 A person who is a graduate or licentiate in dentistry of one of the dental authorities is entitled to be registered in the dentists' register, subject to satisfying the registrar as to good character and so forth. See Dentists Act 1984, s 15; 30 *Halsbury's Laws* (4th edn) para 320ff.

4 The rules no longer require that it be a UK medical school. The IDI Nov/00, Ch 3, Annex J, give details of the General Medical Council requirements for provisional, limited and full registration. Graduates of EEA medical schools may be granted limited registration, and doctors qualifying at certain medical schools in Australia, Hong Kong, New Zealand, Singapore, South Africa and the West Indies may qualify for full registration.

5 HC 395, para 70(i)(a), substituted by HC 338, para 1.

6 HC 395, para 70(i)(a).

7 HC 395, para 70(i)(b). If there is doubt that a doctor or dentist is eligible for full or limited registration with the General Medical Council or General Dental Council but all other requirements are met, leave to enter should be granted for six months pending production of the registration certificate: IDI Nov/00, Ch 3, Annex J.

8 HC 395, para 70(ii).

9 HC 395, para 70(iii). For the definition of public funds see para 6; see chapter 3 above.

10 Participating bodies include the Royal Colleges of Surgeons, Physicians, Anaesthetists and Psychiatrists.

11 IDI Nov/00, Ch 3, Annex J.

12 HC 395, para 71(a).

13 HC 395, para 71(b).

14 HC 395, para 72.

15 HC 395, paras 73–75, as substituted by HC 338, para 1.

16 HC 395, para 73(i)(b)(2).

17 On rare occasions extensions beyond 12 months may be granted exceptionally: IDI Nov/00, Ch 3, Annex J.

18 Intervals for pregnancy or sickness between training should normally be included in the four-year period: IDI Nov/00, Ch 3, Annex J.

19 IDI Nov/00, Ch 3, Annex J.

20 HC 395, para 73(ii).

Spouses and children of students and prospective students

9.35 Spouses and children under 18 of a person admitted or allowed to remain as a student or prospective student[1] are to be given leave to enter in line, if they satisfy the requirements for leave to enter or remain. A spouse may be admitted if the couple are married, the marriage is subsisting and the couple intend living with each other as husband and wife during the student's stay. There must be adequate provision for maintenance and accommodation of the couple and any dependants without recourse to public funds. The spouse may be permitted to take employment if the period of leave granted is 12 months or more,[2] but if not must not intend to seek it, and there must be an intention to leave the UK at the end of any period of leave granted.[3] An unmarried child of a student or prospective student qualifies for admission if he or she has not formed an independent family unit and is not leading an independent life, is under 18 or has leave to enter or remain in the same capacity,[4] can and will be maintained and accommodated adequately without recourse to public funds and will not stay in the UK beyond any period of leave granted to the child's parent.[5] The children of a student may work if admitted for 12 months or more. In practice students admitted to courses at universities, and colleges where courses are run on an annual basis are given 12 months' leave. In such cases the spouse and children will also be given 12 months leave and will be able to take employment. Where the student is on a short course and the period of leave granted is less than 12 months, the spouse and children will not be able to work. Clearly the ability of the spouse to work is a very important factor and may be crucial to the student's continued ability to study and to fulfil the maintenance and accommodation provisions of the Immigration Rules.[6]

1   Under HC 395, paras 57-75 or 82-87.
2   Or if it would have been but for delay in the grant of leave because of queueing and processing times: IDI Nov/00, Ch 3, Annex M.
3   HC 395, paras 76–78, as amended by Cm 4851.
4   This covers a student's child who was under 18 when first admitted with or joining the student, and is now over 18 but still lives with the family and should not be disqualified and required to leave the UK.
5   HC 395 paras 79, 80, as amended by Cm 4851.
6   A spouse's income may be taken into account for this purpose on an application to extend student leave: IDI Nov/00, Ch 3, Annex M.

Registration with the police

9.36 Commonwealth students are not required to register with the police, but foreign nationals[1] admitted for more than six months and the spouse or child over 16 of such a student will be required to register.[2]

1   See Appendix 2 to HC 395.
2   HC 395, para 325(ii) and (iii).

Admission of students - detailed rules

9.37 The Immigration Rules contain a detailed checklist of requirements for admission as students. But, as in the past, the list still leaves plenty of scope for the entry clearance officer or immigration officer to make a fairly subjective assessment of the student's ability and genuineness, and in the end admission is always a matter of discretion. Student admissions have given rise to controversy over whether the immigration service is a better judge of educational ability and potential than an educational establishment. The Rules envisage acceptance on a course of study at three types of educational institution,[1] which are referred to in somewhat obscure terms, and appear to incorporate meanings borrowed from education law. They are set out in the following paragraphs.

1   HC 395, para 57(i).

9.38 *Publicly funded institutions of further and higher education.*[1] Further and higher education are both defined by the Education Act 1996,[2] and are quite distinct types of education.[3] Local education authorities are under a duty to secure for their areas adequate facilities for further education other than for 16- to 18-year-olds, for whom the Further Education Funding Councils of England and Wales are now responsible, and for certain types of courses contained in Schedule 2 to the Further and Higher Education Act 1992.[4] Institutions of further education for which the Funding Councils or local authority are responsible will count as publicly funded, although this is not spelt out anywhere in the Immigration Rules. The position of institutions of higher education is perhaps clearer. The distinction between universities and polytechnics has been abolished and a single funding structure, known as the Higher Education Funding Council for England and Wales, has been set up to channel government money into universities.[5]

1   HC 395, para 57(i)(a).
2   'Higher education' means education provided by means of the following: (i) a course for further training of teachers or youth and community workers; (ii) a postgraduate course (including a higher degree course); (iii) a first degree course; (iv) a course for the diploma of higher education; (v) a course for Higher National Diploma or Higher National Certificate of the Business and Technician Education Council, or the Diploma in Management Studies; (vi) a course for the Certificate in Education; (vii) a course in preparation for a professional examination at a higher level; (viii) a course providing education at a higher level 'whether or not in preparation for an examination': Education Reform Act 1988, s 120(1), Sch 6, paras 1, 2 and 3. 'Further education' means: (a) full-time and part-time education for persons over compulsory school age (including vocational, social, physical and recreational training); and (b) organised leisure-time occupation provided in connection with the provision of such education: Education Act 1996, s 2(3)-(5).
3   Education Act 1996, s 2(3).
4   Education Act 1996, s 15(1).
5   Further and Higher Education Act 1992, ss 62 and 63.

9.39 *Bona fide private education institutions which maintain satisfactory records of enrolment and attendance*[1] are private colleges such as secretarial colleges, language schools and private 'crammers' which may be institutions of further or higher education, but are not under local authority control. They also include US universities offering US degrees and qualifications.[2] Because they are not publicly accountable in the same way as the previous category,[3] entry clearance officers and immigration officers are given latitude to check their bona fides and see that they keep satisfactory records of enrolment and attendance.[4] In addition, students attending such colleges usually have to satisfy stringent requirements as to the number of hours studied each week.[5]

1   HC 395, para 57(i)(b).
2   IDI Nov/00, Ch 3, Annex A.
3   Private providers may apply to the British Accreditation Council for Independent Further and Higher Education for accreditation. English language schools may be recognised by the British Council, which recognises all such schools which are members of the Association of English Language Schools (ARELS) as efficient. All these accredited and recognised institutions should be accepted as bona fide by the Secretary of State: see IDI Nov/00, Ch 3, Annex A.
4   HC 395, para 57(i)(b). See eg *R v Immigration Appeal Tribunal, ex p Idiaro* [1991] Imm AR 546, QBD (investigations into London private college whose principal was eventually jailed for fraud).
5   HC 395, para 57(ii)(b); see **9.41** below.

9.40 *Independent fee-paying schools outside the maintained sector*[1] include preparatory and public schools. But again the more the precise meaning must derive from terms used in education law. According to this,[2] an 'independent school' is a school at which full-time education is provided for five or more pupils of compulsory school age (whether or not such education is also provided for pupils under or over that age), not being a school maintained by a local education authority, a grant-maintained school or a special school not maintained by a local education authority.[3] City Technology Colleges and City Colleges for the Technology of the Arts are not defined as 'maintained'[4] but according to the Home Office,[5] are publicly funded and so not 'independent' for the purpose of the Rules. The IDI include in the 'maintained sector' all publicly-funded schools, including grant-maintained schools, voluntary aided schools, sixth form colleges attached to maintained schools, special schools and nursery schools (as well as the City Technology Colleges and City Colleges for the Technology of the Arts).[6] Independent schools must be registered[7] and an unregistered school will not be regarded as an independent school for the purposes of the Rules.[8] 'Fee paying' describes the school rather than the parent, and a pupil on a free scholarship could presumably qualify for admission as a student under the Immigration Rules.

1 HC 395, para 57(i)(c).
2 A 'maintained school' means: (a) any county or voluntary school; (b) any maintained special school which is not established in a hospital; and (c) except in relation to a local education authority, any grant-maintained school: Education Act 1996, s 350. 'Special schools' are defined as schools which are specially organised to make special educational provision for pupils with special educational needs and which are for the time being approved by the Secretary of State as special schools: Education Act 1996, s 242.
3 Education Act 1996, s 463.
4 Education Act 1996, s 482.
5 IDI Nov/00, Ch 3, Annex A.
6 IDI Nov/00, Ch 3, Annex A.
7 Education Act 1996, s 464ff.
8 IDI Nov/00, Ch 3, Annex A.

Course of study

9.41 Students must have been accepted for a course of study at one of the three types of educational institution above.[1] The course enrolled on may be a degree course or any other full-time course, but the detailed requirements differ according to the type of institution and course attended. Students enrolled on a full-time, recognised degree course at publicly funded institutions of further and higher education do not need to show that the course will involve any particular number of hours' study per week.[2] Similarly, students over 16 attending an independent fee-paying school may be enrolled on any full-time course of study,[3] but if the child is under 16, the course must meet the requirements of the Education Act 1996.[4] Children under five attending nursery or pre-school classes do not qualify for leave to enter or remain as students because the 1996 Act does not cover pre-school education.[5] Acceptance by a university on a full-time degree course or as a pupil at an independent fee-paying school will be sufficient to qualify, without any need to investigate the details of the particular course or the arrangements for attendance at lectures and tutorials. The IDI indicate that the same considerations apply to those following a degree course at a bona fide private education institution where the degree will be awarded by a recognised university, including the Open University.[6] All other students must meet the requirement to spend at least 15 hours per week in organised daytime study. Such students may not enrol on a collection of part-time courses at a number of establishments to make up their 15 hours. They must enrol at a single institution and study a single subject or directly related subjects.[7] Night-time or weekend study will not qualify,[8] but organised classes of less than 15 hours, supplemented by supervised private study which brings the total up to 15 hours, may do.[9] In *Amusu*[10] the Tribunal allowed an appeal by a journalism student whose course was primarily by correspondence but involved outside assignments, projects and tutorials estimated by the school to total 15 hours a week, primarily because of the appellant's proven interest in journalism and because a great deal of study was required to obtain the diploma at the end of the course. It is unlikely that the current Rules allow such leeway.

1 HC 395, para 57(i). A conditional acceptance may be insufficient: see *Chinwo* [1985] Imm AR 74; *Yovsani* (3181).
2 HC 395, para 57(ii)(a). An Open University course with modules requiring 21 hours of study per week does not, however, constitute such a course: *Kagunya* (L36) 2000 6 ILD No 1.
3 HC 395, para 57(ii)(c).
4 HC 395, para 57(iii).The Education Act 1996 contains an obligation to provide efficient and suitable instruction having regard to the ages and sex of the pupils and the Secretary of State for Education and Employment can lay a complaint to an Independent Schools Tribunal if this is not being done: Education Act 1996, s 469. See *Bevan v Shears* [1911] 2 KB 936; *R v West Riding of Yorkshire Justices, ex p Broadbent* [1910] 2 KB 192; *R v Secretary of State for Education and Science, ex p Torah Machzikei Hadass School Trust* (1985) Times, 12 April, QBD.
5 IDI Nov/00, Ch 3, Annex A.
6 IDI Nov/00, Ch 3, Annex A, para 6. But see *Kagunya* (L36), 2000 ILD vol 5, No 1, where an Open University course was not accepted as a 'recognised full-time degree course' despite requiring 21 hours of study per week.
7 HC 395, para 57(ii)(b).
8 *R v Immigration Appeal Tribunal, ex p Idiaro* [1991] Imm AR 546, QBD. Classes starting at or after 6 pm, and weekend classes, will not be counted, although classes beginning in the afternoon and continuing after 6 pm may be acceptable: IDI Nov/00, Ch 3, Annex A, para 6.2.
9 *Awosika* [1989] Imm AR 35.
10 [1974] Imm AR 16.

9.42 Some arrangements for tuition are so vague that they do not qualify. In *Kpoma*[1] it was suggested that to constitute a course of study, there must be something more than a coaching scheme, which is supplementary to some other main field of endeavour, and it must be a course which has a termination point and not one which could be of indefinite length. In *Ex p Kharrazi*[2] the Court of Appeal held that a 'full-time course of study' could include such full-time course of study as a boy of 12 might reasonably expect to follow through to its conclusion (ie the attainment of a degree), even though he had not at that stage been guaranteed a place at a university. It covered not only the course of study for which the prospective student had been accepted, but a coherent and definite educational proposal of more than one course of study which was reasonably capable of being carried out by him or her. Thus arrangements to go to a preparatory school followed by a public school might well be a full-time course of study, since although they would require separate arrangements they would be part of a coherent whole.

1 [1973] Imm AR 25.
2 *R v Chief Immigration Officer, Gatwick Airport, ex p Kharrazi* [1980] 3 All ER 373, [1981] 1 WLR 1396, CA.

Ability and intention

9.43 The immigration authority (the entry clearance officer or the immigration officer on arrival) may scrutinise the applicant's ability and intention to follow the course on which he or she is enrolled.[1] A genuine student is one who is able and intends to follow a particular course.[2] At the entry stage, an immigration officer may have regard to the adequacy of the applicant's qualifications,[3] and inability to converse in English may be relevant if the applicant is proposing immediate study of a complicated subject.[4] However, immigration officers should not normally attempt to second-guess decisions by colleges of enrolment as to the student's ability to follow the course.[5] Later on, it will become easier to assess ability, as students progress and pass or fail examinations.[6]

1 HC 395, para 57(ii).
2 *Pelehroudi* (3798) unreported.
3 *R v Secretary of State for the Home Department, ex p Bhambra* [1985] Imm AR 28, QBD.
4 *R v Secretary of State for the Home Department, ex p Ozkurtulus* [1986] Imm AR 80, QBD; see also *R v Chief Immigration Officer, Bradford Airport, ex p Ashiq Hussain* [1969] 3 All ER 1601, [1970] 1 WLR 9, DC, decided under the old Rules.
5 The IDI Nov/00, Ch 3, Annex A indicate that where an immigration officer is doubtful about a student's ability to follow the course, the principal should be contacted and asked to make an assessment of the student.
6 See 'Extensions of stay' **9.50** below.

Prospective students: genuine and realistic intentions

9.44 Satisfying an entry clearance officer or immigration officer about 'genuine and realistic' intentions is still necessary in those cases where a prospective student is unable to fulfil all the requirements for student admission.[1] An intention will not be 'realistic' if there is an obvious lack of correspondence between the student's previous attainments and the nature of the course proposed and its benefits to the student in terms of future job prospects are uncertain,[2] but will be realistic if the student shows that his or her educational qualifications are acceptable to the proposed college.[3] In *Alexander v Immigration Appeal Tribunal*[4] the House of Lords equated 'genuine and realistic' intentions with the requirement that the student applicant is able and intends to follow a full-time course of study. A student who was found not to be able to follow a course could not be said to have had realistic intentions of so doing.[5] Where an entry clearance officer has assessed these matters and granted a visa, it is not for the immigration officer to go over the same ground again at the point of entry.[6] There is even less cause to do so now that entry clearance stands as leave to enter.[7]

1 HC 395, para 82.
2 *Virdee* [1972] Imm AR 215.
3 *Sharma* [1972] Imm AR 219n. See further *Puri v Secretary of State for the Home Department* [1972] Imm AR 21; *Bhambra* [1973] Imm AR 14; *Islam* [1974] Imm AR 83; *R v Immigration Appeal Tribunal, ex p Khan* [1975] Imm AR 26. DC; *Khan (SGH)* [1975] Imm AR 64.
4 [1982] 2 All ER 766, [1982] 1 WLR 1076.
5 *R v Secretary of State for the Home Department, ex p Bhambra* [1985] Imm AR 28.
6 *Pattuwearachchi* [1991] Imm AR 341.
7 Immigration (Leave to Enter and Remain) Order 2000, SI 2000/1161, art 4(3).

Intention to leave

9.45 The requirement that students will only be admitted if they intend to leave the UK on completion of their studies is intended to emphasise that studying in the UK is not the stepping stone to a future career and settlement in this country. However, the 'intention to leave' clause is not the only way in which immigration law and the Immigration Rules attempt to effect this policy, since checks are made on the student's progress when leave has to be renewed,[1] and there are sanctions for any student who steps out of line. In terms of enforcing an effective immigration control the 'intention to leave' clause is unnecessary, ineffective (since the real evaders will keep quiet about their true intentions) and unfair, disqualifying merely the innocent or naïve.

1 Although IDI Nov/00, Ch 3, Annex A state that after-entry inquiries as to intention need not be made except in cases where there is reason to believe the applicant does not intend to go home, eg if he or she is an unsuccessful asylum applicant, an applicant who has previously been refused in another capacity or one who appears to be moving from course to course without any intention of bringing his or her studies to a close.

9.46 The Rule is satisfied by an intention to leave at the end of the whole of the student's studies, and he or she does not have to intend to leave at the end of the particular course upon which the student is enrolled.[1] So an intention to progress from preparatory school to university does not fall foul of the Rule.[2] An intention to do vocational training or even an apprenticeship following academic studies may also be within the Rule.[3] An intention conditional upon there being no change of circumstances might also satisfy the Immigration Rules.[4] Harbouring a wish to gain work experience at the end of studies, if permitted to do so, does not necessarily disentitle the student from continuing his or her studies.[5] An application for settled status in another capacity is likely to result in refusal under the Rule, but it all depends on the facts.[6]

1 HC 395, para 57(iv); *R v Chief Immigration Officer, Gatwick Airport, ex p Kharrazi* [1980] 3 All ER 373, [1981] 1 WLR 1396, CA.
2 *Kharrazi* above.
3 *Patel v Immigration Appeal Tribunal* [1983] Imm AR 76, CA.
4 *R v Immigration Appeal Tribunal, ex p Perween Khan* [1972] 3 All ER 297, [1972] Imm AR 268, QBD.
5 *R v Immigration Appeal Tribunal, ex p Shaikh* [1981] 3 All ER 29, [1981] 1 WLR 1107, QBD.
6 *Patel v Immigration Appeal Tribunal* [1983] Imm AR 76. See **9.44** fn 1 above.

Proving intention

9.47 The importance attached to a student's intentions is matched by the difficulty in proving what a person's intention is. Statements of intention are not always reliable or to be taken on their face value.[1] They may represent mere aspiration or wishful thinking rather than firm and settled intention,[2] a distinction recognised by the Tribunal and the High Court.[3] A conditional intention to return is not necessarily fatal.[4] In the absence of direct evidence of intention much will rest on the drawing of inferences. The Tribunal has been careful to warn that inferences must be drawn only from the evidence and that mere suspicion is not enough.[5] Where a student is undertaking short courses, the immigration and appellate authorities look for evidence of related employment prospects in the student's own country.[6] In assessing a student's intention to leave at the end of the course of studies, an immigration officer is entitled to take into account all circumstances including a student's academic record.[7]

1 IDI Nov /00, Ch 3, Annex A state that 'any student who expresses the wish to remain in the UK beyond his (sic) studies should not be refused without the opportunity to clarify his intentions'.
2 *Sobanjo* [1978] Imm AR 22, where, despite recognising the difficulties of deciding whether a young appellant's statements should be taken as firm and settled, the Tribunal refused the appeal of a 15-year-old Nigerian girl who had told the entry clearance officer that she wanted to study for eight years in this country and then stay on and work. Contrast *Nakawesa* (3043), where it was held that expressing a hope of remaining after the end of studies does not preclude an intention to leave.
3 *Lai* [1974] Imm AR 98; *R v Immigration Appeal Tribunal, ex p Shaikh* [1981] 3 All ER 29, [1981] 1 WLR 1107; in *Masood v Immigration Appeal Tribunal* [1992] Imm AR 69, CA Glidewell LJ said a wish only became an intention when there was some reasonable prospect of its being fulfilled (at 78).

4 *Sivasubramanian* (13174); *Mdawini* (G0039) IAS 1998 Vol 1 No 11.
5 *Bhambra* [1973] Imm AR 14; *Murgai* [1975] Imm AR 86.
6 'It would be appropriate to ask about his (sic) job opportunities in his country and the material benefits to be gained from the course and to weigh this against the cost of the course which may represent the expenditure of a large sum of money to a person or family of low income': IDI Nov/00, Ch 3, Annex A. See also *Goffar and Dey* [1975] Imm AR 142; *Islam* [1974] Imm AR 83; *Ghosh* [1976] Imm AR 60. Guaranteed employment in the student's own country is not necessary: *Oni* (15886) IAS 1998 Vol 1 No 8.
7 *R v Secretary of State for the Home Department, ex p Mohotty* [1996] Imm AR 256, QBD.

Students and work

9.48 Leave to enter or remain as a student is subject to a condition restricting employment,[1] and students can in general only take part-time or vacation employment.[2] The condition restricting employment imposed on students should be distinguished from the condition prohibiting employment imposed on prospective students.[3] Prospective students, in common with others subject to a condition prohibiting employment, may never work while they remain in this category, but students with a restriction on employment are in a different position. Recently, in an attempt by the government to encourage overseas students to come to the UK, the requirement that students obtain permission from the Department of Employment before working has been relaxed, and students may take any part-time employment (up to 20 hours a week) in term-time, and full-time employment in vacations. They must provide satisfactory evidence from their college that employment will not interfere with their course of study. Graduates of medical schools may take up employment as pre-registration house officers for up to 12 months and doctors and dentists can do postgraduate training in hospitals or community health services for an aggregate of up to four years.[4] Nurses and midwives may accept employment in connection with their training[5] (but not full-time employment on completion of their training, as was previously possible). Leave is only granted if the student or student nurse intends to abide by these Rules.[6]

1 HC 395, paras 58, 61.
2 HC 395, para 57 (v).
3 HC 395, paras 83, 86.
4 HC 395, paras 70–75; see **9.33** above.
5 HC 395, para 64(v).
6 HC 395, paras 57(v), 64 (v).

9.49 Students and student nurses may not engage in business,[1] but the question considered by the Court of Appeal in *Ayoola*,[2] whether students are permitted to transact business, is still open. Our view is that unless clearly prohibited from doing so by the Immigration Rules, they may. Conditions imposed by section 3(1) of the Immigration Act 1971 apply only to employment or occupation, and transacting business is not, in our view, an occupation until it crosses the dividing line into engaging in business. In *Strasburger*[3] the Tribunal held that the sale by a student of her artwork was not to be regarded as a breach of a condition not to engage in business. Provided a student complied with the requirements of the student rules, the fact that he or she sold the occasional picture, or indeed all that he or she produced, could be disregarded. Spouses and children of students are admitted without any employment restriction unless given less than 12 months' leave,[4] and may therefore obtain full-time year-round work without requiring anyone's consent.

1   HC 395, para 57(v), 64(v). This Rule confirms the Tribunal decision in *Durojaiye* [1991] Imm AR 307.
2   *Ayoola v Secretary of State for the Home Department* [1992] Imm AR 170, CA.
3   [1978] Imm AR 165.
4   HC 395, paras 77, 80.

Adequate means

9.50 Students must show that they have adequate means to pay for the course and their accommodation and maintenance costs. Applications may be lost simply because adequate documentary evidence of means has not been produced. Tribunals have indicated a willingness to accept post-decision evidence of means, particularly if this is the only outstanding issue on a student's entry.[1] Evidence of means should be substantiated by production of bank statements, wage slips, employers' letters or similar primary documentary evidence showing an ability to meet the necessary bills.[2] Vague, unsubstantiated assertions in letters are not acceptable. Evidence may also be necessary to show that funds abroad are transferable to the UK. The costs may be met by the student, a sponsoring government or international agency, a parent or close relative abroad, or a sponsor in this country. Occasionally a student may rely on a local education authority grant.[3] The Immigration Rules make it clear that throughout their studies, students must be able to meet the costs of their course and accommodation and the maintenance of themselves and any dependants without taking employment or engaging in business or having recourse to public funds.[4] This means that students may not rely on earnings from part-time or vacation work to satisfy the maintenance and accommodation requirements, but may rely on their spouses' income,[5] at least by the time an extension is sought, when the spouse is in work. Leave should not be refused on the ground of lack of funds alone where the student meets the other requirements of the Rules but is in temporary financial difficulties, for example, because of social or political upheaval at home leading to difficulty in arranging the transfer of funds or the continuance of sponsorship.[6]

1   *Murgai* [1975] Imm AR 86; *Bhagat* [1972] Imm AR 189.
2   *Ayetty* [1972] Imm AR 261. IDI Nov/00, Ch 3, Annex A state that letters or receipts simply showing the balance in an account on a particular day are not sufficient; bank or building society statements should cover a period of approximately three months.
3   IDI Nov/00, Ch 3, Annex A, para 7.3. Refusal should not be based on the grounds that the level of fees charged is low or that the student has a local education authority award. But if the student has not lived in the UK for at least three years in a capacity other than as a student, receipt of a grant may be queried with the local authority concerned.
4   HC 395, paras 57(vi), 60 (ii).
5   This is implicit in the terms of HC 395, para 57(vi). IDI Nov/00, Ch 3, Annex A, state that the potential earnings of the spouse of a student may not be taken into account, but if he or she is already working, actual earnings may be: para 7.4.
6   IDI Nov/00, Ch 3, Annex A, para 7.7.

Extensions for students

9.51 Those admitted as students can have their stay extended to continue a course or begin the next one, and prospective students may extend their stay to continue looking for a course (up to a six-month maximum)[1] and then as students. Non-visa nationals who entered as visitors or in some other temporary capacity can switch to student or student nurse status, but visa nationals may not,[2] unless their application is for postgraduate medical or dental training.[3] To obtain an extension ordinary students must fulfil the following requirements:[4]

(i)   they were admitted to the UK with valid student entry clearance if they are visa nationals.[5] This is mandatory - a visa national who comes in as a visitor may not switch to student status;[6]

(ii)   they meet all the requirements for the admission of a student;[7]

(iii)   they are enrolled for a full-time course of study which meets the requirements for admission as a student;[8]

(iv)   they can produce satisfactory evidence of regular attendance during any course already begun or any other course for which they have been enrolled in the past.[9] Attendance is to be judged at the time of the decision on the application, and not by evidence subsequent to the refusal showing that attendance has improved;[10]

(v)   they can show evidence of satisfactory progress in their course of study,[11] including the taking and passing of any relevant exams.[12] A lack of success in exams[13] or a failure to sit them[14] can be taken into account. But where lack of success has been relied on alone, although there is no obligation to warn the student of the consequences of failure, rejection might be regarded as premature if the student's failure is not balanced against the student's investment in the course and other relevant factors;[15]

(vi)   they would not, as a result of the extension of stay, spend more than four years on short courses (ie courses of less than two years' duration, or longer courses broken off before completion);[16]

(vii)   students whose studies are sponsored by a government or international scholarship agency must show that the sponsorship has not come to an end or, if it has, they have the written consent of their official sponsor for a further period of study and evidence that sufficient sponsorship funding is available.[17] The Rule enables students left stranded by a sponsoring government or agency, often because of a sudden change of government or civil war, to remain if they can find alternative funding and obtain the consent of the official sponsor.[18]

1   HC 395, para 85.
2   HC 395, para 60(i), 67(i). The list of visa countries is set out in HC 395, Appendix 1. Nationals of countries recently added to the visa list are protected by transitional provisions if they did not require visas when they entered. See notes to para 60(i) in *Butterworths Immigration Law Service*, B[364].
3   HC 395, para 73. The visa national dependant of a student who has embarked on a course of studies which overruns the leave granted to his or her spouse must return home to apply for entry clearance in his or her own right: letter Immigration Nationality Directorate to University of Sheffield, 14 December 2000.
4   HC 395, para 60. All relevant parts of the rule need to be satisfied: *Mohey-ud-Din* (15998) IAS 1998 Vol 1 No 6, Immigration Appeal Tribunal.
5   HC 395, para 60(i). See fn 2 above. This will cover entry clearance as a prospective student, although one Immigration Appeal Tribunal decision (which we believe to be wrong) says otherwise: *Ofosu-Oboobah* (00 TH 00586) IAS 2000 Vol 3 No 19.
6   *Okello v Secretary of State for the Home Department* [1995] Imm AR 269, CA.
7   HC 395, para 60(ii). On after-entry inquiries as to a student's intention to leave see **9.45** fn 1 above.
8   HC 395, para 60(iii).
9   HC 395, para 60(iv). An attendance record should always be obtained after a student has been in the UK for three years or, if an English language student, has been studying for 12 months and requests leave to remain to continue English studies: IDI Nov/00, Ch 3, Annex A, para 2.

10 *Juma* [1974] Imm AR 96.

11 A student cannot rely on progress on another course to which he or she has switched without telling the Home Office: *Hoque (Shemeenul)* (18349) IAS 1999 Vol 2 No 18, Immigration Appeal Tribunal.

12 HC 395, para 60(v). As a rule inquiries will be made as to a student's attendance and progress when he or she has been studying in the UK for three years, or sooner if there is any cause for doubt: IDI Nov/00, Ch 3, Annex A, para 9.3. For accountancy and banking students the IDI Annex D describes the entry requirements, structure of courses and examinations of the five main bodies offering qualifications (CIMA, ACCA, AAT, ABE and CIB) against which to track a student's progress.

13 *R v Immigration Appeal Tribunal, ex p Gerami* [1981] Imm AR 187, DC; *Mahendran* [1988] Imm AR 492; *Amer* [1979–80] Imm AR 87; *Mensah* (10855) 1994 ICD vol I No 2. Passing exams is important, but it is not the only factor: *Sayeed* (G0068) IAS 1999 Vol 2 No 9, Immigration Appeal Tribunal.

14 *R v Secretary of State for the Home Department, ex p Adebodin* [1991] Imm AR 60. Dogged persistence over a lengthy period may not be enough to overcome repeated exam failure: *Ofori-Agyemang* (14323) IAS 1997 Vol 3 No 16. See below for rules on resits, para 69A.

15 *Siddiai* (3564) unreported; *Ofoajoku* [1991] Imm AR 68. The IDI (above) state that the student should be asked to provide evidence of all examinations attempted and the results. Where there are doubts as to progress but attendance is satisfactory and all other requirements are met, leave may be granted but with a warning that failure to produce evidence of satisfactory progress could result in a refusal of a further extension.

16 HC 395, para 60(vi). It is not intended to prevent a person from taking short courses which form part of a planned course with a defined educational objective, but inquiries as to a student's educational plans should be considered where he or she has enrolled on a new course bearing no relation to previous studies, or is re-enrolling on the same or similar course without apparently making progress, or breaks off mid-course for no good reason and seeks to commence another course, or where there is any reason to suspect that he or she is making the studies an excuse for remaining in the UK for some other purpose: IDI, Ch 3, Annex A, para 10. Previous short courses may not matter if the extension is for a long course: *Navarthinarajah* (14373) ILD 2000 Vol 6 No 1.

17 HC 395, para 60(vii), amended by Cm 4851, paras 11, 12 (by substituting 'official' sponsor for 'original' sponsor). Failure to obtain written consent may result in refusal: para 39A.

18 Thus an appellant such as *Salah* (20272) 2 February 2000, IAS 2000 Vol 3 No 10, Immigration Appeal Tribunal, whose father was willing to sponsor at the end of an official sponsorship, would no longer qualify unless the official sponsor gave written consent for the switch.

Resits, writing up a thesis, and sabbaticals

9.52 The Immigration Rules enable students to apply for leave to enter or remain to resit examinations provided that they meet the requirements for admission as a student, or, if no longer enrolled and following a course as required by sub-paragraphs 57(i) to (iii), that they met these requirements in the previous academic year and can still fulfil the general requirements in sub-paragraphs 57(iv) to (vi).[1] They must have written confirmation from the school or college concerned that they are required to resit an examination,[2] and evidence of regular attendance on any course currently or previously taken.[3] The sponsorship requirements of the previous paragraph apply,[4] and applicants will be refused if they have previously been granted leave to resit the examination.[5] The wording of this last Rule suggests that a resit leave may be available for each examination, although this will obviously be subject to the general student rules as to satisfactory progress.[6] Students who do not successfully complete access courses preparatory to degree courses (offered by universities as an alternative to meeting the normal educational requirements) are unlikely to satisfy the Secretary of State of their ability to undertake the relevant degree course and refusal of leave to remain to retake the course is likely.[7] The period of leave granted will be whatever is sufficient to enable the student to resit the exam at the first available opportunity, and will be subject to a condition restricting, but not prohibiting, employment.[8]

1 HC 395, paras 69A(i), 69D, inserted by Cm 4851.
2 HC 395, paras 69A(ii), 69D.
3 HC 395, paras 69A(iii), 69D.
4 HC 395, paras 69A(iv), 69D; see above.
5 HC 395, paras 69A(v), 69D.
6 HC 395, para 60(iv); see above.
7 IDI Nov/00, Ch 3, s 1, Annex B, para 1.
8 HC 395, paras 69B, 69E.

9.53 Similar rules apply to students seeking leave to enter or remain to write up a thesis.[1] They need to show that they meet the enrolment requirements, or met them in the previous academic year, and the general requirements (intention to leave and not to work, except part-time, and financial requirements).[2] They must be postgraduate students enrolled as a full-time, part-time or writing-up student at an education institution,[3] which must support the application.[4] If sponsored, they must show continuing sponsorship or alternative funding with the official sponsor's consent.[5] The maximum writing-up period is 12 months and they will be refused leave if they have already had this.[6]

1 HC 395, paras 69G-69L, inserted by Cm 4851.
2 HC 395, paras 69G(i), 69J.
3 HC 395, para 69G(ii).
4 HC 395, para 69G(iii).
5 HC 395, para 69G(iv).
6 HC 395, paras 69H, 69I, 69G(v).

9.54 A student who has been elected as a students' union sabbatical officer may be granted leave to enter or remain for up to two years for the purpose, provided he or she is registered as a student at the establishment where the duties are to be performed and intends to complete a course of study already begun, take up a course which has been deferred for the duration of the sabbatical or leave the UK after the sabbatical.[1] He or she must not engage in business or take employment, except in connection with the post, and must satisfy the maintenance and accommodation and sponsorship criteria.

1 HC 395, paras 87A-F, inserted by Cm 4851.

9.55 An application for an extension of leave should be made on the prescribed form, accompanied by the necessary documentation and other evidence.[1] Failure to complete the form in full or to send the documentation specified will result in no valid application having been made.[2] If the Home Office requests further information, it must be provided promptly, since whatever the merits of the application, it is liable to be refused if there is unreasonable delay in producing the requested documents or evidence.[3] On appeal the Tribunal will consider the substantive merits of the case, but this may not be enough to overcome the adverse effect of the delay. Extensions may be refused if other general considerations apply, for example, if the student has taken full-time employment in breach of conditions.[4]

1 HC 395, para 32. The form for a student variation is FLR(S).

2   HC 395, para 32.
3   HC 395, para 322(9).
4   *Thaker* [1976] Imm AR 114; but see *Strasburger* [1978] Imm AR 165 where it was held
    that casual sales of a student's artwork were not employment which should be taken into
    account.

Student exchange employment programme

9.56   As part of a reciprocal programme of student exchanges between the UK
and the US, any American full-time college student may apply to come to the
UK as part of a Work in Britain Programme. They get a BUNAC 'Blue Card',
which is recognised by the Home Office and the Department for Education and
Employment, which they present to immigration control on entry.[1] They can
enter at any time of the year and stay for up to six months, working as little or
as long as they wish. They have a condition restricting but not prohibiting
employment, which means that they have to get local DfEE approval for each
and every job they take, but normally this is automatic. BUNAC students may
transfer to student status but not to training or work experience.[2]

1   See IDI, Ch 17, s 1. Further information may be obtained from the Council on International
    Exchange, 205 East 42nd Street, New York, NY 10017.
2   IDI, Ch 17, s 1.

Other special cases

9.57   The IDI give guidance on special classes of student or course in Annex B.
Postgraduate students working as researchers require a work permit even where
their research will lead to the award of a higher degree, but higher degree
students who will be awarded degrees by the university at which they are
enrolled, and those enrolled at private colleges or research institutes, whose
studies are validated by a university, should be admitted as students, as should
junior research fellows.[1] Exchange students, normally between the ages of 16
and 18, may be admitted for up to 12 months for attendance at state schools,
on evidence that the local education authority has approved the exchange
scheme and has assigned a school, and subject to suitable arrangements for
support and accommodation (normally satisfied by provision of a host family)
and the intention to leave requirement.[2] The exchange may be arranged by
an organisation which runs such schemes or may be privately arranged. Music
students enrolled at a reputable college of music or under a qualified private
tutor may be admitted despite not meeting the general rule of 15 hours per
week organised daytime study.[3] Similarly, Bar students accepted by an Inn of
Court do not have to meet the 15 hours per week rule for admission.[4] Barristers
taking part in the Crown Prosecution Service-sponsored pupillage scheme,
although paid a wage, should be treated as students, and those who have
completed pupillage and wish to remain for employment with the Crown
Prosecution Service may do so, although applications should normally be
referred to the Work Permits (UK) section fo the DfEE.[5] Articled clerks need a
permit under the Training and Work Experience Scheme. Those who, having
completed articles, wish to work for the Crown Prosecution Service may be
referred to the Work Permits (UK) section in the same way as former pupils.[6]

Agricultural students undertaking practical training on a farm before beginning their course should be admitted as students for up to 12 months if the work is part of the curriculum and the student is supernumerary to the normal labour force.[7] There is also guidance in relation to handicapped children who arrive for education at a special school without entry clearance, nautical students, students attending American Institute for Foreign Study programmes, students on Marshall scholarships, moral rearmament trainees, Pestalozzi children, students attending St George's University School of Medicine, Grenada programmes at affiliated UK teaching hospitals and students at Welbeck college (potential army officers).[8]

1   IDI Nov/00, Ch 3, Annex B, para 13.
2   IDI Nov/00, Ch 3, Annex B, para 4.
3   IDI Nov/00, Ch 3, Annex B, para 9.
4   IDI Nov/00, Ch 3, Annex B, para 6.1.
5   IDI Nov/00, Ch 3, Annex B, para 6.2.
6   IDI Nov/00, Ch 3, Annex B, para 6.3.
7   IDI Nov/00, Ch 3, Annex B, para 2.
8   IDI Nov/00, Ch 3, Annex B, para 2.

Extensions for nurses

9.58 Nursing training will not be extended beyond four years.[1] But within this period student nurses may obtain extensions if they continue to meet all the requirements for admission and can produce satisfactory evidence of regular attendance.[2] If sponsored they must show continuing sponsorship or alternative funding with the official sponsor's written consent.[3]

1   HC 395, para 67(v).
2   HC 395, para 67(ii)–(iv).
3   HC 395, para 67 (vi).

Appeal rights

9.59 Students who arrive in the UK with a visa or entry clearance endorsed with its purpose and conditions are deemed to have leave to enter,[1] and if the leave is cancelled they have a right of appeal to an adjudicator under section 59 of the Immigration and Asylum Act 1999 and can remain here for the hearing of their appeal,[2] as can their dependants.[3] Visa nationals who are refused entry on arrival in the UK without a visa have no right of appeal.[4] Non-visa nationals who arrive without entry clearance and are refused entry, and students, whether or not visa nationals, who are refused entry clearance, have a right of appeal against refusal[5] unless the proposed course is of not more than six months' duration[6] or they are potential students, intending to study but not yet accepted on any course.[7] Where leave to enter is refused and the student is not a holder of a current entry clearance, the appeal right cannot be exercised in-country.[8] A student who switches to an entirely different course after refusal of leave to enter or remain cannot expect to have the merits of a new course dealt with on appeal, since it should form part of a fresh application.[9]

1   Immigration (Leave to Enter and Remain) Order 2000, SI 2000/1161, arts 3, 4(3).
2   Immigration and Asylum Act 1999, Sch 4, para 10.

3   Immigration and Asylum Act 1999, Sch 4, para 15.
4   Immigration and Asylum Act 1999, s 60(7), (8).
5   Immigration and Asylum Act 1999, s 59(1), (2).
6   Immigration and Asylum Act 1999, s 60(4)(b), (5).
7   Immigration and Asylum Act 1999, s 60(4)(c), (5).
8   Immigration and Asylum Act 1999, s 60(3). A prospective student who was granted temporary admission and then refused leave to enter, but who had in the meantime enrolled on a full-time course of study, had become a student with a right of appeal from abroad against the refusal of leave: *Morikawa v Secretary of State for the Home Department* [1995] Imm AR 258, CA.
9   *Thaker* [1976] Imm AR 114 (switch from accountancy to economics); *Muthulakshmi* [1972] Imm AR 231 (English language course substituted for dentistry).

Changing from student status

9.60 Students can switch from one course to another within the limits set out at **9.51** above. An ordinary student can become a student nurse and vice versa. On graduation, medical students can take employment as house officers and undertake postgraduate training.[1] Other students can switch to Department for Education and Employment-approved training or work experience.[2] But the Immigration Rules do not allow the possibility of switching to other temporary categories, such as au pair[3] or working holidaymaker.[4] Nurses may not stay on and take nursing posts after qualifying.[5] As with visitors, the Rules do not permit students to switch to business or employment, subject to various EC Association Agreements (see **9.25** above).[6] The only categories leading to settlement into which students may switch are: (i) Commonwealth citizens with a UK-born grandparent intending to take or seek employment;[7] (ii) close relatives, such as a student child of parents who decide to settle,[8] or a student wishing to remain as a dependent relative on compassionate grounds;[9] and (iii) students who marry someone settled here, or cohabit with an unmarried partner for two years, who may apply for leave to remain as a spouse or unmarried partner.[10]

1   HC 395, para 73. See above **9.34**.
2   HC 395, para 119(i).
3   HC 395, para 92(i).
4   HC 395, para 98(i).
5   HC 395, paras 64(vi) and 67(ii) and (v), subject to the proviso as to shortage areas of nursing: IDI Nov/00, Ch 3, Annex F, para 3.2.
6   But Home Office policy is to permit switching on a discretionary basis for students who obtain a work permit in a shortage occupation: letter from Immigration and Nationality Directorate to Immigration Law Practitioners' Association, 25 October 2000. See **10.56** below.
7   HC 395, para 189.
8   HC 395, paras 298, 311 (adopted child).
9   HC 395, para 317.
10 HC 395, paras 295D and E, inserted by Cm 4851.

AU PAIRS

Nature of the arrangement

9.61 According to the current Immigration Rules, an 'au pair' placement is an arrangement whereby a young person comes to the UK to learn English, lives for a time as a member of an English-speaking family with appropriate opportunities for study, and helps in the home for a maximum of five hours a day in return for a reasonable allowance and two free days a week.[1] The arrangement is open to young men and women from European but non-EEA countries (nationals of EEA countries are dealt with exclusively under EC law and are excluded from the 'au pair' Rule). Apart from the reference to a 'reasonable allowance', the Rules are silent on pay[2] and there is no Department for Education and Employment supervision, so the relationship is open to exploitation and abuse.[3]

1   HC 395, para 88.
2   IDI Nov/00, Ch 4, s 1, Annex A refers (para 4) to an allowance of 'up to £35 a week at 1994 prices. Any sum significantly in excess of this might suggest that the person is filling the position of domestic servant, or similar, which would require a work permit'. At December 2000 prices this would amount to £41.36.
3   Au pairs are not covered by minimum wage legislation. In a publication prepared by the Home Office in 1973 it was stated that an au pair 'receives her keep, entertainment and pocket money and is expected to help with the housework and take care of any children'. It referred to the relationship not as one between employer and employee but between 'the girl and her hostess'. 'Under a proper au pair arrangement the relationship between the hostess and the girl involves acceptance of social equality and is not founded on a mistress/servant basis': *Au pair in Britain* (1973) COI.

The requirements

9.62 The full requirements for entry to the UK as an au pair[1] are that the passenger:

(i)   is seeking entry as an au pair within the definition in HC 395, paragraph 88;
(ii)   is aged between 17 and 27 inclusive when first given leave to enter. Discretion may be exercised in the case of a young person who will be 17 within a few days, but discretion to admit new arrivals aged 28 or over will not be used unless arrival has been delayed by an unexpected domestic crisis, illness or completion of a long-term course of study. In such a case discretion may be exercised to admit someone up to six months over the age of 28;[2]
(iii)   is unmarried;
(iv)   is without dependants;
(v)   is a national of Andorra, Bosnia-Herzegovina, Croatia, Cyprus, Czech Republic, The Faroes, Greenland, Hungary, Macedonia, Malta, Monaco, San Marino, Slovak Republic, Slovenia, Switzerland or Turkey;[3]
(vi)   does not intend to stay in the UK for more than two years as an au pair;
(vii) intends to leave on completion of his or her stay as an au pair; and
(viii) if he or she has already been here as an au pair, is not seeking to remain beyond the two-year period from the date when leave to enter as an au pair was first given;
(ix)   can maintain and accommodate him or herself without recourse to public funds[4]. Being maintained and accommodated by a third party (as will usually be the case) will suffice.[5]

If all these requirements are met, leave of up to two years may be given with a condition prohibiting employment except as an au pair.[6] Visa nationals require a visa, and non-visa nationals are advised to get one.[7] If all the requirements are not met, leave is to be refused.[8] An extension to the au pair arrangement can be obtained provided the person is working as an au pair, meets the main requirements of entry, and the extension would not take them beyond the two-year period, starting from the date of their first leave to enter as an au pair.[9] Previously, persons arriving on a visit could switch to 'au pair' but this is no longer possible under the new Rules.[10] An au pair may switch to a new host family.[11]

1 HC 395, para 89.
2 IDI Nov/00, Ch 4, s 1, Annex A, para 1.
3 The omission from the list of Poland, apparently whimsical, is in fact based on sound historical reasons and is not irrational: *R v CIO, ex p Kasprzykowska* (C/99/8156) 15 May 2000, CA.
4 HC 395, paras 89(ix), 92, as amended by HC 31.
5 *Kaur (Balwinder)* (12838); *Begum* (13489) (1996) 10 INLP 1; *Arman Ali* [2000] INLR 89.
6 HC 395, para 90.
7 HC 395, para 90.
8 HC 395, para 91.
9 HC 395, paras 92–94.
10 HC 395, para 92 (i).
11 IDI Nov/00, Ch 4, s 1, Annex A, para 3.

9.63 There is no need for an au pair to enrol on an educational course to learn English. He or she may improve linguistic skills simply by living in an English-speaking family.[1] Additional guidance is set out in the IDI.[2] The family with whom the au pair is placed should be resident in the UK, but not necessarily settled here.[3] It need not be a nuclear family but a person living alone is not a 'family' for the purposes of the au pair rules. There is nothing preventing a host family from having more than one au pair at a time. An au pair should be free to attend religious services as well as language classes and should have free board and lodging and the use of his or her own room. He or she may be expected to baby-sit for up to two nights a week. The 'reasonable allowance' should not exceed £41.36 at December 2000 prices. A letter from the host family describing the duties, pocket money and arrangements for study should normally be requested.[4]

1 *Soler* (4277), unreported.
2 IDI Nov/00, Ch 4, s 1, Annex A.
3 IDI Nov/00, Ch 4, s 1, Annex A, para 2.
4 IDI No/00, Ch 4, s 1, Annex A, para 4.

9.64 The au pair arrangement is confined to persons from European countries. Now that EEA nationals benefit from free movement under EC law, the au pair arrangement is available mainly to nationals of the so-called accession states.[1] Until 1980 au pairs could come from any country and be any age. The Immigration Rules were tightened in line with the termination of work permits for resident domestic work, so as to prevent non-Europeans using au pair status to come in as resident domestics. The limitations in the present au pair arrangements are, therefore, dictated to some extent by the need to ensure that the discontinuance 20 years ago of work permits for resident domestics remains effective. They were brought about in order to close the door on one of the few ways in which women from poorer countries could come to this country independently of their father, husband or sons.

1 The states of central and eastern Europe which have applied to join the EU and will be allowed to join in the next wave. Turkey's application was also recently approved. Nationals of these countries already have (limited) rights of employment or self-employment in the UK. See chapter 7 above.

WORKING HOLIDAYMAKERS

9.65 Young Commonwealth citizens[1] aged 17 to 27 inclusive[2] may be admitted to the UK for up to two years as working holidaymakers if they satisfy the immigration officer that they are coming to the UK for a working holiday and that they intend to take only employment which will be incidental to their holiday, but not to engage in business or provide services as a professional sportsperson or entertainer or pursue a career in the UK.[3] They must have the means to pay for their onward or return journey[4] and not need to have recourse to public funds,[5] and they must intend to leave the UK at the end of their working holiday.[6] If they have already been in the UK in this capacity, they must not seek to remain beyond the two-year period from the date when leave to enter as a working holidaymaker was first given.[7] A working holidaymaker must be unmarried unless the spouse qualifies in his or her own right and the two are taking a working holiday together.[8] Working holidaymakers may not have children, except for children who will still be under five at the end of the working holiday, and must not have commitments requiring a regular income.[9] Entry clearance is required and leave to enter will be refused without one.[10] A dependent child will only be admitted if both parents are making the trip, except where the working holidaymaker is a sole surviving parent, has sole responsibility for the child's upbringing, or there are serious and compelling family or other considerations and suitable arrangements for the child's care.[11] The child also needs entry clearance in this capacity.[12] If any of these conditions is not met, leave is to be refused.[13]

1 HC 395, para 95(i).
2 HC 395, para 95(ii). There is some discretion on age, although persons over 27 on first arrival should not be admitted more than a week or two over the limit unless their arrival has been delayed through exceptionally compelling or compassionate circumstances, in which case discretion may be exercised up to six months over the 27-years limit: IDI, Ch 4, s 2, Annex C, para 1.2.
3 HC 395, para 95(vi).
4 HC 395, para 95(iv). But see **9.69** below.
5 HC 395, para 95(v). Money in a bank account is relevant to but not conclusive of means: *Tanveer* (L00008) IAS 2000 Vol 3 No 1, Immigration Appeal Tribunal.
6 HC 395, para 95(viii).
7 HC 395, para 95(ix).
8 HC 395, para 95(iii).
9 HC 395, para 95(vii). See **9.66** below.
10 HC 395, paras 96(x), 97.
11 HC 395, para 101(iv).
12 HC 395, para 101(v).
13 HC 395, para 103.

9.66 The rules on working holidaymakers have become much stricter over the years. Up until March 1980 working holidaymakers could be admitted for five years, not just two, and there were no age limits.[1] The present age limit matches those for 'au pairs',[2] although the two Rules otherwise bear no relation to each other. Entry clearance before travelling, not required for non-visa nationals prior to 1994,[3] is mandatory.[4] The core requirement for a working holiday is that there should be a holiday in which employment is allowed but is incidental to the holiday. We look at this in more detail below.

1 HC 79, para 28; HC 80, para 11. For earlier Rules and their effect, see *Clipsham* [1972] Imm AR 35; *Ismail* [1973] Imm AR 62.

2   HC 395, para 89(ii).
3   See HC 251, para 37.
4   HC 395, paras 95(x), 98(i) and 101(v).

Working holiday

9.67 Earlier rules referred to a working holiday as an extended holiday before the holidaymaker settled down in their own country.[1] Although the wording has changed, the idea behind the revised rule is not so different, excluding from its ambit married applicants (except those travelling together) and those with school-age children or other commitments who would be inclined to use the rule to enter the UK for 'career' employment and then try to settle here. The IDI[2] state that a working holidaymaker must not have any commitments (such as other dependent relatives overseas, including children under five, for whom he or she must pay regular maintenance, and property, particularly if it is mortgaged) making it likely that he or she would wish to or have to earn a regular income. A working holidaymaker should have 'sufficient ties and prospects' in his or her own country as to be likely to return after two years.[3]

1   HC 251, para 37. See *Adejumoke* [1993] Imm AR 265. Cf *Rani* (9987) [1993] INLP 140 where a bereaved Indian woman seeking to get over her husband's death and to get experience of the clothing trade was held to be eligible for working holidaymaker status because her job was incidental to her holiday. In *Lana v Secretary of State for the Home Department* [1997] Imm AR 17 the Court of Appeal preferred *Adejumoke* to *Rani* but pointed out that their decision had no relevance to the current Immigration Rules, since the requirement to come as a working holiday-maker 'before settling down in their own countries' had been sensibly dropped from the Rules.
2   IDI Nov/00, Ch 4, s 2, Annex C, para 1.3.
3   IDI Nov/00, Ch 4, s 2, Annex C, para 1.5.

Employment incidental to holiday

9.68 The IDI state that a working holidaymaker must intend to work as part of the holiday, and if he or she does not intend working or has no reasonable prospect of obtaining the type of work envisaged, then he or she will be unlikely to meet the requirements of the Immigration Rules.[1] However, in *Bari v Immigration Appeal Tribunal*[2] the Court of Appeal held that applicants are not disbarred if they intend only to get a job if they become bored or their financial arrangements go wrong. Having realistic proposals for work may be necessary for an applicant to establish the bona fides of the proposed working holiday, but it cannot be a criterion on its own, as it was treated by the Appeal Tribunal in that case. But if it is thought that an applicant's intention is to take full-time employment, employment will not be incidental to an extended holiday and leave will be refused.[3] In *Ranasinghe*[4] a young Sri Lankan woman was refused an entry clearance as she was unable to put forward any coherent plans to visit any places in the UK during her stay. It was held that her wish to 'gain valuable experience of the hotel trade' was the dominant feature of her application. In *Vdofia*[5] the applicant failed because the real purpose was to assist her cousin with child care. In *Mulligan*[6] a Zimbabwean citizen was similarly refused permission to stay as a working holidaymaker on admitting that he could not find employment in his home country. It was held that this indicated that his primary objective would be to work in the UK rather than enjoy a holiday. On the other hand a working holidaymaker is not prevented by the Rules from taking periods of full-time employment during the course of the holiday.[7] As a general rule of thumb work incidental to a holiday means engaging in full-time work for 50 percent or less of the working holiday, although a working holidaymaker may engage in part-time work for over 50 percent of the holiday provided it is clear that he or she will have a holiday.[8] Ownership of a company may, in certain circumstances be permissible[9] but the Rules now expressly forbid a working holidaymaker to engage in business,[10] provide services as a professional sportsman or entertainer,[11] or pursue a career in the UK.[12] A working holidaymaker may engage in some part-time study and short periods of full-time study, but may not engage in full-time study for the whole of his or her stay.[13]

1 IDI Nov/00, Ch 4, s 2, Annex C, para 2.1.
2 [1987] Imm AR 13, CA. In *Acheampong* (18348) IAS 1999 Vol 2 No 6, the Immigration Appeal Tribunal came to the same conclusion notwithstanding that in HC 395, para 95 the word 'only' is omitted from the Rule. In *Singh (Surjit)* (14334) IAS 1997 Vol 3 No 16, the Immigration Appeal Tribunal said that under HC 395, para 97 intention to work is essential and *Bari* is no longer relevant.
3 *Gunatilake* [1975] Imm AR 23; *Munasinge* [1975] Imm AR 79.
4 (4395) unreported.
5 (10829) (1994) IDC, vol 1, No 2.
6 (6022) unreported.
7 *Clive-Lowe* [1992] Imm AR 91.
8 IDI Nov /00, Ch 4, Annex C, para 2.2.
9 IDI Nov/00, Ch 4, Annex C, para 2.2.
10 Temporary self-employment such as window cleaning or working from home as a hairdresser is permitted, but not any activity involving investment in premises, expensive equipment or employing staff, which would be regarded as setting up in business: IDI Nov/00, Ch 4, s 2, Annex C, para 2.4.
11 Amateurs may engage in sport or perform as entertainers for recreational purposes by joining a club, orchestra or theatre group, but professional or semi-professional sportspersons or entertainers intending to engage in such activity in the UK, even temporarily or ostensibly for no pay, should be refused and required to obtain a work permit: IDI Nov/00, Ch 4, s 2, Annex C, para 2.5.
12 HC 395, para 95(vi). The IDI (above) state that a working holidaymaker should not engage in work representing the continuation of his or her career here, and should not take up managerial positions or act as a locum hospital doctor, GP, solicitor or barrister. But temporary work in a profession such as supply teaching, agency nursing, or temporary work as an occupational therapist, physiotherapist, speech therapist or radiographer or locum vet is allowed: para 2.3.
13 IDI Nov/00, Ch 4, s 2, Annex C, para 2.6.

Funds

9.69 Although the Immigration Rules require the working holidaymaker to be able to meet the cost of onward or return travel and fulfil the maintenance and accommodation self-sufficiency rule, the IDI state that 'the requirement to have the means to pay for the return or onward journey should be flexibly applied' where it is reasonably likely that the necessary funds will be earned within the two years.[1] To satisfy the 'no public funds' criterion for entry, the instructions state that working holidaymakers should show they can support themselves for at least the first two months after arrival, or at least one month if they have a job arranged in advance.[2]

1   IDI Nov/00, Ch 4, s 2, Annex C, para 1.4.
2   IDI Nov/00, Ch 4, s 2, Annex C, para 1.4.

9.70 Working holidaymakers must be citizens of independent Commonwealth countries, British Overseas citizens, British Dependent Territories citizens or British Nationals (Overseas).[1] In the past, the Rule was used overwhelmingly by 'old' (ie white) Commonwealth citizens, but this is no longer the case. But, as we commented in the last edition of this work,[2] it is difficult to reconcile this Rule with the general rules for the admission of visitors, who are subject to an express prohibition on employment.

1   IDI Nov/00, Ch 4, s 2, Annex C, para 1.1.
2   9.68.

Chapter 10

COMMERCIAL IMMIGRATION LAW (EMPLOYMENT, BUSINESS, INVESTMENT AND INDEPENDENT MEANS)

INTRODUCTION

10.1 This chapter deals with admission for work and business purposes of non-EEA nationals, both Commonwealth and foreign. The law governing admission to the UK for employment by EEA nationals and their families is dealt with in chapter 7 above, as is the establishment of businesses by nationals of the Central and Eastern European countries with which the EU has concluded Association Agreements (although this is outlined here). This chapter is mostly, but not exclusively, about admission in categories leading to settlement; for business visitors, au pairs and working holidaymakers see chapter 9. In respect of each category, we explain whether an individual may switch in-country to the category concerned and we identify any provision regarding the admission of family members. Save in respect of the work permit scheme administered by the Department for Education and Employment, the question of appeals is dealt with in chapter 18, as the availability of appeal remedies is generally determined not by the category in which an application has been made (eg sole representative), but by the nature of the application (eg entry clearance; variation) and the immigration status of the individual (eg, present with leave; overstayer).

NON-WORK PERMIT EMPLOYEES

10.2 The main categories of non-work permit employment derived from both the Immigration Rules and Immigration Directorate Instructions (IDI) are:

- Seasonal farm workers
- Exchange teachers
- Overseas journalists and broadcasters
- Sole representatives
- Private servants in diplomatic households
- Domestic workers concession
- Overseas government employees
- Ministers of religion, missionaries and members of religious orders
- Operational ground staff of overseas airlines
- Commonwealth citizens with grandparental connections
- Crew members.

Generally, these categories used to be described as the 'permit-free' categories[1] (meaning free of the need to obtain a work permit). Until 1985 the so-called permit-free categories used to include doctors and dentists coming to the UK to work. Their status is now regulated by the work permit scheme, the business provisions of the Immigration Rules and provisions relating to doctors and dentists in training. The term 'permit-free' was abandoned in the current Immigration Rules[2] and in this text the categories concerned are referred to as non-work permit categories, simply to distinguish them as categories involving the immigration authorities alone, *not* the Department for Education and Employment. Foreign nationals coming for non-work permit employment will normally be admitted subject to a condition requiring registration with the police unless they are ministers of religion, missionaries, members of religious orders or private servants in diplomatic households or their employment is for less than six months.[3] In all cases such persons need entry clearance in the appropriate category prior to arrival in the UK. Generally, switching is not allowed into these categories,[4] although there are exceptions and the Home Office is becoming more flexible in practice and so reference should be made to the specific categories discussed below. Persons in these capacities may be accompanied by their spouse or unmarried partner and children,[5] and these dependants will qualify for indefinite leave to remain at the same time as the principal.[6] There are no restrictions on the spouse or children taking employment.

1   HC 251, paras 38–40.
2   HC 395, paras 136–199.
3   HC 395, para 325(i).
4   HC 395, paras 139(i), 147(i), 155(i), 164(i), 173 (i), 181(i).
5   HC 395, paras 194-199, 295J-K, inserted by Cm 4851.
6   HC 395, paras 287, 295G, 298.

Seasonal farm work

10.3 There is a scheme whereby full-time students aged 18 to 25 come to do seasonal work at agricultural camps in the UK.[1] The idea is that they combine farm work with a short visit.[2] Leave is granted with a condition restricting the freedom to take employment for a period not exceeding three months,[3] but extensions may be granted up to a total of six months if further farm work is available.[4] When they first arrive, seasonal farm workers must have a Home Office work card issued by the operator of a government-approved scheme.[5] This category is strictly seasonal and no leave extension is granted beyond

30 November in any year.[6] Students on the scheme can stay on as visitors but cannot switch to any other category,[7] and they may only be admitted if they intend neither to take employment on any other terms nor to stay in the UK at the end of their leave.[8] Non-students may only enter under the scheme if returning at the specific invitation of the farmer. Persons entering in this capacity must be able to maintain and accommodate themselves and any dependants without recourse to public funds.[9] Other students wishing to undertake farm work may obtain permission to work pursuant to the provisions of the training and work experience scheme (TWES), although this is an application which should be made by an employer when the proposed worker is not in the UK or Republic of Ireland.[10] Seasonal farm workers cannot bring with them their spouses or children. If the latter wish to come to the UK at the same time, they must qualify in their own right.

1 HC 395, paras 104–109.
2 Under HC 395, para 44 any period spent in farm work is to be counted as a visit. Thus if four months is spent in farm work, up to two can be spent as a tourist.
3 HC 395, para 105.
4 HC 395, paras 107–108.
5 HC 395, para 104(ii).
6 HC 395, para 105.
7 HC 395, para 104(iii) and (iv).
8 For variation to self-employment under the Association Agreements see *Milenkov* TH/7018/99 and *Barkoci and Malik* C-257/99, **10.93** fn 3 below. See further (1999) 1 IIEL p 4.
9 HC 395, para 104(v).
10 *Department for Education and Employment* leaflet WP2, para 35: see **10.60** below.

Exchange teachers

10.4 Ordinarily, teachers from abroad who are suitably qualified may only come to this country for full-time employment by obtaining a work permit. However, teachers and language assistants can come to the UK for up to two years on a number of different exchange schemes without work permits.[1] This category is steadily becoming redundant as the criteria for a full work permit for teachers are relaxed. Exchange teachers and language assistants must have prior entry clearance[2] and must be coming to a school or educational establishment in the UK under an exchange scheme approved by the Department for Education and Employment or administered by the Central Bureau for Educational Visits and Exchanges[3] or the League for the Exchange of Commonwealth Teachers.[4] They must be prepared to leave the UK at the end of the exchange period,[5] not to take employment except in the terms of this exchange scheme and be able to maintain and accommodate themselves and any dependants without recourse to public funds.[6] Normally leave is given for an initial previous 12 months,[7] and further extensions can be obtained provided this does not mean that the teacher remains in the UK for more than two years from the date when he or she was first given leave to enter.[8] The Immigration Rules provide that only those who enter the UK with a valid work permit may obtain an extension of stay to seek or take work permit employment.[9] This means that exchange teachers cannot normally switch to ordinary employment. However, the Department currently considers teaching to be a shortage occupation and so the Home Office will exceptionally consider in-country applications to switch to work permit status on a case-by-case basis (such consideration is given where an individual with specialised skills has been offered employment and a work permit will be issued on the grounds of acute national shortage of suitably qualified people).[10] Exchange teachers may be accompanied by spouses and children under 18.[11] There are no restrictions on the family members taking employment during the exchange period.

1 HC 395, paras 110–115.
2 HC 395, paras 110(v) and 122.
3 So described in the Immigration Rules (para 110(i)), but now called 'The Central Bureau for International Education and Training' (tel 020 7389 4004).
4 HC 395, para 110(i).
5 HC 395, para 110(ii) and (iii).
6 HC 395, para 110(iv).
7 HC 395, para 111.
8 HC 395, para 113(v).
9 HC 395, para 131 (i).
10 Letter from Home Office to Paul Simon and Co, 30 June 2000.
11 HC 395, paras 122-127. See **10.31** below.

Overseas journalists and broadcasters

10.5 Representatives of overseas newspapers, news agencies and broadcasting organisations on long-term assignment to the UK may qualify for an immigration status as such, and so will not require a work permit. But they must have been engaged by their organisation outside the UK before being posted here, intend to work full-time for the organisation and not to take any other kind of employment, and be able to satisfy the maintenance and accommodation provisions of the Immigration Rules.[1] According to the Home Office the term 'newspaper' is intended to cover not only daily newspapers but also other periodical publications concerned directly with news gathering and reporting.[2] Representatives of some overseas journals or magazines may, therefore, qualify for admission under these arrangements, but others will require work permits if they work for journals which are not directly concerned with news gathering and reporting. Employees other than journalists may be considered under this rule (for example, producers, news cameramen and front-of-camera personnel); secretaries and other administrative staff, however, need work permits.[3] At all times, the newspaper or broadcasting organisation must remain an 'overseas' organisation.[4] This is very much a question of fact. Although a newspaper or broadcasting organisation has its main office overseas, it may cease to be an 'overseas' organisation by having a branch or subsidiary in the UK if the UK activities mean that there is no real presence overseas. A journalist or broadcaster who does not qualify under this rule may qualify in the sole representative category if he or she is in fact the only representative.[5] Alternatively, if there is doubt whether the organisation is an 'overseas' one (because it already has a branch or a subsidiary here), it may be possible to apply for a work permit.

1 HC 395, paras 136–139.
2 Letter dated 9 April 1986 from the Home Office, printed in INLP 1(3) (October 1986).
3 IDI Nov/00, Ch 5, s 2, para 1.
4 HC 395, paras 136–143.
5 See **10.7** below.

10.6 Entry clearance is a mandatory requirement and admission is usually for up to 12 months initially.[1] Journalists and others admitted under this rule qualify for an extension of leave if they are still in the same employment for which they were admitted and their employer certifies that they are still required for the employment in question.[2] Normally the extension will be for three years, if the employer so certifies.[3] After four years they will qualify for settlement and removal of all restrictions.[4]

1   HC 395, para 136(v).
2   HC 395, para 139.
3   HC 395, para 140.
4   HC 395, para 142.

Sole representatives

10.7 Representatives of overseas firms which have no branch, subsidiary or other representative in the UK and have their headquarters and principal place of business outside the UK may qualify for an immigration status as such, and so will not require a work permit. They will need to demonstrate that they have been recruited and taken on as employees outside the UK; are senior employees with full authority to take operational decisions and can set up and operate a registered branch or wholly-owned subsidiary; will be employed full-time as sole representatives; do not intend to take employment except within the terms of the requirements for leave to enter as sole representatives; are not majority shareholders in the overseas firm; and can satisfy the maintenance and accommodation provisions of the Immigration Rules.[1]

1   HC 395, para 144.

10.8 Although entry clearance is mandatory,[1] one of the advantages of sole representative status is that there is no obligation on the entry clearance officer to refer the case to the Home Office, and very often the entry clearance officer will be prepared to deal with an applicant on the spot unless he or she has a complicated immigration history or the case raises difficult and unresolved legal points.[2] In practice, the rule is interpreted flexibly by entry clearance officers and the Home Office. It should be plain that the purpose of the application is the commercial benefit of the overseas business (which may be a sole trader, firm or company),[3] rather than the immigration convenience of the applicant. There must be an operating overseas business in existence, which must remain centred abroad. An employee of a 'brass plate' business will be regarded not as a sole representative but as someone coming to set up in business.[4] Moreover, the application will fail if an overseas business is a one-person business and there will be no one left to run it when the applicant arrives in the UK. The overseas business needs to be an active trading concern overseas apart from its proposed activities in the UK,[5] and a business which has been trading for less than 12 months will be required to justify the need to establish an overseas presence in the UK.[6] But the fact that the UK entity is likely to flourish so vigorously that it might eventually overshadow its parent does not mean that the application will fail.

1   HC 395, paras 144(vii) and 145.
2   Diplomatic Service Procedure Manual.
3   In the case of *Gurung* (TH/7895/98) it was held by an adjudicator that the overseas business is not limited to businesses in the form of companies as the Home Office had argued. The Home Office appears to accept this in practice.

4   *Certilan* (4689).
5   *R v Immigration Appeal Tribunal, ex p Lokko* [1990] Imm AR 539, QBD affirming the Immigration Appeal Tribunal decision at [1990] Imm AR 111.
6   IDI Nov/00, Ch 5, s 3, Annex J, para 1.

10.9 The position of sole representatives who are owners of the overseas business either as shareholders or partners has always caused problems. If they own or partly own the overseas business, they may be considered as business persons seeking to expand their own business, unless they can show that they do not have a majority shareholding in the company or a majority share of the partnership. In *Lokko*[1] the Tribunal said that in principle there was nothing wrong with a majority shareholder or director becoming an overseas representative. However, majority shareholders are now expressly barred from qualifying as sole representatives under the current Immigration Rules.[2] If they wish to come to the UK, they must either divest themselves of control, apply under the business rules or obtain a work permit. The Home Office view is that where an applicant owns more than 30 percent of the overseas business, the application should attract detailed scrutiny.[3] If it is evident that as well as owning a significant share, the applicant is also the driving force behind the overseas business, such that his or her presence in the UK is likely to mean that the centre of operations shifts to the UK, then the application will be refused.[4] However, there is now clear first-instance authority for the proposition that provided the applicant owns no more than 50 percent of the overseas business he or she will not be a majority shareholder.[5]

1   [1990] Imm AR 111, Immigration Appeal Tribunal.
2   HC 395, para 144(iv).
3   IDI Nov/00, Ch 5, s 3, Annex J, para 2.2.
4   IDI Nov/00, Ch 5, s 3, Annex J, para 2.2.
5   *Bakhsh v Entry Clearance Officer (Dubai)* (TH /7096/99); see also (2000) 3 IIEL 6.

10.10 An early Tribunal case ruled that a sole representative must have 'plenipotentiary' powers and not be a mere salesperson on commission.[1] The Immigration Rules now make it clear that sole representatives should be senior employees with full authority to take operational decisions, to set up and operate branches and subsidiaries and should be working full-time. Although sole representatives must have been recruited and taken on as employees outside the UK,[2] they do not have to have been employed by the overseas company for any minimum period. In practice, though, the Home Office prefers to see previous experience.[3] An applicant for entry clearance should be prepared to produce supporting documentation, including a contract of employment or letter of appointment, evidence that the overseas firm is functioning and trading, and an explanation why the firm wishes to appoint him or her and whether it has previously had a UK representative.[4] The application should make clear that decisions by the proposed sole representative generally will *not* have to be made with reference to the employer parent company. If the overseas business already has representation in the UK, the application should be to the Department for Education and Employment for a work permit rather than a sole representative application.

1   *Hope* (832) (14 September 1976). The current IDI indicate that a remuneration package including commission is acceptable provided the salary element satisfies the maintenance and accommodation requirements: IDI Nov/00, Ch 5, s 3, Annex J, para 2.
2   *Baydur* (5442); *Kongar* (5501); *Hope* (832).

3   IDI Nov/00, Ch 5, s 3, Annex J, para 2.
4   IDI Nov/00, Ch 5, s 3, Annex K.

10.11 Leave will be granted for 12 months in the first instance, and during that time the sole representative must establish a branch or subsidiary (unless it is an overseas firm which is incapable of registering a branch).[1] An extension of stay will now only be granted if the sole representative has set up a registered branch or wholly owned subsidiary and is in charge of it.[2] The other requirements of the on-entry rule must continue to be satisfied. An extension is for three years, and at the end of this time the employee will qualify for indefinite leave to remain if he or she has met the sole representative requirements throughout the four-year period and is still needed for the employment in question.[3] Employees brought in from overseas to work in the newly established branch or subsidiary will need a work permit; this in itself will not affect the individual's sole representative status. The Home Office takes the view that every overseas company setting up a branch in the UK must apply to register with Companies House within one month of having opened the branch, or that a subsidiary must be incorporated within that time.[4] The Tribunal has rejected this view, deciding that branch registration or incorporation of a subsidiary need only take place within the first 12 months, and that the Home Office cannot refuse to grant a further three years leave to remain because of a failure to act more promptly, provided the applicant has in fact been employed by the overseas business for the purpose of representing it within the UK and managed to register a branch or incorporate a subsidiary by the end of the initial 12 months.[5] The one-month registration requirement is imposed by company law and not by the Immigration Rules.[6]

1   See *Gurung* at **10.8** fn 3 above.
2   HC 395, para 147(iii).
3   HC 395, para 150. For a discussion of the continuity requirement in this and other work-related rules see **10.91** below.
4   IDI Nov/00, Ch 5, s 3, Annex J, para 1.1.
5   *Trivedi* TH/8202/98 (00 TH 01059).
6   Companies Act 1985, ss 690A, 691 and Sch 21A.

Private servants in diplomatic households

10.12 Domestic workers hired by consular and diplomatic staff and members of their family to work in their households may qualify as 'private servants in diplomatic households' under the Immigration Rules.[1] They may undertake the work of a chauffeur, gardener, cook or nanny if they are providing a personal service relating to the running of the employer's household.[2] Previously, diplomatic servants could be recruited from the age of 16; now the minimum age is 18.[3] A diplomatic household means the household of a member of staff of a diplomatic or consular mission, who enjoys diplomatic privileges and immunity within the meaning of the Vienna Convention, or a member of the family forming part of the household of such a person.[4] Under earlier rules employment could be part-time,[5] but now it must be full-time with no intention to work other than in this capacity.[6] To ensure that the maintenance and accommodation requirements of the Rules are met, the entry clearance officer will require the employer to sign a written undertaking to this effect. A separate bedroom must be provided. The employer must also complete and sign a statement of the main terms and conditions of the servant's employment.[7] The entry clearance officer will also interview the worker alone to ensure that he or she understands the terms or conditions, and if the application is successful will give him or her a leaflet (translated into several languages) explaining the worker's rights under UK law.[8] Initial leave is given for 12 months and extensions are given for 12 months at a time; after four years of continuous stay in this capacity, if the servant is still required for the employment in question, an application may be made for indefinite leave to remain, provided the relevant requirements have been met throughout the four-year period.[9] The Rules do not permit switching to this category,[10] though it is permissible for the servant of a diplomat to change diplomatic employers within the same Embassy. In those circumstances, the new employer will be required to sign a statement relating to the terms and conditions of the employment.[11]

1 HC 395, paras 152-159.
2 IDI Nov/00, Ch 5, s 4, para 1.1.
3 HC 395, para 152(i), replacing HC 251, para 40(a).
4 HC 395, para 152(ii).
5 *Gunaben* (3475).
6 HC 395, para 152(iv).
7 IDI Nov/00, Ch 5, s 4, Annex M, para 5.
8 IDI Nov/00, Ch 5, s 4, Annex M, para 5.
9 HC 395, paras 156 and 158.
10 HC 395, para 155.
11 IDI Nov/00, Ch 5, s 4, Annex M, para 8.3.

10.13 Private servants in diplomatic households are to be distinguished from members of the service staff of a diplomatic mission, as the latter are exempt from immigration control.[1] In practice the distinction is a difficult one to make, as we have already seen.[2] Although not exempt from control, private servants in diplomatic households may enjoy limited immunity under the Vienna Convention.[3]

1 Immigration Act 1971, s 8(3). See *Kandiah* (2699) unreported. A servant of the head of mission employed at the official residence is employed at the mission; see Diplomatic Privileges Act 1964, Sch 1, art 1(i).
2 See **6.46** above.
3 Diplomatic Privileges Act 1964, Sch 1, art 37(4); *Diaz* (2584).

Domestic worker concession

10.14 The rules regarding private servants in diplomatic households must also be distinguished from the concessionary arrangement outside the Immigration Rules,[1] whereby visitors (but not apparently those coming for other temporary purposes) or those coming in a category which will lead to settlement may bring their domestic staff with them to the UK.[2] Under this concession, domestic workers may be permitted entry with their employer,[2] provided they have worked for that employer for 12 months before arrival and will be undertaking specific work at a level exceeding basic International Labour Organisation standards.[3] Only those who are likely to undertake chauffeuring, gardening, cooking and nannying will benefit from the concession; mere washing, cleaning and ironing is no longer sufficient and the concession now requires a servant who is a nanny to have responsibility for a child's care and/or education, the housekeeper/butler to have responsibilities, which include a degree of budgeting or planning, the cook to have particular knowledge and experience of the family's entertaining or dietary needs and the carer to provide attention to a sick, elderly or disabled member of the family.[4] Prior entry clearance is required. Under the concession, the domestic worker must be aged between 18 and 65, must have worked for the employer as a paid employee for the qualifying period referred to above, must not intend to transfer to another employer, and must satisfy the usual maintenance and accommodation requirements. On application a statement of the main terms and conditions of the worker's employment must be produced, and the employer is required to read and understand a document entitled 'Notice to Employers' setting out not only the worker's conditions of stay, but also his or her legal rights in the UK. Domestic workers should be interviewed alone, at least on the first application, to ensure that they understand the terms and conditions and are willing to go to the UK. If the application is successful they will be given a leaflet explaining their rights under UK criminal and employment laws.[5] The worker will initially be given leave in line with the employer and, provided that the employer is in a category leading to settlement, will be able to apply for indefinite leave to remain at the same time as the employer.

1   The Home Office has said it will incorporate the concession into the Immigration Rules, but has not done so yet: see IDI Feb/00, Ch 5, s 12.
2   They may be admitted accompanying the employer, the employer's spouse or his or her minor children: IDI, Ch 5, s 12, Annex AA.
3   These are set out at IDI, Ch 5, s 12, Annex BB.
4   Letter from the Home Office to Bindman and Partners, 2 November 1998; IDI, Ch 5, s 12, Annex AA.
5   IDI, Ch 5, s 12, Annex AA.

10.15   The concession does not provide for individuals to switch in-country to the domestic workers category, but a worker who arrived under the concession may now transfer to another employer. Overstayers who fled their original employer but had initial entry clearance as a domestic worker were formerly permitted to regularise their position up to and including 23 October 1998.[1] The Home Office considers any applications not made within the regularisation deadline on a case-by-case basis.[2] The Home Office has stated that a domestic worker who was granted an initial 12 months' leave under the regularisation programme and subsequently applies for indefinite leave to remain may count his or her continuous domestic employment prior to the date of regularisation in the four-year qualifying period.[3] Where the worker has fled from a private household as a result of abuse or exploitation and has gone into other domestic work but not in a private household, that other work may count towards the four years needed for indefinite leave.

1   Home Office letter to Kingsley Napley, 27 October 1998 and 611 HC Official Report (6th series) written answers col *316*, 23 July 1998.
2   Letter from Home Office to CMS Cameron McKenna, 1 February 2000.
3   Home Office fax of 15 January 2001 to Winstanley-Burgess.

10.16   Employers who employ domestic workers in breach of their landing conditions may be liable to prosecution under section 8 of the Asylum and Immigration Act 1996 (if the employment commenced on or after 27 January 1997). However, the Home Office has indicated that despite the terms of the Act it was never envisaged that any action would be taken against an employer found to be employing a person illegally in his or her private household.[1]

1   Home Office letter to Kingsley Napley, 27 October 1998 and 316 HC Official Report (6th series) written answers, col *611*, 23 July 1998.

Overseas government employees

10.17 Overseas government employees are persons coming to the UK for employment by an overseas government or those employed by the UN or other international organisations of which the UK is a member,[1] but do not include diplomats, members of their service staff and others exempt from immigration control.[2] To obtain entry such employees must be able to produce either a valid entry clearance or satisfactory documentary evidence of their status as overseas government employees.[3] It must be their intention to work full-time and not to take employment in any other capacity, and they must be able to satisfy the maintenance and accommodation requirements of the Immigration Rules.[4] After 12 months, leave will be extended for a further three years if the employee is still in the same employment and the employer certifies that he or she is still needed.[5] If the same conditions are met after four years in the UK in this capacity, the employee qualifies for indefinite leave.[6] This group is also to be distinguished from private servants of diplomats.[7] The key here is that the employment contract should be with the overseas government and not the diplomat.

1 HC 395, para 160, IDI, Ch 5, s 5; IDI, Ch 14, Annex B.
2 See chapter 6 above. The IDI above also refers to governors, directors, alternates, officers and employees of the International Monetary Fund, the Commonwealth Secretariat, the International Bank for Reconstruction and Development, the International Development Agency and similar organisations as exempt from control.
3 HC 395, paras 161(i), 162 and 163.
4 HC 395, para 161(ii)-(iv).
5 HC 395, paras 164 and 165.
6 HC 395, para 167.
7 *Hussain* (5035); see **10.12** above.

Ministers of religion, missionaries and members of religious orders

10.18 Ministers, missionaries and members of religious orders may be admitted for up to 12 months in the first instance if they hold a current entry clearance.[1] Under earlier Rules, the definitions of 'ministers of religion' and so forth were left largely to the appellate authorities and courts. Now such definitions, and the particular qualifications for entry to the UK, are set out in the Immigration Rules and amplified by the IDI.

1 HC 395, paras 170(iv) and 171.

Minister of religion

10.19 A minister of religion is a religious functionary whose main regular duties comprise the leading of a congregation in performing the rites and rituals of the faith and in preaching the essentials of the creed.[1] To qualify for leave a minister must either have worked for at least one year as a minister of religion or (where ordination is prescribed by a religious faith as the sole means of entering the ministry) have been ordained as a minister following at least one year's full-time or two years' part-time training for the ministry.[2] Whether a person is a minister of religion will depend on the structure of the religion in question and the extent to which it is divided into a priesthood and laity, and on the facts of any particular case.[3] Although the criteria for ministry appear to be objective, there is clearly room for discretion, and the IDI make it clear that members of the Church of Scientology and the Church of Unification (the 'Moonies') do not qualify for admission as ministers of religion,[4] although members of the International Society for Krishna Consciousness and Christian Scientists may do.[5] The IDI set out five 'core duties' which a minister of religion will be expected to perform: leading worship; providing religious education for children and adults by preaching and teaching; officiating at marriages, funerals, etc; offering counselling and welfare support to members of the congregation; and recruiting, training and co-ordinating the work of local volunteers and lay preachers.[6] They also contain a long list of additional duties which the minister might or might not be expected to perform.[7]

1 HC 395, para 169(i).
2 HC 395, para 170(i)(a). An understanding of these definitions is assisted by reference to earlier Tribunal decisions, which held that ministers of religion could be defined either by their qualifications, eg ordination, or by their activities, eg leading prayers and responsibility for religious activity in the community: *Mobley* (5368); *Begum (Kalsoon)* [1988] Imm AR 325. Both these elements of the former definition are contained in the Immigration Rules.
3 *Begum (Kalsoon)* above; *Singh (Piara)* [1977] Imm AR 1; *Hamid* [1986] Imm AR 469. IDI Nov/00, Ch 5, s 6, Annex T contains a summary of the beliefs, structures, etc of the major religions.
4 988 HC Official Report (5th series) written answers, col 123 (Scientology); IDI Nov/00, Ch 5, s 6, para 1.
5 IDI Nov/00, Ch 5, s 6, Annex U. The Home Office holds detailed files on a number of religions, which are frequently updated to provide a database to determine whether an employer or applicant qualifies under the Immigration Rules.
6 IDI Nov/00, Ch 5, s 6, Annex Q.
7 IDI Nov/00, Ch 5, s 6, Annex S.

10.20 Whilst the Immigration Rules do not permit switching into this category, the Home Office exercises its discretion in certain circumstances to permit switching if a bona fide minister of religion has been granted a visit entry clearance or leave to enter specifically to attend an interview for a job in the UK as a minister of religion and gets the job.[1] In-country switching may also exceptionally be approved where the individual is granted entry clearance or leave to enter specifically as a *visiting* minister of religion on a preaching tour and is asked to fill a vacant post as a minister of religion in the UK whilst here, and there are good community relations reasons to permit switching.[2]

1 IDI Nov/00, Ch 5, s 6, Annex Q, para 6.
2 IDI Nov/00, Ch 5, s 6, Annex Q, para 6.

Missionaries

10.21 Missionaries are persons who are directly engaged in spreading a religious doctrine and whose work is not in essence administrative or clerical.[1] To obtain entry as a missionary the person must have trained as a missionary or have worked as one and must be sent to the UK by an overseas organisation.[2] In *Begum (Kalsoon)*[3] the Tribunal held that it was wrong to treat the applicant as a 'missionary' bearing in mind that she was seeking to work with committed Muslims rather than preach to prospective converts. On the other hand, a missionary is not restricted to a person engaged full-time in evangelical preaching or counselling, as the Tribunal decision in *Mobley*[4] indicates. There, the applicant wanted to work at the UK-based training centre of a Christian training and missionary society which operated in many countries. She was held to be a missionary even though her duties at the centre involved bookkeeping for 37 hours a week for the international office and 23 hours a week in evangelistic meetings, local church involvement, counselling, bible study and prayer meetings. Under the current Immigration Rules the main question of fact in such a case will be whether the bookkeeping duties make the work essentially administrative or clerical. The IDI give further definition to this rule and state that the duties of a missionary may include the organisation of missionary activity. Working full-time as a teacher in a school run by a Church or missionary organisation would not count as missionary work, but translating the Bible is missionary and not clerical work.[5] Thus a missionary may be doing field work but could be supervising staff and/or co-ordinating the organisation of ministry work or be in charge of a particular activity such as accounts/finance, personnel management or information technology. Those in support posts (clerical, secretarial, etc) should not be considered missionaries unless a substantial amount of time is spent in the UK in active field work. The IDI set out a number of organisations whose staff could be treated as missionaries.[6] Whilst the Rules do not permit switching into this category, the Home Office exercises its discretion in certain circumstances to permit visitors and students to remain as missionaries, but only where a general concession has been agreed with the Home Office on a religion-by-religion basis.[7]

1 HC 395, para 169(ii).
2 HC 395, para 170(i)(b).
3 [1988] Imm AR 325.
4 *Mobley* (5368).
5 IDI Nov/00, Ch 5, s 6, Annex Q, para 7.
6 IDI Nov/00, Ch 5, s 6, Annex U. Mormons, those working with Operation Mobilisation and with St Stephen's Society may be treated as missionaries.
7 IDI Nov/00, Ch 5, s 6, Annex Q, para 9; IDI Nov/00, Ch 5, s 6, Annex U.

Members of a religious order

10.22 Members of a religious order are persons who are coming to live in a community run by that order.[1] To qualify for admission they must be coming to live in a community maintained by the religious order of which they are members, and, if intending to teach, do not intend to do so save at an establishment maintained by their order.[2] According to the Tribunal in *Hamid*,[3] approved in *Begum (Kalsoon)*,[4] a 'religious order' is a monastic order defined in the *codex juris canonici* (canon 487) as a 'stable mode of living in community in which the faithful bind themselves by vow to observe in addition to the precepts of the rule, the evangelical counsels of obedience, chastity and poverty'. The Tribunal believed this definition to be unduly narrow, but made it clear that the term could not extend to persons not in such an order who were simply fulfilling the role of a spiritual guide to a lay congregation. In practice this category is restricted to members of monastic communities, monks and nuns (usually Christian or Buddhist) and similar religious communities involving a permanent commitment.[5] Whilst most of the work undertaken by the member will be within the community itself, the Home Office accepts that some members may undertake outside work directed by their order which will permit teaching within their schools. Teaching in schools not maintained by the order will require a work permit. Novices whose training consists of taking part in the daily community life of an order should be treated as members of a religious order, although anyone taking on a formal course of study in a non-community maintained academic institution will be treated as a student.[6] Whilst the Immigration Rules do not permit switching into this category, the Home Office exercises its discretion in certain circumstances to permit switching exceptionally if the applicant entered the UK to visit or study under the auspices of the order and clearly meets the other requirements of the Rules.[7]

1   HC 395, para 169(iii).
2   HC 395, para 170(i)(c).
3   [1986] Imm AR 469.
4   [1988] Imm AR 325.
5   IDI Nov/00, Ch 5, s 6, Annex Q, para 10. This includes organisations such as the Bruderhof communities in the UK: Annex U.
6   IDI Nov/00, Ch 5, s 6, Annex Q, para 11.
7   IDI Nov/00, Ch 5, s 6, Annex Q, para 12.

Generally applicable requirements

10.23 Admission will only be given to ministers, missionaries and members of religious orders if they are coming to work full-time in their chosen calling,[1] do not intend to take employment other than in that calling,[2] and can maintain and accommodate themselves and any dependants without recourse to public funds.[3] Under the Immigration Rules employment must be full-time, but it is not the task of the entry clearance officer to consider whether the primary purpose of admission is to follow the particular religious calling, as was once held by the Tribunal.[4] But entry clearance officers may have to take into account the general public good,[5] insofar as it may be affected by the existence of a general prohibition such as the one which applies to Scientologists and Moonies, or by the capacity of the religious work of the applicant to stir up inter-communal hatred, lead to public disorder or incite violence.

1   HC 395, para 170(ii).
2   HC 395, para 170(iii).
3   HC 395, para 170(iv).
4   *Singh (Piara)* [1977] Imm AR 1.
5   See HC 395, para 320(19).

10.24 Normally, ministers of religion are admitted for an initial period of 12 months (unless they are here merely for a short mission).[1] At the end of this period extensions are usually for three years to continue their duties.[2] But they must obtain from the leadership of their congregation, their employer or the head of their religious order a certificate that their services are still required.[3] Thereafter they may apply for indefinite leave and removal of all restrictions on their stay.[4] They will need a further certificate that their services are still required.[5]

1   HC 395, para 171.
2   HC 395, para 174.
3   HC 395, para 173(iii).
4   HC 395, para 176.
5   HC 395, para 176(iii).

Concessionary arrangements

10.25 Various concessionary arrangements exist in relation to visiting preachers coming to the UK on a preaching tour, provided the visit is a temporary absence from permanent employment abroad and does not amount to disguised employment as a minister of religion in the UK. Religious musicians may be admitted without a work permit to perform at religious services in the UK.[1] Both these groups will be admitted as visitors for up to six months. Volunteers working for religious organisations are treated like any other charity worker; that is to say, they may be admitted in accordance with a concession which provides that the work must be for a listed[2] or registered charity, the work must be unpaid (save for board, accommodation and pocket money)[3] and directed towards a worthy cause closely related to the aims of the charity, and must be field work involving direct assistance to those the charity has been established to help. If the work is purely manual, clerical or secretarial it will not qualify under the concession.[4]

1   IDI Apr/01, Ch 17, s 3 (religious musicians).
2   In IDI Apr/01, Ch 17, s 3, s 9, Annex B.
3   Currently £35.00 per week: IDI Apr/01, Ch 17, s 9.
4   IDI Apr/01, Ch 17, s 9, Annex C.

Operational ground staff of overseas airlines

10.26   The provisions of the Immigration Rules allowing overseas airlines to send operational ground staff to the UK are first, that there must be a transfer to the UK to take up duties at an international airport as a station manager, security manager or technical manager.[1] Staff who are posted to work outside an airport are excluded, as are airport-based staff such as catering officers. These do not come within the category and will need a work permit.[2] The other conditions applying to operational ground staff of overseas airlines are that the individual must have an intention to work full-time for the airline concerned and not to take employment except within the terms of the requirements for leave to enter under this category; must satisfy a maintenance and accommodation requirement; and must hold a valid entry clearance.[3] Initial leave is normally for 12 months followed by a three-year extension and indefinite leave after four years, provided the employer certifies at each stage that the person is still required for the employment in question.[4]

1   HC 395, para 178(i).
2   See *Attivor v Secretary of State for the Home Department* [1988] Imm AR 109, CA; IDI, Ch 5, s 7.
3   HC 395, para 178(ii)-(iv).
4   HC 395, paras 179-185.

Non-work permit categories outside the Immigration Rules

10.27   There are a number of other categories of persons who may be admitted for work without a work permit, which are listed in the IDI.[1] Most are temporary, such as research assistants to MPs (who are normally overseas students learning about government and politics before resuming studies or entering a career),[2] sportspersons,[3] entertainers,[4] film actors, producers, directors and technicians on location,[5] off-shore workers,[6] overseas insurance company representatives,[7] workers for the Jewish Agency[8] and certain exchange and placement students.[9] Workers qualified in Rudolf Steiner educational methods coming to work at Camphill communities may be admitted with a view to settlement.[10]

1 Currently IDI Dec/00, Ch 17.
2 IDI Dec/00, Ch 17, s 6. They must satisfy the maintenance and accommodation requirement, with reasonable expenses from the UK source. They may be granted up to 12 months' leave.
3 IDI Dec/00, Ch 17, s 8. The IDI are fairly complicated. A permit-free concession enables professional or amateur sportspersons to enter for sporting events such as tournaments and championships for up to six months, provided they satisfy the maintenance and accommodation requirements and can meet the cost of the onward or return journey. Polo grooms and personal coaches may be admitted with them for the same period. But sportspersons need work permits if they are based in the UK for a whole season or are coming to join a British professional team or to give regular coaching, or for over six months.
4 IDI Dec/00, Ch 17, s 3. Those coming for specific types of events, including charity concerts, arts festivals and religious occasions may be admitted under the concession, provided they pose no threat to the domestic labour force, are not using the engagement to establish themselves here and do not intend to remain for more than six months.
5 IDI Dec/00, Ch 17, s 3, para 12.
6 IDI Dec/00, Ch 17, s 4. Entry clearance is not mandatory and no work permit is required if no part of the work is on-shore. Switching is permitted but settlement should normally be refused.
7 IDI Dec/00, Ch 17, s 5.1. The processing of the policy must take place overseas. Leave may be granted for 12 months at a time up to three years.
8 IDI Dec/00, Ch 17, s 5.2. Leave may be granted for a maximum of 12 months.
9 IDI Dec/00, Ch 17, s 5.3 (International Association for Exchange of Students of Technical Experience): placements of up to three months with UK companies and local authorities; British Universities North America Club (BUNAC) (IDI Dec/00, Ch 17, s 1): see chapter 9 above.
10 IDI Dec/00, Ch 17, s 7. A list of establishments is given at Annex A. No work permit or entry clearance is required, but there is no switching into this category. Leave is granted for 12 months at a time.

Crew members

10.28 Leave to enter may be given to crew members of ships, aircraft, hovercraft, hydrofoils or international train services to enable them to join their vessel, for hospital treatment, repatriation or transfer to another vessel, and so forth,[1] if the crew members concerned are not eligible for entry without leave.[2] The period of leave given will only be sufficient for the specific purpose and there is a presumption against extension,[3] unless the crew member is married to a person present and settled in the UK and meets the requirements for an extension of stay as a spouse under the Immigration Rules.

1 IDI, Ch 16, ss 1 and 2.
2 See chapter 6 above.
3 IDI, Ch 16, ss 1 and 2.

Persons with UK ancestry

10.29 A Commonwealth citizen, one of whose grandparents was born in the UK, may come to the UK for the purpose of living and working here.[1] Upon proof that one of his or her grandparents was born in the UK,[2] a Commonwealth citizen aged 17 or over who wishes to seek or take employment[3] in the UK and can satisfy the maintenance and accommodation requirements will be granted an entry clearance for that purpose. On arrival, such a person should be admitted for a period of four years.[4] There is no need to have a specific job to come to.

An intention to seek employment and the ability to perform it[5] may suffice.[6] To prove UK ancestry it will usually be necessary to obtain a certified copy of the grandparent's birth certificate and all necessary marriage and birth certificates to show the connection.[7] An adoptive relationship qualifies under the rule.[8] The word 'grandparents' in HC 395, paragraph 186 refers to both maternal and paternal grandparents. The Immigration Rules expressly provide that the 'parent' of an illegitimate child is not just the mother but includes the father where he is proved to be the father,[9] reversing Tribunal and Court of Appeal authority to the contrary.[10]

1 HC 395, paras 186–193.
2 Or the Channel Islands, the Isle of Man or (before 31 March 1922) the Republic of Ireland.
3 Employment embraces self-employment: HC 395, para 6.
4 HC 395, para 187.
5 Ability in terms of health: IDI, Ch 5, s 8, para 3.
6 Entry clearance officers may require evidence of employment opportunities to ensure that employment is genuinely being sought: IDI, Ch 5, s 8, para 3.
7 The word 'usually' permits an entry clearance officer to accept alternate evidence of the grandparent's birth in the UK, such as a baptismal certificate or other official records.
8 IDI, Ch 5, s 8, para 3.3.
9 HC 395, para 6.
10 *C (an infant)* [1976] Imm AR 165, Immigration Appeal Tribunal; *R v Secretary of State for the Home Department, ex p Crew* [1982] Imm AR 94, CA.

10.30 Earlier rules provided for immediate settlement on arrival, but now a continuous period of four years in the UK in this capacity is required.[1] Continuous employment is not required, but a Commonwealth citizen with a poor or non-existent employment record is likely to be refused indefinite leave in the absence of a good reason.[2] The Home Office will wish to see evidence of the current employment position and an employer's confirmation that current employment will continue. If the Commonwealth citizen is not employed at the time of the application, evidence will be requested of the employment record throughout the four years and of attempts to find employment. There is no bar on in-country switching to this category.[3]

1 HC 395, para 192.
2 IDI, Ch 5, s 8, para 4.3.
3 HC 395, para 190.

Family members

10.31 Spouses, unmarried partners and children under 18, but no other dependants, can accompany or join a principal in any of the above categories except seasonal farm workers, domestic workers under the concession and crew members coming to the UK. The requirements for spouses and children are that:

* the couple intend to cohabit during their stay and the marriage is subsisting;
* the spouse and children do not intend to stay beyond any period given to the non-work permit employee;
* the maintenance and accommodation provisions of HC 395, paragraph 194 are fulfilled; and
* the spouse and children have entry clearance.[1]

Unmarried partners additionally must show that any previous marriage or relationship has broken down; that they are legally unable to marry the worker (other than for reasons of consanguineity, relationship or age); and that a relationship akin to marriage has lasted for two years.[2] A child is not to be admitted to join a principal if the worker's spouse or partner is not also admitted, unless that person is deceased, or the worker has had sole responsibility for the child's upbringing, or there are serious and compelling family or other considerations making exclusion undesirable, and suitable arrangements have been made for the child's care.[3] Children who have married, have formed an independent family unit or lead an independent life will not be admitted. Spouses, partners and children are usually free to take any employment without any need for Home Office or Department for Education and Employment approval. Persons here in a temporary capacity may not switch to family member of a non-work permit holder in the absence of exceptional compassionate circumstances, but the no-switching rule may be waived for dependants of those with UK ancestry.[4] Extensions and indefinite leave to remain are normally given to family members routinely if given to the principal.[5] No provision is made for seasonal farm workers, domestic workers and crew members to bring to the UK or be joined by any family member.

1   HC 395, paras 194 and 197 (paras 122-127 regarding exchange teachers).
2   HC 395, para 295J(ii)–(iv), inserted by Cm 4851.
3   HC 395, para 197(vi).
4   IDI, Ch 5, s 9, para 2.2.
5   HC 395, paras 195, 198, 295K, 295A.

WORK PERMIT EMPLOYEES

Work permit origins and the different types of permit currently available

10.32 Prior to the Immigration Act 1971, work permits were issued only to foreign nationals (then known as aliens). Commonwealth citizens were issued employment vouchers, which gave them a right to immediate settlement. Under the 1971 Act the work permit regime was applied to Commonwealth citizens and foreign nationals alike. The current scheme came into force on 1 January 1980. Since then a number of administrative changes have taken place, but its central purpose has been to strike a balance between enabling employers to recruit or transfer skilled people from abroad and protecting job opportunities for resident workers.[1] The scheme applies to England, Wales and Scotland. It is operated by the Work Permits (UK) (formerly the Overseas Labour Section) of the Department for Education and Employment. Northern Ireland, the Channel Islands and the Isle of Man have a similar scheme designed to protect resident workers; details of those schemes can be obtained by contacting the relevant government departments in those places.

1   WP1 (notes) introductory note. For the current version see the Work Permits (UK) website at www.workpermits.gov.uk. The full set of application forms, guidance notes and other documents are as follows: guidance on applications for work permits (general); application forms and guidance notes WP1 (business and commercial); WP2 (training and work experience scheme); WPSI (student internship); WP3 (sportspeople and entertainers). The guidance notes are in English, Welsh, Bengali, Chinese, Gujarati, Hindi, Punjabi and Urdu. The guidance notes describe detailed criteria for eligibility and set out how to apply (some applications can be made by e-mail) and what evidence to supply.

10.33   The work permit scheme is divided into two distinct sections:

A: The main work permit scheme. This is sub-divided into a number of sections:

(i)   Business and commercial
  (a)   first tier
    •   Intra-company transfers (this used to include a sub-category, not leading to settlement, called 'career development')
    •   board-level positions
    •   inward investment positions
    •   shortage occupation positions
  (b)   second tier
    •   all other applications (this used to include a sub-category, not leading to settlement, called 'key workers')
(ii)   Sportspersons and entertainers

B: The training and work experience scheme

The training part of the training and work experience scheme has already been transferred to the main part of the scheme, although it is still possible to make such an application provided the training is supernumerary: see below.

Discretionary basis of the work permit scheme

10.34   The work permit scheme is a manifestation of policy, similar to Home Office concessions outside the Immigration Rules.[1] This appreciation gives an insight into the sort of judicial challenges to which decisions under the scheme may be prone. Although there are references to work permits in the Immigration Acts, the work permit scheme is a creature of pure policy rather than statute. The Immigration Act 1971 and the Immigration and Asylum Act 1999 both define 'work permit'[2] as:

> 'a permit indicating, in accordance with the immigration rules, that a person named in it is eligible, though not a British citizen,[3] for entry into the United Kingdom for the purpose of taking employment.'

However, neither statute provides a power to establish a work permit scheme or stipulates how the scheme is to operate. The Immigration Rules (HC 395) include a work permit category[4] and a training and work experience scheme category[5] but are similarly silent as to the legal basis for issuing permits and the operational criteria applied. They provide only that holding a valid Department for Education and Employment work permit or training and work experience scheme permit is a requirement for leave to enter for employment or training or work experience, as the case may be.[6] Thus the scheme envisaged by the statute and the Rules is for the Department for Education and Employment to devise, so as to identify those who may work here even though they are subject to immigration control.[7] The schemes that have been devised accordingly comprise pure policy and customarily are notified as guidance notes accompanying the various application forms. Those guidance notes are supplemented by the Work Permits (UK) website, *ad hoc* or seasonal statements of arrangements regarding particular sorts of permit, government evidence to parliamentary proceedings and Work Permits (UK) policy letters. The predominant policy on which the scheme is based is set out clearly at the start of the guidance notes:

> 'The work permit arrangements allow employers based in Great Britain to employ people who are . . . not entitled to work in this country . . . *We aim to strike the right balance between enabling employers to recruit or transfer skilled people from abroad and protecting job opportunities for resident workers.*' (emphasis supplied.)

1 Like concessions, the work permit scheme does not have the strong statutory endorsement of the Immigration Rules generally (Immigration Act 1971, s 3(2)), or for the purposes of an appeal (Immigration and Asylum Act 1999, Sch 4, para 21(1)).
2 See Immigration Act 1971, s 33(1); Immigration and Asylum Act 1999, s 167(2).
3 To be construed as including a reference to anyone with the right of abode in the UK: Immigration Act 1971, s 2(2), as amended by the British Nationality Act 1981, s 39(2) and Immigration Act 1988, s 3(3).
4 HC 395, paras 128-135.
5 HC 395, paras 116-121.
6 HC 395, paras 128(i) and 116(i) respectively.
7 Although possession of a work permit is not conclusive of eligibility to enter: see **10.54** below.

Judicial challenges[1]

10.35 A work permit scheme comprising a complex of policies notified primarily by guidance notes is not *per se* unlawful. However, in certain cases there may be scope for a public law challenge to the way in which a particular policy is applied, a refusal to depart from that policy or even to the legality of the policy itself.

1 See also 'Appealing or reviewing a work permit refusal' at **10.56** below for the limited applicability to Work Permits (UK) refusals of statutory immigration appeal rights and for the system of internal Work Permits (UK) reviews.

10.36 Successful challenges to the legality of a policy are rare but possible; see, for example, *R v Immigration Appeal Tribunal, ex p Manshoora Begum*[1] where a provision of the Immigration Rules was struck down for illegality. There does not appear to be a reported case of a successful challenge to the legality of a provision of the work permit scheme, but that is not to say there has not been the scope for such a challenge. Arguably, for example, a policy to issue seasonal permits rather than back-to-back permits could be challenged if it were to prevent an ordinarily resident worker from ever being in the UK for a 'continuous' period of four years for the purposes of the settlement provisions of the Immigration Rules. There have been several successful challenges to the way in which the Department for Education and Employment has applied its stated policies in a particular case. In *Ex p Ying Fu Chan*[2] Harrison J found the Department had failed to apply its own policy because no account had been taken of experience gained in the UK, even though the relevant guidance notes did not require all such experience to be discounted. In *Ex p Portsmouth FC*[3] McCullough J found, *inter alia*, that the Department ought to have taken into account that but for injury a footballer would have been selected to play in 75 percent of his country's competitive matches.

1 [1986] Imm AR 385 QBD.
2 *R v Secretary of State for Education and Employment, Secretary of State for the Home Department, ex p Ying Fu Chan* (CO/4079/97) 25 March 1999.
3 *R v Secretary of State for Education and Employment, ex p Portsmouth Football Club Ltd* [1998] COD 142.

10.37 Just as the Secretary of State for the Home Department may treat a person more (but not less) favourably than the Immigration Rules or a concession require, so too the Secretary of State for Education and Employment may relax the terms of the work permit scheme. The refusal to depart from policy in such a way may be challenged, for example on grounds of unreasonableness, but such challenges are difficult to sustain. In *Ex p Kwok Shun Yee*[1] it was argued that although, contrary to overseas labour section requirements, no references were available to confirm a chef's expertise, that expertise could easily be confirmed by an examination board. Jowitt J found that:

> 'the Overseas Labour Service has a wide margin of appreciation within *Wednesbury* principles as to whether or not it regards the examination board approach as an acceptable way of demonstrating that Mr Kwok meets the requirements of a key worker and it does not seem to me that it can be faulted in the conclusion that it has reached'.

Overall, there are few work permit judicial reviews relative to the number of immigration judicial reviews, though this may be more a reflection of the reluctance of employers to litigate than of near-perfect Work Permits (UK) legality in formulating and applying its policies and administering the work permit scheme generally.

1   *R v Secretary of State for the Home Department, ex p Kwok Shun Yee* (CO/95/97) 25 June 1998.

Where no work permit is required

10.38 Not all persons who are subject to immigration control need a work permit or Department for Education and Employment approval in order to be able to work lawfully. First, as we have seen, there are those who come to the UK for non-work permit employment. Secondly, there are those who in law cannot be made subject to any condition restricting or prohibiting their employment. These include persons with indefinite leave to enter or remain,[1] EEA nationals exercising free movement rights,[2] some persons arriving in the UK on a local journey from another part of the common travel area[3] and those exempted from immigration control.[4] Thirdly, there are those who under the Immigration Rules are given leave to enter without any condition restricting or prohibiting employment. This category can be altered at any time by changing the Rules. They consist of spouses and dependent children under 18 of the following categories of entrant: students given leave to enter for 12 months or longer;[5] teachers on exchange schemes and trainees;[6] work permit holders and persons in non-work permit employment, including Commonwealth citizens with a grandparent born in the UK;[7] and persons establishing themselves in business, investors, writers, composers and artists.[8] Fourthly, there are those allowed to enter under various concessions outside the Immigration Rules, such as domestic workers accompanying their employers to the UK and charitable volunteers. Fifthly, there are individuals who have claimed to be treated as refugees and have been granted permission to work, refugees and those given exceptional leave to remain. None of these people requires a work permit, although often the only way to prove this to an employer is by production of a passport[9] and applying a detailed knowledge of the Immigration Rules and law.

1   Immigration Act 1971, s 3(1)(b) and (c).
2   Chapter 7 above.
3   Immigration Act 1971, s 1(3); chapter 6 above.
4   Immigration Act 1971, s 8; chapter 6 above.
5   HC 395, paras 77 and 80. Students' dependants admitted for less than 12 months may now ask for and be given the freedom to work: letter from Home Office to UKCOSA, 16 December 1999.
6   HC 395, paras 123 and 126.
7   HC 395, paras 195 and 198.
8   HC 395, paras 241 and 244.
9   See *Dhatt v MacDonald's Hamburgers Ltd* [1991] 3 All ER 692.

The main work permit scheme

10.39 As explained above, 'the work permit scheme' refers to both the 'main' scheme (as it is popularly called) and 'the training and work experience scheme'. We now focus on the main Scheme; training and work experience scheme is discussed separately afterwards.

Who is eligible for a work permit?

10.40 Persons from overseas who are not in one of the 'non-work permit' categories need a work permit if they wish to come to the UK for employment. The Department for Education and Employment only issues work permits for jobs needing relatively high-level skills, but the skills criteria were dramatically reduced on 2 October 2000. Prior to this date the criteria were that the job needed a degree-level qualification and two years' relevant post-qualification experience; had to be a senior executive or senior manager position which needed at least five years' relevant senior management experience; or one which needed high-level technical or similar skills and substantial relevant specialised experience. The new criteria are that the job requires a graduate or someone with an HND-level qualification in the specific field, or an HND (not relevant to the post on offer) with one year's relevant work experience. The employee must also be suitably skilled or experienced. Work permits are still not issued for jobs at manual, craft, clerical, secretarial or similar levels, or for resident domestic work such as nannies or housekeepers. They are also not issued if the employee holds more than a 10 percent share of the employing business. Shares up to this level may be held if they have been or are to be given to the employee as part of a pay package linked to their employment[1] and that this method of remuneration is of a size necessary to recruit the worker.

1   WP1 (notes), para 22.

10.41 Within the main scheme there are a number of important distinctions. There are jobs which require prior advertising and those where this is not necessary. Then there are specialist work permits for top-class entertainers, international sportspersons, those within the hotel and catering industry and those with occupational skills, language or cultural skills not readily available within the EEA. These last two categories used to be in a sub-scheme called 'the key workers' scheme (in which the maximum permitted stay was three years); now such persons can remain for up to five years and seek settlement after four.

Where are the scheme's rules to be found?

10.42 Details of the main work permit scheme are contained in a number of guidance leaflets issued by the Department for Education and Employment. WP1 (notes) is the general guide for employers on work permit applications and WP3 (notes) deals with work permit applications for entertainers and sport persons. Each category requires an application form to be completed (WP1, WP3 for sportspersons, including professional footballers).[1] The work permit scheme is liable to be varied at any time with or without consultation, and care should be taken to ensure that fully up-to-date information on the scheme is obtained before making any work permit application.

1 These guidance notes and application forms are available by from the Department for Education and Employment 24-hour telephone service on 0990 210224 or by downloading them from the Department's internet website at www.workpermits.gov.uk.

What qualifications/experience/skill must the employee have?

10.43 Within the main scheme there are a number of important requirements. First, an employee needs:

- a UK degree-level qualification; or
- an HND-level occupational qualification relevant to the post on offer, eg medical laboratory technician; or
- an HND-level qualification (not relevant to the post of offer) plus one year's relevant work experience; or
- three years' experience using specialist skills acquired by doing the type of job for which the permit is sought. This type of job should be at NVQ level 3 or above. Those who would qualify include head or second chefs, specialist chefs with skills in preparing ethnic cuisine[1] and those with occupational skills and language or cultural skills not readily available in the EEA.

Entertainers only need to prove that they have performed at the highest level and have established a reputation in their profession and are engaged to perform or do work which only they can do. Cultural artists have to be skilled in foreign arts which are rare or unavailable in Great Britain[2] and must be able to make a contribution to the arts, cultural relations or cultural awareness. Sportspersons must be internationally established at the highest level in their sport and must be able to make a significant contribution to the development of that particular sport in Great Britain at the highest level. Their coaches must be suitably qualified to the highest level. Each of the above groups may have technical/support people to accompany them, provided the work is directly related to the employment of an entertainer, cultural artist, sportsperson or a dramatic production in which that person should have proven technical or other specialist skills.[3] Experience gained through working illegally in the UK or through work done whilst the person was in this country as a working holidaymaker or student will not normally be taken into account.

1 WP1 (notes), paras 6–9.
2 The guidance notes refer throughout to 'Great Britain' rather than the United Kingdom. See **10.44** below.
3 WP3 (notes), para 5.

Who should apply for a work permit?

10.44 In general, only an employer based in Great Britain who needs to employ a person to work in England, Scotland or Wales may apply. The employer makes an application for the named person to do a specific job, normally on a full-time basis (perceived by the Department for Education and Employment to be a minimum of 30 hours per week or, if in teaching, 20 hours per week). A work permit is not transferable to a different employer or employee without a fresh work permit application.[1] The person who is the subject of the application must be the employer's employee, though in certain circumstances such as temporary transfer, secondment or provision of services to a UK-based client under contract (other than simply the supply of staff) the employee may remain employed by the overseas employer.[2] Generally, employees employed by their own overseas companies or engaged through other third parties (including overseas companies) whose main involvement with the work is to hire their services to others (a recruitment or employment agency or other similar businesses) cannot obtain work permits.[3]

1 WP1 (notes), para 1.
2 WP1 (notes), paras 2 and 3.
3 WP1 (notes), para 4.

Advertising for the position

10.45 Since one of the central requirements of the scheme is to protect the resident labour force, for certain posts the employer must show that there is no resident labour capable of filling the position. The resident labour force for these purposes means the EEA labour market and those who are settled in the UK.[1] Of course, there are others who are part of the resident labour force, but the Department for Education and Employment is only interested in responses to advertisements from EEA and settled applicants. Under the terms of the scheme not all positions need to be advertised. If they do not, only part 1 of the form WP1 needs completion. Those posts which do not need to be advertised are described in the guidance notes and are:

- intra-company transfers for employees of multinational companies who are transferring to a skilled post in Great Britain where the post needs an established employee who has essential company knowledge and experience and at least six months experience working with the overseas company;
- senior board-level posts or posts at an equivalent level for which there is no other suitable candidate. The person must have personal daily input into the directing of the company at a strategic level and substantial senior board-level experience;
- new posts essential to an inward investment project bringing in jobs and a minimum capital investment of normally £250,000;
- occupations which are acknowledged by the Department to be in very short supply.[2]

Posts which need specific skills, knowledge and experience that are rare will not be considered under this category if the occupation itself is not acknowledged by the Department to be in short supply.[3] In such cases, employers must complete both parts 1 and 2 of the application form and advertise the position. It is, of course, always open to an employer to ask for the advertising requirement exceptionally to be waived and the Department may comply if there are good commercial reasons for so doing. If there is real doubt about the merits of the argument in a particular case, employers should err on the side of caution and start the advertising process, which is time-consuming (the employer must wait for four weeks for the results of any advertising to be known before the application may proceed further).[4]

1   WP1 (notes), para 11.
2   These categories change frequently and are available on the Department for Education and Employment website or via their dedicated telephone line 0114 2594203.
3   WP1 (notes), para 30d.
4   WP1 (notes), para 18.

10.46 Advertising, if required, must be undertaken in a particular way. The Department for Education and Employment expects the advertisement to be placed in the most appropriate medium for reaching suitably qualified resident workers. This will normally be national newspapers or professional journals which are readily available throughout the EEA. It is also possible to advertise on the internet, if this is the most appropriate means of advertising the post, eg if the application refers to an internet-specific job. The Department is concerned that the advertisement display and prominence should reflect the level and nature of the post so that it truly attracts the broadest range of candidates. To ensure that the advertisement trawls the resident labour market effectively, it must give full details of the post, qualifications and experience needed and an indication of the salary or salary range. The employer must wait for four weeks from the date of the advertisement, but no later than six months, before making the application. The application must set out details of the responses received to the advertisement, the number of candidates shortlisted for interview and full reasons why any resident worker was not offered employment, with reference to the job requirements, as well as details of why the chosen candidate met the requirements. The Department expects to see the CVs of all candidates as well as interview notes for those shortlisted.[1] Headhunters may be used[2] for certain senior level or specialist posts, where the headhunter has given advice on suitable candidates after considering candidates within a well-defined group. Evidence of the limited group and of the search undertaken by the headhunter would be of considerable importance.[3] There is no need to advertise the position of entertainers who are internationally established, able to perform in their own right or are cultural artists. The advertising requirement still applies to applications for residencies of three months or more at the same venue or a series of venues, where performers are not normally well known or unique.[4]

1   WP1 (notes), paras 19 and 75-80.
2   But not recruitment consultants or executive search services which find candidates only from persons registered with them.
3   WP1 (notes), paras 20 and 77.
4   WP3 (notes), paras 8-9.

Documents to be sent with the application

10.47 In the case of applications which do not require advertising because they relate to intra-company transfers, board-level positions and posts that are essential for inward investment, there is no need to send copies of the individual's academic or professional qualifications. In respect of all applications, the Department for Education and Employment must be satisfied that the employer exists and is trading. If the employer is not known to the Department or no application has been made in the last four years, the Department will need to see:

- a copy of the employer's latest audited accounts with the accountant's name clearly shown or a copy of the latest annual report, both of which must be signed. If the employer has not been in existence for long enough to have accounts, other evidence must be provided to prove its existence, trading position and contracts. This might include a staff list, publicity material, a certificate of incorporation, and/or contracts entered into showing it is trading; or
- in the case of professional partnerships, such as solicitors, veterinary surgeons, dentists and doctors, the Department will accept a copy of one of the partner's registration details with the appropriate professional body.[1]

Where a position has been advertised or the candidate's relevant experience must be proved, the following additional documents are needed:

- copies of the candidate's academic and professional qualifications;
- statements from past employers on their headed notepaper verifying the candidate's relevant work experience in the last two years. These must be original and accompanied by a certified translation, if necessary. The statements must give start and finish dates of the employment and details of any work and experience making the person qualified to do the job. A general character reference does not prove a candidate's work record. Hotel and catering industry references may be in copy form, as they will be checked independently by the Department through the local British Embassy, Consulate-General or High Commission. In the case of entertainers and sportspersons, copy publicity material should be provided;[2]
- a copy of the advertisement (including any placed by a recruitment agency if one was used). The whole page should be sent, showing the name and date of the publication, with the advertisement clearly marked. If the advertisement is not available, the text of it can be sent with an invoice from the publication in which it was placed. If alternative means such as a headhunter were used, the Department will require details of the terms on which the search was commissioned and the methods used, and supporting evidence.[3] The Department will permit other forms of trawling the resident labour market but these will need to be justified. For example, if the job market is very narrow it might be possible to persuade the Department that all candidates for the position are known and they have been approached personally to fill it. Supporting evidence from those candidates would be essential to justify this approach;
- details of the responses to all methods of recruitment, including the total number of people who apply, the number shortlisted, full reasons why none of the candidates who are resident workers were employed, CVs of all candidates and interviews of all shortlisted candidates.[4]

1 WP1 (notes), para 67(c), 74.
2 WP1 (notes), paras 76-77; also WP3 (notes), paras 66-73.
3 WP1 (notes), paras 75-80.
4 WP1 (notes), para 79.

Timing of applications

10.48 Applications cannot be made more than six months before the employer wishes to engage the overseas national. In the case of someone already here in approved employment, an application should probably be made no earlier than three months and no later than one month before the person's leave to remain expires.[1] Once all necessary advertising procedures have been performed, the employer completes the appropriate application form for the position (WP1 and any annexes, or WP3 and any annexes) and forwards it to the Department for Education and Employment in Sheffield. The Department aims to decide at least 70 percent of applications within one week of receiving all relevant information, and straightforward applications are dealt with in days. If other government departments have to be consulted, a longer period should be allowed, particularly in the case of hotel and catering applications, for which at least three months should be allowed to decide the application because of the need for checks in the home country.[2]

1   WP1 (notes), paras 48–49.
2   See **10.47** above.

Self-certification

10.49 There is, at the date of writing, a pilot scheme for multinational employers to self-certify that a named employee should be issued with a work permit rather than apply for a work permit for employees on intra-company transfers. This scheme, which runs for six months from 1 October 2000, permits such employers to issue their own work permits, provided they meet the requirements of the work permit scheme.

Duration of work permits

10.50 Permits are in principle available for between one day and five years. Until 29 September 2000, work permits were limited to 36 months in respect of career development work permits and work permits for key workers who did not have the occupational skills to meet the criteria required by the work permit scheme. As this distinction has now been abolished, all work permits now potentially lead to settlement. Entertainers and sportspersons are issued with short-term permits to cover the period of engagement, although in principle there is no reason why they may not apply for settlement if they manage to remain in approved employment for a continuous period of four years.[1]

1   IDI, Ch 17, s 8, para 9 provides that indefinite leave to remain may be granted to sportspersons of international reputation who intend to make their home in the UK and have spent four of the last eight years on short-term work permits. For an analysis of the work permit scheme and other Immigration Rules relating to sportspersons and entertainers and their tax position see (2000) 3 IIEL 15–19.

Who must pay the worker?

10.51 As a general rule the employer is responsible for the pay and national insurance and tax deductions of the work permit holder. This rule does not apply if the employer remained overseas or the person is seconded to work for a UK employer from an overseas employer, when the overseas contract of employment may continue.[1] But even in those circumstances, the Department for Education and Employment requires the application form to be signed by the UK employer.[2]

1   See para **10.44** above.
2   WP1 (notes), para 2.

What happens when the work permit is issued?

10.52   Once issued, the work permit is sent to the employer or its representative. The permit is issued for a specified period starting on the date the overseas national enters the UK. If the work permit holder does not enter the UK within six months from the date of issue, the permit loses its validity and must be returned so a new one can be issued. Where the overseas national is already in the UK, whether in approved employment or not, the final decision on whether the individual may work rests with the Home Office, since it is only when the Home Office agrees to grant the necessary leave to enter or remain that the overseas worker is possessed of permission to work. This is endorsed in the overseas national's passport.[1] If the worker is in approved employment, the Department for Education and Employment will endorse the passport (if it is sent with the application) on behalf of the Home Office. If not, it should be endorsed directly by the Home Office. As a result of the Home Office's backlog of undecided cases, emergency provisions have been in place permitting the overseas national to commence work as soon as the letter of permission is sent to the employer, pending a final decision by the Home Office.

1   *Suruk Miah* (1976) Times, 4 February, CA.

Entry to the UK with a work permit

10.53   To qualify for admission under the Immigration Rules, workers must hold a valid work permit; must not be of an age which puts them outside the limits for employment (though the work permit scheme itself no longer has any age limits); must be capable of undertaking the employment specified in the permit; must not intend to take employment except as specified in the permit; must, if the permit is valid for a period of 12 months or less, intend to leave the UK at the end of their approved employment; and must be able to maintain and accommodate themselves and any dependants adequately without recourse to public funds.[1] Normally the period of leave granted will be co-extensive with the period of validity of the work permit, which will not exceed five years.[2] A condition will be imposed restricting the work permit holder to employment approved by the Department for Education and Employment, though it is now possible to undertake supplementary employment without further permission.[3] If the worker has been issued with a work permit valid for four years or more and the employer wishes the job to continue, the worker will become eligible to seek indefinite leave.[4] If the initial leave is less than four years, an extension of leave will only be granted if the Department gives written approval for the continuation of the employment for a further period.[5] The extension will be for a corresponding period.[6] Since extensions depend on the written approval of the Department for Education and Employment, it is that Department, rather than the Home Office, which sets the policy for continued stay in the UK.

1   HC 395, para 128.
2   WP1 (notes), para 27.
3   WP1 (notes), para 40 and WP3 (notes), para 28.
4   HC 395, para 134.
5   HC 395, para 131.
6   HC 395, para 132.

10.54 Possession of a work permit is not conclusive evidence of eligibility for entry for employment. Under the Immigration Rules, immigration officers have a wide discretion to refuse entry. Leave to enter should normally be refused where 'whether or not to the holder's knowledge, false representations were employed or material facts were not disclosed, for the purpose of obtaining a work permit'.[1] An illustration of the way in which the immigration officers' refusal powers operate is provided by the case of *Caballero*.[2] The appellant had a work permit as a domestic worker which had been sent to him in the Philippines. He was unaware that it was his employer's intention that he should be employed by more than one employer. But the immigration officer discovered this and refused him entry. The Tribunal upheld his decision: a work permit was for specific employment with a specific employer. Since this was not the employer's intention here, the permit had been obtained by false representations and the concealment of material facts. Leave to enter was, therefore, properly refused.[3]

1   HC 395, para 320(15). See *R v Secretary of State for the Home Department, ex p Wah Chun Wan* (LTA 96/5916/D) 31 October 1996 for a discussion of the difference between an invalid permit, as in *Chan* [1992] 1 WLR 541, and a permit which is improperly issued but valid, as in *Ku* [1995] QB 364. Even an improperly issued rather than invalid permit is not conclusive evidence of eligibility: see *R v Secretary of State for Education and Employment, Secretary of State for the Home Department, ex p Shu Sang Li* [1999] Imm AR 367.
2   [1974] Imm AR 13.
3   For the effect of improperly issued work permits, see the cases cited in fn 1 above.

Extension of stay in approved employment

10.55 The employer must complete form WP1X or WP3X and have complied with any conditions set out in the letter approving the initial employment, which also details the information required for an extension. Advertising (if originally required) does not need to be repeated, provided the job remains the same.[1] If the application is for the same occupation with a different employer, no advertising needs to be undertaken; only a change of occupation will require fresh advertising.[2] In the case of entertainers and sportspersons, no evidence of their maintenance of an international reputation needs to be provided.[3] If any advertising is undertaken, the same evidence of its results must be provided to the Department for Education and Employment as for the initial application.[4] If the employer had not been trading for sufficient time to have audited accounts available at the time of the initial application, the work permit will have been limited to a period of 18 months, and the Department will expect to see the audited accounts of the business on the extension application. The employee may continue to work whilst the application is pending.

1   WP1 (notes), para 33.
2   WP1 (notes), para 37.
3   WP3 (notes), paras 21–24.
4   See **10.46-10.47** above.

Switching into approved employment

10.56 The main work permit scheme is designed for workers who are abroad at the time the employer makes the application for a permit or already here in approved employment. People admitted as visitors, students or other temporary purposes may occasionally be given leave as a work permit holder outside the Immigration Rules, but the circumstances are very rare. Previously, applications to remain for employment had to be made to the Home Office in the first place and were not accepted by the Department for Education and Employment.[1] The current work permit scheme makes provision for such cases, although the current Immigration Rules contain no provision at all for switching to work permit employment from any other category of leave. Under the scheme, if the overseas national is already in the UK the employer may send the passport to the Department together with the work permit application.[2] The Department acknowledges the application and then makes a decision which is communicated in the form of a recommendation to the Home Office and sent at the same time to the employer. This guidance is in total contradiction to the provisions of the Immigration Rules, which expressly prohibit switching into work permit employment.[3] The Department for Education and Employment guidance suggests that the Home Office must at least consider an application to depart from the Rules, and the provisions for mandatory refusal may be misleading. There are no published IDI dealing generally with switches into approved employment. Home Office policy is to permit switching on a discretionary basis for students who obtain a work permit in a shortage occupation, and once there has been an opportunity to consider the operation of this policy, a rule change will be considered.[4]

1   OW5 (1982), para 13(c).
2   WP1 (notes), para 55.
3   HC 395, paras 131 and 133; 322(1).
4   Letter from Home Office to Immigration Law Practitioners' Association, 25 October 2000.

Appealing a work permit refusal

10.57 There is no provision in the 1971 to 1999 Immigration Acts for an appeal either by the worker or the employer against the refusal of a work permit as such. Under repealed section 14(1) of the Immigration Act 1971, a person already in the UK in another capacity who was refused leave to remain for employment usually had a right of appeal against the refusal to vary leave.[1] If leave is not granted in any other capacity, there will still be a right of appeal under section 61 of the Immigration and Asylum Act 1999. On such an appeal, the appellate authorities cannot consider the exercise of a discretion by the Home Office to refer an application to the Department for Education and Employment,[2] nor can they question the merits of the Department's refusal to issue or continue a work permit.[3] All that the appellate authorities can do is to investigate, on an appeal arising from the refusal of a work permit, whether the Home Office decision is in accordance with the law, and to allow an appeal if it is not.[4] The Department does have its own internal appeals procedure which permits an employer to challenge a refusal. Such an appeal is to be made (or an intention so to appeal must be stated) within 28 days. The procedure gives an independent review of the application by a Department for Education and Employment official senior to the one who took the original decision.[5] A decision of the Department on a work permit may also be challenged by judicial review, on the grounds of illegality, irrationality or procedural impropriety.[6]

1   Subject to the requirement to hold a 'relevant document': see **10.58** below.
2   Old cases on the exercise of the discretion under earlier rules no longer apply: see *Tally* [1975] Imm AR 83; *Stillwaggon* [1975] Imm AR 132; *Pereyra* [1978] Imm AR 13; *Nicolaides* [1978] Imm AR 67; *Sarwar* [1978] Imm AR 190.
3   *Pearson v Immigration Appeal Tribunal* [1978] Imm AR 212, CA.
4   *Bernstein* (4065). The case went on judicial review to the DC (*R v Immigration Appeal Tribunal and Department of Employment, ex p Bernstein* [1987] Imm AR 182) and to the CA [1988] Imm AR 490 on different points. See also G Warr (1987) INLP 68 at 124. The appellate jurisdiction includes human rights and race discrimination: Immigration and Asylum Act 1999, s 65.
5   WP1 (notes), paras 116–118.
6   See *Pearson* above; *Bernstein* above and *R v Department of Employment, ex p Allan* [1991] Imm AR 336, QBD. See also **10.35** above.

10.58 A work permit is a 'relevant document' for the purposes of the Immigration and Asylum Act 1999, the lack of which leads to loss of a right of appeal against the corresponding immigration decision.[1] A person who has applied to remain in a capacity for which a work permit on entry is required will therefore have no appeal. Similarly, a refusal by the Department for Education and Employment to extend a permit probably eliminates the right of appeal against the consequent Home Office decision to refuse an extension of stay, depending on whether the Department's 'written approval' required by paragraph 131(ii) of the Immigration Rules is an 'equivalent document issued after entry' for the purposes of section 62(2)(c) of the 1999 Act.

1   See Immigration and Asylum Act 1999, s 60(8)(c) identifying work permits as a relevant document for the purposes of s 60(7)(a), which limits the s 59 general right of appeal against the refusal of entry clearance and leave to enter; s 62(2)(c) similarly identifies work permits and 'equivalent documents issued after entry' as relevant documents for the purposes of the s 62 limitation on the general right of appeal under s61 to appeal against a refusal to vary leave. The provisions duplicate repealed s 14(2A)(a) and (2B)(c) of the Immigration Act 1971 as amended by s 11 of the Asylum and Immigration Appeals Act 1993.

Family members

10.59 Spouses, unmarried partners and children under 18, but no other dependants, can accompany or join a work permit holder in the UK, provided the maintenance and accommodation provisions of the Immigration Rules are fulfilled.[1] The Home Office will by concession permit over-age dependent children to accompany their parent transferred into approved employment by way of intra-company transfer, provided they have remained part of the family unit. The concession also applies to dependent parents. Other dependent relatives may be admitted at the discretion of the entry clearance officer if there are exceptional compassionate circumstances.[2] This is because the employee is moving at the behest of his employer and not necessarily of his own volition.[3]

Otherwise, the details are the same as those applying to family members of non-work permit employees at **10.31** above. Spouses, partners and children are free to take any employment without the need for Home Office or Department for Education and Employment approval.

1   HC 395, paras 194–199, 295J.
2   Home Office letter to Sturtivant and Co, 6 August 1996.
3   Home Office letter to Bates, Wells and Braithwaite, 16 December 1999.

The training and work experience scheme (TWES)

Introduction and history

10.60 Previous incarnations of this part of the work permit scheme used to state that its aim was to assist businesses and organisations in their international development, and to help other countries by increasing the skills and experience of their citizens. The Department for Education and Employment had a special Eastern European Unit which was set up to deal with nationals from a defined list of countries, whose training in UK businesses was intended to promote the UK, and in particular UK businesses, as natural trading partners. The training and work experience scheme has gone through many superficial changes since then and recently has undergone a major review. A further review was completed in March 2001. The principal consequence of the review is that the availability of resident labour, which used to be irrelevant, becomes crucial. If the post can be filled by a resident worker, the application cannot be made under the training and work experience scheme, which is now only available for trainees who are supernumerary to the main workforce requirements.[1] Furthermore, as a result of the changes in skills thresholds in the main work permit scheme, elements of the old training and work experience scheme have been transferred to the main work permit scheme. Training and work experience scheme permits are available for employers based in Great Britain. Separate arrangements exist for Northern Ireland, the Isle of Man and the Channel Islands.[2]

1   WP2 (notes), introduction.
2   WP2 (notes), paras 137-140.

Who is eligible for a training and work experience scheme (TWES) permit?

10.61 Persons requiring Department for Education and Employment approval[1] need a training and work experience scheme (TWES) permit to enter the UK or to remain for training leading to a professional qualification or for work experience. The Department only issue TWES permits for work-based training for a professional or specialist qualification, or for a period of work experience where the individual will be additional to the employer's normal staffing requirements, and those individuals who are not additional in this sense must apply under the main work permit scheme.[2] So employees who used to be granted TWES permits as graduate trainees, those wishing to undertake training for a professional or specialist qualification, or work experience which is filling a vacancy, must now apply under the main work permit scheme. The Department will not normally issue TWES permits in the sports and entertainment sectors. This is a change from the previous terms of the scheme and there would be some room for making representations to the Department in special cases.[3]

1   See **10.40** above.
2   WP2 (notes), paras 12–13.
3   WP2 (notes), para 11.

Where are the Scheme's rules to be found?

10.62 Details of the training and work experience scheme are contained in guidance leaflets issued by the Department for Education and Employment. WP2 (notes) is the general guide for employers on TWES applications and WP(SI) (notes) deals with internship placements for overseas students who need to complete an internship programme with an employer which has a significant trading presence in the UK and abroad. The employer must be considering recruiting the student as a trainee on completion of his or her course. Each category requires an application form to be completed (WP2 for training and work experience and WP(SI) for internship programme students). The TWES is liable to change at any time with or without consultation, and care should be taken to ensure that fully up-to-date information on the scheme is obtained before making an application for a TWES permit.

Qualifications for TWES permit

10.63 The training and work experience scheme requirements for a permit to train for a professional qualification are as follows:

*   an academic or vocational qualification at UK degree level or National or Scottish Vocational Qualification (NVQ or NSVQ) level 3. This is defined by the National Vocational Qualification Board;
*   the relevant qualifications necessary for the training;
*   the training should lead to a recognised professional or specialist qualification at postgraduate level;
*   the company and the person managing the training should be competent to provide it. This will normally involve being registered or approved by the relevant professional body;
*   the training should be completed in the shortest possible time, interpreted by the Department for Education and Employment as requiring the employee to take an exam at the earliest possible sitting. Two attempts or possible attempts can be made in respect of each exam. Each exam not taken is counted as a possible attempt;
*   a TWES permit is not normally issued for training for a qualification which can be obtained by full-time study. If this is possible, the employee will have to apply to remain as a student and perhaps undertake part-time employment;
*   applications are only approved for the employee to achieve one qualification, but if the employment ends before the qualification is obtained and the employee wishes to continue training with a new employer, a further application can be made on form WP2 within three

months of the end of the previous training. If there is a gap of more than three months, the training will be deemed to have ceased;

- pay and other conditions should be comparable to those normally given to a resident worker doing this level of training and should reflect the person's experience.[1] The pay must meet the national minimum wage which came into effect on 1 April 1999.

1   WP2 (notes), para 12–36.

10.64 The TWES requirements for a work experience permit are as follows:

- the employee should have previous relevant experience or appropriate academic or vocational qualifications to enable him or her to benefit from a work experience programme at this level. Those with neither relevant experience nor academic or vocational qualifications will not normally have their applications approved;
- the work experience should be at managerial level or at least N/SVQ level 3 or equivalent;
- the application should describe the type and level of experience to be gained and how this will be supervised. It should set out a detailed timetable for each stage of the programme, a description of the tasks to be undertaken and who will be supervising the work experience. The more detailed the programme the more likely the period requested will be granted;
- in general the Department for Education and Employment expects that most work experience programmes will not exceed 12 months. If the full 24-month period provided as a maximum in the Immigration Rules[1] is requested, this should be explained in the initial application. As a matter of practice, if a 24-month period is requested and granted, a full 24-month permit is issued immediately. Extensions to a work experience permit are only approved where there are exceptional circumstances, and such a request must be made at the outset;
- the pay and conditions should be no more than those given to a resident worker doing equivalent work experience, although persons coming under an exchange agreement or to be paid by an overseas employer or organisation may receive their normal salary. The pay must meet the national minimum wage which came into effect on 1 April 1999;
- work experience for students studying overseas should be sought through a recognised student exchange body. This limits the period of work experience to a maximum of 12 months.[2]

1   HC 395, para 119(iv).
2   WP2 (notes), paras 29–35.

Procedures for obtaining a TWES permit

10.65 The UK employer applies for the TWES permit and normally pays the worker,[1] and the considerations set out in **10.44** above in relation to the main work permit scheme apply also in respect of the TWES.[2] The same type of documents should be sent with the TWES application to prove that the employer exists.[3] Additionally, in respect of a training application the following should be sent:

- evidence of the person's degree-level qualification;
- evidence of any exemptions from exams;
- a copy of the training plan or programme agreed with the appropriate professional body (if applicable); and
- evidence from the appropriate professional body, where this has not previously been supplied, to show that the trainer is approved to provide the training;
- In respect of a work experience application, the work experience programme should be sent.[4]

The timing of the application is the same as for the main scheme,[5] and the Department for Education and Employment aims to decide at least 70 percent of training and work experience scheme applications submitted with all the relevant information within one week of receiving them.

1   See **10.51** above and WP2 (notes) paras 7–9.
2   See also WP2 (notes), para 68.
3   See **10.47** above.
4   WP2 (notes), paras 69–73.
5   See **10.48** above.

Duration of the TWES permit

10.66 The TWES permit for approved training will be issued for only six months initially if the employer is unable to provide evidence of the person's degree-level qualification. Further periods will be granted to allow the trainee to continue training, attempt examinations and complete the required practical experience leading to the qualification sought.[1] The period the Department for Education and Employment will allow varies from profession to profession, and checks should be made with the Department to identify the appropriate period in a given case. The TWES permit for work experience is issued for an initial period of up to 12 months and, exceptionally, for a further 12-month period, taking the total to 24 months.[2]

1   WP2 (notes), para 25.
2   WP2 (notes), para 33.

Entry to the UK with a TWES permit

10.67 The TWES permit, like the main work permit, is sent to the employer.[1] Under the Immigration Rules, a person seeking admission to the UK for training or work experience must hold a valid TWES permit; not be of an age which puts him or her outside the limits for employment; be capable of undertaking the training or work experience specified in the permit; intend to leave the UK on completion of the training or work experience; not intend to take any other employment; and be able to maintain and accommodate him or herself and any dependants adequately without recourse to public funds.[2] As with work permits, possession of a TWES permit is no guarantee of admission to the UK.[3] The period of leave may be extended if the Department for Education and Employment have given written approval for an extension and the other conditions of admission are met.[4] In the case of work experience, the maximum period of stay is two years.[5] Training is more flexible; on entry up to three years may be given,[6] and this may be extended in suitable cases for a further three years.[7] In both cases changes of employment need Department for Education and Employment permission.[8] Special provision is made for chartered accountants, to whom the Department will approve employment on qualification, usually for two years, to enable them to obtain a practising certificate.[9] For an extension of stay the employer must complete form WP2X and must have complied with any conditions set out in the letter approving the initial employment. That initial letter will also have explained what information needs to be sent with the application for an extension. If the employer had not been trading for sufficient time to have audited accounts available at the time of the initial application, audited accounts will be expected to accompany the extension application. Whilst the application is pending the trainee may continue working, provided the application was received by the Department before the trainee's initial leave expired.[10] Appeal rights for those refused TWES permits, entry with such permits or extensions are the same as for the main work permit scheme.[11]

1 See para **10.52** above and WP2 (notes), para 78.
2 HC 395, paras 116(i)–(vi).
3 See para **10.54** above.
4 HC 395, para 119(ii) and (iii).
5 HC 395, para 119(iv)
6 HC 395, para 117.
7 HC 395, para 120.
8 HC 395, paras 117 and 120.
9 979 HC official report (5th series) written answers col 18.
10 WP2 (notes), para 39.
11 See **10.57** above.

Switching into and out of TWES employment

10.68 Under earlier rules[1] visitors as well as students could switch to training, but under the current Immigration Rules only students may do so.[2] Switching from TWES employment to approved (main work permit) employment is prohibited both under the Rules[3] and under the terms of the training and work experience scheme,[4] both of which provide that trainees would not normally be allowed to transfer to work permit employment in Great Britain and must intend to return overseas at the end of the agreed period.

1 HC 251, para 120.
2 HC 395, para 119(i).
3 HC395, para 116(iv)–(v)
4 WP2 (notes), paras 14–15.

Admission of families

10.69 Those undergoing training or work experience may be joined by their spouses (not their unmarried partners) and their children under 18, provided they can meet the cost of maintenance and accommodation without recourse to public funds.[1] There are no restrictions on family members taking employment.

1 HC395, paras 122-127.

THE SELF-EMPLOYED

Introduction and history

10.70 The Immigration Rules relating to business and self-employment have undergone many changes since 1973. Formerly, there was a broad discretion to admit persons wishing to start or join a business, and to permit visitors or others on a temporary stay in the UK to remain in that capacity.[1] There was no minimum investment required and the application was to be considered in the round, with no one factor being conclusive. This broad brush approach was first put forward by the Divisional Court in *Ex p Joseph*[2] and was endorsed in the later case of *Ex p Peikazadi*[3] and in the unreported Court of Appeal decision in *Mawji*.[4] The Rules in force in 1973 remain important for Turkish nationals, since the European Court of Justice held in *Savas*[5] that under the 'standstill clause' in Article 41 of the Additional Protocol to the EC-Turkey Association Agreement, the parties had agreed not to introduce additional barriers to establishment. Turkish nationals can, therefore, rely on the Rules as they were when the UK acceded to the EEC in January 1973, both in relation to switching from visitor to business status and in respect of the substantive requirements of the business rules.

1   See HC 510, para 21.
2   *R v Immigration Appeal Tribunal, ex p Joseph* [1977] Imm AR 70, QBD.
3   *R v Immigration Appeal Tribunal, ex p Peikazadi* [1979-80] Imm AR 191, QBD.
4   *Mawji v Immigration Appeal Tribunal* (29 October 1984, unreported), CA.
5   *R v Secretary of State for the Home Department, ex p Savas* [2000] INLR 398, C37/98. See chapter 7 above.

10.71 Since 1980 the Immigration Rules have become much more restrictive. The general formula that applications should be 'considered on merit' has been replaced by specific requirements with which the business applicant must comply. The broad brush approach, which overcame some of the 'astonishingly unattractive' results of a literal interpretation,[1] was rejected in *Ex p Rahman*[2] by the majority of the Court of Appeal, who said that although a degree of latitude is allowed in construing the Rules, it does not extend to departing from the plain, ordinary, natural meaning of the language. Business applicants must therefore comply fully with each of the specific requirements of the Rules, however badly geared they may be to the needs of businesses. It is true that in particular cases the Home Office may be persuaded to waive requirements of the Rules, but there is no guarantee of this. So perhaps it is not surprising that business persons and their legal advisers try to avoid the business provisions of the Rules and structure their investments so as to achieve the same result through the work permit scheme or the sole representative or investor categories. In addition, applicants now have the option of making an innovator application.

1   See *R v Immigration Appeal Tribunal, ex p Rahman* [1985] Imm AR 222, QBD, per Woolf J.
2   *R v Immigration Appeal Tribunal, ex p Rahman* [1987] Imm AR 313, CA. The first attack on the 'in the round' approach came from the Tribunal in *Patel* [1987] Imm AR 116.

10.72 It should be noted that business status under the Immigration Rules only applies to those who wish to establish themselves in business. Persons who wish to make business visits to the UK without establishing a business here are free to do so, subject to the restrictions on business visitors already dealt with (chapter 9 above). Different considerations also apply to EEA nationals who wish to set up in business or self-employment in the UK and third country nationals exercising EC law rights (chapter 7 above). But below we deal to some extent with individuals and companies from the Central and Eastern European states with which the EC has concluded Association Agreements. We do so because in this regard EC law is being implemented in the UK by the incorporation of special business provision into the Immigration Rules. These special provisions are an adaptation of the normal business provisions and immediately follow them in HC 395. It is therefore appropriate at least to sketch them in here.

Business status

Requirements

10.73 HC 395, paragraphs 200-223 deal with the admission of those wishing to establish themselves in business; the standard provision is set out in paragraphs 200–210, while paragraphs 211–223 make special provision for business persons seeking admission under the EC Association Agreements. The text that follows focuses on the standard provision; for the position where the Association Agreements apply see **10.93** and chapter 7.

10.74 The first general rule is that a passenger seeking admission must hold a current entry clearance issued for that purpose.[1] All business applications must be referred by the overseas post to the Business Case Unit at the Home Office. Despite the unambiguous requirement for entry clearance, attempts are often made by those already in the UK to switch to business status by making an application direct to the Home Office.[2] Although such applications are to be refused under the Immigration Rules,[3] the entry clearance requirement is sometimes waived on an exceptional basis, for example, if there is no country to which the applicant can safely return; there is no British Embassy or other post issuing entry clearances in the particular country; or the application is a particularly strong one on general business grounds. Decisions of the Tribunal from before 1993 (when lack of entry clearance was fatal to the right of appeal)[4] suggest the Secretary of State for the Home Department is entitled to limit a refusal to the lack of entry clearance and need not deal with the merits,[5] but according to the IDI the decision to refuse must be based on factors in addition to the no switching rule in order to avoid judicial challenge for arbitrariness.[6]

1 HC 395, para 201(xi).
2 IDI Nov/00, Ch 6, s 1.
3 HC 395, para 205.
4 Asylum and Immigration Appeals Act 1993, s 11, which amended Immigration Act 1971, s 13; see chapter 18.
5 *Yousri* (5 April 1989), *Al-Hasini* (4670), *Balluza* (6579), where the Tribunal also held that the question of the fairness or irrationality of the Home Office decision was within their jurisdiction, following the reasoning in the earlier Tribunal decision in *Aujla* (6459).
6 IDI Nov/00, Ch 6, s 1.

10.75 Under the Immigration Rules a business means an enterprise as a sole trader, or a partnership, or a company registered in the UK.[1] The purpose of the Rule is to identify the different forms a business enterprise may take without limiting its activities. For example, 'sole trader' is not intended to limit business activity to trading rather than manufacturing or a profession, but merely refers to persons who engage in business on their own account rather than in partnership or under the umbrella of a company. Where a company is used, it must be registered in the UK. Where the business investment is made through a company it is sometimes difficult to determine whether to apply for a work permit or seek business status. A business application is appropriate in the case of a shareholder with a controlling or equal interest in the business.

1   HC 395, para 200; IDI Nov/00, Ch 6, s 1, Annex C.

10.76 The Immigration Rules have a long list of requirements which must be fulfilled by anyone wishing to set up in business in the UK or join or take over an existing business. They distinguish between new and existing businesses and lay down additional requirements for each. The common requirements are that all business applicants:[1]

- have not less than £200,000 to invest in the business and that this is their own money under their control and disposable in the UK;
- have sufficient additional funds to meet the maintenance and accommodation requirements of the Rules until their business starts to provide an income;
- will be actively involved full-time in the business;
- will maintain a level of financial investment proportional to their interests in the business;
- will have an equal or controlling interest in the business and that any partnership or directorship does not amount to disguised employment;
- will be able to bear their share of the liabilities;
- demonstrate a genuine need for their investment and services in the UK;
- demonstrate that their share of the profits will be sufficient to meet the maintenance and accommodation requirements of the Rules; and
- do not intend to supplement their business activities by taking or seeking employment in the UK other than their work for the business.

1   HC 395, para 201.

10.77 In addition to meeting these common requirements, where the business is already in existence, applicants who wish to take it over, join it or become a director must also produce:[1]

- a written statement of the terms on which they are to take over or join the business;
- audited accounts for the business for previous years; and
- evidence that their services and investment will result in a net increase in the employment provided by the business to persons settled here to the extent of creating at least two new full-time jobs.

Where the business is new, applicants must (in addition to meeting the common requirements) produce evidence that:[2]

- they will be bringing into the country sufficient funds of their own to establish a business; and
- the business will create full-time employment for at least two persons already settled in the UK.

1   HC 395, para 202.
2   HC 395, para 203.

10.78 The Immigration Rules establish a minimum financial requirement of £200,000.[1] Overseas lawyers are exempted from this requirement (and need not create two new jobs for persons settled in the UK). These are persons from abroad who have qualified here as solicitors or barristers or who qualified abroad and wish to practise here as consultants in that overseas law. They must be able to support themselves and their families and meet the costs of establishing themselves in practice (because they must be self-employed, and not employees, to come within the scope of business status).[2] In addition, they must satisfy certain regulatory requirements.[3]

1   HC 395, para 201(ii).
2   IDI Nov/00, Ch 6, s 1, Annex D.
3   IDI Nov/00, Ch 6, s 1, Annex D.

Money of their own, disposable in the UK

10.79 The Rule requires the applicants' investment to be money of their own, which is held in their own name and under their control and disposable in the UK.[1] The purpose is threefold: first, to ensure that the applicant is the investor and not fronting for someone else;[2] secondly, to ensure that the investment is not going to be thwarted because a third party can stop payment or withdraw the funds; thirdly, to ensure that the monies are immediately available for the investment and not tied up elsewhere. The first of these aims is addressed by the requirement that the money must be in the investor's own name and not held in a trust fund or some other investment vehicle. Clearly there will be cases where the applicant's money is tied up, for example, in a trust or off-shore investment company prior to the business investment. What is required is that the money must be unequivocally released into the investor's own name and control in time for the decision on the application. For money to be disposable in the UK it must be immediately available for investment in the business. For this purpose money invested in a house will not usually count (although it may do in respect of the separate categories of retired persons of independent means and investors).[3]

1   HC 395, para 201(ii).
2   *R v Immigration Appeal Tribunal, ex p Peikazadi* [1979–80] Imm AR 191.
3   *Rahman (Hussain)* [1991] Imm AR 102. See **10.106ff** below.

10.80 The term 'under his control' was also used in previous Immigration Rules dealing with persons of independent means and is retained in the current Rules for retired persons of independent means, and additionally applied to investors. The earlier case law therefore remains relevant. In *Ex p Chiew*[1] the Court of Appeal held that 'control' in this context means a right which can be enforced in law against any person who might wish to interfere with it. Thus a wife's money from a legally enforceable separation agreement is money under her control.[2] A continued permission to use and spend family funds in accordance with Chinese family custom is not an enforceable right and will be insufficient.[3] On the other hand money coming from the applicant's family and at the applicant's unfettered disposition will suffice as his or her own money because it is a gift,[4] or because it has been lent on a sufficiently long-term basis.[5] In the case of new businesses, the requirement that applicants will be bringing into the country sufficient funds of their own to establish a business[6] suggests the need for some kind of transfer of funds from overseas, but in practice this is not a substantive additional requirement.[7]

1   *R v Immigration Appeal Tribunal, ex p Chiew* [1981] Imm AR 102, QBD; see also *R v Immigration Appeal Tribunal, ex p Mehra* [1983] Imm AR 156, QBD.
2   *Rohr* [1983] Imm AR 95.
3   *R v Immigration Appeal Tribunal, ex p Chiew* above.
4   *R v Immigration Appeal Tribunal, ex p Chiew* above; *R v Immigration Appeal Tribunal, ex p Kwok on Tong* [1981] Imm AR 214, QBD and IDI Nov/00, Ch 6, s 1, Annex A.
5   *R v Immigration Appeal Tribunal, ex p Peikazadi* **10.79** fn 2 above and IDI Nov/00, Ch 6, s 1, Annex A.
6   HC 395, para 203(i).
7   See *R v Immigration Appeal Tribunal, ex p Rahman* [1987] Imm AR 313 at 317, per Woolf J in QBD, and at 322, per Bingham LJ in CA.

10.81 The investment has to be 'put into the business' and it is, therefore, insufficient if part of the funds goes into the business and part into living accommodation for the applicant's family.[1] If the applicant proposes to buy premises which include residential accommodation for his or her family, the value of this part of the property should be deducted from the business investment.[2] Money already in the business is insufficient, as in *Ex p Rahman*,[3] where the applicant inherited the business as a going concern when his father died. Applicants may make their investment by a direct cash investment, share capital or a combination of the two. A director's loan (unless it is unsecured and fully subordinate to all third-party creditors) and an investment from or through an off-shore company are both unacceptable.[4] In practice the Home Office would expect the full amount to be invested by the time the applicant applies for a first extension of leave, ie within 12 months of the initial entry.[5]

1   *Patel v Entry Clearance Officer, Nairobi* [1987] Imm AR 116 at 126.
2   IDI Nov/00, Ch 6, s 1, Annex A.
3   *R v Immigration Appeal Tribunal, ex p Rahman* [1987] Imm AR 313, CA.
4   IDI Nov/00, Ch 6, s 1, Annex A.
5   This is consistent with *Trivedi v Secretary of State for the Home Department* TH/8202/98 (00 TH 01059), a sole representative case in which the Tribunal held that the 'on entry' requirement need only be satisfied by the end of the initial 12-month period.

Full-time involvement in the business

10.82 The Immigration Rules require a business person to be involved full-time in the business.[1] This does not mean being in the UK full-time, since trips and possibly lengthy periods abroad may be a necessary part of promoting the business. But absences abroad have to be watched, since they may adversely affect a later application for settlement (see **10.92** below). A business which consists of separate and distinct activities may also qualify,[2] but the business applicant must intend to be involved full-time in their management or supervision. The actual wording of the Rules, however, is not quite so clear cut. 'Trading' and 'providing services' are broad and open terms which embrace a full range of business activity including manufacture and research. In the case of company directors, they must be involved in the full-time promotion or management of the company to comply with HC 395, paragraph 201(iv). 'Promotion and management' connote a degree of control and supervision over the aims and objects of the company and must be construed with the requirement of a controlling or equal interest in the business and the ban on disguised employment.[3] Where the business activity involves a lot of promotion or supervision of the company's operations, and in a small company where the director does most of the work and employs very few administrative staff, there is no problem. But where a director does not control but works under the direction of others, that work may be neither promotional nor managerial, and may risk being classified as 'disguised employment.[4] The immigration admission of the applicant must be necessary in the interest of the business, and the business not simply a convenient device for the applicant.[5] The Home Office looks at franchise arrangements particularly closely, to see whether the applicants work full-time and there is a genuine need for their services, as it takes the view that the franchisee often has little say in how the business is run and may not, therefore, have much input except for the investment.

1   HC 395, para 201(iv).
2   *Otani* (3234).
3   HC 395, para 201(vi).
4   An example of disguised employment is provided by *Singh (Pritpal)* [1972] Imm AR 154 where the appellant was a director and secretary of the company with an annual salary. He had loaned money to the company and held £15 shares out of the company share capital of £100; he received no interest on his loan nor dividend on his shareholding. There was no agreement in writing as to his future in the company and he could be removed from the board of directors and from his secretarial duties at any time by the majority shareholders. It was held that he was in reality a paid employee.
5   IDI Nov/00, Ch 6, s 1, Annex A.

Proportionality of investment[1]

10.83 This appears to be a further safeguard against the business rules being used to evade the need to obtain a work permit. A businessman who receives 50 percent of the profits should have an equivalent shareholding or partnership stake in the enterprise. The IDI contend that a person who has a majority or equal financial interest in a business but who nevertheless clearly has no major say in running the business or setting its policy will not have an interest in the business proportional to his investment.[2]

1   HC 395, para 201(v).
2   IDI Nov/00, Ch 6, s 1, Annex A.

Controlling or equal interest

10.84 Applicants need to show that they will have either a controlling or equal interest in the business and that any partnership or directorship does not amount to disguised employment.[1] The purpose of this is to ensure that an investment is not simply used as an entrée to the UK or a front for disguised employment. For example, an investment of £200,000 by a leading motor car designer coming to work for the Ford motor company with a promised seat on the Board would probably not qualify under this Rule, although he or she would be a prime candidate for a work permit.

1   HC 395, para 201(iv) and IDI Nov/00, Ch 6, s 1, Annex A. See also *Singh (Pritpal)* **10.82** above.

Able to bear share of liabilities[1]

10.85 If a business is a limited company, then its liabilities will be limited to the total of its assets and in that sense every promoter of such a business will be able to bear his or her share of liabilities. In *Ex p Hirani*[2] it was held that 'liabilities' referred to those a business is reasonably expected to incur and it was wrong to require an applicant to show a 'capital reserve to cater for any unforeseen liabilities'. The structure of the business may affect an applicant's eventual liability. A sole trader receives all the profit and bears all the losses of the business, is personally responsible for all debts and can be made bankrupt and his or her belongings can be sold to pay creditors.[3] In a partnership each partner is liable without limit for the partnership debts. Creditors may sue an individual partner, a group of partners or the firm itself. A partner who is sued can be made bankrupt if he or she fails to pay the debts or obtain contributions from other partners even if the debts were incurred by another partner.[4]

1   HC 395, para 201(vii).
2   *R v Immigration Appeal Tribunal, ex p Hirani* (2 July 1981, unreported), QBD.
3   IDI Nov/00, Ch 6, s 1, Annex C.
4   IDI Nov/00, Ch 6, s 1, Annex C.

Genuine need for services and investment

10.86 There is uncertainty as to precisely what this provision means. It would be too restrictive to suggest that applicants must identify some market research on the need for their business before receiving entry clearance.[1] However, market research can be helpful to justify the applicant's financial projections.[2] Clearly a business that is wholly unwanted will fail, but this is taken care of by the rules on profitability. Part of the entrepreneurial ethic is to create needs where none existed before. The better meaning of these words, therefore, is that the business must need the service and investment. The needs are those of the business, not the local or national economy. It is no good investing £200,000 in a shop that does not require an investment of that amount. This view accords with the meaning of the phrase under earlier rules, where it was confined to an existing business and clearly related back to the needs of that business and not to some wider economic interest.[3] Tribunal decisions are somewhat ambivalent and contradictory.[4] However, the IDI state that unless there is uncertainty about the *bona fides* of the applicant it will normally be sufficient to concentrate on evidence of funds and the requirement to provide employment.[5] It comes to this: the business must require an investment of at least £200,000, so if it only needs £1,000 for a phone and a desk and the remaining £199,000 will be placed on deposit, the application will fail for want of a 'genuine need' for the investment. But the Home Office is apparently content for only £190,000 to be required in this sense, leaving £10,000 for contingencies.

1   See *Patel* (4895), Immigration Appeal Tribunal.
2   IDI Nov/00, Ch 6, s 1, Annex A.
3   See the comment of the Tribunal in *Otani* (3234).
4   *Patel* above (market research); *Otani* above (no strict commercial test); *Seyed* (5006) (commercial test with an element of general public economic interest).
5   IDI Nov/00, Ch 6, s 1, Annex A.

Profitability

10.87 Applicants need to show that the business will be sufficiently profitable to support them and their families without recourse to employment or public funds.[1] If they intend to supplement their business activity by taking any employment other than their work in the company, sole tradership or partnership, their application will be refused.[2] The applicant must produce a detailed business plan showing the object of the business, the investment and employment involved and financial projections. The IDI set out a comprehensive list of the minimum information that the business plan should contain[3] and the formulae that the Home Office uses to assess the viability of the business.[4]

1 HC 395, para 201(ix).
2 HC 395, para 201(x).
3 IDI Nov/00, Ch 6, s 1, Annex A.
4 IDI Nov/00, Ch 6, s 1, Annex B.

Job creation

10.88 Whether the investment is into a new or existing business, it must lead to the creation of new, paid, full-time employment in the business for two persons already settled in the UK. Employment of part-time workers or temporary trainees would be insufficient.[1] The business plan must identify the number of new jobs expected to be created and the likely pay, hours and duties.[2] The new employees do not need to be in post at the outset or even during the early period of the business,[3] but they will be expected to be so by the end of the initial 12 months.[4] It is employment, not self-employment, which must be created and the use of self-employed contractors is, therefore, insufficient.[5]

1 *Fanous* [1993] Imm AR 200 and IDI Nov/00, Ch 6, s 1, Annex A.
2 IDI Nov/00, Ch 6, s 1, Annex A.
3 *Singh (Inderjit)* (4620).
4 HC 395, para 206(viii), confirming *Jamnadas* (6597). See *Trivedi* TH/8202/98 (00 TH 01059) 10.81 fn 5 above.
5 *Seyed* [1987] Imm AR 303.

10.89 The Immigration Rules refer to employees being recruited from persons 'settled here' and 'already settled in the UK'[1] and are clearly intended to make inroads into UK, rather than continental, unemployment figures. However, where EEA nationals and others exercising EC law rights are in the UK, it is not clear whether they are to be regarded as 'settled' in the UK for these purposes unless they come within regulation 8 of the Immigration (European Economic Area) Regulations.[2] Where an existing business is taken over, the Rules now make it clear that there must be a net increase in employment.[3] Maintaining existing jobs is not enough.

1 HC 395, paras 202(iii) and 203(ii).
2 SI 2000/2326, defining certain categories of EEA nationals and their family members who are to be regarded as being in the UK without being subject to any restriction. They are retired workers and self-employed persons and their families, family members of deceased workers, and persons with indefinite leave to remain.
3 HC395, paras 202(iii) and 206(viii)(b), and IDI Nov/00, Ch 6, s 1, Annex A.

Extensions and settlement

10.90 Applications for extensions of stay by persons established in business will only be granted if the applicant continues to meet the requirements needed to obtain entry.[1] More particularly, applicants must be in a position to show:

- audited accounts proving the precise financial position of the business and confirming that the applicants have made a direct investment into the business of not less than £200,000 of their own money;
- that they are actively involved full-time in the business;
- that their level of financial investment is proportional to their interest in the business;
- that they have an equal or controlling interest in the business and that any partnership or directorship does not amount to disguised employment;
- that they are able to bear their share of liabilities;
- that there is a genuine need for their investment and services in the UK;
- that new full-time paid employment has been created in the business for at least two persons settled in the UK;
- that their share of profits will be sufficient to meet the maintenance and accommodation provisions of the Immigration Rules; and
- that they do not, and do not intend to, supplement their business activities by taking or seeking employment in the UK other than their work for the business.

These provisions suggest that the Home Office will be concerned to see how far the original business proposition has been carried out. The capital will have to have been invested fully and the planned employees will have to be in their posts.[2] The requirement to be able to show audited accounts is not insisted upon at the 12-month stage. At this stage, a business person who has taken over an existing business may be able to produce audited accounts, but in the case of a new enterprise, draft or management accounts will be sufficient.[3] Clearly some business projects will take longer than others to show a return on investment, and where profits appear low or non-existent, leave will be refused unless the slow take-off was anticipated in the original business plan and is covered by the additional funds needed at that time,[4] or there is a good explanation and a realistic expectation of profitability.

1   HC 395, para 206.
2   HC 395, paras 206(ii) and (viii) confirming *Jamnadas* (6597)
3   IDI Nov/00, Ch 6, s 1, para 4.3.
4   HC 395, para 201(iii).

10.91 The initial grant of leave is for 12 months, with a condition restricting employment.[1] Where an application for an extension is successful, the applicant's stay will usually be extended for a further period of three years with a further condition restricting freedom to take employment.[2] If the Home Office is not satisfied that the requirements for a three-year extension have been met but an outright refusal would be inappropriate, it may grant a further 12 months, instead of three years, as a repeat of the initial 12 months. Where such a repeat 12 months is granted, the applicant should be advised that he or she has restarted the four-year period leading to settlement.[3] In *Trivedi*[4] a grant of a 'repeat' 12 months was successfully appealed; however under the Immigration and Asylum Act 1999 this would no longer be possible, and it would have to be challenged by way of judicial review.[5] Business persons qualify for settlement if they have spent a continuous period of four years in the UK in the business capacity and are still engaged in the business in question.[6] They must have met all the requirements of the Immigration Rules throughout the four years,[7] and produce audited accounts for the first three years and management accounts for the fourth year.[8] The Home Office approach is to construe 'continuous' as allowing for short absences abroad such as holidays or business trips consistent with maintaining employment or self-employment in the UK. Longer periods of absence may break the continuity. 'Continuous' must be given a commonsense rather than a literal meaning, with Home Office practice as a guide to what is sensible.

1   HC 395, para 204.
2   HC 395, para 207.
3   IDI Nov/00, Ch 6, s 1, para 4.6; Ch 5, s 1.
4   *Trivedi* (00 TH 01059) **10.81** fn 5 above.
5   An appeal no longer lies against the grant of a lesser leave than that sought, except in asylum cases: Immigration and Asylum Act 1999, s 61.
6   HC 395, para 209(i).
7   HC 395, para 209(ii). See *Fanous* [1993] Imm AR 200 for an example of a failure to do this.
8   HC 395, para 209(iii).

10.92 Where the Home Office considers that a business person has been absent too long or too often to permit settlement to be granted, it may grant a further extension of 12 or 24 months instead. This corresponds with the practice of granting a repeat 12 months at the end of the initial 12 months set out in the previous paragraph, and the considerations there apply. An applicant must specifically apply for settlement at the end of four years; an application for further leave to remain will be treated as such and not as an application for indefinite leave.[1]

1   IDI Nov/00, Ch 6, s 1.

Business status under the EC Association Agreements

10.93 The Immigration Rules make special provision for those who wish to establish themselves in business in the UK under EC Association Agreements.[1] Business persons who can rely on the Agreements are not required to meet the minimum investment provisions applicable to ordinary business status, nor do they need to create new full-time employment. We discuss these Agreements in chapter 7. The rules[2] cover nationals from Bulgaria, the Czech Republic, Estonia, Hungary, Latvia, Lithuania, Poland, Romania, Slovakia and Slovenia.[3] Turkish nationals are in a special position (see **10.70** above).

1   HC 395, paras 211-223.
2   HC 395, as amended, particularly by Cm 4851 on 2 October 2000.
3   For the interpretation of the applicable provisions of the Association Agreements see *Gloszczuk* and *Kondova* (joined Cases C-63/99 and C-235/99; Opinion of A-G Alber delivered 14 September 2000) and *Barkoci and Malik* (Case C-257/99; Opinion of A-G Mischo delivered on 26 September 2000).

Investors

10.94 In October 1994 a new immigration category was introduced for investors.[1] The investor category is aimed at people who wish to make the UK their main home and have substantial funds to invest here. The application will be refused if it appears that the investor does not intend to make his or her main home in the UK and intends only short visits. In this case, it is more appropriate for the applicant to enter as a visitor.[2] An investor may not take employment but can engage full-time or part-time in business or self-employment, for example, as a consultant or non-executive director.[3]

1   HC 395, paras 224–231.
2   IDI Nov/00, Ch 6, s 3, Annex G.
3   HC 395, para 224(iv).

10.95 The amount of money which must be under the investor's control and disposable in the UK is no less than £1,000,000.[1] Capital may be held in a husband and wife's joint names if one spouse is a principal applicant and will be accompanied by the other spouse as a dependant and they both apply for entry clearance at the same time.[2] An investor must intend to invest not less than £750,000 in the UK in the form of UK government bonds, share capital or loan capital in active and trading UK-registered companies (other than those principally engaged in property investment).[3] Investors cannot invest in property companies, banks, building societies or offshore companies.[4] 'Property companies' means companies whose main function is to own or manage land or buildings. It does not include companies principally engaged in construction or in other business areas such as retailing, which happen to own a substantial amount of property.[5] The investor can invest the £750,000 in a regulated collective investment scheme such as a unit trust, provided the funds are invested in companies which meet the requirements of the Immigration Rules. Many standard unit trusts which involve investments in a selection of different companies will include property companies in their portfolio. This investment will be acceptable provided the total value of the investment exceeds £750,000 and £750,000 of the investment can fairly be said to qualify under the Rules. Fund managers' prospectuses may be requested in order to check that a sufficient proportion of the investment qualifies under the Rules.[6] The £750,000 must not be invested through an off-shore company or trust. This is to ensure that maximum tax benefits accrue to the UK.

1   HC 395, para 224(i).
2   IDI Nov/00, Ch 6, s 3, Annex G.
3   HC 395, para 224(ii).
4   HC 395, para 224-(ii) and IDI Nov/00, Ch 6, s 3, Annex G.
5   IDI Nov/00, Ch 6, s 3, Annex G.
6   IDI Nov/00, Ch 6, s 3, Annex G.

10.96 Once an investor has invested at least £750,000 as required under the Immigration Rules, he or she may invest the remaining £250,000 in the UK in property companies or any major durable assets situated here, such as an unmortgaged property or significant works of art. Personal effects such as jewellery and antique furniture do not count as major assets unless it is clear that such items are held for investment purposes.[1] Investors must fulfil the maintenance and accommodation requirements of the Rules.[2] The Home Office will consider carefully the investor's personal circumstances and level of financial commitment; for example, an investor with a number of children who are being privately educated is likely to require a larger disposable income than an investor without children. In the light of current rates of return on government bonds, investors may need substantially more than £1,000,000 to satisfy the Rules. Investors supplementing their investment income by earning money on a self-employed basis will be required to provide details of the intended work.

1   IDI Nov/00, Ch 6, s 3, Annex G.
2   HC 395, para 224(iv).

10.97 The Home Office is concerned to establish the source of the applicant's funds and documentary evidence of the source will assist the application. Entry clearance is mandatory,[1] but in practice the Home Office may allow a switch to investor status in-country if there are compelling reasons why the investor is unable to leave the UK to obtain entry clearance. All investor applications are referred to the Business Case Unit of the Home Office. An investor does not have to bring any money to the UK before the application has been approved, but has to demonstrate that he or she has the requisite amount of money and the intention to invest in accordance with the Immigration Rules. The investor will normally be expected to have transferred capital and made the requisite investments within three months of the application being approved.[2] After the initial period of 12 months, investors may apply to extend leave for a further period of three years if they can demonstrate that no less than £1,000,000 of their own money is under their control in the UK, they have made the UK their main home and have invested not less than £750,000 in accordance with the Rules.[3] An investor who has suffered a major loss in his or her £750,000 portfolio, as a result of which he or she no longer has £1,000,000, may be granted leave to remain for one year only in order to keep the case under close review. After a continuous period of four years in the UK the investor may apply for settlement.[4]

1   HC 395, para 224(v).
2   IDI Dec/00, Ch 6, s 3, Annex G; but the legality of this Home Office expectation is not beyond doubt: see *Trivedi* above **10.81** fn 5.
3   HC 395, para 227.
4   HC 395, para 230; as to the meaning of 'continuous', see **10.91ff** above.

Innovators

10.98 In July 2000 the government announced the launch of a two-year pilot scheme to attract entrepreneurs with innovative business ideas to the UK.[1] The pilot scheme commenced on 4 September 2000. The key distinguishing features of the innovators scheme are that no minimum investment is required, third party funding is permitted and applications will be assessed in order to identify and select 'outstanding entrepreneurs' who will bring exceptional economic benefits to the UK. The pilot scheme is focused in particular on talented entrepreneurs in e-business and other new technology fields, although applicants in other fields may apply. The scheme was introduced in response to government concern that overseas entrepreneurs were being deterred from establishing businesses in the UK as they were unable to qualify for entry under the existing Immigration Rules. Before the introduction of the pilot scheme some innovators were unable to meet the requirements of any other immigration category; in particular, the size of their shareholding made them unsuitable for the work permit scheme and they may have had insufficient money of their own to meet the requirements of the business persons' rules. In addition, they would typically not retain a controlling or equal interest in the venture that is established.

1   Immigration and Nationality Directorate website, 25 July 2000.

10.99 Applications for innovator status must meet three minimum requirements:

- the proposed business must lead to the creation of two full-time jobs (or the equivalent);
- the applicant must maintain a minimum 5 percent shareholding of the equity capital; and
- the applicant must be able to maintain and accommodate him or herself and any dependants without recourse to other employment or public funds until the business provides an income.

Where these minimum requirements are satisfied the application is assessed using a points system, which has some similarity to the system used by the Canadian immigration authorities in respect of an equivalent status. In order to make a successful application, the applicant must achieve a minimum score in each of three separate areas, and a higher overall score. The three areas are personal characteristics (business experience, educational qualifications and proven entrepreneurial ability), the general business plan (including evidence of the technical, commercial and financial viability of the plan and proposals for the establishment of a management team) and the economic benefits of the business plan (the number and skills level of the jobs which will be created and the innovative aspect of the proposals). Each application must be supported by relevant documentation, including academic certificates, employers' references, research, financial and technical references, a full business plan containing a marketing plan and evidence of the individual's shareholding in the proposed company.

10.100 Applicants should normally obtain entry clearance before travelling to the UK, but in practice the Home Office has indicated a willingness to consider an in-country switch. Under the pilot scheme innovators are given leave to remain in the UK for an initial period of 18 months, which can be extended to a total of four years on application. At the end of those four years innovators may apply for settlement.

Writers, composers and artists

10.101 Under the pre-1980 Immigration Rules, writers and artists were not distinguished from other self-employed persons and could be admitted if they were able to support themselves and any dependants without recourse to public funds.[1] From 1980 the self-employed (writers and artists apart) became grouped with, and treated similarly to, business persons. The current Immigration Rules continue this distinction. The category has been expanded to include composers. Writers, composers and artists qualify for admission[2] if they:

- have established themselves outside the UK as a writer, composer or artist primarily engaged in producing original work which has been published (other than exclusively in newspapers or magazines), performed or exhibited for its literary, musical or artistic merit;

- do not intend to work except as related to their self-employment as a writer, composer or artist;
- have been able to support themselves for the preceding year from their own resources without working except as a writer, composer or artist;[3]
- will be able to support themselves and their family from their own resources without working except as a writer, composer or artist and without recourse to public funds; and
- hold a valid entry clearance for entry in this capacity.

1   HC 79, para 36 and HC 81, para 32. No reference was made in the Immigration Rules to support from private sources, but in *Jones* [1978] Imm AR 161 the Tribunal held that the appellant did not meet the requirements of the Rules where he had received no money for his work as a playwright for 18 months and relied upon money sent by his family abroad to cover his living expenses. See now **10.103**.
2   HC 395, para 232.
3   Writers, composers and artists therefore cannot qualify in this category straight from postgraduate studies.

10.102 Immigration law generally distinguishes between the self-employed, including writers, composers and artists, who are dealt with by the Home Office, and employees, who require a work permit and are dealt with by the Department for Education and Employment. This distinction, however, was fudged when it came to dealing with certain artists. In *Stillwaggon*[1] one of the questions for the Tribunal was whether a singer required a work permit as an entertainer or could be treated as a self-employed performing 'artist' . The answer to such a question would surely depend on whether she was an employee or self-employed. The Tribunal, however, begged the question and held that she was an entertainer rather than an artist, since the Rule referred to painters or sculptors rather than to singers. This decision, which is still applied, means that singers of international repute who come to perform in the UK cannot qualify in the writers, composers and artists category. Nor can they qualify as business visitors, because they would be selling services direct to the public, contrary to the visitor requirements (see chapter 9). The only way to enter the UK is therefore via the work permit scheme, and for this there needs to be (a) an employer (usually the promoter) and (b) an entertainer who has performed at the highest level and established an international reputation.[2] The combination of these various requirements makes it virtually impossible for an unknown performer to perform in the UK, unless under a special dispensation from the work permit requirements for recognised festivals and charity concerts.[3] But it does not end there. The distinction the Immigration Rules make between Home Office and Department for Education and Employment applications may also be difficult to apply in the case of musicians who both compose and sing. They face difficulties satisfying the requirements of the writers, composers and artists category since it is clear that (under the *Stillwaggon* doctrine) they intend to do work other than that related to their self-employment (ie sing). It is not always clear whether they should go to the Department or the Home Office or whether they can qualify at all.[4]

1   [1975] Imm AR 132.
2   Department for Education and Employment WP3 application form and WP3 (notes) guidance, and see work permits, **10.39ff** above.
3   See IDI Dec/00, Ch 17, s 3 for a list of such events.

4   Composers may conduct their work provided most of their income is derived from their composing. If they wish to play in a band they require permission from the Department for Education and Employment: IDI Nov/00, Ch 6, s 4, Annex J: guidance on persons who qualify as self-employed writers, composers and artists.

10.103 The Immigration Rules permit writers, composers and artists to meet the maintenance and accommodation requirements from their 'own resources without working except as a writer, composer or artist'.[1] This marks a change from earlier rules which required maintenance and accommodation to come from 'their own resources *including the proceeds of self-employment* without recourse to public funds'.[2] In *Boehm-Bradley*[3] the Tribunal held that the phrase 'including the proceeds of self-employment' meant that an applicant had to be able to generate some income from his or her artistic activities. Now that these words have been removed from the Rules, it is arguable that this class of entrant may be self-supporting from savings, a pension or unearned income, without any need to show earnings from their artistic activities. On the other hand, the IDI state that such persons must support themselves mainly from the proceeds of their work, although they may supplement this with income from their own investments.[4] The point awaits judicial clarification.

1   HC 395, para 232(iii) and (iv).
2   HC 251, para 45 (emphasis supplied).
3   [1986] Imm AR 305.
4   IDI Nov/00, Ch 6, s 4, Annex J.

10.104 Extensions of stay in the writers, composers and artists category are granted if the person continues to meet the requirements for admission. Initial leave will usually be for up to 12 months with a restriction on taking employment,[1] and the subsequent extension will usually be for up to three years on the same conditions.[2] This leads to settlement once the person has spent a four-year continuous period in the UK in this capacity and has met all the requirements during that period.[3]

1   HC 395, para 233.
2   HC 395, para 236.
3   HC 395, para 238; for the meaning of 'continuous', see the discussion in the context of business persons at **10.91ff** above.

RETIRED PERSONS OF INDEPENDENT MEANS

10.105 The current Immigration Rules greatly limit the ambit of the 'person of independent means' category. Prior to October 1994 there was no age limit,[1] but since that date applicants have had to be 60 or over.[2] An income of not less than £25,000 a year is required[3] (net of any overseas tax)[4] and there is no capital alternative.[5] There must also be an intention to make the UK the main home.[6] A verbal or written statement of such an intention is normally sufficient.[7] Applicants must demonstrate a close connection with the UK.[8] There is no longer an alternative requirement that the individual's admission be in the general interests of the UK (as was the case before October 1994).[9] However, the IDI specifically refer to a discretionary category of applicants who may exceptionally be granted leave on the basis that their presence will reflect well on the UK or their abilities are likely directly to benefit people in the UK other than by taking employment.[10] Persons of independent means must be able to support themselves and their families from their own resources with no assistance from any other person and without taking employment or having recourse to public funds.[11] Where applicants satisfy these conditions they will normally be admitted for an initial period of four years with a prohibition on the taking of employment.[12] For the position of British passport holders, see **10.109** below.

1 HC 251, para 44.
2 HC 395, para 263(i).
3 HC 395, para 263(ii)
4 IDI Dec/00, Ch 7, s 4, Annex G.
5 Under earlier rules income of £20,000 or capital of £200,000 was required: HC 251, para 44.
6 HC 395, para 263(v).
7 IDI Dec/00, Ch 7, s 4, Annex H.
8 HC 395, para 263(iv) and IDI Dec/00, Ch 7, s 4, Annex H: see **10.108** below.
9 See HC 251, para 44. The meaning of this phrase was never certain. The suggestion in *Nasby* (3358) that simply being a good citizen was in the interests of the state was rejected in *Wasmouth* [1984] Imm AR 151, and see *Mah* (3511); *Yuen* (4654); and *Sanji* (3524). Bringing in large investments was regarded as possibly sufficient in *Ahmadi* (2770); *Tong* (4960); *Nasnas* (4156); an intention to deploy the wealth in a manner beneficial to the UK was important in *Zandfani* (2945). In fact the Home Office operated a concession that the investment of £500,000 in the UK was *prima facie* in the general interests of the UK, which was withdrawn when the investor category was introduced.
10 IDI Dec/00, Ch 7, s 4, Annex I.
11 HC 395, para 263(iii).
12 HC 395, para 264.

Control of income

10.106 The availability of capital is no longer a consideration for admission as a person of independent means. Income alone is necessary and this must be under the person's control and disposable in the UK. The source of income does not have to be located in the UK provided the income itself is disposable here.[1] Thus problems arise if the income flow is blocked by exchange control regulations.[2] In the case of *Ex p Chiew*[3] the High Court held that the applicant must prove that he or she has a right to a supply of sufficient funds, legally enforceable against any person. Mere permission to use and spend is not control. Thus family funds from which contributions are made to an applicant will not generally count if it cannot be said that the applicant is able to control the advance of funds for the indefinite future.[4] In *Rohr*[5] a legally enforceable maintenance agreement was held to be sufficiently under the person's control for the purpose of the Immigration Rules. If the applicant and his or her spouse or partner are applying to come to the UK together, joint income or income from the spouse or partner can be counted.[6] The standard of proof in these matters is the normal civil one of a balance of probabilities and the Tribunal falls into error if it expresses itself in terms of not being convinced as to the source of funds.[7]

1 *Kotedia* (4977) unreported.
2 See *Ward* [1975] Imm AR 129 and IDI Dec/00, Ch 7, s 4, Annex G.
3 *R v Immigration Appeal Tribunal, ex p Chiew* [1981] Imm AR 102, QBD.
4 See *Gautam* (1891) (guaranteed regular payment from third parties); *Madanipoor* (1969) (voluntary payment from husband to wife).
5 *Rohr* [1983] Imm AR 95.
6 IDI Dec/00, Ch 7, s 4, Annex G.
7 *R v Immigration Appeal Tribunal, ex p Mehra* [1983] Imm AR 156, QBD.

Retirement activity

10.107 Although the Immigration Rules refer to retired persons, the only express requirements suggesting retirement are that applicants must be at least 60 years of age and have sufficient resources without taking employment.[1] A condition prohibiting employment is also attached to leave until such time as settlement is attained.[2] Earlier rules relating to persons of independent means contained the words 'without working' and Tribunal case law established that working covered remunerative activity including self-employment[3] inside or outside the UK.[4] It could be argued that the change of wording to 'without taking employment' is, therefore, significant and indicates that (a) there is no longer any need to make fine distinctions between establishing a business and making investments[5] and (b) there are now no restrictions on persons of independent means keeping their existing business interests going or engaging in new ventures. However, the IDI state that applicants will be expected to have relinquished all work commitments both in the UK and abroad and applications should be refused if an applicant intends to continue running a business abroad.[6] The IDI draw the distinction between overseeing 'business interests' and 'taking an active interest' in a business.[7]

1   HC 395, para 263(i) and (iii).
2   HC 395, para 264.
3   *Jahangard* [1985] Imm AR 69.
4   *Khan (Asadullah)* (2931); *Aalullum* (3056); *Jahangard* above; *Shikley* (4179).
5   See *Nasby* (3358) (a sleeping partner is an investor only); *Mah* (3511) (an exercise of talent as an artist or writer is not establishing a business, if it is not done for profit).
6   IDI Dec/00, Ch 7, s 4 and Annex G.
7   IDI Dec/00, Ch 7, s 4 and Annex G.

Close connection with the UK

10.108 These words are deliberately loose and fall to be interpreted in the light of the particular case. The examples given in earlier rules ('presence of close relatives' and 'periods of previous residence')[1] were examples only and not an exhaustive list. Although the current provision gives no examples at all, undoubtedly those previously given are still relevant.[2] A close relative includes relatives of the blood and by affinity.[3] If a close relative is the eldest son, this may carry more weight than if it is a more distant relative.[4] A close relative present in the UK is not to be discounted simply because he or she is here in a temporary capacity, such as student or visitor, although obviously this will carry less weight.[5] A partner in a gay or lesbian relationship counts.[6] A period of previous residence by the applicant may on its own constitute a close connection,[7] and the quality of the previous residence may be more important than its duration.[8] Thus temporary residence counts. It does not have to constitute settlement to be taken into consideration, nor need it be of any particular duration.[9] The matter must be looked at in the round.[10] Prior British nationality of the applicant or a close relative may also count,[11] but not the constitutional link between the UK and an existing Crown Colony,[12] nor connections with a former UK-mandated territory.[13] It is not necessary to sever connections with another country in order to have close connections with the UK.[14] A strong sense of identity with and belonging to the UK is a significant factor,[15] and speaking or writing English fluently or 'without trace of accent' will help.[16] Property or business connections may be taken into account.[17]

1 HC 251, para 44.
2 See now IDI Dec/00, Ch 7, s 4, Annex H. Examples given are close relatives, periods of previous residence, long-standing possession of substantial property, employment with a British company involving frequent business visits to Britain, or letters of support from eminent British citizens. The possession of British nationality (other than British citizenship) does not constitute a close connection.
3 *Mistry* (3039); *Fung* [1984] Imm AR 159; *Yuen* (4654).
4 *Fung* above.
5 *Bagherzadeh* (2898).
6 *Thong* TH/30896/87 (adjudicator), noted in Mungo Bovey 'UK Immigration Law and the Homosexual' (1984) INLP 8 at 62
7 *R v Immigration Appeal Tribunal, ex p Zandfani* [1984] Imm AR 213; in *Nasby* (3358) eight out of 50 years was insufficient; and see IDI Dec/00, Ch 7, s 4, Annex H.
8 See *Rohr* [1983] Imm AR 95; *Nasby* above.
9 *Zandfani* above; see also *Rohr* above, where residence as a student for six years was part of the reasons for holding that a close connection existed.
10 *Zandfani* above; and see IDI Dec/00, Ch 7, s 4, Annex H.
11 See *Rohr* above; *Fung* above; *Antiglevich* (4661); *Yuen* above. It is insufficient on its own to constitute a close connection: IDI Dec/00, Ch 7, s 4, Annex H.
12 *Chui* (4172); *Yuen* above.
13 *Nasnas* (4156).
14 *Fung* above.
15 *Bagherzadeh* (2898).
16 *Jambuserwara* (2852); *Wasmouth* (3426); *Antiglevich* (4661).
17 *Rohr* above, approved in *Nasnas* above, but not if the property is a purely speculative investment: see *Fung* above; *Sanji* (3524).

10.109 Retired persons of independent means are normally given up to four years' leave on entry.[1] However a British passport holder (British Dependent Territories citizen, British National (Overseas), British Overseas citizen, British subject under the British Nationality Act 1981 or British Protected Person) should be given indefinite leave to remain immediately.[2] If less than four years is given, an extension to take the person up to four years may be granted.[3] Indefinite leave to remain will then be granted on application,[4] provided the applicant has spent a continuous period of four years in the UK in this capacity and has met and continues to meet the requirements of the Immigration Rules.[5]

1 HC 395, para 264.
2 IDI Dec/00, Ch 7, s 4.
3 HC 395, para 267.
4 IDI Dec/00, Ch 7, s 4, and see **10.92** above.
5 HC 395, para 269; for the meaning of 'continuous' see **10.91** above.

SWITCHING TO SELF-EMPLOYMENT OR INDEPENDENT MEANS STATUS

10.110 Although entry clearance is a mandatory requirement of the Immigration Rules in all the categories under discussion,[1] the Home Office exceptionally may consider an in-country switching application. It would normally have to be apparent from the initial application that the applicant meets all the substantive requirements of the Rules.[2] See also the comments in **10.73** (business persons), **10.97** (investors) and **10.100** (innovators). The no-switching provision for dependants may also be waived if they satisfy all the other requirements for entry.[3] Refusal of in-country applications on no-switching grounds must be based on factors additional to the no-switching rule in order to avoid judicial challenge on the ground that the decision is arbitrary.[4] For appeals, see chapter 18.

1 HC 395, para 201(xi) (businesspersons), para 224(v) (investors); Immigration and Nationality Directorate website, 25 July 2000 (innovators), para 232(v) (writers, composers and artists), para 263(vi) (retired persons of independent means).
2 IDI Nov/00, Ch 6, s 1 (business), Immigration and Nationality Directorate website, 25 July 2000 (innovator), IDI Nov/00, Ch 6, s 3 (investors), IDI Nov/00, Ch 6, s 4 (writers, composers and artists), IDI Dec/00, Ch 7, s 4 (retired persons of independent means).
3 IDI Nov/00, Ch 6, s 5 (dependants of businessmen, investors, writers, composers and artists) and IDI Dec/00, Ch 7, s 4, Annex J (dependants of retired persons of independent means).
4 IDI Nov/00, Ch 6, s 1.

FAMILY MEMBERS OF THE SELF-EMPLOYED AND OF RETIRED PERSONS OF INDEPENDENT MEANS

10.111 The spouse, unmarried partner and children under 18 of persons in self-employment (as business persons, investors, innovators or writers, composers and artists), or of retired persons of independent means, may also be admitted to the UK.[1] In all cases they will need to satisfy the maintenance and accommodation provisions of the Immigration Rules which require accommodation which is owned or occupied exclusively by the applicant. In the case of spouses and partners it is essential that the marriage or relationship is subsisting. In the case of children leave will only be granted if they are unmarried, have not formed an independent family unit and are not leading an independent life. Normally, children must be accompanying or joining *both* parents but will be allowed to accompany or join just one parent if the other is deceased, if the parent has had sole responsibility for the child's upbringing, or if there are serious and compelling family or other considerations which make exclusion undesirable and suitable arrangements have been made in such cases for the child's care. As a general rule the spouse, partner and dependent children who have been given permission to accompany or join the principal applicant will be free to take employment or engage in business or other self-employment.[2] Dependants of retired persons of independent means are not permitted to take any form of work,[3] though the Home Office may allow dependent children of retired persons of independent means to undertake training after the first year of residence in the UK.[4]

1 HC 395, paras 240-245 (spouses and children of businesspersons, investors, writers, composers and artists), 271-276 (spouses and children of retired persons of independent means), 295J-K (unmarried partners), Immigration and Nationality Directorate website, 25 July 2000 (spouses and children of innovators).
2 IDI Nov/00, Ch 6, s 5.
3 IDI Dec/00, Ch 7, s 4, Annex J.
4 IDI Dec/00, Ch 7, s 4, Annex J.

FAMILY AND MARRIAGE

INTRODUCTION

11.1 In this chapter we examine the provisions of the Immigration Rules for admission for permanent residence of family members of people settled in the UK. Here, do not cover refugee family reunion (which is dealt with in chapter 12 below) or family members of EEA nationals (dealt with in chapter 7). This chapter will need to be read together with the paragraphs of chapter 8 dealing with Article 8 of the ECHR (right to respect for family and private life): see **8.16**ff above. The most important categories of family members are spouses, fiancé(e)s and unmarried partners, and children under 18.[1] The Rules for other categories such as elderly parents, over-age children and uncles and aunts are highly restrictive.[2] Unmarried partners are now within the Rules on a similar footing as spouses, save that they must have lived together for two years to qualify and must complete a further two years before getting settlement.[3] The most important change for spouses since the last edition (apart from the impact of the Human Rights Act 1998) was the abolition of the primary purpose rule in June 1997.[4] However, the definition of 'sham' marriages under the Immigration and Asylum Act 1999[5] comes uncomfortably close to the old primary purpose rule, and its impact remains to be seen.

1   HC 395, paras 277–316.
2   HC 395, paras 317–319.
3   HC 395, paras 295A-L, as introduced by Cm 4851 from 2 October 2000 See **11.56** below.
4   HC 26, amending HC 395, paras 281, 284 and 290.
5   Immigration and Asylum Act 1999, s 24(5); see **11.45** below.

11.2 The provisions for admission of family members of EU and EEA nationals have been dealt with in chapter 7 above and are not repeated here. It remains an absurd anomaly that the admission of family members of British citizens who have travelled and worked elsewhere in the EC is governed by the generous provisions of EC law,[1] while restrictive domestic Immigration Rules continue to govern the family reunion rights of those who have stayed at home. Practitioners should be astute to search for an EC law solution to family reunion difficulties.

1 See *R v Immigration Appeal Tribunal and Surinder Singh, ex p Secretary of State for the Home Department* [1992] Imm AR 565, [1992] 3 All ER 798 and chapter 7.

11.3 The Immigration Rules were amended on the coming into force of the Human Rights Act 1998 on 2 October 2000[1] to bring them into line with ECHR obligations. A number of extra-rules concessions affecting unmarried partners (heterosexual or same-sex),[2] bereaved spouses[3] and the children of fiancé(e)s[4] have been brought within the Rules, as has the admission of children for adoption.[5] The rules allowing former spouses to enter for access to children of a former marriage, which were heavily criticised in the last edition, have been rewritten to allow for work and settlement.[6] The admission of spouses and children of refugees has also been brought within the Rules.[7] The rules on public funds have been amended in line with the former policy, allowing the UK-settled party to claim in his or her own right so long as the arrival of the family member does not result in additional recourse to public funds.[8] However, other rule changes which require children to be supported by their sponsoring parent or relative[9] appear to entrench Home Office opposition to long-term third party support of children and other family members, attempting to reverse the effect of *Arman Ali*.[10] This limb of the relevant Rules should, to be human rights-compliant, be construed as not precluding third party support to parents, since the amended Rules do not require parental support of children to be from their own resources. Alternatively, it would have to be disapplied in cases involving, for example, disabled parents where support is provided by a third party, so as to avoid discrimination in the enjoyment of family life contrary to Articles 8 and 14 of the ECHR.

1 By Cm 4851.
2 HC 395, as amended, paras 295A–L.
3 HC 395, as amended, para 287(b); bereaved unmarried partners are included at para 295M.
4 HC 395, as amended, paras 303A–F.
5 HC 395, as amended, paras 316A–C.
6 HC 395, as amended, paras 246–248F.
7 HC 395, as amended, paras 352A–F.
8 HC 395, as amended, para 6A.
9 HC 395, as amended, paras 297(v), 298(v), 301(v), 310(v), 311(v), 314(v), 317(v).
10 *R v Secretary of State for the Home Department, ex p Arman Ali* [2000] INLR 89.

11.4 Concessions which operate to prevent the removal of unlawfully resident children, with long residence in the UK,[1] and unlawfully resident spouses or parents of British citizens or UK-settled persons,[2] are still outside the Immigration Rules. Recent government practice has been to apply these concessions strictly, and to require these persons to return home where they have failed to obtain entry clearance prior to arrival.[3] The concession allowing the settlement of spouses and partners who have suffered domestic violence in their probationary period also remains outside the Rules. We examine the remaining concessions affecting family life in **11.53** (domestic violence), **11.59-11.60** (marriage and removal) and **11.106** (children) below.

1 DP69/99 (formerly DP5/96): *Butterworths Immigration Law Service*, D[1121].
2 DP3/96, DP4/96: *Butterworths Immigration Law Service*, D[551] and D[601].
3 See eg *R v Secretary of State for the Home Department, ex p Zighem* [1996] Imm AR 194;
   R v Secretary of State for the Home Department, ex p Gangadeen [1998] INLR 206;
   R v Secretary of State for the Home Department, ex p Kebbeh (CO 1269/98) 30 April
   1999; *R v Secretary of State for the Home Department, ex p Ahmed and Patel* [1998]
   INLR 571 CA; *R v Secretary of State for the Home Department, ex p Isiko* [2001]
   1 FCR 633, CA; *R v Secretary of State for the Home Department, ex p Mahmood* [2001]
   1 WLR 840.

11.5 Sex discrimination in family reunion has now largely disappeared from the Immigration Rules. Working, self-employed[1] and student[2] women can be joined by their husbands, who can now also be deported and removed as family members of women deportees or overstayers.[3] The rules precluding enjoyment of polygamous family life in the UK have been made gender-neutral.[4] The much reviled and now discredited primary purpose rule was withdrawn in 1997, but we have seen in its place a much stricter application of the requirement that the couple intend to live together. Indirect discrimination still operates under the special voucher rules, where only heads of households (normally the husband) will qualify for vouchers to settle as British nationals without the right of abode.[5]

1 HC 395, as amended, paras 194–196, 240–242, 271–273.
2 HC 395, as amended, paras 76–78.
3 HC 395, as amended, paras 363, 365.
4 HC 395, as amended, paras 278-280, 296.
5 HC 395, as amended, paras 249–253. For the explanation of the scheme and the recognition
  of sex discrimination, although the wording of the dependants rule is neutral, see *Re Amin*
  [1983] 2 AC 818, [1983] 2 All ER 864; see also *Kassam v Immigration Appeal Tribunal*
  [1980] 2 All ER 330, [1980] 1 WLR 1037, CA.

11.6 Age limits within the Immigration Rules relating to family settlement may be open to challenge in particular cases where there is dependency, regardless of the age of the applicant, and where the Rules pose a disproportionate obstacle to the right to respect for family life. The requirement that over-age children and other dependent relatives live alone in the most exceptional compassionate circumstances, in order to qualify for settlement with sponsoring relatives in the UK, may be open to challenge as incompatible with Article 8 of the ECHR unless it can be construed and applied purposively in such cases.[1]

1 HC 395, para 317(i)(f); see **11.116** below.

11.7 The provisions for admission of family members considered in this chapter all depend on there being a sponsor who is settled in the UK and wants to bring the family member over.[1] Thus persons admitted as spouses or unmarried partners are dependent on the immigration status of their partner until they obtain settlement.[2] Although entry clearance to join family in the UK stands as leave to enter, a change of circumstances between issue of the entry clearance and arrival here may result in cancellation of leave by an immigration officer.[3] If the sponsoring spouse is found to have obtained entry unlawfully, or doubts are raised about the validity of the marriage, or if the marriage breaks down, or the new arrival has recourse to public funds, an extension of stay may be refused, and a decision to remove will normally follow. A Home Office policy allows the grant of settlement to spouses and unmarried partners who have been victims of domestic violence by their sponsor or a member of his or her family during the probationary period.[4] Spouses and unmarried partners bereaved during their probationary period may now obtain settlement under the Immigration Rules.[5] Once spouses and unmarried partners have been granted settlement they may not be deprived of it, whether or not the marriage or relationship lasts, unless the Home Office can demonstrate that fraud was used to obtain settlement, in which case it may initiate deportation proceedings on the ground that deportation is conducive to the public good.[6]

1 See next section for maintenance, accommodation and third-party support.
2 HC 395, para 321.
3 HC 395, para 283; Immigration (Leave to Enter and Remain) Order 2000, SI 2000/1161, art 6.
4 IDI Dec/00, Ch 8, s 1, Annex C. See **11.53** below.
5 HC 395, as amended by Cm 4851, paras 287(b) (spouses) and 295M (unmarried partners).
6 *R v Immigration Appeal Tribunal, ex p Cheema* [1982] Imm AR 124, CA; *R v Immigration Appeal Tribunal, ex p Patel (Anilkumar Rabindrabhai)* [1988] AC 910, [1988] 2 All ER 378, [1988] 2 WLR 1165; *Yanus Patel v Immigration Appeal Tribunal* [1989] Imm AR 416, CA. See chapter 15 below.

11.8 For those with limited leave to enter or remain as students, workers or business people, family unity is generally confined to spouses and unmarried partners[1] and children under 18.[2] But concessions or waivers may be available for over-age children of certain work permit holders, for example.[3] Family unity provisions for refugees are now included in the Immigration Rules,[4] but those with exceptional leave to remain must still rely on policy.[5]

1 HC 395, as amended, paras 295J-L.
2 See **9.34** for the rules relating to families of students, **10.31** for those of non-work permit holders, **10.59** for work permit holders **10.69** for trainees and **10.105** for the self-employed and persons of independent means.
3 See **10.58** above.
4 HC 395, as amended, paras 352A-F.
5 See policy statement set out in *Butterworths Immigration Law Service* 2B[6]; see also **12.183**ff below.

ENTRY CLEARANCE REQUIREMENTS

11.9 Persons who wish to enter the UK with a view to settlement with a family member, including a spouse or cohabitee, must obtain a prior entry clearance before doing so[1] unless they claim the right of abode. The exceptions are returning residents[2] and children born in the UK who are not British citizens.[3] This requirement is strictly applied. A person who marries while on temporary admission[4] will be required to return home for entry clearance unless there are exceptional compassionate circumstances.[5] The inconvenience or expense of having to travel home to obtain a visa is not considered sufficient reason for waiver,[6] even where the Home Office is satisfied that all other requirements of the Immigration Rules (presence of sponsor; intention to live together; having met; maintenance; and accommodation) are met.[7] Entry clearance as leave to enter may be cancelled if there has been a change of circumstance since its issue (such as the death of a partner or the breakdown of the marriage prior to entry)[8] or it was obtained through false representations or non-disclosure of material circumstances.[9] We have seen that entry clearances are issued in the country of residence and are valid as leave to enter.[10] Those claiming the right of abode need a certificate of entitlement unless they have a passport describing them as a British citizen.[11] Certificates of entitlement can be issued abroad prior to travel or in the UK.[12] There is a duty on the entry clearance officer abroad properly to classify an application as either one for entry clearance or for a certificate of entitlement to the right to abode; this is not the responsibility of the applicant.[13]

1 HC 395, paras 281(vii) (spouses), 290(viii) (fiancé(e)s), 295A(vii) (unmarried partners), 297(v), 301(vi), 310(ix), 314(xii) (children), 317(vi) (other dependent relatives). Leave to enter is to be refused if no such entry clearance is produced on arrival: paras 283, 292, 295C, 300, 303, 313, 316 and 319.
2 HC 395, para 18. See **4.25**ff above.
3 HC 395, para 305.
4 Under Immigration Act 1971, Sch 2, para 21.
5 IDI Dec/00, Ch 8, Annex G, para 2. See *Musu Dyfan v Secretary of State for the Home Department* [1995] Imm AR 206, CA. The case of *R v Secretary of State for the Home Department, ex p Hashim* (12 June 2000), QBD, where this was doubted, was disapproved by the Court of Appeal in *R v Secretary of State for the Home Department, ex p Amjad Mahmood* [2001] 1 WLR 840.
6 See IDI Dec/00, Ch 8, s 2, para 3.2. This refers to the no switching rule for fiancé(e)s (see **11.50** below), but is also applicable to spouses on temporary admission.
7 *R v Secretary of State for the Home Department, ex p Mahmood* [2001] WLR 840, CA, disapproving *R v Secretary of State for the Home Department, ex p Hashim* (CO 2052/99) 12 June 2000.
8 HC 395, para 321(ii).
9 HC 395, para 321(i).
10 See chapter 2; HC 395, para 28. Immigration (Leave to Enter and Remain) Order 2000, SI 2000/1161, arts 3-5.
11 Immigration Act 1971, s 3(9), inserted by Immigration Act 1988, s 3.
12 HC 395, paras 12-14 do not prescribe where a certificate of entitlement must be applied for; see *R v Secretary of State for the Home Department, ex p Phansopkar* [1976] QB 606, [1975] 3 All ER 497, CA.
13 *Khatun (Kessori)* (4272) founded the long-established principle, upheld by the Immigration Appeal Tribunal in *Rahman* (00 TH 00307) 25 January 2000, that an applicant cannot be expected to know or understand the complexities of the immigration and nationality laws of the UK. Note that although the application form is the same, there is now a difference in fee levels between the two applications.

11.10 In *R v Secretary of State for the Home Department, ex p Phansopkar*[1] the Court of Appeal held that where there was considerable delay in processing certificates of entitlement, a person with the right of abode could travel without one and require his or her application to be determined in the UK by the Home Office without having to be removed first. However, the Immigration Act 1988 amended the Immigration Act 1971 to require a person claiming the right of abode to prove it by means of a certificate of entitlement if he or she did not have a British passport,[2] and those without one or other of these documents have no right of appeal against refusal of leave to enter.[3] Arrival without a certificate of entitlement, therefore, will be unwise. It may also be difficult for the person to board an airline to come to the UK without proper documentation.[4] We have already remarked[5] that in the context of family members of EC nationals, a requirement that a family permit should be applied for outside the UK is not compatible with the right of admission granted under EC law.

1 [1976] QB 606, [1975] 3 All ER 497, CA.
2 Immigration Act 1971, s 3(9), as amended by Immigration Act 1988, s 3; HC 395, para 12.
3 Immigration and Asylum Act 1999, s 60(1).
4 See carriers' liability provisions Immigration and Asylum Act 1999, Pt II, ss 40ff, chapter 14 below.
5 See **7.79**ff above and the case of *R v Pieck* [1981] QB 571.

11.11 A person given leave to enter as a visitor, student or in some other temporary capacity may apply to vary that leave to join their relatives in the UK without having first to return to their country of origin.[1] However, this will only apply where there has been a change of circumstances and intention since entry. Someone who had intended to marry or join relatives here permanently when he or she arrived for the visit or temporary stay may well be held to have deceived the immigration officer on entry and runs the risk of refusal or being treated as an illegal entrant.[2]

1 HC 395, paras 284 (spouses), 295D (unmarried partners), 298 (children), 311 (adopted children) and 317(vi) (other dependants), where the distinction is made between the requirement of an entry clearance when seeking leave to enter and leave to remain. This does not apply to fiancé(e)s, who cannot 'switch' from another category.
2 For illegal entry, see chapter 16 below.

PRESENCE OF SPONSOR

11.12 Family settlement claims require a sponsor who is present and settled in the UK, except in cases where all the relevant members of the family will be admitted for settlement at the same time.[1] These conditions will be deemed to be satisfied in the case of a sponsor who is a member of the armed forces serving abroad but based in the UK, or a permanent member of the diplomatic service or a comparable UK-based staff member of the British Council on a tour of duty abroad.[2] In cases of joint sponsorship, both sponsors must be present and settled.[3] 'Settled' means ordinarily resident in the UK without being subject to any restrictions on stay under the immigration laws.[4] When entry clearance officers are considering applications, they are entitled to consider whether these conditions will be met at the time of admission.[5] A fleeting visit will not be sufficient to establish ordinary residence in the UK,[6] but an intention to live here permanently is not required[7] and one can be ordinarily resident in two places at the same time.[8]

1 HC 395, paras 281 (spouses), 290(i) (fiancé(e)s), 295A(i) (unmarried partners), 297(i), 301(i), 305(i), 310(i), 311(i), 314(i) (children), 317(i) (other dependants).
2 HC 395, as amended, para 281.
3 *Shabir (Mohammed)* [1989] Imm AR 185.
4 Immigration Act 1971, s 33(2A), as amended; HC 395, para 6. See further chapter 4 above. The residence must be lawful residence so if the sponsor is an illegal entrant who has obtained leave to remain in a false name, the dependants will not qualify: *Akhtar (Kalsoom)* (10755). An entitlement to reside without actual residence will not suffice: *Wong (Sin Lai Jacqueline)* [1992] Imm AR 180. Those with exceptional leave to remain are not eligible for settlement for four years and so cannot obtain family reunion before then, save in the most exceptional compassionate circumstances. See **12.183** below.
5 *Rashida Bibi v Immigration Appeal Tribunal* [1988] Imm AR 298, CA.
6 *Rashida Bibi v Immigration Appeal Tribunal* [1988] Imm AR 298, CA.
7 *R v Immigration Appeal Tribunal, ex p Rafique* [1990] Imm AR 235.
8 *Shah v Barnet London Borough Council* [1983] 2 AC 309, [1983] 1 All ER 226, HL; *R v Secretary of State for the Home Department, ex p Chugtai* [1995] Imm AR 559.

11.13 The Immigration Rules do not stipulate where the sponsor should be at the time that the application is made. In the case of *R v Immigration Appeal Tribunal, ex p Manek*[1] (decided under earlier rules) the Court of Appeal suggested that a sponsor had to be physically present in the UK at the time of the application, but on the facts of that case the sponsor was not present at the time of decision, which was fatal to the application. It is now sufficient for the sponsor to be ordinarily resident with a right to return to the UK, rather than physically present here at the time of the application, provided that he or she will be present when the sponsored relative arrives.[2] This clarification is important in practice, given the length of time it takes for some applications to be processed and the hardship caused if families have to be divided. However, the sponsor's absence from the UK while the application is being processed may make it more difficult to satisfy maintenance and accommodation criteria at the date of the decision of the entry clearance officer.

1 [1978] Imm AR 131, CA, interpreting HC 79, para 39.
2 *Raheen* (2949), *Bibi (Mokbul)* (4954) unreported, IAT. (1987) 2 INLP 50.

MAINTENANCE AND ACCOMMODATION

11.14 Before admitting family members to join a sponsor, the entry clearance officer will have to be satisfied that there is adequate maintenance and accommodation for them in the UK without recourse to public funds. The spouses and children of refugees are not subject to the maintenance and accommodation requirements.[1] The Home Office has also waived the requirement in particular cases for family members of those with exceptional leave to remain.[2] 'Public funds' are defined[3] as:

- income support or jobseekers' allowance;
- housing and homelessness assistance;
- housing benefit and council tax benefit;
- family credit;[4]
- child benefit;[5]
- attendance allowance;
- severe disablement allowance;
- invalid care allowance;
- disability living allowance;
- disability working allowance.

Neither NHS treatment nor state education counts as recourse to public funds for the purpose of the Rule.[6] A big question was whether the receipt of public funds by sponsors in their own right could disqualify relatives from joining them in circumstances where there would be no additional recourse to public funds, but where the relatives benefited indirectly. This was known as 'indirect reliance on public funds'. After years of divergence between Home Office policy as set out in correspondence[7] and the wording of the Rules, and of conflicting Tribunal and High Court decisions,[8] this issue has been put to rest by an Immigration Rule amendment stating that 'a person is not to be regarded as having (or potentially having) recourse to public funds merely because he is (or will be) reliant in whole or in part on public funds provided to his sponsor, unless, as a result of his presence in the UK, the sponsor is (or would be) entitled to increased or additional public funds'.[9]

1 HC 395, as amended, paras 352A-F.
2 For example, in a policy set out in a Home Office letter of 17 May 1990 and withdrawn on 15 January 1996, a policy specifically for Somali nationals was established which agreed to take a 'flexible approach and consider waiving the requirement in individual

cases; in deciding whether to do this each case is considered on its individual merits, and the decision maker would look, *inter alia*, at the degree of difficulty continuing separation of the family is causing'. 'Somali Family Reunion Policy' [1993] Imm AR 40.

3 HC 395, para 6. This rule is subject to frequent change and an up-to-date version should be consulted.

4 The UK-settled sponsor may claim family credit and child benefit for his or her family if they are entitled to it under social security legislation (see chapter 13 below), and where a foreign wife (sic) is married to a person present and settled in the UK, she may claim family credit on behalf of her husband and family: IDI Dec/00, Ch 8, Annex H.

5 See fn 4 above. Where the only extra benefit being claimed is child benefit, it should not be considered as additional recourse to public funds: IDI Nov/00, Ch 1, s 7, Annex W.

6 IDI Nov/00, Ch 1, s 7.

7 See eg letter from Nicholas Baker to Sir Giles Shaw MP, October 1994, (1995) Legal Action (July) at 21; Nicholas Baker to Max Madden MP, set out in *Kausar* [1998] INLR 141 at 144. The relevant policy statements are also set out in *Butterworths Immigration Law Service*, D[1021].

8 *R v Immigration Appeal Tribunal, ex p Chhinderpal Singh* [1989] Imm AR 69; *R v Secretary of State for the Home Department, ex p Islam Bibi* [1995] Imm AR 157; *Ahmed (Bashir)* [1991] Imm AR 130; *Yousaf* (9190); *Ramzan* (11185); *Scott (Clevon Marcus)* (13389); *Kausar* [1998] INLR 141; *Hussain (Gulam)* (20671); *Khan (Shamima Jaham)* (HX 00663).

9 HC 395, para 6A, inserted by Cm 4851 from 2 October 2000.

11.15 The rules for the admission of spouses and unmarried partners, for children and for other relatives are all slightly different. Spouses and unmarried partners need to show that there will be adequate accommodation for the parties and any dependants without recourse to public funds in accommodation which they own or occupy exclusively, and that they will be able to maintain themselves and any dependants adequately without recourse to public funds.[1] Children must show that they can and will be accommodated adequately by the parent, parents or relative the child is seeking to join without recourse to public funds, in accommodation owned or occupied exclusively by the sponsor, and that they can and will be maintained adequately by the parent or relative without recourse to public funds.[2] Other dependent relatives must show that they can and will be accommodated adequately together with any dependants, without recourse to public funds, in accommodation owned or occupied exclusively by the sponsor, and that they can and will be maintained adequately, together with any dependants, without recourse to public funds.[3] The differences in the wording appear to represent the Home Office view as to who should be responsible for maintaining and accommodating the various relatives. In the case of spouses, the wording of the Rule appears to envisage that the spouses will provide for themselves; children may be accommodated and supported only by their parents or other sponsoring relative; and other dependent relatives may be supported by anyone, and may join sponsors in accommodation provided by others. The October 2000 amendments to the Immigration Rules thus appear to seek to reopen the second big argument in this area, which is whether and to what extent someone other than the sponsor can provide the support and accommodation necessary for family reunion, or 'third party support'. This was also the subject of conflicting decisions in the Tribunal, with some divisions holding that the Rules precluded support from anyone other than the UK sponsor, others that third party support was acceptable so long as it was reliable.[4] After a number of restrictive Tribunal decisions were quashed by consent, the issue seemed to have been resolved with the decision in *Arman Ali*[6] that the maintenance and accommodation requirements of the Rules could be met by long-term third party support.[7] Collins J held that the Rules should be applied sensibly and purposively, to give effect to family life rights. The Rules neither limited third party assistance to family members nor precluded children from supporting themselves from their own resources.[8] However, although the Home Office did not appeal *Arman Ali*, the December 2000 IDI[9] and the October 2000 changes to the rules relating to the admission of children suggest that it is unwilling to accept the court's ruling on third party support and child self-support.[¶] Family life considerations under Article 8 of ECHR mean that the liberal interpretation of the maintenance and accommodation rules, in which any form of support is permissible so long as the family member's arrival does not result in additional recourse to public funds, ought to prevail.[¶]

1 HC 395, paras 281(iv) and (v) (spouses), 295A(v) and (vi) (unmarried partners). Fiancé(e)s may not work before the marriage, so the test for them is that they must be adequately maintained and accommodated until that time, and thereafter the provisions mirror those for spouses: HC 395, para 290(iv)-(vi).
2 HC 395, paras 297(iv) and (v), 298(iv) and (v), 301(iv) and (iva), 310(iv) and (v), 311(iv) and (v), 314(iv) and (iva) (amendments introduced by Cm 4851).
3 HC 395, para 317(iv) and (iva), as amended.
4 *Hussain (Mohammed Jahangir)* [1991] Imm AR 476; *Neesa (Najmun)* (11545): third party support not acceptable; *Khan (Zamal)* (16392); *Nguyen (Thi B)* (18738) IAS 1999, Vol 2, No 9: third party support was acceptable for a very limited period; *Azad* (5993); *Khan* (6283); *Modi* (9714), *Kumar (Rajesh)* (18885) IAS 1999, Vol 2, No 21: acceptable in short to medium term; *Ahmed (Mukhtar)* (9028): long-term third party support acceptable in marriage case, *Njoku* (18520) IAS 1999, Vol 2, No 14: long-term third party support acceptable in principle both in marriage and children cases (sponsors were elderly grandparents who relied on support from relations).
5 eg *Ahmed (Ishaque)* (12292); *Begum (Zabeda)* (16677), rejecting long-term third party support in principle. The consent orders quashing these decisions were not publicised, and so later Tribunals continued to rely on them.
6 *R v Secretary of State for the Home Department, ex p Arman Ali* [2000] INLR 89, QBD.
7 The decision in *Jabeen* [1991] Imm AR 178, that the maintenance rule could not be satisfied when the sponsor was serving a sentence of imprisonment, would not survive if the applicant could rely on third party support or his or her own earnings so as to prevent reliance on public funds.
8 The Tribunal had held in *Begum (Hasna)* (15629) and *Bibi (Sonor)* (19199), IAS 1999, Vol 2, No 17, that earnings of a dependent child could be taken into account in assessing whether there would be sufficient maintenance to avoid recourse to public funds under HC 395, paras 281(v) and (vi) and 297(iv).
9 The IDI relating to spouses say that an undertaking that members of a couple's families will support them until they are able to support themselves from their own resources 'is unacceptable as the Rules require the couple to be able to support themselves . . . from their own resources', although the arrangement may be accepted exceptionally for a limited period. This guidance (IDI Dec/00, Ch 8, s 1, Annex H) is wrong: the Immigration Rules do *not* require self-support from a couple's own resources.

11.16 The Immigration Rules do not require that adequate maintenance and accommodation are available at the date of the decision (which would preclude the entry of spouses and partners and other economically active family members whose own earning power is relied on to satisfy the Rule), but that it is reasonably forseeable that the requirements will be met within six months (the currency of the visa).[1] A written undertaking of support may be required, save in the case of admission of spouses and children under 16, where there is a statutory obligation to support.[2] A refusal to provide such an undertaking may lead to a refusal of the application.[3] Copies of the undertaking are sent to the Department of Social Security, and failure to honour it may lead to a prosecution of the sponsor[4] and/or a refusal to extend stay.[5] However, short-term and emergency recourse to public funds through no fault of the sponsor will not have adverse consequences.[6]

1 *Begum (Momotaz)* (18699), (1999) 5 ILD No 2; *Seen, Arif* (16167).
2 See National Assistance Act 1948, s 42, as amended by Family Law Reform Act 1987, Sch 2; Social Security Administration Act 1992, s 78 (liability to maintain as a result of an undertaking under the Immigration Act 1971).
3 HC 395, para 320(14).
4 Under National Assistance Act 1948, s 51, as amended, in the case of spouse and children, and Social Security Administration Act 1992, s 105 (sponsors who have given an undertaking under the Immigration Act 1971).
5 HC 395, para 322(6). Refusal of an extension is only possible in the case of spouses, partners and children who were admitted for 12 months (or 24 months in the case of partners) in the first instance (paras 284, 293, 295F, 298, 311). Admission on the basis of false representations as to availability of support and accommodation could result in the applicants being referred by the local authority to the Home Office for consideration of whether the person is an illegal entrant (*R v Secretary of State for the Environment, ex p London Borough of Tower Hamlets* [1993] Imm AR 495).
6 IDI Dec/00, Ch 8, s 1, Annex H.

11.17 In determining whether parties or sponsors are able to support themselves and their dependants, information is obtained about their normal income and regular commitments and the case is then assessed to see whether the money available will be sufficient to support the dependants concerned.[1] Where someone is joining a sponsor in the UK, generally there would have to be evidence of an ability to maintain the immigrant from the sponsor's own earnings and savings. Fiancé(e)s are not permitted to work until their leave has been extended after marriage,[2] but persons admitted as spouses can take into account their own anticipated earnings.[3] Applicants' skills and qualifications may suffice without evidence of a job offer if they are of direct value to gaining employment in the UK, but those with few skills might need to show that there is a job open to them in the UK, or that relatives or friends can realistically offer an opening.[4] The IDI state that jobs that are unrealistic in the light of the applicant's skills, or jobs that appear to have been manufactured and lack any prospect of continuing will not suffice. However, they also say that 'care must be taken not to make assumptions'. The fact that unemployment in a certain area is high is not in itself enough to warrant refusal.[5] Adequacy of maintenance should take into account tax obligations,[6] and undeclared earnings may be disregarded.[7] Income support has been held an appropriate comparator to assess whether the income available to the sponsor and his or her family would be adequate.[8] The Tribunal has also accepted that account should be given to the values and habits of the applicants' and sponsors' culture, which may be relatively frugal, with a willingness to assist each other in times of need.[9]

1 In *Uvovo* (00 TH 01450) IAS 2000, Vol 3, No 15, the Tribunal held, disapproving *Osman* (16249), that evidence of a sponsor's regular outgoings was not essential.
2 HC 395, para 291; IDI Dec/00, Ch 8, s 1, Annex H.
3 IDI Dec/00, Ch 8, s 1, Annex H point out that 'it should not be assumed that it is the man who must be the breadwinner', and look for evidence of sufficient independent means, employment or sufficient prospects of employment for one or both of the parties.
4 IDI Dec/00, Ch 8, s 1, Annex H.
5 IDI Dec/00, Ch 8, s 1, Annex H.
6 *Keyani* (5662).
7 *Tedeku* (6024).
8 *Islam* (13183), *Begum (Momotaz)* (18699), (1999) 5 ILS No 2; *Uvovo* (00 TH 01450) IAS 2000, Vol 3, No 15. In the latter case the Tribunal said the sponsor's income must match income support net of accommodation costs and other items such as school meals and prescription charges, to which income support is a gateway.
9 *Khan (Deywan)* (00 TH 02531); *Yasin (Mohammed)* (G0027). However in *Begum (Momotaz)* above, the Tribunal held that family members could not be admitted if their standard of living was going to fall below the minimum considered acceptable nationally.

11.18 The accommodation available for the family member must either be owned or occupied exclusively by the parties or the sponsor; these are alternatives, not cumulative requirements. A freehold interest is not necessary to comply with the requirement of ownership, but there must be some interest in the house, such as a tenancy. Occupation of premises may be as a licensee or lodger. It is doubtful whether boarding children with a neighbour will suffice until the sponsor is the occupier in law,[2] but there is no requirement that the accommodation is the sponsor's sole or main residence. Exclusive occupation does not have to extend to the whole of premises; exclusive occupation of a bedroom will suffice, with shared use of the remainder of the premises. There may be an issue as to whether the Rule is compliant with the ECHR; if durable accommodation is actually available to the family and there will in fact be no recourse to the local authority, then applying the approach in *Arman Ali*,[5] refusal on the basis that occupation is not exclusive may constitute a disproportionate interference with family life contrary to ECHR, Article 8, and if the Rule has disproportionately adverse effects on those from cultures where sleeping in shared accommodation in extended families is the norm, it could violate the anti-discrimination provisions of Article 14 combined with Article 8.

1 *Sokoya* (00 TH 02272) IAS 2000, Vol 3, No 17.
2 *Baidwan* [1975] Imm AR 126; *Jabeen (Musrat)* (4925).
3 *Sokoya* fn 1 above.
4 *Zia (Raja)* [1993] Imm AR 404 at 412; *Kasuji* [1988] Imm AR 587; IDI Dec/00, Ch 8, s 1, Annex H, para 6.
5 [2000] INLR 89. See **11.15** above.

11.19 Like maintenance, accommodation does not have to be available at the time of the application or decision, but only when the family member arrives in the UK.[1] However, the appellate authorities may not admit evidence of available accommodation at an appeal if the arrangement was not in existence or at least canvassed at the time of the decision.[2] The standard of adequacy of the accommodation is that the applicant may live there without breach of the public health laws or statutory overcrowding.[3] An applicant should not, however, be required to produce a report from a local authority as to the fitness of accommodation in every case, since in most cases the issue is not adequacy but availability of accommodation.[4] On an application for settlement, the fact that accommodation does not meet local authority standards does not allow refusal, if the applicant has not received emergency housing prior to the making of the decision, even if it appears likely that the family will require emergency housing in the near future.[5]

1 *Jan (Munir)* (1517); *Begum (Sultan)* (3155). IDI Dec/00, Ch 8, s 1, Annex H accept that accommodation will often be prospective rather than available, and the test should be whether there is a reasonable prospect that adequate accommodation will be available.
2 *Kazmi* (5866); *Azad* (5993); generally for admissibility of evidence not before the decision taker see *R v Immigration Appeal Tribunal, ex p Hassanin* [1987] 1 All ER 74, [1986] 1 WLR 1448, CA. *Rahman* (7228), Immigration Appeal Tribunal.
3 *Begum (Syeda)* (3811); *Thompson (Gayon)* (17926). Congestion is not the same as statutory overcrowding: *Sultana (Nighat)* (19228) IAS 1999, Vol 2, No 2. IDI Dec/00, Ch 8, s 1, Annex H set out guidance on overcrowding at para 6.3 and note that local authorities have the power to licence temporary overcrowding.
4 *Rehman* [1998] INLR 500.
5 IDI Dec/00, Ch 8, s 1, Annex H, para 8.

MARRIAGE

General problems of validity

11.20 In order to obtain admission as a spouse, the applicant must satisfy the entry clearance officer that the marriage is a lawful one and complies with the requirements of the Immigration Rules. A valid marriage requires that both parties had the necessary capacity to marry, and that the celebration was in a valid form. Capacity to marry is normally determined by the ante-nuptial domiciliary law of each party. The formal validity of the marriage is determined by the law of the place of celebration. A detailed review of private international law relating to validity of marriages and divorces is beyond the scope of this work, but we focus on the particular problems likely to be encountered in immigration cases, in particular the rules relating to polygamous marriages and the recognition of talaq divorces.

Polygamous marriages

11.21 Polygamous marriages are those where under the law of the place of the celebration of the marriage (*lex loci celebrationis*) the husband is permitted to marry more than one wife during the subsistence of the marriage, or the wife is permitted to take another husband.[1] Such marriages may be actually or potentially polygamous. It is actually polygamous where the husband has more than one wife or vice versa, and potentially so if the couple have no other wives or husbands but the husband or wife is entitled to take more than one spouse under the local law. A polygamous marriage in England without an English civil ceremony is always invalid.[2] The common law rule was that all marriages celebrated in the UK must be monogamous, whatever the form used.[3] English law used to restrict jurisdiction to granting any relief in respect of a marriage to monogamous marriages, but this has now been modified by Matrimonial Causes Act 1973, section 47. The broad principles of English private international law relating to marriages celebrated abroad follow.

1   The system of marriage where the wife can take a second husband is polyandry. However the amended para 278 of HC 395 uses the word 'polygamous' in a gender-neutral way.
2   *R v Bham* [1966] 1 QB 159, [1965] 3 All ER 124, CCA; *R v Mohammed Ali* [1964] 2 QB 350n.
3   *Chetti v Chetti* [1909] P 67.

11.22 It is the law of the place of the celebration of the marriage which determines whether a marriage is polygamous or monogamous, not the law of the parties' domicile.[1] Marriages which start off as polygamous may be converted into monogamous marriages by subsequent events: the spouses may change their religion;[2] may subsequently marry in an English registry office;[3] the husband may obtain a domicile where polygamous marriage is not allowed;[4] or the local law may change and prohibit polygamy.[5] Under some systems of law the marriage may become a monogamous one once a child is born.[6]

1   *Chetti* above; *Mehta (otherwise Kohn) v Mehta* [1945] 2 All ER 690; *Sinha Peerage Claim* [1946] 1 All ER 348n.
2   *Sinha Peerage Claim* above.
3   *Ohochuku v Ohochuku* [1960] 1 All ER 253, [1960] 1 WLR 183.
4   *Ali v Ali* [1968] P 564, [1966] 1 All ER 664.

5 *Parkasho v Singh* [1968] P 233, [1967] 1 All ER 737.
6 *Cheni v Cheni* [1965] P 85, [1962] 3 All ER 873.

11.23 A man or woman whose personal law does not allow him or her to marry polygamously has no capacity to contract a valid polygamous marriage.[1] Such marriages were not recognised by English law and do not, therefore, bestow on either party the status of husband or wife. The common law rules gave rise to some dispute as to what the appropriate personal law was.[2] For marriages taking place after 31 July 1971, validity is dealt with by statute. The Matrimonial Causes Act 1973, section 11(d) provides that:

> 'A marriage celebrated after 31 July 1971 shall be void on the following grounds only, that is to say . . .
> (d) in the case of a polygamous marriage entered into outside England and Wales, that either party was at the time of the marriage domiciled in England and Wales.
>
> For the purposes of paragraph (d) of this subsection a marriage *is not* polygamous if at its inception neither party has any spouse additional to the other.'[3]

1 *Re Bethell, Bethell v Hildyard* (1888) 38 Ch D 220; *Ali v Ali*, **11.22** fn 4 above.
2 See *Radwan v Radwan (No 2)* [1973] Fam 35, [1972] 3 All ER 1026, which suggested that the test of capacity should be determined by the law of the country of the intended matrimonial home rather than that of the ante-nuptial domicile. See further *Lawrence v Lawrence* [1985] 2 All ER 733 at 740 and 746, CA; *Begum (Ranu)* [1986] Imm AR 461. See also *R v Immigration Appeal Tribunal, ex p Rafika Bibi* [1989] Imm AR 1.
3 The words in italics were inserted by the Private International Law (Miscellaneous Provisions) Act 1995, s 8(2), Sch, para 2(1), (2) (in force January 1996). Prior to this, the sub-section provided that a marriage was polygamous even though at its inception neither party had any additional spouse.

11.24 Prior to the amendment of the Matrimonial Causes Act 1973 on 8 January 1996, section 11(d) provided that a marriage was void for polygamy even if it was only potentially polygamous. In *Hussain v Hussain*[1] the court held that a marriage contracted in a country which permits polygamy could only be potentially polygamous, and hence void under section 11(d), if at least one of the spouses had the capacity to marry polygamously. This protected the position of Muslim men domiciled in the UK who wished to marry abroad in a traditional marriage ceremony with a bride domiciled in that country. This was because under Muslim law women can only have one husband, but a man may have more than one wife at any one time. So a husband with an English domicile contracting an Islamic marriage in Pakistan was not entering a potentially polygamous marriage, since the husband had no capacity in English law to enter such a marriage; the wife, although domiciled in Pakistan, does not have capacity to marry polygamously; so the marriage was valid. The problem was when a Muslim woman domiciled in the UK went back, for example, to Pakistan, to marry a man domiciled there. Applying *Hussain*, the marriage was polygamous since the husband had the capacity under the law of his domicile to take another wife. This would be extremely unfair on British Muslim women. It was Home Office practice to accept the marriage for immigration purposes. However, the amendment of the Matrimonial Causes Act by the Private International Law (Miscellaneous Provisions) Act 1995[2] in force on 8 January 1996, validated marriages which are actually monogamous but are celebrated under a law which permits polygamy. This is fully retrospective, and potentially polygamous marriages which are actually monogamous are therefore now valid under UK law.[3] This should resolve the problem.

1   [1983] Fam 26, [1982] 3 All ER 369, CA.
2   Section 8 and Sch, para 2(1), (2).
3   See IDI Dec/00, Ch 8, s 1, Annex E, para 5.

Polygamous marriages and the Immigration Rules

11.25   Until 1988, entry could be given to a second wife of an actually polygamous marriage if that marriage was recognised as valid by the domiciliary law of the parties.[1] The Immigration Act 1988 provided that no entry clearance or certificate of entitlement would be issued to a woman married under a system of law that allows polygamy, if there was another wife alive who has been to the UK since the marriage or has been granted entry clearance or a certificate of entitlement.[2] The first marriage must be a valid one in order to disqualify the second wife.[3] Women who have the right of abode as Commonwealth citizens married to a CUKC before 1983 may therefore be prevented from exercising the right of abode. The disqualification only applies if the right of abode was obtained as a wife, and will not include people who are British citizens.[4] The provisions do not prevent a wife from returning to the UK if she previously came for settlement as a wife before 1 August 1988,[5] nor do they apply if the wife has been in the UK at any time since her marriage before there was a second wife.[6] Disqualifying presence in the UK by the other spouse will be disregarded if it was as a visitor, as a person on temporary admission or as an illegal entrant.[7] In these cases of actually polygamous marriages, a spouse cannot be admitted to the UK as such until divorce or death removes the other spouse. The IDI provide that entry clearance may not be withheld from a second wife where the husband has divorced the previous wife and the divorce is thought to be one of convenience, even if the husband is still living with the previous wife and to issue the entry clearance would lead to the formation of a polygamous household.[8] The Immigration Rules have now been amended to preclude the admission of a (so-called) polygamous husband of a woman in the same terms as the rules for men.[9] They apply to all applications made after 2 October 2000, regardless of the date of the marriage. The provisions do not prevent polygamous spouses entering the UK in any other capacity.

1   *Begum (Ranu)* [1986] Imm AR 461.
2   Immigration Act 1988, s 2(2); HC 395, para 278. The order in which polygamous spouses marry is not important but the order in which they come to the UK for settlement is. It is the spouse who applies for settlement second, rather than the one who marries second, who will be refused: IDI Dec/00, Ch 8, s 1, Annex E, para 1.
3   The burden of proving the invalidity of a second marriage on the grounds of the existence of a prior valid marriage falls on the party asserting the invalidity, usually in these cases the Home Office: *Mussarat (Rukshana)* (9610).
4   Immigration Act 1988, s 2(1).
5   Immigration Act 1988, s 2(4); HC 395, para 279(i).
6   Immigration Act 1988, s 2(4); HC 395, para 279(ii).
7   Immigration Act 1988, s 2(7) and HC 395, para 280. The IDI has a useful flowchart on the admission of polygamous spouses.
8   IDI Dec/00, Ch 8, s 1, Annex E, para 8.
9   HC 395, as amended by Cm 4851, para 278. Polyandry as a legal system is in fact extremely rare. In *Bibi (Maqsooda)* (G0091) a polyandrous marriage was recognised as giving settlement rights under the Immigration Rules, but this decision was disapproved in *Nadeem* (00 TH 0010) IAS 2000, Vol 3, No 8.

11.26   The fact that a marriage is void as polygamous will not make the children of the marriage illegitimate automatically. Where one of the parties to the marriage is domiciled in the UK the Legitimacy Act 1976 may apply, which provides that if one of the parties to a marriage ceremony believed that the marriage was valid at the time of the child's conception, the child will be legitimate despite the invalidity of the marriage.[1] There may be difficulties in proving the belief at the relevant time.[2] Although illegitimacy is no bar to admission to join a father under the Immigration Rules,[3] citizenship by descent and acquisition of the right of abode through the father still depends on legitimacy.[4] A child of a polygamous marriage who has the right of abode is not prevented from entry to the UK in the same way as a spouse, but where a parent is to be refused entry or leave to remain for settlement on the ground of polygamy, the Rules are not to be construed as permitting a child to be granted entry clearance, leave to enter or remain or a variation of leave.[5]

1   Legitimacy Act 1976, s 1. The belief must be in the validity of the marrigae in the UK, not in the place of its celebration: *Azad v ECO Dhaka* [2001] INLR 109, CA.
2   See *Begum (Dilara)* (10108) where the children were born after a decision that the marriage was polygamous and so invalid, when neither party could have believed in its validity: *Begum (Minara)* (19500). See also *Azad (Misba)* (L00033) IAS 2000, Vol 3, No 8: the presumption of legitimacy introduced by Family Law Reform Act 1987, s 28 did not apply to children born before that Act came into force and the burden of proof was on the appellant.
3   HC 395, para 6 (definition of 'child' for immigration purposes).
4   British Nationality Act 1981, ss 50(9) and 47. Refusal of discretionary registration to an illegitimate child of a British father was upheld in *R (Montana) v Secretary of State for the Home Department* [2001] 1 WLR 552, CA.
5   HC 395, para 296. It is be doubted whether this Rule would prevent the admission of such a child under the 'exclusion undesirable' provisions (see **11.79** below) if abandoned or neglected by its parent abroad.

Domicile

11.27 It will be seen from the above that admission under the Immigration Rules may require the domicile of the relevant parties to be ascertained at material times. Domicile is an important concept in English law.[1] It is one of the key connecting factors determining which country's law governs personal transactions. A person only has one domicile at a time. It is to be distinguished from other connecting factors such as nationality, residence, or the place where a marriage is celebrated, where a contract is entered into or the litigation is being conducted. Originally, domicile meant no more than residence, but over the years it has acquired more complex connotations[2] which were first spelt out by the House of Lords in *Udny v Udny*,[3] a case concerning inheritance. Lord Westbury distinguished between political and civil status. Political status was governed by nationality, but civil status by domicile. Domicile and nationality were quite distinct concepts. Domicile was of two kinds: (i) domicile of origin acquired by birth – the domicile of the father if the child is born legitimate, of the mother if illegitimate; (ii) a domicile of choice acquired by residence in a particular country plus an intention to stay there permanently. He said:

> 'Domicile of choice is a conclusion or inference which the law derives from the fact of a man fixing voluntarily his sole or chief residence in a particular place with an intention of continuing to reside there for an unlimited time . . . it must be a residence not for a limited period or particular purpose, but general and indefinite in its contemplation.'[4]

1   For a full description and recommendations for reform, see Law Commission Report: *Private International Law – The Law of Domicile* (Cm 200, 1987).

2 See now Domicile and Matrimonial Proceedings Act 1973, ss 1–4.
3 (1869) LR 1 Sc & Div 441.
4 (1869) LR 1 Sc & Div 441 at 458.

11.28 Where the intended residence is for a limited period, it is immaterial whether that limitation is expressed in terms of time or is made dependent on the happening of some event or the achievement of a particular task during the person's lifetime. The position was spelt out more clearly by Scarman J in *Re Fuld's Estate (No 3)*:[1]

> 'If a man intends to return to the land of his birth upon a clearly foreseen and reasonably anticipated contingency, the end of his job, the intention required by law is lacking; but, if he has in mind only a vague possibility, such as making a fortune (a modern example might be winning a football pool) . . . such a state of mind is consistent with the intention required by law.'

1 [1968] P 675 at 684–685. See also *Lawrence v Lawrence* [1985] Fam 106, [1985] 2 All ER 733, CA; *R v Immigration Appeal Tribunal, ex p Rafika Bibi* [1989] Imm AR 1, QBD.

11.29 Domicile is to be clearly distinguished from nationality. It is possible to acquire a domicile of choice irrespective of nationality.[1] A person may change his or her nationality without this necessarily affecting domicile.[2] However, although nationality is not conclusive, it may be evidence of a change of domicile, particularly where there has been naturalisation in accordance with the requirements of the British Nationality Act 1981, Schedule 1, paragraph 1(1)(d)(i) (an intention that his or her principal home will be in the UK). Secondly, the requirement of an intention to remain permanently distinguishes domicile from mere residence and in particular from ordinary residence.[3]

1 *Boldrini v Boldrini and Martini* [1932] P 9.
2 *Wahl v A-G* (1932) 147 LT 382: a German national lived in England and became a naturalised British subject, and later returned to Germany to look after his father's estate. Held: although he changed his nationality he had retained his domicile of origin in Germany.
3 See **5.14–5.18** above.

11.30 The distinction between a domicile of origin and domicile of choice is also important. After *Udny v Udny* a tendency arose to apply a very strict test as to evidence of intention with respect to a change of domicile. The cases indicate that 50 years' residence may be insufficient to acquire a domicile of choice unless there is unequivocal proof of an intention to settle.[1] Modern cases may not be quite so strict, but certain elements of the tendency remain.

1 *Winans v A-G* [1904] AC 287, 291; *Bowie (or Ramsay) v Liverpool Royal Infirmary* [1930] AC 588; *A-G v Yule and Mercantile Bank of India* (1931) 145 LT 9. These cases contrast starkly with the expedient approach to wartime divorces, where the acquisition of a domicile of choice was quite readily accepted by the courts in the case of an alien, originally here on a transit visa, who was liable to deportation (*May v May* [1943] 2 All ER 146) or actually under a recommendation for deportation (*Cruh v Cruh* [1945] 2 All ER 545). The Law Commission in its earlier working paper recommended that to establish domicile it should be sufficient to show an intention to make a home in a country indefinitely (Working Paper 80 para 5.17). This suggestion proved controversial and in its final report it recommended that the intention necessary for the acquisition of a new domicile should be determined without reference to any presumption (para 5.22).

11.31 The legal rules may be summarised as follows:

(i)   'There is the strongest possible presumption in favour of the continuance of the domicile of origin. As contrasted with the domicile of choice, "its character is more enduring, its hold stronger and less easily shaken off".'[1]

(ii)   The intention to settle permanently must be ascertained by objective criteria, and statements as to domicile by a testator in a will,[2] by a taxpayer on an Inland Revenue form,[3] or in an application for registration or naturalisation as a British citizen are not necessarily reliable.[4]

(iii)   The burden of proving that a domicile of choice has been acquired rests on the person who asserts that the domicile of origin has been lost.[5] If the burden of proving a change has not been discharged, the domicile of origin will remain.[6]

(iv)   The abandonment of a domicile of choice is easier than its acquisition, although there must be unequivocal evidence of abandonment.[7] One reason for the difference is that abandonment of a domicile of choice does not depend upon the acquisition of a new domicile. If no new domicile of choice is acquired, the domicile of origin revives.[8]

1   Per Lord MacNaughten in *Winans v A-G* [1904] AC 287 at 290. For a modern example see *Cramer v Cramer* [1986] Fam Law 333, CA.
2   *Re Steer* (1858) 3 H & N 594; *A-G v Yule and Mercantile Bank of India* (1931) 145 LT 9.
3   *Buswell v IRC* [1974] 2 All ER 520, [1974] 1 WLR 1631.
4   *Begum (Rokeya)* [1983] Imm AR 163; *Khatun* (9663).
5   *Winans v A-G* [1904] AC 287 at 290 and 291.
6   *Scappaticci v A-G* [1955] P 47, [1955] 1 All ER 193.
7   *Re Lloyd Evans, National Provincial Bank v Evans* [1947] Ch 695 at 703; *Re Raffenel's Goods* (1863) 3 Sw & Tr 49.
8   The Law Commission recommended that the doctrine of revival be abolished, and that an established domicile continues until a new domicile is acquired (Working Paper 80, para 5.25).

11.32 In the case of *Ex p Miah*[1] the problems of domicile were well illustrated. A Bangladesh-born national came to the UK in 1963, where he had worked and lived ever since. He married his first wife in 1972 and a second wife in 1987, who entered the UK before April 1988, albeit claiming to be the sponsor's sister. She subsequently applied for entry clearance from abroad. The entry clearance officer argued that the sponsor had acquired a domicile of choice in the UK, and therefore the second marriage was void. But the evidence that he intended to make his home in the UK was predicated on the ability of the second wife to come here, which was precisely what was excluded if he had a UK domicile. The paradox was to be resolved by the presumption in favour of the domicile of origin, unless it could be shown that the sponsor intended to live in the UK regardless of whether his second wife came.

1   *R v Immigration Appeal Tribunal, ex p Miah* (CO/2100/92) 14 June 1994, QBD. See also *Bibi* (12488), where a seaman in the UK since 1946, who registered as British in 1951, was held to have retained his domicile of origin in Bangladesh, where he maintained a matrimonial home with three wives and their children.

11.33 The IDI[1] set out the factors which will be taken into account in assessing whether someone has acquired a domicile of choice in the UK. They point out that length of residence is not conclusive, and neither is acquisition of nationality, although it is more important if the person has given up his or her former nationality. A statutory declaration made for naturalisation purposes, that an applicant intends to reside permanently in the UK, may be taken into account, as may possession of property, in particular the purchase of a burial ground. The nature and length of the person's employment in this country, registration as an elector, residence of other family members in the UK and children's education in the UK are all relevant. The IDI also point out that the burden is on the Secretary of State to show that a polygamous marriage which took place abroad is invalid because at the time of a marriage one party had acquired a domicile of choice in the UK.[2] A domicile questionnaire to be completed by a sponsor who entered a polygamous marriage abroad is attached to the IDI. In *Ex p Ali*[3] the problems of domicile questionnaires were exposed. The sponsor, not understanding its purpose, had omitted all information which suggested continuing links with Pakistan, which he had left in the late 1960s to work in the UK. Only on the eve of an application for judicial review of the entry clearance officer's refusal of a certificate of entitlement to the children of his second (polygamous) marriage did the sponsor reveal evidence of land purchases, a bank account, frequent long visits and the procreation of more children with his first wife, all of which together negatived the impression given by his answers in the questionnaire that he had lost his domicile of origin in Pakistan and acquired a domicile of choice in the UK by the time of the second marriage. So long as sponsors believe that domicile questionnaires exist to test the sincerity of their desire to live in the UK rather than their domicile and therefore the validity of their second marriage, similar problems are likely to persist.

1   IDI Dec/00, Ch 8, s 1, Annex E, para 5.
2   IDI Dec/00, Ch 8, s 1, Annex E, para 7.
3   *R v Entry Clearance Officer Islamabad, ex p Ali* (CO/3585/97) 20 January 1999, QBD.

Recognition of talaq and other overseas divorces

11.34   The rules relating to recognition of foreign divorces and judicial separations are now to be found in sections 44 to 54 of the Family Law Act 1986[1] and are not set out comprehensively here. The recognition of Islamic talaq divorces is a topic which regularly arises in the immigration context when considering the capacity of the parties to marry. Under Islamic sharia law, a husband is permitted to divorce a wife without recourse to court proceedings simply by declaring unequivocally his intention to repudiate the marriage in the presence of witnesses. This is a bare talaq and involves no proceedings at all. Most Islamic countries have modified pure religious law by some formal requirements as to registration with a court or administrative body and conciliation proceedings. Thus in Pakistan the Muslim Family Law Ordinance requires registration of the talaq with the Chairman of the Union District Council, and the talaq does not become effective until the lapse of a period for reconciliation.[2] A failure to comply with these formalities renders the husband liable to a penalty.[3] In Azad Kashmir, however, the Muslim Family Law Ordinance does not apply.[4]

1   In force on 4 April 1988. See IDI Dec/00, Ch 8, s 1, Annex D on recognition of overseas divorces.
2   Muslim Family Law Ordinance 1961.
3   It may be that a divorce that fails to comply with these provisions is still a valid divorce recognised in Pakistan and may therefore be recognised in the UK under the Immigration Rules where no proceedings have taken place.
4   See *Bi (Maqsood)* (10144), and see **11.36** below.

11.35 Formerly, English common law could give recognition to such a divorce if it were recognised by the law of the parties' domicile, even if the talaq had been pronounced in the UK.[1] The position is now governed by statute, which applies to any divorce, whether obtained before or after April 1988.[2] No talaq pronounced in the UK will be a valid divorce, even if followed by proceedings overseas, for only courts of civil jurisdiction can grant divorces in the UK.[3] This Rule cannot be evaded by divorcing in a foreign embassy, which is considered to be in the UK.[4] Nor can it be evaded by obtaining a foreign court's recognition of the extra-judicial English divorce and seeking to recognise the foreign judgment.[5]

1   *Qureshi v Qureshi* [1972] Fam 173, [1971] 1 All ER 325.
2   Family Law Act 1986, ss 45 and 52; but the Act preserves, *inter alia*, s 6 of the Recognition of Divorces and Legal Separations Act 1971, for the survival of some common law rules on recognition.
3   Family Law Act 1986, s 44; *Re Fatima* [1986] AC 527, [1986] 2 All ER 32, HL; *Hamid* (14314) IAS 1996, Vol 4, No 1.
4   *Radwan v Radwan* [1972] 3 All ER 967; IDI Dec/00, Ch 8, s 1, Annex E, para 4.
5   *Maples v Maples* [1988] Fam 14, [1987] 3 All ER 188.

11.36 Where a divorce is obtained by 'proceedings' outside the UK, it will be recognised if it was effective under the law of the country under which it was obtained and either party to the marriage was habitually resident, domiciled or a national of the country in which the divorce was obtained.[1] Registration of a talaq under the Muslim Family Law Ordinance amounts to proceedings,[2] but a bare talaq does not,[3] even one pronounced in Azad Kashmir at the Union Council offices before two witnesses[4] or one obtained under the Muslim Family Law Ordinance subsequent to a bare talaq in Azad Kashmir.[5]

1   Family Law Act 1986, s 46(1); *Qureshi v Qureshi* [1972] Fam 173, [1971] 1 All ER 325; *R v Registrar General, ex p Minhas* [1977] QB 1, [1976] 2 All ER 246.
2   *Quazi v Quazi* [1980] AC 744, [1979] 3 All ER 897, HL.
3   *Bi (Maqsood)* (10144); *Nadeem* (00 TH 00100) IAS 2000, Vol 3, No 8.
4   *Akhtar (Nahid)* (17071) IAS 1998, Vol 1, No 9.
5   *Akhtar* (15412) IAS 1998, Vol 1, No 2.

11.37 Some provision is now made in UK law for overseas divorces which are obtained without any proceedings at all.[1] The requirements are that the divorce is effective under the law of the country in which it was obtained; that either the two parties were domiciled in the country where the divorce was obtained at the time or one party was so domiciled and the divorce is recognised as valid in the law of the other party's domicile; and that neither party was habitually resident in the UK in the year before the divorce.[2] Thus a West African customary divorce may be recognised if evidence of either dissolution by a customary court or agreement by the heads of the parties' families is available by affidavit, accompanied by a document registering the divorce and a certificate of the Minister for Foreign Affairs.[3]

1   Family Law Act 1986, s 46.
2   Family Law Act 1986, s 46(2).
3   IDI Dec/00, Ch 8, s 1, Annex D, para 6.3.

11.38 The above summary of the legal rules probably suffices for consideration of the validity of divorces for immigration purposes. It should be noted where there is a dispute between parties, a talaq, whether obtained by proceedings or not, may be refused recognition by the English courts in three circumstances:

(a) where notice of proceedings was not given or where a party to the marriage has not been given a reasonable opportunity to take part in the proceedings; (b) where there is no official certificate or document certifying that the divorce without proceedings is effective under the law of that country; or (c) where recognition would be manifestly contrary to public policy.[1] In *Chaudhary v Chaudhary*[2] an alternative ground for non-recognition of a bare talaq was that recognition would be contrary to public policy because the husband pronounced it to defeat the wife's claim to ancillary relief in the UK. Recognition will also be withheld if the foreign divorce conflicts with the judgment of a British court or a court whose judgment is entitled to be recognised in the UK.[3]

1   Family Law Act 1986, s 51(3).
2   [1985] Fam 19.
3   Family Law Act 1986, s 51(1)(b).

Spouses under 16

11.39 The age at which a person can contract a valid marriage varies from country to country. An age requirement will usually be classified as a matter of capacity affecting the essential validity of the marriage. It will therefore fall, under English law, to be dealt with according to the law of the domicile of the particular person. A marriage contracted by a spouse domiciled in the UK is not valid if he or she is under 16.[1] However, in a number of countries marriage under the age of 16 is permitted and marriage by a spouse under this age, domiciled there, is regarded as valid. This means that in the past such wives or husbands would qualify for admission to the UK under the Immigration Rules. Since 1986, the Rules have required that both parties to a marriage be aged 16 on arrival in the UK before an entry certificate or leave to enter or remain is granted. Since the repeal of section 1(5) of the Immigration Act 1971 in 1988, this Rule has applied to all marriages.[2] But a spouse who married validly abroad under the age of 16 will be eligible to enter to join a spouse here on reaching that age, if the other requirements of the Rules are met.

1   Matrimonial Causes Act 1973, s 11(a)(ii).
2   HC 395, para 277.

The validity of the marriage ceremony and proving the marriage

11.40 Apart from the requirement of monogamy, marriages celebrated in the UK must comply with the requirements of the Marriage Acts 1949-94 and subordinate regulations. The marriage should have been celebrated in a building approved for civil marriage by the Marriage Act 1994,[1] and there should be a marriage certificate issued by a registrar or superintendent registrar, a clergyman of the Church of England or Wales, a synagogue, a non-conforming church or the Society of Friends.[2] In *Bath*[3] the Court of Appeal relied on the presumption of validity of marriage[4] to find that a long marriage preceded by an irregular ceremony in an unregistered Sikh temple was valid. If the marriage took place abroad, there is often difficulty in establishing to the satisfaction of the entry clearance officer that the relationship of husband and wife is as claimed.[5] The question is largely one of evidence and of credibility. The onus is on the parties to prove the relationship as claimed. But evidence of a marriage certificate and post-nuptial correspondence may shift the burden of persuasion to the Home Office to disprove the relationship.[6] Previous findings of the appellate authorities carry substantial weight but are not conclusive in the face of fresh evidence.[7]

1 Many buildings, including hotels and foreign embassies may be registered for the purpose: Marriage Act 1994; IDI Dec/00, Ch 8, s 1, Annex D.
2 IDI Dec/00, Ch 8, s 1, Annex D.
3 *Chief Adjudication Officer v Bath* [2000] 1 FCR 419, CA, a case about entitlement to widow's pension.
4 22 *Halsbury's Laws* (4th edn) paras 992 and 993.
5 *Bi (Channo)* [1978] Imm AR 182; *Begum (Inayat)* [1978] Imm AR 174.
6 *Hanison* (5366), *Perez (Aida)* (9636).
7 *Momin Ali v Secretary of State for the Home Department* [1984] 1 All ER 1009, [1984] Imm AR 23; *R v Immigration Appeal Tribunal, ex p Lulu Miah* [1987] Imm AR 143.

11.41 Normally, the best proof of a marriage is a marriage certificate,[1] but this is not always available or there may be doubts as to its authenticity or accuracy, and the existence of the marriage may have to be proved in other ways. The Immigration Appeal Tribunal has accepted that presumptions which go to establish the existence of a marriage in the parties' country of origin can be used. Thus in *Begum (Nazir)*[2] the Tribunal accepted as a presumption of Muslim law that:

'Marriage will be presumed in the absence of direct proof, from:
(a) prolonged and continued cohabitation as husband and wife; or
(b) the fact of the acknowledgment by the man of the child born to the woman, provided all the conditions of a valid acknowledgement . . . are fulfilled; or
(c) the fact of the acknowledgment by the man of the woman as his wife.'[3]

This decision was followed later in *Begum (Inayat)*.[4] The presumption is similar to that applied in the domestic context in the *Bath* case above.[5]

1 Where a marriage certificate is produced, a party disputing the validity of the marriage has to prove to a high degree of probability that the marriage is not valid: *Babir* (16466) IAS 2000, Vol 3, No 7.
2 [1976] Imm AR 31.
3 From Mulla's *Principles of Mohamedan Law* (19th edn, 1990), s 268.
4 [1978] Imm AR 174.
5 *Chief Adjudication Officer v Bath* **11.40**, fn 3 above.

11.42 In *Akhtar*[1] the Tribunal accepted the view of experts on Islamic law that in that tradition the parties need not have met, and so a telephone marriage was valid even though the husband was not present at the marriage ceremony. In *Ur Rehman* the Tribunal held that if both parties are domiciled in a country where a telephone marriage is valid, the marriage is recognised under English law even if one of the parties was resident in the UK on the date of the marriage.[2] The IDI however, say that a telephone marriage is not valid if one party is in the UK at the time.[3] The IDI recognise proxy marriages, provided they are recognised in the country where they are celebrated.[4] The fact that a proxy may be appointed by telephone from England would not detract from recognition of the marriage celebrated elsewhere. However, by the time the application for entry clearance is determined, the couple must have met in order to comply with a specific requirement of the Immigration Rules aimed at arranged marriages.[5] A Pakistan Islamic marriage is complete even if the attendant traditional ceremonial such as the departure of the bride (ruksati) is dispensed with.[6]

1 (2166).
2 *Ur Rehman* (TH 5885/99) IAS 2000, Vol 3, No 15.
3 IDI Dec/00, Ch 8, s 1, Annex D, para 3.
4 IDI Dec/00, Ch 8, s 1, Annex D, para 3.
5 HC 395, para 281(iii); see further **11.49** below.
6 *Hussain (Basharat)* [1991] Imm AR 182.

11.43 In *Khanom*[1] the Tribunal held that it was not essential as a matter of law for the exact date of the marriage to be given. Parties could establish by evidence that they were married without being able to fix the exact date when this took place. Clearly, this would be the situation if the presumptions relating to cohabitation and acknowledgment of paternity operated.[2] But the date of the marriage may be relevant to questions concerning the age and nationality status of children. A marriage that is held to be invalid may nevertheless qualify the applicant for admission as a fiancé(e) if it is demonstrated that the applicant was willing and able to remarry at the date of the decision,[3] or as an unmarried partner if he or she was unable to do so,[4] but there is no jurisdiction to allow an appeal on the basis of the fiancé(e) or unmarried partner rules where the application had been made on the basis of a marriage held to be invalid.[5] The principle is that an applicant must make clear the facts that he or she relies on, but not necessarily all the different potentially applicable rules. When in doubt, therefore, simultaneous applications as a spouse or as a fiancé(e) or an unmarried partner would need to be made in the alternative. A spouse application refused on invalidity grounds could attract an appeal on human rights grounds if the parties had cohabited and family life was established, and if the refusal constituted an interference with family life (because the parties could not live together in the other spouse's country of residence) which was disproportionate to the legitimate aim pursued by the decision.

1 [1979–80] Imm AR 182.
2 See **11.40ff** above.
3 *Ach-Charki* [1991] Imm AR 162.
4 HC 395, para 295A(iii). But parties legally unable to marry on grounds of consanguineous relationships or age may not seek admission as unmarried partners: HC 395, para 295A(ii) and see *R v Secretary of State for the Home Department, ex p Ozminnos* [1994] Imm AR 287, QBD.
5 *R v Immigration Appeal Tribunal, ex p Uddin (Hawa Bibi)* [1991] Imm AR 134, QBD.

11.44 Problems arose when spouses sought admission in false names (to cover up previous tax frauds). The Immigration Appeal Tribunal held, in a series of cases, that a family member could not be granted entry clearance if the name he or she was using was a false one.[1] There is no reason why an appeal cannot be allowed in such cases if the appellate authority finds that, despite the false name, the parties are related as claimed.[2] Greater difficulties could arise with respect to any directions made to give effect to the appeal. A declaratory judgment may be sufficient; alternatively, if the evidence reveals that the 'false name' is an identity of the appellant, directions could be issued; finally directions could be issued for an entry clearance to be granted in a passport in the appellant's true name. Similarly, the fact that lies have been told in the course of an application does not by itself prevent the applicant succeeding, if the relationship claimed at the time of the application is made out to the satisfaction of the authorities.[3]

1 *Khatoon* (2137); *Khanam* (2381); *Akhtar* (2460).
2 In most cases there will be no issue that the applicant for entry clearance and the person recognised as a spouse are the same, but merely a false or assumed name has been used.

3 *R v Immigration Appeal Tribunal, ex p Kulbander Kaur* [1991] Imm AR 107;
   R v Immigration Appeal Tribunal, ex p Gondalia [1991] Imm AR 519; *Haleem* (10048).

Marriages of convenience and 'sham' marriages

11.45 A marriage is not invalid under the general law of England simply because
it is entered for a purpose other than mutual cohabitation,[1] and the parties to such
a marriage have the relationship of man and wife. But the Immigration Rules
require parties to intend to live together permanently as husband and wife,[2] and
the policy generally is only to permit admission as a spouse for the purpose of
matrimonial cohabitation.[3] The old rule on marriages of convenience, in force
between 1977 and 1979, gave no claim to admission to the UK where the
authorities concluded that (a) the marriage was primarily entered into to obtain
settlement *and* (b) there was no intention to live permanently together as husband
and wife.[4] Women who had the right of abode under the original section 2 of the
Immigration Act 1971 and those who were married to Commonwealth citizens
settled here before 1973 could enter or remain notwithstanding that their marriages
were ones of convenience.[5] The Immigration (European Economic Area)
Regulations 2000,[6] like their predecessor the Immigration (EEA) Order 1994,[7]
exclude parties to marriages of convenience from the definition of spouse.[8] The
Tribunal in *Wong*[9] held that the 1994 Order treated the issue as one of the
qualifications as a family member rather than as a public policy ground for
exclusion. In *Chen*,[10] the Tribunal held that it was not in accordance with EC law
to examine on re-entry the marriage on which a residence permit had been granted
to see if it was a marriage of convenience. But the Tribunal clearly believed such
an inquiry legitimate for the decision whether to grant a residence permit in the
first place. In *Yuen*,[11] the Tribunal reiterated that the burden of proof that a
marriage to an EU national is on the Secretary of State, and since the allegation
is one of deceit, the burden is high.

1 In *Vervaeke v Smith* [1983] 1 AC 145, [1982] 2 All ER 144, HL the House of Lords upheld
   the validity of an English marriage which the wife had contracted in 1954 solely in order to
   obtain British nationality and a British passport and to escape the possibility of deportation
   for being a prostitute. The validity of a marriage has also been upheld in other cases where
   it has been contracted with the object of evading immigration control: *Silver v Silver* [1955]
   2 All ER 614, [1955] 1 WLR 728; see also *Martens v Martens* 1952 (3) SA 771, approved by
   Karminski J in *H v H* [1954] P 258, [1953] 2 All ER 1229. See further *Szechter (otherwise
   Karsov) v Szechter* [1971] P 286, [1970] 3 All ER 905. But see *Puttick* below.
2 HC 395, para 281(iii).
3 *Yanus Patel v Immigration Appeal Tribunal* [1989] Imm AR 416, CA.
4 HC 239, para 264, March 1977. See *R v Immigration Appeal Tribunal, ex p Mahmud
   Khan* [1983] QB 790, [1983] 2 All ER 420, CA.
5 *Secretary of State for the Home Department v Huseyin* [1988] Imm AR 129, CA;
   R v Secretary of State for the Home Department, ex p Puttick [1981] QB 767, [1981]
   1 All ER 776.
6 SI 2000/2326, reg 2.
7 SI 1994/1895.
8 See **7.81–7.83** above. The Tribunal in *Kwong* (10661) held that a marriage entered into
   without any intention of living together as husband and wife did not qualify the partner
   for admission under community law. In *Lau* (10859) the Tribunal followed *Kwong* but
   pointed out that the burden of proof lay on the Home Office, and where a couple refused
   to answer questions about their marital intentions, there was insufficient evidence to
   discharge the burden of proof. For reasons set out in **7.81–7.83**, one view is that these
   decisions are of questionable authority.
9 *Wong (Pui-Yu)* (12602), 1996 2 ILD No 16.

10 *Chen* [1998] INLR 642, Immigration Appeal Tribunal.
11 *Yuen* (19283) IAS 1999, Vol 2, No 8.

11.46 The Immigration and Asylum Act 1999[1] imposes a duty on marriage registrars to whom a notice of marriage has been given to report to the Secretary of State for the Home Department suspicions on reasonable grounds that the marriage will be a sham marriage. A 'sham' marriage is defined as:

'a marriage (whether or not void)
(a) entered into between a person ("A") who is neither a British citizen nor a national of an EEA State other than the United Kingdom and another person (whether or not such a citizen or such a national); and
(b) entered into by A for the purpose of avoiding the effect of one or more provisions of the United Kingdom immigration law or the immigration rules.'[2]

A further implicit requirement for a 'sham' marriage must be, we suggest, that the parties do not intend to live together as husband and wife; if it were otherwise there would be no sham, and the provision of the 1999 Act would be re-introducing the reviled primary purpose rule, removed in June 1997, which required parties to a genuine marriage (one in which the parties intended to cohabit) to prove additionally that the primary purpose of the marriage was not settlement for the applicant spouse.[3] Our interpretation of this section accords with the old rule on marriages of convenience, at **11.45** above.

1 Immigration and Asylum Act 1999, s 24.
2 Immigration and Asylum Act 1999, s 24(5).
3 For detailed discussion of the primary purpose rule and the case law to which it gave rise, see the previous edition of this work at **11.54-11.69**.

11.47 A marriage found to be a 'sham' would not give rise to any right to enter or remain, since the requirement of the Immigration Rules that the couple intend to live together would not be fulfilled. In *Choudhry v Metropolitan Police Commissioner*[1] the court went further, suggesting that a representation that a person is married implies that the parties intend to live together as man and wife, thus making the representor liable to prosecution if he or she knew that the parties did not intend to do so. This must be doubted. It would be extraordinary that a representation that was accurate in law should be held to be a misrepresentation in the absence of a specific intent to deceive.[2]

1 *Choudhry v Metropolitan Police Comr* (24 November 1984, unreported), DC, cited in *Patel v Immigration Appeal Tribunal* [1989] Imm AR 416, CA.
2 In *Vervaeke v Smith,* Lord Hailsham suggested that an immigration marriage where payment was made to a stranger to undergo a ceremony of marriage was not what was normally considered a marriage of convenience. This is, however, exactly what a layman would understand by a 'sham' marriage. But note that Immigration and Asylum Act 1999, s 24 requires no payment.

'Intention to live together'

11.48 As indicated above, admission of a spouse is conditional on an intention to live together permanently as husband and wife and the continuing subsistence of the marriage. The abolition of the primary purpose rule in June 1997 was intended to ensure that all those with genuine marriages would be able to live with UK-based spouses, and only those in sham marriages would be excluded.

Practitioners have, however, seen an increase in refusals of entry clearance in cases where formerly the intention to live together was not doubted, although doubts might have been expressed about the primary purpose of the marriage. However, in the vast majority of cases, doubt as to intention to live together is unwarranted, and it should certainly not be inferred from the reluctance or refusal of the UK-based partner to move to the other partner's country.[1] The primary purpose rule should not be reintroduced through the back door by detailed questions as to *where* the parties intend to cohabit, and the fact that a marriage might have economic motivation is of little or no significance in assessing the intention of the parties to live together.[2] Previous cohabitation or the birth of a child would satisfy the requirements of the rule. The relevant date on which an intention to live together as man and wife must be present is the date of the immigration authorities' decision. Fiancé(e)s must show that they intend to live together permanently after the marriage;[3] applicants who are already married must show this is their present intention.[4] On an application for settlement after the probationary period, delays in decision-making may mean that the marriage has broken down while the application is under consideration, even though it survived the probationary period under the rules on variation of leave. This will result in refusal under the variation rule.[5] However, it should be noted that the rule is directed at the permanent intentions of the parties rather than to any temporary quarrels between them which may have interrupted cohabitation. See **11.52** below.

1   *R v Immigration Appeal Tribunal, ex p Lunat* (6 October 1986), unreported, QBD; *R v Secretary of State for the Home Department, ex p Wali* [1989] Imm AR 86, QBD; *R v Immigration Appeal Tribunal, ex p Khatab* [1989] Imm AR 313, QBD; *Iqbal v Immigration Appeal Tribunal* [1988] Imm AR 469, CA; *Zia v Secretary of State for the Home Department* [1993] Imm AR 404. The dicta of Glidewell LJ in *Sumeina Masood v Immigration Appeal Tribunal* [1992] Imm AR 69, CA on conditional intention are to be seen in the factual context of the case, set out in the judgment of Simon Brown J in the DC at [1991] Imm AR 283. Also on conditional intention see Glidewell LJ's dicta in *R v Secretary of State for the Home Department, ex p Brakwah* [1989] Imm AR 366.
2   See eg *Saftar v Secretary of State for the Home Department* [1992] Imm AR 1, CA.
3   HC 395, para 290(iii).
4   HC 395, para 281(iii).
5   For an example of such a case see *R v Immigration Appeal Tribunal, ex p Idrish* (1984) Times, 14 July, QBD; a subsequent appeal against deportation was however successful *Idrish* [1985] Imm AR 155.

OTHER RULES FOR FIANCÉ(E)S, PARTNERS AND SPOUSES

The requirement that the parties have met

11.49 This rule appears to have been directed principally at arranged marriages. The Tribunal has interpreted the paragraph to exclude casual meetings when the parties were very young.[1] There must be a meeting to the extent that the parties recognise and know each other, but it does not have to be a meeting in the context of marriage. It may be sufficient for the parties to have seen each other and there does not have to have been a conversation between them.[2] Refusal on the grounds of not having met will be reconsidered if the parties meet after the original decision to refuse, and entry clearance will be issued if the decision was based solely on that ground.[3]

1 *Raj (Rewal)* [1985] Imm AR 151. See also IDI Dec/00, Ch 8, Annex J: 'if the parties had been childhood friends, it could be acceptable, although the meeting of two infants would not.'
2 *Meharban* [1989] Imm AR 57. IDI Dec/00, Ch 8, Annex J says the parties should have made each others' acquaintance.
3 IDI Dec/00, Ch 8, Annex J, para 2.2.

Leave to enter and remain under the Rules

11.50 Fiancé(e)s and spouses seeking to enter must normally have entry clearance, as we have seen.[1] Fiancé(e)s are given up to six months leave to enter, with a prohibition on taking employment,[2] and spouses are given an initial 12 months, with no such prohibition.[3] If a fiancé(e) fails to marry during the initial period of leave, an explanation will have to be given to the Home Office, and an extension of leave for an appropriate period may be given if the explanation is acceptable and there is evidence that the marriage will take place soon.[4] Once the fiancé(e) has married and has obtained 12 months leave to remain as a spouse, the employment prohibition is lifted. A person admitted in another capacity who marries during his or her stay here can apply for leave to remain as a spouse if, in addition to fulfilling the requirements for entry in that capacity (except for entry clearance), he or she has not remained in breach of the immigration laws and the marriage did not take place after a decision to deport or a recommendation for deportation had been made, or a preparatory notice served.[5] However, no 'switching' is permitted from another temporary capacity to that of fiancé(e), and an application to remain as a fiancé(e) from a person admitted in another capacity will be refused unless there are exceptional compassionate circumstances, such as a serious or terminal illness of one of the parties.[6] It should be noted that fiancé(e)s and spouses are not precluded from coming to the UK as visitors before or even during their settlement application, provided they intend to leave the UK at the end of the particular visit for which entry is sought.

1 See **11.9** above.
2 HC 395, para 291. In cases where the applicant is not sure whether he or she will remain in the UK or return home after the wedding, he or she should be treated as a fiancé(e) rather than as a visitor: IDI Dec/00, Ch 8, Annex K, para 1.
3 HC 395, para 282.
4 HC 395, para 293 and 294.
5 HC 395, para 284(iv) and (v). The IDI appear to allow a two-month 'grace' period after a limited leave has expired, for an application after entry for leave to remain as a spouse: IDI Dec/00, Ch 8, Annex G, para 3.
6 IDI Dec/00, Ch 8, s 2, para 3.2.

Children of fiancé(e)s

11.51 The Immigration Rules were amended in October 2000 to provide for the admission of children of fiancé(e)s.[1] Such children will be granted limited leave to enter if they are accompanying or joining a person who is being or has been admitted in that capacity[2] if: they are under 18, unmarried and not leading an independent life;[3] they can be maintained and accommodated adequately with their parent; there are serious and compelling family or other considerations making their exclusion undesirable; suitable arrangements have been made for their care in the UK; and there is no one outside the UK who could reasonably be expected to care for them.[4] They must have entry clearance.[5]

1   HC 395, para 303A-F.
2   HC 395, para 303A(i).
3   HC 395, para 303A(ii) and (iii). For detailed consideration of the general rules on children see **11.61**ff below.
4   HC 395, para 303A(v); see **11.79** below.
5   HC 395, para 303A(vi).

One year rule

11.52 After 12 months' leave as a spouse, an application can be made for indefinite leave to remain, which should be granted provided the maintenance and accommodation conditions are still met, the marriage is subsisting and each of the parties intends to live permanently with the other as his or her spouse.[1] The language of the rule is discretionary, allowing the Secretary of State to grant further limited leave rather than settlement, but this should only be done when there is reason to doubt the lasting nature of the marriage or where there is real prospect of reconciliation between separated spouses.[2] The IDI indicate that detailed inquiries on the state of the marriage will normally only be made where doubts exist, because of a suspected marriage of convenience, previous refusal of leave to enter or remain, marriage during limited leave to a comparative stranger, information received that the parties are no longer living together, or where the only evidence as to the continued subsistence of the marriage comes from the benefiting spouse.[3] Extensions of stay are subject to the general discretion to refuse on the ground of bad conduct.[4] But it is wrong for an adjudicator, when allowing an appeal, to direct that settlement not be given until four years have elapsed.[5] There is no discretion to grant leave to remain under the Immigration Rules in the case of marriage breakdown,[6] except for the purpose of access to children of the marriage who are remaining with the settled spouse (see **11.54** below). Where a person leaves the UK during the currency of a temporary leave, that person may be re-examined as to the existence of the marriage requirements on a re-entry to the UK during the currency of that leave, and leave may be cancelled if the marriage has broken down.[7] A concessionary policy outside the Rules allows for the grant of settlement if the marriage has broken down due to domestic violence (see **11.53** below). Where the settled spouse has died during the probationary period, indefinite leave will be granted provided that the marriage was still subsisting at the time of the death and the parties intended to continue cohabitation.[8]

1   HC 395, para 287(a).
2   IDI, Ch 8, Annex C, para 2.1. Further limited leave should not be granted where the requirements for settlement are met: *Tanweer* (3490).
3   IDI, Ch 8, Annex C.
4   HC 395, paras 322, 323; *Al Saidi* (5324).
5   *Aslam* (6248).
6   *Patel v Secretary of State for the Home Department* [1986] Imm AR 440.
7   *R v Immigration Appeal Tribunal, ex p Chaudhry* [1983] Imm AR 208, QBD.
8   HC 395, para 287(b), inserted by Cm 4851.

Domestic violence concession

11.53 An overseas national spouse or unmarried partner (see **11.56** below) may be granted indefinite leave to remain provided that there is proof that the applicant has been the victim of domestic violence during the probationary period while the marriage or relationship was subsisting.[1] The concession does not apply to persons admitted to the UK as the spouse or unmarried partner of a sponsor who had only limited leave to remain, or where the sponsor is an EEA national exercising free movement rights under EC law.[2] Nor does it apply to fiancé(e)s. The requirements of proof are stringent, and the Home Office insists on one of the following pieces of evidence to establish a claim of domestic violence:

(i)   an injunction, non-molestation order or other protection order made against the sponsor (but not an *ex parte* or interim order);[3]

(ii)   a relevant court conviction against the sponsor;[4] or

(iii)   full details of a relevant police caution issued against the sponsor.[5]

Where an applicant submits evidence to show that he or she has been subjected to domestic violence from persons other than the sponsor, they may still qualify under the concession if it is clear that this has been the reason for the marriage breakdown, for example, where those abusing the applicant are members of the sponsor's family against whom the sponsor offers no protection.[6] The application should be made while the applicant still has leave to remain as a spouse, but applications made out of time will be considered sympathetically and will not normally be refused solely on this basis, particularly if the applicant only left the sponsor towards the end of the probationary period or that the stress of the situation has led him or her to overlook the need to regularise his or her status.[7]

1   IDI Dec/00, Ch 8, Annex C, para 3. The concession is also published in *Butterworths Immigration Law Service*, D[1131].

2   IDI Dec/00, Ch 8, Annex C, para 3. The rationale is that 'such persons have not been admitted to the UK for the purpose of settlement'.

3   The original or a certified copy of the court order or memorandum of conviction is required: IDI Dec/00, Ch 8, Annex C, para 4.

4   Where a prosecution is pending, indefinite leave will not be granted, but the applicant will be granted further leave to remain for six months at a time until the outcome of the prosecution is known: IDI Dec/00, Ch 8, Annex C, para 4.5.

5   Since there is no documentary evidence of this, the applicant must provide full details of the sponsor to enable inquiries to be carried out with the local police.

6   IDI Dec/00, Ch 8, Annex C, para 4.7.

7   IDI Dec/00, Ch 8, Annex C, para 5.

Leave to remain for the purposes of access

11.54 The provision for entry for access by a former spouse to his or her UK resident child was introduced in 1994.[1] It was substantially amended in October 2000 in order to ensure compliance with ECHR, Article 8 obligations of respect for family life, as set out in the ECHR decision of *Berrehab*.[2] Entry clearance is required for entry in this capacity, but is not required on a variation application made by someone who still has leave to enter or remain as a spouse but whose marriage has broken down.[3] The applicant must have a residence or contact order granting him or her access rights, or a certificate from a district judge confirming his or her intention to maintain contact with the child.[4] In the case of a variation application, the applicant may instead provide a statement from the child's other parent or from a supervisor where access is supervised, confirming his or her intention to maintain contact with the child.[5] The applicant must intend in either case to take an active role in the child's upbringing[6] and satisfy the maintenance and accommodation requirements,[7] but the old prohibition on employment for this category has gone, and while leave is for 12 months in the first instance,[8] settlement in this category is now possible under the Immigration Rules,[9] provided the applicant has completed 12 months in this capacity, enjoys frequent and regular visiting or staying access[10] and continues to meet the other requirements of the Rules. This provision replaces the previous highly restrictive provision which amounted to little more than a specialised visit visa from which very few were able to benefit, given the restrictions on working.[11]

1 HC 395, paras 246-248, now amended by Cm 4851. For our criticisms of the old rule, see previous edition at **11.4**.
2 *Berrehab v Netherlands* (1988) 11 EHRR 322; see also *Ciliz v Netherlands* [2000] 2 FLR 469. Whether there is a breach of art 8 of the ECHR will depend on the degree of contact between parent and child: see *Hlomodor v Secretary of State for the Home Department* [1993] Imm AR 534, CA above; *Iye v Secretary of State for the Home Department* [1994] Imm AR 63 and *R v Secretary of State for the Home Department, ex p Nijjar* [1994] Imm AR 50.
3 HC 395, para 248A(vii), as amended.
4 HC 395, paras 246(iii) and 248A(iii).
5 HC 395, para 248(iii)(c). These provisions for consensual arrangements go some way to meeting the difficulties posed by the previous rule, which required a court order. In *R v Secretary of State for the Home Department, ex p Kebbeh* (above) a removal decision was quashed because, *inter alia*, it prevented the applicant obtaining the necessary order from the family court to enable him to comply with the rule.
6 HC 395, paras 246(iv) and 248A(iv).
7 HC 395, paras 246(ix), (x) and 248A(ix), (x).
8 HC 395, para 248B.
9 HC 395, para 248D, 248E.
10 HC 395, para 248D(iii).
11 See fn 1 above.

11.55 The applicant to remain in this category must not have remained in breach of the immigration laws, and the combination of this much improved new rule with the abolition of deportation for overstayers[1] means that the Home Office will expect overstayers and illegal entrants who seek to remain to exercise access rights to leave the UK and apply for entry clearance, in the absence of exceptional compassionate circumstances. When deportation is being considered (on conducive grounds or after conviction of a criminal offence) the considerations of DP4/96[2] will continue to apply, since the effect of the order would be to prevent parental access in the UK for three years.

1 Immigration and Asylum Act 1999 s 10, see chapter 15.
2 DP4/96, *Butterworths Immigration Law Service*, D[601], para 8, providing that 'it may be unreasonable to expect [the subject of a deportation order] to return abroad to apply for entry clearance . . . in these cases it will be important to assess the quality and the regularity of access to the child in deciding how much weight should be attached to it as a compassionate factor'.

Admission of unmarried and same-sex partners

11.56 The Immigration Rules now make provision for the admission of people who are not married but have a permanent relationship.[1] The Rules replaced hard-won concessions concerning the admission of heterosexual cohabitees and same-sex partners, and were added to give effect to the right to family or private life under Article 8 of the ECHR.[2] They allow for the admission of men and women to join partners of the same or opposite sex who are present and settled or being admitted for settlement here,[3] or who are in the UK with limited leave for work, self-employment or retirement,[4] and with whom they have been living in a relationship akin to marriage for two years.[5] Short breaks apart would be acceptable for good reason, such as work commitments or looking after a relative which takes one partner away for a period of up to six months where it was not possible for the other partner to accompany him or her, and it can be seen that the relationship continued throughout that period.[6] The Rule will not be satisfied by partners merely visiting each other as often as they can during the two years, but where they have been living together in a committed relationship for the two years (barring short breaks) but have divided their time between countries and have used the 'visitor' category to do this, this will be sufficient to meet the requirement.[7] Any previous marriage or similar relationship must have permanently broken down. The parties must also be legally unable to marry in the UK other than for reasons of consanguinity[8] or age.[9] They must intend to live together permanently[10] and be able to satisfy the maintenance and accommodation criteria.[11] On-entry applicants need entry clearance, just as spouses do,[12] and after-entry applicants (those switching from another category such as visitor or student) must not have remained in breach of the immigration laws, and the relationship must have pre-dated any enforcement action (decision to deport, recommendation for deportation or service of notice preparatory to recommendation, or directions for removal as an overstayer under section 10 of the Immigration and Asylum Act 1999).[13] Applicants seeking to enter or remain as the partner of a person with limited leave as an employee, a self-employed or retired person must additionally not intend to remain beyond the period of leave granted to his or her partner.[14] There is no policy for unmarried partners equivalent to DP3/96, but where it is claimed that a decision to remove constitutes an interference with private life rights under ECHR, Article 8 (for example, where homosexuality is illegal or socially unacceptable in the partner's country of nationality or residence, precluding the establishment of the couple there), a human rights appeal under section 65 of the 1999 Act will be available.

1 HC 395, paras 295A–O.
2 See chapter 8 for cases on art 8 in this context.
3 HC 395, para 295A(i).
4 HC 395, para 295J, referring to partners present in the UK under HC 395, paras 128–193 (non-work permit employment), 200–239 (business), or 263–270 (retired persons of independent means).
5 The policy formulated in October 1997 required four years' cohabitation as a threshold period, which made it virtually impossible for someone who began a relationship with a British citizen while here in a temporary capacity, eg as a student, to qualify. The minimum cohabitation period was reduced to two years as from 16 June 1999.
6 IDI Feb/00, Ch 8, Annex AA, para 3.
7 IDI Feb/00, Ch 8, Annex AA, para 3. Evidence of a committed relationship, such as joint commitments, correspondence or official records linking partners to the same address, or record of the births of children born to the relationship, will be required.
8 The Rule gives statutory effect to the decision in *R v Secretary of State for the Home Department, ex p Ozminnos* [1994] Imm AR 287, QBD.
9 HC 395, paras 295A(iii), 295J(iii). For heterosexual couples, this normally means that one party is still married to someone else. Evidence of the legal impediment is required: IDI Feb/00, Ch 8, Annex AA, para 2.
10 HC 395, paras 295A(vii) and 295J(x).
11 HC 395, paras 295A(v) and (vi); 295J(viii) and (ix).

12 In *R v an Immigration Officer, ex p Hashim* (CO 2052/1999) 12 June 2000, Jackson J quashed a refusal of leave to enter and a decision to remove the Malaysian homosexual partner of a British citizen who had no entry clearance, on the ground that the Home Office accepted that he fulfilled all the other requirements of the Immigration Rules and to require him to return to Malaysia served no useful purpose. The Court of Appeal disapproved this approach in *R v Secretary of State for the Home Department, ex p Amjad Mahmood* [2001] 1 WLR 840.
13 HC 395, para 295D(iv) and (vii).
14 HC 395, para 295J(viii).

11.57 Leave to enter to join or accompany an unmarried partner settled in the UK, or leave to remain with such a partner, will be for two years in the first instance,[1] and indefinite leave may be granted at the end of the probationary period, provided the relationship is still subsisting, each of the parties intends to live permanently with the other as his or her partner and the maintenance and accommodation criteria are still met.[2] Indefinite leave may also be granted if the UK-settled partner dies during the probationary period and at the time of the death the relationship was subsisting and the parties intended to live together permanently.[3] Unmarried partners may also benefit from the provisions of the rules relating to access to children,[4] and from the domestic violence concession, just as parties to a marriage.[5]

1 HC 395, paras 295B, 295E.
2 HC 395, paras 295G, 295H. The concession allowing spouses of members of armed forces, of diplomats and of comparable UK-based staff members of the British Council to obtain settlement applies to unmarried partners: see IDI Dec/00, Ch 8, Annex CC.
3 HC 395, paras 295M-O, putting unmarried partners on a par with married couples.
4 HC 395, as amended by Cm 4851, paras 246-248F; see **11.54** above.
5 See **11.53** above.

11.58 Once settlement as a spouse or unmarried partner is achieved, readmission will be as a returning resident rather than a spouse, and thus subsequent marriage or relationship breakdown does not affect immigration status. However, if settlement has been obtained by means of a false representation made by the immigrant, then proceedings can be taken to remove the person on the ground that deportation is conducive to the public good.[1]

1 *Immigration Appeal Tribunal v Patel* [1988] Imm AR 434 where Lord Bridge disapproved his earlier remarks in *Khawaja v Secretary of State for the Home Department* [1984] AC 74; where the false representation has been made by another on behalf of the immigrant, it is doubtful whether deportation is appropriate in the light of Lord Bridge's doubts in *Khawaja*. At the least the Secretary of State would need to be satisfied that the appellant was party to the deception.

Marriage and removal

11.59 There remains the situation of those who marry or enter a relationship while in the UK illegally, or whose stay subsequently becomes unlawful, and who become liable to removal from the UK. As we have seen, the Immigration Rules provide that a person who entered in a temporary capacity and seeks leave to remain for marriage must be in the UK with limited leave and must not have remained in breach of the immigration laws.[1] However, to give effect to the UK's obligations under the ECHR,[2] the Home Office issued internal instructions in 1993 providing guidance on cases where enforcement action against illegal entrants and deportees would not be appropriate bearing in mind their family ties in the

UK. Here, we only deal with those parts of these instructions which affect married and common law relationships. The instructions, DP2/93,[3] provided that persons who had married or begun cohabitation with a partner before enforcement action began, and who had been married or cohabiting for two years before coming to attention, should not as a general rule be forced to leave the UK. When the instructions were leaked, and subsequently published,[4] they gave rise to a large amount of litigation,[5] leading the Secretary of State to replace the policy with a much more restrictive policy, DP3/96,[6] affecting marriages which came to the notice of the Home Office after 13 March 1996.[7] The 1996 policy excluded common-law relationships (same-sex relationships were excluded from both policies), and required a marriage to have taken place two years before the commencement of enforcement action[8] for applicants to avoid removal. The requirement that it is unreasonable to expect the settled spouse to accompany his or her spouse on removal became additional to the requirement that marriage had subsisted for two years,[9] rather than as an alternative, as it had been in DP2/93.

1   HC 395, para 284(i) and (iv).
2   The policy was held to be compatible with ECHR, art 8 in *Gangadeen v Secretary of State for the Home Department; Khan v Secretary of State for the Home Department* [1998] Imm AR 106, CA.
3   Set out in *Butterworths Immigration Law Service*, D[501].
4   In (1993) 7 INLP at 100-102.
5   See eg *R v Secretary of State for the Home Department, ex p Amankwah* [1994] Imm AR 240; *Iye v Secretary of State for the Home Department* [1994] Imm AR 63; *Secretary of State for the Home Department v Hastrup* [1996] Imm AR 616; *Mirza v Secretary of State for the Home Department* [1996] Imm AR 314.
6   Set out in *Butterworths Immigration Law Service*, D[551].
7   DP3/96, set out in *Butterworths Immigration Law Service*, D[551] para 10.
8   'Enforcement action' was defined as including an instruction to leave with a warning of liability to deportation if the subject fails to do so, in addition to the service of a notice of intention to deport or illegal entry papers, or a recommendation for deportation: DP3/96, para 5.
9   DP3/96, para 5(b).

11.60 There may be cases in which a too-rigid application of the policy can give rise to a challenge using Article 8 of the ECHR. The exclusion of an unmarried partner who fulfilled its criteria would almost certainly be held unlawful after the inclusion of unmarried partners into the Immigration Rules. A rigid insistence on marriage two years before enforcement action would be challengeable. However, when considering the impact of a marriage which took place before the commencement of enforcement action, the Secretary of State need not close his eyes to the question of whether or not one spouse was aware that the immigration status of the other was precarious, since such knowledge militates against a finding that removal of the non-resident spouse violates Article 8.[1]

1   *R v Secretary of State for the Home Department, ex p Amjad Mahmood* [2001] 1 WLR 840, CA, per Lord Phillips MR at paras 55 and 61, citing *Poku v UK* (1996) 22 EHRR CD 94.

ADMISSION OF CHILDREN UNDER 18

Introduction

11.61 In this section we examine the rules relating to children under the age of 18 at the time of the application. Older children are only provided for in the residual distressed relatives category.[1] Different age limits for children apply under the special voucher scheme.[2] Although refusal of a special voucher is not appealable under the Immigration Rules,[3] refusal of entry clearance as the child of one is appealable.[4] We examine in turn:

(i)   children with the right of abode;
(ii)   the rules relating to children born in the UK who are not British citizens;
(iii)   the rules for admission of children born abroad who have at least one parent settled or intending to settle here;
(iv)   the 'exclusion undesirable' rule;
(v)   the rules relating to recognition of overseas adoptions for immigration purposes;
(vi)   concessions for the admission of children.

1   HC 395, para 317: see **11.107ff** below. Until 1994, unmarried dependent daughters between 18 and 21 could be admitted to join parents in the UK if they had been living as part of the family unit: HC 251, para 55.
2   Dependent children of any nationality who are under 25 when their parent receives a voucher may be granted entry clearance to join or accompany UK passport-holder heads of household present and settled in the UK or being admitted for settlement under the scheme: IDI Dec/00, Ch 7, s 2, Annex C.
3   *Re Amin* [1983] 2 AC 818. See IDI Dec/00, Ch 7, s 2, Annex C. Judicial review will of course be available to challenge refusal of special vouchers.
4   HC 395, para 252.

Meaning of parent

11.62 HC 395 gave a new and more liberal definition of parent for the purpose of the application of the Immigration Rules generally. A 'parent' now includes both the mother and father of an illegitimate child if paternity is proved.[1] This contrasts with the position in British nationality law, where the father of an illegitimate child is still not able to pass on citizenship.[2] It is thus clear that despite the retention of discrimination on the grounds of parentage in nationality laws, illegitimate children will be treated the same as others for the purposes of all of the Immigration Rules, subject to the question of proof of a relationship.[3]

1   HC 395, para 6.
2   British Nationality Act 1981, s 50(9). The Immigration and Nationality Directorate has a policy of discretionary registration of such children where there are no doubts as to paternity, no reasonable objection from either parent and no character objections: IND letter to Bindmans, 31 March 2000. See **2.37** above.
3   It was this factor which prevented the discrimination in nationality law from being held unlawful under Arts 8 and 14 of the ECHR in *R (Montana) v Secretary of State for the Home Department* [2001] 1 WLR 552, CA.

11.63 Other parts of the definition of parent are more restrictive. First, the previous rule is still retained whereby a step-parent will only qualify as a parent when the natural parent whom the step-parent replaces is dead.[1] Secondly, in the case of children born in the UK who are not British, 'parent' is extended to mean a person to whom there has been a genuine transfer of parental responsibility on the ground of the original parent or parents' inability to care for the child.[2] This could include foster-parents, appointed by local authorities for children in care, as well as other relatives. For the purposes of all the rules, except those relating to children joining parents for settlement, 'parent' includes an adoptive parent, but only where a child was adopted in accordance with a decision taken by the competent administrative authority or court in a country whose adoption orders are recognised by the UK.[3] There are different hurdles to overcome to join adoptive parents in the UK for settlement.[4] Since 1994, *de facto* adoptions have not been recognised, and children whose care has been assumed by other relatives have had to rely on the 'exclusion undesirable' rule for the admission of children,[5] unless their *de facto* carers intended to adopt them in the UK, in which case they might be eligible under the rules relating to entry for settlement as a child for adoption.[6]

1   HC 395, para 6.
2   HC 395, para 6.
3   HC 395, para 6.
4   HC 395, para 310(i)(a)–(f). See **11.92** below.
5   HC 395, paras 297(i)(f) and 298(i)(d).
6   HC 395, paras 316A-C, inserted by Cm 4851, 2 October 2000.

Disputes as to age or identity

11.64 The difficulties in establishing the relationship of parent and child have been largely resolved by DNA-testing,[1] although problems remain where the parents are dead or a full blood comparison is not possible. Past disputed relationships gave rise to the problem of over-age re-applications by children who were initially refused, but later recognised as related as claimed to the parent settled in the UK. The Immigration Rules make no provision for such cases, and the minister's policy outside the Rules is extremely restrictive, requiring that the over-age child remains unmarried and fully dependent on the UK parent, as well as strong compassionate circumstances.[2] The High Court held that the policy was not unreasonable.[3] Other over-age applicants must comply with the distressed relatives rules. Another problem has arisen with children who are claimed as the child of both parents, but after DNA analysis are discovered to be the child of only one of them. Generally, the Rules require the appellate authorities to determine the application on the basis of the facts put forward by the applicant at the time of decision.[4] Although the decision as to which Rule to be applied to those facts can be reviewed by the appellate authorities, a fresh application for admission under some different Rule cannot be first ventilated on appeal.[5] This can create problems where a child becomes over 18 before the true facts are discovered.

1   *DNA Profiling in Immigration Casework: A Progress Report* (February 1989) Home Office B2 Division where guidance for reliance on these tests is set out. Care is taken to prevent impersonation of donors. In 1990 the government announced the scheme for publicly funded DNA-testing in cases of doubt; the costs were to be met by raising the fees for entry clearance applications: see HL Official Report (5th series) written answers col 55, 20 December 1990. See also Legal Action (December 1990) p 25. For the weight to be given to DNA tests see *Ali* (9717) 1993.
2   Ministerial statement, 14 June 1989.
3   *R v Immigration Appeal Tribunal, ex p Ali* [1990] Imm AR 531; *Miah (Hassan) v Secretary of State for the Home Department* [1991] Imm AR 437, CA. Depending on the circumstances, refusal of admission to an over-age child might be a breach of ECHR, art 8.
4   *R v Immigration Appeal Tribunal, ex p Nathwani* [1979–80] Imm AR 9; *R v Immigration Appeal Tribunal, ex p Kotecha* [1983] 1 WLR 487; [1982] Imm AR 88.
5   *R v Immigration Appeal Tribunal, ex p Secretary of State for the Home Department* [1993] Imm AR 298, QBD, affirmed in CA under the name *Hussain (Dilowar and Iqbal) v Secretary of State for the Home Department* [1993] Imm AR 590. See **18.71** below.

11.65 Next, children will have to establish their age. The relevant age for the Settlement Rules is the age of the child when the application is made, rather than at the date of decision,[1] and entry clearance or leave to enter will not be refused merely because the child has become over-age since the application was made.[2] The child's date of birth will have to be established by reference to birth certificates, contemporaneous declarations, the date of marriage if applicable and return visits by sponsors or other credible testimony. Evidence obtained for the purpose of nullity and paternity proceedings is admissible in an immigration appeal if it was read into the record, unless the family court otherwise orders.[3] In the context of asylum, the Home Office normally considers it appropriate to give an applicant the benefit of the doubt unless physical appearance strongly suggests that he or she is over 18.[4] Where there is a real dispute and the applicant can provide no documentary proof, the child or his or her representatives may obtain a medical assessment of age, but it is inappropriate for the Home Office to insist on or request one.[5] Under no circumstances should an applicant be asked to have X-rays taken to determine age.[6] An unwelcome return to age estimation techniques was used in the case of *Khatun (Hamila)*[7] to deny the right of abode to a woman who claimed to have been born after the registration of her father as a British citizen.[8]

1   HC 395, paras 27 and 321(ii). Equally a child who becomes over-age while the Home Office or the appellate authority is considering the application will not suffer: para 298(i); *Mahmood (Fazal)* [1979–80] Imm AR 71n. A person admitted with a view to settlement will still be able to obtain indefinite leave to remain after entry despite becoming over age: see para 298(ii); but a child who enters in some other capacity and then seeks indefinite leave to remain as a dependent child must apply before his or her 18th birthday in order to comply with the Immigration Rules. Note that the relevant age for children accompanying or joining parents for purposes other than settlement is the age at the date of the decision: para 298(ii).
2   An application is only made when any fee payable in respect of a specific application is paid: HC 395, para 30, reversing *Ross* [1992] Imm AR 493. For the previous decisions on what is an application see also *Brown* [1976] Imm AR 119; *R v Immigration Appeal Tribunal, ex p Prajapati* [1981] Imm AR 199, QBD; affd [1982] Imm AR 56, CA; *Soyemi* [1990] Imm AR 564, Immigration Appeal Tribunal.
3   *Hussein* (R.15512) 29 August 1997; CPR 32.12.
4   API Aug/00, Ch 2, s 5, para 3.7.
5   API Aug/00, Ch 2, s 5, para 3.8. The instructions note that paediatricians' reports are subject to a margin of error of up to two years.
6   ADI Jul/98, Ch 2, s 5, para 3.13. This is not reproduced in the current (Aug/00) API.
7   (12492).
8   Age estimation by medical practitioners has proved controversial and unreliable in the past, and the use of X-rays for non-medical purposes is certainly unethical practice. See **3.30** fn 6 above.

Children with the right of abode

11.66 A child who has the right of abode must prove it by a production of either a British passport or a certificate of entitlement.[1] On proof of the right of abode, such a child does not require leave to enter and is dealt with in the same way as any other British citizen. The child will acquire the right of abode if, after 1 January 1983, he or she has been registered as a British citizen, or was born in the UK to a parent who was settled in the UK at the time of birth; or was born abroad to a parent who was a British citizen, otherwise than by descent, at the time of birth.

1   Immigration Act 1971, s 3(9). Without such documents the child may be unable to board an airline or appeal before removal save on human rights grounds: see Immigration and

Asylum Act 1999, s 60(1). See also *R v Secretary of State for the Home Department, ex p Shorzan Bibi* [1987] Imm AR 213. There is a right of appeal against a refusal of a certificate of entitlement: Immigration and Asylum Act 1999, s 59(2).

Non-British children born in the UK

11.67 It has already been noted that children born in the UK after 1 January 1983 will not become British citizens by birth in the UK if neither parent was a British citizen or settled in the UK.[1] A child who remains in the UK continuously for the first ten years of his or her life (with limited provisions for short absences abroad) can obtain registration as a British citizen.[2] A child under 18, one of whose parents becomes settled or acquires British nationality, will also be eligible for registration as a British citizen.[3] Special rules apply to children born in the UK after 1 January 1983 who do not become British citizens.[4] While they remain in the UK without leaving, they do not need leave to remain. Obtaining leave to remain is therefore optional, but advisable if it is expected that the child will travel and seek re-admission, when leave to enter will be required.[5]

1 British Nationality Act 1981, s 1(1). See **2.37** above.
2 British Nationality Act 1981, s 1(4).
3 British Nationality Act 1981, s 1(3).
4 HC 395, paras 304–309.
5 HC 395, para 304.

11.68 The Immigration Rules lay down similar requirements for children seeking either leave to enter or leave to remain. Such children must be born in the UK, under 18, unmarried, not leading an independent life or have formed an independent family unit and not have been away from the UK for more than two years.[1] If the child is accompanied by or seeking to join a parent with limited leave, leave to enter is given for the same period as that of the parents, or the longer of the two periods if each parent has a different period of leave, save where the parents are separated, in which case leave is given for the same period as the parent who has day-to-day control.[2] If neither of the parents has a current leave, leave to enter or remain will normally be refused, unless it is unlikely that the parents will be removed in the immediate future and there is no other person outside the UK who could reasonably be expected to care for the child.[3] In such cases, three months' leave to enter may be given. If one of the parents is a British citizen or if the parental rights and duties in respect of the child are vested in a local authority, indefinite leave to enter or remain is given.[4]

1 HC 395, para 305 (ii)–(v).
2 HC 395, paras 305(i)(a) and 306.
3 HC 395, para 307.
4 HC 395, paras 305(i)(b) and (c) and 308.

11.69 The distinguishing feature of the Immigration Rules for these children compared with those applying to other children is that, provided they return to the UK within two years of leaving, they do not have to satisfy the normal requirements as regards maintenance, accommodation or presence in the UK of both parents. They can obtain prior entry clearance, but do not have to do so, unless they are visa nationals. Children who return after an absence of over two years have to qualify under the ordinary rules, either as a dependent child or in some other capacity, such as a student.

Children under 18 with UK-settled parent, parents or relative

11.70 In the Immigration Rules and practice dealing with the admission of children there is a tremendous conflict between two contrary tendencies. The first is the need to maintain family unity and to recognise that the migration process involves an initial splitting up of the family followed by a reunification. The contrary tendency is to curb and restrict all secondary immigration. In current UK practice, the restrictive tendency finds expression in the limitations as to age and dependency of children, the sole responsibility rule and the restrictions in relation to adoption, as well as in the maintenance and accommodation requirements.

11.71 Children who have no right of abode and were not born in the UK, who are seeking to enter or remain with a UK-settled parent, parents or a relative, must be under 18 at the date of application, unmarried, not leading an independent life[1] or part of an independent family unit,[2] but dependent on the parent, parents or relative in the UK,[3] and capable of being supported and accommodated by them without recourse to public funds.[4] A distinction is then drawn between children both of whose parents (or in the case of death, the surviving parent) live in the UK, and those who have only one such parent or are seeking to join a relative other than a parent.

1   He or she should still be living with parents and siblings unless at boarding school, and should not be employed full-time or for a significant number of hours per week, excluding Saturday and holiday jobs: IDI Dec/00, Ch 8, Annex M, para 3.
2   The IDI interpret this as not currently being in or having previously formed a relationship with another person (such as a common-law or homosexual relationship) which could be said to be the equivalent of being married, except for name and legal recognition: IDI Dec/00, Ch 8, Annex M, para 3.
3   For both financial and emotional support, according to IDI Dec/00, Ch 8, Annex M, para 3.
4   HC 395, para 297(ii)-(vi) as amended by Cm 4851. See above **11.14–11.19** for a discussion of the maintenance and accommodation requirements.

11.72 Children, both of whose natural parents are settled in the UK, and who can comply with the general conditions, qualify for entry clearance, which will operate as indefinite leave to enter[1] unless on arrival in the UK it transpires there has been a change of circumstances since issue. The fact that a child has become over 18 since the issue of the entry clearance does not constitute such a change.[2] The same is true if both parents are being admitted for settlement in the UK at the same time as the child,[3] or one is coming to join the other,[4] or one natural parent is settled or will be admitted for settlement and the other parent (including a parent of an illegitimate child) is dead.[5] Where one natural parent has died and the other parent has remarried, then the step-parent must be settled or admitted for settlement as well as the natural parent,[6] although the relationship of step-parent would terminate on divorce of the parties. The Immigration Rules are the same for adoptive children where the qualifying conditions for adoption are met.[7] A child who enters in some other capacity qualifies for the grant of indefinite leave to remain if the same conditions are met after entry, including the fact that he or she is under 18 at the time of application.[8]

1   HC 395, paras 297(i)(a) and 299; Immigration (Leave to Enter and Remain) Order 2000, SI 2000/1161, arts 2 and 3.
2   HC 395, para 321(ii).
3   HC 395, para 297(i)(b).

4   HC 395, para 297(i)(c).
5   HC 395, para 297(i)(d).
6   HC 395, para 6 (definition of parent); see also *Alam* [1973] Imm AR 79 and *McGillivary*
    [1972] Imm AR 63.
7   HC 395, para 6 (definition of parent), and for adoptions not falling within that paragraph,
    paras 310 and 311. See below **11.84ff** for detailed consideration of adopted children.
8   HC 395, para 298.

11.73 Where one parent is settled and the other parent is given a limited leave to enter with a view to subsequent settlement, the child is given the same leave as the non-settled parent[1] and must apply for indefinite leave when the parent does.[2] The fact that a child has become over 18 since arrival in the UK does not matter if the child was previously admitted by the immigration service with a view to settlement.[3]

1   HC 395, para 301.
2   HC 395, para 298.
3   HC 395, para 298(ii)(b).

Sole responsibility

11.74 Where one parent (including a step-parent where a natural parent is dead) is settled in the UK and the other parent is alive and is not coming to the UK for settlement, then before entry clearance is granted the entry clearance officer must be satisfied that the parent in the UK has had sole responsibility for the child.[1] The same requirement must be satisfied where indefinite leave to remain is sought after entry in another capacity.[2] The phrase is intended to reflect a situation where the chief parental responsibility for the child's upbringing rests to all intents and purposes with one parent. The parent claiming sole responsibility must satisfactorily demonstrate that he or she has, usually for a substantial period, been the chief person exercising responsibility.[3] Where the sole responsibility test is not met, then the child may still qualify under the 'exclusion undesirable' rule considered below, which also permits a child to join a relative other than a parent settled here.[4]

1   HC 395, para 297(i)(e).
2   HC 395, para 298(i)(c).
3   IDI Dec/00, Ch 8, Annex M, para 4.1.
4   HC 395, paras 297(i)(f), 298(i)(d).

11.75 In any case where a parent comes to the UK and leaves the child behind, the person who is looking after the child clearly has some responsibility for the child's upbringing. A literal interpretation of 'sole responsibility' would defeat all claims. This was recognised in *Emmanuel*[1] where the Tribunal found that literal or absolute sole responsibility of the parent in the UK could never be established and there must be, in nearly all such cases, some form of responsibility of the relative with whom the child lives. This does not prevent the parent in the UK having 'sole responsibility'. Sole responsibility is not the same as legal custody. The IDI state that where a residence order has been made (or a custody order exists)[2] giving responsibility for the child to the parent who is settled in the UK or being admitted for settlement, this should normally be accepted as evidence that the 'sole responsibility' requirement is met.[3] In *Nmaju*[4] the Court of Appeal stated that a parent's legal responsibility for the child under the appropriate legal system would be a relevant consideration in deciding sole responsibility, but would not be conclusive. It is necessary to look at what actually was done in relation to the child's upbringing, by whom and whether it had been done under the direction of the parent settled here. In *Sloley*[5] the mother left her son with her mother but had sole financial responsibility and had been continuously consulted about the child's schooling, upbringing and activities. In holding that she had had sole responsibility, the Tribunal considered as relevant, *inter alia*, the source and degree of financial support of the child and whether there was cogent evidence of genuine interest in and affection for the child by the sponsoring parent in the UK. Where responsibility has not been delegated to a grandmother or other relative who is looking after the child, but has been abdicated, then the parent in the UK will not be treated as having sole responsibility.[6] A proper delegation involves a continuing financial and emotional commitment to the child.

1   *Emmanuel* [1972] Imm AR 69.
2   Under the Children Act 1989 custody orders have been replaced by residence orders. The Child Abduction and Custody Act 1985 makes provision for certain overseas custody orders to be recognised under UK law, provided they have been registered with the court. A list of countries whose custody orders are recognised is contained in IDI Dec/00, Ch 8, Annex M, para 4.5.
3   IDI Dec/00, Ch 8, Annex M, para 4.4.
4   *Njamu v Immigration Appeal Tribunal* [2001] INLR 26, CA.
5   [1972] Imm AR 54.
6   *Martin* [1972] Imm AR 71; *McGillivary* [1972] Imm AR 63.

11.76 The IDI[1] suggest the following factors should be considered where the issue is not clear:

(i)   the period for which the parent in the UK has been separated from the child;
(ii)   what the arrangements were for the care of the child before that parent migrated to the UK;
(iii)   who has been entrusted with day-to-day care and control of the child since the sponsor migrated here;
(iv)   who provides the financial support for the child's care and upbringing and in what proportion;
(v)   who takes the important decisions about the child's upbringing, such as where and with whom the child lives, the choice of school, religious practice, etc;
(vi)   the degree of contact that has been maintained between the child and the parent claiming responsibility; and
(vii)   what part in the child's care and upbringing is played by the parent not in the UK and relatives.[2]

1   IDI Dec/00, Ch 8, Annex M, para 4.3.
2   In *Dilliogu* (14045) IAS 1997, Vol 3, No 13, the Tribunal held that the adjudicator was entitled to take into account post-decision facts on these issues lending support to the finding of assumption of responsibility.

11.77 In *Uddin*[1] the High Court stated that the sponsor did not need to have had responsibility for the upbringing of the child for the whole of his or her life, but for a 'not insubstantial period'. In *Nmaju*[2] the Court of Appeal deprecated the Tribunal's attempt to treat the phrase 'a not insubstantial period' as though it were incorporated into the Immigration Rules; time was a relevant, but not conclusive, factor. In that case it upheld the claim of a mother who had had the sole responsibility for her child for two-and-a-half months.

1 *R v Immigration Appeal Tribunal, ex p Uddin* [1986] Imm AR 203, QBD.
2 *Nmaju v Immigration Appeal Tribunal* [2001] INLR 26, CA.

11.78 Construing the meaning in the context of the Immigration Rules as a whole, it might be thought that the word 'sole' refers only to responsibility as between the two parents. It is irrelevant if a child has been left with grandparents during its formative years, if both parents are settled in the UK: so why should a child be disqualified merely because only one parent is so settled? But the Tribunal, the High Court and the Court of Appeal have endorsed the practice of having regard to persons other than parents with whom responsibility could be shared.[1] However, if the child has been living abroad with the other parent, or that parent's relatives, it will be more difficult to establish that the UK-settled parent had sole responsibility than if the child has been living with a relative of the UK-settled parent.[2] In earlier decisions it had been held that daily attention and care by the other natural parent would be fatal to the application of this rule, even though it may have been intermittent and insubstantial.[3] However, this is no longer the case. To disqualify a child for admission, the other parent's involvement needs to have amounted to an independent exercise of responsibility.[4] Certainly distant past responsibility by the other parent should not render the sponsoring parent's responsibility other than sole.[5]

1 *R v Immigration Appeal Tribunal, ex p Mahmood* [1988] Imm AR 121, QBD; *Ramos v Immigration Appeal Tribunal* [1989] Imm AR 148, CA.
2 IDI Dec/00, Ch 8, Annex M, para 4.1 and 4.2. Where two foreign nationals separate and the child remains with the parent abroad for several years and then wishes to join the UK parent to take advantage of the educational system, there is no reason why the child should not remain with the parent abroad, and the UK parent would not be considered to have sole responsibility: IDI Dec/00, Ch 8, Annex M, para 4.1 and 4.2.
3 *Pusey* [1972] Imm AR 240; see also *Eugene* [1975] Imm AR 111.
4 *Nmaju v Immigration Appeal Tribunal*, 11.77 fn 2 above. See also *Annielyn Alagon* [1993] Imm AR 336 CS, Lord Prosser.
5 See *Emmanuel* [1972] Imm AR 69, *Rudolph* [1984] Imm AR 84.

Family or other considerations rendering exclusion undesirable

11.79 Children who fail to qualify under the sole responsibility rule may qualify on the grounds that there are serious and compelling family or other reasons which make their exclusion from the UK undesirable and arrangements have been made for their care.[1] This rule permits such children to join either a parent or a relative other than a parent. 'Relative' is not defined and would presumably be given a broad definition of those related by blood or marriage. It might include legal guardians.[2]

1 HC 395, paras 297(i)(f) and 298(i)(d). Where a child is shown by DNA tests to be the child of only one of its claimed parents, he or she may nevertheless qualify under this paragraph: *R v Immigration Appeal Tribunal, ex p Ali (Iqbal)* [1994] Imm AR 295, CA. For the jurisdiction of the Immigration Appeal Tribunal to entertain a child's application under a different rule than first identified see *Hussain (Shabir)* [1991] Imm AR 483. See **18.71** above.
2 *Shamsuddin* (5366) Immigration Appeal Tribunal. HC 395, para 320(16) makes reference to legal guardians of children under 18.

11.80 The Immigration Rules make it clear that if family or other considerations are to make exclusion undesirable, they must be of a serious and compelling nature. The Rules do not amplify this expression, unlike earlier rules, which gave the example of the other parent's incapacity (physical or mental) to care for the child.[1] The IDI state that where the UK sponsor is a UK-settled parent, the circumstances may relate to the child or the parent, but where the sponsor is not settled or is not a parent, the factors to be considered must relate only to the child.[2] This test is harsher than Tribunal case law, which made no distinction between parents and others in considering the circumstances of the UK sponsor. In *Saluguo*[3] the fact that the child was living comfortably with her aunt and siblings in the Philippines was outweighed by the fact that her mother, a Filipina domestic worker who had worked under poor conditions for a number of years to provide her children with financial security and an education, had a strong desire to bring her youngest child to the UK.

1 HC 251, para 53(f).
2 IDI Dec/00, Ch 8, Annex M, para 1.
3 *Saluguo* (18815).

11.81 In *Campbell*[1] it was said that when considering family or other considerations, the conditions under which the child is living in the home country are not to be weighed against the conditions available for the child in the UK. Conditions in this country are only to be considered if conditions in the overseas country show that exclusion is undesirable. In *Holmes*[2] these tests were satisfied where the child was living in poverty and overcrowded conditions and, importantly, her mother who had been looking after her was about to emigrate to Canada and would not be able to take the child with her. The Tribunal has also considered the death of the carer as being capable of giving rise to compelling and compassionate circumstance. The fact that there are far worse conditions elsewhere in the country is not relevant. Bad conditions are not made better by the existence of worse ones. However, it has also been held that if there is overcrowding it must be shown to be unavoidable.[3] Poverty on its own and unemployment are not enough[4] and the earning potential of the applicant child may be taken into account to relieve temporary difficulties.[5] Initially, the Tribunal set a high standard of 'intolerable' conditions[6] but in *Rudolph*[7] the Tribunal rejected the 'intolerable conditions' test, pointing out that the underlying purpose of the Immigration Rules is to unite families and not divide them and holding that where a father was incapable of caring for a child, that in itself would be grounds for deeming exclusion undesirable. In *Awuko*[8] evidence of a father's failure to care for a child was evidence of his incapacity to do so. Subsequent cases suggest that evidence of voluntary abandonment rather than incapacity to care will be required to make the circumstances compelling.[9] Relevant factors which must be weighed include: the willingness and ability of the overseas adult to look after the child; the living conditions available for the child, although to be able to qualify it is not necessary that these be shown to be intolerable; the greater vulnerability of small children; and the importance of family unity.[10] Contact with a parent overseas which is undesirable may be sufficient to render exclusion of the child from the UK undesirable.[11] In *Patel*[12] the Tribunal posed the question whether the evidence from India as to the circumstances in which the child was living was such that it was in her interests to come to the UK.

1 [1972] Imm AR 115.

2 [1975] Imm AR 20.
3 *Pinnock* [1974] Imm AR 22
4 *Williams* [1972] Imm AR 207.
5 *Needham* [1973] Imm AR 75.
6 *Howard* [1972] Imm AR 93.
7 [1984] Imm AR 84.
8 *Awuko* (4220)
9 *Caballero* (4605); *Darko* (4697); *Anoth* (5954), *Haughton* (4889): all unreported, Immigration Appeal Tribunal.
10 *Hardwood* (00 TH 01522).
11 *Atenaga* (15932). See also *Buendia* (9488).
12 (6961) unreported, 1990.

11.82 With the Immigration Rules precluding recognition of *de facto* adoptions, the 'exclusion undesirable' rule may be the only way in which children in need can be admitted under the rules to join relatives here.[1] Some failed *de facto* adoption cases have succeeded under this Rule.[2] However, as will be seen from the rules relating to adoptive children, these cases are unlikely to succeed where the natural parents continue to exercise parental responsibility up to and during the processing of the application.[3]

1 See IDI Dec/00, Ch 8, Annex R, and for *de facto* adoptions see **11.97** below.
2 *Tariq* (7518) unreported, 1990; *R v Immigration Appeal Tribunal, ex p Tohur Ali* [1988] Imm AR 237, CA.
3 See **11.96** below and Mortimore *Immigration and Adoption* (1994) Trentham pp 52–53.

The 'under 12 concession'

11.83 Where the child seeking to join the UK single parent is under 12 but the sole responsibility rule is not satisfied, entry clearance for settlement may be granted on a concessionary basis if there is adequate accommodation.[1] The IDI state that it may be appropriate to withhold the concession where the UK parent is so handicapped, according to professionally confirmed evidence, as to be incapable of properly caring for the child; or where there are older siblings.[2] The concession cannot be used to get round the prohibition on the entry of certain children of polygamous marriages.[3] The requirement that, where the UK parent is the father, there must be a female relative in the household for the concession to apply seems to have been dropped.

1 IDI Dec/00, Ch 8, Annex M, para 12. In *Alecia* (15337) IAS 1998, Vol 1, No 14, the Tribunal held that the concession had discretionary elements and the adjudicator could not substitute his or her own discretion to allow an appeal outright. Since 2 October 2000 this restriction would not apply in a case such as this in relation to ECHR, art 8 issues, where these are engaged.
2 IDI Dec/00, Ch 8, Annex M, para 12, The detailed guidance for the admission of children with older siblings provides that the numbers of children either side of the dividing line would be relevant, as would whether or not the children have been living together as a group, the arrangements for the care of the children in the UK and the hardship caused by leaving an older sibling alone at home.
3 IDI Dec/00, Ch 8, Annex M, para 12.

ADOPTION OF CHILDREN

11.84 Adoption is of relevance in immigration law in a number of different circumstances and may lead to citizenship, right of abode or settlement. It is a topic of increasing controversy, with the development of a significant divergence in approach between the family courts faced with inter-country adoptions,[1] on the one hand, and the application of the Immigration Rules by the appellate authorities and higher courts on the other. Children, especially babies, are adopted from abroad with increasing frequency[2] and in increasingly unconventional circumstances.[3] Immigration law lags behind in respect of these developments, and is ripe for review and reform.

1 An inter-country adoption is defined by Bevan *Child Law* (1989) Butterworths, p 256 as 'one in which the applicant does not have the same nationality as, or resides in a different country from the child'.
2 A number of measures at international level are attempting to set common standards for the control and regulation of the growing number of children moving between states in inter-country adoptions. See the UN Declaration on Social and Legal principles relating to the Protection and Welfare of Children, with Special Reference to Foster Placement and Adoption Nationally and Internationally (3 December 1986, A/RES/41/85), and the Hague Convention, referred to below.
3 For example through surrogacy arrangements, through the internet, and for gay and lesbian parents.

11.85 To understand the impact in immigration law of adoption it is important to distinguish between:

(i)   adoption by a court in the UK;
(ii)   an 'overseas' adoption for the purposes of section 38(1)(d) of the Adoption Act 1976, namely a legal adoption in a country designated by the Secretary of State under the Adoptions (Designation of Overseas Adoptions) Order 1973;[1]
(iii)   other legal adoptions outside the UK; and
(iv)   informal adoptions.

The consequence of an adoption in the UK or an overseas adoption recognised under the Adoption Act 1976 is that the adopted child is treated in law as if he or she were the legitimate child of the adoptive parents.[2] Such overseas adoptions are recognised automatically without the need for court proceedings in the UK.[3] Recognition of an adoption in a designated country may be denied on public policy grounds.[4] The problem is that the list of countries whose adoptions are recognised is limited,[5] and has not grown since 1973 despite the fact that many non-designated countries have improved their adoption law and procedures in the intervening period. The Hague Convention on the Protection of Children and Co-operation in Respect of Inter-Country Adoptions, signed by the UK in January 1994,[6] has not yet been ratified by the UK and still does not have the force of law within the UK.[7] There are also common law provisions in private international law for recognising overseas adoptions which have not been abrogated by the 1973 Order,[8] although case law is sparse and the precise ambit of these Rules is uncertain.[9] There are, therefore, countries which have a formal adoption procedure but whose adoptions would not be recognised in private international law because the adoptive parents were not domiciled there[10] and they are not designated countries. There are also countries, such as many Muslim countries, where there is no formal system of adoption at all.

1 SI 1973/19, Adoption Act 1976, s 72(2); see Immigration Act 1971, s 33(1).
2 Adoption Act 1976, s 39. The adoption must be made under statute law (and not customary or common law) in respect of a person under 18 who has not been married: Adoptions (Designation of Overseas Adoptions) Order 1973, art 3.

3 Adoption Act 1976, s 38(1)(d)
4 Adoption Act 1976, s 53(2).
5 In March 2001, the designated countries under the 1973 Order, SI 1973/19, were: **A. Commonwealth Countries:** Anguilla; Australia; Bahamas; Barbados; Belize; Bermuda; Botswana; British Virgin Islands; Canada; Cayman Islands; Cyprus; Dominica; Fiji; Ghana; Gibraltar; Guyana; Hong Kong; Jamaica; Kenya; Lesotho; Malaysia; Malawi; Malta; Mauritius; Montserrat; New Zealand; Nigeria; Pitcairn Island; Rhodesia (now known as Zimbabwe); St Christopher and Nevis; St Vincent; Seychelles; Singapore; Sri Lanka; Swaziland; Tanzania; Tonga; Trinidad and Tobago; Uganda; Zambia. **B. Foreign Countries:** Austria; Belgium; Denmark (including Greenland and the Faroes); Finland; France (including Réunion, Martinique, Guadeloupe and French Guyana); Germany; Greece; Iceland; Ireland; Israel; Italy; Luxembourg; The Netherlands (including the Antilles); Norway; Portugal (including the Azores and Madeira), South Africa (including Namibia); Spain (including the Balearic and Canary Islands); Surinam; Sweden; Switzerland; Turkey; The United States of America; Yugoslavia.
6 The number of signatories to this Convention has greatly increased from nine in May 1993 to over 30, but the delay in ratification indicates that, like its predecessor the 1965 Hague Convention, this will not provide a comprehensive solution to legal recognition of adoptions in the foreseeable future. For updated lists of Hague Convention countries and designated countries under the 1973 Order see Clarke Hall and Morrison on Children, [342] and [2001].
7 The Adoption (Intercountry Aspects) Act 1999 was enacted to give effect to the 1993 Hague Convention and will repeal existing arrangements, but it is not currently in force and no date has been specified for it to come into force see s 18(3) of the 1973 Order, SI 1973/19.
8 *Re Valentine's Settlement, Valentine v Valentine* [1965] Ch 831 at 843. Lord Denning suggested the conditions for recognition were that both adoptive parents were domiciled and the child was resident in the country of adoption. This requirement reflected that of English law at the time, but now there is no residence requirement in family law in the UK and only one of the parties need be domiciled: see Mortimore **11.82** fn 3 p 42.
9 *Mathieu* [1979–80] Imm AR 157, see also *Patel (Jesmaben)* [1990] Imm AR 297.
10 See **11.27**ff above.

Adoption by a court in the UK

11.86 Where a court in the UK makes an adoption order in favour of a parent who is a British citizen, the child automatically becomes a British citizen.[1] Even if the adoption order is subsequently annulled, the child's citizenship will not be revoked.[2] An adoption order outside the UK has no automatic effect on citizenship, but may result in the right of abode or be a reason for registration of a minor on application.[3]

1 British Nationality Act 1981, s 1(5).
2 British Nationality Act 1981, s 1(6). The Court of Appeal has held that this does not apply where the Home Office successfully appeals against the making of the order in the first place: *Re K (a minor)* [1994] 3 All ER 553, [1994] 3 WLR 572.
3 See *Lofthouse* [1981] Imm AR 166. For right of abode see chapter 2 and **11.90** below.

11.87 An adoption application can be made by a parent, step-parent or relative in whose home the child has been residing for 13 weeks preceding the application.[1] In other cases (apart from where a child is placed for adoption by an adoption agency) there must be 12 months' residence preceding the application.[2] An adoption order cannot be made where a fee has been paid for a child.[3] The applicant (or one of the applicants in the case of an application by a married couple) must be domiciled in the UK.[4]

1 Adoption Act 1976, s 13(1).
2 Adoption Act 1976, s 13(2).

3 Adoption Act 1976, s 13(2).
4 Adoption Act 1976, ss 14(1) and 15(1).

11.88 Whilst the family courts have recognised that adoption could be used to evade immigration control and that public policy considerations may have to be considered in approving adoptions which have nationality consequences,[1] the earlier cases must be read in the light of the important House of Lords decision in *Re B (adoption order: nationality)*,[2] which is now the leading authority on this issue. The facts were that B's grandparents sought to adopt B, who was 16 at the time of the hearing, after her mother had returned to Jamaica, because if B returned there she would be living in deprived circumstances and her opportunities for education would be greatly reduced. It was accepted that there was a genuine transfer of parental responsibility, but from the outset the case proceeded on the explicit basis that the adoption order was sought to secure British citizenship so that B could remain in the UK, as the Home Office had made it clear that even if the grandparents obtained a residence order, the girl would be removed. The judgment of the House of Lords represents a significant shift from previous Court of Appeal and High Court authorities in relegating the significance of broader policy considerations of maintaining immigration control in adoption cases. It identified from the case law two essential requirements for an inter-country adoption (i) that the purpose of the adoption must be to bring about a genuine transfer of parental responsibility to proposed adopters and not be motivated only by the wish to assist the child to acquire a right of abode (section 12 of the Adoption Act 1976)[3] and (ii) that the adoption, taking account of all the circumstances, would confer real benefits on the child during his or her childhood. Once these requirements were satisfied, the House of Lords held that it would be 'very unlikely that general considerations of "maintaining an effective and consistent immigration policy" could justify the refusal of an order'. It rejected the idea that there could be any real balance between the interests of the child and the public policy considerations. Lord Hoffmann, giving the judgment of the court, acknowledged that the views of the Home Office on this topic should be taken into account by the court as a relevant circumstance, but added that 'It is not easy to see what weight they could be given' and observed that the two considerations were 'hardly commensurable'.[4] Their Lordships gave short shrift to the Court of Appeal's ruling[5] that in considering the question of the welfare of the child under section 6 of the 1976 Act, 'the court must ignore benefits which would result solely from [a] change in immigration status', and, using the words of section 6 itself, requiring the court to have regard to all the circumstances, rejected any distinction between advantages of adoption as such and those flowing from the right of abode.

1 *Re H* [1982] Fam 121 (Hollings J); *Re W* [1986] Fam 54, [1985] 3 All ER 449, CA. For related principles in wardship cases and applications for residence and prohibited steps orders see *Mohamed Arif* [1968] Ch 643; *Re F* [1990] Fam 125; *Re A* [1992] 1 FLR 427, [1991] Imm AR 606; *Re K and S* [1992] 1 FLR 432; *Findlay v Matondo* [1993] Imm AR 541; *Re T* [1994] Imm AR 368, CA.
2 [1999] 2 AC 136, [1999] INLR 125, [1999] 1 FLR 907.
3 This kind of misuse of the adoption procedures has variously been described as an 'accommodation' adoption or a 'sham application' or an 'application of convenience', which 'is solely designed to achieve legal status unsupported by the fundamental foundations which is the creation of the psychological relationship of parent and child'. Thorpe LJ distinguished this situation from 'real' applications tainted by deception, which

would not constitute an abuse of the adoption procedure, in *Re J (Adoption: Non-Patrial)* [1998] INLR 424.

4   *Re B (adoption order: nationality)* [1999] INLR at 128-129.
5   *Re B (adoption order: nationality)* [1998] INLR 505.

11.89   Whilst this case specifically deals with adoption orders, the approach of the House of Lords should, in our view, govern other kinds of applications under the Children Act 1989 for residence and other orders where there is an immigration context to the case.[1] It is, therefore, clear that where natural parents have mistreated, abandoned or rejected the child, or there are other sound family or other reasons for giving the child the stability of membership of a family, as well as other benefits that flow from living in that family in this country, adoption orders can properly be made. In the end, the interests of a child under 18 are the dominant consideration, but the nearer the child is to 18 at the time of the proposed adoption, the more cautious the court is likely to be in approving adoption unless there are clear non-immigration related benefits.[2] Notice should be given to the Home Office who may intervene in the case.[3]

1   On this see *Re E* [1995] Imm AR 475, where a residence order was granted despite the Home Office argument that there was no genuine dispute concerning E other than immigration questions and the court should not be used to try to influence immigration decisions. The order was made under s 3 (1) of the Children Act 1989 because of the actual and practical advantages that would accrue from conferring parental responsibility on a UK-resident sister of a 16-year-old Ecuadorian child, since no one had such responsibility whilst the girl awaited the outcome of her application to stay in the UK, and there were cultural, linguistic and medical benefits. The residence order was made so as to expire when she either voluntarily departed the UK or the Home Office set removal directions.
2   In *Re B* the House of Lords distinguished *Re K (a minor) (adoption order: nationality)* [1995] Fam 38 where an application for adoption was refused in respect of a Sierra Leone national, the niece of a British citizen, who was eight days short of her 18th birthday when the application came before the court. The court was not satisfied that there were any substantial welfare considerations in favour of the adoption. The benefits which would flow from the right of abode would accrue only after her majority. See also *Re H* [1982] Fam 135, [1982] 3 All ER 84; *Re W* [1985] 3 All ER 449; *Re D* [1977] AC 602 at 638. In adoption proceedings the interests of the child are the first consideration and weigh heavier than any other single reason, but are not the paramount reason necessarily outweighing all others: *Re K*.
3   *Re H, Re W* above. See IDI Dec/00, Ch 8, Annex T for flow charts showing that the Home Office will intervene in inter-country adoption proceedings if a child who meets the requirements for leave to remain for the purposes of adoption was not admitted with entry clearance endorsed for adoption, he or she is not being adopted by a couple one of whom is the natural parent, and does not have indefinite leave to remain or leave to remain on the basis of a residence order.

Adoption and right of abode

11.90   Under the provisions of section 2 of the Immigration Act 1971, before amendment by the British Nationality Act 1981, a person who became a citizen of the UK and Colonies (CUKC) by adoption in the UK was a patrial and had a right of abode in the UK. In addition, those who were born to or adopted by a CUKC who was a patrial by birth, adoption, registration or naturalisation in the UK, or by descent from a qualifying parent, became a patrial.[1] Adoption was thus equated with birth for the purpose of linking a child with its new parents and tracing patriality through a parent or grandparent. Whereas it was only adoption in the UK that resulted in citizenship through the territorial link with the UK, the adoption that linked a person to a qualifying parent or grandparent could be outside the UK so long as the person was 'legally adopted'. The 1971 Act defined 'legally adopted' restrictively, confining it to adoptions in designated countries.[2] Now, former CUKC patrials are British citizens and, as we have seen, adoption by a British citizen in the UK bestows British citizenship on the adopted child.[3] Similarly, Commonwealth citizens who have been legally adopted in an overseas adoption by a parent who was born in the UK or Islands were patrials and are now deemed to be British citizens for the purposes of the right of abode.[4]

1 Immigration Act 1971, s 2(1)(b), 2(1)(d). See **2.45** above.
2 Immigration Act 1971, s 33(1).
3 British Nationality Act 1981, s 1(5).
4 Immigration Act 1971, s 2(1)(d), before amendment and s 2(1)(b) as amended by British Nationality Act 1981.

Adoptive parents for the purposes of the Immigration Rules other than settlement

11.91 The general definition of 'parent' for the purposes of the Immigration Rules includes an adoptive parent, but only where a child was adopted in accordance with a decision taken by the competent administrative authority or court in a country whose adoption orders are recognised by the UK.[1] The reference to 'competent administrative authority' reflects the language of the 1993 Hague Convention. It is to be noted that the definition is not restricted to legal adoptions within the meaning of section 33(1) of the Immigration Act 1971 (adoptions in designated countries) and common law principles for recognition of adoption should suffice.[2] Legal adoptions that are not recognised by either statute or common law will not suffice for the purpose of this definition and neither will informal or *de facto* adoptions. The effect is that children of students, workers, business and self-employed persons and the like who are adopted pursuant to a recognised adoption are admissible to join their parents without further inquiry into the circumstances of the adoption.[3]

1 HC 395, para 6. See **11.63** above.
2 The observations to the contrary in *R v Immigration Appeal Tribunal, ex p Uddin* [1989] Imm AR 391 are thus no longer applicable.
3 HC 395, paras 79 (children of students), 101 (children of working holidaymakers), 125 and 197 (children of persons admitted in various categories for employment), 243 (children of investors, the retired and business people). It should be noted that each category except students also permits admission of children where there are serious and compelling family circumstances making exclusion undesirable, which might well be established where there has been an actual transfer of responsibility pursuant to a non-recognised adoption.

Settlement of adopted children under the Immigration Rules

11.92 The general definition of adopted children does not apply to the Immigration Rules for the admission of children for settlement. Instead, a comprehensive package of requirements is identified by HC 395, paragraph 310 and related Rules. This works both ways in terms of the benefits for the immigrant. On the one hand, a potentially broader category of adoptions is permissible under the settlement rule than under the general definition: there is no requirement that the adoption must be recognised in the UK, that is to say that adoptions other than in a designated country or recognised by private international law may qualify,[1] although informal or *de facto* adoptions do not qualify under the Rule.[2] On the other hand, the mere fact of adoption by a court or competent authority is not sufficient by itself to qualify for admission, and a series of other criteria as to the reasons for the adoption and the circumstances surrounding it have to be met.

1 The IDI do not appear to recognise this possibility, defining court adoptions in non-designated countries as *de facto* ones outside the Immigration Rules: IDI Dec/00, Ch 8, Annex R.
2 See **11.97** below.

Adoptions that qualify a child for settlement

11.93 First, the adoption must be by a competent authority or court in the country of origin or residence of the child.[1] Thus *de facto* adoptions, recognised by the Court of Appeal under previous rules relating to settlement of children,[2] are excluded from the Rules. Secondly, the adoptive parents at the time of the adoption must either have both been resident together abroad or one or both of the adoptive parents must have been settled in the UK.[3] As we have previously noted, settlement is to be contrasted with domicile, and ordinary residence in the UK does not require continuous physical presence there.[4] Thirdly, the effect of the decision of the court or the competent authority must be to confer the same rights and obligations as any other child of the marriage.[5] Guardianship or custody orders are thus insufficient; the child must be regarded in law as the child of the adoptive parents. Fourthly, the adoption must be due to the inability of the original parents or any carers at the relevant time to care for the child, and there must have been a genuine transfer of parental responsibility to the adoptive parents.[6] Inability to care should not be interpreted more strictly than in the 'exclusion undesirable' cases,[7] and thus a clearly evidenced rejection of a child by its natural parents or abuse of the child will suffice. Incapability includes not just actual inability but also unwillingness to care.[8] Further the reasons for the adoption cannot sensibly be limited to the death or physical incapacity of all surviving parents and carers. However, an adoption to enable the sponsor to benefit, for example by acquiring a means of support in old age, does not comply with the Rules.[9] Fifthly, the child must have lost or broken all ties with his or her family of origin.[10] Sixthly, the adoption must not be one of convenience arranged to facilitate admission to or stay in the UK.[11]

1 HC 395, as amended by Cm 4851, para 310(vi).
2 *R v Immigration Appeal Tribunal, ex p Tohur Ali* [1987] Imm AR 189, QBD; affd [1988] Imm AR 237, CA. The claim was finally upheld by the Immigration Appeal Tribunal (6596) and followed in *Quijin* (7165).
3 HC 395, as amended by Cm 4851, para 310(vii).
4 See chapter 5 above.
5 HC 395, para 310(viii).
6 HC 395, para 310(ix).
7 See **11.79**ff above.
8 *Kausar (Asima)* (00 TH 1572) IAS 2000, Vol 3, No 15.
9 For observations on the previous Rules see *Singh v Immigration Appeal Tribunal* [1988] Imm AR 510, CA upholding *R v Immigration Appeal Tribunal, ex p Singh* [1987] Imm AR 530.
10 HC 395, para 310(x).
11 HC 395, para 310(xi).

11.94 These requirements are cumulative, and unnecessarily onerous. Adoptions through a court, at the very least those in designated countries, and adoptions by non-British citizens in UK courts, contain enough safeguards to prevent abuse and to protect the welfare of children, yet few would qualify under the stringent criteria of these rules. For example, the requirement that the adoption must be due to the original parent or current carer's 'inability to care' for the child is a more severe test than is applied by the UK (and other) courts which concern themselves with the best interests of the child,[1] and is an unnecessary hurdle given that other rules examine the motives for the adoption and require an actual and genuine transfer of parental responsibility.[2]

1   See *Asif Khan v Immigration Appeal Tribunal* [1984] Imm AR 68; [1985] 1 All ER 40, CA where insistence on a precursor of this rule was held to be unfair in the context of the then policy.
2   In the case of adoptive parents resident in the UK, it is difficult to see how there could be both settlement of the parents at the relevant time, and a transfer abroad to such parents prior to the grant of entry clearance, when the entry clearance process may take many months: *Patel* [1990] Imm AR 297.

11.95 The stark contrast between domestic adoption law and the Immigration Rules is illustrated by the divergence of approach in cases where the adoption is primarily motivated not by the interests of the child but by the infertility of proposed adopted parents. This has arisen predominantly in cases from the Indian sub-continent, where the adoption of a niece or nephew in these circumstances is a long-established custom and social arrangement. This type of adoption cannot, however, satisfy the Rules because of the requirements of inability to care and that family ties have been broken. However, faced with just this scenario in an adoption application made in the UK, the family courts have rejected the Secretary of State's arguments that the adoption application must fail because 'it was not seeking to promote the welfare of the child but to resolve the personal tragedy of infertility'. In *Re H (a minor)*[1] the Court of Appeal declined to apply the requirements of paragraph 310 of HC 395 and held that a genuine adoption application would not be rejected on the ground that it was not primarily motivated by welfare considerations. In *Re J (adoption: non-patrial)*[2] the Court of Appeal went further, rejecting the Secretary of State's reliance on the applicants' conduct in circumventing immigration control by bringing the child to the UK as a visitor, when it was always their intention to seek an adoption order to enable them to keep the child permanently in the UK. The court drew a clear distinction between 'sham' applications and genuine adoptions tainted by deception. The court described the uncompromising terms of the Rules as 'hopeless' in not allowing for this kind of adoption, based as it was upon a widely recognised custom founded on 'a humane response to a sad deprivation'. Giving the judgment of the court, Thorpe LJ observed 'So long as the policy remains as currently expressed, it seems to me that the Secretary of State is to some extent inhibited in criticising those who conclude that the front door is locked and who explore an alternative entry through the rear door.'[3]

1   [1997] 1 WLR 791.
2   [1998] FCR 125, [1998] INLR 424.
3   Mortimore et al (**11.82** fn 3 p 21ff) suggest that in 30 to 40 percent of all adoptions of overseas children in the UK in the early 1990s, the child arrived here without entry clearance, provoking calls for stringent measures including criminal prosecution to deter adoptive parents from bringing in children without prior entry clearance. See Department

of Health *Adoption: the future* (Cm 2288, 1993); and earlier inter-departmental Consultation Paper (1992). Extensive recommendations to remedy this situation were also made; see *Re R (inter-country adoptions)* [1999] INLR 568.

11.96 In the case of *Pawandeep Singh*[1] the *vires* of the rules relating to inability to care and loss of ties with the birth family[2] were challenged in the case of an adoption involving members of an Indian Sikh family where the adoptive parents were infertile. The Court of Appeal refused permission to appeal, rejecting the argument that these rules were *ultra vires* section 1(4) of the Immigration Act 1971 (which requires provision to be made for the admission of dependants) or in conflict with section 6 of the Adoption Act 1976. The court also rejected arguments based on ECHR, Article 8, and the case is currently going to the ECtHR. This issue will no doubt be revisited in the domestic courts with the incorporation of the ECHR, and there are powerful arguments that the rules' absolute bar to adoptions which are not based on the incapacity of the parents has a disproportionate adverse impact on those from countries where this practice prevails, and may breach ECHR, Articles 8 and 14.[3]

1 *Pawandeep Singh v Entry Clearance Officer, Delhi*, 7 December 1999, CA.
2 Then HC 395, para 310(viii) and (ix); now, after amendment by Cm 4851, para 310(ix) and (x).
3 For which see chapter 8 above.

De facto *adoptions*

11.97 Children adopted informally may be admitted to the UK for settlement under Home Office policy outside the Immigration Rules, following the change in 1994 which excluded them from recognition under the Rules.[1] The IDI include in their definition of '*de facto*' adoptions those taking place in a non-designated country, which we suggest is clearly wrong,[2] as well as those where there is no court proceeding.[3] They suggest that a *de facto* adoption should only be considered as having taken place[4] where:

(i)   the adoptive parent(s) have been living and/or working abroad for a substantial period;
(ii)   during their time abroad, they have been caring for the child for a substantial period and have decided to treat the child as their own permanently and to accept all the responsibilities that involves; and
(iii)   the child in turn regards himself or herself as the child of the adoptive parent(s) to the exclusion of the natural parents and their family.

Other criteria set out in the IDI are identical to those for court adoptions. The IDI suggest that the burden of proving a *de facto* adoption will be difficult to discharge in the absence of legal formality or long-standing relationship.[5] Where the adoptive child is related to the sponsors, consideration will be given as to whether the 'exclusion undesirable' rule may be satisfied.[6]

1 HC 395, para 310(vi), as amended by Cm 4851.
2 See **11.92** above.
3 IDI Dec/00, Ch 8, Annex R.
4 IDI Dec/00, Ch 8, Annex R.
5 IDI Dec/00, Ch 8, Annex R.
6 HC 395, paras 297(i)(f), 298(i)(d). See **11.79** above.

Leave to enter and remain

11.98 A child seeking to enter the UK for the purpose of settlement with adoptive parents, who meets the adoption conditions discussed above, will then be treated in the same way as any other child of UK-settled parents. He or she will obtain entry clearance, which will operate as indefinite leave to enter, if both parents are settled or admitted for settlement on the occasion of the entry, or one adoptive parent is dead and the other is settled, or one adoptive parent has had sole responsibility for the child or there are compelling family or other circumstances making exclusion undesirable.[1] Where one parent has been admitted with a view to settlement, then the child is given the same leave.[2] An application for variation of leave to enter to remain for settlement can be made if the 'adoption conditions' are met and both parents are settled in the UK or one parent is dead, or has had sole responsibility or there are compelling circumstances making exclusion undesirable.[3] Maintenance and accommodation provisions must also be met.[4]

1 HC 395, para 310(i).
2 HC 395, para 314.
3 HC 395, para 311(i). See **11.79-11.82** above.
4 See **11.14-11.19** above.

Bringing children to the UK for adoption

11.99 Since 2 October 2000, the Immigration Rules have provided for children to be brought to the UK for the purpose of adoption with a view to settlement. The new paragraph 316A[1] sets out the same conditions as paragraph 310, save that it looks to the future, so, for example, the child need not have lost or broken ties with the natural family provided there is an intention to do so.[2] The new rule effectively incorporates the requirements of the former policy contained in RON 117.[3] The entry clearance officer, the Home Office, the local authority for the area where the adoptive parents live and the Department of Health must all make exhaustive inquiries before entry clearance will be issued for a child to be brought to the UK for adoption. The child will be admitted in the first instance for 12 months,[4] during which time it is anticipated that the adoption application will be made and all the relevant matters will have to be investigated by the UK court, its officers and other relevant bodies. If the new rule is administered efficiently and humanely, it may reduce the incentive to bring the child to the UK in some other capacity, avoiding the risk of the child being removed as an illegal entrant,[5] or more likely, taint what is otherwise a real and genuine adoption with illegality. The incorporation of the criteria into the Rules means that applicants will have a fully effective appeal on the merits of the decision without the restrictions on jurisdiction which limited challenges to decisions under the RON 117 policy.[6]

1 Inserted by Cm 4851.
2 HC 395, para 316A(vii).
3 See *Butterworths Immigration Law Service*, D[401].
4 HC 395, para 316B.
5 See Mortimore, **11.82** fn 3; see also **11.106** below for the policy on removal of children in genuine family relationships.

6 Judicial review was available: *Khan (Asif Mahmood) v Immigration Appeal Tribunal* [1984] Imm AR 68, [1984] 1 WLR 1337, CA where it was held that a refusal of entry clearance was unfair and unreasonable where the provisions of the Immigration Rules relied on had not been indicated in the then policy document handed to applicants. On a statutory appeal, a decision could be held not be in accordance with the law for failure to have regard to the policy: *Abdi v Secretary of State for the Home Department* [1996] Imm AR 288, or failure to categorise the application correctly: *Hassan* (11436); *Ewon* (11392), but the appellate authority could not substitute its own decision. This exacerbated delays which, in the adoption context, could be disastrous.

11.100 The Department of Health[1] is the UK department responsible for decisions relating to adoption, and has responsibility for formulating policy in controversial areas such as the merits of trans-national and trans-racial adoptions and age or health limits on adoptive parents.[2] Its guide to inter-country adoption[3] should be referred to. The Home Office normally seeks the advice of the Department of Health on any application to bring a child into the UK for adoption, because adoption is such an important step in a child's life. The Department of Health needs to have most of the information that the adoption court will need later if the child is admitted. This information would normally be obtained by an adoption agency when considering whether to place a child with adopters. It is necessarily very personal and detailed. The adopters' local authority is asked to prepare a home study report. This means that a social worker will visit the prospective adopters in their home and make the usual adoption inquiries which are made about all adopters and are required by law (including police and health checks). So they must be living in the UK while the home study report is being prepared. The visits will provide an opportunity for them to discuss any matters that may be worrying them and assist them in considering their intention to adopt. An adoption policy panel considers and must make a decision to confirm the adoption.

1 Or the Children and Family Division of the National Assembly for Wales for those living in Wales; the Young People and Looked After Children Division of the Scottish Executive Education Department for those living in Scotland.

2 For a review of the arguments see Mortimore, **11.82** fn 3. They have been stimulated by concern over the adoption of Romanian, Vietnamese and South American babies by European couples. See *Re R (Inter-Country Adoptions)* [1999] INLR 568. Paradoxically, the form of adoption most prevalent in South Asia, where responsibility is transferred inside the family without loss of ethnic identity or all links with the birth family, avoids most of the pitfalls of adoption from a child care viewpoint, yet as we have seen above (**11.95-11.96**) it is the most difficult to achieve under the Immigration Rules. For a critical examination of the policy and the UK's international obligations see *R v Secretary of State for Health, ex p Luff* [1991] Imm AR 382, QBD.

3 Department of Health: *Guide to Inter-country Adoption: Practice and Procedure* (May 1997). See *Re R (Inter-Country Adoptions)* [1999] INLR 568 where a helpful summary of the guide is set out in the judgment of Bracewell J at 569-570. It is particularly tailored to private adoption arrangements rather than arrangements within families but is intended to apply generally.

Bringing a child for adoption: procedure

11.101 The current IDI[1] refer to these provisions as outside the Immigration Rules, but the procedures are unlikely to change now that the applications are within the Rules. A public information leaflet 'Intercountry Adoption' details the evidential and documentary requirements. The form previously used for extra-rules applications, RON 117, has not yet been amended or retitled, so we shall refer to it.[2] As soon as the adopters are able to provide the details of the child, the application for entry clearance should be made on the child's behalf. The questionnaire which is at Appendix 3 of RON 117 should be completed and submitted with all the requested documents attached. The undertaking by intended adopters at Appendix 4 of RON 117 should also be signed and submitted with the other documents. The entry clearance officer will make inquiries into the child's circumstances abroad and then refer the application to the Home Office, which will pass the papers to the Department of Health if there is no reason to believe that the application should be refused at this stage for immigration reasons. The Department of Health will consider whether there are any obvious reasons why the proposed adoption would not safeguard and promote the welfare interests of the child throughout his or her childhood. If satisfied on this point, they will then arrange for a home study report to be made by the local authority and then advise the Home Office whether they consider that there is any welfare reason why an adoption order might not be made.

1   IDI Dec/00, Ch 8, Annex S.
2   See *Butterworths Immigration Law Service* D[401].

11.102 Paragraph 316B of HC 395 stresses that the child must have an entry clearance before travelling, and that such clearance can only be issued at the end of the inquiries listed above. The fact that a child is admitted under these procedures in no way guarantees that a UK court will grant an adoption order in respect of the child. The Home Office should be informed of dates for the hearing. Applicants should apply for an extension of stay if necessary if court proceedings are continuing beyond the initial 12 months granted. Depending on the result of the court decision, the child will acquire the right of abode, be granted indefinite leave, or a limited leave for further inquiries to be made.

OTHER PRACTICES WITH RESPECT TO ADMISSION AND REMOVAL OF CHILDREN

11.103 Unaccompanied children present particular difficulties for immigration control, raising in acute form the divergence between the minimum standards for the protection of children set out in the UN Convention on the Rights of the Child (COROC),[1] and UK immigration policy, which has been held to take precedence.[2] If an unaccompanied child is an asylum seeker, special arrangements apply for their care, investigation of their claim and restraints on removal to a third country.[3] Even if the grounds for coming to the UK may not amount to persecution on the grounds of race, religion, membership of a social group or political opinion (as defined in the 1951 Geneva Convention Relating to the Status of Refugees), such children may be fleeing neglect, abandonment and abuse in their own country. It may well be contrary to ECHR, art 3 or other international obligations to remove them.[4] Even if a child was accompanied on arrival, developments since admission may lead to the same conclusion.[5]

1   20 November1989, A/RES/44/25.
2   Successive UK governments have maintained reservations to this effect: see *R v Secretary of State for the Home Department, ex p Ahmed and Patel* [1998] INLR 570.
3   HC 395, paras 350-352; API Aug/00, Ch 2, s 5. See also the work of the Children's Panel of the Refugee Council.

4   See chapter 8 below; see Commission's decision on admissibility in *FN and BN v Netherlands* (Application 23366/94) Human Rights Case Digest (July–August 1994) p 217.
5   See *Re Sujon Miah* (CO 3391/1994), Ewbank J, Family Division (6 December 1994, unreported) where the court quashed as irrational removal directions in respect of an 11-year-old Bangladeshi child who had been refused leave to enter on arrival in the UK unaccompanied and with a false passport, whose parents in Bangladesh had apparently rejected him and were unwilling to receive him back.

11.104 Unaccompanied children may have been abandoned here by parents and taken into care by the local authority, placed in private foster care, or refused leave to remain. On coming across an unaccompanied child, the Home Office will notify the local authority social services department, whose responsibility it is to care for unaccompanied children.[1] The local authority may support the application of a relative or *de facto* guardian of the child for a residence order under the Children Act 1989, which has the effect of according parental rights to the person with whom the child resides.[2] There has been judicial debate as to the effect of a residence order on the Secretary of State's power to remove.[3] In many cases, the appropriate course will be to make a residence order while the child remains in the UK, but which expires on the giving of removal directions.[4]

1   IDI Dec/00, Ch 8, Annex M. Duties are imposed on local authorities to advise, house and protect the welfare of children in need in the UK: Children Act 1989, ss 17-33.
2   Children Act 1989, ss 8-11.
3   Different views have been expressed in unreported judgments as to whether an unrestricted residence order prevents removal without the consent of the court: see *Toledo Ortega* (CO 528/1994); *Re M (a minor)* [1993] 2 FLR 858; *R v Secretary of State for the Home Department, ex p T* [1995] 1 FLR 293, CA.
4   Section 13(1)(b) of the Children Act 1989 provides that where a residence order is in force no person may remove a child without the written consent of every person who has parental responsibility for the child or the leave of the court. The observations of the Court of Appeal in *Mohamed Arif* [1968] Ch 643 and *Re T* [1994] Imm AR 368 at 375 were not made with these provisions in mind, and the statute makes no exception for removal by lawful excuse or pursuant to other lawful authority.

11.105 If the child is not an asylum claimant, the focus of Home Office inquiries will be how the child came to be in the UK, who looks after him or her, what arrangements have been made with the child's family and how long the arrangement is likely to last; where the child's parent(s) or guardian(s) live, their occupation and their long-term plans for the child; what their material circumstances are in their own country, where siblings are, and the child's own opinion if the child is old enough to express one (normally over seven).[1] The IDI state that children under ten should not be interviewed, and children between ten and 14 should be interviewed only in the presence of an adult who is associated with the child. But any child under 14 who arrives without an older relative or associated adult will have to be interviewed briefly, either to establish immediate admissibility or, if this is not possible, to find out where relatives or friends are located.[2] If the child has no claim to remain in the UK, factors in the decision whether to remove him or her will include the age of the child, the length of his or her stay in the UK, the type of care he or she has had in the UK and the effect of disrupting it, the circumstances abroad and the child's feelings.[3] Generally, the younger the child, and the longer the stay, the less likely is removal.

1   IDI Dec/00, Ch 8, Annex M, para 7.
2   IDI Dec/00, Ch 19, s 1, para 4.
3   IDI Dec/00, Ch 19, s 1, para 4.

11.106 The Home Office has provided guidance to its enforcement section as to when removal of children would be inappropriate. The present policy with respect to children may be summarised:

(i)   children under 16 who are on their own in the UK should not be removed unless their voluntary departure can be arranged;[1]

(ii) no unaccompanied child will be removed from the UK unless the Home Office is satisfied that adequate reception and care arrangements are in place in the country to which he or she is to be removed, and where there is evidence that care arrangements are seriously defective or inadequate, exposing the child to a serious risk of harm, removal should not take place;[2]

(iii) enforcement action will not normally proceed against families with children born here and who have lived here continuously to the age of seven or over, or where, having come to the UK at an early age, children have accumulated seven years or more continuous residence;[3]

(iv) relevant considerations in such a case will be the length of the parents' residence without leave and whether removal has been delayed by protracted and repetitive representations or by parents going to ground, the age of the children, whether any of them were conceived when either parent had leave to remain, whether return to the parents' country would cause extreme hardship to the children or put their health seriously at risk, whether either parent has a history of criminal behaviour or deception;[4]

(v)   in all cases involving potential removal of children the requirements of ECHR, art 8 (family and private life) will have to be complied with.[5]

In *Mobin Jagot* [6] the applicant child had lived in the UK with his grandparents for over seven years, but maintained ties with his parents and siblings in Malawi. The High Court, quashing the decision to remove him, held that the policy DP069/99 contemplated that the requirements of a firm immigration control could not, without strong reason, justify the uprooting of a child who had spent a substantial and formative part of his life in the UK. Neither could disruption to existing family life caused by removal be justified by the possibility of a future effective family life abroad. Although the Home Office is not bound to make the interests of the child the paramount consideration in immigration decisions, they nevertheless represent a primary consideration which must inform such decisions.[7] Thus the potential for conflict between family and immigration law may not be as great as is supposed.

1   DP4/96, para 2 (*Butterworths Immigration Law Service*, D[601]); IDI Dec/00, Ch 8, Annex M, para 7.
2   DP4/96, paras 2 and 3, API Dec/00, Ch 2, s 5, para 3.5; *Re Sujon Miah* **11.103** fn 5 above.
3   DP069/99 (formerly DP5/96).
4   DP069/99.
5   See chapter 8 above.
6   *R v Secretary of State for the Home Department, ex p Mobin Jagot* [2000] INLR 501.
7   In *R v Secretary of State for the Home Department, ex p Ahmed and Patel* [1998] INLR 570 the Court of Appeal accepted the dicta in *MIEA v Teoh* (1995) 128 ALR 353 (Australian High Court) that the ratification of a Convention (the UN Convention on the Rights of the Child) gave rise to a legitimate expectation that the government and its agencies would act in accordance with the Convention, the UK's ratification of the Convention, unlike that of Australia, was expressly subject to an immigration reservation. The court further endorsed the conclusion in *R v Secretary of State for the Home Department, ex p Gangadeen and Khan* [1998] INLR 206 that ECHR, art 8 did not make the interests of the child paramount, but required a balancing exercise: see *Ahmed and Patel* above.

PARENTS, GRANDPARENTS AND OTHER DEPENDENT RELATIVES

The classes of admissible dependent relatives

11.107 The Immigration Rules severely limit the range of dependent relatives other than spouses, fiancé(e)s, unmarried partners and children who may join their relatives in the UK, and the circumstances in which they may do so. All such relatives must be seeking to join or accompany a person who is present and settled in the UK or being admitted for settlement,[1] must be wholly or mainly financially dependent on the relative present and settled in the UK[2] and have no other close relatives in their own country to turn to for financial support.[3] Parents and grandparents of children settled in the UK are allowed to join them only if they are:

(i)   widows or widowers aged 65 or over;[4] or
(ii)   travelling together and at least one of them is aged 65 or over;[5] or
(iii)   aged 65 or over, remarried, but who cannot look to the spouse or children of the second marriage for financial support;[6] or
(iv)   under 65, mainly dependent financially on relatives settled in the UK and living alone in the most exceptional compassionate circumstances.[7]

In *Zanib Bibi*[8] it was held that a separated parent was to be equated with a widow and thus need not comply with the 'most exceptional compassionate circumstances' limb. However, the age requirements still have to be satisfied, and both widowed and separated spouses have to satisfy that limb if they are under 65. The Home Office issued guidance to caseworkers in the UK that all elderly dependent relatives over 65, for whom a sponsor has given an undertaking of support, should be granted indefinite leave to remain without detailed inquires.[9]

1   HC 395, para 317(ii).
2   HC 395, para 317(iii); see **11.111** below.
3   HC 395, para 317(v); see **11.114** below.
4   HC 395, para 317(i)(a) and (b). Previous rules allowed widowed mothers to be under 65, but the other requirements had to be complied with: *R v Immigration Appeal Tribunal, ex p Khan (Azam)* [1993] Imm AR 33, QBD. The rules were 'equalised' downwards in 1994.
5   HC 395, para 317(i)(c).
6   HC 395, para 317(i)(d).
7   HC 395, para 317(i)(e).
8   *R v Immigration Appeal Tribunal, ex p Zanib Bibi* [1987] Imm AR 392; see also *Rosario* (9600) unreported 1993.
9   Memo from B1 Management Unit, January 1994. This is now set out in IDI Sep/98, Ch 8, s 6.

11.108 Sons, daughters, sisters, brothers, uncles and aunts over 18 can qualify for admission to join a sponsor in the UK only if they are living alone outside the UK in the most exceptional compassionate circumstances and mainly financially dependent on relatives settled in the UK.[1] The Rule is clearly intended to be exhaustive of the categories of relative admissible for entry.[2]

1   HC 395, para 317(i)(f).
2   IDI Dec/00, Ch 8, Annex W.

The requirement of entry clearance

11.109 Dependent relatives must always have an entry clearance if seeking leave to enter in that capacity.[1] The position remains that entry clearance is not required for applications for leave to remain as a relative; such applications are to be granted if the other conditions of the Immigration Rules are met.[2]

1 HC 395, para 317(vi). Where a person arrives without entry clearance, the immigration officer will examine him or her to decide whether exceptional compassionate circumstances warrant the exercise of discretion: IDI Sep/98, Ch 8, s 6, para 2.2.
2 HC 395, paras 318 and 319; see also *R v Immigration Appeal Tribunal, ex p Kaur (Mohinder)* [1994] Imm AR 526, QBD confirming that after entry cases must still fulfil the on entry rules.

Maintenance and accommodation

11.110 There must be a sponsor who is present and settled in the UK (or will be on arrival of the relatives), and there must be adequate accommodation owned or occupied by the sponsor, and adequate maintenance for the new arrivals and any dependants of theirs.[1] The wording of the maintenance and accommodation rule suggests that the sponsor does not have to provide the maintenance and accommodation, which can be provided by a third party. This is in contrast to the wording of the rules for children, spouses and partners.[2]

1 HC 395, para 317(iv) and (iva) as amended by Cm 4851.
2 See discussion at **11.14ff** above.

Dependency

11.111 The relative must be wholly or mainly financially dependent on the sponsor.[1] Relatives claiming admission because they live alone in the most exceptional compassionate circumstances have to show they are financially mainly dependent on relatives settled in the UK (not necessarily the sponsor).[2] The relevant question is whether *the relative* is financially mainly dependent upon the sponsor. It is not sufficient to demonstrate that the family with whom the relative lives is so dependent. In *Bibi*[3] the sponsor began to remit money to his brother, with whom the appellant mother lived, when the children's educational needs imposed an impossible burden on the family finances in Bangladesh. Prior to this, the sponsor had not remitted any money and the appellant was dependent upon the family in Bangladesh. It was argued that the family was dependent upon this remittance and therefore the appellant, as a member of the family, was financially dependent mainly on the sponsor. The Court of Appeal, in finding that the appellant was not financially dependent, held that the focus of the examination must be upon the appellant. A connection must be shown between the money provided by the sponsor and the appellant's needs. 'Financially' in the words of the paragraph means money or money's worth, and someone whose needs for accommodation, clothing, food and other necessities, including social comfort and support in old age,[4] are met by another is financially dependent on that person.[5] The case law on dependency under the previous rules will continue to have relevance. Dependency refers to the needs of the applicants, which are not contrived[6] and which they are unable to meet by themselves.[7] Other types of dependency may tip the balance where there is a partial financial dependency; but without financial dependency, this requirement of the Immigration Rules cannot be met. Emotional dependency may turn into financial dependency if expenditure is involved to meet it.[8] There must be some element of material support and a history of close contact for emotional dependency to count.[9] In *Parekh*[10] the Tribunal held that a finding of dependency would normally follow when there was no close relative to turn to. The word 'mainly' is not apt to describe a mathematical calculation, although in some cases arithmetic may provide a useful approach; the phrase calls for a rounded appraisal.[11]

1 HC 395, para 317(iii).
2 HC 395, para 317(i)(e) and (f); *Botan* (18175) 12 May 1999, Immigration Appeal Tribunal. IDI Sep/98, Ch 8, s 6, para 3.2 state that support from two or more relatives in the UK is unacceptable, and applicants in this situation must nominate one sponsor upon whom they have been financially mainly dependent and who will be 'singularly' responsible for their maintenance and accommodation in the UK. The wording of the rules does not necessitate this restrictive interpretation, which is, we suggest, wrong.
3 *Bibi v Entry Clearance Officer Dhaka* [2000] Imm AR 385, CA.
4 *Immigration Appeal Tribunal v Swaran Singh* [1987] Imm AR 563, CA; *R v Immigration Appeal Tribunal, ex p Sayana Khatun* [1989] Imm AR 482, QBD.
5 *Bibi v Entry Clearance Officer Dhaka* above; *Desai v Entry Clearance Officer* [2000] INLR 10, CA.
6 *Chavda* [1978] Imm AR 40; *Zaman* [1973] Imm AR 71; *Musa (Hasan Bibi)* [1976] Imm AR 28; *Grenade* [1978] Imm AR 143.
7 *Bhattacharjee* (3476); *R v Immigration Appeal Tribunal, ex p Patel* (1982) Times, 7 April, QBD; *George* (4184) unreported.
8 *Bi (Rehmat)* (16074) IAS 1998, Vol 1, No 5.
9 *R v Immigration Appeal Tribunal, ex p Bastiampillai* [1983] 2 All ER 844, [1983] Imm AR 1, QBD, where it was said that emotional dependence could tip the balance, but it must mean more than ordinary family affection. See *Dairion* (3356), *Keogh* (5868) and *Ting* (18735) unreported, 5 October 1998, for examples of emotional dependence. For a review of the authorities see *Cheng (Shen)* [1993] Imm AR 81.
10 *Parekh (Hasmuklal)* (14016) IAS 1997, Vol 3, No 14.
11 *Desai v Entry Clearance Officer* above.

11.112 The dependency must be of necessity, not of choice. In *Zaman*[1] an elderly Pakistani farmer and his wife applied to join their son in the UK. The father owned two farms and the income from these was given away to three sons who were still resident in that country, in accordance with custom. This left the parents wholly dependent upon money sent to them by their son in the UK. Nevertheless, the Tribunal held that they were not wholly or mainly dependent, since their dependence was not necessary. This approach was confirmed in *Musa*[2] where two able-bodied teenage sons were held to be capable of supplementing their mother's earnings and it could not, therefore, be said that they were necessarily dependent on the eldest son in the UK. In another case, the Tribunal upheld a refusal of admission where a widowed mother had given up her job voluntarily and without explanation and become dependent on her son in the UK.[3] Where the sponsor's support was for the purposes of keeping up a particular lifestyle, there was no necessary dependency.[4] However, it should be noted that it is only a voluntary act done with intent to become dependent that creates a dependence that is not necessary. Where an act done *bona fide* for other purposes in fact results in dependence, it cannot be said to be a contrived or unnecessary dependence.[5] Where the alternative source of dependence is conditional on the ability of others to find work and support the applicant, dependence on a sponsor in the UK is still necessary.[6]

1 [1973] Imm AR 71. See also *Begum (Fazal)* (15920) IAS 1998, Vol 1, No 8, Immigration Appeal Tribunal.
2 [1976] Imm AR 28.
3 *Grenade* [1978] Imm AR 143; see also *R v Immigration Appeal Tribunal, ex p Coelho* (5 February 1986, unreported).
4 *Sithamparapillai* (15724) IAS 1998, Vol 1, No 6, Immigration Appeal Tribunal. This seems to be using 'necessity' in a different sense; see below.
5 *Bibi v Entry Clearance Officer Dhaka* [2000] Imm AR 385, CA; *George* (4184).
6 *Chavda* [1978] Imm AR 40.

11.113 Difficulties may also arise where the applicants have some assets of their own. Early Tribunal decisions were concerned with when the assets were likely to run out, and held that it was not necessary for applicants to use up all their resources before becoming necessarily dependent on remittances from the UK.[1] An alternative approach is that taken by the Department of Social Security in income support cases where an estimate is made of the income which could reasonably be derived from any capital. In *Bhattacharjee*[2] the Tribunal adopted the guidance of the High Court in *Ex p Patel*[3] and determined that the question was whether there was a deficiency in the applicant's own resources available to meet his or her needs. In *George*[4] the Tribunal applied this test to the value of a house owned in the UK and it was held that there was a deficiency, in that the proceeds would not provide a home and an income for the applicants without substantial recourse to the support of their children. We suggest that the true rationale of *Sithamparapillai*,[5] where the UK sponsor provided support because the pension of a retired government official was not sufficient for the life-style he wished to adopt, was that support which supplements an adequate income does not result in the relative being 'mainly' dependent on the sponsor. The IDI pose the test that 'the payments from the sponsor are essential to help the applicant achieve a reasonable life style'.[6]

1 *Sharma* (227) and *Patel* (506) unreported.
2 (3476) unreported.
3 *R v Immigration Appeal Tribunal, ex p Patel* (1982) Times, 7 April, QBD.
4 (4184) unreported
5 *Sithamparapillai* (15724) IAS 1998 Vol 1 No 6, Immigration Appeal Tribunal. The Tribunal found the dependence was not one of necessity; see **11.112** fn 4 above.
6 IDI Dec/00, Ch 8, Annex V.

Without close relatives to turn to

11.114 The present Immigration Rules require relatives seeking admission to be without close relatives in their own country to whom to turn for financial support.[1] Before the October 1994 change, the Rule simply required that there were no close relatives there 'to turn to'. There are numerous decisions interpreting the phrase in the previous rules. In *Bastiampillai*[2] the High Court held that the Rules imply that the relatives must have the ability to provide shelter or financial support to make it reasonable for the applicant to depend on them rather than the sponsor. This was followed in *Ex p Dadibhai*,[3] where it was held that the phrase implied a willingness to support by the alternative relatives. Relatives who are hostile or indifferent to the applicant could not be relied on. This is accepted by the Home Office.[4] The decisions in *Devshi*[5] and *Yip*[6] are examples of how even close residence with other relatives does not necessarily make them relatives to turn to in this context. The relatives must be in the applicants' own country and this has been interpreted as their country of residence rather than that of nationality.[7]

1 HC 395, para 317(v).
2 *R v Immigration Appeal Tribunal, ex p Bastiampillai* [1983] 2 All ER 844, [1983] Imm AR 1, QBD.
3 *R v Immigration Appeal Tribunal, ex p Dadibhai* (24 October 1983, unreported), QBD.
4 IDI Dec/00, Ch 8, Annex V refer to relatives 'able and willing' to support the applicant at home.
5 *Devshi* (3163).
6 *Yip* (2894).
7 *Levy* [1978] Imm AR 119; *Patel* (20542) IAS 2000, Vol 3, No 2, Immigration Appeal Tribunal.

11.115 In *Swaran Singh*[1] the Court of Appeal indicated that the correct approach to the previous rule was to recognise it as a rule of broad humanity that had not previously been humanely administered. Thus, any kind of need of the appellant that was established by the evidence that could not be met by relatives in the appellant's own country would satisfy the requirements of the rule. Despite the authoritative terms of this Court of Appeal decision, the Home Office sought to argue in *Sayana Khatun*[2] that the court had not meant to include financial need. This viewpoint was rejected once again. It can thus be stated: that before the applicant is disqualified, there must be close relatives in his or her own country to turn to, who are able and willing to meet the needs of the applicant, even if these are supplied by the sponsor in the UK.[3] *Ex p Sayana Khatun*[4] also provides an example of what the unmet needs can include. Here the applicant had spent many years in the household of her daughter-in-law and grandchildren, and was used to living with them. The adjudicator decided that this fact made it reasonable not to turn to her elderly brothers who were willing to support and accommodate her. The Tribunal reversed the adjudicator, but their decision was in turn quashed by the High Court, which held that in the light of the adjudicator's findings there were emotional and social needs of the applicant that only the sponsor in the UK could satisfy. The rule was amended in 1994 to refer explicitly to financial needs.

1 Immigration Appeal Tribunal *v Swaran Singh* [1987] Imm AR 563, CA.
2 [1988] Imm AR 348, Immigration Appeal Tribunal; [1989] Imm AR 482, QBD.
3 *R v Immigration Appeal Tribunal, ex p Kara* [1989] Imm AR 120, QBD.
4 [1989] Imm AR 482, QBD.

Living alone in the most exceptional compassionate circumstances

11.116 The test for admission for those relatives who can only qualify by satisfying this supplementary requirement undoubtedly is a high one, but it must not be interpreted in an unrealistically high way. The rule is intended to assist those who are unable to care for themselves, or suffer isolation and social stigma without the support of their family.[1] However, the financial support from UK-settled relatives, which is necessary for qualification, may mitigate the applicant's circumstances and so take them below the threshold,[2] and the rule is not to be construed as if the financial support was not there.[3] If an applicant is in the UK when an application is made, the rule should be construed as requiring an examination of what the position would have been at the date of decision had the applicant remained where he or she was and had not come here. The Tribunal has held that one can be living alone without necessarily living on one's own.[4] The requirement to be 'living alone' is not restricted to physical isolation and can include those who have been so psychologically isolated as to cut themselves off from those around them.[5] The proper approach to deciding upon the existence of most exceptional compassionate circumstances is to take all the elements of hardship cumulatively,[6] and these have included the existence of a very close relationship between an appellant and her granddaughter;[7] the fact that in the appellant's community a young single woman living alone would be regarded as immoral[8] and the fact that on return to their country appellants would be new re-arrivals in an area of high crime and going to a house which had deteriorated during their absence.[9]

1 *Begum (Iqbal)* (5580). The IDI refer to illness, incapacity, isolation and poverty as capable of constituting most exceptional compassionate circumstances for parents and grandparents under 65: IDI Dec/00, Ch 8, Annex V. For other relatives who are over 18 but not necessarily old and frail, the circumstances the Home Office is looking for will be such that the applicant cannot function (either because of illness or disability) without the help and support of friends or relatives and that no such support is available: IDI Dec/00, Ch 8, Annex W.
2 See *Bibi (Nessa)* (21162A) IAS, Vol 3, No 13, Immigration Appeal Tribunal.
3 *R v Immigration Appeal Tribunal, ex p Manshoora Begum* [1986] Imm AR 385, QBD; *Begum (Zohra) v Immigration Appeal Tribunal* [1994] Imm AR 381. CA.
4 *Paw* (4328) unreported.
5 *Boshir* (10902).
6 *Agoro* (16078) IAS 1998, Vol 1, No 5, Immigration Appeal Tribunal. But see *Nessa (Sharijun)* (16391) IAS 1998, Vol 1, No 23: the factors of dependency and living alone are separate and not to be 'blurred' with the most exceptional compassionate circumstances test. See also *Husna Begum v ECO Dhaka* [2001] INLR 115, CA.
7 *Wu* (12359).
8 *Bayar* (12380). The IDI state that where the applicant is a young single or divorced woman living in a country where it is claimed that it is socially unacceptable for her to live there alone, this may be taken into account when considering whether the test is met, but that such a situation is not on its own sufficient: IDI Sep/98, Ch 8, s 6.
9 *Mohammed* (15454).

Chapter 12

REFUGEES, ASYLUM AND EXCEPTIONAL LEAVE

12.1   Introduction
12.20   The definition of refugee
12.96   Expulsion of refugees
12.100 Consequences of recognition
12.107 UK practice on asylum
12.160 Asylum appeals

INTRODUCTION

Asylum

12.1 In layman's language, refugees are people seeking asylum in a foreign country because of war, civil war or other catastrophic events in their own. It is only in the artificial world of the 1951 Convention Relating to the Status of Refugees, now the major convention used throughout the world for the protection of refugees and signed by 139 states, that generalised catastrophe disqualifies, rather than qualifies, a person from the status of refugee.[1] It is partly this mismatch between 'legal' or 'Convention' refugees and 'actual' or '*de facto*' refugees which has allowed western European governments to enact ever more restrictive measures against refugees, often irresponsibly described as 'bogus' or 'abusive'.[2] Over the past decade the word 'asylum' has almost lost its meaning under the weight of political scaremongering to which it has been subject.

1 The Convention concerning the Specific Aspects of Refugee Problems in Africa 1969 contains a broader definition of the term 'refugee' and one more in keeping with the word's natural meaning, embracing those compelled to leave their place of habitual residence through 'external aggression, occupation, foreign domination or events seriously disturbing public order in either part or the whole of the country' (Plender *Basic Documents on International Migration Law* (2nd revised edn, 1997) p 117).
2 The recognition rate for refugees has less to do with merits than with politics. Thus between 1989 and 1998 Canada granted refugee status to over 80 percent of applicants from Sri Lanka, France to 74 percent, and the UK to 1 percent: Refugee Council response to the Home Secretary's Lisbon Proposals, January 2001.

12.2 Asylum in its ordinary dictionary meaning is a refuge, shelter or protection. Article 14 of the Universal Declaration of Human Rights (UDHR) refers to a right to 'seek and enjoy asylum from persecution' but does not specify the meaning or grounds of persecution. The concept of territorial asylum[1] includes asylum for humanitarian reasons rather than specifically for particular types of refugees. In the UK, the law and the Immigration Rules used to distinguish between asylum and Convention refugee status; that distinction disappeared in 1993[2] and the words are now used synonymously.[3] Thus, in considering appeals against refusal of leave to enter or remain on asylum grounds, the appellate authorities will be confined to considering whether the applicant is a Convention refugee.[4] This chapter is predominantly concerned with the application of the rules relating to asylum, and so references to refugees, asylum and the Convention are references to the statutory definition. Convention refugees are those who seek to escape persecution for reasons of race, religion, nationality, membership of a social group, or political opinion. The scope of this Convention definition is examined in greater detail below (at **12.20ff**).

1   See the Declaration of the Committee of Ministers of the Council of Europe on Territorial Asylum 1977, the Caracas Convention on Territorial Asylum 1954, the Caracas Convention on Diplomatic Asylum 1954 and the Cartagena Declaration on Refugees 1984. See also Recommendation R (1981) 16 on the Harmonisation of National Procedures Relating to Asylum (Plender **12.1** fn 1 above, pp 140, 147).

2   With the Asylum and Immigration Appeals Act 1993, s 1 of which (still in force) for the first time defined 'asylum' as meaning refugee status within the meaning of the Convention Relating to the Status of Refugees (Geneva, 1951) and its 1967 Protocol (collectively the Refugee Convention). However, for the purposes of 'asylum support' in Pt VI of the 1999 Act, a 'claim for asylum' is defined to include a claim that removal would be contrary to the ECHR: see s 94.

3   See Home Office evidence to the House of Commons Home Affairs Committee Sub-Committee on Race and Immigration 1984–85, 72 HC Official Report (6th series) col iv, 17 December 1984. The Education (Mandatory Awards) Regulations 1991, SI 1991/1838 referred to 'refugees or others granted asylum', but the regulations made since 1993 no longer use this terminology. They now refer to 'refugees' and to persons who are not refugees who have been granted leave to enter or remain because 'it is thought right': Education (Mandatory Awards) Regulations 1998, SI 1998/2003.

4   Immigration and Asylum Act 1999, s 69(6). This is of course subject to the one-stop procedure, which will allow other matters including human rights grounds to be litigated in the same proceedings: see chapter 18 below.

12.3   However wide the definition of refugee, there will be those deserving protection under other international instruments who may fall outside it. People may be fleeing torture and inhuman or degrading treatment even though such treatment may not be on the grounds of race, religion, membership of a social group or political opinion.[1] Expulsion of such persons in circumstances where there are substantial grounds to conclude that they face such treatment would be contrary to other international obligations.[2] The distinction is recognised in most EU countries by the grant of a subsidiary status to those who cannot be expected to return to their country of origin for reasons not qualifying them for refugee status.[3] In the UK, such persons historically have been unrecognised in the Immigration Rules, although the Home Office may grant exceptional leave to remain outside the Rules in such cases, and refusal is, since 2 October 2000, appealable by virtue of section 65 of the Immigration and Asylum Act 1999. Until then, the only remedy against a refusal to give effect to ECHR obligations was judicial review.[4] We examined the ECHR in chapter 8 above and will look at the grant of exceptional leave to remain in **12.179** below.

1   See *Ameyaw* [1992] Imm AR 206 (unfair trial); *R v Secretary of State for the Home Department, ex p Zibirila-Alassia* [1991] Imm AR 367, QBD (fear of being selected as

victim of ritual sacrifice); *R v Immigration Appeal Tribunal, ex p Hernandez* [1994] Imm AR 506, QBD (retribution from guerilla groups); *Hamieh* [1993] Imm AR 323 (pressure from extremist groups) for examples of possible persecution for non-Refugee Convention reasons.

2   Most notably art 3 of the ECHR and art 3 of the UN Convention Against Torture: see *R v Secretary of State for the Home Department, ex p Chahal* [1994] Imm AR 107, [1995] 1 All ER 658, CA; *Chahal v UK* (1996) 23 EHRR 413. See also *Mutombo v Switzerland* (1994) 15 HRJ 164; *Alan v Switzerland* [1997] INLR 29. See also Gorlick 'Refugee Protection and the Committee Against Torture' (1995) 7 IJRL 504.

3   In art 63(2)(a) EC, inserted by Treaty of Amsterdam, signed on 2 October 1997 by 15 member states, such persons are described as 'other persons in need of international protection'.

4   See the judgment of Sedley J in *R v Secretary of State for the Home Department, ex p McQuillan* [1995] 4 All ER 400 for a most coherent exposition of *R v Secretary of State for the Home Department, ex p Brind* [1991] 1 AC 696 and the court's jurisdiction to ensure that domestic standards of rationality do not fall out of line with international obligations.

12.4   The present UK practice is that all those who are granted asylum in the UK are recognised as refugees and the appropriate Refugee Convention travel document is given in recognition of this status.[1] But refugees present in the UK do not have to be given asylum here if there is a safe third country to which they can be removed.[2] Where those who do not qualify as refugees are given exceptional leave to remain, the government grants a four-year period of leave, with eligibility for settlement and family reunion rights thereafter. They will not receive a Convention travel document, but will be eligible for a Home Office travel document.[3]

1   Refugee Convention, art 28, Schedule.
2   HC 395, paras 334, 345. We examine the UK's practice on safe third countries at **12.125** below.
3   See **12.182** below.

12.5   The general rule of customary international law is that no individual may assert a right to enter a state of which he or she is not a national, and this rule is normally accepted as applying to refugees as well as ordinary migrants.[1] In accordance with this rule the right of asylum is not a right accorded to an individual refugee (except vis-à-vis 'the country of origin),[2] but is a discretionary right of a state to grant or withhold asylum.[3] The importance of giving states the right to grant asylum was to emphasise that such a grant was not an unfriendly act against the state of which the refugee was a national. These provisions of customary international law are reflected in the international legal instruments that have come into being since 1948. Article 14 of the Universal Declaration of Human Rights 1948 (UDHR) recognised the fundamental right to 'seek and enjoy asylum' but the Convention and Protocol studiously avoid creating any legal right to asylum or any duty to grant asylum or to give a refugee leave to enter a particular territory. However, it is a matter of contention whether 50 years of state practice have modified this position in international customary law.[4]

1   Lauterpacht *Oppenheim's International Law* (7th edn, 1952) p 616; R Plender *International Migration Law* (2nd edn, 1988) p 394; see also F Morgenstern 'The Right of Asylum' (1949) 26 BYBIL 327 at 335; P Weis 'Legal Aspects of the Convention Relating to the Status of Refugees' (1953) 30 BYBIL 478 at 481. See also Goodwin-Gill *The Refugee in International Law* (2nd edn, 1996); Goodwin-Gill's editorial comment 'Asylum: The Law and Politics of Change' (1995) 7 IJRL 1; and Roman Boed, 'The state of the right of asylum in international law', (1994) 5 Duke Journal of Comparative International Law 1.
2   UDHR, art 13(2); International Covenant on Civil and Political Rights, art 12(2).

3   The position in municipal law might be different: see Immigration Rules, HC 395, para 334; *R v Secretary of State for the Home Department, ex p Deniz Mersin* [2000] INLR 511, QBD, at **12.100** below where Elias J held that an asylum seeker who had succeeded on appeal had a right to be granted refugee status and indefinite leave to remain.
4   UNHCR refers to instances of denial of access to protection through closure of borders and non-admission to the territory or to asylum procedures as 'serious breaches of the internationally recognised rights of refugees and asylum seekers' in its *Note on International Protection*, ExCom 50th session, UN doc A/AC.96/914, 7 July 1999, (1999) 11(3) IJRL 557.

The Geneva Convention

12.6 The key international instrument is the Geneva Convention of 1951 Relating to the Status of Refugees, as amended by the Protocol to the Convention 1967 (collectively the Refugee Convention). The original Convention was concerned with the displacement of people as a result of the Second World War and restricted the definition of refugees to those whose fear of persecution arose from events occurring before 1 January 1951. The Protocol removed this time limitation, but enabled parties who had imposed a geographic limitation on the application of the Convention to continue such limitations to post-1951 refugees. Some states made declarations limiting the application of the Convention to refugees fleeing their countries as a result of events occurring in Europe. In the past this included some European countries, but now all EU countries have ratified both Convention and Protocol without temporal or geographical limitations.[1] The Asylum and Immigration Appeals Act 1993 incorporated the Convention into UK law to the extent of providing that it would be unlawful for Immigration Rules to be made that are inconsistent with the Convention.[2]

1   Italy, in particular, used to have a geographical reservation. In 1990 the member states of the EU formulated the Dublin Convention to prevent asylum seekers making multiple applications within the EU. In order to achieve this, signatory states were required to have ratified the Protocol. The Dublin Convention came into force in September 1997. See further **12.146ff** below.
2   Asylum and Immigration Appeals Act 1993, s 2; HC 395, para 334. The House of Lords in *Sivakumaran* [1988] AC 958 took the view that 'the UK having acceded to the Convention and Protocol, their provisions have for all practical purposes been incorporated into UK law'. In *Ex p Adimi* [1999] INLR 490 the Divisional Court held that refugees had a legitimate expectation that the provisions of the Convention would be followed.

12.7 In broad terms the Refugee Convention provides a definition of refugees, creates exclusions from the definition and sets out circumstances when a person may cease to be a refugee,[1] and defines the duties owed to and by refugees vis-à-vis their host states. Where someone is recognised as a refugee and granted asylum, signatory states are under a duty to secure equal treatment in respect of religion, personal status, property, freedom of association, gainful occupation, welfare, administrative measures and the issue of special travel documents to be used in place of the refugee's national passport.[2] It is important to note that refugees are recognised by states rather than created by them: an asylum claimant should thus be treated as a potential refugee unless and until a valid determination is made that he or she is not to be so recognised,[3] but this principle does not preclude the construction of the particular Articles of the Convention which refer to refugees 'lawfully on the territory' as referring to recognised refugees who have been granted leave to stay.[4]

1   Refugee Convention, art 1.

2 Refugee Convention, arts 4-30.
3 See UNHCR *Handbook on Procedures and Criteria for Determining Refugee Status* (1979) para 28; *Khaboka v Secretary of State for the Home Department* [1993] Imm AR 484 at 487, CA, per Nolan LJ.
4 See *R v Secretary of State for the Home Department, ex p Joint Council for the Welfare of Immigrants* [1996] 4 All ER 385, [1997] 1 WLR 275, where the Court of Appeal assumed that art 23 of the Refugee Convention (the right of refugees lawfully staying on the territory to social security on the same basis as nationals) did not apply to asylum seekers.

12.8 The states that are signatories to the Refugee Convention did not surrender their discretionary power to grant or withhold asylum, but in practice the same result is achieved by duties assumed by states signatory to the Convention and the other instruments, such as the UN Convention Against Torture and the ECHR, to those on their territory.[1] Signatory states agreed to abide by Article 33 which prohibited *refoulement* (ie the expulsion or return of refugees in any manner whatsoever to the frontiers of territories where their lives or freedom would be threatened on account of their race, religion, nationality, membership of a particular social group or political opinion). If there is no safe third country to which a person can be sent, the principle of *non-refoulement* effectively requires a state to determine an asylum claim made by someone within its territory (including the border or transit zone at an airport).[2] In the UK, if a person is recognised as a refugee, this results in a grant of asylum. In some other European countries they may have a status short of asylum for failure to meet national criteria for asylum, but are recognised as people who cannot be sent back to their own countries.[3]

1 *T v Secretary of State for the Home Department* [1996] AC 742, [1996] 2 WLR 766, [1996] Imm AR 443 at 446, per Lord Mustill. See also Joan Fitzpatrick 'Revitalising the 1951 Refugee Convention' (1996) 9 Harvard Human Rights Journal 229 at 251: 'The most enduring contribution of the Convention is its elevation of *non-refoulement* to the status of an international norm.'
2 The French attempt to circumvent domestic constraints on detention of asylum seekers by declaring the airport an 'international zone' was thwarted in *Amuur v France* (1996) 22 EHRR 533 where the detention was held to breach art 5 of the ECHR.
3 See IJRL case abstracts No 81 (1994) 6(1) IJRL 113; No 196 (1994) 6(2) IJRL 285; No 198 (1994) 6(3) IJRL 463; No 200 (1994) 6(3) IJRL 474; No 215 (1994) 6(4) IJRL 673; No 226 (1995) 7(1) IJRL 140.

12.9 A big issue in contemporary refugee law is whether the Refugee Convention has extra-territorial effect. The question has assumed great importance as more and more states employ measures, ranging from carrier sanctions and visa controls to airline liaison officers, to prevent undocumented passengers boarding transport in countries of origin, physical interception and return of asylum seekers on the high seas, and increasingly, agreements with countries of origin and transit to prevent asylum seekers leaving for western countries. UNHCR takes the view that the obligation of *non-refoulement*, which is 'progressively acquiring the character of a peremptory rule of international law', extends to all government agents acting in an official capacity, whether within or outside national territory. 'Given the practice of States to intercept persons at a great distance from their own territory, the international refugee protection regime would be rendered ineffective if States' agents abroad were able to act at variance with their obligations under international refugee law and human rights law.'[1] Similarly, Goodwin-Gill has trenchant criticism of the US Supreme Court's decision in *Sale v Haitian Centers Council*[2] upholding the policy of extra-territorial interception and return of Haitian asylum seekers to Haiti by US coastguards without any determination of their claims.[3] In the UK, the High Court concluded in one case that the international obligation only arose when the refugee reached the territory of the state where asylum was claimed.[4] But in other cases it has entertained complaints about obstructive attitudes of British officials abroad. The courts have recognised the effect that carrier sanctions have on refugees' ability to seek asylum, but have not declared them unlawful.[5]

1   UNHCR ExCom Standing Committee, *Interception of asylum seekers and refugees*, 18th meeting, 9 June 2000, EC/50/SC/CRP.17, paras 21-23. See also UNHCR: *The trafficking and smuggling of refugees: the end game in European asylum policy?* July 2000; UNHCR ExCom 50th session, Note on International Protection, UN doc A/AC.96/914, 7 July 1999, in (1999) 11(3) IJRL 557.
2   113 S Ct 2549 (1993).
3   Goodwin-Gill **12.5** fn 1 above, pp 142-144. See also (1994) 6(1) IJRL 68–109.
4   *R v Secretary of State for the Home Department, ex p Sritharan* [1992] Imm AR 184 where a Tamil seeking asylum had been detained in Oman for using false documents to board a plane to come to the UK to claim asylum. It was held that there was no arguable case that the UK owed an obligation to issue a visa to enable him to continue his journey, despite the risk that Oman would return him to Sri Lanka without entertaining an asylum claim.
5   *R v Secretary of State for the Home Department, ex p Yassine* [1990] Imm AR 354, QBD; *R v Uxbridge Magistrates' Court, ex p Adimi* [1999] INLR 490; *R v Secretary of State for the Home Department, ex p Hoverspeed* [1999] INLR 591, at **14.76** below. On the compatibility of carrier sanctions with international law see Erika Feller 'Carrier Sanctions and International Law' (1989) 1 IJRL 48; A Ruff 'The United Kingdom Immigration (Carriers Liability) Act 1987' (1989) 1 IJRL 481. For the background to the enactment of the first carrier sanctions see Nicholas Blake 'The Road to *Sivakumaran*' in (1989) 3 INLP 1 at 12. For detailed consideration of carrier sanctions see **14.68**ff below

12.10 Article 32 of the Refugee Convention gives refugees lawfully within the territory of a contracting state a right not to be expelled, save on grounds of national security or public order. Even then, expulsion is only possible following a decision reached in accordance with due process of law, and there must be a right of appeal and of representation before a competent authority. The UK provisions for deportation now give effect to this requirement, although only since 1998 in cases of removal on grounds relating to national security.[1] Article 32 does not apply to asylum seekers who claim asylum on arrival in the UK, since they cannot claim to be lawfully within the territory of the UK until they have been given leave to enter.[2] It does not, therefore, prevent removal of potential refugees to safe third countries for determination of their claim elsewhere.

1   Following the condemnation of the UK for lack of an effective remedy under art 13 of the ECHR in *Chahal v UK* (1996) 23 EHRR 413, the government set up the Special Immigration Appeals Commission (Special Immigration Appeals Commission Act 1997) which hears all appeals, including asylum appeals, in which there is a national security element. See chapter 18 below.
2   *Bugdaycay v Secretary of State for the Home Department* [1987] AC 514 at 526, per Lord Bridge.

12.11 Article 31(1) of the Refugee Convention precludes a state from imposing penalties on refugees coming directly from territories where they are persecuted on account of their illegal entry and presence, provided they report themselves to the authorities promptly.[1] A refugee is not an illegal entrant simply because he or she arrives without a passport or visa, or may have deceived the carrier in order to travel to the UK,[2] but lies told to the immigration officer on arrival are a different matter.[3] The meaning and application of Article 31(1) was considered by the Divisional Court in *Ex p Adimi and others*,[4] which concerned asylum seekers who had used false passports to enter the UK. Mr Adimi had claimed asylum after being refused leave to enter as a visitor on the basis of a false passport. He had come from Algeria via Italy and France (neither of which recognised persecution by non-state agents as giving rise to a Convention claim), and had spent several weeks in transit. He had been charged with a Forgery and Counterfeiting Act offence and sought judicial review of the magistrates' refusal to stay the proceedings because of Article 31(1) of the Refugee Convention. The other two applicants, Sorani and Kaziu, were Albanians who had entered the UK in transit to Canada, where they hoped to claim asylum. They had been apprehended boarding the onward flight with false passports and had been taken off. They had been similarly charged, convicted and sentenced to several months' imprisonment, which they had served. All three applicants were held to be covered by the protection of Article 31(1). The court held that where illegal entry or the use of false documents or delay can be attributed to a *bona fide* desire to seek asylum, whether here or elsewhere, that conduct should be covered by Article 31(1).[5] As to 'coming directly', some element of choice is, the court held, open to refugees as to where they may properly claim asylum. Any merely short-term stopover *en route* to such intended sanctuary cannot forfeit the protection of the Article. The main touchstones by which exclusion from protection should be judged are the length of stay in the intermediate country, the reasons for delaying there (even a substantial delay in an unsafe third country would be reasonable where the time was spent trying to acquire the means of travelling on), and whether or not the refugee sought or found there protection *de jure* or *de facto* from the persecution they were fleeing.[6] The requirement that the refugee presents himself or herself promptly does not require an asylum seeker to claim on arrival, so long as there is an intention to claim asylum within a short time of arrival having successfully secured entry on false documents.[7] The prohibition on penalties does not prevent the detention of asylum seekers,[8] nor does it prevent their being charged as long as they are not convicted.[9] There is now a statutory defence in section 31 of the Immigration and Asylum Act 1999 to protect asylum seekers against wrongful conviction in breach of the Article: see **14.25**ff. Article 31(2) does not prevent return of asylum seekers to countries through which they have travelled, in accordance with the 1999 Act and the Immigration Rules, or to consult with those countries to ensure that asylum will be offered there.[10]

1 On art 31 of the Refugee Convention, see Hathaway and Neve 'Making International Refugee Law Relevant Again: A Proposal for Collectivized and Solution-Orientated Protection' (1997) 10 Harvard Human Rights J 115 at 161; Rodger Haines 'International Law and Refugees in New Zealand' [1999] NZLR 119 at 128-130.
2 *R v Naillie and Kanesarajah* [1993] AC 674; *Nzamba-Liloneo v Secretary of State for the Home Department* [1993] Imm AR 225, CA.
3 See chapter 16 below.
4 *R v Uxbridge Magistrates' Court, ex p Adimi* [1999] INLR 490.
5 *Adimi* above at 496.
6 *Adimi* above at 497.
7 *Adimi* above at 498.
8 See *A-G v E* [2000] 3 NZLR 257; see also A Davidson 'Article 31(2) of the Refugee Convention and its implementation in New Zealand: Is detention defensible?'.
9 See further **14.24**ff below.
10 Immigration and Asylum Act 1999, ss 11, 12; HC 395, para 345.

United Nations High Commissioner for Refugees

12.12 The Office of the UN High Commissioner for Refugees (UNHCR) was established in 1951 pursuant to a UN General Assembly resolution.[1] The High Commissioner is called upon to provide international protection, under the auspices of the UN, to refugees falling within the competence of the Commissioner's office. This mandate covers all those who are outside their country of nationality or habitual residence and have or have had a well-founded fear of persecution for Refugee Convention reasons,[2] whether or not recognised as refugees. In some countries the determination of refugee status is performed by the UNHCR on behalf of the receiving state. This is not the case in the UK, but full account is taken of the views of the UK representative, particularly in respect of whether a third country is safe or not.

1   General Assembly Resolution 428, December 1950; Goodwin-Gill, **12.5** fn 1, p 241; Plender Documents **12.1** fn 1 above, p 81.
2   Statute of the Office of the UNHCR, arts 6A and 6B (Plender above, 82–83). See also the UK government's paper and the UNHCR reply in (1995) 7(1) IJRL 2.

12.13 The statute setting up the Office of the High Commissioner for Refugees provides that, in the exercise of his or her functions, the Commissioner shall request the opinion of an advisory committee on refugees in matters of difficulty.[1] The advisory committee is composed of representatives of states selected by the Economic and Social Council of the UN 'on the basis of their demonstrated interest in and devotion to the solution of the refugee problem'.[2] The advisory committee is called the Executive Committee of the Programme of the United Nations High Commissioner for Refugees, and is known as ExCom. Its recommendations, conclusions and reports provide valuable guidance on the interpretation of the Refugee Convention and the procedures to be adopted. The collected conclusions are published by the UNHCR. In 1979, at the request of Ex Com, a *Handbook on Procedures and Criteria for Determining Refugee Status* was produced. The *Handbook* is frequently referred to and approved by the UK appellate authorities and the courts,[3] and should form part of the equipment of any lawyer practising in this area of immigration law.[4]

1   See Statute of the Office of UNHCR, Ch 1, para 1; Plender Documents, **12.1** fn 1 above, p 82.
2   Statute of the Office of the UNHCR, para 4.
3   See eg *T v Secretary of State for the Home Department* [1996] AC 742, [1996] 2 All ER 865, [1996] 2 WLR 766, [1996] Imm AR 443, HL; *Adan v Secretary of State for the Home Department* [1999] 1 AC 293; *Secretary of State for the Home Department v Adan and Aitseguer* [2001] INLR 44, HL.
4   The *Handbook* is reproduced in *Butterworths Immigration Law Service*, 2C[73] and is available from the UNHCR (on its website, and see Appendix 2). ExCom's conclusions are published in booklet form; many of them are set out as appendices to Goodwin-Gill **12.5** fn 1 above and all are available on the UNHCR website.

12.14 The UNHCR materials do not have the force of law or form part of the Refugee Convention. Neither the ExCom recommendations and conclusions nor the *Handbook* have been incorporated into UK Immigration Rules, and therefore, although they can provide guidance, they will not override express terms of the Immigration Acts or Rules, and will not be the subject of construction and application by the courts.[1] In *Robinson* the Court of Appeal described the *Handbook* as particularly helpful:

'as a guide to what is the international understanding of the Convention obligations, as worked out in practice, based on the knowledge accumulated by the High Commissioner's Office. This knowledge was derived, *inter alia*, from the practice of states in regard to the determination of refugee status, exchanges of views between the office and the competent authorities of contracting states, and the literature devoted to the subject over the previous quarter of a century.'[2]

The provisions are general rather than specific, and tend to be more exhortatory in tone than directive, although they are nonetheless an authoritative guide to the proper interpretation of the Refugee Convention.[3] The duty of co-operation with the UNHCR imposed by Article 35 of the Convention does not translate into a legally enforceable duty to comply with the recommendations of the High Commissioner and the Executive Committee.[4] The Secretary of State is entitled to have regard to them when deciding whether the UK is an appropriate country of asylum, and it is 'an important source of law, though not having the force of law',[5] but there is no requirement to follow them.[6] In short, the UNHCR materials are useful and authoritative aids to interpretation of the Convention and may be relevant to the exercise of a broad discretion, although not themselves the source of obligations and duties.

1   See *Bugdaycay v Secretary of State for the Home Department* [1987] AC 514 at 524, per Lord Bridge. See also the arguments of the intervener in *R v Secretary of State for the Home Department, ex p Sivakumaran* [1988] AC 958, and at 1000–1001, per Lord Goff, and observations in *T v Secretary of State for the Home Department* [1996] AC 742; *Adan v Secretary of State for the Home Department* [1999] 1 AC 293; *R v Immigration Appeal Tribunal, ex p Shah* [1999] 2 AC 629; *Danian v Secretary of State for the Home Department* [2000] Imm AR 96 at 120.
2   *Robinson v Secretary of State for the Home Department* [1997] Imm AR 568, CA at 11. See also, to similar effect, *R v Secretary of State for the Home Department, ex p Adan, Subaskaran and Aitseguer* [1999] 3 WLR 1274 at 1296.
3   See observations of Purchas LJ in *Alsawaf v Secretary of State for the Home Department* [1988] Imm AR 410 at 419, CA.
4   This argument was advanced and rejected in *R v Secretary of State for the Home Department, ex p Mehari* [1994] QB 474, [1994] Imm AR 151.
5   *T v Secretary of State for the Home Department* [1996] AC 742.
6   See *Miller v Immigration Appeal Tribunal* [1988] Imm AR 358, CA; *R v Secretary of State for the Home Department, ex p Yassine* [1990] Imm AR 354, QBD. See further *Sepet and Bulbul v Secretary of State for the Home Department* [2001] EWCA Civ 681.

Determination of status

12.15 The Refugee Convention sets out no procedures for the determination of refugee status. It is left to contracting states to establish appropriate procedures having regard to their particular constitutional and administrative structures.[1] The wide variation in what was believed appropriate by different contracting states led the Executive Committee to formulate basic requirements for a fair procedure:[2]

(i)   the official (immigration officer or border police) receiving the claim should have clear instructions on how to deal with cases engaging international obligations, must act in accordance with the principle of non-refoulement and refer the case to a higher authority;
(ii)   the applicant should receive necessary guidance on procedure;
(iii)   a clearly identified authority should have responsibility for examining requests and taking first-instance decisions;

(iv)   the applicant should be given the necessary facilities, including a competent interpreter, for submitting the case, and should have the right to contact a UNHCR representative (and be informed of it);

(v)   if recognised as a refugee, the applicant should be informed and issued with appropriate documentation;

(vi)   if not, there should be a right to appeal either to the same or a different authority (administrative or judicial);

(vii)   both the claim (unless established as clearly abusive) and the appeal should be suspensive.

1   UNHCR *Handbook*, **12.13** above, para 189.
2   At its 28th session in 1977: see UNHCR *Handbook* above, para 192. It may be that the demands of fairness are more rigorous a quarter of a century on.

Legislation relating to asylum in the UK

12.16   The UK had a long history of affording asylum before the 1951 Convention and its 1967 Protocol, and both the Extradition Act 1870 and the Aliens Act 1905 contained provisions exempting respectively political offences from extradition and political and religious refugees from refusal of entry.[1] The express enactment of these provisions in 1870 and 1905 meant that it was the UK courts rather than the Secretary of State who decided whether an offence was political or not. This has remained the practice in extradition cases.[2] However, when the Aliens Restriction Acts 1914 and 1919 replaced the 1905 Act, the exemption for refugees was not repeated, and subsequent immigration statutes followed this course until 1993. This omission gave rise to a body of jurisprudence that refugee status was not a matter for the courts but only the Secretary of State,[3] an attitude which passed into the modern decisions under the Immigration Act 1971.[4] In *Bugdaycay*[5] the House of Lords made it clear that in judicial review proceedings whether a person was a 'refugee' was not a matter of jurisdictional fact or law for the courts, but a question for the Secretary of State. However, even before the Asylum and Immigration Appeals Act 1993 restored the statutory recognition of refugees, the appellate authorities could review the merits of certain decisions of the Secretary of State relating to asylum.[6]

1   Extradition Act 1870, s 3(1); Aliens Act 1905, s 1(3); see also Fugitive Offenders Act 1967, s 5(1) and Extradition Act 1989, ss 6, 24. For a full history of policy in this respect see Dummett and Nicol *Subjects, Citizens, Aliens and Others* (1990), in particular, chapters 6 and 8.
2   See *Cheng v Governor of Pentonville Prison* [1973] AC 931 and **12.50** below.
3   See eg *R v Chiswick Police Station Superintendent, ex p Sacksteder* [1918] 1 KB 578, CA; *R v Secretary of State for Home Affairs , ex p Duke of Chateau Thierry* [1917] 1 KB 922, CA; *R v Zausmer* (1911) 7 Cr App Rep 41; *R v Governor of Brixton, ex p Sarno* [1916] 2 KB 742.
4   See *Ali v Immigration Appeal Tribunal* [1973] Imm AR 33 at 35, CA, following *R v Governor of Brixton Prison, ex p Soblen* [1963] 2 QB 243, [1962] 3 All ER 641, CA.
5   [1987] AC 514.
6   There was an in-country appeal against refusal of leave to enter (ie if the passenger held an entry clearance), or a variation or a deportation appeal under ss 13-15 of the Immigration Act 1971, if the appellant had claimed asylum.

12.17   During the 1960s the first Immigration Rules were published and, after representations from the UNHCR, these Rules made reference to asylum and refugees, although not to the 1951 Convention. Considerable advance was achieved in 1980 with the first reference in the Rules to the 1951 Convention and 1967 Protocol. But before 1993 there was tension between the provisions of the Rules giving primacy to the 1951 Convention and the Immigration Act 1971, which made no reference to the Convention and whose provisions were in some respects incompatible with it.[1] People who claimed asylum on arrival and who had no entry clearance had only an out-of-country appeal exercisable on return to the place of feared persecution, and so relied on judicial review for their remedy against removal.[2] Since 1 July 1993 all those refused leave to enter or remain, or who face deportation or removal as illegal entrants or crew members have had a right of appeal to an adjudicator[3] on the ground that their removal would be contrary to the UK's obligations under the Convention.[4] The Immigration Rules made since the passing of the Asylum and Immigration Appeals Act 1993 have attempted to provide a coherent structure in which asylum applications are considered and determined, albeit that the Convention has primacy over the Rules.[5] In addition, since 1998 the Asylum Directorate's instructions to caseworkers (ADI) (now Asylum Policy Instructions or API) have been published, providing a yet more detailed framework within which decisions are taken.[6]

1 See *R v Immigration Appeal Tribunal, ex p Muruganandarajah* [1983] Imm AR 141, QBD, affirmed on appeal [1986] Imm AR 382, CA, for absence of rights of appeal in deportation cases following court recommendations.
2 See *R v Secretary of State for the Home Department, ex p Sivakumaran* [1988] AC 958 where asylum seekers were unsuccessful in judicial review but succeeded on appeal to an adjudicator after removal to Sri Lanka where a number were tortured: *Secretary of State for the Home Department v Immigration Appeal Tribunal* [1990] Imm AR 492. In *Vilvarajah v UK* (1991) 14 EHRR 248 the ECtHR held, reversing the Commission, that judicial review was an effective remedy against the refusal of asylum for the purposes of Art 13 of the ECHR. The decision surprised the British government, which had decided to concede in-country appeal rights to asylum seekers in anticipation of losing on this point.
3 Under the Asylum and Immigration Appeals Act 1993 asylum appeals went to special adjudicators, which no longer exist under the Immigration and Asylum Act 1999.
4 Asylum and Immigration Appeals Act 1993, s 8; see now Immigration and Asylum Act 1999, s 69.
5 HC 395, paras 327–352; Asylum and Immigration Appeals Act 1993, s 2. Laws J in *R v Secretary of State for the Home Department, ex p Mehari* [1994] QB 474, [1994] Imm AR 151, QBD had regard to the Immigration Rules and the statutory instruments 'intended to dovetail with the new regime' in interpreting the 1993 Act.
6 The API, which are regularly updated, are available on the Home Office website (www.ind.homeoffice.gov.uk/) and in hard copy at selected addresses (see Appendix 2).

12.18 People who have had an asylum claim turned down and face removal from the UK, have a right of appeal on the ground that to do so would breach the UK's obligations under the Refugee Convention.[1] The appeal deals with the question of whether the appellant is a refugee.[2] Normally they can appeal to an adjudicator and then to the IAT, but their appeal rights are limited to an adjudicator appeal[3] if the Secretary of State certifies their claim on one of the grounds contravened in para 9 of Sch 4 to the 1999 Act[4] and the adjudicator agrees with the certificate.[5] Repeated applications for asylum on the same basis will not trigger a fresh right of appeal.[6] But the right of an asylum seeker to make a fresh application for asylum has been recognised by the Court of Appeal in *R v Secretary of State for the Home Department, ex p Onibiyo*[7] and is reflected in paragraph 346 of HC 395. An application will not be considered a fresh one if the material in support of it could have been presented at a previous hearing.[8]

1 Immigration and Asylum Act 1999, s 69. Prior to s 69(3) of the 1999 Act port applicants, deportees and illegal entrants granted exceptional leave to remain on refusal of asylum had no right of appeal, while those who were granted exceptional leave to remain between lodging the appeal and its hearing were bound to lose it, as they do not face removal: *Massaquoi v Immigration Appeal Tribunal* C-2000-062, 20 December 2000, CA. See **12.161** below. The only chance of getting refugee status for them was to put in an immediate 'upgrade' application for leave to remain as a refugee; refusal of this application generated a fresh right of appeal. For the advantages of refugee status over exceptional leave to remain see *Adan v Secretary of State for the Home Department* [1997] Imm AR 251 at 256, CA per Simon Brown LJ.

2 Although in form it is against the relevant immigration decision – Immigration and Asylum Act 1999, ss 69(1) (refusal of leave to enter), 69(2) (refusal to grant leave to remain), 69(3) (refusal of Convention status and grant of exceptional leave to remain), 69(4) (deportation decision or refusal to revoke deportation order), 69(5) (removal directions to an overstayer or an illegal immigrant).

3 Immigration and Asylum Act 1999, Sch 4, para 9(2).

4 For a full discussion see **12.165** below.

5 Immigration and Asylum Act 1999, Sch 4, para 9(2).

6 In *R v Secretary of State for the Home Department, ex p Kazmi* [1995] Imm AR 73, Dyson J held that *Kalunga (Lemba) v Secretary of State for the Home Department* [1994] Imm AR 585, CA bound him to apply a judicial review approach to the Secretary of State's decision. An asylum application made after a prior refusal of leave to enter on some other ground must trigger a fresh refusal of leave to enter, however: HC 395, para 332 and *Kazmi* (above). On the judicial review approach see also *Mahmut Cakabay v Secretary of State for the Home Department (No 2)* [1999] Imm AR 176, [1998] INLR 623, CA. *Nassir v Secretary of State for the Home Department* [1999] Imm AR 250; *R v Secretary of State for the Home Department, ex p Bell* [2000] Imm AR 396.

7 [1996] Imm AR 370, CA. The test for a fresh application is whether the claim advanced is sufficiently different from the earlier claim that a favourable view could be taken of it. In considering this, the Secretary of State will disregard material which is not significant or apparently credible, or was previously available: HC 395 para 346. The evidence must be apparently credible though not uncontrovertible: *R v Secretary of State for the Home Department v Boybeyi* [1997] Imm AR 491, CA. See **12.176** below

8 A failure by advisers to obtain evidence earlier did not make the evidence 'previously unavailable': *Kabala v Secretary of State for the Home Department* [1997] Imm AR 517. But 'unavailability' includes psychiatric inability to give evidence: *R v Secretary of State for the Home Department, ex p Molly Ejon* [1998] INLR 195.

12.19 There may be an appeal against the decision to remove the appellant to a safe third country without considering the asylum claim,[1] although those being returned to an EU member state or a designated[2] country no longer have an in-country appeal[3] save on human rights grounds,[4] and not even then if the Secretary of State certifies that the human rights claim is manifestly unfounded.[5] EU member states to which it is proposed to send an asylum seeker under standing arrangements benefit from a statutory presumption that they are safe and will not return the appellant elsewhere save in accordance with the Refugee Convention.[6]

1 Immigration and Asylum Act 1999, s 71. For 'safe third country' removals see **12.125ff** below.

2 Canada, Norway, Switzerland and the US, by the Asylum (Designated Safe Third Countries) Order 2000, SI 2000/2245, art 3.

3 This was removed by the Asylum and Immigration Act 1996, s 2.

4 Immigration and Asylum Act 1999, s 72(2)(b).

5 Immigration and Asylum Act 1999, s 72(2)(a).

6 Immigration and Asylum Act 1999, s 11, inserted after the Court of Appeal held, in *R v Secretary of State for the Home Department, ex p Lul Adan, Aitseguer and Subaskaran* [1999] INLR 362, that the French and German interpretation of the Refugee Convention was unlawful in not recognising persecution from non-state agents. The decision has since been upheld by the House of Lords [2001] INLR 44. For more detailed consideration see **12.135** below.

THE DEFINITION OF REFUGEE

12.20 The definition of refugees for the purposes of the Refugee Convention is contained in Article 1A(2), as amended by the 1967 Protocol. A refugee is any person who:

> 'owing to a well-founded fear of being persecuted for reasons of race religion nationality membership of a particular social group or political opinion, is outside his country of nationality and is unable or, owing to such fear, is unwilling to avail himself of the protection of that country; or who, not having a nationality and being outside the country of his former habitual residence . . . is unable or, owing to such fear, is unwilling to return to it.'[1]

We will now consider the various elements.

1 Convention Relating to the Status of Refugees 1951, art 1A(2), as amended by the 1967 Protocol.

'Owing to a well-founded fear'

The fear

12.21 A genuine fear of persecution must be behind the asylum seeker's absence from his or her country of residence or nationality. This is referred to as the subjective element.[1] Even if objective conditions are such that a reasonable person would have reason to fear persecution, the claimant will not be a refugee unless he or she has such a fear. The use of the term 'fear' was intended to emphasise the forward-looking nature of the test, and not to ground refugee status in an assessment of the refugee claimant's state of mind.[2] The refugee does not have to have left the country because of such a fear, since a person can become a refugee by reason of events after their departure; such a person is referred to as a 'refugee *sur place*'.[3] There is no reason why the fear should not arise from the refugee's activities abroad, even if carried out in bad faith, although a claim based exclusively on such acts will be scrutinised with some scepticism as self-serving and lacking in credibility.[4] The fear must still exist at the date of determination; despite indications in the *travaux préparatoires* of the 1951 Convention which suggested that historic fear may be sufficient to ground refugee status if the refugee is currently unable to return,[5] this interpretation, accepted by the Court of Appeal,[6] was rejected by the House of Lords in *Adan*,[7] which held that while a historic fear may be relevant in providing evidence to establish a present fear, it is the existence or otherwise of a present fear which is determinative. Where objectively it is shown that there is a serious possibility of persecution, then it may well be difficult to refuse an application on the basis that the applicant does not believe the persecution will occur.[8]

1 See UNHCR *Handbook*, **12.13** above, paras 37 and 38; *R v Secretary of State for the Home Department, ex p Singh* [1987] Imm AR 489, DC.
2 James Hathaway *The Law of Refugee Status* (1991) pp 68-69. Hathaway gives one of the most authoritative and highly regarded accounts of the Convention, with particular reference to Canadian and US case law, and is regularly cited with approval in the higher courts. See also, on meaning of 'fear', *Asuming* (11530).
3 UNHCR *Handbook*, **12.13** above, paras 94-96.

4   *Danian v Secretary of State for the Home Department* [2000] Imm AR 96, [1999] INLR 533, CA; HC 395, para 341(vi).
5   See UN Doc E/1818 containing Ecosoc Res 319 (X1 B): 'who has had, or has well founded fear . . . and owing to such fear has had to leave, shall leave or remains outside the country of nationality.' The drafting group's explanatory note of the definition was 'that a person has either been actually a victim of persecution or can show good reason why he [or she] fears persecution'.
6   *Adan and Nooh v Secretary of State for the Home Department* [1997] Imm AR 251, CA.
7   *Secretary of State for the Home Department v Adan* [1999] 1 AC 293, [1998] Imm AR 338, [1998] INLR 325, HL.
8   *Radivojevic* (13372), followed in *Gashi and Nikshiqi (UNHCR intervening)* [1997] INLR 96, IAT.

Well-founded

12.22 The fear of persecution must not only exist but must be well-founded. In *Sivakumaran*[1] the House of Lords, reversing the Court of Appeal, rejected the advice in paragraph 42 of the *Handbook*:

> 'In general the applicant's fear should be considered well-founded if he can establish, to a reasonable degree, that his continued stay in his country of origin has become intolerable to him for the reasons stated in the definition, or would for the same reasons be intolerable if he returned there.'[2]

It held that well-foundedness was an objective test, to be ascertained independently of the appellant's state of mind. But this does not mean that there must have been actual persecution in the past. It is sufficient if there is a well-founded fear of it occurring in the future.[3] Past persecution will always be of great significance. The *travaux* reveal that the drafting group's explanatory note of the Article 1A definition was that 'a person has either been an actual victim of persecution or can show good reason why he [or she] fears persecution'.[4] The House of Lords' decision in *Adan* means, however, that a refugee must have a current risk, as well as a current fear, of persecution.[5] But past persecution means that future persecution is more likely (and the fear of it more likely to be well-founded) unless there has been a significant change of circumstances.[6] The past persecution of an individual may be contrasted with a past generalised risk of violence in an area which has been diminished by government measures to prevent abuse. Thus in *Ex p Ravichandran*[7] the Court of Appeal distinguished the Canadian case of *Thirunavukkarasu*[8] on the safety of Tamils in Colombo, on the basis that it related to a different time.

1   *R v Secretary of State for the Home Department, ex p Sivakumaran* [1988] AC 958 at 996, per Lord Keith.
2   UNHCR *Handbook*, **12.13** above, para 195.
3   Hathaway **12.21** fn 2 above, paras 3.1, p 66, 3.2.3, p 87.
4   Report of the Ad Hoc Committee, 17 February 1950, p 39. See the argument of the intervener in *Sivakumaran* [1988] AC 958 at 976-989 for the drafting history of art 1 of the Refugee Convention and the admissibility of *travaux preparatoires* as an aid to the construction of international instruments. For the relevance of *travaux* in the construction of an international instrument see Vienna Convention on the Law of Treaties (1969), art 32. And as noted at **12.12** above, UNHCR's jurisdiction extends to those who 'have had' a well-founded fear of persecution. Hathaway suggests that the final definition adopted by the drafters intended persecution to be prospective save for those who had suffered pre-1951 persecution and became refugees by reason of art 1A(1) of the Refugee Convention and whose status is not now a matter of present debate: Hathaway above, para 3.1.1 p 66ff.

5   *Adan v Secretary of State for the Home Department* [1999] 1 AC 293, [1998] Imm AR 338; [1998] INLR 325.
6   See eg *Demirkaya v Secretary of State for the Home Department* [1999] INLR 441, CA. Hathaway, above, concludes that 'individualised past persecution is generally a sufficient, though not a mandatory means of establishing prospective risk' (p 88). The German Constitutional Court goes further, stating that where there has been past persecution the test for the determining authority is whether 'future persecution could be excluded with sufficient certainty': Case No 193 (1994) 6(2) IJRL 282.
7   [1996] Imm AR 97.
8   (1993) 109 DLR (4th) 682.

12.23 One of the bases on which the Secretary of State may certify a claim, with the result that appeal rights are potentially curtailed, is that 'the fear is manifestly unfounded or the circumstances which gave rise to the fear no longer subsist'.[1] In our view, certification on this basis can lead to gross injustice, particularly where a decision on refugee status has been delayed for several years, during which time the human rights environment has improved without there being some fundamental alteration in the factors giving rise to the fear. In *Arif*[2] the Court of Appeal decided to proceed by analogy with the cessation clause at Article 1C(5) of the Refugee Convention and held that, since the appellant would have qualified for refugee status had his application been dealt with expeditiously, it was now for the Home Office to demonstrate that a significant change of circumstances had removed the basis for the claim.[3]

1   Immigration and Asylum Act 1999, Sch 4, para 9(4)(b), formerly Asylum and Immigration Act 1996, s 1(4)(b).
2   *Mohammed Arif v Secretary of State for the Home Department* [1999] INLR 327. However, where there is no evidence that the applicant would have so qualified, the shifting evidential burden does not apply: *Nabil Salim v Secretary of State for the Home Department* [2000] Imm AR 503, CA.
3   See **12.84** below for the cessation clause.

The burden of proof

12.24 The burden of establishing a well-founded fear is on the applicant. In *Sivakumaran*[1] the House of Lords held that for a fear to be well-founded, the question was whether there was a 'real and substantial risk' or a 'real likelihood' of persecution for a Refugee Convention reason. It is clear that showing a real likelihood of persecution is a lesser standard than proving that persecution will occur on the balance of probabilities, and the House of Lords approved the words of Lord Diplock in *Fernandez v Government of Singapore*[2] to this effect. Lord Diplock had suggested that the requisite degree of likelihood could be indicated by words such as 'a reasonable chance', 'substantial grounds for thinking', or 'a serious possibility'. In his speech in *Sivakumaran* Lord Keith[3] appeared to approve Stevens J's dictum in the US case of *Immigration and Naturalisation Service v Cardozo Fonseca*[4] that a one in ten chance of being persecuted could amount to a reasonable possibility of persecution. In those circumstances the addition of the word 'substantial' to 'real' ('a real and substantial possibility . . . of persecution') can only be intended to eliminate minimal or mere possibilities rather than to indicate something in the nature of a probability or a prediction. In *Re Adjei and Minister of Employment and Immigration*[5] a Canadian Court of Appeal preferred to follow the language of reasonable possibility rather than some of the alternative formulations mentioned in the speeches in *Sivakumaran*. The Canadian court indicated that use of the word 'would' instead of 'could' in determining the reality of persecution was evidence of a misdirection on burden of proof. This reflects the words of Lord Keith, who had succinctly stated the issue: 'if the examination shows that persecution might indeed take place then the fear is well-founded'. In the case of *Chan*[6] the Australian High Court adopted the test of 'real chance'. To avoid any possibility of confusion in the application of the *Sivakumaran* test, we prefer to state the test in terms of real risk rather than likelihood.[7]

1   [1988] AC 958.
2   [1971] 2 All ER 691, [1971] 1 WLR 987, HL.
3   [1988] AC 958 at 994.
4   94 L ED 2d 434 (1987).
5   (1989) 57 DLR (4th) 153.
6   (1989) 63 ALR 561.
7   In *R v Gough* [1993] AC 646 at 670 Lord Goff noted in the context of the appropriate test for bias, 'for the avoidance of doubt I prefer to state the test in terms of real danger rather than real likelihood, to ensure that the court is thinking in terms of possibility rather than probability of bias'.

12.25   The general human rights background of the country in question is important in assessing the objective foundation for the fear.[1] Background human rights data should be collected from a broad cross-section of official and non-governmental sources in order to supplement the claimant's evidence. The Immigration and Nationality Directorate of the Home Office now has a Country Information Policy Unit which produces sourced country reports on the main refugee-producing countries.[2] The existence of a consistent pattern of gross, flagrant or mass violations of human rights in a country does not as such constitute a sufficient ground for determining that a person would be in danger on return,[3] but where human rights reports substantiate that a real risk of ill-treatment exists, a genuine fear of persecution in a country is likely to be well-founded if it is for a Refugee Convention reason.[4] Where there is a doubt after all the evidence has been placed before the Tribunal of fact, the benefit of it should be given to the applicant.[5]

1   UNHCR *Handbook* **12.13** above, paras 196, 204; *Hathaway* **12.21** fn 2 above, pp 89–90. See cases cited at **18.148** below on evidence of country conditions. See also UN Convention Against Torture, art 3(2); *Mutumbo v Switzerland* (1994) 15 HRLJ 164.
2   See API Aug/00, Ch 3, s 1. Monthly country information round-ups are produced on at least the main 35 refugee-producing countries.
3   *Alan v Switzerland* [1997] INLR 29 (UNCAT).
4   Hathaway **12.21** fn 2 above cites the Federal Court of Appeal in *Benjamin Attakora v Minister for Employment and Immigration* (Decision A-1091-87, 19 May 1989), at para 3.2.1 (p 80) that 'persons who flee countries that are known to commit or acquiesce in persecutory behaviour should benefit from a rebuttable presumption that they have a genuine need for protection'. For an example of a situation where an appellant had not suffered persecution and relied wholly on evidence of country conditions see *Drrias v Secretary of State for the Home Department* [1997] Imm AR 346, CA.
5   UNHCR *Handbook* above, paras 196, 203.

12.26   The correct approach to assessment of past events was authoritatively set out by the Court of Appeal in *Karanakaran*.[1] The Tribunal had been divided on what standard of proof to apply to evidence of past or present facts before the necessary assessment of future risk is undertaken. In *Kaja*[2] the minority had held that historic events should be proven on the normal civil balance and the reduced burden of 'reasonable likelihood' should apply only in respect of future events, while the majority had concluded that the decision-maker should not omit from the assessment of future risk any evidence of past events to which they were prepared to give some credence. They referred to the 'positive role for doubt' in asylum, given the inability of the asylum seeker to produce witnesses from the country of persecution, and the general lack of documentary or other evidence proving either past or future persecution.[3] The Court of Appeal endorsed this approach, which does not lay down a standard of proof for past events but asks the decision-maker to weigh everything for what it is worth in assessing the risk of persecution. Sedley LJ warned that:

> 'the decision-maker must not, by a process of factual findings on particular elements of the material which is provided, foreclose reasonable speculation on the chances of persecution emerging from a consideration of the whole of the material. Everything capable of having a bearing has to be given the weight, great or little, due to it . . . the facts, so far as they can be established, are signposts on the road to a conclusion.'

Brooke LJ, relying on the Australian decision of *Wu Shan Liang*,[4] distinguished between civil litigation, where 'the court has to decide where, on the balance of probabilities, the truth lies as between the evidence the parties to the litigation have thought it in their respective interests to adduce at the trial', and administrative decision-making, where 'a whole range of possible approaches . . . may be correct' and 'the use of such terms provides little assistance'. He reproduced with approval a number of principles derived from the Australian case law:[5]

'(1) There may be circumstances in which a decision-maker must take into account the possibility that alleged past events occurred even though it finds that these events probably did not occur. The reason for this is that the ultimate question is whether the applicant has a real substantial basis for his fear of future persecution. The decision-maker must not foreclose reasonable speculation about the chances of the future hypothetical event occurring.

(2) Although the civil standard of proof is not irrelevant to the fact-finding process, the decision-maker cannot simply apply that standard to all fact-finding. It frequently has to make its assessment on the basis of fragmented, incomplete and confused information. It has to assess the plausibility of accounts given by people who may be understandably bewildered, frightened and, perhaps, desperate, and who often do not understand either the process or the language spoken by the decision-maker/investigator. Even applicants with a genuine fear of persecution may not present as models of consistency or transparent veracity.

(3) In this context, when the decision-maker is uncertain as to whether an alleged event occurred, or finds that although the probabilities are against it, the event may have occurred, it may be necessary to take into account the possibility that the event took place in deciding the ultimate question (for which see question 1 above) . . .

(4) Although the "What if I am wrong?" terminology has gained currency, it is more accurate to see this requirement as simply an aspect of the obligation to apply correctly the principles for determining whether an applicant has a 'well-founded fear of being persecuted' for a Convention reason.

(5) There is no reason in principle to support a general rule that a decision-maker must express findings as to whether alleged past events actually occurred in a manner that makes explicit its degree of conviction or confidence that its findings were correct . . .

(6) If a fair reading of the decision-maker's reasons as a whole shows that it 'had no real doubt' that claimed events did not occur, then there is no warrant for holding that it should have considered the possibility that its findings were wrong.

1 *Karanakaran v Secretary of State for the Home Department* [2000] 3 All ER 449, [2000] INLR 122, [2000] Imm AR 271.
2 *Koyazia Kaja* [1995] Imm AR 1.
3 See UNHCR *Handbook* above, paras 196–197.
4 (1995) 185 CLR 259.
5 *Rajalingam* [1999] FCA 719, per Sackville J, set out in [2000] Imm AR at 290.

12.27 It is, however, for the applicant to establish his or her claim, albeit to a lower than normal civil standard.[1] Thus it is for him or her to establish statelessness, if it forms part of the claim.[2] However, in the context of asylum as elsewhere, where it is the Secretary of State who asserts something, such as that a document produced by an applicant is a forgery, the burden is on him or her to prove it.[3] We have indicated previously that where it is accepted or established that an asylum seeker would have been granted refugee status earlier had it not been for delays in the assessment procedure, the evidential burden shifts to the Secretary of State to show that changes in the country of origin relied on to deny status to the applicant are sufficiently fundamental and durable, by analogy with the cessation clause of the Refugee Convention.[4] *Karanakaran*[5] was a case about the 'internal flight alternative', ie where it is accepted that the applicant faces persecution in part of the country and the issue is whether it would be unduly harsh for him or her to relocate to a safe area.[6] Again, different divisions of the Tribunal had differed on whether the applicant had to show on the balance of probabilities that it would be unduly harsh,[7] or only that it was a 'serious possibility'.[8] The court in *Karanakaran* held that it would be quite impracticable to maintain a regime in which there was one approach to the evidential material relating to historic or existing facts for the purpose of the first part of the definition of 'refugee' in the Convention, and a different approach to such material for the purpose of considering issues of protection and internal relocation.[9] The question was simply 'would it be unduly harsh', but in answering it, only evidence about which there was no doubt that it was not correct should be excluded. The guidance in *Karanakaran* does not, however, disturb the line of jurisprudence to the effect that where there is no real doubt that the whole story of the applicant is unworthy of belief, issues of standard of proof do not arise.[10]

1 The burden is not different or lower for someone with mental problems: *Bolat v Secretary of State for the Home Department* 99/6206/C, 23 February 2000, CA.
2 *Tikhonov* [1998] INLR 737, IAT.
3 *R v Immigration Appeal Tribunal, ex p Shen* [2000] INLR 389, QBD; *Makozo* (20003) 12 February 1999, IAT; *Escobar* (20553) 26 March 1999, IAT. But see *R v Special Adjudicator, ex p Mukhtar Mohammed* [2001] Imm AR 162, QBD.
4 *Mohammed Arif v Immigration Appeal Tribunal* [1999] INLR 327.
5 *Karanakaran v Secretary of State for the Home Department* [2000] 3 All ER 449, [2000] INLR 122, [2000] Imm AR 271.
6 *Robinson v Secretary of State for the Home Department* [1997] Imm AR 568. See **12.43** below.
7 A school of thought exemplified by *Manoharan* [1998] Imm AR 455.
8 *Sachithananthan* [1999] INLR 205.
9 [2000] Imm AR 271 at 293.
10 *R v Secretary of State for the Home Department, ex p Kingori (aka Mypanguli)* [1994] Imm AR 539, CA; *Huseyin Bulut v Secretary of State for the Home Department* [1999] Imm AR 210, CA.

Credibility

12.28 The debate about standard of proof is inextricably linked with issues of credibility. The issue of credibility is one which needs to be addressed seriously, in light of the widespread perception that adverse credibility findings are too easily reached, on too little material, both by the Secretary of State for the Home Department and by the appellate authorities.[1] English courts have not given the same assistance to appellate authorities dealing with asylum claims[2] as has been given by the Canadian courts,[3] which have held that 'when an applicant swears to the truth of certain allegations, this creates a presumption that those allegations are true unless there be reason to doubt their truthfulness',[4] and that 'a reasonable margin of appreciation be applied to any perceived flaws in the claimant's testimony'.[5] But decisions based on adverse credibility are increasingly being subjected to careful scrutiny by the Immigration Appeal Tribunal and the Administrative Court to ensure that they are properly reasoned and take account of relevant evidence,[6] and adjudicators' unsupported assertions that a witness is not credible are no longer acceptable. Questions of credibility are, however, matters for the tribunal of fact, which should be cautious in rejecting as incredible an account by an anxious and inexperienced asylum seeker, whose reasons for seeking asylum may well be expected to contain inconsistencies and omissions in the course of its revelation to the authorities and investigation on appeal.[7] The Tribunal has noted that 'It is perfectly possible for an adjudicator to believe that a witness is not telling the truth about some matters, has exaggerated the story to make his case better, or is simply uncertain about matters, but still to be persuaded that the centrepiece of the story stands'.[8] The API acknowledge this: 'Discrepancies, exaggerated accounts, the addition of new claims of mistreatment may affect credibility. But they may equally reflect a concern on the part of the applicant or his advisers to bolster the claim due to a real fear of return.'[9]

1   See (in a non-asylum context but equally applicable) *R v Immigration Appeal Tribunal, ex p Hussain* (CO 990/1995) 25 April 1996, QBD where Turner J said that 'Credibility is not in itself a valid end to the function of an adjudicator . . . there is a risk .. that overemphasis on the issue of credibility may distort the findings of an adjudicator'. See also *Horvath v Secretary of State for the Home Department* [1999] INLR 7, [1999] Imm AR 121, IAT, and cases cited at **18.147** below. It has been largely left to organisations such as Asylum Aid to draw attention to the 'culture of disbelief' informing Home Office asylum decisions: see Asylum Aid *No reason at all* (1995) and Asylum Aid *Still no reason at all* (1999).
2   The Refugee Legal Centre has produced a useful training document: 'Issues arising from 'credibility', procedure and evidence before the appellate authorities' containing references to Canadian, US, New Zealand and Australian case law to supplement that of the UK courts.
3   The Immigration and Refugee Board has produced a useful guide 'Assessment of credibility in the context of CRDD hearings' (October 1999), setting out all relevant Federal Court of Appeal decisions on various aspects of credibility. It is available on the Immigration and Refugee Board website www.irb.gc.ca.
4   *Maldonado v Canada (Minister of Employment and Immigration)* [1980] 2 FC 302, CA, cited in Hathaway **12.21** fn 2 above, p 84.
5   *Benjamin Attakora v MEI*, FCA Decision A-1091-87, 19 May 1989, cited in Hathaway above, p 85. The UN Committee Against Torture has made the same point, saying that 'complete accuracy is not to be expected from victims of torture', in *Alan v Switzerland* [1997] INLR 29. And in *Hrickova* (00 TH 02034) 9 August 2000, IAT, inconsistencies in the account of a Slovak Roma of stabbing and gang rape were 'properly explained by the nature of human recollection, particularly dealing with traumatic incidents'.
6   See cases cited at **18.147** below.
7   Hathaway above, pp 84-88; *Re SA*, NZRSAA 1/92 (NZ); *Matter of SMJ* Interim Decision 3303 (BIA) 1997 (US); *Kopalapillai v Minister for Immigration and Multicultural Affairs* [1997] 1510 FCA, 24 December 1997 (Aus).
8   *Chiver* (10758); see also *Guo v Minister for Immigration and Ethnic Affairs* (1996) 64 FRC 151 at 194, a decision of the full court of the Federal Court of Australia.
9   API Mar/01, Ch 1, s 2(11).

12.29 Since it is not in the nature of repressive societies to behave reasonably, the strange or unusual cannot be dismissed as incredible or improbable, particularly if there is supporting material of similar accounts in the relevant human rights literature, and decision-makers should constantly be on their guard to avoid implicitly recharacterising the nature of the risk based on their own perceptions of reasonability.[1] An assessment of credibility can only be made on the basis of a complete understanding of the entire picture.[2] The approach of the UN Committee on Torture emphasises the importance of a consistent pattern of gross, flagrant or mass violations of human rights in the assessment of risk.[3] Adjudicators should thus first look at the story and see whether, if it were true, the appeal would succeed, and then proceed to examine it against the background of the country in question.[4] There are equally difficulties in drawing conclusions on credibility from the manner in which evidence is given, usually through an interpreter, by a person from a different society and cultural background.[5] Further judicial guidance on a cautious approach to questions of credibility was given in *Ex p Chunu Miah*.[6]

1   Hathaway **12.21** fn 2 above, p 81. See *Kasolo* (13190); *Mendes* (12183); and cases cited at **18.147** below.
2   *Horvath v Secretary of State for the Home Department* [1997] INLR 7, [1997] Imm AR 121, IAT; *R v Immigration Appeal Tribunal, ex p Sardar Ahmed* [1999] INLR 473. But this only applies where country conditions are relevant: see *R v Immigration Appeal Tribunal, ex p Shokrollahy* [2000] Imm AR 580, QBD; *R v Secretary of State for the Home Department, ex p Befekadu* [1999] Imm AR 467, QBD. API Mar/01, Ch 1, s 2(10)(ii) and (iii) state that a decision on credibility should be based on an objective assessment of the conditions in the proposed country of return at the time of the decision, and that if there is no reason to doubt credibility and no country information contradicting the applicant's statement, he or she must be given the benefit of the doubt.
3   *Mutombo v Switzerland* (Communication No 13/93) unrep, UNCAT (cited in *Alan v Switzerland* [1997] INLR 29).
4   *Guine* (13868).
5   The observations of Webster J in *R v Secretary of State for the Home Department, ex p Patel* [1986] Imm AR 208, QBD are a salutary reminder of the dangers of adverse findings against a person from a different cultural background speaking through an interpreter. See also Lord Bingham's observations on the dangers in assessing credibility from demeanour in *The judge as juror: judicial determination of factual issues* (Current Legal Problems, 1985, p1), and the extra-judicial observations of MacKenna J to similar effect cited in *Guarichico and Sarabia-Molina* (20230) 25 November 1999, IAT.
6   (CO 2318/1994) 12 October 1995, QBD, see *Butterworths Immigration Law Service*, IV[99]. The API also warn caseworkers against making 'irrational judgments' based on, for example, an applicant's family's continued presence in the country of feared persecution. See API Mar/01, Ch 1, s 2(10).

12.30 Before 1993, in the absence of a right of appeal a judicial approach had evolved of ensuring that conclusions founded on credibility were not made without an opportunity for the asylum seeker to comment on specific issues.[1] The introduction of in-country rights of appeal removed direct scrutiny of adverse findings in decision letters by the High Court. Instead, the appellant is required to deal with adverse findings by evidence on the appeal. The test laid down in *Musisi* of 'anxious scrutiny'[2] is now applied by the Administrative Court not so much to the Secretary of State's original decision as to the appellate process.[3] There is a tension between the adjudicator's appellate function[4] and the prospective nature of the question at issue in asylum claims, which makes the appeal hearing part of the determination process.[5] This has surfaced in appeal hearings where credibility is challenged for the first time; if the facts have not been put in issue by the Home Office, the prospective nature of the question should not necessitate a review of those facts.[6] An opportunity to deal with matters of credibility must be given during the appeal hearing, and if fresh issues are to be raised, the appellant will need sufficient time to deal with them, which may require an adjournment.[7]

1 For the principles of fairness in cases where there was no right of appeal see *Secretary of State for the Home Department v Thirukumar* [1989] Imm AR 402, CA; *Gaima v Secretary of State for the Home Department* [1989] Imm AR 205.
2 [1987] AC 514 at 531.
3 *R v Immigration Appeal Tribunal, ex p Omar Ali* [1995] Imm AR 45, QBD.
4 The jurisdiction is to review the 'facts on which the decision or action is based': Immigration and Asylum Act 1999, Sch 4, para 21.
5 *Sandralingham and Ravichandran v Secretary of State for the Home Department* [1996] Imm AR 97 at 112-113.
6 *Ad hoc* challenges to credibility also make a nonsense of the power to give pre-hearing directions to identify and limit the issues in the appeal, in r 30 of the Immigration and Asylum (Procedure) Rules 2000, SI 2000/2333. Where the facts are agreed, or the Secretary of State makes a concession that an appellant is telling the truth about specific matters or generally, the adjudicator should not go behind it: *R (Ganidagli) v Immigration Appeal Tribunal,* [2001] EWHC Admin 70, 5 February 2001, AC; *Carcabuk and Barthelemy,* 18 May 2000, IAT.
7 The Privy Council affirmed the principle that new points originating from the court should not take the parties by surprise in *Hoecheong Products v Cargill Hong Kong Ltd* [1995] 1 WLR 404. See **18.143** below.

12.31 The principle of the benefit of the doubt operates once all the evidence is submitted. In order to benefit from it, the applicant should have co-operated with the investigating authorities and should not attempt to deceive them.[1] Paragraph 341 of HC 395, as amended, sets out specific factors which may damage an asylum applicant's credibility:

(i) the applicant has failed without reasonable explanation to apply forthwith on arrival, unless the application is founded on events which have taken place since arrival;

(ii) the application was delayed until after a refusal of leave to enter or a decision to deport or remove has been taken;

(iii) the applicant adduced and relied on manifestly false evidence or made false representations in support of his application;

(iv) the applicant has failed without reasonable explanation to produce a valid passport or has sought to rely on an invalid one;

(v) the applicant has without reasonable explanation destroyed evidence relevant to his or her claim;

(vi) the applicant has undertaken activities inconsistent with his or her previous beliefs and behaviour which are calculated to create or substantially enhance his or her claim to refugee status;

(vii) the applicant has lodged concurrent applications for asylum in the United Kingdom or in another country.

1 UNHCR *Handbook* **12.13** above, para 205.

12.32 It is important to note that paragraph 341 of HC 395 is discretionary; the listed factors cannot be applied indiscriminately to undermine credibility, and a careful assessment will need to be carried out in relation to the facts of individual cases and the applicant's explanation. Thus, there are many valid reasons why people do not make their asylum claim immediately on arrival:

lack of knowledge of the procedures, arrival in a confused and frightened state, language differences or fear of officialdom may all be insuperable barriers to making any kind of approach to the authorities at the port of entry.[1] Delay in making an application does not necessarily reflect the absence of a fear: asylum seekers who have permission to remain in some other capacity may well not wish to make an asylum claim with all the uncertainties as to eventual outcome, unless it is apparent that they have no other claim to remain and face removal. Further, a refugee may be acting reasonably when deferring making a claim until obtaining advice from relatives, friends or advice organisations. The API acknowledge that an application which contains demonstrably false claims should nevertheless be accepted if there is sufficient evidence to show a reasonable likelihood of future persecution for a Refugee Convention reason.[2] It is often unfair to make adverse credibility findings on the basis of the use of lies or evasion as to the means of escape, false documents or the destruction of documents.[3] In *Yassine*[4] and *Adimi*[5] the Divisional Court has acknowledged that as a result of the carriers' liability legislation, asylum seekers frequently need the assistance of an agent to obtain false papers to smuggle them out of the country,[6] and are obliged to destroy the documents to prevent the escape route being closed down. Such actions have nothing to do with the merits of the asylum claim, and should not be used to diminish credibility.[7]

1   Report of Social Services Advisory Committee (Cm 3062, January 1996) para 38. See also UNHCR *Handbook* **12.13** above, para 198; *R v Uxbridge Magistrates' Court, ex p Adimi* [1999] INLR 490 at 497-498; UNHCR's *Guidelines on applicable Criteria and Standards relating to the Detention of Asylum Seekers* (*Butterworths Immigration Law Service*, 2C[261]); Atle Grahl-Madsen *The Status of Refugees in International Law* Vol II (1972) p 218.
2   API Mar/01, Ch 1, s 2(10)(i). See also UNHCR *Handbook* above, para 199.
3   See *R v Naillie* [1993] AC 674 ; *R v Secretary of State for the Home Department, ex p Sivakumaran (Jayanathan)* [1990] Imm AR 80, QBD; *Nzamba-Liloneo v Secretary of State for the Home Department* [1993] Imm AR 225, QBD.
4   *R v Secretary of State for the Home Department, ex p Yassine* [1990] Imm AR 354, QBD.
5   *R v Uxbridge Magistrates' Court, ex p Adimi* [1999] INLR 490.
6   See **12.9** and **12.11** above, and **14.73**ff below.
7   See *Suleyman* (16242); *Ezzi* (G0003A): genuine refugees may need to adopt ruses or illegal tactics to obtain admission to the country of refuge.

Inconsistent acts

12.33 Issues of credibility are also engaged where a person's claim to asylum is based solely on acts done since leaving the country of feared persecution and these are inconsistent with previous beliefs. In *Danian*[1] the Court of Appeal reviewed earlier authorities which had held that unreasonable activities, or activities performed in bad faith, could not be relied on by an asylum seeker in support of his or her claim.[2] It concluded that a refugee *sur place* who has acted in bad faith did not fall outside the protection of the Refugee Convention and could not be removed if the activities gave rise to a genuine and well-founded fear of persecution.[3] Brooke LJ, noting the decision in *Mbanza*[4] that a fraudulent claim could attract protection, emphasised that the credibility of such an application was likely to be low and would be rigorously scrutinised. Buxton LJ pointed out that the Convention had provided specific exceptions to refugee status (in Articles 1D-F) which should not be added to unless required by a clear international consensus or international practice. Neither criterion was fulfilled in the case of a 'bad faith' claim.[5] Part of the rationale for the decision was the recognition that the applicant would have an irresistible claim to protection under Article 3 of the ECHR.[6] It has been held in other cases that the mere fact of having claimed asylum in another state may put the person at risk for a Convention reason.[7]

1 [2000] Imm AR 96.
2 *R v Immigration Appeal Tribunal, ex p B* [1989] Imm AR 166; *Mustapha Gilgham v Immigration Appeal Tribunal* [1995] Imm AR 129; *Re HB* (1995) 7 IJRL 332 (NZ).
3 *Danian* fn 1 above, at 122.
4 *Mbanza v Secretary of State for the Home Department* [1996] Imm AR 136.
5 *Danian* above, at 130.
6 *Chahal v UK* (1996) 23 EHRR 413, paras 79-80, cited at *Danian* above, at 118.
7 See observations of Laws J in *R v Immigration Appeal Tribunal, ex p Senga* (unreported, 9 March 1994); *Gile* (5641) (relevance of illegal absence from country to persecution claim); see also (1992) 4(3) IJRL 261; Case 111 (where a Polish asylum seeker was held to have been prejudiced by information given in a claim made in Germany). The difficulties in establishing a Convention reason were demonstrated in the case of *Senga* itself when remitted to the Tribunal (12842)-see comment in [1998] 10(3) INLP 110. However, in *Baheldin Mohammed* (13465) a Sudanese claim based on likely inquiries on return succeeded.

12.34 Similarly, in *Iftikhar Ahmed*[1] the question of how far a refugee should voluntarily refrain from exercising fundamental human rights to avoid persecution was revisited. In the earlier cases of *Mendis*[2] and *Ahmad*,[3] it was intimated that a person cannot generally found a claim for asylum solely on future activity he or she might take part in on return to the country of origin, where this might infringe the law. In both of those cases, the applicants had not at that point done any acts which might lead to prosecution in their own countries, and the court rejected their asylum claims on the basis that they would not do in the future what they had not done in the past. The receiving state does not have to grant asylum if the full exercise of human rights cannot be permanently guaranteed in the country of origin, and is entitled to expect some degree of prudence in the activities of the applicant if returned to his or her own country. But, as Simon Brown LJ pointed out in *Iftikhar Ahmed*, while it may well be reasonable to require asylum seekers to refrain from certain political or even religious activities to avoid persecution on return, it is quite another thing to say that, if in fact it appears that the asylum seeker would not refrain from such activities—if in other words it is established that he or she would in fact act unreasonably—he or she is not entitled to refugee status.[4] In the instant case it was established that the appellant, a devout Ahmadi, would continue to proselytise, and however unreasonable that was, it entitled him to protection. This is in accordance with the suggestion in the *Handbook* that refugee status may be based on political opinion as yet unknown to the persecuting government which will become known if the asylum seeker is returned.[5] Asylum seekers cannot be required to give up their religion, racial or sexual identity, or their political opinions, in order to avoid persecution in their own country.[6] In *Ex p Jonah*[7] it was held that to require a former trade union leader to give up his lifelong activities, live apart from his wife and family and withdraw to a remoter part of the country in order to avoid the attention of the authorities was unreasonable and those circumstances amounted to persecution.

1 *Iftikhar Ahmed v Secretary of State for the Home Department* [2000] INLR 1.
2 *Mendis v Immigration Appeal Tribunal and Secretary of State for the Home Department* [1989] Imm AR 6.

3 *Ahmad v Secretary of State for the Home Department* [1990] Imm AR 61; see also *Yavari* [1987] Imm AR 138; *Al Wazah* (6058); *Zadeh* (5424); *Habtu* (5321).
4 *Iftikhar Ahmed* above, at 7.
5 UNHCR *Handbook* **12.13** above, para 82.
6 Clearly there is tension between this proposition and the earlier proposition that the receiving state is not obliged to grant asylum where the full exercise of human rights cannot be guaranteed in the home country; there is, however, a distinction between freedom of conscience (an absolute right) and freedom to manifest beliefs and freedom of expression (both qualified ones). And as Simon Brown LJ said in *Iftikhar Ahmed*, the single question is whether the applicant in the particular case has a well-founded fear of persecution.
7 *R v Immigration Appeal Tribunal, ex p Jonah* [1985] Imm AR 7.

'Outside the country of nationality . . . residence'

12.35 It is fundamental to the definition of a Convention refugee that the person should be outside his or her country owing to the fear of persecution.[1] A person sheltered in a foreign embassy in the country of persecution is outside that country's jurisdiction, but not its territory, and cannot be recognised as a Convention refugee.[2]

1 See UNHCR *Handbook* **12.13** above, para 88. For a discussion of this territorial limitation generally see Hathaway **12.21** fn 2 above, pp 29-33.
2 UNHCR *Handbook* above, para 88, fn.

12.36 It may be necessary to determine what the person's true nationality is, since, if it is not that of the country of feared persecution, the claimant can be returned to the country of nationality.[1] Similarly, a person who is a national of more than one country will be expected to satisfy the refugee definition in respect of each country, or seek protection of that country where persecution is not feared.[2] But the second nationality must be effective, not merely formal, before it disqualifies someone from refugee status vis-à-vis the country of persecution.[3] Where there is a dispute as to nationality, the decision of the country of purported nationality will be decisive, rather than the host country's conclusion as to what the nationality should be.[4] Possession of a passport issued by another state may not be evidence of nationality if it was issued as a travel document to enable the bearer to move elsewhere.[5] However, possession of such a travel document may be evidence that the person can be removed to a safe third country.[6] Arbitrary exclusion from the country of nationality, implying cutting off from the enjoyment of all the benefits and rights enjoyed by citizens, can itself amount to persecution.[7] The Convention definition applies to stateless persons as well as to those who have a nationality. Stateless persons[8] qualify if they flee from the country of habitual residence[9] and cannot go back there because of a fear of persecution,[10] although if they are unable to return to the country of habitual residence, other international law obligations are engaged.[11]

1 *R v Special Adjudicator, ex p Abudine* [1995] Imm AR 60, QBD.
2 Refugee Convention, art 1A(2); UNHCR *Handbook* **12.13** above, paras 106–107; *A-G of Canada v Ward* [1997] INLR 42, S Ct Can.
3 *R (Milisavljevic) v Immigration Appeal Tribunal* [2001] EWHC Admin 203.
4 See *Oppenheimer v Cattermole* [1976] AC 249, [1975] 1 All ER 538, HL; *Stoeck v Public Trustee* [1921] 2 Ch 67; *(Mahaboob) Bibi v Secretary of State for the Home Department* [1987] Imm AR 340, CA. This also accords with the rule of public international law that in general each state may determine who are its nationals: see R Plender *International*

Migration Law (2nd edn, 1988) pp 39ff. But the decision of the purported country of nationality may be ignored if it violates international humanitarian law: *Oppenheimer v Cattermole* [1976] AC 249, HL.

5 (1993) 5(3) IJRL 466, Case No 156.

6 *Alsawaf v Secretary of State for the Home Department* [1988] Imm AR 410, CA.

7 See the decision of the Court of Appeal in *Lazarevic v Secretary of State for the Home Department* [1997] Imm AR 251, CA.

8 See *Samanter* (14520) for circumstances in which statelessness may arise.

9 In *Dag* (01 TH 0075) 14 March 2001 a starred Tribunal held that the Turkish Republic of Northern Cyprus, which was not a state in international law, is not capable of being the country of a person's nationality, and 'tentatively', that although the phrase 'country of former habitual residence' was wider, an area which formed part of a recognised state could not itself be a country of former habitual residence within the meaning of the Refugee Convention.

10 *Revenko v Secretary of State for the Home Department* [2000] Imm AR 610, [2000] INLR 646, where the CA rejected the argument that a stateless person needed only to show inability to return to qualify as a refugee.

11 UN Convention on the Status of Stateless Persons 1954: see **8.91** above. See also *Tjhe Kwet Koe v MIEA* [1997] FCA 912.

12.37 Before the British Nationality Act 1981 came into force in 1983, it was doubtful whether Commonwealth citizens could be afforded refugee status in the UK, because all were 'British subjects'.[1] As such, they might be said to be British nationals for the purposes of international law and thus under British protection. However, in the light of the restricted definition of British subject under the 1981 Act, citizens of independent Commonwealth countries are no longer British nationals. The problem, however, could remain in respect of British Dependent Territories citizens, British Nationals (Overseas) and British Overseas citizens who find themselves persecuted in their country of habitual residence.[2] We have considered the question of international obligations to admit British nationals who are not British citizens at **8.83** above. In one High Court case it was held that where a British Protected person had been rejected elsewhere he or she could be treated as a person without nationality and issues were, therefore, raised under the Refugee Convention.[3] This is a very practical way of bypassing what otherwise might be difficult questions of the UK's International obligations.

1 For British nationality, see chapter 2 above.

2 There are many British Dependent Territories citizens and British Nationals (Overseas) in Hong Kong, although British Nationals (Overseas) with no other nationality may register as British citizens under the British Nationality (Hong Kong) Act 1997, and British Dependent Territories citizens are being offered citizenship under the Partnership for Progress and Prosperity (Cm 4264, March 1999). British Overseas citizens may obtain special vouchers to enter the UK: HC 395, para 249.

3 *R v Chief Immigration Officer, Gatwick Airport, ex p Singh* [1987] Imm AR 346, QBD.

12.38 Although refugees must first leave their own country in order to claim asylum, many of the countries from which refugees are fleeing are visa countries, ie their nationals require visas to enter the UK and other West European countries. While there is nothing in the Refugee Convention that would prevent a contracting state issuing a visa to enable a person to enter as a refugee, there is nothing that obliges them to do so. UK practice, set out in the API, is that entry clearance officers have discretion to accept applications for entry clearance where applicants meet the requirements of the Convention and have close ties with the UK (family, or time spent there as a student) and the UK is the most appropriate country of refuge. The visa application form will be sent to the Home Office.[1] However, the applicant is still required to be outside his or her own country. If a visa is refused or not applied for, but the asylum seekers nevertheless reach the UK, the absence of a visa will not prevent their claims to asylum from being considered. However, the corollary to the imposition of a mandatory visa requirement for most refugee-producing countries has been the enactment of measures penalising the carriers of asylum seekers. This began with the Immigration (Carriers' Liability) Act 1987, which provided for the imposition of a penalty on carriers for each passenger brought into the UK without proper documentation.[2] During the parliamentary debate on the passage of the 1987 Act, amendments to exempt carriers from financial penalties in the case of refugees were rejected. Instead, policy guidelines on the exercise of discretion were adopted (making limited provision for the waiver of fines, *inter alia*, where a passenger was subsequently accepted as a genuine refugee or where the passenger was in 'imminent and self-evident danger of his life').[3] The 1987 Act was repealed by the Immigration and Asylum Act 1999,[4] and re-enacted in amended form in sections 40-42. The 1999 Act also imposes civil penalties on carriers bringing 'clandestine entrants' into the country, whether by design or inadvertently, which force van and lorry drivers and rail freight operators to check their vehicles and containers for stowaways.[5] The government has rejected demands for a waiver of penalties in respect of clandestine entrants recognised as refugees, although it has a policy of waiving penalties imposed on carriers for inadequately documented passengers.[6]

1   See API Oct/00, Ch 2, s 1. Reassuringly, caseworkers are told that an entry clearance issued in this capacity should 'not include any reference to asylum': para 3.2.
2   For the background to the passage of this Act see Nicholas Blake 'The Road to *Sivakumaran*' in (1989) 3 INLP 1 at 12. From 1991 the level of the fine per undocumented passenger was £2,000 (SI 1991/1497); Immigration and Asylum Act 1999, s 40(2) sets the fine at £2,000, or such other sum as may be prescribed (ie, in regulations made by the Secretary of State under s 167(1) of the 1999 Act). For more detailed discussion of carrier sanctions see **14.68ff** below.
3   See **14.75** below, where the guidance is set out in full.
4   Immigration and Asylum Act 1999, Sch 16.
5   See **14.69ff** below.
6   326 HC Official Report (6th series) col 1032.

'Unable or . . . unwilling to avail himself of the protection'

12.39   The failure of state protection is at the heart of refugee law. The refugee definition treats those with nationality and those who are stateless differently. To qualify as refugees, the former must be unable or unwilling to avail themselves of the protection of their country; the latter unable or unwilling to return to the country of habitual residence.[1] At the time of drafting the Refugee Convention it was envisaged that stateless persons, and nationals 'refused passport facilities or other protection by their own governments', would be the main categories qualifying through inability (as opposed to unwillingness) to obtain protection or to return.[2] But the category of refugees who have a nationality but are unable to secure the protection of their country is much wider than originally contemplated. It includes those who are unable through circumstances beyond the control of the state (for example, civil war or grave disturbance) as well as circumstances for which the state is directly responsible (for example, the refusal of passport facilities or denial of admission to the territory, which may itself in particular cases amount to persecution).[3] 'Inability' implies circumstances beyond the control of the person concerned, while unwillingness implies his or her refusal to accept protection because of a fear of persecution.[4] For stateless persons, no question of availment of protection arises and the abandonment of former habitual residence is likely to mean that the person is unable to return.[5] But all categories of refugees, including stateless persons, must demonstrate a current well-founded fear of Convention persecution to fulfil the definition requirements.[6]

1   The meaning of 'country' in each phrase has been held to be different by the Tribunal in *Dag* (01 TH 0075) at **12.36** fn 9 above. See also *Tjhe Kwet Koe v MIEA* [1997] FCA 912 (Aust); *Ahmed Ali Zalzali v MEI* [1991] 3 CF 605, CA (Can).
2   See Goodwin-Gill **12.5** fn 1 above, p 41 citing report of the *Ad Hoc* Committee: UN doc. E/1618, 39.
3   *Lazarevic v Secretary of State for the Home Department* [1997] Imm AR 251 at 272, per Hutchison LJ. The example in that case was the refusal of the Federal Republic of Yugoslavia to permit the return of its nationals who had fled the conflict in former Yugoslavia and sought asylum abroad.
4   UNHCR *Handbook*, **12.13** above, paras 97-100.
5   UNHCR *Handbook* above, para 101; *R v Secretary of State for the Home Department, ex p Adan* [1999] 1 AC 293.
6   *Revenko v Secretary of State for the Home Department* [2000] Imm AR 610, [2000] INLR 646, CA.

12.40   The mere possession of a valid national passport from the country where persecution is feared is not evidence that the person continues to seek protection from that country and is therefore no bar to refugee status; however, refugees who refuse to surrender their national passports to the host country without good reason may throw doubts on their unwillingness to avail themselves of the protection of their own country.[1]

1   UNHCR *Handbook* **12.13** above, paras 48-49, 97-101; *Refugee Appeal No. 67/92 Re BR* (10 November 1992) (NZRSAA).

12.41   In *Adan*[1] the House of Lords considered whether a Somali national who had left his own country because of a well-founded fear of persecution, and who was unable to avail himself of the protection of that country because there was no effective state, was a refugee although he no longer had a well-founded fear of persecution. The Court of Appeal had held by a majority that as long as past persecution or fear of it was still a reason for the refugee's presence in the host country, it was unnecessary to show a current well-founded fear of persecution.[2] The House of Lords disagreed. Lord Lloyd, giving the leading judgment,[3] analysed the refugee definition as comprising a 'fear test' and a 'protection' test', both of which had to be satisfied.[4]

1   *R v Secretary of State for the Home Department, ex p Adan* [1999] 1 AC 293, [1998] INLR 325.
2   [1997] Imm AR 251.
3   Lord Slynn reasoned that the use of the present tense in the definition, '*is* unable or, owing to such fear, unwilling to avail himself of the protection of that country' required a well-founded fear when refugee status was determined. Lords Goff, Nolan and Hope agreed with Lord Lloyd's reasoning.
4   Lord Lloyd's formulation was, however, rejected by the House of Lords in *Horvath v Secretary of State for the Home Department* [2000] INLR 329, HL, in the context of the meaning of 'persecution': see **12.52** below.

12.42 In *Vallaj*[1] the Administrative Court considered and rejected as 'narrowly linguistic' an argument that the protection available to someone to disqualify him or her from refugee status had to be provided by the authorities of the country of nationality, a point which had always been assumed from the language of the refugee definition. The issue arose in relation to ethnic Albanians in the Serbian province of Kosovo, in the Federal Republic of Yugoslavia, who were receiving protection not from the authorities of their own country but from a UN interim administration (known as UNMIK) and by NATO troops, KFOR, mandated by a UN security council resolution. An earlier starred Tribunal case, *Dyli*,[2] had held that the phrase 'the protection of the country' in the refugee definition referred to any protection available in the territory of the country of nationality, whatever its source. In *Vallaj* Dyson J held that as a living instrument, the Refugee Convention should be interpreted in a way which takes account of the realities of the interventionist role that the UN Security Council now adopts when circumstances require it. Protection provided under lawful authority by a body to which all the powers and functions of the state (including the function of protection) have been transferred falls within the definition of 'protection of the country', and a person in receipt of such protection is not, subject to issues of adequacy of protection, a refugee.[3]

1   *R (Vallaj) v Immigration Appeal Tribunal* 21 December 2000, Dyson J.
2   *Dyli* [2000] INLR 372.
3   *Vallaj* above, paras 24-35. Leave to appeal was refused by the CA on 24 May 2001.

Internal flight alternative

12.43 Because the principal concern of refugee law is the provision of international protection to persons unable to receive protection in their own country, a purely localised risk may be insufficient to make someone a refugee. International protection is not needed if the person can obtain protection by moving elsewhere in his or her own country.[1] But if, as the *Handbook* points out, internal flight to another part of the country is not reasonable or safe, it is not necessary to prove that persecution extends to the whole of the country.[2] The EU Joint Position requires assessment of the possibility of finding 'effective protection in another part' of the asylum seeker's own country, to which he or she 'may reasonably be expected to move'.[3] These considerations are reflected in the Immigration Rules,[4] which provide that an asylum claim *may* be refused if there is a part of the country to which it would be reasonable to expect the applicant to go, where he or she does not have a well founded fear of persecution. The option of internal flight only arises if the asylum seeker has a well-founded fear of persecution in his or her home area, or if he or she cannot return there without a real risk of persecution on the way.[5] The Tribunal has held that internal flight is not possible where the state is the agent of feared persecution.[6]

1   See *Florianowicz* (15333), IAT.
2   UNHCR *Handbook* **12.13** above, para 91.
3   EU Joint Position (96/196/JHA) of 4 March 1996 on harmonised application of definition of the term 'refugee': *Butterworths Immigration Law Service*, 2D[138].
4   HC 395, para 343.
5   *Dyli* [2000] INLR 372, IAT (starred Tribunal); *R (Vallaj) v Immigration Appeal Tribunal*, 21 December 2000, QBD, para 65, upheld by the CA on 24 May 2001. In *Canaj* (24 May 2001) the CA rejected the argument that the fear of persecution could relate to any part of the country of nationality, even if the applicant had never been there.

6   *Kumaran* (00 TH 01459) 7 June 2000; *Orechkov* (18330). This accords with the views of
     academics including Hathaway in the Michigan Colloquium of April 1999: see the Michigan
     Guidelines on the internal protection alternative, 1999.

12.44 In *Robinson*[1] the Court of Appeal considered the appellate authorities'
jurisdiction to decide on the reasonableness of relocation to an area of the
country where there was no fear of persecution. The Tribunal had been divided
on whether it could consider the issue, with one division holding that its
jurisdiction was limited to the issue whether returning the appellant would
breach the UK's obligations under the Refugee Convention[2] and that the wording
of paragraph 343 of the Immigration Rules reflected an unreviewable discretion,[3]
and another that the possibility of internal flight was part of the refugee
definition.[4] The Court of Appeal, after reviewing Commonwealth jurisprudence
and the views of academics, held that both the safety and the reasonableness of
the 'internal flight alternative' went to ability and willingness to accept protection
within the Convention, and thus were within the appellate authorities'
jurisdiction. As to what would be 'reasonable', the court emphasised that decision-
makers must consider 'all relevant circumstances against the backcloth that the
issue is whether the claimant is entitled to the status of refugee'. Such
circumstances might include whether as a practical matter (for financial,
logistical or other good reason) the 'safe' part of the country is reasonably
accessible; whether the claimant is required to encounter great physical danger
or to undergo undue hardship in travelling there or staying there, and whether
the quality of the internal protection fails to meet basic norms of civil, political
and socio-economic human rights.[5] The court approved the test by Linden JA in
Thirunavukkarasu:[6] 'Would it be unduly harsh to expect this person to move to
another less hostile part of the country?'[7] In *Canaj*[8] the CA has suggested that
Robinson should now be read together with the New Zealand decision in Refugee
Appeal No 71684/99.[9]

1   *R v Secretary of State for the Home Department, Immigration Appeal Tribunal,
     ex p Robinson* [1997] INLR 182, [1997] Imm AR 568.
2   Asylum and Immigration Appeals Act 1993, s 8 (now Immigration and Asylum Act 1999,
     s 69); *R v Secretary of State for the Home Department, ex p Mehari* [1994] QB 474.
3   *Dupovac* (11846); *Ahmed* (13371); *Nirmalan* (14361).
4   *Ikhlaq* (13679).
5   *Robinson* above, para 18, referring to the Preamble to the Refugee Convention.
6   *Thirunavukkarasu v Minister of Employment and Immigration* (1993) 109 DLR (4th) 682
     per Linden JA at 687, (Can Fed Ct).
7   *Robinson* above, para 29.
8   *Canaj v Secretary of State for the Home Department, Vallaj v Special Adjudicator*,
     24 May 2001, para 31.
9   [2000] INLR 165.

12.45 The second difficulty with internal flight related to the burden and standard
of proving whether internal relocation was reasonable or 'unduly harsh'. Who
had to prove what, to which standard? In *Manoharan*[1] a tribunal had held that
the burden was on the applicant to show on balance of probabilities that it
would be unduly harsh to return him; in *Sachithananthan*[2] a tribunal held
(following *Thirunavukkarasu*)[3] that the test was whether there was a serious
possibility that it would be unduly harsh. The issue was resolved in *Karanakaran*[4]
where the Court of Appeal decided that no 'standard of proof' as such applied;
the question was simply whether, taking all relevant[5] matters into account,
return of the claimant would be unduly harsh. Everything capable of having a

bearing on the question was to be taken into account (which might include the need to consider the cumulative effect of a whole range of disparate considerations).[6] The court commended the methodology of the Tribunal in the case of *Sayandan* where, in considering whether return would be unduly harsh, it had set out some 11 disparate risks as matters worthy of attention and had evaluated both the likelihood of a risk eventuating and the seriousness of the consequences.[7]

1   *Manoharan* [1998] INLR 519.
2   *Sachitananthan* [1999] INLR 205.
3   *Thirunavukkarasu v MEI* (1993) 109 DLR (4th) 682.
4   *Karanakaran v Secretary of State for the Home Department* [2000] INLR 122, CA.
5   In *Gnanam v Secretary of State for the Home Department* [1999] INLR 219, CA Tuckey LJ emphasised that what may be relevant factors in one case would not necessarily be so in another, whether considered individually or cumulatively.
6   *Gnanam* above, at 145, per Brooke LJ. Sedley LJ observed at 154-155 that the correct approach coincided with that advocated by Simon Brown LJ in *Ravichandran v Secretary of State for the Home Department* [1996] Imm AR 97 at 109, ie consideration of the 'single composite question' whether a person has a 'well-founded fear of being persecuted for Convention reasons' in the round and with all relevant circumstances brought into account. In Australia a similar wide-ranging approach to internal flight has been adopted: see eg *Randhawa v MILGEA* (1994) 52 FCR 437; *Franco-Buitrago v MIMA* [2000] FCA 1525.
7   *Sayandan* (16312) 5 March 1998. The risks identified in returning a Tamil to Colombo were arrest and return to the North East because of lack of documents; repeated arrest in round-ups; being subject to extortion; unduly harsh treatment before accessing judicial process; dreadful prison conditions if detained; not being able to find or retain accommodation; not being able to find employment because of discrimination; where the appellant could not speak Sinhalese; being subjected to a regime where racial discrimination was part of everyday life; having no real contacts or ties in Colombo; and previous ill-treatment in Sri Lanka by both the LTTE and the security forces.

Persecution for Convention reasons

State persecution[1]

12.46   The Refugee Convention does not define persecution and, although the term, like the entire refugee definition, has an autonomous meaning,[2] there is no universally accepted definition. As we shall see in relation to persecution by non-state agents, its meaning is linked to the availability of state protection, at least so far as the UK is concerned.[3] The *Handbook* indicates that, while a threat to life or freedom for the relevant reason will always amount to persecution,[4] persecution does not have to involve threats to life or freedom; other serious violations of human rights will also qualify.[5] In *R v Immigration Appeal Tribunal, ex p Jonah*[6] Nolan J ruled that the word must be given its ordinary dictionary definition 'to pursue with malignancy or injurious action, especially to oppress for holding a heretical opinion or belief'. The case law reveals a tension between (i) the approach which sees the issue solely as one of fact for the decision maker and the adjudicator, subject to challenge in the Administrative Court solely on *Wednesbury* principles,[7] and (ii) attempts to provide a coherent framework for persecution based on human rights law. The human rights approach dictated by the preamble of the Refugee Convention has been propounded by James Hathaway, who in his seminal book *The Law of Refugee Status* defined persecution as 'the sustained or systemic failure of state protection in relation to one of the core entitlements which has been recognised by the international community'.[8] In the influential case of *Gashi*,[9] the Tribunal adopted UNHCR's analysis of persecution,[10] which drew heavily on Hathaway's definition,[11] in relation to three categories of human rights. Breaches of 'inviolable human rights such as the right of life and the prohibition against torture, cruel, inhuman or degrading treatment would always be persecution. Violation of rights whose limited derogation or curtailment by the state could be justified only in time of public emergency (freedom from arbitrary arrest and detention and freedom of expression) would be persecution if unjustified. The denial of rights reflecting goals for social, economic or cultural development, such as the right to a livelihood, could amount to persecution if it was systematic and discriminatory. More recently, Goodwin-Gill[12] has stated that the 'core meaning' of persecution 'readily includes the threat of deprivation of life or physical freedom' although 'less overt measures may suffice, such as the imposition of serious economic disadvantage, denial of access to employment, to the professions, or to education, or other restrictions on the freedoms traditionally guaranteed in a democratic society'.[13] Although mere discrimination is probably not enough, evidence of discrimination will make it easier to demonstrate persecution. And where discrimination is so severe, frequent or protracted that it inhibits freedom to exercise basic human rights such as the right to a livelihood or to practice a religion, it may amount to persecution.[14] The downside to linking the definition of persecution to core human rights is that if the asylum seeker cannot establish the existence of the core right, there will be no persecution.[15]

1 This section considers the meaning of persecution when it comes from the state. Following *Horvath v Secretary of State for the Home Department* [2000] INLR 239, a different meaning is required where the allegation relates to persecution by non-state agents: see *Persecution by non-state agents* at **12.51**ff below.

2 See *R v Secretary of State for the Home Department, ex p Adan, R v Secretary of State for the Home Department, ex p Aitseguer* [2001] INLR 44.

3 *Horvath* fn 1 above, at **12.51**ff.

4 This is clear from the '*non-refoulement*' provision in art 33, which prohibits the return of a refugee to the frontiers of territories 'where his life or freedom would be threatened' for a Refugee Convention reason.

5 UNHCR *Handbook* **12.13** above, para 52; *R v Secretary of State for the Home Department, ex p Sivakumaran* [1988] AC 958, per Lord Goff; *Horvath* above, at 215H, per Lord Lloyd.

6 [1985] Imm AR 7.

7 See *Kagema v Secretary of State for the Home Department* [1997] Imm AR 137; *Faraj v Secretary of State for the Home Department* [1999] INLR 451. In *Horvath* above Lord Lloyd described the proposition that persecution should be given its ordinary dictionary meaning as 'settled law' (at 251).

8 See **12.21** fn 2 above.

9 *Gashi and Nikshiqi* [1997] INLR 96. See also Schiemann LJ in *Blanusa v Secretary of State for the Home Department*, 18 May 1998, CA.

10 UNHCR appeared as intervener in the case.

11 In Hathaway's formulation, the types of harm to be protected against include the breach of any right within the first category, a discriminatory or non-emergency abrogation of a right within the second category, or the failure to implement a right within the third category which is either discriminatory or not grounded in the absolute lack of resources.

12 *The Refugee in International Law*, **12.5** fn 1 above, pp 66–68.

13 Whether such restrictions amount to persecution requires assessment of a complex of factors, including (1) the nature of the freedom threatened, (2) the nature and severity of the restriction, and (3) the likelihood of the restriction eventuating in the individual case: Goodwin-Gill fn 11 above. See *Chen Shi Hai v Minister for Immigration* [2000] INLR 455, Aust HC (adverse treatment which a 'black child' is likely to receive in China—denial of access to food, education and health care—could amount to persecution.

14 UNHCR *Handbook* **12.13** above, paras 54–55; *Chen* above, at 24; *Ahmad v Secretary of State for the Home Department* [1990] Imm AR 61 at 66, per Farquarson LJ. Examples of Tribunal determinations in which findings of persecution have been made in 'third category' cases include *Padhu* (12318) (inability to work and deprivation of state benefits) and *Lucreteanu* (12126) (threatening phone calls in Romania). In *Kadham v Canada* IMM-652-97, 8 January 1998, FC Moulden J observed that harassment could constitute persecution if it was sufficiently serious or long-lasting as to threaten the claimant's physical or moral integrity.

15 *Sepet and Bulbul v Secretary of State for the Home Department* [2001] EWCA Civ 681.

12.47 In *Ravichandran*[1] the Court of Appeal found Hathaway's human rights-based analysis of persecution instructive. In *Adan v Secretary of State for the Home Department*[2] Hutchinson LJ saw no reason not to accept it. And in *Horvath*[3] it received the seal of approval from Lord Hope. *Ravichandran* held that the arbitrary detention of young Tamils for periods of a few days following terrorist atrocities did not amount to persecution, although long-term detention, or detention accompanied by ill-treatment, would have been a different matter.[4] The court held that the question whether an individual's fear is one of persecution for a Convention reason is a single composite question to be determined in the round with all relevant circumstances being taken into account.[5] Breaches of rights other than absolute rights probably require an element of persistence to constitute 'persecution'.[6] But the question of whether persistence is a necessary element of physical ill-treatment has been the subject of conflicting decisions. While the reference in Hathaway to 'sustained or systemic denial of core human rights' is meant to refer to country practices underlying individual claims, it was adopted in *Ravichandran*[7] as an individual requirement by Staughton LJ, who observed that 'persecution must at least be persistent and serious ill-treatment without just cause by the state, or from which the state can provide protection but chooses not to'. His remarks have become detached from their context (short-term but arbitrary and unlawful detention of Tamils as terrorist suspects) and wrongly applied as a rigid legal criterion regardless of the nature of the feared persecution.[8] It would, however, be absurd to deny refugee status to someone with a well-founded fear of life-threatening torture on the ground that the torture would not be repeated. Freedom from torture is an absolute right which can never be balanced or qualified, and its violation must always constitute persecution.[9] This was accepted by the Court of Appeal in *Demirkaya*,[10] although apparently not by a different division of the court in *Faraj*.[11] The Australian and New Zealand courts regard any requirement of systematic conduct aimed at the claimant as a misdirection.[12] Back in the UK, the higher courts have held that the threshold of 'serious harm' is a high one,[13] although regard should be had to the individual's characteristics and expectations in deciding what the refugee from a troubled part of the world ought to be able to put up with.[14] There is no requirement that a person be 'singled out' for persecution to be a refugee.[15]

1 *Sandralingham and Ravichandran v Secretary of State for the Home Department; Rajendrakumar v Immigration Appeal Tribunal* [1996] Imm AR 97 at 107. It had already been accepted by La Forest J in the leading Canadian case of *A-G of Canada v Ward* [1993] 2 SCR 689 at 709.

2 [1997] 1 WLR 1107 at 1126E.

3 *Horvath v Secretary of State for the Home Department* [2000] 3 WLR 379 at 383E-F.

4 'If there remained a practice of torturing those detained, I very much doubt whether a finding of persecution on Convention grounds would be precluded merely because the torture was intended to discourage terrorism or to persuade detainees to inform on their associates rather than inflicted for purposes of oppression': Simon Brown LJ at 109.

5 *Ravichandran* above; see also *Karanakaran v Secretary of State for the Home Department* [2000] INLR 122 CA.

6 See the reference to 'cumulative grounds' in UNHCR *Handbook* **12.13** above, para 53.
7 *Sandralingham and Ravichandran v Secretary of State for the Home Department; Rajendrakumar v Immigration Appeal Tribunal* [1996] Imm AR 97 at 114.
8 Simon Brown LJ understood this distinction; see his reference in *Ravichandran* above to a 'practice of torturing those detained' as opposed to an individual requirement of repetitive ill-treatment.
9 See UNHCR *Handbook* above, para 51.
10 *Demirkaya v Secretary of State for the Home Department* [1999] INLR 441. This accords with the EU Joint Position, which states at para 4: 'It is generally agreed that, in order to constitute 'persecution' . . . acts suffered or feared must be sufficiently serious, by their nature *or* their repetition (emphasis added).
11 *Faraj v Secretary of State for the Home Department* [1999] INLR 451, CA. But even on the analysis of Peter Gibson LJ, a claimant might be a refugee based on a single incident 'if there are other incidents affecting a group of which that person is a member' (at 456E). See also the obiter remark of Lord Clyde in *Horvath v Secretary of State for the Home Department* [2000] INLR 239, HL quoting Hathaway ('sustained or systemic') when stating that persecution appeared to carry with it 'some element of persistence' (at 261F).
12 See *Chan v MIEA* (1989) 169 CLR 379, 430; *Abdalla v MIMA* (1998) 51 ALD 666 at 671–673; *Anjum v MIMA* (1998) 52 ALD 225 at 230-232; *Refugee Appeal No 71462/99* [2000] INLR 311, para 78 (NZRSAA). See also *Doymus* (00 TH 01748), 19 July 2000, IAT: 'persistence is usual but not universal'; *Foughali* (00 TH 01514) 2 June 2000, IAT.
13 See *Horvath v Secretary of State for the Home Department* [2000] INLR 15, CA, at 50, per Ward LJ: 'anything short of a really serious flouting of the citizen's human rights and dignities will not do'.
14 UNHCR *Handbook* above, para 52.
15 *Jeyakumaran v Secretary of State for the Home Department* [1994] Imm AR 45.

Prosecution

12.48 Persecution must be distinguished from prosecution, and the *Handbook* points out that fugitives from common law offences are unlikely to be refugees.[1] But prosecution is not always inconsistent with persecution and may be good evidence of it. The nature of the allegations against the applicant and procedural safeguards to ensure a fair trial will have to be examined with care. The conclusion of persecution may be drawn where a fair trial would be denied; where punishment is excessive; where a particular political viewpoint or religion is expressly prohibited or the state's laws prohibit other normal and reasonable human activity guaranteed by fundamental human rights; or where there is other reason to suspect that the prosecution is being conducted for political reasons.[2] In deciding whether arrangements in the country of origin breach the Refugee Convention, the principles of comity have no place.[3] Of course, a persecutory prosecution must also relate to a Convention reason to found refugee status.[4] In this connection a number of cases raise the question whether a prosecution under a law of general application amounts to persecution for a Convention reason. The question is posed in an acute way in cases of conscientious objection to military service. Why is a prosecution persecution? Is the person being prosecuted for merely breaking the law, or being persecuted for a Convention reason? The Court of Appeal held in *Sepet and Bulbul v Secretary of State for the Home Department*[5] that unless and until the right to conscientious objection to military service becomes a recognised human right, prosecution for refusing to bear arms does not amount to persecution. In Canada, the courts have adopted a test of looking at the intent of the law of general application to see whether it is 'neutral' or 'persecutory'.[6]

1 UNHCR *Handbook* **12.13** above, paras 56-60; *R v Secretary of State for the Home Department, ex p Bilged Singh* [1994] Imm AR 42. See also Goodwin-Gill **12.5** fn 1 above, at 4.3.2.

2 Hathaway **12.21** fn 2 above, para 5.6.1, p169; EU Joint Action (OJ L 63) para 5.1.2. Prosecution for participation in a protest march is likely to be persecution: *R (Tientchu) v IAT*, 18 October 2000, CA.

3 *Zaitz v Secretary of State for the Home Department* [2000] INLR 346 at 39–41, per Buxton LJ; *Islam v Secretary of State for the Home Department* [1999] INLR 144 at 166B–C, per Lord Hoffmann.

4 Trials of smugglers before a Tribunal condemned as unfair did not give rise to a Refugee Convention claim in *Ameyaw v Secretary of State for the Home Department* [1992] Imm AR 206; but contrast 4(3) IJRL 261, Case 111 where the risk of prosecution for revealing state secrets was held to be Convention persecution.

5 *Sepet and Bulbul v Secretary of State for the Home Department (UNHCR intervening)* [2001] EWCA Civ 681.

6 *Zolfagharkani v Canada* [1993] 3 FC 540 at 552, per MacGuigan JA; *Ciric v Canada* [1994] 2 CF 65.

12.49 The distinction between prosecution and persecution is also relevant to a consideration of the exclusion from protection of refugees who have committed serious non-political offences.[1] UK practice on extradition gives a generous interpretation to the political offence exemptions in the Extradition Act 1871 and Fugitive Offenders Act 1967, and (although the scope for the exemption has been narrowed by the Suppression of Terrorism Act 1978)[2] the Extradition Act 1989 still enables a fugitive to demonstrate that extradition was sought for an offence of a political character, or that:

> 'the request for his return (though purporting to be made on an account of an extradition crime) is in fact made for the purpose of prosecuting or punishing him on account of his race, religion, nationality, or political opinions;'

or that:

> 'he might if surrendered be prejudiced at his trial or punished, detained or restricted in his personal liberty by reason of his race religion nationality or political opinions.'[3]

These considerations are equally relevant to the determination of refugee status.

1 See *Re Castioni* [1891] 1 QB 149; *Re Meunier* [1894] 2 QB 415; *Schtraks v Government of Israel* [1964] AC 556, [1962] 3 All ER 529, HL; *Re Gross* [1968] 3 All ER 804, [1969] 1 WLR 12; *Fernandez v Government of Singapore* [1971] 2 All ER 691, [1971] 1 WLR 987; *Cheng v Governor of Pentonville Prison* [1973] AC 931, [1973] 2 All ER 204, HL; *R v Governor of Winson Green Prison, ex p Littlejohn* [1975] 3 All ER 208, [1975] 1 WLR 893. But see *T v Immigration Officer* [1996] AC 742; see also **12.94-12.95** below.

2 This Act gives effect to the European Convention on the Suppression of Terrorism 1977: see Archbold *Criminal Pleading, Evidence and Practice* 2001, 25-147ff.

3 Extradition Act 1989, ss 6, 24.

12.50 Prosecution for an offence which is political in itself (such as sedition) or for contravention of laws which themselves infringe human rights, will give rise to an inference of persecution more easily than common law offences which are committed for a relevant political purpose,[1] unless in the latter case the accused is likely to be prejudiced in the trial or during lawful punishment for a Convention reason.[2] Even where there is such a risk, the decision of the House of Lords in *T v Immigration Officer*[3] means that Convention protection can be lost if the crime is an atrocious one or the violence inflicted is considered too remote from an effective political objective to be said to be political, although the offender could be exempted from extradition because of the prohibition on extradition for a political offence. In these circumstances, the broader protection against torture and inhuman and degrading treatment offered by the ECHR and other international instruments will be very relevant.[4] For discussion of the problems raised by evasion of military service see **12.72** below.

1   *O v Immigration Appeal Tribunal* [1995] Imm AR 494, where the Court of Appeal rejected a submission that prosecution for the offence of stockpiling arms to foment a tribal insurrection was in itself persecution for a political reason. But the court's reference to a latter-day Guy Fawkes confuses the issue, since a member of a persecuted religious minority who tried to end the persecution by eliminating the government would have a case for Convention status if he or she faced brutal torture and gruesome execution in a prosecution for high treason.
2   Goodwin-Gill **12.5** fn 1 above, p 52; EU Joint Position 96/196/JHA, 4 March 1996, para 5.1.2.
3   [1996] AC 742, [1996] 2 WLR 766, sub nom *T v Secretary of State for the Home Department* [1996] Imm AR 443.
4   *Chahal v UK* (1996) 23 EHRR 413; see chapter 8 above.

Persecution by non-state agents

12.51 The *Handbook* states that although:

> 'persecution is normally related to action by the authorities of a country [it] may also emanate from sections of the population that do not respect the standards established by the laws of the country concerned . . . where serious discriminatory or other offensive acts are committed by the local populace, they can be considered as persecution if they are knowingly tolerated by the authorities, or if the authorities refuse, or prove unable, to offer effective protection'.[1]

The authorities of a country include regional or local government, or parties which control the state. Where legal authority is breaking down, anyone purporting to exercise government authority may be an agent of persecution, whether the state is legally recognised internationally or not. The security forces of a country do not cease to be agents of official persecution merely because it is not the policy of central government to persecute the victims in question.[2] It is equally persecution when the authorities condone, tolerate or fail to protect against persecution by one section of the population against another. In *Jeyakumaran*[3] Tamils resident in Colombo were the victims of reprisal by the local Sinhalese population and received no protection from the state. The High Court held it irrelevant to the merits of the claim that the victims were not 'singled out' for persecution by the government. The House of Lords in *Adan and Aitseguer*[4] affirmed the principle established in *Ward*[5] and *Adan v Secretary of State for the Home Department*[6] that the autonomous meaning of 'persecution' does not limit the concept to conduct which can be attributed to a state, but includes circumstances where the state is not complicit in the persecution, whether because it is unwilling or unable to afford protection.[7]

1   UNHCR *Handbook* **12.13** above, para 65.
2   Hathaway **12.21** fn 2 above, para 4.5.1; *R v Secretary of State for the Home Department, ex p Chahal* [1995] 1 WLR 526 at 536, per Staughton LJ.
3   *R v Secretary of State for the Home Department, ex p Jeyakumaran* [1994] Imm AR 45.
4   *R v Secretary of State for the Home Department, ex p Adan, R v Secretary of State for the Home Department, ex p Aitseguer* [2001] INLR 44, HL.
5   *A-G of Canada v Ward* (1993) 103 DLR (4th) 1, [1993] 2 SCR 689, [1997] INLR 42, Canada Sup Ct.
6   *Adan v Secretary of State for the Home Department* [1999] 1 AC 293 at 305-306: 'if for whatever reason the state is unable to afford protection against factions within the state, the qualifications for refugee status are complete.'
7   Lord Steyn in *Adan and Aitseguer* disapproved the EU Joint Position of 4 March 1996 96/196/JHA para 5.2 on this point.

12.52 The appellant in *Horvath*[1] was a Roma from Slovakia who feared persecution by skinheads against whom, he said, the Slovak police were unable to provide protection. He also alleged discrimination in the field of employment, the right to marry and education. The principal focus of the judgments in the House of Lords was on whether the word 'persecution' denotes merely sufficiently serious ill-treatment, or sufficiently severe ill-treatment against which the state fails to afford protection. The House of Lords upheld the Tribunal's conclusion that the fear of violence at the hands of non-state agents was not a fear of 'persecution', since the authorities were neither involved nor failed to provide a 'sufficiency of protection'.[2] In the leading judgment, Lord Hope pointed out that:

> 'the obligation to afford refugee status arises only if the person's own state is unable or unwilling to discharge its own duty to protect its own nationals ... to satisfy the 'fear' test in a non-state agent case, the applicant must show that the persecution which he fears consists of acts of violence or ill-treatment against which the state is unable or unwilling to provide protection. The applicant may have a well-founded fear of threats to his life due to famine or civil war or of isolated acts of violence *or of ill-treatment for a Convention reason which may be perpetrated against him*. But the risk, however severe, and the fear, however well-founded, do not entitle him to the status of refugee. The Convention has a more limited objective, the limits of which are identified by the list of Convention reasons and by the principle of surrogacy.'[3]

He thus assimilated ill-treatment for a Refugee Convention reason with famine and civil war, and concluded that ill-treatment for a Convention reason does not amount to persecution unless there is a failure of state protection. This was the majority view. Lord Lloyd disagreed with this approach, holding that the ordinary meaning of the word 'persecution' does not involve a failure of state protection. 'The text of the Convention does not suggest that anything other than the ordinary meaning should be used, nor is there any hint that the failure of state protection is an ingredient in the meaning of the word.'[4] We agree.

1   *Horvath v Secretary of State for the Home Department* [2000] INLR 239, HL.
2   [1999] INLR 7. There had been a line of Tribunal decisions on what was a 'sufficiency of protection' which would disqualify the victim of non-state persecution from international protection: see eg *Jaworski* (17152); *Debrah* [1998] INLR 383; *Chinder Singh* [1998] Imm AR 551; *Mojka* (18265); *Dymiter* (18467).
3   *Horvath* above, at 247-248. Our emphasis.
4   *Horvath* above at 251-252.

12.53 The standard of protection which disqualifies victims of non-state violence from international protection is not one which would eliminate all risk; rather, it is a 'practical standard' taking proper account of the duty owed by the state to all its own nationals. Lord Clyde cited the ECHR case of *Osman*[1] to the effect that the obligation to protect must not be so interpreted as to impose an impossible or disproportionate burden on the authorities. For him, what was required was 'a system of domestic protection and machinery for the detection, prosecution and punishment of actings contrary to the purposes which the Convention requires to have protected', and 'more importantly . . . an ability and a readiness to operate that machinery'.[2] He approved Stuart Smith LJ's formulation in the Court of Appeal:[3]

> 'There must be in force in the country in question a criminal law which makes the violent attacks by the persecutors punishable by sentences commensurate with the gravity of the crimes. The victims as a class must not be exempt from

the protection of the law. There must be a reasonable willingness by the law enforcement agencies, that is to say the police and courts, to detect, prosecute and punish offenders . . .'

Further, inefficiency and incompetence is not the same as unwillingness, there may be various sound reasons why criminals may not be brought to justice, and the corruption, sympathy or weakness of some individuals in the system of justice does not mean that the state is unwilling to afford protection. It will require cogent evidence that the state which is able to afford protection is unwilling to do so, especially in the case of a democracy.[4]

1   *Osman v UK* (1998) 29 EHRR 245.
2   *Horvath* **12.52** fn 1 above, at 259.
3   [2000] INLR 15, para 22.
4   *Horvath* **12.52** fn 1 above, at 260A-D.

12.54   A further question considered in *Horvath* concerned the phrase 'unwilling, owing to such fear, to avail himself of the protection' of the country of nationality, and its application to non-state cases. Lord Hope considered that the fear which prevented recourse to state protection in such cases had to be fear of reprisals from the persecutors. In other words, the fear had to be a well-founded fear of being persecuted *because* he or she had sought the state's protection.[1]

1   *Horvath* **12.52** fn 1 above. Lord Hope and Lord Clyde delivered the two main judgments. Lord Hobhouse agreed with Lord Hope (266G); Lord Browne-Wilkinson (249G) agreed with Lords Hope and Clyde. Lord Lloyd (249H-256D) disagreed with the majority on the first question.

12.55   The majority in *Horvath* have, we believe, adopted a strained and difficult definition of 'persecution' in non-state cases which could lead to the rejection of cases deserving of international protection.[1] The test for sufficiency of protection has moved perilously close to the 'attribution' test rejected by the Lords in *Adan and Aitseguer*.[2] New Zealand's Refugee Status Appeals Authority has suggested[3] that the House of Lords' decision in *Horvath* enables an individual to be returned to his or her country of origin notwithstanding a well-founded fear of persecution for a Convention reason, and has commented that:

'[T]his interpretation of the Refugee Convention is at odds with the fundamental obligation of non-refoulement . . . [which] cannot be avoided by a process of interpretation which measures the sufficiency of state protection not against the absence of a real risk of persecution, but against the availability of a system for the protection of the citizen and a reasonable willingness by the state to operate that system. The point which emerges from *Ward* is that the refugee inquiry is not an inquiry into blame. Rather the purpose of refugee law is to identify those who have a well-founded fear of persecution for a Convention reason. If the net result of a state's 'reasonable willingness' to operate a system for the protection of the citizen is that it is incapable of preventing a real chance of persecution of a particular individual, refugee status cannot be denied that individual. The persecuted clearly do not enjoy the protection of their country of origin.'

1   The House of Lords accepted that persons with a well-founded fear of serious harm for a Convention reason – like the Slovakian Roma family in the case before them—would not, on their formulation, be entitled to protection, because the state is 'reasonably willing' to operate the machinery of protection: see below; so what the family fears is not 'persecution'.
2   The attribution test confines persecution to conduct which can be attributed to a state. *R v Secretary of State for the Home Department, ex p Adan, R v Secretary of State for the Home Department, ex p Aitseguer* [2001] INLR 44, HL, see **12.51** above.

3 Refugee Appeal No. 71427/99 [2000] INLR 608 (R P G Haines QC and L Tremewan), NZRSAA.

12.56 However, in post-*Horvath* cases, the courts and the Tribunal have made it clear that, while it will always be relevant to ask whether or not there is in general sufficiency of protection in a country, the crucial question remains whether there is a reasonable likelihood of Convention persecution in the individual case.[1] The axiom of refugee determination, that one examines both the general situation and the situation of the individual claimant, does not lose force simply because the focus of the examination is the protection issue.[2] In *Noune* the Court of Appeal held that if a decision-maker interpreted *Horvath* to mean that where the law enforcement agencies are doing their best and are not being either generally inefficient or incompetent, this was enough to disqualify a potential victim from being a refugee, this interpretation would be an error of law.[3] The Tribunal has held that the crucial part of any case involving non-state agents is precisely where the general system of protection in force is tested against how it actually worked in the individual case.[4] Jews targeted by anti-Semites in Russia and Roma from the Czech Republic and some areas of Poland have been held to be refugees.[5]

1 *Souad Noune v Secretary of State for the Home Department* (CO 2000/2669), 6 December 2000, CA (Algerian civil servant targeted by Islamists); *Koudriachov* (00 TH 02254) (Jews and their families in Russia).
2 Refugee Appeal No 71427/99, above.
3 *Souad Noune* above, at para 28, per Schiemann LJ.
4 *Harangova* (00 TH 01325) 8 November 2000.
5 *Doudetski* (00 TH 01768); *Koudriachov* above; *Franczak* CC-10255-00. In *Harakal v Secretary of State for the Home Department*, 10 May 2001, the CA allowing a Czech Roma appeal, held that it was not necessary to have exhausted all possible domestic remedies to demonstrate failure of protection.

12.57 In *Fadli*[1] the Court of Appeal held that the risk to a soldier or ex-soldier of being killed by a terrorist group was not a risk of persecution for a Refugee Convention reason. The reasoning of the court was that the Convention does not distinguish between soldiers engaged on the battlefield in combat against others observing the rules of war and those engaged on internal security duties against terrorists who breach the laws of war. It held that to allow soldiers' claims for asylum based on the failure of the state to provide practical protection to the soldiers would strengthen the terrorists' hand and 'hinder the home state in providing the very protection for the generality of its citizens which the definition of refugee in the Convention assumes that the home state should provide'.

1 *R (Fadli) v Secretary of State for the Home Department* [2001] 02 LS Gaz R 40, CA.

Civil war

12.58 The House of Lords held in *Adan and Aitseguer*[1] that for someone to qualify for refugee status, there need be no effective state authority and that the state does not have to encourage or tolerate the feared persecution.[2] The inability of the state to provide protection against Convention persecution, for any reason, including civil war or internal armed conflict, founds refugee status. But in an earlier *Adan* case,[3] the House of Lords, reversing the Court of Appeal, held that:

'the language of the Convention did not apply to those caught up in a civil war where law and order had broken down and every group was fighting some other group or groups in an endeavour to gain power. What the members of each group may have is a well-founded fear not so much of persecution by other groups as of death or injury or loss of freedom due to the fighting between the groups. In such a situation the individual or group has to show a well-founded fear of persecution over and above the risk to life and liberty inherent in the civil war'.[4]

Lord Lloyd referred to it as 'differential impact'.[5]

1   *R v Secretary of State for the Home Department, ex p Adan, ex p Aitseguer* [2001] INLR 44, HL.
2   The former was the situation in Somalia in *Adan*, the latter in Algeria in *Aitseguer*.
3   *Secretary of State for the Home Department v Adan* [1999] 1 AC 293, [1998] Imm AR 338, [1998] INLR 325, HL.
4   *Adan* above [1998] INLR 325 at 327, per Lord Slynn.
5   *Adan* above [1998] INLR 325 at 336.

12.59   The decision in *Adan* is hard to comprehend where the basis of the civil war (and therefore the risk of persecution) is a Convention reason. In the Court of Appeal Simon Brown LJ appreciated the 'floodgates' consequences of holding that all who may be identified with the interests of either side are potential refugees, but considered that his conclusion more faithfully reflected the Convention and gave better effect to its broad humanitarian instincts.[1] We agree. If a refugee claimant from a civil war is at risk of persecution because of his or her race, it is not legitimate to ignore that fact simply because the source of the risk is a civil war, and to require a fear of something over and above 'the ordinary risks of clan warfare'. Once the claimant has shown a real risk of persecution for reasons of one of the five Convention reasons he or she is a refugee and nothing more can be required.[2]   The danger inherent in the House of Lords' approach is that it reintroduces in a civil war situation the requirement of being 'singled out'.[3]

The Canadian case of *Salibian* on which Lord Lloyd relied[4] supports this proposition.

1   [1997] Imm AR 251 at 264-265.
2   See decision of New Zealand Refugee Status Appeals Authority in Refugee Appeal No 71462/99 [2000] INLR 311, declining to follow *Adan* for these reasons (paras 67–86 at 328).
3   What the NZRSAA calls 'the old heresy ([2000] INLR 311, para 69), following Crawford and Hyndman 'Three heresies in the application of the Geneva Convention' (1989) 1 IJRL 155. The reasoning in *Adan* was also rejected by the full court of the Australian FCA in *MIMA v Abdi* (1999) 162 ALR 105; see also *MIMA v Ibrahim* [2000] HCA 55.
4   *Salibian v Canada (MEI)* [1990] 73 DLR (4th) 551.

12.60   It is important, however, to realise how limited the application of *Adan* is. Their Lordships were not concerned to exclude from the refugee definition those at risk of death, torture or imprisonment on suspicion of siding with one party in territory under the effective control of the other. They are concerned only with a situation where 'the fear is felt indiscriminately by all citizens as a consequence of the civil war', or where law and order have completely broken down[1] and state authority has ceased to exist, as in Somalia in the circumstances of that case.[2] Lord Lloyd, citing Goodwin-Gill,[3] contrasted the civil war in Somalia with that in Liberia 'on the ground that in the former country none of the competing clans has yet emerged *as an authority in fact, controlling territory and possessing a minimum of organisation*'.[4] The distinction reflects the rules of international law on the recognition of a government of a state.[5] *Adan* does not apply, for example, to Sri Lanka, Algeria or Angola, where, although engaged against insurrectionary movements, fully functioning states continue to exist.[6]

1 *Adan* above, at 327H–328A, per Lord Slynn (**12.58** above).
2 In *R v Secretary of State for the Home Department, ex p Aitsegeur* at first instance, 18 December 1998, Sullivan J held *Adan* applicable in civil war situations 'where state authority had ceased to exist', and in *R v Secretary of State for the Home Department, ex p Lul Adan* [1999] INLR 84, the Secretary of State for the Home Department accepted that it applied to situations 'where civil war has destroyed state authority'
3 Goodwin-Gill **12.5** fn 1 above, p 76.
4 *Adan* above at 336.
5 See *Republic of Somalia v Woodhouse, Drake & Carey (Suisse) SA* [1993] QB 54 where Hobhouse J held (at 67-68) that factors to be taken into account in recognition were (a) whether it is the constitutional government of the state; (b) the degree, nature and stability of administrative control, if any, that it exercises over the territory of the state; (c) whether Her Majesty's Government has any dealings with it and if so the nature of those dealings; and (d) in marginal cases, the extent of international recognition that it has as the government of the state.
6 See, for example, *Matondo v Secretary of State for the Home Department*, 15 March 1999, where leave to appeal was granted against a Tribunal decision purporting to apply *Adan* to the situation in Angola. The appeal was allowed by consent on the appellant being recognised as a refugee. But see *Kibiti v Secretary of State for the Home Department* [2000] Imm AR 594, CA, where the Immigration Appeal Tribunal's application of *Adan* to Congo was upheld. See also Theodor Meron *Human Rights in Internal Strife* (1987); von Sternberg 'Political Asylum and the Law of Internal Armed Conflict' (1993) 5(2) IJRL 153. See also UNHCR Executive Committee Conclusion (October 1994) (1995) 7(1) IJRL 142; and decision of German Constitutional Court in a Bosnian case: (1995) 7(1) IJRL case 226.

'For reasons of'

12.61 The definition of refugee requires consideration of the reasons for the persecution. It is not enough to face persecution; it must be connected to one of the reasons assigned by the Refugee Convention. The issue of causation raises difficult questions. Should the proper focus of attention be the fear of the applicant or the motives of the persecutor? To what extent does the motivation of the persecutor need to be established? Persecutory conduct may have more than one motive, and it is established that so long one motive is a Convention ground, the requirement is satisfied.[1] It is not necessary that the Convention ground is the sole reason for the fear.[2]

1 *Harpinder Singh v Ilchert* 63 F 3d at 1501 (US 9th Cir).
2 *Jahazi v MIEA* (1995) 133 ALR 437, 443 (French J); approved in *MIMA v Abdi* (1999) 162 ALR 105, 112 (FC).

12.62 The humanitarian obligation is to be interpreted broadly: a refugee may well not be aware of the reasons for the persecution, and it is not his or her duty to identify or analyse the reasons in detail.[1] The focus therefore is on the acts of the persecutors. Thus a person who is not in fact involved in any political opposition to the government may nevertheless be persecuted by the government for perceived or imputed opinions.[2] The Convention ground does not have to be the sole cause of the persecution,[3] and the fact that the persecutor may have some ulterior motive, such as suppression of disorder or terrorism, does not necessarily remove it from the realm of Convention persecution if acts of sufficient gravity are done against a person or group identified by race, religion, nationality, social group or political opinion.[4] The test of Canadian law is whether the applicant's personal status exposes him or her to heightened risk so that persecution would not arise *but for* race, religion or another Convention ground. Other international cases adopt the approach of whether the persecution is 'related' to Convention reasons.[5]

1   UNHCR *Handbook* **12.13** above, para 66.
2   *Asante* [1991] Imm AR 78; *R v Secretary of State for the Home Department and Special Adjudicators, ex p Stefan, Chiper and Ionel* [1995] Imm AR 410 at 413. See also *Ward v A-G Canada* [1993] 2 SCR 689.
3   Hathaway **12.21** fn 2 above, p 140. See also *Harpinder Singh v Ilchert* 63 F 3d at 1501 (US 9th Cir), and the Australian cases of *Jahazi v MIEA* (1995) 133 ALR 437, 443 (French, J) and *MIMA v Abdi* (1999) 162 ALR 105, 112 (FC; FC).
4   *Sandralingham and Ravichandaran* [1996] Imm AR 97 at 109. See also (1993) 5(2) IJRL 154: sexual abuse linked to political opinion or other characteristics; (1993) 5(3) IJRL, Case 161 *Veeravagu v Canada* (1992) FCJ No 468 where the Canadian Court of Appeal held that irrespective of whether young Tamils constituted a social group there was racial persecution if a person faced real risk of oppression because he belonged to a group one of whose defining characteristics was race.
5   See (1992) 4(2) IRJL, Case 109, Case 110; (1993) 5(2) IJRL, Case 154.

12.63   The issue of causation was considered by the House of Lords in *Shah and Islam*[1] where Lord Hoffmann rejected the Canadian 'but for' test[2] as too simplistic and noted that the meaning of any statutory notion of causation depends on the context. He gave the example of women vulnerable to sexually motivated attacks by marauding men during a time of civil unrest. While the *but for* test would be satisfied (the women would not be subject to rape but for their gender), in a context where attacks and failure of protection alike were indiscriminate, their treatment was not *for reasons of* their gender. By contrast, a Jew in Germany in 1935 who was punished for contravening racial laws (by failing to wear a yellow star) was persecuted on ground of race; so was a Jewish shopkeeper attacked for reasons of commercial rivalry in a climate of impunity, because the authorities' failure to provide protection was based on race.

1   *R v Immigration Appeal Tribunal, Secretary of State for the Home Department, ex p Shah; Islam v Immigration Appeal Tribunal* [1999] 2 AC 629, [1999] INLR 144.
2   Ie the women would not have feared persecution *but for* their gender: see above.

12.64   In *Shah and Islam* the House of Lords used the touchstone of discrimination in deciding that the women's persecution was for reasons of their membership of the particular social group (Pakistani women). The House concluded that a fundamental purpose of the Refugee Convention was counteracting discrimination[1] and that the concept of discrimination was central to an understanding of the Convention.[2] It was concerned with persecution based on discrimination, or with making distinctions inconsistent with the right of every human being to equal treatment and respect. All Convention reasons are grounds upon which a person may be discriminated against by society.[3] Persecution must be discriminatory.[4] In the light of this formidable array of authority it is difficult to assert that discrimination is not necessary in establishing causation.[5] Where there is evidence of discrimination, it will not be difficult to establish the necessary causal link between the fear and the Convention reason. But it will not always be necessary to prove conscious discrimination by the persecutor. In *Omoruyi*[6] the facts of the case meant that there needed to be an element of conscious discrimination, because the case concerned the motives of a criminal gang. It did not deal with state persecution. In his judgment Simon Brown LJ suggested that some element of conscious discrimination, based on a Convention reason, is a necessary ingredient of

Convention persecution. But he also noted that 'discrimination, *at least in the sense that the substantive law or its enforcement in practice bears unequally upon different people or different groups,*[7] is essential to the concept of persecution under the Convention'. This objective approach, looking at the discriminatory impact of persecutory laws or practices, is in line with UK domestic law in the context of the Race Relations and Sex Discrimination Acts.[8] In *Sepet and Bulbul*[9] the Court of Appeal held that conscious discrimination was not a necessary element of persecution for a Convention reason, although it would be strong evidence of it.

1 [1999] INLR 144 at 150E, per Lord Steyn.
2 [1999] INLR at 161G-H, per Lord Hoffmann.
3 [1999] INLR, per Lord Hope.
4 [1999] INLR at 170A, per Lord Millett.
5 See Goodwin-Gill, in his commentary on *Shah and Islam* in (1999) 11 IJRL.
6 *Omoruyi v Secretary of State for the Home Department* [2001] Imm AR 175, CA.
7 Our emphasis.
8 These laws recognise direct and indirect discrimination, and the case law makes it clear that direct discrimination does not need to be conscious or intentional: *Nagarajan v London Regional Transport* [1999] IRLR 572, HL; *R v Birmingham City Council, ex p Equal Opportunities Commission* [1989] IRLR 173, HL; *James v Eastleigh Borough Council* [1990] IRLR 288, HL; *Pereira v Civil Service* [1982] IRLR 147, EAT.
9 *Sepet and Bulbul v Secretary of State for the Home Department* [2001] EWCA Civ 681.

12.65 The Australian High Court has held that proof of the persecutor's motives is unnecessary. *Chen Shi Hai*[1] concerned a Chinese child born in contravention of the one-child policy and likely to be denied access to food, shelter, medical treatment and education under Chinese law. The Court decisively rejected any requirement of personal animus, enmity or malignancy to the Refugee Convention attribute as a necessary ingredient of causation.[2] Such attribution, it held, 'risks a fictitious personification of the abstract and the impersonal'. The Court also took into account the extreme difficulty or impossibility of an inquiry into the motives and feelings of the alleged persecutors in a foreign country.[3] It rejected any formula, rule or principle which could be substituted for the Convention language. As Kirby J said, 'In the end it is necessary . . . to return to the broad expression of the Convention . . . the decision-maker must evaluate the postulated connection between the asserted fear of persecution and the ground suggested to give rise to the fear.'

1 *Chen Shi Hai v MIMA*, Aust HC [2000] INLR 455.
2 Goodwin-Gill does not accept that motivation is a necessary condition of persecution: *The Refugee in International Law* (2nd ed, 1996) pp 50–51.
3 *Chen Shi Hai v MIMA*, Aust HC [2000] INLR 455, para 64.

Race

12.66 A broad definition of race that includes membership of ethnic groups is to be adopted.[1] The EU Joint position[2] states that:

> 'persecution should be deemed to be founded on racial grounds where the persecutor regards the victim of his persecution as belonging to a racial group other than his own, by reason of a real or supposed difference, and this forms the grounds for his action.'

Article 1 of the Convention on the Elimination of All Forms of Racial Discrimination 1965 (CERD) defines 'racial discrimination' as 'any distinction, exclusion, restriction or preference based on race, colour, descent, or national or ethnic origin'. The House of Lords in *Shah and Islam*[3] emphasised that counteracting discrimination was a fundamental purpose of the Convention. Racial discrimination represents an important element in determining the existence of racial persecution, and may be a sufficient foundation for recognition if it affects human dignity to the extent of incompatibility with inalienable or elementary rights.[4]

1   *King-Ansell v Police* [1979] 2 NZLR 531, 533; *Sewa Singh Mandla v Dowell Lee* [1983] 2 AC 548 at 563-564.
2   EU Joint Position (96/196/JHA), 4 March 1996, para 7.1.
3   *R v Immigration Appeal Tribunal, Secretary of State for the Home Department, ex p Shah; Islam v Immigration Appeal Tribunal* [1999] 2 AC 629, [1999] INLR 144 at 150, per Lord Steyn.
4   UNHCR *Handbook* **12.13** above, paras 68–69.

Religion

12.67 Persecution may take the form of a total ban on worship and religious instruction, or severe discrimination in the profession of a religion which renders life unbearable.[1] Apostate Muslims who convert to Christianity have been held to have a well-founded fear of persecution on account of the severity of the penalties for conversion.[2] Punishment for proselytising has created difficulties. The Universal Declaration of Human Rights proclaims the right to manifest a religion in public, but a state has some margin of appreciation that would preclude causing offence to others.[3] A number of cases concern the Ahmadi sect, regarded as heretical by orthodox Pakistani Muslims, whose members are subjected to severe punishments for proselytising.[4] In *Iftikhar Ahmed* the Court of Appeal held that if an Ahmadi would proselytise on return and would therefore be at risk of persecution, a claim for refugee status would not be defeated on the basis that the claimant is inviting persecution and should refrain.[5] In so holding, the court put to rest the suggestion found in *Mendis*[6] and *Ahmad*,[7] that a claim could not be founded on deliberate conduct inviting persecution (at least where the conduct is an exercise of fundamental rights of freedom of conscience).[8] Punishment for conscientious objection to military service based on religious conviction could be Refugee Convention persecution.[9]

1   UNHCR *Handbook* **12.13** above, paras 71–73; EU Joint Position (above) para 7.2. Two German cases show that the link to religions need not be direct: in one, membership of a Christian social club was viewed with suspicion by the authorities (1993) 5 IJRL Case 164; similarly where an Iranian Muslim would face measures for having married a Catholic Polish woman: (1993) 5 IJRL Case 165.
2   *R v Secretary of State for the Home Department, ex p Kazmi* [1994] Imm AR 94, QBD. For a US decision that an Iranian convicted drug smuggler who converted to Christianity in prison had a well-founded fear, see (1993) 5 IJRL Case 220.
3   See the discussion of prosecution and persecution above. Religions which have proselytising as the essence of their witness will more rapidly lead to recognition *Ahmad v Secretary of State for the Home Department* [1990] Imm AR 61, CA, per Farquarson LJ. See also *Iftikhar Ahmed* below.
4   See *inter alia Ahmed* (12774); *Khan* (18982); *R v Secretary of State for the Home Department, ex p Arshad* (C/2000/5154) 14 July 2000, QBD.
5   *Iftikhar Ahmed v Secretary of State for the Home Department* [2000] INLR 1, reinstating the decision of a Special Adjudicator (reversed on appeal by the Tribunal on the grounds that the claimant should 'make some allowances for the situation in Pakistan and . . . exercise a measure of discretion in his conduct and in the profession of his faith').
6   *Mendis v Immigration Appeal Tribunal* [1989] Imm AR 6, CA.
7   *Ahmad* [1990] Imm AR 61.

8   See also *Danian v Secretary of State for the Home Department* [1999] INLR 533, CA.
9   *Kokkinakis v Greece* (1993) 17 EHRR 397; *Thrimmenos v Greece*, App 34369/97, see **8.66** fn 6 above. Cf *Sepet and Bulbul v Secretary of State for the Home Department* [2001] EWCA Civ 681.

Nationality

12.68 Like race, 'nationality' should be interpreted broadly to include a specific cultural or linguistic minority identifying itself as such.[1] The persecution of Gypsies may be on grounds of race or nationality.[2] Denial of full citizenship in a person's own country may ground refugee status if this puts him or her at risk of persecution.[3] The right to return is one of the normal incidents of 'nationality' and where citizens are arbitrarily deprived of their right to return this can amount to persecution (although there may be overlap with other Convention reasons in such cases).[4]

1   UNHCR *Handbook* **12.13** above, paras 74–76; EU Joint Position (above) para 7.3.
2   Nowadays it is more likely to be described as persecution on grounds of race or ethnicity. See eg *Harangova* (00 TH 01325) 8 November 2000; *Franczak* CC-10255-00. See *CRE v Dutton* [1989] QB 783, CA (Gypsies are an ethnic group for the purposes of the Race Relations Act 1976).
3   Hathaway **12.21** fn 2 above, p 144.
4   See *Adan, Lazarevic v Secretary of State for the Home Department* [1997] Imm AR 251, CA where Hutchison LJ stated that 'if a state arbitrarily excludes one of its citizens, thereby cutting him off from enjoyment of all those benefits and rights enjoyed by citizens and duties owed by a state to its citizens, there is in my view no difficulty in accepting that such conduct *can* amount to persecution' (at 272). Certain nationals of the former Yugoslavia have been denied the right to return to the Federal Republic of Yugoslavia (Serbia) since 1994. See eg *Stula* (14622), where a Tribunal found persecution by reason of the Federal Republic of Yugoslavia's deprivation of citizenship and the denial of her right to return. (The case was quashed by the CA on grounds not affecting the Tribunal's discussion of the principles.)

Political opinion

12.69 Freedom of expression is a core value of democratic societies,[1] and freedom of thought, conscience, opinion, expression, assembly and association are human rights protected by various international instruments.[2] These considerations, together with the need to adopt a broad purposive construction to all Refugee Convention grounds,[3] provide the context for the construction of the term 'political opinion'. For Goodwin-Gill, 'political opinion' covers 'any opinion on any matter in which the machinery of state, government and policy may be engaged',[4] while Hathaway defines political opinion as 'any action perceived to challenge governmental authority'.[5] The latter definition was approved by a 'starred' Tribunal in *Gomez*,[6] which involved a Colombian citizen who was threatened by guerrillas, after assisting a victim of extortion. At issue was whether, as a differently constituted tribunal found in *Acero-Garces*,[7] persecution by non-state actors of persons obstructing their aims and activities was for reasons of political opinion.[8] In the Colombian context, this involved scrutiny of the relationship between political and criminal activity. The Tribunal held that this was not necessarily so, in a decision which reviewed international jurisprudence. Looking at the definition of political opinion, the Tribunal in *Gomez* observed that where non-state actors are involved, the phrase had to be given 'a more inclusive, multi-sided definition' than one limited by reference to party politics[9] or to government or governmental authority,[10] but doubted whether it would embrace power relationships at all levels of society. Save in very unusual circumstances political opinion would not be established 'at the purely domestic or interpersonal level'.[11]

1 See *Handyside v UK* (1976) 1 EHRR 737.
2 See UDHR, arts 18-20; International Covenant on Civil and Political Rights, arts 19, 20, 21, 22; ECHR, arts 9-11.
3 *R v Secretary of State for the Home Department, Immigration Appeal Tribunal, ex p Shah; Islam v Immigration Appeal Tribunal* [1999] Imm AR 283 at 293, HL.
4 Hathaway **12.21** fn 2 above, p 49. The Tribunal in *Gomez (Emila del Socorro Gutierrez)* [2000] INLR 549 doubted whether the definition was wide enough.
5 Hathaway above, p 154.
6 *Gomez* above.
7 *Acero-Garces v Secretary of State for the Home Department* [1999] INLR 460; see also *Mezal* (14377).
8 *Gomez* above, para 4.
9 As in the 'classical' definition of Lord Diplock in *Cheng v Governor of Pentonville Prison* [1973] AC 931; *Gomez* above, para 28.
10 *Gomez* above, para 31ff, referring to *V v Minister for Immigration and Multicultural Affairs* [1999] FCA 428, Federal Court of Australia.
11 To engage the Refugee Convention, power relationships must in some way link up to the major power transactions that take place in government or related sectors such as industry and the media. Politics at the 'micro' level must be in some way relate to politics at the 'macro' level: *Gomez* above, para 38.

12.70 The Convention ground of political opinion refers both to the holding of the opinion and the expression of it.[1] Having an opinion implies the right to express it and persecution will not usually be alleged on the ground of having the opinion alone;[2] but political *action* or *activity,* although possibly an important indication of political opinion, are not necessary to found a claim.[3] Political opinion may be express, implied or imputed,[4] and in establishing an imputed political opinion it is not the persecutor's political opinions but those attributed, rightly or wrongly, to the victims which are considered.[5] Thus a civil servant accused of politically motivated sabotage may have been performing functions negligently rather than expressing a political opinion, but the imputation of such an opinion by persecutors would establish the Convention reason.[6] In *Ward* [7] the Supreme Court of Canada held that punishment of a former member of a terrorist political group for failing to execute hostages could amount to persecution for the political opinion that placed humanitarian obligation over the orders of the group.[8] In certain circumstances, as the Tribunal in *Gomez* recognised, neutrality may constitute a political opinion.[9] Trade union activists and those working against the power of organised cartels may have political opinions attributed to them in particular situations.[10] But there is no universal proposition that those on the side of law and order and justice who face persecution from non-state actors, be they guerrilla organisations or political or criminal gangs, will have a political opinion attributed to them.[11] All would depend on the relationship between crime and power in a particular country at a particular time.[12] While non-state actors would necessarily have political objectives, persecutors do not always attribute political opinions to victims or opponents,[13] and not all persecution by political groups is for political reasons; sometimes it is simple extortion of money or drugs.[14]

1 UNHCR *Handbook* **12.13** above, para 80ff.
2 UNHCR *Handbook* above, para 81.
3 *Minister of Immigration and Ethnic Affairs v Guo* (1997) 191 CLR 559, High Court of Australia; *Gomez (Emila del Socorro Gutierrez)* [2000] INLR 549, para 24; see also *Orlov* (18505).

4 See eg *Adan and Lazarevic v Secretary of State for the Home Department* [1997] Imm AR 251; *Secretary of State for the Home Department v Otchere* [1988] Imm AR 21; *Asante* [1991] Imm AR 78; *A-G (Canada) v Ward* [1993] 103 DLR (4th) 1, [1993] 2 SCR 689.
5 *Sanga v INS* 103 F 3d 1482 (9th Cir, 1997), US; *Allie* (14814); *Galvis* (22502).
6 See *Asante* [1991] Imm AR 21.
7 (1993) 103 DLR (4th) 1, [1993] 2 SCR 689, [1997] INLR 42.
8 Cited, together with *Klinko v Canada (Minister of Citizenship and Immigration)* 22 February 2000, FCA, in *Gomez* above, para 32.
9 *Sanga v INS* above.
10 *Gomez* above, paras 48, 51; *R v Secretary of State for the Home Department, ex p Walteros-Castenada* (CO/2383/99) 27 June 2000, QBD;
11 *Gomez* above, para 47. To this extent the Tribunal disapproved *Acero-Garces* (above).
12 In *Storozhenko* (19935) a Tribunal held that those on the side of law and order in the Ukraine would not have a political opinion imputed to them.
13 *Gomez* above, para 52.
14 *Gomez* above, at para 54; *R v Secretary of State for the Home Department, ex p Hernandez* [1994] Imm AR 506; *R v Secretary of State for the Home Department, ex p Gedrimas* [1999] Imm AR 486; *R v Special Adjudicator, ex p Sigitas Roznys* [2000] Imm AR 57; *Quijano* (10699); *Re Jeah* (Refugee Appeal No 2507/95), NZRSAA; *INS v Elias-Zacarias* 112 S Ct 812 (1992) (US).

12.71 Thus the term 'political opinion' needs to be a flexible one, since the boundaries between the political and the non-political will change in historical time and place.[1] What makes an opinion political is the social structure and social context of the asylum seeker's country of origin.[2] There is little doubt that feminism qualifies as a political opinion,[3] and the Home Office Asylum Policy Instructions recognise that 'if a woman resists gendered oppression, her resistance is political'.[4] Transgression of social roles and behaviour,[5] such as violation of dress codes in a fundamentalist Muslim country,[6] seeking exercise of a fundamental human right, as in the case of China's one-child policy, or unauthorised travel abroad, may establish a sufficient link with a political opinion, depending on all the circumstances.[7] Working in local government will not normally provide the basis of itself for the imputation of political opinions, although this may be the case where there is a major armed conflict between the authorities and guerrilla groups.[8] Similarly, there are no fixed distinctions between what is political and what is criminal,[9] nor between what is political and economic,[10] nor between actions motivated by personal interests and by political opinions.[11] A person who has not previously expressed his political dislike of the regime may be exposed by the very fact of flight and claiming asylum.[12] A claim may be based on the future expression of political opinion.[13]

1 The Refugee Convention is a living instrument constantly adapting to meet changing times: see Sedley J in *R v Immigration Appeal Tribunal, ex p Shah* [1997] Imm AR 145 at 152 and Schiemann LJ in *Jain v Secretary of State for the Home Department* [2000] INLR 71 at 77C.
2 Berkowitz and Jarvis *Immigration Appellate Authority Asylum Gender Guidelines* (Nov 2000) paras 3.18, 3.22ff.
3 *Fatin v INS* 12 F 3d 1233 (3rd Cir, 1993) (US).
4 API, Mar/01, Ch 1, s 2, para 9.5.
5 *Fathi and Ahmady* (14264).
6 *Re MN*, Refugee Appeal No 2039/93, 12 February 1996 (NZRSAA); *Gomez* **12.70** fn 3 above, para 40.
7 Canada: *Cheung v MEI* (1993) 102 DLR (4th) 214; *Chan v MEI* 128 DLR (4th) 213 SCJ; Australia: *Minister for Immigration and Ethnic Affairs v A* (24 February 1997, unreported); New Zealand: *Re ZWD Refugee Appeal 3/91* (20 October 1992). See also Goodwin-Gill **12.5**

fn 1 above, pp 52-53, 359. Gender guidelines for the application of the Refugee Convention to women who face compulsory abortions have been established in Canada, US, Australia and New Zealand as well as in the UK, although the ambit of the protection has proved politically controversial in the US and Australia. See *Asylum Gender Guidelines* above, para 2A.17.

8   *Gomez* above, para 40. See *Doufani* (14798) and *Woldemichael* (17663).
9   *Gomez* above, paras 41-42 and cases there discussed. Participation in a banned demonstration is clearly political rather than criminal: *R (Tientchu) v IAT*, 18 October 2000, CA.
10 *Gomez* above, para 43.
11 *Gomez* above, para 44
12 UNHCR *Handbook* **12.13** above, paras 82-83; Hathaway **12.21** fn 2 above, pp 149ff. See *Mbanza* [1996] Imm AR 136, CA: where the act of claiming asylum is perceived by a regime as expressing hostile political opinions towards it, the act of putting forward a baseless claim for asylum (and thereby establishing risk on return) could itself found a claim based on imputed political opinion.
13 *Omar v MIMA* [2000] FCA 1430, drawing on *Iftikhar Ahmed v Secretary of State for the Home Department* [2000] INLR 1; *Danian v Secretary of State for the Home Department* [2000] Imm AR 96; *MIMA v Mohammed* [2000] FCA 576, Fed CA (Aust).

Refusal to perform military service

12.72 Generally, those who claim refugee status on the basis of a refusal to perform military service[1] are not refugees *per se*, since a state may require compulsory military service of its nationals and prosecution and punishment arising from refusal may be seen not as persecution but as prosecution and punishment under a law of general application.[2] However, draft evaders and deserters are not excluded from refugee status either; the state's right to demand military service is not absolute and there are important exceptions to the general rule. Objection to military service may engage the Refugee Convention if the refusal to serve is treated as an expression of political opinion or religious conviction, or because conscientious objectors are part of a social group. It is certainly open to states to regard prosecution and punishment as persecutory if they override a genuine and deeply held conviction on conscientious or other principled grounds,[3] and the UK courts may follow suit, if they find that the right of conscientious objection to military service is now recognised as a fundamental human right.[4]

1   See generally UNHCR *Handbook* **12.13** above, paras 167–170; Hathaway **12.21** fn 2 above, pp 179–185; Goodwin-Gill, **12.5** fn 1 above pp 54–59.
2   UNHCR *Handbook* above, para 167.
3   UNHCR *Handbook* above, paras 168–172.
4   See **12.61**ff above.

12.73 In *Foughali*[1] the Tribunal analysed the principles and identified four broad exceptions to the general rule that draft evasion or desertion does not ground refugee status:

(i)   persecution due to the conditions of life in the military service in question;
(ii)   persecution due to the repugnant nature of military duty likely to be performed;
(iii)   persecution due solely to genuine political, religious or moral convictions, or to valid reasons of conscience;[2] and
(iv)   persecution due to likely disproportionate punishment.

Paragraphs (i), (ii) and (iv) are not in dispute. The area of contention is (iii), the CA having held in *Sepet and Bulbul* that it is not yet a proper basis for a finding of persecution.[3] Whilst the traditional conscientious objector (such as the pacifist

Quaker) may or may not yet have a right to object based on freedom of conscience which takes priority over the state's right to require performance of military service,[4] it is not only those who object absolutely, but also those who object to fighting on other principled grounds whose fundamental rights may or may not be violated by the requirement to perform military service. For example, they may object to the use of chemical weapons,[5] or to fighting an oppressed minority or their own people.[6] There is uncertainty, however, as to whether the holding of a genuine and principled objection to the performance of military service can of itself substantiate a claim. The language of the UNHCR's 1979 *Handbook on Procedures and Criteria for Determining Refugee Status* is somewhat cautious, merely stating that it is open to contracting states to grant refugee status to 'persons who object to performing military service for genuine reasons of conscience'.[7]

1 (00 TH 01513).
2 See UNHCR *Handbook* **12.13** above, para 170. Note in this context that the listing of particular types of conscientious objection has given way to what the Tribunal in *Foughali* described as 'a more flexible "compelling reasons of conscience"' definition. See eg Council of Europe Committee of Ministers Recommendation R(87)8; UN Commission on Human Rights report 2 March 1995, E/CN.4/1995/L.82, noting the general comment No 22(48) of the Human Rights Committee that 'there should be no differentiation between conscientious objectors on the basis of the nature of their particular beliefs'.
3 [2001] EWCA Civ 681.
4 See ECHR Art 9 or the views of Commission members in *Thlimmenos v Greece* (App 34369/97, 4 Dec 1998) at paras 44-45.
5 *Zolfagharkani v Canada* [1993] 3 FC 540.
6 *Ciric v Canada* [1994] 2 CF 65.
7 See also Goodwin-Gill **12.5** fn 1 above, p 55ff.

12.74 In *Zaitz*[1] the Court of Appeal recognised that the appellant, a Polish national asylum seeker sentenced to nine months' imprisonment for refusal to perform military service, was 'a genuine pacifist who for reasons of conscience considers military service to be anathema'. The court stated, without the matter being argued, that the right to hold a conscientious objection to the performance of military service was a 'primary' right which had to be protected under the Refugee Convention. Once a conscientious objection was established, a well-founded fear of persecution could arise without any need to consider the proportionality of punishment.[2]

1 *Zaitz v Secretary of State for the Home Department* [2000] INLR 346.
2 *Zaitz* above, para 33.

12.75 In *Sepet and Bulbul*,[1] a case involving Turkish Kurds who objected to performing military service because it was likely to involve fighting fellow Kurds, the Tribunal dismissed the appeals on the ground that they could not properly consider the appellants' objection because it was partial and contained unacceptable discrimination against non-Kurds. In the CA,[2] the Tribunal decision was upheld, but on quite different grounds. First, the Court held that, in order for prosecution for refusal to bear arms to amount to persecution, a right to conscientious objection had to have become a recognised fundamental human right and the majority held it had not. Secondly, if it was such a right, it was not necessary to prove that the prosecuting state was motivated by a Convention reason to prosecute and punish the objectors. Punishment for the assertion of rights by the objector could be seen as persecution for a political reason.

1 *Sepet and Bulbul* [2000] Imm AR 455, IAT.
2 [2001] EWCA Civ 681.

12.76 In *Adan and Lazarevic*[1] the Court of Appeal stated that a person who faces prosecution for a genuine objection to the performance of military service involving action contrary to basic rules of human conduct is expressing a political opinion and is a refugee.[2] Although paragraph 171 of the UNHCR *Handbook* refers to military action 'condemned by the international community', proof of condemnation is not required, but the phrase indicates the need for evidence of the abhorrent nature of the military action.[3] The Canadian case of *Zolfagharkani*[4] is authority for the proposition that the applicant does not have to prove actual participation in acts contrary to Article 1F of the Refugee Convention, if the army he or she refuses to join carries out such acts.

1   *Adan, Lazarevic v Secretary of State for the Home Department* [1997] 1 WLR 1107. See further *Altun v Secretary of State for the Home Department* (1999/0845/C), 28 January 2000, where the Court of Appeal accepted that the interpretation of art 1A(2) of the Refugee Convention required recognition in such circumstances.
2   UNHCR *Handbook* 12.13 above, para 171. See also (in the context of the Yugoslavian conflicts) *Azapovic* (13611) and *Drvis* (13129); *Tallah* [1998] INLR 258 (Algeria); *Zolfagarkhani v Canada* [1993] 3 FC 540 (use of chemical weapons in Iran-Iraq war).
3   See *Sepet and Bulbul* [2000] Imm AR 455, paras 61-62.
4   [1993] 3 FC 540 above.

12.77 It will always be important for asylum seekers who base their claims on a wish to avoid the performance of military service to give detailed and cogent evidence.[1] In *Adan and Lazarevic*[2] the issue was whether refugee status could be granted to draft evaders from an army engaged in an internationally condemned conflict, regardless of whether their objection to fighting was genuine or (as the adjudicator had found) opportunistic. Hutchison LJ held that the fact that they were opportunists and not genuine objectors was fatal to their claim.

1   See eg UNHCR *Handbook* 12.13 above, para 174, referring to the need for 'a thorough investigation of . . . personality and background' to establish the genuineness of the objection. Adjudicators tend to draw adverse conclusions on credibility more readily where the appellant's views are not explained in detail. See also *Kulet* (00 TH 00391).
2   *Adan and Lazarevic v Secretary of State for the Home Department* [1997] Imm AR 251, CA above

Membership of a particular social group

12.78 This last category has been the most litigated of all the Refugee Convention reasons and the one where the necessity to see the Convention as a living thing, constant in motive but mutable in form,[1] is most apparent. The cases have raised controversial issues as to the limits of Convention protection. However, those limits can be stated with a far greater degree of certainty following *Shah and Islam*[2] in which the House of Lords held that women in Pakistan constituted a particular social group. Lord Steyn approved the following passage from the decision of the US Board of Immigration Appeals in *Acosta*:[3]

> 'We find the well-established doctrine of *ejusdem generis* . . . to be most helpful in construing the phrase . . . Each of [the other grounds] describes persecution aimed at an immutable characteristic: a characteristic that either is beyond the power of an individual to change or is so fundamental to individual identity or conscience that it ought not to be required to be changed . . .
> Applying the doctrine of *ejusdem generis*, we interpret the phrase . . . to mean persecution that is directed toward an individual who is a member of a group of persons all of whom share a common, immutable characteristic. The

shared characteristic might be an innate one such as sex, colour, or kinship ties, or in some circumstances it might be a shared experience such as former military leadership or land ownership . . . By construing [the phrase] in this manner we preserve the concept that refugee status is restricted to individuals who are either unable by their own actions, or as a matter of conscience should not be required, to avoid persecution.'[4]

Whether a number of people sharing particular characteristics constitute a 'particular social group' depends on the factual situation in the particular country. Westernised women may be seen as a distinct social group in the Middle East but not in Israel, just as landowners were such a group in pre-revolutionary Russia but would not be in England today.[5] The following underlying principles emerge from the judgments:

(i)   interpretation of the phrase 'particular social group' must be seen in the context of the fundamental purpose of the Refugee Convention of counteracting discrimination;[6]

(ii)   the social group must exist independently of, and not be defined by, the persecution, otherwise anyone persecuted for whatever reason would qualify;[7]

(iii)   however, this does not mean that discrimination against members is irrelevant as a means of identifying the group.[8] On the contrary, women in Pakistan were held to be a particular social group precisely because as a group distinguished by gender, they were discriminated against and unprotected by the state;[9]

(iv)   although cohesiveness may prove the existence of a particular social group, it is not a requirement for the existence of the group.[10]

1 *R v Immigration Appeal Tribunal and Secretary of State for the Home Department, ex p Shah* [1997] Imm AR 145 at 152, per Sedley J.
2 *R v Immigration Appeal Tribunal and Secretary of State for the Home Department, ex p Shah; Islam v Immigration Appeal Tribunal* [1999] 2 AC 629, [1999] Imm AR 283, [1999] INLR 144.
3 (1985) 19 I & N 211.
4 See also LA Forest J's (similar) formulation in *Ward* above.
5 *Shah and Islam* above, per Lord Millett.
6 [1999] INLR 144 at 150A–F, 161E–162D, 167B-C. In *A v MIEA* [1998] INLR 1 at 15, Dawson J said that where a persecutory law or practice applies to all members of society, it cannot create a particular social group consisting of all who bring themselves within its terms (referring to China's one-child policy).
7 [1999] INLR 144 at 151A–151C, 156D–G, 167C. But this does not mean that the actions of the persecutors cannot 'identify or even cause the creation of a particular social group in society': see Lord Steyn at 156D-G, endorsing McHugh J in *A v MIEA* [1998] INLR 1.
8 [1999] INLR 144 at 167E–F.
9 In the words of Lord Hoffmann, 'discrimination was the critical element in the persecution' ([1999] INLR 144 at 164H–165A).
10 Staughton LJ had held that cohesiveness (or interdependence or co-operation) was an essential prerequisite of a 'particular social group' in the Court of Appeal ([1998] INLR 97). Lord Steyn at 151D–154H and Lord Hoffmann at 162E–H rejected this ([1999] INLR 144), approving the decision of La Forest J in *Ward* (social group could include 'such bases as gender, linguistic background and sexual orientation'—none of which implied interdependence or co-operation).

12.79   Prior to *Shah and Islam* gender[1] had not been accepted in practice as the basis of a particular social group,[2] although it had been cited as one of the immutable characteristics which *could* found such a group in *Acosta* and *Ward*.

Particular sub-groups defined partly by gender and partly by another characteristic (such as transgressing social mores) had been recognised.[3] Women who faced compulsory sterilisation or abortion because of China's one-child policy had been held to be refugees on the grounds of social group[4] or political opinion.[5] A divorced Somali woman who had no effective state protection from abuse by her husband and whose daughter might face mutilation was recognised as a refugee.[6] Western-educated Afghani,[7] Algerian[8] and Iranian[9] women had been held to have a well-founded fear of persecution arising from Islamic opposition to their identities and way of life.[10] A number of Canadian decisions had recognised as refugees women fleeing domestic violence,[11] forced marriage[12] or sexual exploitation[13] from which their state would or could not protect them. Rape and severe sexual harassment had been recognised in some cases as constituting Convention persecution,[14] and the Home Office had recognised that rape, forcible abortion, forcible sterilisation, acts involving genital mutilation or allied practices 'probably always' constitute torture.[15] But gender-based social groups had been rejected in a number of cases.[16]

1 See for discussion of gender persecution UNHCR Symposium on Gender-based Persecution, February 1996, IJRL (Autumn 1997); H Crawley *Women as Asylum Seekers: A legal handbook* (1993); 'Women as a social group: Recognising sex-based persecution as grounds for asylum' (1998) 20(1) HRLR 203; Kelly 'Guidelines for Women's Asylum Claims' (1994) 6(4) IJRL 517. The Canadian Board's Guidelines on Gender Related Persecution are reproduced in (1993) 5(2) IJRL 278, 240. See now Berkowitz and Jarvis *Immigration Appellate Authority Asylum Gender Guidelines* (Nov 2000).

2 UNHCR's Executive Committee had issued a recommendation, No 39 of 1985, indicating that states *could* recognise women at risk for transgressing social mores as refugees; see also UNHCR *Guidelines on the Protection of Refugee Women* (1991) paras 54–57; Canadian Immigration and Refugee Board Guidelines above; US INS *Considerations for Asylum Officers Adjudicating Asylum Claims from Women* (May 1995); Australian Dept of Imm and Multicultural Affairs, Refugee and Humanitarian Visa applicants *Guidelines on Gender Issues for Decision Makers* (July 1996).

3 See UNHCR ExCom conclusion 39 (1985) above.

4 *Cheung v Minister of Immigration* (1993) FCJ No 309 digested in (1994) 6(1) 118, IJRL case 184. But contrast *Yu (Chang Zheng)* (15469) where a tribunal held that the one-child policy could not provide the basis of a social group. And see also *A v MIEA* [1997] 142 ALR 331, [1998] INLR 1, High Court of Australia: a husband and wife who feared forced sterilisation under the 'one-child policy' were not members of a social group. Lord Steyn in *Shah and Islam* ([1999] INLR 144 at 153B–D) said that the uniform application of the policy meant that there was 'no obvious element of discrimination'.

5 *Guo v Carroll* 62 US Law Week 2473.

6 (1994) 6(4) IJRL 662 Case 207.

7 *Shaysta Ameer-Ali v Minister of Citizenship and Immigration* Imm-3404-95, 23 September 1996 (Can).

8 (1994) 6(4) IJRL Case 209.

9 (1993) 5(4) IJRL 611, Case 170.

10 See eg *Fatin v INS* 12 F 3d 1233; *Fisher v INS* 37 F 3d 1371.

11 *Mayers v Minister of Employment and Immigration* (1992) 97 DLR (4th) 729; *Narvaez v Canada* [1995] 2 CF 55; *Tahusi*, CRDD T9802494, 7 September 1999 (Georgia).

12 *Vidhani v Canada (Minister of Citizenship and Immigration)* TD Imm-3528-94, 8 June 1995.

13 *Cen v Canada (Minister of Citizenship and Immigration)* TD Imm-1023-95, 1995.

14 (1995) 5(4) IJRL 613 Case 173; (1994) 6(4) IJRL, Case 211; *Eustaquio Ransell* CRDD T98-04880, 20 October 1999 (Romania).

15 API Jul/98, Ch 3, para 2.1.

16 See eg *Khan (Nafees Parveen)* (15884) (unprotected Pakistani widow); *Safraz (Lubna)* (16179) (Pakistani woman at risk from husband); *Gomez v INS* 947 F 2d 660 (1991) (women previously raped by guerrillas).

12.80 Since *Shah and Islam* the Tribunal has upheld a number of gender-based claims, including: an Iranian woman who feared prosecution for adultery after leaving her violent husband;[1] a Pakistani woman whose illegitimate children would be seen as evidence of sexual immorality;[2] a single Pakistani woman without male protection at risk from the Mohajirs;[3] and a Ukrainian woman forced into prostitution.[4] In the latter case there was evidence that the Ukraine was 'an important source country of girls and women trafficked for sexual exploitation'. The particular social group was defined as 'women in the Ukraine forced into prostitution against their will', whose defining characteristics included gender and lack of state protection. On the other hand, attempts to establish Jaffna Tamil women at risk of arrest and rape in Colombo as a social group have failed for lack of evidence of 'differential gender victimisation'.[5] And a citizen of Latvia subjected to violent assault by her ex-husband was unable to establish a social group of Latvian ex-wives on the evidence, because of the system in place in Latvia to help battered wives.[6] Forced marriage[7] and domestic violence[8] have grounded claims in the US.[9]

1 *Fatemeh (Miriam)* (00 TH 00921) (for reasons mirroring those in *Shah and Islam*, given the similar position of women in Iran).
2 *Altaf (Robina)* (00 TH 01370). Cf *Babalola (Olayinka Adebukola)* (00 TH 00926) where the social group contended for was divorced women in Nigeria. But since the claimant could establish no well-founded fear of persecution, the tribunal did not consider the evidence on the position of divorced women in Nigeria.
3 *Begum (Syeda)* (21257).
4 *Dzhygun* (00 TH 00728).
5 See eg *Thangarajah (Vathana)* (16414) where the Tribunal held that Tamil women from Jaffna were not a social group because it was not established that they were being raped or sexually assaulted as such, nor with impunity; *Muralitharali* (B20813).
6 *Mortuleva* (00 TH 02064).
7 A76-512-001, Imm Ct Chicago, 18 October 2000.
8 *Aguirre-Cervantes v INS*, 21 March 2001, US CA (9th Cir).
9 See the comprehensive treatment of gender issues in H Crawley *Refugees and gender: law and process* (2001).

12.81 The decision in *Shah and Islam* also makes it clear that homosexuals may constitute a particular social group if, as a group defined by their sexuality (an immutable characteristic), they suffer discrimination.[1] There had been contradictory decisions of differently constituted Tribunals on this question.[2] In *Jain*[3] it was common ground before the Court of Appeal that homosexuals in India constitute a particular social group, since Indian law makes sodomy an offence, thus discriminating against the group on grounds of sexuality.[4] Since *Shah and Islam*, homosexuals in Romania have been held to constitute a particular social group because of the combination of societal and legal discrimination against them.[5]

1 [1999] INLR 144 per Lord Steyn at 154D-F; Lord Hoffmann at 162H; Lord Millett at 173F–H. Note Lord Steyn's express endorsement of the decision of the New Zealand Refugee Status Authority in *Re GJ* [1998] INLR 387.
2 See for example *Vrachiu* (11559); *Golchin* (7623); *Jacques* (11580); *Saddegh* (13124): see also *R v Secretary of State for the Home Department, ex p Binbasi* [1989] Imm AR 595 where the court had assumed, without deciding, that homosexuals could form a social group.
3 *Jain v Secretary of State for the Home Department* [2000] INLR 71.
4 Being a member of a particular social group does not, however, necessarily mean there is a well-founded fear of persecution, and the CA rejected the appeal in *Jain* for this reason.
5 In *Beteringhe* (18120), where the claim succeeded, and in *Dumitru* (00 TH 00945) where the claim failed on the facts, the Tribunal holding that the evidence fell short of establishing risk to homosexuals of a 'widespread and systematic pattern of abuses of their human rights'. See also in relation to Romania *Tanase* (16136), no well-founded fear of persecution on the facts, and *Vitali* (17528; remitted for assessment of risk where a presenting officer

accepted the existence of the social group), both pre-dating *Shah and Islam*. In *Apostolov* (18547) a Tribunal accepted that a Bulgarian homosexual was a member of a social group, although dismissing the appeal on the facts.

12.82 Although *Shah and Islam* resolved many issues of principle on particular social group, difficulties still occur in areas such as what characteristics are 'immutable', what is included in 'individual identity or conscience' and the relationship between persecution and the existence of the group. Previously, in *Savchenkov*,[1] the Court of Appeal had held that those refusing to join a Russian mafia were not a social group because they did not exist independently of the persecution feared. Attempts since *Shah and Islam* to persuade Tribunals to reach a different conclusion and to identify groups by reference to risks from criminal gangs or corrupt officials have failed on the same basis: civic conscience is not, in most cases, enough to constitute a particular social group.[2] In *Montoya*[3] the Tribunal summarised the jurisprudence on particular social groups, in the context of a claim by a landowner targeted by guerrillas in Columbia. In *Ouanes*[4] an Algerian government-employed midwife whose work involved giving advice on contraception (which put her at risk of persecution from fundamentalists) was held not to be employed in an occupation having 'that impact upon individual identities or conscience necessary to constitute employees a particular social group'. The court accepted that certain employments could reflect identity and conscience, citing membership of a religious order.[5] We suggest that this is an overly restrictive approach; many professions engage identity and conscience sufficiently to be capable of constituting a particular social group. Opportunist draft-evaders were held not to constitute a particular social group in *Lazarevic*.[6] 'Conscientious objectors', on the other hand, have been held in a number of cases to constitute a particular social group (their views are so fundamental to conscience that they ought not to be required to change). Refugees[7] have been held not to constitute a social group, although it is hard to see why not, if they suffer marginalisation and discrimination as a group defined by the shared experience of exile.

1   [1996] Imm AR 28, CA.
2   See eg *Storozhenko* (19935) (citizens of Ukraine conscientiously fulfilling their civic duty by seeking redress against the illegal actions of agents of the state are not a social group in the absence of discrimination or inability or unwillingness of the state to provide protection); *R v Immigration Appeal Tribunal, ex p Gedrimas* [1999] Imm AR 486 (Lithuanian businessmen at risk from Mafia not arguably a social group); *Jegorovas* (00 TH 00724) (adjudicator's acceptance as social group 'Lithuanians who challenge the power of the Mafia' reversed on appeal as group identified by persecution - there was no evidence of an identifiable group); *Stankeviciute* (00 TH 01321) (attempts by embezzling ex-mayor to have Lithuanian claimant killed was a private vendetta); *Kayani* (19646) (informants in Pakistan about suspected crimes and drugs criminals not a social group because such group defined only by persecution). See also *Diallo* (00 TH 01231) (wealthy educated Sierra Leonean mine owner not member of social group where there were no immutable characteristics and risk was from generalised effects of civil war). Cf *Osorio-Bonilla* (11451) (pre-*Shah and Islam*): those with criminal records *could* establish a social group if, because of their record, they were viewed by society in a particular way.
3   (00 TH 00161).
4   *R v Secretary of State for the Home Department, ex p Ouanes* [1998] Imm AR 76.
5   *Ouanes* above, at 82.
6   *R v Secretary of State for the Home Department, ex p Lazarevic* [1997] Imm AR 251, CA.
7   *R v Secretary of State for the Home Department, ex p Natando* Immigration Law Digest, Vol 1 no 4.

12.83 The family is the social group *par excellence*, and family membership may form the basis of a 'particular social group'.[1] The question which has emerged from the case law is whether it is enough to be persecuted because of membership of a family regardless of the reason for that family's original persecution, or whether another Convention reason must be behind the initial persecution. There are conflicting decisions. In *Ex p De Melo and De Arujo*[2] Laws J adopted the reasoning of the Tribunal in *Hernandez*[3] to the effect that although the murder of the head of the family by drug gangs might not be for a Convention reason, persecution of family members because of their family relationship to the dead man could be. He rejected the Secretary of State's argument that the non-Convention reason advanced against the principal continued to operate against the family, and concluded that membership of a social group was a distinct Convention reason and not a sub-group that had to be qualified by another Convention reason such as political opinion. The Court of Appeal in *Quijano*,[4] however, narrowed the application of the definition to exclude circumstances where ill-treatment of family members by a drug cartel was a fortuitous by-product of criminal activities, as likely to have been directed at employees as family members, and persecution was not therefore for reasons of membership of the family. Much depends on the reason for the targeting. Thus in *Jaramillo-Aponte*[5] (another case involving Colombian asylum seekers) a tribunal found Convention persecution because the claimants were at risk 'as members of the Escobar family'.

1   A kinship tie plainly is an immutable characteristic: see **12.78** above. A family as a social group was readily accepted by the Court of Appeal in *Quijano* below. See also *Kagedan*, CRDD A99-00215, 9 September 1999.
2   *R v Secretary of State for the Home Department ex p De Melo and De Arujo* [1997] Imm AR 43.
3   *Hernandez* (12773) was not followed by the Immigration Appeal Tribunal in *Quijano* (13693).
4   *Quijano v Secretary of State for the Home Department* [1997] Imm AR 227, upholding IAT (13693). See also *Obikwelu* (15343) where the claimant's child was at risk of sacrifice not as a member of the husband's family but for random and opportunistic reasons.
5   *Jaramillo-Aponte and Ayala* (00 TH 00428).

Cessation

12.84 A person who is a refugee may cease to qualify for international recognition if circumstances arise to bring about the operation of the cessation clauses of the Refugee Convention.[1] These are:

(i)   voluntary reavailment of protection of country of nationality;
(ii)   voluntary reacquisition of old nationality;
(iii)   acquisition of a new nationality and enjoyment of the protection of the country of new nationality;
(iv)   voluntary reestablishment in country where persecution was feared;
(v)   change of circumstances giving rise to recognition as a refugee.

1   Refugee Convention, art 1C.

12.85 Refugees who apply for and obtain a fresh passport from the authorities from whom they feared persecution may be acting inconsistently with their fear and raise the question of voluntary reavailment. They will have been granted a Refugee Convention travel document with which to travel abroad. If they voluntarily obtain a fresh passport from the country from which they fled, or entry permits with a view to returning there, they will be presumed to intend to avail themselves of their country's protection in the absence of proof to the contrary.[1] But renewal of a national passport without more does not automatically give rise to such a presumption.[2] If the country of asylum instructs individuals to apply for a national passport, that will not be counted against them as it would not be a voluntary reavailment of protection.[3] There may be circumstances beyond their control which require them to have recourse to some measure of protection. This may particularly arise when the refugee is awaiting recognition and has not yet received a Convention travel document or any other document issued by the country where asylum is claimed. Obtaining other official documents such as marriage or birth certificates is less likely to give rise to a presumption of voluntary reacquisition of protection.[4] Acquisition of a new nationality means cessation of status. But where the new nationality is lost, depending on the circumstances of the loss, refugee status may be revived.[5]

1 UNHCR *Handbook* **12.13** above, paras 120-124. See also *Thi Xuan Mai Phan*, Commission des recours des réfugiés, France, No 57165, 15 Sep 1989 (UNHCR Refworld) (obtaining national passport and using it for tourist visit was inconsistent with refugee status).
2 *Thevarayan*, Conseil d'Etat, France, No 78.055, 13 Jan 1989 (UNHCR Refworld).
3 UNHCR *Handbook* above, para 120.
4 UNHCR *Handbook* above, para 121; *Sellathurai Paramanathan*, Commission des recours des réfugiés No 247916, 7 July 1995 (going to Sri Lankan consulate in Singapore for documents in order to marry did not constitute 'reavailment of protection').
5 UNHCR *Handbook* above, para 132.

12.86 Questions of voluntary re-establishment may arise if refugees visit their country of nationality on their Refugee Convention travel document. There clearly is a risk that the country of asylum will regard that as evidence that there is no longer a well-founded fear of persecution. Where exceptional leave to remain has been granted for protection reasons, holders of such a status are also vulnerable to a cancellation of such leave and refusal of readmission to the UK.[1] A temporary visit, however, usually falls far short of reestablishment,[2] and before any inference of voluntary re-acquisition of protection is drawn, regard should be had to the particular circumstances, such as the need to visit sick relatives or business associates.[3]

1 See *R v Secretary of State for the Home Department, ex p Ibrahim Zib* [1993] Imm AR 350.
2 UNHCR *Handbook* **12.13** above, para 134; see also Decision A 1008308-479, 20 March 1992, Bundesamt für die Anerkennung ausländischer Flüchtlinge (brief visit to country of origin without notifying local authorities did not constitute reestablishment).
3 UNHCR *Handbook* above, para 125. See also Goodwin-Gill **12.5** fn 1 above, para 3.1, pp 80-83.

12.87 If the circumstances in the country of nationality or, in the case of stateless persons, former habitual residence, have so changed that refugees can no longer refuse to avail themselves of the protection of that country, Refugee Convention refugee status will cease.[1] This rule is subject to an exception in the case of what the Convention terms 'statutory refugees' (essentially, pre-1939 refugees), who do not lose refugee status 'where there are compelling reasons arising out of previous persecution for refusing to avail themselves' of such protection.[2] The UNHCR *Handbook* suggests that similar considerations could also apply to post-1951 refugees on the general humanitarian principle that those who have suffered particularly atrocious forms of persecution should never be expected to repatriate.[3] A cessation of circumstances refers to fundamental changes rather than merely transitory ones.[4] A refugee's status should not be subject to frequent review since this would jeopardise a sense of security which the Convention was designed to provide.[5] Proof that the circumstances of persecution have ceased to exist would fall upon the receiving state.[6] When the authority takes a long time to determine the claim of someone who would have been accepted as a refugee if the claim had been dealt with promptly, and circumstances change in the meantime, the Court of Appeal has held that the situation is analogous to Refugee Convention, Article 1C(5) cessation. The state bears an evidential burden to show that the change is sufficiently fundamental to deny status.[7] Cessation of refugee status will not automatically mean repatriation, since many refugees will have acquired settlement rights in their country of refuge.[8]

1 Refugee Convention, art 1C(5).
2 Refugee Convention, art 1C(5), para 2.
3 UNHCR *Handbook* **12.13** above, para 136.
4 UNHCR *Handbook* above, para 135. See eg Decision V97/07790, 31 March 1998, Refugee Review Tribunal (Aus) (Austlii website: see Appendix 2).
5 UNHCR *Handbook* above, para 135.
6 Hathaway **12.21** fn 2 above, p 199. 'In the absence of compelling evidence to the contrary it should not be inferred that the grounds for fear had dissipated . . . In the absence of facts indicating a material change in the state of affairs in the country of nationality, an applicant should not be compelled to provide justification for his continuing to possess a fear which he has established was well-founded at the time when he left the country of his nationality': *Chan v MIEA* (1989) 169 CLR 379 (Aus).
7 *Mohammed Arif v Secretary of State for the Home Department* [1999] INLR 327, CA. But see *Nabil Salim v Secretary of State for the Home Department* [2000] Imm AR 503, CA: this only applies where it is accepted that the applicant would have qualified as a refugee; see also *Dyli* [2000] Imm AR 652, IAT. See the discussion in Goodwin-Gill **12.5** fn 1 above, pp 86-87 and *Yusuf v Canada* [1995] FCJ No 35: the issue of changed circumstances is in danger of being elevated in a question of law, when at bottom it is simply one of fact; the fundamental issue is the possibility or risk of persecution.
8 See two German cases reported in (1995) 7(1) IJRL, Cases 218 and 224. In the latter case the change of regime in Ethiopia removed the claim to Convention persecution but expulsion was not permitted because there was still fighting that made a compulsory return contrary to art 3 of the ECHR.

Exclusion

12.88 The Refugee Convention will not apply to refugees in circumstances where protection of another state is unnecessary or the person is not deserving of protection. Article 1D of the Convention provides that refugees who are in receipt of assistance from a branch of the UN other than the UNHCR are outside the terms of the Convention until such assistance ceases.[1] This exclusion has to date been applied only to refugees under UN Relief and Works Agency (UNRWA) protection.[2] However, Article 1D has been held not to be exhaustive of all the circumstances in which the role of international agencies is relevant for the purposes of the Convention definition.[3]

1 Refugee Convention, art 1D; UNHCR *Handbook* **12.13** above, paras 142-143.
2 Thus a Palestinian registered with the UNRWA in the Gaza strip was held to qualify as a refugee *ipso facto* when he could not return there because of Israeli military occupation: (1992) 4(3) IJRL 387. Case 120. In *Dyli* [2000] Imm AR 652, the Tribunal held that art 1D of the Refugee Convention did not apply to protection inside the country of persecution (UNMIK and KFOR in Kosovo).

3 R *(Vallaj) v Immigration Appeal Tribunal* 21 December 2000, para 44 where the protection of KFOR troops and a UN interim administration in the country of persecution was held relevant to the issue of protection and well-founded fear of persecution. See also the CA judgment of 24 May 2001.

12.89 People are not entitled to Refugee Convention protection if they do not need it because the authorities of the territory in which they have taken up residence recognise them as having the rights and obligations attached to the possession of nationality of that country.[1] This exception is of limited application. The person's status must be largely assimilated to that of a national of the receiving country for the exclusion to apply; for example, he or she must be fully protected against deportation or expulsion.[2] The UNHCR *Handbook* suggests that the drafters had in mind refugees of German extraction settling in Germany and recognised there as having the rights and obligations of Germans. In UK terms this would suggest that a grant of settlement or of a subsidiary British nationality which did not confer full citizenship rights would not be enough to bring a person within the exception.

1 Refugee Convention, art 1E; UNHCR *Handbook* **12.13** above, paras 144-146.
2 See *Seare* (3853) unreported: refugee status in Sudan afforded to an Ethiopian national did not exclude the person from the Refugee Convention when he travelled to the UK. See also Hathaway **12.21** fn 2 above, para 6.2.3.

Exclusion for criminal activity

12.90 The protection of the Refugee Convention does not apply where there are serious reasons for considering that a refugee has committed:

(i)   a war crime or a crime against humanity as defined in the relevant international instruments;[1]
(ii)   an act contrary to the purposes and principles of the UN or
(iii)   a serious non-political crime committed outside the country of refuge prior to admission to that country.[2]

The terms of Article 1F of the Convention are mandatory; the protective provisions of the Convention 'shall not' apply in these cases.

1 These are listed in the UNHCR *Handbook* (**12.13** above) at Annex VI and include the London Agreement 1945, the charter of the Nuremberg International Military Tribunal (extract in Annex V of the UNHCR *Handbook*), and the Geneva Conventions and additional Protocol relating to the protection of victims of war and international armed conflicts.
2 Refugee Convention, art 1F.

12.91 The UNHCR *Handbook* points out that in view of the serious consequences of a decision to exclude from protection Article 1F must be interpreted restrictively.[1] The same point is made by the EU Joint Position, which stresses that the exclusion clause is applied only in very exceptional cases after thorough and careful consideration.[2] The Tribunal has decided that one should first determine whether a person is a refugee and then consider whether there are grounds to exclude the person from protection.[3] Serious reasons for a belief are not the same as proof of guilt beyond doubt; it is enough that 'there is sufficient proof warranting the assumption of the (claimant's) guilt of such a crime'.[4]

1 UNHCR *Handbook* above, para 149. See also the Netherlands Council of State decision of *JMS v Staatsecretaris van Justitie* 17 December 1992 (NAV 1993, 1), digested in (1995) 7(1) IJRL 129.

2 Joint Position of 4 March 1996, para 13.
3 *Singh* (10860). See also *JMS v Staatsecretaris van Justitie* fn 1 above. But the Canadian Federal Court of Appeal held it was not an error for the Tribunal to apply the exclusion clause without making any explicit finding on inclusion, in *Gonzalez v MEI* [1994] FCJ 765. See Goodwin-Gill **12.5** fn 1 above, para 4.1.2, p 97.
4 See *Dhayakpa v MIEA* (1995) 62 FCR 556 (Aus): 'Serious reasons for considering' means it is unnecessary for the state to make a positive or concluded finding about the commission of the crime or the act of the class referred to. See also Robinson 'Convention relating to the Status of Refugees' (1953) cited in Hathaway **12.21** fn 2 above, para 6.3, p 215.

12.92 The Canadian courts have held that the burden of establishing that the exclusion clause applies rests on the state denying protection in reliance on these provisions.[1] This accords with the view that determination of whether a person is a refugee within Article 1A of the Refugee Convention must be carried out in every case. The issue has not been authoritatively resolved in the UK; it did not arise in the case of *T v Immigration Officer* since there were undisputed admissions of participation in activity there.[2] The case of *Ramirez* also considered the extent of participation required for an applicant to be excluded under Article 1F of the Convention. It was held that some personal activity must be shown, whether as a leader, organiser or accomplice participating in the planning as well as the execution of the crime; mere membership of a group which from time to time commits international offences is not normally sufficient for exclusion from refugee status.[3] But where an organisation is principally directed to a limited, brutal purpose, such as a secret police activity, mere membership may by necessity involve personal and knowing participation in persecutory acts.[4] The Dutch Council of State has held that Article 1F of the Convention is to be interpreted restrictively and primarily focused on persons who had acted as organs of the state. Private persons would only come within the scope of the Article if they had committed flagrant human rights violations.[5]

1 *Ramirez v Minister of Employment and Immigration* (1992) FCJ 109.
2 *T v Immigration Officer* [1996] AC 742, [1996] 2 WLR 766.
3 This is highly relevant in the light of the proscription of 21 organisations to which exiles might belong, including the LTTE and the PKK, under the provisions of the Terrorism Act 2000.
4 *Ramirez* above; see also *Nantnakumar* (11619), IAT; W97/164, AAT No 12974 [1998] AATA 618, 10 June 1998 (Aus).
5 *JMS v Staatsecretaris van Justitie* **12.91** fn 1 above.

12.93 There have been almost no UK cases concerned with war crimes, crimes against humanity[1] or crimes against the purposes and principles of the UN.[2] In *Amberber* the Tribunal, allowing an appeal of an Ethiopian accused of 'wars of aggression' for participation in attacks by Ethiopian organisations, said that Article 1F(a) of the Refugee Convention only applied to waging war across international boundaries.[3] There is an extensive Canadian and Australian case law on both sub-paragraphs. The former has been applied to exclude former government officials who have resorted to barbaric methods against civilians in the repression of disorder.[4] The killing of civilians in the course of internal conflict does not engage the exclusion clause,[5] but torture, genocide, and arbitrary reprisals do.[6] It is not sufficient that the act alleged could be a crime against humanity; it must be established that it would be.[7] In *Pushpanathan*[8] the Canadian Supreme Court held that narcotics trafficking was not an act 'contrary to the purposes and principles of the UN'. It reasoned that the rationale of Article 1F was that those responsible for the persecution which creates refugees should not enjoy the benefits of the Convention designed to protect those refugees. The purpose of Article 1F(c) was 'to exclude those individuals responsible for serious, sustained or systemic violations of fundamental human rights which amount to persecution in a non-war setting'. It may be applicable to non-state actors although it may be more difficult for non-state actors to perpetrate human rights violations on a scale amounting to persecution without the state thereby implicitly adopting the acts.[9] The UK government's endeavours to exclude promoters of international terrorism from refugee status, described in the Supplement to the last edition of this work,[10] are reflected in the terms of a Declaration annexed to a UN General Assembly Resolution,[11] re-affirming that acts, methods and practices of terrorism are contrary to the purposes and principles of the UN, and declaring that 'knowingly financing, planning and inciting terrorist acts are also contrary to [those] purposes and principles'.[12] It calls on states to take appropriate measures to ensure that asylum seekers have not participated in terrorist acts before granting asylum and do not use the grant of asylum to do so.[13] The draft Convention on International Terrorism[14] prepared by the *Ad Hoc* Committee set up by the General Assembly[15] expressly calls on states not to grant asylum to any person in respect of whom there are reasonable grounds indicating involvement in such acts.[16] Such persons would be excluded from Convention protection in any event (in the UK at least) by virtue of their participation in 'serious non-political crimes'.[17] But they would not be removable to a country of feared persecution, by virtue of Article 3 of the EHCR.[18]

1 Refugee Convention, art 1F(a).
2 Refugee Convention 1F(c).
3 *Amberber* (00 TH 01570) 13 June 2000, IAT. The European jurisprudence on Article 1F(a) of the Refugee Convention is set out in Jean-Yves Carlier et al (eds) *Who is a Refugee?* (1997).
4 See article by Feisman (1996) 8 IJRL 111. Goodwin-Gill **12.5** fn 1 above, pp 95–100 suggests a somewhat narrower basis for exclusion under this head relying on the *travaux* and their reference to the principles established by the London Charter of the International Military Tribunal
5 *Polyukhovich v Commonwealth of Australia* (1991) 172 CLR 501 at 669, per Toohey J.
6 *Gonzalez v MEI* (1994) FCJ 765.
7 *Moreno v MEI* (1993) 159 NR 210.
8 *Pushpanathan v MCI* [1998] 1 SCR 982, [1999] INLR 36. The refugee could not be excluded under Art 1F(b) of the Refugee Convention ('serious non-political crime') because the acts were committed inside Canada after recognition.
9 *Pushpanathan* above.
10 At **12.63A**.
11 Declaration to supplement the Declaration on Measures to Eliminate International Terrorism 1994, A/RES/51/210 of 16 January 1997.
12 A/RES/51/210, para 2.
13 A/RES/51/210, para 3.
14 Draft Comprehensive Convention on International Terrorism (working document) A/C.6/55/1, 28 August 2000.
15 Resolution A/RES/51/210, para 9ff.
16 Draft Comprehensive Convention above, art 7.
17 *T v Immigration Officer* [1996] AC 742, [1996] 2 WLR 766; see below.
18 *Chahal v UK* (1996) 23 EHRR 413.

Serious non-political crime

12.94 It is only serious offences that will bring this limb of the exclusion clause into operation. The UNHCR *Handbook* suggests that they will have to be capital crimes or very grave punishable acts.[1] What constitutes a 'non-political offence' has given rise to difficulty. The drafters of the Refugee Convention intended a link with the international principles of extradition and the extradition case law is likely to be relevant.[2] The fact that violence is used in support of a political objective does not render the case outside the political offence exception.[3] In the case of *T v Immigration Officer*[4] the House of Lords had to consider the exclusion clause in relation to someone who had been an organiser of a group which had planted a bomb at a civilian airport, killing a number of innocent people. Lord Lloyd, delivering the principal judgment, held that a crime is a political crime for the purposes of Article 1F(b) of the Refugee Convention if, and only if, it is committed for a political purpose (ie with the object of overthrowing or subverting or changing the government of a state or inducing it to change its policy), and there is a sufficiently close and direct link between the crime and the alleged political purpose. In determining whether such a link exists, the court will bear in mind the means used to achieve the political end, the target (whether civilian or military) and whether it involved indiscriminate killing. The House disapproved observations in the *Handbook*[5] to the effect that a balance of the acts alleged against the consequences to the applicant was any part of deciding whether the acts constituted serious non-political crimes.[6]

1   UNHCR *Handbook* **12.13** above, para 155. See also Hathaway **12.21** fn 2 above, p 224; Goodwin-Gill **12.5** fn 1 above, para 4.2.1, pp 101-108.
2   Hathaway above, pp 221-222. It was drawn on extensively in *T v Immigration Officer*: see below.
3   *Handbook* above, para 152. A hijacking was held not to fall under the exclusion clause in the Dutch case of *YYA v Staatsecretaris van Justitie*, R 02880417, 8 April 1991 (Council of State). On the other hand, rioting in which buses were burned, stones thrown and stores looted was held capable doing so in the US SC case of *INS v Juan Anibal Aguirre-Aguirre* [2000] INLR 60, on the basis that the criminal outweighed the political aspect of the offence. The decision of the Board of Immigration Appeals (BIA), which had held the acts disproportionate to the aim (protest against government failure to investigate disappearances and rise in bus fares), was approved, and the court said it was not necessary for the acts to be atrocities for them to be disproportionate and so lose their political character.
4   [1996] AC 742, [1996] 2 WLR 766.
5   UNHCR *Handbook* above, para 156; see also Hathaway above, p 224; *SAM v BFF* (1994) 6(4) IJRL 672 Case 215.
6   [1996] 2 All ER 865 at 882.

12.95 The exclusion clause is unlikely to apply if the offence has been the subject of an amnesty or is no longer capable of prosecution.[1] It can only apply to conduct committed before entry to the country of asylum.[2] Conduct arising after admission to the country of asylum is considered in the next paragraph.

1   Hathaway **12.21** fn 2 above, pp 222-223; see also *JMS v Staatsecretaris van Justitie* **12.91** fn 1 above.
2   *Pushpanathan v MCI* [1998] 1 SCR 982, [1999] INLR 36 above.

EXPULSION OF REFUGEES

12.96 Article 33 of the Refugee Convention imposes an express duty on receiving states that may result in the grant of asylum. It provides:

'1. No Contracting State shall expel or return (*'refouler'*) a refugee in any manner whatsoever to the frontiers of territories where his life or freedom would be threatened on account of his race, religion, nationality, membership of a particular social group or political opinion.

2. The benefit of the present provision may not, however, be claimed by a refugee whom there are reasonable grounds for regarding as a danger to the security of the country in which he is, or who, having been convicted by a final judgment of a particularly serious crime, constitutes a danger to the community of that country.'

As far as the courts in the UK are concerned, the reference to 'would be threatened' does not import a higher standard of proof than under Article 1 of the Convention.[1] This is consistent with the purpose of the Convention, which is to prevent the removal of potential refugees to the place where they fear persecution. Unless there is a prior proper determination that a person is not a refugee, he or she may be one, and so removal without determination of refugee status can only be effected to a country where there is no risk of persecution or of onward removal to the country of persecution.[2]

1 See *R v Secretary of State for the Home Department, ex p Sivakumaran* [1988] AC 958, HL where Lord Keith distinguished *INS v Cardozo-Fonseca*, 480 US 421, a US case where the different standard of proof arose from the terms of the US statute.
2 *Re Musisi* [1987] AC 514 at 526.

12.97 The only exceptions to the prohibition on *refoulement* under the Refugee Convention[1] are (i) where there are reasonable grounds for regarding the refugee as a danger to the security of the country in which he or she is,[2] or (ii) the refugee constitutes a danger to the community in that country having been convicted of a particularly serious crime. The weight of opinion is that these are two separate requirements, ie that the conviction of a particularly serious crime is not conclusive, and whether the commission of such a crime makes the refugee a danger to the community is a question of fact. The application of Article 33(2) of the Convention is not mechanistic, and will always involve a question of proportionality, with account taken of the consequences likely to befall the refugee on return.[3] The Canadian approach is to look both to the context of the crime and to the degree of persecution faced in the home country.[4] In *A v MIMA*[5] the Australian Federal Court of Appeal held that the provision was concerned with the perils represented by the refugee, and thus the nature of the crime committed was not conclusive.[6] Article 33(2) applies both to recognised refugees and to asylum seekers, but while those of Article 1F above are mandatory, this is discretionary.

1 But even if Article 33(2) of the Refugee Convention applies, art 3 of the ECHR prevents removal to torture or inhuman or degrading treatment or punishment, whatever the person has done and whatever threat he or she represents: *Chahal v UK* (1996) 23 EHRR 413.
2 See **12.99** below.
3 See Goodwin-Gill **12.5** fn 1 above, para 3.2, p 140.
4 *Re Chu and MCI* 161 DLR 4th 499, 1 June 1998.
5 [1999] FCA 227, 16 March 1999, Australian Federal Court of Appeals.
6 See also *Betkoshabeh v MIMA* (1998) 157 ALR 95. This appears analogous to the EC provisions on deportation, where the criminal offences committed are not conclusive of deportation.

12.98 A refugee who has already been recognised and granted admission to the UK can only be expelled in accordance with the provisions of Article 32 of the Refugee Convention. First, this means that the grounds of expulsion can only be national security or public order. Secondly, except where compelling reasons of national security otherwise require, 'the refugee shall be allowed to submit evidence to clear himself, and to appeal to and be represented before competent authority'. Previous UK practice provided an appeal only where the person was lawfully in the country at the date of the decision,[1] but following *Chahal*[2] there will always be an appeal against expulsion, at least where asylum or human rights issues are raised, whether to the adjudicator under the Immigration and Asylum Act 1999 or by virtue of section 2 of the Special Immigration Appeals Commission Act 1997. Where a receiving country intends to remove a refugee lawfully, an opportunity should be afforded for an alternative country of refuge to be found.[3]

1   *NSH v Secretary of State for the Home Department* [1988] Imm AR 389, CA.
2   (1996) 23 EHRR 413, see below.
3   Refugee Convention, article 32(3). An attempt to expel a leading Saudi dissident, Mohammed al-Masari, to Dominica failed in March 1996 when the appellate authority held that Dominica was not safe. The attempt was notorious for the exposure of the close links between diplomatic staff and arms salesmen (sometimes the same people), and by ministers' admission that the motivation was fear that billions of pounds' worth of arms contracts would be lost by Mr al-Masari's continued presence in the UK.

National security

12.99 National security can thus ground expulsion of asylum seekers and of recognised refugees by virtue of Articles 33(2) and 32 of the Refugee Convention. But the phrase is not defined in the Convention. In *Rehman*[1] the Court of Appeal gave an extremely broad meaning to the phrase 'national security' in the context of a non-asylum deportation; see **15.32** below. However, the ECHR in *Chahal v UK*[2] confirmed that even where there are national security grounds to expel an asylum claimant, Article 3 of the EHCR prohibits expulsion to a territory where there is a real risk of torture. And it is to *Chahal* that the edifice of the Special Immigration Appeals Commission is owed; the Strasbourg court roundly condemned the 'advisory panel' procedure in national security expulsions as not providing the necessary safeguards to the appellant - legal representation, information about the grounds for the expulsion decision, and not sufficiently independent or open, to constitute a court or an effective remedy for a potential breach of Article 3.[3] Now, section 2 of the Special Immigration Appeals Commission Act 1997 provides an appeal against expulsion, including on asylum grounds, and section 2A of the 1997 Act provides a human rights appeal. The special procedure adopted there means that the refugee or asylum seeker does not hear all the evidence but his or her interests are represented in closed sessions by the special advocate. The system is certainly a vast improvement on the discredited advisory procedure.

1   *Secretary of State for the Home Department v Shafiq ur Rehman* [2000] INLR 531, CA.
2   (1996) 23 EHRR 413.
3   (1996) 23 EHRR 413, para 130.

CONSEQUENCES OF RECOGNITION

12.100 Where the authorities recognise someone within their territory as a Convention refugee, they must issue identity papers or a travel document to enable the refugee to travel outside the country of asylum.[1] The charge for its issue must not exceed the lowest scale of fees for national passports.[2] Refugees must be readmitted to the state which issued the document at any time during its validity.[3] The Convention requires that refugees are granted the 'most favourable treatment accorded to nationals of a foreign country' as regards trade union membership (Article 15), entry to wage-earning employment (Article 17), self-employment (Article 18) and membership of the liberal professions (Article 19). They should be given 'treatment as favourable as possible' as regards housing (Article 21) and education (Article 22) and approximately the same treatment as nationals with respect to public relief and assistance (Article 23), labour legislation and social security (Article 24).[4] Their freedom of movement within the country of asylum is guaranteed by Article 26. The policy of the Convention is that after asylum has been given, refugees shall as far as possible be integrated into their country of asylum and to that end contracting states are urged to expedite naturalisation procedures.[5] There is a debate in the UK appellate authorities as to whether refugee status can be backdated on an appeal against refusal of asylum being allowed.[6] But the Divisional Court has condemned the delays in the grant of status following a successful appeal, which can be severely prejudicial to refugees.[7]

1 Refugee Convention, art 28.
2 Refugee Convention, Sch, para 3.
3 Refugee Convention, Sch, para 13. Thus a Somali refugee with indefinite leave to remain who had stayed in Ethiopia for over two years caring for a sick relative was wrongly refused re-entry as a returning resident since his refugee travel document was still valid: *R v Secretary of State for the Home Department, ex p Sherreh* (CO 2194/1997) 15 August 1997, QBD (permission; the case was conceded by the Home Office).
4 In UK practice community support, housing, education (including language learning) access to health services, social security benefits and employment are perceived as the essential elements of refugee integration: Home Office Immigration and Nationality Directorate *The Integration of Recognised Refugees in the UK* (1999). Refugees are treated as own nationals for the purpose of health care, social security and housing, and as home students for education fees and grants purposes. There are no employment restrictions on recognised refugees.
5 Refugee Convention, art 34.
6 *Haibe* [1997] INLR 119 says that because refugee status is not granted but recognised, in an appropriate case it is open to the appellate authority to declare that the status of refugee existed at the date of the decision or other appropriate date, and a direction can be given to that effect. *Altun* (16628) 17 July 1998 disapproves *Haibe*, saying that nothing in the Immigration Act 1971 allows directions of a retrospective nature and that it is no part of the appellate authorities' function nor does the Refugee Convention require them to determine exactly when a person became a refugee.
7 'It would wholly undermine the rule of law if the Secretary of State could simply ignore a ruling without appealing it, nor could he deliberately delay giving effect to it': Elias J in *R v Secretary of State for the Home Department, ex p Deniz Mersin* [2000] INLR 511, QBD. The applicant had a right to be granted refugee status unless or until there was a change in the position.

12.101 Where a refugee has left the country of refuge and entered another territory and stayed there lawfully for a period of time, the Refugee Convention envisages that the responsibility for the issue of a further travel document may become that of the second country of residence.[1] The circumstances when this might happen are uncertain; a refugee has no right to have asylum transferred to a country in which he or she has temporary residence. In order to eliminate ambiguity, member states of the Council of Europe drew up the European Agreement on Transfer of Responsibility for Refugees[2] which provides for the transfer of responsibility after two years' continuous lawful residence other than for the purposes of study, training, medical visit, or a period of imprisonment,[3] or if the refugee has been permitted to stay beyond the validity of his or her travel document from the first state (unless the extension beyond validity was for study or training, or the refugee is still re-admissible to the first state). The Agreement does not, however, assist in cases of unlawful residence, nor does it provide any mechanism or criteria for transfer of lawful residence.[4] Current Home Office policy is to consider cases falling outside the European Agreement on a case-by-case basis, accepting responsibility only where the UK clearly is the most appropriate place of long-term refuge. Factors which will be considered include the length of time spent in the first country, the strength of ties there compared with the UK and any compelling compassionate circumstances.[5] For short-term visa-free travel, the European Agreement on the Abolition of Visas for Refugees 1959[6] enables refugees resident in a contracting state and possessing a valid travel document issued under the Refugee Convention to travel without a visa to any other contracting state[7] for visits of up to three months.[8]

1 Refugee Convention, Sch, para 11.
2 16 October 1980, Cmnd 8127.
3 European Agreement on Transfer of Responsibility for Refugees 1980 above, art 2.
4 See *Rahman* [1989] Imm AR 325 for a case where the appellate authority exercised a broad discretion on a transfer of status case. Now, an appeal under s 65 of the Immigration and Asylum Act 1999 would be available where, for example, refusal to transfer status meant continued separation from close family members.
5 API Oct/00 Ch 2, s 2(3).
6 [376] UNTS 85, reproduced in *Butterworths Immigration Law Service*, 2D[1].
7 Belgium, Denmark, France, Germany, Iceland, Ireland, Italy, Liechtenstein, Luxembourg, the Netherlands, Norway, Portugal, Spain, Sweden and Switzerland.
8 See also *Shramir v Secretary of State for the Home Department* [1992] Imm AR 542.

Refugees in the EU

12.102 Until refugees obtain the nationality of the country of refuge, they will not be entitled to freedom of movement rights as EC nationals. Article 39 (ex art 48) of the EEC Treaty dealing with the freedom of movement of workers does not apply to refugees. Apart from the European Agreements noted above, adopted within the framework of the Council of Europe in 1959 and 1980, the only other measure designed to give refugees rights within Europe was the 1964 EEC Council of Ministers' declaration that:

> 'the entry to their territories for the purpose of engaging in a paid activity there, of refugees recognised as such within the meaning of the Convention of 1951 and established in the territory of another member state of the community should be examined with particular favour, particularly so as to afford to such refugees within their territories the most favourable treatment possible.'

Further to this declaration, Council Regulation (EC) 1408/71[1] provided that refugees resident in the territory of a member state are entitled to the same social security benefits as nationals of that state, a measure which did no more than Europeanise Article 24 of the Refugee Convention.

1 Article 2(3).

12.103 From the mid-1980s EU member states' asylum policy was restricted to trying to stop 'irregular movements' – in practice, all movement of refugees into EU territory, by treating asylum seekers as essentially a policing problem.

12.103 *Refugees, asylum and exceptional leave*

Thus, the brief of the *Ad Hoc* Group on Immigration set up in 1986 was to stem 'abuses of the asylum procedures'. The immediate results were, in April 1987, the first (unofficial) agreement on carrier sanctions for airlines bringing in undocumented passengers,[1] the beginnings of co-ordinated visa policies[2] and a rudimentary 'early warning system', whereby members states alerted each other to large numbers of asylum seekers coming from particular countries so that visa requirements could be imposed.[3] The group (also known as the Working Group on Immigration) produced the Dublin Convention (Convention Determining the State Responsible for Examining Applications for Asylum Lodged in One of the Member States of the European Communities), signed by member states in June 1990,[4] which precluded multiple asylum claims in EU territory without ensuring the uniform criteria and procedures to remove the need for them; the Resolution on manifestly unfounded applications for asylum,[5] which established the principle and criteria of accelerated procedures; the Resolution on a harmonised approach to questions concerning host third countries,[6] which laid the foundations for the 'third safe country' procedures; the Conclusions on countries in which there is generally no serious risk of persecution,[7] the foundation of the 'safe countries of origin' procedures.

1 The UK's own Immigration (Carriers' Liability) Act was passed in May 1987.
2 Visa policies (common list of countries whose nationals require visas, common criteria, common form) went into Community competence under the Treaty on European Union in 1993.
3 This evolved into CIREA, the central clearing house on information on asylum within the EU, which produces and exchanges country information on the main refugee-producing countries as well as monitoring 'flows'.
4 In force 1 September 1997, reproduced in *Butterworths Immigration Law Service*, 2D[81].
5 Approved at the EU Council of Ministers' meeting of 30 November 1992, known as the London Resolution.
6 Approved at the same meeting.
7 The third item approved at the London ministers' meeting of 30 November 1992. All these were approved as non-binding inter-governmental agreements, which meant they were subject to no scrutiny by either national or European Parliament, although they have influenced policy profoundly in the UK and throughout Europe since. See Bunyan and Webber *Intergovernmental cooperation on immigration and asylum* (1995) and Guild *The Developing Immigration and Asylum Policies of the European Union* (1996) for these pre-Maastricht agreements.

12.104 After 1993, when the Treaty on European Union institutionalised the inter-governmental character of immigration and asylum issues (apart from visa policy) in the Third Pillar of the Treaty, there was an attempt to harmonise criteria, procedures,[1] reception conditions[2] and refugees' rights[3] within the EU. The non-binding Joint Position of March 1996[4] was the main fruit of this process. It was the first attempt to reconcile the varying interpretations of the Convention by the member states. Although welcomed in *Robinson*,[5] the Joint Position was dismissed in *Adan and Aitseguer* [6] as no more than a political agreement which was not particularly useful.

1 See eg Resolution on minimum guarantees for asylum seekers and refugees, 21 June 1995, OJ 1996 C 274, 19 September 1996.
2 Draft Joint Action on the minimum conditions for the reception of asylum seekers, 17 August 1995, ASIM 223.
3 Draft Council Act adopting a common action on certain aspects on the status of refugees recognised by the member states of the EU, 6784/95.
4 Joint Position of 4 March 1996 defined by the Council on the basis of art K3 of the Treaty on European Union on the harmonised application of the term 'refugee' of art 1

of the Convention relating to the status of refugees (Geneva, 28 July 1951), 96/196/
JHA, reproduced in *Butterworths Immigration Law Service*, **2D[138]**.
5   *Robinson v Secretary of State for the Home Department* [1997] Imm AR 568.
6   On the issue of agents of persecution: *R v Secretary of State for the Home Department,
    ex p Adan and Aitseguer* [1999] Imm AR 521, [1999] INLR 362, CA. See also Lord
    Steyn [2001] INLR 44 at 57, HL.

12.105 The Treaty of Amsterdam[1] saw immigration and asylum policy as a
whole being taken into Community competence. Title IV inserts visas, asylum,
immigration and other policies related to free movement of persons into the
EC Treaty. It contains the provisions previously dealt with under Articles K1
to K3 and K6 of the Treaty on European Union. Regulations and directives
are expected from the Council up to April 2004.[2]

1   Signed on 2 October 1997 by 15 member states.
2   According to the Commission Scoreboard of March 2000. See Chapter 7 above.

12.106 EU nationals are not prevented from applying for asylum in another
member state, but their claims must be assessed against the presumption
contained in the Protocol to the EC Treaty[1] that 'given the level of protection
of fundamental rights and freedoms . . . Member States shall be regarded as
constituting safe countries of origin in respect of each other for all legal and
practical purposes in relation to asylum matters'. Applications may be
considered or declared admissible only if the applicant's member state has
taken measures derogating from the ECHR, or the Council determines that
the member state in question is in serious and persistent breach of principles
of liberty, democracy, respect for human rights and fundamental freedoms,[2]
or if the procedure for such a determination has been initiated. If a member
state unilaterally decides to consider an asylum claim and none of these
conditions apply, the Council must be immediately informed, and the
application will be dealt with as manifestly unfounded.

1   Protocol on asylum for nationals of Member States of the European Union, added by the
    Treaty of Amsterdam.
2   Treaty on European Union, arts 6 and 7 (ex F and F.1).

UK PRACTICE ON ASYLUM

The application

12.107 An asylum application is defined as a claim that it would be contrary
to the UK's obligations under the Refugee Convention for the person to be
removed from or required to leave the UK.[1] The asylum application will be
determined in accordance with the UK's obligations under the Convention
and will be granted if the applicant is in the UK or has arrived at a port of
entry in the UK, is a Convention refugee, and refusing his or her application
would result (whether immediately or after the expiry of leave) in *refoulement*
contrary to the Convention.[2] In all other cases the application will be refused.[3]

1   Asylum and Immigration Appeals Act 1993, s 1; Immigration and Asylum Act 1999,
    s 69(6); HC 395, para 327.
2   HC 395, para 334.
3   HC 395, para 336.

Applications at the port

12.108 A person arriving at a port of entry who intends to seek asylum will normally ask for it from an immigration officer on arrival. No particular form of words is required, and if a person expresses unwillingness to return to their country of nationality or habitual residence because they believe they would be in danger, it should be assumed that they are making an asylum application.[1] Arrangements whereby passengers without visas are prevented from leaving the aircraft and making a claim to an immigration officer are contrary to the UK's obligations under the Refugee Convention.[2] Facilities at the port of entry must include an interpreter so that an applicant can make a claim. In the rare case where an entry clearance has been granted in order for a claim for asylum to be made, the immigration officer may grant a leave to enter.[3] In all other cases, the claim will be referred to the Immigration and Nationality Directorate (IND) of the Home Office for determination.[4] Current practice in port cases is to conduct screening immediately (this will include taking identity details, fingerprinting[5] and, if the applicant is potentially returnable to a safe third country, questioning about the route of travel and any periods of stay in third countries). After screening there are different procedures depending on the nationality of the applicant:[6]

(i)   asylum seekers from countries deemed safe by the Home Office[7] are given their substantive asylum interview on or within one or two days of arrival. They are likely to be detained.[8] After interview they have five days (two days if detained) to submit material in support of the application. The Immigration and Nationality Directorate aims to make the decision within six days of the person's arrival;

(ii)   others are given a Statement of Evidence form to complete and return within ten working days.[9] On return of the form, if asylum is not granted an interview will be fixed for five days ahead, and a decision will be taken immediately after that.

1   Asylum Policy Instructions (API) Aug/00 Ch 1 s 1.2. See also *R v Uxbridge Magistrates' Court, ex p Adimi* [1999] INLR 490 at 499, 506.
2   A number of cases of such practices came to light in 1990; judicial review proceedings were settled after the grant of permission. Similarly, cases have come to light of stowaways being removed without being able to make contact with an immigration officer. The EU Draft Minimum Guarantees for Asylum seekers and Refugees (Presidency Proposals submitted by the Home Office to Parliament, 10 November 1994) para 20 provides: 'Member States shall adopt administrative measures ensuring that no asylum seeker arriving at their frontier is refused admission without being afforded an opportunity to file an asylum application.'.
3   See below, [**12.112**].
4   HC 395, para 328.
5   Immigration and Asylum Act 1999 s 141 gives power to fingerprint asylum seekers: s 141(7)(e); their dependants: s 141(7)(f) and 141(14); and anyone else without a valid passport or a reasonable excuse: s 141(7)(a), (10). The High Court has held that a policy of fingerprinting unaccompanied children whose identity is in doubt is lawful: *R v Secretary of State for the Home Department, ex p Ahmed Tabed* [1994] Imm AR 468.
6   These procedures are set out in a document from Immigration and Nationality Directorate headed 'Asylum process pilots and procedures', 25 January 2000. But procedures are subject to variation, and the IND frequently runs pilot schemes.
7   Claims are no longer certified on the basis that the claimant comes from a country designated as one in which there is in general no serious risk of persecution (as was formerly the case: Asylum and Immigration Act 1996, s 1). Instead their claims are subjected to an unofficial accelerated procedure. Discrimination by immigration officers

in exercising immigration functions on the basis of nationality is exempted from the reach of the Race Relations Act 1976: see s 19D, inserted by Race Relations Amendment Act 2000.

8 Many port asylum seekers believed on the basis of their nationality to have unfounded claims are detained at Oakington, near Cambridge. See chapter 17 below. They receive legal assistance at interview and assistance with completing Statement of Evidence forms from Immigration Advisory Service and Refugee Legal Centre staff.

9 The period was changed from 14 days to synchronise with the one-stop statement of additional evidence forms, handed to port claimants with the Statement of Evidence form and to be returned within ten working days: Immigration and Nationality Directorate to Asylum Processes Stakeholder Group, 29 November 2000. The deadline is impossibly tight given that most asylum seekers who are not detained are dispersed all over the country for asylum support, with no infrastructure of legal, linguistic or medical expertise to assist in completing the Statement of Evidence forms. The Home Office has refused to allow more time, however, and is adamant that the forms can be completed without legal assistance. They must be completed in full and in English, and returned with translations of all evidence relied on. See further **12.122** below.

12.109 Port asylum seekers will either be detained[1] or granted temporary admission[2] pending consideration of the claim. Temporary admission is given by immigration officers at ports to allow applicants physically to enter the UK while their application is being dealt with.[3] The Home Office guidelines on detention[4] stress that this is used only where there is no alternative and there are good grounds for believing that the person will not keep in touch voluntarily. When deciding whether or not to detain someone factors such as whether there is a sponsor, satisfactory evidence of identity and past immigration history, and whether detention is available will be considered.[5] The 1994 instructions said that the case for detaining an asylum seeker immediately on the claim being made must be particularly strong;[6] the current API go further, suggesting that port applicants will only be detained if they are identified as illegal entrants. Detained persons have a right to apply to an adjudicator for bail if seven days have elapsed since arrival and no decision has been taken.[7] Part III of the 1999 Act[8] contains provisions for automatic bail hearings and a presumption in favour of bail.[9]

1 The power to detain is pursuant to Immigration Act 1971, Sch 2, para 16. To comply with art 5 of the ECHR (right to liberty) it must not be exercised arbitrarily and may only be exercised 'to prevent unauthorised entry into the country' or 'pending deportation', with rigorous judicial scrutiny: *Amuur v France* (1996) 22 EHRR 533. See further Blake *The international principles governing detention of asylum seekers* in Blake and Fransman (eds) *A guide to the Human Rights Act 1998* (1999); see chapter 17 below.

2 The power to admit temporarily is governed by Immigration Act 1971, Sch 2, para 21.

3 Immigration Act 1971, s 11. This fiction means that a person can be refused 'leave to enter' after living in the UK for years, something which, in the context of EC law, was not acceptable: see *R v Secretary of State for the Home Department, ex p Yiadom* Case C-357/98 [2001] All ER (EC) 267, ECJ; see further **7.141** above.

4 API Aug/00, Ch 1, s 1(4). These coexist with the Immigration Service Instruction on Detention 3 December 1991; Immigration Service Instruction on Detention 20 September 1994, (reproduced in *Butterworths Immigration Law Service*, D[971]); see chapter 17 below.

5 API Aug/00, Ch 1, s 1(4).

6 Immigration Serive Instruction on Detention 1994 above, para 2. See the UNHCR Guidelines on applicable criteria and standard relating to the detention of asylum seekers, 1995, reproduced in *Butterworths Immigration Law Service*, 2C[261]. Concern has been expressed by *inter alia* UNHCR, Amnesty International and the UN Committee Against Torture on the detention of asylum seekers.

7 Immigration Act 1971, Sch 2, para 22(1).

8 Immigration and Asylum Act 1999, ss 44, 46, due to enter into force in October 2001.

9 See further chapter 17 below.

12.110 Those granted temporary admission will be referred to the National Asylum Support Service (NASS) for assistance if they appear destitute. They may be subject to stringent conditions of residence[1] and reporting,[2] and will not be permitted to take employment unless their claim remains outstanding for more than six months, or has been refused and they have lodged an appeal.[3]

1 Immigration Act 1971, Sch 2, para 21(2B)ff; Asylum Support Regulations 2000, SI 2000/704. Asylum seekers may be prohibited from living in certain areas, as well as being directed to stay in particular accommodation. See further chapter 13 below.
2 Immigration Act 1971, Sch 2, para 21(2).
3 API Nov/00, Ch 8, s 3.

Applications made in-country

12.111 Asylum applications may be made by applying for variation of a leave already granted (as a visitor or a student), or on apprehension as an illegal entrant,[1] or by someone facing removal for overstaying or breach of conditions. An in-country application may be made by post or in person. Current practice is to invite postal applicants in for screening and then to give them a Statement of Evidence form to complete and return within ten working days.[2] If asylum is not granted an interview will be fixed as for port applicants.[3] There is no power to detain someone who is applying for a variation of leave, but such an application made shortly after entry as a visitor or a student may result in an interview under caution and a decision to treat the applicant as an illegal entrant, who may be detained.[4] The previous provision for curtailment of leave on refusal of an asylum claim has been dropped.[5] The power to detain illegal entrants and those facing removal as overstayers or deportation is not affected by the making of an asylum claim which precludes immediate removal,[6] but must not be exercised capriciously, unreasonably or contrary to policy.[7] Since 1996 there has been a right to apply for bail pending removal.[8]

1 Those apprehended as illegal entrants at ports are generally treated as in-country applicants.
2 The period was changed in November 2000: Immigration and Nationality Directorate to Asylum Processes Stakeholder Group, 29 November 2000.
3 Asylum process pilots and procedures, Immigration and Nationality Directorate 25 January 2000.
4 Immigration Act 1971, Sch 2, para 16. Note the new power to detain on suspicion of illegal entry in para 16(2). During the asylum interview of all known and potential illegal entrants, the interviewing officer will ask the applicant about his or her reasons for travelling to the UK and method of entry, to ascertain whether deception was used: API Aug/00 Ch 2, s 8(4) and (5). There is nothing unfair about the same immigration officer conducting both an illegal entry interview and an asylum interview: *R v Secretary of State for the Home Department, ex p Range* [1991] Imm AR 505, QBD; see also *Odishu (Yousuf) v Secretary of State for the Home Department* [1994] Imm AR 475, CA. But in the Scottish case of *Sofia Kim v Secretary of State for the Home Department* 2000 SLT 249, OHCS, an asylum interview which turned into an illegal entry interview without a caution being administered was held inadmissible to prove illegal entry.
5 Asylum and Immigration Appeals Act 1993, s 7; in the vast majority of cases leave was only extant by virtue of the statutory provisions of the Immigration (Variation of Leave) Order 1976, SI 1976/1572 in any event, so the only purpose of the curtailment power was to turn variation appeals into deportation appeals, to prevent a further appeal being available. The same purpose is served by abolishing deportation (and thus the deportation appeal) for overstaying and by the one-stop appeals system.
6 *R v Secretary of State for the Home Department, ex p Khan* [1995] Imm AR 348, [1995] NLJR 216, CA.
7 *Re Vilvarajah's application* (1987) Times, 31 October; [1990] Imm AR 457; see also *R v Governor of Haslar Prison, ex p Egbe* (1991) Times, 4 June. Current policy is that

asylum applicants may be detained at port, when they have been identified as illegal entrants; applicants may also be detained after directions have been set to remove them, when leave has been curtailed (but see fn 3 above) or when applications are made following the commencement of enforcement action for overstaying: API Aug/00, Ch 1, s 1(4).

8   Immigration Act 1971, Sch 2, para 22(1)(b), as amended by Asylum and Immigration Act 1996, Sch 2, para 11.

Special cases

12.112 We have referred above to the possibility of making a claim for asylum abroad in exceptional circumstances,[1] and the criteria for the grant of entry clearance as a refugee. In addition, mandate refugees (ie refugees recognised by UNHCR abroad) may be referred by the British Red Cross on nomination for resettlement by UNHCR.[2] Such cases attract priority, and should be granted if the UK is the most appropriate country of refuge.[3] Another scheme run by the British Red Cross is the 'ten or more plan', established by UNHCR for the resettlement of disabled refugees in need of medical attention. Under it, host countries accept ten or more disabled refugees and their families annually. Again, refugee status has already been granted and entry for settlement should be granted if the severity of the disability and the applicant's circumstances in the present country of refuge warrant it, and if the UK is the most appropriate country of resettlement.[4] Applications for transfer of refugee status have been considered above.[5] Applications made in the UK from persons currently exempt from control (eg diplomats or consular staff) are dealt with as special cases,[6] as are claims by EU nationals.[7]

1   At **12.38** above.
2   In addition there is a policy in relation to stateless Palestinian refugees assisted by UNWRA under art 1D of the Refugee Convention, who have family ties in the UK: see API Aug/00, Ch 2, s 3.
3   API Aug/00, Ch 2, s 3(4).
4   API Aug/00, Ch 2, s 4.
5   See **12.74** above.
6   API Aug/00, Ch 2, s 6.
7   API Oct/00, Ch 2, s 9; see **12.106** above.

Children

12.113 There are special provisions for dealing with claims by children, both accompanied and unaccompanied.[1] A child is defined as a person who is under 18 or who, in the absence of documentary evidence, appears to be under that age. In assessing an application from a child (whether accompanied or not) more weight should be given to objective indications of risk than to the child's state of mind. An asylum application from or on behalf of a child should not be refused solely because the child is too young to understand his or her situation or to have formed a fear of persecution.[2] When an unaccompanied child comes to the attention of immigration officers at the port or at the asylum unit at the Home Office, or where a child becomes unaccompanied during the asylum process (by being abandoned or taken into care, for example) they will notify the Refugee Council's non-statutory Panel of Advisers,[3] whose members act as a 'friend' to the child in his or her dealings with the Home Office and other central and local government agencies. Where there are disputes over age, the Panel will be informed without prejudice, even if the application is proceeded with as for an adult.[4] Applications from children (accompanied or not) receive priority at all stages.[5] It will rarely be acceptable to hold an application from an unaccompanied child with no action on it for longer than six months.[6] Children should not be interviewed about the substance of their asylum claim unless it is impossible to obtain by written inquiries or other sources sufficient information to determine the claim.[7] Where an interview is essential it must be conducted in the presence of an appropriate adult.[8] Particular care is needed in assessing the evidence of minors, and a more liberal interpretation of the benefit of the doubt is called for.[9] No unaccompanied child will be removed from the UK unless adequate reception and care arrangements are in place in the country to which he or she is to be removed.[10]

1　HC 395, paras 349, 350-352; API Aug/00 Ch 2, s 5, reflecting the concerns expressed in the UNHCR *Handbook* **12.13** above, paras 213-219.
2　HC 395, para 351; API Aug/00, Ch 2, s 5, para 2.2.
3　API Aug/00, Ch 2, s 5, para 3.9. Ministers agreed to fund this panel on a non-statutory basis during the passage of the Asylum and Immigration Appeals Act 1993.
4　API Aug/00, Ch 2, s 5, para 3.9.
5　HC 395, para 350.
6　API Aug/00, Ch 2, s 5, para 3.9. In other cases applications may be held awaiting clarification of country conditions: ibid.
7　HC 395, para 352. But in *Orman* [1998] Imm AR 224 the Tribunal doubted the wisdom of this approach and suggested that a preferable course would be to allow the child to be interviewed with the Panel adviser.
8　Not an immigration officer, a police officer or a Home Office civil servant: API Ch 2, s 5, para 2.3. Interviews conducted in the absence of a responsible adult are to be excluded from consideration in assessing the claim and on appeal: *Ehalaivan* (00 TH 01749) 3 August 2000, IAT; *Omotayo* (00 TH 00854) 12 April 2000, IAT; *Rajanathan* (18418) 20 July 1999.
9　UNHCR *Handbook* **12.13** above, para 219; *Jakitay* (12658) 15 November 1995, IAT.
10　*Re Sujon Miah* (CO 3391/1994, 6 December 1994); API Aug/00, Ch 2, s 5, para 3.5. See also the recommendation given by the Tribunal in *Afrifa* (18392) 24 March 2000, that before removal of the appellant whose asylum appeal it had rejected, International Social Services, International Red Cross and the British High Commission be asked to report on reception and care arrangements.

12.114 The determination of age is controversial. In principle the burden is on the applicant to demonstrate that he or she is a minor, but in practice it would normally be appropriate to give the applicant the benefit of the doubt unless his or her physical appearance strongly suggests that he or she is over 18.[1] It is open to an applicant to obtain a medical assessment of age, but this must be voluntary and it is not appropriate to insist or even to request that one is obtained.[2] It is inappropriate for X-rays to be used merely to assist in age determination for immigration purposes.[3]

1　API Aug/00, Ch 2, s 5, para 3.7.
2　API Aug/00, Ch 2, s 5, para 3.8. In cases where an applicant had initially claimed to be an adult and only later claimed to be under-age, the burden on the applicant would be discharged only if his or her appearance clearly supported the claim: para 3.7. Otherwise, in some circumstances it might be appropriate to request a medical assessment of age.
3　ADI Jul/98, Ch 2, s 5, para 3.13. This instruction marked a change from former practice, particularly in the context of family reunion applications from the Indian sub-continent, where 'bone-age testing' by X-ray was sometimes conducted at the behest of the immigration authorities. It has been ommitted from the recent API of August 2000.

Investigation of asylum claims

12.115 As a result of the particular difficulties experienced by those fleeing persecution, and the likely lack of documentary evidence in support of claims, the UNHCR *Handbook*[1] indicates that the duty to ascertain and evaluate all the relevant facts is shared between the applicant and the examiner. The applicant should tell the truth and assist the examiner to the full in establishing the facts of his or her case, make an effort to support his or her statements by any available evidence, give a satisfactory explanation for any lack of evidence, and if necessary make an effort to procure additional evidence. He or she should supply as much detail as is necessary about him- or herself and should answer any questions put. The examiner should ensure that the applicant presents his or her case as fully as possible, with all available evidence; assess his or her credibility and evaluate the evidence, if necessary giving the applicant the benefit of the doubt, in order to establish the objective and subjective elements of the claim, and relate the elements to the relevant criteria of the Refugee Convention to arrive at a correct conclusion on the applicant's refugee status.[2]

1   **12.13** above, paras 195-205.
2   UNHCR *Handbook* above, Summary, para 205.

12.116 The White Paper *Fairer, faster and firmer: a modern approach to immigration and asylum*[1] contained an undertaking to reduce the time taken on determination of asylum claims to a total of six months: two months for the initial determination and four months for the appeal. Previous delays of several years were unjust; they denied refugees the prompt determination of status which they deserved, and created difficulties for those who were ultimately found not to need international protection. But the implementation of the commitment to reduce delays has caused its own problems. The conditions under which asylum determination is now carried out in the UK – in particular, the pernicious combination of an overly ambitious and over-rigid timetable for determining claims and the dispersal or detention of asylum seekers (neither of which is conducive to clarity of recollection or articulation) – make compliance with the duties set out in the *Handbook* extremely difficult, if not impossible, for both the applicant and the examiner. As we have seen above, in many port cases applicants are interviewed immediately on arrival,[2] or are detained and interviewed within a day or two, and are given between two and five days (depending on whether or not they are detained) to submit evidence in support of the claim.[3] The five-day post-interview period for receipt of further evidence will only be extended in exceptional circumstances, such as to await receipt of a Medical Foundation report.[4] Many other applicants are sent hundreds of miles to areas where legal, medical, social and linguistic support is scarce and living conditions squalid, and are given 14 days to complete evidence forms in full and in English, obtain all relevant documents and get them translated. The time limit will not be extended except in the rarest of cases.[5] Illness (evidenced by medical certificate) or a postal strike would constitute good reason for extension, but not the illness or absence of a representative or solicitor, since the view of the Home Office remains that applicants do not need legal assistance in filling the form.[6]

1   July 1998.
2   Despite the wealth of evidence presented to the Home Office showing how exhaustion, fear, linguistic difficulties, confusion and unfamiliarity all combine to render on-arrival interviews less than comprehensive or reliable see **12.32** above. The UNHCR *Handbook*

12.13 above, para 198 points out that non-disclosure at a first interview should not be held against the asylum seeker; see further below.

3 *Asylum process pilots and procedures* Immigration and Nationality Directorate, 25 January 2000.

4 Home Office minister to Medical Foundation, 14 October 1998, confirmed by Immigration and Nationality Directorate, 20 April 2000.

5 Immigration and Nationality Directorate to Asylum Processes Stakeholder Group 15 September 2000. See **12.122** below.

6 Minutes of Asylum Processes Stakeholder Group, April 2000.

12.117 The Immigration Rules are silent on the procedural safeguards to be adopted during investigation, with the exception of specific provision for unaccompanied children.[1] Despite the absence of particular rules for adults, it is recognised that the procedures must be fair: there must be an opportunity for contact with the UNHCR or voluntary advice agencies such as the Refugee Legal Centre; there must be competent interpreters skilled in the applicant's language. The practice of interviewing on arrival cuts across the principle that applicants may have access to a lawyer throughout the asylum procedures. Legal assistance at the asylum interview has been recommended by UNHCR[2] and recognised by (*inter alia*) the Lord Chancellor's Department and the Legal Services Commission.[3] There is no right to legal representation at interview, but the immigration officer's discretion to admit or exclude a legal representative must be exercised properly.[4] A draft protocol on interviewing indicates that a representative may be excluded from the interview if he or she refuses to provide evidence of identity or is illegally in the UK or has an outstanding asylum claim or a history of disruptive behaviour. The same rule applies to the admission of the applicant's own interpreter.[5] The draft protocol also says that representatives should not interrupt the interview except over interpretation problems.[6] Previous Asylum Directorate Instructions emphasised the importance of agreeing the transcript of the interview with the applicant at the end of the interview,[7] which is clearly desirable in the interests of fairness and accuracy; in June 2000 however the Home Office announced the end of the 'read-over' procedure except in cases involving illiterate or traumatised applicants, where the immigration officer retains a discretion.[8] The interviewer has a duty to elicit details of the claim, to enable the applicant to do justice to it.[9] The extent to which a failure to mention aspects of the claim at an initial screening interview should be allowed adversely to affect credibility remains controversial.[10]

1 As to which see **12.113** above.

2 'Where national legislation provides for the participation of legal or other counsel to assist an applicant in the presentation of his or her claim, it is essential to allow such counsel to participate in the interview. The presence of a legal representative or other counsel who is familiar with the refugee criteria, local jurisprudence and the applicant's claim is helpful not only to the applicant but also to the interviewer.' UNHCR Guidelines 1995, para 15.

3 ACLEC *Improving the quality of immigration advice and representation: A report* (1998), para 2.23. See also ILPA *Breaking down the barriers: a report on the conduct of asylum interviews at ports* (1999). Former immigration minister Mike O'Brien said that the Home Office 'aim to arrange the interview process so that advisers are available to accompany the applicant at interview' (letter to ILPA, 27 July 1999). Legal help is now available for asylum interviews.

4 *R v Secretary of State for the Home Department, ex p Vera Lawson* [1994] Imm AR 58. Home Office policy is to defer substantive asylum interviews where the applicant has a representative who is not present, but otherwise to hold such interviews immediately after screening interviews (which ascertain whether an applicant is returnable to a third country): Immigration and Nationality Directorate to ILPA, 11 December 2000.

5 *R v Secretary of State for the Home Department, ex p Bostanci* [1999] Imm AR 411.
6 Draft Protocol between Immigration and Nationality Directorate and representatives, April 2000. The Refugee Legal Centre's proposed guidance for representatives, on the other hand, says the representative 'should clarify ambiguous or misleading questions or comments, prompt the immigration officer when relevant inquiries are curtailed or not pursued, ensure the record of interview is correct and read over at the end . . . ensure that breaks are taken' as well as ensuring that interpretation problems are dealt with immediately.
7 ADI Jul/98, Ch 16, s 3, para 6.4, Annex A, para 4: 'The read back is an essential part of the interview.' The section on interviewing is omitted from the current API.
8 Immigration and Nationality Directorate letter, 23 June 2000. The justification cited is that completion of the Statement of Evidence Form 'lessens the scope for omissions and misunderstandings' at interview, while in non-Statement of Evidence form cases where there is no read-over, the applicant has five days after interview to make representations. For read-over in torture claims see API Nov/00, Ch 3, s 2, Annex A.
9 *R v Secretary of State for the Home Department, ex p Akdogan* [1995] Imm AR 176, QBD.
10 In *Salim* (13202) and *Simsek* (13202) the Tribunal held that great care was needed in weighing discrepancies between the first, unsigned interview, at which 'basic details only' were sought, and the full asylum interview. See also *Mayisokele* (13039); *Vimaleswaran* (15493); *Jeevaponkalan* (17742). But failure to mention a central feature of the claim may affect credibility: *R v Secretary of State for the Home Department, ex p Agbonmenio* [1996] Imm AR 69.

12.118 Since the elaboration of gender guidelines by the Refugee Women's Legal Group in 1998,[1] the Immigration and Nationality Directorate has begun to recognise the importance of gender-sensitive procedures and is elaborating its own gender guidelines for caseworkers.[2] Instructions to staff on interviewing are no longer published,[3] but in correspondence the Immigration and Nationality Directorate has indicated that requests for an interviewer or interpreter of the same sex as the applicant 'will be complied with as far as operationally possible' and consideration will be given to deferring interviews if it is not possible to comply.[4] The instructions to caseworkers acknowledge that victims of torture might be reluctant to talk in detail about their experiences,[5] a reluctance recognised by the High Court in *Ejon*,[6] but also indicate that a late claim to have been tortured may adversely affect credibility. Similarly, while the lack of a medical report cannot ground a dismissal of a claim of torture, and applicants should never be invited to provide a medical report if one is not already available, credibility 'may be undermined' if the applicant describes fairly recent brutal or severe torture of a nature likely to leave scars but admits there are none.[7] If a medical report is submitted, caseworkers may disagree with the conclusions, but are 'not normally in a position to dismiss the medical assessment out of hand', bearing in mind that the report is prepared by a specialist.[8] An extension of time for submission of supporting evidence should normally be granted to enable a medical report to be submitted.[9] There is no reflection in the Immigration Rules or the API of the UNHCR *Handbook*'s guidance for investigation of the claims of mentally disturbed persons.[10] But the Tribunal has held that it is totally wrong, especially for a person with a known mental condition, to conduct an interview by asking a series of leading questions. It is much better to allow an applicant with such a condition to tell his or her story in their own way. Interviewers must be sensitive to these matters.[11]

1 Refugee Women's Legal Group *Gender Guidelines for the Determination of Asylum Claims in the United Kingdom* (July 1998). The guidelines were referred to with approval by Lord Hoffmann in *Islam v Secretary of State for the Home Department; R v Immigration Appeal Tribunal and Secretary of State for the Home Department, ex p Shah* [1999]

2 AC 629; [1999] INLR 144, HL. See now the Asylum Gender Guidelines issued by the IAA in November 2000, and see also H Crawley *Refugees and gender: law and process* (Jordans, 2001) chapters 1 and 10.

2 See Crawley above and IAA, Asylum Gender Guidelines above, s 5 on procedural and evidential issues for women refugees.

3 The previous guidance on interviewing (ADI Jul/98, Ch 16, s 3) had no reference to gender. That on torture (API Nov/00, Ch 3, s 2) notes that 'where there are grounds for considering that the interview might be particularly sensitive, every effort should be made to ensure that the interviewer, interpreter and applicant are of the same sex': Annex A.

4 Immigration and Nationality Directorate to ILPA, 27 March 2000.

5 API Nov/00, Ch 3, s 2, para 3.1, Annex A.

6 *R v Secretary of State for the Home Department ex p Molly Ejon* [1998] INLR 195, QBD: just as a person may be unable, due to physical injury, to disclose evidence at an earlier stage, so they may be unable to do so because of psychiatric damage.

7 API Nov/00, Ch 3, s 2, para 4.

8 API Nov/00, Ch 3, s 2, para 4.

9 Home Office concession 14 October 1998, confirmed in correspondence June 2000.

10 UNHCR *Handbook* **12.13** above, paras 206-212.

11 *Ibrahim v Secretary of State for the Home Department* [1998] INLR 511, IAT. See also *Ermias* (HX00312) 11 August 1999, where the Tribunal agreed that an interview with an applicant who was not fit to be interviewed had no evidential value.

12.119 The Immigration Rules are also silent on the actual practice of obtaining relevant information. In *Musisi* Lord Bridge found it 'strange that such an important interview as this should be entrusted to an immigration officer at a port of entry with no knowledge of conditions in the country of origin of a claimant for asylum'.[1] Port interviews are still conducted by Immigration Service staff and so his comments are still apposite. This contrasts with asylum claims made after entry which are usually conducted by specialist asylum staff. Claims are determined against the background of information about countries of origin provided by the Country Information Policy Unit, which produces detailed, sourced and publicly available assessments of the main refugee-producing countries,[2] and sometimes, information from the Foreign and Commonwealth Office.

1 *Re Musisi* [1987] AC 514.
2 Currently 35. These are sometimes misleading, however, and it remains important to check the sources cited.

12.120 A significant development has been the Home Office practice of giving full reasons for rejection of asylum claims.[1] It is now recognised generally in administrative law that even in the absence of statutory obligation, reasons will be required for a decision which will have significant effects on the rights of individuals affected.[2] Once the giving of reasons became standard practice it was apparent that in a number of cases adverse inferences were being drawn on matters that were capable of reply and had never been canvassed in interview. In a series of cases the courts held that such an approach was a breach of the duty of fairness.[3] In *Ex p Thirukumar*[4] the Court of Appeal held that if an opportunity to make representations was to be meaningful an applicant should be informed of the matters to which his or her attention needed to be directed, and, where time had elapsed since the interview, to be reminded of what had been said. The introduction of a right of appeal in July 1993 put an end to the provisional decision to refuse which invited observations as to why a different course should be adopted. Now, if adverse inferences are wrongly drawn in a refusal letter, the remedy is to address them at the statutory appeal, and failure to do so will mean that they stand.[5] Now that there is power to serve refusal of leave to enter by post after adjourning examination of an applicant for further inquiries,[6] there is no longer an expectation of a final interview at which the refusal letter will be served and the applicant asked for comments. Refusals will be sent by first class, recorded delivery post to the applicant's last known address and nine days will be allowed for lodging appeals (seven days plus two 'posting days').[7]

1 Since the case of *R v Secretary of State for the Home Department, ex p Gurmeet Singh* [1987] Imm AR 489 in which the Divisional Court indicated that the giving of reasons was highly desirable in asylum cases.
2 *R v Secretary of State for the Home Department, ex p Doody* [1994] 1 AC 531; *Stefan v General Medical Council* [1999] 1 WLR 1293; *R v Secretary of State for the Home Department, ex p Zighem* [1996] Imm AR 194. However, Dyson J held in *R (Vallaj) v IAA* (CO 2738/2000) 21 December 2000, that the Secretary of State for is not bound to give reasons for certifying a claim as manifestly unfounded: paras 59–60.
3 *R v Secretary of State for the Home Department, ex p Yemoh* [1988] Imm AR 595; *Gaima v Secretary of State for the Home Department* [1989] Imm AR 205, CA; *R v Secretary of State, ex p Oran (Ayse)* [1991] Imm AR 290.
4 [1989] Imm AR 402, CA, upholding the QBD at [1989] Imm AR 270.
5 See **18.143** below.
6 Immigration (Leave to Enter and Remain) Order 2000, SI 2000/1161, art 12. In the past, the provisions of Immigration Act 1971, Sch 2, para 6(1) (six months' leave to enter deemed given where notice of decision not given within 24 hours of final examination) meant that, in port cases, immigration officers had to complete examination by calling the applicant to a final interview where the refusal letter was served.
7 UK Immigration Service HQ Asylum Liaison Unit, 9 May 2000.

12.121 Refusal letters usually set out a summary of the applicant's claim and contain a number of standard paragraphs referring to credibility issues such as failure to claim in a country of transit or on arrival, and to conditions in the country of feared persecution. Following complaints about unsourced assertions and unfair credibility findings in refusal letters, the Immigration and Nationality Directorate promised in May 2000 that paragraphs on country conditions would be sourced by reference to the Country Immigration Policy Unit assessments, that credibility would not be given disproportionate weight and letters would properly explain, with bullet-pointed discrepancies, clear findings on what was and was not accepted.[1] Specific matters to which the decision-maker is entitled to have regard are set out in the Immigration Rules.[2] There is nothing in the Rules relating to confidentiality of asylum claims, but the Immigration and Nationality Directorate respects the principle of confidentiality in general in asylum claims, and that principle is given added weight by the fact that respect for confidential information is a vital aspect of the right to respect for privacy under Article 8 of the ECHR.[3] It is not permissible for a decision to refer to information provided in confidence by another applicant, including a spouse, unless that information is already in the public domain.[4] Details from forgery reports relied on to discredit documents produced by an asylum claimant will not normally be disclosed.[5]

1 Asylum Processes Stakeholders' Group meeting, May 2000.
2 HC 395, para 341: see **12.31** above.
3 *Z v Finland* (1997) 25 EHRR 371. Previous Asylum Directive instructions indicated that the information in an asylum claim may be disclosed to other government departments or agencies, local authorities, international organisations and other bodies to ensure that they carry out their functions: ADI Jul/98, Ch 16, s 2. They are no longer published.
4 Asylum claims enter the public domain once an appeal has been heard in public.
5 ADI Jul/98, Ch 16, s 2, para 2.7 (no longer published); see also Immigration and Asylum Act 1999, Sch 4, para 6 and Immigration and Asylum (Procedure) Rules 2000, SI 2000/2333, r 40.

Non-compliance refusal

12.122 HC 395, paragraph 340 provides that a failure without reasonable explanation to make a prompt disclosure of material facts or to assist the Secretary of State in establishing the facts of the case may lead to refusal. It includes failure to complete an asylum questionnaire. The actions of an agent may be taken into account for these purposes.[1] Failure to return Statement of Evidence forms in time[2] leads to refusal of the claim for non-compliance,[3] even where the asylum seeker concerned was in hospital having a baby when the form was due.[4] Receipt of the form even days late does not result in cancellation of the refusal decision or to interview on the claim, merely to 'consideration' of the material in the form.[5] Failure to attend or late attendance for interview will also lead to non-compliance refusal unless exceptional circumstances prevented attendance.[6] In *Ali Hoddad*, a starred Tribunal held that an application may not be refused on non-compliance ground alone; in each case the Home Office is obliged to decide the asylum claim, and the appellate authority the appeal, on the material available.[7] In *Busuulwa* the Tribunal lamented that the words of the statute forced the appellate authority to exercise original jurisdiction over asylum claims which have never been considered substantively,[8] although it was wrong in priniple for the primary decision to be taken other than in accordance with the UNHCR guidelines. It called on the Secretary of State to withdraw non-compliant refusals which failed to review the merits of the asylum claim.[9] Otherwise, the only remedy was judical review.

1   HC 395, para 342.
2   The Statement of Evidence form must be returned within ten working days. Requests to extend the time limit will only be granted in the most exceptional circumstances, and not to enable the applicant to instruct a representative to complete the form: API Aug/00, Ch 4, s 1, para 4.2. In practice, applicants and representatives are unable to get access to caseworkers to request an extension of time: see correspondence between ILPA and Barbara Roche, 24 October 2000.
3   HC 395, para 341. It was widely believed that the flood of non-compliance refusals during 2000, including many issued when forms had been returned either within or only just outside the period, had more to do with political priorities (statistics showing the rate of decision-making was rapidly improving) than with proper refugee determination.
4   Judicial review proceedings were lodged but were withdrawn when the Home Office accepted the late Statement of Evidence and issued a reasoned decision in place of the non-compliance one.
5   See correspondence between ILPA and Barbara Roche, 24 October 2000.
6   HC 395, para 341; API Aug/00, Ch 4, s 1, para 3 cite medical evidence of inability to attend through hospitalisation, or serious disruption to public transport.
7   *Haddad (Ali) v Secretary of State for the Home Department* [2000] INLR 117. Earlier cases such as *Davies (Sandra)* (17797), which had held that the correct course for the appellate authority finding good reason for non-compliance was to allow the appeal and remit to the Secretary of State for substantive consideration of the asylum claim, were not referred to. In *Shreef* (01 TH 00476) another Tribunal held that the course adopted in *Davies* was correct. See also API Aug/00, Ch 4, s 1, para 2.2.
8   *Busuulwa* (01 TH 00239). By March 2001, nearly one-third of all claims were refused without consideration of the merits, for alleged non-compliance with time limits. A fair proportion of these were erroneous, ie there was evidence that the Statement of Evidence form had been returned in time.
9   The API indicate that an incorrect refusal on these grounds will be withdrawn as fatally flawed and substantive consideration of the asylum application will continue: API Aug/00, Ch 4, s 1, para 8.1. The policy of withdrawal of the flawed decision (and not merely the reasons for it) was confirmed in April 2001.

Asylum and the one-stop procedure

12.123 Port asylum applicants and their relevant family members,[1] and those claiming asylum as illegal entrants or persons liable to removal, are given a one-stop notice under section 75 of the Immigration and Asylum Act 1999 when they make their claim, asking for any additional grounds on which they seek to remain.[2] The Statement of Additional Grounds must be completed in full and in English and returned within ten working days.[3] The preparation and service of the additional grounds has given rise to similar difficulties as has that of the Statement of Evidence form.[4] In each case, beleaguered representatives in dispersal areas complain that it is impossible, given the severe lack of legal and interpretation assistance in these areas, for the forms to be submitted in time. In each case the Home Office responds that all that is required is a simple factual statement whose preparation requires no legal assistance. It is certainly the case that what the procedure contemplates is that the facts on which any human rights claim to remain is based, rather than any legal elaboration, are put before the decision-maker. Thus a fear of torture or of arbitrary or prolonged imprisonment in insanitary conditions, or the presence of family members in the UK would not need to be couched in the language of Articles of the ECHR.[5] But what the Home Office position signally fails to recognise (apart from the need for interpreting facilities to complete the form in English) is the legal knowledge required to know which facts among a myriad of reasons for wanting to remain are relevant and cogent and which are not. It takes little experience in the field to know that unrepresented applicants frequently do not know what in their histories, lives and futures has cogency in immigration law terms. Many would never, for example, think of referring to a same-sex relationship, or wish to refer to domestic violence, let alone seeking to rely on these matters to remain in the country. The publicly declared view of Home Office ministers that asylum claimants are cynical opportunists is often the opposite of the truth.

1 'Relevant family member' is defined as a person making a claim to remain as a dependant of the asylum claimant, who appears to be the spouse of the claimant, the child of the claimant or of the spouse, a cohabitee for two of the preceding three years, a person dependent on the claimant or on whom the claimant is dependent: Immigration and Asylum Appeals (One-Stop Procedure) Regulations 2000, SI 2000/2244, reg 7.

2 The same applies to those claiming that removal would breach their human rights. For details of the one-stop procedure and its application in asylum and human rights appeals see **18.108**ff below.

3 See **18.114** below.

4 See non-compliance **12.122** fn 2 above.

5 Although Home Office staff are reportedly ignoring claims which fail to refer in terms to the ECHR Article relied on.

12.124 The one-stop procedure applies slightly differently to in-country asylum claimants. They will only be served with a one-stop notice on refusal of their asylum claim. The one-stop notice, served on the claimant and relevant family members under section 74 of the Immigration and Asylum Act 1999 will ask for a statement of additional grounds on which they wish to remain in the UK. Thereafter the procedures are similar. Failure to set out relevant grounds for wishing to remain affect the scope of matters which can be raised on the appeal and in future appeals. Similarly, those refused entry or stay in another capacity who wish to claim asylum will be expected to raise asylum grounds in the section 74 statement of additional grounds they will have to serve in response to the one-stop notice they will be given with the refusal decision. Details are given at **18.108ff** below.

Removal to safe third countries

12.125 The Asylum and Immigration Appeals Act 1993 was the first statutory provision[1] incorporating and extending an international practice whereby claims for asylum made in one state could be refused without substantive consideration on the basis that the claimant could be removed to a country other than the country of feared persecution, which would be responsible for determining the asylum claim. The practice was based upon the 'first country of asylum' principle of international law whereby neighbouring countries were expected to take refugees fleeing a persecuting state.[2] In modern times, governments have turned the principle round so as to expect a refugee to find refuge locally wherever possible.[3] Removal to 'safe third countries' is a controversial practice[4] and one that resulted in substantial and protracted litigation during the 1990s, and consequential significant statutory amendment in the Asylum and Immigration Act 1996 and Immigration and Asylum Act 1999. This section reviews the case law under the previous statutory provisions, as the issues raised continue to be relevant and will inform any challenge to certificates under the new regime.

1 Prior to the Asylum and Immigration Appeals Act 1993, removal of an asylum seeker on third country grounds had been entirely a matter of administrative discretion subject only to the requirement in the Immigration Rules that the rules should lay down no practice which was not in accordance with the Refugee Convention. The landmark and foundation case of *Re Musisi* [1987] AC 514, in which the removal of a Ugandan to Kenya was quashed because of Kenya's practice of returning Ugandans home, had established that art 33 of the Refugee Convention prevented indirect as well as direct *refoulement*: *Musisi* at 532C–E.
2 See references in Goodwin-Gill **12.5** fn 1 above.
3 See eg Preamble to Resolution on a harmonised approach to questions concerning host third countries, approved by EU ministers 30 November 1992 under Third Pillar.
4 See UNHCR 'The "safe third country" policy in the light of the international obligations of countries vis-à-vis refugees and asylum seekers' London, July 1993. See also Amnesty International *Playing human pinball: Home Office practice in 'safe third country' asylum cases* (June 1995); ECRE *Safe third countries: myths and realities* (February 1995). In *R v Uxbridge Magistrates' Court, ex p Adimi* [1999] INLR 490, the Divisional Court held, rejecting the submission of the Home Office to the contrary, that asylum seekers had an element of choice as to where they might claim asylum: per Simon Brown LJ at 496H–497A–C and Newman J at 507C.

12.126 A third country removal engages the UK's obligations under the Refugee Convention only if it exposes the claimant (directly or indirectly)[1] to a real risk of *refoulement*;[2] there is no breach if removal may be ineffective in the sense that the third country returns the applicant to the UK.[3] However, repeated ineffective removals would be oppressive and might constitute inhuman treatment[4] and in practice the Home Office normally only operates the third country procedure once, dealing with the claim substantively if the person is returned here. If the third state removes the claimant to a fourth state, that in itself would not breach the UK's obligations under the Convention if it were a safe country and a procedure was in place in the third state to assess the safety of the fourth state,[5] but where a removal by the UK instigated a real risk of *refoulement* via a chain of states then the UK's obligation would still be engaged.

1 *Re Musisi* **12.125** fn 1 above.
2 Ie return to the borders of the territory where persecution is feared. See Goodwin-Gill **12.5** fn 1 above, Ch 4.
3 *R v Secretary of State for the Home Department, ex p Dursun (Huseyin)* [1991] Imm AR 297; *R v Secretary of State for the Home Department, ex p Mehari* [1994] QB 474; *Thavathevathasan v Secretary of State for the Home Department* [1994] Imm AR 249; *Mohamed Jafar v Secretary of State for the Home Department* [1994] Imm AR 497.
4 *Karali (Kemal) v Secretary of State for the Home Department* [1991] Imm AR 199.
5 *Martinas v Special Adjudicator and the Secretary of State for the Home Department* [1995] Imm AR 190, CA.

The Asylum and Immigration Appeals Act 1993

12.127 Section 6 of the Asylum and Immigration Appeals Act 1993[1] prohibited the removal of asylum seekers until their claims were determined. Third country removals were not mentioned in the Act, but an asylum claim by a person deemed removable to a third country was determined by the Secretary of State without consideration of the merits and certified 'without foundation' as not engaging the UK's obligations under the Refugee Convention.[2] The Immigration Rules provide that the Secretary of State may decide not to consider the substance of the person's claim to asylum if he or she is satisfied that the person's removal to a third country does not raise any issue as to the UK's obligations under the Convention and Protocol.[3] The claim does not raise any such issue if the removal was:

- to a country of which the applicant is not a national or citizen;
- where his or her life or freedom is not threatened contrary to Article 33 of the Refugee Convention;
- from where he or she would not be sent elsewhere in a manner inconsistent with the Convention; and, either:
    - the applicant has not arrived directly in the UK from the place where persecution is feared and has had an opportunity to make contact with the authorities of another country to seek their protection; or
    - there is clear evidence of his or her admissibility to a third country.[4]

A separate Rule[5] dealt with removals to third countries of claimants who had already sought and been refused asylum. The removal could be to the country which was a party to the Convention and had refused the asylum claim, or to another country meeting the criteria above. On removal to the state which had refused the claim, the claimant was expected to raise any new circumstances with its authorities. An in-country appeal against refusal on third country grounds was provided, with its own special procedures.[6]

1 Re-enacted as Immigration and Asylum Act 1999, s 15.
2 Asylum and Immigration Appeals Act 1993, Sch 2, para 5(2).
3 HC 395, para 337, now deleted.
4 HC 395, para 345.
5 HC 395, para 347, now deleted.
6 Asylum Appeals (Procedure) Rules 1993, SI 1993/1661. Rules 5, 6, 9 and 11 provided shorter time limits, envisaging the determination of these appeals within seven days. In fact, appeals under the so-called 'fast track' could take over a year to be heard.

12.128 The whole procedure was predicated on speedy removals[1] and an underlying assumption that there would be little if any basis for challenging the certificates, since most third-country returns were to European, usually EU, states. But the reverse of what was anticipated occurred – in large measure due to thorough research and effective representation by the then newly established Refugee Legal Centre – and many certificates were overturned on appeal or on judicial review. During the period between 1993 and 1996, special adjudicators[2] on occasion rejected certificates of the Secretary of State relating to every member state of the EU, and consistently rejected certificates relating to removals to France[3] and Belgium.[4] The Secretary of State desisted from removing asylum seekers to Italy, Greece and Portugal following adverse decisions and in the light of the evidence produced at appeals as to practice in these states.

1   *R v Secretary of State for the Home Department, ex p Mehari* [1994] Imm AR 151, QBD; *Abdi and Gawe v Secretary of State for the Home Department* [1994] Imm AR 402, CA, [1996] Imm AR 288, HL.
2   Special Adjudicators were adjudicators designated under Asylum and Immigration Appeals Act 1993, s 8(5) to hear asylum appeals.
3   See *Canbolat v Secretary of State for the Home Department* [1997] Imm AR 442 at 454.
4   *R v Special Adjudicator, ex p Bostem* [1996] Imm AR 388 at 393.

The Asylum and Immigration Act 1996

12.129 The Asylum and Immigration Act 1996 expressly excluded asylum claimants removable to third countries from the protection from removal provided in section 6 of the Asylum and Immigration Appeals Act 1993[1] and put into statutory form the criteria for certification on 'third country' grounds previously only contained in the Immigration Rules. The criteria themselves remained the same: the Secretary of State had to be satisfied that:

•   the person was not a national of that territory;[2]
•   his or her life or liberty would not be threatened there on Refugee Convention grounds;[3] and
•   the authorities would not send him to another country otherwise than in accordance with the Convention.[4]

In addition, other provisions of the Rules continued to apply, that the claimant must have had an opportunity to claim protection in the third country or there must be other clear evidence of his or her admissibility there.[5] The Immigration Rules were amended to reflect the provisions of the 1996 Act and rule 347 was entirely deleted, so that claims previously refused in a third country were assimilated to the general 'third country' provisions.

1   Asylum and Immigration Act 1996, s 2(2).
2   Asylum and Immigration Act 1996, s 2(2)(a).
3   Asylum and Immigration Act 1996, s 2(2)(b).
4   Asylum and Immigration Act 1996, s 2(2)(c).
5   HC 395, para 345(2).

12.130 The substantial change brought about by the Asylum and Immigration Act 1996 was, however, in respect of appeal rights. The right of appeal against the issue of the certificate was restricted to the ground that the statutory conditions were not met when the certificate was issued or had since ceased to be fulfilled, until the certificate was set aside on appeal.[1] But where the third state was a member state of the EU, or designated by a statutory instrument,[2] the in-country right of appeal was abolished.[3] Since the vast majority of asylum claimants removed to third countries were to EU states or the designated countries, this provision virtually abolished statutory appeals against third country removal at a stroke. It was highly controversial, given the success rates of third country appeals under the Asylum and Immigration Appeals Act 1993. But the effective ending of the statutory appeal did not put an end to challenges to the issue of certificates in such cases. Following the coming into force of the 1996 Act the Secretary of State resumed third country removals to all EU member states, and evidence of those countries' interpretation of the Refugee Convention and their practices gleaned for the purposes of the 1993 Act appeals now formed the basis of many challenges to the lawfulness of the Secretary of State's certificates by judicial review. These cases will be considered below.

1   Asylum and Immigration Act 1996, s 3(1).
2   Asylum and Immigration Act 1996, s 2(3).
3   Asylum and Immigration Act 1996, s 3(2). The countries designated under s 2(3) as safe third countries are Canada, Norway, Switzerland and the US: Asylum (Designated Countries of Destination and Designated Safe Third Countries) Order 1996, SI 1996/2671, in force 1 October 1996. The same four countries are designated under the Asylum (Designated Safe Third Countries) Order 2000, SI 2000/2245.

The issues raised

Refoulement by the third country

12.131 The possibility that the third country will remove the claimant in a manner inconsistent with its Refugee Convention obligations has been the central issue in most third country cases. The fact that the country has signed the Refugee Convention or other relevant international agreements that reaffirm its Convention obligations, that it co-operates with the UNHCR and has procedures in place to give effect to its obligations, has been held to constitute some evidence on which the Secretary of State could rely to conclude that removal would not be contrary to the UK's obligations. But these factors were held to create a rebuttable presumption of safety which could be displaced by examination of the actual practice and procedures of the country.

12.132 Before the coming into force of the Dublin Convention in 1997, the UK, not being part of the Schengen system, was bound by no multilateral obligations ordering responsibility for asylum determination, and nor was any other country bound to accept those returned from the UK. The Immigration Rules imposed no obligation on the Secretary of State to consult the third country's authorities to ensure the admission of the claimant to an asylum procedure. The lack of any guarantee of admission meant that examination of state practice was required in individual cases. On appeals under the Asylum and Immigration Appeals Act 1993, evidence was produced which indicated that despite the laws and international obligations of those countries, aspects of practice in third states, particularly relating to admissibility procedures and the actions of border officials or others, was inconsistent with Convention obligations and could create a real risk that the country was not safe. In many EU states admissibility procedures were restrictively cast to exclude a large number of returnees from gaining access to the procedure (often precisely because claimants had travelled through third countries and not sought asylum[1] and/or had failed to claim asylum within a specified time when passing through the third country).[2] Additionally, disturbing evidence was produced of actual *refoulement* by border officials from a number of third countries including Italy, Austria, Greece, Portugal and France, leading to expressions of concern by UNHCR and other organisations.

1   Eg Austria.
2   See eg the 'eight-day rule' in Belgium, and Portuguese admissibility procedures.

12.133 *Canbolat*[1] was the first reported challenge to a removal under the Asylum and Immigration Act 1996.[2] The challenge was founded on the frequent refusal of French border officials to admit would-be applicants to asylum procedures and their attempts to remove them. While noting the consistent views of adjudicators[3] that France could not be certified as a safe third country because of these concerns, the Court of Appeal rejected the application for judicial review for want of recent evidence of malpractice by the French border police.[4] The court gave general guidance that has been applied in subsequent cases:

(i)   the statutory test requires that the Secretary of State be satisfied that there is 'no real risk' that the claimant would be sent to another country otherwise than in accordance with the Refugee Convention;

(ii)   the Secretary of State must demonstrate to the court that such steps as are reasonable in the circumstances to acquaint himself with the relevant facts have been taken;

(iii)   the opinion of the Secretary of State would be reviewed on a *Wednesbury* basis with the heightened scrutiny required by reference to the fundamental rights engaged.[5]

1   *Canbolat v Secretary of State for the Home Department* [1997] Imm AR 442.
2   The challenge was to the Secretary of State's certificate that he was satisfied that France would not send the applicant to another country otherwise than in accordance with the Refugee Convention.
3   In the six months prior to the coming into force of the Asylum and Immigration Act 1996, special adjudicators upheld certificates in only two of 80 cases heard on removal to France: *Canbolat* above at 454; see also *Butterworths Immigration Law Service*, 2E[514]-[520].
4   Permission for judicial review was granted where contemporary evidence was obtained of attempted *refoulement* by French officials: *R v Secretary of State for the Home Department, ex p Cicek* (CO 873/1997) (permission granted 27 June 1997).
5   *Bugdaycay v Secretary of State for the Home Department* [1987] AC 514; *R v Ministry of Defence, ex p Smith* [1996] QB 517.

12.134 Applying these principles, the Court of Appeal rejected challenges to certificates in respect of the safety[1] of Belgium[2] and Greece,[3] and the High Court has dismissed applications in respect of Italy[4] and the US.[5] However, in the case of *Besnik Gashi*[6] the Court of Appeal quashed a certificate in respect of the removal of two Kosovar Albanians to Germany on the basis that the Secretary of State could not demonstrate that adequate inquires had been made which would explain the gross disparity in outcome of claims from ethnic Albanians in the UK, where they were universally recognised as refugees,[7] and Germany, where only a tiny percentage were given refugee status and many were returned to the Federal Republic of Yugoslavia.[8] The Secretary of State withdrew an appeal to the House of Lords, and *Gashi* remains good law on the standard of inquires expected of the Secretary of State in such cases.[9]

1　Under Asylum and Immigration Act 1996, s 2(2)(c), ie on whether the Secretary of State could reasonably be satisfied that the third country concerned would not send the applicant to another country otherwise than in accordance with the Refugee Convention.

2　*R v Secretary of State for the Home Department, ex p James Mbanja* [1999] Imm AR 508.

3　*R v Secretary of State for the Home Department, ex p Elshani and Berisha* [1999] INLR 265, [1999] Imm AR 400.

4　*R v Secretary of State for the Home Department, ex p Sharifi and Kahsay*, 10 June 1997.

5　*R v Secretary of State for the Home Department, ex p Salas* [2001] Imm AR 105, Sullivan J. This case is on appeal to the Court of Appeal and may be approached differently by the court in light of the judgment of the House of Lords in *Adan and Aitseguer* [2001] INLR 44 because it includes a challenge to the US interpretation of arts 1A(2) and 33 of the Refugee Convention.

6　*Besnik Gashi v Secretary of State for the Home Department* [1999] INLR 276; revsd [1999] Imm AR 415.

7　This was because of the Immigration Appeal Tribunal's decision in *Gashi and Nikshiqi* [1997] INLR 96, which had ruled that ethnic Albanians were victims of systematic group persecution by the Serbian authorities and that the general experience of discrimination was sufficient to found a claim for refugee status.

8　Many were refused on the basis of an internal flight alternative within the Federal Republic of Yugoslavia to Montenegro, regardless of the fact that this approach was facilitating the Serbian policy of ridding Kosovo of Albanians.

9　The change in circumstances in Kosovo meant that after June 1999 the disparity in treatment requiring explanation disappeared and the Secretary of State could resume the issue of certificates in such cases: *R v Secretary of State for the Home Department, ex p Artan Gjoka and Shefki Gashi*, 15 June 2000, Collins J. More controversially the Secretary of State sought to maintain certificates that were issued in cases which had been stayed pending the resolution of the litigation in *Besnik Gashi*. In *R (Zeqiri) v Secretary of State for the Home Department* [2001] EWCA Civ 342, the Court of Appeal held that, although the Secretary of State was entitled to re-certify that Germany was a safe third country after a change in circumstances, given the time delay and the Secretary of State's conduct in treating *Gashi* as a test case, it was unfair and a breach of a legitimate expectation to treat such claimants differently.

Different approaches to the Refugee Convention

12.135 The question of whether or not removal of an asylum claimant to a third country would be in accordance with the Refugee Convention as required by the Asylum and Immigration Act 1996[1] if that country did not apply the Convention in the same way as the UK led to complex litigation, which has now been largely settled by the House of Lords in *Adan and Aitseguer.*[2] In these cases a clear difference of interpretation of the Refugee Convention between the UK and the receiving states Germany and France led to differential treatment of cases based on fear of non-state persecution. Ms Adan feared persecution as a female member of a minority clan in the civil war in Somalia, where there was no functioning state authority. Mr Aitseguer feared reprisals by armed Islamic groups in Algeria, where the state was unable to provide adequate protection. It was accepted that if their accounts were established they would be entitled to refugee status in the UK (applying the 'protection' theory), but that if removed to Germany and France respectively, they would be denied refugee status in those countries. Both France and Germany interpreted the Refugee Convention as providing protection only to those who feared persecution in which the state was implicated in some way (the accountability theory). A fear of persecution by 'non-state agents' *simpliciter* was not regarded in either country as sufficient to qualify for refugee status.[3] The issue was whether there was one true meaning of the Convention or whether there was a permissible range of interpretations. If there was one true meaning, a state which did not subscribe to it and so wrongly denied refugee status would not be one to which the Secretary of State could legitimately remove an asylum claimant. If on the other hand there was a permissible range of meanings, as had been assumed by the Court of Appeal in two earlier cases of *Ex p Kerrouche*[4] and *Ex p Iyadurai*,[5] the issue for the court would be whether the Secretary of State's conclusion on the third country's compliance with the Convention was reasonable.

1   Asylum and Immigration Act 1996, s 2(2)(c); the same test applies under the Immigration and Asylum Act 1999, see s 12(7). See **12.152** below.
2   *Secretary of State for the Home Department v Adan, Secretary of State for the Home Department v Aitseguer* [2001] INLR 44, HL.
3   A similar interpretation of the Refugee Convention is adopted by Italy.
4   *R v Secretary of State for the Home Department, ex p Kerrouche* [1997] Imm AR 610 at 615.
5   *R v Secretary of State for the Home Department, ex p Iyadurai* [1998] Imm AR 470 at 476.

12.136 The House of Lords upheld the judgment of the Court of Appeal[1] and rejected the Secretary of State's argument that there is a permissible range of interpretations of the Refugee Convention and the court could not interfere with a decision to remove if his conclusion that the French and German interpretations of the Convention were within that permissible range was a reasonable one. In so doing the House of Lords overruled the Court of Appeal decisions in *Kerrouche* and *Iyadurai*[2] insofar as they proceeded on the basis that there was such a permissible range of interpretations (variously described as 'a margin of discretion' or 'range of tolerance').[3] Instead, the House of Lords ruled that the wording of section 2(2)(c) of the Asylum and Immigration Act 1996, 'in accordance with the Convention', refers to the meaning of the Refugee Convention properly interpreted and that the refugee definition in Article 1A(2) of the Convention has only one true interpretation or 'autonomous' meaning,[4] which is a matter of law to be determined by international principles of interpretation of treaties.[5] In issuing a certificate the Secretary of State must satisfy himself that the third state properly interprets the Convention in accordance with this meaning. The court reviewing any such conclusion determines as a matter of law whether the Secretary of State has properly directed him- or herself that the third state applies the correct interpretation of the Convention. The true meaning of Article 1A(2) did not require state complicity for harm inflicted by non-state agents to constitute persecution; the protection of the Convention extends to those persecuted by non-state agents where 'for whatever reason the state in question is unable to afford protection against factions within the state'.[6]

1   *R v Secretary of State for the Home Department, ex p Adan* [1999] 4 All ER 774.
2   *R v Secretary of State for the Home Department, ex p Kerrouche* [1997] Imm AR 610; *R v Secretary of State for the Home Department, ex p Iyadurai* [1998] Imm AR 470.
3   *Adan and Aitseguer* above, per Lord Steyn, at 56 and Lord Hobhouse, 71 (with whose judgments Lord Scott agreed: 72).
4   *Adan and Aitseguer* above, per Lord Steyn.
5   See Vienna Convention on the Law of Treaties, arts 31, 32. The UNHCR *Handbook* **12.13** above, in particular was identified as of 'high persuasive authority' (per Steyn *Adan and Aitseguer* above, 59H), whilst the EU Joint Position upon which the Secretary of State for the Home Department placed great reliance was rejected (57D).
6   Affirming *Adan v Secretary of State for the Home Department* [1999] 1 AC 293, per Lord Lloyd of Berwick at 306A-B, see **12.51** above.

12.137 The foundation for the House of Lords judgment in *Adan and Aitseguer* was the principle established in *Musisi*[1] that Article 33 of the Refugee Convention prohibits indirect as well as direct *refoulement*. As the Law Lords pointed out, the consequence of the Secretary of State's approach was fundamentally to undermine the protection from indirect *refoulement*.[2] The Secretary of State had accepted that to return the claimants directly to Somalia or Algeria would not be in accordance with the UK's obligation under the Convention, but claimed he was entitled to allow just that result to occur if they went back via Germany or France. Clear words in the statute were required to achieve such a 'remarkable result'.[3]

1   *Re Musisi* [1987] AC 514.
2   *TI v UK* [2000] INLR 211.
3   *Adan and Aitseguer* above, per Lord Steyn at 55A.

12.138 The Court of Appeal had drawn a clear distinction between cases that involved third countries' interpretation of the Refugee Convention and those involving their application of it. While the interpretation of the Convention was a question of law to be decided on the basis of the true meaning of its terms, its application involved an area of discretion, where there was no one answer and to which *Wednesbury* review was appropriate. This approach had been required to make sense of and to distinguish the earlier cases of *Canbolat*,[1] *Kerrouche*[2] and *Iyadurai*,[3] cases involving procedures, safeguards and practices in the third states. The House of Lords did not adopt such a strict delineation between the interpretation of the Convention and its application.[4] Its approach was to require the Secretary of State to decide in each case whether the third state may decide to return the asylum claimant to the country from which he or she originally fled and if so, whether that decision could be described as in accordance with the Convention.

1   *Canbolat v Secretary of State for the Home Department* [1997] Imm AR 442.
2   *R v Secretary of State for the Home Department, ex p Kerrouche* [1997] Imm AR 610.
3   *R v Secretary of State for the Home Department, ex p Iyadurai* [1998] Imm AR 470.
4   The distinction between interpretation and application may be difficult in practice. The Secretary of State pointed out that the distinction did not always hold good; the standard of proof, which was an issue in *Iyadurai* (above) was treated in *Sivakumaran* [1988] AC 958 as a question of interpretation of the refugee definition. This issue may be clarified in the Court of Appeal in *R v Secretary of State for the Home Department, ex p Salas* (reported in the DC at [2001] Imm AR 105), where one issue is the standard of proof applied to art 33 of the Convention, treated in the Divisional Court as involving the application of the Convention.

De facto protection

12.139 In *Adan and Aitseguer* the House of Lords, like the Court of Appeal, left open for another case the question of whether the conditions for removal were satisfied by alternative forms of protection in the receiving state despite differences in interpretation which would exclude asylum seekers from recognition as refugees there. We suggest that any such alternative protection would have to be measured against the protection requirements of the Refugee Convention, so that equivalent protection would be necessary to avoid a breach of Article 33. This must mean protection from removal, guaranteed by an enforceable and durable status obtained on the basis of equivalent qualifying facts, without a more onerous substantive or procedural requirement for eligibility (for example, the harm feared should not need to be established to a higher degree than a real risk). An alternative status cannot be dependent on administrative discretion to withhold removal: this is not equivalent to the judicially enforceable right that refugee status provides.[1] Temporary inability to remove an asylum seeker because of practical difficulties patently does not fall into the category of equivalent protection.[2] The Court of Appeal accepted in *Adan*[3] that non-removal obligations could be violated if *de facto* protection involved such a reduction in social and economic rights that the claimant was presented with an effective choice of destitution or reluctant return to the country of origin.

1   In *R v Secretary of State for the Home Department, ex p Aitseguer* [1999] INLR 176 the High Court rejected (at 196E-H) the Secretary of State's reliance on alternative protection in France because it was based upon 'the broadest possible political discretion', no reasons for refusal nor right of appeal were given, and an application to the ECtHR would not prevent removal.
2   In *R v Secretary of State for the Home Department, ex p Adan* [1999] Imm AR 114 at 120 the Divisional Court rejected the Secretary of State's reliance upon mere factual inability to remove to Somalia as a valid basis for certification. The assertion that she would have obtained 'tolerated status' in Germany was rejected on the evidence.
3   *R v Secretary of State for the Home Department, ex p Adan* [1999] 3 WLR 1274, CA, at 1300.

12.140 Following the Court of Appeal judgment in *Adan and Aitseguer,* in *Ex p Bouheraoua and Kerkeb*[1] a certificate was quashed in respect of removal to Greece where there was a dispute as to the position in Greek law on non-state persecution. Dyson J held that the Secretary of State's conclusion that Greece applied the protection theory was contrary to the evidence and/or, applying *Gashi*,[2] that inadequate inquiries had been made. The Secretary of State's reliance on the availability of alternative protection was rejected on the evidence.

1   *R v Secretary of State for the Home Department, ex p Bouheraoua and Kerkeb*, 22 May 2000, QBD, upheld in the CA on 8 May 2001.
2   *Besnik Gashi v Secretary of State for the Home Department* [1999] INLR 276, [1999] Imm AR 415.

Previous refusal

12.141 In cases where a claimant has been refused asylum in the third country, a decision to return may also be successfully challenged where the determination of the asylum claim involved a breach of natural justice[1] or was perverse.[2] In *Ex p Dahmas*[3] in the Court of Appeal, the Secretary of State confirmed that the approach to this category of third country cases included satisfying himself on the evidence that a decision refusing a claim for asylum in the third country 'is [not] flawed by reason of some manifest irrationality or serious procedural irregularity, such that it might not be appropriate to issue a certificate in the particular case'. This approach reflects the case law and is, we suggest, a proper approach to cases where a claim had been refused and no issues of the correct approach to the Refugee Convention arise.[4] Where fresh material is available or new matters arise which were not presented to authorities of the third country, an issue may arise if evidence discloses that it will be impossible for that new material to be considered on return.[5]

1   *R v Special Adjudicator, ex p Stefan and Chiper* [1995] Imm AR 410.
2   *R v Special Adjudicator, ex p Ionel* [1995] Imm AR 410 (decision held not to be perverse); *R v Secretary of State for the Home Department, ex p Dahmas*, 17 November 1999, CA (reversing the QBD decision reported at [2000] Imm AR 151), where the dismissal of an asylum appeal by a Danish court was held to be perverse on the facts.

3   *R v Secretary of State for the Home Department, ex p Dahmas* above.
4   See *R (Agoroh) v Secretary of State for the Home Department* [2001] EWHC Admin 273, Jackson J: proposed return of Togolese asylum seeker to Germany quashed because of failure of Secretary of State to make adequate inquiries into alleged procedural deficiencies in German courts.
5   *Stefan and Chiper* above.

Chain removals

12.142 Chain removals have been an issue in many cases, with third states passing asylum claimants on without adequate consideration of the safety of fourth or fifth states.[1] In *Ex p Sherebayani*[2] permission was granted in respect of the proposed removal of three Iraqi Kurds to the Netherlands-Germany-Czech Republic. Permission was also granted in *Ex p Ozaci*,[3] a case involving a removal to Germany where a 1993 amendment to the asylum law had created an irrebuttable presumption of safety in respect of other member states of the EU, using the concept of 'normative certainty'.[4] The applicant had travelled to Germany from Turkey via Austria – then generally accepted as unsafe because, *inter alia*, of its strict interpretation of the requirement that the claimant come 'directly' from the country of feared persecution, and its practice of returning asylum claimants to neighbouring unsafe countries such as Romania and Hungary. These cases were both conceded by the Secretary of State shortly before the full hearing because it was anticipated that the Dublin Convention, which was about to come into effect, would make these issues academic. However, the UK's Refugee Convention obligations would plainly be engaged where a third state automatically sends a claimant on to a country which the UK would not consider safe, whether or not the states concerned are Dublin signatories.[5]

1   *R v Secretary of State for the Home Department, ex p de Carvalho* [1996] Imm AR 435 (quashing an appellate decision relating to a chain removal to Portugal via Spain); *R v Special Adjudicator, ex p Srikantharajah* [1996] Imm AR 326.
2   *R v Secretary of State for the Home Department, ex p Sherebayani*, 30 August 1996, QBD.
3   *R v Secretary of State for the Home Department, ex p Ozaci*, 1996, QBD.
4   See review of the decision by the Federal Constitutional Court upholding these laws by Marx and Lumpp, in (1996) 8(3) IJRL 419.
5   *Martinas v Special Adjudicator and Secretary of State for the Home Department* [1995] Imm AR 190, CA following *Musisi* [1987] AC 514.

Opportunity to claim in the third state

12.143 In considering whether the asylum claimant had the opportunity to claim asylum in the third country or at its borders, one of the alternative conditions precedent to removal under the Immigration Rules,[1] opportunity is to be objectively assessed. It does not mean a knowing opportunity in the sense that the claimant was aware of the third country's procedures for receiving refugee applications and could form a judgment as to whether it was appropriate to apply there. The question is whether the claimant could have approached the authorities at the border or internally and could have had an asylum claim received.[2] Of course, opportunity is only relevant if the country is safe. The courts have held that the fact that an agent planned the journey and for all intents and purposes dictated the claimant's actions does not preclude the claimant from having an opportunity to make a claim *en route*.[3] But there will be no opportunity if the claimant was transported clandestinely through a country in a vehicle, or the method or duration of the transit is such that no immigration officials were met. The Rule does not import the concept of 'constructive opportunity': it must be the claimant who has the opportunity , not some third party over whom he or she has no control.

1 HC 395, para 345(2)(i).
2 *R v Special Adjudicator, ex p Kandasamy (Linsam)* [1994] Imm AR 333, QBD.
3 *Dursun v Secretary of State for the Home Department* [1993] Imm AR 169, CA; *R v Secretary of State for the Home Department, ex p Musa* [1993] Imm AR 210,QBD.

Clear evidence of admissibility

12.144 This is the alternative 'condition precedent' for third country removal, where the Secretary of State cannot prove that the asylum claimant had an opportunity to claim asylum in the third country to which removal is proposed.[1] 'Clear evidence of admissibility' is a higher threshold than 'reason to believe he would be admitted' which is the criterion for selecting removal destination in other refusal of entry cases,[2] but authorities on the latter test have some relevance. In *Ex p Alsawaf* [3] the court held that claimants do not have to be admitted for settlement in the third country for the test to be satisfied; it is enough if they are accepted for a temporary period while their asylum claim and other relevant circumstances are considered. This approach was followed and applied in *Ex p de Carvalho*.[4] In *Yassine*[5] Lebanese claimants with tourist visas for Brazil, who claimed asylum while in transit in the UK, were refused asylum on the assumption that they could travel on to Brazil; the decision was quashed as the Secretary of State had not demonstrated that the claimants would be admitted to Brazil. The visas had been obtained by misrepresentation: the claimants were refuges, not tourists, and they had no other connection with Brazil apart from the visa. However, in *Shah*[6] Collins J held that a Portuguese visa on a passport which had been obtained by deception and to which the holder was not entitled was a 'valid' visa for the purposes of the Dublin Convention, enabling the applicant to be returned to Portugal.

1 HC 395, para 345(2)(ii).
2 Immigration Act 1971, Sch 2, para 8(1)(c)(iv).
3 *Alsawaf v Secretary of State for the Home Department* [1988] Imm AR 410, CA, at 422, per Staughton LJ.
4 *R v Secretary of State for the Home Department, ex p de Carvalho* [1996] Imm AR 435.
5 *R v Secretary of State for the Home Department, ex p Yassine* [1990] Imm AR 354, QBD.
6 *R (Shah) v Secretary of State for the Home Department* [2001] EWHC Admin 197, para 31.

12.145 In most cases of removal to the EU, the terms of the Dublin Convention, which came into force in September 1997, provide sufficient evidence of admissibility, and for the most part it is no longer a live issue. Admissibility is relevant to cases of removal to non-designated countries. Other forms of re-admission agreements could provide evidence of admissibility, along with residence permits, a valid visa, or other evidence of a right of entry.[1]

1 *Miller v Immigration Appeal Tribunal* [1988] Imm AR 358, CA. An attempt to avoid removal to Belgium by withdrawing an asylum claim was rejected in *R (Zajmi) v Secretary of State for the Home Department*, 15 November 2000, CA.

Dublin Convention

12.146 The Dublin Convention[1] was one of the first agreements between states to delineate responsibility for examining asylum applications. Its main purposes were on the one hand to prevent multiple claims and 'forum-shopping' by asylum seekers,[2] and on the other to prevent the situation of refugees 'in orbit', passed between states with no one state having responsibility for examining the asylum application, by guaranteeing a determination of the asylum claim in one country. All EU member states are parties to the Convention, so in the following text we will refer to 'member states' rather than 'contracting states'. The Convention provides that normally an application for asylum will be considered by one member state in accordance with its national law and international obligations,[3] although another member state has the right to examine the claim if the claimant agrees even when it is not responsible.[4] Article 3(7) of the Convention provides for the return of a claimant to a member state in which he or she has previously lodged a claim for asylum. The criteria for determining which member state is responsible for examining an asylum application are set out in Articles 4-8 of the Convention. The Articles apply in the order in which they appear.

(i) *Family member*: The first criterion or connecting factor is where a claimant has a family member who has been recognised as a refugee and is legally resident in a member state. That state shall be responsible, provided the persons concerned agree.[5] Family member is strictly defined as spouse, unmarried child under 18 or, in the case of an unmarried claimant under 18, parents. The definition excludes those recognised only as *de facto* refugees or with exceptional leave, and in this respect UK practice is more generous and consistent with the concept of family unity and respect for family life.

(ii) *Visa*: The second connecting factor is where a claimant possesses a valid residence permit or visa issued by a member state.[6] That state is responsible unless it issued the visa at the request of another member state, or the visa is a transit visa only and the claimant either lodges the application in another member state where there is no visa requirement or there is written confirmation that the claimant fulfils the conditions for entry into that state.[7] Rules also determine which state is responsible where there is more than one visa or residence permit.[8]

(iii) *Illegal Entry*: The third connecting factor is illegal entry. Where a refugee has made an irregular entry into a member state from outside the Community, that state is responsible unless the application is made in another member state in which the asylum applicant has been living for at least six months prior to making the application.[9]

(iv) *Lawful entry without a visa*: The fourth connecting factor deals with lawful entry without a visa. It places responsibility for examining applications on the state responsible for controlling the entry of the claimant into the territory of the member states,[10] except where the claimant chooses to lodge the application in another member state to which he or she is entitled to go without a visa. A member state which authorises transit without a visa through the transit zone of its airports is not to be regarded as responsible for control on entry in respect of travelers who do not leave the transit zone. But if an application for asylum is made in transit in an airport of a member state, that state is responsible for examining the claim.[11]

(v)   *Place where the application is lodged*: The fifth connecting factor operates where no state can be designated on the basis of the other criteria listed in the Dublin Convention. Then the first member state in which an application is lodged will be responsible.[12] If an application is lodged in one member state but the claimant is in the territory of another, the latter is regarded as the state where the application is lodged, provided there is prompt notification of the claim by the first state.[13]

(vi)   Another member state may also be requested by the receiving state to examine the application although not responsible under the above criteria. It may do so for humanitarian reasons based on family or cultural grounds, if the claimant so desires.[14] But responsibility will only transfer when the requested state agrees.

1 The Convention Determining the State Responsible For Examining Applications For Asylum Lodged in One of the Member States of the European Community [1990] Imm AR 604. It came into force on 1 September 1997. See A Nicol and S Harrison 'The law and practice in the application of the Dublin Convention in the UK' (1999) 1 EJML 465.

2 As has been pointed out repeatedly by non-governmental organisations since the Dublin Convention was signed, when the protection offered by contracting states varies, there is profound injustice if asylum claimants have no choice over their country of asylum. For discussion of this problem see Gregor Noll 'Formalism vs. empiricism: some reflections on the Dublin Convention on the occasion of recent European case law' (2001) ECRAN weekly update, 25 January.

3 Dublin Convention, art 3(2) and (3.)

4 Dublin Convention, art 3(4). In *R v Secretary of State for the Home Department, ex p S* [1998] Imm AR 416 Forbes J held that the UK had not assumed responsibility under Article 3(4) for examination of the claim, even though the claimant had been interviewed about the merits of the claim on two occasions for a total of nine hours. In the absence of some positive statement that the UK has accepted the unconditional or exclusive right to examine the claim, the actual examination of the claim was not sufficient.

5 Dublin Convention, art 4.

6 See *R v Secretary of State for the Home Department, ex p Yassine* [1990] Imm AR 354, *R (Shah) v Secretary of State for the Home Department* [2001] EWHC Admin 197, at **12.144** above as to validity of visa.

7 Dublin Convention, art 5(1) and (2).

8 Dublin Convention, art 5(3).

9 Dublin Convention, art 6.

10 Dublin Convention, art 7(1).

11 Dublin Convention, art 7(2) and (3). See *R v Secretary of State for the Home Department, ex p Behluli* [1998] INLR 594, CA where a dispute arose between the UK and Italian governments as to the application of art 7, when 53 Kosovo Albanians were held in transit in an Italian airport for over 24 hours while officials argued about whether they could travel on to the UK. The dispute centred on whether asylum claims had been made in Italy. The Italian government denied it was responsible under art 7, but agreed to the Kosovans' return as a matter of discretion.

12 Dublin Convention, art 8.

13 Dublin Convention, art 12.

14 Dublin Convention, art 9.

12.147 The Dublin Convention establishes a procedure for determining responsibility and resolving disputes between states. Importantly it also provides a timetable for resolution of these issues. The process of determination must start as soon as the application for asylum is lodged.[1] The transfer request must be made as quickly as possible and in any event within six months. If it is not, responsibility will rest with the state in which the application was lodged.[2] The receiving state must respond to the request within three months; if not, it is deemed to accept it.[3] Once it is determined that the responsible state is not the one where the application was lodged, the next stage is to transfer the claimant to the responsible state. This must be done within one month of the acceptance of the claim by the responsible state.[4] In cases where a return is to a member state in which a previous claim for asylum was made, the time limits are stricter, requiring the receiving state to respond to the request within eight days and to take the claimant back as quickly as possible and no later than one month after agreeing to do so.[5] These time limits are mandatory.[6] The responsible state is obliged to take charge of the claimant until the asylum claim is determined.[7] Responsibility for processing an application ceases if another member state grants a residence permit of more than three months or if the claimant leaves EU territory for at least three months.[8]

1   Dublin Convention, art 3(6).
2   Dublin Convention, art 11(1).
3   Dublin Convention, art 11(4).
4   Dublin Convention, art 11(5)
5   Dublin Convention, art 13(1)(b).
6   Dublin Convention, art 10(1)(a) and (c); but the time limits do not give rise to a legitimate expectation in the applicant that he or she will not be removed thereafter: see *R v Secretary of State for the Home Department, ex p Akhbari* [2000] Imm AR 436, CA.
7   Dublin Convention, art 10(1)(a); see *R (Zajmi) v Secretary of State for the Home Department* (CO 2607/2000) 15 November 2000, holding that the Dublin Convention obliges the state which rejected a claim to take the claimant back.
8   Dublin Convention, art 10(2) and (3).

12.148 States agree to exchange information about general practices[1] and specific information about an individual[2] where this information is necessary to determine the asylum claim or the state responsible for its determination. Certain of this information can be exchanged only with the consent of the asylum claimant,[3] who has the right on request to receive the information concerned.[4]

1   Dublin Convention, art 14.
2   Dublin Convention, art 15. Personal details (as defined) may be exchanged and details of the asylum claim.
3   Dublin Convention, art 15(3). The information about the asylum claim needs the asylum seeker's consent for its exchange; identifying and route details do not.
4   Dublin Convention, art 15(7).

Status of the Dublin Convention in domestic law

12.149 The Dublin Convention was adopted under the Third Pillar of the EU[1] and has no direct effect in the UK.[2] In the case of *Ex p Behluli*[3] the Court of Appeal ruled that as an international treaty the Dublin Convention did not give rise to enforceable rights and duties in domestic law.[4] Statements and actions indicating that the Home Office intended to treat relevant third-country cases in accordance with the Dublin Convention were not sufficiently clear, unambiguous representations to create a legitimate expectation that claimants would only be removed in accordance with its criteria.[5] Attempts to distinguish this case on the basis of later authority on legitimate expectation[6] have not succeeded in ensuring compliance with the Dublin Convention; its limiting provisions have been held not to fetter the broad powers in the statute and the rules.[7] A legitimate expectation can arise from specific assurances made to a particular claimant.[8] This jurisprudence is now overtaken by the Immigration and Asylum Act 1999, section 11 of which incorporates the Dublin Convention,[9] but it may still be relevant to removals involving other inter-state readmission agreements.

1 Co-operation in the fields of justice and home affairs.

2 The legal basis for any future Convention performing the same function is the consolidated art 63(1)(a) (ex art 73k) EC. Any measure passed under art 63 will be a first pillar measure and will have direct effect.

3 *R v Secretary of State for the Home Department, ex p Behluli* [1998] INLR 594, CA.

4 *R v Secretary of State for the Home Department, ex p Altan Gjoka and Shefki Gashi*, 15 June 2000, QBD; *Zeqiri v Secretary of State for the Home Department* [2001] EWCA Civ 342.

5 On the basis of *R v Secretary of State for the Home Department, ex p Brind* [1991] 1 AC 696 and *Chundawadra v Immigration Appeal Tribunal* [1988] Imm AR 161, that ratification of the Dublin Convention itself did not give rise to a legitimate expectation of compliance with it.

6 *R v Secretary of State for the Home Department, ex p Ahmed and Patel* [1998] INLR 570, where the Court of Appeal, adopting the approach of the Australian High Court in *Minister for Immigration and Ethnic Affairs v Teoh* (1995) 183 CLR 273, held that in the absence of an express statement to the contrary, ratification of an international Treaty was an adequate foundation for a legitimate expectation that its terms would be complied with.

7 In *R v Secretary of State for the Home Department, ex p Akhbari* [2000] Imm AR 165, Hooper J was prepared to distinguish *Behluli* by applying *Ahmed and Patel* but held that no expectation could arise that the time limit provisions of the Dublin Convention would be adhered to because the statute made no reference to time limits and constituted an express statement of policy. The Court of Appeal refused permission to appeal on 23 March 2000. See also *R (Shah) v Secretary of State for the Home Department* [2001] EWHC Admin 197.

8 In *R v Secretary of State for the Home Department, ex p Mohamed Ourad*, 5 July 1999, the Court of Appeal granted permission to challenge a removal to Portugal where the Secretary of State had previously agreed not to proceed on third-country grounds, since the immigration authorities arguably could not resile from their previous position and an opportunity to make representations was arguably insufficient. The Secretary of State agreed to consider the claim substantively.

9 Immigration and Asylum Act 1999, ss 11(2), (4). The 'standing arrangements' are at present those contained in the Dublin Convention, although in future they will be under art 63(1)(a) EC; see **12.105** above.

Discretionary cases

12.150 Articles 3(4) and 9 are important provisions of the Dublin Convention, in that they preserve the member states' sovereign discretion to consider asylum claims for which they are not responsible according to the other criteria, at claimants' request or with their agreement. Article 3(4) is, of course, necessary in cases where a domestic court rules that the responsible state is not 'safe' and the asylum seeker may not be returned there. These provisions also appear to recognise the element of choice afforded to refugees in seeking international protection[1] and alleviate some of the hardship that third-country removals can cause. Although the Home Office, in common with its European counterparts, usually refuses to accept this, asylum seekers make rational choices (if they are able) about the country in which to seek asylum, most obviously on the basis of their perception of the safety of the country, but also because of family ties, for reasons of language and culture and other connections to the country. The ability to depart from the normal practice by reference to these factors also promotes a subsidiary purpose of the Refugee Convention, which is the integration of refugees into the host community – an aim more likely to be achieved if they have pre-existing connections with it.

1 *R v Uxbridge Magistrates' Court, ex p Adimi* [1999] INLR 490.

12.151 The Secretary of State's policy only partially reflects these considerations. A claimant will not normally be removed on third-country grounds if (i) he or she has a spouse or minor children in the UK or (ii) he or she is a minor with a parent in the UK (other relatives can be considered if the claimant is dependent upon them). A restrictive approach to the exercise of discretion in this area has not always been approved by the courts.[1] In *Ex p Nicholas*[2] a decision to remove a claimant who had married after arrival, pursuant to a policy distinction between pre- and post-arrival marriage, was quashed as unreasonable where there was no issue as to the genuineness of the marriage. This reasoning should also apply to unmarried partners in subsisting relationships. However, adult claimants with parents and/or siblings in the UK have rarely had discretion exercised in their favour, and the policy will need to be reassessed generally and in particular cases to ensure conformity with Article 8 of the ECHR. Permission was granted to challenge the removal of an Indian woman who, prior to her last entry into the UK, had been continuously resident for nine years in the UK, had been educated, employed and established a substantial network of supportive friends here and was vulnerable to mental illness if deprived of these support networks.[3]

1 In *R v Secretary of State for the Home Department, ex p B* (CO 1818/1998) 24 June 1999, removal of a minor was held 'cruel'. See also *R v Secretary of State for the Home Department, ex p Asif Islam* (CO 628/1999) 1 February 2000.
2 *R v Secretary of State for the Home Department, ex p Nicholas* [2000] Imm AR 334. This case may be useful in other circumstances where the Home Office takes a restrictive approach to marriages entered into post-arrival or (in the context of asylum) post-flight. If the relationship is genuine, no rational distinction appears possible, nor can it justify interference with family unity.
3 *R v Secretary of State for the Home Department, ex p Reena Raj* (CO 2630/1998) 30 November 1999. The case was conceded at the close of the claimant's submissions at the full hearing after the judge, Sullivan J, gave clear indications that he thought removal perverse. However in *R v Secretary of State for the Home Department, ex p Ahmed (Marion)*, 1 February 1999, the Court of Appeal held that the applicant could not rely on connections made during delays caused by her own representations or litigation against removal.

The Immigration and Asylum Act 1999

12.152 Sections 11 and 12 of the Immigration and Asylum Act 1999 replace the provisions of the Asylum and Immigration Appeals Act 1993 and Asylum and Immigration Act 1996 in respect of all third-country cases: removals to member states of the EU under standing arrangements,[1] removals to EU member states otherwise than under standing arrangements[2] and to designated countries,[3] and removals to non-EU and non-designated countries.[4]

1 Immigration and Asylum Act 1999, s 11.
2 Immigration and Asylum Act 1999, s 12(1)(a).
3 Immigration and Asylum Act 1999, s 12(1)(b). The countries designated under the 1999 Act are, as before, Canada, Norway, Switzerland and the US: Asylum (Designated Safe Third Countries) Order 2000, SI 2000/2245.
4 Immigration and Asylum Act 1999, s 12(4), (5).

Removals to EU countries under standing arrangements

12.153 Section 11(2) of the Immigration and Asylum Act 1999 allows asylum seekers to be removed notwithstanding the statutory protection against removal[1] if the Secretary of State has certified that: (i) that a member state has accepted that, under standing arrangements, it is the responsible state;[2] (ii) in his or her opinion, the claimant is not a national or citizen of the member state to which he or she is to be sent;[3] and (iii) the certificate has not been set aside on an appeal under section 65 (ie on human rights grounds).[4] This suggests a return to the scheme of statutory appeal before removal. However, there are two unpleasant shocks.

1 See Immigration and Asylum Act 1999, s 15 (re-enacting Asylum and Immigration Appeals Act 1993, s 6).
2 Immigration and Asylum Act 1999, s 11(2)(a)(i). Standing arrangements are defined in s 11(4) and though not specifically named, currently means the Dublin Convention. See **12.149** above.
3 Immigration and Asylum Act 1999, s 11(2)(a)(ii).
4 Immigration and Asylum Act 1999, s 11(2)(b).

12.154 The first is that section 11(1) of the Immigration and Asylum Act 1999 provides that in determining whether the person will be removed under the standing arrangements, a member state is to be regarded as a place where life and liberty is not threatened for Refugee Convention reasons[1] and from which the person will not be sent to another country otherwise than in accordance with the Refugee Convention.[2] This is a radical provision giving effect to a statutory presumption of safety, like the German concept of 'normative certainty' described at **12.142** above. The idea is to meet and defeat challenges to removal by reference to the statutory presumption with no investigation by the courts into the member state's interpretation or application of the Convention. The presumption was inserted during the passage of the Act in direct response to the Court of Appeal's decision in *Adan*.[3]

1 Immigration and Asylum Act 1999, s 11(1)(a).
2 Immigration and Asylum Act 1999, s 11(1)(b)
3 Announcing the amendment in July 2000, the minister explained that it was based on 'the principle that member states trust each other to consider asylum claims in accordance with the 1951 Convention'. But the lesson of the litigation since 1993 is that trust alone cannot ensure compliance with the UK's obligations to refugees.

12.155 The second shock is that the appeal under section 65 of the Immigration and Asylum Act 1999 can effectively be prevented by the service of another certificate by the Secretary of State. Section 72(2)(a) of the 1999 Act provides that there is no in-country right of appeal if the Secretary of State certifies that the allegation that the removal will give rise to a breach of human rights is manifestly unfounded. The provisions work together in this way:

(i) The Secretary of State decides to return the claimant to a member state under the Dublin Convention, and certifies the claim under section 11(2) of the 1999 Act;

(ii) The claimant appeals under section 65 on the basis that the member state's application or interpretation of the Refugee Convention will result in his or her being sent to another country (most usually the country of persecution) in breach of the Refugee Convention, which will give rise to a breach by the UK of Article 3 of the ECHR;

(iii) The Secretary of State certifies the appeal under section 72(2)(a) of the 1999 Act, relying on the statutory presumption of safety under section 11(1) of the Act, with the result that there is no in-country appeal;

(iv) The only remedy for the claimant is judicial review; but the statutory presumption of safety in section 11(1) of the 1999 Act applies there too.

12.156 Since the presumption of the EU member states' safety is a statutory one, it could only be overridden by the appellate authority reading in the words 'unless the contrary is proved',[1] in accordance with the interpretative obligation of the Human Rights Act 1998[2] to interpret legislation in a way which gives effect to rather than defeats human rights, and allowing the asylum seeker to adduce evidence disproving it in a particular case.[3] In practice, if there were evidence that a country's interpretation or application of the Dublin Convention made return unsafe, the Secretary of State would be unlikely to block the human rights appeal by a 'manifestly unfounded' certificate under section 72(2)(a) of the Immigration and Asylum Act 1999.[4] Cogent evidence that the statutory presumption of safety is not justified in an individual case or category of case would provide a basis for challenge of the use of the section 72 certificate on judicial review.[5] In cases where there is a real risk of *refoulement* from the third state, such as *Adan and Aitseguer*,[6] it would not be open to the Secretary of State to assert that the UK will not be in breach of its human rights obligations because the state responsible for the violation will be the third state.[7] Nor can the Secretary of State argue that the risk of *refoulement* from the third state is remediable by the ECtHR. These submissions were rejected by the ECHR in *TI v UK*[8] where the court ruled that removal through an intermediary country, which was also a contracting state, did not affect the UK's obligation to ensure that the claimant was not exposed to treatment contrary to Article 3 of the ECHR. Nor did the Dublin Convention, as an international agreement for attribution of responsibility between European countries for deciding claims in the related area of asylum, absolve the UK from its responsibility under the ECHR.[9]

1 See by analogy the court's approach to an irrebuttable presumption of service in *R v Secretary of State for the Home Department, ex p Saleem* [2000] INLR 413, CA.
2 Human Rights Act 1998, s 3. See also *R v DPP, ex p Kebilene* [2000] 2 AC 326, [1999] 4 All ER 801, HL.
3 Otherwise, the Divisional Court might have make a declaration of incompatibility under s 4 of the Human Rights Act 1998, on the basis that preventing an asylum seeker from proving the existence of facts which make his or her removal potentially in breach of art 3 of the ECHR is itself a breach of that article together with art 13 of the ECHR (the right to an effective remedy). See chapter 8 above.
4 For a period in October and November 2000 the Secretary of State refrained from certifying as manifestly unfounded s 65 appeals against Dublin Convention removals to Germany because of pending litigation over the safety of German admissibility procedures.
5 For an example of a successful challenge to the similar statutory presumption of safety in s 1(2) of the Asylum and Immigration Act 1996 (now repealed), which had a similar effect to s 11(1) of the Immigration and Asylum Act 1999 in respect of the designation of generally safe countries of origin, in this case Pakistan, see *R v Secretary of State for the Home Department, ex p Javed and Ali* [2001] EWCA Admin 7, 19 January 2001 upheld in the CA in May 2001.
6 See **12.135–12.137** above.
7 *Soering v UK* [1989] 11 EHRR 439; *TI v UK* [2000] INLR 211.
8 *TI v UK* above, an important ruling asserting the primary obligation of the sending state and rejecting reliance on inter-state agreements such as the Dublin Convention to provide the necessary safeguards for protecting the fundamental rights of those seeking protection.
9 *TI v UK* above, at 228-229.

12.157 If the Secretary of State certifies that the removal is under standing arrangements, ie, the Dublin Convention, we suggest that he or she must properly interpret and comply with it, and these questions are reviewable as matters of law.[1] This applies both to the substantive Articles governing criteria for responsibility and to the procedural provisions. If time limits under the Convention are exceeded, arguably the removal cannot properly be said to be 'under standing arrangements'.

1 *Secretary of State for the Home Department v Adan and Aitseguer* [2001] INLR 44, **12.135** above; *R v Secretary of State for the Home Department, ex p Launder* [1997] 1 WLR 839.

12.158 Issues of *refoulement* are not the only possible arguments on a section 65 appeal[1] or judicial review in a Dublin Convention removal case. Family life considerations which go beyond the Home Office policy (set out at **12.151** above) could also be argued in the human rights appeal, as well as factors relating to the health of the claimant if the effect of removal is of sufficient severity to engage Article 3 of the ECHR[2] and/or the moral and physical integrity of the person protected by Article 8 of the ECHR.[3] In a case such as *Reena Raj*[4] where there was previous long residence and close connection with the UK, private life considerations may also be engaged[5] in a third-country removal that could form the basis of a section 65 appeal. Judicial review would also be available to challenge removal where issues arise on the unlawful exercise of discretion under the close connections policy which do not engage human rights obligations.

1 Immigration and Asylum Act 1999, s 65.
2 See **8.41-8.46** above.
3 *X and Y v The Netherlands* (see chapter 8 above).
4 *R v Secretary of State for the Home Department, ex p Reena Raj* (CO 2630/1998) 30 November 1999, QBD, at **12.151** above.
5 *Beldjoudi v France* (1992) 14 EHRR 801, concurring judgment of Martens J, **8.62–8.64** above.

Other removals

12.159 Section 12 of the Immigration and Asylum Act 1999 applies to removals to (i) EU member states other than in accordance with standing arrangements[1] and (ii) designated countries[2] and countries which are neither member states nor designated.[3] The conditions for certification on third-country grounds are identical to those contained in section 2 of the Asylum and Immigration Act 1996.[4] There is no statutory presumption of safety of the third state in these cases. So in cases involving non-Dublin Convention removals to EU states, and all other removals, the full range of arguments on the third state's interpretation and application of the Convention, the likelihood of *refoulement* or chain removal from there, are open on a section 65 appeal in addition to family life grounds for challenging the removal.[5] In addition, the in-country right of appeal on the merits of the certificate is preserved in cases of removal to non-EU, non-designated countries.[6] The person cannot be removed until the time for giving notice of appeal has expired,[7] or (in the case of a section 65 appeal) the Secretary of State has certified that the allegation of breach of human rights is manifestly unfounded.[8]

1 Immigration and Asylum Act 1999, s 12(1)(a).
2 Currently Canada, Norway, Switzerland and the US: Immigration and Asylum Act 1999, s 12(1)(b); Asylum (Designated Safe Third Countries) Order 2000, SI 2000/2245.

3 Immigration and Asylum Act 1999, s 12(4).
4 Immigration and Asylum Act 1999, s 12(7). See **12.129** above.
5 The provisions in s 11 of the Immigration and Asylum Act 1999 relating to the s 65 appeal and their certification as 'manifestly unfounded' under s 72(2)(a) are replicated in s 12(2), (3) and (5) of the 1999 Act.
6 Immigration and Asylum Act 1999, ss 12(5)(b), 71.
7 Immigration and Asylum Act 1999, ss 11(3), 12(3) and (5).
8 Immigration and Asylum Act 1999, ss 11(3), 12(3) and (6). But an ECHR Article 3 claim raised 'well after the eleventh hour' on a case involving removal to Germany did not entitle the victim of a mistaken removal to an order for his return to the UK; *R (Akpinar) v Secretary of State for the Home Department* [2001] EWHC Admin 287.

ASYLUM APPEALS

12.160 Asylum appeals are covered in section 69 of the Immigration and Asylum Act 1999 and section 2(1) of the Special Immigration Appeals Commission Act 1997. They are to an adjudicator[1] or, in appropriate cases, to the Commission. An asylum claim must have been made for an appeal to be brought.[2] Asylum appeals are kept conceptually separate from human rights appeals, although a one-stop appeal under section 74 or 75 of the 1999 Act might contain both elements. The 'Convention' referred to in section 69 of the 1999 Act is the Refugee Convention, and does not include the ECHR. The 1999 Act provides for an appeal in the following circumstances:

(i)   against refusal of leave to enter, on the ground that removal in consequence of the refusal would be contrary to the Refugee Convention;[3]

(ii) against any variation of or refusal to vary a limited leave to enter or remain, which would result in the person being required to leave the UK within 28 days of notification of the decision, on the ground that the requirement to leave would be contrary to the Convention;[4]

(iii) against a refusal of asylum and a grant of limited leave to enter or remain, on the ground that a requirement to leave after the expiry of that leave would be contrary to the Convention;[5]

(iv) against a decision to deport or refusal to revoke a deportation order, on the ground that removal in pursuance of such an order would be contrary to the Convention;[6]

(v)   against directions for removal from the UK as an illegal entrant, an overstayer, a person remaining by deception, an entrant in breach of a deportation order, or under the special rules for removal of crew members of a ship or aircraft, on the ground that removal in pursuance of the directions would be contrary to the Convention.[7]

1 Special Adjudicators, introduced by the Asylum and Immigration Appeals Act 1993, have now disappeared.
2 Immigration and Asylum Act 1999, s 70(7).
3 Immigration and Asylum Act 1999, s 69(1), or Special Immigration Appeals Commission Act 1997, s 2 where national security is engaged.
4 Immigration and Asylum Act 1999, s 69(2) or Special Immigration Appeals Commission Act 1997, s 2 if national security is engaged.
5 Immigration and Asylum Act 1999, s 69(3) or Special Immigration Appeals Commission Act 1997, if the reason for the refusal of asylum was exclusion under art 1F of the Refugee Convention, ie where there are serious reasons for considering that a refugee has committed a war crime or crime against humanity, an act contrary to the purposes and principles of the UN, or a serious non-political crime, and where disclosure of the material grounding the refusal is not in the interests of national security: see s 70(4) of the 1999 Act.

6   Immigration and Asylum Act 1999, s 69(4) or Special Immigration Appeals Commission Act 1997, s 2 if s 70(5) or (6) of the 1999 Act applies (national security based decisions).
7   Immigration and Asylum Act 1999, s 69(5).

12.161 The appeal rights under the Immigration and Asylum Act 1999 preserve the scheme of the Asylum and Immigration Appeals Act 1993 in making not the refusal of asylum, but the immigration decision consequent on that refusal, the subject of the appeal. The 1999 Act deals with one problem to which this scheme had given rise. There was considerable litigation about the appeal rights under the 1993 Act of persons who applied for asylum but were granted exceptional leave to remain instead. The right of appeal attaches not to the refusal of asylum, but to the accompanying immigration decision: the decision to refuse leave to enter and issue removal directions; to refuse to extend leave; to deport; to remove as an illegal entrant.[1] The ground of the appeal in port, illegal entry and deportation cases is that removal in consequence of the decision would be contrary to the UK's obligations under the Refugee Convention. In *Massaquoi*[2] the appellant appealed against a deportation decision on asylum and non-asylum grounds, and succeeded on the non-asylum but not the asylum grounds at first instance. She was granted exceptional leave to remain while the Tribunal appeal was pending. She pursued the asylum appeal because she needed the right to family reunion to rescue her young son from Sierra Leone. The Court of Appeal held, upholding the Tribunal, that her appeal could not succeed since she was not going to be deported, so that there was 'nothing left to argue about'.[3] The result would be the same in any port, deportation or illegal entry removal appeal if the effect of the grant of exceptional leave to remain was that there would be no removal. This logic was not applied to appeals against a refusal to vary leave by the grant of asylum, because the wording of the appeal ground there was different: the appeal was against a requirement 'to leave the UK after the time limited by the leave', and the grant of exceptional leave to remain did not preclude such a requirement to leave at a later stage. Section 69(3) of the 1999 Act resolves this problem by providing an express right of appeal against a refusal of asylum combined with a grant of limited leave.[4] Only those granted indefinite leave to remain but not refugee status would be excluded from appealing, on the *Massaquoi* interpretation of the section, since the grant of indefinite leave to remain means they would never be required to leave. They would have to seek judicial review of the refusal of refugee status.[5]

1   Previously Asylum and Immigration Appeals Act 1993, ss 8(1)-(4); now Immigration and Asylum Act 1999, s 69(1), (2), (4), (5).
2   (19542) 23 November 1999, IAT, upheld in the Court of Appeal on 20 December 2000 (C/2000/0622) para30.
3   See *Laftaly v Home Secretary* [1993] Imm AR 284. In *Meles* (00 TH 2433) the Tribunal agreed that *Massaquoi* did not apply to a variation appeal, but refused to consider the merits of an Ethiopian asylum appeal on the basis that it could not tell what the situation would be in four years' time (the period of exceptional leave to remain granted).
4   If the appellate authority takes the attitude taken by the Tribunal in *Meles* above, this would clearly frustrate the statutory purpose, and would, we suggest, be susceptible to a mandatory order of the Administrative Court requiring it to determine the appeal.
5   *R v Secretary of State for the Home Department, ex p Ramarajah* [1994] Imm AR 472, not following *R v Secretary of State for the Home Department, ex p Kaygusuz* [1991] Imm AR 300. Adequate reasons for the refusal of asylum would have to be given despite the grant of exceptional leave to remain; currently this does not happen, so there would need to be a specific request for reasons.

12.162 No one may appeal on asylum grounds unless they have made a claim for asylum.[1] But not every asylum claim necessarily gives rise to an appeal,[2] and certainly not every claim gives rise to an appeal on the merits or even an in-country appeal. As we have seen, protection against removal given to asylum claimants by section 15 of the Immigration and Asylum Act 1999[3] does not apply where it is intended to remove them to a 'safe' third country. If the Secretary of State certifies that an asylum seeker is removable to such a country, the existence, scope and suspensive effect of the right of appeal against such a certificate depend on the country to which he or she is intended to be removed. There are three different scenarios:

(i)   The Secretary of State intends to remove the asylum seeker to an EU member state under standing arrangements (ie under the Dublin Convention).[4] In such a case, the member state in question is deemed 'safe', ie a country where the claimant's life and liberty would not be threatened for a Refugee Convention reason, and one whose government would not *refoule* the claimant contrary to the Refugee Convention.[5] The Secretary of State's certificate is limited to the fact that the relevant state has accepted responsibility for determining the claim, and that the claimant is not a national of that state.[6] The claimant may challenge these facts on appeal, but not in-country.[7] The only possible appeal before removal is a human rights appeal under section 65 of the 1999 Act, which may be prevented if the Secretary of State certifies that the allegation of breach of human rights is manifestly unfounded.[8]

(ii)   The Secretary of State intends to remove the asylum seeker to an EU member state otherwise than under standing arrangements, or to a state designated by Order.[9] Countries designated by Order under the 1999 Act are Canada, Norway, Switzerland and the US.[10] In such a case, if the Secretary of State certifies that the three conditions (non-nationality, safety and non-*refoulement*) are satisfied in relation to the country concerned,[11] there is a right of appeal on the ground that the conditions were not satisfied then or have since ceased to be satisfied,[12] but only once the asylum claimant has left the UK.[13] The only possible appeal before removal, as in the previous case, is a human rights appeal under section 65, which can be precluded if the Secretary of State certifies that the allegation of breach of human rights is manifestly unfounded.[14] The difference between this and the previous case is that on appeal there is no presumption that the proposed country of destination (whether or not an EU state) fulfils the safety and non-*refoulement* conditions.

(iii)   The Secretary of State intends to send the asylum claimant to a country which is not an EU member state, nor a state designated by order. In such a case, if the Secretary of State certifies that the three conditions (non-nationality, safety and non-*refoulement*) are satisfied in relation to the country concerned,[15] there is a right of appeal on the ground that the conditions were not satisfied then or have since ceased to be satisfied,[16] and in this case the appeal is suspensive of removal. There is also a human rights appeal.

In each of these cases, there is no substantive consideration of the asylum claim, and no substantive asylum appeal, or any other appeal 'in respect of matters arising before [the appellant's] removal from the UK', unless or until the Secretary of State's certificate under section 11 or 12 of the 1999 Act (the third-country certificate) is set aside on appeal.[17] If it is set aside, the claim returns to the

Secretary of State for substantive consideration, if the appellant is in the UK. If not, the adjudicator may issue directions requiring the Secretary of State to facilitate the return of the appellant to the UK (by eg the issue of entry clearance) to enable the asylum claim to be determined.[18]

1 Immigration and Asylum Act 1999, s 70(7)(a).
2 For the impact of one-stop appeals on repeat claims for asylum, see **12.176** and **18.20** below.
3 Reproducing Asylum and Immigration Appeals Act 1993, s 6.
4 See Immigration and Asylum Act 1999, s 11(4).
5 Immigration and Asylum Act 1999, s 11(1).
6 Immigration and Asylum Act 1999, s 11(2)(a).
7 Immigration and Asylum Act 1999, s 72(2)(b).
8 Immigration and Asylum Act 1999, s 72(2)(a).
9 Immigration and Asylum Act 1999, s 12(1).
10 The Asylum (Designated Safe Third Countries) Order 2000, SI 2000/2245, art 3.
11 Immigration and Asylum Act 1999, s 12(7).
12 Immigration and Asylum Act 1999, s 71.
13 Immigration and Asylum Act 1999, s 72(2)(b).
14 Immigration and Asylum Act 1999, s 72(2)(a).
15 Immigration and Asylum Act 1999, s 12(7).
16 Immigration and Asylum Act 1999, s 71.
17 Immigration and Asylum Act 1999, s 72(1).
18 See **18.84** below for directions which the adjudicator may issue.

Certified asylum (and human rights or discrimination) claims

12.163 Apart from the 'third country' cases where appeal rights are limited and do not usually suspend removal, the other category of asylum appeals which attract special treatment (apart from one-stop appeals) are appeals in relation to certified claims. These used to be called 'without foundation' claims under the Asylum and Immigration Appeals Act 1993,[1] and were cases which either raised no issue as to the UK's obligations under the Refugee Convention (usually because the asylum seeker was returnable to a third-country, see above)[2] or were otherwise 'frivolous and vexatious'.[3] The effects of certification of a claim as without foundation were that the claim and appeal were subjected to rigorous time limits, that (in the case of third country claims) the merits of the asylum claim were not explored on appeal, and that if the adjudicator agreed with the characterisation of the claim as manifestly unfounded, there was no right of appeal to the Tribunal.

1 Asylum and Immigration Appeals Act 1993, Sch 2, para 5(3). The 'accelerated procedure for manifestly unfounded claims for asylum' arose after intensive efforts at the inter-governmental level to reduce the numbers of asylum seekers entering Europe, culminating in the London Resolution on manifestly unfounded applications for asylum, adopted at the immigration ministers' meeting of 30 November 1992. See Bunyan and Webber 'Intergovernmental co-operation on immigration and asylum' (1995).
2 *R v Secretary of State for the Home Department, ex p Mehari* [1994] 2 All ER 494.
3 *R v Special Adjudicator, ex p Paulino and Edoukou* [1996] Imm AR 122.

12.164 The grounds for certifying a claim expanded dramatically in 1996, while the 'third country' cases were separated off into another category. The first category of certified claims was those where the country or territory to which the appellant was to be sent was designated by statutory instrument as one in which it appeared to the Secretary of State that there was in general no serious risk of persecution.[1] The countries so designated in 1996 – the so-called 'white list' – were Bulgaria,

Cyprus, Ghana, India, Pakistan, Poland and Romania.[2] The designation power was very controversial,[3] as was its use, particularly in relation to Pakistan in the light of the difficulties faced there by Christians, Ahmadis and women among others, and to countries of eastern Europe where the Roma faced continuing racist attacks and systematic marginalisation. If a claim was certified on this ground the adjudicator could not discharge the certificate in the absence of evidence of torture, on the ground that the claim should not have been certified.[4] The challenge to designation and to certification had to be by way of judicial review.[5] Such a challenge was successful in *Javed and Ali*[6] where the Court of Appeal held that the Secretary of State's decision to designate Pakistan as a country in which there is in general no serious risk of persecution was made on an erroneous view of the facts or the law. Claims can no longer be certified on the basis that they relate to designated 'safe countries of destination', under the provisions of the Immigration and Asylum Act 1999.

1   Asylum and Immigration Appeals Act 1993, as amended, Sch 2, para 5(2).
2   Asylum (Designated Countries of Destination and Designated Safe Third Countries) Order 1996, SI 1996/2671.
3   In that it tended to undermine the principle of individual determination of claims required by the Refugee Convention.
4   *R v Special Adjudicator, ex p Mohammed Zaman* [2000] Imm AR 68; *Talat Bajwa v Secretary of State for the Home Department* [2000] Imm AR 364, CA.
5   *R v Special Adjudicator and Secretary of State for the Home Department, ex p Dhanoa* 1999/7535/C, 21 January 2000, CA.
6   *Javed and Ali v Secretary of State for the Home Department* [2001] EWCA Admin 7, upheld in the CA on 17 May 2001, [2001] EWCA Civ 789.

12.165   However, the Immigration and Asylum Act 1999 preserves and extends to human rights and discrimination appeals[1] all the other categories of certified claims included in the Asylum and Immigration Act 1996. Thus, an asylum, human rights or discrimination claim may now be certified if the evidence does not establish a reasonable likelihood that the appellant has been tortured in the country of proposed removal[2] and:

(i)   the applicant failed to produce a valid passport on request, without a reasonable explanation, or produced an invalid passport without saying so;[3]

(ii)   the claim was made after refusal of leave to enter, a decision to deport or recommendation for deportation, or notification of removal as an illegal entrant;[4]

(iii)   the claim under the Refugee Convention does not show a fear of persecution for a Convention reason, or the fear it shows is manifestly unfounded or the circumstances giving rise to it no longer exist;[5]

(iv)   the claim under the ECHR does not disclose a right under the Convention or is manifestly unfounded;[6]

(v)   the claim is manifestly fraudulent or any of the evidence adduced in support is manifestly false;[7]

(vi)   the claim is frivolous or vexatious.[8]

Unlike third-country cases, certified claims are considered substantively by the Secretary of State, but if, when rejecting a claim on the ground that he or she is not satisfied that the applicant has a well-founded fear of persecution or (in a human rights case) of treatment contrary to the ECHR) he or she is also satisfied that a ground for certification applies, the refusal letter will contain such certification. There is no 'certificate' as such, merely a paragraph or two in the decision letter refusing asylum. Claims are certified only after substantive consideration.[9] A claim will not be certified if any of the issues raised by it are complex, or if exceptional leave has been granted, or where the claim is refused on non-compliance grounds.[10] Where the claim contains more than one element, eg an asylum and a human rights element, both parts should be certified.[11]

1 Immigration and Asylum Act 1999, Sch 4, para 9.
2 Immigration and Asylum Act 1999, Sch 4, para 9(7).
3 Immigration and Asylum Act 1999, Sch 4, para 9(3).
4 Immigration and Asylum Act 1999, Sch 4, para 9(6)(a).
5 Immigration and Asylum Act 1999, Sch 4, para 9(4).
6 Immigration and Asylum Act 1999, Sch 4, para 9(5).
7 Immigration and Asylum Act 1999, Sch 4, para 9(6)(b).
8 Immigration and Asylum Act 1999, Sch 4, para 9(6)(c).
9 API Jul/98, Ch 5, s 2, para 1.
10 API Jul/98, Ch 5, s 2, para 2.2.
11 *Zenovics* (01 TH 00631*), IAT.

12.166 If the adjudicator dismisses the asylum, human rights or discrimination appeal and agrees with the Secretary of State's certificate, the appellant has no right of appeal to the Tribunal.[1] But the Secretary of State may appeal in a case where the substantive appeal succeeds although the certificate is upheld, because of the way the word 'appellant' is used in the provisions. In certifying a claim under these provisions, the Secretary of State is obliged to refer specifically to the ground relied on and must advert to the question of torture. A certificate which failed to do so was held invalid in *Salah Ziar*,[2] in which the Tribunal held that an amendment could not be permitted which reduced appeal rights and that, since certification could affect the preparation of a case and the adjudicator's whole approach to it, the adjudicator had to consider whether the preparation of the case had been affected to such a degree that it ought to be adjourned and considered in the framework of a non-certified case. Later Tribunal decisions have differed on whether a letter of refusal which incorrectly or defectively certifies the claim (by eg neglecting to deal with the issue of torture) may or may not be amended.[3] The Court of Appeal has held that certification does not have to be in the exact words of the statute to be valid.[4]

1 Immigration and Asylum Act 1999, Sch 4, para 9(2). Where an appeal contains both asylum and human rights or discrimination grounds, the Adjudicator can only agree if both elements are properly certified. He or she may not uphold the certification in respect of one part only: *Zenovics* (01 TH 00631*).
2 [1997] INLR 221, [1997] Imm AR 456.
3 In *Khan* [1999] INLR 309 a different division of the Tribunal distinguished *Ziar* and held that certification could be amended at any time prior to the hearing, provided the appellant was not prejudiced and in *Nanthakumar* (01 TH 02261) the Tribunal held that the adjudicator should not decide on whether the applicant has been tortured for the purposes of certification in advance of deciding the asylum claim. But in *Meflah* [1998] INLR 150 and *Zolele* [1999] INLR 422, the Tribunal held that where a decision was not certified in accordance with the statute the defect could not be cured by amendment.
4 *R v Secretary of State for the Home Department, ex p Djeugone* 1999/8135/C, 22 May 2000, CA.

12.167 While some of the certification categories clearly go to the merits of the asylum or human rights claim, others appear to be purely punitive in nature. A refugee claim based solely on economic considerations such as poverty or unemployment at home certainly raises no Refugee Convention issues and could validly be certified.[1] But there is no correlation between the failure to produce valid travel documents and the genuineness of an asylum claim; indeed the Divisional Court has accepted the need for genuine refugees to travel on false documents and the reasonableness in many cases of their seeking entry on such documents rather than making a port asylum claim.[2] It is therefore wrong in principle to certify a claim on such grounds. Certification on grounds of failure to make a claim prior to refusal of leave in another capacity, or enforcement action, is also arguably punitive, in the absence of evidence that claims made when there is no lawful alternative basis for stay in the country are *ipso facto* less likely to be true ones.[3]

1   See the debate on the 1996 Bill, HC Official Report SC D (Asylum and Immigration Bill), 11 January 1996, cols 92-93 and 99; 570 HL Official Report (5th series) col 960.
2   See eg *R v Secretary of State for the Home Department, ex p Yassine* [1990] Imm AR 354; *R v Uxbridge Magistrates' Court, ex p Adimi* [1999] INLR 490.
3   Note the evidence presented in *R v Secretary of State for Social Security, ex p Joint Council for the Welfare of Immigrants* [1997] 1 WLR 275, CA indicating that the proportion of port and in-country applications which were successful was similar.

Failure to produce valid travel document

12.168 A passport or travel document means a document satisfactorily establishing identity and nationality or citizenship.[1] A passport with pages missing is not a 'valid' passport for these purposes.[2] In *Naillie*[3] the House of Lords accepted that inability to produce a passport was a good reason for not doing so. A reasonable explanation for the failure to produce a passport does not necessarily mean that the applicant's behaviour had to be reasonable. The surrender by a young person of 16 or 18 of his passport to an agent is capable of being a reasonable explanation.[4] On the other hand, an incredible explanation is not a reasonable one.[5] The adjudicator must give reasons for rejecting the explanation given for the failure to produce a valid passport as not reasonable.[6] Certification on these grounds is inappropriate in cases of clandestine entry, since there is no request to produce a passport in such cases.[7]

1   As in Immigration Act 1971, Sch 2, para 4(2).
2   *R v Secretary of State for the Home Department, ex p Karafu* [2001] Imm AR 26; *R v Special Adjudicator, ex p Githuma* (CO 1649/2000) 14 November 2000, AC.
3   [1993] AC 674.
4   *R v Special Adjudicator, ex p Naguleswaran* (CO 3968/1999) 3 December 1999, distinguishing *R v Secretary of State for the Home Department, ex p Sivaharan* (4 March 1999, Owen J).
5   *R v Special Adjudicator, ex p Vasanthasivan* 1999/6534/C, 31 January 2000 CA (renewed permission application).
6   *R v Special Adjudicator, ex p Islam* (CO 583/2000) 16 October 2000, QBD; *Naguleswaran* above; *R (Kaman) v Special Adjudicator* [2001] EWHC Admin 326.
7   *Hua* (G0077) 21 April 1999, IAT.

Late claim

12.169 The Secretary of State's decision to certify a claim for this reason is only challengeable on appeal if it is wrong in fact, ie, if the claim was in fact made before refusal of leave to enter or the beginning of enforcement action. In other words, if a claim is certified on this basis, the adjudicator may not disagree with the certification on the basis that the claim is *bona fide* regardless of the fact that it was made after refusal of leave to enter or a decision to deport.

No fear of Refugee Convention persecution

12.170 A claim may be certified under paragraph 9(4) of Schedule 4 to the Immigration and Asylum Act 1999 on the ground that it does not show a fear of persecution on one of the grounds set out in the Refugee Convention. However, if it shows a fear of torture or inhuman or degrading treatment contrary to Article 3 of the ECHR, or a threat to life contrary to Article 2, or threats to other fundamental rights such as liberty (Article 5), it will give rise to a full (ie, non-certified) human rights appeal under section 65 of the 1999 Act (either consecutively or, if the relevant notices have been served and procedures complied with, as a one-stop appeal under section 77 of the 1999 Act).

Fear manifestly unfounded or circumstances giving rise to it have ceased to exist

12.171 The change of circumstances ground of certification is clearly based on the cessation clauses in the Refugee Convention.[1] The change of circumstances must be fundamental and permanent, and temporary amelioration or a change of government by itself should not result in certification. The 'manifestly unfounded' ground for certification reveals a considerable degree of overlap between the categories. UNHCR defines claims which are manifestly unfounded as those which are clearly fraudulent or not related to the criteria for the granting of refugee status laid down in the Refugee Convention nor to any other criteria justifying the grant of asylum.[2] The EU ministers' December 1992 Resolution on manifestly unfounded applications for asylum, claiming inspiration from the UNHCR Conclusion, states that an application for asylum shall be regarded as

> 'manifestly unfounded because it clearly raises no substantive issue under the Geneva Convention . . . for one of the following reasons: (i) there is clearly no substance to the applicant's claim to fear persecution in his (sic) own country; or (ii) the claim is based on deliberate deception or is an abuse of asylum procedures.'[3]

Examples of claims with no substance are that the grounds are outside the scope of the Convention or that the application is 'totally lacking in substance or credibility'.[4] In *Gavira*[5] the Administrative Court held that a claim should not be certified manifestly unfounded on credibility grounds. The dangers of doing so are obvious, in the light of the known correlation between post-traumatic stress and failure of recollection. Examples in the Resolution of claims clearly based on deceit reflect fairly closely all the grounds for certifying claims in UK domestic law, including reliance on false identity documents, late timing etc, and include other grounds, such as lodging a repeat application following rejection in another country which has adequate procedures. These grounds for holding a claim manifestly unfounded have been criticised above.[6] They bear no necessary relation to the genuineness of an asylum claim. In *Vallaj*[7] Dyson J held that a manifestly unfounded claim is different from a fraudulent or abusive one; it is simply one which, on a reasonably quick appraisal, can be seen to be plainly and obviously without foundation.[8] A claim is not 'manifestly unfounded', he held, if the answer only becomes plain after a lengthy and detailed consideration.[9] Dyson J also held in that case that it was not always necessary to give reasons for certifying a claim manifestly unfounded, where full reasons had been given for refusing a claim, since it will often be obvious why the claim has been certified. It follows, we suggest, that where it is not so obvious why the claim has been certified, reasons must be given in accordance with the duty of fairness.[10]

1 See **12.87** above.
2 ExCom Conclusion 30 of 1983.
3 SN 4822/92 1282 ASIM 146, set out in full in Bunyan *Key texts on justice and home affairs in the European Union* Vol 1 (1976–1993) (1997).
4 EEC Ministers' Resolution, para 6.
5 *R (Gavira) v Secretary of State for the Home Department* (CO 2326/2000) 4 April 2001.
6 See **12.167** above.
7 *R (Vallaj) v IAA* 21 December 2000.
8 *Vallaj* para 55.
9 *Vallaj* para 53.
10 *Vallaj* para 59. See *R v Higher Education Funding Council ex p Institute of Dental Surgery* [1994] 1 WLR 242.

Manifestly fraudulent claim or evidence

12.172 A manifestly fraudulent claim is one which is wholly fabricated, while a claim in which manifestly false evidence is adduced does not have to depend solely on such evidence, although we suggest that for a claim to be certified the false evidence must be central as well as very obviously false. The burden of proving fraud or falsity lies on the Secretary of State.

Frivolous or vexatious

12.173 In the House of Lords debate on the Bill which became the Asylum and Immigration Appeals Act 1993 (in which this category first appeared), Earl Ferrers suggested that boredom with one's country or conflict with one's mother-in-law were examples of frivolous or vexatious asylum claims.[1] But in *Paulino and Edoukou*[2] the Divisional Court, accepting that there was overlap between this and other grounds for certification, held that a claim could be frivolous or vexatious either because on its face it did not engage the Refugee Convention at all, or because the applicant's account was totally incredible, or because there was an attempt to relitigate decided issues.[3]

1 Cited in *R v SA, ex p Paulino and Edoukou* [1996] Imm AR 122 at 128.
2 [1996] Imm AR 122 at 128.
3 [1996] Imm AR 122 at 130. See also *Ahmad* [1994] Imm AR 454, QBD.

12.174 The proviso in respect of torture prevents the certified claims procedure being used in respect of those who, notwithstanding other reasons for certification, have in their history a strong *prima facie* reason against return. Removal to a real risk of torture is contrary to the UK's obligations under a number of Conventions, including the UN and European Conventions against Torture as well as the ECHR and the Refugee Convention. Torture is not defined in the Immigration and Asylum Act 1999, although it is defined in the UN Torture

Convention.[1] In *Roszkowski*[2] the Secretary of State accepted that to constitute torture, the ill-treatment did not have to be officially instigated or sanctioned (as it does in the Torture Conventions).[3] But the court held it must be related to the asylum claim.[4] It could be relatively minor physical force if used for the purpose of putting a person in fear or extracting information.[5] Whether particular treatment constitutes torture is not to be assessed according to the degree of blame attaching to those meting out the treatment.[6] But where there was evidence before the Secretary of State that an applicant was severely beaten by police in his home country to extract information, the claim should not have been certified.[7] All the appellant's evidence must do is show that it is reasonably likely that he or she was tortured, to avoid certification or have the certificate discharged on appeal. The adjudicator must properly direct him- or herself on the standard of proof of torture.[8] He or she must look at all the evidence, no matter by whom produced, in determining the question of torture.[9]

1   UN Convention Against Torture and other cruel or inhuman and degrading treatment or punishment, art 1. This definition is incorporated into domestic criminal law by the Criminal Justice Act 1988, s 134.
2   *R (Roszkowski) v Special Adjudicator* (CO 2609/1999) 31 October 2000, QBD.
3   See also *Nanthakumar* (00 TH 02261). In the context of the UN Torture Convention see *Elmi v Australia* [1999] INLR 341, holding that Somali clans could be *de facto* 'public officials or other persons acting in an official capacity' for the purposes of the torture definition.
4   See also *R v Immigration Appeal Tribunal, ex p Brylewicz*, 26 March 1999, QBD.
5   *R v Secretary of State for the Home Department, ex p Singh*, 3 March 2000, QBD.
6   *R v Secretary of State for the Home Department, ex p Sarbjit Singh* [1999] INLR 632, Keene J, who declined to adopt a particular definition of torture while holding that its definition as 'totally reprehensible behaviour' was a misdirection.
7   *Singh (Sukhdeep)* (G0081) 21.4.99, IAT.
8   *R v Special Adjudicator, ex p Chohan* (CO 2042/1999) 10 October 2000, QBD.
9   *Nanthakumar v Secretary of State for the Home Department* [2000] INLR 480, CA.

Procedure on asylum appeals

12.175 Asylum appeals used to be subject to different time limits and procedures, and had their own procedure rules.[1] The current procedure rules embrace all immigration and asylum appeals, and details of procedure are to be found at **18.90ff** below.

1   Asylum Appeals (Procedure) Rules 1993, SI 1993/1661; Asylum Appeals (Procedure) Rules 1996, SI 1996/2070.

12.176 A person who has previously been refused asylum in the UK and who has not thereafter left the UK and returned will not normally have an appeal against refusal of a second application. There are two situations where a second application may generate a further appeal:

(i)   Under the Immigration Rules, the second application may be accepted as a fresh claim for asylum, as opposed to further representations on the old claim, in order to generate a further right of appeal.[1] Where an asylum applicant has previously been refused asylum in the UK, the Secretary of State will decide whether further representations should be treated as a fresh claim for asylum. Representations will be treated as a fresh claim if the claim advanced in them is sufficiently different from the earlier claim that there is a realistic prospect that the conditions for recognition are satisfied. But in assessing the fresh representations the Secretary of State may disregard any material which is not significant, is not credible or was available for the previous application or appeal.[2] It is for the Secretary of State to decide if a fresh claim has been made, subject to *Wednesbury* review,[3] although some authorities suggest that where evidence of a relevant and substantial change in circumstances, or new evidence is advanced which could not reasonably have been advanced earlier, the Secretary of State is obliged to entertain the new claim, whatever the reasons for rejecting the previous one, unless the new evidence is not credible or is not capable of producing a different outcome.[4] The new evidence would need to have an important influence on the result of the case, although it need not be decisive, and it must be apparently credible, although it need not be incontrovertible.[5] The requirement that the claim be 'sufficiently different' from the old one does not require a change in the factual basis of the application; convincing fresh evidence of the same persecution previously alleged is capable of giving rise to a fresh claim.[6] The failure of advisers to obtain evidence earlier does not make that evidence 'previously unavailable';[7] but evidence was not 'available' if the giver of it was physically or psychologically unable to give it.[8]

(ii)   The Secretary of State has a policy as to when fairness requires a subsequent application to trigger further appeal rights even where the application is not regarded as a fresh one. It includes previous loss of appeal rights by error or a serious miscarriage in procedure.[9] The policy may be prayed in aid where there is no change in the nature of the application or the evidence adduced, but where it would be unjust not to give the applicant an opportunity to appeal. A request for the Secretary of State to issue a fresh refusal to give rise to a fresh appeal on *Kazmi* grounds should be made promptly after the claimed miscarriage of procedure.[10] The case law on section 21 of the Immigration Act 1971, now repealed, is also relevant. This allowed the Secretary of State to refer a dismissed appeal back to the appellate authority for an advisory opinion in certain circumstances.[11] If the statutory appeal route had failed because of an adverse decision following a full hearing or because the applicant had taken a calculated risk in not attending, probably nothing short of potentially decisive evidence, reasonably capable of acceptance, would be required to prompt further consideration of the claim. Where, however, it had or may have failed because of lack of notice for which the applicant bore no personal or imputed blame, that was a relevant, though not a decisive, consideration for the Secretary of State in deciding whether to exercise the power.[12]

1   Unless and until the Secretary of State accepts the application as a fresh claim, no decision falls within the section and no right of appeal arises: *R v Immigration Appellate Authority, ex p Secretary of State for the Home Department* [1998] Imm AR 52.

2   HC 395, para 346, as amended after *Onibiyo v Secretary of State for the Home Department* [1996] Imm AR 370, CA, which established the test of 'a reasonable prospect that a favourable view could be taken of the new claim'.

3   *R v Secretary of State for the Home Department, ex p Ravichandran (No 3)* [1997] Imm AR 74; *Cakabay v Secretary of State for the Home Department (No 3)* [1999] Imm AR 176, [1998] INLR 623, CA; *R v Secretary of State for the Home Department, ex p Bell* [2000] Imm AR 396.

4   *R v Secretary of State for the Home Department, ex p Habibi* [1997] Imm AR 391, QBD.

5   *R v Secretary of State for the Home Department, ex p Boybeyi* [1997] Imm AR 491; [1997] INLR 130, CA.

6 *R v Secretary of State for the Home Department, ex p Ravichandran (No 2)* [1996] Imm AR 418; *Yolanda Ward v Secretary of State for the Home Department* [1997] Imm AR 236; *R (Senkoy) v Secretary of State for the Home Department* [2001] EWCA Civ 328.

7 *Kabala v Secretary of State for the Home Department* [1997] Imm AR 517, CA.

8 *R v Secretary of State for the Home Department, ex p Molly Ejon* [1998] INLR 195 (traumatised rape victim). Contrast *R v Secretary of State for the Home Department, ex p Saleem Khan* (CO 647/1999) 17 May 1999, QBD where Collins J held that evidence of the applicant's homosexuality was 'previously available' despite the taboo in Muslim society and the fact that the applicant's family (who were unaware of his sexuality) helped with the first claim, making it impossible for him to disclose it.

9 Home Office letter, 22 July 1994, cited in *R v Secretary of State for the Home Department, ex p Kazmi* [1995] Imm AR 73.

10 *R v Secretary of State for the Home Department, ex p Kone* [1998] Imm AR 291.

11 See *R v Secretary of State for the Home Department, ex p Bello* [1995] Imm AR 537, QBD; *Khaldoun v Secretary of State for the Home Department* [1996] Imm AR 200, CA.

12 *R v Secretary of State for the Home Department, ex p Yousaf, Jamil* [2000] INLR 432, CA.

12.177 A further appeal could be prevented by a certificate from the Secretary of State under section 73(9) of the Immigration and Asylum Act 1999 that the only purpose of making the further application was to delay the removal from the UK of the appellant or any member of his or her family.[1] This is unlikely to happen in (i) above, where the Secretary of State has accepted that representations made after the dismissal of an appeal amount to a fresh claim warranting a further appeal, but could happen where an applicant seeks a further appeal on the ground of miscarriage of procedure.

1 See one-stop appeals, **18.20, 18.111** below.

Leave to remain

Refugees

12.178 A person who is recognised as a refugee is now normally granted indefinite leave to remain immediately.[1] This contrasts with the previous grant of limited leave for four years with the possibility of applying for indefinite leave thereafter. The dependants of the claimant will be granted leave in line.[2] The practice of the Secretary of State is not normally to review the status of refugees from particular countries or groups to assess whether the cessation clause in Article 1C(5) of the Refugee Convention applies, and the only application of any of the clauses is when refugees come to the attention of the immigration authorities by travelling to their country of origin or for some similar reason.[3] It would be open to the Secretary of State to apply the cessation clause and seek to deport the person on conducive grounds in such a situation. Where concurrent applications are made for refugee status and in some other capacity, current policy is to decide the non-asylum application first and to invite the applicant to withdraw the asylum claim if leave to enter or remain in another capacity is granted.[4] A person granted exceptional leave is granted leave to enter or remain which is more carefully reviewed from time to time in the light of prevailing conditions.[5]

1 White paper *Fairer, Faster, Firmer*, July 1998. Indefinite leave to remain might not be granted to a refugee who has committed a serious criminal offence and about whom the Home Office wishes to have more time to consider whether his or her continued presence

in the UK is conducive to the public good: Home Office letter to Asylum Aid, 18 March 1998, reproduced in *Butterworths Immigration Law Service*, **2B[13]**.
2 HC 395, para 349. See below for family reunion.
3 Answers to questions put by the French delegation on the application of the cessation clause in Article 1C(5) of the Refugee Convention, Telex No 4480 of 14 October 1998, SN 5054/98, 17 November 1998.
4 API, Ch 2, s 7, paras 2, 3. The policy applies only to concurrent in-country applications.
5 See eg *Arulanandam v Secretary of State for the Home Department* [1996] Imm AR 587, CA.

Exceptional leave to remain

12.179 The grant of exceptional leave has not been regulated by the Immigration Rules. However, Home Office policy is to grant exceptional leave in two broad categories: to individuals who are not refugees but who are in need of protection (including ECHR protection); and for compassionate or practical reasons unrelated to protection.[1] The API indicate that exceptional leave to enter or remain must be granted in the following circumstances:[2]

(i)   if return to the country of origin would result in the applicant being tortured or subjected to cruel, inhuman or degrading treatment;[3] or the removal would result in an unjustifiable break-up of family life;[4] for example:

    (a)   where there are substantial grounds for believing that the applicant would suffer a serious and wholly disproportionate punishment for a criminal offence;

    (b)   where there is credible medical evidence that return, due to the medical facilities in the country, would reduce the applicant's life expectancy and subject him or her to acute physical and mental suffering, in circumstances where the UK can be regarded as having assumed responsibility for his or her care;[5]

(ii)   where the applicant does not satisfy the Refugee Convention criteria but there are compassionate or humanitarian reasons for not requiring him or her to return;

(iii)   where ministers have agreed that, for humanitarian reasons, a general country policy will apply.[6]

1 Letter from Immigration and Nationality Directorate to Law for All 27 April 2000.
2 API Jul/98, Ch 5, s 1, para 2.1, reproduced in *Butterworths Immigration Law Service*, **2B[12]**.
3 Ie treatment contrary to art 3 of the ECHR.
4 Contrary to art 8 of the ECHR.
5 *D v UK* (1997) 24 EHRR 423; *R v Secretary of State for the Home Department, ex p Kebbeh* (CO 1269/1998) 30 April 1999 (deporting disabled man to Gambia where he would have no treatment and face destitution), QBD; *R v Secretary of State for the Home Department, ex p M*, 23 July 1999, QBD (AIDs patient). But see *I v Secretary of State for the Home Department* [1997] Imm AR 172 (not unreasonable to return HIV positive mother and child to Uganda, where treatment was available); *Bensaid v Secretary of State for the Home Department* [1998] Imm AR 525 (returning mental patient to Algeria not unreasonable).
6 Currently Liberia and Sierra Leone are subject to country policies for the grant of exceptional leave to remain.

12.180 Additionally, asylum seekers who have been waiting for a considerable period for their claims to be assessed may be eligible for leave to remain. The general policy is to grant exceptional leave after a claim has been outstanding for seven years.[1] Under the backlog clearance policy[2] asylum applications outstanding on 27 July 1998 were eligible for exceptional leave unless the applicant was subject to enforcement action or his or her presence in the UK was not considered conducive to the public good. Applicants who had claimed asylum before 1 July 1993 were normally granted indefinite leave to remain. Those who had claimed before 31 December 1995 would be considered for four years' exceptional leave depending on compassionate factors such as family ties and community connections with the UK.[3] Four years is now the normal period of exceptional leave which is granted, after which the applicant is eligible for settlement. Previously settlement could be sought only after seven years.[4]

1　API, Ch 5, s 1, para 2.1 above.
2　New measures for dealing with asylum claims, Asylum and Appeals Policy Directorate, April 1999, reproduced in *Butterworths Immigration Law Service*, **2B[14]**.
3　A person who had claimed in 1993 as a dependant but had made a claim in her own right when the relationship broke down was eligible under the scheme as claiming in 1993: letter from Peter Kandler to ILPA 23 July 1999.
4　New measures, fn 2 above. See the table in the section headed 'Reducing the Qualifying Period for Settlement' for transitional measures for those previously granted exceptional leave.

12.181 In deciding whether to grant exceptional leave to a refused asylum claimant, the Secretary of State is bound by the factual findings made after hearing evidence on the appeal, unless they are perverse or relate solely to country conditions which he or she is in as good a position to judge as the adjudicator.[1] Thus in *Danaie*[2] the adjudicator had rejected an Iranian man's asylum appeal but had found the appellant to be an adulterer; this made him vulnerable to execution in Iran and the Court of Appeal held that the Secretary of State was bound by the finding.

1　For cases on country conditions where the Secretary of State is not bound, see *R v Secretary of State for the Home Department, ex p Alakesan* [1997] Imm AR 315; *R v Secretary of State for the Home Department, ex p Elhasoglu* [1997] Imm AR 380.
2　*R v Secretary of State for the Home Department, ex p Danaie* [1998] Imm AR 84, [1998] INLR 124, CA.

Travel documents

12.182 A refugee is entitled to a Convention travel document as evidence of his or her status under the Refugee Convention.[1] The holder is entitled to re-admission to the country of refuge at any time during the validity of the document, so if the document is valid for more than two years, the two-year rule for returning residents cannot be applied to refuse readmission.[2] A person granted exceptional leave is not entitled to such a document, but current policy[3] is that those granted exceptional leave on refusal of asylum after 26 July 1993, and those who applied for asylum before 1 July 1993 and qualified under the backlog clearance scheme, are granted a Home Office travel document (certificate of identity) on request[4] and payment of the prescribed fee.[5] However, persons granted exceptional leave to remain in line with a spouse or partner, rather than on refusal of asylum, would not normally be eligible for a travel document unless they have been formally and unreasonably refused one by the authorities of their own country, or there are exceptional circumstances (for example, the country concerned has no UK diplomatic representation).[6] Neither a Convention travel document nor a national travel document (certificate of identity) is normally valid for the country of origin.[7]

1 Refugee Convention, art 28 and Sch: see **12.100** above. Note that the fee payable should not exceed the minimum payable for a national passport. The fee payable for a Convention travel document is currently £28. See also fn 3 below.

2 *R v Secretary of State for the Home Department, ex p Shirreh* (CO 2194/1997) 15 August 1997, QBD (permission; the case was then conceded by the Home Office).

3 Letter, Immigration and Nationality Directorate to Refugee Council 13 April 1999.

4 They do not have to demonstrate that they cannot obtain a passport from their national authorities or other exceptional circumstances, which those who obtained exceptional leave to remain before 1 July 1993 do. The policy of requiring pre-July 1993 recipients of exceptional leave to remain to demonstrate that they could not obtain a passport from their national authorities or other exceptional circumstances was upheld as not irrational in the absence of evidence of feared danger in *R v Secretary of State for the Home Department, ex p Najem* [1999] Imm AR 107, QBD.

5 The fee for a certificate of identity is £67. In February 1999 the government was advised that there was no power in domestic law to charge for travel documents and it introduced a refund scheme for those who had paid. There is now a statutory foundation for charges in Immigration and Asylum Act 1999, s 27, which is retrospective.

6 Immigration and Nationality Directorate letter to Fisher Meredith, 13 September 2000.

7 See **12.86** above for application of cessation clause to refugees who return to their own country. Similar considerations apply to those granted exceptional leave to remain on a protection basis.

Family reunion

12.183 The Final Act of the Conference which adopted the 1951 Convention recommended that governments took measures to ensure the unity of the refugee's family.[1] 'Family' usually means spouse and unmarried dependent children,[2] unless special circumstances exist, such as recognition of a broader family unit in certain societies.[3] The Refugee Convention does not incorporate family unity in the definition of the refugee, and family unity is not an obligation of the UK under the Convention,[4] but the UK and most other signatory states nevertheless makes provision for family reunion in its practices. Since October 2000 the Immigration Rules have made provision for the admission of the pre-existing spouse and minor children of a refugee.[5] The normal maintenance and accommodation criteria are not applied to them. The parents and minor siblings of children recognised as refugees are also admissible immediately, but not under the Rules.[6] The family reunion rights of those granted exceptional leave to remain are not set out in the Immigration Rules either, but under the Home Office policy they have to wait for four years before exercising them, unless there are compelling compassionate circumstances justifying waiver of the qualifying period.[7] They normally have to show they can maintain and accommodate their dependants, but this condition too can be waived.[8] Entry clearance fees may also be waived for family reunion with both refugee sponsors and those with exceptional leave to remain.[9]

1 UNHCR *Handbook* **12.13** above, Annex I.

2 UNHCR *Handbook* above, Annex I.

3 See UNHCR *Handbook* above, para 185; Somali Family Reunion Policy, set out in [1993] Imm AR 40; *Butterworths Immigration Law Service*, 2B[4]. The UNHCR has formulated a very broad definition including anyone in fact dependent on the principal: see 'Family Protection Issues', ExCom Sub-Committee 15th meeting, para 3, in (1999) 11(3) IJRL 582. See also ExCom Conclusion No 88(L) 1999 'Conclusion on the Protection of the Refugee's Family', which calls on states to consider 'liberal criteria in identifying those family members who can be admitted, with a view to promoting a comprehensive reunification of the family'.

4   The Final Act of the UN Conference producing the Convention recommended that governments 'take necessary measures . . . to ensure that the unity of the refugee's family is maintained'. See *D S Abdi v Secretary of State for the Home Department* [1996] Imm AR 148, disapproving *Ali* (10520), where the Tribunal had held that refugee family reunion was an obligation under the Refugee Convention and therefore within the rules (HC 395 para 327). The debate is no longer so important now that refugee family reunion has been brought within the Immigration Rules.
5   HC 395, paras 352A–F.
6   Letter from Immigration Minister to Lord Archer, 30 June 2000.
7   See *Warsame v Entry Clearance Officer Nairobi* [2000] Imm AR 155.
8   Immigration and Nationality Directorate statement of policy 20 January 2000.
9   In *R v Entry Clearance Officer Addis Ababa, ex p Jama (Zainab Ali)* (CO 3338/1999) 15 December 1999, QBD, permission was granted to challenge the refusal of the Embassy to waive visa fees on a settlement application from Somali family members whose sponsor had exceptional leave to remain and was on income support, where the children were in a refugee camp with no access to any income. The refusal was quashed by consent on 30 May 2000, and the entry clearance officer agreed to waive the fee and treat the application urgently.

12.184 In cases involving the admission of relatives other than pre-existing spouses and minor children of refugees, and the admission of any relatives of sponsors with exceptional leave to remain,[1] the appellate authorities have no jurisdiction to conduct a merits review of refusals of entry clearances to family members outside the rules relating to settled family members (although they will of course have jurisdiction under section 65 of the Immigration and Asylum Act 1999, which comes very close to a full merits review). But where a refusal is inconsistent with a published policy on family unity, the appellate authorities can consider whether a failure to apply the policy is in accordance with the law.[2] For that purpose they may review the facts on which any refusal was based and decide whether on the true facts there has been a misapplication of any policy. The Tribunal can construe the published policy in the exercise of this jurisdiction.[3]

1   See *Hersi v Secretary of State for the Home Department* [1996] Imm AR 569; *Darbiye v Entry Clearance Officer, Nairobi* [1998] Imm AR 64, CA.
2   See eg *Karshe* (18486), IAT (failure to consider relevant factors); *Mohammed (Asha)* (13170), IAT.
3   See *Osman* (13757) applying *Paw* (4328) on 'living alone'; *Sabriye* (13673), *Munim* (HX00367) reaching contrary conclusions on 'dependent member of the refugee's immediate family unit'.

12.185 The best known policy on family reunion, and the one giving rise to most litigation, has been the Somali family reunion policy which operated between 1988 and 17 January 1996.[1] It is still relevant for applications made before (and in some cases after) January 1996. The policy had two aspects. By a procedural concession, the Home Office in London would advise sponsors on request as to the eligibility of family members so that the family members did not have to make the arduous journey to a British post in Kenya or Ethiopia to determine their eligibility, at a time when the Mogadishu post was closed.[2] The advice that a relative was ineligible to join the sponsor for family reunion was not a refusal of entry clearance and did not give rise to appeal rights.[3] Family members who wished to appeal had to apply for entry clearance to the entry clearance officer abroad and be refused. Family members deemed eligible by the Home Office still had to apply to the entry clearance officer to be issued with entry clearance, which was forthcoming provided the facts presented to the entry clearance officer were as the sponsor had related them to the Home

Office. This concession was ended in January 1994. The substantive policy divided applicants into four categories: immediate family of refugees;[4] dependants under the normal Immigration Rules;[5] refugees for whom the UK is the most appropriate country of refuge;[6] and exceptional cases.[7] Relatives other than the sponsor's spouse and minor children could be considered under the policy if they had been dependent members of the refugee's immediate family unit before the refugee came to the UK. Much of the Tribunal's jurisprudence in this area turns on the meaning of this phrase, and many cases have been remitted to the Secretary of State on the appellate authority establishing that the necessary dependency and membership of the family unit existed.[8] In *Hersi*[9] the Court of Appeal held that relatives of sponsors with exceptional leave were not to be equated with relatives of refugees under the policy.[10] A relative who applies as such and not as a refugee is not entitled to consideration as a refugee for whom the UK is the most appropriate country of refuge under paragraph 8.3 of the policy.[11] The substantive Somali family reunion policy ended on 17 January 1996 and applications made thereafter are considered under the normal family reunion policies for refugees[12] and those on exceptional leave. But an application for entry clearance made after 17 January 1996, referring back to an approach to the Home Office before that date, is to be considered under the provisions of the Somali family reunion policy.[13]

1 Its terms are set out in a letter from the Home Office to Tower Hamlets Law Centre and others dated 17 May 1990; see *Butterworths Immigration Law Service*, 2B[4] [1993] Imm AR 40.
2 A similar concession allowed Vietnamese nationals who were refugees in the UK to apply direct to the Home Office by letter for relatives in Vietnam to join them. This concession was withdrawn on 1 November 1999. See API Aug/00, Ch 6, s 2, para 4.
3 *Secretary of State for the Home Department v Abdi and Dahir* [1995] Imm AR 570, CA.
4 Somali family reunion policy fn 1 above, para 8.1.
5 Somali family reunion policy above, para 8.2.
6 Somali family reunion policy above, para 8.3.
7 Somali family reunion policy above, para 8.4.
8 See eg *Munim* (HX00367) 1 January 2000; *Karshe* (18486) 20 March 1999.
9 *Hersi v Secretary of State for the Home Department* [1996] Imm AR 569.
10 In *Ahmed (Isse)* (18759) 24 June 1999 the Tribunal held that where a sponsor was on exceptional leave to remain at the time of the family reunion application but was later recognised as a refugee, recognition could not be backdated so that the provisions in the policy for relatives of refugees applied.
11 *Darbiye v Entry Clearance Officer, Nairobi* [1998] Imm AR 64, CA. The Tribunal held that family members who described themselves as 'urban refugees' and gave information relevant to establishing refugee status to the entry clearance officer, had no intention of claiming refugee status and were not entitled to consideration under para 8.3 of the Somali family reunion policy, in *Abdi (Farah Mohamed)*, (17113) 20 May 1998.
12 And of course under the Immigration Rules (HC 395, paras 352A-F) if the decision on the application postdates 1 October 2000.
13 *Mohamed (Mohamed Ahmed)* (22545) 6 January 2000, IAT.

12.186 In *Gasmelsid*[1] the Tribunal held that where a refugee married following recognition, the family reunion policy included his or her spouse, so that the normal rules did not apply. The couple in that case had been engaged before the refugee fled and the Tribunal emphasised that they had been unable to marry at that time through no fault of their own. A construction of the family reunion policy excluding such persons would 'give an artificial, strained and unjust construction to a rule the underlying purpose of which is to unite family members rather than keep them apart'. In *Onen* the Tribunal by a majority held that it was unfair to rely on the prolonged separation of family members who had fled to different countries to hold that the relationship between spouses was no longer subsisting.[2]

1 (13261) 29 April 1996, IAT.
2 *Onen* (22101) 8 October 1999, IAT.

12.187 Where one member of a family is in the UK and wants to be joined by others, the following practices apply:

(i) where a person is recognised as a refugee, immediate application for entry clearance can be made for other family members (as above) without any need for the maintenance and accommodation provisions of the Immigration Rules to be met;[1]

(ii) family members other than the pre-existing spouse and minor children of a refugee may not be admitted under the Rules, but refusal to admit them will be appealable if the refusal is not in accordance with the law (including failing to give effect to an established policy and on human rights grounds);

(iii) where a person has exceptional leave to enter or remain, an application for entry clearance for other family members normally will have to wait for four years and normally will have to satisfy the maintenance and accommodation provisions. Refusal is appealable as in (ii) above;[2]

(iv) family members who arrive in the UK without entry clearance to claim asylum in their own right or as a dependant will be able to rely on the presence in the UK of a 'qualifying' family member (spouse or minor child, or parent if the new arrival is a child), to prevent removal to a safe third country under the Dublin convention[3] or otherwise. The Dublin Convention requires the qualifying member to be in the country as a refugee, but Home Office policy does not require this.[4]

1 HC 395, paras 352A-F.
2 *Warsame v Entry Clearance Officer, Nairobi* [2000] Imm AR 155.
3 Article 4.
4 The UK relative may be in the UK on exceptional leave to remain or even on temporary admission as an asylum seeker: see *Conteh v Secretary of State for the Home Department* [1992] Imm AR 594, CA.

12.188 A husband or wife or minor children accompanying a principal asylum applicant may be included in the application, and will be granted leave to enter or remain in line with the principal.[1] Family members may claim asylum in their own right, and if they have a separate claim and wish to do so, they should do so as soon as possible, as failure to claim promptly will be taken into account and may damage credibility.[2] The rule provides that where the principal claimant is refused asylum and a dependant has already been refused in his or her own right, the dependant may be removed immediately, regardless of any right of that the principal asylum seeker wishes to exercise.[3] Now, it is likely that appeals will be synchronised, since all dependent members of the asylum seeker's family will be served with one-stop notices and if any have independent asylum claims they will be expected to say so in response to the notices. If they do not do so they run the risk of having any later application for asylum certified abusive, with the result that there will be no appeal.[4]

1 HC 395, para 349. This is also applied to unmarried partners, where there is evidence of a stable pre-existing relationship.

2   HC 395, para 349. Unless there is a good reason, eg a couple have separated since arrival.
3   HC 395, para 349. Where serial asylum claims are made by a husband and wife, a decision to remove the husband after the dismissal of his appeal but before his wife's was held not to be *Wednesbury* unreasonable or a breach of arts 6 or 8 of the ECHR in *R v Secretary of State for the Home Department, ex p Polat*, 7 November 1996, QBD. See also *R v Secretary of State for the Home Department, ex p Uzun* [1998] Imm AR 314; *R v Secretary of State for the Home Department, ex p Yolamba* [1997] Imm AR 564, QBD.
4   Immigration and Asylum Act 1999, ss 75, 73(8), 76(5).

Chapter 13

WELFARE PROVISION

ACCESS TO SOCIAL SECURITY BENEFITS

Non-contributory benefits

13.1 Access to social security benefits by those subject to immigration control was radically restructured from 3 April 2000. Persons 'subject to immigration control' are excluded by statute from that date from access to most non-contributory social security benefits.[1] These social security benefits are: income-based jobseeker's allowance; severe disablement allowance; invalid care allowance; disability living allowance; income support; working families' tax credit; disabled person's tax credit; social fund payments; child benefit; housing benefit; and council tax benefit. The non-contributory benefits which are not subject to the exclusion are industrial injuries benefits, category D retirement pensions and guardian's allowance. Prescribed categories of persons are, however, exempted by regulations[2] which exempt different persons in respect of the different benefits[3] and also apply transitional protection. Certain benefits— income support, income-based jobseeker's allowance, housing benefit and council

584

tax benefit—require claimants to satisfy the 'habitual residence' test as well, whether they are British citizens, EEA nationals or third country nationals.[4] We consider below first, who is 'subject to immigration control', next, who is exempted from the test, and for which benefits, and who gets transitional protection, and finally, the habitual residence test and who is exempted from it.

1　Under the Social Security Contributions and Benefits Act 1992, Social Security Contributions and Benefits (Northern Ireland) Act 1992, Jobseekers Act 1995, Jobseekers (Northern Ireland) Order 1995 SI 1995/2705: Immigration and Asylum Act 1999, s 115(1), (2), (9).
2　Social Security (Immigration and Asylum) Consequential Amendments Regulations 2000, SI 2000/636, made under Immigration and Asylum Act 1999, s 115(3)–(8).
3　Immigration and Asylum Act 1999, s 115(4).
4　See **13.21-13.23** below.

Subject to immigration control

13.2 Those who fall within the definition of being 'subject to immigration control' are:

- non-EEA nationals who require leave to enter or remain in the UK but have no such leave;[1]
- non-EEA nationals whose leave is subject to a condition of no recourse to public funds;[2]
- those given leave as the result of a 'maintenance undertaking';[3]
- those with a statutory leave pending appeal under the Immigration and Asylum Act 1999.[4]

No British or EEA nationals[5] are 'subject to immigration control'. A mistaken grant of leave to enter to a person who does not require it will *not* render that person 'subject to immigration control'.[6]

1　Immigration and Asylum Act 1999, s 115(9)(a).
2　Immigration and Asylum Act 1999, s 115(9)(b). The Home Office's decision as to the conditions upon which leave is granted is conclusive: Commissioner's Decisions R(SB) 25/85 and R(SB) 2/85.
3　Immigration and Asylum Act 1999, s 115(9)(c).
4　Immigration and Asylum Act 1999, s 115(9)(d).
5　Ie nationals of the EU member states (Austria, Belgium, Denmark, Finland, France, Germany, Greece, Republic of Ireland, Italy, Luxembourg, the Netherlands, Portugal, Spain, Sweden and the UK) together with Norway, Liechtenstein and Iceland: Immigration and Asylum Act 1999, s 167(1).
6　Commissioner's Decision R(SB) 11/88 (under earlier regulations).

13.3 EEA nationals are excluded from the definition whether or not they are exercising Treaty rights. This contrasts with the previous benefits regime, which defined as 'persons from abroad' those EEA nationals who were 'required by the Secretary of State to leave the United Kingdom'.[1] From April 1993,[2] the Secretary of State for the Home Department issued letters to those in the UK not exercising Treaty rights,[3] for example, those who had been in the UK as work-seekers for over six months without finding work or any genuine chance of doing so,[4] requiring them to leave the UK, which had the effect of excluding them from entitlement to benefit. In the cases of *Remelien and Wolke*[5] the House of Lords held that the letters lacked the necessary degree of compulsion to amount to a 'requirement' to leave so as to exclude EEA nationals from entitlement to benefits. What the regulations envisaged was an order for removal.[6] The Secretary of State has now relinquished the attempt to exclude from entitlement EEA nationals not exercising Treaty rights. This has diminished the need to rely on directly effective rights to social security benefit derived from EU law which are not described here.[7]

1 Income Support (General) Regulations 1987, SI 1987/1967, reg 21(1)(h).
2 When the amendment to the regs came into force: Income-related Benefits Schemes (Miscellaneous Amendments) Regulations 1993, SI 1993/315, reg 4.
3 See chapter 7 above.
4 *R v Immigration Appeal Tribunal, ex p Antonissen* [1991] ECR I-745.
5 *Remelien v Secretary of State for Social Security, Chief Adjudication Officer v Wolke* [1998] 1 All ER 129.
6 Under art 15(2) of the Immigration (European Economic Area) Order 1994, SI 1994/1895; see now Immigration (European Economic Area) Regulations 2000, SI 2000/2326, reg 21(3). A deportation order would also suffice.
7 For a treatment of EU law relating to the 'co-ordination' of social security benefits and the 'protection of social advantages', see CPAG's *Migration & Social Security Handbook* (2001) 3rd edn.

Those who require but who are without leave to enter or remain

13.4 Most non-British and non-EEA citizens require leave to enter. Apart from British citizens, a small number of Commonwealth nationals have the right of abode.[1] There are other categories who are exempt from requiring leave to enter, including certain members of the crew of a ship or aircraft, certain diplomats and their families, members of certain visiting armed forces and of Her Majesty's forces.[2] When they cease to be exempt, most need leave but do not have it, but former diplomats are treated as having been granted leave for 90 days after their exemption expires[3] and will not be 'subject to immigration control' for benefits purposes during that period.

1 Immigration Act 1971, ss 1(1), (2), 2(1), (2), and see chapter 2 above.
2 Immigration Act 1971, ss 8(1), (3)-(6), 8A, 8B; see chapter 6 above.
3 Immigration Act 1971, s 8A, inserted by Immigration and Asylum Act 1999, s 7. Such leave is not subject to conditions (save as to duration) and is not caught by s 115(9)(b) or (c) of the 1999 Act. See **6.49** above.

Leave subject to a condition of no recourse to public funds

13.5 Those who have leave to enter or remain in the UK which is subject to a condition of no recourse to public funds are 'subject to immigration control' for benefits purposes.[1] Only someone whose leave is subject to this express condition is 'subject to immigration control' under this head. The definition of 'public funds' has expanded over the years and is contained in the Immigration Rules.[2] The Rules require persons seeking leave to enter or remain in the UK for most purposes to show that they can maintain and accommodate themselves and their dependants without recourse to public funds.[3] No such requirement is imposed on refugees and their dependants,[4] transit visitors,[5] returning residents,[6] holders of special vouchers,[7] bereaved spouses and unmarried partners of persons who were settled in the UK who are seeking indefinite leave to remain,[8] and non-British citizen children born in the UK and now seeking leave to enter or remain.[9] Showing there will be no recourse to public funds in order to gain entry is not the same as having leave subject to this condition, however. Since November

1996, the immigration authorities have been able to attach a condition to leave that the recipient will not have recourse to public funds.[10] There is no guidance as to when such a condition should be imposed. A person with indefinite leave cannot be 'subject to immigration control' on this basis, since this leave by definition has no conditions attached to it.[11] But someone with indefinite leave could be 'subject to immigration control' if their leave was give as the result of a maintenance undertaking (below).

1 Immigration and Asylum Act 1999, s 115(9)(b).
2 HC 395, para 6. For discussion of the entries see **11.14**ff above.
3 Eg for visits, study, work, family reunion. For the substantive requirements of these rules, see chapters 9-11 above.
4 HC 395, Pt XI.
5 HC 395, paras 47-50.
6 HC 395, paras 18-20, although the applicant must not have received assistance from public funds towards previous departure from the UK: para 18(iii).
7 HC 395, paras 249-254.
8 HC 395, paras 287(b) and 295M, inserted by Cm 4851, paras 31 and 32.
9 HC 395, para 305-309.
10 Immigration Act 1971, s 3(1)(c); HC 395, para 8, as amended by Cm 3365, para 3.
11 Immigration Act 1971, s 3(1)(c), (3)(a).

Leave given as the result of a maintenance undertaking

13.6 A person given leave to enter or remain in the UK as the result of a maintenance undertaking is 'subject to immigration control'.[1] A maintenance undertaking for these purposes means a 'written undertaking given by another person in pursuance of the immigration rules to be responsible for that person's maintenance and accommodation'.[2] This wording is almost identical to that used under the regulations in force prior to 3 April 2000.[3] Only formal undertakings entered into under the Immigration Rules exclude a person from benefit entitlement.[4] Informal declarations of the kind often volunteered by well-meaning sponsors will not be effective for the statutory purpose.

1 Immigration and Asylum Act 1999, s 115(9)(c).
2 Immigration and Asylum Act 1999, s 115(10).
3 See, *inter alia*, Income Support (General) Regulations 1987, SI 1987/1967, reg 21(3)(i); the change from the words 'upon' an undertaking being given to 'as a result of [an undertaking]' emphasises the requisite causal connection; see Commissioner's decision CIS/6608/1999.
4 HC 395, para 35. A maintenance undertaking resulting in the grant of leave outside the Immigration Rules (for example, where one of the Rules is waived) is unlikely to be effective for this purpose. The form annexed to the prescribed application forms under para 32 of the rules, must also be counter-signed on behalf of the Secretary of State.

Leave pending appeal

13.7 Persons who have leave only by statutory extension pending appeal under the Immigration and Asylum Act 1999 are 'subject to immigration control'.[1] This does not apply to those whose leave has been extended by statute pending determination of an application,[2] nor to appellants awaiting old variation appeals under section 14(1) of the Immigration Act 1971 or section 8(2) of the Asylum and Immigration Appeals Act 1993, who are not covered by the statutory extension in the 1999 Act[3] and do not require leave, so should not be 'subject to immigration control' for benefit purposes unless the lease is subject to a public funds condition or was given as the result of a maintenance undertaking.[4]

13.7 Welfare provision

1 Immigration and Asylum Act 1999, s 115(9)(d), with reference to Sch 4, para 17(1) (continuation of leave, in force from 2 October 2000).
2 Immigration Act 1971, s 3C, inserted by Immigration and Asylum Act 1999, s 3 from 2 October 2000, applying to decisions made after 2 October 2000 whether the application for variation is made before or after that date (Commencement No 6 Order, art 2, Sch 2, para 2(2)).
3 The transitional provisions in the Commencement No 6 Order 2000, arts 3(1), 4(1), Sch 2 paras 1(5), (11)(b), 2(5), 3(2)(b), retained the Immigration Act 1971 provisions for appeals against pre-2 October 2000 decisions, and did not extend the statutory continuation of leave pending appeal to them.
4 The exclusion under Immigration and Asylum Act 1999, s 115(9)(d) applies to those who have leave 'only' as a result of Sch 4, para 17.

Exemptions from 'subject to immigration control' test

13.8 The exemptions from the 'subject to immigration control' test vary between the benefits, although there is some overlap, as appears below, and it is therefore convenient to consider the benefits in groups.

Income-based jobseeker's allowance, income support, social fund payments, housing benefit, council tax benefit

13.9 There are three groups of people who are exempted from the 'subject to immigration control' test and are therefore eligible to claim these benefits.[1] The first exemption applies to those who have been given leave within the Immigration Rules having satisfied a requirement that they will not have recourse to or be a charge on public funds[2] and who are temporarily without funds owing to the disruption of remittances from abroad.[3] There must, however, be a 'reasonable expectation' that the supply of funds will be resumed. The classic case is of a student whose funds from their home sponsor have been disrupted by, for example, short-term banking problems in that country.

1 Social Security (Immigration and Asylum) Consequential Amendments Regulations 2000, SI 2000/636 reg 2(1) and Sch, Pt I.
2 SI 2000/636, Sch, para 1(a).
3 SI 2000/636, Sch, para 1(b).

13.10 The next exempt group consists of certain persons granted leave to enter or remain under a maintenance undertaking.[1] Such persons are exempt if either the sponsor who gave the undertaking has died[2] or the person has been resident in the UK for a period of five years since either the date of entry into the UK or the date of the undertaking (whichever date is later).[3]

1 Primarily excluded by Immigration and Asylum Act 1999, s 115(9)(c), (10): see **13.6** above.
2 Social Security (Immigration and Asylum) Consequential Amendments Regulations 2000, SI 2000/636, Sch, Pt I, para 2.
3 SI 2000/636, para 3.

13.11 The final exempt group are nationals of states which have ratified either of two Treaties of the Council of Europe, the European Convention on Social and Medical Assistance (ECSMA)[1] or the Council of Europe Social Charter (CESC)[2] and who are 'lawfully present' in the UK.[3] Other than EEA member states, Cyprus, Czech Republic, Hungary, Malta, Poland, Slovakia, Turkey and Ukraine have ratified the Social Charter, and Malta and Turkey have in addition ratified ECSMA.

Their nationals must also be 'lawfully present' in the UK to benefit from this exemption. Those lawfully present for temporary purposes (visitors, students, au pairs, etc) are protected.[4] The government interprets the phrase 'lawfully present' as requiring a person to have a 'valid leave to enter or remain in the UK'[5] which would exclude a potentially large class of asylum seekers and others granted temporary admission, temporary release or bail pending resolution of their applications for leave. As Simon Brown LJ observed in *Ex p O*,[6] the 'concept of illegality under the 1971 Act is not an entirely satisfactory one: there is an obvious tension between the sections criminalising conduct such as overstaying and other provisions which ... operate to stay removal directions in the event of an appeal'. In the different context of access to community care services, he distinguished asylum seekers who claim asylum on entry and are granted temporary admission, or who claim during an extant leave, who, he said, are in the UK 'lawfully', from those who enter illegally, overstay or otherwise breach their conditions of leave.[7] However, in *Kaya v London Borough of Haringey*[8] the CA held that post asylum claimants on temporary admission were not 'lawfully present' for the purposes of ECSMA. The Court relied principally upon the interpretation of 'lawfully in' the territory for the purposes of article 32(1) 1951 Convention in *Musisi* [1987] AC 514 HL at 522-526 and noted that no material had been placed before the Court to suggest that a different approach should be adopted for the purposes of ECSHA or CESC.[9]

1   European Treaty Series (ETS) No 14, Paris, 11 December 1953.
2   ETS No 35, Turin, 18 October 1961.
3   Social Security (Immigration and Asylum) Consequential Amendments Regulations 2000, SI 2000/636, Sch 1, para 4.
4   See Lenia Samuel *Fundamental Social Rights: Case law of the European Social Charter* (1997) Council of Europe p 325 citing the Conclusions of the Committee of Experts at Conclusions XIII-2, p 142, Norway; Conclusions XIII-3, p 367, Finland.
5   Department of Environment, Transport and the Regions letter to all Chief Executives of housing authorities in England, 14 March 2000; see also Income Support *Bulletin* 41/00.
6   *R v Wandsworth London Borough Council, ex p O, R v Leicester City Council, ex p Bhikha* [2000] 4 All ER 590 at 601. See also Hale LJ at 607.
7   A distinction not drawn *R v Brent London Borough Council, ex p D* [1998] 31 HLR 10, DC, where Moses J decided that all asylum seekers' presence is lawful as they may not be returned pending the determination of their claim. *D* was followed in *R v Lambeth London Borough Council, ex p Sarhangi* [1999] LGR 641, and see *R v London Borough of Hammersmith and Fulham London Borough Council, ex p M* [1997] 1 CCLR 69 in which Collins J referred to asylum seekers as 'entitled' to remain in the UK. The point was not taken in the CA ([1997] 1 CCLR 85). Overstayers, etc were held excluded from duties owed by local housing authorities in *R v Hillingdon Borough Council, ex p Streeting* [1980] 3 All ER 413 and *R v Secretary of State for the Environment, ex p Tower Hamlets Borough Council* [1993] 3 All ER 439 at 447; for the yet more problematical category of persons who enter lawfully without requiring leave but who subsequently lose the exemption and require leave, see *R v Westminster City Council, ex p Castelli and Tristan-Garcia* [1996] 3 FCR 383.
8   [2001] EWCA Civ 677.
9   The conclusions of the European Committee of Social Rights (formerly the Committee of Experts) assessing compliance with the Social Charter might have constituted just such material; see in particular their conclusions at XII-1 p 197, XII-2 p 198, XIII-4 pp 60-62, 210-212.

13.12 Transitional provisions protect certain claimants from the regime in force from 3 April 2000 and preserve eligibility for these benefits. There are provisions continuing existing transitional protection from previous changes made in 1996 and others preserving entitlement under the regime in force from 1996 to April 2000.

Those entitled to benefit before 5 February 1996

13.13 There are two categories of person who are exempt from the 'subject to immigration control' test for income support, social fund payments, housing and council tax benefits[1] as a result of previous transitional provisions in regulations in force from 5 February 1996.[2] First is a diminishing class of asylum seekers who claimed asylum, whether on arrival or not, prior to 5 February 1996 and who have not since then received the next decision on their claim (whether of the Secretary of State for the Home Department or of the appellate authorities on appeal).[3] To benefit from this protection, the claimant must have been entitled to benefit immediately before 5 February 1996.[4] For a long time there remained uncertainty as to whether a claimant remains protected following a break in entitlement after 5 February 1996 (for example, where the asylum seeker obtains and then loses work after that date).[5] The Court of Appeal has now decided that entitlement continues in these circumstances.[6] Members of an asylum seeker's family who were receiving the benefit concerned on 4 February 1996 who claim asylum in their own right after that date are also transitionally protected under this rule.[7] Also protected are persons in respect of whom a sponsor gave a maintenance undertaking before 5 February 1996 and who were receiving, or entitled to receive, income support, housing benefit or council tax benefit immediately[8] before that date.[9]

1   But not income-based jobseeker's allowance.
2   Social Security (Immigration and Asylum) Consequential Amendments Regulations 2000, SI 2000/636, reg 2(4).
3   SI 2000/636, regs 2(4)(a), 12(11)(b) applying Social Security (Persons from Abroad) Miscellaneous Amendments Regulations 1996, SI 1996/30, reg 12(1), and see CIS/3108/1997.
4   See *R v Secretary of State for Social Security, ex p Vijeikis, Zaheer and Okito*, 10 July 1997, QBD, Dyson J, upheld 5 March 1998, CA; see also CIS/16992/96, CIS/2809/97, CFC/1580/97.
5   The Commissioner in CIS/1115/1999 held that protection ended in these circumstances, applying *R v Adjudication Officer, ex p B*, CA (which dealt with different provisions); however in *R v Secretary of State for Social Security, ex p Markovic* (CO 3855/1999), 24 May 2000 it was conceded as arguable that a break in entitlement does not end transitional protection under SI 2000/636, reg 12(1). The application for permission was dismissed on other grounds.
6   *Yildiz v Secretary of State for Social Security* (C/00/3093) 28 February 2001, CA .
7   SI 1996/30, reg 12(1), as amended by Asylum and Immigration Act 1996, Sch 1, para 5.
8   Commissioner's Decision CIS/16992/96
9   SI 2000/636, regs 2(4)(a), 12(11)(b); SI 1996/30, reg 21(2).

Those entitled to benefit before 3 April 2000

13.14 There is also transitional protection for persons entitled to income support, income-based jobseeker's allowance,[1] social fund payments, housing and council tax benefit before 3 April 2000. The first protected group are persons who submitted a claim for asylum 'on arrival in the UK' on or before 2 April 2000.[2] The claim must have been made to the Secretary of State for the Home Department, and 'recorded by the Secretary of State as having been made before that date.[3] A claim for asylum in this context means a claim under the Refugee Convention, not the ECHR. For what constitutes a 'claim' to the 'Secretary of State' and a 'record', see **13.37-13.40** below. To be eligible for jobseeker's allowance as opposed to income support, the claimant must hold a work permit or have written authorisation to work in the UK from the Secretary of State.[4]

1 Both paid at the 'urgent cases' rate of 90 per cent of the claimant's ordinary 'applicable amount' calculated under the Income Support (General) Regulations 1987, SI 1987/1967, reg 21, Jobseekers Allowance Regulations 1996, SI 1996/207, reg 128.
2 Social Security (Immigration and Asylum) Consequential Amendments Regulations 2000, SI 2000/636, regs 2(5), (6), 12(3), (7).
3 SI 2000/636, regs 2(5), (6), 12(3), (7).
4 SI 2000/636, reg 12(4)(c).

13.15 Before the Social Security (Immigration and Asylum) Consequential Amendments Regulations 2000,[1] the phrase 'on arrival' was used in the Social Security (Persons from Abroad) Miscellaneous Amendments Regulations 1996,[2] and has led to considerable difficulty and divergent case law in the decisions of the Social Security Commissioners. During the passage of the 1996 legislation, an attempt was made in the House of Lords to incorporate a three-day period of grace in which a person might claim asylum without losing access to benefits.[3] The defeat of the amendment left open whether Parliament intended the somewhat elliptical phrase 'on arrival' to be sufficiently flexible to avoid injustice.[4] The Secretary of State interprets 'on arrival' as synonymous with 'clearing immigration control', and the issue is whether more flexibility was intended. No case has reached the higher courts[5] and divergent views have been taken by different social security Commissioners. Even on the flexible approach, where the claimant has entered through immigration control, a compelling reason has been required for not taking the opportunity of claiming asylum there. In one case the Commissioner commented: 'If, as I accept, the words "on his arrival" were used because they may be applied flexibly, it seems wrong to try to find another simple formula which may be applied in all cases ... I would therefore accept that "clearing immigration control" is not a universal test applicable in all cases.'[6] That approach was followed by other Commissioners where claimants sought to claim asylum after passing through controls but while still at the port[7] and where a claimant submitted a claim for asylum two or three days after entering, alleging that he had been too ill to claim at the immigration desk.[8] In the latter case, the Commissioner cited his own earlier dismissal of the appeal of a clandestine entrant who claimed asylum in Wales near his brother's home after being released from the back of a lorry in central London.[9] Other Commissioners have upheld the Secretary of State's approach and in so doing have taken the term 'arrival' to have some statutory resonance under the Immigration Act 1971,[10] citing *Naillie*[11] as authority for the proposition that arrival must precede entry and construing the regulation as relating to the application for leave to enter.[12] The result of this approach is that only a claim for asylum made to the immigration officer before passing through controls will bring a claimant within the regulations; claims made in any other manner, including all claims made by clandestine entrants[13] exclude the claimant from eligibility. Yet a further Commissioner, having regard to comments made by the sponsoring minister[14] under the principle in *Pepper v Hart*[15] decided that, in order to satisfy the test, the claimant had to have claimed asylum while within the perimeter of the port of entry, although not necessarily before passing through immigration controls.[16]

1 SI 2000/636.
2 SI 1996/30.
3 Referred to in Commissioner's Decisions CIS/143/97, para 7 and CIS/4117/97, para 19.
4 Bonner et al *Social Security: Legislation 2000* (Sweet & Maxwell, 2000).
5 Appeals were not pursued in CIS/2719/97 and CIS/3231/97, noted below.

6   CIS/4117/97, para 20, the Commissioner applying a different approach to that in his earlier Decision CIS/143/97. The appeal was rejected on the facts (young female asylum seeker acting under the control of an agent at port, claiming asylum three days later), demonstrating the difficulty of satisfying the test even applied with some flexibility. The same Commissioner allowed the appeal in CIS/4439/98, where a claim was submitted very shortly after the claimant came through immigration controls. The Commissioner noted (paras 12-18) that to interpret 'on arrival' in the manner contended for by the respondent would be inconsistent with the UK's obligations under the Refugee Convention, art 31, which precludes the imposition of penalties on refugees 'provided they present themselves without delay to the authorities and show good cause for their illegal entry or presence': see **12.11** above, **14.24**ff below. The Commissioner accepted (para 16) that civil penalties as well as criminal penalties fell within art 31, and that denial as well as removal of a right was a 'penalty'. Thus, he reasoned, construing 'on his arrival' to be of similar effect to 'without delay' in art 31 would render consistency between the provision and the UK's international obligations. This interpretation of art 31 has been questioned in decisions adopting a less benign interpretation of the regulations: see CIS/3646/98, para 9, CIS/1671/97.
7   CIS/4341/98, paras 2, 13.
8   CIS/3803/98, para 5. The Commissioner remitted the matter to the appeal tribunal for a proper investigation of the facts.
9   CIS/3231/97, paras 3, 10. It is to be assumed that these two decisions of the same Commissioner are consistent and adhere to the somewhat clearer analysis of the Commissioner in CIS/3803/98.
10 Immigration Act 1971, ss 3-4, 11, Sch 2, para 2.
11 *R v Naillie* [1993] AC 674 at 679G-680B.
12 CIS/3867/98, para 16-18, heard with CIS/259/99.
13 See CIS/2918/98, para 7.
14 281 HC Official Report (6th series) cols 844-879, 15 July 1996.
15 [1993] AC 593.
16 CIS/1137/97, joined with CIS/2719/97.

13.16 Asylum seekers who claimed asylum before 3 April 2000 and within three months of what has become known as a 'declaration of upheaval' are also transitionally protected for these benefits.[1] There have only been two declarations that a country 'is subject to such a fundamental change of circumstances that [the Secretary of State] would not normally order the return of a person to that country': in respect of former Zaire (now the Democratic Republic of Congo) on 16 May 1997, and in respect of Sierra Leone on 1 July 1997. Claimants must have submitted a claim for asylum to the Secretary of State within three months from the date of the declaration and the claim must have been recorded by the Secretary of State as having been made.[2] Where a claimant arrived in the UK after the declaration had been made but was nevertheless present in the UK and claimed asylum within three months of it, the Commissioner dismissed an appeal, holding that it was necessary for the claimant actually to have been in the UK at the time of the declaration.[3]

1   Social Security (Immigration and Asylum) Consequential Amendments Regulations 2000, SI 2000/636, regs 2(5), 12(3), (4)(b), (6), (7)(b).
2   SI 2000/636, reg 12(4)(b)(ii), (iii), (6)(ii), (iii).
3   CIS/3864/98. Leave to appeal to the Court of Appeal was granted but the appeal was not pursued.

13.17 Both 'on arrival' and 'declaration of upheaval' claimants lose entitlement when the asylum claim is recorded as having been determined (by the Secretary of State, not on appeal), or is 'abandoned'.[1] The courts have held that this requires a reliable document by way of an unprovisional note on the relevant file that the claim has been determined,[2] regardless of whether the claimant has been notified of the decision and regardless of whether the Secretary of State is considering fresh representations.[3] When the decision could be said to have been made was, in turn, complicated by the two-stage process operated by the Secretary of State.[4] The Secretary of State has reverted to the practice of issuing 'holding letters' to asylum seekers informing them that their claim for asylum has been recorded as determined, prior to the service of the 'immigration decision' consequent on the refusal of asylum (refusal of leave, removal directions, etc). This avoids the (previously common) situation of asylum seekers learning from the Benefits Agency that their asylum claim has been refused and their benefit terminated. An asylum seeker who was in receipt of benefit and whose claim was recorded as determined prior to 25 September 2000 became eligible to apply for interim asylum support on refusal if he or she appealed or had a child living as part of the household. If the claim was recorded as determined after that date he or she would be similarly eligible for NASS support.[5]

1 Social Security (Immigration and Asylum) Consequential Amendments Regulations 2000, SI 2000/636, reg 12(5)(8).
2 *R v Secretary of State for the Home Department, ex p Karaoui and Abbad*, 11 March 1997, QBD.
3 *R v Secretary of State for the Home Department, ex p Salem* [1999] 2 WLR 1 at 22D-G, 26E-27F overruling the decision of Potts J in *R v Secretary of State for the Home Department, ex p Bawa* 27 October 1997. Leave to appeal to the House of Lords was granted but the appeal was never heard as the point became academic prior to hearing.
4 A case-worker initially assesses the asylum claim, minutes the file with a *proposed* decision and sends the file to a supervising officer, who takes the final decision: see affidavit of David Laubach, Higher Executive Officer in the Asylum Directorate Policy Unit set out in *Salem* above at 25F-26D.
5 Immigration and Asylum Act 1999, s 94. Regrettably some asylum seekers have experienced difficulties in accessing NASS support where the asylum decision has been recorded yet the 'immigration decision' has not been served.

Rates of benefit and dependants in respect of income support and jobseeker's allowance

13.18 The pre-3 April 2000 claimants benefiting from transitional benefits, having claimed on arrival or within three months of an upheaval declaration, are eligible for income support and income-based jobseeker's allowance, not at the full rate but at the 'urgent cases' rate of 90 per cent of a claimant's ordinary weekly applicable amount.[1] The reduced rate also applies to those exempted from the 'subject to immigration control' test on the basis that they are temporarily without funds or were granted leave under a sponsorship undertaking and the sponsor has died.[2] However, these groups may at least obtain benefit for their spouses and children, whether or not the latter are 'subject to immigration control',[3] whereas those entitled to these benefits at the ordinary rates may not obtain benefit in respect of their spouses who are subject to immigration control nor, if such a spouse is present, for any children who are subject to control. However, where the claimant is a single parent or the *spouse* is not subject to immigration control, additional benefit is due, regardless of their immigration status.[4]

1 Income Support (General) Regulations 1987, SI 1987/1967, reg 71, Jobseeker's Allowance Regulations 1996, SI 1996/207, reg 148.
2 SI 1987/1967, reg 70(1), (2), (2A); SI 1996/207, reg 147(1), (2), (2A).
3 SI 1987/1967, reg 71(1)(a)(i), (ii) with reference to Sch 2, paras 1, 2; SI 1996/207, reg 148(1)(a)(i), (ii) with reference to Sch 1, paras 1, 2.
4 SI 1987/1967, reg 21, Sch 7 para 16; SI 1996/207, reg 85, Sch 5, para 13A.

Attendance allowance, severe disablement allowance, invalid care allowance, disability living allowance, social fund payments, child benefit

13.19 Three classes of people are exempted from the 'subject to immigration control' test for these benefits:[1]

(i)   Those given leave to enter or remain in the UK upon a maintenance undertaking.[2] This wide exemption re-includes that whole class of claimant primarily excluded by one of the limbs of section 115 of the Immigration and Asylum Act 1999;

(ii)   Family members of EEA nationals;[3]

(iii)   Those nationals, and their family members who are living with them, of countries with which the EC has concluded an agreement'[4] which provides for the equal treatment of workers who are nationals of the signatory state in the area of social security.[5] The exemption extends to association agreements and to Association Council decisions made under them.[6]

In addition, transitional protection applies to persons entitled to or receiving the benefits as a result of transitional protection from the February 1996 changes.[7] The claimant must have been entitled to the benefit in question prior to 5 February 1996,[8] and protection continues until *either* any claim to asylum is recorded as having been determined or is abandoned *or* entitlement to that benefit is revised or superseded by the social security determining authorities.[9] Unlike income support, protection only applies to the benefit award made before 5 February 1996 and not to renewal claims made after that date.[10] For child benefit, the claimant needs to have been paid the benefit immediately prior to 7 October 1996,[11] and the conditions for cessation of benefit are similar.[12]

1   Social Security (Immigration and Asylum) Consequential Amendments Regulations 2000, SI 2000/636, reg 2(2), Sch, Pt II.
2   SI 2000/636, Sch, Pt II, para 4. See **13.6** above. The exemption applies to a person 'given leave to enter or remain ... by the Secretary of State', failing to recognise that the immigration officer, not the Secretary of State is responsible for on-entry decisions: see chapter 3 above.
3   Sch, Pt II, para 1. 'Family members' is not defined, but it is suggested that it should be understood to include at least those who are treated as family members under EU free movement provisions.
4   Under art 310 EC (ex art 238).
5   Social Security (Immigration and Asylum) Consequential Amendments Regulations 2000, SI 2000/636, Sch, Pt II, paras 2-3.
6   Commissioner's Decision CFC/2613/97. The exemption applies to nationals of Algeria, Morocco, Slovenia, Tunisia and Turkey.
7   SI 2000/636, regs 2(4), 12(10) and Social Security (Persons From Abroad) Miscellaneous Amendments Regulations 1996, SI 1996/30, reg 12(3).
8   *R v Secretary of State for Social Security, ex p Vijeikis, Zaheer and Okito*, 10 July 1997, QBD, Dyson J, upheld by the Court of Appeal on 5 March 1998; for the need for entitlement immediately prior to 5 February 1996 see Commissioner's Decisions CIS/16992/96, CIS/2809/97, CFC/1580/97.
9   SI 2000/636, reg 12(10), Social Security Act 1998, ss 9-10.
10 *R v Chief Adjudication Officer, ex p B*, 9 December 1998.
11 When the Asylum and Immigration Act 1996 removed entitlement from anyone 'subject to immigration control' by inserting s 146A into the Social Security Contributions and Benefits Act 1992.
12 SI 2000/636, regs 2(4)(b), 12(10), Child Benefit (General) Regulations 1976, SI 1976/965, reg 14B(g).

Child benefit, attendance allowance, disability living allowance

13.20 Attendance allowance, disability living allowance and child benefit are payable under another exemption from section 115 of the Immigration and Asylum Act 1999. The UK has certain reciprocal agreements with both EEA and non-EEA countries which are given effect by Orders in Council.[1] Where an agreement is in effect in respect of any of these benefits, nationals of (or in some cases, migrants coming from) the contracting state are exempted from the 'subject to immigration control test' and are eligible to claim that benefit.[2]

1 Made under s 179 of the Social Security Administration Act 1992. Among the non-EEA countries and territories which have concluded agreements in respect of any of these benefits are Australia, Barbados, Canada, Israel, Jersey and Guernsey, Mauritius, New Zealand, Switzerland, Federal Republic of Yugoslavia.
2 Social Security (Immigration and Asylum) Consequential Amendments Regulations 2000, SI 2000/626, reg 2(3). The provisions of the agreements are too detailed to set out here. See Cox et al *Migration and Social Security Benefits Handbook* CPAG, (2nd edn, 1997) pp 372-378.

Habitual residence

13.21 The 'habitual residence' test applies an additional obstacle to eligibility for income support, income-based jobseeker's allowance, housing benefit and council tax benefit,[1] subject to the exemptions below. It was introduced in August 1994 in order to combat what the then government viewed as 'benefit tourism'[2] on the part of EEA nationals and is retained in the regime applicable to these benefits from 3 April 2000. In principle it applies to nationals of all countries, including EEA nationals and British citizens, who must be habitually resident in the common travel area.[3] In other areas of law, the concept of habitual residence has been seen as synonymous with 'ordinary residence', ie the claimant must be lawfully resident for a settled purpose, which was a question of fact to be determined in the light of all the circumstances.[4] It is clearly distinct from that of domicile[5] as it is possible to be habitually resident in more than one country at the same time.

1 Income Support (General) Regulations 1987, SI 1987/1967, reg 21(3), Jobseeker's Allowance Regulations 1996, SI 1996/207, reg 85(4), Housing Benefit (General) Regulations 1987, SI 1987/1971, reg 7A(4)(e), Council Tax Benefit (General) Regulations 1992, SI 1992/1814, reg 4A(4)(e).
2 See eg the speech of Rt Hon Peter Lilley MP, Secretary of State for Social Security, to Conservative Party annual conference, Autumn 1993.
3 Ie the UK, Channel Islands, Isle of Man, Republic of Ireland: see chapter 6 above.
4 *Shah v Barnet London Borough Council* [1983] 2 AC 309; see chapter 5 above. The Social Security Commissioner has recognised that asylum seekers awaiting resolution of their claims may be habitually resident: CIS/564/94.
5 R(U) 8/88; see **11.27-11.33** above.

13.22 In *Nessa*,[1] the Commissioner endorsed the view of an earlier case[2] that an 'appreciable period' of residence by the claimant was required to establish habitual residence.[3] The Court of Appeal (by a majority) and the House of Lords agreed, although the Lords accepted that the 'appreciable period' may be as short as a month,[4] and that there may be 'special cases', such as resumption of earlier residence.[5] A different meaning was given to the term by the ECJ in *Swaddling*,[6] where the court considered that no minimum period of residence in the member state in which the claimant had applied for social security benefit was necessary to establish habitual residence there for the purposes of Council Regulation 1408/71 (EEC), although the reasons for a person's presence, its duration and the claimant's intentions were all relevant factors.

1   CIS/2326/95, *Nessa v Chief Adjudication Officer* [1998] 2 All ER 728.
2   R(IS) 6/96.
3   Contrast, in another context, *Macrae v Macrae* [1949] 2 All ER 34.
4   By reference to *Re F (a minor)* [1994] FLR 548.
5   See further CIS/1304/97 and, for retention of habitual residence during a period of absence, CIS/14591/96.
6   Case C-90/97 *Swaddling v Adjudication Officer* [1999] All ER (EC) 217.

Exemptions from habitual residence test

13.23   The following persons are exempt from the habitual residence test:

•   'workers' within the meaning of Council Regulations 1612/68 (EEC) or 1251/70 (EEC),
•   persons with a right to reside in the UK pursuant to Council Directives 68/360 (EEC) or 73/148 (EEC),
•   refugees within the meaning of Article 1A(2) of the Refugee Convention,
•   persons who have been granted exceptional leave to enter or remain.[1]

In addition, persons who are not 'subject to immigration control' for the purposes of the Immigration and Asylum Act 1999,[2] and who are in the UK as a result of their deportation, or other removal by compulsion from another country to the UK, are exempt from the habitual residence test for the purposes of income support and income-based jobseekers' allowance.[3] Once in *receipt* of income support or income-based jobseeker's allowance, such a claimant may receive housing benefit and council tax benefit regardless of the habitual residence test.[4]

1   Income Support (General) Regulations 1987, SI 1987/1967, reg 21(3), Jobseeker's Allowance Regulations 1996, SI 1996/207, reg 85(4), Housing Benefit (General) Regulations 1987, SI 1987/1971, reg 7A(4)(e), Council Tax Benefit (General) Regulations 1992, SI 1992/1814, reg 4A(4)(e).
2   Immigration and Asylum Act 1999, s 115.
3   SI 1987/1967, reg 21(3), SI 1996/207, reg 85(4).
4   SI 1987/1971, reg 7A(4)(5), SI 1992/1814, reg 4A(4)(5).

Backdating of benefits for refugees

13.24   There are two regimes in force for the backdating of income support for asylum seekers who are subsequently granted refugee status.

(i)   Those who claimed asylum before 3 April 2000, provided they claim income support within 28 days of notification that they have been recorded as a refugee by the Secretary of State, are entitled to backdated payments of benefit *at the urgent case*s *rate* from the date that the claim to asylum was refused (if the asylum claim was made on arrival)[1] or from the date of the claim, or 5 February 1996 if that is later, if the claim was made in country,[2] up until the date they are recorded by the Secretary of State as a refugee.[3]

(ii)   Those who claimed asylum on or after 3 April 2000 and who are subsequently recognised as refugees, and who claim income support within

28 days of notification of being recorded as a refugee, are entitled to backdated benefit paid at the *full rate* from the date of the claim for asylum.[4] However, for these claimants, as opposed to the pre-3 April claimants, the award of income support is subject to an express deduction representing asylum support received under either NASS or the interim scheme.[5] Similar provisions apply in respect of the back-dating of awards of housing benefit and council tax benefit.[6]

1 This category were eligible for benefits until refusal of their claim.
2 This category lost eligibility on 5 February 1996, see above.
3 Income Support (General) Regulations 1987, SI 1987/1967, reg 21ZA, now superseded by Social Security (Immigration and Asylum) Consequential Amendments Regulations 2000, SI 2000/636, reg 3(5) but preserved for pre-3 April 2000 asylum applicants by reg 12(1), (2).
4 SI 1987/1967, reg 21ZB, inserted by SI 2000/636, reg 3(5).
5 SI 1987/1967, reg 21ZB(3).
6 Housing Benefit (General) Regulations 1987, SI 1987/1971, reg 7B, Sch A1, Council Tax Benefit (General) Regulations 1992, SI 1992/1814, reg 4D, Sch A1; as amended respectively by SI 2000/636, regs 6(4)-(6), 7(4)-(6) with transitional arrangements for pre-3 April 2000 claimants contained in SI 2000/636, reg 12(2)(c), (d).

Further residence requirements and contributory benefits

13.25 Some of the benefits referred to above have additional residence tests, which cannot be set out within the scope of this text, which may require presence in the UK for a certain specified period of time and/or ordinary residence in the UK.[1] The benefits to which additional requirements are added are: attendance allowance, child benefit/guardian's allowance (for which the rules are most complex), disability living allowance, disabled person's tax credit, working families' tax credit, invalid care allowance, category D retirement pension, severe disablement allowance. Access to the contributory benefits—contribution-based jobseeker's allowance, incapacity benefit, maternity allowance, widow's payment, widowed mother's allowance, widow's pension, category A and B retirement pensions—does not depend upon immigration status, but they are payable only in those cases in which sufficient national insurance contributions have been paid. In practice, this may exclude many who are coming or who have recently come to the UK.

1 See CPAG's *Migration and Social Security Handbook* (3rd edition, 2001).

THE ASYLUM SUPPORT SCHEME

13.26 In July 1998 the government announced the introduction of a new national system of support for asylum seekers and their dependants.[1] The new system that was finally introduced took shape in the form of two distinct, although similar, structures for providing asylum support, both enacted through the provisions of the Immigration and Asylum Act 1999.[2] The stated aim of the government was to ensure that genuine asylum seekers were not left destitute while at the same time containing the cost to the public purse of providing for asylum seekers.[3] One means of achieving this was to provide 'incentives' to asylum seekers to look first to their own communities for support.[4] A key disincentive to applying for asylum support, and one of the most controversial aspects of the scheme, has been the provision of accommodation on a 'no-choice' basis outside the London area. This system of dispersing asylum seekers reflected the aim of the government to reduce both the costs of support—by using empty social housing in different parts of the country—and the perceived burden on authorities in London and the south-east. Equally controversial was the government's decision to implement a largely cashless system requiring asylum seekers to present vouchers redeemable for goods at participating retail outlets.[5] The additional and explicit policy aim was to reduce the 'incentive to economic migration'.[6]

1   See Home Office White Paper *Fairer, Faster, Firmer: A Modern Approach to Asylum and Immigration* (Cm 4018, July 1998).
2   Immigration and Asylum Act 1999, Pt VI and Schs 8-10.
3   White Paper above.
4   Asylum Seekers Support Project Team, Immigration Nationality Directorate *Asylum Seekers Support* (March 1999) para 1.1.
5   The main participating supermarket chains have been Tesco, Sainsbury's, Asda and Somerfield.
6   *Asylum Seekers Support* above, paras 1.1, 1.4.

13.27   These two features of the system, in particular, have attracted persistent criticism both during the passage of the Immigration and Asylum Act 1999[1] and since the new system has been in operation.[2] In June 2000, the Audit Commission reported[3] that the lack of effective support for asylum seekers in the areas of dispersal could lead them to become trapped in a cycle of social exclusion and dependency in those areas, or to their drifting back to London (as did resettled Vietnamese refugees two decades earlier). The Commission's report highlighted, in particular, the absence outside the capital of sufficient legal support (less than half the law firms contracted by the Legal Services Commission to provide immigration advice are outside London), mental health services, English language support and refugee community organisations. Also significant was the hostile media coverage given to asylum seekers, which was likely to prove inflammatory to public opinion and encourage violent attack.[4] By the end of 2000, the warnings made by the Commission appeared to have been borne out. The dispersal system was reported to be in a state of collapse as large numbers of asylum seekers abandoned dispersed accommodation, where they were fearful of racial harassment and unable to access necessary support, for cramped accommodation with relatives in and around London.[5] As for the voucher system, by October 2000, in the face of mounting criticism,[6] the government had been forced to agree to review its operation.[7]

1   See for example Memorandum from the African-Caribbean and Refugee Support Project on the 'distressing and humiliating' effect of vouchers, and evidence of the Hackney Churches Refugee Network, to the House of Commons Special Standing Committee on the 1999 Bill. The Local Government Association told the Committee that vouchers could be 'costly, bureaucratic and stigmatising' and that an unofficial market had developed by their being sold on at under face value by asylum seekers needing to buy essential non-food items.
2   In October 2000 the report of the Commission on the future of multi-ethnic Britain, set up by the Runnymede Trust in January 1998 to propose ways of countering racial discrimination and disadvantage and to promote racial justice, proposed a return to a cash system of support for asylum seekers at no less than the basic level of income support and a choice of available housing.
3   Audit Commission *Another Country: Implementing dispersal under the IAA 1999* (June 2000); the early difficulties faced by the dispersal scheme are further apparent from the 'Asylum Seekers Voluntary Dispersal Scheme' Bulletins 1-6 (on the Local Government Association website www.lga.gov.uk).

4   The Commission found that only 6% of 161 local press articles analysed between October and November 1999 referred to the positive contribution made by asylum seekers and refugees.

5   See 'Refugees pour back to London', 'Nowhere left to run' Observer, 31 December 2000.

6   A report by Oxfam GB, the Refugee Council and the Transport and General Workers Union 'Token Gestures—the effects of the voucher scheme on asylum seekers and organisations in the UK' (December 2000) contains the views of over 50 organisations working with asylum seekers across the UK. Eighty-two per cent of the organisations found the level of support insufficient to allow asylum seekers to buy enough food, 96 per cent that it was not enough to purchase other essential items, 70 per cent that asylum seekers had reported poor treatment from shops accepting vouchers and 62 per cent that asylum seekers had reported hostility from other shoppers. The report recommended the return to a cash-based system pitched at a 'realistic' level of support. The difficulties encountered by asylum seekers using the voucher system have also been noted by the UNCHR: *Reception standards for asylum seekers in the European Union* (2000).

7   Parliamentary answer of Secretary of State for the Home Department, 355 HC Official Report (6th series) col 210W, 26 October 2000.

13.28 In addition, the asylum statistics belie the proposition that the new system limits costs by acting as a disincentive to asylum claims as the Home Office had predicted.[1] In fact, since the withdrawal in February 1996 of means-tested cash benefits for in-country and refused asylum seekers, after an initial fall,[2] asylum applications have risen steadily.[3] There were substantial year on year increases in the number of applications from 29,500 in 1996 to 32,500 (1997), 46,000 (1998), 71,000 (1999), 77,000 (2000).[4] The figures represent a level of claims greatly in excess of the 42,000 expected over the first year of the NASS scheme[5] and reflects, we suggest, the self-evident reality that the level of asylum seekers depends on the level of international human rights abuse rather than the nature of welfare provision available in host countries.

1   Asylum seeker support: estimates of public expenditure, Home Office Research Development and Statistics Directorate, Immigration and Nationality Directorate, Departments of Education and Employment, Health, Social Security, at Appendix E, paras 5, 6, 11. The other policy measures cited were the increase in airline liaison officers, increased Dublin Convention co-operation and action against facilitators of clandestine entry by lorry. A full breakdown of the Research Directorate's projection is cited in, Asylum Seekers Support Project Team, IND *Asylum Seeker Support* (March 1999) chapter 2 and in the Home Office paper *Cluster Areas: Role of local organisations*.

2   *Asylum Seeker Support* above, Appendix E, paras 3, 5.

3   *Asylum Seeker Support* above, Appendix E, Chart 1: The effect of changing support provision for in-country applicants in 1996.

4   Immigration Research and Statistics Service, Research and Statistics Directorate of the Home Office, see Bulletins HOSB 14/98, 10/99, 17/00, 22/00 and paper 'Asylum Statistics: November 2000'.

5   In fact the rate of claims since April 2000 exceeded even the Home Office's 'high variant' forecast of 51,000 for the year 2000-01 and its comparative forecast of 57,000 claims over that year if no policy changes had been made: *Asylum Seeker Support* above, estimates of public expenditure at Appendix E, para 11.

13.29 Another important point is that the new support scheme was intended to dovetail with operational improvements within the Immigration and Nationality Department of the Home Office aimed at reducing the time taken to determine asylum applications. The Home Office's aim was that, by April 2001, decisions would take two months on average, and appeals resolved in a further four months on average.[1] Underlying decisions as to the nature of support provided, therefore, is the intention that it is for a short, temporary period.[2] The adequacy of the support provided may therefore be called into question where the resolution of the application is delayed significantly beyond these targets.[3]

1 White Paper **13.26** fn 1 above (Cm 4018, July 1998).
2 332 HC Official Report (6th series) written answers col 334, 9 June 1999; this is expressly reflected in the statutory criteria for the exercise of powers to provide accommodation in Immigration and Asylum Act 1999, s 97(1)(a).
3 The system of 'additional single payments' is an attempt to deal with this criticism (see **13.84** below).

Two schemes

13.30 There are, in effect, two schemes in operation. From 6 December 1999 a new 'interim' support scheme for asylum seekers and their dependants, operated by local authorities, was introduced in England and Wales (not in Scotland or Northern Ireland).[1] The introduction of the interim scheme coincided with the exclusion from many community care services of most asylum seekers and others 'subject to immigration control' within the meaning of section 115 of the Immigration and Asylum Act 1999.[2] Most asylum seekers who were in receipt of support under section 21 of the National Assistance Act 1948 or section 17 of the Children Act 1989 did not notice or experience any change in their support with the introduction of the interim scheme, as they were deemed to have been accepted for support by the local authority under the interim provisions.[3] The government's intention was to ensure that local authorities had a 'purpose-designed' statutory duty of support until its main scheme could be introduced, rather than the ill-fitting duties under the community care and Children Act legislation.[4]

1 Immigration and Asylum Act 1999, Sch 9; Asylum Support (Interim Provisions) Regulations 1999, SI 1999/3056.
2 Immigration and Asylum Act 1999, ss 116-117.
3 SI 1999/3056, reg 11.
4 NASS Director's circular to all Chief Executives of local authorities in England and Wales, 19 November 1999, para 6.

13.31 From 3 April 2000 the national scheme was introduced, administered by the National Asylum Support Service of the Home Office (the 'NASS scheme').[1] Although under this scheme NASS is charged with the responsibility for deciding whether a person is entitled to support and what forms of support are appropriate,[2] the Secretary of State may arrange for the actual delivery of the support by another agency.[3] In particular, although not exclusively, local authorities are empowered to provide support under such arrangements[4] and may form companies and enter into contracts with the Secretary of State, either alone or with other agencies such as registered social landlords, housing associations and the private and voluntary sectors, for the provision of support services to asylum seekers.[5] By October 2000 three contracts had been signed between NASS and regional consortia of such agencies for the provision of accommodation to asylum seekers.[6] NASS works closely with voluntary sector agencies[7] which act as 'assistants' in identifying and assessing applicants for asylum support.

1 Immigration and Asylum Act 1999, Pt VI, and Schs 8, 10.
2 See ss 95(1), (5), (7), 96(2), (3), 97(1), (2), (4), (5), (7), 98(1) of the Immigration and Asylum Act 1999 and the decision-making functions devolved to the Secretary of State in the Asylum Support Regulations 2000, SI 2000/704.
3 Immigration and Asylum Act 1999, ss 95(1), 98(1).

4   Immigration and Asylum Act 1999, s 99(1), (2), (3).
5   Immigration and Asylum Act 1999, s 99(4), (5).
6   Scottish, North-East and Yorkshire and Humberside Consortia; see Parliamentary Answer of Secretary of State, 355 HC Official Report (6th series) col 209W, 26 October 2000.
7   Refugee Arrivals Project, Migrants Helpline, Refugee Action, the Refugee Council and the Scottish and Welsh Refugee Councils.

13.32 The purpose of the NASS scheme is to provide comprehensively for the support for asylum seekers in the absence of a general right to community care services and benefits. NASS will eventually take over responsibility for all those currently supported under the interim scheme (the life-span of the interim scheme is from 6 December 1999 to 1 April 2002,[1] although it could be extended if necessary).[2] The Secretary of State may give directions to local authorities to treat the interim period as ending for certain classes of asylum seekers on dates earlier than 1 April 2002.[3] Where the interim period is treated as having ended for any particular asylum seeker, that person cannot be provided with support under the interim scheme,[4] and may therefore apply for NASS support.[5] Four such directions have been given, which had the general effect of rendering different classes of new asylum seekers and different classes of newly 'disbenefitted' asylum seekers[6] eligible for NASS rather than interim support between April and September 2000.[7] The directions brought new asylum seekers, and asylum seekers who had hitherto been entitled to social security, into the NASS scheme where responsibility would otherwise have lain with the local authorities under the interim scheme. They have not had the effect of literally 'moving' classes of asylum seeker already supported under the interim scheme, into the NASS scheme.

1   Immigration and Asylum Act 1999, Sch 9, para 15 and Asylum Support (Interim Provisions) Regulations 1999, SI 1999/3056, regs 1(1), 2(5).
2   The time span of the interim period is set by SI 1999/3056 and could be changed by amending regulations.
3   Immigration and Asylum Act 1999, Sch 15, para 14(1), (4); this provision enables the Secretary of State for the Home Department to direct local authorities to 'treat the interim period' as coming to an end earlier than 1 April 2002: for specified purposes; in relation to a specified area or locality; or in relation to persons of a specified description.
4   SI 1999/3056, reg 3(1) provides in terms that an authority '... must provide support during the interim period to eligible persons'.
5   Asylum Support Regulations 2000, SI 2000/704, reg 4(5)(a).
6   Ie those who have received a negative decision by the Secretary of State having up to that point been entitled to social security benefit.
7   Direction Nos 1, 2, 2A, 3 of the Secretary of State for the Home Department issued on 13 March, 10 April, 10 April and 11 July 2000 respectively, see **13.153**ff below.

Further powers

13.33 The Secretary of State has powers to require local authorities, registered social landlords and housing associations to provide assistance in the provision of NASS accommodation.[1] This includes putting suitable spare accommodation at the Secretary of State's disposal in return for appropriate reimbursement[2] as well as providing the Secretary of State with information about their housing stock on request.[3] The Secretary of State also has powers to designate areas consisting of one or more local authorities as 'reception zones' in which local authorities may be directed to make available to NASS, or to another agency with which NASS has contracted to provide support, a specified amount of accommodation.[4] The Secretary of State has indicated that these powers will only be used if local authorities refuse to co-operate voluntarily in providing accommodation for asylum seekers.[5]

1   Immigration and Asylum Act 1999, s 100.
2   Explanatory Notes to the Immigration and Asylum Act 1999, para 310.
3   Immigration and Asylum Act 1999, s 100(4).
4   Immigration and Asylum Act 1999, s 101; if such powers are implemented, further regulations would be required dealing, *inter alia*, with the management of such housing accommodation; see s 101(10)-(14).
5   See Explanatory Notes to Immigration and Asylum Act 1999, para 312.

Other changes

13.34   The new system of asylum support must be seen in the context of simultaneous changes in provision of community care and social security benefits with particular ramifications for asylum seekers. From 6 December 1999 those who fall within a new statutory definition of being 'subject to immigration control' are *prima facie* excluded from access to many community care services and, from 3 April 2000, from social security benefits.[1]

1   Immigration and Asylum Act 1999, ss 115-117; see paras **13.2-13.20** (for social security) and paras **13.164-13.167** (for community care services).

COMMON ASPECTS OF THE TWO SCHEMES FOR SUPPORT

13.35   Although the detail of the two schemes of support is provided for in separate secondary legislation,[1] important elements of the primary provision made for the two schemes in the Immigration and Asylum Act 1999 overlap so that many of the key conditions relating to entitlement are the same.[2] The general conditions of eligibility for support under the schemes are that the person is an 'asylum seeker' or the 'dependant of an asylum seeker' within the meaning of Part VI of the 1999 Act and is either destitute or likely to become destitute within a limited period.[3] We deal now with these common general conditions of eligibility.

1   The Asylum Support (Interim Provisions) Regulations 1999, SI 1999/3056 regulate interim support and the Asylum Support Regulations 2000, SI 2000/704 and Asylum Support Appeals (Procedure) Rules 2000, SI 2000/541 provide for the main scheme of support.
2   Immigration and Asylum Act 1999, ss 94, 95, Sch 9, paras 1, 3.
3   Immigration and Asylum Act 1999, ss 94(1), 95(1), Sch 9, paras 1-3; SI 1999/3056, regs 2(1), 3; SI 2000/704, reg 3.

'Asylum seekers' under the support schemes

13.36   An 'asylum seeker' for the purposes of the asylum support schemes is a person aged 18 or over who has made a 'claim for asylum', which has been 'recorded' by the Secretary of State and which has not been 'determined'.[1] It is necessary to consider these ingredients in turn.

1   Immigration and Asylum Act 1999, ss 94(1), 95(1), Sch 9 para 1(1), (2); Asylum Support (Interim Provisions) Regulations 1999, SI 1999/3056, reg 2(1); SI 2000/704, reg 3(1).

Claim for asylum

13.37 An asylum claim under the support regime is a claim by a person that it would be a breach of the UK's obligations under the Refugee Convention or Article 3 of the ECHR for him or her to be removed from or required to leave the UK.[1] Unlike the Refugee Convention,[2] Article 3 of the ECHR contains no express prohibition on returning persons to a country where they may face ill-treatment, but a claim under Article 3 is nevertheless predicated on the assumption that it will be a breach of the UK's obligations under the Convention to remove a person to a country where they face a real risk of it.[3] The protection offered by Article 3 is appreciably wider than that available under the Refugee Convention.[4] A claim under Article 3 may re-engage eligibility for asylum support after entitlement has ceased by the final determination of a claim under the Refugee Convention.[5] Similarly, a fresh claim for asylum may re-engage eligibility for asylum support in such circumstances.[6] This is of particular importance to those asylum seekers without dependent children under 18 who, because of new dangers or fresh evidence, make a fresh claim after the original claim has been finally determined. Those who have child dependants continue to qualify for asylum support for as long as they and the child remain in the UK.[7]

1 Immigration and Asylum Act 1999, s 94(1).
2 1951 Convention relating to the Status of Refugees, arts 32, 33.
3 *Soering v UK* (1989) 11 EHRR 439; *D v UK* (1997) 24 EHRR 423.
4 See chapters 8 and 12 above.
5 In *R v London Borough of Lambeth, ex p Tekeste* (CO/77/00) 11 January 2000, Maurice Kay J granted interim relief to the asylum seeker in judicial review proceedings turning on this point, but the applicant was granted exceptional leave before the full hearing.
6 The jurisprudence on 'fresh claims' to asylum (*Singh (Manvinder) v Secretary of State for the Home Department*, 8 December 1995, CA; *Onibiyo v Secretary of State for the Home Department* [1996] Imm AR 370, CA) is based on an analysis of the term 'claim to asylum' as defined in the Asylum and Immigration Appeals Act 1993, s 1, a definition in identical terms to that used in Immigration and Asylum Act 1999, s 94 (aside from the addition of ECHR, art 3 claims). Thus, the same approach should govern the question of fresh claims for support purposes regardless of the lack of specific provision in the Immigration and Asylum Act 1999 or the regulations.
7 Immigration and Asylum Act 1999, s 94(5).

13.38 There is no particular form in which a claim for asylum must be made. The Home Office accepts that a claim has been made when a person asserts that it would be 'contrary to the Refugee Convention to require him (sic) to leave the UK,'[1] or 'where it appears to the immigration officer as a result of information given that he may be eligible for asylum.'[2] The Home Office API adopt a wide and flexible approach which recognises that it is not necessary for the terms 'asylum' or 'refugee' to be used; an expression of unwillingness to return to the country of nationality or habitual residence as a result of some perceived danger is sufficient. The merits of a claim are irrelevant (even where the claim, on its face, does not engage the Convention) and any doubt must be resolved in favour of a claim having been made.[3] Case law of the Social Security Commissioners construing the phrase 'claim for asylum' in the context of determining whether such a claim was made 'on arrival' in the UK is to similar effect: there is no need for a person to have completed any particular forms[4] and 'an indication of a desire to claim asylum is itself a claim for asylum'.[5] The claim may be oral (even over the telephone) or in writing,[6] and may be made on behalf of the asylum seeker by someone with the authority to act for him or her.[7] The claim for asylum need not be submitted to the Secretary of State for the Home Department.[8] There is no reason in principle why a claim made to a police officer or Department of Social Security official should not qualify as a claim to asylum. However, the claim must have been recorded by the Secretary of State (see below).[9]

1   The current Immigration Rules, HC 395, para 327.
2   The formulation under earlier Immigration Rules, HC 251, para 75, uncontroversially cited on this point in *R v Uxbridge Magistrates' Court, ex p Adimi* [1999] 4 All ER 520 at 530D–F.
3   ADI Oct/00, Ch 1, s 1, para 1.2.
4   Commissioner's Decision CIS/4341/98, para 10.
5   Commissioners' Decision CIS/4439/98, para 7; see also CIS/3867/98, para 9 and CIS/259/99, para 9.
6   Commissioner's Decision CIS/4439/98, para 7, CIS/3867/98, para 6(4).
7   Commissioner's Decision CIS/4439/98, para 7. An asylum support adjudicator has held that the burden of demonstrating that an asylum claim has been made rests with the claimant: ASA 00/11/0111, para 8.
8   Contrast previous reg 70(3A)(a) of the Income Support (General) Regulations 1987, SI 1987/1967 and similar social security provisions, which expressly required claims to asylum to be made to the Secretary of State.
9   Immigration and Asylum Act 1999, s 94(1).

Claim for asylum has been 'recorded by the Secretary of State'

13.39 The claim to asylum must have been 'recorded by the Secretary of State'.[1] All that is necessary for a claim to have been recorded, we suggest, is that there is in the Home Office some note made by an officer of the Secretary of State which identifies the person making the claim and which is sufficient to indicate that a claim to asylum has been made by that person. Again, the case law of the Social Security Commissioners dealing with claims recorded as having been made for benefits purposes may be applicable in this context. In one case, a Commissioner held that there was no specified manner in which the record of the claim had to be made, and relied on a letter from the Secretary of State issued in response to a complaint as to how a person had been treated on entry to the UK as either a sufficient record of the claim in itself or as secondary evidence of a Home Office record.[2] There is no requirement that the asylum seeker has been notified of the recording of the claim. In another case, the Commissioner was satisfied that a record of the claim to asylum had been made during the course of a telephone conversation between the asylum applicant and an immigration officer before the applicant was issued with a Standard Acknowledgment Letter.[3] From the language of the provision we suggest that it does not matter if the record of the claim is subsequently lost, for example, if the Home Office loses the relevant file, provided that it can be established that the claim was originally made and recorded.[4]

1   Immigration and Asylum Act 1999, s 94(1).
2   Commissioner's Decision CIS/4439/98, paras 3, 7, 8.
3   Commissioner's Decisions CIS/3867/98, paras 6(3), (4) and CIS/259/99, para 7(2).
4   Section 94(1) of the Immigration and Asylum Act 1999 uses the perfect tense: 'a claim for asylum which has been recorded by the Secretary of State'.

13.40 Further guidance may be obtained from the decisions of the courts on the question of the recording of the determination of a claim to asylum.[1] It has been held that a 'record' exists if there is a reliable document by way of an unprovisional note on the relevant file that the claim had been determined,[2] regardless of whether the applicant has been notified that the claim had been determined and regardless of whether the Secretary of State is considering fresh representations.[3] The circumstances of those cases are not, however, directly analogous, as the 'record' had to show that a particular decision had been made by the Secretary of State, namely a decision to refuse asylum—a question complicated by the internal two-stage process which the Secretary of State operates when making such decisions.[4]

1 Under previous reg 70(3A)(b)(i) of the Income Support (General) Regulations 1987, SI 1987/1967.
2 *R v Secretary of State for the Home Department, ex p Karaoui and Abbad* (1997) Times, 11 March, QBD.
3 *R v Secretary of State for the Home Department, ex p Salem* [1999] 2 WLR 1 at 22D-G, 26E-27F, overruling the decision of Potts J in *R v Secretary of State for the Home Department, ex p Bawa*, 27 October 1997, QBD.
4 A case-worker initially assesses the claim for asylum, minutes the file as to a proposed decision and sends it to a supervising officer, who takes the final decision: affidavit of David Laubach, Higher Executive Officer in the Asylum Directorate Policy Unit, set out in *Salem* above at 25F-26D.

Claim for asylum has not been determined

13.41 A person remains an 'asylum seeker' for support purposes until the claim for asylum 'has been determined'.[1] The one exception to this rule is that if there is a dependent child in the asylum seeker's household, the person does not cease to be an asylum seeker while the child remains under 18 and both remain in the UK.[2] In all other cases, a person ceases to be an asylum seeker 14 days after[3] either[4] the day on which the Secretary of State notifies him or her in writing[5] of the decision on the claim for asylum or, if there is an appeal against the decision, the day on which the time limit for a further appeal expires.[6] Thus a person remains an asylum seeker, for these purposes, throughout the period during which there is no decision on the asylum application and, if the Secretary of State's decision is negative, throughout the entire appeals process.

1 Immigration and Asylum Act 1999, s 94(1).
2 Immigration and Asylum Act 1999, s 94(5).
3 Asylum Support Regulations 2000, SI 2000/704, reg 2(2), (3), Asylum Support (Interim Provisions) Regulations 1999, SI 1999/3056, reg 2(6).
4 Immigration and Asylum Act 1999, s 93(3)(4).
5 Immigration and Asylum Act 1999, s 94(8).
6 Immigration Act 1971, s 33(4) as amended by Immigration and Asylum Act 1999, Sch 14, para 55; Immigration and Asylum Act 1999, ss 94(4), 167.

13.42 Viewing the determination of an asylum claim as inclusive of the appeal process both accords with the case law[1] and avoids the situation which arose in 1996 where asylum seekers had, in theory, important appeal rights but were, in practice, unable to exercise them because of destitution.[2] Eligibility for social security benefits and community care services is restored when asylum seekers are successful on appeal and are recognised as refugees and granted leave by the Home Office accordingly. There have, unfortunately, been very severe delays in the Home Office granting refugee status to successful appellants, which has caused prejudice in terms of access to conventional social security benefits and housing, naturalisation, travel documents and entitlement to work. The High Court has declared such delays unlawful.[3]

1 Which sees the asylum appellate process as an extension of the original asylum decision-making process: see *Ravichandran v Secretary of State for the Home Department* [1996] Imm AR 97, CA.
2 See observations in *R v Secretary of State for Social Security, ex p Joint Council for the Welfare of Immigrants* [1996] 4 All ER 385.
3 *R v Secretary of State for the Home Department, ex p Mersin (Deniz)* [2000] INLR 511, Elias J; timely notification of decisions was a further factor identified by the Audit Commission as critical for the proper and efficient functioning of the dispersal system in *Another Country: Implementing dispersal under the Immigration and Asylum Act 1999* June 2000.

Dependants of asylum seekers

13.43 Both schemes provide for support to be provided not only to asylum seekers but also to the dependants of asylum seekers.[1] There are some minor differences in the wording of the regulations defining dependants for the two schemes.[2] The general definition of dependants which applies to both NASS and the interim scheme is set out below, with the differences between the two schemes discussed immediately afterwards. A person is the 'dependant of an asylum seeker' if he or she is related or connected to the asylum seeker in one of the following ways:[3]

(a) is the spouse of the asylum seeker (almost certainly in a marriage recognised by UK law);[4]

(b) is the child of the asylum seeker *or* of his or her spouse, who is under 18 and dependent on the asylum seeker;

(c) is a member of the asylum seeker's or his or her spouse's 'close family'[5] who is under 18;

(d) has been living as part of the asylum seeker's household *either* for at least six of the 12 months before the day on which the claim for support was made *or* since birth and, in either case, is under 18;

(e) is in need of care and attention from the asylum seeker or a member of his or her household by reason of a disability *and is either* a member of the asylum seeker's or their spouse's close family *or* has been living as part of the asylum seeker's household for six of the 12 months before the date on which the claim to support was made *or* since birth;

(f) has been living with the asylum seeker as a member of an unmarried couple for at least two of the three years before the day on which the claim to support was made;

(g) is living with the asylum seeker as part of his or her household and was receiving assistance from a local authority under section 17 of the Children Act 1989 immediately before 6 December 1999;[6]

(h) has made a claim for leave to enter or remain in the UK, or to vary such leave, which is being considered on the basis that the person is the dependant of an asylum seeker. Under the Immigration Rules[7], only the spouse and minor children of asylum seekers are to be considered as dependants on the asylum claim, but the Secretary of State may, as a matter of discretion, treat other family members as dependent on the asylum seeker for the purposes of the asylum claim;[8]

(i) is an asylum seeker, in circumstances where his or her dependant has claimed support.

1 Immigration and Asylum Act 1999, ss 94(1)(a)-(c), 95(1), Sch 9, para 1(2); Asylum Support (Interim Provisions) Regulations 1999, SI 1999/3056, reg 2(1); Asylum Support Regulations 2000, SI 2000/704, reg 3(3).

2 SI 2000/704, reg 2(9) prevents the definition of dependant under NASS from being applied to the interim scheme.
3 SI 1999/3056, reg 2(1); SI 2000/704, reg 2(4).
4 See **11.20**ff above.
5 'Close family' remains undefined in the regulations.
6 The date on which the interim regulations (Asylum Support, SI 1999/3056) came into force, and thus the beginning of the 'interim period' for SI 1999/3056, reg 1(1), 2(1)(g), 2(5); ASR, SI 2000/704, reg 2(4)(g).
7 HC 395, para 349.
8 The acceptance of the spouse and minor child is the 'minimum requirement' of the policy on family reunion of the United Nations High Commission for Refugees and the Final Act of the Conference which adopted the Refugee Convention, and other family members may be accepted. This policy is followed by the government: see API, Aug/00, Ch 6, s 1, para 3.

13.44 In addition to the categories referred to above, a person qualifies as a dependant under NASS if he or she is living as a part of the asylum seeker's household and, immediately before 3 April 2000, was receiving support from a local authority in Scotland or Northern Ireland under provisions equivalent to the Children Act 1989.[1] This category ensures that dependants in Scotland and Northern Ireland are provided for by NASS rather than by the social services, as the interim scheme has never applied in Scotland and Northern Ireland.[2]

1 Asylum Support Regulations 2000, SI 2000/704, reg 2(4)(h).
2 Asylum Support (Interim Provisions) Regulations 1999, SI 1999/3056, reg 1(2).

13.45 The regulations for the NASS scheme expressly provide that, in categories (b), (c) and (d) above, a person counts as a dependant if he or she was under 18 at the time that the application for support for him/her was made, or when he or she joined her a supported asylum seeker in the UK,[1] and so will continue to receive support after their 18th birthday, provided all the other conditions continue to be met. The interim provisions contain no such express protection for dependants after they reach 18.

1 Asylum Support Regulations 2000, SI 2000/704, reg 2(4)(b), (c), (d), (6).

13.46 In category (f), under the NASS scheme, those joining a partner in the UK while the latter was being supported, must have lived with him or her as a couple for two of the three previous years.[1] The interim scheme makes no separate provision for this situation. Further, the NASS regulations define an 'unmarried couple' as a man and woman who, though not married to each other, are living together as if married,[2] in contrast to the interim regulations, which do not define 'unmarried couple'. In the interim scheme it could therefore be argued that a same-sex couple living together in a relationship akin to marriage are an 'unmarried couple' and that the non-asylum seeker partner qualifies as a dependant.

1 Asylum Support Regulations 2000, SI 2000/704, reg 2(4)(f), (6).
2 SI 2000/704, reg 2(1).

'Destitute' or likely shortly to become 'destitute'

13.47 In order for asylum seekers to obtain support under either scheme, they must appear to be either destitute or likely to become destitute[1] within 14 days.[2] A person is destitute if he or she either[3] does not have 'adequate accommodation' or the means to secure it or has adequate accommodation or the means of getting it but cannot meet his or her other 'essential living needs'. Statutory rules set out what may and what may not be taken into account in determining this issue and they are different for the two schemes of support (they are therefore dealt with separately in the sections below),[4] so the case law under the community care provisions which the schemes replace will not be directly applicable.[5] The needs which are referred to in the asylum support provisions are generally current needs. The concept of 'entitlement' over a particular period, which exists in social security law, does not form part of the scheme of asylum support, so that asylum seekers may face difficulties in seeking to 'backdate' entitlement.[6]

1   Immigration and Asylum Act 1999, s 95(1), Sch 9, para 1(2).
2   Asylum Support (Interim Provisions) Regulations 1999, SI 1999/3056, reg 2(1); Asylum Support Regulations 2000, SI 2000/704, reg 7(a).
3   Immigration and Asylum Act 1999, s 95(2), Sch 9, para 3.
4   Immigration and Asylum Act 1999, s 95(5), (6), as applied by Sch 9, para 3 (interim scheme); s 95(5)-(8) and SI 2000/704, regs 6, 8-9 (NASS scheme).
5   See *R v Westminster City Council, ex p M, P, A and X* [1997] 1 CCLR 85, CA; *R v London Borough of Hammersmith and Fulham, ex p M; R v London Borough of Lambeth, ex p P and X, R v Westminster City Council, ex p A* [1997] 1 CCLR 69, QBD (combination of lack of food or accommodation, inability to speak English as first language, stress of fleeing persecution and inexperience of UK will inevitably result in a person requiring 'care and attention' under s 21 of the National Assistance Act 1948 where other assistance is unavailable; the longer an asylum seeker remains in such a situation, the more compelling his or her claim for assistance becomes; further, an authority could anticipate the deterioration that would otherwise take place in the condition of the asylum seeker by providing support); *R v Newham London Borough Council, ex p Gorenkin (Mikhail)* [1998] 1 CCLR 309 (authority able to conclude that a person was 'in need of care and attention' within the meaning of s 21 of the National Assistance Act 1948 even where he was not actually or imminently homeless); *R v Southwark London Borough Council, ex p Cui (Hong)* [1999] 2 CCLR 86 (authority must arguably look beyond questions of principle - whether applicant for support had permission to work - to the practical realities to whether there was any realistic possibility that she would find it).
6   *R v Hammersmith London Borough Council, ex p Isik*, 19 September 2000, CA. But see ASA 01/02/0202, paras 4 and 14 where an adjudicator held an asylum seeker legally entitled to amounts due from the date of the asylum support application to the date when he was granted indefinite leave to remain and became entitled to social security benefit, subject only to deduction for backdated income support (as to which see **13.24** above).

Differences between the two schemes

13.48 Despite their common features, there are many differences between the two schemes. The obvious difference is that under the interim scheme, local authorities are responsible for determining who is entitled to support and for making arrangements to provide it,[1] whereas under NASS, it is the Secretary of State for the Home Department who is responsible for determining eligibility and ensuring that support is provided.[2] There are also differences in the procedures for making applications for support, the operation of temporary support, what may be provided, decisions on dispersal of asylum seekers, rules excluding persons from support and the procedures for challenging decisions.

1   Immigration and Asylum Act 1999, Sch 9, para 2(1); Asylum Support (Interim Provisions) Regulations 1999, SI 1999/3056, reg 3(2).
2   Immigration and Asylum Act 1999, s 95(1), Asylum Support Regulations 2000, SI 2000/704, reg 5.

NATIONAL ASYLUM SUPPORT SCHEME

13.49 The National Asylum Support Service (NASS) is a body established as part of the Home Office to be responsible for providing comprehensive support to destitute asylum seekers. It has been operational since 3 April 2000, when it took on responsibility for the support of certain new asylum applicants.[1] The intention is that, eventually, all destitute asylum seekers will have recourse to NASS rather than to the interim scheme, community care services or social security benefits.[2] By the end of August 2000, all new asylum seekers were eligible to apply for NASS support, and in April 2002, when the interim scheme is set to end, NASS will be responsible for all asylum seekers.[3]

1 The system of support provided by NASS is set out in Immigration and Asylum Act 1999, Pt VI and Schs 8 and 10; the key provisions were brought into force from 3 April 2000 (Immigration and Asylum Act 1999 (Commencement No 3) Order 2000, SI 2000/464, art 2 and Sch), on which date the regulations which set out the detailed machinery of the scheme also came into force: Asylum Support Regulations 2000, SI 2000/704, reg 1; Asylum Support Appeals (Procedure) Rules 2000, SI 2000/541, reg 1.
2 See **13.146ff** below for a detailed description of which asylum seekers are eligible to apply NASS support and which for interim support.
3 Asylum Support (Interim Provisions) Regulations 1999, SI 1999/3056, regs 1(1) and 2(5). Local authorities will retain community care responsibilities for those whose need for care and attention does not arise solely from destitution, however: *R (Westminster City Council) v NASS* [2001] EWCA Civ 512; see **13.164** below.

Procedures under the NASS scheme

Applications for support

13.50 The NASS scheme, unlike the interim scheme, requires an application to NASS for support.[1] The application must be in a specified form, NASS1 (attached to the Asylum Support Regulations), or in similar form.[2] Asylum seekers may receive assistance completing the form from the voluntary sector 'assistants'[3] which help to identify and convey relevant information to NASS. The application may be for a sole applicant or for the applicant and his or her dependants,[4] and a group application may be made on one application form. A new or newly arrived dependant of a person who is already being supported by NASS does not need to complete another application, and NASS will consider providing additional support when notified of his or her existence.[5] The form is mandatory and if it is not used NASS may not consider the application for support.[6] The application may be sent to NASS by fax or post, but if sent by fax the original should also be sent by post.[7] A person in detention who is awaiting the hearing of a bail application may make an application for support in anticipation of release.[8] NASS may make further inquiries of the asylum seeker in connection with any of the details contained in the application form.[9]

1 Asylum Support Regulations 2000, SI 2000/704, reg 3(1).
2 SI 2000/704, reg 3(3).
3 Refugees Arrival Project, Migrants Helpline, Refugee Action, the Refugee Council, Scottish and Welsh Refugee Councils.
4 SI 2000/704, reg 3(2).
5 SI 2000/704, reg 3(6).
6 SI 2000/704, reg 3(4).

7   SI 2000/704, explanatory notes to Sch.
8   SI 2000/704, notes to NASS1 Form 'Do you live in any other kind of accommodation ?'
9   SI 2000/704, reg 3(5).

13.51 The Asylum Support Regulations 2000[1] contain no express time limits for making the decision on support, but we may infer that the process should be extremely speedy.[2] There is no requirement in the regulations that decisions must be in writing, but clearly it is intended that a written explanation will be provided of a decision refusing all support, with details of how to appeal.[3]

1   SI 2000/704.
2   See the very strict and short time limits for appealing refusal of asylum support at **13.111** below.
3   SI 2000/704, Sch, Notes 'What happens next ?'

Persons entitled to NASS support

13.52 In order to be entitled to NASS support a person must satisfy the general conditions of entitlement, ie, that a person is an asylum seeker or a dependant of an asylum seeker[1] and is destitute or likely to become so.

1   See **13.36**, **13.43** above.

Deciding whether a person is destitute under NASS

13.53 To determine whether an applicant for support and any dependants are 'destitute' or 'likely to become destitute', NASS must consider whether they have 'adequate accommodation' or any means of obtaining it, and whether or not they can meet their other 'essential living needs'.[1] In relation to both accommodation and essential living needs, NASS must take into account any of the following in relation to the applicant *or* his or her dependants:[2]

*   any income they have or which they may reasonably be expected to have;
*   any other support which is available or which may reasonably be expected to be available;[3] and
*   any of the following assets which might reasonably be expected to be available: cash, savings, investments, land, vehicles, goods for trade or business.

Assets which do not fall into these categories, NASS support or temporary support and items of jewellery, personal clothing, bedding and medical or optical items must be disregarded.[4] Applicants are, however, required to disclose items of jewellery or watches worth over £1,000 and to inform NASS immediately if they are sold and how much was received for them, so that the level of support may be adjusted accordingly.[5] NASS uses its own internal threshold tables, based loosely on what it would provide, a rule of thumb for the different categories of asylum seeker (below) to determine whether they are able to meet their essential living or accommodation requirements.[6] If support is applied for by more than one person, NASS will consider whether the group taken as a whole is destitute or likely to become so.[7] NASS applies the same approach when considering whether to continue to provide support for those already supported, and their dependants who are already being supported or are being added to the application for support.[8]

1 Immigration and Asylum Act 1999, s 95(1), (3).
2 Asylum Support Regulations 2000, SI 2000/704, reg 6(4), (5).
3 For example, the asylum support adjudicators have held that 'emergency money' provided by a relative and not returned may be taken into account (ASA 00/05/0011), as may money which the asylum seeker has had, if he or she cannot provide a reasonable explanation of its disposal (ASA 00/06/0017) (drawing on conventional social security law: Commissioner's Decision R(SB) 38/85); ASA 00/06/0020).
4 SI 2000/704, reg 6(3), (6), Sch, Notes to NASS1 'Cash savings and assets'.
5 SI 2000/704, Notes to NASS1 'Jewellery'.
6 NASS Policy Bulletin No. 4 where the threshold tables are set out.
7 Immigration and Asylum Act 1999, s 95(4), SI 2000/704, reg 5(1).
8 SI 2000/704, reg 5(2).

Determining whether a person can meet their 'essential living needs'

13.54 For the purposes of deciding whether a person can meet their essential living needs, certain items are treated as not essential. Inability to pay for sending or receiving faxes, photocopying, buying or using computer facilities and travelling expenses are not relevant to determining destitution[1] (although if a person is found to be destitute, these costs may be met by NASS either as expenses incurred in connection with the asylum claim or 'exceptional' circumstances). The regulations appear to exclude *any* travelling requirements which a person may have[2] except the costs of the initial journey to NASS accommodation, or to the applicant's notified address if he or she is not going to NASS accommodation.[3] The fact that any other need that a person may have is not expressly excluded does not automatically convert it into an 'essential living need', so that an inability to meet it must be taken into account by NASS in deciding destitution.[4] NASS will decide for itself whether any claimed need is essential for the person's living. In determining this question, the individual circumstances of the applicant for support are important.

1 Immigration and Asylum Act 1999, s 95(8), Asylum Support Regulations 2000, SI 2000/704, reg 9(3), (4).
2 SI 2000/704, reg 9(4)(d).
3 SI 2000/704, reg 9(4)(d), (5).
4 SI 2000/704, reg 9(6).

Clothing

13.55 In deciding whether a person can meet their essential living needs as regards clothing, NASS cannot take into account personal clothing preferences.[1] The rule is designed to prevent applications based on inability to buy clothing which is more expensive than that which is reasonably required, such as fashion items or designer wear. NASS must, however, take into account individual circumstances, including health or cultural needs and weather and hygiene requirements, in deciding whether a person can meet their clothing needs.[2]

1 Immigration and Asylum Act 1999, s 95(7)(b); Asylum Support Regulations 2000, SI 2000/704, reg 9(1)(2).
2 SI 2000/704, reg 9(2).

Determining whether a person has 'adequate' accommodation

13.56 If a person applies for support, including accommodation, but already has accommodation, NASS must decide whether the existing accommodation is 'adequate'. Similarly, if a person, who is already being supported by NASS without the provision of accommodation, requests it, NASS will need to decide whether the accommodation available to the applicant is adequate or whether NASS should be providing accommodation. In deciding either of these questions,[1] NASS must have regard to whether:[2]

- it is 'reasonable' for the person to continue to occupy the accommodation;
- the person can afford to pay for the accommodation;
- the accommodation is provided as temporary support under NASS or on any other emergency basis while the claim for asylum support is being determined;
- entry to the accommodation may be gained by the asylum seeker;
- if the accommodation is a houseboat, caravan or some other moveable structure which may be lived in, there is somewhere where the person is able to place it and live in it;
- the person may live in the accommodation together with his or her dependants;
- the asylum seeker or a dependant is likely to suffer domestic violence if he or she continues to live in the accommodation.

NASS may ignore any of the above matters, except the affordability of the accommodation and whether it is temporary NASS or other emergency accommodation, if the asylum seeker wishes to stay there.[3] There are also certain matters which *cannot* be taken into account in determining whether a person has adequate accommodation,[4] namely: the fact that the person does not have a legal right to stay in the accommodation; that it is shared or temporary; and its location.

1   The regulations apply to either situation: Asylum Support Regulations 2000, SI 2000/704, reg 8(1)(a), (b).
2   Immigration and Asylum Act 1999, s 95(5)(a); SI 2000/704, reg 8(1)(a), (b), (3).
3   SI 2000/704, reg 8(2).
4   Immigration and Asylum Act 1999, s 95(5), (6).

Reasonable to continue to occupy

13.57 In deciding whether it is reasonable for an asylum seeker to continue to occupy accommodation,[1] NASS may have regard to the general housing circumstances which exist in the district[2] of the local government housing authority in which the accommodation is situated.[3]

1   Asylum Support Regulations 2000, SI 2000/704, reg 8(3)(a).
2   By SI 2000/704, reg 8(6)(b), 'district' for these purposes is given the same meaning as in s 217(3) of the Housing Act 1996.
3   SI 2000/704, reg 8(4).

Affordability of the accommodation

13.58 In determining whether the asylum seeker can afford to pay for the accommodation,[1] NASS must take account of his or her assets and savings, the costs of the accommodation and other reasonable living expenses.[2]

1   Asylum Support Regulations 2000, SI 2000/704, reg 8(3)(b).
2   SI 2000/704, reg 8(5)(a), (b).

Domestic violence

13.59 NASS must decide whether it is 'probable' that continued occupation of the accommodation will lead to domestic violence against the asylum seeker or any dependant.[1] Domestic violence for these purposes must be from a close family member, and must be in the form of actual violence or threats of violence which are likely to be carried out.[2] There is no definition of close family member, but it is suggested that it may cover spouses or unmarried partners and ex-partners, those to whom the asylum seeker has a blood relationship, in-laws, relatives of the asylum seeker's partner and others who have lived or live in the household.[3]

1   Asylum Support Regulations 2000, SI 2000/704, reg 8(3)(g).
2   SI 2000/704, reg 8(6)(a).
3   See NASS Policy *Bulletin No 18* 'Dealing with Allegations of Racial Harassment, General Harassment and Domestic Violence'.

EXCLUSION FROM SUPPORT

13.60 The following categories of people are or can be excluded from NASS support:[1]

(1)   persons not excluded from obtaining social security benefits by their immigration status;
(2)   persons not treated by the Home Office as having claimed asylum or as the dependants of an asylum seeker;
(3)   persons eligible to obtain interim support;
(4)   persons in respect of whom there are reasonable grounds for suspecting that they have breached the conditions upon which support was given;
(5)   persons in respect of whom there are reasonable grounds for suspecting that they have committed a criminal offence connected to the provision of support;
(6)   persons in respect of whom there are reasonable grounds to suspect that they have intentionally made themselves and their dependants destitute;
(7)   persons who are absent from their address for certain periods of time without permission;
(8)   persons who have permanently stopped living at their address.

These categories are discussed in turn below, but some general comments can be made first and two specific points made in respect of the exclusions under categories (1) to (3). The first three categories are also excluded from temporary NASS support,[2] but the others are apparently not.[3] Categories (1) to (3) *must* be excluded from NASS support,[4] and since NASS has no power to provide support for people in these categories, support will be refused or brought to an end as soon as one of them applies. However, NASS has a discretion whether to exclude those in categories (4) to (8),[5] and may, in these cases, either 'suspend or discontinue' support or continue to provide it.[6] The existence of reasonable grounds for suspecting the asylum seeker to be guilty of the relevant conduct may trigger suspension of support, which could be lifted if the asylum seeker were able to allay the suspicions. Suspension or discontinuance of support does not, however, depend on reasonable grounds in categories (7) and (8), which must be established as facts.

1 Immigration and Asylum Act 1999, s 95(2); Asylum Support Regulations 2000, SI 2000/704, regs 4, 20.
2 SI 2000/704, reg 4(8), (9).
3 SI 2000/704, reg 20, dealing with the other exclusions, makes no reference to s 98 of the Immigration and Asylum Act 1999 (temporary support), in contrast with reg 4(8), (9).
4 By exclusion from the provisions of the Immigration and Asylum Act 1999 which give NASS the power to provide support: see Immigration and Asylum Act 1999, s 95(1), (2); Asylum Support (Interim Provisions) Regulations 1999, SI 1999/3056, reg 4(1).
5 SI 2000/704, reg 20(1); and see ASA 00/09/0066, para 9: the use of the word 'may' imports a discretion. See also ASA 00/11/0100.
6 SI 2000/704, reg 20(1).

13.61 By their nature and from the statutory language employed, exclusion under categories (5) to (8) appears to apply only to persons already supported by NASS.[1] It may be that asylum seekers cannot be refused support under these rules on the basis, for example, that they were intentionally destitute at the time they applied for support.[2] Support for this proposition lies in the notable absence of an equivalent exclusionary provision under NASS to deal with these circumstances as compared to the interim scheme.[3] However, there is discrete provision[4] for refusing a further application for support where support has previously been discontinued or suspended under any of these four categories. Where an application for support is made and the person applying, or any other person to whom the application relates, has previously had asylum support suspended or discontinued,[5] NASS may refuse to consider the application for support if, firstly,[6] there has been no material change in circumstances since the original decision to suspend or discontinue the support and, secondly, there are no exceptional circumstances which justify considering the new application. A change of circumstances as defined for these purposes is one which a claimant is required in any event to notify to NASS[7] during any period when support is being provided. If NASS decides to consider the new application for support, it may ultimately still refuse support if the general conditions are not satisfied.[8]

1 Asylum Support Regulations 2000, SI 2000/704, reg 20(1) refers to a 'supported person' (or dependants), defined as an 'asylum seeker' (or dependant) who has applied for support and for whom NASS support has been provided (s 94(1) of the Immigration and Asylum Act 1999); also, the reference to suspension or discontinuation of support presupposes current provision.
2 A person arguably cannot be said to be intentionally destitute on the basis of conduct which took place before the interim scheme came into effect: *Fetiti v London Borough of Islington* (C/OO/2748) 19 October 2000, CA, Laws LJ (permission). Similar reasoning can be applied to the NASS scheme.
3 See Asylum Support (Interim Provisions) Regulations 1999, SI 1999/3056, regs 7(3), 8(1). But Asylum Support Regulations 2000, SI 2000/704, reg 20(2) (period for becoming destitute for the purposes of intentional destitution) refers in general terms to reg 7, which suggests that the exclusion covers acts committed before and after the support is provided: see reg 7(a).
4 SI 2000/704, reg 21.
5 Ie under SI 2000/704, reg 20.
6 SI 2000/704, reg 21(1).
7 SI 2000/704, reg 21(1)(c), (2), with reference to reg 15.
8 SI 2000/704, reg 21(3).

13.62 For category (4) (breach of conditions), NASS may take into account breaches of conditions in deciding whether to provide support in the first instance or to continue to provide support.[1] Thus it is clear that in this category, previous breaches may be taken into account as relevant to the initial decision to provide support as well as to its continued provision.

1   Asylum Support Regulations 2000, SI 2000/704, reg 19.

Exclusions in group applications for support in categories 1–3

13.63 Persons applying for NASS support not for themselves alone but for others as well, or included in a joint application, are only excluded if every person who is included in that application is excluded from NASS support for any of the three reasons in categories (1) to (3).[1] On its face, the purpose of this provision appears to be to ensure that groups containing 'mixed' applicants are brought within NASS. However, households should in fact access all other available means of support before asylum support is made available,[2] and so asylum seekers whose spouses may claim social security benefit or interim support may apply for asylum support, but deductions will be made reflecting the amount of the benefit.[3] Accommodation will only be provided by NASS if what is otherwise available is inadequate (see **13.56** above).

1   Asylum Support Regulations 2000, SI 2000/704, reg 4(3), (4); in particular because reg 4(3)(c) refers to each person as falling within any of the categories in reg 4(4); this exclusion only applies to applications for support, not once support has been approved: ASA 00/06/0018.
2   See NASS Policy *Bulletin No 11*, 28 July 2000, 'Mixed Households', complete with examples and draft decision letters.
3   This is the approach which has been applied by the asylum support adjudicators: ASA 00/07/0039; 00/08/0033; 00/09/0054, ASA 01/02/0202, citing SI 2000/704, reg 6, which requires NASS to take into account any other support which is available to the principal or any dependant.

Exclusion where applicant is the dependant of a supported asylum seeker in categories 1–3

13.64 A person is not excluded under categories (1) to (3), whether applying for themselves alone or as part of a joint application, if, when the application is made, the person is the dependant of a person already receiving asylum support.[1]

1   Asylum Support Regulations 2000, SI 2000/704, reg 4(7). 'Dependant' for these purposes bears precisely the same meaning as dependant of asylum seeker: reg 2(4). See **13.43** above.

(1)   Persons not excluded from obtaining social security benefits by their immigration status

13.65 An asylum seeker is excluded from support if, as a sole applicant, he or she is not excluded from obtaining income-based jobseeker's allowance, income support, housing benefit or council tax benefit through his or her immigration status.[1] Those affected by this exclusion are asylum seekers who, for the purpose of these social security benefits, are exempted from the 'subject to immigration control' test. They are set out at **13.8ff** above. The regulations do not exclude from access to asylum support all the possible categories of asylum seekers who might be able to obtain these benefits.[2] For example, they do not exclude persons who, although they have applied for asylum, still have leave to enter or remain in the UK which is not subject to a condition of not having recourse to public funds nor as the result of an undertaking, nor leave automatically granted by the law while an appeal is pending.[3] Thus, a person who claims asylum while in the UK as a student may be eligible for social security benefits and NASS support. Nor do the regulations exclude EEA nationals (although asylum claims are virtually never made by such nationals). NASS might nevertheless refuse support to persons falling into these latter categories on the basis that they are not destitute, given that social security benefits are available to them. NASS may require proof from the Benefits Agency that benefit has been refused before providing support to asylum seekers who were previously entitled.[4]

1 Asylum Support Regulations 2000, SI 2000/704, reg 4(2), (4)(b), (6)(a); by reg 4(6)(b), this also includes income-based jobseeker's allowance or income support, housing benefit in Northern Ireland provided under the Jobseekers (Northern Ireland) Order 1995, SI 1995/2705 and the Social Security Contributions and Benefits (Northern Ireland) Act 1992.
2 These are persons who may be seeking asylum in the UK but are not excluded from benefit generally by s 115(9) of the Immigration and Asylum Act 1999.
3 See Immigration and Asylum Act 1999, Sch 4, para 17.
4 NASS Policy *Bulletin No 16* 4 August 2000.

(2) Persons not treated by the Home Office as having claimed asylum or as the dependants of an asylum seeker[1]

13.66 Those excluded from NASS support under this provision are sole applicants who are not treated by the Home Office as 'an asylum seeker or dependent on an asylum seeker' for immigration purposes.[2] Since the definition of 'asylum seeker' under the asylum support provisions is wide, no asylum seeker should be excluded from support under this provision. But it might prevent support being provided, potentially, to a large group of persons who are 'dependants' for support purposes[3] but not for immigration purposes. A spouse and minor children who accompany an asylum seeker to the UK, or who are mentioned by the asylum seeker in interview or written application, are always considered by the Home Office as dependants of the asylum claim.[4] A dependent child who reaches 18 before a decision is made on the asylum seeker's application will continue to be treated as a dependant pending the decision and during the appeals process.[5] However, other relatives and those who do not arrive with the principal applicant may be treated as dependants on the asylum claim at the discretion of the Home Office, provided there has been no decision on the asylum application.[6]

1 This exclusion relates to people who have not made a 'claim for leave to enter or remain in the UK or for variation of any such leave' in which they are being considered an asylum seeker or dependent on one. A claim for asylum or as the dependant of an asylum seeker is simultaneously a claim for leave to enter or remain in that capacity: see HC 395, paras 327–328, 330, 335, 349.
2 Asylum Support Regulations 2000, SI 2000/704, reg 4(2), (4)(c).
3 SI 2000/704, reg 2(4) and see **13.43** above.
4 HC 395, para 349; ADI Aug/00, Ch 6, s 1, para 2; in the latter case Home Office caseworkers will assume that they are applying for leave to enter or remain in the UK as dependants of the asylum seeker, although confirmation will later be sought from him or her.

5 ADI Aug/00, Ch 6, s 1, para 3.
6 ADI Aug/00, Ch 2, s 1, paras 1-3.

(3) Persons eligible to obtain interim support

13.67 A person applying for NASS support as a sole applicant will be excluded if he or she is eligible to obtain support under the interim scheme from a local authority.[1] For obvious reasons, this exclusion extends to persons whose application to a local authority has been rejected or whose support has been discontinued or suspended on grounds other than qualification for NASS support.[2]

1 Asylum Support Regulations 2000, SI 2000/704, reg 4(2), (4)(a), (5).
2 SI 2000/704, reg 4(5)(b), (c); Asylum Support (Interim Provisions) Regulations 1999, SI 1999/3056, regs 7, 8.

(4) Persons for whom there are 'reasonable grounds' for suspecting that they have breached the conditions upon which support was given without reasonable excuse

13.68 NASS may provide support subject to conditions.[1] Any conditions which are made must be set out in writing[2] and given to the person who is being supported.[3] Exclusion may follow if NASS reasonably suspects that an asylum seeker or any of his or her dependants has failed, without reasonable excuse, to comply with any condition subject to which the support is provided.[4] Although there has only to be a 'reasonable suspicion' of breach of conditions,[5] NASS cannot rely upon mere speculation, and there must be some evidence in support of the suspicion. For exclusion on these grounds, the conditions must have been set out in writing and given to the asylum seeker;[6] even if it were possible in principle to remove from support an asylum seeker not given the conditions in writing, there will almost certainly be a 'reasonable excuse' for failure to comply in these circumstances.

1 Immigration and Asylum Act 1999, s 95(9). No examples are given or limits set in the regulations, but it is suggested that conditions must be reasonable, eg that accommodation is not sublet or that noise is kept down to a reasonable level in the interests of neighbours. In ASA 00/09/0063 the adjudicator found that an allegation of a physical attack on a fellow asylum seeker at the premises gave NASS 'reasonable grounds to suspect' a breach of conditions before criminal proceedings were resolved.
2 Immigration and Asylum Act 1999, s 95(1).
3 Immigration and Asylum Act 1999, s 95(11); ASA 00/10/1174 at para 14 and ASA 00/10/0077.
4 SI 2000/704, reg 20(1)(a). See by analogy *R v Royal Borough of Kensington and Chelsea, ex p Kujtim* (1999) 32 HLR 579, where the Court of Appeal indicated that a 'persistent and unequivocal refusal to observe reasonable requirements' of a local authority would be needed before its duty under s 21 of the National Assistance Act 1948 was discharged. But an authority should not seek to apply the detailed and specific legislative provisions of the asylum support scheme to the support it provides under its community care duties: *R v London Borough of Lambeth, ex p Shazady and Maksoudian*, CO 532/2000, 1 March 2000 (permission).
5 Unlike the interim scheme, where the local authority must show that the asylum seeker has in fact breached a condition before exclusion operates: Asylum Support (Interim Provisions) Regulations 1999, SI 1999/3056, reg 8(2)(a).
6 Immigration and Asylum Act 1999, ss 95(1), (11) and see Asylum Support Regulations 2000, SI 2000/704, reg 19(1),(2) which refer to 'relevant conditions' subject to which asylum support has been provided.

13.69 A condition regularly imposed by NASS requires the asylum seeker to attend in order to travel to the accommodation provided as part of the support package, or to return to accommodation which has been left. There have been a considerable number of decisions of asylum support adjudicators on the circumstances which constitute a reasonable excuse for breach of this condition. Many have concerned previous racial harassment. Asylum support adjudicators have held the nature, degree, frequency, persistence and organisation of harassement and its effect on the asylum seeker all relevant,[1] and whether it has been reported to the police and if so, whether police action has been effective.[2] The 'sufficiency of protection' test of refugee status itself[3] has even been applied to deciding whether a refusal to return to the site of previous racist harassment was reasonable in the light of the police response.[4] These decisions suggest that there is such a thing as an acceptable level of racial harassment (or a level of harassment which asylum seekers must accept, which is the same thing). In our view, a 'sufficiency of protection' test has no place in this area of the law. Reasonable excuse may also derive from a combination of factors such as ill-health, single parenthood with young children, language difficulties and lack of proof that NASS had notified details of the travel arrangements.[5] Emotional trauma at the prospect of dispersal,[6] lack of awareness of the travel arrangements[7] or finding alternative accommodation[8] have been held good reasons for not travelling to accommodation provided by NASS.

1 ASA 00/08/0034; 00/08/0036; 00/09/0044. In ASA 00/09/0066 and 00/08/0036, verbal abuse and gesturing was held insufficient. Frequent racist taunts were held sufficient to constitute reasonable excuse in 00/07/0024.
2 ASA 00/09/0044.
3 See *Horvath v Secretary of State for the Home Department* [2000] Imm AR 552.
4 ASA 00/09/0044.
5 ASA 00/09/0046.
6 ASA 00/09/0057.
7 ASA 00/09/0058.
8 ASA 00/09/0067.

(5)   Persons for whom there are 'reasonable grounds' for suspecting that the person has committed a criminal offence connected to the provision of support[1]

13.70 An asylum seeker can be excluded from NASS support, if there are reasonable grounds to suspect that he or she or a dependant has committed a criminal offence under the Immigration and Asylum Act 1999, which is connected to the provision of support,[2] such as[3] making false representations or producing false documents or false information,[4] or failure to notify a relevant change of circumstances,[5] or obstructing a person administering support,[6] or refusal or failure to answer questions, give information or produce documents,[7] or refusal or failure to maintain a person in respect of whom an undertaking was given so that support is provided to that person.[8] It is not necessary that an asylum seeker or dependant has been convicted or even charged with an offence for this ground of exclusion to operate, as NASS needs only 'reasonable grounds' for suspecting that an offence has been committed.

1 Asylum Support Regulations 2000, SI 2000/704, reg 20(1)(b).
2 Arguably, offences committed in respect of interim support rather than NASS support do not disqualify someone from NASS support, since the provision refers to offences in relation to support under Part VI rather than under Sch 9. The interim regulations contain no equivalent exclusion from interim support. This is not, however, an attractive argument.

3   All the relevant offences are contained in Immigration and Asylum Act 1999, Pt VI.
4   Immigration and Asylum Act 1999, ss 105(1)(a), (b), 106(1)(a), (b).
5   Immigration and Asylum Act 1999, ss 105(1)(c), (d), 106(1)(c), (d).
6   Immigration and Asylum Act 1999, s 107(1)(a).
7   Immigration and Asylum Act 1999, s 107(1); SI 2000/704, reg 3(2), (3), (5), Sch, requiring applicants for support to provide the information contained in the prescribed form and authorising the making of further inquiries into any matter 'connected with the application'.
8   Immigration and Asylum Act 1999, s 108(1).

(6)   Persons for whom there are 'reasonable grounds' to suspect that they have 'intentionally' made themselves and their dependants destitute

13.71   Exclusion from support may follow if there is a 'reasonable suspicion' that an asylum seeker has 'intentionally' made himself or herself and any dependants destitute.[1] An asylum seeker is intentionally destitute for these purposes if the asylum seeker, *or any dependant*, while in the UK, deliberately and without reasonable excuse, commits some act or makes some omission which has that result within a period of eight weeks.[2] These constituent elements are discussed below. The following discussion applies equally to interim support but for the following notable differences. Under NASS, exclusion may result from a 'reasonable suspicion'[3] that a person is intentionally destitute, rather than definite proof; support may be 'suspended' rather than ended irrevocably; and, unlike under the interim scheme, exclusion is not automatic.[4] Further, since this provision (unlike that in the interim scheme) relates to the suspension and discontinuation of existing support rather than the initial refusal of support,[5] the period within which the asylum seeker must, if not already destitute, be likely to become so following the act or omission, is 56 days (as opposed to the 14 days prescribed under the interim scheme).[6]

1   Asylum Support Regulations 2000, SI 2000/704, reg 20(1)(c).
2   SI 2000/704, reg 20(2) read with reg 7, assuming that an asylum seeker may only be excluded from support under this head when actually in receipt of support, see para **13.61** above.
3   SI 2000/704, reg 20(1)(c).
4   Support 'may' be suspended or discontinued: SI 2000/704, reg 20(1).
5   See **13.126** below.
6   Asylum Support (Interim Provisions) Regulations 1999, SI 1999/3056, reg 7(1)(a).

13.72   The definition of intentional destitution is very similar to the definition of intentional homelessness in housing law, where a finding of intentionality reduces the housing duties owed by a local authority.[1] Intentional destitution will most often arise in relation to leaving accommodation, but a finding of intentionality affects the entirety of the support.[2] Case law on intentional homelessness will clearly be relevant, and we refer to the most important homelessness cases below. There are, however, three important distinctions between intentional destitution and intentional homelessness.[3] In the support scheme, intentional destitution expressly includes the conduct of dependants; the support scheme exempts those who have a 'reasonable excuse' for acts or omissions which cause destitution; and the support scheme considers only acts or omissions *in the UK* as potentially causing intentional destitution.

1   See Housing Act 1996, ss 190-191; a person is intentionally homeless if '... he deliberately does or fails to do anything in consequence of which he ceases to occupy accommodation which is available for his occupation and which it would have been reasonable for him to continue to occupy'. But 'an act or omission in good faith on the part of a person who was unaware of any relevant fact shall not be treated as deliberate'.

2   *R (Adam Wisniewski) v Wakefield Metropolitan District Council and Secretary of State for the Home Department* CO 3827/2000, 27 October 2000, QBD.
3   There are other less important distinctions in the language used in the two legislative definitions. For example, certain conduct is deemed automatically to constitute intentional homelessness in housing law by Housing Act 1996, s 191(3), (4).

Deliberate act or omission

13.73 To be excluded from support, the act or omission causing destitution must be a deliberate one. This does not mean that the person must be destitute deliberately[1] but simply that the act which resulted in destitution was deliberate. The housing cases are often concerned with loss of accommodation for reasons such as persistent failure to make mortgage or rent payments, provoking questions on whether the failure to make the payments was deliberate or whether in reality it was caused by lack of financial resources and the need to give priority to other essential living needs such as food and service bills.[2] The deliberate act or omission could also be the breach of other terms upon which previous accommodation was held or other conduct which provided grounds for eviction such as causing a nuisance to neighbours,[3] or a decision to move out of secure accommodation to accommodation which was less settled and which is subsequently lost,[4] or the failure to take legal action following unlawful eviction (this could not apply to accommodation the asylum seeker had no legal right to occupy). A refusal to accept an offer of accommodation in another area after transfer of the claim for support might also constitute a deliberate act, although there may be a reasonable excuse[5] for the refusal.[6] Destitution in terms of loss of essential living needs could be caused by loss of employment in circumstances where the asylum seeker was responsible, for example by conduct which inevitably led to dismissal and inability to obtain further employment. In housing law, intentional homelessness can come about through misconduct at work leading to the loss of tied accommodation.[7]

1   *R v Salford City Council, ex p Devenport* (1983) 8 HLR 54.
2   See *R v Wandsworth London Borough Council, ex p Hawthorne* (1994) 27 HLR 59, CA; *R v Hillingdon London Borough Council, ex p Tinn* (1988) 20 HLR 305, CA.
3   *Ex p Devenport*, above.
4   See *R v Brent London Borough Council, ex p Awua* [1996] AC 55.
5   See **13.78** below.
6   The Secretary of State's guidance, in a letter of NASS to Chief Executives 1 December 1999, para 10, indicates that support will not be forthcoming in these circumstances, without explaining why. An alternative basis of refusal might be lack of destitution (Immigration and Asylum Act 1999, s 95(3)) or that the refused support 'might reasonably be expected to be available' to the asylum seeker and so is taken into account in providing support (Asylum Support (Interim Provisions) Regulations 1999, SI 1999/3056, reg 6(1)(b); Asylum Support Regulations 2000, SI 2000/704, reg 6(4)(b)).
7   See *R v Thanet District Council, ex p Reeve* (1981) 6 HLR 31.

13.74 Unlike in the housing legislation, an act done or an omission made in 'good faith' on the part of someone who was unaware of any relevant fact is not excluded from intentional destitution.[1] But an honest and reasonable misunderstanding by a person leading him or her to act in a certain way which then causes the loss of accommodation or essential living needs, could not be said to be deliberate behaviour amounting to intentional destitution,[2] and even if it could, there would be a 'reasonable excuse' so that the asylum seeker could not be held intentionally destitute.

1 Cf Housing Act 1996, s 191(2).
2 See (in homelessness) *R v Hammersmith and Fulham London Borough Council, ex p Lusi* (1991) 23 HLR 260.

Act or omission must cause destitution or likely destitution

13.75 Before the act or omission can be said to give rise to intentional destitution, it must be shown that destitution actually resulted. A common situation in the housing cases occurs where the loss of the original accommodation was by deliberate conduct but, before needing assistance, some other accommodation is found but then lost through no fault. The courts have held that the original act causing the homelessness may, depending on the circumstances, still be said to be the cause of the later homelessness even though there was an intervening period when the person was not homeless.[1] The authority may therefore be entitled to look to see what is the real, underlying and continuing cause of any destitution rather than simply the most immediate cause.[2] But in housing cases, the 'chain of causation' between the act causing the initial homelessness and the later homelessness may be broken by other events. The easiest way for the chain to be broken is by the person finding 'settled' accommodation during the intervening period, for example a tenancy,[3] but other events can also break the chain of causation.[4] Remarkably, a person remains intentionally homeless because of earlier actions even if by the date of the application for housing that person would have lost their accommodation anyway due to other events.[5] It remains to be seen whether the same approach will be applied for support purposes.

1 *R v Brent London Borough Council, ex p Awua* [1996] AC 55.
2 *R v Hackney London Borough Council, ex p Ajayi* (1997) 30 HLR 473.
3 See *R v Rochester-upon-Medway City Council, ex p Williams* (1994) 26 HLR 588.
4 See *Ex p Awua* above; *R v Harrow London Borough Council, ex p Fahia* [1998] 1 WLR 1396, HL; *R v Basingstoke and Deane Borough Council, ex p Basset* (1983) 10 HLR 125; *R v Camden London Borough Council, ex p Aranda* (1997) 30 HLR 76, CA.
5 See *Din v Wandsworth London Borough Council* [1983] 1 AC 657

Acts or omissions of asylum seeker or dependants

13.76 Unlike in homelessness, a person may be intentionally destitute as a result of the act or omission of a dependant.[1] The conduct of those who are not the dependants of an asylum seeker may also be considered relevant. In the housing context, authorities have been held entitled to take into account the acts of nuisance of an applicant's lodgers which had led to the eviction of the applicant, where the applicant could be said to be responsible by not preventing the behaviour or failing to evict the offending lodgers.[2] But because the support regulations, unlike the housing legislation, expressly set out whose conduct is to be taken into account (the dependants), arguably the conduct of other persons should not be taken into account. Asylum seekers are unlikely in any event to have lodgers; if they do they are likely to be in breach of conditions of support.

1 Contrast the position in housing: *R v North Devon District Council, ex p Lewis* [1981] 1 WLR 328; *R v Nottingham City Council, ex p Caine* (1995) 28 HLR 374, CA. But the housing authority is entitled to consider whether the applicant had acquiesced in the conduct of the other family member so as to be party to that conduct and therefore also intentionally homeless: *Ex p Lewis*. See also *R v Tower Hamlets London Borough Council,*

ex p Khatun (1993) 27 HLR 344: if a wife leaves important decisions to her husband, for cultural or other reasons, she may be taken to have acquiesced.
2   See *Smith v Bristol City Council* [1981] LAG Bulletin 287, CA; *R v Cardiff City Council, ex p John* (1982) 9 HLR 56.

Act or omission in the UK

13.77   The act or omission of the asylum seeker or dependant must have taken place in the UK. In contrast to the position regarding intentional homelessness for housing purposes,[1] the act of leaving another country to come to the UK or anything else done abroad which resulted in loss of accommodation and other resources there, cannot be relevant in determining intentional destitution. If it were otherwise, NASS would be determining applicants' asylum claims.

1   See eg *De Falco, Silvestri v Crawley Borough Council* [1980] QB 460.

Reasonable excuse for the act or omission

13.78   A person will not be treated as intentionally destitute under the asylum support scheme if there is a reasonable excuse for their act or omission. No examples are given, but certainly, we suggest, a genuine misunderstanding on the part of the asylum seeker or their dependant as to the consequences of an action or of any material fact relevant to the conduct, should constitute a reasonable excuse.[1] Another example would be giving up accommodation which was in such a state of disrepair as to be damaging to health, since it would not be reasonable to expect the asylum seeker to continue living there.[2] In this case the asylum seeker can argue either that the act of leaving did not cause the destitution, which was constituted by the lack of 'adequate' accommodation[3] *or* that he or she had a reasonable excuse for leaving the accommodation. In either event, the asylum seeker is not intentionally destitute. Similarly, an asylum seeker who leaves a job because of intolerable working conditions, so losing all his or her income, can rely on the 'reasonable excuse' exception to intentional destitution. A real risk of violence may constitute a reasonable excuse.[4]

1   In homelessness law, this is deemed incapable of amounting to intentional homelessness (Housing Act 1996, s 191(2)).
2   Again this is dealt with expressly in homelessness law, and cannot give rise to intentional homelessness (Housing Act 1996, s 191(1)).
3   See definition of destitution, Immigration and Asylum Act 1999, s 95(3), and **13.56** above.
4   *R (Adam Wisniewski) v Wakefield Metropolitan District Council and Secretary of State for the Home Department* CO 3827/2000, 27 October 2000, QBD.

(7)   Absence from authorised address for specified period without permission

13.79   Absence from the 'authorised address' can give rise to suspension or discontinuance of support.[1] The authorised address for these purposes is either the accommodation NASS is providing[2] or, where it is not providing accommodation, the address notified to the Home Office or a change of address given to the Home Office or NASS since the person has been provided with support.[3] It is not necessary for the Home Office to have granted temporary admission on the basis that the asylum seeker will live at the notified address, although a notice of temporary admission with the address on it will constitute the clearest evidence of the address notified to the Home Office by the asylum seeker. A person can only be excluded from support on this basis if he or she has been absent from the address for more than seven consecutive days and nights[4] or a total of more than 14 days and nights in any six-month period,[5] in either case without the permission of the Secretary of State.[6]

1 Asylum Support Regulations 2000, SI 2000/704, reg 20(1)(e).
2 SI 2000/704, reg 20(3)(a).
3 SI 2000/704, reg 20(3)(b) with reference to reg 15(2)(n).
4 SI 2000/704, reg 20(1)(e)(i).
5 SI 2000/704, reg 20(1)(e)(ii).
6 SI 2000/704, reg 20(1)(e).

(8) Persons who have stopped residing at their address

13.80 Support may be suspended or discontinued if the asylum seeker or any dependant stops 'residing' at the authorised address.[1] 'Authorised address' has the same meaning as above. There is no definition of 'reside' for these purposes. If the case law on ordinary residence is adopted, a person could remain resident in the authorised accommodation although also 'residing' elsewhere.[2] A likely approach would be one similar to that adopted to determine whether a person is 'normally occupying' a property as their home for housing benefit purposes[3] under which the following factors are significant: the amount of time the claimant spends at the property as opposed to anywhere else, the reason for absences from the property, where personal belongings are kept, where the claimant regards as his/her 'home', the claimant's other connections with the area, for example where he or she is registered with a doctor or dentist. This exclusion is simultaneously broader and narrower than the previous one. A person may be absent from the home for particular reasons for the relevant periods yet not cease to reside there; on the other hand, a person could cease to reside at a certain place, having made a complete move away, before the expiry of the specified periods above.

1 Asylum Support Regulations 2000, SI 2000/704, reg 20(1)(d).
2 See eg *IRC v Lysaght* [1928] AC 234 HL and see above chapter 5.
3 Housing Benefit (General) Regulations 1987, SI 1987/1971, reg 5.

PROVISION OF SUPPORT

Temporary NASS support

13.81 NASS may provide support or arrange for temporary support to be provided to an asylum seeker or the dependant of an asylum seeker who it appears may be destitute.[1] Various voluntary agencies funded by NASS to provide this support employ 'reception assistants' who are responsible for placing asylum seekers in temporary accommodation. Temporary support is an emergency form of support which is to be provided on an application for support being made, until NASS decides whether to provide support.[2] If NASS refuses support, temporary support ends immediately. As with full NASS support, temporary support may be provided subject to conditions but those conditions must be given in writing to the person or persons being provided with temporary support.[3] There are no rules governing what can and cannot be provided by way of temporary support,[4] but a similar approach to that for full NASS support ought to be adopted.

1 Immigration and Asylum Act 1999, s 98(1). The same definition of destitution applies as with full NASS support.
2 Immigration and Asylum Act 1999, s 98(2).
3 Immigration and Asylum Act 1999, s 98(3), applying s 95(11).
4 The Immigration and Asylum Act 1999, ss 96-97 and the Asylum Support Regulations 2000, SI 2000/704, deal with support provided under the full NASS scheme (Immigration and Asylum Act 1999, s 95) rather than support provided as a temporary measure (Immigration and Asylum Act 1999, s 98).

Support provided under NASS

13.82 NASS may provide the following kinds of support to eligible asylum seekers and their dependants:[1]

- essential living needs; and/or
- accommodation which is adequate; and/or
- expenses, other than legal expenses, in connection with the asylum claim; and/or
- expenses in attending bail hearings where the asylum seeker or their dependants are detained for immigration purposes;
- services in the form of education, English language lessons, sporting or other developmental activities;[2]
- *if the circumstances of the particular case are exceptional*, any other form of support which NASS thinks necessary to enable the asylum seeker and their dependants to be supported.[3]

In providing for either essential living needs or for accommodation or other forms of support, NASS must provide the majority of the support otherwise than by cash payments.[4] The Secretary of State may change this rule by order[5] and, in the first year of the scheme there has been significant lobbying to return to a cash-based system, leading to a review of the voucher system.[6] The rule does not, however, apply where the circumstances of a particular case are 'exceptional'.[7] In addition, NASS may meet all the 'expenses' and 'services' referred to above by making cash payments, which do not count for the purposes of calculating the manner in which support is provided to meet the other needs.[8]

1 Immigration and Asylum Act 1999, s 96(1).
2 Immigration and Asylum Act 1999, Sch 8, para 4; Asylum Support Regulations 2000, SI 2000/704, reg 14.
3 Immigration and Asylum Act 1999, s 96(2).
4 Immigration and Asylum Act 1999, s 96(3).
5 Immigration and Asylum Act 1999, s 96(4).
6 See **13.27** above.
7 Immigration and Asylum Act 1999, s 96(3); it is unclear why the cashless 'majority' rule is applied to the other forms of support referred to in s 96(2) since, by definition, such support may only be accessed where the circumstances of a particular case are 'exceptional', which leads to the disapplication of the rule under s 96(3).
8 Immigration and Asylum Act 1999, s 96(1)(c)-(d), (3).

13.83 NASS may disregard any preference which an asylum seeker or dependant may have as to the way support is given.[1] In deciding on the level and kind of support to provide to an applicant and his or her dependants or to anyone already being provided with support, NASS must take into account income, support which may be reasonably expected to be available and any assets such as cash or savings.[2] It may take into account previous breach of any conditions on which the support has been or is being provided,[3] but must have regard to the seriousness or triviality of the breach in deciding whether to alter the level of support and by how much.[4]

1 Immigration and Asylum Act 1999, s 97(7).
2 Asylum Support Regulations 2000, SI 2000/704, reg 12(3).
3 SI 2000/704, reg 19(1).
4 SI 2000/704, reg 19(1) allows the Secretary of State to take into account the extent to which conditions have been complied with.

Providing essential living needs

13.84 Where NASS decides that a person needs support in relation to essential living needs, the general rule is that he or she will be provided with vouchers some of which may be exchanged for goods and services, and others which may be exchanged for cash.[1] The vouchers are provided on a weekly basis[2] and the value of those redeemable for cash is not expected to exceed £10.00 per person per week.[3] Additionally, after every period of six months, an asylum seeker will be likely to be provided with an additional 'single payment' voucher which may be exchanged for cash to the value of £50.00.[4] The single payments provision is in case of delay beyond Home Office targets in determining the asylum application, including any appeal. But if in NASS's view, the delay is the fault of the asylum seeker, who has no reasonable excuse for it, the qualifying period for the additional payment may be extended commensurately.[5] A single, one-off 'maternity' payment of £300.00 may be provided to asylum seekers to assist with the costs of a newborn baby.[6] A written application must be lodged by the father or mother close to the date of the birth, and the child must, generally, have been born to a NASS-supported person.[7] If vouchers are lost or stolen, emergency backdated vouchers may be issued from the date NASS receives written confirmation of a police report with relevant particulars.[8] Vouchers which have not arrived as a result of official error may be backdated to the full extent of the loss. In all circumstances, however, backdated payments are made in the form of non-cash redeemable emergency vouchers only.[9]

1 Asylum Support Regulations 2000, SI 2000/704, reg 10(2).
2 SI 2000/704.
3 SI 2000/704, reg 10(6).
4 SI 2000/704, reg 11.
5 SI 2000/704, reg 11(6).
6 NASS Policy *Bulletin 37* (13 November 2000) 'Maternity Payments'.
7 The provisions of the instruction are detailed and should be obtained by those advising asylum seekers in this position.
8 The crime reference number, the name of the officer who recorded the theft and the name of the police station to which it was reported.
9 NASS Policy *Bulletin 5*.

Amounts provided

13.85 Regulation 10 of the Asylum Support Regulations sets out the total weekly value of the vouchers that an asylum seeker and any dependants will be provided with.[1] For the purposes of payment, to count as a married couple, the couple must be a man and a woman who are married to each other and who are members of the same household;[2] to count as an unmarried couple, the couple must be a man and a woman who, although not married, are living together as though they are married;[3] a 'lone parent' is a person who is not a part of a married or unmarried couple who is the parent of a child under 18 and support is being provided for the child;[4] a 'single person' is a person who is neither a member of a married or unmarried couple nor the parent of a child under 18 for whom support is being provided.[5] The amounts payable will be reduced where NASS provides accommodation as part of the support which includes some provision for essential living needs, such as bed and breakfast or full board.[6]

1 The rates as at May 2001 are as follows (Asylum Support Regulations 2000, SI 2000/704, reg 10(2) as amended by Asylum Support (Amendment) Regs 2000, SI 2000/3053, regs 1-2): Married or unmarried couple at least one of whom is 18 or over but where neither is under 16: £57.37.
Lone parent aged 18 or over, or single person aged 25 or over: £36.54;
Single person aged 18–24: £28.95;
Person aged 16–17 (except a member of a married or unmarried couple as referred to above): £31.75;
Person aged under 16: £30.95.
2 Asylum Support Regulations 2000, SI 2000/704, reg 2(1).
3 SI 2000/704, reg 2(1).
4 SI 2000/704, reg 10(4)(b), (d).
5 SI 2000/704, reg 10(4)(c).
6 SI 2000/704, reg 10(5).

13.86 The amounts payable are less than the 'applicable amounts' of income support which similarly situated persons would be entitled to if they qualified, reflecting approximately 70 per cent of the applicable amounts of income support.[1] This is partly in recognition of the fact that the support is to be temporary[2] and does not need to include the cost of service bills, replacement items of clothing and household items which are usually provided.[3] The rules on provision for essential living needs are, however, all rules of thumb[4] which set out what an asylum seeker can generally expect to receive. In appropriate cases, NASS may provide more, or less, or make provision in a different form.

1 Applicable amounts for income support are provided pursuant to the Social Security Contributions and Benefits Act 1992, s 124(4).
2 Immigration and Asylum Act 1999, s 97(5).
3 See para 305 of Explanatory Notes to the Immigration and Asylum Act 1999.
4 See Asylum Support Regulations 2000, SI 2000/704, regs 10(2), (6), 11(1).

Providing accommodation

13.87 The system of 'dispersal' is one of the most controversial new departures of the Immigration and Asylum Act 1999.[1] In deciding upon the location and nature of the accommodation which a person will be given, NASS must have regard to the fact that support by way of accommodation is only being provided on a temporary basis until the claim to asylum (including any appeal) has been dealt with, and that it is desirable to provide accommodation for asylum seekers in those areas where there is a good supply of accommodation.[2] But NASS may not have regard to any preferences of the asylum seeker as to the area in which he or she wishes the accommodation to be located, the nature of the accommodation to be provided;[3] or the nature and standard of the fixtures and fittings in the accommodation.[4] It may, however, take into account the asylum seeker's and his or her dependants' individual circumstances as they relate to their accommodation needs.[5] The court has been fairly generous in its approach, holding in *ex p Mahida* that location close to a mosque was not merely a matter of preference, but was relevant to the applicant's religious and emotional needs and so to his or her welfare, in assessing adequacy of the accommodation.[6]

1   See above **13.26-13.27**. For dispersal under the interim scheme see **13.145-13.149** below.
2   Immigration and Asylum Act 1999, s 97(1)(a) with reference to ss 94(3), (4), 97(1)(b).
3   Asylum Support Regulations 2000, SI 2000/704, reg 13(2)(a).
4   SI 2000/704, reg 13(2)(b).
5   SI 2000/704, reg 13(2), and see ASA 00/11/0110 at para 9, enabling consideration of the asylum seeker's family-related concerns.
6   *R v London Borough of Islington, ex p Fatah Mahida* CO 2519/2000, 14 August 2000, QBD, on the similar provisions under interim support provisions (Asylum Support (Interim Provisions) Regulations 1999, SI 1999/3056, reg 6(2)).

13.88 Applying the above statutory criteria, NASS general policy is to seek to disperse asylum seekers away from London and the south-east.[1] In allocating accommodation to someone who seeks to remain in that area, NASS will consider whether it is reasonable to disperse, whether such an allocation will meet the person's needs and whether the decision is compatible with the Human Rights Act 1998. In determining what is reasonable in a particular case, consideration should be given to medical treatment, special needs, family ties, education, ethnic group, religion, employment, legal advice and language.

1   NASS Policy *Bulletin 31* (12 October 2000) paras 2.1-2.2, referring to s 97 of the Immigration and Asylum Act 1999, which requires NASS to have regard, in general, to the desirability of providing accommodation in areas in which there is a ready supply. Current policy, however, is that where an asylum seeker applies for asylum in a 'dispersal area' and asks to be accommodated in that area, the request will normally be met, subject to the availability of accommodation: *Bulletin 31* at para 2.3.

13.89 Family ties are clearly a key factor in the light of Article 8 of the ECHR. Although the instruction recognises the need to consider each case on its merits, NASS is of the view that 'in the absence of exceptional circumstances' relating to this factor, dispersal will normally be appropriate.[1] So far as education is concerned, where an asylum seeker has children of school age and has been resident in an area for twelve months or more, dispersal will generally not be appropriate.[2] The existence of an ethnic community in the preferred area is normally insufficient to militate against dispersal, as NASS accommodation is all supposed to be in areas which boast an established ethnic minority community and are 'able to sustain a new ethnic group and voluntary and community infrastructures'.[3] If there is only one area where an asylum seeker can properly worship, then his or her request may be accommodated having regard to Article 9 ECHR (freedom of thought, conscience and religion).[4] In the case of new port and in-country applicants, where a referral[5] is made to the Medical Foundation for the Care of the Victims of Torture, NASS must give careful consideration to deferring dispersal from the south-east, and where, after initial assessment, the Medical Foundation accepts the applicant for treatment, NASS must give sympathetic consideration to providing local accommodation. The same applies to those already receiving treatment.[6]

1   NASS Policy *Bulletin 31* (12 October 2000), para 4.
2   NASS Policy *Bulletin 31* (12 October 2000), para 5.3.
3   NASS Policy *Bulletin 31* (12 October 2000), para 6.1.
4   NASS Policy *Bulletin 31* (12 October 2000), at para 7.2.
5   Normally the referral should be made by the reception assistant using the standard form at Annex A to NASS Policy *Bulletin 19* (August 2000), 'The Medical Foundation For the Care of Victims of Torture'.
6   NASS Policy *Bulletin 19* (August 2000).

13.90 If, applying the above factors, a decision is made to disperse an asylum seeker, he or she will be likely to be provided with a document providing details, and stating that the support is provided on condition that the asylum seeker travels there in accordance with the enclosed travel instructions. A warning letter advises the person that travel will only be rearranged where there are exceptional reasons for not travelling at the appointed time. Failure to travel to the accommodation without good reason is likely to result in the termination of support and the refusal of any further application on the basis that support has previously been discontinued.[1] It is not known how many people have been excluded from support for failure to arrive, under this astonishingly draconian provision.

1   Asylum Support Regulations 2000, SI 2000/704, regs 19-21, and see NASS Policy *Bulletin 17* (4 August 2000), a casework instruction on 'failure to travel' and NASS Policy *Bulletin 28* (26 September 2000) 'Travel'.

Racial harassment and domestic violence

13.91 NASS has developed internal guidelines on the subject of racial harassment and domestic violence which detail the investigations needed to determine whether a person who has left the accommodation provided should be offered alternative accommodation.[1] The central factor is whether there is a significant risk of violence and the extent of the individual's vulnerability. Where a person leaves dispersed accommodation and presents to reception assistants in the south-east once more, NASS will only approve funding for further temporary accommodation 'where there is good *prima facie* evidence either that someone has been the victim of serious assault or has good reason to believe they would be a victim if they remained in the area'.[2]

1   NASS Policy *Bulletin 18* (16 August 2000) 'Dealing with Allegations of Racial Harassment, General Harassment and Domestic Violence'. But see **13.69** above on the approach of asylum support adjudicators to racial harassment as a 'reasonable excuse' for breach of conditions requiring an asylum seeker to attend for dispersal.
2   NASS Policy *Bulletin 18* (16 August 2000).

Expenses in connection with asylum claim

13.92 NASS may meet expenses connected with the asylum claim,[1] excluding 'legal' expenses such as the costs of paying a lawyer for preparation or for representation. Included are travel expenses of the asylum seeker (or those of witnesses) in attending the appeal or interviews or examinations in connection with the claim.[2] Expenses in preparing and copying documents,[3] sending letters and faxes in order to obtain further evidence are also included. Travel expenses for a Medical Foundation assessment in connection with the asylum application or where referred by a GP should generally be met.[4]

1   Immigration and Asylum Act 1999, s 96(1)(c).
2   These are expressly included in the interim scheme (Asylum Support (Interim Provisions) Regulations 1999, SI 1999/3056, reg 5(3)), and it would be anomalous if they were to be left out for the purposes of NASS.
3   See Explanatory Notes to the Immigration and Asylum Act 1999, at para 300.
4   See NASS Policy *Bulletin 19* (August 2000), 'The Medical Foundation For the Care of Victims of Torture' and NASS Policy *Bulletin 28* (26 September 2000) 'Travel' for the procedures for obtaining payment.

Other services

13.93 NASS may provide education services (including English language classes) and sporting or other developmental activities to any person who is receiving NASS support.[1] These services are not provided automatically, but may only be provided in order to 'maintain good order' among supported asylum seekers.[2] This does not require that good order has broken down before these services are provided, but that without the stimulation of sport, education and developmental activities, and the access to and integration with the wider community these activities entail, morale and thus 'good order' could be jeopardised.

1   Immigration and Asylum Act 1999, Sch 8, para 4, Asylum Support Regulations 2000, SI 2000/704, reg 14.
2   SI 2000/704, reg 14(1).

Contributions to support

13.94 In deciding what level of support to provide to a destitute asylum seeker, NASS must take into account the income, support and assets which are available or might reasonably be expected to be available to him or her.[1] As an alternative to reducing the level of support, NASS may require that the asylum seeker makes a contribution from their own income or assets to the support being provided.[2] In these circumstances, the asylum seeker will be required to make payments directly to NASS.[3] Where support is provided with a requirement of a contribution by the asylum seeker, NASS may make it a condition of the provision of support that 'prompt payments' are made.[4]

1   Asylum Support Regulations 2000, SI 2000/704, reg 12(3).
2   SI 2000/704, reg 16(2).
3   SI 2000/704, reg 16(3).
4   SI 2000/704, reg 16(4).

National Health Service prescriptions/dental treatment/sight tests

13.95 When an application for asylum support is accepted, NASS will simultaneously issue the individual with an HC2 certificate entitling the holder to free NHS prescriptions, dental treatment, sight tests and wigs.[1] The asylum seeker may also be eligible for vouchers towards the costs of glasses, contact lenses and refunds on the costs of travel to and from hospital for NHS treatment.[2]

1   See NASS Policy *Bulletin 43* (30 November 2000), 'HC2 Certificates'.
2   See below, para **13.181**.

Conditions

13.96 NASS may provide support subject to conditions.[1] Any conditions must be set out in writing[2] and given to the person who is being supported.[3] Breach of conditions upon which support is provided may be taken into account in deciding whether to provide or continue support and the level or kind of support provided.[4]

1   Immigration and Asylum Act 1999, s 95(9), see para **13.68** above.
2   Immigration and Asylum Act 1999, s 95(1).
3   Immigration and Asylum Act 1999, s 95(11).
4   Asylum Support Regulations 2000, SI 2000/704, reg 19.

Changes of circumstances

13.97 Supported persons are required to notify NASS of relevant changes in their circumstances.[1] NASS must be notified if the asylum seeker or any dependant:[2]

- is joined in the UK by a dependant;
- receives or obtains access to any money or savings, investments, land, cars or other vehicles, or goods for the purposes of trade or other business which have not previously been declared to NASS;
- becomes unemployed;
- changes his or her name;
- gets married;
- begins living with another person as if married to that person;
- gets divorced;
- separates from a spouse or from a person with whom they have been living as if married;
- becomes pregnant;
- has a child;
- leaves school;
- begins to share accommodation with another person;
- moves to a different address or otherwise leaves accommodation;
- goes into hospital;
- goes to prison or some other form of custody;
- leaves the UK; or
- dies.

Where, as a result of notification of a change in circumstances, NASS believes that asylum support should be provided for a person for whom it is not currently provided (for example a new dependant arriving or the birth of a child) or should not be provided for an existing recipient, or that asylum support is otherwise affected, it may make further inquiries to determine what support should now be provided.[3] It may change the nature or level of the existing support or provide or withdraw support.

1   Asylum Support Regulations 2000, SI 2000/704, reg 15(1).
2   SI 2000/704, reg 15(2).
3   SI 2000/704, reg 15(3), (4).

Further applications for support

13.98 In most circumstances, there is nothing to prevent repeat claims for support and NASS must consider the application unless it is not made in the prescribed form,[1] or the person has previously had his or her support suspended or discontinued,[2] or a further application for support is made after an appeal to the Asylum Support Adjudicator is dismissed,[3] and there has been no 'material change in circumstances'.[4]

1 Asylum Support Regulations 2000, SI 2000/704, reg 3(3), (4).
2 SI 2000/704, reg 21.
3 Immigration and Asylum Act 1999, s 103(6).
4 SI 2000/704, reg 21; Immigration and Asylum Act 1999, s 103(6).

PREVENTING ABUSE

13.99 There are various safeguards to prevent abuse of the NASS scheme. First, there are the grounds on which people, although destitute, may be excluded from obtaining asylum support by their own conduct.[1] Secondly, criminal charges may be brought against persons who, in relation to asylum support, make false representations/produce false documents or information,[2] fail to notify a required change of circumstances,[3] delay or obstruct a person administering the support scheme,[4] fail to provide required information,[5] or fail, as a sponsor, to maintain a sponsored person who is then provided with asylum support.[6] Thirdly, there are ways to recover asylum support to which asylum seekers were not entitled.[7]

1 See **13.68**ff above.
2 Immigration and Asylum Act 1999, ss 105(1)(a), (b), 106(1)(a), (b).
3 Immigration and Asylum Act 1999, ss 105(1)(c), (d), 106(1)(c), (d).
4 Immigration and Asylum Act 1999, s 107(1)(a).
5 Immigration and Asylum Act 1999, s 107(1).
6 Immigration and Asylum Act 1999, s 108(1).
7 See para **13.102** below.

13.100 To detect and act on abuses of the system, NASS has a number of further powers. It may obtain a warrant from a justice of the peace (or, in Scotland, a sheriff) to enter premises provided as temporary or ordinary NASS support where there is reason to believe that the person/s who are supposed to be supported there are not in fact resident there or the accommodation is being used for other purposes, or other persons are residing there.[1] Reasonable force may be used to enter the accommodation with a warrant.[2] NASS may also require the owner or manager of property provided by way of ordinary NASS support[3] to provide information about the premises and those living there.[4] The power might be used to require landlords to notify the Secretary of State when an asylum seeker has left or is subletting property.[5] NASS may further require the Royal Mail or others delivering post, to provide information about redirection requests.[6] With the exception of the power to obtain information about the re-direction of mail, it is doubtful whether these powers apply to support under the interim scheme, and there is an argument that the criminal charges do not apply either,[7] although there may be other measures available in respect of interim support. The grounds on which persons may be excluded from interim support are described below, **13.125**ff.

1 Immigration and Asylum Act 1999, s 125.
2 Immigration and Asylum Act 1999, s 125(3)(b).
3 This power does not extend to temporary NASS support because it relates only to accommodation which has been provided for 'supported persons' (Immigration and Asylum Act 1999, s 126(1)), defined in s 94(1) of the 1999 Act as asylum seekers or their dependants in receipt of support under s 95.
4 Immigration and Asylum Act 1999, s 126.
5 Explanatory Notes to the IAA 1999, para 126.
6 Immigration and Asylum Act 1999, s 127.
7 The criminal offences in ss 105-109 relate to support provided 'under Part VI' of the Immigration and Asylum Act 1999. Interim support is provided under Sch 9. Albeit certain of the key provisions of Part VI are applied to that support, it is not support which is provided 'under' Part VI. Similarly, the provisions relating to recovery, ss 112–114 Immigration and Asylum Act 1999, Sch 8, para 11(1) read with Asylum Support Regulations 2000, SI 2000/704, reg 17, refer to recovery of support under either or both s 95 and s 98 of the 1999 Act but not to interim support under Sch 9. Entry of premises (s 125) is only permitted in relation to support provided under s 95 or s 98, information from property owners may only be obtained in respect of persons who have been provided with ordinary NASS support (s 126(1) refers to 'supported persons' who are defined in s 94(1) as persons provided with support under s 95) but information about redirection relates to support under Part VI or for 'for any other purpose relating to the provision of support to asylum seekers' (see s 127(1)(c)), which may allow that power to be used in relation to interim support as well.

Eviction from accommodation

13.101 One of the government's aims was to ensure that the asylum support scheme is untrammelled by the procedural safeguards operating in the general law. So when the time comes for asylum support to be terminated, the legislation makes provision for tenancies or licences provided by way of asylum support to come to an end before they would have done in line with the general law. Thus, where asylum support is terminated for any reason, any tenancy or licence granted during the period of support is brought to an end at the end of the period specified in the 'notice to quit',[1] 'regardless of when it could otherwise be brought to an end'.[2] Notices to quit must be given in writing.[3]

1 Seven days or less in the case of any termination of support other than due to the determination of the claim to asylum (Asylum Support Regulations 2000, SI 2000/704, reg 22(3)(a)); or where the termination of the support is due to the determination of the asylum claim, fourteen days after the determination by the Secretary of State or fourteen days after the time limit for further appeal expires (reg 22(3)(b)(i), (ii) read with Immigration and Asylum Act 1999, s 94(3), (4) and Sch 14, para 55 and SI 2000/704, regs 2(2), (3) and Asylum Support (Interim Provisions) Regulations 1999, SI 1999/3056, reg 2(6); or, in any case, less than seven days, when the 'circumstances of the case are such that that notice period is justified' (SI 2000/704, reg 22(4)).
2 SI 2000/704, reg 22(1).
3 SI 2000/704, reg 22(3), (4)(a).

Recovery of support

13.102 There are four circumstances in which support which has been provided may be recovered:

(1)   where a supported person is later able to realise assets held at the time of the support application;[1]

(2)   where a person was overpaid support as a result of an error;[2]

(3)   where a person obtained support as the result of a misrepresentation or
failure to disclose a material fact;[3]

(4)   recovery from a person who sponsored the stay in the UK of a person
who subsequently resorted to asylum support.[4]

These circumstances are considered in more detail below, but the following
general comments can be made. In the first two cases, the recovery is, at least
initially, made directly by NASS, whereas in the last two cases NASS makes an
application to the court (in the third case, to the county court and in the last, to
the magistrates, or in Scotland, to the sheriff in either case).

1   Asylum Support Regulations 2000, SI 2000/704, reg 17.
2   Immigration and Asylum Act 1999, s 114.
3   Immigration and Asylum Act 1999, s 112.
4   Immigration and Asylum Act 1999, s 113.

13.103 Overpayments made as a result of an error, misrepresentation or failure
to disclose may be recovered under ordinary and temporary NASS support,[1]
while recovery from realised assets or from a sponsor is available only under
ordinary NASS support.[2] Where assets becoming realisable or where overpayment
has been made in error, recovery may take the form of deductions from NASS
support[3] or the sums may be recovered as a 'debt' due to NASS in ordinary
court proceedings.[4] Where overpayment resulted from a misrepresentation or a
failure to disclose or from a sponsor's default, recovery starts and ends with the
courts.[5] NASS appears to have a discretion as to whether to pursue recovery of
an overpayment in all cases.[6]

1   Immigration and Asylum Act 1999, ss 112(1)(b), 114(1).
2   The former is referred to only in Asylum Support Regulations 2000, SI 2000/704, reg 17(3)(a),
which does not refer to temporary support, and the enabling provisions refer solely to s 95:
Sch 8, para 11(1); in the latter case, s 113(1)(b) refers only to s 95 (asylum support); cfs
s 112(1)(b) and 114(1), which refer to both s 95 and s 98 (temporary asylum support).
3   The deductions themselves may only be made from NASS support: Immigration and
Asylum Act 1999, s 114(4), Sch 8, para 11(2)(b), SI 2000/704, regs 17(4) and 18.
4   Immigration and Asylum Act 1999, s 114(2), Sch 8, para 11(2)(a), (b); SI 2000/704,
regs 17(4), 18.
5   Immigration and Asylum Act 1999, ss 112-113.
6   The discretion is explicit in Immigration and Asylum Act 1999, ss 113(2), 114(2) and
SI 2000/704, reg 17(2), but must be inferred in respect of misrepresentation and failure to
disclose in s 112.

Convertible assets

13.104 NASS may require the repayment of the value of any asylum support
which has been provided if, at the time when the supported person applied for
support, he or she had assets (in the UK or elsewhere) such as savings, investments,
property or shares, which could not then be converted into money, but have
become realisable since (even if they have not in fact been converted).[1] NASS
may require repayment up to the total money value of the assets concerned or
the total money value of all the support provided (whichever is less).[2]

1   Immigration and Asylum Act 1999, Sch 8, para 11, Asylum Support Regulations 2000,
SI 2000/704, reg 17(1). NASS has a discretion to recover less than the recoverable amount,
see SI 2000/704, reg 17(2): ' ... a sum not exceeding'. It is unclear whether NASS can
require a person who is no longer being supported to repay the value of the support, since

these provisions contain no wording equivalent to s 114(2) (recovery of overpayments made in error from a person who is or has been a supported person).
2   SI 2000/704, reg 17(2), (3), (5).

Recovery of overpayments of support as a result of error

13.105 NASS may require the repayment of any temporary support or asylum support which has been provided as a result of its own error,[1] up to the total money value of the overpayment.[2] For recovery of these overpayments (in contrast to the position with most social security benefits), there is no need for the supported person to be responsible for the overpayment or at fault in any way. The overpayment may be recovered even after support ends.[3]

1   Immigration and Asylum Act 1999, s 114(1).
2   Immigration and Asylum Act 1999, s 114(2).
3   Immigration and Asylum Act 1999, s 114(2).

Recovery following misrepresentation or failure to disclose

13.106 If NASS determines that a person has received support (temporary or ordinary) as a result of a misrepresentation or failure to disclose a material fact, it may apply to a county court for an order that the person who made the misrepresentation or who was responsible for the failure to disclose, repay the amount.[1] Recovery may be made from any person who made the misrepresentation or failed to disclose, not only from the asylum seeker or dependant who received the support. The amount which the court can order repaid is the total money value of the support paid as a result of the misrepresentation or failure to disclose which would not otherwise have been provided.[2]

1   Immigration and Asylum Act 1999, s 112.
2   Immigration and Asylum Act 1999, s 112(2), (3).

Recovery from sponsor

13.107 Support may be recovered from a sponsor of a person in receipt of (ordinary) asylum support,[1] ie the person who gave a written undertaking for the purposes of the immigration rules to be responsible for the maintenance and accommodation of that person when he or she sought to enter or remain in the UK.[2] This form of recovery is intended to deal with the situation where a person obtains admission to the UK under a sponsorship agreement in a non-asylum capacity and then seeks to remain in the UK as a refugee and becomes entitled to asylum support during the process. The sponsor can only be made liable to make payments covering the period over which the undertaking has effect.[3] Thus, if a person is granted six months' visitor leave on the strength of an undertaking by a sponsor, and claims asylum (and obtains asylum support) after a month, the sponsor could be made liable to repay five months' support. If the same visitor claims asylum after five months, the liability of the sponsor would be limited to a month. If the visitor overstays and then claims asylum and support a year later, we suggest the sponsor is not liable, since no asylum support payment has been made over the period of the undertaking. The same applies if the visitor obtains leave to remain as a student (with no further undertaking) and then claims asylum and support; there would be no liability.

1   Immigration and Asylum Act 1999, s 113.
2   Immigration and Asylum Act 1999, s 113.
3   Immigration and Asylum Act 1999, s 113(1)(b).

13.108 The procedure for recovery is that NASS must make a complaint to a magistrates' court (in Scotland, a sheriff) for an order. The court may order the sponsor to make weekly payments to NASS of an amount which the court thinks appropriate having regard to all the circumstances of the case and, in particular, to the sponsor's own income.[1] The weekly sum must not be more than the weekly value of the support being provided to the asylum seeker.[2] The court may order repayment of support already paid before the date of the complaint but, if it does so, it must have regard to the sponsor's income during the period concerned rather than their current income.[3] The order can be enforced in the same way as a maintenance order.[4]

1   Immigration and Asylum Act 1999, s 113(3).
2   Immigration and Asylum Act 1999, s 113(4).
3   Immigration and Asylum Act 1999, s 113(5).
4   Immigration and Asylum Act 1999, s 113(6).

APPEALS UNDER THE NATIONAL ASYLUM SUPPORT SCHEME

Rights of appeal

13.109 There are rights of appeal against certain NASS decisions to an asylum support adjudicator, who is appointed by the Secretary of State.[1] Given that the Secretary of State (through NASS) is a party to the appeals, there is an issue as to whether the adjudicators are sufficiently independent to comply with the requirements of art 6 of the ECHR.[2] Additionally, the circumstances in which an asylum seeker or dependant may appeal are extremely limited.[3] A person may only appeal if NASS decides that the person is not entitled to any support at all,[4] or terminates all support for reasons other than the person ceasing to be an asylum seeker.[5] The only means of challenging any other decision relating to asylum support or any decision relating to interim support will be by way of judicial review.[6] Asylum support adjudicators have been at pains to stress that they have no jurisdiction to hear complaints about location of accommodation,[7] and the way this issue has come before them has been in appeals against termination of support for breach of conditions, where the breach is failing to attend for return to dispersed accommodation and appellants have argued that features of the location give rise to a reasonable excuse for the breach. See **13.69** above.

1   Immigration and Asylum Act 1999, Sch 10, paras 1-3, 5.
2   See chapter 8 above. A preliminary issue arises as to whether asylum support is capable of falling within the scope of 'civil right' under ECHR art 6. Rights to health insurance benefits under contributory social security schemes, and a statutory entitlement to disability allowance amount to 'civil rights': *Feldbrugge* (1986) 8 EHRR 425, para 29; *Salesi* (1993) 26 EHRR 187, para 19, as does criminal injuries compensation: *Rolf Gustavson v Sweden* (1997) 25 EHRR 623. Asylum support is provided as of right if certain general conditions

are met (destitution etc), although the means of providing support (in respect of which appeals under the NASS scheme do not lie) contain a large discretionary element. Asylum support adjudicators have questioned whether asylum support falls within art 6, on the basis that it involves arguments over discretion rather than obligation on the part of the Secretary of State, but accept that the minimum standards of fairness set out in art 6 should be applied: ASA 00/09/0063, and have endeavoured to ensure that the substance of their decisions is compliant with s 6(1) of the Human Rights Act 1998: ASA 00/09/0063 para 36; ASA 00/10/0087 para 5; ASA 00/10/0089.

3   Immigration and Asylum Act 1999, s 103(7) allows the Secretary of State to extend by regulations the scope of appeal rights so as to cover decisions on location of support, but the regulations made so far have not done this.
4   Immigration and Asylum Act 1999, s 103(1).
5   Immigration and Asylum Act 1999, s 103(2); where a decision is made to stop providing support the appeal may be made before support actually ends.
6   The lack of appeal rights in these cases may also raise issues under ECHR, art 6 (although administrative decisions in respect of a person's civil rights may not always require a merits appeal on the facts of the case: *Kaplan v UK* (1980) 4 EHRR 64 at para 61; *Bryan v UK* (1995) 21 EHRR 342, *W v UK* (1987) 10 EHRR 29. Other concerns are the lack of legal aid for representation: *Airey v Ireland* (1979) 2 EHRR 305), particularly if appeals where an appellant's personal conduct are at issue are determined in the appellant's absence: *Muyldermans* (1991) 15 EHRR 204 at para 64.
7   ASA 00/09/0046; 00/09/0066; 00/10/0087; although adjudicators have directed NASS not to return asylum seekers to particular locations: ASA 00/07/0024, para 11.

Appeal procedures

13.110 The main emphasis in the rules on asylum support appeals is speed.[1] The appeal procedures set out in the rules are not detailed, but the adjudicator has a general power to give directions on matters connected with the appeal where he or she considers that it is in the interests of justice to do so.[2] In addition, a failure to comply with the following rules does not automatically mean that the appeal or the decision on the appeal has no effect.[3] If, however, a party has been disadvantaged as a result of a failure to comply with the rules, the adjudicator must do whatever he or she can to reduce the disadvantage.[4] Appellants may be represented throughout the appeal procedure by any person who they choose to represent them whether legally qualified or not,[5] in which case, provided they are notified, relevant documents sent by NASS or the adjudicator to the appellant must be copied also to the representative.[6]

1   See Immigration and Asylum Act 1999, s 104(3); Asylum Support Appeals (Procedure) Rules 2000, SI 2000/541, Preamble.
2   SI 2000/541, r 14. The asylum support adjudicator has also used this power to direct NASS to expedite consideration of a second application for asylum support: ASA 00/06/0017.
3   SI 2000/541, r 19(1).
4   SI 2000/541, r 19(2). When an asylum seeker arrived too late for a hearing, having taken the specific train directed, the adjudicator used r 19, the interpretative provisions of s 3 of the Human Rights Act and fair hearing standards of ECHR, art 6 to set aside the decision and re-list the appeal: ASA 00/11/0106.
5   SI 2000/541, r 2(2)(d), 15.
6   SI 2000/541, r 2(2)(c).

Notice of appeal

13.111 Any decision against which an appeal lies must be communicated by NASS by letter.[1] Notice of appeal must be sent so that it is received by the adjudicator no later than two days after the day on which the notice of the decision was received.[2] It is given by filling out the standard form which is issued by NASS or a self-made form substantially the same as the NASS form.[3] The standard form itself is attached to the Asylum Support Appeals Rules.[4] The form must be signed by the appellant or his or her representative.[5] In particular, the form requests details of the grounds of appeal and whether the appellant requires an oral hearing and if so, whether an interpreter would be required. The form must be completed in full and in English.[6] Any information or evidence which has not been submitted may be sent in with the form.[7]

1   The Asylum Support Regulations 2000, SI 2000/704, contains no express requirement that these decisions must be communicated by letter but the Asylum Support Appeals (Procedure) Rules 2000, SI 2000/541, assume that they will be: see definition of 'appeal bundle' and 'decision letter' in SI 2000/541, rr 2(1) and 3(3); see also NASS Policy *Bulletin 12* (28 July 2000), referring to a generic refusal letter and a reasons letter to be sent to both the applicant and the reception assistant.
2   SI 2000/541, r 3(3).
3   SI 2000/541, r 3(1).
4   SI 2000/541, Sch. Any changes in the form require its re-issue as a new Schedule: SI 2000/541, r 3(1).
5   SI 2000/541, r 3(2).
6   SI 2000/541, r 3(1).
7   See form.

13.112 The adjudicator may be asked to extend the time limit for appealing, either before or after its expiry, but may only do so if: (i) it is in the interests of justice; and (ii) the asylum seeker or the representative could not comply with the time limit due to circumstances beyond their control.[1] The strength of the case is relevant to the question of whether it is in the interests of justice to extend time.[2] The second limb is more difficult to meet, as there needs to be some practical reason for the inability to submit a notice of appeal in time, for which the would-be appellant was not responsible. If an adjudicator refuses to extend time, the remedies will be either a new application for support or a judicial review of the refusal. It may or may not be possible in these circumstances to seek judicial review of the NASS decision.[3]

1   Asylum Support Appeals (Procedure) Rules 2000, SI 2000/541, rule 3(4). The asylum support adjudicators have so far applied a liberal approach to the extension of time, where an appellant appeared not to have had access to an interpreter (ASA 00/04/0003); where a notice of appeal was submitted with a page missing (ASA 00/06/0017); where NASS was unable to confirm that the decision had been sent by first class post (ASA 00/07/0021); where no reference to the right of appeal was contained in the decision letter, although the explanatory notes to the application forms said this would be the case (ASA 00/07/0030); and where there had been postal delays (ASA 00/08/0037).
2   See *R v Immigration Appeal Tribunal, ex p Mehta* [1976] Imm AR 38, CA, and **18.103** below. In ASA 00/00/0056 no reasons for extending time were given, but the merits appear to have been relevant.
3   In judicial review proceedings, the court may refuse to interfere with the decision where an applicant has failed to exercise a statutory right of appeal. See chapter 18 below.

Preparation of the appeal bundle

13.113 On the same day that the adjudicator receives notice of appeal, or, if that is not reasonably practicable, as soon as possible on the next day, the adjudicator must fax a copy of the notice of appeal and any supporting documents to NASS.[1] On the day following receipt of the notice of appeal, NASS must deliver (by fax or hand) to the adjudicator and (by fax or first class post) to the appellant, copies of the form on which support was claimed and any supporting documentation which was attached to that form (where the appeal is against a refusal as opposed to a withdrawal of support), the decision letter refusing support, and any other evidence which NASS took into account in refusing support.[2]

1 Asylum Support Appeals (Procedure) Rules 2000, SI 2000/541, r 4(1).
2 SI 2000/541, r 4(2), and see definition of 'appeal bundle' in r 2(1).

Decision of the adjudicator whether to hold a hearing of the appeal

13.114 On the day after NASS sends the documentation to the adjudicator, the adjudicator must consider the documents, decide whether to hold an oral hearing of the appeal or to determine it without a hearing and, in either case, set a date for determination of the appeal.[1] If the adjudicator decides to hold an oral hearing, he or she must, on the same day, notify NASS and the appellant of the time, date and place of the hearing.[2] The adjudicator must hold an oral hearing if it was requested in the notice of appeal or, if he or she thinks it necessary to fairly decide the appeal.[3] This would be the case where, for example, the appellant disputed allegations about breach of conditions or other conduct resulting in termination of support. The adjudicator may also decide to hold an oral hearing of the appeal for any other reason.[4] Where an oral hearing is decided upon, it must be held and the appeal determined within four days of the decision to hold it.[5] If the adjudicator decides not to hold an oral hearing, he or she must determine the appeal on the same day or 'as soon as possible' thereafter and in any event within four days.[6]

1 Asylum Support Appeals (Procedure) Rules 2000, SI 2000/541, r 4(3)(a), (b), (4).
2 SI 2000/541, r 4(3)(c), (4), 7.
3 SI 2000/541, r 4(3), 5(1).
4 SI 2000/541, r 5(2).
5 SI 2000/541, r 6(1).
6 SI 2000/541, r 6(2).

Further evidence before determination of the appeal

13.115 If there is further evidence in support of the appeal which was not submitted with the notice of appeal, it may be submitted subsequently for consideration by the adjudicator, within the extremely tight time limits above. The evidence must, at the same time, be sent to NASS.[1] If no oral hearing is to be held, the adjudicator will be determining the appeal, at most, five days after the notice of appeal was received. If NASS wishes to rely on any further evidence which was not submitted after it received the notice of appeal, it may submit it to the adjudicator before the appeal is determined, and must send it to the appellant at the same time.[2] The adjudicator may admit evidence showing a change in the appellant's circumstances since the NASS decision.[3]

1 Asylum Support Appeals (Procedure) Rules 2000, SI 2000/541, r 8(1), (2).
2 SI 2000/541, r 8(3), (4).
3 SI 2000/541, r 10(2).

Oral hearings

13.116 Oral hearings before the adjudicator generally take place in public,[1] although the adjudicator may exclude the public or particular persons from all or part of the hearing if he or she considers it in the public interest.[2] The appellant's interests or desire for the appeal to be heard in private is not decisive. There are no rules setting out the procedure to be adopted at the oral hearing, and the adjudicator has a broad discretion, but fairness requires that appellants are allowed to give oral evidence, call witnesses in support,[3] question any witnesses relied on by NASS, and address the adjudicator on the law and the facts (by themselves or their representatives). If witnesses are called, the adjudicator may require that their evidence is given under oath or affirmation.[4] NASS should meet an appellant's reasonable travelling expenses to attend the oral hearing.[5] If either party adduces new evidence at the hearing, the other party must be given the opportunity of looking at that evidence and photocopying it in order to comment on it.[6] If the appellant fails to attend despite notification of the date, time and place of the hearing, or indicated in the notice of appeal that he or she did not wish to attend or be represented at the hearing, the appeal may be heard in the absence of the appellant.[7] The appeal may also go ahead in the absence of a NASS representative.[8] The adjudicator must ensure that a written record is made of the proceedings.[9] Appellants may obtain a refund of their travel costs for attending an asylum support appeal.[10]

1 Asylum Support Appeals (Procedure) Rules 2000, SI 2000/541, r 12(1).
2 SI 2000/541, r 12(2).
3 SI 2000/541, r 10(5) assumes that witnesses may be called.
4 SI 2000/541, r 10(4).
5 Immigration and Asylum Act 1999, s 103(9).
6 Asylum Support Appeals (Procedure) Rules 2000, SI 2000/541, r 10(6).
7 SI 2000/541, r 9(1), (2).
8 SI 2000/541, r 9(3).
9 SI 2000/541, r 11.
10 ASA 00/07/0027, para 3.

Decision and reasons

13.117 Whether an appeal is dealt with orally or without a hearing, the adjudicator must give reasons for his or her decision in writing.[1] On an oral hearing, the adjudicator must inform the parties of the decision at the end of the hearing.[2] If a party is neither present nor represented at the hearing, the adjudicator must send notice of the decision to that party on the day the appeal is heard.[3] Whether or not the parties attended, the adjudicator must send them a statement containing reasons for the decision no later than two days after the hearing.[4] If no oral hearing is held, the adjudicator must send notice of the decision, with a statement of reasons, on the day the appeal is determined.[5] Asylum support adjudicators are not bound by their own decisions.[6]

1 Immigration and Asylum Act 1999, s 103(4).
2 Asylum Support Appeals (Procedure) Rules 2000, SI 2000/541, r 13(1).
3 SI 2000/541, r 13(1)(b) and (d).
4 SI 2000/541, r 13(1)(d), (4). Asylum support adjudicators' 'reasons statements' are carefully monitored by NASS: NASS Policy *Bulletin 9* (19 June 2000).
5 SI 2000/541, r 13(2), (4).
6 ASA 00/08/0034, para 14.

Evidence and burden of proof

13.118 In deciding the appeal, the adjudicator may take into account any changes of circumstances since the decision.[1] There are no rules on who bears the burden of proof in asylum support appeals but, applying ordinary legal principles, the person who makes a particular assertion must prove it. The burden may, therefore, rest with the person claiming support to establish matters such as destitution, but if NASS has sought to exclude someone from support despite *prima facie* entitlement, it should establish the ground of exclusion. The asylum support adjudicators have generally applied the balance of probabilities as the appropriate standard of proof,[2] although arguably a higher civil standard applies where NASS alleges particularly egregious conduct in breach of conditions, or an offence under Part VI of the Immigration and Asylum Act 1999, in order to exclude a person from support.[3]

1 Asylum Support Appeals (Procedure) Rules 2000, SI 2000/541, r 10(2).
2 See eg ASA 00/04/0003.
3 Asylum Support Regulations 2000, SI 2000/704, regs 19, 20.

Adjudicator's powers

13.119 On deciding the appeal, the asylum support adjudicator may require NASS to reconsider the question of whether the appellant should be provided with support, replace the NASS decision with his or her own decision or dismiss the appeal so that the decision of NASS stands.[1] The extent of the asylum support adjudicators' powers is not specified in the 1999 Act, in contrast to ordinary immigration adjudicators, but it is clear that they must apply the provisions of the Act and the asylum support regulations, and they have also shown themselves willing to consider whether decisions are in accordance with the Secretary of State's policy, as set out, *inter alia*, in the NASS Policy *Bulletins*.[2] Asylum support adjudicators have endeavoured to ensure that their decisions do not constitute or adopt a breach of the appellant's human rights, by, for example, considering whether the termination of support following breach of conditions will leave an appellant exposed to levels of suffering which would engage ECHR, art 3, or breach rights to home and physical integrity under ECHR, art 8.[3] In one case an adjudicator allowed an appeal with reference to ECHR, art 3 (in the context of reasonable excuse for breach of conditions) where an appellant with heart trouble had to go without food if he missed the hostel meals which were provided at rigidly enforced times.[4]

1 Immigration and Asylum Act 1999, s 103(3).
2 ASA 00/09/0044; 00/09/0049; 00/11/0095.
3 See eg ASA 00/10/0089.
4 ASA 00/11/0106.

13.120 The adjudicator's decision is effective from the day on which it is made.[1] Therefore, where the parties are notified at the hearing that the appeal has been successful, NASS must, as far as possible, take immediate steps to implement the decision rather than wait for the written reasons. It is not apparent from the legislation whether the adjudicator should focus on the date of the NASS decision or the date of hearing. The power to require NASS to reconsider the decision suggests the latter.[2] There are no express rules as to the backdating of support or compensating an asylum seeker who has been without support as a result of an erroneous earlier decision.[3] The interim period will be very short but where no temporary support has been provided during that period, NASS should presumably take into account the effect of being without support for that period in meeting the asylum seeker's current needs.

1 Asylum Support Appeals (Procedure) Rules 2000, SI 2000/541, r 13(3).
2 See Immigration and Asylum Act 1999, s 103(3)(a). But see ASA 00/10/0071, where an adjudicator dismissed an appeal on destitution although by the time of the decision the appellant's capital would have diminished sufficiently to qualify. See also ASA 00/11/0105, paras 9 and 15.
3 Although the asylum support adjudicator has held that an asylum seeker is legally entitled to amounts due from the date of the asylum application subject to deduction for backdated social security benefit: ASA 01/02/0202, paras 4 and 14; but see also *R v Hammersmith LBC, ex p Isik* 19 September 2000, CA.

Procedures following an appeal

13.121 There is no further appeal against the decision of the asylum support adjudicator and no provision for a review by the adjudicator.[1] An appellant dissatisfied with a decision of an asylum support adjudicator must proceed by way of judicial review. If the appeal is dismissed, NASS may not consider any further application for support from the appellant unless satisfied that there is a 'material' change of circumstances.[2] Relevant changes would include, but are not limited to, those about which a supported asylum seeker must notify NASS.[3]

1 Immigration and Asylum Act 1999, s 103(5).
2 Immigration and Asylum Act 1999, s 103(6).
3 See Asylum Support Regulations 2000, SI 2000/704, reg 15. Other relevant changes might include disentitlement to social security benefits by refusal of an asylum claim.

Ending the appeal by withdrawal

13.122 An appellant may decide at any stage not to proceed with an appeal, in which case NASS and the adjudicator should be notified as soon as possible.[1] If NASS decides at any time to withdraw the decision against which the appeal is brought, it must notify the appellant and the adjudicator as soon as possible.[2] In either case, the appeal is treated as having come to an end.[3] On the face of the regulation, if NASS withdraws its decision, it is required to make a fresh decision on the application for support, which may be the subject of a further appeal. But in one case[4] the adjudicator treated the further decision as an amendment of the earlier one, so avoiding the delay created by the need to lodge a further appeal.[5]

1 Asylum Support Appeals (Procedure) Rules 2000, SI 2000/541, r 16(2).
2 SI 2000/541, r 16(1).
3 SI 2000/541, r 16(3).
4 ASA 00/11/0116.
5 Such delay could deprive the appellant of the right to a hearing within a reasonable time required by ECHR, art 6, read with Human Rights Act 1998, s 3.

INTERIM SUPPORT SCHEME

13.123 Designed as a temporary stop-gap, the interim scheme for the support of asylum seekers had effect from 6 December 1999[1] and operates during what has been called the 'interim period'[2] which is to run from that date to 1 April 2002.[3] The Secretary of State for the Home Department has taken steps between April and September 2000 to give responsibility to NASS for the support of asylum seekers who would otherwise have made initial applications for support to local authorities under the interim scheme.[4] The interim scheme does not extend to Scotland or Northern Ireland[5] and the community care provisions under which asylum seekers were supported continued in those countries until the introduction of the NASS scheme in April 2000. The local authorities which may owe duties under the interim scheme are, therefore,[6] in England: a county council, metropolitan district council, a district council, a London borough council, the Common Council of the City of London and the Council of the Isles of Scilly and, in Wales, a county council or a county borough council.

1 The provisions enabling the scheme came into force on 11 November 1999, the day the Immigration and Asylum Act 1999 received Royal Assent (see s 170(3)(g), (r)), the duty upon local authorities to provide support for destitute asylum seekers was introduced from 6 December 1999: see Immigration and Asylum Act 1999 (Commencement No 1) Order 1999, SI 1999/3190, Sch, art 2, commencing s 95(3)-(8) of the 1999 Act for the purposes of the interim scheme and Asylum Support (Interim Provisions) Regulations 1999, SI 1999/3056, reg 1(1).
2 Immigration and Asylum Act 1999, Sch 9, paras 1(1), 15.
3 Asylum Support (Interim Provisions) Regulations 1999, SI 1999/3056, regs 1(1), 2(5) and Explanatory Note.
4 See **13.151**ff below.
5 SI 1999/3056, reg 1(2).
6 SI 1999/3056, reg 2(1).

13.124 To be entitled to support under the interim scheme, an asylum seeker must satisfy the general conditions of entitlement,[1] be eligible for interim support as opposed to NASS support,[2] and must not be excluded from interim support.[3]

1 See **13.35–13.47** above.
2 See **13.151**ff below.
3 See Asylum Support (Interim Provisions) Regulations 1999, SI 1999/3056, regs 7 and 8.

Exclusions from interim support

13.125 Overall, it is intended to exclude from interim support persons able to obtain other forms of support; persons who are, in truth, the responsibility of another authority; and persons whose conduct disqualifies them. An authority *must* refuse support to the following persons:[1]

- persons who are 'intentionally destitute';
- persons who have made a claim for support to another authority;
- persons who have made a claim for support to an authority other than one from which, in the previous year, they sought assistance under section 21 of the National Assistance Act 1948 or section 17 of the Children Act 1989;
- certain persons who are not prevented from getting income support because of their immigration status;
- persons whom the Home Office is not treating as asylum seekers or as dependent on the asylum claim of another for immigration purposes.

An authority *may* suspend or discontinue support to the following:

- persons who fail, without reasonable excuse, to comply with the conditions on which the support is provided;
- persons who, without reasonable excuse, leave the accommodation in which support is granted for more than seven days.

Some of these exclusions mirror the exclusions from NASS set out at **13.60–13.80** above. The grounds for exclusion are dealt with separately below but some general comments can be made. The last two refer to people who have already been granted support by the local authority. In those cases withdrawal of support is discretionary[2] and may be temporary (suspension) or indefinite (discontinuance).[3] For example, an authority might suspend the provision of support until the asylum seeker has remedied the breach of conditions or returned to their accommodation. All the other categories of exclusion appear mandatory rather than discretionary in their operation. They provide that in such cases support must be refused, but they do not appear to allow support to be withdrawn once provided,[4] unless the authority then becomes aware of disqualifying circumstances which were unknown at the time of the decision to provide support.[5] The authority may not be able to rely on disqualifying circumstances which it knew, or perhaps which it ought with reasonable diligence to have known, nor on matters that arise after support has been provided.[6] For example, if the authority discovers, after providing support, that the asylum seeker had failed to take up a reasonable job offer and so was 'intentionally destitute' when he or she applied for support, it can rely on this to withdraw support, but if it knew this when it provided support, it should not be able to withdraw support later on that basis. If the asylum seeker fails to take a reasonable job offer after support is provided, the authority cannot withdraw support on the ground of intentional destitution.[7] Further, arguably a person cannot be declared intentionally destitute on the basis of conduct which took place before the interim scheme came into effect.[8]

1   Asylum Support (Interim Provisions) Regulations 1999, SI 1999/3056, regs 7(1), 8.
2   Contrast SI 1999/3056, reg 8(2)(a) 'Support may be suspended or discontinued' with Reg 7(1)(a) 'support must be refused' where other exclusions apply.
3   SI 1999/3056, reg 8(2).
4   See the wording of SI 1999/3056, reg 7(1).
5   SI 1999/3056, regs 8(1) and 7(3).
6   SI 1999/3056, regs 8(1) and 7(3).
7   SI 1999/3056, regs 7(1), (3), 8(1), which do not admit of circumstances post-dating the granting of support forming the basis of exclusion of support, although the authority could argue that the person is no longer destitute, having the means of obtaining accommodation (Immigration and Asylum Act 1999, s 95(3)(a)) or support/assets reasonably expected to be available to them (SI 1999/3056, reg 6(1)(b)).
8   *Fetiti v Islington London Borough* (C/OO/2748) 19 October 2000, per Laws LJ, CA (permission hearing, case subsequently settled).

Intentional destitution

13.126   Where a person has intentionally made himself or herself and any dependants destitute, he or she is to be refused support.[1] The meaning of intentional destitution is almost identical to the NASS scheme, and is analysed at **13.71–13.78** above. The main difference is that in the interim scheme exclusion under this head is mandatory, which may render the interim regulations in breach of the European Convention of Human Rights.[2] A person is intentionally destitute if he or she 'appears to be, or likely within fourteen days to become, destitute'[3] as a result of relevant act or omission, while under the NASS scheme the period is 56 days.

1 Asylum Support (Interim Provisions) Regulations 1999, SI 1999/3056, reg 7(1)(a).
2 *Fetiti v Islington London Borough* (C/OO/2748) 19 October 2000, CA.
3 SI 1999/3056, reg 7(2).

A claim for support to another local authority

13.127 If a person claims support from one local authority and then makes a claim to another authority, the second authority must refuse support.[1] This rule is intended to prevent 'shopping around' between authorities. The exclusion rule clearly does not apply if one authority transfers a claim for support to another local authority.[2]

1 Asylum Support (Interim Provisions) Regulations 1999, SI 1999/3056, reg 7(1)(b).
2 SI 1999/3056, reg 9.

A previous National Assistance Act or Children Act claim to another authority

13.128 If in the 12 months before the claim for interim support, the asylum seeker has claimed assistance from a different local authority under either section 21 of the National Assistance Act 1948 or section 17 of the Children Act 1989, the second local authority must refuse the claim for interim support.[1] This does not mean that the asylum seeker will not be entitled to support at all, merely that the claim for interim support must be made instead to an authority from which the assistance was earlier claimed.

1 Asylum Support (Interim Provisions) Regulations 1999, SI 1999/3056, reg 7(1)(c).

Immigration status does not preclude income support

13.129 The purpose of this exclusion is apparently to prevent those who are asylum seekers for support purposes from getting interim support when they may obtain income support (and housing benefit and council tax benefit).[1] As with NASS, persons falling into this category could also be excluded on the basis that they are not 'destitute',[2] and could also be excluded as intentionally destitute if they failed to claim benefit. The regulations do not exclude from access to asylum support all the possible categories of asylum seekers who might be able to obtain these benefits. The situations not accounted for are set out at **13.65** above. The rules for exclusion from interim support on this basis[3] are more complicated than the equivalent rules under NASS support.[4]

1 See Social Security (Immigration and Asylum) Consequential Amendments Regulations 2000, SI 2000/636, regs 2(1), (4)(a), 12(6)-(8), Sch, Part 1, para 4 (formerly Housing Benefit (General) Regulations 1987, SI 1987/1971, reg 7A(3)(a), Council Tax Benefit (General) Regulations 1992, SI 1992/1814, reg 4A(3)(a).
2 Because they have the 'means of obtaining' adequate accommodation and essential living needs: Immigration and Asylum Act 1999, s 95(3); additionally, the authority must have regard to any income or assets which the asylum seeker 'might reasonably be expected to have': reg 6(1)(b).
3 SI 1999/3056, reg 7(1)(d).
4 Asylum Support Regulations 2000, SI 2000/704, reg 4(4), (6), see **13.65** above.

13.130 The regulations are poorly drafted. The intention is to exclude from interim support persons defined as 'asylum seekers' for benefit purposes who remain entitled to benefit, and nationals of states which have signed the European Convention on Social and Medical Assistance (ECSMA) or the Council of Europe Social Charter (CESC). These categories are dealt with separately below. Unhelpfully, the definitions used in the interim support regulations refer to welfare benefits regulations which have now been repealed.[1] A literal reading would mean that no-one could be excluded from interim support on this basis. But since the definitions have been repeated with minor modifications in more recent regulations, the interim support regulations must probably be read as referring to the definitions in the later regulations.[2] This is reasonable where there is only minor modification ('asylum seekers' refer to those who claimed prior to 2 April 2000 in the later regulations).[3] But for nationals of signatory states to ECSMA or CESC, the change is not so minor. To obtain income support (and so be excluded from interim support) their state must now not merely have signed but also ratified ECSMA or CESC,[4] and instead of having leave subject to a 'no recourse to public funds' condition, they need only be lawfully present in the UK.[5] The difficulty for these nationals is that, although they may not be excluded from income support by their *immigration status*, they may still be unable to access income support even though they are destitute,[6] and may access income-based jobseeker's allowance[7] instead only if, as asylum seekers, they have been given permission to work by the Home Office and so are available for and actively seeking employment.[8] These nationals could therefore find themselves excluded from both social security and interim support.

1   The Income Support (General) Regulations 1987, SI 1987/1967, reg 70 (definition of asylum seeker) has been repealed by Social Security (Immigration and Asylum) Consequential Amendments Regulations 2000, SI 2000/636, reg 3(7)(c), and SI 1987/1967, reg 21(3)(a) (exemption from the definition of 'persons from abroad' for certain nationals of states signatory to the European Convention on Social and Medical Assistance or the Council of Europe Social Charter) by SI 2000/636, reg 3(4)(b).
2   See Bennion *Statutory Interpretation* (3rd edn) at pp 230 s 21; *Britnell v Secretary of State for Social Security* [1991] 2 All ER 726 as to the meaning of 'modification'.
3   SI 2000/636, reg 12(3)-(5) (transitional provisions).
4   For a list of non-EEA states which have ratified the Convention and the Charter see **13.11** above.
5   SI 1987/1967, reg 21(3)(a); SI 2000/636, Sch, para 4.
6   These nationals appear to be excluded from the 'prescribed categories' of people who may claim income support: Social Security Contributions and Benefits Act 1992, s 124(1)(e), SI 1987/1967, reg 4ZA(1) and para 21 (as amended), referring to the persons to whom SI 1987/1967, reg 70(2A) applies. Persons to whom SI 2000/636, Sch, Part 1, para 4 applies (nationals of ratifying states to the European Convention on Social and Medical Assistance or the Council of Europe Social Charter) are excluded.
7   SI 2000/636, reg 2(1), Sch, Part 1, para 4.
8   Jobseekers Act 1995, s 1(2).

Asylum seekers for benefit purposes

13.131 Persons who are 'asylum seekers' for the purposes of income support and therefore able to claim income support are not entitled to support under the interim scheme.[1] This can only apply to people who claimed asylum on or before 3 April 2000.[2] The definition of 'asylum seekers' for these purposes is identical to that in the NASS scheme and is set out at **13.36** above.

1   Asylum Support (Interim Provisions) Regulations 1999, SI 1999/3056, reg 7(1)(d).

2   This is because the Income Support (General) Regulations 1987, 1987/1967 have been amended so that the only persons who remain asylum seekers for income support purposes are those who were asylum seekers for those purposes before 3 April 2000; see Social Security (Immigration and Asylum) Consequential Amendments Regulations 2000, SI 2000/636, regs 2(4)(a), 3(7)(a)-(c), 12(4), (5); Social Security (Persons from Abroad) Miscellaneous Amendments Regulations 1996, SI 1996/30, reg 12(1).

Nationals of states signatories of the European Convention on Social and Medical Assistance or the Council of Europe Social Charter

13.132 The regulations exclude from interim support those able to access benefit by being exempted from the definition of 'persons from abroad'.[1] These were defined as nationals of a state which has signed the European Convention on Social and Medical Assistance or the Council of Europe Social Charter, who have leave to enter or remain in the UK subject to a condition that they have no recourse to public funds.[2] The new exemption from the definition of 'persons from abroad' refers to nationals of states which have *ratified* ECSMA or CESC, not simply signed it, who are 'lawfully present' (broader than 'having leave to remain') in the UK.[3] It is not at all clear whether the regulations cover those who fall into the new or the old definition or whether they manage to cover persons falling into both.

1   Asylum Support (Interim Provisions) Regulations 1999, SI 1999/3056, reg 7(1)(d)(iii).
2   Income Support (General) Regulations 1987, SI 1987/1967, reg 21(3)(a).
3   Social Security (Immigration and Asylum) Consequential Amendments Regulations 2000, SI 2000/636, reg 2(1), Sch, para 4. See **13.131** above. Past asylum claimants on temporary admission have been held not to be lawfully present 'for this purpose': *Kaya v London Borough of Haringey* [2001] EWCA Civ 677.

Persons the Home Office are not treating as asylum seekers or as dependants on a claim for asylum

13.133 Where the Home Office does not accept that a person is an asylum seeker or his or her dependant for the purpose of an asylum claim, the local authority must refuse interim support.[1] This exclusion is identical to that under the NASS scheme, set out at **13.66** above. It may well be important where a fresh claim is made which the Home Office does not accept as such,[2] as well as where the dependants for support purposes[3] do not match those accepted by the Home Office for the purposes of the asylum claim. An unmarried common-law partner who has been living with the asylum seeker for two of the last three years, for example, is a 'dependant' for support purposes[4] but not for the purposes of the asylum claim,[5] unless discretion is exercised in his or her favour.

1   Asylum Support (Interim Provisions) Regulations 1999, SI 1999/3056, reg 7(1)(e).
2   See **13.37** above.
3   See **13.43** above.
4   SI 1999/3056, reg 2(1)(f).
5   See HC 395, para 349.

Persons who fail to comply with conditions on which the support is provided

13.134 The local authority, like NASS, may provide support subject to conditions,[1] which similarly must be in writing[2] and given to the person who is being supported,[3] and may suspend or discontinue support for breach of those conditions by the asylum seeker or a dependant.[4] Unlike NASS, however, the authority must prove breach of conditions and may not remove support on reasonable suspicion.[5]

1 Asylum Support (Interim Provisions) Regulations 1999, SI 1999/3056, reg 5(6).
2 SI 1999/3056, reg 5(7).
3 SI 1999/3056, reg 5(8).
4 SI 1999/3056, reg 8(2).
5 See **13.68** above.

Persons who leave the accommodation on which support is granted for more than seven days

13.135 Support may be suspended or discontinued if an asylum seeker, or any dependant, leaves the accommodation provided as part of such support for more than seven consecutive days without reasonable excuse.[1] Arguably, accommodation which is damaging to health, or good family reasons for leaving, constitutes a reasonable excuse. In *Fetiti v Islington London Borough*,[2] the court declared arguable the common-sense proposition that the accommodation must have been provided under the interim scheme, and not under different powers before the interim scheme came into effect on 6 December 1999.

1 Asylum Support (Interim Provisions) Regulations 1999, SI 1999/3056, reg 8(2)(b).
2 C/OO/2748, 19 October 2000, CA (permission). The case subsequently settled.

Procedures for obtaining interim support

13.136 The regulations do not prescribe any particular procedures for applying for and obtaining interim support or for reviewing decisions relating to entitlement.

Claims and decision relating to interim support

13.137 The scheme requires a claim for support to be made to a local authority[1] but does not specify how. 'Claim' suggests an active process and it is unlikely that an authority has duties to persons who come to its attention otherwise than by making an application.[2] The authority has a responsibility to determine whether a person claiming support is an 'eligible person', namely he or she is an asylum seeker or the dependant of one and is destitute.[3]

1 See eg Immigration and Asylum Act 1999, Sch 9, paras 2(2), 9(6), 10(1), 12; Asylum Support (interim Provisions) Regulations 1999, SI 1999/3056, regs 3(3), 4(2), 9. The Secretary of State has not used the powers under the Immigration and Asylum Act 1999, Sch 9, para 12 to make rules about how to claim support and how claims for support will be determined.
2 SI 1999/3056, reg 3(3).
3 SI 1999/3056, reg 2(1), 3(2), (3).

13.138 If the asylum seeker is eligible for support and not excluded from support or entitled to apply for NASS rather than interim support, then, if the local authority cannot transfer the claim for support to another local authority, it must provide support.[1] If the authority transfers the claim for support to another local authority, it need not decide whether the person is eligible for support or not. That decision, and the duty to provide support if eligibility is determined,[2] become the responsibility of the authority to whom the claim for support has been transferred.[3] Pending a decision on eligibility for support or transfer to another authority, the local authority must provide temporary support.[4]

1 Asylum Support (Interim Provisions) Regulations 1999, SI 1999/3056, reg 3(1).
2 SI 1999/3056, reg 3(1).
3 SI 1999/3056, reg 3(1)-(3),
4 SI 1999/3056, reg 4, see **13.142** below.

13.139 There are no rights of appeal to an independent body against decisions concerning interim support.[1] Because the availability of adequate support is fundamental to the ability of asylum seekers to pursue their claims for asylum,[2] authorities must proceed with a high degree of care, thoroughness and with high standards of fairness in making their decisions.[3] In particular, if an authority conducting inquiries into the circumstances of applicants comes across matters of particular concern which will affect the decision whether and how to provide support, it should put them to the applicants or their advisers for their comments or explanations before taking a decision.[4] Procedural fairness is particularly important where the authority believes that the asylum seeker has more resources available than have been disclosed, and on matters such as intentional destitution and breach of conditions. Although the regulations do not stipulate that reasons for a decision refusing support are required, it is likely that the courts will impose such a duty because of the nature and subject matter of the decision.[5]

1 This may raise issues as to whether the scheme complies with ECHR, art 6, see **13.109** fnn 2 and 6 above.
2 See *R v Secretary of State for Social Security, ex p JCWI* [1997] 1 WLR 275, CA.
3 See *Secretary of State for the Home Department v Thirukumar* [1989] Imm AR 402, CA; *Re Musisi* [1987] AC 514.
4 The general legal principle that fair decision-making requires that a person must have a proper opportunity of being heard before a decision affecting their interests is made, has been applied in the field of social welfare law: see *R v Gravesham Borough Council, ex p Winchester* (1986) 18 HLR 207 at 214; *R v Wyre Borough Council, ex p Joyce* (1983) 11 HLR 73; *R v Nottingham County Council, ex p Edwards* (1998) 31 HLR 33.
5 See *R v Higher Education Funding Council, ex p Institute of Dental Surgery* [1994] 1 WLR 242.

Reviewing support

13.140 The regulations do not deal with how support decisions may be reviewed following a change in circumstances after the award of support. But since the authority is only required to provide support for an asylum seeker who is destitute or likely to become destitute within 14 days[1] and it is for the authority to determine this issue,[2] it is implicit that an authority may review the question of destitution if there is a relevant change of circumstances—if, for example, the asylum seeker finds work. The changes which are likely to be material will be similar to those which a person supported by NASS is required to notify.[3] Similarly, where the resources available to an asylum seeker have increased (or decreased) although he or she remains within the definition of destitution,[4] it is implicit that the authority may review the nature and the level of support provided.[5] The local authority may also review the support provided if it appears that there are grounds to discontinue or to suspend support.

1 Immigration and Asylum Act 1999, Sch 9, para 1(1), (2); Asylum Support (Interim Provisions) Regulations 1999, SI 1999/3056, regs 2(1), 3(1.)
2 Immigration and Asylum Act 1999, Sch 9, para 2(1); SI 1999/3056, reg 3(2).
3 See **13.97** above.
4 Immigration and Asylum Act 1999, s 95(3), Sch 9, para 3; see **13.47**, **13.53**ff above.
5 This is also implicit from the wording of SI 1999/3056, reg 5(1)(a), (b).

Determining destitution

13.141 The general common criteria relating to destitution are set out at **13.47** above. Unlike the NASS scheme, no additional rules have been made under the interim scheme prescribing what may or may not be taken into account in deciding whether a person cannot meet their essential living needs.[1] However, under the statute, in determining whether a person has adequate accommodation, no account may be taken of the fact that the asylum seeker has no legal right to stay there, or that the accommodation or part of it is shared with other persons; or that it is temporary, or its location.[2]

1 The Secretary of State has not used his rule-making powers for these purposes (Immigration and Asylum Act 1999, Sch 9, para 3). Contrast the NASS rules; see **13.53**ff above.
2 Immigration and Asylum Act 1999, s 95(5)(6), as applied to the interim scheme by Sch 9, para 3.

Temporary interim support

13.142 An authority to which a claim for support has been made[1] or transferred[2] is under a duty to provide temporary support pending its decision on transfer or eligibility for support. Temporary support must be adequate to meet the needs of the applicant and his or her dependants.[3] It may include accommodation, essential living needs and any other necessary support.[4]

1 Asylum Support (Interim Provisions) Regulations 1999, SI 1999/3056, reg 4(2)(a).
2 SI 1999/3056, reg 4(1), (2)(b).
3 SI 1999/3056, reg 4(3); 'dependants' has the same meaning as in interim support: SI 1999/3056, reg 2(1).
4 It is unclear whether 'temporary support' in SI 1999/3056, reg 4 is constrained by the limitations set out in SI 1999/3056, reg 5 or whether, for example, support but no accommodation may be offered on a temporary basis.

Provision of interim support

Forms of support provided

13.143 An authority is bound to provide to destitute asylum seekers[1] accommodation which appears to the local authority to be adequate for them and their dependants (if any), and support to meet what appear to be the essential living needs of the asylum seeker and their dependants and to meet reasonable travel expenses incurred in attending interviews with the Home Office concerning the asylum application and the hearing of an asylum appeal. The regulations require the local authority to provide both accommodation and support to meet essential living needs.[2] Thus a person who already has adequate accommodation but no means of meeting his or her needs for food and clothing, a fairly common situation,[3] must be given both. This provision, which replicates the case law under section 21 of the National Assistance Act that it was unlawful for an authority to provide food vouchers alone to an asylum seeker without also the provision of residential accommodation,[4] prejudices both the asylum seeker, who may face unnecessary and unwanted dispersal in order to meet essential living needs, and the public purse.[5] The motive for this indissoluble package is not unwonted generosity but a desire to force asylum seekers out of accommodation which is too big or too expensive (such as flats) and into hostels.

1 Asylum Support (Interim Provisions) Regulations 1999, SI 1999/3056, reg 5(1)(3).
2 SI 1999/3056, reg 5(1).
3 Or vice versa, which is not at all common.
4 *R v Newham London Borough Council, ex p Gorenkin (Mikhail)* [1998] 1 CCLR 309.
5 The apparently unnecessary cost implications were referred to by Hooper J in *R v Camden London Borough, ex p Diirshe* (CO/5069/99) 24 February 2000, para 8.

13.144 There are two exceptions to this unfortunate regime. First, accommodation may be separated from support where the asylum seeker's household includes a dependent child who is under 18.[1] The second exception is that, if the circumstances of a particular case are 'exceptional', support may be provided 'in such other ways as are necessary to enable the assisted person and his dependants ... to be supported'[2]—sufficiently wide words to enable the authority to split the package and offer support or accommodation only where appropriate.[3] In practice, if a person already has adequate accommodation, the authority may fulfil its statutory duty by providing essential living needs and making arrangements with the accommodation provider (including payment) to continue to provide it. Where essential living needs are already being met, the authority could fulfil its duty by taking over the support or by meeting any deficiency in it. There is, however, no power simply not to provide one or other form of support because it is not wanted.

1 Asylum Support (Interim Provisions) Regulations 1999, SI 1999/3056, reg 5(2); for definition of 'dependant' see reg 2(1) and **13.43** above. In *R v Camden London Borough, ex p Diirshe* (CO/5069/99) 24 February 2000 the court held that the child could fall within any of the listed categories of dependant in SI 1999/3056, reg 2(1), rejecting the local authority's argument that the child had to fall within the narrow definition in SI 1999/3056, reg 2(1)(b) ('a child of his ... who is under 18 and dependent on him'). The Administrative Court has held that even where there are dependants under 18, the authority is entitled to provide accommodation and essential living needs as a package, and is not obliged to provide solely essential living needs if the family reject the dispersal accommodation: *R v Hammersmith and Fulham London Borough Council, ex p Isik*, CO 1945/2000, 26 June 2000. Leave to appeal was granted but the matter became academic.
2 SI 1999/3056, reg 5(4).
3 This interpretation is supported by the Secretary of State's Guidance, in NASS letter to Chief Executives of Local Authorities in England and Wales, 1 December 1999, at para 9, and has generally been accepted by local authorities.

Level and nature of support

13.145 In deciding what to provide by way of accommodation and essential living needs, the local authority must have regard[1] to income or assets which the asylum seeker and his or her dependants have or might reasonably be expected to have,[2] the welfare of the asylum seeker and their dependants and the costs of providing support. But in providing accommodation, it must not have regard to the asylum seeker's preferences as to the locality in which the accommodation is provided, its nature or the nature and standard of fixtures and fittings in it.[3] There is a clear tension between the requirement to ignore a person's preferences on the location of the accommodation and the requirement to take into account the asylum seeker's welfare, since in most cases preference and welfare will coincide. For example, the welfare of the individual claimant may only be properly safeguarded by placing them near appropriate medical facilities, other family members or the children's school—all of which will be reflected in the person's preferences. The discretion as to locality is a further disguised form of dispersal which may be operated by local authorities in addition to the formal dispersal scheme, by way of transfer (below). In one case,[4] an authority was prevented from moving asylum seekers to whom it was already providing support, until it had at least consulted them.

1   Asylum Support (Interim Provisions) Regulations 1999, SI 1999/3056, reg 6(1).
2   An authority is entitled to take into account evidence (electronic entertainment and communication equipment) of other income from sub-letting in reducing support for essential living needs: *R v Camden London Borough, ex p Kwiek* 12 April 2000, QBD, upheld by the Court of Appeal on 12 October 2000 (C/00/1699; renewed permission).
3   SI 1999/3056, reg 6(2).
4   *R v Newham London Borough, ex p Ally (Samira Said)*, 21 January 2000; an injunction was granted, after which the authority consulted.

13.146 The accommodation provided must be adequate.[1] In the context of the immigration rules, the Immigration Appeal Tribunal has held that, to be adequate, accommodation must not be statutorily overcrowded or unfit for human habitation.[2] We suggest that the standard of adequacy here is higher, as it is framed in terms which involve a subjective element of adequacy 'for the needs of the assisted person'.[3] To comply with the local authority's duty, it must meet any particular needs which the asylum seeker has. As for the provision of essential living needs, there are no 'rule of thumb' rates of support for those eligible, as in NASS.[4] But comparison may be made with those rates to determine the kind of levels payable, although authorities should bear in mind that NASS rates exclude household bills and assume an additional payment of £50 per person every six months.[5] Support for essential living needs may be made by way of vouchers redeemable in certain shops or cash payments or both, but cash payments are limited to £10 per person per week unless either the claimant's household includes a child under 18 who is dependent upon them or the circumstances of the case are exceptional.[6]

1   Asylum Support (Interim Provisions) Regulations 1999, SI 1999/3056, reg 5(1)(a).
2   See **11.19** above.
3   SI 1999/3056, reg 5(1)(a). See *R v Islington London Borough, ex p Fatah Mahida*, CO 2519/2000, 14 August 2000, QBD: location of accommodation near mosque was relevant to applicant's welfare and so to adequacy of accommodation.
4   See **13.85** above.
5   Since the two schemes are both provided for under the same principal Act and aim to achieve the same legislative purpose, they should generally not give rise to different provision where the cases are otherwise identical and only distinguishable by the day on which a person became eligible for the support in question: *R v Derby City Council, ex p Bajric* CO/1139/00 14 August 2000. In *R v Camden London Borough Council, ex p Kwiek*, C/00/1699, 12 October 2000, the Court of Appeal left open the question whether an authority could be required to disclose the scale rates it used to calculate the level of support it provided in any particular case.
6   SI 1999/3056, reg 5(5).

Transferring claims for support

13.147 In certain circumstances, a local authority may transfer a claim for support to another local authority without deciding whether the applicant is eligible for interim support. The authority to which the claim is transferred then has the responsibility for determining whether the asylum seeker is eligible for support and for providing support accordingly.[1] These circumstances are not set out in the regulations; instead, local authorities may make their own arrangements.[2] The Secretary of State may make rules to force certain authorities to accept referrals and provide support where a claim is made to an authority which is already supporting a specified maximum number of asylum seekers,[3] or to prevent authorities from providing support in particular areas.[4] At the request of the local authorities, the Secretary of State has so far refrained from making any such rules, in the hope that the agreed arrangements between the local authorities will work to relieve the pressure on the areas where most asylum seekers are concentrated, London and the south-east.[5] Authorities are able not only to transfer claims for support to another authority under their own agreements but may also transfer their duty to provide support or further support.[6]

1 Asylum Support (Interim Provisions) Regulations 1999, SI 1999/3056, reg 3.
2 SI 1999/3056, reg 9.
3 Immigration and Asylum Act 1999, Sch 9, paras 9(1)-(4).
4 SI 1999/3056, Sch 9, para 8.
5 Letter from Bob Eagle, Director of NASS, to Chief Executives of local authorities in England and Wales, 19 November 1999, para 20. An annex to the letter consists of a draft form of regulations to be brought in if the voluntary arrangements do not work.
6 Immigration and Asylum Act 1999, Sch 9, para 9(6), (7); SI 1999/3056, regs 9 and 3(1)(b) all make this clear.

13.148 The agreements between the local authorities developed out of a cooperative process between the local authorities, the Local Government Association, the Home Office and the Association of London Government. Transfer may take place in the following circumstances:[1]

- the applicant for support is aged eighteen or over; and
- the claim for support has been made in London or Kent; and
- the asylum seeker has made an in-country asylum claim and is awaiting an initial Home Office appointment or is a port asylum applicant who has received a negative decision from the Home Office and is appealing against such decision; and
- the applicant is destitute in accordance with the standard applied by the relevant local authority;[2] and
- the claim for support discloses a need for the provision of accommodation, not just essential living needs; and
- neither the applicant nor his or her dependants have any 'exceptional reasons' for needing to be accommodated in London or Kent; and
- the asylum seeker was not in receipt of accommodation and help with essential living needs before 6 December 1999 (when the interim scheme came into force).[3]

In addition, where it is apparent that the applicant and his or her dependants have 'special needs', a comprehensive assessment and investigation must be completed before a decision is made as to whether transfer of the claim is appropriate.

1 The details are set out (although very poorly) in the 'Guidance Note to Local Authorities in England and Wales: Interim Arrangements for Asylum Seeker Support' issued by the Home Office, ss 1 (final page), 2 (parts 3 and 4), and Annex 2.
2 This criterion cuts across Asylum Support (Interim Provisions) Regulations 1999, SI 1999/3056, which does not require the transferring authority to determine eligibility: SI 1999/3056, reg 3(1)(a), (3).
3 In general, this excludes from transferral people who were supported under the National Assistance Act 1948, s 21 by a local social services department before 6 December 1999.

13.149 In transferring claims for support, local authorities must have regard to the guidance issued by the Secretary of State as to when claims can and cannot be transferred.[1] The Secretary of State's guidance[2] suggests that authorities should undertake an assessment to determine whether there are exceptional reasons why asylum seekers should remain in the authority where they claimed support. Exceptional reasons for remaining in London and Kent are expressed to include (but are not limited to) circumstances where the asylum seeker has particular medical needs which can only be met locally. The example given is access to the Medical Foundation for the Care of Victims of Torture, which provides specialist counselling and treatment, and prepares reports for use in asylum claims. The guidance also cites close family members already living in the area as exceptional reasons. It also sets out criteria for local authorities receiving transferred asylum seekers on where to place them,[3] which is intended to cohere with the approach to dispersal under the NASS scheme.[4] Local authorities placing transferred asylum seekers are required to take into account:

• the culture and language of the asylum seeker;
• his or her particular needs regarding the type of accommodation required (the examples given are accommodation suitable for families, those with special needs or disabilities);
• accessibility of other forms of services and support needed by asylum seekers;
• the possibilities for developing support provided by existing voluntary and community groups in the area;
• whether there is likely to be suitable accommodation available in the particular location;
• whether there is an existing multi-ethnic population or infrastructure able to assist asylum seekers there.

1 Immigration and Asylum Act 1999, Sch 9, para 9(7).
2 Letter of Judith Simpson, NASS to all Chief Executives of Local Authorities in England and Wales, 1 December 1999. Paragraphs 1 and 2 make it clear that the letter constitutes 'guidance' under the Immigration and Asylum Act 1999 to which the local authorities are legally obliged to have regard.
3 See NASS Guidance 1 December 1999, paras 1-6; but the legal force of this guidance is doubtful, since Immigration and Asylum Act 1999, Sch 9, para 9(7) requires authorities to have regard to it in exercising any 'power under the regulations to refer or transfer', not after transfer.
4 Asylum seekers should not be placed in isolated surroundings but in 'cluster areas' where there already exists a multi-cultural population: see the Home Office document 'Cluster Areas: Role of local organisations', September 1999.

Challenges to interim support decisions

13.150 There are no rights of appeal against decisions on interim support, in contrast to the appeal rights under NASS against refusal or withdrawal of support.[1] The only means of challenging decisions on interim support (and decisions on NASS asylum support which are not susceptible to appeal), is by way of judicial review.[2]

1 See **13.109ff** above.
2 The alternative remedy for maladministration (as opposed to an unlawful decision) is a complaint to the local government Ombudsman, but this would probably not be sufficiently speedy for cases concerning support. For a discussion of this possibility see *R v Lambeth London Borough Council, ex p Crookes* (1995) 29 HLR 28 at 35ff.

WHICH SUPPORT? ELIGIBILITY FOR INTERIM OR NASS SUPPORT

13.151 Since September 2000, no new asylum claimant, wherever he or she makes the application, has been eligible for interim support and all have been entitled to apply for NASS. However, many asylum claimants who previously obtained or were eligible for interim support, will continue to receive it or will remain eligible to apply for it. The important dates are not the dates on which support was claimed but the date of the asylum claim and (if applicable) its rejection or withdrawal. The interim support scheme came into force on 6 December 1999 and the scheme for NASS support on 3 April 2000. Between those two dates, all destitute asylum seekers who were without social security or community care provision were required to apply to their local authority for interim support. Those who, on 5 December 1999, were already receiving support under section 21 of the National Assistance Act or under the Children Act 1989 were generally transferred into the interim support scheme.[1] These forms of assistance are however different in scope and in their qualifying criteria. The effect of the 'transitional provision'[2] was not to require local authorities to make exactly the same provision as previously, but to assess asylum seekers under the terms of the interim provisions to determine the nature and level of support appropriate.[3] The situation became more complex on 3 April 2000, from which date the two schemes continued in tandem.

1 Asylum Support (Interim Provisions) Regulations 1999, SI 1999/3056, reg 11. See also letter from Director of NASS, to all Chief Executives of local authorities in England and Wales, 19 November 1999.
2 SI 1999/3056, reg 11.
3 *R v Derby City Council, ex p Bajric* (CO/1139/00), 14 August 2000 per Newman J at paras 43-45.

13.152 On their face, the Interim Support Regulations appear to operate so that all destitute asylum seekers and their dependants are able to get interim support.[1] However, asylum seekers can only be provided with interim support during what is called the 'interim period',[2] which in general terms runs from 6 December 1999 to 1 April 2002.[3] But the Secretary of State may direct local authorities to treat the interim period as ending for certain classes of asylum seekers on a date earlier than 1 April 2002,[4] with the effect that interim support ends for them on that date[5] and they become eligible for NASS support.[6] The Secretary of State may specify different dates for the ending of the interim period for different classes of case.[7]

1 Asylum Support (Interim Provisions) Regulations 1999, SI 1999/3056, reg 2(1).
2 SI 1999/3056, reg 3(1); Immigration and Asylum Act 1999, Sch 9, paras 1(1) and 15.
3 SI 1999/3056, regs 1(1), 2(5).
4 Immigration and Asylum Act 1999, Sch 15, para 14(1) enables the Secretary of State to direct local authorities to 'treat the interim period' as coming to an end earlier than 1 April 2002: for specified purposes; in relation to a specified area or locality; or in relation to

persons of a specified description. See below for such directions and see, summarising the 'phased roll-out', NASS Policy *Bulletin 15* (4 August 2000).
5   SI 1999/3056, reg 3(1) provides that an authority '... must provide support during the interim period to eligible persons'.
6   Asylum Support Regulations 2000, SI 2000/704, reg 4(5)(a), (b), (c).
7   Immigration and Asylum Act 1999, Sch 15, para 14(1), read with para 14(4).

Those ineligible for interim support, but eligible for NASS support

13.153 The following groups of people are unable to get interim support and so able to apply for NASS support because the interim period is treated as having ended for them on the date given.

Post-2 April 2000 port/declaration asylum seekers/Oakington Reception Centre detainees/ cases in Scotland and Northern Ireland

13.154 From 3 April 2000, the following asylum seekers are ineligible for interim support and so able to apply for NASS support:

(a)   persons who apply for asylum on or after 3 April 2000 who *either* claim asylum on their arrival in the UK; *or* within three months of a declaration of upheaval by the Secretary of State;[1]
(b)   persons who make a claim for asylum in-country on or after 3 April 2000 and are, at any time after making that claim, detained at Oakington Reception Centre;[2]
(c)   persons who claim asylum on or after 3 April 2000 in Scotland or Northern Ireland.[3]

1   A declaration of upheaval is a declaration that the country from which the applicant is seeking asylum is subject to such a fundamental change of circumstances that the Secretary of State would not normally order the return of any person to that country. Direction No 1 of Secretary of State, March 2000, paras (a), (b).
2   Direction No 1 of Secretary of State, March 2000, para (d).
3   The interim scheme does not extend to Scotland or Northern Ireland: Asylum Support (Interim Provisions) Regulations 1999, SI 1999/3056, reg 1(2), and so asylum seekers in these areas are not people to whom interim support applies for the purposes of Asylum Support Regulations 2000, SI 2000/704, reg 4(5) (exclusion from NASS support).

Pre-3 April 2000 port/declaration asylum claimants after refusal ('disbenefitted' cases)

13.155 Persons who made claims for asylum before 3 April 2000 either on arrival or within three months of a declaration of upheaval and who either:

(a)   abandon their asylum claim on or after 25 September 2000; *or*
(b)   have their claim to asylum recorded as decided by the Secretary of State on or after 25 September

are no longer entitled to interim support from the date of abandonment or decision, but may instead apply for NASS support.[1] These asylum seekers would have received social security benefit, rather than interim support, both before and, as a result of the transitional provisions, after 1 April 2000.

1   Direction No 3 of Secretary of State, 11 July 2000, para 5.

13.156 *Welfare provision*

Kent and Medway asylum seekers

13.156 Special provisions were made for local authorities of Kent and Medway. Kent County Council and Medway District Council have no power to provide support for asylum seekers who claimed asylum in the circumstances above (on arrival or after an upheaval declaration) and who receive a notice of decision on the claim for asylum on or after 17 April 2000.[1] Asylum seekers who are refused asylum on or after 17 April 2000 while in Kent or Medway, cannot be provided with interim support from any other local authority either.[2] The Direction requires the 'Kent and Medway' asylum seekers to have received notice of the decision on the asylum claim, in contrast to the non-Kent or Medway cases, which only require a decision to have been recorded but not necessarily received.[3] These 'Kent and Medway' asylum seekers are also all eligible for NASS rather than for interim support from local authorities.

1   Direction No 2A of Secretary of State, 10 April 2000, para (b).
2   Direction No 2 of Secretary of State, 10 April 2000, para (b).
3   *R v Secretary of State for the Home Department, ex p Salem* [1999] QB 805.

In-country asylum seekers

13.157 Those who made in-country applications for asylum after certain dates shown below are not entitled to interim support from the authorities shown. They are entitled to apply for NASS support instead. The directions, as set out below, provide a cut-off date for interim support for all the local authorities in England and Wales.

(a)   Those who claim asylum in-country on or after 17 April 2000, may not obtain interim support from Kent County Council or Medway District Council.[1]

(b)   Those who claim asylum in-country on or after 24 July 2000 may not obtain interim support from a London borough council or the Common Council of the City of London.[2]

(c)   Those who claim asylum in-country on or after 31 July 2000 may not obtain interim support from a local authority in the North East, Yorkshire and Humberside or Wales.[3]

(d)   Those who claim asylum in-country on or after 14 August 2000 may not obtain interim support from a local authority in the North West, East Midlands, Eastern, South West or South Central England.[4]

(e)   Those who claim asylum in-country on or after 29 August 2000 may not obtain interim support from a local authority in the West Midlands or Sussex.[5]

The directions achieve this by stating that the relevant authority is to treat the interim period as having come to an end for those asylum seekers. If an asylum seeker applies in-country after the relevant cut-off date for the authority to which it later applies for interim support, the application must be refused by that authority,[6] and the asylum seeker would be able to apply for NASS support as there would be no local authority which must provide interim support.[7]

1   Direction No 2A of Secretary of State, 10 April 2000, para (a).
2   Direction No 3 of the Secretary of State, 11 July 2000, para 1.
3   Direction No 3 of the Secretary of State, 11 July 2000, para 2 and Sch Part I.

4   Direction No 3 of the Secretary of State, 11 July 2000, para 3 and Sch Part II.
5   Direction No 3 of the Secretary of State, 11 July 2000, para 4 and Sch Part III.
6   Asylum Support (Interim Provisions) Regulations 1999, SI 1999/3056, reg 3(1).
7   Asylum Support Regulations 2000, SI 2000/704, reg 4(5).

Those eligible for interim support

13.158 It may be apparent from the above that all new asylum seekers after 29 August 2000, wherever they claimed asylum, are now entitled to apply for NASS rather than interim support whether they claimed on arrival, within three months of a declaration of upheaval or in-country. The persons who are still entitled to get interim support rather than social security benefits or NASS support are the following:

Port/declaration asylum seekers

13.159 Asylum seekers who, before 3 April 2000, claimed asylum at port or within three months of a declaration of upheaval and who were recorded as having their claim to asylum determined by the Secretary of State prior to 25 September 2000[1] unless they received notice of refusal of their asylum claim on or after 17 April 2000 while they were living in the area of Kent County Council or Medway District Council,[2] in which case they are eligible for NASS support.

1   Direction No 3 of Secretary of State, 11 July 2000, para 5, only ends interim support for those whose claim is abandoned or refused on or after 25 September 2000.
2   The combined effect of Direction No 2 of the Secretary of State of 10 April 2000, para (b) and Direction No 2A of Secretary of State of 10 April 2000, para (b) precludes any local authority from providing interim support for such asylum seekers. An asylum seeker in this group who receives notice of decision while living in Kent or Medway continues to be entitled to interim support after 17 April 2000 only if the notice was received before 17 April 2000.

In-country asylum seekers

13.160 Persons who claimed asylum in-country before the relevant cut-off date for the local authority to whom they apply for interim support. The cut-off date refers to claims for asylum, not for support.[1] It doesn't matter whether these in-country asylum seekers claimed asylum before or after 3 April 2000, the only relevant date is that which relates to in-country asylum claims for the local authority concerned.

1   See ASA 00/11/0016 and ASA 00/11/0115 at para 9, where the adjudicator laments that the local authority may well have committed precisely this error.

13.161 Those entitled to interim support as a result of the above rules continue to be entitled after the relevant cut-off dates. Thus, a person in the first group above, who was entitled to interim support rather than NASS support when his or her pre-April 2000, port claim to asylum was recorded as being determined before 25 September 2000, remains entitled to interim support thereafter pending the hearing of any appeal. Similarly, a person in the second group who made an in-country asylum claim before the cut-off date for his or her local authority, remains entitled to receive, apply for and obtain interim support from that authority after the authority's cut-off date.[1]

1 The cut-off dates depend on the date of the asylum claim or its refusal or notification of refusal, not when asylum support was claimed: see Directions 2, 2A and 3 of the Secretary of State above. See also letter of NASS to all Chief Executives and Directors of Social Services in England and Wales, 10 July 2000, accompanying Direction No 3: 'Nothing in this letter or the Direction applies to asylum seekers being supported under the interim arrangements prior to the relevant date. They continue to be so supported.'

HARD CASES

13.162 The other controversial area of asylum support is the complete termination of all support—interim or NASS—to those without dependent children under 18, once all appeals have been exhausted.[1] There are many asylum seekers thus excluded from all support, who cannot leave the UK because of civil war or turmoil in their home country[2] or severe illness or other compelling compassionate circumstances, or who are in the process of judicially reviewing a refusal of leave to appeal. In response to the concerns expressed during the passage of the Immigration and Asylum Act 1999, the Secretary of State was empowered[3] to make grants available to voluntary sector organisations, on restrictive terms and conditions,[4] to allow them to assist former asylum seekers and their dependants. The voluntary sector, alarmed at the prospect of judicial review challenges by former asylum seekers refused support, was unwilling to administer the proposed scheme, and as a result, NASS initiated its own 'hard cases' fund under section 4 of the Immigration and Asylum Act 1999. Under the section the Secretary of State may provide, or arrange for the provision of facilities for the accommodation of anyone who is temporarily admitted to the UK, released from detention by the immigration authorities or released on bail from immigration detention. It thus covers, but is not limited to, former asylum seekers.

1 See definition of 'asylum seeker', **13.36** above.
2 It has not been the invariable practice of the Home Office to grant exceptional leave to people in this situation; a more common response is to suspend their removal without granting them any status, leaving them in a limbo which could be contrary to ECHR, arts 3 and 13: *HLR v France* (1997) 26 EHRR 29.
3 Immigration and Asylum Act 1999, s 111.
4 Immigration and Asylum Act 1999, s 111(2).

13.163 NASS has indicated that it proposes to provide support under this section to former asylum seekers and their dependants in very limited circumstances.[1] The criteria for eligibility are that the asylum seeker has been supported by NASS or by a local authority, is no longer an asylum seeker, appears to the Secretary of State to be destitute and has no other avenue of support (from friends or family, NHS or community care). While each case will be considered on its merits, support will not normally be made available unless it is not practicable for the person to travel to any other country, by reason of a physical impediment (for example, illness or late pregnancy) or the circumstances of the case are exceptional.[2] The support which may be provided is primarily accommodation, but NASS has accepted that it will be 'full board'.[3] Meals rather than vouchers and cash will be provided.[4] At present, all accommodation provided under these powers is outside London[5] but there is no reason why this should be so. It is envisaged that the immigration authorities will be able to impose residence and curfew conditions on temporary admission for persons provided with support under section 4, which would enable those breaking conditions to be arrested.[6]

1 Letter of NASS dated 3 April 2000 to 'Assistant' voluntary sector organisations involved in administering 'NASS' support scheme, Annex A.
2 In *R v Immigration Appeal Tribunal, ex p Mohamed* CO 2234 1999, 2 August 2000, Dyson J held that it was not unreasonable to use section 4 support for asylum seekers awaiting a test case on third country removals, whose asylum claims were not being considered substantively.
3 NASS letter 3 April 2000 (see fn 1 above).
4 NASS letter 3 April 2000 (see fn 1 above) para 3.
5 NASS letter 3 April 2000 (see fn 1 above).
6 Immigration and Asylum Act 1999, Sch 14, para 62, inserting new sub-paras (2A) and (2C) after para 21(2) of the Immigration Act 1971, Sch 2.

COMMUNITY CARE PROVISION FOR THOSE SUBJECT TO IMMIGRATION CONTROL

13.164 One of the stated purposes behind the Immigration and Asylum Act 1999 was to reduce the perceived incentive provided by the availability of welfare benefits, which was thought to attract economic migrants, as opposed to asylum seekers, to make applications for asylum in the UK.[1] Section 116 of the 1999 Act was designed to amend Section 21 of the National Assistance Act 1948 in order to prevent local authorities giving assistance to destitute asylum seekers or to anyone who was subject to immigration control.[2] But an asylum seeker who has a need for care and attention because of age, illness, disability or other circumstances, which is not being met, will still be entitled to assistance under the 1948 Act, unless the need arises solely because he or she is destitute or is suffering from physical, or anticipated physical effects, of such destitution.[3] In that case, the local authority will have no power to provide assistance under the Act and he or she will have to rely on NASS to provide accommodation and essential living needs. But in the circumstances referred to in *ex p O, ex p Bhikha*,[4] the duty to provide support and assistance arising under section 21 of the 1948 Act relieves any duty which would otherwise arise under the asylum support provisions, thus imposing the burden on the local authority rather than on NASS.[5]

1 'Basis of a Safety Net Scheme' in White Paper 'Fairer, Faster and Firmer—A Modern Approach to Immigration and Asylum', July 1998, chapter 8, p 39.
2 Immigration and Asylum Act 1999, s 115(9).
3 *R v Wandsworth London Borough Council, ex p O, R v Leicester City Council, ex p Bhikha* [2000] 4 All ER 590, CA.
4 [2000] 4 All ER 590, CA.
5 See also *R (Westminster) v NASS* [2001] EWCA Civ 512.

13.165 Persons who are subject to immigration control and who are not asylum seekers may also be entitled to support under the National Assistance Act 1948 if their need arose for those same reasons and not merely because of an inability to access benefits or to obtain permission to work, or otherwise support themselves.[1] In particular, illegal entrants and overstayers will be entitled to assistance, if they are unfit to return to their country of origin.[2] If they are prevented from returning to their country of origin by factors outside their own control, a duty may also arise.[3]

1 *R v Newham London Borough Council, ex p Plastin* (1997) 30 HLR 261, [1998] 1 CCLR 305; *R v Southwark London Borough Council, ex p Hong Cui* (1998) 31 HLR 639, [1998] 2 CCLR 86.
2 *R v Brent London Borough Council, ex p D* [1998] 1 CCLR 234.
3 *R v Lambeth London Borough Council, ex p Sarhangi* [1998] 2 CCLR 145

13.166 Section 117 of the Immigration and Asylum Act 1999 similarly partially removes the duties placed on local authorities, which arise from section 45 of the Health Services and Public Health Act 1968 (the duty to promote the welfare of the elderly) and paragraph 2 of Schedule 8 to the National Health Service Act 1977 (the duty to make arrangements to prevent illness and to provide care and after-care), when the need arises solely from destitution or the physical effects of such destitution. The extent of the residual duties was not discussed in *R v Wandsworth London Borough Council, ex p O*,[1] but it would be reasonable to assume that the same principles will apply. Paragraph 341 of the Explanatory Notes to the 1999 Act would also suggest that this is the correct interpretation.

1 *R v Wandsworth London Borough Council, ex p O, R v Leicester City Council, ex p Bhikha* [2000] 4 All ER 590.

13.167 Where a person is still entitled to assistance under the National Assistance Act 1948, existing case law relating to it will still be applicable. Therefore, local authorities will have no power to give assistance in cash.[1] Neither do they have the power to provide an individual with food vouchers, if they are not also providing accommodation. However, in that situation, the person could be in need of care and attention because he or she had no food (although there would have to be another reason, or no duty would arise) and the local authority should therefore consider whether it should secure residential accommodation for the person, even if he or she is not yet threatened with eviction.[2] The local authority does not have to provide residential accommodation within an institutional setting and can provide ancillary services, appropriate to the individual's needs, including board, as part of an overall package.[3] Neither is it restricted to providing bed and breakfast accommodation.[4] Health and social services authorities have a duty to provide residential accommodation, free of charge to anyone who has been discharged from detention under section 3 of the Mental Health Act 1983.[5]

1 *R v Secretary of State for Health, ex p Hammersmith and Fulham London Borough Council M and K* [1997] 1 CCLR 495.
2 *R v Newham London Borough Council, ex p Gorenkin (Mikhail)* [1998] 1 CCLR 309.
3 *R v Newham London Borough Council, ex p Medical Foundation for the Care of Victims of Torture* [1997] 1 CCLR 227. For guidance on when the duty is discharged see *R v Royal Borough of Kensington and Chelsea, ex p Kujtim* (1999) 32 HLR 579, CA.
4 *R v Newham London Borough Council, ex p C* (1998) 31 HLR 567
5 Mental Health Act 1983, s 117; *R v Richmond upon Thames London Borough Council, ex p Watson* [2001] QB 370, CA.

CHILDREN ACT 1989

13.168 Local authorities have duties towards children which might involve the provision of accommodation and financial support of children, and sometimes their families. The Children Act 1989 requires local authorities to safeguard and promote the welfare of children within their area who are in need, by providing a range of services appropriate to the child's needs, and to promote the upbringing of such children by their families wherever that is consistent with promoting the child's welfare.[1] Asylum-seeking families with children are supported by NASS or by local authorities under asylum support provisions until they leave the country, but the duties of local authorities under the Children Act 1989 are owed to other families in need who are not claiming asylum but who are excluded from benefits or other welfare provision by virtue of being subject to immigration control. Support and accommodation may be provided under the Children Act 1989 not only to the child but also to the family.[2] In certain circumstances, an authority may offer to fund the return of the family to the country from which they came, where it believes the needs of the child may best be met.[3]

1   Children Act 1989, s 17.
2   *R v Tower Hamlets London Borough, ex p Bradford* [1998] 1 CCLR 294; *R v Lambeth London Borough, ex p K*, CO 5095/98, 14 September 1999; *G's application for judicial review* [2001] EWCA Civ 540, [2001] 2 FCR 193.
3   *R v Hammersmith and Fulham London Borough Council, ex p Damoah* [1999] 2 CCLR 18. But see also *G's application for judicial review* above.

ACCESS TO HOUSING

13.169 A person who is subject to immigration control[1] has the right to own property in the UK and to enter into a private tenancy agreement. As a private sector tenant, he or she has the same rights to security of tenure, access to civil remedies in cases of disrepair or excessive rent rises as any other private tenant and may rely on the Protection from Eviction Act 1977.[2] He or she is also protected from discrimination on the basis of race, when seeking accommodation.[3] However, there is no eligibility for housing benefit[4] except for certain categories of asylum seeker. Those who claimed asylum on arrival before 3 April 2000 whose applications are not yet recorded by the Secretary of State as having been decided or abandoned, are still entitled to housing benefit[5] even if they did not apply for housing benefit on arrival. They are also entitled to housing benefit, if they are entitled to income support or income-based jobseeker's allowance for some other reason.[6] They will not generally be eligible for public sector housing.[7] Access to such housing is obtained by either applying to join a local authority's housing register[8] or by being accepted as homeless and therefore in need of rehousing. Local authorities have a broad discretion when deciding what classes of person may qualify to join their housing register. However, the Secretary of State for the Environment, Transport and the Regions may also issue regulations to limit this discretion.[9] He has exercised this power and defined which categories of persons who are subject to immigration control, may be added to a register.[10] These are:

- refugees and persons with exceptional leave to remain (since they are not excluded from having recourse to public funds);
- persons who have indefinite leave to remain and are habitually resident in the common travel area and who are not sponsored immigrants who have been here for less than five years and whose sponsor is still alive;
- persons over 18, who left Montserrat after 1 November 1995 because of the effect on that territory of a volcanic eruption; and

- nationals of a state which has ratified[11] the European Convention on Social and Medical Assistance or the Council of Europe Social Charter and who are lawfully present and habitually resident here.[12] Prior to 3 April 2000, nationals of states which had signed the Convention and Charter and who were habitually resident here were also entitled to join the housing register, but this right has now been removed, unless they are owed an extant duty under Part III of the Housing Act 1985 (housing the homeless) or Part VII of the Housing Act 1996 (homelessness).

Nationals of EEA states must be excluded from a register unless they are habitually resident in the common travel area and are also workers[13] or persons with the right to reside pursuant to the Immigration (European Economic Area) Regulations 2000 and the relevant council directives.[14]

1 Immigration and Asylum Act 1999, s 118(6).
2 *Akinbolu v Hackney London Borough Council* (1996) 29 HLR 259.
3 Race Relations Act 1976, ss 20-21.
4 Immigration and Asylum Act 1999, s 115(1)(j).
5 Social Security (Immigration and Asylum) Consequential Amendments Regulations 2000, SI 2000/636, regs 12(6), (7)(a), (8).
6 Housing Benefit (General) Regulations, 1987, SI 1987/1971, reg 7A(5)(f).
7 Immigration and Asylum Act 1999, s 118.
8 The Homes Bill before the previous Parliament was intended to abolish the housing register. This Bill is likely to be revised.
9 Housing Act 1996, s 161(3). When the housing register has been abolished (fn 8 above), the mandatory disentitlement of persons from abroad will be continued: Homes Bill.
10 Allocation of Housing (England) Regulations 2000, SI 2000/702, reg 4; Persons Subject to Immigration Control (Housing Authority Accommodation and Homelessness) Order 2000, SI 2000/706.
11 For non-EEA states which have ratified these agreements see **13.11** above.
12 Allocation of Housing (England) Regulations 2000, SI 2000/702, reg 4(e). See also the Allocation of Housing (Wales) Regulations 2000, SI 2000/1080 (W.73). For 'lawfully present' see *Kaya v London Borough of Haringey* [2001] EWCA Civ 677, **13.11** above.
13 Council Regulation (EEC) 1612/68 or 1251/70.
14 Council Directives (EEC) No 68/360 and 73/148.

13.170 Section 118 of the Immigration and Asylum Act 1999, which reenacts section 9(1) of the Asylum and Immigration Act 1996, requires housing authorities to ensure that, so far as is practicable, tenancies and licences are not granted under Part II of the Housing Act 1985 (provision of housing accommodation) to a person who is subject to immigration control. Certain classes within this category are however entitled to tenancies and licences.[1] The regulations consolidate previous provisions made under section 9 of the 1996 Act. However, from 3 April 2000, regulations also permit housing authorities to use hard to let accommodation held under Part II of the Housing Act 1985 for overseas students, as long as they are not granted secure tenancies.[2] Also from 3 April 2000, nationals of states which have signed, but not ratified, the European Convention on Social and Medical Assistance or the Council of Europe Social Charter do not qualify for housing under Part II of the Housing Act l985, and nationals of ratifying states must be lawfully present[3] in order to qualify. Section 118 does not apply to secure tenancies allocated through the housing register under Part VI of the Housing Act l996, but few persons subject to immigration control can qualify for inclusion on the housing register in any event.

1 Persons Subject to Immigration Control (Housing Authority Accommodation and Homelessness) Order 2000, SI 2000/706, para 3.

2 SI 2000/706, para 4(e). See also the Persons Subject to Immigration Control (Housing Authority Accommodation) (Wales) Order 2000, SI 2000/1036 (W67).
3 See **13.11** above.

13.171 From 3 April 2000, asylum seekers became ineligible for housing authority accommodation if they were homeless, even if they were in priority need and not intentionally homeless.[1] They must instead apply to NASS for a decision on whether they are destitute.[2] If they have accommodation but it is in a very poor state of disrepair, it is unlikely to be deemed adequate so as to preclude a finding of destitution.[3] If they are facing eviction from previous accommodation, NASS will only deem them destitute, if the actual eviction is due to take place in 14 days or less.[4] In order to provide accommodation for asylum seekers, NASS enters into contractual arrangements with local authorities, registered social landlords and private landlords and companies. It does not enter into a contract with the asylum seekers themselves. The accommodation provider does not provide them with a tenancy agreement, but enters into an occupation agreement. Asylum seekers provided with accommodation by NASS are, therefore, not secure tenants, unless their landlord expressly notifies them that they have been given a secure tenancy.[5] This is the case even if they are occupying local authority accommodation. Neither can they be assured tenants.[6] In addition, they will not benefit from the Protection against Eviction Act 1977.[7] Once an asylum application has been finally determined, the asylum seeker is expected to leave the accommodation provided by NASS within 14 days. However, if NASS does evict a person from accommodation it has previously provided to him or her, it would be expected to act reasonably in doing so.[8]

1 Immigration and Asylum Act 1999, Sch 16, amending Housing Act 1996, s 183(2); Homelessness (England) Regulations 2000, SI 2000/701, reg 3(f); NASS Policy *Bulletin 10*. See also the Homelessness (Wales) Regulations 2000, SI 2000/1079 (W.72).
2 See above **13.53ff**.
3 *Lismane v Hammersmith and Fulham London Borough Council* (1998) 31 HLR 427; see **13.56** above.
4 Asylum Support Regulations 2000, SI 2000/704, reg 7(a).
5 Housing Act 1985, Sch 1, para 4A; Housing (Scotland) Act 1987, Sch 2, para 5A.
6 Housing Act 1988, Sch 1, para 12A; Housing (Scotland) Act 1988, Sch 4, para 11B.
7 Immigration and Asylum Act 1999, Sch 14, para 73 excludes asylum seekers from security of tenure.
8 See *R v Newham London Borough Council, ex p Ojuri (No 5)* (1998) 31 HLR 631 and *R v Secretary of State for the Environment, ex p Shelter and the Refugee Council*, 23 August 1996, QBD.

13.172 Accommodation provided by NASS should be adequate for the needs of the asylum seeker.[1] Ministerial statements suggest that the adequacy of the accommodation should be judged on the same basis as the suitability of accommodation provided to homeless persons under housing legislation.[2] It is likely that the need to access specialist hospital services, to ensure the safety, welfare and protection of children and to protect public health will be taken into account.[3] Other factors which may be taken into account are the location of members of the same ethnic or religious group, health needs, disability and dietary needs.[4] As asylum seekers do not hold the accommodation which they occupy under a tenancy, they are not protected by any implied repairing obligation if the property is in disrepair.[5] Occupation agreements drawn up by accommodation providers are unlikely to include express repairing obligations.

However, if the accommodation is in such a state of disrepair that it could be said to be prejudicial to the health of asylum seekers or their dependants, they can seek an abatement order in the county court against a local authority, a registered social landlord or a private landlord.[6] If the accommodation is provided by a registered social landlord or a private landlord, they could also request inspection by an environmental health officer and, if appropriate, ask the local authority to serve a statutory notice.[7] If there is a significant risk of violence occurring to the asylum seeker or one of his or her dependants, as a result of racial harassment directed towards them, NASS should provide alternative accommodation.[8]

1   Immigration and Asylum Act 1999, s 96(1)(a).
2   Barbara Roche (Parliamentary Under-Secretary of State), Written Answer, 348 HC Official Report (6th series), col 593, 20 April 2000. See **13.87ff** above.
3   Lord Williams of Mostyn, 605 HL Official Report (5th series), col 1163, 20 October 1999.
4   NASS Application Form, note 11.
5   Under Landlord and Tenant Act 1985, s 11.
6   Environmental Protection Act 1990, s 82.
7   Environmental Protection Act 1990, s 80.
8   NASS Policy *Bulletin 18* 'Dealing with Allegations of Racial Harassment, General Harassment and Domestic Violence', see **13.91** above.

13.173   Those persons who claimed asylum on arrival in the UK before 3 April 2000 and whose applications are not yet recorded as having been decided (other than on appeal) or abandoned, are still eligible for temporary accommodation as homeless persons under Part VII of the Housing Act 1996 if they are homeless, in priority need and not intentionally homeless.[1] They may also apply for housing benefit.[2] If they are homeless but not in priority need,[3] the local authority is not obliged to house them, but has a duty to provide advice and assistance in relation to finding alternative housing.[4] This may involve access to a rent deposit scheme, a hostel placement, a lodger scheme or fast tracking of housing benefit. An asylum seeker whose application is recorded as having been made within three months of a declaration of fundamental upheaval and whose claim is not yet recorded as having been decided (other than on appeal) or abandoned, will also be entitled to accommodation under homelessness legislation[5] and to housing benefit.[6] Such an asylum seeker will be deemed to be in priority need if he or she is vulnerable on grounds of age, illness, pregnancy or disability or has dependent children or a pregnant partner.[7] If a single asylum seeker, who was eligible for housing but for the fact that he or she was not in priority need, is joined by a dependant with such needs on or after 3 April 2000, he or she will become eligible, if they enter as his or her dependants and if his or her application has not yet been recorded as decided.[8]

1   Homelessness (England) Regulations 2000, SI 2000/701, reg 3(f); NASS Policy *Bulletin 10*.
2   Social Security (Immigration and Asylum) Consequential Amendments Regulations 2000, SI 2000/636, reg 12(6), (7)(a).
3   The most usual example of this is a single person in good health, with no dependants.
4   Housing Act 1996, s 192.
5   SI 2000/701, reg 3(g).
6   SI 2000/636, reg 12(6), (7)(b).
7   Housing Act 1996, s 189.
8   SI 2000/701, reg 3(f).

13.174   Amendments to Part VII of the Housing Act 1996 (homelessness) have also been introduced to enable local authorities to disperse asylum seekers to areas outside London and the south-east and for the receiving local authorities to place them in housing authority accommodation.[1] These regulations came into force on 6 December 1999 and will continue in force whilst local authorities need to exercise such powers.[2]

1   The Homelessness (Asylum-Seekers) (Interim Period) (England) Order 1999, SI 1999/3126.
2   See **13.147ff** above.

13.175 Prior to 3 April 2000, nationals of countries which had signed the European Convention on Social and Medical Assistance or the Council of Europe Social Charter, who were in the UK with leave to enter or remain, were entitled to housing under homelessness legislation. Now entitlement depends on whether the country in question has ratified the Charter or the Convention. However, nationals of countries which had signed either the Charter or the Convention and who were owed a duty, which was extant, under either Part III of the Housing Act 1985 or Part VII of the Housing Act 1996, retain their entitlement.[1]

1   Homelessness (England) Regulations 2000, SI 2000/701, reg 3(e).

13.176 Persons who are subject to immigration control, but who qualify for public sector housing under housing legislation, will be allocated long-term accommodation by a local authority or a registered social landlord.[1] Their applications will be considered in accordance with the provisions of Part VI of the Housing Act 1996 or the equivalent parts of the appropriate housing legislation in Wales. Housing is allocated according to housing need and local authorities are required to draw up procedures by which they prioritise the allocation of their available housing stock.[2] If a person who is subject to immigration control, is wrongfully excluded or removed from a housing register, he or she is still entitled to have his or her case reviewed.[3]

1   A housing association, trust or co-operative or limited company, which is registered with the Housing Corporation under Housing Act 1996, Part I.
2   Housing Act 1996, s 167; DoE. DoH Code of Guidance on the Housing Act 1996, Parts VI and VII.
3   Housing Act 1996, s 164; Allocation of Housing and Homelessness (Review Procedures) Regulations 1999, SI 1999/71.

ACCESS TO EDUCATIONAL PROVISION

Secondary education

13.177 Although children may not be admitted to the UK for the purpose of state education,[1] access to state education for children between 5 and 16 is not subject to any restriction in the immigration legislation. Even if an adult's leave to remain is subject to the condition that they do not rely on public funds, they are entitled to send their children to school. Local authorities have a duty to provide school places to any child residing, temporarily or permanently, in their area.[2] Local authorities and governors of maintained schools are also required to admit children to the school of their parents' choice, subject to resource considerations.[3] These duties are not qualified by the immigration status of parents.[4] Children of asylum seekers will also be entitled to free school meals. Unaccompanied minors, who are asylum seekers or refugees, are entitled to free access to state education.[5] Other unaccompanied children, who are in care or accommodated by local authorities, are also entitled to education. In any event, the local authority would be failing in its statutory obligations, if it did not ensure that they received an education.[6]

1 HC 395, para 57; see chapter 9 above.
2 Education Act 1944, s 8(1).
3 Education Act 1996, s 411.
4 Department of Education Circulars 11/88 and 6/93; 'Our Children's Education', the Updated Parents Charter, 1994.
5 Education Act 1944, s 8(1); Convention on the Status of Refugees, art 22.
6 Children Act 1989, s 22.

Student fees

13.178 Colleges are permitted to charge higher fees for students of further and higher education, who do not qualify as 'home students'.[1] To qualify as a home student, the student must be settled in the UK and Islands and must have been ordinarily resident in the UK throughout the three-year period preceding the start of his or her course, and that ordinary residence must not have been wholly or mainly for the purpose of receiving full time education. Local authorities may lawfully impose eligibility criteria for awards to meet a student's maintenance costs and tuition fees, which exclude those subject to immigration control.[2]

1 Education (Fees and Awards) Act 1983, s 1; Education (Fees and Awards) Regulations 1997, SI 1997/1972.
2 Education (Mandatory Awards) Regulations 1997, SI 1997/431, reg 13.

ACCESS TO THE NATIONAL HEALTH SERVICE

13.179 The founding principle of the National Health Service was the provision of treatment which was free at the point of delivery, comprehensive and provided on the basis of need.[1] But inroads were made into the principle of free treatment in the late 1970s, when the Secretary of State was empowered to make regulations imposing charges for non-emergency treatment on people who are not ordinarily resident.[2] Subsequent regulations permitted charges to be made.[3] There is, however, a presumption that health services will be provided free of charge unless charges are expressly prescribed by statute.

1 See now National Health Service Act 1977, s 1(1)(b).
2 National Health Service Act 1977, s 121. For ordinary residence see chapter 5 above.
3 National Health Service (Charges to Overseas Visitors) Regulations 1989, SI 1989/306, as amended by SI 1991/438 and SI 1994/1535.

13.180 Persons entering the UK as visitors for medical treatment are required to pay privately as a condition of entry and further leave to remain.[1] In such cases, the NHS can withhold treatment pending payment in advance for any treatment or an acceptable guarantee of the future payment for any such treatment.[2] Nevertheless, in particularly compassionate circumstances, the Secretary of State will grant exceptional leave to remain even if treatment is being obtained under the NHS.

1   HC 395, paras 51–56; see chapter 9 above.
2   *R v Hammersmith Hospitals NHS Trust, ex p Reffell* (2000) 55 BMLR 130.

Persons not subject to charge

13.181 A person living here for a settled purpose may be accepted as being ordinarily resident and, therefore, be exempt from charges.[1] This includes anyone who has resided in the UK for more than one year, and anyone who is employed or self-employed or is a student on a course which includes work experience of more than 12 weeks in the first year of the course.[2] Others exempt from charges are asylum seekers, refugees and persons detained in prison or immigration detention centres.[3]

1   NHS Executive *Patients Guide to National Health Service.*
2   National Health Service (Charges to Overseas Visitors) Regulations 1989, SI 1989/306, as amended, reg 4.
3   SI 1989/306, reg 4. Asylum seekers and refugees in particular suffer a high rate of medical problems, exacerbated by poverty, poor housing, and loss of status and family support. See Refugee Health Consortium *Promoting the Health of Refugees* (November 1998) published by ILPA. The incidence of mental illness is particularly high. See eg Brent and Harrow HA 'Brent and Harrow Refugee Survey' (1995); Carey Wood and others 'The settlement of refugees in Britain' HO Research Study No 1441 (HMSO, 1995); Health of Londoners Project 'Refugee Health in London—Key issues for public health' HOLP, c/o East London and City HA (1999).

13.182 Nationals of EEA member states who are temporarily working or studying in the UK and in possession of a form E128, are eligible for free medical treatment of all types, as are their families.[1] In contrast, EEA nationals in possession of a form E112 are eligible only for treatment for the particular condition specified on the form. EEA nationals in possession of a form E111 will be entitled to emergency health care[2] (as will those without one, and anyone else requiring emergency treatment).[3] Oxygen therapy and renal dialysis are available free of charge to nationals of EU and EEA member states.[4] Nationals of a number of other states, which have entered into reciprocal arrangements with the UK, are entitled to treatment for needs which arise during their visit to the UK or when they are referred here for treatment.[5] So are nationals of Cyprus and Turkey, who have not entered into a reciprocal agreement, but have ratified the Council of Europe Social Charter.

1   Regulation (EEC) 1408/71; Health Services Circular HSC 1999/018.
2   Regulation (EEC) 1408/71.
3   National Health Service (Charges to Overseas Visitors) Regulations 1989, SI 1989/306, as amended, reg 3.
4   Regulation (EEC) 1408/71, art 21(1)(a).
5   *Patients' Guide to National Health Service Hospital Charges to Overseas Visitors*, May 1999.

13.183 The National Health Service (Charges to Overseas Visitors) Regulations 1989[1] do not apply to general practitioners, who are technically self-employed. GPs may therefore decide to treat overseas visitors free of charge, on an exceptional basis. So may general dental practitioners, who however may not accept a patient on to their list on a temporary basis, in the same way that GPs may.[2] Ophthalmic opticians also have a discretion to provide free treatment, subject to certain eligibility criteria.[3] Persons accepted as eligible for NHS treatment will be entitled to a free eye test and, if eligible under further regulations,[4] will be issued with an optical voucher if required. Asylum seekers on a low income may also qualify for free optical and dental treatment and free prescriptions, even when they are not in receipt of income support, by completing a form HCI, which can be obtained from the NHS, the Benefits Agency or the Health Benefits Division. General practitioners should also offer them permanent registration to ensure that the practice is able to obtain their past medical records and that they are integrated into ongoing health promotions.[5] It is unethical to refuse to register a patient because he or she may require expensive treatment.[6]

1   SI 1989/306, as amended by SI 1991/438 and SI 1994/1535.
2   Health Service Circular HSCV 1999/018, DoH 1 February 1999, para 31.
3   NHS (General Ophthalmic Services) Regulations 1986, SI 1986/975.
4   NHS (Optical Charges and Payment) Regulations 1997, SI 997/818.
5   *The Health of Refugees: A Guide for GPs* (Kings Fund 1999).
6   British Medical Association, *Access to Health Care for Asylum Seekers Following the Implementation of the Asylum and Immigration Act 1996* (January 1997).

Services for which no charge can be made

13.184 Treatment in accident and emergency and casualty departments is free of charge.[1] So is the diagnosis and treatment of certain diseases, including malaria, TB and whooping cough, family planning services, the treatment of sexually transmitted diseases, the diagnosis of Human Immunodeficiency Virus (HIV) and AIDS and any related counselling, and the treatment of those detained under the Mental Health Act 1983 or the Powers of the Criminal Courts Act 1973.[2] It is not clear whether combination therapy for the treatment of HIV positive and AIDS patients can be defined as emergency or preventative treatment. But refusal to treat such a patient with no means to pay for private treatment, could possibly give rise to a breach of Article 3 ECHR by analogy with *D v UK*.[3]

1   But organ transplants are allocated strictly according to immigration status: see NHS Directions on the Allocation of Human Organs for Transplantation, 12 February 1996.
2   National Health Service (Charges to Overseas Visitors) Regulations 1989, SI 1989/306 as amended, reg 3.
3   24 EHHR 423.

Chapter 14

PENAL AND CARRIER SANCTIONS

INTRODUCTION

14.1 Enforcement of immigration control has become the major policy issue preoccupying UK ministers and their EU counterparts. There are a number of overlapping enforcement mechanisms. For example, in a case where leave to enter has been obtained by deception, an immigrant might be summarily removed as an illegal entrant by the immigration service,[1] deported on conducive to the public good grounds by the Secretary of State[2] or prosecuted in the courts by the police,[3] with a possibility of a recommendation for deportation as part of the sentence.[4] We deal with deportation and removal in the following chapters. In this chapter we deal with arrests by police and immigration officers, their ancillary powers, and criminal sanctions aimed at immigrants and asylum seekers and those who assist them. We also deal with the burgeoning civil sanctions designed to prevent the arrival of immigrants and asylum seekers in the UK.

1   Immigration Act 1971, Sch 2, para 9; *Khawaja v Secretary of State for the Home Department* [1984] AC 74, [1983] 1 All ER 765, HL.
2   Immigration Act 1971, s 3(5)(b); *Immigration Appeal Tribunal v Patel* [1988] Imm AR 434, HL.
3   Immigration Act 1971, s 24A (as amended by Immigration and Asylum Act 1999, s 28), 26(1)(c) of the 1971 Act.
4   Immigration Act 1971, s 3(6).

14.2 From the immigrant's point of view, the existence of a parallel set of criminal and administrative sanctions means that there is no knowing which way they are going to be dealt with. Unlike other sections of the population, those subject to immigration control are always in double jeopardy. The fact that they have been arrested by the police and charged with a criminal offence is no guarantee that they will not be summarily removed as an illegal entrant under the administrative powers.[1] The principle of double jeopardy is enshrined in section 28(4) of the Immigration Act 1971, which provides that:

> 'Any powers exercisable under this Act in the case of any person may be exercised notwithstanding that proceedings for an offence under this Part of this Act have been taken against them.'

In practice, the use of the criminal law is rare where immediate removal is a viable option. The use of criminal sanctions against overstayers virtually ceased when rights of appeal against deportation were restricted in 1988.[2] IDI on overstayers who come to notice while embarking indicate that they 'should not be detained for prosecution'.[3] Although recent years have seen an increased emphasis on criminal sanctions, these are directed mainly at preventing the entry of immigrants and asylum seekers to the UK and at deterring employers from employing them.

1   See *Mohammed Anwar* DC No 448/77 (19 January 1978, unreported), where the Divisional Court held that the abandonment of criminal proceedings for illegal entry in favour of administrative removal of a suspected impostor was not an unreasonable exercise of the Secretary of State's discretion.
2   By Immigration Act 1988, s 5.
3   IDI Dec/00, Ch 20 (Evasion of control), para 3.1. However, the IDI are silent on criteria for prosecution of those overstayers and illegal entrants discovered prior to embarkation. The detailed instructions from the Immigration Service Enforcement Directorate (ISED) covering evasion of control, illegal entry, deportation work, offences against the immigration laws and procedures for investigation, remain confidential.

14.3 In addition to the alternative procedures—criminal or administrative—for dealing with an offender against the immigration laws, immigrants also face the possibility of being held in detention under widely different powers. First there are the normal criminal law powers of detention in custody on suspicion of having committed an offence. These carry all the normal safeguards of the criminal law—the need to charge and bring before a court. But then there are the additional powers of detention contained in Schedules 2 and 3 to the Immigration Act 1971 pending a decision on whether the person is to be refused entry, or be removed as an illegal entrant or overstayer, or be made subject to a deportation order. Here there are few of the safeguards normally given to those suspected of a criminal offence. We deal with detention in chapter 17 below.

POLICE AND IMMIGRATION OFFICERS' POWERS

14.4 The police have a number of different functions relating to immigration which can be summarised as:

(i)   investigating criminal offences;
(ii)   performing duties given to them under the Immigration Act 1971 in connection with the administration of immigration control;
(iii)   conducting civil inquiries for the Home Office;
(iv)   intelligence gathering.

We have already referred to their general powers under immigration law in **1.54** above. Here we only deal with their arrest powers under the Immigration Act 1971. The Immigration and Asylum Act 1999 has extended the powers of arrest of immigration officers considerably, and has given them powers of search, entry and seizure in respect of immigration offences equivalent to those of the police.[1] They have the power to use reasonable force if necessary in carrying out any of their functions.[2] The aim of the increase in their powers is to reduce dependency on the police, who in practice have always carried out arrests and removals under the 1971 Act, by enabling immigration officers to perform these functions alone.[3]

1 Immigration and Asylum Act 1999, ss 128–139.
2 Immigration and Asylum Act 1999, s 146(1).
3 Explanatory Note to Immigration and Asylum Act 1999, Pt VII; Mike O'Brien speech to Special Standing Committee, 13 May 1999.

14.5 Broadly, there are three types of arrest power under the Immigration Act 1971, as amended by the Immigration and Asylum Act 1999: (a) without a warrant on reasonable suspicion of certain immigration offences; (b) with a warrant on reasonable suspicion of immigration offences; and (c) administrative arrests for the purpose of detention and removal of persons refused leave to enter, absconders from temporary admission, illegal entrants, overstayers and persons in breach of conditions, and for the purpose of deportation on conducive grounds or following a recommendation.

14.6 A police or immigration officer has a power of arrest without warrant in respect of offences under section 24 of the Immigration Act 1971, such as illegal entry, overstaying and related offences including breach of conditions, or failure to observe restrictions on temporary admission[1] and for facilitating entry contrary to section 25(1) of the Act.[2] Section 25(1) offences are arrestable offences, but in the case of the section 24 ones, although there is a statutory power of arrest, these are not arrestable offences under section 24 of the Police and Criminal Evidence Act 1984 and therefore, arrest is confined to police and immigration officers, but not the general public.[3] The power is exercisable on suspicion of an offence based on reasonable belief.[4] An immigration officer also has a power of arrest for harbouring.[5] Since this is not an arrestable offence, a police officer can only arrest for this offence if it would be impracticable or inappropriate for specified reasons to proceed by way of summons.[6] Immigration officers also have a power of arrest for the offence of obstruction, but only where it would be impracticable to proceed by way of summons.[7] There is no power of arrest for failing to report to a medical officer[8] or for offences (other than obstruction) connected with the administration of the 1971 Act, or by captains of ships or aircraft or operators of trains.[9]

1 Immigration Act 1971, s 28A(1), inserted by Immigration and Asylum Act 1999, s 128.
2 The police power of arrest comes from Police and Criminal Evidence Act 1984, s 24(1)(b), that of immigration officers from Immigration Act 1971, s 28A(3), inserted by Immigration and Asylum Act 1999, s 128.
3 Police and Criminal Evidence Act 1984, s 24(4), (5).
4 'Reasonable grounds for suspicion' require the officer to have formed a genuine suspicion (subjective element), and there must be reasonable grounds for it (objective element): *O'Hara v Chief Constable of RUC* [1997] AC 286, HL. It is curious and disturbing that para A.1.7 of the PACE Code of Practice on Stop and Search, which says that reasonable suspicion can never be based on a person's colour or on stereotyped images of certain persons or groups as more likely to be committing offences, is disapplied to immigration officers by the Immigration (PACE Codes of Practice) Direction 2000.
5 Immigration Act 1971, s 25(2), 28A(4), inserted by Immigration and Asylum Act 1999, s 128.
6 Police and Criminal Evidence Act 1984, s 25. See further *Archbold* (Sweet & Maxwell, 2001) paras 15–172 to 15–175.

7 Immigration Act 1971, s 26(1)(g); s 28A(5) of the 1971 Act, inserted by s 128 of the Immigration and Asylum Act 1999.
8 Immigration Act 1971, s 24(1)(d).
9 Immigration Act 1971, ss 26, 27.

14.7 Police and immigration officers have powers to enter and search without a warrant any premises where they believe on reasonable grounds that a suspect is, in order to make an arrest for an offence of assisting illegal entry or the entry of asylum claimants or assisting remaining by deception under section 25(1) of the Immigration Act 1971.[1] With a warrant issued by a magistrate, they may enter premises to search for and arrest a suspect for illegal entry, overstaying, breach of conditions, failure to report for medical examination, failure to comply with conditions of temporary admission, unlawful disembarkation, entry or remaining by deception, or for harbouring.[2]

1 Police power comes from Police and Criminal Evidence Act 1984, s 17; immigration officer's from Immigration Act 1971, s 28C, inserted by Immigration and Asylum Act 1999, s 130.
2 Immigration Act 1971, s 28B, inserted by Immigration and Asylum Act 1999, s 129. The offences for which the power of entry and search by warrant is available have been expanding inexorably since its introduction by Asylum and Immigration Act 1996, s 7.

14.8 Police and immigration officers also have powers of arrest under Schedules 2 and 3 of the Immigration Act 1971 in support of the administration of the Act. Persons who are required to submit to examination by an immigration officer on arrival in the UK, those who have been refused leave to enter the country, members of the crew of a ship or aircraft who desert ship and overstay their leave or who are reasonably suspected of so doing, illegal entrants who have not been given leave to remain, overstayers liable to removal, persons suspected of belonging to any of these categories and those awaiting deportation may all be detained under the authority of an immigration officer or the Secretary of State for the purpose of examination, a decision on removal or being given removal directions.[1] All these people may be arrested without warrant by an immigration officer or a police officer.[2] If they cannot be found, a magistrate may issue a warrant to the police to enter premises where any of them is reasonably believed to be for the purpose of searching for and arresting that person. Reasonable force may be used in the execution of the warrant.[3] There is also a power to arrest those who have broken or are about to break bail conditions imposed by the appellate authorities,[4] or restrictions imposed by a court on those recommended for deportation.[5]

1 Immigration Act 1971, Sch 2, para 16(1), (IA) and (2), applied to overstayers by Immigration and Asylum Act 1999, s 10(7) (save those falling within the transitional 'regularisation' provisions of s 9), and Sch 3, para 2 for deportees. Note Sch 2, para 16(2) which empowers detention on suspicion; previously, being in one of the categories, eg an illegal entrant, was a condition precedent for detention, and damages could be (and were) awarded for the detention of a person reasonably but incorrectly suspected of being an illegal entrant and detained under Sch 2.
2 Immigration Act 1971, Sch 2, para 17.
3 Immigration Act 1971, Sch 2, para 17(2); strangely, immigration officers appear to have no power to obtain a warrant for a person's arrest under the Schedule.
4 Immigration Act 1971, Sch 2, paras 24(1), 33(1).
5 Immigration Act 1971, Sch 3, para 7.

14.9 The administrative powers under Schedules 2 and 3 to the Immigration Act 1971 are not concerned with the task of catching and prosecuting offenders, but to facilitate examination of new arrivals and the removal of persons without leave to enter (including illegal entrants and overstayers). The extensive powers of examination, and the duty to reply and to furnish information,[1] are confined to new arrivals seeking to enter the country and those leaving or about to leave, but have no application after entry.[2]

1   The powers of examination are conferred by Immigration Act 1971, Sch 2, paras 2, 2A (inserted by Immigration and Asylum Act 1999, Sch 14, para 57) and 3. The duty to furnish information is imposed by para 4.
2   The decision to the contrary in *Baljinder Singh v Hammond* [1987] 1 All ER 829, [1987] 1 WLR 283, QBD is, with respect, *per incuriam* in so far as it interprets Sch 2 to the Immigration Act 1971, since the court did not refer to s 11 of the 1971 Act, which would have enabled them to understand that these special powers of examination under Sch 2 terminate on entry.

Ancillary powers: search and seizure of evidence

14.10 Offences including illegal entry, obtaining entry or stay by deception, overstaying and breach of conditions, facilitating entry and harbouring are now assimilated with 'serious arrestable offences' under the Police and Criminal Evidence Act 1984,[1] so as to enable police to obtain a warrant from a magistrate to enter premises to search for and seize evidence.[2] Immigration officers were included in the power by the Immigration and Asylum Act 1999, which also extended it to include even more minor offences, such as failure to report to a medical officer.[3] Police and immigration officers may also, on arrest of a suspect, search the premises where the suspect was, at or immediately before arrest, for evidence relating to the offence;[4] and, with the prior authorisation of a chief immigration officer (or, if impracticable, the subsequent notification of that officer), an immigration officer may enter and search any premises controlled by a suspect after arrest for an offence of assisting under section 25(1) of the Immigration Act 1971.[5] The suspect may be searched, outside or in the police station, for weapons, escape tools, evidence and documents.[6]

1   'Serious arrestable offences' are defined in Police and Criminal Evidence Act 1984, s 116 and Sch 5.
2   Police and Criminal Evidence Act 1984, s 8, as applied by Immigration and Asylum Act 1999, ss 28D(4) and 25 to offences under Immigration Act 1971, ss 24 and 25. See the 1999 Act, s 169 and Sch 14, para 80(1), (2).
3   Immigration and Asylum Act 1999, s 131, inserting Immigration Act 1971, s 28D.
4   Police have power under Police and Criminal Evidence Act 1984, s 32; immigration officers under Immigration Act 1971, s 28E, inserted by Immigration and Asylum Act 1999, s 132(1). For immigration officers, the power covers all offences under Pt III of the 1971 Act.
5   Immigration Act 1971, s 28F, inserted by Immigration and Asylum Act 1999, s 133. Police have this power in respect of arrestable offences (including s 25 offences) by virtue of Police and Criminal Evidence Act 1984, s 18.
6   Police powers of search of persons derive from Police and Criminal Evidence Act 1984, ss 32, 54, 55; immigration officers are given equivalent powers under Immigration Act 1971, ss 28G and 28H, inserted by Immigration and Asylum Act 1999, ss 134(1) and 135(1). Immigration officers have no powers to conduct intimate body searches.

14.11 Similar powers exist on arrest or detention under the administrative provisions of Schedule 2 to the Immigration Act 1971, to search the arrested person,[1] or (with the authority of a chief immigration officer) premises controlled or occupied by the arrested person, for (*inter alia*) documents which might establish the person's identity, nationality, citizenship, his or her country of embarkation and of destination.[2] Additionally, but only for the purpose of examining new arrivals, immigration officers have the power to search a newly arrived ship or aircraft or anything on board it, or any vehicle taken off it, to find passengers.[3] They may search passengers and their luggage, their vehicle, and the ship, vehicle or aircraft on or in which they arrived, to check whether they have or have had documents (such as passports, which many asylum seekers destroy or hide to prevent return).[4] Immigration officers also have extensive powers of examination and search under the Terrorism Act 2000.[5]

1 Immigration Act 1971, Sch 2, paras 25B and 25C, inserted by Immigration and Asylum Act 1999, ss 134(2) and 135(2). Immigration officers have no power to conduct an intimate body search.
2 Immigration Act 1971, Sch 2, para 25A, inserted by Immigration and Asylum Act 1999, s 132(2).
3 Immigration Act 1971, Sch 2, para 1(5).
4 Immigration Act 1971, Sch 2, para 4(3).
5 See **6.32** above.

14.12 There are in addition powers to detain vehicles, including small ships and aircraft, in which illegal entrants, clandestine entrants and asylum claimants have arrived, either pending a criminal prosecution, or pending the payment of a civil penalty. In criminal cases the vehicle may be forfeited on conviction, and in civil cases it may be sold if the penalty remains unpaid.[1]

1 See **14.31** and **14.72** below.

Search powers under asylum support provisions

14.13 To enforce the draconian provisions on compulsory dispersal of asylum seekers and their dependants, the Immigration and Asylum Act 1999 contains powers of search of premises in which accommodation has been provided by 'a person authorised by the Secretary of State' (who could be a private hotel-owner) on a warrant, where there is reason to believe that the supported person or his or her dependants for whom the accommodation is provided are not living there, or the accommodation is being used for any other purpose, or any unauthorised person is living there.[1] This would presumably include putting up another family member or friend, running a small business (for example, as a mechanic or seamstress) from the room, as well as unauthorised sub-letting.

1 Immigration and Asylum Act 1999, s 125. See further **13.100** above.

Fingerprinting

14.14 Police (but not immigration officers) have powers to take fingerprints from those charged with criminal offences.[1] Police, immigration officers and anyone else so authorised may take fingerprints, photographs or other identification measures in respect of anyone detained under the administrative provisions of Schedule 2 to the Immigration Act 1971.[2] Immigration officers were given powers to fingerprint asylum seekers and their dependants (defined as spouse and children under 18) by the Asylum and Immigration Appeals Act 1993, with powers of arrest without warrant for those who failed to comply with a notice requiring their attendance for the purpose.³ These powers are extended to other classes of persons by the Immigration and Asylum Act 1999:

(i)   those failing on request by the immigration officer to produce a passport or other satisfactory evidence of identity;

(ii)   those refused leave to enter, who have been granted temporary admission, who the immigration officer reasonably suspects will breach conditions of residence or reporting;

(iii)   those in respect of whom there are directions for their removal as illegal entrants or overstayers, or after a deportation order;

(iv)   those arrested under paragraph 17 of Schedule 2 (persons liable to be detained under paragraph 16);

(v)   asylum claimants;

(vi)   dependants of any of the above.⁴

The Secretary of State may require any of the above persons by written notice to attend for fingerprinting at a specified place, on seven days' notice, and police and immigration officers have the power of arrest for a failure to comply. Fingerprints may then be forcibly taken.⁵ There are detailed provisions for the destruction of fingerprints within specified periods.⁶ The Secretary of State retains the power to make regulations allowing immigration officers to collect data on external physical characteristics in any other way.⁷

1   Police and Criminal Evidence Act 1984, ss 27, 61. They may be taken without consent at a police station in order to confirm or disprove involvement in an offence, on charge or after conviction of a recordable offence.
2   Immigration Act 1971, Sch 2, para 18(2); *R v Secretary of State for the Home Department, ex p Irawo-Osan* [1992] Imm AR 337.
3   Asylum and Immigration Appeals Act 1993, s 3.
4   Immigration and Asylum Act 1999, s 141, in force 11 December 2000, SI 2000/3099.
5   Immigration and Asylum Act 1999, s 142.
6   Immigration and Asylum Act 1999, s 143.
7   Immigration and Asylum Act 1999, s 144.

14.15   The purpose of the broad fingerprinting powers in relation to asylum seekers is to detect those who have made a claim before, in another identity, or in another EU member state. Under the proposed EU Eurodac regulation (formerly a draft Convention, now part of EC law under the provisions of the Treaty of Amsterdam),¹ the fingerprints of all asylum seekers over 14 will be sent to a central unit, set up by the European Commission, for matching.² The draft extends this centralised matching of fingerprints to certain other third country nationals who are apprehended crossing borders irregularly³ or are found 'illegally present' in any member state,⁴ paving the way for concerted expulsion measures.⁵

1   See European Commission: *Amended Proposal for a Council Regulation concerning the establishment of "Eurodac" for the comparison of fingerprints of applicants for asylum and certain other third-country nationals to facilitate the implementation of the Dublin Convention* COM(2000) 100 final, Brussels, 15 March 2000.
2   COM (2000) 100 final, art 4.
3   COM (2000) 100 final, art 8.
4   COM (2000) 100 final, art 11.
5   See eg the Initiative of the Republic of Finland with a view to the adoption of a Council Regulation determining obligations as between the member states for the readmission of third-country nationals 12488/99, Brussels, 22 November 1999, which proposes the application of Dublin Convention principles of responsibility to expulsion of illegal entrants in the EU territory.

Codes of Practice

14.16 The Codes of Practice issued under the Police and Criminal Evidence Act 1984 have always applied to persons who are not police officers who are investigating offences,[1] and have been held to apply to immigration officers exercising administrative powers in relation to illegal entrants and overstayers, at least if a criminal offence was potentially involved.[2] Now, in the exercise of powers of arrest, questioning, search, fingerprinting, entry and seizure—whether investigating criminal offences or in the course of their Immigration Act 1971, Schedule 2 functions—immigration officers are statutorily obliged to have regard to certain specified (but not all) provisions of the Codes of Practice.[3] Thus, when arresting a suspect without a warrant for an offence of illegal entry, overstaying, deception, breach of conditions, assisting entry or obstruction, immigration officers must have regard to all the provisions of Codes C, D and E.[4] When conducting interviews, they should not refuse access to solicitors, and questioning should be under caution and contemporaneously recorded.[5] But when arresting without warrant under the administrative provisions of the Schedule, none of the provisions of Code C relating to the conduct of interviews apply, according to the Codes of Practice Direction.[6] Where there is a Code breach, this does not necessarily mean that the immigration officer or Secretary of State cannot subsequently rely on what is said at an interview.[7] If it is not voluntary, has been obtained by force, inducement or oppression, or a statement has been made at a time of stress, it may be ruled out.[8] But if there is simply a failure to inform the applicant that his or her solicitor is available, all the court or Secretary of State need do is to be very careful to test the reliability of the answers.[9]

1 Police and Criminal Evidence Act 1984, s 67(9).
2 *R v Secretary of State for the Home Department, ex p Ibrahim* [1993] Imm AR 124, QBD.
3 Immigration and Asylum Act 1999, s 145, Immigration (PACE Codes of Practice) Direction 2000.
4 The Detention, Treatment and Questioning of Persons by Police Officers; The Identification of Persons by Police Officers; Tape Recording of Interviews with Suspects.
5 See PACE Code C as applied by the Immigration (PACE Codes of Practice) Direction 2000, paras 6, 10, 11, and 12. Illegal entry interviews where no caution was administered were held inadmissible in the Scottish cases of *Oghonoghor v Secretary of State for the Home Department* 1995 SLT 733, OHCS and *Sofia Kim v Secretary of State for the Home Department* 2000 SLT 249, OH.
6 Immigration (PACE Codes of Practice) Direction 2000, Sch 1. In practice, immigration officers are likely to adhere to the relevant Code, as (broadly speaking) they have done in the past.
7 But see *Oghonoghor v Secretary of State for the Home Department, Sofia Kim v Secretary of State for the Home Department*, fn 5 above.
8 Evidence of a police interview was excluded by an adjudicator in a deportation appeal (breach of conditions) in *Oyefuwa* (18035).
9 *Ibrahim*, above at 129. In addition it should be recalled that Police and Criminal Evidence Act 1984, ss 76 and 78 (exclusion of evidence obtained unfairly or by oppression) do not apply to civil proceedings.

14.17 To conform with the ECHR, powers of entry and search of premises, seizure of documents and search of the person, and similarly intrusive measures, all of which constitute interference with privacy under Article 8 of the ECHR, must be not only in accordance with the law but also must have a legitimate aim and be proportionate to the aim pursued.[1] If they are not (an extreme example might be a midnight, intrusive search causing damage looking for someone who has failed to report to a medical officer) damages would be recoverable.[2] Breaches of Article 8 would also be relevant to admissibility of evidence in criminal proceedings.

1   *Chappell v UK* (1989) 12 EHRR 1; *Niemietz v Germany* (1992) 16 EHRR 97. See **8.65** above.
2   Human Rights Act 1998, s 8.

14.18 Complaints about immigration officers' exercise of their new powers of arrest, search and seizure under Part VII of the Immigration and Asylum Act 1999 will be referred to the Immigration Service Complaints Unit for consideration of whether an investigation is required; investigations will be supervised by a Complaints Audit Committee.

CRIMINAL OFFENCES

Illegal entry and deception

14.19 The criminal offence of illegal entry is defined in section 24(1)(a) of the Immigration Act 1971. The offence cannot be committed by a British citizen.[1] It occurs if contrary to the Act a person knowingly enters the UK without the leave of an immigration officer or in breach of a deportation order. It requires actual entry, and can only be committed on the day of entry.[2] It is a purely summary offence punishable with a fine on level 5 or imprisonment up to six months.[3] The extended time limit for prosecution applies.[4] Suspected offenders can be arrested without warrant.[5] Normally the burden of proving an illegal entry is on the prosecution, but an exception is made in cases brought within six months of the date of entry, where the defendant must prove that he or she had leave to enter.[6] Proof in such cases will be on the balance of probabilities, in accordance with the normal rule of criminal law where the burden of proof is reversed.[7]

1   Immigration Act 1971, s 24(1), as amended by British Nationality Act 1981, Sch 4, para 2(a).
2   *Grant v Borg* [1982] 2 All ER 257, [1982] 1 WLR 638, HL.
3   Immigration Act 1971, s 24(1), as amended by Criminal Justice Act 1982, ss 38 and 46, and by Asylum and Immigration Act 1996, s 6(a). A level 5 fine is presently £5,000: Criminal Justice Act 1982, s 37 as amended by Criminal Justice Act 1991, s 17.
4   Immigration Act 1971, ss 24(3), 28(1).
5   Immigration Act 1971, s 28A, added by Immigration and Asylum Act 1999, s 128.
6   Immigration Act 1971, s 24(4)(b). It is questionable whether this reversal of the legal (as opposed to the evidential) burden of proof can long survive the coming into force of the Human Rights Act 1998, because of the presumption of innocence in art 6(2) of the ECHR: see *R v DPP, ex p Kebilene* [2000] 2 AC 326, HL.
7   *R v Carr-Briant* [1943] KB 607, [1943] 2 All ER 156.

14.20 The offence of using deception to enter or remain was added in 1996 and expanded in scope in 1999. It is set out in section 24A of the Immigration Act 1971. Again, it cannot be committed by a British citizen.[1] It occurs if, by means which include deception by him or her, a person:

(a)   obtains or seeks to obtain leave to enter or remain in the United Kingdom;[2] or

(b)   secures or seeks to secure the avoidance, postponement or revocation of enforcement action against him.[3]

The wording of the offence makes clear that the deception must be by the immigrant him- or herself. It must be material, ie instrumental in obtaining leave to enter, remain, etc,[4] although it does not have to be the sole effective means of obtaining entry, stay, etc. Deception can be carried out by conduct or conduct accompanied by silence as to a material fact, such as the silent presentation of a false passport.[5] 'Enforcement action' is defined to include removal directions, the making of a deportation order or removal in consequence of either. The offence is considerably broader in certain respects than the offence of illegal entry. It can be committed by seeking to enter, as well as by actually doing so. It extends to embrace action taken to remain in the UK, and to prevent or defer removal, as well as action taken to enter.[6] It would thus cover a false asylum claim, adduced to obtain leave to remain or to avoid removal, but clearly there is all the difference in the world between a rejected claim and a false one, and stringent proof of fabrication would be required. The offence of deception is triable either way, with penalties of a fine up to the statutory maximum and/or up to six months' imprisonment on summary conviction, or a fine and/or two years' imprisonment on indictment.[7] The extended time limit for prosecutions applies to offences under the section.[8]

1 Immigration Act 1971, s 24A(1), inserted by Immigration and Asylum Act 1999, s 28.
2 This sub-s was previously enacted as Immigration Act 1971, s 24(1)(aa), added by Asylum and Immigration Act 1996, s 4.
3 This sub-s was added by the Immigration and Asylum Act 1999.
4 See discussion in the House of Lords during passage of the Asylum and Immigration Act 1996, which created the offence: 571 HL Official Report (5th series) col 1633, 1996.
5 *Choudhry v Metropolitan Police Comr* (24 November 1984, unreported), QBD; *R v Secretary of State for the Home Department, ex p Patel* [1986] Imm AR 515, CA (cases relating to false representations under Immigration Act 1971, s 26(1)(c)). See **16.20** below.
6 Immigration Act 1971, s 24A(2).
7 Immigration Act 1971, s 24A(3). When the offence was created in 1996 it was summary only.
8 Immigration Act 1971, s 24A(4).

14.21 It is important to distinguish the offences of illegal entry and entry by deception from the status of an illegal entrant. The status of illegal entrant requires no intention, or even knowledge, of a breach of immigration law, and includes those who enter without realising that they require and have no leave to enter or are subject to a deportation order.[1] The criminal offence, on the other hand, is only committed if done knowingly. Illegal entrants also include those who have obtained leave by another person's deception,[2] but entry by means of another person's deception cannot ground a criminal prosecution. Thus, persons who do not realise that they have no leave, and those who were brought in (usually as children) by the deception of another person (usually a relative), or those wrongly believed to be British citizens and so not granted leave to enter, can be removed summarily as illegal entrants, even though they cannot be prosecuted.[3]

1 See *R v Governor of Ashford Remand Centre, ex p Bouzagou* [1983] Imm AR 69, CA; *R v Secretary of State for the Home Department, ex p Yeboah* [1986] Imm AR 52 at 59, QBD. See **16.9**ff below.
2 Immigration Act 1971, s 33 as amended by Asylum and Immigration Act 1996, Sch 2, para 4); *Khawaja v Secretary of State for the Home Department* [1984] AC 74, [1983] 1 All ER 765, HL.
3 *Ex p Bouzagou* above; *R v Secretary of State for the Home Department, ex p Khaled* [1987] Imm AR 67, QBD; *Mokuolo v Secretary of State for the Home Department* [1989] Imm AR 51, CA.

14.22 The use of criminal sanctions against those entering the UK illegally has given rise to issues relating to the UK's obligations under EC law and under international law relating to refugees.

EC nationals

14.23 The ECJ has ruled that illegal entry or a failure to report their presence to the authorities does not affect an EC national's right of residence under Community law. However, these rights do not prevent any member state from prosecuting such persons, provided that the penalty imposed is not so disproportionate to the gravity of the infringement that it becomes an obstacle to the free movement of persons.[1] EU nationals exercising community rights do not require leave to enter,[2] and will very rarely be illegal entrants, although an EU national entering the UK after an exclusion order was made against him, which had not been set aside, was held to have been properly characterised as an illegal entrant in the *Shingara* case.[3]

1 Case 118/75 *Watson and Belmann* [1976] ECR 1185, ECJ (failure to report); Case 48/75 *Royer* [1976] ECR 497, ECJ (clandestine entry). Case C-157/79 *R v Pieck* [1981] QB 571, ECJ.
2 By virtue of Immigration Act 1988 s 7.
3 *R v Secretary of State for the Home Department, ex p Mann Singh Shingara* [1999] Imm AR 257, CA.

Refugees

14.24 The criminal sanctions laid down in the Immigration Act 1971 made no allowance for refugees who entered the UK illegally. But the combined effect of visa requirements and carrier sanctions has forced refugees to adopt illegal methods of finding safety, and in response to the growing numbers of asylum seekers and intending asylum seekers found using false documents, either on entry or in transit via the UK to Canada and the US, criminal prosecutions under the Forgery and Counterfeiting Act 1981 and under section 24A and 26(1)(d) of the 1971 Act (falsification of documents)[1] became frequent, with custodial sentences of up to nine months being imposed (and upheld by the Court of Appeal).[2] In *Ex p Adimi*[3] the Divisional Court denounced this practice as contrary to Article 31(1) of the Refugee Convention. This provides that contracting states should not impose penalties on refugees who enter their territory illegally, provided they present themselves without delay to the authorities. The court recognised that 'the combined effect of visa regimes and carriers' liability has made it well-nigh impossible for refugees to travel to countries of refuge without false documents'.[4] The broad purpose sought to be achieved by Article 31(1), it held, was 'to provide immunity for genuine refugees whose quest for asylum reasonably involved them in breaching the law', so that 'where the illegal entry or use of false documents or delay can be attributed to a *bona fide* desire to seek asylum whether here or elsewhere, that conduct should be covered by Article 31'.[5] The protection of Article 31(1) applies not only to those ultimately recognised as refugees, but to those claiming asylum in good faith, and to those using false documents as well as clandestine entrants.[6] Since some element of choice is open to refugees as to where they may properly claim asylum, the phrase 'coming directly' should be interpreted in such a way that any merely short-term stopover en route to the intended sanctuary cannot forfeit the protection of the Article. The main touchstones by which exclusion from protection should be judged are the length of stay in the intermediate country, the reasons for delaying there (even a substantial delay in an unsafe third country would be reasonable were the time spent trying to acquire the means of travelling on), and whether or not the refugee sought or found there protection *de jure* or *de facto* from the persecution they were fleeing.[7] The requirement in the Article to 'present themselves without delay' was not necessarily breached by a failure to claim asylum on arrival.[8] Simon Brown LJ expressed the hope that prosecutions would be conducted only 'where the offence itself appears manifestly unrelated to a genuine quest for asylum'.[9] The court was divided on the issue of responsibility for ensuring compliance with Article 31; Newman J held that the Secretary of State for the Home Department should determine entitlement to the protection of Article 31(1) since it was analogous to a pardon, which was an executive act;[10] Simon Brown LJ did not feel able to impose such an obligation on the executive and believed that the magistrates' abuse of process jurisdiction could be invoked.[11]

1 See **14.48** and **14.52ff** below.
2 A sentence of eight months was held appropriate in *Daljit Singh* [1999] 1 Cr App Rep (S) 490, a 'guideline case' involving a guilty plea to using a false instrument in respect of an attempt to travel to Canada using a false passport. The court said that cases involving the use of false passports will almost always merit a significant period of custody (six to nine months).
3 *R v Uxbridge Magistrates' Court, ex p Adimi; R v Crown Prosecution Service, Secretary of State for the Home Department, ex p Sorani; R v Secretary of State for the Home Department, ex p Kaziu* [1999] INLR 490.
4 [1999] INLR 490 at 492G, per Simon Brown LJ.
5 [1999] INLR 490 at 496D–E.
6 [1999] INLR 490 at 496F.
7 [1999] INLR 490 at 497A–C.
8 [1999] INLR 490 at 498E.
9 [1999] INLR 490 at 504C.
10 [1999] INLR 490 at 513F.
11 [1999] INLR 490 at 503C.

14.25 After the judgment in *Adimi* a statutory defence was enacted to charges of deception under section 24A of the Immigration Act 1971 or falsification of documents under section 26(1)(d) of the Act, and to charges under the Forgery and Counterfeiting Act 1981 (forgery, use and possession of false instruments) by the Immigration and Asylum Act 1999, section 31. The statutory defence is significantly narrower in its scope than the protection afforded by Article 31(1) of the Refugee Convention according to *Adimi*. It applies only to those ultimately recognised as refugees;[1] requires refugees to have made a claim for asylum as soon as was reasonably practicable after arrival in the UK (in addition to presenting themselves to the authorities without delay);[2] and excludes the defence where refugees have stopped en route to the UK in another country, unless they could not reasonably have expected to be given protection in that country.[3] It provides that those wrongly convicted before the commencement of the section may apply to the Criminal Cases Review Commission for their cases to be referred to the Court of Appeal.[4] In practice section 31 of the 1999 Act removes much of the protection which the court held was provided by Article 31(1) of the Refugee Convention, and is potentially challengeable as giving rise to unlawful deprivation of liberty contrary to Article 5 of the ECHR.[5]

1 Immigration and Asylum Act 1999, s 31(1), (6). A refused asylum seeker can seek to avail himself of the defence, but the burden of proof is on him or her to show that he or she is in fact a refugee: s 31(7).
2 Immigration and Asylum Act 1999, s 31(1)(a) and (c).
3 Immigration and Asylum Act 1999, s 31(2).
4 Immigration and Asylum Act 1999, s 31(8). In fact most convictions were in the magistrates' court, and could be reopened under Magistrates' Courts Act 1980, s 142(2), to enable the Crown to offer no evidence.
5 By way of proceedings in the Divisional Court for a declaration of incompatibility under Human Rights Act 1998, s 4.

14.26 A joint Memorandum of Good Practice compiled by representatives of the police, the Home Office, the Crown Prosecution Service and the Law Society indicates that immigration officers, police and prosecutors should apply both Article 31(1) of the Refugee Convention and the statutory defence in deciding whether to investigate, initiate or continue a prosecution.[1] The Memorandum sets out procedures for liaison between immigration officers, the police and crown prosecutors. The police are to notify an immigration officer in any case where a suspect for an offence relating to false travel documents might raise Article 31(1) of the Refugee Convention or section 31 of the Immigration and Asylum Act 1999, for example, by claiming asylum, indicating that he or she has previously claimed asylum, or by saying anything which suggests a possible claim to refugee status. The immigration officer is to provide details of the suspect's immigration history and an opinion as to whether the suspect might be a refugee and whether Article 31(1) or section 31 might apply. Only in the clearest of cases (for example, where the suspect is a British citizen or says nothing to suggest any fear of persecution) should police proceed to charge.[2] If Article 31(1) or section 31 clearly applies, the police should take no further action. Where the immigration officer believes that Article 31(1) or the statutory defence might apply he or she must notify the police and the suspect should be given police bail pending resolution of the asylum claim. If asylum is granted, police should take no further action.[3] If asylum is refused, the Immigration and Nationality Directorate (IND) should be asked whether nevertheless Article 31(1) or section 31 applies. The guidance for Crown prosecutors in the Memorandum indicates that the prosecutor must consider carefully whether prosecution is in the public interest in cases where the defendant is a refugee but the IND does not accept that Article 31(1) or section 31 applies, and where asylum is refused but the defendant has been granted exceptional leave to remain or faces removal to a safe third country, or where the asylum claim would have been accepted but for post-arrival changes in the country of persecution.[4] The accompanying Protocol for liaison indicates that 'where the Immigration Service is of the view that the defendant is a genuine asylum seeker, it is highly unlikely to be in the public interest to proceed to a criminal prosecution. This can apply even where the defendant may have failed to comply with the conditions of "coming directly" or presenting himself to the authorities "without delay" as interpreted by the High Court in *Adimi*'.[5] Meanwhile, asylum seekers who were wrongly convicted and imprisoned have received compensation averaging £40,000.

1 *The prosecution of persons who may have a claim to refugee status, for offences involving the obtaining, use or possession of false travel documents: A memorandum of good practice for liaison between the Association of Chief Police Officers, the Immigration and Nationality Directorate, the Crown Prosecution Service and the Law Society*, Third Draft, 8.3.2000.
2 Memorandum above, para 3.11.

3   Memorandum above, para 3.14.
4   Memorandum above, paras 6.9–6.10.
5   *Protocol for Liaison between the Association of Chief Police Officers, the Immigration Service, the Crown Prosecution Service, the Law Society Immigration Sub-Committee and UNHCR*, para 4.4.

Offences of assisting entry and deception, and harbouring

14.27 Section 25(1) of the Immigration Act 1971 covers the smuggling of immigrants into the UK, bringing asylum seekers to the country for gain, and helping people enter, remain or avoid removal by deception. These are the most serious offences in the Act. On summary trial they carry a fine up to the statutory maximum[1] and imprisonment of up to six months, but it is rare for magistrates to accept jurisdiction, and on indictment a prison sentence of up to ten years can be given.[2] They are arrestable offences within the meaning of the Police and Criminal Evidence Act 1984, section 24(1)(b).[3]

1   The statutory maximum is presently £5,000: Magistrates' Courts Act 1980, s 32(9); Criminal Justice Act 1991, s 17.
2   Immigration Act 1971, s 25(1), as amended by Immigration and Asylum Act 1999, s 29(2). The 1999 Act increased the maximum sentence from seven years, and there is no provision restricting the application of the increased penalty to offences committed after the date of commencement, 14 February 2000. A sentence which is based on the new statutory maximum for an offence committed before then would offend against ECHR, art 7.
3   See **14.6** above.

14.28 Section 25(1)(a) of the Immigration Act 1971 makes it an offence knowingly to be concerned in making or carrying out arrangements for securing or facilitating the entry into the UK of anyone known or reasonably believed to be an illegal entrant. Acts to facilitate entry into the UK can be committed even though the illegal entrants have already passed through that part of the port of entry which is under the control of the immigration authorities.[1] The offence is only made out if the persons assisted are in fact illegal entrants,[2] and the accused knew or had reasonable cause for believing that this was so. The prosecution may have difficulty in proving this. Production of Home Office records on their own may not be enough. It will almost always be necessary in such cases to call a Home Office official to give an explanation of their significance.[3] In *R v Naillie*[4] it was held that in a section 25(1)(a) prosecution it was necessary to determine whether the persons whose entry was assisted were illegal entrants; a distinction was to be drawn between arrival and entry, and mere disembarkation without a passport was not enough to make the asylum seekers illegal entrants; that they did not seek to enter the UK in breach of the laws until they presented a false passport to an immigration officer or tried to pass out of the immigration control area without submitting to examination at all; that by requesting asylum without any attempt to deceive, they did not seek to enter in breach, and were not illegal entrants. But the offence is committed if the intending immigrants are discovered before entry in circumstances indicating their intention to enter illegally.[5] There is scope for the defence of necessity, which has been used on occasion at first instance when those smuggled in were refugees and smuggling was the only way to secure their safety from a threat of death or serious injury,[6] and an argument based on abuse of process succeeded where a charge under section 25(1)(b) of the 1971 Act was brought but dropped in favour of section 25(1)(a) when the Crown realised it could not prove gain.[7]

1 *R v Singh* [1973] 1 All ER 122, [1972] 1 WLR 1600, CA.
2 *R v Naillie* [1993] AC 674, HL.
3 *R v Patel* [1981] 3 All ER 94, CA; see *Myers v DPP* [1965] AC 1001, [1964] 2 All ER 881.
4 See fn 2 above.
5 *R v Adams* [1996] Crim LR 593; *R v Eyck, R v Hadakoglu* [2000] INLR 277, CA.
6 See *R v Martin* [1989] 88 Cr App Rep 343, CA at 345–346, per Simon Brown J; *R v Pommell* [1995] 2 Cr App Rep 601, CA; *R v Abdul-Hussain* [1999] Crim LR 570; *R v Cairns* [1999] 2 Cr App Rep 137, CA.
7 *R v KS*, Middlesex Guildhall, 3 October 1999, HHJ Blacksall. See (2000) Legal Action February p 21.

14.29 Section 25(1)(b) of the Immigration Act 1971, added in 1996,[1] created the offence of facilitating the entry of asylum claimants. No element of smuggling is required to make out the offence; the asylum seekers do not need to be illegal entrants. The offence is aimed at those who, for gain, bring asylum seekers to the UK to enable them to claim asylum; it was intended to plug the gap disclosed by *R v Naillie*.[2] Since the right to seek and enjoy asylum is declared a fundamental human right by Article 14 of the UDHR, the criminalisation of those who assist asylum seekers to enter the UK lawfully was a controversial move and the government was at pains to stress that it was aimed at 'illegal racketeering activity' of 'those who make profit by facilitating the entry of asylum seekers'.[3] The definition of the offence is being knowingly concerned in making or carrying out arrangements for securing or facilitating the entry into the UK of anyone known or reasonably believed to be an asylum claimant. An 'asylum claimant' is given an extended meaning by section 25(1D) of the 1971 Act,[4] and is a person who intends to make a claim that it would be contrary to the UK's obligations under the Refugee Convention or the ECHR for him or her to be removed from or required to leave the UK. It does not apply to acts done otherwise than for gain,[5] or in the course of employment by a *bona fide* organisation, if the purposes of that organisation include assistance to persons in the position of the asylum claimant.[6] Nor does it apply to acts done in relation to asylum claimants who have been detained or granted temporary admission;[7] this proviso prevents the criminalisation of lawyers advising and assisting with asylum claims, who would otherwise be caught because such advice and assistance would facilitate the grant of leave to enter.[8] It does not cover advice given abroad on the criteria and procedures for claiming asylum in the UK, which would be 'too remote from the immigration control in the UK to fall within the scope of the ... offence'.[9]

1 By Asylum and Immigration Act 1996, s 5(1).
2 **14.28** fn 2 above.
3 See HL Official Report (5th series) cols 570–574, 20 June 1996.
4 Inserted by Immigration and Asylum Act 1999, s 29(3).
5 Immigration Act 1971, s 25(1B), as amended. Despite the wording of this provision, it is clear that gain is an essential ingredient of the offence and the burden of proof remains on the Crown to prove gain. See *R v Hunt* [1987] AC 352; *R v Duibi* (Harrow Crown Court, 30 March 1999, (2000) Legal Action February, p 21.
6 Immigration Act 1971, s 25(1C), as amended.
7 Immigration Act 1971, s 25(1A), as amended by Immigration and Asylum Act 1999, s 29(3).
8 See the distinction between 'arrival' and 'entry' in Immigration Act 1971, s 11 relied on in *R v Naillie* (**14.28** fn 2 above).
9 Letter from Immigration and Nationality Directorate to ILPA, 2 August 1996.

14.30 Since a large part of the arrangements for illegal immigration and for bringing asylum claimants will be made outside the UK, it is provided that acts committed abroad are triable in the UK, if committed by British citizens, British Dependent Territories citizens, British Overseas citizens, British Protected Persons, and all other classes of British subject, other than citizens of independent Commonwealth countries.[1] The extended time limit for prosecution applies.[2]

1   Immigration Act 1971, s 25(5), as amended by British Nationality Act 1981, Sch 4, para 6, and Immigration and Asylum Act 1999, s 29(4).
2   Immigration Act 1971, ss 25(4) and 28.

14.31 The courts have, regrettably, been unwilling to apply the principle behind Article 31(1) of the Refugee Convention to allow those who smuggle in refugees for purely humanitarian reasons to escape penalty. But in sentencing for the offence of facilitating illegal entry, the courts must have regard to whether, in particular, the motivation was commercial or humanitarian, as well as to whether the offence was an isolated act or repeated, the degree of organisaton and the defendant's role. However, the Court of Appeal has deemed an immediate custodial sentence appropriate for all but the most minor offences.[1] Reported sentences range from six months for smuggling a husband[2] to five years for a central role in a conspiracy involving the recruitment of couriers, the arrangement of transport and the acquisition of ferry tickets and passports.[3] In addition to the penalties of fines and imprisonment, the Crown Court has very wide powers to order the forfeiture of any ship, aircraft or other vehicle used to bring illegal immigrants into the UK,[4] which can be detained under the authority of a police or senior immigration officer pending prosecution, conviction and forfeiture.[5]

1   *R v Le and Stark* [1999] 1 Cr App Rep (S) 422. A suspended sentence of 18 months was imposed in *R v Belliki* [1998] 1 Cr App Rep (S) 135 (driving through immigration control with an illegal entrant concealed in van), because of exceptionally difficult domestic circumstances.
2   *R v Ozdemir* [1996] 2 Cr App Rep (S) 64.
3   *R v Ali (Ashik)* [1996] CLY 1935.
4   Immigration Act 1971, s 25(6)–(8), amended by Immigration and Asylum Act 1999, s 38(1).
5   Immigration Act 1971, s 25A, inserted by Immigration and Asylum Act 1999, s 38(2).

14.32 The offence under section 25(1)(c) of the Immigration Act 1971 of facilitating deception is defined as being knowingly concerned in making or carrying out arrangements for securing or facilitating the obtaining of leave to remain in the UK by means which include deception. It covers helping people to stay by providing false documents, and could cover helping people enter into sham marriages. Those assisted would normally be guilty of an offence under section 24A of the 1971 Act.[1] The extended time limit for prosecution applies to this offence,[2] but unlike the two other section 25(1) offences, it cannot be committed abroad, since it does not relate to entry but to stay in the UK. Maximum sentences are the same as for the other two section 25(1) offences, but there are no reported cases on sentencing for this offence, and it seems its use is rare.

1   For which see **14.20** above.
2   Immigration Act 1971, ss 25(4), 28.

Harbouring

14.33 Section 25(2) of the Immigration Act 1971 creates separate offences for anyone knowingly to harbour anyone whom they know or have reasonable cause for believing to be:

(1) an illegal entrant;
(2) a person who has committed the offence of overstaying; or
(3) a person who has committed the offence of breaching a condition of leave.[1]

An information which does not specify which allegation is relied on is bad for duplicity.[2] The offence is triable summarily only and the penalty is a fine of not more than level 5 or up to six months' imprisonment.[3] The extended time limit applies,[4] and there is power to arrest without warrant.[5]

1 Leave may be granted subject to conditions restricting work, precluding recourse to public funds, or requiring registration with the police: Immigration Act 1971, s 3(3)(c), as amended by Asylum and Immigration Act 1996, Sch 2, para 1.
2 *Rahman and Qadir v DPP* [1993] Crim LR 874.
3 Immigration Act 1971, s 25(2). Level 5 is presently £5,000: Criminal Justice Act 1982, s 37, Criminal Justice Act 1991, s 17.
4 Immigration Act 1971, ss 25(4), 28.
5 Immigration Act 1971, s 28A(4), inserted by Immigration and Asylum Act 1999, s 128.

14.34 According to the dictionary, harbouring means 'to provide a lodging for; to shelter; lodge; entertain';[1] 'to give shelter to'.[2] In *Darch v Weight*[3] a narrower definition was suggested. It means to provide shelter or support rather than mere entertainment or assistance without such shelter or support. Shelter can be afforded or provided irrespective of the accused's interest in the premises. He or she need not be the owner or landlord, but some element of control is presumably necessary. In all cases the prosecution must prove that the person harboured was an illegal entrant or a person guilty of the criminal offence of overstaying or breach of a condition.

1 *Shorter Oxford English Dictionary.*
2 *Concise Oxford English Dictionary.*
3 [1984] 2 All ER 245, [1984] 1 WLR 659, citing with approval *R v Mistry* [1980] Crim LR 177, CA.

Breach of conditions and overstaying

14.35 A person who is not a British citizen commits a criminal offence if, having only a limited leave to enter or remain in the UK, he or she knowingly either:

(i)   remains beyond the time limited by the leave; or
(ii) fails to observe a condition of the leave.[1]

Both these offences are summary only. The maximum penalty is six months' imprisonment and a fine at level 5,[2] and police and immigration officers may arrest suspected offenders without warrant.[3]

1 Immigration Act 1971, s 24(1)(b), as amended by British Nationality Act 1981, Sch 4, para 2.

2 Set at £5,000: Criminal Justice Act 1982, s 37(2), as amended by Criminal Justice Act 1991, s 17.
3 Immigration Act 1971, s 28A, inserted by Immigration and Asylum Act 1999, s 128.

Overstaying

14.36 Overstaying used to be the most common immigration offence but since overstayers' rights of appeal against deportation were restricted in 1988,[1] it has rarely been used. The wording of the offence gives rise to difficulty: 'having' a limited leave does not readily fit an offence of remaining beyond the leave. It is entirely appropriate for the second limb of the offence, where there must be an extant leave in order for there to be a breach of conditions.[2] To make sense of the wording, 'having' has to be interpreted as meaning 'having had', although such an interpretation of identical words in section 14 of the Immigration Act 1971 was rejected by the House of Lords in the case of *Suthendran*.[3] The offence of overstaying is defined as a continuing offence which is committed at any time when the immigrant knows that the time limited by his or her leave has expired and nevertheless remains in the UK.[4] There is no need for any provision to extend the time limits for prosecution. But a person cannot be prosecuted more than once in respect of the same limited leave.[5]

1 By Immigration Act 1988, s 5.
2 *Gurdev Singh v R* [1974] 1 All ER 26, [1973] 1 WLR 1444, DC.
3 *Suthendran v Immigration Appeal Tribunal* [1977] AC 359, [1976] 3 All ER 611, HL.
4 Immigration Act 1971, s 24(1A), inserted by Immigration Act 1988, s 6, except in relation to persons whose leave had expired before 10 July 1988, for whom the offence could only be committed on the day following the expiry of their leave: *Grant v Borg* [1982] 2 All ER 257, [1982] 1 WLR 638, HL.
5 Immigration Act 1971, s 24(1A), as amended.

14.37 Persons who applied before the expiry of their leave for further leave and who remain awaiting a decision on their application are not overstayers because their leave is to be treated as continuing until the end of the period allowed for the bringing of an appeal.[1] Leave is then deemed to continue pending the appeal,[2] including any further appeal.[3] These considerations give rise to evidential difficulties in that the expiry date on the leave stamp in a passport is not conclusive evidence that the accused has overstayed.[4]

1 Immigration Act 1971, s 3C, inserted by Immigration and Asylum Act 1999, s 3. The period allowed under Sch 4, para 3 of the 1999 Act for the bringing of an appeal is ten days: Immigration and Asylum (Procedure) Rules 2000, SI 2000/2333, r 6.
2 Immigration and Asylum Act 1999, Sch 4, para 17.
3 Immigration and Asylum Act 1999, s 58(6), (7).
4 See *Zoltak v Sussex Constabulary* [1983] CLY 1923 where a conviction for overstaying was quashed where the defendant had applied for an extension, and the application was date-stamped as received two days after his leave expired. The court held that since the application was made when it was posted (following *Lubetkin* [1979–80] Imm AR 162) the prosecutor had not established that on the date of the alleged offence the defendant was not covered by art 3(1) of the Immigration (Variation of Leave) Order 1976, SI 1976/1572.

14.38 A conviction for overstaying requires proof of knowledge. A belief that one's leave expires on a different date is a mistake of fact; so also is the belief that another person—a friend or agent—has made an application for an extension when this is not the case. There may be cases of illiterate persons or persons whose comprehension of English is so poor that they do not appreciate that their leave has expired, or persons whose employer has retained their passport and has never shown the employee the endorsement. Sheer forgetfulness, and oversight owing to the stress caused by bereavement, may be capable of providing good defences.[1]

1 *Immigration Appeal Tribunal v Chelliah* [1985] Imm AR 192, CA; *R v Bello* (1978) 67 Cr App Rep 288, [1978] Crim LR 551, CA (dismissed on the facts).

Breach of conditions

14.39 Conditions can only be attached to a limited leave to remain, and the only conditions that can be attached are a restriction on employment or occupation in the UK, a condition requiring an immigrant to maintain and accommodate him or herself and any dependants without recourse to public funds, or to register with the police, or all three.[1] Thus there is no power to attach conditions to an indefinite leave, and where a limited leave is extended to become an indefinite leave any conditions automatically cease.[2] Where a limited leave is subject to conditions, an automatic extension of leave under the statutory provisions also extends the conditions.[3] However, a person can only be guilty of the offence of a breach of conditions during a period in which the conditions apply; where the leave itself has run out and is not extended by statute (whether by an application or by an appeal) there is nothing for the conditions to attach to and the conditions will lapse.[4] Thereafter a person may be guilty of overstaying the leave but not of contravening restrictions attached to it.[5] Thus a person who takes employment after the expiry of leave is not committing any additional offence by doing so (although his or her employer is: see **14.64ff** below). The same principles apply to persons who are required to register with the police; this requirement attaches to a leave and expires with the leave.[6] The offence is a continuing one in that the Crown is not confined to the first occasion of the breach of condition.[7] The extended time limit for prosecutions does not apply to an offence of breach of conditions, and a prosecution must, therefore, be brought within six months of the commission of the offence. Knowledge of the conditions is a prerequisite of the offence.

1 Immigration Act 1971, s 3(1)(c), as amended by Asylum and Immigration Act 1996, Sch 2, para 1(1).
2 Immigration Act 1971, s 3(3)(a).
3 Immigration Act 1971, s 3C, inserted by Immigration and Asylum Act 1999, s 3; para 17 of Sch 4 to the 1999 Act; *Shaukat Ali v Chief Adjudication Officer* (1985) Times, 24 December, CA; *Rajendran v Secretary of State for the Home Department* [1989] Imm AR 512.
4 *Suthendran v Immigration Appeal Tribunal* [1977] AC 359, [1976] 3 All ER 611, HL.
5 *Gurdev Singh v R* [1974] 1 All ER 26, [1973] 1 WLR 1444, DC.
6 *R v Naik* (1978) Times, 26 July, CA.
7 *Manickavsagar v Metropolitan Police Comr* [1987] Crim LR 50, DC. See further *Gurdev Singh* above.

EA nationals

14.40 Since the right of entry and residence of EEA nationals flows directly from the provisions of EC law and the EEA Treaty and is not subject to the requirements of the Immigration Act 1971 to obtain leave to enter or remain,[1] it is difficult to see how an EEA national covered by the free movement provisions of the EC Treaty can commit the offence of overstaying under section 24(1)(b) of the 1971 Act by remaining after his or her residence permit expires. The 'no visa' rule, however, does not apply to members of the EEA worker's family who are not EEA nationals. They are required to obtain a family permit confirming their rights of entry under EC law (see chapter 7 above). But their rights flow from EC law and provided they continue to qualify as members of the family, they should not be liable to criminal or administrative action for remaining beyond the time limited by their permit.

1   Case C-157/79 *R v Pieck* [1981] QB 571, [1981] 3 All ER 46, ECJ; Immigration Act 1988, s 7, in force 20 July 1994.

Seamen and air and train crews who overstay

14.41   Under section 8(1) of the Immigration Act 1971,[1] as we have seen, crews of ships, international trains and aircraft are allowed entry without leave until their ship, train or aircraft leaves the country again. Under section 24(1)(c) of the 1971 Act it is an offence if seamen or air or train crews stay longer than the temporary period of admission normally allowed under section 8(1) when their ship, train or aircraft docks, arrives or lands here. The extended time limit applies to such offences,[2] and they may be arrested without warrant by the police or immigration officers if with reasonable cause they are suspected of having committed such an offence.[3] This offence was intended in particular to catch seamen who deserted ship when it arrived in the UK, but it is a less effective way, from the authorities' point of view, than the extensive administrative powers of removal under Schedule 2 to the 1971 Act.

1   Modified in relation to international trains by the Channel Tunnel (International Arrangements) Order 1993, SI 1993/1813, Sch 4, para 1(4).
2   Immigration Act 1971, ss 24(3), 28.
3   Immigration Act 1971, s 28A, inserted by Immigration and Asylum Act 1999, s 128.

Breach of directions

14.42   A variety of miscellaneous offences exist to back up the immigration officer's powers on examination and removal, although they are rarely, if ever, used. Thus it is an offence to fail to comply with a direction to report to a medical officer of health, as directed, or to fail to attend or to submit to an examination required by such an officer.[1] There is a defence of reasonable excuse, which might apply, for example, to a refusal to undergo an examination which was not conducted by properly qualified medical staff. There is no power of arrest for this offence—although, as we have seen, immigration officers may search premises to effect an arrest with a warrant[2]—and, in reality, as it only applies to persons seeking entry, the authorities have a more effective measure at their disposal: refusal of entry and removal.

1   Immigration Act 1971, s 24(1)(d).
2   Immigration Act 1971, s 28B, inserted by Immigration and Asylum Act 1999, s 129.

14.43   Where a person is given temporary admission—either pending a further examination on entry, or pending removal as an illegal entrant, overstayer or deportee—it is an offence to fail to observe any requirements as to residence, employment or occupation, or reporting to the police or an immigration officer, without reasonable excuse.[1] A person who has been placed on board a ship or aircraft pursuant to removal directions commits an offence if he or she disembarks, as does a person who embarks in contravention of an Order in Council made under the provision of the Immigration Act 1971 to permit retaliatory measures or hostage orders.[2] The extended time limits do not apply to any of the offences considered in this section.

1   Immigration Act 1971, s 24(1)(e). Immigration officers may arrest for this and the following offences by warrant: s 28B, **14.42** fn 2 above.
2   Immigration Act 1971, s 24(1)(f) and (g).

Offences in connection with the administration of the Immigration Acts

14.44   There are a number of offences which serve to emphasise the extensive powers of immigration officers when conducting an examination on entry. Persons who refuse or fail to submit to such an examination,[1] who refuse or fail to produce information in their possession, or documents under their control which they are required to produce, or fail to complete a landing card or embarkation card, commit offences if they have no reasonable excuse.[2] It is also an offence to fail without lawful excuse to comply with any regulations regarding registering with the police or keeping hotel records.[3]

1   Immigration Act 1971, s 26(1)(a). The maximum penalties are now six months' imprisonment or a level 5 fine. The offences are summary only.
2   Immigration Act 1971, s 26(1)(b).
3   Immigration Act 1971, s 26(1)(f).

14.45   Two offences bear closer examination. The first is that of making a false statement under section 26(1)(c) of the Immigration Act 1971. It is an offence to make a return, statement, or representation which is known to be false or not believed to be true to an immigration officer or other person acting in the execution of a 'relevant enactment', either on a 1971 Act, Schedule 2 examination or otherwise. The 'relevant enactments' are defined as the Immigration Act 1971, the Immigration Act 1988, the Asylum and Immigration Appeals Act 1993 or the Immigration and Asylum Act 1999 (apart from Part VI).[1] 'Otherwise' means otherwise acting in execution of the relevant Act. So the phrase qualifies both the person to whom the statement is made and the circumstances in which it is made. A great many people act in the course of their employment in functions which promote the purposes of the Acts, but they are not acting in the execution of the 'relevant enactments'.[2] The offence is committed where the false statement is addressed to a person pursuing a right or duty under one of the relevant Acts to receive information, such as immigration officers, entry clearance officers,[3] medical inspectors, police officers acting under the 1971 Act, Home Office officials who process applications to vary and the appellate authorities. Prior to 1999, the offence could only be committed in relation to a person exercising functions under the 1971 Act. The amendment in 1999 broadened the scope of the offence to cover functions under the 1988, 1993 and 1999 Acts. The change means that the offence can now be committed by telling lies to a wider range of people—a detainee custody officer in a contracted-out detention centre[4] or to a marriage registrar,[5] for instance, and can be committed by a much wider range

14.45 *Penal and carrier sanctions*

of people in respect of a vastly wider range of functions. Lies told by a third party to an immigration officer who is searching a property for a person or for documents could be covered, since such a search is now a statutory function. Thus does the 1999 Act make immigration officers or offenders of us all—or at least, of many more of us.

1   The phrase 'relevant enactments' was inserted and defined by Immigration and Asylum Act 1999, s 30.
2   *R v Clarke* [1985] AC 1037, [1985] 2 All ER 777, HL in which lies told to police investigating an offence under the Immigration Act 1971 were held not to constitute the offence since the officers were not acting 'in the execution of the Act'.
3   *R v Secretary of State for the Home Department, ex p Saffu-Mensah* [1991] Imm AR 43, QBD, affd on different grounds in CA [1992] Imm AR 185. Though made abroad, such representations may be prosecutable in the UK as an act done to obtain a benefit here, or having a real and substantial link with the UK: *R v Baxter* [1972] 1 QB 1, [1971] 2 All ER 359, CA; *DPP v Stonehouse* [1977] 2 All ER 909 at 913; *Liangsiriprasert v Government of the United States of America* [1991] 1 AC 225, PC.
4   In respect of the functions performed under Immigration and Asylum Act 1999, Pt VIII in contracted-out detention centres.
5   In respect of the power to require evidence of nationality under IAA 1999, s 162, although there might be an issue as to whether the registrar is acting in the execution of the Marriage Act 1949 (which s 162 amends) or the 1999 Act.

14.46 The Crown does not need to prove that the false representation concerned was effective in obtaining leave to enter, only that it was likely to influence the decision to allow entry.[1] Nowadays, making false representations to immigration officers giving leave to enter, or to Home Office officials giving leave to remain or deciding on removal or deportation, is more likely to be charged as deception (if performed by the immigrant) or facilitating deception or obstruction (if performed by third parties). These offences are committed if the means of entry, remaining, etc included deception.[2] Charging deception also gets round the technical problems described in **14.45** above and discussed in *R v Clarke*[3] as to when a person was acting in the execution of the relevant Act.

1   *R v Secretary of State for the Home Department, ex p Castro* [1996] Imm AR 540. This is not a criminal case but a judicial review of a decision that the person was an illegal entrant, following *Khawaja v Secretary of State for the Home Department* [1984] AC 74, [1983] 1 All ER 765, [1983] 2 WLR 321, [1982] Imm AR 139, HL, which held that the offence was at the heart of illegal entry by deception. See **16.21**ff below.
2   See **14.20** above.
3   [1985] AC 1037, [1985] 2 All ER 777, HL.

14.47 There is also an offence of obstructing an immigration officer or other person acting in execution of the Immigration Act 1971.[1] By analogy with the offence of obstructing a police officer, the offence would require some physical or other unlawful activity which prevents or impedes a person from carrying out some particular duty entrusted to them by the Act.[2] Where the obstruction consists of a refusal to do something requested by an immigration official, the offence will only be committed if there is a duty under the Act to do what is requested, such as permitting inspection of luggage by an immigration officer.[3] There is a restricted power of arrest without warrant for obstruction, on failure of the suspect to provide a reliable name or address.[4]

1   Immigration Act 1971, s 26(1)(g).
2   See *R v Clarke* [1985] AC 1037, [1985] 2 All ER 777, HL.
3   Immigration Act 1971, Sch 2, para 4.
4   Immigration Act 1971, s 28A(5), inserted by Immigration and Asylum Act 1999, s 128.

14.48 The final offences in connection with the administration of the Immigration Acts are in respect of documents. It is an offence to alter a certificate of entitlement, entry clearance, work permit or other document issued or made under and for the purposes of the 1971 Act. This latter might include police registration books. These are all documents emanating from the UK authorities. Furthermore it is an offence to use for the purposes of the 1971 Act, or to possess with intent to use, any passport, certificate of entitlement, entry clearance, work permit or other document which a person knows to be false or has reasonable cause to believe to be false.[1] The category of documents here is wider, and might include any document presented to an immigration officer or Home Office official for the purpose of obtaining leave to enter or remain. The reference to a document being false must be a reference to a false particular of a material kind to give the general character of falsity to the document.[2] The document concerned must actually be false for the offence to be committed;[3] the reasonable cause for belief in its falsity is necessary but not sufficient for the offence to be made out. It is likely that the defendant must actually believe the document to be false.[4] The penalties for this, as for the other 1971 Act, section 26 offences, are a fine on level 5 and six months' imprisonment.[5] If the possession or use of the false document is related to a *bona fide* quest for asylum, the section 31/Article 31(1) defence is available.[6]

1 Immigration Act 1971, s 26(1)(d).
2 See Webster J in *R v Secretary of State for the Home Department, ex p Patel* [1986] Imm AR 208, QBD; affd [1986] Imm AR 515, CA.
3 By analogy with the facilitation offences of s 25 of the Immigration Act 1971, which have the same wording—those assisted must actually be illegal entrants or asylum claimants: see *R v Naillie* [1993] AC 674.
4 By analogy with 'reasonable grounds for suspicion', which requires actual suspicion: *O'Hara v Chief Constable of RUC* [1997] AC 286, HL. See discussion in *R v Secretary of State for the Home Department, ex p Rouse and Shrimpton* (13 November 1985, unreported), QBD.
5 Immigration Act 1971, s 26. The fine is currently £5,000: Criminal Justice Act 1982, s 37, as amended by Criminal Justice Act 1991, s 17.
6 Immigration and Asylum Act, s 31, Refugee Convention, art 31(1): see **14.24–14.26** above.

14.49 All the offences discussed in this section can be committed by British as well as non-British citizens. There is no power of arrest without warrant, and the offences must be prosecuted within six months, save the offences of false statements and false documents, in respect of which the extended time limit applies.

Extended time limit

14.50 Normally the time limit for bringing a prosecution for a summary offence is six months.[1] This normal time limit applies to most immigration offences, but, as already indicated, there are a number of offences to which the extended time limit, set out in section 28 of the Immigration Act 1971, applies. In particular, it applies to the offences of illegal entry, overstaying,[2] deception,[3] facilitating entry or deception, harbouring[4] and making a false statement or altering a document.[5] In England and Wales the extended time limit enables a magistrate's court to try an information if it is laid within three years after the commission of the offence and not more than two months after the date certified by a chief officer of police to be the date on which evidence sufficient to justify proceedings came to the notice of an officer of that police force.[6] In Scotland the certifying officer is the Lord Advocate[7] and in Northern Ireland, a police officer not below the rank of assistant chief constable.[8] The 'trial' of the information begins with the hearing of the information, not with the plea of not guilty, which only marks the need for a trial.[9] 'Evidence' means more than information given over the telephone, which would be inadmissible in proceedings.[10]

1 Magistrates' Courts Act 1980, s 127.
2 Immigration Act 1971, s 24(3).
3 Immigration Act 1971, s 24A(3).
4 Immigration Act 1971, s 25(4).
5 Immigration Act 1971, s 26(2).
6 Immigration Act 1971, s 28(1)(a).
7 Immigration Act 1971, s 28(1)(b).
8 Immigration Act 1971, s 28(1)(c).
9 *Quazi v DPP* (1988) 152 JP 385.
10 *Enaas v Dovey* (1986) Times, 25 November

14.51 The operation of the extended time limit was illustrated in *Ex p Offei*,[1] where a certificate to enable an extended time limit to apply had been signed by the chief constable, but officers from the same force had interviewed the applicant in connection with his overstaying at least 18 months earlier than the two-month period to which the certificate related. As a result of the earlier interview, all the evidence needed to prosecute him for an offence against section 24(1)(b) of the Immigration Act 1971 was to hand. The Divisional Court quashed his conviction, holding that by reason of the earlier interview there was evidence sufficient to justify proceedings and the certificate was therefore a nullity. The court held that there would not have been sufficient evidence if the overstayer's whereabouts were unknown. In that case it held that the challenge to the validity of the certificate was for the High Court rather than the magistrates,[2] although a different view was taken in *Enaas v Dovey*,[3] which held that magistrates could go behind the certificate to see whether the decision of the chief of police was reasonable. Resolution of these conflicting views is awaited. The sufficiency of evidence is a matter for the chief of police's judgment, which can only be successfully challenged if it is unreasonable in a *Wednesbury*[4] sense. The extended time limit for prosecution is no longer of importance in relation to the offence of overstaying, since it can be prosecuted at any time until the person leaves the country, but it is still important in offences which are not continuing, such as illegal entry and using a false document.

1 *R v Clerk to Birmingham Justices, ex p Offei* (28 November 1985, unreported), QBD.
2 By analogy with the absence of the Director of Public Prosecutions' consent in *R v Angel* [1968] 2 All ER 607n, [1968] 1 WLR 669, CA.
3 (1986) Times, 25 November.
4 *Associated Provincial Picture Houses Ltd v Wednesbury Corpn* [1948] 1 KB 223, [1947] 2 All ER 680, CA.

Offences in relation to passports and acquisition of nationality

14.52 It is an offence punishable on summary conviction by a level 5 fine[1] or three months' imprisonment, or both, for any person, for the purpose of procuring anything to be done or not to be done under the British Nationality Act 1981, knowingly or recklessly to make any statement which is false in a material particular.[2] The offence would be committed by a person lying about the length of his or her residence in the UK to obtain naturalisation, for example. The extended time limit for prosecution applies.[3]

1 Set at £5000: Criminal Justice Act 1982, s 37(2), as amended by Criminal Justice Act 1991, s 17.
2 British Nationality Act 1981, s 46(1).
3 British Nationality Act 1981, s 46(3).

14.53 Making a statement which is to the person's knowledge untrue for the purpose of procuring a passport for him or herself or for any other person[1] is a more serious offence, triable either way and punishable on summary conviction by the statutory maximum fine and/or six months' imprisonment, and on indictment by two years' imprisonment. A custodial sentence has been held appropriate for a first offence.[2]

1 Criminal Justice Act 1925, s 36.
2 *R v Walker* [1999] 1 Cr App Rep (S) 42, where an overstayer applied for a passport using a false name, date and place of birth. The sentence of 18 months was however reduced to nine months.

14.54 A passport is an 'instrument' for the Forgery and Counterfeiting Act 1981.[1] Relevant offences are forgery (making a false instrument),[2] using a false instrument,[3] possession of a false instrument with intent,[4] and possession of a false instrument without lawful authority or excuse.[5] All the offences are triable either way, punishable on summary conviction by a fine up to the statutory maximum or six months' imprisonment, and on indictment by ten years' imprisonment, save for possession without lawful authority when the maximum sentence on indictment is two years.[6] Persons presenting false passports at immigration control are frequently charged with the possession offences. The statutory defence under the Immigration and Asylum Act 1999, section 31, and Refugee Convention, Article 31 argument, apply to these offences.[7]

1 Forgery and Counterfeiting Act 1981, ss 8(1)(a), 5(5)(f).
2 Forgery and Counterfeiting Act 1981, s 1.
3 Forgery and Counterfeiting Act 1981, s 3.
4 Forgery and Counterfeiting Act 1981, s 5(1).
5 Forgery and Counterfeiting Act 1981, s 5(2).
6 Forgery and Counterfeiting Act 1981, s 6; the statutory maximum is £5000: Magistrates' Courts Act 1980, s 32(9).
7 Immigration and Asylum Act 1999, s 31(3) and (4); see **14.24–14.26** above.

Offences by persons connected with ships, aircraft, ports or trains

14.55 Captains of ships or aircraft, and managers of Eurostar through trains and shuttle trains, commit an offence if they allow people to disembark or leave the transport when required to prevent it, or fail to provide passenger information and information on non-EEA arrivals as required, or fail without reasonable excuse to comply with directions for a person's removal.[1] In the last-mentioned case, the owner or agent is also liable. Whether a demonstration by anti-deportation protesters or other passengers' refusal to travel on a flight with a deportee (both of which activities are on the increase with the recent intensification of enforcement action) constitute 'reasonable excuse' for failure to comply with directions for a passenger's removal has yet to be tested in the courts. Additionally, an owner or agent who arranges for a ship or aircraft to call at an unauthorised port, or who without reasonable excuse fails to provide landing or embarkation cards, commits an offence. The offences are all summary only and punishable by a fine up to level 5 and/or six months' imprisonment.[2]

1   Immigration Act 1971, s 27, modified in relation to Channel Tunnel trains by the Channel Tunnel (International Arrangements) Order 1993, SI 1993/1813, Sch 4, para 1(9). The requirement to provide passenger lists and times of arrival is contained in SI 1993/1813, Sch 2, para 27B, and 27C, inserted by Immigration and Asylum Act 1999, ss 18 and 19 (modified in relation to Channel Tunnel trains by the Channel Tunnel (International Arrangements) (Amendment) Order 2000, SI 2000/913).
2   Immigration Act 1971, s 27.

Offences in relation to asylum support

14.56 The Immigration and Asylum Act 1999 removed virtually everyone subject to immigration control from the scope of social security benefits and created a new Home Office department which provides workhouse-type subsistence to destitute asylum seekers.[1] This support regime is enforced by a number of new offences modelled on offences relating to social security:[2] false representations; dishonest representations and obstruction; and failure by a sponsor to maintain. They can be committed by corporate bodies, whose officers and even members may be liable if they have consented or connived in the offence, or it is attributable to neglect on their part.[3] In Scotland, partnerships and partners may be liable in corresponding circumstances.[4] The powers of entry and search on a warrant issued by a magistrate to check for the presence of unauthorised persons or the absence of authorised ones[5] are of relevance in relation to these offences.

1   See chapter 13 above.
2   The new offences are in Immigration and Asylum Act 1999, ss 105–108, and are based on Social Security Administration Act 1992, ss 105 and 111–113.
3   Immigration and Asylum Act 1999, s 109(1).
4   Immigration and Asylum Act 1999, s 109(4).
5   Immigration and Asylum Act 1999, s 125: see **14.13** above.

14.57 The offence of false representations is committed by a person who, with a view to obtaining support for him- or herself or for any other person, makes a statement or representation he or she knows to be false in a material particular,[1] gives a document or information he or she knows to be false to someone performing asylum support functions,[2] fails to notify a relevant change of circumstances[3] or without reasonable excuse, knowingly causes another person to fail to notify such a change.[4] It is a summary offence, punishable by a level 5 fine or three months' imprisonment, or both.[5] The offence is likely to be used in respect of false information given in the asylum support application form which applicants are required to complete 'in full and in English'.[6] There is no power of arrest without warrant.

1   Immigration and Asylum Act 1999, s 105(1)(a).
2   Immigration and Asylum Act 1999, s 105(1)(b). Persons performing functions under Pt VI of the Act include officers of NASS and of local authorities who process applications for support. They could also include officers of registered social landlords and housing associations by virtue of s 100, and asylum support adjudicators by virtue of ss 102–103.

3   Immigration and Asylum Act 1999, s 105(1)(c). The relevant changes are set out in the
     Asylum Support Regulations 2000, SI 2000/704, reg 15(2), and include being joined by a
     dependant, receiving or getting access to any previously undeclared money or other asset,
     becoming employed or unemployed, changing one's name, marrying, divorcing, separating,
     becoming pregnant, having a child, leaving school, sharing, moving or leaving
     accommodation, going into hospital or prison, leaving the UK and dying.
4   Immigration and Asylum Act 1999, s 105(1(d).
5   Immigration and Asylum Act 1999, s 105(2).
6   Asylum Support Regulations 2000, SI 2000/704, reg 3.

14.58 The offence of dishonest representations is committed by performing the
same acts, but with a view to obtaining any benefit or advantage under Part VI
of the Immigration and Asylum Act 1999 for him- or herself or any other person.
The acts must have been performed dishonestly.[1] The offence is thus broader
and could be committed by landlords or providers of other services attempting
to defraud NASS. The section is directed at cases of serious and calculated
fraud, such as where a person makes a plan to extract as much from the Home
Office as possible by deception.[2] This is evident from the penalties: it is triable
either way, and punishable on summary conviction by a fine up to the statutory
maximum or six months' imprisonment, or both, and on indictment by a fine
and/or seven years' imprisonment.[3] It is an arrestable offence within the meaning
of section 24(1)(b) of the Police and Criminal Evidence Act 1984.

1   Immigration and Asylum Act 1999, s 106(1).
2   Explanatory notes to Immigration and Asylum Act 1999, s 106.
3   Immigration and Asylum Act 1999, s 106(2).

14.59 The offence of delay or obstruction is committed by intentionally delaying
or obstructing someone exercising asylum support functions, or refusing or
neglecting to answer a question, give information or produce a document when
required to do so.[1] It is summary only and punishable by a fine up to level 3.[2]
There is no power of arrest without warrant.

1   Immigration and Asylum Act 1999, s 107(1). For persons exercising functions under Pt VI
     of the Act see chapter 13 and **14.57** fn 2 above.
2   Immigration and Asylum Act 1999, s 107(2).

14.60 The offence of failure to maintain is committed by a sponsor (a person
who has given a written undertaking under the Immigration Rules to be
responsible for the maintenance and accommodation of another person) who,
during the period covered by the undertaking, persistently refuses or neglects,
without reasonable excuse, to maintain the person in accordance with the
undertaking, with the result that support has to be provided under Part VI of the
Immigration and Asylum Act 1999.[1] A sponsor is not to be taken to have refused
or neglected to maintain another person by reason only of anything done or
omitted in furtherance of a trade dispute.[2] The proviso that the refusal or neglect
must be without reasonable excuse was added at Report stage, after the minister
had made clear that 'it is not our intention to catch people who might become
ill or unable to support the person for a genuine reason'.[3] Sponsored immigrants
are not entitled to social security benefits for at least five years unless their
sponsor dies,[4] and so the offence, which requires receipt of support in consequence
of the failure to maintain, can, it appears, only be committed if the sponsored
immigrant concerned applies for asylum as a refugee or under Article 3 of the
ECHR[5] and receives asylum support because of the sponsor's failure. The offence

is summary only and punishable by a fine up to level 4 or three months' imprisonment, or both.[6] There is no power of arrest without warrant.

1 Immigration and Asylum Act 1999, s 108(1).
2 Immigration and Asylum Act 1999, s 108(3).
3 HC Official Report, Special SC (Immigration and Asylum Bill), 21st sitting, 11 May 1999, col 1422; 606 HL Official Report (5th series) cols 839–842, 2 November 1999.
4 By Immigration and Asylum Act 1999, s 115 and the Social Security (Immigration and Asylum) Consequential Amendments Regulations 2000, SI 2000/636, Sch, paras 2 and 3.
5 See interpretation section, Immigration and Asylum Act 1999, s 94(1).
6 Immigration and Asylum Act 1999, s 108(2). Level 4 is currently £2,500: Criminal Justice Act 1982, s 37(2), as amended by Criminal Justice Act 1991, s 17.

Offences in relation to provision of immigration advice or services

14.61 The Immigration and Asylum Act 1999 polices not just immigrants and asylum seekers, but also those who advise and represent them. In response to widespread disquiet at the abuse and exploitation of immigrants and asylum seekers by lawyers and by unqualified consultants, Part V of the Act creates a structure of authorisation or registration within which advice and services are to be provided.[1] Essentially, no one may provide immigration advice or services unless he or she is registered with the Immigration Services Commissioner[2] (or employed or supervised by a person or body so registered) or is authorised by a designated professional body[3] (or employed or supervised by a person or body so authorised),[4] or is exempt. The Commissioner has a duty to investigate complaints regarding the competence or fitness of persons providing advice, and breaches of Commissioners' rules and Code of Practice,[5] and may decline or cancel registration.[6] The Immigration Services Tribunal, which hears appeals and disciplinary charges arising from the Commissioner's decisions, or the disciplinary body with jurisdiction over the service provider (if he or she is a solicitor, legal executive or barrister), may make a restraining order restricting, suspending or prohibiting the advice or services of the individual or firm concerned.[7] In the course of investigating a complaint, the Commissioner has power to enter and search premises where it is believed on reasonable grounds that advice is being provided, and may require the production of documents or information held on a computer, which may be copied or removed.[8]

1 Immigration and Asylum Act 1999, s 84.
2 Immigration and Asylum Act 1999, s 84(2)(a) and (b). The Commissioner is created by s 83.
3 Defined in Immigration and Asylum Act 1999, s 86(1) as the Law Society, the Law Society of Scotland, the Law Society of Northern Ireland, the Institute of Legal Executives, the General Council of the Bar, the Faculty of Advocates and the General Council of the Bar of Northern Ireland. There is provision to amend the list after consultation: s 86(2)–(7).
4 Immigration and Asylum Act 1999, s 84(2)(c) and (f). Paras (d) and (e) deal with those registered or authorised in another EEA state.
5 Immigration and Asylum Act 1999, Sch 5, para 5.
6 Immigration and Asylum Act 1999, Sch 5, para 6(3), Sch 6, paras 2 and 3.
7 Immigration and Asylum Act 1999, ss 89(8), 90(1), Sch 5, para 9(3).
8 Immigration and Asylum Act 1999, Sch 5, para 7.

14.62 It is an offence for an unqualified person (one who is not registered, authorised or exempt), or for one subject to a restraining order, to provide immigration advice or services.[1] The offence is triable either way, and is punishable on summary conviction with a fine up to the statutory maximum or six months' imprisonment, or both, and on indictment by a fine or two years' imprisonment, or both.[2] Where it is committed by a corporate body, the company's officers (director, manager, secretary, etc) or members may be liable if they are proved to have connived in the offence or it is attributable to neglect on their part.[3] In Scotland, partners are liable in corresponding circumstances where the offence is committed by a partnership.[4]

1   Immigration and Asylum Act 1999, s 91(1).
2   Immigration and Asylum Act 1999 s 91(1).
3   Immigration and Asylum Act 1999, s 91(3)–(5).
4   Immigration and Asylum Act 1999, s 91(6)–(7).

Offences of disclosure

14.63 Finally, there are offences of wrongfully disclosing sensitive information. A person who is or has been the Immigration Services Commissioner, or an agent or staff member of a Commissioner, commits an offence if, without lawful authority, he or she knowingly or recklessly discloses information relating to an identified or identifiable individual or business which was obtained by the Commissioner for the purposes of the Immigration and Asylum Act 1999 and is not in the public domain.[1] The offence is triable either way and punishable by a fine. The penalties are steeper for a private sector employee at a detention centre or on escort duties who makes unauthorised disclosure of information relating to a particular detainee acquired in the course of his or her employment.[2] The penalty for this offence, also triable either way, is a fine up to the statutory maximum or six months' imprisonment or both on summary conviction, and on indictment, up to two years' imprisonment.

1   Immigration and Asylum Act 1999, s 93(4).
2   Immigration and Asylum Act 1999, s 158.

EMPLOYER SANCTIONS

14.64 The Asylum and Immigration Act 1996 created a new offence for employers who employ persons aged 16 or over subject to immigration control who are not entitled to work in the UK. Employers (including individuals, companies, directors, managers and other officers)[1] commit an offence punishable by a fine on level 5[2] if they employ someone subject to immigration control[3] who has not been granted leave to enter or remain in the UK, or whose leave is not valid and subsisting, or is subject to a condition precluding that employment.[4] The first category includes persons who entered clandestinely and those on temporary admission. The second includes overstayers, although it cannot include those whose leave was obtained by deception.[5] The third category includes those with leave to enter as visitors (the leave is subject to a condition prohibiting employment), and business people and those of independent means, and work permit holders who need the permission of the Department for Education and Employment to change jobs. There are certain statutory exceptions to these categories of illegal employees, such as asylum seekers who have Home Office written permission to work,[6] employees with a pending appeal whose previous leave did not preclude the employment,[7] and persons granted bail by an adjudicator whose bail conditions do not preclude employment.[8]

14.64 *Penal and carrier sanctions*

1 Asylum and Immigration Act 1996, s 8(5) covers officers of corporate bodies.
2 Asylum and Immigration Act 1996, s 8(4).
3 Broadly speaking this means anyone except British citizens, Commonwealth citizens with the right of abode, EEA nationals and their non-EEA family members, and the family members of exempt persons such as diplomats.
4 Asylum and Immigration Act 1996, s 8(1). Now that statutory leave (together with any conditions) continues pending a variation appeal, under Immigration and Asylum Act 1999, Sch 4, para 17(1), the offence can be committed by someone awaiting appeal if his or her previous leave was subject to a prohibition on employment.
5 Immigration Act 1971, Sch 2, para 9(2) provides that leave to enter obtained by deception is to be disregarded *for the purposes of the paragraph* (setting removal directions); but following *Khawaja v Secretary of State for the Home Department* [1984] AC 74, for other purposes leave is not nullified until discovery of the deception by the immigration authorities, and remains valid and subsisting. To expect an employer to know that an apparently valid leave was obtained by deception would in any event be absurd.
6 Home Office policy is to allow asylum seekers to seek permission to take employment if their case is not decided, including appeal, within six months: API Nov/00, Ch 8, s 3.
7 Immigration (Restrictions on Employment) Order 1996, SI 1996/3225, Sch, Pt I.
8 Letter from Immigration and Nationality Directorate to Gill & Co, 11 December 2000.

14.65 The offence is one of strict liability, so that proof of knowledge of the employee's ineligibility to work is unnecessary to found a conviction. But neither does the employer have to prove positive belief that the employee was entitled to work. The statutory defence available[1] to employers requires them to prove that, before the employment began, they saw, and retained or copied, one of a list of specified documents,[2] including a document issued by a previous employer, the Benefits Agency or other relevant agency[3] which contains the employee's national insurance number, a passport describing the holder as a British citizen or as having the right of abode in or an entitlement to readmission in the UK; a passport endorsed with a certificate of entitlement to the right of abode; a registration or naturalisation certificate;[4] a UK or Republic of Ireland birth certificate;[5] an EEA passport or identity card;[6] a passport endorsed with indefinite leave to remain or showing the holder as exempt from immigration control; a passport, travel document or Home Office letter showing that the holder has current leave to remain and is not precluded from taking the employment; a UK residence permit of an EEA national[7] or a family permit issued to the family member of such a national;[8] a Home Office letter indicating that the holder is a British citizen or has permission to work;[9] or a Department for Education and Employment work permit or proof of British Dependent Territories citizenship through Gibraltar. Employers are not obliged to check the authenticity of the document or the employee's entitlement to it, provided the document appears to relate to the employee and to be one of the listed documents.[10] However, actual knowledge that the employee was not entitled to work cancels out the statutory defence afforded by the provision and retention of the specified document.[11]

1 Under Asylum and Immigration Act 1996, s 8(2).
2 Immigration (Restriction on Employment) Order 1996, SI 1996/3225, Sch, Pt II.
3 Such as the Contributions Agency, the Employment Service or their Northern Ireland equivalents. This would include a P45, P60, a pay slip, a NINO card or a letter issued by one of the statutory agencies. A document showing only a temporary national insurance number (format TN followed by employee's date of birth and F or M for their sex) would not suffice.
4 If issued before 1983, it would describe the holder as a citizen of the UK and colonies, otherwise as a British citizen.
5 Including short and standard certificates, and certified copies issued some time after the birth.

698

6 EEA states are Austria, Belgium, Denmark, Finland, France, Germany, Greece, Iceland, Ireland, Italy, Liechtenstein, Luxembourg, Netherlands, Norway, Portugal, Spain, Sweden.
7 A blue document carrying a photograph and brief details of the holder.
8 Making it clear that the holder has the right of residence in the UK.
9 Including a Standard Acknowledgement letter issued to an asylum seeker, or a standard letter confirming the grant of refugee status or exceptional leave to remain.
10 See Baroness Blatch, HL Official Report, 2nd reading of Asylum and Immigration Bill, 14 March 1996.
11 Asylum and Immigration Act 1996, s 8(3).

14.66 The offence is not retrospective, and it is therefore not an offence to continue to employ someone ineligible to work whom the employer has employed since before 27 January 1997, when section 8 of the Asylum and Immigration Act 1996 came into force. Additionally, it does not cover using the services of a self-employed person under a contract for services.[1] Voluntary work is unlikely to constitute a contract of service, so organisations assisted by volunteers normally would have no liability. Only in cases of a legally binding obligation to work in exchange for remuneration would section 8 apply.[2] By the end of 1999 there had only been one successful prosecution, of a firm called Labour Force (UK) Ltd, which was convicted on nine charges after nine Lithuanian nationals were found working without permission in a nursery in Kent. The company was fined £500 for each worker, a total of £4,500.[3]

1 Asylum and Immigration Act 1996, s 8(8). There could be difficulties over employment *versus* self-employment in marginal cases; also over agency staff, as to whether the agency or the employer to whom staff are sent is liable. See Berkowitz 'Employer sanctions and their impact on asylum seekers' in *United Kingdom Asylum law in its European context*, (1999).
2 Letter from Immigration and Nationality Directorate to Commission for Racial Equality, 7 July 1997.
3 Letter from Immigration and Nationality Directorate to Mishcon de Reya, 15 May 2000.

14.67 The creation of the offence was deeply controversial, with many believing it would exacerbate and entrench racial discrimination in employment while not preventing illegal working but driving it further underground to yet more exploitative conditions. Section 8A of the Asylum and Immigration Act 1996, added by the Immigration and Asylum Act 1999,[1] obliges the Secretary of State to issue a Code of Practice for employers to avoid racial discrimination in complying with the requirements of the statutory defence under section 8(2).[2] Failure on the part of an employer to observe a provision of the code, while not itself creating liability for unlawful racial discrimination, is admissible in proceedings for race discrimination.[3]

1 Immigration and Asylum Act 1999, s 22, in force 19 February 2001 for the purpose of laying a draft code before Parliament: Immigration and Asylum Act 1999 (Commencement No 9) Order 2001, SI 2001/239.
2 The Code of Practice was issued in May 2001.
3 Asylum and Immigration Act 1996, s 8A(9), (10).

CARRIERS' LIABILITY

14.68 Ever since the first carriers' liability legislation in the UK, passed in 1987 in a panic response to the arrival of a flight containing 58 Sri Lankan Tamils with no visas, carrier sanctions have been one of the favourite and well-used weapons in the armoury against illegal entrants and asylum seekers (too often seen as synonymous).[1] Despite concerns that they undermine the fundamental right to seek and enjoy asylum set out in Article 14 of the UDHR and the right to leave ones own country conferred by Article 12 of the International Covenant on Civil and Political Rights,[2] and despite overwhelming evidence that carrier sanctions do not deter immigration or the quest for asylum but merely drive up the price and the human cost,[3] the UK government, in common with its European partners, continues the restrictive policies which both make legal entry well-nigh impossible and penalise all those involved, however inadvertently, in illegal entry.[4] The latest turn of the screw is the penalties for carriers of clandestine entrants, introduced in 1999 to join the original penalties for carriers of inadequately documented passengers— themselves extended to cover almost all forms of transport. A formidable range of powers is deployed to enforce carrier sanctions. The provisions are all contained in Part II of the Immigration and Asylum Act 1999, and the Immigration (Carriers' Liability) Act 1987 has been repealed.[5]

1   See for example the Resolution on manifestly unfounded applications for asylum drafted by the Ad Hoc Group on Immigration and adopted at the Council of Ministers' meeting of 30 November 1992, which described as 'unlawful' the actions of asylum seekers who travelled to another continent rather than availing themselves of local protection. See **12.103** fn 7 above.
2   Among the vast critical literature see James Hathaway 'Harmonizing for Whom? The Devaluation of Refugee Protection in the Era of European Economic Integration' (1993) 26 Cornell International Law Journal 719; UNHCR Position on Conventions Recently Concluded in Europe (Dublin and Schengen Conventions), Aug 16 1991; International Law Association International Committee on the Status of Refugees, *Restrictive Measures in Europe* 21 (1992).
3   On 31 July 2000 58 Chinese would-be asylum claimants were found dead in a lorry in Dover. Every year hundreds of would-be asylum claimants from sub-Saharan Africa, Iraq, Afghanistan and other refugee-producing areas of the world die attempting to cross the sea to Europe in small boats, or hiding in the holds of ships or in the undercarriages of aircraft or in lorries.
4   See John Morrison *The trafficking and smuggling of refugees* UNHCR (July 2000).
5   See Immigration and Asylum Act 1999, Sch 16.

Liability for clandestine entrants

14.69 Section 32 of the Immigration and Asylum Act 1999 imposes a penalty on persons responsible for a clandestine entrant. A clandestine entrant is defined as someone who either claims asylum or evades or tries to evade immigration control, having:

(a)   arrived in the UK concealed in a vehicle, ship or aircraft;

(b)   passed or tried to pass through immigration control concealed in a vehicle; or

(c)   arrived in the UK on a ship or aircraft, after embarking outside the UK concealed in a vehicle.[1]

Aircraft includes hovercraft and a vehicle includes a trailer, semi-trailer, caravan or anything else designed for towing.[2] A 'responsible person' is defined as the owner or captain of the ship or aircraft if sub-section (1)(a) applies, and in all cases, the owner, hirer or driver of the vehicle (or operator, if the vehicle was a trailer) in or on which the clandestine entrant was concealed.[3] All 'responsible persons' are jointly and severally liable for a penalty (currently £2,000)[4] in respect of each clandestine entrant carried.[5] 'Immigration control' for the purposes of the section includes any UK immigration control operated in a prescribed control zone outside the UK.[6] Section 39 of the 1999 Act empowers the Secretary of State by regulation to extend liability for clandestine entrants to persons responsible for rail freight wagons in which they conceal themselves. Regulations and a Code of Practice followed and came into force in March 2001.[7]

1 Immigration and Asylum Act 1999, s 32(1).
2 Immigration and Asylum Act 1999, s 43.
3 Immigration and Asylum Act 1999, s 32(5) and (6).
4 The penalty is set out in the Carriers' Liability (Clandestine Entrants and Sale of Transporters) Regulations 2000, SI 2000/685, reg 3.
5 Immigration and Asylum Act 1999, s 32(2) and (4).
6 Immigration and Asylum Act 1999, s 32(10). The part of France situated at Coquelles, which is a control zone for international purposes, is prescribed by SI 2000/685, reg 5.
7 See the Carriers' Liability (Clandestine Entrants) (Application to Rail Freight) Order 2001, SI 2001/280; the Carriers' Liability (Clandestine Entrants and Sale of Transporters) (Amendment) Regulations 2001, SI 2001/311; and the Carriers' Liability (Clandestine Entrants) (Code of Practice for Rail Freight) Order 2001, SI 2001/312.

14.70 The statutory definition of 'clandestine entrants' for whom responsible persons are liable for penalties is far broader than its everyday usage. It includes not just those who try to enter without seeing (or being seen by) an immigration officer, but also those who present themselves at immigration control and claim asylum after stowing away on a ship or aircraft, or hidden in a lorry or rail freight wagon for the journey. In such a case the owner and captain of the ship or aircraft or manager of the train in which they stowed away, or the owner, hirer and driver or operator of the lorry or trailer would all be potentially liable to pay the penalty. It also includes asylum seekers who present themselves at immigration control in, say, Dover having hidden in a vehicle to embark on a cross-Channel ferry and got out of the vehicle during the crossing to leave the boat as a foot passenger. In such a situation, the owner, hirer or the driver of the vehicle in which they hid at Calais would be liable, although not the owner or captain of the ferry.[1] The provisions apply to private as well as public vehicles, so all car drivers must check that their vehicles are not concealing extra passengers, that windows are fully closed and doors and car boots fully locked before driving on to the cross-Channel ferry on their return from a continental holiday, to avoid liability.

1 See Immigration and Asylum Act 1999, s 32(8) and (9).

14.71 There are two statutory defences:

(i)   duress;[1] or
(ii)   the carrier did not know and had no reasonable grounds for suspecting that a clandestine entrant might be concealed in the transporter; an effective system for preventing the carriage of clandestine entrants was in operation in relation to the transporter; and that system was properly operated on the occasion in question.[2]

If duress is successfully relied on, it discharges the liability of all responsible persons for that occasion, whereas the liability of the other responsible persons is not discharged by a successful reliance by one of them on the 'effective system' defence.[3] Codes of Practice have been issued which detail the precautions which should be taken by owners, hirers, operators and drivers of road haulage and other commercial vehicles, buses and coaches and private vehicles;[4] and those operating rail freight transport. Regard will be had to its provisions in determining whether the system in operation is effective for the purposes of the Immigration and Asylum Act 1999, section 34(3) defence.[5]

1 Immigration and Asylum Act 1999, s 34(2).
2 Immigration and Asylum Act 1999, s 34(3).
3 Immigration and Asylum Act 1999, s 34(5) and (6).
4 The Immigration and Asylum Act 1999: Civil Penalty: Code of Practice for Vehicles was brought into force by the Carriers' Liability (Clandestine Entrants) (Code of Practice) Order 2000, SI 2000/684, on 3 April 2000. The Code of Practice for Rail Freight was brought into force by the Carriers' Liability (Clandestine Entrants) (Code of Practice for Rail Freight) Order 2001, SI 2001/312, on 1 March 2001.
5 Immigration and Asylum Act 1999, s 34(4).

14.72 Once the responsible persons are served with a penalty notice, payment must be made within 60 days[1] unless a notice of objection is served within 30 days,[2] in which case the Secretary of State decides whether the penalty is payable.[3] Senior officers have the power to detain any relevant vehicle, small ship or small aircraft ('the transporter') pending payment of the penalty if there is a significant risk that the penalty will not be paid without such detention.[4] Application may be made to the County Court or the High Court[5] by any interested person for release of the transporter.[6] Subject to any court order for release, the Secretary of State is empowered to sell the transporter after 12 weeks if the penalty is not paid.[7] The Administrative Court held in *Balbo Auto Transporti*[8] that the appropriate line of defence for a penalty imposed under section 35 of the Immigration and Asylum Act 1999 is to wait for the Secretary of State to sue, and then to raise a defence under section 34 of the Act in the proceedings, which are likely to be in the County Court. Judicial review is not an appropriate remedy.

1 Period defined by the Carriers' Liability (Clandestine Entrants and Sale of Transporters) Regulations 2000, SI 2000/685, reg 4 (applied to rail freight by SI 2001/311).
2 Period defined by SI 2000/685, reg 6.
3 Immigration and Asylum Act 1999, s 35.
4 Immigration and Asylum Act 1999, s 36.
5 In England, Wales and Northern Ireland; in Scotland, the sheriff or the Court of Session: Immigration and Asylum Act 1999, s 43.
6 Immigration and Asylum Act 1999, s 37(2) and (3).
7 Immigration and Asylum Act 1999, s 37(4) and Sch 1. The Carriers' Liability (Clandestine Entrants and Sale of Transporters) Regulations 2000, SI 2000/685, set out the procedures for service of notices and sale of transporters and the application of the proceeds of sale.
8 *R (Balbo B&C Auto Transporti Internazionali) v Secretary of State for the Home Department* [2001] EWHC Admin 195.

Liability for inadequately documented passengers

14.73 Section 40 of the Immigration and Asylum Act 1999 consolidates the carriers' liability provisions of the Immigration (Carriers' Liability) Act 1987 and subsequent legislation, and extends them to bus and coach operators. The owner of a ship, aircraft or road passenger vehicle[1] or the operator of a train[2] is liable to pay a charge, currently £2000, in respect of each passenger who requires leave to enter the UK (ie, not a British citizen or national of the EEA, or exempt) and arrives in the UK without a valid passport or other travel document satisfactorily establishing his or her identity and nationality or citizenship, or without a valid visa of the required kind.[3] The required kind may be an entry visa or a transit visa.[4] Where a false document or visa is presented, or a passenger is not the person to whom the document relates, the owner or operator is liable only if the falsity or impersonation is reasonably apparent.[5] This imposes on carriers the responsibility to ensure not only that passengers are carrying genuine documents but also that they have requisite visas, which is extremely difficult where the passengers are not visa nationals. Such passengers will require visas if they are entering the UK for some purposes (mainly with a view to settlement) but not for others (visits, studies or resuming residence). Guidance has been issued to carriers on passport and visa requirements.[6]

1 Defined as one used commercially and adapted to carry more than eight passengers, or one not so adapted but where passengers are charged separate fares: Immigration and Asylum Act 1999, s 40(11). This definition excludes taxis from liability.
2 Defined in Immigration and Asylum Act 1999, s 43 to exclude shuttle services, since through a bilateral agreement between the UK and France, the effective UK frontier for immigration control is at the point of embarkation in France. See also s 40(9) and (10).
3 Immigration and Asylum Act 1999, s 40(1) and (2).
4 Immigration and Asylum Act 1999, s 40(12). The power to require transit passengers to hold a transit visa is now contained in s 41 (not yet in force). Persons requiring transit visas are set out in the Immigration (Transit Visas) Order 1993 and Amendment Orders 1998, SI 1993/1678, SI 1998/55, SI 1998/1014 and SI 1999/2483, 1999, SI 1999/3086, and 2000, SI 2000/1381. They are nationals of Afghanistan, China, Colombia, Democratic Republic of Congo (formerly Zaire), Ecuador, Eritrea, Ethiopia, Ghana, Iran, Iraq, Libya, Nigeria, the Slovak Republic, Somalia, Sri Lanka, Turkey, Uganda, Federal Republic of Yugoslavia, and persons holding travel documents issued by the 'Turkish Republic of Northern Cyprus' or the former Socialist Federal Republic of Yugoslavia. These are all countries from which refugees come.
5 Immigration and Asylum Act 1999, s 40(6).
6 *Passports and Visas: A Guide for Carriers* (1998 edition), known as the *Blue Guide*.

14.74 The owner or operator is not liable if the passenger produced the required document on embarkation.[1] It is for the carrier to establish that a purported travel document was produced; if that burden is discharged, the Secretary of State can only charge if he or she proves the document's falsity to have been reasonably apparent.[2] Liability is not incurred where the owner or operator was not lawfully able to carry out checks in the country where the passenger embarked, that satisfactory arrangements were in place to prevent the carriage of inadequately documented passengers, and that everything practicable had been done in accordance with those arrangements to establish that passengers had the required documentation and to prevent those who did not from arriving in the UK. This defence was introduced for railway services providers in 1998, and is extended to bus and coach operators by the Immigration and Asylum Act 1999, because of prohibitions on identity checks in French law. It does not apply where document checks lawfully may be performed in the country of embarkation.[3] Where a passenger was carried by bus on a ship or hovercraft, a charge may be imposed either on the owner of the bus or the captain of the ship or hovercraft, but not both.[4] Powers of detention and sale of transporters apply to carriers of inadequately documented passengers as they do to carriers of clandestine entrants.[5]

1 Immigration and Asylum Act 1999, s 40(4).

2   *R v Secretary of State for the Home Department, ex p Hoverspeed* [1999] INLR 591 at 601.
3   Immigration and Asylum Act 1999, s 40(5). One of the complaints in the *Hoverspeed* case (see **14.76** below) was that under French law it is a criminal offence for unauthorised persons, including carriers, to conduct identity checks, as opposed to documentary checks, but this did not allow the company to claim the benefit of the defence under this sub-section.
4   Immigration and Asylum Act 1999, s 40(7), (8). The section applies to vehicles carried on ships and aircraft.
5   Immigration and Asylum Act 1999, s 42, Sch 1. See **14.72** above.

14.75   The Immigration and Nationality Directorate issued guidance for carriers under the Immigration (Carriers' Liability) Act 1987 and, pending its replacement, was issued information for bus and coach owners and operators on the working of the provisions.[1] The guidance sets out some of the situations in which immigration inspectors will normally be prepared to waive a charge:

- the passenger is a child travelling as part of an organised school group;
- the passenger has arrived on a flight or ship which, following departure, has been diverted to the UK;
- the passenger is a stowaway and the carrier has done everything possible to ensure that no unauthorised persons use the service (but a carrier regularly carrying stowaways may find the charge maintained);
- the carrier has no realistic alternative to bringing the passenger to or via the UK, eg where the law or government of another country requires it (unless the carrier has taken the passenger there through the UK without the requisite documents);
- the carrier acted on the advice of a UK government representative and it was reasonable to rely on that advice;[2]
- the case is the first to arise in respect of the particular carrier from that port;
- at the time of check-in the passenger was in imminent and self-evident danger of his or her life, and had no reasonable means of obtaining the necessary documents, and the UK was the only or clearly the most appropriate destination, and the carrier had no opportunity to verify his or her acceptability with the UK authorities;
- there are exceptional compelling compassionate reasons or other compelling circumstances justifying waiver.[3]

In addition, the Secretary of State routinely exercises discretion to waive or cancel the charge in respect of passengers ultimately granted full refugee status (a concession not extended to those granted exceptional leave to remain)[4] and in respect of EEA nationals.[5] Charges will also be waived for visa nationals relying on used visas which have not been properly endorsed by the immigration officer, and for visa nationals arriving by air who qualified for a visa waiver under the Transit without Visa concession, where the carrier genuinely believed that their sole purpose was to pass through the UK in onward passage, unless the passenger is subsequently denied onward carriage by the airline while in the UK owing to detection of inadequate documentation.[6] Carriers may also escape liability by achieving and retaining Approved Gate Check (AGC) Status, for which they have to fulfil stringent criteria for checking passengers' documentation prior to embarkation.[7] As of January 1998, 46 carriers at 163 operating locations worldwide had registered for Approved Gate Check status.[8]

1   *Charging Procedures, a Guide for Carriers* (1996 edition, as revised), known as the *Green Guide*; *Information for Bus and Coach Owners and Operators: Carriers' Liability Provisions in respect of Inadequately Documented Passengers* (1999).

2   A number of ports and airports overseas now have UK liaison immigration officers (LIOs) or airline liaison officers (ALOs) permanently based there, advising carriers on passengers' eligibility to travel and authenticity of their documentation. They are responsible for preventing many hundreds of passengers, including refugees, from embarking on journeys to the UK. See Morrison *The Trafficking and Smuggling of Refugees*, UNHCR (July 2000) p 40; UNHCR *Interception of Asylum seekers and Refugees: The international framework and recommendations for a comprehensive approach* Standing Committee, 9 June 2000 [EC/50/SC/CRP.17].

3   *Charging Procedures, a Guide for Carriers* above, Appendix A.

4   See the list in *Hoverspeed* **14.76** fn 2 below, at 595G.

5   See the list in *Hoverspeed* below, at 595G.

6   See *Charging Procedures, a Guide for Carriers* above, Appendix A for detailed requirements of this concession. See **14.73** fn 4 above for a list of countries whose nationals require transit visas.

7   See *Charging Procedures, a Guide for Carriers* above, para 7.

8   J Morrison *The cost of survival* (1998).

14.76 In the *Hoverspeed* case[1] the company, which had incurred (disputed) liabilities of almost £500,000 for carrying inadequately documented passengers, mostly relating to passengers without a valid or current visa, sought declarations that the carriers' liability legislation offended against EC law in two distinct ways: (i) it constituted an unlawful restriction on the company's right to provide services, contrary to Article 49 EC (ex Article 59); (ii) it constituted an unlawful interference with the free movement rights of EEA nationals and their families who were subjected to documentary checks, an interference which the company was entitled to rely on. The Divisional Court rejected both arguments. Simon Brown LJ made the point that the Schengen Convention,[2] incorporated into EU law via the Amsterdam Treaty, obliged member states (except the UK, Ireland and Denmark, which have opted out) to impose carrier sanctions, making it realistic to assume that it was compatible with EC law,[3] and held that the legislation did not impose measures so disproportionate as to thwart the central purpose of the EC Treaty, the free movement of persons, and so did not constitute a restriction for the purposes of Article 49 EC (ex Article 59).[4] If it did amount to a restriction, it was justified on public policy grounds, in the interests of immigration control, as an essential adjunct to the effective operation of the visa system.[5] Nor did it impede free movement of EEA nationals, who suffered only a brief though careful documentary check which had no perceptible effect on their freedom to travel.[6] In the course of his judgment he accepted implicitly that carrier sanctions deprived asylum seekers of any choice as to the country of asylum,[7] a choice which he held in the later *Adimi* case[8] to be open to asylum seekers on a limited basis as part of the international obligations towards refugees.

1   *R v Secretary of State for the Home Department, ex p Hoverspeed* [1999] INLR 591.

2   Article 26(2) of the Schengen Convention.

3   *Hoverspeed* above, at 603A.

4   *Hoverspeed* above, at 607H.

5   *Hoverspeed* above, at 608D.

6   *Hoverspeed* above, at 612H.

7   *Hoverspeed* above, at 599H.

8   *R v Uxbridge Magistrates' Court, ex p Adimi* [1999] INLR 490 at 496H–497F.

14.77 It is clear from the terms of the Immigration and Asylum Act 1999 and the guidance that exacting the penalty is a matter of discretion. How should it be exercised, and what is the threshold for challenging a decision to impose a penalty? In *Hoverspeed* Simon Brown LJ said that it is for the court, not the

Home Office, to say whether liability is established.[1] This suggests that the court can substitute its own view on liability on the merits. However he qualified this by stating that 'it is ultimately for the court to decide, in any given case, whether the Secretary of State is, by his officials, setting impermissibly high standards for the detection of forged or otherwise inadequate travel documents'[2]—a formulation in classic administrative law terms. In *Naraine v Hoverspeed*[3] a British citizen of Asian/Caribbean origin holding a British visitor's passport (BVP), who was refused access to a hovercraft to France on a day trip, lost his claim against Hoverspeed on the ground that the company's action was dictated by French insistence on visas for BVP holders and its carrier sanction regime, which were not in breach of EC law, and there was no racial discrimination since all BVP holders were treated in the same way. But in *Farah v British Airways and Home Office*,[4] an appeal against the striking out of a negligence claim, Somali nationals, who had been refused access to a British Airways flight in Cairo on the advice of an airline liaison officer and were subsequently deported to Ethiopia, were held entitled to pursue a claim against the Home Office for the wrong advice, since loss, including non-economic loss, was eminently forseeable and it was arguable that the airline liaison officer owes a duty of care to passengers to give correct and accurate advice to airlines as to the validity of documents issued at a British diplomatic post overseas.

1 *Hoverspeed* **14.76** fn 1 above, at 602A.
2 *Hoverspeed* above, at 602C.
3 (1999) Independent, 18 November; [1999] CLY 2273.
4 *Farah v British Airways and Home Office* (2000) Times, 26 January, CA.

The future

14.78 This area of the law is marked by intensive activity in Europe, and proposals for directives and framework decisions on strengthening the penal framework to prevent the facilitation of unauthorised entry and residence, and on harmonisation of financial penalties imposed on carriers, are at the time of writing, undergoing refinement under Articles 61(a) and 63(3)(b) of the consolidated EC Treaty.[1] The UK has 'opted in' to these provisions,[2] over which there are serious concerns, particularly in the failure of the facilitation measures to protect humanitarian, church and community groups from criminalisation, and the absence of any indication that the right to asylum will be protected. There is no agreement within the Council of the EU as to whether humanitarian 'smuggling' activities should be criminalised. The UK is also signed up to the Schengen Information System, a computer-aided data collection and retrieval system for searches for persons and objects in the contracting states. Under the Schengen Information System, personal data are stored in the central computer in Strasbourg and simultaneously on linked-up national systems for searches with a view to arrest, remand in custody, tracing people, discreet surveillance, or with a view to returning a person to the external borders of the contracting states, or introducing measures to terminate residence and expel persons apprehended on the territory of a contracting state. This will enable persons sought for immigration offences to be arrested in any EU member state.

1   Documents 10186/00, 10675/00 and 10676/00.
2   See **7.27** above. It has been accepted for participation in art 27 of the Schengen
     Implementing Convention, which provides for jurisdiction over offences of assisting entry
     or residence in the Schengen area. See Home Office explanatory memorandum on Justice
     and Home Affairs matters, 29 September 2000.

Chapter 15

DEPORTATION AND REPATRIATION

DEPORTATION

Introduction

15.1 Deportation is the process whereby a non-British citizen can be compulsorily removed from the UK and prevented from returning unless the deportation order is revoked.[1] There is no power to deport a person who has already left the UK. A deportation order operates to cancel leave to remain.[2] But deportation has an effect long after the removal. It continues in force until revoked. Deportation is thus to be distinguished from other forms of compulsory removal which only bring a particular application or entry to an end, although they may create difficulties for an immigrant seeking to enter in the future. These various powers are not mutually exclusive: being an illegal entrant or a psychiatric patient does not prevent the exercise of the power to deport, provided the conditions for deportation exist.[3]

1 Immigration Act 1971, s 5(1) and (2).
2 Immigration Act 1971, s 5(1).
3 See *Patel v Immigration Appeal Tribunal* [1989] Imm AR 416, CA. As to the alternative use of deportation or Mental Health Act 1983 powers see *R v Immigration Appeal Tribunal, ex p Alghali* [1986] Imm AR 376, *X v Secretary of State for the Home Department,* [2001] 1 WLR 740, [2001] INLR 205, CA, and see **16.67** below.

History of the power to deport

15.2 Deportation was a power originally confined to aliens,[1] or foreign nationals. Its origins were in the prerogative powers of the Crown relating to aliens, but came to be regulated by statute. For example, there was power under the Aliens Order 1953 to deport aliens on the ground that to do so was conducive to the public good.[2] In 1962 the first provisions enabling the deportation of Commonwealth citizens were introduced. But at first deportation was only available on the recommendation of a criminal court following a conviction, including convictions for immigration offences under the Commonwealth

Immigrants Act 1962.[3] In 1969 the Secretary of State for the Home Department was given the power to initiate deportation proceedings against Commonwealth citizens who were in breach of their conditions of admission.[4] With the coming into force of the Immigration Act 1971 in 1973, the position of Commonwealth immigrants and aliens was made broadly the same. Anyone (except exempt persons including certain Commonwealth citizens, see below) could be deported for overstaying or breaching conditions of leave; on grounds that it was conducive to the public good; for belonging to the family of someone being deported on these grounds; or on a recommendation in a criminal case.[5]

1   Ie not Commonwealth citizens. Defined in British Nationality Act 1981, s 50(1).
2   Aliens Order 1953, art 20(2)(b), now repealed.
3   Commonwealth Immigrants Act 1962 and 1968, s 6 now repealed.
4   Immigration Appeals Act 1969, s 16, now repealed.
5   Immigration Act 1971, unamended, s 3(5), (6).

15.3 The law distinguished between illegal entrants, who (like those refused leave to enter) could be removed without further ado,[1] and those who had entered lawfully but had breached conditions or overstayed. The latter were made subject to deportation (connoting not just removal but prohibition on re-entry), but had the protection of an in-country appeal right before this was done. In one of its more dramatic reforms, the Immigration and Asylum Act 1999 removed this distinction. From 2 October 2000, overstayers, those breaching conditions of their leave and persons obtaining leave by deception, together with their families, became subject to administrative removal procedures identical to those applying to illegal entrants.[2] Only those protected by transitional provisions and those participating in a so-called regularisation programme are excepted.[3]

1   Immigration Act 1971, Sch 2, para 9.
2   Immigration and Asylum Act 1999, s 10. See chapter 16 below.
3   Immigration and Asylum Act 1999, s 9, Sch 15, para 12.

Liability to be deported

Non-British citizens

15.4 A British citizen cannot be deported.[1] If someone becomes a citizen (or acquires the right of abode and is therefore deemed to be a citizen for the purposes of the Immigration Acts) any deportation order ceases to have effect.[2] The term 'British citizen' includes a Commonwealth citizen who had the right of abode in the UK before 1983.[3] Thus a Commonwealth woman married to a British citizen before 1983 is not liable to be deported.[4] There is no legal bar in UK domestic law to deporting a British Dependent Territories citizen or a British Overseas citizen,[5] and in the case of British Overseas citizen visitors there can be no legitimate expectation that they will not be deported.[6] In practice, however, it is extremely difficult as there appears to be little obligation on the country of former residence to receive them back.[7] Equally, there is no bar on the deportation of EEA nationals, but special rules apply, as we have seen in chapter 7 above.[8] There is no statutory bar on the deportation of Convention refugees, although the Immigration Rules preclude the making of a deportation order against anyone whose removal would breach the UK's obligations under the Refugee Convention or the ECHR.[9]

1   Immigration Act 1971, ss 3(5), 6(2).
2   Immigration Act 1971, s 5(2). This contrasts with the position under the old law of an alien who became a British subject after the making of a deportation order: see *C v E* (1946) 62 TLR 326.
3   Immigration Act 1971, s 2, as amended by British Nationality Act 1981.
4   Immigration Act 1971, ss 2(2) and 5(2). But if the marriage took place after a deportation order had been signed, then she would not be deemed to be a British citizen.
5   See *R v Immigration Appeal Tribunal, ex p Sunsara* [1995] Imm AR 15.
6   *Patel v Secretary of State for the Home Department* [1993] Imm AR 392, CA.
7   See *R v Chief Immigration Officer, Gatwick Airport, ex p Harjendar Singh* [1987] Imm AR 346, QBD. The absence of evidence that the country specified in the removal direction would accept a person did not remove the Secretary of State's power to deport: *Sunsara* above.
8   See also **15.42** below.
9   HC 395, para 380, as amended by Cm 4851. See *Raziastaraie v Secretary of State for the Home Department* [1995] Imm AR 459.

Exemption from deportation

Diplomatic exemption

15.5 Under section 8(3) of the Immigration Act 1971 and the Immigration (Exemption from Control) Order 1972[1] made under section 8(2), as we have seen in chapter 6 above, exemption from immigration control is given to diplomats and international functionaries. In some cases full immunity is given, including immunity from deportation, but in other cases the exempted category of person can still be deported on grounds conducive to the public good. Where someone is subject to an exemption, normally the exemption will extend to members of their family who form part of their household.[2] Whether someone falls within this category sometimes can be difficult to determine.[3]

1   SI 1972/1613.
2   See chapter 6 above.
3   *Gupta v Secretary of State for the Home Department* [1979–80] Imm AR 52 at 57; *R v Secretary of State for the Home Department, ex p Bagga* [1990] Imm AR 413, CA.

Five-year rule for Irish and Commonwealth citizens

15.6 Certain Commonwealth and Irish citizens, who were ordinarily resident in the UK when the Immigration Act 1971 came into force, are exempted from liability for deportation.[1] Under earlier laws, Commonwealth or Irish citizens could not be deported if they had completed five years ordinary residence, excluding any long periods spent in prison.[2] At the same time, no Commonwealth or Irish citizen could be deported on conducive to the public good grounds. These exemptions were continued in the circumstances set out in section 7 of the 1971 Act for Commonwealth and Irish citizens who became ordinarily resident in the UK on or before 1 January 1973, when the 1971 Act came into force, and were Commonwealth or Irish citizens at that time.[3] The burden of proving entitlement to the exemption is on the proposed deportee, and not the authorities.[4] Essentially this means showing that they have been 'ordinarily resident' for the requisite period.

1   Immigration Act 1971, s 7(1)(b). The subsection was modified by Immigration and Asylum Act 1999, Sch 14, para 46, applying the exemption to those who would formerly have been deported but are now subject to administrative removal by virtue of s 10.
2   Commonwealth Immigrants Act 1962, s 7(2), now repealed, and see *R v Edgehill* [1963] 1 QB 593, [1963] 1 All ER 181, CCA.

3   Immigration Act 1971, s 7(1), as amended by Immigration and Asylum Act 1999, Sch 14, para 46.
4   Immigration Act 1971, s 7(5).

15.7 Those Commonwealth and Irish citizens who became ordinarily resident on or before 1 January 1973 and have continued to be ordinarily resident at all times since that date cannot be deported on conducive to the public good grounds.[1] Commonwealth and Irish citizens cannot be deported on any ground (conducive to the public good, membership of deportee's family, or recommendation by a criminal court) if they were ordinarily resident at 1 January 1973 and have been so for the five years prior to the decision or recommendation.[2] The conditions are not cumulative, but separate heads of exemption.[3] The five years must have been completed at the time of the decision or recommendation for deportation, not the date of the actual making of the order.[4] The date on which a decision to deport is made is a matter of fact, not law, and is not necessarily the date when notice of it is given to or reaches the potential deportee.[5]

1   Immigration Act 1971, s 7(1)(a).
2   Immigration Act 1971, s 7(1)(b) and (c). See *R v Secretary of State for the Home Department, ex p Olashehinde* [1992] Imm AR 443, QBD.
3   *Kane (Lawrence)* [2000] Imm AR 250, IAT.
4   *Mehmet v Secretary of State for the Home Department* [1977] Imm AR 68, CA.
5   *Rehman v Secretary of State for the Home Department* [1978] Imm AR 80. Contrast *Robina Rafiq v Secretary of State for the Home Department* [1998] Imm AR 193: a grant of leave is not effective until communicated. The practice of serving deportation decisions on the file when the person's whereabouts were unknown, prevalent until 1986, meant that many long-term overstayers were not aware of deportation decisions, and even deportation orders, against them for many years. See **16.44** below.

15.8 Normally a person is not to be treated as ordinarily resident at a time when he or she is in this country 'in breach of the immigration laws'.[1] But for the purposes of this exemption from deportation, the position is different. Section 7(2) of the Immigration Act 1971 provides that a person who has at any time become ordinarily resident is not to be treated for the purposes of the exemption as having ceased to be so by reason only of having remained in breach of the immigration laws. Deserting seamen[2] and illegal entrants[3] will not gain exemption, only those who have overstayed. For example, in the case of *R v Immigration Appeal Tribunal, ex p Perdikos*[4] the applicant returned to this country while he was still subject to a deportation order. Woolf J held that he never acquired ordinary residence, and so could not benefit from the deportation exemption.

1   Immigration Act 1971, s 33(1); see chapter 5 above.
2   *Re Abdul Manan* [1971] 2 All ER 1016, [1971] 1 WLR 859, CA: a deserting seaman had never become ordinarily resident since he was guilty of an offence when he deserted ship, and continued to be so during the whole period of his stay in this country.
3   *R v Bangoo* [1977] Imm AR 33n, CA; *Perdikos* (1981) 131 NLJ 477.
4   (1981) 131 NLJ 477, following *Manan* above. See further *R v Secretary of State for the Home Department, ex p Margueritte* [1983] QB 180, [1982] 3 All ER 909, CA; *Immigration Appeal Tribunal v Chelliah* [1985] Imm AR 192, CA; *R v Secretary of State for the Home Department, ex p Oni* (CO 2863/1998) 25 October 1999.

Section 1(5) cases

15.9 Until August 1988, a Commonwealth woman married to a Commonwealth man settled here before 1 January 1973 was not liable to be deported, even if the marriage was a sham one.[1] Children under 16 at the time of the decision to deport also benefitted.[2] This exemption has disappeared with the repeal of section 1(5) of the Immigration Act 1971 by the Immigration Act 1988,[3] and it is doubtful if any privilege or right under section 1(5) was preserved by section 16 of the 1988 Act after the repeal.[4]

1 This was because of the saving provision of s 1(5) of the Immigration Act 1971 combined with provisions allowing such women to register as British on marriage. See *Secretary of State for the Home Department v Huseyin* [1988] Imm AR 129, CA; this did not apply to alien wives of Commonwealth citizens: see *O'Shea v Secretary of State for the Home Department* [1988] Imm AR 484, CA. It did not apply if the marriage took place after the deportation order had been signed: *R v Secretary of State for the Home Department, ex p Hayden* [1988] Imm AR 555, QBD. Nor did it apply to husbands of women settled here: *Singh v Immigration Appeal Tribunal* [1988] Imm AR 582.
2 *Menn v Secretary of State for the Home Department* [1992] Imm AR 245, CA.
3 Immigration Act 1988, s 1.
4 *Menn* above; *R v Secretary of State for the Home Department, ex p Delpratt* [1991] Imm AR 5n, QBD; see also *R v Secretary of State for the Home Department, ex p Ovakkouche* [1991] Imm AR 5, QBD.

Application to citizens of Pakistan and South Africa

15.10 Pakistan withdrew from the Commonwealth on 30 January 1972. Section 1 of the Pakistan Act 1973, passed on 25 July 1973 and in force on 1 September 1973, enacted that citizens of Pakistan ceased to be Commonwealth citizens at commencement. But transitional provisions enabled citizens of Pakistan to retain some of their rights as Commonwealth citizens for long enough to register as citizens of the UK and colonies (CUKC).[1] In 1989 Pakistan rejoined the Commonwealth.[2] Thus from 1 October 1989 its citizens have been able to claim exemption again if they fulfilled the residence conditions set out above.[3] In 1994 South Africa rejoined the Commonwealth, and its citizens became able to claim exemption if they fulfilled the residence conditions set out above.

1 By deeming them Commonwealth citizens until 31 August 1974, giving one year to apply for registration as a CUKC. If such an application was made, deemed Commonwealth citizenship continued pending its determination. Those not applying in time lost eligibility for the exemption.
2 British Nationality (Pakistan) Order 1989, SI 1989/1331.
3 In *Siddique* (16050) 7 January 1998, IAT, a Pakistan national relied on the transitional provisions to found exemption from deportation on the ground of ordinary residence on 1 January 1973 and for five years preceding the decision.

Grounds of deportation

15.11 A person who is not a British citizen and not exempt is liable to deportation from the UK in the following circumstances:

(i)   the Secretary of State deems his or her deportation to be conducive to the public good;[1]
(ii)   another member of the family to which he or she belongs is to be deported;[2]
(iii)   a court recommends deportation after conviction of an offence punishable by imprisonment.[3]

1 Immigration Act 1971, s 3(5)(a), as amended by Immigration and Asylum Act 1999, Sch 14, para 44(2).

2   Immigration Act 1971, s 3(5)(b), as amended.
3   Immigration Act 1971, s 3(6).

Deportation conducive to public good

15.12 The power to deport on public good grounds has existed in the case of foreign nationals for most of the last century, and probably before, under the prerogative powers of the Crown. There was no right of appeal until 1969 and the decided cases in the High Court all favoured the executive, although the judges proclaimed their ability to protect the liberty of the subject.[1] The power is now contained in section 3(5)(a) of the Immigration Act 1971, as amended. A special regime applies to political cases, as we shall see.[2] The most frequent use of the powers is against convicted criminals who have not been recommended for deportation by the court which sentenced them,[3] as the section 3(5)(a) power is available without a prior court recommendation. The 1971 Act retained the criminal courts' power to make recommendations for deportation, which can then be acted on without an appeal in the immigration system. There is little benefit and some procedural unfairness in retaining both avenues, but Parliament has not sought to reform the system by way of amendment in the Immigration and Asylum Act 1999. The inequalities of this system were reduced to an extent by the regime of asylum appeals introduced in 1993, and by the Human Rights Act 1998, which affects the duties of the criminal court in considering recommendations and led to a human rights appeal, introduced by section 65 of the 1999 Act. Where the deportee is an EC national, the Secretary of State in practice always follows the administrative route, regardless of whether a criminal court has made a recommendation.[4]

1   *R v Governor of Brixton Prison, ex p Sarno* [1916] 2 KB 742 at 749 and 752 ('if it was clear that an act was done by the executive with the intention of misusing those powers, this court would have jurisdiction to deal with the matter'); *R v Chiswick Police Station Supt, ex p Sacksteder* [1918] 1 KB 578 at 586-587, CA ('if that order is ... practically a sham ... it seems to me the court can go behind it'); cf *R v Brixton Prison, ex p Bloom* (1920) 85 JP 87 at 88. See further *R v Secretary of State for Home Affairs, ex p Duke of Chateau Thierry* [1917] 1 KB 922; *R v Home Secretary, ex p Bressler* (1924) 88 JP 89; see *C v E* (1946) 62 TLR 326; *R v Governor of Brixton Prison, ex p Soblen* [1963] 2 QB 243, [1962] 3 All ER 641. See A W Brian Simpson *In the Highest Degree Odious* (1994) for an illuminating review of the treatment of aliens under wartime and emergency regulations.
2   See **15.32** below.
3   The failure or refusal of a criminal court to make a recommendation does not prevent the minister initiating deportation proceedings under s 3(5)(a): see *Martin* [1993] Imm AR 161, IAT; *R v Secretary of State for the Home Department, ex p Figueiredo* [1993] Imm AR 606, QBD.
4   Presumably because of the requirements of arts 3 and 9 of Council Directive (EEC) 64/221, see **7.140ff** above.

Criminal conviction

15.13 The existence of the power to deport on public good grounds based on a past criminal conviction is not in doubt.[1] It has been suggested that the power should only be exercised on specific and positive grounds,[2] and the Court of Appeal has suggested that the provisions of Council Directive 64/221 (EEC), which prevent deportation based on the mere fact of conviction, made good sense and were equally applicable in UK domestic law.[3] The Tribunal has endorsed this view.[4] The Court of Appeal has on occasion adopted a more insular view,[5] confining such dicta to recommendations by the criminal courts[6] and underlining the differences between the Immigration Act 1971, section 3(5)(a) regime and the EC public policy directive. Indeed in one case the Court of Appeal went so far as to say that the power does not require there to be a discernible public interest other than the deterrence of others.[7]

1 *R v Immigration Appeal Tribunal, ex p Florent* [1985] Imm AR 141, CA.
2 *Khawaja v Secretary of State for the Home Department* [1984] AC 74, per Lord Bridge.
3 *R v Secretary of State for the Home Department, ex p Santillo* [1981] QB 778, [1981] 2 All ER 897, CA. In *Goremsandu v Secretary of State for the Home Department* [1996] Imm AR 250 the CA assimilated the EC approach to the municipal law approach but dismissed the appeal.
4 *Fernandez* (12016) 12 April 1995.
5 *R v Secretary of State for the Home Department, ex p Al-Sabah* [1992] Imm AR 223, CA; *R v Secretary of State for the Home Department, ex p Samaroo* (CO 4973/1999) 20 December 2000.
6 *R v Escauriaza* (1987) 87 Cr App Rep 344, CA; *R v Spura* (1988) 10 Cr App Rep (S) 376, CA.
7 *Goremsandu v Secretary of State for the Home Department* [1996] Imm AR 250, CA.

15.14 Nevertheless, it is not every conviction that could legitimately result in a deportation decision being taken. The acts proved must impinge on the public domain in a real sense.[1] There must be some public interest at stake in favour of removal. The power is not meant to be merely a supplement to punishment. It is not the label attached to an offence but its factual circumstances that best indicate the nature of the conduct and its repercussions on the public domain.[2] Although recidivism and a propensity to commit further offences are not essential preconditions to the exercise of the power to deport under section 3(5)(a) of the Immigration Act 1971,[3] they are generally material considerations when considering the merits of a decision.[4] However, cases do arise, exceptionally, where the personal conduct of a proposed deportee has been such that, whilst not necessarily evincing any clear propensity to re-offend, it causes such deep public revulsion that public policy requires deportation.[5] Convictions for importing or supplying dangerous drugs[6] for example, or for rape,[7] incest,[8] violent robbery[9] and arson[10] have been held to be in themselves a sufficient threat to public order as to give rise to the exercise of the power, although compassionate or other relevant circumstances may outweigh the public good.[11]

1 Per Woolf J in *R v Immigration Appeal Tribunal, ex p Ullah* (19 February 1982, unreported), QBD; affd [1982] Imm AR 124, CA.
2 *Ex p Florent* above. See also *Ennis* (12393) 9 August 1995.
3 *Said v Immigration Appeal Tribunal* [1989] Imm AR 372, CA; *Martinez-Tobon v Immigration Appeal Tribunal* [1988] Imm AR 319, CA.
4 Except where the deportee is an EU national, where propensity to re-offend is generally crucial to the exercise of the deportation power. See **15.42** below and **7.128ff** above.
5 *Ex p Florent* above; *Said v Immigration Appeal Tribunal* [1989] Imm AR 372, CA.
6 *Marchon* [1993] Imm AR 384, CA; *R v Secretary of State for the Home Department, ex p Samaroo* (CO 4973/1999) 20 December 2000; *Thompson* (17777) (supply of crack cocaine); *Salvi* (17823) (EU national, possession of a ton of cannabis); *Roger* (17891) (EU national, importation of ecstasy and cocaine, no previous convictions). But see **15.42** below.
7 *Galoo* (00 TH 0009): 'rape strikes at the roots of society, including the sanctity of the family'.
8 *Goremsandu v Secretary of State for the Home Department* [1996] Imm AR 250, CA.
9 *Florent* above.
10 *Escudero* (20525) 8 March 1999.
11 *Bouchereau* [1978] QB 732, particularly AG Warner at 742b-c; but see Case C-348/96 *Calfa* [1999] ECR I-11.

Political cases

15.15 Deportation may be deemed conducive to the public good as being in the interests of national security or of the relations between the UK and another country, or for other reasons of a political nature. In *Rehman*[1] the Court of Appeal held that 'national security', 'international relations' and 'other political reasons' may overlap. The power to deport on these grounds is not confined to grounds touching the public good of the people in the UK.[2] The planning and organisation in the UK of terrorist acts abroad could found deportation,[3] since the promotion of terrorism against any state is capable of being a threat to the UK's national security, although the Secretary of State would have to show that there was a real possibility of adverse repercussions in terrorist cases.[4] Grounds may also include assisting the proliferation of another country's nuclear capability contrary to international treaty.[5]

1   *Secretary of State for the Home Department v Shafiq ur Rehman* [2000] INLR 531.
2   *R v Secretary of State for the Home Department, ex p Raghbir Singh* [1995] Imm AR 446, QBD.
3   *Ex p Raghbir Singh* [1996] Imm AR 507, CA, at 510.
4   *Rehman* above. See **15.32** below.
5   *R v Secretary of State for the Home Department, ex p Saleem*, 23 July 1996.

Other conducive grounds

15.16 The circumstances other than criminal behaviour (apart from political cases) where the public good power can be exercised are not defined. Whatever they are, it is for the Secretary of State to prove the detrimental conduct complained of and to demonstrate that it impinges on the public domain. It has been held that a sham marriage qualifies because it undermines a fundamental institution of society,[1] though the appellate body must be careful that all the elements of a sham marriage are proved.[2] Criminal associations which have not led to a conviction might be a further basis, but here, although the Secretary of State may rely on inferences,[3] there may be difficulty in proving the acts complained of. The standard is the civil burden of proof, but flexibly applied, so that the graver the allegation the more certain the proof required.[4] The commission of offences abroad might be a ground for a public good deportation,[5] so long as it is not disguised extradition and does not engage human rights considerations.[6]

1   *R v Immigration Appeal Tribunal, ex p Cheema* [1982] Imm AR 134.
2   *R v Immigration Appeal Tribunal, ex p Khan* [1983] QB 790.
3   *Martinez-Tobon v Immigration Appeal Tribunal* [1988] Imm AR 319, CA.
4   *Khawaja v Secretary of State for the Home Department* [1984] AC 74.
5   *El-Awam* (12807) 14 December 1995.
6   See **15.36** below.

Deception of the Home Office

15.17 Where the Home Office has been misled into granting an indefinite leave to remain, it can base a decision to deport under section 3(5)(a) of the Immigration Act 1971 on that ground.[1] This may involve false allegations as to marital status, or as to the continued existence of cohabitation at a time when the parties are living separately. Whether there has been a deception is a matter of fact to be proved to the satisfaction of the Tribunal on a civil balance of proof, flexibly applied to take into account the gravity of the allegation.[2] Where the Tribunal was not satisfied of the allegation of a bigamous marriage, but was nevertheless satisfied that there was a history of deception, it was entitled to dismiss the appeal and not remit the matter for reconsideration by the Home Office. In *Patel*[3] Lord Bridge reconsidered and withdrew his dictum in *Khawaja*[4] that the power could not be used to deport someone who told lies on entry if his or her conduct thereafter was perfectly satisfactory, and lies on entry may now form the basis of a later deportation on conducive grounds,[5] although administrative removal is easier[6] and therefore far more likely.

1　*Re Owusu-Sekyere* [1987] Imm AR 425, CA; *Patel* (4719); *Siew (Nang Fong)* (18293), IAT.
2　*Tahir v Immigration Appeal Tribunal* [1989] Imm AR 98, CA.
3　*R v Immigration Appeal Tribunal, ex p Patel (Anilkumar Ravindrabhai)* [1988] AC 910, [1988] Imm AR 434; see also *R v Immigration Appeal Tribunal, ex p Karim* [1986] Imm AR 428 (use of a false identity).
4　*Khawaja v Secretary of State for the Home Department* [1984] AC 74, [1983] 1 All ER 765, HL.
5　*R v Secretary of State for the Home Department, ex p Chaumun* [1999] INLR 479
6　See Immigration Act 1971, Sch 2, para 9; chapter 16 below.

Deportation of family members

15.18 The power to deport on public good grounds has applied to members of a family for the best part of a century.[1] Under section 3(5)(b) of the Immigration Act 1971,[2] the Secretary of State possesses the power to deport the dependent spouse and dependent children of an immigrant where the spouse or parent respectively (hereafter called the principal deportee) has been deported or is ordered to be deported. In practice this power is only likely to be used where the family are all settled in the UK. Where the family have a limited leave in consequence of the principal's status, then an extension of that leave will normally be refused on a decision to deport the principal deportee. Where the principal has been ordered to be deported, his or her spouse and any children under 18 may also be deported, even where they are the children of the dependent spouse and not the principal's own.[3] Adopted and illegitimate children may also be deported, but not natural children who have been adopted by someone else.[4] For the purposes of this section, 'wife' includes each of two or more wives.[5]

1　Aliens Restriction Act 1914, s 1(1); *R v Home Secretary, ex p Bressler* (1924) 88 JP 89, where the courts upheld the decision of the Secretary of State to deport Mrs Bressler because of her husband's deportation following a criminal conviction.
2　As amended by Immigration and Asylum Act 1999, Sch 14, para 46.
3　Immigration Act 1971, s 5(4)(a), (b).
4　Immigration Act 1971, s 5(4).
5　Immigration Act 1971, s 5(4).

15.19 The power can be exercised where a decision to deport has been taken against the head of the family. No actual deportation order is necessary.[1] But there are limits on family deportation. If a principal deportee leaves the country after the deportation order and eight weeks elapse, no family deportation order can be made against any family members.[2] But in calculating the period of eight weeks, any period during which an appeal is pending is to be disregarded.[3] Similarly, if someone ceases to belong to the family of the deportee (because a marriage is dissolved or a child reaches 18), a family deportation order ceases to have effect against him or her.[4] A dependent spouse who is merely separated from the principal would still be liable to family deportation, although the rules make it clear that he or she would not in practice be deported.[5] If the deportation order against the principal deportee ceases to have effect, for example, because it is revoked, any family deportation order also lapses.[6]

1   *Ibrahim v Immigration Appeal Tribunal* [1989] Imm AR 111, CA, reversing the earlier case of *R v Immigration Appeal Tribunal, Ekrem Mehmet* [1977] Imm AR 56.
2   Immigration Act 1971, s 5(3).
3   Immigration and Asylum Act 1999, Sch 4, para 19. For decisions to deport before 2 October 2000 see Immigration Act 1971, s 15(2).
4   Immigration Act 1971, s 5(3).
5   HC 395, para 365(ii).
6   Immigration Act 1971, s 5(3).

Deportation recommended by court

15.20   The third head of deportation arises where a non-citizen over 17 years of age[1] is convicted[2] of an offence punishable with imprisonment[3] and is recommended for deportation by the court.[4] The recommendation may be made by any court having power to sentence him or her for the offence, unless the court commits the person to be sentenced or further dealt with for that offence by another court.[5] Thus, the recommendation may be made by the magistrates' court, a Crown Court, or the Court of Appeal.[6] There is no statutory restriction on the combination of a recommendation with other any other sentence;[7] it may be made in respect of an offender who is sentenced to imprisonment for life[8] or one who is sentenced to a fine, although it is unlikely a non-custodial sentence would reach the entry-point criteria for demonstrating 'potential detriment'. A recommendation may also be made in respect of youth custody, although such a sentence, intended to rehabilitate and train, may mean that it is not a proper case for a recommendation.[9]

1   A person is deemed to have attained the age of 17 if, on consideration of any available evidence, he or she appears to the court to have done so: Immigration Act 1971, s 6(3)(a).
2   A person is convicted of an offence for deportation purposes if he or she is found to have committed it, notwithstanding any enactment to the contrary and notwithstanding that the court does not proceed to conviction: Immigration Act 1971, s 6(3).
3   Whether an offence is punishable with imprisonment is to be determined without regard to any enactment restricting imprisonment of young offenders, or first offenders: Immigration Act 1971, s 6(3)(b).
4   Immigration Act 1971, s 3(6).
5   Immigration Act 1971, s 6(1), in which special provision is made for Scotland.
6   In Scotland a recommendation may be made by a Sheriff or the High Court of Justiciary (subject to provisos): see Immigration Act 1971, s 6(1).
7   Notwithstanding any rule of practice restricting the matters which ought to be taken into account in dealing with an offender sentenced to imprisonment: Immigration Act 1971, s 6(4) and see *R v Assa Singh* [1965] 2 QB 312, [1965] 1 All ER 938, CCA.
8   *R v Akan* [1973] QB 491.
9   See *R v Flynn* [1963] Crim LR 647.

15.21   A recommendation is to be treated as a sentence for the purposes of appealing against sentence.[1] In England an appeal may be made to the Crown Court or the Court of Appeal against a recommendation for deportation, even if this is the only part of the sentence against which an appeal is made.[2] But in those cases in which no appeal lies to the Court of Appeal from a sentence of a lower court, no appeal can be made to that court against a recommendation.[3] A recommendation can be challenged only in the criminal courts, and there is no further deportation appeal[4] if the Secretary of State decides to follow the recommendation, except on human rights or race discrimination grounds.[5] An asylum appeal can be invoked by applying to revoke the deportation order on asylum grounds and appealing refusal.[6]

1   Immigration Act 1971, s 6(5)(a), as amended by Race Relations Amendment Act 2000.
2   See *R v Edgehill* [1963] 1 QB 593, [1963] 1 All ER 181, CCA on a similar provision in the repealed Commonwealth Immigrants Act 1962.
3   *R v Lynch* [1965] 3 All ER 925, [1966] 1 WLR 92, CCA.
4   Under Immigration and Asylum Act 1999, s 63.
5   Under Immigration and Asylum Act 1999, s 65; see chapter 8.
6   Under Immigration and Asylum Act 1999, s 69(4).

15.22 No court may recommend a person for deportation unless he or she has been given seven days' notice in writing.[1] If the notice has not been served in time, the hearing may be adjourned, even after conviction, to enable the notice to be served.[2] The court needs a 'full inquiry into all the circumstances' and counsel should be invited to address the court specifically on the issue of a recommendation.[3] Where a court decides to make a recommendation, full reasons for the decision should be given, in fairness to the offender and in order to assist the Secretary of State with the ultimate decision as to whether to proceed with deportation.[4] A failure by the sentencing court to provide any, or any adequate, reasoning does not automatically lead to a recommendation being quashed, however, since the Court of Appeal has the power to give its own reasons where it is considers deportation appropriate.[5]

1   Immigration Act 1971, s 6(2).
2   Immigration Act 1971, s 6(2).
3   *R v Nazari* (1980) 71 Cr App Rep 87; *R v Escauriaza* (1987) 9 Cr App Rep (S) 542; *R v Omojudi* (1992)13 Cr App Rep (S) 346; *R v Frank* (1991) 13 Cr App Rep (S) 500.
4   *R v Nazari* above; *R v Rodney* [1998] INLR 118, [1996] Cr App Rep (S) 230; *R v Bozat* [1997] 1 Cr App Rep (S) 270.
5   *R v Bozat* above; *R v Dudeye* [1998] 2 Cr App Rep (S) 430.

Guidelines for criminal courts

15.23 The power to make a recommendation must be exercised judicially and is concerned with criminal behaviour rather than the enforcement of an immigration policy.[1] The court is not under an obligation to recommend deportation in serious cases concerning evasion of immigration controls (such as forging passports or organising illegal entry)[2] and the question whether to recommend deportation should be decided quite independently of the immigration status of the offender.[3] The basic statement of principle to guide the criminal courts was set out in the decision in *R v Caird*.[4] In quashing a recommendation for deportation against one of the defendants, the court stated that it wished to emphasise:

> 'that the courts when considering a recommendation for deportation are normally concerned simply with crime committed and the individual's past record and the question as to what is their effect on the question of potential detriment to this country of the appellant remaining here. It does not embark, and indeed is in no position to embark, upon the issue as to what is likely to be his life if he goes back to his country of origin. That is a matter for the Home Secretary.'

Caird was cited with approval and amplified in the leading case of *R v Nazari*,[5] where the widely differing cases of four appellants were dealt with together and the Court of Appeal set out a series of guidelines for courts. The criminal courts are concerned with potential detriment to the UK, and assessing potential detriment is a question of fact in each case, involving consideration of matters other than the gravity of the offence. Detriment refers to the potential harm caused by the defendant's criminal behaviour, and not such matters as receipt of welfare benefits[6] or immigration status.[7] A comparatively minor offence will not make continued presence a detriment;[8] the important issue is the defendant's likely future conduct.[9] The likelihood of re-offending is always relevant; indeed the EC criteria have to all intents and purposes been assimilated into domestic law.[10] It may include mental instability connected with or resulting in the commission of a serious criminal offence.

1 See Arthur Rogerson 'Deportation' [1963] PL 305 at 309; Graham Zellick 'The Power of The Courts To Recommend Deportation' [1973] Crim LR 612; the Wilson Committee on Immigration Appeals (1967) Cmnd 2739, para 94.
2 *R v Akan* (1972) 56 Cr App Rep 716, CA.
3 The relevant considerations were the offender's history, particularly criminal history, and the gravity of the offence: *R v Khandri*, 24 April 1979, Bridge LJ. A similar view was expressed in *Miller v Lenton* (1981) 3 Cr App Rep (S) 171; *R v Nunu* (1991) 12 Cr App Rep (S) 752, CA.
4 (1970) 54 Cr App Rep 499, CA.
5 [1980] 3 All ER 880 at 885-886, 71 Cr App Rep 87.
6 *R v Serry* (1980) 2 Cr App Rep (S) 336, [1980] LS Gaz R 1181, CA.
7 See fn 3 above.
8 *R v Kraus* (1982) 4 Cr App Rep (S) 113, CA; *R v Compassi* (1987) 9 Cr App Rep (S) 270, CA; *R v Okelola* (1992) 13 Cr App Rep (S) 560, CA.
9 *R v David* (1980) 2 Cr App Rep (S) 362, CA; *R v Tshuma* (1981) 3 Cr App Rep (S) 97; *R v Altawel* (1981) 3 Cr App Rep (S) 281 and other cases cited in Thomas *Current Sentencing Practice* part K.
10 *R v Escauriaza* (1987) 87 Cr App Rep 344, CA; *R v Spura* (1988) 10 Cr App Rep (S) 376, CA. Note the different approach under Immigration Act 1971, s 3(5)(a), for which see *R v Secretary of State for the Home Department, ex p Samaroo* (CO 4973/1999) 20 December 2000.

15.24 The second guideline from *Nazari* and *Caird*, that the courts are not concerned with the political system in the offender's home country, or with what is likely to be the offender's life there, must now be modified in the light of the court's primary obligation under the Human Rights Act 1998.[1] The criminal court cannot make a recommendation which could result in an offender being persecuted or subjected to torture or other violation of his or her fundamental human rights in another country.[2] It would be contrary to the Human Rights Act to recommend for deportation an AIDS sufferer where medical facilities in his own country are inadequate.[3] There has, however, been no litigation yet on the scope of their duty, and it is possible (but unlikely) that they will pursue their insular approach on the basis that they only recommend and the final decision is with the Secretary of State for the Home Department. It was adopted because of the difficulties and undesirability of their making such an assessment, particularly if there may be a long period of imprisonment between the conviction and the execution of the deportation order, during which time there may be a change of circumstances.[4] However, where there was cogent evidence of the consequences of deportation, and where the anticipated deportation was reasonably proximate to the decision, such material was considered.[5] The difficulties for those claiming asylum caused by the court's reluctance to deal with political issues were resolved by the creation of an asylum appeal in 1993.

1 As a public authority under Human Rights Act 1998, s 6.
2 See chapter 8 above.
3 *R v Secretary of State for the Home Department, ex p M* [1999] Imm AR 548 concerning the Secretary of State's decision following a court recommendation.
4 *R v Uddin* [1971] Crim LR 663, CA; *R v Caird* (1970) 54 Cr App Rep 499, CA.
5 And in other circumstances too: see eg *R v Said Dudeye* [1998] 2 Cr App Rep (S) 430 (recommendation against young Somali refugee for robbery quashed in light of circumstances in Somalia).

15.25 The third *Nazari* guideline[1] is that the criminal courts will have regard to the effect of any recommendation on innocent third parties. The courts have no desire to break up families and force spouses to choose between the interests of their children or the future of their marriage.[2] Since October 2000 the test is broader. For the purpose of compliance with Article 8 of the ECHR, the courts must consider whether deportation would result in interference with family or private life (ie whether the proposed deportee has family or other ties in the UK which would be interfered with by deportation, eg if family members could not reasonably be expected to accompany the deportee abroad) and if such interference would result, whether it is proportionate to the legitimate aim of preventing crime or disorder.[3] Generally, the criminal courts can be expected to take the same approach as the Secretary of State and the appellate authorities in deciding on an Immigration Act 1971, section 3(5)(a) deportation. Either authority must decide whether the proposed interference with family or private life is, in the circumstances of the case, no more than that necessary to pursue the legitimate object of prevention of crime or disorder or the protection of health and morals. For this purpose it would be necessary to consider the prevalence of the crime, its gravity and the effect it has on society and health, the deterrent effect of deportation to future offending, and decide what weight must be given to family or private life considerations and the degree of interference which would be caused. The Divisional Court has held that the sheer gravity of an offence, absent the propensity to repeat it, can in certain circumstances satisfy the test allowing interference with family or private life under Article 8(2) of the ECHR.[4]

1 [1980] 3 All ER 880 at 886, 71 Cr App Rep 87.
2 *R v Craviato* (1990) 12 Cr App Rep (S) 71; *R v Odendaal* (1991) 13 Cr App Rep (S) 341; *R v Shittu* (1992) 14 Cr App Rep (S) 283.
3 See *B v Secretary of State for the Home Department* [2000] Imm AR 478; [2000] INLR 361 (on a decision under s 3(5)(a) of the Immigration Act 1971).
4 *R v Secretary of State for the Home Department, ex p Samaroo* (CO 4973/1999) 20 December 2000.

15.26 *Nazari* did not deal with the position of EC nationals and others deriving rights from EC law,[1] and the restrictions on the court's powers to recommend deportation (see chapter 7 above). But the courts have remedied this by indicating that British law provides the same standards as EC law and so there has to be a continuing threat to some identifiable element of public interest that requires deportation.[2] Thus a recommendation for deportation may be made against a person protected by the EC Treaty, provided the conditions set down in Articles 3 and 9 of Council Directive (EEC) 64/221 have been met.[3]

1 Such as Turkish nationals enjoying rights under the Ankara Agreement: Case C-340/97 *Nazli v Stadt Nurnberg* [2000] ECR I-957.
2 *R v Escauriaza* (1987) 87 Cr App Rep 344, CA; *R v Spura* (1988) 10 Cr App Rep (S) 376, CA.

3 Article 3 of Council Directive (EEC) 64/221 provides that measures of expulsion taken on grounds of public policy or public security must be based exclusively on the personal conduct of the individual, and that previous criminal convictions should not in themselves constitute grounds for taking such measures. See also Case C-348/96 *Calfa* [1999] ECR I-11. Article 9 provides for review by an independent competent authority before expulsion. See further **7.137** above.

Decisions to deport and appeals

Making and notifying a decision

15.27 In two of the three cases where a person is liable to deportation, the initiative is taken by the Secretary of State for the Home Department. Save where a decision is required by statute to be taken by the Secretary of State personally,[1] administrative arrangements can be made for departmental officers to exercise these powers. The Secretary of State is entitled to act through departmental civil servants, pursuant to the *Carltona* principles,[2] including immigration officers.[3] Decisions to deport on the grounds of public good other than political cases, and decisions to deport family members, are taken by the officials at the enforcement section of the Home Office at Croydon.

1 Eg Immigration and Asylum Act 1999, s 63(2)(b). The decision need not be signed personally: *Re Amanullah Khan* [1986] Imm AR 485.
2 *Carltona Ltd v Works Comrs* [1943] 2 All ER 560, CA.
3 *Oladehinde and Alexander v Secretary of State for the Home Department* [1991] 1 AC 254, [1990] 3 All ER 393, [1990] 3 WLR 797, HL.

15.28 A decision to deport which carries a right of appeal[1] must be notified in accordance with the Immigration and Asylum Appeals (Notices) Regulations 2000,[2] and the notice must state the reason for the decision, indicate the country to which removal directions will be given, and indicate the right of appeal and how it may be exercised.[3] Amplification of the reasons for a decision to deport is permissible consequent to notification,[4] although a decision-maker may not switch to a different statutory category.[5] An adjudicator may not allow an appeal solely on the basis of a defect in the notice, if the decision itself was in accordance with the law and the rules.[6] The Regulations allow service of the notice at the last known address of *either* the proposed deportee *or* the representative,[7] and the election is that of the Secretary of State, so a notice may be sent to the deportee's last known address even if it is known that he or she no longer lives there or has asked for the notice to be sent to a representative.[8] Service may be achieved by fax transmission in addition to the traditional methods of hand and postal delivery.[9] Under the old rules, if the Secretary of State or his officers had no knowledge of the whereabouts or place of abode of a prospective deportee, service could be dispensed with altogether, and there was no necessity for re-service of the notice if the deportee was subsequently located.[10] Although deemed *intra vires* by the courts,[11] the power was abandoned in 1986 as unfair and ineffective,[12] and it has not been replicated in the 2000 Regulations. For a detailed discussion of notice and service, see **18.93**ff below.

1 Where the decision follows a recommendation and the only right of appeal exercisable is on human rights or race discrimination grounds, there is no obligation on the Secretary of State to give notice: Immigration and Asylum Appeals (Notices) Regulations 2000,

SI 2000/2246, reg 4(4) as amended by SI 2000/868. Where however an allegation is made that deportation would breach human rights or the Race Relations Act 1976 (as amended), notice must be given on receipt of the allegation, to enable an appeal to be brought under Immigration and Asylum Act 1999, s 65.

2   SI 2000/2246. These replace the Immigration Appeals (Notices) Regulations 1984, SI 1984/2040. The new Regulations apply to deportation appeals generated under s 15 of the Immigration Act 1971 which have arisen as a result of the regularisation procedures under s 9 of the Immigration and Asylum Act 1999: see reg 3.

3   SI 2000/2246, reg 5.

4   *R v Immigration Appeal Tribunal, ex p Hubbard* [1985] Imm AR 110; *R v Immigration Appeal Tribunal, ex p Dukobo* [1990] Imm AR 390.

5   *Yau Yak Wah v Home Office* [1982] Imm AR 16, CA; *R v Immigration Appeal Tribunal, ex p Ekrem Mehmet* [1977] Imm AR 56, QBD; *Parsaiyan v Visa Officer, Karachi* [1986] Imm AR 155. For further discussion see **18.71** below.

6   *R v Immigration Appeal Tribunal, ex p Jeyeanthan* [2000] 1 WLR 354, [1999] Imm AR 10, [1999] INLR 241, CA.

7   SI 2000/2246, reg 7(c)(ii).

8   *Singh (Pargat) v Secretary of State for the Home Department* [1993] Imm AR 112, HL; *Tongo v Secretary of State for the Home Department* [1995] Imm AR 109, CA.

9   SI 2000/2246, reg 7. Where notice is given by post it is deemed received two days after posting: Immigration and Asylum Act 1999, Sch 4, para 2.

10 SI 1984/2040, reg 3(4); *Pargat Singh* above at 117; *R v Secretary of State for the Home Department, ex p Brew* [1988] Imm AR 93, QBD.

11 *Singh (Pargat)* above; *Rhemtulla v Immigration Appeal Tribunal* [1979–80] Imm AR 168, CA

12 Under a policy DP5/86; see *R v Secretary of State for the Home Department, ex p Popatia and Chew* [2000] INLR 587 **16.44** below.

Right of appeal

15.29 Where a decision to deport is taken on conducive grounds (other than political cases) or on family grounds, there is a right of appeal under section 63 of the Immigration and Asylum Act 1999. Notice of appeal should be served within ten days of the decision being notified,[1] though there is provision for an extension of time where 'special circumstances' can be demonstrated.[2] All appeals are to the adjudicator in the first instance.[3] The right of appeal comes after the decision to deport, but before the making of a deportation order. The sequence is thus decision, appeal, deportation order. The clear distinction between a 'decision to deport' and a 'deportation order' should be noted. The right of appeal under section 63 of the Immigration and Asylum Act 1999 mirrors that formerly pertaining under section 15 of the Immigration Act 1971, embracing both an appeal against a decision to deport[4] and an appeal against a refusal to revoke an order for deportation.[5] The latter cannot be invoked while the appellant is in the UK.[6]

1   Immigration and Asylum Appeals (Procedure) Rules 2000, SI 2000/2333, r 6(1). In political cases the appeal is to the Special Immigration Appeals Commission: Immigration and Asylum Act 1999, s 64(1), Special Immigration Appeals Commission Act 1997, s 2.

2   SI 2000/2333, r 7. See also **18.102ff** below.

3   This marks a change from the old regime, where 'conducive' and 'family' deportation appeals both went to the Tribunal: Immigration Act 1971, s 15(7).

4   Immigration and Asylum Act 1999, s 63(1)(a).

5   Immigration and Asylum Act 1999, s 63(1)(b).

6   Immigration and Asylum Act 1999, s 64(3). This does not of course prevent an asylum appeal against refusal to revoke a deportation order (s 69(4)(b)), or a human rights appeal under s 65, both of which would be in-country.

15.30 While an appeal is pending, a deportation order cannot be made against a person under section 5(1) of the Immigration Act 1971.[1] An appeal is pending until it is either 'finally determined' or has been withdrawn or treated as abandoned.[2] Where a decision is being challenged on judicial review the appeal is no longer pending, but the Home Office will usually stay its hand pending the determination of the Administrative Court, although the practice does not of itself give rise to a legitimate expectation that a deportation order will not be made.[3] The decision to deport enables the immigrant to be detained in custody or subjected to restrictions.[4] If it has been served on the deportee, it stops the clock for the purpose of the long residence policy.[5] Although a deportation order will not be signed without further consideration of whether to maintain enforcement action by the Home Office, many people used to leave voluntarily before this happened, and a number were removed because they waived their appeal rights and did not wish to be detained in custody.[6] Those with in-country appeal rights may submit a challenge to destination,[7] but this aspect of the appeal will be effective only where an alternative destination has been specified.[8]

1   Immigration and Asylum Act 1999, s 63(2). See further Sch 4, para 18, in relation to ss 63(1)(a) and 69(4)(a) (asylum) appeals.
2   Immigration and Asylum Act 1999, s 58(5)-(10). See Immigration and Asylum Act, Sch 14, amending Immigration Act 1971, s 33(4).
3   *R v Secretary of State for the Home Department, ex p Yesufu* [1987] Imm AR 366, QBD.
4   Immigration Act 1971, Sch 3, para 2(2).
5   *Musah v Secretary of State for the Home Department* [1995] Imm AR 236, CA; *R v Secretary of State for the Home Department, ex p Popatia and Chew* [2000] INLR 587.
6   They were mostly overstayers seeking to avoid the prohibition on re-entry. Now that deportation has been abolished for this group, those making a voluntary departure will be fewer.
7   Immigration and Asylum Act 1999, s 63(3)–(4).
8   See further **16.64–16.66** below.

Transitional provisions and regularisation scheme

15.31   Where a decision to deport was reached before 2 October 2000, and an appeal was lodged under section 15 of the Immigration Act 1971 or section 5 of the Immigration Act 1988, the appeal continued to have effect notwithstanding the repeal of those sections.[1] Section 9 of the Immigration and Asylum Act 1999 allowed those who had become overstayers prior to 2 October 2000 to preserve their right to be deported rather than summarily removed, and so their right of appeal against deportation, provided they applied for regularisation before that date.[2] If they last entered the UK within seven years of the date of the decision, the appeal was limited to the ground that the Secretary of State did not possess 'power in law' to make an order;[3] otherwise they had a full appeal on the merits of the decision. The appeals were however governed by the 2000 procedure rules.[4]

1   Immigration and Asylum Act 1999, Sch 15, para 11; Commencement Order No 6, Sch 2, para 1(2).
2   Immigration and Asylum Act 1999, s 9, Sch 15, para 12.
3   Immigration and Asylum Act 1999, Sch 15, para 12; Immigration Act 1988, s 5; Immigration (Restricted Right of Appeal against Deportation) (Exemption) Order 1993, SI 1993/1656.
4   Immigration and Asylum Appeals (Procedure) Rules 2000, SI 2000/2333.

Political cases

15.32   There is no appeal to the appellate authority against a decision that a person's deportation is conducive to the public good as being in the interests of national security or of the relations between the UK and any other country or for other reasons of a political nature,[1] nor against a refusal to revoke a deportation order where the Secretary of State has personally certified that the person's exclusion is conducive to the public good.[2] In each case the right of appeal is to the Special Immigration Appeals Commission (SIAC), under section 2(1) and (1A) of the Special Immigration Appeals Commission Act 1997. The history of the Commission and its procedures are set out at **18.186ff** below. For the previous procedures involving an advisory panel, see the last edition of this work at **15.52–15.56**. In *Rehman*[3] the Court of Appeal gave an extremely broad meaning to the phrase 'national security', rejecting the approach of the Special Immigration Appeals Commission which had held that offending against national security required engagement in, promotion or encouragement of violent activity targeted at the UK, its system of government or its people.[4] Lord Woolf MR accepted the Secretary of State's submission that 'increasingly the security of one country is dependent upon the security of other countries', and that 'it is essential in the interests of national security that the UK fosters such ties with as many states as possible against the day when any of them may be able directly to safeguard the UK's security interests'. This made any activity likely to create a risk of adverse repercussions, including conduct which could have an adverse effect on the UK's relationship with a friendly state, potentially a risk to national security. Therefore, the logical conclusion reached by the court was that 'the promotion of terrorism *against any state* is capable of being a threat to our own national security'.[5] Not since the majority decision in *Liversidge v Anderson*[6] has the executive been given such deference; one can hear the Secretary of State saying 'I can make national security mean anything I want it to mean'. To assist the executive further, the court went on to say there was no need to go to the trouble of proving that the individual had endangered national security by any specific act; it sufficed if, on a 'global approach', he or she was 'a danger' to national security.[7] Thus did the Court of Appeal fire across the Special Immigration Appeals Commission's bows on its first case.[8]

1   Immigration and Asylum Act 1999, s 64(1).
2   Immigration and Asylum Act 1999, s 64(2).
3   *Secretary of State for the Home Department v Shafiq ur Rehman* [2000] INLR 531, CA.
4   *Shafiq ur Rehman v Secretary of State for the Home Department* [1999] INLR 517 (SIAC).
5   [2000] INLR 531 at para 40. This has been followed up by the proscription of 21 organisations under the provisions of the Terrorism Act 2000, s 3, the logic being that membership of, or even support for any of them (including the PKK and the LTTE), in itself justifies national security expulsion.
6   [1942] AC 206, HL.
7   [2000] INLR 531 at para 44. It held that the Special Immigration Appeals Commission's approach was in both respects (approach to national security and approach to the evidence) flawed.
8   The case is going to the House of Lords and its decision will be awaited with interest.

Consideration of merits

15.33   The general rule for deportations is now contained in HC 395, para 364. It applies to all decisions to deport. It reads:

'In considering whether deportation is the right course on the merits, the public interest will be balanced against any compassionate circumstances of the case. While each case will be considered in the light of the particular circumstances, the aim is the exercise of the power of deportation that is consistent and fair as between one person and another, although one case will rarely be identical with another in all material respects. In cases to which [the transitional provisions] apply,[1] deportation will normally be the proper course for a person who has failed to comply with or has contravened a condition or has remained without authority. Before a decision to deport is reached the Secretary of State will take into account all relevant factors known to him including:

(i)   age;
(ii)   length of residence in the UK;
(iii)   strength of connections with the UK;
(iv)   personal history, including character, conduct and employment record;
(v)   domestic circumstances;
(vi)   previous criminal record and the nature of any offence of which the person has been convicted;
(vii)   compassionate circumstances;
(viii) any representations received on the person's behalf.'

1   HC 395, para 363A, inserted by Cm 4851.

Consistent and fair

15.34 This rule indicates that the task in a deportation case is one of discretion rather than the application of a precise code having mandatory effect. The paragraph characterises the essential issue in most cases but it is not intended to be exhaustive or comprehensive. It is not designed to restrict what are relevant factors or to limit the consideration of factors simply to compassionate ones.[1] In *Idrish*[2] the Tribunal held that the strength of the public interest in deporting could and should be assessed in the light of all circumstances. The reference to the power being exercised consistently and fairly as between one person and another is more than a mere requirement that the Home Office apply the Immigration Rules to all deportees,[3] and means that they must be even-handed between a particular applicant and others, and disparate treatment may found a successful appeal.[4] Where one party who has played the principal part in some criminal enterprise is allowed to stay, it would be inconsistent and unfair to allow another whose involvement is minor to be deported, unless there is some other weighty or distinguishing feature in their two cases.[5] Such comparisons of individual cases will occur relatively rarely because, as the rule says, one case is rarely identical with another. But where the minister makes general statements as to how the power will be exercised, such statements can be relied on by an appellant. In judicial review terms the publication of the policy will no doubt give rise to a legitimate expectation that it will be applied consistently as between all applicants who apply to regularise their position.[6] If it is unpublished, unexplained departure from it would be inconsistent and unfair, and therefore irrational.[7]

1   *Singh v Immigration Appeal Tribunal* [1986] 2 All ER 721, [1986] Imm AR 352, HL.
2   *Idrish* [1985] Imm AR 155, IAT.
3   *Alsawaf v Secretary of State for the Home Department* [1988] Imm AR 410, CA.
4   See *R v Secretary of State for the Home Department, ex p Shafat Ahmed Sheikh*, DC/260/81, 4 February 1982, QBD, in which the inconsistent treatment of two brothers, both innocent beneficiaries of corruptly obtained leave, founded a successful challenge.
5   *R v Immigration Appeal Tribunal, ex p Alavi-Veighoe* (CO 1431/1988) 20 July 1989, QBD; *Secretary of State for the Home Department v Yasin* [1995] Imm AR 118, CA; *Arshad* (9888), IAT; *Cardona* (14949), IAT.

6 *Khan v Immigration Appeal Tribunal* [1984] Imm AR 68, CA (refusal of entry clearance); *Gyeabour* [1989] Imm AR 94, IAT; *Hussain v Immigration Appeal Tribunal* [1991] Imm AR 413, CA.
7 *R v Secretary of State for the Home Department, ex p Amankwah* [1994] Imm AR 240, QBD (Home Office 'marriage and children policy' DP2/93); *R v Secretary of State for the Home Department, ex p Urmaza* [1996] COD 479, (1996) Times, 23 July. The policy and its successors are now published, but initially it was not.

All relevant circumstances

15.35 The listed circumstances are far broader than simple compassionate circumstances; they include everything that is properly persuasive for or against deportation, including the background situation in the country to which deportees are to be deported.[1] The impact of the proposed deportation on third parties, whether family, work colleagues, employees,[2] police[3] or members of a local community, is always a relevant circumstance and it does not have to be squeezed into the category of compassionate circumstances.[4] Only what is irrelevant to a decision to deport should be excluded (such as the threat of industrial action or other forms of unrest either in support of or against deportation, matters to which it would be improper for the minister to have regard).[5]

1 *Kamara (Elizabeth)* (20155); *Kamara (Mohammed)* (21814); *Kapusnik* (00 TH 01897).
2 *Leong* (5055), IAT where deportation would have resulted in a loss of employment for persons settled here.
3 But the desire of police officers to retain the services of a valuable informer was held not decisive against deportation in *CM* [1997] Imm AR 336.
4 *Bakhtaur Singh v Immigration Appeal Tribunal* [1986] 2 All ER 721, [1986] Imm AR 352, HL.
5 *Bakhtaur Singh* above, per Lord Bridge.

15.36 The Secretary of State and the appellate authority must ensure that the decision complies with the ECHR.[1] Previously, the Convention had been held not to be part of the relevant circumstances to be taken into account in considering whether deportation is the right course on the merits,[2] but in practice it had become so in cases involving the deportation of spouses and children of persons settled in the UK, through the policy adopted in purported compliance with the ECHR after *Berrehab*.[3] A decision made without reference to the policy was unlawful,[4] but a policy is not a rule and need not be followed rigidly provided reasons are given for not following it in a particular case.[5] The original policy, DP2/93, applied to all proposed deportees and illegal entrants who had married prior to enforcement action and whose marriages or common-law relationships had lasted for two years and had been notified to the Secretary of State before 16 March 1996.[6] Thereafter a more restrictive policy applied, which is contained in three documents: DP/3/96, DP/4/95 and DP/5/96. A proposed deportee who marries after a deportation or removal decision or recommendation is made cannot benefit.[7] The earlier policy was held compliant with Article 8 of the ECHR[8] but the point has not yet been decided in respect of the later policies. The court reviewing the decision to deport may still consider these policies, but will have to decide whether on the facts of the particular case the decision to deport is a proportionate response in the light of countervailing human rights considerations.[9] In judicial review the courts have held that the Secretary of State's decision in deportation deserves some deference,[10] but on an appeal to the appellate authority the adjudicator or tribunal decides for itself, as it always has. It has previously shown itself willing to rule against deportation, even where serious offences have been committed, where the consequences of return would be disproportionately severe.[11] For the approach to deportation in cases involving family or private life see **15.25** and **8.56–8.64** above.

1 Under Human Rights Act 1998, s 6.
2 *Chundawadra v Immigration Appeal Tribunal* [1988] Imm AR 161, CA.
3 *Berrehab v Netherlands* (1988) 11 EHtRR 322, ECHR where the expulsion of a Moroccan father enjoying regular contact with his Dutch child was held a disproportionate interference with the parties' rights to respect for family life. See also *Ciliz v Netherlands* [2000] 2 FLR 469, ECtHR.
4 *R v Secretary of State for the Home Department, ex p Amankwah* [1994] Imm AR 240, QBD (a reasons challenge).
5 *Secretary of State for the Home Department v Hastrup* [1996] Imm AR 616, CA.
6 *R v Secretary of State for the Home Department, ex p Ekewuba* [1995] Imm AR 89, QBD; *R v Secretary of State for the Home Department, ex p Jonah* [1995] Imm AR 120. See **11.59** above.
7 *Sekhon v Secretary of State for the Home Department* [1995] Imm AR 507, CA; *Hing Fai Tong v Secretary of State for the Home Department* [1996] Imm AR 551, CA; *R v Secretary of State for the Home Department, ex p Zighem* [1996] Imm AR 194, QBD.
8 *R v Secretary of State for the Home Department, ex p Gangadeen, Khan* [1998] INLR 206, CA.
9 See *B v Secretary of State for the Home Department* [2000] Imm AR 478, [2000] INLR 361, CA.
10 *R v Secretary of State for the Home Department, ex p Isiko* [2001] INLR 175; *R v Secretary of State for the Home Department, ex p Amjad Mahmood* [2001] 1 WLR 840, [2001] INLR 1; *R v Secretary of State for the Home Department, ex p Samaroo* (CO 4973/1999) 20 December 2000. But see now *R (Daly) v Secretary of State for the Home Department* [2001] UKHL 26, [2001] 2 WLR 1622.
11 *Kim* (11041) (Korean national convicted of several homicides, appeal allowed on basis of double jeopardy and possibility of execution). See also *Oyedeji* (19618) (drugs, serious possibility of arrest and charge on return, which would be double jeopardy, and life-threatening detention conditions).

15.37 Where representations have been made, the minister must have regard to them.[1] The representations may be ones made during the course of an interview and in certain cases fairness may require such an interview.[2] If there is no opportunity to make representations before the decision is taken, this is not fatal since the appellate authorities can hear evidence of any factor in existence at the date of the decision even though unknown to the Home Office.[3] Representations may take the form of letters from members of Parliament or members of the public, or petitions. The Tribunal has suggested[4] that it is not the number of such representations but their content that should be persuasive. In *Bakhtaur Singh*[5] the testimonials and letters from hundreds of local people, the presence of a large number at the appeal and the fact that the appellant, a Sikh priest and musician, had given much pleasure and service to his community were taken into consideration. But the desire of police officers to retain the services of an informer cannot be decisive.[6]

1 HC 395, para 364; for the duty to have regard to relevant circumstances see *Baktaur Singh v Immigration Appeal Tribunal* [1986] 2 All ER 721, [1986] Imm AR 352, HL.
2 *Afful* [1986] Imm AR 230, IAT (yes); *Agyemang* [1988] Imm AR 519, IAT (no).
3 *R v Immigration Appeal Tribunal, ex p Hassanin* [1987] 1 All ER 74, [1986] 1 WLR 1448, CA.
4 *Pereira* (3203) 1984, IAT.
5 [1986] 2 All ER 721, [1986] Imm AR 352, HL.
6 *CM* [1997] Imm AR 336.

15.38 Since there is (subject to the transitional provisions) no merits appeal against removal as an overstayer, it is likely to be extremely rare that a proposed deportee has no claim to remain under the Immigration Rules. The old overstaying cases indicate that the fact that a proposed deportee has or had no claim to remain in the country under the Rules does not mean that he or she must be deported,[1] and a marriage or other relationship which has not satisfied the Immigration Rules for the purposes of settlement may nevertheless give rise to compassionate factors or family life considerations militating against deportation.[2] In addition the Immigration Rules expressly provide that a deportation order will not be made against a person with a well-founded fear of persecution, or a person whose removal would be in breach of the UK's obligations under the ECHR.[3]

1   *Idrish* [1985] Imm AR 155.
2   *R v Secretary of State for the Home Department, ex p Arora* [1990] Imm AR 89, QBD.
3   HC 395, para 380. This does not prevent the deportation of a refugee, simply because he or she has in the past been granted refugee status, if by his or her criminal activities the protection of the Refugee Convention has been lost: *Raziastaraie v Secretary of State for the Home Department* [1995] Imm AR 459, CA. But no removal could take place if a real risk engaging the ECHR exists.

Length of residence in the UK

15.39 Strength of connections with the UK and length of residence are matters of degree. Past UK citizenship (being a former UK and colonies citizen) would be of little significance as it would not necessarily amount to a connection with the UK as opposed to a former colony. But a past claim to the right of abode may be of weight.[1] Length of residence is a stronger factor if the residence has been lawful; a long period of overstaying is sometimes considered more heinous than a short one.[2] The Home Office policy on long residence, sometimes known as the 'ten year rule' and the 'fourteen year rule', is of more relevance in cases of overstaying, and is set out at **16.43-16.44** below.

1   *Lawrence* (3171).
2   *Idrish* [1985] Imm AR 155.

Special rules for family deportations

15.40 On a family deportation appeal, appellants cannot claim that they do not belong to a principal deportee's family by disputing the truth of any statement made with a view to obtaining leave for them to enter or remain in the UK, unless it was made by another person, not their agent, and they did not know of it, or they were under 18 at the time.[1] This includes statements made to obtain entry clearance. Thus a sponsorship declaration, a tax return or an affidavit from a village elder proving a relationship and used to gain admission cannot be disputed when it comes to deportation if the appellant was an adult and knew of the contents of these documents. This rather complicated rule might work as follows. A tax return made out by a father in the UK might give the age of his child as 14, when in fact he is 15. The return is used to gain admission for the child and three years later the question of deportation arises. According to the tax return the child is 17 and deportable as a family member. In fact he is 18. Under the Immigration and Asylum Act 1999 the child is allowed to adduce evidence of his or her real age. On the other hand, if the tax return (falsely) makes out that the appellant is the wife of the taxpayer in the UK and (on the strength of it) she is admitted as his wife, she cannot dispute the validity of the statement if steps are then taken to deport her as his wife. Her only defence would be that she did not know of the original statement.

1   Immigration and Asylum Act 1999, s 64(5), formerly Immigration Act 1971, s 15(6).

15.41 The decision to deport the family members must be taken independently and considered on its merits rather than following as a matter of course.[1] A dependent spouse remains a member of the family of the principal deportee until divorced. However, the Immigration Rules make plain that the Secretary of State will not deport a dependent spouse who has qualified for settlement in his or her own right or has been living apart from the principal deportee.[2] Children will not normally be considered for deportation where they are living apart from the deportee or have left home and established themselves on an independent basis, or married before deportation came into prospect.[3] Apart from the usual considerations which apply to all deportations, the following additional considerations apply to family deportations:

(i)   the ability of the spouse to maintain himself or herself and any children in the UK, or to be maintained by relatives or friends without charge to public funds for the foreseeable future;

(ii)   in the case of a child of school age, the effect of removal on his or her education;[4]

(iii) the practicability of any plans for a child's care and maintenance in this country if one or both of the child's parents were deported; and

(iv) any representations made by or on behalf of the spouse or child.[5]

Where a decision is made to deport someone as a member of the principal deportee's family, the right of appeal will be notified and at the same time the procedure of voluntary departure will be explained.[6] Deported family members may be able to seek re-admission to the UK under the Immigration Rules when a child reaches 18, when the marriage to the principal deportee comes to an end;[7] or when the deportation order against the principal deportee is revoked.

1   *Yau Yak Wah v Home Office* [1982] Imm AR 16, CA.
2   HC 395, para 365.
3   HC 395, para 366.
4   *Ozter* [1978] Imm AR 137, IAT; *Mustafa* [1979–80] Imm AR 33, IAT. See now ECHR, Protocol 1, art 2, and see *R v Secretary of State for the Home Department, ex p Holub*, 20 December 2000, CA (no breach of right to education to remove child to Poland, which had a well-established education system).
5   HC 395, para 367.
6   HC 395, para 368.
7   HC 395, para 389.

Deportation of EEA nationals

15.42 The deportation of EEA nationals exercising Treaty rights is subject to special rules which provide both procedural safeguards and more rigorous justification for deportation. This is dealt with in detail at **7.120ff** above. The most important points are first, that the decision to deport must be reviewed by an independent competent authority before it is implemented.[1] This reviewing body may be the court making a recommendation or the appellate authority or Special Immigration Appeals Commission on an administrative deportation.

Secondly, a measure interfering with EC freedom of movement rights must be taken only on grounds of public policy, public security or public health,[2] must be based exclusively on the personal conduct of the individual concerned, which must constitute a present threat to the requirements of public policy;[3] and the measure must be a proportionate response to the risk posed by the person's conduct. This means that there can be no automatic deportation based simply on the gravity of an offence[4] without consideration of propensity to re-offend and all the individual's circumstances.[5]

1 Council Directive (EEC) 64/221, art 9; *Adoui and Cornuaille v Belgium* [1982] ECR 1665, [1982] 3 CMLR 631.
2 Article 39(3) EC (ex art 48(3)); art 46 EC (ex art 56).
3 Council Directive 64/221, art 3.
4 Case C-348/96 *Calfa* [1999] ECR I-11.
5 *B v Secretary of State for the Home Department* [2000] Imm AR 478, [2000] INLR 361, CA.

Successful appeals

15.43 If the appeal is allowed, the decision is reversed but an adjudicator has no power to direct the grant of leave to remain. He or she may recommend this course, however.[1] If the proposed deportee's leave has expired, and the Home Office has not renewed it pending appeal, leave to remain will normally be granted in order to regularise the position. But this does not follow as a matter of course. Immigrants who succeed in an appeal should not, therefore, leave the country for a celebratory holiday until leave has been obtained.[2] If they do they have no right to be treated as a returning resident and would have no other claim to re-enter. An adjudicator has no power to grant a stay of deportation, for example because of the political situation then pertaining in a country,[3] but a determination that deportation is not currently the right course on the merits could be properly made without prejudice to a future exercise of the power if the person's behaviour merits deportation. In one case an adjudicator allowed the appeal on the grounds that the applicant was a genuine student who should be given a further opportunity to progress with his studies.[4] But where an appeal was unsuccessful but an appellant was given a period of grace to allow him to finish a course and make a voluntary departure, that did not constitute fresh leave, and the Secretary of State was entitled to sign a deportation order when he did not leave.[5]

1 *R v Immigration Appeal Tribunal, ex p Mahendra Singh* [1984] Imm AR 1, QBD. See **18.52** below.
2 *R v Secretary of State for the Home Department, ex p Botta* [1987] Imm AR 80, QBD.
3 *Yuksel* [1976] Imm AR 91, IAT.
4 *Youssef* (TH 114300 Adjudicator); see also *Dexter* (4980) unreported.
5 *R v Secretary of State for the Home Department, ex p Smith* [1996] Imm AR 331.

Signing and revocation of deportation orders

Detaining deportees

15.44 The power to detain deportees arises at three stages; first when the decision to deport is made, secondly when the court recommends deportation;[1] and thirdly when the deportation order is signed. At all three stages there is also the option of bail or release on temporary admission, subject to requirements as to residence and so forth.[2] The position can be quite complicated and we deal with it more fully in the chapter on detention (chapter 17 below). As a matter of policy, the Home Office will not detain EC nationals on the strength of a court recommendation, but will instead serve notice of intention to deport and order detention by virtue of the notice.[3]

1 For the legality of detention pending the implementation of a recommendation to deport, see *Re Nwafor* [1994] Imm AR 91, QBD.
2 Immigration Act 1971, Sch 3; HC 395, para 382.
3 IDI Dec/00, Ch 13, s 1, para 2.8.

Voluntary or supervised departure

15.45 Persons liable to deportation who are not detained may leave the UK voluntarily, paying for their own passage and leaving under their own auspices, at any time before a deportation order is signed. This may require liaison with the port if travel documents are held. The advantage of this option is that it does not preclude a future return under the Immigration Rules, since the power to sign a deportation order can only be exercised when the person is in the UK.[1] If it is known that a person has embarked, enforcement action will cease.[2] For this reason it may be unfair to reject representations to remain on compassionate grounds and sign a deportation order before giving the opportunity for a voluntary departure.[3] However, the reason for the decision to deport could operate to exclude the person from the UK on an attempt to re-enter.[4] Voluntary departure is to be contrasted with supervised departure. Section 5(6) of the Immigration Act 1971 refers to persons liable to deportation who leave the UK to live permanently abroad and enables the Secretary of State to meet their expenses. Undoubtedly such funding will be a relevant consideration if the person seeks to return. Reference to supervised departure has been deleted from the current Immigration Rules, but it remains in the IDI, which suggest that it would be appropriate where a person agrees to leave immediately and signs a waiver regarding appeal rights.[5]

1 Immigration Act 1971, s 5(1).
2 IDI Dec/00, Ch 13, s 1, para 9.1.
3 The argument was unsuccessful on its facts in *R v Secretary of State for the Home Department, ex p Brew* [1988] Imm AR 93.
4 See HC 395, para 320(18), (19).
5 IDI Dec/00, Ch 13, s 1, para 9.2.

Signing the deportation order

15.46 In criminal cases, where a recommendation has been made by the courts, the next stage is for the Secretary of State to consider whether effect should be given to the recommendation. He or she cannot, however, make a deportation order until the convicted person has exhausted all rights of appeal or until the time for bringing an appeal has expired (in Scotland, until the expiry of 28 days from the date of the recommendation).[1] The factors to be taken into account by the Secretary of State in exercising his or her discretion are the same as in conducive to the public good cases.[2] Although a recommendation by a sentencing judge carries real and in many cases decisive weight and affords a presumption in favour of deportation, and although the reasoning of the sentencing judge is a material factor for the Secretary of State, the recommendation simply initiates the Secretary of State's task; the sentencing judge's reasons and decision should not be substituted for what the Secretary of State has to decide.[3] If the Secretary of State decides to make an order, he or she can do so before the end of any sentence passed by the court,[4] but the usual practice is to wait until the sentence has been served.[5] It will then be necessary to review the case in the light of any changed circumstances before a deportation order is signed.[6] Inviting further representations from a deportee does not mean that the original decision is flawed.[7] The minister can take into account fresh circumstances without having to start the deportation process over again.[8] In non-recommendation cases where no appeal is lodged or if the appeal is dismissed, the order for deportation is submitted to the minister for signature.[9] Earlier Immigration Rules stated that the submission would include a summary of the facts of the case, written confirmation of the dismissal of any appeal, and a note of any other relevant information, whether or not it was available to the courts or the appellate authorities.[10] It is believed that the practice remains the same. In *Sanusi*[11] the Court of Appeal held that the Secretary of State could not sign a deportation order between the making of an asylum application and the notification of a decision on it, because of the prohibition on removal in section 6 of the Asylum and Immigration Appeals Act 1993. The case has been reversed by section 15 of the Immigration and Asylum Act 1999.[12] If a deportation order is signed while the proposed deportee is in the UK but he or she leaves without becoming aware of it, it is still effective. A failure to serve the order and the return of the person's passport with an uncancelled indefinite leave stamp does not give rise to a legitimate expectation that the order will not be enforced.[13]

1 Immigration Act 1971, s 6(6).
2 HC 395 para 364; see **15.33-15.39** above.
3 *R v Secretary of State for the Home Department, ex p Dinc* [1999] Imm AR 380, [1999] INLR 256, CA.
4 The Secretary of State is entitled to decide when to make the order in pursuance of the recommendation: *R (Sezek) v Secretary of State for the Home Department* (CO 283/2000) 21 December 2000.
5 For the effect of lapse of time, see Case 131/79 *R v Secretary of State for the Home Department, ex p Santillo* [1980] ECR 1585, [1980] 2 CMLR 308.
6 *Ayo v Immigration Appeal Tribunal* [1990] Imm AR 461, CA.
7 *R v Secretary of State for the Home Department, ex p Amoa* [1992] Imm AR 218, QBD.
8 *Charles v Secretary of State for the Home Department (No 2)* [1992] Imm AR 503, CA.
9 Normally the order is signed by the Home Office immigration minister, but contentious cases may be referred to the Secretary of State for the Home Department for signature: IDI Dec/00, Ch 13, s 1, para 5.
10 HC 251, para 157.
11 *R v Secretary of State for the Home Department, ex p Sanusi* [1999] INLR 198, [1999] Imm AR 334.
12 See also Immigration and Asylum Act 1999, Sch 4, para 20, which makes the same provision in respect of human rights appeals, ie a deportation order may be signed while such an appeal is pending, but not implemented.
13 *Sri Kumar Dey v Secretary of State for the Home Department* [1996] Imm AR 521, CA.

Removal of deportees

15.47 Following the making of a deportation order, removal directions will be set. Where the person is serving a prison sentence, arrangements for removal will be made to coincide with his or her release wherever possible.[1] For removal see chapter 16 below.

1   IDI Dec/00, Ch 13, s 1, para 6.

Revocation of deportation orders

15.48 The effect of a deportation order is to invalidate any leave to enter or remain in the UK given before the order is made or while it is in force.[1] A deportation order comes into force on the day it is signed rather than when it is served.[2] There are statutory provisions for when it ceases to apply. The order ceases to have effect automatically:

(1)   if the deportee becomes a British citizen;[3]
(2)   if a spouse, deported under a family order, is divorced from the principal deportee;[4]
(3)   in the case of children deported under a family order, as soon as they reach the age of 18.[5]

An order may also be invalid if the deportee has become a family member of an EEA national exercising Treaty rights in the UK.[6] In all other circumstances a deportation order continues in force until it is revoked by a further order of the Secretary of State.[7] Revocation of a deportation order, however, does not entitle the person to re-enter the UK, but merely to qualify for admission under the Immigration Rules.[8] Application for revocation can be made to the entry clearance officer or the Home Office.[9] Normally, three years must have elapsed.[10] Time runs from the date the order was signed, not the date of removal, although time spent out of the UK is relevant.[11]

1   Immigration Act 1971, s 5(1).
2   *Peerbocus* [1987] Imm AR 331; *Sri Kumar Dey v Secretary of State for the Home Department* [1996] Imm AR 521, CA.
3   Immigration Act 1971, s 5(2). But an order is not revoked merely because a Commonwealth citizen marries a British citizen after the order is signed: *R v Secretary of State for the Home Department, ex p Hayden* [1988] Imm AR 555, QBD.
4   Immigration Act 1971, s 5(3), (4).
5   Immigration Act 1971, s 5(3), (4).
6   IDI Dec/00, Ch 13, s 5, para 2; see chapter 7 above.
7   Immigration Act 1971, s 5(2). A deportation order cannot be impliedly revoked and the grant of entry clearance while the order is in existence does not have this effect: *Watson* [1986] Imm AR 75.
8   HC 395, para 392.
9   HC 395, para 392.
10 HC 395, para 391; but since the question of revocation is a matter of the minister's discretion, shorter or longer periods are possible: (*Udoh* [1972] Imm AR 89 where it was held that one year was a sufficient time for atonement; and see further *Dervish* [1972] Imm AR 48 where it was felt that 12 months was too soon to revoke the order, but that a further seven months led the Tribunal to recommend an early consideration of revocation.
11 *Dosieah* (4944) unreported; *Peerbocus* [1987] Imm AR 331, IAT.

15.49 An application for revocation of a deportation order will be considered in the light of all the circumstances, including the grounds on which the order was made, any representations in support of revocation, the interests of the community, including the maintenance of an effective immigration control, and the interests of the applicant including any compassionate circumstances.[1] The Immigration Rules dictate that in the case of an applicant with a serious criminal record, continued exclusion for a long term of years will normally be the proper course.[2] Where the order was founded on a criminal conviction which has become spent under the Rehabilitation of Offenders Act 1974, revocation should normally be granted.[3] In other cases, revocation of the order will not normally be authorised unless the situation has been materially altered, either by a change of circumstances since the order was made, or by fresh information coming to light.[4] A failure by counsel to advise of the possibility of an appeal against a recommendation for deportation is not such a circumstance.[5] The passage of time since the person was deported may also, in itself, amount to such a change of circumstances as to warrant revocation of the order.[6] The IDI indicate that revocation would normally be appropriate three years after departure in cases involving overstayers deported under the earlier provisions, and family members, while serious offences (violence against the person including homicide, sexual offences, armed robbery, persistent or large-scale burglary or theft, serious public order offences, drug trafficking and forgery) would normally require a ten-year wait before revocation.[7]

1   HC 395, para 390.
2   HC 395, para 391.
3   IDI Dec/00, Ch 13, s 5, para 3.3.
4   The IDI state that cases should be decided on their known circumstances, but further inquiries might be appropriate where further offences may have been committed abroad or, in a case where less than three years have elapsed since the order was enforced, where there appears to have been a material change, such as marriage after deportation or the sickness of a relative in the UK.
5   *Osu* (4851) unreported, IAT.
6   HC 395, para 391. See *Sanusi* [1975] Imm AR 114.
7   IDI Dec/00, Ch 13, Annex A.

15.50 If an application for revocation is refused there is a right of appeal against the refusal, to an adjudicator in the first instance.[1] Where the Secretary of State personally decides that continued exclusion from the UK is 'conducive to the public good', the appeal lies to the Special Immigration Appeals Commission.[2] No revocation appeal is possible so long as the person is in the UK (either because they have not left or because they have returned illegally).[3] However, a refusal to revoke a deportation order may be appealed on asylum or human rights grounds before departure.[4]

1   Immigration and Asylum Act 1999, s 63(1)(b).
2   Immigration and Asylum Act 1999, s 64(2); Special Immigration Appeals Commission Act 1997, s 2(1), (1A).
3   Immigration and Asylum Act 1999, s 64(3).
4   Immigration and Asylum Act 1999, ss 69(4)(b), 65.

Returned deportees

15.51 Where someone returns to the UK in breach of a deportation order, he or she may lawfully be deported under the original order.[1] But every case should be considered in the light of all the relevant circumstances.[2] A person who enters in breach of a deportation order is an illegal entrant[3] and a person who does so knowingly is, in addition, guilty of a criminal offence.[4] There is a limited, and ineffectual, right of appeal against a decision to remove, exercisable only from abroad, on the limited ground that on the facts of the case there is in law no power to remove him or her from the UK.[5]

1   Immigration Act 1971, s 5(5).
2   HC 395, para 388; *Alsawaf v Secretary of State for the Home Department* [1988] Imm AR 410, where the country of proposed destination refused to accept the deportee.
3   Immigration Act 1971, s 33(1).
4   Immigration Act 1971, s 24(1)(a); *R v Secretary of State for the Home Department, ex p Yeboah* [1986] Imm AR 52, QBD.
5   Immigration and Asylum Act 1999, s 66(1)(a). It does not allow the appellant to dispute the validity of the original deportation order: s 66(4).

REPATRIATION

Voluntary repatriation

15.52 Section 29 of the Immigration Act 1971 makes provision for financial assistance to be given towards the travel costs of people who are not British citizens[1] and who wish to leave this country permanently, if that is in their best interests. The scheme is administered by the International Social Services of the UK, and is intended to help those persons who have failed to settle satisfactorily in the UK and who wish to leave but lack the means to do so.[2] Persons whose stay here is subject to a time condition will not normally be referred to the International Social Services of the UK; the scheme is not meant to provide a facility for repatriating visitors.[3] The provision in the 1971 Act for this kind of voluntary repatriation caused some concern at the time that a future government might want to use repatriation assistance as a deliberate policy of substantially reducing the immigrant (meaning 'black') population of this country.[4] There were, however, built-in safeguards in that the scheme was only available for those who wanted to leave,[5] and these fears have not materialised. A person settled in this country who makes use of public funds for resettlement will not be able to claim re-entry as a returning resident.[6]

1   Although the fact that some members of the household or family are British does not disqualify them, provided the head of the family is subject to immigration control.
2   IDI Dec/00, Ch 13, s 6.
3   IDI Dec/00, Ch 13, s 6.
4   HC Official Report, SC B (Immigration Bill), 25 May 1971, col 1302.
5   Immigration Act 1971, s 29(2). The Habeas Corpus Act of 1679, s 11 forbids the sending of any person as a prisoner out of the realm and imposes the penalty of life imprisonment upon anyone taking part in such illegal repatriation or deportation. But s 12 exempts from this prohibition any persons, who 'by contract in writing agree with ... any merchant or owner of any plantation, or other persons whatsoever, to be transported to any parts beyond the seas'.
6   HC 395, para 18(iii).

Prison repatriation

15.53 The Council of Europe Convention on the Repatriation of Prisoners 1983 provided for repatriation to enable prisoners sentenced abroad to serve their sentences in their home country, with the consent of the prisoner and the agreement of the two countries concerned. Under the Convention the prisoner must have at least six months of his or her sentence left to serve and be a national of the state to which he or she is to be transferred. There should be no outstanding appeal to a higher court against sentence or conviction. The Repatriation of Prisoners Act 1984 was enacted to give effect to the Convention in UK law. British prisoners convicted overseas may be repatriated to complete their sentence in a British jail or other institution, and overseas prisoners in UK jails may be sent back to their own countries to complete their sentences. Under the 1984 Act any repatriation must take place under an international arrangement, such as the Council of Europe Convention or some bilateral arrangement between the UK and another government,[1] and consent must be given by the prisoner and the two countries concerned.[2] Transfer in and out is effected at the British end by a warrant issued by the Secretary of State for the Home Department. In outward transfers this authorises the taking of a prisoner to any place in any part of the UK, his or her delivery at a place of departure to the custody of an agent of the transfer country and the removal of the prisoner from the UK.[3] In inward transfers the 1984 Act authorises the return of prisoners to the UK and their subsequent detention in a prison, hospital or other institution as authorised by the Secretary of State's warrant.[4] A prisoner who is in the UK or on board a British ship, aircraft or hovercraft is deemed to be in the legal custody of the Secretary of State.[5] A prisoner who escapes can be arrested by the police without warrant.[6]

1 Repatriation of Prisoners Act 1984, ss 1(1) and 8(1).
2 Repatriation of Prisoners Act 1984, s 1(1)(b) and (c).
3 Repatriation of Prisoners Act 1984, s 2.
4 Repatriation of Prisoners Act 1984, s 3.
5 Repatriation of Prisoners Act 1984, s 5(2).
6 Repatriation of Prisoners Act 1984, s 5(5).

Inducements to depart

15.54 A person liable to be sentenced by a criminal court or punished for contempt of court may be encouraged to avoid punishment by agreeing to a voluntary departure and not to return to the UK. This inducement was used in the nineteenth century for convicted prisoners, who were offered free pardons if they left the UK.[1] There were a number of contempt cases where the application to commit was adjourned *sine die* on the agreement to depart.[2] The more frequent technique of persuasion has been the use of a bind-over at common law to come up for judgment when called on to do so upon terms that the person leaves the UK within a specified time and does not return within a specified number of years.[3] There is no power to make such a condition under the Justices of the Peace Act 1361[4] or a probation order,[5] and it can only be made in lieu of and not in addition to a sentence of the court.[6] The Court of Appeal has held that consent remains free even though given in the face of the alternative of imprisonment.[7] The making of such a bind-over was considered to be a purely internal situation and therefore not contrary to community law in the case of *R v Saunders*.[8] But it is unlikely to survive scrutiny under the Human Rights Act 1998.[9]

1 O Higgins 'Voluntary Deportation' [1963] Crim LR 680.
2 *Yager v Musa* [1962] Crim LR 240; *Smith v Smith* (1963) Times, 23 August.

3   See D Williams 'Suspended Sentence at Common Law' [1963] PL 441; Supreme Court Act 1981, s 79.
4   *R v Ayu* [1958] 3 All ER 636, [1958] 1 WLR 1264.
5   *R v McCartan* [1958] 3 All ER 140, [1958] 1 WLR 933.
6   *R v Ayu* above; *R v Governor of Brixton Prison, ex p Havilde* [1969] 1 All ER 109, [1969] 1 WLR 42.
7   *R v Carl Williams* [1982] 3 All ER 1092, [1982] 1 WLR 1398.
8   Case C-175/78 [1980] QB 72.
9   On bind-overs see *Steel v UK* (1998) 28 EHRR 603. On the prohibition of exile in international law see Nuala Mole 'Constructive deportation' (1995) EHRLR 64.

Chapter 16

REMOVAL AND OTHER EXPULSION

INTRODUCTION

16.1 In this chapter we examine the grounds for administrative removal from the UK and the means by which it is achieved. The main categories of persons liable to removal are those refused leave to enter; overstayers, those in breach of their conditions of stay, or who have used deception to remain; members of their families; and illegal entrants. The powers of removal of persons refused leave to enter and illegal entrants are set out in Schedule 2 to the Immigration Act 1971;[1] of overstayers and those in breach of conditions, in section 10 of the Immigration and Asylum Act 1999 and the Immigration (Removal Directions) Regulations 2000.[2] Removal of asylum claimants to 'safe third countries' under sections 11 and 12 of the 1999 Act is dealt with in chapter 12 above. In addition, there are provisions for the summary removal of sea, air and train crews who are in the UK illegally, and for detained psychiatric patients and members of visiting forces. We examine each of these categories in turn. Although the arrangements differ slightly according to the category of person being removed, the 1999 Act has introduced greater uniformity, in particular in subjecting overstayers, persons in breach of conditions of leave and others formerly eligible for deportation, to administrative removal procedures without the process of deportation.[3] The most complicated arrangements relate to the removal of persons refused entry, for reasons mainly to do with costs.[4]

1   Immigration Act 1971, Sch 2, paras 8–15.
2   SI 2000/2243.

3   See chapter 15 above; see also **16.32** below.
4   See **16.54** below.

REMOVAL OF ILLEGAL ENTRANTS AND OVERSTAYERS

16.2   Historically, the treatment of illegal entrants liable to summary removal[1] was in stark contrast to the position of those who had entered lawfully but breached conditions or remained beyond the time limited by their leave. The latter previously had a full right of appeal on the merits of the decision to deport, before it was implemented, either if they had been here for more than seven years or if the decision to deport followed a curtailment decision.[2] Illegal entrants had to resort to judicial review to challenge their treatment as illegal entrants or their removal directions, since there has never been a merits appeal which suspended removal,[3] unless the illegal entrant had an asylum claim.[4] Since 'illegal entrants' and 'overstayers' may both have long-established roots in the community, the distinction in available remedies was difficult to justify. Now, section 10 of the Immigration and Asylum Act 1999 levels down the treatment of the two groups by subjecting overstayers to the same summary removal process as illegal entrants, with the safeguard of a suspensive appeal against removal on human rights grounds under section 65 of the Act.

1   Immigration Act 1971, Sch 2, para 9 as amended by para 6 of Sch 2 to the Asylum and Immigration Act 1996; see Lord Bridge in *Khawaja v Secretary of State for the Home Department* [1984] AC 74.
2   Immigration Act 1971, s 15, as amended by Immigration Act 1988 s 5; see also Immigration (Restricted Right of Appeal Against Deportation) (Exemption) Order 1993, SI 1993/1656.
3   The appeal against removal directions under s 66 of the Immigration and Asylum Act 1999 (formerly s 16 of the Immigration Act 1971) is exercisable only after removal, and jurisdiction is limited to whether the power in law exists.
4   By Asylum and Immigration Appeals Act 1993, s 8(4), now Immigration and Asylum Act 1999, s 69(5).

Definition of illegal entry

16.3   An illegal entrant is defined in section 33(1) of the Immigration Act 1971 as:[1]

'a person:
   unlawfully entering or seeking to enter in breach of a deportation order or of the immigration laws; or
   entering or seeking to enter to enter by means which include deception by another person,
and includes also a person who has entered as mentioned in paragraph (a) or (b) above.'

The definition of 'illegal entrants' thus covers three stages:

• those who enter;
• those who seek to enter;
• those who have entered.

1   As amended by Asylum and Immigration Act 1996 Sch 2, para 4. See also Immigration and Asylum Act 1999, s 167(2), which provides that 'illegal entrant' has the same meaning as in the Immigration Act 1971.

16.4 By section 11(1) of the Immigration Act 1971 'entry' is distinguished from 'arrival'.[1] Usually passengers 'arriving' at a port or airport are deemed not to 'enter' the UK until they have (1) embarked from their ship, aircraft or Channel Tunnel train; and (2) left the areas reserved for immigration control.[2] If detained or temporarily admitted or released while liable to detention under Schedule 2 of the Act (including release on bail under Part III of the Immigration and Asylum Act 1999), they are deemed not to have 'entered'. By contrast, those who try to evade immigration control by arriving at a remote beach or private landing strip away from a designated port or airport are treated as 'entering' as soon as they leave their ship or aircraft.[3] These statutory distinctions between 'arriving' and 'entering' may help distinguish between someone seeking to enter and someone who has entered.

1   See also **3.4** above.
2   The area is defined by s 11(1) of the Immigration Act 1971 as such area at the port 'as may be approved for this purpose by an immigration officer'. Thus, stowaways who claimed asylum before the ferry bringing them to the UK docked were not illegal entrants: *Ex p Karakoc, ex p Karatas* (C0 695/2000), 16 May 2000, and stowaways in a lorry on the Eurostar shuttle who took steps to alert the immigration service of their presence and to make an asylum claim immediately on entering the UK, and before leaving the designated control area, were not illegal entrants: *Ex p Uzun, ex p Karadag* (CO 2090/2000) 10 July 2000, (permission granted, Home Office conceded that such persons could not be treated as having entered or having sought to enter illegally).
3   Immigration Act 1971, s 11(1), as amended by the Immigration and Asylum Act 1999, Sch 14, para 48 with the addition of the words at the end of s 11(1) 'or by Part III of the Immigration and Asylum Act 1999'. The effect of the 1999 Act amendment is simply to make clear that release on bail similarly displaces the presumption of entry by leaving immigration control. For the provisions relating to Channel Tunnel trains see the Channel Tunnel (International Arrangements) Order 1993, SI 1993/1813; s 11(1) is modified by Sch 4, para 1(5) of the Order.

16.5 The provisions of the Immigration and Asylum Act 1999 and Orders made under it to grant or refuse leave to enter 'before arrival in the United Kingdom' and for entry clearance 'to have effect as leave to enter the United Kingdom'[1] mean that a person who has obtained leave to enter by deception, becomes an illegal entrant before leaving his or her own country. He or she would then be liable to removal on arrival in the UK.[2]

1   Section 1 of the Immigration and Asylum Act 1999 inserts a new s 3A into the Immigration Act 1971, making 'further provision as to leave to enter'. See Immigration (Leave to Enter and Remain) Order 2000, SI 2000/1161 which provides for an entry clearance to 'have effect as leave to enter the United Kingdom'. See Ch 3 above.
2   Immigration Act 1971, Sch 2, para 9(1), (2).

16.6 It is not entirely clear why those seeking to enter should be classed as illegal entrants (unless it is in order to prosecute anyone assisting them under section 25 of the Immigration Act 1971). For if they are caught before they succeed in entering, they can be examined by immigration officers and, if necessary, refused entry and removed without being classified as illegal entrants.[1] However, there are two differences which may follow from classifying someone seeking to enter as an illegal entrant:

(i)   the safeguards given to those seeking to enter lawfully do not apply; an illegal entrant is not entitled to a notice of refusal of entry within 24 hours of examination or further examination and a deemed leave to enter if this provision is not fulfilled;[2]

(ii)   an illegal entrant has no right of appeal on the merits under section 59 of the Immigration and Asylum Act 1999 against a refusal of leave to enter, only the narrower right of appeal under section 66 of the Immigration and Asylum Act 1999 on the legality of the right to remove as an illegal entrant.[3]

A person who arrives at immigration control without a valid passport (whether an asylum seeker or not) is not seeking to enter in breach of the Act unless he or she intends to deceive the immigration officer, and so cannot be treated as an illegal entrant.[4]

1   Immigration Act 1971, Sch 2, para 8.
2   Immigration Act 1971, Sch 2, para 6(1), as amended by Immigration Act 1988. In *Re Maqbool Hussain* (4 May 1976, unreported), DC the Divisional Court said that the time limit in this para does not apply to an illegal entrant; but this was a case of someone who had entered illegally rather than someone seeking to enter. But see **3.65**ff above.
3   Such differences have little practical impact in relation to refugees and persons making 'human rights' claims. Illegal entrants who claim asylum can appeal against removal directions under Immigration and Asylum Act 1999, s 69(5), and s 65 provides an in-country right of appeal on human rights grounds.
4   *R v Naillie* [1993] AC 674, [1993] 2 All ER 782, [1993] Imm AR 462, HL.

16.7 An illegal entrant is a person (a) unlawfully entering or seeking to enter the UK in breach of a deportation order or of the immigration laws or (b) entering or seeking to enter by means which include deception by another person. The 'immigration laws' means the Immigration Act 1971and any law for purposes similar to this Act.[1] In order to sustain an allegation of illegal entry, it is therefore necessary to show that the person has entered in breach of some statutory provision. To enter clandestinely without leave is, of course, such a case, if entry is in breach of the requirement of section 3(1) of the 1971 Act that a person 'shall not enter unless given leave to do so in accordance with the Act'. Entry in breach of the immigration laws is a wider concept than entry in breach of section 3(1), and will include (most commonly) entry by deception in breach of sections 24A and 26(1)(c) of the Act. It now seems clear that breach of other criminal sections of the Act would also constitute illegal entry. The use of the word 'unlawfully' in the definition does not appear to add anything, since it is difficult to envisage any entry in breach of the immigration laws which would be regarded as lawful. This was the view of the Court of Appeal in *Ex p Bouzagou*,[2] which concerned a man who had crossed over from the Republic of Ireland to the UK. The inference, accepted by the court, was that he had not known that he was entering in breach of the immigration law. But the court rejected the argument that the word 'unlawfully' imported into the definition a requirement of *mens rea* (ie an awareness of illegality), and held that the applicant was an illegal entrant. In the light of this decision it appears that the only possible entry in breach of the immigration laws but not unlawful is an involuntary act or one compelled by necessity,[3] as where an aircraft develops a fault and is forced to land or a boat is forced ashore by bad weather.

1   Immigration Act 1971, s 33(1). See also Immigration and Asylum Act 1999, s 167(1) defining 'the Immigration Acts' as meaning the 1971 Act, the Immigration Act 1988, the Asylum and Immigration Appeals Act 1993, the Asylum and Immigration Act 1996 and the Immigration and Asylum Act 1999.
2   *R v Governor of Ashford Remand Centre, ex p Bouzagou* [1983] Imm AR 69, CA. See also *Ifzal Ali v Secretary of State for the Home Department* [1994] Imm AR 69.
3   See the criminal case *R v Bourne* [1939] 1 KB 687, [1938] 3 All ER 615 where the word was held to refer to the defence of necessity; see Glanville Williams *Criminal Law: The*

General Part (3rd edn, 1963) para 8. Normally 'unlawfully' means 'without lawful justification or excuse', and does not connote a mental element: see *Archbold Criminal Pleading, Evidence and Practice* (Sweet & Maxwell, 2001) para 17.44.

16.8 There are four kinds of possible illegal entry under the Immigration Act 1971:

- entry without leave;
- entry in breach of a deportation order;
- entry through the common travel area; and
- entry by deception, use of false documents and corruption.

Effectively, the first three are 'no leave' cases and in the fourth leave is granted but deception is involved. The entry without leave and subsequent overstay of crew members is dealt with at **16.46** below.[1]

1   For the history of the powers of removal of illegal entrants see the previous edition at 16.1–16.6.

NO LEAVE CASES

Entry without leave

16.9 Entry to the UK without leave normally constitutes a breach of section 3(1)(a) of the Immigration Act 1971, which requires that, unless otherwise provided, a person who is not a British citizen shall not enter the UK unless given leave to enter in accordance with the Act. Such persons will be illegal entrants within the statutory definition (having entered the UK in breach of the immigration laws). However, the spectrum of persons who are illegal entrants on this basis varies greatly. At one end are clandestine entrants, who evade immigration control and knowingly enter without leave; at the other end are the entirely blameless victims of someone else's fraud or mistake. Clandestine entrants who enter without leave will include those who come in the back of container lorries, slip through the airport terminal,[1] or land on a remote beach at night.[2] There are also those the circumstances of whose entry are unknown, but who cannot show that leave was granted,[3] or can only point to a leave which is forged.[4]

1   See *Re Wajid Hassan* [1976] 2 All ER 123, DC.
2   See *R v Governor of Brixton Prison, ex p Ahsan* [1969] 2 QB 222, [1969] 2 All ER 347, DC.
3   Leave no longer has to be in writing in every case: Immigration (Leave to Enter and Remain) Order 2000, SI 2000/1161, art 8. But the burden of proof as to the date and manner of entry is on the entrant: see SI 2000/1161, art 11. See **3.65** above.
4   *R v Secretary of State for the Home Department, ex p Musawwir* [1989] Imm AR 297, QB.

16.10 Particular problems arise over mistakes or ignorance of the law. There are considerable numbers of people who do not need leave to enter, in view of their citizenship, the common travel area, EEA, diplomatic exemptions and so forth.[1] Because of the complexity of the law and the Immigration Rules, it is easy for both travellers and immigration officers to make mistakes. For example, people come from Ireland not knowing that their particular group needs leave to enter; others are wrongly allowed through immigration control by immigration officers who mistakenly think that they do not need leave. The law is harsh. They are all illegal entrants.[2] It was formerly thought that people who submitted to immigration control and were mistakenly passed through by the immigration service had been examined and were the beneficiaries of a deemed leave under the Immigration Act 1971, Schedule 2, paragraph 6.[3] But the case law makes it clear that such a deemed leave only arises where an immigration officer carries out an examination intending to give a limited leave or to refuse leave, but fails to record the decision within the appropriate time limits.[4] Thus persons who are wrongly assumed to be British citizens may find themselves being treated as illegal entrants through no fault of their own.[5] Yet others become illegal entrants even though they have been examined and an open date stamp has been placed in their passport.[6] Again the law is harsh, since here it is the immigration officer's mistake in allowing them entry without leave which founds the illegality.[7] These cases are to be contrasted with the case where the immigration officer's mistaken grant of leave is valid.[8]

1   The list of exemptions from leave is at **3.3** above. See *R v Secretary of State for the Home Department, ex p Wuan* [1989] Imm AR 501.
2   *R v Governor of Ashford Remand Centre, ex p Bouzagou* [1983] Imm AR 69, CA; *R v Secretary of State for the Home Department, ex p Mohan* [1989] Imm AR 436.
3   *R v Secretary of State for the Home Department, ex p Malik* (2 October 1987, unreported), QBD. See **3.65**ff above.
4   *Secretary of State for the Home Department v Thirukumar* [1989] Imm AR 402, CA; *Rehal v Secretary of State for the Home Department* [1989] Imm AR 576, CA; *R v Secretary of State for the Home Department, ex p Kumar* [1990] Imm AR 265.
5   *Rehal* above; *R v Secretary of State for the Home Department, ex p Khaled* [1987] Imm AR 67; *Mokuolo and Ogunbiyi v Secretary of State for the Home Department* [1989] Imm AR 51, CA.
6   *Mokuolo* above; *R v Secretary of State for the Home Department v Bagga* [1990] Imm AR 413, CA. See **3.70** above.
7   In view of the more relaxed requirements for notice of leave under the Immigration and Asylum Act 1999, there is doubt whether these decisions remain relevant: see **3.65** above.
8   *R v Secretary of State for the Home Department, ex p Ram* [1979] 1 All ER 687, [1979] 1 WLR 148, DC.

16.11 The case of *Noor Nawal Khan*[1] illustrates the absurdities of this doctrine. At the time of his birth in Pakistan in 1971, Mr Khan was a citizen of the UK and colonies by descent. He became a British Dependent Territories citizen on the coming into force of the British Nationality Act 1981. On arrival in the UK in 1992, he presented his passport describing him (correctly) as a British Dependent Territories citizen, although he believed himself entitled to enter and depart from the UK freely by reason of his father's registration as a CUKC in 1965 at the British Sovereign Base in Cyprus. Initially granted temporary admission whilst his claim was investigated, he later received a letter from a chief immigration officer informing him that his 'British nationality had been resolved', that he was 'deemed to be a British citizen' and that he could apply for a British passport describing him as such. His subsequent application for registration as a British citizen, however, was rejected and the letter from the chief immigration officer held incorrect, although he was told he could re-apply for registration later. When he applied for leave to remain as a working holidaymaker, the Home Office responded by informing him that he was an illegal entrant with no claim to remain and that he should 'now make arrangements to return to Pakistan'. Fortunately, on judicial review McCullough J held that the decision declaring Mr Khan to be an illegal entrant and telling him that he should 'now' leave the country was 'altogether excessive and out of proportion to the occasion'. Once it had been decided that he was not going to be allowed to remain to enable him to apply again for British citizenship, 'fairness demanded that he should have been invited to make representations to argue the contrary'.

1 *R v Secretary of State for the Home Department , ex p Noor Nawal Khan* (9 May 1997, unreported) (McCullough J).

Breach of deportation order

16.12 A deportation order is defined by section 5(1) of the Immigration Act 1971 as an order requiring a person to leave and prohibiting him or her from entering the UK. The section provides that a deportation order against a person invalidates any leave to enter or remain in the UK given before the order was made or while it is in force. What this means is that if someone subject to a deportation order still in force manages to obtain leave to enter, this will be invalidated by section 5(1). Questions of deception do not arise. The statutory invalidation of leave operates whether the deportee obtained it by deception or through the immigration officer's mistake.[1] The immigration authorities can make arrangements for the removal of deportees under the existing deportation order.[2] The only gain from removing them as illegal entrants is that sometimes the airline or shipping company can be made to pay their return fare, whereas in a deportation it is the British government which pays.

1 *R v Secretary of State for the Home Department, ex p Yeboah* [1986] Imm AR 52.
2 Immigration Act 1971, Sch 3, para 1; on procedure see Immigration Rules, HC 395, para 388. As to appeal rights, see ss 65 (human rights appeal) and 66 (appeal against validity of directions for removal) of the Immigration and Asylum Act 1999. Note the availability of the s 65 appeal right irrespective as to whether directions are given under Sch 2 or 3 to the 1971 Act.

16.13 Most returning deportees will be illegal entrants because they have no leave.[1] They would still be illegal entrants if the words 'in breach of a deportation order' were omitted from the definition of illegal entrants in section 33(1) of the Immigration Act 1971. But these words are essential for those who do not need leave to enter the UK, such as Irish citizens and deportees of other nationalities who return through Ireland, or EEA nationals exercising free movement rights.[2] The operation of the deportation order is unaffected by the leave-free travel provisions of the EEA or common travel area.[3] Deportees of other nationalities who return to the UK on a local journey from Ireland do not need leave to enter, but are illegal entrants because their return is in breach of the deportation order. Where someone has been deported from the Channel Islands or the Isle of Man the order has the same effect as if it was a UK deportation order,[4] and the person who tries to enter the UK in breach of it would be an illegal entrant.

1 Immigration Act 1971, s 5(1).
2 See eg *Shingara v Secretary of State for the Home Department* [1999] Imm AR 257, CA.
3 Immigration Act 1971, ss 1(3) and 9(4).
4 Immigration Act 1971, Sch 4, para 3(1).

Entry through the common travel area

16.14 Those who arrive in this country after a local journey[1] from Ireland, the Channel Islands or Isle of Man—all parts of the common travel area—do not normally require leave to enter[2] and so unless they have arrived in breach of a deportation order they will not usually be illegal entrants.[3] But there are a number of exceptions. Those arriving from the Channel Islands or the Isle of Man will be illegal entrants if:

- their presence there was unlawful;[4] or
- they have previously been refused entry to the UK and have not been given a later leave to enter or remain.[5]

1 For the definition of a local journey, see Immigration Act 1971, s 11(4).
2 Immigration Act 1971, s 1(3). Generally on the common travel area see chapter 6 above.
3 By Immigration Act 1971, s 9(4) leave-free travel within the common travel area under s 1(3) does not affect the operation of a deportation order.
4 Immigration Act 1971, Sch 4, para 4.
5 Immigration Act 1971, s 9(4)(b).

16.15 For arrivals from Ireland the position is more complicated. A distinction has to be made between citizens of the Republic and other nationals who come via Ireland. Citizens of the Republic will only be illegal entrants if: (1) they are returning deportees; or (2) they return after being refused entry for national security reasons.[1] Other nationals who come via Ireland will be illegal entrants if they need leave to enter the UK under the Immigration (Control of Entry through Republic of Ireland) Order 1972[2] and enter without it.[3] Even if they are unaware that they ought to have obtained leave,[4] they can nevertheless be treated as illegal entrants in the following circumstances:[5]

(i)   they have previously been refused entry to the UK and have not been given later leave to enter or remain;[6]
(ii)   although arriving on an aircraft which began its flight in the Republic they entered the Republic in transit from another country and did not obtain leave to land;[7]
(iii)   they are visa nationals who have no valid visa to enter the UK;[8]
(iv)   they entered the Republic unlawfully from a place outside the common travel area;[9]
(v)   they entered the Republic from the UK or Northern Ireland having been illegal entrants or overstayers there;[10]
(vi)   directions have been given to exclude them from the UK on the ground that their exclusion is conducive to the public good.[11]

1 Immigration Act 1971, s 9(4)(a). Here, the EC law public policy derogation will apply: see **7.125**ff above.
2 SI 1972/1610.
3 They 'enter' the UK as soon as they leave their ship or plane and immigration officers do not usually travel on board: see Immigration Act 1971, s 11(1) and (2). So unless they obtain leave before leaving Ireland, they will already have become illegal entrants by the time they find an immigration officer on arrival.
4 *R v Governor of Ashford Remand Centre, ex p Bouzagou* [1983] Imm AR 69, CA; *R v Secretary of State for the Home Department, ex p Mohan* [1989] Imm AR 436.
5 See further **6.24** above.
6 Immigration Act 1971, s 9(4)(b).
7 SI 1972/1610, art 3(1)(a).
8 SI 1972/1610, arts 2(1) and 3(1)(b)(i).
9 SI 1972/1610, art 3(1)(b)(ii).
10 SI 1972/1610, art 3(1)(b)(iii), as amended by the Immigration (Control of Entry through Republic of Ireland) (Amendment) Order 1979, SI 1979/730. In *R v Secretary of State for the Home Department, ex p Wuan* [1989] Imm AR 501 a British Dependent Territories citizen from Hong Kong entered the UK when exempt from control as a member of the armed forces; he left for the Republic of Ireland after he ceased to be exempt; it was held that he was not excluded from the common travel area as an overstayer and had accordingly been given a deemed leave on his re-entry to the UK.
11 SI 1972/1610, art 3(1)(b)(iv).

DECEPTION, FALSE DOCUMENTS AND CORRUPTION

Entry by deception

16.16 Entry by deception occurs where the entrant: (i) makes or causes to be made a false representation contrary to section 26(1)(c) of the Immigration Act 1971 and such deception is the effective means of entry; (ii) enters the UK by means including deception, contrary to section 24A of the 1971 Act; or (iii) enters or seeks to enter by means which include deception by another person. The landmark decision in the House of Lords in *Khawaja*[1] established that leave to enter is obtained in breach of the Act if the effective means of obtaining it is the commission of the offence of making a false representation under section 26(1)(c) of the 1971 Act.[2] The court held that the entrant had no duty of candour,[3] and is not deemed to be aware of all the Immigration Rules and conditions for entry. They doubted whether a person who was personally innocent of any fraud could be removed as an illegal entrant by the section 26(1)(c) route.[4] This part of the judgment has been superseded by the extension of the definition of illegal entry to include entry by means of deception by a third party.[5] The creation of a new criminal offence of obtaining or seeking to obtain leave to enter by deception[6] provides a clear statutory foundation for illegal entry by deception.

1   *Khawaja v Secretary of State for the Home Department* [1984] AC 74, [1984] 1 All ER 765, HL.
2   *Khawaja* above at 118–119, per Lord Bridge.
3   Imposed on immigrants in the 1979 case of *Zamir v Secretary of State for the Home Department* [1980] AC 930, [1980] 2 All ER 768, HL.
4   *Khawaja* above at 199, per Lord Bridge.
5   Immigration Act 1971, s 33(1) as amended by Asylum and Immigration Act 1996, Sch 2, para 4. This statutory creation put an end to 20 years' debate in the courts: see *Khan v Secretary of State for the Home Department* [1977] 3 All ER 538, [1977] 1 WLR 1466, CA; *Khawaja v Secretary of State for the Home Department* [1984] AC 74, [1984] 1 All ER 765, HL; *Chan v Secretary of State for the Home Department* [1992] Imm AR 233, CA; *Hamid v Secretary of State for the Home Department* [1993] Imm AR 216, CA; *Kuet v Secretary of State for the Home Department* [1995] Imm AR 274, CA.
6   Immigration Act 1971, s 24A, inserted by Asylum and Immigration Act 1996, s 4 and amended by Immigration and Asylum Act 1999, s 28.

16.17 Deception in illegal entry cases involves representations made to the immigration officer at the port of entry and to an entry clearance officer at an overseas post.[1] Knowledge of falsehood is a key element. The deception may take a variety of forms. It may involve landing cards filled out on the plane, answers given to questions by an immigration officer, an entry clearance officer or medical inspector, as well as a whole host of representations which the courts have implied from the mere presentation of a passport, and representations by conduct.[2]

1   *R v Secretary of State for the Home Department, ex p Saffu Mensah* [1991] Imm AR 43, QBD.
2   See *Akinde v Secretary of State for the Home Department* [1993] Imm AR 512, CA; *Rasmiah Al-Zahrany v Secretary of State for the Home Department* [1995] Imm AR 510, CA; *R v Secretary of State for the Home Department, ex p Zahide Awan* [1996] Imm AR 354, QBD; *R v Secretary of State for the Home Department, ex p Kuteesa* [1997] Imm AR 194, QBD.

16.18 The fact that leave no longer lapses when the holder leaves the common travel area[1] means that, if leave was obtained by deception, the holder enters illegally each time he or she enters the UK using it. What of the situation where leave obtained by deception lapses and fresh leave is sought on entry? For example, a returning resident seeking entry after more than two years away presents a passport endorsed with a previous indefinite leave to enter; strictly, the representation of indefinite leave, and thus eligibility as a returning resident, is accurate, as leave is not vitiated or rendered non-existent by deception; but if the presenter of the passport knows that the previous leave was improperly obtained, the judges will infer an implied representation that the leave was a lawful one.[2] Offering a passport containing a student leave implies a representation that the holder had validly been granted leave as a student.[3]

1   Immigration (Leave to Enter and Remain) Order 2000, SI 2000/1161, art 13: see **4.4** above.
2   *R v Secretary of State for the Home Department, ex p Patel* [1986] Imm AR 515, CA; *R v Secretary of State for the Home Department, ex p Salim* [1990] Imm AR 316, QBD.
3   *Durojaiye v Secretary of State for the Home Department* [1991] Imm AR 307, CA.

16.19 Where the passport contains an entry clearance, a representation is implied: (i) that entry clearance was validly obtained; and (ii) that the person seeks entry for that purpose and no other.[1] The representation may be a silent one; although the duty of candour has gone, judicial enthusiasm for implying representations from the silent presentation of a passport has almost plugged the gap.[2] Each case will depend on its own facts, however, and an entrant who has reason to believe that a previous irregularity has been cured or pardoned will not be guilty of misrepresentation as to the nature of a previous leave.[3] Where there has been no contact at all between the immigrant and the immigration officer or entry clearance officer, there is no representation of any kind.[4] In *Doldur*[5] (where between the grant of a settlement visa as a dependant son and entry the applicant had married) the Court of Appeal held (by majority) that it was not an irresistible inference that he failed to reveal his marriage because he knew that to do so would affect his chances of entry. Rather, it was a reasonable inference that the applicant believed his marriage did not alter the fact that he entered as his father's dependant and would remain so until he found a job and could provide for his wife himself. The applicant had been asked no questions on arrival by the immigration officer and (in the words of Evans LJ) seeking to rely on his failure to volunteer information as a positive misrepresentation came very close to contending that he owed a duty of candour.[6] In *James* two adult twins who were mentally impaired were brought to the UK as visitors by their aunt, who subsequently died. The twins' admission that they had always wanted to live in the UK did not make them illegal entrants, because there was no evidence that this was the aunt's intention and they themselves had had no dealings with the immigration officer.[7]

1   *R v Secretary of State for the Home Department, ex p Saffu-Mensah* [1991] Imm AR 43, QBD (husband intending to join wife permanently if she would have him obtains entry clearance as visitor). See also *Rasmiah AL Zahrany v Secretary of State for the Home Department* [1995] Imm AR 510, CA; *R v Secretary of State for the Home Department, ex p Awan* [1996] Imm AR 354, QBD.
2   See cases referred to at **16.17** fn 2 above. Presentation of a passport showing an earlier leave to enter obtained by false representations amounts to a fresh false representation: *R v Secretary of State for the Home Department, ex p Patel* [1986] Imm AR 515, CA. Re-entry on the basis of leave to enter obtained by a false representation is a fresh false representation which carries forward from one trip to the next *ad infinitum*: see *Layla Khatun* [1993] Imm AR 616, IAT (false representation made in 1969 still effective in 1992).

3   *R v Secretary of State for the Home Department, ex p Addo* (1985) Times, 18 April, QBD, followed in *R v Secretary of State for the Home Department, ex p Okunbowa* (19 November 1985, unreported), QBD.

4   *R v Secretary of State for the Home Department, ex p Dordas* [1992] Imm AR 99, QBD (ill-treated domestic servant, who decided before she left Kuwait to run away in the UK if the opportunity arose, was not an illegal entrant where her entry clearance was obtained by her employer and at the port her passport was also presented by him).

5   *Doldur v Secretary of State for the Home Department* [1998] Imm AR 352. For a case on the other side of the line see *Jahangir v Secretary of State for the Home Department* (11 December 1996, unreported), CA.

6   See also *R (Wilson) v Secretary of State for the Home Department* [2001] EWHC Admin 115, in which visit leave was held not to have been obtained by deception, although an intention to remain with a settled spouse existed, because there were no questions on the length of the visit and the applicant was unaware of the visa requirement for family reunion.

7   *R v Secretary of State for the Home Department, ex p James* (27 May 1994, unreported), QBD (Sedley J).

16.20 In *Choudhry v Metropolitan Police*[1] the Divisional Court found that an application to the Home Office to remain on the ground of marriage carried with it an implied representation that it was a 'genuine' marriage and not a marriage of convenience entered into solely to persuade the Home Office to grant leave. The judgment was given on the basis that the implied representation was of general application and not confined to the particular defendant, with his particular knowledge of the Immigration Rules relating to husbands. Unfortunately, the court did not refer to older cases dealing with marriages of convenience.[2] A marriage solely for immigration and nationality purposes is nevertheless a valid one; it is for the Home Office to consider whether it also complies with the Rules.[3] The decision in *Choudhry* turns a perfectly accurate statement of the law into a deception. The fact of marriage is by no means conclusive of immigration and nationality status; such matters as the purpose of the marriage[4] and the parties' intention to cohabit and their financial security are further criteria which may need to be satisfied. To import into a statement that the parties are married further representations that the marriage has qualities required to give the spouse admission under the Rules is to turn application and investigation upside down. It is strongly arguable that the decision in *Choudhry* was wrong. Too great a readiness to find false representations risks bringing back the duty of candour via the back door. It is to be hoped that the issue may fall for reconsideration.

1   (24 November 1984, unreported), QBD.

2   *Silver v Silver* [1955] 2 All ER 614, [1955] 1 WLR 728; *Vervaeke v Smith* [1983] 1 AC 145, [1982] 2 All ER 144, HL; *Puttick v A-G* [1980] Fam 1, [1979] 3 All ER 463.

3   Until the British Nationality Act 1981 came into force on 1 January 1983, Commonwealth citizens marrying patrial men automatically became patrial, no matter what the purpose of the marriage, provided merely that it was a valid one. If, however, fraud had been used, the courts might refuse to grant any relief: see *Puttick v A-G* above

4   The 'primary purpose' element of the marriage rules was withdrawn from 5 June 1997 (one of the first acts of the new Labour government in honouring a manifesto commitment): see HC 26, amending Pt 8 of HC 395.

Effective deception

16.21 In *Khawaja* the House of Lords held that deception or fraud must be the effective means, or one of the means, of obtaining leave to enter so as to make the contravention of the Immigration Act 1971 and the obtaining of leave two inseparable elements in the single process of entry.[1] It was thought that a useful guide as to what constituted effective means was the earlier case of *Jayakody*.[2] There the court held that the fraud must be decisive of the application, *ie* in all probability the leave would have been refused but for the deception. Thus a failure to reveal one of the purposes of an otherwise genuine visit, or to tell the immigration officer that a spouse was resident in the UK, may not be decisive of the grant or refusal of leave to enter. But the binding effect of the Court of Appeal's decision has been watered down by subsequent cases, which have moved the focus away from 'effective means' to mere 'materiality'. First, in *Bugdaycay*[3] the House of Lords held that the question of whether a fraud was effective in obtaining entry could only be considered in the light of the application actually made and it was irrelevant that the person might have been admitted in some other capacity. Then in *Durojaiye v Secretary of State for the Home Department*[4] Staughton LJ said that false answers to questions about a student's hours of attendance at college plainly were 'material in the sense it was likely to influence the decision'. This was followed by Laws J in *Ex p Ming*,[5] holding that a representation was material if, on revelation of the truth, 'at the very least further inquiries would have been made'. And in *Kaur v Secretary of State for the Home Department*[6] (an appeal against refusal of leave to enter on the ground that material facts were not disclosed for the purpose of obtaining a visa) Ward LJ stated that the time had come 'to put the *Jayakody* test to rest' as being 'quite inconsistent' with *Bugdaycay*[7] and *Durojaiye*.[8] He agreed expressly with Staughton LJ's analysis in *Durojaiye*[9] as being the 'appropriate test'. The wording of the 1971 Act, section 24A offence puts it beyond doubt that the deception employed need only have been one of the factors leading to the grant of leave to enter, not necessarily the decisive one, and represents a clear endorsement of the shift from *Jayakody* to the materiality test.

1   *Khawaja v Secretary of State for the Home Department* [1984] AC 74 at 118E, per Lord Bridge.
2   *R v Secretary of State for the Home Department, ex p Jayakody* [1982] 1 All ER 461, [1982] 1 WLR 405, CA.
3   [1987] AC 514, where a visitor failed to disclose his intention of applying for asylum. He was held to be an illegal entrant despite the fact that he would not have been removable had he claimed asylum.
4   [1991] Imm AR 307, CA.
5   *R v Secretary of State for the Home Department, ex p Ming* [1994] Imm AR 216, Laws J. See also *R v Secretary of State for the Home Department, ex p Castro* [1996] Imm AR 540 where Dyson J was satisfied that deception was the effective means of obtaining leave to enter, but thought it 'may' have been sufficient for the Secretary of State to show that deception was material in the sense of being likely to influence the decision.
6   [1998] Imm AR 1, CA.
7   [1987] 1 AC 514, see fn 3 above.
8   [1991] Imm AR 307, CA.
9   Fn 3 above.

16.22   There is substantial case law on the application of a material deception.[1] Particular problems were created where the Immigration Rules allowed a switch in categories from visitor to student or dependent relative status. It is not permissible to come in with leave in one category with a fixed intention of applying to vary to another.[2] Although there is a difference between a wish and an intention, the courts are prepared to draw the inference of deception where all the circumstances warrant it.[3]

1 See, for example, *Re Olusanya* [1988] Imm AR 117, QBD (intending student gained entry as visitor); *R v Secretary of State for the Home Department, ex p Mahoney* [1992] Imm AR 275, QBD (visitor, always intended to study); *Tadimi v Secretary of State for the Home Department* [1993] Imm AR 90, CA (doing work inconsistent with student status); *R v Secretary of State for the Home Department, ex p Ahmed* [1993] Imm AR 242, QBD and *R v Secretary of State for the Home Department, ex p Miah* [1994] Imm AR 279, QBD (son pretending to be single when in fact married); *R v Secretary of State for the Home Department, ex p Zeenat Bibi* [1994] Imm AR 326, QBD (spouse posing as unmarried visitor). For instances where a deception was immaterial, see *R v Secretary of State for the Home Department, ex p Miah* [1989] Imm AR 559, CA; *R v Secretary of State for the Home Department, ex p Khan (Hiram)* [1990] Imm AR 327, CA.

2 *Adesina v Secretary of State for the Home Department* [1988] Imm AR 442, CA; *Ex p Mahoney* above. Cf *R v Immigration Appeal Tribunal, ex p Coomasaru* [1983] 1 All ER 208, [1982] Imm AR 77 (returning residents entering as visitors, fixed intention to settle qualifies them as returning residents rather than as illegal entrants). This scenario is much less likely in any event since the Immigration (Leave to Enter and Remain) Order 2000, SI 2000/1161, art 13.

3 *R v Secretary of State for the Home Department, ex p Brakwah* [1989] Imm AR 366, QBD; *R v Secretary of State for the Home Department, ex p Nwanurue* [1992] Imm AR 39, QBD.

Invalid documents and third party deception

16.23 Before the enactment of section 24A in 1996,[1] there were differences of judicial opinion as to whether illegal entry was constituted by obtaining a leave in breach of criminal sections of the Immigration Act 1971 other than section 26(1)(c), in particular section 26(1)(d) which deals with the possession and use of false passports, entry clearances, work permits and other documents.[2] To be guilty of this offence the person must know or have reasonable cause to believe that the document is false. It is unclear whether an unreasonable but genuine belief in a document's authenticity grounds the section 26(1)(d) offence. Woolf J in *Rouse and Shrimpton*[3] held that this offence was not necessarily one of fraud so as to make a person who obtained leave to enter an illegal entrant. However, it is all now academic, since the knowing use of a false passport or other document will in any event amount to a representation by conduct that the document is genuine and come within section 24A or section 26(1)(c). The amendment of the statutory definition of illegal entrant puts beyond doubt that the innocent proffering of false documents renders entry illegal after 1 November 1996,[4] since the use of a false document, the falsity of which is unknown to the entrant, will now be dealt with as 'means which include deception by another'. But the person must have entered or be seeking to enter by means of the false documents, so where someone travels on forged documents but claims asylum at the immigration desk without seeking entry on the basis of the documents, the person is not an illegal entrant.[5]

1 By the Asylum and Immigration Act 1996.
2 Woolf J in *Ex p Rouse and Shrimpton* (13 November 1985, unreported), QBD, thought a breach of s 26(1)(d) of the Immigration Act 1971 did not make someone an illegal entrant; Webster J came to a different conclusion in *R v Secretary of State for the Home Department, ex p Patel* [1986] Imm AR 208, QBD.
3 (13 November 1985, unreported), QBD.
4 Ie when the Asylum and Immigration Act 1996 amendment came into force.
5 *R v Naillie* [1993] AC 674, [1993] 2 All ER 782, HL. However, intending immigrants discovered before entry in circumstances indicating an intention to enter illegally have been treated as illegal entrants for the purpose of convicting a facilitator in *R v Eyck, R v Hadakoglu* [2000] INLR 277.

Breaking conditions of temporary admission

16.24 Where a person's examination is left unfinished for further inquiries to be made, he or she is normally given temporary admission under paragraph 21 of Schedule 2 to the Immigration Act 1971. Under section 11 of the Act persons under temporary admission are not deemed to have 'entered' the UK unless they have 'otherwise entered'. Absconders and those in breach of conditions of temporary admission may be detained, refused leave and summarily removed,[1] but they may also be treated as illegal entrants, according to the Court of Appeal in *Ex p Akhtar*,[2] either on the basis that they were seeking entry by deception or that by breaking conditions of temporary admission they have 'otherwise entered' the UK without obtaining leave to enter.[3] But not every breach of temporary admission will make a person an illegal entrant, or at least liable to removal, unless the breach is sufficiently serious and deliberate to amount to an entry or an attempt to enter without leave.[4]

1   Immigration Act 1971, Sch 2, paras 6, 8 and 21(1) and (4).
2   *Akhtar v Governor of Pentonville Prison* [1993] Imm AR 424, CA; see also *R v Secretary of State for the Home Department, ex p Taj Khan* [1985] Imm AR 104, CA. See **16.29** below.
3   See *Ex p Akhtar* above at 431, per Sir Thomas Bingham MR.
4   *Ex p Akhtar* above at 431, per Evans LJ. We suggest that only absconding, and not breach of employment restrictions or of the draconian residence conditions which are envisaged in Immigration Act 1971, Sch 2, para 21(2B), would constitute illegal entry, since the latter does not indicate an intention to 'enter'.

Leave to enter obtained by corruption or forgery

16.25 A forged leave to enter is clearly no leave at all.[1] A leave to enter obtained in knowing reliance on an entry clearance or a work permit itself obtained by corruption would be a leave obtained by fraud (because the proffering of such a permit or endorsement carries a representation that it was duly obtained).[2] But what if the entrant was unaware of the corruption? In the previous edition of this work[3] we raised the possibility of an innocent entrant (not party to any false or corrupt procurement of leave to enter) being able to rely on such leave if it was issued by someone who had the authority to do so, particularly since an immigrant is not to be penalised for the errors or dishonesty of public officials.[4] If an innocent immigrant presents an entry clearance or work permit obtained by corruption to which he or she has not been a party, it is hard to see why such document, issued by a person with authority to do so, cannot be relied on, since neither it nor any leave obtained in reliance on it has been obtained by deception on anyone's part—unless it could be said that the endorsement of the passport by the corrupt official constitutes third-party deception just as forgery of a visa does.

1   *R v Secretary of State for the Home Department, ex p Musawwir* [1989] Imm AR 297.
2   See **16.19** above.
3   Fourth edition at para **16.34**.
4   *Kuet v Secretary of State for the Home Department* [1995] Imm AR 274, CA, observations of Sir Thomas Bingham MR.

Persons claiming to be British citizens

16.26 Persons who are British citizens cannot be removed as illegal entrants, even if they entered under some other nationality.[1] The difficulty may lie in proving the entitlement. The burden of proof rests on the immigrant concerned.[2] Section 3(9) of the Immigration Act 1971 requires proof of the right of abode by means either of a UK passport describing the holder as a British citizen (or a CUKC with the right of abode), or a certificate of entitlement certifying such right of abode. This will satisfy the initial burden and it will then be for the Home Office to demonstrate that the documents were improperly obtained or that the holder was not entitled to them.[3] In *Obi*[4] the burden of proof was everything (since it was accepted that if it lay on the Secretary of State it was not one he could discharge). The applicant had produced a UK passport describing him as a British citizen. The Secretary of State accepted that the passport described Mr Obi as a British citizen, but contended that until the applicant proved that he was Mr Obi, the passport was not one describing 'him' as a British citizen. The physical possession of a UK passport alone would not satisfy the section 3(9) test (for example, if it was believed to be stolen or forged the burden could not be discharged until the bearer could show him- or herself to be the person described in the passport). But here it was undisputed both that the person described in the passport as a British citizen had applied for it in Liverpool and that that person was the applicant (the photograph being indisputably his). Sedley J held that no further burden lay on the applicant. Where such an allegation is made in the course of illegal entry proceedings, the case is one within *Khawaja* principles. It should be noted that production of a birth certificate in the name of the applicant[5] or an identity document is not proof of British citizenship, so as to shift the burden of proof on to the Secretary of State.[6]

1   Immigration Act 1971, s 1(1).
2   Immigration Act 1971, s 3(8); see *Re Bamgbose* [1990] Imm AR 135, CA where a birth certificate did not discharge the burden as there was a dispute as to whether it truly related to the applicant. In *Mokuolo v Secretary of State for the Home Department* [1989] Imm AR 51, CA a statement as to birth in the UK in a Nigerian passport was similarly not sufficient.
3   A passport or certificate of entitlement are the means specified in the Immigration Act 1971 for proving citizenship: see s 3(9); Sch 2, para 3.
4   *R v Secretary of State for the Home Department, ex p Obi* [1997] Imm AR 420 QBD.
5   *Re Bamgbose* [1990] Imm AR 135, CA.
6   *Minta v Secretary of State for the Home Department* [1992] Imm AR 380, CA (British visitors passport (BVP), now discontinued).

EEA nationals

16.27 Similar considerations apply to EEA nationals. Under the Immigration (European Economic Area) Regulations 2000[1] EEA nationals must be admitted to the UK if, on arrival, they produce a valid national identity card or passport issued by another EEA state,[2] unless there are public policy reasons for their exclusion.[3] Community rights, as we have seen, flow from EC law and do not need any grant of leave under the Immigration Act 1971.[4] Add the removal of internal frontiers, and entry in breach of the immigration laws will be a rare and exceptional thing. It could occur if someone enters clandestinely without any intention of exercising free movement rights, for example, to land a consignment of drugs, or if someone enters in breach of a deportation order. The Court of Appeal held in *Shingara*[5] that it occurred when an EEA national entered after being excluded pursuant to a validly imposed exclusion order which complied with Council Directive (EEC) 64/221. Where an EEA national has entered illegally, removal can only take place in accordance with the public policy provisions of Council Directive (EEC) 64/221 and must not be discriminatory or disproportionate to the limited rights of member states to impose penalties for infringements of their national procedures.[6]

1   SI 2000/2326.
2   SI 2000/2326, reg 12.
3   SI 2000/2326, reg 21.
4   *R v Pieck* [1981] QB 571; Immigration Act 1988, s 7(1); see chapter 7 above.
5   *Shingara v Secretary of the State Department* [1999] Imm AR 257, CA.
6   *Re Belgian Passport Control: EC Commission v Belgium* [1990] 2 CMLR 492, ECJ; *Royer* [1976] 2 CMLR 619, ECJ; *Watson and Belmann* [1976] 2 CMLR 552, ECJ.

Refugees

16.28 Illegal entrants who are refugees cannot be removed to a country where they have a well-founded fear of persecution,[1] but it is not contrary to the Immigration Acts or the UK's international obligations to treat asylum claimants who obtained leave to enter by deception (eg by presenting themselves as visitors) as illegal entrants.[2]

1   See chapter 12 above; Refugee Convention, art 33.
2   *Bugdaycay v Secretary of State for the Home Department* [1987] AC 514, [1987] 1 All ER 940, HL.

Treating someone as an illegal entrant

16.29 Although the decision that a person is to be treated as an illegal entrant is taken by an immigration officer, in practice it will often be made by the Home Office, either because of instructions given to the immigration officer or because the main decision is whether to grant leave to remain, and that decision is for the Secretary of State for the Home Department, rather than the immigration officer, under section 4(1) of the Immigration Act 1971. Where the authorities purport to set aside a previous grant of leave in order to remove someone as an illegal entrant, the burden of proving that entry was in breach of the laws falls on the Home Office, and in any judicial proceedings the court inquires whether the facts precedent to the exercise of the administrative power have been proven.[1] However, the fact that a person has entered illegally, eg by obtaining leave to enter as a visitor intending to claim asylum, does not oblige the Secretary of State to treat him or her as such.[2] The difficulty here is that a number of policy statements[3] have conferred benefits on illegal entrants and overstayers which have not been available to those seeking leave to enter, because of the failure to recognise that many persons seeking leave to enter have physically been in the country (on temporary admission), forming relationships and ties with the country, for many years. Thus it has been, paradoxically, necessary for persons to be 'recognised'[4] as illegal entrants rather than 'mere' port applicants to obtain the benefit of policies on family life. Where (for example) a person who claims asylum at the port on arrival marries whilst on temporary admission (pending consideration of the asylum claim) he or she is unambiguously a 'port' case and potentially would not benefit from the marriage policy (DP/3/96) applicable to persons 'liable to be removed as illegal entrants'.[5] But what is the position if the person is as a matter of law an illegal entrant (for example having breached temporary admission by absconding)?[6] In *Afunyah*[7] Lord Woolf MR approved the statement of Laws J (at first instance) that in such circumstances the Secretary of State was entitled to treat the applicant as a port case. Laws J had considered it to be 'entirely plain' that if the applicant could insist that she be treated as an illegal entrant she would be 'building rights on an edifice consisting of nothing but her own wrongdoing'. Where the policy concerned gives effect to human rights (eg the right to respect for family or private life), these problems should no longer arise since the introduction of the free-standing human rights appeal under section 65 of the Immigration and Asylum Act 1999, which will be available to port applicants and illegal entrants equally.[8]

1 *Khawaja v Secretary of State for the Home Department* [1984] AC 74, HL.
2 See *Afunyah v Secretary of State for the Home Department* [1998] Imm AR 201, fn 7 below. Contrast *R v Secretary of State for the Home Department, ex p Urmaza* [1996] COD 479 (seaman deserter was illegal entrant and it was not open to Secretary of State not to treat him as one). See further, on the need for an immigration official to exercise discretion whether or not to treat a person who *is* an illegal entrant as such, *Cakmak v Secretary of State for the Home Department* [2001] INLR 194.
3 See for example statements on 'the long residence concession'; the marriage policy (DP/3/96) and the policies on children (DP/4/95 and DP 5/96), for which see *Butterworths Immigration Law* Service, D[551]; see also the IDI and the ADI (available on the Internet at www.homeoffice.gov.uk).
4 *Abu Shahed v Secretary of State for the Home Department* [1995] Imm AR 303.
5 See **11.59-11.60** above.
6 In *Akhtar v Governor of Pentonville Prison* [1993] Imm AR 424 the Court of Appeal held (by majority, Evans LJ reserving his position) that breach of conditions of temporary admission made the applicant an illegal entrant.
7 *Afunyah v Secretary of State for the Home Department* [1998] Imm AR 201, CA followed in *R v Secretary of State for the Home Department, ex p Olawole* (FC3/000/6002/C, 18 April 2000, CA; contrast decision of Sedley J in *R v Secretary of State for the Home Department, ex p Urmaza* [1996] COD 479.
8 See **16.51** below and **8.71ff** above.

16.30 Once it is established that the person is an illegal entrant and that the immigration officer or Secretary of State is going to treat the person as such, the practice is to serve an IS 151A notice to an illegal entrant. However there is no statutory provision requiring such notice to be given. It is not a decision to give or refuse leave, and so is not regulated by section 4(1) of the Immigration Act 1971. The service of such notice is significant, however, in that it may unlock the benefit of a particular policy, and it also dates the 'commencement of enforcement action' for the purposes of policies and concessions based on long residence, marriage or other ties which the person may seek to rely on to argue that he or she should not be removed.[1]

1 See **11.59-11.60** above for the policies relating to marriage; **11.106** for those relating to children, and **16.43** below for the long-residence concession.

Later leave to enter or remain

16.31 Under paragraph 9 of Schedule 2 to the Immigration Act 1971 the power of removal only arises where the illegal entrant has not been given 'leave to enter or remain':[1]

> '9(1) Where an illegal entrant is not given leave to enter or remain in the United Kingdom, an immigration officer may give any such directions in respect

of him as in a case within paragraph 8 above as are authorised by paragraph 8(1);

9(2) any leave to enter the United Kingdom which is obtained by deception shall be disregarded for the purposes of this paragraph.'

This reflects the discretion of the immigration officer or Secretary of State for the Home Department to decide whether or not to allow an illegal entrant to remain in the UK. Section 9(2) was added to resolve the difficulty caused by the decision in *Khawaja*[2] to the effect that leave obtained by deception remained valid.[3] However, leave granted on a completely different basis (eg as a refugee) in ignorance of initial illegal entry (as, say, a visitor) cannot be disregarded, and would prevent removal, since the initial deception played no role in the grant of the new leave. The paragraph does not, however, cover the position of those who entered lawfully, but who subsequently obtained leave to remain by deception. Persons in this category who have left the UK and re-entered are clearly illegal entrants on re-entry with their original leave. But those who have obtained leave to remain by deception and have not left the country since are not illegal entrants. Previously, these persons had to be deported on 'conducive to the public good' grounds. Section 10 of the Immigration and Asylum Act 1999 now provides that they may be summarily removed.[4]

1 Immigration Act 1971, Sch 2, para 9(1), as amended by Asylum and Immigration Act 1996, Sch 2, para 6.
2 *Khawaja v Secretary of State for the Home Department* [1984] AC 74, HL.
3 The section gives statutory effect to the Court of Appeal decision in *R v Secretary of State for the Home Department, ex p Lapinid* [1984] 3 All ER 257, [1984] 1 WLR 1269, that para 9 of the Immigration Act 1971 must exclude leave obtained by deception, or any extension of it. Following *Azam v Secretary of State for the Home Department* [1974] AC 18, HL, an extension of leave granted by the Home Office prevented removal under para 9 even if based on the initial deception—a construction now excluded by para 9(2).
4 See **16.40** below.

OVERSTAYERS AND OTHERS

16.32 From 2 October 2000 the following categories of individual who were formerly subject to deportation action are subject to administrative removal procedures identical to those which apply to illegal entrants and those refused leave to enter:

- persons overstaying their limited leave;
- persons breaching a condition of their limited leave;
- those whose continued stay was obtained by deception; and
- family members of any of the above.[1]

Of these, only overstayers and those in breach who applied before 2 October 2000 for leave to remain in accordance with a specially constituted regularisation scheme are excluded from the new procedures.[2] Those so qualifying will, together with their dependants, remain subject to pre-existing arrangements.[3] Deportation action continues to apply where the Secretary of State deems deportation to be conducive to the public good, and following a court recommendation, and to dependants in these cases,[4] and procedures remain fundamentally unchanged for these persons.[5] Under the new removal provisions for the four categories listed above, the person to be removed will be given written notice of the decision,[6] following which the immigration officer may authorise detention or make an order restricting residence, employment or occupation, or imposing reporting conditions pending removal.[7]

1   Immigration and Asylum Act 1999, s 10(1); HC 395, para 395B as amended by Cm 4851. The first two categories were formerly liable to deportation under old s 3(5)(a) of the Immigration Act 1971, the third under s 3(5)(aa) and the last under s 3(5)(c) of the 1971 Act.
2   Immigration and Asylum Act 1999, s 10(2). The regularisation scheme is set out in s 9 of the 1999 Act.
3   Immigration and Asylum Act 1999, s 10(2).
4   Immigration Act 1971,s 3(5)(a), as amended by Immigration and Asylum Act 1999, Sch 14, para 44, and 3(6). See chapter 15 above.
5   See **17.29** below.
6   HC 395, para 395E as amended by Cm 4851.
7   HC 395, para 395F as amended by Cm 4851.

Overstaying and breach of conditions

16.33 Leave to enter the UK may be given for a limited period, and may be subject to a condition restricting employment or occupation, precluding recourse to public funds in maintenance or accommodation, or requiring registration with the police. Failing to observe any of these conditions or remaining beyond the time limited by the leave makes a person liable to removal under section 10. Thereafter, there needs to be a decision to remove, which involves the exercise of a discretion; see **16.42** below. The burden of proving overstaying or breach of conditions is on the Home Office. The Secretary of State must establish the facts which give rise to the power to remove, although reasonable suspicion is enough to justify detention. There are, however, one or two areas of difficulty. What are the ingredients of overstaying and breach of conditions which need to be proved in order to justify removal under section 10 of the Immigration and Asylum Act 1999?

16.34 The words in section 10(1)(a) of the Immigration and Asylum Act 1999 referring to persons 'having only a limited leave to remain' suggest the existence of a current leave either at the time of the breach or of the decision to remove, but this would make the provision inoperative as far as overstaying is concerned. The words are confusing, and in the context of overstaying the established view is that they need to be read as 'having had' leave.[1] To establish overstaying, the date of the expiry of leave will clearly need to be proved. Normally this can be done by looking at the passport, but where the passport is not available, or where leave was granted by other means, such as orally or by e-mail, no assumption may be made as to the date and duration of any leave granted. While the Home Office must prove overstaying as a precedent fact to the exercise of the power to remove, the provisions of the Immigration (Leave to Enter and Remain) Order 2000[2] impose a burden on the recipient of an oral leave, or a leave granted through a responsible third party, to establish the manner and date of his or her entry into the UK. The date of expiry of leave is not conclusive on the issue of overstaying, since if a valid in-time application for a variation was made prior to the expiry of limited leave, that leave is deemed to continue until after the decision on the variation application[3] and, if the decision is negative and the person appeals, the leave is further deemed to continue pending the appeal.[4]

1   See *Suthendran v Immigration Appeal Tribunal* [1977] AC 359, [1977] Imm AR 44, HL where this argument failed in relation to the similar construction of appeal rights under s 14 of the Immigration Act 1971. See further *Sabbagh* [1986] Imm AR 244.

2 SI 2000/1161, art 11.
3 Immigration Act 1971, s 3C, inserted by Immigration and Asylum Act 1999, s 3. Leave continues until the last date for putting in an appeal.
4 Immigration and Asylum Act 1999, Sch 4, para 17(1).

16.35 An issue which arose in the earlier case law on deportation was whether past overstaying or breach of conditions justifies removal.[1] The use of the present tense in the reference to not observing a condition of leave or remaining beyond the time limited suggests that only current overstaying and breach of conditions founds liability to removal, not a historical breach, so that someone who has been granted further leave to remain after overstaying cannot be removed. In our view this is the only sensible construction; it is inconceivable that the grant of a fresh leave after overstaying could leave a residual liability to summary removal under section 10 of the Immigration and Asylum Act 1999 because of a past overstay or breach of conditions. It would be different if there were further overstaying or breaches. If a fresh leave was granted in ignorance of past overstay or breach, summary removal would in any event result, if it were shown that the failure to refer to the past breaches constituted deception. If no deception was employed to obtain the fresh leave, and the past breaches were sufficiently severe to warrant enforcement action, we suggest the right course would be to make a decision to deport under section 3(5)(a) of the Immigration Act 1971 (deportation conducive to the public good). This would at least give rise to an appeal on the merits.

1 See *Sabir* [1993] Imm AR 477.

16.36 Past breaches of conditions were held to found liability for deportation in *Sabir*,[1] but different considerations may arise now that the penalty is summary removal with no such appeal. In addition, the Tribunal failed in that case to address whether liability to removal for breach of conditions continues once fresh leave, which is not subject to the relevant condition, is granted. Further, if there is no extant leave, no conditions attach to it, so there can be no liability to removal for breach of conditions where the alleged breach occurs after leave expires. However, any conditions attached to leave are deemed to continue with the leave pending an appeal against a refusal to vary leave under Part IV of the Immigration and Asylum Act 1999.[2] Thus, if a person who had leave, with a condition prohibiting employment, works while an appeal against refusal of an extension is pending, he or she becomes liable to removal under section 10 of the 1999 Act.

1 [1993] Imm AR 477.
2 Immigration and Asylum Act 1999, Sch 4, para 17(1). A s 61 appeal is an ordinary variation appeal, and a s 69(2) appeal is a variation appeal on asylum grounds.

16.37 What happens if someone overstays or breaches conditions and then becomes exempt from immigration control under section 8(1) of the Immigration Act 1971? Cases under the old law established that exemption simply removed the person from control for the period of the exemption, so that liability to removal arising before the exemption continued to exist after the exemption ended.[1] But if leave was still current on termination of the exemption there was no continuing liability to enforcement action.[2] The position is not clear now that statutory leave of 90 days operates automatically at the end of the exemption if the person requires leave and does not have it.[3] One view is that removal could be enforced in this situation, since removal directions under section 10 of the Immigration and Asylum Act 1999 invalidate any leave granted before they were made, or while they are in force.[4] Another view is that the pre-1999 Act position still holds. Alternatively, since the 90-day leave is statutory, it is unaffected by what happened pre-exemption.

1   See *Sabbagh* [1986] Imm AR 244; *Noorhu* [1984] Imm AR 190, IAT.
2   *Ashiwaju* [1994] Imm AR 233, IAT.
3   Immigration Act 1971, s 8A(2).
4   Immigration and Asylum Act 1999, s 10(8).

16.38 In cases of breach of conditions, the Home Office must show that the conditions are ones which may be lawfully imposed, and that they have been properly notified.[1] This is particularly important with visit leave, which may be granted orally, and normally will be subject to conditions restricting working and precluding recourse to public funds. However, a person does not need to be knowingly an overstayer or in breach of conditions to be liable to removal (knowledge founds liability to criminal prosecution),[2] although in considering whether removal is justified by reference to the factors set out in the Immigration Rules, lack of knowledge will clearly be relevant.[3]

1   Immigration Act 1971, s 4(1). Conditions are an integral part of leave and must be notified in writing along with the leave, unless the leave is visit leave granted orally by Immigration (Leave to Enter and Remain) Order 2000, SI 2000/1161, art 8(3).
2   Immigration Act 1971, s 24(1)(b).
3   HC 395, para 395C, as amended by Cmd 4851; see *Hanif* [1985] Imm AR 57, IAT.

16.39 Another issue is whether every overstay or breach of conditions, however trivial, gives rise to liability to removal under section 10 of the Immigration and Asylum Act 1999. The likely answer is that all breaches give rise to liability, but trivial breaches are likely to be condoned.[1] A decision to remove always involves the exercise of a discretion, and could be challenged where, for example, Home Office policy is to overlook a minor breach or a short overstay, since it would be inconsistent with good administration and unfair to remove someone on that basis. For example, anyone whose leave is subject to a condition of no recourse to public funds may be summarily removed if he or she claims any welfare or social security benefits or homeless persons housing.[2] However, Home Office policy in relation to extension of stay is not to refuse in the case of strictly temporary recourse to public funds;[3] it would thus be unreasonable to remove someone on this basis. Similar considerations apply to an overstay of a few weeks.

1   See *R v Secretary of State for the Home Department, ex p Amoa* [1992] Imm AR 218, QBD; *R v Secretary of State for the Home Department, ex p Ajayi*, 12 May 1994 (deportation).
2   For the definition of public funds see HC 395, para 6. A person is not, however, to be regarded as relying on public funds if they rely wholly or in part on public funds provided to their sponsor and their presence results in no additional recourse to public funds: HC 395, para 6A, inserted by Cm 4851, para 4.
3   See eg IDI Dec/00, Ch 8, Annex H.

Obtaining leave to remain by deception

16.40 A person who obtains leave to remain by deception is liable to removal under section 10 of the Immigration and Asylum Act 1999.[1] This provision is new. It would include someone who makes any false representation or uses false documentation, but it does not contemplate third-party deception, so the applicant would need to be aware that the documentation or representation was false to be liable to be removed. The discussion at **16.16-16.22** above on what constitutes deception, and what is a material deception, is relevant here.

1   Immigration and Asylum Act 1999, s 10(1)(b).

Family members

16.41 Where directions have been given for the removal of a person under section 10 of the Immigration and Asylum Act 1999, his or her family members are also liable to removal under section 10 provided those family members were notified no more than eight weeks after the departure of the first person.[1] The detailed criteria for removal of family members mirror those for deportation of family members, at **15.18-15.19** and **15.40-15.41**, to which reference should be made.

1   Immigration and Asylum Act 1999, ss 10(1)(c), 10(3).

Use of discretion in removal cases

16.42 The fact that a person is liable to be removed as an illegal entrant, or an overstayer and so on, does not always mean that he or she should be removed. In relation to those who are liable to removal as illegal entrants, the Immigration Rules are silent on the exercise of discretion. But in the case of overstayers, the rules set out factors which the Secretary of State must take into account, which are identical to the factors required to be considered in deportation cases.[1] This requires consideration of all relevant circumstances, including: age; length of residence and strength of connections with the UK; personal history, including character, conduct and employment record; domestic circumstances; criminal record; compassionate circumstances; and representations made on the person's behalf. They are discussed in detail at **15.33**ff above. In the case of family members, the factors listed in HC 395, paras 365-368 will also be taken into account.[2] In addition there are policies which the Secretary of State must have regard to in deciding whether to remove illegal entrants and overstayers—in particular, those relating to marriage and children,[3] which are described at **11.59** and **11.106** above, and policies on long residence. No one may be removed as an illegal entrant or as an overstayer, etc if removal would be contrary to the Refugee Convention or the ECHR.[4]

1   See HC 395, para 395A-D, as amended by Cmd 4851.
2   HC 395, para 395C. These relate to the degree of independence of the principal of the family members the Secretary of State proposes to remove.
3   See, *inter alia*, *R v Secretary of State for the Home Department, ex p Amankwah* [1994] Imm AR 240, QBD; *R v Secretary of State for the Home Department, ex p Zeenat Bibi* [1994] Imm AR 326, QBD; *R v Secretary of State for the Home Department, ex p Kumar* [1996] Imm AR 190, QBD; *Secretary of State for the Home Department v Hastrup* [1996] Imm AR 616, CA; *Adebiyi v Secretary of State for the Home Department* [1997] Imm AR 57, CA; *R v Secretary of State for the Home Department, ex p Zellouf* [1997] Imm AR 120, QBD; *R v Secretary of State for the Home Department, ex p Balwant Singh* [1997] Imm AR 331, QBD; and *R v Secretary of State for the Home Department, ex p Ahmed and Patel* [1998] Imm AR 375, [1998] INLR 546, QBD; on appeal [1998] INLR 570, CA.
4   HC 395, para 395D as amended.

The 'long residence concession'

16.43 The 'long residence' concession, previously known as the 'ten and 14 year rule' is amongst the most litigated of the Secretary of State's discretionary policies. Its origins lie in the UK's ratification in 1969 of the European Convention on Establishment, Article 3(3) of which provides that nationals of any contracting state who have been lawfully resident for over ten years in the territory of another party may only be expelled for reasons of national security or for particularly serious reasons relating to public order, public health or morality. Home Office practice has been to extend this provision in three respects:

- to include all foreign nationals;
- to grant indefinite leave rather than simply refrain from removal; and
- to allow those who have been in the UK illegally to benefit.

The policy as originally formulated benefited all those with ten years' continuous residence, making no distinction between lawful and unlawful residence. It was amended in 1987 to make ten years' continuous lawful residence, or 14 years' continuous residence of any legality, the qualifying condition. Indefinite leave to remain will normally be granted in the absence of any strong countervailing factors, such as an extant criminal record, apart from minor non-custodial offences, or deliberate and blatant attempts to evade or circumvent immigration control, for example, by using forged documents, absconding or contracting a marriage of convenience.[1] Where a person has completed between ten and 14 years' residence which is not all lawful, the length of the residence and the strength of ties to the UK, particularly family ties, will be the guiding factors.[2] Residence can be considered lawful if there were short delays in submitting an application provided it was successful, and the period between the submission and determination of an appeal counts as lawful residence if the appeal was successful, or if leave was granted following the adjudicator's recommendation.[3] Continuity of residence will not be broken by short absences (up to six months at any one time), but will be broken by removal or deportation from the UK, evidence of no intention to return or a lengthy absence which severed ties.[4]

1 IDI Dec/00, Ch 18.
2 IDI Dec/00, Ch 18, para 4.
3 IDI Dec/00, Ch 18, para 3.
4 IDI Dec/00, Ch 18, para 5. See, *inter alia, Miah v Secretary of State for the Home Department* [1992] Imm AR 106, CA; *R v Secretary of State for the Home Department, ex p Ali (F)* [1992] Imm AR 316, QB (continuous residence is not ordinary residence); *R v Secretary of State for the Home Department, ex p Ali (Akin)* [1993] Imm AR 610, QBD ('continuous' residence); *R v Secretary of State for the Home Department, ex p Mannan* [1996] Imm AR 215, QBD.

16.44 Service of a notice to an illegal entrant, or removal directions (previously a notice of intention to deport) to an overstayer, putting the recipient on notice of his or her removability, 'stops the clock' for the purpose of computing length of residence,[1] but only when the person concerned became aware of the notice.[2] Previous Home Office policy of 'service on the file' of the notice, where the person's whereabouts were unknown, was abandoned in 1986 as unfair and ineffective.[3] A person who qualifies by residence will have a reasonable expectation of being granted indefinite leave.[4]

1   *R v Secretary of State for the Home Department, ex p Ofori* [1994] Imm AR 34, CA; *Musah v Secretary of State for the Home Department* [1995] Imm AR 236, *Hussain v Immigration Appeal Tribunal and Secretary of State for the Home Department* [1991] Imm AR 413.
2   *R v Secretary of State for the Home Department, ex p Popatia and Chew* [2000] INLR 587.
3   See Home Office policy DP5/86, referred to in *Popatia and Chew* above, paras 46ff. See previous edition of this work at **15.32-15.34**.
4   *Zeriba* (L17077) (1999) 5 ILD 2, IAT. See also *Gyeabour* [1989] Imm AR 94, IAT.

16.45   To the so-called 'ten year rule' and 'fourteen year rule' we now have to add the 'seven year rule', a separate concession embodying a general presumption against removal of families with children who were born in the UK and have lived here continuously to the age of seven or over, or where, having come to the UK at an early age, they have accumulated seven years' or more continuous residence.[1] There may be circumstances where enforcement action is still considered appropriate, for example, where the parents have a particularly poor immigration history and have deliberately caused serious delay to the consideration of their case. Relevant factors will include the length of the parents' residence without leave, whether removal has been delayed through protracted and repetitive representations, or by going to ground; the age of the children; whether they were conceived when either parent had leave to remain; whether return to the parents' country of origin would cause extreme hardship for the children or put their health seriously at risk; and whether either parent has a history of criminal behaviour or deception.[2]

1   Policy DP069/99, previously known as DP5/96, modified on 24 February 1999, see *Butterworths Immigration Law Service*, D[1121]. It does not apply where the child is over 18 at the time the case is considered, or is unaccompanied; these cases will be considered on their merits.
2   Policy DP069/99.

SEA, AIR AND TRAIN CREWS

16.46   Seamen and air and train crews are in a special category. As we have seen[1] section 8(1) of the Immigration Act 1971 provides that they may enter the UK without leave and remain until the departure of the ship, aircraft or train in which they are required by their engagement to leave. This concession is subject to exceptions, and means that crew members can be treated as illegal entrants if they require leave to enter and enter without it. They also become illegal entrants if they desert their ship, plane or train and remain in this country. This is because of the provisions of section 11(5) of the Act which provide that someone who enters the UK lawfully under section 8(1) and seeks to remain beyond the section 8(1) time limit is to be treated as 'seeking to enter the UK'.[2] However, these distinctions are somewhat academic because Schedule 2 to the Act gives immigration officers powers to order the removal of crew members who overstay, or who the immigration officer reasonably suspects of intending to do so.[3] In view of these draconian powers there is perhaps no need to declare seamen or air or train crews illegal entrants and to treat them as such.

1   See **6.31** above.
2   See *R v Secretary of State for the Home Department, ex p Urmaza* [1996] COD 479 where Sedley J held that a seaman deserter was an illegal entrant on the analysis identified in the preceding paragraph. DP/2/93 applied to 'all illegal entry cases' and on the plain and ordinary meaning of such words it was not open to the Secretary of State to contend

that it did not apply to the applicant as a seaman deserter. Contrast this approach with *Afunyah* and *Olawole* (**16.29** fn 7 above).
3   Immigration Act 1971, Sch 2, paras 12 and 13, modified in relation to Channel Tunnel trains by SI 1993/1813, Sch 4, para 1(11)(n).

CHALLENGING LIABILITY FOR REMOVAL

Appeal rights

16.47   A restricted right of appeal against the validity of directions for removal has been afforded by section 66 of the Immigration and Asylum Act 1999, which permits challenge on the limited basis that there is 'no power in law to give them on the grounds given'.[1] The right of appeal is not exercisable in-country, however, save where it is brought in conjunction with appeals against removal on human rights grounds,[2] or on the basis that the proposed removal would contravene the Refugee Convention.[3] It follows that where human rights or asylum grounds are adduced, the appellant may also challenge the finding of illegal entry, overstay etc. A person appealing under section 66 against directions issued pursuant to a deportation order may not dispute the validity of the original order.[4]

1   Immigration and Asylum Act 1999, s 66. The right of appeal was formerly contained in s 16 of the Immigration Act 1971.
2   Immigration and Asylum Act 1999, s 66(3), referring to s 65.
3   Immigration and Asylum Act 1999, referring to s 69(5).
4   Immigration and Asylum Act 1999, s 66(4).

Judicial review or habeas corpus

16.48   Where no in-country appeal lies against the validity of removal directions (because there are no human rights or asylum grounds) the only way to challenge the finding of illegal entry, overstay, etc before removal takes place is by way of *habeas corpus* or judicial review. Before 1999, on a challenge to the detention for removal of a person believed to be an illegal entrant, the court was bound to ensure that the jurisdictional facts (that the applicant was an illegal entrant) had been established. But the 1999 amendments to the powers of detention mean that anyone may now be detained if he or she is *reasonably suspected* of being someone in respect of whom removal directions may be given.[1] Those suspected of being illegal entrants, overstayers, in breach of conditions, or guilty of remaining by deception may be detained under the amended provisions of the Immigration Act 1971, and a *habeas corpus* application to secure their release would fail, provided reasonable suspicion could be made out, such suspicion being the only condition precedent to lawful detention. Effectively, this change sounds the death-knell for *habeas corpus* in removal cases, save where there is no reasonable suspicion (ie *mala fides* is alleged) or where detention is excessively lengthy (the *Hardial Singh* situation).[2]

1   Immigration Act 1971, Sch 2, para 16(2), as amended by s 140(1) of the Immigration and Asylum Act 1999.
2   *R v Governors of Durham Prison, ex p Hardial Singh* [1984] 1 All ER 983, QBD. See **17.18** below.

16.49 However, on a plain reading of the Immigration 1971 and Immigration and Asylum Act 1999, the power to *remove* illegal entrants, overstayers, etc is still contingent on their actually being such, and not on reasonable suspicion.[1] On any challenge to proposed removal by way of judicial review, the Secretary of State must establish the factual basis for the jurisdiction to remove, ie, that the person to be removed is an illegal entrant, or is someone who had a limited leave and overstayed, or breached conditions of stay, obtained leave to remain by deception, or is a family member of a person liable to removal. The court must arrive at its own conclusion on the evidence before it.[2] Once the party seeking relief has discharged the initial burden of showing that he or she has a case fit to be considered by the court (in illegal entry cases a burden discharged by a leave stamp in the person's passport or other evidence that leave was granted,[3] or by the production of a British passport),[4] the burden of proving the necessary facts lies on the immigration officer or Secretary of State.[5] The distinction between the removal of overstayers or illegal entrants and the removal of those refused leave to enter is that the refusal of leave to enter is never in dispute, only the reasons for it, which involve the exercise of discretion by an immigration officer.[6] In the illegal entry and overstaying cases, the dispute is whether the person entered illegally, whether they have overstayed, whether they breached conditions or whether they used deception to remain.

1 Immigration Act 1971, Sch 2, para 9; Immigration and Asylum Act 1999, s 10(1). Contrast Sch 2, para 12(2) of the 1971 Act, which allows removal of those reasonably suspected of being overstaying sea or air crew members.
2 *Khawaja v Secretary of State for the Home Department* [1984] AC 74, [1983] 1 All ER 765.
3 Immigration (Leave to Enter and Remain) Order 2000, SI 2000/1161, art 8.
4 *R v Secretary of State for the Home Department, ex p Obi* [1997] INLR 173.
5 *Khawaja, Obi* above.
6 *Khawaja* above at 790.

Standard of proof and evidential issues

16.50 If the Secretary of State for the Home Department must discharge the burden of showing that an applicant is an illegal entrant, an overstayer, etc if removal directions are challenged, how and to what standard is it done? In *Khawaja* Lords Bridge and Scarman concluded that the civil standard of proof applied, but that where fraud was alleged 'the Court should not be satisfied with anything less than probability of a high degree'. The Court of Appeal followed this in *Rahman*.[1] Where the immigration appellate authority has decided a disputed issue of identity or relationship after hearing oral evidence, and the Secretary of State later treats the person as an illegal entrant on new information on the disputed issue, the starting point is the binding decision of an appropriate Tribunal in favour of the applicant, so the standard of proof to establish illegality is even higher.[2] However, the facts may (and in the vast majority of cases will) be established by way of written statements, although cross-examination may be permitted by a judge when justice so demands.[3] In *Ex p Patel*[4] Webster J thought that very little assistance would be gained from the cross-examination of witnesses who could only give their evidence through an interpreter or in English as their second or third language. He considered at length the difficulties of assessing the demeanour and credibility of such witnesses—reflections which should be borne in mind by the appellate authority. In *Doldur v Secretary of*

State for the Home Department[5] Thorpe LJ commented that it was incumbent on the Secretary of State to face the applicant with the challenge of cross-examination where the allegation of deceit was based on failure to volunteer information, since, following *Khawaja*, there was no duty of candour, and deception could not be irresistibly inferred. The court should examine all the evidence, including hearsay evidence, on which the Secretary of State or the immigration officer relied in reaching the decision, to decide whether the conclusion of illegal entry, overstay, etc was justified.[6] Because of the erratic and haphazard way illegal entry interviews were recorded by Home Office officials, Woolf J recommended[7] proper safeguards such as contemporaneous notes and readovers, and most if not all illegal entry interviews are now tape-recorded. An allegation that a caution was not properly administered does not render an interview inadmissible, but goes to the weight to be attached to any admissions contained in it.[8] But the Scottish courts have held that interviews not conducted under caution may not be relied on to establish illegal entry by deception.[9]

1   *Re Rahman* [1997] Imm AR 197, CA.
2   *R v Secretary of State for the Home Department, ex p Miah* [1983] Imm AR 91; *Ali v Secretary of State for the Home Department* [1984] 1 All ER 1009, [1984] Imm AR 23.
3   *Khawaja v Secretary of State for the Home Department* [1984] AC 74 at 124. See also *R v Secretary of State for the Home Department, ex p Rouse and Shrimpton* (13 November 1985, unreported), DC where Woolf J said that cross-examination should not be used to shore up a weak case.
4   *R v Secretary of State for the Home Department, ex p Patel* [1986] Imm AR 208, affirmed at [1986] Imm AR 515, CA.
5   [1998] Imm AR 352.
6   *Khawaja* above, per Lord Templeman [1983] 1 All ER 765 at 794–795 and [1984] AC 74 at 128; *R v Secretary of State for the Home Department, ex p Rahman* [1996] 4 All ER 945, QBD; affd [1997] Imm AR 197, CA.
7   In *R v Secretary of State for the Home Department, ex p Govinden* (1985) Times, 12 July.
8   *Yasin v Secretary of State for the Home Department* [1997] Imm AR 97, CA.
9   *Oghonoghor v Secretary of State for the Home Department* 1995 SLT 733, OACS; *Sofia Kim v Secretary of State for the Home Department* 2000 SLT 249.

CHALLENGING EXERCISE OF DISCRETION TO REMOVE

Human rights appeal

16.51 Most challenges to removal accept the liability to remove (ie the fact that the person concerned is an illegal entrant, an overstayer, etc) but seek to argue that removal breaches fundamental human rights, usually under Article 8 of the ECHR, as being a disproportionate interference with family or private life.[1] This will be done by an appeal against removal directions to the immigration appellate authorities under section 65 of the Immigration and Asylum Act 1999.[2] The removal directions will not indicate that such an appeal is available unless the person concerned has made 'an allegation that an authority had acted in breach of his human rights'.[3] On a statutory appeal, the appellate authority must decide for itself whether the interference is proportionate in any given case,[4] and policies such as DP3/96, which requires a marriage to have been entered two years prior to enforcement action, should have less weight. However, the date of commencement of enforcement action will still be important, since family relationships entered in full knowledge of the liability to removal may not be enough to engage state responsibility under the ECHR.[5]

1   See **8.54ff** above for detailed consideration of art 8 of the ECHR.
2   See **8.66ff** above.
3   Immigration and Asylum Appeals (Notices) Regulations 2000, SI 2000/2246, reg 4(4).
4   See **8.30** above.
5   *Abdulaziz, Cabales and Balkandali v UK* (1985) 7 EHRR 471; *Poku v UK* (1996) 22 EHRR CD 94; *Ajayi v UK* Application 27663/95, 20 June 1999; *R v Secretary of State for the Home Department, ex p Amjad Mahmood* [2001] 1 WLR 840, CA.

16.52   For those cases that do not engage human rights, challenges in respect of this exercise of discretion will be based on normal judicial review principles.[1] Where it is accepted that a person had a legitimate expectation of entry and is personally innocent of any irregularity, this is a relevant consideration in deciding whether removal should follow;[2] this remains the position even though 'innocent' entrants may be illegal entrants on the basis of third-party deception.[3] For an illustrative example of a successful challenge of this exercise of discretion see the decision of McCullough J in *Noor Nawal Khan*.[4]

1   See eg the cases mentioned in **16.44** fn 4 above in relation to the long residence concession.
2   Donaldson J in *R v Secretary of State for the Home Department, ex p Hassan* (1981) Times, 22 July, CA; see also *R v Secretary of State for the Home Department, ex p Sheikh* (4 February 1982, unreported), DC; Sir Thomas Bingham MR in *Ex p Kuet* [1995] Imm AR 274; *Rehal v Secretary of State for the Home Department* [1989] Imm AR 576, CA, but the court will not necessarily grant leave for the issue of innocence to be judicially resolved.
3   Immigration Act 1971, s 33(1), as amended by Asylum and Immigration Act 1996, Sch 2, para 4
4   (1997) unreported, 9 May; see **16.11** above.

REMOVAL DIRECTIONS

16.53   Removal can only take place if directions are properly given in accordance with the 1971 Act. They are not mere notifications to the carrier of its obligations, but are part of the machinery for removal. An immigrant affected by a direction is, therefore, entitled, in appropriate circumstances, to challenge its validity.[1] A direction is only valid if it indicates clearly that the immigrant is then, and not at some future unspecified date, required to be removed. So in *R v Immigration Officer, ex p Shah*[2] a direction directing the airline to remove the applicant to India 'as soon as his application to enter the UK is finally resolved' was held invalid. In a recent Tribunal case,[3] the Secretary of State has sought to argue that it is unnecessary to specify the time and place of removal, which may be flexible, and it is sufficient that he possess an intention to remove at the conclusion of the appeal process. An issue which arose in the context of asylum appeals under the Asylum and Immigration Appeals Act 1993 was whether, in the frequent case where removal directions are set, deferred or cancelled and then re-set, the second set constitute new removal directions against which the rejected appellant has a second right of appeal. In *ex p Manwinder Singh*[4] counsel for the Secretary of State conceded in the High Court that removal directions are deemed to be given each time a new flight or ship departure is specified (thus potentially giving rise to more than one asylum claim under section 69(5) of the Immigration and Asylum Act 1999).[5] The concession was withdrawn before the Court of Appeal.[6]

1   *R v Immigration Officer, ex p Shah* [1982] 2 All ER 264, [1982] 1 WLR 544; *Parshotam Singh v Secretary of State for the Home Department* [1989] Imm AR 469, CA.
2   *R v Immigration Officer, ex p Shah* [1982] 2 All ER 264, [1982] 1 WLR 544, DC.

3   *Teymori* (IAT) 2001.
4   *R v Secretary of State for the Home Department, ex p Manwinder Singh* [1996] Imm AR 41, QBD, Carnwath J.
5   Then Asylum and Immigration Appeals Act 1993, s 8(4).
6   Unreported, 8 December 1995. In *Onibiyo v Secretary of State for the Home Department* [1996] QB 768 the CA held that a second right of appeal against refusal of asylum was possible, but it is implicit in the decision that this right does not depend on the issue of further removal directions, but on the Refugee Convention requirement (which constitutes the ground of an asylum appeal) that removal to a country where there is a well-founded fear of persecution on the grounds set out in the Convention is prohibited. This reasoning applies equally to ECHR, art 3 cases: see chapters 8 and 12 above.

Removal after refusal of leave to enter

16.54 Where passengers arriving in the UK are refused leave to enter, an immigration officer may arrange for their removal by the owners or agents of the aircraft or ship which brought them in.[1] If such arrangements are made within two months the carriers must bear the costs of removal, and they are also liable if removal is not effected within this timescale but the IO has given them written notice of the intention to remove.[2] In calculating the period of two months, any period during which an appeal is pending against refusal of leave to enter, destination or asylum (under sections 59, 67 or 69(1) of the Immigration and Asylum Act 1999) is to be disregarded.[3] While an appeal is pending, removal directions cannot be made and any directions already given cease to have effect, except in so far as they have already been carried out.[4] The failure to remove a person refused leave to enter within two months, or to make arrangements or give notice to the carriers of proposed removal, does not, however, prevent later removal.[5] But after two months the Secretary of State for the Home Department takes responsibility for the removal and must pay for it.[6] The government also pays the cost of removal when removal under the normal procedure is 'not practicable' or would be 'ineffective' and special arrangements have to be made.[7] A captain of a ship or airline who is told to remove someone and fails, without reasonable excuse, to comply, commits a criminal offence and is liable to a fine or imprisonment.[8] In this context it is also material to note that the 1999 Act for the first time provides that directions for removal may include provision that the person being removed have an escort, which the carrier may be required to pay for.[9]

1   Immigration Act 1971, Sch 2, para 8(1). There is no specific provision for the removal of persons whose advance leave to enter is cancelled under Sch 2, para 2A(8), who are left in limbo, unable to enter the UK without leave but apparently irremovable.
2   Immigration Act 1971, Sch 2, para 8(2), as amended by Immigration Act 1988, Sch, para 9.
3   Immigration and Asylum Act 1999, Sch 4, Pt II, para 13, replacing Immigration Act 1971, Sch 2, para 28(4).
4   Immigration and Asylum Act 1999, Sch 4, Pt II, para 10, replacing Immigration Act 1971, Sch 2, para 28(1), (2). See *R v Immigration Appeal Tribunal, ex p Alghali* [1984] Imm AR 106, QBD.
5   Immigration Act 1971, Sch 2, para 10(1)(b). See *Mohammed Rahman v Secretary of State for the Home Department* [1995] Imm AR 488, CA; *R v Secretary of State for the Home Department, ex p Al Zahrany* [1995] Imm AR 283.
6   Immigration Act 1971, Sch 2, para 10(3).
7   Immigration Act 1971, Sch 2, para 10(1)(a).
8   Immigration Act 1971, s 27(a). This measure forms part of the range of measures, including carriers' liability, penalties for inadvertent carriage of stowaways and employer sanctions, which implicate private companies and individuals in the enforcement of immigration control.
9   Immigration and Asylum Act 1999, s 14. Regulations under the section may require the carrier to arrange for the escort's return to the UK and for his or her remuneration.

16.55 Apart from the time limit which determines who is to pay for removal, there is no express requirement on the part of the authorities to act quickly. In *Ex p Mohammed Rafiq*[1] the Divisional Court held that it was entirely reasonable to delay for six weeks the giving of directions for removal, until the Home Office had discovered whether or not the applicant would be admitted to Pakistan. The alternative course would have been to direct his removal without establishing whether the directions would be effective. But where a person is in custody pending removal, there is a requirement to act reasonably promptly; otherwise detention may become unlawful.[2]

1   *R v Secretary of State for the Home Department, ex p Rafiq* [1970] 3 All ER 821.
2   *R v Governor of Durham Prison, ex p Hardial Singh* [1983] Imm AR 198, QBD: see **17.18** below.

Removal of illegal entrants

16.56 Precisely the same removal procedure operates in the case of illegal entrants (assuming of course that the illegal entrant can in fact be removed),[1] save that the two-month time limit for immigration officers' directions does not apply.[2] Illegal entrants who are discovered as stowaways coming off a particular ferry may clearly be the subject of directions to the captain, but in the case of illegal entrants who are not detected at the port, it will rarely be 'practicable' or 'effective' to identify or issue directions to the company which brought them in, in which case responsibility falls on the Secretary of State, who bears the costs.[3]

1   See *R v Secretary of State for the Home Department, ex p Yu and Lin* (CO 393/1999, CO 4621/1999) where permission was granted for judicial review of the failure to remove or to regularise Chinese illegal entrants for over four years while travel documents were awaited from the Chinese authorities. The matter never reached full hearing because the travel documents were finally issued and removal was effected.
2   Immigration Act 1971, Sch 2 para 9, referring to para 8(1). See *Rahman v Secretary of State for the Home Department* [1995] Imm AR 488, CA.
3   Immigration Act 1971, Sch 2, para 10(1)(a), 10(3).

Removal under section 10 of the Immigration and Asylum Act 1999

16.57 For the new categories of persons subject to administrative removal, directions are now set just as they are after refusal of leave and for illegal entrants.[1] Issue of removal directions immediately invalidates any extant leave.[2] The costs of removal, so far as reasonably incurred, will be borne by the Secretary of State.[3] If removal of dependants is proposed, separate notice of intention to remove must be issued, which must be served within eight weeks of the departure of the principal in accordance with the first directions.[4] Failure by the Secretary of State to comply with the time limit invalidates removal directions against family members.

1   Immigration and Asylum Act 1999, s 10(7); see the Immigration (Removal Directions) Regulations 2000, SI 2000/2243.
2   Immigration and Asylum Act 1999, s 10(8). Leave may be extant although obtained by deception, or in cases of breach of conditions.
3   Immigration and Asylum Act 1999, s 10(9).
4   Immigration and Asylum Act 1999, s 10(3).

Removal of deportees

16.58 For persons still subject to deportation action, the arrangements for removal are set out in Schedule 3 to the Immigration Act 1971.[1] The cost again falls on the Secretary of State for the Home Department, except where the deportees are made to pay for their own removal.[2] A deportation order is not to be made whilst an appeal against deportation under section 63(1)(a) of the Immigration and Asylum Act 1999, or an asylum appeal under section 69(4)(a) of the 1999 Act following a decision to deport, may be brought.[3] This does not preclude a deportation order being made against a person who has claimed asylum.[4] Thus a person who does not claim asylum until his or her deportation appeal has been dismissed may have an order made, provided it is not carried out while the claim is being determined. The subsection was brought in to reverse the effect of *Sanusi*.[5] Similarly, a deportation order may be made while an appeal against removal on human rights grounds under section 65 of the 1999 Act is pending, although the subject of the order may not actually be removed.[6]

1   Immigration Act 1971, Sch 3, para 1.
2   Immigration Act 1971, para 1(4).
3   Immigration and Asylum Act 1999, s 63(2), Sch 4, para 18.
4   Immigration and Asylum Act 1999, s 15(2)(b).
5   *R v Secretary of State for the Home Department, ex p Sanusi* [1999] INLR 198, CA.
6   Immigration and Asylum Act 1999, Sch 4, para 20(2)(b).

Removal of sea, air and train crews

16.59 Here the removal arrangements are very similar to those of persons refused entry. Initially, responsibility for removal and its costs are borne by the owners or agents of the ship or aircraft or train manager of whose crew the person to be removed is a member, but if this is not practicable or would be ineffective the alternative removal arrangements are paid for by the government.[1] In the case of *Ex p Urmaza*,[2] Sedley J had to consider when enforcement action began against a deserting seaman who had married and resided in this country. He concluded that it was when removal directions were given and not when the exemption from obtaining leave to enter was revoked, and thus the enforcement policy applied in the same way as other cases.

1   Immigration Act 1971, Sch 2, paras 12–14.
2   *R v Secretary of State for the Home Department, ex p Urmaza* [1996] COD 479, (1996) Times, 23 July.

Carrying out removal

16.60 To ensure that directions for removal are effective against the captain of a ship or airline or against the owners or agents, it is made a criminal offence for them to disobey directions without reasonable excuse.[1] Where directions for removal have been given, the person to be removed may be placed under the authority of an immigration officer or the Secretary of State on board any ship or aircraft in which that person is to be removed in accordance with those directions.[2] There is no express power to use force to put someone on board an aircraft or ship, although it may be implied, and it has certainly been used, on occasion with fatal effects.[3] Once the person is on board, it becomes the responsibility of the captain of the ship or aircraft to prevent them escaping. For this purpose they may be detained until removal is fulfilled.[4] A captain who knowingly lets such person disembark, commits a criminal offence and is liable to a fine or imprisonment.[5] Where a person who is being removed threatens suicide, or gives any indication that he or she may attempt suicide, immigration officers are under instruction to seek the port medical inspector's opinion of the person's state of mind and not to pursue removal without reference to the passenger casework section of the Immigration Service.[6] The Immigration and Asylum Act 1999 has provision for escorts to accompany the removed person, to be specified in the removal directions.[7] The section empowers the Secretary of State to make regulations regarding the costs of such escorts.

1   Immigration Act 1971, s 27(a)(ii) and (b)(iii).
2   Immigration Act 1971, Sch 2, paras 11 and 15; Sch 3, para 1(3).
3   In the case of Joy Gardner, who died after being gagged with 13 feet of tape in addition to being manacled and handcuffed in August 1993. Other deportees have been seriously injured by the use of inappropriate restraint, and protests by passengers at excessive physical restraint of deportees on aircraft increasingly are becoming common. See eg Amnesty International: *Cruel, inhuman or degrading treatment during forcible deportation* (July 1994).
4   Immigration Act 1971, Sch 2, para 16(4)—this is a very clumsily worded paragraph and our interpretation involves placing the words 'or before the directions for his removal have been fulfilled ...' after 'an immigration officer'.
5   Immigration Act 1971, s 27(a)(i). This is an absolute offence with no room for 'reasonable excuse'. Where the condition of a deportee or other compelling factors such as an on-board protest dictate removal of the deportee from the aircraft, the captain would have to obtain the permission of the immigration officer or the Secretary of State to avoid criminal liability.
6   IDI Dec/00, Ch 9, s 6, para 5.
7   Immigration and Asylum Act 1999, s 14.

16.61 Those liable to be removed from the UK, particularly illegal entrants, will often possess no valid travel documents (or none at all) and no proof of identity or nationality. The authorities of the state to which removal is proposed may, not unreasonably, require production of identification data to enable them to confirm the person's nationality before issuing a travel document. Although under the Immigration Act 1971 wide powers existed to deal with this situation,[1] the process usually required the co-operation of the proposed returnee, which was not always forthcoming.[2] To overcome the impasse which could frustrate removal and lead to prolonged detention, the Immigration and Asylum Act 1999 empowers the Secretary of State to release to the authorities of the proposed country of removal identification data on the returnee.[3] At present the data concerned is confined to fingerprints, but the Secretary of State may make regulations permitting collation of data on other external physical characteristics,[4] which may also be released.[5] Provisions of the Data Protection Act 1988 forbidding transfer of personal data to states outside the EEA are avoided by deeming the transfer of such personal data 'necessary for reasons of substantial public interest'.[6] The only express limitation is that the Secretary of State must not disclose whether or not an asylum claim has been made.[7] This miserable sole safeguard is wholly inadequate to protect those whose national authorities are made aware by the transfer of identification data that they are in the UK without travel documents and that they are shortly to be returned home. A number of repressive states keep surveillance on political opponents abroad; some hunt them down for assassination; some carry out reprisals on families once they become aware that their quarry has fled the country; and many inflict excessive and inhuman punishment for the mere act of leaving the country without permission.

1 Immigration Act 1971, Sch 2, para 18(2), allowing immigration officers, police, prison officers and anyone else authorised by the Secretary of State to photograph, measure and otherwise identify detainees, and para 18(3), allowing them to take detainees anywhere necessary to establish their citizenship, and to make arrangements for their admission to another country.
2 In *R v Secretary of State for the Home Department, ex p Z* [1998] Imm AR 516 the Secretary of State had sought information from an undocumented Algerian whose asylum application had failed, with a view to preparation of a travel document. Moses J rejected the applicant's contention that such information could only be required of a detained person, finding that the power to make removal directions implied a power to obtain the information required to implement the directions, and failure to co-operate would empower the Secretary of State to detain him under Immigration Act 1971, Sch 2, para 18(2).
3 Immigration and Asylum Act 1999, s 13.
4 Immigration and Asylum Act 1999, s 144.
5 Immigration and Asylum Act 1999, s 13(5)(b).
6 Immigration and Asylum Act 1999, s 13(4). This section renders inapplicable the eighth principle of Sch 1 to the Data Protection Act 1998 which prohibits transfer of personal data to countries outside the EEA unless an adequate level of protection in relation to its processing is guaranteed.
7 Immigration and Asylum Act 1999, s 13(3).

Countries to which removal is possible

16.62 The range of countries to which removal may be effected varies according to the immigration status of the person being removed. Overstayers etc and deportees may only be removed to a country:

• of which they are nationals or citizens; or
• to which there is reason to believe they will be admitted.[1]

Illegal entrants and those refused entry can be removed to a wider range of countries:

• of which they are nationals or citizens;
• in which they obtained a passport or identity documents;
• from which they embarked for the UK; or
• to which there is reason to believe they will be admitted.[2]

The power to return those refused leave to enter to the country of embarkation or any country to which there is reason to believe that they will be admitted provides the statutory basis for the removal of asylum claimants to 'safe' third countries without determining their claim under sections 11 and 12 of the Immigration and Asylum Act 1999. Members of a ship or aircrew additionally may be removed to the country where they were engaged.[3]

1 Immigration (Removal Directions) Regulations 2000, SI 2000/2243, reg 4(2); Immigration Act 1971, Sch 3, para 1.
2 Immigration Act 1971, Sch 2, paras 8(1)(c)(i)-(iv) and 10(1). 'Admitted' does not mean admitted for an indefinite period: *Alsawaf v Secretary of State for the Home Department* [1988] Imm AR 410, CA.
3 Immigration Act 1971, Sch 2, para 12(2)(c)(iv).

16.63 The country of nationality or citizenship may under the rules of international law be bound to receive its own nationals.[1] There is, therefore, usually no problem about admission.[2] But where persons are being removed to other countries, there may be difficulties. There is nothing in the 1971 or 1999 Acts which suggests that the immigration authorities must check on whether a person will be admitted before directing their removal to that country. But it is not enough for the Secretary of State to conclude that a person ought to be admitted to a country which is not obliged to accept him or her if there is no evidence that admission is likely to be granted.[3]

1   See chapter 8 above.
2   This is subject to proof of nationality: see discussion at **16.61** above on measures related to the provision of travel documents for removal.
3   *R v Secretary of State for the Home Department, ex p Yassine* [1990] Imm AR 354.

Appeals objecting to destination

16.64 Appeals objecting to destination, in common with all other immigration appeals, have been subject to reorganisation under the Immigration and Asylum Act 1999. But the repeal of section 17 of the Immigration Act 1971 (the source of the destination appeal in non-asylum cases), and section 8 of the Asylum and Immigration Appeals Act 1993 (which provided an appeal against removal directions on asylum grounds), and their replacement under the 1999 Act, changes little of substance. An appeal against destination may be made in the following cases:

(i)   in certain cases of refusal of leave to enter;[1]
(ii)   on a deportation order being made;[2]
(iii)   on entry to the UK in breach of a deportation order.[3]

The right to object to destination exists both as part of the substantive appeal right against a decision to remove following refusal of leave to enter or to deport and as a discrete appeal against destination under section 67 of the 1999 Act, which reflects the appeal right previously contained in section 17 of the 1971 Act. If a person has a right of appeal against refusal of leave or a decision to deport and has been notified of the destination, he or she should raise any objection to the destination in that appeal; otherwise the right of appeal against destination will be lost.[4] The section 67 right exists in these cases only where destination has not been notified prior to the hearing of the substantive appeal. The section 67 destination appeal stands alone in the case of removal of a person who has entered in breach of a deportation order, who has no substantive appeal in which destination can be challenged.

1   Immigration and Asylum Act 1999, ss 59(4), 67(1)(a), (2).
2   Immigration and Asylum Act 1999, ss 63(4), 67(1)(b).
3   Immigration and Asylum Act 1999, s 67(1)(c).
4   Immigration and Asylum Act 1999, s 68(2).

16.65 The parameters of the destination appeal continue to be severely circumscribed in various other ways. First, in refusal of entry cases it applies only to those who have a right of appeal on the ground that they are British citizens and do not require leave, and holders of entry clearance or work permits.[1] Secondly, illegal entrants are excluded apart from those entering in breach of a deportation order. Finally, the grounds upon which an appeal can be successfully mounted are extremely narrow, the only issue being whether the appellant ought to be removed to a different territory specified by him or her.[2] Inclusion of the bracketed words ('if at all') in the various subsections does not permit challenge to the substantive decision to remove.[3] It is an argument as to one destination over another. Previously, most appeals against destination have been in deportation cases,[4] but now that deportation has been superseded by administrative removal in most cases, this pattern is unlikely to continue.

1   Immigration and Asylum Act 1999, s 68(1).
2   If no alternative country is put forward by an appellant, there is no valid appeal: *R v An Adjudicator, ex p Umeloh* [1991] Imm AR 602, QBD.
3   *R v Immigration Appeal Tribunal, ex p Murugarandarajah* [1986] Imm AR 382.
4   *Alsawaf v Secretary of State for the Home Department* [1988] Imm AR 410, CA; *R v Secretary of State for the Home Department, ex p Akram* [1994] Imm AR 8, QBD.

16.66 While the Immigration Act 1971 was silent as to the appellant's need to prove that the country or territory specified is willing to receive him or her, the rules relating to removal on deportation provide that normally the power should be exercised so as to secure the person's return to the country of which they are a national, or which has most recently provided them with a travel document, unless they can show that another country will receive them notwithstanding their deportation from the UK.[1] Now, section 68(3) of the Immigration and Asylum Act 1999 puts into statutory form and extends to all destination appeals the requirement that a person seeking to be removed elsewhere than to the country of nationality must show that the preferred country will admit him or her. Where an appellant claims nationality of another state, he or she bears the burden of proving it or, otherwise, proving admissibility there.[2] A clear, unequivocal intention to relocate to the proposed third country is essential, and expression of a 'contingent' desire to be removed to a third state, conditional, for example, on the exhaustion of all appeals against removal, has been held not to satisfy the statutory criterion.[3] The Appeal Tribunal has held that there must be cogent reasons for seeking a departure from the normal arrangements for a return to the country of citizenship. Having lived for 19 years in another country was not compelling enough in one case.[4] The Immigration Rules also require the appellate authorities, in considering any departure from normal arrangements, to have regard to the public interest generally and to any additional expense that may fall on public funds,[5] including the additional expense that continued detention in custody would involve while inquiries were being made on his or her behalf as to an alternative destination.[6] The Secretary of State is entitled to decline to stay removal directions while efforts are made to secure entry to a third country.[7]

1   HC 395, para 385.
2   *Mouncife v Secretary of State for the Home Department* [1996] Imm AR 265, CA. The Tribunal's obligation to investigate the claimed nationality is not more onerous merely because an EC right is claimed: HC 395, para 385.
3   *R v Secretary of State for the Home Department, ex p Withane* [1997] Imm AR 246 where the appellant wished to be removed to Ireland, where her husband had said he would go in exercise of his EC free movement rights if her deportation appeal did not succeed.
4   *Croning* [1972] Imm AR 51, IAT.
5   HC 395, para 385.
6   *Kroohs* [1978] Imm AR 75.

7   *R v Secretary of State for the Home Department, ex p Kudaisi* [2000] Imm AR 46 where
a deportee's spouse, a British citizen, was seeking to go to Ireland in exercise of free
movement rights, which would have entitled the deportee to join her. Tucker J held that
the EC law requirement in Council Directive (EEC) 68/361 that 'Member States facilitate
the grant of visas to family members' of EC workers did not impose obligations on the UK
in this situation, but on Ireland.

Compulsory removal of psychiatric patients

16.67 Section 86 of the Mental Health Act 1983 empowers the Secretary of
State for the Home Department to authorise the removal to any country abroad
of certain detained patients who have been given leave to enter or remain, but
do not have a right of abode in the UK and who are receiving in-patient
treatment for psychiatric illness. The power originated with the Lunacy Act
1890, under which aliens detained as persons of unsound mind could be returned
to their own country at the request of their family or friends, a right of initiative
removed by the Mental Health Act 1959. The Secretary of State's powers of
removal of mental patients were increased by the Immigration Act 1971[1] and
the British Nationality Act 1981[2] to embrace all patients without the right of
abode. The main purpose of the power, according to the government, is to
'enable patients who are either irrationally opposed to their removal, or are
unable to express a view, to be compulsorily removed to another country
when this is judged to be in their best interests. It is also used to enable
patients to be kept under escort on their journey home if this is necessary.'[3]
Before exercising these powers the Secretary of State must have obtained the
approval of a Mental Health Review Tribunal[4] and must be satisfied that
proper arrangements have been made for the removal of patients and for their
care or treatment, and that removal is in their interests.[5] Where a psychiatric
patient is liable to removal under some other provision of the 1971 Act, for
example because he or she is on temporary admission, the Secretary of State
is not obliged to use this procedure for removal of psychiatric patients, so the
safeguard of the Mental Health Review Tribunal does not apply.[6] As removal
under the section is not pursuant to a decision to deport, there is no right of
appeal[7] except on human rights grounds. On arrival at their destination, any
orders or directions made in respect of them will cease to have effect,[8] and
there is nothing to prevent patients who have been removed from applying for
re-admission to the UK at any time.[9] The removal powers are, however,
draconian and need very rigorous adherence to the safeguards to avoid non-
compliance with due process and private life requirements of the ECHR.

1   Immigration Act 1971, s 30(1).
2   British Nationality Act 1981, s 39(7).
3   White Paper *The Review of the Mental Health Act 1959* (Cmd 7320) para 8.26. Powers of
escort are now expressly contained in Immigration and Asylum Act 1999, s 14, and are not
confined to psychiatric patients.
4   Mental Health Act 1983, s 86(3).
5   Mental Health Act 1983, s 86(2).
6   *R (X) v Secretary of State for the Home Department* [2001] 1 WLR 740, [2001] INLR
205, CA.
7   *R v Immigration Appeal Tribunal and the Secretary of State for the Home Department,
ex p Alghali* [1986] Imm AR 376, QBD.
8   Mental Health Act 1983, s 91.
9   But a compulsory order under s 37 of the Mental Health Act 1983 takes effect on a
patient's return.

Removal of deserters from friendly forces

16.68 The position of deserters or absentees without leave in the UK from friendly foreign forces is governed by the Visiting Forces Act 1952, under which deserters can be arrested, detained and removed from the UK.[1] Arrest must be by warrant granted either to the police or army personnel. The person is then brought before a court which decides whether they should be handed over for trial as a deserter to the country concerned. Court proceedings can be dispensed with if the deserter surrenders voluntarily at a police station. As in extradition proceedings the magistrates courts' powers are subject to *habeas corpus* proceedings or judicial review. This is how the provisions work.

1 The Visiting Forces Act 1952 applies to the forces of Antigua and Barbuda, Australia, Bahamas, Bangladesh, Barbados, Belize, Botswana, Brunei, Canada, Dominica, Fiji, Ghana, Grenada, Guyana, India, Jamaica, Kenya, Kiribati, Lesotho, Malawi, Malaysia, Maldives, Malta, Mauritius, Namibia, New Hebrides, New Zealand, Nigeria, Pakistan, Papua New Guinea, Republic of Cyprus, Saint Christopher and Nevis, Seychelles, Sierra Leone, Singapore, Solomon Islands, South Africa, Sri Lanka, St Lucia, St Vincent and the Grenadines, Swaziland, Tanzania, The Gambia, Tonga, Trinidad and Tobago, Tuvalu, Uganda, Western Samoa and Nauru, Zambia, Zanzibar, Zimbabwe. It also applies under designation orders made under s 1(2) of the 1952 Act to Armenia, Azerbaijan, Belarus, Belgium, Denmark, Finland, Former Yugoslav Republic of Macedonia, France, Georgia, Germany, Greece, Italy, Kazakhstan, Kyrgystan, Luxembourg, Moldova, Netherlands, Norway, Portugal, Russia, Spain, Switzerland, Turkey, Turkmenistan, Ukraine, United States of America and Uzbekistan (see VF (Designation) Orders SI 1954/634, SI 1954/637; SI 1956/2041; SI 1958/1261; SI 1961/1511; SI 1962/170; SI 1962/1639; SI 1989/1329; SI 1997/1779; SI 1998/1268. See 3 *Halsbury's Laws* (4th edn) p 936. The Act also applies, with adaptations, to any headquarters or organisation set up in pursuance of arrangements for defence (International Headquarters And Defence Organisations Act 1964, s 5).

16.69 Section 13(1) of the Visiting Forces Act 1952 applies the Army Act 1955, sections 186–188[1] and 190 (which allows for the apprehension, detention and delivery into military custody of deserters and absentees without leave from the regular forces)[2] to deserters and absentees from forces of any country to which the section applies. But first there must be a request (either specific or general) of the appropriate authority of the country to which the person belongs and a certificate that he or she is a deserter or absentee. Section 13(3) states that references in the sections of the 1955 Act to the delivery of a person into military custody shall be construed as references to the handing over of that person to such authority of the country to which he or she belongs, at such place in the UK as may be designated by the appropriate authority of that country.

1 Section 186 of the Army Act 1955 gives power to arrest suspected deserters/absentees to a constable, or if none is available, any officer, warrant officer, NCO or soldier of the regular forces. A warrant for the arrest of a suspect as aforesaid can be issued by anyone having authority to issue warrants for arrest of persons charged with crime. A person in custody by virtue of s 186 shall be brought before a court of summary jurisdiction as soon as practicable. If the person admits being a deserter and the court is satisfied with the truth of the admission, or if he denies it but the court is satisfied that (a) he is under military law and (b) that there is sufficient evidence for him to be tried for desertion, the court shall deliver him into military custody, but otherwise discharge him (s 187). If a person surrenders himself to the police as a deserter and it appears to the police that he is telling the truth, the police may deliver him into military custody without taking him to court (s 188). Governors of police stations and persons in charge of prisons are under a duty to receive deserters and detain them until they can be delivered into military custody (s 190).

2 Visiting Forces Act 1952, s 13(2). Under s 14 the magistrates' court will require two certificates: (1) stating that the country concerned has made a request for the exercise of the 1952 Act (this is signed by either the Secretary of the Admiralty, Army Council or Air Council); and (2) stating that the person is a deserter (this is signed by the officer commanding a unit or detachment of any of the forces of the country concerned).

16.70 Section 13 of the Visiting Forces Act 1952 does not apply just to deserters from visiting forces (ie those stationed in the UK) but also to all the forces of a country to which the section applies. In *R v Thames Justices, ex p Brindle*[1] an American citizen resident in England returned to the US, joined the army and was posted to Germany, deserted and came to England where he was arrested for other offences and ordered by the magistrate to be handed into the custody of the US military authorities on completion of his sentence. The Court of Appeal held that although Part I of the 1952 Act (sections 1–12) applied just to visiting forces as defined in section 12(1), section 13 applied to deserters from the 'forces of any designated country' without a limitation to visiting forces.

1 [1975] 3 All ER 941, [1975] 1 WLR 1400, CA.

16.71 The procedure and standard of proof to be applied by a magistrates' court in such cases was spelt out by the Divisional Court in *R v Tottenham Magistrates' Court, ex p Williams*.[1] Mr W, a Nigerian lawfully settled in the UK, was arrested as a deserter from the Nigerian airforce, but claimed that his engagement had terminated before he came to the UK. The magistrate had ordered his surrender on the basis that he was the person named in a certificate signed by an officer commanding a unit of the Nigerian forces who stated that Mr W was a deserter. She did not take into account the evidence and statement of Mr W. The Divisional Court quashed the decision. Donaldson LJ pointed out that there was a very heavy onus and that no one was to be imprisoned or delivered into the custody of any authority, whether British or Nigerian, save in strict compliance with the law. As Mr W did not admit he was legally absent, two things had to be proved under the Visiting Forces Act 1952 procedure:

• that Mr W was subject to Nigerian military law. The magistrates had to be satisfied beyond reasonable doubt—the criminal standard of proof; and

• if so, that there was sufficient evidence to justify his being tried in Nigeria for desertion.

This is the less onerous test applied to committal proceedings. In deciding both questions magistrates had to consider all the evidence tendered and not just that of the prosecution. In *Re Narinder Singh Virdee*[2] the Divisional Court held that proceedings under the Visiting Forces Act 1952 were quasi-criminal, like the exercise of extradition powers, and so not affected by Article 48 EC (now Article 39), since the purpose both of extradition and of handover under section 13 was a trial by a foreign court with a view to punishment, rather than exclusion from the UK.

1 [1982] 2 All ER 705, DC.
2 [1980] 1 CMLR 709, DC.

EXTRADITION

16.72 Extradition is another form of compulsory removal from this country and is a topic beyond the scope of this work.[1] There may be an overlapping of extradition and immigration law where a fugitive offender is refused leave to enter the country and enters unlawfully, or resists extradition on the ground of being a refugee. In those circumstances, as long as immigration powers are used lawfully and *bona fide* and not with the intention of circumventing extradition rules, removal could be ordered to any country permitted under the Immigration Acts,[2] including the country requesting extradition.

1 See Jones *Extradition* (1995); Stanbrook and Stanbrook *Extradition Law and Practice* (2000).
2 Immigration Act 1971, Sch 2, paras 8(1)(c) (persons refused entry and illegal entrants), 12(2)(c) and 13(2) (sea, air and international train crews) (Channel Tunnel (International Arrangements) Order 1993, SI 1993/1813, Sch 4, para 1(11)(n)), Sch 3, para 1(1) (deportees); Immigration (Removal Directions) Regulations 2000, SI 2000/2243, reg 4(2) (those removed under s 10 of the Immigration and Asylum Act 1999). Removal powers would be subject to the UK's international obligations under the Refugee Convention and the ECHR.

Chapter 17

DETENTION AND BAIL

INTRODUCTION

17.1 The use of detention for immigrants and asylum seekers is growing inexorably.[1] At the same time, administrative powers of detention of immigrants, pending examination on arrival or following a decision to remove from the UK, are evolving away from the virtually untrammelled executive discretion of the past. These powers are increasingly limited by principles of international human rights law, by Home Office policy and by statutory restriction, and subject to increasing judicial scrutiny. We will examine in this chapter the limits to the power to detain and the power to grant bail by immigration officers and adjudicators, and review the exercise of the Administrative Court bail jurisdiction while proceedings are pending before it.

1 By the end of 2000 an average of approximately 1,100 persons were held in immigration detention (excluding 120 asylum seekers held at Oakington Reception Centre), in eight detention centres and 45 prisons all over the UK, an increase of 300 a month from the late 1990s. The government has announced its intention considerably to increase its detention capacity (current holding capacity 1,352).

17.2 The powers to detain immigrants are ancillary to other immigration decisions; they are holding powers until the next step in the procedure is reached. Detention in connection with immigration is a lawful purpose under Article 5 of the ECHR, if used to prevent someone effecting an unauthorised entry into the country or with a view to removal, but the power to detain is (both under the ECHR and at common law) limited to the proper statutory function. Excessive delay, or detention pending removal when there is no practical prospect of removal, will render the use of the power unlawful.[1] On arrival in the UK detention is used pending examination or further examination, pending a decision to grant, cancel or refuse leave to enter, and after refusal or cancellation of leave pending removal. At this stage it is likely to take place in the immigration control areas of sea and airports and its duration is likely to be short, except for those detained pending consideration of asylum claims, where inordinate periods of detention in unacceptable conditions are still regrettably common. In overstaying and illegal entry cases detention is quite likely to start in a police station and end in prison awaiting removal. In deportation cases, where public good grounds are relied on or a recommendation for deportation is made by a criminal court, the same thing may happen. But where the deportee is of fixed abode and has family, there may be little or no detention throughout the whole deportation or removal process.

1   *R v Governor of Durham Prison, ex p Hardial Singh* [1983] Imm AR 198; followed in *Re Wasfi Suleiman Mahmood* [1995] Imm AR 311, QBD where Laws J said: 'While of course Parliament is entitled to confer power of administrative detention without trial, the courts will see to it that ... the statute that confers it will be strictly and narrowly construed and its operation and effect will be supervised by the court according to high standards.'

17.3   There is no doubt that the power to detain is wide and the safeguards, while vastly enhanced as a result of ECHR decisions and the new statutory scheme under the Immigration and Asylum Act 1999, are still inadequate. We shall deal with bail, temporary admission and release on conditions and note that, while a statutory presumption in favour of release is a new feature of the English and Welsh system (although of much older vintage in Scotland), there is still no statutory time limit set on the period of detention.[1] The 1999 Act[2] and detention rules made under it[3] for the first time regulate immigration detention centres and the powers and duties of custodians, and provide a regulated basis (albeit not in primary legislation) for the giving of written reasons for detention.[4]

1   A statutory time limit on Immigration Act detention was considered and rejected during the passage of the Immigration and Asylum Act 1999: see 603 HL Official Report (5th series) col 220, 29 June 1999; 605 HL Official Report (5th series) col 1248, 20 October 1999.
2   See Pt VIII of the Immigration and Asylum Act 1999 (ss 147-159).
3   The Detention Centre Rules 2001, SI 2001/238.
4   SI 2000/238, r 9.

IMMIGRATION OFFICERS' POWERS TO DETAIN

17.4   The code for regulating the examination and admission of non-nationals to UK territory is contained within the Immigration Acts 1971 to 1999. Incidental to the power to examine or remove a non-national is the ancillary power to detain pending the conclusion of such examination or removal. Under paragraph 16 of Schedule 2 to the Immigration Act 1971, immigration officers are authorised to detain the following categories of person:

(i)   persons arriving in the UK may be detained pending examination by an immigration officer to establish whether they need or should be granted leave to enter.[1] There is no equivalent power to detain those who are seeking to leave the UK, even though such persons may be examined in order to establish whether they are British citizens or to check their identity;[2]

(ii)   those who, on arrival in the UK with leave to enter granted prior to arrival, have been examined under paragraph 2A of the 1971 Act[3] and had their leave suspended,[4] may be detained pending completion of the examination and a decision on whether to cancel leave;

(iii)   those refused leave to enter and those reasonably suspected of having been refused leave to enter[5] may be detained pending the giving of directions for their removal from the UK;[6]

(iv)   illegal entrants and those reasonably suspected of being illegal entrants may be detained, pending a decision on whether to issue removal directions and pending removal in pursuance of directions;[7]

(v)   those who, having limited leave to enter or remain, do not observe a condition attached to their leave or remain beyond their leave or obtained leave by deception, or are reasonably suspected of being such persons, may be detained pending a decision on removing them or pending removal;[8] and those belonging to a family a member of which has been given removal directions under the section;[9]

(vi)   members of the crew of a ship, aircraft or train who remain beyond the leave granted to enable them to join their ship, aircraft or train, or abscond having lawfully entered without leave, or are reasonably suspected of doing so, may also be detained.[10]

Persons may be detained under Schedule 2, paragraph 16 anywhere the Secretary of State directs.[11]

1 Immigration Act 1971, Sch 2, para 16(1).
2 Immigration Act 1971, Sch 2, para 3(1).
3 Immigration Act 1971, Sch 2, para 2A (inserted by Immigration and Asylum Act 1999, Sch 14, para 57) allows examination on entry of those granted leave prior to entry, to establish (i) if there has been a change circumstances since that leave was given; (ii) whether that leave was obtained as a result of false information or a failure to disclose material facts; (iii) if there are medical grounds on which that leave should be cancelled; and (iv) if it would be conducive to the public good for that leave to be cancelled.
4 Immigration Act 1971, Sch 2, para 16(1A), inserted by Immigration and Asylum Act 1999, Sch 14, para 60.
5 Ie suspected of having absconded from temporary admission having been refused leave to enter.
6 Immigration Act 1971, Sch 2, paras 8, 16(2), as amended by Immigration and Asylum Act 1999, s 140(1).
7 Immigration Act 1971, paras 9, and 16(2), as amended. Note that the amended wording of para 16(2) allows detention of suspected illegal entrants as well as those who actually are illegal entrants, although actual illegal entry will still be a precedent fact founding the power to remove.
8 Immigration and Asylum Act 1999, s 10(1)(a), (b) and (7). The latter applies the provisions of para 16.
9 Immigration and Asylum Act 1999, s 10(1)(c) and (7).
10 Immigration Act 1971, Sch 2, paras 12-14, 16(2), modified in relation to Channel Tunnel train crews by the Channel Tunnel (International Arrangements) Order 1993, SI 1993/1813, Sch 4, para 1(11)(n) and (p).
11 Immigration Act 1971, Sch 2, para 18(1). The Immigration (Places of Detention) Direction 1999 sets out a list of places where detention under para 16 is authorised. After five consecutive days' detention (or seven after removal directions are issued), any further detention must be at either a prison, remand centre, approved hospital, place of safety in respect of children or at one of the authorised detention centres in England or Wales or an authorised police cell in Scotland. During the passage of the Immigration and Asylum Act 1999, ministers gave assurances that those who would more properly be detained under the Mental Health Act 1983 would be transferred to hospital.

17.5 In the case of a port or illegal entrant asylum claimant, the examination referred to in Schedule 2 to the Immigration Act 1971 embraces the whole asylum determination procedure, which has frequently taken years to complete: indeed, it has not been unknown for asylum claimants to be detained for the whole of this period, although the incorporation of the ECHR may make this increasingly difficult to justify. Whilst section 15 of the Immigration and Asylum Act 1999 reproduces the protection against removal pending the determination of an asylum claim formerly contained in section 6 of the Asylum and Immigration Appeals Act 1993,[1] it also provides that directions for removal may be given during that period and that a deportation order can also be served.[2] The amendment to paragraph 16(2) of the 1971 Act[3] ensures that the prohibition on removal does not preclude the power to detain.[4]

1 Repealed by Immigration and Asylum Act 1999, Sch 14, para 102. Section 15 of the Act is to be treated as having come into force on 26 July 1993 (the date of entry into force of the Asylum and Immigration Appeals Act 1993).
2 Ministers confirmed however, during the passage of the 1999 Act, that no directions or deportation order would be served until a negative determination: Lord Williams of Mostyn, 605 HL Official Report (5th series) col 785; 606 HL Official Report (5th series) cols 766–767.
3 By Immigration and Asylum Act 1999, s 140(1), see fn 2 above.
4 *Secretary of State for the Home Department v Khan* [1995] Imm AR 348, CA.

Temporary admission

17.6 As an alternative to detention such persons may be temporarily admitted to the UK without being detained, or be released from detention, and in such cases may be subject to such restrictions as to residence, employment or occupation, and reporting to the police or an immigration officer as the immigration officer notifies to them in writing from time to time.[1] The restrictions may be varied and the grant of temporary admission is without prejudice to the exercise of the power to detain. The power to re-detain does not require breach of conditions of temporary admission, but could be condemned as arbitrary if there is no such breach, actual or anticipated. The residence restrictions may include prohibitions on residence in a specified area, or a condition requiring residence in specified accommodation provided under section 4 of the Immigration and Asylum Act 1999,[2] and prohibiting absence from it, in accordance with regulations.[3] An employment restriction will ordinarily be imposed on asylum seekers, but will be lifted on request if the application is not dealt with (including appeal) within six months.[4] Illegal entrants and overstayers who are granted temporary release may not be made subject to an employment restriction if consideration of their case is likely to be protracted and the person is supporting his or her family by employment.[5] Reporting should not normally be required more than once a month, and if a case remains unresolved for three years, should be lifted.[6]

1 Immigration Act 1971, Sch 2, para 21(1), (2), as amended by Immigration Act 1988, Sch, para 10.
2 Section 4 of the Immigration and Asylum Act 1999 empowers the Secretary of State to provide accommodation for persons temporarily admitted or released from detention, the immigration equivalent of bail hostels.
3 Immigration Act 1971, Sch 2, para 21(2A)-(2E), inserted by Immigration and Asylum Act 1999, Sch 14, para 62. No regulations are yet in force under these paragraphs.
4 See **12.110** above.
5 Operational Enforcement Manual (21 December 2000) para 38.19.
6 Operational Enforcement Manual above, para 38.19.

Criteria for detention or release

17.7 The criteria for detention are based on the policy set out in Immigration Service Instructions to staff on detention dated 3 December 1991 and 20 September 1994,[1] although these now have to be read with the additional factors in the White Paper,[2] incorporated through the Operational Enforcement Manual[3] and the API.[4] The 1991 and 1994 criteria were previously confidential and only came to the attention of practitioners through accidental disclosure. The policy is to 'grant temporary admission/release whenever possible and to authorise detention only where there is no alternative. The aim is to free detention space for all those who have shown a real disregard for the immigration laws and whom we expect to remove within a realistic timetable'.[5] The factors identified in the policy statements as relevant to the exercise of the power to detain are as follows:

(i) previous absconding from detention;

(ii) previous failure to comply with conditions of temporary admission or bail;

(iii) evidence of previous disregard for the immigration laws (eg entry in breach of a deportation order, attempted or actual clandestine entry);

(iv) previous attempts to gain entry by presenting falsified documentation;

(v) history of compliance with the requirements of immigration control— eg by applying for a visa, further leave, etc;

(vi) the likelihood of removal and its timescale;

(vii) the ties with the UK evidenced by a settled address, employment, close relatives (including dependants) in the country;

(viii) the individual's expectations about the outcome of the case and any factors which would provide an incentive to keep in contact with the department, such as an outstanding application for judicial review, representations or an appeal;

(ix) compassionate factors such as a medical condition of the subject or of a dependent relative;[6]

(x) the duration of the detention - the longer a person has been detained, particularly if it is the result of a failure on the part of the Home Office to resolve the case, the greater the onus on the Secretary of State to justify continuation of detention.[7]

The 1994 instructions, which focus particularly on the detention of asylum seekers, provide a general presumption in favour of release prior to the determination of a claim and any appeal,[8] and an express presumption in favour of release for those who brought themselves to the attention of the immigration service at the first reasonable opportunity, including illegal entrants (provided they did not enter clandestinely).[9] The courts have held that the policy embodies a presumption in favour of release[10] and have held the Secretary of State to the policy in determining whether detention is lawful. In *Ex p B*[11] Kay J held unlawful the continued detention of an asylum seeker for two months after his identity had been established and sureties offered, by reference to the policy criteria.

1 Cited in *R v Secretary of State for the Home Department, ex p Brezinski and Glowacka* (CO 4251/1995) and (CO 4237/1995) (19 July 1996, unreported), Kay J.

2 See **17.8** below.

3 Operational Enforcement Manual (21 December 2000) relevant paragraphs of which are referred to below.

4 API Aug/00, Ch 1, s 1, para 4.

5   For the way in which decisions to detain are actually taken see Leanne Weber's valuable study *Deciding to detain* (University of Cambridge Institute of Criminology, 2000).
6   These factors are all set out in the 1991 policy, ISC 26/1991: see *Butterworths Immigration Law Service*, D[971].
7   The additional factor set out in the 1994 statement, which deals largely (but not exclusively) with detention of asylum seekers.
8   'The case for detaining an asylum seeker when he first makes his claim needs to be particularly strong': Immigration Service Instruction on Detention dated 20 September 1994, para 2: see *Butterworths Immigration Law Service*, D[977].
9   Immigration Service Instruction on Detention above, para 3. The presumption does not apply where an application is judged without foundation (now certified: see Immigration and Asylum Act 1999, Sch 4, para 9), but even then detention should be authorised 'only when it is judged essential to do so'.
10 See eg *Lamin Minteh* (396/5400/D), 8 March 1996, CA [1996] 3 ILD.
11 *R v Special Adjudicator and Secretary of State for the Home Department, ex p B* [1998] INLR 315, following *R v Secretary of State for the Home Department, ex p Brezinski and Glowacka*, fn 4 above.

17.8 The government confirmed the presumption in favour of temporary admission or release in its 1998 White Paper,[1] which set out the occasions for detention: to effect removal; initially to establish true identity or the basis of a claim to enter; or where there was reason to believe that the person would fail to comply with conditions attached to temporary admission or release. It gave additional guidance in relation to particular categories. In respect of asylum seekers, evidence of a history of torture should weigh strongly in favour of temporary admission whilst an asylum claim is being considered. It referred to the need to exercise particular care in considering a person's physical or mental health in deciding to detain.[2] It stated that unaccompanied minors should never be detained other than in the most exceptional circumstances, and then only overnight with appropriate care if they, for example, arrive unaccompanied at an airport.[3] In all cases, children under the age of 18 are to be referred to the Refugee Council Children's Panel. Where reliable medical evidence indicates that a person is under 18 years of age they will be treated as minors. Detention of families with young children should be effected (if at all) as close to removal as possible so as to ensure that families normally are not detained for more than a few days.[4] The Detention Centre Rules[5] now provide for medical examination of all immigration detainees within 24 hours of admission to the detention centre and oblige the medical practitioner to report to the manager, who must send a copy of the report to the Secretary of State, in any case where the detainee may have been the victim of torture, or is potentially suicidal, or whose health is likely to be injuriously affected by detention or detention conditions, or who becomes seriously ill or is removed to hospital on account of mental disorder.[6]

1   *Fairer Faster and Firmer – A Modern Approach to Immigration and Asylum* (Cm 4018, July 1998).
2   These factors are reflected in the Operational Enforcement Manual, which indicates that persons who are elderly, or pregnant, who suffer serious physical or mental ill-health or a serious disability, or who have independent evidence of torture, should not be detained: Manual 21 December 2000, para 38. However at 38.8 it says that emotionally disturbed or suicidal detainees should be sent to prison!
3   The Manual (above) also indicates that minors should be detained only in a 'place of safety' as defined in the Children and Young Persons Act 1933, the Social Work (Scotland) Act 1958 or the Children and Young Persons (Northern Ireland) Act 1968. In England and Wales this includes local authority accommodation, a remand home, a police station, a hospital, a surgery or an 'other suitable place'. In Scotland and Northern Ireland the statutory definition is narrower.
4   The White Paper (fn 1 above) policy informs the statutory criteria for bail in the Immigration and Asylum Act 1999: see **17.40** below.

5   The Detention Centre Rules 2001, SI 2001/238, rr 35 and 36.
6   A number of reputable organisations including the Medical Foundation for the Care of Victims of Torture and Bail for Immigration Detainees report that torture victims are still being detained too frequently. See eg Alison Harvey 'The detention of asylum seekers', a conference paper given at the University of Cambridge Institute of Criminology, 20 March 2001. See also Leanne Weber *Deciding to detain* **17.7** fn 5 above.

17.9 The criteria for detention in the API indicate that detention is only used when there is no alternative and there are good grounds for believing that the person will not keep in touch voluntarily. Factors such as whether there is a sponsor, evidence of identity and past immigration history, and the availability of detention accommodation, are relevant. Detention may be appropriate where the applicant has been identified as an illegal entrant.[1] However, a much wider use of detention appears to be sanctioned by the parliamentary answer[2] amending the White Paper[3] criteria in respect of detention at Oakington, a detention centre for holding asylum seekers whose claims are expected to be processed swiftly.[4] Asylum applicants will be detained at Oakington if it appears their applications can be decided quickly, including a certification as manifestly unfounded. Those *not* to be detained at Oakington are defined in the Enforcement Manual as:[5]

- persons not belonging to one of the nationalities listed in the regular instructions to staff;[6]
- persons whose claims cannot be decided quickly;
- persons whose claims raise complicating factors;
- persons claiming to be minors, whose age is disputed, unless there is clear and irrefutable evidence they are over 18;
- persons with special medical needs which cannot be met by a GP;
- persons unsuitable for the 'relaxed' regime at Oakington, including those likely to abscond.

1   API Aug/00, Ch 1, s 1, para 4.
2   346 HC Official Report (6th series) written answers col 263N, 16 March 2000, Barbara Roche.
3   Cm 4018, **17.8** fn 1 above.
4   Detention there is to be for a period of seven days, while applicants are interviewed and an initial decision made. If a decision has not been taken, the applicant will be granted temporary admission or transferred to longer-term detention; if refused, a decision about further detention will be made in accordance with normal criteria: ibid.
5   Operational Enforcement Manual (21 December 2000) para 38.3.1.
6   The list in February 2001 was: Albania, Bangladesh, China, Czech Republic, Estonia, Ghana, India, Iraq, Kosovo, Latvia, Lithuania, Nigeria, Pakistan, Poland, Romania, Slovakia, Tanzania, Uganda, Zimbabwe. The Race Relations Act 1976, s 19D (inserted by the RR(Amendment) Act 2000) makes discrimination based on nationality, or ethnic or national origin, lawful in respect of immigration functions. See **1.28** above.

17.10 The UNHCR has issued guidelines relating to the detention of asylum seekers.[1] These guidelines include the general principle that asylum seekers should not be detained.[2] The only permissible exceptions[3] are:

(i)   for the purposes of a preliminary interview to verify identity where this is undetermined or in dispute or to determine the elements on which the claim for refugee status or asylum is based;
(ii)   where an individual has destroyed or used fraudulent travel or identity documents in order to mislead the authorities of the receiving country;
(iii) to protect national security and public order.

Unaccompanied minors should not be detained,[4] and unaccompanied elderly persons, torture or trauma victims, or persons with mental or physical disabilities should only be detained on the certification of a qualified medical practitioner that detention will not adversely affect their health and well being.[5] The Guidelines also refer to the UN Body of Principles for the Protection of all Persons under any form of Detention or Imprisonment 1988,[6] which set out indispensable procedural safeguards for detainees. These include reasons for detention in a language the detainee can understand; medical screening to identify trauma or torture victims; the segregation of asylum seekers from criminal prisoners; the segregation of men and women, and children from adults, unless they are part of a family group; rights to communicate with the outside world, with family, friends and consular officials; the right to challenge detention, with appropriate legal advice and assistance; the right to prompt medical attention; and educational, social, religious and cultural rights.

1   UNHCR *Guidelines on applicable Criteria and Standards relating to the Detention of Asylum Seekers* (February 1999) set out in *Butterworths Immigration Law Service*, 2C[261].
2   UNHCR *Guidelines* above, Guideline 2.
3   Set out in UNHCR *Guidelines* above, Guideline 3.
4   UNHCR *Guidelines* above, Guideline 6. The UN Working Group on Arbitrary Detention states that unaccompanied minors should never be detained: Commission on Human Rights, 55th Session, 18 December 1998, E/CN.4/1999/63 Add.3, para 37.
5   UNHCR *Guidelines* above, Guideline 7. See now Detention Centre Rules 2001, SI 2001/238, rr 35 and 36, **17.8** above.
6   UNGA 43/173, 1988.

SECRETARY OF STATE'S POWERS TO DETAIN

17.11 In addition to the powers of detention by immigration officers, the Secretary of State has wide powers to detain persons liable to deportation. This may occur in the following situations:

(i)   *After a court recommendation.* Where a recommendation for deportation made by a court is in force and the person is not in custody[1] or on bail,[2] that person must be detained pending the making of a deportation order, unless *either* the court by which the recommendation is made or an appeal court otherwise directs, *or* the Secretary of State directs that the person be released pending further consideration of the case, *or* (when section 54 of the Immigration and Asylum Act 1999 is in force) he or she is released on bail.[3]

(ii) *Decision to deport.* Where notice has been given to a person of a decision to make a deportation order under section 3(5) of the Immigration Act 1971,[4] and that person is not in custody or on bail, he or she may be detained under the authority of the Secretary of State pending the making of the deportation order.[5]

(iii) *Deportation order made.* Persons against whom a deportation order is in force may be detained under the authority of the Secretary of State pending their removal or departure from the UK. If they are already detained under either of the previous provisions they shall continue to be detained unless the Secretary of State directs otherwise *or* (when section 54 of the 1999 Act is in force) unless they are released on bail.[6]

1   The paragraph has no application where the person is serving a sentence or on remand to a criminal court: see *Re Nwafor* [1994] Imm AR 91, QBD.

2   In *R v Governor of Holloway Prison, ex p Giambi* [1982] 1 All ER 434, [1982] 1 WLR 535 the Divisional Court stated that this referred only to bail granted by a court which was seized of the question of deportation, ie the recommending court, the Crown Court or a High Court judge exercising the court's inherent jurisdiction. See, however, Immigration Act 1971, Sch 3, para 2(2) where this narrow construction clearly cannot apply to similar words, dealing with detention of those against whom an administrative *decision* to deport has been made. See fn 5 below.

3   Immigration Act 1971, Sch 3, para 2(1), (1A), inserted by Criminal Justice Act 1982, Sch 10. The provision on release on bail in this para is contained in the amendment to para 2(1) by Immigration and Asylum Act 1999, s 54(1) (not yet in force), which equates the position of detainees awaiting deportation with those detained under the authority of an immigration officer for the purposes of immigration officer bail: see **17.30** below.

4   Deportation deemed conducive to the public good, and of family members of deportees. There may also still be a few overstayers served with notices of intended deportation under the old s 3(5)(a) IA 1971 because of the transitional protection provided by Immigration and Asylum Act 1999, s 9.

5   Immigration Act 1971, Sch 3, para 2(2). *The Enforcement Manual* (21 December 2000) para 38.9.3 states that for the purposes of this provision, the grant of bail by a criminal court on a wholly unrelated case precludes detention by the Secretary of State on service of the notice of intention to deport, in contrast with the position where a deportation order is made.

6   Immigration Act 1971, Sch 3, para 2(3), as amended by Immigration and Asylum Act 1999, s 54(3) (the bail provision, not yet in force).

17.12 In each of these cases, including the case of recommendations by the courts, an alternative to detention is provided. On the Secretary of State's direction, the person may instead be subjected to a restriction order which places him or her under such restrictions as to residence, employment or occupation and as to reporting to the police or immigration officer as the Secretary of State may from time to time notify in writing.[1] The restrictions mirror those which an immigration officer may impose on temporary admission, for which see **17.6** above.

1   Immigration Act 1971, Sch 3, para 2(5) and (6), as amended by IA 1988, Sch, para 10; Asylum and Immigration Act 1996, Sch 2, para 13.

17.13 The qualified requirement to detain those recommended for deportation pending the decision of the Secretary of State was the subject of considerable criticism, on the grounds that it resulted in unnecessary detention in custody of such persons, either at the end of a prison sentence or immediately where a non-custodial sentence had been given. In July 1978, partly in response to these criticisms, the Home Office issued a circular to the courts[1] reminding them that because of appeal rights, a person recommended for deportation may spend at least five weeks in detention; that the Secretary of State would not necessarily be in a position to decide whether to exercise his or her discretion to release the person if the court had not already done so; and that courts might wish to bear in mind, when considering whether or not to release, the principal grounds for withholding bail in criminal proceedings under the Bail Act 1976. The circular also reminded the courts of the importance of submitting a certificate of recommendation without delay to the Home Office. The clear intention of the circular was to make release the rule rather than the exception. Section 54 of the Immigration and Asylum Act 1999 (when in force) assimilates the position of persons detained for deportation (whether after a recommendation, a notice of intention to deport or a deportation order) to that of persons detained by immigration officers, for the purpose of release on immigration officer or adjudicator bail.[2]

1 Home Office Circular No 113/1978 'Immigration Act 1971: Detention Pending Deportation'.
2 Immigration Act 1971, Sch 3, para 4A, inserted by Immigration and Asylum Act 1999, s 54(4) as from a date to be notified. For bail under para 22 of the 1971 Act, see **17.30** below.

17.14 In cases where persons are liable to detention either under the authority of the Secretary of State or of an immigration officer, they may be arrested without warrant by a police or immigration officer.[1] In addition, warrants may be issued to the police for the purpose of searching for and arresting those persons.[2]

1 Immigration Act 1971, Sch 2, para 17 and Sch 3, para 2(4). This does not, however, apply to those recommended for deportation by a court, presumably because if they are not detained, it is by direction of the Secretary of State or because they have been released on bail; see fn 2 above. The powers of arrest are additional to arrest powers of those who have failed to answer to bail, see below.
2 Immigration Act 1971, Sch 2, para 17 and Sch 3, para 2(4). Note that immigration officers may not obtain search warrants for persons liable to detention for removal, although the Immigration and Asylum Act 1999 gave them considerable new powers to search premises for immigration offenders: see chapter 14 above.

Reasons for detention

17.15 There is no requirement in primary legislation for reasons to be given for detention, despite the obligation in Article 5(2) of the ECHR.[1] The 1999 White Paper contained a commitment for written reasons to be given on initial detention and at monthly intervals thereafter, or shorter periods in cases involving families.[2] Since October 1999 immigration officers have served written reasons in the form of a checklist.[3] They are instructed to ensure that the contents of the checklist are interpreted into the detainee's language.[4] Rule 9 of the Detention Centre Rules 2001[5] represents the first statutory requirement for written reasons for detention, and incorporates the commitment that reasons be given monthly and not just on first detention.

1 See **17.24** below.
2 *Fairer, Faster and Firmer - a Modern Approach to Immigration and Asylum* (Cm 4018, July 1998).
3 The use of a checklist has been criticised as contrary to UNHCR's requirements of individualised written reasons, and there are indications that the checklist often masks the real reasons for detention: see Weber *Deciding to detain* **17.7** fn 5 above.
4 *Operational Enforcement Manual*, 21 December 2000, para 38.5.2.
5 SI 2001/238.

LIMITS TO THE POWER TO DETAIN

17.16 The lawfulness of a detention depends on a number of considerations:

(i) whether it is or continues to be for the statutory purpose for which the power is given;

(ii) whether the detention has gone on for longer than is reasonably necessary for the purpose for which it is authorised;

(iii)   whether the exercise or continued exercise of the power is reasonable when balanced against the alternative of interim liberation or temporary admission;

(iv)   whether there has been a failure to follow Home Office policy;[1]

(v)   as an overriding consideration embracing some of the above factors, whether the detention is for a lawful purpose, is prescribed by law and is proportionate to its legitimate aim under Article 5(1)(f) of the ECHR.

Prior to the amendment of paragraph 16(2) of Schedule 2 to the Immigration Act 1971,[2] actual (as opposed to suspected) illegal entry was a condition precedent to the power to detain an illegal entrant for removal, and the lawfulness of the detention in such a case was dependent on whether the precedent facts giving rise to the jurisdiction to detain were established.[3] Now, the only precedent fact required is a suspicion on reasonable grounds that the person is liable to be removed.

1   *R v A Special Adjudicator and Secretary of State for the Home Department, ex p B* [1998] INLR 315.
2   By Immigration and Asylum Act 1999, s 140(1).
3   See *Khawaja v Secretary of State for the Home Department* [1984] AC 74, HL.

17.17 The purpose for which detention is authorised is spelt out in the immigration laws. As we have seen above, administrative detention under the Immigration Act 1971 is authorised pending examination or further examination for a decision on the grant, refusal or cancellation of leave, pending the making of a deportation order, the giving of removal directions and pending the removal of the person from the UK. Detention is not authorised for any other purpose.[1] Thus, a practice of routine detention of particular nationalities, of heads of households or of undocumented passengers which was not for one of the above purposes would be unlawful in domestic law as well as under Article 5 of the ECHR.[2]

1   See Immigration Act 1971, Sch 2, paras 2, 2A and 16; Sch 3, para 2(2).
2   Police have no power to detain an asylum seeker not carrying identity documents to check immigration status, and a four-hour detention sounded in damages of £2,000 in *Okot v Metropolitan Police Comr*, 1 September 1995, Central London Trial Centre (reported in (1996) Legal Action, February, p 12).

17.18 The limits of the power to detain were spelt out in *Ex p Hardial Singh*.[1] The case concerned the power given to the Secretary of State authorising the detention of a person against whom a deportation order had been made. The principles set out in the case apply to all administrative detentions. It was held that this particular power authorised the detention of the applicant only pending his removal and could not be used for any other purpose. Secondly, the power of detention was implicitly limited to the period reasonably necessary for the purpose. Thirdly, it was implicit that the Secretary of State should exercise all reasonable expedition to ensure that all necessary steps were taken for the removal of the applicant within a reasonable time. A failure by the immigration authority responsible for detention to take the action it should take, or to take it sufficiently promptly, renders the detention unlawful.[2] *Hardial Singh* was followed by the High Court in the case of *Wasfi Mahmood*[3] where a ten-month detention to obtain travel documents to effect removal was held to be excessive, and was approved by the Privy Council when reviewing the lengthy detention of Vietnamese asylum seekers in Hong Kong.[4] However, prolongation of detention pending exhaustion of the judicial process is not necessarily unlawful,[5] and neither is prolonged detention caused by the immigrant's refusal to co-operate in verification of identity for the procurement of travel documents for his or her removal. An undertaking to 'take no steps to remove' an applicant once judicial review proceedings had been issued was held not to preclude detention.[6]

1   *R v Governor of Durham Prison, ex p Hardial Singh* [1984] 1 All ER 983, [1984] 1 WLR 704, [1983] Imm AR 198, QBD.
2   In *R v Special Adjudicator and Secretary of State for the Home Department, ex p B* [1998] INLR 315 continued detention after an asylum seeker had established his identity was held unlawful on the basis, *inter alia*, that the Home Office had had long enough to check the information he provided.
3   *Re Wasfi Mahmood* [1995] Imm AR 311.
4   *Tan Te Lam v Superintendent of Tai A Chau Detention Centre* [1997] AC 97, [1996] 4 All ER 256, PC.
5   *R v Secretary of State for the Home Department, ex p Chahal* [1996] Imm AR 205. A 30-month detention of a long-term overstayer which appeared 'inordinate and inexcusable' was held not unreasonable in *R v Secretary of State for the Home Department, ex p Ghaly* (CO 4303/1997) 11 November 1997 because it was largely due to the applicant's applications to adjourn his hearing before the appellate authorities.
6   *R v Secretary of State for the Home Department, ex p Jaswinder Singh* [1997] Imm AR 166, OHCS.

17.19 Detention is unlawful if it is an unreasonable exercise of the power to detain. The UN Working Group on Arbitrary Detention observed that it was 'inherently unjust' to detain people who had been in the UK for ten or 12 years and had put down roots.[1] In *Sokha*[2] Lord Prosser highlighted the difference between the Scottish courts' approach to detention and that in England. In Scotland the risk of absconding, which is an inevitable concomitant of liberty, was, he said, not normally regarded by the Secretary of State as justifying continued detention, so that for such detention to be reasonable there had to be some feature in the particular case which indicated that there was a greater risk of absconding than usual. The decision was followed in *Rafaqat Ali*[3] where the Outer House of the Court of Session found detention lawful on the basis that the particular applicant had not employed a 'normal' degree of deception, but a 'degree and duration going far beyond the normal case of illegal immigration'. A continued detention also may be inherently unreasonable having regard to the circumstances of the case or it may be so because of the absence of any material distinction between the case in hand and those 'normal' cases in which conditional release is granted.[4] Since then, the English courts have gradually begun to accept a presumption of liberty at common law, through the application of Home Office policy and through the provisions of the ECHR, which should lead to a convergence of approach in the two jurisdictions. An exercise of the power to detain which fails to have regard to the Home Office policy on criteria for detention is unlawful.[5]

1   UN Commission on Human Rights, 55th Session, 18 December 1998, E/CN.4/1999/Add.3, paras 22–23.
2   *Sokha v Secretary of State for the Home Department* [1992] Imm AR 14, CS.
3   *Rafaqat Ali v Secretary of State for the Home Department* [1999] SCLR 555, OHCS.
4   For an unreasonable exercise of the discretion to detain in the English courts but in another context, see *Holgate-Mohammed v Duke* [1984] AC 437 at 444, 446 where Lord Diplock's comments on the unreasonable exercise by a police officer of a lawful power of arrest could also apply to immigration officers. See also *R v Special Adjudicator and Secretary of State for the Home Department, ex p B* [1998] INLR 315.
5   *R v SA and Secretary of State for the Home Department, ex p B* **17.18** fn 2 above.

17.20 Detention must also be compatible with Article 5 of the ECHR to be lawful. Whilst contracting states to the Convention have a right to control the entry into and residence in their territory, this right must be exercised in accordance with Article 5, so that any deprivation of liberty in the context of immigration must be for one of the purposes set out in Article 5(1)(f), ie for the prevention of unlawful entry or for removal, and in accordance with the law and proportionate to the aim pursued. Article 5 is concerned with the deprivation of liberty rather than its mere restriction, but the distinction is a matter of degree rather than substance, depending on factors such as the nature of the interference with liberty, its duration and the effect on the individual.[1] Thus, the interference with liberty involved in a short examination at the port to establish identity and qualifications for entry would probably not constitute detention so as to engage Article 5. But an equally short detention for fingerprinting or a compulsory medical examination would be of a nature and effect on the individual which would probably attract the protection of the Article, because of the element of compulsion and intrusion on privacy.[2] In the seminal case of *Amuur v France*[3] the ECHR considered the detention of asylum seekers at the port. It rejected the French government's contentions that an airport contained an 'international zone' where the safeguards of domestic law did not apply, and that deprivation of liberty was 'voluntary' and did not attract the protection of the Convention, since the detainees were free to leave the territory.

1   *Guzzardi v Italy* (1980) 3 EHRR 333, para 92; *Amuur v France* (1996) 22 EHRR 533, para 42.
2   See eg App 8278/78 18 DR 154.
3   *Amuur v France* above.

17.21 It is for the detaining authority to justify detention by showing that:

(i)   it is to prevent unlawful entry or to remove a person liable to expulsion, or for another purpose expressly permitted by Article 5 of the ECHR (such as prevention of the commission of crime,[1] lawful detention for non-compliance with an order of a court,[2] lawful detention of a minor for educational supervision[3] or lawful detention of persons of unsound mind)[4];

(ii)   it is in accordance with domestic law and with the requirements of precision and predictability;

(iii)   it is proportionate to its aim.

The establishment of the purpose of the detention is vital to show that detention is not arbitrary. The purpose of Article 5 is to protect the individual from arbitrariness.[5] In *A v Australia*[6] the UN Human Rights Committee, applying the equivalent provisions of the International Covenant on Civil and Political Rights, held that detention of an asylum seeker can be considered arbitrary if it is 'not necessary in all the circumstances of the case, for example to prevent flight or interference with evidence: the element of proportionality becomes relevant in this context'. In *Amuur*[7] the court accepted some confinement of asylum seekers to enable states to prevent unlawful immigration, but held that states must ensure the presence of suitable safeguards[8] and that the length of confinement was proportionate to the process of examination.[9] Confinement should not 'above all ... deprive the asylum seeker of the right to gain effective access to the procedure for determining refugee status'.[10] In *Litwa v Poland*, a case involving the detention of a drunk, the court emphasised that 'detention of an individual is such a serious measure that it is only justified where other, less severe, measures have been considered and found to be insufficient to safeguard the individual or the public interest'.[11]

1 ECHR, art 5(1)(c).
2 ECHR, art 5(1)(b).
3 ECHR, art 5(1)(d).
4 ECHR, art 5(1)(e).
5 *Winterwerp v Netherlands* (1979) 2 EHRR 387, paras 37-39; *Kemmache v France (No 3)* (1994) 19 EHRR 349; *Amuur v France* (1996) 22 EHRR 533, para 50.
6 *A v Australia* [1997] Communication No 560/1993.
7 *Amuur v France* above.
8 *Amuur v France* above, para 43.
9 *Amuur v France* above, para 42.
10 *Amuur v France* above, para 43.
11 *Litwa v Poland*, Appn No 26629/95, 4 April 2000.

17.22 Detention to prevent unlawful entry should not encompass asylum seekers who use false documents to travel, and who arrive undocumented, since they would not be attempting to effect an unlawful entry.[1] In *Ferko*[2] it was held that the practice of detaining heads of household so as to deter other family members from absconding was only lawful so long as it was based on reasonable apprehension that the person who is being detained is likely to abscond otherwise.[3] Similar considerations apply to detention of particular nationalities. The so-called 'special exercises', involving detention of nationals of particular countries,[4] and the nationality criteria for detention at Oakington,[5] give rise to concern that detention is not justified by the facts of the particular case but by reference to a policy, which cannot be justified under Article 5 of the ECHR. Other concerns about arbitrariness in UK practice on detention include the very wide disparities in the proportion of those detained on arrival at different ports. Thirty-two per cent of all arrivals at Manchester airport's Terminal 2 are detained overnight, compared with 1.5 per cent of arrivals at London Heathrow's Terminal 1. Stansted airport detains 18 per cent of arrivals for over five days; Felixstowe only 1.5 per cent.[6] The UN Human Rights Commission's Working Group on Arbitrary Detention, which visited the UK in 1998, was concerned at the fact that availability of detention accommodation was a criterion, making detention somewhat arbitrary. The Working Group also expressed concern, *inter alia*, at the length of detention, the lack of written grounds or judicial supervision, and that the decision to detain an asylum seeker is made by an immigration officer who may not have sufficient training in refugee law or the human rights situation in refugee-producing countries.[7]

1 *R v Naillie* [1993] AC 674.
2 *R v Secretary of State for the Home Department, ex p Andrej Ferko* (CO 4205/1997) 11 December 1997, Kay J.
3 The *Operational Enforcement Manual* (21 December 2000) para 38.1.1.1 acknowledges that 'detention for purposes such as deterrence to others where detention is not necessary for the purposes of removal of the individual is not compatible with Article 5'. It also accepts that such detention may offend art 8 of the ECHR by separating families, although it may be justifiable to enforce immigration control, and that it would be disproportionate to detain whole families: para 38.1.1.2.
4 See exchange of correspondence between Bail for Immigration Detainees and the Immigration Service Enforcement Directorate, 26 and 30 October 2000.
5 *Operational Enforcement Manual* para 38.3.1. See **17.9** above.

6   Leanne Weber *Deciding to Detain* (2000); see **17.7** fn 5 above.
7   See Report of the visit of the Working Group to the UK on the issue of immigrants and asylum seekers EC/CN.4/1999/Add.3, 18 December 1998, para 18(h).

17.23   The exceptions to the statutory right to bail under the Immigration and Asylum Act 1999[1] appear, on their face, generally compatible with Article 5 of the ECHR, if applied fairly and proportionately on the facts. To justify detention with a view to deportation, all that is required is that 'action is being taken with a view to deportation',[2] but as at common law, any deprivation of liberty under the second limb of Article 5(1)(f) will be justified only whilst deportation proceedings are in progress, and if removal is a remote and impractical prospect for the foreseeable future, or is not prosecuted with due diligence, the detention can no longer be said to be for the purpose of removal.[3] However, in *Chahal*[4] a six-year detention pending deportation was held not to violate Article 5(1) of the Convention, since there were sufficient guarantees against arbitrariness.

1   Immigration and Asylum Act 1999, s 46. See **17.40** below.
2   *Chahal v UK* (1996) 23 EHRR 413, para 413.
3   *R v Secretary of State for the Home Department, ex p Hardial Singh* [1984] 1 WLR 704; *Chahal v UK* above, at para 113. See the criticisms of the UN Working Group on Arbitrary Detention of December 1998, to the effect that sometimes detention was so prolonged as to become arbitrary: UN Commission on Human Rights, 55th Session, 18 December 1998, E/CN.4/1999/Add.3, para 18.
4   *Chahal* above, at paras 109 and 117.

17.24   Article 5 of the ECHR requires that any detention conform to the substantive and procedural rules of national law, which themselves must be sufficiently accessible and precise.[1] The statutory right to bail and exceptions to it comply in this respect with Article 5; unpublished criteria for detention such as the 1991 and 1994 instructions (now published)[2] would not. Article 5(2) requires reasons to be given for detention in a language the detainee understands. In determining whether the detention of immigrants and asylum seekers is arbitrary, the UN Working Group on Arbitrary Detention considers whether the person concerned is able to enjoy all or some of the following guarantees:

(1)   to be informed, at least orally, in a language he or she understands, of the grounds for proposed refusal at the border;

(2)   to have the detention decision taken by an authorised official with a sufficient level of responsibility;

(3)   determination of the lawfulness of the detention by automatic and prompt recourse to a judge or body of equivalent competence, independence and impartiality, or the possibility of appealing to a judge or such a body;

(4)   entitlement to review of detention by higher court or equivalent body;

(5)   written and reasoned notification of detention measure in a language understood by the applicant;

(6)   the possibility of communicating effectively by phone, fax or e-mail with, in particular, a lawyer, consular representative and relatives;

(7)   assistance by counsel (of the detainee's choice or officially appointed) through visits in the place of custody and at any hearing;

(8)   detention in dedicated detention centres or separation from criminal prisoners;

(9)   up-to-date register of those detained with reasons;

(10)   not to be held for an excessive or unlimited period, with a maximum statutory period;

(11)   information of guarantees provided in disciplinary rules;
(12)   procedure for incommunicado detention;
(13)   alternatives to administrative detention;
(14)   access to places of custody by UNHCR, International Committee of the Red Cross and specialised NGOs.[3]

UNHCR's view of required safeguards in respect of detention of asylum seekers[4] includes (i) prompt and full communication of any order of detention, together with the reasons for the order, and the rights in connection with the order, in a language and in terms they understand; (ii) to be informed of the right to legal counsel. Where possible, they should receive free legal assistance; (iii) to have the decision subjected to an automatic review before a judicial or administrative body independent of the detaining authorities, followed by regular periodic reviews of the necessity to continue detention; (iv) either personally or through a representative, the right to challenge the necessity of the deprivation of liberty at the review hearing.

1   *Zamir v UK* (1983) 40 DR 42; *Steel v UK* (1999) 28 EHRR 603; *Amuur v France* (1996) 22 EHRR 533, para 50; *Kawka v Poland* Appn No 25874/94, 9 January 2001, para 49.
2   *Butterworths Immigration Law Service*, D[971]; see **17.7** above.
3   *Civil and political rights, including questions of torture and detention* UN Commission on Human Rights, 55th Session, 18 December 1998, E/CN.4/1999/63, para 69.
4   UNHCR *Guidelines on applicable criteria and standards relating to the detention of asylum seekers* (February 1999), Guideline 5 *Butterworths Immigration Law Service*, 2C[261].

17.25 Article 5(4) of the ECHR requires rapid access to a court to determine the lawfulness of detention, and release if the detention is not lawful.[1] The procedure must be adversarial and ensure equality of arms.[2] Those detained for removal or deportation on national security grounds had no such access to a court until the ECtHR in *Chahal*[3] held that the national security advisory panel set up to advise the Secretary of State in such cases did not qualify as a 'court' and that the UK was in breach of Article 5(4) of the ECHR. This ruling led to the establishment of the Special Immigration Appeals Commission to hear national security appeals and related bail applications.[4] The Court in *Amuur*[5] held that deprivation of liberty is not compatible with the Convention if the courts are unable to review the conditions under which individuals are being held, or to impose a limit on the length of detention or to provide legal, humanitarian or social assistance.[6] The court stressed that 'account should be taken of the fact that detention is applied 'not to those who have committed criminal offences but to aliens who, often fearing for their lives, have fled from their own country'.[7] In this connection, the seven-day bar on bail applications for new arrivals contained in the Immigration Act 1971, and the eight- and 36-day delay in automatic bail references under the Immigration and Asylum Act 1999, compare unfavourably with the review afforded to detained criminal suspects and may not be compatible with Article 5(4). The requirement of the Secretary of State's consent for adjudicator bail pending appeal in cases where removal directions have been given is unlikely to withstand scrutiny.[8] Another cause for concern is the absence on any statutory limit to the duration of detention.[9] However, free legal assistance in challenging detention is available, both by grants to voluntary organisations, which provide advice and assistance for detained persons,[10] and by the grant of legal aid by way of controlled legal help for representation on bail hearings.

1 The court must be able to examine not only whether conditions precedent for detention under domestic law are met (which the High Court does in *habeas corpus*) but also whether detention is necessary or proportionate: *Amuur* **17.21** fn 5 above, para 53. See also *X v UK* (1981) 4 EHRR 188; *Brogan v UK* (1988) 11 EHRR 117, para 65.
2 *Sanchez-Reisse v Switzerland* (1986) 9 EHRR 71; *Toth v Austria* Series (1991) 14 EHRR 551; *Kampanis v Greece* (1995) 21 EHRR 43; *Nikolova v Bulgaria* App No 31195/96, 25 March 1999.
3 *Chahal v UK* (1996) 23 EHRR 413.
4 See **17.33** and chapter 18 below.
5 *Amuur* above.
6 *Amuur* above, para 53.
7 *Amuur* above, para 43.
8 Immigration Act 1971, Sch 2, para 30(1).
9 The criticisms of the UN Working Group on Arbitrary Detention included the lack of immediate access to a court or a quick judicial remedy, the lack of judicial supervision, and the lack of a specified time limit within which the applicant was required to be produced before an adjudicator: UN Commission on Human Rights, 55th Session, 18 December 1998, E/CN.4/1999/Add.3, para 18.
10 Immigration and Asylum Act 1999, s 55.

17.26 Everyone who has been the victim of arrest or detention in contravention of the provisions of Article 5 of the ECHR must have an enforceable right to compensation.[1] Damages for breaches of section 6 of the Human Rights Act 1998 may not be awarded against a court or appellate authority for judicial acts done in good faith, but there is an exception where the award is for compensation for breaches of Article 5, since it is required by Art 5(5). Thus damages may be recoverable against an adjudicator who unnecessarily and disproportionately prolonged detention by refusing bail. However, in *Chahal v UK* the ECHR declined to award monetary compensation for the applicant despite finding a breach of Article 5(4) by the lack of judicial supervision of the detention,[2] and a challenge by judicial review of the Secretary of State's refusal to provide compensation was rejected by the Court of Appeal on the basis that the lack of judicial supervision did not affect the lawfulness of the actual detention.[3] In the past damages have been awarded against the Home Office for unlawful detention on a scale similar to that obtaining in actions against the police.[4]

1 ECHR, art 5(5). See *W v Home Office* [1997] Imm AR 302.
2 *Chahal v UK* (1996) 23 EHRR 413, para 158.
3 *R v Secretary of State for the Home Department, ex p Chahal (Karamjit Singh)* QBCOF 1998/1537/4 (1999) Times, 10 November, CA.
4 £17,000 was awarded for detention of a British citizen and her infant child for approximately five days following a successful judicial review of her detention in *R v Ejaz (Naheed)* [1994] Imm AR 300, CA. The same amount was awarded for a four-day detention over Christmas of Peter Honegan following a judgment that the refusal of leave to enter on which the detention depended was irrational: *R v Secretary of State for the Home Department, ex p Honegan*, 13 March 1995, QBD. £2,000 was awarded against police for a four-hour detention for immigration status check in *Okot v Metropolitan Police Comr*, 1 September 1995, CLCC (1996) Legal Action February, p 12.

CHALLENGING DETENTION IN THE HIGH COURT

17.27 A challenge to detention in the High Court may be made either by *habeas corpus* or judicial review. In *B v Barking, Havering and Brentwood Community Health Care NHS Trust*[1] Lord Woolf MR expressed his hope that in the future it would be possible to make an order for *habeas corpus* on an application for judicial review, to avoid two sets of proceedings, and added that until that time every effort should be made to harmonise the proceedings. In *Sheikh* the Court of Appeal held that a *habeas corpus* application seeking to challenge a determination of illegal entry which founded a detention, made some time after the failure of a renewed application for judicial review, itself years out of time, undermined the principle of finality in litigation and was an abuse of process.[2] There are, however, clear procedural advantages in seeking *habeas corpus*.[3] First, there is the high priority traditionally given to getting such applications into court and, secondly, a refusal to issue a writ is potentially appealable to the House of Lords, whereas a refusal of permission to apply for judicial review is not. But a *habeas corpus* application, while appropriate where the challenge is to the jurisdiction to detain, may not be the appropriate vehicle to challenge the compatibility of detention with ECHR, Article 5 requirements of proportionality.[4] In *Ex p Muboyayi*[5] the Court of Appeal made it clear that *habeas corpus* is not available if the real challenge is to an underlying administrative decision, such as a refusal of entry, which involves making a judgment after consideration of a number of circumstances and factors. The appropriate remedy in such a case is judicial review. It is also not appropriate to use *habeas corpus* to challenge an adjudicator's conclusion that he or she had no jurisdiction to grant bail pending an appeal.[6] Where there is a challenge to the legality of a detention made under paragraph 16 of Schedule 2 to the Immigration Act 1971, it is no answer to an application for *habeas corpus* to rely on the provision of paragraph 18(4) of that Schedule, which provides that 'a person shall be deemed to be in legal custody at any time when he is detained under paragraph 16'. Criticism of views to the contrary expressed in a number of cases[7] was accepted 'unreservedly' in *Ex p Muboyayi*. The object of paragraph 18 is to provide that once an order of detention is made the person named in that order may be kept in custody anywhere the Secretary of State directs.[8] The bail jurisdiction of the Special Immigration Appeals Commission does not oust the *habeas corpus* jurisdiction of the High Court.[9]

1 *B v Barking, Havering and Brentwood Community Health Care NHS Trust* [1999] 1 FLR 106.
2 *R v Secretary of State for the Home Department, ex p Sheikh* (2000) Times, 7 December, CA, upholding Scott-Baker J, 28 July 2000, QBD. See also *R v Governor of Pentonville Prison, ex p Tarling* [1979] 1 WLR 1417; *R v Secretary of State for the Home Department, ex p Momin Ali* [1984] 1 WLR 663.
3 Although see Woolf LJ in *B v Barking* above.
4 Although proportionality is, as has been seen, central to the legality of the detention, and the court is used to examining the duration and purpose of detention as well as jurisdiction to detain, on *habeas corpus*: see *Wasfi Mahmood* [1995] Imm AR 311.
5 *R v Secretary of State for the Home Department, ex p Muboyayi* [1991] 3 WLR 442 at 448F. See also *R v Secretary of State for the Home Department, ex p Cheblak* [1991] 2 All ER 319, CA.
6 *Re Maybasan* [1991] Imm AR 89, QBD.
7 *Cheblak* above; *Re Olusanya* [1988] Imm AR 117, DC.
8 *R v Secretary of State for the Home Department, ex p Greene* [1942] 1 KB 87 at 117, per Goddard LJ.
9 *In the matter of Youseff* (CO 706/1999) 2 March 1999, QBD [2000] 6 (1) ILD.

Paying for detention

17.28 The expense of detention will normally be the responsibility of the immigration authorities. However, carriers may be required to pay the detention costs (up to a maximum of 14 days) of those who are removed after being refused leave to enter,[1] except those passengers holding a certificate of entitlement, entry clearance or work permit,[2] or any person who successfully appeals.[3] Carriers may also be required to pay the detention costs of illegal entrants[4] or absconding or overstaying crew members who are facing removal.[5] No liability arises in the case of those held to be illegal entrants by deception whose leave was not cancelled within 24 hours of its grant.[6] A person facing deportation may find his or her money used to defray the costs of detention.[7]

1   Immigration Act 1971, Sch 2, para 19(1). The 14-day limitation was inserted by the Asylum and Immigration Act 1996, Sch 2, para 8.
2   Immigration Act 1971, Sch 2, para 19(2).
3   Immigration Act 1971, Sch 2, para 19(3).
4   Immigration Act 1971, Sch 2, para 20(1)(a).
5   Immigration Act 1971, Sch 2, para 20(1)(b).
6   Immigration Act 1971, Sch 2, para 20(1A) (inserted by Asylum and Immigration Act 1996 Sch 2, para 9), referring to para 6(2) (cancellation of leave within 24 hours of grant by immigration officer).
7   Immigration Act 1971, Sch 3, para 1(4).

PROVISIONS FOR RELEASE OR BAIL

17.29 In all cases where the Secretary of State or immigration officer have a power to detain, they also have a power to release. The power to grant temporary admission as an alternative to detention has been described in **17.6** and **17.12** above. In addition, almost everyone detained under the Immigration Act 1971 may seek bail under paragraph 22 of Schedule 2 to the 1971 Act (as amended by the Asylum and Immigration Act 1996 and Immigration and Asylum Act 1999), in addition to having a right to two automatic references to the magistrates' court for bail under the provisions of Part III of the 1999 Act (when in force). Those awaiting appeal may apply for bail to the immigration appellate authorities, and there are in addition possibilities of obtaining bail in judicial review or *habeas corpus* proceedings. The grant of bail is distinct from the issue of the lawfulness of the detention[1] (although the issues of eligibility for bail and lawfulness of detention are sometimes difficult to separate). We describe below the provisions for release on bail under the 1971 and 1999 Acts, and in *habeas corpus* and judicial review proceedings.

1   See *In the matter of Yousseff* **17.27** fn 9 above. See also *R v Secretary of State for the Home Department, ex p Gedaine and Demere* (CO 3694/1997) 10 December 1997, QBD, a permission application where continued bail was held arguably unlawful in respect of someone who arguably should not have been detained as an illegal entrant.

New arrivals and those detained for removal: bail under the Immigration Act 1971

17.30 The right to apply for bail has been achieved through the accretion of amendments to Schedule 2 to the Immigration Act 1971 by the Asylum and Immigration Act 1996 and the Immigration and Asylum Act 1999. It applies to new arrivals detained for more than seven days pending examination,[1] and anyone detained pending a decision on cancellation of leave,[2] or after refusal of leave to enter (pending removal directions),[3] or as a suspected illegal entrant or overstayer detained pending the giving of directions,[4] or persons detained following a decision to deport or (when section 54 of the 1999 Act enters into force) a recommendation for deportation or a deportation order.[5] Bail may be granted by a chief immigration officer[6] or police officer not below the rank of inspector[7] or by an adjudicator,[8] on the person's own recogisance (or bail bond in Scotland), with a condition to appear before an immigration officer at a time and place notified in writing,[9] and other conditions may be imposed to secure the appearance of the person bailed at the requisite time and place.[10] Immigration officers and police may arrest those in breach of bail or those they reasonably believe will breach, are breaching or have breached conditions,[11] or on notice in writing of a surety that the released person is likely to breach a condition and that the surety wishes to withdraw.[12] There is provision for the forfeiture of the recognisance or bail bond in case of breach of bail.[13] Bail may also be granted to persons against whom removal directions have been set.[14]

1 Immigration Act 1971, Sch 2, para 22(1)(a), (1B), as amended by Asylum and Immigration Act 1996, Sch 2, para 11(1)- (3).
2 Immigration Act 1971, Sch 2, para 22(1)(aa), inserted by Immigration and Asylum Act 1999, Sch 14, para 63. There is no seven-day waiting requirement in relation to this category, or indeed to anyone except new arrivals seeking leave to enter.
3 Immigration Act 1971, Sch 2, para 22(1)(b).
4 Immigration Act 1971, Sch 2, para 22(1)(b).
5 Immigration and Asylum Act 1999, s 54, extending paras 22-25 of Sch 2 to the Immigration Act 1971 to those detained under the relevant provisions of Sch 3, para 2. Until s 54 is in force, only the court seised of the question of deportation, ie the sentencing court or the appeal court, or the High Court in its inherent jurisdiction, may release on bail: *R v Governor of Holloway Prison, ex p Giambi* [1982] 1 All ER 434. The Court of Appeal may grant bail pending an appeal against a recommendation, under Criminal Appeal Act 1968, s 19: *R v Ofori and Tackie* (1993) 99 Cr App Rep 219.
6 The *Operational Enforcement Manual* (21 December 2000) para 39 sets out criteria for CIO bail including the likelihood of absconding, the likely delay pending a decision or disposal of an appeal, any special reasons for detention, the reliability and standing of sureties and (in deportation cases) the views of the caseworker. It stipulates that normally two sureties will be required, and professional sureties suspected of acting for financial gain, or with a view to evasion, will be rejected. It expects sureties to have a personal connection with the applicant or to be acting on behalf of a reputable organisation with an interest in the detainee's welfare. The 'normal' requirement for two sureties may be unlawful if applied without proper regard to its necessity in individual cases: see **17.35** below.
7 Immigration Act 1971, Sch 2, para 22(1A).
8 Immigration Act 1971, Sch 2, para 22(1A).
9 Immigration Act 1971, Sch 2, para 22(1A).
10 Immigration Act 1971, Sch 2, para 22(2).
11 Immigration Act 1971, Sch 2, para 24(1)(a).
12 Immigration Act 1971, Sch 2, para 24(1)(b).
13 Immigration Act 1971, Sch 2, para 24.
14 Immigration Act 1971, Sch 2, para 34, applying the provisions of paras 22 as to release on bail, and 23-25 relating to arrest, forfeiture of recognisance and bail procedures.

Bail pending appeal

17.31 Persons detained under Schedules 2 and 3 to the Immigration Act 1971 are eligible for bail if they have an in-country appeal pending before the appellate authority. The appeal may be against refusal of leave to enter, a human rights appeal, an appeal against the validity of directions for removal, a destination appeal, an asylum appeal against refusal of leave to enter or removal directions, or an appeal against removal to a 'safe' third country.[1] As with bail pending examination, bail on appeal may be granted by a chief immigration officer or police inspector[2] as well as by an adjudicator[3] or, on appeal to the Immigration Appeal Tribunal, by the Tribunal.[4] There is a statutory right to be released on bail by an adjudicator or the Tribunal where leave to appeal to the Tribunal has been granted (or where leave is not required and the appellant has given notice of appeal to the Tribunal),[5] subject to exceptions on grounds of previous non-compliance, prevention of crime, public health, and necessity to protect those vulnerable by reason of mental health or youth.[6] Otherwise the grant of bail is discretionary. In any case it may be subject to the giving of sureties or recognisance and to conditions.[7] Where removal directions are in force or the power to give directions is exercisable, the consent of the Secretary of State to bail must be obtained.[8] In *Ex p Alghali*[9] the court held that, since directions for removal are of no effect while an appeal is pending, the consent of the Secretary of State is not needed. However, the Immigration and Asylum Act 1999 provides that, although removal directions may not be given pending appeal against refusal of leave to enter[10] and may not be effected pending appeals on validity of removal directions, destination and deportation,[11] the detention and bail provisions of the Immigration Act 1971 apply as if removal directions were in force.[12] The effect of this provision would appear to be to make virtually all bail pending appeal subject to the Secretary of State's consent. Such an interpretation would be an unwarranted restriction on the powers of the appellate authorities to grant bail, and would in all likelihood offend against Art 5(4) of the ECHR, which requires the lawfulness of detention to be decided by a court. We suggest that the better interpretation of the provision is to limit its effect to those cases where, prior to the appeal being lodged, directions for removal had actually been set.[13] Immigration officers and police officers may arrest persons released on bail pending appeal on reasonable grounds for believing that the person is likely to break the conditions of bail, or is breaking or has broken such conditions,[14] or on written notice by a surety that he or she no longer wishes to stand surety because of a belief that the person on bail will not appear.[15] There are powers for the adjudicator or the Tribunal to forfeit any recognisance in whole or in part,[16] in which case a magistrates' court is specified to recover the sum.[17]

1 Immigration Act 1971, Sch 2, para 29(1), as amended by Immigration and Asylum Act 1999, s 169(1), Sch 14, paras 43, 66.
2 Immigration Act 1971, Sch 2, para 29(2).
3 Immigration Act 1971, Sch 2, para 29(3).
4 Immigration Act 1971, Sch 2, para 29(4).
5 Immigration Act 1971, Sch 2, para 29A.
6 These statutory exceptions are set out at Immigration Act 1971, Sch 2, para 30(2), which also provides that release is not mandatory without a proper recognisance or sufficient or satisfactory sureties (or bail in Scotland).
7 Immigration Act 1971, Sch 2, para 29(2), (3) and (5).
8 Immigration Act 1971, Sch 2, para 30(1).
9 *R v Immigration Appeal Tribunal, ex p Alghali* [1984] Imm AR 106, QBD.
10 Immigration and Asylum Act 1999, Sch 4, para 10, referring to appeals under ss 59 and 69(1) of that Act.
11 Immigration and Asylum Act 1999, Sch 4, para 11.
12 Immigration and Asylum Act 1999, Sch 4, para 12.
13 This would be consistent with the heading of this part of the Schedule, 'Stay on directions for removal'.
14 Immigration Act 1971, Sch 2, para 33(1)(a). Even this could offend against the requirements of Art 5(4) of the EHCR; see above.
15 Immigration Act 1971, Sch 2, para 33(1)(b).

16 Immigration Act 1971, Sch 2, para 31(1).
17 Immigration Act 1971, Sch 2, para 31(2)-(5).

17.32 Bail pending appeal to the Court of Appeal from the Tribunal[1] is provided for in section 9A of the Asylum and Immigration Appeals Act 1993. Bail may be granted by a chief immigration officer, a police inspector or the Immigration Appeal Tribunal pending an appeal or an application for leave to appeal.[2] There is a statutory right to bail where leave to appeal has been granted or where the immigrant or asylum seeker is the respondent to the Secretary of State's appeal.[3] The right to bail is subject to the same exceptions as that pending appeal to the Tribunal,[4] and the provisions for arrest for breach of bail and for forfeiture of recognisances also apply.[5]

1 Under Asylum and Immigration Appeals Act 1993, s 9.
2 Asylum and Immigration Appeals Act 1993, s 9A(1), (2), (3).
3 Asylum and Immigration Appeals Act 1993, s (3)(a) and (b).
4 Asylum and Immigration Appeals Act 1993, s 9A(4) applies the relevant provisions of Immigration Act 1971, Sch 2, paras 29 and 30(2) to bail pending appeal to the Court of Appeal.
5 Asylum and Immigration Appeals Act 1993, s 9A(5), applying the provisions of Immigration Act 1971, Sch 2, paras 31-33 (see **17.31** above).

Bail before the Special Immigration Appeals Commission

17.33 The provisions of the Immigration Act 1971 in relation to bail are modified in respect of the following persons:

(i)   those detained under provisions of the Immigration Act 1971 whose detention has been certified by the Secretary of State as necessary in the interests of national security;[1]

(ii)   those detained following a decision to refuse leave to enter on the ground that exclusion is in the interests of national security;[2]

(iii)   those detained following a decision to deport on national security grounds.[3]

The modifications are set out in Schedule 3 to the Special Immigration Appeals Commission Act 1997. In national security cases it is the Special Immigration Appeals Commission which has the power to grant bail, not immigration or police officers or adjudicators.[4] This applies both to new arrivals and to appellants.[5] Provisions as to arrest for breach of bail and forfeiture of recognisances are modified accordingly.[6]

1 Special Immigration Appeals Commission Act 1997, s 3(1), (2)(a).
2 Special Immigration and Appeals Commission Act 1997, s 3(2)(b).
3 Special Immigration and Appeals Commission Act 1997, s 3(2)(c).
4 Special Immigration and Appeals Commission Act 1997, Sch 3, para 1.
5 Special Immigration and Appeals Commission Act 1997, Sch 3, para 4, substituting references to the adjudicator or Tribunal with references to the Commission.
6 Special Immigration and Appeals Commission Act 1997, Sch 3, paras 2-8.

Bail procedure before immigration appellate authority

17.34 The procedure governing bail applications before the immigration appellate authority is governed by Rule 34 of the Immigration and Asylum

(Appeals) Procedure Rules 2000.[1] The application may be made orally or in writing to an immigration officer, a police officer or to the appellate authority.[2] An application in writing must give the full name and date of birth of the applicant; the address where he or she is detained; whether an appeal is pending; a bail address; the amount of any recognisance offered; the names, addresses and occupations of two potential sureties and the amounts offered by them; the grounds of the application; and, if a previous application has been refused, details of any change in circumstances.[3] The application must be signed by the applicant or a representative or (if the detainee is a minor) a person acting on his or her behalf.[4] The rules envisage release without the necessity in all cases of a recognisance or surety.[5] Forms may be prescribed for the recognisance and sureties.[6] There are further detailed provisions on the recording and transmission of decisions to grant bail[7] and for bail in Scotland.[8]

1 SI 2000/2333.
2 Immigration and Asylum (Procedure) Rules 2000 SI 2000/2333, r 34(1).
3 SI 2000/2333, r 34(3).
4 SI 2000/2333, r 34(4).
5 SI 2000/2333, r 34(8).
6 SI 2000/2333, r 34(5).
7 See SI 2000/2333, r 34(6)-(7).
8 SI 2000/2333, r 34(9).

17.35 Guidance Notes for Adjudicators from the Chief Adjudicator on applications for bail[1] refer to a 'common law presumption in favour of bail'.[2] The burden of proof that detention is necessary therefore lies on the Secretary of State, to the standard of balance of probabilities.[3] The notes request adjudicators to have regard to the Immigration Service Instructions,[4] the UNHCR guidelines on detention[5] and the White Paper.[6] The Chief Adjudicator stresses that 'sureties are only required if [the Adjudicator] cannot otherwise be satisfied that the applicant will comply with any conditions imposed and a sense of obligation would reinforce them'.[7] Where sureties are considered necessary then the assessment of the amount of recognisance to be taken from a surety should be based upon the means of that surety.[8] In *Lamin Minteh* the Court of Appeal held unlawful the declared practice of an adjudicator not to grant bail if there were no sureties regardless of whether there was evidence that the applicant was likely to abscond.[9] In *AKB* it was held that an adjudicator had to justify his decision to refuse bail; it was not good enough to say merely that there was a chance the applicant might abscond.[10] The Guidance Notes advise adjudicators to consider bail in three stages: whether bail should be granted in principle, subject to satisfactory conditions; whether sureties are necessary; and whether those offered are satisfactory.[11] The applicant should attend all hearings for renewal of bail, but sureties need not do so if they have been given permission not to attend and have written indicating their willingness to continue.[12] A failure to comply with a residence or reporting condition is not a reason for instituting forfeiture proceedings, but an adjudicator may take such a failure into account in renewing bail.[13]

1 Bail: Guidance notes for Adjudicators from the Chief Adjudicator, communicated to Immigration Law Practitioners' Association, 22 September 2000.
2 Guidance notes above, para 1.4
3 Guidance notes above, para 2.51
4 See **17.7** above.
5 See **17.10** above.

6 See **17.8** above.
7 Guidance notes above, para 2.2.2.
8 Guidance notes above, para 2.3.2.
9 *R v Secretary of State for the Home Department, ex p Lamin Minteh* (396/5400/D) 8 March 1996, CA.
10 *R v Secretary of State for the Home Department, ex p AKB* [1996] 3 (2)ILD, QBD.
11 Guidance notes above, para 2.7.3.
12 Guidance notes above, para 3.1.
13 Guidance notes above, para 3.2.

Procedures before the Special Immigration Appeals Commission

17.36 Procedures for bail hearings before the Special Immigration Appeals Commission are more formal than other bail hearings, and are contained in the Commission's Procedure Rules.[1] The Rules provide that within 42 days the Secretary of State provides a summary of the facts relating to the decision and reasons for it, with grounds of opposition and a statement of evidence, and takes any objection to the disclosure of material to the applicant, with reasons.[2] A bail application must be in writing and must contain particulars of the full name of the applicant, the address where and reasons why he or she is detained, the date of any notice of appeal, a bail address, the amount of any recognisance offered, the names, addresses and occupations of two potential sureties and the amounts they might offer, the grounds of the application and any change in circumstances since a previous unsuccessful application.[3] There is no power to detain simply on national security grounds,[4] although the statutory presumption in favour of bail contained in section 46 of the Immigration and Asylum Act 1999 does not apply,[5] and national security concerns have been held relevant to the lawfulness of continued detention.[6]

1 Special Immigration Appeals Commission (Procedure) Rules 1998, SI 1998/1881, rr 26 and 27.
2 SI 1998/1881, r 26(4), applying r 10 (time limit for Secretary of State's reply).
3 SI 1998/1881, r 26(5)
4 The applicants in *R v Secretary of State for the Home Department, ex p Hany Youssef* (CO 706/1999, CO 1649/1999), Egyptian nationals detained under national security certificates, were detained for removal, as was Mr Chahal; all were released, Mr Chahal immediately following the ECtHR's ruling that removal would breach art 3 of the ECHR: *Chahal v UK* (1996) 23 EHRR 413.
5 Immigration and Asylum Act 1999, s 46(4).
6 *R v Secretary of State for the Home Department, ex p Ben Taher*, 24 September 1999, QBD.

17.37 The Immigration and Asylum Act 1999 empowers the Secretary of State for the Home Department by regulation to make new provisions in relation to bail applications for those detained under the Immigration Act 1971.[1] The regulations may confer a right to bail in prescribed circumstances[2] (to end the anomaly of a right to bail on a reference[3] but none on an application), may create or transfer jurisdiction for bail hearings,[4] provide where bail applications may be held,[5] the procedure to be followed[6] and the circumstances and conditions where an applicant may be released on bail.[7] They may amend or repeal any enactment.[8] The Lord Chancellor must approve the regulations.[9] None have been made, since this Part of the Act was not in force at the time of writing.

1 Immigration and Asylum Act 1999, s 53(1) (not yet in force). The Secretary of State must have regard to the desirability of making provision similar to those relating to references under s 44, in making regs: s 53(5).

2 Immigration and Asylum Act 1999, s 53(2).
3 See **17.40** below.
4 Immigration and Asylum Act 1999, s 53(3)(a).
5 Immigration and Asylum Act 1999, s 53(3)(b).
6 Immigration and Asylum Act 1999, s 53(3)(c).
7 Immigration and Asylum Act 1999, s 53(3)(d).
8 Immigration and Asylum Act 1999, s 53(3)(e).
9 Immigration and Asylum Act 1999, s 53(6). In Scotland the consent of the Scottish Ministers must be obtained.

Bail under the Immigration and Asylum Act 1999

17.38 The Immigration and Asylum Act 1999 gives a statutory right to bail to most people detained under the Immigration Act 1971, effected (i) by a system of automatic bail hearings and (ii) by a statutory presumption in favour of bail.[1] Section 44 of the 1999 Act provides for automatic bail hearings for anyone detained under the 1971 Act except for:

- those also detained under provisions other than the Immigration Act 1971[2] (for example, in police custody, in custody pursuant to a criminal court order or sentence or in Mental Health Act detention);
- those liable to deportation as a result of a recommendation by a court;[3] and
- those who have given written notice that they do not wish their case to be referred to a court for a routine bail hearing.[4]

The automatic referrals are additional to existing rights to apply for bail under the 1971 Act.[5] The bail hearings are in the appellate authority if an appeal is pending,[6] otherwise in the magistrates' court.[7] Those detained on national security grounds benefit from automatic referrals, but in such cases all bail hearings are in the Special Immigration Appeals Commission.[8] No time limits are prescribed by the Act for making a reference or holding a hearing before the Special Immigration Appeals Commission,[9] but in all other cases the Secretary of State must refer the question of bail to the court by the eighth day after detention,[10] and the first bail hearing must take place before the tenth day following detention.[11] If that application is unsuccessful, and there is no request to dispense with a second referral,[12] such a referral must be made between the 33rd and the 36th day of detention,[13] and the hearing must take place before the 38th day following detention.[14] If a reference is not made within the statutory time limits, the Secretary of State must refer it and the court must deal with it as soon as reasonably practicable.[15] Regulations may modify the requirements of the section where a court adjourns for medical or other reports or for any other reason,[16] and may dispense with the second referral in defined circumstances.[17]

1 The government announced that this part (Pt III) of the Immigration and Asylum Act 1999 would come into force in October 2001.
2 Immigration and Asylum Act 1999, s 44(3)(a).
3 Immigration and Asylum Act 1999, s 44(3)(b).
4 Immigration and Asylum Act 1999, s 44(3)(c).
5 Immigration and Asylum Act 1999, s 44(16).
6 Immigration and Asylum Act 1999, s 44(12)(a).
7 Immigration and Asylum Act 1999, s 44(12)(c). In Scotland this residual category of automatic bail hearings is before an adjudicator.
8 Immigration and Asylum Act 1999, s 44(12)(b).

9 See Immigration and Asylum Act 1999, s 44(4)(a), (5)(a), (8)(a), all of which provide that
   the reference must be made and heard in accordance with the Commission's own rules,
   which have not yet been amended to cover bail referrals.
10 Immigration and Asylum Act 1999, s 44(4)(b). Time runs from the day following that on
   which the person was detained: see wording of sections.
11 Immigration and Asylum Act 1999, s 44(7)(b).
12 See Immigration and Asylum Act 1999, s 44(9).
13 See Immigration and Asylum Act 1999, s 44(6), (5)(b).
14 Immigration and Asylum Act 1999, s 44(8)(b).
15 This applies to both the first and the second reference: Immigration and Asylum Act 1999,
   s 44(10), (11).
16 Under Immigration and Asylum Act 1999, s 44(14).
17 Immigration and Asylum Act 1999, s 44(15).

17.39 Bail hearings under the referral provisions may be heard in any place
specified in directions issued by the Secretary of State with the approval of the
Lord Chancellor,[1] including detention centres and prisons.[2] Rules of procedure
for bail hearings under Part III of the Immigration and Asylum Act 1999[3] must
require the Secretary of State to notify the detained person and any representative
of the date, time and place of the hearing.[4] A magistrates' court hearing a
reference under section 44 must sit in open court unless the detained person is
an asylum seeker and the court considers there are compelling reasons for sitting
in private, or the court considers it necessary in the interests of justice to sit in
private.[5] But the detained person does not have to be physically present at the
court hearing the reference if he or she is able to see, hear and be seen and
heard by means of a live TV link; in such a case the court may, following
representations from the parties, direct that the detainee is to be treated as
present.

1 Immigration and Asylum Act 1999, s 45(1), (4).
2 Immigration and Asylum Act 1999, s 45(2)(c) and (d).
3 Made by the Lord Chancellor under s 144 of the Magistrates Courts Act 1980 or northern
   Ireland equivalent: Immigration and Asylum Act 1999, s 51(7).
4 Immigration and Asylum Act 1999, s 51(1).
5 Immigration and Asylum Act 1999, s 51(4). These provisions are similar to (although not
   identical with) the exceptions to a public hearing in art 6 of the ECHR.

17.40 Section 46 of the Immigration and Asylum Act 1999 enacts a general
right to bail in references under section 44 of the Act. But there are many
statutory exceptions. Bail need not be granted to those whose detention has
been authorised on national security grounds,[1] nor where a recognisance, bail
bond or security has been imposed for the detainee's release[2] which has not
been complied with.[3] Bail need not be granted where the court is satisfied that
there are substantial grounds for believing that if released on bail a detainee
would:

(i)   fail to comply with a condition of bail or of a recognisance or bail bond;[4]
(ii)   commit an offence punishable by imprisonment;[5]
(iii)   be likely to cause a danger to public health;[6] or
(iv)   alone or with others, be a serious threat to the maintenance of public
        order.[7]

1 Immigration and Asylum Act 1999, s 46(4), referring to Special Immigration Appeals
   Commission Act 1997, s 3(2).
2 Under Immigration and Asylum Act 1999, s 47(1); see below.
3 Immigration and Asylum Act 1999, s 46(1)(b).

4   Immigration and Asylum Act 1999, s 46(2)(a).
5   Immigration and Asylum Act 1999, s 46(2)(b). The question whether an offence is punishable with imprisonment is to be decided without reference to statutory restrictions on the imprisonment of young or first offenders: s 46(5).
6   Immigration and Asylum Act 1999, s 46(2)(c).
7   Immigration and Asylum Act 1999, s 46(2)(d).

17.41 Further exceptions to the right to bail apply where the court is satisfied that the detainee:

(i)   is or has been knowingly involved with others in a concerted attempt by all or some of them to enter the UK in breach of immigration law;[1]
(ii)   is suffering from a psychiatric disorder and continued detention is necessary for the protection of him- or herself or others;[2]
(iii)   is under 18 and no satisfactory arrangements have been made for his or her care on release;[3]
(iv)   is required to submit to an examination by an immigration officer under paragraph 2 or 2A of Schedule 2 to the Immigration Act 1971[4] and there is no relevant decision which the officer is in a position to take;[5]
(v)   is the subject of directions for removal which are in force.[6]

The Secretary of State for the Home Department may add or restrict these exceptions to the right to bail, by order.[7]

1   Immigration and Asylum Act 1999, s 46(3)(a).
2   Immigration and Asylum Act 1999, s 46(3)(b).
3   Immigration and Asylum Act 1999, s 46(3)(c). Local authority social services departments have a duty under the Children Act 1989 towards unaccompanied minors and this exception should only apply where the appropriate social services have failed in their statutory duty. See the policy set out in the White Paper *Fairer, Faster and Firmer—A Modern Approach to Immigration and Asylum* **17.8** fn 1 above.
4   To determine whether leave to enter is required, will be granted, or (if leave has been granted before entry) should be cancelled.
5   This rather clumsily drafted exception appears to apply in all circumstances where a decision on leave to enter is outstanding. Clarification was provided by Lord Falconer of Thoronton (605 HL Official Report (5th series) col 894) that it would not apply where the Home Office has simply failed to make a decision, but 'might apply in the case of a person who claims asylum on arrival and fails to give his true identity or where there is no suitable release address. Such a person could not be given or refused leave and would not, on the information available, be suitable for the grant of temporary admission.'
6   Immigration and Asylum Act 1999, s 46(3)(e). This could not apply where an appeal has been lodged, whose effect is to suspend removal directions: see Sch 4, para 11 (although arguably the deeming provision of para 12 applies here to override the right to bail).
7   Immigration and Asylum Act 1999, s 46(8).

17.42 Section 47 of the Immigration and Asylum Act 1999 empowers the court to require a recognisance or bail bond when releasing a person under section 46 of the Act.[1] The court may additionally require a security from a surety (money to be paid into the court prior to the applicant's release), a power not contained in the Immigration Act 1971.[2] It may also impose conditions requiring the person to appear before the court, Commission, authority or immigration officer at specified times and places,[3] and other conditions appearing to the court to be necessary to secure the appearance of the bailed person.[4] A person released on bail under section 46 may be subject to restrictions as to employment and occupation as a condition of bail.[5] Where an individual fails to comply with mandatory bail conditions,[6] a court may declare the recognisance forfeit and order the surety to pay part or all of the sum offered.[7] In the case of a bail bond, the sum can be forfeited if any of the conditions, not just mandatory conditions, are breached.[8] As in the 1971 Act provisions, if the court ordering forfeiture is not a magistrates' court, the matter must be transferred to one (or the sheriff court, in Scotland), for recovery of the sum.[9] There are further detailed provisions for forfeiture of securities.[10] The powers of arrest for breach of bail under the 1999 Act[11] reflect the provisions contained in the Immigration Act 1971.[12]

1 Immigration and Asylum Act 1999, s 47(1)(a).
2 Immigration and Asylum Act 1999, s 47(1)(b). These powers must only be imposed if the court considers it necessary to secure compliance with a condition of appearance before the court or the immigration officer: s 47(2).
3 Immigration and Asylum Act 1999, s 47(3), (4), (5). The conditions are slightly different depending on the circumstances.
4 Immigration and Asylum Act 1999, s 47(6).
5 Immigration and Asylum Act 1999, s 47(11), (12).
6 Defined by s 48(2) as conditions to appear before the court, Commission, authority or immigration officer (ie not conditions of residence or occupation).
7 Immigration and Asylum Act 1999, s 48(1).
8 Immigration and Asylum Act 1999, s 48(6).
9 Immigration and Asylum Act 1999, s 48(3), (7).
10 Immigration and Asylum Act 1999, s 49.
11 Immigration and Asylum Act 1999, s 50.
12 Immigration Act 1971, Sch 2, paras 24 and 33.

Second and subsequent applications or references

17.43 If a person is refused bail on a reference under section 44 of the Immigration and Asylum Act 1999, or on an application to the appellate authority under the Immigration Act 1971 or the Asylum and Immigration Appeals Act 1993, or to the Commission, on the second reference or application the applicant is not restricted in the legal or factual arguments in support of bail, but on any subsequent reference or application, the court need not hear any argument (whether on the facts or on the law) which the applicant has raised previously.[1]

1 Immigration and Asylum Act 1999, s 51(2) and (3).

Bail pending judicial review or habeas corpus

17.44 The statutory scheme for release on bail is, as has been seen above, fairly comprehensive, and will be even more so once the bail provisions of Part III of the Immigration and Asylum Act 1999 are in force. But there are notable *lacunae*, such as the inability to apply for bail for new arrivals until seven days have elapsed.[1] In the past the higher courts have shown themselves willing to entertain bail applications pursuant to their inherent jurisdiction pending the hearing of an application for judicial review, notwithstanding the availability of bail from the appellate authority. In *Ex p Turkoglu*[2] the Court of Appeal reviewed the position regarding bail in judicial review cases and held that the High Court has jurisdiction to grant bail on an application for permission to apply for judicial review or a substantive application. Where the High Court judge refuses bail in such a case, appeal lies to the Court of Appeal. But bail must be ancillary to some other proceeding, and if the High Court refuses permission for judicial review it is *functus officio* and therefore has no jurisdiction to grant bail. The Court of Appeal has its own inherent jurisdiction on a renewed application for permission. Where there is a statutory right to apply for bail, it should generally be sought from the appellate authority, but in *Ex p Kelso*,[3] Collins J held that, where such an application could result in a further application for judicial review if returned to an adjudicator who refused bail or imposed unsatisfactory conditions, it was appropriate for the High Court to entertain the application.

1   Immigration Act 1971, Sch 2, para 22(1B).
2   *R v Secretary of State for the Home Department, ex p Turkoglu* [1988] QB 398, [1987] 2 All ER 823.
3   *R v Secretary of State for the Home Department, ex p Kelso* [1998] INLR 603, QBD.

17.45   In *Kelso*[1] Collins J also retrieved the High Court's original jurisdiction to grant bail on the merits (as opposed to a jurisdiction to determine the reasonableness of detention on *Wednesbury* grounds), by adverting to the distinction drawn in *Vilvarajah*[2] between detention in respect of which statutory bail was not available and detention in respect of which it was. Only in the former case, where the discretion to grant temporary admission was not subject to appeal, was the jurisdiction to be limited to *Wednesbury* review. In the latter case, the court's inherent jurisdiction allowed it to decide for itself on the material before it whether bail should be granted as an adjunct to the proceedings, and virtually every immigration detention now fell within that category.[3] *Kelso* was approved by the Court of Appeal in *Doku*,[4] a case involving detention pursuant to a recommendation for deportation.

1   *R v Secretary of State for the Home Department, ex p Kelso* [1998] INLR 603, QBD.
2   *Vilvarajah v Secretary of State for the Home Department* [1990] Imm AR 457, CA.
3   *Kelso* above, at 606.
4   *R (Doku) v Secretary of State for the Home Department* (C/2000/3360) 30 November 2000, CA.

Chapter 18

IMMIGRATION APPEALS

BACKGROUND AND STRUCTURE OF THE APPEALS SYSTEM

Background

18.1 'In this day and age a right of access to a tribunal or other adjudicative mechanism established by the state is as important and fundamental as a right of access to the ordinary courts.'[1] These words of the Court of Appeal in striking down a procedural rule for unfairness demonstrate how vital appellate procedures have become in the field of immigration and asylum in the 30-odd years since their creation. The current system of immigration appeals, with its proliferation of appeal rights, exclusions, restrictions, jurisdictions and procedures, bears little resemblance to the primitive and informal system created by the Immigration Appeals Act 1969, although its basic skeleton, the two tiers of Immigration Appeal Tribunal and adjudicators, survives. The 1969 Act, passed in response to the Wilson Committee report,[2] provided Commonwealth citizens (but not aliens) with appeals against exclusion at ports; refusal to grant entry certificates or visas; refusal to withdraw a standing instruction for a person's removal; refusal to vary conditions favourably to the immigrant; variation of conditions unfavourably to the immigrant; decisions to deport or remove; and refusal to revoke deportation orders. The appellate system thus set up was not intended in any way to undermine an effective immigration control. It was calculated to ease the fears of racial discrimination that immigration restrictions, imposed on Commonwealth immigrants for the first time only seven years previously in 1962, had provoked by seeing that the controls were imposed fairly; to provide 'a sense of protection against

806

oppression and injustice, and ... reassurance against fears of arbitrary action on the part of the Immigration Service',[3] and to ensure a more consistent and rational decision-making process. It was intended to be informal and largely inquisitorial; legal representation was not envisaged as necessary; it was for Commonwealth citizens only; and it did not provide appeals against deportation or other restrictive action 'on grounds which are primarily of a political nature'.[4]

1 *R v Secretary of State for the Home Department, ex p Saleem (Asifa)* [2000] Imm AR 529, [2000] INLR 413, upholding Hooper J at [1999] INLR 621. See **18.171** below.
2 Committee on Immigration Appeals, set up in 1966, chaired by Sir Roy Wilson QC (Cmnd 3387, 1967).
3 Cmnd 3387 (fn 2 above) para 85.
4 Cmnd 3387 (fn 2 above) para 191.

18.2 The Immigration Act 1971 adopted the scheme of the Immigration Appeals Act 1969 and extended it to aliens, who had hitherto had no appeal rights. There were, however, important gaps in the scheme. Those who were refused leave to enter and had no entry clearance could exercise their rights of appeal only from abroad - a devastating disadvantage in asylum cases. There was no appeal against a proposed deportation where the decision had been made following a recommendation of a criminal court, nor against a decision to remove those deemed illegal entrants. Persons excluded, refused leave to enter or remain or subjected to deportation action on national security or political grounds had no right of appeal, only a right to an extra-advisory procedure involving no disclosure of the grounds of proposed exclusion.[1]

1 See below **18.186** and the fourth edition of this book **15.52-15.57**.

18.3 The Immigration Act 1971 provided suspensive appeal rights to everyone who was subject to deportation as an overstayer or for breaching conditions of stay, in acknowledgment of the fact that, unlike illegal entrants, they had been admitted to the UK lawfully and so had a right to be heard before removal. The undermining of that distinction began in 1988, with the introduction of restricted rights of appeal for those whose last entry to the UK was within seven years of the decision to deport.[1] Adjudicators were henceforth precluded from reviewing the merits of the deportation decision in such cases.[2]

1 Immigration Act 1988, s 5; exceptions to the seven-year rule were laid by statutory instrument, but resulted in arbitrary distinctions between those who had a right of appeal and those who did not.
2 For a salutary case of the exercise of such discretion, see *Idrish* [1985] Imm AR 155. The removal of a right of appeal immediately led to harsher decisions being taken: see observations of Lord Griffiths in *R v Secretary of State for the Home Department, ex p Oladehinde* [1991] 1 AC 254, [1990] 3 All ER 393, [1990] 3 WLR 797.

18.4 By 1993 the big issue in immigration law was asylum. The lack of suspensive appeal rights for refused asylum seekers who claimed on arrival had led to litigation at the European Court of Human Rights.[1] The Asylum and Immigration Appeals Act 1993 introduced rights of appeal before removal for nearly all asylum seekers, including those who were to be removed to an EU member state through which they had travelled to get to the UK, but removed the appeal rights of rejected visitors, short-term students and all applicants who did not possess either the requisite documents or the necessary age or nationality qualifications.

1   *Vilvarajah v UK* (1991) 14 EHRR 248. The judgment, which appeared after the 1993 Bill was published, in fact upheld the government's submission that judicial review of an adverse asylum decision was an effective remedy for the purposes of art 13 to prevent a breach of art 3 (exposure to torture or inhuman or degrading treatment by return to Sri Lanka), reversing the Commission on this point.

18.5 The accelerating integration of the UK into Europe marked in 1993 by the Treaty of European Union, and by proliferating inter-governmental measures on immigration and, more particularly, on asylum, had its impact on immigration appeals. The Immigration (EEA) Order 1994, SI 1994/1895 partially resolved the problem of EEA nationals and their families who, by virtue of the fact of not requiring leave to enter under the Immigration Act 1971, found themselves deprived of appeal rights against exclusion, removal and deportation. The embarrassing number of successful appeals against the removal of asylum seekers to the 'safe' countries of the EU,[1] on the grounds that *refoulement* from these countries to the country of persecution could not be ruled out, led to the abolition of the in-country appeal for this group of asylum seekers in the Asylum and Immigration Act 1996.[2] That Act, the first product of a co-ordinated European approach to asylum,[3] also curtailed the appeal rights of others, whose appeals were 'certified' for a variety of reasons, including the country they fled from, the timing of their claim and its nature.[4] The latter group of claimants had a first instance appeal but none to the Immigration Appeal Tribunal. Neither the Asylum and Immigration Appeals Act 1993 nor the Asylum and Immigration Act 1996 brought appeal rights to persons who could not claim to be refugees but whose removal arguably breached fundamental human rights, an omission which led to the proliferation of challenges to removal by judicial review, with particular reference to Article 3 and Article 8 of the ECHR.[5]

1   Under *ad hoc* arrangements preceding the Dublin Convention, which came into force in 1997: see **12.125**ff.
2   Sections 2–3.
3   See eg the Resolution on manifestly unfounded applications for asylum, anticipating the coming into force of the Dublin Convention, produced by the EU member states' Ad Hoc Group on Immigration and agreed at the immigration ministers' meeting of 30 November 1992, whose principles were reflected in Asylum and Immigration Act 1996, s 1 (now Immigration and Asylum Act 1999, Sch 4, para 9).
4   Asylum and Immigration Act 1996, s 1, amending Asylum and Immigration Appeals Act 1993, Sch 2, para 5.
5   See eg *R v Secretary of State for the Home Department, ex p Kebbeh* (30 April 1998, Hidden J) on removal of disabled applicant to destitution and despair in Gambia (Art 3); *Ahmed and Patel v Secretary of State for the Home Department* [1998] INLR 570; *R v Secretary of State for the Home Department, ex p Gangadeen* [1998] Imm AR 106; *R v Secretary of State for the Home Department, ex p Ali (Arman)* [1999] INLR 89 (art 8).

18.6 In response to the European Court of Human Rights' condemnation in *Chahal*[1] of the lack of judicial scrutiny of national security-based deportation and detention, and similar criticisms by the European Court of Justice in *Shingara and Radiom*,[2] an appeal against exclusion, refusal of leave to enter or remain, or deportation on political or security grounds was introduced by the Special Immigration Appeals Commission Act 1997.[3] The intention was specifically to protect the UK against further findings of violations of ECHR Article 3 in such cases—although the machinery for a direct human rights appeal (as opposed to an asylum appeal) was not provided until the Human

Rights Act 1998 and the human rights appeal of the Immigration and Asylum Act 1999 came simultaneously into force on 2 October 2000.

1   *Chahal v UK* (1996) 23 EHRR 413.
2   C-65/95, C-111/95, [1997] 3 CMLR 703.
3   See **18.186** below.

18.7 The Immigration and Asylum Act 1999 completed the process, begun in 1988, of removing the distinction between illegal entrants on the one hand, and overstayers and those in breach of conditions on the other, by taking the latter out of the deportation process altogether, in the process removing rights of appeal. Only those who complain that their removal will breach their human rights or is racially discriminatory will have an appeal, benefitting from the free-standing human rights appeal introduced into the 1999 Act as a result of the long overdue incorporation of the rights set out in the European Convention on Human Rights[1] into UK law and the consequential amendments of the Race Relations Act 1976. Section 65 brings a human rights and anti-discrimination jurisdiction to all immigration appeals, to be exercised where the effect of any immigration decision is to breach the appellant's human rights or where it constitutes race discrimination.[2] To prevent what are seen as abusive and repetitious applications and multiple appeals, the 1999 Act introduces, in tandem with the human rights appeal (but not limited to it), the one-stop appeal system, whose governing idea is the simple one that all issues relating to a person's right to stay in the UK should be dealt with, wherever possible, in one appeal. The idea is simple but the procedures designed to effect it, in the Act[3] and the regulations,[4] give rise to complication and obscurity.

1   Convention for the protection of human rights and fundamental freedoms 1950. Articles 2–12, 14, 16–18 and the First and Sixth Protocols form Sch 1 to the Human Rights Act 1998.
2   Immigration and Asylum Act 1999, s 65 as amended by the Race Relations (Amendment) Act 2000.
3   Immigration and Asylum Act 1999, ss 73–77.
4   The Immigration and Asylum Appeals (One-stop Procedure) Regulations 2000, SI 2000/2244.

18.8 The human rights appeal bridges the gap in international protection in that (subject to procedural requirements) it ensures that human rights or discrimination arguments can be aired in all cases prior to removal. The appellate authorities' jurisdiction is enhanced by their role as public authorities for the purposes of the Human Rights Act 1998, which obliges them to disregard subordinate legislation (immigration regulations and procedural rules) which are incompatible with Convention rights.[1] Another effect of incorporation may be increased scrutiny of appeal procedures by the higher courts to ensure that they fulfil the criteria of independence and fairness required not only by the common law but by the ECHR; if not via Article 6,[2] then by the necessity for procedural safeguards to protect the substantive rights.[3]

1   Human Rights Act 1998, s 6. The duty does not apply if the secondary legislation is in those terms because of primary legislation.
2   The jurisprudence of the European Court of Human Rights has consistently failed to recognise the admission and expulsion of aliens, including asylum, as a 'civil right' under Art 6: from *Uppal v UK* (1979) 3 EHRR 391 to *Maaouia v France* (App No 39652, 5 October 2000). See **8.51** above.
3   See *Chahal v UK* (1996) 23 EHRR 413; *Huvig v France* (1990) 12 EHRR 528, paras 31–35.

Structure of the appeal system

18.9 In ordinary cases (those not involving national security) there are two tiers of appeals. The first-instance appeal is in all cases to an adjudicator, sitting at Taylor House in London or at one of the regional centres located in Feltham, Birmingham, Bromley, Glasgow, Havant, Leeds and Manchester. There are periodic sittings in Cardiff, Belfast and Edinburgh. In addition, there are satellite centres in many Crown, county and magistrates' courts.[1] Thereafter, in all cases save certified asylum appeals,[2] there is a further appeal to a tribunal of up to three members which usually sits in London. Generally, leave to appeal to the Tribunal is required,[3] with the possibility of judicial review if leave is refused. Thereafter, where there has been a final decision there is a right of appeal to the Court of Appeal or Court of Session on a point of law if leave is granted.[4] There is power both at adjudicator and Tribunal level to review their own decisions to pre-empt judicial review challenges.[5]

1 The full list is available on the Immigration Appellate Authority website: www.iaa.gov.uk/Locations.
2 See Immigration and Asylum Act 1999, Sch 4, para 9(2); **12.163** above.
3 Immigration and Asylum Appeals (Procedure) Rules 2000, SI 2000/2333, r 16; leave to appeal must be given where a person seeking entry holds an entry clearance or certificate of entitlement (Immigration and Asylum Act 1999, Sch 4, para 7).
4 Immigration and Asylum Act 1999, Sch 4, para 23.
5 SI 2000/2244, rr 14, 17.

Adjudicators

18.10 Adjudicators were originally appointed by the Home Office, leading to concerns about their independence. The Lord Chancellor's Department took over the appointments in 1987.[1] They are required to be barristers, advocates, or solicitors of seven years' standing, or to have appropriate legal experience.[2] Full-time adjudicators may work until the age of 70,[3] while part-time adjudicators are appointed on one-year renewable contracts (now seen as potentially problematic in relation to the issue of independence).[4] The Chief Adjudicator is responsible for the allocation of cases to adjudicators and other administrative matters and also hears appeals. His or her powers and duties include the issue of practice directions,[5] including directions that in a specified case or class of cases an appeal is to be heard by more than one adjudicator,[6] review of a non-appealable decision which is subject to judicial review,[7] and setting aside determinations in cases remitted by the Tribunal and making arrangements for their rehearing.[8] The Lord Chancellor must appoint a Chief Adjudicator[9] and may appoint a Deputy Chief Adjudicator and Regional Adjudicators, with duties assigned by the Chief Adjudicator.[10] During 2001, the establishment for immigration appeals is one Chief Adjudicator, one Deputy Chief Adjudicator, 82 full-timers and approximately 300 part-timers who are expected to serve a minimum of 50 days per annum. This marks a considerable increase in the establishment since 1990, when there were 13 full-timers and 70 part-timers. The 1993 Act provided for Special Adjudicators (adjudicators given training in refugee law) to determine asylum appeals but the 1999 Act removed this category and returned to the uniform status of adjudicator to hear all appeals including those with asylum or human rights or discrimination elements.

1 The Transfer of Functions (Immigration Appeals) Order 1987, S1 1987/465. The argument as to independence on this basis has now re-emerged over the appointment by the Home Office of asylum support adjudicators to hear appeals from the refusal of Home Office-provided support under the Immigration and Asylum Act 1999, Pt VI.
2 A new requirement contained in the Immigration and Asylum Act 1999, Sch 2, para 2, although in practice only legally qualified adjudicators have been appointed since 1987.
3 Extendable to 75: see Immigration and Asylum Act 1999, Sch 2, para 3.
4 See *Starrs v Procurator Fiscal (Linlithgow)* 1999 SCCR 1052, 8 BHCR 1. The European Court of Justice held that immigration adjudicators were held to have sufficient guarantees of independence to constitute 'a court or tribunal' in *Nour El-Yassini v Secretary of State for the Home Department* [1999] INLR 131.
5 Immigration and Asylum Act 1999, Sch 4, para 5(2).
6 Reversing *Mebratu* (15537), IAT.
7 Immigration and Asylum Appeals (Procedure) Rules 2000, SI 2000/2333, r 14.
8 SI 2000/2333, r 21(2).
9 Immigration and Asylum Act 1999, s 77(2).
10 Immigration and Asylum Act 1999, Sch 3, para 1.

Immigration Appeal Tribunal

18.11 Members of the Immigration Appeal Tribunal are appointed by the Lord Chancellor.[1] There is a President and a Deputy President,[2] and as many members as the Lord Chancellor determines.[3] Some members are without legal qualifications, but the rest are barristers, advocates or solicitors of at least seven years' standing, or persons with appropriate legal experience (usually academic lawyers).[4] The President may issue practice directions,[5] including directions as to the number and qualification of members exercising the Tribunal's jurisdiction in specified cases or classes of cases.[6] A legally qualified member must conduct the review of a Tribunal decision which is challenged by judicial review,[7] and such a member or the President, acting alone, decides applications for leave to appeal from the Tribunal to the Court of Appeal or the Court of Session.[8]

1 Immigration and Asylum Act 1999, Sch 2, para 1.
2 Immigration and Asylum Act 1999, Sch 2, para 2.
3 The current establishment is 11 vice-presidents, 13 full-time and six part-time legally qualified chairs, and 34 members, most of whom are legally qualified. (Figures from Court Service website at www.iaa.gov.uk.)
4 Immigration and Asylum Act 1999, Sch 2, para 1.
5 Immigration and Asylum Act 1999, Sch 4, para 5(1).
6 Immigration and Asylum Act 1999, Sch 2, para 6.
7 Immigration and Asylum (Procedure) Rules 2000, SI 2000/2333, r 17(3).
8 SI 2000/2244, r 25(4).

The Special Appeals Commission

18.12 The Lord Chancellor also appoints members of the Commission, established in 1997 to hear appeals involving national security.[1] It is 'duly constituted' by three members, of whom one holds or has held high judicial office,[2] and one is or has been Chief Adjudicator or a legally qualified member of the Immigration Appeal Tribunal.[3] The third member of the Commission needs no particular qualification by statute, but during the passage of the Bill the minister indicated that the third member would 'have some experience of national security matters and will be familiar with the evidence that is likely to be presented to the commission'.[4]

1 Special Immigration Appeals Commission Act 1997, Sch 1, para 1.
2 Special Immigration Appeals Commission Act 1997, Sch 1, para 5(a). This means a High Court or Court of Appeal judge. The current incumbent is Potts J.
3 Special Immigration Appeals Commission Act 1997, Sch 1, para 5(b).
4 301 HC Official Report (6th series) col 1033, 26 November 1997.

RIGHTS OF APPEAL

18.13 The circumstances in which an appeal may be made are set out in sections 59–71 of and Schedule 4 to the Immigration and Asylum Act 1999, Regulations 29–31 of the Immigration (European Economic Area) Regulations 2000,[1] and in national security cases, the Special Immigration Appeals Commission Act 1997, sections 2 and 2A. The rules of procedure for both adjudicators and the Tribunal are contained in the Immigration and Asylum Appeals (Procedure) Rules 2000[2] and (for the one-stop procedure) the Immigration and Asylum Appeals (One-Stop Procedure) Regulations 2000.[3] Rules regarding the service of notices are contained in the Immigration Appeals (Notices) Regulations 2000.[4] Appeals to the Special Immigration Appeals Commission have their own special procedure rules.[5] Subject to the exceptions and qualifications discussed below, appeals can be made in the following cases:

(1)   against refusal of entry, entry clearance and other exclusions from the UK (Immigration and Asylum Act 1999, section 59);

(2)   against refusals to extend leave and curtailment of leave (Immigration and Asylum Act 1999, section 61);

(3)   against decisions to deport on conducive grounds and refusals to revoke deportation orders (Immigration and Asylum Act 1999, section 63);

(4)   against the validity of directions to remove someone as an illegal entrant, an overstayer, for breach of conditions of stay, or as an overstaying member of a ship or aircrew (Immigration and Asylum Act 1999, section 66);

(5)   against removal to a particular country or destination (Immigration and Asylum Act 1999, section 67);

(6)   against refusal of asylum (Immigration and Asylum Act 1999, section 69);

(7)   against a certificate that an asylum claimant may make his or her claim in another country (Immigration and Asylum Act 1999, section 71, referring to sections 11 and 12);

(8)   against a decision relating to any of the above which is in breach of the appellant's human rights or racially discriminates (Immigration and Asylum Act 1999, section 65).

1 SI 2000/2326.
2 SI 2000/2333.
3 SI 2000/2244.
4 SI 2000/2246, as amended by the Immigration Appeals (Notices) (Amendment) Regulations 2001, SI 2001/868.
5 Special Immigration Appeals Commission (Procedure) Rules 1998, SI 1998/1881, as amended by the Special Immigration Appeals Commission (Procedure) (Amendment) Rules 2000, SI 2000/1849.

18.14 In addition, EEA nationals and their family members have rights of appeal in the following cases:

(9)   against refusal of admission to and removal from the UK;[1]

(10)   against refusal to grant or withdrawal of a residence permit or document.[2]

1   Immigration (European Economic Area) Regulations 2000, SI 2000/2326, reg 29.
2   SI 2000/2326, reg 29.

18.15 A small number of people are excluded from the normal system of appeals because of the political or national security grounds of the decision. The excluded decisions are:

(1)   a personal decision of the Secretary of State to refuse entry to the UK (or entry clearance) on conducive grounds (Immigration and Asylum Act 1999, section 60(9));

(2)   a personal decision by the Secretary of State to refuse to vary leave on conducive grounds based on national security, diplomatic or political reasons (Immigration and Asylum Act 1999, section 62(4));

(3)   a decision to deport on conducive grounds based on national security, diplomatic or political reasons (Immigration and Asylum Act 1999, section 64(1));

(4)   a personal decision by the Secretary of State to refuse to revoke a deportation order (Immigration and Asylum Act 1999, section 64(2));

(5)   a refusal of asylum on national security grounds (Immigration and Asylum Act 1999, sections 70(1)-(3) and (5)-(6));

(6)   a refusal of asylum coupled with the grant of exceptional leave, on the ground that the applicant is excluded from refugee status by Article 1F, on the basis of material which is non-disclosable on national security grounds (Immigration and Asylum Act 1999, section 70(4));

(7)   decisions in respect of EEA nationals and their family members relating to refusal of admission, removal, refusal or withdrawal of residence permits or documents on national security grounds.[1]

These decisions are, with one exception, appealable to the Special Immigration Appeals Commission under section 2 of the Special Immigration Appeals Commission Act 1997.[2] A personal decision by the Secretary of State to refuse entry clearance on conducive grounds is only appealable if the appellant seeks to rely on an enforceable Community right or any provision made under section 2(2) of the European Communities Act 1972, or seeks entry to exercise rights of access to a child, or as a spouse, fiancé(e), parent, grandparent or other dependent relative.[3] An appeal on human rights or discrimination grounds in respect of, or combined with, any of the above decisions is appealable in the Special Immigration Appeals Commission rather than to the ordinary appellate authority, by section 2A of the 1997 Act.[4]

1   Immigration (European Economic Area) Regulations 2000, SI 2000/2326, reg 31(2) relating to removal conducive to the public good for national security, diplomatic or political reasons. Regulation 31(4) relates to exclusion and reg 31(6) to removal on refusal of admission.
2   As amended by Immigration and Asylum Act 1999, Sch 14, para 119.
3   Special Immigration Appeals Commission Act 1997, s 2(2).
4   Inserted by Immigration and Asylum Act 1999, Sch 14, para 121.

Exclusion of the right of appeal

18.16 There is no right of appeal at all under the 1999 Act in respect of a decision on an application which was not made on a prescribed form on which it was required to be made, nor where the applicant was required to take prescribed steps in relation to an application, or to do so within a prescribed period or at a prescribed time, but has failed to do so.[1] 'Prescribed' means 'prescribed by regulations,[2] so although all applications for variation of leave are required by the immigration rules to be made on forms (except for asylum and human rights applications)[3] applications made otherwise would not forfeit appeal rights, since the forms requirement is not 'prescribed' within the meaning of the Act. On the other hand, all applications made by way of additional grounds for wishing to enter or remain under the one-stop procedure, including asylum and human rights applications, must be made on the statement form specified in the regulations,[4] and returned within a specified period, since these are prescribed by regulations.

1   Immigration and Asylum Act 1999, s 72(3).
2   See definition of 'prescribed' in Immigration and Asylum Act 1999, s 167.
3   HC 395, para 32, inserted by HC 329, para 2.
4   Immigration and Asylum Appeals (One-Stop Procedure) Regulations 2000, SI 2000/ 2244 reg 4(1).

18.17 The Home Office has given assurances that this section will not be used to exclude asylum and human rights claimants who fail to attend for interview or to complete their evidence forms in the time set by the immigration officer, by prescribing periods for these steps in regulations.[1] The section should be interpreted in a way that gives effect to fundamental rights,[2] and its use in a way which deprived asylum seekers or human rights claimants of appeal rights for minor non-compliance, particularly if the fault is not theirs,[3] would be incompatible with the ECHR.

1   See exchange of correspondence between ILPA and Home Office minister Barbara Roche, October 2000.
2   By Human Rights Act 1998, s 3.
3   The huge disparity between demand and supply of legal assistance in the areas to which asylum seekers are dispersed is behind most non-compliance, particularly failure to get SEF and SAG forms back to the Home Office in time: see **12.122** above.

18.18 The non-compliance exclusions apply in principle to all appeals including those based on asylum or human rights or race discrimination grounds. The right of appeal is also excluded in the following cases, except where an asylum, human rights or discrimination claim is made:

(1)   against a refusal of entry clearance as a visitor, except a family visitor;[1]
(2)   against a refusal of leave to enter as a visitor, unless the person holds a current entry clearance at the time of refusal;[2]
(3)   against a refusal of entry clearance or leave to enter for short-term study or as a prospective student, unless the person holds a current entry clearance at the time of refusal;[3]
(4)   against a refusal of entry clearance or leave to enter as a dependant of any of the persons in (1)-(3) above;[4]
(5)   against a refusal of entry clearance or leave to enter because the person does not have the right passport or identity document or the necessary entry clearance or work permit;[5]
(6)   against a refusal of entry clearance or leave to enter because the person does not satisfy a requirement of the Immigration Rules as to age, nationality or citizenship;[6]

(7) against a refusal of entry clearance or leave to enter because the person seeks entry for a period exceeding that permitted by the Immigration Rules;[7]

(8) as a dependant of a person refused entry clearance or leave to enter on grounds in (5)-(7) above;[8]

(9) against a refusal of entry clearance on the personal decision of the Secretary of State on conducive grounds, unless the application was under Community law or for specified family purposes;[9]

(10) against a decision that the person does not have the right of abode and requires leave to enter, except for holders of a British passport or certificate of entitlement;[10]

(11) against a decision that leave to enter is required for a person claiming exemption from the requirement, except for holders of documents required by the rules or by order;[11]

(12) against refusal of, delay in issuing or the method of allocating special vouchers to British Overseas citizens;[12]

(13) against the refusal by the DfEE to grant a work permit,[13]

(14) against a variation of leave or a refusal to vary it if the application to vary was made after the expiry of the existing limited leave;[14]

(15) against the imposition of conditions of leave or the refusal to revoke conditions;[15]

(16) against the grant of a lesser period of leave than that sought;[16]

(17) against a refusal to vary leave for lack of entry clearance in the appropriate capacity, or a passport or work permit or equivalent after-entry permission;[17]

(18) against a refusal to vary leave for failure to satisfy a requirement of the immigration rules relating to age, nationality or citizenship;[18]

(19) against a refusal to vary leave because the variation would result in the duration of leave exceeding the maximum permitted under the rules;[19]

(20) against a refusal to vary leave because the fee has not been paid;[20]

(21) against a variation of, or refusal to vary leave made by statutory instrument, such as might occur under a 'hostage order' made under section 3(7) of the Immigration Act 1971;[21]

(22) against the cancellation of leave when the holder is outside the common travel area;[22]

(23) against a decision to deport on a recommendation by a criminal court;[23]

(24) against an EEA decision, if the appellant cannot produce a valid national identity card or passport issued by an EEA state other than the UK.[24]

1 Immigration and Asylum Act 1999, s 60(5)(a). The 'family visitor' appeal is contingent on payment of a required fee (£125 with a hearing, £50 without: Immigration Appeals (Family Visitor) (No 2) Regulations 2000, SI 2000/2446, amended by the Immigration Appeals (Family Visitor) (Amendment) Regulations 2001, SI 2001/52. The original fee levels imposed were excessive, and possibly contravened ECHR, art 6 (access to a court): *Ait-Mouhoub v France* (2000) 30 EHRR 382; *R v Lord Chancellor, ex p Witham* [1998] QB 575.
2 Immigration and Asylum Act 1999, s 60(5)(b).
3 Immigration and Asylum Act 1999, s 60(4), (5).
4 Immigration and Asylum Act 1999, s 60(4)(d).
5 Immigration and Asylum Act 1999, s 60(7)(a), (8).
6 Immigration and Asylum Act 1999, s 60(7)(b).
7 Immigration and Asylum Act 1999, s 60(7)(c).
8 Immigration and Asylum Act 1999, s 60(7).
9 Immigration and Asylum Act 1999, s 60(9), Special Immigration Appeals Commission Act 1997, s 2(1), (2).

10 Immigration and Asylum Act 1999, s 60(1).
11 Immigration and Asylum Act 1999, s 60(2).Various groups including consular officials, representatives of international associations are exempted from the requirement of leave to enter by the Immigration Act 1971, s 8(2). In addition, Commonwealth citizens and citizens of Ireland may be exempted from the requirement, either generally or in relation to day trips, providing they carry specific documents; see Immigration (Exemption from Control) Order 1972, art 5 (SI 1972/1613) and **6.41**ff above. This provision makes the right of appeal against refusal of readmission contingent on their carrying the requisite document.
12 See *R v Entry Clearance Officer, Bombay, ex p Amin* [1980] 2 All ER 837, [1980] 1 WLR 1530, QBD.
13 *Pearson v Immigration Appeal Tribunal* [1978] Imm AR 212, CA.
14 See *Suthendran v Immigration Appeal Tribunal* [1977] AC 359, [1976] 3 All ER 611, HL; *Wa-Selo v Secretary of State for the Home Department* [1990] Imm AR 76, CA, in relation to Immigration Act 1971, s 14, and would also apply to Immigration and Asylum Act 1999, s 61, whose wording is similar. Section 3C, inserted by s 3 of the Immigration and Asylum Act 1999, has the same effect as the Immigration (Variation of Leave) Order 1976, SI 1976/1572 in extending leave until the decision on the application, to enable an appeal to be lodged while limited leave is extant.
15 Immigration and Asylum Act 1999, s 61.
16 Immigration and Asylum Act 1999, s 61.
17 Immigration and Asylum Act 1999, s 62(1)(a), (2).
18 Immigration and Asylum Act 1999, s 62(1)(b).
19 Immigration and Asylum Act 1999, s 62(1)(c).
20 Immigration and Asylum Act 1999, s 62(1)(d). An administrative fee for handling applications is unobjectionable, but must be applied in accordance with policy criteria: *R v FCO, ex p Jamma (Zaineb Ali)*, CO 3338/99, 15 December 1999, where refusal to waive entry clearance fees where the sponsor was on income support and applicants had no other income was held arguably in breach of policy of waiving fees in cases of 'proven destitution'.
21 Immigration and Asylum Act 1999, s 62(5).
22 Under the Immigration (Leave to Enter and Remain) Order 2000, SI 2000/1161, art 13(7).
23 Immigration and Asylum Act 1999, s 63(1), which provides for an appeal only against a decision under the Immigration Act 1971, s 3(5), not under s 3(6). There is, however, an appeal, using the criminal ladder to the Court of Appeal (Criminal Division) or to the Crown Court, the recommendation being classed for these purposes as a sentence: Criminal Appeal Act 1968, ss 9, 10 and 50(1); Magistrates' Courts Act 1980, s 108.
24 Immigration and Asylum Act 1999, s 80(12).

18.19 Asylum appeals are excluded in two situations outside the one-stop procedure (below). There is no appeal on asylum grounds unless the person has actually claimed asylum.[1] In addition, there will be no appeal against refusal to revoke a deportation order on asylum grounds if the appellant had the right of appeal on asylum grounds against the decision to make the deportation order, whether or not it was exercised.[2]

1 Immigration and Asylum Act 1999, s 70(7). A claim for asylum can be informal: **12.108** above.
2 Immigration and Asylum Act 1999, s 70(8). This is tougher than the equivalent provision under the Asylum and Immigration Appeals Act 1993, which prevented an actual appeal under both limbs (decision to deport and refusal to revoke). It could have the effect of penalising appellants for the negligence of their advisers. There is no 'reasonable excuse' exception. But see **12.176** above for '*Kazmi*' discretion.

The one-stop appeal

18.20 In a number of situations, the issues that can be raised on appeal may be restricted, and a second appeal by the same appellant or a member of that appellant's family may be prevented or treated as finally determined by a certificate from the Secretary of State. By the Immigration and Asylum Act 1999, section 74, when any decision is taken (refusal of leave to enter or remain, or a decision to deport) which is appealable by virtue of sections 59-63 or under the Special Immigration Appeals Commission Act 1997, the appellant and any relevant member of the family[1] will be served with a notice asking for any additional grounds they have for wishing to enter or remain. By section 75, a person refused entry with no UK right of appeal, or subject to removal as an overstayer, for breach of conditions or deception, or as an illegal entrant, who claims asylum or makes a human rights or discrimination claim, is served with a section 75 notice requiring the applicant to state any additional grounds for wishing to stay.

(1) Failure to mention a particular ground (other than an asylum or human rights or discrimination ground) for wishing to enter or remain in the UK, in a section 74 or section 75 statement prevents the appellant from relying on that ground on appeal, unless the Secretary of State considers that there was a reasonable excuse for the omission.[2]

(2) If a human rights or discrimination claim is not made in the section 74 statement (after refusal of leave to enter or remain in another capacity) and an appeal proceeds without reference to human rights or discrimination issues, a subsequent human rights or discrimination appeal can be treated as finally determined if the Secretary of State certifies under section 73 that the human rights or discrimination claim could reasonably have been included in the section 74 statement or in the previous appeal but was not. The Secretary of State must however also certify that there is no other legitimate purpose for the human rights or discrimination claim than delaying the appellant's, or his or her family member's removal.[3]

(3) Failure to mention a human rights or discrimination claim in a section 75 statement prevents reliance on that ground in the asylum appeal, if the Secretary of State certifies that it could reasonably have been included in the statement and that there is no other legitimate purpose for the human rights or discrimination claim than delaying the appellant's, or his or her family member's removal.[4]

(4) Similarly, if a claim for asylum is not made in the section 74 statement (or in a section 75 statement, in the case of a human rights claimant), a subsequent asylum claim may be refused with no right of appeal if the Secretary of State (or immigration officer, in the case of a section 75 case) certifies that the appellant has no legitimate purpose for making the asylum claim other than delaying removal of him- or herself or a family member.[5]

(5) If a human rights or discrimination appeal raises an issue which is certified by the Secretary of State as having been considered in the original one-stop appeal, the appeal is to be treated as finally determined in relation to that issue.[6]

(6) Finally, any application made after an earlier appeal may be certified as having no legitimate purpose other than to delay the removal of the appellant or any family member, and if so certified the decision on it will not attract a right of appeal.[7]

1 Defined as a person who is the subject of the decision but is not an applicant, or someone appearing to be a spouse, a child of the appellant or the spouse, a cohabitee for two of the previous three years, a dependant or a person on whom the appellant depends (Immigration and Asylum Appeals (One-Stop Procedure) Regulations 2000, SI 2000/2244, reg 6. A far more generous definition than that used for family settlement, it could do with transplanting.

2   Immigration and Asylum Act 1999 as amended by the Race Relations (Amendment) Act 2000, Sch 2, s 76, modified in relation to section 75 statements by SI 2000/2244, reg 5(5) as amended by the Immigration and Asylum (One-Stop Procedure) (Amendment) Regulations 2001, SI 2001/867. It is hard to see what non-asylum or human rights or discrimination claim would give rise to an appeal right anyway in the case of s 75, which applies to claims made in the context of non-appealable decisions.
3   Immigration and Asylum Act 1999, s 73(3).
4   Immigration and Asylum Act 1999 as amended, as applied to s 75 by the Immigration and Asylum Appeals (One-Stop Procedure) Regulations 2000, SI 2000/2244, reg 5(1)–(4) as amended by SI 2001/867.
5   Immigration and Asylum Act 1999, s 76(5), modified in relation to section 75 cases by SI 2000/2244, reg 5(5).
6   Immigration and Asylum Act 1999, s 73(4)–(6), applied to section 75 cases by SI 2000/2244, reg 5(4).
7   Immigration and Asylum Act 1999, s 73(7)–(9).

18.21 The one-stop procedure does not apply to applications for entry clearance. The intention of the one-stop procedure is clear: to ensure that all relevant issues are dealt with before removal from the UK. But its specific effects in particular cases, and in particular the use made of the certifying power, remain to be seen. The broad effect can be illustrated by example. A student who has married and has a UK-born child, and is refused further leave to remain as a student, will on refusal be served with a section 74 notice. If he or she responds with a statement including an intention to remain as a spouse, the appeal will include this matter. If the appeal is rejected, and he or she subsequently applies to remain by virtue of ECHR, Article 8 (right to family life), the Secretary of State may certify that this was dealt with in the original appeal (section 73(5)), in which case the human rights appeal is treated as finally determined. If, on the other hand, he or she fails to respond to the section 74 notice, the spouse application under the immigration rules cannot be raised on the appeal unless the Secretary of State accepts that there was a reasonable excuse for the failure, but as an Article 8 claim, it may be raised on the original appeal (section 76(2) and (3)). If the appellant fails to refer to domestic circumstances at all on the original appeal, despite service with the section 74 notice, and applies to remain on that basis later, he or she could be prevented from appealing against refusal by a certificate that the new application is merely an attempt to delay removal (section 73(1)–(3)).

18.22 A port asylum claimant will not have an in-country right of appeal against refusal of entry on non-asylum grounds, so will be served with a section 75 notice on lodging his or her asylum claim, as will his or her family members.[1] The main purpose of section 75 is to prevent serial asylum claims by different members of the same family. But it could also prevent an ECHR claim being raised on the asylum appeal unless this has been flagged up by the section 75 notice, which would be a draconian (and possibly unlawful) use of the procedure. The one-stop procedure applies equally to claims which are not dealt with substantively but refused on third-country grounds.

1   For definition of relevant family members in this context, see Immigration and Asylum Appeals (One-Stop Procedure) Regulations 2000, SI 2000/2244, reg 7, and see **18.20** above.

18.23 The effect of the certification of an appeal as 'finally determined'[1] is to put an end to any appeal proceedings.[2] This is not likely to be susceptible to any preliminary issue jurisdiction and could probably only be challenged by judicial review.[3] It is not so clear that the certificate relating to a late and allegedly abusive asylum claim[4] or a similar certificate in respect of any other application[5] could not be challenged in the appellate authority as a preliminary issue.[6] This remains to be seen.[7]

1 Under Immigration and Asylum Act 1999, s 73(3) and (6).
2 See definition of 'finally determined' in Immigration and Asylum Act 1999, s 58(6) and (7).
3 Because of the difference in wording between an appeal deemed determined and the denial of a right of appeal; see fn 6 below. A definitive answer to this question of the scope of the adjudicator's preliminary jurisdiction awaits litigation.
4 Under Immigration and Asylum Act 1999, s 76(5).
5 Under Immigration and Asylum Act 1999, s 73(8).
6 Note that the Immigration and Asylum (Procedure) Rules 2000, SI 2000/2333, r 12(1)(a)(i) specifically includes within the preliminary jurisdiction the respondent's allegation that by virtue of a provision of the Immigration and Asylum Act 1999 the appellant is not entitled to appeal.
7 See discussion at **18.127–18.128** below.

Other restrictions on scope or subject-matter of appeals

18.24 An asylum seeker's right of appeal against a certificate that another country has accepted responsibility for the claim is restricted in that, if the country concerned is a member state and the removal is to take place under standing arrangements, that state is deemed safe (ie, a place where the claimant's life or liberty is not under threat by reason of race, religion, nationality, membership of a particular social group or political opinion, and which will not send the claimant elsewhere otherwise than in accordance with the Refugee Convention).[1] This restriction is discussed at **12.153** above.

1 Immigration and Asylum Act 1999, s 11(1).

18.25 In certain cases of removal, where there is no asylum or human rights or discrimination claim, the right of appeal is restricted to arguing that on the facts of the case the immigration authority had no power in law to remove for the reasons stated in the notice. This applies in the following cases:

(1) removal for overstaying or failing to comply with a condition attached to leave or being a family member of such a person;[1]
(2) removal for obtaining leave to remain by deception, or as the family member of a person being removed on this ground;[2]
(3) removal as an illegal entrant or a person who has entered the UK in breach of a deportation order;[3]
(4) removal of overstaying crew members of a ship or aircraft.[4]

1 Immigration and Asylum Act 1999, s 66(1)(b), s 10(1)(a) and (c). Overstaying or breach of conditions are precedent facts for the exercise of the jurisdiction to remove, however, and so on a judicial review of a decision to remove on these grounds the Secretary of State would be required to establish the facts, although probably not to as high a standard as in *Khawaja v Secretary of State for the Home Department* [1984] AC 74, unless deception were alleged.
2 Immigration and Asylum Act 1999, s 66(1)(b), s 10(1)(b) and (c). The comments in the previous footnote apply. Here the burden would on the Secretary of State would be a high one, since the allegation is one of deception.
3 Immigration and Asylum Act 1999, s 66(1)(a).
4 Immigration and Asylum Act 1999, s 66(1)(c).

18.26 Where the appeal is restricted in this way, the effect is to limit the adjudicator to considering whether or not the appellant has overstayed, breached conditions of stay, is an illegal entrant etc. In determining that issue he or she can examine the facts and come to a decision (the burden of proof is on the Secretary of State) but has no broad jurisdiction to review the merits of the decision to remove. The adjudicator is concerned only with the existence of the power and not the exercise of it.[1] An example of there being no power to remove would be where there is no country to which an appellant is removable under Schedule 2, paragraph 8 of the Immigration Act 1971. In practice, this appellate jurisdiction is seldom exercised, not least because it is exercisable only after removal unless combined with a human rights or asylum claim.[2]

1   *R v Secretary of State for the Home Department, ex p Malhi* [1990] Imm AR 275, CA; judgment approved and adopted by the House of Lords in *R v Secretary of State for the Home Department, ex p Oladehinde* [1991] 1 AC 254, [1990] 3 All ER 393.
2   Immigration and Asylum Act 1999, s 66(3).

Presence of appellants in the UK

18.27 Appellants who have been refused entry clearance have no right to come to the UK for the purpose of attending their appeal and giving evidence.[1] There is, however, no reason under the immigration rules why they should not be admitted as visitors for this purpose, and it is wrong for entry clearance officers automatically to assume that someone who has applied to remain permanently will not leave at the conclusion of the appeal, if the facts justify such a conclusion.[2]

1   The Immigration Rules are silent on entry for the purposes of attending an appeal, but see *R v Immigration Officer (Heathrow), ex p Ali* (1982) Times, 25 October, CA.
2   *Patel (Chhaganbai)* [1991] Imm AR 97, IAT; *Patel (Aiyub)* [1991] Imm AR 273, IAT. The Immigration and Asylum Act 1999, s 59(2) does not require an appellant to be out of the UK when the appeal is heard.

18.28 In other cases the appeal can only go ahead if the appellant has left the UK, unless before removal they appeal on human rights or discrimination or asylum grounds. These are mainly cases of refusal of entry, but also include refusal to revoke deportation orders and removal as illegal entrants. Even where entry clearance is not mandatory, these appellants will not be entitled to appeal so long as they remain in the UK unless they have an entry clearance or work permit which is current at the time of the decision.[1] Appeals against the following decisions are out-of-country:

(1)   refusal to grant entry clearance or a certificate of entitlement (Immigration and Asylum Act 1999, section 59(2));

(2)   refusal of entry, except where the person arrives in possession of an entry clearance or work permit or claims not to require leave to enter (Immigration and Asylum Act 1999, section 60(3));

(3)   refusal to revoke a deportation order (Immigration and Asylum Act 1999, section 64(3));

(4)   directions to remove someone as an overstayer, for breach of conditions or remaining by deception, as an illegal entrant or overstaying member of the crew of a ship or aircraft (Immigration and Asylum Act 1999, section 66(3)).

The need to have left the UK before appealing used to be particularly serious for returning residents who found their expectation of settlement frustrated because an immigration officer was of the view that a previous leave was obtained by deception. It also imposed severe difficulties on students returning from short holidays abroad, accused by immigration officers of having worked without permission and so refused re-entry. The introduction by the Immigration and Asylum Act 1999 of leave which does not lapse on leaving the common travel area has largely removed the problem. The only leave which does lapse is a leave of six months or less.[2] Where removal would be in breach of the UK's obligation under the Refugee Convention or the Human Rights Convention or would unlawfully discriminate, and there is an appeal on this ground under sections 65 or 69, there is an in-country right of appeal.

1   *Ashraf v Immigration Appeal Tribunal* [1989] Imm AR 234, CA: where a second application for entry is made after the entry clearance has ceased to be current there is still a right of appeal from abroad. See further *R v Immigration Appeal Tribunal, ex p Secretary of State for the Home Department* [1990] 1 WLR 1126, CA.

2   Immigration Act 1971, ss 3A (2)(d) and 3B(2)(c), inserted by Immigration and Asylum Act 1999, ss 1 and 2; Immigration (Leave to Enter and Remain) Order 2000, SI 2000/1161, art 13.

18.29   Asylum claimants have no in-country right of appeal against removal to a member state or a designated country which is not their country of nationality, save on human rights or discrimination grounds,[1] and not even then if the Secretary of State certifies that the human rights or discrimination claim is manifestly unfounded.[2] See **12.162** above.

1   Immigration and Asylum Act 1999, s 72(2)(b)

2   Immigration and Asylum Act 1999, s 72(2)(a) as amended by Race Relations (Amendment) Act 2000, Sch 2, para 36. In autumn 2000 Secretary of State indicated how this process is likely to work by indicating in correspondence that while litigation as to Germany's treatment of a second asylum claim was outstanding *(R v Secretary of State for the Home Department, ex p Karasoylu (Gulbahar)* 23 November 2000), he could not certify human rights claims in relation to Germany as manifestly unfounded. This suggests that the certifying power will be used only where the statutory presumption of safety of Dublin states is uncontradicted by evidence or events.

18.30   EEA nationals may not appeal in the UK against a decision:

(1)   to refuse admission to the UK, or a decision to remove someone consequent on refusal;[1]

(2)   to refuse to revoke a deportation order;

(3)   to refuse to issue an EEA family permit

unless, in the case of a refusal or decision to remove, either the person held an EEA family permit, a residence permit or a residence document on arrival, or the appeal raises human rights or discrimination grounds, or the appeal is to the Special Immigration Appeals Commission.[2] This restriction may be incompatible with Community law.[3]

1   But removal of EEA nationals pursuant to a leave to enter after several months on temporary admission was expulsion, not refusal of entry: *Yiadom*, Case C-357/98 [2001] All ER (EC) 267, ECJ.

2   Immigration (European Economic Area) Regulations 2000, SI 2000/2326, reg 30 (made under Immigration and Asylum Act 1999, s 80(6)).

3   In *R v Secretary of State for the Home Department, ex p Darwiche*, CO 413/98, the Secretary of State for the Home Department accepted that a decision to refuse leave to enter to a person with EEA residence rights should be treated as a removal decision so as to attract the protection of Directive 64/221 (including suspensive appeal). See Chapter 7 above.

Suspensory effect of an appeal

18.31 If some appeal rights may be exercised only from outside the UK, others are exercisable only from within the UK. In such a case, the effect of a pending appeal is to freeze the position of appellant and suspend any requirement to leave the UK or the power to remove. Any removal directions previously given on refusal of leave to enter cease to have effect, and no directions may be given while the appeal is pending. This applies to appeals against refusal of leave to enter (where an in-country right of appeal exists),[1] and to appeals against refusal of asylum where the claim was made on arrival.[2] In the case of destination appeals, and asylum and human rights appeals brought by illegal entrants, overstayers and proposed deportees, there is no prohibition on the issuing of removal directions pending an appeal, but they are to have no effect.[3] In the case of human rights appeals against refusal of entry or removal (where there is otherwise no suspensive right of appeal), removal directions may be given and a deportation order signed pending the appeal, so long as they are not effected.[4] In cases where there is a dispute as to whether the right of appeal is in-country or out-of-country (eg a dispute as to whether the appellant had a current entry clearance when refused leave to enter) and a notice of appeal is lodged, removal may only be effected once the dispute is finally determined against the appellant by the appellate authority under its preliminary jurisdiction.[5]

1   Immigration and Asylum Act 1999, Sch 4, para 10.
2   Immigration and Asylum Act 1999, Sch 4, para 10.
3   Immigration and Asylum Act 1999, Sch 4, para 11.
4   Immigration and Asylum Act 1999, Sch 4, para 20.
5   Immigration and Asylum Appeals (Procedure) Rules 2000, SI 2000/2333, rule 12. See *Lokko* [1990] Imm AR 111.

18.32 An appeal is pending, and so the freeze continues, and no removal directions may be given or implemented, while any further appeal is brought and, if it is brought, until it is determined.[1] However, this provision is qualified in relation to non-asylum appeals by the requirement to give notice of appeal to the Tribunal (or, in an appropriate case, to apply for leave to appeal to the adjudicator) immediately after an adjudicator dismisses the appeal.[2] If this is not done, the appeal is no longer regarded as pending, and removal directions may be given and implemented. This draconian provision applies to human rights or discrimination appeals, including appeals concerning Article 3; only asylum appeals under section 69 are excluded.[3] The freeze on removal directions pending appeal against removal applies not just to an appeal by the principal but to appeals brought by family members under the one-stop procedure. So if a visitor is refused leave to enter and the visitor's spouse then claims that his or her removal engages ECHR Article 3,[4] removal directions for the whole family are suspended.[5] The ban on removal pending appeal does not however prevent detention under the administrative provisions of Schedules 2 and 3 to the Immigration Act 1971.[6]

1   Immigration and Asylum Act 1999, s 58(5)–(7).
2   Immigration and Asylum Act 1999, Sch 4, para 14.
3   Thus, in the case of asylum appeals, the appeal remains 'pending' after an adjudicator has dismissed it, while an appeal may still be brought to the Immigration Appeal Tribunal.
4   Prohibition on torture or inhuman or degrading treatment or punishment.

5   Immigration and Asylum Act 1999, Sch 4, para 15.
6   Immigration and Asylum Act 1999, Sch 4, para 12.

18.33 An appeal against the refusal to vary leave, or against a variation which curtails leave, has similar effect. A variation is not to take effect so long as an appeal is pending against the variation.[1] But the effect of a section 61 appeal, or an asylum appeal under section 69(2) of the Immigration and Asylum Act 1999,[2] is to continue the leave to which the appeal relates and any conditions attached to it until the appeal is finally determined, withdrawn or abandoned.[3] An appeal is abandoned if the appellant leaves the UK,[4] if he or she is granted leave to enter or remain (other than exceptional leave in an asylum case),[5] or (in the case of a non-asylum variation appeal) if a deportation order is made against the appellant.[6] In deportation cases, on the other hand, the effect of an appeal is to suspend the Secretary of State's power to sign a deportation order while the appeal is pending.[7]

1   Immigration and Asylum Act 1999, Sch 4, para 16.
2   A refusal to vary leave on asylum grounds.
3   Immigration and Asylum Act 1999, Sch 4, para 17. Under the previous law a variation appeal did not continue leave but the person concerned could not be required to leave the UK. The situation was akin to that of a squatter awaiting eviction proceedings: see *Mesirionye v Immigration Appeal Tribunal* [1993] Imm AR 119, where it was held that this was not lawful residence for the purpose of computing continuous 'lawful residence' under the long residence concession.
4   Immigration and Asylum Act 1999, s 58(8).
5   Immigration and Asylum Act 1999, s 58(9).
6   Immigration and Asylum Act 1999, s 58(10).
7   Immigration and Asylum Act 1999, Sch 4, para 18.

18.34 An appeal against an EEA decision to refuse to admit a person to the UK, or to remove the person, freezes removal directions in respect of the appellant in the same way as for a non-EEA decision. No directions may be given while an appeal against exclusion is pending,[1] and directions for the removal of the appellant after revocation of the residence permit or in situations analogous with section 10 of the Immigration and Asylum Act 1999 or Schedule 3 to the Immigration Act 1971, are not to take effect while the appeal is pending.[2] This means that in quasi-deportation cases, and in cases analogous to overstayer removal, directions may be given during the period while the appeal is pending so long as they are not acted on. The detention powers contained in Schedules 2 and 3 to the Immigration Act 1971 continue to apply despite the freezing of removal directions.[3] No deportation order is to be made against an EEA national while the deportation appeal is pending.[4]

1   Immigration (European Economic Area) Regulations 2000, SI 2000/2326, reg 34(1).
2   SI 2000/2326, reg 34(2).
3   SI 2000/2326, reg 34(3).
4   SI 2000/2326, reg 34(5). For EEA deportations, see **18.49** below.

Human rights and race discrimination appeals

18.35 The Immigration and Asylum Act 1999 provides a specific human rights appeal in section 65 against any decision under the Immigration Acts relating to the appellant's entitlement to enter or remain in the UK. Human rights appeals are dealt with in Chapter 8: see **8.71**ff above, and race discrimination appeals at **1.30** above.

Asylum appeals

18.36 Asylum appeals are covered in section 69 of the Immigration and Asylum Act 1999 and section 2(1) of the Special Immigration Appeals Commission Act 1997. They are dealt with in Chapter 12, at **12.160ff** above.

Other appeals against exclusion from UK

18.37 Apart from asylum, race discrimination human rights appeals, and EEA appeals (see **18.41, 18.47, 18.49** and **18.51**), a person may appeal to an adjudicator against exclusion from the UK (ie refusal to admit) in three situations: (1) refusal or cancellation of leave to enter;[1] (2) refusal to grant a certificate of entitlement or an entry clearance,[2] and (3) a decision that the person requires leave to enter.[3] In the first and third group of cases an appeal against the decision may be combined with an appeal objecting to the country to which the appellant is to be removed.[4] The first point to make is that there is no appeal against refusal of leave to enter if the person does not hold entry clearance or a work permit, or other relevant document (passport or identity document), if required by the rules.[5] In the case of visitors, short-term students,[6] would-be students,[7] and the dependants of all these groups, lack of an entry clearance means no right of appeal, whether or not they are visa nationals and so require entry clearance under the rules.[8] This means that all visa nationals,[9] all visitors, short-term students, would-be students, and all persons seeking entry for any purpose leading to settlement (ie work, setting up in business, joining family in the UK),[10] and the dependants of all these groups, must have the necessary pre-entry permission in order to have a right of appeal at all against refusal of leave to enter. Entry clearance is in most situations to be treated as leave to enter under the provisions of the Immigration (Leave to Enter and Remain) Order 2000.[11] Others who have no right of appeal against refusal of leave to enter are those not satisfying a requirement of the rules as to age, nationality or citizenship. This might affect a non-visa national seeking entry as an au pair, for example; while there is no requirement for entry clearance in this capacity, there are requirements as to age and nationality.[12] Finally, persons seeking entry for a period exceeding the maximum have no appeal against refusal;[13] this would cover au pairs who seek leave to enter for more than two years, for example. None of these persons, nor their dependants, have any appeal right against the refusal of leave to enter (save on asylum or human rights or discrimination grounds).

1 Immigration and Asylum Act 1999, s 59(1)(b), Immigration Act 1971, Sch 2, para 2A(9), inserted by Immigration and Asylum Act 1999, Sch 14, para 57.
2 Immigration and Asylum Act 1999, s 59(2).
3 Immigration and Asylum Act 1999, s 59(1(a).
4 Immigration and Asylum Act 1999, ss 59(3) and (4), 67(1)(a), 68(1).
5 Immigration and Asylum Act 1999, s 60(7). Since the rules require everyone seeking entry to the UK (including those coming through the Channel Tunnel) to provide evidence of identity and nationality (HC 395, para 11), anyone arriving without such documentation would have no appeal under this section against refusal of leave to enter.
6 Ie those seeking entry for a course of not more than six months.
7 Ie those who intend to study but have not yet been accepted on a course.
8 Immigration and Asylum Act 1999, s 60(5)(b).
9 Listed in the Appendix to the Immigration Rules (currently HC 395).
10 Because everyone seeking entry for a purpose leading to settlement requires entry clearance.
11 SI 2000/1161, arts 2–6.

12 HC 395 para 89.
13 Immigration and Asylum Act 1999, s 60(7)(c).

18.38 Second, even if entry clearance is not required by the rules, only those who in fact have entry clearance or a work permit, or who are appealing against cancellation of leave, are entitled to remain and be present at their appeal.[1] This requirement has led to great injustice and hardship in the past. First, before the Asylum and Immigration Appeals Act 1993, refugees claiming asylum at the port had no in-country right of appeal against refusal, unless they had obtained entry clearance (usually as a visitor, since visas are not issued to refugees). Second, because all leave lapsed on leaving the common travel area prior to the Immigration and Asylum Act 1999,[2] long-term students and returning residents who did not require entry clearance and who were refused entry on return to the UK after a short trip abroad were required to leave the UK to exercise appeal rights.[3] These defects have been remedied by the in-country asylum and human rights appeal and by the provisions of the Immigration (Leave to Enter and Remain) Order 2000,[4] whereby those with more than six months' leave may go abroad without their leave lapsing. Returnees who find their leave cancelled on return are treated as if they were refused leave to enter and had a current entry clearance.[5] Persons refused leave to enter on the Secretary of State's personal decision, on the ground that their exclusion is conducive to the public good, have no appeal right to the adjudicator,[6] but may appeal to the Special Immigration Appeals Commission if they would have been entitled to appeal to the adjudicator.[7]

1   Immigration and Asylum Act 1999, s 60(3), Immigration Act 1971, Sch 2, para 2A(9), inserted by Immigration and Asylum Act 1999, Sch 14, para 57. This would apply where entry clearance was not treated as leave to enter by virtue of Immigration (Leave to Enter and Remain) Order 2000, SI 2000/1161, art 3.
2   Immigration Act 1971, s 3(4).
3   To get round these difficulties, ingenious arguments had been mounted to the effect that a previous stamp granting leave was an entry clearance (rejected by the Divisional Court in *R v Immigration Officer, ex p Oyo* [1995] Imm AR 553), or that it gave rise to a legitimate expectation of re-entry (rejected by the Court of Appeal in *Katoorah v Secretary of State for the Home Department* [1996] Imm AR 595).
4   SI 2000/1161, art 13.
5   See fn 1 above.
6   Immigration and Asylum Act 1999, s 60(9).
7   Special Immigration Appeals Commission Act 1997, s 2 as amended by Immigration and Asylum Act 1999, Sch 4, para 119 (superseded by SI 2000/2326).

18.39 The second situation concerns refusal of certificates of entitlement and entry clearance. The appellants will almost invariably be abroad, since applications for entry clearance, and most applications for certificates of entitlement, are made to British posts overseas.[1] The exclusion from appeal rights for want of relevant documents, or for failing to satisfy a requirement of the rules as to age, nationality or citizenship, or for seeking a period of leave exceeding that permitted by the rules, applies to refusal of entry clearance as it applies to refusal of leave to enter.[2] Visitors (except family visitors) and short-term and would-be students, and their dependants, have no appeal against refusal of entry clearance.[3] The family visitor appeal is contingent on payment of a prescribed fee.[4] A refusal of entry clearance by a personal decision of the Secretary of State that exclusion is conducive to the public good is not appealable to the adjudicator under section 59,[5] nor is it appealable to the Special Immigration

Appeals Commission unless the application relates to an enforceable Community right, or to family rights, eg access to a child resident in the UK, or to join a spouse or fiancé(e), or to join family as a parent, grandparent or other dependent relative.[6] A special voucher issued to a British Overseas citizen is not 'entry clearance' and there is no right of appeal against the refusal to issue it[7] (save now on human rights or race discrimination grounds). A decision by the Secretary of State in the context of the Somali family reunion policy, that a visa was unlikely to be granted if a formal application was made, was not appealable, since it was only a preliminary assessment given before the subject of the request was required to do anything by way of travelling to the post or payment of the application fees.[8]

1   HC 395, para 28 requires entry clearance applicants to be outside the UK. Certificates of entitlement may be applied for in the UK but persons claiming entitlement to the right of abode on entry must hold a certificate of entitlement if they do not hold a British passport: Immigration Act 1971, s 3(9).
2   Immigration and Asylum Act 1999, s 60(7).
3   Immigration and Asylum Act 1999, s 60(5)(a)
4   Immigration and Asylum Act 1999, s 60(6). See **18.18** fn 1 above.
5   Immigration and Asylum Act 1999, s 60(9).
6   Special Immigration Appeals Commission Act 1997, s 2(2).
7   *Re Amin* [1983] 2 AC 818, HL.
8   *Secretary of State for the Home Department v Abdi and Dahir* [1995] Imm AR 570, CA. The policy recognised the difficulties for family members of refugees and other asylees in the UK of travelling to a British post in Ethiopia or Kenya for interview and returning for entry clearance if the application was successful, by providing for a preliminary assessment to be made on application by the sponsor to the Home Office in the UK. If the assessment was positive, the applicant was called to the post and after a short interview to establish identity, was normally granted entry clearance on the spot; if negative, a formal application had to be made, following *Abdi and Dahir*, to attract a right of appeal.

18.40 Appeals in the third group are by those claiming they do not require leave to enter because they have the right of abode or are otherwise exempt from immigration control. Those claiming the right of abode have a right of appeal against the decision that they require leave only if they hold a British passport or a certificate of entitlement.[1] Since the right of appeal is predicated on the holding of one of these documents, it follows that the appeal will in most cases be concerned with the person's entitlement to hold it. The passport must be a full and current one, not a British visitors' passport[2] and not expired.[3] Similarly, a person who claims not to require leave on the ground of a particular exemption will not have a right of appeal unless he or she holds a document required by the rules or by the Immigration (Exemption from Control) Order 1972,[4] eg a British visitors' passport or an identity document. The appellant is entitled to be present for the appeal. An argument that leave has not lapsed will ground an in-country right of appeal against a decision that leave to enter is required.[5]

1   Immigration and Asylum Act 1999, s 60(1).
2   *Minta v Secretary of State for the Home Department* [1992] Imm AR 380, CA. British visitors' passports have now been abolished: See **2.14** above.
3   *Akewushola v Secretary of State for the Home Department* [1999] Imm AR 594, [1999] INLR 433, CA.
4   SI 1972/1613. The 1972 order exempts diplomatic staff, members of defined international organisations and their families and households from control, but in addition it provides for various persons not to require leave to enter, including Commonwealth citizens returning from excursions to France and Belgium with identity documents instead of a passport, and citizens of the UK and colonies holding British visitors' passports; see art 5.

5 *Khan (Mohammed Arshad)* (12404) 2 August 1995, IAT. In that case the argument was that the appellant had not left the common travel area (he had travelled to Ireland) and did not therefore require leave to enter on his return.

EEA appeals against exclusion

18.41 Since EEA nationals and their family members[1] do not require leave to enter, and must be admitted unless there are good reasons based on public policy, public security or public health for their exclusion, the appeals regime which applies to them is a modified one. An EEA national or a family member of an EEA national (or a person claiming to be an EEA national or a family member) may appeal to an adjudicator or, in appropriate cases, to the Special Immigration Appeals Commission, against a refusal to admit to the UK or an ECO's refusal to grant a family permit.[2] Persons claiming to be EEA nationals may not appeal against exclusion or refusal to issue a residence permit unless they produce a valid passport or national identity card issued by an EEA government.[3] The appeal against refusal of admission is not in-country unless there is an appeal to the Special Immigration Appeals Commission, or a human rights or discrimination appeal, or where the appellant held an EEA family permit or residence permit or document on arrival.[4] This must be read subject to the judgment in *Yiadom,*[5] that where a Community national has been physically present in the UK on temporary admission for a period of several months pending the refusal, the decision refusing admission constitutes a decision concerning expulsion rather than entry, and so must attract a right of appeal or review before implementation by removal.[6] An EEA national producing a valid identity card or passport may not be refused admission save on grounds of public policy, public security or public health.[7] A family member of an EEA national producing a valid EEA family permit or residence document (if a visa national) or documentary proof of the relationship may not be refused admission save on public policy, security or health grounds or if the immigration officer disputes that he or she is the family member of a qualified person.[8] In that situation the officer may revoke the family permit or residence document,[9] and the decision attracts an in-country appeal right,[10] together with the right to object to destination on removal.[11] In the case of both EEA nationals and family members, if the decision is a personal decision of the Secretary of State on grounds that exclusion is conducive to the public good, there is an in-country appeal to the Special Immigration Appeals Commission.[12]

1 For definition of family member see Immigration (European Economic Area) Regulations 2000, SI 2000/2326, reg 6. Note that this includes family members of UK nationals only in specified circumstances, essentially after the UK national has genuinely exercised a Community right (SI 2000/2326, reg 11), and does not include a spouse in a marriage of convenience (SI 2000/2326, reg 2). See *Chang* (01 TH 00100*), IAT; and **7.84** above.
2 SI 2000/2326, reg 29.
3 Immigration and Asylum Act 1999, s 80(12).
4 Immigration (European Economic Area) Regulations 2000, SI 2000/2326, reg 30(1)(a), (3).
5 *R v Secretary of State for the Home Department, ex p Nana Yiadom,* Case C-357/98 [2001] All ER (EC) 267. See also *R v Secretary of State for the Home Department, ex p Darwiche* CO 413/98, **18.30** above.
6 By virtue of Council Directive (EEC) 64/221, art 9.
7 SI 2000/2326, reg 12(1), 21(1). Schedule 1 to the regulations lists the diseases and disabilities which may justify a decision taken on grounds of public health (very infectious diseases), and those which may justify a decision on public policy or public security grounds (drug addiction and profound mental or psychotic disturbances). See **7.136** above.

8 SI 2000/2326, regs 12(2), 21(1), (2).
9 SI 2000/2326, reg 22(3) and (4).
10 SI 2000/2326, reg 30(3)(c).
11 Immigration and Asylum Act 1999, ss 67, 68; SI 2000/2326, reg 25(3)(c).
12 SI 2000/2326, reg 31.

18.42 While EEA nationals and their families may obtain residence permits and residence documents respectively as proof of their right of residence in the UK,[1] the EEA family permit is the clearest equivalent of entry clearance for family members of EEA nationals. An EEA family permit must be issued to family members of qualified persons and potential qualified persons, unless there are public policy, public security or public health reasons for excluding either the principal (the qualified person) or the applicant.[2] Refusal attracts an out-of-country appeal.[3]

1 See chapter 7 above; for appeals against refusal to issue, and revocation of, these documents see **18.47** below.
2 Immigration (European Economic Area) Regulations 2000, SI 2000/2326, reg 13.
3 SI 2000/2326, reg 30(1)(c).

Appeals against variation or refusal to vary leave

18.43 Section 61 gives the right of appeal to an adjudicator to persons with a limited leave against a variation of leave or refusal to vary if, as a result of the decision, the person may be required to leave the UK within 28 days. In practice this means that curtailment of leave, or a refusal to vary leave, may be appealed, but not a grant of lesser leave than that sought, or the grant of a limited leave after a period of exemption, or the imposition of, or refusal to lift, conditions. In these respects the appeal under the section is considerably narrower in scope than its predecessor under the Immigration Act 1971. The parliamentary intention was to provide appeals 'only for the most adverse decisions and ... [those requiring] departure from the UK'.[1]

1 Explanatory notes to the Immigration and Asylum Act 1999, para 198.

18.44 The right of appeal against a refusal to vary leave is limited to situations where there is an existing leave at the time of the lodging of the appeal.[1] In *Subramaniam* in the Court of Appeal[2] and in *Suthendran* in the House of Lords[3] it was decided by a majority of the judges that on its true construction the Immigration Act 1971, section 14(1), the precursor of section 61 of the Immigration and Asylum Act 1999, and in similar terms, gave a right of appeal to 'a person who has a limited leave under this Act' and not to 'a person who has had' such limited leave. So there is no right of appeal under section 61 of the 1999 Act for a person whose limited leave to remain in the UK has expired at the time of applying for a variation.[4] But the interpretation adopted by the majority in the House of Lords also meant that someone whose application was made in time, but whose limited leave expired before the Home Office reached a decision, would also have no right of appeal. The majority of the House of Lords realised this, but said that the injustice could be cured by administrative means. The 'leave gap' was closed by the Variation of Leave Order 1976;[5] it is now dealt with by section 3C of the 1971 Act.[6] This provides that if a person with limited leave to enter or remain applies before the expiry of the leave for variation and when it expires no decision has been taken, the leave is to be treated as continuing until the end of the period allowed for appealing the decision. The section also provides that during this period of deemed leave, no further application for variation may be made, although the original application, which gave rise to the deemed leave, may be varied.[7] This allows for notice of a statement under the one-stop procedure detailing further grounds for seeking to remain in the UK, after the decision on the original application.[8] If an appeal is lodged during the period of deemed leave, the leave (and any conditions attached to it) continues until the appeal is finally determined, withdrawn or abandoned.[9]

1   *Akhtar v Secretary of State for the Home Department* [1991] Imm AR 232, CA; see *also Wa-Selo v Secretary of State for the Home Department* [1990] Imm AR 76, CA.
2   *R v Immigration Appeal Tribunal, ex p Subramaniam* [1977] QB 190, [1976] 3 All ER 604.
3   *Suthendran v Immigration Appeal Tribunal* [1977] AC 359, [1976] 3 All ER 611.
4   Since all applications except asylum and human rights or discrimination ones must be on prescribed forms, which must be completed in full and sent with all requisite documents to constitute a valid application, the effect of a letter seeking further leave, or (a common previous practice among students) the sending in of a passport to the Home Office for further endorsement, will be that no valid application has been made prior to expiry of leave, and so no right of appeal will accrue. See HC 395, para 32 as amended by HC 329, para 2.
5   SI 1976/1572, as amended by SI 1989/1005.
6   Inserted by Immigration and Asylum Act 1999, s 3.
7   Immigration Act 1971, s 3C(3) and (4).
8   Under Immigration and Asylum Act 1999, s 74(4)-(7).
9   Immigration and Asylum Act 1999, s 58, Sch 4 para 17. For 'finally determined', 'withdrawn' and 'abandoned' see **18.120–18.122** below.

18.45   There is no right of appeal (by a principal or a dependant) against a refusal to vary leave on the ground that the applicant does not hold the required entry clearance, passport or work permit or after-entry equivalent,[1] or does not satisfy a requirement of the immigration rules as to age, nationality or citizenship,[2] or seeks leave in excess of the maximum permitted,[3] or has not paid a required fee.[4] The 'required' entry clearance is that in the category for which the applicant seeks leave to remain.[5] There is no right of appeal against the refusal of further leave to remain as a visitor for a person whose leave has already exceeded the maximum because of the grant of exceptional leave.[6] But a refusal of exceptional leave to a person with visit leave has been held to attract the right of appeal because what was sought was outside the rules.[7]

1   Immigration and Asylum Act 1999, s 62(1)(a), (2).
2   Immigration and Asylum Act 1999, s 62(1)(b).
3   Immigration and Asylum Act 1999, s 62(1)(c).
4   Immigration and Asylum Act 1999, s 62(1)d).
5   *R v Secretary of State for the Home Department, ex p Ahmed* [1995] Imm AR 590; on appeal [1996] Imm AR 260, CA.
6   *R v Immigration Appeal Tribunal, ex p Sam* [1996] Imm AR 272, QBD.
7   *Namwinga* (15496) 29 August 1997, IAT.

18.46   There is no appeal to the adjudicator against a personal decision by the Secretary of State to refuse to vary leave on the ground that the appellant's departure from the UK would be conducive to the public good in the interests of national security, diplomatic relations or other political reasons.[1] In such a case an appeal lies to the Special Immigration Appeals Commission.[2]

1   Immigration and Asylum Act 1999, s 62(4).
2   Special Immigration Appeals Commission Act 1997, s 2, replaced by Immigration and Asylum Act 1999, Sch 14, para 119; Immigration (European Economic Area) Regulations 2000, SI 2000/2326, reg 32.

Appeals by EEA nationals: refusal to issue or to renew, or revocation of residence documents

18.47 Refusal to issue or to renew a residence permit or document to an EEA national or family member in the UK, or revocation of such a document, is the EEA equivalent of variation or refusal to vary leave to enter or remain. The refusal to issue a residence permit to an EEA national (which is proof of entitlement to be in the UK),[1] or to a family member producing a family permit or other proof of eligibility,[2] may be grounded on public policy, public security or public health; the refusal to renew the permit, or a decision to revoke it, may additionally be grounded on a dispute as to whether the applicant is (or has ceased to be) a qualified person, the family member of such a person or satisfies conditions of dependency.[3] There is a right of appeal to the adjudicator against a refusal or revocation, exercisable in the UK. If the decision is on conducive grounds relating to national security, diplomatic or political reasons and is followed by a decision to remove, there is a right of appeal to the Special Immigration Appeals Commission instead.[4] The retention of the passport of the spouse of an EEA national who entered with a residence permit is capable of constituting implied withdrawal or withdrawal by conduct of the permit, which attracts a right of appeal.[5] In *Boukssid v Secretary of State for the Home Department*, the Court of Appeal held that an EEA national or family member, seeking indefinite leave to remain but granted a five-year residence permit instead, has no right of appeal under the domestic law, because that depends on having limited leave under UK law, and there is no refusal of a residence permit so as to bring into play the appeal provisions of the Regulations. The only remedy in this situation is judicial review.[6] However, in *Baumbast* the Tribunal accepted an argument based on paragraph 255 of HC 395 that the only method of granting indefinite leave under paragraph 255 was to endorse the residence permit to show permission to remain in the UK indefinitely and therefore by necessary inference, to grant a permit. If that endorsement was refused, that amounted to a refusal of a residence permit, against which there was a right of appeal.[7]

1   Immigration (European Economic Area) Regulations 2000, SI 2000/2326, reg 15(1).
2   SI 2000/2326, reg 15(2).
3   SI 2000/2326, regs 10(3), 22.
4   SI 2000/2326, regs 27(2)(c), 31(5) and (6).
5   SI 2000/2326, reg 29.
6   *Boukssid v Secretary of State for the Home Department* [1998] INLR 275, CA, decided under equivalent provisions of the 1971 Act and the Immigration (European Economic Area) Order 1994, SI 1994/1895.
7   *Baumbast* (21263) 8 June 1999, IAT.

Appeals in deportation cases

18.48 Since overstayers and those in breach of conditions of leave are no longer deported but removed from the UK,[1] subject to transitional provisions affecting those served with a deportation notice or who applied to regularise their stay before 2 October 2000,[2] the range of people who are deported, and so enjoy a right of appeal before removal, has shrunk dramatically. Now, apart from persons recommended for deportation by a criminal court, only those whose deportation the Secretary of State deems to be conducive to the public good, and their family members, are to be deported and have corresponding appeal rights.[3] The majority of appeals are in relation to those convicted of criminal offences, who were not made subject to a recommendation for deportation at sentencing.[4] The appeal is to an adjudicator,[5] and no order is to be made while such an appeal may be brought[6] or while it is pending.[7] However, once a deportation order is made, any pending appeal under section 61 of the Immigration and Asylum Act 1999 (variation of leave or refusal to vary it) is to be treated as abandoned.[8] The proposed deportee may object to the proposed destination in the deportation appeal.[9] In a family deportation appeal, the appellant may not dispute statements as to family relationships made to obtain entry clearance, leave to enter or remain, in order to show that he or she is not part of that family,[10] unless they were not made by him or her or an agent, or they were made without his or her knowledge, or he or she was a child at the time.[11] If the grounds for the decision to deport are national security, diplomatic or political, the appeal is not to the adjudicator[12] but to the Special Immigration Appeals Commission.[13] There is no in-country appeal under section 63 of the Immigration and Asylum Act 1999 against a refusal to revoke a deportation order,[14] and a refusal to revoke based on a personal decision by the Secretary of State that the applicant's exclusion from the UK would be conducive to the public good is not appealable to the adjudicator but may be appealed to the Special Immigration Appeals Commission.[15]

1 Immigration and Asylum Act 1999, s 10.
2 Immigration and Asylum Act 1999, s 9 and Sch 15, paras 11 and 12, Immigration (Regularisation Period for Overstayers) Regulations 2000, SI 2000/265.
3 Immigration Act 1971, s 3(5) as amended by Immigration and Asylum Act 1999, Sch 15, para 44(2); Immigration and Asylum Act 1999, s 63.
4 There is no appeal (save on human rights or discrimination grounds, or asylum grounds if an asylum claim has been made) against a decision to deport following a recommendation, pursuant to the Immigration Act 1971, s 3(6), despite promises that such decisions would be subject to appeal during the passage of the Immigration and Asylum Act 1999.
5 Immigration and Asylum Act 1999, s 63(1). Previously, 'conducive' deportations went to the Immigration Appeal Tribunal as a first-instance appellate body.
6 Immigration and Asylum Act 1999, s 63(2).
7 Immigration and Asylum Act 1999, Sch 4, para 18.
8 Immigration and Asylum Act 1999, s 58(9).
9 Immigration and Asylum Act 1999, s 63(3), (4).
10 Immigration and Asylum Act 1999, s 64(4), (5).
11 Immigration and Asylum Act 1999, s 64(6).
12 Immigration and Asylum Act 1999, s 64(1).
13 Special Immigration Appeals Commission Act 1997, s 2(1), as amended by the Immigration (European Economic Area) Regulations 2000, SI 2000/2326, reg 32(2).
14 Immigration and Asylum Act 1999, s 64(3).
15 See fn 13 above.

EEA public policy decisions to remove

18.49 Removal of an EEA national or family member on public policy, public security or public health grounds[1] is equivalent to a deportation on conducive grounds, and section 5 of and Schedule 3 to the Immigration Act 1971 apply.[2] Where national security, diplomatic or political reasons underly the decision, the appeal is to the Special Immigration Appeals Commission,[3] otherwise it is to an adjudicator.[4] The appeal is in-country and suspends removal.[5] An appeal against a refusal to revoke a deportation order is, however, out-of-country.[6]

1 Immigration (European Economic Area) Regulations 2000, SI 2000/2326, reg 21(3)(b).
2 SI 2000/2326, reg 26(3).
3 SI 2000/2326, reg 31(2).
4 SI 2000/2326, reg 29(3).

5   SI 2000/2326, reg 34(2) for suspensive effect. It is in-country by virtue of its omission from
    the list of out-of-country appeals at SI 2000/2326, reg 30.
6   SI 2000/2326, reg 30(1)(b).

Appeals against removal: overstayers, illegal entrants, ship and aircrews

18.50 Illegal entrants,[1] overstayers, those in breach of conditions, persons who
have remained in the UK by deception, and seamen or air crew members who
overstay their 'shore' leave or come to the UK to join a ship or aircraft and then
abscond may be summarily removed from the UK under directions given by the
immigration officer or the Secretary of State.[2] In such cases there is a restricted
right of appeal against the existence of the power to remove on the grounds
stated in the notice,[3] only exercisable after removal[4] unless there is an asylum,
race discrimination or human rights appeal.[5] Where removal directions have
been given by virtue of a deportation order, the appellant is not allowed to
dispute the original validity of the deportation order on the appeal.[6]

1   See chapter 15 above.
2   Under Immigration Act 1971, Sch 2, paras 9, 10, 13(2), 14, and Immigration and Asylum
    Act 1999, s 10.
3   See **18.25–18.26** above.
4   Immigration and Asylum Act 1999, s 66.
5   Immigration and Asylum Act 1999, s 66(3).
6   Immigration and Asylum Act 1999, s 66(4).

EEA decisions to remove on grounds of non-qualification

18.51 A person may be removed from the UK if he or she is not, or has ceased to
be, a qualified person or a family member of such a person.[1] Removal of this
group is equivalent to removal of overstayers under section 10(1)(a) of the
Immigration and Asylum Act 1999, which is to apply.[2] There is no right of appeal
on the ground that the person is an EEA national unless the appellant produces a
valid national identity card or passport issued by an EEA state.[3] A person claiming
to be a family member for the purposes of an appeal must produce a family
permit or other proof of relationship.[4] An appeal against removal may be made
on human rights or discrimination grounds.[5] It could also be made on asylum
grounds, although the regulations are silent on this; nothing in the Act or the
regulations prevents asylum applications by EEA nationals.[6]

1   Immigration (European Economic Area) Regulations 2000, SI 2000/2326, reg 21(3)(a).
2   SI 2000/2326, reg 26(2).
3   Immigration and Asylum Act 1999, s 80(12).
4   SI 2000/2326, reg 33.
5   SI 2000/2326, reg 29(2).
6   An asylum claim by an EEA national is, however, to be deemed manifestly unfounded
    except in particular circumstances, by virtue of Protocol 29 to the Amsterdam Treaty.
    See **12.106** above.

Appeals objecting to destination

18.52 An appeal to an adjudicator which consists essentially of an objection to
the country or territory to which the appellant is to be removed may be made in
certain cases:

(1)   on removal directions following refusal of leave to enter, where the appellant has an in-country appeal right under the Immigration and Asylum Act 1999, section 59;[1]

(2)   on a deportation order being made;[2]

(3)   on removal for entry in breach of a deportation order.[3]

There is no right to object to destination if the appellant has had the opportunity to do so in an in-country appeal[4] (against refusal of leave to enter, a decision that he or she requires leave to enter, or a decision to deport) and either did not do so or was unsuccessful in the objection.[5] This is likely to apply to (1) and (2) above, so that only those who are to be removed for entry in breach of a deportation order are likely to have a 'free-standing' destination appeal. Appellants cannot use a destination appeal to argue that they should not be removed at all.[6] They must produce evidence that there is another country which will admit them.[7] Evidence of a conditional intention by the deportee's EEA national spouse to move to Ireland if the deportation appeal was unsuccessful, so that the deportee would be admissible there, has been held insufficient to fulfil this requirement.[8]

1   Immigration and Asylum Act 1999, ss 67(1)(a), 68(1).
2   Immigration and Asylum Act 1999, s 67(1)(b).
3   Immigration and Asylum Act 1999, s 67(1)(c).
4   By service of removal directions specifying the destination before or after the substantive appeal is lodged: Immigration and Asylum Act 1999, s 59(3), 63(3).
5   Immigration and Asylum Act 1999, s 68(2).
6   *R v Immigration Appeal Tribunal, ex p Muruganandarajah and Sureshkumar* [1986] Imm AR 382, CA.
7   Immigration and Asylum Act 1999, s 68(3), placing the decisions in *R v an Adjudicator, ex p Umeloh* [1991] Imm AR 602, QBD and *Mounciffe v Secretary of State for the Home Department* [1996] Imm AR 265, CA on a statutory footing. See also HC 395, para 385.
8   *R v Secretary of State for the Home Department, ex p Withane* [1997] Imm AR 246, QBD, leave application.

One-stop appeals

18.53 Where a decision attracts an in-country right of appeal, whether on refusal of entry, refusal to vary leave or on a decision to deport, and a statement of additional grounds for seeking to enter or remain in the UK is served in response to the one-stop notice under the Immigration and Asylum Act 1999, section 74, the appeal will embrace not just the original application but the additional grounds too.[1] The additional grounds could be further grounds for leave to enter or remain under the immigration rules, under a relevant Home Office policy, asylum or human rights or discrimination grounds. The appeal would also embrace further grounds not contained in the one-stop statement, if they are human rights or discrimination grounds, or if the appellant was not aware of them on completing the one-stop statement, or if the Secretary of State considers there was a reasonable excuse for failing to mention them.[2] So for example, a person refused leave to enter or remain under the rules, with a right of appeal, who has been living with someone settled in the UK for two years at the date of refusal, may also appeal under the Home Office policy on cohabitation if he or she raises this in the one-stop statement, and under ECHR, Article 8 (right to respect for private and family life) even if he or she does not raise it in the statement. The adjudicator will deal with all the heads of appeal in one proceeding. An asylum ground raised after the date for submission of the one-stop statement will be embraced in the appeal unless the Secretary of State certifies that the only purpose of the claim was to delay the applicant's or a family member's removal.[3]

1   Immigration and Asylum Act 1999, s 77(2). See **18.20** above.
2   Immigration and Asylum Act 1999, s 76(2), (3).
3   Immigration and Asylum Act 1999, s 76(4) and (5).

18.54   The one-stop procedure also embraces reasons other family members[1] have for wanting to stay in the UK, since family members are also served with one-stop notices when the principal is the subject of a decision appealable in the UK.[2] Thus, if a visitor is refused leave to enter but, by virtue of possession of entry clearance, has an in-country appeal, a member of the visitor's family may raise a claim for admission under the rules or a Home Office policy, an asylum claim or a human rights claim in the one-stop statement. This would give rise to a separate appeal by the relevant family member, which is justiciable in the principal's visit appeal.

1   See **18.20** above for definition of 'relevant family member'.
2   Immigration and Asylum Act 1999, s 74(4).

18.55   Similar provisions apply when a person who is the subject of a decision not appealable in the UK—refusal of leave to enter to someone without entry clearance, or removal of an overstayer or an illegal entrant—seeks to raise an asylum or human rights or discrimination ground against removal. That person is served with a one-stop notice under the Immigration and Asylum Act 1999, section 75, and the asylum or human rights appeal will then embrace the further grounds on which the appellant seeks to argue against removal, in so far as they are themselves appealable. In practice the section 75 procedure will allow human rights or discrimination and asylum grounds to be heard together, as for example when an asylum seeker wishes to argue an ECHR, Article 3 ground in the alternative (eg, because there is doubt as to whether the persecution faced is for a Convention reason). The one-stop appeal would also cover the situation of a port asylum seeker who marries in the UK while the asylum claim is being processed, and seeks to raise Article 8 issues arising from the marriage in his or her appeal. Like the procedure under the Immigration and Asylum Act 1999, section 74, the one-stop procedure under section 75 also embraces grounds that other family members apart from the original appellant might have for not being removed. A one-stop statement of a child of an asylum claimant might cite ties to the UK through schooling, friends, health and putting down roots in the UK, giving rise to Article 8 considerations[1] if the family had been in the UK for some time before the decision to remove which sparked the asylum claim.

1   'Private life' in the sense used by Judge Martens, concurring, in *Beldjoudi v France* (1992) 14 EHRR 801: see **8.62**ff above.

18.56   There is at the time of writing no case law on how these provisions will work. But the case law on mixed appeals under the Asylum and Immigration Appeals Act 1993 (mixed asylum and deportation appeals) may be relevant. On a mixed appeal, an adjudicator was obliged to deal with both issues in the same proceedings, and a determination dealing with only one of the issues—the appellant's liability to deportation—was held a nullity.[1] On the other hand, where an adjudicator simply dealt with one part of the mixed appeal inadequately, as opposed to not dealing with it at all, the Tribunal could rectify the failure itself rather than having to remit the matter for *de novo* hearing.[2]

1   *Angus* (17706) 8 July 1998, IAT. See also *Ousman* (12957) 30 January 1996, IAT.
2   *Dragica* (13288) 28 April 1996, IAT.

18.57 The one-stop procedure applies equally to appeals in the Special Immigration Appeals Commission.[1] It does not appear to apply as such to appeals against EEA decisions, although there is provision for human rights or discrimination grounds in all such appeals, and such a ground converts an out-of-country appeal into an in-country one.[2]

1   See Immigration and Asylum Act 1999, s 74(1)(b), (2)(b), (3)(b).
2   Immigration (European Economic Area) Regulations 2000, SI 2000/2326, regs 29(2), 30(3)(b).

POWERS OF APPELLATE AUTHORITIES

18.58 On an appeal, the power of an adjudicator to decide the appeal one way or the other is contained in Schedule 4, para 21 to the Immigration and Asylum Act 1999.[1] The Tribunal no longer has any first-instance jurisdiction,[2] and on an appeal from an adjudicator to the Tribunal, the Tribunal can affirm the determination or make any other determination which could have been made by the adjudicator, or can remit the appeal for determination by the same or another adjudicator.[3] The appellate authorities also have a jurisdiction to determine as a preliminary issue whether an out-of-time appeal should be allowed to proceed, and whether there is a right of appeal at all. We deal with this preliminary issue jurisdiction, and the Tribunal's power to hear an appeal from preliminary issue determinations of adjudicators at **18.127–18.128** and **18.169** below. Both the Tribunal and the adjudicators have powers to make directions and recommendations consequent on their determinations. Both have power in certain circumstances to review or rescind certain of their decisions.[4]

1   In identical terms (although written in New English, with 'must' for 'shall' and 'if' for 'where') to Immigration Act 1971, s 19, the old jurisdiction section.
2   The Tribunal had such jurisdiction in deportation appeals, in 'conducive' cases and 'family' cases, by Immigration Act 1971, s 15(7). Conducive cases and surviving family cases now go to the adjudicator; most family cases involved family members of overstayers, who are no longer subject to the deportation process.
3   Immigration and Asylum Act 1999, Sch 4, para 22; Immigration and Asylum Appeals (Procedure) Rules 2000, SI 2000/2333, r 23.
4   SI 2000/2333, r 16 (adjudicator); r 19 (Tribunal, limited to reviewing refusal of leave to appeal). See **18.168, 18.175** below.

18.59 In certain cases the adjudicator is bound to dismiss an appeal, for example in an appeal against a refusal of leave to enter, if he or she is satisfied that the appellant was an illegal entrant at the time of the refusal.[1] An appeal against a refusal of an entry clearance must also be dismissed if the adjudicator is satisfied that there was a deportation order in force in respect of the appellant at the time of the refusal.[2] Similarly, members of the crew of a ship or aircraft may have succeeded in showing that there was no power on the facts of the case to remove them as crew-members under Schedule 2 to the Immigration Act 1971.

Nevertheless, the adjudicator must dismiss a crew-member's appeal if he or she is satisfied that there was power to give directions for their removal on the alternative ground that the appellant was an illegal entrant.[3] This duty to dismiss appeals must of course be read subject to any human rights or discrimination or asylum grounds raised.

1   Immigration and Asylum Act 1999, Sch 4, para 24(1).
2   Immigration and Asylum Act 1999, Sch 4, para 24(2).
3   Immigration and Asylum Act 1999, Sch 4, para 24(3).

18.60 Subject to these cases, and subject to any restriction on the grounds of appeal, Schedule 4, para 21 to the Immigration and Asylum Act 1999 provides that an adjudicator must allow the appeal if he or she considers:

(1)   that the decision or action against which the appeal is brought was not in accordance with the law or with any immigration rule applicable to the case;[1] or

(2)   where the decision or action involved the exercise of a discretion by the Secretary of State or an officer, that the discretion should have been exercised differently.[2]

Otherwise, the adjudicator must dismiss the appeal. In exercising these functions an adjudicator may review any determination of a question of fact on which a decision was based. A decision by the Secretary of State not to depart from the rules may not be reviewed on the merits, but may be reviewed to see whether it is in accordance with the law.[3]

1   Immigration and Asylum Act 1999 Sch 4 para 21(1)(a).
2   Immigration and Asylum Act 1999, Sch 4, paras 21(1)(b) and 21(4). See *Pearson v Secretary of State for the Home Department* [1978] Imm AR 211, CA.
3   Immigration and Asylum Act 1999, Sch 4, paras 21(1)(a), (b) and 21(4). See **18.62**ff below.

18.61 Where an appeal is allowed, the adjudicator must give requisite directions for giving effect to the determination,[1] and may make recommendations with respect to any other action which he or she considers should be taken in the case under the Immigration Acts.[2] Where such directions are given, and are not in suspense pending a further appeal, it is the duty of the Secretary of State and any officer to whom the directions are given to comply with them.[3] These, in outline, are the normal powers of adjudicators. We now look in more detail at the various requirements.

1   Immigration and Asylum Act 1999, Sch 4, para 21(5)(a).
2   Immigration and Asylum Act 1999, Sch 4, para 21(5)(b).
3   Immigration and Asylum Act 1999, Sch 4, paras 21(6), 22(4).

In accordance with the law

18.62 An adjudicator must allow an appeal if the decision or action in question is not in accordance with the law. The ambit of this jurisdiction has given rise to much litigation. The law is clearly something distinct from and much wider than the immigration rules or the 'immigration laws', both of which are terms of art used and defined in the Immigration Act 1971.[1] Little difficulty is encountered where an appellate authority is called upon to construe and interpret the immigration or nationality laws, or some other applicable statutory provision, or to refer to the common law for the meaning of such terms as domicile, ordinary residence and the like. Equally clearly, their task extends to interpreting and applying European Community law, the Refugee Convention[2] and, since October 2000, the European Convention on Human Rights. More difficult has been the question of how far the appellate authorities can and must have regard to the general principles of administrative law when considering the actions and decisions of the Secretary of State or an immigration officer, where these involve the exercise of a discretion.

1 Immigration Act 1971, s 33. If the intention of parliament had been to confine the appellate jurisdiction to checking whether the decision or action was in accordance with the immigration laws, the use of that phrase would have been entirely apt.

2 The Tribunal in *Mehareb* (12982) 2 February 1996 had to remind an adjudicator that a decision could not be in accordance with the law if it was not in accordance with the Refugee Convention 1951.

18.63 In the case of *Bakhtaur Singh*[1] the House of Lords held that the appellate authorities were not precluded from examining any aspect of the Secretary of State's broad discretion in deportation cases. Lord Bridge reasoned that the adjudicator's jurisdiction to determine whether a decision was in accordance with the law had to embrace the general requirements of administrative law and so an appeal would be allowed if the Secretary of State had failed to have regard to all relevant circumstances.[2] He equated the adjudicator's jurisdiction with the supervisory jurisdiction of the High Court in such circumstances. The difficulty since then has been to ascertain how far these principles, and the appellate authorities' powers, go, in the absence of powers to issue quashing orders or to give declaratory relief (although they may give directions where an appeal is allowed: see **18.84ff** below).

1 *Singh v Immigration Appeal Tribunal* [1986] 2 All ER 721, [1986] Imm AR 352, HL.

2 *Associated Provincial Picture Houses Ltd v Wednesbury Corpn* [1948] 1 KB 223, [1948] 2 All ER 680 - the origin of the '*Wednesbury* unreasonable' test in administrative law.

18.64 After two decades of litigation on the scope of the appellate authorities' jurisdiction, the following principles have been established:

(1) If an application called for the exercise of a discretion which has not in fact been exercised, the decision is not in accordance with the law, and an appeal would be allowed to the extent that the Secretary of State should reconsider the case.[1] This is based on the principle that an adjudicator is not an original decision taker and, therefore, cannot determine an application which has been made to the Secretary of State but not determined prior to appeal.[2] Similarly, where the Secretary of State misinterprets the application and fails to apply the correct rule to it, or applies only one of the applicable rules,[3] the case should be remitted for consideration under the proper rule or outside the rules altogether, if that was what was sought.[4] In *Yau Yak Wah*[5] the Court of Appeal held that a decision was not in accordance with the law where the Secretary of State had failed to give separate consideration to the case of each appellant in a case involving different members of a family, and thus failed to exercise discretion.

(2) A decision taken outside the immigration rules which fails to take account of or give effect to the Secretary of State's own published policy outside

the rules is not in accordance with the law.[6] The decision of the Court of Appeal in *Abdi*,[7] while observing that 'it is not obvious that Parliament intended adjudicators to have the power to examine the validity of the Home Secretary's decision by reference to all the matters that would be relevant for a judicial review of that decision', went on to 'proceed on the footing that if it can be shown that the Home Secretary failed to act in accordance with established principles of administrative or common law, for example if he did not take account of or give effect to his own published policy, that was 'not in accordance with the law'.[8] This was the position which had been taken for several years by one division of the Tribunal, which in a number of important and carefully reasoned decisions had held that the 'law applicable to the case' in section 19(1) of the Immigration Act 1971 (the precursor to Schedule 4, paragraph 21 to the Immigration and Asylum Act 1999), meant the law which the appellate authority must apply whatever the source of that law.[9] The Court of Appeal's endorsement of this principle in *Abdi* was followed in *Hersi*[10] and is now well established.[11]

(3)   The exercise of discretion outside the rules, whether under a policy, or under section 4(1) of Immigration Act 1971,[12] which is predicated on a misapprehension of material facts, is not in accordance with the law. This was the *ratio* of *Abdi*[13] and again is now well established.[14] This requires the appellate authority to determine material questions of fact.[15] And where the appellate authority has determined that the Secretary of State reached a conclusion excluding an appellant from the benefit of a policy under a misapprehension of material facts, its own findings on the facts relevant to the inquiry, made within its statutory jurisdiction, bind the Secretary of State.[16]

(4)   The appellate authorities have jurisdiction to consider whether the conduct of the Secretary of State or an officer has given rise to a legitimate expectation to which effect ought to be given. This was Professor Jackson's view in *Odozi*,[17] which won more general, if not universal, acceptance in the Tribunal.[18] It certainly follows from the logic of *Abdi*.

1   Sometimes this is expressed as the matter remaining outstanding before the decision-maker: see eg *Ibeakanma* (18632) 25 September 1998, IAT; *Adeyemi* (17115) 20 May 1998, IAT.
2   *R v Immigration Appeal Tribunal, ex p Malik* (1981) Times, 16 November, Forbes J.
3   *Tohur Ali v Secretary of State for the Home Department* [1987] Imm AR 189.
4   *Livingstone* (10964) April 1994.
5   *Wah (Yau Yak) v Home Office* [1982] Imm AR 16, CA
6   *Gyeabour* [1989] Imm AR 94; *Van Liew* [1989] Imm AR 62; *Patel (Dawood)* [1990] Imm AR 478.
7   *Abdi (Dhudi Saleban) v Secretary of State for the Home Department* [1996] Imm AR 148.
8   [1996] Imm AR 148 at 157.
9   *Odozi* (9582); *Andereh* (9331); *Patel (Dawood)* [1990] Imm AR 478; *Saemian* [1991] Imm AR 489; *Bernstein* (4063) (reported on other issues in the Court of Appeal at [1988] Imm AR 449).
10 *Hersi v Secretary of State for the Home Department* [1996] Imm AR 569.
11 See eg *Kausar* [1998] INLR 141, IAT; *Adeyemi* (17115) 20 May 1998, IAT; *Botan* (18175) 12 May 1999, IAT; *Adeniran* (18883) 20 May 1999, IAT; *Scott (Clevon Marcus)* (13389), IAT.
12 General discretion of immigration officers and the Secretary of State: see **18.73** below.
13 See fn 7 above.
14 See also *Onen* (14501) 4 February 1997, IAT.
15 See **18.78** below.

16 *Onen* (22101) 8 October 1999, IAT, following *Secretary of State for the Home Department, ex p Danaie* [1998] Imm AR 84.
17 (9582).
18 See eg *Dave (Sangita)* (11313) 6 September 1994; *Aboutalebi* (14012) 17 October 1996; *Suleman* (16371) 11 August 1998.

18.65 Issues which remain unresolved by the higher courts include:

(1)   whether the appellate authority may look at the underlying rule on which a decision was based, and declare that rule invalid;

(2)   whether a Tribunal can set aside a decision as 'not in accordance with the law' for procedural impropriety, eg a failure to deal properly or fairly with an application before issuing a decision, or for *Wednesbury* unreasonableness;

(3)   what powers the appellate authority has, if any, to substitute its own decision for an impugned extra-rules decision of the Secretary of State.

18.66 On the issue of the *vires* of a rule relied on by the Secretary of State in reaching a decision, in *Chief Adjudication Officer v Foster*[1] the House of Lords, considering an analogous power possessed by the Chief Adjudication Officer on an appeal from a Social Security Appeal Tribunal, ruled that the Social Security Commissioner could determine the vires of a regulation under his or her 'erroneous in point of law' jurisdiction. In *Bugg v DPP*[2] the Divisional Court held that a magistrates' court could determine the issue of the substantive invalidity of a byelaw on which the Crown relied, if the byelaw was bad on its face (although it could not inquire into procedural invalidity, since such an inquiry required investigation into whether the bylaw was improperly made). In the immigration field those issues have never been definitively decided. In *Manshoora Begum*,[3] where a provision in an immigration rule was struck down in the Divisional Court as unreasonable, the court assumed, without deciding the point, that the Tribunal could not have decided the issue. One division of the Tribunal has held that *Manshoora Begum* has been superseded by the subsequent decision in *Foster*, and that it has jurisdiction to consider the *vires* of immigration rules.[4] Another division of the Tribunal has disagreed, saying it did not see how jurisdiction could be given to the appellate authority to strike down a paragraph of the immigration rules because it undermines another statute (in that case, the Adoption Act 1976).[5] A starred Tribunal in *Pardeepan* suggested without deciding that the *vires* of a commencement order under the 1999 Act were a matter for the High Court,[6] and in *Koprinov*[7] a Tribunal chaired by the President held it had no jurisdiction to decide whether a rule was *ultra vires*.

1   [1993] AC 754, [1993] 1 All ER 705.
2   [1993] QB 473.
3   *R v Immigration Appeal Tribunal, ex p Begum (Manshoora)* [1986] Imm AR 385.
4   *Shafique (Qaisar)* (18448) 16 September 1998, IAT.
5   *Singh (Pawandeep)* (18465) 16 March 1999, IAT. In refusing leave to appeal, however, Buxton LJ was prepared to accept, without deciding, that the tribunal would have jurisdiction to enter upon that inquiry in an appropriate case, although in this case the rule was not *ultra vires*: SLJ 99/6917/4, 2 December 1999.
6   *Pardeepan* [2000] INLR 447. It proceeded on the basis that the order was *intra vires*.
7   (01 TH 00091) 5 February 2001.

18.67 Many cases which involve an allegation of unfairness or procedural impropriety involve the exercise of a discretion within the immigration rules, and the appellate authorities can consider whether the discretion should have been exercised differently in view of the facts as found by them[1] and do not, therefore, need to base their decision on unfairness or other illegality. In *Mumin's case*[2] the Divisional Court was confronted squarely with the issue of unfairness in the exercise of discretion outside the rules. The Tribunal had held that a decision on an application to switch from visitor to student (which was subject to mandatory refusal under the rules) was reached unfairly because the Secretary of State had not identified the criteria on which he would be prepared to depart from the rule and had not, therefore, granted the appellant a fair opportunity of meeting those criteria. Thus, it held, the decision was not in accordance with the law. The Divisional Court decided it was unnecessary to resolve this issue, in view of its finding that there was in fact no unfairness, but stated that 'it would be prudent of chairmen of tribunals to leave such matters to this court which is accustomed to dealing with them'. The issue of procedural unfairness in relation to applications outside the rules has not been revisited since, although the dicta in *Abdi*[3] should apply equally in this situation. The new human rights jurisdiction is likely to have an impact here, insofar as procedural unfairness detracts from the safeguards required as an ingredient of rights under the ECHR.

1   Under Immigration and Asylum Act 1999, Sch 4, para 21(1)(b).
2   *R v Immigration Appeal Tribunal, ex p Secretary of State for the Home Department* [1992] Imm AR 554, QBD.
3   *Abdi (Dhudi Saleban) v Secretary of State for the Home Department* [1996] Imm AR 148.

18.68   On the question of whether the appellate authority can substitute its own decision for a decision of the Secretary of State that it finds to be not in accordance with the law, the Tribunal's answer depends on the degree of discretion to be exercised. While the appellate authority cannot exercise the Secretary of State's discretion itself,[1] it may give effect to a substantive legitimate expectation in an appropriate case.[2] And where the application of a policy depends solely on a particular factual situation and as a matter of law is not dependent on the exercise of discretion by the Secretary of State, it is open to the appellate authority to determine the matter itself. Where an appellant fulfilled the criteria of the long residence concession and there were no countervailing factors, the Tribunal has held that that was just such a case.[3]

1   See eg *Kausar* [1998] INLR 141; *Kaur (Harvinder)* (13700) 25 July 1996; *Ali (Ayad)* (14176) 15 November 1996; *Botan* (18175) 12 May 1999.
2   *Odozi* (9582); *Dave (Sangita)* (11313) 6 September 1994; *Suleman* (16371) 11 August 1998, IAT.
3   *Umujakporne* (12448) 18 August 1995, IAT.

Scottish or English law

18.69   The Immigration Acts and Rules apply throughout the UK and there is a unified appellate authority. This should mean that the law is the same in both Scotland and England. There are divergences in higher court decisions, particularly in areas such as detention,[1] in the exclusion of unfairly obtained evidence in illegal entry decisions,[2] and over the issue of delay in judicial review,[3] but in asylum cases at least, the distinctions between Scottish and English decisions are more apparent than real. Two questions arise. The first is a choice of law and the second a choice of jurisdiction. First, if there is a conflict between the

Scottish and English decisions, which law should the adjudicator or Tribunal apply? In *Akbar*[4] the Tribunal suggested that if the judicial approach differs in any material way, it will be for the appellate authority to decide with which legal system the case is most closely connected. Secondly, can appellants choose whether to litigate in Scotland or England? At adjudicator or Tribunal level, the matter does not arise, since there is no distinct appellate unit in either jurisdiction. In appeals from final determinations by the Tribunal on questions of law the choice of jurisdiction is determined by statute. The appeal goes to the Court of Session where the determination of the Tribunal is *made* in Scotland and in all other cases to the Court of Appeal.[5]

1   *Sokha v Secretary of State for the Home Department* [1992] Imm AR 14, Ct of Sess.
2   *Oghonoghor v Secretary of State for the Home Department* 1995 SLT 733; *Kim (Sofia) v Secretary of State for the Home Department* 2000 SLT 249, OHCS, Lord Abernethy.
3   *Singh (Gurjit)* 14 March 2000, OH CS, Lord Nimmo Smith.
4   (8670) IAT.
5   Immigration and Asylum Act 1999, Sch 4, para 23(3).

18.70 In applications for judicial review, the question is not so easily determined. Where the challenge is to a decision of the Secretary of State, the English High Court or the Scottish Court of Session may each have or claim jurisdiction. In *Sokha*[1] the Court of Session resolved the matter by the application of the doctrine of *forum non conveniens,* and rejected jurisdiction in a case with no Scottish connection. Although strong preference should be given to the forum chosen by the applicant, particularly where the alternative jurisdiction is another part of the UK, rather than a wholly foreign country, this preference may be overcome if the respondent can 'establish that there is another available forum which is clearly and distinctly more appropriate', although less advantageous.[2]

1   *Sokha v Secretary of State for the Home Department* [1992] Imm AR 14, Ct of Sess.
2   *Spiliada Maritime Corpn v Cansulex Ltd, The Spiliada* [1987] AC 460, per Lord Goff; *Trendtex Trading Corpn v Crédit Suisse* [1982] AC 679; *Abidin Daver, The* [1984] AC 398 at 411.

In accordance with the immigration rules

18.71 An adjudicator must allow an appeal if the decision or action appealed against is not in accordance with the immigration rules. This applies where the wrong rule is applied, and the decision is based on grounds which are inapplicable to the applicant,[1] or where the evidence before the adjudicator establishes the appellant's eligibility for entry under the relevant rule.[2] Because of this provision the immigration rules have the force of law for the purposes of appeals, though not for other purposes.[3] The case law reflects some conflict between two principles: on the one hand, the appellate authority must ensure that the decision is in accordance with any applicable rule, implying a broad jurisdiction;[4] on the other, it is only entitled to determine that which is before it for determination.[5] The position may be summarised as follows:

(1)   The adjudicator is not restricted to the particular rule or part of a rule relied on in the notice of decision or explanatory statement, but, having found the facts, is entitled to apply the immigration rules applicable to the case having regard to the facts that he or she has found.[6] This applies whether the new rule involves mandatory refusal or the exercise of discretion;[7]

(2)   The adjudicator is not entitled, however, to go behind a finding of fact of the Secretary of State favourable to the appellant;[8]

(3)   Similarly, the respondent may seek to rely on a new rule applicable to the facts, subject to providing the appellant with a fair opportunity to deal with the new rule, by amendment of the refusal decision or the issue of a new explanatory statement.[9] It is not contrary to the two-tier system of appeals for the Secretary of State to raise a point at Tribunal level for the first time, as the appellate authority must be satisfied that the decision is in accordance with the law and the rules to allow the appeal. But where the Secretary of State has so conducted the case as to lead the appellant and the appellate authority to believe that no point was to be taken on a particular ground, the appellate authority should be slow to raise the point of its own motion;[10]

(4)   The respondent may not seek to alter the statutory basis of its decision, eg by relying on a wholly different deportation power in the Immigration Act 1971 from that originally exercised;[11]

(5)   If adjudicators are minded to take points themselves they should say so, and provide a opportunity to the parties to deal with them;[12]

(6)   Subject to this, where the new rule is mandatory or its proper application is readily ascertainable once the facts have been determined, the adjudicator may go on to consider it at once, although where the new rule involves the exercise of a discretion which has not been exercised or purported to be exercised by the Secretary of State, the better course may be to allow the appeal and remit the case for the Secretary of State to exercise discretion on the facts as found, with regard to the relevant rule;[13]

(7)   The principle for appellants is that if they make clear the facts that they rely on when making their application, they are not required to set out all the different potentially applicable immigration rules.[14] They must be permitted to ventilate on appeal eligibility under rules other than those previously considered by the respondent, provided the fact found forms part of the basis of the decision, since to hold otherwise would mean that the scope of the right of appeal would be confined to the basis on which the respondent chose to frame it.[15] But there is no jurisdiction to allow an appeal against a decision on the basis that if the application had been made on another ground it might have qualified under another section of the rules,[16] particularly if the grounds are mutually exclusive;[17]

(8)   Adjudicators may on their own initiative have regard to any particular rule that bears on the case put forward by the appellant with regard to the decision or action appealed against,[18] but they are not required to conduct a roving inquiry into whether the facts could fit any conceivable rule in the absence of submissions to that effect;[19]

(9)   If the appellant wishes to raise wholly new matters, the ability to do so on appeal will be subject to the provisions of section 76 of the Immigration and Asylum Act 1999.[20] Since there can be no asylum appeal if there has been no asylum claim, an appeal on family reunion issues cannot be used to argue that the appellant is a refugee.[21]

1   *R v Immigration Appeal Tribunal, ex p Khan* [1975] Imm AR 26. This happens most frequently in cases involving family settlement, where for example the 'living alone in the most exceptional compassionate circumstances' test is wrongly applied to an appellant.
2   For a case which illustrates both the 'law' and 'rules' jurisdiction neatly, see *Ibeakanma* (18632) 25 September 1998.

3 *Pearson v Immigration Appeal Tribunal* [1978] Imm AR 212; *R v Secretary of State for the Home Department, ex p Hosenball* [1977] 3 All ER 452, [1977] 1 WLR 766, CA; *Singh v Immigration Appeal Tribunal* [1986] 2 All ER 721, [1986] Imm AR 352, HL.

4 *R v Immigration Appeal Tribunal, ex p Khan* [1975] Imm AR 26; *R v Immigration Appeal Tribunal, ex p Hubbard* [1985] Imm AR 110, QBD.

5 *R v Immigration Appeal Tribunal, ex p Akhtar* (1982) 126 Sol Jo 430, QBD.

6 *R v Immigration Appeal Tribunal, ex p Hubbard* [1985] Imm AR 110; *R v Immigration Appeal Tribunal, ex p Malik* (1981) Times, 16 November, QBD.

7 *Tahir (Nadeem) v Immigration Appeal Tribunal* [1989] Imm AR 98, CA.

8 *R v Immigration Appeal Tribunal, ex p Hubbard* [1985] Imm AR 110.

9 *R v Immigration Appeal Tribunal, ex p Hubbard* [1985] Imm AR 110; *Parsaiyan* [1986] Imm AR 155, IAT; *Uddin v Immigration Appeal Tribunal* [1991] Imm AR 134, CA; *Aboutalebi* (14012) 17 October 1996.

10 *Ahmed* (13371) 15 May 1996, IAT. However, in *Kathiripillai* (12250a) 16 December 1996, the Tribunal declined to allow the Secretary of State to raise a new ground of refusal of asylum based on Art 1F.

11 *R v Immigration Appeal Tribunal, ex p Mehmet* [1978] Imm AR 46.

12 *R v Immigration Appeal Tribunal, ex p Hubbard* [1985] Imm AR 110. But see also *Agyen-Frempong v Immigration Appeal Tribunal* [1988] Imm AR 262, CA; Immigration Appeal Tribunals can deal with a rule applied by the Secretary of State but not dealt with by the adjudicator, without necessarily calling further evidence or remitting to the adjudicator: *Hussain* (5783).

13 *Parsaiyan* [1986] Imm AR 155, following *R v Immigration Appeal Tribunal, ex p Malik* (1981) Times, 16 November, QBD: *Yau Yak Wah v Home Office* [1982] Imm AR 16, CA; but see *R v Immigration Appeal Tribunal, ex p Mohan (Surinder)* [1985] Imm AR 84, CA.

14 *Khatun (Kessori)* (4272).

15 *Rahman (Aklakur)* (00TH00307) 10 March 2000.

16 *Uddin (Hawa Bibi) v Immigration Appeal Tribunal* [1991] Imm AR 134, CA (application on the basis of marriage which was found invalid; appeal raised issue of common law relationship).

17 *Hussain (Shabir)* [1991] Imm AR 483 (IAT).

18 *Uddin (Hawa Bibi) v Immigration Appeal Tribunal* [1991] Imm AR 134, CA; *R v Immigration Appeal Tribunal, ex p Tohur Ali* [1987] Imm AR 189, QBD; whether the adjudicator ought to do so was reserved in Court of Appeal [1988] Imm AR 237.

19 *Mohammed Frazor Ali v Secretary of State for the Home Department* [1988] Imm AR 274, CA; *R v Immigration Appeal Tribunal, ex p Hawa Uddin* [1990] Imm AR 309, QBD; on appeal [1991] Imm AR 134, CA; *Robinson v Immigration Appeal Tribunal* [1997] Imm AR 568, CA.

20 See **18.53**ff above and **18.108**ff below.

21 *Hersi v Secretary of State for the Home Department* [1996] Imm AR 569; *Darbiye v ECO Nairobi* [1998] Imm AR 64.

18.72 Where a rule has been waived by the Secretary of State, whether in the individual case or in the particular class of case to which the appellant belongs, it cannot be applied to the appellant without good cause and a decision which did so would be not in accordance with the law as it would breach a legitimate expectation.[1]

1 Eg the waiver of maintenance and accommodation requirements in refugee family reunion cases. See eg *Aboutalebi* (14012) 17 October 1996, and cases cited at **18.64** fn 6 above.

Discretion should be exercised differently

18.73 Where persons are subject to immigration control, the Secretary of State for the Home Department and immigration officers have a general discretion as to who should be admitted and in what circumstances. Section 4(1) of the Immigration Act 1971 gives the responsibility to immigration officers of granting leave to enter and that of leave to remain to the Secretary of State. Under section 3(2) of the 1971 Act, the Secretary of State is empowered to make immigration rules as to the practice to be followed in the administration of the Act for regulating the entry into and stay in the UK of persons required by the Act to have leave to enter. Thus, it is clear that under the 1971 Act the Secretary of State has a general and wide discretion to determine who can be admitted to the UK and in what circumstances, both through the guidelines set out in the immigration rules and in particular cases or situations not covered by the rules.[1] The Immigration Directorate Instructions (IDI) and the Asylum Policy Instructions (API), and other published material such as ministerial statements and parliamentary answers, provide detailed guidelines as to the exercise of discretion both inside and outside the immigration rules. There are many published policies dealing with matters outside the rules such as the admission of children for adoption, the admission and stay of domestic workers, the treatment of spouses who have suffered domestic violence during their 'probationary period' in the UK, the bringing of enforcement action against family members of those with residence rights in the UK, or the grant of indefinite leave and family reunion rights to those with exceptional leave to remain. There are also cases where the Secretary of State will allow someone to remain exceptionally, in the exercise of his or her general discretion, although the immigration rules expressly say that they should not qualify.

1   In *R v Secretary of State for the Home Department, ex p Ahmed and Patel* [1998] INLR 570 there was an inconclusive discussion on whether the extra-rules discretion in relation to the admission of aliens was derived from the statute or the prerogative. See *R v Secretary of State for the Home Department, ex p Immigration Appeal Tribunal* [1990] Imm AR 166.

Discretion under the rules

18.74 In cases where the application of an immigration rule involves the exercise of a discretion, Schedule 4, paragraph 21(1)(b) to the Immigration and Asylum Act 1999 empowers the appellate authorities to review the exercise of the discretion on the merits. In other words adjudicators and the Tribunal are not limited to determining whether the original decision was in accordance with the law and the immigration rules applicable to the case, but are required to consider whether the discretion should be exercised differently.[1] Whether there has been fresh evidence or not,[2] whether the evidence discloses a different factual situation to that before the original decision-maker or not, the adjudicator may exercise discretion differently and allow the appeal, or may uphold the decision on different grounds.[3] Where the focus of the decision-making process has been on how the discretion should be exercised, the Adjudicator can go straight to this aspect of the case without being bound to make a finding on the lawfulness of decision under Schedule 4, paragraph 21(1)(a) to the 1999 Act.[4]

1   *R v Immigration Appeal Tribunal, ex p Desai* [1987] Imm AR 18.
2   *Begum (Zakia)* [1988] Imm AR 465.
3   *Nadeem Tahir v Immigration Appeal Tribunal* [1989] Imm AR 98, CA.
4   *R v Immigration Appeal Tribunal, ex p Razaque* [1989] Imm AR 451, QBD.

18.75 This is clearly a very wide power and it is perhaps not surprising that Schedule 4, paragraph 21(4) to the Immigration and Asylum Act 1999 should impose limits on its use. This provides that no decision or action which is in accordance with the immigration rules is to be treated as having involved the exercise of a discretion by the Secretary of State by reason only of the fact that he or she has been requested to depart, or to authorise an officer to depart, from the immigration rules and has refused to do so. The adjudicator's jurisdiction to review the decision in such a case is limited to whether it is not in accordance with the law.[1] A question which has given rise to difficulty is what constitutes a request to depart from the rules and a refusal to do so. There used to be a fruitful distinction between decisions involving a request to depart from the rules, and decisions outside the rules. In the latter situation, where there was no relevant rule, for example in cases involving transfer of refugees, applications to stay to continue same-sex relationships, and in a number of other factual scenarios for which no immigration rule had been devised, there was no request to depart from the rules, and so the adjudicator had an unfettered review of the merits of the decision.[2] In 1994, with the advent of comprehensive rules providing for mandatory refusal of anyone not falling within any of the categories of eligibility set out,[3] this gap disappeared and the jurisprudence it had given rise to ceased to be of more than historical interest.

1   This was held in *Singh (Nachhtar)* [1991] Imm AR 195 to apply to an application for further exceptional leave to remain, following the grant of a period of exceptional leave to remain: the Secretary of State was entitled to refuse under the rules, limiting the adjudicator's jurisdiction on appeal.
2   Eg *R v Immigration Appeal Tribunal, ex p Prajapati* [1981] Imm AR 199, QBD (see the fourth edition of this book, **18.49** fn 6, for relevant citation, omitted from the report of the case); *Wirdestedt v Secretary of State for the Home Department* [1982] Imm AR 186; *Livingstone* (10964), IAT; *Dzexter* (4980) 19 February 1987, IAT; *Rahman (Jinnah)* [1989] Imm AR 325; *Curic (Stjepan)* (10934) 10 May 1994, IAT.
3   HC 395, paras 320 (1) and 322 (1).

18.76 Now, every decision outside the rules is a response to a request—implicit or explicit—to depart from the rules. There may be an express request to depart from the rules, or a necessary implication where the application can only succeed if there is a departure from the rules. A request to depart arises where there is a rule requiring mandatory refusal of the application. This applies even where the Secretary of State has a policy outside the rules, thereby indicating that the discretion will normally be exercised within the terms of the policy and not the rules. A discretion exercised under the rules instead of the policy will, in such a situation, be 'not in accordance with the law' but the appellate authority cannot substitute its own decision on the merits. In *Abdi*[1] the Court of Appeal rejected the argument that a policy constituted a revised legal framework whereby the Secretary of State has agreed to depart from the rules. In *Kausar*[2] the Tribunal agreed that the policy of the Secretary of State—in applying the maintenance and accommodation criteria in family reunion cases so as to exclude only those whose arrival would cause additional recourse to public funds—appeared a *de facto* amendment to the rules by way of concession, but insisted that, while the adjudicator should make formal findings on the evidence, it could not take the decision itself on the basis of the concession. However, in *Scott*[3] the Tribunal exercised a full merits review on the exercise of discretion under the rule as *de facto* amended.

1   *Dhudi Saleban Abdi v Secretary of State for the Home Department* [1996] Imm AR 148, CA.
2   *Kausar* [1998] INLR 141, IAT.
3   (13389), IAT.

18.77 Where on appeal it has been determined that a discretion outside the rules has not been exercised properly, or at all, so that the decision is 'not in accordance with the law', the appellate authorities may not substitute their own discretion. They may substitute their own decision only where the correct legal framework gives rise to no possibility of an adverse decision—the opposite of a discretionary situation.[1] Their proper role is to make relevant factual findings and allow the appeal, remitting it to the primary decision-maker for decision in accordance with those facts and the correct legal framework.[2]

1 See **18.68** above.
2 *Kausar* [1998] INLR 141, IAT.

Reviewing questions of fact

18.78 In order to reach a decision whether or not to allow an appeal under the Immigration and Asylum Act 1999, Schedule 4, paragraph 21, adjudicators can review any determination of a question of fact on which the decision or action was based.[1] This means that as far as questions of fact are concerned adjudicators are not confined to the evidence which was before the immigration authority when they reached their decision or took action, but they can consider all the evidence, including any further evidence found since the decision was taken. In doing so, adjudicators and the Tribunal perform a different function from that of the High Court either on judicial review or when dealing with statutory appeals, where the court is confined to the material which the minister or other body had before them.[2] In immigration appeals the appellate authority goes into the facts again,[3] and can correct factual errors made by the immigration authority,[4] and hear of facts which were unknown to the decision-maker.[5] By reason of this jurisdiction, and the power to determine exercises of discretion, the appellate authority can correct irrationality (eg failures to take into account important and relevant facts) and procedural unfairness (eg a failure to interview) without having to classify them as errors of law. But there are certain important limitations on the review powers of adjudicators when dealing with questions of fact. First, they are reviewing questions of fact on which the decision or action is based, and therefore only evidence which relates to such facts is relevant or inadmissible. Secondly, any fresh evidence must normally relate to facts in existence at the time of the decision (this is dealt with below). Thirdly, in appeals against refusal of entry clearance and other decisions taken abroad, they must pay respect to the views of the entry clearance officer who has interviewed the appellant.[6] But adjudicators do not need to have fresh evidence before reversing the entry clearance officer.[7]

1 Immigration and Asylum Act 1999, Sch 4, para 21(3).
2 See *Ashbridge Investments Ltd v Minister of Housing* [1965] 3 All ER 371 at 374, CA. But see **8.71**ff above for the new role of the courts in human rights cases.
3 *R v Immigration Appeal Tribunal, ex p Hubbard* [1985] Imm AR 110, QBD.
4 *R v Secretary of State for the Home Department, ex p Husbadak* [1982] Imm AR 8.
5 *R v Immigration Appeal Tribunal, ex p Hassanin* [1987] 1 All ER 74 [1986] 1 WLR 1448, CA.
6 See *R v Immigration Appeal Tribunal, ex p Kwok On Tong* [1981] Imm AR 214, DC; *R v Immigration Appeal Tribunal, ex p Mahendra Singh* [1984] Imm AR 1, QBD.
7 *Begum (Zakia)* [1988] Imm AR 465; *Ahmad (Zafar)* [1989] Imm AR 254.

18.79 At the Tribunal level, findings of fact reached by an adjudicator do not have to be perverse or *Wednesbury* unreasonable for the Tribunal to differ, especially where no question arises as to credibility, but the question is as to the proper inference to draw,[1] although the Tribunal will give great weight to an adjudicator's credibility findings based on oral evidence.[2] The principle that the Tribunal may review the evidence *de novo* applies most particularly in asylum appeals and those raising ECHR, Article 3 issues, where the focus of the inquiry is the future.

1　*Ikhlaq v Secretary of State for the Home Department* [1997] Imm AR 404; *R v Immigration Appeal Tribunal, ex p Balendran and Katheeskumaran* [1998] Imm AR 170, QBD; *Sarker v Secretary of State for the Home Department* (9 November 2000, unreported), CA.
2　*Borissor v Secretary of State for the Home Department* [1996] Imm AR 524; *Balendran* above; *Alam Bi v Immigration Appeal Tribunal* [1979–80] Imm AR 146, *Chiver* [1997] INLR 212; *R v Immigration Appeal Tribunal, ex p Jeyeanthan* [1998] Imm AR 369, QBD (reversed on other grounds).

18.80 The adjudicator's power of factual review extends to situations where it is claimed that a decision outside the rules is not in accordance with the law because of a material misapprehension of the facts.[1] A redetermination of facts on appeal after hearing oral evidence binds the Secretary of State unless the adjudicator's factual findings are perverse or relate solely to the conditions in a particular country.[2]

1　*Dhudi Saleban Abdi v Secretary of State for the Home Department* [1996] Imm AR 148, CA; *Onen* (14501) 2 February 1997 (ruling), (22101) 8 October 1999.
2　*R v Secretary of State for the Home Department, ex p Danaie* [1998] INLR 124, [1998] Imm AR 84, CA; *Onen* (14501) 2 February 1997 (ruling), (22101) 8 October 1999.

Determining illegal entry

18.81 If the adjudicator determines that a person appealing against refusal of leave to enter is an illegal entrant, the appeal must be dismissed[1] (subject to asylum or human rights or discrimination grounds). In *Khawaja*[2] the House of Lords held that a person only became an illegal entrant by deception when the Home Office declared them to be such, and thus, in cases where the Secretary of State did not assert illegal entry, adjudicators should not attempt to usurp this function.[3] The fact that a local authority can determine questions of illegal entry for the purpose of their housing functions should not alter the approach of adjudicators or Tribunals in immigration appeals.[4]

1　Immigration and Asylum Act 1999, Sch 4, para 24(1) and (3).
2　*Khawaja v Secretary of State for the Home Department* [1984] AC 74, [1983] 1 All ER 765, HL.
3　*Watson* [1986] Imm AR 75, IAT. See also *R v Secretary of State for the Home Department, ex p Jayakody* [1982] 1 All ER 461, [1982] 1 WLR 405, CA; *R v Immigration Appeal Tribunal, ex p Akhtar and Bowen* (1982) 126 Sol Jo 430, QBD.
4　*R v Secretary of State for the Environment, ex p Tower Hamlets London Borough Council* [1993] Imm AR 495, CA.

The appellate jurisdiction in asylum appeals

18.82 While the jurisdiction of the adjudicator set out in Schedule 4, paragraph 21 to the Immigration and Asylum Act 1999 applies equally to an asylum appeal, the ground of appeal is that the appellant's removal or requirement that he or she leave the UK would be contrary to the Refugee Convention.[1] This has positive and negative consequences for the appellate authorities' jurisdiction on appeal. One the one hand, even where the Secretary of State has failed to consider a claim substantively but has refused an application for failure to attend an interview or complete a statement of evidence form, the adjudicator on appeal must decide whether the appellant's removal is in breach of the Convention.[2] On the other hand, the Tribunal has held that the limitation on the appellate jurisdiction precludes consideration of discretion under the rule relating to the return of an asylum seeker to a third safe country,[3] nor would it allow an asylum appeal and remit it to the Secretary of State in a case where an unaccompanied minor was interviewed in breach of the requirements of the rules, since an appeal may only be allowed on the statutory ground.[4] In *Massaquoi*[5] it decided that the grant of exceptional leave pending an appeal against a decision to deport on asylum grounds resulted in the appeal, if proceeded with, being dismissed. The rationale of the decision was that to succeed, an appellant had to show that a deportation order or removal directions could lawfully be made or implemented as a result of the appealed decision, and that such removal would be contrary to the Convention, to succeed on the appeal. Where the former condition was not satisfied the decision was not 'not in accordance with the law'. The resulting denial of the possibility of recognition to those accorded an inferior status has been remedied by statute.[6] For the appellate jurisdiction in human rights and asylum appeals see **8.71ff** and **12.160ff** above.

1 Immigration and Asylum Act 1999, s 69.
2 *Haddad (Ali)* [2000] INLR 117, Busuulwa (01 TH 00239) IAT.
3 *Munchula* (12986), IAT. This is now subject to the human rights jurisdiction, under which the exercise of discretion is clearly amenable to appeal.
4 *Orman (Bektas)* [1998] Imm AR 224; *Rajanathan* (18418) 20 July 1999, IAT.
5 (19542) 23 November 1999, IAT upheld by the CA on 20 December 2000; see **12.161** above.
6 Immigration and Asylum Act 1999, s 69(3).

Restricted jurisdiction: 'no power in law'

18.83 On appeal against a decision to remove a person as an illegal entrant, an overstayer, a person who has breached conditions or remained by deception, or a family member of such a person,[1] the jurisdiction of the appellate authority is limited to deciding whether the Secretary of State has power in law to make the order for the reasons stated in the notice. This does not allow a review of the merits of the decision to remove, nor does it allow the adjudicator to decide that the decision was 'not in accordance with the law'[2] for failure to comply with the ordinary principles of administrative law. The principle was settled in *Malhi*[3] and *Oladehinde*[4] in relation to restricted deportation appeals under the Immigration Act 1988, was upheld by the Tribunal following *Foster*[5] in *Dharam Singh*,[6] and applies equally to the restricted post-removal appeal in section 66 of the Immigration and Asylum Act 1999. On such an appeal the adjudicator cannot claim a jurisdiction to protect the individual from the unfettered power of the executive.[7]

1 See **18.25-18.26** above.
2 See **18.62ff** above.
3 *R v Secretary of State for the Home Department, ex p Malhi* [1990] Imm AR 275, CA.
4 *R v Secretary of State for the Home Department, ex p Oladehinde* [1991] 1 AC 254, [1990] 3 All ER 393, HL.
5 *Chief Adjudication Officer v Foster* [1993] AC 754, [1993] 1 All ER 705, HL.
6 *Singh (Dharam)* [1998] INLR 747.
7 *Robina Rafiq v Secretary of State for the Home Department* [1998] Imm AR 193, CA.

Giving directions where an appeal is allowed

18.84 Under Schedule 4, paragraph 21(5) to the Immigration and Asylum Act 1999,[1] where an appeal is allowed, adjudicators must give such directions for giving effect to the determination as they think requisite. The Tribunal has the same power on appeal.[2] They may also make recommendations with respect to any other action which they consider should be taken in the case under the Immigration Acts. Except where there is a further appeal from the adjudicator to the Tribunal, the Secretary of State and any other officer to whom directions have been given are under a duty to comply with them. The paragraph does not appear to impose any limitations on the power to give directions other than that (i) they can only be given where an appeal is allowed,[3] (ii) in order to give effect to the determination.[4] The difficulty is in defining when it is necessary to give directions. Where an application for entry clearance is made for settlement and an appeal against a refusal is allowed, there is little difficulty in directing that entry clearance should be issued in the capacity sought. This is because all relevant issues will now have been determined in favour of an appellant. The entry clearance officer will be bound by this direction in the absence of an appeal. But where the appeal is against a refusal of entry in some limited capacity, as a family visitor, an au pair or a student, it is likely that the passage of time since the decision will have led to a change of circumstances. The Tribunal has suggested that entry clearances should not generally be directed in these cases.[5] If the immigrant still seeks entry, the matter should be remitted for reconsideration by the entry clearance officer in the light of the decision.[6] In such circumstances the entry clearance officer would be bound by the positive findings in favour of the appellant unless it can be proved to a high civil balance of probabilities that the findings were obtained by fraud,[7] but other issues such as *present* intentions or ability to maintain may be considered. The direction given for the grant of entry clearance on a successful appeal is spent when such entry clearance is granted, and the failure of an appellant to use it does not oblige an entry clearance officer to grant another years later without a further decision.[8]

1 Immigration and Asylum Act 1999, Sch 4, para 21(5).
2 Immigration and Asylum Act 1999, Sch 4, para 22(5)-(7).
3 An adjudicator cannot direct the Secretary of State to issue a fresh refusal letter as a condition of allowing the Home Office to defend a decision on appeal. The asylum rules are procedural, not substantive: *Mwanza v Secretary of State for the Home Department* (2000) Independent, 9 November, CA.
4 Otherwise, they are of no effect: *Fardy* [1972] Imm AR 192; *R v Immigration Appeal Tribunal, ex p Mahendra Singh* [1984] Imm AR 1, QBD.
5 *Obeid* [1986] Imm AR 341, in effect overruling the earlier practice in *Narand* (5207).
6 An alternative approach might be to direct entry clearance conditional on the production of up to date documents; *Thabel* [1977] Imm AR 75; *Rasiah* (3245) unreported.
7 *R v Immigration Appeal Tribunal, ex p Miah* [1987] Imm AR 143, QBD.
8 *R v Secretary of State for the Home Department, ex p Moon* [1997] INLR 165, QBD. See also *Hashim* (6421), where directions were quashed by consent because there had been a change of circumstances and a fresh application for entry between the original decision and the appeal.

18.85 If on appeal an adjudicator finds that an appellant is a British citizen, directions may be given to the respondent for the issue of a certificate of entitlement to the right of abode.[1] In deportation cases, the question whether indefinite leave to remain or exceptional leave should be given is one for the Secretary of State.[2] A recommendation can be made to this effect but no direction.[3] The question of what directions it is lawful or appropriate to give on allowing an asylum appeal is unresolved, with divisions of the Tribunal holding on the one hand that the appellate authorities are entitled to give directions declaring that the appellant was a refugee at the date of decision, as well as the date of hearing,[4] and on the other, that it is not necessary for giving effect to the determination (which is whether removal would be contrary to the Convention) to direct the grant of status or its backdating, since the only direction required is leave to enter.[5] In our view, the latter view cannot be correct given that the withholding of refugee status would be contrary to the Convention, and effect is given to a successful asylum appeal not merely by the grant of leave, but specifically by granting recognition, whether or not that recognition must be backdated.[6] Where an asylum appeal was allowed but the appellant had by then been returned to the country of persecution (in a pre-1993 case, when an appeal was not suspensive), the question arose whether directions should order his return to the UK.[7] The Tribunal decided that in view of the time that had passed since his removal and the lack of current knowledge of his circumstances, the appropriate direction was that, should he apply to a British post abroad, consideration should be given to the application as if he were in the UK. Clearly in such a case the entry clearance officer would be bound by the factual findings as to the past treatment of the appellant. It is submitted that the same reasoning should apply where an asylum seeker leaves the UK voluntarily before promulgation of the determination of his or her appeal.[8]

1   *Rahman and Akhter* (00307) 10 March 2000, IAT.
2   *R v Immigration Appeal Tribunal, ex p Botta* [1987] Imm AR 80; *Rathiesh* (14648) 14 March 1997, IAT.
3   *R v Secretary of State for the Home Department, ex p Mahendra Singh* [1984] Imm AR 1.
4   *Haibe* [1997] INLR 119, IAT; *Belvue* (11834a), in accordance with the fact that refugees are recognised, not created, by the grant of refugee status: *Khaboka v Secretary of State for the Home Department* [1993] Imm AR 484, CA.
5   *Merzouk* [1999] INLR 468, IAT.
6   In *Altun (Guluzar)* (16628) 17 July 1998, the Tribunal held that 'there is nothing in the 1951 Convention which requires the determination of a notional point at which [an appellant] became a refugee', but accepted that the adjudicator could declare the appellant to be one.
7   *Kondo* (10413).
8   Since pending in-country appeals lapse by departure from the UK, this is the only scenario where the case may have relevance.

18.86 Directions may be given in extra-rules cases. Thus appropriate directions where the Secretary of State has failed to give effect to a policy will be that the respondent give consideration to the case in accordance with the relevant policy and in the light of the evidence available to him or her and the facts found by the adjudicator. It may well be right to add, as part of the direction, that the respondent give that consideration as an extended part of the original decision on the application, so that the appellant has no new fee to pay and the date of the application remains unchanged. It would not be appropriate for the adjudicator to direct the grant of entry clearance: the appellant's right is for the case to be considered in accordance with the policy, not an eventual decision in his or her favour.[1]

1   *Kausar* [1998] INLR 141. See also *Antonipillai* (16588) 12 May 1998, IAT.

18.87 The Tribunal has declared that directions should normally be given only when requested by a party to the appeal.[1] They should not be given without the parties having an opportunity to make submissions,[2] and if necessary to call evidence.[3] Directions need not be given at the same time as the decision allowing the appeal.[4] This is sensible as most decisions are delivered by post when there is no opportunity for oral argument on what directions are necessary. Thus a successful appellant can return to the appellate authority within a reasonable time after the appeal has been allowed to seek directions. This may provide some sanction against an obdurate entry clearance officer or immigration officer. The most prudent course is for directions to be asked for by appellants to be reserved in cases of anticipated difficulty, so a hearing can be reconvened for argument before there is any question of the authority becoming *functus*. Directions to give effect to a determination under Schedule 4, paragraph 21 to the Immigration and Asylum Act 1999 (which are matters of substance) should not be confused with procedural directions under the Procedure Rules.[5] These are matters of procedure to which we now turn. Equally, they should not be confused with recommendations made to the Secretary of State when an adjudicator dismisses an appeal. These are purely gratuitous and have no basis in the Act or procedure rules.

1   *Yousuf* [1990] Imm AR 191.
2   *Adac-Bosompra* [1992] Imm AR 579.
3   *Yousuf* [1990] Imm AR 191.
4   *Parry* (6123); *Hashim* (6421), IAT; *Yousuf* [1990] Imm AR 191.
5   Immigration and Asylum (Procedure) Rules 2000, SI 2000/2333, r 30.

18.88 The Tribunal has no jurisdiction to entertain an appeal against the giving or refusal to give directions in a particular case, since it has been held that the directions are not part of the 'determination on the appeal' but made to give effect to it.[1] There is an appeal, however, against an adjudicator's determination that he or she has no power to give directions.[2]

1   *Haydar* (12127) 19 May 1995. The Tribunal exercised jurisdiction in *Nahid* (12308), notwithstanding *Haydar*, but dismissed the appeal against the refusal of the adjudicator to give directions after the entry clearance officer refused to grant entry clearance on the basis of 'total divergence' of statements made at various times.
2   *Yousuf* [1990] Imm AR 191, above.

Recommendations when an appeal is dismissed

18.89 There is no statutory power to make a recommendation when a case is dismissed, and a recommendation forms no part of the adjudicator's determination,[1] but the adjudicator and the Tribunal can make their extra-statutory comments as to any appropriate future course of action if they think fit. The discretion is practically unfettered. Adjudicators can hear evidence which is relevant only to a hoped-for recommendation, but if they decline to do so, or to adjourn the case so that such evidence can be called at a later date, or refuse to consider making a recommendation, or refuse to make one on the basis of the evidence which they have already heard, neither the Tribunal nor the High Court can or will intervene.[2] This is so even where the refusal to make a recommendation is based on a material misapprehension of the facts, since the remedy lies against the Secretary of State if he or she adopts flawed findings of fact.[3] How and when a recommendation should be made is left entirely to the good sense of adjudicators. Previously, recommendations were used where the adjudicator's hands were tied by restrictions on the scope of the appeal but there were nevertheless important considerations militating against removal or for entry, such as family or private life, or risks of harm on return which did not fall within the scope of the Refugee Convention. These considerations are now the subject of appeal rights by virtue of section 65 of the Immigration and Asylum Act 1999, so the scope for extra-statutory recommendations is correspondingly narrower. There is still a place for them where, for example, there has been a change of circumstances subsequent to the date of decision which qualifies the person for leave, or where there are very strong compassionate circumstances which do not fall within the scope of the rights protected by either the Refugee Convention or the ECHR but which might qualify a person for leave outside the rules.

1   *R v Immigration Appeal Tribunal, ex p Chavrimootoo* [1995] Imm AR 267, QBD;
    R v Immigration Appeal Tribunal, ex p Anderson (CO 1048/99) 14 March 2000, QBD;
    Khatib-Shahidi v Immigration Appeal Tribunal [2001] Imm AR 124, [2000] INLR 491,
    CA.
2   *R v Immigration Appeal Tribunal, ex p Chavrimootoo* [1995] Imm AR 267, QBD;
    R v Immigration Appeal Tribunal, ex p Nalongo [1994] Imm AR 536; *Wadia* [1977] Imm
    AR 92; *Gillegao* [1989] Imm AR 174; *R v Secretary of State for the Home Department,
    ex p Kumar* [1993] Imm AR 401, QBD; *R v Immigration Appeal Tribunal, ex p Anderson*
    (CO 1048/99) 14 March 2000; *Khatib-Shahidi v Immigration Appeal Tribunal* [2001]
    Imm AR 124, CA.
3   *Khatib-Shahidi v Immigration Appeal Tribunal* [2001] Imm AR 124, CA.

18.90 The policy of the Secretary of State is to accept an adjudicator's recommendation in dismissed or withdrawn appeals 'only where the written determination discloses clear exceptional compassionate circumstances which have not been previously considered and which would merit the exercise of my discretion outside the immigration rules'.[1] Even the former, far more generous, policy (that the 'normal practice' was to follow a recommendation)[2] was held to give rise to no legitimate expectation that a recommendation would be followed, only that it will be given very serious consideration by the Secretary of State. A failure to follow a recommendation did not betray any promise made on behalf of the Department.[3] However, a refusal to follow a recommendation was irrational where it involved a possible breach of ECHR, Article 8 and where the Secretary of State was misapplying the rules relating to third-party support.[4] And in considering any recommendation or further application, the Secretary of State is bound by factual findings of the adjudicator after oral evidence (although not by the adjudicator's assessment of the objective conditions in the country of origin of an asylum seeker),[5] unless these factual findings are themselves unsustainable.[6]

1   42 HC Official Report (6th series) col 173, 23 July 1996.
2   See fourth edition of this book at **18.117**.
3   *R v Secretary of State for the Home Department, ex p Sakala* [1994] Imm AR 143, CA;
    R v Secretary of State, ex p Alakesan [1997] Imm AR 315, QBD; *R v Secretary of State
    for the Home Department, ex p Gardian* (1996) Times, 1 April, CA; *R v Secretary of State
    for the Home Department, ex p Maya Banu* [1999] Imm AR 161.
4   *R v Secretary of State for the Home Department, ex p Arman Ali* [2000] Imm AR 134,
    [2000] INLR 89, QBD.
5   *Elhasoglu v Secretary of State for the Home Department* [1997] Imm AR 380; *Kamara
    v Secretary of State for the Home Department* [1997] Imm AR 105, CA.
6   *R v Secretary of State for the Home Department, ex p Danaie* [1998] Imm AR 84, [1998]
    INLR 124, CA.

PROCEDURE ON APPEALS

18.91 Adjudicators, the Immigration Appeal Tribunal and the Special Immigration Appeals Commission are public authorities under the Human Rights Act 1998, and are therefore subject to an overriding duty to ensure that their procedures comply with the rights guaranteed by the Human Rights Convention.[1] Although the European Court of Human Rights (ECtHR) has held on several occasions that 'the right of an alien to reside in a country is a matter of public law' and is thus not a 'civil right' for the purposes of ECHR, Article 6 (fair trial in determination of civil rights and obligations),[2] the ECtHR has consistently held procedural safeguards to be vital ingredients of substantive Convention rights.[3] The higher courts in the UK have also consistently applied high common law standards of fairness to immigration appeals of all kinds, and particularly to those raising issues of international protection.[4] Since, in any event, the duty of the courts is to have regard to, rather than slavishly to follow, Strasbourg jurisprudence,[5] the result of the incorporation of the ECHR through the 1998 Act should be a fruitful marriage of its requirements and the common law in this area.

1   See Human Rights Act 1998, s 6(3).
2   *Agee v UK* (1977) 7 DR 164; *P v UK* (13162/87), (1987) 54 DR 211, *Bozano v France* (1984) 39 DR 119; *Maaouia v France*, App 39652/98, 5 October 2000; *Ilic v Croatia* App 42389/98, 19 September 2000.
3   See eg *Chahal v UK* (1996) 23 EHRR 413; *McCann v UK* (1995) 21 EHRR 97; *Kaya v Turkey* (1998) 28 EHRR 1. The European Court has also emphasised the importance of effective remedies under ECHR, Art 13 (deemed incorporated in practice and so not set out in the Schedule to the Human Rights Act).
4   See eg *R v Secretary of State for the Home Department, ex p Asifa Saleem* [2000] Imm AR 529, [2000] INLR 413, CA; *Ravichandran and Jeyeanthan v Secretary of State for the Home Department* [2000] Imm AR 10, CA.
5   By virtue of Human Rights Act 1998, s 2.

18.92 Subject to that overriding duty, the procedure on appeals is governed by the Immigration and Asylum Appeals (Notices) Regulations 2000,[1] the Immigration and Asylum Appeals (Procedure) Rules 2000,[2] and the Immigration and Asylum Appeals (One-Stop Procedure) Regulations 2000.[3] Separate consideration will be given to the procedures at the Special Immigration Appeals Commission.[4]

1   SI 2000/2246 as amended by the Immigration and Asylum Appeals (Notices) (Amendment) Regulations 2001, SI 2001/868, made under Immigration and Asylum Act 1999, s 166(3) and Sch 4, para 1.
2   SI 2000/2333, made under Immigration and Asylum Act 1999, s 58(2), 166(3), Sch 4, paras 3, 4.
3   SI 2000/2244 as amended by the Immigration and Asylum Appeals (One-Stop Procedure) (Amendment) Regulations 2001, SI 2001/867, made under Immigration and Asylum Act 1999, ss 74, 75, 76, 166 and 167.
4   See **18.186ff** below.

Notices of action or decision

18.93 The first stage in the appeal procedure is for notice of the decision or action of the immigration authority in question to be given to the immigrant. Under the Notices Regulations,[1] a written notice of any appealable decision or action must be given to the person in respect of whom the decision or action is taken.[2] Written notice does not have to be given if the only appeal would be on human rights or discrimination grounds,[3] but it must be given if it is alleged that the decision is in breach of the applicant's human rights or is racially discriminatory.[4] Thus, an unappealable refusal of leave to enter as a visitor with no entry clearance requires no written notice, but if the applicant then says that removal would breach rights to family life, or would be racially discriminatory, the duty to serve written notice is engaged if the refusal is maintained. A decision may be given by hand or sent by recorded delivery post or fax[5] to the applicant or his or her representative[6] (either the last known or usual address or a correspondence address), and a standard-form refusal of leave to enter under the Immigration Act 1971 will be deemed in accordance with the regulations if accompanied by the prescribed information,[7] which must otherwise be contained in the notice. The information prescribed is:

(1)   the reasons for the decision or action;
(2)   the country or territory to which the person is to be removed, where the notice refers to the giving of directions for removal from the UK;
(3)   information to the person of his or her right of appeal, the statutory provision on which the right of appeal is based, manner in which the appeal should be brought, the actual, postal or fax address to which a notice of appeal should be taken or sent, the time limit for appealing, and the facilities available for advice and assistance.[7]

1   Immigration and Asylum Appeals (Notices) Regulations 2000, SI 2000/2246.
2   SI 2000/2246, reg 4(1).
3   Under Immigration and Asylum Act 1999, s 65 (as amended by Race Relations (Amendment) Act 2000) or Special Immigration Appeals Commission Act 1997, s 2A.
4   SI 2000/2246, reg 4(4), as amended by SI 2001/868.
5   SI 2000/2246, reg 7(b); Immigration (Leave to Enter and Remain) Order 2000, SI 2000/1161, Art 8(2).
6   SI 2000/2246, reg 7(c)(ii).
7   SI 2000/2246, reg 6(2).
8   SI 2000/2246, reg 5.

18.94   Where a notice fails to comply with any of these requirements, do the defects invalidate the notice, or is the notice still good? Guidance on this question was given by the Court of Appeal in *Jeyeanthan*,[1] a case about a notice of application to appeal to the Tribunal without the necessary declaration. The Master of the Rolls said that:

'the important question [is] what the legislator should be judged to have intended should be the consequence of non-compliance. This has to be assessed on a consideration of the language of the legislation against the factual circumstances of the non-compliance. In the majority of cases it provides limited, if any, assistance to inquire whether the requirement is mandatory or directory ... Procedural requirements are designed to further the interests of justice and any consequence which would achieve a result contrary to those interests should be treated with considerable reservation.'

He suggested that three questions were likely to arise:

(a)   Is the statutory requirement fulfilled if there has been substantial compliance with the requirement and, if so, has there been substantial compliance in the case in issue even though there has not been strict compliance? (The substantial compliance question.)
(b)   Is the non-compliance capable of being waived, and if so, has it been, or can it and should it be waived in this particular case? (The discretionary question.)

(c)   If it is not capable of being waived or is not waived then what is the consequence of the non-compliance? (The consequences question.)[2]

These considerations were expressed to apply to procedural requirements for both sides and at all stages of the appeal process. But this careful judicial solution to the non-compliance problem is precluded by statute in the case of appellants' notices.[3] If the draconian provisions of s 72(3) of the Immigration and Asylum Act 1999 are applied, issues of fairness and equality of arms are likely to arise. A notice which fails to tell an appellant of a right of appeal is likely to be held invalid, so that time would not begin to run for the purposes of appealing.[4]

1   *R v Immigration Appeal Tribunal, ex p Jeyeanthan; Ravichandran v Secretary of State for the Home Department* [2000] 1 WLR 354, [2000] Imm AR 10, [2000] INLR 241.
2   *R v Immigration Appeal Tribunal, ex p Jeyeanthan; Ravichandran v Secretary of State for the Home Department* [2000] INLR 241 at 247. The court held that the Secretary of State's failure to make a declaration of truth on the form meant there was not substantial compliance (disapproving *R v Immigration Appeal Tribunal, ex p Nicholapillai* [1998] Imm AR 232) but that the non-compliance had in one case been waived and in the other had had no adverse consequences.
3   By Immigration and Asylum Act 1999, s 72(3).
4   See *Akhuemonkhan v Secretary of State for the Home Department* [1998] INLR 265, where an appeal was allowed against a notice from the appellate authority of 'abandonment of appeal' with no indication of appeal rights. See also *Odomusu* (17109) 22 May 1998, IAT, a decision involving failure to serve notices on the children of a proposed deportee including rights of voluntary departure and of appeal.

Service of notice of decision

18.95 The Notices Regulations,[1] unlike their 1984 predecessor[2] contain no requirement that notice be served 'as soon as practicable' after a decision is taken. Cases under the old regulations indicated that the notice could be sent to the last-known or usual place of abode even when the Home Office knew that the appellant was not there,[3] or had been asked to send it to the appellant's legal representative.[4] In *ex p Yeboah* and *Draz*,[5] where a letter was sent by post but not received by its intended recipient, the Court of Appeal held that the Interpretation Act 1978, section 7 did not enable the appellant to disprove the presumption of receipt by evidence of actual non receipt. This harsh decision has been reversed by statute,[6] following another Court of Appeal decision, *Saleem*,[7] which made it clear that such irrebuttable presumptions which deprived appellants of appeal rights were no longer acceptable in the new climate. The new procedure rules require the notice of the decision to be 'received' in most cases before time limits for appealing start to run.[8] There is deemed receipt of a notice of a decision which was sent by first class recorded delivery post, on the second day after it is posted, unless the contrary is proved.[9] Notices sent abroad are deemed received on the 28th day after the day of posting.[10]

1   Immigration Appeals (Notices) Regulations 2000, SI 2000/2246.
2   Immigration Appeals (Notices) Regulations 1984, SI 1984/2040.
3   *Singh (Pargat) v Secretary of State for the Home Department* [1993] Imm AR 112 at 118, HL.
4   *Tongo v Secretary of State for the Home Department* [1995] Imm AR 109, CA.
5   *R v Secretary of State for the Home Department, ex p Yeboah and Draz* [1987] Imm AR 414, CA.
6   Immigration and Asylum Act 1999, Sch 4, para 2; Immigration and Asylum Appeals (Procedure) Rules 2000, SI 2000/2333, r 6.
7   *R v Secretary of State for the Home Department, ex p Asifa Saleem* [2000] Imm AR 529, [2000] INLR 413.

8 SI 2000/2333, reg 6.
9 Immigration and Asylum Act 1999, Sch 4, para 2.
10 Immigration and Asylum Appeals (Notices) Regulations 2000, SI 2000/2246, as amended by the Immigration and Asylum Appeals (Notices) (Amendment) Regulations 2001, SI 2001/868, reg 8.

18.96 The old Notices Regulations[1] also allowed the Home Office to dispense with service altogether if the decision-maker had no knowledge of the whereabouts of the person who was the subject of the decision. The decision could, in those circumstances, be 'served on the file'. This provision, which gave rise to considerable litigation, has not been reproduced. In fact, in deportation cases the practice of dispensing with service was abandoned in 1986,[2] and the High Court has held that 'service on the file' of a deportation decision did not 'stop the clock' for the purpose of the long residence concession.[3] The Tribunal has held that evidence of sending a notice to a prison was insufficient to establish that a proposed deportee, an inmate, was served, in the absence of evidence of personal service on him, in a decision that emphasised the harsh consequences of non-compliance with the strict requirements of service of refusal or deportation decisions.[4] A notice which was not properly served could not give rise to a valid dismissal of an appeal on the ground that it was out of time or that the appellant did not appear.[5]

1 Immigration Appeals (Notices) Regulations 1984, SI 1984/2040.
2 By a little-known Home Office policy, DP5/86, quoted in *R v Secretary of State for the Home Department, ex p Chew, ex p Popatia* [2000] INLR 587, QBD.
3 *R v Secretary of State for the Home Department, ex p Chew, ex p Popatia* [2000] INLR 587, QBD.
4 *Jaroudy* (20063) 9 February 1999, IAT.
5 *R v Secretary of State for the Home Department, ex p Kondo* [1992] Imm AR 326; *Babar* (18302) 2 October 1998, IAT, where *R v Secretary of State for the Home Department, ex p Lateef* [1991] Imm AR 334 was distinguished.

One-stop notice

18.97 In a case where the decision on an application for leave to enter or remain, a variation application or a decision to deport attracts an in-country appeal, the decision-maker must also serve a 'one-stop notice' under section 74 of the Immigration and Asylum Act 1999 on the applicant and on all relevant members of his or her family, giving each of them the opportunity to state any additional grounds they may have for wishing to enter or remain in the UK.[1] The relevant family members are those subject of the decision but not an applicant (ie dependants whose application falls to be refused with that of the principal), and who appears to be a spouse, a child of the applicant or the spouse, a cohabitee for two of the past three years; and a person dependent on the applicant or on whom the applicant is dependent[2] (ie someone who might have rights to remain dependent on that of the applicant or on whom the applicant might claim a parasitic right to remain). The notice must be in the form set out in the regulations.[3]

1 Immigration and Asylum Act 1999, s 74(4).
2 Immigration and Asylum Appeals (One-stop Procedure) Regulations 2000, SI 2000/2244 (as amended by the Immigration and Asylum Appeals (One-Stop Procedure) (Amendment) Regulations 2001, SI 2001/867), reg 6.
3 SI 2000/2244, Schedule, Pt I.

Grounds for decision

18.98 Where a statement of the reasons for the decision or action is included in a notice, it 'shall be conclusive of the person by whom and of the ground on which any decision or action was taken'.[1] This provision has also given rise to considerable litigation. The case law establishes that where the grounds given reflect the immigration rules, the statutory finality does not prevent the immigration officer or Secretary of State amending the notice by varying or amplifying the reasons for the decision.[2] If, and only if, a decision is based on a statutory ground, the notice is in reality 'conclusive'. This principle is illustrated in the old case law on deportation. There used to be various statutory grounds for deportation: overstaying; breach of conditions; conducive to the public good; being a family member of a proposed deportee. A decision-maker could not switch between these statutory categories.[3] This is particularly important where the appellate jurisdiction is confined to deciding whether there is power to implement the decision for the reason stated in the notice: in such a case the Secretary of State cannot amend the notice so as to increase the jurisdiction of the appellate authority to take into account reasons not initially stated in the grounds of decision.[4] The principle applies with full effect in relation to restricted appeals against removal, either under sections 66 (overstayers etc) or 11 and 12 (asylum seekers' removal to 'safe' third countries) of the Immigration and Asylum Act 1999—both situations where appeal rights are restricted.

1   Immigration and Asylum Act 1999, Sch 4, para 1(2).
2   For a recent example, see *Ibeakanma* (18632) 25 September 1998, IAT. *In R v Immigration Appeal Tribunal, ex p Hubbard* [1985] Imm AR 110 Woolf J doubted whether it was right or sensible to draw a distinction between grounds and reasons and held that the appellate authorities were not restricted on an appeal to the grounds or reasons specified in the notice of refusal. See **18.71** above.
3   *R v Immigration Appeal Tribunal, ex p Mehmet (Ekrem)* [1977] Imm AR 56, QBD; *Parsaiyan v Visa Officer, Karachi* [1986] Imm AR 155. See also *R v Secretary of State for the Home Department, ex p Cheblak* [1991] 2 All ER 319.
4   *Lindsay* (10673); *Egbale* [1997] INLR 88, IAT.

Certified appeals

18.99 The principle of finality set out in the statute applies to certification in asylum and human rights appeals, preventing amendment of a certificate and also resulting in invalidity if the certificate is defective. In *Salah Ziar*[1] the Tribunal held that a notice certifying an asylum claim as one to which the accelerated appeals procedure applied, which did not set out both statutory reasons required to certify the claim— the paragraph under which the claim was certified and the absence of evidence of torture—meant that the certificate was invalid. An amendment could not be allowed so as to reduce the appellant's appeal rights. Since the criteria for certification are statutory, the Tribunal was simply applying the statutory provision. However, the decision has not been adhered to by all Tribunal divisions.[2]

1   *Ziar (Salah)* [1997] Imm AR 456, [1997] INLR 221, IAT. See further **12.166** above.
2   It was followed in *Meflah* [1998] INLR 180, but distinguished in *Khan* [1999] INLR 309, where *Ziar* was distinguished on the ground that the amendment had been made in plenty of time to allow the appellant an opportunity to deal with it. The point of principle in *Ziar* was perhaps not understood. In *Zolele* [1999] INLR 422 Professor Jackson made the point: 'The conclusion in *Khan* is contrary to the statutory framework. It is not open to the adjudicator to remedy a defective certificate.'

Time limits for appealing

18.100 The time for appealing against any decision or action of an immigration authority varies according to whether the appellant is in the UK or abroad. Where the appeal is in-country, notice of appeal must be given no later than ten working days after the notice of decision was received.[1] Where the appellant was in the UK at the date of decision but the appeal is out-of-country, the notice of appeal must be given not later than 28 days after departure from the UK.[2] And where the appellant was not in the UK when the decision was made, the notice of appeal must be submitted no later than 28 days after the decision was received.[3] Notices of appeal are deemed given when actually received at the address or fax number specified for return.[4] When time *runs out*, the notice of appeal should have *reached* the respondent. It is no good if it has merely been posted by that time.[5] Any notices or documents sent to the appellate authority are deemed received when actually received.[6] For in-country appeals, weekends and public holidays are not included in the time for appealing;[7] for all appeals, where time for serving notice runs out on a weekend or a public holiday, an appeal lodged on the next working day is in time.[8]

1 Immigration and Asylum Appeals (Procedure) Rules 2000, SI 2000/2333, r 6(1). The period is to be calculated from the expiry of the day on which notice is received: SI 2000/2333, r 48(6).
2 SI 2000/2333, r 6(2)(a).
3 SI 2000/2333, r 6(2)(b).
4 SI 2000/2333, r 48(4).
5 *R v Immigration Appeal Tribunal, ex p Rocha* [1982] Imm AR 12, QBD.
6 SI 2000/2333, r 48(3).
7 SI 2000/2333, r 48(8).
8 SI 2000/2333, r 48(7).

18.101 The existence of a time limit for appealing against the actions or decisions of the immigration authorities can also mislead would-be appellants into thinking that if they merely adhere to the time limit they will be able to enjoy their full right of appeal. There are several situations where this may not be the case. For example, persons refused entry have a right of appeal without having to leave the UK if they had an entry clearance or work permit on arrival.[1] But the existence of a right of appeal does not in itself operate as a stay on removal, and if such appellants delay giving notice of appeal they may in fact find themselves being removed from the UK.[2] They still have a right of appeal, but can only exercise it from abroad,[3] whereas if they had given notice of appeal before their departure they would have been allowed to remain until their appeal was heard.

1 Immigration and Asylum Act 1999, s 60(3).
2 The stay on directions for removal in Immigration and Asylum Act 1999, Sch 4, para 10 provides that 'any directions previously given by virtue of the refusal for his [sic] removal from the UK cease to have effect, *except insofar as they have already been carried out ...*'
3 28 days after departure: Immigration and Asylum Appeals (Procedure) Rules 2000, SI 2000/2333, r 6(2)(a). .

Out-of-time appeals

18.102 The Procedure Rules[1] allow two procedures for entertaining out-of-time appeals. The first is by consent of the responsible immigration authority and the second is at the discretion of an adjudicator or the Tribunal. Unlike other jurisdictions, notices of appeal in immigration cases are sent to the responsible immigration authority, who will be the respondent in the appeal, rather than to the adjudicator or Tribunal. Under the rules a respondent is able to accept an out-of-time notice of appeal without reference to the appellate authorities. The appeal papers are then forwarded in the normal way and the appeal proceeds as if notice had been given in time. The respondent, however, will only adopt this course if it is satisfied that because of special circumstances it is just to do so.[2]

1 Immigration and Asylum Appeals (Procedure) Rules 2000, SI 2000/2333.
2 SI 2000/2333, r 7(1).

18.103 Where a respondent refuses to accept a notice of appeal because it is out of time the matter is referred to the adjudicator for determination as a preliminary issue. Under rule 12(5) of the Procedure Rules[1] the adjudicator must first determine whether or not the notice of appeal is out of time. He or she may then allow the appeal to proceed (unless a deportation order is in force against the appellant) if satisfied that because of special circumstances, it is just to do so. The notice of appeal will then be treated as having been served in time.[2] A failure by the respondent to raise the question of the timeliness of an appeal does not deprive the appellate authority of jurisdiction to investigate whether a notice of appeal was properly served or whether it would be right to extend time.[3]

1 Immigration and Asylum Appeals (Procedure) Rules 2000, SI 2000/2333.
2 SI 2000/2333, r 12(6).
3 *Jaroudy* (20063) 9 February 1999, IAT.

18.104 The criterion of whether it is 'just' for time for appealing to be extended under the new procedure rule is essentially the same as that of whether it is 'just and right' to do so under the old immigration procedure rules.[1] The leading Court of Appeal decision on the question held that the rule should be liberally interpreted so as not to let an appellant suffer unfairly.[2] There was no reason in law why the appellate authority should not take into account the substantive merits of the case, or the fact that the failure was due to a mistake by the applicant's legal advisers, or that the applicant had been lulled into a false sense of security. However, in a later case[3] the court emphasised that, although all these matters might be taken into account, it was still a matter of discretion whether to allow a late appeal to proceed and, therefore, the appellate authority should decide in each case what weight (if any) should be given to such factors. The later case attempted to explain more clearly what adjudicators and the Tribunal should do in assessing the substantive merits of an appeal and stated that this could only mean making, at best, a provisional assessment of the chances of success of the appeal.[4] The Tribunal has followed the liberal line of authority, particularly in asylum appeals, despite the more restrictive wording that obtained until October 2000, where it had to be shown that the failure was due to circumstances beyond the appellant's control.[5] Lord Denning's principle in *ex p Mehta*[6] that the court 'would never let a party suffer because his solicitors had made a mistake and are a day or two late' has been held to extend to cases where the delay was longer, in the context of a leisurely decision-making process where an applicant could not be expected to make constant inquiries about the progress of the application.[7] The danger of pre-judging the merits in refusing an extension has been emphasised,[8] as has the fact that there is no requirement to show 'exceptional' circumstances.[9] An adjudicator dealing with the issue of extension of time in relation to a certified appeal should not deal with the question of certification at the same time.[10] A decision on the preliminary issue of time was held to be a determination under the 1971 Act (making it appealable) and to require reasons.[11] 'Determination' was not defined under the 1971 Act or the Procedure Rules, and the case law established that it was a decision other than an interlocutory one, ie a decision which was capable of putting an end to the proceedings.[12] However, the new Procedure Rules define determination as 'the decision of the appellate authority to allow or dismiss an appeal and the reasons for that decision'.[13] On the face of it, this excludes the determination of a preliminary issue as to whether there is an entitlement to appeal at all, suggesting that decisions refusing an extension of time to appeal will be reviewable only by the Administrative Court on judicial review.[14]

1 Immigration Appeals (Procedure) Rules 1984, SI 1984/2041, r 11(4). The test under the Asylum Appeals (Procedure) Rules 1996, SI 1996/2070, was more stringent (r 41(2), reflecting the very tight time limits for asylum appeals under the 1996 rules). These, which were always honoured in the breach by respondent and appellate authority, have now been removed.

2 *R v Immigration Appeal Tribunal, ex p Mehta* [1976] Imm AR 38, CA.

3 *R v Immigration Appeal Tribunal, ex p Mehta* (VM) [1976] Imm AR 174 at 184-185 CA, per Browne LJ.

4 It should be noted that this part of the test is similar to that used for late appeals under the Sex Discrimination Act 1975 and the Race Relations Act 1976: see *Hutchison v Westward Television Ltd* [1977] ICR 279, EAT.

5 Advisers' negligence or simple mistakes was usually grounds to allow an out-of-time appeal to proceed: *Sonoiki* (12424) 9 August 1995; *Mahmood* (13290) 30 April 1996; *Minta-Ampofo* (15024) 15 May 1997; *Khatib* (15676) 31 October 1997, IAT.

6 [1976] Imm AR 38 at 42 CA.

7 *Abaci* (16605) 2 December 1998, where a long delay in lodging an asylum appeal because of a solicitor's mistake was seen in the context of a six-year delay in making the asylum decision.

8 *Oremnle* (15844) 24 November 1997, where the Tribunal allowed an appeal against the refusal of an extension of time on a student appeal, lodged a day late, because the student had not passed many exams.

9 *McNulty* (14204) 22 November 1996.

10 *Grozdas* (19532) 26 October 1999, IAT.

11 *Jaayeola* (14819) 2 April 1997, IAT.

12 *Akhuemonkhan* [1998] INLR 265, IAT.

13 SI 2000/2333, r 2(1).

14 Since only a 'determination' is appealable to the Tribunal: Immigration and Asylum Act 1999, Sch 4, para 22.

18.105 In the case of a variation appeal, there used to be an absolute maximum 'grace' period of 14 days for a late appeal. This is because, as has already been noted, whether a decision to refuse to vary leave is appealable at all depends on whether there is a limited leave in existence at the date of the decision and the notice of appeal.[1] To deal with this problem, the Variation of Leave Order 1976[2] extended leave for 28 days after a decision, and the limit for appealing was then 14 days.[3] Now, when someone makes an application for variation of their leave, section 3C of the Immigration and Asylum Act 1999 continues the extant leave 'until the end of the period allowed under [the] rules ... for bringing an appeal against the decision'. On a literal reading, any appeal lodged after the period allowed for appealing is lodged after the expiry of leave and there would be no jurisdiction to hear it. This result is avoided by providing that a notice of appeal not given within the appropriate time limit shall be treated 'for all purposes' as having been given in time if the Secretary of State or the adjudicator is satisfied that it is just to do so.

1 *Suthendran v Immigration Appeal Tribunal* [1977] AC 359, [1977] Imm AR 44, *Fernando v Secretary of State for the Home Department* [1991] Imm AR 232. Section 61 of the Immigration and Asylum Act 1999 is in sufficiently similar terms to s 14 of the Immigration Act 1971 for the House of Lords' interpretation of the latter to apply to the former.
2 Immigration (Variation of Leave) Order 1976, SI 1976/1572, art 3.
3 SI 1976/1572. Immigration Appeals (Procedure) Rules 1984, SI 1984/2041, r 4(6).

Notice of appeal

18.106 A notice of appeal has to be in the appropriate prescribed form[1] or a similar form with variations that the circumstances might require.[2] The rules require that the notice sets out the grounds for the appeal,[3] the name and address of the appellant and of his or her representative (if any).[4] The form itself contains many more questions including details of the appellant's age, citizenship or nationality and of previous appeals. The appellant in a family visitor appeal under section 59 of the Immigration and Asylum Act 1999 must specify in the notice all matters he or she wishes to be considered for the purposes of the appeal.[5] Where a person intends to object to a destination on removal the notice of appeal should specify why he or she objects, the alternative country to which the appellant wishes to be removed, and some indication why it is thought that such a country would admit the appellant. The notice must be signed by the appellant or the appellant's representative.[6] Cases under the old rules suggest that many of the requirements in the notice are not mandatory, and failure to include some of the information would not invalidate an appeal.[7] The guidance provided by the Court of Appeal case of *Jeyeanthan*[8] has resonance here.

1 Immigration and Asylum Appeals (Procedure) Rules 2000, SI 2000/2333, r 8(1). The forms are set out in the Schedule to the rules. There are distinct forms for UK and overseas appeals, and for family visitors.
2 SI 2000/2333, r 2(1).
3 SI 2000/2333, r 8(3).
4 SI 2000/2333, r 8(5).
5 SI 2000/2333, r 8(4).
6 SI 2000/2333, r 8(6).
7 *Jarvis* [1994] Imm AR 102; *R v Immigration Appeal Tribunal, ex p Begum (Hamida)* [1988] Imm AR 199, QBD; *Sogunle* [1994] Imm AR 554. In *R v an Adjudicator, ex p Umeloh* [1991] Imm AR 602, QBD, it was held that a notice of appeal in a destination appeal was invalid where an alternative destination was not specified: see now Immigration and Asylum Act 1999, s 68(3). But the Immigration and Asylum Appeals (Procedure) Rules 2000, SI 2000/2333 do not require this information to be specified in the notice, and it is therefore arguable that there is a valid appeal so long as the notice contains an indication that it will be specified.
8 *R v Immigration Appeal Tribunal, ex p Jeyeanthan; Ravichandran v Secretary of State for the Home Department* [2000] 1 WLR 354, [2000] Imm AR 10, [2000] INLR 241. See **18.94** above.

18.107 Notice is then served on the person prescribed in the notice of decision.[1] An appellant in custody may serve the notice on the person with custody of him or her.[2] The prescribed forms themselves indicate that they must be sent to both the Home Office and the appellate authority (in-country appeals) and to the entry clearance officer in overseas appeals. The notice must be accompanied by a copy of the decision notice or letter with reasons, and a statement of additional grounds in one-stop appeals, for which see below.[3] The notice and its accompanying documents may be delivered by hand, or sent by post or by fax, to an address or a fax number specified by the person or authority to whom the notice or document is directed.[4] A notice of appeal sent by post or fax to the address or fax number specified in the decision notice is deemed to be given on the day it was received.[5]

1   Immigration and Asylum Appeals (Procedure) Rules 2000, SI 2000/2333, r 8(1).
2   SI 2000/2333, r 8(2).
3   SI 2000/2333, r 8(7).
4   SI 2000/2333, r 46(1). If it is sent to the wrong address and cannot be traced, the Secretary of State is entitled to conclude that no valid appeal has been lodged: *Adeniyi v Secretary of State for the Home Department* [1995] Imm AR 23, CA; *Shaffi* [1990] Imm AR 468.
5   SI 2000/2333, r 48(4).

One-stop appeals

18.108 One of the aims of the Immigration and Asylum Act 1999 is to put an end to the possibilities of sequential appeals under the Immigration Act 1971 and Asylum and Immigration Appeals Act 1993. Under those Acts it was possible for an applicant to enjoy an appeal under the rules (eg a student appeal), then a deportation appeal for overstaying, and finally an appeal against a refusal to revoke a deportation order, on asylum grounds. It was also possible for a member of the principal applicant's family to apply for asylum after the principal's claim had been rejected, in most cases preventing the removal of the whole family. These possibilities were used by a number of desperate appellants and families. We have seen how section 10 of the 1999 Act put an end to deportation and its concomitant in-country appeal rights for overstayers. The one-stop procedure is the main mechanism by which the government seeks to ensure that all possible grounds of appeal, including asylum and human rights or discrimination grounds, by the principal applicant and all members of the family, are dealt with together. It has no application to overseas appeals.

18.109 Broadly speaking, a ground on which the principal appellant or a member of his or her family seeks to stay in the UK cannot be (a) ventilated or (b) made the subject of a further application or appeal, unless it has been the subject of a one-stop statement, or 'statement of additional grounds' served in response to a one-stop notice. A one-stop notice is served[1] in two situations:

(1)   when an application for leave to enter or remain is refused and the refusal attracts an in-country right of appeal,[2]
(2)   when a person who is to be removed from the UK with no right of appeal makes an application for asylum or under the Human Rights Convention.[3]

In response to a one-stop notice under section 74 of the Immigration and Asylum Act 1999, the applicant and relevant family members on whom a notice has been served must set out additional grounds for wishing to stay in the UK. To the extent that those grounds are appealable, the appellate authority will consider them too.[4] An asylum claim, race discrimination claim, or a human rights claim must be included in the statement.[5] Grounds not set out in the notice will not be considered on the appeal[6] unless they are asylum or human rights or discrimination grounds,[7] or the appellant was not aware of them at the time the one-stop notice was served,[8] or the Secretary of State considers that the appellant had a reasonable excuse for omitting to refer to them.[9] If the appellant subsequently claims asylum and has not mentioned asylum grounds in the one-stop statement, the Secretary of State may prevent the asylum claim being ventilated on appeal by a certificate that the claim had no legitimate purpose other than delaying the removal from the UK of the appellant or a member of his or her family (ie, certifies the claim as abusive).[10] The effect of certifying the claim abusive is to prevent an asylum appeal being made.[11]

1 Immigration and Asylum Act 1999, s 74(4), 75(2).
2 Immigration and Asylum Act 1999, s 74(1), (2), (3), dealing respectively with refusal of leave to enter, variation or refusal to vary, and deportation decisions (on conducive grounds).
3 Immigration and Asylum Act 1999, s 75.
4 Whether, in the case of relevant family members, in the same proceedings or in different ones is considered at **18.157** below.
5 Immigration and Asylum Act 1999, s 74(7) as amended by Race Relations (Amendment) Act 2000, Sch 2, para 37.
6 Immigration and Asylum Act 1999, s 76(2).
7 Immigration and Asylum Act 1999, s 76(3)(a) as amended by Race Relations (Amendment) Act 2000, Sch 2, para 38.
8 Immigration and Asylum Act 1999, s 76(2(b).
9 Immigration and Asylum Act 1999, s 76(3)(b).
10 Immigration and Asylum Act 1999, s 76(5).
11 Immigration and Asylum Act 1999, s 76(5).

18.110 In a one-stop appeal, that is, an in-country appeal to which the provisions of section 74 of the Immigration and Asylum Act 1999 apply,[1] the appellant is to be treated as appealing on the additional grounds mentioned in the one-stop statement,[2] and grounds not mentioned but that he or she is not precluded from relying on by section 76.[3] Thus, a student refused a variation who is served with a one-stop notice and indicates a wish to stay under the long residence concession will enjoy an appeal in which the adjudicator will consider the refusal of leave to remain as a student and the long residence policy,[4] but (unless specifically requested) probably not the human rights aspects of long residence (ie private life under ECHR, Article 8).[5] One who does not refer to the long residence policy but refers instead to ECHR, Article 8 will enjoy an appeal in which the adjudicator will consider the residence under ECHR, Article 8 but not under the policy (unless the Secretary of State accepts that there was a reasonable excuse for the failure to mention the policy). A student in a similar situation who fears return home on asylum grounds but fails to refer to that fear in a one-stop statement will not be able to raise asylum for the first time on the student appeal[6] and, even if he or she makes a late asylum claim, may be prevented from relying on the asylum ground on the student appeal if the Secretary of State certifies that the claim is abusive, but could not be prevented from arguing that return would be contrary to ECHR, Article 3, since that is a human rights claim protected by section 76(3) of the Immigration and Asylum Act 1999, despite the statutory requirement to include it in the one-stop statement.[7]

1 See Immigration and Asylum Act 1999, s 77(1) and the Immigration and Asylum Appeals (One-stop Procedure) Regulations 2000, SI 2000/2244, reg 5(6).
2 Immigration and Asylum Act 1999, s 77(5) and SI 2000/2244 .
3 This is the wording of and clear intention of the Immigration and Asylum Act 1999, s 77(2), but 'additional grounds' as defined in s 77(5) appears to restrict the appellant to the grounds in the one-stop statement, contrary to the statutory intention. This will have to be construed sensibly and purposively so that all grounds not precluded are considered, whether or not in the statement.

4   The adjudicator can only allow an appeal in relation to the policy if the refusal is 'not in accordance with the law' (see **18.62** above); but most policies encapsulate human rights issues in respect of which an adjudicator must look at the merits of the decision to see whether it interferes with a Convention right, and if so whether it does so for a legitimate aim and is proportionate to that aim; see **8.75** above.

5   Following dicta in a concurring opinion in *Beldjoudi v France* (1992) 14 EHRR 801 to the effect that private life is the sum of all the ties a person builds in the country of residence: see **8.63** above.

6   There can be no asylum appeal without an asylum claim: Immigration and Asylum Act 1999, s 70(7)(a).

7   Immigration and Asylum Act 1999, s 74(7).

18.111 The provisions in respect of Immigration and Asylum Act 1999, section 75 one-stop notices are similar. A person who is refused leave to enter with no in-country appeal, or someone to be removed as an illegal entrant or overstayer, who claims asylum or makes a claim that removal would be in breach of his or her human rights or is racially discriminatory, and relevant family members of that person,[1] must be served with a one-stop notice under section 75(2) asking for any additional grounds on which the person seeks to remain. The additional grounds set out in the statement would be considered on the asylum or human rights appeal if the claim was refused.[2] It is hard to see that someone with no in-country right of appeal could have additional grounds which were not asylum or human rights or discrimination grounds,[3] but the same provisions apply to section 75 one-stop appeals as those under section 74 of the 1999 Act, ie grounds other than human rights or discrimination or asylum grounds of which the appellant was aware cannot be relied on appeal unless the decision-maker accepts there was a reasonable excuse for not mentioning them in the statement; there can be no asylum appeal if there has been no asylum claim; and an asylum appeal can be prevented by the decision-maker certifying that a post-statement claim is abusive.[4] An asylum seeker or member of his or her family would thus be precluded from raising a wholly new asylum claim on appeal, and could be prevented from relying on one which had been put in late, by a certificate of an abusive claim, but could not be prevented from raising an Article 3 or other new human rights or discrimination issue on appeal for the first time because of the protective effect of section 76(3)(a). However, these restrictions on appeal grounds would not apply to an asylum seeker whose asylum claim was determined before the section 75 statement had to be served.[5]

1   Defined as someone who has made a claim to remain but is not the claimant (ie claims as a dependant), and who appears to be the spouse of the claimant, the child of the claimant or of the spouse, a cohabitee for two of the preceding three years, a person dependent on the claimant or the person on whom the claimant is dependent: Immigration and Asylum Appeals (One-stop Procedure) Regulations 2000, SI 2000/2244, reg 7.

2   Immigration and Asylum Act 1999, s 77(6), as modified by SI 2000/2244, reg 5(6).

3   By definition, Immigration and Asylum Act 1999, s 75 applies where there is no in-country appeal right, so an asylum seeker who asserts in a statement of additional grounds that he or she wishes to enter as a student, for example, would not be able to appeal against a refusal of that decision. The one-stop appeal does not give rights of appeal where none exist under the 1999 Act; it merely compresses all those an appellant has, including asylum and human rights or discrimination ones.

4   Immigration and Asylum Act 1999, s 76 as modified by SI 2000/2244, reg 5(5).

5   SI 2000/2244, reg 5(2).

18.112 In most cases, it is anticipated that all appealable issues, including in particular asylum and human rights or discrimination issues, would be dealt with in one appeal. Once an appeal is determined, there is no opportunity to raise human rights or discrimination issues in another appeal if the Secretary of State certifies either that the claim could have been included in the original one-stop notice, or raised in the original appeal, and that the only purpose for making it now is to delay the appellant's or a family member's removal from the UK,[1] or that the claim was dealt with in the original one-stop appeal.[2] In either case, a certificate from the Secretary of State puts an end to the appeal, so far as that claim is concerned.[3] An even broader power exists, exercisable not only by the Secretary of State but also by the immigration officer, to certify as abusive on refusal any post-appeal application which would otherwise attract a right of appeal, thereby precluding an appeal.[4]

1   Immigration and Asylum Act 1999, s 73(2).
2   Immigration and Asylum Act 1999, s 73(4) and (5).
3   Immigration and Asylum Act 1999, s 73(3), (6), subject, of course, to the adjudicator's jurisdiction to investigate the accuracy of the certificate under the Immigration and Asylum Appeals (Procedure) Rules 2000, SI 2000/2333, r 12(1)(a)(i). The adjudicator does not appear to have any residual discretion to allow a second appeal to go ahead on the condemned ground, however.
4   Immigration and Asylum Act 1999, s 73(8) and (9). This power is likely to be used most often in relation to fresh post-appeal claims for asylum or on human rights grounds, either by a previous appellant or a member of his or her family.

One-stop notice and statement of additional grounds

18.113 In a one-stop appeal (ie all in-country appeals against refusal of leave to enter, remain, variation of leave, and deportation), as we have seen, when the decision-maker serves notice of refusal, he or she must also serve on the applicant and any relevant family member[1] a notice requiring the recipient to state any additional grounds for wishing to enter or remain in the UK. Similarly, when a person who is to be removed as an illegal entrant, overstayer or on refusal of leave to enter makes an asylum or human rights claim, the claimant and any relevant family member[2] is served with a one-stop notice under section 75 of the Immigration and Asylum Act 1999. This notice does not await the refusal of the asylum or human rights claim, and so is not attached to any notice of refusal. The notice, whether under section 74 or section 75, must be in the form set out in the Immigration and Asylum Appeals (One-Stop Procedure) Regulations.[3] It must provide addresses to which the statement of additional grounds may be delivered by hand or sent by post, and a fax number to which the statement may be sent by fax.[4] The one-stop notice may be served by hand, by recorded delivery post to the last known or usual address of the person concerned or the representative, or a correspondence address provided.[5] If sent by post it is deemed received on the second day after posting, unless the contrary is proved.[6]

1   Defined in the Immigration and Asylum Appeals (One-Stop Procedure) Regulations 2000, SI 2000/2244, reg 6, as someone who is the subject of a decision but is not the applicant, and who appears to be the spouse of the applicant the child of the applicant or of the spouse, a cohabitee for two of the preceding three years, a person dependent on the applicant or the person on whom the applicant is dependent.
2   Defined in SI 2000/2244, reg 7, as someone who has made a claim to remain but is not the claimant, and who appears to be the spouse of the claimant, the child of the claimant or of the spouse, a cohabitee for two of the preceding three years, a person dependent on the claimant or the person on whom the claimant is dependent.

3   SI 2000/2244, reg 3.
4   SI 2000/2244, reg 3(3).
5   SI 2000/2244, reg 3(4).
6   SI 2000/2244, reg 3(6).

18.114 The one-stop notice under section 74 or 75 of the Immigration and Asylum Act 1999 is accompanied by a form 'Statement of additional grounds' and contains instructions on how to fill it in, and when and where to send it. The statement of additional grounds must be made by completing the statement form (or a form to like effect)[1] in full and in English,[2] and signed by the requisite person or his or her representative.[3] It must be returned to the address or fax number provided within ten working[4] days,[5] and is served when received there.[6] If the person is in custody and the notice does not relate to a national security appeal, the statement may be served by giving it to the custodian.[7] Time for putting in the statement runs from midnight on the date of receipt of the notice by the person or the representative.[8]

1   Immigration and Asylum Appeals (One-stop Procedure) Regulations 2000, SI 2000/2244, reg 2(2).
2   SI 2000/2244, reg 4(1).
3   SI 2000/2244, reg 4(2).
4   The effect of SI 2000/2244, reg 4(5) and (11).
5   SI 2000/2244, reg 4(3), unless it relates to a national security appeal to the Special Immigration Appeals Commission, when the period is five days.
6   SI 2000/2244, reg 4(7). In response to widespread complaints by representatives that the period is too short, particularly in dispersal areas where the shortage of legal help leads to months of waiting for asylum seekers, the Home Office insists that legal help is not needed to fill in the Statement of Additional Grounds, which can be a short factual statement such as 'I fear torture'. The problem is, of course, that the issue is not so much the phrasing (although language clearly is a problem) as the legal training required to know what is relevant.
7   SI 2000/2244, reg 4(8) and (9).
8   SI 2000/2244, reg 4(5).

18.115 In a section 74 case (ie where the right of appeal already exists) the statement of additional grounds is attached to the notice of appeal form and its accompanying documents.[1] In a section 75 case, the statement is sent on its own. The decision-maker may grant leave to enter or remain on an additional ground. If not, in a section 74 case, a supplementary refusal notice will be served on the 'requisite person' (who might be the original applicant or a family member). An appellant has five days to put in a variation of grounds of appeal in response to the supplementary refusal.[2] The next stage is for the respondent to send the notice of appeal, any documents attached to it, supplementary refusal grounds,[3] variation of grounds of appeal, notes of asylum interview (if any) and any other document referred to in the decision letter or notice,[4] apart from statutory or public materials[5] to the adjudicator, the appellant and the appellant's representative.

1   Immigration and Asylum Appeals (Procedure) Rules 200, SI 2000/2333, r 8(7)(b).
2   SI 2000/2333, r 9.
3   These are not always served, where for example the statement of additional grounds raises no new matters of substance.
4   SI 2000/2333, r 10(1).
5   SI 2000/2333, r 10(2). The exception refers to legislative material 'or other published or publicly available material'. In asylum appeals this could be Country Information and Policy Unit (CIPU) documentation, reports from Amnesty International, the US State Department etc.

18.116 The respondent's duty to send the documents on is regardless of whether the notice of appeal is served in time or not. The appellant must serve the notice on the decision-maker rather than the appellate body because the power to remove an appellant or a member of his or her family from the UK is suspended once notice of appeal is given.[1] But this does not give the Secretary of State or other immigration authority the right to declare that an appeal is 'forfeited' either because it is out of time or for some other reason. Under the Immigration and Asylum Act 1999, the right of appeal depends on the statutory provisions and the lodging of a notice of appeal, and it is for the appellate authority to determine whether or not it has jurisdiction, not the Secretary of State.[2] This is done under the preliminary issue jurisdiction.[3] If the notice of appeal is not referred to the appropriate appellate authority, it is open to an individual who has duly lodged notice of appeal to request that the appeal be set down for an adjudicator,[4] or alternatively to seek judicial review of the failure to refer it.[5]

1   Immigration and Asylum Act 1999, Sch 4, paras 10-11, 15. In the case of a variation appeal, the variation does not take effect and the leave the appellant had continues, subject to the same conditions: Sch 4, paras 16, 17.
2   *Ken'aan* [1990] Imm AR 544, decided under the Immigration Act 1971. This principle has been eroded by the decisions of the Divisional Court and the Court of Appeal in *R v Secretary of State for the Home Department, ex p Ravichandran, Sandralingham (No 3)* [1997] Imm AR 74; *Yolanda Ward v Secretary of State for the Home Department* [1997] Imm AR 236; *Secretary of State for the Home Department v Boybeyi* [1997] Imm AR 491, [1997] INLR 130; *R v IAA, ex p Secretary of State for the Home Department* [1998] Imm AR 52, to the effect that the Secretary of State's decision whether there was enough new material to constitute a fresh asylum claim was subject to judicial review rather than to the preliminary issue jurisdiction of the adjudicator. But these questions may now be contained within the one-stop provisions of the Immigration and Asylum Act 1999, and so may fall within the adjudicator's preliminary issue jurisdiction under the new procedure rules: see **18.127**ff below.
3   Immigration and Asylum Appeals (Procedure) Rules 2000, SI 2000/2333, r 12.
4   *Lokko* [1990] Imm AR 111.
5   *Akhtar* [1991] Imm AR 232, CA.

18.117 After a notice of appeal has been given, a number of further steps may be taken before the appeal comes on for a hearing or is determined. A preliminary issue may arise as to the appellant's entitlement to appeal.[1] The adjudicator may issue directions as to the conduct of the appeal, to determine the form of the appeal, whether there is to be a hearing, the time it will take, the evidence, documentary and oral, that will be given and the issues to be addressed.[2] There is provision to allow the grounds of appeal to be varied during the course of the appeal.[3] The immigration authorities may reverse, withdraw or vary their action—which will lead to the appeal being treated as abandoned[4] unless it is a grant of exceptional leave to remain in response to an asylum appeal, in which case the appellant will need to serve a fresh notice of appeal.[5] The appellate authority may decide to treat an appeal as abandoned for a number of reasons,[6] or may decide to determine the appeal without considering its merits because of failure to comply with procedural requirements.[7] Some of these steps will now be examined more closely.

1   Immigration and Asylum Appeals (Procedure) Rules 2000, SI 2000/2333, r 12.
2   SI 2000/2333, r 30.
3   SI 2000/2333, r 11.
4   Immigration and Asylum Act 1999, s 58(9).
5   Under Immigration and Asylum Act 1999, s 69(3).
6   SI 2000/2333, r 32.
7   SI 2000/2333, r 33.

Parties to an appeal

18.118 Normally, the parties to an appeal will be the appellant and the respondent.[1] In adjudicator appeals the appellant is the person appealing against an immigration decision.[2] In human rights appeals it is this person whose human rights must have been breached by the decision.[3] This should not cause undue difficulty since, even in those family cases in which the purpose of the appellant's presence in the UK is to care for a dependent relative, both family members' rights under ECHR, Article 8 are engaged. The respondent is not defined in the rules but will be either the Secretary of State, an immigration officer or an entry clearance officer, as before. In asylum appeals, the UK representative of the UNHCR may become a party, if he or she gives notice to the appellate authority at any time.[4] The advantage of being a party is that the persons become entitled to receive copies of all notices and documents relating to the appeal,[5] including notice of the time and place of the hearing[6] or adjourned hearing[7] of the appeal, and can appear or be represented at the hearing with all the attendant rights of a party.[8] Where there is more than one applicant, all must serve notices of appeal and be identified thereafter.[9] A person who appeals in a false name does not cease to be an appellant although the falsity may go to credibility.[10]

1 Immigration and Asylum Appeals (Procedure) Rules 2000, SI 2000/2333, r 29(1).
2 SI 2000/2333, r 5(2).
3 Immigration and Asylum Act 1999, s 65(1).
4 SI 2000/2333, r 29(2).
5 SI 2000/2333, r 30(5).
6 SI 2000/2333, r 13.
7 SI 2000/2333, r 31(4).
8 SI 2000/2333, r 35.
9 *Caballero* [1986] Imm AR 409. The identification of an appellant by name in the ground, although not in the heading to the notice, was held sufficient to give rise to an appeal under the Immigration Act 1971: *Miah (Bashir)* (4940) unreported, IAT. It is, however, a moot point as to whether this decision can survive mandatory appeal and statement forms.
10 *Begum (Anwara)* (4936) unreported, IAT.

Amending the grounds of appeal

18.119 After service of the notice of appeal, and of any variation or addition to the grounds after a supplementary refusal under the one-stop procedure, grounds of appeal can only be varied with leave of the adjudicator.[1] In all but asylum and human rights cases, the adjudicator may only give leave to vary the grounds of appeal if satisfied that special circumstances make it just to do so. No such limitation applies in appeals under the Immigration and Asylum Act 1999, sections 65 (human rights and discrimination) or 69 (asylum). This reflects the spirit of the one-stop system, and more fundamentally, the fact that the adjudicator is a 'public authority' for the purpose of compliance with the Human Rights Convention, and has to give effect to the Refugee Convention, and so has primary duties to prevent breaches of either Convention. Clearly the rule should not be read as meaning that legal arguments cannot be refined on the appeal; what the rule is designed to prevent, except in special circumstances, is wholly new applications being made by way of amendment to grounds of appeal.[2]

1 Immigration and Asylum Appeals (Procedure) Rules 2000, SI 2000/2333, r 11.
2 See the old cases of *Francis* [1972] Imm AR 162 and *Muthalakshmi* [1972] Imm AR 231, IAT.

Withdrawal of appeals

18.120 All appeals may be withdrawn or abandoned. Likewise the immigration authority may reverse or withdraw the decision appealed against. What are the distinctions between withdrawal and abandonment, and what are the consequences? Withdrawal implies a positive act, while abandonment suggests a passive failure to prosecute the appeal. There are statutory provisions concerning abandonment, in some cases deeming it; there are none relating to withdrawal. Much of the case law deals with the issue of who decides whether an appeal has been withdrawn, how is the decision made, and whether it is appealable. An appeal may be withdrawn at any time,[1] and may be withdrawn orally at the hearing, a pre-hearing review or directions hearing.[2] It is clear that whether an appeal has been withdrawn is a matter for the appellate authority and the courts, not exclusively for the Secretary of State.[3] Once an appeal has been lodged it is for that authority to decide whether a purported withdrawal is so, and an appeal is not withdrawn until the appellate authority is notified by the appellant or with his or her authority.[4] It follows that where the withdrawal of an appeal is contested, the appellate authority must allow the appellant an opportunity to put the case against withdrawal, and should issue a determination with reasons.[5] On the other hand, where an appeal is validly withdrawn prior to the hearing, it does not go into a state of suspended animation but ceases to exist,[6] and any determination of the appeal (on the merits) is a nullity.[7]

1 See *Rahman (Akikur) v Immigration Appeal Tribunal* [1995] Imm AR 372, CA, for an analysis of the position under the Immigration Act 1971. Section 58(5) of the Immigration and Asylum Act 1999 is in identical terms.
2 *Saleh* [1975] Imm AR 154; *Rahman (Akikur) v Immigration Appeal Tribunal* [1995] Imm AR 372, CA.
3 *Boutari* (7349) 14 August 1990, IAT; *Patel (Idris)* (13444) 8 May 1996, IAT.
4 *Boutari* (7349) 14 August 1990, IAT and *Patel (Idris)* (13444) 8 May 1996, IAT; *Singh (Sohan Kaur)* (17473) 17 June 1998, IAT.
5 *El-Tuyeb* (12643) 30 October 1995, IAT; *Patel (Idris)* (13444) 8 May 1996, IAT.
6 *Adewole* (18538) 22 September 1998; IAT; *R v Hampstead and St Pancras Rent Tribunal, ex p Goodman* [1951] 1 KB 541; *Singh (Nachtar)* [1991] Imm AR 195; *Osman (Ayse)* [1993] Imm AR 417.
7 *Kirungi* (13111) 20 March 1996, IAT.

18.121 The main difficulty in practice has been whether the person withdrawing has the necessary instructions and authority to do so.[1] The general rule that a retainer of a solicitor includes authority to compromise an action or withdraw unless contrary instructions are expressly given,[2] does not appear to apply in immigration appeals,[3] and a solicitor without instructions has been held to have no authority to withdraw an appeal.[4] Where there is authority, withdrawal will be effective.[5] The old case law indicates that an employer or someone who has no right of audience at the appeal may validly withdraw an appeal.[6] This is unlikely to apply to a representative who is not registered or exempt under Part V of the 1999 Act.[7] The issue in all cases however is likely to be whether it is clear that the appellant intended to withdraw the appeal. If appellants have signed a letter of withdrawal, the burden is on them to show that they instructed their representative not to present it, or to withdraw it.[8]

1 See *Rahmani v Diggines* [1985] QB 1109, [1986] Imm AR 195; *R v Immigration Appeal Tribunal, ex p Pollicino* [1989] Imm AR 531, QBD; *Nessa v Secretary of State for the Home Department* [1985] Imm AR 131, CA.

2   44 *Halsbury's Laws* (4th edn) para 116.
3   See *Rahmani v Diggines* [1985] QB 1109, [1986] Imm AR 195.
4   *Singh* [1991] Imm AR 195.
5   *Attivor* [1988] Imm AR 109.
6   *Tanakloe* [1991] Imm AR 611.
7   See also Immigration and Asylum Appeals (Procedure) Rules 2000, SI 2000/2333, r 35 below.
8   *Adewole* (18538) 22 September 1998, IAT.

Abandonment of appeal

18.122 An appeal is deemed abandoned by statute in three specific situations. The first is when an appellant leaves the UK.[1] Obviously this only applies to in-country appeals. It does not apply to cases involving EEA nationals.[2] The adverse effect of the provision, making appellants effective prisoners in the UK for years in the past, will be mitigated if the waiting time for appeals is further reduced in line with government promises.[3] The second situation where an appeal is treated as abandoned is where an appellant is granted leave to enter or remain.[4] This does not apply to asylum claimants granted exceptional leave, who will be able to appeal in order to assert their rights to refugee status.[5] The third situation applies only to variation appeals, which are to be treated as abandoned if a deportation order is made against the appellant.[6]

1   Immigration and Asylum Act 1999, s 58(8), putting an end to litigation as to the meaning of the provisions of s 33(4) of the Immigration Act 1971 (as amended by the Asylum and Immigration Act 1996): *Dupovac v Secretary of State for the Home Department* [2000] Imm AR 265.
2   See *Baumbast* (21263) 8 June 1999, IAT.
3   See *Fairer, Faster, Firmer: a modern approach to immigration and asylum* (July 1998) paras 8.9: 'the government is aiming to ensure that ... most asylum decisions will be made within two months of receipt'; and 7.16: 'the intention is that in most cases the appeal before the adjudicator should produce finality and that the entire process should be completed within six months.'
4   Immigration and Asylum Act 1999, s 58(9).
5   Immigration and Asylum Act 1999, s 69(3).
6   Immigration and Asylum Act 1999, s 58(10).

18.123 Apart from these three situations, an adjudicator is entitled to treat an appeal as abandoned where a party has failed to comply with any directions given for the conduct of the appeal (such as filing of evidence etc), or with a procedural requirement of the rules, or has failed to appear at a hearing of which he or she has been properly notified, if the appellate authority is satisfied in all the circumstances, including the extent of the failure and any reasons for it, that the party is not pursuing the appeal.[1] The case law under the old rules makes it clear that mere non-appearance or non-compliance with directions is not sufficient for an appeal to be treated as abandoned,[2] although escape from custody and failure to make contact with the authorities may well be.[3] In *Ali*,[4] the court emphasised that the abandonment rule is meant only for cases where an appellant clearly has no intention of pursuing an appeal. It is thus clear that an investigation will have to be carried out. If an appellate authority decides to treat an appeal as abandoned it must inform the parties in writing, with reasons for the decision.[5] The Tribunal held that such a decision was a 'determination' under the Immigration Act 1971 attracting a right of appeal to it;[6] and a starred Tribunal has held that the same applies under the 1999 Act and 2000 Procedure Rules.[7]

1 Immigration and Asylum Appeals (Procedure) Rules 2000, SI 2000/2333, r 32.
2 *Akhuemonkhan* [1998] INLR 265, IAT, *Tahmouresy* (13540) 12 June 1996, IAT; *Salim* (14001) 15 October 1996, IAT; *Awan* (14827) 3 April 1997, IAT.
3 *Khamis* (13854) 2 September 1996, IAT.
4 *R v Immigration Appeal Tribunal and Lord Chancellor, ex p Mohammed Sarif Ali* [1998] INLR 526, [1999] Imm AR 48.
5 Immigration and Asylum Appeals (Procedure) Rules 2000, SI 2000/2333, r 32(2); *Adeyemi* (14825) 12 April 1997; *Singh (Nirmal)* (14875) 4 April 1997; *Sesay* (14870) 3 April 1997, IAT.
6 *Nzinga* (00536) 3 November 1999.
7 *Gremesty* [2001] INLR 132, a starred case, where the Tribunal however advised adjudicators to determine appeals under rule 33 where there has been non-compliance with directions. See definition of 'determination' under Immigration and Asylum Appeals (Procedure) Rules 2000, SI 2000/2333, r 2.

Defining the issues pre-hearing

18.124 There is no longer any requirement for the respondent immigration authority to serve an explanatory statement. The requirement for an explanatory statement was removed in asylum appeals in 1993, and since then the decision letter has set out in detail the evidential foundation and reasoning behind the refusal. At present, in non-asylum and non-human rights appeals, explanatory statements are still being issued, rather than detailed decision letters. But whether by decision letter or by case summary or explanatory statement, the respondent must set out in some document the facts of the case relied on by the immigration authority. The old explanatory statement had been held to be evidence rather than simply a pleading,[1] so that a summary of an interview contained in it was acceptable as evidence without production of the notes of interview[2] (except in asylum cases).[3] The modern practice is to supply copies of interview notes and other documents relied on by the immigration authority, in accordance with the principles of fairness under ECHR, Article 6 and at common law.[4] In non-asylum appeals the documents can be obtained, if necessary, in a variety of ways. Although there is (surprisingly) no express power of discovery[5] under the Procedure Rules,[6] much the same result can be obtained through other provisions of the procedure rules. The appellate authority, in exercise of its powers to give directions to secure the 'just, timely and effective disposal of appeals'[7] may require the furnishing of particulars which appear requisite for determining the appeal,[8] as well as requiring statements of evidence,[9] chronologies[10] and bundles of all documents to be relied on[11] to be filed and served on all other parties.[12] The list of possible directions is not exhaustive. While their use has been mainly to control appellants' cases, they are apt to extract from the respondent in advance all evidence on which it seeks to rely.

1 *R v Immigration Appeal Tribunal, ex p Weerasuriya* [1983] 1 All ER 195, QBD; *R v Immigration Appeal Tribunal, ex p Hassanin* [1987] 1 All ER 74, [1986] 1 WLR 1448, CA.
2 *Manjit Singh v Entry Clearance Officer, New Delhi* [1986] Imm AR 219.
3 Where the respondent must send the interview notes to the adjudicator with the notice of appeal and its attachments: Immigration and Asylum Appeals (Procedure) Rules 2000, SI 2000/2333, r 10(1)(d).
4 See eg *R v Secretary of State for the Home Department, ex p Thirukumar* [1989] Imm AR 270, DC.
5 *R v Adjudicator (RG Care), ex p Secretary of State for the Home Department* [1989] Imm AR 423, QBD.
6 Immigration and Asylum Appeals (Procedure) Rules 2000, SI 2000/2333
7 SI 2000/2333, r 30(1).
8 SI 2000/2333, r 30(4)(c)(iii).

9 SI 2000/2333, r 30(4)(d)(i).
10 SI 2000/2333, r 30(4)(d)(vi).
11 SI 2000/2333, r 30(4)(d)(ii).
12 SI 2000/2333, r 30(5).

18.125 An application for particulars is particularly important in cases where the Secretary of State makes a positive assertion, eg that the unauthorised disclosure of an asylum claim to the authorities of the appellant's country will not affect his or her safety on return,[1] or that a particular practice operates at the airport of a particular country, or that a document is not genuine. In addition, the appellate authority is obliged to give all parties the opportunity to inspect and copy any documentary evidence which is taken into consideration,[2] except that, if the document is a passport, other travel document, certificate of entitlement, work permit or entry clearance which is alleged to be forged, and disclosure of the method of detection of the forgery would be contrary to the public interest, there is provision for the evidence to be withheld from the appellant and his or her representative.[3] Under the Procedure Rules,[4] rule 36 it is also possible to obtain documents by summoning a witness to produce them, subject only to the limitation in rule 37(2) regarding circumstances when a person cannot be compelled to give evidence or produce documents.[5] Where the respondent is asserting some matter, such as fraud or forgery of documents, the burden of proof is on the respondent, and the more serious the allegation, the clearer and more direct the proof should be.[6] In such cases a failure to produce or call evidence in support of the allegations should result in the respondent's allegations remaining unproven or of very little weight.[7]

1 *R v Immigration Appeal Tribunal, ex p Agbenyenu* [1999] Imm AR 460, QBD.
2 SI 2000/2333, r 38.
3 Immigration and Asylum Act 1999, Sch 4, para 6.
4 Immigration and Asylum Appeals (Procedure) Rules 2000, SI 2000/2333.
5 See *Bharg* (7084) unreported, IAT: in principle a senior civil servant could be summoned to produce documents held by the Home Office relating to an asylum claim.
6 *Ali v Secretary of State for the Home Department* [1984] 1 All ER 1009, [1984] Imm AR 23, CA. See **18.146, 18.153** below.
7 See *R v Immigration Appeal Tribunal, ex p Cheema* [1982] Imm AR 124 at 133, CA.

Reasons for the decision or action appealed

18.126 The giving of reasons is a substantial matter. The Notices Regulations[1] require that reasons should be given when the decision or action is notified to the appellant, as seen above. The giving of reasons for an administrative decision adversely affecting rights of residence, family life, and even more fundamental rights embodied in the Refugee Convention, is increasingly seen as vital for compliance with standards of fairness at common law,[2] and for compatibility with the Human Rights Convention.[3] It is for this reason thought that unless the notice of refusal is amended, it is not possible for the immigration authority to rely upon an entirely different reason for refusal at the hearing. The extent to which the reasons may be amended to reflect the true reasons for the decision and the extent to which an adjudicator and Tribunal are tied to the reasons contained in the notice and decision letter, when it comes to the hearing of the appeal, have already been considered.[4] The position under the Immigration Act 1971 was that the notice of decision and explanatory statement were preliminary definitions of the issues between the parties on appeal, but with the probable exception of statutory grounds (eg for deportation), not necessarily conclusive.[5] Certainly, the jurisdiction of the appellate authorities is wide enough in all appeals to place a duty on them to measure their view of the facts[6] against the applicable statutes, rules, policies, Conventions and administrative law standards, whether or not these have been expressly referred to, with the Court of Appeal decision in *Robinson*[7] providing the parameters of this duty.[8] So, where an asylum claim has been refused on non-compliance grounds, the Tribunal has held that the appellate authority has an obligation to decide for itself whether the appellant's removal would be contrary to the Convention.[9] Again, there will be exceptions to such a wide duty where the respondent relies on a specific statutory ground, whether for deportation or for certification of human rights and asylum appeals.[10] But equally, a fair hearing demands a proper opportunity to meet the case made. In this connection it is important to recall that the adjudicator has power to limit the issues on appeal.[11] This provides an opportunity to agree facts and legal issues which once agreed, should not be reopened unless patently wrong.[12]

1 Immigration Appeals (Notices) Regulations 2000, SI 2000/2246.
2 See eg *Stefan v General Medical Council* [1999] 1 WLR 1293; *R v Secretary of State for the Home Department, ex p Zighem* [1996] Imm AR 194.
3 *Stefan v General Medical Council* [1999] 1 WLR 1293; *R v Higher Education Funding Council, ex p Institute of Dental Surgery* [1994] 1 WLR 242.
4 See **18.71**, **18.98** above.
5 Woolf J in *R v Immigration Appeal Tribunal, ex p Hubbard* [1985] Imm AR 110.
6 Immigration and Asylum Act 1999, Sch 4, para 21(3).
7 *Robinson v Secretary of State for the Home Department* [1997] Imm AR 568, CA.
8 *Rahman and Akhter* (00307) 10 March 2000, IAT; *Kaur (Sukhinder) v Secretary of State for the Home Department* [1998] Imm AR 1, CA.
9 *Haddad (Ali)* [2000] INLR 117, IAT; *Diai* (00149) 11 February 2000, IAT, *Adeeb* (16665) 12 August 1998, IAT.
10 Immigration and Asylum Act 1999, Sch 4, para 9. See **18.99** above (certified appeals).
11 Immigration and Asylum Appeals (Procedure) Rules 2000, SI 2000/2333, r 30(4)(e)(iv).
12 See *R v Immigration Appeal Tribunal, ex p Akhtar and Bowen* (1982) 126 Sol Jo 430, QBD.

Preliminary issues

18.127 The preliminary issue jurisdiction applies where the respondent immigration authority has alleged under rule 12(1) of the Procedure Rules[1] that either the appellant is not entitled to appeal or the notice of appeal was out of time. Where a preliminary issue falls within rule 12(1) the validity of the allegation must then be determined as a preliminary issue if the respondent has submitted a written, reasoned allegation and so requests. If the allegation is made but no request is submitted for a preliminary issue determination, the appellate authority has a discretion whether to do so.[2] This is a surprising provision, since it means that the adjudicator may proceed to hear an appeal even if the jurisdictional basis is in doubt, if the respondent does not take the point. Apart from the allegation that the appeal is out of time,[3] the respondent may rely on one of four separate grounds for alleging that there is no appeal right:

(1) By virtue of a provision of the Immigration and Asylum Act 1999.[4] This could be an issue as to whether the appellant held a document required by the rules,[5] about whether an asylum claimant seeking to revoke a deportation order had an opportunity to appeal against the deportation decision,[6] or as to non-compliance with prescribed steps,[7] or an argument about the certifying of a claim as abusive under the one-stop procedure,[8] or if the

> Secretary of State certifies a human rights claim in a third-country case manifestly unfounded.[9]

(2) On an EEA appeal, by virtue of a provision of regulations made under the European Communities Act and section 80 of the Immigration and Asylum Act 1999.[10] This refers to provisions of the EEA Order denying appeal rights to those without relevant documents proving their status.[11]

(3) By virtue of the fact that a passport, travel document, certificate of entitlement, entry clearance or work permit relied on by the appellant is a forgery or the appellant is not the rightful holder of it.[12] The adjudicator would have to reach a conclusion on the genuineness of the document, perhaps in a hearing closed in part even to the appellant and his or her representative.[13]

(4) By reason of the failure of the appellant or his or her representative to sign the notice of appeal.[14]

1 Immigration and Asylum Appeals (Procedure) Rules 2000, SI 2000/2333.
2 SI 2000/2333, r 12(3).
3 SI 2000/2333, r 12(1)(b); see **18.103** above.
4 SI 2000/2333, r 12(1)(a)(i).
5 Immigration and Asylum Act 1999, s 60(2) or s 62(1)(a).
6 Immigration and Asylum Act 1999, s 70(8).
7 Immigration and Asylum Act 1999, s 72(3).
8 Immigration and Asylum Act 1999, s 73(8), 76(5).
9 Immigration and Asylum Act 1999, s 72(2)(a).
10 SI 2000/2333, r 12(1)(a)(ii).
11 Immigration (European Economic Area) Regulations 2000, SI 2000/2326, reg 29.
12 SI 2000/2333, r 12(1)(a)(iii).
13 Immigration and Asylum Act 1999, Sch 4, para 6.
14 SI 2000/2333, r 12(1)(a)(iv).

18.128 In relation to the certificates of abusive claims or appeals under the one-stop procedure, the wording of the statute draws a distinction between those whose effect is that the appeal is treated as finally determined, and those whose effect is that 'no appeal may be made'. But it appears to be a distinction without a difference, since in either case there is probably no appeal right, although only in the latter cases this is expressly stated. Can the certificates be challenged in the preliminary issue jurisdiction? This issue remains to be resolved through the courts. In practice, given that the certificate would be issued in response to a notice of appeal, there seems to be no reason why the adjudicator could not deal with it and make a ruling. Issues of jurisdiction are for the appellate authority, not the Secretary of State, and should be dealt with under the preliminary issue jurisdiction.[1] However, what is not yet clear is how much scope the adjudicator has for disagreeing with the Secretary of State's assessment, for example, that a repeat human rights or asylum claim is abusive or a human rights claim in respect of a third safe country manifestly unfounded. It would be very surprising if the adjudicator's jurisdiction on a preliminary issue hearing was limited to ascertaining that the certificate had been duly issued, without being able to inquire into the underlying merits, ie whether it *should* have been issued on the facts. It is also unclear what if any discretion the adjudicator has to allow an appeal to proceed even if (in the fourth scenario) an appeal notice has not been signed. None is apparent from the wording of the rule save in respect of out-of-time appeals.[2] But it will surely be necessary to read some discretion in, particularly in such a case, to ensure compliance with ECHR and basic fairness.[3] The tribunal has also held that it can hear appeals on these preliminary issues,[4] since if the adjudicator determines that the appellant is not entitled to appeal, the consequence will be that the appeal will be dismissed.[5] The position where the Secretary of State decides there is no appeal and refuses to forward the notice of appeal has already been considered.[6] The preliminary issue jurisdiction does not, however, cover the question of whether the appellant has an *in-country* appeal right: it is limited to the question of whether there is an appeal at all. A dispute over whether there is an in-country appeal would have to be taken to the High Court on judicial review.

1 *Lokko* [1990] Imm AR 111; *Ken'aan* [1990] Imm AR 544.
2 As to which see **18.102** above.
3 See the Court of Appeal's discussion of the proper consequences of non-compliance for appeal rights in *R v Immigration Appeal Tribunal, ex p Jeyeanthan; Ravichandran v Secretary of State for the Home Department* [2000] 1 WLR 354, [1999] INLR 241.
4 *Omishore* [1990] Imm AR 582.
5 *Ibrahim* [1994] Imm AR 1.
6 See **18.116** above.

18.129 The procedure for a preliminary issue determination is that the respondent sets out the allegation in writing with reasons and relevant facts and sends it with the appeal documents to the adjudicator, with a copy of the allegation and reasons to the appellant and his or her representative.[1] The appellant may send a written statement in reply.[2] At a hearing, the adjudicator gives the parties the opportunity to explain and respond respectively.[3] There need not be a hearing if the appellant has failed to take the opportunity to rebut the respondent's allegation, or if the adjudicator decides that the matters put forward by the appellant in the rebuttal statement do not warrant a hearing.[4] If the preliminary issue is whether a notice of appeal is out of time, the appellate authority must, having decided that the notice was out of time, exercise discretion in deciding whether to allow the appeal to proceed.[5] The only occasion in which the appellate authorities are unable to allow an out-of-time appeal to proceed is where a deportation order is in force against the appellant.[6]

1 Immigration and Asylum Appeals (Procedure) Rules 2000, SI 2000/2333, r 12(1).
2 SI 2000/2333, r 12(2).
3 SI 2000/2333, r 12(4).
4 SI 2000/2333, r 43(1)(c).
5 SI 2000/2333, r 12(5).
6 SI 2000/2333. See **18.102** above for detailed discussion of out-of-time appeals.

Notice of hearing and directions

18.130 The appellate authority must serve on the appellant or his or her representative, and on any other party, notice of the date, time and place fixed for the hearing and any directions for the conduct of the hearing.[1] Directions may not be given to an unrepresented party unless the appellate authority is satisfied that he or she is able to comply with them.[2] The power to give directions, which was introduced in an attempt to streamline asylum appeals, has been extended under the Procedure Rules[3] to all appeals. It applies at both levels of the appellate authority and the overriding objective is to secure the just, timely and effective disposal of the appeal.[4] Directions may be given orally or in writing.[5] They may provide for matters to be dealt with as preliminary issues (which might include, but is not limited to, the issues referred to above). The power to request the furnishing of particulars has been dealt with above.[6] There may be a direction as to whether there should be a hearing of the appeal[7] and if so, the witnesses to be heard, if any, and how the evidence is to be given (eg with an interpreter).[8] Their main use is in directing witness statements, skeleton arguments, chronologies and bundles of the documentary evidence to be relied on to be served within specified time limits.[9] Time estimates are often ordered, and occasionally directions are given limiting the number or length of documents to be submitted (particularly useful in asylum appeals where 'standard bundles' of over 300 pages are frequently served).[10] Anything lodged in response to directions must be served on all other parties.[11] Directions may be given limiting the length of oral submissions and limiting the time allowed for examination of witnesses, for example by allowing witness statements to stand as evidence in chief.[12] This power is not subject to the appellant's consent, although this does not mean that at the hearing the appellant should not have the opportunity of adding to the witness statement anything necessarily supplementary to it to bring it to life.[13] Directions may limit the issues to be addressed at the hearing,[14] and should facilitate the holding of combined hearings.[15]

1 Immigration and Asylum Appeals (Procedure) Rules 2000, SI 2000/2333, r 13.
2 SI 2000/2333, r 30(6).
3 Immigration and Asylum Appeals (Procedure) Rules 2000, SI 2000/2333.
4 SI 2000/2333, r 30(2).
5 SI 2000/2333, r 30(3).
6 See **18.124** above. In *Gimedhin* (14019) 21 October 1996, the Tribunal contemplated the use of this power to direct the submission of medical reports. This could present serious difficulties, as the tribunal itself recognised.
7 As to which see **18.131** below.
8 SI 2000/2333, r 30(4)(c)(v) and (vi).
9 SI 2000/2333, r 30(4)(a), (d).
10 SI 2000/2333, r 30(4)(e). The Chief Adjudicator has issued Guidance Notes for good practice on the preparation of trial bundles (February 2000), which contains the following instructions relating to asylum appeals: Illegible or handwritten documents or translations should be typed. The bundle should be indexed and paginated and preferably agreed between the parties. The skeleton and chronology or summary should be cross-referenced to the relevant page of the bundle, which should include (where relevant) the pro-forma, asylum questionnaire or statement of evidence form, interview record, asylum statement, refusal letter, explanatory statement, notice of decision, medical reports and responses to them, expert reports and responses to them, relevant country reports, other necessary and relevant documents. Adjudicators will take judicial notice of reports from the US State Department, the Home Office Country Information Policy Unit, Amnesty International and Human Rights Watch annual reports, Europa World yearbooks, so only the relevant page of these should be included. Bundles should be lodged 7-28 days before the hearing.
11 SI 2000/2333, r 30(5).
12 SI 2000/2333, r 30(4)(e)(iii).
13 *R v Secretary of State for the Home Department, ex p Singh* [1998] INLR 608, CA (permission).
14 See **18.126** above.
15 See **18.157** below. But an adjudicator has no power to direct the Secretary of State to issue a fresh refusal letter, failing which the original refusal would be treated as withdrawn: *Mwanza v Secretary of State for the Home Department* (2000) Independent, 9 November, CA.

18.131 What effect does non-compliance with directions have on the appeal? As we have seen above, an adjudicator may treat an appeal as abandoned where a party has without satisfactory explanation failed to comply with a direction, but only if the failure is such that the adjudicator can be satisfied that the party is not pursuing the appeal.[1] If satisfied that it is necessary to have regard to the overriding objective of just, timely and effective disposal of appeals,[2] the adjudicator faced with non-compliance may dismiss or allow the appeal without considering the merits,[3] determine the appeal without a hearing on the evidence before him or her,[4] or prohibit a party from relying on a document, statement or evidence not submitted.[5] The adjudicator must have regard to all the circumstances, including the extent of the failure and the reasons for it, before taking any of these steps. The power to determine an appeal without a hearing for non-compliance with directions should be exercised with extreme caution and will rarely if ever be appropriate if the party in default is present;[6] this caution would apply to an even greater extent to the power to dispose of the appeal without consideration of the merits. Where the failure to comply does not go to an essential part of the case, the use of the guillotine powers would be unsustainable.[7]

1   See **18.122**ff above.
2   Immigration and Asylum Appeals (Procedure) Rules 2000, SI 2000/2333, r 33(1).
3   SI 2000/2333, r 33(2)(a).
4   SI 2000/2333, r 33(2)(b).
5   SI 2000/2333, r 33(2)(c).
6   *Meflah* [1997] Imm AR 555, IAT; *R v Immigration Appeal Tribunal, ex p S* [1998] Imm AR 252, [1998] INLR 168. Although these cases were decided before an express power existed to dispense with a hearing, or with consideration on the merits, for non-compliance with directions, the overriding objective, and so the framework within which the appellate authority must exercise its discretion, remains the same.
7   *Meflah* [1997] Imm AR 555.

ADJUDICATOR HEARINGS

Dispensing with a hearing

18.132   The adjudicator has separate powers to determine an appeal without a hearing,[1] and to determine the appeal in the absence of a party.[2] Here we consider determination of an appeal without a hearing at all (apart from the determination of preliminary issues, considered above at **18.127**). The situations where this can be done are set out in rule 43 of the Procedure Rules.[3] Under this rule an appellate authority can determine an appeal without a hearing if:

(1)   no party to the appeal has requested a hearing;[4]
(2)   the appellate authority has decided, after giving every other party to the appeal an opportunity of replying to any representations submitted in writing by or on behalf of the appellant, to allow the appeal;[5] or
(3)   the appellate authority is satisfied that the appellant (not the Secretary of State or an officer) is outside the UK or that it is impracticable to give him or her notice of a hearing and, in either case, that no person is authorised to represent him or her at a hearing;[6] or
(4)   the appellate authority is satisfied, having given every party the opportunity to make representations and having regard to the material before it and the nature of the issues raised, that the appeal could be disposed of justly without a hearing;[7] or
(5)   there has been non-compliance with a direction or a provision of the procedure rules of an extent and for a reason making it necessary to have regard to the overriding objective of disposing of the appeal justly, effectively and in a timely manner.[8]

In addition, the appellate authority must determine a family visitor appeal without a hearing if the fee for the hearing has not been paid.[9]

1 Immigration and Asylum Appeals (Procedure) Rules 2000, SI 2000/2333, r 43.
2 SI 2000/2333, r 41. The adjudicator should be clear to distinguish between the two situations and should make it clear which procedure he or she is adopting: *Abali* (15543) 6 October 1997, IAT.
3 Immigration and Asylum Appeals (Procedure) Rules 2000, SI 2000/2333.
4 SI 2000/2333, r 43(1)(e).
5 SI 2000/2333, r 43(1)(a).
6 SI 2000/2333, r 43(1)(b). See *R v Diggines, ex p Rahmani* [1985] QB 1109, [1986] Imm AR 195, HL, where it was held that UKIAS had not ceased to act for the appellant, although they had lost her new address; before proceeding under this rule, the adjudicator should have required an unambiguous declaration from UKIAS either that their instructions had been withdrawn or that they had no instructions.
7 SI 2000/2333, r 43(1)(d).
8 SI 2000/2333, r 43(1)(f).
9 SI 2000/2333, r 43(2). The fee is set at £125 if the appellant elects a hearing, and £50 without one: Immigration Appeals (Family Visitor) (No 2) Regulations 2000, SI 2000/2446, reg 3(1), as amended by SI 2001/52. For court fees and ECHR, Art 6 rights, see *R v Lord Chancellor, ex p Witham* [1998] QB 575.

18.133 These powers are significantly broader than under the pre-2000 procedure rules, particularly in respect of non-compliance and the general power based on the nature of the issues raised. We have dealt above with dispensing with a hearing for non-compliance with directions.[1] This power should clearly be used very sparingly, in cases indicative of abandonment, and probably not at all when parties have appeared for the hearing. The power to dispense with a hearing because of the material put in and the nature of the issues raised would clearly never be used where credibility was in issue.[2] Both parties should have had an opportunity to ask for a hearing or respond to any representations made and evidence submitted[3] and the power must be exercised by the adjudicator personally rather than a member of the administrative staff.[4] Where indications have been given that the appellant wishes to give oral evidence it is signally inappropriate that directions be given to determine the appeal without a hearing.[5] An adjudicator cannot decide to determine an appeal without a hearing and then receive submissions from counsel.[6]

1 See **18.131** above.
2 See *Federation of Canadian Sikh Societies v Canadian Council of Churches* [1985] 1 SCR 178 (cited in *R v Immigration Appeal Tribunal, ex p S* [1998] Imm AR 252 at 267.
3 *Jan* (7063) IAT.
4 *Singh (Piara)* (7069), IAT.
5 *Gioshev* (15801) 24 November 1997.
6 *Sivayokam* (16015) 8 January 1998, IAT.

Summary determination

18.134 Another form of appeal without a hearing is provided for in rule 44 of the Procedure Rules.[1] A summary determination of the appeal without a hearing can be made where it appears to the appellate authority that the issues raised on an appeal have been determined in a previous appeal, to which the appellant or a family member[2] was a party, and there is no material difference in the facts.[3] The previous rule limited the application of summary hearings to the situation where appellants themselves had been parties to previous appeals on the same facts. This did not preclude family members from having full consecutive appeals relying on the same facts. For example, the issue of the validity of a marriage could be litigated first by the spouse in a marriage appeal and then by the children in certificate of entitlement appeals.[4] The amendment, which is another element in the one-stop procedure, will make the use of combined hearings more common for family members whose applications rest on the same factual foundation, who could otherwise find themselves bound by a determination to which they were not party.

1 Immigration and Asylum Appeals (Procedure) Rules 2000, SI 2000/2333.
2 Defined as a person served with a notice under s 74(4) (as a relevant family member).
3 See *Ahmed* [1977] Imm AR 25; *Bibi (Taj)* [1977] Imm AR 25; *Ahmed* (5247), unreported, IAT.
4 As happened in *R v Secretary of State for the Home Department, ex p Sattar* (CO 2555/99), September 2000, where a dismissal of an appeal by summary hearing was quashed by consent when it was realised that the appellants in the case were the children and the original appellant had been their mother.

18.135 A request that the appeal be dealt with summarily can be made at the start of the hearing, where the case has been listed for oral hearing. The appellate authority must give the parties an opportunity of making representations before proceeding to a summary determination of an appeal.[1] Where an appeal is dealt with in this way the appellate authority must give the parties written notice that the appeal has been so determined and must include a statement of the issues raised and specify the previous proceedings in which those issues were determined.[2] The adjudicator should then consider the parties' representations on the application and may then, if the conditions of rule 44 are fulfilled, to determine the appeal summarily.[3] Rule 44 is a discretionary provision, and in a suitable case an adjudicator may proceed to a full hearing even though there has been a previous appeal raising the same issue and doing so on facts not materially different.[4] However, such a previous adjudication would be a highly relevant circumstance in considering whether to deal with the appeal summarily. The doctrine of *res judicata* does not apply in this sphere.

1 Immigration and Asylum Appeals (Procedure) Rules 2000, SI 2000/2333, r 44(2).
2 SI 2000/2333, r 44(3).
3 *Ramzan* [1978] Imm AR 111.
4 *R v Immigration Appeal Tribunal, ex p Taj and Riaz* [1981] Imm AR 81, QBD.

The hearing

18.136 Except where the appeal is to be determined without a hearing under rules 43 or 44 of the Procedure Rules, all appeals will be dealt with by way of a hearing, including those which proceed in a party's absence.[1] There is provision in the rules for hearings to be conducted, evidence given or representations made by video link or other electronic means,[2] opening up for the first time the possibility of appellants giving evidence in their own out-of-country appeals. All appeals (save those not listed for hearing) are allocated to a fast track or a first hearing track.[3] Those listed in the fast track are:

(1) asylum appeals where the claim has been certified;[4]
(2) appeals where the appellant is detained;
(3) appeals remitted for re-hearing by the Tribunal or the Administrative Court;
(4) asylum appeals where the claimant has dependent family members with him or her in the UK;
(5) immigration appeals against refusal of leave to enter on general grounds;[5]

(6)   family visit appeals listed for hearing;
(7)   appeals listed for hearing in Belfast.

Other appeals are listed for first hearing, and will not be heard then, unless there is a failure to return the reply form and to attend, and no satisfactory explanation has been given; or it is not proposed to call oral evidence; or the appeal is conceded and the appellant merely seeks a recommendation.[6] The immigration appeals listed in rule 43(1)(a)–(e) of the Procedure Rules[7] are not listed unless in the light of representations from the parties, the interests of justice require it.[8] There is nothing in the procedure rules as to where hearings may take place. The appellate authority is not required to list an appeal at the hearing centre which is closest or most convenient for the appellant, but should transfer an appeal where there is a good reason.[9] An appellant has no legitimate expectation that the date of the hearing will not be brought forward, only that it will not be changed without reasonable notice.[10]

1 Immigration and Asylum Appeals (Procedure) Rules 2000, SI 2000/2333, r 14(1).
2 SI 2000/2333, r 14(2).
3 Practice Direction CA4/2000 [2000] INLR 687, in force 2 October 2000.
4 Ie under the Immigration and Asylum Act 1999, Sch 4, para 9, as not disclosing a Convention claim or made after refusal or enforcement decisions or fraudulent or frivolous claims.
5 Those listed at HC 395, para 321, which could be loosely characterised as public policy, public security and public health grounds.
6 Practice Direction, CA4/2000 [2000] INLR 687. For recommendations when an appeal is dismissed see **18.89** above.
7 See **18.132** above.
8 Practice Direction CA4/2000 [2000] INLR 687, para 4.
9 *Ahmad* (12033) 21 April 1995; *Kaur* (13052) 1 March 1996, IAT. *In R v Secretary of State for the Home Department, ex p Semaane* [1998] Imm AR 48, the High Court held that the listing of an appeal in Birmingham necessitating travel from London was not unreasonable where the appellant had some means and had sought a transfer from Glasgow, from where he had lived, distinguishing *Adedayo* (14940), where the Tribunal allowed an appeal after an adjudicator decided a transferred case in the absence of an appellant with no means who had been unable to travel. An unpublished instruction, the 'Marylebone Directive', issued in 1993 or 1994, required appeals of appellants with an address north of Marylebone Road in London to be listed in Birmingham to alleviate pressure on the lists, 'where judicial capacity at London hearing centres is fully committed'.
10 *R v Immigration Appeal Tribunal, ex p Shandar* [2000] Imm AR 181.

Proceeding in a party's absence

18.137 Rule 41 enables the appellate authority in proper circumstances to hear an appeal in the absence of a party, when it is satisfied, *inter alia*, that he or she is not in the UK;[1] is suffering from a communicable disease or a mental disorder;[2] cannot attend through accident or illness;[3] is unrepresented at the hearing and it is impracticable to give notice;[4] or has notified the appellate authority that he or she does not wish to attend. The appellate authority may also proceed if the party has failed to appear despite notification of the time and place of the hearing,[5] and must proceed if there is no satisfactory explanation for absence.[6] This is a mandatory requirement and applies equally to both parties: an adjudicator may not adjourn for the respondent to be present if there is no explanation for a Home Office presenting officer's absence.[7] A party, for the purposes of the rule, includes a representative.[8] This provision does not entitle an adjudicator to proceed as if the appellant were absent when he or she is present but the representative is absent.[9] The Tribunal has set out guidelines for adjudicators on how to proceed where the Home Office is not represented, attached to the starred case of MNM.[10]

1 SI 2000/2333, r 41(1)(a).
2 SI 2000/2333, r 41(1)(b).
3 SI 2000/2333, r 41(1)(c).
4 SI 2000/2333, r 41(1)(d).
5 SI 2000/2333, r 41(2). An adjudicator is not entitled to proceed under this rule without checking the correctness of the address of the representative, particularly where the address for the appellant is apparently incorrect: *Alabi* (12975) 6 February 1996.
6 SI 2000/2333, r 41(3).
7 *R v Special Adjudicator, ex p Demeter* [2000] Imm AR 424, QBD: 'To give the impression of allowing special favours to the Home Office by allowing an adjournment without an explanation for absence is dangerous.' The earlier case of *Kozar* (18831) 7 July 1999, where the Tribunal allowed an appeal by the Secretary of State after the adjudicator had proceeded in the absence of a presenting officer who had offered no explanation for absence, should no longer be followed.
8 But SI 2000/2333, r 46(2), deeming service on a representative good service on the party represented, does not require a notice of hearing to be served on both the appellant and the representative: *R v Secretary of State for the Home Department, ex p Ogunsowo* (1999/6315/4), CA, 11 August 1999, CA (permission); *Awadh* [1997] INLR 39, IAT.
9 *Singh (Santokh)* (13002) 22 February 1996, IAT.
10 (00 TH 02423*) 1 November 2000, IAT ('the *Surerdran* guidelines').

18.138 Most of the case law concerns allegations of non-receipt of notices of hearing, leading to hearings in the absence of appellants. Parties are obliged to notify the appellate authority of the address for service of documents and until change of address is notified documents sent to that address are deemed to have been properly served.[1] They also have a duty to maintain contact with representatives, and notify them of any change of address. The representatives have a duty to keep the appellate authority informed of any change of representation.[2] Notice to the immigration authorities is not enough;[3] the respondent is under no duty to notify the appellate authority of an appellant's change of address or representative.[4] But all deemed service must arguably be subject to a proviso, whether or not expressly stated, allowing proof of non-receipt.[5] The Tribunal is obliged to consider an allegation of non-receipt of the notice of hearing in an application for leave to appeal.[6] Service of a notice of hearing is not legally adequate if the name on the envelope is incorrect.[7] Where a direction requires a certificate of readiness to be submitted, failing which the party is to appear on the date in the notice, and a certificate of 'unreadiness' is sent in, the adjudicator is entitled to proceed in the absence of the appellant and the representative.[8]

1 Immigration and Asylum Appeals (Procedure) Rules 2000, SI 2000/2333, r 47. The same rule applies to representatives.
2 SI 2000/2333, r 35(2)-(6).
3 *R v Secretary of State for the Home Department, ex p Hannach* [1997] Imm AR 162, QBD.
4 *R v Secretary of State for the Home Department, ex p Hannach* [1997] Imm AR 162, QBD, and see *R v Secretary of State for the Home Department, ex p Ladipo* [1997] Imm AR 51, CA.
5 Following *R v Secretary of State for the Home Department, ex p Asifa Saleem*, [2000] Imm AR 529, [2000] INLR 413, upholding Hooper J at [1999] INLR 621.
6 *R v Immigration Appeal Tribunal, ex p Susikanth* [1998] INLR 185, CA.
7 *Choudhry* (15911) 7 January 1998, IAT.
8 *R v Secretary of State for the Home Department, ex p Butt* [1999] Imm AR 341, QBD; *R v Special Adjudicator, ex p Arshad* (CO 1145/97), 15 April 1997, QBD.

18.139 In exercising the power to proceed in a party's absence, adjudicators must act fairly,[1] but are not obliged to accept any excuse for non-attendance at face value. In particular, the adjudicator is not obliged to accept a medical certificate which does not explain why a party is unable to attend.[2] If in such circumstances neither the appellant nor the respondent is represented, the appeal is determined upon such evidence as has been received.[3] Adjudicators must specify precisely why they are proceeding in the absence of a party, ie which limb of the rule they are relying on.[4] If they proceed, they must allow or dismiss the appeal.[5]

1 *Singh (Reshan) and Kaur* [1993] Imm AR 382 (if hearing is described as pre-hearing review, it is unfair to proceed in the absence of appellant, as if it was the final hearing).
2 *R v Immigration Appeal Tribunal, ex p Baira* [1994] Imm AR 487, QBD; *Deen-Koroma v Immigration Appeal Tribunal* [1997] Imm AR 242, CA; *R v Secretary of State for the Home Department, ex p Lal Singh* [1998] Imm AR 320, QBD.
3 Immigration and Asylum Appeals (Procedure) Rules 2000, SI 2000/2333, r 41(4).
4 *Jan* (7063) unreported, IAT; *Deb* [1990] Imm AR 14.
5 *Ali (Shaharia)* [1999] INLR 108, IAT. Additionally, if the adjudicator accepts material from the party in whose absence he or she are proceeding, that is tantamount to reopening the hearing, obliging the adjudicator to reconsider whether it is appropriate to proceed in the party's absence: *Feghali* (16602) 25 November 1998, IAT.

Representation

18.140 Parties to an appeal may appear in person or be represented.[1] Appellants may be represented by any person not prohibited from acting by section 84 of the Immigration and Asylum Act 1999;[2] the Secretary of State or any officer can be represented by an authorised advocate or any officer of the Home Department (known as presenting officers).[3] The UK Representative of the UN High Commissioner for Refugees can be represented by any person appointed as such. A representative has all the powers of the party he or she is representing, such as the giving or receipt of notices etc.[4] The parties have a duty to maintain contact with their representative until the appeal is finally determined, and to notify the representative of changes of address.[5] Both have a duty to notify the appellate authority of changes in representation. Until such notification, documents served on the first representative are deemed properly served on the party he or she was representing.[6]

1 Immigration and Asylum Appeals (Procedure) Rules 2000, SI 2000/2333, r 35(1).
2 Qualified lawyers or registered or exempted immigration service providers: see **1.58** above.
3 A Home Office Presenting Officer has authority to concede the appeal, but counsel representing the Secretary of State does not.
4 SI 2000/2333, r 35(2).
5 SI 2000/2333, r 35(3).
6 SI 2000/2333, r 35(5).

Controlled legal representation (CLR)

18.141 From 1 January 2000, legal aid in the form of Controlled Legal Representation (CLR) has been available for hearings, to immigration service providers which have a contract with or a franchise from the Legal Services Commission (LSC).[1] Previously, appellants were eligible for legal help (advice and assistance) in preparing the appeal, but not for representation before the appellate authority. Now, subject to means and merits testing, funding for representation at the hearing is available, covering adjudicator and Immigration

Appeal Tribunal hearings including bail and interlocutory directions hearings. Funding for representation covers the fee for appealing.[2] However, funding does not extend to representation before the Special Immigration Appeals Commission,[3] and appellants before the Commission are eligible only for a discretionary grant of public funding.[4]

1 Community Legal Service (Funding) Order 2000, SI 2000/627.
2 Lord Chancellor's Department to ILPA 14 September 2000.
3 See Access to Justice Act 1999, Sch 2, para 2.
4 Access to Justice Act 1999, s 6(8)(b). Discretionary legal funding was refused in both Special Immigration Appeals Commission cases. The second case, *Singh (Mukhtiar) and Singh (Paramjit)*, was determined in the appellants' favour on ECHR, Art 3 grounds on 31 July 2000.

Adjournments

18.142 The appellate authority has power to adjourn a hearing but may not do so unless satisfied that refusing the adjournment would prevent the just disposal of the appeal.[1] This is a similar criterion to that contained in the 1996 Asylum Procedure Rules.[2] There are two main reasons for seeking an adjournment: health, and need for representation. In the former situation, the higher courts have generally been content to leave it to the adjudicator's judgment,[3] so long as the adjudicator has given an adequate opportunity to respond to objections to medical evidence.[4] In the latter, the higher courts have recently frowned on the more liberal approach of the tribunal,[5] which in asylum appeals such as *Ajeh*[6] had said that 'whether or not an appellant is articulate, the need for representation at the hearing ... appears almost axiomatic given the obligation to give the most anxious scrutiny to cases of this kind'.[7] But in *ex p Ghaly*[8] Sedley J issued a reminder that 'the question of adjournment ... frequently throws up fundamental issues of fairness. If the maxim "both sides are to be fairly heard" is to have any effect, it means that each side has to have a fair opportunity of preparing to deal with what the other side is going to say'.[9] In *Okiji*[10] the Tribunal deprecated the refusal of an adjournment when counsel was taken ill and the adjudicator had, in refusing, referred to the 'normal practice of the Bar' in sending a replacement 'even at one moment's notice'. It observed that the traditions of the Bar were 'not always consistent with the interests of the appellant'.[11] The withdrawal of a representative at a hearing (other than when an appellant withdraws instructions) is a good reason to adjourn.[12] An adjournment should be granted if the appellant requests it, where there is evidence that a refusal on non-compliance grounds was erroneous.[13] When a party—or the adjudicator—wishes to rely on evidence, or on a ground, not previously sent to the other party, there must be an adjournment if necessary to avoid prejudice.[14] An adjournment should be granted to adduce evidence not reasonably available at the hearing,[15] or where a new, binding decision on the point at issue is imminent.[16] In *Kimbesa*,[17] a refusal to adjourn was quashed where, shortly before an asylum appeal hearing, the appellant's brothers, whose claims rested on the same facts, had arrived in the UK. Ognall J held that it was unfair to expect the brothers to have their accounts tested in an appeal hearing before they had been interviewed on their claim. In *Rajan*,[18] a starred Tribunal case, Collins J said, distinguishing *Kimbesa*, that it was not authority for the proposition that wherever there was a concurrent application by a relative an adjournment was in the interests of justice, although the existence of concurrent applications by family members was a relevant consideration which may point to an adjournment in an appropriate case.

1 Immigration and Asylum Appeals (Procedure) Rules 2000, SI 2000/2333, r 31(1).
2 Asylum Appeals (Procedure) Rules 1996, SI 1996/2070.
3 See eg *R v Secretary of State for the Home Department, ex p Odubanjo* [1996] Imm AR 504, QBD (adjudicator entitled to use common sense regarding a pregnant appellant who felt unwell at the hearing); *R v Immigration Appeal Tribunal, ex p Choudhury (Kawsar)* (1999/6451/C), 2 November 1999, CA (adjudicator entitled to refuse adjournment having regard to medical evidence and appellant's demeanour and ability to answer questions at the hearing).
4 *Chisthi* (14953) 12 May 1997; *Awadh* (12783) 7 December 1995; *Gheorghiu* (12850) 28 December 1995.
5 In *R v Secretary of State for the Home Department and Immigration Appeal Tribunal, ex p Bogou* [2000] Imm AR 494, Maurice Kay J pointed to the tightening of the criteria for adjourning between the Asylum Appeals (Procedure) Rules 1993 and 1996, SI 1993/1661 and SI 1996/2070 and to the failure of Tribunal jurisprudence to reflect that change. In *R v Special Adjudicator, ex p Nitcheu* (00/5158/C) 7 March 2000, CA (renewed permission application) a refusal to adjourn for legal representation for an appellant who had lost his representation through compulsory dispersal was upheld. See also *R v SA, ex p Kotovas* [2000] Imm AR 26; *R v Immigration Appeal Tribunal, ex p Adrees* (95/5564/D) 18 April 1996, CA; *R v Secretary of State for the Home Department, ex p Janneh* [1997] Imm AR 154; *R v Secretary of State for the Home Department, ex p Twaha* (CO/4073/98) 1 December 1999, QBD.
6 (13853) 30 August 1996, IAT, followed in *(inter alia) Cabrera* (17123) 21 May 1998; *Kyeyune* (18153) 25 November 1998.
7 The Tribunal's view reflected those of the Genn Report, *Representation before Tribunals* (1989) Hazel and Yvette Genn, the Legal Aid Board (now Legal Services Commission), *Access to quality services in the immigration category* (May 1999), and of the Lord Chancellor's Advisory Committee on Legal Education and Conduct, *Improving the quality of immigration advice and representation: A report*, ACLEC (July 1998).
8 *R v Secretary of State for the Home Department, ex p Ghaly* (27 June 1996), unreported, QBD.
9 See also the guidance in *R v Kingston-upon-Thames Justices, ex p Martin* [1994] Imm AR 172, DC.
10 (13079) 7 March 1996, IAT.
11 See also *Bozkurt* (11783) 19 January 1995; *Muia* (17223), 29 May 1998, IAT.
12 *Kandeepan* (15124), IAT.
13 In *Busuulwa* (01 TH 00239) the Tribunal indicated that the proper course was for the respondent to withdraw the decision; otherwise the only remedy was judicial review.
14 *Macharia v Immigration Appeal Tribunal* [2000] INLR 156, CA.
15 *R v Medical Appeal Tribunal, ex p Corrarini* [1966] 1 WLR 883; *Kondo* (10413) 12 November 1993, IAT; *Sarica* (15363) 21 August 1997, IAT; or to obtain a translation: *Getener* (14799), IAT.
16 *Glowacki* (R.16139) 19 January 1998, IAT.
17 *R v Secretary of State for the Home Department, ex p Kimbesa*, 29 January 1997, Ognall J.
18 *Rajan (Munigesu)* (01 TH 00244), 8 February 2001.

Procedure at the hearing

18.143 At the hearing each party may address the appellate authority, give evidence and call witnesses, and put questions to any person giving live evidence. Each party should also be given an opportunity of making representations on the evidence (if any) and on the subject matter of the appeal generally but, where evidence is taken, the representations are normally made after the evidence is completed. The issues addressed, the oral and documentary evidence received and the submissions entertained may be limited in accordance with directions previously given and with the time estimate put in by the parties.[1] The appellate authority has power to conduct the proceedings in such manner as it considers appropriate in the circumstances for ascertaining the matters in dispute and determining the appeal. In doing so the adjudicator must act fairly,[2] and should give an appellant a chance to comment on any adverse material in the evidence.[3] Provisional conclusions should not be indicated at the outset of the hearing.[4] If the adjudicator has access to relevant evidence not cited by the parties, their attention should be drawn to it.[5] Similarly, the parties should be given an opportunity to deal with any case they have not referred to which appears to be determinative or call for argument.[6] In an asylum appeal, the adjudicator may introduce the issue of internal flight even if the Secretary of State has not done so, but should be cautious about doing so and must give the parties an opportunity to deal with it.[7] All representatives, including respondents', are under a duty to assist adjudicators by presenting them with all relevant case law, including that contrary to the argument put forward.[8] The respondent must put to a witness any matter said to undermine the witness' credibility,[9] and must not knowingly mislead the court by not disclosing material which detracts from its case.[10] It may be that asylum and human rights are a field where, since the court has an overriding obligation to ensure the highest standards of fairness, litigation privilege would not allow a party to refuse production of an expert report.[11] The court has a reasonable inquisitorial function to make its own inquiries in the context of full disclosure and discussion of all relevant issues at the hearing, and is entitled to control the hearing by making interventions,[12] but should exercise the power sparingly.[13]

1 See **18.130** above and *R v Secretary of State for the Home Department, ex p Singh* [1998] INLR 608, CA, upholding an adjudicator's refusal to allow a witness to add orally to her statement, which was the subject of a direction that it stand as evidence in chief.
2 So, for example, where an appellant put in a report from Amnesty International concerning the dangers facing failed asylum seekers from Algeria, which was unchallenged by the presenting officer, the adjudicator should not have rejected the evidence without allowing the appellant to adduce further evidence to confirm it: *Kriba v Secretary of State for the Home Department* 1998 SLT 1113, OHCS (Scot).
3 *Ahmed v Secretary of State for the Home Department* [1994] Imm AR 457, CA; *R v Immigration Appeal Tribunal, ex p Seri* (CO/2135/99) 27 June 2000; *R v Immigration Appeal Tribunal, ex p Gunn*, 22 January 1998, QBD. This obligation does not extend to obvious discrepancies on matters central to the appellant's case and already drawn to the appellant's attention in the refusal letter: *R v Immigration Appeal Tribunal, ex p Williams* [1995] Imm AR 518; *Sahota v Immigration Appeal Tribunal* [1995] Imm AR 500; *Ezzi*(G0003A) 29 May 1997, IAT, nor must an adjudicator foresee and put at the hearing every aspect of the evidence which goes into his or her findings on the facts: *R v Immigration Appeal Tribunal, ex p Hansford* [1992] Imm AR 407.
4 *Rajah* (15159) 24 June 1997, IAT.
5 *Gimedhin* (14019), IAT; *R v Secretary of State for the Home Department, ex p Fortunato* [1996] Imm AR 366, QBD; *Aygun* (12331) 14 July 1995; *Norbert* [1995] Imm AR 64; *R v Immigration Appeal Tribunal, ex p Kang* (CO 497/2000), 6 October 2000, QBD.
6 *R v Immigration Appeal Tribunal, ex p Sui Rong Suen* [1997] Imm AR 355.
7 *He (Bai Hai)* (00 TH 00744), IAT; *Mehta* (17861), IAT.
8 *Choudhury* (10646), 11 February 1994, IAT.
9 *Ezzi* (G0003A) 29 May 1997, IAT.
10 *Kerrouche v Secretary of State for the Home Department* [1997] Imm AR 610, CA; *Konan v Secretary of State for the Home Department* (IATRF 00/0020/C) 20 March 2000, CA. The majority conclusion in *Abdi and Gawe* [1996] Imm AR 288, HL, of no general disclosure duty of country information, does not undermine this principle.
11 *Besnik Gashi v Secretary of State for the Home Department* [1999] Imm AR 415, CA.
12 *R v Immigration Appeal Tribunal and Special Adjudicator, ex p Kumar* (CO 5073/98) 17 April 2000, QBD; *Moala* (16409) 29 June 1999, IAT; *Gimedhin* (14019) 21 October 1996, IAT.
13 There is a fine line between legitimate inquiry and stepping into the respondent's shoes; see eg *Bahar v Secretary of State for the Home Department* [1988] Imm AR 534; *Muwyngyi* (00052) IAT; *R v Special Adjudicator, ex p Demeter* [2000] Imm AR 424, QBD; *Sababathi* (19572) 5 August 1999, IAT.

18.144 The adjudicator should not dictate to representatives which witnesses to call,[1] or stop re-examination on the basis that a matter had been dealt with in chief.[2] At appeal hearings it is the usual practice to exclude witnesses (other than parties) from the hearing room until they give their evidence, a practice which it has been said adjudicators are entitled to follow by virtue of the general control over proceedings given to them by rule 30 of the Procedure Rules,[3] but which is not a rule of law.[4] In the vast majority of cases the decision whether an interpreter should be used is for the appellant and his or her advisers, and it is not the function of the adjudicator to disagree or express any view on the matter.[5] The adjudicator must ensure that unrepresented appellants are aware of their entitlement to give evidence.[6] Women appellants alleging sexual abuse ought to be allowed an all-female Tribunal if requested.[7]

1 *Nabhani* (13195) 17 April 1996, IAT; *Petre* (12998) 13 February 1996, IAT; *Riasat* (13256) 17 April 1996, IAT; *Biley* (11579) 22 November 1994, IAT.
2 *Kamara* (11984) 3 April 1996, IAT.
3 Immigration and Asylum Appeals (Procedure) Rules 2000, SI 2000/2333; *Wadia* [1977] Imm AR 92.
4 *Moore v Registrar Lambeth County Court* [1969] 1 All ER 782 at 783–784, DC; *R v Immigration Appeal Tribunal, ex p Jebunisha Patel* [1996] Imm AR 161, QBD.
5 *Cavusoglu* (15357) 28 May 1997. But there is no absolute right to an interpreter wholly irrespective of need: *R v Special Adjudicator, ex p Naqvi*, 23 February 2000, CA.
6 *Singh (Santokh)* (13002) 22 February 1996; *Tamba* (13525) 12 June 1996.
7 *Tiganov* (11193) 29 July 1994; *Akyol* (14745) 25 March 1997, IAT. See Berkowitz and Jouvis: *Asylum Gender Guidelines*, IAA, November 2000; H Crawley, *Refugees and gender: law and process* (2001).

Evidence

18.145 The appellate authority may issue a witness summons for the purposes of any appeal to require anyone in the UK to attend the hearing to answer questions and to produce relevant documents.[1] If a witness has important evidence to give but neither party wishes to call him or her, the appellate authority has the power to do so, although it should hesitate long before using it.[2] Where witnesses are called they may be required to give evidence on oath or affirmation,[3] and no witness can be compelled to give any evidence or produce any document which that witness could not be compelled to give or produce in a court of law.[4] Furthermore, except where the method of detecting forgeries might be disclosed, the normal rule is that where an appellate authority takes documentary evidence into consideration every party should have an opportunity of inspecting the documents and taking copies.[5]

1 Immigration and Asylum Appeals (Procedure) Rules 2000, SI 2000/2333, r 36. A witness need not attend unless the expenses of attending are paid.
2 *Kesse v Secretary of State for the Home Department* [2001] EWCA Civ 177, CA, differing from *Jamali* (TH/131186/84) 25 April 1986, in which the Immigration Appeal Tribunal held that the appellate authority could only call witnesses if the parties assented.
3 SI 2000/2333, r 37(3). This is left to adjudicators' discretion and is fairly rare.
4 SI 2000/2333, r 37(2).
5 SI 2000/2333, r 38. See *Odusanwo* [1992] Imm AR 430; *Hettierarachchi v Secretary of State for the Home Department* [1991] Imm AR 499, CA.

18.146 In appeal hearings the rules of evidence applicable in a court of law are relaxed. Rule 37(1) of the Procedure Rules provides that an appellate authority may receive oral, documentary or other evidence of any fact which appears to be relevant to the appeal, notwithstanding that it would be inadmissible in a court of law.[1] Explanatory statements[2] and refusal letters[3] have been held to be evidence. The judge's summing up in a criminal trial has been received in a deportation appeal.[4] Where the respondent asserts a fact, little if any weight can be given to such assertion without evidence in support.[5] It is for the respondent to make good an allegation of forgery with evidence.[6] But a Home Office presenting officer cannot give evidence in the case he or she is presenting.[7] An entry clearance officer who is trying to establish the truth as to a claimed relationship is entitled to take into account information obtained from villagers selected at random on a visit to the sponsor's village.[8] Evidence in rebuttal may be admitted from a witness who has carried out a village visit on behalf of an appellant.[9] Although the appellate authority cannot normally receive evidence of post-decision facts, as will be seen, evidence of facts not known to the decision-maker is admissible.[10] The weight to be attached to such evidence is, within reasonable limits, a matter for the adjudicator or Tribunal.[11] But a witness's evidence supporting an appellant's case must be addressed.[12]

1　Ie, hearsay evidence is admissible: *R v Immigration Appeal Tribunal, ex p Miah* [1987] Imm AR 143, QBD.
2　*R v Immigration Appeal Tribunal, ex p Weerasuriya* [1983] 1 All ER 195, QBD.
3　*Abdi and Gawe* [1996] Imm AR 288, HL, in the context of the accelerated procedure for certified appeals. These were third country appeals and it is arguable that the majority were swayed by the need for particular speed in such cases.
4　*Ayo v Immigration Appeal Tribunal* [1990] Imm AR 461, CA
5　*Gebretensae* (14794) 27 March 1997; *Lakew* (13214) 17 April 1996; *Oni* (15886) 2 December 1997, IAT.
6　*R v Immigration Appeal Tribunal, ex p Shen* [2000] INLR 389, QBD; *Chowdhury (Ahmed Hafiz)* (11721) 30 December 1994; *Findik* (17029) 12 May 1998; *Escobar* (20553) 26 March 1999; *A, B, C and D* (R17367, R21180, R16463, R21181) 3 August 1999, IAT. See, however, *Kongo-Kongo* (0064) 3 March 2000, *Waimatha* (16575) 18 August 1998, IAT; *R v Special Adjudicator, ex p Mohammed (Mukhtar)* [2001] Imm AR 162, QBD, where documentary evidence was patently not genuine on its face.
7　*Aitsaid* (11391).
8　*Altaf (Mohammed)* [1979–80] Imm AR 141. A previous grant of entry clearance to a woman as wife of the sponsor, although not an estoppel, is evidence relevant to the claimed relationship when another woman later applies for admission in the same capacity: *Bi (Channo)* [1978] Imm AR 182. Where affidavit evidence about an event is tendered by an applicant or sponsor and is disputed by the Home Office, the matter should be tested in cross-examination and evidence in rebuttal should be tendered: *Kassam* [1976] Imm AR 20.
9　*R v Immigration Appeal Tribunal, ex p Hussain* [1982] Imm AR 74, QBD.
10　*R v Immigration Appeal Tribunal, ex p Hassanin* [1987] 1 All ER 74, [1986] 1 WLR 1448, CA.
11　*R v Immigration Appeal Tribunal, ex p Kandiya* [1989] Imm AR 491, QBD; *R v Immigration Appeal Tribunal, ex p Aurangzeb Khan* [1989] Imm AR 524, QBD.
12　*R (Sugur) v Secretary of State for the Home Department* (CO 279/2000) 1 November 2000, CA.

Credibility of witnesses

18.147 Credibility is not in itself a valid end to the function of an adjudicator, and over-emphasis on the issue may distort his or her findings.[1] An adverse credibility finding should not be based solely on the fact that no oral evidence was called at the hearing,[2] or on lack of corroboration for an appellant's evidence.[3]

But the appellant must make a case,[4] and where credibility has been put in issue by the respondent, an appellant who does not give evidence cannot complain of an adverse credibility finding.[5] Where there is corroboration, it should be taken into account.[6] Supporting evidence should not be dismissed out of hand as 'self-serving'.[7] Prejudicial evidence of little probative value should not be the basis of an adverse credibility finding.[8] Caution should be exercised in relying on the demeanour of a witness whose language and culture is different,[9] and on relying on past deception.[10] It is perfectly possible for a witness not to be telling the truth or to be exaggerating about certain matters, but for the centre-piece of his or her story to stand.[11] Whether an adjudicator is entitled to make an adverse finding on the credibility of a witness whose evidence was not challenged at the hearing appears to depend on how obvious the discrepancies giving rise to the adverse finding are, or whether (in the case of an appellant) the respondent had already referred to them in the refusal letter.[12] In assessing credibility, the interview record should be approached with caution where there have been breaches of PACE codes[13] or defective[14] or confrontational questioning,[15] or where the record of interview was written substantially later,[16] or where the interview was a preliminary one[17] or where the applicant had felt unwell or tired.[18] Decisions on credibility must be reasoned, just as decisions on other aspects of the case.[19] For credibility in the context of the burden of proof in asylum appeals, see **12.28**ff above.

1 *R v Immigration Appeal Tribunal, ex p Hussain* (CO/990/95) 25 April 1996, QBD; *Guine* (13868) 9 September 1996; *Jawaid* (17159) 20 May 1998, IAT.
2 *Ahmed (Kaleem)* (12774) 8 November 1995, IAT; *Gok* (15971) 7 January 1998; *Coskuner* (16769) 23 July 1998; *Sad-Chaouche* (17423) 19 June 1998, IAT. Contra when potential witness who could have given highly relevant evidence was sitting in court but was not called: *R v Secretary of State for the Home Department, ex p Kajenthra* [1998] Imm AR 158, QBD.
3 *Kasolo* (13190) 1 April 1996; *Saspo* (14759) 24 March 1997; *Ozer (Nazim)* (14698) 13 March 1997, IAT.
4 *Amrik Singh v Secretary of State for the Home Department* [2000] Imm AR 340, CA; *Adebola* (16731) 19 August 1998, IAT.
5 *Nassir v Secretary of State for the Home Department* (1999/5682/4) 9 June 1999, CA (permission). See also *Carcabuk and Bla* (00 TH 0146), distinguishing between a concession or agreement on the facts, which an adjudicator should not disturb, and mere failure to challenge, which does not bind the adjudicator.
6 *Mirani* [1990] Imm AR 132; *Atwal* (13948) 7 October 1996; *Aygun* (14091) 11 November 1996, IAT.
7 *Quijano* (13693) 16 July 1996; *Malakar* (16540) 23 September 1998, IAT. See also the useful remarks in *Re RS*, 135/92, New Zealand Refugee Status Appeals Authority, 27 August 1991, and *John Meadows v MIMA* [1998] 1706 FCA, 23 December 1998, Canada.
8 *Iqbal v Immigration Appeal Tribunal* [1988] Imm AR 469, CA.
9 *Daniel* (13623) 2 July 1996; *Guarichico and Sarabia-Molina* (20230) 25 November 1999, IAT.
10 *R v Immigration Appeal Tribunal, ex p Chunnu Miah*, 12 October 1995, QBD; *Mahmood* (10629) 3 February 1994; *Majri* (12406) 9 August 1995; *Fernando* (11878) 23 February 1995; *Ibrahim* (17270) 17 June 1998.
11 *Chiver* [1997] INLR 212, IAT.
12 See cases cited at **18.143** above and see *Carcabuk and Bla*, fn 5 above.
13 *Ziraret* (12024) 19 April 1995, IAT.
14 *R v Secretary of State for the Home Department, ex p Akdogan* [1995] Imm AR 176; *Risan* (12551) 26 September 1995, IAT.
15 *Uruthiran* (21813) 8 March 2000, IAT.
16 *Singh (Daya Pal)* (14829) 3 April 1997, IAT.
17 *Salim* (13202) 17 April 1996; *Mayisokele* (13039) 23 February 1996; *Vimaleswaran* (15493) 26 August 1997; *Jeevaponkalan* (17742) 24 July 1998; *Adong* (20404) 15 November 1999, IAT. The adjudicator may, however, take into account a failure to mention a matter of great importance at the initial interview: *R v Secretary of State for the Home Department, ex p Agbonmenio* [1996] Imm AR 69, QBD (leave).

18 *Velasco* (HX00476) 11 October 1999, IAT.
19 *R v Immigration Appeal Tribunal, ex p Senol Adin* (CO 4533/98) 13 July 2000, QBD;
    R v Secretary of State for the Home Department, ex p Chugtai [1995] Imm AR 559;
    Mecheti v Secretary of State for the Home Department [1999] SCLR 998.

18.148 In asylum and human rights appeals, medical evidence capable of supporting an appellant's claim deserves careful and specific consideration,[1] and adjudicators should not make credibility findings in isolation from it.[2] A lay person cannot express a view on a medical matter without the benefit of medical evidence.[3] An experienced adjudicator must have regard to the possibility that the quality of a witness' evidence may be affected by his or her mental state, which might explain inconsistency and forgetfulness.[4] All documentary evidence in support of the claim must be considered,[5] and there must be a satisfactory basis for rejecting its authenticity.[6] Credibility findings can only really be made on the basis of a complete understanding of the entire picture, placing a claim into the context of the background information regarding the country of origin,[7] although going into detail about the background circumstances will not always be necessary or fruitful,[8] and an adjudicator is not required to set out in detail all the background evidence he or she has read.[9] Where the background evidence is in conflict, the Tribunal and the courts have expressed a preference for independent, sourced reports,[10] but where there are divergent opinions from reputable human rights organisations about the conditions in a country, there should be an in-depth examination to see if the evidence can be reconciled,[11] and a real attempt to balance them.[12] If they cannot be reconciled, the adjudicator should give reasons for preferring one report over another.[13] Expert witnesses' duty is to the court and it is important that they appreciate that, comply with it, believe in the truth of the facts in the report and the accuracy of the opinions given, cover all relevant matters and set out any matters affecting its validity.[14] The adjudicator need not invite oral evidence from an expert witness whose report he or she is minded to reject,[15] but expert evidence should not be rejected merely because it has not been tested in cross-examination,[16] not should it be rejected as 'mere speculation'.[17] The Court of Appeal has been critical of the cursory and at times contemptuous way the appellate authorities have treated the evidence of reputable experts, and has pointed out that such evidence should not be lightly rejected.[18] The Tribunal has deprecated the practice of putting in evidence in one case expert reports prepared for a different case.[19] Foreign law is a question of fact which should be determined, in the absence of agreement between the parties, by expert evidence,[20] but in the absence of such evidence the appellate authority may review questions of foreign law for itself.[21]

1 *Mohammed (Swaleh)* (12412) 4 August 1995; *Adanir* (12601) 11 October 1995; *Faustino* (13020) 1 March 1996; *Njehia* (16523) 14 May 1999; *Guney* (19159) 4 August 1999; *Sivakarathas* (01056) 12 May 2000, IAT.
2 *Kitshi* (11920) 23 March 1995; *Salami* (12053) 25 April 1995.
3 *R v Secretary of State for the Home Department, ex p Khaira* [1998] INLR 731. See too *Mensah* (17472), IAT.
4 *Mageto v Immigration Appeal Tribunal* [1996] Imm AR 56, CA. However, in *Amrik Singh v Secretary of State for the Home Department* [2000] Imm AR 340 the Court of Appeal held that psychiatric evidence of the effect of an appellant's mental state on his ability to recall reliably entitled the Tribunal to find his evidence unreliable and so reject his claim—an illustration of the double-edged nature of such evidence. The UNHCR Handbook recommends reliance on other sources of evidence in the case of mentally disturbed asylum claimants (paras 206–212).

5 *Okwu* (14518) 6 March 1997; *Yilmaz* (11896) 13 March 1995.

6 *Naqeeb* (15385) 20 August 1997; *Belayneh* (15216) 20 August 1997, IAT; *Jaswinder Singh v Secretary of State for the Home Department* 1998 SLT 1370, OHCS.

7 Handbook paras 42–43; *R v Immigration Appeal Tribunal, ex p Sardar Ahmed* [1999] INLR 473 (QBD); *Horvath* [1999] Imm AR 121, [1999] INLR 7 (IAT); *Acero-Garces* (14075) 22 January 1997; *Suleyman* (16242) 11 February 1998; *Yildirim* (12811) 20 December 1995; *Tharunalingam* (18452). For an example of the danger of assessing credibility in isolation, see *R v Immigration Appeal Tribunal, ex p Pratheepan* (CO 1102/98) 27 April 1999, QBD (adjudicator dismissed advocate's letter on basis of ignorance of legal procedures in Sri Lanka). See also *R (Gulbudek) v Immigration Appeal Tribunal* (CO 2174/2000) 21 November 2000, where an adjudicator's conclusion that the Turkish authorities would investigate rape and torture allegations was quashed as perverse; and *R (Vuckovic) v Special Adjudicator* CO 3021/2000, 18 December 2000 (adjudicator unfair to determine case without Home Office country assessment which lent support to appellant's case).

8 *R v Secretary of State for the Home Department, ex p Befekadu* [1999] Imm AR 467, QBD.

9 *R v Immigration Appeal Tribunal, ex p Shokrollahy* [2000] Imm AR 580, QBD.

10 *Mario* [1998] Imm AR 281, [1998] INLR 306, IAT; *Singh (Chinder)* (G0055), IAT (need for circumspection in accepting evidence from sources connected with the authorities); *Drrias v Secretary of State for the Home Department* [1997] Imm AR 346, CA (value of 'bland' FCO letter questioned); *X* (98/0474/4) 24 July 1998, CA (UNHCR report might deserve more weight than that of a national immigration authority). UNHCR reports are seen as the most reliable: see *Kumarlingam* (14685) 13 March 1997; *Ragavan* (15350) 21 August 1997; *Teshome* (15693); *Pasupathipillai* (14057) 4 November 1996, IAT. The Tribunal preferred the US State Department in *Panainte* (11767) 11 January 1995 and *Ionescu* (11914) 21 March 1995.

11 *Hassen* (15558) 3 October 1997; see also *Lahori* (G0062) 7 October 1998, IAT.

12 *Mulumba* (14760) 24 March 1997.

13 *Thillarajah* (14606) 10 March 1997; *Vasikaran* (15241) 4 July 1997, IAT.

14 *Thambiah* (01372) 10 May 2000, IAT.

15 *R v Secretary of State for the Home Department, ex p Khanafer* [1996] Imm AR 212.

16 *Tarlochan Singh v Secretary of State for the Home Department* [2000] Imm AR 36. But the testimony of an expert witness who did attend court would be highly important: *Zheng* (20271) 1 April 1999, IAT.

17 *Karanakaran v Secretary of State for the Home Department* [2000] Imm AR 271, CA. On expert evidence, see also *Gomez* [2000] INLR 549; *Kapela v Secretary of State for the Home Department* [1998] Imm AR 294.

18 *Karanakaran* above; see also CA's observations in granting permission to appeal in *R v Immigration Appeal Tribunal, ex p Es-Eldin* (C/00/2681) 29 November 2000, subsequently allowing by consent the appeal against the QBD decision reported in [2001] Imm AR 98. See also *Tarlochan Singh v Secretary of State for the Home Department* [2000] Imm AR 36.

19 *Armardeep Singh* (00943) 28 April 2000; *Zheng* (20271) 1 April 1999, IAT; *Habteselassie* (00308) 28 February 2000. Expert reports should show the status of their author and be specifically relevant to the case: *R v Immigration Appeal Tribunal, ex p Keziban Kilinc* [1999] Imm AR 588.

20 *Bradshaw* [1994] Imm AR 359; *Tikhonov* [1998] INLR 737, IAT.

21 *R v Special Adjudicator, ex p Turus* [1996] Imm AR 388, QBD.

Evidence of post-decision facts

18.149 It has been emphasised on a number of occasions that, except in appeals raising asylum or ECHR issues, adjudicators are appellate authorities and not some kind of super entry clearance or immigration officers.[1] They are not an extension of the original decision-making function, but a process for enabling the decision of the Secretary of State to be reviewed.[2] This means that although their power to review facts is similar to that of a body conducting a hearing at first instance,[3] they have to judge the validity of an immigration decision on the basis of the facts as they were at the time of the decision and not as they are at the date of the determination.[4] So, in deportation cases, the relevant circumstances that an adjudicator can take into account are those in existence at the date of decision and events that have happened subsequently (such as a fresh marriage) are not admissible,[5] although new evidence of pre-existing facts is admissible.[6] This position has been given statutory effect in relation to one-stop appeals in section 77 of the Immigration and Asylum Act 1999, which provides that in considering non-asylum and non-Article 3 grounds, the appellate authority may take into account only evidence available to the Secretary of State when the decision appealed against was taken, or which relates to relevant facts as at that date.[7] Whether or not the 'decision' here will include any amended or further decision in response to the statement of additional grounds is a moot point. An amended decision notice has been held to give rise to a new date of decision, thus extending the adjudicator's scope for factual investigation.[8] But the submission of fresh evidence to the decision-maker post-decision, and the review of that evidence in a supplementary refusal letter, does not give rise to a new date of decision, so that the evidence does not lose its quality of inadmissible post-decision evidence.[9] However, a number of decisions under the rules involve predictions: whether a business will succeed,[10] whether a couple will live together as man and wife,[11] whether the parties will have accommodation available,[12] whether a student will be able to pursue a course with reasonable success.[13] In these cases, post-decision facts that throw light on the decision will be admissible.[14]

1 *R v Immigration Appeal Tribunal, ex p Weerasuriya* [1983] 1 All ER 195, [1982] Imm AR 23, DC; *Sae-Heng* [1979–80] Imm AR 69; *R v Secretary of State for the Home Department, ex p Madoris Miah* [1998] Imm AR 44, QBD.
2 *R v Immigration Appeal Tribunal, ex p Hassanin* [1987] 1 All ER 74, [1986] 1 WLR 1448, CA, per Dillon LJ.
3 See *R v Secretary of State for the Home Department, ex p Husbadak* [1982] Imm AR 8, QBD.
4 *Rahman v Secretary of State for the Home Department* (30 April 1997), CA.
5 *Ex p Weerasuriya* fn 1 above; *Ashraf v Immigration Appeal Tribunal* [1988] Imm AR 101, CA.
6 *Rahman* (7228) (unreported), IAT.
7 Immigration and Asylum Act 1999, s 77(4). See **18.150** fn 3 below.
8 *Rajendran* [1989] Imm AR 512 at 519.
9 *R v Immigration Appeal Tribunal and Secretary of State for the Home Department, ex p Maya Banu* [1999] Imm AR 161, [1999] INLR 226, QBD.
10 *R v Immigration Appeal Tribunal, ex p Amir Beaggi* (1982) Times, 25 May, QBD; *Thaker* [1976] Imm AR 114.
11 *Patel* [1986] Imm AR 440, IAT.
12 *Azad* (5993), IAT.
13 *Rajendran* [1989] Imm AR 512.
14 *R v Immigration Appeal Tribunal, ex p Kwok On Tong* [1981] Imm AR 214; *R v Immigration Appeal Tribunal, ex p Amir Beaggi* fn 10 above. The admission of post-decision evidence in these cases is, however, strictly limited to that purpose and still looks back to the date of decision.

18.150 The big exception to the rule against evidence of post-decision facts is in asylum and ECHR Article 3 cases. The Court of Appeal held in *Ravichandran*[1] that the appellate authority is an extension of the decision-making process because of the nature of the question to be asked in asylum cases, looking at whether projected removal would bring a real risk of harm contrary to the Refugee Convention, rather than fixing on a past situation. The decision has been given statutory effect in the Immigration and Asylum Act 1999,[2] and extended to Article 3 cases, where the same perspective is adopted.[3] We suggest that it is not only in ECHR Article 3 cases that post-decision facts are relevant, but in all cases where expulsion will give rise to a real risk of violation of an ECHR right.[4] In *Arif*,[5] the

Court of Appeal dealt with the potential injustice this could give rise to in cases where recognition as a refugee would have been forthcoming but for delays in the determination process during which there has been change in the country of origin, by placing an evidential burden on the Secretary of State to show that the change is sufficiently fundamental to warrant deprivation of the expected status.[6]

1 *Ravichandran v Secretary of State for the Home Department* [1996] Imm AR 97, CA.
2 Immigration and Asylum Act 1999, s 77(3).
3 See *R v Secretary of State for the Home Department, ex p Turgut* [2000] Imm AR 306, CA.
4 See discussion in *Kacaj*, a starred Tribunal case heard in May 2001 (CC/23044/2000) on 'extra-territorial affect' of other ECHR articles.
5 *Mohammed Arif v Secretary of State for the Home Department* [1999] Imm AR 271, [1999] INLR 327.
6 See **18.153** below.

Evidence of like facts in other appeals

18.151 In asylum appeals evidence of the situation in a particular country may be common to a number of appeals and there may exist a number of determinations, for example, on whether in a particular country, members of a particular minority face persecution. A special adjudicator is certainly entitled to take into account evidence on country conditions presented in an earlier appeal. But the case law has retreated from its high point in *Gnanavarathan*,[1] where the Court of Appeal held that, although adjudicators have no duty to search files to find other relevant decisions not put to them by the parties, they were arguably under an obligation to give full reasons, if they came to conclusions different to other adjudicators. In *Sinnathamby Kumar*[2] the Court of Appeal did not accept that the differing adjudicator had to give reasons, only that he or she had to consider the material in the instant appeal and explain his or her conclusions. This has been the line adopted by the Tribunal since. The importance of the adjudicator reaching his or her own conclusion has been emphasised over the need for consistent treatment of those emanating from a particular country.[3] If adjudicators choose to rely on any determination not put to them, they should draw the parties' attention to such determinations and invite submissions. This is also the case where an adjudicator wishes to draw upon information obtained in the course of his or her experience or from data available generally to special adjudicators.[4] The problem identified in the last edition of this work, that of the respondent's failure to provide the parties or the adjudicator with all the information available to it,[5] has been resolved to a large extent by the introduction of Home Office 'country bundles' which are produced on most asylum appeals,[6] and by the introduction of legal aid for immigration and asylum appeals,[7] enabling appellants to be properly represented by persons who have access to the material the Home Office sees.

1 *Gnanavatharan* [1995] Imm AR 64.
2 *Sinnathamby Kumar* [1996] Imm AR 548.
3 *Pasupathipillai* (14115) 11 November 1996; *Avtar Singh* (14191) 25 November 1996; *Kelecha* (15038) 15 May 1997; *Kapela* (16283) 29 April 1998.
4 See **18.143** above.
5 See *Macdonald* (4th edn) and Supplement, **18.104**; *Secretary of State for the Home Department v Abdi and Gawe* [1996] Imm AR 288.
6 From the Country Information and Policy Unit of the IND, CIPU. The reports are sourced and rely mainly on UNHCR, US State Department, Amnesty International and Europa World Year Book. The sources should always be inspected, to check the accuracy of the summaries in the CIPU reports.
7 Controlled legal representation, from 1 January 2000: see **18.141** above.

Evidence after remittal from the Tribunal

18.152 On appeals from adjudicators, the Tribunal has power to remit a case for further determination by an adjudicator, although this power should not be exercised unless the Tribunal considers that it is necessary in the interests of justice and would save time and avoid expense.[1] On remittal the adjudicator can hear further evidence. The extent to which this power is exercisable will depend on the terms of the remit by the Tribunal. If the appeal is remitted to be considered in the light of fresh evidence, normally the adjudicator will be confined to hearing that evidence and submission on it,[2] but if the remit is to a different adjudicator to be redetermined and heard afresh, the evidence receivable will be as in any first instance appeal.[3] Remittal to the same adjudicator has been held appropriate where fresh documentary evidence requires a reassessment of the current political situation[4] or of the appellant's personal situation.[5] When the case is remitted for hearing *de novo* the adjudicator rehearing the case is entitled and in some cases obliged to have regard to the evidence given in the previous proceedings,[6] and to the Tribunal's determination. The adjudicator should then apply his or her mind afresh to the issues, the law and the evidence involved, without regard to the previous adjudicator's determination or assessments of the credibility of the appellant or other witnesses.[7] When writing the determination following a rehearing the adjudicator should record specifically what he or she had disregarded and to what he or she had paid attention in relation to the material on file relating to the earlier hearing.

1   Immigration and Asylum Appeals (Procedure) Rules 2000, SI 2000/2333, r 23.
2   Where the factual findings are unclear, the adjudicator can be directed on remittal as to what issues to consider and what findings of fact are required: *Birru v Secretary of State for the Home Department* [1998] Imm AR 212, CA.
3   *Bibi (Rohima)* [1986] Imm AR 103; *Karim (Mohammed)* [1986] Imm AR 224, IAT. See *R v Immigration Appeal Tribunal, ex p Nalokweza* [1996] Imm AR 230, QBD.
4   *Lewis* (15485) 26 August 1997; *Raicu* (14195) 25 November 1996, IAT.
5   *Kapay* (12723) 20 November 1995; *Kodjo* (13186) 1 April 1996; *Chadouli* (15284) 16 July 1997, IAT.
6   When credibility is in issue, the adjudicator should take account of the evidence given at the previous hearing, since consistency relates to the appellant's credibility: *Boakye-Yiadom* (11654), IAT.
7   *Patel* [1991] Imm AR 147. The second adjudicator may reach adverse credibility findings without oral evidence although the first adjudicator made positive findings: *R v Immigration Appeal Tribunal, ex p Nalokweza* [1996] Imm AR 230, QBD. It is desirable for the first determination to be removed from the file, although it is not unlawful for the second adjudicator to read it so long as he or she is not influenced by it: *R v Secretary of State for the Home Department, ex p Aissaoui* [1997] Imm AR 184, QBD.

Burden and standard of proof

18.153 The rules relating to the burden of proof in appeals may be summarised as follows:

(1)   The burden of proving British citizenship or any exemption from statutory provisions is on the person who makes the assertion.[1] Usually this will be the applicant, but not always.[2]

(2)   In an appeal, an appellant who wishes to assert that he or she has a right of abode or is exempt and, therefore, that the decision or action should not have been taken, must prove it.[3]

(3) Most claims to enter or remain will depend on the applicant satisfying the immigration officer or Home Office of the necessary facts which will qualify them in the appropriate category, and consequently in an appeal the burden of proving such a claim is on the party making it.[4]

(4) This applies equally to asylum and human rights or discrimination claims, where the burden of proof is on the applicant to make his or her case.[5]

(5) But where it is accepted that at the date of the decision on the claim an asylum seeker did in fact qualify for refugee status, but the Secretary of State contends that by the date of the hearing the circumstances have changed, then by analogy with Article 1C(5) of the Refugee Convention (where proof that the circumstances of persecution have ceased to exist falls on the receiving state) there is an evidential burden on the Secretary of State to establish that the appellant can safely return home.[6]

(6) So far as concerns the burden of proof where an internal flight option is alleged by the Secretary of State, in *Tharumakulasingham*,[7] Jowitt J approached the question on the basis that it is for the Secretary of State to show that it would be reasonable to expect an applicant to go to another part of the country, but that there was an evidential burden to put forward matters indicating that it would be unduly harsh to expect him or her to do so.[8] But in *Karanakaran*,[9] the Court of Appeal held that no question of burden or standard of proof arises; the question is simply whether, taking all relevant matters into account, it would be unduly harsh to expect the applicant to relocate.

(7) Where the Secretary of State seeks to deport someone under section 3(5) of the 1971 Act, it will fall on the Secretary of State to prove the facts necessary to establish a ground for deporting. This will also be the case where the Home Office are relying on non-disclosure of material facts to justify the refusal of entry,[10] or on one of the general grounds for refusal, such as character, conduct, associations, criminal convictions and so forth, and in an asylum or ECHR, Article 3 case, where the Secretary of State seeks to rely on a ground for certification.[11] It falls on the party who asserts to prove.

(8) There will also be a heavy burden on the Secretary of State if it is sought to contradict a finding as to relationship made in a previous appeal, although the concept of *res judicata* does not apply to the determination of the immigration appellate authorities.[12]

(9) Where the respondent asserts that documents relied on by an appellant are false, it is for him or her to prove it.[13]

1 Immigration Act 1971, s 3(8).

2 An example would be where the applicant wishes to rely on a stamp on his or her passport giving indefinite leave, but the Home Office asserts that the stamp does not apply because the applicant had a diplomatic exemption at the time.

3 Immigration and Asylum Appeals (Procedure) Rules 2000, SI 2000/2333, r 39, reflecting Immigration Act 1971, s 3(8).

4 SI 2000/2333, r 39(2). See *R v Secretary of State for the Home Department, ex p Mughal* [1974] QB 313, [1974] 3 All ER 796, CA. See also *Bi (Channo)* [1978] Imm AR 182 where, although the appellant had previously been granted entry clearance as the wife of the sponsor, she still had the burden of proving she was his wife on a later occasion when she sought readmission.

5 *Adebola* (16731) 19 August 1998, IAT. So in an appeal to the Tribunal, the fact that the Secretary of State, as the appellant, had to show that the adjudicator had erred in law or fact was held quite separate from proof by an asylum seeker of the basic elements

needed to satisfy the criteria of a refugee claim: *Tikhonov* [1998] INLR 737, IAT. For burden and standard of proof in asylum appeals see **12.24ff** above.

6 *Mohammed Arif v Secretary of State for the Home Department* [1999] INLR 327, CA. The court used the cessation provisions of Art 1C(5), where the legal burden falls on the state to show that the circumstances creating the need for flight have ceased to exist, by way of analogy. The court and the Tribunal respectively distinguished *Arif* in *Salim v Secretary of State for the Home Department* [2000] Imm AR 503, CA and *Dyli* [2000] Imm AR 652 (starred), where it was not accepted that the appellant would have qualified for refugee status on arrival. In *Sijakovic* (01 TH 00632) the Tribunal said it was unhelpful to talk of a burden, whether legal or evidential, on the Secretary of State: the issue was whether there was a well-founded fear of persecution.

7 *R v Immigration Appeal Tribunal, ex p Tharumakulasingham* [1997] Imm AR 550, QBD

8 But there was some confusion about this; see *R v Secretary of State for the Home Department, ex p Salim* [1999] INLR 628, QBD, where the burden was held to be on the appellant to show that internal flight does not apply.

9 *Karanakaran v Secretary of State for the Home Department* [2000] Imm AR 271 at 305.

10 *Ghati* (19707) 27 July 1999, IAT.

11 Under Immigration and Asylum Act 1999, Sch 4, para 9.

12 *Momin Ali v Secretary of State for the Home Department* [1984] 1 All ER 1009, [1984] Imm AR 23, CA; *R v Immigration Appeal Tribunal, ex p Lulu Miah* [1987] Imm AR 143.

13 *R v Immigration Appeal Tribunal, ex p Shen* [2000] INLR 389, QBD; *Makozo* (20033) 12 February 1999, IAT; *Escobar* (20553) 26 March 1999, IAT. See cases cited at **18.146** fn 6 above.

18.154 The standard of proof is generally that which applies in all civil proceedings – proof on balance of probabilities. This is so even when questions of citizenship and right of abode are at stake. So where the Tribunal stated that they were not 'convinced' of the appellant's means, this indicated that they were applying too high a standard of proof, more akin to that in criminal cases, and their determination was quashed.[1] The civil standard is, however, flexible and has regard to the nature of the allegation and its consequences. Where the allegation is fraud or corruption and the consequences for the appellant are correspondingly serious, proof to a high degree of probability is required.[2] So where the allegation is conduct leading to deportation, a very high standard is required.[3] Where there has already been a binding decision of an appropriate tribunal in favour of the applicant the standard is even higher.[4]

1 *R v Immigration Appeal Tribunal, ex p Mehra* [1983] Imm AR 156 at 162.

2 *Khawaja v Secretary of State for the Home Department* [1984] AC 74, [1983] 1 All ER 765, HL.

3 *Offeh* (9662), unreported.

4 *Momin Ali v Secretary of State for the Home Department* [1984] 1 All ER 1009, [1984] Imm AR 23, CA.

18.155 In asylum cases where the onus is to show a well-founded fear of persecution, it is inappropriate to apply a test of balance of probabilities to what is likely to happen in the future and it will be sufficient if a reasonable likelihood of persecution is established.[1] The Court of Appeal gave guidance in *Karanakaran*[2] on how to apply this lower standard of proof, in the process illuminating the meaning of decision in *Kaja*, in which the majority of the Tribunal had held that the lower standard applies to all aspects of proving that a person is a Convention refugee, including the assessment of accounts of past events.[3] This is dealt with in detail at **12.26ff** above. Similar considerations apply in ECHR, Article 3 cases where the onus is to show a serious risk of the relevant harm.[4] The burden is the same for someone with mental or psychological problems.[5]

1 *R v Secretary of State for the Home Department, ex p Sivakumaran* [1988] AC 958.
2 *Karanakaran v Secretary of State for the Home Department* [2000] 3 All ER 449, [2000] INLR 122, [2000] Imm AR 271, CA.
3 *Kaja* [1995] Imm AR 1, a majority decision of the Tribunal
4 *Kacaj* (starred Tribunal) (CC/23044/2000) 21 May 2001. See **18.159** fn 3 above.
5 *Bolat v Secretary of State for the Home Department* (99/6206/C), 23 February 2000, CA (leave to appeal).

18.156 Where the burden of proof lies on a party, he or she may adduce sufficient *prima facie* evidence to discharge that burden in the absence of reasons to the contrary or evidence in rebuttal. What is sufficient *prima facie* evidence will vary from case to case; the quality of documentation relied on as proof of events may be variable; for example later birth certificates will be less weighty than contemporaneous ones. In an asylum or Article 3 case, the Handbook indicates that evidence of past maltreatment is an excellent indicator of the fate that may await an applicant on return.[1]

1 Handbook para 45; see also *Demirkaya v Secretary of State for the Home Department* [1999] Imm AR 498, [1999] INLR 441, CA; *R v Secretary of State for the Home Department, ex p Dahmas* (17 November 1999), CA (overturning [2000] Imm AR 151). See also EU Joint Position of 4 March 1996. The court in *Demirkaya* also pointed out that the Tribunal's statement that it was 'reasonably likely that the appellant would be released after one or two days' was an incorrect application of the burden of proof. The proper question was whether there was a real risk that he would *not* be released.

Combined hearings

18.157 The one-stop system is designed to ensure that all appeal grounds are dealt with together in one hearing. The system applies not only to applicants but also to members of their family, as we have seen. One-stop notices must be served on all members of the family of the principal applicant or the person who received the appealable decision refusing leave to enter or remain. Any of them may raise a ground for wishing to remain in the UK, and refusal of leave to stay on that ground may itself be appealable (although in practice it is likely to be only asylum or human rights or discrimination grounds which give rise to an appealable decision by a family member).[1] Neither the Procedure Rules[2] nor the One-Stop Procedure Regulations[3] expressly deal with this situation. Should the family member's one-stop appeal be heard in a combined hearing with that of the principal appellant? What of the situation where family members arrive in the UK and claim asylum at different times or for some other reason do not fall within the one-stop procedure?[4] And in what other circumstances may hearings be combined? The Procedure Rules[5] follow the 1996 Asylum Procedure Rules[6] in dispensing with the consent of all the parties as a prerequisite for a combined hearing of a number of appeals. The appellate authority may hear appeals together if a common question of law or fact arises in them, or they relate to decisions or actions taken against members of the same family,[7] or for some other reason it is desirable to hear them together.[8] All the parties must be given the opportunity of being heard before a decision to hear the appeals together.[9] An adjudicator is not entitled to hear appeals together without either a request by the appellants or affording them this opportunity.[10] In hearing a combined appeal, it is crucial that the appellate authority give separate consideration to the case for each appellant.[11] Appellants' appeals should not fail solely because they differ in their testimony at a combined hearing.[12] It is inappropriate to exclude a principal appellant from the hearing room from any part of the combined appeal.[13] If two or more appeals are heard together it is preferable to issue separate determinations, unless the appeals are interdependent.[14]

1 See **18.108** above.
2 Immigration and Asylum Appeals (Procedure) Rules 2000, SI 2000/2333.
3 Immigration and Asylum Appeals (One-Stop Procedure) Regulations 2000, SI 2000/2244.
4 See *Tahir* (01307) 7 June 2000, IAT, where the Tribunal considered the situation where one person's asylum appeal was completely interwined with that of another family member whose claim was still outstanding. One suggestion was for the adjudicator to delay the hearing of the appeal until the decision on the related application was known and then, if it was adverse, to ensure that the appeals were heard together or sequentially. The preferred solution was for the Secretary of State for the Home Department to withdraw the first decision so that a fresh application could be made and considered at the same time as the linked application.
5 SI 2000/2333, r 42.
6 Asylum Appeals (Procedure) Rules 1996, SI 1996/2070, r 34.
7 It is inappropriate to list the principal's appeal with that of a divorced spouse who had no knowledge of the welfare of the child: *Aderibgbe* (16659) 12 May 1998, IAT.
8 SI 2000/2333, r 42.
9 SI 2000/2333, r 42.
10 *Agyawaa* (15965) 4 December 1997, IAT.
11 *Yau Yak Wah v Home Office* [1982] Imm AR 16, CA; *R v Immigration Appeal Tribunal, ex p Hamida Begum* [1988] Imm AR 199.
12 *Tabores and Munoz* (17819) 24 July 1998, IAT, where dismissal on the basis that they 'cannot both be telling the truth' was set aside.
13 *Tabores and Munoz* (17819) 24 July 1998, IAT.
14 *Twum* [1986] Imm AR 316; *Ahmed* (7903), unreported.

Hearings in public

18.158 Reflecting the principle of open justice enshrined in ECHR, Article 6,[1] the general rule for immigration and asylum appeals is that hearings take place in public. The exceptions to the rule set out in rule 40 of the Procedure Rules[2] mirror those permitted by ECHR, Article 6(1). There is a discretion to exclude a particular member of the public, or the public generally, from a hearing or part of a hearing, where:

(1)   in the opinion of the authority, it is necessary in the interests of morals, public order or national security;
(2)   in the opinion of the authority, the interests of minors or the protection of the private life of the parties so require; or
(3)   in special circumstances publicity would prejudice the interests of justice, but only to the extent strictly necessary in the opinion of the authority.

There is no longer a power to hold a hearing in private merely because a party requests it, and it will therefore be for an appellant to justify a closed hearing by reference to one of these public interest criteria. The exceptions are likely to be invoked by asylum seekers who will argue that publicity prejudices the interests of justice in inhibiting them from giving a full account of their claim, or indeed proceeding with the hearing at all, for fear of reprisals, and those who have psychological conditions which could be exacerbated by reporting of their cases.[3] Regrettably, many asylum seekers are not aware that the cloak of confidentiality which surrounds their claim is lifted for the appeal unless they make a case for retaining it. If they do make such a case, however, the appellate authority may direct that the appellant be known by initial only and may make other directions necessary for preserving confidentiality.[4]

1 'A fair and public hearing': see eg *R v Secretary of State for Health, ex p Associated Newspapers* [2001] 1 WLR 292, CA.
2 Immigration and Asylum Appeals (Procedure) Rules 2000, SI 2000/2333, r 40(3), expressed to be without prejudice to the right of members of the Council of Tribunals or its Scottish Committee from attending appeals.
3 See *R v Legal Aid Board, ex p Kaim Todner* [1999] QB 966. For general principles underlying withholding of identity, see *A-G v Leveller* [1979] AC 440; see also *R v Westminster City Council, ex p Castelli* (1995) 7 Admin LR at 845.
4 SI 2000/2333, r 30, which gives wide powers to regulate the conduct of hearings.

18.159 In addition to these circumstances, there is a duty to exclude the public (and indeed the appellant and his or her representative) where evidence is being given of the method of detection of a forgery of a passport, other travel document or work permit and it is alleged that it would be contrary to the public interest to disclose the methods of detection.[1] This is a very wide power (although rarely if ever used) and it is difficult to see why it has been retained. Such evidence is given in the presence of the parties in a criminal trial, and should also be given in an immigration matter, particularly when the burden of proving such an allegation falls on the Home Office and it will be impossible to challenge it, if the appellant does not know how the Home Office are proving it.

1 Immigration and Asylum Appeals (Procedure) Rules 2000, SI 2000/2333, r 40(2), referring to Immigration and Asylum Act 1999, Sch 4, para 6(1).

Transfer of proceedings

18.160 It sometimes happens that an appeal goes part-heard and events conspire to prevent its return to the adjudicator who started hearing the case within a reasonable time[1] or at all. The Chief Adjudicator or a deputy has power to step in and arrange for the appeal to be heard by another adjudicator if it appears that it is not practicable without undue delay for the proceedings to be completed by the first adjudicator or for some other good reason they cannot be completed justly by that adjudicator.[2] Transfer was held not unfair and justified when there had been a delay of ten months in a part-heard appeal, although the effect was that the appellant lost the benefit of provisional positive credibility findings.[3] On transfer the second adjudicator stands in the shoes of the first as regards documents, notices and powers.[4] The Chief Adjudicator must transfer proceedings to the Special Immigration Appeals Commission if notified by the Secretary of State that section 78 of the Immigration and Asylum Act 1999 applies (where an appeal turns into a deportation or one-stop case involving national security).[5]

1 A delay of four months between hearings led to the determination being ruled unsafe in *Kissi* (11873) 27 February 1995, IAT, and five months in *Jeyanthan* (11975) 30 March 1995, IAT.
2 Immigration and Asylum Appeals (Procedure) Rules 2000, SI 2000/2333, r 45(1).
3 *R v Special Adjudicator, ex p Hasan Akdogan* (CO 1357/99) 11 February 2000, QBD.
4 SI 2000/2333, r 45(2).
5 SI 2000/2333, r 45(3).

After the hearing

18.161 An adjudicator may indicate during the hearing that he or she is prepared to receive further evidence and/or submissions within a specified time, in order to do justice between the parties and ensure that all issues are not only ventilated but that all the requisite evidence and arguments are deployed in their support. The first guiding rule is equality of treatment; if an appellant is given extra time to submit a document which has not arrived in time for the hearing, the respondent must be afforded an opportunity to deal with it, in writing or even, if necessary, by reconvening the hearing. The course to be adopted will depend on the circumstances of the case, the approach of the parties and the adjudicator to the hearing itself.[1] The second guiding rule is that if an adjudicator has allowed time for further submissions, they must not be ignored if they are sent within the specified time.[2]

1 *Bwamiki* (17710) 10 July 1998, IAT.
2 *Singh (Billa)* (G0071) 21 January 1999, IAT.

Irregularities in procedure

18.162 An irregularity resulting from failure to comply with the rules does not render the proceedings void, and an appellate authority which considers that prejudice may have occurred has power to cure any irregularities resulting from failure to comply with the rules before reaching its decision.[1] This would normally be done either by amendment of documents or the giving of any notice, but it is not confined to such steps. This rule cannot be used to extend time limits or to give jurisdiction where none exists.[2] Procedural irregularities discovered after the adjudicator's decision can normally only be dealt with on appeal. If the decision is unappealable (ie a certified asylum or human rights or discrimination appeal where the adjudicator has upheld the certificate) the Procedure Rules allow the Chief Adjudicator to review a determination which was wrongly made as a result of administrative or procedural error.[3] Otherwise, where a hearing before the adjudicator is flawed by inadmissible evidence, or procedural impropriety, the proper course would be for the Tribunal to remit for a *de novo* hearing rather than 'excuse' the conduct which has effectively deprived the appellant of a fair first instance appeal.

1 Immigration and Asylum Appeals (Procedure) Rules 2000, SI 2000/2333, r 49.
2 *R v Immigration Appeal Tribunal, ex p Secretary of State for the Home Department* [1990] Imm AR 166; *Wa-Selo v Secretary of State for the Home Department* [1990] Imm AR 76, CA.
3 SI 2000/2333, r 16; see **18.168** below.

Keeping a record of proceedings

18.163 The appellate authority no longer has a duty to cause a summary of the proceedings before it to be taken, which it had under the 1984 and 1996 Procedure Rules.[1] If a record is kept, the Tribunal is entitled to rely on a rebuttable presumption that it is accurate.[2] The abolition of the duty to keep a record seems on the face of it extraordinary, unless it is intended finally[3] to equip all hearing rooms with recording equipment to allow for the recording of hearings: if not, how is an appellant to challenge the accuracy of the adjudicator's summary of the evidence in the determination, if no record of evidence is kept or can be called for? Perhaps in such a case the proper course would be for true copies of the original notes of the hearing taken by the representative to be annexed to a statement of truth to form grounds of appeal. The respondent would clearly be required to compare the appellant's note with his or her own, and presumably the dispute would go to the adjudicator for comment, but it would have to be resolved by the Tribunal.

1   Immigration Appeals (Procedure) Rules 1984, SI 1984/2041; Asylum Appeals (Procedure) Rules 1996, SI 1996/2070.
2   *Ning* (9863), IAT.
3   The Tribunal has been asking for mechanical recording for a number of years: see *Goonawardene* (13487), IAT.

Making a determination

18.164 The determination is the decision of the appellate authority to allow or dismiss an appeal and the reasons for that decision.[1] Written notice of the adjudicator's determination must be sent to every party and the appellant's representative, if any.[2] Adjudicators must allow or dismiss an appeal,[3] and cannot allow it on a conditional basis,[4] but an appeal may be allowed to the extent that the matter is remitted to the Secretary of State for consideration in accordance with the law and the correct facts as found by the adjudicator.[5] A question arises as to whether the definition of 'determination' in the Procedure Rules excludes a decision that there is no right of appeal under rule 12, and a decision that the appeal had been abandoned under rule 32—both decisions which had previously been held to constitute determinations and thus appealable to the Tribunal.[6] On the face of it, neither of these decisions would appear to be a 'dismissal' of the appeal, but in *Akhuemonkhan*[7] the Tribunal held that abandonment and failure to lodge the appeal in time meant that the appeal was dismissed, and in *Gremesty*[8] a starred Tribunal held that a decision that an appeal had been abandoned was a determination under the new rules. An adjudicator is obliged to make a formal determination in every case where he or she purports to dispose of the appeal.[9]

1   Immigration and Asylum Appeals (Procedure) Rules 2000, SI 2000/2333, r 2.
2   SI 2000/2333, r 15. The new rules contain no express power to promulgate a determination orally at the end of the hearing, although it would clearly be within the power of an adjudicator to give the decision, while reserving the reasons. Where a written determination contradicted the oral decision to allow the appeal issued at the end of the hearing, the remedy was not mandamus to compel a written decision in accordance with the oral one, but certiorari to quash the written determination for the whole matter to be reconsidered de novo: *R v Special Adjudicator, ex p Bashir* (CO 4643/98) 6 December 1999, QBD.
3   *Hamdan* (12338) 24 July 1995, IAT: there is no power to remit to the Secretary of State as an alternative to allowing or dismissing an appeal, although the adjudicator may adjourn to enable the respondent to deal with an issue arising in the course of a hearing.
4   *Khalil* [1993] Imm AR 481; *Aryee* (8707), IAT.
5   *Kanahalashmi* (10007), IAT.
6   An adjudicator's decision on the preliminary issue of extension of time had been held by an all-legal Tribunal to be a 'determination' and thus require reasons: *Jaayeola* (14819) 2 April 1997; similarly, under the previous rules a decision that an appeal had been abandoned was held to be a determination: *Akhuemonkhan* [1998] INLR 265, IAT. See also *Ibrahim* [1994] Imm AR 1; *Munchula* [1996] Imm AR 344; *R v Immigration Appeal Tribunal, ex p Lila* [1978] Imm AR 50.

7 [1998] INLR 265, IAT.
8 [2001] INLR 132.
9 *Kouchalieva* (10259) 2 September 1993, IAT, where the adjudicator on a spouse entry clearance appeal decided that the appellant was a British citizen and made no formal determination.

18.165 Determinations of the appellate authorities must not only get the law right and keep within the proper sphere of the appellate jurisdiction, but they must also be properly reasoned. Inadequate reasons may form the basis for a successful appeal from adjudicator to Tribunal or be the subject of an application for judicial review. An appeal to the Tribunal should first be attempted if a right of appeal exists, in order to exhaust this avenue before any High Court application. The adequacy of reasons has been dealt with in a number of decisions of the higher courts dealing with a variety of jurisdictions, including planning appeals and employment tribunals as well as immigration adjudicators. A determination must state what the issues are, the adjudicator's decision on them, and the evidence by which he or she comes to that conclusion.[1] On a reasons challenge in judicial review the applicant will need to show substantial prejudice, which can arise through ignorance as to the real basis of the decision.[2] In immigration appeals, as in other appeals,[3] the degree of particularity will vary according to the issues. In a deportation appeal the deportee should be able to follow the basis of the conclusion, and the determination should show that the adjudicator has taken account of all the relevant factors and carried out the balancing act required by the rules.[4] In family reunion, asylum and human rights appeals, where much may turn on credibility, the *locus classicus* of the adjudicator's obligation is *Mohammed Amin*:[5] 'An adjudicator should set out with some clarity what evidence was accepted, what rejected, on what evidence no conclusion could be reached and what evidence was irrelevant.' Findings must be consistent[6] and adequate.[7] Material facts must be the subject of clear findings.[8] A general statement that the appellant is not credible is insufficient.[9] In asylum and Article 3 appeals an adjudicator must make a clear statement as to the standard of proof to be applied.[10] A mechanical recitation of a certain formula to show matters have been taken into account may also be inadequate.[11]

1 *R v Immigration Appeal Tribunal, ex p Mahmud Khan* [1983] QB 790, [1983] 2 All ER 420, CA. But an adjudicator need not give reasons for each conclusion reached in the course of the decision: *R v CICB, ex p Cook* [1996] 1 WLR 1037; *Bolton Metropolitan District Council v Secretary of State for the Environment* (1995) 71 P & CR 309; *Arulanandam v Secretary of State for the Home Department* [1996] Imm AR 587, CA.
2 *Save Britain's Heritage v Number 1 Poultry Ltd* [1991] 1 WLR 153, HL, per Lord Bridge
3 *Union of Construction Allied Trades and Technicians v Brain* [1981] ICR 542, CA, per Lord Denning MR.
4 *R v Immigration Appeal Tribunal, ex p Dhaliwal* [1994] Imm AR 387, QBD.
5 *R v Immigration Appeal Tribunal, ex p Amin* [1992] Imm AR 367, QBD; see also *Jaswinder Singh v Secretary of State for the Home Department* 1998 SLT 1370; *Mecheti v Secretary of State for the Home Department* [1996] SCLR 998; *Konate* (16418) 7 August 1998, IAT.
6 *Singh (Avtar)* (12547) 26 September 1995, IAT; *Tadesse* (15079) 19 May 1997, IAT.
7 All material aspects of a claim should be the subject of clear findings: *Habtegiorgis* (14446) 13 January 1997; *Arega* (14772) 26 March 1997; *Rai* (00048) 17 February 2000, IAT.
8 *Yelocagi v Secretary of State for the Home Department*, 16 May 2000, CA.
9 *Nicu* (11615) 7 December 1994; *Gharbi* (11791) 23 January 1995; *Ayinde* (13015) 20 February 1996; *Muthengi* (13571) 24 June 1996; *Aboud* (15127) 23 June 1997, IAT.
10 *Banica* (10789) 5 April 1994, IAT.
11 *R v Immigration Appeal Tribunal, ex p Iram Iqbal* [1993] Imm AR 270, QBD; *Khan (Ajaib)* [1993] Imm AR 68; *Saini* [1993] Imm AR 96.

18.166 A misdirection of fact in the determination will ground an appeal if it affects the general conclusion,[1] although a factual error on one issue does not necessarily vitiate the determination.[2] There is nothing objectionable in an adjudicator adopting the Secretary of State's decision letter but there is a risk that any error in the letter will infect the adjudicator's decision.[3] But adjudicators must reach independent decisions following their own assessment of the evidence.[4] It is incumbent on adjudicators to deal with all the issues before them,[5] and in relation to the old mixed appeals jurisdiction, the Tribunal has held that a determination dealing only with one aspect of a mixed appeal (eg deportation and not asylum) is a nullity.[6]

1 *Manzeke v Secretary of State for the Home Department* [1997] Imm AR 524, CA; *R (Judes) v Secretary of State for the Home Department* 10 November 2000, HC; *Joginder Paul* (11071) 20 June 1994; *Mehertab* (11809) 27 January 1995; *Mulumba* (14760) 24 March 1997; *Fatai* (15241) 9 July 1997, IAT.
2 *R v Secretary of State for the Home Department, ex p Yasun* [1998] Imm AR 215, QBD; *Wahome* (12755) 21 November 1995. See also *El-Mahdi* (11591); *Bamadevan* (11790): 'it is difficult to support a determination in which a finding of credibility is dependent on a mistaken view of the consistency of the story told by the appellant.'
3 *R v Immigration Appeal Tribunal, ex p Peranantham* (20 June 1996), QBD; remitted *de novo* by IAT at (13752) 29 July 1996.
4 *Xie* (14644) 14 March 1997 (adoption of Secretary of State letter rendered decision flawed); *Al-Musshadi* (11254) 15 August 1994; *Randhawa* (11514) 3 November 1994; *Atwal* (12229) 27 June 1995 (adoption of previous determination of same appeal rendered decision flawed).
5 *Stefanescu* (11491); *Sakota* (13576) 24 June 1996, IAT.
6 *Angus* (17706) 8 July 1998; *Dragica* (13288) 29 April 1996, IAT.

18.167 Delay in the promulgation of the determination may render the determination unsafe of itself. The Tribunal has said that normally, a period of over three months between the date of hearing and promulgation is unacceptable where credibility is in issue,[1] although this is only a guide which is not applicable where there is no prejudice, for example where the delay is administrative or where credibility findings were contemporaneously recorded, or where the decision was justified on grounds which did not depend on recollection and assessment of oral evidence[2] or where, because of the nature of the evidence or other material before the adjudicator, its falsehood or absurdity was plain.[3] There was a practice, which was given the blessing of the Tribunal, of repromulgating a determination when it appeared to have gone astray or where it was otherwise in the interests of justice to do so,[4] but the practice may have been unlawful.[5] But a determination not properly served and never received has not been promulgated, and on proof of non-receipt should be sent again.[6]

1 Memorandum to Tribunal chairs, referred to in *Waiganjo* (R.15717) 17 October 1997, IAT. See *Mario* [1998] Imm AR 281.
2 *Sad Chaouche* (17423), IAT; *Behre v Secretary of State for the Home Department* (8 May 2000), CA.
3 *Sambasivan v Secretary of State for the Home Department* [2000] Imm AR 85, [2000] INLR 105, CA. So a delay of nine months did not give rise to concern since it did not depend on oral evidence, there had been no material change, and nothing else had been put forward suggesting prejudice to the appellant: *R v Immigration Appeal Tribunal, ex p Shandar* [2000] Imm AR 181, QB. But in *Ehalaivan* (4275/99) 14 June 2000, CA, a delay of two months before dictating a determination should have been addressed by the Tribunal in considering leave to appeal.
4 *Raza (Hushard)* (16238); *Ahmed* (00 TH 00485); *Korsak and Pawlowska* (15855), IAT. The purpose of the practice, described at an Immigration Appellate Authority users' meeting of 10 July 1997, was to mitigate the harshness of the non-extendable time-limit

for applying to the Tribunal for leave to appeal, which has now been resolved by allowing the Tribunal to extend time for good reason: see SI 2000/2333, r 18(3).
5   *Akewnshola v Secretary of State for the Home Department* [1999] Imm AR 594, CA. The assumption that the practice was unlawful formed the basis of a consent order in *R v Immigration Appeal Tribunal, ex p Nicoue* (CO 654/2000) 15 May 2000.
6   See *Korsak and Pawlowska* (15855) IAT; *R v Secretary of State for the Home Department, ex p Asifa Saleem* [2000] Imm AR 529, [2000] INLR 413.

Review of a determination

18.168 In a case where there is no right of appeal to the Tribunal (ie a certified asylum or human rights or discrimination appeal where the adjudicator has upheld the certificate),[1] the Chief Adjudicator may review the determination on the basis that it was wrongly made as a result of an administrative or procedural error by the adjudicator.[2] This can be done on the written application of the appellant (the application to be made within ten days of the determination),[3] or of the Chief Adjudicator's own motion,[4] where the time limit is also ten days. The determination may be confirmed or set aside on review;[5] if the latter a rehearing must be directed. Written notice must be sent to the parties in either case, with summary reasons.[6] The power, a new one in the 2000 Procedure Rules, will be used to correct injustice where, for example, relevant information showing that an appeal had not been abandoned, or that the appellant had a reasonable excuse for non-attendance, or that directions had been complied with, never reached the adjudicator's file and the appeal was determined without the benefit of that information; where the adjudicator wrongly refused an adjournment so that relevant evidence could be obtained or where there was any other procedural irregularity which resulted in prejudice to either party.

1   See **12.163**ff above.
2   Immigration and Asylum Appeals (Procedure) Rules 2000, SI 2000/2333, r 16.
3   SI 2000/2333, r 16(1) and (2).
4   SI 2000/2333, r 16(3).
5   SI 2000/2333, r 16(4).
6   SI 2000/2333, r 16(5)–(7).

IMMIGRATION APPEAL TRIBUNAL

Appeals to the Tribunal from the adjudicator

18.169 Subject to the restrictions in the Immigration and Asylum Act 1999 relating to certified and third country appeals,[1] and to the rules regarding leave to appeal, any party dissatisfied with an adjudicator's determination may appeal to the Immigration Appeal Tribunal.[2] On the appeal the Tribunal may affirm the determination, make any other determination which could have been made by the adjudicator,[3] or remit the case back to an adjudicator.[4] The Tribunal, however, is only entitled to review the completed determination of an adjudicator and cannot entertain appeals relating to incidental or interlocutory matters arising in the course of the appeal. In such cases the dissatisfied party must either wait until the whole appeal has been determined or else apply for judicial review to the High Court.[5] There is no appeal from the adjudicator on whether directions should or should not have been given.[6] The distinction between interlocutory rulings, which were not appealable, and determinations of preliminary issues, which were,[7] may not have survived the new definition of 'determination' in the procedure rules. The issue in all cases will be whether the appeal has been allowed or dismissed. If it has been disposed of in either of these ways, an appeal will lie. If not, it is hard to see how a right of appeal to the Tribunal can ensue.[8] The rules may need amendment, or judicial clarification, to ensure that the Tribunal has clear jurisdiction to consider whether a right of appeal to itself and to the adjudicator exists,[9] although the Tribunal has accepted jurisdiction on the issue of whether an appeal has been abandoned.[10]

1 There is no appeal to the Tribunal from an adjudicator's determination of an appeal in a third country case under Immigration and Asylum Act 1999, s 71: see Immigration and Asylum Act 1999, Sch 4, para 22(1), nor for an applicant in an asylum or Art 3 appeal where the adjudicator agrees that the conditions in Immigration and Asylum Act 1999, Sch 4, para 9(1) applies: Immigration and Asylum Act 1999, Sch 4, para 9(2). The Secretary of State, however, retains the right of appeal in the latter situation: *Secretary of State for the Home Department v Khan* [1999] INLR 309. Whether there is a right of appeal to the Immigration Appeal Tribunal in a one-stop appeal of which a certified asylum or human rights claim forms a part is the subject of an appeal in *Zanovic, Hrbac* (11 April 2001), IAT.
2 Immigration and Asylum Act 1999, Sch 4, para 22.
3 Immigration and Asylum Act 1999, Sch 4, para 22(2).
4 *Secretary of State for the Home Department v Zengin* [2000] Imm AR 518. But there is a presumption against remittal: SI 2000/2333, para 23. See **18.184** below.
5 *R v Immigration Appeal Tribunal, ex p Lila* [1978] Imm AR 50, QBD.
6 *Gulsen* (12127) IAT.
7 *Egbale v Secretary of State for the Home Department* [1997] INLR 88: the Immigration Appeal Tribunal accepted jurisdiction to decide an appeal from an adjudicator's preliminary decision that grounds for a deportation decision could be amended.
8 See **18.164** above.
9 *Secretary of State for the Home Department v Khan* [1999] INLR 309
10 *Gremesty* (starred case) [2001] INLR 132; see also (under the old rules) *Akhuemonkhan v Secretary of State for the Home Department* [1998] INLR 265, IAT.

Leave to appeal

18.170 At present, leave is required from the Tribunal in all cases,[1] although provisions of the 1999 Act appear to envisage a different future.[2] Leave to appeal must be given:

(1)   where the appellant is the holder of a certificate of entitlement who has been refused entry without leave;[3]
(2)   where the appellant is the holder of a current entry clearance, and not an illegal entrant or the subject of a deportation order, who has been refused leave to enter.[4]

Otherwise, leave to appeal will be granted only where the Tribunal is satisfied that the appeal would have a real prospect of success;[5] or there is some other compelling reason why the appeal should be heard.[6] These criteria replace those in the old procedure rules for the grant of leave.[7] The applicant for leave must identify in the application the alleged errors of fact or law in the determination which would have made a material difference to the outcome, together with all the grounds relied on for the appeal.[8] The criteria for the grant of leave are broad enough to encompass situations where no error of law is alleged but significant new evidence is available, for example, and in such a case the requirement to identify errors would appear inapplicable. However, it would be necessary not only to submit the evidence but also a statement explaining why it was not previously available, to make good the compelling reason for the grant of leave.[9] If an error of law or fact is alleged, the first question the legal member will usually have to consider and form a preliminary view on is whether the allegation is arguably correct, and if so, they will have to ask themselves whether the error arguably made a material difference to the outcome. If so, then leave must be granted, for the prospects of success on appeal are good. If, however, the Tribunal concludes that the adjudicator could properly have come to the same determination, then leave must be refused unless there is another compelling reason for hearing the appeal.[10] The 'compelling reason' jurisdiction thus supplements the 'legal' jurisdiction to encompass appeals on procedural grounds, for example where an appeal has been dismissed without consideration of the merits through no fault of the appellant. Leave must be granted regardless of the prospects of success of the appeal in this case. Another example might be where the adjudicator has erred in his or her treatment of an issue which is not determinative of the appeal and the appellant needs correction of the flawed determination to ground a request for a recommendation or a further application. For example, an adjudicator might have reached a flawed decision on the intention of parties to a marriage, where although the appeal could not succeed on maintenance and accommodation grounds, those criteria can now be satisfied.[11] The resolution of a complex issue of law may well constitute a compelling reason for granting leave.[12] The grounds of appeal must be specified with some care, since leave is required to amend them.[13] In addition, judicial review will not lie against a refusal of leave on grounds not before the Tribunal unless they raise an obvious point or one with a strong prospect of success.[14]

1 SI 2000/2333, r 18(1).
2 In particular Immigration and Asylum Act 1999, s 79(3) (penalty for continuing unmeritorious appeal), and Sch 4 para 7.
3 Immigration and Asylum Act 1999, Sch 4, para 7(a).
4 Immigration and Asylum Act 1999, Sch 4, para 7(b).
5 SI 2000/2333, r 18(7)(a).
6 SI 2000/2333, r 18(7)(b).
7 Immigration Appeals (Procedure) Rules 1984, r 14(1), which required leave to be granted where the determination of the appeal involved an arguable point of law, unless the adjudicator could properly have made the determination in any event. There was a discretion to grant leave in any other case.
8 SI 2000/2333, r 18(4)(c).
9 SI 2000/2333, r 18(11); Practice Direction [2001] Imm AR 172, [2001] INLR 216, para 2(ii). This is subject to Immigration and Asylum Act 1999, s 77, ie in asylum and ECHR, Art 3 appeals, the evidence can have arisen post-decision or even post-adjudicator determination. See also *R v Secretary of State for the Home Department, ex p Herida* [1998] Imm AR 71, QBD, under the old rules.
10 *Slimaui* (01 TH 00092*), IAT. A material error of fact will ground an application, where it would have made a difference: *Manzeke v Secretary of State for the Home Department* [1997] Imm AR 524, CA; *R (Judes) v Immigration Appeal Tribunal* (10 November 2000), QBD.
11 See *R v Immigration Appeal Tribunal, ex p Amin* [1992] Imm AR 367; *R v Immigration Appeal Tribunal, ex p Khan* [1995] Imm AR 19; *R v Immigration Appeal Tribunal, ex p Jan* [1995] Imm AR 440, QBD, decisions under the old rules.
12 *R v Immigration Appeal Tribunal, ex p Tewelde* (CO 1687/99) 18 May 2000, QBD (decision under the old rules).
13 SI 2000/2333, r 21.
14 *Robinson v Immigration Appeal Tribunal* [1997] Imm AR 568, [1997] INLR 182; *R v Secretary of State for the Home Department, ex p Kerrouche* [1998] INLR 88; *Taore v Secretary of State for the Home Department* [1998] Imm AR 450.

18.171 The application for leave must be made in a prescribed form,[1] which must be signed by the appellant or representative, be sent with the adjudicator's determination, and state whether a hearing of the appeal is desired.[2] A failure to comply with these requirements would have to be judged against the tests in *Jeyeanthan*[3] of substantial compliance, waiver and consequences to determine whether leave should be granted. The application may be delivered or sent by post or fax before the expiry of the prescribed period,[4] to the office referred to in the form for receipt of the application, not to any Tribunal office.[5] It must be made no later than ten days (or if the application is made from outside the UK, 28 days) after the appellant received the written notice of the determination.[6] The determination will be deemed to have been received on the second day after it was sent (28 days if outside the UK), unless the contrary is proved.[7] The time limit may be extended by the Tribunal if it is satisfied that because of special circumstances it is just to do so.[8] However, it should be noted that in non-asylum cases, an appeal is no longer pending, and so removal directions can be set, once the adjudicator has dismissed the appeal unless *immediately* after the dismissal the appellant gives notice of appeal.[9]

1   The form is annexed to SI 2000/2333 and is sent out with the determination.
2   SI 2000/2333, r 18(4)(a), (b), (d).
3   *R v Immigration Appeal Tribunal, ex p Jeyeanthan* [2000] 1 WLR 354, [2000] INLR 241, CA; see **18.94** above.
4   SI 2000/2333, r 46(1).
5   *R v Secretary of State for the Home Department, ex p Thakar Singh* [2000] INLR 208, QBD.
6   SI 2000/2333, r 18(2). In the case of an in-country appeal, this means ten working days and excludes the period between Christmas and New Year: SI 2000/2333, r 48(8). Time does not start to run if the appellate authority errs in stating that no right of appeal exists or fails to send a covering letter informing an appellant of their right: *Zolele v Secretary of State for the Home Department* [1999] INLR 422. The Practice Direction states that applications for leave will be considered in time if, but only if, they are made within 12 days (if from the UK) or 56 days (if from abroad) after the date of the notice accompanying the adjudicator's determination: *Practice Direction 4 (IAT)* [2000] Imm AR 172, [2001] INLR 216, para 2(iv). See also **18.167** above.
7   SI 2000/2333, r 48(2), replacing the old rule which deemed such receipt 'regardless of when or whether it was received', a formula deemed *ultra vires* in *R v Secretary of State for the Home Department, ex p Asifa Saleem* [2000] Imm AR 529, [2000] INLR 413, CA. See *Practice Direction (No 3) (IAT)* [2000] INLR 686.
8   SI 2000/2333, r 18(3). This is a welcome new provision, giving the Tribunal parallel jurisdiction with that of the adjudicator to extend time, using the same criteria. It puts an end to much hardship caused by neglectful representatives. See cases cited at **18.104** above.
9   Immigration and Asylum Act 1999, Sch 4, para 14.

18.172 The application for leave will be decided by a legally qualified member without a hearing,[1] and there is no obligation to consider grounds not included in the application.[2] This provision appears designed to put an end to the submission of the appeal form with 'grounds to follow' or the submission of additional grounds separately but before the expiry of the period for applying.[3] It also appears designed to prevent judicial review of refusal of leave to appeal on grounds not put to the Tribunal but important and apparent on the face of the determination.[4] In asylum and human rights cases the procedure rule cannot, however, properly be read to limit the obligation of the appellate authority to ensure compliance with the relevant Conventions.[5] We suggest that, in asylum and human rights appeals, this means that the Tribunal should be astute to pick up plain errors of construction of a statute or misunderstanding of the immigration rules in the adjudicator's determination, obvious unfairness or failure of proper procedures before the adjudicator, and clear self-contradiction on the facts on the face of the determination, and that judicial review should lie on these grounds notwithstanding the absence of such matters from the grounds of appeal.

1   SI 2000/2333, r 18(8).
2   SI 2000/2333, r 18(6).
3   The *Practice Direction 4* [2001] Imm AR 172 expressly states that 'further grounds will not be considered'. See under the old rules *R v Immigration Appeal Tribunal, ex p Wanyoike* [2000] Imm AR 389; *Mubassir* [1998] Imm AR 304, [1998] INLR 446, holding that the Tribunal did not have jurisdiction to reconsider a determination of leave when further grounds were submitted, although they were submitted in time. But in *R v Immigration Appeal Tribunal, ex p Njenga* (14 June 2000), the High Court held that a legitimate expectation was created by the Tribunal's practice of waiting to the end of the period for the submission of grounds before deciding an application which said 'further grounds to follow'. See also *R v Immigration Appeal Tribunal, ex p Ishola* (CO/4204/98) 5 March 1999, QBD, (consent order).
4   *Robinson v Secretary of State for the Home Department* [1997] Imm AR 568, CA; *R v Immigration Appeal Tribunal, ex p Sui Rong Suen* [1997] Imm AR 355. In *R v Immigration Appeal Tribunal, ex p Kang* (CO 497/2000), the Court of Appeal held that extraneous considerations not referred to by the parties clearly flawed the determination, and the refusal of leave was quashed despite the failure of the grounds of appeal to raise the point.
5   *Robinson v Secretary of State for the Home Department* [1997] Imm AR 568, CA; definition of 'public authority' in Human Rights Act 1998, s 6.

18.173 The Tribunal has a duty to notify the other parties where an application for leave to appeal is made,[1] although there is no provision for the receipt of representations by them in relation to the grant of leave. There is provision for the Tribunal to send written notice to the parties of the decision on the application,[2] with summary reasons for refusal.[3] The Tribunal is not required to consider evidence not submitted to the adjudicator unless satisfied that there were good reasons for its non-submission.[4] This is, however, subject to section 77 of the Immigration and Asylum Act 1999, which refers to the reception of post-decision evidence on asylum and ECHR, Article 3 appeals.[5] The effect of this proviso is to oblige the Tribunal to have regard to any fresh material relied on in an application for leave in an asylum or Article 3 appeal.[6] But the process of appeal to the Tribunal is not intended to provide applicants with a chance to present evidence which they could reasonably have produced to the adjudicator at the appropriate time and had failed to produce despite directions,[7] so appellants' representatives will not have *carte blanche* to avoid the consequences of their own neglect by an appeal. The Tribunal is obliged to investigate an allegation of unfairness or procedural irregularity at an adjudicator hearing before refusing leave.[8]

1   Immigration and Asylum Appeals (Procedure) Rules 2000, SI 2000/2333, r 18(5).
2   SI 2000/2333, r 18(9).
3   SI 2000/2333, r 18(10).
4   SI 2000/2333, r 18(11).
5   Immigration and Asylum Act 1999, s 77(3).
6   See eg *R v Immigration Appeal Tribunal, ex p Aziz* [1999] INLR 355, QBD, where Latham J said that it was not appropriate to apply the criteria in *Ladd v Marshall* [1954] 3 All ER 745, CA (significance, credibility and previous unavailability) in asylum appeals and that where evidence was credible and sufficiently cogent to be capable of affecting the decision, the Tribunal should be slow to refuse to allow it to support an application for leave to appeal.
7   *R v Immigration Appeal Tribunal, ex p Chen Liu Guang* [2000] Imm AR 59, QBD.
8   *R v Immigration Appeal Tribunal, ex p Susikanth* [1998] INLR 185, CA; *R (Koncek) v Immigration Appeal Tribunal* (CO 1109/2000) 20 November 2000, QBD.

18.174 The extent of the Tribunal's duty to give adequate reasons addressing the issues raised in grounds of appeal has been the subject of considerable jurisprudence. The position seems to be that where a first instance appeal truly depended on its own facts and on the adjudicator's assessment of the evidence, which has been carried out carefully and reasonably, standard-form reasons for refusal are acceptable.[1] But for consistency and transparency the Tribunal should give clear reasons why it is refusing leave when unusual points have been put to it,[2] and should address specific arguments on legal issues and procedural irregularities in the decision, as well as fresh evidence adduced.[3] Necessary minimum reasons must be given so that they can be examined for rationality and so that the appellant, as a matter of justice, can know what has become of his or her application.[4]

1 *Sahota v Immigration Appeal Tribunal* [1995] Imm AR 500, CA; *R v Secretary of State for the Home Department, ex p Thiruchchelvam* [1999] Imm AR 217.
2 *Robinson v Secretary of State for the Home Department* [1997] Imm AR 568 at 582.
3 *R v Immigration Appeal Tribunal, ex p Ehalaivan* (CO 4275/99) 14 June 2000, CA.
4 *R v Immigration Appeal Tribunal, ex p Jasvir Pal* (CO 2282/98) 15 June 2000; *R v Immigration Appeal Tribunal, ex p Swaleh Mohammed* (CO 1472/95) 18 May 1995; *R v Secretary of State for the Home Department, ex p Kabuiku* (CO 546/95) 24 February 1995; *R v Secretary of State for the Home Department, ex p Bamra* (CO 1904/94) 24 February 1995; *R v Immigration Appeal Tribunal, ex p Pratheepan* (CO 1102/98) 27 April 1999; *R v Secretary of State for the Home Department, ex p Prialgauskiene* (CO 1514/99) 15 September 1999; *R v Immigration Appeal Tribunal, ex p Sendiwalla* (CO 4604/98) 17 February 2000, QBD.

18.175 The Tribunal has power to review a refusal of leave to appeal, either on application or of its own motion, on the ground that the refusal was wrongly made as a result of an administrative or procedural error by the Tribunal.[1] An application must be made in writing within ten days of receipt of the notice of refusal of leave and must identify all the matters relied on and include copies of all relevant documents.[2] The Tribunal's own motion jurisdiction, on grounds that the interests of justice require review, must also be exercised within ten days.[3] It is not yet known how this is likely to occur—whether, for example, refusals of leave will be monitored regularly to identify those requiring review. A legally qualified member conducts the review without a hearing, and may confirm or set aside and reconsider the decision.[4] Written notice of the decision and summary reasons must be sent to the parties.[5] These reasons would supplement the original reasons for the purposes of any judicial review of the refusal of leave. The review relates only to procedural and administrative errors by the Tribunal, and is thus limited to matters such as failure by administrative staff to attach relevant documents to the file, or other procedural errors—not errors of law.

1 Immigration and Asylum Appeals (Procedure) Rules 2000, SI 2000/2333, r 19. This remedies the unsatisfactory situation where judicial review had to be obtained to quash a refusal of leave which all parties recognised was erroneous, since previously, once the Tribunal had refused leave it was *functus officio* and had no discretion to reopen the matter: *R v Immigration Appeal Tribunal, ex p Frederick Nelson* (CO 3392/1999) 29 June 2000.
2 SI 2000/2333, r 19(1), (2). No particular form is required, but the applicant must specify the procedural or administrative error relied on, and enclose any documents relied on: *Practice Direction 4* [2001] Imm AR 172, [2001] INLR 216, para 3.
3 SI 2000/2333, r 19(3).
4 SI 2000/2333, r 19(4), (5).
5 SI 2000/2333, r 19(6).

18.176 The grant of leave by the Tribunal is not reviewable at the suit of the other party, either under the procedure rules or by way of judicial review.[1] If the Tribunal grants leave, it may limit the grounds to be argued by setting out in its

notice of decision the grounds on which the appellant may appeal.[2] The grounds
are then deemed to be the notice of appeal.[3] They may be amended, but only
with the Tribunal's leave.[4]

1 *R v Secretary of State for the Home Department, ex p Fadia Nader* [1998] Imm AR 33;
   R v Immigration Appeal Tribunal, ex p Balendran, Katheeskumaran [1998] Imm AR 162.
2 Immigration and Asylum Appeals (Procedure) Rules 2000, SI 2000/2333, r 18(9). The
   Tribunal was divided on the compatibility of limiting grounds which can be argued with
   its *de novo* jurisdiction: see *Kimbesa* (13127) 25 March 1996; *Lukusa* (14353) 23 December
   1996. In *Guccuk* (18460) 26 February 1999, it held that the statement of reasons attached
   to a consent order quashing a decision superseded the original grounds to become the only
   arguable grounds. This must be wrong as a general proposition, since it would effectively
   give the respondent in the judicial review proceedings the power to decide what could be
   argued in the Tribunal (by the terms of the consent order).
3 SI 2000/2333, r 20(1).
4 SI 2000/2333, r 21. There are detailed requirements for the application for leave, in
   Practice Direction 4 [2001] Imm AR 172, [2001] INLR 216, para 4.

Parties

18.177 The parties to an appeal are the same as those who were parties before
the adjudicator. However, the appellant and respondent may change places,
depending on who initiates the appeal. In addition, the UK representative of the
UN High Commissioner for Refugees may become a party to the appeal at any
stage. Notice of hearing is sent to the parties and their representatives.[1]

1 Immigration and Asylum Appeals (Procedure) Rules 2000, SI 2000/2333, r 20(2).

Evidence

18.178 Appeals to the Tribunal are not confined to questions of law, but also
cover questions of fact. However, although fresh evidence can be called before
the Tribunal, and will usually be necessary in cases in which an adjudicator's
credibility finding is challenged, it functions more as a review body of questions
of fact, and a total rehearing of the appeal is unusual. The Tribunal will normally
take the facts from the summary of evidence contained in the determination, or
any note or record of proceedings made by the adjudicator. The latter may be
received as evidence by the Tribunal.[1] Other than that, the Tribunal may consider
evidence which was not before the adjudicator, either on application or of its
own motion,[2] although it may not consider any evidence not served in a timely
manner in accordance with the rules or any directions unless there are good
reasons for doing so.[3] A party wishing to call additional evidence before the
Tribunal must give written notice to this effect and indicate the nature of the
evidence.[4] This must be done 'as soon as practicable' after the grant of leave to
appeal.[5] Evidence which had been in the hands of the party below but not
called would not normally be admitted.[6] In receiving any additional evidence
the Tribunal can direct that this be given orally or in writing, and if orally, it
may remit the appeal to an adjudicator (either the one who heard the original
appeal or another).[7] Any additional documents not already supplied to the parties
should be supplied, other than documents which might involve disclosure of the
method of detecting forgeries,[8] and the Tribunal may not rely on any evidence
not so supplied.[9] Rules 36 and 37 of the Procedure Rules which deal with the

summoning of witnesses and the admission of evidence, also apply in the Tribunal.

1   Immigration and Asylum Appeals (Procedure) Rules 2000, SI 2000/2333, r 22(1).
2   SI 2000/2333, r 22(2).
3   SI 2000/2333, r 22(3). See *Practice Direction 4* [2001] Imm AR 172, [2001] INLR 216, para 6.
4   SI 2000/2333, r 22(5)
5   SI 2000/2333, r 22(6). The phrase is elastic enough to cover a situation where early notice is not given through no fault of the party, and also to cover the situation of documents coming into existence later: *Shanthakunavadivel* (16744) 23 July 1998.
6   *Aghakhani* (13717) 22 July 1996; *Kavuako* (15615) 7 October 1997; *Hussein* (R.15512) 29 August 1997; *Murugiath* (15807) 20 November 1997, IAT. This would not apply where an appellant had been taken by surprise by the course of the hearing below given the terms of the refusal notice: *Ahmad* (11649) 14 December 1994, IAT.
7   SI 2000/2333, r 22(7).
8   SI 2000/2333, r 38.
9   SI 2000/2333, r 22(4). But the Tribunal can admit further evidence even after hearing the appeal, prior to promulgation of its decision, in the interests of justice, provided the parties have an opportunity to make further submissions: *Keskin* (15381) 2 September 1997, IAT.

18.179   The Tribunal has the same powers to give directions for the conduct of the appeal as does the adjudicator.[1] The Tribunal notice of hearing form contains standard directions about filing of evidence. In addition to these standard directions and any individual directions, the procedure before the Tribunal is regulated by Practice Directions[2] issued by the President. Practice Direction No 1[3] provides for service of bundles of documents on the Tribunal and on the respondent. It indicates that the Tribunal will rarely allow oral evidence and sets out the procedure for requesting permission to give oral evidence and for interpreters, which should be made as early as possible, preferably in the application for leave to appeal. A challenge to the conduct of the adjudicator must always be supported by evidence.[4]

1   Immigration and Asylum Appeals (Procedure) Rules 2000, SI 2000/2333, r 30. See **18.130** above.
2   Issued under Immigration and Asylum Act 1999, Sch 4, para 5(1).
3   (3 March 2000) [2000] Imm AR 407.
4   *Yerlikaya* (21477) 16 June 1999; *Aftab Ahmed* (00230) 1 March 2000, IAT.

Hearing

18.180   The hearing usually takes place before a three-person tribunal, of which the chairman is legally qualified, although the Immigration and Asylum Act 1999 makes provision for hearings to take place before differently constituted panels or a single member on the President's direction.[1] It is inappropriate for a member who has previously made adverse credibility findings on the appellant to sit on the panel hearing his or her appeal.[2] Where there are a number of conflicting Tribunal decisions, the Tribunal may sit as an all-legal panel, which may be headed by the President. A decision of such a panel is usually a 'starred' case, to be followed by all Tribunals and adjudicators.[3]

1   Immigration and Asylum Act 1999, Sch 3, para 6(3), (4).
2   *Huang* (14058) 4 November 1996. But it is not improper for the chair who refused leave to appeal to sit on the appeal after the refusal of leave was quashed: *Mwakulna v Secretary of State for the Home Department* (98/7306/4) 4 March 1999, CA.
3   *Haddad (Ali)* [2000] INLR 117; *Sivakarathas* (01056) 12 May 2000, IAT.

18.181 A hearing may be conducted, or evidence or representations given or made, by video link or other electronic means.[1] The time and place of hearing are notified as in the case of adjudicator appeals.[2] The Tribunal has the same powers to dispose of an appeal without a hearing under rules 43 and 44 of the Procedure Rules as an adjudicator.[3] It may dispense with a hearing if the parties agree an outcome, but it is not obliged to.[4] The rules relating to abandonment of appeals,[5] hearing an appeal in the absence of a party[6] and the power to dismiss an appeal without consideration of the merits[7] apply to Tribunal appeals as to those before adjudicators. The criteria for adjournment are the same,[8] and the Tribunal's Practice Direction sets out the procedure to be adopted in applying for one.[9] Adjournment is appropriate to avoid prejudice to a party.[10]

1 Immigration and Asylum Appeals (Procedure) Rules 2000, SI 2000/2333, r 24(2).
2 SI 2000/2333, r 20(2).
3 SI 2000/2333, r 24(1). See **18.132**, **18.134** above.
4 *Yelocagi v Secretary of State for the Home Department* (C/99/7970) 16 May 2000, CA (Tribunal not bound by parties' agreement to remit case).
5 SI 2000/2333, r 32: see **18.122** above. See also *Ghouti* (17937) 13 May 1999, IAT.
6 SI 2000/2333, r 41: see **18.137** above.
7 SI 2000/2333, r 33: see **18.131** above.
8 SI 2000/2333, r 31: see **18.142** above.
9 *Practice Direction No 2* [2000] INLR 238, [2000] Imm AR 435. It requires 48 hours' notice unless there are compelling reasons such as last-minute illnesses, and reminds representatives of the importance of attending if no response has been received or the request is made late.
10 *Pasupathipillai* (R.13732) 29 July 1996. But where an appeal was properly before it the Tribunal would not adjourn because the *vires* of the relevant rule was under challenge in unrelated judicial review proceedings: *Kalejaiye* (17097) 21 May 1998, IAT.

The decision

18.182 The Tribunal has the same powers as an adjudicator relating to appeals,[1] and is not limited to correcting errors of law. The extent to which the Tribunal may review the facts found by the adjudicator has been the subject of considerable litigation. The Court of Appeal has ruled in a number of cases that where, on examination of the evidence, the adjudicator's conclusions on the facts were unsustainable, the Tribunal is entitled to reverse those findings in reaching its own conclusions,[2] although the power would be used sparingly, and the Tribunal would be most reluctant to interfere with a finding of primary fact by the adjudicator which was dependent on his or her assessment of the credibility of a witness who had given oral evidence.[3] It has warned that the Tribunal must avoid the impression of being more prepared to overturn findings of fact favourable to the immigrant than unfavourable ones.[4] The Tribunal is in as good a position as the adjudicator to review documentary evidence of country conditions and draw its own inferences.[5] It is also open to the Tribunal to reverse the adjudicator's decision on the basis of further evidence.[6] A Scottish decision has held that, unless the mistake of the adjudicator is *de minimis*, the Tribunal is bound to consider the matter *de novo*, following *Zaman*,[7] ie it must discard the adjudicator's reasoning and consider the primary issue in the light of all the evidence.[8] The Tribunal, like the adjudicator, must give sufficient and adequate reasons for its determination. In asylum appeals, the Tribunal's promulgation of its decision used to be subject to tight time limits,[9] but these have now been abolished.

1   Immigration and Asylum Act 1999, Sch 4, para 22(2).
2   *Alam Bi v Immigration Appeal Tribunal* [1979–80] Imm AR 146.
3   *Borissov v Secretary of State for the Home Department* [1996] Imm AR 524; *Assah v Immigration Appeal Tribunal* [1994] Imm AR 519; *Ikhlaq v Secretary of State for the Home Department* [1997] Imm AR 404. The Tribunal followed these principles in *Horvath v Secretary of State for the Home Department* [1999] INLR 7, reversing an adjudicator's adverse credibility findings (although dismissing the appeal).
4   *R (Arshad) v Secretary of State for the Home Department* [2001] EWCA Civ 587.
5   *R v Immigration Appeal Tribunal, ex p Balendran, Katheeskumaran* [1998] Imm AR 162, QBD; *Sarker v Secretary of State for the Home Department* (9 November 2000), CA.
6   In *Sachitananthan* (16860) the Tribunal held that, in an asylum appeal, following *Ravichandran v Secretary of State for the Home Department* [1996] Imm AR 97, CA, it had to look at the position at the date of the appeal before it.
7   *R v Immigration Appeal Tribunal, ex p Zaman* [1982] Imm AR 61.
8   *Hanif v Secretary of State for the Home Department* 1999 SC 337.
9   Asylum Appeals (Procedure) Rules 1996, SI 1996/2070, r 19: a ten-day promulgation period was prescribed. In *Berhe v Secretary of State for the Home Department* [2000] Imm AR 463, CA, an 11-month delay was held not to render the decision a nullity. But delays such as this brought the appellate authority into disrepute.

18.183   If an adjudicator has allowed an appeal and given directions for giving effect to the determination, these are suspended so long as an appeal to the Tribunal is pending.[1] If the Tribunal affirms the adjudicator's determination allowing the appeal, it can alter or add to the directions and recommendations already given or replace them with its own directions and recommendation.[2] Directions must be complied with by the Secretary of State or any officer to whom they are given. Where an appeal is dismissed by an adjudicator but allowed by the Tribunal, the Tribunal can give directions and make recommendations in the same way as an adjudicator.[3] Like the adjudicator, it may make an extra-statutory recommendation on dismissing an appeal.

1   Immigration and Asylum Act 1999, Sch 4, para 22(3), (4).
2   Immigration and Asylum Act 1999, Sch 4, para 22(5).
3   Immigration and Asylum Act 1999, Sch 4, para 22(7).

18.184   In an appropriate case the Tribunal may remit the matter for further determination to an adjudicator,[1] although the rules contain a presumption against remittal.[2] The adjudicator may be the same or different from the one who heard the original appeal.[3] Remittal *de novo* may be appropriate where the appellant was previously deprived of a fair first-instance hearing[4] or findings on credibility are inadequate.[5] Remittal to the same adjudicator is appropriate where there has been a positive finding on credibility but the adjudicator misdirected him- or herself on the law.[6] On remittal the adjudicator can hear further evidence.[7]

1   In *Secretary of State for the Home Department v Immigration Appeals Tribunal* [2001] EW HC Admin 261, the High Court held, overturning *Zengin* [2000] Imm AR 518, that remittal is never 'a final determination' of an appeal to give rise to an appeal to the CA. See also *Hussein Kara v Secretary of State for the Home Department* [1995] Imm AR 584, CA).
2   Immigration and Asylum Appeals (Procedure) Rules 2000, SI 2000/2333, r 23.
3   *R v Immigration Appeal Tribunal, ex p Fadia Nader* [1998] Imm AR 33.
4   *Kose* (14110) 11 November 1996; *Demirkaya* (12023) 19 April 1995; *Brown* (12928) 22 January 1996; *Mario* [1998] INLR 306. The Tribunal has articulated the importance of not depriving the appellant of the first tier of the two-tier appeal system in cases such as *Muia* (15155) 24 June 1997; *Hamadou* (16217) 11 February 1998. This is an important principle even where there is a presumption against remittal.
5   *Singh (Devinder)* (15265) 9 July 1997; *Rameswaran* (17621) 6 August 1998, IAT.

6 *Youssef* (12140) 19 May 1995; *Arun* (13718) 22 July 1996; *Macit* (16154) 29 January 1998; *Doutlik* (16152) 29 January 1998, IAT.
7 See **18.152** above.

18.185 After the Tribunal has made its determination, it has one further power of review, exercisable on a party applying for leave to appeal to the Court of Appeal.[1] The legally qualified member considering the application may, if he or she intends to grant leave to appeal, instead set aside the determination and direct that the appeal to the Tribunal be reheard.[2] The parties must be given an opportunity to make representations before this course is taken.[3] This is a much broader power of review than the Chief Adjudicator's to set aside an adjudicator's determination, or the Tribunal's to set aside a refusal of leave to appeal to itself, both of which are limited to procedural or administrative errors. What is envisaged here is a full legal review such as that the Court of Appeal itself would undertake.

1 See **18.192** below.
2 Immigration and Asylum Appeals (Procedure) Rules 2000, SI 2000/2333, r 27(5).
3 SI 2000/2333, r 27(5).

APPEALS TO THE SPECIAL IMMIGRATION APPEALS COMMISSION

18.186 There is no appeal to the adjudicator or the Tribunal if the grounds for any decision—refusal of entry or of leave to remain, a decision to curtail leave, to remove or to deport, or a refusal of asylum—are national security or political grounds. The full list of matters excluded from the normal appeals system is set out at **18.15** above. In such cases, before 1998 the only recourse for those thus fingered for exclusion was an extra-statutory advisory procedure known as the 'three wise men', whose outstanding feature was the absence of elementary rules of natural justice. There were no particulars about the case to be met, not even the names of witnesses, there was no right to representation, no right even to know the advice tendered to the Secretary of State at the end of the procedure.[1] In *Chahal v UK*[2] the European Court of Human Rights concluded that the advisory panel was not a 'court' within the meaning of ECHR, Article 5(4) (which guarantees the right to have the lawfulness of detention decided speedily by a court). The Court deprecated the use of the shibboleth of 'national security' by the executive to attempt to free itself from effective control by the domestic courts and commended the arrangements in Canada which 'both accommodate legitimate security concerns ... and yet accord the individual a substantial measure of protection'.[3]

1 The procedure is set out in detail in the fourth edition of this book, at **15.55-15.56**.
2 (1996) 23 EHRR 413.
3 (1996) 23 EHRR 413, para 130.

18.187 The Special Immigration Appeals Commission Act 1997 was the government's response. It provides rights of appeal in respect of all the excluded decisions with one exception—a refusal of entry clearance which does not relate either to EU rights or to family life.[1] The rights of appeal, which are set out in section 2(1) of the 1997 Act, include a right of appeal against a refusal of asylum but a grant of exceptional leave on the ground that the appellant is excluded from refugee status by Article 1F of the Refugee Convention (ie by virtue of a war crime, a serious non-political crime or acts contrary to the purposes of the UN).[2] The human rights and discrimination appeal—the equivalent of section 65—is set out in section 2A of the 1997 Act.[3] There is provision in section 78 of the Immigration and Asylum Act 1999 for transfer of an extant appeal before the appellate authority where the appellant is served with a decision to deport or a refusal to revoke a deportation order on national security or political grounds, or where a supplementary refusal after a one-stop statement under section 74 or 75 raises such issues.[4] The effects of an appeal are the same as for ordinary appeals. An appeal is treated as pending from when notice of appeal is given to when it is finally determined, withdrawn or abandoned,[5] in provisions mirroring those of section 58 in ordinary appeals, and the suspensory effect of an appeal on removal directions is the same.[6] Appellants to the Special Immigration Appeals Commission are not entitled to a grant of controlled legal representation.[7]

1 See **18.15** above.
2 See chapter 12 above. Only if the Secretary of State certifies that disclosure of the material on which the refusal of asylum is based is not in the interests of national security: Immigration and Asylum Act 1999, s 70(4)(b); otherwise the appeal is before the adjudicator.
3 Inserted by Immigration and Asylum Act 1999, Sch 14, para 121.
4 See also Immigration and Asylum Appeals (Procedure) Rules 2000, SI 2000/2333, r 45(4); Special Immigration Appeals Commission Procedure Rules 1998, SI 1998/1881, r 6, as amended by the Special Immigration Appeals Commission (Procedure) Amendment Rules 2000, SI 2000/1849, r 5 provides that steps already taken before any such transfer are not prejudiced.
5 Special Immigration Appeals Commission Act 1997, s 7A, inserted by Immigration and Asylum Act 1999, Sch 14, para 124.
6 Special Immigration Appeals Commission Act 1997, Sch 2, paras 1-3G, mirroring the provisions of Immigration and Asylum Act 1999, Sch 4, Part II (paras 10-20). See **18.31** above for suspensory effect of appeals.
7 See **18.141** above.

Jurisdiction, procedure and evidence before the Special Immigration Appeals Commission

18.188 The Commission, on an appeal under the Special Immigration Appeals Commission Act 1997, must allow the appeal if it considers that the decision appealed is not in accordance with the law or the immigration rules, or that the discretion of the Secretary of State or an officer should have been exercised differently, and otherwise must dismiss the appeal.[1] The powers of the Commission are greater than those of the adjudicator and Tribunal, embracing a merits review of a refusal to exercise discretion outside the rules. Although the section does not contain an express power to review the facts on which the decision is based, the Court of Appeal in *Rehman*[2] agreed with the Commission that its role was a full merits review including reviewing the facts. The Commission has the same power to give directions and make recommendations where an appeal is allowed as do the appellate authorities in normal appeals.[3] In an appeal against refusal of asylum but grant of exceptional leave on the ground of exclusion from refugee status under Article 1F of the Refugee Convention, the Commission may, instead of allowing or dismissing the appeal, quash the Secretary of State's certificate that disclosure of the evidence supporting the decision would be contrary to the public interest, and may remit the appeal to the adjudicator for hearing.[4]

1 Special Immigration Appeals Commission Act 1997, s 4.
2 *Secretary of State for the Home Department v Shafiq Ur Rehman* [2000] INLR 531, CA.
   For the Commission decision see [1999] INLR 517.
3 Special Immigration Appeals Commission Act 1997, s 4(2).
4 Special Immigration Appeals Commission Act 1997, s 4(1A), inserted by Immigration and
   Asylum Act 1999, Sch 14, para 122.

18.189 The balancing exercise which has to be performed, and to which the
Lord Chancellor is obliged to have regard in making procedural rules, is between
the need for a proper review of an executive decision and the need to secure that
information is not disclosed contrary to the public interest.[1] This is reflected in
the Special Immigration Appeals Procedure Rules 1998, which set out the
Commission's general duties in similar terms (but in reverse order).[2] To that
end the special advocate system has been devised. In order to protect national
security, there is evidence which even the appellant and his or her representative
may not hear.[3] This may include material obtained through interception of
communications.[4] So, when the Secretary of State is served with a notice of
appeal under the 1997 Act, unless it is intended to concede the appeal or not to
object to the disclosure of any material on which the decision is based, the
appropriate law officer[5] must be notified,[6] with a view to appointing a special
advocate, a security-vetted lawyer who represents the appellant's interests on
the appeal but is not instructed by or responsible to the appellant,[7] and cannot
have any direct contract with him or her after seeing the 'closed' material,
without the leave of the court.[8] The procedure in a nutshell is thus: a national
security decision is made; the appellant appeals[9] (and the one-stop procedure
applies here too, so there may be a section 74 or 75 statement, a supplementary
refusal and additional grounds of appeal).[10] If the Secretary of State intends to
rely on 'closed material' on the appeal he or she informs the appropriate law
officer, who appoints a special advocate;[11] the appellant and his or her
representative are served with the 'open' material and the special advocate
with the material which the Secretary of State does not wish to disclose to the
appellant (the 'closed material').[12] The Commission must test the Secretary of
State's assertion that material should not be disclosed.[13] On the hearing of the
appeal the appellant and his or her representative are excluded while that evidence
is given[14] and the special advocate stays in the hearing to represent the appellant's
interests by cross-examination, submissions and representations.[15] But none of
that cross-examination or submissions is on instructions, since as soon as the
special advocate receives the 'closed material' his or her contact with the
appellant is at an end.[16] The appellant is entitled to a summary of the evidence
and submissions given in the closed hearing.[17]

1 Special Immigration Appeals Commission Act 1997, s 5 (rule-making power).
2 Special Immigration Appeals Procedure Rules 1998, SI 1998/1881, as amended by the
   Special Immigration Appeals Commission (Procedure) (Amendment) Rules 2000,
   SI 2000/1849, r 3.
3 Special Immigration Appeals Commission Act 1997, s 5(3)(a)
4 Special Immigration Appeals Commission Act 1997, s 5(7) provides that the exclusionary
   rule of evidence in the Interception of Communications Act 1985, s 9 does not apply in
   proceedings before the Commission.
5 The Attorney-General in England and Wales, the Lord Advocate in Scotland and the
   Attorney General for Northern Ireland in Northern Ireland: Special Immigration Appeals
   Commission Act 1997, s 6(2).
6 SI 1998/1881, r 7(2).
7 Special Immigration Appeals Commission Act 1997, s 6. See the comments of Lord Williams
   during the passage of the Act, 580 HL Official Report (5th series) col 1437.

8 SI 1998/1881, r 7.
9 SI 1998/1881, r 8, 9. The time limit for appealing is five days if in-country, 28 if overseas (as amended by the Special Immigration Appeals Commission (Procedure) (Amendment) Rules 2000, SI 2000/1849). The notice of appeal is not in a prescribed form but must contain the information in SI 1998/1881, r 9 (name, address, representative, grounds and signature) and must attach a copy of the decision appealed.
10 See SI 1998/1881, r 9A (inserted by SI 2000/1849).
11 The rules are couched as discretionary terms, but in practice this must be mandatory to comply with ECHR, Art 6 and the *Chahal* judgment.
12 SI 1998/1881, r 10.
13 In a procedure which the appellant does not participate in but the special advocate does, by written and (if necessary, at the request of the Commission) oral submissions: SI 1998/1881, r 11.
14 SI 1998/1881, r 19.
15 SI 1998/1881, r 7(4).
16 SI 1998/1881, r 7(5)-(6). There is power to seek directions from the Commission authorising the special advocate to obtain information from the appellant after receipt of the 'closed material' but the Secretary of State must be notified of the application and may object: SI 1998/1881, r 7(7)-(9).
17 SI 1998/1881, r 22.

18.190 The Commission must send its determination to the special advocate and the parties,[1] but its duty to give reasons is circumscribed once more by public interest considerations.[2] In *Rehman*[3] the Court of Appeal rejected the Secretary of State's argument that there should be two determinations, an open and a 'closed' one. They said it would make for confusion, and approved the Commission's decision in that case to issue a determination which enabled the appellant to make sense of the decision while disclosing no dangerous details. This is in accordance with the principle that the normal procedures should be applied so far as possible in national security appeals—a principle reflected in the Commission's Procedure Rules, which are familiar in most respects. The power to give directions for the conduct of the appeal[4] is in similar terms to rule 30 of the normal Procedure Rules,[5] except that there is no power to require the furnishing of particulars nor to demand a bundle of the evidence relied on. On non-compliance with directions the Commission has the power to issue an 'unless' order requiring compliance with a stated period; the sanction is that the appeal proceeds without the relevant evidence.[6] The Commission also has the power to extend time for doing anything, presumably including service of the notice of appeal.[7] On an asylum appeal UNHCR is entitled to be joined as a party, but on the same terms as the appellant as regards access to closed material.[8]

1 Special Immigration Appeals Commission (Procedure) Rules 1998, SI 1998/1881, r 23(2).
2 SI 1998/1881, r 23(1).
3 *Secretary of State for the Home Department v Shafiq ur Rehman* [2000] INLR 531, CA.
4 SI 1998/1881, r 13.
5 Immigration and Asylum Appeals (Procedure) Rules 2000, SI 2000/2333.
6 SI 1998/1881, r 14.
7 SI 1998/1881, r 13(3).
8 SI 1998/1881, r 17.

18.191 An appeal lies from the Commission's decision to the Court of Appeal, with the leave of the Commission or of the Court of Appeal. An application for leave to appeal must be lodged with the Commission within ten days of the determination, and normally will be determined without a hearing.[1] On an appeal from the Commission, the Court of Appeal will only accept a departure from the normal appellate procedure if it is necessary in the interests of justice with regard to the issues before the court. If there is such a departure the interests of the individual will be protected to the best of the court's ability.[2]

1 Special Immigration Appeals Commission (Procedure) Rules 1998, SI 1998/1881, r 24.
2 *Secretary of State for the Home Department v Shafiq ur Rehman* [2000] INLR 531, CA, directions hearing.

STATUTORY APPEALS AND JUDICIAL REVIEW

Appeal to Court of Appeal and Court of Sessions

18.192 Where the Immigration Appeal Tribunal (or the Special Immigration Appeals Commission: see above) has made a final determination of an appeal, any party may bring a further appeal to the Court of Appeal or the Court of Sessions on any question of law material to that determination.[1] Such an appeal may only be brought with the leave of the Tribunal, or if such leave is refused, with the leave of the Court of Appeal or Court of Sessions, as appropriate.[2] Cases decided in Scotland go to the Court of Session and all others to the Court of Appeal. An application to the Tribunal for leave to appeal must be made within ten days of receipt of the written determination of the Tribunal.[3] The application must be in writing on a prescribed form, signed by the appellant or representative, and must include the grounds of appeal.[4] It is determined by a legal member acting alone, and will be without a hearing.[5] Reasons must be given for the refusal in summary form.[6] If leave is refused by the Tribunal, the applicant can go direct to the Court of Appeal or Court of Session for leave. In England and Wales the procedure is governed by Civil Procedure Rules, Part 52, and is dealt with by a single judge on the papers in the first instance with a renewal to the full court. The single judge might issue a preliminary 'minded to refuse' decision and list the matter for hearing before him or herself. If so, the applicant should address the reasons for the judge being 'minded to refuse'.[7]

1 Immigration and Asylum Act 1999, Sch 4, para 23(1).
2 Immigration and Asylum Act 1999, Sch 4, para 23(2) and (3).
3 Immigration and Asylum Appeals (Procedure) Rules 2000, SI 2000/2333, r 27(1).
4 SI 2000/2333, r 27(2), (3).
5 SI 2000/2333, r 27(4).
6 SI 2000/2333, r 27(7). Usually it is the legal member of the Tribunal which dismissed the appeal who decides the application for leave to appeal. The Tribunal very rarely grants leave to appeal and its refusals are usually in standard form such as 'the grounds disclose no point of law'.
7 *Mohammed Sad-Chaouche v Secretary of State for the Home Department* (29 March 2000), CA (leave hearing).

18.193 Only a 'final determination' of the Tribunal goes to the Court of Appeal or Court of Session. A decision to remit an appeal to an adjudicator is not a final determination,[1] and does not therefore give rise to an appeal to the CA.[2] But remittal is expressly stated in the Procedure Rules to be an alternative to determining the appeal itself.[3] The Court of Appeal decided in *Abdi and Dahir*[4] that there is no right of appeal to it against a ruling on a preliminary issue, which is not a final determination. With the consent of the parties, the case was treated as an application for judicial review, which is the appropriate remedy where no statutory appeal exists. Where there is doubt as to whether the decision is itself a 'final decision' it may be necessary first to renew the application to the Court of Appeal or the Court of Session before judicial review is taken.[5]

1 See IAA 1999, Sch 4, para 23(1).
2 *Secretary of State for the Home Department v Immigration Appeals Tribunal (Re Zengin)* [2001] EWHC Admin 261, following *Kara v Secretary of State for the Home Department* [1995] Imm AR 584.
3 Immigration and Asylum Appeals (Procedure) Rules 2000, SI 2000/2333, r 23.
4 [1995] Imm AR 570.
5 *R v Immigration Appeal Tribunal, ex p Mukendi* (CO 06694) (1994, unreported), QBD.

18.194 The Court of Appeal has jurisdiction to decide 'a question of law material to the determination' of the Tribunal.[1] This is a narrower jurisdiction than that of the High Court, which can review decisions on all the grounds of administrative law (see below). Issues of procedural impropriety marring the Tribunal determination should therefore go by way of judicial review rather than statutory appeal.[2] The Court of Appeal is not a fact-finding court, and will only review factual conclusions if they are perverse and so unlawful.[3] It is inappropriate for fresh evidence to be presented to the Court of Appeal, since it is confined to deciding whether the Tribunal erred on the facts and material before it.[4] It may, however, on agreed facts, decide that an asylum claimant fulfils the criteria for refugee status, as an alternative to remitting a successful appeal to the Tribunal or the adjudicator.[5] It may restore an adjudicator's determination when allowing an appeal from the Tribunal.[6] The court will not hear academic appeals (ie where a respondent has abandoned a claim, as happened in *Dahir*,[7] or an appellant cannot be found, having been unlawfully removed from the country, as happened in *Re M*)[8] unless there is a good reason in the public interest for doing so, for example, the case raises questions of general importance which can be decided irrespective of the facts of individual appeals and would affect a large number of similar cases.[9] Nor will it hear an appeal on a point not argued at the Immigration Appeal Tribunal by agreement but raised before it in order to obtain a remittal to the Tribunal.[10]

1 Immigration and Asylum Act 1999, Sch 4, para 23(1).
2 *Macharia v Immigration Appeal Tribunal* [2000] Imm AR 190.
3 See eg *X v Secretary of State for the Home Department* (24 July 1998), CA.
4 *Kibiti v Secretary of State for the Home Department* [2000] Imm AR 594, CA.
5 As the House of Lords did in *Islam v Immigration Appeal Tribunal* [1999] 2 AC 629.
6 See *Drrias v Secretary of State for the Home Department* [1997] Imm AR 346; *Mohammed Arif v Secretary of State for the Home Department* [2000] INLR 327; *Harakal v Secretary of State for the Home Department* 10 May 2001, CA.
7 *Abdi and Dahir* [1995] Imm AR 570, CA.
8 *Re M* [1994] 1 AC 377, where the issue was whether the Secretary of State was in contempt of court for removing and failing to return to the jurisdiction an asylum seeker in respect of whom an undertaking had been given not to remove him.
9 *R v Secretary of State for the Home Department, ex p Salem* [1999] 1 AC 450, HL.
10 *Srimanoharan v Secretary of State for the Home Department* (13 June 2000); *Zaitz v Secretary of State for the Home Department* [2000] INLR 346.

Judicial review

18.195 Judicial review is the High Court procedure to challenge the validity of a decision of a body exercising public law administrative functions. The branch of the High Court dealing with it is, since November 2000, known as the Administrative Court. An application for judicial review can only be started with the permission of the court (in immigration cases usually a single High Court judge). The procedure is set out in Part 54 of the CPR. Immigration cases take up a very large proportion of all applications for judicial review. In 2000, immigration cases, at 2119, made up half the total number of judicial review applications for permission.[1] This is not a book about judicial review and we merely flag up points pertinent to immigration law.[2]

1   Figures from the Administrative Court. See the Bowman report. For the growth of immigration judicial review see Law Commission *Administrative Law: Judicial Review and Statutory Appeals* (HC669) p 12; Sunlin, Bridges and Meszaros *Judicial Review in Perspective* (1993) p 52.
2   See further de Smith, Woolf and Jowell *Judicial Review of Administrative Action*; Fordham. Judicial Review Handbook (1997) Harti. Wade and Forsyth *Administrative Law* 8th ed, 2000; Gordon *Judicial Review and Crown Office Practice* 1999, Sweet & Maxwell, Clayton & Tomlinson *Judicial Review Procedure* 1997, Wiley.

18.196 Most immigration decisions are potentially subject to judicial review, whether those of an entry clearance officer, an immigration officer, an adjudicator, a Tribunal, or a criminal court dealing with immigration offences.[1] In *Secretary of State for the Home Department v Javed* [2] the CA confirmed that a statutory instrument which had been approved by both Houses of Parliament was vulnerable to judicial review. Decisions of the Secretary of State are reviewable, including prerogative acts such as the grant or refusal of a passport,[3] and even where statute makes express provision to the contrary.[4] Equally, failures and delays by administrative bodies are challengeable by judicial review.[5] However, the potential for review is limited by the need to have suitable grounds upon which relief can be granted in the particular case and also by the principle that alternative remedies must first be exhausted. In removal cases the High Court can investigate the truth of an allegation that entry was obtained by deception or was otherwise illegal, because illegal entry is a precedent fact to the exercise of the power to remove[6] (although no longer to the exercise of the power to detain).[7] This has already been dealt with in chapter 16. In other cases the court's role is not a fact-finding one, although evidence will be carefully scrutinised in asylum and human rights cases.[8]

1   *R v Clerk to Birmingham Justices, ex p Offei* (28 November 1985, unreported), DC, where a successful challenge was made to the validity of a police certificate extending the time limit for bringing magistrates' court proceedings for an immigration offence under Immigration Act 1971, s 28. This led to the quashing of the applicant's conviction and recommendation for deportation.
2   [2001] EWCA Civ 789.
3   *R v Secretary of State for Foreign and Commonwealth Affairs, ex p Everett* [1989] QB 811, [1989] 1 All ER 655, CA.
4   *R v Secretary of State for the Home Department, ex p Ejaz* [1994] QB 496; *R v Secretary of State for the Home Department, ex p Fayed* [1997] 1 All ER 228, [1997] INLR 138, CA (statutory exclusion of judicial review of decisions on grant or withholding of nationality does not oust court's jurisdiction where decision is unlawful on administrative law grounds).
5   See eg *R v Secretary of State for the Home Department, ex p Phansopkar* [1976] QB 606; *Cheng Poh v Public Prosecutor of Malaysia* [1980] AC 458, PC; *Engineers and Managers' Association v ACAS* [1980] 1 WLR 302; *R v Secretary of State for the Home Department, ex p Mersin (Deniz)* [2000] INLR 511.
6   *Khawaja v Secretary of State for the Home Department* [1984] AC 74, [1983] 1 All ER 765, HL.
7   Immigration Act 1971, Sch 2, para 16(2), as amended by Immigration and Asylum Act 1999, s 140.
8   *Bugdaycay v Secretary of State for the Home Department* [1987] AC 514; *Turgut v Secretary of State for the Home Department* [2000] Imm AR 306, [2000] INLR 292, CA. See **18.151** above.

Statutory appeals and judicial review

18.197 While final determinations of the Appeal Tribunal are appealable to the Court of Appeal or Court of Session, the appeal is limited to questions of law material to the Tribunal's determination. The ambit of the Appeal Tribunal's jurisdiction is, therefore, determinative of the question whether to proceed by the appeal route or by judicial review. Thus in the case of a removal appeal restricted by section 66 of the Immigration and Asylum Act 1999 to the question of the power of removal rather than its exercise, the appeal route to the Court of Appeal or Court of Session is similarly restricted, and questions of unfair procedure and *Wednesbury* unreasonableness will have to be dealt with by way of judicial review.[1] In *Macharia*[2] Sedley LJ expressed the view that the Administrative Court is the natural forum for questions of natural justice arising from tribunal proceedings. Thus, allegations of procedural impropriety or unfairness in any Tribunal hearing should be the subject of an application for judicial review, not statutory appeal.

1 *R v Secretary of State for the Home Department, ex p Oladehinde* [1991] 1 AC 254, [1990] 3 All ER 393, [1993] 3 WLR 797, HL; *R v Secretary of State for the Home Department, ex p Malhi* [1992] 2 All ER 357, [1990] 2 WLR 932, [1990] Imm AR 275, CA.
2 *Macharia v Immigration Appeal Tribunal* [2000] INLR 156 at 165.

18.198 The case of *D S Abdi*[1] resolved that the appellate authorities' jurisdiction in statutory appeals encompasses some administrative law issues such as failure to give effect to or have regard to a published policy, although not all heads of judicial review challenge.[2] Some former policies have now been incorporated into the immigration rules,[3] but many have not, and the exact parameters of their power of review of extra-rules discretion are still to be defined. Their jurisdiction has also been enlarged to embrace review of all decisions, inside and outside the rules, for compliance with the ECHR. As the relationship between the enlarged appellate jurisdiction and judicial review develops, it seems likely that judicial review will be the route to challenge:

(1) decisions of the Tribunal which are not final determinations, such as a decision to remit to an adjudicator,[4] or a ruling on a preliminary issue[5] such as a refusal to extend time;

(2) the Tribunal's refusal of leave to appeal from an adjudicator;[6]

(3) decisions of the adjudicator on interlocutory issues, or on the giving of directions, which are not 'determinations' and so attract no right of appeal to the Tribunal;[7]

(4) decisions of the adjudicator on preliminary issues upholding the Secretary of State's certificate that an application or a late asylum claim is abusive and gives rise to no right of appeal;[8]

(5) decisions of the adjudicator dismissing an asylum or Article 3 ECHR or race discrimination claim and upholding the Secretary of State's certificate on it, depriving the appellant of a right of appeal to the Tribunal;[9]

(6) decisions of the Secretary of State within the one-stop system that a claim is abusive, with the result that an appeal in relation to that claim is to be treated as finally determined;[10]

(7) decisions of the Secretary of State to remove an asylum claimant to a member state or other designated country, which give rise to no in-country right of appeal, where the basis of challenge does not engage human rights;

(8)   other decisions of the Secretary of State which give rise to no appeal rights, such as refusal of leave to enter of a visitor who is not a family visitor, or removal of an overstayer or an illegal entrant, where the basis of challenge does not engage human rights.

(9)   decisions of the Secretary of State to detain, or of the adjudicator to refuse bail. But the appropriate course is *habeas corpus* where it is alleged that the detention is unlawful.[11]

1 [1996] Imm AR 148, CA.
2 See **18.62-18.67** above.
3 Some policies giving effect to family life rights, eg the cohabitees' concession, and that allowing a parent to stay for a child's schooling, have been incorporated into the rules, others, like the policy on exceptional leave to remain, now give rise to a statutory appeal under Immigration and Asylum Act 1999, s 65.
4 *Kara v Secretary of State for the Home Department* [1995] Imm AR 584.
5 *Secretary of State for the Home Department v Abdi, Secretary of State for the Home Department v Dahir* [1995] Imm AR 570.
6 By far the largest category of judicial review applications challenge the Tribunal's refusal of leave.
7 See discussion at **18.164** above.
8 Under Immigration and Asylum Act 1999, s 73(9) and 76(5). The issue of whether an appeal lies should be the subject of the adjudicator's preliminary jurisdiction under Immigration and Asylum Appeals (Procedure) Rules 2000, SI 2000/2333, r 12, although this is not yet litigated. See discussion at **18.128** above.
9 Immigration and Asylum Act 1999, Sch 4, para 9(2). If the adjudicator allows the appeal but upholds the certificate, the Secretary of State can appeal to the Tribunal in the ordinary way and the case will follow the appeal route: *R v Immigration Appeal Tribunal, ex p Khan* (18 August 1998), QBD. See further *R v Secretary for the Home Department, ex p Mehari* [1994] Imm AR 151, QBD; *Secretary of State for the Home Department v Abdi and Gawe* [1994] Imm AR 402, CA.
10 Immigration and Asylum Act 1999, s 73(3), (6). This, by definition, must be outside the adjudicator's preliminary jurisdiction, and so amenable only to judicial review.
11 It may be an abuse of process to bring two separate proceedings (ie judicial review and *habeas corpus*) directed at the same issue: *R v Secretary of State for the Home Department, ex p Sheikh* [2001] INLR 98, CA.

18.199 Where there is a statutory remedy the court will normally expect that remedy to have been exhausted before granting relief.[1] Judicial review may lie where the statutory remedy is defective,[2] but not merely where it is less convenient.[3] Where an appeal has been lodged but not determined, it has been held that judicial review will not lie, even where the issue is whether or not there is a right of appeal.[4] Judicial review relief may be refused where an immigrant has failed to take advantage of an appeal opportunity[5] or has withdrawn an appeal,[6] or elected on advice not to pursue it,[7] but not where the opportunity was lost through unintentional error.[8] If an appeal was lost through the fault of the legal representative and not the appellate authority or the Secretary of State, no judicial review will lie to challenge the determination of the appeal.[9] Relief may also be refused where a point is not taken in an appeal, but is raised for the first time in representations to a minister whose decision it is then sought to review.[10] Relief may also be refused in a judicial review application, where the passage of time or a change of circumstances gives rise to a new appeal before an immigration appellate authority. Thus relief was refused where a fiancé case came to be heard on its merits, but by then the fiancé had married and had a husband appeal pending before an adjudicator.[11]

1 *Rehman v Secretary of State for the Home Department* [1987] Imm AR 602, CA; *R v Secretary of State for the Home Department, ex p Ozkurtulus* [1986] Imm AR 80,

QBD; *R v Secretary of State for the Home Department, ex p Fernando* [1987] Imm AR 377, QBD.

2 For example, an out-of-country appeal in an asylum case: *Canbolat v Secretary of State for the Home Department* [1997] Imm AR 442, CA.

3 *R v Secretary of State for the Home Department, ex p Swati* [1986] 1 All ER 717, [1986] Imm AR 88, CA; *R v Secretary of State for the Home Department, ex p Soon Ok Ryoo* [1992] Imm AR 59.

4 *R v Secretary of State for the Home Department, ex p Abdi* [1993] Imm AR 35, QBD. But an extant asylum appeal does not prevent judicial review of a refusal to grant exceptional leave to remain: *R v Secretary of State for the Home Department, ex p Erdogan* [1995] Imm AR 430.

5 *R v Secretary of State for the Home Department, ex p Luciani* [1996] Imm AR 558; *Sakala v Secretary of State for the Home Department* [1994] Imm AR 227 at 231, CA, but see *R v Immigration Appeal Tribunal, ex p Secretary of State for the Home Department* [1990] Imm AR 166.

6 *Hardeep Singh Sangha v Secretary of State for the Home Department* [1996] Imm AR 493, OH.

7 *R v Secretary of State for the Home Department, ex p Allegret* [1989] Imm AR 211, QBD; but *see Alagon v Secretary of State for the Home Department* 1995 SLT 381, where failure to appeal to the tribunal did not preclude judicial review.

8 *R v Immigration Appeal Tribunal, ex p Secretary of State for the Home Department* [1990] Imm AR 166 (application for leave to appeal sent to wrong address); *R v Special Adjudicator, ex p Amina Ahmed* 1999/62313/C (10 November 1999), CA (application for leave to appeal a day late because of miscalculation). Now that the Tribunal may extend time for appealing, judicial review would only lie of its refusal to extend time in such a case.

9 *Al-Mehdawi v Secretary of State for the Home Department* [1990] Imm AR 140, HL

10 *Rukshanda Begum v Secretary of State for the Home Department* [1990] Imm AR 1, CA.

11 *R v Immigration Appeal Tribunal, ex p Saeed* [1993] Imm AR 109, QBD.

18.200 On a judicial review from the appellate authority, the decision reviewed is the final decision, that is the decision of the Tribunal refusing leave to appeal (if any), not that of the adjudicator.[1] But the Tribunal, while a party, is not the substantive respondent, who remains the decision-maker (Secretary of State, immigration officer or entry clearance officer).[2] An application for judicial review must be made promptly[3] and in any event within three months of the decision complained of. The time limit cannot be artificially extended by making further representations which contain no new material in order to generate a fresh formal decision; time starts to run at the date of the operative decision.[4] On the other hand, Lord Woolf said in *Ahmad and Simba*[5] that in the case of asylum claimants the court would normally be circumspect about being too rigorous in relation to delay, appreciating that to refuse an application solely on the ground of delay may have very grave consequences. This would apply equally to human rights claims. A late applicant for judicial review cannot rely on matters that have occurred during the period of delay, however.[6]

1 *R v Immigration Appeal Tribunal, ex p Said* [1989] Imm AR 372. But see *R (Ganidagli) v Immigration Appeals Tribunal* [2001] EWHC Admin 70, where Elias J quashed both the IAT and the adjudicator's decision.

2 Attorney-General's statement, 1989.

3 In *R v Secretary of State for the Home Department, ex p Ondiek* (CO 4/2000) 25 February 2000, QBD, Owen J discharged an injunction preventing the applicant's removal when he failed to seek judicial review promptly of the Tribunal's decision that his appeal was out of time but had let a month go by, despite previous proceedings being compromised on the basis that he would not be removed while the appeal was pending. The applicant had a history of delays in making applications.

4 *R v Secretary of State for the Home Department, ex p Foster* (13 October 1998, unreported), QBD.

5 *Ahmad and Simba v Secretary of State for the Home Department* [1999] Imm AR 356, CA.

6 *Almad and Simba* above.

18.201 Judicial review of a refusal of leave to appeal to the Tribunal may succeed on grounds not before the Tribunal, where the point was an obvious one or one with a strong prospect of success.[1] Where the Tribunal has refused leave to appeal on a manifestly erroneous basis, the respondent would have to show that no Tribunal could reasonably have granted leave to appeal in order to resist judicial review.[2]

1 *Robinson v Immigration Appeal Tribunal* [1997] Imm AR 568, [1997] INLR 182; *R v Secretary of State for the Home Department, ex p Kerrouche* [1998] INLR 88.
2 *R v Immigration Appeal Tribunal, ex p Deldadeh* (CO 69/2000) 5 July 2000.

18.202 When, following the issue of proceedings, the Secretary of State withdraws the decision under review, or other events supervene, should the court continue to hear the application? In *Canbolat*[1] and in *Abdi and Dahir*[2] the Court of Appeal heard the applications although in the former case there was no longer any question of the applicant's removal and in the latter one of the persons who was the object of the application had disappeared, because of the general importance of the issues and the number of other cases affected by the legal point at issue. The principles are set out in *Salem*,[3] and apply equally to statutory appeals to the Court of Appeal and to judicial review applications. Whether judicial review of a refusal of leave to enter as a visitor should be pursued after the applicant has returned home and the Home Office has undertaken to decide any further application on its merits has been the subject of conflicting decisions.[4] In *Alabi* the Court of Appeal dealt with an agreement to reconsider the decision under review. Simon Brown LJ held that it would be inappropriate in all but the rarest of cases involving a point of general importance and wide application to proceed to a substantive hearing while the decision-maker is undertaking to consider a decision afresh. Generally, such an agreement would exhaust whatever rights an applicant had in the challenge and bring an end to proceedings. But, he continued, where a *Wednesbury* irrationality challenge may lie against any future adverse decision however it comes to be reasoned, the right course is to put the judicial review on hold, with no further evidence and no steps to bring to substantive hearing, and a fresh decision should be reached as soon as possible, so that the future course of proceedings can be reviewed. If the parties cannot agree that the applicant may use the leave already obtained to advance a challenge the respondent thinks impossible, the respondent should apply to set aside the leave and strike out the proceedings.[5] Following that decision, it has been held that where the decision-maker agrees to reconsider during judicial review proceedings, he or she should make it clear what material has been considered and the reasons for rejecting it.[6]

1 *Canbolat v Secretary of State for the Home Department* [1997] Imm AR 442, CA
2 *Secretary of State for the Home Department v Dahir, Secretary of State for the Home Department v Suleiman Ege Abdi* [1995] Imm AR 570, CA.
3 *R v Secretary of State, ex p Salem* [1999] 1 AC 450, HL. See **18.194** above.
4 In *R v Secretary of State for the Home Department, ex p Kekana* [1998] Imm AR 136, the judge refused to hear the application. In the earlier case of *R v Immigration Officer, ex p Honegan* (13 March 1995), QBD, the application was heard, the refusal of leave to enter quashed and subsequently, damages of £17,000 awarded for the detention arising from the unlawful refusal.
5 *R v Secretary of State for the Home Department, ex p Alabi* [1997] INLR 124, CA.
6 *R v FCO, ex p Nwanya* (CO 1772/99) 17 February 2000, QBD.

18.203 Evidential issues do not arise frequently on judicial review. But the courts have held that in a challenge in which the Secretary of State must establish the existence of precedent facts to justify the decision, the court will hear oral evidence and cross-examination if necessary,[1] but hearsay evidence is admissible.[2] So interviews in relation to variation of leave, for entry clearance and at the port may be admitted, as may confidential medical records which resolve the issue of whether someone is an impostor.[3] Discovery should be unnecessary in an application for judicial review, since it is the obligation of the respondent public body in its evidence to make frank disclosure to the court of the decision-making process. The absence of a requirement to give reasons cannot be prayed in aid to avoid discovery or the usual 'cards on the table' approach.[4]

1   *Khawaja v Secretary of State for the Home Department* [1984] AC 74; *R v Secretary of State for the Home Department, ex p Yasmeen* (CO 2930/99) 29 September 1999, QBD.
2   *R v Secretary of State for the Home Department, ex p Yilmaz* [1993] Imm AR 359; *Re Saidur Rahman* [1997] Imm AR 197, CA
3   *R v Secretary of State for the Home Department, ex p Taj* (CO 1084/99), 20 October 1999, QBD. This clearly engages ECHR, Art 8 privacy issues and there would have to be a balancing exercise to see whether the interference was necessary in the circumstances.
4   *R v Secretary of State for the Home Department, ex p Fayed* [1997] INLR 138, CA.

18.204 In *Turgut v Secretary of State for the Home Department*,[1] a case decided before the coming into force of the Human Rights Act 1998, the Court of Appeal examined the standard of review and the correct approach to the evidence required in a human rights case. It held that on an ECHR, Article 3 challenge the court had an obligation to subject the Secretary of State's decision to rigorous examination by reference to the underlying factual material on which the decision was based. Although the court's role was still supervisory, it would pay no special deference to the Secretary of State's conclusions on the facts, since the right involved is absolute and fundamental. The court was hardly less well placed than the decision-maker to evaluate the risk once the relevant material was before it, and the discretionary area of judgment of the Secretary of State was decidedly narrow. Since the material date for the assessment of risk is the time of the court's consideration of the case (following *Chahal*),[2] the Secretary of State had to reconsider the decision repeatedly, and the High Court would not shut out evidence, might order disclosure of evidence, and was not limited to the evidence before the Secretary of State at the time of the decision. And in *Daly*[3] the House of Lords affirmed that the *Wednesbury* test of irrationality has no place in cases engaging fundamental human rights.

1   *Turgut v Secretary of State for the Home Department* [2000] Imm AR 306, CA.
2   *Chahal v UK* (1996) 23 EHRR 413, para 97: 'the notion of an effective remedy under Article 13 requires independent scrutiny of the claim that there exist substantial grounds for fearing a real risk of treatment contrary to Article 3.'
3   *R (Daly) v Secretary of State for the Home Department* [2001] EWHL 26, [2001] 2 WLR 1622, HL.

18.205 Costs normally follow the event on a judicial review which goes to full hearing. The most common problem is where the Secretary of State concedes after the grant of permission or, as frequently happens, before the permission hearing, once an application has been lodged after a number of letters before action. The court has held that if the concession was made for administrative convenience, costs should not be awarded, while if the decision under challenge was withdrawn in recognition of the inevitability of final defeat, a costs order would be appropriate.[1] The court will not be persuaded that the concession represented a bowing to the inevitable unless the respondent admits it or there is clear and unequivocal evidence that this is the case; otherwise no order for costs will be made. The applicant's representatives have a duty to the court not to pursue hopeless applications and may be penalised in wasted costs orders if they ignore this duty.[2] A similar duty rests on the Secretary of State's representative, who is likewise concerned with the spending of public funds, not to continue to defend indefensible decisions.

1 *R v Kensington and Chelsea, ex p Ghebregiorgis* [1994] COD 502; *R v Liverpool City Council, ex p Newman* [1993] COD 65.
2 *R v Secretary of State for the Home Department, ex p Samuel Yeboah* (CO 3166/99) 8 September 1999, QBD.

APPENDIX 1
UK AND EC LEGISLATION

UK STATUTES

IMMIGRATION ACT 1971

1971 CHAPTER 77

An Act to amend and replace the present immigration laws, to make certain related changes in the citizenship law and enable help to be given to those wishing to return abroad, and for purposes connected therewith

[28th October 1971]

BE IT ENACTED by the Queen's most Excellent Majesty, by and with the advice and consent of the Lords Spiritual and Temporal, and Commons, in this present Parliament assembled, and by the authority of the same, as follows:–

PART I

REGULATION OF ENTRY INTO AND STAY IN UNITED KINGDOM

1   General principles

(1)   All those who are in this Act expressed to have the right of abode in the United Kingdom shall be free to live in, and to come and go into and from, the United Kingdom without let or hindrance except such as may be required under and in accordance with this Act to enable their right to be established or as may be otherwise lawfully imposed on any person.

(2)   Those not having that right may live, work and settle in the United Kingdom by permission and subject to such regulation and control of their entry into, stay in and departure from the United Kingdom as is imposed by this Act; and indefinite leave to enter or remain in the United Kingdom shall, by virtue of this provision be treated as having been given under this Act to those in the United Kingdom at its coming into force, if they are then settled there (and not exempt under this Act from the provisions relating to leave to enter or remain).

(3)   Arrival in and departure from the United Kingdom on a local journey from or to any of the Islands (that is to say, the Channel Islands and Isle of Man) or the Republic of Ireland shall not be subject to control under this Act, nor shall a person require leave to enter the United Kingdom on so arriving, except in so far as any of those places is for any purpose excluded from this subsection under the powers conferred by this Act; and in this Act the United Kingdom and those places, or such of them as are not so excluded, are collectively referred to as "the common travel area".

(4)   The rules laid down by the Secretary of State as to the practice to be followed in the administration of this Act for regulating the entry into and stay in the United Kingdom of persons not having the right of abode shall include provision for admitting (in such cases and subject to such restrictions as may be provided by the rules, and subject or not to conditions as to length of stay or otherwise) persons coming for the purpose of taking employment, or for purposes of study, or as visitors, or as dependants of persons lawfully in or entering the United Kingdom.

(5)   ...

NOTES

Appointment
Commencement order: SI 1972/1514.

Amendment
Sub-s (5): repealed by the Immigration Act 1988, s 1.

[2   Statement of right of abode in United Kingdom]

[(1)   A person is under this Act to have the right of abode in the United Kingdom if—

   (a)   he is a British citizen; or
   (b)   he is a Commonwealth citizen who—
      (i)   immediately before the commencement of the British Nationality Act 1981 was a Commonwealth citizen having the right of abode in the United Kingdom by virtue of section 2(1)(d) or section 2(2) of this Act as then in force; and
      (ii)   has not ceased to be a Commonwealth citizen in the meanwhile.

(2)   In relation to Commonwealth citizens who have the right of abode in the United Kingdom by virtue of subsection (1)(b) above, this Act, except this section and [section 5(2)], shall apply as if they were British citizens; and in this Act (except as aforesaid) "British citizen" shall be construed accordingly.]

NOTES

Amendment
Substituted by the British Nationality Act 1981, s 39(2).
Sub-s (2): words in square brackets substituted by the Immigration Act 1988, s 3(3).

3   General provisions for regulation and control

(1)   Except as otherwise provided by or under this Act, where a person is not [a British citizen]—

   (a)   he shall not enter the United Kingdom unless given leave to do so in accordance with [the provisions of, or made under,] this Act;
   (b)   he may be given leave to enter the United Kingdom (or, when already there, leave to remain in the United Kingdom) either for a limited or for an indefinite period;
   [(c)   if he is given limited leave to enter or remain in the United Kingdom, it may be given subject to all or any of the following conditions, namely—
      (i)   a condition restricting his employment or occupation in the United Kingdom;
      (ii)   a condition requiring him to maintain and accommodate himself, and any dependants of his, without recourse to public funds; and
      (iii)   a condition requiring him to register with the police.]

(2)   The Secretary of State shall from time to time (and as soon as may be) lay before Parliament statements of the rules, or of any changes in the rules, laid down by him as to the practice to be followed in the administration of this Act for regulating the entry into and stay in the United Kingdom of persons required by this Act to have leave to enter, including any rules as to the period for which leave is to be given and the conditions to be attached in different circumstances; and section 1(4) above shall not be taken to require uniform provision to be made by the rules as regards admission of persons for a purpose or in a capacity specified in section 1(4) (and in particular, for this as well as other purposes of this Act, account may be taken of citizenship or nationality).
   If a statement laid before either House of Parliament under this subsection is disapproved by a resolution of that House passed within the period of forty days beginning with the date of laying (and exclusive of any period during which Parliament is dissolved or prorogued or during which both Houses are adjourned for more than four days), then the Secretary of State shall as soon as may be make such changes or further changes in the rules as appear to him to be required in the circumstances, so that the statement of those changes be laid before Parliament at latest by the end of the period of forty days beginning with the date of the resolution (but exclusive as aforesaid).

(3)   In the case of a limited leave to enter or remain in the United Kingdom,—

(a) a person's leave may be varied, whether by restricting, enlarging or removing the limit on its duration, or by adding, varying or revoking conditions, but if the limit on its duration is removed, any conditions attached to the leave shall cease to apply; and

(b) the limitation on and any conditions attached to a person's leave [(whether imposed originally or on a variation) shall], if not superseded, apply also to any subsequent leave he may obtain after an absence from the United Kingdom within the period limited for the duration of the earlier leave.

(4) A person's leave to enter or remain in the United Kingdom shall lapse on his going to a country or territory outside the common travel area (whether or not he lands there), unless within the period for which he had leave he returns to the United Kingdom in circumstances in which he is not required to obtain leave to enter; but, if he does so return, his previous leave (and any limitation on it or conditions attached to it) shall continue to apply.

[(5) A person who is not a British citizen is liable to deportation from the United Kingdom if—

(a) the Secretary of State deems his deportation to be conducive to the public good; or

(b) another person to whose family he belongs is or has been ordered to be deported.]

(6) Without prejudice to the operation of subsection (5) above, a person who is not [a British citizen] shall also be liable to deportation from the United Kingdom if, after he has attained the age of seventeen, he is convicted of an offence for which he is punishable with imprisonment and on his conviction is recommended for deportation by a court empowered by this Act to do so.

(7) Where it appears to Her Majesty proper so to do by reason of restrictions or conditions imposed on [British citizens, British Dependent Territories citizens or British Overseas citizens] when leaving or seeking to leave any country or the territory subject to the government of any country, Her Majesty may by Order in Council make provision for prohibiting persons who are nationals or citizens of that country and are not [British citizens] from embarking in the United Kingdom, or from doing so elsewhere than at a port of exit, or for imposing restrictions or conditions on them when embarking or about to embark in the United Kingdom; and Her Majesty may also make provision by Order in Council to enable those who are not [British citizens] to be, in such cases as may be prescribed by the Order, prohibited in the interests of safety from so embarking on a ship or aircraft specified or indicated in the prohibition.

Any Order in Council under this subsection shall be subject to annulment in pursuance of a resolution of either House of Parliament.

(8) When any question arises under this Act whether or not a person is [a British citizen], or is entitled to any exemption under this Act, it shall lie on the person asserting it to prove that he is.

[(9) A person seeking to enter the United Kingdom and claiming to have the right of abode there shall prove that he has that right by means of either—

(a) a United Kingdom passport describing him as a British citizen or as a citizen of the United Kingdom and Colonies having the right of abode in the United Kingdom; or

(b) a certificate of entitlement issued by or on behalf of the Government of the United Kingdom certifying that he has such a right of abode.]

NOTES

Appointment
Commencement order: SI 1972/1514.

Amendment

Sub-s (1): words "a British citizen" in square brackets substituted by the British Nationality Act 1981, s 39(6), Sch 4, paras 2, 4.

Sub-s (1): in para (a) words "the provisions of, or made under," in square brackets inserted by the Immigration and Asylum Act 1999, s 169(1), Sch 14, paras 43, 44(1).

Date in force: 14 February 2000: see SI 2000/168, art 2, Schedule.

Sub-s (1): para (c) substituted by the Asylum and Immigration Act 1996, s 12(1), Sch 2, para 1(1).

Sub-s (3): words in square brackets substituted by the Immigration Act 1988, s 10, Schedule, para 1.

Sub-s (5): substituted by the Immigration and Asylum Act 1999, s 169(1), Sch 14, paras 43, 44(2).

Date in force: 2 October 2000: see SI 2000/2444, art 2, Sch 1.

Sub-ss (6)–(8): words in square brackets substituted by the British Nationality Act 1981, s 39(6), Sch 4, paras 2, 4.

Sub-s (9): substituted for existing sub-ss (9), (9A) by the Immigration Act 1988, s 3(1).

Modification

Modified, in relation to France and the United Kingdom, by the Channel Tunnel (International Arrangements) Order 1993, SI 1993/1813, art 7(1), Sch 4, para 1(2).

Modified, in relation to its application to frontier controls between the United Kingdom, France and Belgium, by the Channel Tunnel (Miscellaneous Provisions) Order 1994, SI 1994/1405, art 7.

Subordinate Legislation

Immigration (Variation of Leave) (Amendment) Order 2000, SI 2000/2445 (made under sub-s (3)(a)).

[3A   Further provision as to leave to enter]

[(1)   The Secretary of State may by order make further provision with respect to the giving, refusing or varying of leave to enter the United Kingdom.

(2)   An order under subsection (1) may, in particular, provide for—

    (a)   leave to be given or refused before the person concerned arrives in the United Kingdom;

    (b)   the form or manner in which leave may be given, refused or varied;

    (c)   the imposition of conditions;

    (d)   a person's leave to enter not to lapse on his leaving the common travel area.

(3)   The Secretary of State may by order provide that, in such circumstances as may be prescribed—

    (a)   an entry visa, or

    (b)   such other form of entry clearance as may be prescribed,

is to have effect as leave to enter the United Kingdom.

(4)   An order under subsection (3) may, in particular—

    (a)   provide for a clearance to have effect as leave to enter—

        (i)   on a prescribed number of occasions during the period for which the clearance has effect;

        (ii)   on an unlimited number of occasions during that period;

        (iii)   subject to prescribed conditions; and

    (b)   provide for a clearance which has the effect referred to in paragraph (a)(i) or (ii) to be varied by the Secretary of State or an immigration officer so that it ceases to have that effect.

(5)   Only conditions of a kind that could be imposed on leave to enter given under section 3 may be prescribed.

(6)   In subsections (3), (4) and (5) "prescribed" means prescribed in an order made under subsection (3).

(7)   The Secretary of State may, in such circumstances as may be prescribed in an order made by him, give or refuse leave to enter the United Kingdom.

(8)   An order under subsection (7) may provide that, in such circumstances as may be prescribed by the order, paragraphs 2, 4, 6, 7, 8, 9 and 21 of Part I of Schedule 2 to this Act are to be read, in relation to the exercise by the Secretary of State of functions which he has as a result of the order, as if references to an immigration officer included references to the Secretary of State.

(9)   Subsection (8) is not to be read as affecting any power conferred by subsection (10).

(10) An order under this section may—

(a)   contain such incidental, supplemental, consequential and transitional provision as the Secretary of State considers appropriate; and
(b)   make different provision for different cases.

(11) This Act and any provision made under it has effect subject to any order made under this section.

(12) An order under this section must be made by statutory instrument.

(13) But no such order is to be made unless a draft of the order has been laid before Parliament and approved by a resolution of each House.]

NOTES

Amendment
Inserted by the Immigration and Asylum Act 1999, s 1; for transitional provisions see Sch 15, para 1(1).
Date in force: 14 February 2000: see SI 2000/168, art 2, Schedule.

Subordinate Legislation
Immigration (Leave to Enter and Remain) Order 2000, SI 2000/1161 (made under sub-ss (1)–(4), (6), (10)).

[3B Further provision as to leave to remain]

[(1)   The Secretary of State may by order make provision as to further provision with respect to the giving, refusing or varying of leave to remain in the United Kingdom.

(2)   An order under subsection (1) may, in particular, provide for—

(a)   the form or manner in which leave may be given, refused or varied;
(b)   the imposition of conditions;
(c)   a person's leave to remain in the United Kingdom not to lapse on his leaving the common travel area.

(3)   An order under this section may—

(a)   contain such incidental, supplemental, consequential and transitional provision as the Secretary of State considers appropriate; and
(b)   make different provision for different cases.

(4)   This Act and any provision made under it has effect subject to any order made under this section.

(5)   An order under this section must be made by statutory instrument.

(6)   But no such order is to be made unless a draft of the order has been laid before Parliament and approved by a resolution of each House.]

NOTES

Amendment
Inserted by the Immigration and Asylum Act 1999, s 2; for transitional provisions see Sch 15, para 1(2).
Date in force: 14 February 2000: see SI 2000/168, art 2, Schedule.

Subordinate Legislation
Immigration (Leave to Enter and Remain) Order 2000, SI 2000/1161 (made under sub-ss (2)(a), (c), (3)(a)).

[3C Continuation of leave pending decision]

[(1) This section applies if—

    (a)   a person who has limited leave to enter or remain in the United Kingdom applies to the Secretary of State, before his leave expires, for it to be varied; and
    (b)   when it expires, no decision has been taken on the application.

(2) His leave is to be treated as continuing until the end of the period allowed under rules made under paragraph 3 of Schedule 4 to the Immigration and Asylum Act 1999 for bringing an appeal against a decision on the application.

(3) An application for variation of a person's leave to enter or remain in the United Kingdom may not be made while that leave is treated as continuing as a result of this section.

(4) But subsection (3) does not prevent the variation of an application mentioned in subsection (1).]

NOTES

Amendment
Inserted by the Immigration and Asylum Act 1999, s 3.
Date in force: 2 October 2000: see SI 2000/2444, art 2, Sch 1; for transitional provisions see art 3, Sch 2, para 2(2) thereof.

4   Administration of control

(1) The power under this Act to give or refuse leave to enter the United Kingdom shall be exercised by immigration officers, and the power to give leave to remain in the United Kingdom, or to vary any leave under section 3(3)(a) (whether as regards duration or conditions), shall be exercised by the Secretary of State; and, unless otherwise [allowed by or under] this Act, those powers should be exercised by notice in writing given to the person affected, except that the powers under section 3(3)(a) may be exercised generally in respect of any class of persons by order made by statutory instrument.

(2) The provisions of Schedule 2 to this Act shall have effect with respect to—

    (a)   the appointment and powers of immigration officers and medical inspectors for purposes of this Act;
    (b)   the examination of persons arriving in or leaving the United Kingdom by ship or aircraft [. . .], and the special powers exercisable in the case of those who arrive as, or with a view to becoming, members of the crews of ships and aircraft; and
    (c)   the exercise by immigration officers of their powers in relation to entry into the United Kingdom, and the removal from the United Kingdom of persons refused leave to enter or entering or remaining unlawfully; and
    (d)   the detention of persons pending examination or pending removal from the United Kingdom;

and for other purposes supplementary to the foregoing provisions of this Act.

(3)   The Secretary of State may by regulations made by statutory instrument, which shall be subject to annulment in pursuance of a resolution of either House of Parliament, make provision as to the effect of a condition under this Act requiring a person to register with the police; and the regulations may include provision—

(a)   as to the officers of police by whom registers are to be maintained, and as to the form and content of the registers;

(b)   as to the place and manner in which anyone is to register and as to the documents and information to be furnished by him, whether on registration or on any change of circumstances;

(c)   as to the issue of certificates of registration and as to the payment of fees for certificates of registration;

and the regulations may require anyone who is for the time being subject to such a condition to produce a certificate of registration to such persons and in such circumstances as may be prescribed by the regulations.

(4)   The Secretary of State may by order made by statutory instrument, which shall be subject to annulment in pursuance of a resolution of either House of Parliament, make such provision as appears to him to be expedient in connection with this Act for records to be made and kept of persons staying at hotels and other premises where lodging or sleeping accommodation is provided, and for persons (whether [British citizens] or not) who stay at any such premises to supply the necessary information.

NOTES

Appointment
Commencement order: SI 1972/1514.

Amendment
Sub-s (1): words "allowed by or under" in square brackets substituted by the Immigration and Asylum Act 1999, s 169(1), Sch 14, paras 43, 45.
Date in force: 14 February 2000: see SI 2000/168, art 2, Schedule.
Sub-s (2): words omitted, originally inserted by SI 1990/2227, art 3, Sch 1, Part I, para 1, repealed by SI 1993/1813, art 9, Sch 6, Part I.
Sub-s (4): words in square brackets substituted by the British Nationality Act, s 39(6), Sch 4, para 2.

Modification
Modified, in relation to France and the United Kingdom, by the Channel Tunnel (International Arrangements) Order 1993, SI 1993/1813, art 7(1), Sch 4, para 1(3).
Modified, in relation to its application to frontier controls between the United Kingdom, France and Belgium, by the Channel Tunnel (Miscellaneous Provisions) Order 1994, SI 1994/1405, art 7.

Subordinate Legislation
Immigration (Variation of Leave) (Amendment) Order 2000, SI 2000/2445 (made under sub-s (1)).

5   Procedure for, and further provisions as to, deportation

(1)   Where a person is under section 3(5) or (6) above liable to deportation, then subject to the following provisions of this Act the Secretary of State may make a deportation order against him, that is to say an order requiring him to leave and prohibiting him from entering the United Kingdom; and a deportation order against a person shall invalidate any leave to enter or remain in the United Kingdom given him before the order is made or while it is in force.

(2)   A deportation order against a person may at any time be revoked by a further order of the Secretary of State, and shall cease to have effect if he becomes [a British citizen].

(3)   A deportation order shall not be made against a person as belonging to the family of another person if more than eight weeks have elapsed since the other person left the United Kingdom after the making of the deportation order against him; and a deportation order made against a person on that ground shall cease to have effect if he ceases to belong to the family of the other person, or if the deportation order made against the other person ceases to have effect.

(4)   For purposes of deportation the following shall be those who are regarded as belonging to another person's family—

    (a)   where that other person is a man, his wife and his or her children under the age of eighteen; and

    [(b)   where that other person is a woman, her husband and her or his children under the age of eighteen;]

and for purposes of this subsection an adopted child, whether legally adopted or not, may be treated as the child of the adopter and, if legally adopted, shall be regarded as the child only of the adopter; an illegitimate child (subject to the foregoing rule as to adoptions) shall be regarded as the child of the mother; and "wife" includes each of two or more wives.

(5)   The provisions of Schedule 3 to this Act shall have effect with respect to the removal from the United Kingdom of persons against whom deportation orders are in force and with respect to the detention or control of persons in connection with deportation.

(6)   Where a person is liable to deportation under section [3(5)] or (6) above but, without a deportation order being made against him, leaves the United Kingdom to live permanently abroad, the Secretary of State may make payments of such amounts as he may determine to meet that person's expenses in so leaving the United Kingdom, including travelling expenses for members of his family or household.

NOTES

Appointment
Commencement order: SI 1972/1514.

Amendment
Sub-s (2): words in square brackets substituted by the British Nationality Act 1981, s 39(6), Sch 4, para 2.
Sub-s (4): para (b) substituted by the Asylum and Immigration Act 1996, s 12(1), Sch 2, para 2.
Sub-s (6): figures in square brackets substituted by the Immigration Act 1988, s 10, Schedule, para 2.

6   Recommendations by court for deportation

(1)   Where under section 3(6) above a person convicted of an offence is liable to deportation on the recommendation of a court, he may be recommended for deportation by any court having power to sentence him for the offence unless the court commits him to be sentenced or further dealt with for that offence by another court:
   . . .

(2)   A court shall not recommend a person for deportation unless he has been given not less than seven days notice in writing stating that a person is not liable to deportation if he is [a British citizen], describing the persons who are [British citizens] and stating (so far as material) the effect of section 3(8) above and section 7 below; but the powers of adjournment conferred by [section 10(3) of the Magistrates' Courts Act 1980], [section 179 or 380 of the Criminal Procedure (Scotland) Act 1975] or any corresponding enactment for the time being in force in Northern Ireland shall include power to adjourn, after convicting an offender, for the purpose of enabling a notice to

be given to him under this subsection or, if a notice was so given to him less than seven days previously, for the purpose of enabling the necessary seven days to elapse.

(3)   For purposes of section 3(6) above—

(a)   a person shall be deemed to have attained the age of seventeen at the time of his conviction if, on consideration of any available evidence, he appears to have done so to the court making or considering a recommendation for deportation; and

(b)   the question whether an offence is one for which a person is punishable with imprisonment shall be determined without regard to any enactment restricting the imprisonment of young offenders or [persons who have not previously been sentenced to imprisonment];

and for purposes of deportation a person who on being charged with an offence is found to have committed it shall, notwithstanding any enactment to the contrary and notwithstanding that the court does not proceed to conviction, be regarded as a person convicted of the offence, and references to conviction shall be construed accordingly.

(4)   Notwithstanding any rule of practice restricting the matters which ought to be taken into account in dealing with an offender who is sentenced to imprisonment, a recommendation for deportation may be made in respect of an offender who is sentenced to imprisonment for life.

(5)   Where a court recommends or purports to recommend a person for deportation, the validity of the recommendation shall not be called in question except on an appeal against the recommendation or against the conviction on which it is made; but—

(a)   . . . the recommendation shall be treated as a sentence for the purpose of any enactment providing an appeal against sentence; . . .

(b)   . . .

(6)   A deportation order shall not be made on the recommendation of a court so long as an appeal or further appeal is pending against the recommendation or against the conviction on which it was made; and for this purpose an appeal or further appeal shall be treated as pending (where one is competent but has not been brought) until the expiration of the time for bringing that appeal or, in Scotland, until the expiration of twenty-eight days from the date of the recommendation.

(7)   . . .

NOTES

Appointment
Commencement order: SI 1972/1514.

Amendment
Sub-s (1): words omitted apply to Scotland only.
Sub-s (2): first and second words in square brackets substituted by the British Nationality Act 1981, s 39(6), Sch 4, para 2; third words in square brackets substituted by the Magistrates' Courts Act 1980, s 154, Sch 7, para 105; final words in square brackets substituted by the Criminal Procedure (Scotland) Act 1975, s 461(1), Sch 9, para 47.
Sub-s (3): words in square brackets substituted by the Criminal Justice Act 1972, s 64(1), Sch 5, and the Criminal Justice Act 1982, s 77, Sch 15.
Sub-s (5): words omitted repealed by the Criminal Justice (Scotland) Act 1980, s 83(3), Sch 8, and the Criminal Justice Act 1982, ss 77, 78, Sch 15, para 15, Sch 16.
Sub-s (7): applies to Scotland only.

7   Exemption from deportation for certain existing residents

(1)   Notwithstanding anything in section 3(5) or (6) above but subject to the provisions of this section, a Commonwealth citizen or citizen of the Republic of Ireland who was

such a citizen at the coming into force of this Act and was then ordinarily resident in the United Kingdom—

   (a)   shall not be liable to deportation under section [3(5)(a)] if at the time of the Secretary of State's decision he had at all times since the coming into force of this Act been ordinarily resident in the United Kingdom and Islands; and
   (b)   shall not be liable to deportation under section 3(5)(a) [or (b) or 10 of the Immigration and Asylum Act 1999] if at the time of the Secretary of State's decision he had for the last five years been ordinarily resident in the United Kingdom and Islands; and
   (c)   shall not on conviction of an offence be recommended for deportation under section 3(6) if at the time of the conviction he had for the last five years been ordinarily resident in the United Kingdom and Islands.

(2)   A person who has at any time become ordinarily resident in the United Kingdom or in any of the Islands shall not be treated for the purposes of this section as having ceased to be so by reason only of his having remained there in breach of the immigration laws.

(3)   The "last five years" before the material time under subsection (1)(b) or (c) above is to be taken as a period amounting in total to five years exclusive of any time during which the person claiming exemption under this section was undergoing imprisonment or detention by virtue of a sentence passed for an offence on a conviction in the United Kingdom and Islands, and the period for which he was imprisoned or detained by virtue of the sentence amounted to six months or more.

(4)   For purposes of subsection (3) above—

   (a)   "sentence" includes any order made on conviction of an offence; and
   (b)   two or more sentences for consecutive (or partly consecutive) terms shall be treated as a single sentence; and
   (c)   a person shall be deemed to be detained by virtue of a sentence—
      (i)   at any time when he is liable to imprisonment or detention by virtue of the sentence, but is unlawfully at large; and
      (ii)   (unless the sentence is passed after the material time) during any period of custody by which under any relevant enactment the term to be served under the sentence is reduced.

   In paragraph (c)(ii) above "relevant enactment" means *section 67 of the Criminal Justice Act 1967* [section 87 of the Powers of Criminal Courts (Sentencing) Act 2000] (or, before that section operated, section 17(2) of the Criminal Justice Administration Act 1962) and any similar enactment which is for the time being or has (before or after the passing of this Act) been in force in any part of the United Kingdom and Islands.

(5)   Nothing in this section shall be taken to exclude the operation of section 3(8) above in relation to an exemption under this section.

NOTES

Appointment
Commencement order: SI 1972/1514.

Amendment
Sub-s (1): in para (a) reference relating to "3(5)(a)" in square brackets substituted by the Immigration and Asylum Act 1999, s 169(1), Sch 14, paras 43, 46(a).
Date in force: 2 October 2000: see SI 2000/2444, art 2, Sch 1.
Sub-s (1): in para (b) words "or (b) or 10 of the Immigration and Asylum Act 1999" in square brackets substituted by the Immigration and Asylum Act 1999, s 169(1), Sch 14, paras 43, 46(b).
Date in force: 2 October 2000: see SI 2000/2444, art 2, Sch 1.

Sub-s (4): words "section 67 of the Criminal Justice Act 1967" in italics repealed and subsequent words in square brackets substituted by the Crime (Sentences) Act 1997, Sch 4, para 7 (as amended by the Powers of Criminal Courts (Sentencing) Act 2000, s 165(1), Sch 9, para 187(1), (3)).
Date in force: to be appointed: see the Crime (Sentences) Act 1997, s 57(2).

8 Exceptions for seamen, aircrews and other special cases

(1) Where a person arrives at a place in the United Kingdom as a member of the crew of a ship or aircraft under an engagement requiring him to leave on that ship as a member of the crew, or to leave within seven days on that or another aircraft as a member of its crew, then unless either—

(a) there is in force a deportation order made against him; or

(b) he has at any time been refused leave to enter the United Kingdom and has not since then been given leave to enter or remain in the United Kingdom; or

(c) an immigration officer requires him to submit to examination in accordance with Schedule 2 to this Act;

he may without leave enter the United Kingdom at that place and remain until the departure of the ship or aircraft on which he is required by his engagement to leave.

(2) The Secretary of State may by order exempt any person or class of persons, either unconditionally or subject to such conditions as may be imposed by or under the order, from all or any of the provisions of this Act relating to those who are not [British citizens].

An order under this subsection, if made with respect to a class of persons, shall be made by statutory instrument, which shall be subject to annulment in pursuance of a resolution of either House of Parliament.

(3) [Subject to subsection (3A) below,] the provisions of this Act relating to those who are not [British citizens] shall not apply to any person so long as he is a member of a mission (within the meaning of the Diplomatic Privileges Act 1964), a person who is a member of the family and forms part of the household of such a member, or a person otherwise entitled to the like immunity from jurisdiction as is conferred by that Act on a diplomatic agent.

[(3A) For the purposes of subsection (3), a member of a mission other than a diplomatic agent (as defined by the 1964 Act) is not to count as a member of a mission unless—

(a) he was resident outside the United Kingdom, and was not in the United Kingdom, when he was offered a post as such a member; and

(b) he has not ceased to be such a member after having taken up the post.]

(4) The provisions of this Act relating to those who are not [British citizens], other than the provisions relating to deportation, shall also not apply to any person so long as either—

(a) he is subject, as a member of the home forces, to service law; or

(b) being a member of a Commonwealth force or of a force raised under the law of any . . . colony, protectorate or protected state, is undergoing or about to undergo training in the United Kingdom with any body, contingent or detachment of the home forces; or

(c) he is serving or posted for service in the United Kingdom as a member of a visiting force or of any force raised as aforesaid or as a member of an international headquarters or defence organisation designated for the time being by an Order in Council under section 1 of the International Headquarters and Defence Organisations Act 1964.

(5) Where a person having a limited leave to enter or remain in the United Kingdom becomes entitled to an exemption under this section, that leave shall continue to apply after he ceases to be entitled to the exemption, unless it has by then expired; and a

person is not to be regarded for purposes of this Act as having been [settled in the United Kingdom at any time when he was entitled under the former immigration laws to any exemption corresponding to any of those afforded by subsection (3) or (4)(b) or (c) above or by any order under subsection (2) above.]

[(5A) An order under subsection (2) above may, as regards any person or class of persons to whom it applies, provide for that person or class to be in specified circumstances regarded (notwithstanding the order) as settled in the United Kingdom for the purposes of section 1(1) of the British Nationality Act 1981.]

(6)   In this section "the home forces" means any of Her Majesty's forces other than a Commonwealth force or a force raised under the law of any associated state, colony, protectorate or protected state; "Commonwealth force" means a force of any country to which provisions of the Visiting Forces Act 1952 apply without an Order in Council under section 1 of the Act; and "visiting force" means a body, contingent or detachment of the forces of a country to which any of those provisions apply, being a body, contingent or detachment for the time being present in the United Kingdom on the invitation of Her Majesty's Government in the United Kingdom.

NOTES

Appointment
Commencement order: SI 1972/1514.

Amendment
Sub-ss (2), (5): words in square brackets substituted by the British Nationality Act 1981, s 39(6), Sch 4, paras 2, 5.
Sub-s (3): first words in square brackets inserted by the Immigration Act 1988, s 4; second words in square brackets substituted by the British Nationality Act 1981, s 39(6), Sch 4, para 2.
Sub-s (3A) (as originally inserted by the Immigration Act 1988, s 4, except in relation to a person who has taken up the post before 1 August 1988): substituted by the Immigration and Asylum Act 1999, s 6.
Date in force: 1 March 2000: see SI 2000/168, art 2, Schedule.
Sub-s (4): words in square brackets substituted by the British Nationality Act 1981, s 39(6), Sch 4, paras 2, 5; in para (b) words omitted repealed by the Statute Law (Repeals) Act 1995.
Sub-s (5A): inserted by the British Nationality Act 1981, s 39(4).

Modification
Modified, in relation to France and the United Kingdom, by the Channel Tunnel (International Arrangements) Order 1993, SI 1993/1813, art 7(1), Sch 4, para 1(4).
Modified, in relation to its application to frontier controls between the United Kingdom, France and Belgium, by the Channel Tunnel (Miscellaneous Provisions) Order 1994, SI 1994/1405, art 7.

[8A   Persons ceasing to be exempt]

[(1)   A person is exempt for the purposes of this section if he is exempt from provisions of this Act as a result of section 8(2) or (3).

(2)   If a person who is exempt—

   (a)   ceases to be exempt, and
   (b)   requires leave to enter or remain in the United Kingdom as a result,

he is to be treated as if he had been given leave to remain in the United Kingdom for a period of 90 days beginning on the day on which he ceased to be exempt.

(3)   If—

   (a)   a person who is exempt ceases to be exempt, and
   (b)   there is in force in respect of him leave for him to enter or remain in the United Kingdom which expires before the end of the period mentioned in subsection (2),

his leave is to be treated as expiring at the end of that period.]

NOTES

Amendment
Inserted by the Immigration and Asylum Act 1999, s 7.
Date in force: 1 March 2000: see SI 2000/168, art 2, Schedule.

[8B Persons excluded from the United Kingdom under international obligations]

[(1) An excluded person must be refused—

   (a)   leave to enter the United Kingdom;
   (b)   leave to remain in the United Kingdom.

(2) A person's leave to enter or remain in the United Kingdom is cancelled on his becoming an excluded person.

(3) A person's exemption from the provisions of this Act as a result of section 8(1), (2) or (3) ceases on his becoming an excluded person.

(4) "Excluded person" means a person—

   (a)   named by or under, or
   (b)   of a description specified in,

a designated instrument.

(5) The Secretary of State may by order designate an instrument if it is a resolution of the Security Council of the United Nations or an instrument made by the Council of the European Union and it—

   (a)   requires that a person is not to be admitted to the United Kingdom (however that requirement is expressed); or
   (b)   recommends that a person should not be admitted to the United Kingdom (however that recommendation is expressed).

(6) Subsections (1) to (3) are subject to such exceptions (if any) as may specified in the order designating the instrument in question.

(7) An order under this section must be made by statutory instrument.

(8) Such a statutory instrument shall be laid before Parliament without delay.]

NOTES

Amendment
Inserted by the Immigration and Asylum Act 1999, s 8.
Date in force: 1 March 2000: see SI 2000/168, art 2, Schedule.

Subordinate Legislation
Immigration (Designation of Travel Bans) Order 2000, SI 2000/2724 (made under sub-ss (5), (6)).
Immigration (Designation of Travel Bans) (Amendment) Order 2000, SI 2000/3338 (made under sub-s (5)).

9   Further provisions as to common travel area

(1) Subject to subsection (5) below, the provisions of Schedule 4 to this Act shall have effect for the purpose of taking account in the United Kingdom of the operation in any of the Islands of the immigration laws there.

(2) Persons who lawfully enter the United Kingdom on a local journey from a place in the common travel area after having either—

   (a)   entered any of the Islands or the Republic of Ireland on coming from a place outside the common travel area; or

   (b)   left the United Kingdom while having a limited leave to enter or remain which has since expired;

if they are not [British citizens] (and are not to be regarded under Schedule 4 to this Act as having leave to enter the United Kingdom), shall be subject in the United Kingdom to such restrictions on the period for which they may remain, and such conditions restricting their employment or occupation or requiring them to register with the police or both, as may be imposed by an order of the Secretary of State and may be applicable to them.

(3)   Any provision of this Act applying to a limited leave or to conditions attached to a limited leave shall, unless otherwise provided, have effect in relation to a person subject to any restriction or condition by virtue of an order under subsection (2) above as if the provisions of the order applicable to him were terms on which he had been given leave under this Act to enter the United Kingdom.

(4)   Section 1(3) above shall not be taken to affect the operation of a deportation order; and, subject to Schedule 4 to this Act, a person who is not [a British citizen] may not by virtue of section 1(3) enter the United Kingdom without leave on a local journey from a place in the common travel area if either—

   (a)   he is on arrival in the United Kingdom given written notice by an immigration officer stating that, the Secretary of State having issued directions for him not to be given entry to the United Kingdom on the ground that his exclusion is conducive to the public good as being in the interests of national security, he is accordingly refused leave to enter the United Kingdom; or

   (b)   he has at any time been refused leave to enter the United Kingdom and has not since then been given leave to enter or remain in the United Kingdom.

(5)   If it appears to the Secretary of State necessary so to do by reason of differences between the immigration laws of the United Kingdom and any of the Islands, he may by order exclude that island from section 1(3) above for such purposes as may be specified in the order, and references in this Act to the Islands . . . shall apply to an island so excluded so far only as may be provided by order of the Secretary of State.

(6)   The Secretary of State shall also have power by order to exclude the Republic of Ireland from section 1(3) for such purposes as may be specified in the order.

(7)   An order of the Secretary of State under this section shall be made by statutory instrument, which shall be subject to annulment in pursuance of a resolution of either House of Parliament.

NOTES

Appointment
Commencement order: SI 1972/1514.

Amendment
Sub-ss (2), (4): words in square brackets substituted by the British Nationality Act 1981, s 39(6), Sch 4, para 2.
Sub-s (5): words omitted repealed by the British Nationality Act 1981, s 52(8), Sch 9.

Subordinate Legislation
Immigration (Control of Entry through Republic of Ireland) (Amendment) Order 2000, SI 2000/1776 (made under sub-s (2)).

10   Entry otherwise than by sea or air

(1)   Her Majesty may by Order in Council direct that any of the provisions of this Act shall have effect in relation to persons entering or seeking to enter the United Kingdom on arrival otherwise than by ship or aircraft [. . .] as they have effect in the case of a person arriving by ship or aircraft [. . .]; *and any such Order may make such adaptations*

or modifications of those provisions, and such provisions supplementary thereto, as appear to Her Majesty to be necessary or expedient for the purposes of the Order.

[(1A) Her Majesty may by Order in Council direct that paragraph 27B or 27C of Schedule 2 shall have effect in relation to trains or vehicles as it has effect in relation to ships or aircraft.

(1B) Any Order in Council under this section may make—

    (a) such adaptations or modifications of the provisions concerned, and
    (b) such supplementary provisions,

as appear to Her Majesty to be necessary or expedient for the purposes of the Order.]

(2) The provision made by an Order in Council under *this section* [subsection (1)] may include provision for excluding the Republic of Ireland from section 1(3) of this Act either generally or for any specified purposes.

(3) No recommendation shall be made to Her Majesty to make an Order in Council under this section unless a draft of the Order has been laid before Parliament and approved by a resolution of each House of Parliament.

NOTES

Appointment
Commencement order: SI 1972/1514.

Amendment
Sub-s (1): words omitted inserted by SI 1990/2227, art 3, Sch 1, Part I, para 2, repealed by SI 1993/1813, art 9, Sch 6.
Sub-s (1): words from "any such order" to "of the Order" in italics repealed by the Immigration and Asylum Act 1999, s 169(1), (3), Sch 14, paras 43, 47(1), (2), Sch 16.
Date in force: to be appointed: see the Immigration and Asylum Act 1999, s 170(4).
Sub-ss (1A), (1B): inserted by the Immigration and Asylum Act 1999, s 169(1), Sch 14, paras 43, 47(1), (3).
Date in force: to be appointed: see the Immigration and Asylum Act 1999, s 170(4).
Sub-s (2): words "this section" in italics repealed and subsequent words in square brackets substituted by the Immigration and Asylum Act 1999, s 169(1), Sch 14, paras 43, 47(1), (4).
Date in force: to be appointed: see the Immigration and Asylum Act 1999, s 170(4).

11 Construction of references to entry, and other phrases relating to travel

(1) A person arriving in the United Kingdom by ship or aircraft shall for purposes of this Act be deemed not to enter the United Kingdom unless and until he disembarks, and on disembarkation at a port shall further be deemed not to enter the United Kingdom so long as he remains in such area (if any) at the port as may be approved for this purpose by an immigration officer; and a person who has not otherwise entered the United Kingdom shall be deemed not to do so as long as he is detained, or temporarily admitted or released while liable to detention, under the powers conferred by Schedule 2 to this Act [or by Part III of the Immigration and Asylum Act 1999].

[(1A) ...]

(2) In this Act "disembark" means disembark from a ship or aircraft, and "embark" means embark in a ship or aircraft; and, except in subsection (1) above,—

    (a) references to disembarking in the United Kingdom do not apply to disembarking after a local journey from a place in the United Kingdom or elsewhere in the common travel area; and
    (b) references to embarking in the United Kingdom do not apply to embarking for a local journey to a place in the United Kingdom or elsewhere in the common travel area.

(3)   Except in so far as the context otherwise requires, references in this Act to arriving in the United Kingdom by ship shall extend to arrival by any floating structure, and "disembark" shall be construed accordingly; but the provisions of this Act specially relating to members of the crew of a ship shall not by virtue of this provision apply in relation to any floating structure not being a ship.

(4)   For purposes of this Act "common travel area" has the meaning given by section 1(3), and a journey is, in relation to the common travel area, a local journey if but only if it begins and ends in the common travel area and is not made by a ship or aircraft which—

(a)   in the case of a journey to a place in the United Kingdom, began its voyage from, or has during its voyage called at, a place not in the common travel area; or

(b)   in the case of a journey from a place in the United Kingdom, is due to end its voyage in, or call in the course of its voyage at, a place not in the common travel area.

(5)   A person who enters the United Kingdom lawfully by virtue of section 8(1) above, and seeks to remain beyond the time limited by section 8(1), shall be treated for purposes of this Act as seeking to enter the United Kingdom.

NOTES

Appointment
Commencement order: SI 1972/1514.

Amendment
Sub-s (1): words "or by Part III of the Immigration and Asylum Act 1999" in square brackets inserted by the Immigration and Asylum Act 1999, s 169(1), Sch 14, paras 43, 48.
Date in force: to be appointed: see the Immigration and Asylum Act 1999, s 170(4).
Sub-s (1A): inserted by SI 1990/2227, art 3, Sch 1, Part I, para 3; repealed by SI 1993/1813, art 9, Sch 6.

Modification
Modified, in relation to France and the United Kingdom, by the Channel Tunnel (International Arrangements) Order 1993, SI 1993/1813, art 7(1), Sch 4, para 1(5).
Modified, in relation to its application to frontier controls between the United Kingdom, France and Belgium, by the Channel Tunnel (Miscellaneous Provisions) Order 1994, SI 1994/1405, art 7.

PART II
APPEALS

NOTES

Amendment
Repealed by the Immigration and Asylum Act 1999, s 169(1), (3), Sch 14, paras 43, 49, Sch 16.
Date in force: 2 October 2000 (for certain purposes): see SI 2000/2444, art 2, Sch 1; for transitional provisions see art 3, Sch 2 thereto.

. . .

NOTES

Amendment
Repealed by the Immigration and Asylum Act 1999, s 169(1), (3), Sch 14, paras 43, 49, Sch 16.
Date in force: 14 February 2000: see SI 2000/168, art 2, Schedule.

12   . . .

. . .

NOTES

Amendment
Repealed by the Immigration and Asylum Act 1999, s 169(1), (3), Sch 14, paras 43, 49, Sch 16.
Date in force: 14 February 2000: see SI 2000/168, art 2, Schedule.

. . .

NOTES

Amendment
Repealed by the Immigration and Asylum Act 1999, s 169(1), (3), Sch 14, paras 43, 49, Sch 16.
Date in force: 2 October 2000 (except in relation to events which took place before that date):
see SI 2000/2444, art 2, Sch 1; for transitional provisions see art 3, Sch 2, para 2 thereof.

13 . . .

. . .

NOTES

Amendment
Repealed by the Immigration and Asylum Act 1999, s 169(1), (3), Sch 14, paras 43, 49, Sch 16.
Date in force: 2 October 2000 (except in relation to events which took place before that date):
see SI 2000/2444, art 2, Sch 1; for transitional provisions see art 3, Sch 2, para 2(4) thereof.

14 . . .

. . .

NOTES

Amendment
Repealed by the Immigration and Asylum Act 1999, s 169(1), (3), Sch 14, paras 43, 49, Sch 16.
Date in force: 2 October 2000 (except in relation to events which took place before that date):
see SI 2000/2444, art 2, Sch 1; for transitional provisions see art 3, Sch 2, para 2(5) thereof
and SI 2000/3099, art 5.

15 . . .

. . .

NOTES

Amendment
Repealed by the Immigration and Asylum Act 1999, s 169(1), (3), Sch 14, paras 43, 49, Sch 16.
Date in force: 2 October 2000 (except in relation to events which took place before that date):
see SI 2000/2444, art 2, Sch 1; for transitional provisions see art 3, Sch 2, para 2(6) thereof.

16 . . .

. . .

NOTES

Amendment
Repealed by the Immigration and Asylum Act 1999, s 169(1), (3), Sch 14, paras 43, 49, Sch 16.
Date in force: 2 October 2000 (except in relation to events which took place before that date):
see SI 2000/2444, art 2, Sch 1; for transitional provisions see art 3, Sch 2, para 2(7) thereof.

17 . . .

. . .

NOTES

Amendment

Repealed by the Immigration and Asylum Act 1999, s 169(1), (3), Sch 14, paras 43, 49, Sch 16. Date in force: 2 October 2000 (except in relation to events which took place before that date): see SI 2000/2444, art 2, Sch 1; for transitional provisions see art 3, Sch 2, para 2(8) thereof.

18 ...

...

NOTES

Amendment

Repealed by the Immigration and Asylum Act 1999, s 169(1), (3), Sch 14, paras 43, 49, Sch 16. Date in force: 2 October 2000 (except in relation to events which took place before that date): see SI 2000/2444, art 2, Sch 1; for transitional provisions see art 3, Sch 2 thereto.

19 ...

...

NOTES

Amendment

Repealed by the Immigration and Asylum Act 1999, s 169(1), (3), Sch 14, paras 43, 49, Sch 16. Date in force: 2 October 2000 (except in relation to events which took place before that date): see SI 2000/2444, art 2, Sch 1; for transitional provisions see art 3, Sch 2 thereto.

...

NOTES

Amendment

Repealed by the Immigration and Asylum Act 1999, s 169(1), (3), Sch 14, paras 43, 49, Sch 16. Date in force: 2 October 2000 (except in relation to events which took place before that date): see SI 2000/2444, art 2, Sch 1; for transitional provisions see art 3, Sch 2, para 2 thereof.

20 ...

...

NOTES

Amendment

Repealed by the Immigration and Asylum Act 1999, s 169(1), (3), Sch 14, paras 43, 49, Sch 16. Date in force: 2 October 2000 (except in relation to events which took place before that date): see SI 2000/2444, art 2, Sch 1; for transitional provisions see art 3, Sch 2 thereto.

21 ...

...

NOTES

Amendment

Repealed by the Immigration and Asylum Act 1999, s 169(1), (3), Sch 14, paras 43, 49, Sch 16. Date in force: 2 October 2000 (except in relation to events which took place before that date): see SI 2000/2444, art 2, Sch 1; for transitional provisions see art 3, Sch 2, para 2(9) thereof.

Supplementary

NOTES

Amendment
Repealed by the Immigration and Asylum Act 1999, s 169(1), (3), Sch 14, paras 43, 49, Sch 16.
Date in force: 2 October 2000 (for certain purposes): see SI 2000/2444, art 2, Sch 1; for
transitional provisions see art 3, Sch 2 thereto.

22 Procedure

(1)   The [Lord Chancellor] may make rules (in this Act referred to as "rules of
procedure")—

    (a)   for regulating the exercise of the rights of appeal conferred by this Part of this Act;

    (b)   for prescribing the practice and procedure to be followed on or in connection
with appeals thereunder, including the mode and burden of proof and
admissibility of evidence on such an appeal; and

    (c)   for other matters preliminary or incidental to or arising out of such appeals,
including proof of the decisions of adjudicators or the Appeal Tribunal.

(2)   Rules of procedure may include provision—

    (a)   enabling the Tribunal, on an appeal from an adjudicator, to remit the appeal to
an adjudicator for determination by him in accordance with any directions of
the Tribunal, or for further evidence to be obtained with a view to determination
by the Tribunal; or

    (b)   enabling any functions of the Tribunal which relate to matters preliminary or
incidental to an appeal, or which are conferred by Part II of Schedule 2 to this
Act, to be performed by a single member of the Tribunal; or

    (c)   conferring on adjudicators or the Tribunal such ancillary powers as the [Lord
Chancellor] thinks necessary for the purposes of the exercise of their functions.

(3)   The rules of procedure shall provide that any appellant shall have the right to be
legally represented.

(4)   Where on an appeal under this Part of this Act it is alleged—

    (a)   that a passport or other travel document, [certificate of entitlement], entry
clearance or work permit (or any part thereof or entry therein) on which a
party relies is a forgery; and

    (b)   that the disclosure to that party of any matters relating to the method of
detection would be contrary to the public interest;

then (without prejudice to the generality of the power to make rules of procedure) the
adjudicator or Tribunal shall arrange for the proceedings to take place in the absence of
that party and his representatives while the allegation at (b) above is inquired into by
the adjudicator or Tribunal and, if it appears to the adjudicator or Tribunal that the
allegation is made out, for such further period as appears necessary in order to ensure
that those matters can be presented to the adjudicator or Tribunal without any disclosure
being directly or indirectly made contrary to the public interest.

(5)   If under the rules of procedure leave to appeal to the Tribunal is required in cases
where an adjudicator dismisses an appeal under section 13 above, then the authority
having power to grant leave to appeal shall grant it—

    (a)   in any case where the appeal was against a decision that the appellant required
leave to enter the United Kingdom, and the authority is satisfied that at the
time of the decision he held a [certificate of entitlement]; and

    (b)   in any case where the appeal was against a refusal of leave to enter, and the
authority is satisfied that at the time of the refusal the appellant held an entry

clearance and that the dismissal of the appeal was not required by section 13(4).

(6)   A person who is required under or in accordance with rules of procedure to attend and give evidence or produce documents before an adjudicator or the Tribunal, and fails without reasonable excuse to comply with the requirement, shall be guilty of an offence and liable on summary conviction to a fine not exceeding [level 3 on the standard scale].

(7)   The power to make rules of procedure shall be exercisable by statutory instrument, which shall be subject to annulment in pursuance of a resolution of either House of Parliament.

NOTES

Appointment
Commencement order: SI 1972/1514.

Amendment
Repealed by the Immigration and Asylum Act 1999, s 169(1), (3), Sch 14, paras 43, 49, Sch 16. Date in force: 2 October 2000 (for certain purposes): see SI 2000/2444, art 2, Sch 1; for transitional provisions see art 3, Sch 2 thereto.
Sub-ss (1), (2): words in square brackets substituted by SI 1987/465, art 3.
Sub-ss (4), (5): words in square brackets substituted by the British Nationality Act 1981, s 39(6), Sch 4, para 3(1).
Sub-s (6): maximum fine increased and converted to a level on the standard scale by virtue of the Criminal Justice Act 1982, ss 37, 38, 46.

Modification
This section has effect as if the Asylum and Immigration Appeals Act 1993, s 8, were contained in this Part: see the Asylum and Immigration Appeals Act 1993, s 8(6), Sch 2.
Sub-ss (1)–(4), (6), (7) have effect as if the Asylum and Immigration Act 1996, s 3, were contained in this Part: see the Asylum and Immigration Act 1996, s 3(4).

Subordinate Legislation
Immigration and Asylum Appeals (Procedure) Rules 2000, SI 2000/2333.

23   ...

...

NOTES

Amendment
Repealed by the Immigration and Asylum Act 1999, s 169(1), (3), Sch 14, paras 43, 49, Sch 16. Date in force: 2 October 2000 (except in relation to events which took place before that date): see SI 2000/2444, art 2, Sch 1; for transitional provisions see art 3, Sch 2 thereto.

PART III
CRIMINAL PROCEEDINGS

24   Illegal entry and similar offences

(1)   A person who is not [a British citizen] shall be guilty of an offence punishable on summary conviction with a fine of not more than [[level 5] on the standard scale] or with imprisonment for not more than six months, or with both, in any of the following cases:—

    (a)   if contrary to this Act he knowingly enters the United Kingdom in breach of a deportation order or without leave;

    [(aa)...]

    (b)   if, having only a limited leave to enter or remain in the United Kingdom, he knowingly either—

      (i)   remains beyond the time limited by the leave; or

      (ii)   fails to observe a condition of the leave;

(c)   if, having lawfully entered the United Kingdom without leave by virtue of section 8(1) above, he remains without leave beyond the time allowed by section 8(1);

(d)   if, without reasonable excuse, he fails to comply with any requirement imposed on him under Schedule 2 to this Act to report to a medical officer of health, or to attend, or submit to a test or examination, as required by such an officer;

(e)   if, without reasonable excuse, he fails to observe any restriction imposed on him under Schedule 2 or 3 to this Act as to residence[, as to his employment or occupation] or as to reporting to the police or to an immigration officer;

(f)   if he disembarks in the United Kingdom from a ship or aircraft after being placed on board under Schedule 2 or 3 to this Act with a view to his removal from the United Kingdom;

(g)   if he embarks in contravention of a restriction imposed by or under an Order in Council under section 3(7) of this Act.

[(1A) A person commits an offence under subsection (1)(b)(i) above on the day when he first knows that the time limited by his leave has expired and continues to commit it throughout any period during which he is in the United Kingdom thereafter; but a person shall not be prosecuted under that provision more than once in respect of the same limited leave.]

(2) ...

(3) The extended time limit for prosecutions which is provided for by section 28 below shall apply to offences under [subsection (1)(a) and (c)] above.

(4) In proceedings for an offence against subsection (1)(a) above of entering the United Kingdom without leave,—

(a)   any stamp purporting to have been imprinted on a passport or other travel document by an immigration officer on a particular date for the purpose of giving leave shall be presumed to have been duly so imprinted, unless the contrary is proved;

(b)   proof that a person had leave to enter the United Kingdom shall lie on the defence if, but only if, he is shown to have entered within six months before the date when the proceedings were commenced.

NOTES

Appointment
Commencement order: SI 1972/1514.

Amendment
Sub-s (1): words "a British citizen" in square brackets substituted by the British Nationality Act 1981, s 39(6), Sch 4, para 2.
Sub-s (1): words "level 5" in square brackets substituted by the Asylum and Immigration Act 1996, s 6.
Sub-s (1): words ending with the words "on the standard scale" in square brackets substituted by virtue of the Criminal Justice Act 1982, ss 37, 38, 46.
Sub-s (1): para (aa) (as originally inserted by the Asylum and Immigration Act 1996, s 4) repealed by the Immigration and Asylum Act 1999, s 169(1), (3), Sch 14, paras 43, 50, Sch 16.
Date in force: 14 February 2000: see SI 2000/168, art 2, Schedule.
Sub-s (1): in para (e) words ", as to his employment or occupation" in square brackets inserted by the Immigration Act 1988, s 10, Schedule, para 10(3), (4).
Sub-s (1A): inserted by the Immigration Act 1988, s 6(1), except in relation to a person whose leave expired before 10 July 1988.
Sub-s (2): repealed by the Immigration and Asylum Act 1999, s 169(1), (3), Sch 14, paras 43, 50, Sch 16.
Date in force: 14 February 2000: see SI 2000/168, art 2, Schedule.

Sub-s (3): words in square brackets substituted by the Immigration Act 1988, s 6(2), except in relation to a person whose leave expired before 10 July 1988.

Modification
Modified, in relation to France and the United Kingdom, by the Channel Tunnel (International Arrangements) Order 1993, SI 1993/1813, art 7(1), Sch 4, para 1(7).
Modified, in relation to its application to frontier controls between the United Kingdom, France and Belgium, by the Channel Tunnel (Miscellaneous Provisions) Order 1994, SI 1994/1405, art 7.

[24A   Deception]

[(1)   A person who is not a British citizen is guilty of an offence if, by means which include deception by him—

   (a)   he obtains or seeks to obtain leave to enter or remain in the United Kingdom; or
   (b)   he secures or seeks to secure the avoidance, postponement or revocation of enforcement action against him.

(2)   "Enforcement action", in relation to a person, means—

   (a)   the giving of directions for his removal from the United Kingdom ("directions") under Schedule 2 to this Act or section 10 of the Immigration and Asylum Act 1999;
   (b)   the making of a deportation order against him under section 5 of this Act; or
   (c)   his removal from the United Kingdom in consequence of directions or a deportation order.

(3)   A person guilty of an offence under this section is liable—

   (a)   on summary conviction, to imprisonment for a term not exceeding six months or to a fine not exceeding the statutory maximum, or to both; or
   (b)   on conviction on indictment, to imprisonment for a term not exceeding two years or to a fine, or to both.

(4)   The extended time limit for prosecutions which is provided for by section 28 applies to an offence under this section.]

NOTES

Amendment
Inserted by the Immigration and Asylum Act 1999, s 28.
Date in force: 14 February 2000: see SI 2000/168, art 2, Schedule.

25   Assisting illegal entry, and harbouring

(1)   Any person knowingly concerned in making or carrying out arrangements for securing or facilitating—

   [(a)   the entry into the United Kingdom of anyone whom he knows or has reasonable cause for believing to be an illegal entrant;
   (b)   the entry into the United Kingdom of anyone whom he knows or has reasonable cause for believing to be an asylum claimant; or
   (c)   the obtaining by anyone of leave to remain in the United Kingdom by means which he knows or has reasonable cause for believing to include deception,]

shall be guilty of an offence, punishable on summary conviction with a fine of not more than [the prescribed sum] or with imprisonment for not more than six months, or with both, or on conviction on indictment with a fine or with imprisonment for not more than [ten] years, or with both.

[(1A)   Nothing in subsection (1)(b) applies to anything done in relation to a person who—

(a) has been detained under paragraph 16 of Schedule 2 to this Act; or

(b) has been granted temporary admission under paragraph 21 of that Schedule.

(1B) Nothing in subsection (1)(b) applies to anything done by a person otherwise than for gain.

(1C) Nothing in subsection (1)(b) applies to anything done to assist an asylum claimant by a person in the course of his employment by a bona fide organisation, if the purposes of that organisation include assistance to persons in the position of the asylum claimant.

(1D) "Asylum claimant" means a person who intends to make a claim that it would be contrary to the United Kingdom's obligations under the Refugee Convention or the Human Rights Convention for him to be removed from, or required to leave, the United Kingdom.

(1E) "Refugee Convention" and "Human Rights Convention" have the meaning given in the Immigration and Asylum Act 1999.]

(2) Without prejudice to subsection (1) above a person knowingly harbouring anyone whom he knows or has reasonable cause for believing to be either an illegal entrant or a person who has committed an offence under section 24(1)(b) or (c) above, shall be guilty of an offence, punishable on summary conviction with a fine of not more than [level 5 on the standard scale] or with imprisonment for not more than six months, or with both.

(3) ...

(4) The extended time limit for prosecutions which is provided for by section 28 below shall apply to offences under this section.

(5) [Paragraphs (a) and (b) of subsection (1)] above shall apply to things done outside as well as to things done in the United Kingdom where they are done—

[(a) by a British citizen, a British Dependent Territories citizen, or a British Overseas citizen;

(b) by a person who under the British Nationality Act 1981 is a British subject; or

(c) by a British protected person (within the meaning of that Act)].

(6) Where a person convicted on indictment of an offence under [subsection (1)(a) or (b)] above is at the time of the offence—

(a) the owner or one of the owners of a ship, aircraft or vehicle used or intended to be used in carrying out the arrangements in respect of which the offence is committed; or

(b) a director or manager of a company which is the owner or one of the owners of any such ship, aircraft or vehicle; or

(c) captain of any such ship or aircraft; [or

(d) the driver of any such vehicle;]

then subject to subsections (7) and (8) below the court before which he is convicted may order the forfeiture of the ship, aircraft or vehicle.

In this subsection (but not in subsection (7) below) "owner" in relation to a ship, aircraft or vehicle which is the subject of a hire-purchase agreement, includes the person in possession of it under that agreement and, in relation to a ship or aircraft, includes a charterer.

(7) A court shall not order a ship or aircraft to be forfeited under subsection (6) above on a person's conviction, unless—

(a) in the case of a ship, it is of less than 500 tons gross tonnage or, in the case of an aircraft (not being a hovercraft), it is of less than 5,700 kilogrammes operating weight; or

(b) the person convicted is at the time of the offence the owner or one of the owners, or a director or manager of a company which is the owner or one of the owners, of the ship or aircraft; or

(c) the ship or aircraft, under the arrangements in respect of which the offence is committed, has been used for bringing more than 20 persons at one time to the United Kingdom as illegal entrants, and the intention to use the ship or aircraft in bringing persons to the United Kingdom as illegal entrants was known to, or could by the exercise of reasonable diligence, have been discovered by, some person on whose conviction the ship or aircraft would have been liable to forfeiture in accordance with paragraph (b) above.

In this subsection "operating weight" means in relation to an aircraft the maximum total weight of the aircraft and its contents at which the aircraft may take off anywhere in the world, in the most favourable circumstances, in accordance with the certificate of airworthiness in force in respect of the aircraft.

(8) A court shall not order a ship, aircraft or vehicle to be forfeited under subsection (6) above, where a person claiming to be the owner of the ship, aircraft or vehicle or otherwise interested in it applies to be heard by the court, unless an opportunity has been given to him to show cause why the order should not be made.

NOTES

Appointment
Commencement order: SI 1972/1514.

Amendment
Sub-s (1): words from "(a) the entry into" to "to include deception," in square brackets substituted by the Asylum and Immigration Act 1996, s 5(1).
Sub-s (1): words "the prescribed sum" in square brackets substituted by virtue of the Magistrates' Courts Act 1980, s 32(2).
Sub-s (1): word "ten" in square brackets substituted by the Immigration and Asylum Act 1999, s 29(1), (2).
Date in force: 14 February 2000: see SI 2000/168, art 2, Schedule.
Sub-ss (1A)–(1E): substituted, for sub-s (1A) (as inserted by the Asylum and Immigration Act 1996, s 5(2)), by the Immigration and Asylum Act 1999, s 29(1), (3).
Date in force: 2 October 2000: see SI 2000/2444, art 2, Sch 1.
Sub-s (2): maximum fine increased and converted to a level on the standard scale by virtue of the Criminal Justice Act 1982, ss 37, 38, 46.
Sub-s (3): repealed by the Immigration and Asylum Act 1999, s 169(1), (3), Sch 14, paras 43, 50, Sch 16.
Date in force: 14 February 2000: see SI 2000/168, art 2, Schedule.
Sub-s (5): words "Paragraphs (a) and (b) of subsection (1)" in square brackets substituted by the Immigration and Asylum Act 1999, s 29(1), (4).
Date in force: 14 February 2000: see SI 2000/168, art 2, Schedule.
Sub-s (5): words from "(a) by a British citizen" to "of that Act)" in square brackets substituted by the British Nationality Act 1981, s 39(6), Sch 4, para 6.
Sub-s (6): words "subsection (1)(a) or (b)" in square brackets substituted by the Asylum and Immigration Act 1996, s 5(4).
Sub-s (6): para (d) inserted by the Immigration and Asylum Act 1999, s 38(1), (3).
Date in force: 3 April 2000 (in relation to offences committed after that date): see SI 2000/464, art 2, Schedule.

Modification
Modified, in relation to France and the United Kingdom, by the Channel Tunnel (International Arrangements) Order 1993, SI 1993/1813, art 7(1), Sch 4, para 1(8).
Modified, in relation to its application to frontier controls between the United Kingdom, France and Belgium, by the Channel Tunnel (Miscellaneous Provisions) Order 1994, SI 1994/1405, art 7.

[25A Detention of ships, aircraft and vehicles in connection with offences under section 25(1)]

[[(1)   If a person has been arrested for an offence under section 25(1)(a) or (b), a senior officer or a constable may detain a relevant ship, aircraft or vehicle—

(a)   until a decision is taken as to whether or not to charge the arrested person with that offence; or

(b)   if the arrested person has been charged—
  (i)   until he is acquitted, the charge against him is dismissed or the proceedings are discontinued; or
  (ii)   if he has been convicted, until the court decides whether or not to order forfeiture of the ship, aircraft or vehicle.

(2)   A ship, aircraft or vehicle is a relevant ship, aircraft or vehicle, in relation to an arrested person, if it is one which the officer or constable concerned has reasonable grounds for believing could, on conviction of the arrested person for the offence for which he was arrested, be the subject of an order for forfeiture made under section 25(6).

(3)   A person (other than the arrested person) who claims to be the owner of a ship, aircraft or vehicle which has been detained under this section may apply to the court for its release.

(4)   The court to which an application is made under subsection (3) may, on such security or surety being tendered as it considers satisfactory, release the ship, aircraft or vehicle on condition that it is made available to the court if—]

(a)   the arrested person is convicted; and

(b)   an order for its forfeiture is made under section 25(6).

(5)   In the application to Scotland of subsection (1), for paragraphs (a) and (b) substitute—

"(a)   until a decision is taken as to whether or not to institute criminal proceedings against the arrested person for that offence; or

(b)   if criminal proceedings have been instituted against the arrested person—
  (i)   until he is acquitted or, under section 65 or 147 of the Criminal Procedure (Scotland) Act 1995, discharged or liberated or the trial diet is deserted simpliciter;
  (ii)   if he has been convicted, until the court decides whether or not to order forfeiture of the ship, aircraft or vehicle,

and for the purposes of this subsection, criminal proceedings are instituted against a person at whichever is the earliest of his first appearance before the sheriff on petition, or the service on him of an indictment or complaint."

(6)   "Court" means—

(a)   in England and Wales—
  (i)   if the arrested person has not been charged, the magistrates' court for the petty sessions area in which he was arrested;
  (ii)   if he has been charged but proceedings for the offence have not begun to be heard, the magistrates' court for the petty sessions area in which he was charged;
  (iii)   if he has been charged and proceedings for the offence are being heard, the court hearing the proceedings;

(b)   in Scotland, the sheriff; and

(c)   in Northern Ireland—
  (i)   if the arrested person has not been charged, the magistrates' court for the county court division in which he was arrested;

    (ii)   if he has been charged but proceedings for the offence have not begun to be heard, the magistrates' court for the county court division in which he was charged;

    (iii) if he has been charged and proceedings for the offence are being heard, the court hearing the proceedings.

(7)   "Owner" has the same meaning as it has in section 25(6).

(8)   "Senior officer" means an immigration officer not below the rank of chief immigration officer.]

NOTES

Amendment
Inserted by the Immigration and Asylum Act 1999, s 38(2), (4).
Date in force: 3 April 2000 (in relation to persons arrested for offences alleged to have been committed after that date): see SI 2000/464, art 2, Schedule.

26   General offences in connection with administration of Act

(1)   A person shall be guilty of an offence punishable on summary conviction with a fine of not more than [[level 5] on the standard scale] or with imprisonment for not more than six months, or with both, in any of the following cases—

    (a)   if, without reasonable excuse, he refuses or fails to submit to examination under Schedule 2 to this Act;

    (b)   if, without reasonable excuse, he refuses or fails to furnish or produce any information in his possession, or any documents in his possession or control, which he is on an examination under that Schedule required to furnish or produce;

    (c)   if on any such examination or otherwise he makes or causes to be made to an immigration officer or other person lawfully acting in the execution of [a relevant enactment] a return, statement or representation which he knows to be false or does not believe to be true;

    (d)   if, without lawful authority, he alters any [certificate of entitlement], entry clearance, work permit or other document issued or made under or for the purposes of this Act, or uses for the purposes of this Act, or has in his possession for such use, any passport, [certificate of entitlement], entry clearance, work permit or other document which he knows or has reasonable cause to believe to be false;

    (e)   if, without reasonable excuse, he fails to complete and produce a landing or embarkation card in accordance with any order under Schedule 2 to this Act;

    (f)   if, without reasonable excuse, he fails to comply with any requirement or regulations under section 4(3) or of an order under section 4(4) above;

    (g)   if, without reasonable excuse, he obstructs an immigration officer or other person lawfully acting in the execution of this Act.

(2)   The extended time limit for prosecutions which is provided for by section 28 below shall apply to offences under subsection (1)(c) and (d) above.

[(3)   "Relevant enactment" means—

    (a)   this Act;

    (b)   the Immigration Act 1988;

    (c)   the Asylum and Immigration Appeals Act 1993 (apart from section 4 or 5); or

    (d)   the Immigration and Asylum Act 1999 (apart from Part VI).]

NOTES

Appointment
Commencement order: SI 1972/1514.

Amendment
Sub-s (1): words ending with "on the standard scale" in square brackets substituted by virtue of the Criminal Justice Act 1982, ss 37, 38, 46.
Sub-s (1): words "level 5" in square brackets substituted by the Asylum and Immigration Act 1996, s 6.
Sub-s (1): in para (c) words "a relevant enactment" in square brackets substituted by the Immigration and Asylum Act 1999, s 30(1), (2).
Date in force: 14 February 2000: see SI 2000/168, art 2, Schedule.
Sub-s (1): in para (d) words "certificate of entitlement" in square brackets, in both places they occur, substituted by the British Nationality Act 1981, s 39(6), Sch 4, para 3(1).
Sub-s (3): inserted by the Immigration and Asylum Act 1999, s 30(1), (3).
Date in force: 14 February 2000: see SI 2000/168, art 2, Schedule.

27 Offences by persons connected with ships or aircraft or with ports

A person shall be guilty of an offence punishable on summary conviction with a fine of not more than [[level 5] on the standard scale] or with imprisonment for not more than six months, or with both, in any of the following cases—

(a) if, being the captain of a ship or aircraft,—
    (i) he knowingly permits a person to disembark in the United Kingdom when required under Schedule 2 or 3 to this Act to prevent it, or fails without reasonable excuse to take any steps he is required by or under Schedule 2 to take in connection with the disembarkation or examination of passengers or for furnishing a passenger list or particulars of members of the crew; or
    (ii) he fails, without reasonable excuse, to comply with any directions given him under Schedule 2 or 3 [or under the Immigration and Asylum Act 1999] with respect to the removal of a person from the United Kingdom;

(b) if, as owner or agent of a ship or aircraft,—
    (i) he arranges, or is knowingly concerned in any arrangements, for the ship or aircraft to call at a port other than a port of entry contrary to any provision of Schedule 2 to this Act; or
    (ii) he fails, without reasonable excuse, to take any steps required by an order under Schedule 2 for the supply to passengers of landing or embarkation cards; or
    (iii) he fails, without reasonable excuse, to make arrangements for [or in connection with] the removal of a person from the United Kingdom when required to do so by directions given under Schedule 2 or 3 to this Act [or under the Immigration and Asylum Act 1999; or
    (iv) he fails, without reasonable excuse, to comply with the requirements of paragraph 27B or 27C of Schedule 2];

(c) if, as owner or agent of a ship or aircraft or as a person concerned in the management of a port, he fails, without reasonable excuse, to take any steps required by Schedule 2 in relation to the embarkation or disembarkation of passengers where a control area is designated.

[(d) . . .]

NOTES

Appointment
Commencement order: SI 1972/1514.

Amendment
Words "level 5" in square brackets substituted by the Asylum and Immigration Act 1996, s 6.

Words ending with the words "on the standard scale" in square brackets substituted by virtue of the Criminal Justice Act 1982, ss 37, 38, 46.

Para (a): in sub-para (ii) words "or under the Immigration and Asylum Act 1999" in square brackets inserted by the Immigration and Asylum Act 1999, s 169(1), Sch 14, paras 43, 52(1), (2). Date in force: 2 October 2000: see SI 2000/2444, art 2, Sch 1.

Para (b): in sub-para (iii) words "or in connection with" in square brackets inserted by the Immigration and Asylum Act 1999, s 169(1), Sch 14, paras 43, 52(1), (3)(a). Date in force: 1 March 2000: see SI 2000/464, art 2, Schedule.

Para (b): words "or under the Immigration and Asylum Act 1999; or" in square brackets and sub-para (iv) inserted by the Immigration and Asylum Act 1999, s 169(1), Sch 14, paras 43, 52(1), (3)(b). Date in force: 3 April 2000: see SI 2000/464, art 2, Schedule.

Para (d): inserted by SI 1990/2227, art 3, Sch 1, Pt I, para 4, repealed by SI 1993/1813, art 9, Sch 6.

Modification
Modified, in relation to France and the United Kingdom, by the Channel Tunnel (International Arrangements) Order 1993, SI 1993/1813, art 7(1), Sch 4, para 1(9).
Modified, in relation to its application to frontier controls between the United Kingdom, France and Belgium, by the Channel Tunnel (Miscellaneous Provisions) Order 1994, SI 1994/1405, art 7.

28   Proceedings

(1)   Where the offence is one to which, under section 24, [24A,] 25 or 26 above, an extended time limit for prosecutions is to apply, then—

   (a)   an information relating to the offence may in England and Wales be tried by a magistrates' court if it is laid within six months after the commission of the offence, or if it is laid within three years after the commission of the offence and not more than two months after the date certified by [an officer of police above the rank of chief superintendent] to be the date on which evidence sufficient to justify proceedings came to the notice of an officer of [the police force to which he belongs]; and

   (b)   . . .

   (c)   a complaint charging the commission of the offence may in Northern Ireland be heard and determined by a magistrates' court if it is made within six months after the commission of the offence, or if it is made within three years after the commission of the offence and not more than two months after the date certified by an officer of police not below the rank of assistant chief constable to be the date on which evidence sufficient to justify the proceedings came to the notice of the police in Northern Ireland.

(2)   . . .

(3)   For the purposes of the trial of a person for an offence under this Part of this Act, the offence shall be deemed to have been committed either at the place at which it actually was committed or at any place at which he may be.

(4)   Any powers exercisable under this Act in the case of any person may be exercised notwithstanding that proceedings for an offence under this Part of this Act have been taken against him.

NOTES

Appointment
Commencement order: SI 1972/1514.

Amendment
Sub-s (1): reference to "24A" in square brackets inserted by the Immigration and Asylum Act 1999, s 169(1), Sch 14, paras 43, 53.
Date in force: 14 February 2000: see SI 2000/168, art 2, Schedule.

Sub-s (1): in para (a) words "an officer of police above the rank of chief superintendent" and "the police force to which he belongs" in square brackets substituted by the Immigration Act 1988, s 10, Schedule, para 4.
Sub-s (1): para (b) applies to Scotland only.
Sub-s (2): applies to Scotland only.

[28A   Arrest without warrant]

[(1)   A constable or immigration officer may arrest without warrant a person—

   (a) who has committed or attempted to commit an offence under section 24 or 24A; or
   (b) whom he has reasonable grounds for suspecting has committed or attempted to commit such an offence.

(2)   But subsection (1) does not apply in relation to an offence under section 24(1)(d).

(3)   An immigration officer may arrest without warrant a person—

   (a) who has committed an offence under section 25(1); or
   (b) whom he has reasonable grounds for suspecting has committed that offence.

(4)   An immigration officer may arrest without warrant a person—

   (a) who has committed or attempted to commit an offence under section 25(2); or
   (b) whom he has reasonable grounds for suspecting has committed or attempted to commit that offence.

(5)   An immigration officer may arrest without warrant a person ("the suspect") who, or whom he has reasonable grounds for suspecting—

   (a) has committed or attempted to commit an offence under section 26(1)(g); or
   (b) is committing or attempting to commit that offence.

(6)   The power conferred by subsection (5) is exercisable only if either the first or the second condition is satisfied.

(7)   The first condition is that it appears to the officer that service of a summons (or, in Scotland, a copy complaint) is impracticable or inappropriate because—

   (a) he does not know, and cannot readily discover, the suspect's name;
   (b) he has reasonable grounds for doubting whether a name given by the suspect as his name is his real name;
   (c) the suspect has failed to give him a satisfactory address for service; or
   (d) he has reasonable grounds for doubting whether an address given by the suspect is a satisfactory address for service.

(8)   The second condition is that the officer has reasonable grounds for believing that arrest is necessary to prevent the suspect—

   (a) causing physical injury to himself or another person;
   (b) suffering physical injury; or
   (c) causing loss of or damage to property.

(9)   For the purposes of subsection (7), an address is a satisfactory address for service if it appears to the officer—

   (a) that the suspect will be at that address for a sufficiently long period for it to be possible to serve him with a summons (or copy complaint); or
   (b) that some other person specified by the suspect will accept service of a summons (or copy complaint) for the suspect at that address.

(10)   In relation to the exercise of the powers conferred by subsections (3)(b), (4)(b) and (5), it is immaterial that no offence has been committed.

(11) In Scotland the powers conferred by subsections (3), (4) and (5) may also be exercised by a constable.]

NOTES

Amendment
Inserted by the Immigration and Asylum Act 1999, s 128.
Date in force: 14 February 2000: see SI 2000/168, art 2, Schedule.

[28B   Search and arrest by warrant]

[(1)   Subsection (2) applies if a justice of the peace is, by written information on oath, satisfied that there are reasonable grounds for suspecting that a person ("the suspect") who is liable to be arrested for a relevant offence is to be found on any premises.

(2)   The justice may grant a warrant authorising any immigration officer or constable to enter, if need be by force, the premises named in the warrant for the purpose of searching for and arresting the suspect.

(3)   Subsection (4) applies if in Scotland the sheriff or a justice of the peace is by evidence on oath satisfied as mentioned in subsection (1).

(4)   The sheriff or justice may grant a warrant authorising any immigration officer or constable to enter, if need be by force, the premises named in the warrant for the purpose of searching for and arresting the suspect.

(5)   "Relevant offence" means an offence under section 24(1)(a), (b), (c), (d), (e) or (f), section 24A or section 25(2).]

NOTES

Amendment
Inserted by the Immigration and Asylum Act 1999, s 129.
Date in force: 14 February 2000: see SI 2000/168, art 2, Schedule.

[28C   Search and arrest without warrant]

[(1)   An immigration officer may enter and search any premises for the purpose of arresting a person for an offence under section 25(1).

(2)   The power may be exercised—

   (a)   only to the extent that it is reasonably required for that purpose; and
   (b)   only if the officer has reasonable grounds for believing that the person whom he is seeking is on the premises.

(3)   In relation to premises consisting of two or more separate dwellings, the power is limited to entering and searching—

   (a)   any parts of the premises which the occupiers of any dwelling comprised in the premises use in common with the occupiers of any such other dwelling; and
   (b)   any such dwelling in which the officer has reasonable grounds for believing that the person whom he is seeking may be.

(4)   The power may be exercised only if the officer produces identification showing that he is an immigration officer (whether or not he is asked to do so).]

NOTES

Amendment
Inserted by the Immigration and Asylum Act 1999, s 130.
Date in force: 14 February 2000: see SI 2000/168, art 2, Schedule.

[28D   Entry and search of premises]

[(1) If, on an application made by an immigration officer, a justice of the peace is satisfied that there are reasonable grounds for believing that—

(a)   a relevant offence has been committed,
(b)   there is material on premises specified in the application which is likely to be of substantial value (whether by itself or together with other material) to the investigation of the offence,
(c)   the material is likely to be relevant evidence,
(d)   the material does not consist of or include items subject to legal privilege, excluded material or special procedure material, and
(e)   any of the conditions specified in subsection (2) applies,

he may issue a warrant authorising an immigration officer to enter and search the premises.

(2)   The conditions are that—

(a)   it is not practicable to communicate with any person entitled to grant entry to the premises;
(b)   it is practicable to communicate with a person entitled to grant entry to the premises but it is not practicable to communicate with any person entitled to grant access to the evidence;
(c)   entry to the premises will not be granted unless a warrant is produced;
(d)   the purpose of a search may be frustrated or seriously prejudiced unless an immigration officer arriving at the premises can secure immediate entry to them.

(3)   An immigration officer may seize and retain anything for which a search has been authorised under subsection (1).

(4)   "Relevant offence" means an offence under section 24(1)(a), (b), (c), (d), (e) or (f), section 24A or section 25.

(5)   In relation to England and Wales, expressions which are given a meaning by the Police and Criminal Evidence Act 1984 have the same meaning when used in this section.

(6)   In relation to Northern Ireland, expressions which are given a meaning by the Police and Criminal Evidence (Northern Ireland) Order 1989 have the same meaning when used in this section

(7)   In the application of subsection (1) to Scotland—

(a)   read the reference to a justice of the peace as a reference to the sheriff or a justice of the peace; and
(b)   in paragraph (b), omit the reference to excluded material and special procedure material.]

NOTES

Amendment
Inserted by the Immigration and Asylum Act 1999, s 131.
Date in force: 14 February 2000: see SI 2000/168, art 2, Schedule.

[28E   Entry and search of premises following arrest]

[[(1) This section applies if a person is arrested for an offence under this Part at a place other than a police station.

(2)   An immigration officer may enter and search any premises—

(a)   in which the person was when arrested, or

(b)   in which he was immediately before he was arrested,

for evidence relating to the offence for which the arrest was made ("relevant evidence").

(3)   The power may be exercised—

(a)   only if the officer has reasonable grounds for believing that there is relevant evidence on the premises; and

(b)   only to the extent that it is reasonably required for the purpose of discovering relevant evidence.

(4)   In relation to premises consisting of two or more separate dwellings, the power is limited to entering and searching—

(a)   any dwelling in which the arrest took place or in which the arrested person was immediately before his arrest; and]

(b)   any parts of the premises which the occupier of any such dwelling uses in common with the occupiers of any other dwellings comprised in the premises.

(5)   An officer searching premises under subsection (2) may seize and retain anything he finds which he has reasonable grounds for believing is relevant evidence.

(6)   Subsection (5) does not apply to items which the officer has reasonable grounds for believing are items subject to legal privilege.]

NOTES

Amendment
Inserted by the Immigration and Asylum Act 1999, s 132(1).
Date in force: 14 February 2000: see SI 2000/168, art 2, Schedule.

[28F   Entry and search of premises following arrest under section 25(1)]

[(1)   An immigration officer may enter and search any premises occupied or controlled by a person arrested for an offence under section 25(1).

(2)   The power may be exercised—

(a)   only if the officer has reasonable grounds for suspecting that there is relevant evidence on the premises;

(b)   only to the extent that it is reasonably required for the purpose of discovering relevant evidence; and

(c)   subject to subsection (3), only if a senior officer has authorised it in writing.

(3)   The power may be exercised—

(a)   before taking the arrested person to a place where he is to be detained; and

(b)   without obtaining an authorisation under subsection (2)(c),

if the presence of that person at a place other than one where he is to be detained is necessary for the effective investigation of the offence.

(4)   An officer who has relied on subsection (3) must inform a senior officer as soon as is practicable.

(5)   The officer authorising a search, or who is informed of one under subsection (4), must make a record in writing of—

(a)   the grounds for the search; and

(b)   the nature of the evidence that was sought.

(6)   An officer searching premises under this section may seize and retain anything he finds which he has reasonable grounds for suspecting is relevant evidence.

(7) "Relevant evidence" means evidence, other than items subject to legal privilege, that relates to the offence in question.

(8) "Senior officer" means an immigration officer not below the rank of chief immigration officer.]

NOTES

Amendment
Inserted by the Immigration and Asylum Act 1999, s 133.
Date in force: 14 February 2000: see SI 2000/168, art 2, Schedule.

[28G   Searching arrested persons]

[(1)   This section applies if a person is arrested for an offence under this Part at a place other than a police station.

(2)   An immigration officer may search the arrested person if he has reasonable grounds for believing that the arrested person may present a danger to himself or others.

(3)   The officer may search the arrested person for—

(a)   anything which he might use to assist his escape from lawful custody; or
(b)   anything which might be evidence relating to the offence for which he has been arrested.

(4)   The power conferred by subsection (3) may be exercised—

(a)   only if the officer has reasonable grounds for believing that the arrested person may have concealed on him anything of a kind mentioned in that subsection; and
(b)   only to the extent that it is reasonably required for the purpose of discovering any such thing.

(5)   A power conferred by this section to search a person is not to be read as authorising an officer to require a person to remove any of his clothing in public other than an outer coat, jacket or glove; but it does authorise the search of a person's mouth.

(6)   An officer searching a person under subsection (2) may seize and retain anything he finds, if he has reasonable grounds for believing that that person might use it to cause physical injury to himself or to another person.

(7)   An officer searching a person under subsection (3) may seize and retain anything he finds, if he has reasonable grounds for believing—

(a)   that that person might use it to assist his escape from lawful custody; or
(b)   that it is evidence which relates to the offence in question.

(8)   Subsection (7)(b) does not apply to an item subject to legal privilege.]

NOTES

Amendment
Inserted by the Immigration and Asylum Act 1999, s 134(1).
Date in force: 14 February 2000: see SI 2000/168, art 2, Schedule.

[28H   Searching persons in police custody]

[(1)   This section applies if a person—

(a)   has been arrested for an offence under this Part; and
(b)   is in custody at a police station or in police detention at a place other than a police station.

(2)   An immigration officer may, at any time, search the arrested person in order to see whether he has with him anything—

    (a)   which he might use to—
        (i)   cause physical injury to himself or others;
        (ii)   damage property;
        (iii) interfere with evidence; or
        (iv) assist his escape; or
    (b)   which the officer has reasonable grounds for believing is evidence relating to the offence in question.

(3)   The power may be exercised only to the extent that the custody officer concerned considers it to be necessary for the purpose of discovering anything of a kind mentioned in subsection (2).

(4)   An officer searching a person under this section may seize anything he finds, if he has reasonable grounds for believing that—

    (a)   that person might use it for one or more of the purposes mentioned in subsection (2)(a); or
    (b)   it is evidence relating to the offence in question.

(5)   Anything seized under subsection (4)(a) may be retained by the police.

(6)   Anything seized under subsection (4)(b) may be retained by an immigration officer.

(7)   The person from whom something is seized must be told the reason for the seizure unless he is—

    (a)   violent or appears likely to become violent; or
    (b)   incapable of understanding what is said to him.

(8)   An intimate search may not be conducted under this section.

(9)   The person carrying out a search under this section must be of the same sex as the person searched.

(10) "Custody officer"—

    (a)   in relation to England and Wales, has the same meaning as in the Police and Criminal Evidence Act 1984;
    (b)   in relation to Scotland, means the officer in charge of a police station; and
    (c)   in relation to Northern Ireland, has the same meaning as in the Police and Criminal Evidence (Northern Ireland) Order 1989.

(11) "Intimate search"—

    (a)   in relation to England and Wales, has the meaning given by section 65 of the Act of 1984;
    (b)   in relation to Scotland, means a search which consists of the physical examination of a person's body orifices other than the mouth; and
    (c)   in relation to Northern Ireland, has the same meaning as in the 1989 Order.

(12) "Police detention"—

    (a)   in relation to England and Wales, has the meaning given by section 118(2) of the 1984 Act; and
    (b)   in relation to Northern Ireland, has the meaning given by Article 2 of the 1989 Order.

(13) In relation to Scotland, a person is in police detention if—

    (a)   he has been taken to a police station after being arrested for an offence; or

(b) he is arrested at a police station after attending voluntarily at the station, accompanying a constable to it or being detained under section 14 of the Criminal Procedure (Scotland) Act 1995,

and is detained there or is detained elsewhere in the charge of a constable, but is not in police detention if he is in court after being charged.]

NOTES

Amendment
Inserted by the Immigration and Asylum Act 1999, s 135(1).
Date in force: 14 February 2000: see SI 2000/168, art 2, Schedule.

[28I Seized material: access and copying]

[(1) If a person showing himself—

(a) to be the occupier of the premises on which seized material was seized, or
(b) to have had custody or control of the material immediately before it was seized,

asks the immigration officer who seized the material for a record of what he seized, the officer must provide the record to that person within a reasonable time.

(2) If a relevant person asks an immigration officer for permission to be granted access to seized material, the officer must arrange for him to have access to the material under the supervision—

(a) in the case of seized material within subsection (8)(a), of an immigration officer;
(b) in the case of seized material within subsection (8)(b), of a constable.

(3) An immigration officer may photograph or copy, or have photographed or copied, seized material.

(4) If a relevant person asks an immigration officer for a photograph or copy of seized material, the officer must arrange for—

(a) that person to have access to the material for the purpose of photographing or copying it under the supervision—
   (i) in the case of seized material within subsection (8)(a), of an immigration officer;
   (ii) in the case of seized material within subsection (8)(b), of a constable; or
(b) the material to be photographed or copied.

(5) A photograph or copy made under subsection (4)(b) must be supplied within a reasonable time.

(6) There is no duty under this section to arrange for access to, or the supply of a photograph or copy of, any material if there are reasonable grounds for believing that to do so would prejudice—

(a) the exercise of any functions in connection with which the material was seized; or
(b) an investigation which is being conducted under this Act, or any criminal proceedings which may be brought as a result.

(7) "Relevant person" means—

(a) a person who had custody or control of seized material immediately before it was seized, or
(b) someone acting on behalf of such a person.

(8) "Seized material" means anything—

(a)   seized and retained by an immigration officer, or

(b)   seized by an immigration officer and retained by the police,

under this Part.]

NOTES

Amendment
Inserted by the Immigration and Asylum Act 1999, s 136(1).
Date in force: 14 February 2000: see SI 2000/168, art 2, Schedule.

[28J Search warrants: safeguards]

[(1)   The entry or search of premises under a warrant is unlawful unless it complies with this section and section 28K.

(2)   If an immigration officer applies for a warrant, he must—

(a)   state the ground on which he makes the application and the provision of this Act under which the warrant would be issued;

(b)   specify the premises which it is desired to enter and search; and

(c)   identify, so far as is practicable, the persons or articles to be sought.

(3)   In Northern Ireland, an application for a warrant is to be supported by a complaint in writing and substantiated on oath.

(4)   Otherwise, an application for a warrant is to be made ex parte and supported by an information in writing or, in Scotland, evidence on oath.

(5)   The officer must answer on oath any question that the justice of the peace or sheriff hearing the application asks him.

(6)   A warrant shall authorise an entry on one occasion only.

(7)   A warrant must specify—

(a)   the name of the person applying for it;

(b)   the date on which it is issued;

(c)   the premises to be searched; and

(d)   the provision of this Act under which it is issued.

(8)   A warrant must identify, so far as is practicable, the persons or articles to be sought.

(9)   Two copies of a warrant must be made.

(10)   The copies must be clearly certified as copies.

(11)   "Warrant" means a warrant to enter and search premises issued to an immigration officer under this Part or under paragraph 17(2) of Schedule 2.]

NOTES

Amendment
Inserted by the Immigration and Asylum Act 1999, s 137.
Date in force: 14 February 2000: see SI 2000/168, art 2, Schedule.

[28K   Execution of warrants]

[[(1) A warrant may be executed by any immigration officer.

(2)   A warrant may authorise persons to accompany the officer executing it.

(3)   Entry and search under a warrant must be—

(a)   within one month from the date of its issue; and

(b) at a reasonable hour, unless it appears to the officer executing it that the purpose of a search might be frustrated.

(4) If the occupier of premises which are to be entered and searched is present at the time when an immigration officer seeks to execute a warrant, the officer must—

(a) identify himself to the occupier and produce identification showing that he is an immigration officer;
(b) show the occupier the warrant; and
(c) supply him with a copy of it.]

(5) If—

(a) the occupier is not present, but
(b) some other person who appears to the officer to be in charge of the premises is present,

subsection (4) has effect as if each reference to the occupier were a reference to that other person.

(6) If there is no person present who appears to the officer to be in charge of the premises, the officer must leave a copy of the warrant in a prominent place on the premises.

(7) A search under a warrant may only be a search to the extent required for the purpose for which the warrant was issued.

(8) An officer executing a warrant must make an endorsement on it stating—

(a) whether the persons or articles sought were found; and
(b) whether any articles, other than articles which were sought, were seized.

(9) A warrant which has been executed, or has not been executed within the time authorised for its execution, must be returned—

(a) if issued by a justice of the peace in England and Wales, to the justices' chief executive appointed by the magistrates' court committee whose area includes the petty sessions area for which the justice acts;
(b) if issued by a justice of the peace in Northern Ireland, to the clerk of petty sessions for the petty sessions district in which the premises are situated;
(c) if issued by a justice of the peace in Scotland, to the clerk of the district court for the commission area for which the justice of the peace was appointed;
(d) if issued by the sheriff, to the sheriff clerk.

(10) A warrant returned under subsection (9)(a) must be retained for 12 months by the justices' chief executive.

(11) A warrant issued under subsection (9)(b) or (c) must be retained for 12 months by the clerk.

(12) A warrant returned under subsection (9)(d) must be retained for 12 months by the sheriff clerk.

(13) If during that 12 month period the occupier of the premises to which it relates asks to inspect it, he must be allowed to do so.

(14) "Warrant" means a warrant to enter and search premises issued to an immigration officer under this Part or under paragraph 17(2) of Schedule 2.]

NOTES

Amendment
Inserted by the Immigration and Asylum Act 1999, s 138; for transitional provisions see Sch 15, para 4(b) thereto.
Date in force: 14 February 2000: see SI 2000/168, art 2, Schedule.

[28L   Interpretation of Part III]

[In this Part, "premises" and "items subject to legal privilege" have the same meaning—

    (a)   in relation to England and Wales, as in the Police and Criminal Evidence Act 1984;

    (b)   in relation to Northern Ireland, as in the Police and Criminal Evidence (Northern Ireland) Order 1989"; and

    (c)   in relation to Scotland, as in section 33 of the Criminal Law (Consolidation) (Scotland) Act 1995.]

NOTES

Amendment
Inserted by the Immigration and Asylum Act 1999, s 139(1).
Date in force: 14 February 2000: see SI 2000/168, art 2, Schedule.

PART IV
SUPPLEMENTARY

29   Contributions for expenses of persons returning abroad

(1)   The Secretary of State may, in such cases as he may with the approval of the Treasury determine, make payments of such amount as may be so determined to meet or provide for expenses of persons who are not [British citizens] in leaving the United Kingdom for a country or territory where they intend to reside permanently, including travelling expenses for members of their families or households.

(2)   The Secretary of State shall, so far as practicable, administer this section so as to secure that a person's expenses in leaving the United Kingdom are not met by or out of a payment made by the Secretary of State unless it is shown that it is in that person's interest to leave the United Kingdom and that he wishes to do so.

NOTES

Amendment
Sub-s (1): words in square brackets substituted by the British Nationality Act 1981, s 39(6), Sch 4, para 2.

31   Expenses

There shall be defrayed out of moneys provided by Parliament any expenses incurred [by the Lord Chancellor under Schedule 5 to this Act or] by a Secretary of State under or by virtue of this Act—

    (a)   by way of administrative expenses . . . ; or

    (b)   in connection with the removal of any person from the United Kingdom under Schedule 2 or 3 to this Act or the departure with him of his dependants, or his or their maintenance pending departure; or

    (c)   . . .

    (d)   on the making of any grants or payments under section 23 or 29 above.

NOTES

Amendment
Words in square brackets inserted, and para (c) repealed, by SI 1987/465, art 3(4); words omitted from para (a) repealed by the British Nationality Act 1981, s 52(8), Sch 9.

[31A   Procedural requirements as to applications]

[(1)   If a form is prescribed for a particular kind of application under this Act, any application of that kind must be made in the prescribed form.

(2) If procedural or other steps are prescribed in relation to a particular kind of application under this Act, those steps must be taken in respect of any application of that kind.

(3) "Prescribed" means prescribed in regulations made by the Secretary of State.

(4) The power to make regulations under this section is exercisable by statutory instrument.

(5) Any such statutory instrument shall be subject to annulment in pursuance of a resolution of either House of Parliament.]

NOTES

Amendment
Inserted by the Immigration and Asylum Act 1999, s 165.
Date in force (for the purpose of enabling subordinate legislation to be made): 22 May 2000: see SI 2000/1282, art 2, Schedule.
Date in force (for remaining purposes): to be appointed: see the Immigration and Asylum Act 1999, s 170(4).

32   General provisions as to Orders in Council, etc

(1) Any power conferred by Part I of this Act to make an Order in Council or order (other than a deportation order) or to give any directions includes power to revoke or vary the Order in Council, order or directions.

(2) Any document purporting to be an order, notice or direction made or given by the Secretary of State for the purposes of [the Immigration Acts] and to be signed by him or on his behalf, and any document purporting to be a certificate of the Secretary of State so given and to be signed by him [or on his behalf], shall be received in evidence, and shall, until the contrary is proved, be deemed to be made or issued by him.

(3) Prima facie evidence of any such order, notice, direction or certificate as aforesaid may, in any legal proceedings or [other proceedings under the Immigration Acts], be given by the production of a document bearing a certificate purporting to be signed by or on behalf of the Secretary of State and stating that the document is a true copy of the order, notice, direction or certificate.

(4) Where an order under section 8(2) above applies to persons specified in a schedule to the order, or any directions of the Secretary of State given for the purposes of [the Immigration Acts] apply to persons specified in a schedule to the directions, prima facie evidence of the provisions of the order or directions other than the prima facie evidence of the provisions of the order or directions other than the schedule and of any entry contained in the schedule may, in any legal proceedings or [other proceedings under the Immigration Acts], be given by the production of a document purporting to be signed by or on behalf of the Secretary of State and stating that the document is a true copy of the said provisions and of the relevant entry.

[(5) "Immigration Acts" has the same meaning as in the Immigration and Asylum Act 1999.]

NOTES

Amendment
Sub-s (2): words "the Immigration Acts" in square brackets substituted by the Immigration and Asylum Act 1999, s 169(1), Sch 14, paras 43, 54(1), (2)(a); for the application of this amendment see para 54(6) thereto.
Date in force: 6 December 1999: see SI 1999/3190, art 2, Schedule.
Sub-s (2): words "or on his behalf" in square brackets inserted by the Immigration and Asylum Act 1999, s 169(1), Sch 14, paras 43, 54(1), (2)(b).

Date in force: 6 December 1999: see SI 1999/3190, art 2, Schedule.
Sub-s (3): words "other proceedings under the Immigration Acts" in square brackets substituted by the Immigration and Asylum Act 1999, s 169(1), Sch 14, paras 43, 54(1), (3).
Date in force: 6 December 1999: see SI 1999/3190, art 2, Schedule.
Sub-s (4): words "the Immigration Acts" and "other proceedings under the Immigration Acts" in square brackets substituted by the Immigration and Asylum Act 1999, s 169(1), Sch 14, paras 43, 54(1), (4).
Date in force: 6 December 1999: see SI 1999/3190, art 2, Schedule.
Sub-s (5): inserted by the Immigration and Asylum Act 1999, s 169(1), Sch 14, paras 43, 54(1), (5); for the application of this amendment see para 54(6) thereto.
Date in force: 6 December 1999: see SI 1999/3190, art 2, Schedule.

Subordinate Legislation
Immigration (Control of Entry through Republic of Ireland) (Amendment) Order 2000, SI 2000/1776 (made under sub-s (1)).

33   Interpretation

(1)   For purposes of this Act, except in so far as the context otherwise requires—
"aircraft" includes hovercraft, "airport" includes hoverport and "port" includes airport;
"captain" means master (of a ship) or commander (of an aircraft);
"certificate of [entitlement]" means such a certificate as is referred to in section 3(9) above;
["Convention adoption" has the same meaning as in the Adoption Act 1976 and the Adoption (Scotland) Act 1978;]
[...]
"crew", in relation to a ship or aircraft, means all persons actually employed in the working or service of the ship or aircraft, including the captain, and "member of the crew" shall be construed accordingly;
["entrant" means a person entering or seeking to enter the United Kingdom and "illegal entrant" means a person—
(a)   unlawfully entering or seeking to enter in breach of a deportation order or of the immigration laws, or
(b)   entering or seeking to enter by means which include deception by another person,
and includes also a person who has entered as mentioned in paragraph (a) or (b) above;]
"entry clearance" means a visa, entry certificate or other document which, in accordance with the immigration rules, is to be taken as evidence [or the requisite evidence] of a person's eligibility, though not [a British citizen], for entry into the United Kingdom (but does not include a work permit);
"immigration laws" means this Act and any law for purposes similar to this Act which is for the time being or has (before or after the passing of this Act) been in force in any part of the United Kingdom and Islands;
"immigration rules" means the rules for the time being laid down as mentioned in section 3(2) above;
"the Islands" means the Channel Islands and the Isle of Man, and "the United Kingdom and Islands" means the United Kingdom and the Islands taken together;
"legally adopted" means adopted in pursuance of an order made by any court in the United Kingdom and Islands[, under a Convention adoption] or by any adoption specified as an overseas adoption by order of the Secretary of State under [section 72(2) of the Adoption Act 1976];
"limited leave" and "indefinite leave" mean respectively leave under this Act to enter or remain in the United Kingdom which is, and one which is not, limited as to duration;
"settled" shall be construed in accordance [with subsection (2A) below];
"ship" includes every description of vessel used in navigation;

[. . .]

["United Kingdom passport" means a current passport issued by the Government of the United Kingdom, or by the Lieutenant-Governor of any of the Islands or by the Government of any territory which is for the time being a dependent territory within the meaning of the British Nationality Act 1981;]
"work permit" means a permit indicating, in accordance with the immigration rules, that a person named in it is eligible, though not [a British citizen], for entry into the United Kingdom for the purpose of taking employment.

(2)   It is hereby declared that, except as otherwise provided in this Act, a person is not to be treated for the purposes of any provision of this Act as ordinarily resident in the United Kingdom or in any of the Islands at a time when he is there in breach of the immigration laws.

[(2A)   Subject to section 8(5) above, references to a person being settled in the United Kingdom are references to his being ordinarily resident there without being subject under the immigration laws to any restriction on the period for which he may remain.]

(3)   The ports of entry for purposes of this Act, and the ports of exit for purposes of any Order in Council under section 3(7) above, shall be such ports as may from time to time be designated for the purpose by order of the Secretary of State made by statutory instrument.

[(4) For the purposes of this Act, the question of whether an appeal is pending shall be determined—

(a)   in relation to an appeal to the Special Immigration Appeals Commission, in accordance with section 7A of the Special Immigration Appeals Commission Act 1997;
(b)   in any other case, in accordance with section 58(5) to (10) of the Immigration and Asylum Act 1999.]

(5)   This Act shall not be taken to supersede or impair any power exercisable by Her Majesty in relation to aliens by virtue of Her prerogative.

NOTES

Amendment
Sub-s (1): in definition "certificate of entitlement" word "entitlement" in square brackets substituted by the British Nationality Act 1981, s 39(6), Sch 4, para 2.
Sub-s (1): definition "Convention adoption" inserted by the Adoption (Intercountry Aspects) Act 1999, s 15(1), Sch 2, para 2(a).
Date in force: to be appointed: see the Adoption (Intercountry Aspects) Act 1999, s 18(3).
Sub-s (1): definitions omitted inserted by SI 1990/2227, art 3, Sch 1, Pt I, repealed by SI 1993/1813, art 9, Sch 6.
Sub-s (1): definitions "entrant" and "illegal entrant" substituted by the Asylum and Immigration Act 1996, s 12(1), Sch 2, para 4(1).
Sub-s (1): in definition "entry clearance" words "or the requisite evidence" in square brackets inserted by the Immigration Act 1988, s 10, Schedule, para 5.
Sub-s (1): in definition "entry clearance" words "a British citizen" in square brackets substituted by the British Nationality Act 1981, s 39(6), Sch 4, para 2.
Sub-s (1): in definition "legally adopted" words ", under a Convention adoption" in square brackets inserted by the Adoption (Intercountry Aspects) Act 1999, s 15(1), Sch 2, para 2(b).
Date in force: to be appointed: see the Adoption (Intercountry Aspects) Act 1999, s 18(3).
Sub-s (1): in definition "legally adopted" words "section 72(2) of the Adoption Act 1976" in square brackets substituted by the Adoption Act 1976, s 73(2), Sch 6, para 17.
Sub-s (1): in definition "settled" words "with subsection (2A) below" in square brackets substituted by the British Nationality Act 1981, s 39(6), Sch 4, para 3.
Sub-s (1): definition "United Kingdom passport" inserted by the British Nationality Act 1981, s 39(6), Sch 4, para 7.
Sub-s (1): in definition "work permit" words "a British citizen" in square brackets substituted by the British Nationality Act 1981, s 39(6), Sch 4, para 7.

Sub-s (2A): inserted by the British Nationality Act 1981, s 39(6), Sch 4, para 7.
Sub-s (4): substituted by the Immigration and Asylum Act 1999, s 169(1), Sch 14, paras 43, 55.
Date in force: 2 October 2000: see SI 2000/2444, art 2, Sch 1.

Modification
Modified, in relation to France and the United Kingdom, by the Channel Tunnel (International Arrangements) Order 1993, SI 1993/1813, art 7(1), Sch 4, para 1(10).
Modified, in relation to its application to frontier controls between the United Kingdom, France and Belgium, by the Channel Tunnel (Miscellaneous Provisions) Order 1994, SI 1994/1405, art 7.

34   Repeal, transitional and temporary

(1)   Subject to the following provisions of this section, the enactments mentioned in Schedule 6 to this Act are hereby repealed, as from the coming into force of this Act, to the extent mentioned in column 3 of the Schedule; and—

(a)   this Act, as from its coming into force, shall apply in relation to entrants or others arriving in the United Kingdom at whatever date before or after it comes into force; and

(b)   after this Act comes into force anything done under or for the purposes of the former immigration laws shall have effect, in so far as any corresponding action could be taken under or for the purposes of this Act, as if done by way of action so taken, and in relation to anything so done this Act shall apply accordingly.

(2)   Without prejudice to the generality of subsection (1)(a) and (b) above, a person refused leave to land by virtue of the Aliens Restriction Act 1914 shall be treated as having been refused leave to enter under this Act, and a person given leave to land by virtue of that Act shall be treated as having been given leave to enter under this Act; and similarly with the Commonwealth Immigrants Acts 1962 and 1968.

(3)   A person treated in accordance with subsection (2) above as having leave to enter the United Kingdom—

(a)   shall be treated as having an indefinite leave, if he is not at the coming into force of this Act subject to a condition limiting his stay in the United Kingdom; and

(b)   shall be treated, if he is then subject to such a condition, as having a limited leave of such duration, and subject to such conditions (capable of being attached to leave under this Act), as correspond to the conditions to which he is then subject, but not to conditions not capable of being so attached.
   This subsection shall have effect in relation to any restriction or requirement imposed by Order in Council under the Aliens Restriction Act 1914 as if it had been imposed by way of a landing condition.

(4)   Notwithstanding anything in the foregoing provisions of this Act, the former immigration laws shall continue to apply, and this Act shall not apply,—

(a)   in relation to the making of deportation orders and matters connected therewith in any case where a decision to make the order has been notified to the person concerned before the coming into force of this Act;

(b)   in relation to removal from the United Kingdom and matters connected therewith (including detention pending removal or pending the giving of directions for removal) in any case where a person is to be removed in pursuance of a decision taken before the coming into force of this Act or in pursuance of a deportation order to the making of which paragraph (a) above applies;

(c)   in relation to appeals against any decision taken or other thing done under the former immigration laws, whether taken or done before the coming into force of this Act or by virtue of this subsection.

(5)   Subsection (1) above shall not be taken as empowering a court on appeal to recommend for deportation a person whom the court below could not recommend for

deportation, or as affecting any right of appeal in respect of a recommendation for deportation made before this Act comes into force, or as enabling a notice given before this Act comes into force and not complying with section 6(2) to take the place of the notice required by section 6(2) to be given before a person is recommended for deportation.

(6) ...

NOTES

Amendment
Sub-s (6): repealed by the Statute Law (Repeals) Act 1993.

35 Commencement, and interim provisions

(1) Except as otherwise provided by this Act, Parts I to III of this Act shall come into force on such day as the Secretary of State may appoint by order made by statutory instrument; and references to the coming into force of this Act shall be construed as references to the beginning of the day so appointed.

(2) Section 25 above, except section 25(2), and section 28 in its application to offences under section 25(1) shall come into force at the end of one month beginning with the date this Act is passed.

(3)–(5) ...

NOTES

Amendment
Sub-ss (3)–(5): repealed by the Statute Law (Repeals) Act 1986.

36 Power to extend to Islands

Her Majesty may by Order in Council direct that any of the provisions of this Act shall extend, with such exceptions, adaptations and modifications, if any, as may be specified in the Order, to any of the Islands; and any Order in Council under this subsection may be varied or revoked by a further Order in Council.

37 Short title and extent

(1) This Act may be cited as the Immigration Act 1971.

(2) It is hereby declared that this Act extends to Northern Ireland, and (without prejudice to any provision of Schedule 1 to this Act as to the extent of that Schedule) where an enactment repealed by this Act extends outside the United Kingdom, the repeal shall be of like extent.

SCHEDULE 2
Administrative Provisions as to Control on Entry etc

Section 4

PART I
GENERAL PROVISIONS

Immigration officers and medical inspectors

1   (1) Immigration officers for the purposes of this Act shall be appointed by the Secretary of State, and he may arrange with the Commissioners of Customs and Excise for the employment of officers of customs and excise as immigration officers under this Act.

(2)   Medical inspectors for the purposes of this Act may be appointed by the Secretary of State or, in Northern Ireland, by the Minister of Health and Social Services or other appropriate Minister of the Government of Northern Ireland in pursuance of arrangements made between that Minister and the Secretary of State, and shall be fully qualified medical practitioners.

(3)   In the exercise of their functions under this Act immigration officers shall act in accordance with such instructions (not inconsistent with the immigration rules) as may be given them by the Secretary of State, and medical inspectors shall act in accordance with such instructions as may be given them by the Secretary of State or, in Northern Ireland, as may be given in pursuance of the arrangements mentioned in sub-paragraph (2) above by the Minister making appointments of medical inspectors in Northern Ireland.

(4)   An immigration officer or medical inspector may board any ship [or aircraft] for the purpose of exercising his functions under this Act.

(5)   An immigration officer, for the purpose of satisfying himself whether there are persons he may wish to examine under paragraph 2 below, may search any ship [or aircraft] and anything on board it, or any vehicle taken off a ship or aircraft in which it has been brought to the United Kingdom.

Examination by immigration officers, and medical examination

2   (1)   An immigration officer may examine any persons who have arrived in the United Kingdom by ship [or aircraft] (including transit passengers, members of the crew and others not seeking to enter the United Kingdom) for the purpose of determining—

  (a)   whether any of them is or is not [a British citizen]; and
  (b)   whether, if he is not, he may or may not enter the United Kingdom without leave; and
  [(c)   whether, if he may not—
     (i)   he has been given leave which is still in force,
     (ii)   he should be given leave and for what period or on what conditions (if any), or
     (iii) he should be refused leave].

(2)   Any such person, if he is seeking to enter the United Kingdom, may be examined also by a medical inspector or by any qualified person carrying out a test or examination required by a medical inspector.

(3)   A person, on being examined under this paragraph by an immigration officer or medical inspector, may be required in writing by him to submit to further examination; but a requirement under this sub-paragraph shall not prevent a person who arrives as a transit passenger, or as a member of the crew of a ship or aircraft, or for the purpose of joining a ship or aircraft as a member of the crew, from leaving by his intended ship or aircraft.

[Examination of persons who arrive with continuing leave

2A   (1)   This paragraph applies to a person who has arrived in the United Kingdom with leave to enter which is in force but which was given to him before his arrival.

(2)   He may be examined by an immigration officer for the purpose of establishing—

  (a)   whether there has been such a change in the circumstances of his case, since that leave was given, that it should be cancelled;
  (b)   whether that leave was obtained as a result of false information given by him or his failure to disclose material facts; or
  (c)   whether there are medical grounds on which that leave should be cancelled.

(3)   He may also be examined by an immigration officer for the purpose of determining whether it would be conducive to the public good for that leave to be cancelled.

(4)   He may also be examined by a medical inspector or by any qualified person carrying out a test or examination required by a medical inspector.

(5)   A person examined under this paragraph may be required by the officer or inspector to submit to further examination.

(6)   A requirement under sub-paragraph (5) does not prevent a person who arrives—

(a)   as a transit passenger,
(b)   as a member of the crew of a ship or aircraft, or
(c)   for the purpose of joining a ship or aircraft as a member of the crew,

from leaving by his intended ship or aircraft.

(7)   An immigration officer examining a person under this paragraph may by notice suspend his leave to enter until the examination is completed.

(8)   An immigration officer may, on the completion of any examination of a person under this paragraph, cancel his leave to enter.

(9)   Cancellation of a person's leave under sub-paragraph (8) is to be treated for the purposes of this Act and Part IV of the Immigration and Asylum Act 1999 as if he had been refused leave to enter at a time when he had a current entry clearance.

(10) A requirement imposed under sub-paragraph (5) and a notice given under sub-paragraph (7) must be in writing.]

3   (1) An immigration officer may examine any person who is embarking or seeking to embark in the United Kingdom [. . .] for the purpose of determining whether he is [a British citizen] and, if he is not, for the purpose of establishing his identity.

(2)   So long as any Order in Council is in force under section 3(7) of this Act, an immigration officer may examine any person who is embarking or seeking to embark in the United Kingdom [. . .] for the purpose of determining—

(a)   whether any of the provisions of the Order apply to him; and
(b)   whether, if so, any power conferred by the Order should be exercised in relation to him and in what way.

Information and documents

4   (1) It shall be the duty of any person examined under paragraph 2[, 2A] or 3 above to furnish to the person carrying out the examination all such information in his possession as that person may require for the purpose of his functions under that paragraph.

(2)   A person on his examination under paragraph 2[, 2A] or 3 above by an immigration officer shall, if so required by the immigration officer—

(a)   produce either a valid passport with photograph or some other document satisfactorily establishing his identity and nationality or citizenship; and
(b)   declare whether or not he is carrying or conveying[, or has carried or conveyed,] documents of any relevant description specified by the immigration officer, and produce any documents of that description which he is carrying or conveying.
In paragraph (b), "relevant description" means any description appearing to the immigration officer to be relevant for the purposes of the examination.

[(2A)   An immigration officer may detain any passport or other document produced pursuant to sub-paragraph (2)(a) above until the person concerned is given leave to enter the United Kingdom or is about to depart or be removed following refusal of leave.]

(3) Where under sub-paragraph (2)(b) above a person has been required to declare whether or not he is carrying or conveying[, or has carried or conveyed,] documents of any description—

> [(a) he and any baggage or vehicle belonging to him or under his control; and
> (b) any ship, aircraft or vehicle in which he arrived in the United Kingdom,]

may be searched with a view to ascertaining whether he is doing [or, as the case may be, has done] so by the immigration officer or a person acting under the directions of that officer:
> Provided that no woman or girl shall be searched except by a woman.

(4) An immigration officer may examine any documents produced pursuant to sub-paragraph (2)(b) above or found on a search under sub-paragraph (3), and may for that purpose detain them for any period not exceeding seven days; and if on examination of any document so produced or found the immigration officer is of the opinion that it may be needed in connection with proceedings on an appeal under this Act or for an offence, he may detain it until he is satisfied that it will not be so needed.

5   The Secretary of State may by order made by statutory instrument make provision for requiring passengers disembarking or embarking in the United Kingdom, or any class of such passengers, to produce to an immigration officer, if so required, landing or embarkation cards in such form as the Secretary of State may direct, and for requiring the owners or agents of ships and aircraft to supply such cards to those passengers.

Notice of leave to enter or of refusal of leave

6   (1) Subject to sub-paragraph (3) below, where a person examined by an immigration officer under paragraph 2 above is to be given a limited leave to enter the United Kingdom or is to be refused leave, the notice giving or refusing leave shall be given not later than [twenty-four hours] after the conclusion of his examination (including any further examination) in pursuance of that paragraph; and if notice giving or refusing leave is not given him before the end of those [twenty-four hours], he shall (if not [a British citizen]) be deemed to have been given [leave to enter the United Kingdom for a period of six months subject to a condition prohibiting his taking employment] and the immigration officer shall as soon as may be give him written notice of that leave.

(2) Where on a person's examination under paragraph 2 above he is given notice of leave to enter the United Kingdom, then at any time before the end of [twenty-four hours] from the conclusion of the examination he may be given a further notice in writing by an immigration officer cancelling the earlier notice and refusing him leave to enter.

(3) Where in accordance with this paragraph a person is given notice refusing him leave to enter the United Kingdom, that notice may at any time be cancelled by notice in writing given by an immigration officer; and where a person is given a notice of cancellation under this sub-paragraph, [and the immigration officer does not at the same time give him indefinite or limited leave to enter, he shall be deemed to have been given leave to enter for a period of six months subject to a condition prohibiting his taking employment and the immigration officer shall as soon as may be give him written notice of that leave.]

(4) Where an entrant is a member of a party in charge of a person appearing to the immigration officer to be a responsible person, any notice to be given in relation to that entrant in accordance with this paragraph shall be duly given if delivered to the person in charge of the party.

[Power to require medical examination after entry

7 (1) This paragraph applies if an immigration officer examining a person under paragraph 2 decides—

(a) that he may be given leave to enter the United Kingdom; but
(b) that a further medical test or examination may be required in the interests of public health.

(2) This paragraph also applies if an immigration officer examining a person under paragraph 2A decides—

(a) that his leave to enter the United Kingdom should not be cancelled; but
(b) that a further medical test or examination may be required in the interests of public health.

(3) The immigration officer may give the person concerned notice in writing requiring him—

(a) to report his arrival to such medical officer of health as may be specified in the notice; and
(b) to attend at such place and time and submit to such test or examination (if any), as that medical officer of health may require.

(4) In reaching a decision under paragraph (b) of sub-paragraph (1) or (2), the immigration officer must act on the advice of—

(a) a medical inspector; or
(b) if no medical inspector is available, a fully qualified medical practitioner.]

Removal of persons refused leave to enter and illegal entrants

8 (1) Where a person arriving in the United Kingdom is refused leave to enter, an immigration officer may, subject to sub-paragraph (2) below—

(a) give the captain of the ship or aircraft in which he arrives directions requiring the captain to remove him from the United Kingdom in that ship or aircraft; or
(b) give the owners or agents of that ship or aircraft directions requiring them to remove him from the United Kingdom in any ship or aircraft specified or indicated in the directions, being a ship or aircraft of which they are the owners or agents; or
(c) give those owners or agents [. . .] directions requiring them to make arrangements for his removal from the United Kingdom in any ship or aircraft specified or indicated in the direction to a country or territory so specified being either—
   (i) a country of which he is a national or citizen; or
   (ii) a country or territory in which he has obtained a passport or other document of identity; or
   (iii) a country or territory in which he embarked for the United Kingdom; or
   (iv) a country or territory to which there is reason to believe that he will be admitted.

(2) No directions shall be given under this paragraph in respect of anyone after the expiration of two months beginning with the date on which he was refused leave to enter the United Kingdom [except that directions may be given under sub-paragraph (1)(b) or (c) after the end of that period if the immigration officer has within that period given written notice to the owners or agents in question of his intention to give directions to them in respect of that person].

9 [(1)] Where an illegal entrant is not given leave to enter or remain in the United Kingdom, an immigration officer may give any such directions in respect of him as in a case within paragraph 8 above are authorised by paragraph 8(1).

[(2) Any leave to enter the United Kingdom which is obtained by deception shall be disregarded for the purposes of this paragraph.]

10   (1) Where it appears to the Secretary of State either—

- (a) that directions might be given in respect of a person under paragraph 8 or 9 above, but that it is not practicable for them to be given or that, if given, they would be ineffective; or
- (b) that directions might have been given in respect of a person under paragraph 8 above [but that the requirements of paragraph 8(2) have not been complied with];

then the Secretary of State may give to the owners or agents of any ship or aircraft any such directions in respect of that person as are authorised by paragraph 8(1)(c).

(2)   Where the Secretary of State may give directions for a person's removal in accordance with sub-paragraph (1) above, he may instead give directions for his removal in accordance with arrangements to be made by the Secretary of State to any country or territory to which he could be removed under sub-paragraph (1).

(3)   The costs of complying with any directions given under this paragraph shall be defrayed by the Secretary of State.

11   A person in respect of whom directions are given under any of paragraphs 8 to 10 above may be placed, under the authority of an immigration officer, on board any ship or aircraft in which he is to be removed in accordance with the directions.

Seamen and aircrews

12   (1) If, on a person's examination by an immigration officer under paragraph 2 above, the immigration officer is satisfied that he has come to the United Kingdom for the purpose of joining a ship or aircraft as a member of the crew, then the immigration officer may limit the duration of any leave he gives that person to enter the United Kingdom by requiring him to leave the United Kingdom in a ship or aircraft specified or indicated by the notice giving leave.

(2)   Where a person (not being [a British citizen]) arrives in the United Kingdom for the purpose of joining a ship or aircraft as a member of a crew and, having been given leave to enter as mentioned in sub-paragraph (1) above, remains beyond the time limited by that leave, or is reasonably suspected by an immigration officer of intending to do so, an immigration officer may—

- (a) give the captain of that ship or aircraft directions requiring the captain to remove him from the United Kingdom in that ship or aircraft; or
- (b) give the owners or agents of that ship or aircraft directions requiring them to remove him from the United Kingdom in any ship or aircraft specified or indicated in the directions, being a ship or aircraft of which they are the owners or agents; or
- (c) give those owners or agents directions requiring them to make arrangements for his removal from the United Kingdom in any ship or aircraft specified or indicated in the directions to a country or territory so specified, being either—
  - (i) a country of which he is a national or citizen; or
  - (ii) a country or territory in which he has obtained a passport or other document of identity; or
  - (iii) a country or territory in which he embarked for the United Kingdom; or
  - (iv) a country or territory where he was engaged as a member of the crew of the ship or aircraft which he arrived in the United Kingdom to join; or
  - (v) a country or territory to which there is reason to believe that he will be admitted.

13 (1) Where a person being a member of the crew of a ship or aircraft is examined by an immigration officer under paragraph 2 above, the immigration officer may limit the duration of any leave he gives that person to enter the United Kingdom—

(a) in the manner authorised by paragraph 12(1) above; or

(b) if that person is to be allowed to enter the United Kingdom in order to receive hospital treatment, by requiring him, on completion of that treatment, to leave the United Kingdom in accordance with arrangements to be made for his repatriation; or

(c) by requiring him to leave the United Kingdom within a specified period in accordance with arrangements to be made for his repatriation.

(2) Where a person (not being [a British citizen]) arrives in the United Kingdom as a member of the crew of a ship or aircraft, and either—

(A) having lawfully entered the United Kingdom without leave by virtue of section 8(1) of this Act, he remains without leave beyond the time allowed by section 8(1), or is reasonably suspected by an immigration officer of intending to do so; or

(B) having been given leave limited as mentioned in sub-paragraph (1) above, he remains beyond the time limited by that leave, or is reasonably suspected by an immigration officer of intending to do so;

an immigration officer may—

(a) give the captain of the ship or aircraft in which he arrived directions requiring the captain to remove him from the United Kingdom in that ship or aircraft; or

(b) give the owners or agents of that ship or aircraft directions requiring them to remove him from the United Kingdom, being a ship or aircraft specified or indicated in the directions, being a ship or aircraft of which they are the owners or agents; or

(c) give those owners or agents directions requiring them to make arrangements for his removal from the United Kingdom in any ship or aircraft specified or indicated in the directions to a country or territory so specified, being either—

(i) a country of which he is a national or citizen; or

(ii) a country or territory in which he has obtained a passport or other document of identity; or

(iii) a country in which he embarked for the United Kingdom; or

(iv) a country or territory in which he was engaged as a member of the crew of the ship or aircraft in which he arrived in the United Kingdom; or

(v) a country or territory to which there is reason to believe that he will be admitted.

14 (1) Where it appears to the Secretary of State that directions might be given in respect of a person under paragraph 12 or 13 above, but that it is not practicable for them to be given or that, if given, they would be ineffective, then the Secretary of State may give to the owners or agents of any ship or aircraft any such directions in respect of that person as are authorised by paragraph 12(2)(c) or 13(2)(c).

(2) Where the Secretary of State may give directions for a person's removal in accordance with sub-paragraph (1) above, he may instead give directions for his removal in accordance with arrangements to be made by the Secretary of State to any country or territory to which he could be removed under sub-paragraph (1).

(3) The costs of complying with any directions given under this paragraph shall be defrayed by the Secretary of State.

15 A person in respect of whom directions are given under any of paragraphs 12 to 14 above may be placed, under the authority of an immigration officer, on board any ship or aircraft in which he is to be removed in accordance with the directions.

Detention of persons liable to examination or removal

16 (1) A person who may be required to submit to examination under paragraph 2 above may be detained under the authority of an immigration officer pending his examination and pending a decision to give or refuse him leave to enter.

[(1A) A person whose leave to enter has been suspended under paragraph 2A may be detained under the authority of an immigration officer pending—

(a) completion of his examination under that paragraph; and
(b) a decision on whether to cancel his leave to enter.]

[(2) If there are reasonable grounds for suspecting that a person is someone in respect of whom directions may be given under any of paragraphs 8 to 10 or 12 to 14, that person may be detained under the authority of an immigration officer pending—

(a) a decision whether or not to give such directions;
(b) his removal in pursuance of such directions.]

(3) A person on board a ship or aircraft may, under the authority of an immigration officer, be removed from the ship or aircraft for detention under this paragraph; but if an immigration officer so requires the captain of a ship or aircraft shall prevent from disembarking in the United Kingdom any person who has arrived in the United Kingdom in the ship or aircraft and been refused leave to enter, and the captain may for that purpose detain him in custody on board the ship or aircraft.

(4) The captain of a ship or aircraft, if so required by an immigration officer, shall prevent from disembarking in the United Kingdom or before the directions for his removal have been fulfilled any person placed on board the ship or aircraft under paragraph 11 or 15 above, and the captain may for that purpose detain him in custody on board the ship or aircraft.

[(4A) . . .]

17 (1) A person liable to be detained under paragraph 16 above may be arrested without warrant by a constable or by an immigration officer.

(2) If—

(a) a justice of the peace is by written information on oath satisfied that there is reasonable ground for suspecting that a person liable to be arrested under this paragraph is to be found on any premises; or
(b) . . .

he may grant a warrant [authorising any immigration officer or constable to enter, if need be] by force, the premises named in the warrant for the purposes of searching for and arresting that person.

18 (1) Persons may be detained under paragraph 16 above in such places as the Secretary of State may direct (when not detained in accordance with paragraph 16 on board a ship or aircraft).

(2) Where a person is detained under paragraph 16, any immigration officer, constable or prison officer, or any other person authorised by the Secretary of State, may take all such steps as may be reasonably necessary for photographing, measuring or otherwise identifying him.

[(2A) The power conferred by sub-paragraph (2) includes power to take fingerprints.]

(3) Any person detained under paragraph 16 may be taken in the custody of a constable, or of any person acting under the authority of an immigration officer, to and from any place where his attendance is required for the purpose of ascertaining his

citizenship or nationality or of making arrangements for his admission to a country or territory other than the United Kingdom, or where he is required to be for any other purpose connected with the operation of this Act.

(4) A person shall be deemed to be in legal custody at any time when he is detained under paragraph 16 or is being removed in pursuance of sub-paragraph (3) above.

19 (1) Where a person is refused leave to enter the United Kingdom and directions are given in respect of him under paragraph 8 or 10 above, then subject to the provisions of this paragraph the owners or agents of the ship or aircraft in which he arrived [. . .] shall be liable to pay the Secretary of State on demand any expenses incurred by the latter in respect of the custody, accommodation or maintenance of that person [for any period (not exceeding 14 days)] after his arrival while he was detained or liable to be detained under paragraph 16 above.

(2) Sub-paragraph (1) above shall not apply to expenses in respect of a person who, when he arrived in the United Kingdom, held a [certificate of entitlement] or a current entry clearance or was the person named in a current work permit; and for this purpose a document purporting to be a [certificate of entitlement], entry clearance or work permit is to be regarded as being one unless its falsity is reasonably apparent.

(3) If, before the directions for a person's removal under paragraph 8 or 10 above have been carried out, he is given leave to enter the United Kingdom, or if he is afterwards given that leave in consequence of the determination in his favour of an appeal under this Act (being an appeal against a refusal of leave to enter by virtue of which the directions were given), or it is determined on an appeal under this Act that he does not require leave to enter (being an appeal occasioned by such a refusal), no sum shall be demanded under sub-paragraph (1) above for expenses incurred in respect of that person and any sum already demanded and paid shall be refunded.

(4) Sub-paragraph (1) above shall not have effect in relation to directions which, in consequence of an appeal under this Act, have ceased to have effect or are for the time being of no effect; and the expenses to which that sub-paragraph applies include expenses in conveying the person in question to and from the place where he is detained or accommodated unless the journey is made for the purpose of attending an appeal by him under this Act.

20 (1) Subject to the provisions of this paragraph, in either of the following cases, that is to say,—

(a) where directions are given in respect of an illegal entrant under paragraph 9 or 10 above; and

(b) where a person has lawfully entered the United Kingdom without leave by virtue of section 8(1) of this Act, but directions are given in respect of him under paragraph 13(2)(A) above or, in a case within paragraph 13(2)(A), under paragraph 14;

the owners or agents of the ship or aircraft in which he arrived in the United Kingdom [. . .] shall be liable to pay the Secretary of State on demand any expenses incurred by the latter in respect of the custody, accommodation or maintenance of that person [for any period (not exceeding 14 days)] after his arrival while he was detained or liable to be detained under paragraph 16 above.

[(1A) Sub-paragraph (1) above shall not apply to expenses in respect of an illegal entrant if he obtained leave to enter by deception and the leave has not been cancelled under paragraph 6(2) above.]

(2) If, before the directions for a person's removal from the United Kingdom have been carried out, he is given leave to remain in the United Kingdom, no sum shall be demanded under sub-paragraph (1) above for expenses incurred in respect of that person and any sum already demanded and paid shall be refunded.

(3)   Sub-paragraph (1) above shall not have effect in relation to directions which, in consequence of an appeal under this Act, are for the time being of no effect; and the expenses to which that sub-paragraph applies include expenses in conveying the person in question to and from the place where he is detained or accommodated unless the journey is made for the purpose of attending an appeal by him under this Act.

Temporary admission or release of persons liable to detention

21   (1)   A person liable to detention or detained under paragraph 16 above may, under the written authority of an immigration officer, be temporarily admitted to the United Kingdom without being detained or be released from detention; but this shall not prejudice a later exercise of the power to detain him.

(2)   So long as a person is at large in the United Kingdom by virtue of this paragraph, he shall be subject to such restrictions as to residence[, as to his employment or occupation] and as to reporting to the police or an immigration officer as may from time to time be notified to him in writing by an immigration officer.

[(2A)   The provisions that may be included in restrictions as to residence imposed under sub-paragraph (2) include provisions of such a description as may be prescribed by regulations made by the Secretary of State.

(2B)   The regulations may, among other things, provide for the inclusion of provisions—

    (a)   prohibiting residence in one or more particular areas;
    (b)   requiring the person concerned to reside in accommodation provided under section 4 of the Immigration and Asylum Act 1999 and prohibiting him from being absent from that accommodation except in accordance with the restrictions imposed on him.

(2C) The regulations may provide that a particular description of provision may be imposed only for prescribed purposes.

(2D) The power to make regulations conferred by this paragraph is exercisable by statutory instrument and includes a power to make different provision for different cases.

(2E) But no regulations under this paragraph are to be made unless a draft of the regulations has been laid before Parliament and approved by a resolution of each House.]

[(3) Sub-paragraph (4) below applies where a person who is at large in the United Kingdom by virtue of this paragraph is subject to a restriction as to reporting to an immigration officer with a view to the conclusion of his examination under paragraph 2 [or 2A] above.

(4)   If the person fails at any time to comply with that restriction—

    (a)   an immigration officer may direct that the person's examination . . . shall be treated as concluded at that time; but
    (b)   nothing in paragraph 6 above shall require the notice giving or refusing him leave to enter the United Kingdom to be given within twenty-four hours after that time.]

22   [(1) The following, namely—

    (a)   a person detained under paragraph 16(1) above pending examination;
    [(aa) a person detained under paragraph 16(1A) above pending completion of his examination or a decision on whether to cancel his leave to enter;] and
    (b)   a person detained under paragraph 16(2) above pending the giving of directions,

may be released on bail in accordance with this paragraph.

(1A) An immigration officer not below the rank of chief immigration officer or an adjudicator may release a person so detained on his entering into a recognizance or, in Scotland, bail bond conditioned for his appearance before an immigration officer at a time and place named in the recognizance or bail bond or at such other time and place as may in the meantime be notified to him in writing by an immigration officer.

(1B) Sub-paragraph (1)(a) above shall not apply unless seven days have elapsed since the date of the person's arrival in the United Kingdom.]

(2) The conditions of a recognizance or bail bond taken under this paragraph may include conditions appearing to the [immigration officer or adjudicator] to be likely to result in the appearance of the person bailed at the required time and place; and any recognizance shall be with or without sureties as the [officer or adjudicator] may determine.

(3) In any case in which an [immigration officer or adjudicator] has power under this paragraph to release a person on bail, the [officer or adjudicator] may, instead of taking the bail, fix the amount and conditions of the bail (including the amount in which any sureties are to be bound) with a view to its being taken subsequently by any such person as may be specified by the adjudicator; and on the recognizance or bail bond being so taken the person to be bailed shall be released.

23 (1) Where a recognizance entered into under paragraph 22 above appears to an adjudicator to be forfeited, the adjudicator may by order declare it to be forfeited and adjudge the persons bound thereby, whether as principal or sureties, or any of them, to pay the sum in which they are respectively bound or such part of it, if any, as the adjudicator thinks fit; and an order under this sub-paragraph shall specify a magistrates' court or, in Northern Ireland court of summary jurisdiction, and—

(a) the recognizance shall be treated for the purposes of collection, enforcement and remission of the sum forfeited as having been forfeited by the court so specified; and

(b) the adjudicator shall, as soon as practicable, give particulars of the recognizance to the [proper officer] of that court.

[(1A) In sub-paragraph (1) "proper officer" means—

(a) in relation to a magistrates' court in England and Wales, the justices' chief executive for the court; and

(b) in relation to a court of summary jurisdiction in Northern Ireland, the clerk of the court.]

(2) . . .

(3) Any sum the payment of which is enforceable by a magistrates' court in England and Wales by virtue of this paragraph shall be treated for the [purposes of the Justices of the Peace Act 1997 and, in particular, section 60 of that Act, as being] due under a recognizance forfeited by such a court . . .

(4) Any sum the payment of which is enforceable by virtue of this paragraph by a court of summary jurisdiction in Northern Ireland shall, for the purposes of section 20(5) of the Administration of Justice Act (Northern Ireland) 1954, be treated as a forfeited recognizance.

24 (1) An immigration officer or constable may arrest without warrant a person who has been released by virtue of paragraph 22 above—

(a) if he has reasonable grounds for believing that that person is likely to break the condition of his recognizance or bail bond that he will appear at the time and place required or to break any other condition of it, or has reasonable grounds to suspect that that person is breaking or has broken any such other condition; or

(b)   if, a recognizance with sureties having been taken, he is notified in writing by any sureties of the surety's belief that that person is likely to break the first-mentioned condition, and of the surety's wish for that reason to be relieved of his obligation as a surety;

and paragraph 17(2) above shall apply for the arrest of a person under this paragraph as it applies for the arrest of a person under paragraph 17.

(2)   A person arrested under this paragraph—

(a)   if not required by a condition on which he was released to appear before an immigration officer within twenty-four hours after the time of his arrest, shall as soon as practicable be brought before an adjudicator or, if that is not practicable within those twenty-four hours, before a justice of the peace acting for the petty sessions area in which he is arrested or, in Scotland, the sheriff; and

(b)   if required by such a condition to appear within those twenty-four hours before an immigration officer, shall be brought before that officer.

(3)   An adjudicator, justice of the peace or sheriff before whom a person is brought by virtue of sub-paragraph (2)(a) above—

(a)   if of the opinion that that person has broken or is likely to break any condition on which he was released, may either—
   (i)   direct that he be detained under the authority of the person by whom he was arrested; or
   (ii)   release him, on his original recognizance or on a new recognizance, with or without sureties, or, in Scotland, on his original bail or on new bail; and

(b)   if not of that opinion, shall release him on his original recognizance or bail.

25   The power to make rules of procedure conferred by section 22 of this Act shall include power to make rules with respect to applications to an adjudicator under paragraphs 22 to 24 above and matters arising out of such applications.

[Entry and search of premises

25A (1)   This paragraph applies if—

(a)   a person is arrested under this Schedule; or
(b)   a person who was arrested by a constable (other than under this Schedule) is detained by an immigration officer under this Schedule.

(2)   An immigration officer may enter and search any premises—

(a)   occupied or controlled by the arrested person, or
(b)   in which that person was when he was arrested, or immediately before he was arrested,

for relevant documents.

(3)   The power may be exercised—

(a)   only if the officer has reasonable grounds for believing that there are relevant documents on the premises;
(b)   only to the extent that it is reasonably required for the purpose of discovering relevant documents; and
(c)   subject to sub-paragraph (4), only if a senior officer has authorised its exercise in writing.

(4)   An immigration officer may conduct a search under sub-paragraph (2)—

   (a)   before taking the arrested person to a place where he is to be detained; and

   (b)   without obtaining an authorisation under sub-paragraph (3)(c),

if the presence of that person at a place other than one where he is to be detained is necessary to make an effective search for any relevant documents.

(5)   An officer who has conducted a search under sub-paragraph (4) must inform a senior officer as soon as is practicable.

(6)   The officer authorising a search, or who is informed of one under sub-paragraph (5), must make a record in writing of—

   (a)   the grounds for the search; and

   (b)   the nature of the documents that were sought.

(7)   An officer searching premises under sub-paragraph (2)—

   (a)   may seize and retain any documents he finds which he has reasonable grounds for believing are relevant documents; but

   (b)   may not retain any such document for longer than is necessary in view of the purpose for which the person was arrested.

(8)   But sub-paragraph (7)(a) does not apply to documents which the officer has reasonable grounds for believing are items subject to legal privilege.

(9)   "Relevant documents" means any documents which might—

   (a)   establish the arrested person's identity, nationality or citizenship; or

   (b)   indicate the place from which he has travelled to the United Kingdom or to which he is proposing to go.

(10) "Senior officer" means an immigration officer not below the rank of chief immigration officer.]

[Searching persons arrested by immigration officers

25B (1)   This paragraph applies if a person is arrested under this Schedule.

(2)   An immigration officer may search the arrested person if he has reasonable grounds for believing that the arrested person may present a danger to himself or others.

(3)   The officer may search the arrested person for—

   (a)   anything which he might use to assist his escape from lawful custody; or

   (b)   any document which might—

      (i)   establish his identity, nationality or citizenship; or

      (ii)   indicate the place from which he has travelled to the United Kingdom or to which he is proposing to go.

(4)   The power conferred by sub-paragraph (3) may be exercised—

   (a)   only if the officer has reasonable grounds for believing that the arrested person may have concealed on him anything of a kind mentioned in that sub-paragraph; and

   (b)   only to the extent that it is reasonably required for the purpose of discovering any such thing.

(5)   A power conferred by this paragraph to search a person is not to be read as authorising an officer to require a person to remove any of his clothing in public other than an outer coat, jacket or glove; but it does authorise the search of a person's mouth.

(6)   An officer searching a person under sub-paragraph (2) may seize and retain anything he finds, if he has reasonable grounds for believing that the person searched might use it to cause physical injury to himself or to another person.

(7)   An officer searching a person under sub-paragraph (3)(a) may seize and retain anything he finds, if he has reasonable grounds for believing that he might use it to assist his escape from lawful custody.

(8)   An officer searching a person under sub-paragraph (3)(b) may seize and retain anything he finds, other than an item subject to legal privilege, if he has reasonable grounds for believing that it might be a document falling within that sub-paragraph.

(9)   Nothing seized under sub-paragraph (6) or (7) may be retained when the person from whom it was seized—

(a)   is no longer in custody, or
(b)   is in the custody of a court but has been released on bail.]

[Searching persons in police custody

25C (1)   This paragraph applies if a person—

(a)   has been arrested under this Schedule; and
(b)   is in custody at a police station.

(2)   An immigration officer may, at any time, search the arrested person in order to ascertain whether he has with him—

(a)   anything which he might use to—
    (i)   cause physical injury to himself or others;
    (ii)   damage property;
    (iii)   interfere with evidence; or
    (iv)   assist his escape; or
(b)   any document which might—
    (i)   establish his identity, nationality or citizenship; or
    (ii)   indicate the place from which he has travelled to the United Kingdom or to which he is proposing to go.

(3)   The power may be exercised only to the extent that the officer considers it to be necessary for the purpose of discovering anything of a kind mentioned in sub-paragraph (2).

(4)   An officer searching a person under this paragraph may seize and retain anything he finds, if he has reasonable grounds for believing that—

(a)   that person might use it for one or more of the purposes mentioned in sub-paragraph (2)(a); or
(b)   it might be a document falling within sub-paragraph (2)(b).

(5)   But the officer may not retain anything seized under sub-paragraph (2)(a)—

(a)   for longer than is necessary in view of the purpose for which the search was carried out; or
(b)   when the person from whom it was seized is no longer in custody or is in the custody of a court but has been released on bail.

(6)   The person from whom something is seized must be told the reason for the seizure unless he is—

(a)   violent or appears likely to become violent; or
(b)   incapable of understanding what is said to him.

(7)   An intimate search may not be conducted under this paragraph.

(8)   The person carrying out a search under this paragraph must be of the same sex as the person searched.

(9)   "Intimate search" has the same meaning as in section 28H(11).]

[Access and copying

25D (1) If a person showing himself—

(a)   to be the occupier of the premises on which seized material was seized, or
(b)   to have had custody or control of the material immediately before it was seized,

asks the immigration officer who seized the material for a record of what he seized, the officer must provide the record to that person within a reasonable time.

(2)   If a relevant person asks an immigration officer for permission to be granted access to seized material, the officer must arrange for that person to have access to the material under the supervision of an immigration officer.

(3)   An immigration officer may photograph or copy, or have photographed or copied, seized material.

(4)   If a relevant person asks an immigration officer for a photograph or copy of seized material, the officer must arrange for—

(a)   that person to have access to the material under the supervision of an immigration officer for the purpose of photographing or copying it; or
(b)   the material to be photographed or copied.

(5)   A photograph or copy made under sub-paragraph (4)(b) must be supplied within a reasonable time.

(6)   There is no duty under this paragraph to arrange for access to, or the supply of a photograph or copy of, any material if there are reasonable grounds for believing that to do so would prejudice—

(a)   the exercise of any functions in connection with which the material was seized; or
(b)   an investigation which is being conducted under this Act, or any criminal proceedings which may be brought as a result.

(7)   "Relevant person" means—

(a)   a person who had custody or control of seized material immediately before it was seized, or
(b)   someone acting on behalf of such a person.

(8)   "Seized material" means anything which has been seized and retained under this Schedule.]

[25E   Section 28L applies for the purposes of this Schedule as it applies for the purposes of Part III.]

Supplementary duties of those connected with ships or aircraft or with ports

26   (1)   The owners or agents of a ship or aircraft employed to carry passengers for reward shall not, without the approval of the Secretary of State, arrange for the ship or aircraft to call at a port in the United Kingdom other than a port of entry for the purpose of disembarking passengers, if any of the passengers on board may not enter the United Kingdom without leave . . ., or for the purpose of embarking passengers unless the owners or agents have reasonable cause to believe all of them to be [British citizens].

[(1A)   Sub-paragraph (1) does not apply in such circumstances, if any, as the Secretary of State may by order prescribe.]

(2)   The Secretary of State may from time to time give written notice to the owners or agents of any ships or aircraft designating control areas for the embarkation or disembarkation of passengers in any port in the United Kingdom and specifying the conditions and restrictions (if any) to be observed in any control area; and where by notice given to any owners or agents a control area is for the time being designated for the embarkation or disembarkation of passengers at any port, the owners or agents shall take all reasonable steps to secure that, in the case of their ships or aircraft, passengers do not embark or disembark, as the case may be, at the port outside the control area and that any conditions or restrictions notified to them are observed.

(3)   The Secretary of State may also from time to time give to any persons concerned with the management of a port in the United Kingdom written notice designating control areas in the port and specifying conditions or restrictions to be observed in any control area; and any such person shall take all reasonable steps to secure that any conditions or restrictions as notified to him are observed.

[(3A)   The power conferred by sub-paragraph (1A) is exercisable by statutory instrument; and any such instrument shall be subject to annulment by a resolution of either House of Parliament.]

27   (1)   The captain of a ship or aircraft arriving in the United Kingdom—

  (a)   shall take such steps as may be necessary to secure that persons on board do not disembark there unless either they have been examined by an immigration officer, or they disembark in accordance with arrangements approved by an immigration officer, or they are members of the crew who may lawfully enter the United Kingdom without leave by virtue of section 8(1) of this Act; and
  (b)   where the examination of persons on board is to be carried out on the ship or aircraft, shall take such steps as may be necessary to secure that those to be examined are presented for the purpose in an orderly manner.

(2)   The Secretary of State may by order made by statutory instrument make provision for requiring captains of ships or aircraft arriving in the United Kingdom or of such of them as arrive from or by way of countries or places specified in the order, to furnish to immigration officers—

  (a)   a passenger list showing the names and nationality or citizenship of passengers arriving on board the ship or aircraft;
  (b)   particulars of members of the crew of the ship or aircraft;

and for enabling an immigration officer to dispense with the furnishing of any such list or particulars.

[27A   ...]

[Passenger information

27B (1)   This paragraph applies to ships or aircraft—

  (a)   which have arrived, or are expected to arrive, in the United Kingdom; or
  (b)   which have left, or are expected to leave, the United Kingdom.

(2)   If an immigration officer asks the owner or agent ("the carrier") of a ship or aircraft for passenger information, the carrier must provide that information to the officer.

(3)   The officer may ask for passenger information relating to—

    (a)   a particular ship or particular aircraft of the carrier;
    (b)   particular ships or aircraft (however described) of the carrier; or
    (c)   all of the carrier's ships or aircraft.

(4)   The officer may ask for—

    (a)   all passenger information in relation to the ship or aircraft concerned; or
    (b)   particular passenger information in relation to that ship or aircraft.

(5)   A request under sub-paragraph (2)—

    (a)   must be in writing;
    (b)   must state the date on which it ceases to have effect; and
    (c)   continues in force until that date, unless withdrawn earlier by written notice by an immigration officer.

(6)   The date may not be later than six months after the request is made.

(7)   The fact that a request under sub-paragraph (2) has ceased to have effect as a result of sub-paragraph (5) does not prevent the request from being renewed.

(8)   The information must be provided—

    (a)   in such form and manner as the Secretary of State may direct; and
    (b)   at such time as may be stated in the request.

(9)   "Passenger information" means such information relating to the passengers carried, or expected to be carried, by the ship or aircraft as may be specified.

(10) "Specified" means specified in an order made by statutory instrument by the Secretary of State.

(11) Such an instrument shall be subject to annulment in pursuance of a resolution of either House of Parliament.]

[*Notification of non-EEA arrivals*

27C (1) If a senior officer, or an immigration officer authorised by a senior officer, gives written notice to the owner or agent ("the carrier") of a ship or aircraft, the carrier must inform a relevant officer of the expected arrival in the United Kingdom of any ship or aircraft—

    (a)   of which he is the owner or agent; and
    (b)   which he expects to carry a person who is not an EEA national.

(2)   The notice may relate to—

    (a)   a particular ship or particular aircraft of the carrier;
    (b)   particular ships or aircraft (however described) of the carrier; or
    (c)   all of the carrier's ships or aircraft.

(3)   The notice—

    (a)   must state the date on which it ceases to have effect; and
    (b)   continues in force until that date, unless withdrawn earlier by written notice given by a senior officer.

(4)   The date may not be later than six months after the notice is given.

(5)   The fact that a notice under sub-paragraph (1) has ceased to have effect as a result of sub-paragraph (3) does not prevent the notice from being renewed.

(6)   The information must be provided—

(a)   in such form and manner as the notice may require; and

(b)   before the ship or aircraft concerned departs for the United Kingdom.

(7)   If a ship or aircraft travelling to the United Kingdom stops at one or more places before arriving in the United Kingdom, it is to be treated as departing for the United Kingdom when it leaves the last of those places.

(8)   "Senior officer" means an immigration officer not below the rank of chief immigration officer.

(9)   "Relevant officer" means—

(a)   the officer who gave the notice under sub-paragraph (1); or

(b)   any immigration officer at the port at which the ship or aircraft concerned is expected to arrive.

(10)   "EEA national" means a national of a State which is a Contracting Party to the Agreement on the European Economic Area signed at Oporto on 2nd May 1992 as it has effect for the time being.]

NOTES

Appointment
Commencement order: SI 1972/1514.

Amendment
Para 1: words in square brackets in sub-paras (4), (5) substituted by SI 1993/1813, art 8, Sch 5, Part I, para 1(a).
Para 2: in sub-para (1) words "or aircraft" in square brackets substituted by SI 1993/1813, art 8, Sch 5, Pt I, para 1(b).
Para 2: in sub-para (1)(a) words "a British citizen" in square brackets substituted by the British Nationality Act 1981, s 39(6), Sch 4, para 2.
Para 2: sub-para (1)(c) substituted by the Immigration and Asylum Act 1999, s 169(1), Sch 14, paras 43, 56.
Date in force: 14 February 2000: see SI 2000/168, art 2, Schedule.
Para 2A: inserted by the Immigration and Asylum Act 1999, s 169(1), Sch 14, paras 43, 57.
Date in force: 14 February 2000: see SI 2000/168, art 2, Schedule.
Para 3: words omitted, originally inserted by SI 1990/2227, art 3, Sch 1, Part I, para 8, repealed by SI 1993/1813, art 9, Sch 6, Part I.
Para 3: second words in square brackets substituted by the British Nationality Act 1981, s 39(6), Sch 4, para 2.
Para 4: in sub-para (1) reference to ", 2A" in square brackets inserted by the Immigration and Asylum Act 1999, s 169(1), Sch 14, paras 43, 58.
Date in force: 14 February 2000: see SI 2000/168, art 2, Schedule.
Para 4: in sub-para (2) reference to ", 2A" in square brackets inserted by the Immigration and Asylum Act 1999, s 169(1), Sch 14, paras 43, 58.
Date in force: 14 February 2000: see SI 2000/168, art 2, Schedule.
Para 4: in sub-para (2)(b) words ", or has carried or conveyed," in square brackets inserted by the Asylum and Immigration Act 1996, s 12(1), Sch 2, para 5(1).
Para 4: sub-para (2A) inserted by the Immigration Act 1988, s 10, Schedule, paras 6, 10.
Para 4: in sub-para (3) words ", or has carried or conveyed," in square brackets inserted by the Asylum and Immigration Act 1996, s 12(1), Sch 2, para 5(2)(a).
Para 4: sub-para (3)(a), (b) substituted by the Asylum and Immigration Act 1996, s 12(1), Sch 2, para 5(2)(b).
Para 4: in sub-para (3) words "or, as the case may be, has done" in square brackets inserted by the Asylum and Immigration Act 1996, s 12(1), Sch 2, para 5(2)(c).
Para 6: first, second and final words in square brackets in sub-para (1) substituted by the Immigration Act 1988, s 10, Schedule, paras 7, 8.
Para 6: third words in square brackets in sub-para (1) substituted by the British Nationality Act 1981, s 39, Sch 4, para 2.
Para 6: words in square brackets in sub-paras (2), (3) substituted by the Immigration Act 1988, s 10, Schedule, paras 7, 8.
Para 7: substituted by the Immigration and Asylum Act 1999, s 169(1), Sch 14, paras 43, 59.

Date in force: 14 February 2000: see SI 2000/168, art 2, Schedule.

Para 8: words omitted from sub-para (1), originally inserted by SI 1990/2227, art 3, Sch 1, Part I, para 9, repealed by SI 1993/1813, art 9, Sch 6, Part I.

Para 8: words in square brackets in sub-para (2) inserted by the Immigration Act 1988, s 10, Schedule, para 9.

Para 9: sub-para (1) numbered as such, and sub-para (2) inserted, by the Asylum and Immigration Act 1996, s 12(1), Sch 2, para 6.

Para 10: words in square brackets in sub-para (1) substituted by the Immigration Act 1988, s 10, Schedule, para 9.

Paras 12, 13: words "a British citizen" in square brackets substituted by the British Nationality Act 1981, s 39(6), Sch 4, para 2.

Para 16: sub-para (1A) inserted by the Immigration and Asylum Act 1999, s 169(1), Sch 14, paras 43, 60.

Date in force: 14 February 2000: see SI 2000/168, art 2, Schedule.

Para 16: sub-para (2) substituted by the Immigration and Asylum Act 1999, s 140(1).

Date in force: 11 November 1999: see the Immigration and Asylum Act 1999, s 170(3)(m).

Para 16: sub-para (4A) inserted by SI 1990/2227, art 3, Sch 1, Part I, para 10, repealed by SI 1993/1813, art 9, Sch 6, Part I.

Para 17: first words omitted apply to Scotland only, repealed in part by the Asylum and Immigration Act 1996, ss 12(1), (3), Sch 2, para 7, Sch 4.

Para 17: in sub-para (2) words from "authorising any" to "if need be" in square brackets substituted by the Immigration and Asylum Act 1999, s 140(2).

Date in force: 11 November 1999: see the Immigration and Asylum Act 1999, s 170(3)(m).

Para 18: sub-para (2A) inserted by the Immigration and Asylum Act 1999, s 169(1), Sch 14, paras 43, 61.

Date in force: 11 December 2000: see SI 2000/3099, art 3, Schedule.

Para 19: words omitted from sub-para (1) inserted by SI 1990/2227, Sch 1, Part I, para 11, repealed by SI 1993/1813, art 9, Sch 6, Part I.

Para 19: words in square brackets in sub-para (1) substituted by the Asylum and Immigration Act 1996, s 12(1), Sch 2, para 8.

Para 19: words in square brackets in sub-para (2) substituted by the British Nationality Act 1981, s 39(6), Sch 4, para 3(1).

Para 20: words omitted from sub-para (1) inserted by SI 1990/2227, Sch 1, Part I, para 12, repealed by SI 1993/1813, art 9, Sch 6, Part I.

Para 20: words in square brackets in sub-para (1) substituted by the Asylum and Immigration Act 1996, s 12(1), Sch 2, para 9(1).

Para 20: sub-para (1A) inserted by the Asylum and Immigration Act 1996, s 12(1), Sch 2, para 9(2).

Para 21: words in square brackets in sub-para (2) inserted by the Immigration Act 1988, s 10, Schedule, paras 6, 10.

Para 21: sub-paras (2A)–(2E) inserted by the Immigration and Asylum Act 1999, s 169(1), Sch 14, paras 43, 62(1), (2).

Date in force: 11 November 1999: see the Immigration and Asylum Act 1999, s 170(3)(s).

Para 21: sub-paras (3), (4) inserted by the Asylum and Immigration Act 1996, s 12(1), Sch 2, para 10.

Para 21: in sub-para (3) words "or 2A" in square brackets inserted by the Immigration and Asylum Act 1999, s 169(1), Sch 14, paras 43, 62(1), (3).

Date in force: 14 February 2000: see SI 2000/168, art 2, Schedule.

Para 21: in sub-para (4)(a) words omitted repealed by the Immigration and Asylum Act 1999, s 169(1), (3), Sch 14, paras 43, 62(1), (4), Sch 16.

Date in force: 14 February 2000: see SI 2000/168, art 2, Schedule.

Para 22: sub-paras (1), (1A), (1B) substituted, for sub-para (1) as originally enacted, by the Asylum and Immigration Act 1996, s 12(1), Sch 2, para 11(1).

Para 22: sub-para (1)(aa) inserted by the Immigration and Asylum Act 1999, s 169(1), Sch 14, paras 43, 63.

Date in force: 14 February 2000: see SI 2000/168, art 2, Schedule.

Para 22: in sub-paras (2), (3) words "immigration officer or adjudicator" and "office or adjudicator" in square brackets substituted by the Asylum and Immigration Act 1996, s 12(1), Sch 2, para 11(2).

Para 23: in sub-para (1)(b) words in square brackets substituted by the Access to Justice Act 1999, s 90(1), Sch 13, para 70(1), (2).

Date in force: 1 April 2001: see SI 2001/916, art 2(a)(ii).

Para 23: sub-para (1A) inserted by the Access to Justice Act 1999, s 90(1), Sch 13, para 70(1), (3).
Date in force: 1 April 2001: see SI 2001/916, art 2(a)(ii).
Para 23: sub-para (2) applies to Scotland only.
Para 23: in sub-para (3) words from "purposes of the" to "Act, as being" in square brackets substituted by the Justices of the Peace Act 1997, s 73(2), Sch 5, para 10.
Para 23: in sub-para (3) words omitted repealed by the Criminal Justice Act 1972, ss 64(2), 66(7), Sch 6, Pt II.
Para 25A: inserted by the Immigration and Asylum Act 1999, s 132(2).
Date in force: 14 February 2000: see SI 2000/168, art 2, Schedule.
Para 25B: inserted by the Immigration and Asylum Act 1999, s 134(2).
Date in force: 14 February 2000: see SI 2000/168, art 2, Schedule.
Para 25C: inserted by the Immigration and Asylum Act 1999, s 135(2).
Date in force: 14 February 2000: see SI 2000/168, art 2, Schedule.
Para 25D: inserted by the Immigration and Asylum Act 1999, s 136(2).
Date in force: 14 February 2000: see SI 2000/168, art 2, Schedule.
Para 25E: inserted by the Immigration and Asylum Act 1999, s 139(2).
Date in force: 14 February 2000: see SI 2000/168, art 2, Schedule.
Para 26: in sub-para (1) words omitted repealed by the Immigration and Asylum Act 1999, s 169(1), (3), Sch 14, paras 43, 64(1), (2), Sch 16.
Date in force: 14 February 2000: see SI 2000/168, art 2, Schedule.
Para 26: in sub-para (1) words "British citizens" in square brackets substituted by the British Nationality Act 1981, s 39(6), Sch 4, para 2.
Para 26: sub-para (1A) inserted by the Immigration and Asylum Act 1999, s 169(1), Sch 14, paras 43, 64(1), (3).
Date in force: 14 February 2000: see SI 2000/168, art 2, Schedule.
Para 26: sub-para (3A) inserted by the Immigration and Asylum Act 1999, s 169(1), Sch 14, paras 43, 64(1), (4).
Date in force: 14 February 2000: see SI 2000/168, art 2, Schedule.
Para 27A: inserted by SI 1990/2227, art 3, Sch 1, Part I, para 13; repealed by SI 1993/1813, art 9, Sch 6, Part I.
Para 27B: inserted by the Immigration and Asylum Act 1999, s 18.
Date in force (for certain purposes): 1 March 2000: see SI 2000/464, art 2, Schedule.
Date in force (for remaining purposes): 3 April 2000: see SI 2000/464, art 2, Schedule.
Para 27C: inserted by the Immigration and Asylum Act 1999, s 19.
Date in force: 3 April 2000: see SI 2000/464, art 2, Schedule.

Modification
Modified, in relation to France and the United Kingdom, by the Channel Tunnel (International Arrangements) Order 1993, SI 1993/1813, art 7(1), Sch 4, para 1(11).
Modified, in relation to its application to frontier controls between the United Kingdom, France and Belgium, by the Channel Tunnel (Miscellaneous Provisions) Order 1994, SI 1994/1405, art 7.
Paras 22–24 modified, in relation to a person detained on certain grounds relating to national security, by the Special Immigration Appeals Commission Act 1997, Sch 3, paras 1–3.
The Northern Ireland Act 1998 makes new provision for the government of Northern Ireland for the purpose of implementing the Belfast Agreement (the agreement reached at multi-party talks on Northern Ireland and set out in Command Paper 3883). As a consequence of that Act, any reference in this Schedule to the Parliament of Northern Ireland or the Assembly established under the Northern Ireland Assembly Act 1973, s 1, certain office-holders and Ministers, and any legislative act and certain financial dealings thereof, shall, for the period specified, be construed in accordance with Sch 12, paras 1–11 to the 1998 Act.

Transfer of Functions
Functions under this section: certain functions under para 1 are transferred, in so far as they are exercisable in or as regards Scotland, to the Scottish Ministers, by the Scotland Act 1998 (Transfer of Functions to the Scottish Ministers etc) Order 1999, SI 1999/1750, art 2, Sch 1.

Subordinate Legislation
Immigration (Passenger Information) Order 2000, SI 2000/912 (made under para 27B(9), (10)).

PART II
EFFECT OF APPEALS

. . .

28 ...

Grant of bail pending appeal

29 (1) Where a person (in the following provisions of this Schedule referred to as "an appellant") has an appeal pending under section [59, 65, 66, 67, 69(1) or (5) or 71 of the Immigration and Asylum Act 1999] and is for the time being detained under Part I of this Schedule, he may be released on bail in accordance with this paragraph.

(2) An immigration officer not below the rank of chief immigration officer or a police officer not below the rank of inspector may release an appellant on his entering into a recognizance or, in Scotland, bail bond conditioned for his appearance before an adjudicator or the Appeal Tribunal at a time and place named in the recognizance or bail bond.

(3) An adjudicator may release an appellant on his entering into a recognizance or, in Scotland, bail bond conditioned for his appearance before that or any other adjudicator, or the Appeal Tribunal at a time and place named in the recognizance or bail bond; and where an adjudicator dismisses an appeal but grants leave to the appellant to appeal to the Tribunal, or, in a case in which leave to appeal is not required, the appellant has duly given notice of appeal to the Tribunal, the adjudicator shall, if the appellant so requests, exercise his powers under this sub-paragraph.

(4) Where an appellant has duly applied for leave to appeal to the Appeal Tribunal, the Tribunal may release him on his entering into a recognizance or, in Scotland, bail bond conditioned for his appearance before the Tribunal at a time and place named in the recognizance or bail bond; and where—

    (a)   the Tribunal grants leave to an appellant to appeal to the Tribunal; or

    (b)   in a case in which leave to appeal is not required, the appellant has duly given notice of appeal to the Tribunal;

the Tribunal shall, if the appellant so requests, release him as aforesaid.

(5) The conditions of a recognizance or bail bond taken under this paragraph may include conditions appearing to the person fixing the bail to be likely to result in the appearance of the appellant at the time and place named; and any recognizance shall be with or without sureties as that person may determine.

(6) In any case in which an adjudicator or the Tribunal has power or is required by this paragraph to release an appellant on bail, the adjudicator or Tribunal may, instead of taking the bail, fix the amount and conditions of the bail (including the amount in which any sureties are to be bound) with a view to its being taken subsequently by any such person as may be specified by the adjudicator or the Tribunal; and on the recognizance or bail bond so taken the appellant shall be released.

Restrictions on grant of bail

30 (1) An appellant shall not be released under paragraph 29 above without the consent of the Secretary of State if directions for the removal of the appellant from the United Kingdom are for the time being in force, or the power to give such directions is for the time being exercisable.

(2) Notwithstanding paragraph 29(3) or (4) above, an adjudicator and the Tribunal shall not be obliged to release an appellant unless the appellant enters into a proper recognizance, with sufficient and satisfactory sureties if required, or in Scotland sufficient

and satisfactory bail is found if so required; and an adjudicator and the Tribunal shall not be obliged to release an appellant if it appears to the adjudicator or the Tribunal, as the case may be—

(a) that the appellant, having on any previous occasion been released on bail (whether under paragraph 24 or under any other provision), has failed to comply with the conditions of any recognizance or bail bond entered into by him on that occasion;

(b) that the appellant is likely to commit an offence unless he is retained in detention;

(c) that the release of the appellant is likely to cause danger to public health;

(d) that the appellant is suffering from mental disorder and that his continued detention is necessary in his own interests or for the protection of any other person; or

(e) that the appellant is under the age of seventeen, that arrangements ought to be made for his care in the event of his release and that no satisfactory arrangements for that purpose have been made.

Forfeiture of recognizances

31 (1) Where under paragraph 29 above (as it applies in England and Wales or in Northern Ireland) a recognizance is entered into conditioned for the appearance of an appellant before an adjudicator or the Tribunal, and it appears to the adjudicator or the Tribunal, as the case may be, to be forfeited, the adjudicator or Tribunal may by order declare it to be forfeited and adjudge the persons bound thereby, whether as principal or sureties, or any of them, to pay the sum in which they are respectively bound or such part of it, if any, as the adjudicator or Tribunal thinks fit.

(2) An order under this paragraph shall, for the purposes of this sub-paragraph, specify a magistrates' court or, in Northern Ireland, court of summary jurisdiction; and the recognizance shall be treated for the purposes of collection, enforcement and remission of the sum forfeited as having been forfeited by the court so specified.

(3) Where an adjudicator or the Tribunal makes an order under this paragraph the adjudicator or Tribunal shall, as soon as practicable, give particulars of the recognizance to the [proper officer] of the court specified in the order in pursuance of sub-paragraph (2) above.

[(3A) In sub-paragraph (3) "proper officer" means—

(a) in relation to a magistrates' court in England and Wales, the justices' chief executive for the court; and

(b) in relation to a court of summary jurisdiction in Northern Ireland, the clerk of the court.]

(4) Any sum the payment of which is enforceable by a magistrates' court in England or Wales by virtue of this paragraph shall be treated for the [purposes of the Justices of the Peace Act 1997 and, in particular, section 60 of that Act, as being] due under a recognizance forfeited by such a court . . .

(5) Any sum the payment of which is enforceable by virtue of this paragraph by a court of summary jurisdiction in Northern Ireland shall, for the purposes of section 20(5) of the Administration of Justice Act (Northern Ireland) 1954, be treated as a forfeited recognizance.

32 . . .

Arrest of appellants released on bail

33 (1) An immigration officer or constable may arrest without warrant a person who has been released by virtue of this Part of this Schedule—

(a) if he has reasonable grounds for believing that that person is likely to break the condition of his recognizance or bail bond that he will appear at the time and place required or to break any other condition of it, or has reasonable ground to suspect that that person is breaking or has broken any such other condition; or

(b) if, a recognizance with sureties having been taken, he is notified in writing by any surety of the surety's belief that that person is likely to break the first-mentioned condition, and of the surety's wish for that reason to be relieved of his obligations as a surety;

and paragraph 17(2) above shall apply for the arrest of a person under this paragraph as it applies for the arrest of a person under paragraph 17.

(2) A person arrested under this paragraph—

(a) if not required by a condition on which he was released to appear before an adjudicator or Tribunal within twenty-four hours after the time of his arrest, shall as soon as practicable be brought before an adjudicator or, if that is not practicable within those twenty-four hours, before a justice of the peace acting for the petty sessions area in which he is arrested or, in Scotland, the sheriff; and

(b) if required by such a condition to appear within those twenty-four hours before an adjudicator or before the Tribunal, shall be brought before that adjudicator or before the Tribunal, as the case may be.

(3) An adjudicator, justice of the peace or sheriff before whom a person is brought by virtue of sub-paragraph (2)(a) above—

(a) if of the opinion that that person has broken or is likely to break any condition on which he was released, may either—
  (i) direct that he be detained under the authority of the person by whom he was arrested; or
  (ii) release him on his original recognizance or on a new recognizance, with or without sureties, or, in Scotland, on his original bail or on new bail; and

(b) if not of that opinion, shall release him on his original recognizance or bail.

[Grant of bail pending removal

34 (1) Paragraph 22 above shall apply in relation to a person—

(a) directions for whose removal from the United Kingdom are for the time being in force; and

(b) who is for the time being detained under Part I of this Schedule,

as it applies in relation to a person detained under paragraph 16(1) above pending examination[, detained under paragraph 16(1A) above pending completion of his examination or a decision on whether to cancel his leave to enter] or detained under paragraph 16(2) above pending the giving of directions.

(2) Paragraphs 23 to 25 above shall apply as if any reference to paragraph 22 above included a reference to that paragraph as it applies by virtue of this paragraph.]

NOTES

Appointment
Commencement order: SI 1972/1514.

Amendment
Para 28: repealed by the Immigration and Asylum Act 1999, s 169(1), (3), Sch 14, paras 43, 65, Sch 16.

Date in force: 2 October 2000 (except in relation to an event which took place before that date): see SI 2000/2444, art 2, Sch 1; for transitional provisions see art 3, Sch 2, para 2(10) thereof.

Para 29: in sub-para (1) words "59, 65, 66, 67, 69(1) or (5) or 71 of the Immigration and Asylum Act 1999" in square brackets substituted by the Immigration and Asylum Act 1999, s 169(1), Sch 14, paras 43, 66.

Date in force: 2 October 2000 (except in relation to an event which took place before that date): see SI 2000/2444, art 2, Sch 1; for transitional provisions see art 3, Sch 2, para 2(10) thereof.

Para 31: in sub-para (3) words in square brackets substituted by the Access to Justice Act 1999, s 90(1), Sch 13, para 70(1), (4).

Date in force: 1 April 2001: see SI 2001/916, art 2(a)(ii).

Para 31: sub-para (3A) inserted by the Access to Justice Act 1999, s 90(1), Sch 13, para 70(1), (5).

Date in force: 1 April 2001: see SI 2001/916, art 2(a)(ii).

Para 31: in sub-para (4) words from "purposes of the" to "Act, as being" in square brackets substituted by the Justices of the Peace Act 1997, s 73(2), Sch 5, para 10.

Para 31: in sub-para (4) words omitted repealed by the Criminal Justice Act 1972, s 64(2), Sch 6, Pt II.

Para 32: applies to Scotland only.

Para 34: inserted by the Asylum and Immigration Act 1996, s 12(1), Sch 12, para 12.

Para 34: in para (1) words from ", detained under" to "leave to enter" in square brackets inserted by the Immigration and Asylum Act 1999, s 169(1), Sch 14, paras 43, 67.

Date in force: 14 February 2000: see SI 2000/168, art 2, Schedule.

Modification

Modified by the Asylum and Immigration Appeals Act 1993, s 8(6), Sch 2, para 9.

Modification: para 29 modified by the Asylum and Immigration Act 1996, s 3(6).

Paras 29–33 modified, in relation to a person detained on certain grounds relating to national security, by the Special Immigration Appeals Commission Act 1997, Sch 3, paras 4–8.

SCHEDULE 3
Supplementary Provisions as to Deportation

Section 5

Removal of persons liable to deportation

1   (1) Where a deportation order is in force against any person, the Secretary of State may give directions for his removal to a country or territory specified in the directions being either—

(a)   a country of which he is a national or citizen; or

(b)   a country or territory to which there is reason to believe that he will be admitted.

(2)   The directions under sub-paragraph (1) above may be either—

(a)   directions given to the captain of a ship or aircraft about to leave the United Kingdom requiring him to remove the person in question in that ship or aircraft; or

(b)   directions given to the owners or agents of any ship or aircraft requiring them to make arrangements for his removal in a ship or aircraft specified or indicated in the directions; or

(c)   directions for his removal in accordance with arrangements to be made by the Secretary of State.

(3)   In relation to directions given under this paragraph, paragraphs 11 and 16(4) of Schedule 2 to this Act shall apply, with the substitution of references to the Secretary of State for references to an immigration officer, as they apply in relation to directions for removal given under paragraph 8 of that Schedule.

(4) The Secretary of State, if he thinks fit, may apply in or towards payment of the expenses of or incidental to the voyage from the United Kingdom of a person against whom a deportation order is in force, or the maintenance until departure of such a person and his dependants, if any, any money belonging to that person; and except so far as they are paid as aforesaid, those expenses shall be defrayed by the Secretary of State.

Detention or control pending deportation

2 (1) Where a recommendation for deportation made by a court is in force in respect of any person, and that person is neither detained in pursuance of the sentence or order of any court nor for the time being released on bail by any court having power so to release him, he shall, unless the court by which the recommendation is made otherwise directs, [or a direction is given under sub-paragraph (1A) below,] be detained pending the making of a deportation order in pursuance of the recommendation, unless the Secretary of State directs him to be released pending further consideration of his case [or he is released on bail].

[(1A)   Where—

- (a) a recommendation for deportation made by a court on conviction of a person is in force in respect of him; and
- (b) he appeals against his conviction or against that recommendation,

the powers that the court determining the appeal may exercise include power to direct him to be released without setting aside the recommendation.]

(2) Where notice has been given to a person in accordance with regulations under section 18 of this Act of a decision to make a deportation order against him, and he is neither detained in pursuance of the sentence or order of a court nor for the time being released on bail by a court having power so to release him, he may be detained under the authority of the Secretary of State pending the making of the deportation order.

(3) Where a deportation order is in force against any person, he may be detained under the authority of the Secretary of State pending his removal or departure from the United Kingdom (and if already detained by virtue of sub-paragraph (1) or (2) above when the order is made, shall continue to be detained unless [he is released on bail or] the Secretary of State directs otherwise).

(4) In relation to detention under sub-paragraph (2) or (3) above, paragraphs 17[, 18 and 25A to 25E] of Schedule 2 to this Act shall apply as they apply in relation to detention under paragraph 16 of that Schedule.

[(4A)   Paragraphs 22 to 25 of Schedule 2 to this Act apply in relation to a person detained under sub-paragraph (1), (2) or (3) as they apply in relation to a person detained under paragraph 16 of that Schedule.]

[(5) A person to whom this sub-paragraph applies shall be subject to such restrictions as to residence[, as to his employment or occupation] and as to reporting to the police [or an immigration officer] as may from time to time be notified to him in writing by the Secretary of State.]

[(6) The persons to whom sub-paragraph (5) above applies are—

- (a) a person liable to be detained under sub-paragraph (1) above, while by virtue of a direction of the Secretary of State he is not so detained; and
- (b) a person liable to be detained under sub-paragraph (2) or (3) above, while he is not so detained.]

Effect of appeals

3   Part II of Schedule 2 to this Act, so far as it relates to appeals under section [66 or 67 of the Immigration and Asylum Act 1999], shall apply for purposes of this Schedule as if the references ... in paragraph 29(1) to Part I of that Schedule were references to this Schedule; and paragraphs 29 to 33 shall apply in like manner in relation to appeals under section [63(1)(a) or 69(4)(a) of the Immigration and Asylum Act 1999].

[Powers of courts pending deportation

4   Where the release of a person recommended for deportation is directed by a court, he shall be subject to such restrictions as to residence[, as to his employment or occupation] and as to reporting to the police as the court may direct.

5   (1)   On an application made—

(a)   by or on behalf of a person recommended for deportation whose release was so directed; or
(b)   by a constable; or
(c)   by an immigration order,

the appropriate court shall have the powers specified in sub-paragraph (2) below.

(2)   The powers mentioned in sub-paragraph (1) above are—

(a)   if the person to whom the application relates is not subject to any such restrictions imposed by a court as are mentioned in paragraph 4 above, to order that he shall be subject to any such restrictions as the court may direct; and
(b)   if he is subject to such restrictions imposed by a court by virtue of that paragraph or this paragraph—
     (i)   to direct that any of them shall be varied or shall cease to have effect; or
     (ii)   to give further directions as to his residence and reporting.

6   (1)   In this Schedule "the appropriate court" means except in a case to which sub-paragraph (2) below applies, the court which directed release.

(2)   This sub-paragraph applies where the court which directed release was—

(a)   the Crown Court;
(b)   the Court of Appeal;
(c)   the High Court of Justiciary;
(d)   the Crown Court in Northern Ireland; or
(e)   the Court of Appeal in Northern Ireland.

(3)   Where the Crown Court or the Crown Court in Northern Ireland directed release, the appropriate court is—

(a)   the court that directed release; or
(b)   a magistrates' court acting for the commission area or county court division where the person to whom the application relates resides.

(4)   Where the Court of Appeal or the Court of Appeal in Northern Ireland gave the direction, the appropriate court is the Crown Court or the Crown Court in Northern Ireland, as the case may be.

(5)   Where the High Court of Justiciary directed release, the appropriate court is—

(a)   that court; or
(b)   in a case where release was directed by that court on appeal, the court from which the appeal was made.

7 (1) A constable or immigration officer may arrest without warrant any person who is subject to restrictions imposed by a court under this Schedule and who at the time of the arrest is in the relevant part of the United Kingdom—

(a) if he has reasonable grounds to suspect that that person is contravening or has contravened any of those restrictions; or

(b) if he has reasonable grounds for believing that that person is likely to contravene any of them.

(2) In sub-paragraph (1) above "the relevant part of the United Kingdom" means—

(a) England and Wales, in a case where a court with jurisdiction in England or Wales imposed the restrictions;

(b) Scotland, in a case where a court with jurisdiction in Scotland imposed them; and

(c) Northern Ireland, in a case where a court in Northern Ireland imposed them.

8 (1) A person arrested in England or Wales or Northern Ireland in pursuance of paragraph 7 above shall be brought as soon as practicable and in any event within 24 hours after his arrest before a justice of the peace for the petty sessions area or district in which he was arrested.

(2) In reckoning for the purposes of this paragraph any period of 24 hours, no account shall be taken of Christmas Day, Good Friday or any Sunday.

9 (1) A person arrested in Scotland in pursuance of paragraph 7 above shall wherever practicable be brought before the appropriate court not later than in the course of the first day after his arrest, such day not being a Saturday, a Sunday or a court holiday prescribed for that court under section 10 of the Bail etc. (Scotland) Act 1980.

(2) Nothing in this paragraph shall prevent a person arrested in Scotland being brought before a court on a Saturday, a Sunday or such a court holiday as is mentioned in sub-paragraph (1) above where the court is, in pursuance of section 10 of the said Act of 1980, sitting on such day for the disposal of criminal business.

10 Any justice of the peace or court before whom a person is brought by virtue of paragraph 8 or 9 above—

(a) if of the opinion that that person is contravening, has contravened or is likely to contravene any restriction imposed on him by a court under this Schedule, may direct—
   (i) that he be detained; or
   (ii) that he be released subject to such restrictions as to his residence and reporting to the police as the court may direct; and

(b) if not of that opinion, shall release him without altering the restrictions as to his residence and his reporting to the police.]

NOTES

Appointment
Commencement order: SI 1972/1514.

Amendment
Para 2: in sub-para (1) words "or a direction is given under sub-paragraph (1A) below," in square brackets substituted by the Criminal Justice Act 1982, s 64, Sch 10.
Para 2: in sub-para (1) words "or he is released on bail" in square brackets inserted by the Immigration and Asylum Act 1999, s 54(1), (2).
Date in force: to be appointed: see the Immigration and Asylum Act 1999, s 170(4).
Para 2: sub-paras (1A), (6) inserted by the Criminal Justice Act 1982, s 64, Sch 10.
Para 2: in sub-para (3) words "he is released on bail or" in square brackets inserted by the Immigration and Asylum Act 1999, s 54(1), (3).

Date in force: to be appointed: see the Immigration and Asylum Act 1999, s 170(4).
Para 2: in sub-para (4) words ", 18 and 25A to 25E" in square brackets substituted by the Immigration and Asylum Act 1999, s 169(1), Sch 14, paras 43, 68.
Date in force: 14 February 2000: see SI 2000/168, art 2, Schedule.
Para 2: sub-para (4A) inserted by the Immigration and Asylum Act 1999, s 54(1), (4).
Date in force: to be appointed: see the Immigration and Asylum Act 1999, s 170(4).
Para 2: sub-para (5) substituted by the Criminal Justice Act 1982, s 64, Sch 10.
Para 2: in sub-para (5) words ", as to his employment or occupation" in square brackets inserted by the Immigration Act 1988, s 10, Schedule.
Para 2: in sub-para (5) words "or an immigration officer" in square brackets inserted by the Asylum and Immigration Act 1996, s 12(1), Sch 2, para 13.
Para 3: words "66 or 67 of the Immigration and Asylum Act 1999" and "63(1)(a) or 69(4)(a) of the Immigration and Asylum Act 1999" in square brackets substituted by the Immigration and Asylum Act 1999, s 169(1), Sch 14, paras 43, 69(a), (c).
Date in force: 2 October 2000 (except in relation to an event which took place before that date): see SI 2000/2444, art 2, Sch 1; for transitional provisions see art 3, Sch 2, para 2(10) thereof.
Para 3: words omitted repealed by the Immigration and Asylum Act 1999, s 169(1), (3), Sch 14, paras 43, 69(b), Sch 16.
Date in force: 2 October 2000 (except in relation to an event which took place before that date): see SI 2000/2444, art 2, Sch 1; for transitional provisions see art 3, Sch 2, para 2(10) thereof.
Para 4: inserted, together with paras 5–10, by the Criminal Justice Act 1982, s 64, Sch 10, para 2.
Para 4: words in square brackets inserted by the Immigration Act 1988, s 10, Schedule, para 10.
Paras 5–10: inserted, together with para 4, by the Criminal Justice Act 1982, s 64, Sch 10, para 2.

Modification
Para 1 modified, in relation to France and the United Kingdom, by the Channel Tunnel (International Arrangements) Order 1993, SI 1993/1813, art 7(1), Sch 4, para 1(12).
Para 3 modified by the Asylum and Immigration Appeals Act 1993, s 8(6), Sch 2, para 9.
Modified, in relation to its application to frontier controls between the United Kingdom, France and Belgium, by the Channel Tunnel (Miscellaneous Provisions) Order 1994, SI 1994/1405, art 7.

SCHEDULE 4
Integration with United Kingdom Law of Immigration Law of Islands

Section 9

Leave to enter

1   (1) Where under the immigration laws of any of the Islands a person is or has been given leave to enter or remain in the island, or is or has been refused leave, this Act shall have effect in relation to him, if he is not [a British citizen], as if the leave were leave (of like duration) given under this Act to enter or remain the United Kingdom, or, as the case may be, as if he had under this Act been refused leave to enter the United Kingdom.

(2)   Where under the immigration laws of any of the Islands a person has a limited leave to enter or remain in the Island subject to any such conditions as are authorised in the United Kingdom by section 3(1) of this Act (being conditions imposed by notice given to him, whether the notice of leave or a subsequent notice), then on his coming to the United Kingdom this Act shall apply, if he is not [a British citizen], as if those conditions related to his stay in the United Kingdom and had been imposed by notice under this Act.

(3)   Without prejudice to the generality of sub-paragraphs (1) and (2) above, anything having effect in the United Kingdom by virtue of either of those sub-paragraphs may in relation to the United Kingdom be varied or revoked under this Act in like manner, and subject to the like appeal (if any), as if it had originated under this Act as mentioned in that sub-paragraph.

(4)   Where anything having effect in the United Kingdom by virtue of sub-paragraph (1) or (2) above ceases to have effect or is altered in effect as mentioned in sub-paragraph (3) or otherwise by anything done under this Act, sub-paragraph (1) or (2) shall not thereafter apply to it or, as the case may be, shall apply to it as so altered in effect.

(5)   Nothing in this paragraph shall be taken as conferring on a person a right of appeal under this Act against any decision or action taken in any of the Islands.

2   Notwithstanding section 3(4) of this Act, leave given to a person under this Act to enter or remain in the United Kingdom shall not continue to apply on his return to the United Kingdom after an absence if he has during that absence entered any of the Islands in circumstances in which he is required under the immigration laws of that island to obtain leave to enter.

Deportation

[**3**   (1)   This Act has effect in relation to a person who is subject to an Islands deportation order as if the order were a deportation order made against him under this Act.

(2)   Sub-paragraph (1) does not apply if the person concerned is—

   (a)   a British citizen;
   (b)   an EEA national;
   (c)   a member of the family of an EEA national; or
   (d)   a member of the family of a British citizen who is neither such a citizen nor an EEA national.

(3)   The Secretary of State does not, as a result of sub-paragraph (1), have power to revoke an Islands deportation order.

(4)   In any particular case, the Secretary of State may direct that paragraph (b), (c) or (d) of sub-paragraph (2) is not to apply in relation to the Islands deportation order.

(5)   Nothing in this paragraph makes it unlawful for a person in respect of whom an Islands deportation order is in force in any of the Islands to enter the United Kingdom on his way from that island to a place outside the United Kingdom.

(6)   "Islands deportation order" means an order made under the immigration laws of any of the Islands under which a person is, or has been, ordered to leave the island and forbidden to return.

(7)   Subsections (10) and (12) to (14) of section 80 of the Immigration and Asylum Act 1999 apply for the purposes of this section as they apply for the purposes of that section.]

Illegal entrants

4   Notwithstanding anything in section 1(3) of this Act, it shall not be lawful for a person who is not [a British citizen] to enter the United Kingdom from any of the Islands where his presence was unlawful under the immigration laws of that island, unless he is given leave to enter.

NOTES

Appointment
Commencement order: SI 1972/1514.

Amendment
Para 1: in sub-paras (1), (2) words "a British Citizen" in square brackets substituted by the British Nationality Act 1981, s 39(6), Sch 4, para 2.
Para 3: substituted by the Immigration and Asylum Act 1999, s 169(1), Sch 14, paras 43, 70.

Date in force: 2 October 2000: see SI 2000/2444, art 2, Sch 1.
Para 4: words "a British Citizen" in square brackets substituted by the British Nationality Act 1981, s 39(6), Sch 4, para 2.

SCHEDULE 5

. . .

NOTES

Amendment
Repealed by the Immigration and Asylum Act 1999, s 169(3), Sch 16.
Date in force: 14 February 2000: see SI 2000/168, art 2, Schedule.

. . .

NOTES

Amendment
Repealed by the Immigration and Asylum Act 1999, s 169(3), Sch 16.
Date in force: 14 February 2000: see SI 2000/168, art 2, Schedule.

PART I

. . .

NOTES

Amendment
Repealed by the Immigration and Asylum Act 1999, s 169(3), Sch 16.
Date in force: 14 February 2000: see SI 2000/168, art 2, Schedule.

. . .

NOTES

Amendment
Repealed by the Immigration and Asylum Act 1999, s 169(3), Sch 16.
Date in force: 14 February 2000: see SI 2000/168, art 2, Schedule.

PART II

. . .

NOTES

Amendment
Repealed by the Immigration and Asylum Act 1999, s 169(3), Sch 16.
Date in force: 14 February 2000: see SI 2000/168, art 2, Schedule.

. . .

NOTES

Amendment
Repealed by the Immigration and Asylum Act 1999, s 169(3), Sch 16.
Date in force: 14 February 2000: see SI 2000/168, art 2, Schedule.

PART III

. . .

NOTES

Amendment
Repealed by the Immigration and Asylum Act 1999, s 169(3), Sch 16.
Date in force: 14 February 2000: see SI 2000/168, art 2, Schedule.

. . .

NOTES

Amendment
Repealed by the Immigration and Asylum Act 1999, s 169(3), Sch 16.
Date in force: 14 February 2000: see SI 2000/168, art 2, Schedule.

IMMIGRATION ACT 1988

1988 CHAPTER 14

An Act to make further provision for the regulation of immigration into the United Kingdom; and for connected purposes

[10th May 1988]

BE IT ENACTED by the Queen's most Excellent Majesty, by and with the advice and consent of the Lords Spiritual and Temporal, and Commons, in this present Parliament assembled, and by the authority of the same, as follows:–

1 Termination of saving in respect of Commonwealth citizens settled before 1973

. . .

NOTES

Appointment
Commencement order: SI 1988/1133.

Amendment
This section repeals the Immigration Act 1971, s 1(5).

2 Restriction on exercise of right of abode in cases of polygamy

(1) This section applies to any woman who—

    (a) has the right of abode in the United Kingdom under section 2(1)(b) of the principal Act as, or as having been, the wife of a man ("the husband")—
        (i) to whom she is or was polygamously married; and
        (ii) who is or was such a citizen of the United Kingdom and Colonies, Commonwealth citizen or British subject as is mentioned in section 2(2)(a) or (b) of that Act as in force immediately before the commencement of the British Nationality Act 1981; and
    (b) has not before the coming into force of this section and since her marriage to the husband been in the United Kingdom.

(2) A woman to whom this section applies shall not be entitled to enter the United Kingdom in the exercise of the right of abode mentioned in subsection (1)(a) above or

1003

to be granted a certificate of entitlement in respect of that right if there is another woman living (whether or not one to whom this section applies) who is the wife or widow of the husband and who—

(a) is, or at any time since her marriage to the husband has been, in the United Kingdom; or

(b) has been granted a certificate of entitlement in respect of the right of abode mentioned in subsection (1)(a) above or an entry clearance to enter the United Kingdom as the wife of the husband.

(3) So long as a woman is precluded by subsection (2) above from entering the United Kingdom in the exercise of her right of abode or being granted a certificate of entitlement in respect of that right the principal Act shall apply to her as it applies to a person not having a right of abode.

(4) Subsection (2) above shall not preclude a woman from re-entering the United Kingdom if since her marriage to the husband she has at any time previously been in the United Kingdom and there was at that time no such other woman living as is mentioned in that subsection.

(5) Where a woman claims that this section does not apply to her because she had been in the United Kingdom before the coming into force of this section and since her marriage to the husband it shall be for her to prove that fact.

(6) For the purposes of this section a marriage may be polygamous although at its inception neither party has any spouse additional to the other.

(7) For the purposes of subsections (1)(b), (2)(a), (4) and (5) above there shall be disregarded presence in the United Kingdom as a visitor or an illegal entrant and presence in circumstances in which a person is deemed by section 11(1) of the principal Act not to have entered the United Kingdom.

(8) In subsection (2)(b) above the reference to a certificate of entitlement includes a reference to a certificate treated as such a certificate by virtue of section 39(8) of the British Nationality Act 1981.

(9) No application by a woman for a certificate of entitlement in respect of such a right of abode as is mentioned in subsection (1)(a) above or for an entry clearance shall be granted if another application for such a certificate or clearance is pending and that application is made by a woman as the wife or widow of the same husband.

(10) For the purposes of subsection (9) above an application shall be regarded as pending so long as it and any appeal proceedings relating to it have not been finally determined.

NOTES

Appointment
Commencement order: SI 1988/1133.

3   Proof of right of abode

. . .

NOTES

Appointment
Commencement order: SI 1988/1133.

Amendment
This section amends the Immigration Act 1971, ss 2, 3, 13, and the British Nationality Act 1981, s 39.

4   Members of diplomatic missions

. . .

NOTES

Appointment
Commencement order: SI 1988/1133.

Amendment
This section amends the Immigration Act 1971, s 8.

5   . . .

. . .

NOTES

Amendment
Repealed by the Immigration and Asylum Act 1999, s 169(1), (3), Sch 14, paras 83, 84, Sch 16.
Date in force: 2 October 2000: see SI 2000/2444, art 2, Sch 1.

6   Knowingly overstaying limited leave

(1), (2) . . .

(3)   These amendments do not apply in relation to a person whose leave has expired
before the coming into force of this section.

NOTES

Amendment
Sub-ss (1), (2): amend the Immigration Act 1971, s 24.

7   Persons exercising Community rights and nationals of member States

(1)   A person shall not under the principal Act require leave to enter or remain in the
United Kingdom in any case in which he is entitled to do so by virtue of an enforceable
Community right or of any provision made under section 2(2) of the European
Communities Act 1972.

(2)   The Secretary of State may by order made by statutory instrument give leave to
enter the United Kingdom for a limited period to any class of persons who are nationals
of member States but who are not entitled to enter the United Kingdom as mentioned
in subsection (1) above; and any such order may give leave subject to such conditions
as may be imposed by the order.

(3)   References in the principal Act to limited leave shall include references to leave
given by an order under subsection (2) above and a person having leave by virtue of
such an order shall be treated as having been given that leave by a notice given to him
by an immigration officer within the period specified in paragraph 6(1) of Schedule 2 to
that Act.

NOTES

Appointment
Commencement order: SI 1994/1923.

8   Examination of passengers prior to arrival

(1)   This section applies to a person who arrives in the United Kingdom with a passport
or other travel document bearing a stamp which—

(a)   has been placed there by an immigration officer before that person's departure on his journey to the United Kingdom or in the course of that journey; and

(b)   states that the person may enter the United Kingdom either for an indefinite or a limited period and, if for a limited period, subject to specified conditions.

(2)   A person to whom this section applies shall for the purposes of the principal Act be deemed to have been given on arrival in the United Kingdom indefinite or, as the case may be, limited leave in terms corresponding to those of the stamp.

(3)   A person who is deemed to have leave by virtue of this section shall be treated as having been given it by a notice given to him by an immigration officer within the period specified in paragraph 6(1) of Schedule 2 to the principal Act.

(4)   A person deemed to have leave by virtue of this section shall not on his arrival in the United Kingdom be subject to examination under paragraph 2 of Schedule 2 to the principal Act but may be examined by an immigration officer for the purpose of establishing that he is such a person.

(5)   The leave which a person is deemed to have by virtue of this section may, at any time before the end of the period of twenty-four hours from his arrival at the port at which he seeks to enter the United Kingdom or, if he has been examined under subsection (4) above, from the conclusion of that examination, be cancelled by an immigration officer by giving him a notice in writing refusing him leave to enter.

(6)   Sub-paragraphs (3) and (4) of paragraph 6 of Schedule 2 to the principal Act shall have effect as if any notice under subsection (5) above were a notice under that paragraph.

(7)   References in this section to a person's arrival in the United Kingdom are to the first occasion on which he arrives after the time when the stamp in question was placed in his passport or travel document, being an occasion not later than seven days after that time.

[(8) ...]

NOTES

Amendment
Repealed by the Immigration and Asylum Act 1999, s 169(1), (3), Sch 14, paras 83, 85, Sch 16.
Date in force: to be appointed: see the Immigration and Asylum Act 1999, s 170(4).
Sub-s (8): inserted by SI 1990/2227, art 3, Sch 1, Part II; repealed by SI 1993/1813, art 9, Sch 6, Part I.

9   Charges

(1)   The Secretary of State may with the consent of the Treasury make regulations prescribing fees to be paid, at such times as may be prescribed, in connection with any application for indefinite leave to remain in the United Kingdom or the grant of such leave; and no such leave shall be granted unless any fee payable in connection with the grant of that leave has been paid.

(2)   Regulations under subsection (1) above may make different provision for different cases, including provision for cases in which no fee is to be paid.

(3)   The power to make regulations under subsection (1) above shall be exercisable by statutory instrument subject to annulment in pursuance of a resolution of either House of Parliament.

(4)   The Secretary of State may, at the request of any person and in consideration of such charges as he may determine, make arrangements for the provision at any port of additional immigration officers or for the provision of immigration officers for dealing with passengers of a particular description or in particular circumstances.

NOTES

Amendment

Repealed by the Immigration and Asylum Act 1999, s 169(1), (3), Sch 14, paras 83, 86, Sch 16.

Date in force: to be appointed: see the Immigration and Asylum Act 1999, s 170(4).

10 Miscellaneous minor amendments

The principal Act shall have effect with the amendments specified in the Schedule to this Act.

11 Expenses and receipts

(1)   There shall be paid out of money provided by Parliament any expenses incurred by the Secretary of State in consequence of this Act.

(2)   Any sums received by the Secretary of State by virtue of this Act shall be paid into the Consolidated Fund.

12 Short title, interpretation, commencement and extent

(1)   This Act may be cited as the Immigration Act 1988.

(2)   In this Act "the principal Act" means the Immigration Act 1971 and any expression which is also used in that Act has the same meaning as in that Act.

(3)   Except as provided in subsection (4) below this Act shall come into force at the end of the period of two months beginning with the day on which it is passed.

(4)   Sections 1, 2, 3, 4, 5 and 7(1) and paragraph 1 of the Schedule shall come into force on such day as may be appointed by the Secretary of State by an order made by statutory instrument; and such an order may appoint different days for different provisions and contain such transitional provisions and savings as the Secretary of State thinks necessary or expedient in connection with any provision brought into force.

(5)   This Act extends to Northern Ireland and section 36 of the principal Act (power to extend any of its provisions to the Channel Islands or the Isle of Man) shall apply also to the provisions of this Act.

SCHEDULE
Minor Amendments

Section 10

1–5 ...

Power to detain passport etc

6   (1) ...

(2)   This amendment does not apply in relation to any person whose examination under paragraph 2 or 3 of Schedule 2 began before the coming into force of this paragraph.

Time-limit for giving, refusing or cancelling leave to enter

7   (1) ...

(2)   This amendment does not apply in relation to any person whose examination under paragraph 2 began before the coming into force of this paragraph.

Leave in default of notice giving or refusing leave or cancelling refusal

8   (1), (2)   ...

(3)   The amendment in sub-paragraph (1) above does not apply in relation to any person in whose case the time-limit in paragraph 6(1) of Schedule 2 has expired before the coming into force of this paragraph; and the amendment in sub-paragraph (2) above does not apply in relation to a person given a notice of cancellation under paragraph 6(3) of Schedule 2 before the coming into force of this paragraph.

Time-limit for removal directions

9   (1)–(3)   ...

(4)   These amendments do not apply in relation to any person refused leave to enter the United Kingdom before the coming into force of this paragraph.

Restriction on work in case of persons temporarily admitted etc

10   (1)–(3)   ...

(4)   These amendments apply in relation to persons granted temporary admission or released from detention under paragraph 21 of Schedule 2, becoming liable to detention under paragraph 2(2) or (3) of Schedule 3, or directed to be released as mentioned in paragraph 4 of that Schedule, as the case may be, before as well as after the coming into force of this paragraph.

NOTES

Appointment
Commencement order: SI 1991/1001.

Amendment
Paras 1–5: amend the Immigration Act 1971, ss 3(3)(b), 5(6), 14, 28(1)(a), 33(1).
Para 6: sub-para (1) amends the Immigration Act 1971, Sch 2, para 4.
Para 7: sub-para (1) amends the Immigration Act 1971, Sch 2, para 6(1), (2).
Para 8: sub-paras (1), (2) amend the Immigration Act 1971, Sch 2, para 6(1), (3).
Para 9: sub-paras (1)–(3) amend the Immigration Act 1971, Sch 2, paras 8(2), 10(1)(b), 28(4).
Para 10: sub-paras (1)–(3) amend the Immigration Act 1971, s 24(1)(e), Sch 2, para 21(2), Sch 3, paras 2(5), 4.

ASYLUM AND IMMIGRATION APPEALS ACT 1993

1993 CHAPTER 23

An Act to make provision about persons who claim asylum in the United Kingdom and their dependants; to amend the law with respect to certain rights of appeal under the Immigration Act 1971; and to extend the provisions of the Immigration (Carriers' Liability) Act 1987 to transit passengers

[1st July 1993]

Introductory

1   Interpretation

In this Act—

"the 1971 Act" means the Immigration Act 1971;

"claim for asylum" means a claim made by a person (whether before or after the coming into force of this section) that it would be contrary to the United Kingdom's obligations under the Convention for him to be removed from, or required to leave, the United Kingdom; and

"the Convention" means the Convention relating to the Status of Refugees done at Geneva on 28th July 1951 and the Protocol to that Convention.

NOTES

Appointment
Commencement order: SI 1993/1655.

2 Primacy of Convention

Nothing in the immigration rules (within the meaning of the 1971 Act) shall lay down any practice which would be contrary to the Convention.

15 Extent

(1) Her Majesty may by Order in Council direct that any of the provisions of this Act shall extend, with such modifications as appear to Her Majesty to be appropriate, to any of the Channel Islands or the Isle of Man.

(2) This Act extends to Northern Ireland.

16 Short title

This Act may be cited as the Asylum and Immigration Appeals Act 1993.

ASYLUM AND IMMIGRATION ACT 1996

1996 CHAPTER 49

An Act to amend and supplement the Immigration Act 1971 and the Asylum and Immigration Appeals Act 1993; to make further provision with respect to persons subject to immigration control and the employment of such persons; and for connected purposes

[24th July 1996]

Miscellaneous and supplemental

12 Other amendments and repeals

(1) Schedule 2 to this Act (which contains amendments of the 1971 Act and a related amendment of the Immigration Act 1988) shall have effect.

(2) Schedule 3 to this Act (which contains amendments of the 1993 Act) shall have effect.

(3) The enactments specified in Schedule 4 to this Act are hereby repealed to the extent specified in the third column of that Schedule.

13 Short title, interpretation, commencement and extent

(1) This Act may be cited as the Asylum and Immigration Act 1996.

(2)   In this Act—
>   "the 1971 Act" means the Immigration Act 1971;
>   "the 1993 Act" means the Asylum and Immigration Appeals Act 1993;
>   "person subject to immigration control" means a person who under the 1971 Act requires leave to enter or remain in the United Kingdom (whether or not such leave has been given).

(3)   This Act, except section 11 and Schedule 1, shall come into force on such day as the Secretary of State may by order made by statutory instrument appoint, and different days may be appointed for different purposes.

(4)   An order under subsection (3) above may make such transitional and supplemental provision as the Secretary of State thinks necessary or expedient.

(5)   Her Majesty may by Order in Council direct that any of the provisions of this Act shall extend, with such modifications as appear to Her Majesty to be appropriate, to any of the Channel Islands or the Isle of Man.

(6)   This Act extends to Northern Ireland.

SCHEDULE 1

. . .

NOTES

Amendment
Repealed by the Immigration and Asylum Act 1999, s 169(1), (3), Sch 14, paras 108, 113.
Date in force: 3 April 2000: see SI 2000/464, art 2, Schedule.

. . .

NOTES

Amendment
Repealed by the Immigration and Asylum Act 1999, s 169(1), (3), Sch 14, paras 108, 113.
Date in force: 3 April 2000: see SI 2000/464, art 2, Schedule.

PART I

. . .

NOTES

Amendment
Repealed by the Immigration and Asylum Act 1999, s 169(1), (3), Sch 14, paras 108, 113.
Date in force: 3 April 2000: see SI 2000/464, art 2, Schedule.

. . .

NOTES

Amendment
Repealed by the Immigration and Asylum Act 1999, s 169(1), (3), Sch 14, paras 108, 113.
Date in force: 3 April 2000: see SI 2000/464, art 2, Schedule.

PART II

. . .

NOTES

Amendment
Repealed by the Immigration and Asylum Act 1999, s 169(1), (3), Sch 14, paras 108, 113.
Date in force: 3 April 2000: see SI 2000/464, art 2, Schedule.

. . .

NOTES

Amendment
Repealed by the Immigration and Asylum Act 1999, s 169(1), (3), Sch 14, paras 108, 113.
Date in force: 3 April 2000: see SI 2000/464, art 2, Schedule.

SCHEDULE 2
Amendments of the 1971 Act and the Immigration Act 1988

Section 12(1)

. . .

NOTES

Amendment
This Schedule amends the Immigration Act 1988, s 5(1), the Immigration Act 1971, ss 3(1), (5), 5(4), 14, 33(1), (4), Sch 2, paras 4, 9, 17, 19–22, Sch 3, para 2, and adds Sch 2, para 34. Repealed in part by the Immigration and Asylum Act 1999, s 169(1), (3), Sch 14, paras 108, 114, Sch 16.
Date in force: 2 October 2000: see SI 2000/2444, art 2, Sch 1.

SCHEDULE 3
Amendments of the 1993 Act

Section 12(2)

1–5 ...

NOTES

Amendment
This Schedule amends the Asylum and Immigration Appeals Act 1993, ss 7, 8, Sch 1, para 6, Sch 2, para 4(2) and adds s 9A.
Paras 1, 2, 5: repealed by the Immigration and Asylum Act 1999, s 169(1), (3), Sch 14, paras 99, 115, Sch 16.
Date in force: 2 October 2000: see SI 2000/2444, art 2, Sch 1.

SPECIAL IMMIGRATION APPEALS COMMISSION ACT 1997

1997 CHAPTER 68

An Act to establish the Special Immigration Appeals Commission; to make provision with respect to its jurisdiction; and for connected purposes.

[17th December 1997]

1   Establishment of the Commission

(1)   There shall be a commission, known as the Special Immigration Appeals Commission, for the purpose of exercising the jurisdiction conferred by this Act.

(2)   Schedule 1 to this Act shall have effect in relation to the Commission.

NOTES

Initial Commencement
To be appointed
To be appointed: see s 9(2).

Appointment
Appointment: 3 August 1998: see SI 1998/1892, art 2.

2   Jurisdiction: appeals

[(1)   A person may appeal to the Special Immigration Appeals Commission against a decision which he would be entitled to appeal against under Part IV of the Immigration and Asylum Act 1999 ("the 1999 Act") but for a public interest provision.

(1A) Subsection (1) does not apply to an appeal under section 59(2) of the 1999 Act.

(1B) "Public interest provision" means any of sections 60(9), 62(4), 64(1) or (2) or 70(1) to (6) of the 1999 Act.

(1C) A reference in this Act to an appeal under this section includes a reference to an appeal under regulation 29(1) of the Immigration (European Economic Area) Regulations 2000 (other than on the ground mentioned in paragraph (2) of that regulation) which lies to the Commission as a result of regulation 31 of those Regulations.]

(2)   A person may appeal to the Special Immigration Appeals Commission against the refusal of an entry clearance if he would be entitled to appeal against the refusal under [section 59(2) of the 1999 Act but for section 60(9) of that Act] (exclusion conducive to public good), and—

    (a)   he seeks to rely on an enforceable Community right or any provision made under section 2(2) of the European Communities Act 1972, or
    (b)   he seeks to enter the United Kingdom under immigration rules making provision about entry—
        (i)   to exercise rights of access to a child resident there,
        (ii)   as the spouse or fiance of a person present and settled there, or
        (iii)   as the parent, grandparent or other dependent relative of a person present and settled there.

(3)   Schedule 2 to this Act (which makes supplementary provision relating to appeals under this section) shall have effect.

(4)   In this section, "immigration rules" has the same meaning as in the Immigration Act 1971.

NOTES

Initial Commencement
To be appointed
To be appointed: see s 9(2).

Appointment
Appointment: 3 August 1998: see SI 1998/1892, art 2.

Amendment
Sub-ss (1)–(1C): substituted for sub-s (1) as originally enacted by SI 2000/2326, reg 32(1), (2).

Date in force: 2 October 2000 (except in relation to any decision made before that date): see SI 2000/2326, reg 1(1); for transitional provisions see s 36 thereof.

Sub-s (2): words from "section 59(2) of the 1999 Act but for section 60(9) of that Act" in square brackets substituted by the Immigration and Asylum Act 1999, s 169(1), Sch 14, paras 118, 120.

Date in force: 2 October 2000 (except in relation to events which took place before that date): see SI 2000/2444, art 2, Sch 1; for transitional provisions see art 3, Sch 2, para 5(1) thereof.

[2A Jurisdiction: [racial discrimination and] human rights]

[(1) A person who alleges that an authority has, in taking an appealable decision, [racially discriminated against him or] acted in breach of his human rights may appeal to the Commission against that decision.

(2) For the purposes of this section[—

    (a)   an authority racially discriminates against a person if he acts, or fails to act, in relation to that other person in a way which is unlawful by virtue of section 19B of the Race Relations Act 1976; and

    (b)] an authority acts in breach of a person's human rights if he acts, or fails to act, in relation to that other person in a way which is made unlawful by section 6(1) of the Human Rights Act 1998.

(3) Subsections (4) and (5) apply if, in any appellate proceedings being heard by the Commission, a question arises as to whether an authority has, in taking a decision which is the subject of the proceedings, [racially discriminated against the appellant or] acted in breach of the appellant's human rights.

(4) The Commission has jurisdiction to consider the question.

(5) If the Commission decides that the authority concerned[—

    (a)   racially discriminated against the appellant; or

    (b)] acted in breach of the appellant's human rights, the appeal may be allowed on [the ground in question].

(6) "Authority" means—

    (a)   the Secretary of State;

    (b)   an immigration officer;

    (c)   a person responsible for the grant or refusal of entry clearance.]

[(7) "Appealable decision" means a decision against which a person would be entitled to appeal under Part IV of the 1999 Act but for a public interest provision.

(8) "The 1999 Act" and "public interest provision" have the same meaning as in section 2.

(9) A reference in this Act to an appeal under this section includes a reference to an appeal under regulation 29(1) of the Immigration (European Economic Area) Regulations 2000, on the ground mentioned in paragraph (2) of that regulation, which lies to the Commission as a result of regulation 31 of those Regulations.]

NOTES

Amendment

Provision heading: words "racial discrimination and" in square brackets inserted by the Race Relations (Amendment) Act 2000, s 9(1), Sch 2, para 27.

Inserted by the Immigration and Asylum Act 1999, s 169(1), Sch 14, paras 118, 121.

Date in force (in so far as it relates to sub-ss (1)–(6)): 2 October 2000 (except in relation to events which took place before that date): see SI 2000/2444, art 2, Sch 1; for transitional provisions see art 3, Sch 2, para 5 thereof.

Sub-s (1): words "racially discriminated against him or" in square brackets inserted by the Race Relations (Amendment) Act 2000, s 9(1), Sch 2, para 23.

Date in force: 2 April 2001: see SI 2001/566, art 2(1).
Sub-s (2): words in square brackets from "— (a)" to "b" inserted by the Race Relations (Amendment) Act 2000, s 9(1), Sch 2, para 24.
Date in force: 2 April 2001: see SI 2001/566, art 2(1).
Sub-s (3): words "racially discriminated against the appellant or" in square brackets inserted by the Race Relations (Amendment) Act 2000, s 9(1), Sch 2, para 25.
Date in force: 2 April 2001: see SI 2001/566, art 2(1).
Sub-s (5): words in square brackets from "— (a)" to "b" inserted by the Race Relations (Amendment) Act 2000, s 9(1), Sch 2, para 26(a).
Date in force: 2 April 2001: see SI 2001/566, art 2(1).
Sub-s (5): in para (b) words "that ground" in italics repealed and subsequent words in square brackets substituted by the Race Relations (Amendment) Act 2000, s 9(1), Sch 2, para 26(b).
Date in force: 2 April 2001: see SI 2001/566, art 2(1).
Sub-ss (7)–(9): original sub-ss (7), (8) inserted by the Immigration and Asylum Act 1999, s 169(1), Sch 14, paras 118, 121 (as noted above); new sub-ss (7)–(9) inserted by the Immigration (European Economic Area) Regulations 2000, SI 2000/2326, reg 32, which also provided for the repeal of the Immigration and Asylum Act 1999, Sch 14, para 121 in so far as it related to the original insertion of sub-ss (7), (8).
Date in force: 2 October 2000 (except in relation to any decision made before that date): see SI 2000/2326, reg 1(1); for transitional provisions see s 36 thereof.

3   Jurisdiction: bail

(1)   In the case of a person to whom subsection (2) below applies, the provisions of Schedule 2 to the Immigration Act 1971 specified in Schedule 3 to this Act shall have effect with the modifications set out there.

(2)   This subsection applies to a person who is detained under the Immigration Act 1971 if—

> (a)   the Secretary of State certifies that his detention is necessary in the interests of national security,
> (b)   he is detained following a decision to refuse him leave to enter the United Kingdom on the ground that his exclusion is in the interests of national security, or
> (c)   he is detained following a decision to make a deportation order against him on the ground that his deportation is in the interests of national security.

NOTES

Initial Commencement
To be appointed
To be appointed: see s 9(2).

Appointment
Appointment: 3 August 1998: see SI 1998/1892, art 2.

4   Determination of appeals

(1)   The Special Immigration Appeals Commission on an appeal to it under this Act—

> (a)   shall allow the appeal if it considers—
> > (i)   that the decision or action against which the appeal is brought was not in accordance with the law or with any immigration rules applicable to the case, or
> > (ii)   where the decision or action involved the exercise of a discretion by the Secretary of State or an officer, that the discretion should have been exercised differently, and
> (b)   in any other case, shall dismiss the appeal.

[(1A)   If a certificate under section 70(4)(b) of the Immigration and Asylum Act 1999 has been issued, the Commission on an appeal to it under this Act may, instead of determining the appeal, quash the certificate and remit the appeal to an adjudicator.]

(2)   Where an appeal is allowed, the Commission shall give such directions for giving effect to the determination as it thinks requisite, and may also make recommendations with respect to any other action which it considers should be taken in the case under the Immigration Act 1971; and it shall be the duty of the Secretary of State and of any officer to whom directions are given under this subsection to comply with them.

(3)   In this section, "immigration rules" has the same meaning as in the Immigration Act 1971.

NOTES

Initial Commencement
To be appointed
To be appointed: see s 9(2).

Appointment
Appointment: 3 August 1998: see SI 1998/1892, art 2.

Amendment
Sub-s (1A): inserted by the Immigration and Asylum Act 1999, s 169(1), Sch 14, paras 118, 122.
Date in force: 2 October 2000: see SI 2000/2444, art 2, Sch 1.

5   Procedure in relation to jurisdiction under sections 2 and 3

(1)   The Lord Chancellor may make rules—

- (a)   for regulating the exercise of the rights of appeal conferred by section 2 [or 2A] above,
- (b)   for prescribing the practice and procedure to be followed on or in connection with appeals under [section 2 or 2A above], including the mode and burden of proof and admissibility of evidence on such appeals, and
- (c)   for other matters preliminary or incidental to or arising out of such appeals, including proof of the decisions of the Special Immigration Appeals Commission.

(2)   Rules under this section shall provide that an appellant has the right to be legally represented in any proceedings before the Commission on an appeal under section 2 [or 2A] above, subject to any power conferred on the Commission by such rules.

(3)   Rules under this section may, in particular—

- (a)   make provision enabling proceedings before the Commission to take place without the appellant being given full particulars of the reasons for the decision which is the subject of the appeal,
- (b)   make provision enabling the Commission to hold proceedings in the absence of any person, including the appellant and any legal representative appointed by him,
- (c)   make provision about the functions in proceedings before the Commission of persons appointed under section 6 below, and
- (d)   make provision enabling the Commission to give the appellant a summary of any evidence taken in his absence.

(4)   Rules under this section may also include provision—

- (a)   enabling any functions of the Commission which relate to matters preliminary or incidental to an appeal, or which are conferred by Part II of Schedule 2 to the Immigration Act 1971, to be performed by a single member of the Commission, or
- (b)   conferring on the Commission such ancillary powers as the Lord Chancellor thinks necessary for the purposes of the exercise of its functions.

(5)   The power to make rules under this section shall include power to make rules with respect to applications to the Commission under paragraphs 22 to 24 of Schedule 2 to the Immigration Act 1971 and matters arising out of such applications.

(6)   In making rules under this section, the Lord Chancellor shall have regard, in particular, to—

    (a)   the need to secure that decisions which are the subject of appeals are properly reviewed, and

    (b)   the need to secure that information is not disclosed contrary to the public interest.

(7)   ...

(8)   The power to make rules under this section shall be exercisable by statutory instrument.

(9)   No rules shall be made under this section unless a draft of them has been laid before and approved by resolution of each House of Parliament.

NOTES

Initial Commencement
To be appointed
To be appointed: see s 9(2).

Appointment
Appointment: 11 June 1998: see SI 1998/1336, art 2.

Amendment
Sub-s (1): in para (a) words "or 2A" in square brackets inserted by the Race Relations (Amendment) Act 2000, s 9(1), Sch 2, para 28(a).
Date in force: 2 April 2001: see SI 2001/566, art 2(1).
Sub-s (1): in para (b) words in square brackets substituted by the Race Relations (Amendment) Act 2000, s 9(1), Sch 2, para 28(b).
Date in force: to be appointed: 2 April 2001: see SI 2001/566, art 2(1).
Sub-s (2): words "or 2A" in square brackets inserted by the Race Relations (Amendment) Act 2000, s 9(1), Sch 2, para 28(c).
Date in force: 2 April 2001: see SI 2001/566, art 2(1).
Sub-s (7): repealed by the Regulation of Investigatory Powers Act 2000, s 82(2), Sch 5.
Date in force: 2 October 2000: see SI 2000/2543, art 3.

Subordinate Legislation
Special Immigration Appeals Commission (Procedure) (Amendment) Rules 2000, SI 2000/1849.

6   Appointment of person to represent the appellant's interests

(1)   The relevant law officer may appoint a person to represent the interests of an appellant in any proceedings before the Special Immigration Appeals Commission from which the appellant and any legal representative of his are excluded.

(2)   For the purposes of subsection (1) above, the relevant law officer is—

    (a)   in relation to proceedings before the Commission in England and Wales, the Attorney General,

    (b)   in relation to proceedings before the Commission in Scotland, the Lord Advocate, and

    (c)   in relation to proceedings before the Commission in Northern Ireland, the Attorney General for Northern Ireland.

(3)   A person appointed under subsection (1) above—

    (a)   if appointed for the purposes of proceedings in England and Wales, shall have a general qualification for the purposes of section 71 of the Courts and Legal Services Act 1990,

(b) if appointed for the purposes of proceedings in Scotland, shall be—
    (i) an advocate, or
    (ii) a solicitor who has by virtue of section 25A of the Solicitors (Scotland) Act 1980 rights of audience in the Court of Session and the High Court of Justiciary, and

(c) if appointed for the purposes of proceedings in Northern Ireland, shall be a member of the Bar of Northern Ireland.

(4) A person appointed under subsection (1) above shall not be responsible to the person whose interests he is appointed to represent.

NOTES

Initial Commencement
To be appointed
To be appointed: see s 9(2).

Appointment
Appointment: 3 August 1998: see SI 1998/1892, art 2.

Transfer of Functions
By virtue of the Scotland Act 1998, s 44(1)(c), the Lord Advocate ceased, on 20 May 1999 (see SI 1998/3178), to be a Minister of the Crown and became a member of the Scottish Executive. Accordingly, certain functions of the Lord Advocate are transferred to the Secretary of State (or as the case may be the Secretary of State for Scotland), or the Advocate General for Scotland: see the Transfer of Functions (Lord Advocate and Secretary of State) Order 1999, SI 1999/678 and the Transfer of Functions (Lord Advocate and Advocate General for Scotland) Order 1999, SI 1999/679.

7 Appeals from the Commission

(1) Where the Special Immigration Appeals Commission has made a final determination of an appeal, any party to the appeal may bring a further appeal to the appropriate appeal court on any question of law material to that determination.

(2) An appeal under this section may be brought only with the leave of the Commission or, if such leave is refused, with the leave of the appropriate appeal court.

(3) In this section "the appropriate appeal court" means—

(a) in relation to a determination made by the Commission in England and Wales, the Court of Appeal,

(b) in relation to a determination made by the Commission in Scotland, the Court of Session, and

(c) in relation to a determination made by the Commission in Northern Ireland, the Court of Appeal in Northern Ireland.

(4) ...

NOTES

Initial Commencement
To be appointed
To be appointed: see s 9(2).

Appointment
Appointment: 3 August 1998: see SI 1998/1892, art 2.

Amendment
Sub-s (4): repealed by the Immigration and Asylum Act 1999, s 169(1), (3), Sch 14, paras 118, 123, Sch 16.
Date in force: 2 October 2000: see SI 2000/2444, art 2, Sch 1.

[7A   Pending appeals]

[(1)   For the purposes of this Act, an appeal to the Commission is to be treated as pending during the period beginning when notice of appeal is given and ending when the appeal is finally determined, withdrawn or abandoned.

(2)   An appeal is not to be treated as finally determined while a further appeal may be brought.

(3)   If a further appeal is brought, the original appeal is not to be treated as finally determined until the further appeal is determined, withdrawn or abandoned.

(4)   A pending appeal to the Commission is to be treated as abandoned if the appellant leaves the United Kingdom.

(5)   A pending appeal to the Commission is to be treated as abandoned if the appellant is granted leave to enter or remain in the United Kingdom.

(6)   But subsection (5) does not apply to an appeal brought under section 2(1) as a result of section 70(4) of the Immigration and Asylum Act 1999.

(7)   A pending appeal brought under section 2(1) as a result of section 62(3) of that Act is to be treated as abandoned if a deportation order is made against the appellant.]

NOTES

Amendment
Inserted by the Immigration and Asylum Act 1999, s 169(1), Sch 14, paras 118, 124.
Date in force: 2 October 2000: see SI 2000/2444, art 2, Sch 1.

8   Procedure on applications to the Commission for leave to appeal

(1)   The Lord Chancellor may make rules regulating, and prescribing the procedure to be followed on, applications to the Special Immigration Appeals Commission for leave to appeal under section 7 above.

(2)   Rules under this section may include provision enabling an application for leave to appeal to be heard by a single member of the Commission.

(3)   The power to make rules under this section shall be exercisable by statutory instrument.

(4)   No rules shall be made under this section unless a draft of them has been laid before and approved by resolution of each House of Parliament.

NOTES

Initial Commencement
To be appointed
To be appointed: see s 9(2).

Appointment
Appointment: 11 June 1998: see SI 1998/1336, art 2.

9   Short title, commencement and extent

(1)   This Act may be cited as the Special Immigration Appeals Commission Act 1997.

(2)   This Act, except for this section, shall come into force on such day as the Secretary of State may by order made by statutory instrument appoint; and different days may be so appointed for different purposes.

(3)   Her Majesty may by Order in Council direct that any of the provisions of this Act shall extend, with such modifications as appear to Her Majesty to be appropriate, to any of the Channel Islands or the Isle of Man.

(4)   This Act extends to Northern Ireland.

NOTES

Initial Commencement
Royal Assent
Royal Assent: 17 December 1997: (no specific commencement provision).

SCHEDULE 1
The Commission

Section 1

Members

1   (1)   The Special Immigration Appeals Commission shall consist of such number of members appointed by the Lord Chancellor as he may determine.

(2)   A member of the Commission shall hold and vacate office in accordance with the terms of his appointment and shall, on ceasing to hold office, be eligible for re-appointment.

(3)   A member of the Commission may resign his office at any time by notice in writing to the Lord Chancellor.

Chairman

2   The Lord Chancellor shall appoint one of the members of the Commission to be its chairman.

Payments to members

3   (1)   The Lord Chancellor may pay to the members of the Commission such remuneration and allowances as he may determine.

(2)   The Lord Chancellor may, if he thinks fit in the case of any member of the Commission pay such pension, allowance or gratuity to or in respect of the member, or such sums towards the provision of such pension, allowance or gratuity, as he may determine.

(3)   If a person ceases to be a member of the Commission and it appears to the Lord Chancellor that there are special circumstances which make it right that the person should receive compensation, he may pay to that person a sum of such amount as he may determine.

Proceedings

4   The Commission shall sit at such times and in such places as the Lord Chancellor may direct and may sit in two or more divisions.

5   The Commission shall be deemed to be duly constituted if it consists of three members of whom—

(a)   at least one holds or has held high judicial office (within the meaning of the Appellate Jurisdiction Act 1876), and

(b) at least one is or has been—
  (i) appointed as chief adjudicator under [section 57(2) of the Immigration and Asylum Act 1999], or
  (ii) a member of the Immigration Appeal Tribunal qualified as mentioned in [paragraph 1(3) of Schedule 2 to that Act].

6   The chairman or, in his absence, such other member of the Commission as he may nominate, shall preside at sittings of the Commission and report its decisions.

Staff

7   The Lord Chancellor may appoint such officers and servants for the Commission as he thinks fit.

Expenses

8   The Lord Chancellor shall defray the remuneration of persons appointed under paragraph 7 above and such expenses of the Commission as he thinks fit.

NOTES

Initial Commencement
To be appointed
To be appointed: see s 9(2).

Appointment
Appointment: 3 August 1998: see SI 1998/1892, art 2.

Amendment
Para 5: in sub-para (b) words "section 57(2) of the Immigration and Asylum Act 1999" and "paragraph 1(3) of Schedule 2 to that Act" in square brackets substituted by the Immigration and Asylum Act 1999, s 169(1), Sch 14, paras 118, 125.
Date in force: 14 February 2000: see SI 2000/168, art 2, Schedule.

SCHEDULE 2
Appeals: Supplementary

Section 2

[Stay on directions for removal

1   If a person in the United Kingdom appeals under section 2(1) above on being refused leave to enter, any directions previously given by virtue of the refusal for his removal from the United Kingdom cease to have effect, except in so far as they have already been carried out, and no directions may be so given so long as the appeal is pending.

2   If a person in the United Kingdom appeals under section 2(1) above against any directions given under Part I of Schedule 2 or Schedule 3 to the 1971 Act for his removal from the United Kingdom, those directions except in so far as they have already been carried out, have no effect while the appeal is pending.

3   But the provisions of Part I of Schedule 2 or, as the case may be, Schedule 3 to the 1971 Act with respect to detention and persons liable to detention apply to a person appealing under section 2(1) above as if there were in force directions for his removal from the United Kingdom, except that he may not be detained on board a ship or aircraft so as to compel him to leave the United Kingdom while the appeal is pending.

3A   In calculating the period of two months limited by paragraph 8(2) of Schedule 2 to the 1971 Act for the giving of directions under that paragraph for the removal of a person from the United Kingdom and for the giving of a notice of intention to give such directions, any period during which there is pending an appeal by him under section 2(1) above is to be disregarded.

3B If directions are given under Part I of Schedule 2 or Schedule 3 to the 1971 Act for anyone's removal from the United Kingdom, and directions are also so given for the removal with him of persons belonging to his family, then if any of them appeals under section 2(1) above, the appeal has the same effect under paragraphs 1 to 3A in relation to the directions given in respect of each of the others as it has in relation to the directions given in respect of the appellant.

Suspension of variation of limited leave

3C A variation is not to take effect while an appeal is pending under section 2(1) above against the variation.

Continuation of leave

3D (1) While an appeal under section 2(1) above is pending, the leave to which the appeal relates, and any conditions subject to which it was granted continue to have effect.

(2) A person may not make an application for a variation of his leave to enter or remain while that leave is treated as continuing to have effect as a result of sub-paragraph (1).

(3) For the purposes of section 2(1), in calculating whether, as a result of a decision, a person may be required to leave the United Kingdom within twenty-eight days, a continuation of leave under this paragraph is to be disregarded.

Deportation orders

3E A deportation order is not to be made against a person under section 5 of the 1971 Act while an appeal duly brought under section 2(1) above against the decision to make it is pending.

3F In calculating the period of eight weeks set by section 5(3) of the 1971 Act for making a deportation order against a person as belonging to the family of another person, there is to be disregarded any period during which an appeal under section 2(1) above against the decision to make the order is pending.

Appeals under section 2A

3G (1) A person is not to be required to leave, or be removed from, the United Kingdom if an appeal under section 2A is pending against the decision on which that requirement or removal would otherwise be based.

(2) That does not prevent—

    (a) directions for his removal being given during that period;
    (b) a deportation order being made against him during that period.

(3) But no such direction or order is to have effect during that period.]

Construction of references to pending appeal

4 For the purposes of [this Schedule], an appeal under section 2 [or 2A] above shall be treated as pending during the period beginning when notice of appeal is duly given and ending when the appeal is finally determined or withdrawn; and an appeal shall not be treated as finally determined so long as a further appeal can be brought by virtue of section 7 above, nor, if such an appeal is duly brought, until it is determined or withdrawn.

. . .

5   . . .

[Notice of appealable decision and statement of appeal rights etc

6   Paragraph 1 of Schedule 4 to the Immigration and Asylum Act 1999 has effect as if section 2 [and 2A] of this Act were contained in Part IV of that Act.

Financial support for organisations helping persons with rights of appeal

7   Section 81 of the Immigration and Asylum Act 1999 shall have effect as if section 2 [and 2A] above were contained in Part IV of that Act.]

NOTES

Initial Commencement
To be appointed
To be appointed: see s 9(2).

Appointment
Appointment: 3 August 1998: see SI 1998/1892, art 2.

Amendment
Paras 1–3, 3A–3G: substituted, for paras 1–3 as originally enacted, by the Immigration and Asylum Act 1999, s 169(1), Sch 14, paras 118, 126.
Date in force: 2 October 2000: see SI 2000/2444, art 2, Sch 1.
Para 4: words "this Schedule" in square brackets substituted by the Immigration and Asylum Act 1999, s 169(1), Sch 14, paras 118, 127.
Date in force: 2 October 2000: see SI 2000/2444, art 2, Sch 1.
Para 4: words "or 2A" in square brackets inserted by the Race Relations (Amendment) Act 2000, s 9(1), Sch 2, para 29(a).
Date in force: 2 April 2001: see SI 2001/566, art 2(1).
Para 5: repealed by the Immigration and Asylum Act 1999, s 169(1), (3), Sch 14, paras 118, 128, Sch 16.
Date in force: 2 October 2000: see SI 2000/2444, art 2, Sch 1.
Paras 6, 7: substituted by the Immigration and Asylum Act 1999, s 169(1), Sch 14, paras 118, 129.
Date in force: 1 August 2000: see SI 2000/1985, art 2, Schedule; for transitional provisions see art 3 thereof.
Para 6: words "and 2A" in square brackets inserted by the Race Relations (Amendment) Act 2000, s 9(1), Sch 2, para 29(b).
Date in force: 2 April 2001: see SI 2001/566, art 2(1).
Para 7: words "and 2A" in square brackets inserted by the Race Relations (Amendment) Act 2000, s 9(1), Sch 2, para 29(b).
Date in force: 2 April 2001: see SI 2001/566, art 2(1).

SCHEDULE 3
Bail: Modifications of Schedule 2 to the Immigration Act 1971

Section 3

1   (1) Paragraph 22 shall be amended as follows.

(2) In sub-paragraph (1A), for the words from the beginning to "adjudicator" there shall be substituted "The Special Immigration Appeals Commission .

(3) In sub-paragraph (2)—

    (a) for the words "immigration officer or adjudicator" there shall be substituted "Special Immigration Appeals Commission", and

    (b) for the words "officer or adjudicator" there shall be substituted "Commission".

(4) In sub-paragraph (3)—

    (a) for "an immigration officer or adjudicator" there shall be substituted "the Special Immigration Appeals Commission", and

    (b) for "officer or adjudicator", in both places, there shall be substituted "Commission".

2 (1) Paragraph 23 shall be amended as follows.

(2) In sub-paragraph (1)—

    (a) for "an adjudicator" there shall be substituted "the Special Immigration Appeals Commission", and

    (b) for "the adjudicator", in each place, there shall be substituted "the Commission".

(3) In sub-paragraph (2)—

    (a) for "an adjudicator" there shall be substituted "the Special Immigration Appeals Commission", and

    (b) for "the adjudicator" there shall be substituted "the Commission".

3 (1) Paragraph 24 shall be amended as follows.

(2) For sub-paragraph (2), there shall be substituted—

"(2) A person arrested under this paragraph shall be brought before the Special Immigration Appeals Commission within twenty-four hours."

(3) In sub-paragraph (3), for the words from the beginning to "above" there shall be substituted "Where a person is brought before the Special Immigration Appeals Commission by virtue of sub-paragraph (2) above, the Commission—"

4 (1) Paragraph 29 shall be amended as follows.

(2) For sub-paragraphs (2) to (4) there shall be substituted—

"(2) The Special Immigration Appeals Commission may release an appellant on his entering into a recognizance or, in Scotland, bail bond conditioned for his appearance before the Commission at a time and place named in the recognizance or bail bond."

(3) For sub-paragraph (6) there shall be substituted—

"(6) In any case in which the Special Immigration Appeals Commission has power to release an appellant on bail, the Commission may, instead of taking the bail, fix the amount and conditions of the bail (including the amount in which any sureties are to be bound) with a view to its being taken subsequently by any such person as may be specified by the Commission; and on the recognizance or bail bond being so taken the appellant shall be released."

5 Paragraph 30(2) shall be omitted.

6 (1) Paragraph 31 shall be amended as follows.

(2) In sub-paragraph (1)—

    (a) for "an adjudicator or the Tribunal" there shall be substituted "the Special Immigration Appeals Commission",

    (b) for "the adjudicator or the Tribunal, as the case may be," there shall be substituted "the Commission", and

    (c) for "the adjudicator or Tribunal", in both places, there shall be substituted "the Commission".

(3) In sub-paragraph (3)—

    (a) for "an adjudicator or the Tribunal" there shall be substituted "the Special Immigration Appeals Commission", and

    (b) for "the adjudicator or Tribunal" there shall be substituted "it".

7   Paragraph 32 shall be amended as follows—

    (a) for "an adjudicator or the Tribunal" there shall be substituted "the Special Immigration Appeals Commission",

    (b) for "the adjudicator or Tribunal" there shall be substituted "the Commission", and

    (c) for "the adjudicator or the Tribunal" there shall be substituted "the Commission".

8   (1) Paragraph 33 shall be amended as follows.

(2) For sub-paragraph (2), there shall be substituted—

"(2) A person arrested under this paragraph shall be brought before the Special Immigration Appeals Commission within twenty-four hours."

(3) In sub-paragraph (3), for the words from the beginning to "above" there shall be substituted "Where a person is brought before the Special Immigration Appeals Commission by virtue of sub-paragraph (2) above, the Commission—".

NOTES

Initial Commencement
To be appointed
To be appointed: see s 9(2).

Appointment
Appointment: 3 August 1998: see SI 1998/1892, art 2.

IMMIGRATION AND ASYLUM ACT 1999

1999 CHAPTER 33

An Act to make provision about immigration and asylum; to make provision about procedures in connection with marriage on superintendent registrar's certificate; and for connected purposes.

[11th November 1999]

PART I
IMMIGRATION: GENERAL

Leave to enter, or remain in, the United Kingdom

1   Leave to enter

In the 1971 Act, after section 3, insert—

"3A Further provision as to leave to enter

(1)   The Secretary of State may by order make further provision with respect to the giving, refusing or varying of leave to enter the United Kingdom.

(2)   An order under subsection (1) may, in particular, provide for—

   (a)   leave to be given or refused before the person concerned arrives in the United Kingdom;
   (b)   the form or manner in which leave may be given, refused or varied;
   (c)   the imposition of conditions;
   (d)   a person's leave to enter not to lapse on his leaving the common travel area.

(3)   The Secretary of State may by order provide that, in such circumstances as may be prescribed—

   (a)   an entry visa, or
   (b)   such other form of entry clearance as may be prescribed,

is to have effect as leave to enter the United Kingdom.

(4)   An order under subsection (3) may, in particular—

   (a)   provide for a clearance to have effect as leave to enter—
      (i)   on a prescribed number of occasions during the period for which the clearance has effect;
      (ii)   on an unlimited number of occasions during that period;
      (iii)   subject to prescribed conditions; and
   (b)   provide for a clearance which has the effect referred to in paragraph (a)(i) or (ii) to be varied by the Secretary of State or an immigration officer so that it ceases to have that effect.

(5)   Only conditions of a kind that could be imposed on leave to enter given under section 3 may be prescribed.

(6)   In subsections (3), (4) and (5) "prescribed" means prescribed in an order made under subsection (3).

(7)   The Secretary of State may, in such circumstances as may be prescribed in an order made by him, give or refuse leave to enter the United Kingdom.

(8)   An order under subsection (7) may provide that, in such circumstances as may be prescribed by the order, paragraphs 2, 4, 6, 7, 8, 9 and 21 of Part I of Schedule 2 to this Act are to be read, in relation to the exercise by the Secretary of State of functions which he has as a result of the order, as if references to an immigration officer included references to the Secretary of State.

(9)   Subsection (8) is not to be read as affecting any power conferred by subsection (10).

(10)   An order under this section may—

   (a)   contain such incidental, supplemental, consequential and transitional provision as the Secretary of State considers appropriate; and
   (b)   make different provision for different cases.

(11)   This Act and any provision made under it has effect subject to any order made under this section.

(12)   An order under this section must be made by statutory instrument.

(13)   But no such order is to be made unless a draft of the order has been laid before Parliament and approved by a resolution of each House."

NOTES

Initial Commencement
To be appointed
To be appointed: see s 170(4).

Appointment
Appointment: 14 February 2000: see SI 2000/168, art 2, Schedule.

2 Leave to remain

In the 1971 Act, after section 3A, insert—

"3B Further provision as to leave to remain

(1) The Secretary of State may by order make provision as to further provision with respect to the giving, refusing or varying of leave to remain in the United Kingdom.

(2) An order under subsection (1) may, in particular, provide for—

    (a) the form or manner in which leave may be given, refused or varied;
    (b) the imposition of conditions;
    (c) a person's leave to remain in the United Kingdom not to lapse on his leaving the common travel area.

(3) An order under this section may—

    (a) contain such incidental, supplemental, consequential and transitional provision as the Secretary of State considers appropriate; and
    (b) make different provision for different cases.

(4) This Act and any provision made under it has effect subject to any order made under this section.

(5) An order under this section must be made by statutory instrument.

(6) But no such order is to be made unless a draft of the order has been laid before Parliament and approved by a resolution of each House."

NOTES

Initial Commencement
To be appointed
To be appointed: see s 170(4).

Appointment
Appointment: 14 February 2000: see SI 2000/168, art 2, Schedule.

3 Continuation of leave pending decision

In the 1971 Act, after section 3B, insert—

"3C Continuation of leave pending decision

(1) This section applies if—

    (a) a person who has limited leave to enter or remain in the United Kingdom applies to the Secretary of State, before his leave expires, for it to be varied; and
    (b) when it expires, no decision has been taken on the application.

(2) His leave is to be treated as continuing until the end of the period allowed under rules made under paragraph 3 of Schedule 4 to the Immigration and Asylum Act 1999 for bringing an appeal against a decision on the application.

(3) An application for variation of a person's leave to enter or remain in the United Kingdom may not be made while that leave is treated as continuing as a result of this section.

(4) But subsection (3) does not prevent the variation of an application mentioned in subsection (1)."

NOTES

Initial Commencement
To be appointed
To be appointed: see s 170(4).

Appointment
Appointment: 2 October 2000: see SI 2000/2444, art 2, Sch 1.

4   Accommodation for those temporarily admitted or released from detention

The Secretary of State may provide, or arrange for the provision of, facilities for the accommodation of persons—

(a)   temporarily admitted to the United Kingdom under paragraph 21 of Schedule 2 to the 1971 Act;
(b)   released from detention under that paragraph; or
(c)   released on bail from detention under any provision of the Immigration Acts.

NOTES

Initial Commencement
Royal Assent
Royal Assent: 11 November 1999: see s 170(3)(a).

5   Charges

(1) The Secretary of State may, with the approval of the Treasury, make regulations prescribing fees to be paid in connection with applications for—

(a)   leave to remain in the United Kingdom;
(b)   the variation of leave to enter, or remain in, the United Kingdom;
(c)   an indefinite leave stamp to be fixed on the applicant's passport (or travel document) as the result of the renewal or replacement of his previous passport (or travel document).

(2) If a fee prescribed in connection with an application of a particular kind is payable, no such application is to be entertained by the Secretary of State unless the fee has been paid in accordance with the regulations.

(3) But—

(a)   a fee prescribed in connection with such an application is not payable if the basis on which the application is made is that the applicant is—
  (i)   a person making a claim for asylum which claim either has not been determined or has been granted; or
  (ii)   a dependant of such a person; and
(b)   the regulations may provide for no fee to be payable in prescribed circumstances.

(4) If no fee is payable in respect of some part of the application, the Secretary of State must entertain that part of the application.

(5) "Indefinite leave stamp" means a stamp which indicates that the applicant has been granted indefinite leave to enter, or remain in, the United Kingdom.

(6)   "Claim for asylum" has the meaning given in subsection (1) of section 94; and subsection (3) of that section applies for the purposes of this section as it applies for the purposes of Part VI.

(7)   "Dependant" has such meaning as may be prescribed.

NOTES

Initial Commencement
To be appointed
To be appointed: see s 170(4).

Exemption from immigration control

6   Members of missions other than diplomatic agents

In the 1971 Act, in section 8 (exceptions for certain categories of person), for subsection (3A) (members of diplomatic missions) substitute—

"(3A)   For the purposes of subsection (3), a member of a mission other than a diplomatic agent (as defined by the 1964 Act) is not to count as a member of a mission unless—

(a)   he was resident outside the United Kingdom, and was not in the United Kingdom, when he was offered a post as such a member; and
(b)   he has not ceased to be such a member after having taken up the post."

NOTES

Initial Commencement
To be appointed
To be appointed: see s 170(4).

Appointment
Appointment: 1 March 2000: see SI 2000/168, art 2, Schedule.

7   Persons ceasing to be exempt

In the 1971 Act, after section 8, insert—

"8A Persons ceasing to be exempt

(1)   A person is exempt for the purposes of this section if he is exempt from provisions of this Act as a result of section 8(2) or (3).

(2)   If a person who is exempt—

(a)   ceases to be exempt, and
(b)   requires leave to enter or remain in the United Kingdom as a result,

he is to be treated as if he had been given leave to remain in the United Kingdom for a period of 90 days beginning on the day on which he ceased to be exempt.

(3)   If—

(a)   a person who is exempt ceases to be exempt, and
(b)   there is in force in respect of him leave for him to enter or remain in the United Kingdom which expires before the end of the period mentioned in subsection (2),

his leave is to be treated as expiring at the end of that period."

NOTES

Initial Commencement
To be appointed
To be appointed: see s 170(4).

Appointment
Appointment: 1 March 2000: see SI 2000/168, art 2, Schedule.

8 Persons excluded from the United Kingdom under international obligations

In the 1971 Act, after section 8A, insert—

"8B Persons excluded from the United Kingdom under international obligations

(1) An excluded person must be refused—

    (a) leave to enter the United Kingdom;
    (b) leave to remain in the United Kingdom.

(2) A person's leave to enter or remain in the United Kingdom is cancelled on his becoming an excluded person.

(3) A person's exemption from the provisions of this Act as a result of section 8(1), (2) or (3) ceases on his becoming an excluded person.

(4) "Excluded person" means a person—

    (a) named by or under, or
    (b) of a description specified in,

a designated instrument.

(5) The Secretary of State may by order designate an instrument if it is a resolution of the Security Council of the United Nations or an instrument made by the Council of the European Union and it—

    (a) requires that a person is not to be admitted to the United Kingdom (however that requirement is expressed); or
    (b) recommends that a person should not be admitted to the United Kingdom (however that recommendation is expressed).

(6) Subsections (1) to (3) are subject to such exceptions (if any) as may specified in the order designating the instrument in question.

(7) An order under this section must be made by statutory instrument.

(8) Such a statutory instrument shall be laid before Parliament without delay."

NOTES

Initial Commencement
To be appointed
To be appointed: see s 170(4).

Appointment
Appointment: 1 March 2000: see SI 2000/168, art 2, Schedule.

Removal from the United Kingdom

9 Treatment of certain overstayers

(1) During the regularisation period overstayers may apply, in the prescribed manner, for leave to remain in the United Kingdom.

(2)   The regularisation period begins on the day prescribed for the purposes of this subsection and is not to be less than three months.

(3)   The regularisation period ends—

(a)   on the day prescribed for the purposes of this subsection; or
(b)   if later, on the day before that on which section 65 comes into force.

(4)   Section 10 and paragraph 12 of Schedule 15 come into force on the day after that on which the regularisation period ends.

(5)   The Secretary of State must publicise the effect of this section in the way appearing to him to be best calculated to bring it to the attention of those affected.

(6)   "Overstayer" means a person who, having only limited leave to enter or remain in the United Kingdom, remains beyond the time limited by the leave.

NOTES

Initial Commencement
Royal Assent
Royal Assent: 11 November 1999: see s 170(3)(b).

Subordinate Legislation
Immigration (Regularisation Period for Overstayers) Regulations 2000, SI 2000/265 (made under sub-ss (1), (2), (3)).

10   Removal of certain persons unlawfully in the United Kingdom

(1)   A person who is not a British citizen may be removed from the United Kingdom, in accordance with directions given by an immigration officer, if—

(a)   having only a limited leave to enter or remain, he does not observe a condition attached to the leave or remains beyond the time limited by the leave;
(b)   he has obtained leave to remain by deception; or
(c)   directions ("the first directions") have been given for the removal, under this section, of a person ("the other person") to whose family he belongs.

(2)   Directions may not be given under subsection (1)(a) if the person concerned has made an application for leave to remain in accordance with regulations made under section 9.

(3)   Directions may not be given under subsection (1)(c) unless the Secretary of State has given the person concerned written notice, not more than eight weeks after the other person left the United Kingdom in accordance with the first directions, that he intends to remove the person concerned from the United Kingdom.

(4)   If such a notice is sent by the Secretary of State by first class post, addressed to the person concerned's last known address, it is to be taken to have been received by that person on the second day after the day on which it was posted.

(5)   Directions for the removal of a person under subsection (1)(c) cease to have effect if he ceases to belong to the family of the other person.

(6)   Directions under this section—

(a)   may be given only to persons falling within a prescribed class;
(b)   may impose any requirements of a prescribed kind.

(7)   In relation to any such directions, paragraphs 10, 11, 16 to 18, 21 and 22 to 24 of Schedule 2 to the 1971 Act (administrative provisions as to control of entry), apply as they apply in relation to directions given under paragraph 8 of that Schedule.

(8)   Directions for the removal of a person given under this section invalidate any leave to enter or remain in the United Kingdom given to him before the directions are given or while they are in force.

(9)   The costs of complying with a direction given under this section (so far as reasonably incurred) must be met by the Secretary of State.

NOTES

Initial Commencement
To be appointed
To be appointed (in accordance with s 9): see s 170(4).

Appointment
Sub-ss (1)–(5), (7)–(9): Appointment: 2 October 2000: see SI 2000/2444, art 2, Sch 1; for transitional provisions see art 3, Sch 2, para 1(2), thereof.
Sub-s (6): Appointment: 22 May 2000: see SI 2000/1282, art 2, Schedule.

Subordinate Legislation
Immigration (Removal Directions) Regulations 2000, SI 2000/2243.

11   Removal of asylum claimants under standing arrangements with member States

(1)   In determining whether a person in relation to whom a certificate has been issued under subsection (2) may be removed from the United Kingdom, a member State is to be regarded as—

(a)   a place where a person's life and liberty is not threatened by reason of his race, religion, nationality, membership of a particular social group, or political opinion; and

(b)   a place from which a person will not be sent to another country otherwise than in accordance with the Refugee Convention.

(2)   Nothing in section 15 prevents a person who has made a claim for asylum ("the claimant") from being removed from the United Kingdom to a member State if—

(a)   the Secretary of State has certified that—
(i)   the member State has accepted that, under standing arrangements, it is the responsible State in relation to the claimant's claim for asylum; and
(ii)   in his opinion, the claimant is not a national or citizen of the member State to which he is to be sent;

(b)   the certificate has not been set aside on an appeal under section 65.

(3)   Unless a certificate has been issued under section 72(2)(a) in relation to a person, he is not to be removed from the United Kingdom—

(a)   if he has an appeal under section 65 against the decision to remove him in accordance with this section pending; or

(b)   before the time for giving notice of such an appeal has expired.

(4)   "Standing arrangements" means arrangements in force as between member States for determining which state is responsible for considering applications for asylum.

NOTES

Initial Commencement
To be appointed
To be appointed: see s 170(4).

Appointment
Appointment: 2 October 2000: see SI 2000/2444, art 2, Sch 1.

12   Removal of asylum claimants in other circumstances

(1)   Subsection (2) applies if the Secretary of State intends to remove a person who has made a claim for asylum ("the claimant") from the United Kingdom to—

  (a)   a member State, or a territory which forms part of a member State, otherwise than under standing arrangements; or

  (b)   a country other than a member State which is designated by order made by the Secretary of State for the purposes of this section.

(2)   Nothing in section 15 prevents the claimant's removal if—

  (a)   the Secretary of State has certified that, in his opinion, the conditions set out in subsection (7) are fulfilled;

  (b)   the certificate has not been set aside on an appeal under section 65.

(3)   Unless a certificate has been issued under section 72(2)(a) in relation to a person, he is not to be removed from the United Kingdom—

  (a)   if he has an appeal under section 65 against the decision to remove him in accordance with subsection (2) pending; or

  (b)   before the time for giving notice of such an appeal has expired.

(4)   Subsection (5) applies if the Secretary of State intends to remove a person who has made a claim for asylum ("the claimant") from the United Kingdom to a country which is not—

  (a)   a member State; or

  (b)   a country designated under subsection (1)(b).

(5)   Nothing in section 15 prevents the claimant's removal if—

  (a)   the Secretary of State has certified that, in his opinion, the conditions set out in subsection (7) are fulfilled;

  (b)   the certificate has not been set aside on an appeal under section 65 or 71; and

  (c)   the time for giving notice of such an appeal has expired and no such appeal is pending.

(6)   For the purposes of subsection (5)(c), an appeal under section 65 is not to be regarded as pending if the Secretary of State has issued a certificate under section 72(2)(a) in relation to the allegation on which it is founded.

(7)   The conditions are that—

  (a)   he is not a national or citizen of the country to which he is to be sent;

  (b)   his life and liberty would not be threatened there by reason of his race, religion, nationality, membership of a particular social group, or political opinion; and

  (c)   the government of that country would not send him to another country otherwise than in accordance with the Refugee Convention.

(8)   "Standing arrangements" has the same meaning as in section 11.

NOTES

Initial Commencement
To be appointed
To be appointed: see s 170(4).

Appointment
Sub-s (1): Appointment (for the purpose of enabling subordinate legislation to be made): 22 May 2000: see SI 2000/1282, art 2, Schedule.
Sub-s (1): Appointment (for remaining purposes): 2 October 2000: see SI 2000/2444, art 2, Sch 1.
Sub-ss (2)–(8): Appointment: 2 October 2000: see SI 2000/2444, art 2, Sch 1.

Subordinate Legislation
Asylum (Designated Safe Third Countries) Order 2000, SI 2000/2245 (made under sub-s (1)(b)).

13 Proof of identity of persons to be removed or deported

(1) This section applies if a person—

(a) is to be removed from the United Kingdom to a country of which he is a national or citizen; but

(b) does not have a valid passport or other document establishing his identity and nationality or citizenship and permitting him to travel.

(2) If the country to which the person is to be removed indicates that he will not be admitted to it unless identification data relating to him are provided by the Secretary of State, he may provide them with such data.

(3) In providing identification data, the Secretary of State must not disclose whether the person concerned has made a claim for asylum.

(4) For the purposes of paragraph 4(1) of Schedule 4 to the Data Protection Act 1998, the provision under this section of identification data is a transfer of personal data which is necessary for reasons of substantial public interest.

(5) "Identification data" means—

(a) fingerprints taken under section 141; or

(b) data collected in accordance with regulations made under section 144.

(6) "Removed" means removed as a result of directions given under section 10 or under Schedule 2 or 3 to the 1971 Act.

NOTES

Initial Commencement
To be appointed
To be appointed: see s 170(4).

Appointment
Appointment: 11 December 2000: see SI 2000/3099, art 3, Schedule.

14 Escorts for persons removed from the United Kingdom under directions

(1) Directions for, or requiring arrangements to be made for, the removal of a person from the United Kingdom may include or be amended to include provision for the person who is to be removed to be accompanied by an escort consisting of one or more persons specified in the directions.

(2) The Secretary of State may by regulations make further provision supplementing subsection (1).

(3) The regulations may, in particular, include provision—

(a) requiring the person to whom the directions are given to provide for the return of the escort to the United Kingdom;

(b) requiring him to bear such costs in connection with the escort (including, in particular, remuneration) as may be prescribed;

(c) as to the cases in which the Secretary of State is to bear those costs;

(d) prescribing the kinds of expenditure which are to count in calculating the costs incurred in connection with escorts.

NOTES

Initial Commencement
To be appointed
To be appointed: see s 170(4).

Appointment
Appointment: 1 March 2000: see SI 2000/168, art 2, Schedule.

15   Protection of claimants from removal or deportation

(1)   During the period beginning when a person makes a claim for asylum and ending when the Secretary of State gives him notice of the decision on the claim, he may not be removed from, or required to leave, the United Kingdom.

(2)   Subsection (1) does not prevent—

(a)   directions for his removal being given during that period;
(b)   a deportation order being made against him during that period.

(3)   But no such direction or order is to have effect during that period.

(4)   This section is to be treated as having come into force on 26 July 1993.

NOTES

Initial Commencement
Royal Assent
Royal Assent: 11 November 1999, with effect from 26 July 1993; see sub-s (4) above and s 170(3)(c).

Provision of financial security

16   Security on grant of entry clearance

(1)   In such circumstances as may be specified, the Secretary of State may require security to be given, with respect to a person applying for entry clearance, before clearance is given.

(2)   In such circumstances as may be specified—

(a)   the Secretary of State may accept security with respect to a person who is applying for entry clearance but for whom security is not required; and
(b)   in determining whether to give clearance, account may be taken of any security so provided.

(3)   "Security" means—

(a)   the deposit of a sum of money by the applicant, his agent or any other person, or
(b)   the provision by the applicant, his agent or any other person of a financial guarantee of a specified kind,

with a view to securing that the applicant will, if given leave to enter the United Kingdom for a limited period, leave the United Kingdom at the end of that period.

(4)   Immigration rules must make provision as to the circumstances in which a security provided under this section—

(a)   is to be repaid, released or otherwise cancelled; or
(b)   is to be forfeited or otherwise realised by the Secretary of State.

(5)   No security provided under this section may be forfeited or otherwise realised unless the person providing it has been given an opportunity, in accordance with immigration rules, to make representations to the Secretary of State.

(6) Immigration rules may, in particular—

    (a) fix the maximum amount that may be required, or accepted, by way of security provided under this section;

    (b) specify the form and manner in which such a security is to be given or may be accepted;

    (c) make provision, where such a security has been forfeited or otherwise realised, for the person providing it to be reimbursed in such circumstances as may be specified;

    (d) make different provision for different cases or descriptions of case.

(7) "Specified" means specified by immigration rules.

(8) Any security forfeited or otherwise realised by the Secretary of State under this section must be paid into the Consolidated Fund.

NOTES

Initial Commencement
To be appointed
To be appointed: see s 170(4).

17 Provision of further security on extension of leave

(1) This section applies if security has been provided under section 16(1) or (2) with respect to a person who, having entered the United Kingdom (with leave to do so), applies—

    (a) to extend his leave to enter the United Kingdom; or

    (b) for leave to remain in the United Kingdom for a limited period.

(2) The Secretary of State may refuse the application if security of such kind as the Secretary of State considers appropriate is not provided, or continued, with respect to the applicant.

(3) Immigration rules must make provision as to the circumstances in which a security provided under this section—

    (a) is to be repaid, released or otherwise cancelled; or

    (b) is to be forfeited or otherwise realised by the Secretary of State.

(4) No security provided under this section may be forfeited or otherwise realised unless the person providing it has been given an opportunity, in accordance with immigration rules, to make representations to the Secretary of State.

(5) Subsection (7) of section 16 applies in relation to this section as it applies in relation to that section.

(6) Any security forfeited or otherwise realised by the Secretary of State under this section must be paid into the Consolidated Fund.

NOTES

Initial Commencement
To be appointed
To be appointed: see s 170(4).

Information

18 Passenger information

In the 1971 Act, in Schedule 2, after paragraph 27, insert—

"Passenger information

27B (1) This paragraph applies to ships or aircraft—

    (a)   which have arrived, or are expected to arrive, in the United Kingdom; or

    (b)   which have left, or are expected to leave, the United Kingdom.

(2) If an immigration officer asks the owner or agent ("the carrier") of a ship or aircraft for passenger information, the carrier must provide that information to the officer.

(3) The officer may ask for passenger information relating to—

    (a)   a particular ship or particular aircraft of the carrier;

    (b)   particular ships or aircraft (however described) of the carrier; or

    (c)   all of the carrier's ships or aircraft.

(4) The officer may ask for—

    (a)   all passenger information in relation to the ship or aircraft concerned; or

    (b)   particular passenger information in relation to that ship or aircraft.

(5) A request under sub-paragraph (2)—

    (a)   must be in writing;

    (b)   must state the date on which it ceases to have effect; and

    (c)   continues in force until that date, unless withdrawn earlier by written notice by an immigration officer.

(6) The date may not be later than six months after the request is made.

(7) The fact that a request under sub-paragraph (2) has ceased to have effect as a result of sub-paragraph (5) does not prevent the request from being renewed.

(8) The information must be provided—

    (a)   in such form and manner as the Secretary of State may direct; and

    (b)   at such time as may be stated in the request.

(9) "Passenger information" means such information relating to the passengers carried, or expected to be carried, by the ship or aircraft as may be specified.

(10) "Specified" means specified in an order made by statutory instrument by the Secretary of State.

(11) Such an instrument shall be subject to annulment in pursuance of a resolution of either House of Parliament."

NOTES

Initial Commencement
To be appointed
To be appointed: see s 170(4).

Appointment
Appointment (for the purpose of enabling subordinate legislation to be made): 1 March 2000: see SI 2000/464, art 2, Schedule.
Appointment (for remaining purposes): 3 April 2000: see SI 2000/464, art 2, Schedule.

19   Notification of non-EEA arrivals

In the 1971 Act, in Schedule 2, after paragraph 27B, insert—

"Notification of non-EEA arrivals

27C (1) If a senior officer, or an immigration officer authorised by a senior officer, gives written notice to the owner or agent ("the carrier") of a ship or aircraft, the carrier must inform a relevant officer of the expected arrival in the United Kingdom of any ship or aircraft—

(a) of which he is the owner or agent; and

(b) which he expects to carry a person who is not an EEA national.

(2) The notice may relate to—

(a) a particular ship or particular aircraft of the carrier;

(b) particular ships or aircraft (however described) of the carrier; or

(c) all of the carrier's ships or aircraft.

(3) The notice—

(a) must state the date on which it ceases to have effect; and

(b) continues in force until that date, unless withdrawn earlier by written notice given by a senior officer.

(4) The date may not be later than six months after the notice is given.

(5) The fact that a notice under sub-paragraph (1) has ceased to have effect as a result of sub-paragraph (3) does not prevent the notice from being renewed.

(6) The information must be provided—

(a) in such form and manner as the notice may require; and

(b) before the ship or aircraft concerned departs for the United Kingdom.

(7) If a ship or aircraft travelling to the United Kingdom stops at one or more places before arriving in the United Kingdom, it is to be treated as departing for the United Kingdom when it leaves the last of those places.

(8) "Senior officer" means an immigration officer not below the rank of chief immigration officer.

(9) "Relevant officer" means—

(a) the officer who gave the notice under sub-paragraph (1); or

(b) **any immigration officer at the port at which the ship or aircraft concerned is expected to arrive.**

(10) "EEA national" means a national of a State which is a Contracting Party to the Agreement on the European Economic Area signed at Oporto on 2nd May 1992 as it has effect for the time being."

NOTES

Initial Commencement
To be appointed
To be appointed: see s 170(4).

Appointment
Appointment: 3 April 2000: see SI 2000/464, art 2, Schedule.

20 Supply of information to Secretary of State

(1) This section applies to information held by—

(a) a chief officer of police;

(b) the Director General of the National Criminal Intelligence Service;

(c) the Director General of the National Crime Squad;

(d) the Commissioners of Customs and Excise, or a person providing services to them in connection with the provision of those services;

(e)   a person with whom the Secretary of State has made a contract or other arrangements under section 95 or 98 or a sub-contractor of such a person; or

(f)   any specified person, for purposes specified in relation to that person.

(2)   The information may be supplied to the Secretary of State for use for immigration purposes.

(3)   "Immigration purposes" means any of the following—

(a)   the administration of immigration control under the Immigration Acts;

(b)   the prevention, detection, investigation or prosecution of criminal offences under those Acts;

(c)   the imposition of penalties or charges under Part II;

(d)   the provision of support for asylum-seekers and their dependants under Part VI;

(e)   such other purposes as may be specified.

(4)   "Chief officer of police" means—

(a)   the chief officer of police for a police area in England and Wales;

(b)   the chief constable of a police force maintained under the Police (Scotland) Act 1967;

(c)   the *Chief Constable of the Royal Ulster Constabulary* [Chief Constable of the Police Service of Northern Ireland].

(5)   "Specified" means specified in an order made by the Secretary of State.

(6)   This section does not limit the circumstances in which information may be supplied apart from this section.

NOTES

Initial Commencement
To be appointed
To be appointed: see s 170(4).

Appointment
Appointment: 1 January 2000: see SI 1999/3190, art 2, Schedule.

Amendment
Sub-s (4): in para (c) words "Chief Constable of the Royal Ulster Constabulary" in italics repealed and subsequent words in square brackets substituted by the Police (Northern Ireland) Act 2000, s 78(2)(a).
Date in force: to be appointed: see the Police (Northern Ireland) Act 2000, s 79(1).

21   Supply of information by Secretary of State

(1)   This section applies to information held by the Secretary of State in connection with the exercise of functions under any of the Immigration Acts.

(2)   The information may be supplied to—

(a)   a chief officer of police, for use for police purposes;

(b)   the Director General of the National Criminal Intelligence Service, for use for NCIS purposes;

(c)   the Director General of the National Crime Squad, for use for NCS purposes;

(d)   the Commissioners of Customs and Excise, or a person providing services to them, for use for customs purposes; or

(e)   any specified person, for use for purposes specified in relation to that person.

(3)   "Police purposes" means any of the following—

(a)   the prevention, detection, investigation or prosecution of criminal offences;

(b)   safeguarding national security;
(c)   such other purposes as may be specified.

(4)   "NCIS purposes" means any of the functions of the National Criminal Intelligence Service mentioned in section 2 of the Police Act 1997.

(5)   "NCS purposes" means any of the functions of the National Crime Squad mentioned in section 48 of that Act.

(6)   "Customs purposes" means any of the Commissioners' functions in relation to—

(a)   the prevention, detection, investigation or prosecution of criminal offences;
(b)   the prevention, detection or investigation of conduct in respect of which penalties which are not criminal penalties are provided for by or under any enactment;
(c)   the assessment or determination of penalties which are not criminal penalties;
(d)   checking the accuracy of information relating to, or provided for purposes connected with, any matter under the care and management of the Commissioners or any assigned matter (as defined by section 1(1) of the Customs and Excise Management Act 1979);
(e)   amending or supplementing any such information (where appropriate);
(f)   legal or other proceedings relating to anything mentioned in paragraphs (a) to (e);
(g)   safeguarding national security; and
(h)   such other purposes as may be specified.

(7)   "Chief officer of police" and "specified" have the same meaning as in section 20.

(8)   This section does not limit the circumstances in which information may be supplied apart from this section.

NOTES

Initial Commencement
To be appointed
To be appointed: see s 170(4).

Appointment
Appointment: 1 January 2000: see SI 1999/3190, art 2, Schedule.

Employment: code of practice

22   Restrictions on employment: code of practice

In the Asylum and Immigration Act 1996, after section 8, insert—

"8A Code of practice

(1)   The Secretary of State must issue a code of practice as to the measures which an employer is to be expected to take, or not to take, with a view to securing that, while avoiding the commission of an offence under section 8, he also avoids unlawful discrimination.

(2)   "Unlawful discrimination" means—

(a)   discrimination in contravention of section 4(1) of the Race Relations Act 1976 ("the 1976 Act"); or
(b)   in relation to Northern Ireland, discrimination in contravention of Article 6(1) of the Race Relations (Northern Ireland) Order 1997 ("the 1997 Order").

(3)   Before issuing the code, the Secretary of State must—

    (a)   prepare and publish a draft of the proposed code; and

    (b)   consider any representations about it which are made to him.

(4)   In preparing the draft, the Secretary of State must consult—

    (a)   the Commission for Racial Equality;

    (b)   the Equality Commission for Northern Ireland; and

    (c)   such organisations and bodies (including organisations or associations of organisations representative of employers or of workers) as he considers appropriate.

(5)   If the Secretary of State decides to proceed with the code, he must lay a draft of the code before both Houses of Parliament.

(6)   The draft code may contain modifications to the original proposals made in the light of representations to the Secretary of State.

(7)   After laying the draft code before Parliament, the Secretary of State may bring the code into operation by an order made by statutory instrument.

(8)   An order under subsection (7)—

    (a)   shall be subject to annulment in pursuance of a resolution of either House of Parliament;

    (b)   may contain such transitional provisions or savings as appear to the Secretary of State to be necessary or expedient in connection with the code.

(9)   A failure on the part of any person to observe a provision of the code does not of itself make him liable to any proceedings.

(10) But the code is admissible in evidence—

    (a)   in proceedings under the 1976 Act before an employment tribunal;

    (b)   in proceedings under the 1997 Order before an industrial tribunal.

(11) If any provision of the code appears to the tribunal to be relevant to any question arising in such proceedings, that provision is to be taken into account in determining the question.

(12) The Secretary of State may from time to time revise the whole or any part of the code and issue the code as revised.

(13) The provisions of this section also apply (with appropriate modifications) to any revision, or proposed revision, of the code."

NOTES

Initial Commencement
To be appointed
To be appointed: see s 170(4).

Appointment
Appointment (for the purpose of laying a draft code before Parliament and the making of subordinate legislation under the Asylum and Immigration Act 1996, s 8A): 19 February 2001: see SI 2001/239, art 2, Schedule.

Monitoring entry clearance

23   Monitoring refusals of entry clearance

(1)   The Secretary of State must appoint a person to monitor, in such a manner as the Secretary of State may determine, refusals of entry clearance in cases where there is, as a result of section 60(5), no right of appeal.

(2) But the Secretary of State may not appoint a member of his staff.

(3) The monitor must make an annual report on the discharge of his functions to the Secretary of State.

(4) The Secretary of State must lay a copy of any report made to him under subsection (3) before each House of Parliament.

(5) The Secretary of State may pay to the monitor such fees and allowances as he may determine.

NOTES

Initial Commencement
To be appointed
To be appointed: see s 170(4).

Appointment
Appointment: 2 October 2000: see SI 2000/2444, art 2, Sch 1.

Reporting suspicious marriages

24 Duty to report suspicious marriages

(1) Subsection (3) applies if—

    (a) a superintendent registrar to whom a notice of marriage has been given under section 27 of the Marriage Act 1949,

    (b) any other person who, under section 28(2) of that Act, has attested a declaration accompanying such a notice,

    (c) a district registrar to whom a marriage notice or an approved certificate has been submitted under section 3 of the Marriage (Scotland) Act 1977, or

    (d) a registrar or deputy registrar to whom notice has been given under section 13 of the Marriages (Ireland) Act 1844 or section 4 of the Marriage Law (Ireland) Amendment Act 1863,

has reasonable grounds for suspecting that the marriage will be a sham marriage.

(2) Subsection (3) also applies if—

    (a) a marriage is solemnized in the presence of a registrar of marriages or, in relation to Scotland, an authorised registrar (within the meaning of the Act of 1977); and

    (b) before, during or immediately after solemnization of the marriage, the registrar has reasonable grounds for suspecting that the marriage will be, or is, a sham marriage.

(3) The person concerned must report his suspicion to the Secretary of State without delay and in such form and manner as may be prescribed by regulations.

(4) The regulations are to be made—

    (a) in relation to England and Wales, by the Registrar General for England and Wales with the approval of the Chancellor of the Exchequer;

    (b) in relation to Scotland, by the Secretary of State after consulting the Registrar General of Births, Deaths and Marriages for Scotland;

    (c) in relation to Northern Ireland, by the Secretary of State after consulting the Registrar General in Northern Ireland.

(5) "Sham marriage" means a marriage (whether or not void)—

(a)   entered into between a person ("A") who is neither a British citizen nor a national of an EEA State other than the United Kingdom and another person (whether or not such a citizen or such a national); and

(b)   entered into by A for the purpose of avoiding the effect of one or more provisions of United Kingdom immigration law or the immigration rules.

NOTES

Initial Commencement
To be appointed
To be appointed: see s 170(4).

Appointment
Appointment: 1 January 2001: see SI 2000/2698, art 2, Schedule.

Immigration control: facilities and charges

25   Provision of facilities for immigration control at ports

(1)   The person responsible for the management of a control port ("the manager") must provide the Secretary of State free of charge with such facilities at the port as the Secretary of State may direct as being reasonably necessary for, or in connection with, the operation of immigration control there.

(2)   Before giving such a direction, the Secretary of State must consult such persons likely to be affected by it as he considers appropriate.

(3)   If the Secretary of State gives such a direction, he must send a copy of it to the person appearing to him to be the manager.

(4)   If the manager persistently fails to comply with the direction (or part of it), the Secretary of State may—

(a)   in the case of a control port which is not a port of entry, revoke any approval in relation to the port given under paragraph 26(1) of Schedule 2 to the 1971 Act;

(b)   in the case of a control port which is a port of entry, by order revoke its designation as a port of entry.

(5)   A direction under this section is enforceable, on the application of the Secretary of State—

(a)   by injunction granted by a county court; or

(b)   in Scotland, by an order under section 45 of the Court of Session Act 1988.

(6)   "Control port" means a port in which a control area is designated under paragraph 26(3) of Schedule 2 to the 1971 Act.

(7)   "Facilities" means accommodation, facilities, equipment and services of a class or description specified in an order made by the Secretary of State.

NOTES

Initial Commencement
To be appointed
To be appointed: see s 170(4).

26   Charges: immigration control

(1)   The Secretary of State may, at the request of any person and in consideration of such charges as he may determine, make arrangements—

(a) for the provision at any control port of immigration officers or facilities in addition to those (if any) needed to provide a basic service at the port;

(b) for the provision of immigration officers or facilities for dealing with passengers of a particular description or in particular circumstances.

(2) "Control port" has the same meaning as in section 25.

(3) "Facilities" includes equipment.

(4) "Basic service" has such meaning as may be prescribed.

NOTES

Initial Commencement
To be appointed
To be appointed: see s 170(4).

Charges: travel documents

27 Charges: travel documents

(1) The Secretary of State may, with the approval of the Treasury, make regulations prescribing fees to be paid in connection with applications to him for travel documents.

(2) If a fee is prescribed in connection with an application of a particular kind, no such application is to be entertained by the Secretary of State unless the fee has been paid in accordance with the regulations.

(3) In respect of any period before the coming into force of this section, the Secretary of State is to be deemed always to have had power to impose charges in connection with—

(a) applications to him for travel documents; or

(b) the issue by him of travel documents.

(4) "Travel document" does not include a passport.

NOTES

Initial Commencement
Royal Assent
Royal Assent: 11 November 1999: see s 170(3)(d).

Subordinate Legislation
Travel Documents (Fees) Regulations 1999, SI 1999/3339.

Offences

28 Deception

In the 1971 Act, after section 24, insert—

"24A Deception

(1) A person who is not a British citizen is guilty of an offence if, by means which include deception by him—

(a) he obtains or seeks to obtain leave to enter or remain in the United Kingdom; or

(b) he secures or seeks to secure the avoidance, postponement or revocation of enforcement action against him.

1043

(2)   "Enforcement action", in relation to a person, means—

    (a)   the giving of directions for his removal from the United Kingdom ("directions") under Schedule 2 to this Act or section 10 of the Immigration and Asylum Act 1999;

    (b)   the making of a deportation order against him under section 5 of this Act; or

    (c)   his removal from the United Kingdom in consequence of directions or a deportation order.

(3)   A person guilty of an offence under this section is liable—

    (a)   on summary conviction, to imprisonment for a term not exceeding six months or to a fine not exceeding the statutory maximum, or to both; or

    (b)   on conviction on indictment, to imprisonment for a term not exceeding two years or to a fine, or to both.

(4)   The extended time limit for prosecutions which is provided for by section 28 applies to an offence under this section."

NOTES

Initial Commencement
To be appointed
To be appointed: see s 170(4).

Appointment
Appointment: 14 February 2000: see SI 2000/168, art 2, Schedule.

29   Facilitation of entry

(1)   Section 25 of the 1971 Act (assisting illegal entry) is amended as follows.

(2)   In subsection (1), for "seven" substitute "ten".

(3)   For subsection (1A) substitute—

"(1A)   Nothing in subsection (1)(b) applies to anything done in relation to a person who—

    (a)   has been detained under paragraph 16 of Schedule 2 to this Act; or

    (b)   has been granted temporary admission under paragraph 21 of that Schedule.

(1B) Nothing in subsection (1)(b) applies to anything done by a person otherwise than for gain.

(1C) Nothing in subsection (1)(b) applies to anything done to assist an asylum claimant by a person in the course of his employment by a bona fide organisation, if the purposes of that organisation include assistance to persons in the position of the asylum claimant.

(1D) "Asylum claimant" means a person who intends to make a claim that it would be contrary to the United Kingdom's obligations under the Refugee Convention or the Human Rights Convention for him to be removed from, or required to leave, the United Kingdom.

(1E) "Refugee Convention" and "Human Rights Convention" have the meaning given in the Immigration and Asylum Act 1999."

(4)   In subsection (5), for "Subsection (1)(a)" substitute "Paragraphs (a) and (b) of subsection (1)".

NOTES

Initial Commencement
To be appointed
To be appointed: see s 170(4).

Appointment

Sub-s (1): Appointment (for certain purposes): 14 February 2000: see SI 2000/168, art 2, Schedule.
Sub-s (1): Appointment (for remaining purposes): 2 October 2000: see SI 2000/2444, art 2, Sch 1.
Sub-ss (2), (4): Appointment: 14 February 2000: see SI 2000/168, art 2, Schedule.
Sub-s (3): Appointment: 2 October 2000: see SI 2000/2444, art 2, Sch 1.

30   False statements etc

(1)   Section 26 of the 1971 Act (general offences in connection with administration of the Act) is amended as follows.

(2)   In subsection (1)(c), for "this Act" substitute "a relevant enactment".

(3)   After subsection (2), insert—

"(3) "Relevant enactment" means—

   (a)   this Act;
   (b)   the Immigration Act 1988;
   (c)   the Asylum and Immigration Appeals Act 1993 (apart from section 4 or 5); or
   (d)   the Immigration and Asylum Act 1999 (apart from Part VI)."

NOTES

Initial Commencement
To be appointed
To be appointed: see s 170(4).

Appointment
Appointment: 14 February 2000: see SI 2000/168, art 2, Schedule.

31   Defences based on Article 31(1) of the Refugee Convention

(1)   It is a defence for a refugee charged with an offence to which this section applies to show that, having come to the United Kingdom directly from a country where his life or freedom was threatened (within the meaning of the Refugee Convention), he—

   (a)   presented himself to the authorities in the United Kingdom without delay;
   (b)   showed good cause for his illegal entry or presence; and
   (c)   made a claim for asylum as soon as was reasonably practicable after his arrival in the United Kingdom.

(2)   If, in coming from the country where his life or freedom was threatened, the refugee stopped in another country outside the United Kingdom, subsection (1) applies only if he shows that he could not reasonably have expected to be given protection under the Refugee Convention in that other country.

(3)   In England and Wales and Northern Ireland the offences to which this section applies are any offence, and any attempt to commit an offence, under—

   (a)   Part I of the Forgery and Counterfeiting Act 1981 (forgery and connected offences);
   (b)   section 24A of the 1971 Act (deception); or
   (c)   section 26(1)(d) of the 1971 Act (falsification of documents).

(4)   In Scotland, the offences to which this section applies are those—

   (a)   of fraud,
   (b)   of uttering a forged document,
   (c)   under section 24A of the 1971 Act (deception), or
   (d)   under section 26(1)(d) of the 1971 Act (falsification of documents),

and any attempt to commit any of those offences.

(5)   A refugee who has made a claim for asylum is not entitled to the defence provided by subsection (1) in relation to any offence committed by him after making that claim.

(6)   "Refugee" has the same meaning as it has for the purposes of the Refugee Convention.

(7)   If the Secretary of State has refused to grant a claim for asylum made by a person who claims that he has a defence under subsection (1), that person is to be taken not to be a refugee unless he shows that he is.

(8)   A person who—

    (a)   was convicted in England and Wales or Northern Ireland of an offence to which this section applies before the commencement of this section, but

    (b)   at no time during the proceedings for that offence argued that he had a defence based on Article 31(1),

may apply to the Criminal Cases Review Commission with a view to his case being referred to the Court of Appeal by the Commission on the ground that he would have had a defence under this section had it been in force at the material time.

(9)   A person who—

    (a)   was convicted in Scotland of an offence to which this section applies before the commencement of this section, but

    (b)   at no time during the proceedings for that offence argued that he had a defence based on Article 31(1),

may apply to the Scottish Criminal Cases Review Commission with a view to his case being referred to the High Court of Justiciary by the Commission on the ground that he would have had a defence under this section had it been in force at the material time.

(10)   The Secretary of State may by order amend—

    (a)   subsection (3), or
    (b)   subsection (4),

by adding offences to those for the time being listed there.

(11)   Before making an order under subsection (10)(b), the Secretary of State must consult the Scottish Ministers.

NOTES

Initial Commencement
Royal Assent
Royal Assent: 11 November 1999: see s 170(3)(e).

PART II
CARRIERS' LIABILITY

Clandestine entrants

32   Penalty for carrying clandestine entrants

(1)   A person is a clandestine entrant if—

    (a)   he arrives in the United Kingdom concealed in a vehicle, ship or aircraft,
    (b)   he passes, or attempts to pass, through immigration control concealed in a vehicle, or
    (c)   he arrives in the United Kingdom on a ship or aircraft, having embarked—

      (i)   concealed in a vehicle; and
      (ii)   at a time when the ship or aircraft was outside the United Kingdom,

and claims, or indicates that he intends to seek, asylum in the United Kingdom or evades, or attempts to evade, immigration control.

(2)   The person (or persons) responsible for a clandestine entrant is (or are together) liable to—

    (a)   a penalty of the prescribed amount in respect of the clandestine entrant; and
    (b)   an additional penalty of that amount in respect of each person who was concealed with the clandestine entrant in the same transporter.

(3)   A penalty imposed under this section must be paid to the Secretary of State before the end of the prescribed period.

(4)   Payment of the full amount of a penalty by one or more of the persons responsible for the clandestine entrant discharges the liability of each of the persons responsible for that entrant.

(5)   In the case of a clandestine entrant to whom subsection (1)(a) applies, each of the following is a responsible person—

    (a)   if the transporter is a ship or aircraft, the owner or captain;
    (b)   if it is a vehicle (but not a detached trailer), the owner, hirer or driver of the vehicle;
    (c)   if it is a detached trailer, the owner, hirer or operator of the trailer.

(6)   In the case of a clandestine entrant to whom subsection (1)(b) or (c) applies, each of the following is a responsible person—

    (a)   if the transporter is a detached trailer, the owner, hirer or operator of the trailer;
    (b)   if it is not, the owner, hirer or driver of the vehicle.

(7)   Subject to any defence provided by section 34, it is immaterial whether a responsible person knew or suspected—

    (a)   that the clandestine entrant was concealed in the transporter; or
    (b)   that there were one or more other persons concealed with the clandestine entrant in the same transporter.

(8)   Subsection (9) applies if a transporter ("the carried transporter") is itself being carried in or on another transporter.

(9)   If a person is concealed in the carried transporter, the question whether any other person is concealed with that person in the same transporter is to be determined by reference to the carried transporter and not by reference to the transporter in or on which it is carried.

(10) "Immigration control" means United Kingdom immigration control and includes any United Kingdom immigration control operated in a prescribed control zone outside the United Kingdom.

NOTES

Initial Commencement
To be appointed
To be appointed: see s 170(4).

Appointment
Appointment (for certain purposes): 3 April 2000: see SI 2000/464, art 2, Schedule.
Appointment (for certain purposes): 18 September 2000: see SI 2000/2444, art 2, Sch 1.

Sub-ss (2)(a), (3), (10): Appointment (for the purpose of enabling subordinate legislation to be made): 6 December 1999: see SI 1999/3190, art 2, Schedule.

Subordinate Legislation
Carriers' Liability (Clandestine Entrants and Sale of Transporters) Regulations 2000, SI 2000/685 (made under sub-ss (2), (3), (10)).

33   Code of practice

(1)   The Secretary of State must issue a code of practice to be followed by any person operating a system for preventing the carriage of clandestine entrants.

(2)   Before issuing the code, the Secretary of State must—

    (a)   consult such persons as he considers appropriate; and
    (b)   lay a draft before both Houses of Parliament.

(3)   The requirement of subsection (2)(a) may be satisfied by consultation before the passing of this Act.

(4)   After laying the draft code before Parliament, the Secretary of State may bring the code into operation by an order.

(5)   The Secretary of State may from time to time revise the whole or any part of the code and issue the code as revised.

(6)   Subsections (2) and (4) also apply to any revision, or proposed revision, of the code.

NOTES

Initial Commencement
To be appointed
To be appointed: see s 170(4).

Appointment
Appointment: 6 December 1999: see SI 1999/3190, art 2, Schedule.

Subordinate Legislation
Carriers' Liability (Clandestine Entrants) (Code of Practice) Order 2000, SI 2000/684.
Carriers' Liability (Clandestine Entrants) (Code of Practice for Rail Freight) Order 2001, SI 2001/312.

34   Defences to claim that penalty is due under section 32

(1)   This section applies if it is alleged that a person ("the carrier") is liable to a penalty under section 32.

(2)   It is a defence for the carrier to show that he, or an employee of his who was directly responsible for allowing the clandestine entrant to be concealed, was acting under duress.

(3)   It is also a defence for the carrier to show that—

    (a)   he did not know, and had no reasonable grounds for suspecting, that a clandestine entrant was, or might be, concealed in the transporter;
    (b)   an effective system for preventing the carriage of clandestine entrants was in operation in relation to the transporter; and
    (c)   that on the occasion in question the person or persons responsible for operating that system did so properly.

(4)   In determining, for the purposes of this section, whether a particular system is effective, regard is to be had to the code of practice issued by the Secretary of State under section 33.

(5)   If there are two or more persons responsible for a clandestine entrant, the fact that one or more of them has a defence under subsection (3) does not affect the liability of the others.

(6)   But if a person responsible for a clandestine entrant has a defence under subsection (2), the liability of any other person responsible for that entrant is discharged.

NOTES

Initial Commencement
To be appointed
To be appointed: see s 170(4).

Appointment
Appointment (for certain purposes): 3 April 2000: see SI 2000/464, art 2, Schedule.
Appointment (for certain purposes): 18 September 2000: see SI 2000/2444, art 2, Sch 1.

35   Procedure

(1)   If the Secretary of State decides that a person ("P") is liable to one or more penalties under section 32, he must notify P of his decision.

(2)   A notice under subsection (1) (a "penalty notice") must—

- (a)   state the Secretary of State's reasons for deciding that P is liable to the penalty (or penalties);
- (b)   state the amount of the penalty (or penalties) to which P is liable;
- (c)   specify the date before which, and the manner in which, the penalty (or penalties) must be paid; and
- (d)   include an explanation of the steps—
  - (i)   that P must take if he objects to the penalty;
  - (ii)   that the Secretary of State may take under this Part to recover any unpaid penalty.

(3)   Subsection (4) applies if more than one person is responsible for a clandestine entrant.

(4)   If a penalty notice is served on one of the responsible persons, the Secretary of State is to be taken to have served the required penalty notice on each of them.

(5)   The Secretary of State must nevertheless take reasonable steps, while the penalty remains unpaid, to secure that the penalty notice is actually served on each of those responsible persons.

(6)   If a person on whom a penalty notice is served, or who is treated as having had a penalty notice served on him, alleges that he is not liable for one or more, or all, of the penalties specified in the penalty notice, he may give written notice of his allegation to the Secretary of State.

(7)   Notice under subsection (6) ("a notice of objection") must—

- (a)   give reasons for the allegation; and
- (b)   be given before the end of such period as may be prescribed.

(8)   If a notice of objection is given before the end of the prescribed period, the Secretary of State must consider it and determine whether or not any penalty to which it relates is payable.

(9)   The Secretary of State may by regulations provide, in relation to detached trailers, for a penalty notice which is served in such manner as may be prescribed to have effect as a penalty notice properly served on the responsible person or persons concerned under this section.

(10) Any sum payable to the Secretary of State as a penalty under section 32 may be recovered by the Secretary of State as a debt due to him.

NOTES

Initial Commencement
To be appointed
To be appointed: see s 170(4).

Appointment
Appointment (for certain purposes): 3 April 2000: see SI 2000/464, art 2, Schedule.
Appointment (for certain purposes): 18 September 2000: see SI 2000/2444, art 2, Sch 1.
Sub-ss (7)–(9): Appointment (for the purpose of enabling subordinate legislation to be made): 6 December 1999: see SI 1999/3190, art 2, Schedule.

Subordinate Legislation
Carriers' Liability (Clandestine Entrants and Sale of Transporters) Regulations 2000, SI 2000/685 (made under sub-ss (7)–(9)).

36   Power to detain vehicles etc in connection with penalties under section 32

(1)   If a penalty notice has been given under section 35, a senior officer may detain any relevant—

- (a)   vehicle,
- (b)   small ship, or
- (c)   small aircraft,

until all penalties to which the notice relates, and any expenses reasonably incurred by the Secretary of State in connection with the detention, have been paid.

(2)   That power—

- (a)   may be exercised only if, in the opinion of the senior officer concerned, there is a significant risk that the penalty (or one or more of the penalties) will not be paid before the end of the prescribed period if the transporter is not detained; and
- (b)   may not be exercised if alternative security which the Secretary of State considers is satisfactory, has been given.

(3)   If a transporter is detained under this section, the owner, consignor or any other person who has an interest in any freight or other thing carried in or on the transporter may remove it, or arrange for it to be removed, at such time and in such way as is reasonable.

(4)   The detention of a transporter under this section is lawful even though it is subsequently established that the penalty notice on which the detention was based was ill-founded in respect of all or any of the penalties to which it related.

(5)   But subsection (4) does not apply if the Secretary of State was acting unreasonably in issuing the penalty notice.

NOTES

Initial Commencement
To be appointed
To be appointed: see s 170(4).

Appointment
Appointment (for certain purposes): 3 April 2000: see SI 2000/464, art 2, Schedule.
Appointment (for certain purposes): 18 September 2000: see SI 2000/2444, art 2, Sch 1.
Sub-s (2)(a): Appointment (for the purpose of enabling subordinate legislation to be made): 6 December 1999: see SI 1999/3190, art 2, Schedule.

Subordinate Legislation
Carriers' Liability (Clandestine Entrants and Sale of Transporters) Regulations 2000, SI 2000/685
(made under sub-s (2)).

37 Effect of detention

(1) This section applies if a transporter is detained under section 36.

(2) The person to whom the penalty notice was addressed, or the owner or any other person claiming an interest in the transporter, may apply to the court for the transporter to be released.

(3) The court may release the transporter if it considers that—

    (a) satisfactory security has been tendered in place of the transporter for the payment of the penalty alleged to be due and connected expenses;

    (b) there is no significant risk that the penalty (or one or more of the penalties) and any connected expenses will not be paid; or

    (c) there is a significant doubt as to whether the penalty is payable and the applicant has a compelling need to have the transporter released.

(4) If the court has not ordered the release of the transporter, the Secretary of State may sell it if the penalty in question and connected expenses are not paid before the end of the period of 84 days beginning with the date on which the detention began.

(5) "Connected expenses" means expenses reasonably incurred by the Secretary of State in connection with the detention.

(6) Schedule 1 applies to the sale of transporters under this section.

NOTES

Initial Commencement
To be appointed
To be appointed: see s 170(4).

Appointment
Appointment (for certain purposes): 3 April 2000: see SI 2000/464, art 2, Schedule.
Appointment (for certain purposes): 18 September 2000: see SI 2000/2444, art 2, Sch 1.
Sub-s (6): Appointment (for certain purposes): 6 December 1999: see SI 1999/3190, art 2, Schedule.

38 Assisting illegal entry and harbouring

(1) In section 25 of the 1971 Act (assisting illegal entry and harbouring), at the end of paragraph (c) of subsection (6), insert—

    "or
    (d) the driver of any such vehicle;".

(2) After section 25, insert—

"25A Detention of ships, aircraft and vehicles in connection with offences under section 25(1)

(1) If a person has been arrested for an offence under section 25(1)(a) or (b), a senior officer or a constable may detain a relevant ship, aircraft or vehicle—

    (a) until a decision is taken as to whether or not to charge the arrested person with that offence; or

    (b) if the arrested person has been charged—

        (i) until he is acquitted, the charge against him is dismissed or the proceedings are discontinued; or

    (ii)   if he has been convicted, until the court decides whether or not to order forfeiture of the ship, aircraft or vehicle.

(2) A ship, aircraft or vehicle is a relevant ship, aircraft or vehicle, in relation to an arrested person, if it is one which the officer or constable concerned has reasonable grounds for believing could, on conviction of the arrested person for the offence for which he was arrested, be the subject of an order for forfeiture made under section 25(6).

(3) A person (other than the arrested person) who claims to be the owner of a ship, aircraft or vehicle which has been detained under this section may apply to the court for its release.

(4) The court to which an application is made under subsection (3) may, on such security or surety being tendered as it considers satisfactory, release the ship, aircraft or vehicle on condition that it is made available to the court if—

    (a)   the arrested person is convicted; and
    (b)   an order for its forfeiture is made under section 25(6).

(5) In the application to Scotland of subsection (1), for paragraphs (a) and (b) substitute—

    "(a) until a decision is taken as to whether or not to institute criminal proceedings against the arrested person for that offence; or
    (b) if criminal proceedings have been instituted against the arrested person—
        (i)   until he is acquitted or, under section 65 or 147 of the Criminal Procedure (Scotland) Act 1995, discharged or liberated or the trial diet is deserted *simpliciter*;
        (ii)   if he has been convicted, until the court decides whether or not to order forfeiture of the ship, aircraft or vehicle,

and for the purposes of this subsection, criminal proceedings are instituted against a person at whichever is the earliest of his first appearance before the sheriff on petition, or the service on him of an indictment or complaint."

(6) "Court" means—

    (a)   in England and Wales—
        (i)   if the arrested person has not been charged, the magistrates' court for the petty sessions area in which he was arrested;
        (ii)   if he has been charged but proceedings for the offence have not begun to be heard, the magistrates' court for the petty sessions area in which he was charged;
        (iii)   if he has been charged and proceedings for the offence are being heard, the court hearing the proceedings;
    (b)   in Scotland, the sheriff; and
    (c)   in Northern Ireland—
        (i)   if the arrested person has not been charged, the magistrates' court for the county court division in which he was arrested;
        (ii)   if he has been charged but proceedings for the offence have not begun to be heard, the magistrates' court for the county court division in which he was charged;
        (iii)   if he has been charged and proceedings for the offence are being heard, the court hearing the proceedings.

(7) "Owner" has the same meaning as it has in section 25(6).

(8) "Senior officer" means an immigration officer not below the rank of chief immigration officer."

(3) Subsection (1) has effect in relation to offences committed after the coming into force of that subsection.

(4) Subsection (2) has effect in relation to persons arrested for offences alleged to have been committed after the coming into force of that subsection.

NOTES

Initial Commencement
To be appointed
To be appointed: see s 170(4).

Appointment
Appointment: 3 April 2000: see SI 2000/464, art 2, Schedule.

39 Rail freight

(1) The Secretary of State may make regulations applying (with or without modification) any provision of this Part for the purpose of enabling penalties to be imposed in respect of a person ("a clandestine entrant") who—

(a) arrives in the United Kingdom concealed in a rail freight wagon; and
(b) claims, or indicates that he intends to seek, asylum in the United Kingdom or evades, or attempts to evade, immigration control.

(2) The regulations may, in particular, make provision—

(a) enabling additional penalties to be imposed in respect of persons concealed with the clandestine entrant;
(b) as to which person is (or which persons are together) liable to penalties in respect of the clandestine entrant;
(c) for conferring on a senior officer a power to detain any relevant rail freight wagon in prescribed circumstances;
(d) for conferring on the Secretary of State a power to sell in prescribed circumstances a rail freight wagon which has been detained.

(3) Before making any regulations under this section, the Secretary of State must consult, in the way he considers appropriate, persons appearing to him to be likely to be affected by the imposition of penalties under the regulations.

NOTES

Initial Commencement
To be appointed
To be appointed: see s 170(4).

Appointment
Appointment: 6 December 1999: see SI 1999/3190, art 2, Schedule.

Subordinate Legislation
Carriers' Liability (Clandestine Entrants) (Application to Rail Freight) Regulations 2001, SI 2001/280 (made under sub-s (1)).

Passengers without proper documents

40 Charges in respect of passengers without proper documents

(1) This section applies if a person requiring leave to enter the United Kingdom arrives in the United Kingdom by ship, aircraft, road passenger vehicle or train and, on being required to do so by an immigration officer, fails to produce—

    (a)   a valid passport with photograph or some other document satisfactorily establishing his identity and nationality or citizenship; and

    (b)   if he requires a visa, a valid visa of the required kind.

(2)   The Secretary of State may charge the owner of the ship, aircraft or vehicle or the train operator, in respect of that person, the sum of £2,000 or such other sum as may be prescribed.

(3)   The charge is payable to the Secretary of State on demand.

(4)   No charge is payable in respect of any person who is shown by the owner or train operator to have produced the required document or documents to him or his representative when embarking—

    (a)   on the ship or aircraft for the voyage or flight to the United Kingdom; or

    (b)   on the vehicle or train for the journey to the United Kingdom.

(5)   No charge is payable by a train operator, or by the owner of a road passenger vehicle, in respect of a person ("A"), if he shows that—

    (a)   neither he nor his representative was permitted, under the law applicable to the place where A embarked on the journey to the United Kingdom, to require A to produce to him when embarking the required document or documents;

    (b)   he had in place satisfactory arrangements (including, where appropriate, arrangements with other persons) designed to ensure that he did not carry passengers who did not, or might not, have documents of the required kind;

    (c)   all such steps as were practicable were taken in accordance with the arrangements to establish whether A had the required document or documents; and

    (d)   all such steps as were practicable were taken in accordance with the arrangements to prevent A's arrival in the United Kingdom where—

        (i)   A refused to produce the required document or documents to a person acting in accordance with the arrangements; or

        (ii)   for other reasons it appeared to that person that A did not, or might not, have the required document or documents.

(6)   For the purposes of subsections (4) and (5), a document—

    (a)   is to be regarded as being what it purports to be unless its falsity is reasonably apparent; and

    (b)   is to be regarded as relating to the person producing it unless it is reasonably apparent that it relates to another person.

(7)   Subsection (8) applies if—

    (a)   a person arrives in the United Kingdom in circumstances in which the Secretary of State is entitled to impose on the owner of a road passenger vehicle a charge under this section in respect of that person; and

    (b)   the vehicle arrived in the United Kingdom in a ship or aircraft.

(8)   The Secretary of State may impose a charge in respect of the arrival of the vehicle, or a charge in respect of the arrival of the ship or aircraft, but not in respect of both.

(9)   The Secretary of State may by order provide that this section is not to apply in relation to passengers arriving in the United Kingdom on a train who embarked on the journey to the United Kingdom—

    (a)   in a country specified in the order; or

    (b)   at places so specified within a country so specified.

(10) The Secretary of State may make an order under subsection (9) only if he is satisfied that there is in force between the United Kingdom and the country concerned

an agreement providing for the operation of United Kingdom immigration control in that country or for the checking of passports and visas there.

(11) "Road passenger vehicle" means a vehicle—

(a) which is adapted to carry more than eight passengers and is being used for carrying passengers for hire or reward; or

(b) which is not so adapted but is being used for carrying passengers for hire or reward at separate fares in the course of a business of carrying passengers.

(12) For the purposes of this section a person requires a visa if—

(a) under the immigration rules he requires a visa for entry into the United Kingdom; or

(b) as a result of section 41 he requires a visa for passing through the United Kingdom.

(13) "Representative", in relation to a person, means an employee or agent of his.

NOTES

Initial Commencement
To be appointed
To be appointed: see s 170(4).

Appointment
Sub-ss (9), (10): Appointment: 6 December 1999: see SI 1999/3190, art 2, Schedule.

41   Visas for transit passengers

(1) The Secretary of State may by order require transit passengers to hold a transit visa.

(2) "Transit passengers" means persons of any description specified in the order who on arrival in the United Kingdom pass through to another country without entering the United Kingdom; and "transit visa" means a visa for that purpose.

(3) The order—

(a) may specify a description of persons by reference to nationality, citizenship, origin or other connection with any particular country but not by reference to race, colour or religion;

(b) may not provide for the requirement imposed by the order to apply to any person who under the 1971 Act has the right of abode in the United Kingdom;

(c) may provide for any category of persons of a description specified in the order to be exempt from the requirement imposed by the order;

(d) may make provision about the method of application for visas required by the order.

NOTES

Initial Commencement
To be appointed
To be appointed: see s 170(4).

42   Power to detain vehicles etc in connection with charges under section 40

(1) A senior officer may, pending payment of any charge imposed under section 40, detain—

(a) the transporter in which the person in respect of whom the charge was imposed was carried; or

   (b)   any other transporter used (on any route) in the course of providing a service of carriage of passengers by sea, air or land by the person on whom the charge was imposed.

(2)   If a transporter is detained under subsection (1) it may continue to be detained pending payment of any connected expenses.

(3)   The court may release the transporter if it considers that—

   (a)   satisfactory security has been tendered in place of the transporter for the payment of the charge alleged to be due and connected expenses;
   (b)   there is no significant risk that the charge and any connected expenses will not be paid; or
   (c)   there is a significant doubt as to whether the charge is payable and the applicant has a compelling need to have the transporter released.

(4)   If the court has not ordered the release of the transporter, the Secretary of State may sell it if the charge in question and connected expenses are not paid before the end of the period of 84 days beginning with the date on which the detention began.

(5)   The detention of a transporter under this section is lawful even though it is subsequently established that the imposition of the charge on which the detention was based was ill-founded.

(6)   But subsection (5) does not apply if the Secretary of State was acting unreasonably in imposing the charge.

(7)   "Connected expenses" means expenses reasonably incurred by the Secretary of State in connection with the detention.

(8)   Schedule 1 applies to the sale of transporters under this section.

NOTES

Initial Commencement
To be appointed
To be appointed: see s 170(4).

Appointment
Sub-s (8): Appointment (for certain purposes): 6 December 1999: see SI 1999/3190, art 2, Schedule.

Interpretation

43   Interpretation of Part II

In this Part—
         "aircraft" includes hovercraft;
         "captain" means the master of a ship or commander of an aircraft;
         "concealed" includes being concealed in any freight, stores or other thing carried in or on the vehicle, ship or aircraft concerned;
         "court" means—
         (a)   in England and Wales, the county court or the High Court;
         (b)   in Scotland, the sheriff or the Court of Session;
         (c)   in Northern Ireland, the county court or the High Court;
         "detached trailer" means a trailer, semi-trailer, caravan or any other thing which is designed or adapted for towing by a vehicle but which has been detached for transport—
         (a)   in or on the vehicle concerned; or
         (b)   in the ship or aircraft concerned (whether separately or in or on a vehicle);
         "equipment", in relation to an aircraft, includes—

(a) any certificate of registration, maintenance or airworthiness of the aircraft;

(b) any log book relating to the use of the aircraft; and

(c) any similar document;

"hirer", in relation to a vehicle, means any person who has hired the vehicle from another person;

"operating weight", in relation to an aircraft, means the maximum total weight of the aircraft and its contents at which the aircraft may take off anywhere in the world, in the most favourable circumstances, in accordance with the certificate of airworthiness in force in respect of the aircraft;

"owner" includes—

(a) in relation to a ship or aircraft, the agent or operator of the ship or aircraft; and

(b) in relation to a road passenger vehicle, the operator of the vehicle; and in relation to a transporter which is the subject of a hire-purchase agreement, includes the person in possession of it under that agreement;

"penalty notice" has the meaning given in section 35(2);

"rail freight wagon" has such meaning as may be prescribed;

"senior officer" means an immigration officer not below the rank of chief immigration officer;

"ship" includes every description of vessel used in navigation;

"small aircraft" means an aircraft which has an operating weight of less than 5,700 kilogrammes;

"small ship" means a ship which has a gross tonnage of less than 500 tonnes;

"train" means a train which—

(a) is engaged on an international service as defined by section 13(6) of the Channel Tunnel Act 1987; but

(b) is not a shuttle train as defined by section 1(9) of that Act;

"train operator", in relation to a person arriving in the United Kingdom on a train, means the operator of trains who embarked that person on that train for the journey to the United Kingdom;

"transporter" means a vehicle, ship or aircraft together with—

(a) its equipment; and

(b) any stores for use in connection with its operation;

"vehicle" includes a trailer, semi-trailer, caravan or other thing which is designed or adapted to be towed by another vehicle.

NOTES

Initial Commencement
To be appointed
To be appointed: see s 170(4).

Appointment
Appointment: 6 December 1999: see SI 1999/3190, art 2, Schedule.

Subordinate Legislation
Carriers' Liability (Clandestine Entrants) (Application to Rail Freight) Regulations 2001, SI 2001/280.

PART III
BAIL

Routine bail hearings

44 Bail hearings for detained persons

(1) This section applies if a person is detained under any provision of the 1971 Act.

(2)   The Secretary of State must arrange a reference to the court for it to determine whether the detained person should be released on bail.

(3)   The duty under this section to arrange a reference does not apply if the detained person—

    (a)   is also detained otherwise than under a provision of the 1971 Act;
    (b)   is liable (under section 3(6) of that Act) to deportation as a result of the recommendation of a court; or
    (c)   has given to the Secretary of State, and has not withdrawn, written notice that he does not wish his case to be referred to a court under this section.

(4)   The Secretary of State must secure that a first reference to the court is made—

    (a)   in the case of a reference to the Commission, in accordance with rules; and
    (b)   in any other case, no later than the eighth day following that on which the detained person was detained.

(5)   If the detained person remains in detention, the Secretary of State must secure that a second reference to the court is made—

    (a)   in the case of a reference to the Commission, in accordance with rules; and
    (b)   in any other case, no later than the thirty-sixth day following that on which the detained person was detained.

(6)   A reference under subsection (5) may not be heard by the court before the thirty-third day following that on which the detained person was detained.

(7)   The court hearing a case referred to it under this section must proceed as if the detained person had made an application to it for bail.

(8)   The court must determine the matter—

    (a)   in the case of a reference to the Commission, in accordance with rules; and
    (b)   in any other case—
        (i)   on a first reference, before the tenth day following that on which the person concerned was detained; and
        (ii) on a second reference, before the thirty-eighth day following that on which he was detained.

(9)   Subsection (8) does not apply if the detained person has been released or has given notice under subsection (3)(c).

(10) If it appears to the Secretary of State that there has been a failure to comply with subsection (4) or (5), he must refer the matter to the court, and the court must deal with the reference, as soon as is reasonably practicable.

(11) If it appears to the Secretary of State that there has been a failure to comply with subsection (8), he must notify the court concerned, and the court must deal with the matter, as soon as is reasonably practicable.

(12) In this Part "court" means—

    (a)   if the detained person has brought an appeal under the Immigration Acts, the court or other appellate authority dealing with his appeal;
    (b)   in the case of a detained person to whom section 3(2) of the Special Immigration Appeals Commission Act 1997 applies (jurisdiction in relation to bail for persons detained on grounds of national security), the Commission; and
    (c)   in any other case, such magistrates' court as the Secretary of State considers appropriate or, in Scotland, an adjudicator.

(13) Rules made by the Lord Chancellor under section 5 of the Special Immigration Appeals Commission Act 1997 may include provision made for the purposes of this

section; and in subsections (4), (5) and (8) "rules" means rules made by virtue of this subsection.

(14) The Secretary of State may by regulations make provision modifying the application of this section in relation to cases where the proceedings on a reference under this section are adjourned to enable medical or other reports to be obtained or for any other reason.

(15) The regulations may, in particular, provide for the requirement for there to be a second reference not to apply in prescribed circumstances.

(16) This section does not affect any other provision under which the detained person may apply for, or be released on, bail.

NOTES

Initial Commencement
To be appointed
To be appointed: see s 170(4).

45 Location of bail hearings

(1) The Secretary of State may, in relation to a particular case or class of case, direct that the hearing of a reference under section 44 is to be at a specified place.

(2) The places that may be specified include, in particular—

    (a)   any place at which a court sits;
    (b)   any place at which appeals under this Act are heard;
    (c)   detention centres;
    (d)   prisons; or
    (e)   any particular premises or rooms within a place of a kind mentioned in paragraphs (a) to (d).

(3) A direction under subsection (1) has effect notwithstanding any other direction which may be given as to the place in which the court is to sit.

(4) A direction under subsection (1) requires the approval of the Lord Chancellor.

(5) "Specified" means specified in the direction.

NOTES

Initial Commencement
To be appointed
To be appointed: see s 170(4).

46 General right to be released on bail

(1) On a reference under section 44, the court must release the detained person on bail unless—

    (a)   subsection (2), (3) or (4) applies; or
    (b)   the court has imposed a requirement under section 47(1) which has not been complied with.

(2) The detained person need not be granted bail if the court is satisfied that there are substantial grounds for believing that if released on bail he would—

    (a)   fail to comply with one or more of the conditions of bail or of any recognizance or bail bond;
    (b)   commit an offence while on bail which is punishable with imprisonment;

1059

   (c)   be likely to cause danger to public health; or

   (d)   alone or with others, be a serious threat to the maintenance of public order.

(3)   The detained person need not be granted bail if the court is satisfied that—

   (a)   he is or has been knowingly involved with others in a concerted attempt by all or some of them to enter the United Kingdom in breach of immigration law;

   (b)   he is suffering from mental disorder and his continued detention is necessary in his own interests or for the protection of any other person;

   (c)   he is under the age of 18 and, while arrangements ought to be made for his care in the event of his release from detention, no satisfactory arrangements have been made;

   (d)   he is required to submit to an examination by an immigration officer under paragraph 2 or 2A of Schedule 2 to the 1971 Act and there is no relevant decision which the officer is in a position to take; or

   (e)   directions for his removal from the United Kingdom are in force.

(4)   The detained person need not be granted bail if the court is satisfied that he is a person to whom section 3(2) of the Special Immigration Appeals Commission Act 1997 (national security cases) applies.

(5)   For the purposes of this section, the question whether an offence is one which is punishable with imprisonment is to be determined without regard to any enactment prohibiting or restricting the imprisonment of young offenders or first offenders.

(6)   "Immigration law" means any provision of the Immigration Acts or any similar provision in force in any part of the British Islands.

(7)   Each of the following is a relevant decision—

   (a)   a decision as to whether, and if so how, to exercise the powers conferred by paragraph 21 of Schedule 2 to the 1971 Act;

   (b)   a decision as to whether to grant the person concerned leave to enter, or remain in, the United Kingdom;

   (c)   a decision as to whether to cancel his leave to enter the United Kingdom under paragraph 2A(8) of that Schedule.

(8)   The Secretary of State may by order amend subsection (2) or (3) by adding to or restricting the circumstances in which the subsection applies.

(9)   If bail is granted under this section, the appropriate court may, on an application by or on behalf of the person released, vary any condition on which it was granted.

(10) If bail is granted under this section, the appropriate court may, on an application by or on behalf of the Secretary of State, vary any condition on which it was granted or impose conditions on it.

(11) "Appropriate court" means—

   (a)   if the person released has brought an appeal under the Immigration Acts, the court or other appellate body dealing with his appeal;

   (b)   in any other case, the court which released the person concerned on bail.

NOTES

Initial Commencement
To be appointed
To be appointed: see s 170(4).

47   Powers exercisable on granting bail

(1)   Before releasing a person on bail under section 46, the court may require—

(a) a recognizance or, in Scotland, a bail bond to be entered into; or

(b) security to be given by the person bailed or on his behalf.

(2) The court may impose a requirement under subsection (1) only if it considers that its imposition is necessary to secure compliance with any condition to which bail granted under section 46 will be subject as a result of subsection (3), (4) or (5).

(3) Bail granted under section 46 by the Commission is subject to a condition requiring the person bailed to appear before it at a specified time and place.

(4) Bail granted under section 46 by a court or other appellate authority (other than the Commission) dealing with an appeal by the person bailed is subject to a condition requiring him—

(a) to appear before the court or authority at a time and place specified by it; and

(b) if the appeal is dismissed, withdrawn or abandoned, to appear before an immigration officer at such time and place as may be notified to him in writing by an immigration officer.

(5) In any other case, bail granted under section 46 is subject to a condition requiring the person bailed to appear before an immigration officer—

(a) at a time and place specified by the court; or

(b) at such other time and place as may be notified to him in writing by an immigration officer.

(6) Bail granted under section 46 may be subject to such other conditions as appear to the court to be likely to result in the appearance of the person bailed at the required time and place.

(7) A recognizance taken under this section may be with or without sureties, as the court may determine.

(8) Subsections (9) and (10) apply if, on a reference under section 44, the court has power to release the detained person on bail but is not required to do so by section 46.

(9) The court may, instead of releasing him—

(a) fix the amount of any recognizance, bail bond or security to be taken on his release on bail (including the amount in which any sureties are to be bound); and

(b) settle the terms of any conditions to be imposed on his release on bail.

(10) The person concerned must be released on bail on the recognizance or bond being taken, or the security being given.

(11) A person released on bail under section 46 is to be subject to such restrictions (if any) as to his employment or occupation while he is in the United Kingdom as may from time to time be notified to him in writing by an immigration officer.

(12) Any restriction imposed on a person under subsection (11) has effect for the purposes of this Part as a condition of his bail.

NOTES

Initial Commencement
To be appointed
To be appointed: see s 170(4).

48 Forfeiture

(1) If it appears to a court that a mandatory bail condition has been broken, it may—

    (a)   by order declare the recognizance to be forfeited; and

    (b)   order any person bound by the recognizance (whether as principal or surety) to pay the sum in which he is bound or such part of that sum, if any, as the court thinks fit.

(2)   "Mandatory bail condition" means a condition—

    (a)   to which bail granted under section 46 is subject as a result of section 47(3), (4) or (5); and

    (b)   in relation to which the court has taken a recognizance under section 47.

(3)   If the court which makes an order under subsection (1) is not a magistrates' court, it must—

    (a)   specify a magistrates' court which is, for the purposes of collection, enforcement and remission of the sum forfeited, to be treated as the court which ordered the forfeiture; and

    (b)   as soon as practicable give particulars of the recognizance to—

        (i)   in England and Wales, the justices' chief executive appointed by the magistrates' court committee whose area includes the petty sessions area, or

        (ii) in Northern Ireland, the clerk of petty sessions for the petty sessions district,

        for which the specified court acts.

(4)   Any sum collected as a result of subsection (3)(a) must be paid to the Lord Chancellor.

(5)   The Lord Chancellor may, with the approval of the Treasury, make regulations as to the times at which and the manner in which accounts for, and payments of, sums collected as a result of subsection (3)(a) must be made and for the keeping and auditing of accounts in relation to such sums.

(6)   If a person fails to comply with any of the conditions of a bail bond taken by a court under section 47, the court may declare the bail to be forfeited.

(7)   Any bail forfeited by a court under subsection (6)—

    (a)   must be transmitted to the sheriff court having jurisdiction in the area where the proceedings took place; and

    (b)   is to be treated as having been forfeited by that court.

NOTES

Initial Commencement
To be appointed
To be appointed: see s 170(4).

49   Forfeiture of securities

(1)   If a court is satisfied that a person ("A") by whom, or on whose behalf, security has been given under section 47 has broken a mandatory bail condition, it may order the security to be forfeited unless it appears that A had reasonable cause for breaking the condition.

(2)   The order may provide for the forfeiture to extend to a specified amount which is less than the value of the security.

(3)   An order under subsection (1) takes effect, unless previously revoked, at the end of the period of 21 days beginning with the day on which it is made.

(4)   Any sum forfeited as a result of this section must be paid to the Lord Chancellor.

(5)   Subsection (6) applies if a court which has made an order under subsection (1) is satisfied, on an application made by or on behalf of the person who gave the security, that A did after all have reasonable cause for breaking the condition.

(6)   The court may by order—

(a)   remit the forfeiture; or
(b)   provide for it to extend to a specified amount which is less than the value of the security.

(7)   An application under subsection (5)—

(a)   may be made before or after the order for forfeiture has taken effect; but
(b)   may not be entertained unless the court is satisfied that the Secretary of State was given reasonable notice of the applicant's intention to make the application.

(8)   The Lord Chancellor may, with the approval of the Treasury, make regulations as to the times at which and the manner in which accounts for, and payments of, sums forfeited as a result of this section must be made and for keeping and auditing of accounts in relation to such sums.

(9)   "Mandatory bail condition" means a condition—

(a)   to which bail granted under section 46 is subject as a result of section 47(3), (4) or (5); and
(b)   in relation to which a person has given security under section 47.

NOTES

Initial Commencement
To be appointed
To be appointed: see s 170(4).

50   Power of arrest

(1)   An immigration officer or constable who has reasonable grounds for believing that a person released on a reference under section 44 has broken or is likely to break any condition on which he was bailed, may arrest him without a warrant.

(2)   Subsection (3) applies if a person other than the person bailed ("a third party")—

(a)   has agreed to act as a surety in relation to a recognizance entered into under section 47; or
(b)   has given security on behalf of the person bailed under that section.

(3)   If an immigration officer or constable is notified in writing by a third party—

(a)   of his belief that a person released on a reference under section 44 is likely to break the condition that he must appear at the time and place required; and
(b)   of the third party's wish, for that reason, to be relieved of his obligations as a surety or to have the security given returned to him,

the officer or constable may arrest the person released without a warrant.

(4)   Subsection (5) applies if—

(a)   a justice of the peace is, by written information on oath, satisfied that there are reasonable grounds for suspecting that a person liable to be arrested under this section is to be found on any premises;
(b)   in Scotland, the sheriff or a justice of the peace is by evidence on oath so satisfied; or
(c)   in Northern Ireland, a justice of the peace is by written complaint on oath so satisfied.

(5)   The justice of the peace or the sheriff may grant a warrant authorising any immigration officer or constable to enter, if need be by reasonable force, the premises named in the warrant for the purpose of searching for and arresting the person concerned.

(6)   A person arrested under this section must, if required by a condition on which he was released to appear before an immigration officer within 24 hours after his arrest, be brought before an immigration officer within that period.

(7)   A person arrested under this section must, if he was released under section 46 by the Commission, be brought before it within twenty-four hours after his arrest.

(8)   Subsection (9) applies if a person has been arrested under this section and—

    (a)   neither subsection (6) nor subsection (7) applies to him; or
    (b)   he has been brought before an immigration officer under subsection (6) but has not been released.

(9)   The arrested person must be brought before—

    (a)   a justice of the peace acting for the petty sessions area in which he was arrested;
    (b)   in Scotland, an adjudicator or, if that is not practicable within 24 hours after his arrest, the sheriff; or
    (c)   in Northern Ireland, a magistrates' court acting for the county court division in which he was arrested.

(10) If subsection (9) applies, the arrested person must be brought before the person or court concerned—

    (a)   as soon as is practicable after his arrest; and
    (b)   if subsection (9)(a) or (c) applies, in any event within 24 hours after his arrest.

(11) Subsections (12) and (13) apply in relation to an arrested person dealt with under subsection (7) or (9).

(12) The court or person dealing with the matter may, if of the opinion that the arrested person has broken or is likely to break any condition on which he was released—

    (a)   give a direction that the arrested person be detained under the authority of the person by whom he was arrested;
    (b)   release him on his original bail; or
    (c)   release him on a new recognizance (with or without sureties) or on new bail.

(13) If not of that opinion, that court or person must release the arrested person on his original bail.

(14) In reckoning any period of 24 hours for the purposes of this section, no account is to be taken of Christmas Day, Good Friday or any Sunday.

NOTES

Initial Commencement
To be appointed
To be appointed: see s 170(4).

Procedure

51   Procedure

(1)   Any rules made in connection with bail hearings resulting from any provision of, or made under, this Part must include provision requiring the Secretary of State to notify—

(a) the detained person who is the subject of the hearing of a reference under section 44, and

(b) if the Secretary of State is aware that that person will be represented at the hearing (whether or not by an authorised advocate), the person who will be representing him at the hearing,

of the date, place and time of the hearing as soon as is reasonably practicable after the Secretary of State is given that information by the magistrates' court.

(2) If a person has been refused bail—

(a) on a reference under section 44, or

(b) on an application under the 1971 Act, the Asylum and Immigration Appeals Act 1993 or the Special Immigration Appeals Commission Act 1997,

he may, on the first subsequent such reference or application, advance any argument as to fact or law.

(3) But on any subsequent such reference or application the court need not hear any argument as to fact or law that that court has heard previously.

(4) A magistrates' court dealing with a reference under section 44 must sit in open court unless—

(a) the detained person has made a claim for asylum and the court considers that there are compelling reasons why it should sit in private; or

(b) the court considers that the interests of the administration of justice require it to sit in private.

(5) Any proceedings before a magistrates' court or the sheriff under this Part may be conducted—

(a) on behalf of the Secretary of State, by a person authorised by him, or

(b) on behalf of the detained person, by a person nominated by him,

even though that person is not an authorised advocate.

(6) "Authorised advocate"—

(a) in relation to England and Wales, has the meaning given by section 119 of the Courts and Legal Services Act 1990;

(b) in relation to Scotland, means an advocate or solicitor;

(c) in relation to Northern Ireland, means a barrister or solicitor.

(7) "Rules" means rules made by the Lord Chancellor under section 144 of the Magistrates' Courts Act 1980 or under any corresponding provision having effect in Northern Ireland.

NOTES

Initial Commencement
To be appointed
To be appointed: see s 170(4).

52   Use of live television links at bail hearings

(1) On a reference under section 44, the court may, after hearing representations from the parties, direct that the detained person is to be treated as being present in the court if he is able (whether by means of a live television link or otherwise) to see and hear the court and to be seen and heard by it.

(2) If the detained person wishes to make representations under subsection (1) he must do so by using the facilities that will be used if the court decides to give the proposed direction.

(3)   If, after hearing representations from the parties, the court decides not to give a direction, it must give its reasons for refusing.

(4)   The court may not give a direction unless—

(a)   it has been notified by the Secretary of State that facilities are available in the relevant institution which will enable the detained person to see and hear the court and to be seen and heard by it; and

(b)   the notice has not been withdrawn.

(5)   "Relevant institution" means the institution in which the detained person will be detained at the time of the bail hearing.

NOTES

Initial Commencement
To be appointed
To be appointed: see s 170(4).

Bail hearings under other enactments

53   Applications for bail in immigration cases

(1)   The Secretary of State may by regulations make new provision in relation to applications for bail by persons detained under the 1971 Act.

(2)   The regulations may confer a right to be released on bail in prescribed circumstances.

(3)   The regulations may, in particular, make provision—

(a)   creating or transferring jurisdiction to hear an application for bail by a person detained under the 1971 Act;

(b)   as to the places in which such an application may be held;

(c)   as to the procedure to be followed on, or in connection with, such an application;

(d)   as to circumstances in which, and conditions (including financial conditions) on which, an applicant may be released on bail;

(e)   amending or repealing any enactment so far as it relates to such an application.

(4)   The regulations must include provision for securing that an application for bail made by a person who has brought an appeal under any provision of this Act or the Special Immigration Appeals Commission Act 1997 is heard by the appellate authority hearing that appeal.

(5)   When exercising his power under subsection (1), the Secretary of State must have regard to the desirability, in relation to applications for bail by persons detained under the 1971 Act, of making provision similar to that which is made by this Part in relation to references to the court under section 44.

(6)   Regulations under this section require the approval of the Lord Chancellor.

(7)   In so far as regulations under this section relate to the sheriff or the Court of Session, the Lord Chancellor must obtain the consent of the Scottish Ministers before giving his approval.

NOTES

Initial Commencement
To be appointed
To be appointed: see s 170(4).

54 Extension of right to apply for bail in deportation cases

(1)   Paragraph 2 of Schedule 3 to the 1971 Act (detention or control pending deportation) is amended as follows,

(2)   In sub-paragraph (1), at the end insert "or he is released on bail".

(3)   In sub-paragraph (3), after "unless" insert "he is released on bail or".

(4)   After sub-paragraph (4) insert—

"(4A)   Paragraphs 22 to 25 of Schedule 2 to this Act apply in relation to a person detained under sub-paragraph (1), (2) or (3) as they apply in relation to a person detained under paragraph 16 of that Schedule."

NOTES

Initial Commencement
To be appointed
To be appointed: see s 170(4).

Grants

55 Grants to voluntary organisations

(1)   The Secretary of State may, with the approval of the Treasury, make grants to any voluntary organisation which provides advice or assistance for detained persons in connection with proceedings under this Part.

(2)   Grants may be made on such terms, and subject to such conditions, as the Secretary of State may determine.

NOTES

Initial Commencement
To be appointed
To be appointed: see s 170(4).

PART IV
APPEALS

The appellate authorities

56 The Immigration Appeal Tribunal

(1)   There is to continue to be an Immigration Appeal Tribunal.

(2)   Schedule 2 makes further provision about the Tribunal.

NOTES

Initial Commencement
To be appointed
To be appointed: see s 170(4).

Appointment
Appointment: 14 February 2000: see SI 2000/168, art 2, Schedule; for transitional provisions see art 3 thereof.

57   Adjudicators

(1)   There are to be such number of adjudicators for the purposes of this Act as the Lord Chancellor may determine.

(2)   The Lord Chancellor must appoint one of the adjudicators as Chief Adjudicator.

(3)   Schedule 3 makes further provision about the adjudicators.

NOTES

Initial Commencement
To be appointed
To be appointed: see s 170(4).

Appointment
Appointment: 14 February 2000: see SI 2000/168, art 2, Schedule; for transitional provisions see art 3 thereof.

Appeals

58   General

(1)   The right of appeal given by a particular provision of this Part is to be read with any other provision of this Part which restricts or otherwise affects that right.

(2)   Part I of Schedule 4 makes provision with respect to the procedure applicable in relation to appeals under this Part.

(3)   Part II of Schedule 4 makes provision as to the effect of appeals.

(4)   Part III of Schedule 4 makes provision—

    (a)   with respect to the determination of appeals under this Part; and
    (b)   for further appeals.

(5)   For the purposes of the Immigration Acts, an appeal under this Part is to be treated as pending during the period beginning when notice of appeal is given and ending when the appeal is finally determined, withdrawn or abandoned.

(6)   An appeal is not to be treated as finally determined while a further appeal may be brought.

(7)   If such a further appeal is brought, the original appeal is not to be treated as finally determined until the further appeal is determined, withdrawn or abandoned.

(8)   A pending appeal under this Part is to be treated as abandoned if the appellant leaves the United Kingdom.

(9)   A pending appeal under any provision of this Part other than section 69(3) is to be treated as abandoned if the appellant is granted leave to enter or remain in the United Kingdom.

(10) A pending appeal under section 61 is to be treated as abandoned if a deportation order is made against the appellant.

NOTES

Initial Commencement
To be appointed
To be appointed: see s 170(4).

Appointment
Sub-ss (1), (3)–(10): Appointment: 2 October 2000: see SI 2000/2444, art 2, Sch 1; for transitional provisions in relation to sub-ss (5)–(10) see art 3, Sch 2, para 1(3) thereof.

Sub-s (2): Appointment (for certain purposes): 14 February 2000: see SI 2000/168, art 2, Schedule.
Sub-s (2): Appointment (for certain purposes): 22 May 2000: see SI 2000/1282, art 2, Schedule.
Sub-s (2): Appointment (for remaining purposes): 2 October 2000: see SI 2000/2444, art 2, Sch 1.

Modification
Sub-s (2): references to Part IV of this Act shall include references to the Immigration Act 1971, Pt II, the Asylum and Immigration Act 1993, s 8, Sch 2, and the Asylum and Immigration Act 1996, s 3 as from 1 August 2000: see SI 2000/1985, art 3(1)(a), (3).

Subordinate Legislation
Immigration and Asylum Appeals (Procedure) Rules 2000, SI 2000/2333 (made under sub-s (2)).

Leave to enter

59 Leave to enter the United Kingdom

(1)   A person who is refused leave to enter the United Kingdom under any provision of the 1971 Act may appeal to an adjudicator against—

    (a)   the decision that he requires leave; or
    (b)   the refusal.

(2)   A person who, on an application duly made, is refused a certificate of entitlement or an entry clearance may appeal to an adjudicator against the refusal.

(3)   Subsection (4) applies if a person appeals under this section on being refused leave to enter the United Kingdom and—

    (a)   before he appeals, directions have been given for his removal from the United Kingdom; or
    (b)   before or after he appeals, the Secretary of State or an immigration officer serves on him notice that any directions which may be given for his removal as a result of the refusal will be for his removal to a country or one of several countries specified in the notice.

(4)   The appellant may—

    (a)   object to the country to which he would be removed in accordance with the directions, or
    (b)   object to the country specified in the notice (or to one or more of those specified),

and claim that he ought to be removed (if at all) to a different country specified by him.

NOTES

Initial Commencement
To be appointed
To be appointed: see s 170(4).

Appointment
Appointment: 2 October 2000: see SI 2000/2444, art 2, Sch 1; for transitional provisions see art 3, Sch 2, para 1(4) thereof.

60 Limitations on rights of appeal under section 59

(1)   Section 59 does not entitle a person to appeal, on the ground that he has a right of abode in the United Kingdom, against a decision that he requires leave to enter the United Kingdom if he does not hold—

    (a)   a United Kingdom passport describing him as a British citizen or as a citizen of the United Kingdom and Colonies having the right of abode in the United Kingdom; or
    (b)   a certificate of entitlement.

(2)   Section 59 does not entitle a person to appeal, on the ground that he does not require leave to enter the United Kingdom, against a decision that he does require such leave if he is required by immigration rules or an order under section 8(2) of the 1971 Act to hold a specified document but does not do so.

(3)   Section 59 does not entitle a person to appeal against a refusal of leave to enter while he is in the United Kingdom unless, at the time of the refusal, he held a current entry clearance or was a person named in a current work permit.

(4)   Subsection (5) applies to a person who seeks to enter the United Kingdom—

    (a)   as a visitor;
    (b)   in order to follow a course of study of not more than six months' duration for which he has been accepted;
    (c)   with the intention of studying but without having been accepted for any course of study; or
    (d)   as a dependant of a person within paragraph (a), (b) or (c).

(5)   That person—

    (a)   is not entitled to appeal under section 59 against a refusal of an entry clearance unless he is a family visitor; and
    (b)   is not entitled to appeal against a refusal of leave to enter if he does not hold a current entry clearance at the time of the refusal.

(6)   The Secretary of State may by regulations make provision—

    (a)   requiring a family visitor appealing under section 59 to pay such fee as may be fixed by the regulations;
    (b)   for such an appeal not to be entertained unless the required fee has been paid by the appellant;
    (c)   for the repayment of any such fee if the appeal is successful.

(7)   Section 59 does not entitle a person to appeal against a refusal of leave to enter, or against a refusal of an entry clearance, if the refusal is on the ground that he or any person whose dependant he is—

    (a)   does not hold a relevant document required by the immigration rules;
    (b)   does not satisfy a requirement of the immigration rules as to age or nationality or citizenship; or
    (c)   seeks entry for a period exceeding that permitted by the immigration rules.

(8)   The following are relevant documents—

    (a)   entry clearances;
    (b)   passports or other identity documents; and
    (c)   work permits.

(9)   Section 59 does not entitle a person to appeal against a refusal of leave to enter, or against a refusal of an entry clearance, if—

    (a)   the Secretary of State certifies that directions have been given by the Secretary of State (and not by a person acting under his authority) for the appellant not to be given entry to the United Kingdom on the ground that his exclusion is conducive to the public good; or
    (b)   the leave to enter, or entry clearance, was refused in compliance with any such directions.

(10)   "Family visitor" has such meaning as may be prescribed.

NOTES

Initial Commencement

To be appointed
To be appointed: see s 170(4).

Appointment
Sub-ss (1)–(5), (7)–(9): Appointment: 2 October 2000: see SI 2000/2444, art 2, Sch 1.
Sub-ss (6), (10): Appointment: 22 May 2000: see SI 2000/1282, art 2, Schedule.

Subordinate Legislation
Immigration Appeals (Family Visitor) (Amendment) Regulations 2001, SI 2001/52 (made under sub-s (6)).

Variation of limited leave to enter or remain

61   Variation of limited leave to enter or remain

A person may appeal against a decision to vary, or to refuse to vary, any limited leave to enter or remain in the United Kingdom which he has if, as a result of that decision, he may be required to leave the United Kingdom within 28 days of being notified of the decision.

NOTES

Initial Commencement
To be appointed
To be appointed: see s 170(4).

Appointment
Appointment: 2 October 2000: see SI 2000/2444, art 2, Sch 1; for transitional provisions see art 3, Sch 2, para 1(5) thereof.

62   Limitations on rights of appeal under section 61

(1)   Section 61 does not entitle a person or a person whose dependant he is to appeal against a refusal to vary leave if the refusal is on the ground that—

    (a)   a relevant document which is required by the immigration rules has not been issued;

    (b)   the person does not satisfy a requirement of the immigration rules as to age or nationality or citizenship;

    (c)   the variation would result in the duration of a person's leave exceeding that permitted by the immigration rules; or

    (d)   any fee required by or under any enactment has not been paid.

(2)   The following are relevant documents—

    (a)   entry clearances;

    (b)   passports or other identity documents; and

    (c)   work permits or equivalent documents issued after entry.

(3)   Section 61 does not entitle a person to appeal against a refusal to vary leave if either of the following conditions is satisfied.

(4)   The conditions are—

    (a)   that the Secretary of State has certified that the appellant's departure from the United Kingdom would be conducive to the public good as being in the interests of national security, the relations between the United Kingdom and any other country or for other reasons of a political nature; or

    (b)   that the decision questioned by the appeal was taken on that ground by the Secretary of State (and not by a person acting under his authority).

(5)   A person is not entitled to appeal under section 61 against—

(a)   a variation made by statutory instrument; or

(b)   a refusal of the Secretary of State to make a statutory instrument.

NOTES

Initial Commencement
To be appointed
To be appointed: see s 170(4).

Appointment
Appointment: 2 October 2000: see SI 2000/2444, art 2, Sch 1.

Deportation

63   Deportation orders

(1)   A person may appeal to an adjudicator against—

(a)   a decision of the Secretary of State to make a deportation order against him under section 5(1) of the 1971 Act as a result of his liability to deportation under section 3(5) of that Act; or

(b)   a refusal by the Secretary of State to revoke a deportation order made against him.

(2)   A deportation order is not to be made against a person under section 5(1) of the 1971 Act while an appeal may be brought against the decision to make it.

(3)   Subsection (4) applies if—

(a)   a person appeals under this section; and

(b)   before or after he appeals, the Secretary of State serves on him notice that any directions which may be given for his removal as a result of the deportation order will be for his removal to a country or one of several countries specified in the notice.

(4)   The appellant may object to the country specified in the notice (or to one or more of those specified), and claim that he ought to be removed (if at all) to a different country specified by him.

NOTES

Initial Commencement
To be appointed
To be appointed: see s 170(4).

Appointment
Appointment: 2 October 2000: see SI 2000/2444, art 2, Sch 1; for transitional provisions see art 3, Sch 2, para 1(6) thereof.

64   Limitations on rights of appeal under section 63

(1)   Section 63 does not entitle a person to appeal against a decision to make a deportation order against him if the ground of the decision was that his deportation is conducive to the public good as being in the interests of national security or of the relations between the United Kingdom and any other country or for other reasons of a political nature.

(2)   Section 63 does not entitle a person to appeal against a refusal to revoke a deportation order, if—

(a)   the Secretary of State has certified that the appellant's exclusion from the United Kingdom would be conducive to the public good; or

(b)   revocation was refused on that ground by the Secretary of State (and not by a person acting under his authority).

(3)   Section 63 does not entitle a person to appeal against a refusal to revoke a deportation order while he is in the United Kingdom, whether because he has not complied with the requirement to leave or because he has contravened the prohibition on entering.

(4)   Subsection (5) applies to—

(a)   an appeal against a decision to make a deportation order against a person as belonging to the family of another person; or
(b)   an appeal against a refusal to revoke a deportation order so made.

(5)   The appellant is not to be allowed, for the purpose of showing that he does not or did not belong to another person's family, to dispute any statement made with a view to obtaining leave for the appellant to enter or remain in the United Kingdom (including any statement made to obtain an entry clearance).

(6)   But subsection (5) does not apply if the appellant shows—

(a)   that the statement was not so made by him or by any person acting with his authority; and
(b)   that, when he took the benefit of the leave, he did not know any such statement had been made to obtain it or, if he did know, he was under the age of eighteen.

NOTES

Initial Commencement
To be appointed
To be appointed: see s 170(4).

Appointment
Appointment: 2 October 2000: see SI 2000/2444, art 2, Sch 1.

Human rights

65   [Racial discrimination and breach of human rights]

(1)   A person who alleges that an authority has, in taking any decision under the Immigration Acts relating to that person's entitlement to enter or remain in the United Kingdom, [racially discriminated against him or] acted in breach of his human rights may appeal to an adjudicator against that decision unless he has grounds for bringing an appeal against the decision under the Special Immigration Appeals Commission Act 1997.

(2)   For the purposes of this Part[—

(a)   an authority racially discriminates against a person if he acts, or fails to act, in relation to that other person in a way which is unlawful by virtue of section 19B of the Race Relations Act 1976; and
(b)]   an authority acts in breach of a person's human rights if he acts, or fails to act, in relation to that other person in a way which is made unlawful by section 6(1) of the Human Rights Act 1998.

(3)   Subsections (4) and (5) apply if, in proceedings before an adjudicator or the Immigration Appeal Tribunal on an appeal, a question arises as to whether an authority has, in taking any decision under the Immigration Acts relating to the appellant's entitlement to enter or remain in the United Kingdom, [racially discriminated against the appellant or] acted in breach of the appellant's human rights.

(4)   The adjudicator, or the Tribunal, has jurisdiction to consider the question.

(5)   If the adjudicator, or the Tribunal, decides that the authority concerned[—

- (a)   racially discriminated against the appellant; or
- (b)]   acted in breach of the appellant's human rights, the appeal may be allowed on [the ground in question].

(6)   No appeal may be brought under this section by any person in respect of a decision if—

- (a)   that decision is already the subject of an appeal brought by him under the Special Immigration Appeals Commission Act 1997; and
- (b)   the appeal under that Act has not been determined.

(7)   "Authority" means—

- (a)   the Secretary of State;
- (b)   an immigration officer;
- (c)   a person responsible for the grant or refusal of entry clearance.

NOTES

Initial Commencement
To be appointed
To be appointed: see s 170(4).

Appointment
Appointment: 2 October 2000: see SI 2000/2444, art 2, Sch 1; for transitional provisions see art 3, Sch 2, para 1(7) thereof.

Amendment
Provision heading: substituted by the Race Relations (Amendment) Act 2000, s 9(1), Sch 2, para 34.
Sub-s (1): words "racially discriminated against him or" in square brackets inserted by the Race Relations (Amendment) Act 2000, s 6(3).
Date in force: 2 April 2001: see SI 2001/566, art 2(1).
Sub-s (2): words in square brackets from "— (a)" to "(b)" inserted by the Race Relations (Amendment) Act 2000, s 6(4).
Date in force: 2 April 2001: see SI 2001/566, art 2(1).
Sub-s (3): words "racially discriminated against the appellant or" in square brackets inserted by the Race Relations (Amendment) Act 2000, s 9(1), Sch 2, para 32.
Date in force: 2 April 2001: see SI 2001/566, art 2(1).
Sub-s (5): words in square brackets from "— (a)" to "(b)" inserted by the Race Relations (Amendment) Act 2000, s 9(1), Sch 2, para 33(a).
Date in force: 2 April 2001: see SI 2001/566, art 2(1).
Sub-s (5): in para (b) words in square brackets substituted by the Race Relations (Amendment) Act 2000, s 9(1), Sch 2, para 33(b).
Date in force: 2 April 2001: see SI 2001/566, art 2(1).

Directions for removal

66   Validity of directions for removal

(1)   This section applies if directions are given for a person's removal from the United Kingdom—

- (a)   on the ground that he is an illegal entrant;
- (b)   under section 10; or
- (c)   under the special powers conferred by Schedule 2 to the 1971 Act in relation to members of the crew of a ship or aircraft or persons coming to the United Kingdom to join a ship or aircraft as a member of the crew.

(2) That person may appeal to an adjudicator against the directions on the ground that on the facts of his case there was in law no power to give them on the ground on which they were given.

(3) This section does not entitle a person to appeal while he is in the United Kingdom unless he is appealing under section 65 or 69(5).

(4) If a person appeals under this section against directions given by virtue of a deportation order, he may not dispute the original validity of that order.

NOTES

Initial Commencement
To be appointed
To be appointed: see s 170(4).

Appointment
Appointment: 2 October 2000: see SI 2000/2444, art 2, Sch 1; for transitional provisions see art 3, Sch 2, para 1(8) thereof.

Objection to destination

67 Removal on objection to destination

(1) This section applies if directions are given under the 1971 Act for a person's removal from the United Kingdom—

    (a)   on his being refused leave to enter,
    (b)   on a deportation order being made against him, or
    (c)   on his having entered the United Kingdom in breach of a deportation order.

(2) That person may appeal to an adjudicator against the directions on the ground that he ought to be removed (if at all) to a different country specified by him.

NOTES

Initial Commencement
To be appointed
To be appointed: see s 170(4).

Appointment
Appointment: 2 October 2000: see SI 2000/2444, art 2, Sch 1; for transitional provisions see art 3, Sch 2, para 1(9) thereof.

68 Limitations on rights of appeal under section 67

(1) Section 67 does not entitle a person to appeal against directions given on his being refused leave to enter the United Kingdom unless—

    (a)   he is also appealing under section 59(1) against the decision that he requires leave to enter; or
    (b)   he was refused leave at a time when he held a current entry clearance or was a person named in a current work permit.

(2) If a person is entitled to object to a country on an appeal under section 59 or 63 and—

    (a)   he does not object to it on that appeal, or
    (b)   his objection to it on that appeal is not sustained,

section 67 does not entitle him to appeal against any directions subsequently given as a result of the refusal or order in question, if their effect will be his removal to that country.

(3)   A person who claims that he ought to be removed to a country other than one he has objected to on an appeal under section 59, 63 or 67 must produce evidence, if he is not a national or citizen of that other country, that that country will admit him.

NOTES

Initial Commencement
To be appointed
To be appointed: see s 170(4).

Appointment
Appointment: 2 October 2000: see SI 2000/2444, art 2, Sch 1; for transitional provisions see art 3, Sch 2, para 1(10) thereof.

Asylum

69   Claims for asylum

(1)   A person who is refused leave to enter the United Kingdom under the 1971 Act may appeal against the refusal to an adjudicator on the ground that his removal in consequence of the refusal would be contrary to the Convention.

(2)   If, as a result of a decision to vary, or to refuse to vary, a person's limited leave to enter or remain in the United Kingdom, he may be required to leave the United Kingdom within 28 days of being notified of the decision, he may appeal against the decision to an adjudicator on the ground that such a requirement would be contrary to the Convention.

(3)   A person who—

    (a)   has been refused leave to enter or remain in the United Kingdom on the basis of a claim for asylum made by him, but

    (b)   has been granted (whether before or after the decision to refuse leave) limited leave to enter or remain,

may, if that limited leave will not expire within 28 days of his being notified of the decision, appeal to an adjudicator against the refusal on the ground that requiring him to leave the United Kingdom after the time limited by that leave would be contrary to the Convention.

(4)   If the Secretary of State—

    (a)   has decided to make a deportation order against a person under section 5(1) of the 1971 Act, or

    (b)   has refused to revoke such an order,

that person may appeal to an adjudicator against the decision or refusal on the ground that his removal in pursuance of the order would be contrary to the Convention.

(5)   If directions are given as mentioned in section 66(1) for the removal of a person from the United Kingdom, he may appeal to an adjudicator on the ground that his removal in pursuance of the directions would be contrary to the Convention.

(6)   "Contrary to the Convention" means contrary to the United Kingdom's obligations under the Refugee Convention.

NOTES

Initial Commencement
To be appointed
To be appointed: see s 170(4).

Appointment
Appointment: 2 October 2000: see SI 2000/2444, art 2, Sch 1; for transitional provisions see art 3, Sch 2, para 1(11) thereof.

70 Limitations on rights of appeal under section 69

(1)   Section 69(1) does not entitle a person to appeal against a refusal of leave to enter if—

    (a)   the Secretary of State certifies that directions have been given by the Secretary of State (and not by a person acting under his authority) for the appellant not to be given entry to the United Kingdom on the ground that his exclusion is in the interests of national security; or

    (b)   the leave to enter was refused in compliance with any such directions.

(2)   Section 69(2) does not entitle a person to appeal against—

    (a)   a variation of his leave which reduces its duration, or

    (b)   a refusal to enlarge or remove the limit on its duration,

if either of the following conditions is satisfied.

(3)   The conditions are—

    (a)   that the Secretary of State has certified that the appellant's departure from the United Kingdom would be in the interests of national security; or

    (b)   that the decision questioned by the appeal was taken on that ground by the Secretary of State (and not by a person acting under his authority).

(4)   Section 69(3) does not entitle a person to appeal against a refusal mentioned in paragraph (a) of that subsection if—

    (a)   the reason for the refusal was that he was a person to whom the Refugee Convention did not apply by reason of Article 1(F) of that Convention; and

    (b)   the Secretary of State has certified that the disclosure of material on which the refusal was based is not in the interests of national security.

(5)   Section 69(4)(a) does not entitle a person to appeal against a decision to make a deportation order against him if the ground of the decision was that his deportation is in the interests of national security.

(6)   Section 69(4)(b) does not entitle a person to appeal against a refusal to revoke a deportation order, if—

    (a)   the Secretary of State has certified that the appellant's exclusion from the United Kingdom would be in the interests of national security; or

    (b)   if revocation was refused on that ground by the Secretary of State (and not by a person acting under his authority).

(7)   A person may not bring an appeal on any of the grounds mentioned in subsections (1) to (5) of section 69—

    (a)   if, before the time of the refusal, variation, decision or directions (as the case may be) he has not made a claim for asylum;

    (b)   otherwise than under that section.

(8)   A person may not appeal under section 69(4)(b) if he has had the right to appeal under section 69(4)(a) (whether or not he has exercised it).

NOTES

Initial Commencement
To be appointed
To be appointed: see s 170(4).

Appointment

Appointment: 2 October 2000: see SI 2000/2444, art 2, Sch 1; for transitional provisions see art 3, Sch 2, para 1(12) thereof.

Removal to safe countries

71   Removal of asylum claimants to safe third countries

(1)   This section applies if a certificate has been issued under section 11 or 12.

(2)   The person in respect of whom the certificate was issued may appeal against it to an adjudicator on the ground that any of the conditions applicable to that certificate was not satisfied when it was issued, or has since ceased to be satisfied.

NOTES

Initial Commencement
To be appointed
To be appointed: see s 170(4).

Appointment
Appointment: 2 October 2000: see SI 2000/2444, art 2, Sch 1.

Miscellaneous

72   Miscellaneous limitations on rights of appeal

(1)   Unless a certificate issued under section 11 or 12 has been set aside on an appeal under section 65 or 71 or otherwise ceases to have effect, the person in respect of whom the certificate was issued is not entitled to appeal under this Act as respects any matter arising before his removal from the United Kingdom.

(2)   A person who has been, or is to be, sent to a member State or to a country designated under section 12(1)(b) is not, while he is in the United Kingdom, entitled to appeal—

   (a)   under section 65 if the Secretary of State certifies that his allegation that a person acted in breach of his human rights [or racially discriminated against him] is manifestly unfounded; or
   (b)   under section 71.

(3)   No appeal under this Part may be made in relation to a decision made on an application if—

   (a)   the application was required to be made in a prescribed form but was not made in that form; or
   (b)   the applicant was required to take prescribed steps in relation to the application, or to take such steps at a prescribed time or within a prescribed period, but failed to do so.

NOTES

Initial Commencement
To be appointed
To be appointed: see s 170(4).

Appointment
Sub-ss (1), (2): Appointment: 2 October 2000: see SI 2000/2444, art 2, Sch 1.
Sub-s (3): Appointment (for the purposes of enabling subordinate legislation to be made): 22 May 2000: see SI 2000/1282, art 2, Schedule.

Amendment

Sub-s (2): in para (a) words "or racially discriminated against him" in square brackets inserted by the Race Relations (Amendment) Act 2000, s 9(1), Sch 2, para 35.

Date in force: to be appointed: see the Race Relations (Amendment) Act 2000, s 10(2).

73 Limitation on further appeals

(1) This section applies where a person ("the appellant") has appealed under the Special Immigration Appeals Commission Act 1997 or this Act and that appeal ("the original appeal") has been finally determined.

(2) If the appellant serves a notice of appeal making a claim that [in taking a decision, a decision-maker racially discriminated against the appellant or that] a decision of a decision-maker was in breach of the appellant's human rights, the Secretary of State may certify that in his opinion—

    (a)   the appellant's claim—
        (i)   could reasonably have been included in a statement required from him under section 74 but was not so included, or
        (ii) could reasonably have been made in the original appeal but was not so made;
    (b)   one purpose of such a claim would be to delay the removal from the United Kingdom of the appellant or of any member of his family; and
    (c)   the appellant had no other legitimate purpose for making the claim.

(3) On the issuing of a certificate by the Secretary of State under subsection (2), the appeal, so far as relating to that claim, is to be treated as finally determined.

(4) Subsection (5) applies if a notice under section 74 was served on the appellant before the determination of his original appeal and the appellant has served a further notice of appeal.

(5) The Secretary of State may certify that grounds contained in the notice of appeal were considered in the original appeal.

(6) On the issuing of a certificate by the Secretary of State under subsection (5), the appeal, so far as relating to those grounds, is to be treated as finally determined.

(7) Subsection (8) applies if, on the application of the appellant, an immigration officer or the Secretary of State makes a decision in relation to the appellant.

(8) The immigration officer or, as the case may be, the Secretary of State may certify that in his opinion—

    (a)   one purpose of making the application was to delay the removal from the United Kingdom of the appellant or any member of his family; and
    (b)   the appellant had no other legitimate purpose for making the application.

(9) No appeal may be brought under the Special Immigration Appeals Commission Act 1997 or this Act against a decision on an application in respect of which a certificate has been issued under subsection (8).

(10) Nothing in section 58(6) affects the operation of subsections (3) and (6).

NOTES

Initial Commencement
To be appointed
To be appointed: see s 170(4).

Appointment
Appointment: 2 October 2000: see SI 2000/2444, art 2, Sch 1.

Amendment
Sub-s (2): words from "in taking a" to "appellant or that" in square brackets inserted by the
Race Relations (Amendment) Act 2000, s 9(1), Sch 2, para 36.
Date in force: 2 April 2001: see SI 2001/566, art 2(1).

"One-stop" procedure

74   Duty to disclose the grounds for appeal etc

(1)   This section applies if—

    (a)   the decision on an application for leave to enter or remain in the United
Kingdom is that the application be refused; and

    (b)   the applicant, while he is in the United Kingdom, is entitled to appeal against
the refusal under the Special Immigration Appeals Commission Act 1997 or
this Act.

(2)   This section also applies if—

    (a)   as a result of a decision to vary, or to refuse to vary, any limited leave to enter
or remain in the United Kingdom which a person has, he may be required to
leave the United Kingdom within 28 days of being notified of the decision;
and

    (b)   that person is entitled to appeal against the decision under the Special
Immigration Appeals Commission Act 1997 or this Act.

(3)   This section also applies if—

    (a)   the Secretary of State has decided to make a deportation order against a
person under section 5(1) of the 1971 Act as a result of his liability to
deportation under section 3(5) of that Act; and

    (b)   that person, while he is in the United Kingdom, is entitled to appeal against
that decision under the Special Immigration Appeals Commission Act 1997
or this Act.

(4)   The decision-maker must serve on the applicant and on any relevant member of
his family a notice requiring the recipient of the notice to state any additional grounds
which he has or may have for wishing to enter or remain in the United Kingdom.

(5)   "Decision-maker" means the Secretary of State or (as the case may be) an
immigration officer.

(6)   The statement must be—

    (a)   in writing; and

    (b)   served on the Secretary of State before the end of such period as may be
prescribed.

(7)   A statement required under this section must—

    (a)   if the person making it wishes to claim asylum, include a claim for asylum;

    [(aa) if he claims that he was racially discriminated against, include notice of that
claim;] and

    (b)   if he claims that an act breached his human rights, include notice of that
claim.

(8)   Regulations may prescribe the persons who, in relation to an applicant, are
relevant members of his family.

(9)   Regulations may prescribe the procedure to be followed in connection with
notices given and statements made in accordance with this section and, in particular,
may prescribe the form in which such notices and statements are to be given or made.

NOTES

Initial Commencement
To be appointed
To be appointed: see s 170(4).

Appointment
Appointment (for the purposes of enabling subordinate legislation to be made): 22 May 2000: see SI 2000/1282, art 2, Schedule.
Appointment (for remaining purposes): 2 October 2000: see SI 2000/2444, art 2, Sch 1.

Amendment
Sub-s (7): para (aa) inserted by the Race Relations (Amendment) Act 2000, s 9(1), Sch 2, para 37. Date in force: 2 April 2001: see SI 2001/566, art 2(1).

Subordinate Legislation
Immigration and Asylum Appeals (One-Stop Procedure) Regulations 2000, SI 2000/2244.

75 Duty to disclose grounds for entering etc the United Kingdom

(1) This section applies if a person who—

    (a)   is an illegal entrant,
    (b)   is liable to be removed under section 10, or
    (c)   has arrived in the United Kingdom without—
        (i)   leave to enter;
        (ii)   an entry clearance; or
        (iii)   a current work permit in which he is named,

makes a claim for asylum or a claim that it would be contrary to the United Kingdom's obligations under the Human Rights Convention for him to be removed from, or required to leave, the United Kingdom.

(2) The person responsible for the determination of the claim must serve on the claimant and on any relevant member of his family a notice requiring the recipient of the notice to state any additional grounds which he has or may have for wishing to enter or remain in the United Kingdom.

(3) The statement must be—

    (a)   in writing; and
    (b)   served on the person who is responsible for the determination of the claim before the end of such period as may be prescribed.

(4) Regulations may prescribe the procedure to be followed in connection with notices given and statements made in accordance with this section and, in particular, may prescribe the form in which such notices and statements are to be given or made.

(5) Regulations may prescribe the persons who, in relation to a claimant, are relevant members of his family.

(6) Regulations may provide that, if a claim is determined against the claimant, prescribed provisions of section 73, 76, or 77 are to apply to an appeal against that determination by a person on whom a notice has been served under subsection (2), with such modifications (if any) as may be prescribed.

NOTES

Initial Commencement
To be appointed
To be appointed: see s 170(4).

Appointment
Appointment (for the purposes of enabling subordinate legislation to be made): 22 May 2000: see SI 2000/1282, art 2, Schedule.

Appointment (for remaining purposes): 2 October 2000: see SI 2000/2444, art 2, Sch 1.

Subordinate Legislation
Immigration and Asylum Appeals (One-Stop Procedure) Regulations 2000, SI 2000/2444.

76   Result of failure to comply with section 74

(1)   In this section—

    (a)   "the applicant" means the person on whom a notice has been served under section 74(4);

    (b)   "notice" means a notice served under that section; and

    (c)   "statement" means the statement which the notice requires the applicant to make to the Secretary of State.

(2)   If the applicant's statement does not mention a particular ground—

    (a)   on which he wishes to enter or remain in the United Kingdom, and

    (b)   of which he is aware at the material time,

he may not rely on that ground in any appeal under the Special Immigration Appeals Commission Act 1997 or this Part.

(3)   Subsection (2) does not apply if—

    (a)   the ground is a claim for asylum or a claim that an act [racially discriminated against the applicant or breached his] human rights; or

    (b)   the Secretary of State considers that the applicant had a reasonable excuse for the omission.

(4)   Subsection (5) applies if the applicant's statement does not include a claim for asylum.

(5)   If the applicant claims asylum after the end of the period prescribed under section 74(6)(b), no appeal may be made under section 69 if the Secretary of State has certified that in his opinion—

    (a)   one purpose of making the claim for asylum was to delay the removal from the United Kingdom of the applicant or of any member of his family; and

    (b)   the applicant had no other legitimate purpose for making the application.

(6)   "Member of the family" has such meaning as may be prescribed.

NOTES

Initial Commencement
To be appointed
To be appointed: see s 170(4).

Appointment
Sub-ss (1)–(5): Appointment: 2 October 2000: see SI 2000/2444, art 2, Sch 1.
Sub-s (6): Appointment: 22 May 2000: see SI 2000/1282, art 2, Schedule.

Amendment
Sub-s (3): in para (a) words "breached the applicant's" in italics repealed and subsequent words in square brackets substituted by the Race Relations (Amendment) Act 2000, s 9(1), Sch 2, para 38.
Date in force: 2 April 2001: see SI 2001/566, art 2(1).

Subordinate Legislation
Immigration and Asylum Appeals (One-Stop Procedure) Regulations 2000, SI 2000/2444.

77   "One-stop" appeals

(1)   This section applies in relation to—

(a) an appeal brought on any of the grounds mentioned in section 69;

(b) any other appeal against a decision—

  (i) to refuse an application for leave to enter or remain in the United Kingdom;

  (ii) to vary, or to refuse to vary, any limited leave to enter or remain in the United Kingdom, which has the result mentioned in section 74(2)(a); or

  (iii) to make a deportation order against a person under section 5(1) of the 1971 Act as a result of his liability to deportation under section 3(5) of that Act.

(2) Subject to section 72(2), the appellant is to be treated as also appealing on any additional grounds—

(a) which he may have for appealing against the refusal, variation, decision or directions in question under any other provision of this Act; and

(b) which he is not prevented (by any provision of section 76) from relying on.

(3) In considering—

(a) any ground mentioned in section 69, or

(b) any question relating to the appellant's rights under Article 3 of the Human Rights Convention,

the appellate authority may take into account any evidence which it considers to be relevant to the appeal (including evidence about matters arising after the date on which the decision appealed against was taken).

(4) In considering any other ground, the appellate authority may take into account only evidence—

(a) which was available to the Secretary of State at the time when the decision appealed against was taken; or

(b) which relates to relevant facts as at that date.

(5) "Additional grounds", in relation to an appeal, means any grounds specified in a statement made to the Secretary of State under section 74(4) other than those on which the appeal has been brought.

(6) "Appellate authority" means an adjudicator, the Tribunal or the Special Immigration Appeals Commission.

NOTES

Initial Commencement
To be appointed
To be appointed: see s 170(4).

Appointment
Appointment: 2 October 2000: see SI 2000/2444, art 2, Sch 1.

78   Transfer of appellate proceedings

(1) Subsection (3) applies if—

(a) a person who has brought an appeal under this Part has been notified of the Secretary of State's decision to make a deportation order against him; and

(b) as a result of section 64(1), he is not entitled to appeal against that decision under section 63.

(2) Subsection (3) also applies if—

(a) a person who has brought an appeal under this Part has been notified of the Secretary of State's decision to refuse to revoke a deportation order made against him; and

(b)   as a result of section 64(2), he is not entitled to appeal against that refusal under section 63.

(3)   If he appeals against that decision under section 2(1) or 2A of the Special Immigration Appeals Commission Act 1997, any appeal under this Part is transferred to, and must be heard by, the Commission.

(4)   Subsection (5) applies if a person, in a statement required by a notice under section 74 or 75, states an additional ground which relates to a matter which may be the subject of an appeal under section 2(1) or 2A of the Special Immigration Appeals Commission Act 1997.

(5)   The appeal under this Part is transferred to, and must be heard by, the Commission.

NOTES

Initial Commencement
To be appointed
To be appointed: see s 170(4).

Appointment
Appointment: 2 October 2000: see SI 2000/2444, art 2, Sch 1.

Appeals without merit

79   Penalty on continuing an appeal without merit

(1)   If, at any time before it determines an appeal, the Immigration Appeal Tribunal considers that the appeal has no merit it may notify the appellant of its opinion.

(2)   A notice under subsection (1) must—

(a)   include an explanation of the Tribunal's powers under this section; and
(b)   be made in such form as may be required by rules made under paragraph 3 of Schedule 4.

(3)   Subsection (1) does not apply if leave for appeal to the Tribunal was required.

(4)   Subsection (5) applies if an appeal which has been continued by the appellant after he has been given a notice under subsection (1) is dismissed.

(5)   The Tribunal may impose on the appellant, or on his representative, a penalty of the specified amount.

(6)   "Specified" means specified by an order made by the Lord Chancellor.

(7)   The Lord Chancellor may by order make such provision as he considers appropriate as to—

(a)   the enforcement in England and Wales and Northern Ireland, and
(b)   the payment and application,

of penalties imposed under this section.

(8)   Such an order may, in particular, make provision similar to that made by sections 129 and 130 of the County Courts Act 1984.

(9)   An order imposing a penalty under subsection (5) may be enforced in Scotland as if it were an extract registered decree arbitral bearing a warrant for execution issued by the sheriff court of any sheriffdom in Scotland.

NOTES

Initial Commencement
To be appointed
To be appointed: see s 170(4).

EEA nationals

80 EEA nationals

(1) The Secretary of State may by regulations make provision for appeals against any immigration decision in relation to—

    (a)   an EEA national;
    (b)   a member of the family of an EEA national;
    (c)   a member of the family of a United Kingdom national who is neither such a national nor an EEA national.

(2) "Immigration decision" means a decision concerning a person's removal from the United Kingdom or his entitlement—

    (a)   to be admitted to the United Kingdom;
    (b)   to reside, or to continue to reside, in the United Kingdom; or
    (c)   to be issued with, or not to have withdrawn, a residence permit.

(3) The regulations may also make provision for appeals against any decision concerning the matters mentioned in subsection (1) taken in relation to a citizen of any other State on whom any such entitlement has been conferred by an agreement to which the United Kingdom is a party or by which it is bound.

(4) An appeal under the regulations lies to an adjudicator or, in such circumstances as may be prescribed, to the Commission.

(5) The regulations may provide for appeals from the adjudicator or the Commission.

(6) The regulations may prescribe cases, or classes of case, in which a person is not entitled to appeal while he is in the United Kingdom.

(7) The regulations may make provision under which an appellant may be required to state, in such manner as may be prescribed, any grounds he has or may have for wishing to be admitted to, or to remain in, the United Kingdom additional to those on which he is appealing and for the consequences of such a requirement.

(8) The regulations may—

    (a)   amend sections 2 and 2A of the Special Immigration Appeals Commission Act 1997 (appellate jurisdiction of the Commission);
    (b)   amend or revoke the Immigration (European Economic Area) Order 1994.

(9) Part IV has effect subject to any regulations made under this section.

(10) "EEA national" means a person who is, or claims to be, a national of an EEA State (other than the United Kingdom).

(11) "United Kingdom national" means a person who falls to be treated as a national of the United Kingdom for the purposes of the Community Treaties.

(12) If a person claims to be an EEA national, he may not appeal under the regulations unless he produces—

    (a)   a valid national identity card, or
    (b)   a valid passport,

issued by an EEA State other than the United Kingdom.

(13) For the purposes of subsection (12), a document—

    (a)   is to be regarded as being what it purports to be unless its falsity is reasonably apparent; and

    (b)   is to be regarded as relating to the person producing it unless it is reasonably apparent that it relates to another person.

(14) The regulations may—

    (a)   prescribe the persons who, for the purposes of this section, are the members of a person's family; and

    (b)   make provision as to the manner in which membership of a person's family is to be established.

(15) "Residence permit" means any permit or other document issued by the Secretary of State as proof of the holder's right of residence in the United Kingdom.

NOTES

Initial Commencement
To be appointed
To be appointed: see s 170(4).

Appointment
Appointment: 22 May 2000: see SI 2000/1282, art 2, Schedule.

Subordinate Legislation
Immigration (European Economic Area) Regulations 2000, SI 2000/2326.

Grants

81   Grants to voluntary organisations

(1)   The Secretary of State may, with the approval of the Treasury, make grants to any voluntary organisation which provides advice or assistance for, or other services for the welfare of, persons who have rights of appeal under this Act.

(2)   Grants may be made on such terms, and subject to such conditions, as the Secretary of State may determine.

NOTES

Initial Commencement
To be appointed
To be appointed: see s 170(4).

Appointment
Appointment: 2 October 2000: see SI 2000/2444, art 2, Sch 1.

PART V
IMMIGRATION ADVISERS AND IMMIGRATION SERVICE PROVIDERS

Interpretation

82   Interpretation of Part V

(1)   In this Part—

    "claim for asylum" means a claim that it would be contrary to the United Kingdom's obligations under—

(a) the Refugee Convention, or
(b) Article 3 of the Human Rights Convention,
for the claimant to be removed from, or required to leave, the United Kingdom;

"the Commissioner" means the Immigration Services Commissioner;

"the complaints scheme" means the scheme established under paragraph 5(1) of Schedule 5;

"designated judge" has the same meaning as in section 119(1) of the Courts and Legal Services Act 1990;

"designated professional body" has the meaning given by section 86;

"immigration advice" means advice which—
(a) relates to a particular individual;
(b) is given in connection with one or more relevant matters;
(c) is given by a person who knows that he is giving it in relation to a particular individual and in connection with one or more relevant matters; and
(d) is not given in connection with representing an individual before a court in criminal proceedings or matters ancillary to criminal proceedings;

"immigration services" means the making of representations on behalf of a particular individual—
(a) in civil proceedings before a court, tribunal or adjudicator in the United Kingdom, or
(b) in correspondence with a Minister of the Crown or government department,
in connection with one or more relevant matters;

"Minister of the Crown" has the same meaning as in the Ministers of the Crown Act 1975;

"qualified person" means a person who is qualified for the purposes of section 84;

"registered person" means a person who is registered with the Commissioner under section 85;

"relevant matters" means any of the following—
(a) a claim for asylum;
(b) an application for, or for the variation of, entry clearance or leave to enter or remain in the United Kingdom;
(c) unlawful entry into the United Kingdom;
(d) nationality and citizenship under the law of the United Kingdom;
(e) citizenship of the European Union;
(f) admission to Member States under Community law;
(g) residence in a Member State in accordance with rights conferred by or under Community law;
(h) removal or deportation from the United Kingdom;
(i) an application for bail under the Immigration Acts or under the Special Immigration Appeals Commission Act 1997;
(j) an appeal against, or an application for judicial review in relation to, any decision taken in connection with a matter referred to in paragraphs (a) to (i); and

"the Tribunal" means the Immigration Services Tribunal.

(2) In this Part, references to the provision of immigration advice or immigration services are to the provision of such advice or services by a person—

(a) in the United Kingdom (regardless of whether the persons to whom they are provided are in the United Kingdom or elsewhere); and
(b) in the course of a business carried on (whether or not for profit) by him or by another person.

NOTES

Initial Commencement
To be appointed
To be appointed: see s 170(4).

Appointment
Appointment: 22 May 2000: see SI 2000/1282, art 2, Schedule.

The Immigration Services Commissioner

83   The Commissioner

(1)   There is to be an Immigration Services Commissioner (referred to in this Part as "the Commissioner").

(2)   The Commissioner is to be appointed by the Secretary of State after consulting the Lord Chancellor and the Scottish Ministers.

(3)   It is to be the general duty of the Commissioner to promote good practice by those who provide immigration advice or immigration services.

(4)   In addition to any other functions conferred on him by this Part, the Commissioner is to have the regulatory functions set out in Part I of Schedule 5.

(5)   The Commissioner must exercise his functions so as to secure, so far as is reasonably practicable, that those who provide immigration advice or immigration services—

  (a)   are fit and competent to do so;
  (b)   act in the best interests of their clients;
  (c)   do not knowingly mislead any court, tribunal or adjudicator in the United Kingdom;
  (d)   do not seek to abuse any procedure operating in the United Kingdom in connection with immigration or asylum (including any appellate or other judicial procedure);
  (e)   do not advise any person to do something which would amount to such an abuse.

(6)   The Commissioner—

  (a)   must arrange for the publication, in such form and manner and to such extent as he considers appropriate, of information about his functions and about matters falling within the scope of his functions; and
  (b)   may give advice about his functions and about such matters.

(7)   Part II of Schedule 5 makes further provision with respect to the Commissioner.

NOTES

Initial Commencement
To be appointed
To be appointed: see s 170(4).

Appointment
Sub-ss (1)–(3), (6), (7): Appointment: 22 May 2000: see SI 2000/1282, art 2, Schedule.
Sub-ss (4), (5): Appointment (for certain purposes): 22 May 2000: see SI 2000/1282, art 2, Schedule.
Sub-ss (4), (5): Appointment (for remaining purposes): 30 October 2000: see SI 2000/1985, art 2, Schedule.

The general prohibition

84 Provision of immigration services

(1)   No person may provide immigration advice or immigration services unless he is a qualified person.

(2)   A person is a qualified person if—

   (a)   he is registered with the Commissioner or is employed by, or works under the supervision of, such a person;

   (b)   he is a member or employee of a body which is a registered person, or works under the supervision of such a member or employee;

   (c)   he is authorised by a designated professional body to practise as a member of the profession whose members are regulated by that body, or works under the supervision of such a person;

   (d)   he is registered with, or authorised by, a person in another EEA State responsible for regulating the provision in that EEA State of advice or services corresponding to immigration advice or immigration services or would be required to be so registered or authorised were he not exempt from such a requirement;

   (e)   he is authorised by a body regulating the legal profession, or any branch of it, in another EEA State to practise as a member of that profession or branch; or

   (f)   he is employed by a person who falls within paragraph (d) or (e) or works under the supervision of such a person or of an employee of such a person.

(3)   If a registered person's registration has limited effect (by virtue of paragraph 2(2) of Schedule 6), neither paragraph (a) nor (b) of subsection (2) authorises the provision of advice or services falling outside the scope of that registration.

(4)   Subsection (1) does not apply to a person who—

   (a)   is certified by the Commissioner as exempt ("an exempt person");

   (b)   is employed by an exempt person;

   (c)   works under the supervision of an exempt person or an employee of an exempt person; or

   (d)   who falls within a category of person specified in an order made by the Secretary of State for the purposes of this subsection.

(5)   A certificate under subsection (4)(a) may relate only to a specified description of immigration advice or immigration services.

(6)   Subsection (1) does not apply to a person—

   (a)   holding an office under the Crown, when acting in that capacity;

   (b)   employed by, or for the purposes of, a government department, when acting in that capacity;

   (c)   acting under the control of a government department; or

   (d)   otherwise exercising functions on behalf of the Crown.

(7)   An exemption given under subsection (4) may be withdrawn by the Commissioner.

NOTES

Initial Commencement
To be appointed
To be appointed: see s 170(4).

Appointment
Sub-s (2)(a), (b): Appointment (for certain purposes): 30 October 2000: see SI 2000/1985, art 2, Schedule.

Sub-s (4)(a): Appointment (for certain purposes): 30 October 2000: see SI 2000/1985, art 2, Schedule.
Sub-s (4)(d): Appointment (for the purposes of enabling subordinate legislation to be made): 30 October 2000: see SI 2000/1985, art 2, Schedule.
Sub-ss (5), (7): Appointment: 30 October 2000: see SI 2000/1985, art 2, Schedule.

85   Registration exemption by the Commissioner

(1)   The Commissioner must prepare and maintain a register for and the purposes of section 84(2)(a) and (b).

(2)   The Commissioner must keep a record of the persons to whom he has issued a certificate of exemption under section 84(4)(a).

(3)   Schedule 6 makes further provision with respect to registration.

NOTES

Initial Commencement
To be appointed
To be appointed: see s 170(4).

Appointment
Sub-ss (1), (2): Appointment: 30 October 2000: see SI 2000/1985, art 2, Schedule.
Sub-s (3): Appointment (for certain purposes): 1 August 2000: see SI 2000/1985, art 2, Schedule.
Sub-s (3): Appointment (for remaining purposes): 30 October 2000: see SI 2000/1985, art 2, Schedule.

Subordinate Legislation
Immigration Services Commissioner (Registration Fee) Order 2000, SI 2000/2735 (made under sub-s (3)).

86   Designated professional bodies

(1)   "Designated professional body" means—

    (a)   The Law Society;
    (b)   The Law Society of Scotland;
    (c)   The Law Society of Northern Ireland;
    (d)   The Institute of Legal Executives;
    (e)   The General Council of the Bar;
    (f)   The Faculty of Advocates; or
    (g)   The General Council of the Bar of Northern Ireland.

(2)   If the Secretary of State considers that a designated professional body has consistently failed to provide effective regulation of its members in their provision of immigration advice or immigration services, he may by order amend subsection (1) to remove the name of that body.

(3)   If a designated professional body asks the Secretary of State to amend subsection (1) so as to remove its name, the Secretary of State may by order do so.

(4)   If the Secretary of State is proposing to act under subsection (2) he must, before doing so—

    (a)   consult the Commissioner;
    (b)   consult the Legal Services Ombudsman, if the proposed order would affect a designated professional body in England and Wales;
    (c)   consult the Scottish Legal Services Ombudsman, if the proposed order would affect a designated professional body in Scotland;

(d) consult the lay observers appointed under Article 42 of the Solicitors (Northern Ireland) Order 1976, if the proposed order would affect a designated professional body in Northern Ireland;

(e) notify the body concerned of his proposal and give it a reasonable period within which to make representations; and

(f) consider any representations so made.

(5) An order under subsection (2) requires the approval of—

(a) the Lord Chancellor, if it affects a designated professional body in England and Wales or Northern Ireland;

(b) the Scottish Ministers, if it affects a designated professional body in Scotland.

(6) Before deciding whether or not to give his approval under subsection (5)(a), the Lord Chancellor must consult—

(a) the designated judges, if the order affects a designated professional body in England and Wales;

(b) the Lord Chief Justice of Northern Ireland, if it affects a designated professional body in Northern Ireland.

(7) Before deciding whether or not to give their approval under subsection (5)(b), the Scottish Ministers must consult the Lord President of the Court of Session.

(8) If the Secretary of State considers that a body which—

(a) is concerned (whether wholly or in part) with regulating the legal profession, or a branch of it, in an EEA State,

(b) is not a designated professional body, and

(c) is capable of providing effective regulation of its members in their provision of immigration advice or immigration services,

ought to be designated, he may by order amend subsection (1) to include the name of that body.

(9) The Commissioner must—

(a) keep under review the list of designated professional bodies set out in subsection (1); and

(b) report to the Secretary of State if he considers that a designated professional body is failing to provide effective regulation of its members in their provision of immigration advice or immigration services.

(10) For the purpose of meeting the costs incurred by the Commissioner in discharging his functions under this Part, each designated professional body must pay to the Commissioner, in each year and on such date as may be specified, such fee as may be specified.

(11) Any unpaid fee for which a designated professional body is liable under subsection (10) may be recovered from that body as a debt due to the Commissioner.

(12) "Specified" means specified by an order made by the Secretary of State.

NOTES

Initial Commencement
To be appointed
To be appointed: see s 170(4).

Appointment
Sub-ss (1)–(9): Appointment: 22 May 2000: see SI 2000/1282, art 2, Schedule.
Sub-ss (10)–(12): Appointment (for the purposes of enabling subordinate legislation to be made): 30 October 2000: see SI 2000/1985, art 2, Schedule.

The Immigration Services Tribunal

87   The Tribunal

(1)   There is to be a tribunal known as the Immigration Services Tribunal (referred to in this Part as "the Tribunal").

(2)   Any person aggrieved by a relevant decision of the Commissioner may appeal to the Tribunal against the decision.

(3)   "Relevant decision" means a decision—

- (a)   to refuse an application for registration made under paragraph 1 of Schedule 6;
- (b)   to withdraw an exemption given under section 84(4)(a);
- (c)   under paragraph 2(2) of that Schedule to register with limited effect;
- (d)   to refuse an application for continued registration made under paragraph 3 of that Schedule;
- (e)   to vary a registration on an application under paragraph 3 of that Schedule; or
- (f)   which is recorded under paragraph 9(1)(a) of Schedule 5.

(4)   The Tribunal is also to have the function of hearing disciplinary charges laid by the Commissioner under paragraph 9(1)(e) of Schedule 5.

(5)   Schedule 7 makes further provision with respect to the Tribunal and its constitution and functions.

NOTES

Initial Commencement
To be appointed
To be appointed: see s 170(4).

Appointment
Sub-ss (1)–(4): Appointment: 30 October 2000: see SI 2000/1985, art 2, Schedule.
Sub-s (5): Appointment (for certain purposes): 1 August 2000: see SI 2000/1985, art 2, Schedule.
Sub-s (5): Appointment (for remaining purposes): 30 October 2000: see SI 2000/1985, art 2, Schedule.

88   Appeal upheld by the Tribunal

(1)   This section applies if the Tribunal allows an appeal under section 87.

(2)   If the Tribunal considers it appropriate, it may direct the Commissioner—

- (a)   to register the applicant or to continue the applicant's registration;
- (b)   to make or vary the applicant's registration so as to have limited effect in any of the ways mentioned in paragraph 2(2) of Schedule 6;
- (c)   to restore an exemption granted under section 84(4)(a); or
- (d)   to quash a decision recorded under paragraph 9(1)(a) of Schedule 5 and the record of that decision.

NOTES

Initial Commencement
To be appointed
To be appointed: see s 170(4).

Appointment
Appointment: 30 October 2000: see SI 2000/1985, art 2, Schedule.

89 Disciplinary charge upheld by the Tribunal

(1) This section applies if the Tribunal upholds a disciplinary charge laid by the Commissioner under paragraph 9(1)(e) of Schedule 5 against a person ("the person charged").

(2) Subsection (3) applies if the person charged is—

    (a) a registered person;

    (b) a person employed by, or working under the supervision of, a registered person;

    (c) a member or employee of a body which is a registered person; or

    (d) a person working under the supervision of such a member or employee.

(3) The Tribunal may—

    (a) direct the Commissioner to record the charge and the Tribunal's decision on it for consideration when the registered person next applies for continued registration; or

    (b) direct the registered person to apply to the Commissioner for continued registration without delay.

(4) If the person charged is certified by the Commissioner as exempt under section 84(4)(a), the Tribunal may direct the Commissioner to consider whether to withdraw his exemption.

(5) If the person charged is found to have charged unreasonable fees for immigration advice or immigration services, the Tribunal may direct him to repay to the clients concerned such portion of those fees as it may determine.

(6) The Tribunal may direct the person charged to pay a penalty to the Commissioner of such sum as it considers appropriate.

(7) A direction given by the Tribunal under subsection (5) (or under subsection (6)) may be enforced by the clients concerned (or by the Commissioner)—

    (a) as if it were an order of a county court; or

    (b) in Scotland, as if it were an extract registered decree arbitral bearing a warrant for execution issued by the sheriff court of any sheriffdom in Scotland.

(8) The Tribunal may direct that the person charged or any person employed by him or working under his supervision is to be—

    (a) subject to such restrictions on the provision of immigration advice or immigration services as the Tribunal considers appropriate;

    (b) suspended from providing immigration advice or immigration services for such period as the Tribunal may determine; or

    (c) prohibited from providing immigration advice or immigration services indefinitely.

(9) The Commissioner must keep a record of the persons against whom there is in force a direction given by the Tribunal under subsection (8).

NOTES

Initial Commencement
To be appointed
To be appointed: see s 170(4).

Appointment
Appointment: 30 October 2000: see SI 2000/1985, art 2, Schedule.

90   Orders by disciplinary bodies

(1)   A disciplinary body may make an order directing that a person subject to its jurisdiction is to be—

(a)   subject to such restrictions on the provision of immigration advice or immigration services as the body considers appropriate;

(b)   suspended from providing immigration advice or immigration services for such period as the body may determine; or

(c)   prohibited from providing immigration advice or immigration services indefinitely.

(2)   "Disciplinary body" means any body—

(a)   appearing to the Secretary of State to be established for the purpose of hearing disciplinary charges against members of a designated professional body; and

(b)   specified in an order made by the Secretary of State.

(3)   The Secretary of State must consult the designated professional body concerned before making an order under subsection (2)(b).

(4)   For the purposes of this section, a person is subject to the jurisdiction of a disciplinary body if he is an authorised person or works under the supervision of an authorised person.

(5)   "Authorised person" means a person who is authorised by the designated professional body concerned to practise as a member of the profession whose members are regulated by that body.

NOTES

Initial Commencement
To be appointed
To be appointed: see s 170(4).

Appointment
Appointment (for the purposes of enabling subordinate legislation to be made): 1 August 2000: see SI 2000/1985, art 2, Schedule.

Enforcement

91   Offences

(1)   A person who provides immigration advice or immigration services in contravention of section 84 or of a restraining order is guilty of an offence and liable—

(a)   on summary conviction, to imprisonment for a term not exceeding six months or to a fine not exceeding the statutory maximum, or to both; or

(b)   on conviction on indictment, to imprisonment for a term not exceeding two years or to a fine, or to both.

(2)   "Restraining order" means—

(a)   a direction given by the Tribunal under section 89(8) or paragraph 9(3) of Schedule 5; or

(b)   an order made by a disciplinary body under section 90(1).

(3)   If an offence under this section committed by a body corporate is proved—

(a)   to have been committed with the consent or connivance of an officer, or

(b)   to be attributable to neglect on his part,

the officer as well as the body corporate is guilty of the offence and liable to be proceeded against and punished accordingly.

(4) "Officer", in relation to a body corporate, means a director, manager, secretary or other similar officer of the body, or a person purporting to act in such a capacity.

(5) If the affairs of a body corporate are managed by its members, subsection (3) applies in relation to the acts and defaults of a member in connection with his functions of management as if he were a director of the body corporate.

(6) If an offence under this section committed by a partnership in Scotland is proved—

(a) to have been committed with the consent or connivance of a partner, or
(b) to be attributable to neglect on his part,

the partner as well as the partnership is guilty of the offence and liable to be proceeded against and punished accordingly.

(7) "Partner" includes a person purporting to act as a partner.

NOTES

Initial Commencement
To be appointed
To be appointed: see s 170(4).

92 Enforcement

(1) If it appears to the Commissioner that a person—

(a) is providing immigration advice or immigration services in contravention of section 84 or of a restraining order, and
(b) is likely to continue to do so unless restrained,

the Commissioner may apply to a county court for an injunction, or to the sheriff for an interdict, restraining him from doing so.

(2) If the court is satisfied that the application is well-founded, it may grant the injunction or interdict in the terms applied for or in more limited terms.

(3) "Restraining order" has the meaning given by section 91.

NOTES

Initial Commencement
To be appointed
To be appointed: see s 170(4).

Miscellaneous

93 Information

(1) No enactment or rule of law prohibiting or restricting the disclosure of information prevents a person from—

(a) giving the Commissioner information which is necessary for the discharge of his functions; or
(b) giving the Tribunal information which is necessary for the discharge of its functions.

(2) No relevant person may at any time disclose information which—

    (a)   has been obtained by, or given to, the Commissioner under or for purposes of this Act,

    (b)   relates to an identified or identifiable individual or business, and

    (c)   is not at that time, and has not previously been, available to the public from other sources,

unless the disclosure is made with lawful authority.

(3)   For the purposes of subsection (2), a disclosure is made with lawful authority only if, and to the extent that—

    (a)   it is made with the consent of the individual or of the person for the time being carrying on the business;

    (b)   it is made for the purposes of, and is necessary for, the discharge of any of the Commissioner's functions under this Act or any Community obligation of the Commissioner;

    (c)   it is made for the purposes of any civil or criminal proceedings arising under or by virtue of this Part, or otherwise; or

    (d)   having regard to the rights and freedoms or legitimate interests of any person, the disclosure is necessary in the public interest.

(4)   A person who knowingly or recklessly discloses information in contravention of subsection (2) is guilty of an offence and liable—

    (a)   on summary conviction, to a fine not exceeding the statutory maximum; or

    (b)   on conviction on indictment, to a fine.

(5)   "Relevant person" means a person who is or has been—

    (a)   the Commissioner;

    (b)   a member of the Commissioner's staff; or

    (c)   an agent of the Commissioner.

NOTES

Initial Commencement
To be appointed
To be appointed: see s 170(4).

Appointment
Appointment: 22 May 2000: see SI 2000/1282, art 2, Schedule.

PART VI
SUPPORT FOR ASYLUM-SEEKERS

Interpretation

94   Interpretation of Part VI

(1)   In this Part—

        "adjudicator" has the meaning given in section 102(2);
        "asylum-seeker" means a person who is not under 18 and has made a claim for asylum which has been recorded by the Secretary of State but which has not been determined;
        "claim for asylum" means a claim that it would be contrary to the United Kingdom's obligations under the Refugee Convention, or under Article 3 of the Human Rights Convention, for the claimant to be removed from, or required to leave, the United Kingdom;

"the Department" means the Department of Health and Social Services for Northern Ireland;

"dependant", in relation to an asylum-seeker or a supported person, means a person in the United Kingdom who—

(a) is his spouse;

(b) is a child of his, or of his spouse, who is under 18 and dependent on him; or

(c) falls within such additional category, if any, as may be prescribed;

"the Executive" means the Northern Ireland Housing Executive;

"housing accommodation" includes flats, lodging houses and hostels;

"local authority" means—

(a) in England and Wales, a county council, a county borough council, a district council, a London borough council, the Common Council of the City of London or the Council of the Isles of Scilly;

(b) in Scotland, a council constituted under section 2 of the Local Government etc (Scotland) Act 1994;

"supported person" means—

(a) an asylum-seeker, or

(b) a dependant of an asylum-seeker,

who has applied for support and for whom support is provided under section 95.

(2) References in this Part to support provided under section 95 include references to support which is provided under arrangements made by the Secretary of State under that section.

(3) For the purposes of this Part, a claim for asylum is determined at the end of such period beginning—

(a) on the day on which the Secretary of State notifies the claimant of his decision on the claim, or

(b) if the claimant has appealed against the Secretary of State's decision, on the day on which the appeal is disposed of,

as may be prescribed.

(4) An appeal is disposed of when it is no longer pending for the purposes of the Immigration Acts or the Special Immigration Appeals Commission Act 1997.

(5) If an asylum-seeker's household includes a child who is under 18 and a dependant of his, he is to be treated (for the purposes of this Part) as continuing to be an asylum-seeker while—

(a) the child is under 18; and

(b) he and the child remain in the United Kingdom.

(6) Subsection (5) does not apply if, on or after the determination of his claim for asylum, the asylum-seeker is granted leave to enter or remain in the United Kingdom (whether or not as a result of that claim).

(7) For the purposes of this Part, the Secretary of State may inquire into, and decide, the age of any person.

(8) A notice under subsection (3) must be given in writing.

(9) If such a notice is sent by the Secretary of State by first class post, addressed—

(a) to the asylum-seeker's representative, or

(b) to the asylum-seeker's last known address,

it is to be taken to have been received by the asylum-seeker on the second day after the day on which it was posted.

NOTES

Initial Commencement
Royal Assent
Royal Assent: 11 November 1999: see s 170(3)(f).

Subordinate Legislation
Asylum Support (Interim Provisions) Regulations 1999, SI 1999/3056.
Asylum Support Regulations 2000, SI 2000/704.

Provision of support

95   Persons for whom support may be provided

(1)   The Secretary of State may provide, or arrange for the provision of, support for—

(a)   asylum-seekers, or
(b)   dependants of asylum-seekers,

who appear to the Secretary of State to be destitute or to be likely to become destitute within such period as may be prescribed.

(2)   In prescribed circumstances, a person who would otherwise fall within subsection (1) is excluded.

(3)   For the purposes of this section, a person is destitute if—

(a)   he does not have adequate accommodation or any means of obtaining it (whether or not his other essential living needs are met); or
(b)   he has adequate accommodation or the means of obtaining it, but cannot meet his other essential living needs.

(4)   If a person has dependants, subsection (3) is to be read as if the references to him were references to him and his dependants taken together.

(5)   In determining, for the purposes of this section, whether a person's accommodation is adequate, the Secretary of State—

(a)   must have regard to such matters as may be prescribed for the purposes of this paragraph; but
(b)   may not have regard to such matters as may be prescribed for the purposes of this paragraph or to any of the matters mentioned in subsection (6).

(6)   Those matters are—

(a)   the fact that the person concerned has no enforceable right to occupy the accommodation;
(b)   the fact that he shares the accommodation, or any part of the accommodation, with one or more other persons;
(c)   the fact that the accommodation is temporary;
(d)   the location of the accommodation.

(7)   In determining, for the purposes of this section, whether a person's other essential living needs are met, the Secretary of State—

(a)   must have regard to such matters as may be prescribed for the purposes of this paragraph; but
(b)   may not have regard to such matters as may be prescribed for the purposes of this paragraph.

(8)   The Secretary of State may by regulations provide that items or expenses of such a description as may be prescribed are, or are not, to be treated as being an essential living need of a person for the purposes of this Part.

(9) Support may be provided subject to conditions.

(10) The conditions must be set out in writing.

(11) A copy of the conditions must be given to the supported person.

(12) Schedule 8 gives the Secretary of State power to make regulations supplementing this section.

(13) Schedule 9 makes temporary provision for support in the period before the coming into force of this section.

NOTES

Initial Commencement
Royal Assent
Sub-s (13): Royal Assent: 11 November 1999: see s 170(3)(g).
To be appointed
Sub-ss (1)–(12): To be appointed: see s 170(4).

Appointment
Sub-ss (1)–(11): Appointment (for the purposes of enabling subordinate legislation to be made): 1 January 2000: see SI 1999/3190, art 2, Schedule.
Sub-ss (1)–(11): Appointment (for remaining purposes): 3 April 2000: see SI 2000/464, art 2, Schedule.
Sub-ss (3)–(8): Appointment (for certain purposes): 6 December 1999: see SI 1999/3190, art 2, Schedule.
Sub-s (12): Appointment: 1 January 2000: see SI 1999/3190, art 2, Schedule.

Subordinate Legislation
Asylum Support Regulations 2000, SI 2000/704.

96 Ways in which support may be provided

(1) Support may be provided under section 95—

    (a) by providing accommodation appearing to the Secretary of State to be adequate for the needs of the supported person and his dependants (if any);

    (b) by providing what appear to the Secretary of State to be essential living needs of the supported person and his dependants (if any);

    (c) to enable the supported person (if he is the asylum-seeker) to meet what appear to the Secretary of State to be expenses (other than legal expenses or other expenses of a prescribed description) incurred in connection with his claim for asylum;

    (d) to enable the asylum-seeker and his dependants to attend bail proceedings in connection with his detention under any provision of the Immigration Acts; or

    (e) to enable the asylum-seeker and his dependants to attend bail proceedings in connection with the detention of a dependant of his under any such provision.

(2) If the Secretary of State considers that the circumstances of a particular case are exceptional, he may provide support under section 95 in such other ways as he considers necessary to enable the supported person and his dependants (if any) to be supported.

(3) Unless the circumstances of a particular case are exceptional, support provided by the Secretary of State under subsection (1)(a) or (b) or (2) must not be wholly or mainly by way of payments made (by whatever means) to the supported person or to his dependants (if any).

(4) But the Secretary of State may by order provide for subsection (3) not to apply—

    (a) in all cases, for such period as may be specified;

    (b) in such circumstances as may be specified;

    (c)   in relation to specified categories of person; or

    (d)   in relation to persons whose accommodation is in a specified locality.

(5)   The Secretary of State may by order repeal subsection (3).

(6)   "Specified" means specified in an order made under subsection (4).

NOTES

Initial Commencement
To be appointed
To be appointed: see s 170(4).

Appointment
Appointment: 3 April 2000: see SI 2000/464, art 2, Schedule.

97   Supplemental

(1)   When exercising his power under section 95 to provide accommodation, the Secretary of State must have regard to—

    (a)   the fact that the accommodation is to be temporary pending determination of the asylum-seeker's claim;

    (b)   the desirability, in general, of providing accommodation in areas in which there is a ready supply of accommodation; and

    (c)   such other matters (if any) as may be prescribed.

(2)   But he may not have regard to—

    (a)   any preference that the supported person or his dependants (if any) may have as to the locality in which the accommodation is to be provided; or

    (b)   such other matters (if any) as may be prescribed.

(3)   The Secretary of State may by order repeal all or any of the following—

    (a)   subsection (1)(a);

    (b)   subsection (1)(b);

    (c)   subsection (2)(a).

(4)   When exercising his power under section 95 to provide essential living needs, the Secretary of State—

    (a)   must have regard to such matters as may be prescribed for the purposes of this paragraph; but

    (b)   may not have regard to such other matters as may be prescribed for the purposes of this paragraph.

(5)   In addition, when exercising his power under section 95 to provide essential living needs, the Secretary of State may limit the overall amount of the expenditure which he incurs in connection with a particular supported person—

    (a)   to such portion of the income support applicable amount provided under section 124 of the Social Security Contributions and Benefits Act 1992, or

    (b)   to such portion of any components of that amount,

as he considers appropriate having regard to the temporary nature of the support that he is providing.

(6)   For the purposes of subsection (5), any support of a kind falling within section 96(1)(c) is to be treated as if it were the provision of essential living needs.

(7)   In determining how to provide, or arrange for the provision of, support under section 95, the Secretary of State may disregard any preference which the supported person or his dependants (if any) may have as to the way in which the support is to be given.

NOTES

Initial Commencement
To be appointed
To be appointed: see s 170(4).

Appointment
Appointment (for the purpose of enabling subordinate legislation to be made): 1 January 2000: see SI 1999/3190, art 2, Schedule.
Appointment (for remaining purposes): 3 April 2000: see SI 2000/464, art 2, Schedule.

Subordinate Legislation
Asylum Support Regulations 2000, SI 2000/704.

98 Temporary support

(1) The Secretary of State may provide, or arrange for the provision of, support for—

    (a) asylum-seekers, or
    (b) dependants of asylum-seekers,

who it appears to the Secretary of State may be destitute.

(2) Support may be provided under this section only until the Secretary of State is able to determine whether support may be provided under section 95.

(3) Subsections (2) to (11) of section 95 apply for the purposes of this section as they apply for the purposes of that section.

NOTES

Initial Commencement
To be appointed
To be appointed: see s 170(4).

Appointment
Sub-ss (1), (2): Appointment: 3 April 2000: see SI 2000/464, art 2, Schedule.
Sub-s (3): Appointment (for the purpose of enabling subordinate legislation to be made under s 95 as applied by this subsection): 1 March 2000: see SI 2000/464, art 2, Schedule.
Sub-s (3): Appointment (for remaining purposes): 3 April 2000: see SI 2000/464, art 2, Schedule.

Support and assistance by local authorities etc

99 Provision of support by local authorities

(1) A local authority may provide support for asylum-seekers and their dependants (if any) in accordance with arrangements made by the Secretary of State under section 95.

(2) Such support may be provided by the local authority—

    (a) in one or more of the ways mentioned in section 96(1) and (2);
    (b) whether the arrangements in question are made with the authority or with another person.

(3) The Executive may provide support by way of accommodation for asylum-seekers and their dependants (if any) in accordance with arrangements made by the Secretary of State under section 95, whether the arrangements in question are made with the Executive or with another person.

(4) A local authority may incur reasonable expenditure in connection with the preparation of proposals for entering into arrangements under section 95.

(5) The powers conferred on a local authority by this section include power to—

  (a) provide services outside their area;
  (b) provide services jointly with one or more bodies who are not local authorities;
  (c) form a company for the purpose of providing services;
  (d) tender for contracts (whether alone or with any other person).

NOTES

Initial Commencement
Royal Assent
Sub-ss (4), (5): Royal Assent: 11 November 1999: see s 170(3)(h).
To be appointed
Sub-ss (1)–(3): To be appointed: see s 170(4).

Appointment
Sub-ss (1)–(3): Appointment: 3 April 2000: see SI 2000/464, art 2, Schedule.

100 Local authority and other assistance for Secretary of State

(1)   This section applies if the Secretary of State asks—

  (a) a local authority,
  (b) a registered social landlord,
  (c) a registered housing association in Scotland or Northern Ireland, or
  (d) the Executive,

to assist him to exercise his power under section 95 to provide accommodation.

(2)   The person to whom the request is made must co-operate in giving the Secretary of State such assistance in the exercise of that power as is reasonable in the circumstances.

(3)   Subsection (2) does not require a registered social landlord to act beyond its powers.

(4)   A local authority must supply to the Secretary of State such information about their housing accommodation (whether or not occupied) as he may from time to time request.

(5)   The information must be provided in such form and manner as the Secretary of State may direct.

(6)   "Registered social landlord" has the same meaning as in Part I of the Housing Act 1996.

(7)   "Registered housing association" has the same meaning—

  (a) in relation to Scotland, as in the Housing Associations Act 1985; and
  (b) in relation to Northern Ireland, as in Part II of the Housing (Northern Ireland) Order 1992.

NOTES

Initial Commencement
To be appointed
To be appointed: see s 170(4).

Appointment
Appointment: 3 April 2000: see SI 2000/464, art 2, Schedule.

101 Reception zones

(1)   The Secretary of State may by order designate as reception zones—

  (a) areas in England and Wales consisting of the areas of one or more local authorities;

   (b)   areas in Scotland consisting of the areas of one or more local authorities;

   (c)   Northern Ireland.

(2)   Subsection (3) applies if the Secretary of State considers that—

   (a)   a local authority whose area is within a reception zone has suitable housing accommodation within that zone; or

   (b)   the Executive has suitable housing accommodation.

(3)   The Secretary of State may direct the local authority or the Executive to make available such of the accommodation as may be specified in the direction for a period so specified—

   (a)   to him for the purpose of providing support under section 95; or

   (b)   to a person with whom the Secretary of State has made arrangements under section 95.

(4)   A period specified in a direction under subsection (3)—

   (a)   begins on a date so specified; and

   (b)   must not exceed five years.

(5)   A direction under subsection (3) is enforceable, on an application made on behalf of the Secretary of State, by injunction or in Scotland an order under section 45(b) of the Court of Session Act 1988.

(6)   The Secretary of State's power to give a direction under subsection (3) in respect of a particular reception zone must be exercised by reference to criteria specified for the purposes of this subsection in the order designating that zone.

(7)   The Secretary of State may not give a direction under subsection (3) in respect of a local authority in Scotland unless the Scottish Ministers have confirmed to him that the criteria specified in the designation order concerned are in their opinion met in relation to that authority.

(8)   Housing accommodation is suitable for the purposes of subsection (2) if it—

   (a)   is unoccupied;

   (b)   would be likely to remain unoccupied for the foreseeable future if not made available; and

   (c)   is appropriate for the accommodation of persons supported under this Part or capable of being made so with minor work.

(9)   If housing accommodation for which a direction under this section is, for the time being, in force—

   (a)   is not appropriate for the accommodation of persons supported under this Part, but

   (b)   is capable of being made so with minor work,

the direction may require the body to whom it is given to secure that that work is done without delay.

(10) The Secretary of State must make regulations with respect to the general management of any housing accommodation for which a direction under subsection (3) is, for the time being, in force.

(11) Regulations under subsection (10) must include provision—

   (a)   as to the method to be used in determining the amount of rent or other charges to be payable in relation to the accommodation;

   (b)   as to the times at which payments of rent or other charges are to be made;

   (c)   as to the responsibility for maintenance of, and repairs to, the accommodation;

    (d) enabling the accommodation to be inspected, in such circumstances as may be prescribed, by the body to which the direction was given;

    (e) with respect to the condition in which the accommodation is to be returned when the direction ceases to have effect.

(12) Regulations under subsection (10) may, in particular, include provision—

    (a) for the cost, or part of the cost, of minor work required by a direction under this section to be met by the Secretary of State in prescribed circumstances;

    (b) as to the maximum amount of expenditure which a body may be required to incur as a result of a direction under this section.

(13) The Secretary of State must by regulations make provision ("the dispute resolution procedure") for resolving disputes arising in connection with the operation of any regulations made under subsection (10).

(14) Regulations under subsection (13) must include provision—

    (a) requiring a dispute to be resolved in accordance with the dispute resolution procedure;

    (b) requiring the parties to a dispute to comply with obligations imposed on them by the procedure; and

    (c) for the decision of the person resolving a dispute in accordance with the procedure to be final and binding on the parties.

(15) Before—

    (a) designating a reception zone in Great Britain,

    (b) determining the criteria to be included in the order designating the zone, or

    (c) making regulations under subsection (13),

the Secretary of State must consult such local authorities, local authority associations and other persons as he thinks appropriate.

(16) Before—

    (a) designating Northern Ireland as a reception zone, or

    (b) determining the criteria to be included in the order designating Northern Ireland,

the Secretary of State must consult the Executive and such other persons as he thinks appropriate.

(17) Before making regulations under subsection (10) which extend only to Northern Ireland, the Secretary of State must consult the Executive and such other persons as he thinks appropriate.

(18) Before making any other regulations under subsection (10), the Secretary of State must consult—

    (a) such local authorities, local authority associations and other persons as he thinks appropriate; and

    (b) if the regulations extend to Northern Ireland, the Executive.

NOTES

Initial Commencement
To be appointed
To be appointed: see s 170(4).

Appointment
Appointment: 3 April 2000: see SI 2000/464, art 2, Schedule.

Appeals

102 Asylum Support Adjudicators

(1) There are to be adjudicators to hear appeals under this Part.

(2) A person appointed as an adjudicator under this Part is to be known as an Asylum Support Adjudicator (but is referred to in this Part as "an adjudicator").

(3) Schedule 10 makes further provision with respect to adjudicators.

NOTES

Initial Commencement
To be appointed
To be appointed: see s 170(4).

Appointment
Appointment: 3 April 2000: see SI 2000/464, art 2, Schedule.

103 Appeals

(1) If, on an application for support under section 95, the Secretary of State decides that the applicant does not qualify for support under that section, the applicant may appeal to an adjudicator.

(2) If the Secretary of State decides to stop providing support for a person under section 95 before that support would otherwise have come to an end, that person may appeal to an adjudicator.

(3) On an appeal under this section, the adjudicator may—

    (a) require the Secretary of State to reconsider the matter;
    (b) substitute his decision for the decision appealed against; or
    (c) dismiss the appeal.

(4) The adjudicator must give his reasons in writing.

(5) The decision of the adjudicator is final.

(6) If an appeal is dismissed, no further application by the appellant for support under section 95 is to be entertained unless the Secretary of State is satisfied that there has been a material change in the circumstances.

(7) The Secretary of State may by regulations provide for decisions as to where support provided under section 95 is to be provided to be appealable to an adjudicator under this Part.

(8) Regulations under subsection (7) may provide for any provision of this section to have effect, in relation to an appeal brought by virtue of the regulations, subject to such modifications as may be prescribed.

(9) The Secretary of State may pay any reasonable travelling expenses incurred by an appellant in connection with attendance at any place for the purposes of an appeal under this section.

NOTES

Initial Commencement
To be appointed
To be appointed: see s 170(4).

Appointment
Appointment: 3 April 2000: see SI 2000/464, art 2, Schedule.

104 Secretary of State's rules

(1)   The Secretary of State may make rules regulating—

    (a)   the bringing of appeals under this Part; and

    (b)   the practice and procedure of the adjudicators.

(2)   The rules may, in particular, make provision—

    (a)   for the period within which an appeal must be brought;

    (b)   as to the burden of proof on an appeal;

    (c)   as to the giving and admissibility of evidence;

    (d)   for summoning witnesses;

    (e)   for an appeal to be heard in the absence of the appellant;

    (f)   for determining an appeal without a hearing;

    (g)   requiring reports of decisions of adjudicators to be published;

    (h)   conferring such ancillary powers on adjudicators as the Secretary of State considers necessary for the proper discharge of their functions.

(3)   In making the rules, the Secretary of State must have regard to the desirability of securing, so far as is reasonably practicable, that appeals are brought and disposed of with the minimum of delay.

NOTES

Initial Commencement
To be appointed
To be appointed: see s 170(4).

Appointment
Appointment: 1 January 2000: see SI 1999/3190, art 2, Schedule.

Subordinate Legislation
Asylum Support Appeals (Procedure) Rules 2000, SI 2000/541.

Offences

105 False representations

(1)   A person is guilty of an offence if, with a view to obtaining support for himself or any other person under any provision made by or under this Part, he—

    (a)   makes a statement or representation which he knows is false in a material particular;

    (b)   produces or gives to a person exercising functions under this Part, or knowingly causes or allows to be produced or given to such a person, any document or information which he knows is false in a material particular;

    (c)   fails, without reasonable excuse, to notify a change of circumstances when required to do so in accordance with any provision made by or under this Part; or

    (d)   without reasonable excuse, knowingly causes another person to fail to notify a change of circumstances which that other person was required to notify in accordance with any provision made by or under this Part.

(2)   A person guilty of an offence under this section is liable on summary conviction to imprisonment for a term not exceeding three months or to a fine not exceeding level 5 on the standard scale, or to both.

NOTES

Initial Commencement
Royal Assent
Royal Assent: 11 November 1999: see s 170(3)(i).

106 Dishonest representations

(1)   A person is guilty of an offence if, with a view to obtaining any benefit or other payment or advantage under this Part for himself or any other person, he dishonestly—

    (a)   makes a statement or representation which is false in a material particular;

    (b)   produces or gives to a person exercising functions under this Part, or causes or allows to be produced or given to such a person, any document or information which is false in a material particular;

    (c)   fails to notify a change of circumstances when required to do so in accordance with any provision made by or under this Part; or

    (d)   causes another person to fail to notify a change of circumstances which that other person was required to notify in accordance with any provision made by or under this Part.

(2)   A person guilty of an offence under this section is liable—

    (a)   on summary conviction, to imprisonment for a term not exceeding six months or to a fine not exceeding the statutory maximum, or to both; or

    (b)   on conviction on indictment, to imprisonment for a term not exceeding seven years or to a fine, or to both.

(3)   In the application of this section to Scotland, in subsection (1) for "dishonestly" substitute "knowingly".

NOTES

Initial Commencement
Royal Assent
Royal Assent: 11 November 1999: see s 170(3)(i).

107 Delay or obstruction

(1)   A person is guilty of an offence if, without reasonable excuse, he—

    (a)   intentionally delays or obstructs a person exercising functions conferred by or under this Part; or

    (b)   refuses or neglects to answer a question, give any information or produce a document when required to do so in accordance with any provision made by or under this Part.

(2)   A person guilty of an offence under subsection (1) is liable on summary conviction to a fine not exceeding level 3 on the standard scale.

NOTES

Initial Commencement
Royal Assent
Royal Assent: 11 November 1999: see s 170(3)(i).

108 Failure of sponsor to maintain

(1)   A person is guilty of an offence if, during any period in respect of which he has given a written undertaking in pursuance of the immigration rules to be responsible for the maintenance and accommodation of another person—

    (a)   he persistently refuses or neglects, without reasonable excuse, to maintain that person in accordance with the undertaking; and

    (b)   in consequence of his refusal or neglect, support under any provision made by or under this Part is provided for or in respect of that person.

(2)   A person guilty of an offence under this section is liable on summary conviction to imprisonment for a term not exceeding 3 months or to a fine not exceeding level 4 on the standard scale, or to both.

(3)   For the purposes of this section, a person is not to be taken to have refused or neglected to maintain another person by reason only of anything done or omitted in furtherance of a trade dispute.

NOTES

Initial Commencement
Royal Assent
Royal Assent: 11 November 1999: see s 170(3)(i).

109 Supplemental

(1)   If an offence under section 105, 106, 107 or 108 committed by a body corporate is proved—

    (a)   to have been committed with the consent or connivance of an officer, or
    (b)   to be attributable to neglect on his part,

the officer as well as the body corporate is guilty of the offence and liable to be proceeded against and punished accordingly.

(2)   "Officer", in relation to a body corporate, means a director, manager, secretary or other similar officer of the body, or a person purporting to act in such a capacity.

(3)   If the affairs of a body corporate are managed by its members, subsection (1) applies in relation to the acts and defaults of a member in connection with his functions of management as if he were a director of the body corporate.

(4)   If an offence under section 105, 106, 107 or 108 committed by a partnership in Scotland is proved—

    (a)   to have been committed with the consent or connivance of a partner, or
    (b)   to be attributable to neglect on his part,

the partner as well as the partnership is guilty of the offence and liable to be proceeded against and punished accordingly.

(5)   "Partner" includes a person purporting to act as a partner.

NOTES

Initial Commencement
Royal Assent
Royal Assent: 11 November 1999: see s 170(3)(i).

Expenditure

110 Payments to local authorities

(1)   The Secretary of State may from time to time pay to any local authority or Northern Ireland authority such sums as he considers appropriate in respect of expenditure incurred, or to be incurred, by the authority in connection with—

    (a)   persons who are, or have been, asylum-seekers; and
    (b)   their dependants.

(2)   The Secretary of State may from time to time pay to any—

  (a)   local authority,
  (b)   local authority association, or
  (c)   Northern Ireland authority,

such sums as he considers appropriate in respect of services provided by the authority or association in connection with the discharge of functions under this Part.

(3)   The Secretary of State may make payments to any local authority towards the discharge of any liability of supported persons or their dependants in respect of council tax payable to that authority.

(4)   The Secretary of State must pay to a body to which a direction under section 101(3) is given such sums as he considers represent the reasonable costs to that body of complying with the direction.

(5)   The Secretary of State must pay to a directed body sums determined to be payable in relation to accommodation made available by that body under section 101(3)(a).

(6)   The Secretary of State may pay to a directed body sums determined to be payable in relation to accommodation made available by that body under section 101(3)(b).

(7)   In subsections (5) and (6)—
      "determined" means determined in accordance with regulations made by virtue of subsection (11)(a) of section 101, and
      "directed body" means a body to which a direction under subsection (3) of section 101 is given.

(8)   Payments under subsection (1), (2) or (3) may be made on such terms, and subject to such conditions, as the Secretary of State may determine.

(9)   "Northern Ireland authority" means—

  (a)   the Executive; or
  (b)   a Health and Social Services Board established under Article 16 of the Health and Personal Social Services (Northern Ireland) Order 1972.

NOTES

Initial Commencement
Royal Assent
Sub-ss (1), (2): Royal Assent: 11 November 1999: see s 170(3)(j).
Sub-s (8): Royal Assent (for certain purposes): 11 November 1999: see s 170(3)(j).

To be appointed
Sub-ss (3)–(7), (9): To be appointed: see s 170(4).
Sub-s (8): To be appointed (for remaining purposes): see s 170(4).

Appointment
Sub-ss (3)–(7): Appointment: 3 April 2000: see SI 2000/464, art 2, Schedule.
Sub-s (8): Appointment (for remaining purposes): 3 April 2000: see SI 2000/464, art 2, Schedule.
Sub-s (9): Appointment: 6 December 1999: see SI 1999/3190, art 2, Schedule.

111 Grants to voluntary organisations

(1)   The Secretary of State may make grants of such amounts as he thinks appropriate to voluntary organisations in connection with—

  (a)   the provision by them of support (of whatever nature) to persons who are, or have been, asylum-seekers and to their dependants; and
  (b)   connected matters.

(2)   Grants may be made on such terms, and subject to such conditions, as the Secretary of State may determine.

NOTES

Initial Commencement
Royal Assent
Royal Assent: 11 November 1999: see s 170(3)(k).

112 Recovery of expenditure on support: misrepresentation etc

(1)   This section applies if, on an application made by the Secretary of State, the court determines that—

(a)   a person ("A") has misrepresented or failed to disclose a material fact (whether fraudulently or otherwise); and

(b)   as a consequence of the misrepresentation or failure, support has been provided under section 95 or 98 (whether or not to A).

(2)   If the support was provided by the Secretary of State, the court may order A to pay to the Secretary of State an amount representing the monetary value of the support which would not have been provided but for A's misrepresentation or failure.

(3)   If the support was provided by another person ("B") in accordance with arrangements made with the Secretary of State under section 95 or 98, the court may order A to pay to the Secretary of State an amount representing the payment to B which would not have been made but for A's misrepresentation or failure.

(4)   "Court" means a county court or, in Scotland, the sheriff.

NOTES

Initial Commencement
To be appointed
To be appointed: see s 170(4).

Appointment
Appointment: 3 April 2000: see SI 2000/464, art 2, Schedule.

113 Recovery of expenditure on support from sponsor

(1)   This section applies if—

(a)   a person ("the sponsor") has given a written undertaking in pursuance of the immigration rules to be responsible for the maintenance and accommodation of another person; and

(b)   during any period in relation to which the undertaking applies, support under section 95 is provided to or in respect of that other person.

(2)   The Secretary of State may make a complaint against the sponsor to a magistrates' court for an order under this section.

(3)   The court—

(a)   must have regard to all the circumstances (and in particular to the sponsor's income); and

(b)   may order him to pay to the Secretary of State such sum (weekly or otherwise) as it considers appropriate.

(4)   But such a sum is not to include any amount attributable otherwise than to support provided under section 95.

(5)   In determining—

(a)   whether to order any payments to be made in respect of support provided under section 95 for any period before the complaint was made, or

(b)   the amount of any such payments,

the court must disregard any amount by which the sponsor's current income exceeds his income during that period.

(6) An order under this section is enforceable as a magistrates' court maintenance order within the meaning of section 150(1) of the Magistrates' Courts Act 1980.

(7) In the application of this section to Scotland—

(a) omit subsection (6);
(b) for references to a complaint substitute references to an application; and
(c) for references to a magistrates' court substitute references to the sheriff.

(8) In the application of this section to Northern Ireland, for references to a magistrates' court substitute references to a court of summary jurisdiction and for subsection (6) substitute—

"(6) An order under this section is an order to which Article 98(11) of the Magistrates' Courts (Northern Ireland) Order 1981 applies."

NOTES

Initial Commencement
To be appointed
To be appointed: see s 170(4).

Appointment
Appointment: 3 April 2000: see SI 2000/464, art 2, Schedule.

114 Overpayments

(1) Subsection (2) applies if, as a result of an error on the part of the Secretary of State, support has been provided to a person under section 95 or 98.

(2) The Secretary of State may recover from a person who is, or has been, a supported person an amount representing the monetary value of support provided to him as a result of the error.

(3) An amount recoverable under subsection (2) may be recovered as if it were a debt due to the Secretary of State.

(4) The Secretary of State may by regulations make provision for other methods of recovery, including deductions from support provided under section 95.

NOTES

Initial Commencement
To be appointed
To be appointed: see s 170(4).

Appointment
Appointment (for the purpose of enabling subordinate legislation to be made): 1 January 2000: see SI 1999/3190, art 2, Schedule.
Appointment (for remaining purposes): 3 April 2000: see SI 2000/464, art 2, Schedule.

Subordinate Legislation
Asylum Support Regulations 2000, SI 2000/704.

Exclusions

115 Exclusion from benefits

(1) No person is entitled to income-based jobseeker's allowance under the Jobseekers Act 1995 or to—

(a)   attendance allowance,
(b)   severe disablement allowance,
(c)   invalid care allowance,
(d)   disability living allowance,
(e)   income support,
(f)   working families' tax credit,
(g)   disabled person's tax credit,
(h)   a social fund payment,
(i)   child benefit,
(j)   housing benefit, or
(k)   council tax benefit,

under the Social Security Contributions and Benefits Act 1992 while he is a person to whom this section applies.

(2)   No person in Northern Ireland is entitled to—

(a)   income-based jobseeker's allowance under the Jobseekers (Northern Ireland) Order 1995, or
(b)   any of the benefits mentioned in paragraphs (a) to (j) of subsection (1),

under the Social Security Contributions and Benefits (Northern Ireland) Act 1992 while he is a person to whom this section applies.

(3)   This section applies to a person subject to immigration control unless he falls within such category or description, or satisfies such conditions, as may be prescribed.

(4)   Regulations under subsection (3) may provide for a person to be treated for prescribed purposes only as not being a person to whom this section applies.

(5)   In relation to the benefits mentioned in subsection (1)(f) or (g), "prescribed" means prescribed by regulations made by the Treasury.

(6)   In relation to the matters mentioned in subsection (2) (except so far as it relates to the benefits mentioned in subsection (1)(f) or (g)), "prescribed" means prescribed by regulations made by the Department.

(7)   Section 175(3) to (5) of the Social Security Contributions and Benefits Act 1992 (supplemental powers in relation to regulations) applies to regulations made by the Secretary of State or the Treasury under subsection (3) as it applies to regulations made under that Act.

(8)   Sections 133(2), 171(2) and 172(4) of the Social Security Contributions and Benefits (Northern Ireland) Act 1992 apply to regulations made by the Department under subsection (3) as they apply to regulations made by the Department under that Act.

(9)   "A person subject to immigration control" means a person who is not a national of an EEA State and who—

(a)   requires leave to enter or remain in the United Kingdom but does not have it;
(b)   has leave to enter or remain in the United Kingdom which is subject to a condition that he does not have recourse to public funds;
(c)   has leave to enter or remain in the United Kingdom given as a result of a maintenance undertaking; or
(d)   has leave to enter or remain in the United Kingdom only as a result of paragraph 17 of Schedule 4.

(10)   "Maintenance undertaking", in relation to any person, means a written undertaking given by another person in pursuance of the immigration rules to be responsible for that person's maintenance and accommodation.

NOTES

Initial Commencement
To be appointed
Sub-ss (1), (2): To be appointed (in accordance with the first regulations made under Sch 8): see
s 170(2), (4).
Sub-ss (3)–(10): To be appointed: see s 170(4).

Appointment
Sub-ss (1), (2): Appointment: 3 April 2000 (in accordance with SI 2000/704, the first regulations
made under Sch 8): see s 170(2), (4).
Sub-ss (3)–(10): Appointment (for the purpose of enabling subordinate legislation to be made):
1 January 2000: see SI 1999/3190, art 2, Schedule.
Sub-ss (3)–(10): Appointment (for remaining purposes): 3 April 2000: see SI 2000/464, art 2,
Schedule.

Subordinate Legislation
Social Security (Immigration and Asylum) Consequential Amendments Regulations 2000,
SI 2000/636 (made under sub-ss (3), (4), (7)).
Immigration (Eligibility for Assistance) (Scotland and Northern Ireland) Regulations 2000,
SI 2000/705 (made under sub-ss (3), (4)).

116 Amendment of section 21 of the National Assistance Act 1948

In section 21 of the National Assistance Act 1948 (duty of local authorities to provide
accommodation), after subsection (1), insert—

"(1A)   A person to whom section 115 of the Immigration and Asylum Act 1999
(exclusion from benefits) applies may not be provided with residential accommodation
under subsection (1)(a) if his need for care and attention has arisen solely—

(a)   because he is destitute; or
(b)   because of the physical effects, or anticipated physical effects, of his being destitute.

(1B) Subsections (3) and (5) to (8) of section 95 of the Immigration and Asylum Act
1999, and paragraph 2 of Schedule 8 to that Act, apply for the purposes of subsection (1A)
as they apply for the purposes of that section, but for the references in subsections (5)
and (7) of that section and in that paragraph to the Secretary of State substitute references
to a local authority."

NOTES

Initial Commencement
To be appointed
To be appointed: see s 170(4).

Appointment
Appointment: 6 December 1999: see SI 1999/3190, art 2, Schedule.

117 Other restrictions on assistance: England and Wales

(1)   In section 45 of the Health Services and Public Health Act 1968 (promotion by local
authorities of the welfare of old people), after subsection (4), insert—

"(4A)   No arrangements under this section may be given effect to in relation to a
person to whom section 115 of the Immigration and Asylum Act 1999 (exclusion from
benefits) applies solely—

(a)   because he is destitute; or
(b)   because of the physical effects, or anticipated physical effects, of his being destitute.

(4B) Subsections (3) and (5) to (8) of section 95 of the Immigration and Asylum Act
1999, and paragraph 2 of Schedule 8 to that Act, apply for the purposes of subsection (4A)

as they apply for the purposes of that section, but for the references in subsections (5) and (7) of that section and in that paragraph to the Secretary of State substitute references to a local authority."

(2)   In paragraph 2 of Schedule 8 to the National Health Service Act 1977 (arrangements by local authorities for the prevention of illness and for care and after-care), after sub-paragraph (2), insert—

"(2A)   No arrangements under this paragraph may be given effect to in relation to a person to whom section 115 of the Immigration and Asylum Act 1999 (exclusion from benefits) applies solely—

   (a)   because he is destitute; or
   (b)   because of the physical effects, or anticipated physical effects, of his being destitute.

(2B) Subsections (3) and (5) to (8) of section 95 of the Immigration and Asylum Act 1999, and paragraph 2 of Schedule 8 to that Act, apply for the purposes of subsection (2A) as they apply for the purposes of that section, but for the references in subsections (5) and (7) of that section and in that paragraph to the Secretary of State substitute references to a local social services authority."

(3)   In section 161 of the Housing Act 1996 (allocation of housing accommodation only to qualifying persons), after subsection (2), insert—

"(2A)   Regulations may not be made under subsection (2) so as to include in a prescribed class any person to whom section 115 of the Immigration and Asylum Act 1999 (exclusion from benefits) applies."

(4)   In section 185 of the 1996 Act (persons from abroad not eligible for housing assistance), after subsection (2), insert—

"(2A)   Regulations may not be made under subsection (2) so as to include in a prescribed class any person to whom section 115 of the Immigration and Asylum Act 1999 (exclusion from benefits) applies."

(5)   In the 1996 Act, omit section 186 (asylum-seekers and their dependants).

(6)   In section 187(1) of the 1996 Act (provision of information by Secretary of State), in paragraph (a), for "or has become an asylum-seeker, or a dependant of an asylum-seeker" substitute "a person to whom section 115 of the Immigration and Asylum Act 1999 (exclusion from benefits) applies".

NOTES

Initial Commencement
To be appointed
To be appointed: see s 170(4).

Appointment
Sub-ss (1), (2): Appointment: 6 December 1999: see SI 1999/3190, art 2, Schedule.
Sub-ss (3), (4), (6): Appointment: 3 April 2000: see SI 2000/464, art 2, Schedule.

118 Housing authority accommodation

(1)   Each housing authority must secure that, so far as practicable, a tenancy of, or licence to occupy, housing accommodation provided under the accommodation provisions is not granted to a person subject to immigration control unless—

   (a)   he is of a class specified in an order made by the Secretary of State; or
   (b)   the tenancy of, or licence to occupy, such accommodation is granted in accordance with arrangements made under section 95.

(2) "Housing authority" means—

(a) in relation to England and Wales, a local housing authority within the meaning of the Housing Act 1985;

(b) in relation to Scotland, a local authority within the meaning of the Housing (Scotland) Act 1987; and

(c) in relation to Northern Ireland, the Executive.

(3) "Accommodation provisions" means—

(a) in relation to England and Wales, Part II of the Housing Act 1985;

(b) in relation to Scotland, Part I of the Housing (Scotland) Act 1987;

(c) in relation to Northern Ireland, Part II of the Housing (Northern Ireland) Order 1981.

(4) "Licence to occupy", in relation to Scotland, means a permission or right to occupy.

(5) "Tenancy", in relation to England and Wales, has the same meaning as in the Housing Act 1985.

(6) "Person subject to immigration control" means a person who under the 1971 Act requires leave to enter or remain in the United Kingdom (whether or not such leave has been given).

(7) This section does not apply in relation to any allocation of housing to which Part VI of the Housing Act 1996 (allocation of housing accommodation) applies.

NOTES

Initial Commencement
To be appointed
To be appointed: see s 170(4).

Appointment
Appointment (for the purpose of enabling subordinate legislation to be made): 1 January 2000: see SI 1999/3190, art 2, Schedule.
Appointment (for remaining purposes): 1 March 2000: see SI 2000/464, art 2, Schedule.

Subordinate Legislation
Persons subject to Immigration Control (Housing Authority Accommodation and Homelessness) Order 2000, SI 2000/706.
Persons Subject to Immigration Control (Housing Authority Accommodation) (Wales) Order 2000, SI 2000/1036.

119 Homelessness: Scotland and Northern Ireland

(1) A person subject to immigration control—

(a) is not eligible for accommodation or assistance under the homelessness provisions, and

(b) is to be disregarded in determining for the purposes of those provisions, whether another person—

(i) is homeless or is threatened with homelessness, or

(ii) has a priority need for accommodation,

unless he is of a class specified in an order made by the Secretary of State.

(2) An order under subsection (1) may not be made so as to include in a specified class any person to whom section 115 applies.

(3) "The homelessness provisions" means—

(a) in relation to Scotland, Part II of the Housing (Scotland) Act 1987; and

    (b)   in relation to Northern Ireland, Part II of the Housing (Northern Ireland) Order 1988.

(4)   "Person subject to immigration control" has the same meaning as in section 118.

NOTES

Initial Commencement
To be appointed
To be appointed: see s 170(4).

Appointment
Appointment (for the purpose of enabling subordinate legislation to be made): 1 January 2000: see SI 1999/3190, art 2, Schedule.
Appointment (for remaining purposes): 1 March 2000: see SI 2000/464, art 2, Schedule.

Subordinate Legislation
Persons subject to Immigration Control (Housing Authority Accommodation and Homelessness) Order 2000, SI 2000/706.

120 Other restrictions on assistance: Scotland

(1)   In section 12 of the Social Work (Scotland) Act 1968 (general social welfare services of local authorities), after subsection (2) insert—

"(2A)   A person to whom section 115 of the Immigration and Asylum Act 1999 (exclusion from benefits) applies is not to receive assistance under subsection (1) of this section (whether by way of residential accommodation or otherwise) if his need for assistance has arisen solely—

    (a)   because he is destitute; or
    (b)   because of the physical effects, or anticipated physical effects, of his being destitute.

(2B) Subsections (3) and (5) to (8) of section 95 of the Immigration and Asylum Act 1999, and paragraph 2 of Schedule 8 to that Act, apply for the purposes of subsection (2A) as they apply for the purposes of that section, but for the references in subsections (5) and (7) of that section and in that paragraph to the Secretary of State substitute references to a local authority."

(2)   In section 13A of that Act (provision of residential accommodation with nursing), after subsection (3) insert—

"(4) No arrangements under subsection (1) above may be given effect to in relation to a person to whom section 115 of the Immigration and Asylum Act 1999 (exclusion from benefits) applies solely—

    (a)   because he is destitute; or
    (b)   because of the physical effects, or anticipated physical effects, of his being destitute.

(5)   Subsections (3) and (5) to (8) of section 95 of the Immigration and Asylum Act 1999, and paragraph 2 of Schedule 8 to that Act, apply for the purposes of subsection (4) above as they apply for the purposes of that section, but for the references in subsections (5) and (7) of that section and in that paragraph to the Secretary of State substitute references to a local authority."

(3)   In section 13B of that Act (provision of care and after-care), after subsection (2) insert—

"(3) No arrangements under subsection (1) above may be given effect to in relation to a person to whom section 115 of the Immigration and Asylum Act 1999 (exclusion from benefits) applies solely—

    (a)   because he is destitute; or

    (b)   because of the physical effects, or anticipated physical effects, of his being destitute.

(4)   Subsections (3) and (5) to (8) of section 95 of the Immigration and Asylum Act 1999, and paragraph 2 of Schedule 8 to that Act, apply for the purposes of subsection (3) above as they apply for the purposes of that section, but for the references in subsections (5) and (7) of that section and in that paragraph to the Secretary of State substitute references to a local authority."

(4)   In section 7 of the Mental Health (Scotland) Act 1984 (functions of local authorities), after subsection (2) insert—

"(3) No arrangements under paragraph (a) or (c) of subsection (1) above may be given effect to in relation to a person to whom section 115 of the Immigration and Asylum Act 1999 (exclusion from benefits) applies solely—

    (a)   because he is destitute; or

    (b)   because of the physical effects, or anticipated physical effects, of his being destitute.

(4)   Subsections (3) and (5) to (8) of section 95 of the Immigration and Asylum Act 1999, and paragraph 2 of Schedule 8 to that Act, apply for the purposes of subsection (3) above as they apply for the purposes of that section, but for the references in subsection (5) and (7) of that section and in that paragraph to the Secretary of State substitute references to a local authority."

(5)   In section 8 of that Act (provision of after-care services), after subsection (3) insert—

"(4) After care services may not be provided under subsection (1) above in respect of any person to whom section 115 of the Immigration and Asylum Act 1999 (exclusion from benefits) applies solely—

    (a)   because he is destitute; or

    (b)   because of the physical effects, or anticipated physical effects, of his being destitute.

(5)   Subsections (3) and (5) to (8) of section 95 of the Immigration and Asylum Act 1999, and paragraph 2 of Schedule 8 to that Act, apply for the purposes of subsection (4) above as they apply for the purposes of that section, but for the references in subsection (5) and (7) of that section and in that paragraph to the Secretary of State substitute references to a local authority."

(6)   In the Asylum and Immigration Appeals Act 1993, omit sections 4 and 5 and Schedule 1 (provisions relating to housing of asylum-seekers).

NOTES

Initial Commencement
To be appointed
To be appointed: see s 170(4).

Appointment
Appointment (for the purpose of enabling subordinate legislation to be made under s 95 as applied by any provision inserted by this section): 1 March 2000: see SI 2000/464, art 2, Schedule.
Appointment (for remaining purposes): 3 April 2000: see SI 2000/464, art 2, Schedule.

121 Other restrictions on assistance: Northern Ireland

(1)   In Article 7 of the Health and Personal Social Services (Northern Ireland) Order 1972 (prevention of illness, care and after-care), after paragraph (2) insert—

"(3) No arrangements made under paragraph (1) may be given effect to in relation to a person to whom section 115 of the Immigration and Asylum Act 1999 applies solely—

(a) because he is destitute; or

(b) because of the physical effects, or anticipated physical effects, of his being destitute.

(3A) Subsections (3) and (5) to (8) of section 95 of the Immigration and Asylum Act 1999, and paragraph 2 of Schedule 8 to that Act, apply for the purposes of paragraph (3) as they apply for the purposes of that section, but for the references in subsections (5) and (7) of that section and in paragraph 2 of that Schedule to the Secretary of State substitute references to the Department."

(2) In Article 15 of that Order (general social welfare), after paragraph (5) insert—

"(6) Assistance may not be provided under paragraph (1) in respect of any person to whom section 115 of the Immigration and Asylum Act 1999 applies if his need for assistance has arisen solely—

(a) because he is destitute, or

(b) because of the physical effects, or anticipated physical effects, of his being destitute.

(7) Subsections (3) to (8) of section 95 of the Immigration and Asylum Act 1999, and paragraph 2 of Schedule 8 to that Act, apply for the purposes of paragraph (6) as they apply for the purposes of that section, but for references to the Secretary of State in subsections (5) and (7) of that section and in paragraph 2 of that Schedule substitute references to the Department."

(3) In the Asylum and Immigration Appeals Act 1993, omit sections 4 and 5 and Schedule 1 (provisions relating to housing of asylum-seekers).

NOTES

Initial Commencement
To be appointed
To be appointed: see s 170(4).

Appointment
Appointment (for the purpose of enabling subordinate legislation to be made under s 95 as applied by any provision inserted by this section): 1 March 2000: see SI 2000/464, art 2, Schedule.
Appointment (for remaining purposes): 3 April 2000: see SI 2000/464, art 2, Schedule.

122 Support for children

(1) In this section "eligible person" means a person who appears to the Secretary of State to be a person for whom support may be provided under section 95.

(2) Subsections (3) and (4) apply if an application for support under section 95 has been made by an eligible person whose household includes a dependant under the age of 18 ("the child").

(3) If it appears to the Secretary of State that adequate accommodation is not being provided for the child, he must exercise his powers under section 95 by offering, and if his offer is accepted by providing or arranging for the provision of, adequate accommodation for the child as part of the eligible person's household.

(4) If it appears to the Secretary of State that essential living needs of the child are not being met, he must exercise his powers under section 95 by offering, and if his offer is accepted by providing or arranging for the provision of, essential living needs for the child as part of the eligible person's household.

(5) No local authority may provide assistance under any of the child welfare provisions in respect of a dependant under the age of 18, or any member of his family, at any time when—

(a) the Secretary of State is complying with this section in relation to him; or

(b) there are reasonable grounds for believing that—

    (i) the person concerned is a person for whom support may be provided under section 95; and

    (ii) the Secretary of State would be required to comply with this section if that person had made an application under section 95.

(6) "Assistance" means the provision of accommodation or of any essential living needs.

(7) "The child welfare provisions" means—

(a) section 17 of the Children Act 1989 (local authority support for children and their families);

(b) section 22 of the Children (Scotland) Act 1995 (equivalent provision for Scotland); and

(c) Article 18 of the Children (Northern Ireland) Order 1995 (equivalent provision for Northern Ireland).

(8) Subsection (9) applies if accommodation provided in the discharge of the duty imposed by subsection (3) has been withdrawn.

(9) Only the relevant authority may provide assistance under any of the child welfare provisions in respect of the child concerned.

(10) "Relevant authority" means—

(a) in relation to Northern Ireland, the authority within whose area the withdrawn accommodation was provided;

(b) in any other case, the local authority within whose area the withdrawn accommodation was provided.

(11) In such circumstances as may be prescribed, subsection (5) does not apply.

NOTES

Initial Commencement
To be appointed
To be appointed: see s 170(4).

Appointment
Appointment (for the purpose of enabling subordinate legislation to be made): 1 March 2000: see SI 2000/464, art 2, Schedule.
Appointment (for remaining purposes): 3 April 2000: see SI 2000/464, art 2, Schedule.

Subordinate Legislation
Immigration (Eligibility for Assistance) (Scotland and Northern Ireland) Regulations 2000, SI 2000/705 (made under sub-s (11)).

123 Back-dating of benefits where person recorded as refugee

(1) This section applies if—

(a) a person is recorded by the Secretary of State as a refugee within the meaning of the Refugee Convention; and

(b) before the refugee was so recorded, he or his dependant was a person to whom section 115 applied.

(2) Regulations may provide that a person mentioned in subsection (1)(b) may, within a prescribed period, claim the whole, or any prescribed proportion, of any benefit to which he would have been entitled had the refugee been so recorded when he made his claim for asylum.

(3)   Subsections (5) and (6) apply if the refugee has resided in the areas of two or more local authorities and he or his dependant makes a claim under the regulations in relation to housing benefit.

(4)   Subsections (5) and (6) also apply if the refugee has resided in the areas of two or more local authorities in Great Britain and he or his dependant makes a claim under the regulations in relation to council tax benefit.

(5)   The claim must be investigated and determined, and any benefit awarded must be paid or allowed, by such one of those authorities as may be prescribed by the regulations ("the prescribed authority").

(6)   The regulations may make provision requiring a local authority who are not the prescribed authority to supply that authority with such information as they may reasonably require in connection with the exercise of their functions under the regulations.

(7)   The regulations may make provision in relation to a person who has received support under this Part or who is a dependant of such a person—

    (a)   for the determination, or for criteria for the calculation, of the value of that support; and
    (b)   for the sum which he would be entitled to claim under the regulations to be reduced by the whole, or any prescribed proportion, of that valuation.

(8)   The reductions permitted by subsection (7) must not exceed the amount of the valuation.

(9)   "Regulations" means—

    (a)   in relation to jobseeker's allowance under the Jobseekers Act 1995, regulations made by the Secretary of State under that Act or the Social Security Administration Act 1992;
    (b)   in relation to jobseeker's allowance under the Jobseekers (Northern Ireland) Order 1995, regulations made by the Department under that Order or the Social Security Administration (Northern Ireland) Act 1992;
    (c)   in relation to a benefit under the Social Security Contributions and Benefits Act 1992, regulations made by the Secretary of State under that Act or the Social Security Administration Act 1992;
    (d)   in relation to a benefit under the Social Security Contributions and Benefits (Northern Ireland) Act 1992, regulations made by the Department under that Act or the Social Security Administration (Northern Ireland) Act 1992.

NOTES

Initial Commencement
To be appointed
To be appointed: see s 170(4).

Appointment
Appointment (for the purpose of enabling subordinate legislation to be made): 1 January 2000: see SI 1999/3190, art 2, Schedule.
Appointment (for remaining purposes): 3 April 2000: see SI 2000/464, art 2, Schedule.

Subordinate Legislation
Social Security (Immigration and Asylum) Consequential Amendments Regulations 2000, SI 2000/636 (made under sub-ss (5), (6)).

Miscellaneous

124 Secretary of State to be corporation sole for purposes Part VI

(1)   For the purpose of exercising his functions under this Part, the Secretary of State is a corporation sole.

(2) Any instrument in connection with the acquisition, management or of disposal of property, real or personal, heritable or moveable, by the Secretary of State under this Part may be executed on his behalf by a person authorised by him for that purpose.

(3) Any instrument purporting to have been so executed on behalf of the Secretary of State is to be treated, until the contrary is proved, to have been so executed on his behalf.

NOTES

Initial Commencement
Royal Assent
Royal Assent: 11 November 1999: see s 170(3)(l).

125 Entry of premises

(1) This section applies in relation to premises in which accommodation has been provided under section 95 or 98 for a supported person.

(2) If, on an application made by a person authorised in writing by the Secretary of State, a justice of the peace is satisfied that there is reason to believe that—

(a) the supported person or any dependants of his for whom the accommodation is provided is not resident in it,

(b) the accommodation is being used for any purpose other than the accommodation of the asylum-seeker or any dependant of his, or

(c) any person other than the supported person and his dependants (if any) is residing in the accommodation,

he may grant a warrant to enter the premises to the person making the application.

(3) A warrant granted under subsection (2) may be executed—

(a) **at any reasonable time;**

(b) using reasonable force.

(4) In the application of subsection (2) to Scotland, read the reference to a justice of the peace as a reference to the sheriff or a justice of the peace.

NOTES

Initial Commencement
To be appointed
To be appointed: see s 170(4).

Appointment
Appointment: 3 April 2000: see SI 2000/464, art 2, Schedule.

126 Information from property owners

(1) The power conferred by this section is to be exercised with a view to obtaining information about premises in which accommodation is or has been provided for supported persons.

(2) The Secretary of State may require any person appearing to him—

(a) to have any interest in, or

(b) to be involved in any way in the management or control of,

such premises, or any building which includes such premises, to provide him with such information with respect to the premises and the persons occupying them as he may specify.

(3) A person who is required to provide information under this section must do so in accordance with such requirements as may be prescribed.

(4) Information provided to the Secretary of State under this section may be used by him only in the exercise of his functions under this Part.

NOTES

Initial Commencement
To be appointed
To be appointed: see s 170(4).

Appointment
Appointment: 3 April 2000: see SI 2000/464, art 2, Schedule.

127 Requirement to supply information about redirection of post

(1) The Secretary of State may require any person conveying postal packets to supply redirection information to the Secretary of State—

  (a) for use in the prevention, detection, investigation or prosecution of criminal offences under this Part;
  (b) for use in checking the accuracy of information relating to support provided under this Part; or
  (c) for any other purpose relating to the provision of support to asylum-seekers.

(2) The information must be supplied in such manner and form, and in accordance with such requirements, as may be prescribed.

(3) The Secretary of State must make payments of such amount as he considers reasonable in respect of the supply of information under this section.

(4) "Postal packet" has the same meaning as in the Post Office Act 1953.

(5) "Redirection information" means information relating to arrangements made with any person conveying postal packets for the delivery of postal packets to addresses other than those indicated by senders on the packets.

NOTES

Initial Commencement
To be appointed
To be appointed: see s 170(4).

Appointment
Appointment: 3 April 2000: see SI 2000/464, art 2, Schedule.

PART VII
POWER TO ARREST, SEARCH AND FINGERPRINT

Power to arrest

128 Arrest without warrant

In the 1971 Act, after section 28, insert—

"28A Arrest without warrant

(1) A constable or immigration officer may arrest without warrant a person—

  (a) who has committed or attempted to commit an offence under section 24 or 24A; or

(b) whom he has reasonable grounds for suspecting has committed or attempted to commit such an offence.

(2) But subsection (1) does not apply in relation to an offence under section 24(1)(d).

(3) An immigration officer may arrest without warrant a person—

(a) who has committed an offence under section 25(1); or
(b) whom he has reasonable grounds for suspecting has committed that offence.

(4) An immigration officer may arrest without warrant a person—

(a) who has committed or attempted to commit an offence under section 25(2); or
(b) whom he has reasonable grounds for suspecting has committed or attempted to commit that offence.

(5) An immigration officer may arrest without warrant a person ("the suspect") who, or whom he has reasonable grounds for suspecting—

(a) has committed or attempted to commit an offence under section 26(1)(g); or
(b) is committing or attempting to commit that offence.

(6) The power conferred by subsection (5) is exercisable only if either the first or the second condition is satisfied.

(7) The first condition is that it appears to the officer that service of a summons (or, in Scotland, a copy complaint) is impracticable or inappropriate because—

(a) he does not know, and cannot readily discover, the suspect's name;
(b) he has reasonable grounds for doubting whether a name given by the suspect as his name is his real name;
(c) the suspect has failed to give him a satisfactory address for service; or
(d) he has reasonable grounds for doubting whether an address given by the suspect is a satisfactory address for service.

(8) The second condition is that the officer has reasonable grounds for believing that arrest is necessary to prevent the suspect—

(a) causing physical injury to himself or another person;
(b) suffering physical injury; or
(c) causing loss of or damage to property.

(9) For the purposes of subsection (7), an address is a satisfactory address for service if it appears to the officer—

(a) that the suspect will be at that address for a sufficiently long period for it to be possible to serve him with a summons (or copy complaint); or
(b) that some other person specified by the suspect will accept service of a summons (or copy complaint) for the suspect at that address.

(10) In relation to the exercise of the powers conferred by subsections (3)(b), (4)(b) and (5), it is immaterial that no offence has been committed.

(11) In Scotland the powers conferred by subsections (3), (4) and (5) may also be exercised by a constable."

NOTES

Initial Commencement
To be appointed
To be appointed: see s 170(4).

Appointment
Appointment: 14 February 2000: see SI 2000/168, art 2, Schedule.

Power to search and arrest

129 Search and arrest by warrant

In the 1971 Act, after section 28A, insert—

"28B Search and arrest by warrant

(1)   Subsection (2) applies if a justice of the peace is, by written information on oath, satisfied that there are reasonable grounds for suspecting that a person ("the suspect") who is liable to be arrested for a relevant offence is to be found on any premises.

(2)   The justice may grant a warrant authorising any immigration officer or constable to enter, if need be by force, the premises named in the warrant for the purpose of searching for and arresting the suspect.

(3)   Subsection (4) applies if in Scotland the sheriff or a justice of the peace is by evidence on oath satisfied as mentioned in subsection (1).

(4)   The sheriff or justice may grant a warrant authorising any immigration officer or constable to enter, if need be by force, the premises named in the warrant for the purpose of searching for and arresting the suspect.

(5)   "Relevant offence" means an offence under section 24(1)(a), (b), (c), (d), (e) or (f), section 24A or section 25(2)."

NOTES

Initial Commencement
To be appointed
To be appointed: see s 170(4).

Appointment
Appointment: 14 February 2000: see SI 2000/168, art 2, Schedule.

130 Search and arrest without warrant

In the 1971 Act, after section 28B, insert—

"28C Search and arrest without warrant

(1)   An immigration officer may enter and search any premises for the purpose of arresting a person for an offence under section 25(1).

(2)   The power may be exercised—

    (a)   only to the extent that it is reasonably required for that purpose; and
    (b)   only if the officer has reasonable grounds for believing that the person whom he is seeking is on the premises.

(3)   In relation to premises consisting of two or more separate dwellings, the power is limited to entering and searching—

    (a)   any parts of the premises which the occupiers of any dwelling comprised in the premises use in common with the occupiers of any such other dwelling; and
    (b)   any such dwelling in which the officer has reasonable grounds for believing that the person whom he is seeking may be.

(4)   The power may be exercised only if the officer produces identification showing that he is an immigration officer (whether or not he is asked to do so)."

NOTES

Initial Commencement
To be appointed
To be appointed: see s 170(4).

Appointment
Appointment: 14 February 2000: see SI 2000/168, art 2, Schedule.

Power to enter and search premises

131 Entry and search of premises

In the 1971 act, after section 28C, insert—

"28D Entry and search of premises

(1) If, on an application made by an immigration officer, a justice of the peace is satisfied that there are reasonable grounds for believing that—

    (a) a relevant offence has been committed,

    (b) there is material on premises specified in the application which is likely to be of substantial value (whether by itself or together with other material) to the investigation of the offence,

    (c) the material is likely to be relevant evidence,

    (d) the material does not consist of or include items subject to legal privilege, excluded material or special procedure material, and

    (e) any of the conditions specified in subsection (2) applies,

he may issue a warrant authorising an immigration officer to enter and search the premises.

(2) The conditions are that—

    (a) it is not practicable to communicate with any person entitled to grant entry to the premises;

    (b) it is practicable to communicate with a person entitled to grant entry to the premises but it is not practicable to communicate with any person entitled to grant access to the evidence;

    (c) entry to the premises will not be granted unless a warrant is produced;

    (d) the purpose of a search may be frustrated or seriously prejudiced unless an immigration officer arriving at the premises can secure immediate entry to them.

(3) An immigration officer may seize and retain anything for which a search has been authorised under subsection (1).

(4) "Relevant offence" means an offence under section 24(1)(a), (b), (c), (d), (e) or (f), section 24A or section 25.

(5) In relation to England and Wales, expressions which are given a meaning by the Police and Criminal Evidence Act 1984 have the same meaning when used in this section.

(6) In relation to Northern Ireland, expressions which are given a meaning by the Police and Criminal Evidence (Northern Ireland) Order 1989 have the same meaning when used in this section

(7) In the application of subsection (1) to Scotland—

    (a) read the reference to a justice of the peace as a reference to the sheriff or a justice of the peace; and

    (b) in paragraph (b), omit the reference to excluded material and special procedure material."

NOTES

Initial Commencement
To be appointed
To be appointed: see s 170(4).

Appointment
Appointment: 14 February 2000: see SI 2000/168, art 2, Schedule.

132 Entry and search of premises following arrest

(1) In the 1971 Act, after section 28D, insert—

"28E Entry and search of premises following arrest

(1) This section applies if a person is arrested for an offence under this Part at a place other than a police station.

(2) An immigration officer may enter and search any premises—

(a) in which the person was when arrested, or
(b) in which he was immediately before he was arrested,

for evidence relating to the offence for which the arrest was made ("relevant evidence").

(3) The power may be exercised—

(a) only if the officer has reasonable grounds for believing that there is relevant evidence on the premises; and
(b) only to the extent that it is reasonably required for the purpose of discovering relevant evidence.

(4) In relation to premises consisting of two or more separate dwellings, the power is limited to entering and searching—

(a) any dwelling in which the arrest took place or in which the arrested person was immediately before his arrest; and
(b) any parts of the premises which the occupier of any such dwelling uses in common with the occupiers of any other dwellings comprised in the premises.

(5) An officer searching premises under subsection (2) may seize and retain anything he finds which he has reasonable grounds for believing is relevant evidence.

(6) Subsection (5) does not apply to items which the officer has reasonable grounds for believing are items subject to legal privilege."

(2) In the 1971 Act, in Schedule 2 after paragraph 25, insert—

"Entry and search of premises

25A (1) This paragraph applies if—

(a) a person is arrested under this Schedule; or
(b) a person who was arrested by a constable (other than under this Schedule) is detained by an immigration officer under this Schedule.

(2) An immigration officer may enter and search any premises—

(a) occupied or controlled by the arrested person, or
(b) in which that person was when he was arrested, or immediately before he was arrested,

for relevant documents.

(3) The power may be exercised—

(a) only if the officer has reasonable grounds for believing that there are relevant documents on the premises;

(b) only to the extent that it is reasonably required for the purpose of discovering relevant documents; and

(c) subject to sub-paragraph (4), only if a senior officer has authorised its exercise in writing.

(4) An immigration officer may conduct a search under sub-paragraph (2)—

(a) before taking the arrested person to a place where he is to be detained; and

(b) without obtaining an authorisation under sub-paragraph (3)(c),

if the presence of that person at a place other than one where he is to be detained is necessary to make an effective search for any relevant documents.

(5) An officer who has conducted a search under sub-paragraph (4) must inform a senior officer as soon as is practicable.

(6) The officer authorising a search, or who is informed of one under sub-paragraph (5), must make a record in writing of—

(a) the grounds for the search; and

(b) the nature of the documents that were sought.

(7) An officer searching premises under sub-paragraph (2)—

(a) may seize and retain any documents he finds which he has reasonable grounds for believing are relevant documents; but

(b) may not retain any such document for longer than is necessary in view of the purpose for which the person was arrested.

(8) But sub-paragraph (7)(a) does not apply to documents which the officer has reasonable grounds for believing are items subject to legal privilege.

(9) "Relevant documents" means any documents which might—

(a) establish the arrested person's identity, nationality or citizenship; or

(b) indicate the place from which he has travelled to the United Kingdom or to which he is proposing to go.

(10) "Senior officer" means an immigration officer not below the rank of chief immigration officer."

NOTES

Initial Commencement
To be appointed
To be appointed: see s 170(4).

Appointment
Appointment: 14 February 2000: see SI 2000/168, art 2, Schedule.

133 Entry and search of premises following arrest under section 25(1) of the 1971 Act

In the 1971 Act, after section 28E, insert—

"28F Entry and search of premises following arrest under section 25(1)

(1) An immigration officer may enter and search any premises occupied or controlled by a person arrested for an offence under section 25(1).

(2) The power may be exercised—

(a)   only if the officer has reasonable grounds for suspecting that there is relevant evidence on the premises;

(b)   only to the extent that it is reasonably required for the purpose of discovering relevant evidence; and

(c)   subject to subsection (3), only if a senior officer has authorised it in writing.

(3)   The power may be exercised—

(a)   before taking the arrested person to a place where he is to be detained; and

(b)   without obtaining an authorisation under subsection (2)(c),

if the presence of that person at a place other than one where he is to be detained is necessary for the effective investigation of the offence.

(4)   An officer who has relied on subsection (3) must inform a senior officer as soon as is practicable.

(5)   The officer authorising a search, or who is informed of one under subsection (4), must make a record in writing of—

(a)   the grounds for the search; and

(b)   the nature of the evidence that was sought.

(6)   An officer searching premises under this section may seize and retain anything he finds which he has reasonable grounds for suspecting is relevant evidence.

(7)   "Relevant evidence" means evidence, other than items subject to legal privilege, that relates to the offence in question.

(8)   "Senior officer" means an immigration officer not below the rank of chief immigration officer."

NOTES

Initial Commencement
To be appointed
To be appointed: see s 170(4).

Appointment
Appointment: 14 February 2000: see SI 2000/168, art 2, Schedule.

Power to search persons

134 Searching arrested persons

(1)   In the 1971 Act, after section 28F, insert—

"28G Searching arrested persons

(1)   This section applies if a person is arrested for an offence under this Part at a place other than a police station.

(2)   An immigration officer may search the arrested person if he has reasonable grounds for believing that the arrested person may present a danger to himself or others.

(3)   The officer may search the arrested person for—

(a)   anything which he might use to assist his escape from lawful custody; or

(b)   anything which might be evidence relating to the offence for which he has been arrested.

(4)   The power conferred by subsection (3) may be exercised—

    (a)   only if the officer has reasonable grounds for believing that the arrested person may have concealed on him anything of a kind mentioned in that subsection; and

    (b)   only to the extent that it is reasonably required for the purpose of discovering any such thing.

(5)   A power conferred by this section to search a person is not to be read as authorising an officer to require a person to remove any of his clothing in public other than an outer coat, jacket or glove; but it does authorise the search of a person's mouth.

(6)   An officer searching a person under subsection (2) may seize and retain anything he finds, if he has reasonable grounds for believing that that person might use it to cause physical injury to himself or to another person.

(7)   An officer searching a person under subsection (3) may seize and retain anything he finds, if he has reasonable grounds for believing—

    (a)   that that person might use it to assist his escape from lawful custody; or

    (b)   that it is evidence which relates to the offence in question.

(8)   Subsection (7)(b) does not apply to an item subject to legal privilege."

(2)   In the 1971 Act, in Schedule 2 after paragraph 25A, insert—

"Searching persons arrested by immigration officers

25B (1)   This paragraph applies if a person is arrested under this Schedule.

(2)   An immigration officer may search the arrested person if he has reasonable grounds for believing that the arrested person may present a danger to himself or others.

(3)   The officer may search the arrested person for—

    (a)   anything which he might use to assist his escape from lawful custody; or

    (b)   any document which might—

        (i)   establish his identity, nationality or citizenship; or

        (ii)   indicate the place from which he has travelled to the United Kingdom or to which he is proposing to go.

(4)   The power conferred by sub-paragraph (3) may be exercised—

    (a)   only if the officer has reasonable grounds for believing that the arrested person may have concealed on him anything of a kind mentioned in that sub-paragraph; and

    (b)   only to the extent that it is reasonably required for the purpose of discovering any such thing.

(5)   A power conferred by this paragraph to search a person is not to be read as authorising an officer to require a person to remove any of his clothing in public other than an outer coat, jacket or glove; but it does authorise the search of a person's mouth.

(6)   An officer searching a person under sub-paragraph (2) may seize and retain anything he finds, if he has reasonable grounds for believing that the person searched might use it to cause physical injury to himself or to another person.

(7)   An officer searching a person under sub-paragraph (3)(a) may seize and retain anything he finds, if he has reasonable grounds for believing that he might use it to assist his escape from lawful custody.

(8)   An officer searching a person under sub-paragraph (3)(b) may seize and retain anything he finds, other than an item subject to legal privilege, if he has reasonable grounds for believing that it might be a document falling within that sub-paragraph.

(9)   Nothing seized under sub-paragraph (6) or (7) may be retained when the person from whom it was seized—

(a)   is no longer in custody, or
(b)   is in the custody of a court but has been released on bail."

NOTES

Initial Commencement
To be appointed
To be appointed: see s 170(4).

Appointment
Appointment: 14 February 2000: see SI 2000/168, art 2, Schedule.

135 Searching persons in police custody

(1)   In the 1971 Act, after section 28G, insert—

"28H Searching persons in police custody

(1)   This section applies if a person—

(a)   has been arrested for an offence under this Part; and
(b)   is in custody at a police station or in police detention at a place other than a police station.

(2)   An immigration officer may, at any time, search the arrested person in order to see whether he has with him anything—

(a)   which he might use to—
    (i)   cause physical injury to himself or others;
    (ii)   damage property;
    (iii) interfere with evidence; or
    (iv)   assist his escape; or
(b)   which the officer has reasonable grounds for believing is evidence relating to the offence in question.

(3)   The power may be exercised only to the extent that the custody officer concerned considers it to be necessary for the purpose of discovering anything of a kind mentioned in subsection (2).

(4)   An officer searching a person under this section may seize anything he finds, if he has reasonable grounds for believing that—

(a)   that person might use it for one or more of the purposes mentioned in subsection (2)(a); or
(b)   it is evidence relating to the offence in question.

(5)   Anything seized under subsection (4)(a) may be retained by the police.

(6)   Anything seized under subsection (4)(b) may be retained by an immigration officer.

(7)   The person from whom something is seized must be told the reason for the seizure unless he is—

(a)   violent or appears likely to become violent; or
(b)   incapable of understanding what is said to him.

(8)   An intimate search may not be conducted under this section.

(9)   The person carrying out a search under this section must be of the same sex as the person searched.

(10) "Custody officer"—

  (a) in relation to England and Wales, has the same meaning as in the Police and Criminal Evidence Act 1984;
  (b) in relation to Scotland, means the officer in charge of a police station; and
  (c) in relation to Northern Ireland, has the same meaning as in the Police and Criminal Evidence (Northern Ireland) Order 1989.

(11) "Intimate search"—

  (a) in relation to England and Wales, has the meaning given by section 65 of the Act of 1984;
  (b) in relation to Scotland, means a search which consists of the physical examination of a person's body orifices other than the mouth; and
  (c) in relation to Northern Ireland, has the same meaning as in the 1989 Order.

(12) "Police detention"—

  (a) in relation to England and Wales, has the meaning given by section 118(2) of the 1984 Act; and
  (b) in relation to Northern Ireland, has the meaning given by Article 2 of the 1989 Order.

(13) In relation to Scotland, a person is in police detention if—

  (a) he has been taken to a police station after being arrested for an offence; or
  (b) he is arrested at a police station after attending voluntarily at the station, accompanying a constable to it or being detained under section 14 of the Criminal Procedure (Scotland) Act 1995,

and is detained there or is detained elsewhere in the charge of a constable, but is not in police detention if he is in court after being charged."

(2) In the 1971 Act, in Schedule 2 after paragraph 25B, insert—

"Searching persons in police custody

25C (1) This paragraph applies if a person—

  (a) has been arrested under this Schedule; and
  (b) is in custody at a police station.

(2) An immigration officer may, at any time, search the arrested person in order to ascertain whether he has with him—

  (a) anything which he might use to—
     (i)   cause physical injury to himself or others;
     (ii) damage property;
     (iii) interfere with evidence; or
     (iv) assist his escape; or
  (b) any document which might—
     (i)   establish his identity, nationality or citizenship; or
     (ii) indicate the place from which he has travelled to the United Kingdom or to which he is proposing to go.

(3) The power may be exercised only to the extent that the officer considers it to be necessary for the purpose of discovering anything of a kind mentioned in sub-paragraph (2).

(4) An officer searching a person under this paragraph may seize and retain anything he finds, if he has reasonable grounds for believing that—

- (a) that person might use it for one or more of the purposes mentioned in sub-paragraph (2)(a); or
- (b) it might be a document falling within sub-paragraph (2)(b).

(5)   But the officer may not retain anything seized under sub-paragraph (2)(a)—

- (a) for longer than is necessary in view of the purpose for which the search was carried out; or
- (b) when the person from whom it was seized is no longer in custody or is in the custody of a court but has been released on bail.

(6)   The person from whom something is seized must be told the reason for the seizure unless he is—

- (a) violent or appears likely to become violent; or
- (b) incapable of understanding what is said to him.

(7)   An intimate search may not be conducted under this paragraph.

(8)   The person carrying out a search under this paragraph must be of the same sex as the person searched.

(9)   "Intimate search" has the same meaning as in section 28H(11)."

NOTES

Initial Commencement
To be appointed
To be appointed: see s 170(4).

Appointment
Appointment: 14 February 2000: see SI 2000/168, art 2, Schedule.

Seized material: access and copying

136 Access and copying

(1)   In the 1971 Act, after section 28H, insert—

"28I   Seized material: access and copying

(1)   If a person showing himself—

- (a) to be the occupier of the premises on which seized material was seized, or
- (b) to have had custody or control of the material immediately before it was seized,

asks the immigration officer who seized the material for a record of what he seized, the officer must provide the record to that person within a reasonable time.

(2)   If a relevant person asks an immigration officer for permission to be granted access to seized material, the officer must arrange for him to have access to the material under the supervision—

- (a) in the case of seized material within subsection (8)(a), of an immigration officer;
- (b) in the case of seized material within subsection (8)(b), of a constable.

(3)   An immigration officer may photograph or copy, or have photographed or copied, seized material.

(4)   If a relevant person asks an immigration officer for a photograph or copy of seized material, the officer must arrange for—

- (a) that person to have access to the material for the purpose of photographing or copying it under the supervision—

      (i)   in the case of seized material within subsection (8)(a), of an immigration officer;

      (ii) in the case of seized material within subsection (8)(b), of a constable; or

  (b) the material to be photographed or copied.

(5) A photograph or copy made under subsection (4)(b) must be supplied within a reasonable time.

(6) There is no duty under this section to arrange for access to, or the supply of a photograph or copy of, any material if there are reasonable grounds for believing that to do so would prejudice—

  (a) the exercise of any functions in connection with which the material was seized; or

  (b) an investigation which is being conducted under this Act, or any criminal proceedings which may be brought as a result.

(7) "Relevant person" means—

  (a) a person who had custody or control of seized material immediately before it was seized, or

  (b) someone acting on behalf of such a person.

(8) "Seized material" means anything—

  (a) seized and retained by an immigration officer, or

  (b) seized by an immigration officer and retained by the police,

under this Part."

(2) In the 1971 Act, in Schedule 2 after paragraph 25C, insert—

"*Access and copying*

25D (1) If a person showing himself—

  (a) to be the occupier of the premises on which seized material was seized, or

  (b) to have had custody or control of the material immediately before it was seized,

asks the immigration officer who seized the material for a record of what he seized, the officer must provide the record to that person within a reasonable time.

(2) If a relevant person asks an immigration officer for permission to be granted access to seized material, the officer must arrange for that person to have access to the material under the supervision of an immigration officer.

(3) An immigration officer may photograph or copy, or have photographed or copied, seized material.

(4) If a relevant person asks an immigration officer for a photograph or copy of seized material, the officer must arrange for—

  (a) that person to have access to the material under the supervision of an immigration officer for the purpose of photographing or copying it; or

  (b) the material to be photographed or copied.

(5) A photograph or copy made under sub-paragraph (4)(b) must be supplied within a reasonable time.

(6) There is no duty under this paragraph to arrange for access to, or the supply of a photograph or copy of, any material if there are reasonable grounds for believing that to do so would prejudice—

   (a)   the exercise of any functions in connection with which the material was seized;
         or
   (b)   an investigation which is being conducted under this Act, or any criminal
         proceedings which may be brought as a result.

(7)   "Relevant person" means—

   (a)   a person who had custody or control of seized material immediately before it
         was seized, or
   (b)   someone acting on behalf of such a person.

(8)   "Seized material" means anything which has been seized and retained under this
Schedule."

NOTES

Initial Commencement
To be appointed
To be appointed: see s 170(4).

Appointment
Appointment: 14 February 2000: see SI 2000/168, art 2, Schedule.

Search warrants

137 Search warrants: safeguards

In the 1971 Act, after section 28I, insert—

"28J Search warrants: safeguards

(1)   The entry or search of premises under a warrant is unlawful unless it complies
with this section and section 28K.

(2)   If an immigration officer applies for a warrant, he must—

   (a)   state the ground on which he makes the application and the provision of this
         Act under which the warrant would be issued;
   (b)   specify the premises which it is desired to enter and search; and
   (c)   identify, so far as is practicable, the persons or articles to be sought.

(3)   In Northern Ireland, an application for a warrant is to be supported by a complaint
in writing and substantiated on oath.

(4)   Otherwise, an application for a warrant is to be made ex parte and supported by
an information in writing or, in Scotland, evidence on oath.

(5)   The officer must answer on oath any question that the justice of the peace or
sheriff hearing the application asks him.

(6)   A warrant shall authorise an entry on one occasion only.

(7)   A warrant must specify—

   (a)   the name of the person applying for it;
   (b)   the date on which it is issued;
   (c)   the premises to be searched; and
   (d)   the provision of this Act under which it is issued.

(8)   A warrant must identify, so far as is practicable, the persons or articles to be
sought.

(9)   Two copies of a warrant must be made.

(10) The copies must be clearly certified as copies.

(11) "Warrant" means a warrant to enter and search premises issued to an immigration officer under this Part or under paragraph 17(2) of Schedule 2."

NOTES

Initial Commencement
To be appointed
To be appointed: see s 170(4).

Appointment
Appointment: 14 February 2000: see SI 2000/168, art 2, Schedule.

138 Execution of warrants

In the 1971 Act, after section 28J, insert—

"28K Execution of warrants

(1)   A warrant may be executed by any immigration officer.

(2)   A warrant may authorise persons to accompany the officer executing it.

(3)   Entry and search under a warrant must be—

    (a)   within one month from the date of its issue; and
    (b)   at a reasonable hour, unless it appears to the officer executing it that the purpose of a search might be frustrated.

(4)   If the occupier of premises which are to be entered and searched is present at the time when an immigration officer seeks to execute a warrant, the officer must—

    (a)   identify himself to the occupier and produce identification showing that he is an immigration officer;
    (b)   show the occupier the warrant; and
    (c)   supply him with a copy of it.

(5)   If—

    (a)   the occupier is not present, but
    (b)   some other person who appears to the officer to be in charge of the premises is present,

subsection (4) has effect as if each reference to the occupier were a reference to that other person.

(6)   If there is no person present who appears to the officer to be in charge of the premises, the officer must leave a copy of the warrant in a prominent place on the premises.

(7)   A search under a warrant may only be a search to the extent required for the purpose for which the warrant was issued.

(8)   An officer executing a warrant must make an endorsement on it stating—

    (a)   whether the persons or articles sought were found; and
    (b)   whether any articles, other than articles which were sought, were seized.

(9)   A warrant which has been executed, or has not been executed within the time authorised for its execution, must be returned—

    (a)   if issued by a justice of the peace in England and Wales, to the justices' chief executive appointed by the magistrates' court committee whose area includes the petty sessions area for which the justice acts;

    (b)   if issued by a justice of the peace in Northern Ireland, to the clerk of petty sessions for the petty sessions district in which the premises are situated;

    (c)   if issued by a justice of the peace in Scotland, to the clerk of the district court for the commission area for which the justice of the peace was appointed;

    (d)   if issued by the sheriff, to the sheriff clerk.

(10) A warrant returned under subsection (9)(a) must be retained for 12 months by the justices' chief executive.

(11) A warrant issued under subsection (9)(b) or (c) must be retained for 12 months by the clerk.

(12) A warrant returned under subsection (9)(d) must be retained for 12 months by the sheriff clerk.

(13) If during that 12 month period the occupier of the premises to which it relates asks to inspect it, he must be allowed to do so.

(14) "Warrant" means a warrant to enter and search premises issued to an immigration officer under this Part or under paragraph 17(2) of Schedule 2."

NOTES

Initial Commencement
To be appointed
To be appointed: see s 170(4).

Appointment
Appointment: 14 February 2000: see SI 2000/168, art 2, Schedule.

139 Interpretation

(1)   In the 1971 Act, after section 28K, insert—

"28L   Interpretation of Part III

In this Part, "premises" and "items subject to legal privilege" have the same meaning—

    (a)   in relation to England and Wales, as in the Police and Criminal Evidence Act 1984;

    (b)   in relation to Northern Ireland, as in the Police and Criminal Evidence (Northern Ireland) Order 1989"; and

    (c)   in relation to Scotland, as in section 33 of the Criminal Law (Consolidation) (Scotland) Act 1995."

(2)   In the 1971 Act, in Schedule 2, after paragraph 25D insert—

"25E   Section 28L applies for the purposes of this Schedule as it applies for the purposes of Part III."

NOTES

Initial Commencement
To be appointed
To be appointed: see s 170(4).

Appointment
Appointment: 14 February 2000: see SI 2000/168, art 2, Schedule.

Detention

140 Detention of persons liable to examination or removal

(1)   In paragraph 16 of Schedule 2 to the 1971 Act, for sub-paragraph (2) substitute—

"(2) If there are reasonable grounds for suspecting that a person is someone in respect of whom directions may be given under any of paragraphs 8 to 10 or 12 to 14, that person may be detained under the authority of an immigration officer pending—

    (a)   a decision whether or not to give such directions;

    (b)   his removal in pursuance of such directions."

(2) In paragraph 17(2) of that Schedule (power to grant constable a warrant to search and arrest), for the words from "authorising any constable" to "if need be" substitute "authorising any immigration officer or constable to enter, if need be".

NOTES

Initial Commencement
Royal Assent
Royal Assent: 11 November 1999: see s 170(3)(m).

Fingerprinting

141 Fingerprinting

(1) Fingerprints may be taken by an authorised person from a person to whom this section applies.

(2) Fingerprints may be taken under this section only during the relevant period.

(3) Fingerprints may not be taken under this section from a person under the age of sixteen ("the child") except in the presence of a person of full age who is—

    (a)   the child's parent or guardian; or

    (b)   a person who for the time being takes responsibility for the child.

(4) The person mentioned in subsection (3)(b) may not be—

    (a)   an officer of the Secretary of State who is not an authorised person;

    (b)   an authorised person.

(5) "Authorised person" means—

    (a)   a constable;

    (b)   an immigration officer;

    (c)   a prison officer;

    (d)   an officer of the Secretary of State authorised for the purpose; or

    (e)   a person who is employed by a contractor in connection with the discharge of the contractor's duties under a detention centre contract.

(6) In subsection (5)(e) "contractor" and "detention centre contract" have the same meaning as in Part VIII.

(7) This section applies to—

    (a)   any person ("A") who, on being required to do so by an immigration officer on his arrival in the United Kingdom, fails to produce a valid passport with photograph or some other document satisfactorily establishing his identity and nationality or citizenship;

    (b)   any person ("B") who has been refused leave to enter the United Kingdom but has been temporarily admitted under paragraph 21 of Schedule 2 to the 1971 Act if an immigration officer reasonably suspects that B might break any condition imposed on him relating to residence or as to reporting to the police or an immigration officer;

    (c)   any person ("C") in respect of whom—

    (i)   an immigration officer has given directions under paragraph 9(1) of Schedule 2 to the 1971 Act or under section 10;

    (ii)   the Secretary of State has given directions under paragraph 10(1) of Schedule 2 to the 1971 Act (but only in a case where it appears to the Secretary of State that the person is a person in respect of whom directions under paragraph 9 of that Schedule might be given); or

    (iii)   the Secretary of State has given directions under paragraph 1(1) of Schedule 3 to that Act;

(d)   any person ("D") who has been arrested under paragraph 17 of Schedule 2 to the 1971 Act;

(e)   any person ("E") who has made a claim for asylum;

(f)   any person ("F") who is a dependant of any of those persons.

(8) "The relevant period" begins—

(a)   for A, on his failure to produce the passport or other document;

(b)   for B, on the decision to admit him temporarily;

(c)   for C, on the direction being given;

(d)   for D, on his arrest;

(e)   for E, on the making of his claim for asylum; and

(f)   for F, at the same time as for the person whose dependant he is.

(9) "The relevant period" ends on the earliest of the following—

(a)   the grant of leave to enter or remain in the United Kingdom;

(b)   for A, B, C or D, his removal or deportation from the United Kingdom;

(c)   for C, if a deportation order has been made against him, its revocation or otherwise ceasing to have effect;

(d)   for D, his release if he is no longer liable to be detained under paragraph 16 of Schedule 2 to the 1971 Act;

(e)   for E, the final determination or abandonment of his claim for asylum; and

(f)   for F, at the same time as for the person whose dependant he is.

(10) No fingerprints may be taken from A if the immigration officer considers that A has a reasonable excuse for the failure concerned.

(11) No fingerprints may be taken from B unless the decision to take them has been confirmed by a chief immigration officer.

(12) An authorised person may not take fingerprints from a person under the age of sixteen unless his decision to take them has been confirmed—

(a)   if he is a constable, by a person designated for the purpose by the chief constable of his police force;

(b)   if he is a person mentioned in subsection (5)(b) or (e), by a chief immigration officer;

(c)   if he is a prison officer, by a person designated for the purpose by the governor of the prison;

(d)   if he is an officer of the Secretary of State, by a person designated for the purpose by the Secretary of State.

(13) Neither subsection (3) nor subsection (12) prevents an authorised person from taking fingerprints if he reasonably believes that the person from whom they are to be taken is aged sixteen or over.

(14) For the purposes of subsection (7)(f), a person is a dependant of another person if—

(a)   he is that person's spouse or child under the age of eighteen; and

(b)   he does not have a right of abode in the United Kingdom or indefinite leave to enter or remain in the United Kingdom.

(15) "Claim for asylum" has the same meaning as in Part VI.

NOTES

Initial Commencement
To be appointed
To be appointed: see s 170(4).

Appointment
Appointment: 11 December 2000: see SI 2000/3099, art 3, Schedule.

142 Attendance for fingerprinting

(1) The Secretary of State may, by notice in writing, require a person to whom section 141 applies to attend at a specified place for fingerprinting.

(2) The notice—

(a) must give the person concerned a period of at least seven days within which to attend, beginning not earlier than seven days after the date of the notice; and
(b) may require him to attend at a specified time of day or during specified hours.

(3) A constable or immigration officer may arrest without warrant a person who has failed to comply with a requirement imposed on him under this section (unless the requirement has ceased to have effect).

(4) Before a person arrested under subsection (3) is released—

(a) he may be removed to a place where his fingerprints may conveniently be taken; and
(b) his fingerprints may be taken (whether or not he is so removed).

(5) A requirement imposed under subsection (1) ceases to have effect at the end of the relevant period (as defined by section 141).

NOTES

Initial Commencement
To be appointed
To be appointed: see s 170(4).

Appointment
Appointment: 11 December 2000: see SI 2000/3099, art 3, Schedule.

143 Destruction of fingerprints

(1) If they have not already been destroyed, fingerprints must be destroyed before the end of the specified period beginning with the day on which they were taken.

(2) If a person from whom fingerprints were taken proves that he is—

(a) a British citizen, or
(b) a Commonwealth citizen who has a right of abode in the United Kingdom as a result of section 2(1)(b) of the 1971 Act,

the fingerprints must be destroyed as soon as reasonably practicable.

(3) If a person from whom fingerprints were taken—

(a) in the case of E, is given indefinite leave to enter or remain in the United Kingdom, or
(b) in any other case, is given leave to enter or remain in the United Kingdom,

the fingerprints must be destroyed as soon as reasonably practicable.

(4)   Fingerprints taken from B must be destroyed as soon as reasonably practicable after his removal from the United Kingdom.

(5)   But subsection (4) does not apply if it appears to the Secretary of State that B has failed to comply with a restriction imposed on him under paragraph 21(2) of Schedule 2 to the 1971 Act.

(6)   Fingerprints taken from C must, if the directions cease to have effect, be destroyed as soon as reasonably practicable.

(7)   If a deportation order made against C is revoked, any fingerprints taken from him must be destroyed as soon as reasonably practicable.

(8)   If D ceases to be liable to be detained under paragraph 16 of Schedule 2 to the 1971 Act, fingerprints taken from him must be destroyed as soon as reasonably practicable.

(9)   Fingerprints taken from F must be destroyed when fingerprints taken from the person whose dependant he is have to be destroyed.

(10) The obligation to destroy fingerprints under this section applies also to copies of fingerprints.

(11) The Secretary of State must take all reasonably practicable steps to secure—

   (a)   that data which are held in electronic form and which relate to fingerprints which have to be destroyed as a result of this section are destroyed or erased; or
   (b)   that access to such data is blocked.

(12) The person to whom the data relate is entitled, on request, to a certificate issued by the Secretary of State to the effect that he has taken the steps required by subsection (11).

(13) A certificate under subsection (12) must be issued within three months of the date of the request for it.

(14) "Fingerprints" means fingerprints taken under section 141 and references to B, C, D, E and F are to the persons so described in that section.

(15) "Specified period" means—

   (a)   such period as the Secretary of State may specify by order;
   (b)   if no period is so specified, ten years.

NOTES

Initial Commencement
To be appointed
To be appointed: see s 170(4).

Appointment
Appointment: 11 December 2000: see SI 2000/3099, art 3, Schedule.

144 Other methods of collecting data about physical characteristics

The Secretary of State may make regulations containing provisions equivalent to sections 141, 142 and 143 in relation to such other methods of collecting data about external physical characteristics as may be prescribed.

NOTES

Initial Commencement
To be appointed
To be appointed: see s 170(4).

Appointment
Appointment: 11 December 2000: see SI 2000/3099, art 3, Schedule.

Codes of practice

145 Codes of practice

(1)   An immigration officer exercising any specified power to—

    (a)   arrest, question, search or take fingerprints from a person,
    (b)   enter and search premises, or
    (c)   seize property found on persons or premises,

must have regard to such provisions of a code as may be specified.

(2)   Subsection (1) also applies to an authorised person exercising the power to take fingerprints conferred by section 141.

(3)   Any specified provision of a code may have effect for the purposes of this section subject to such modifications as may be specified.

(4)   "Specified" means specified in a direction given by the Secretary of State.

(5)   "Authorised person" has the same meaning as in section 141.

(6)   "Code" means—

    (a)   in relation to England and Wales, any code of practice for the time being in force under the Police and Criminal Evidence Act 1984;
    (b)   in relation to Northern Ireland, any code of practice for the time being in force under the Police and Criminal Evidence (Northern Ireland) Order 1989.

(7)   This section does not apply to any person exercising powers in Scotland.

NOTES

Initial Commencement
Royal Assent
Royal Assent: 11 November 1999: see s 170(3)(n).

Use of force

146 Use of force

(1)   An immigration officer exercising any power conferred on him by the 1971 Act or this Act may, if necessary, use reasonable force.

(2)   Any person exercising a power conferred by section 141 or 142 or regulations under section 144 may, if necessary, use reasonable force.

NOTES

Initial Commencement
Royal Assent
Sub-s (1): Royal Assent: 11 November 1999: see s 170(3)(o).

To be appointed
Sub-s (2): To be appointed: see s 170(4).

PART VIII
DETENTION CENTRES AND DETAINED PERSONS

Interpretation

147 Interpretation of Part VIII

In this Part—

"certificate of authorisation" means a certificate issued by the Secretary of State under section 154;

"certified prisoner custody officer" means a prisoner custody officer certified under section 89 of the Criminal Justice Act 1991, or section 114 of the Criminal Justice and Public Order Act 1994, to perform custodial duties;

"contract monitor" means a person appointed by the Secretary of State under section 149(4);

"contracted out detention centre" means a detention centre in relation to which a detention centre contract is in force;

"contractor", in relation to a detention centre which is being run in accordance with a detention centre contract, means the person who has contracted to run it;

"custodial functions" means custodial functions at a detention centre;

"detained persons" means persons detained or required to be detained under the 1971 Act;

"detainee custody officer" means a person in respect of whom a certificate of authorisation is in force;

"detention centre" means a place which is used solely for the detention of detained persons but which is not a short-term holding facility, a prison or part of a prison;

"detention centre contract" means a contract entered into by the Secretary of State under section 149;

"detention centre rules" means rules made by the Secretary of State under section 153;

"directly managed detention centre" means a detention centre which is not a contracted out detention centre;

"escort arrangements" means arrangements made by the Secretary of State under section 156;

"escort functions" means functions under escort arrangements;

"escort monitor" means a person appointed under paragraph 1 of Schedule 13;

"prisoner custody officer"—

(a) in relation to England and Wales, has the same meaning as in the Criminal Justice Act 1991;

(b) in relation to Scotland, has the meaning given in section 114(1) of the Criminal Justice and Public Order Act 1994;

(c) in relation to Northern Ireland, has the meaning given in section 122(1) of that Act of 1994;

"short-term holding facility" means a place used solely for the detention of detained persons for a period of not more than seven days or for such other period as may be prescribed.

NOTES

Initial Commencement
To be appointed
To be appointed: see s 170(4).

Appointment
Appointment: 1 August 2000: see SI 2000/1985, art 2, Schedule.

Detention centres

148 Management of detention centres

(1) A manager must be appointed for every detention centre.

(2) In the case of a contracted out detention centre, the person appointed as manager must be a detainee custody officer whose appointment is approved by the Secretary of State.

(3) The manager of a detention centre is to have such functions as are conferred on him by detention centre rules.

(4) The manager of a contracted out detention centre may not—

    (a)   enquire into a disciplinary charge laid against a detained person;

    (b)   conduct the hearing of such a charge; or

    (c)   make, remit or mitigate an award in respect of such a charge.

(5) The manager of a contracted out detention centre may not, except in cases of urgency, order—

    (a)   the removal of a detained person from association with other detained persons;

    (b)   the temporary confinement of a detained person in special accommodation; or

    (c)   the application to a detained person of any other special control or restraint (other than handcuffs).

NOTES

Initial Commencement
To be appointed
To be appointed: see s 170(4).

Appointment
Sub-ss (1), (2), (4), (5): Appointment: 2 April 2001: see SI 2001/239, art 2, Schedule.
Sub-s (3): Appointment (for the purposes of enabling subordinate legislation to be made): 1 August 2000: see SI 2000/1985, art 2, Schedule.
Sub-s (3): Appointment (for remaining purposes): 2 April 2001: see SI 2001/239, art 2, Schedule.

Subordinate Legislation
Detention Centre Rules 2001, SI 2001/238 (made under sub-s (3)).

149 Contracting out of certain detention centres

(1) The Secretary of State may enter into a contract with another person for the provision or running (or the provision and running) by him, or (if the contract so provides) for the running by sub-contractors of his, of any detention centre or part of a detention centre.

(2) While a detention centre contract for the running of a detention centre or part of a detention centre is in force—

    (a)   the detention centre or part is to be run subject to and in accordance with the provisions of or made under this Part; and

    (b)   in the case of a part, that part and the remaining part are to be treated for the purposes of those provisions as if they were separate detention centres.

(3) If the Secretary of State grants a lease or tenancy of land for the purposes of a detention centre contract, none of the following enactments applies to the lease or tenancy—

    (a)   Part II of the Landlord and Tenant Act 1954 (security of tenure);

    (b)   section 146 of the Law of Property Act 1925 (restrictions on and relief against forfeiture);

(c) section 19(1), (2) and (3) of the Landlord and Tenant Act 1927 and the Landlord and Tenant Act 1988 (covenants not to assign etc);

(d) the Agricultural Holdings Act 1986;

(e) sections 4 to 7 of the Law Reform (Miscellaneous Provisions) (Scotland) Act 1985 (irritancy clauses);

(f) the Agricultural Holdings (Scotland) Act 1991;

(g) section 14 of the Conveyancing Act 1881;

(h) the Conveyancing and Law of Property Act 1892;

(i) the Business Tenancies (Northern Ireland) Order 1996.

(4) The Secretary of State must appoint a contract monitor for every contracted out detention centre.

(5) A person may be appointed as the contract monitor for more than one detention centre.

(6) The contract monitor is to have—

(a) such functions as may be conferred on him by detention centre rules;

(b) the status of a Crown servant.

(7) The contract monitor must—

(a) keep under review, and report to the Secretary of State on, the running of a detention centre for which he is appointed; and

(b) investigate, and report to the Secretary of State on, any allegations made against any person performing custodial functions at that centre.

(8) The contractor, and any sub-contractor of his, must do all that he reasonably can (whether by giving directions to the officers of the detention centre or otherwise) to facilitate the exercise by the contract monitor of his functions.

(9) "Lease or tenancy" includes an underlease, sublease or sub-tenancy.

(10) In relation to a detention centre contract entered into by the Secretary of State before the commencement of this section, this section is to be treated as having been in force at that time.

NOTES

Initial Commencement
To be appointed
To be appointed: for effect see sub-s (10) above and s 170(4).

Appointment
Sub-ss (1), (3), (6)(a), (9): Appointment: 1 August 2000: see SI 2000/1985, art 2, Schedule.
Sub-ss (2), (4), (5), (6)(b), (7), (8), (10): Appointment: 2 April 2001: see SI 2001/239, art 2, Schedule.

Subordinate Legislation
Detention Centre Rules 2001, SI 2001/238 (made under sub-s (6)).

150 Contracted out functions at directly managed detention centres

(1) The Secretary of State may enter into a contract with another person—

(a) for functions at, or connected with, a directly managed detention centre to be performed by detainee custody officers provided by that person; or

(b) for such functions to be performed by certified prisoner custody officers who are provided by that person.

(2) For the purposes of this section "detention centre" includes a short-term holding facility.

NOTES

Initial Commencement
To be appointed
To be appointed: see s 170(4).

Appointment
Appointment: 2 April 2001: see SI 2001/239, art 2, Schedule.

151 Intervention by Secretary of State

(1) The Secretary of State may exercise the powers conferred by this section if it appears to him that—

    (a) the manager of a contracted out detention centre has lost, or is likely to lose, effective control of the centre or of any part of it; or

    (b) it is necessary to do so in the interests of preserving the safety of any person, or of preventing serious damage to any property.

(2) The Secretary of State may appoint a person (to be known as the Controller) to act as manager of the detention centre for the period—

    (a) beginning with the time specified in the appointment; and

    (b) ending with the time specified in the notice of termination under subsection (5).

(3) During that period—

    (a) all the functions which would otherwise be exercisable by the manager or the contract monitor are to be exercisable by the Controller;

    (b) the contractor and any sub-contractor of his must do all that he reasonably can to facilitate the exercise by the Controller of his functions; and

    (c) the staff of the detention centre must comply with any directions given by the Controller in the exercise of his functions.

(4) The Controller is to have the status of a Crown servant.

(5) If the Secretary of State is satisfied that a Controller is no longer needed for a particular detention centre, he must (by giving notice to the Controller) terminate his appointment at a time specified in the notice.

(6) As soon as practicable after making an appointment under this section, the Secretary of State must give notice of the appointment to those entitled to notice.

(7) As soon as practicable after terminating an appointment under this section, the Secretary of State must give a copy of the notice of termination to those entitled to notice.

(8) Those entitled to notice are the contractor, the manager, the contract monitor and the Controller.

NOTES

Initial Commencement
To be appointed
To be appointed: see s 170(4).

Appointment
Appointment: 2 April 2001: see SI 2001/239, art 2, Schedule.

152 Visiting Committees and inspections

(1) The Secretary of State must appoint a committee (to be known as the Visiting Committee) for each detention centre.

(2)   The functions of the Visiting Committee for a detention centre are to be such as may be prescribed by the detention centre rules.

(3)   Those rules must include provision—

    (a)   as to the making of visits to the centre by members of the Visiting Committee;
    (b)   for the hearing of complaints made by persons detained in the centre;
    (c)   requiring the making of reports by the Visiting Committee to the Secretary of State.

(4)   Every member of the Visiting Committee for a detention centre may at any time enter the centre and have free access to every part of it and to every person detained there.

(5)   In section 5A of the Prison Act 1952 (which deals with the appointment and functions of Her Majesty's Chief Inspector of Prisons), after subsection (5), insert—

"(5A)   Subsections (2) to (5) apply to detention centres (as defined by section 147 of the Immigration and Asylum Act 1999 and including any in Scotland) and persons detained in such detention centres as they apply to prisons and prisoners."

NOTES

Initial Commencement
To be appointed
To be appointed: see s 170(4).

Appointment
Sub-ss (1), (4), (5): Appointment: 2 April 2001: see SI 2001/239, art 2, Schedule.
Sub-ss (2), (3): Appointment (for the purposes of enabling subordinate legislation to be made): 1 August 2000: see SI 2000/1985, art 2, Schedule.
Sub-ss (2), (3): Appointment (for remaining purposes): 2 April 2001: see SI 2001/239, art 2, Schedule.

Subordinate Legislation
Detention Centre Rules 2001, SI 2001/238 (made under sub-ss (2), (3)).

153 Detention centre rules

(1)   The Secretary of State must make rules for the regulation and management of detention centres.

(2)   Detention centre rules may, among other things, make provision with respect to the safety, care, activities, discipline and control of detained persons.

NOTES

Initial Commencement
To be appointed
To be appointed: see s 170(4).

Appointment
Appointment (for the purposes of enabling subordinate legislation to be made): 1 August 2000: see SI 2000/1985, art 2, Schedule.
Appointment (for remaining purposes): 2 April 2001: see SI 2001/239, art 2, Schedule.

Subordinate Legislation
Detention Centre Rules 2001, SI 2001/238.

Custody and movement of detained persons

154 Detainee custody officers

(1)   On an application made to him under this section, the Secretary of State may certify that the applicant—

(a) is authorised to perform escort functions; or

(b) is authorised to perform both escort functions and custodial functions.

(2) The Secretary of State may not issue a certificate of authorisation unless he is satisfied that the applicant—

(a) is a fit and proper person to perform the functions to be authorised; and

(b) has received training to such standard as the Secretary of State considers appropriate for the performance of those functions.

(3) A certificate of authorisation continues in force until such date, or the occurrence of such event, as may be specified in the certificate but may be suspended or revoked under paragraph 7 of Schedule 11.

(4) A certificate which authorises the performance of both escort functions and custodial functions may specify one date or event for one of those functions and a different date or event for the other.

(5) If the Secretary of State considers that it is necessary for the functions of detainee custody officers to be conferred on prison officers or prisoner custody officers, he may make arrangements for that purpose.

(6) A prison officer acting under arrangements made under subsection (5) has all the powers, authority, protection and privileges of a constable.

(7) Schedule 11 makes further provision about detainee custody officers.

NOTES

Initial Commencement
To be appointed
To be appointed: see s 170(4).

Appointment
Sub-ss (1)–(6): Appointment: 2 April 2001: see SI 2001/239, art 2, Schedule.
Sub-s (7): Appointment (for certain purposes): 3 April 2000: see SI 2000/464, art 2, Schedule.
Sub-s (7): Appointment (for certain purposes): 1 August 2000: see SI 2000/1985, art 2, Schedule.
Sub-s (7): Appointment (for remaining purposes): 2 April 2001: see SI 2001/239, art 2, Schedule.

155 Custodial functions and discipline etc at detention centres

(1) Custodial functions may be discharged at a detention centre only by—

(a) a detainee custody officer authorised, in accordance with section 154(1), to perform such functions; or

(b) a prison officer, or a certified prisoner custody officer, exercising functions in relation to the detention centre—

(i) in accordance with arrangements made under section 154(5); or

(ii) as a result of a contract entered into under section 150(1)(b).

(2) Schedule 12 makes provision with respect to discipline and other matters at detention centres and short-term holding facilities.

NOTES

Initial Commencement
To be appointed
To be appointed: see s 170(4).

Appointment
Sub-s (1): Appointment: 2 April 2001: see SI 2001/239, art 2, Schedule.
Sub-s (2): Appointment (for certain purposes): 1 August 2000: see SI 2000/1985, art 2, Schedule.
Sub-s (2): Appointment (for remaining purposes): 2 April 2001: see SI 2001/239, art 2, Schedule.

156 Arrangements for the provision of escorts and custody

(1)   The Secretary of State may make arrangements for—

    (a)   the delivery of detained persons to premises in which they may lawfully be detained;

    (b)   the delivery of persons from any such premises for the purposes of their removal from the United Kingdom in accordance with directions given under the 1971 Act or this Act;

    (c)   the custody of detained persons who are temporarily outside such premises;

    (d)   the custody of detained persons held on the premises of any court.

(2)   Escort arrangements may provide for functions under the arrangements to be performed, in such cases as may be determined by or under the arrangements, by detainee custody officers.

(3)   "Court" includes—

    (a)   adjudicators;

    (b)   the Immigration Appeal Tribunal;

    (c)   the Commission.

(4)   Escort arrangements may include entering into contracts with other persons for the provision by them of—

    (a)   detainee custody officers; or

    (b)   prisoner custody officers who are certified under section 89 of the Criminal Justice Act 1991, or section 114 or 122 of the Criminal Justice and Public Order Act 1994, to perform escort functions.

(5)   Schedule 13 makes further provision about escort arrangements.

(6)   A person responsible for performing a function of a kind mentioned in subsection (1), in accordance with a transfer direction, complies with the direction if he does all that he reasonably can to secure that the function is performed by a person acting in accordance with escort arrangements.

(7)   "Transfer direction" means a transfer direction given under—

    (a)   section 48 of the Mental Health Act 1983 or section 71 of the Mental Health (Scotland) Act 1984 (removal to hospital of, among others, persons detained under the 1971 Act); or

    (b)   in Northern Ireland, article 54 of the Mental Health (Northern Ireland) Order 1986 (provision corresponding to section 48 of the 1983 Act).

NOTES

Initial Commencement
To be appointed
To be appointed: see s 170(4).

Appointment
Sub-ss (1)–(4), (6), (7): Appointment: 2 April 2001: see SI 2001/239, art 2, Schedule.
Sub-s (5): Appointment (for certain purposes): 1 August 2000: see SI 2000/1985, art 2, Schedule.
Sub-s (5): Appointment (for remaining purposes): 2 April 2001: see SI 2001/239, art 2, Schedule.

157 Short-term holding facilities

(1)   The Secretary of State may by regulations extend any provision made by or under this Part in relation to detention centres (other than one mentioned in subsection (2)) to short-term holding facilities.

(2)   Subsection (1) does not apply to section 150.

(3)   The Secretary of State may make rules for the regulation and management of short-term holding facilities.

NOTES

Initial Commencement
To be appointed
To be appointed: see s 170(4).

Appointment
Appointment (for the purposes of enabling subordinate legislation to be made): 1 August 2000: see SI 2000/1985, art 2, Schedule.
Appointment (for remaining purposes): 2 April 2001: see SI 2001/239, art 2, Schedule.

Miscellaneous

158 Wrongful disclosure of information

(1)   A person who is or has been employed (whether as a detainee custody officer, prisoner custody officer or otherwise)—

(a)   in accordance with escort arrangements,
(b)   at a contracted out detention centre, or
(c)   to perform contracted out functions at a directly managed detention centre,

is guilty of an offence if he discloses, otherwise than in the course of his duty or as authorised by the Secretary of State, any information which he acquired in the course of his employment and which relates to a particular detained person.

(2)   A person guilty of such an offence is liable—

(a)   on conviction on indictment, to imprisonment for a term not exceeding two years or to a fine or to both;
(b)   on summary conviction, to imprisonment for a term not exceeding six months or to a fine not exceeding the statutory maximum or to both.

(3)   "Contracted out functions" means functions which, as the result of a contract entered into under section 150, fall to be performed by detainee custody officers or certified prisoner custody officers.

NOTES

Initial Commencement
To be appointed
To be appointed: see s 170(4).

Appointment
Appointment: 2 April 2001: see SI 2001/239, art 2, Schedule.

159 Power of constable to act outside his jurisdiction

(1)   For the purpose of taking a person to or from a detention centre under the order of any authority competent to give the order, a constable may act outside the area of his jurisdiction.

(2)   When acting under this section, the constable concerned retains all the powers, authority, protection and privileges of his office.

NOTES

Initial Commencement
To be appointed
To be appointed: see s 170(4).

Appointment
Appointment: 2 April 2001: see SI 2001/239, art 2, Schedule.

PART IX
REGISTRAR'S CERTIFICATES: PROCEDURE

160 Abolition of certificate by licence

(1)   In the Marriage Act 1949, in section 26, omit subsection (2) (marriage under superintendent registrar's certificate to be by licence issued by the registrar or without licence).

(2)   In section 27 of the 1949 Act—

   (a)   in subsection (1), omit "without licence";
   (b)   omit subsection (2);
   (c)   in subsection (3), in paragraph (a), omit "in the case of a marriage intended to be solemnized without licence,";
   (d)   in subsection (3), omit paragraph (b).

(3)   Section 32 of the 1949 Act (marriage under certificate by licence) shall cease to have effect.

(4)   In section 31 of the 1949 Act (marriage under certificate without licence requiring 21 days' notice)—

   (a)   in subsection (1), omit "without licence" and for "twenty-one" substitute "15";
   (b)   in subsection (2), for "twenty-one" substitute "15";
   (c)   in subsection (4), omit "without licence" and for "said period of twenty-one days" substitute "waiting period in relation to each notice of marriage".

(5)   In section 31 of the 1949 Act, after subsection (4) insert—

"(4A)   "The waiting period", in relation to a notice of marriage, means—

   (a)   the period of 15 days, or
   (b)   such shorter period as may be determined by the Registrar General under subsection (5A) or by a superintendent registrar under any provision of regulations made under subsection (5D),

after the day on which the notice of marriage was entered in the marriage notice book."

(6)   In section 31 of the 1949 Act, insert at the end—

"(5A)   If, on an application made to the Registrar General, he is satisfied that there are compelling reasons for reducing the 15 day period because of the exceptional circumstances of the case, he may reduce that period to such shorter period as he considers appropriate.

(5B)   "The 15 day period" means the period of 15 days mentioned in subsections (1) and (2).

(5C)   If the Registrar General reduces the 15 day period in a particular case, the reference to 15 days in section 75(3)(a) is to be treated, in relation to that case, as a reference to the reduced period.

(5D)   The Registrar General may by regulations make provision with respect to the making, and granting, of applications under subsection (5A).

(5E)   The regulations—

   (a)   may provide for the power conferred by subsection (5A) to be exercised by a superintendent registrar on behalf of the Registrar General in cases falling within a category prescribed in the regulations;

(b) may provide for the making of an appeal to the Registrar General against a decision taken by a superintendent registrar in accordance with regulations made by virtue of paragraph (a);

(c) may make different provision in relation to different cases;

(d) require the approval of the Chancellor of the Exchequer.

(5F) The Chancellor of the Exchequer may by order provide for a fee, of such an amount as may be specified in the order, to be payable on an application under subsection (5A).

(5G) The order may make different provision in relation to different cases.

(5H) The power to make regulations under subsection (5D) or an order under subsection (5F) is exercisable by statutory instrument.

(5I) Any statutory instrument made under subsection (5F) shall be subject to annulment in pursuance of a resolution of either House of Parliament."

NOTES

Initial Commencement
To be appointed
To be appointed: see s 170(4).

Appointment
Appointment: 1 January 2001: see SI 2000/2698, art 2, Schedule.

161 Notice of marriage

(1) In the Marriage Act 1949, in section 27(1) (persons by whom notice of marriage must be given)—

(a) in paragraph (a), for "either" substitute "each";

(b) in paragraph (b), for "either" substitute "each" and for "each registration district in which one of them has resided" substitute "the registration district in which he or she has resided".

(2) In section 27 of the 1949 Act, in subsection (3) (matters to be stated in notice of marriage), for "and place of residence" substitute ", place of residence and nationality".

(3) In the 1949 Act, in section 26(1) (marriages which may be solemnized on authority of a certificate of a superintendent registrar), for "a certificate" substitute "two certificates".

(4) In the Marriage Law (Ireland) Amendment Act 1863, in section 2(3) (matters to be stated in notice of marriage), after "dwelling place" insert "and the nationality".

NOTES

Initial Commencement
To be appointed
To be appointed: see s 170(4).

Appointment
Appointment: 1 January 2001: see SI 2000/2698, art 2, Schedule.

162 Power to require evidence

(1) In the Marriage Act 1949, after section 28, insert—

"28A Power to require evidence

(1) A superintendent registrar to whom a notice of marriage is given under section 27, or any other person attesting a declaration accompanying such a notice, may require the person giving the notice to provide him with specified evidence—

    (a)   relating to that person; or

    (b)   if the superintendent registrar considers that the circumstances are exceptional, relating to each of the persons to be married.

(2)   Such a requirement may be imposed at any time—

    (a)   on or after the giving of the notice of marriage; but

    (b)   before the superintendent registrar issues his certificate under section 31.

(3)   "Specified evidence", in relation to a person, means such evidence of that person's—

    (a)   name and surname,

    (b)   age,

    (c)   marital status, and

    (d)   nationality,

as may be specified in guidance issued by the Registrar General."

(2)   In the Marriage Law (Ireland) Amendment Act 1863, after section 3, insert—

"3A Power to require evidence

(1)   A registrar to whom a notice of marriage, mentioned in section 2 is given may require the person giving the notice to provide him with specified evidence relating to each of the persons to be married.

(2)   Such a requirement may be imposed at any time—

    (a)   on or after the giving of the notice of marriage; but

    (b)   before the registrar issues his certificate.

(3)   "Specified evidence", in relation to a person, means such evidence of that person's—

    (a)   name and surname,

    (b)   age,

    (c)   marital status, and

    (d)   nationality,

as may be specified in guidance issued by the Registrar General."

NOTES

Initial Commencement
To be appointed
To be appointed: see s 170(4).

Appointment
Appointment: 1 January 2001: see SI 2000/2698, art 2, Schedule.

163 Refusal to issue certificate

(1)   In the Marriage Act 1949, in section 31(2) (issue of marriage certificate), for paragraph (a) substitute—

    "(a) the superintendent registrar is not satisfied that there is no lawful impediment to the issue of the certificate; or".

(2)   In the 1949 Act, after section 31, insert—

"31A Appeal on refusal under section 31(2)(a)

(1)   If, relying on section 31(2)(a), a superintendent registrar refuses to issue a certificate, the person applying for it may appeal to the Registrar General.

(2)   On such an appeal, the Registrar General must—

    (a)   confirm the refusal; or

    (b)   direct that a certificate be issued.

(3) If—

    (a)   relying on section 31(2)(a), a superintendent registrar refuses to issue a certificate as a result of a representation made to him, and

    (b)   on an appeal against the refusal, the Registrar General declares the representation to have been frivolous and to be such that it ought not to obstruct the issue of a certificate,

the person making the representation is liable for the costs of the proceedings before the Registrar General and for damages recoverable by the applicant for the certificate.

(4) For the purpose of enabling a person to recover any such costs and damages, a copy of the declaration of the Registrar General purporting to be sealed with the seal of the General Register Office is evidence that the Registrar General has declared the representation to have been frivolous and to be such that it ought not to obstruct the issue of a certificate."

(3) In the Marriages (Ireland) Act 1844, in section 16 (issue of marriage certificate), for "provided that no lawful impediment be shown to the satisfaction of the registrar why such certificate should not issue" substitute "unless the registrar is not satisfied that there is no lawful impediment to the issue of the certificate".

(4) In the 1844 Act, after section 16, insert—

"16A Appeal on refusal under section 16

(1) If the registrar refuses to issue a certificate under section 16 on the ground that he is not satisfied that there is no lawful impediment to the issue of the certificate, the party by whom the notice was given may appeal to the Registrar General.

(2) On such an appeal, the Registrar General must—

    (a)   confirm the refusal; or

    (b)   direct that a certificate be issued.

(3) If—

    (a)   the registrar refuses to issue a certificate under section 16 on the ground specified in subsection (1) as a result of a representation made to him, and

    (b)   on an appeal against the refusal, the Registrar General declares the representation to have been frivolous and to be such that it ought not to obstruct the issue of a certificate,

the person making the representation is liable for the costs of the proceedings before the Registrar General and for damages recoverable by the applicant for the certificate.

(4) For the purpose of enabling a person to recover any such costs and damages, a copy of the declaration of the Registrar General purporting to be sealed with the seal of the General Register Office is evidence that the Registrar General has declared the representation to have been frivolous and to be such that it ought not to obstruct the issue of a certificate."

NOTES

Initial Commencement
To be appointed
To be appointed: see s 170(4).

Appointment
Appointment: 1 January 2001: see SI 2000/2698, art 2, Schedule.

PART X
MISCELLANEOUS AND SUPPLEMENTAL

164 Institution of proceedings

In section 3(2) of the Prosecution of Offences Act 1985 (proceedings which must be conducted by the Director of Public Prosecutions), after paragraph (a) insert—

> "(aa) to take over the conduct of any criminal proceedings instituted by an immigration officer (as defined for the purposes of the Immigration Act 1971) acting in his capacity as such an officer;".

NOTES

Initial Commencement
To be appointed
To be appointed: see s 170(4).

165 Procedural requirements as to applications

In the 1971 Act, after section 31, insert—

"31A Procedural requirements as to applications

(1) If a form is prescribed for a particular kind of application under this Act, any application of that kind must be made in the prescribed form.

(2) If procedural or other steps are prescribed in relation to a particular kind of application under this Act, those steps must be taken in respect of any application of that kind.

(3) "Prescribed" means prescribed in regulations made by the Secretary of State.

(4) The power to make regulations under this section is exercisable by statutory instrument.

(5) Any such statutory instrument shall be subject to annulment in pursuance of a resolution of either House of Parliament."

NOTES

Initial Commencement
To be appointed
To be appointed: see s 170(4).

Appointment
Appointment (for certain purposes): 22 May 2000: see SI 2000/1282, art 2, Schedule.

166 Regulations and orders

(1) Any power to make rules, regulations or orders conferred by this Act is exercisable by statutory instrument.

(2) But subsection (1) does not apply in relation to rules made under paragraph 1 of Schedule 5 or immigration rules.

(3) Any statutory instrument made as a result of subsection (1) may—

(a) contain such incidental, supplemental, consequential and transitional provision as the person making it considers appropriate;
(b) make different provision for different cases or descriptions of case; and
(c) make different provision for different areas.

(4)   No order is to be made under—

(a)   section 20,
(b)   section 21,
(c)   section 31(10),
(d)   section 86(2),
(e)   section 96(5),
(f)   section 97(3),
(g)   section 143(15), or
(h)   paragraph 4 of Schedule 5,

unless a draft of the order has been laid before Parliament and approved by a resolution of each House.

(5)   No regulations are to be made under—

(a)   section 9,
(b)   section 46(8),
(c)   section 53, or
(d)   section 144,

unless a draft of the regulations has been laid before Parliament and approved by a resolution of each House.

(6)   Any statutory instrument made under this Act, apart from one made—

(a)   under any of the provisions mentioned in subsection (4) or (5), or
(b)   under section 24(3) or 170(4) or (7),

shall be subject to annulment by a resolution of either House of Parliament.

NOTES

Initial Commencement
Royal Assent
Royal Assent: 11 November 1999: see s 170(3)(p).

Subordinate Legislation
Asylum Support (Interim Provisions) Regulations 1999, SI 1999/3056.
Homelessness (Asylum-Seekers) (Interim Period) (England) Order 1999, SI 1999/3126 (made under sub-s (3)).
Travel Documents (Fees) Regulations 1999, SI 1999/3339.
Immigration and Asylum Act 1999 (Commencement No 2 and Transitional Provisions) Order 2000, SI 2000/168 (made under sub-s (3)).
Immigration (Regularisation Period for Overstayers) Regulations 2000, SI 2000/265 (made under sub-s (3)).
Asylum Support Appeals (Procedure) Rules 2000, SI 2000/541 (made under sub-s (3)).
Social Security (Immigration and Asylum) Consequential Amendments Regulations 2000, SI 2000/636 (made under sub-s (3)).
Carriers' Liability (Clandestine Entrants) (Code of Practice) Order 2000, SI 2000/684 (made under sub-s (3)).
Carriers' Liability (Clandestine Entrants and Sale of Transporters) Regulations 2000, SI 2000/685 (made under sub-s (3)).
Asylum Support Regulations 2000, SI 2000/704.
Immigration (Eligibility for Assistance) (Scotland and Northern Ireland) Regulations 2000, SI 2000/705.
Persons subject to Immigration Control (Housing Authority Accommodation and Homelessness) Order 2000, SI 2000/706 (made under sub-s (3)).
Persons Subject to Immigration Control (Housing Authority Accommodation) (Wales) Order 2000, SI 2000/1036 (made under sub-s (3)).
Immigration and Asylum Act 1999 (Commencement No 5 and Transitional Provisions) Order 2000, SI 2000/1985 (made under sub-s (3)).
Immigration and Asylum Appeals (One-Stop Procedure) Regulations 2000, SI 2000/2244.

Immigration and Asylum Appeals (Notices) Regulations 2000, SI 2000/2246 (made under sub-s (3)).
Immigration and Asylum Appeals (Procedure) Rules 2000, SI 2000/2333 (made under sub-s (3)).
Immigration and Asylum Act 1999 (Commencement No 6, Transitional and Consequential Provisions) Order 2000, SI 2000/2444 (made under sub-s (3)).
Asylum Support (Amendment) Regulations 2000, SI 2000/3053 (made under sub-s (3)).
Immigration and Asylum Act 1999 (Commencement No 8 and Transitional Provisions) Order 2000, SI 2000/3099 (made under sub-s (3)).
Immigration Appeals (Family Visitor) (Amendment) Regulations 2001, SI 2001/52 (made under sub-s (3)).
Detention Centre Rules 2001, SI 2001/238 (made under sub-s (3)).

167 Interpretation

(1)   In this Act—
"the 1971 Act" means the Immigration Act 1971;
"adjudicator" (except in Part VI) means an adjudicator appointed under section 57;
"Chief Adjudicator" means the person appointed as Chief Adjudicator under section 57(2);
"claim for asylum" (except in Parts V and VI and section 141) means a claim that it would be contrary to the United Kingdom's obligations under the Refugee Convention for the claimant to be removed from, or required to leave, the United Kingdom;
"the Commission" means the Special Immigration Appeals Commission;
"country" includes any territory;
"EEA State" means a State which is a Contracting Party to the Agreement on the European Economic Area signed at Oporto on 2nd May 1992 as it has effect for the time being;
"the Human Rights Convention" means the Convention for the Protection of Human Rights and Fundamental Freedoms, agreed by the Council of Europe at Rome on 4th November 1950 as it has effect for the time being in relation to the United Kingdom;
"the Immigration Acts" means—
(a)   the 1971 Act;
(b)   the Immigration Act 1988;
(c)   the Asylum and Immigration Appeals Act 1993;
(d)   the Asylum and Immigration Act 1996; and
(e)   this Act;
"prescribed" means prescribed by regulations made by the Secretary of State;
"the Refugee Convention" means the Convention relating to the Status of Refugees done at Geneva on 28 July 1951 and the Protocol to the Convention;
"voluntary organisations" means bodies (other than public or local authorities) whose activities are not carried on for profit.

(2)   The following expressions have the same meaning as in the 1971 Act—
"certificate of entitlement";
"entry clearance";
"illegal entrant";
"immigration officer";
"immigration rules";
"port";
"United Kingdom passport";
"work permit".

NOTES

Initial Commencement
Royal Assent
Royal Assent: 11 November 1999: see s 170(3)(p).

Subordinate Legislation
Immigration (Regularisation Period for Overstayers) Regulations 2000, SI 2000/265.
Social Security (Immigration and Asylum) Consequential Amendments Regulations 2000, SI 2000/636.
Carriers' Liability (Clandestine Entrants and Sale of Transporters) Regulations 2000, SI 2000/685.
Asylum Support Regulations 2000, SI 2000/704.
Immigration (Eligibility for Assistance) (Scotland and Northern Ireland) Regulations 2000, SI 2000/705.
Immigration (Removal Directions) Regulations 2000, SI 2000/2243.
Immigration and Asylum Appeals (One-Stop Procedure) Regulations 2000, SI 2000/2244.
Reporting of Suspicious Marriages (Scotland) Regulations 2000, SI 2000/3232 (made under sub-s (1)).
Reporting of Suspicious Marriages (Northern Ireland) Regulations 2000, SI 2000/3233 (made under sub-s (1)).
Carriers' Liability (Clandestine Entrants) (Application to Rail Freight) Regulations 2001, SI 2001/280 (made under sub-s (1)).

168 Expenditure and receipts

(1)   There is to be paid out of money provided by Parliament—

   (a)   any expenditure incurred by the Secretary of State or the Lord Chancellor in consequence of this Act; and

   (b)   any increase attributable to this Act in the sums so payable by virtue of any other Act.

(2)   Sums received by the Secretary of State under section 5, 32, 40, 112 or 113 or by the Lord Chancellor under section 48(4) or 49(4) must be paid into the Consolidated Fund.

NOTES

Initial Commencement
Royal Assent
Royal Assent: 11 November 1999: see s 170(3)(p).

169 Minor and consequential amendments, transitional provisions and repeals

(1)   Schedule 14 makes minor and consequential amendments.

(2)   Schedule 15 contains transitional provisions and savings.

(3)   The enactments set out in Schedule 16 are repealed.

NOTES

Initial Commencement
To be appointed
To be appointed: see s 170(4).

Appointment
Sub-ss (1), (2): Appointment (for certain purposes): 6 December 1999: see SI 1999/3190, art 2, Schedule.
Sub-ss (1)–(3): Appointment (for certain purposes): 14 February 2000: see SI 2000/168, art 2, Schedule.
Sub-ss (1), (3): Appointment (for certain purposes): 1 March 2000: see SI 2000/464, art 2, Schedule.
Sub-ss (1), (3): Appointment (for certain purposes): 3 April 2000: see SI 2000/464, art 2, Schedule.
Sub-ss (1), (3): Appointment (for certain purposes): 1 January 2001: see SI 2000/2698, art 2, Schedule.
Sub-ss (1), (3): Appointment (for certain purposes): 11 December 2000: see SI 2000/3099, art 3, Schedule.

Sub-s (1): Appointment (for certain purposes): 1 August 2000: see SI 2000/1985, art 2, Schedule.
Sub-s (1): Appointment (for certain purposes): 2 October 2000: see SI 2000/2444, art 2, Sch 1.
Sub-s (2): Appointment (for certain purposes): 2 October 2000: see SI 2000/2444, art 2, Sch 1.
Sub-s (3): Appointment (for certain purposes): 2 October 2000: see SI 2000/2444, art 2, Sch 1.

170 Short title, commencement and extent

(1)   This Act may be cited as the Immigration and Asylum Act 1999.

(2)   Subsections (1) and (2) of section 115 come into force on the day on which the first regulations made under Schedule 8 come into force.

(3)   The following provisions come into force on the passing of this Act—

- (a) section 4;
- (b) section 9;
- (c) section 15;
- (d) section 27;
- (e) section 31;
- (f) section 94;
- (g) section 95(13);
- (h) section 99(4) and (5);
- (i) sections 105 to 109;
- (j) section 110(1), (2) and (8) (so far as relating to subsections (1) and (2));
- (k) section 111;
- (I) section 124;
- (m) section 140;
- (n) section 145;
- (o) section 146(1);
- (p) sections 166 to 168;
- (q) this section;
- (r) Schedule 9;
- (s) paragraphs 62(2), 73, 78, 79, 81, 82, 87, 88 and 102 of Schedule 14;
- (t) paragraphs 2 and 13 of Schedule 15.

(4)   The other provisions of this Act, except section 10 and paragraph 12 of Schedule 15 (which come into force in accordance with section 9), come into force on such day as the Secretary of State may by order appoint.

(5)   Different days may be appointed for different purposes.

(6)   This Act extends to Northern Ireland.

(7)   Her Majesty may by Order in Council direct that any of the provisions of this Act are to extend, with such modifications (if any) as appear to Her Majesty to be appropriate, to any of the Channel Islands or the Isle of Man.

NOTES

Initial Commencement
Royal Assent
Royal Assent: 11 November 1999: see sub-s (3)(q) above.

Subordinate Legislation
Immigration and Asylum Act 1999 (Commencement No 1) Order 1999, SI 1999/3190 (made under sub-ss (4), (5)).
Immigration and Asylum Act 1999 (Commencement No 2 and Transitional Provisions) Order 2000, SI 2000/168 (made under sub-ss (4), (5)).
Immigration and Asylum Act 1999 (Commencement No 3) Order 2000, SI 2000/464 (made under sub-ss (4), (5)).
Immigration and Asylum Act 1999 (Commencement No 4) Order 2000, SI 2000/1282 (made under sub-ss (4), (5)).

Immigration and Asylum Act 1999 (Commencement No 5 and Transitional Provisions) Order 2000, SI 2000/1985 (made under sub-ss (4), (5)).
Immigration and Asylum Act 1999 (Commencement No 9) Order 2001, SI 2001/239 (made under sub-ss (4), (5)).

SCHEDULE 1
Sale of Transporters

Sections 37(6) and 42(8)

Leave of court required

1 (1) The sale of a transporter requires the leave of the court.

(2) The court is not to give its leave except on proof—

  (a) that the penalty or charge is or was due;
  (b) that the person liable to pay it or any connected expenses has failed to do so; and
  (c) that the transporter which the Secretary of State seeks leave to sell is liable to sale.

Notice of proposed sale

2 Before applying for leave to sell a transporter, the Secretary of State must take such steps as may be prescribed—

  (a) for bringing the proposed sale to the notice of persons whose interests may be affected by a decision of the court to grant leave; and
  (b) for affording to any such person an opportunity of becoming a party to the proceedings if the Secretary of State applies for leave.

Duty to obtain best price

3 If leave for sale is given, the Secretary of State must secure that the transporter is sold for the best price that can reasonably be obtained.

Effect of failure to comply with paragraph 2 or 3

4 Failure to comply with any requirement of paragraph 2 or 3 in respect of any sale—

  (a) is actionable against the Secretary of State at the suit of any person suffering loss in consequence of the sale; but
  (b) after the sale has taken place, does not affect its validity.

Application of proceeds of sale

5 (1) Any proceeds of sale arising from a sale under section 37 or 42 must be applied—

  (a) in making prescribed payments; and
  (b) in accordance with such provision as to priority of payments as may be prescribed.

(2) The regulations may, in particular, provide for proceeds of sale to be applied in payment—

(a)   of customs or excise duty,
(b)   of value added tax,
(c)   of expenses incurred by the Secretary of State,
(d)   of any penalty or charge which the court has found to be due,
(e)   in the case of the sale of an aircraft, of charges due as a result of regulations made under section 73 of the Civil Aviation Act 1982,
(f)   of any surplus to or among the person or persons whose interests in the transporter have been divested as a result of the sale,

but not necessarily in that order of priority.

NOTES

Initial Commencement
To be appointed
To be appointed: see s 170(4).

Appointment
Paras 1, 3, 4: Appointment (for certain purposes): 3 April 2000: see SI 2000/464, art 2, Schedule.
Paras 2, 5: Appointment: 6 December 1999: see SI 1999/3190, art 2, Schedule.

Subordinate Legislation
Carriers' Liability (Clandestine Entrants and Sale of Transporters) Regulations 2000, SI 2000/685 (made under paras 2, 5).

SCHEDULE 2
The Immigration Appeal Tribunal

Section 56(2)

Members

1   (1)   The members of the Tribunal are to be appointed by the Lord Chancellor.

(2)   The Lord Chancellor may appoint such number of legally qualified members and of other members as he considers appropriate.

(3)   A person is legally qualified if—

(a)   he has a 7 year general qualification, within the meaning of section 71 of the Courts and Legal Services Act 1990;
(b)   he is an advocate or solicitor in Scotland of at least 7 years' standing;
(c)   he is a member of the Bar of Northern Ireland or solicitor of the Supreme Court of Northern Ireland of at least 7 years' standing; or
(d)   he has such legal and other experience as appears to the Lord Chancellor to make him suited for appointment as a legally qualified member.

President and Deputy President

2   (1)   The Lord Chancellor must appoint one legally qualified member to be President of the Tribunal and another such member to be Deputy President.

(2)   The Deputy President is to have such functions in relation to the Tribunal as the President may assign to him.

(3)   If the President is temporarily absent or otherwise unable to act, the Deputy President may act on his behalf.

Term of office

3   (1)   Each member of the Tribunal—

(a)   is to hold and vacate his office in accordance with the terms of his appointment;

(b)   is, on ceasing to hold office, eligible for re-appointment;

(c)   may resign his office at any time by giving written notice to the Lord Chancellor;

(d)   must vacate his office on the day on which he reaches the age of 70.

(2)   But sub-paragraph (1)(d) is subject to subsections (4) to (6) of section 26 of the Judicial Pensions and Retirement Act 1993 (power to authorise continuance in office up to the age of 75).

Remuneration

4   The Lord Chancellor must pay to the members such remuneration and allowances as he may determine.

Compensation

5   If a person ceases to be a member and it appears to the Lord Chancellor that there are special circumstances which make it right that he should receive compensation, the Lord Chancellor may pay him a sum of such amount as the Lord Chancellor may determine.

Proceedings

6   (1) For the purpose of hearing and determining appeals under this Act or any matter preliminary or incidental to such an appeal, the Tribunal must sit at such times and in such place or places as the Lord Chancellor may direct.

(2)   The Tribunal may sit in two or more divisions.

(3)   The jurisdiction of the Tribunal may be exercised by such number of members as the President may direct.

(4)   A direction under sub-paragraph (3) may—

(a)   be given in relation to a specified case or category of case;

(b)   provide for the jurisdiction to be exercised by a single member;

(c)   require the member exercising the jurisdiction, or a specified number of the members exercising the jurisdiction, to be legally qualified;

(d)   be varied at any time by a further direction given by the President.

(5)   "Specified" means specified in the direction.

Staff

7   (1) The Lord Chancellor may appoint such staff for the Tribunal as he may determine.

(2)   The remuneration of the Tribunal's staff is to be defrayed by the Lord Chancellor.

(3)   Such expenses of the Tribunal as the Lord Chancellor may determine are to be defrayed by the Lord Chancellor.

NOTES

Initial Commencement
To be appointed
To be appointed: see s 170(4).

Appointment
Appointment: 14 February 2000: see SI 2000/168, art 2, Schedule; for transitional provisions see art 3 thereof.

SCHEDULE 3
Adjudicators

Section 57(3)

Deputy Chief Adjudicator and Regional Adjudicators

1　(1)　The Lord Chancellor may appoint one of the adjudicators as Deputy Chief Adjudicator.

(2)　The Lord Chancellor may appoint as Regional Adjudicators such number of the adjudicators as he may determine.

(3)　A person appointed under sub-paragraph (1) or (2) is to have such functions as the Chief Adjudicator may assign to him.

(4)　If the Chief Adjudicator is temporarily absent or otherwise unable to act, the Deputy Chief Adjudicator may act on his behalf.

Qualification for appointment

2　A person is qualified for appointment as an adjudicator only if—

(a)　he has a 7 year general qualification, within the meaning of section 71 of the Courts and Legal Services Act 1990;
(b)　he is an advocate or solicitor in Scotland of at least 7 years' standing;
(c)　he is a member of the Bar of Northern Ireland or solicitor of the Supreme Court of Northern Ireland of at least 7 years' standing; or
(d)　he has such legal and other experience as appears to the Lord Chancellor to make him suited for appointment as an adjudicator.

Term of office

3　(1)　Each adjudicator—

(a)　is to hold and vacate his office in accordance with the terms of his appointment;
(b)　is, on ceasing to hold office, eligible for re-appointment;
(c)　may resign his office at any time by giving written notice to the Lord Chancellor;
(d)　must vacate his office on the day on which he reaches the age of 70.

(2)　But sub-paragraph (1)(d) is subject to subsections (4) to (6) of section 26 of the Judicial Pensions and Retirement Act 1993 (power to authorise continuance in office up to the age of 75).

Remuneration

4　The Lord Chancellor must pay to the adjudicators such remuneration and allowances as he may determine.

Compensation

5　If a person ceases to be an adjudicator and it appears to the Lord Chancellor that there are special circumstances which make it right that he should receive compensation, the Lord Chancellor may pay him a sum of such amount as the Lord Chancellor may determine.

Proceedings

6　(1)　The adjudicators must sit at such times and at such places as the Lord Chancellor may direct.

(2)   The Chief Adjudicator—

(a)   must allocate duties among the adjudicators; and
(b)   is to have such other functions as may be conferred on him by the Lord Chancellor.

(3)   The Chief Adjudicator may direct that, in a specified case or category of case, an appeal to an adjudicator is to be heard by such number of adjudicators as may be specified.

(4)   "Specified" means specified in the direction.

Staff

7   (1)   The Lord Chancellor may appoint such staff for the adjudicators as he may determine.

(2)   The remuneration of the adjudicators' staff is to be defrayed by the Lord Chancellor.

(3)   Such expenses of the adjudicators as the Lord Chancellor may determine are to be defrayed by the Lord Chancellor.

NOTES

Initial Commencement
To be appointed
To be appointed: see s 170(4).

Appointment
Appointment: 14 February 2000: see SI 2000/168, art 2, Schedule; for transitional provisions see art 3 thereof.

SCHEDULE 4
Appeals

Section 58(2) to (4)

PART I
PROCEDURE

Notice of appealable matters

1   (1)   The Secretary of State may by regulations provide—

(a)   for written notice to be given to a person of any such decision or action taken in respect of him as is appealable under Part IV (whether or not in his particular case he is entitled to appeal) or would be so appealable but for the ground on which it was taken;
(b)   for any such notice to include a statement of the reasons for the decision or action and, where the action is the giving of directions for the removal of the person from the United Kingdom, of the country to which he is to be removed;
(c)   for any such notice to be accompanied by a statement containing particulars of the rights of appeal available under Part IV and of the procedure by which those rights may be exercised;
(d)   for the form of any such notice or statement and the way in which a notice is to be, or may be, given.

(2)   For the purpose of any proceedings under Part IV, a statement included in a notice in accordance with the regulations is conclusive as to the person by whom and the ground on which any decision or action was taken.

Service of notices

2   If a notice given under regulations made under paragraph 1 is sent by first class post, addressed to the person to whom the notice is required to be given, it is to be taken to have been received by that person on the second day after the day on which it was posted unless the contrary is proved.

Lord Chancellor's rules of procedure

3   The Lord Chancellor may make rules—

(a)   for regulating the exercise of the rights of appeal conferred by Part IV;
(b)   for prescribing the practice and procedure to be followed on or in connection with appeals under Part IV, including the mode and burden of proof and admissibility of evidence on such an appeal; and
(c)   for other matters preliminary or incidental or arising out of such appeals, including proof of the decisions of the adjudicator or the Immigration Appeal Tribunal.

4   (1) The rules may include provision—

(a)   enabling appeals to be determined without a hearing;
(b)   enabling an adjudicator or the Tribunal to allow or dismiss an appeal without considering its merits—
    (i)   if there has been a failure by one of the parties to comply with a provision of the rules or with a direction given under the rules; or
    (ii)   if one of the parties has failed to attend at a hearing;
(c)   enabling or requiring an adjudicator or the Tribunal to treat an appeal as abandoned in specified circumstances;
(d)   enabling the Tribunal, on an appeal from an adjudicator, to remit the appeal to an adjudicator for determination by him in accordance with any directions of the Tribunal, or for further evidence to be obtained with a view to determination by the Tribunal;
(e)   as to the circumstances in which—
    (i)   a decision of an adjudicator may be set aside by an adjudicator; or
    (ii)   a decision of the Tribunal may be set aside by the Tribunal;
(f)   conferring on adjudicators or the Tribunal such ancillary powers as the Lord Chancellor thinks necessary for the purposes of the exercise of their functions;
(g)   as to the procedure to be followed on applications to the Tribunal for leave to appeal under paragraph 23.

(2)   The rules must provide that any appellant is to have the right to be legally represented at any hearing of his appeal.

(3)   Nothing in this paragraph affects the scope of the power conferred by paragraph 3.

(4)   In this Schedule "rules" means rules under this paragraph.

Practice directions

5   (1) The President of the Tribunal may give directions as to the practice and procedure to be followed by the Tribunal in relation to appeals and applications to it.

(2)   The Chief Adjudicator may give directions as to the practice and procedure to be followed by adjudicators in relation to appeals and applications to them.

Hearings in private

6   (1) Sub-paragraph (2) applies if, on an appeal under Part IV, it is alleged—

(a) that a passport or other travel document, certificate of entitlement, entry clearance or work permit (or any part of it or entry in it) on which a party relies is a forgery, and

(b) that the disclosure to that party of any matters relating to the method of detection would be contrary to the public interest.

(2) The adjudicator or Tribunal must arrange—

(a) for the proceedings to take place in the absence of that party and his representatives while the allegation mentioned in sub-paragraph (1)(b) is inquired into by the adjudicator or Tribunal; and

(b) if it appears to the adjudicator or Tribunal that the allegation is made out, for such further period as appears necessary in order to ensure that those matters can be presented to the adjudicator or Tribunal without any disclosure being directly or indirectly made contrary to the public interest.

Leave to appeal

7 If, under the rules, leave to appeal to the Tribunal is required in cases in which an adjudicator dismisses an appeal under section 59, the authority having power to grant leave must grant it—

(a) if the appeal was against a decision that the appellant required leave to enter the United Kingdom and the authority is satisfied that at the time of the decision he held a certificate of entitlement; and

(b) if the appeal was against a refusal of leave to enter and the authority is satisfied that—

(i) at the time of the refusal the appellant held an entry clearance; and

(ii) the dismissal of the appeal was not required by paragraph 24.

Offences

8 A person who is required under or in accordance with the rules to attend and give evidence or produce documents before an adjudicator or the Tribunal, and fails without reasonable excuse to comply with the requirement is guilty of an offence and liable on summary conviction to a fine not exceeding level three on the standard scale.

Convention cases

9 (1) This paragraph applies to an appeal under Part IV of this Act by a person who claims that it would be contrary to the Convention for him to be removed from, or to be required to leave, the United Kingdom, if the Secretary of State has certified that, in his opinion, that claim is one to which—

(a) sub-paragraph (3), (4), (5) or (6) applies; and

(b) sub-paragraph (7) does not apply.

(2) If, on an appeal to which this paragraph applies, the adjudicator agrees [with the opinion expressed in the Secretary of State's certificate], paragraph 22 does not confer on the appellant any right to appeal to the Immigration Appeal Tribunal.

(3) This sub-paragraph applies to a claim if, on his arrival in the United Kingdom, the appellant was required by an immigration officer to produce a valid passport and—

(a) he failed to do so, without giving a reasonable explanation for his failure; or

(b) he produced an invalid passport and failed to inform the officer that it was not valid.

(4)   This sub-paragraph applies to a claim under the Refugee Convention if—

   (a)   it does not show a fear of persecution by reason of the appellant's race, religion, nationality, membership of a particular social group, or political opinion; or
   (b)   it shows a fear of such persecution, but the fear is manifestly unfounded or the circumstances which gave rise to the fear no longer subsist.

(5)   This sub-paragraph applies to a claim under the Human Rights Convention if—

   (a)   it does not disclose a right under the Convention; or
   (b)   it does disclose a right under the Convention, but the claim is manifestly unfounded.

(6)   This sub-paragraph applies to a claim if—

   (a)   it is made at any time after the appellant—
      (i)   has been refused leave to enter the United Kingdom under the 1971 Act;
      (ii)   has been recommended for deportation by a court empowered by that Act to do so;
      (iii)   has been notified of the Secretary of State's decision to make a deportation order against him under section 5(1) of the 1971 Act as a result of his liability to deportation; or
      (iv)   has been notified of his liability to removal under paragraph 9 of Schedule 2 to that Act;
   (b)   it is manifestly fraudulent, or any of the evidence adduced in its support is manifestly false; or
   (c)   it is frivolous or vexatious.

(7)   This sub-paragraph applies to a claim if the evidence adduced in its support establishes a reasonable likelihood that the appellant has been tortured in the country to which he is to be sent.

(8)   "Contrary to the Convention" means contrary to the United Kingdom's obligations under the Refugee Convention or the Human Rights Convention.

[Racial discrimination

9A   (1)   This paragraph applies to an appeal under Part IV of this Act by a person who claims that he has been racially discriminated against, if the Secretary of State has certified that, in his opinion, the claim is manifestly unfounded.

(2)   If, on an appeal to which this paragraph applies, the adjudicator agrees with the opinion expressed in the Secretary of State's certificate, paragraph 22 does not confer on the appellant any right to appeal to the Immigration Appeal Tribunal.]

NOTES

Initial Commencement
To be appointed
To be appointed: see s 170(4).

Appointment
Para 1: Appointment: 22 May 2000: see SI 2000/1282, art 2, Schedule.
Paras (6)–(9): Appointment: 2 October 2000: see SI 2000/2444, art 2, Sch 1; for transitional provisions see art 3, Sch 2, para 1(13), (14) thereof.
Para 2: Appointment: 2 October 2000: see SI 2000/2444, art 2, Sch 1.
Paras 3, 4: Appointment: 14 February 2000: see SI 2000/168, art 2, Schedule.
Para 5: Appointment: 14 February 2000: see SI 2000/168, art 2, Schedule; for transitional provisions see art 3 thereof.

Amendment
Para 9: in sub-para (2) words in square brackets substituted by the Race Relations (Amendment) Act 2000, s 9(1), Sch 2, para 39.
Date in force: 2 April 2001: see SI 2001/566, art 2(1).
Para 9A: inserted by the Race Relations (Amendment) Act 2000, s 9(1), Sch 2, para 40.
Date in force: 2 April 2001: see SI 2001/566, art 2(1).

Modification
Paras 1, 3, 4: references to Part IV of this Act shall include references to the Immigration Act 1971, Pt II, the Asylum and Immigration Act 1993, s 8, Sch 2, and the Asylum and Immigration Act 1996, s 3 as from 1 August 2000: see SI 2000/1985, art 3(1)(a), (3).
Para 1: in sub-para (2) reference to "the regulations" includes a reference to regulations made under the Immigration Act 1971, s 18 as from 1 August 2000: see SI 2000/1985, art 3(1)(b), (3).

Subordinate Legislation
Immigration and Asylum Appeals (Procedure) Rules 2000, SI 2000/2333 (made under paras 3, 4).

PART II
EFFECT OF APPEALS

Stay on directions for removal

10 If a person in the United Kingdom appeals under section 59 or 69(1) on being refused leave to enter, any directions previously given by virtue of the refusal for his removal from the United Kingdom cease to have effect, except in so far as they have already been carried out, and no directions may be so given while the appeal is pending.

11 If a person in the United Kingdom appeals under section 66, 67 or 69(5) against any directions given under—

(a) section 10,
(b) Part I of Schedule 2 to the 1971 Act, or
(c) Schedule 3 to that Act,

for his removal from the United Kingdom, those directions except in so far as they have already been carried out, are to have no effect while the appeal is pending.

12 But the provisions of Part I of Schedule 2 or, as the case may be, Schedule 3 to the 1971 Act with respect to detention and persons liable to detention apply to a person appealing under section 59, 66, 67 or 69(1) or (5), as if there were in force directions for his removal from the United Kingdom, except that he may not be detained on board a ship or aircraft so as to compel him to leave the United Kingdom while the appeal is pending.

13 **In calculating the period of two months limited by paragraph 8(2) of Schedule 2 to the 1971 Act for—**

(a) the giving of directions under that paragraph for the removal of a person from the United Kingdom, and
(b) the giving of a notice of intention to give such directions,

any period during which there is pending an appeal by him under section 59, 67 or 69(1) of this Act is to be disregarded.

14 For the purposes of paragraphs 10 to 12 (but not for purposes of paragraph 13), except in so far as those paragraphs apply to appeals under section 69, where an appeal to an adjudicator is dismissed, an appeal is not to be regarded as pending unless immediately after the dismissal—

(a) the appellant gives notice of appeal against the determination of the adjudicator; or

(b)   in a case in which leave to appeal against that determination is required and the adjudicator has power to grant leave, the appellant applies for and obtains the leave of the adjudicator.

15   If directions are given under Part I of Schedule 2 or Schedule 3 to the 1971 Act for a person's removal from the United Kingdom, and directions are also so given for the removal with him of persons belonging to his family, then if any of them appeals under section 59, 63, 66, 67 or 69(1) or (5), the appeal is to have the same effect under paragraphs 10 to 14 in relation to the directions given in respect of each of the others as it has in relation to the directions given in respect of the appellant.

Suspension of variation of limited leave

16   A variation is not to take effect while an appeal against the variation is pending under section 61 or 69(2).

Continuation of leave

17   (1)   While an appeal under section 61 or 69(2) is pending, the leave to which the appeal relates and any conditions subject to which it was granted continue to have effect.

(2)   A person may not make an application for a variation of his leave to enter or remain while that leave is treated as continuing to have effect as a result of sub-paragraph (1).

(3)   For the purposes of section 61 or 69(2), in calculating whether, as a result of a decision, a person may be required to leave the United Kingdom within 28 days, a continuation of leave under this paragraph is to be disregarded.

Deportation orders

18   A deportation order is not to be made against a person under section 5 of the 1971 Act while an appeal duly brought under section 63(1)(a) or 69(4)(a) against the decision to make it is pending.

19   In calculating the period of 8 weeks set by section 5(3) of the 1971 Act for making a deportation order against a person as belonging to the family of another person, there is to be disregarded any period during which an appeal under section 63(1)(a) or 69(4)(a) against the decision to make the order is pending.

Appeals under section 65

20   (1)   A person is not to be required to leave, or be removed from, the United Kingdom if an appeal under section 65 is pending against the decision on which that requirement or removal would otherwise be based.

(2)   That does not prevent—

(a)   directions for his removal being given during that period;
(b)   a deportation order being made against him during that period.

(3)   But no such direction or order is to have effect during that period.

NOTES

Initial Commencement
To be appointed
To be appointed: see s 170(4).

Appointment
Appointment: 2 October 2000: see SI 2000/2444, art 2, Sch 1.

PART III
DETERMINATION OF APPEALS

Determination of appeals

21 (1) On an appeal to him under Part IV, an adjudicator must allow the appeal if he considers—

(a) that the decision or action against which the appeal is brought was not in accordance with the law or with any immigration rules applicable to the case, or

(b) if the decision or action involved the exercise of a discretion by the Secretary of State or an officer, that the discretion should have been exercised differently,

but otherwise must dismiss the appeal.

(2) Sub-paragraph (1) is subject to paragraph 24 and to any restriction on the grounds of appeal.

(3) For the purposes of sub-paragraph (1), the adjudicator may review any determination of a question of fact on which the decision or action was based.

(4) For the purposes of sub-paragraph (1)(b), no decision or action which is in accordance with the immigration rules is to be treated as having involved the exercise of a discretion by the Secretary of State by reason only of the fact that he has been requested by or on behalf of the appellant to depart, or to authorise an officer to depart, from the rules and has refused to do so.

(5) If an appeal is allowed, the adjudicator—

(a) must give such directions for giving effect to the determination as he thinks are required; and

(b) may also make recommendations with respect to any other action which he considers should be taken in the case under any of the Immigration Acts.

(6) The duty to comply with directions given under this paragraph is subject to paragraph 22.

Appeals to Immigration Appeal Tribunal

22 (1) Subject to any requirement of rules made under paragraph 3 as to leave to appeal, any party to an appeal, other than an appeal under section 71, to an adjudicator may, if dissatisfied with his determination, appeal to the Immigration Appeal Tribunal.

(2) The Tribunal may affirm the determination or make any other determination which the adjudicator could have made.

(3) Sub-paragraphs (4) to (6) apply if directions have been given by an adjudicator under paragraph 21.

(4) The directions need not be complied with—

(a) so long as an appeal can be brought against his determination; and

(b) if such an appeal is duly brought, so long as the appeal is pending.

(5) If the Tribunal affirm the adjudicator's determination allowing the appeal, they may alter or add to his directions and recommendations under paragraph 21 or replace them with their own directions and recommendations.

(6)   The provisions of paragraph 21 are to apply accordingly.

(7)   If an appeal is dismissed by an adjudicator but allowed by the Tribunal, paragraph 21 applies with the substitution of references to the Tribunal for references to the adjudicator.

Appeals from Immigration Appeal Tribunal

23   (1)   If the Immigration Appeal Tribunal has made a final determination of an appeal brought under Part IV, any party to the appeal may bring a further appeal to the appropriate appeal court on a question of law material to that determination.

(2)   An appeal under this section may be brought only with the leave of the Immigration Appeal Tribunal or, if such leave is refused, of the appropriate appeal court.

(3)   "Appropriate appeal court" means—

    (a)   if the appeal is from the determination of an adjudicator made in Scotland, the Court of Session; and

    (b)   in any other case, the Court of Appeal.

Appeals which must be dismissed

24   (1)   An appeal against a refusal of leave to enter the United Kingdom must be dismissed by the adjudicator if he is satisfied that the appellant was at the time of the refusal an illegal entrant.

(2)   An appeal against a refusal of an entry clearance must be dismissed by the adjudicator if he is satisfied that a deportation order was at the time of the refusal in force in respect of the appellant.

(3)   An appeal under section 66 against directions given as mentioned in subsection (1)(c) of that section must be dismissed by the adjudicator, even though the ground of appeal is made out, if he is satisfied that there was power to give the same directions on the ground that the appellant was an illegal entrant.

NOTES

Initial Commencement
To be appointed
To be appointed: see s 170(4).

Appointment
Appointment: 2 October 2000: see SI 2000/2444, art 2, Sch 1; for transitional provisions see art 3, Sch 2, para 1(13), (15)–(18) thereof.

SCHEDULE 5
The Immigration Services Commissioner

Section 83

Part I
Regulatory Functions

The Commissioner's rules

1   (1)   The Commissioner may make rules regulating any aspect of the professional practice, conduct or discipline of—

(a)   registered persons, and

(b)   those employed by, or working under the supervision of, registered persons,

in connection with the provision of immigration advice or immigration services.

(2)   Before making or altering any rules, the Commissioner must consult such persons appearing to him to represent the views of persons engaged in the provision of immigration advice or immigration services as he considers appropriate.

(3)   In determining whether a registered person is competent or otherwise fit to provide immigration advice or immigration services, the Commissioner may take into account any breach of the rules by—

(a)   that person; and

(b)   any person employed by, or working under the supervision of, that person.

(4)   The rules may, among other things, make provision requiring the keeping of accounts or the obtaining of indemnity insurance.

2   (1)   The Commissioner's rules must be made or altered by an instrument in writing.

(2)   Such an instrument must specify that it is made under this Schedule.

(3)   Immediately after such an instrument is made, it must be printed and made available to the public.

(4)   The Commissioner may charge a reasonable fee for providing a person with a copy of the instrument.

(5)   A person is not to be taken to have contravened a rule made by the Commissioner if he shows that at the time of the alleged contravention the instrument containing the rule had not been made available in accordance with this paragraph.

(6)   The production of a printed copy of an instrument purporting to be made by the Commissioner on which is endorsed a certificate signed by an officer of the Commissioner authorised by him for that purpose and stating—

(a)   that the instrument was made by the Commissioner,

(b)   that the copy is a true copy of the instrument, and

(c)   that on a specified date the instrument was made available to the public in accordance with this paragraph,

is evidence (or in Scotland sufficient evidence) of the facts stated in the certificate.

(7)   A certificate purporting to be signed as mentioned in sub-paragraph (6) is to be treated as having been properly signed unless the contrary is shown.

(8)   A person who wishes in any legal proceedings to rely on an instrument containing the Commissioner's rules may require him to endorse a copy of the instrument with a certificate of the kind mentioned in sub-paragraph (6).

Code of Standards

3   (1)   The Commissioner must prepare and issue a code setting standards of conduct which those to whom the code applies are expected to meet.

(2)   The code is to be known as the Code of Standards but is referred to in this Schedule as "the Code".

(3)   The Code is to apply to any person providing immigration advice or immigration services other than—

(a)   a person who is authorised by a designated professional body to practise as a member of the profession whose members are regulated by that body;

1171

(b)   a person who works under the supervision of such a person; or

(c)   a person mentioned in section 84(6).

(4)   It is the duty of any person to whom the Code applies to comply with its provisions in providing immigration advice or immigration services.

(5)   If the Commissioner alters the Code, he must re-issue it.

(6)   Before issuing the Code or altering it, the Commissioner must consult—

(a)   each of the designated professional bodies;

(b)   the designated judges;

(c)   the Lord President of the Court of Session;

(d)   the Lord Chief Justice of Northern Ireland; and

(e)   such other persons appearing to him to represent the views of persons engaged in the provision of immigration advice or immigration services as he considers appropriate.

(7)   The Commissioner must publish the Code in such form and manner as the Secretary of State may direct.

Extension of scope of the Code

4   (1)   The Secretary of State may by order provide for the provisions of the Code, or such provisions of the Code as may be specified by the order, to apply to—

(a)   persons authorised by any designated professional body to practise as a member of the profession whose members are regulated by that body; and

(b)   persons working under the supervision of such persons.

(2)   If the Secretary of State is proposing to act under sub-paragraph (1) he must, before doing so, consult—

(a)   the Commissioner;

(b)   the Legal Services Ombudsman, if the proposed order would affect a designated professional body in England and Wales;

(c)   the Scottish Legal Services Ombudsman, if the proposed order would affect a designated professional body in Scotland;

(d)   the lay observers appointed under Article 42 of the Solicitors (Northern Ireland) Order 1976, if the proposed order would affect a designated professional body in Northern Ireland.

(3)   An order under sub-paragraph (1) requires the approval of—

(a)   the Lord Chancellor, if it affects a designated professional body in England and Wales or Northern Ireland;

(b)   the Scottish Ministers, if it affects a designated professional body in Scotland.

(4)   Before deciding whether or not to give his approval under sub-paragraph (3)(a), the Lord Chancellor must consult—

(a)   the designated judges, if the order affects a designated professional body in England and Wales;

(b)   the Lord Chief Justice of Northern Ireland, if it affects a designated professional body in Northern Ireland.

(5)   Before deciding whether or not to give their approval under sub-paragraph (3)(b), the Scottish Ministers must consult the Lord President of the Court of Session.

Investigation of complaints

5   (1) The Commissioner must establish a scheme ("the complaints scheme") for the investigation by him of relevant complaints made to him in accordance with the provisions of the scheme.

(2)   Before establishing the scheme or altering it, the Commissioner must consult—

(a)   each of the designated professional bodies; and
(b)   such other persons appearing to him to represent the views of persons engaged in the provision of immigration advice or immigration services as he considers appropriate.

(3)   A complaint is a relevant complaint if it relates to—

(a)   the competence or fitness of a person to provide immigration advice or Immigration services,
(b)   the competence or fitness of a person employed by, or working under the supervision of, a person providing immigration advice or immigration services,
(c)   an alleged breach of the Code,
(d)   an alleged breach of one or more of the Commissioner's rules by a person to whom they apply, or
(e)   an alleged breach, by a person who falls within paragraph (c), (d), (e) or (f) of section 84(2), of one or more of the rules of the relevant regulatory body,

but not if it relates to a person who is excluded from the application of subsection (1) of section 84 by subsection (6) of that section.

(4)   The Commissioner may, on his own initiative, investigate any matter which he would have power to investigate on a complaint made under the complaints scheme.

(5)   In investigating any such matter on his own initiative, the Commissioner must proceed as if his investigation were being conducted in response to a complaint made under the scheme.

6   (1) The complaints scheme must provide for a person who is the subject of an investigation under the scheme to be given a reasonable opportunity to make representations to the Commissioner.

(2)   Any person who is the subject of an investigation under the scheme must—

(a)   take such steps as are reasonably required to assist the Commissioner in his investigation; and
(b)   comply with any reasonable requirement imposed on him by the Commissioner.

(3)   If a person fails to comply with sub-paragraph (2)(a) or with a requirement imposed under sub-paragraph (2)(b) the Commissioner may—

(a)   in the case of a registered person, cancel his registration;
(b)   in the case of a person certified by the Commissioner as exempt under section 84(4)(a), withdraw his exemption; or
(c)   in the case of a person falling within paragraph (c), (d), (e) or (f) of section 84(2), refer the matter to the relevant regulatory body.

Power to enter premises

7   (1) This paragraph applies if—

(a)   the Commissioner is investigating a complaint under the complaints scheme;
(b)   the complaint falls within paragraph 5(3)(a), (b) or (d); and

(c)   there are reasonable grounds for believing that particular premises are being used in connection with the provision of immigration advice or immigration services by a registered person.

(2)   The Commissioner, or a member of his staff authorised in writing by him, may enter the premises at reasonable hours.

(3)   Sub-paragraph (2) does not apply to premises to the extent to which they constitute a private residence.

(4)   A person exercising the power given by sub-paragraph (2) ("the investigating officer") may—

(a)   take with him such equipment as appears to him to be necessary;
(b)   require any person on the premises—
    (i)   to produce any document which he considers relates to any matter relevant to the investigation; and
    (ii)   if the document is produced, to provide an explanation of it;
(c)   require any person to state, to the best of his knowledge and belief, where any such document is to be found;
(d)   take copies of, or extracts from, any document which is produced;
(e)   require any information which is held in a computer and is accessible from the premises and which the investigating officer considers relates to any matter relevant to the investigation, to be produced in a form—
    (i)   in which it can be taken away; and
    (ii)   in which it is visible and legible.

(5)   Instead of exercising the power under sub-paragraph (2), the Commissioner may require such person as he may determine ("his agent") to make a report on the provision of immigration advice or immigration services from the premises.

(6)   If the Commissioner so determines, his agent may exercise the power conferred by sub-paragraph (2) as if he were a member of the Commissioner's staff appropriately authorised.

(7)   If a registered person fails without reasonable excuse to allow access under sub-paragraph (2) or (6) to any premises under his occupation or control, the Commissioner may cancel his registration.

(8)   The Commissioner may also cancel the registration of a registered person who—

(a)   without reasonable excuse fails to comply with a requirement imposed on him under sub-paragraph (4);
(b)   intentionally delays or obstructs any person exercising functions under this paragraph; or
(c)   fails to take reasonable steps to prevent an employee of his from obstructing any person exercising such functions.

Determination of complaints

8   (1)   On determining a complaint under the complaints scheme, the Commissioner must give his decision in a written statement.

(2)   The statement must include the Commissioner's reasons for his decision.

(3)   A copy of the statement must be given by the Commissioner to—

(a)   the person who made the complaint; and
(b)   the person who is the subject of the complaint.

9   (1)   On determining a complaint under the complaints scheme, the Commissioner may—

    (a)   if the person to whom the complaint relates is a registered person or a person employed by, or working under the supervision of, a registered person, record the complaint and the decision on it for consideration when that registered person next applies for his registration to be continued;

    (b)   if the person to whom the complaint relates is a registered person or a person employed by, or working under the supervision of, a registered person and the Commissioner considers the matter sufficiently serious to require immediate action, require that registered person to apply for continued registration without delay;

    (c)   if the person to whom the complaint relates falls within paragraph (c), (d), (e) or (f) of section 84(2), refer the complaint and his decision on it to the relevant regulatory body;

    (d)   if the person to whom the complaint relates is certified by the Commissioner as exempt under section 84(4)(a) or is employed by, or working under the supervision of, such a person, consider whether to withdraw that person's exemption;

    (e)   lay before the Tribunal a disciplinary charge against a relevant person.

(2)   Sub-paragraph (3) applies if—

    (a)   the Tribunal is considering a disciplinary charge against a relevant person; and

    (b)   the Commissioner asks it to exercise its powers under that sub-paragraph.

(3)   The Tribunal may give directions (which are to have effect while it is dealing with the charge)—

    (a)   imposing such restrictions in connection with the provision—
        (i)   by the relevant person, or
        (ii) by any person employed by him or working under his supervision,
        of immigration advice or immigration services as the directions may specify; or

    (b)   prohibiting him, or any person employed by him or working under his supervision, from providing immigration advice or immigration services.

(4)   "Relevant person" means a person providing immigration advice or immigration services who is—

    (a)   a registered person;
    (b)   a person employed by, or working under the supervision of, a registered person;
    (c)   a member or employee of a body which is a registered person;
    (d)   a person working under the supervision of a member or employee of such a body;
    (e)   a person certified by the Commissioner as exempt under section 84(4)(a);
    (f)   a person to whom section 84(4)(d) applies; or
    (g)   a person employed by, or working under the supervision of, a person to whom paragraph (e) or (f) applies.

Complaints referred to designated professional bodies

10 (1) This paragraph applies if the Commissioner refers a complaint to a designated professional body under paragraph 9(1)(c).

(2)   The Commissioner may give directions setting a timetable to be followed by the designated professional body—

    (a)   in considering the complaint; and
    (b)   if appropriate, in taking disciplinary proceedings in connection with the complaint.

(3)   In making his annual report to the Secretary of State under paragraph 21, the Commissioner must take into account any failure of a designated professional body to comply (whether wholly or in part) with directions given to it under this paragraph.

(4)   Sub-paragraph (5) applies if the Commissioner or the Secretary of State considers that a designated professional body has persistently failed to comply with directions given to it under this paragraph.

(5)   The Commissioner must take the failure into account in determining whether to make a report under section 86(9)(b) and the Secretary of State must take it into account in determining whether to make an order under section 86(2).

NOTES

Initial Commencement
To be appointed
To be appointed: see s 170(4).

Appointment
Paras 1(1), (2), (4), 2(1)–(4), (6)–(8), 3(1)–(3), (5)–(7), 4, 5(1)–(3), 6(1): Appointment: 22 May 2000: see SI 2000/1282, art 2, Schedule.
Paras 1(3), 2(5), 3(4), 5(4), (5), 6(2), (3), 7–10: Appointment: 30 October 2000: see SI 2000/1985, art 2, Schedule.

PART II
COMMISSIONER'S STATUS, REMUNERATION AND STAFF ETC

Status

11   (1)   The Commissioner is to be a corporation sole.

(2)   The Commissioner and the members of the Commissioner's staff are not to be regarded as the servants or agents of the Crown or as having any status, privilege or immunity of the Crown.

Period of office

12   (1)   The Commissioner—

(a)   is to hold office for a term of five years; but
(b)   may resign at any time by notice in writing given to the Secretary of State.

(2)   The Secretary of State may dismiss the Commissioner—

(a)   on the ground of incapacity or misconduct; or
(b)   if he is satisfied—
    (i)   that he has been convicted of a criminal offence; or
    (ii)   that a bankruptcy order has been made against him, or his estate has been sequestrated, or he has made a composition or arrangement with, or granted a trust deed for, his creditors.

(3)   The Commissioner is eligible for re-appointment when his term of office ends.

Terms and conditions of appointment

13   Subject to the provisions of this Schedule, the Commissioner is to hold office on such terms and conditions as the Secretary of State may determine.

Remuneration, expenses and pensions

14 (1) There is to be paid to the Commissioner such remuneration and expenses as the Secretary of State may determine.

(2) The Secretary of State may pay, or provide for the payment of, such pensions, allowances or gratuities to or in respect of the Commissioner as he may determine.

Compensation

15 If a person ceases to be the Commissioner, otherwise than when his term of office ends, and it appears to the Secretary of State that there are special circumstances which make it right for him to receive compensation, the Secretary of State may make a payment to him of such amount as the Secretary of State may determine.

Deputy Commissioner

16 (1) The Secretary of State must appoint a person to act as Deputy Commissioner.

(2) During any vacancy in the office of Commissioner, or at any time when he is unable to discharge his functions, the Deputy Commissioner may act in his place.

(3) Paragraphs 11(2) and 12 to 15 apply to the Deputy Commissioner as they apply to the Commissioner.

Staff

17 (1) Subject to obtaining the approval of the Secretary of State as to numbers and terms and conditions of service, the Commissioner may appoint such staff as he considers appropriate.

(2) Subject to obtaining the approval of the Secretary of State, the Commissioner may pay, or provide for the payment of, such pensions, allowances or gratuities (including by way of compensation for loss of office or employment) to or in respect of his staff as he considers appropriate.

(3) Any functions of the Commissioner may, to the extent authorised by him, be performed by the Deputy Commissioner or any of his staff.

(4) The Employers' Liability (Compulsory Insurance) Act 1969 is not to require insurance to be effected by the Commissioner.

Expenditure

18 The Secretary of State may pay to the Commissioner—

(a) any expenses incurred or to be incurred by the Commissioner in respect of his staff; and
(b) with the approval of the Treasury, such other sums for enabling the Commissioner to perform his functions as the Secretary of State thinks fit.

Receipts

19 (1) Subject to any general or specific directions given to him by the Secretary of State, sums received by the Commissioner in the exercise of his functions must be paid to the Secretary of State.

(2) Sums received by the Secretary of State under this paragraph must be paid into the Consolidated Fund.

(3)   The approval of the Treasury is required for any direction given under this paragraph.

Accounts and records

20   (1)   The Commissioner must—

(a)   keep proper accounts and proper records in relation to his accounts;

(b)   prepare a statement of accounts for each financial year; and

(c)   send copies of the statement to the Secretary of State and to the Comptroller and Auditor General on or before the specified date.

(2)   The statement of accounts must be in such form as the Secretary of State may, with the approval of the Treasury, direct.

(3)   The Comptroller and Auditor General must—

(a)   examine, certify and report on each statement received by him under this paragraph; and

(b)   lay copies of each statement and of his report before each House of Parliament.

(4)   "Financial year" means the period of 12 months beginning with 1st April.

(5)   "Specified date" means—

(a)   31st August next following the end of the year to which the statement relates; or

(b)   such earlier date after the end of that year as the Treasury may direct.

Annual report

21   (1)   The Commissioner must, as soon as is practicable after the end of each financial year, report to the Secretary of State on the performance of his functions in that year.

(2)   The report must, in particular, set out the Commissioner's opinion as to the extent to which each designated professional body has provided effective regulation of its members in their provision of immigration advice or immigration services.

(3)   The Secretary of State must lay a copy of the report before each House of Parliament.

(4)   "Financial year" has the same meaning as in paragraph 20.

Proof of instruments

22   A document purporting to be an instrument issued by the Commissioner and to be signed by or on behalf of the Commissioner is to be received in evidence and treated as such an instrument unless the contrary is shown.

Disqualification for House of Commons

23   In Part III of Schedule 1 to the House of Commons Disqualification Act 1975 (offices disqualifying for membership), insert at the appropriate place—

"The Immigration Services Commissioner

The Deputy Immigration Services Commissioner".

Disqualification for Northern Ireland Assembly

24 In Part III of Schedule 1 to the Northern Ireland Assembly Disqualification Act 1975 (offices disqualifying for membership), insert at the appropriate place—

"The Immigration Services Commissioner

The Deputy Immigration Services Commissioner".

The Parliamentary Commissioner Act 1967 (c 13)

25 In Schedule 2 of the Parliamentary Commissioner Act 1967 (departments and authorities subject to investigation) insert, at the appropriate place, "The Immigration Services Commissioner".

NOTES

Initial Commencement
To be appointed
To be appointed: see s 170(4).

Appointment
Appointment: 22 May 2000: see SI 2000/1282, art 2, Schedule.

SCHEDULE 6
Registration

Section 85(3)

Applications for registration

1 (1) An application for registration under section 84(2)(a) or (b) must—

(a)   be made to the Commissioner in such form and manner, and
(b)   be accompanied by such information and supporting evidence,

as the Commissioner may from time to time determine.

(2) When considering an application for registration, the Commissioner may require the applicant to provide him with such further information or supporting evidence as the Commissioner may reasonably require.

Registration

2 (1) If the Commissioner considers that an applicant for registration is competent and otherwise fit to provide immigration advice and immigration services, he must register the applicant.

(2) Registration may be made so as to have effect—

(a)   only in relation to a specified field of advice or services;
(b)   only in relation to the provision of advice or services to a specified category of person;
(c)   only in relation to the provision of advice or services to a member of a specified category of person; or
(d)   only in specified circumstances.

Review of qualifications

3 (1) At such intervals as the Commissioner may determine, each registered person must submit an application for his registration to be continued.

(2)   Different intervals may be fixed by the Commissioner in relation to different registered persons or descriptions of registered person.

(3)   An application for continued registration must—

  (a)   be made to the Commissioner in such form and manner, and
  (b)   be accompanied by such information and supporting evidence,

as the Commissioner may from time to time determine.

(4)   When considering an application for continued registration, the Commissioner may require the applicant to provide him with such further information or supporting evidence as the Commissioner may reasonably require.

(5)   If the Commissioner considers that an applicant for continued registration is no longer competent or is otherwise unfit to provide immigration advice or immigration services, he must cancel the applicant's registration.

(6)   Otherwise, the Commissioner must continue the applicant's registration but may, in doing so, vary the registration—

  (a)   so as to make it have limited effect in any of the ways mentioned in paragraph 2(2); or
  (b)   so as to make it have full effect.

(7)   If a registered person fails, without reasonable excuse—

  (a)   to make an application for continued registration as required by sub-paragraph (1) or by a direction given by the Tribunal under section 89(3)(b), or
  (b)   to provide further information or evidence under sub-paragraph (4),

the Commissioner may cancel the person's registration as from such date as he may determine.

Disqualification of certain persons

4   A person convicted of an offence under section 25 or 26(1)(d) or (g) of the 1971 Act is disqualified for registration under paragraph 2 or for continued registration under paragraph 3.

Fees

5   (1) The Secretary of State may by order specify fees for the registration or continued registration of persons on the register.

(2)   No application under paragraph 1 or 3 is to be entertained by the Commissioner unless it is accompanied by the specified fee.

Open registers

6   (1) The register must be made available for inspection by members of the public in a legible form at reasonable hours.

(2)   A copy of the register or of any entry in the register must be provided—

  (a)   on payment of a reasonable fee;
  (b)   in written or electronic form; and
  (c)   in a legible form.

(3)   Sub-paragraphs (1) and (2) also apply to—

    (a) the record kept by the Commissioner of the persons to whom he has issued a certificate of exemption under section 84(4)(a); and

    (b) the record kept by the Commissioner of the persons against whom there is in force a direction given by the Tribunal under section 89(8).

NOTES

Initial Commencement
To be appointed
To be appointed: see s 170(4).

Appointment
Paras 1–4, 5(2), 6: Appointment: 30 October 2000: see SI 2000/1985, art 2, Schedule.
Para 5(1): Appointment (for the purposes of enabling subordinate legislation to be made): 1 August 2000: see SI 2000/1985, art 2, Schedule.
Para 5(1): Appointment (for remaining purposes): 30 October 2000: see SI 2000/1985, art 2, Schedule.

Subordinate Legislation
Immigration Services Commissioner (Registration Fee) Order 2000, SI 2000/2735 (made under para 5(1)).

SCHEDULE 7
The Immigration Services Tribunal

Section 87(5)

Members

1   (1) The Tribunal is to consist of such number of members as the Lord Chancellor may determine.

(2)   The members are to be appointed by the Lord Chancellor.

(3)   A person may be appointed as a member only if—

    (a) he is legally qualified; or
    (b) he appears to the Lord Chancellor to have had substantial experience in immigration services or in the law and procedure relating to immigration.

The President

2   The Tribunal is to have a President appointed by the Lord Chancellor from among those of its members who are legally qualified.

Terms and conditions of appointment

3   (1) Each member is to hold and vacate office in accordance with the terms of his appointment.

(2)   A member is eligible for re-appointment when his term of office ends.

(3)   A member may resign at any time by notice in writing given to the Lord Chancellor.

(4)   The Lord Chancellor may dismiss a member on the ground of incapacity or misconduct.

Remuneration and expenses

4   The Lord Chancellor may pay to any member such remuneration and expenses as he may determine.

Proceedings

5   The Tribunal is to sit at such times and in such places as the Lord Chancellor may direct.

6   (1) The Commissioner is entitled to be represented before the Tribunal, in relation to the hearing of appeals or disciplinary charges, by such persons as he may authorise.

(2)   The Commissioner may authorise a person to represent him before the Tribunal in relation to—

(a)   specified proceedings; or
(b)   all or specified categories of proceedings.

(3)   "Specified" means specified by the Commissioner.

Rules of procedure

7   (1) The Lord Chancellor may make rules as to the procedure and practice to be followed in relation to the exercise of the Tribunal's functions.

(2)   Before making or altering any such rules, the Lord Chancellor must consult the Scottish Ministers.

(3)   Subject to the provisions of this Schedule and the rules, the Tribunal may determine its own procedure.

(4)   The rules must make provision for any person appealing to the Tribunal or otherwise subject to its jurisdiction to be entitled to be legally represented.

(5)   The rules may, in particular, make provision—

(a)   as to the mode and burden of proof and the giving and admissibility of evidence;
(b)   for proceedings before the Tribunal to be capable of being determined in the absence of any party to the proceedings if that party has failed, without reasonable excuse, to appear before the Tribunal or has failed to comply with any reasonable directions given by the Tribunal as to the conduct of the proceedings;
(c)   with respect to other matters preliminary or incidental to, or arising out of, any matter with respect to which the Tribunal is or may be exercising functions;
(d)   as to the period within which an appeal against a decision of the Commissioner can be brought;
(e)   authorising such functions of the Tribunal as may be specified in the rules to be exercised by a single member.

Suspending the effect of a relevant decision

8   (1) A relevant decision of the Commissioner is not to have effect while the period within which an appeal may be brought against the decision is running.

(2)   If the appellant applies to the Tribunal under this paragraph, the Tribunal may direct that while the appeal is being dealt with—

(a)   no effect is to be given to the decision appealed against; or
(b)   only such limited effect is to be given to it as may be specified in the direction.

(3)   Rules under paragraph 7 must include provision requiring the Tribunal to consider applications by the Commissioner for the cancellation or variation of directions given under this paragraph.

Staff

9   (1) The Lord Chancellor may appoint such staff for the Tribunal as he considers appropriate.

(2)   The Lord Chancellor may pay, or provide for the payment of, such pensions, allowances or gratuities (including by way of compensation for loss of office or employment) to or in respect of the Tribunal's staff as he considers appropriate.

Expenditure

10   The Lord Chancellor may pay such other expenses of the Tribunal as he considers appropriate.

Meaning of "legally qualified"

11   A person is legally qualified for the purposes of this Schedule if—

(a)   he has a 7 year general qualification, within the meaning of section 71 of the Courts and Legal Services Act 1990;

(b)   he is an advocate or solicitor in Scotland of at least 7 years' standing; or

(c)   he is a member of the Bar of Northern Ireland or solicitor of the Supreme Court of Northern Ireland of at least 7 years' standing.

Disqualification for House of Commons

12   In Part I of Schedule 1 to the House of Commons Disqualification Act 1975 (offices disqualifying for membership), insert at the appropriate place—

"Member of the Immigration Services Tribunal".

Disqualification for Northern Ireland Assembly

13   In Part I of Schedule 1 to the Northern Ireland Assembly Disqualification Act 1975 (offices disqualifying for membership), insert at the appropriate place—

"Member of the Immigration Services Tribunal".

NOTES

Initial Commencement
To be appointed
To be appointed: see s 170(4).

Appointment
Paras 1–6, 8(1), (2), 9–13: Appointment: 30 October 2000: see SI 2000/1985, art 2, Schedule.
Paras 7, 8(3): Appointment: 1 August 2000: see SI 2000/1985, art 2, Schedule.

Subordinate Legislation
Immigration Services Tribunal Rules 2000, SI 2000/2739 (made under paras 7, 8(3)).

SCHEDULE 8
Provision of Support: Regulations

Section 95(12)

General regulation-making power

1   The Secretary of State may by regulations make such further provision with respect to the powers conferred on him by section 95 as he considers appropriate.

Determining whether a person is destitute

2   (1) The regulations may provide, in connection with determining whether a person is destitute, for the Secretary of State to take into account, except in such circumstances (if any) as may be prescribed—

(a)   income which the person concerned, or any dependant of his, has or might reasonably be expected to have, and

(b)   support which is, or assets of a prescribed kind which are, or might reasonably be expected to be, available to him or to any dependant of his,

otherwise than by way of support provided under section 95.

(2) The regulations may provide that in such circumstances (if any) as may be prescribed, a person is not to be treated as destitute for the purposes of section 95.

Prescribed levels of support

3   The regulations may make provision—

(a)   as to the circumstances in which the Secretary of State may, as a general rule, be expected to provide support in accordance with prescribed levels or of a prescribed kind;

(b)   as to the circumstances in which the Secretary of State may, as a general rule, be expected to provide support otherwise than in accordance with the prescribed levels.

Provision of items and services

4   The regulations may make provision for prescribed items or services to be provided or made available to persons receiving support under section 95 for such purposes and in such circumstances as may be prescribed.

Support and assets to be taken into account

5   The regulations may make provision requiring the Secretary of State, except in such circumstances (if any) as may be prescribed, to take into account, when deciding the level or kind of support to be provided—

(a)   income which the person concerned, or any dependant of his, has or might reasonably be expected to have, and

(b)   support which is, or assets of a prescribed kind which are, or might reasonably be expected to be, available to him or to any dependant of his,

otherwise than by way of support provided under section 95.

Valuation of assets

6   The regulations may make provision as to the valuation of assets.

Breach of conditions

7   The regulations may make provision for the Secretary of State to take into account, when deciding—

(a)   whether to provide, or to continue to provide, support under section 95, or

(b)   the level or kind of support to be provided,

the extent to which any condition on which support is being, or has previously been, provided has been complied with.

Suspension or discontinuation of support

8 (1) The regulations may make provision for the suspension or discontinuance of support under section 95 in prescribed circumstances (including circumstances in which the Secretary of State would otherwise be under a duty to provide support).

(2) The circumstances which may be prescribed include the cessation of residence—

(a) in accommodation provided under section 95; or
(b) at an address notified to the Secretary of State in accordance with the regulations.

Notice to quit

9 (1) The regulations may provide that if—

(a) as a result of support provided under section 95, a person has a tenancy or a licence to occupy accommodation,
(b) one or more of the conditions mentioned in sub-paragraph (2) are satisfied, and
(c) he is given such notice to quit as may be prescribed by the regulations,

his tenancy or licence is to be treated as ending with the period specified in that notice, regardless of when it could otherwise be brought to an end.

(2) The conditions are that—

(a) the support provided under section 95 is suspended or discontinued as a result of any provision of a kind mentioned in paragraph 8;
(b) the relevant claim for asylum has been determined;
(c) the supported person has ceased to be destitute;
(d) he is to be moved to other accommodation.

Contributions to support

10 The regulations may make provision requiring a supported person to make payments to the Secretary of State, in prescribed circumstances, by way of contributions to the cost of the provision of that support.

Recovery of sums by Secretary of State

11 (1) The regulations may provide for the recovery by the Secretary of State of sums representing the whole or part of the monetary value of support provided to a person under section 95 where it appears to the Secretary of State—

(a) that that person had, at the time when he applied for support, assets of any kind in the United Kingdom or elsewhere which were not capable of being realised; but
(b) that those assets have subsequently become, and remain, capable of being realised.

(2) An amount recoverable under regulations made by virtue of sub-paragraph (1) may be recovered—

(a) as if it were a debt due to the Secretary of State; or
(b) by such other method of recovery, including by deduction from support provided under section 95 as may be prescribed.

Procedure

12 The regulations may make provision with respect to procedural requirements including, in particular, provision as to—

(a) the procedure to be followed in making an application for support;
(b) the information which must be provided by the applicant;
(c) the circumstances in which an application may not be entertained;
(d) the making of further enquiries by the Secretary of State;
(e) the circumstances in which, and person by whom, a change of circumstances of a prescribed description must be notified to the Secretary of State.

NOTES

Initial Commencement
To be appointed
To be appointed: see s 170(4).

Appointment
Appointment: 1 January 2000: see SI 1999/3190, art 2, Schedule.

Subordinate Legislation
Asylum Support Regulations 2000, SI 2000/704.
Asylum Support (Amendment) Regulations 2000, SI 2000/3053 (made under para 3(a)).

SCHEDULE 9
Asylum Support: Interim Provisions

Section 95(13)

1 (1) The Secretary of State may by regulations make provision requiring prescribed local authorities or local authorities falling within a prescribed description of authority to provide support, during the interim period, to eligible persons.

(2) "Eligible persons" means—

(a) asylum-seekers, or
(b) their dependants,

who appear to be destitute or to be likely to become destitute within such period as may be prescribed.

(3) For the purposes of sub-paragraph (1), in Northern Ireland, a Health and Social Services Board established under Article 16 of the Health and Personal Social Services (Northern Ireland) Order 1972 is to be treated as a local authority.

2 (1) The regulations must provide for the question whether a person is an eligible person to be determined by the local authority concerned.

(2) The regulations may make provision for support to be provided, before the determination of that question, to a person making a claim for support under the regulations by the Secretary of State or such local authority as may be prescribed.

(3) "The local authority concerned" has such meaning as may be prescribed.

3 Subsections (3) to (8) of section 95 apply for the purposes of the regulations as they apply for the purposes of that section, but for the references in subsections (5) and (7) to the Secretary of State substitute references to the local authority concerned.

4 The regulations may prescribe circumstances in which support for an eligible person—

(a) must be provided;
(b) must or may be refused; or
(c) must or may be suspended or discontinued.

5 The regulations may provide that support—

(a) is to be provided in prescribed ways;

(b) is not to be provided in prescribed ways.

6 The regulations may include provision—

(a) as to the level of support that is to be provided;

(b) for support to be provided subject to conditions;

(c) requiring any such conditions to be set out in writing;

(d) requiring a copy of any such conditions to be given to such person as may be prescribed.

7 The regulations may make provision that, in providing support, a local authority—

(a) are to have regard to such matters as may be prescribed;

(b) are not to have regard to such matters as may be prescribed.

8 The regulations may include provision—

(a) prescribing particular areas, or descriptions of area, (which may include a locality within their own area) in which a local authority may not place asylum-seekers while providing support for them;

(b) prescribing circumstances in which a particular area, or description of area, (which may include a locality within their own area) is to be one in which a local authority may not place asylum-seekers while providing support for them;

(c) as to the circumstances (if any) in which any such provision is not to apply.

9 (1) The regulations may make provision for the referral by one local authority to another of a claim for support made under the regulations if the local authority to whom the claim is made consider that it is not manifestly unfounded but—

(a) they are providing support for a number of asylum-seekers equal to, or greater than, the maximum number of asylum-seekers applicable to them; or

(b) they are providing support for a number of eligible persons equal to, or greater than, the maximum number of eligible persons applicable to them.

(2) For the purposes of any provision made as a result of sub-paragraph (1), the regulations may make provision for the determination by the Secretary of State of—

(a) the applicable maximum number of asylum-seekers;

(b) the applicable maximum number of eligible persons.

(3) The regulations may make provision for any such determination to be made—

(a) for local authorities generally;

(b) for prescribed descriptions of local authority; or

(c) for particular local authorities.

(4) The regulations may provide that a referral may not be made—

(a) to a prescribed local authority;

(b) to local authorities of a prescribed description; or

(c) in prescribed circumstances.

(5) The regulations may make provision for the payment by a local authority of any reasonable travel or subsistence expenses incurred as a result of a referral made by them.

(6) The regulations may make provision for the transfer of a claim for support, or responsibility for providing support, under the regulations from one local authority to another on such terms as may be agreed between them.

(7) In exercising any power under the regulations to refer or transfer, a local authority must have regard to such guidance as may be issued by the Secretary of State with respect to the exercise of the power.

10   (1) The regulations may make provision for the referral of claims for support made to the Secretary of State to prescribed local authorities or local authorities of a prescribed description.

(2)   The regulations may make provision for the payment by the Secretary of State of any reasonable travel or subsistence expenses incurred as a result of a referral made by him as a result of provision made by virtue of sub-paragraph (1).

11   The regulations may make provision requiring prescribed local authorities or other prescribed bodies to give reasonable assistance to local authorities providing support under the regulations.

12   The regulations may make provision for the procedure for making and determining claims for support.

13   The regulations may make provision for an asylum-seeker or a dependant of an asylum-seeker who has received, or is receiving, any prescribed description of support from a local authority to be taken to have been accepted for support under the regulations by a prescribed local authority.

14   A person entitled to support under the regulations is not entitled to any prescribed description of support, except to such extent (if any) as may be prescribed.

15   "The interim period" means the period—

(a)   beginning on such day as may be prescribed for the purposes of this paragraph; and

(b)   ending on such day as may be so prescribed.

NOTES

Initial Commencement
Royal Assent
Royal Assent: 11 November 1999: see s 170(3)(r).

Subordinate Legislation
Asylum Support (Interim Provisions) Regulations 1999, SI 1999/3056 (made under paras 1, 2, 4–7, 9, 11, 13–15).

SCHEDULE 10
Asylum Support Adjudicators

Section 102(3)

Adjudicators

1   (1) The Secretary of State must—

(a)   appoint such number of adjudicators as he considers necessary;
(b)   appoint one of the adjudicators to be the Chief Asylum Support Adjudicator; and
(c)   appoint one of the adjudicators to be the Deputy Chief Asylum Support Adjudicator ("the Deputy").

(2)   The adjudicators are to exercise their functions under the direction of the Chief Asylum Support Adjudicator.

(3)   The Chief Asylum Support Adjudicator is to have such other functions as the Secretary of State may from time to time direct.

(4)   During any vacancy in the office of Chief Asylum Support Adjudicator, or at any time when he is unable to discharge his functions, the Deputy may act in his place.

Terms and conditions of appointment

2 (1) Each adjudicator is to hold and vacate office in accordance with the terms of his appointment.

(2) An adjudicator is eligible for re-appointment when his term of office ends.

(3) An adjudicator may resign at any time by notice in writing given to the Secretary of State.

Remuneration, expenses and pensions

3 (1) The Secretary of State may pay to any adjudicator such remuneration and expenses as he may determine.

(2) The Secretary of State may pay, or provide for the payment of, such pensions, allowances or gratuities to or in respect of any adjudicator as he may determine.

Compensation

4 If a person ceases to be an adjudicator, otherwise than when his term of office ends, and it appears to the Secretary of State that there are special circumstances which make it right for him to receive compensation, the Secretary of State may make a payment to him of such amount as the Secretary of State may determine.

Staff

5 (1) The Secretary of State may appoint such staff for the adjudicators as he considers appropriate.

(2) The Secretary of State may pay, or provide for the payment of, such pensions, allowances or gratuities (including by way of compensation for loss of office or employment) to or in respect of the adjudicators' staff as he considers appropriate.

Expenditure

6 The Secretary of State may pay such other expenses of the adjudicators as he considers appropriate.

Proceedings

7 For the purpose of discharging their functions, adjudicators are to sit at such times and in such places as the Secretary of State may direct.

NOTES

Initial Commencement
To be appointed
To be appointed: see s 170(4).

SCHEDULE 11
Detainee Custody Officers

Section 154(7)

Obtaining certificates of authorisation by false pretences

1 A person who, for the purpose of obtaining a certificate of authorisation for himself or for any other person—

(a)   makes a statement which he knows to be false in a material particular, or
(b)   recklessly makes a statement which is false in a material particular,

is guilty of an offence and liable on summary conviction to a fine not exceeding level 4 on the standard scale.

Powers and duties of detainee custody officers

2   (1)   A detainee custody officer exercising custodial functions has power—

(a)   to search (in accordance with rules made by the Secretary of State) any detained person in relation to whom the officer is exercising custodial functions; and
(b)   to search any other person who is in, or is seeking to enter, any place where any such detained person is or is to be held, and any article in the possession of such a person.

(2)   The power conferred by sub-paragraph (1)(b) does not authorise requiring a person to remove any of his clothing other than an outer coat, jacket or glove.

(3)   As respects a detained person in relation to whom he is exercising custodial functions, it is the duty of a detainee custody officer—

(a)   to prevent that person's escape from lawful custody;
(b)   to prevent, or detect and report on, the commission or attempted commission by him of other unlawful acts;
(c)   to ensure good order and discipline on his part; and
(d)   to attend to his wellbeing.

(4)   The powers conferred by sub-paragraph (1), and the powers arising by virtue of sub-paragraph (3), include power to use reasonable force where necessary.

Short-term holding facilities

3   (1)   A detainee custody officer may perform functions of a custodial nature at a short-term holding facility (whether or not he is authorised to perform custodial functions at a detention centre).

(2)   When doing so, he is to have the same powers and duties in relation to the facility and persons detained there as he would have if the facility were a detention centre.

Assaulting a detainee custody officer

4   A person who assaults a detainee custody officer who is—

(a)   acting in accordance with escort arrangements,
(b)   performing custodial functions, or
(c)   performing functions of a custodial nature at a short-term holding facility,

is guilty of an offence and liable on summary conviction to a fine not exceeding level 5 on the standard scale or to imprisonment for a term not exceeding six months or to both.

Obstructing detainee custody officers

5   A person who resists or wilfully obstructs a detainee custody officer who is—

(a)   acting in accordance with escort arrangements,
(b)   performing custodial functions, or
(c)   performing functions of a custodial nature at a short-term holding facility,

is guilty of an offence and liable on summary conviction to a fine not exceeding level 3 on the standard scale.

Uniforms and badges

6   For the purposes of paragraphs 4 and 5, a detainee custody officer is not to be regarded as acting in accordance with escort arrangements at any time when he is not readily identifiable as such an officer (whether by means of a uniform or badge which he is wearing or otherwise).

Suspension and revocation of certificates of authorisation

7   (1) If it appears to the Secretary of State that a detainee custody officer is not a fit and proper person to perform escort functions or custodial functions, he may revoke that officer's certificate so far as it authorises the performance of those functions.

(2) If it appears to the escort monitor that a detainee custody officer is not a fit and proper person to perform escort functions, he may—

(a)   refer the matter to the Secretary of State; or
(b)   in such circumstances as may be prescribed, suspend the officer's certificate pending a decision by the Secretary of State as to whether to revoke it.

(3) If it appears to the contract monitor for the detention centre concerned that a detainee custody officer is not a fit and proper person to perform custodial functions, he may—

(a)   refer the matter to the Secretary of State; or
(b)   in such circumstances as may be prescribed, suspend the officer's certificate pending a decision by the Secretary of State as to whether to revoke it.

NOTES

Initial Commencement
To be appointed
To be appointed: see s 170(4).

Appointment
Paras 1, 7(1): Appointment: 3 April 2000: see SI 2000/464, art 2, Schedule.
Paras 2(1)(a), 7(2), (3): Appointment (for the purposes of enabling subordinate legislation to be made): 1 August 2000: see SI 2000/1985, art 2, Schedule.
Paras 2(1)(a), 7(2), (3): Appointment (for remaining purposes): 2 April 2001: see SI 2001/239, art 2, Schedule.
Paras 2(1)(b), (2)–(4), 3–6: Appointment: 2 April 2001: see SI 2001/239, art 2, Schedule.

Subordinate Legislation
Detention Centre Rules 2001, SI 2001/238 (made under para 2).
Immigration (Suspension of Detainee Custody Officer Certificate) Regulations 2001, SI 2001/241 (made under para 7(2), (3)).

SCHEDULE 12
Discipline etc at Detention Centres

Section 155(2)

Measuring and photographing detained persons

1   (1) Detention centre rules may (among other things) provide for detained persons to be measured and photographed.

(2)   The rules may, in particular, prescribe—

    (a)   the time or times at which detained persons are to be measured and photographed;

    (b)   the manner and dress in which they are to be measured and photographed; and

    (c)   the numbers of copies of measurements or photographs that are to be made and the persons to whom they are to be sent.

Testing for drugs or alcohol

2   (1)   If an authorisation is in force, a detainee custody officer may, at the centre to which the authorisation applies and in accordance with detention centre rules, require a detained person who is confined in the centre to provide a sample for the purpose of ascertaining—

    (a)   whether he has a drug in his body; or

    (b)   whether he has alcohol in his body.

(2)   The sample required may be one or more of the following—

    (a)   a sample of urine;

    (b)   a sample of breath;

    (c)   a sample of a specified description.

(3)   Sub-paragraph (2)(c)—

    (a)   applies only if the authorisation so provides; and

    (b)   does not authorise the taking of an intimate sample.

(4)   "Authorisation" means an authorisation given by the Secretary of State for the purposes of this paragraph in respect of a particular detention centre.

(5)   "Drug" means a drug which is a controlled drug for the purposes of the Misuse of Drugs Act 1971.

(6)   "Specified" means specified in the authorisation.

(7)   "Intimate sample"—

    (a)   in relation to England and Wales, has the same meaning as in Part V of the Police and Criminal Evidence Act 1984;

    (b)   in relation to Scotland, means—

        (i)   a sample of blood, semen or any other tissue fluid, urine or pubic hair;

        (ii)   a dental impression;

        (iii)   a swab taken from a person's body orifice other than the mouth; and

    (c)   in relation to Northern Ireland, has the same meaning as in Part VI of the Police and Criminal Evidence (Northern Ireland) Order 1989.

Medical examinations

3   (1)   This paragraph applies if—

    (a)   an authorisation is in force for a detention centre; and

    (b)   there are reasonable grounds for believing that a person detained in the centre is suffering from a disease which is specified in an order in force under sub-paragraph (7).

(2)   A detainee custody officer may require the detained person to submit to a medical examination at the centre.

(3)   The medical examination must be conducted in accordance with detention centre rules.

(4)   A detained person who fails, without reasonable excuse, to submit to a medical examination required under this paragraph is guilty of an offence.

(5)   A person guilty of an offence under sub-paragraph (4) is liable on summary conviction to imprisonment for a term not exceeding six months or to a fine not exceeding level 5 on the standard scale.

(6)   "Authorisation" means an authorisation given by the manager of the detention centre for the purpose of this paragraph.

(7)   The Secretary of State may by order specify any disease which he considers might, if a person detained in a detention centre were to suffer from it, endanger the health of others there.

Assisting detained persons to escape

4   (1)   A person who aids any detained person in escaping or attempting to escape from a detention centre or short-term holding facility is guilty of an offence.

(2)   A person who, with intent to facilitate the escape of any detained person from a detention centre or short-term holding facility—

- (a)   conveys any thing into the centre or facility or to a detained person,
- (b)   sends any thing (by post or otherwise) into the centre or facility or to a person detained there,
- (c)   places any thing anywhere outside the centre or facility with a view to its coming into the possession of a person detained there,

is guilty of an offence.

(3)   A person guilty of an offence under this section is liable—

- (a)   on summary conviction, to imprisonment for a term not exceeding six months or to a fine not exceeding the statutory maximum or to both; or
- (b)   on conviction on indictment, to imprisonment for a term not exceeding two years or to a fine or to both.

Alcohol

5   (1)   A person who, contrary to detention centre rules, brings or attempts to bring any alcohol into a detention centre, or to a detained person, is guilty of an offence.

(2)   A person who places alcohol anywhere outside a detention centre, intending that it should come into the possession of a detained person there, is guilty of an offence.

(3)   A detainee custody officer or any other person on the staff of a detention centre who, contrary to detention centre rules, allows alcohol to be sold or used in the centre is guilty of an offence.

(4)   A person guilty of an offence under this paragraph is liable on summary conviction to imprisonment for a term not exceeding six months or to a fine not exceeding level 3 on the standard scale or to both.

(5)   "Alcohol" means any spirituous or fermented liquor.

Introduction of other articles

6   (1)   A person who—

(a) conveys or attempts to convey any thing into or out of a detention centre or to a detained person, contrary to detention centre rules, and

(b) is not as a result guilty of an offence under paragraph 4 or 5,

is guilty of an offence under this paragraph.

(2)   A person who—

(a) places any thing anywhere outside a detention centre, intending it to come into the possession of a detained person, and

(b) is not as a result guilty of an offence under paragraph 4 or 5,

is guilty of an offence under this paragraph.

(3)   A person guilty of an offence under this paragraph is liable on summary conviction to a fine not exceeding level 3 on the standard scale.

Notice of penalties

7   (1) In the case of a contracted out detention centre, the contractor must cause a notice setting out the penalty to which a person committing an offence under paragraph 4, 5 or 6 is liable to be fixed outside the centre in a conspicuous place.

(2)   In the case of any other detention centre, the Secretary of State must cause such a notice to be fixed outside the centre in a conspicuous place.

8   (1) In the case of a contracted out short-term holding facility, the contractor must cause a notice setting out the penalty to which a person committing an offence under paragraph 4 is liable to be fixed outside the facility in a conspicuous place.

(2)   In the case of any other short-term holding facility, the Secretary of State must cause such a notice to be fixed outside the facility in a conspicuous place.

NOTES

Initial Commencement
To be appointed
To be appointed: see s 170(4).

Appointment
Paras 1, 2, 3(7): Appointment (for the purposes of enabling subordinate legislation to be made): 1 August 2000: see SI 2000/1985, art 2, Schedule.
Paras 1, 2, 3(7): Appointment (for remaining purposes): 2 April 2001: see SI 2001/239, art 2, Schedule.
Paras 3(1)–(6), 4–8: Appointment: 2 April 2001: see SI 2001/239, art 2, Schedule.

Subordinate Legislation
Detention Centre Rules 2001, SI 2001/238 (made under paras 1–3).
Detention Centre (Specified Diseases) Order 2001, SI 2001/240 (made under para 3(7)).

SCHEDULE 13
Escort Arrangements

Section 156(5)

Monitoring of escort arrangements

1   (1) Escort arrangements must include provision for the appointment of a Crown servant as escort monitor.

(2)   The escort monitor must—

   (a)   keep the escort arrangements under review and report on them to the Secretary of State as required in accordance with the arrangements;

   (b)   from time to time inspect the conditions in which detained persons are transported or held in accordance with the escort arrangements;

   (c)   make recommendations to the Secretary of State, with a view to improving those conditions, whenever he considers it appropriate to do so;

   (d)   investigate, and report to the Secretary of State on, any allegation made against a detainee custody officer or prisoner custody officer in respect of any act done, or failure to act, when carrying out functions under the arrangements;

(3)   Paragraph (d) of sub-paragraph (2) does not apply in relation to—

   (a)   detainee custody officers employed as part of the Secretary of State's staff; or

   (b)   an act or omission of a prisoner custody officer so far as it falls to be investigated by a prisoner escort monitor under section 81 of the Criminal Justice Act 1991 or under section 103 or 119 of the Criminal Justice and Public Order Act 1994.

Powers and duties of detainee custody officers

2   (1)   A detainee custody officer acting in accordance with escort arrangements has power—

   (a)   to search (in accordance with rules made by the Secretary of State) any detained person for whose delivery or custody the officer is responsible in accordance with the arrangements; and

   (b)   to search any other person who is in, or is seeking to enter, any place where any such detained person is or is to be held, and any article in the possession of such a person.

(2)   The power conferred by sub-paragraph (1)(b) does not authorise requiring a person to remove any of his clothing other than an outer coat, jacket or glove.

(3)   As respects a detained person for whose delivery or custody he is responsible in accordance with escort arrangements, it is the duty of a detainee custody officer—

   (a)   to prevent that person's escape from lawful custody;

   (b)   to prevent, or detect and report on, the commission or attempted commission by him of other unlawful acts;

   (c)   to ensure good order and discipline on his part; and

   (d)   to attend to his wellbeing.

(4)   The Secretary of State may make rules with respect to the performance by detainee custody officers of their duty under sub-paragraph (3)(d).

(5)   The powers conferred by sub-paragraph (1), and the powers arising by virtue of sub-paragraph (3), include power to use reasonable force where necessary.

Breaches of discipline

3   (1)   Sub-paragraph (2) applies if a detained person for whose delivery or custody a person ("A") has been responsible in accordance with escort arrangements is delivered to a detention centre.

(2)   The detained person is to be treated, for the purposes of such detention centre rules as relate to disciplinary offences, as if he had been in the custody of the director of the detention centre at all times while A was so responsible.

(3)   Sub-paragraph (4) applies if a detained person for whose delivery or custody a person ("B") has been responsible in accordance with escort arrangements is delivered to a prison.

(4)   The detained person is to be treated, for the purposes of such prison rules as relate to disciplinary offences, as if he had been in the custody of the governor or controller of the prison at all times while B was so responsible.

(5)   "Director" means—

(a)   in the case of a contracted out detention centre, the person appointed by the Secretary of State in relation to the centre under section 149 or such other person as the Secretary of State may appoint for the purposes of this paragraph;
(b)   in the case of any other detention centre, the manager of the detention centre.

(6)   This paragraph does not authorise the punishment of a detained person under detention centre rules or prison rules in respect of any act or omission of his for which he has already been punished by a court.

(7)   "Prison rules" means—

(a)   rules made under section 47 of the Prison Act 1952;
(b)   rules made under section 19 of the Prisons (Scotland) Act 1989;
(c)   rules made under section 13 of the Prison Act (Northern Ireland) 1953.

NOTES

Initial Commencement
To be appointed
To be appointed: see s 170(4).

Appointment
Paras 1, 2(1)(b), (2), (3), (5), 3: Appointment: 2 April 2001: see SI 2001/239, art 2, Schedule.
Para 2(1)(a), (4): Appointment (for the purposes of enabling subordinate legislation to be made): 1 August 2000: see SI 2000/1985, art 2, Schedule.
Para 2(1)(a), (4): Appointment (for remaining purposes): 2 April 2001: see SI 2001/239, art 2, Schedule.

Subordinate Legislation
Detention Centre Rules 2001, SI 2001/238 (made under para 2).

SCHEDULE 14
Consequential Amendments

Section 169(1)

The Marriages (Ireland) Act 1844 (c 81)

1   In Schedule (B) to the Marriages (Ireland) Act 1844, in the fifth column, after "Dwelling Place" insert "and Nationality".

The Marriage Law (Ireland) Amendment Act 1863 (c 27)

2   In Schedule (A) to the Marriage Law (Ireland) Amendment Act 1863, in the fifth column, after "Dwelling Place" insert "and Nationality".

The Marriage Act 1949 (c 76)

3   The Marriage Act 1949 is amended as follows.

4   In section 3(1) (marriages of persons under 21)—

(a)   for "a certificate" substitute "certificates"; and
(b)   omit "whether by licence or without licence,".

5   In section 5 (methods of authorising marriages), in paragraph (d), for "a certificate" substitute "certificates".

6   In section 17 (marriage under superintendent registrar's certificate)—

   (a)   for "a certificate" substitute "certificates"; and
   (b)   for "notice of marriage and certificate" substitute "notices of marriage and certificates".

7   In section 25 (void marriages)—

   (a)   in paragraph (b), for "a certificate" substitute "certificates";
   (b)   in paragraph (c), for "a certificate of a superintendent registrar which is" substitute "certificates of a superintendent registrar which are"; and
   (c)   in paragraph (d), for "a certificate" substitute "certificates" and for "notice of marriage and certificate" substitute "notices of marriage and certificates".

8   In section 27(1) (notice of marriage), for "a certificate" substitute "certificates".

9   In section 27A (additional information required in certain cases)—

   (a)   in subsections (2) and (3), for the first "the notice" substitute "each notice";
   (b)   in subsection (4), for the first "The person" substitute "Each person"; and
   (c)   in subsection (6), for "either" substitute "each".

10   In section 27B (provisions relating to section 1(3) marriages)—

   (a)   in subsection (1), for "a certificate" substitute "certificates";
   (b)   in subsections (4) and (6), omit "or licence"; and
   (c)   in subsection (5), omit ", or certificate and licence,".

11   In section 28(1) (declaration to accompany notice of marriage), omit "or licence" and for paragraph (b) substitute—

   "(b)   that the persons to be married have for the period of 7 days immediately before the giving of the notice had their usual places of residence within the registration district or registration districts in which notice is given;".

12   In section 29 (caveat against issue of certificate or licence), omit every "or licence".

13   In section 30 (provision for issue of certificate to be forbidden) for first "a certificate" substitute "certificates".

14   In section 31 (marriage certificates)—

   (a)   in subsections (1) and (4), for "a certificate" substitute "certificates"; and
   (b)   in subsection (5), for "one of the persons to be married" substitute "the person by whom notice of marriage was given".

15   For section 33 substitute—

"33 Period of validity of certificate

(1)   A marriage may be solemnized on the authority of certificates of a superintendent registrar at any time within the period which is the applicable period in relation to that marriage.

(2)   If the marriage is not solemnized within the applicable period—

   (a)   the notices of marriage and the certificates are void; and
   (b)   no person may solemnize the marriage on the authority of those certificates.

(3)   The applicable period, in relation to a marriage, is the period beginning with the day on which the notice of marriage was entered in the marriage notice book and ending—

(a) in the case of a marriage which is to be solemnized in pursuance of section 26(1)(dd), 37 or 38, on the expiry of three months; and

(b) in the case of any other marriage, on the expiry of twelve months.

(4) If the notices of marriage given by each person to be married are not given on the same date, the applicable period is to be calculated by reference to the earlier of the two dates."

16 For section 34 substitute—

"34 Marriages normally to be solemnized in registration district in which one party resides

Subject to section 35, a superintendent registrar may not issue a certificate for the solemnization of a marriage elsewhere in than within a registration district in which one of the persons to be married has resided for 7 days immediately before the giving of the notice of marriage."

17 (1) Section 35 (marriages in registration district in which neither party resides) is amended as follows.

(2) In subsection (1)—

(a) omit ", or if the marriage is to be by licence, a certificate and a licence,"; and

(b) for "or certificate and licence is issued" substitute "is issued in respect of each of the persons to be married".

(3) In subsections (2) and (4), omit "or, if the marriage is to be by licence, a certificate and a licence,".

(4) In subsections (2A) and (2B), omit "or, if the marriage is to be by licence, a certificate and licence,".

(5) In subsection (5)—

(a) for "a certificate" substitute "certificates";

(b) for "the notice" substitute "each notice"; and

(c) for "the certificate" substitute "each certificate".

18 Omit section 36 (superintendent registrar not normally to issue licences for marriages in registered buildings outside his district).

19 In section 37(1) (one party resident in Scotland)—

(a) for first "a certificate" substitute "certificates"; and

(b) omit "without licence".

20 (1) Section 38 (one party resident in Northern Ireland) is amended as follows.

(2) In subsection (1)—

(a) for "a certificate" substitute "certificates"; and

(b) omit "without licence".

(3) In subsection (2), for "and place of residence" substitute ", place of residence and nationality".

(4) In subsection (3), for "twenty-one" substitute "15".

21 In section 39(1) (issue of certificates on board Her Majesty's ships)—

(a) for first "a certificate" substitute "certificates"; and

(b) omit "without licence".

22 In section 40 (forms of certificates for marriage), omit subsection (2).

23 In section 44(1) (solemnization of marriage in registered buildings), for "a notice of marriage and certificate" substitute "the notices of marriage and certificates".

24 In section 45(1) (solemnization of marriage in register office)—

    (a) for "a certificate" substitute "certificates";
    (b) for first "notice" substitute "notices";
    (c) for "notice has" substitute "notices have"; and
    (d) for "certificate or certificate and licence, as the case may be, has or" substitute "certificates".

25 In section 47(2) (marriages according to usages of Society of Friends), in paragraph (a), for "the person" substitute "each person".

26 In section 48(1) (proof of certain matters not necessary to validity of marriages), in paragraph (a), for "notice" substitute "notices".

27 In section 49 (void marriages)—

    (a) in paragraph (b), after "issued" insert ", in respect of each of the persons to be married,";
    (b) omit paragraph (c);
    (c) in paragraph (d), for "a certificate which is" substitute "certificates which are"; and
    (d) in paragraph (e), for "notice" substitute "notices" and for "certificate" substitute "certificates".

28 In section 50 (person to whom certificate to be delivered)—

    (a) in subsection (1), for "a certificate" substitute "certificates" and omit "the certificate or, if notice of marriage has been given to more than one superintendent registrar,";
    (b) omit subsection (2); and
    (c) in subsection (3), for "certificate or certificate and licence, as the case may be," substitute "certificates".

29 In section 51(1) (fees of registrars for attending marriages), omit from first "the sum" to "case,".

30 (1) Section 75 (offences relating to solemnization of marriages) is amended as follows.

(2) In subsection (1)(b), for "a certificate" substitute "certificates".

(3) In subsection (2)—

    (a) in paragraph (a)(ii), for "notice of marriage and certificate" substitute "notices of marriage and certificates";
    (b) in paragraph (d), for "a certificate" substitute "certificates" and for from "(not being" to "book" substitute "before the expiry of the waiting period in relation to each notice of marriage"; and
    (c) in paragraph (e), for "a certificate" substitute "certificates".

(4) After subsection (2), insert—

"(2A) In subsection (2)(d) "the waiting period" has the same meaning as in section 31(4A)."

(5) In subsection (3), for paragraph (a) substitute—

"(a) issues any certificate for marriage before the expiry of 15 days from the day on which the notice of marriage was entered in the marriage notice book;".

(6) In subsection (3), in paragraph (b), omit "or licence".

31   In section 78(3) (interpretation), in paragraph (a), for "the notice" substitute "each notice".

32   In Schedule 4 (provisions of Act which are excluded or modified in their application to naval, military and air force chapels), in Part III (exclusion of provisions relating to marriages otherwise than according to the rites of the Church of England), omit "The proviso to subsection (2) of section twenty-six".

The Prison Act 1952 (c 52)

33   In section 55 of the Prison Act 1952 (provisions extending to Scotland) at the end insert—

"(4A)   Subsections (2) to (5) of section 5A, as applied by subsection (5A) of that section, extend to Scotland."

The Firearms Act 1968 (c 27)

34   The Firearms Act 1968 is amended as follows.

35   In Schedule 1 (offences for which there is an additional penalty if committed when in possession of a firearm), after paragraph 5B insert—

"5C An offence under paragraph 4 of Schedule 11 to the Immigration and Asylum Act 1999 (assaulting a detainee custody officer)."

36   In Schedule 2 (which lists corresponding Scottish offences), after paragraph 13A insert—

"13B   An offence under paragraph 4 of Schedule 11 to the Immigration and Asylum Act 1999 (assaulting a detainee custody officer)."

The Family Law Reform Act 1969 (c 46)

37   In section 2(3) (provisions relating to marriage), omit "or licence" in both cases.

The Marriage (Registrar General's Licence) Act 1970 (c 34)

38   The Marriage (Registrar General's Licence) Act 1970 is amended as follows.

39   In section 1(1) (marriages which may be solemnised by Registrar General's licence), for "a certificate" substitute "certificates".

40   In section 5 (caveat against issue of Registrar General's licence), omit "or licence".

41   In section 6 (marriage of persons under 18), for "a certificate" substitute "certificates".

42   In section 13 (void marriages)—

   (a)   in paragraph (a), for ""certificate" substitute ""certificates" and for ""Registrar" substitute ""a Registrar"; and
   (b)   omit paragraph (b).

The Immigration Act 1971 (c 77)

43   The 1971 Act is amended as follows.

44   (1) In section 3 (general provisions for regulation and control), in subsection (1)(a), after "in accordance with" insert "the provisions of, or made under,".

(2)   In section 3, for subsection (5) substitute—

"(5) A person who is not a British citizen is liable to deportation from the United Kingdom if—

> (a)   the Secretary of State deems his deportation to be conducive to the public good; or
> (b)   another person to whose family he belongs is or has been ordered to be deported."

45   In section 4(1) (giving or refusal of leave to enter or remain to be in writing except where allowed by the Act) for "allowed by" substitute "allowed by or under".

46   In section 7(1) (exemption of certain residents from deportation)—

> (a)   in paragraph (a), for "3(5)(b)" substitute "3(5)(a)"; and
> (b)   in paragraph (b), for ", (b) or (c)" substitute "or (b) or 10 of the Immigration and Asylum Act 1999".

47   (1)   Section 10 (entry otherwise than by sea or air) is amended as follows.

(2)   In subsection (1), omit from "and any such Order" to the end.

(3)   After subsection (1), insert—

"(1A)   Her Majesty may by Order in Council direct that paragraph 27B or 27C of Schedule 2 shall have effect in relation to trains or vehicles as it has effect in relation to ships or aircraft.

(1B) Any Order in Council under this section may make—

> (a)   such adaptations or modifications of the provisions concerned, and
> (b)   such supplementary provisions,

as appear to Her Majesty to be necessary or expedient for the purposes of the Order."

(4)   In subsection (2), for "this section" substitute "subsection (1)".

48   In section 11(1) (entry to the United Kingdom), at the end insert "or by Part III of the Immigration and Asylum Act 1999".

49   Omit Part II.

50   In section 24 (illegal entry and similar offences), omit subsections (1)(aa) and (2).

51   In section 25 (assisting illegal entry and harbouring), omit subsection (3).

52   (1)   Section 27 (offences by persons connected with ships or aircraft) is amended as follows.

(2)   In paragraph (a)(ii), after "Schedule 2 or 3" insert "or under the Immigration and Asylum Act 1999".

(3)   In paragraph (b)(iii)—

> (a)   after "arrangements for" insert "or in connection with"; and
> (b)   at the end insert—
> "or under the Immigration and Asylum Act 1999; or
> (iv)   he fails, without reasonable excuse, to comply with the requirements of paragraph 27B or 27C of Schedule 2;".

53   In section 28(1) (time limits for proceedings) after "24," insert "24A,".

54   (1)   Section 32 (proof of documents) is amended as follows.

(2)   In subsection (2)—

(a) for "this Act" substitute "the Immigration Acts"; and

(b) after second "by him" insert "or on his behalf".

(3)   In subsection (3), for "proceedings under Part II of this Act" substitute "other proceedings under the Immigration Acts".

(4)   In subsection (4)—

(a) for first "this Act" substitute "the Immigration Acts"; and

(b) for "proceedings under Part II of this Act" substitute "other proceedings under the Immigration Acts".

(5)   After subsection (4) insert—

"(5) "Immigration Acts" has the same meaning as in the Immigration and Asylum Act 1999."

(6)   The amendments made by sub-paragraphs (2)(a) and (5) apply whenever the document in question was made or issued.

55   In section 33 (interpretation), for subsection (4) substitute—

"(4) For the purposes of this Act, the question of whether an appeal is pending shall be determined—

(a) in relation to an appeal to the Special Immigration Appeals Commission, in accordance with section 7A of the Special Immigration Appeals Commission Act 1997;

(b) in any other case, in accordance with section 58(5) to (10) of the Immigration and Asylum Act 1999".

56   In Schedule 2 (administrative provisions as to control on entry), in paragraph 2(1) (purposes for which persons arriving in the United Kingdom may be examined), for paragraph (c) substitute—

"(c) whether, if he may not—
  (i) he has been given leave which is still in force,
  (ii) he should be given leave and for what period or on what conditions (if any), or
  (iii) he should be refused leave."

57   In Schedule 2, after paragraph 2, insert—

"Examination of persons who arrive with continuing leave

2A   (1)   This paragraph applies to a person who has arrived in the United Kingdom with leave to enter which is in force but which was given to him before his arrival.

(2)   He may be examined by an immigration officer for the purpose of establishing—

(a) whether there has been such a change in the circumstances of his case, since that leave was given, that it should be cancelled;

(b) whether that leave was obtained as a result of false information given by him or his failure to disclose material facts; or

(c) whether there are medical grounds on which that leave should be cancelled.

(3)   He may also be examined by an immigration officer for the purpose of determining whether it would be conducive to the public good for that leave to be cancelled.

(4)   He may also be examined by a medical inspector or by any qualified person carrying out a test or examination required by a medical inspector.

(5) A person examined under this paragraph may be required by the officer or inspector to submit to further examination.

(6) A requirement under sub-paragraph (5) does not prevent a person who arrives—

(a) as a transit passenger,
(b) as a member of the crew of a ship or aircraft, or
(c) for the purpose of joining a ship or aircraft as a member of the crew,

from leaving by his intended ship or aircraft.

(7) An immigration officer examining a person under this paragraph may by notice suspend his leave to enter until the examination is completed.

(8) An immigration officer may, on the completion of any examination of a person under this paragraph, cancel his leave to enter.

(9) Cancellation of a person's leave under sub-paragraph (8) is to be treated for the purposes of this Act and Part IV of the Immigration and Asylum Act 1999 as if he had been refused leave to enter at a time when he had a current entry clearance.

(10) A requirement imposed under sub-paragraph (5) and a notice given under sub-paragraph (7) must be in writing."

58 In Schedule 2, in paragraph 4(1) and (2) (production of information and documents in connection with examinations), after "paragraph 2" insert ", 2A".

59 In Schedule 2, for paragraph 7 substitute—

"Power to require medical examination after entry

7 (1) This paragraph applies if an immigration officer examining a person under paragraph 2 decides—

(a) that he may be given leave to enter the United Kingdom; but
(b) that a further medical test or examination may be required in the interests of public health.

(2) This paragraph also applies if an immigration officer examining a person under paragraph 2A decides—

(a) that his leave to enter the United Kingdom should not be cancelled; but
(b) that a further medical test or examination may be required in the interests of public health.

(3) The immigration officer may give the person concerned notice in writing requiring him—

(a) to report his arrival to such medical officer of health as may be specified in the notice; and
(b) to attend at such place and time and submit to such test or examination (if any), as that medical officer of health may require.

(4) In reaching a decision under paragraph (b) of sub-paragraph (1) or (2), the immigration officer must act on the advice of—

(a) a medical inspector; or
(b) if no medical inspector is available, a fully qualified medical practitioner."

60 In Schedule 2, in paragraph 16 (detention of persons liable to examination), after sub-paragraph (1), insert—

"(1A) A person whose leave to enter has been suspended under paragraph 2A may be detained under the authority of an immigration officer pending—

(a)   completion of his examination under that paragraph; and
(b)   a decision on whether to cancel his leave to enter."

61   In Schedule 2, in paragraph 18 (treatment of persons detained), after sub-paragraph (2) insert—

"(2A)   The power conferred by sub-paragraph (2) includes power to take fingerprints."

62   (1)   In Schedule 2, paragraph 21 (temporary admission of persons liable to detention) is amended as follows.

(2)   After sub-paragraph (2) insert—

"(2A)   The provisions that may be included in restrictions as to residence imposed under sub-paragraph (2) include provisions of such a description as may be prescribed by regulations made by the Secretary of State.

(2B) The regulations may, among other things, provide for the inclusion of provisions—

(a)   prohibiting residence in one or more particular areas;
(b)   requiring the person concerned to reside in accommodation provided under section 4 of the Immigration and Asylum Act 1999 and prohibiting him from being absent from that accommodation except in accordance with the restrictions imposed on him.

(2C) The regulations may provide that a particular description of provision may be imposed only for prescribed purposes.

(2D) The power to make regulations conferred by this paragraph is exercisable by statutory instrument and includes a power to make different provision for different cases.

(2E) But no regulations under this paragraph are to be made unless a draft of the regulations has been laid before Parliament and approved by a resolution of each House."

(3)   In sub-paragraph (3), after "2" insert "or 2A".

(4)   In sub-paragraph (4)(a), omit "under paragraph 2 above".

63   In Schedule 2, in paragraph 22 (temporary release of persons liable to detention), in sub-paragraph (1)(a), after "examination;" insert—

"(aa)   a person detained under paragraph 16(1A) above pending completion of his examination or a decision on whether to cancel his leave to enter;".

64   (1)   In Schedule 2, paragraph 26 (supplementary duties of those connected with ships or aircraft or with ports) is amended as follows.

(2)   In sub-paragraph (1), omit "and have not been given leave".

(3)   After sub-paragraph (1) insert—

"(1A)   Sub-paragraph (1) does not apply in such circumstances, if any, as the Secretary of State may by order prescribe."

(4)   After sub-paragraph (3) insert—

"(3A)   The power conferred by sub-paragraph (1A) is exercisable by statutory instrument; and any such instrument shall be subject to annulment by a resolution of either House of Parliament."

65   In Schedule 2, omit paragraph 28.

66 In Schedule 2, in paragraph 29, for "13(1), 16 or 17 of this Act" substitute "59, 65, 66, 67, 69(1) or (5) or 71 of the Immigration and Asylum Act 1999".

67 In Schedule 2, in paragraph 34 (grant of bail pending removal), in sub-paragraph (1), after "examination" insert ", detained under paragraph 16(1A) above pending completion of his examination or a decision on whether to cancel his leave to enter".

68 In Schedule 3, in paragraph 2(4) (application of certain provisions if person detained under Schedule 3), for "and 18" substitute ", 18 and 25A to 25E".

69 In Schedule 3 (supplementary provision as to deportation), in paragraph 3—

(a) for "16 or 17" substitute "66 or 67 of the Immigration and Asylum Act 1999";

(b) omit "in paragraph 28(2), (3) and (6) and"; and

(c) for "15(1)(a)" substitute "63(1)(a) or 69(4)(a) of the Immigration and Asylum Act 1999".

70 In Schedule 4 (integration of United Kingdom and Islands immigration law), for paragraph 3 (deportation) substitute—

"**3** (1) This Act has effect in relation to a person who is subject to an Islands deportation order as if the order were a deportation order made against him under this Act.

(2) Sub-paragraph (1) does not apply if the person concerned is—

(a) a British citizen;

(b) an EEA national;

(c) a member of the family of an EEA national; or

(d) a member of the family of a British citizen who is neither such a citizen nor an EEA national.

(3) The Secretary of State does not, as a result of sub-paragraph (1), have power to revoke an Islands deportation order.

(4) In any particular case, the Secretary of State may direct that paragraph (b), (c) or (d) of sub-paragraph (2) is not to apply in relation to the Islands deportation order.

(5) Nothing in this paragraph makes it unlawful for a person in respect of whom an Islands deportation order is in force in any of the Islands to enter the United Kingdom on his way from that island to a place outside the United Kingdom.

(6) "Islands deportation order" means an order made under the immigration laws of any of the Islands under which a person is, or has been, ordered to leave the island and forbidden to return.

(7) Subsections (10) and (12) to (14) of section 80 of the Immigration and Asylum Act 1999 apply for the purposes of this section as they apply for the purposes of that section."

The House of Commons Disqualification Act 1975 (c 24)

71 In Part III of Schedule 1 to the House of Commons Disqualification Act 1975 (disqualifying offices)—

(a) omit—

"Adjudicator appointed for the purposes of the Immigration Act 1971";
and

(b) at the appropriate places, insert—

"Adjudicator appointed for the purposes of the Immigration and Asylum Act 1999";
and

"Asylum Support Adjudicator".

The Northern Ireland Assembly Disqualification Act 1975 (c 25)

72   In Part III of Schedule 1 to the Northern Ireland Assembly Disqualification Act 1975 (disqualifying offices)—

    (a)   omit—

"Adjudicator appointed for the purposes of the Immigration Act 1971";
and
    (b)   at the appropriate places, insert—

"Adjudicator appointed for the purposes of the Immigration and Asylum Act 1999";
and

"Asylum Support Adjudicator".

The Protection from Eviction Act 1977 (c 43)

73   In section 3A of the Protection from Eviction Act 1977 (excluded tenancies and licences), after subsection (7), insert—

"(7A)   A tenancy or licence is excluded if it is granted in order to provide accommodation under Part VI of the Immigration and Asylum Act 1999."

The Education (Scotland) Act 1980 (c 44)

74   Section 53 of the Education (Scotland) Act 1980 (requirement to provide school meals etc) is amended as follows—

    (a)   in subsection (3)—
        (i)   for the words from the beginning to "an", where it occurs for the second time, substitute—

"(3) Subsection (3AA) below applies in relation to a pupil—

    (a)   whose parents are in receipt of—
        (i)   income support;
        (ii)   an income-based jobseeker's allowance (payable under the Jobseekers Act 1995); or
        (iii)   support provided under Part VI of the Immigration and Asylum Act 1999; or
    (b)   who is himself in receipt of income support or an income-based jobseeker's allowance.

(3AA)   An";
and
        (ii)   for "him", where it occurs for the first time, substitute "the pupil"; and
    (b)   in subsection (3A), for "Subsections (1), (2) and (3)" substitute "Subsections (1) to (3AA)".

The Firearms (Northern Ireland) Order 1981 (SI 1981/155 (NI 2))

75   In Schedule 1 to the Firearms (Northern Ireland) Order 1981 (offences for which there is an additional penalty if committed when in possession of a firearm), after paragraph 4 insert—

"**4A** An offence under paragraph 4 of Schedule 11 to the Immigration and Asylum Act 1999 (assaulting a detainee custody officer)."

The Magistrates' Courts (Northern Ireland) Order 1981 (SI 1981/1675 (NI 26))

76 In Article 98(11) of the Magistrates' Courts (Northern Ireland) Order 1981 (enforcement of orders for periodical payment of money), at the end, insert—

"(k) section 113 of the Immigration and Asylum Act 1999."

The Marriage Act 1983 (c 32)

77 In section 1 of the Marriage Act 1983 (marriages of house-bound and detained persons in England and Wales)—

    (a)   in subsection (1), for "a superintendent registrar's certificate" substitute "certificates of a superintendent registrar"; and

    (b)   in subsection (2)(a), for "the notice" substitute "each notice".

The Housing (Northern Ireland) Order 1983 (SI 1983/1118 (NI 15))

78 In Schedule 2 to the Housing (Northern Ireland) Order 1983 (tenancies which are not secure tenancies), after paragraph 3, insert—

"Accommodation for asylum-seekers

3A (1) A tenancy is not a secure tenancy if it is granted in order to provide accommodation under Part VI of the Immigration and Asylum Act 1999.

(2) A tenancy mentioned in sub-paragraph (1) becomes a secure tenancy if the landlord notifies the tenant that it is to be regarded as a secure tenancy."

The Rent (Scotland) Act 1984 (c 58)

79 In section 23A of the Rent (Scotland) Act 1984 (excluded tenancies and occupancy rights), after subsection (5) insert—

"(5A) Nothing in section 23 of this Act applies to a tenancy or right of occupancy if it is granted in order to provide accommodation under Part VI of the Immigration and Asylum Act 1999."

The Police and Criminal Evidence Act 1984 (c 60)

80 (1) The Police and Criminal Evidence Act 1984 is amended as follows.

(2) In section 8 (power of justice to authorise entry and search of premises), at the end insert—

"(6) This section applies in relation to a relevant offence (as defined in section 28D(4) of the Immigration Act 1971) as it applies in relation to a serious arrestable offence."

(3) In section 22 (retention), at the end insert—

"(6) This section also applies to anything retained by the police under section 28H(5) of the Immigration Act 1971."

(4) In section 61 (fingerprints), in subsection (9)(a), after "1971" insert ", section 141 of the Immigration and Asylum Act 1999 or regulations made under section 144 of that Act".

The Housing Act 1985 (c 68)

81   In Schedule 1 to the Housing Act 1985 (tenancies which cannot be secure tenancies), after paragraph 4, insert—

"Accommodation for asylum-seekers

4A   (1)   A tenancy is not a secure tenancy if it is granted in order to provide accommodation under Part VI of the Immigration and Asylum Act 1999.

(2)   A tenancy mentioned in sub-paragraph (1) becomes a secure tenancy if the landlord notifies the tenant that it is to be regarded as a secure tenancy."

The Housing (Scotland) Act 1987 (c 26)

82   In Schedule 2 to the Housing (Scotland) Act 1987 (tenancies which cannot be secure tenancies), after paragraph 5 insert—

"Accommodation for asylum-seekers

5A   (1)   A tenancy shall not be a secure tenancy if it is granted in order to provide accommodation under Part VI of the Immigration and Asylum Act 1999.

(2)   A tenancy mentioned in sub-paragraph (1) becomes a secure tenancy if the landlord notifies the tenant that it is to be regarded as a secure tenancy."

The Immigration Act 1988 (c 14)

83   The Immigration Act 1988 is amended as follows.

84   Omit section 5 (restricted right of appeal against deportation in cases of breach of limited leave).

85   Omit section 8 (examination of passengers before arrival).

86   Omit section 9 (charges).

The Housing (Scotland) Act 1988 (c 43)

87   In Schedule 4 to the Housing (Scotland) Act 1988 (tenancies which cannot be assured tenancies), after paragraph 11A insert—

"Accommodation for asylum-seekers

11B A tenancy granted under arrangements for the provision of support for asylum-seekers or dependants of asylum-seekers made under Part VI of the Immigration and Asylum Act 1999."

The Housing Act 1988 (c 50)

88   In Schedule 1 to the Housing Act 1988 (tenancies which are not assured tenancies), after paragraph 12, insert—

"Accommodation for asylum-seekers

12A (1)   tenancy granted by a private landlord under arrangements for the provision of support for asylum-seekers or dependants of asylum-seekers made under Part VI of the Immigration and Asylum Act 1999.

(2) "Private landlord" means a landlord who is not within section 80(1) of the Housing Act 1985."

The Prevention of Terrorism (Temporary Provisions) Act 1989 (c 4)

89 *(1) Paragraph 10 of Schedule 5 to the Prevention of Terrorism (Temporary Provisions) Act 1989 (requirements on captain of ship or aircraft with respect to passengers and crew) is amended as follows.*

(2) In sub-paragraph (4), for "unless he is subject to the requirements of an order under paragraph 27(2) of Schedule 2 to the Immigration Act 1971 and subject to sub-paragraph (6)" substitute "subject to sub-paragraphs (5A) and (6)".

(3) After sub-paragraph (5), insert—

"(5A) Sub-paragraph (4) above does not apply to the extent that the information mentioned in sub-paragraph (5) above is the subject of—

> *(a) an order under paragraph 27(2) of Schedule 2 to the Immigration Act 1971 in relation to the arrival of the ship or aircraft, or*
> *(b) a request made to the owner or agent of the ship or aircraft under paragraph 27B of that Schedule in relation to the arrival of the ship or aircraft."*

The Police and Criminal Evidence (Northern Ireland) Order 1989 (SI 1989/1341 (NI 12))

90 (1) The Police and Criminal Evidence (Northern Ireland) Order 1989 is amended as follows.

(2) In Article 10 (provision for Northern Ireland corresponding to section 8 of the 1984 Act), at the end insert—

"(6) This Article applies in relation to a relevant offence (as defined in section 28D(4) of the Immigration Act 1971) as it applies in relation to a serious arrestable offence."

(3) In Article 24 (provision for Northern Ireland corresponding to section 22 of the 1984 Act), at the end insert—

"(6) This Article also applies to anything retained by the police under section 28H(5) of the Immigration Act 1971."

(4) In Article 61 (fingerprints) in paragraph (9)(a), after "1971" insert ", section 141 of the Immigration and Asylum Act 1999 or regulations made under section 144 of that Act".

The Courts and Legal Services Act 1990 (c 41)

91 (1) The Courts and Legal Services Act 1990 is amended as follows.

(2) In Schedule 10 (judicial and other appointments), omit paragraph 34.

(3) In Schedule 11 (judges etc barred from legal practice), in the entry relating to the Immigration Appeal Tribunal, omit "appointed under Schedule 5 to the Immigration Act 1971" and after that entry insert—

"Adjudicator for the purposes of the Immigration and Asylum Act 1999 (other than Asylum Support Adjudicator)".

The Social Security Contributions and Benefits Act 1992 (c 4)

92 In the Social Security Contributions and Benefits Act 1992, omit section 146A (persons subject to immigration control).

The Social Security Contributions and Benefits (Northern Ireland) Act 1992 (c 7)

93 In the Social Security Contributions and Benefits (Northern Ireland) Act 1992, omit section 142A (persons subject to immigration control).

The Tribunals and Inquiries Act 1992 (c 53)

94 The Tribunals and Inquiries Act 1992 is amended as follows.

95 In Schedule 1 (tribunals under the supervision of the Council on Tribunals), after paragraph 2 insert—

"Asylum-seekers support   2A Asylum Support Adjudicators established under section 102 of the Immigration and Asylum Act 1999."

96 In Schedule 1, in paragraph 22—

    (a) in sub-paragraph (a), for "12 of the Immigration Act 1971" substitute" 57 of the Immigration and Asylum Act 1999"; and
    (b) in sub-paragraph (b), for "that section" substitute "section 56 of that Act".

97 In Schedule 1, after paragraph 22, insert—

"Asylum-seekers support   2A Asylum Support Adjudicators established under section 102 of the Immigration and Asylum Act 1999."

The Judicial Pensions and Retirement Act 1993 (c 8)

98 (1) The Judicial Pensions and Retirement Act 1993 is amended as follows.

(2) In Schedule 1 (offices which may be qualifying judicial offices), in Part II, for "Chief, or any other, immigration adjudicator under the Immigration Act 1971" substitute "Adjudicator for the purposes of the Immigration and Asylum Act 1999 (other than Asylum Support Adjudicator)".

(3) In Schedule 5 (relevant offices in relation to the retirement provisions), for "Immigration Adjudicator" substitute "Adjudicator for the purposes of the Immigration and Asylum Act 1999 (other than Asylum Support Adjudicator)".

(4) In Schedule 6 (retirement date for certain judicial offices), omit paragraphs 37 and 38.

The Asylum and Immigration Appeals Act 1993 (c 23)

99 The Asylum and Immigration Appeals Act 1993 is amended as follows.

100 Omit section 3 (fingerprinting).

101 Omit sections 4 and 5 and Schedule 1 (housing of asylum-seekers and their dependants).

102 (1) Omit section 6 (protection of asylum claimants from deportation etc).

(2) This paragraph is to be treated as having come into force on 26th July 1993.

103 Omit section 7 (curtailment of leave).

104 Omit sections 8, 9, 10 and 11 and Schedule 2 (which relate to appeals).

105 For paragraph (a) of section 9A(1) (bail pending appeal from Immigration Appeal Tribunal), substitute—

    "(a) has an appeal under Part IV of the Immigration and Asylum Act 1999 which is pending by reason of an appeal, or an application for leave to appeal;".

106 In section 9A(6), for "section 9 above" substitute "paragraph 23 of Schedule 4 of the Immigration and Asylum Act 1999".

107 Omit section 12 (carriers' liability).

The Asylum and Immigration Act 1996 (c 49)

108 The Asylum and Immigration Act 1996 is amended as follows.

109 Omit section 7 (power of arrest and search warrants).

110 Omit section 9 (entitlement to housing accommodation and assistance).

111 Omit section 10 (entitlement to child benefit).

112 Omit section 11 (saving for social security regulations).

113 Omit Schedule 1 (modifications of social security regulations).

114 In Schedule 2, omit sub-paragraphs (2) and (3) of paragraph 1, paragraph 3 and paragraph 4(2) (which are spent as a result of this Act).

115 In Schedule 3, omit paragraphs 1, 2 and 5 (which are spent as a result of this Act).

The Housing Act 1996 (c 52)

116 In section 183(2) of the Housing Act 1996 (interpretation of expressions related to assistance), in the definition of "eligible for assistance", omit "or section 186 (asylum seekers and their dependants)".

The Education Act 1996 (c 56)

117 In section 512(3) of the Education Act 1996 (requirement to provide school meals)—

    (a)   for the words from the beginning to "a", where it occurs for the second time, substitute—

"(3) Subsection (3A) applies in relation to a pupil—

    (a)   whose parents are in receipt of—
        (i)   income support;
        (ii)   an income-based jobseeker's allowance (payable under the Jobseekers Act 1995); or
        (iii)   support provided under Part VI of the Immigration and Asylum Act 1999; or
    (b)   who is himself in receipt of income support or an income-based jobseeker's allowance.

(3A) A";

         and
    (b)   in paragraph (a), for "him" substitute "the pupil".

The Special Immigration Appeals Commission Act 1997 (c 68)

118 The Special Immigration Appeals Commission Act 1997 is amended as follows.

119 . . .

120 In section 2(2) for "subsection (2) of section 13 of the Immigration Act 1971, but for subsection (5) of that section" substitute "section 59(2) of the 1999 Act but for section 60(9) of that Act".

121 After section 2 insert—

"2A Jurisdiction: human rights

(1)   A person who alleges that an authority has, in taking an appealable decision, acted in breach of his human rights may appeal to the Commission against that decision.

(2)   For the purposes of this section, an authority acts in breach of a person's human rights if he acts, or fails to act, in relation to that other person in a way which is made unlawful by section 6(1) of the Human Rights Act 1998.

(3)   Subsections (4) and (5) apply if, in any appellate proceedings being heard by the Commission, a question arises as to whether an authority has, in taking a decision which is the subject of the proceedings, acted in breach of the appellant's human rights.

(4)   The Commission has jurisdiction to consider the question.

(5)   If the Commission decides that the authority concerned acted in breach of the appellant's human rights, the appeal may be allowed on that ground.

(6)   "Authority" means—

    (a)   the Secretary of State;
    (b)   an immigration officer;
    (c)   a person responsible for the grant or refusal of entry clearance.

(7)   . . .

(8)   . . ."

122 In section 4 (determination of appeals), after subsection (1) insert—

"(1A)   If a certificate under section 70(4)(b) of the Immigration and Asylum Act 1999 has been issued, the Commission on an appeal to it under this Act may, instead of determining the appeal, quash the certificate and remit the appeal to an adjudicator."

123 In section 7 (appeals from Commission), omit subsection (4).

124 After section 7, insert—

"7A Pending appeals

(1)   For the purposes of this Act, an appeal to the Commission is to be treated as pending during the period beginning when notice of appeal is given and ending when the appeal is finally determined, withdrawn or abandoned.

(2)   An appeal is not to be treated as finally determined while a further appeal may be brought.

(3)   If a further appeal is brought, the original appeal is not to be treated as finally determined until the further appeal is determined, withdrawn or abandoned.

(4)   A pending appeal to the Commission is to be treated as abandoned if the appellant leaves the United Kingdom.

(5)   A pending appeal to the Commission is to be treated as abandoned if the appellant is granted leave to enter or remain in the United Kingdom.

(6)   But subsection (5) does not apply to an appeal brought under section 2(1) as a result of section 70(4) of the Immigration and Asylum Act 1999.

(7)   A pending appeal brought under section 2(1) as a result of section 62(3) of that Act is to be treated as abandoned if a deportation order is made against the appellant."

125 In Schedule 1 (supplementary provision as to Commission), in paragraph 5(b)—

(a) in sub-paragraph (i), for "paragraph 1 of Schedule 5 to the Immigration Act 1971" substitute "section 57(2) of the Immigration and Asylum Act 1999"; and

(b) in sub-paragraph (ii), for "paragraph 7 of that Schedule" substitute "paragraph 1(3) of Schedule 2 to that Act".

126 In Schedule 2 (supplementary provisions as to appeals) for paragraphs 1 to 3 substitute—

"Stay on directions for removal

1   If a person in the United Kingdom appeals under section 2(1) above on being refused leave to enter, any directions previously given by virtue of the refusal for his removal from the United Kingdom cease to have effect, except in so far as they have already been carried out, and no directions may be so given so long as the appeal is pending.

2   If a person in the United Kingdom appeals under section 2(1) above against any directions given under Part I of Schedule 2 or Schedule 3 to the 1971 Act for his removal from the United Kingdom, those directions except in so far as they have already been carried out, have no effect while the appeal is pending.

3   But the provisions of Part I of Schedule 2 or, as the case may be, Schedule 3 to the 1971 Act with respect to detention and persons liable to detention apply to a person appealing under section 2(1) above as if there were in force directions for his removal from the United Kingdom, except that he may not be detained on board a ship or aircraft so as to compel him to leave the United Kingdom while the appeal is pending.

3A   In calculating the period of two months limited by paragraph 8(2) of Schedule 2 to the 1971 Act for the giving of directions under that paragraph for the removal of a person from the United Kingdom and for the giving of a notice of intention to give such directions, any period during which there is pending an appeal by him under section 2(1) above is to be disregarded.

3B   If directions are given under Part I of Schedule 2 or Schedule 3 to the 1971 Act for anyone's removal from the United Kingdom, and directions are also so given for the removal with him of persons belonging to his family, then if any of them appeals under section 2(1) above, the appeal has the same effect under paragraphs 1 to 3A in relation to the directions given in respect of each of the others as it has in relation to the directions given in respect of the appellant.

Suspension of variation of limited leave

3C   A variation is not to take effect while an appeal is pending under section 2(1) above against the variation.

Continuation of leave

3D   (1) While an appeal under section 2(1) above is pending, the leave to which the appeal relates, and any conditions subject to which it was granted continue to have effect.

(2) A person may not make an application for a variation of his leave to enter or remain while that leave is treated as continuing to have effect as a result of sub-paragraph (1).

(3) For the purposes of section 2(1), in calculating whether, as a result of a decision, a person may be required to leave the United Kingdom within twenty-eight days, a continuation of leave under this paragraph is to be disregarded.

Deportation orders

3E   A deportation order is not to be made against a person under section 5 of the 1971 Act while an appeal duly brought under section 2(1) above against the decision to make it is pending.

3F   In calculating the period of eight weeks set by section 5(3) of the 1971 Act for making a deportation order against a person as belonging to the family of another person, there is to be disregarded any period during which an appeal under section 2(1) above against the decision to make the order is pending.

Appeals under section 2A

3G   (1)   A person is not to be required to leave, or be removed from, the United Kingdom if an appeal under section 2A is pending against the decision on which that requirement or removal would otherwise be based.

(2)   That does not prevent—

(a)   directions for his removal being given during that period;
(b)   a deportation order being made against him during that period.

(3)   But no such direction or order is to have effect during that period."

127 In Schedule 2, in paragraph 4, for "the Immigration Act 1971 as applied by paragraphs 1 to 3 above" substitute "this Schedule".

128 In Schedule 2, omit paragraph 5.

129 In Schedule 2, for paragraphs 6 and 7 substitute—

"Notice of appealable decision and statement of appeal rights etc

6   Paragraph 1 of Schedule 4 to the Immigration and Asylum Act 1999 has effect as if section 2 of this Act were contained in Part IV of that Act.

Financial support for organisations helping persons with rights of appeal

7   Section 81 of the Immigration and Asylum Act 1999 shall have effect as if section 2 above were contained in Part IV of that Act."

NOTES

Initial Commencement
Royal Assent
Paras 62(2), 73, 78, 79, 81, 82, 87, 88, 102: Royal Assent: 11 November 1999: see s 170(3)(s).

To be appointed
Paras 1–61, 62(1), (3), (4), 63–72, 74–77, 80, 83–86, 89–101, 103–129: To be appointed: see s 170(4).

Appointment
Paras 1–32, 37–42, 77: Appointment: 1 January 2001: see SI 2000/2698, art 2, Schedule.
Para 43: Appointment (for certain purposes) by virtue of the appointment of para 54: 6 December 1999: see SI 1999/3190, art 2, Schedule.
Paras 43, 49, 80(1), 90(1), 94, 108, 118: Appointment (for certain purposes): 14 February 2000: see SI 2000/168, art 2, Schedule.
Paras 43, 52(1), 108: Appointment (for certain purposes): 1 March 2000: see SI 2000/464, art 2, Schedule.
Paras 43, 52(1), 99, 108: Appointment (for certain purposes): 3 April 2000: see SI 2000/464, art 2, Schedule.

Paras 43, 83, 99, 118: Appointment (for certain purposes): 2 October 2000: see SI 2000/2444, art 2, Sch 1; for transitional provisions see art 3, Sch 2 thereof.

Paras 44(1), 45, 50, 51, 53, 56–60, 62(1), (3), (4), 63, 64, 67, 68, 80(2), (3), 90(2), (3), 95, 96, 109, 125: Appointment: 14 February 2000: see SI 2000/168, art 2, Schedule.

Paras 44(2), 46, 55, 65, 66, 69, 70, 84, 103–106, 114, 115, 120, 122–124, 126–128: Appointment: 2 October 2000: see SI 2000/2444, art 2, Sch 1; for transitional provisions see art 3, Sch 2 thereto.

Paras 49, 121: Appointment (for certain purposes): 2 October 2000: see SI 2000/2444, art 2, Sch 1; for transitional provisions see art 3, Sch 2, para 2 thereto.

Paras 52(1), 108: Appointment (for remaining purposes): 2 October 2000: see SI 2000/2444, art 2, Sch 1.

Paras 52(3)(a), 110: Appointment: 1 March 2000: see SI 2000/464, art 2, Schedule.

Paras 52(3)(b), 74, 76, 92, 93, 101, 111–113: Appointment: 3 April 2000: see SI 2000/464, art 2, Schedule.

Paras 54, 117: Appointment: 6 December 1999: see SI 1999/3190, art 2, Schedule.

Para 61: Appointment: 11 December 2000: see SI 2000/3099, art 3, Schedule.

Paras 71, 72, 91, 98: Appointment: 14 February 2000: see SI 2000/168, art 2, Schedule; for transitional provisions see art 3 thereof.

Para 118: Appointment (for certain purposes): 1 August 2000: see SI 2000/1985, art 2, Schedule.

Para 129: Appointment: 1 August 2000: see SI 2000/1985, art 2, Schedule.

Amendment

Para 89: repealed by the Terrorism Act 2000, s 125(2), Sch 16, Pt I.

Date in force: to be appointed: see the Terrorism Act 2000, s 128.

Para 119: repealed by SI 2000/2326, reg 32(4)(a).

Date in force: 2 October 2000: see SI 2000/2326, reg 1(1).

Para 121: repealed (in so far as it relates to the insertion of the Special Immigration Appeals Commission Act 1997, s 2A(7), (8)) by SI 2000/2326, reg 32(1), (4)(b).

Date in force: 2 October 2000: see SI 2000/2326, reg 1(1).

SCHEDULE 15
Transitional Provisions and Savings

Section 169(2)

Leave to enter or remain

1 (1) An order made under section 3A of the 1971 Act may make provision with respect to leave given before the commencement of section 1.

(2) An order made under section 3B of the 1971 Act may make provision with respect to leave given before the commencement of section 2.

Section 2 of the Asylum and Immigration Act 1996

2 (1) This paragraph applies in relation to any time before the commencement of the repeal by this Act of section 2 of the Asylum and Immigration Act 1996.

(2) That section has effect, and is to be deemed always to have had effect, as if the reference to section 6 of the Asylum and Immigration Appeals Act 1993 were a reference to section 15, and any certificate issued under that section is to be read accordingly.

Adjudicators and the Tribunal

3 (1) Each existing member of the Tribunal is to continue as a member of the Tribunal as if he had been duly appointed by the Lord Chancellor under Schedule 2.

(2) Each existing adjudicator is to continue as an adjudicator as if he had been duly appointed by the Lord Chancellor under Schedule 3.

(3)   The terms and conditions for a person to whom sub-paragraph (1) or (2) applies remain those on which he held office immediately before the appropriate date.

(4)   The provisions of Schedule 7 to the Judicial Pensions and Retirement Act 1993 (transitional provisions for retirement dates), so far as applicable in relation to an existing member or adjudicator immediately before the appropriate date, continue to have effect.

(5)   The repeal by this Act of Schedule 5 to the 1971 Act (provisions with respect to adjudicators and the Tribunal) does not affect any entitlement which an existing member or adjudicator had immediately before the appropriate date as a result of a determination made under paragraph 3(1)(b) or 9(1)(b) of that Schedule.

(6)   "The appropriate date" means—

    (a)   in relation to existing members of the Tribunal, the date on which section 56 comes into force; and

    (b)   in relation to existing adjudicators, the date on which section 57 comes into force.

(7)   "Existing member" means a person who is a member of the Tribunal immediately before the appropriate date.

(8)   "Existing adjudicator" means a person who is an adjudicator immediately before the appropriate date.

References to justices' chief executive

4   At any time before the coming into force of section 90 of the Access to Justice Act 1999—

    (a)   the reference in section 48(3)(b) to the justices' chief executive appointed by the magistrates' court committee whose area includes the petty sessions area for which the specified court acts is to be read as a reference to the clerk of that court; and

    (b)   the reference in section 28K(9)(a) and (10) of the 1971 Act (inserted by section 138) to the justices' chief executive appointed by the magistrates' court committee whose area includes the petty sessions area for which the justice acts is to be read as a reference to the clerk to the justices for the petty sessions area for which the justice acts.

Duties under National Assistance Act 1948

5   Section 116 has effect, in relation to any time before section 115 is brought into force, as if section 115 came into force on the passing of this Act.

Duties under Health Services and Public Health Act 1968

6   Section 117(1) has effect, in relation to any time before section 115 is brought into force, as if section 115 came into force on the passing of this Act.

Duties under Social Work (Scotland) Act 1968

7   Subsections (1) to (3) of section 120 have effect, in relation to any time before section 115 is brought into force, as if section 115 came into force on the passing of this Act.

Duties under Health and Personal Social Services (Northern Ireland) Order 1972

8 Subsections (1) and (2) of section 121 have effect, in relation to any time before section 115 is brought into force, as if section 115 came into force on the passing of this Act.

Duties under National Health Service Act 1977

9 Section 117(2) has effect, in relation to any time before section 115 is brought into force, as if section 115 came into force on the passing of this Act.

Duties under Mental Health (Scotland) Act 1984

10 Subsections (4) and (5) of section 120 have effect, in relation to any time before section 115 is brought into force, as if section 115 came into force on the passing of this Act.

Appeals relating to deportation orders

11 Section 15 of the 1971 Act, section 5 of the Immigration Act 1988 and the Immigration (Restricted Right of Appeal against Deportation) (Exemption) Order 1993 are to continue to have effect in relation to any person on whom the Secretary of State has, before the commencement of the repeal of those sections, served a notice of his decision to make a deportation order.

12 (1) Sub-paragraph (2) applies if, on the coming into force of section 10, sections 15 of the 1971 Act and 5 of the Immigration Act 1988 have been repealed by this Act.

(2) Those sections are to continue to have effect in relation to any person—

(a) who applied during the regularisation period fixed by section 9, in accordance with the regulations made under that section, for leave to remain in the United Kingdom, and

(b) on whom the Secretary of State has since served a notice of his decision to make a deportation order.

Assistance under Part VII of the Housing Act 1996

13 (1) The Secretary of State may by order provide for any provision of Part VII of the Housing Act 1996 (homelessness) to have effect in relation to section 185(2) persons, during the interim period, with such modifications as may be specified in the order.

(2) An order under this paragraph may, in particular, include provision—

(a) for the referral of section 185(2) persons by one local housing authority to another by agreement between the authorities;

(b) as to the suitability of accommodation for such persons;

(c) as to out-of-area placements of such persons.

(3) "Interim period" means the period beginning with the passing of this Act and ending on the coming into force of the repeal of section 186 of the Act of 1996 (asylum-seekers and their dependants) by this Act (as to which see section 117(5)).

(4) "Local housing authority" has the same meaning as in the Act of 1996.

(5) "Section 185(2) person" means a person who—

(a)   is eligible for housing assistance under Part VII of the Act of 1996 as a result of regulations made under section 185(2) of that Act; and

(b)   is not made ineligible by section 186 (or any other provision) of that Act.

(6)   The fact that an order may be made under this paragraph only in respect of the interim period does not prevent it from containing provisions of a kind authorised under section 166(3)(a) which are to have continuing effect after the end of that period.

Provision of support

14   (1)   The Secretary of State may, by directions given to a local authority to whom Schedule 9 applies, require the authority to treat the interim period fixed for the purposes of that Schedule as coming to an end—

(a)   for specified purposes,

(b)   in relation to a specified area or locality, or

(c)   in relation to persons of a specified description,

on such earlier day as may be specified.

(2)   The Secretary of State may, by directions given to an authority to whom an amended provision applies, provide for specified descriptions of person to be treated—

(a)   for specified purposes, or

(b)   in relation to a specified area or locality,

as being persons to whom section 115 applies during such period as may be specified.

(3)   Directions given under this paragraph may—

(a)   make such consequential, supplemental or transitional provision as the Secretary of State considers appropriate; and

(b)   make different provision for different cases or descriptions of case.

(4)   "Specified" means specified in the directions.

(5)   "Amended provision" means any provision amended by—

(a)   section 116;

(b)   section 117(1) or (2);

(c)   section 120; or

(d)   section 121.

NOTES

Initial Commencement
Royal Assent
Paras 2, 13: Royal Assent: 11 November 1999: see s 170(3)(t).

To be appointed
Paras 1, 3–11, 14: To be appointed: see s 170(4).
Para 12: To be appointed (in accordance with s 9): see s 170(4).

Appointment
Paras 1, 3, 4(b), 14: Appointment: 14 February 2000: see SI 2000/168, art 2, Schedule.
Paras 5, 6, 9: Appointment: 6 December 1999: see SI 1999/3190, art 2, Schedule.
Paras 11, 12: Appointment: 2 October 2000: see SI 2000/2444, art 2, Sch 1.

Subordinate Legislation
Homelessness (Asylum-Seekers) (Interim Period) (England) Order 1999, SI 1999/3126 (made under para 13).

SCHEDULE 16
Repeals

Section 169(3)

Chapter	Short title	Extent of repeal
1949 c 76	The Marriage Act 1949	In section 3(1), "whether by licence or without licence,".
		Section 26(2).
		In section 27, in subsection (1) "without licence", subsection (2), in subsection (3)(a) "in the case of a marriage intended to be solemnized without licence,", and subsection (3)(b).
		In section 27B, in subsections (4) and (6) "or licence", and in subsection (5) "or certificate and licence,".
		In section 28(1), "or licence".
		In section 29, every "or licence".
		In section 31, in subsection (1) "without licence", and in subsection (4) "without licence".
		Section 32.
		In section 35, in subsection (1) ", or if the marriage is to be by licence, a certificate and a licence," in subsections (2) and (4) "or, if the marriage is to be by licence, a certificate and a licence,", and in subsections (2A) and (2B) "or, if the marriage is to be by licence, a certificate and licence,".
		Section 36.
		In section 37(1), "without licence".
		In section 38(1), "without licence".
		In section 39(1), "without licence".
		Section 40(2).
		Section 49(c).
		In section 50, in subsection (1) "the certificate or, if notice of marriage has been

Chapter	Short title	Extent of repeal
1949 c 76 *(cont'd)*	The Marriage Act 1949 *(cont'd)*	given to more than one superintendent registrar", and subsection (2).
		In section 51(1), from first "the sum" to "case,".
		In section 75(3), in paragraph (b) "or licence".
		In Schedule 4, in Part III, "The proviso to subsection (2) of section twenty-six".
1969 c 46	The Family Law Reform Act 1969	In section 2(3), "or licence" in both cases.
1970 c 34	The Marriage (Registrar General's Licence) Act 1970	In section 5, "or licence". Section 13(b).
1971 c 77	The Immigration Act 1971	In section 10(1), from "and any such Order" to the end.
		Part II.
		In section 24, subsections (1)(aa) and (2).
		Section 25(3).
		In Schedule 2, in paragraph 21(4)(a) "under paragraph 2 above", in paragraph 26(1) "and have not been given leave" and paragraph 28.
		In Schedule 3, in paragraph3, "in paragraph 28(2), (3) and (6) and".
		Schedule 5.
1975 c 24	The House of Commons Disqualification Act 1975	In Schedule 1, in Part III, "Adjudicator appointed for the purposes of the Immigration Act 1971".
1975 c 25	The Northern Ireland Assembly Disqualification Act 1975	In Schedule 1, in Part III, "Adjudicator appointed for the purposes of the Immigration Act 1971".
1987 c 24	The Immigration (Carriers' Liability) Act 1987	The whole Act.

Chapter	Short title	Extent of repeal
1988 c 14	The Immigration Act 1988	Section 5. Section 8. Section 9.
1990 c 41	The Courts and Legal Services Act 1990	In Schedule 10, paragraph 34. In Schedule 11, in the entry relating to the Immigration Appeal Tribunal, "appointed under Schedule 5 to the Immigration Act 1971".
1992 c 4	The Social Security and Benefits Act Contributions 1992	Section 146A.
1992 c 7	The Social Security Contributions and Benefits (Northern Ireland) Act 1992	Section 142A.
1993 c 8	The Judicial Pensions and Retirement Act 1993	In Schedule 6, paragraphs 37 and 38.
1993 c 23	The Asylum and Immigration Appeals Act 1993	Section 3. Section 4. Section 5. Section 6. Section 7. Section 8. Section 9. Section 10. Section 11. Section 12. Schedule 1. Schedule 2.
1996 c 49	The Asylum and Immigration Act 1996	Section 1. Section 2. Section 3. Section 4. Section 7. Section 9. Section 10. Section 11. In Schedule 2, paragraphs 1(2) and (3), 3 and 4(2). In Schedule 3, paragraphs 1, 2 and 5.

Chapter	Short title	Extent of repeal
1996 c 52	The Housing Act 1996	In section 183(2), in the definition "eligible for assistance", "or section 186 (asylum seekers and their dependants)".
		Section 186.
		In Schedule 16, paragraph 3.
1997 c 68	The Special Immigration Appeals Commission Act 1997	Section 7(4).
		In Schedule 2, paragraph 5.

NOTES

Initial Commencement
To be appointed
To be appointed: see s 170(4).

Appointment
Appointment (in part): 14 February 2000: see SI 2000/168, art 2, Schedule.
Appointment (in part): 1 March 2000: see SI 2000/464, art 2, Schedule.
Appointment (in part): 3 April 2000: see SI 2000/464, art 2, Schedule.
Appointment (in part): 2 October 2000: see SI 2000/2444, art 2, Sch 1; for transitional provisions see art 3, Sch 2 thereto.
Appointment (in part): 1 January 2001: see SI 2000/2698, art 2, Schedule.
Appointment (in part): 11 December 2000: see SI 2000/3099, art 3, Schedule.

NATIONAL ASSISTANCE ACT 1948

1948 CHAPTER 29

An Act to terminate the existing poor law and to provide in lieu thereof for the assistance of persons in need by the National Assistance Board and by local authorities; to make further provision for the welfare of disabled, sick, aged and other persons and for regulating homes for disabled and aged persons and charities for disabled persons; to amend the law relating to non-contributory old age pensions; to make provision as to the burial or cremation of deceased persons; and for purposes connected with the matters aforesaid

[13th May 1948]

PART III
LOCAL AUTHORITY SERVICES

Provision of Accommodation

21   Duty of local authorities to provide accommodation

(1)   [Subject to and in accordance with the provisions of this Part of this Act, a local authority may with the approval of the Secretary of State, and to such extent as he may direct shall, make arrangements for providing]—

(a) residential accommodation for persons [aged eighteen or over] who by reason of age, [illness, disability] or any other circumstances are in need of care and attention which is not otherwise available to them; [and

(aa) residential accommodation for expectant and nursing mothers who are in need of care and attention which is not otherwise available to them.]

(b) ...

[(1A) A person to whom section 115 of the Immigration and Asylum Act 1999 (exclusion from benefits) applies may not be provided with residential accommodation under subsection (1)(a) if his need for care and attention has arisen solely—

(a) because he is destitute; or

(b) because of the physical effects, or anticipated physical effects, of his being destitute.

(1B) Subsections (3) and (5) to (8) of section 95 of the Immigration and Asylum Act 1999, and paragraph 2 of Schedule 8 to that Act, apply for the purposes of subsection (1A) as they apply for the purposes of that section, but for the references in subsections (5) and (7) of that section and in that paragraph to the Secretary of State substitute references to a local authority.]

(2) In [making any such arrangements] a local authority shall have regard to the welfare of all persons for whom accommodation is provided, and in particular to the need for providing accommodation of different descriptions suited to different descriptions of such persons as are mentioned in the last foregoing subsection.

[(2A) In determining for the purposes of paragraph (a) or (aa) of subsection (1) of this section whether care and attention are otherwise available to a person, a local authority shall disregard so much of the person's capital as does not exceed the capital limit for the purposes of section 22 of this Act.

(2B) For the purposes of subsection (2A) of this section—

(a) a person's capital shall be calculated in accordance with assessment regulations in the same way as if he were a person for whom accommodation is proposed to be provided as mentioned in subsection (3) of section 22 of this Act and whose ability to pay for the accommodation falls to be assessed for the purposes of that subsection; and

(b) "the capital limit for the purposes of section 22 of this Act" means the amount for the time being prescribed in assessment regulations as the amount which a resident's capital (calculated in accordance with such regulations) must not exceed if he is to be assessed as unable to pay for his accommodation at the standard rate;

and in this subsection "assessment regulations" means regulations made for the purposes of section 22(5) of this Act.]

(3) ...

(4) [Subject to the provisions of section 26 of this Act] accommodation provided by a local authority in the exercise of their [functions under this section] shall be provided in premises managed by the authority or, to such extent as may be [determined in accordance with the arrangements] under this section, in such premises managed by another local authority as may be agreed between the two authorities and on such terms, including terms as to the reimbursement of expenditure incurred by the said other authority, as may be so agreed.

(5) References in this Act to accommodation provided under this Part thereof shall be construed as references to accommodation provided in accordance with this and the five next following sections, and as including references to board and other services,

amenities and requisites provided in connection with the accommodation except where in the opinion of the authority managing the premises their provision is unnecessary.

(6)   References in this Act to a local authority providing accommodation shall be construed, in any case where a local authority agree with another local authority for the provision of accommodation in premises managed by the said other authority, as references to the first-mentioned local authority.

(7)   Without prejudice to the generality of the foregoing provisions of this section, a local authority may—

(a)   provide, in such cases as they may consider appropriate, for the conveyance of persons to and from premises in which accommodation is provided for them under this Part of the Act;

[(b)   make arrangements for the provision on the premises in which accommodation is being provided of such other services as appear to the authority to be required.]

. . .

(8)   < . . . > nothing in this section shall authorise or require a local authority to make any provision authorised or required to be made (whether by that or by any other authority) by or under any enactment not contained in this Part of this Act [or authorised or required to be provided under the National Health Service Act 1977].

NOTES

Amendment
Repealed in relation to Scotland by the Social Work (Scotland) Act 1968, s 95(2), Sch 9, Part I.
Sub-s (1): first words in square brackets substituted by the Local Government Act 1972, s 195, Sch 23, para 2; second words in square brackets inserted by the Children Act 1989, s 108(5), Sch 13, para 11(1); third words in square brackets substituted, and final words in square brackets inserted, by the National Health Service and Community Care Act 1990, s 42(1); para (b) repealed by the Housing (Homeless Persons) Act 1977, s 20(4), Schedule.
Sub-ss (1A), (1B): inserted by the Immigration and Asylum Act 1999, s 116; for transitional provisions see Sch 15, para 5 thereto.
Date in force: 6 December 1999: see SI 1999/3190, art 2, Schedule.
Sub-s (2): words "making any such arrangements" in square brackets substituted by the Local Government Act 1972, s 195, Sch 23, para 2.
Sub-ss (2A), (2B): inserted by the Community Care (Residential Accommodation) Act 1998, s 1.
Date in force: 11 August 1998: see the Community Care (Residential Accommodation) Act 1998, s 3(2).
Sub-s (3): repealed by the Local Government Act 1972, ss 195, 272, Sch 23, para 2, Sch 30.
Sub-s (4): first words in square brackets inserted by the National Health Service and Community Care Act 1990, s 66(1), Sch 9, para 5(1); other words in square brackets substituted by the Local Government Act 1972, s 195, Sch 23, para 2.
Sub-s (7): para (b) substituted, for paras (b), (c) as originally enacted, by the National Health Service and Community Care Act 1990, s 66(1), Sch 9, para 5(2); words omitted repealed by the National Health Service Reorganisation Act 1973, s 58, Sch 5.
Sub-s (8): words omitted repealed, and words in square brackets inserted, by the National Health Service and Community Care Act 1990, s 66(1), (2), Sch 9, para 5(3), Sch 10.

Transfer of Functions
Functions of a Minister of the Crown, so far as exercisable in relation to Wales, transferred to the National Assembly for Wales, by the National Assembly for Wales (Transfer of Functions) Order 1999, SI 1999/672, art 2, Sch 1.
SI 1968/1699 and SI 1988/1843.

Welfare Services

29 Welfare arrangements for blind, deaf, dumb and crippled persons, etc

(1)   A local authority [may, with the approval of the Secretary of State, and to such extent as he may direct in relation to persons ordinarily resident in the area of the local authority shall] make arrangements for promoting the welfare of persons to whom this section applies, that is to say persons [aged eighteen or over] who are blind, deaf or dumb [or who suffer from mental disorder of any description], and other persons [aged eighteen or over] who are substantially and permanently handicapped by illness, injury, or congenital deformity or such other disabilities as may be prescribed by the Minister.

(2), (3)   . . .

(4)   Without prejudice to the generality of the provisions of subsection (1) of this section, arrangements may be made thereunder—

  (a)   for informing persons to whom arrangements under that subsection relate of the services available for them thereunder;
  (b)   for giving such persons instruction in their own homes or elsewhere in methods of overcoming the effects of their disabilities;
  (c)   for providing workshops where such persons may be engaged (whether under a contract of service or otherwise) in suitable work, and hostels where persons engaged in the workshops, and other persons to whom arrangements under subsection (1) of this section relate and for whom work or training is being provided in pursuance of the Disabled Persons (Employment) Act 1944 [or the Employment and Training Act 1973] may live;
  (d)   for providing persons to whom arrangements under subsection (1) of this section relate with suitable work (whether under a contract of service or otherwise) in their own homes or elsewhere;
  (e)   for helping such persons in disposing of the produce of their work;
  (f)   for providing such persons with recreational facilities in their own homes or elsewhere;
  (g)   for compiling and maintaining classified registers of the persons to whom arrangements under subsection (1) of this section relate.

[(4A)   Where accommodation in a hostel is provided under paragraph (c) of subsection (4) of this section—

  (a)   if the hostel is managed by a local authority, section 22 of this Act shall apply as it applies where accommodation is provided under section 21;
  (b)   if the accommodation is provided in a hostel managed by a person other than a local authority under arrangements made with that person, subsections (2) to (4A) of section 26 of this Act shall apply as they apply where accommodation is provided under arrangements made by virtue of that section; and
  (c)   sections 32 and 43 of this Act shall apply as they apply where accommodation is provided under sections 21 to 26;

and in this subsection references to "accommodation" include references to board and other services, amenities and requisites provided in connection with the accommodation, except where in the opinion of the authority managing the premises or, in the case mentioned in paragraph (b) above, the authority making the arrangements their provision is unnecessary.]

(5)   . . .

(6)   Nothing in the foregoing provisions of this section shall authorise or require—

  (a)   the payment of money to persons to whom this section applies, other than persons for whom work is provided under arrangements made by virtue of paragraph (c) or paragraph (d) of subsection (4) of this section or who are engaged in work which they are enabled to perform in consequence of anything done in pursuance of arrangements made under this section; or

(b)   the provision of any accommodation or services required to be provided under the [National Health Service Act 1977] . . .

(7)   A person engaged in work in a workshop provided under paragraph (c) of subsection (4) of this section, or a person in receipt of a superannuation allowance granted on his retirement from engagement in any such workshop, shall be deemed for the purposes of this Act to continue to be ordinarily resident in the area in which he was ordinarily resident immediately before he [was accepted for work in that workshop; and for the purposes of this subsection a course of training in such a workshop shall be deemed to be work in that workshop].

NOTES

Amendment

Repealed in relation to Scotland by the Social Work (Scotland) Act 1968, s 95(2), Sch 9, Part I.

Sub-s (1): first words in square brackets substituted by the Local Government Act 1972, s 195, Sch 23, para 2; second and final words in square brackets inserted by the Children Act 1989, s 108(5), (6), Sch 13, para 11(2), Sch 14, para 1; third words in square brackets substituted by the Mental Health (Scotland) Act 1960, ss 113(1), 114, Sch 4.

Sub-ss (2), (3): repealed by the Local Government Act 1972, ss 195, 272(1), Sch 23, para 2, Sch 30.

Sub-s (4): words in square brackets inserted by the Employment and Training Act 1973, s 14(1), Sch 3, para 3.

Sub-s (4A): inserted by the National Health Service and Community Care Act 1990, s 44(7).

Sub-s (5): repealed by the Health and Social Services and Social Security Adjudications Act 1983, s 30, Sch 10, Part I.

Sub-s (6): words in square brackets substituted by the National Health Service Act 1977, s 129, Sch 15, para 6; words omitted repealed by the Social Work (Scotland) Act 1968, s 95(2), Sch 9, Part I.

Sub-s (7): words in square brackets substituted retrospectively by the National Assistance (Amendment) Act 1959, s 1(2).

Transfer of Functions

Functions of the Minister of Health transferred to the Secretary of State for Health by virtue of the Secretary of State for Social Services Order 1968, SI 1968/1699, and the Transfer of Functions (Health and Social Services) Order 1988, SI 1988/1843.

Functions under this section, so far as exercisable in relation to Wales, transferred to the National Assembly for Wales, by the National Assembly for Wales (Transfer of Functions) Order 1999, SI 1999/672, art 2, Sch 1.

HEALTH SERVICES AND PUBLIC HEALTH ACT 1968

1968 CHAPTER 46

An Act to amend the National Health Service Act 1946 and the National Health Service (Scotland) Act 1947 and make other amendments connected with the national health service; to make amendments connected with local authorities' services under the National Assistance Act 1948; to amend the law relating to notifiable diseases and food poisoning; to amend the Nurseries and Child-Minders Regulation Act 1948; to amend the law relating to food and drugs; to enable assistance to be given to certain voluntary organisations; to enable the Minister of Health and Secretary of State to purchase goods for supply to certain authorities; to make other amendments in the law relating to the public health; and for purposes connected with the matters aforesaid

[26th July 1968]

45 Promotion, by local authorities of the welfare of old people

(1)   A local authority may with the approval of [the Secretary of State], and to such extent as he may direct shall, make arrangements for promoting the welfare of old people.

(2)   . . .

(3)   A local authority may employ as their agent for the purposes of this section [any voluntary organisation or any person carrying on, professionally or by way of trade or business, activities which consist of or include the provision of services for old people, being an organisation or person appearing to the authority to be capable of promoting the welfare of old people].

(4)   No arrangements under this section shall provide—

   (a)   for the payment of money to old people except in so far as the arrangements may provide for the remuneration of old people engaged in suitable work in accordance with the arrangements;
   (b)   for making available any accommodation or services required to be provided under the [National Health Service Act 1977].

[(4A)   No arrangements under this section may be given effect to in relation to a person to whom section 115 of the Immigration and Asylum Act 1999 (exclusion from benefits) applies solely—

   (a)   because he is destitute; or
   (b)   because of the physical effects, or anticipated physical effects, of his being destitute.

(4B) Subsections (3) and (5) to (8) of section 95 of the Immigration and Asylum Act 1999, and paragraph 2 of Schedule 8 to that Act, apply for the purposes of subsection (4A) as they apply for the purposes of that section, but for the references in subsections (5) and (7) of that section and in that paragraph to the Secretary of State substitute references to a local authority.]

(5)   The National Assistance Act 1948 shall have effect as if the following references included a reference to this section, that is to say,—

   (a)   the reference, in section 32, to section 29 of that Act;
   (b)   the references, in sections 35, . . . 45, 52 . . . , to Part III of that Act;
   (c)   the references, in sections . . . 56 and 59, to that Act.

(6)–(8)   . . .

(9)   The Health Visiting and Social Work (Training) Act 1962 shall have effect in relation to functions of local authorities under this section as it does in relation to functions of local authorities under Part III of the National Assistance Act 1948.

(10) ...

(11) In this section "local authority" (except where used in the expression "public or local authority") means the council of a county, [other than a metropolitan county, or of a [county borough,] metropolitan district] or London borough or the Common Council of the City of London, and "voluntary organisation" means a body the activities of which are carried on otherwise than for profit but does not include any public or local authority.

(12) ...

NOTES

Appointment
Commencement order: SI 1971/423.

Amendment
Repealed, in relation to Scotland, by the Social Work (Scotland) Act 1968, ss 14(4), 95(2), Sch 9, Pt I.
Sub-s (1): words in square brackets substituted by virtue of SI 1968/1699, art 5(4).
Sub-s (2): repealed by the Health and Social Services and Social Security Adjudications Act 1983, s 30, Sch 10, Part I.
Sub-s (3): words in square brackets substituted by the National Health Service and Community Care Act 1990, s 42(7).
Sub-s (4): words in square brackets substituted by the National Health Service Act 1977, s 129, Sch 15, para 43.
Sub-ss (4A), (4B): inserted by the Immigration and Asylum Act 1999, s 117(1); for transitional provisions see Sch 15, para 6 thereto.
Date in force: 6 December 1999: see SI 1999/3190, art 2, Schedule.
Sub-s (5): words omitted repealed by the Statute Law (Repeals) Act 1978, the Local Authority Social Services Act 1970, s 14(2), Sch 3, and the National Health Service and Community Care Act 1990, s 66(2), Sch 10.
Sub-ss (6)–(8): repealed by the Local Authority Social Services Act 1970, s 14(2), Sch 3.
Sub-s (10): repealed by the Residential Homes Act 1980, s 11(5), Sch 2.
Sub-s (11): first words in square brackets substituted by the Local Government Act 1972, s 195, Sch 23, para 15(3), words in square brackets therein inserted by the Local Government (Wales) Act 1994, s 22(4), Sch 10, para 5(1).
Sub-s (12): repealed by the Social Work (Scotland) Act 1968, ss 14(4), 95(2), Sch 9, Pt I.

Transfer of Functions
Functions of the Minister of Health and the Secretary of State, so far as exercisable in relation to Wales, transferred to the National Assembly for Wales, by the National Assembly for Wales (Transfer of Functions) Order 1999, SI 1999/672, art 2, Sch 1.

CHRONICALLY SICK AND DISABLED PERSONS ACT 1970

1970 CHAPTER 44

An Act to make further provision with respect to the welfare of chronically sick and disabled persons; and for connected purposes

[29th May 1970]

BE IT ENACTED by the Queen's most Excellent Majesty, by and with the advice and consent of the Lords Spiritual and Temporal, and Commons, in this present Parliament assembled, and by the authority of the same, as follows:–

Welfare and housing

2 Provision of welfare services

(1) Where a local authority having functions under section 29 of the National Assistance Act 1948 are satisfied in the case of any person to whom that section applies who is ordinarily resident in their area that it is necessary in order to meet the needs of that person for that authority to make arrangements for all or any of the following matters, namely-

(a) the provision of practical assistance for that person in his home;

(b) the provision for that person of, or assistance to that person in obtaining, wireless, television, library or similar recreational facilities;

(c) the provision for that person of lectures, games, outings or other recreational facilities outside his home or assistance to that person in taking advantage of educational facilities available to him;

(d) the provision for that person of facilities for, or assistance in, travelling to and from his home for the purpose of participating in any services provided under arrangements made by the authority under the said section 29 or, with the approval of the authority, in any services provided otherwise than as aforesaid which are similar to services which could be provided under such arrangements;

(e) the provision of assistance for that person in arranging for the carrying out of any works of adaptation in his home or the provision of any additional facilities designed to secure his greater safety, comfort or convenience;

(f) facilitating the taking of holidays by that person, whether at holiday homes or otherwise and whether provided under arrangements made by the authority or otherwise;

(g) the provision of meals for that person whether in his home or elsewhere;

(h) the provision for that person of, or assistance to that person in obtaining, a telephone and any special equipment necessary to enable him to use a telephone,

then, . . . subject . . . [. . . to the provisions of section 7(1) of the Local Authority Social Services Act 1970 (which requires local authorities in the exercise of certain functions, including functions under the said section 29, to act under the general guidance of the Secretary of State)] [and to the provisions of section 7A of that Act (which requires local authorities to exercise their social services functions in accordance with directions given by the Secretary of State)], it shall be the duty of that authority to make those arrangements in exercise of their functions under the said section 29.

(2) . . .

NOTES

Amendment
Sub-s (1): first words omitted repealed by the Local Government Act 1972, s 272(1), Sch 30; first words in square brackets inserted by the Local Authority Social Services Act 1970, s 14(1), Sch 2, para 12; second words in square brackets inserted, and second and final words omitted repealed, by the National Health Service and Community Care Act 1990, s 66, Sch 9, para 12, Sch 10.
Sub-s (2): repealed by the Local Government Act 1972, s 272(1), Sch 30.

EUROPEAN COMMUNITIES ACT 1972

1972 CHAPTER 68

An Act to make provision in connection with the enlargement of the European Communities to include the United Kingdom, together with (for certain purposes) the Channel Islands, the Isle of Man and Gibraltar

[17th October 1972]

PART I
GENERAL PROVISIONS

1 Short title and interpretation

(1)   This Act may be cited as the European Communities Act 1972.

(2)   In this Act . . . —

"the Communities" means the European Economic Community, the European Coal and Steel Community and the European Atomic Energy Community;
"the Treaties" or "the Community Treaties" means, subject to subsection (3) below, the pre-accession treaties, that is to say, those described in Part I of Schedule 1 to this Act, taken with—

(a)   the treaty relating to the accession of the United Kingdom to the European Economic Community and to the European Atomic Energy Community, signed at Brussels on the 22nd January 1972; and

(b)   the decision, of the same date, of the Council of the European Communities relating to the accession of the United Kingdom to the European Coal and Steel Community; [and

(c)   the treaty relating to the accession of the Hellenic Republic to the European Economic Community and to the European Atomic Energy Community, signed at Athens on 28th May 1979; and

(d)   the decision, of 24th May 1979, of the Council relating to the accession of the Hellenic Republic to the European Coal and Steel Community;] [and

(e)   the decisions of the Council of 7th May 1985, 24th June 1988, and 31st October 1994, on the Communities' system of own resources; and][

(g)   the treaty relating to the accession of the Kingdom of Spain and the Portuguese Republic to the European Economic Community and to the European Atomic Energy Community, signed at Lisbon and Madrid on 12th June 1985; and

(h)   the decision, of 11th June 1985, of the Council relating to the accession of the Kingdom of Spain and the Portuguese Republic to the European Coal and Steel Community;] [and

(j)   the following provisions of the Single European Act signed at Luxembourg and The Hague on 17th and 28th February 1986, namely Title II (amendment of the treaties establishing the Communities) and, so far as they relate to any of the Communities or any Community institution, the preamble and Titles I (common provisions) and IV (general and final provisions);] [and

(k)   Titles II, III and IV of the Treaty on European Union signed at Maastricht on 7th February 1992, together with the other provisions of the Treaty so far as they relate to those Titles, and the Protocols adopted at Maastricht on that date and annexed to the Treaty establishing the European

Community with the exception of the Protocol on Social Policy on page 117 of Cm 1934] [and

(l) the decision, of 1st February 1993, of the Council amending the Act concerning the election of the representatives of the European Parliament by direct universal suffrage annexed to Council Decision 76/787/ECSC, EEC, Euratom of 20th September 1976] [and

(m) the Agreement on the European Economic Area signed at Oporto on 2nd May 1992 together with the Protocol adjusting that Agreement signed at Brussels on 17th March 1993] [and

(n) the treaty concerning the accession of the Kingdom of Norway, the Republic of Austria, the Republic of Finland and the Kingdom of Sweden to the European Union, signed at Corfu on 24th June 1994;] [and

(o) the following provisions of the Treaty signed at Amsterdam on 2nd October 1997 amending the Treaty on European Union, the Treaties establishing the European Communities and certain related Acts—
   (i) Articles 2 to 9,
   (ii) Article 12, and
   (iii) the other provisions of the Treaty so far as they relate to those Articles,
   and the Protocols adopted on that occasion other than the Protocol on Article J.7 of the Treaty on European Union]
   and any other treaty entered into by any of the Communities, with or without any of the member States, or entered into, as a treaty ancillary to any of the Treaties, by the United Kingdom;

and any expression defined in Schedule 1 to this Act has the meaning there given to it.

(3) If Her Majesty by Order in Council declares that a treaty specified in the Order is to be regarded as one of the Community Treaties as herein defined, the Order shall be conclusive that it is to be so regarded; but a treaty entered into by the United Kingdom after the 22nd January 1972, other than a pre-accession treaty to which the United Kingdom accedes on terms settled on or before that date, shall not be so regarded unless it is so specified, nor be so specified unless a draft of the Order in Council has been approved by resolution of each House of Parliament.

(4) For purposes of subsections (2) and (3) above, "treaty" includes any international agreement, and any protocol or annex to a treaty or international agreement.

NOTES

Amendment
Sub-s (2): words omitted repealed by the Interpretation Act 1978, s 25(1), Sch 3.
Sub-s (2): in definition ""the Treaties" or "the Community Treaties"" paras (c), (d) inserted by the European Communities (Greek Accession) Act 1979, s 1.
Sub-s (2): in definition ""the Treaties" or "the Community Treaties"" para (e) substituted for existing paras (e), (f) (as inserted by the European Communities (Finance) Act 1985, s 1), by the European Communities (Finance) Act 1995, s 1.
Sub-s (2): in definition ""the Treaties" or "the Community Treaties"" paras (g), (h) inserted by the European Communities (Spanish and Portuguese Accession) Act 1985, s 1.
Sub-s (2): in definition ""the Treaties" or "the Community Treaties"" para (j) inserted by the European Communities (Amendment) Act 1986, s 1.
Sub-s (2): in definition ""the Treaties" or "the Community Treaties"" para (k) inserted by the European Communities (Amendment) Act 1993, s 1(1).
Sub-s (2): in definition ""the Treaties" or "the Community Treaties"" para (l) inserted by the European Parliamentary Elections Act 1993, s 3(2).
Sub-s (2): in definition ""the Treaties" or "the Community Treaties"" para (m) inserted by the European Economic Area Act 1993, s 1.
Sub-s (2): in definition ""the Treaties" or "the Community Treaties"" para (n) inserted by the European Union (Accessions) Act 1994, s 1.

Sub-s (2): in definition ""the Treaties" or "the Community Treaties"" para (o) inserted by the European Communities (Amendment) Act 1998, s 1.
Date in force: 11 June 1998: (no specific commencement provision).

2 General implementation of Treaties

(1) All such rights, powers, liabilities, obligations and restrictions from time to time created or arising by or under the Treaties, and all such remedies and procedures from time to time provided for by or under the Treaties, as in accordance with the Treaties are without further enactment to be given legal effect or used in the United Kingdom shall be recognised and available in law, and be enforced, allowed and followed accordingly; and the expression "enforceable Community right" and similar expressions shall be read as referring to one to which this subsection applies.

(2) Subject to Schedule 2 to this Act, at any time after its passing Her Majesty may by Order in Council, and any designated Minister or department may by regulations, make provision—

> (a) for the purpose of implementing any Community obligation of the United Kingdom, or enabling any such obligation to be implemented, or of enabling any rights enjoyed or to be enjoyed by the United Kingdom under or by virtue of the Treaties to be exercised; or
>
> (b) for the purpose of dealing with matters arising out of or related to any such obligation or rights or the coming into force, or the operation from time to time, of subsection (1) above;

and in the exercise of any statutory power or duty, including any power to give directions or to legislate by means of orders, rules, regulations or other subordinate instrument, the person entrusted with the power or duty may have regard to the objects of the Communities and to any such obligation or rights as aforesaid.

In this subsection "designated Minister or department" means such Minister of the Crown or government department as may from time to time be designated by Order in Council in relation to any matter or for any purpose, but subject to such restrictions or conditions (if any) as may be specified by the Order in Council.

(3) There shall be charged on and issued out of the Consolidated Fund or, if so determined by the Treasury, the National Loans Fund the amounts required to meet any Community obligation to make payments to any of the Communities or member States, or any Community obligation in respect of contributions to the capital or reserves of the European Investment Bank or in respect of loans to the Bank, or to redeem any notes or obligations issued or created in respect of any such Community obligation; and, except as otherwise provided by or under any enactment,—

> (a) any other expenses incurred under or by virtue of the Treaties or this Act by any Minister of the Crown or government department may be paid out of moneys provided by Parliament; and
>
> (b) any sums received under or by virtue of the Treaties or this Act by any Minister of the Crown or government department, save for such sums as may be required for disbursements permitted by any other enactment, shall be paid into the Consolidated Fund or, if so determined by the Treasury, the National Loans Fund.

(4) The provision that may be made under subsection (2) above includes, subject to Schedule 2 to this Act, any such provision (of any such extent) as might be made by Act of Parliament, and any enactment passed or to be passed, other than one contained in this Part of this Act, shall be construed and have effect subject to the foregoing provisions of this section; but, except as may be provided by any Act passed after this Act, Schedule 2 shall have effect in connection with the powers conferred by this and the following sections of this Act to make Orders in Council and regulations.

(5)   . . . and the references in that subsection to a Minister of the Crown or government department and to a statutory power or duty shall include a Minister or department of the Government of Northern Ireland and a power or duty arising under or by virtue of an Act of the Parliament of Northern Ireland.

(6)   A law passed by the legislature of any of the Channel Islands or of the Isle of Man, or a colonial law (within the meaning of the Colonial Laws Validity Act 1865) passed or made for Gibraltar, if expressed to be passed or made in the implementation of the Treaties and of the obligations of the United Kingdom thereunder, shall not be void or inoperative by reason of any inconsistency with or repugnancy to an Act of Parliament, passed or to be passed, that extends to the Island or Gibraltar or any provision having the force and effect of an Act there (but not including this section), nor by reason of its having some operation outside the Island or Gibraltar; and any such Act or provision that extends to the Island or Gibraltar shall be construed and have effect subject to the provisions of any such law.

NOTES

Amendment
Sub-s (5): words omitted repealed by the Northern Ireland Constitution Act 1973, s 41(1), Sch 6, Part I.

Modification
Modified by the Scotland Act 1998, s 125, Sch 8, para 15.
The Northern Ireland Act 1998 makes new provision for the government of Northern Ireland for the purpose of implementing the Belfast Agreement (the agreement reached at multi-party talks on Northern Ireland and set out in Command Paper 3883). As a consequence of that Act, any reference in this section to the Parliament of Northern Ireland or the Assembly established under the Northern Ireland Assembly Act 1973, s 1, certain office-holders and Ministers, and any legislative act and certain financial dealings thereof, shall, for the period specified, be construed in accordance with Sch 12, paras 1–11 to the 1998 Act.

Transfer of Functions
Functions under this section: by the Scotland Act 1998 (Transfer of Functions to the Scottish Ministers etc) Order 1999, SI 1999/1750, art 3, Sch 2, certain functions under sub-s (2) which were exercisable by a Minister of the Crown are, in so far as they are exercisable in or as regards Scotland, exercisable by the Scottish Ministers acting concurrently with the Minister of the Crown concerned. See also art 7(4) of the 1999 Order.

3 Decisions on, and proof of, Treaties and Community instruments, etc

(1)   For the purposes of all legal proceedings any question as to the meaning or effect of any of the Treaties, or as to the validity, meaning or effect of any Community instrument, shall be treated as a question of law (and, if not referred to the European Court, be for determination as such in accordance with the principles laid down by and any relevant [decision of the European Court or any court attached thereto)].

(2)   Judicial notice shall be taken of the Treaties, of the Official Journal of the Communities and of any decision of, or expression of opinion by, the European Court [or any court attached thereto] on any such question as aforesaid; and the Official Journal shall be admissible as evidence of any instrument or other act thereby communicated of any of the Communities or of any Community institution.

(3)   Evidence of any instrument issued by a Community institution, including any judgment or order of the European Court [or any court attached thereto], or of any document in the custody of a Community institution, or any entry in or extract from such a document, may be given in any legal proceedings by production of a copy certified as a true copy by an official of that institution; and any document purporting to be such a copy shall be received in evidence without proof of the official position or handwriting of the person signing the certificate.

(4) Evidence of any Community instrument may also be given in any legal proceedings—

- (a) by production of a copy purporting to be printed by the Queen's Printer;
- (b) where the instrument is in the custody of a government department (including a department of the Government of Northern Ireland), by production of a copy certified on behalf of the department to be a true copy by an officer of the department generally or specially authorised so to do;

and any document purporting to be such a copy as is mentioned in paragraph (b) above of an instrument in the custody of a department shall be received in evidence without proof of the official position or handwriting of the person signing the certificate, or of his authority to do so, or of the document being in the custody of the department.

(5) ...

NOTES

Amendment
Sub-ss (1)–(3): words in square brackets substituted or inserted by the European Communities (Amendment) Act 1986, s 2.
Sub–s (5): applies to Scotland only.

Modification
Modified, so as to have effect as if references to a government department include any part of the Scottish Administration, by the Scotland Act 1998, s 125, Sch 8, para 15(4).

PART II
AMENDMENT OF LAW

4 General provision for repeal and amendment

(1)   The enactments mentioned in Schedule 3 to this Act (being enactments that are superseded or to be superseded by reason of Community obligations and of the provision made by this Act in relation thereto or are not compatible with Community obligations) are hereby repealed, to the extent specified in column 3 of the Schedule, with effect from the entry date or other date mentioned in the Schedule; and in the enactments mentioned in Schedule 4 to this Act there shall, subject to any transitional provision there included, be made the amendments provided for by that Schedule.

(2)   Where in any Part of Schedule 3 to this Act it is provided that repeals made by that Part are to take effect from a date appointed by order, the orders shall be made by statutory instrument, and an order may appoint different dates for the repeal of different provisions to take effect, or for the repeal of the same provision to take effect for different purposes; and an order appointing a date for a repeal to take effect may include transitional and other supplementary provisions arising out of that repeal, including provisions adapting the operation of other enactments included for repeal but not yet repealed by that Schedule, and may amend or revoke any such provisions included in a previous order.

(3)   Where any of the following sections of this Act, or any paragraph of Schedule 4 to this Act, affects or is construed as one with an Act or Part of an Act similar in purpose to provisions having effect only in Northern Ireland, then—

- (a) unless otherwise provided by Act of the Parliament of Northern Ireland, the Governor of Northern Ireland may by Order in Council make provision corresponding to any made by the section or paragraph, and amend or revoke any provision so made; and
- (b) ...

(4)   Where Schedule 3 or 4 to this Act provides for the repeal or amendment of an enactment that extends or is capable of being extended to any of the Channel Islands or the Isle of Man, the repeal or amendment shall in like manner extend or be capable of being extended thereto.

NOTES

Amendment
Sub-s (3): para (b) repealed by the Northern Ireland Constitution Act 1973, s 41(1), Sch 6, Part I.

Modification
The Northern Ireland Act 1998 makes new provision for the government of Northern Ireland for the purpose of implementing the Belfast Agreement (the agreement reached at multi-party talks on Northern Ireland and set out in Command Paper 3883). As a consequence of that Act, any reference in this section to the Parliament of Northern Ireland or the Assembly established under the Northern Ireland Assembly Act 1973, s 1, certain office-holders and Ministers, and any legislative act and certain financial dealings thereof, shall, for the period specified, be construed in accordance with Sch 12, paras 1–11 to the 1998 Act.

Appointed Day
Appointed Day, for the purposes of sub-s (2): 16 August 1982 (for certain purposes), see SI 1982/1048; 1 September 1981 (for certain purposes), see SI 1981/1192; 1 September 1978 (for certain purposes), see SI 1978/1003; 1 January 1978 (for certain purposes), see SI 1977/2028; 1 December 1976 (for certain purposes), see SI 1976/2016; 1 September 1976 (for certain purposes), see SI 1976/1304; 5 May 1976 (for certain purposes), see SI 1976/548; 1 August 1975 (for certain purposes), see SI 1975/1164; 1 January 1974 (for certain purposes), see SI 1973/2176; 1 July 1973 (for certain purposes), see SI 1973/1019; 1 February 1973 (for remaining purposes), see SI 1973/135.

RACE RELATIONS ACT 1976

1976 CHAPTER 74

An Act to make fresh provision with respect to discrimination on racial grounds and relations between people of different racial groups; and to make in the Sex Discrimination Act 1975 amendments for bringing provisions in that Act relating to its administration and enforcement into conformity with the corresponding provisions in this Act

[22nd November 1976]

BE IT ENACTED by the Queen's most Excellent Majesty, by and with the advice and consent of the Lords Spiritual and Temporal, and Commons, in this present Parliament assembled, and by the authority of the same, as follows:–

[Public authorities]

[19B Discrimination by public authorities]

[(1) It is unlawful for a public authority in carrying out any functions of the authority to do any act which constitutes discrimination.

(2)   In this section "public authority"—

    (a)   includes any person certain of whose functions are functions of a public nature; but

    (b)   does not include any person mentioned in subsection (3).

(3)   The persons mentioned in this subsection are—

(a)   either House of Parliament;
(b)   a person exercising functions in connection with proceedings in Parliament;
(c)   the Security Service;
(d)   the Secret Intelligence Service;
(e)   the Government Communications Headquarters; and
(f)   any unit or part of a unit of any of the naval, military or air forces of the Crown which is for the time being required by the Secretary of State to assist the Government Communications Headquarters in carrying out its functions.

(4)   In relation to a particular act, a person is not a public authority by virtue only of subsection (2)(a) if the nature of the act is private.

(5)   This section is subject to sections 19C to 19F.

(6)   Nothing in this section makes unlawful any act of discrimination which—

(a)   is made unlawful by virtue of any other provision of this Act; or
(b)   would be so made but for any provision made by or under this Act.]

NOTES
Amendment
Inserted by the Race Relations (Amendment) Act 2000, s 1.
Date in force: 2 April 2001: see SI 2001/566, art 2(1).

[19C Exceptions or further exceptions from section 19B for judicial and legislative acts etc]

[(1)   Section 19B does not apply to—

(a)   any judicial act (whether done by a court, tribunal or other person); or
(b)   any act done on the instructions, or on behalf, of a person acting in a judicial capacity.

(2)   Section 19B does not apply to any act of, or relating to, making, confirming or approving any enactment or Order in Council or any instrument made by a Minister of the Crown under an enactment.

(3)   Section 19B does not apply to any act of, or relating to, making or approving arrangements, or imposing requirements or conditions, of a kind falling within section 41.

(4)   Section 19B does not apply to any act of, or relating to, imposing a requirement, or giving an express authorisation, of a kind mentioned in section 19D(3) in relation to the carrying out of immigration and nationality functions.

(5)   In this section—

"immigration and nationality functions" has the meaning given in section 19D; and
"Minister of the Crown" includes the National Assembly for Wales and a member of the Scottish Executive.]

NOTES
Amendment
Inserted by the Race Relations (Amendment) Act 2000, s 1.
Date in force: 2 April 2001: see SI 2001/566, art 2(1).

[19D Exception from section 19B for certain acts in immigration and nationality cases]

[(1)   Section 19B does not make it unlawful for a relevant person to discriminate against another person on grounds of nationality or ethnic or national origins in carrying out immigration and nationality functions.

(2) For the purposes of subsection (1), "relevant person" means—

    (a) a Minister of the Crown acting personally; or

    (b) any other person acting in accordance with a relevant authorisation.

(3) In subsection (2), "relevant authorisation" means a requirement imposed or express authorisation given—

    (a) with respect to a particular case or class of case, by a Minister of the Crown acting personally;

    (b) with respect to a particular class of case—

        (i) by any of the enactments mentioned in subsection (5); or

        (ii) by any instrument made under or by virtue of any of those enactments.

(4) For the purposes of subsection (1), "immigration and nationality functions" means functions exercisable by virtue of any of the enactments mentioned in subsection (5).

(5) Those enactments are—

    (a) the Immigration Acts (within the meaning of the Immigration and Asylum Act 1999 but excluding sections 28A to 28K of the Immigration Act 1971 so far as they relate to offences under Part III of that Act);

    (b) the British Nationality Act 1981;

    (c) the British Nationality (Falkland Islands) Act 1983;

    (d) the British Nationality (Hong Kong) Act 1990;

    (e) the Hong Kong (War Wives and Widows) Act 1996;

    (f) the British Nationality (Hong Kong) Act 1997; and

    (g) the Special Immigration Appeals Commission Act 1997;

and include any provision made under section 2(2) of the European Communities Act 1972, or any provision of Community law, which relates to the subject-matter of any of the enactments mentioned above.]

NOTES

Amendment
Inserted by the Race Relations (Amendment) Act 2000, s 1.
Date in force (for the purpose of the imposition of requirements or giving of express authorisations by a Minister of the Crown acting personally in accordance with sub-s (3) above): 26 March 2001: see SI 2001/566, art 2(2).
Date in force (for remaining purposes): 2 April 2001: see SI 2001/566, art 2(1).

[19E Monitoring of exception in relation to immigration and nationality cases]

[(1) The Secretary of State shall appoint a person who is not a member of his staff to act as a monitor.

(2) Before appointing any such person, the Secretary of State shall consult the Commission.

(3) The person so appointed shall monitor, in such manner as the Secretary of State may determine—

    (a) the likely effect on the operation of the exception in section 19D of any relevant authorisation relating to the carrying out of immigration and nationality functions which has been given by a Minister of the Crown acting personally; and

    (b) the operation of that exception in relation to acts which have been done by a person acting in accordance with such an authorisation.

(4) The monitor shall make an annual report on the discharge of his functions to the Secretary of State.

(5)   The Secretary of State shall lay a copy of any report made to him under subsection (4) before each House of Parliament.

(6)   The Secretary of State shall pay to the monitor such fees and allowances (if any) as he may determine.

(7)   In this section "immigration and nationality functions" and "relevant authorisation" have the meanings given to them in section 19D.]

NOTES

Amendment
Inserted by the Race Relations (Amendment) Act 2000, s 1.
Date in force: 2 April 2001: see SI 2001/566, art 2(1).

[19F Exceptions from section 19B for decisions not to prosecute etc]

[Section 19B does not apply to—

    (a)   a decision not to institute criminal proceedings and, where such a decision has been made, any act done for the purpose of enabling the decision whether to institute criminal proceedings to be made;

    (b)   where criminal proceedings are not continued as a result of a decision not to continue them, the decision and, where such a decision has been made—

        (i)   any act done for the purpose of enabling the decision whether to continue the proceedings to be made; and

        (ii)   any act done for the purpose of securing that the proceedings are not continued.]

NOTES

Amendment
Inserted by the Race Relations (Amendment) Act 2000, s 1.
Date in force: 2 April 2001: see SI 2001/566, art 2(1).
ch 3, Part I.

NATIONAL HEALTH SERVICE ACT 1977

1977 CHAPTER 49

An Act to consolidate certain provisions relating to the health service for England and Wales; and to repeal certain enactments relating to the health service which have ceased to have any effect

[29th July 1977]

Co-operation and assistance

21 Local social services authorities

(1)   Subject to paragraphs (d) and (e) of section 3(1) above, the services described in Schedule 8 to this Act in relation to—

    (a)   care of mothers . . .,
    (b)   prevention, care and after-care,
    (c)   home help and laundry facilities,

are functions exercisable by local social services authorities, and that Schedule has effect accordingly.

(2) A local social services authority who provide premises, furniture or equipment for any of the purposes of this Act may permit the use of the premises, furniture or equipment—

    (a)   by any other local social services authority, or
    (b)   by any of the bodies constituted under this Act, or
    (c)   by a local education authority.

This permission may be on such terms (including terms with respect to the services of any staff employed by the authority giving permission) as may be agreed.

(3) A local social services authority may provide (or improve or furnish) residential accommodation—

    (a)   for officers employed by them for the purposes of any of their functions as a local social services authority, or
    (b)   for officers employed by a voluntary organisation for the purposes of any services provided under this section and Schedule 8.

NOTES

Derivation
Sub-ss (2), (3) derived from the National Health Service Act 1946, ss 63, 65.

Amendment
Sub-s (1): words omitted in para (a) repealed by the Children Act 1989, s 108(7), Sch 15.

Extent
This section does not extend to Scotland.

SCHEDULE 8
Local Social Services Authorities

Section 21

Care of mothers and young children

1 (1) A local social services authority may, with the Secretary of State's approval, and to such extent as he may direct shall, make arrangements for the care of expectant and nursing mothers [(other than for the provision of residential accommodation for them)] . . .

(2) . . .

Prevention, care and after-care

2 (1) A local social services authority may, with the Secretary of State's approval, and to such extent as he may direct shall, make arrangements for the purpose of the prevention of illness and for the care of persons suffering from illness and for the after-care of persons who have been suffering and in particular for—

    (a)   . . .
    (b)   the provision, for persons whose care is undertaken with a view to preventing them from becoming ill, persons suffering from illness and persons who have been so suffering, of centres or other facilities for training them or keeping them suitably occupied and the equipment and maintenance of such centres;

(c) the provision, for the benefit of such persons as are mentioned in paragraph (b) above, of ancillary or supplemental services; and

[(d) for the exercise of the functions of the authority in respect of persons suffering from mental disorder who are received into guardianship under Part II or III of the Mental Health Act 1983 (whether the guardianship of the local social services authority or of other persons)].

Such an authority shall neither have the power nor be subject to a duty to make under this paragraph arrangements to provide facilities for any of the purposes mentioned in section 15(1) of the Disabled Persons (Employment) Act 1944.

(2)   No arrangements under this paragraph shall provide for the payment of money to persons for whose benefit they are made except—

(a) in so far as they may provide for the remuneration of such persons engaged in suitable work in accordance with the arrangements; . . .

(b) . . .

of such amounts as the local social services authority think fit in respect of their occasional personal expenses where it appears to that authority that no such payment would otherwise be made.

[(2A)   No arrangements under this paragraph may be given effect to in relation to a person to whom section 115 of the Immigration and Asylum Act 1999 (exclusion from benefits) applies solely—

(a) because he is destitute; or

(b) because of the physical effects, or anticipated physical effects, of his being destitute.

(2B) Subsections (3) and (5) to (8) of section 95 of the Immigration and Asylum Act 1999, and paragraph 2 of Schedule 8 to that Act, apply for the purposes of subsection (2A) as they apply for the purposes of that section, but for the references in subsections (5) and (7) of that section and in that paragraph to the Secretary of State substitute references to a local social services authority.]

(3)   The Secretary of State may make regulations as to the conduct of premises in which, in pursuance of arrangements made under this paragraph, are provided for persons whose care is undertaken with a view to preventing them from becoming sufferers from mental disorder within the meaning of [that Act of 1983] or who are, or have been, so suffering, . . . facilities for training them or keeping them suitably occupied.

(4) . . .

[(4A)   This paragraph does not apply in relation to persons under the age of 18.]

[(4AA)   No authority is authorised or may be required under this paragraph to provide residential accommodation for any person.]

(5) . . .

Home help and laundry facilities

3   (1)   It is the duty of every local social services authority to provide on such a scale as is adequate for the needs of their area, or to arrange for the provision on such a scale as is so adequate, of home help for households where such help is required owing to the presence of . . . a person who is suffering from illness, lying-in, an expectant mother, aged, handicapped as a result of having suffered from illness or by congenital deformity, . . . and every such authority has power to provide or arrange for the provision of laundry facilities for households for which home help is being, or can be, provided under this sub-paragraph.

(2) . . .

[*Research*

4 Without prejudice to any powers conferred on them by any other Act, a local social services authority may conduct or assist other persons in conducting research into matters relating to the functions of local social services authorities under this Schedule.]

NOTES

Derivation
Paras 1–3 derived from the National Health Service Act 1946, s 22(1), (2), and the Health Services and Public Health Act 1968, ss 12(1)–(5), 13(1), (2).

Amendment
Para 1: in sub-para (1) words in square brackets inserted by the National Health Service and Community Care Act 1990, s 66(1), Sch 9, para 18(14)(a); words omitted repealed by the Children Act 1989, s 108(7), Sch 15; sub-para (2) repealed by the Health and Social Security Adjudications Act 1983, s 30, Sch 10, Part I.
Para 2: sub-para (1)(a) repealed by the National Health Service and Community Care Act 1990, s 66, Sch 9, para 18(14)(b)(i), Sch 10.
Para 2: sub-para (1)(d) substituted by the Mental Health Act 1983, s 148, Sch 4, para 47(e)(i).
Para 2: in sub-para (2) words omitted repealed by the Children Act 1989, s 108(7), Sch 15.
Para 2: sub-paras (2A), (2B) inserted by the Immigration and Asylum Act 1999, s 117(2); for transitional provisions see Sch 15, para 9 thereto.
Date in force: 6 December 1999: see SI 1999/3190, art 2, Schedule.
Para 2: in sub-para (3) words "that Act of 1983" in square brackets substituted by the Mental Health Act 1983, s 148, Sch 4, para 47(e)(iii).
Para 2: in sub-para (3) words omitted repealed by the National Health Service and Community Care Act 1990, s 66, Sch 9, para 18(14)(b)(i), Sch 10.
Para 2: sub-para (4) repealed by the National Health Service and Community Care Act 1990, s 66, Sch 9, para 18(14)(b)(i), Sch 10.
Para 2: sub-para (4A) inserted by the Children Act 1989, s 108(4), Sch 12, para 34.
Para 2: sub-para (4AA) inserted by the National Health Service and Community Care Act 1990, s 66(1), Sch 9, para 18(14)(b)(ii).
Para 2: sub-para (5) repealed by the Health and Social Security Adjudications Act 1983, s 30, Sch 10, Pt I.
Para 3: words omitted from sub-para (1) repealed by the Children Act 1989, s 108(7), Sch 15; sub-para (2) repealed by the Health and Social Security Adjudications Act 1983, s 30, Sch 10, Part I.
Para 4: inserted by the Health and Social Security Adjudications Act 1983, s 29, Sch 9, para 23.

Transfer of Functions
Functions of the Secretary of State in matters concerning only Wales to be exercised by the Secretary of State for Wales, by virtue of SI 1969/388, art 2(1).
Functions of the Secretary of State for Wales, transferred to the National Assembly for Wales, by the National Assembly for Wales (Transfer of Functions) Order 1999, SI 1999/672, art 2, Sch 1.

Extent
This Schedule does not extend to Scotland.

CHILDREN ACT 1989

1989 CHAPTER 41

An Act to reform the law relating to children; to provide for local authority services for children in need and others; to amend the law with respect to children's homes, community homes, voluntary homes and voluntary organisations; to make provision with respect to fostering, child minding and day care for young children and adoption; and for connected purposes

[16th November 1989]

PART III
LOCAL AUTHORITY SUPPORT FOR CHILDREN AND FAMILIES

Provision of services for children and their families

17 Provision of services for children in need, their families and others

(1)   It shall be the general duty of every local authority (in addition to the other duties imposed on them by this Part)—

    (a)   to safeguard and promote the welfare of children within their area who are in need; and

    (b)   so far as is consistent with that duty, to promote the upbringing of such children by their families,

by providing a range and level of services appropriate to those children's needs.

(2)   For the purpose principally of facilitating the discharge of their general duty under this section, every local authority shall have the specific duties and powers set out in Part I of Schedule 2.

(3)   Any service provided by an authority in the exercise of functions conferred on them by this section may be provided for the family of a particular child in need or for any member of his family, if it is provided with a view to safeguarding or promoting the child's welfare.

(4)   The Secretary of State may by order amend any provision of Part I of Schedule 2 or add any further duty or power to those for the time being mentioned there.

(5)   Every local authority—

    (a)   shall facilitate the provision by others (including in particular voluntary organisations) of services which the authority have power to provide by virtue of this section, or section 18, 20, 23 *or* 24 [23, 23B to 23D, 24A or 24B]; and

    (b)   may make such arrangements as they see fit for any person to act on their behalf in the provision of any such service.

(6)   The services provided by a local authority in the exercise of functions conferred on them by this section may include giving assistance in kind or, in exceptional circumstances, in cash.

(7)   Assistance may be unconditional or subject to conditions as to the repayment of the assistance or of its value (in whole or in part).

(8)   Before giving any assistance or imposing any conditions, a local authority shall have regard to the means of the child concerned and of each of his parents.

(9) No person shall be liable to make any repayment of assistance or of its value at any time when he is in receipt of income support[, working families' tax credit] [or disabled person's tax credit] under the [Part VII of the Social Security Contributions and Benefits Act 1992] [or of an income-based jobseeker's allowance].

(10) For the purposes of this Part a child shall be taken to be in need if—

(a) he is unlikely to achieve or maintain, or to have the opportunity of achieving or maintaining, a reasonable standard of health or development without the provision for him of services by a local authority under this Part;

(b) his health or development is likely to be significantly impaired, or further impaired, without the provision for him of such services; or

(c) he is disabled,

and "family", in relation to such a child, includes any person who has parental responsibility for the child and any other person with whom he has been living.

(11) For the purposes of this Part, a child is disabled if he is blind, deaf or dumb or suffers from mental disorder of any kind or is substantially and permanently handicapped by illness, injury or congenital deformity or such other disability as may be prescribed; and in this Part—

"development" means physical, intellectual, emotional, social or behavioural development; and

"health" means physical or mental health.

NOTES

Appointment
Commencement order: SI 1991/828.

Amendment
Sub-s (5): in para (a) words "23 or 24" in italics repealed and subsequent words in square brackets substituted by the Children (Leaving Care) Act 2000, s 7(1), (2).
Date in force: to be appointed: see the Children (Leaving Care) Act 2000, s 8(2).
Sub-s (9): words ", working families' tax credit" in square brackets substituted by virtue of the Tax Credits Act 1999, s 1(2), Sch 1, paras 1(a), 6(d)(i).
Date in force: 5 October 1999: see the Tax Credits Act 1999, s 20(2).
Sub-s (9): words "or disabled person's tax credit" in square brackets substituted by virtue of the Tax Credits Act 1999, s 1(2), Sch 1, paras 1(b), 6(d)(i).
Date in force: 5 October 1999: see the Tax Credits Act 1999, s 20(2).
Sub-s (9): words from "Part VII of" to "Benefits Act 1992" in square brackets substituted by the Social Security (Consequential Provisions) Act 1992, s 4, Sch 2, para 108(a).
Sub-s (9): words "or of an income-based jobseeker's allowance" in square brackets inserted by the Jobseekers Act 1995, s 41(4), Sch 2, para 19(2).

Transfer of Functions
Functions of the Secretary of State, so far as exercisable in relation to Wales, transferred to the National Assembly for Wales, by the National Assembly for Wales (Transfer of Functions) Order 1999, SI 1999/672, art 2, Sch 1.

Extent
This section does not extend to Scotland.

Provision of accommodation for children

20 Provision of accommodation for children: general

(1) Every local authority shall provide accommodation for any child in need within their area who appears to them to require accommodation as a result of—

(a) there being no person who has parental responsibility for him;

(b)   his being lost or having been abandoned; or

(c)   the person who has been caring for him being prevented (whether or not permanently, and for whatever reason) from providing him with suitable accommodation or care.

(2)   Where a local authority provide accommodation under subsection (1) for a child who is ordinarily resident in the area of another local authority, that other local authority may take over the provision of accommodation for the child within—

(a)   three months of being notified in writing that the child is being provided with accommodation; or

(b)   such other longer period as may be prescribed.

(3)   Every local authority shall provide accommodation for any child in need within their area who has reached the age of sixteen and whose welfare the authority consider is likely to be seriously prejudiced if they do not provide him with accommodation.

(4)   A local authority may provide accommodation for any child within their area (even though a person who has parental responsibility for him is able to provide him with accommodation) if they consider that to do so would safeguard or promote the child's welfare.

(5)   A local authority may provide accommodation for any person who has reached the age of sixteen but is under twenty-one in any community home which takes children who have reached the age of sixteen if they consider that to do so would safeguard or promote his welfare.

(6)   Before providing accommodation under this section, a local authority shall, so far as is reasonably practicable and consistent with the child's welfare—

(a)   ascertain the child's wishes regarding the provision of accommodation; and

(b)   give due consideration (having regard to his age and understanding) to such wishes of the child as they have been able to ascertain.

(7)   A local authority may not provide accommodation under this section for any child if any person who—

(a)   has parental responsibility for him; and

(b)   is willing and able to—

(i)   provide accommodation for him; or

(ii)   arrange for accommodation to be provided for him,
objects.

(8)   Any person who has parental responsibility for a child may at any time remove the child from accommodation provided by or on behalf of the local authority under this section.

(9)   Subsections (7) and (8) do not apply while any person—

(a)   in whose favour a residence order is in force with respect to the child; or

(b)   who has care of the child by virtue of an order made in the exercise of the High Court's inherent jurisdiction with respect to children,

agrees to the child being looked after in accommodation provided by or on behalf of the local authority.

(10) Where there is more than one such person as is mentioned in subsection (9), all of them must agree.

(11) Subsections (7) and (8) do not apply where a child who has reached the age of sixteen agrees to being provided with accommodation under this section.

NOTES

Appointment
Commencement order: SI 1991/828.

Extent
This section does not extend to Scotland.

SCHEDULE 2
Local Authority Support for Children and Families

Sections 17, 23, 29

PART I
PROVISION OF SERVICES FOR FAMILIES

Identification of children in need and provision of information

Assessment of children's needs

3   Where it appears to a local authority that a child within their area is in need, the authority may assess his needs for the purposes of this Act at the same time as any assessment of his needs is made under—

(a)   the Chronically Sick and Disabled Persons Act 1970;
(b)   [Part IV of the Education Act 1996];
(c)   the Disabled Persons (Services, Consultation and Representation) Act 1986; or
(d)   any other enactment.

NATIONAL HEALTH SERVICE AND COMMUNITY CARE ACT 1990

1990 CHAPTER 19

An Act to make further provision about health authorities and other bodies constituted in accordance with the National Health Service Act 1977; to provide for the establishment of National Health Service trusts; to make further provision about the financing of the practices of medical practitioners; to amend Part VII of the Local Government (Scotland) Act 1973 and Part III of the Local Government Finance Act 1982; to amend the National Health Service Act 1977 and the National Health Service (Scotland) Act 1978; to amend Part VIII of the Mental Health (Scotland) Act 1984; to make further provision concerning the provision of accommodation and other welfare services by local authorities and the powers of the Secretary of State as respects the social services functions of such authorities; to make provision for and in connection with the establishment of a Clinical Standards Advisory Group; to repeal the Health Services Act 1976; and for connected purposes

[29th June 1990]

General provisions concerning community care services

46 Local authority plans for community care services

(1)   Each local authority—

(a)   shall, within such period after the day appointed for the coming into force of this section as the Secretary of State may direct, prepare and publish a plan for the provision of community care services in their area;

(b)   shall keep the plan prepared by them under paragraph (a) above and any further plans prepared by them under this section under review; and

(c)   shall, at such intervals as the Secretary of State may direct, prepare and publish modifications to the current plan, or if the case requires, a new plan.

(2)   In carrying out any of their functions under paragraphs (a) to (c) of subsection (1) above, a local authority shall consult—

(a)   any [Health Authority the whole or any part of whose area] lies within the area of the local authority;

(b)   ...

(c)   in so far as any proposed plan, review or modifications of a plan may affect or be affected by the provision or availability of housing and the local authority is not itself a local housing authority, within the meaning of the Housing Act 1985, every such local housing authority whose area is within the area of the local authority;

(d)   such voluntary organisations as appear to the authority to represent the interests of persons who use or are likely to use any community care services within the area of the authority or the interests of private carers who, within that area, provide care to persons for whom, in the exercise of their social services functions, the local authority have a power or a duty to provide a service;

(e)   such voluntary housing agencies and other bodies as appear to the local authority to provide housing or community care services in their area; and

(f)   such other persons as the Secretary of State may direct.

(3)   In this section—

"local authority" means the council of a county, [a county borough,] a metropolitan district or a London borough or the Common Council of the City of London;

"community care services" means services which a local authority may provide or arrange to be provided under any of the following provisions—

(a)   Part III of the National Assistance Act 1948;

(b)   section 45 of the Health Services and Public Health Act 1968;

(c)   section 21 of and Schedule 8 to the National Health Service Act 1977; and

(d)   section 117 of the Mental Health Act 1983; and

"private carer" means a person who is not employed to provide the care in question by any body in the exercise of its functions under any enactment.

NOTES

Appointment
Commencement order: SI 1990/2218.

Amendment
Sub-s (2): words omitted repealed and words in square brackets substituted by the Health Authorities Act 1995, ss 2(1), 5(1), Sch 1, para 80, Sch 3.
Sub-s (3): in definition "local authority" words in square brackets inserted by the Local Government (Wales) Act 1994, s 22(4), Sch 10, para 14.

Transfer of Functions
Functions of the Secretary of State, so far as exercisable in relation to Wales, transferred to the National Assembly for Wales, by the National Assembly for Wales (Transfer of Functions) Order 1999, SI 1999/672, art 2, Sch 1.

Extent
This section does not extend to Scotland.

47 Assessment of needs for community care services

(1) Subject to subsections (5) and (6) below, where it appears to a local authority that any person for whom they may provide or arrange for the provision of community care services may be in need of any such services, the authority—

(a) shall carry out an assessment of his needs for those services; and
(b) having regard to the results of that assessment, shall then decide whether his needs call for the provision by them of any such services.

(2) If at any time during the assessment of the needs of any person under subsection (1)(a) above it appears to a local authority that he is a disabled person, the authority—

(a) shall proceed to make such a decision as to the services he requires as is mentioned in section 4 of the Disabled Persons (Services, Consultation and Representation) Act 1986 without his requesting them to do so under that section; and
(b) shall inform him that they will be doing so and of his rights under that Act.

(3) If at any time during the assessment of the needs of any person under subsection (1)(a) above, it appears to a local authority—

(a) that there may be a need for the provision to that person by such [Health Authority] as may be determined in accordance with regulations of any services under the National Health Service Act 1977, or
(b) that there may be a need for the provision to him of any services which fall within the functions of a local housing authority (within the meaning of the Housing Act 1985) which is not the local authority carrying out the assessment,

the local authority shall notify that [Health Authority] or local housing authority and invite them to assist, to such extent as is reasonable in the circumstances, in the making of the assessment; and, in making their decision as to the provision of the services needed for the person in question, the local authority shall take into account any services which are likely to be made available for him by that [Health Authority] or local housing authority.

(4) The Secretary of State may give directions as to the manner in which an assessment under this section is to be carried out or the form it is to take but, subject to any such directions and to subsection (7) below, it shall be carried out in such manner and take such form as the local authority consider appropriate.

(5) Nothing in this section shall prevent a local authority from temporarily providing or arranging for the provision of community care services for any person without carrying out a prior assessment of his needs in accordance with the preceding provisions of this section if, in the opinion of the authority, the condition of that person is such that he requires those services as a matter of urgency.

(6) If, by virtue of subsection (5) above, community care services have been provided temporarily for any person as a matter of urgency, then, as soon as practicable thereafter, an assessment of his needs shall be made in accordance with the preceding provisions of this section.

(7)   This section is without prejudice to section 3 of the Disabled Persons (Services, Consultation and Representation) Act 1986.

(8)   In this section—

"disabled person" has the same meaning as in that Act; and
"local authority" and "community care services" have the same meanings as in section 46 above.

NOTES

Appointment
Commencement order: SI 1992/2975.

Amendment
Sub-s (3): words in square brackets substituted by the Health Authorities Act 1995, s 2(1), Sch 1, para 81.

Transfer of Functions
Functions of the Secretary of State, so far as exercisable in relation to Wales, transferred to the National Assembly for Wales, by the National Assembly for Wales (Transfer of Functions) Order 1999, SI 1999/672, art 2, Sch 1.

Extent
This section does not extend to Scotland.

SOCIAL SECURITY CONTRIBUTIONS AND BENEFITS ACT 1992

1992 CHAPTER 4

An Act to consolidate certain enactments relating to social security contributions and benefits with amendments to give effect to recommendations of the Law Commission and the Scottish Law Commission

[13th February 1992]

146 Persons outside Great Britain

(1)   Regulations may modify the provisions of this Part of this Act in their application to persons who are or have been outside Great Britain at any prescribed time or in any prescribed circumstances.

(2)   Subject to any regulations under subsection (1) above, no child benefit shall be payable in respect of a child for any week unless—

(a)   he is in Great Britain in that week; and
(b)   either he or at least one of his parents has been in Great Britain for more than 182 days in the 52 weeks preceding that week.

(3)   Subject to any regulations under subsection (1) above, no person shall be entitled to child benefit for any week unless—

(a)   he is in Great Britain in that week; and
(b)   he has been in Great Britain for more than 182 days in the 52 weeks preceding that week.

NOTES

Derivation
This section derived from the Child Benefit Act 1975, s 13.

Subordinate Legislation
Child Benefit (Residence and Persons Abroad) Amendment Regulations 1999, SI 1999/198 (made under sub-s (1)).

[146A . . .]

. . .

NOTES

Amendment
Inserted by the Asylum and Immigration Act 1996, s 10.
Repealed by the Immigration and Asylum Act 1999, s 169(1), (3), Sch 14, para 92, Sch 16.
Date in force: 3 April 2000: see SI 2000/464, art 2, Schedule.

HOUSING ACT 1996

1996 CHAPTER 52

An Act to make provision about housing, including provision about the social rented sector, houses in multiple occupation, landlord and tenant matters, the administration of housing benefit, the conduct of tenants, the allocation of housing accommodation by local housing authorities and homelessness; and for connected purposes

[24th July 1996]

The housing register

161 Allocation only to qualifying persons

(1)   A local housing authority shall allocate housing accommodation only to persons ("qualifying persons") who are qualified to be allocated housing accommodation by that authority.

(2)   A person subject to immigration control within the meaning of the Asylum and Immigration Act 1996 is not qualified to be allocated housing accommodation by any authority in England and Wales unless he is of a class prescribed by regulations made by the Secretary of State.

[(2A)   Regulations may not be made under subsection (2) so as to include in a prescribed class any person to whom section 115 of the Immigration and Asylum Act 1999 (exclusion from benefits) applies.]

(3)   The Secretary of State may by regulations prescribe other classes of persons who are, or are not, qualifying persons in relation to local housing authorities generally or any particular local housing authority.

(4)   Subject to subsection (2) and any regulations under subsection (3) a local housing authority may decide what classes of persons are, or are not, qualifying persons.

(5)   The prohibition in subsection (1) extends to the allocation of housing accommodation to two or more persons jointly if any of them is excluded from being a qualifying person by subsection (2) or regulations under subsection (3).

(6)   The prohibition does not otherwise extend to the allocation of housing accommodation to two or more persons jointly if one or more of them are qualifying persons.

NOTES

Amendment
Sub-s (2A): inserted by the Immigration and Asylum Act 1999, s 117(3).
Date in force: 3 April 2000: see SI 2000/464, art 2, Schedule.

Subordinate Legislation
Allocation of Housing (England) Regulations 2000, SI 2000/702 (made under sub-ss (2), (3)).
Allocation of Housing (Wales) Regulations 2000, SI 2000/1080 (made under sub-ss (2), (3)).
Allocation of Housing and Homelessness (Amendment) (England) Regulations 1999, SI 1999/2135 (made under sub-ss (2), (3)).

Extent
This section does not extend to Scotland.

164 Notification of adverse decision and right to review

(1)   If a local housing authority decide—

  (a)   not to put a person on their housing register who has applied to be put on, or
  (b)   to remove a person from their housing register otherwise than at his request,

they shall notify him of their decision and of the reasons for it.

(2)   The notice shall also inform him of his right to request a review of the decision and of the time within which such a request must be made.

(3)   A request for review must be made before the end of the period of 21 days beginning with the day on which he is notified of the authority's decision and reasons, or such longer period as the authority may in writing allow.

(4)   There is no right to request a review of the decision reached on an earlier review.

(5)   On a request being duly made to them, the authority shall review their decision.

(6)   Notice required to be given to a person under this section shall be given in writing and, if not received by him, shall be treated as having been given if it is made available at the authority's office for a reasonable period for collection by him.

NOTES

Extent
This section does not extend to Scotland.

The allocation scheme

167 Allocation in accordance with allocation scheme

(1)   Every local housing authority shall have a scheme (their "allocation scheme") for determining priorities, and as to the procedure to be followed, in allocating housing accommodation.
  For this purpose "procedure" includes all aspects of the allocation process, including the persons or descriptions of persons by whom decisions are to be taken.

(2)   As regards priorities, the scheme shall be framed so as to secure that reasonable preference is given to—

(a)   people occupying insanitary or overcrowded housing or otherwise living in unsatisfactory housing conditions,

(b)   people occupying housing accommodation which is temporary or occupied on insecure terms,

(c)   families with dependent children,

(d)   households consisting of or including someone who is expecting a child,

(e)   households consisting of or including someone with a particular need for settled accommodation on medical or welfare grounds, and

(f)   households whose social or economic circumstances are such that they have difficulty in securing settled accommodation.

The scheme shall also be framed so as to secure that additional preference is given to households within paragraph (e) . . . who cannot reasonably be expected to find settled accommodation for themselves in the foreseeable future.

(3)   The Secretary of State may by regulations—

(a)   specify further descriptions of people to whom preference is to be given as mentioned in subsection (2), or

(b)   amend or repeal any part of subsection (2).

(4)   The Secretary of State may by regulations specify factors which a local housing authority shall not take into account in allocating housing accommodation.

(5)   As regards the procedure to be followed, the scheme shall be framed in accordance with such principles as the Secretary of State may prescribe by regulations.

(6)   Subject to the above provisions, and to any regulations made under them, the authority may decide on what principles the scheme is to be framed.

(7)   Before adopting an allocation scheme, or making an alteration to their scheme reflecting a major change of policy, a local housing authority shall—

(a)   send a copy of the draft scheme, or proposed alteration, to every registered social landlord with which they have nomination arrangements (see section 159(4)), and

(b)   afford those persons a reasonable opportunity to comment on the proposals.

(8)   A local housing authority shall not allocate housing accommodation except in accordance with their allocation scheme.

NOTES

Amendment
Sub-s (2): words omitted repealed by SI 1997/1902, reg 3.
Date in force: 1 November 1997: see SI 1997/1902, reg 1.

Extent
This section does not extend to Scotland.

Application for assistance in case of homelessness or threatened homelessness

183 Application for assistance

(1)   The following provisions of this Part apply where a person applies to a local housing authority for accommodation, or for assistance in obtaining accommodation, and the authority have reason to believe that he is or may be homeless or threatened with homelessness.

(2)   In this Part—

> "applicant" means a person making such an application,
> "assistance under this Part" means the benefit of any function under the following provisions of this Part relating to accommodation or assistance in obtaining accommodation, and
> "eligible for assistance" means not excluded from such assistance by section 185 (persons from abroad not eligible for housing assistance) *or section 186 (asylum seekers and their dependants)*.

(3)   Nothing in this section or the following provisions of this Part affects a person's entitlement to advice and information under section 179 (duty to provide advisory services).

NOTES

Amendment
Sub-s (2): in definition "eligible for assistance" words "or section 186 (asylum seekers and their dependants)" in italics repealed by the Immigration and Asylum Act 1999, s 169(1), (3), Sch 14, para 116, Sch 16.
Date in force: to be appointed: see the Immigration and Asylum Act 1999, s 170(4).

Extent
This section does not extend to Scotland.

189 Priority need for accommodation

(1)   The following have a priority need for accommodation—

(a)   a pregnant woman or a person with whom she resides or might reasonably be expected to reside;

(b)   a person with whom dependent children reside or might reasonably be expected to reside;

(c)   a person who is vulnerable as a result of old age, mental illness or handicap or physical disability or other special reason, or with whom such a person resides or might reasonably be expected to reside;

(d)   a person who is homeless or threatened with homelessness as a result of an emergency such as flood, fire or other disaster.

(2)   The Secretary of State may by order—

(a)   specify further descriptions of persons as having a priority need for accommodation, and

(b)   amend or repeal any part of subsection (1).

(3)   Before making such an order the Secretary of State shall consult such associations representing relevant authorities, and such other persons, as he considers appropriate.

(4)   No such order shall be made unless a draft of it has been approved by resolution of each House of Parliament.

NOTES

Subordinate Legislation
Homeless Persons (Priority Need) (Wales) Order 2001, SI 2001/607 (made under sub-s (2)).

Extent
This section does not extend to Scotland.

192 Duty to persons not in priority need who are not homeless intentionally

(1)   This section applies where the local housing authority—

   (a)   are satisfied that an applicant is homeless and eligible for assistance, and
   (b)   are not satisfied that he became homeless intentionally,

but are not satisfied that he has a priority need.

(2)   The authority shall provide the applicant with advice and such assistance as they consider appropriate in the circumstances in any attempts he may make to secure that accommodation becomes available for his occupation.

NOTES

Extent
This section does not extend to Scotland.

HUMAN RIGHTS ACT 1998

1998 CHAPTER 42

An Act to give further effect to rights and freedoms guaranteed under the European Convention on Human Rights; to make provision with respect to holders of certain judicial offices who become judges of the European Court of Human Rights; and for connected purposes.

[9th November 1998]

BE IT ENACTED by the Queen's most Excellent Majesty, by and with the advice and consent of the Lords Spiritual and Temporal, and Commons, in this present Parliament assembled, and by the authority of the same, as follows:—

Introduction

1 The Convention Rights

(1)   In this Act "the Convention rights" means the rights and fundamental freedoms set out in—

   (a)   Articles 2 to 12 and 14 of the Convention,
   (b)   Articles 1 to 3 of the First Protocol, and
   (c)   Articles 1 and 2 of the Sixth Protocol,

as read with Articles 16 to 18 of the Convention.

(2)   Those Articles are to have effect for the purposes of this Act subject to any designated derogation or reservation (as to which see sections 14 and 15).

(3)   The Articles are set out in Schedule 1.

(4)   The Secretary of State may by order make such amendments to this Act as he considers appropriate to reflect the effect, in relation to the United Kingdom, of a protocol.

(5)   In subsection (4) "protocol" means a protocol to the Convention—

   (a)   which the United Kingdom has ratified; or
   (b)   which the United Kingdom has signed with a view to ratification.

(6)   No amendment may be made by an order under subsection (4) so as to come into force before the protocol concerned is in force in relation to the United Kingdom.

NOTES

Initial Commencement
To be appointed
To be appointed: see s 22(3).

Appointment
Appointment: 2 October 2000: see SI 2000/1851, art 2.

2 Interpretation of Convention rights

(1)   A court or tribunal determining a question which has arisen in connection with a Convention right must take into account any—

- (a)   judgment, decision, declaration or advisory opinion of the European Court of Human Rights,
- (b)   opinion of the Commission given in a report adopted under Article 31 of the Convention,
- (c)   decision of the Commission in connection with Article 26 or 27(2) of the Convention, or
- (d)   decision of the Committee of Ministers taken under Article 46 of the Convention,

whenever made or given, so far as, in the opinion of the court or tribunal, it is relevant to the proceedings in which that question has arisen.

(2)   Evidence of any judgment, decision, declaration or opinion of which account may have to be taken under this section is to be given in proceedings before any court or tribunal in such manner as may be provided by rules.

(3)   In this section "rules" means rules of court or, in the case of proceedings before a tribunal, rules made for the purposes of this section—

- (a)   by the Lord Chancellor or the Secretary of State, in relation to any proceedings outside Scotland;
- (b)   by the Secretary of State, in relation to proceedings in Scotland; or
- (c)   by a Northern Ireland department, in relation to proceedings before a tribunal in Northern Ireland—
  - (i)   which deals with transferred matters; and
  - (ii)   for which no rules made under paragraph (a) are in force.

NOTES

Initial Commencement
To be appointed
To be appointed: see s 22(3).

Appointment
Appointment: 2 October 2000: see SI 2000/1851, art 2.

Subordinate Legislation
Act of Adjournal (Criminal Procedure Rules Amendment No 2) (Human Rights Act 1998) 2000, SSI 2000/315.
Act of Sederunt (Rules of the Court of Session Amendment No 6) (Human Rights Act 1998) 2000, SSI 2000/316.

Legislation

3 Interpretation of legislation

(1) So far as it is possible to do so, primary legislation and subordinate legislation must be read and given effect in a way which is compatible with the Convention rights.

(2) This section—

(a) applies to primary legislation and subordinate legislation whenever enacted;
(b) does not affect the validity, continuing operation or enforcement of any incompatible primary legislation; and
(c) does not affect the validity, continuing operation or enforcement of any incompatible subordinate legislation if (disregarding any possibility of revocation) primary legislation prevents removal of the incompatibility.

NOTES

Initial Commencement
To be appointed
To be appointed: see s 22(3).

Appointment
Appointment: 2 October 2000: see SI 2000/1851, art 2.

4 Declaration of incompatibility

(1) Subsection (2) applies in any proceedings in which a court determines whether a provision of primary legislation is compatible with a Convention right.

(2) If the court is satisfied that the provision is incompatible with a Convention right, it may make a declaration of that incompatibility.

(3) Subsection (4) applies in any proceedings in which a court determines whether a provision of subordinate legislation, made in the exercise of a power conferred by primary legislation, is compatible with a Convention right.

(4) If the court is satisfied—

(a) that the provision is incompatible with a Convention right, and
(b) that (disregarding any possibility of revocation) the primary legislation concerned prevents removal of the incompatibility,

it may make a declaration of that incompatibility.

(5) In this section "court" means—

(a) the House of Lords;
(b) the Judicial Committee of the Privy Council;
(c) the Courts-Martial Appeal Court;
(d) in Scotland, the High Court of Justiciary sitting otherwise than as a trial court or the Court of Session;
(e) in England and Wales or Northern Ireland, the High Court or the Court of Appeal.

(6) A declaration under this section ("a declaration of incompatibility")—

(a) does not affect the validity, continuing operation or enforcement of the provision in respect of which it is given; and
(b) is not binding on the parties to the proceedings in which it is made.

NOTES

Initial Commencement
To be appointed
To be appointed: see s 22(3).

Appointment
Appointment: 2 October 2000: see SI 2000/1851, art 2.

5 Right of Crown to intervene

(1)   Where a court is considering whether to make a declaration of incompatibility, the Crown is entitled to notice in accordance with rules of court.

(2)   In any case to which subsection (1) applies—

(a)   a Minister of the Crown (or a person nominated by him),
(b)   a member of the Scottish Executive,
(c)   a Northern Ireland Minister,
(d)   a Northern Ireland department,

is entitled, on giving notice in accordance with rules of court, to be joined as a party to the proceedings.

(3)   Notice under subsection (2) may be given at any time during the proceedings.

(4)   A person who has been made a party to criminal proceedings (other than in Scotland) as the result of a notice under subsection (2) may, with leave, appeal to the House of Lords against any declaration of incompatibility made in the proceedings.

(5)   In subsection (4)—

"criminal proceedings" includes all proceedings before the Courts-Martial Appeal Court; and
"leave" means leave granted by the court making the declaration of incompatibility or by the House of Lords.

NOTES

Initial Commencement
To be appointed
To be appointed: see s 22(3).

Appointment
Appointment: 2 October 2000: see SI 2000/1851, art 2.

Transfer of Functions
The function under sub-s (2) shall be exercisable by the National Assembly for Wales concurrently with any Minister of the Crown by whom it is exercisable, in so far as it relates to any proceedings in which a court is considering whether to make a declaration of incompatibility within the meaning of s 4 of this Act, in respect of subordinate legislation made by the National Assembly, and subordinate legislation made, in relation to Wales, by a Minister of the Crown in the exercise of a function which is exercisable by the National Assembly: see the National Assembly for Wales (Transfer of Functions) (No 2) Order 2000, SI 2000/1830, art 2.

Subordinate Legislation
UK
Criminal Appeal (Amendment) Rules 2000, SI 2000/2036.
Scotland
Act of Adjournal (Criminal Procedure Rules Amendment No 2) (Human Rights Act 1998) 2000, SSI 2000/315.
Act of Sederunt (Rules of the Court of Session Amendment No 6) (Human Rights Act 1998) 2000, SSI 2000/316.

Public authorities

6 Acts of public authorities

(1)   It is unlawful for a public authority to act in a way which is incompatible with a Convention right.

(2)   Subsection (1) does not apply to an act if—

  (a)   as the result of one or more provisions of primary legislation, the authority could not have acted differently; or

  (b)   in the case of one or more provisions of, or made under, primary legislation which cannot be read or given effect in a way which is compatible with the Convention rights, the authority was acting so as to give effect to or enforce those provisions.

(3)   In this section "public authority" includes—

  (a)   a court or tribunal, and

  (b)   any person certain of whose functions are functions of a public nature,

but does not include either House of Parliament or a person exercising functions in connection with proceedings in Parliament.

(4)   In subsection (3) "Parliament" does not include the House of Lords in its judicial capacity.

(5)   In relation to a particular act, a person is not a public authority by virtue only of subsection (3)(b) if the nature of the act is private.

(6)   "An act" includes a failure to act but does not include a failure to—

  (a)   introduce in, or lay before, Parliament a proposal for legislation; or

  (b)   make any primary legislation or remedial order.

NOTES

Initial Commencement
To be appointed
To be appointed: see s 22(3).

Appointment
Appointment: 2 October 2000: see SI 2000/1851, art 2.

7 Proceedings

(1)   A person who claims that a public authority has acted (or proposes to act) in a way which is made unlawful by section 6(1) may—

  (a)   bring proceedings against the authority under this Act in the appropriate court or tribunal, or

  (b)   rely on the Convention right or rights concerned in any legal proceedings,

but only if he is (or would be) a victim of the unlawful act.

(2)   In subsection (1)(a) "appropriate court or tribunal" means such court or tribunal as may be determined in accordance with rules; and proceedings against an authority include a counterclaim or similar proceeding.

(3)   If the proceedings are brought on an application for judicial review, the applicant is to be taken to have a sufficient interest in relation to the unlawful act only if he is, or would be, a victim of that act.

(4)   If the proceedings are made by way of a petition for judicial review in Scotland, the applicant shall be taken to have title and interest to sue in relation to the unlawful act only if he is, or would be, a victim of that act.

(5)   Proceedings under subsection (1)(a) must be brought before the end of—

    (a)   the period of one year beginning with the date on which the act complained of took place; or

    (b)   such longer period as the court or tribunal considers equitable having regard to all the circumstances,

but that is subject to any rule imposing a stricter time limit in relation to the procedure in question.

(6)   In subsection (1)(b) "legal proceedings" includes—

    (a)   proceedings brought by or at the instigation of a public authority; and

    (b)   an appeal against the decision of a court or tribunal.

(7)   For the purposes of this section, a person is a victim of an unlawful act only if he would be a victim for the purposes of Article 34 of the Convention if proceedings were brought in the European Court of Human Rights in respect of that act.

(8)   Nothing in this Act creates a criminal offence.

(9)   In this section "rules" means—

    (a)   in relation to proceedings before a court or tribunal outside Scotland, rules made by the Lord Chancellor or the Secretary of State for the purposes of this section or rules of court,

    (b)   in relation to proceedings before a court or tribunal in Scotland, rules made by the Secretary of State for those purposes,

    (c)   in relation to proceedings before a tribunal in Northern Ireland—

        (i)   which deals with transferred matters; and

        (ii)   for which no rules made under paragraph (a) are in force,
           rules made by a Northern Ireland department for those purposes,

and includes provision made by order under section 1 of the Courts and Legal Services Act 1990.

(10)   In making rules, regard must be had to section 9.

(11)   The Minister who has power to make rules in relation to a particular tribunal may, to the extent he considers it necessary to ensure that the tribunal can provide an appropriate remedy in relation to an act (or proposed act) of a public authority which is (or would be) unlawful as a result of section 6(1), by order add to—

    (a)   the relief or remedies which the tribunal may grant; or

    (b)   the grounds on which it may grant any of them.

(12)   An order made under subsection (11) may contain such incidental, supplemental, consequential or transitional provision as the Minister making it considers appropriate.

(13)   "The Minister" includes the Northern Ireland department concerned.

NOTES

Initial Commencement
To be appointed
To be appointed: see s 22(3).

Appointment
Appointment: 2 October 2000: see SI 2000/1851, art 2.

Subordinate Legislation
UK
Proscribed Organisations Appeal Commission (Human Rights Act Proceedings) Rules 2001, SI 2001/127 (made under sub-s 7(9)(a), (b)).
Scotland
Human Rights Act 1998 (Jurisdiction) (Scotland) Rules 2000, SSI 2000/301.

8 Judicial remedies

(1)   In relation to any act (or proposed act) of a public authority which the court finds is (or would be) unlawful, it may grant such relief or remedy, or make such order, within its powers as it considers just and appropriate.

(2)   But damages may be awarded only by a court which has power to award damages, or to order the payment of compensation, in civil proceedings.

(3)   No award of damages is to be made unless, taking account of all the circumstances of the case, including—

(a)   any other relief or remedy granted, or order made, in relation to the act in question (by that or any other court), and
(b)   the consequences of any decision (of that or any other court) in respect of that act,

the court is satisfied that the award is necessary to afford just satisfaction to the person in whose favour it is made.

(4)   In determining—

(a)   whether to award damages, or
(b)   the amount of an award,

the court must take into account the principles applied by the European Court of Human Rights in relation to the award of compensation under Article 41 of the Convention.

(5)   A public authority against which damages are awarded is to be treated—

(a)   in Scotland, for the purposes of section 3 of the Law Reform (Miscellaneous Provisions) (Scotland) Act 1940 as if the award were made in an action of damages in which the authority has been found liable in respect of loss or damage to the person to whom the award is made;
(b)   for the purposes of the Civil Liability (Contribution) Act 1978 as liable in respect of damage suffered by the person to whom the award is made.

(6)   In this section—

"court" includes a tribunal;
"damages" means damages for an unlawful act of a public authority; and
"unlawful" means unlawful under section 6(1).

NOTES

Initial Commencement
To be appointed
To be appointed: see s 22(3).

Appointment
Appointment: 2 October 2000: see SI 2000/1851, art 2.

9 Judicial acts

(1)   Proceedings under section 7(1)(a) in respect of a judicial act may be brought only—

    (a)   by exercising a right of appeal;

    (b)   on an application (in Scotland a petition) for judicial review; or

    (c)   in such other forum as may be prescribed by rules.

(2)   That does not affect any rule of law which prevents a court from being the subject of judicial review.

(3)   In proceedings under this Act in respect of a judicial act done in good faith, damages may not be awarded otherwise than to compensate a person to the extent required by Article 5(5) of the Convention.

(4)   An award of damages permitted by subsection (3) is to be made against the Crown; but no award may be made unless the appropriate person, if not a party to the proceedings, is joined.

(5)   In this section—

> "appropriate person" means the Minister responsible for the court concerned, or a person or government department nominated by him;
> "court" includes a tribunal;
> "judge" includes a member of a tribunal, a justice of the peace and a clerk or other officer entitled to exercise the jurisdiction of a court;
> "judicial act" means a judicial act of a court and includes an act done on the instructions, or on behalf, of a judge; and
> "rules" has the same meaning as in section 7(9).

NOTES

Initial Commencement
To be appointed
To be appointed: see s 22(3).

Appointment
Appointment: 2 October 2000: see SI 2000/1851, art 2.

Subordinate Legislation
Human Rights Act 1998 (Jurisdiction) (Scotland) Rules 2000, SSI 2000/301.

Remedial action

10 Power to take remedial action

(1)   This section applies if—

    (a)   a provision of legislation has been declared under section 4 to be incompatible with a Convention right and, if an appeal lies—

        (i)   all persons who may appeal have stated in writing that they do not intend to do so;

        (ii)   the time for bringing an appeal has expired and no appeal has been brought within that time; or

        (iii)   an appeal brought within that time has been determined or abandoned; or

    (b)   it appears to a Minister of the Crown or Her Majesty in Council that, having regard to a finding of the European Court of Human Rights made after the coming into force of this section in proceedings against the United Kingdom, a provision of legislation is incompatible with an obligation of the United Kingdom arising from the Convention.

(2)   If a Minister of the Crown considers that there are compelling reasons for proceeding under this section, he may by order make such amendments to the legislation as he considers necessary to remove the incompatibility.

(3)   If, in the case of subordinate legislation, a Minister of the Crown considers—

(a)   that it is necessary to amend the primary legislation under which the subordinate legislation in question was made, in order to enable the incompatibility to be removed, and

(b)   that there are compelling reasons for proceeding under this section,

he may by order make such amendments to the primary legislation as he considers necessary.

(4)   This section also applies where the provision in question is in subordinate legislation and has been quashed, or declared invalid, by reason of incompatibility with a Convention right and the Minister proposes to proceed under paragraph 2(b) of Schedule 2.

(5)   If the legislation is an Order in Council, the power conferred by subsection (2) or (3) is exercisable by Her Majesty in Council.

(6)   In this section "legislation" does not include a Measure of the Church Assembly or of the General Synod of the Church of England.

(7)   Schedule 2 makes further provision about remedial orders.

NOTES

Initial Commencement
To be appointed
To be appointed: see s 22(3).

Appointment
Appointment: 2 October 2000: see SI 2000/1851, art 2.

Other rights and proceedings

11 Safeguard for existing human rights

A person's reliance on a Convention right does not restrict—

(a)   any other right or freedom conferred on him by or under any law having effect in any part of the United Kingdom; or

(b)   his right to make any claim or bring any proceedings which he could make or bring apart from sections 7 to 9.

NOTES

Initial Commencement
To be appointed
To be appointed: see s 22(3).

Appointment
Appointment: 2 October 2000: see SI 2000/1851, art 2.

12 Freedom of expression

(1)   This section applies if a court is considering whether to grant any relief which, if granted, might affect the exercise of the Convention right to freedom of expression.

(2)   If the person against whom the application for relief is made ("the respondent") is neither present nor represented, no such relief is to be granted unless the court is satisfied—

(a)   that the applicant has taken all practicable steps to notify the respondent; or

(b)   that there are compelling reasons why the respondent should not be notified.

(3)   No such relief is to be granted so as to restrain publication before trial unless the court is satisfied that the applicant is likely to establish that publication should not be allowed.

(4)   The court must have particular regard to the importance of the Convention right to freedom of expression and, where the proceedings relate to material which the respondent claims, or which appears to the court, to be journalistic, literary or artistic material (or to conduct connected with such material), to—

(a)   the extent to which—

(i)   the material has, or is about to, become available to the public; or

(ii)   it is, or would be, in the public interest for the material to be published;

(b)   any relevant privacy code.

(5)   In this section—

"court" includes a tribunal; and

"relief" includes any remedy or order (other than in criminal proceedings).

NOTES

Initial Commencement
To be appointed
To be appointed: see s 22(3).

Appointment
Appointment: 2 October 2000: see SI 2000/1851, art 2.

13 Freedom of thought, conscience and religion

(1)   If a court's determination of any question arising under this Act might affect the exercise by a religious organisation (itself or its members collectively) of the Convention right to freedom of thought, conscience and religion, it must have particular regard to the importance of that right.

(2)   In this section "court" includes a tribunal.

NOTES

Initial Commencement
To be appointed
To be appointed: see s 22(3).

Appointment
Appointment: 2 October 2000: see SI 2000/1851, art 2.

Derogations and reservations

14 Derogations

(1)   In this Act "designated derogation" means—

. . .

any derogation by the United Kingdom from an Article of the Convention, or of any protocol to the Convention, which is designated for the purposes of this Act in an order made by the Secretary of State.

(2)   . . .

(3)   If a designated derogation is amended or replaced it ceases to be a designated derogation.

(4) But subsection (3) does not prevent the Secretary of State from exercising his power under subsection (1)... to make a fresh designation order in respect of the Article concerned.

(5) The Secretary of State must by order make such amendments to Schedule 3 as he considers appropriate to reflect—

(a) any designation order; or
(b) the effect of subsection (3).

(6) A designation order may be made in anticipation of the making by the United Kingdom of a proposed derogation.

NOTES

Initial Commencement
To be appointed
To be appointed: see s 22(3).

Appointment
Appointment: 2 October 2000: see SI 2000/1851, art 2.

Amendment
Sub-s (1): words omitted repealed by SI 2001/1216, art 2(a).
Date in force: 1 April 2001: see SI 2001/1216, art 1.
Sub-s (2): repealed by SI 2001/1216, art 2(b).
Date in force: 1 April 2001: see SI 2001/1216, art 1.
Sub-s (4): reference omitted repealed by SI 2001/1216, art 2(c).
Date in force: 1 April 2001: see SI 2001/1216, art 1.

15 Reservations

(1) In this Act "designated reservation" means—

(a) the United Kingdom's reservation to Article 2 of the First Protocol to the Convention; and
(b) any other reservation by the United Kingdom to an Article of the Convention, or of any protocol to the Convention, which is designated for the purposes of this Act in an order made by the Secretary of State.

(2) The text of the reservation referred to in subsection (1)(a) is set out in Part II of Schedule 3.

(3) If a designated reservation is withdrawn wholly or in part it ceases to be a designated reservation.

(4) But subsection (3) does not prevent the Secretary of State from exercising his power under subsection (1)(b) to make a fresh designation order in respect of the Article concerned.

(5) The Secretary of State must by order make such amendments to this Act as he considers appropriate to reflect—

(a) any designation order; or
(b) the effect of subsection (3).

NOTES

Initial Commencement
To be appointed
To be appointed: see s 22(3).

Appointment
Appointment: 2 October 2000: see SI 2000/1851, art 2.

16 Period for which designated derogations have effect

(1) If it has not already been withdrawn by the United Kingdom, a designated derogation ceases to have effect for the purposes of this Act—

> . . .
>
> at the end of the period of five years beginning with the date on which the order designating it was made.

(2) At any time before the period—

(a) fixed by subsection (1). . ., or
(b) extended by an order under this subsection,

comes to an end, the Secretary of State may by order extend it by a further period of five years.

(3) An order under section 14(1). . . ceases to have effect at the end of the period for consideration, unless a resolution has been passed by each House approving the order.

(4) Subsection (3) does not affect—

(a) anything done in reliance on the order; or
(b) the power to make a fresh order under section 14(1). . ..

(5) In subsection (3) "period for consideration" means the period of forty days beginning with the day on which the order was made.

(6) In calculating the period for consideration, no account is to be taken of any time during which—

(a) Parliament is dissolved or prorogued; or
(b) both Houses are adjourned for more than four days.

(7) If a designated derogation is withdrawn by the United Kingdom, the Secretary of State must by order make such amendments to this Act as he considers are required to reflect that withdrawal.

NOTES

Initial Commencement
To be appointed
To be appointed: see s 22(3).

Appointment
Appointment: 2 October 2000: see SI 2000/1851, art 2.

Amendment
Sub-s (1): words omitted repealed by SI 2001/1216, art 3(a).
Date in force: 1 April 2001: see SI 2001/1216, art 1.
Sub-s (2): in para (b) words omitted repealed by SI 2001/1216, art 3(b).
Date in force: 1 April 2001: see SI 2001/1216, art 1.
Sub-s (3): reference omitted repealed by SI 2001/1216, art 3(c).
Date in force: 1 April 2001: see SI 2001/1216, art 1.
Sub-s (4): in para (b) reference omitted repealed by SI 2001/1216, art 3(d).
Date in force: 1 April 2001: see SI 2001/1216, art 1.

Subordinate Legislation
Human Rights Act (Amendment) Order 2001, 2001/1216 (made under sub-s (7)).

17 Periodic review of designated reservations

(1) The appropriate Minister must review the designated reservation referred to in section 15(1)(a)—

(a) before the end of the period of five years beginning with the date on which section 1(2) came into force; and

(b) if that designation is still in force, before the end of the period of five years beginning with the date on which the last report relating to it was laid under subsection (3).

(2) The appropriate Minister must review each of the other designated reservations (if any)—

(a) before the end of the period of five years beginning with the date on which the order designating the reservation first came into force; and

(b) if the designation is still in force, before the end of the period of five years beginning with the date on which the last report relating to it was laid under subsection (3).

(3) The Minister conducting a review under this section must prepare a report on the result of the review and lay a copy of it before each House of Parliament.

NOTES

Initial Commencement
To be appointed
To be appointed: see s 22(3).

Appointment
Appointment: 2 October 2000: see SI 2000/1851, art 2.

Judges of the European Court of Human Rights

18 Appointment to European Court of Human Rights

(1) In this section "judicial office" means the office of—

(a) Lord Justice of Appeal, Justice of the High Court or Circuit judge, in England and Wales;

(b) judge of the Court of Session or sheriff, in Scotland;

(c) Lord Justice of Appeal, judge of the High Court or county court judge, in Northern Ireland.

(2) The holder of a judicial office may become a judge of the European Court of Human Rights ("the Court") without being required to relinquish his office.

(3) But he is not required to perform the duties of his judicial office while he is a judge of the Court.

(4) In respect of any period during which he is a judge of the Court—

(a) a Lord Justice of Appeal or Justice of the High Court is not to count as a judge of the relevant court for the purposes of section 2(1) or 4(1) of the Supreme Court Act 1981 (maximum number of judges) nor as a judge of the Supreme Court for the purposes of section 12(1) to (6) of that Act (salaries etc);

(b) a judge of the Court of Session is not to count as a judge of that court for the purposes of section 1(1) of the Court of Session Act 1988 (maximum number of judges) or of section 9(1)(c) of the Administration of Justice Act 1973 ("the 1973 Act") (salaries etc);

(c) a Lord Justice of Appeal or judge of the High Court in Northern Ireland is not to count as a judge of the relevant court for the purposes of section 2(1) or 3(1) of the Judicature (Northern Ireland) Act 1978 (maximum number of judges) nor as a judge of the Supreme Court of Northern Ireland for the purposes of section 9(1)(d) of the 1973 Act (salaries etc);

(d)   a Circuit judge is not to count as such for the purposes of section 18 of the Courts Act 1971 (salaries etc);

(e)   a sheriff is not to count as such for the purposes of section 14 of the Sheriff Courts (Scotland) Act 1907 (salaries etc);

(f)   a county court judge of Northern Ireland is not to count as such for the purposes of section 106 of the County Courts Act (Northern Ireland) 1959 (salaries etc).

(5)   If a sheriff principal is appointed a judge of the Court, section 11(1) of the Sheriff Courts (Scotland) Act 1971 (temporary appointment of sheriff principal) applies, while he holds that appointment, as if his office is vacant.

(6)   Schedule 4 makes provision about judicial pensions in relation to the holder of a judicial office who serves as a judge of the Court.

(7)   The Lord Chancellor or the Secretary of State may by order make such transitional provision (including, in particular, provision for a temporary increase in the maximum number of judges) as he considers appropriate in relation to any holder of a judicial office who has completed his service as a judge of the Court.

NOTES

Initial Commencement
Royal Assent
Royal Assent: 9 November 1998: see s 22(2).

Parliamentary procedure

19 Statements of compatibility

(1)   A Minister of the Crown in charge of a Bill in either House of Parliament must, before Second Reading of the Bill—

(a)   make a statement to the effect that in his view the provisions of the Bill are compatible with the Convention rights ("a statement of compatibility"); or

(b)   make a statement to the effect that although he is unable to make a statement of compatibility the government nevertheless wishes the House to proceed with the Bill.

(2)   The statement must be in writing and be published in such manner as the Minister making it considers appropriate.

NOTES

Initial Commencement
To be appointed
To be appointed: see s 22(3).

Appointment
Appointment: 24 November 1998: see SI 1998/2882, art 2.

Supplemental

20 Orders etc under this Act

(1)   Any power of a Minister of the Crown to make an order under this Act is exercisable by statutory instrument.

(2)   The power of the Lord Chancellor or the Secretary of State to make rules (other than rules of court) under section 2(3) or 7(9) is exercisable by statutory instrument.

(3) Any statutory instrument made under section 14, 15 or 16(7) must be laid before Parliament.

(4) No order may be made by the Lord Chancellor or the Secretary of State under section 1(4), 7(11) or 16(2) unless a draft of the order has been laid before, and approved by, each House of Parliament.

(5) Any statutory instrument made under section 18(7) or Schedule 4, or to which subsection (2) applies, shall be subject to annulment in pursuance of a resolution of either House of Parliament.

(6) The power of a Northern Ireland department to make—

    (a) rules under section 2(3)(c) or 7(9)(c), or
    (b) an order under section 7(11),

is exercisable by statutory rule for the purposes of the Statutory Rules (Northern Ireland) Order 1979.

(7) Any rules made under section 2(3)(c) or 7(9)(c) shall be subject to negative resolution; and section 41(6) of the Interpretation Act (Northern Ireland) 1954 (meaning of "subject to negative resolution") shall apply as if the power to make the rules were conferred by an Act of the Northern Ireland Assembly.

(8) No order may be made by a Northern Ireland department under section 7(11) unless a draft of the order has been laid before, and approved by, the Northern Ireland Assembly.

NOTES

Initial Commencement
Royal Assent
Royal Assent: 9 November 1998: see s 22(2).

21 Interpretation, etc

(1) In this Act—

    "amend" includes repeal and apply (with or without modifications);
    "the appropriate Minister" means the Minister of the Crown having charge of the appropriate authorised government department (within the meaning of the Crown Proceedings Act 1947);
    "the Commission" means the European Commission of Human Rights;
    "the Convention" means the Convention for the Protection of Human Rights and Fundamental Freedoms, agreed by the Council of Europe at Rome on 4th November 1950 as it has effect for the time being in relation to the United Kingdom;
    "declaration of incompatibility" means a declaration under section 4;
    "Minister of the Crown" has the same meaning as in the Ministers of the Crown Act 1975;
    "Northern Ireland Minister" includes the First Minister and the deputy First Minister in Northern Ireland;
    "primary legislation" means any—
    (a) public general Act;
    (b) local and personal Act;
    (c) private Act;
    (d) Measure of the Church Assembly;
    (e) Measure of the General Synod of the Church of England;
    (f) Order in Council—
        (i) made in exercise of Her Majesty's Royal Prerogative;

> (ii)   made under section 38(1)(a) of the Northern Ireland Constitution Act 1973 or the corresponding provision of the Northern Ireland Act 1998; or
>
> (iii)   amending an Act of a kind mentioned in paragraph (a), (b) or (c); and includes an order or other instrument made under primary legislation (otherwise than by the National Assembly for Wales, a member of the Scottish Executive, a Northern Ireland Minister or a Northern Ireland department) to the extent to which it operates to bring one or more provisions of that legislation into force or amends any primary legislation;
>
> "the First Protocol" means the protocol to the Convention agreed at Paris on 20th March 1952;
>
> "the Sixth Protocol" means the protocol to the Convention agreed at Strasbourg on 28th April 1983;
>
> "the Eleventh Protocol" means the protocol to the Convention (restructuring the control machinery established by the Convention) agreed at Strasbourg on 11th May 1994;
>
> "remedial order" means an order under section 10;
>
> "subordinate legislation" means any—
>
> (a)   Order in Council other than one—
>
>> (i)   made in exercise of Her Majesty's Royal Prerogative;
>>
>> (ii)   made under section 38(1)(a) of the Northern Ireland Constitution Act 1973 or the corresponding provision of the Northern Ireland Act 1998; or
>>
>> (iii)   amending an Act of a kind mentioned in the definition of primary legislation;
>
> (b)   Act of the Scottish Parliament;
>
> (c)   Act of the Parliament of Northern Ireland;
>
> (d)   Measure of the Assembly established under section 1 of the Northern Ireland Assembly Act 1973;
>
> (e)   Act of the Northern Ireland Assembly;
>
> (f)   order, rules, regulations, scheme, warrant, byelaw or other instrument made under primary legislation (except to the extent to which it operates to bring one or more provisions of that legislation into force or amends any primary legislation);
>
> (g)   order, rules, regulations, scheme, warrant, byelaw or other instrument made under legislation mentioned in paragraph (b), (c), (d) or (e) or made under an Order in Council applying only to Northern Ireland;
>
> (h)   order, rules, regulations, scheme, warrant, byelaw or other instrument made by a member of the Scottish Executive, a Northern Ireland Minister or a Northern Ireland department in exercise of prerogative or other executive functions of Her Majesty which are exercisable by such a person on behalf of Her Majesty;
>
> "transferred matters" has the same meaning as in the Northern Ireland Act 1998; and
>
> "tribunal" means any tribunal in which legal proceedings may be brought.

(2)   The references in paragraphs (b) and (c) of section 2(1) to Articles are to Articles of the Convention as they had effect immediately before the coming into force of the Eleventh Protocol.

(3)   The reference in paragraph (d) of section 2(1) to Article 46 includes a reference to Articles 32 and 54 of the Convention as they had effect immediately before the coming into force of the Eleventh Protocol.

(4)   The references in section 2(1) to a report or decision of the Commission or a decision of the Committee of Ministers include references to a report or decision made as provided by paragraphs 3, 4 and 6 of Article 5 of the Eleventh Protocol (transitional provisions).

(5) Any liability under the Army Act 1955, the Air Force Act 1955 or the Naval Discipline Act 1957 to suffer death for an offence is replaced by a liability to imprisonment for life or any less punishment authorised by those Acts; and those Acts shall accordingly have effect with the necessary modifications.

NOTES

Initial Commencement
Royal Assent
Sub-s (5): Royal Assent: 9 November 1998: see s 22(2).
To be appointed
Sub-ss (1)–(4): To be appointed: see s 22(3).

Appointment
Sub-ss (1)–(4): Appointment: 2 October 2000: see SI 2000/1851, art 2.

22 Short title, commencement, application and extent

(1) This Act may be cited as the Human Rights Act 1998.

(2) Sections 18, 20 and 21(5) and this section come into force on the passing of this Act.

(3) The other provisions of this Act come into force on such day as the Secretary of State may by order appoint; and different days may be appointed for different purposes.

(4) Paragraph (b) of subsection (1) of section 7 applies to proceedings brought by or at the instigation of a public authority whenever the act in question took place; but otherwise that subsection does not apply to an act taking place before the coming into force of that section.

(5) This Act binds the Crown.

(6) This Act extends to Northern Ireland.

(7) Section 21(5), so far as it relates to any provision contained in the Army Act 1955, the Air Force Act 1955 or the Naval Discipline Act 1957, extends to any place to which that provision extends.

NOTES

Initial Commencement
Royal Assent
Royal Assent: 9 November 1998: see s 22(2).

Subordinate Legislation
Human Rights Act 1998 (Commencement) Order 1998, SI 1998/2882 (made under sub-s (3)).
Human Rights Act 1998 (Commencement No 2) Order 2000, SI 2000/1851 (made under sub-s (3)).

SCHEDULE 1
The Articles

Section 1(3)

PART I
THE CONVENTION

RIGHTS AND FREEDOMS

Article 2
Right to life

1   Everyone's right to life shall be protected by law. No one shall be deprived of his life intentionally save in the execution of a sentence of a court following his conviction of a crime for which this penalty is provided by law.

2   Deprivation of life shall not be regarded as inflicted in contravention of this Article when it results from the use of force which is no more than absolutely necessary:

(a)   in defence of any person from unlawful violence;
(b)   in order to effect a lawful arrest or to prevent the escape of a person lawfully detained;
(c)   in action lawfully taken for the purpose of quelling a riot or insurrection.

Article 3
Prohibition of torture

No one shall be subjected to torture or to inhuman or degrading treatment or punishment.

Article 4
Prohibition of slavery and forced labour

1   No one shall be held in slavery or servitude.

2   No one shall be required to perform forced or compulsory labour.

3   For the purpose of this Article the term "forced or compulsory labour" shall not include:

(a)   any work required to be done in the ordinary course of detention imposed according to the provisions of Article 5 of this Convention or during conditional release from such detention;
(b)   any service of a military character or, in case of conscientious objectors in countries where they are recognised, service exacted instead of compulsory military service;
(c)   any service exacted in case of an emergency or calamity threatening the life or well-being of the community;
(d)   any work or service which forms part of normal civic obligations.

Article 5
Right to liberty and security

1   Everyone has the right to liberty and security of person. No one shall be deprived of his liberty save in the following cases and in accordance with a procedure prescribed by law:

(a) the lawful detention of a person after conviction by a competent court;

(b) the lawful arrest or detention of a person for non-compliance with the lawful order of a court or in order to secure the fulfilment of any obligation prescribed by law;

(c) the lawful arrest or detention of a person effected for the purpose of bringing him before the competent legal authority on reasonable suspicion of having committed an offence or when it is reasonably considered necessary to prevent his committing an offence or fleeing after having done so;

(d) the detention of a minor by lawful order for the purpose of educational supervision or his lawful detention for the purpose of bringing him before the competent legal authority;

(e) the lawful detention of persons for the prevention of the spreading of infectious diseases, of persons of unsound mind, alcoholics or drug addicts or vagrants;

(f) the lawful arrest or detention of a person to prevent his effecting an unauthorised entry into the country or of a person against whom action is being taken with a view to deportation or extradition.

2   Everyone who is arrested shall be informed promptly, in a language which he understands, of the reasons for his arrest and of any charge against him.

3   Everyone arrested or detained in accordance with the provisions of paragraph 1(c) of this Article shall be brought promptly before a judge or other officer authorised by law to exercise judicial power and shall be entitled to trial within a reasonable time or to release pending trial. Release may be conditioned by guarantees to appear for trial.

4   Everyone who is deprived of his liberty by arrest or detention shall be entitled to take proceedings by which the lawfulness of his detention shall be decided speedily by a court and his release ordered if the detention is not lawful.

5   Everyone who has been the victim of arrest or detention in contravention of the provisions of this Article shall have an enforceable right to compensation.

Article 6
Right to a fair trial

1   In the determination of his civil rights and obligations or of any criminal charge against him, everyone is entitled to a fair and public hearing within a reasonable time by an independent and impartial tribunal established by law. Judgment shall be pronounced publicly but the press and public may be excluded from all or part of the trial in the interest of morals, public order or national security in a democratic society, where the interests of juveniles or the protection of the private life of the parties so require, or to the extent strictly necessary in the opinion of the court in special circumstances where publicity would prejudice the interests of justice.

2   Everyone charged with a criminal offence shall be presumed innocent until proved guilty according to law.

3   Everyone charged with a criminal offence has the following minimum rights:

(a) to be informed promptly, in a language which he understands and in detail, of the nature and cause of the accusation against him;

(b) to have adequate time and facilities for the preparation of his defence;

(c) to defend himself in person or through legal assistance of his own choosing or, if he has not sufficient means to pay for legal assistance, to be given it free when the interests of justice so require;

(d) to examine or have examined witnesses against him and to obtain the attendance and examination of witnesses on his behalf under the same conditions as witnesses against him;

(e)   to have the free assistance of an interpreter if he cannot understand or speak the language used in court.

Article 7
No punishment without law

1   No one shall be held guilty of any criminal offence on account of any act or omission which did not constitute a criminal offence under national or international law at the time when it was committed. Nor shall a heavier penalty be imposed than the one that was applicable at the time the criminal offence was committed.

2   This Article shall not prejudice the trial and punishment of any person for any act or omission which, at the time when it was committed, was criminal according to the general principles of law recognised by civilised nations.

Article 8
Right to respect for private and family life

1   Everyone has the right to respect for his private and family life, his home and his correspondence.

2   There shall be no interference by a public authority with the exercise of this right except such as is in accordance with the law and is necessary in a democratic society in the interests of national security, public safety or the economic well-being of the country, for the prevention of disorder or crime, for the protection of health or morals, or for the protection of the rights and freedoms of others.

Article 9
Freedom of thought, conscience and religion

1   Everyone has the right to freedom of thought, conscience and religion; this right includes freedom to change his religion or belief and freedom, either alone or in community with others and in public or private, to manifest his religion or belief, in worship, teaching, practice and observance.

2   Freedom to manifest one's religion or beliefs shall be subject only to such limitations as are prescribed by law and are necessary in a democratic society in the interests of public safety, for the protection of public order, health or morals, or for the protection of the rights and freedoms of others.

Article 10
Freedom of expression

1   Everyone has the right to freedom of expression. This right shall include freedom to hold opinions and to receive and impart information and ideas without interference by public authority and regardless of frontiers. This Article shall not prevent States from requiring the licensing of broadcasting, television or cinema enterprises.

2   The exercise of these freedoms, since it carries with it duties and responsibilities, may be subject to such formalities, conditions, restrictions or penalties as are prescribed by law and are necessary in a democratic society, in the interests of national security, territorial integrity or public safety, for the prevention of disorder or crime, for the protection of health or morals, for the protection of the reputation or rights of others, for preventing the disclosure of information received in confidence, or for maintaining the authority and impartiality of the judiciary.

Article 11
Freedom of assembly and association

1 Everyone has the right to freedom of peaceful assembly and to freedom of association with others, including the right to form and to join trade unions for the protection of his interests.

2 No restrictions shall be placed on the exercise of these rights other than such as are prescribed by law and are necessary in a democratic society in the interests of national security or public safety, for the prevention of disorder or crime, for the protection of health or morals or for the protection of the rights and freedoms of others. This Article shall not prevent the imposition of lawful restrictions on the exercise of these rights by members of the armed forces, of the police or of the administration of the State.

Article 12
Right to marry
Men and women of marriageable age have the right to marry and to found a family, according to the national laws governing the exercise of this right.

Article 14
Prohibition of discrimination
The enjoyment of the rights and freedoms set forth in this Convention shall be secured without discrimination on any ground such as sex, race, colour, language, religion, political or other opinion, national or social origin, association with a national minority, property, birth or other status.

Article 16
Restrictions on political activity of aliens
Nothing in Articles 10, 11 and 14 shall be regarded as preventing the High Contracting Parties from imposing restrictions on the political activity of aliens.

Article 17
Prohibition of abuse of rights
Nothing in this Convention may be interpreted as implying for any State, group or person any right to engage in any activity or perform any act aimed at the destruction of any of the rights and freedoms set forth herein or at their limitation to a greater extent than is provided for in the Convention.

Article 18
Limitation on use of restrictions on rights
The restrictions permitted under this Convention to the said rights and freedoms shall not be applied for any purpose other than those for which they have been prescribed.

NOTES

Initial Commencement
To be appointed
To be appointed: see s 22(3).

Appointment
Appointment: 2 October 2000: see SI 2000/1851, art 2.

PART II
THE FIRST PROTOCOL

Article 1
Protection of property

Every natural or legal person is entitled to the peaceful enjoyment of his possessions. No one shall be deprived of his possessions except in the public interest and subject to the conditions provided for by law and by the general principles of international law.

The preceding provisions shall not, however, in any way impair the right of a State to enforce such laws as it deems necessary to control the use of property in accordance with the general interest or to secure the payment of taxes or other contributions or penalties.

Article 2
Right to education

No person shall be denied the right to education. In the exercise of any functions which it assumes in relation to education and to teaching, the State shall respect the right of parents to ensure such education and teaching in conformity with their own religious and philosophical convictions.

Article 3
Right to free elections

The High Contracting Parties undertake to hold free elections at reasonable intervals by secret ballot, under conditions which will ensure the free expression of the opinion of the people in the choice of the legislature.

NOTES

Initial Commencement
To be appointed
To be appointed: see s 22(3).

Appointment
Appointment: 2 October 2000: see SI 2000/1851, art 2.

PART III
THE SIXTH PROTOCOL

Article 1
Abolition of the death penalty

The death penalty shall be abolished. No one shall be condemned to such penalty or executed.

Article 2
Death penalty in time of war

A State may make provision in its law for the death penalty in respect of acts committed in time of war or of imminent threat of war; such penalty shall be applied only in the instances laid down in the law and in accordance with its provisions. The State shall communicate to the Secretary General of the Council of Europe the relevant provisions of that law.

NOTES

Initial Commencement
To be appointed
To be appointed: see s 22(3).

Appointment
Appointment: 2 October 2000: see SI 2000/1851, art 2.

SCHEDULE 2
Remedial Orders

Section 10

Orders

1   (1)   A remedial order may—

(a)   contain such incidental, supplemental, consequential or transitional provision as the person making it considers appropriate;
(b)   be made so as to have effect from a date earlier than that on which it is made;
(c)   make provision for the delegation of specific functions;
(d)   make different provision for different cases.

(2)   The power conferred by sub-paragraph (1)(a) includes—

(a)   power to amend primary legislation (including primary legislation other than that which contains the incompatible provision); and
(b)   power to amend or revoke subordinate legislation (including subordinate legislation other than that which contains the incompatible provision).

(3)   A remedial order may be made so as to have the same extent as the legislation which it affects.

(4)   No person is to be guilty of an offence solely as a result of the retrospective effect of a remedial order.

Procedure

2   No remedial order may be made unless—

(a)   a draft of the order has been approved by a resolution of each House of Parliament made after the end of the period of 60 days beginning with the day on which the draft was laid; or
(b)   it is declared in the order that it appears to the person making it that, because of the urgency of the matter, it is necessary to make the order without a draft being so approved.

Orders laid in draft

3   (1)   No draft may be laid under paragraph 2(a) unless—

(a)   the person proposing to make the order has laid before Parliament a document which contains a draft of the proposed order and the required information; and
(b)   the period of 60 days, beginning with the day on which the document required by this sub-paragraph was laid, has ended.

(2)   If representations have been made during that period, the draft laid under paragraph 2(a) must be accompanied by a statement containing—

(a)   a summary of the representations; and
(b)   if, as a result of the representations, the proposed order has been changed, details of the changes.

Urgent cases

4 (1)   If a remedial order ("the original order") is made without being approved in draft, the person making it must lay it before Parliament, accompanied by the required information, after it is made.

(2)   If representations have been made during the period of 60 days beginning with the day on which the original order was made, the person making it must (after the end of that period) lay before Parliament a statement containing—

    (a)   a summary of the representations; and

    (b)   if, as a result of the representations, he considers it appropriate to make changes to the original order, details of the changes.

(3)   If sub-paragraph (2)(b) applies, the person making the statement must—

    (a)   make a further remedial order replacing the original order; and

    (b)   lay the replacement order before Parliament.

(4)   If, at the end of the period of 120 days beginning with the day on which the original order was made, a resolution has not been passed by each House approving the original or replacement order, the order ceases to have effect (but without that affecting anything previously done under either order or the power to make a fresh remedial order).

Definitions

5   In this Schedule—

"representations" means representations about a remedial order (or proposed remedial order) made to the person making (or proposing to make) it and includes any relevant Parliamentary report or resolution; and
"required information" means—

    (a)   an explanation of the incompatibility which the order (or proposed order) seeks to remove, including particulars of the relevant declaration, finding or order; and

    (b)   a statement of the reasons for proceeding under section 10 and for making an order in those terms.

Calculating periods

6   In calculating any period for the purposes of this Schedule, no account is to be taken of any time during which—

    (a)   Parliament is dissolved or prorogued; or

    (b)   both Houses are adjourned for more than four days.

[**7**   (1)   This paragraph applies in relation to—

    (a)   any remedial order made, and any draft of such an order proposed to be made,—

       (i)   by the Scottish Ministers; or

       (ii)   within devolved competence (within the meaning of the Scotland Act 1998) by Her Majesty in Council; and

    (b)   any document or statement to be laid in connection with such an order (or proposed order).

(2)   This Schedule has effect in relation to any such order (or proposed order), document or statement subject to the following modifications.

(3)   Any reference to Parliament, each House of Parliament or both Houses of Parliament shall be construed as a reference to the Scottish Parliament.

(4)   Paragraph 6 does not apply and instead, in calculating any period for the purposes of this Schedule, no account is to be taken of any time during which the Scottish Parliament is dissolved or is in recess for more than four days.]

NOTES

Initial Commencement
To be appointed
To be appointed: see s 22(3).

Appointment
Appointment: 2 October 2000: see SI 2000/1851, art 2.

Amendment
Para 7: inserted by SI 2000/2040, art 2(1), Schedule, Pt I, para 21.
Date in force: 27 July 2000: see SI 2000/2040, art 1(1).

SCHEDULE 3
Derogation and Reservation

Sections 14 and 15

PART I
. . .

NOTES

Amendment
Repealed by SI 2001/1216, art 4.
Date in force: 1 April 2001: see SI 2001/1216, art 1.

. . .

NOTES

Amendment
Repealed by SI 2001/1216, art 4.
Date in force: 1 April 2001: see SI 2001/1216, art 1.

PART II
RESERVATION

At the time of signing the present (First) Protocol, I declare that, in view of certain provisions of the Education Acts in the United Kingdom, the principle affirmed in the second sentence of Article 2 is accepted by the United Kingdom only so far as it is compatible with the provision of efficient instruction and training, and the avoidance of unreasonable public expenditure.

Dated 20 March 1952. Made by the United Kingdom Permanent Representative to the Council of Europe.

NOTES

Initial Commencement
To be appointed
To be appointed: see s 22(3).

Appointment
Appointment: 2 October 2000: see SI 2000/1851, art 2.

SCHEDULE 4
Judicial Pensions

Section 18(6)

Duty to make orders about pensions

1 (1)   The appropriate Minister must by order make provision with respect to pensions payable to or in respect of any holder of a judicial office who serves as an ECHR judge.

(2)   A pensions order must include such provision as the Minister making it considers is necessary to secure that—

(a)   an ECHR judge who was, immediately before his appointment as an ECHR judge, a member of a judicial pension scheme is entitled to remain as a member of that scheme;

(b)   the terms on which he remains a member of the scheme are those which would have been applicable had he not been appointed as an ECHR judge; and

(c)   entitlement to benefits payable in accordance with the scheme continues to be determined as if, while serving as an ECHR judge, his salary was that which would (but for section 18(4)) have been payable to him in respect of his continuing service as the holder of his judicial office.

Contributions

2   A pensions order may, in particular, make provision—

(a)   for any contributions which are payable by a person who remains a member of a scheme as a result of the order, and which would otherwise be payable by deduction from his salary, to be made otherwise than by deduction from his salary as an ECHR judge; and

(b)   for such contributions to be collected in such manner as may be determined by the administrators of the scheme.

Amendments of other enactments

3   A pensions order may amend any provision of, or made under, a pensions Act in such manner and to such extent as the Minister making the order considers necessary or expedient to ensure the proper administration of any scheme to which it relates.

Definitions

4   In this Schedule—

"appropriate Minister" means—

(a)   in relation to any judicial office whose jurisdiction is exercisable exclusively in relation to Scotland, the Secretary of State; and

(b)   otherwise, the Lord Chancellor;

"ECHR judge" means the holder of a judicial office who is serving as a judge of the Court;

"judicial pension scheme" means a scheme established by and in accordance with a pensions Act;

"pensions Act" means—

(a)   the County Courts Act (Northern Ireland) 1959;

(b)   the Sheriffs' Pensions (Scotland) Act 1961;

(c)   the Judicial Pensions Act 1981; or

(d)   the Judicial Pensions and Retirement Act 1993; and

"pensions order" means an order made under paragraph 1.

NOTES

Initial Commencement
Royal Assent
Royal Assent: 9 November 1998: see s 22(2).

IMMIGRATION RULES

IMMIGRATION RULES

STATEMENT OF CHANGES IN IMMIGRATION RULES (HC 395)

Date   Laid before Parliament 23 May 1994.

Authority   Immigration Act 1971, s 3(2).

Note   This incorporates amending Statements laid before, or presented to, Parliament on 20 September 1994 (Cmnd 2663), 26 October 1995 (HC 797), 4 January 1996 (Cmnd 3073), 7 March 1996 (HC 274), 2 April 1996 (HC 329), 30 August 1996 (Cmnd 3365), 31 October 1996 (HC 31), 27 February 1997 (HC 338), 29 May 1997 (Cmnd 3669), 5 June 1997 (HC 26), 30 July 1997 (HC 161), 11 May 1998 (Cmnd 3953), October 1998 (Cmnd 4065), 18 November 1999 (HC 22), 28 July 2000 (HC 704) and 2 October 2000 (Cmnd 4851).

Contents

Refusal of leave to enter in relation to a person in possession of an entry clearance (rr 321–321A)
Refusal of variation of leave to enter or remain or curtailment   of leave (rr 322–323)
Crew members (r 324)

Part 10:   Registration with the police (rr 324A–326)

Part 11:   Asylum (rr 327–352F)

Part 12:   Rights of appeal (rr 353–361)   (*Deleted by CM 4851*)

Part 13:   Deportation [and Administrative Removal under Section 10 of the 1999 Act] (rr 362–395F)

Appendix 1
Visa requirements for the United Kingdom

Appendix 2

Introduction

1   The Home Secretary has made changes in the Rules laid down by him as to the practice to be followed in the administration of the Immigration Acts for regulating entry into and the stay of persons in the United Kingdom and contained in the statement laid before Parliament on 23 March 1990 (HC251) (as amended). This statement contains the Rules as changed and replaces the provisions of HC251 (as amended).

2   Immigration Officers, Entry Clearance Officers and all staff of the Home Office Immigration and Nationality [Directorate] will carry out their duties without regard to the race, colour or religion of persons seeking to enter or remain in the United Kingdom [and in compliance with the provisions of the Human Rights Acts 1998].

3   In these Rules words importing the masculine gender include the feminine unless the contrary intention appears.

Note   Words in square brackets inserted by CM 4851.

Implementation and transitional provisions

4   These Rules come into effect on 1 October 1994 and will apply to all decisions taken on or after that date save that any application made before 1 October 1994 for entry clearance, leave to enter or remain or variation of leave to enter or remain [, other than an application for leave by a person seeking asylum,] shall be decided under the provisions of HC 251, as amended, as if these Rules had not been made.

Application

[5   Save where expressly indicated, these Rules do not apply to those persons who are entitled to enter or remain in the United Kingdom by virtue of the provisions of the Immigration (European Economic Area) Regulations 2000 or Commission Regulation 1251/70. But any person who is not entitled to rely on the provisions of those Regulations is covered by these Rules.]

Note   Substituted by CM 4851.

Interpretation

6   In these Rules the following interpretations apply:

> 'the Immigration Acts' mean the Immigration Act 1971 and the Immigration Act 1988.
> 'the 1993 Act' is the Asylum and Immigration Appeals Act 1993.
> ['the 1996 Act' is the Asylum and Immigration Act 1996.]

['the 2000 EEA Regulations' are the Immigration (European Area) Regulations 2000.]

'United Kingdom passport' bears the meaning it has in the Immigration Act 1971.

'Immigration Officer' includes a Customs Officer acting as an Immigration Officer.

['public funds' means:

(a)   housing under Part II or III of the Housing Act 1985, Part I or II of the Housing (Scotland)Act 1987, Part II of the Housing (Northern Ireland) Order 1988;

(b)   attendance allowance, severe disablement allowance, invalid care allowance and disability living allowance under Part III, income support, family credit, council tax benefit, disability working allowance and housing benefit under Part VII and child benefit under Part IX of the Social Security Contribution and Benefits Act 1992;

(c)   attendance allowance, severe disablement allowance, invalid care allowance and disability living allowance under Part III, income support, family credit, disability working allowance, housing benefit under Part VII and child benefit under Part IX of the Social Security Contributions and Benefits (Northern Ireland) Act 1992; and

(d)   income-based jobseeker's allowance under the Jobseekers Act 1995.]

['Department of Employment' means the Department for Education and Employment and includes, where appropriate, the equivalent Government Department for Northern Ireland;]

'settled in the United Kingdom' means that the person concerned:

(a)   is free from any restriction on the period for which he may remain save that a person entitled to an exemption under Section 8 of the Immigration Act 1971 (otherwise than as a member of the home forces) is not to be regarded as settled in the United Kingdom except in so far as Section 8(5A) so provides; and

(b)   is either:

(i)   ordinarily resident in the United Kingdom without having entered or remained in breach of the immigration laws; or

(ii)   despite having entered or remained in breach of the immigration laws, has subsequently entered lawfully or has been granted leave to remain and is ordinarily resident.

'a parent' includes:

(a)   the stepfather of a child whose father is dead;

(b)   the stepmother of a child whose mother is dead;

(c)   the father as well as the mother of an illegitimate child where he is proved to be the father;

(d)   an adoptive parent but only where a child was adopted in accordance with a decision taken by the competent administrative authority or court in a country whose adoption orders are recognised by the United Kingdom (except where an application for leave to enter or remain is made under paragraphs 310–316);

(e)   in the case of a child born in the United Kingdom who is not a British citizen, a person to whom there has been a genuine transfer of parental responsibility on the ground of the original parent(s)' inability to care for the child.

'visa nationals' are the persons specified in the [Appendix 1] to these Rules who need a visa for the United Kingdom.

'employment', unless the contrary intention appears, includes paid and unpaid employment, self-employment and engaging in business or any professional activity.

[. . .]

['the Human Rights Convention' means the Convention for the Protection of Human Rights and Fundamental Freedoms, agreed by the Council of Europe at Rome on 4th November 1950 as it has effect for the time being in relation to the United Kingdom.]

Note Frequent amendments to this paragraph makes it important to note the following. Before 4 April 1996 the definition covered: housing under the Housing Act 1985; income support family credit, council tax benefit and housing benefit. After 3 April 1996, HC 329 added: attendance allowance, severe disablement allowance, invalid care allowance, disability living allowance, disability working allowance. The position (as at March 1997) is that since 30 October 1996 HC 31 has added child benefit. It also replaces income support with income-based jobseeker's allowance (JSA). This definition does not include contributions-based JSA. The definition of 'visa national' was amended with effect from 11 May 1998 (Cmnd 3953). On each occasion the definitions have included the equivalent provisions under legislation for Scotland and Northern Ireland.

Words in square brackets beginning 'the 2000 EEA Regulations' substituted by CM 4851.

Definitions of 'EEA national' and 'family member' following the definition of 'employment' omitted by CM 4851.

Words in square brackets beginning 'the Human Rights Convention' inserted by CM 4851.

[**6A** For the purpose of these Rules, a person is not to be regarded as having (or potentially having) recourse to public funds merely because he is (or will be) reliant in whole or in part on public funds provided to his sponsor, unless, as a result of his presence in the United Kingdom, the sponsor is (or would be) entitled to increased or additional public funds).]

Note Inserted by CM 4851.

PART 1: GENERAL PROVISIONS REGARDING LEAVE TO ENTER OR REMAIN IN THE UNITED KINGDOM

Leave to enter the United Kingdom

[**7** A person who is neither a British citizen nor a Commonwealth citizen with the right of abode nor a person who is entitled to enter or remain in the United Kingdom by virtue of the provisions of the Immigration (European Economic Area) Regulations 2000 or Commission Regulation 1251/70 requires leave to enter the United Kingdom.]

Note Substituted by CM 4851.

[**8** Under Sections 3 and 4 of the Immigration Act 1971 an Immigration Officer when admitting to the United Kingdom a person subject to control under that Act may give leave to enter for a limited period and, if he does, may impose all or any of the following conditions:

    (i)   a condition restricting employment or occupation in the United Kingdom;

    (ii)   a condition requiring the person to maintain and accommodate himself, and any dependants of his, without recourse to public funds; and

    (iii) a condition requiring the person to register with the police.

He may also require him to report to the appropriate Medical Officer of Environmental Health. Under Section 24 of the 1971 Act it is an offence knowingly to remain beyond the time limit or to fail to comply with such a condition or requirement.]

[**9** The time limit and any conditions attached will normally be made known to the person concerned:

    (i)   by written notice given to him or endorsed by the immigration officer in his passport or travel document; or

    (ii)   in any other manner permitted by the Immigration (Leave to Enter and Remain) Order 2000.]

Note Paragraph 9 substituted by HC 704.

[Exercise of the power to refuse leave to enter the United Kingdom or to cancel leave to enter or remain which is in force]

10 The power to refuse leave to enter the United Kingdom [or to cancel leave to enter or remain which is already in force] is not to be exercised by an Immigration Officer acting on his own. The authority of a Chief Immigration Officer or of an Immigration Inspector must always be obtained.

[Suspension of leave to enter or remain in the United Kingdom

10A Where a person has arrived in the United Kingdom with leave to enter or remain which is in force but which was given to him before his arrival he may be examined by an Immigration Officer under paragraph 2A of Schedule 2 to the Immigration Act 1971. An Immigration Officer examining a person under paragraph 2A may suspend that person's leave to enter or remain in the United Kingdom until the examination is completed.

Cancellation of leave to enter or remain in the United Kingdom

10B Where a person arrived in the United Kingdom with leave to enter or remain in the United Kingdom which is already in force, an Immigration Officer may cancel that leave.]

Note Sub-heading of paragraph 10 substituted, words in square brackets in para 10 inserted and paragraphs 10A and B inserted by HC 704.

Requirement for persons arriving in the United Kingdom or seeking entry through the Channel Tunnel to produce evidence of identity and nationality

11 A person must, on arrival in the United Kingdom or when seeking entry through the Channel Tunnel, produce on request by the Immigration Officer:

(i) a valid national passport or other document satisfactorily establishing his identity and nationality; and

(ii) such information as may be required to establish whether he requires leave to enter the United Kingdom and, if so, whether and on what terms leave to enter should be given.

Requirement for a person not requiring leave to enter the United Kingdom to prove that he has the right of abode

12 A person claiming to be a British citizen must prove that he has the right of abode in the United Kingdom by producing either:

(i) a United Kingdom passport describing him as a British citizen or as a citizen of the United Kingdom and Colonies having the right of abode in the United Kingdom; or

(ii) a certificate of entitlement duly issued by or on behalf of the Govern-ment of the United Kingdom certifying that he has the right of abode.

13 A person claiming to be a Commonwealth citizen with the right of abode in the United Kingdom must prove that he has the right of abode by producing a certificate of entitlement duly issued to him by or on behalf of the Government of the United Kingdom certifying that he has the right of abode.

14 A Commonwealth citizen who has been given limited leave to enter the United Kingdom may later claim to have the right of abode. The time limit on his stay may be removed if he is able to establish a claim to the right of abode, for example by showing that:

(i) immediately before the commencement of the British Nationality Act 1981 he was a Commonwealth citizen born to or legally adopted by a parent who at the time of his birth had citizenship of the United Kingdom and Colonies by his birth in the United Kingdom or any of the Islands; and

(ii) he has not ceased to be a Commonwealth citizen in the meanwhile.

Common Travel Area

15 The United Kingdom, the Channel Islands, the Isle of Man and the Republic of Ireland collectively form a common travel area. A person who has been examined for the purpose of immigration control at the point at which he entered the area does not normally require leave to enter any other part of it. However certain persons subject to the Immigration (Control of Entry through the Republic of Ireland)Order 1972 (as amended) who enter the United Kingdom through the Republic of Ireland do require leave to enter. This includes:

(i)   those who merely passed through the Republic of Ireland;
(ii)   persons requiring visas;
(iii) persons who entered the Republic of Ireland unlawfully;
(iv)   persons who are subject to directions given by the Secretary of State for their exclusion from the United Kingdom on the ground that their exclusion is conducive to the public good;
(v)   persons who entered the Republic from the United Kingdom and Islands after entering there unlawfully or overstaying their leave.

Admission of certain British passport holders

16 A person in any of the following categories may be admitted freely to the United Kingdom on production of a United Kingdom passport issued in the United Kingdom and Islands or the Republic of Ireland prior to 1 January 1973, unless his passport has been endorsed to show that he was subject to immigration control:

(i)   a British Dependent Territories citizen;
(ii)   a British National (Overseas);
(iii) a British Overseas citizen;
(iv)   a British protected person;
(v)   a British subject by virtue of Section 30(*a*) of the British Nationality Act 1981, (who, immediately before the commencement of the 1981 Act, would have been a British subject not possessing citizenship of the United Kingdom and Colonies or the citizenship of any other Commonwealth country or territory).

17 British Overseas citizens who hold United Kingdom passports wherever issued and who satisfy the Immigration Officer that they have, since 1 March 1968, been given indefinite leave to enter or remain in the United Kingdom may be given indefinite leave to enter.

[Persons outside the United Kingdom

17A Where a person is outside the United Kingdom but wishes to travel to the United Kingdom an Immigration Officer may give or refuse him leave to enter. An Immigration Officer may exercise these powers whether or not he is, himself, in the United Kingdom. However, an Immigration Officer is not obliged to consider an application for leave to enter from a person outside the United Kingdom.

17B Where a person, having left the common travel area, has leave to enter the United Kingdom which remains in force under article 13 of the Immigration (Leave to Enter and Remain) Order 2000, an Immigration Officer may cancel that leave. An Immigration Officer may exercise these powers whether or not he is, himself, in the United Kingdom. If a person outside the United Kingdom has leave to remain in the United Kingdom which is in force in this way, the Secretary of State may cancel that leave.]

Note   Paragraphs 17A and B inserted by HC 704.

Returning residents

18 A person seeking leave to enter the United Kingdom as a returning resident may be admitted for settlement provided the Immigration Officer is satisfied that the person concerned:

(i) had indefinite leave to enter or to remain in the United Kingdom when he last left; and

(ii) has not been away from the United Kingdom for more than 2 years; and

(iii) did not receive assistance from public funds towards the cost of leaving the United Kingdom; and

(iv) now seeks admission for the purpose of settlement.

19 A person who does not benefit from the preceding paragraph by reason only of having been away from the United Kingdom too long may nevertheless be admitted as a returning resident if, for example, he has lived here for most of his life.

[**19A** Where a person who has infinite leave to enter or remain in the United Kingdom accompanies, on a tour of duty abroad, a spouse who is a member of HM Forces serving overseas, or a permanent member of HM Diplomatic Service or a comparable UK-based staff member of the British Council, sub-paragraphs (ii) and (iii) of paragraph 18 shall not apply.]

Note Paragraph 19A inserted by CM 4851.

20 The leave of a person whose stay in the United Kingdom is subject to a time limit lapses on his going to a country or territory outside the common travel area [if the leave was given for a period of six months or less or conferred by a visit visa. In other cases, leave lapses on the holder remaining outside the United Kingdom for a continuous period of more than two years]. [A person whose leave has lapsed and] who returns after a temporary absence abroad within the period of this earlier leave has no claim to admission as a returning resident. His application to re-enter the United Kingdom should be considered in the light of all the relevant circumstances.The same time limit and any conditions attached will normally be reimposed if he meets the requirements of these Rules, unless he is seeking admission in a different capacity from the one in which he was last given leave to enter or remain.

Note Words in first set of square brackets in paragraph 20 inserted and those in second set of square brackets substituted by HC 704.

[**Non-lapsing leave**

20A Leave to enter or remain in the United Kingdom will usually lapse on the holder going to a country or territory outside the common travel area. However, under article 13 of the Immigration (Leave to Enter and Remain) Order 2000 such leave will not lapse where it was given for a period exceeding six months or where it was conferred by means of an entry clearance (other than a visit visa).]

Note Inserted by HC 704.

Holders of restricted travel documents and passports

21 The leave to enter or remain in the United Kingdom of the holder of a passport or travel document whose permission to enter another country has to be exercised before a given date may be restricted so as to terminate at least 2 months before that date.

22 If his passport or travel document is endorsed with a restriction on the period for which he may remain outside his country of normal residence, his leave to enter or remain in the United Kingdom may be limited so as not to extend beyond the period of authorised absence.

23 The holder of a travel document issued by the Home Office should not be given leave to enter or remain for a period extending beyond the validity of that document. This paragraph and paragraphs 21–22 do not apply to a person who is eligible for admission for settlement or to a spouse who is eligible for admission under paragraph 282 or to a person who qualifies for the removal of the time limit on his stay.

Entry clearance

24 A visa national and any other person who is seeking entry for a purpose for which prior entry clearance is required under these Rules must produce to the Immigration Officer a valid passport or other identity document endorsed with a United Kingdom entry clearance issued to him for the purpose for which he seeks entry. Such a person will be refused leave to enter if he has no such current entry clearance. Any other person who wishes to ascertain in advance whether he is eligible for admission to the United Kingdom may apply for the issue of an entry clearance.

25 Entry clearance takes the form of a visa (for visa nationals) or an entry certificate (for non-visa nationals). These documents are to be taken as evidence of the holder's eligibility for entry into the United Kingdom, and accordingly accepted as 'entry clearances' within the meaning of the Immigration Act 1971.

[**25A** An entry clearance which satisfies the requirements set out in article 3 of the Immigration (Leave to Enter and Remain) Order 2000 will have effect as leave to enter the United Kingdom. The requirements are that the entry clearance must specify the purpose for which the holder wants to enter the United Kingdom and should be endorsed with the conditions to which it is subject or with a statement that it has effect as indefinite leave to enter the United Kingdom. The holder of such an entry clearance will not require leave to enter on arrival in the United Kingdom and, for the purposes of the Rules, will be treated as a person who has arrived in the United Kingdom with leave to enter the United Kingdom which is in force but which was given to him before his arrival.]

Note Inserted by HC 704.

26 An application for entry clearance will be considered in accordance with the provisions in these Rules governing the grant or refusal of leave to enter. Where appropriate, the term 'Entry Clearance Officer' should be substituted for 'Immigration Officer'.

27 An application of entry clearance is to be decided in the light of the circumstances existing at the time of the decision, except that an applicant will not be refused an entry clearance where entry is sought in one of the categories contained in paragraphs 296–316 solely on account of his attaining the age of 18 years between receipt of his application and the date of the decision on it.

28 An applicant for an entry clearance must be outside the United Kingdom and Islands at the time of the application. An applicant for an entry clearance who is seeking entry as a visitor must apply to a post designated by the Secretary of State to accept applications for entry clearance for that purpose and from that category of applicant. Any other application must be made to the post in the country or territory where the applicant is living which has been designated by the Secretary of State to accept applications for entry clearance for that purpose and from that category of applicant. Where there is no such post the applicant must apply to the appropriate designated post outside the country or territory where he is living.

29 For the purposes of paragraph 28 'post' means a British Diplomatic Mission, British Consular post or the office of any person outside the United Kingdom and

Islands who has been authorised by the Secretary of State to accept applications for entry clearance. A list of designated posts is published by the Foreign and Commonwealth Office.

30   An application for an entry clearance is not made until any fee required to be paid under the Consular Fees Act 1980 (including any Regulations or Orders made under that Act) has been paid.

[30A   An entry clearance may be revoked if the Entry Clearance Officer is satisfied that:

(i)   whether or not to the holder's knowledge, false representations were employed or material facts were not disclosed, either in writing or orally, for the purpose of obtaining the entry clearance; or

(ii)   a change in circumstances since the entry clearance was issued has removed the basis of the holder's claim to be admitted to the United Kingdom, except where the change of circumstances amounts solely to his exceeding the age for entry in one of the categories contained in paragraphs 296–316 of these Rules since the issue of the entry clearance; or

(iii)   the holder's exclusion from the United Kingdom would be conducive to the public good.]

[30B   An entry clearance shall cease to have effect where the entry clearance has effect as leave to enter and an Immigration Officer cancels that leave in accordance with paragraph 2A(8) of Schedule 2 to the Immigration Act 1971.

30C   An Immigration Officer may cancel an entry clearance which is capable of having effect as leave to enter if the holder arrives in the United Kingdom before the day on which the entry clearance becomes effective of if the holder seeks to enter the United Kingdom for a purpose other than the purpose specified in the entry clearance.]

Note   Paragraph 30A inserted by HC 31 and paragraphs 30B and 30C inserted by HC 704.

Variation of leave to enter or remain in the United Kingdom

31   Under Section 3(3) of the 1971 Act a limited leave to enter or remain in the United Kingdom may be varied by extending or restricting its duration, by adding, varying or revoking conditions or by removing the time limit (whereupon any condition attached to the leave ceases to apply). When leave to enter or remain is varied an entry is to be made in the applicant's passport or travel document (and his registration certificate where appropriate) or the decision may be made known in writing or some other appropriate way.

[31A   Where a person has arrived in the United Kingdom with leave to enter or remain in the United Kingdom which is in force but was given to him before his arrival, he may apply, on arrival at a port of entry in the United Kingdom, for variation of that leave. An Immigration Officer acting on behalf of the Secretary of State may vary the leave at the port of entry but is not obliged to consider an application for variation made at the port of entry. If an Immigration Officer acting on behalf of the Secretary of State has declined to consider an application for variation of leave at a port of entry but the leave has not been cancelled under paragraph 2A(8) of Schedule 2 to the Immigration Act 1971, the person seeking variation should apply to the Home Office under paragraph 32.]

Note   Paragraph 31A inserted by HC 704.

32   After admission to the United Kingdom any application for an extension of the time limit on or variation of conditions attached to a person's stay in the United Kingdom must be made to the Home Office before the applicant's current leave to enter or remain expires.

[With the exception of applications made under [paragraph 31A (applications at the port of entry),] paragraph 33 (work permits), [33A (applications made outside the United Kingdom),] paragraphs 255 to 257 (EEA nationals) and Part 11 (asylum), all applications for variation of leave to enter or remain must be made using the form prescribed for the purpose by the Secretary of State, which must be completed in the manner required by the form and be accompanied by the documents and photographs specified in the form. An application for such a variation made in any other way is not valid.]

33 Where the application is in respect of employment for which a work permit or a permit for training or work experience is required or is in respect of the spouse or child or a person who is making such an application, the application should be made direct to the Department of Employment Overseas Labour Service.

[**33A** Where a person, having left the common travel area, has leave to enter or remain in the United Kingdom which remains in force under article 13 of the Immigration (Leave to Enter and Remain) Order 2000, his leave may be varied (including any conditions to which it is subject) in such form and manner as permitted for the giving of leave to enter. However, the Secretary of State is not obliged to consider an application for variation of leave to enter or remain from a person outside the United Kingdom.]

Note Words in first set of square brackets in para 32 added by HC329, para 2 with effect from 3 June 1996. Words in square brackets within first set in para 32, and the whole of para 33A, inserted by HC 704.

Withdrawn applications for variation of leave to enter or remain in the United Kingdom

34 Where a person whose application for variation of leave to enter or remain is being considered requests the return of his passport for the purpose of travel outside the common travel area, the application for variation of leave shall, provided it has not already been determined, be treated as withdrawn as soon as the passport is returned in response to that request [. . .]

Note Words deleted by CM 4851.

Undertakings

35 A sponsor of a person seeking leave to enter or variation of leave to enter or remain in the United Kingdom may be asked to give an undertaking in writing to be responsible for that person's maintenance and accommodation for the period of any leave granted, including any further variation. Under the Social Security Administration Act 1992 and the Social Security Administration (Northern Ireland) Act 1992, the Department of Social Security or, as the case may be, the Department of Health and Social Services in Northern Ireland may seek to recover from the person giving such an undertaking any income support paid to meet the needs of the person in respect of whom the undertaking has been given.

[Under the Immigration and Asylum Act 1999 the Home Office may seek to recover from the person giving such an undertaking amounts attributable to any support provided under section 95 of the Immigration and Asylum Act 1999 (support for asylum seekers) to, or in respect of, the person in respect of whom the undertaking has been given. Failure by the sponsor to maintain that person on accordance with the undertaking, may also be an offence under section 105 of the Social Security Administration Act 1992 and/or under section 108 of the Immigration and Asylum Act 1999 if, as a consequence asylum support and/or income support is provided to or in respect of, that person.]

Note Words in square brackets inserted by CM 4851.

Medical

36   A person who intends to remain in the United Kingdom for more than 6 months should normally be referred to the Medical Inspector for examination. If he produces a medical certificate he should be advised to hand it to the Medical Inspector. Any person seeking entry who mentions health or medical treatment as a reason for his visit, or who appears not to be in good mental or physical health, should also be referred to the Medical Inspector; and the Immigration Officer has discretion, which should be exercised sparingly, to refer for examination in any other case.

37   Where the Medical Inspector advises that a person seeking entry is suffering from a specified disease or condition which may interfere with his ability to support himself or his dependants, the Immigration Officer should take account of this, in conjunction with other factors, in deciding whether to admit that person. The Immigration Officer should also take account of the Medical Inspector's assessment of the likely course of treatment in deciding whether a person seeking entry for private medical treatment has sufficient means at his disposal.

38   A returning resident should not be refused leave to enter [or have existing leave to enter or remain cancelled] on medical grounds. But where a person would be refused leave to enter [or have existing leave to enter or remain cancelled] on medical grounds if he were not a returning resident, or in any case where it is decided on compassionate grounds not to exercise the power to refuse leave to enter [or to cancel existing leave to enter or remain], or in any other case where the Medical Inspector so recommends, the Immigration Officer should give the person concerned a notice requiring him to report to the Medical Officer of Environmental Health designated by the Medical Inspector with a view to further examination and any necessary treatment.

39   The Entry Clearance Officer has the same discretion as an Immigration Officer to refer applicants for entry clearance for medical examination and the same principles will apply to the decision whether or not to issue an entry clearance.

Note   Words in square brackets in paragraph 38 inserted by HC 704.

[Students

39A   An application for a variation of leave to enter or remain made by a student who is sponsored by a government or international sponsorship agency may be refused if the sponsor has not given written consent to the proposed variation.]

PART 2:   PERSONS SEEKING TO ENTER OR REMAIN IN THE UNITED KINGDOM FOR VISITS

VISITORS

Requirements for leave to enter as a visitor

40   For the purpose of paragraphs 41–46 a visitor includes a person living and working outside the United Kingdom who comes to the United Kingdom to transact business (such as attending meetings and briefings, fact finding, negotiating or making contracts with United Kingdom businesses to buy or sell goods or services). A visitor seeking leave to enter or remain for private medical treatment must meet the requirements of paragraphs 51 or 54.

41   The requirements to be met by a person seeking leave to enter the United Kingdom as a visitor are that he:

   (i)   is genuinely seeking entry as a visitor for a limited period as stated by him, not exceeding 6 months; and

(ii) intends to leave the United Kingdom at the end of the period of the visit as stated by him; and

(iii) does not intend to take employment in the United Kingdom; and

(iv) does not intend to produce goods or provide services within the United Kingdom, including the selling of goods or services direct to members of the public; and

(v) does not intend to study at a maintained school; and

(vi) will maintain and accommodate himself and any dependants adequately out of resources available to him without recourse to public funds or taking employment; or will, with any dependants, be maintained and accommodated adequately by relatives or friends; and

(vii) can meet the cost of the return or onward journey.

Leave to enter as a visitor

42 A person seeking leave to enter the United Kingdom as a visitor may be admitted for a period not exceeding 6 months, subject to a condition prohibiting employment, provided the Immigration Officer is satisfied that each or the requirements of paragraph 41 is met.

Refusal of leave to enter as a visitor

43 Leave to enter as a visitor is to be refused if the Immigration Officer is not satisfied that each of the requirements of paragraph 41 is met.

Requirements for an extension of stay as a visitor

44 Six months is the maximum permitted leave which may be granted to a visitor. The requirements for an extension of stay as a visitor are that the applicant:

(i) meets the requirements of paragraph 41(ii)–(vii); and

(ii) has not already spent, or would not as a result of an extension of stay spend, more than 6 months in total in the United Kingdom as a visitor.

Any period spent as a seasonal agricultural worker is to be counted as a period spent as a visitor.

Extension of stay as a visitor

45 An extension of stay as a visitor may be granted, subject to a condition prohibiting employment, provided the Secretary of State is satisfied that each of the requirements of paragraph 44 is met.

Refusal of extension of stay as a visitor

46 An extension of stay as a visitor is to be refused if the Secretary of State is not satisfied that each of the requirements of paragraph 44 is met.

VISITORS IN TRANSIT

Requirements for admission as a visitor in transit to another country

47 The requirements to be met by a person (not being a member of the crew of a ship, aircraft, hovercraft, hydrofoil or train) seeking leave to enter the United Kingdom as visitor in transit to another country are that he:

(i) is in transit to a country outside the common travel area; and

(ii) has both the means and the intention of proceeding at once to another country; and

(iii) is assured of entry there; and
(iv) intends and is able to leave the United Kingdom within 48 hours.

Leave to enter as a visitor in transit

48 A person seeking leave to enter the United Kingdom as a visitor in transit may be admitted for a period not exceeding 48 hours with a prohibition on employment provided the Immigration Officer is satisfied that each of the requirements of paragraph 47 is met.

Refusal of leave to enter as a visitor in transit

49 Leave to enter as a visitor in transit is to be refused if the Immigration Officer is not satisfied that each of the requirements of paragraph 47 is met.

Extension of stay as a visitor in transit

50 The maximum permitted leave which may be granted to a visitor in transit is 48 hours. An application for an extension of stay beyond 48 hours from a person admitted in this category is to be refused.

VISITORS SEEKING TO ENTER OR REMAIN FOR PRIVATE MEDICAL TREATMENT

Requirements for leave to enter as a visitor for private medical treatment

51 The requirements to be met by a person seeking leave to enter the United Kingdom as a visitor for private medical treatment are that he:

(i) meets the requirements set out in paragraph 41(iii)–(vii) for entry as a visitor; and
(ii) in the case of a person suffering from a communicable disease, has satisfied the Medical Inspector that there is no danger to public health; and
(iii) can show, if required to do so, that any proposed course of treatment is of finite duration; and
(iv) intends to leave the United Kingdom at the end of his treatment; and
(v) can produce satisfactory evidence, if required to do so, of:
  (a) the medical condition requiring consultation or treatment; and
  (b) satisfactory arrangements for the necessary consultation or treatment at his own expense; and
  (c) the estimated costs of such consultation or treatment; and
  (d) the likely duration of his visit; and
  (e) sufficient funds available to him in the United Kingdom to meet the estimated costs of his undertaking to do so.

Leave to enter as a visitor for private medical treatment

52 A person seeking leave to enter the United Kingdom as a visitor for private medical treatment may be admitted for a period not exceeding 6 months, subject to a condition prohibiting employment, provided the Immigration Officer is satisfied that each of the requirements of paragraph 51 is met.

Refusal of leave to enter as a visitor for private medical treatment

53 Leave to enter as a visitor for private medical treatment is to be refused if the Immigration Officer is not satisfied that each of the requirements of paragraph 51 is met.

Requirements for an extension of stay as a visitor for private medical treatment

54 The requirements for an extension of stay as a visitor to undergo or continue private medical treatment are that the applicant:

(i) meets the requirements set out in paragraph 41(ii)–(vii) and paragraph 51(ii)–(v); and

[(ii) has produced evidence from a registered medical practitioner who holds an NHS consultant post or who appears in the Specialist Register of the General Medical Council of satisfactory arrangements for private medical consultation or treatment and its likely duration; and, where treatment has already begun, evidence as to its progress; and](iii)   can show that he has met, out of the resources available to him, any costs and expenses incurred in relation to his treatment in the United Kingdom; and

(iv) has sufficient funds available to him in the United Kingdom to meet the likely costs of his treatment and intends to meet those costs.

Note Para 54(ii) substituted by CM 4851.

Extension of stay as a visitor for private medical treatment

55 An extension of stay to undergo or continue private medical treatment may be granted, with a prohibition on employment, provided the Secretary of State is satisfied that each of the requirements of paragraph 54 is met.

Refusal of extension of stay as a visitor for private medical treatment

56 An extension of stay as a visitor to undergo or continue private medical treatment is to be refused if the Secretary of State is not satisfied that each of the requirements of paragraph 54 is met.

[PARENT OF A CHILD AT SCHOOL

Requirements for leave to enter or remain as the parent of a child at school

56A The requirements to be met by a person seeking leave to enter or remain in the United Kingdom as the parent of a child at school are that:

(i) the parent meets the requirements set out in paragraph 41 (ii)-(iv); and

(ii) the child is attending an independent fee paying day school and meets the requirements set out in paragraph 57 (i)-(vi); and

(iii) the child is under 12 years of age; and

(iv) the parent can provide satisfactory evidence of adequate and reliable funds for maintaining a second home in the United Kingdom; and

(v) the parent is not seeking to make the United Kingdom his main home.

Leave to enter or remain as the parent of a child at school

56B A person seeking leave to enter or remain in the United Kingdom as the parent of a child at school may be admitted or allowed to remain for a period not exceeding 12 months, subject to a condition prohibiting employment, providing the Immigration Officer or, in the case of an application for limited leave to remain, the Secretary of State is satisfied that each of the requirements of paragraph 56A is met.

Refusal of leave to enter or remain as the parent of a child at school

56C Leave to enter or remain in the United Kingdom as the parent of a child at school is to be refused if the Immigration Office or, in the case of an application for limited leave to remain, the Secretary of State, is not satisfied that each of the requirements of paragraph 56A is met.]

Notes   Words in square brackets inserted by CM 4851.

PART 3:   PERSONS SEEKING TO ENTER OR REMAIN IN THE UNITED KINGDOM FOR STUDIES

STUDENTS

Requirements for leave to enter as a student

57   The requirements to be met by a person seeking leave to enter the United Kingdom as a student are that he:

- (i)   has been accepted for a course of study at:
    - (*a*)   a publicly funded institution of further or higher education; or
    - (*b*)   a *bona fide* private education institution which maintains satisfactory records of enrolment and attendance; or
    - (*c*)   an independent fee paying school outside the maintained sector; and
- (ii)   is able and intends to follow either:
    - (*a*)   a recognised full-time degree course at a publicly funded institution of further or higher education; or
    - (*b*)   a weekday full-time course involving attendance at a single institution for a minimum of 15 hours organised daytime study per week of a single subject or directly related subjects; or
    - (*c*)   a full-time course of study at an independent fee paying school; and
- (iii)   if under the age of 16 years is enrolled at an independent fee paying school on a full-time course of studies which meets the requirements of the Education Act 1944; and
- (iv)   intends to leave the United Kingdom at the end of his studies; and
- (v)   does not intend to engage in business or to take employment, except part-time or vacation work undertaken with the consent of the Secretary of State for Employment; and
- (vi)   is able to meet the costs of his course and accommodation and the maintenance of himself and any dependants without taking employment or engaging in business or having recourse to public funds.

Note   Paras 57–62 replace HC 251, paras 26, 27 and 108–112.

Leave to enter as a student

58   A person seeking leave to enter the United Kingdom as a student may be admitted for an appropriate period depending on the length of his course of study and his means, and with a condition restricting his freedom to take employment, provided the Immigration Officer is satisfied that each of the requirements of paragraph 57 is met.

Refusal of leave to enter as a student

59   Leave to enter as a student is to be refused if the Immigration Officer is not satisfied that each of the requirements of paragraph 57 is met.

Requirements for an extension of stay as student

60   The requirements for an extension of stay as a student are that the applicant:

- (i)   was admitted to the United Kingdom with a valid student entry clearance if he is a person specified in [Appendix 1] to these Rules; and

(ii)   meets the requirements for admission as a student set out in paragraph 57(i)–(vi); and

(iii) has produced evidence of his enrolment on a course which meets the requirements of paragraph 57; and

(iv)   can produce satisfactory evidence of regular attendance during any course which he has already begun; or any other course for which he has been enrolled in the past; and

(v)   can show evidence of satisfactory progress in his course of study including the taking and passing of any relevant examinations; and

(vi)   would not, as a result of an extension of stay, spend more than 4 years on short courses (ie courses of less than 2 years duration, or longer courses broken off before completion); and

(vii) has not come to the end of a period of government or international scholarship agency sponsorship, or has the written consent of his [official] sponsor for a further period of study in the United Kingdom and satisfactory evidence that sufficient sponsorship funding is available.

Note   Paragraph 60(i) amended with effect from 11 May 1998 (Cmnd 3953). Words in square brackets in paragraph 60(vii) substituted by CM 4851.

Extension of stay as a student

61   An extension of stay as a student may be granted, subject to a restriction on his freedom to take employment, provided the Secretary of State is satisfied that the applicant meets each of the requirements of paragraph 60.

Refusal of extension of stay as a student

62   An extension of stay as a student is to be refused if the Secretary of State is not satisfied that each of the requirements of paragraph 60 is met.

STUDENT NURSES

Definition of student nurse

63   For the purposes of these Rules the term student nurse means a person accepted for training as a student nurse or midwife leading to a registered nursing qualification; or an overseas nurse or midwife who has been accepted on an adaptation course leading to registration as a nurse with the United Kingdom Central Council for Nursing, Midwifery and Health Visiting.

Requirements for leave to enter as a student nurse

64   The requirements to be met by a person seeking leave to enter the United Kingdom as a student nurse are that the person:

(i)   comes within the definition set out in paragraph 63 above; and

(ii)   has been accepted for a course of study in a recognised nursing educational establishment offering nursing training which meets the requirements of the United Kingdom Central Council for Nursing, Midwifery and Health Visiting; and

(iii) did not obtain acceptance by misrepresentation; and

(iv)   is able and intends to follow the course; and

(v)   does not intend to engage in business or take employment except in connection with the training course; and

(vi)   intends to leave the United Kingdom at the end of the course; and

(vii) has sufficient funds available for accommodation and maintenance for himself and any dependants without engaging in business or taking employment (except in connection with the training course) or having recourse to public funds. The possession of a Department of Health bursary may be taken into account in assessing whether the student meets the maintenance requirement.

Leave to enter the United Kingdom as a student nurse

65   A person seeking leave to enter the United Kingdom as a student nurse may be admitted for the duration of the training course, with a restriction on his freedom to take employment, provided the Immigration Officer is satisfied that each of the requirements of paragraph 64 is met.

Refusal of leave to enter as a student nurse

66   Leave to enter as a student nurse is to be refused if the Immigration Officer is not satisfied that each of the requirements of paragraph 64 is met.

Requirements for an extension of stay as a student nurse

67   The requirements for an extension of stay as a student nurse are that the applicant:

  (i)   was admitted to the United Kingdom with a valid student entry clearance if he is a person specified in [Appendix 1] to these Rules; and
  (ii)   meets the requirements set out in paragraphs 64(i)–(vii); and
  (iii) has produced evidence of enrolment at a recognised nursing educational establishment; and
  (iv) can provide satisfactory evidence of regular attendance during any course which he has already begun; or any other course for which he has been enrolled in the past; and
  (v)   would not, as a result of an extension of stay, spend more than 4 years in obtaining the relevant qualification; and
  (vi) has not come to the end of a period of government or international scholarship agency sponsorship, or has the written consent of his [official] sponsor for a further period of study in the United Kingdom and evidence that sufficient sponsorship funding is available.

Note   Paragraph 67(i) amended with effect from 11 May 1998 (Cmnd 3953).
Words in square brackets in para 67(vi) substituted by CM 4851.

Extension of stay as a student nurse

68   An extension of stay as a student nurse may be granted, subject to a restriction on his freedom to take employment, provided the Secretary of State is satisfied that the applicant meets each of the requirements of paragraph 67.

Refusal of extension of stay as student nurse

69   An extension of stay as a student nurse is to be refused if the Secretary of State is not satisfied that each of the requirements of paragraph 67 is met.

[RE-SITS OF EXAMINATIONS

Requirements for leave to enter to re-sit an examination

69A   The requirements to be met by a person seeking leave to enter the United Kingdom in order to re-sit an examination are that the applicant:

(i)   (*a*)   meets the requirements for admission as a student set out in paragraph 57 (i)-(vi); or

      (*b*)   met the requirements for admission as a student set out in paragraph 57 (i)-(iii) in the previous academic year and continues to meet the requirements of paragraph 57 (iv)-(vi); and

(ii)   has produced written confirmation from the education institution or independent fee paying school which he attends or attended in the previous academic year that he is required to re-sit an examination; and

(iii)   can provide satisfactory evidence of regular attendance during any course which he has already begun; or any other course for which he has been enrolled in the past; and

(iv)   has not come to the end of a period of government or international scholarship agency sponsorship, or has the written consent of his official sponsor for a further period of study in the United Kingdom and satisfactory evidence that sufficient sponsorship funding is available; and

(v)   has not previously been granted leave to re-sit the examination.

Leave to enter to re-sit an examination

69B   A person seeking leave to enter the United Kingdom in order to re-sit an examination may be admitted for a period sufficient to enable him to re-sit the examination at the first available opportunity with a condition restricting his freedom to take employment, provided the Immigration Officer is satisfied that each of the requirements of paragraph 69A is met.

Refusal of leave to enter to re-sit an examination

69C   Leave to enter to re-sit an examination is to be refused if the Immigration Officer is not satisfied that each of the requirements of paragraph 69A is met.

Requirements for an extension of stay to re-sit an examination

69D   The requirements for an extension of stay to re-sit an examination are that the applicant:

(i)   was admitted to the United Kingdom with a valid student entry clearance if he was then a visa national; and

(ii)   meets the requirements set out in paragraph 69A (i)-(v).

Extension of stay to re-sit an examination

69E   An extension of stay to re-sit an examination may be granted for a period sufficient to enable the applicant to re-sit the examination at the first available opportunity, subject to a restriction on his freedom to take employment, provided the Secretary of State is satisfied that the applicant meets each of the requirements of paragraph 69D.

Refusal of extension of stay to re-sit an examination

69F   An extension of stay to re-sit an examination is to be refused if the Secretary of State is not satisfied that each of the requirements of paragraph 69D is met.

WRITING UP A THESIS

Requirements for leave to enter to write up a thesis

69G   The requirements to be met by a person seeking leave to enter the United Kingdom in order to write up a thesis are that the applicant:

    (i)   (a meets the requirements for admission as a student set out in paragraph 57 (i)-(vi); or
(b) met the requirements for admission as a student set out in paragraph 57 (i)-(iii) in the previous academic year and continues to meet the requirements of paragraph 57 (iv)-(vi); and

    (ii)   can provide satisfactory evidence that he is a postgraduate student enrolled at an education institution as either a full time, part time or writing up student; and

    (iii) can demonstrate that his application is supported by the education institution; and

    (iv) has not come to the end of a period of government or international scholarship agency sponsorship, or has the written consent of his official sponsor for a further period of study in the United Kingdom and satisfactory evidence that sufficient sponsorship funding is available; and

    (v)   has not previously been granted 12 months leave to write up the same thesis.

Leave to enter to write up a thesis

69H A person seeking leave to enter the United Kingdom in order to write up a thesis may be admitted for 12 months with a condition restricting his freedom to take employment, provided the Immigration Officer is satisfied that each of the requirements of paragraph 69G is met.

Refusal of leave to enter to write up a thesis

69I Leave to enter to write up a thesis is to be refused if the Immigration Officer is not satisfied that each of the requirements of paragraph 69G is met.

Requirements for an extension of stay to write up a thesis

69J The requirements for an extension of stay to write up a thesis are that the applicant:

    (i)   was admitted to the United Kingdom with a valid student entry clearance if he was then a visa national; and

    (ii)   meets the requirements set out in paragraph 69G (i)-(v).

Extension of stay to write up a thesis

69K An extension of stay to write up a thesis may be granted for 12 months subject to a restriction on his freedom to take employment, provided the Secretary of State is satisfied that the applicant meets each of the requirements of paragraph 69J.

Refusal of extension of stay to write up a thesis

69L An extension of stay to write up a thesis is to be refused if the Secretary of State is not satisfied that each of the requirements of paragraph 69J is met.]

Note *[Paras 63–69 replace HC251, para 29.]*
Paragraphs 69A to 69L inserted by CM 4851.

POSTGRADUATE DOCTORS AND DENTISTS

Requirements for leave to enter as a postgraduate doctor or dentist

[**70** The requirements for leave to enter the United Kingdom for the purpose of training as a postgraduate doctor or dentist are that the applicant:

(i)   (*a*) is a graduate from a medical school, who is eligible for provisional or limited registration with the General Medical Council, and who
  (1)   intends to undertake pre-registration House Officer employment for up to 12 months, and
  (2)   has not spent more than 12 months in aggregate in pre-registration House Officer employment; or
(*b*)   is a doctor or dentist eligible for full or limited registration with the General Medical Council or the General Dental Council, who intends to undertake post-graduate training in a hospital or the Community Health Services or both;
(ii)   intends to leave the United Kingdom on completion of his training period; and
(iii)   is able to maintain and accommodate himself and any dependants without recourse to public funds.]

Note   Substituted by HC 338, r 1 with effect from 1 April 1997.

[Leave to enter as a postgraduate doctor or dentist

71   A person seeking leave to enter the United Kingdom to undertake:

(*a*)   pre-registration House Officer employment may be admitted for a period not exceeding 12 months; and
(*b*)   postgraduate training as a doctor or dentist in a hospital or the Community Health services, or both, may be admitted for a period not exceeding three years,

if the Immigration Officer is satisfied that each of the requirements of paragraph 70 is met.]

Note   Substituted by HC 338, r 1 with effect from 1 April 1997.

Refusal of leave to enter as a postgraduate doctor or dentist

72   Leave to enter as a postgraduate doctor or dentist is to be refused if the Immigration Officer is not satisfied that each of the requirements of paragraph 70 is met.

Requirements for extension of stay as a postgraduate doctor or dentist

[**73**   The requirements for an extension of stay as a postgraduate doctor or dentist are that the applicant:

(i)   (*a*) is a graduate from a medical school who is eligible for provisional or limited registration with the General Medical Council, and who
  (1)   intends to undertake pre-registration House Officer employment for up to 12 months, and
  (2)   would not, as a result of an extension of stay, spend more than 12 months in aggregate in pre-registration House Officer employment; or
(*b*)   is a doctor or dentist, who can provide evidence of limited or full registration with the General Medical Council or registration with the General Dental Council and who—
  (1)   intends to undertake or continue postgraduate training in a hospital or the Community Health Services or both, and
  (2)   can show evidence of satisfactory progress in his postgraduate training including the passing of any relevant examinations.
(ii)   intends to leave the United Kingdom on completion of his training period; and
(iii)   is able to maintain and accommodate himself and any dependants without recourse to public funds.]

Note   Substituted by HC 338, r 1 with effect from 1 April 1997.

Extension of stay as a postgraduate doctor or dentist

[74   An extension of stay may be granted—

    (*a*)   as a pre-registration House Officer for a period not exceeding 12 months, and

    (*b*)   as a doctor or dentist undertaking postgraduate training in a hospital or the Community Health Service or both for a period not exceeding three years,

if the Secretary of State is satisfied that—

    (i)   each of the requirements of paragraph 73 is met, and

    (ii)   no more than four years in aggregate will be spent in Senior House Officer (basic specialist training) or equivalent posts.]

Note   Substituted by HC 338, r 1 with effect from 1 April 1997.

Refusal of extension of stay as a postgraduate doctor or dentist

75   An extension of stay as a postgraduate doctor or dentist is to be refused if the Secretary of State is not satisfied that each of the requirements of paragraph 73 is met.

SPOUSES OF STUDENTS

Requirements for leave to enter or remain as the spouse of a student [or prospective student]

76   The requirements to be met by a person seeking leave to enter or remain in the United Kingdom as the spouse of a student are that:

    (i)   the applicant is married to a person admitted to or allowed to remain in the United Kingdom under paragraphs 57–75 [or 82–87]; and

    (ii)   each of the parties intends to live with the other as his or her spouse during the applicant's stay and the marriage is subsisting; and

    (iii)   there will be adequate accommodation for the parties and any dependants without recourse to public funds; and

    (iv)   the parties will be able to maintain themselves and any dependants adequately without recourse to public funds; and

    (v)   the applicant does not intend to take employment except as permitted under paragraph 77 below; and

    (vi)   the applicant intends to leave the United Kingdom at the end of any period of leave granted to him.

Leave to enter or remain as the spouse of a student [or prospective student]

77   A person seeking leave to enter or remain in the UnitedKingdom as the spouse of a student may be admitted or allowed to remain for a period not in excess of that granted to the student provided the Immigration Officer or, in the case of an application for limited leave to remain, the Secretary of State, is satisfied that each of the requirements of paragraph 76 is met. [Employment may be permitted] where the period of leave being granted is [, or was,] 12 months or more.

Note   Words in square brackets substituted and inserted by CM 4851.

Refusal of leave to enter or remain as the spouse of a student [or prospective student]

78   Leave to enter or remain as the spouse of a student is to be refused if the Immigration Officer or, in the case of an application for limited leave to remain, the Secretary of State is not satisfied that each of the requirements of paragraph 76 is met.

CHILDREN OF STUDENTS

Requirements for leave to enter or remain as the child of a student [or prospective student]

79   The requirements to be met by a person seeking leave to enter or remain in the United Kingdom as the child of a student are that he:

  (i)   is the child of a parent admitted to or allowed to remain in the United Kingdom as a student under the paragraphs 57–75 [or 82–87]; and
  (ii) is under the age of 18 or has current leave to enter or remain in this capacity; and(iii)   is unmarried, has not formed an independent family unit and is not leading an independent life; and
  (iv) can, and will, be maintained and accommodated adequately without recourse to public funds; and
  (v)   will not stay in the United Kingdom beyond any period of leave granted to his parent.

Leave to enter or remain as the child of a student [or prospective student]

[80   A person seeking leave to enter or remain in the United Kingdom as the child of a student may be admitted or allowed to remain for a period not in excess of that granted to the student provided the Immigration Officer or, in the case of an application for limited leave to remain, the Secretary of State is satisfied that each of the requirements of paragraph 79 is met. Employment may be permitted where the period of leave being granted is, or was, 12 months or more.]

Note   Substituted by CM 4851.

Refusal of leave to enter or remain as the child of a student [or prospective student]

81   Leave to enter or remain in the United Kingdom as the child of a student is to be refused if the Immigration Officer or, in the case of an application for limited leave to remain, the Secretary of State, is not satisfied that each of the requirements of paragraph 79 is met.

PROSPECTIVE STUDENTS

Requirements for leave to enter as a prospective student

82   The requirements to be met by a person seeking leave to enter the United Kingdom as a prospective student are that he:

  (i)   can demonstrate a genuine and realistic intention of undertaking, within 6 months of his date of entry, a course of study which would meet the requirements for an extension of stay as a student set out in paragraphs 60 or 67; and
  (ii) intends to leave the United Kingdom on completion of his studies or on the expiry of his leave to enter if he is not able to meet the requirements for an extension of stay as a student set out in paragraphs 60 or 67; and
  (iii) is able without working or recourse to public funds to meet the costs of his intended course and accommodation and the maintenance of himself and any dependants while making arrangements to study and during the course of his studies.

Leave to enter as a prospective student

83   A person seeking leave to enter the United Kingdom as a prospective student may be admitted for a period not exceeding 6 months with a condition prohibiting

employment, provided the Immigration Officer is satisfied that each of the requirements of paragraph 82 is met.

Refusal of leave to enter as a prospective student

84   Leave to enter as a prospective student is to be refused if the Immigration Officer is not satisfied that each of the requirements of paragraph 82 is met.

Requirements for extension of stay as a prospective student

85   Six months is the maximum permitted leave which may be granted to a prospective student. The requirements for an extension of stay as a prospective student are that the applicant:

(i)   was admitted to the United Kingdom with a valid prospective student entry clearance if he is a person specified in [Appendix 1] to these Rules; and

(ii)   meets the requirements of paragraph 82; and

(iii)   would not, as a result of an extension of stay, spend more than 6 months in the United Kingdom.

Note   Paragraph 85(i) amended with effect from 11 May 1998 (Cmnd 3953).

Paragraph 85(i) of HC 395 of 1994 shall not apply to any application for an extension of stay for the purpose of studying made by a national of the SlovakRepublic whose current leave to enter and remain was granted before 8 October 1998 or by a national of the Republic of Croatia whose current leave to enter and remain was granted before 19 November 1999.

Extension of stay as a prospective student

86   An extension of stay as a prospective student may be granted, with a prohibition on employment, provided the Secretary of State is satisfied that each of the requirements of paragraph 85 is met.

Refusal of extension of stay as a prospective student

87   An extension of stay as a prospective student is to be refused if the Secretary of State is not satisfied that each of the requirements of paragraph 85 is met.

[STUDENTS' UNIONS SABBATICAL OFFICERS]

Requirements for leave to enter as a sabbatical officer

87A   The requirements to be met by a person seeking leave to enter the United Kingdom as a sabbatical officer are that the person:

(i)   has been elected to a full-time salaried post as a sabbatical officer at an educational establishment at which he is registered as a student;

(ii)   meets the requirements set out in paragraph 57 (i)-(ii) or met the requirements set out in paragraph 57 (i)-(ii) in the academic year prior to the one in which he took up or intends to take up sabbatical office; and

(iii)   does not intend to engage in business or take employment except in connection with his sabbatical post; and

(iv)   is able to maintain and accommodate himself and any dependants adequately without recourse to public funds; and

(v)   at the end of the sabbatical post he intends to:

(*a*)   complete a course of study which he has already begun; or

(*b*)   take up a further course of study which has been deferred to enable the applicant to take up the sabbatical post; or

(*c*)   leave the United Kingdom; and

(vi) has not come to the end of a period of government or international scholarship agency sponsorship, or has the written consent of his official sponsor to take up a sabbatical post in the United Kingdom; and

(vii) has not already completed 2 years as a sabbatical officer.

Leave to enter the United Kingdom as a sabbatical officer

87B A person seeking leave to enter the United Kingdom as a sabbatical officer may be admitted for a period not exceeding 12 months on conditions specifying his employment provided the Immigration Officer is satisfied that each of the requirements of paragraph 87A is met.

Refusal of leave to enter the United Kingdom as a sabbatical officer

87C Leave to enter as a sabbatical officer is to be refused if the Immigration Officer is not satisfied that each of the requirements of paragraph 87A is met.

Requirements for an extension of stay as a sabbatical officer

87D The requirements for an extension of stay as a sabbatical officer are that the applicant:

(i) was admitted to the United Kingdom with a valid student entry clearance if he was then a visa national; and

(ii) meets the requirements set out in paragraph 87A (i)-(vi); and

(iii) would not, as a result of an extension of stay, remain in the United Kingdom as a sabbatical officer to a date beyond 2 years from the date on which he was first given leave to enter the United Kingdom in this capacity.

Extension of stay as a sabbatical officer

87E An extension of stay as a sabbatical officer may be granted for a period not exceeding 12 months on conditions specifying his employment provided the Secretary of State is satisfied that the applicant meets each of the requirements of paragraph 87D.

Refusal of extension of stay as a sabbatical officer

87F An extension of stay as a sabbatical officer is to be refused if the Secretary of State is not satisfied that each of the requirements of paragraph 87D is met.]

Note   Paragraphs 87A–87F inserted by CM 4851.

PART 4:   PERSONS SEEKING TO ENTER OR REMAIN IN THE UNITED KINGDOM IN AN 'AU PAIR' PLACEMENT, AS A WORKING HOLIDAYMAKER, OR FOR TRAINING OR WORK EXPERIENCE

'AU PAIR' PLACEMENTS

Definition of an 'au pair' placement

88 For the purposes of these Rules an 'au pair' placement is an arrangement whereby a young person:

(*a*) comes to the United Kingdom for the purpose of learning the English language; and

(*b*) lives for a time as a member of an English speaking family with appropriate opportunities for study; and

(*c*) helps in the home for a maximum of 5 hours per day in return for a reasonable allowance and with two free days per week.

Requirements for leave to enter as an 'au pair'

89   The requirements to be met by a person seeking leave to enter the United Kingdom as an 'au pair' are that he:

(i) is seeking entry for the purpose of taking up an arranged placement which can be shown to fall within the definition set out in paragraph 88; and

(ii) is aged between 17–27 inclusive or was so aged when first given leave to enter in this capacity; and

(iii) is unmarried; and

(iv) is without dependants; and

(v) is a national of one of the following countries: Andorra, Bosnia-Herzegovina, Croatia, Cyprus, Czech Republic, [The Faroes], Greenland, Hungary, . . . Macedonia, Malta, Monaco, San Marino, Slovak Republic, Slovenia, Switzerland, or Turkey; and

(vi) does not intend to stay in the United Kingdom for more than 2 years as an 'au pair'; and

(vii) intends to leave the United Kingdom on completion of his stay as an 'au pair'; and

(viii) if he has previously spent time in the United Kingdom as an 'au pair', is not seeking leave to enter to a date beyond 2 years from the date on which he was first given leave to enter the United Kingdom in this capacity.
[; and

(ix) is able to maintain and accommodate himself without recourse to public funds.]

Leave to enter as an 'au pair'

90   A person seeking leave to enter the United Kingdom as an 'au pair' may be admitted for a period not exceeding 2 years with a prohibition on employment except as an 'au pair', provided the Immigration Officer is satisfied that each of the requirements of paragraph 89 is met. (A non-visa national who wishes to ascertain in advance whether a proposed 'au pair' placement is likely to meet the requirements of paragraph 89 is advised to obtain entry clearance before travelling to the United Kingdom).

Refusal of leave to enter as an 'au pair'

91   An application for leave to enter as an 'au pair' is to be refused if the Immigration Officer is not satisfied that each of the requirements of paragraph 89 is met.

Requirements for an extension of stay as an 'au pair'

92   The requirements for an extension of stay as an 'au pair' are that the applicant:

(i) was given leave to enter the United Kingdom as an 'au pair' under paragraph 90; and

(ii) is undertaking an arranged 'au pair' placement which can be shown to fall within the definition set out in paragraph 88; andi

(iii) meets the requirements of paragraph [89(ii)–(ix)]; and

(iv) would not, as a result of an extension to stay, remain in the United Kingdom as an 'au pair' to a date beyond 2 years from the date on which he was first given leave to enter the United Kingdom in this capacity.

Extension of stay as an 'au pair'

93   An extension of stay as an 'au pair' may be granted with a prohibition on employment except as an 'au pair', provided the Secretary of State is satisfied that each of the requirements of paragraph 92 is met.

Refusal of extension of stay as an 'au pair'

94   An extension of stay as an 'au pair' is to be refused if the Secretary of State is not satisfied that each of the requirements of paragraph 92 is met.

WORKING HOLIDAYMAKERS

Requirements for leave to enter as a working holidaymaker

95   The requirements to be met by a person seeking leave to enter the United Kingdom as a working holidaymaker are that he:

(i)   is a Commonwealth citizen; and

(ii)   is aged 17–27 inclusive or was so aged when first given leave to enter in this capacity; and

(iii)   is unmarried or is married to a person who meets the requirements of this paragraph and the parties to the marriage intend to take a working holiday together; and

(iv)   has the means to pay for his return or onward journey; and

(v)   is able and intends to maintain and accommodate himself without recourse to public funds; and

(vi)   is intending to take employment incidental to a holiday but not to engage in business, provide services as a professional sportsman or entertainer or pursue a career in the United Kingdom; and

(vii)   does not have dependent children any of whom are 5 years of age or over or who will reach 5 years of age before the applicant completes his working holiday; or commitments which would require him to earn a regular income; and

(viii)   intends to leave the United Kingdom at the end of his working holiday; and

(ix)   if he has previously spent time in the United Kingdom as a working holidaymaker, is not seeking leave to enter to a date beyond 2 years from the date he was first given leave to enter in this capacity; and

(x)   holds a valid United Kingdom entry clearance for entry in this capacity.

Leave to enter as a working holidaymaker

96   A person seeking leave to enter the United Kingdom as a working holidaymaker may be admitted for a period not exceeding 2 years with a condition restricting his freedom to take employment, provided he is able to produce to the Immigration Officer, on arrival, a valid United Kingdom entry clearance for entry in this capacity.

Refusal of leave to enter as a working holidaymaker

97   Leave to enter as a working holidaymaker is to be refused if a valid United Kingdom entry clearance for entry in this capacity is not produced to the Immigration Officer on arrival.

Requirements for an extension of stay as a working holidaymaker

98   The requirements for an extension of stay as a working holidaymaker are that the applicant:

(i)   entered the United Kingdom with a valid United Kingdom entry clearance as a working holidaymaker; and

(ii)   meets the requirements of paragraph 95(i)–(viii); and

(iii)   would not, as a result of an extension of stay, remain in the United Kingdom as a working holidaymaker to a date beyond 2 years from the date on which he was first given leave to enter the United Kingdom in this capacity.

Extension of stay as a working holidaymaker

99 An extension of stay as a working holidaymaker may be granted with a condition restricting his freedom to take employment, provided the Secretary of State is satisfied that the applicant meets each of the requirements of paragraph 98.

Refusal of extension of stay as a working holidaymaker

100 An extension of stay as a working holidaymaker is to be refused if the Secretary of State is not satisfied that each of the requirements of paragraph 98 is met.

CHILDREN OF WORKING HOLIDAYMAKERS

Requirements for leave to enter or remain as the child of a working holidaymaker

101 The requirements to be met by a person seeking leave to enter or remain in the United Kingdom as the child of a working holidaymaker are that:

(i) he is the child of a parent admitted to or allowed to remain in the United Kingdom as a working holidaymaker; and

(ii) he is under the age of 5 and will leave the United Kingdom before reaching that age; and

(iii) he can and will be maintained and accommodated adequately without recourse to public funds or without his parent(s) engaging in business or taking employment except as provided by paragraph 95 above; and

(iv) both parents are being or have been admitted to or allowed to remain in the United Kingdom save where:

(a) the parent he is accompanying or joining is his sole surviving parent; or

(b) the parent he is accompanying or joining has had the sole responsibility for his upbringing; or

(c) there are serious and compelling family or other considerations which make exclusion from the United Kingdom undesirable and suitable arrangements have been made for his care; and

(v) if seeking leave to enter, he holds a valid United Kingdom entry clearance for entry in this capacity or, if seeking leave to remain, was admitted with a valid United Kingdom entry clearance for entry in this capacity.

Leave to enter or remain as the child of a working holidaymaker

102 A person seeking leave to enter or remain in the United Kingdom as the child of a working holidaymaker may be admitted or allowed to remain for the same period of leave as that granted to the working holidaymaker provided that, in relation to an application for leave to enter, a valid United Kingdom entry clearance for entry in this capacity is produced to the Immigration Officer on arrival or, in the case of an application for leave to remain, he was admitted with a valid United Kingdom entry clearance for entry in this capacity and is able to satisfy the Secretary of State that each of the requirements of paragraph 101(i)–(iv) is met.

Refusal of leave to enter or remain as the child of a working holidaymaker

103 Leave to enter or remain in the United Kingdom as the child of a working holidaymaker is to be refused if, in relation to an application for leave to enter, a valid United Kingdom entry clearance for entry in this capacity is not produced to the Immigration Officer on arrival or, in the case of an application for leave to remain, the applicant was not admitted with a valid United Kingdom entry clearance for entry in this capacity or is unable to satisfy the Secretary of State that each of the requirements of paragraph 101(i)–(iv) is met.

Requirements for leave to enter as a seasonal worker at an agricultural camp

104 The requirements to be met by a person seeking leave to enter the United Kingdom as a seasonal worker at an agricultural camp are that he:

(i) is a student in full-time education aged between 18–25 years inclusive, except if returning for another season at the specific invitation of a farmer; and

(ii) holds a valid Home Office work card issued by the operator of a scheme approved by the Secretary of State; and

(iii) intends to leave the United Kingdom at the end of his period of leave as a seasonal worker; and

(iv) does not intend to take employment except in the terms of this paragraph. [; and

(v) is able to maintain and accommodate himself and any dependants without recourse to public funds.]

Leave to enter as a seasonal worker at an agricultural camp

[**105** A person seeking leave to enter the United Kingdom as a seasonal worker at an agricultural camp may be admitted with a condition restricting his freedom to take employment, until 30 November of the year in question, if the Immigration Officer is satisfied that each of the requirements of paragraph 104 is met.]

Note Substituted by HC 338, r 2 with effect from 1 April 1997.

Refusal of leave to enter as a seasonal worker at an agricultural camp

106 Leave to enter the United Kingdom as a seasonal worker at an agricultural camp is to be refused if the Immigration Officer is not satisfied that each of the requirements of paragraph 104 is met.

Requirements for extension of stay as a seasonal worker at an agricultural camp

107 The requirements for an extension of stay as a seasonal worker at an agricultural camp are that the applicant:

(i) entered the United Kingdom as a seasonal worker with a valid Home Office work card under paragraph 105; and

(ii) meets the requirements of paragraph [104(iii)–(v)]; and

(iii) can show that there is further farm work available under the approved scheme; and

(iv) would not, as a result of an extension of stay, remain in the United Kingdom as a seasonal worker for longer than 6 months in aggregate or beyond 30 November of the year in question, whichever is the shorter period.

Extension of stay as a seasonal worker at an agricultural camp

108 An extension of stay as a seasonal worker may be granted with a condition restricting his freedom to take employment for a further period not exceeding 3 months or until 30 November of the year in question, whichever is the shorter period, provided the Secretary of State is satisfied that the applicant meets each of the requirements of paragraph 107.

Refusal of extension of stay as a seasonal worker in an agricultural camp

109 An extension of stay as a seasonal worker at an agricultural camp is to be refused if the Secretary of State is not satisfied that each of the requirements of paragraph 107 is met.

Requirements for leave to enter as a teacher or language assistant under an approved exchange scheme

110   The requirements to be met by a person seeking leave to enter the United Kingdom as a teacher or language assistant on an approved exchange scheme are that he:

(i)   is coming to an educational establishment in the United Kingdom under an exchange scheme approved by the Education Departments or administered by the Central Bureau for Educational Visits and Exchanges or the League for the Exchange of Commonwealth Teachers; and
(ii)   intends to leave the United Kingdom at the end of his exchange period; and
(iii) does not intend to take employment except in the terms of this paragraph; and
(iv)   is able to maintain and accommodate himself and any dependants without recourse to public funds; and
(v)   holds a valid United Kingdom entry clearance for entry in this capacity.

Leave to enter as a teacher or language assistant under an exchange scheme

111   A person seeking leave to enter the United Kingdom as a teacher or language assistant under an approved exchange scheme may be given leave to enter for a period not exceeding 12 months provided he is able to produce to the Immigration Officer, on arrival, a valid United Kingdom entry clearance for entry in this capacity.

Refusal of leave to enter as a teacher or language assistant under an approved exchange scheme

112   Leave to enter the United Kingdom as a teacher or language assistant under an approved exchange scheme is to be refused if a valid United Kingdom entry clearance for entry in this capacity is not produced to the Immigration Officer on arrival.

Requirements for extension of stay as a teacher or language assistant under an approved exchange scheme

113   The requirements for an extension of stay as a teacher or language assistant under an approved exchange scheme are that the applicant:

(i)   entered the United Kingdom with a valid United Kingdom entry clearance as a teacher or language assistant; and
(ii)   is still engaged in the employment for which his entry clearance was granted; and(iii)   is still required for the employment in question, as certified by the employer; and
(iv)   meets the requirements of paragraph 110(ii)–(iv); and
(v)   would not, as a result of an extension of stay, remain in the United Kingdom as an exchange teacher or language assistant for more than 2 years from the date on which he was first given leave to enter the United Kingdom in this capacity.

Extension of stay as a teacher or language assistant under an approved exchange scheme

114   An extension of stay as a teacher or language assistant under an approved exchange scheme may be granted for a further period not exceeding 12 months provided the Secretary of State is satisfied that each of the requirements of paragraph 113 is met.

Refusal of extension of stay as a teacher or language assistant under an approved exchange scheme

115   An extension of stay as a teacher or language assistant under an approved exchange scheme is to be refused if the Secretary of State is not satisfied that each of the requirements of paragraph 113 is met.

Requirements for leave to enter for Department of Employment approved training or work experience

116   The requirements to be met by a person seeking leave to enter the United Kingdom for Department of Employment approved training or work experience are that he:

- (i)   holds a valid work permit from the Department of Employment issued under the Training and Work Experience Scheme; and
- (ii)   is not of an age which puts him outside the limits for employment; and
- (iii)   is capable of undertaking the training or work experience as specified in his work permit; and
- (iv)   intends to leave the United Kingdom on the completion of his training or work experience; and(v)   does not intend to take employment except as specified in his work permit; and
- (vi)   is able to maintain and accommodate himself and any dependants adequately without recourse to public funds.

Leave to enter for Department of Employment approved training or work experience

117   A person seeking leave to enter the United Kingdom for approved training may be admitted to the United Kingdom for a period not exceeding 3 years and a person seeking entry for approved work experience may be admitted for a period not exceeding 12 months, provided the Immigration Officer is satisfied that each of the requirements of paragraph 116 is met. Leave to enter is to be subject to a condition permitting the person to take or change employment only with the permission of the Department of Employment.

Refusal of leave to enter for Department of Employment approved training or work experience

118   Leave to enter the United Kingdom for Department of Employment approved training or work experience is to be refused if the Immigration Officer is not satisfied that each of the requirements of paragraph 116 is met.

Requirements for extension of stay for Department of Employment approved training or work experience

119   The requirements for an extension of stay for Department of Employment approved training or work experience are that the applicant:

- (i)   entered the United Kingdom with a valid work permit under paragraph 117 or was admitted or allowed to remain in the United Kingdom as a student; and
- (ii)   has written approval from the Department of Employment for an extension of stay in this category; and
- (iii)   meets the requirements of paragraph 116(ii)–(vi); and
- (iv)   would not as a result of an extension of stay spend more than 2 years in the United Kingdom for Department of Employment approved work experience.

Extension of stay for Department of Employment approved training or work experience

120   An extension of stay for approved training may be granted for a further period not exceeding 3 years; and an extension of stay for approved work experience may be granted for a further period not exceeding 12 months provided the Secretary of State is satisfied that each of the requirements of paragraph 119 is met. An extension of stay is to be subject to a condition permitting the applicant to take or change employment only with the permission of the Department of Employment.

Refusal of extension of stay for Department of Employment approved training or work experience

121   An extension of stay for Department of Employment approved training or work experience is to be refused if the Secretary of State is not satisfied that each of the requirements of paragraph 119 is met.

Spouses of persons with limited leave to enter or remain under paragraphs 110–121

Requirements for leave to enter or remain as the spouse of a person with limited leave to enter or remain in the United Kingdom under paragraphs 110–121

122   The requirements to be met by a person seeking leave to enter or remain in the United Kingdom as the spouse of a person with limited leave to enter or remain in the United Kingdom under paragraphs 110–121 are that:

  (i)   the applicant is married to a person with limited leave to enter or remain in the United Kingdom under paragraphs 110–121; and
  (ii)   each or the parties intends to live with the other as his or her spouse during the applicant's stay and the marriage is subsisting; and
  (iii) there will be adequate accommodation for the parties and any dependants without recourse to public funds in accommodation which they own or occupy exclusively; and
  (iv)   the parties will be able to maintain themselves and any dependants adequately without recourse to public funds; and
  (v)   the applicant does not intend to stay in the United Kingdom beyond any period of leave granted to his spouse; and
  (vi)   if seeking leave to enter, the applicant holds a valid United Kingdom entry clearance for entry in this capacity or, if seeking leave to remain, was admitted with a valid United Kingdom entry clearance for entry in this capacity.

Leave to enter or remain as the spouse of a person with limited leave to enter or remain in the United Kingdom under paragraphs 110–121

123   A person seeking leave to enter or remain in the United Kingdom as the spouse of a person with limited leave to enter or remain in the United Kingdom under paragraphs 110–121 may be given leave to enter or remain in the United Kingdom for a period of leave not in excess of that granted to the person with limited leave to enter or remain under paragraphs 110–121 provided that, in relation to an application for leave to enter, he is able, on arrival, to produce to the Immigration Officer a valid United Kingdom entry clearance for entry in this capacity or, in the case of an application for limited leave to remain, was admitted with a valid United Kingdom entry clearance for entry in this capacity and is able to satisfy the Secretary of State that each of the requirements of paragraph 122(i)–(v) is met.

Refusal of leave to enter or remain as the spouse of a person with limited leave to enter or remain in the United Kingdom under paragraphs 110–121

124   Leave to enter or remain in the United Kingdom as the spouse of a person with limited leave to enter or remain in the United Kingdom under paragraphs 110–121 is to be refused if, in relation to an application for leave to enter, a valid United Kingdom entry clearance for entry in this capacity is not produced the the Immigration Officer on arrival or, in the case of an application for limited leave to remain, if the applicant was not admitted with a valid United Kingdom entry clearance for entry in this capacity or is unable to satisfy the Secretary of State that each of the requirements of paragraph 122(i)–(v) is met.

Requirements for leave to enter or remain as the child of a person with limited leave to enter or remain in the United Kingdom under paragraphs 110–121

125 The requirements to be met by a person seeking leave to enter or remain in the United Kingdom as the child of a person with limited leave to enter or remain in the United Kingdom under paragraphs 110–121 are that:

(i) he is the child of a parent who has limited leave to enter or remain in the United Kingdom under paragraphs 110–121; and

(ii) he is under the age of 18 or has current leave to enter or remain in this capacity; and

(iii) he is unmarried, has not formed an independent family unit and is not leading an independent life; and

(iv) he can, and will, be maintained and accommodated adequately without recourse to public funds in accommodation which his parent(s) own or occupy exclusively; and

(v) he will not stay in the United Kingdom beyond any period of leave granted to his parent(s); and

(vi) both parents are being or have been admitted to or allowed to remain in the United Kingdom save where:

    (*a*) the parent he is accompanying or joining is his sole surviving parent; or

    (*b*) the parent he is accompanying or joining has had sole responsibility for his upbringing; or

    (*c*) there are serious and compelling family or other considerations which make exclusion from the United Kingdom undesirable and suitable arrangements have been made for his care; and

(vii) if seeking leave to enter, he holds a valid United Kingdom entry clearance for entry in this capacity of, if seeking leave to remain, was admitted with a valid United Kingdom entry clearance for entry in this capacity.

Leave to enter or remain as the child of a person with limited leave to enter or remain in the United Kingdom under paragraphs 110–121

126 A person seeking leave to enter or remain in the United Kingdom as the child of a person with limited leave to enter or remain in the United Kingdom under paragraphs 110–121 may be given leave to enter or remain in the United Kingdom for a period of leave not in excess of that granted to the person with limited leave to enter or remain under paragraphs 110–121 provided that, in relation to an application for leave to enter, he is able, on arrival, to produce to the Immigration Officer a valid United Kingdom entry clearance for entry in this capacity or, in the case of an application for limited leave to remain, he was admitted with a valid United Kingdom entry clearance for entry in this capacity and is able to satisfy the Secretary of State that each of the requirements of paragraph 125(i)–(vi) is met.

Refusal of leave to enter or remain as the child of a person with limited leave to enter or remain in the United Kingdom under paragraphs 110–121

127 Leave to enter or remain in the United Kingdom as the child of a person with limited leave to enter or remain in the United Kingdom under paragraphs 110–121 is to be refused if, in relation to an application for leave to enter, a valid United Kingdom entry clearance for entry in this capacity is not produced to the Immigration Officer on arrival or, in the case of an application for limited leave to remain, if the applicant was not admitted with a valid United Kingdom entry clearance for entry in this capacity or is unable to satisfy the Secretary of State that each of the requirements of paragraph 125(i)–(vi) is met.

PART 5:   PERSONS SEEKING TO ENTER OR REMAIN IN THE UNITED KINGDOM FOR
EMPLOYMENT

WORK PERMIT EMPLOYMENT

Requirements for leave to enter the United Kingdom for work permit employment

128   The requirements to be met by a person coming to the United Kingdom to seek or take employment (unless he is otherwise eligible for admission for employment under these Rules or is eligible for admission as a seaman under contract to join a ship due to leave British waters) are that he:

(i)   holds a valid Department of Employment work permit; and
(ii)   is not of an age which puts him outside the limits for employment; and
(iii)   is capable of undertaking the employment specified in the work permit; and
(iv)   does not intend to take employment except as specified in his work permit; and
(v)   is able to maintain and accommodate himself and any dependants adequately without recourse to public funds; and
(vi)   in the case of a person in possession of a work permit which is valid for a period of 12 months or less, intends to leave the United Kingdom at the end of his approved employment.

Leave to enter for work permit employment

129   A person seeking leave to enter the United Kingdom for the purpose of work permit employment may be admitted for a period not exceeding 4 years (normally as specified in his work permit), subject to a condition restricting him to employment approved by the Department of Employment, provided the Immigration Officer is satisfied that each of the requirements of paragraph 128 is met.

Refusal of leave to enter for employment

130   Leave to enter for the purpose of employment is to be refused if the Immigration Officer is not satisfied that each of the requirements of paragraph 128 is met (unless he is otherwise eligible for admission for employment under these Rules or is eligible for admission as a seaman under contract to join a ship due to leave British waters).

Requirements for an extension of stay for work permit employment

131   The requirements for an extension of stay to seek or take employment (unless the applicant is otherwise eligible for an extension of stay for employment under these Rules) are that the applicant:

(i)   entered the United Kingdom with a valid work permit under paragraph 129; and
(ii)   has written approval from the Department of Employment for the continuation of his employment; and
(iii)   meets the requirements of paragraph 128(ii)–(v).

Extension of stay for work permit employment

132   An extension of stay for work permit employment may be granted for a period not exceeding the period of approved employment recommended by the Department of Employment provided the Secretary of State is satisfied that each of the requirements of paragraph 131 is met. An extension of stay is to be subject to a condition restricting the applicant to employment approved by the Department of Employment.

Refusal of extension of stay for employment

133 An extension of stay for employment is to be refused if the Secretary of State is not satisfied that each of the requirements of paragraph 131 is met (unless the applicant is otherwise eligible for an extension of stay for employment under these Rules).

Indefinite leave to remain for a work permit holder

134 Indefinite leave to remain may be granted, on application, to a person admitted as a work permit holder provided:

(i) he has spent a continuous period of 4 years in the United Kingdom in this capacity; and
(ii) he has met the requirements of paragraph 131 throughout the 4 year period; and
(iii) he is still required for the employment in question, as certified by his employer.

Refusal of indefinite leave to remain for a work permit holder

135 Indefinite leave to remain in the United Kingdom for a work permit holder is to be refused if the Secretary of State is not satisfied that each of the requirements of paragraph 134 is met.

REPRESENTATIVES OF OVERSEAS NEWSPAPERS, NEWS AGENCIES AND BROADCASTING ORGANISATIONS

Requirements for leave to enter as a representative of an overseas newspaper, news agency or broadcasting organisation

136 The requirements to be met by a person seeking leave to enter the United Kingdom as a representative of an overseas newspaper, news agency or broadcasting organisation are that he:

(i) has been engaged by that organisation outside the United Kingdom and is being posted to the United Kingdom on a long-term assignment as a representative; and
(ii) intends to work full-time as a representative of that overseas newspaper, news agency or broadcasting organisation; and
(iii) does not intend to take employment except within the terms of this paragraph; and
(iv) can maintain and accommodate himself and any dependants adequately without recourse to public funds; and
(v) holds a valid United Kingdom entry clearance for entry in this capacity.

Leave to enter as a representative of an overseas newspaper, news agency or broadcasting organisation

137 A person seeking leave to enter the United Kingdom as a representative of an overseas newspaper, news agency or broadcasting organisation may be admitted for a period not exceeding 12 months provided he is able to produce to the Immigration Officer, on arrival, a valid United Kingdom entry clearance for entry in this capacity.

Refusal of leave to enter as a representative of an overseas newspaper, news agency or broadcasting organisation

138 Leave to enter as a representative of an overseas newspaper, news agency or broadcasting organisation is to be refused if a valid United Kingdom entry clearance for entry in this capacity is not produced to the Immigration Officer on arrival.

Requirements for an extension of stay as a representative of an overseas newspaper, news agency or broadcasting organisation

139   The requirements for an extension of stay as a representative of an overseas newspaper, news agency or broadcasting organisation are that the applicant:

(i)   entered the United Kingdom with a valid United Kingdom entry clearance as a representative of an overseas newspaper, news agency or broadcasting organisation; and

(ii)   is still engaged in the employment for which his entry clearance was granted; and

(iii)   is still required for the employment in question, as certified by his employer; and

(iv)   meets the requirements of paragraph 136(ii)–(iv).

Extension of stay as a representative of an overseas newspaper, news agency or broadcasting organisation

140   An extension of stay as a representative of an overseas newspaper, news agency or broadcasting organisation may be granted for a period not exceeding 3 years provided the Secretary of State is satisfied that each of the requirements of paragraph 139 is met.

Refusal of extension of stay as a representative of an overseas newspaper, news agency or broadcasting organisation

141   An extension of stay as a representative of an overseas newspaper, news agency or broadcasting organisation is to be refused if the Secretary of State is not satisfied that each of the requirements of paragaph 139 is met.

Indefinite leave to remain for a representative of an overseas newspaper, news agency or broadcasting organisation

142   Indefinite leave to remain may be granted, on application, to a representative of an overseas newspaper, news agency or broadcasting organisation provided:

(i)   he has spent a continuous period of 4 years in the United Kingdom in this capacity; and

(ii)   he has met the requirements of paragraph 139 throughout the 4 year period; and

(iii)   he is still required for the employment in question, as certified by his employer.

Refusal of indefinite leave to remain for a representative of an overseas newspaper, news agency or broadcasting organisation

143   Indefinite leave to remain in the United Kingdom for a representative of an overseas newspaper, news agency or broadcasting organisation is to be refused if the Secretary of State is not satisfied that each of the requirements of paragraph 142 is met.

REPRESENTATIVES OF OVERSEAS FIRMS WHICH HAVE NO BRANCH, SUBSIDIARY OR OTHER REPRESENTATIVE IN THE UNITED KINGDOM (SOLE REPRESENTATIVES)

Requirements for leave to enter as a sole representative

144   The requirements to be met by a person seeking leave to enter the United Kingdom as a sole representative are that he:

(i)   has been recruited and taken on as an employee outside the United Kingdom as a representative of a firm which has its headquarters and principal place of business outside the United Kingdom and which has no branch, subsidiary or other representative in the United Kingdom; and

(ii) seeks entry to the United Kingdom as a senior employee with full authority to take operational decisions on behalf of the overseas firm for the purpose of representing it in the United Kingdom by establishing and operating a registered branch or wholly owned subsidiary of that overseas firm; and

(iii) intends to be employed full time as a representative of that overseas firm; and

(iv) is not a majority shareholder in that overseas firm; and

(v) does not intend to take employment except within the terms of this paragraph; and

(vi) can maintain and accommodate himself and any dependants adequately without recourse to public funds; and

(vii) holds a valid United Kingdom entry clearance for entry in this capacity.

Leave to enter as a sole representative

145 A person seeking leave to enter the United Kingdom as a sole representative may be admitted for a period not exceeding 12 months provided he is able to produce to the Immigration Officer, on arrival, a valid United Kingdom entry clearance for entry in this capacity.

Refusal of leave to enter as a sole representative

146 Leave to enter as a sole representative is to be refused if a valid United Kingdom entry clearance for entry in this capacity is not produced to the Immigration Officer on arrival.

Requirements for an extension of stay as a sole representative

147 The requirements for an extension of stay as a sole representative are that the applicant:

(i) entered the United Kingdom with a valid United Kingdom entry clearance as a sole representative of an overseas firm; and

(ii) can show that the overseas firm still has its headquarters and principal place of business outside the United Kingdom; and

(iii) is employed full-time as a representative of that overseas firm and has established and is in charge of its registered branch or wholly-owned subsidiary; and

(iv) is still required for the employment in question, as certified by his employer; and

(v) meets the requirements of paragraph 144(iii)–(vi).

Extension of stay as a sole representative

148 An extension of stay not exceeding 3 years as a sole representative may be granted provided the Secretary of State is satisfied that each of the requirements of paragraph 147 is met.

Refusal of extension of stay as a sole representative

149 An extension of stay as a sole representative is to be refused if the Secretary of State is not satisfied that each of the requirements of paragraph 147 is met.

Indefinite leave to remain for a sole representative

150 Indefinite leave to remain may be granted, on application, to a sole representative provided:

(i)   he has spent a continuous period of 4 years in the United Kingdom in this capacity; and

(ii)   he has met the requirements of paragraph 147 throughout the 4 year period; and

(iii) he is still required for the employment in question, as certified by his employer.

Refusal of indefinite leave to remain for a sole representative

151   Indefinite leave to remain in the United Kingdom for a sole representative is to be refused if the Secretary of State is not satisfied that each of the requirements of paragraph 150 is met.

PRIVATE SERVANTS IN DIPLOMATIC HOUSEHOLDS

Requirements for leave to enter as a private servant in a diplomatic household

152   The requirements to be met by a person seeking leave to enter the United Kingdom as a private servant in a diplomatic household are that he:

(i)   is aged 18 or over; and

(ii)   is employed as a private servant in the household of a member of staff of a diplomatic or consular mission who enjoys diplomatic privileges and immunity within the meaning of the Vienna Convention on Diplomatic and Consular Relations or a member of the family forming part of the household of such a person; and

(iii) intends to work full-time as a private servant within the terms of this paragraph; and

(iv)   does not intend to take employment except within the terms of this paragraph; and

(v)   can maintain and accommodate himself and any dependants adequately without recourse to public funds; and

(vi)   holds a valid United Kingdom entry clearance for entry in this capacity.

Leave to enter as a private servant in a diplomatic household

153   A person seeking leave to enter the United Kingdom as a private servant in a diplomatic household may be given leave to enter for a period not exceeding 12 months provided he is able to produce to the Immigration Officer, on arrival, a valid United Kingdom entry clearance for entry in this capacity.

Refusal of leave to enter as a private servant in a diplomatic household

154   Leave to enter as a private servant in a diplomatic household is to be refused if a valid United Kingdom entry clearance for entry in this capacity is not produced to the Immigration Officer on arrival.

Requirements for an extension of stay as a private servant in a diplomatic household

155   The requirements for an extension of stay as a private servant in a diplomatic household are that the applicant:

(i)   entered the United Kingdom with a valid United Kingdom entry clearance as a private servant in a diplomatic household; and

(ii)   is still engaged in the employment for which his entry clearance was granted; and

(iii) is still required for the employment in question, as certified by the employer; and

(iv)   meets the requirements of paragraph 152(iii)–(v).

Extension of stay as a private servant in a diplomatic household

156 An extension of stay as a private servant in a diplomatic household may be granted for a period not exceeding 12 months provided the Secretary of State is satisfied that each of the requirements of paragraph 155 is met.

Refusal of extension of stay as a private servant in a diplomatic household

157 An extension of stay as a private servant in a diplomatic household is to be refused if the Secretary of State is not satisfied that each of the requirements of paragraph 155 is met.

Indefinite leave to remain for a servant in a diplomatic household

158 Indefinite leave to remain may be granted, on application, to a private servant in a diplomatic household provided:

(i) he has spent a continuous period of 4 years in the United Kingdom in this capacity; and

(ii) he has met the requirements of paragraph 155 throughout the 4 year period; and

(iii) he is still required for the employment in question, as certified by his employer.

Refusal of indefinite leave to remain for a servant in a diplomatic household

159 Indefinite leave to remain in the United Kingdom for a private servant in a diplomatic household is to be refused if the Secretary of State is not satisfied that each of the requirements of paragraph 158 is met.

OVERSEAS GOVERNMENT EMPLOYEES

Requirements for leave to enter as an overseas government employee

160 For the purposes of these Rules an overseas government employee means a person coming for employment by an overseas government or employed by the United Nations Organisation or other international organisation of which the United Kingdom is a member.

161 The requirements to be met by a person seeking leave to enter the United Kingdom as an overseas government employee are that he:

(i) is able to produce either a valid United Kingdom entry clearance for entry in this capacity or satisfactory documentary evidence of his status as an overseas government employee; and

(ii) intends to work full time for the government or organisation concerned; and

(iii) does not intend to take employment except within the terms of this paragraph; and

(iv) can maintain and accommodate himself and any dependants adequately without recourse to public funds.

Leave to enter as an overseas government employee

162 A person seeking leave to enter the United Kingdom as an overseas government employee may be given leave to enter for a period not exceeding 12 months, provided he is able, on arrival, to produce to the Immigration Officer a valid United Kingdom entry clearance for entry in this capacity or satisfy the Immigration Officer that each of the requirements of paragraph 161 is met.

Refusal of leave to enter as an overseas government employee

163   Leave to enter as an overseas government employee is to be refused if a valid United Kingdom entry clearance for entry in this capacity is not produced to the Immigration Officer on arrival or if the Immigration Officer is not satisfied that each of the requirements of paragraph 161 is met.

Requirements for an extension of stay as an overseas government employee

164   The requirements to be met by a person seeking an extension of stay as an overseas government employee are that the applicant:

   (i)   was given leave to enter the United Kingdom under paragraph 162 as an overseas government employee; and
  (ii)   is still engaged in the employment in question; and
 (iii) is still required for the employment is question, as certified by the employer; and
 (iv) meets the requirements of paragraph 161(ii)–(iv).

Extension of stay as an overseas government employee

165   An extension of stay as an overseas government employee may be granted for a period not exceeding 3 years provided the Secretary of State is satisfied that each of the requirements of paragraph 164 is met.

Refusal of extension of stay as an overseas government employee

166   An extension of stay as an overseas government employee is to be refused if the Secretary of State is not satisfied that each of the requirements of paragraph 164 is met.

Indefinite leave to remain for an overseas government employee

167   Indefinite leave to remain may be granted, on application, to an overseas government employee provided:

   (i)   he has spent a continuous period of 4 years in the United Kingdom in this capacity; and
  (ii)   he has met the requirements of paragraph 164 throughout the 4 year period; and
 (iii) he is still required for the employment in question, as certified by his employer.

Refusal of indefinite leave to remain for an overseas government employee

168   Indefinite leave to remain in the United Kingdom for an overseas government employee is to be refused if the Secretary of State is not satisfied that each of the requirements of paragraph 167 is met.

MINISTERS OF RELIGION, MISSIONARIES AND MEMBERS OF RELIGIOUS ORDERS

169   For the purposes of these Rules:

   (i)   a minister of religion means a religious functionary whose main regular duties comprise the leading of a congregation in performing the rites and rituals of the faith and in preaching the essentials of the creed;
  (ii)   a missionary means a person who is directly engaged in spreading a religious doctrine and whose work is not in essence administrative or clerical;
 (iii) a member of a religious order means a person who is coming to live in a community run by that order.

Requirements for leave to enter as a minister or religion, missionary or member of a religious order

170   The requirements to be met by a person seeking leave to enter the United Kingdom as a minister of religion, missionary or member of a religious order are that he:

(i) (a) if seeking leave to enter as a minister of religion has either been working for at least one year as a minister of religion or, where ordination is prescribed by a religious faith as the sole means of entering the ministry, has been ordained as a minister of religion following at least one year's full-time or two years' part-time training for the ministry; or

(b) if seeking leave to enter as a missionary has been trained as a missionary or has worked as a missionary and is being sent to the United Kingdom by an overseas organisation; or

(c) if seeking leave to enter as a member of a religious order is coming to live in a community maintained by the religious order of which he is a member and, if intending to teach, does not intend to do so save at an establishment maintained by his order; and

(ii) intends to work full-time as a minister of religion, missionary or for the religious order of which he is a member; and

(iii) does not intend to take employment except within the terms of this paragraph; and

(iv) can maintain and accommodate himself and any dependants adequately without recourse to public funds; and

(v) holds a valid United Kingdom entry clearance for entry in this capacity.

Leave to enter as a minister or religion, missionary or member of a religious order

171   A person seeking leave to enter the United Kingdom as a minister of religion, missionary or member of a religious order may be admitted for a period not exceeding 12 months provided he is able to produce to the Immigration Officer, on arrival, a valid United Kingdom entry clearance for entry in this capacity.

Refusal of leave to enter as a minister of religion, missionary or member of a religious order

172   Leave to enter as a minister of religion, missionary or member of a religious order is to be refused if a valid United Kingdom entry clearance for entry in this capacity is not produced to the Immigration Officer on arrival.

Requirements for an extension to stay as a minister of religion, missionary or member of a religious order

173   The requirements for an extension of stay as a minister of religion, missionary or member of a religious order are that the applicant:

(i) entered the United Kingdom with a valid United Kingdom entry clearance as a minister of religion, missionary or member of a religious order; and

(ii) is still engaged in the employment for which his entry clearance was granted; and

(iii) is still required for the employment in question as certified by the leadership of his congregation, his employer or the head of his religious order; and

(iv) meets the requirements of paragraph 170(ii)–(iv).

Extension of stay as a minister of religion, missionary or member of a religious order

174   An extension of stay as a minister of religion, missionary or member of a religious order may be granted for a period not exceeding 3 years provided the Secretary of State is satisfied that each of the requirements of paragraph 173 is met.

Refusal of extension of stay as a minister of religion, missionary or member of a religious order

175 An extension of stay as a minister of religion, missionary or member of a religious order is to be refused if the Secretary of State is not satisfied that each of the requirements of paragraph 173 is met.

Indefinite leave to remain for a minister of religion, missionary or member of a religious order

176 Indefinite leave to remain may be granted, on application, to a person admitted as a minister of religion, missionary or member of a religious order   provided:

- (i) he has spent a continuous period of 4 years in the United Kingdom in this capacity; and
- (ii) he has met the requirements of paragraph 173 throughout the 4 year period; and
- (iii) he is still required for the employment in question as certified by the leadership of his congregation, his employer or the head of the religious order to which he belongs.

Refusal of indefinite leave to remain for a minister of religion, missionary or member of a religious order

177 Indefinite leave to remain in the United Kingdom for a minister of religion, missionary or member of a religious order is to be refused if the Secretary of State is not satisfied that each of the requirements of paragraph 176 is met.

AIRPORT-BASED OPERATIONAL GROUND STAFF OF OVERSEAS-OWNED AIRLINES

Requirements for leave to enter the United Kingdom as a member of the operational ground staff of an overseas-owned airline

178 The requirements to be met by a person seeking leave to enter the United Kingdom as a member of the operational ground staff of an overseas-owned airline are that he:

- (i) has been transferred to the United Kingdom by an overseas-owned airline operating services to and from the United Kingdom to take up duty at an international airport as station manager, security manager or technical manager; and
- (ii) intends to work full-time for the airline concerned; and
- (iii) does not intend to take employment except within the terms of this paragraph; and
- (iv) can maintain and accommodate himself and any dependants without recourse to public funds; and
- (v) holds a valid United Kingdom entry clearance for entry in this capacity.

Leave to enter as a member of the operational ground staff of an overseas-owned airline

179 A person seeking leave to enter the United Kingdom as a member of the operational staff of an overseas-owned airline may be given leave to enter for a period not exceeding 12 months, provided he is able to produce to the Immigration Officer, on arrival, a valid United Kingdom entry clearance for entry in this capacity.

Refusal of leave to enter as a member of the operational ground staff of an overseas-owned airline

180 Leave to enter as a member of the operational ground staff of an overseas-owned airline is to be refused if a valid United Kingdom entry clearance for entry in this capacity is not produced to the Immigration Officer on arrival.

Requirements for an extension of stay as a member of the operational ground staff of an overseas-owned airline

181 The requirements to be met by a person seeking an extension of stay as a member of the operational ground staff of an overseas-owned airline are that the applicant:

    (i)   entered the United Kingdom with a valid United Kingdom entry clearance as a member of the operational ground staff of an overseas-owned airline; and

    (ii)   is still engaged in the employment for which entry was granted; and

    (iii) is still required for the employment in question, as certified by the employer; and

    (iv) meets the requirements of paragraph 178(ii)–(iv).

Extension of stay as a member of the operational ground staff of an overseas-owned airline

182 An extension of stay as a member of the operational ground staff of an overseas-owned airline may be granted for a period not exceeding 3 years, provided the Secretary of State is satisfied that each of the requirements of paragraph 181 is met.

Refusal of extension of stay as a member of the operational ground staff of an overseas-owned airline

183 An extension of stay as a member of the operational staff of an overseas-owned airline is to be refused if the Secretary of State is not satisfied that each of the requirements of paragraph 181 is met.

Indefinite leave to remain for a member of the operational ground staff of an overseas-owned airline

184 Indefinite leave to remain may be granted, on application, to a member of the operational ground staff of an overseas-owned airline provided:

    (i)   he has spent a continuous period of 4 years in the United Kingdom in this capacity; and

    (ii)   he has met the requirements of paragraph 181 throughout the 4 year period; and

    (iii) he is still required for the employment in question, as certified by the employer.

Refusal of indefinite leave to remain for a member of the operational ground staff of an overseas-owned airline

185 Indefinite leave to remain in the United Kingdom for a member of the operational ground staff of an overseas-owned airline is to be refused if the Secretary of State is not satisfied that each of the requirements of paragraph 184 is met.

PERSONS WITH UNITED KINGDOM ANCESTRY

Requirements for leave to enter on the grounds of United Kingdom ancestry

186 The requirements to be met by a person seeking leave to enter the United Kingdom on the grounds of his United Kingdom ancestry are that he:

(i)   is a Commonwealth citizen; and
(ii)   is aged 17 or over; and
(iii) is able to provide proof that one of his grandparents was born in the United Kingdom and Islands; and
(iv)   is able to work and intends to take or seek employment in the United Kingdom; and
(v)   will be able to maintain and accommodate himself and any dependants adequately without recourse to public funds; and
(vi)   holds a valid United Kingdom entry clearance for entry in this capacity.

Leave to enter the United Kingdom on the grounds of United Kingdom ancestry

187   A person seeking leave to enter the United Kingdom on the grounds of his United Kingdom ancestry may be given leave to enter for a period not exceeding 4 years provided he is able to produce to the Immigration Officer, on arrival, a valid United Kingdom entry clearance for entry in this capacity.

Refusal of leave to enter on the grounds of United Kingdom ancestry

188   Leave to enter the United Kingdom on the grounds of United Kingdom ancestry is to be refused if a valid United Kingdom entry clearance for entry in this capacity is not produced to the Immigration Officer on arrival.

Requirements for an extension of stay on the grounds of United Kingdom ancestry

189   The requirements to be met by a person seeking an extension of stay on the grounds of United Kingdom ancestry are that he is able to meet each of the requirements of paragraph 186(i)–(v).

Extension of stay on the grounds of United Kingdom ancestry

190   An extension of stay on the grounds of United Kingdom ancestry may be granted for a period not exceeding 4 years provided the Secretary of State is satisfied that each of the requirements of paragraph 186(i)–(v) is met.

Refusal of extension of stay on the grounds of United Kingdom ancestry

191   An extension of stay on the grounds of United Kingdom ancestry is to be refused if the Secretary of State is not satisfied that each of the requirements of paragraph 186(i)–(v) is met.

Indefinite leave to remain on the grounds of United Kingdom ancestry

192   Indefinite leave to remain may be granted, on application, to a Commonwealth citizen with a United Kingdom born grandparent provided:

(i)   he meets the requirements of paragraph 186(i)–(v); and
(ii)   he has spent a continuous period of 4 years in the United Kingdom in this capacity.

Refusal of indefinite leave to remain on the grounds of United Kingdom ancestry

193   Indefinite leave to remain in the United Kingdom on the grounds of a United Kingdom born grandparent is to be refused if the Secretary of State is not satisfied that each of the requirements of paragraph 192 is met.

Requirements for leave to enter or remain as the spouse of a person with limited leave to enter or remain in the United Kingdom under paragraphs 128–193

194 The requirements to be met by a person seeking leave to enter or remain in the United Kingdom as the spouse of a person with limited leave to enter or remain in the United Kingdom under paragraphs 128–193 are that:

(i) the applicant is married to a person with limited leave to enter or remain in the United Kingdom under paragraphs 128–193; and

(ii) each of the parties intends to live with the other as his or her spouse during the applicant's stay and the marriage is subsisting; and

(iii) there will be adequate accommodation for the parties and any dependants without recourse to public funds in accommodation which they own or occupy exclusively; and

(iv) the parties will be able to maintain themselves and any dependants adequately without recourse to public funds; and

(v) the applicant does not intend to stay in the United Kingdom beyond any period of leave granted to his spouse; and

(vi) if seeking leave to enter, the applicant holds a valid United Kingdom entry clearance for entry in this capacity or, if seeking leave to remain, was admitted with a valid United Kingdom entry clearance for entry in this capacity.

Leave to enter or remain as the spouse of a person with limited leave to enter or remain in the United Kingdom under paragraphs 128–193

195 A person seeking leave to enter or remain in the United Kingdom as the spouse of a person with limited leave to enter or remain in the United Kingdom under paragraphs 128–193 may be given leave to enter or remain in the United Kingdom for a period of leave not in excess of that granted to the person with limited leave to enter or remain under paragraphs 128–193 provided that, in relation to an application for leave to enter, he is able, on arrival, to produce to the Immigration Officer a valid United Kingdom entry clearance for entry in this capacity or, in the case of an application for limited leave to remain, he was admitted with a valid United Kingdom entry clearance for entry in this capacity and is able to satisfy the Secretary of State that each of the requirements of paragraph 194(i)–(v) is met. An application for indefinite leave to remain in this category may be granted provided the applicant was admitted with a valid United Kingdom entry clearance for entry in this capacity and is able to satisfy the Secretary of State that each of the requirements of paragraph 194(i)–(v) is met and provided indefinite leave to remain is, at the same time, being granted to the person with limited leave to enter or remain under paragraphs 128–193.

Refusal of leave to enter or remain as the spouse of a person with limited leave to enter or remain in the United Kingdom under paragraphs 128–193

196 Leave to enter or remain in the United Kingdom as the spouse of a person with limited leave to enter or remain in the United Kingdom under paragraphs 128–193 is to be refused if, in relation to an application for leave to enter, a valid United Kingdom entry clearance for entry in this capacity is not produced to the Immigration Officer on arrival or, in the case of an application for limited leave to remain, if the applicant was not admitted with a valid United Kingdom entry clearance for entry in this capacity or is unable to satisfy the Secretary of State that each of the requirements of paragraph 194(i)–(v) is met. An application for indefinite leave to remain in this category is to be refused if the applicant was not admitted with a valid United Kingdom entry clearance for entry in this capacity or is unable to satisfy the Secretary of State that each of the requirements of paragraph 194(i)–(v) is met or if indefinite leave to remain is not, at the same time, being granted to the person with limited leave to enter or remain under paragraphs 128–193.

CHILDREN OF PERSONS WITH LIMITED LEAVE TO ENTER OR REMAIN IN THE UNITED KINGDOM UNDER PARAGRAPHS 128–193

Requirements for leave to enter or remain as the child of a person with limited leave to enter or remain in the United Kingdom under paragraphs 128–193

197   The requirements to be met by a person seeking leave to enter or remain in the United Kingdom as a child of a person with limited leave to enter or remain in the United Kingdom under paragraphs 128–193 are that:

  (i)   he is the child of a parent with limited leave to enter or remain in the United Kingdom under paragraphs 128–193; and
 (ii)   he is under the age of 18 or has current leave to enter or remain in this capacity; and
(iii)   he is unmarried, has not formed an independent family unit and is not leading an independent life; and
 (iv)   he can and will be maintained and accommodated adequately without recourse to public funds in accommodation which his parent(s) own or occupy exclusively; and
  (v)   he will not stay in the United Kingdom beyond any period of leave granted to his parent(s); and
 (vi)   both parents are being or have been admitted to or allowed to remain in the United Kingdom save where:
      (*a*)   the parent he is accompanying or joining is his sole surviving parent; or
      (*b*)   the parent he is accompanying or joining has had sole responsibility for his upbringing; or
      (*c*)   there are serious and compelling family or other considerations which make exclusion from the United Kingdom undesirable and suitable arrangements have been made for his care; and
(vii)   if seeking leave to enter, he holds a valid United Kingdom entry clearance for entry in this capacity or, if seeking leave to remain, was admitted with a valid United Kingdom entry clearance for entry in this capacity.

Leave to enter or remain as the child of a person with limited leave to enter or remain in the United Kingdom under paragraphs 128–193

198   A person seeking leave to enter or remain in the United Kingdom as the child of a person with limited leave to enter or remain in the United Kingdom under paragraphs 128–193 may be given leave to enter or remain in the United Kingdom for a period of leave not in excess of that granted to the person with limited leave to enter or remain under paragraphs 128–193 provided that, in relation to an application for leave to enter, he is able to produce to the Immigration Officer, on arrival, a valid United Kingdom entry clearance for entry in this capacity or, in the case of an application for limited leave to remain, he was admitted with a valid United Kingdom entry clearance for entry in this capacity and is able to satisfy the Secretary of State that each of the requirements of paragraph 197(i)–(vi) is met. An application for indefinite leave to remain in this category may be granted provided the applicant was admitted with a valid United Kingdom entry clearance for entry in this capacity and is able to satisfy the Secretary of State that each of the requirements of paragraph 197(i)–(vi) is met and provided indefinite leave to remain is, at the same time, being granted to the person with limited leave to enter or remain under paragraphs 128–193.

Refusal of leave to enter or remain as the child of a person with limited leave to enter or remain in the United Kingdom under paragraphs 128–193

199 Leave to enter or remain in the United Kingdom as the child of a person with limited leave to enter or remain in the United Kingdom under paragraphs 128–193 is to be refused if, in relation to an application for leave to enter, a valid United Kingdom entry clearance for entry in this capacity is not produced to the Immigration Officer on arrival or, in the case of an application for limited leave to remain, if the applicant was not admitted with a valid United Kingdom entry clearance for entry in this capacity or is unable to satisfy the Secretary of State that each of the requirements of paragraph 197(i)–(vi) is met. An application for indefinite leave to remain in this category is to be refused if the applicant was not admitted with a valid United Kingdom entry clearance for entry in this capacity or is unable to satisfy the Secretary of State that each of the requirements of paragraph 197(i)–(vi) is met or if indefinite leave to remain is not, at the same time, being granted to the person with limited leave to enter or remain under paragraphs 128–193.

PART 6: PERSONS SEEKING TO ENTER OR REMAIN IN THE UNITED KINGDOM AS A BUSINESSMAN, SELF-EMPLOYED PERSON, INVESTOR, WRITER, COMPOSER OR ARTIST

PERSONS INTENDING TO ESTABLISH THEMSELVES IN BUSINESS

Requirements for leave to enter the United Kingdom as a person intending to establish himself in business

200 For the purpose of paragraphs 201–210 a business means an enterprise as:

- a sole trader; or
- a partnership; or
- a company registered in the United Kingdom.

201 The requirements to be met by a person seeking leave to enter the United Kingdom to establish himself in business are:

(i) that he satisfies the requirements of either paragraph 202 or paragraph 203; and

(ii) that he has not less than £200,000 of his own money under his control and disposable in the United Kingdom which is held in his own name and not by a trust or other investment vehicle and which he will be investing in the business in the United Kingdom; and

(iii) that until his business provides him with an income he will have sufficient additional funds to maintain and accommodate himself and any dependants without recourse to employment (other than his work for the business) or to public funds; and

(iv) that he will be actively involved full-time in trading or providing services on his own account or in partnership, or in the promotion and management of the company as a director; and

(v) that his level of financial investment will be proportional to his interest in the business; and

(vi) that he will have either a controlling or equal interest in the business and that any partnership or directorship does not amount to disguised employment; and

(vii) that he will be able to bear his share of liabilities; and

(viii) that there is a genuine need for his investment and services in the United Kingdom; and

(ix) that his share of the profits of the business will be sufficient to maintain and accommodate himself and any dependants without recourse to employment (other than his work for the business) or to public funds; and

(x)   that he does not intend to supplement his business activities by taking or seeking employment in the United Kingdom other than his work for the business; and

(xi) that he holds a valid United Kingdom entry clearance for entry in this capacity.

202   Where a person intends to take over or join as a partner or director an existing business in the United Kingdom he will need, in addition to meeting the requirements at paragraph 201, to produce:

(i)   a written statement of the terms on which he is to take over or join the business; and

(ii) audited accounts for the business for previous years; and

(iii) evidence that his services and investment will result in a net increase in the employment provided by the business to persons settled here to the extent of creating at least 2 new full-time jobs.

203   Where a person intends to establish a new business in the United Kingdom he will need, in addition to meeting the requirements at paragraph 201 above, to produce evidence:

(i)   that he will be bringing into the country sufficient funds of his own to establish a business; and

(ii) that the business will create full-time paid employment for at least 2 persons already settled in the United Kingdom.

Leave to enter the United Kingdom as a person seeking to establish himself in business

204   A person seeking leave to enter the United Kingdom to establish himself in business may be admitted for a period not exceeding 12 months with a condition restricting his freedom to take employment provided he is able to produce to the Immigration Officer, on arrival, a valid United Kingdom entry clearance for entry in this capacity.

Refusal of leave to enter the United Kingdom as a person seeking to establish himself in business

205   Leave to enter the United Kingdom as a person seeking to establish himself in business is to be refused if a valid United Kingdom entry clearance for entry in this capacity is not produced to the Immigration Officer on arrival.

Requirements for an extension of stay in order to remain in business

206   The requirements for an extension to stay in order to remain in business in the United Kingdom are that the applicant can show:

(i)   that he entered the United Kingdom with a valid United Kingdom entry clearance as a businessman; and

(ii)   audited accounts which show the precise financial position of the business and which confirm that he has invested not less than £200,000 of his own money directly into the business in the United Kingdom; and

(iii) that he is actively involved on a full-time basis in trading or providing services on his own account or in partnership or in the promotion and management of the company as a director; and

(iv)   that his level of financial investment is proportional to his interest in the business; and

(v)   that he has either a controlling or equal interest in the business and that any partnership or directorship does not amount to disguised employment; and

(vi)   that he is able to bear his share of any liability the business may incur; and

(vii) that there is a genuine need for his investment and services in the United Kingdom; and

(viii) (*a*)   that where he has established a new business, new full-time paid employment has been created in the business for at least 2 persons settled in the United Kingdom; or

      (*b*)   that where he has taken over or joined an existing business, his services and investment have resulted in a net increase in the employment provided by the business to persons settled here to the extent of creating at least 2 new full-time jobs; and

(ix)   that his share of the profits of the business is sufficient to maintain and accommodate him and any dependants without recourse to employment (other than his work for the business) or to public funds; and

(x)   that he does not and will not have to supplement his business activities by taking or seeking employment in the United Kingdom other than his work for the business.

Extension of stay in order to remain in business

207   An extension of stay in order to remain in business with a condition restricting his freedom to take employment may be granted for a period not exceeding 3 years provided the Secretary of State is satisfied that each of the requirements of paragraph 206 is met.

Refusal of extension of stay in order to remain in business

208   An extension of stay in order to remain in business is to be refused if the Secretary of State is not satisfied that each of the requirements of paragraph 206 is met.

Indefinite leave to remain for a person established in business

209   Indefinite leave to remain may be granted, on application, to a person established in business provided he:

(i)   has spent a continuous period of 4 years in the United Kingdom in this capacity and is still engaged in the business in question; and

(ii)   has met the requirements of paragraph 206 throughout the 4 year period; and

(iii)   submits audited accounts for the first 3 years of trading and management accounts for the 4th year.

Refusal of indefinite leave to remain for a person established in business

210   Indefinite leave to remain in the United Kingdom for a person established in business is to be refused if the Secretary of State is not satisfied that each of the requirements of paragraph 209 is met.

PERSONS INTENDING TO ESTABLISH THEMSELVES IN BUSINESS UNDER PROVISIONS OF EC ASSOCIATION AGREEMENTS

Requirements for leave to enter the United Kingdom as a person intending to establish himself in business under the provisions of an EC Association Agreement

211   For the purpose of paragraphs 212–223 a business means an enterprise as:

-   a sole trader; or
-   a partnership; or
-   a company registered in the United Kingdom.

212   The requirements to be met by a person seeking leave to enter the United Kingdom to establish himself in business are that:

(i)   he satisfies the requirements of either paragraph 213 or paragraph 214; and

(ii)   the money he is putting into the business is under his control and sufficient to establish himself in business in the UnitedKingdom; and

(iii) until his business provides him with an income he will have sufficient additional funds to maintain and accommodate himself and any dependants without recourse to employment (other than his work for the business) or to public funds; and

(iv)   his share of the profits of the business will be sufficient to maintain and accommodate himself and any dependants without recourse to employment (other than his work for the business) or to public funds; and

(v)   he does not intend to supplement his business activities by taking or seeking employment in the United Kingdom other than his work for the business; and

(vi)   he holds a valid United Kingdom entry clearance for entry in this capacity.

213   Where a person intends to establish himself in a company in the United Kingdom which he effectively controls he will need, in addition to meeting the requirements at paragraph 212, to show:

[(i)   that he is a national of Bulgaria, the Czech Republic, Estonia, Hungary, Latvia,   Poland, Romania, Slovakia or Slovenia; and]

(ii)   that he will have a controlling interest in the company; and

(iii) that he will be actively involved in the promotion and management of the company; and

(iv)   that the company will be registered in the United Kingdom and be trading or providing services in the United Kingdom; and

(v)   that the company will be the owner of the assets of the business; and

(vi)   where he is taking over an existing company, a written statement of the terms on which he is to take over the business and audited accounts for the business for previous years.

Note   Paragraph 213(i) substituted by CM 4851.

214   Where a person intends to establish himself in self-employment or in partnership in the United Kingdom he will need, in addition to meeting the requirements at 212 above, to show:

[(i)   that he is a national of Bulgaria, the Czech Republic, Estonia, Hungary, Latvia, Lithuania, Poland, Romania or Slovakia; and]

(ii)   that he will be actively involved in trading or providing services on his own account or in partnership in the United Kingdom; and

(iii) that he, or he together with his partners, will be the owner of the assets of the business; and

(iv)   in the case of a partnership, that his part in the business will not amount to disguised employment; and

(v)   where he is taking over or joining an existing business a written statement of the terms on which he is to take over or join the business and audited accounts for the business for previous years.

Note   Paragraph 214(i) substituted by CM 4851.

Leave to enter the United Kingdom as a person seeking to establish himself in business under the provisions of an EC Association Agreement

215   A person seeking leave to enter the United Kingdom to establish himself in business may be admitted for a period not exceeding 12 months with a condition restricting his freedom to take employment provided he is able to produce to the Immigration Officer, on arrival, a valid United Kingdom entry clearance for entry in this capacity.

Refusal of leave to enter the United Kingdom as a person seeking to establish himself in business under the provisions of an EC Association Agreement

216 Leave to enter the United Kingdom as a person seeking to establish himself in business is to be refused if a valid United Kingdom entry clearance for entry in this capacity is not produced to the Immigration Officer on arrival.

Requirements for an extension of stay in order to remain in business under the provisions of an EC Association Agreement

217 The requirements for an extension of stay in order to remain in business in the United Kingdom are that the applicant can show that:

- (i) he has established himself in business in the United Kingdom; and
- (ii) his share of the profits of the business is sufficient to maintain and accommodate himself and any dependants without recourse to employment (other than his work for the business) or to public funds; and
- (iii) he does not and will not supplement his business activities by taking or seeking employment in the United Kingdom other than his work for the business; and
- (iv) in addition he satisfies the requirements of either paragraph 218 or paragraph 219.

218 Where a person has established himself in a company in the United Kingdom which he effectively   controls he will need, in addition to meeting the requirements at paragraph 217 above, to show:

- [(i) that he is a national of Bulgaria, the Czech Republic, Estonia, Hungary, Latvia, Lithuania, Poland, Romania, Slovakia or Slovenia; and]
- (ii) that he is actively involved in the promotion and management of the company; and
- (iii) that he has a controlling interest in the company; and
- (iv) that the company is registered in the United Kingdom and trading or providing services in the United Kingdom; and
- (v) that the company is the owner of the assets of the business; and
- (vi) the current financial position in the form of audited accounts for the company.

Note   Paragraph 218(i) substituted by CM 4851.

219 Where a person has established himself as a sole trader or in partnership in the United Kingdom he will need, in addition to meeting the requirements at 217 above, to show:

- [(i) that he is a national of Bulgaria, the Czech Republic, Estonia, Hungary, Latvia, Lithuania, Poland, Romania or Slovakia; and]
- (ii) that he is actively involved in trading or providing services on his own account or in partnership in the United Kingdom; and
- (iii) that he, or he together with his partners, is the owner of the assets of the business; and
- (iv) in the case of a partnership, that his part in the business does not amount to disguised employment; and
- (v) the current financial position in the form of audited accounts for the business.

Note   Paragraph 219(i) substituted by CM 4851.

Extension of stay in order to remain in business under the provisions of an EC Association Agreement

220 An extension of stay in order to remain in business with a condition restricting his freedom to take employment may be granted for a period not exceeding 3 years provided the Secretary of State is satisfied that each of the requirements of paragraphs 217 and 218 or 219 is met.

Refusal of extension of stay in order to remain in business under the provisions of an EC Association Agreement

221   An extension of stay in order to remain in business is to be refused if the Secretary of State is not satisfied that each of the requirements of paragraphs 217 and 218 or 219 is met.

Indefinite leave to remain for a person established in business under the provisions of an EC Association Agreement

222   Indefinite leave to remain may be granted, on application, to a person established in business provided he:

(i)   has spent a continuous period of 4 years in the United Kingdom in this capacity and is still so engaged; and

(ii)   has met the requirements of paragraphs 217 and 218 or 219 throughout the 4 years; and

(iii)   submits audited accounts for the first 3 years of trading and management accounts for the 4th year.

Refusal of indefinite leave to remain for a person established in business under the provisions of an EC Association Agreement

223   Indefinite leave to remain in the United Kingdom for a person established in business is to be refused if the Secretary of State is not satisfied that each of the requirements of paragraph 222 is met.

INVESTORS

Requirements for leave to enter the United Kingdom as an investor

224   The requirements to be met by a person seeking leave to enter the United Kingdom as an investor are that he:

(i)   has money of his own under his control and disposable in the UnitedKingdom amounting to no less than £1 million; and

(ii)   intends to invest not less than £750,000 of his capital in the United Kingdom by way of United Kingdom Government bonds, share capital or loan capital in active and trading United Kingdom registered companies (other than those principally engaged in property investment and excluding investment by the applicant by way of deposits with a bank, building society or other enterprise whose normal course of business includes the acceptance of deposits); and

(iii)   intends to make the United Kingdom his main home; and

(iv)   is able to maintain and accommodate himself and any dependants without taking employment (other than self-employment or business) or recourse to public funds; and

(v)   holds a valid United Kingdom entry clearance for entry in this capacity.

Leave to enter as an investor

225   A person seeking leave to enter the United Kingdom as an investor may be admitted for a period not exceeding 12 months with a restriction on his right to take employment, provided he is able to produce to the Immigration Officer, on arrival, a valid United Kingdom entry clearance for entry in this capacity.

Refusal of leave to enter as an investor

226 Leave to enter as an investor is to be refused if a valid United Kingdom entry clearance for entry in this capacity is not produced to the Immigration Officer on arrival.

Requirements for an extension of stay as an investor

227 The requirements for an extension of stay as an investor are that the applicant:

(i) entered the United Kingdom with a valid United Kingdom entry clearance as an investor; and

(ii) has no less than £1 million of his own money under his control in the United Kingdom; and

(iii) has invested not less than £750,000 of his capital in the United Kingdom on the terms set out in paragraph 224(ii) above and intends to maintain that investment on the terms set out in paragraph 224(ii); and

(iv) has made the United Kingdom his main home; and

(v) is able to maintain and accommodate himself and any dependants without taking employment (other than his self-employment or business) or recourse to public funds.

Extension of stay as an investor

228 An extension of stay as an investor, with a restriction on the taking of employment, may be granted for a maximum period of 3 years, provided the Secretary of State is satisfied that each of the requirements of paragraph 227 is met.

Refusal of extension of stay as an investor

229 An extension of stay as an investor is to be refused if the Secretary of State is not satisfied that each of the requirements of paragraph 227 is met.

Indefinite leave to remain for an investor

230 Indefinite leave to remain may be granted, on application, to a person admitted as an investor provided he:

(i) has spent a continuous period of 4 years in the United Kingdom in this capacity; and

(ii) has met the requirements of paragraph 227 throughout the 4 year period including the requirement as to the investment of £750,000 and continues to do so.

Refusal of indefinite leave to remain for an investor

231 Indefinite leave to remain in the United Kingdom for an investor is to be refused if the Secretary of State is not satisfied that each of the requirements of paragraph 230 is met.

WRITERS, COMPOSERS AND ARTISTS

Requirements for leave to enter the United Kingdom as a writer, composer or artist

232 The requirements to be met by a person seeking leave to enter the United Kingdom as a writer, composer or artist are that he:

(i) has established himself outside the United Kingdom as a writer, composer or artist primarily engaged in producing original work which has been published (other than exclusively in newspapers or magazines), performed or exhibited for its literary, musical or artistic merit; and

(ii)   does not intend to work except as related to his self-employment as a writer, composer or artist; and

(iii) has for the preceding year been able to maintain and accommodate himself and any dependants from his own resources without working except as a writer, composer or artist; and

(iv)   will be able to maintain and accommodate himself and any dependants from his own resources without working except as a writer, composer or artist and without recourse to public funds; and

(v)   holds a valid United Kingdom entry clearance for entry in this capacity.

Leave to enter as a writer, composer or artist

233   A person seeking leave to enter the United Kingdom as a writer, composer or artist may be admitted for a period not exceeding 12 months, subject to a condition restricting his freedom to take employment, provided he is able to produce to the Immigration Officer, on arrival, a valid United Kingdom entry clearance for entry in this capacity.

Refusal of leave to enter as a writer, composer or artist

234   Leave to enter as a writer, composer or artist is to be refused if a valid United Kingdom entry clearance for entry in this capacity is not produced to the Immigration Officer on arrival.

Requirements for an extension of stay as a writer, composer or artist

235   The requirements for an extension of stay as a writer, composer or artist are that the applicant:

(i)   entered the United Kingdom with a valid United Kingdom entry clearance as a writer, composer or artist; and

(ii)   meets the requirements of paragraph 232(ii)–(iv).

Extension of stay as a writer, composer or artist

236   An extension of stay as writer, composer or artist may be granted for a period not exceeding 3 years with a restriction on his freedom to take employment, provided the Secretary of State is satisfied that each of the requirements of paragraph 235 is met.

Refusal of extension of stay as a writer, composer or artist

237   An extension of stay as a writer, composer or artist is to be refused if the Secretary of State is not satisfied that each of the requirements of paragraph 235 is met.

Indefinite leave to remain for a writer, composer or artist

238   Indefinite leave to remain may be granted, on application, to a person admitted as a writer, composer or artist provided he:

(i)   has spent a continuous period of 4 years in the United Kingdom in this capacity; and

(ii)   has met the requirements of paragraph 235 throughout the 4 year period.

Refusal of indefinite leave to remain for a writer, composer or artist

239   Indefinite leave to remain for a writer, composer or artist is to be refused if the Secretary ofState is not satisfied that each of the requirements of paragraph 238 is met.

Requirements for leave to enter or remain as the spouse of a person with limited leave to enter or remain under paragraphs 200–239

240 The requirements to be met by a person seeking leave to enter or remain in the United Kingdom as the spouse of a person with limited leave to enter or remain in the United Kingdom under paragraphs 200–239 are that:

(i) the applicant is married to a person with limited leave to enter or remain in the United Kingdom under paragraphs 200–239; and

(ii) each of the parties intends to live with the other as his or her spouse during the applicant's stay and the marriage is subsisting; and

(iii) there will be adequate accommodation for the parties and any dependants without recourse to public funds in accommodation which they own or occupy exclusively; and

(iv) the parties will be able to maintain themselves and any dependants adequately without recourse to public funds; and

(v) the applicant does not intend to stay in the United Kingdom beyond any period of leave granted to his spouse; and

(vi) if seeking leave to enter, the applicant holds a valid United Kingdom entry clearance for entry in this capacity or, if seeking leave to remain, was admitted with a valid United Kingdom entry clearance for entry in this capacity.

Leave to enter or remain as the spouse of a person with limited leave to enter or remain in the United Kingdom under paragraphs 200–239

241 A person seeking leave to enter or remain in the United Kingdom as the spouse of a person with limited leave to enter or remain in the United Kingdom under paragraphs 200–239 may be given leave to enter or remain in the United Kingdom for a period of leave not in excess of that granted to the person with limited leave to enter or remain under paragraphs 200–239 provided that, in relation to an application for leave to enter, he is able, on arrival, to produce to the Immigration Officer a valid United Kingdom entry clearance for entry in this capacity or, in the case of an application for limited leave to remain, he was admitted with a valid UnitedKingdom entry clearance for entry in this capacity and is able the satisfy the Secretary of State that each of the requirements of paragraph 240(i)–(v) is met. An application for indefinite leave to remain in this category may be granted provided the applicant was admitted with a valid United Kingdom entry clearance for entry in this capacity and is able to satisfy the Secretary of State that each of the requirements of paragraph 240(i)–(v) is met and provided indefinite leave to remain is, at the same time, being granted to the person with limited leave to remain under paragraphs 200–239.

Refusal of leave to enter or remain as the spouse of a person with limited leave to enter or remain in the United Kingdom under paragraphs 200–239

242 Leave to enter or remain in the United Kingdom as the spouse of a person with limited leave to enter or remain in the United Kingdom under paragraphs 200–239 is to be refused if, in relation to an application for leave to enter, a valid United Kingdom entry clearance for entry in this capacity is not produced to the Immigration Officer on arrival or, in the case of an application for limited leave to remain, if the applicant was not admitted with a valid United Kingdom entry clearance for entry in this capacity or is unable to satisfy the Secretary of State that each of the requirements of paragraph 240(i)–(v) is met. An application for indefinite leave to remain in this category is to be refused if the applicant was not admitted with a valid United Kingdom entry clearance for entry in this capacity or is unable to satisfy the Secretary of State

that each of the requirements of paragraph 240(i)–(v) is   met or if indefinite leave to remain is not, at the same time, being granted to the person with limited leave to remain under paragraphs 200–239.

CHILDREN OF PERSONS WITH LIMITED LEAVE TO ENTER OR REMAIN UNDER PARAGRAPHS 200–239

Requirements for leave to enter or remain as the child of a person with limited leave to enter or remain in the United Kingdom under paragraphs 200–239

243   The requirements to be met by a person seeking leave to enter or remain in the United Kingdom as a child of a person with limited leave to enter or remain in the United Kingdom under paragraphs 200–239 are that:

(i)   he is the child of a parent who has leave to enter or remain in the United Kingdom under paragraphs 200–239; and

(ii)   he is under the age of 18 or has current leave to enter or remain in this capacity; and

(iii)   he is unmarried, has not formed an independent family unit and is not leading an independent life; and

(iv)   he can and will be maintained and accommodated adequately without recourse to public funds in accommodation which his parent(s) own or occupy exclusively; and

(v)   he will not stay in the United Kingdom beyond any period of leave granted to his parent(s); and

(vi)   both parents are being or have been admitted to or allowed to remain in the United Kingdom save where:

(*a*)   the parent he is accompanying or joining is his sole surviving parent; or

(*b*)   the parent he is accompanying or joining has had sole responsibility for his upbringing; or

(*c*)   there are serious and compelling family or other considerations which make exclusion from the United Kingdom undesirable and suitable arrangements have been made for his care; and

(vii)   if seeking leave to enter, he holds a valid United Kingdom entry clearance for entry in this capacity or, if seeking leave to remain, was admitted with a valid United Kingdom entry clearance for entry in this capacity.

Leave to enter or remain as the child of a person with limited leave to enter or remain in the United Kingdom under paragraphs 200–239

244   A person seeking leave to enter or remain in the United Kingdom as the child of a person with limited leave to enter or remain in the United Kingdom under paragraphs 200–239 may be admitted to or allowed to remain in the United Kingdom for the same period of leave as that granted to the person given limited leave to enter or remain under paragraphs 200–239 provided that, in relation to an application for leave to enter, he is able to produce to the Immigration Officer, on arrival, a valid United Kingdom entry clearance for entry in this capacity or, in the case of an application for limited leave to remain, he was admitted with a valid UnitedKingdom entry clearance for entry in this capacity and is able the satisfy the Secretary of State that each of the requirements of paragraph 243(i)–(vi) is met. An application for indefinite leave to remain in this category may be granted provided the applicant was admitted with a valid United Kingdom entry clearance for entry in this capacity and is able to satisfy the Secretary of State that each of the requirements of paragraph 243(i)–(vi) is met and provided indefinite leave to remain is, at the same time, being granted to the person with limited leave to remain under paragraphs 200–239.

Refusal of leave to enter or remain as the child of a person with limited leave to enter or remain in the United Kingdom under paragraphs 200–239

245 Leave to enter or remain in the United Kingdom as the child of a person with limited leave to enter or remain in the United Kingdom under paragraphs 200–239 is to be refused if, in relation to an application for leave to enter, a valid United Kingdom entry clearance for entry in this capacity is not produced to the Immigration Officer on arrival or, in the case of an application for limited leave to remain, if the applicant was not admitted with a valid United Kingdom entry clearance for entry in this capacity or is unable to satisfy the Secretary of State that each of the requirements of paragraph 243(i)–(vi) is met. An application for indefinite leave to remain in this capacity is to be refused if the applicant was not admitted with a valid United Kingdom entry clearance for entry in this capacity or is unable to satisfy the Secretary of State that each of the requirements of paragraph 243(i)–(vi) is met or if indefinite leave to remain is not, at the same time, being granted to the person with limited leave to remain under paragraphs 200–239.

PART 7: OTHER CATEGORIES

PERSONS EXERCISING RIGHTS OF ACCESS TO A CHILD RESIDENT IN THE UNITED KINGDOM

[Requirements for leave to enter the United Kingdom as a person exercising rights of access to a child resident in the United Kingdom

246 The requirements to be met by a person seeking leave to enter the United Kingdom to exercise access rights to a child resident in the United Kingdom are that:

(i)   the applicant is the parent of a child who is resident in the United Kingdom; and

(ii) the parent or carer with whom the child permanently resides is resident in the United Kingdom; and

(iii) the applicant produces evidence that he has access rights to the child in the form of:
  (*a*) a Residence Order or a Contact Order granted by a Court in the United Kingdom; or
  (*b*) a certificate issued by a district judge confirming the applicant's intention to maintain contact with the child; and

(iv) the applicant intends to continue to take an active role in the child's upbringing; and

(v)   the child is under the age of 18; and

(vi) there will be adequate accommodation for the applicant and any dependants without recourse to public funds in accommodation which the applicant owns or occupies exclusively; and

(vii) the applicant will be able to maintain himself and any dependants adequately without recourse to public funds; and

(viii) the applicant holds a valid United Kingdom entry clearance for entry in this capacity.

Leave to enter the United Kingdom as a person exercising rights of access to a child resident in the United Kingdom

247 Leave to enter as a person exercising access rights to a child resident in the United Kingdom may be granted for 12 months in the first instance, provided that a valid United Kingdom entry clearance for entry in this capacity is produced to the Immigration Officer on arrival.

Refusal of leave to enter the United Kingdom as a person exercising rights of access to a child resident in the United Kingdom

248   Leave to enter as a person exercising rights of access to a child resident in the United Kingdom is to be refused if a valid United Kingdom entry clearance for entry in this capacity is not produced to the Immigration Officer on arrival.]

[Requirements for leave to remain in the United Kingdom as a person exercising rights of access to a child resident in the United Kingdom

248A   The requirements to be met by a person seeking leave to remain in the United Kingdom to exercise access rights to a child resident in the United Kingdom are that:

- (i)   the applicant is the parent of a child who is resident in the United Kingdom; and
- (ii)   the parent or carer with whom the child permanently resides is resident in the United Kingdom; and
- (iii)   the applicant produces evidence that he has access rights to the child in the form of:
  - (*a*) a Residence Order or a Contact Order granted by a Court in the United Kingdom; or
  - (*b*) a certificate issued by a district judge confirming the applicant's intention to maintain contact with the child; or
  - (*c*) a statement from the child's other parent (or, if contact is supervised, from the supervisor) that the applicant is maintaining contact with the child; and
- (iv)   the applicant takes and intends to continue to take an active role in the child's upbringing; and
- (v)   the child visits or stays with the applicant on a frequent and regular basis and the applicant intends this to continue; and
- (vi)   the child is under the age of 18; and
- (vii) the applicant has limited leave to remain in the United Kingdom as the spouse or unmarried partner of a person present and settled in the United Kingdom who is the other parent of the child; and
- (viii) the applicant has not remained in breach of the immigration laws; and
- (ix)   there will be adequate accommodation for the applicant and any dependants without recourse to public funds in accommodation which the applicant owns or occupies exclusively; and
- (x)   the applicant will be able to maintain himself and any dependants adequately without recourse to public funds.

Leave to remain in the United Kingdom as a person exercising rights of access to a child resident in the United Kingdom

248B Leave to remain as a person exercising access rights to a child resident in the United Kingdom may be granted for 12 months in the first instance, provided the Secretary of State is satisfied that each of the requirements of paragraph 248A is met.

Refusal of leave to remain in the United Kingdom as a person exercising rights of access to a child resident in the United Kingdom

248C   Leave to remain as a person exercising rights of access to a child resident in the United Kingdom is to be refused if the Secretary of State is not satisfied that each of the requirements of paragraph 248A is met.

Indefinite leave to remain in the United Kingdom as a person exercising rights of access to a child resident in the United Kingdom

248D   The requirements for indefinite leave to remain in the United Kingdom as a person exercising rights of access to a child resident in the United Kingdom are that:

(i)   the applicant was admitted to the United Kingdom or granted leave to remain in the United Kingdom for a period of 12 months as a person exercising rights of access to a child and has completed a period of 12 months as a person exercising rights of access to a child; and

(ii)   the applicant takes and intends to continue to take an active role in the child's upbringing; and

(iii)   the child visits or stays with the applicant on a frequent and regular basis and the applicant intends this to continue; and

(iv)   there will be adequate accommodation for the applicant and any dependants without recourse to public funds in accommodation which the applicant owns or occupies exclusively; and

(v)   the applicant will be able to maintain himself and any dependants adequately without recourse to public funds; and

(vi)   the child is under 18 years of age.

Indefinite leave to remain as a person exercising rights of access to a child resident in the United Kingdom

248E   Indefinite leave to remain as a person exercising rights of access to a child may be granted provided the Secretary of State is satisfied that each of the requirements of paragraph 248D is met.

Refusal of indefinite leave to remain in the United Kingdom as a person exercising rights of access to a child resident in the United Kingdom

248F   Indefinite leave to remain as a person exercising rights of access to a child is to be refused if the Secretary of State is not satisfied that each of the requirements of paragraph 248D is met.]

Note   Paragraphs 246–248 substituted by CM 4851.
Paragraphs 248A–248F inserted by CM 4851.

Holders of special vouchers

Requirements for indefinite leave to enter as the holder of a special voucher

249   The requirements for indefinite leave to enter as the holder of a special voucher are that the person concerned:

(i)   is a British Overseas citizen; and

(ii)   is in possession of a special voucher issued to him by a British Government representative overseas or a valid United Kingdom entry clearance for settlement in the United Kingdom in this capacity.

Indefinite leave to enter as the holder of a special voucher

250   A BritishOverseas citizen may be granted indefinite leave to enter the United Kingdom provided he is able to produce to the Immigration Officer, on arrival, either a special voucher issued to him by a British Government representative or a valid United Kingdom entry clearance for settlement in this capacity.

Refusal of indefinite leave to enter as the holder of a special voucher

251   Indefinite leave to enter as the holder of a special voucher is to be refused if neither a special voucher issued by a British Government representative nor a valid United Kingdom entry clearance for settlement in this capacity is produced to the Immigration Officer on arrival.

Requirements for indefinite leave to enter as the spouse or child of a special voucher holder

252   The requirements for indefinite leave to enter the UnitedKingdom as the spouse or child of a special voucher holder are that the person concerned:

(i)   is in possession of a valid United Kingdom entry clearance for settlement in the United Kingdom in this capacity; and

(ii)   can and will be maintained and accommodated adequately by the special voucher holder without recourse to public funds.

Indefinite leave to enter as the spouse or child of a special voucher holder

253   Indefinite leave to enter as the spouse or child of a special voucher holder may be granted provided a valid United Kingdom entry clearance for settlement is produced to the Immigration Officer on arrival.

Refusal of indefinite leave to enter as the spouse or child of a special voucher holder

254   Indefinite leave to enter as the spouse or child of a special voucher holder is to be refused if a valid United Kingdom entry clearance for settlement is not produced to the Immigration Officer on arrival.

EEA NATIONALS AND THEIR FAMILIES

Settlement

[**255**   Any person (other than a student) who under, either the Immigration (European Economic Area) Order 1994, or the 2000 EEA Regulations has been issued with a residence permit or residence document valid for 5 years, and who has remained in the United Kingdom in accordance with the provisions of that Order or those Regulations (as the case may be) for 4 years and continues to do so may, on application, have his residence permit or residence document (as the case may be) endorsed to show permission to remain in the United Kingdom indefinitely.]

Note   Substituted by CM 4851.

256   [. . .].

Note   Paragraph 256 deleted by CM 4851.

257   In addition, the following persons will be permitted to remain in the United Kingdom indefinitely [in accordance with Commission Regulation 1251/70]:

(i)   an EEA national who has been continuously resident in the United Kingdom for at least 3 years, has been in employment in the United Kingdom or any other Member State of the EEA for the preceding 12 months, and has reached the age of entitlement to a state retirement pension;

(ii)   an EEA national who has ceased to be employed owing to a permanent incapacity for work arising out of an accident at work or an occupational disease entitling him to a state disability pension;

(iii) an EEA national who has been continuously resident in the United Kingdom for at least 2 years, and who has ceased to be employed owing to a permanent incapacity for work;

(iv)   a member of the family of an EEA national [. . .] to whom (i), (ii) or (iii) above applies;(v)   a member of the family of an EEA national   [. . .] who dies during his working life after having resided continuously in the United Kingdom for at least 2 years, or whose death results from an accident at work or an occupational disease.

[For the purposes of this paragraph:

'EEA national' means a national of a State other than the United Kingdom which is a Contracting Party to the European Economic Area Agreement, but for the purposes of (iv) and (v) includes a national of the United Kingdom where the conditions set out in regulation 11 of the 2000 EEA Regulations are satisfied.

A 'member of the family' is a family member as defined in regulation 6 of the 2000 EEA Regulations, or a person whom it has been decided to treat as a family member in accordance with the principles set out in regulation 10 of those Regulations.]

Notes   Words deleted and words in square brackets inserted by CM 4851.

258–261 [. . .].

Note   Paragraphs 258–261 deleted by CM 4851.

Registration with the police for family members of EEA nationals

262   [*Deleted with effect from 11 May 1998 by Cmnd 3953.*]

RETIRED PERSONS OF INDEPENDENT MEANS

[Requirements for leave to enter the United Kingdom as a retired person of independent means

263   The requirements to be met by a person seeking leave to enter the United Kingdom as a retired person of independent means are that he:

(i)   is at least 60 years old; and
(ii)   has under his control and disposable in the United Kingdom an income of his own of not less than £25,000 per annum; and
(iii) is able and willing to maintain and accommodate himself and any dependants indefinitely in the United Kingdom from his own resources with no assistance from any other person and without taking employment or having recourse to public funds; and
(iv)   can demonstrate a close connection with the United Kingdom; and
(v)   intends to make the United Kingdom his main home; and
(vi)   holds a valid United Kingdom entry clearance for entry in this capacity.

Leave to enter as a retired person of independent means

264   A person seeking leave to enter the United Kingdom as a retired person of independent   means may be admitted subject to a condition prohibiting employment for a period not exceeding 4 years, provided he is able to produce to the Immigration Officer, on arrival, a valid United Kingdom entry clearance for entry in this capacity.

Refusal of leave to enter as a retired person of independent means

265   Leave to enter as a retired person of independent means is to be refused if a valid UnitedKingdom entry clearance for entry in this capacity is not produced to the Immigration Officer on arrival.

Requirements for an extension of stay as a retired person of independent means

266   The requirements for an extension of stay as a retired person of independent means are that the applicant:

    (i)   entered the United Kingdom with a valid United Kingdom entry clearance as a retired person of independent means; and

    (ii)   meets the requirements of paragraph 263(ii)–(iv); and

    (iii) has made the United Kingdom his main home.

Extension of stay as a retired person of independent means

267   An extension of stay as a retired person of independent means, with a prohibition on the taking of employment, may be granted so as to bring the person's stay in this category up to a maximum of 4 years in aggregate, provided the Secretary of State is satisfied that each of the requirements of paragraph 266 is met.

Refusal of extension of stay as a retired person of independent means

268   An extension of stay as a retired person of independent means is to be refused if the Secretary of State is not satisfied that each of the requirements of paragraph 266 is met.

Indefinite leave to remain for a retired person of independent means

269   Indefinite leave to remain may be granted, on application, to a person admitted as a retired person of independent means provided he:

    (i)   has spent a continuous period of 4 years in the United Kingdom in this capacity; and

    (ii)   has met the requirements of paragraph 266 throughout the 4 year period and continues to do so.

Refusal of indefinite leave to remain for a retired person of independent means

270   Indefinite leave to remain in the United Kingdom for a retired person of independent means is to be refused if the Secretary of State is not satisfied that each of the requirements of paragraph 26[9] is met.

Spouses of persons with limited leave to enter or remain in the United Kingdom as retired persons of independent means

Requirements for leave to enter or remain as the spouse of a person with limited leave to enter or remain in the United Kingdom as a retired person of independent means

271   The requirements to be met by a person seeking leave to enter or remain in the United Kingdom as the spouse of a person with limited leave to enter or remain in the United Kingdom as a retired person of independent means are that:

    (i)   the applicant is married to a person with limited leave to enter or remain in the United Kingdom as a retired person of independent means; and

    (ii)   each of the parties intends to live with the other as his or her spouse during the applicant's stay and the marriage is subsisting; and

    (iii) there will be adequate accommodation for the parties and any dependants without recourse to public funds in accommodation which they own or occupy exclusively; and

    (iv) the parties will be able to maintain themselves and any dependants adequately without recourse to public funds; and

    (v)   the applicant does not intend to stay in the United Kingdom beyond any period of leave granted to his spouse; and

    (vi) if seeking leave to enter, the applicant holds a valid United Kingdom entry clearance for entry in this capacity or, if seeking leave to remain, was admitted with a valid United Kingdom entry clearance for entry in this capacity.

Leave to enter or remain as the spouse of a person with limited leave to enter or remain in the United Kingdom as a retired person of independent means

272 A person seeking leave to enter or remain in the United Kingdom as the spouse of a person with limited leave to enter or remain in the United Kingdom as a retired person of independent means may be given leave to enter or remain in the United Kingdom for a period not in excess of that granted to the person given limited leave to enter or remain as a retired person of independent means provided that, in relation to an application for leave to enter, he is able to produce to the Immigration Officer, on arrival, a valid United Kingdom entry clearance for entry in this capacity, or, in the case of an application for limited leave to remain, he was admitted with a valid United Kingdom entry clearance for entry in this capacity and is able to satisfy the Secretary of State that each of the requirements of paragraph 271(i)–(v) is met. An application for indefinite leave to remain in this category may be granted provided the applicant was admitted with a valid United Kingdom entry clearance for entry in this capacity and is able to satisfy the Secretary of State that each of the requirements of paragraph 271(i)–(v) is met and provided indefinite leave to remain is, at the same time, being granted to the person with limited leave to enter or remain as a retired person of independent means. Leave to enter or remain is to be subject to a condition prohibiting employment except in relation to the grant of indefinite leave to remain.

Refusal of leave to enter or remain as the spouse of a person with limited leave to enter or remain in the United Kingdom as a retired person of independent means

273 Leave to enter or remain in the United Kingdom as the spouse of a person with limited leave to enter or remain in the United Kingdom as a retired person of independent means is to be refused if, in relation to an application for leave to enter, a valid United Kingdom entry clearance for entry in this capacity is not produced to the Immigration Officer on arrival or, in the case of an application for limited leave to remain, if the applicant was not admitted with a valid United Kingdom entry clearance for entry in this capacity or is unable to satisfy the Secretary of State that each of the requirements of paragraph 271(i)–(v) is met. An application for indefinite leave to remain in this category is to be refused if the applicant was not admitted with a valid United Kingdom entry clearance for entry in this capacity or is unable to satisfy the Secretary of State that each of the requirements of paragraph 271(i)–(v) is met or if indefinite leave to remain is not, at the same time, being granted to the person with limited leave to enter or remain as a retired person of independent means.

CHILDREN OF PERSONS WITH LIMITED LEAVE TO ENTER OR REMAIN IN THE UNITED KINGDOM AS RETIRED PERSONS OF INDEPENDENT MEANS

Requirements for leave to enter or remain as the child of a person with limited leave to enter or remain in the United Kingdom as a retired person of independent means

274 The requirements to be met by a person seeking leave to enter or remain in the United Kingdom as the child of a person with limited leave to enter or remain in the United Kingdom as a retired person of independent means are that:

(i)   he is the child of a parent who has been admitted to or allowed to remain in the United Kingdom as a retired person of independent means; and

(ii) he is under the age of 18 or has current leave to enter or remain in this capacity; and

(iii) he is unmarried, has not formed an independent family unit and is not leading an independent life; and

(iv) he can, and will, be maintained and accommodated adequately without recourse to public funds in accommodation which his parent(s) own or occupy exclusively; and

    (v)   he will not stay in the United Kingdom beyond any period of leave granted to his parent(s); and

    (vi) both parents are being or have been admitted to or allowed to remain in the United Kingdom save where:

        (*a*) the parent he is accompanying or joining is his sole surviving parent; or

        (*b*) the parent he is accompanying or joining has had sole responsibility for his upbringing; or

        (*c*) there are serious and compelling family or other considerations which make exclusion from the United Kingdom undesirable and suitable arrangements have been made for his care; and

    (vii) if seeking leave to enter, he holds a valid United Kingdom entry clearance for entry in this capacity or, if seeking leave to remain, was admitted with a valid United Kingdom entry clearance for entry in this capacity.

Leave to enter or remain as the child of a person with limited leave to enter or remain in the United Kingdom as a retired person of independent means

275   A person seeking leave to enter or remain in the United Kingdom as the child of a person with limited leave to enter or remain in the United Kingdom as a retired person of independent means may be given leave to enter or remain in the UnitedKingdom for a period of leave not in excess of that granted to the person with limited leave to enter or remain as a retired person of independent means provided that, in relation to an application for leave to enter, he is able to produce to the Immigration Officer, on arrival, a valid United Kingdom entry clearance for entry in this capacity or, in the case of an application for limited leave to remain, he was admitted with a valid United Kingdom entry clearance for entry in this capacity and is able to satisfy the Secretary of State that each of the requirements of paragraph 274(i)–(vi) is met. An application for indefinite leave to remain in this category may be granted provided the applicant was admitted to the United Kingdom with a valid United Kingdom entry clearance for entry in this capacity and is able to satisfy the Secretary of State that each of the requirements of paragraph 274(i)–(vi) is met and provided indefinite leave to remain is, at the same time, being granted to the person with limited leave to enter or remain as a retired person of independent means. Leave to enter or remain is to be subject to a condition prohibiting employment except in relation to the grant of indefinite leave to remain.

Refusal of leave to enter or remain as the child of a person with limited leave to enter or remain in the United Kingdom as a retired person of independent means

276   Leave to enter or remain in the United Kingdom as the child of a person with limited leave to enter or remain in the United Kingdom as a retired person of independent means is to be refused if, in relation to an application for leave to enter, a valid United Kingdom entry clearance for entry in this capacity is not produced to the Immigration Officer on arrival, or in the case of an application for limited leave to remain, if the applicant was not admitted with a valid United Kingdom entry clearance for entry in this capacity or is unable to satisfy the Secretary of State that each of the requirements of paragraph 274(i)–(vi) is met. An application for indefinite leave to remain in this category is to be refused if the applicant was not admitted with a valid United Kingdom entry clearance for entry in this capacity or is unable to satisfy the Secretary of State that each of the requirements of paragraph 274(i)–(vi) is met or if indefinite leave to remain is not, at the same time, being granted to the person with limited leave to enter or remain as a retired person of independent means.

Spouses

277 Nothing in these Rules shall be construed as permitting a person to be granted entry clearance, leave to enter, leave to remain or variation of leave as a spouse of another if either party to the marriage will be aged under 16 on the date of arrival in the United Kingdom or (as the case may be) on the date on which the leave to remain or variation of leave would be granted.

[**278** Nothing in these Rules shall be construed as allowing a person to be granted entry clearance, leave to enter, leave to remain or variation of leave as the spouse of a man or woman (the sponsor) if:

- (i)   his or her marriage to the sponsor is polygamous; and
- (ii) there is another person living who is the husband or wife of the sponsor and who:
  - (*a*) is, or at any time since his or her marriage to the sponsor has been, in the United Kingdom; or
  - (*b*) has been granted a certificate of entitlement in respect of the right of abode mentioned in Section 2(1)(a) of the Immigration Act 1988 or an entry clearance to enter the United Kingdom as the husband or wife of the sponsor.

For the purpose of this paragraph a marriage may be polygamous although at its inception neither party had any other spouse.]

Note   Paragraph 278 substituted by CM 4851.

[**279**   Paragraph 278 does not apply to any person who seeks entry clearance, leave to enter, leave to remain or variation of leave where:

- (i)   he or she has been in the United Kingdom before 1 August 1988 having been admitted for the purpose of settlement as the husband or wife of the sponsor; or
- (ii) he or she has, since their marriage to the sponsor, been in the United Kingdom at any time when there was no such other spouse living as is mentioned in paragraph 278 (ii).

But where a person claims that paragraph 278 does not apply to them because they have been in the United Kingdom in circumstances which cause them to fall within sub-paragraphs (i) or (ii) of that paragraph, it shall be for them to prove that fact.]

Note   Paragraph 279 substituted by CM 4851.

[**280**   For the purposes of paragraphs 278 and 279 the presence of any wife or husband in the United Kingdom in any of the following circumstances shall be disregarded:

- (i)   as a visitor; or
- (ii) an illegal entrant; or
- (iii) in circumstances whereby a person is deemed by Section 11(1) of the Immigration Act 1971 not to have entered the United Kingdom.]

Note   Paragraph 280 substituted by CM 4851.

Requirements for leave to enter the United Kingdom with a view to settlement as the spouse of a person present and settled in the United Kingdom or being admitted on the same occasion for settlement

[281   The requirements to be met by a person seeking leave to enter the United Kingdom with a view to settlement as the spouse of a person present and settled in the United Kingdom or who is on the same occasion being admitted for settlement are that:

- (i)   the applicant is married to a person present and settled in the United Kingdom or who is on the same occasion being admitted for settlement; and
- (ii)   the parties to the marriage have met; and
- (iii)   each of the parties intends to live permanently with the other as his or her spouse and the marriage is subsisting; and
- (iv)   there will be adequate accommodation for the parties and any dependants without recourse to public funds in accommodation which they own or occupy exclusively; and
- (v)   the parties will be able to maintain themselves and any dependants adequately without recourse to public funds; and
- (vi)   the applicant holds a valid United Kingdom entry clearance for entry in this capacity.[For the purposes of this paragraph and paragraphs 282-289 a member of HM Forces serving overseas, or a permanent member of HM Diplomatic Service or a comparable UK-based staff member of the British Council on a tour of duty abroad, is to be regarded as present and settled in the United Kingdom.]

Note   Substituted by HC26, para 1 with effect from 5 June 1997.
Words in second set of square brackets subtituted by CM 4851.

Leave to enter as the spouse of a person present and settled in the United Kingdom or being admitted for settlement on the same occasion

282   A person seeking leave to enter the United Kingdom as the spouse of a person present and settled in the United Kingdom or who is on the same occasion being admitted for settlement may be admitted for an initial period not exceeding 12 months provided a valid United Kingdom entry clearance for entry in this capacity is produced to the Immigration Officer on arrival.

Refusal of leave to enter as the spouse of a person present and settled in the United Kingdom or being admitted on the same occasion for settlement

283   Leave to enter the United Kingdom as the spouse of a person present and settled in the United Kingdom or who is on the same occasion being admitted for settlement is to be refused if a valid United Kingdom entry clearance for entry in this capacity is not produced to the Immigration Officer on arrival.

Requirements for an extension of stay as the spouse of a person present and settled in the United Kingdom

[284   The requirements for an extension of stay as the spouse of a person present and settled in the United Kingdom are that:

- (i)   the applicant has limited leave to remain in the United Kingdom; and
- (ii)   is married to a person present and settled in the United Kingdom; and
- (iii)   the parties to the marriage have met; and
- (iv)   the applicant has not remained in breach of the immigration laws; and

(v) the marriage has not taken place after a decision has been made to deport the applicant or he has been recommended for deportation or been given notice under Section 6(2) of the Immigration Act 1971; and

(vi) each of the parties intends to live permanently with the other as his or her spouse and the marriage is subsisting; and

(vii) there will be adequate accommodation for the parties and any dependants without recourse to public funds in accommodation which they own or occupy exclusively; and

(viii) the parties will be able to maintain themselves and any dependants adequately without recourse to public funds.]

Note Substituted by HC 26, para 2 with effect from 5 June 1997.

Extension of stay as the spouse of a person present and settled in the United Kingdom

285 An extension of stay as the spouse of a person present and settled in the United Kingdom may be granted for a period of 12 months in the first instance, provided the Secretary of State is satisfied that each of the requirements of paragraph 284 is met.

Refusal of extension of stay as the spouse of a person present and settled in the United Kingdom

286 An extension of stay as the spouse of a person present and settled in the United Kingdom is to be refused if the Secretary of State is not satisfied that each of the requirements of paragraph 284 is met.

Requirements for indefinite leave to remain for the spouse of a person present and settled in the United Kingdom

[**287**(*a*) The requirements for indefinite leave to remain for the spouse of a person present and settled in the United Kingdom are that:

    (i) the applicant was admitted to the United Kingdom or given an extension of stay for a period of 12 months and has completed a period of 12 months as the spouse of a person present and settled in the United Kingdom; and

    (ii) the applicant is still the spouse of the person he or she was admitted or granted an extension of stay to join and the marriage is subsisting; and

    (iii) each of the parties intends to live permanently with the other as his or her spouse; and

    (iv) there will be adequate accommodation for the parties and any dependants without recourse to public funds in accommodation which they own or occupy exclusively; and

    (v) the parties will be able to maintain themselves and any dependants adequately without recourse to public funds.

  (*b*) The requirements for indefinite leave to remain for the bereaved spouse of a person who was present and settled in the United Kingdom are that:

    (i) the applicant was admitted to the United Kingdom or given an extension of stay for a period of 12 months as the spouse of a person present and settled in the United Kingdom; and

    (ii) the person whom the applicant was admitted or granted an extension of stay to join died during that 12 month period; and

    (iii) the applicant was still the spouse of the person he or she was admitted or granted an extension of stay to join at the time of the death; and

    (iv) each of the parties intended to live permanently with the other as his or her spouse and the marriage was subsisting at the time of the death.]

Note Paragraph 287 substituted by CM 4851.

Indefinite leave to remain for the spouse of a person present and settled in the United Kingdom

288   Indefinite leave to remain for the spouse of a person present and settled in the United Kingdom may be granted provided the Secretary of State is satisfied that each of the requirements of paragraph 287 is met.

Refusal of indefinite leave to remain for the spouse of a person present and settled in the United Kingdom

289   Indefinite leave to remain for the spouse of a person present and settled in the United Kingdom is to be refused if the Secretary of State is not satisfied that each of the requirements of paragraph 287 is met.

FIANCE(E)S

Requirements for leave to enter the United Kingdom as a fiance(e) (ie with a view to marriage and permanent settlement in the United Kingdom)

[290   The requirements to be met by a person seeking leave to enter the United Kingdom as a fiance(e) are that:

(i)   the applicant is seeking leave to enter the United Kingdom for marriage to a person present and settled in the United Kingdom or who is on the same occasion being admitted for settlement; and

(ii)   the parties to the proposed marriage have met; and

(iii)   each of the parties intends to live permanently with the other as his or her spouse after the marriage; and

(iv)   adequate maintenance and accommodation without recourse to public funds will be available for the applicant until the date of the marriage; and

(v)   there will, after the marriage, be adequate accommodation for the parties and any dependants without recourse to public funds in accommodation which they own or occupy exclusively; and

(vi)   the parties will be able after the marriage to maintain themselves and any dependants adequately without recourse to public funds; and

(vii)   the applicant holds a valid United Kingdom entry clearance for entry in this capacity.]

Note   Substituted by HC 26, para 3 with effect from 5 June 1997.

Leave to enter as a fiance(e)

291   A person seeking leave to enter the United Kingdom as a fiance(e) may be admitted, with a prohibition on employment, for a period not exceeding 6 months to enable the marriage to take place provided a valid United Kingdom entry clearance for entry in this capacity is produced to the Immigration Officer on arrival.

Refusal of leave to enter as a fiance(e)

292   Leave to enter the United Kingdom as a fiance(e) is to be refused if a valid UnitedKingdom entry clearance for entry in this capacity is not produced to the Immigration Officer on arrival.

Requirements for an extension of stay as a fiance(e)

293   The requirements for an extension of stay as a fiance(e) are that:

(i)   the applicant was admitted to the United Kingdom with a valid United Kingdom entry clearance as a fiance(e); and

    (ii)   good cause is shown why the marriage did not take place within the initial period of leave granted under paragraph 291; and

   (iii)   there is satisfactory evidence that the marriage will take place at an early date; and

   (iv)   the requirements of paragraph 290(ii)–(vi) are met.]

Note   Sub-para (iv) substituted by HC26, para 4 with effect from 5 June 1997.

Extension of stay as a fiance(e)

294   An extension of stay as a fiance(e) may be granted for an appropriate period with a prohibition on employment to enable the marriage to take place provided the Secretary of State is satisfied that each of the requirements of paragraph 293 is met.

Refusal of extension of stay as a fiance(e)

295   An extension of stay is to be refused if the Secretary of State is not satisfied that each of the requirements of paragraph 293 is met.

[LEAVE TO ENTER AS THE UNMARRIED PARTNER OF A PERSON PRESENT AND SETTLED IN THE UNITED KINGDOM OR BEING ADMITTED ON THE SAME OCCASION FOR SETTLEMENT

Requirements for leave to enter the United Kingdom with a view to settlement as the unmarried partner of a person present and settled in the United Kingdom or being admitted on the same occasion for settlement

295A   The requirements to be met by a person seeking leave to enter the United Kingdom with a view to settlement as the unmarried partner of a person present and settled in the United Kingdom or being admitted on the same occasion for settlement, are that:

    (i)   the applicant is the unmarried partner of a person present and settled in the United Kingdom or who is on the same occasion being admitted for settlement; and

   (ii)   any previous marriage (or similar relationship) by either partner has permanently broken down; and

   (iii)   the parties are legally unable to marry under United Kingdom law (other than by reason of consanguineous relationships or age); and

   (iv)   the parties have been living together in a relationship akin to marriage which has subsisted for two years or more; and

   (v)   there will be adequate accommodation for the parties and any dependants without recourse to public funds in accommodation which they own or occupy exclusively; and

   (vi)   the parties will be able to maintain themselves and any dependants adequately without recourse to public funds; and

   (vii) the parties intend to live together permanently; and

   (viii) the applicant holds a valid United Kingdom entry clearance for entry in this capacity.

Leave to enter the United Kingdom with a view to settlement as the unmarried partner of a person present and settled in the United Kingdom or being admitted on the same occasion for settlement

295B   Leave to enter the United Kingdom with a view to settlement as the unmarried partner of a person present and settled in the United Kingdom or being admitted on the same occasion for settlement, may be granted for an initial period not exceeding 2 years provided that a valid United Kingdom entry clearance for entry in this capacity is produced to the Immigration Officer on arrival.

Refusal of leave to enter the United Kingdom with a view to settlement as the unmarried partner of a person present and settled in the United Kingdom or being admitted on the same occasion for settlement

295C   Leave to enter the United Kingdom with a view to settlement as the unmarried partner of a person present and settled in the United Kingdom or being admitted on the same occasion for settlement, is to be refused if a valid United Kingdom entry clearance for entry in this capacity is not produced to the Immigration Officer on arrival.

LEAVE TO REMAIN AS THE UNMARRIED PARTNER OF A PERSON PRESENT AND SETTLED IN THE UNITED KINGDOM

Requirements for leave to remain as the unmarried partner of a person present and settled in the United Kingdom

295D   The requirements to be met by a person seeking leave to remain as the unmarried partner of a person present and settled in the United Kingdom are that:

(i) the applicant has limited leave to remain in the United Kingdom; and
(ii) any previous marriage (or similar relationship) by either partner has permanently broken down; and
(iii) the applicant is the unmarried partner of a person who is present and settled in the United Kingdom; and
(iv) the applicant has not remained in breach of the immigration laws; and
(v) the parties are legally unable to marry under United Kingdom law (other than by reason of consanguineous relationships or age); and
(vi) the parties have been living together in a relationship akin to marriage which has subsisted for two years or more; and
(vii) the parties' relationship pre-dates any decision to deport the applicant, recommend him for deportation, give him notice under Section 6(2) of the Immigration Act 1971, or give directions for his removal under section 10 of the Immigration and Asylum Act 1999; and
(viii) there will be adequate accommodation for the parties and any dependants without recourse to public funds in accommodation which they own or occupy exclusively; and -
(ix) the parties will be able to maintain themselves and any dependants adequately without recourse to public funds; and
(x) the parties intend to live together permanently.

Leave to remain as the unmarried partner of a person present and settled in the United Kingdom

295E   Leave to remain as the unmarried partner of a person present and settled in the United Kingdom may be granted for a period of 2 years in the first instance provided that the Secretary of State is satisfied that each of the requirements of paragraph 295D are met.

Refusal of leave to remain as the unmarried partner of a person present and settled in the United Kingdom

295F   Leave to remain as the unmarried partner of a person present and settled in the United Kingdom is to be refused if the Secretary of State is not satisfied that each of the requirements of paragraph 295D is met.

Requirements for indefinite leave to remain as the unmarried partner of a person present and settled in the United Kingdom

295G The requirements to be met by a person seeking indefinite leave to remain as the unmarried partner of a person present and settled in the United Kingdom are that:

(i) the applicant was admitted to the United Kingdom or given an extension of stay for a period of 2 years and has completed a period of 2 years as the unmarried partner of a person present and settled here; and

(ii) the applicant is still the unmarried partner of the person he was admitted or granted an extension of stay to join and the relationship is still subsisting; and

(iii) each of the parties intends to live permanently with the other as his partner; and

(iv) there will be adequate accommodation for the parties and any dependants without recourse to public funds in accommodation which they own or occupy exclusively; and

(v) the parties will be able to maintain themselves and any dependants adequately without recourse to public funds.

Indefinite leave to remain as the unmarried partner of a person present and settled in the United Kingdom

295H Indefinite leave to remain as the unmarried partner of a person present and settled in the United Kingdom may be granted provided that the Secretary of State is satisfied that each of the requirements of paragraph 295G is met.

Refusal of indefinite leave to remain as the unmarried partner of a person present and settled in the United Kingdom

295I Indefinite leave to remain as the unmarried partner of a person present and settled in the United Kingdom is to be refused if the Secretary of State is not satisfied that each of the requirements of paragraph 295G is met.

LEAVE TO ENTER OR REMAIN AS THE UNMARRIED PARTNER OF A PERSON WITH LIMITED LEAVE
TO ENTER OR REMAIN IN THE UNITED KINGDOM UNDER PARAGRAPHS 128-193;
200-239; OR 263-270

Requirements for leave to enter or remain as the unmarried partner of a person with limited leave to enter or remain in the United Kingdom under paragraphs 128-193; 200-239; or 263-270

295J The requirements to be met by a person seeking leave to enter or remain as the unmarried partner of a person with limited leave to enter or remain in the United Kingdom under paragraphs 128-193; 200-239; or 263-270; are that:

(i) the applicant is the unmarried partner of a person who has limited leave to enter or remain in the United Kingdom under paragraphs 128-193; 200-239; or 263-270; and

(ii) any previous marriage (or similar relationship) by either partner has permanently broken down; and

(iii) the parties are legally unable to marry under United Kingdom law (other than by reason of consanguineous relationship or age); and

(iv) the parties have been living together in a relationship akin to marriage which has subsisted for 2 years or more; and

(v) each of the parties intends to live with the other as his partner during the applicant's stay; and

(vi) there will be adequate accommodation for the parties and any dependants without recourse to public funds in accommodation which they own or occupy exclusively; and

(vii) the parties will be able to maintain themselves and any dependants adequately without recourse to public funds; and

(viii) the applicant does not intend to stay in the United Kingdom beyond any period of leave granted to his partner; and

(ix) if seeking leave to enter, the applicant holds a valid United Kingdom entry clearance for entry in this capacity or, if seeking leave to remain, was admitted with a valid United Kingdom entry clearance for entry in this capacity.

Leave to enter or remain as the unmarried partner of a person with limited leave to enter or remain in the United Kingdom under paragraphs 128-193; 200-239; or 263-270

295K Leave to enter as the unmarried partner of a person with limited leave to enter or remain in the United Kingdom under paragraphs 128-193; 200-239; or 263-270; may be granted provided that a valid United Kingdom entry clearance for entry in this capacity is produced to the Immigration Officer on arrival. Leave to remain as the unmarried partner of a person with limited leave to enter or remain in the United Kingdom under paragraphs 128-193; 200-239; or 263-270; may be granted provided that the Secretary of State is satisfied that each of the requirements of paragraph 295J is met.

Refusal of leave to enter or remain as the unmarried partner of a person with limited leave to enter or remain in the United Kingdom under paragraphs 128-193; 200-239; or 263-270

295L Leave to enter as the unmarried partner of a person with limited leave to enter or remain in the United Kingdom under paragraphs 128-193; 200-239; or 263-270; is to be refused if a valid United Kingdom entry clearance for entry in this capacity is not produced to the Immigration Officer on arrival. Leave to remain as the unmarried partner of a person with limited leave to enter or remain in the United Kingdom under paragraphs 128-193; 200-239; or 263-270; is to be refused if the Secretary of State is not satisfied that each of the requirements of paragraph 295J is met.

INDEFINITE LEAVE TO REMAIN FOR THE BEREAVED UNMARRIED PARTNER OF A PERSON PRESENT AND SETTLED IN THE UNITED KINGDOM

Requirements for indefinite leave to remain for the bereaved unmarried partner of a person present and settled in the United Kingdom

295M The requirements to be met by a person seeking indefinite leave to remain as the bereaved unmarried partner of a person present and settled in the United Kingdom, are that:

(i) the applicant was admitted to the United Kingdom or given an extension of stay for a period of 2 years as the unmarried partner of a person present and settled in the United Kingdom; and

(ii)   the person whom the applicant was admitted or granted an extension of stay to join died during that 2 year period; and

(iii)   the applicant was still the unmarried partner of the person he was admitted or granted extension of stay to join at the time of the death; and

(iv)   each of the parties intended to live permanently with the other as his partner and the relationship was subsisting at the time of the death.

Indefinite leave to remain for the bereaved unmarried partner of a person present and settled in the United Kingdom

295N   Indefinite leave to remain for the bereaved unmarried partner of a person present and settled in the United Kingdom, may be granted provided that the Secretary of State is satisfied that each of the requirements of paragraph 295M is met.

Refusal of indefinite leave to remain for the bereaved unmarried partner of a person present and settled in the United Kingdom

295O   Indefinite leave to remain for the bereaved unmarried partner of a person present and settled in the United Kingdom, is to be refused if the Secretary of State is not satisfied that each of the requirements of paragraph 295M is met.]

Note   Paragraphs 295A–295O inserted by CM 4851.

CHILDREN

[**296**   Nothing in these Rules shall be construed as permitting a child to be granted entry clearance, leave to enter or remain, or variation of leave where his mother is party to a polygamous marriage and any application by that parent for admission or leave to remain for settlement or with a view to settlement would be refused pursuant to paragraphs 278 or 278A].

Note   Paragraphs 296 substituted by CM 4851.

LEAVE TO ENTER OR REMAIN IN THE UNITED KINGDOM AS THE CHILD OF A PARENT, PARENTS OR A RELATIVE PRESENT AND SETTLED OR BEING ADMITTED FOR SETTLEMENT IN THE UNITED KINGDOM

Requirements for indefinite leave to enter the United Kingdom as the child of a parent, parents or a relative present and settled or being admitted for settlement in the United Kingdom

297   The requirements to be met by a person seeking indefinite leave to enter the United Kingdom as the child of a parent, parents or a relative present and settled or being admitted for settlement in the United Kingdom are that he:

(i)   is seeking leave to enter to accompany or join a parent, parents or a relative in one of the following circumstances:

(*a*)   both parents are present and settled in the United Kingdom; or

(*b*)   both parents are being admitted on the same occasion for settlement; or

(*c*)   one parent is present and settled in the United Kingdom and the other is being admitted on the same occasion for settlement; or

(*d*)   one parent is present and settled in the United Kingdom or being admitted on the same occasion for settlement and the other parent is dead; or

(*e*)   one parent is present and settled in the United Kingdom or being admitted on the same occasion for settlement and has had sole responsibility for the child's upbringing; or (*f*)   one parent or a relative is present and settled in the United Kingdom or being admitted on the same occasion for settlement and there are serious and compelling family or other considerations which make exclusion of the child undesirable and suitable arrangements have been made for the child's care; and

(ii)   is under the age of 18; and

(iii)   is not leading an independent life, is unmarried, and has not formed an independent family unit; and

[(iv)   can, and will, be accommodated adequately by the parent, parents or relative the child is seeking to join without recourse to public funds in accommodation which the parent, parents or relative the child is seeking to join, own or occupy exclusively; and

(v)   can, and will, be maintained adequately by the parent, parents or relative the child is seeking to join, without recourse to public funds; and

(vi)   holds a valid United Kingdom entry clearance for entry in this capacity.]

Note   Paragraph 297 (iv)-(v) substituted and paragraph 297 (vi) inserted by CM 4851.

Requirements for indefinite leave to remain in the United Kingdom as the child of a parent, parents or a relative present and settled or being admitted for settlement in the United Kingdom

298   The requirements to be met by a person seeking indefinite leave to remain in the United Kingdom as the child of a parent, parents or a relative present and settled in the United Kingdom are that he:

(i)   is seeking to remain with a parent, parents or a relative in one of the following circumstances:

(*a*)   both parents are present and settled in the United Kingdom; or

(*b*)   one parent is present and settled in the United Kingdom and the other parent is dead; or

(*c*)   one parent is present and settled in the United Kingdom and has had sole responsibility for the child's upbringing; or

(*d*)   one parent or a relative is present and settled in the United Kingdom and there are serious and compelling family or other considerations which make exclusion of the child undesirable and suitable arrangements have been made for the child's care; and

(ii)   has limited leave to enter or remain in the United Kingdom, and

(*a*)   is under the age of 18; or

(*b*)   was given leave to enter or remain with a view to settlement under paragraph 302; and

(iii)   is not leading an independent life, is unmarried, and has not formed an independent family unit; and

[(iv)   can, and will, be accommodated adequately by the parent, parents or relative the child was admitted to join, without recourse to public funds in accommodation which the parent, parents or relative the child was admitted to join, own or occupy exclusively; and

(v)   can, and will, be maintained adequately by the parent, parents or relative the child was admitted to join, without recourse to public funds.]

Note   Paragraph 298 (iv) substituted and paragraph 298 (v) inserted   by CM 4851.

Indefinite leave to enter or remain in the United Kingdom as the child of a parent, parents or a relative present and settled or being admitted for settlement in the United Kingdom

299   Indefinite leave to enter the United Kingdom as the child of a parent, parents or a relative present and settled or being admitted for settlement in the United Kingdom may be granted provided a valid United Kingdom entry clearance for entry in this capacity is produced to the Immigration Officer on arrival. Indefinite leave to remain in the United Kingdom as the child of a parent, parents or a relative present and settled in the United Kingdom may be granted provided the Secretary of State is satisfied that each of the requirements of paragraph 298 is met.

Refusal of indefinite leave to enter or remain in the United Kingdom as the child of a parent, parents or a relative present and settled or being admitted for settlement in the United Kingdom

300   Indefinite leave to enter the United Kingdom as the child of a parent, parents or a relative present and settled or being admitted for settlement in the United Kingdom is to be refused if a valid United Kingdom entry clearance for entry in this capacity is not produced to the Immigration Officer on arrival. Indefinite leave to remain in the United Kingdom as the child of a parent, parents or a relative present and settled in the United Kingdom is to be refused if   the Secretary of State is not satisfied that each of the requirements of paragraph 298 is met.

Requirements for limited leave to enter or remain in the United Kingdom with a view to settlement as the child of a parent or parents given limited leave to enter or remain in the United Kingdom with a view to settlement

301   The requirements to be met by a person seeking limited leave to enter or remain in the United Kingdom with a view to settlement as the child of a parent or parents given limited leave to enter or remain in the United Kingdom with a view to settlement are that he:

(i)   is seeking leave to enter to accompany or join or remain with a parent or parents in one of the following circumstances:
   (*a*)   one parent is present and settled in the United Kingdom or being admitted on the same occasion for settlement and the other parent is being or has been given limited leave to enter or remain in the United Kingdom with a view to settlement; or
   (*b*)   one parent is being or has been given limited leave to enter or remain in the United Kingdom with a view to settlement and has had sole responsibility for the child's upbringing; or
   (*c*)   one parent is being or has been given limited leave to enter or remain in the United Kingdom with a view to settlement and there are serious and compelling family or other considerations which make exclusion of the child undesirable and suitable arrangements have been made for the child's care; and
(ii)   is under the age of 18; and
(iii)   is not leading an independent life, is unmarried, and has not formed an independent family unit; and
[(iv)   can, and will, be accommodated adequately without recourse to public funds, in accommodation which the parent or parents own or occupy exclusively; and
(iva) can, and will, be maintained adequately by the parent or parents without recourse to public funds; and]
(v)   (where an application is made for limited leave to remain with a view to settlement) has limited leave to enter or remain in the United Kingdom; and
(vi)   if seeking leave to enter, holds a valid United Kingdom entry clearance for entry in this capacity or, if seeking leave to remain, was admitted with a valid United Kingdom entry clearance for entry in this capacity.

Note   Paragraph 301(iv) substituted and paragraph 301(iva) inserted   by CM 4851.

Limited leave to enter or remain in the United Kingdom with a view to settlement as the child of a parent or parents given limited leave to enter or remain in the United Kingdom with a view to settlement

302   A person seeking limited leave to enter the United Kingdom with a view to settlement as the child of a parent or parents given limited leave to enter or remain in the United Kingdom with a view to settlement may be admitted for a period not exceeding 12 months provided he is able, on arrival, to produce to the Immigration Officer a valid United Kingdom entry clearance for entry in this capacity. A person seeking limited leave to remain in the United Kingdom with a view to settlement as the child of a parent or parents given limited leave to enter or remain in the United Kingdom with a view to settlement may be given limited leave to remain for a period not exceeding 12 months provided the Secretary of State is satisfied that each of the requirements of paragraph 301(i)–(v) is met.

Refusal of limited leave to enter or remain in the United Kingdom with a view to settlement as the child of a parent or parents given limited leave to enter or remain in theUnited Kingdom with a view to settlement

303   Limited leave to enter the United Kingdom with a view to settlement as the child of a parent or parents given limited leave to enter or remain in the United Kingdom with a view to settlement is to be refused if a valid United Kingdom entry clearance for entry in this capacity is not produced to the Immigration Officer on arrival. Limited leave to remain in the United Kingdom with a view to settlement as the child of a parent or parents given limited leave to enter or remain in the United Kingdom with a view to settlement is to be refused if the Secretary of State is not satisfied that each of the requirements of paragraph 301(i)–(v) is met.

[LEAVE TO ENTER AND EXTENSION OF STAY IN THE UNITED KINGDOM AS THE CHILD OF A PARENT WHO IS BEING, OR HAS BEEN ADMITTED TO THE UNITED KINGDOM AS A FIANCÉ(E)

Requirements for limited leave to enter the United Kingdom as the child of a fiancé(e)

303A   The requirements to be met by a person seeking limited leave to enter the United Kingdom as the child of a fiancé(e), are that:

(i)   he is seeking to accompany or join a parent who is, on the same occasion that the child seeks admission, being admitted as a fiancé(e), or who has been admitted as a fiancé(e); and

(ii)   he is under the age of 18; and

(iii)   he is not leading an independent life, is unmarried, and has not formed an independent family unit; and

(iv)   he can, and will, be maintained and accommodated adequately without recourse to public funds with the parent admitted or being admitted as a fiancé(e); and(v)   there are serious and compelling family or other considerations which make the child's exclusion undesirable, that suitable arrangements have been made for his care in the United Kingdom, and there is no other person outside the United Kingdom who could reasonably be expected to care for him; and

(vi)   he holds a valid United Kingdom entry clearance for entry in this capacity.

Limited leave to enter the United Kingdom as the child of a parent who is being, or has been admitted to the United Kingdom as a fiancé(e)

303B   A person seeking limited leave to enter the United Kingdom as the child of a fiancé(e), may be granted limited leave to enter the United Kingdom for a period not in excess of that granted to the fiancé(e), provided that a valid United Kingdom entry clearance for entry in this capacity is produced to the Immigration Officer on arrival. Where the period of limited leave granted to a fiancé(e) will expire in more than 6 months, a person seeking limited leave to enter as the child of the fiancé(e) should be granted leave for a period not exceeding six months.

Refusal of limited leave to enter the United Kingdom as the child of a parent who is being, or has been admitted to the United Kingdom as a fiancé(e)

303C Limited leave to enter the United Kingdom as the child of a fiancé(e), is to be refused if a valid United Kingdom entry clearance for entry in this capacity is not produced to the Immigration Officer on arrival.

Requirements for an extension of stay in the United Kingdom as the child of a fiancé(e)

303D The requirements to be met by a person seeking an extension of stay in the United Kingdom as the child of a fiancé(e) are that:

(i)   the applicant was admitted with a valid United Kingdom entry clearance as the child of a fiancé(e); and

(ii) the applicant is the child of a parent who has been granted limited leave to enter, or an extension of stay, as a fiancé(e); and

(iii) the requirements of paragraph 303A (ii)-(v) are met.

Extension of stay in the United Kingdom as the child of a fiancé(e)

303E An extension of stay as the child of a fiancé(e) may be granted provided that the Secretary of State is satisfied that each of the requirements of paragraph 303D is met.

Refusal of an extension of stay in the United Kingdom as the child of a fiancé(e)

303F An extension of stay as the child of a fiancé(e) is to be refused if the Secretary of State is not satisfied that each of the requirements of paragraph 303D is met.]

Note Paragraphs 303A-303F inserted by CM 4851.

Children born in the United Kingdom who are not British citizens

304 This paragraph and paragraphs 305–309 apply only to unmarried dependent children under 18 years of age who were born in the United Kingdom on or after 1 January 1983 (when the British Nationality Act 1981 came into force) but who, because neither of their parents was a British citizen or settled in the United Kingdom at the time of their birth, are not British citizens and are therefore subject to immigration control. Such a child requires leave to enter where admission to the United Kingdom is sought, and leave to remain where permission is sought for the child to be allowed to stay in the United Kingdom.If he qualifies for entry clearance, leave to enter or leave to remain under any other part of these Rules, a child who was born in the United Kingdom but is not a British citizen may be granted entry clearance, leave to enter or leave to remain in accordance with the provisions of that other part.

Requirements for leave to enter or remain in the United Kingdom as the child of a parent or parents given leave to enter or remain in the United Kingdom

305 The requirements to be met by a child born in the United Kingdom who is not a British citizen who seeks leave to enter or remain in the United Kingdom as the child of a parent or parents given leave to enter or remain in the United Kingdom are that he:

(i) (*a*)   is accompanying or seeking to join or remain with a parent or parents who have, or are given, leave to enter or remain in the United Kingdom; or

(*b*)   is accompanying or seeking to join or remain with a parent or parents one of whom is a British citizen or has the right of abode in the United Kingdom; or

(*c*)   is a child in respect of whom the parental rights and duties are vested solely in a local authority; and

(ii)   is under the age of 18; and

(iii)   was born in the United Kingdom; and

(iv)   is not leading an independent life, is unmarried, and has not formed an independent family unit; and

(v)   (where an application is made for leave to enter) has not been away from the United Kingdom for more than 2 years.

Leave to enter or remain in the United Kingdom

306   A child born in the United Kingdom who is not a British citizen and who requires leave to enter or remain in the circumstances set out in paragraph 304 may be given leave to enter for the same period as his parent or parents where paragraph 305(i)(*a*) applies, provided the Immigration Officer is satisfied that each of the requirements of paragraph 305(ii)–(v) is met. Where leave to remain in sought, the child may be granted leave to remain for the same period as his parent or parents where paragraph 305(i)(*a*) applies, provided the Secretary of State is satisfied that each of the requirements of paragraph 305(ii)–(iv) is met. Where the parent or parents have or are given periods of leave of different duration, the child may be given leave to whichever period is longer except that if the parents are living apart the child should be given leave for the same period as the parent who has day to day responsibility for him.

307   If a child does not qualify for leave to enter or remain because neither of his parents has a current leave (and neither of them is a British citizen or has the right of abode), he will normally be refused leave to enter or remain, even if each of the requirements of paragraph 305(ii)–(v) has been satisfied. However, he may be granted leave to enter or remain for a period not exceeding 3 months if both of his parents are in the United Kingdom and it appears unlikely that they will be removed in the immediate future, and there is no other person outside the United Kingdom who could reasonably be expected to care for him.

308   A child born in the United Kingdom who is not a British citizen and who requires leave to enter or remain in the United Kingdom in the circumstances set out in paragraph 304 may be given indefinite leave to enter where paragraph 305(i)(*b*) or (i)(*c*) applies provided the Immigration Officer is satisfied that each of the requirements of paragraph 305(ii)–(v) is met. Where an application is for leave to remain, such a child may be granted indefinite leave to remain where paragraph 305(i)(*b*) or (i)(*c*) applies, provided the Secretary of State is satisfied that each of the requirements of paragraph 305(ii)–(iv) is met.

Refusal of leave to enter or remain in the United Kingdom

309   Leave to enter the United Kingdom where the circumstances set out in paragraph 304 apply is to be refused if the Immigration Officer is not satisfied that each of the requirements of paragraph 305 is met. Leave to remain for such a child is to be refused if the Secretary of State is not satisfied that each of the requirements of paragraph 305(i)–(iv) is met.

ADOPTED CHILDREN

Requirements for indefinite leave to enter the United Kingdom as the adopted child of a parent or parents present and settled or being admitted for settlement in the United Kingdom

310   The requirements to be met in the case of a child seeking indefinite leave to enter the United Kingdom as the adopted child of a parent or parents present and settled or being admitted for settlement in the United Kingdom are that he:

(i)   is seeking leave to enter to accompany or join an adoptive parent or parents in one of the following circumstances:
   (*a*)   both parents are present and settled in the United Kingdom; or
   (*b*)   both parents are being admitted on the same occasion for settlement; or
   (*c*)   one parent is present and settled in the United Kingdom and the other is being admitted on the same occasion for settlement; or
   (*d*)   one parent is present and settled in the United Kingdom or being admitted on the same occasion for settlement and the other parent is dead; or
   (*e*)   one parent is present and settled in the United Kingdom or being admitted on the same occasion for settlement and has had sole responsibility for the child's upbringing; or
   (*f*)   one parent is present and settled in the United Kingdom or being admitted on the same occasion for settlement and there are serious and compelling family or other considerations which make exclusion of the child undesirable and suitable arrangements have been made for the child's care; and

(ii)   is under the age of 18; and

(iii)   is not leading an independent life, is unmarried, and has not formed an independent family unit; and

[(iv)   can, and will, be accommodated adequately without recourse to public funds in accommodation which the adoptive parent or parents own or occupy exclusively; and

(v)   can, and will, be maintained adequately by the adoptive parent or parents without recourse to public funds; and]

(vi)   was adopted in accordance with a decision taken by the competent administrative authority or court in his country of origin or the country in which he is resident; and

(vii)   was adopted at a time when:
   (*a*)   both adoptive parents were resident together abroad; or
   (*b*)   either or both adoptive parents were settled in the United Kingdom; and

(viii) has the same rights and obligations as any other child of the marriage; and

(ix)   was adopted due to the inability of the original parent(s) or current carer(s) to care for him and there has been a genuine transfer of parental responsibility to the adoptive parents; and

(x)   has lost or broken his ties with his family of origin; and

(xi)   was adopted, but the adoption is not one of convenience arranged to facilitate his admission to or remaining in the United Kingdom; and

(xii) holds a valid United Kingdom entry clearance for entry in this capacity.

Note Paragraph 310(iv) substituted, paragraph 310(v) inserted and subsequent paragraphs renumbered by CM 4851.

Requirements for indefinite leave to remain in the United Kingdom as the adopted child of a parent or parents present and settled in the United Kingdom

311   The requirements to be met in the case of a child seeking indefinite leave to remain in the United Kingdom as the adopted child of a parent or parents present and settled in the United Kingdom are that he:

  (i) is seeking to remain with an adoptive parent or parents in one of the following circumstances:
- (*a*) both parents are present and settled in the United Kingdom; or
- (*b*) one parent is present and settled in the United Kingdom and the other parent is dead; or
- (*c*) one parent is present and settled in the United Kingdom and has had sole responsibility for the child's upbringing; or
- (*d*) one parent is present and settled in the United Kingdom and there are serious and compelling family or other considerations which make exclusion of the child undesirable and suitable arrangements have been made for the child's care; and

  (ii) has limited leave to enter or remain in the United Kingdom, and
- (*a*) is under the age of 18; or
- (*b*) was given leave to enter or remain with a view to settlement under paragraph 315 [or paragraph 316B]; and

  (iii) is not leading an independent life, is unmarried, and has not formed an independent family unit; and

  [(iv) can, and will, be accommodated adequately without recourse to public funds in accommodation which the adoptive parent or parents own or occupy exclusively; and

  (v) can, and will, be maintained adequately by the adoptive parent or parents without recourse to public funds; and]

  (vi) was adopted in accordance with a decision taken by the competent administrative authority or court in his country of origin or the country in which he is resident; and

  (vii) was adopted at a time when:
- (*a*) both adoptive parents were resident together abroad; or
- (*b*) either or both adoptive parents were settled in the United Kingdom; and

  (viii) has the same rights and obligations as any other child of the marriage; and

  (ix) was adopted due to the inability of the original parent(s) or current carer(s) to care for him and there has been a genuine transfer of parental responsibility to the adoptive parents; and

  (x) has lost or broken his ties with his family of origin; and

  (ix) was adopted, but the adoption is not one of convenience arranged to facilitate his admission to or remaining in the United Kingdom.

Note Words in square brackets in paragraph 311(ii)(b) and paragraph 311(v) inserted, paragraph 311(iv) substituted and subsequent paragraphs renumbered by CM 4851.

Indefinite leave to enter or remain in the United Kingdom as the adopted child of a parent or parents present and settled or being admitted for settlement in the United Kingdom

312   Indefinite leave to enter the United Kingdom as the adopted child of a parent or parents present and settled or being admitted for settlement in the United Kingdom may be granted provided a valid United Kingdom entry clearance for entry in this capacity is produced to the Immigration Officer on arrival. Indefinite leave to remain in the United Kingdom as the adopted child of a parent or parents present and settled in the United Kingdom may be granted provided the Secretary of State is satisfied that each of the requirements of paragraph 311 is met.

Refusal of indefinite leave to enter or remain in the United Kingdom as the adopted child of a parent or parents present and settled or being admitted for settlement in the United Kingdom

313   Indefinite leave to enter the United Kingdom as the adopted child of a parent or parents present and settled or being admitted for settlement in the UnitedKingdom is

to be refused if a valid United Kingdom entry clearance for entry in this capacity is not produced to the Immigration Officer on arrival. Indefinite leave to remain in the United Kingdom as the adopted child of a parent or parents present and settled in the United Kingdom is to be refused if the Secretary of State is not satisfied that each of the requirements of paragraph 311 is met.

Requirements for limited leave to enter or remain in the United Kingdom with a view to settlement as the adopted child of a parent or parents given limited leave to enter or remain in the United Kingdom with a view to settlement

314 The requirements to be met in the case of a child seeking limited leave to enter or remain in the United Kingdom with a view to settlement as the adopted child of a parent or parents given limited leave to enter or remain in the United Kingdom with a view to settlement are that he:

- (i) is seeking leave to enter to accompany or join or remain with a parent or parents in one of the following circumstances:
  - (a) one parent is present and settled in the United Kingdom or being admitted on the same occasion for settlement and the other parent is being or has been given limited leave to enter or remain in the United Kingdom with a view to settlement; or
  - (b) one parent is being or has been given limited leave to enter or remain in the United Kingdom with a view to settlement and has had sole responsibility for the child's upbringing; or
  - (c) one parent is being or has been given limited leave to enter or remain in the United Kingdom with a view to settlement and there are serious and compelling family or other considerations which make exclusion of the child undesirable and suitable arrangements have been made for the child's care; and
- (ii) is under the age of 18; and
- (iii) is not leading an independent life, is unmarried, and has not formed an independent family unit; and
- [(iv) can, and will, be accommodated adequately without recourse to public funds in accommodation which the adoptive parent or parents own or occupy exclusively; and
- (iva) can, and will, be maintained adequately by the adoptive parent or parents without recourse to public funds; and]
- (v) was adopted in accordance with a decision taken by the competent administrative authority or court in his country of origin or the country in which he is resident; and
- (vi) was adopted at a time when:
  - (a) both adoptive parents were resident together abroad; or
  - (b) either or both adoptive parents were settled in the United Kingdom; and
- (vii) has the same rights and obligations as any other child of the marriage; and
- (viii) was adopted due to the inability of the original parent(s) or current carer(s) to care for him and there has been a genuine transfer of parental responsibility to the adoptive parents; and
- (ix) has lost or broken his ties with his family of origin; and
- (x) was adopted, but the adoption is not one of convenience arranged to facilitate his admission to the United Kingdom; and
- (xi) (where an application is made for limited leave to remain with a view to settlement) has limited leave to enter or remain in the United Kingdom; and
- (xii) if seeking leave to enter, holds a valid United Kingdom entry clearance for entry in this capacity.

Note Paragraph 314(iv) substituted and paragraph 314(iva) inserted by CM 4851.

Limited leave to enter or remain in the United Kingdom with a view to settlement as the adopted child of a parent or parents given limited leave to enter or remain in the United Kingdom with a view to settlement

315   A person seeking limited leave to enter the United Kingdom with a view to settlement as the adopted child of a parent or parents given limited leave to enter or remain in the United Kingdom with a view to settlement may be admitted for a period not exceeding 12 months provided he is able, on arrival, to produce to the Immigration Officer a valid United Kingdom entry clearance for entry in this capacity. A person seeking limited leave to remain in the United Kingdom with a view to settlement as the adopted child of a parent or parents given limited leave to enter or remain in the United Kingdom with a view to settlement may be granted limited leave for a period not exceeding 12 months provided the Secretary of State is satisfied that each of the requirements of paragraph 314(i)–(xi) is met.

Refusal of limited leave to enter or remain in the United Kingdom with a view to settlement as the adopted child of a parent or parents given limited leave to enter or remain in the United Kingdom with a view to settlement

316   Limited leave to enter the United Kingdom with a view to settlement as the adopted child of a parent or parents given limited leave to enter or remain in the United Kingdom with a view to settlement is to be refused if a valid United Kingdom entry clearance for entry in this capacity is not produced to the Immigration Officer on arrival. Limited leave to remain in the United Kingdom with a view to settlement as the adopted child of a parent or parents given limited leave to enter or remain in the United Kingdom with a view to settlement is to be refused if the Secretary of State is not satisfied that each of the requirements of paragraph 314(i)–(xi) is met.

[Requirements for limited leave to enter the United Kingdom with a view to settlement as a child for adoption

316A   The requirements to be satisfied in the case of a child seeking limited leave to enter the United Kingdom for the purpose of being adopted in the United Kingdom are that he:

(i)   is seeking limited leave to enter to accompany or join a person or persons who wish to adopt him in the United Kingdom (the 'prospective parent(s)'), in one of the following circumstances:

   (*a*)   both prospective parents are present and settled in the United Kingdom; or

   (*b*)   both prospective parents are being admitted for settlement on the same occasion that the child is seeking admission; or

   (*c*)   one prospective parent is present and settled in the United Kingdom and the other is being admitted for settlement on the same occasion that the child is seeking admission; or

   (*d*)   one prospective parent is present and settled in the United Kingdom and the other is being given limited leave to enter or remain in the United Kingdom with a view to settlement on the same occasion that the child is seeking admission, or has previously been given such leave; or

   (*e*)   one prospective parent is being admitted for settlement on the same occasion that the other is being granted limited leave to enter with a view to settlement, which is also on the same occasion that the child is seeking admission; or

   (*f*)   one prospective parent is present and settled in the United Kingdom or is being admitted for settlement on the same occasion that the child is seeking admission, and has had sole responsibility for the child's upbringing; or(g)   one prospective parent is present and settled in the United Kingdom or is being admitted for settlement on the same occasion that the child is seeking admission, and there are serious and compelling family or other considerations which would make the child's exclusion undesirable, and suitable arrangements have been made for the child's care; and

(ii)   is under the age of 18; and

(iii)   is not leading an independent life, is unmarried, and has not formed an independent family unit; and

(iv)   can, and will, be maintained and accommodated adequately without recourse to public funds in accommodation which the prospective parent or parents own or occupy exclusively; and

(v)   will have the same rights and obligations as any other child of the marriage; and

(vi)   is being adopted due to the inability of the original parent(s) or current carer(s) (or those looking after him immediately prior to him being physically transferred to his prospective parent or parents) to care for him, and there has been a genuine transfer of parental responsibility to the prospective parent or parents; and

(vii) has lost or broken or intends to lose or break his ties with his family of origin; and

(viii) will be adopted in the United Kingdom by his prospective parent or parents, but the proposed adoption is not one of convenience arranged to facilitate his admission to the United Kingdom.

Limited leave to enter the United Kingdom with a view to settlement as a child for adoption

316B   A person seeking limited leave to enter the United Kingdom with a view to settlement as a child for adoption may be admitted for a period not exceeding 12 months provided he is able, on arrival, to produce to the Immigration Officer a valid United Kingdom entry clearance for entry in this capacity.

Refusal of limited leave to enter the United Kingdom with a view to settlement as a child for adoption

316C   Limited leave to enter the United Kingdom with a view to settlement as a child for adoption is to be refused if a valid United Kingdom entry clearance for entry in this capacity is not produced to the Immigration Officer on arrival.]

Note   Paragraphs 316A–316C inserted by CM 4851.

PARENTS, GRANDPARENTS AND OTHER DEPENDENT RELATIVES OF PERSONS PRESENT AND SETTLED IN THE UNITED KINGDOM

Requirements for indefinite leave to enter or remain in the United Kingdom as the parent, grandparent or other dependent relative of a person present and settled in the United Kingdom

317   The requirements to be met by a person seeking indefinite leave to enter or remain in the United Kingdom as the parent, grandparent or other dependent relative of a person present and settled in the United Kingdom are that the person:

(i)   is related to a person present and settled in the United Kingdom in one of the following ways:

   (a)   mother or grandmother who is a widow aged 65 years or over; or (*b*)   father or grandfather who is a widower aged 65 years or over; or

      (*c*)   parent or grandparents travelling together of whom at least one is aged 65 or over; or

      (*d*)   a parent or grandparent aged 65 or over who has remarried but cannot look to the spouse or children of the second marriage for financial support; and where the person settled in the United Kingdom is able and willing to maintain the parent or grandparent and any spouse or child of the second marriage who would be admissible as a dependent; or

      (*e*)   a parent or grandparent under the age of 65 if living alone outside the United Kingdom in the most exceptional compassionate circumstances and mainly dependent financially on relatives settled in the United Kingdom; or

      (*f*)   the son, daughter, sister, brother, uncle or aunt over the age of 18 if living alone outside the United Kingdom in the most exceptional compassionate circumstances and mainly dependent financially on relatives settled in the United Kingdom; and

  (ii)   is joining or accompanying a person who is present and settled in the United Kingdom or who is on the same occasion being admitted for   settlement; and

  (iii) is financially wholly or mainly dependent on the relative present and settled in the United Kingdom; and

  [(iv) can, and will, be accommodated adequately, together with any dependants, without recourse to public funds, in accommodation which the sponsor owns or occupies exclusively; and

  (iva) can, and will, be maintained adequately, together with any dependants, without recourse to public funds; and]

  (v)   has no other close relatives in his own country to whom he could turn for financial support; and

  (vi) if seeking leave to enter, holds a valid UnitedKingdom entry clearance for entry in this capacity.

Note   Paragraph 317(iv) substituted and paragraph 317(iva) inserted by CM 4851.

Indefinite leave to enter or remain as the parent, grandparent or other dependent relative of a person present and settled in the United Kingdom

318   Indefinite leave to enter the United Kingdom as the parent, grandparent or other dependent relative of a person present and settled in the United Kingdom may be granted provided a valid United Kingdom entry clearance for entry in this capacity is produced to the Immigration Officer on arrival. Indefinite leave to remain in the United Kingdom as the parent, grandparent or other dependent relative of a person present and settled in the United Kingdom may be granted provided the Secretary of State is satisfied that each of the requirements of paragraph 317(i)–(v) is met.

Refusal of indefinite leave to enter or remain in the United Kingdom as the parent, grandparent or other dependent relative of a person present and settled in the United Kingdom

319   Indefinite leave to enter the United Kingdom as the parent, grandparent or other dependent relative of a person settled in the United Kingdom is to be refused if a valid United Kingdom entry clearance for entry in this capacity is not produced to the Immigration Officer on arrival. Indefinite leave to remain in the United Kingdom as the parent, grandparent or other dependent relative of a person present and settled in the United Kingdom is to be refused if the Secretary of State is not satisfied that each of the requirements of paragraph 317(i)–(v) is met.

PART 9:   GENERAL GROUNDS FOR THE REFUSAL OF ENTRY CLEARANCE, LEAVE TO ENTER OR
VARIATION OF LEAVE TO ENTER OR REMAIN IN THE UNITED KINGDOM

REFUSAL OF ENTRY CLEARANCE OR LEAVE TO ENTER THE UNITED KINGDOM

320   In addition to the grounds for refusal of entry clearance or leave to enter set out
in Parts 2–8 of these Rules, and subject to paragraph 321   below, the following grounds
for the refusal of entry clearance or leave to enter apply:

Grounds on which entry clearance or leave to enter the United Kingdom is to
be refused
(1)   the fact that entry is being sought for a purpose not covered by these Rules;
(2)   the fact that the person seeking entry to the United Kingdom is currently
the subject of a deportation order;
(3)   failure by the person seeking entry to the United Kingdom to produce to
the Immigration Officer a valid national passport or other document
satisfactorily establishing his identity and nationality;
(4)   failure to satisfy the Immigration Officer, in the case of a person arriving
in the United Kingdom or seeking entry through the Channel Tunnel
with the intention of entering any other part of the common travel area,
that he is acceptable to the immigration authorities there;
(5)   failure, in the case of a visa national, to produce to the Immigration
Officer a passport or other identity document endorsed with a valid and
current United Kingdom entry clearance issued for the purpose for which
entry is sought;
(6)   where the Secretary of State has personally directed that the exclusion of
a person from the United Kingdom is conducive to the public good;
(7)   save in relation to a person settled in the United Kingdom or where the
Immigration Officer is satisfied that there are strong compassionate
reasons justifying admission, confirmation from the Medical Inspector
that, for medical reasons, it is undesirable to admit a person seeking
leave to enter the United Kingdom.

Grounds on which entry clearance or leave to enter the United Kingdom should
normally be refused
(8)   failure by a person arriving in the United Kingdom to furnish the
Immigration Officer with such information as may be required for the
purpose of deciding whether he requires leave to enter and, if so, whether
and on what terms leave should be given;
[(8A) where the person seeking leave is outside the United Kingdom, failure by
him to supply any information, documents, copy documents or medical
report requested by an Immigration Officer;]
(9)   failure by a person seeking leave to enter as a returning resident to satisfy
the Immigration Officer that he meets the requirements of paragraph 18
of these Rules [or that he seeks leave to enter for the same purpose as
that for which his earlier leave was granted];
(10) production by the person seeking leave to enter the United Kingdom of a
national passport or travel document issued by a territorial entity or
authority which is not recognised by Her Majesty's Government as a
state or is not dealt with as a government by them, or which does not
accept valid United Kingdom passports for the purpose of its own
immigration control; or a passport or travel document which does not
comply with international passport practice;
(11) failure to observe the time limit or conditions attached to any grant of
leave to enter or remain in the United Kingdom;
(12) the obtaining of a previous leave to enter or remain by deception;

(13) failure, except by a person eligible for admission to the United Kingdom for settlement or a spouse eligible for admission under paragraph 282, to satisfy the Immigration Officer that he will be admitted to another country after a stay in the United Kingdom;

(14) refusal by a sponsor of a person seeking leave to enter the United Kingdom to give, if requested to do so, an undertaking in writing to be responsible for that person's maintenance and accommodation for the period of any leave granted;

(15) whether or not to the holder's knowledge, the making of false representations or the failure to disclose any material fact for the purpose of obtaining a work permit;

(16) failure, in the case of a child under the age of 18 years seeking leave to enter the United Kingdom otherwise than in conjunction with an application made by his parent(s) or legal guardian, to provide the Immigration Officer, if required to do so, with written consent to the application from his parent(s) or legal guardian; save that the requirement as to written consent does not apply in the case of a child seeking admission to the United Kingdom as an asylum seeker;

(17) save in relation to a person settled in the United Kingdom, refusal to undergo a medical examination when required to do so by the Immigration Officer;

(18) save where the Immigration Officer is satisfied that admission would be justified for strong compassionate reasons, conviction in any country including the United Kingdom of an offence which, if committed in the United Kingdom, is punishable with imprisonment for a term of 12 months or any greater punishment or, if committed outside the United Kingdom, would be so punishable if the conduct constituting the offence had occurred in the United Kingdom;

(19) where from information available to the Immigration Officer, it seems right to refuse leave to enter on the ground that exclusion from the United Kingdom is conducive to the public good; if, for example, in the light of the character, conduct or associations of the person seeking leave to enter it is undesirable to give him leave to enter.

Note   Sub-paragraph 8A inserted by HC 704.

Refusal of leave to enter in relation to a person in possession of an entry clearance

321   A person seeking leave to enter the United Kingdom who holds an entry clearance which was duly issued to him and is still current may be refused leave to enter only where the Immigration Officer is satisfied that:

(i) whether or not to the holder's knowledge, false representations were employed or material facts were not disclosed, either in writing or orally, for the purpose of obtaining the entry clearance; or

(ii) a change of circumstances since it was issued has removed the basis of the holder's claim to admission, except where the change of circumstances amounts solely to the person becoming over age for entry in one of the categories contained in paragraphs 296–316 of these Rules since the issue of the entry clearance; or

(iii) refusal is justified on grounds of restricted returnability; on medical   grounds; on grounds of criminal record; because the person seeking leave to enter is the subject of a deportation order or because exclusion would be conducive to the public good.

[Grounds on which leave to enter or remain which is in force is to be cancelled at port or while the holder is outside the United Kingdom

321A The following grounds for the cancellation of a person's leave to enter or remain which is in force on his arrival in, or whilst he is outside, the United Kingdom apply:

(1) there has been such a change in the circumstances of that person's case, since the leave was given, that it should be cancelled; or

(2) the leave was obtained as a result of false information given by that person or by that person's failure to disclose material facts; or

(3) save in relation to a person settled in the United Kingdom or where the Immigration Officer or the Secretary of State is satisfied that there are strong compassionate reasons justifying admission, where it is apparent that, for medical reasons, it is undesirable to admit that person to the United Kingdom; or

(4) where the Secretary of State has personally directed that the exclusion of that person from the United Kingdom is conducive to the public good; or

(5) where from information available to the Immigration officer or the Secretary of State, it seems right to cancel leave on the ground that exclusion from the United Kingdom is conducive to public good; if, for example, in the light of the character, conduct or associations of that person it is undesirable for him to have leave to enter the United Kingdom; or

(6) where that person is outside the United Kingdom, failure by that person to supply any information, documents, copy documents or medical report requested by an Immigration Officer or the Secretary of State.]

Note   Para 321A inserted by HC 704.

Refusal of variation of leave to enter or remain or curtailment of leave

322   In addition to the grounds for refusal of extension of stay set out in Parts 2–8 of these Rules, the following provisions apply in relation to the refusal of an application for variation of leave to enter or remain or, where appropriate, the curtailment of leave:

Grounds on which an application to vary leave to enter or remain in the United Kingdom is to be refused

(1) the fact that variation of leave to enter or remain is being sought for a purpose not covered by these Rules.

Grounds on which an application to vary leave to enter or remain in the United Kingdom should normally be refused

(2) the making of false representations or the failure to disclose any material fact for the purpose of obtaining leave to enter or a previous variation of leave;

(3) failure to comply with any conditions attached to the grant of leave to enter or remain;

(4) failure by the person concerned to maintain or accommodate himself and any dependants without recourse to public funds;

(5) the undesirability of permitting the person concerned to remain in the United Kingdom in the light of his character, conduct or associations or the fact that he represents a threat to national security;

(6) refusal by a sponsor of the person concerned to give, if requested to do so, an undertaking in writing to be responsible for his maintenance and accommodation in the United Kingdom or failure to honour such an undertaking once given;

(7) failure by the person concerned to honour any declaration or undertaking given orally or in writing as to the intended duration and/or purpose of his stay;

    (8) failure, except by a person who qualifies for settlement in the United Kingdom or by the spouse of a person settled in the United Kingdom, to satisfy the Secretary of State that he will be returnable to another country if allowed to remain in the United Kingdom for a further period;

    (9) failure by an applicant to produce within a reasonable time documents or other evidence required by the Secretary of State to establish his claim to remain under these Rules;

  (10) failure, without providing a reasonable explanation, to comply with a request made on behalf of the Secretary of State to attend for interview;

  (11) failure, in the case of a child under the age of 18 years seeking a variation of his leave to enter or remain in the United Kingdom otherwise than in conjunction with an application by his parent(s) or legal guardian, to provide the Secretary of State, if required to do so, with written consent to the application from his parent(s) or legal guardian; save that the requirement as to written consent does not apply in the case of a child who has been admitted to the United Kingdom as an asylum seeker.

Grounds on which leave to enter or remain may be curtailed

[323   A person's leave to enter or remain may be curtailed:

    (i)   on any of the grounds set out in paragraph 322 (2)–(5) above; or

   (ii)   if he ceases to meet the requirements of the Rules under which his leave to enter or remain was granted; or

  (iii) if he is the dependant, or is seeking leave to remain as the dependant, of an asylum applicant whose claim has been refused and whose leave has been curtailed under section 7 of the 1993 Act, and he does not qualify for leave to remain in his own right.]

Crew members

324   A person who has been given leave to enter to join a ship, aircraft, hovercraft, hydrofoil or international train service as a member of its crew, or a crew member who has been given leave to enter for hospital treatment, repatriation or transfer to another ship, aircraft, hovercraft, hydrofoil or international train service in the United Kingdom, is to be refused leave to remain unless an extension of stay is necessary to fulfil the purpose for which he was given leave to enter or unless he meets the requirements for an extension of stay as a spouse in paragraph 284.

PART 10:   REGISTRATION WITH THE POLICE

[324A   For the purposes of paragraphs 325 and 326, a 'relevant foreign national' is a person aged 16 years or over who is:

    (i)   a national or citizen of a country or territory listed in Appendix 2 to these Rules;

   (ii)   a stateless person; or

  (iii) a person holding a non-national travel document.

325   (1) A condition requiring registration with the police should normally be imposed on any relevant foreign national who is given limited leave to enter the United Kingdom:

    (i)   for employment for longer than 6 months unless he has been admitted for permit free employment as:

        (*a*)   a seasonal worker at an agricultural camp;

        (*b*)   a private servant in a diplomatic household; or

        (*c*)   a minister of religion, missionary or member of a religious order; or

   (ii)   for longer than 6 months under the following categories of these Rules:

(*a*)   students;
(*b*)   'au pair';
(*c*)   businessmen and self-employed persons;
(*d*)   investors or persons of independent means;
(*e*)   creative artists; or
(iii)   as the spouse or child of a person required to register with the police.

(2)   Such a condition should also be imposed on any foreign national aged 16 years or over who is given limited leave to enter the United Kingdom where, exceptionally, the Immigration Officer considers it necessary to ensure that he complies with the terms of the leave.

326   A condition requiring registration with the police should also normally be imposed when a relevant foreign national on whom a registration requirement was not imposed on arrival is granted an extension of stay which has the effect of allowing him to remain in the United Kingdom for longer than 6 months, reckoned from the date of his arrival, save where the extension of stay was granted:

(i)   as a private servant in a diplomatic household;
(ii)   as a minister of religion, missionary or member of a religious order;
(iii)   on the basis of marriage to a person settled in the United Kingdom; or
(iv)   following the grant of asylum.]

PART 11:   ASYLUM

Definition of asylum applicant

327   Under these Rules an asylum applicant is a person who claims that it would be contrary to the United Kingdom's obligations under the United Nations Convention and Protocol relating to the Status of Refugees for him to be removed from or required to leave the United Kingdom. All such cases are referred to in these Rules as asylum applications.

Applications for asylum

328   All asylum applications will be determined by the Secretary of State in accordance with the United Kingdom's obligations under the United Nations Convention and Protocol relating to the Status of Refugees. Every asylum application made by a person at a port or airport in the United Kingdom will be referred by the Immigration Officer for determination by the Secretary of State in accordance with these Rules.

[329   Until an asylum application has been determined by the Secretary of State or the Secretary of State has issued a certificate under section 11 or section 12 of the Immigration and Asylum Act 1999, no action will be taken to require the departure of the asylum applicant or his dependants from the United Kingdom.]

Note   Amended by CM 4851.

330   If the Secretary of State decides to grant asylum and the person has not yet been given leave to enter, the Immigration Officer will grant limited leave to enter.

331   [If a person seeking leave to enter is refused asylum, the Immigration Officer will consider whether or not he is in a position to decide to give or refuse leave to enter without interviewing the person further. If the Immigration Officer decides that a further interview is not required he may serve the notice giving or refusing leave to enter by post. If the Immigration Officer decides that a further interview is required, he will then resume his examination to determine whether or not to grant the person] leave to enter without interviewing the person further. If the Immigration Officer

decides that a further interview is not required he may serve the notice giving or refusing leave to enter by post. If the Immigration Officer decides that a further interview is required, he will then resume his examination to determine whether or not to grant the person leave to enter under any other provision of these Rules. If the person fails at any time to comply with a requirement to report to an Immigration Officer for examination, the Immigration Officer may direct that the person's examination shall be treated as concluded at that time. The Immigration Officer will then consider any outstanding applications for entry on the basis of any evidence before him.

Note   Paragraph 331 substituted by CM 3365. Words in square brackets in para 331 substituted by HC 704.

332   If a person who has been refused leave to enter applies for asylum and that application is refused, leave to enter will again be refused unless the applicant qualifies for admission under any other provision of these Rules.

333   . . .

Note   Paragraph 333 is deleted by CM 4851.

Grant of asylum

334   An asylum applicant will be granted asylum in the United Kingdom if the Secretary of State is satisfied that:

(i)   he is in the United Kingdom or has arrived at a port of entry in the United Kingdom; and

(ii)   he is a refugee, as defined by the Convention and Protocol; and

(iii)   refusing his application would result in his being required to go (whether immediately or after the time limited by an existing leave to enter or remain) in breach of the Convention and Protocol, to a country in which his life or freedom would be threatened on account of his race, religion, nationality, political opinion or membership of a particular social group.

335   If the Secretary of State decides to grant asylum to a person who has been given leave to enter (whether or not the leave has expired) or to a person who has entered without leave, the Secretary of State will vary the existing leave or grant limited leave to remain.

Refusal of asylum

336   An application which does not meet the criteria set out in paragraph 334 will be refused.

337   . . .

338   When a person in the United Kingdom is notified that asylum has been refused he may, if he is liable to removal as an illegal entrant [, removal under section 10 of the IAA 1999] or to deportation, at the same time be notified of removal directions, served with a notice of intention to make a deportation order, or served with a deportation order, as appropriate.

Note   Words in square brackets inserted by CM 4851.

339   . . .

Note   Paragraph 339 is deleted by CM 4851.

Consideration of cases

[340 A failure, without reasonable explanation, to make a prompt and full disclosure of material facts, either orally or in writing, or otherwise to assist the Secretary of State in establishing the facts of the case may lead to refusal of an asylum application. This includes failure to comply with a notice issued by the Secretary of State or an Immigration Officer requiring the applicant to report to a designated place to be fingerprinted, or failure to complete an asylum questionnaire, or failure to comply with a request to attend an interview concerning the application, or failure to comply with a requirement to report to an Immigration Officer for examination.]

[341 In determining an asylum application the Secretary of State will have regard to matters which may damage an asylum applicant's credibility. Among such matters are:

(i) that the applicant has failed without reasonable explanation to apply forthwith upon arrival in the United Kingdom, unless the application is founded on events which have taken place since his arrival in the United Kingdom;

(ii) that the application is made after the applicant has been refused leave to enter under the 1971 Act, or has been recommended for deportation by a court empowered by the 1971 Act to do so, or has been notified of the Secretary of State's decision to make a deportation order against him or has been notified of his liability for removal;

(iii) that the application has adduced manifestly false evidence in support of his application, or has otherwise made false representations, either orally or in writing;

(iv) that on his arrival in the United Kingdom the applicant was required to produce a passport in accordance with paragraph 11(i) and either:
   (*a*) failed to do so without providing a reasonable explanation; or
   (*b*) produced a passport which was not in fact valid, and failed to inform the immigration officer of that fact;

(v) that the applicant has otherwise, without reasonable explanation, destroyed, damaged or disposed of any passport, other document, or ticket relevant to his claim;

(vi) that the applicant has undertaken any activities in the United Kingdom before or after lodging his application which are inconsistent with his previous beliefs and behaviour and calculated to create or substantially enhance his claim to refugee status;

(vii) that the applicant has lodged concurrent applications for asylum in the United Kingdom or in another country.

If the Secretary of State concludes for these or any other reasons that an asylum applicant's account is not credible, the application will be refused.]

342 The actions of anyone acting as an agent of the asylum applicant may also be taken into account in regard to the matters set out in paragraphs 340 and 341.

343 If there is a part of the country from which the applicant claims to be a refugee in which he would not have a well-founded fear of persecution, and to which it would be reasonable to expect him to go, the application may be refused.

344 Cases will normally be considered on an individual basis but if an applicant is part of a group whose claims are clearly not related to the criteria for refugee status in the Convention and Protocol he may be refused without examination of his individual claim. However, the Secretary of State will have regard to any evidence produced by an individual to show that his claim should be distinguished from those of the rest of the group.

Third country cases

[345 (1) In a case where the Secretary of State is satisfied that the conditions set out in [either section 11(2) or section 12(7) of the IAA 1999] are fulfilled, he will normally refuse the asylum application and issue a certificate under [section 11 or section 12 of the IAA 1999 (as the case may be)] without substantive consideration of the applicant's claim to refugee status. The conditions are:

(i)   that the applicant is not a national or citizen of the country or territory to which he is to be sent;

(ii)   that the applicant's life and liberty would not be threatened in that country by reason of his race, religion, nationality, membership of a particular social group, or political opinion; and

(iii)   that the government of that country or territory would not send him to another country or territory otherwise than in accordance with the Convention.

(2) The Secretary of State shall not remove an asylum applicant without substantive consideration of his claim unless:

(i)   the asylum applicant has not arrived in the United Kingdom directly from the country in which he claims to fear persecution and has had an opportunity at the border or within the third country or territory to make contact with the authorities of that third country or territory in order to seek their protection; or

(ii)   there is other clear evidence of his admissibility to a third country or territory.

Provided that he is satisfied that a case meets these criteria, the Secretary of State is under no obligation to consult the authorities of the third country or territory before the removal of an asylum applicant to that country or territory.]

Note   Amendment made by CM 4851.

Previously rejected applications

[346   Where an asylum applicant has previously been refused asylum during his stay in the United Kingdom, the Secretary of State will determine whether any further representations should be treated as a fresh application for asylum. The Secretary of State will treat representations as a fresh application for asylum if the claim advanced in the representations is sufficiently different from the earlier claim that there is a realistic prospect that the conditions set out in paragraph 334 will be satisfied. In considering whether to treat the representations as a fresh claim, the Secretary of State will disregard any material which:

(i)   is not significant; or

(ii)   is not credible; or

(iii)   was available to the applicant at the time when the previous application was refused or when any appeal was determined.]

347   . . .

Rights of appeal

348   . . .

Note   Paragraph 348 is deleted by CM 4851.

Dependants

[349   A husband or wife or minor children accompanying a principal applicant may be included in an application for asylum. If the principal applicant is granted asylum any such dependants will be granted leave to enter or remain for the same duration. The case of any dependant who claims asylum in his own right and who would otherwise be refused leave to enter or remain will be considered individually in accordance with paragraph 334 above. If the dependant has a claim in his own right, it should be made at the earliest opportunity. Any failure to do so will be taken into account and may damage credibility if no reasonable explanation for it is given. Where the principal applicant is refused asylum and the dependant has previously been refused asylum in his own right, the dependant may be removed forthwith, notwithstanding any outstanding right of appeal that may be available to the principal applicant. At the same time that asylum is refused the applicant may be notified of removal directions or served with a notice of the Secretary of State's intention to deport him, as appropriate.]

[In this paragraph and paragraphs 350–352, a child means a person who is under 18 years of age or who, in the absence of documentary evidence, appears to be under that age.]

Note   Amendment made by CM 4851.

Unaccompanied children

350   Unaccompanied children may also apply for asylum and, in view of their potential vulnerability, particular priority and care is to be given to the handling of their cases.

351   A person of any age may qualify for refugee status under the Convention and the criteria in paragraph 334 apply to all cases. However, account should be taken of the applicant's maturity and in assessing the claim of a child more weight should be given to objective indications of risk than to the child's state of mind and understanding of his situation. An asylum application made on behalf of a child should not be refused solely because the child is too young to understand his situation or to have formed a well-founded fear of persecution. Close attention should be given to the welfare of the child at all times.

352   A child will not be interviewed about the substance of his claim to refugee status if it is possible to obtain by written enquiries or from other sources sufficient information properly to determine the claim. When an interview is necessary it should be conducted in the presence of a parent, guardian, representative or another adult who for the time being takes responsibility for the child and is not an Immigration Officer, an officer of the Secretary of State or a police officer. The interviewer should have particular regard to the possibility that a child will feel inhibited or alarmed. The child should be allowed to express himself in his own way and at his own speed. If he appears tired or distressed, the interview should be stopped.

[**352A**   The requirements to be met by a person seeking leave to enter or remain in the United Kingdom as the spouse of a refugee are that:

(i)   the applicant is married to a person granted asylum in the United Kingdom; and

(ii)   the marriage did not take place after the person granted asylum had left the country of his former habitual residence in order to seek asylum; and

(iii) the applicant would not be excluded from protection by virtue of article 1F of the United Nations Convention and Protocol relating to the Status of Refugees if he were to seek asylum in his own right; and

(iv) if seeking leave to enter, the applicant holds a valid United Kingdom entry clearance for entry in this capacity.

352B   Limited leave to enter the United Kingdom as the spouse of a refugee may be granted provided a valid United Kingdom entry clearance for entry in this capacity is produced to the Immigration Officer on arrival. Limited leave to remain in the United Kingdom as the spouse of a refugee may be granted provided the Secretary of State is satisfied that each of the requirements paragraph 352A (i)-(iii) are met.

352C   Limited leave to enter the United Kingdom as the spouse of a refugee is to be refused if a valid United Kingdom entry clearance for entry in this capacity is not produced to the Immigration Officer on arrival. Limited leave to remain as the spouse of a refugee is to be refused if the Secretary of State is not satisfied that each of the requirements of paragraph 352A (i)-(iii) are met.

352D   The requirements to be met by a person seeking leave to enter or remain in the United Kingdom as the child of a refugee are that the applicant:

(i)   is the child of a parent who has been granted asylum in the United Kingdom; and

(ii)   is under the age of 18; and

(iii)   is not leading an independent life, is unmarried, and has not formed an independent family unit; and

(iv)   was part of the family unit of the person granted asylum at the time that the person granted asylum left the country of his habitual residence in order to seek asylum; and

(v)   would not be excluded from protection by virtue of article 1F of the United Nations Convention and Protocol relating to the Status of Refugees if he were to seek asylum in his own right; and

(vi)   if seeking leave to enter, holds a valid United Kingdom entry clearance for entry in this capacity.

352E   Limited leave to enter the United Kingdom as the child of a refugee may be granted provided a valid United Kingdom entry clearance for entry in this capacity is produced to the Immigration Officer on arrival. Limited leave to remain in the United Kingdom as a child of a refugee may be granted provided the Secretary of State is satisfied that each of the requirements of paragraph 352D (i)-(v) are met.

352F   Limited leave to enter the United Kingdom as the child of a refugee is to be refused if a valid United Kingdom entry clearance for entry in this capacity is not produced to the Immigration Officer on arrival. Limited leave to remain as the child of a refugee is to be refused if the Secretary of State is not satisfied that each of the requirements of paragraph 352D (i)-(v) are met.

Note   Paragraphs 352A-352F inserted by Cm 4851.

PART 12:   RIGHTS OF APPEAL

353–361   [. . .]

Note   Paragraphs 353 to 361 deleted by CM 4851.

PART 13:   DEPORTATION [AND ADMINISTRATIVE REMOVAL UNDER SECTION 10 OF THE 1999 ACT]

A DEPORTATION ORDER

362   A deportation order requires the subject to leave the United Kingdom and authorises his detention until he is removed. It also prohibits him from re-entering the country for as long as it is in force and invalidates any leave to enter or remain in the United Kingdom given him before the order was made or while it is in force.

[**363**   The circumstances in which a person is liable to deportation include:

(i)   where the Secretary of State deems the person's deportation to be conducive the public good;

(ii) where the person is the spouse or child under 18 of a person ordered to be deported; and

(iii) where a court recommends deportation in the case of a person over the age of 17 who has been convicted of an offence punishable with imprisonment.]

[363A   Prior to 2 October 2000, a person would have been liable to deportation in certain circumstances in which he is now liable to administrative removal. These circumstances are listed in paragraph 394B below. However, such a person remains liable to deportation, rather than administrative removal where:

(i) a decision to make a deportation order against him was taken before 2 October 2000; or

(ii) the person has made a valid application under the Immigration (Regularisation Period for Overstayers) Regulations 2000.]

364   [Subject to paragraph 380] in considering whether deportation is the right course on the merits, the public interest will be balanced against any compassionate circumstances of the case. While each case will be considered in the light of the particular circumstances, the aim is an exercise of the power of deportation which is consistent and fair as between one person and another, although one case will rarely be identical with another in all material respects.

[In the cases detailed in paragraph 363A,] deportation will normally be the proper course where a person has failed to comply with or has contravened a condition or has remained without authority. Before a decision to deport is reached the Secretary of State will take into account all relevant factors known to him including:

(i)   age;

(ii)   length of residence in the United Kingdom;

(iii)   strength of connections with the United Kingdom;

(iv)   personal history, including character, conduct and employment record;

(v)   domestic circumstances;

(vi)   previous criminal record and the nature of any offence of which the person has been convicted;

(vii)   compassionate circumstances;

(viii) any representations received on the person's behalf.

Notes   Words in square brackets in the title to Part 13 inserted by CM 4851.
Paragraph 363 substituted and paragraph 363A and words in square brackets in paragraph 364 inserted by CM 4851.

Deportation of family members

[365   Section 5 of the Immigration Act 1971 gives the Secretary of State power in certain circumstances to make a deportation order against the spouse or child of a person against whom a deportation order has been made. The Secretary of State will not normally decide to deport the spouse of a deportee where:

(i)   he has qualified for settlement in his own right; or

(ii)   he has been living apart from the deportee.]

[366   The Secretary of State will not normally decide to deport the child of a deportee where:

(i)   he and his mother or father are living apart from the deportee; or

(ii)   he has left home and established himself on an independent basis; or

(iii)   he married before deportation came into prospect.]

[367   In considering whether to require a spouse or child to leave with the deportee, the Secretary of State will take account of the factors listed in paragraph 364 as well as the following:

    (i)   the ability of the spouse to maintain herself and any children in the United Kingdom, or to be maintained by relatives or friends without charge to public funds, not merely for a short period but for the foreseeable future; and

    (ii) in the case of a child of school age, the effect of removal on his education; and

    (iii) the practicability of any plans for a child's care and maintenance in this country if one or both of his parents were deported; and

    (iv) any representations made by or on behalf of the spouse or child.]

368 Where the Secretary of State decides that it would be appropriate to deport a member of a family as such, the decision, and the right of appeal, will be notified and it will at the same time be explained that it is open to the member of the family to leave the country voluntarily if he does not wish to appeal or if he appeals and his appeal is dismissed.

369–374 [. . .].

Note   Paragraph 369 to 374 deleted by CM 4851.

Hearing of appeals

376 . . .

377 [. . .]

[**378** A deportation order may not be made while it is still open to the person to appeal against the Secretary of State's decision, or while an appeal is pending. There is no appeal within the immigration appeal system against the making of a deportation order on the recommendation of a court; but there is a right of appeal to a higher court against the recommendation itself. A deportation order may not be made while it is still open to the person to appeal against the relevant conviction, sentence or recommendation, or while such an appeal is pending.]

Note   Paragraph 377 deleted and paragraph 378 substituted by CM 4851.

Persons who have claimed asylum

379–379A [. . .]:

Note   Paragraphs 379 and 379A deleted by CM 4851.

380 A deportation order will not be made against any person if his removal in pursuance of the order would be contrary to the United Kingdom's obligations under the Convention and Protocol relating to the Status of Refugees [or the Human Rights Convention].

Note   Words in square brackets inserted by CM 4851.

Procedure

381 When a decision to make a deportation order has been taken (otherwise than on the recommendation of a court) a notice will be given to the person concerned informing him of the decision and of his right of appeal [. . .].

382 [Following the issue of such a notice the Secretary of State may authorise detention or make an order restricting a person as to residence, employment or occupation and requiring him to report to the police, pending the making of a deportation order.]

383 [. . .].

384   If a notice of appeal is given within the period allowed, a summary of the facts of the case on the basis of which the decision was taken will be sent to the [appropriate] appellate authorities, who will notify the appellant of the arrangements for the appeal to be heard.

Notes   Words in paragraph 381 deleted, paragraph 382 substituted, paragraph 383 deleted and words in square brackets in paragraph 384 inserted by CM 4851.

Arrangements for removal

385   A person against whom a deportation order has been made will normally be removed from the United Kingdom. The power is to be exercised so as to secure the person's return to the country of which he is a national, or which has most recently provided him with a travel document, unless he can show that another country will receive him. In considering any departure from the normal arrangements, regard will be had to the public interest generally, and to any additional expense that may fall on public funds.

386   The person will not be removed as the subject of a deportation order while an appeal may be brought against the removal directions or such an appeal is pending.

Supervised departure

387   [. . .].

Note   Paragraph 387 deleted by CM 4851.

Returned deportees

388   Where a person returns to this country when a deportation order is in force against him, he may be deported under the original order. The Secretary of State will consider every such case in the light of all the relevant circumstances before deciding whether to enforce the order.

Returned family members

389   Persons deported in the circumstances set out in paragraph 365–368 above (deportation of family members) may be able to seek re-admission to the United Kingdom under the Immigration Rules where:

(i)   a child reaches 18 (when he ceases to be subject to the deportation order); or

(ii)   in the case of a wife, the marriage comes to an end.

Revocation of deportation order

390   An application for revocation of a deportation order will be considered in the light of all the circumstances including the following:

(i)   the grounds on which the order was made;

(ii)   any representations made in support of revocation;

(iii)   the interests of the community, including the maintenance of an effective immigration control;

(iv)   the interests of the applicant, including any compassionate circumstances.

391   In the case of an applicant with a serious criminal record continued exclusion for a long term of years will normally be the proper course. In other cases revocation of the order will not normally be authorised unless the situation has been materially altered, either by a change of circumstances since the order was made, or by fresh information coming to light which was not before the court which made the recommendation or the appellate authorities or the Secretary of State. The passage of time since the person was deported may also in itself amount to such a change of circumstances as to warrant revocation of the order. However, save in the most exceptional circumstances, the Secretary of State will not revoke the order unless the person has been absent from the United Kingdom for a period of at least 3 years since it was made.

392   Revocation of a deportation order does not entitle the person concerned to re-enter the United Kingdom; it renders him eligible to apply for admission under the Immigration Rules. Application for revocation of the order may be made to the Entry Clearance Officer or direct to the Home Office.

Rights of appeal in relation to a decision not to revoke a deportation order

393–394   [. . .].

395   [There may be a right of appeal against refusal to revoke a deportation order.] Where an appeal does lie the right of appeal will be notified at the same time as the decision to refuse to revoke the order.

[Administrative Removal

395A   A person is now liable to administrative removal in certain circumstances in which he would, prior to 2 October 2000, have been liable to deportation.

395B   These circumstances are set out in section 10 of the 1999 Act. They are:

(i)   failure to comply with a condition attached to his leave to enter or remain, or remaining beyond the time limited by the leave;
(ii)   where the person has obtained leave to remain by deception; and
(iii)   where the person is the spouse or child under 18 of someone in respect of whom directions for removal have been given under section 10.

395C   Before directions for removal under section 10 are given, regard will be had to any compassionate circumstances of the case, taking into account all the relevant factors known to the Secretary of State, as listed in paragraph 364. In the case of family members, the factors listed in paragraphs 365—368 will also be taken into account.

395D   No one shall be removed under section 10 if his removal' would be contrary to the United Kingdom's obligations under the Convention and Protocol relating to the Status of Refugees or under the Human Rights Convention.

Procedure

395E   When directions for a person's removal under section 10 have been given, a notice will be given to the person concerned informing him of the decision.

395F   Following the issue of such a notice an Immigration Officer may authorise detention or make an order restricting a person as to residence, employment or occupation and requiring him to report to the police, pending the removal.]

Note   Paragraphs 393 and 394 deleted, words in square brackets in paragraph 395 inserted and paragraphs 395A to 395F inserted by CM 4851.

[APPENDIX 1]

[**Visa requirements for the United Kingdom**

1 Subject to paragraph 2 below the following persons need a visa for the United Kingdom:

(*a*) Nationals or citizens of the following countries or territorial entities

Afghanistan	Ethiopia	Papua New Guinea
Albania	Fiji	Peru
Algeria	Gabon	Philippines
Angola	Georgia	Qatar
Armenia	Ghana	Romania
Azerbaijan	Guinea	Russia
Bahrain	Guinea-Bissau	Rwanda
Bangladesh	Guyana	Sao Tome e Principe
Belarus	Haiti	Saudi Arabia
Benin	India	Senegal
Bhutan	Indonesia	Sierra Leone
Bosnia-Herzegovina	Iran	[SlovakRepublic]
Bulgaria	Iraq	Somalia
Burkina Faso	Ivory Coast	Sri Lanka
Burma	Jordan	Sudan
Burundi	Kazakhstan	Surinam
Cambodia	Kenya	Syria
Cameroon	Kirgizstan	Taiwan
Cape Verde	Korea (North)	Tajikistan
Central African	Laos	Tanzania
Republic	Lebanon	Thailand
Chad	Liberia	Togo
China	Libya	Tunisia
[Colombia]	Macedonia	Turkey
Comoros	Madagascar	Turkmenistan
Congo	Maldives	Uganda
[Republic of Croatia]	Mali	Ukraine
Cuba	Mauritania	United Arab Emirates
[Democratic Republic	Moldova	Uzbekistan
of the Congo	Mongolia	Vietnam
(Zaire)]	Morocco	Yemen
Djibouti	Mozambique	The territories
Dominican Republic	Nepal	formerly comprising
Ecuador	Niger	the Socialist Federal
Egypt	Nigeria	Republic of Yugoslavia
Equatorial Guinea	Oman	excluding Croatia and
Eritrea	Pakistan	Slovenia

b) Persons who hold passports or travel documents issued by the former Soviet Union or by the former Socialist Federal Republic of Yugoslavia.

(*c*) Stateless persons.

(*d*) Persons who hold non-national documents.

2 The following persons do not need a visa for the United Kingdom:

(*a*) those who qualify for admission to the United Kingdom as returning residents in accordance with paragraph 18;

[(*b*) those who seek leave to enter the United Kingdom within the period of their earlier leave and for the same purpose as that for which leave was granted, unless it:
  (i)   was for a period of six months or less; or
  (ii) was extended by statutory instrument;]
(*c*) those holding refugee travel documents issued under the 1951 Convention relating to the Status of Refugees by countries which are signatories of the Council of Europe Agreement of 1959 on the Abolition of Visas for Refugees if coming on visits of 3 months or less.]

Note   Appendix amended by Statement of Changes in Immigration Rules with effect from 4 April 1996. Renamed Appendix 1 with effect from 11 May 1998 (Cmnd 3953). Republic of Croatia added by HC 22.
Readers are warned that in relation to this Appendix in particular amendments are made periodically and often without prior warning.

[APPENDIX 2

(Paragraph 324A)

Countries or territories whose nationals or citizens are relevant foreign nationals for the purposes of Part 10 of these rules (registration with the police)

Afghanistan	Iran	Peru
Algeria	Iraq	Qatar
Argentina	Israel	Russia
Armenia	Jordan	Saudi Arabia
Azerbaijan	Kazakhstan	Sudan
Bahrain	Kirgizstan	Syria
Belarus	Kuwait	Tajikistan
Bolivia	Lebanon	Tunisia
Bhutan	Libya	Turkey
Brazil	Moldova	Turkmenistan
China	Morocco	United Arab Emirates
Colombia	North Korea	Ukraine
Cuba	Oman	Uzbekistan
Egypt	Palestine	Yemen]
Georgia		

Note   Appendix 2 added with effect from 11 May 1998 by Cmnd 3953.

STATUTORY INSTRUMENTS

IMMIGRATION (CONTROL OF ENTRY THROUGH REPUBLIC OF IRELAND) ORDER 1972

1972 No 1610

Made - - - 23rd October 1972

Authority: Immigration Act 1971, s 9(2), (6)

1 This Order may be cited as the Immigration (Control of Entry through Republic of Ireland) Order 1972 and shall come into operation on 1st January 1973.

2 (1) In this Order—
"the Act" means the Immigration Act 1971; and
"visa national" means a person who, in accordance with the immigration rules, is required on entry into the United Kingdom to produce a passport or other document of identity endorsed with a United Kingdom visa and includes a stateless person.

(2) In this Order any reference to an Article shall be construed as a reference to an Article of this Order and any reference in an Article to a paragraph as a reference to a paragraph of that Article.

(3) The Interpretation Act 1889 shall apply to the interpretation of this Order as it applies to the interpretation of an Act of Parliament.

3 (1) This Article applies to—

(a) any person (other than a citizen of the Republic of Ireland) who arrives in the United Kingdom on an aircraft which began its flight in that Republic if he entered that Republic in the course of a journey to the United Kingdom which began outside the common travel area and was not given leave to land in that Republic in accordance with the law in force there;

(b) any person (other than a person to whom sub-paragraph (a) of this paragraph applies) who arrives in the United Kingdom on a local journey from the Republic of Ireland if he satisfies any of the following conditions, that is to say:—

(i) he is a visa national who has no valid visa for his entry into the United Kingdom;

(ii) he entered that Republic unlawfully from a place outside the common travel area;

(iii) he entered that Republic from a place in the United Kingdom and Islands after entering there unlawfully, [or, if he had a limited leave to enter or remain there, after the expiry of the leave, provided that in either case] he has not subsequently been given leave to enter or remain in the United Kingdom or any of the Islands; or

(iv) he is a person in respect of whom directions have been given by the Secretary of State for him not to be given entry to the United Kingdom on the ground that his exclusion is conducive to the public good.

(2) In relation only to persons to whom this Article applies, the Republic of Ireland shall be excluded from section 1(3) of the Act (provisions relating to persons travelling on local journeys in the common travel area).

NOTES

Amendment
Para (1): words in square brackets substituted by SI 1979/730, art 2.

4   (1) Subject to paragraph (2), this Article applies to [any person who does not have the right of abode in the United Kingdom under section 2 of the Act] and is not a citizen of the Republic of Ireland who enters the United Kingdom on a local journey from the Republic of Ireland after having entered that Republic—

(a)   on coming from a place outside the common travel area; or

(b)   after leaving the United Kingdom whilst having a limited leave to enter or remain there which has since expired.

(2)   This Article shall not apply to any person [who arrives in the United Kingdom with leave to enter or remain in the United Kingdom which is in force but which was given to him before his arrival or] who requires leave to enter the United Kingdom by virtue of Article 3 or section 9(4) of the Act.

(3)   A person to whom this Article applies by virtue only of paragraph (1)(a) shall, unless he is a visa national who has a visa containing the words "short visit", be subject to the restriction and to the condition set out in paragraph (4).

(4)   The restriction and the condition referred to in paragraph (3) are—

(a)   the period for which he may remain in the United Kingdom shall not be more than three months from the date on which he entered the United Kingdom; and

[(b)   unless he is a national of a state which is a member of the European Economic Community he shall not engage in any occupation for reward; and

(c)   unless he is a national of a state which is a member of the European Economic Community other than . . . [, Portugal or Spain] he shall not engage in any employment.]

(5)   In relation to a person who is a visa national and has a visa containing the words "short visit" the restriction and the conditions set out in paragraph (6) shall have effect instead of the provisions contained in paragraph (4).

(6)   The restriction and the conditions referred to in paragraph (5) are—

(a)   the period for which he may remain in the United Kingdom shall not be more than one month from the date on which he entered the United Kingdom;

(b)   he shall not engage in any occupation for reward or any employment; and

(c)   he shall, unless he is under the age of 16 years, be required to register with the police.

(7)   The preceding provisions of this Article shall have effect in relation to a person to whom this Article applies by virtue of sub-paragraph (b) of paragraph (1) (whether or not he is also a person to whom this Article applies by virtue of sub-paragraph (a) thereof) as they have effect in relation to a person to whom this Article applies by virtue only of the said sub-paragraph (a), but as if for the references in paragraphs (4) and (6) to three months and one month respectively there were substituted a reference to seven days.

NOTES

Amendment

Para (1): words in square brackets substituted by SI 1982/1028, art 2.

Para (2): words from "who arrives in" to "his arrival or" in square brackets inserted by SI 2000/1776, art 2.

Date in force: 30 July 2000: see SI 2000/1776, art 1.

Para (4): sub-paras (b), (c) substituted by SI 1980/1859, art 2; in para (c), word omitted revoked by SI 1987/2092, art 2, words in square brackets inserted by SI 1985/1854, art 2.

IMMIGRATION (EXEMPTION FROM CONTROL) ORDER 1972

1972 No 1613

Made - - - 24th October 1972

Authority: Immigration Act 1971, s 8(2)

1 This Order may be cited as the Immigration (Exemption from Control) Order 1972 and shall come into operation on 1st January 1973.

2 (1) In this Order—
"the Act" means the Immigration Act 1971; and
"consular employee" and "consular officer" have the meanings respectively assigned to them by Article 1 of the Vienna Convention on Consular Relations as set out in Schedule 1 to the Consular Relations Act 1968.

(2) In this Order any reference to an Article or to the Schedule shall be construed as a reference to an Article of this Order or, as the case may be, to the Schedule thereto and any reference in an Article to a paragraph as a reference to a paragraph of that Article.

(3) In this Order any reference to an enactment is a reference to it as amended, and includes a reference to it as applied, by or under any other enactment and any reference to an instrument made under or by virtue of any enactment is a reference to any such instrument for the time being in force.

(4) The Interpretation Act 1889 shall apply to the interpretation of this Order as it applies to the interpretation of an Act of Parliament.

3 (1) The following persons shall be exempt from any provision of the Act relating to those who are not [British citizens], that is to say:—

(a) any consular officer in the service of any of the states specified in the Schedule (being states with which consular conventions have been concluded by Her Majesty);
(b) any consular employee in such service as is mentioned in sub-paragraph (a) of this paragraph; and
(c) any member of the family of a person exempted under sub-paragraph (a) or (b) of this paragraph forming part of his household.

(2) In paragraph (1) and in Article 4 any reference to a consular employee shall be construed as a reference to such an employee who is in the full-time service of the state concerned and is not engaged in the United Kingdom in any private occupation for gain.

NOTES

Amendment
Para (1): words in square brackets substituted by SI 1982/1649, art 2.

4 The following persons shall be exempt from any provision of the Act relating to those who are not [British citizens] except any provision relating to deportation, that is to say:—

(a) unless the Secretary of State otherwise directs, any member of the government of a country or territory outside the United Kingdom and Islands who is visiting the United Kingdom on the business of that government;

(b)   any person entitled to immunity from legal process with respect to acts performed by him in his official capacity under any Order in Council made under section 3(1) of the Bretton Woods Agreements Act 1945 (which empowers Her Majesty by Order in Council to make provision relating to the immunities and privileges of the governors, executive directors, alternates, officers and employees of the International Monetary Fund and the International Bank for Reconstruction and Development);

(c)   any person entitled to immunity from legal process with respect to acts performed by him in his official capacity under any Order in Council made under section 3(1) of the International Finance Corporation Act 1955 (which empowers Her Majesty by Order in Council to make provision relating to the immunities and privileges of the governors, directors, alternates, officers and employees of the International Finance Corporation);

(d)   any person entitled to immunity from legal process with respect to acts performed by him in his official capacity under any Order in Council made under section 3(1) of the International Development Association Act 1960 (which empowers Her Majesty by Order in Council to make provision relating to the immunities and privileges of the governors, directors, alternates, officers and employees of the International Development Association);

(e)   any person (not being a person to whom section 8(3) of the Act applies) who is the representative or a member of the official staff of the representative of the government of a country to which section 1 of the Diplomatic Immunities (Conferences with Commonwealth Countries and Republic of Ireland) Act 1961 applies (which provides for representatives of certain Commonwealth countries and their staff attending conferences in the United Kingdom to be entitled to diplomatic immunity) so long as he is included in a list compiled and published in accordance with that section;

(f)   any person on whom any immunity from jurisdiction is conferred by any Order in Council made under section 12(1) of the Consular Relations Act 1968 (which empowers Her Majesty by Order in Council to confer on certain persons connected with the service of the government of Commonwealth countries or the Republic of Ireland all or any of the immunities and privileges which are conferred by or may be conferred under that Act on persons connected with consular posts);

(g)   any person (not being a person to whom section 8(3) of the Act applies) on whom any immunity from suit and legal process is conferred by any Order in Council made under section 1(2), 5(1) or 6(2) of the International Organisations Act 1968 (which empower Her Majesty by Order in Council to confer certain immunities and privileges on persons connected with certain international organisations and international tribunals and on representatives of foreign countries and their staffs attending certain conferences in the United Kingdom) except any such person as is mentioned in section 5(2)(c) to (e) of the said Act of 1968 [or by any Order in Council continuing to have effect by virtue of section 12(5) of the said Act of 1968];

(h)   any consular officer (not being an honorary consular officer) in the service of a state other than such a state as is mentioned in the Schedule;

(i)   any consular employee in such service as is mentioned in paragraph (h);

[(j)   any officer or servant of the Commonwealth Secretariat falling within paragraph 6 of the Schedule to the Commonwealth Secretariat Act 1966 (which confers certain immunities on those members of the staff of the Secretariat who are not entitled to full diplomatic immunity);

[(k)   any person to whom any immunity from suit and legal process is conferred by the European Communities (Immunities and Privileges of the North Atlantic Salmon Conservation Organisation) Order 1985 (which confers certain immunities and privileges on the representatives and officers of the North Atlantic Salmon Conservation Organisation);

[(l) any member of the Hong Kong Economic and Trade Office as defined by paragraph 8 of the Schedule to the Hong Kong Economic and Trade Office Act 1996,

[(m)

    (i) Any member or servant of the Independent International Commission on Decommissioning ("the Commission") established under an Agreement between the Government of the United Kingdom of Great Britain and Northern Ireland and the Government of the Republic of Ireland concluded on 26th August 1997,

    (ii) in sub-paragraph (i) above, "servant" includes any agent of or person carrying out work for or giving advice to the Commission,

(n) any member of the family of a person exempted under any of the preceding paragraphs forming part of his household]]]].

NOTES

Amendment

First words in square brackets substituted by SI 1982/1649, art 2; in para (g) words in square brackets inserted by SI 1977/693, art 3(a); paras (j), (k) substituted for para (j), as originally enacted, by SI 1977/693, art 3(b), paras (k), (l) substituted, for existing para (k), by SI 1985/1809, art 4, paras (l), (m) substituted, for existing para (l), by SI 1997/1402, art 3, paras (m), (n) prospectively substituted for existing para (m), by SI 1997/2207, art 3, as from 1st September 1997.

5 (1) Subject to the provisions of this Article the following persons who are not [British citizens] shall, on arrival in the United Kingdom, be exempt from the provisions of section 3(1)(a) of the Act (which requires persons who are not [British citizens] to obtain leave to enter the United Kingdom), that is to say—

(a) any citizen of the United Kingdom and Colonies who holds a passport issued to him in the United Kingdom and Islands and expressed to be a British Visitor's Passport;

(b) any Commonwealth citizen who is included in a passport issued in the United Kingdom by the Government of the United Kingdom or in one of the Islands by the Lieutenant-Governor thereof which is expressed to be a Collective Passport;

(c) any Commonwealth citizen or citizen of the Republic of Ireland returning to the United Kingdom from an excursion to France or Belgium [or the Netherlands] who holds a valid document of identity issued in accordance with arrangements approved by the United Kingdom Government and in a form authorised by the Secretary of State and enabling him to travel on such an excursion without a passport;

(d) any Commonwealth citizen who holds a British seaman's card or any citizen of the Republic of Ireland if (in either case) he was engaged as a member of the crew of a ship in a place within the common travel area and, on arrival in the United Kingdom, is, or is to be, discharged from his engagement;

(e) any person who, having left the United Kingdom after having been given a limited leave to enter, returns to the United Kingdom within the period for which he had leave as a member of the crew of an aircraft under an engagement requiring him to leave on that or another aircraft as a member of its crew within a period exceeding seven days.

(2) Paragraph (1) shall not apply so as to confer any exemption on any person against whom there is a deportation order in force or who has previously entered the United Kingdom unlawfully and has not subsequently been given leave to enter or remain in the United Kingdom and sub-paragraphs (d) and (e) of that paragraph shall not apply to a person who is required by an immigration officer to submit to examination in accordance with Schedule 2 to the Act.

(3)   In this Article any reference to a Commonwealth citizen shall be construed as including a reference to a British protected person and in paragraph (1)(d) "British seaman's card" means a valid card issued under any regulations in force under section 70 of the Merchant Shipping Act 1970 or any card having effect by virtue of the said regulations as a card so issued and "holder of a British seaman's card" has the same meaning as in the said regulations.

NOTES

Amendment
Para (1): first and second words in square brackets substituted by SI 1982/1649, art 2; final words in square brackets inserted by SI 1975/617, art 2.

[6]   [(1) For the purposes of section 1(1) of the British Nationality Act 1981 (which relates to acquisition of British citizenship by birth in the United Kingdom), a person to whom a child is born in the United Kingdom on or after 1st January 1983 is to be regarded (notwithstanding the preceding provisions of this Order) as settled in the United Kingdom at the time of the birth if—

(a)   he would fall to be so regarded but for his being at that time entitled to an exemption by virtue of this Order; and
(b)   immediately before he became entitled to that exemption he was settled in the United Kingdom; and
(c)   he was ordinarily resident in the United Kingdom from the time when he became entitled to that exemption to the time of the birth;

but this Article shall not apply if at the time of the birth the child's father or mother is a person on whom any immunity from jurisdiction is conferred by or under the Diplomatic Privileges Act 1964.

(2)   Expressions used in this Article shall be construed in accordance with section 50 of the British Nationality Act 1981.]

NOTES

Amendment
Inserted by SI 1982/1649, art 3.

SCHEDULE
States with which Consular Conventions have been concluded by Her Majesty

Articles 3, 4

Austria
Belgium
Bulgaria
[Czechoslovakia]
Denmark
France
[German Democratic Republic]
Greece
Federal Republic of Germany
Hungary
Italy
Japan
Mexico
[Mongolia]
Norway
Poland

Roumania
Sweden
Spain
Union of Soviet Socialist Republics
United States of America
Yugoslavia

NOTES

Amendment
Words in square brackets inserted by SI 1977/693, art 4.

IMMIGRATION (REVOCATION OF EMPLOYMENT RESTRICTIONS) ORDER 1972

1972 No 1647

Made - - - 1st November 1972

Authority: Immigration Act 1971, ss 3(3), 4(1)

1   This Order may be cited as the Immigration (Revocation of Employment Restrictions) Order 1972 and shall come into operation on 1st January 1973.

2   In this Order "the Order of 1953" means the Aliens Order 1953, as amended.

3   (1) Any employment restriction which, by virtue of section 34(3) of the Immigration Act 1971, applies to an alien who is a national of a state which is a member of the European Economic Community is hereby revoked.

(2)   In this Article "employment restriction" means—

    (a) any landing condition imposed under Article 5 of the Order of 1953 or any condition treated as a landing condition so imposed by virtue of Article 6 of that Order;

    (b) any restriction imposed by any Order made under Article 22 of the Order of 1953; or

    (c) any restriction imposed by virtue of paragraph 3 of Schedule 1 to the Order of 1953,

which prohibits an alien from or imposes restrictions on taking employment or engaging in any occupation in the United Kingdom.

IMMIGRATION (PARTICULARS OF PASSENGERS AND CREW) ORDER 1972

1972 No 1667

Made - - - 1st November 1972

Authority: Immigration Act 1971, Sch 2, para 27(2)

1   This Order may be cited as the Immigration (Particulars of Passengers and Crew) Order 1972 and shall come into operation on 1st January 1973.

2   The Interpretation Act 1889 shall apply to the interpretation of this Order as it applies to the interpretation of an Act of Parliament[; and in this Order the expressions "shuttle train", "through train" and "train manager" have the same meanings as in the Channel Tunnel (International Arrangements) Order 1993].

NOTES

Amendment
Words in square brackets inserted by SI 1993/1813, art 8, Sch 5, Part II, para 1(a).

3   (1) This Article applies to a ship which arrives in the United Kingdom from or after calling at a place outside the common travel area or an aircraft which arrives there from or after calling at a place outside the United Kingdom and Islands.

[(1A)   This article also applies to through trains and shuttle trains arriving in the United Kingdom.]

(2)   Subject to the following provisions of this Article, the captain of a ship or aircraft to which this Article applies shall—

  (a)   if so required by an immigration officer, furnish to that officer a list of the names and nationalities of all passengers arriving on the ship or aircraft, as the case may be; and

  (b)

    (i)   in the case of a ship, furnish to an immigration officer within 12 hours of the arrival of the ship, a return in the form set out in the Schedule to this Order containing particulars of all members of the crew arriving on the ship;

    (ii)   in the case of an aircraft, if so required by an immigration officer, furnish to that officer a list of the names, dates of birth and nationalities of all members of the crew arriving on the aircraft as soon as practicable after the arrival of the aircraft.

(3)   In relation to an aircraft which started its flight in the Republic of Ireland, paragraph (2) of this Article shall have effect as if—

  (a)   for the reference in sub-paragraph (a) to all passengers arriving on the aircraft there were substituted a reference to any passengers so arriving (not being citizens of that Republic) who entered that Republic in the course of a journey to the United Kingdom which began outside the common travel area and were not given leave to land in that Republic in accordance with the law in force there; and

  (b)   sub-paragraph (b)(ii) were omitted.

[(3A)   In relation to a train to which this article applies, paragraph (2) of this article shall have effect as if the reference to the captain of a ship or aircraft were a reference to the train manager, and—

(a) in the case of a shuttle train, as if sub-paragraph (a) were omitted;
(b) in the case of a through train, as if the reference in sub-paragraph (a) to the ship or aircraft were a reference to the train; and
(c) in each case, as if the reference in sub-paragraph (b)(ii) to an aircraft were a reference to a through train or as the case may be a shuttle train and references to the aircraft were references to the train.]

(4)   An immigration officer may by notice given to the captain of a ship or aircraft [or the train manager of a train] dispense with the requirements of paragraph (2)(b) of this Article either in respect of all members of the crew or in respect of such classes of persons as he may specify.

(5)   Any passenger on a ship or aircraft [or through train] shall furnish to the captain of the ship or aircraft [or the train manager of a train], as the case may be, any information required by him for the purpose of complying with the provisions of this Article.

NOTES

Amendment
Paras (1A), (3A): inserted by SI 1993/1813, art 8, Sch 5, Part II, para 1(b), (c).
Paras (4), (5): words in square brackets inserted by SI 1993/1813, art 8, Sch 5, Part II, para 1(d), (e).

[SCHEDULE
Particulars of Members of the Crew of a ship arriving in the United Kingdom]

NOTES

Amendment
Substituted by SI 1975 No 980, art 2, Schedule.

Article 3

[(This Form deals with the return required by an immigration officer. Due to its complexity, it has proved impossible to obtain a satisfactory reproduction on the database. It has therefore been omitted. Please see the original.)]

NOTES

Amendment
Substituted by SI 1975/980, art 2, Schedule.

IMMIGRATION (HOTEL RECORDS) ORDER 1972

1972 No 1689

Made - - - 7th November 1972

Authority: Immigration Act 1971, s 4(4)

1   Citation and commencement

This Order may be cited as the Immigration (Hotel Records) Order 1972 and shall come into operation on 1st January 1973.

2   Interpretation and transitional provisions

(1)   In this Order the following expressions have the meanings hereby respectively assigned to them, that is to say:—

"alien" has the same meaning as in the [British Nationality Act 1981];

"certificate of registration" means a certificate issued, or treated as issued, in pursuance of regulations from time to time in force under section 4(3) of the Immigration Act 1971;

"keeper", in relation to any premises, includes any person who for reward receives any other person to stay in the premises, whether on his own behalf or as manager or otherwise on behalf of any other person;

"nationality" includes the status of a stateless alien;

"stay" means lodge or sleep, for one night or more, in accommodation provided for reward.

(2)   The Interpretation Act 1889 shall apply to the interpretation of this Order as it applies to the interpretation of an Act of Parliament.

(3)   Any information required by this Order to be given by or to any person may be given by or to any other person acting on his behalf.

(4)   Anything done under, or for the purposes of, Article 19 of the Aliens Order 1953, as amended, shall have effect as if done under, or for the purposes of, this Order and, in particular, any information given or record maintained under or for the purposes of the said Article 19 shall be treated as if it had been given or maintained under, or for the purposes of, this Order.

NOTES

Amendment
Para (1): in definition "alien" words in square brackets substituted by SI 1982/1025, art 2.

3   Application of Order

This Order shall apply in the case of any hotel or other premises, whether furnished or unfurnished, where lodging or sleeping accommodation is provided for reward, not being premises certified by the chief officer of police of the area in which they are situate to be occupied for the purposes of a school, hospital, club or other institution or association.

4   Provision of information by visitors

(1)   Every person of or over the age of 16 years who stays at any premises to which this Order applies shall, on arriving at the premises, inform the keeper of the premises of his full name and nationality.

(2)   Every such person who is an alien shall also—

(a)   on arriving at the premises, inform the keeper of the premises of the number and place of issue of his passport, certificate of registration or other document establishing his identity and nationality; and

(b)   on or before his departure from the premises, inform the keeper of the premises of his next destination and, if it is known to him, his full address there.

5   Records to be maintained by keeper of premises

The keeper of any premises to which this Order applies shall—

(a)   require all persons of or over the age of 16 years who stay at the premises to comply with their obligations under the foregoing Article; and

(b) keep for a period of at least 12 months a record in writing of the date of arrival of every such person and of all information given to him by any such person in pursuance of the foregoing Article;

and every record shall at all times be open to inspection by any constable or by any person authorised by the Secretary of State.

IMMIGRATION (REGISTRATION WITH POLICE) REGULATIONS 1972

1972 No 1758

Made - - - 14th November 1972

Authority: Immigration Act 1971, s 4(3)

1 Citation and commencement

These Regulations may be cited as the Immigration (Registration with Police) Regulations 1972 and shall come into operation on 1st January 1973.

2 Interpretation and transitional provisions

(1) In these Regulations, except where the context otherwise requires, the following expressions have the meanings hereby respectively assigned to them, that is to say:—

"the Act" means the Immigration Act 1971;
"alien" has the same meaning as in the [British Nationality Act 1981];
"certificate of registration" means a certificate issued in pursuance of Regulation 10(1) to the alien concerned;
"local register" means a register kept in pursuance of Regulation 4;
"nationality" includes the status of a stateless alien;
"registration officer" and "appropriate registration officer" have the meanings assigned thereto by Regulation 4;
"a residence" means a person's private dwelling-house or other premises in which he is ordinarily resident but does not include any premises in which he is not ordinarily resident.

(2) In these Regulations any reference to a Regulation is a reference to a Regulation contained therein and any reference in a Regulation to a paragraph is a reference to a paragraph of that Regulation.

(3) Where an alien has failed to comply with any requirement made by a provision of these Regulations within a period specified in that provision he shall, without prejudice to any liability in respect of that failure under section 26(1)(f) of the Act, continue to be subject to that requirement notwithstanding the expiry of that period.

(4) The Interpretation Act 1889 shall apply to the interpretation of these Regulations as it applies to the interpretation of an Act of Parliament.

(5) Anything done, or having effect as if done, under or for the purposes of, any provision of the Aliens Order 1953, as amended, corresponding to a provision of these Regulations shall have effect as if done under, or for the purposes of, that corresponding provision and, in particular—

(a) any register kept under Article 13 of the said Order shall be treated as part of the local register kept under Regulation 4(2);

(b)   particulars furnished under Article 14(2) of the said Order shall be treated as furnished under Regulation 5, and

(c)   a certificate of registration supplied in pursuance of Article 13(3)(b) of the said Order shall be treated as a certificate of registration issued in pursuance of Regulation 10(1).

NOTES

Amendment
Para (1): in definition "alien" words in square brackets substituted by SI 1982/1024, reg 2.

3   Application of Regulations

These Regulations shall apply in the case of an alien who has a limited leave to enter or remain in the United Kingdom which is for the time being subject to a condition requiring him to register with the police and in the case of an alien who, by virtue of section 34 of the Act or paragraph 1 of Schedule 4 thereto, is treated as having such a limited leave.

4   Registration officers etc

(1)   For the purposes of these Regulations the chief officer of police for each police area shall be the registration officer for that area, and the police area shall be the registration area; and any reference to the appropriate registration officer is a reference—

(a)   in the case of an alien who has a residence in the United Kingdom, to the registration officer for the area in which that residence is situated;

(b)   in any other case, to the registration officer for the area in which, for the time being, he happens to be.

(2)   Every registration officer shall keep for his registration district a local register of aliens containing the particulars specified in the Schedule hereto:
    Provided that if a registration officer is not satisfied as to the nationality of an alien he may describe that alien in the local register as being of uncertain nationality or may describe him as having such nationality as appears to that officer to be the probable nationality of the alien.

(3)   Anything required or authorised by these Regulations to be done by or to a registration officer may be done by or to any constable or other person who is authorised by that officer to act for the purposes of these Regulations.

5   Duty to register etc

(1)   Within 7 days of these Regulations becoming applicable to him, an alien shall, subject to Regulation 6, attend at the office of the appropriate registration officer and furnish to that officer such information, documents and other particulars (including a recent photograph) relating to him as are required by that officer for the purposes of the local register kept by him or the issue of a certificate of registration to the alien.

(2)   Without prejudice to the generality of paragraph (1) an alien attending as aforesaid shall either—

(a)   produce to the appropriate registration officer a passport furnished with a photograph of himself or some other document satisfactorily establishing his identity and nationality; or

(b)   give to that officer a satisfactory explanation of the circumstances which prevent him from producing such a passport or document.

6 Exemption from registration in certain cases

(1) An alien shall not be required to attend and furnish particulars under Regulation 5 if—

    (a) immediately before these Regulations becoming applicable to him, he was ordinarily resident in the United Kingdom, and

    (b) he had previously, during that period of ordinary residence, attended and furnished particulars under Regulation 5.

(2) Without prejudice to paragraph (1) or the provisions of Regulation 2(5), an alien shall not be required to attend and furnish particulars under Regulation 5 if—

    (a) on the coming into operation of these Regulations they become applicable to him,

    (b) immediately before their coming into operation he was resident in the United Kingdom, and

    (c) he had previously, during that period of residence, attended and furnished particulars under Article 14(2) of the Aliens Order 1953, as amended.

7 Duty to notify changes of residence or address etc

(1) Every alien to whom these Regulations apply who has furnished particulars under Regulation 5 shall be under a duty to notify any changes therein in accordance with this Regulation.

(2) Such an alien who for the time being has a residence in the United Kingdom shall, if he adopts a new residence within the United Kingdom, report his arrival at his new residence to the appropriate registration officer before the expiration of the period of 7 days beginning with the day of his arrival.

(3) Such an alien who for the time being has a residence in the United Kingdom, if he is absent from his residence for a continuous period exceeding 2 months (without adopting a new residence)—

    (a) shall forthwith notify the appropriate registration officer of his address for the time being (whether within or outside the United Kingdom);

    (b) subject to paragraph (5), shall notify the appropriate registration officer of any subsequent change of address within the United Kingdom before the expiration of 8 days beginning with the day of his arrival at the new address; and

    (c) shall, on returning to his residence, notify the appropriate registration officer of his return (whether or not he has throughout the period of absence remained in the United Kingdom).

(4) Subject to paragraphs (5) and (6), such an alien who for the time being has not a residence in the United Kingdom shall, if he moves from one address to another (in the same or a different registration district), notify the appropriate registration officer of his arrival thereat before the expiration of 8 days beginning with the day of his arrival.

(5) Such an alien need not, under paragraph (3)(b) or (4), notify the appropriate registration officer of his address unless he remains or intends to remain at that address for a longer period than 7 days beginning with the day of his arrival thereat.

(6) If such an alien who for the time being has not a residence in the United Kingdom supplies to a registration officer the name and address of a referee, being a person resident within the United Kingdom who is willing to act, and in the opinion of that officer is a suitable person to act, as a referee under this paragraph, the officer shall include the referee's name and address among the entries relating to the alien in the local register kept by him; and in such case, the following provisions shall apply in substitution for those of paragraph (4), that is to say:—

(a) the alien shall keep the referee informed as to his address from time to time and shall notify the registration officer of any change in the referee's address; and

(b) the referee shall, if so required by the registration officer, furnish to that officer any information in his possession as to the alien which is required by that officer for the purposes of his duties under these Regulations.

8   Duty to notify other changes in particulars etc

Every alien to whom these Regulations apply who has furnished particulars under Regulation 5—

(a) shall notify the appropriate registration officer of any change in his case in the particulars specified as items 1, 3, 5, 6, 7 and 14 in the Schedule hereto, before the expiration of 8 days beginning with that on which the change, or the event occasioning the change, occurs; and

(b) if so required by the appropriate registration officer, shall furnish to that officer by such date as he may specify such information, documents and other particulars (including, where so required, a recent photograph) relating to him which are required by that officer for the purposes of his duties under these Regulations.

9   Provisions supplemental to Regulations 5, 7 and 8

(1) An alien required under Regulation 5(1) or 8(b) to furnish a photograph of himself shall furnish 2 copies of the same photograph; and, if he fails to furnish such copies, the registration officer may cause him to be photographed.

(2) An alien required under Regulation 7 or 8(a) to notify the appropriate registration officer of any change in his residence or address or of any change in his case in the particulars mentioned in Rule 8(a) shall either attend for the purpose at the office of the registration officer or send written notice of the change to that officer by post so, however, that where written notice is given the alien shall also send to the registration officer his certificate of registration.

(3) An alien required under Regulation 8(b) to furnish information, documents or other particulars to the appropriate registration officer (whether or not in connection with a change of which written notice has been given in pursuance of paragraph (2)) shall attend for the purpose at the office of the registration officer if that officer so requires.

[10   Issue of registration certificates]

[(1) Every registration officer shall issue certificates of registration to aliens of whom particulars are entered in the local register kept by him.

(2) A certificate of registration shall be independent of, and shall not be included in, any other document.

(3) An alien to whom a certificate of registration is issued shall pay to the registration officer concerned a fee of [£34] except where the requirement to register is a condition of leave granted to an alien after an absence from the United Kingdom of a period of less than one year immediately following an earlier period of leave which was subject to the same condition.]

NOTES

Amendment
Substituted by SI 1990/400, reg 2.
Para (3): sum in square brackets substituted by SI 1995/2928, reg 2.

11   Production of registration certificates

(1)   On the making of any alteration or addition to the local register, the registration officer may require the alien concerned to produce his certificate of registration in order that any necessary amendment may be made thereto.

(2)   Any immigration officer or constable may—

(a)   require an alien to whom these Regulations apply, forthwith, to either produce a certificate of registration or give to the officer or constable a satisfactory reason for his failure to produce it;

(b)   where the alien fails to produce a certificate of registration in pursuance of such a requirement (whether or not he gives a satisfactory reason for his failure), require him, within the following 48 hours, to produce a certificate of registration at a police station specified by the officer or constable,

so, however, that a requirement under sub-paragraph (b) to produce a certificate of registration at a police station shall have effect in substitution for the requirement under sub-paragraph (a) so as to cause that previous requirement to cease to have effect.

SCHEDULE
Particulars to be entered in Local Register

1   Name in full.

2   Sex.

3   Matrimonial status (married or single).

4   (a) Date of birth.
(b) Country of birth.

5   (a) Present nationality.
(b) How and when acquired.
(c) Previous nationality (if any).

6   Particulars of passport or other document establishing nationality.

7   Business, profession or occupation.

8   Residence in the United Kingdom (or address if no residence).

9   Name and address of referee (if any) supplied under Regulation 7(b).

10   Last residence outside the United Kingdom.

11   (a) Date of arrival in the United Kingdom.
(b)   Place of arrival in the United Kingdom.
(c)   Mode of arrival in the United Kingdom.

12   Duration of limited leave and conditions attached thereto.

13   Restrictions or conditions, if any, applicable by virtue of section 9(2) of the Act.

14   (a) If employed in the United Kingdom—
(i)   name and address of employer;
(ii) address at which employed, if different.
(b) If engaged in business or profession in the United Kingdom—
(i)   name under which business or profession is carried on;
(ii) address at which business or profession is carried on.

15   Signature (or fingerprints if unable to write in the characters of the English language).

16   Photograph.

IMMIGRATION (LANDING AND EMBARKATION CARDS) ORDER 1975

1975 No 65

Made - - - 21st January 1975

Authority: Immigration Act 1971, Sch 2, para 5

1   This Order may be cited as the Immigration (Landing and Embarkation Cards) Order 1975 and shall come into operation on 1st March 1975.

2   The Interpretation Act 1889 shall apply to the interpretation of this Order as it applies to the interpretation of an Act of Parliament.

4   (1)   Except as provided by Article 5 a person aged 16 years or over who disembarks or embarks in the United Kingdom[, or leaves or boards in the United Kingdom a train which for the purposes of sections 11 and 12 of the Channel Tunnel Act 1987 is engaged on an international service,] shall, unless he has a right of abode there under section 2 of the Immigration Act 1971 and produces a current passport issued by the Government of the United Kingdom not acting on behalf of another Government, produce to an Immigration Officer, if required, a landing card or embarkation card, as the case may be, duly completed.

(2)   The card shall be in such form as the Secretary of State may direct, and it shall be supplied by the owners or agents of the ship or aircraft concerned [or, as the case may be, by the person operating the international service].

NOTES

Amendment
Paras (1), (2): words in square brackets inserted by SI 1993/1813, art 8, Sch 5, Part II, para 3.

5   This Order shall not apply to a person disembarking from or embarking on a ship or aircraft coming from or going to a place in the common travel area unless he is a person who, disembarking from an aircraft coming from the Republic of Ireland, entered the Republic on a journey to the United Kingdom which had begun outside the common travel area and was not given leave to land in the Republic in accordance with the law in force there.

IMMIGRATION (VARIATION OF LEAVE) ORDER 1976

1976 No 1572

Made - - - 22nd September 1976

Authority: Immigration Act 1971, ss 3(3), 4(1)

1   Citation and Operation

This Order may be cited as the Immigration (Variation of Leave) Order 1976 and shall come into operation on 27th September 1976.

2   Interpretation

The Interpretation Act 1889 shall apply to the interpretation of this Order as it applies to the interpretation of an Act of Parliament.

3   Variation of limited leave to enter or remain in the United Kingdom

(1)   Where a person has leave to enter or remain in the United Kingdom for a limited period and applies to the Secretary of State before the expiry of that period for such limited leave to be varied, then, except in a case falling within paragraph (2) below, the duration of his leave shall, by virtue of this Order, be extended until the expiration of the twenty-eighth day after [either the date of the decision on the application or, if the application is withdrawn, the date of the withdrawal of the application].

(2)   Paragraph (1) above shall not apply—

(a)   in a case in which the date of the decision is earlier than 28 days before the expiration of the period of limited leave;

(b)   in a case in which the period of limited leave had expired before the coming into operation of this Order;

(c)   in a case in which the application is made at a time when, by virtue of the previous operation of this Order, an extension of the applicant's period of leave is taking effect [and he has no other concurrent period of leave];

[(d)   in a case in which the duration of a person's limited leave to enter or remain has been curtailed by the Secretary of State under section 7(1) of the Asylum and Immigration Appeals Act 1993];

[(e)   in a case in which the date of the decision is 2nd October 2000 or later].

(3)   For the purposes of this Article the date of the decision shall have the same meaning as in Rule 4(11) of the Immigration Appeals (Procedure) Rules 1972, that is to say, shall—

(a)   where notice of the decision is sent by post, be deemed to be the day on which such notice is sent;

(b)   in any other case, be deemed to be the day on which notice of the decision is served.

NOTES

Amendment
Para (1): words in square brackets substituted by SI 1989/1005, art 2(a).
Para (2): in sub-para (c) words "and he has no other concurrent period of leave" in square brackets inserted by SI 1989/1005, art 2(b).
Para (2): sub-para (d) inserted by SI 1993/1657, art 2(a).
Para (2): sub-para (e) inserted by SI 2000/2445, art 2.
Date in force: 2 October 2000: see SI 2000/2445, art 1.

[4]   [Where—

(a)   the duration of a person's limited leave to enter or remain in the UK has been extended by the operation of article 3(1); and

(b)   the duration of that leave has been curtailed by the Secretary of State under section 7(1) of the Asylum and Immigration Appeals Act 1993,

the extension shall not have effect beyond the date to which the leave is curtailed.]

NOTES

Amendment
Inserted by SI 1993/1657, art 2(b).

IMMIGRATION (PORTS OF ENTRY) ORDER 1987

1987 No 177

Made - - - 10th February 1987

Authority: Immigration Act 1971, s 33(3)

1   (1) This Order may be cited as the Immigration (Ports of Entry) Order 1987 and shall come into force on 1st March 1987.

(2)   . . .

NOTES

Amendment
Para (2): revokes SI 1972/1668, SI 1975/2221 and SI 1979/1635.

2   The ports specified in the Schedule to this Order shall be ports of entry for the purposes of the Immigration Act 1971.

SCHEDULE
Ports of Entry

Article 2

Seaports and Hoverports

Dover	Plymouth
Felixstowe	Portsmouth
Folkestone	Ramsgate
Harwich	Sheerness
Hull	Southampton
London	Tyne
Newhaven	

Airports

Aberdeen	Leeds/Bradford
Belfast	Liverpool
Birmingham	Luton
Bournemouth (Hurn)	Manchester
Bristol	Newcastle
Cardiff (Wales)	Norwich
East Midlands	Prestwick
Edinburgh	Southampton
Gatwick–London	Southend
Glasgow	Stansted–London
Heathrow–London	Tees-side

IMMIGRATION (TRANSIT VISA) ORDER 1993

1993 No 1678

Made - - - 2nd July 1993

In exercise of the powers conferred upon me by section 1A(1) and (2) of the Immigration (Carriers' Liability) Act 1987, I hereby make the following order

1 This Order may be cited as the Immigration (Transit Visa) Order 1993 and shall come into force on 22nd July 1993.

[1A] [In this Order, "EEA State" means a country which is a Contracting Party to the Agreement on the European Economic Area signed at Oporto on 2nd May 1992 as adjusted by the Protocol signed at Brussels on 17th March 1993.]

NOTES

Amendment
Inserted by SI 2000/1381, art 2(1).
Date in force: 14 June 2000: see SI 2000/1381, art 1(2).

2 A national or citizen of one or more of the countries or territories specified in the Schedule to this Order[, or a person holding a travel document issued by the purported "Turkish Republic of Northern Cyprus",] [or the former Socialist Federal Republic of Yugoslavia,] who on arrival in the United Kingdom passes through to another country or territory without entering the United Kingdom shall hold a visa for that purpose (a transit visa) unless he:

    (a) has the right of abode in the United Kingdom under the Immigration Act 1971; or

    (b) is also a national of [an EEA State].

NOTES

Amendment
Words ", or a person holding a travel document issued by the purported "Turkish Republic of Northern Cyprus"," in square brackets inserted by SI 1998/55, art 2.
Date in force: 5 February 1998: see SI 1998/55, art 1.
Words "or the former Socialist Federal Republic of Yugoslavia," in square brackets inserted by SI 1998/1014, art 3.
Date in force: 10 April 1998: see SI 1998/1014, art 1.
In para (b) words "an EEA State" in square brackets substituted by SI 2000/1381, art 2(2).
Date in force: 14 June 2000: see SI 2000/1381, art 1(2).

3 An application for a transit visa shall be made to any British High Commission, Embassy or Consulate which accepts such applications.

[Schedule
Countries or Territories whose Nationals or Citizens Need a Visa for Passing
Through the United Kingdom]

NOTES

Amendment
Substituted by SI 2000/1381, art 3, Schedule.
Date in force: 25 May 2000: see SI 2000/1381, art 1(2).

[Article 3]

NOTES

Amendment
Substituted by SI 2000/1381, art 3, Schedule.
Date in force: 25 May 2000: see SI 2000/1381, art 1(2).

[Afghanistan
Colombia
Democratic Republic of the Congo
Ecuador
Eritrea
Ethiopia
Federal Republic of Yugoslavia
Ghana
Iran
Iraq
Libya
Nigeria
People's Republic of China
Republic of Croatia
Slovak Republic
Somalia
Sri Lanka
Turkey
Uganda]

NOTES

Amendment
Substituted by SI 2000/1381, art 3, Schedule.
Date in force: 25 May 2000: see SI 2000/1381, art 1(2).

IMMIGRATION (RESTRICTIONS ON EMPLOYMENT) ORDER 1996

1996 No 3225

Made - - - *18th December 1996*

Laid before Parliament - - - 23rd December 1996

Coming into force - - - 27th January 1997

The Secretary of State, in exercise of the powers conferred upon him by section 8(1) and (2) of the Asylum and Immigration Act 1996, hereby makes the following Order:

1 (1) This Order may be cited as the Immigration (Restrictions on Employment) Order 1996 and shall come into force on 27th January 1997.

(2) In this Order "the Act" means the Asylum and Immigration Act 1996.

NOTES

Initial Commencement
Specified date
Specified date: 27 January 1997: see para (1) above.

2 (1) The conditions set out in Part I of the Schedule to this Order are the conditions specified under section 8(1) of the Act (no offence committed in employing a person who satisfies such conditions).

(2) The documents described in Part II of that Schedule are the documents specified under section 8(2)(a) of the Act (defence for an employer to show that a specified document was produced before employment began).

(3) The manner of copying or recording specified documents described in Part III of that Schedule is the manner specified under section 8(2)(b) of the Act (specified document to be retained by employer or a copy or other record to be made in a specified manner).

NOTES

Initial Commencement
Specified date
Specified date: 27 January 1997: see art 1(1).

Ann Widdecombe

Minister of State

Home Office

18th December 1996

SCHEDULE

PART I
CONDITIONS SPECIFIED UNDER SECTION 8(1) OF THE ACT

Article 2(1)

1 The employee has made a claim for asylum, which has not been finally determined or abandoned, and has been given written permission to work by the Home Office.

2 The employee's appeal under Part II of the Immigration Act 1971 is pending and, before notice of appeal was given, he had leave to enter or remain in the United Kingdom which did not preclude his taking the employment in question.

3 The employee is permitted to work under the Immigration Rules.

NOTES

Initial Commencement
Specified date
Specified date: 27 January 1997: see art 1(1).

PART II
DOCUMENTS SPECIFIED UNDER SECTION 8(2)(A) OF THE ACT

Article 2(2)

1 A document issued by a previous employer, the Inland Revenue, the Benefits Agency, the Contributions Agency, the Employment Service, the Training and Employment

Agency (Northern Ireland) or the Northern Ireland Social Security Agency which contains the National Insurance number of the person named in the document.

2   A passport which describes the holder as a British citizen or as having the right of abode in, or an entitlement to readmission to, the United Kingdom.

3   A passport which contains a Certificate of Entitlement issued by, or on behalf of, the Government of the United Kingdom certifying that the holder has the right of abode in the United Kingdom.

4   A certificate of registration or naturalisation as a British citizen.

5   A birth certificate issued in the United Kingdom, the Republic of Ireland, the Channel Islands or the Isle of Man.

6   A passport or national identity card, issued by a State which is a party to the European Economic Area Agreement, which describes the holder as a national of a State which is a party to that Agreement.

7   A passport or other travel document which is endorsed to show that the holder is exempt from immigration control, has indefinite leave to enter, or remain in, the United Kingdom or has no time limit on his stay; or a letter issued by the Home Office which contains that information.

8   A passport or other travel document which is endorsed to show that the holder has current leave to enter, or remain in, the United Kingdom and is not precluded from taking the employment in question; or a letter issued by the Home Office which contains that information.

9   A United Kingdom residence permit issued to a national of a State which is a party to the European Economic Area Agreement.

10   A passport or other travel document which is endorsed to show that the holder has a current right of residence in the United Kingdom as the family member of a named national of a State which is a party to the European Economic Area Agreement and who is resident in the United Kingdom.

11   A letter issued by the Home Office which indicates that the person named in it is a British citizen or has permission to take employment.

12   A work permit or other approval to take employment issued by the Department for Education and Employment or the Training and Employment Agency (Northern Ireland).

13   A passport which describes the holder as a British Dependent Territories citizen and which indicates that that status derives from a connection with Gibraltar.

NOTES

Initial Commencement
Specified date
Specified date: 27 January 1997: see art 1(1).

PART III
Manner of Keeping or Recording A Document Specified Under Section 8(2)(b) of the Act

Article 2(3)

1   In the case of a passport or other travel document, the following parts are to be photocopied or scanned into a computer database, using the technology known as "Write Once Read Many"—

(a) the front cover;
(b) the pages containing the holder's personal details including nationality;
(c) the page containing the holder's photograph or signature; and
(d) the pages containing the information referred to in paragraphs 2 (other than citizenship), 3, 7, 8 or 10 of Part II of this Schedule.

2 All other documents are to be photocopied or scanned into a computer database, using the technology known as "Write Once Read Many".

NOTES

Initial Commencement
Specified date
Specified date: 27 January 1997: see art 1(1).

SPECIAL IMMIGRATION APPEALS COMMISSION (PROCEDURE) RULES 1998

1998 No 1881

Made - - - 30th July 1998

Coming into force - - - 31st July 1998

The Lord Chancellor, in exercise of the powers conferred by sections 5 and 8 of the Special Immigration Appeals Commission Act 1997, makes the following Rules of which a draft has, in accordance with sections 5(9) and 8(4), been laid before and approved by resolution of each House of Parliament:—

PART I
GENERAL PROVISIONS

These Rules may be cited as the Special Immigration Appeals Commission (Procedure) Rules 1998 and shall come into force on the day after the day on which they are made.

NOTES

Initial Commencement
Specified date
Specified date: 31 July 1998: see above.

2 **Interpretation**

In these Rules—
"the 1971 Act" means the Immigration Act 1971;
"the 1997 Act" means the Special Immigration Appeals Commission Act 1997;
["the 1999 Act" means the Immigration and Asylum Act 1999;]
"the chairman" means the chairman of the Commission;
"the Commission" means the Special Immigration Appeals Commission; and
"the special advocate" means a person appointed under section 6(1) of the 1997 Act to represent the interests of the appellant.

NOTES

Initial Commencement
Specified date
Specified date: 31 July 1998: see r 1.

Amendment
Definition ""the 1999 Act"" inserted by SI 2000/1849, r 3.
Date in force: 2 October 2000: see SI 2000/1849, r 1(1).

3   General duty of Commission

(1)   When exercising its functions, the Commission shall secure that information is not disclosed contrary to the interests of national security, the international relations of the United Kingdom, the detection and prevention of crime, or in any other circumstances where disclosure is likely to harm a public interest.

(2)   Where the Rules require information not to be disclosed contrary to the public interest, the requirement shall be construed in accordance with paragraph (1).

(3)   Subject to paragraphs (1) and (2), the Commission must satisfy itself that the material available to it enables it properly to review decisions.

NOTES

Initial Commencement
Specified date
Specified date: 31 July 1998: see r 1.

4   Delegated powers

(1)   The powers of the Commission under the following provisions may be exercised by the chairman or by any other member of the Commission who falls within paragraph 5(a) or (b) of Schedule 1 to the 1997 Act:—

    (a)   rule 12(1) and (3) (amendment and supplementary grounds);
    (b)   rule 13 (directions);
    (c)   rule 25 (application for leave to appeal);
    (d)   rules 26 and 27 (bail proceedings).

(2)   Instead of exercising a power under paragraph (1), the chairman or member may remit the matter to be dealt with by the Commission.

(3)   Where the chairman or member exercises any power of the Commission, references to the Commission in the Rules shall as appropriate include references to him.

NOTES

Initial Commencement
Specified date
Specified date: 31 July 1998: see r 1.

5   Notices etc

(1)   Any document required or authorised to be given or sent to—

    (a)   the Commission, shall be directed to the Secretary to the Commission;
    (b)   the Secretary of State, shall be directed to [an address or fax number specified by him].

(2)   The appellant must inform the Commission if an address given under rule 9(3) changes.

NOTES

Initial Commencement
Specified date
Specified date: 31 July 1998: see r 1.

Amendment
Para (1): in sub-para (b) words "an address or fax number specified by him" in square brackets substituted by SI 2000/1849, r 4.
Date in force: 2 October 2000: see SI 2000/1849, r 1(1).

PART II
APPEALS

[6 Application of Part II]

[(1) Subject to paragraph (2), this Part applies to appeals brought under section 2 of the 1997 Act and to appeals transferred to the Commission under subsection (3) or (5) of section 78 of the 1999 Act where an appeal has been or may be made under section 2(1) of the 1997 Act.

(2) The provisions of this Part shall not—

(a) prejudice steps already taken in respect of an appeal transferred under either of those subsections, or
(b) require any step to be taken under these Rules which is equivalent to a step which has already been taken in respect of such an appeal.]

NOTES

Amendment
Substituted by SI 2000/1849, r 5.
Date in force: 2 October 2000: see SI 2000/1849, r 1(1).

7 The special advocate

(1) On receiving . . . the notice of appeal, the Secretary of State shall inform the relevant law officer of the proceedings before the Commission, with a view to the law officer, if he thinks fit to do so, appointing a special advocate to represent the interests of the appellant in the proceedings.

(2) Paragraph (1) applies unless—

(a) the Secretary of State does not intend to oppose the appeal, or
(b) he does not intend to object to the disclosure of material to the appellant.

(3) If at any stage in proceedings before the Commission, paragraph (2)(b) ceases to apply, the Secretary of State shall immediately notify the relevant law officer as in paragraph (1).

(4) The function of the special advocate is to represent the interests of the appellant by—

(a) making submissions to the Commission in any proceedings from which the appellant and his representative are excluded;
(b) cross-examining witnesses at any such proceedings; and
(c) making written submissions to the Commission.

(5) Except in accordance with paragraphs (6) to (9), the special advocate may not communicate directly or indirectly with the appellant or his representative on any matter connected with proceedings before the Commission.

(6) The special advocate may communicate with the appellant and his representative at any time before the Secretary of State makes material available to him under rule 10(3).

(7) At any time after the Secretary of State has made material available under rule 10(3), the special advocate may seek directions from the Commission authorising him to seek information in connection with the proceedings from the appellant or his representative.

(8) The Commission shall notify the Secretary of State of a request for directions under paragraph (7) and the Secretary of State must, within a period specified by the Commission, give the Commission notice of any objection which he has to the request for information being made or to the form in which it is proposed to be made.

(9) Where the Secretary of State makes an objection under paragraph (8), rule 11 shall apply as appropriate.

NOTES

Initial Commencement
Specified date
Specified date: 31 July 1998: see r 1.

Amendment
Para (1): words omitted revoked by SI 2000/1849, r 6.
Date in force: 2 October 2000: see SI 2000/1849, r 1(1).

[8   Time limit for appealing]

[(1) The appellant shall give notice of an appeal no later than—

  (a) 5 days after receiving the notice of the decision being appealed against, where the appellant appeals in the United Kingdom; or
  (b) 28 days after receiving the notice of the decision being appealed against, where the appellant appeals from outside the United Kingdom.

(2) The period specified in paragraph (1) shall begin from the end of the day on which the notice of the decision being appealed against was received.

(3) Where the period specified under paragraph (1) expires on an excluded day, the notice of appeal shall be taken to have been served as required if served on the next day that is not an excluded day.

(4) Where the period specified under paragraph (1)(a) includes an excluded day, that day shall be discounted.

(5) The notice of appeal shall be taken to have been served as required on the day on which it is received at the address or fax number specified in the notice of the decision against which the appeal is made.

(6) "Excluded day" means a Saturday, a Sunday, a bank holiday, Christmas Day, 27th to 31st December or Good Friday.

(7) "Bank holiday" means a day that is specified in, or appointed under, the Banking and Financial Dealings Act 1971.]

NOTES

Amendment
Substituted by SI 2000/1849, r 7.
Date in force: 2 October 2000: see SI 2000/1849, r 1(1).

[9 Notice of appeal]

[(1) An appeal to the Commission shall be made by sending to the Secretary of State a notice of appeal by hand, by fax or by post to the address or fax number specified in the document which informed him of the decision against which he is appealing.

(2) The notice of appeal shall set out the grounds for the appeal.

(3) The notice of appeal shall state the name and address of the appellant and the name and address of any representative of the appellant.

(4) The appellant or his representative shall sign the notice of appeal.

(5) The appellant shall attach to the notice of appeal—

    (a) a copy of the document which informed him of the decision against which he is appealing; and

    (b) where a notice has been served on the appellant under section 74(4) of the 1999 Act, a statement form, on which additional grounds which he has or may have for wishing to enter or remain in the United Kingdom may be stated, whether or not that form has been completed.

(6) As soon as practicable after he receives a notice of appeal in a case where no such grounds have been stated, the Secretary of State shall send that notice, together with any documents attached to it under paragraph (5), to the Commission.]

NOTES

Amendment
Substituted by SI 2000/1849, r 8.
Date in force: 2 October 2000: see SI 2000/1849, r 1(1).

[9A Additional grounds for appealing]

[(1) Where the appellant is treated as appealing on additional grounds by virtue of section 77(2) of the 1999 Act, he shall serve any variation of his grounds of appeal on the Secretary of State no later than 5 days after he received the supplementary grounds of refusal.

(2) As soon as practicable after this period, the Secretary of State shall send to the Commission—

    (a) the notice of appeal, together with any documents attached to it under rule 9(5),

    (b) any supplementary grounds for refusal, and

    (c) any variation of the grounds of appeal.

(3) For the purpose of calculating the period specified in paragraph (1), paragraphs (2) to (7) of rule 8 shall apply as if the variation of grounds of appeal were a notice of appeal and the supplementary grounds of refusal were the notice of the decision against which the appeal is made.

(4) In this rule, "supplementary grounds of refusal" means the reasons given by the Secretary of State for maintaining the decision being appealed against after consideration by him of the additional grounds.]

NOTES

Amendment
Inserted by SI 2000/1849, rr 2, 9.
Date in force: 2 October 2000: see SI 2000/1849, r 1(1).

10   Secretary of State's reply

(1)   If the Secretary of State intends to oppose the appeal, he must. . .,—

(a)   provide the Commission with a summary of the facts relating to the decision being appealed and the reasons for the decision;

(b)   inform the Commission of the grounds on which he opposes the appeal; and

(c)   provide the Commission with a statement of the evidence which he relies upon in support of those grounds.

(2)   Where the Secretary of State objects to material referred to in paragraph (1) being disclosed to the appellant or his representative, he must also—

(a)   state the reasons for his objection; and

(b)   if and to the extent it is possible to do so without disclosing information contrary to the public interest, provide a statement of that material in a form which can be shown to the appellant.

(3)   Where he makes an objection under paragraph (2), the Secretary of State must make available to the special advocate, as soon as it is practicable to do so, the material which he has provided to the Commission under paragraphs (1) and (2).

NOTES

Initial Commencement
Specified date
Specified date: 31 July 1998: see r 1.

Amendment
Para (1): words omitted revoked by SI 2000/1849, r 10.
Date in force: 2 October 2000: see SI 2000/1849, r 1(1).

11   Consideration of Secretary of State's objection

(1)   Proceedings under this rule shall take place in the absence of the appellant and his representative.

(2)   The Commission shall decide whether to uphold the Secretary of State's objection.

(3)   Before doing so, it must invite the special advocate to make written representations.

(4)   After considering representations made under paragraph (3), the Commission may—

(a)   invite the special advocate to make oral representations; or

(b)   uphold the Secretary of State's objection without requiring further representations from the special advocate.

(5)   Where the Commission is minded to overrule the Secretary of State's objection, or to require him to provide material in a different form from that in which he has provided it under rule 10(2)(b), the Commission must invite the Secretary of State and the special advocate to make oral representations.

(6)   Where—

(a)   the Commission overrules the Secretary of State's objection or requires him to provide material in a different form from that which he has provided under rule 10(2)(b), and

(b)   the Secretary of State wishes to continue to oppose the appeal,
he shall not be required to disclose any material which was the subject of his unsuccessful objection if he chooses not to rely upon it in opposing the appeal.

NOTES

Initial Commencement
Specified date
Specified date: 31 July 1998: see r 1.

12 Amendment and supplementary grounds

[(1) Subject to paragraph (1A), the appellant may amend his notice of appeal or deliver supplementary grounds of appeal.

(1A) Where the Secretary of State has provided material under rule 10, the appellant shall obtain the leave of the Commission before amending his notice of appeal or delivering supplementary grounds of appeal under paragraph (1).

(2) The appellant shall send any proposed amended notice of appeal or supplementary grounds of appeal to the Secretary of State who shall, as soon as practicable, send a copy to the Commission.]

(3) With the leave of the Commission, the Secretary of State may amend or supplement the material which he has provided under rule 10.

(4) Where the Secretary of State provides further objections under paragraph (3), the Commission shall consider them in accordance with rule 11.

NOTES

Initial Commencement
Specified date
Specified date: 31 July 1998: see r 1.

Amendment
Paras (1), (1A), (2): substituted, for paras (1), (2) as originally enacted, by SI 2000/1849, r 11.
Date in force: 2 October 2000: see SI 2000/1849, r 1(1).

13 Directions

(1) Subject to any decision which it makes under rule 11 and to the need to secure that information is not disclosed contrary to the public interest, the Commission may give directions for the conduct of proceedings.

(2) Directions may—

    (a) provide for a particular matter to be dealt with as a preliminary issue and for a pre-hearing review to be held;

    (b) limit the length of oral submissions and the time allowed for the examination and cross-examination of witnesses;

    (c) require any party to the appeal to give to the Commission—

        (i) statements of facts and statements of the evidence which will be called at any hearing, including such statements provided in a modified or edited form;

        (ii) a skeleton argument which summarises the submissions which will be made and cites all the authorities which will be relied upon, identifying any particular passages to be relied upon;

        (iii) an estimate of the time which will be needed for any hearing;

        (iv) a list of the witnesses who will be called to give evidence;

        (v) a chronology of events;

        (vi) a statement of any interpretation requirements,
        and to serve any such material on the other parties to the appeal.

[(3) The Commission may—

    (a)   subject to any specific provision of the Rules, specify time limits for steps to be taken in the proceedings; and

    (b)   extend any time limit.]

(4)   The power to give directions may be exercised in the absence of the parties.

NOTES

Initial Commencement
Specified date
Specified date: 31 July 1998: see r 1.

Amendment
Para (3): substituted by SI 2000/1849, r 12.
Date in force: 2 October 2000: see SI 2000/1849, r 1(1).

14   Failure to comply with directions

(1)   Where a party fails to comply with a direction, the Commission may send him a notice which states—

    (a)   the respect in which he has failed to comply with the relevant direction;

    (b)   the time limit for complying with the direction; and

    (c)   that the Commission may proceed to determine the appeal on the material available to it if the party fails to comply with the relevant direction within the time specified.

(2)   Where the party in default fails to comply with the notice under paragraph (1), the Commission may proceed in accordance with paragraph (1)(c).

NOTES

Initial Commencement
Specified date
Specified date: 31 July 1998: see r 1.

15   Applications by Secretary of State

(1)   This rule applies to the notification to the appellant by the Commission of—

    (a)   any order or direction made or given in the absence of the Secretary of State,

    (b)   any summary prepared under rule 22, and

    (c)   its determination under rule 23.

(2)   Before the Commission notifies the appellant as mentioned in paragraph (1), it must first notify the Secretary of State.

(3)   If the Secretary of State considers that compliance by him with an order or direction or notification to the appellant of any matter under paragraph (1) would cause information to be disclosed contrary to the public interest, he may apply to the Commission to reconsider the order or direction or to review the proposed summary or determination.

(4)   At the same time as he makes his application, or as soon as practicable afterwards, the Secretary of State must send a copy of it to the special advocate.

(5)   An application by the Secretary of State must be made within 14 days of receipt of notification under paragraph (2), and the Commission shall not notify the appellant as mentioned in paragraph (1) before the time for applying has expired.

(6)   Rule 11 shall apply as appropriate to the Commission's consideration of the Secretary of State's application.

NOTES

Initial Commencement
Specified date
Specified date: 31 July 1998: see r 1.

16 Notification of hearing

The Secretary to the Commission must send notice of the date, time and place fixed for any hearing to the special advocate and every party entitled to attend that hearing.

NOTES

Initial Commencement
Specified date
Specified date: 31 July 1998: see r 1.

17 Parties

(1) The parties to an appeal shall be the appellant and the Secretary of State.

(2) If the United Kingdom Representative of the United Nations High Commissioner for Refugees (the "United Kingdom Representative") gives written notice that he wishes to be treated as a party to the appeal, he shall be so treated from the date of the notice.

(3) Any restriction imposed by or under these Rules in relation to the appellant as to the disclosure of material, attendance at hearings, notification of directions or decisions and communications with the special advocate, applies to the United Kingdom Representative.

NOTES

Initial Commencement
Specified date
Specified date: 31 July 1998: see r 1.

18 Representation of parties

(1) The appellant may act in person or be represented or appear by—

- (a) a person having a qualification referred to in section 6(3) of the 1997 Act,
- (b) a person appointed by any voluntary organisation for the time being in receipt of a grant under section 23 of the 1971 Act, or
- (c) with the leave of the Commission, any other person.

(2) The Secretary of State and the United Kingdom Representative may be represented by any person appointed by them respectively for that purpose.

NOTES

Initial Commencement
Specified date
Specified date: 31 July 1998: see r 1.

19 Proceedings in private

(1) Where the Commission considers it necessary for the appellant and his representative to be excluded from the proceedings or any part of them in order to secure that information is not disclosed contrary to the public interest, it must—

- (a) direct accordingly, and
- (b) hear the proceedings, or that part of it from which the appellant and his representative are excluded, in private.

(2)   The Commission may hear the proceedings or part of them in private for any other good reason.

NOTES

Initial Commencement
Specified date
Specified date: 31 July 1998: see r 1.

20   Evidence

(1)   In any proceedings on an appeal, the evidence of witnesses may be given either—

(a)   orally, before the Commission, or
(b)   in writing, in which case it shall be given in such a manner and at such time as the Commission has directed.

(2)   The Commission may also receive evidence in documentary or any other form.

(3)   The Commission may receive evidence that would not be admissible in a court of law.

(4)   No person shall be compelled to give evidence or produce a document which he could not be compelled to give or produce on the trial of an action in the part of the United Kingdom in which the proceedings before the Commission are taking place.

(5)   Every party shall be entitled to adduce evidence and to cross-examine witnesses during any part of the hearing of the appeal from which he and his representative are not excluded.

(6)   The Commission may require a witness to give evidence on oath.

NOTES

Initial Commencement
Specified date
Specified date: 31 July 1998: see r 1.

21   Summoning of witnesses

(1)   Subject to rules 3 and 20(4) and paragraph (2) of this rule, the Commission may require any person in the United Kingdom to attend as a witness at any proceedings before the Commission and to answer any questions or produce any documents in his custody or under his control which relate to any matter in question in the appeal.

(2)   No person shall be required to travel more than 16 kilometres from his place of residence unless the necessary expenses of his attendance are paid or tendered to him.

(3)   Where a party requests the attendance of a witness, that party must pay or tender those expenses.

NOTES

Initial Commencement
Specified date
Specified date: 31 July 1998: see r 1.

22   Notification to appellant before determination

(1)   Where the appellant or his representative have been excluded from the hearing of the appeal or any part of it, the Commission must, before it [determines the appeal], give the appellant a summary of the submissions and evidence received in his absence

if and to the extent it is possible to do so without disclosing information contrary to the public interest.

(2) Where the Commission provides such a summary, it shall afford the special advocate and the parties an opportunity to make representations and adduce evidence or further evidence to the Commission in respect of the material contained in it.

NOTES

Initial Commencement
Specified date
Specified date: 31 July 1998: see r 1.

Amendment
Para (1): words "determines the appeal" in square brackets substituted by SI 2000/1849, r 13.
Date in force: 2 October 2000: see SI 2000/1849, r 1(1).

23 Promulgation of determination

(1) The Commission must record its determination and, if and to the extent it is possible to do so without disclosing information contrary to the public interest, the reasons for it.

(2) The Commission shall publish its determination and send written notice of it to the special advocate and the parties.

NOTES

Initial Commencement
Specified date
Specified date: 31 July 1998: see r 1.

PART III
LEAVE TO APPEAL FROM COMMISSION

24 Application of Part III

This Part applies to applications for leave to appeal, on a question of law, to the Court of Appeal, the Court of Session or the Court of Appeal in Northern Ireland, as the case may be, from a final determination of an appeal by the Commission.

NOTES

Initial Commencement
Specified date
Specified date: 31 July 1998: see r 1.

25 Application for leave to appeal

(1) An application to the Commission for leave to appeal shall be made not later than 10 days after the party seeking to appeal has received written notice of the determination.

(2) The Commission may decide an application for leave without a hearing unless it considers there are special circumstances which make a hearing necessary or desirable.

NOTES

Initial Commencement
Specified date
Specified date: 31 July 1998: see r 1.

Part IV
Bail Applications

26   Application for bail: procedure

(1)   Subject to the provisions of this rule and rule 27, these Rules apply to—

    (a)   applications for bail by a person who brings an appeal under section 2 of the 1997 Act, and

    (b)   applications to the Commission under paragraphs 22 to 24 of Schedule 2 to the 1971 Act,

with appropriate modifications.

(2)   References in the Rules to the appellant shall be read, in relation to bail applications, as if they were references to the applicant.

[(3)   Rules 8, 9 and 9A shall not apply to bail applications.]

(5)   An application to the Commission to be released on bail must be made in writing and shall contain the following particulars—

    (a)   the full name of the applicant;

    (b)   the address of the place where, and the reason why, the applicant is detained at the time when the application is made;

    (c)   the date of any notice of appeal which has been given;

    (d)   the address where the applicant would reside if his application for bail were to be granted;

    (e)   the amount of the recognizance in which he would agree to be bound;

    (f)   the full names, addresses and occupations of two persons who might act as sureties for the applicant if his application for bail were to be granted, and the amounts of the recognizances in which those persons might agree to be bound; and

    (g)   the grounds on which the application is made and, where a previous application has been refused, particulars of any change in circumstances which has occurred since that refusal.

(6)   In its application to Scotland, this rule shall have effect as if, for paragraph (5)(e) and (f), there were substituted—

    "(e)   the amount, if any, to be deposited if bail is granted;

    (f)   the full names, addresses and occupations of such persons if any, who offer to act as cautioners if the applicant's application for bail were to be granted;".

(7)   A bail application shall be signed by the applicant or by a person duly authorised by him for that purpose or, in the case of an applicant who is a minor or who is for any reason incapable of acting, by any person acting on his behalf.

(8)   The application must be delivered, or sent by post, to the Commission.

NOTES

Initial Commencement
Specified date
Specified date: 31 July 1998: see r 1.

Amendment
Para (3): substituted, for paras (3), (4) as originally enacted, by SI 2000/1849, r 14.
Date in force: 2 October 2000: see SI 2000/1849, r 1(1).

27   Release on bail

(1)   Where the Commission directs the release of an applicant on bail and the taking of the recognizance is postponed under paragraph 22(3) or 29(6) of Schedule 2 to the

1971 Act, it shall certify in writing that the applicant has been granted bail and shall include in the certificate—

(a) particulars of the conditions to be endorsed on the recognizance with a view to the recognizance being taken subsequently;

(b) the amounts in which the applicant and any sureties are to be bound; and

(c) the date of issue of the certificate.

(2) The person having custody of an applicant shall release him—

(a) on receipt of a certificate signed by the Commission stating that the recognizances of any sureties required have been taken or on being otherwise satisfied that all such recognizances have been taken, and

(b) on being satisfied that the applicant has entered into his recognizance.

(3) In its application to Scotland, this rule shall have effect as if for paragraph (2), there were substituted—

"(2) The person having custody of an appellant shall release him—

(a) on receipt of a certified copy of the decision to grant bail, and

(b) on being satisfied that the amount, if any, to be deposited has been so deposited.".

NOTES

Initial Commencement
Specified date
Specified date: 31 July 1998: see r 1.

Irvine of Lairg, C

Dated 30th July 1998

ASYLUM SUPPORT (INTERIM PROVISIONS) REGULATIONS 1999

1999 No 3056

Made - - - 13th November 1999

Laid before Parliament - - - 15th November 1999

Coming into force - - - 6th December 1999

The Secretary of State, in exercise of the powers conferred on him by sections 94 and 166 of, and paragraphs 1, 2, 4 to 7, 9, 11 and 13 to 15 of Schedule 9 to, the Immigration and Asylum Act 1999, hereby makes the following Regulations:

1   Citation, commencement and extent

(1) These Regulations may be cited as the Asylum Support (Interim Provisions) Regulations 1999 and shall come into force on 6th December 1999.

(2) These Regulations do not extend to Scotland or Northern Ireland.

NOTES

Initial Commencement
Specified date
Specified date: 6 December 1999: see para (1) above.

2 Interpretation

(1)   In these Regulations—
"assisted person" means an asylum-seeker, or a dependant of an asylum-seeker, who has applied for support and for whom support is provided;
"dependant", in relation to an asylum-seeker, an assisted person or a person claiming support, means a person in the United Kingdom who:
(a)   is his spouse;
(b)   is a child of his, or of his spouse, who is under 18 and dependent on him;
(c)   is under 18 and is a member of his, or his spouse's, close family;
(d)   is under 18 and had been living as part of his household:
(i)   for at least six of the 12 months before the day on which his claim for support was made; or
(ii)   since birth;
(e)   is in need of care and attention from him or a member of his household by reason of a disability and would fall within sub-paragraph (c) or (d) but for the fact that he is not under 18;
(f)   had been living with him as a member of an unmarried couple for at least two of the three years before the day on which his claim for support was made;
(g)   is a person living as part of his household who was receiving assistance from a local authority under section 17 of the Children Act 1989 immediately before the beginning of the interim period;
(h)   has made a claim for leave to enter or remain in the United Kingdom, or for variation of any such leave, which is being considered on the basis that he is dependent on the asylum-seeker; or
(i)   in relation to an assisted person or a person claiming support who is himself a dependant of an asylum-seeker, is the asylum-seeker;
"eligible persons" means asylum-seekers or their dependants who appear to be destitute or to be likely to become destitute within 14 days;
"local authority" means:
(a)   in England, a county council, a metropolitan district council, a district council with the functions of a county council, a London borough council, the Common Council of the City of London or the Council of the Isles of Scilly;
(b)   in Wales, a county council or a county borough council.

(2)   Any reference in these Regulations to support is to support under these Regulations.

(3)   Any reference in these Regulations to assistance under section 21 of the National Assistance Act 1948 is to assistance, the need for which has arisen solely:

(a)   because of destitution; or
(b)   because of the physical effects, or anticipated physical effects, of destitution.

(4)   Any reference in these Regulations to assistance under section 17 of the Children Act 1989 is to the provision of accommodation or of any essential living needs.

(5)   The interim period begins on the day on which these Regulations come into force and ends on 1st April 2002.

(6)   For the purposes of section 94(3) of the Immigration and Asylum Act 1999 (day on which a claim for asylum is determined), the period of 14 days is prescribed for any case to which these Regulations apply.

NOTES

Initial Commencement
Specified date
Specified date: 6 December 1999: see reg 1(1).

Extent
These Regulations do not extend to Scotland; see reg 1(2).

3 Requirement to provide support

(1) Subject to regulations 7 and 8:

    (a)   the local authority concerned, or

    (b)   the local authority to whom responsibility for providing support is transferred under regulation 9,

must provide support during the interim period to eligible persons.

(2) The question whether a person is an eligible person is to be determined by the local authority concerned.

(3) For the purposes of these Regulations, the local authority concerned are the local authority to whom a claim for support is made, except where a claim for support is transferred by a local authority in accordance with regulation 9, in which case the local authority concerned are the local authority to whom the claim is transferred.

NOTES

Initial Commencement
Specified date
Specified date: 6 December 1999: see reg 1(1).

Extent
These Regulations do not extend to Scotland; see reg 1(2).

4 Temporary support

(1) This regulation applies to support to be provided before it has been determined whether a person is an eligible person ("temporary support").

(2) Temporary support is to be provided to a person claiming support:

    (a)   by the local authority to whom the claim is made until such time (if any) as the claim is transferred under regulation 9;

    (b)   where the claim is so transferred, by the local authority to whom the claim is transferred.

(3) Temporary support must appear to the local authority by whom it is provided to be adequate for the needs of the person claiming support and his dependants (if any).

NOTES

Initial Commencement
Specified date
Specified date: 6 December 1999: see reg 1(1).

Extent
These Regulations do not extend to Scotland; see reg 1(2).

5 Provision of support

(1) Subject to paragraph (2), support is to be provided by providing:

(a)   accommodation appearing to the local authority by whom it is provided to be adequate for the needs of the assisted person and his dependants (if any) ("accommodation"); and

(b)   what appear to the local authority by whom it is provided to be essential living needs of the assisted person and his dependants (if any) ("essential living needs").

(2)   Where an assisted person's household includes a child who is under 18 and a dependant of his, support is to be provided:

(a)   in accordance with paragraph (1);
(b)   by providing accommodation; or
(c)   by providing essential living needs.

(3)   Support is to be provided to enable the assisted person (if he is the asylum-seeker) to meet reasonable travel expenses incurred in attending:

(a)   a hearing of an appeal on his claim for asylum; or
(b)   an interview in connection with his claim for asylum which has been requested by the Secretary of State.

(4)   Where the circumstances of a particular case are exceptional, support is to be provided in such other ways as are necessary to enable the assisted person and his dependants (if any) to be supported.

(5)   Support provided by way of payments made (by whatever means) to the assisted person and his dependants (if any) is not to exceed £10 per person in any one week, unless:

(a)   the assisted person's household includes a child who is under 18 and a dependant of his; or
(b)   the circumstances of a particular case are exceptional.

(6)   A local authority may provide support subject to conditions.

(7)   Such conditions are to be set out in writing.

(8)   A copy of the conditions is to be given to the assisted person.

NOTES

Initial Commencement
Specified date
Specified date: 6 December 1999: see reg 1(1).

Extent
These Regulations do not extend to Scotland; see reg 1(2).

6   Matters to which the local authority are to have regard

(1)   In providing support, the local authority are to have regard to:

(a)   income which the assisted person has, or his dependants (if any) have, or might reasonably be expected to have;
(b)   support which is, or assets which are, or might reasonably be expected to be, available to the assisted person, or to his dependants (if any);
(c)   the welfare of the assisted person and his dependants (if any); and
(d)   the cost of providing support.

(2)   In providing accommodation under these Regulations, the local authority are not to have regard to any preference that the assisted person or his dependants (if any) may have as to:

(a) the locality in which the accommodation is to be provided;
(b) the nature of the accommodation to be provided; or
(c) the nature and standard of fixtures and fittings in that accommodation.

NOTES

Initial Commencement
Specified date
Specified date: 6 December 1999: see reg 1(1).

Extent
These Regulations do not extend to Scotland; see reg 1(2).

7 Refusal of support

(1) Unless this paragraph does not apply, support must be refused in the following circumstances:

(a) where the person claiming support has intentionally made himself and his dependants (if any) destitute;
(b) where the person claiming support has made a claim for support to another local authority, except where the claim is one to which regulation 9 applies;
(c) where the claim for support is made by a person to a local authority other than one to whom, in the previous 12 months, he has made a claim for assistance under section 21 of the National Assistance Act 1948 or under section 17 of the Children Act 1989;
(d) where the person claiming support—
    (i) is an asylum-seeker within the meaning of paragraph (3A)(a) or (aa) of regulation 70 of the Income Support (General) Regulations 1987 who has not ceased to be an asylum-seeker by virtue of sub-paragraph (b) of that paragraph;
    (ii) is a person who became an asylum-seeker under paragraph (3A)(a) of regulation 70 of the Income Support (General) Regulations 1987 and who has not ceased to be an asylum-seeker by virtue of sub-paragraph (b) of that paragraph, as saved by regulation 12(1) of the Social Security (Persons from Abroad) Miscellaneous Amendments Regulations 1996;
    (iii) is not a person from abroad within the meaning of sub-paragraph (a) of regulation 21(3) of the Income Support (General) Regulations 1987 by virtue of the exclusions specified in that sub-paragraph;
(e) where neither the person claiming support nor any of his dependants is an asylum-seeker or has made a claim for leave to enter or remain in the United Kingdom, or for variation of any such leave, which is being considered on the basis that he is dependent on an asylum-seeker.

(2) For the purposes of paragraph (1)(a), a person has intentionally made himself destitute if he appears to be, or likely within 14 days to become, destitute as a result of an act or omission deliberately done or made by him or any dependant of his without reasonable excuse while in the United Kingdom.

(3) Paragraph (1) does not apply where the local authority concerned did not know, or could not with reasonable diligence have known, of any circumstance set out in that paragraph.

NOTES

Initial Commencement
Specified date
Specified date: 6 December 1999: see reg 1(1).

Extent
These Regulations do not extend to Scotland; see reg 1(2).

8   Suspension and discontinuation of support

(1)   Support for the assisted person and his dependants (if any) must be discontinued as soon as the local authority by whom it is provided become aware of any circumstance which, if they had known of it when the claim was made, would have led to the claim being refused in accordance with regulation 7(1).

(2)   Support may be suspended or discontinued:

   (a)   where the assisted person, or any dependant of his, fails without reasonable excuse to comply with any condition subject to which the support is provided;
   (b)   where the assisted person, or any dependant of his, leaves accommodation provided as part of such support for more than seven consecutive days without reasonable excuse.

NOTES

Initial Commencement
Specified date
Specified date: 6 December 1999: see reg 1(1).

Extent
These Regulations do not extend to Scotland; see reg 1(2).

9   Transfer of a claim for support or responsibility for providing support by a local authority

A local authority may transfer a claim for support made to them, or responsibility for providing support, to another local authority on such terms as may be agreed between the two authorities.

NOTES

Initial Commencement
Specified date
Specified date: 6 December 1999: see reg 1(1).

Extent
These Regulations do not extend to Scotland; see reg 1(2).

10   Assistance to those providing support

Reasonable assistance to a local authority providing support is to be given by:

   (a)   any district council for an area any part of which lies within the area of the local authority providing support, and
   (b)   any registered social landlord, within the meaning of Part I of the Housing Act 1996, which manages any house or other property which is in the area of the local authority providing support,

who is requested to provide such assistance by the local authority providing support.

NOTES

Initial Commencement
Specified date
Specified date: 6 December 1999: see reg 1(1).

Extent
These Regulations do not extend to Scotland; see reg 1(2).

11   Transitional provision

Where an asylum-seeker or a dependant of an asylum-seeker is receiving assistance from a local authority under section 21 of the National Assistance Act 1948 or under section 17 of the Children Act 1989 immediately before the beginning of the interim period, he is to be taken to have been accepted for support by the local authority providing such assistance.

NOTES

Initial Commencement
Specified date
Specified date: 6 December 1999: see reg 1(1).

Extent
These Regulations do not extend to Scotland; see reg 1(2).

12   Entitlement to claim support

A person entitled to support under these Regulations is not entitled to assistance under section 17 of the Children Act 1989.

NOTES

Initial Commencement
Specified date
Specified date: 6 December 1999: see reg 1(1).

Extent
These Regulations do not extend to Scotland; see reg 1(2).

Barbara Roche
Minister of State
Home Office
13th November 1999

TRAVEL DOCUMENTS (FEES) REGULATIONS 1999

1999 No 3339

Made - - - 13th December 1999

Laid before Parliament - - - 14th December 1999

Coming into force - - - 16th December 1999

The Secretary of State, in exercise of the powers conferred on him by sections 27 and 166 of the Immigration and Asylum Act 1999 and section 56(1) of the Finance Act 1973, and with the approval of the Treasury, hereby makes the following Regulations:

1 Title and commencement

These Regulations may be cited as the Travel Documents (Fees) Regulations 1999 and shall come into force on 16th December 1999.

NOTES

Initial Commencement

Specified date
Specified date: 16 December 1999: see above.

2 Interpretation

In these Regulations—

"Convention travel document" means a travel document issued in accordance with Article 28 of the Refugee Convention (travel documents) or Article 28 of the Stateless Persons Convention (travel documents);

"document of identity" means a travel document issued in the United Kingdom to a person who is not a British citizen which enables the holder to make one journey out of the United Kingdom;

"the Refugee Convention" means the Convention relating to the Status of Refugees done at Geneva on 28th July 1951 and the Protocol to the Convention; and

"the Stateless Persons Convention" means the Convention relating to the Status of Stateless Persons done at New York on 28th September 1954.

NOTES

Initial Commencement

Specified date
Specified date: 16 December 1999: see reg 1.

3 Prescription of fees

(1)   A fee of £28 is to be paid in connection with an application to the Secretary of State for a Convention travel document or a document of identity.

(2)   A fee of £67 is to be paid in connection with an application to the Secretary of State for any other Home Office travel document.

NOTES

Initial Commencement

Specified date
Specified date: 16 December 1999: see reg 1.

4 Payment into the Consolidated Fund

A fee received by the Secretary of State under these Regulations is to be paid into the Consolidated Fund.

NOTES

Initial Commencement

Specified date
Specified date: 16 December 1999: see reg 1.

5 Revocation

The Travel Documents (Refugees and Stateless Persons) (Fees) Regulations 1999 are hereby revoked.

NOTES

Initial Commencement

Specified date
Specified date: 16 December 1999: see reg 1.

Barbara Roche
Minister of State
Home Office
9th December 1999
We approve,
Bob Ainsworth
Jim Dowd
Two of the Lords Commissioners of Her Majesty's Treasury
13th December 1999

IMMIGRATION AND ASYLUM ACT 1999 (COMMENCEMENT NO 2 AND TRANSITIONAL PROVISIONS) ORDER 2000

2000 No 168

Made - - - 21st January 2000

In exercise of the powers conferred upon him by sections 166(3) and 170(4) and (5) of the Immigration and Asylum Act 1999, the Secretary of State hereby makes the following Order:

1 Citation and interpretation

(1) This Order may be cited as the Immigration and Asylum Act 1999 (Commencement No 2 and Transitional Provisions) Order 2000.

(2) In this Order "the Act" means the Immigration and Asylum Act 1999.

NOTES

Initial Commencement
Date Made
Date made: 21 January 2000: (no specific commencement provision).

2 Commencement of provisions

The provisions of the Act specified in column 1 of the Schedule to this Order shall come into force on the date specified in column 2 of that Schedule, but where a particular purpose is specified in relation to any such provision in column 3 of that Schedule, the provision concerned shall come into force on that date only for that purpose.

NOTES

Initial Commencement
Date Made
Date made: 21 January 2000: (no specific commencement provision).

3 Transitional provisions relating to the appeals provisions commenced by this Order

(1) The adjudicators and the Immigration Appeal Tribunal for the purposes of the Act are to be treated as the adjudicators and the Immigration Appeal Tribunal for the purposes of the previous Immigration Acts.

(2)   Accordingly:

    (a)   references (however expressed) to the Act in the appeals provisions, or in any enactment as amended by those provisions, are to be construed as including a reference to the previous Immigration Acts;

    (b)   references (however expressed) in any Act or in any subordinate legislation (within the meaning of section 21(1) of the Interpretation Act 1978) to adjudicators or the Immigration Appeal Tribunal for the purposes of any of the previous Immigration Acts are to be construed as including references to the adjudicators (other than Asylum Support Adjudicators) or (as the case may be) the Immigration Appeal Tribunal for the purposes of the Act; and

    (c)   the designation of an adjudicator as a special adjudicator under (and for the purposes of) any provision of the previous Immigration Acts shall continue notwithstanding the commencement of the appeals provisions.

(3)   For the purposes of this article:

"the appeals provisions" means sections 56 and 57 of the Act; Schedules 2 and 3 to the Act; paragraph 5 of Schedule 4 to the Act; and paragraphs 71, 72, 91 and 98 of Schedule 14 to the Act; and

"the previous Immigration Acts" means the Immigration Act 1971, the Immigration Act 1988, the Asylum and Immigration Appeals Act 1993, and the Asylum and Immigration Act 1996.

(4)   This article is without prejudice to the operation of the Interpretation Act 1978.

NOTES

Initial Commencement
Date Made
Date made: 21 January 2000: (no specific commencement provision).

Jack Straw
One of Her Majesty's Principal Secretaries of State
Home Office
21st January 2000

SCHEDULE

Article 2

Column 1	Column 2	Column 3
Sections 1 and 2 (Leave to enter; leave to remain).	14th February 2000	
Sections 6 and 7 (Members of Missions other than diplomatic agents; Persons ceasing to be exempt).	1st March 2000	
Section 8 (Persons excluded from the United Kingdom under International Obligations).	1st March 2000	

Section 14 (Escorts for persons removed from the United Kingdom under directions).	1st March 2000	
Sections 28, 29(1), (2) and (4) and 30 (Offences).	14th February 2000	Section 29(1) is commenced so far as it relates to section 29(2) and (4).
Sections 56 (The Immigration Appeal Tribunal) and 57 (Adjudicators).	14th February 2000	
Section 58(2) (Part I of Schedule 4 to the Act).	14th February 2000	Commenced for the purposes of the provisions of Part I of Schedule 4 to the Act commenced by this Order.
Sections 128 to 139 (Powers to arrest and search).	14th February 2000	
Section 169.	14th February 2000	Commenced for the purposes of the provisions of Schedules 14 to 16 to the Act commenced by this Order.
Schedules 2 (The Immigration Appeal Tribunal) and 3 (Adjudicators).	14th February 2000	
In Schedule 4 (Appeals), paragraphs 3 to 5.	14th February 2000	
In Schedule 14, paragraphs 43, 44(1), 45, 49, 50, 51, 53, 56 to 60, 62(1), (3) and (4), 63, 64, 67, 68, 71, 72, 80(1), (2) and (3), 90(1), (2) and (3), 91, 94 to 96, 98, 108, 109, 118 and 125 (Provisions consequential on the provisions of the Act commenced by this Order).	14th February 2000	Paragraph 43 is commenced so far as it relates to paragraphs 44(1), 45, 49, 50, 51, 53, 56 to 60, 62 to 64, 67 and 68 of the Schedule; paragraph 49 is commenced so far it repeals section 12 of the Immigration Act 1971; paragraphs 80(1) and 90(1) are commenced so far as they relate to paragraphs 80(2) and (3) and 90(2) and (3) respectively; paragraph 94 is commenced so far as it relates to paragraphs 95 and 96; paragraph 108 is commenced so far as it relates to paragraph 109; and paragraph 118 is commenced so far as it relates to paragraph 125.
In Schedule 15, paragraphs 1, 3, 4(b) and 14 (Transitional provisions).	14th February 2000	

In Schedule 16, the following 14th February 2000 entries: in the entry relating to the Immigration Act 1971, the entries in the third column concerning Part II of, sections 24 and 25 of, and Schedules 2 and 5 to, that Act; the entries relating to the House of Commons Disqualification Act 1975, the Northern Ireland Assembly Disqualification Act 1975, the Courts and Legal Services Act 1990 and the Judicial Pensions and Retirement Act 1993; and, in the entry relating to the Asylum and Immigration Act 1996, the entry in the third column concerning section 7 of that Act.

In the case of the entry relating to Part II of the Immigration Act 1971, it is commenced so far as it repeals section 12 of that Act; and in the case of the entry relating to Schedule 2 to that Act, it is commenced so far as it repeals words in paragraphs 21 and 26 of that Schedule.

NOTES

Initial Commencement
Date Made
Date made: 21 January 2000: (no specific commencement provision).

IMMIGRATION (REGULARISATION PERIOD FOR OVERSTAYERS) REGULATIONS 2000

2000 No 265

Made - - - 7th February 2000

Coming into force - - - 8th February 2000

Whereas a draft of these Regulations has been laid before Parliament and approved by a resolution of each House in accordance with section 166(5) of the Immigration and Asylum Act 1999;

Now, therefore, the Secretary of State, in exercise of the powers conferred upon him by sections 9(1), (2) and (3), 166(3) and 167 of that Act, hereby makes the following Regulations:

1 Citation, commencement and interpretation

(1) These Regulations may be cited as the Immigration (Regularisation Period for Overstayers) Regulations 2000 and shall come into force on the day after the day on which they are made.

(2) In these Regulations "the Act" means the Immigration and Asylum Act 1999.

NOTES

Initial Commencement
Specified date
Specified date: 8 February 2000: see para (1) above.

2 Manner of application

(1)   An application under section 9(1) of the Act shall be made in the following manner.

(2)   The application shall be made in writing, setting out the information required by paragraph (4), and attaching the material required by paragraph (5).

(3)   The application shall either:

   (a)   be sent by post to the following address:
         Regularisation Scheme for Overstayers
         Initial Consideration Unit
         Immigration and Nationality Directorate
         Block C
         Whitgift Centre
         Croydon
         CR9 1AT; or

   (b)   be delivered by hand to the Home Office at:
         The Public Caller Unit
         Immigration and Nationality Directorate
         Block C
         Whitgift Centre
         Wellesley Road
         Croydon.

(4)   The information referred to in paragraph (2) is:

   (a)   the applicant's full name, date of birth and nationality;
   (b)   the applicant's home address or, if none, an address where he may be contacted;
   (c)   the name and address of any representative who is acting on behalf of the applicant;
   (d)   the date of each occasion on which leave to enter or remain has been granted to the applicant since his first arrival in the United Kingdom, if known;
   (e)   in relation to each date specified in accordance with sub-paragraph (d), the period for which leave was granted, if known;
   (f)   the applicant's Home Office reference, if known;
   (g)   the fact that the application is made under section 9 of the Act; and
   (h)   all the circumstances which the applicant wishes the Secretary of State to take into account when considering his application, including:
      (i)   his length of residence in the United Kingdom;
      (ii)   the strength of his connections with the United Kingdom;
      (iii) his personal history, including character, conduct and employment record;
      (iv)   his domestic circumstances; and
      (v)   any compassionate circumstances.

(5)   The material referred to in paragraph (2) is:

   (a)   the applicant's current passport, if he has one and it is available to him;
   (b)   any other passports (whether expired or not) which have been used by the applicant and which are available to him; and
   (c)   any document or copy document which the applicant considers is evidence supporting his application.

NOTES

Initial Commencement
Specified date
Specified date: 8 February 2000: see reg 1(1).

3 Prescribed days

(1)   The day prescribed for the purposes of section 9(2) of the Act (the start of the regularisation period) is the day on which these Regulations come into force or, if later, 1st February 2000.

(2)   The day prescribed for the purposes of section 9(3) of the Act (the end of the regularisation period in certain circumstances) is 1st October 2000.

NOTES

Initial Commencement
Specified date
Specified date: 8 February 2000: see reg 1(1).

4 Delivery of applications

(1)   Paragraph (2) applies to an application sent by recorded delivery, addressed to the address set out in regulation 2(3)(a).

(2)   Such an application shall be taken to have been delivered for the purposes of these Regulations and section 9 of the Act on the second day after the day on which it was posted, if not received earlier.

NOTES

Initial Commencement
Specified date
Specified date: 8 February 2000: see reg 1(1).

Barbara Roche

Minister of State

Home Office

7th February 2000

ASYLUM SUPPORT APPEALS (PROCEDURE) RULES 2000

2000 No 541

Made - - - 2nd March 2000

Laid before Parliament - - - 10th March 2000

Coming into force - - - 3rd April 2000

The Secretary of State, in exercise of the powers conferred on him by sections 104 and 166(3) of the Immigration and Asylum Act 1999, after consultation with the Council on Tribunals in accordance with section 8 of the Tribunals and Inquiries Act 1992, and having regard to the desirability of securing, so far as is reasonably practicable, that appeals are brought and disposed of with the minimum of delay, hereby makes the following Rules:

General

1 Title and commencement

These Rules may be cited as the Asylum Support Appeals (Procedure) Rules 2000 and shall come into force on 3rd April 2000.

NOTES

Initial Commencement
Specified date
Specified date: 3 April 2000: see above.

2 Interpretation

(1)   In these Rules—

"the Act" means the Immigration and Asylum Act 1999;

"adjudication" means a decision of an adjudicator made in accordance with section 103(3) of the Act;

"appeal bundle" means a bundle prepared by the Secretary of State containing copies of the following documents:

(a)   the form on which the appellant made a claim for support under section 95 of the Act, if the appeal is made under section 103(1) of the Act;

(b)   any supporting documentation attached to that form;

(c)   the decision letter; and

(d)   other material relied on by the Secretary of State in reaching his decision;

"appellant" means a person who appeals under section 103 of the Act against a decision of the Secretary of State;

"bank holiday" means a day that is specified in, or appointed under, the Banking and Financial Dealings Act 1971;

"consideration day" has the meaning given to it by rule 4(4);

"decision letter" means a letter from the Secretary of State giving notice of a decision that gives rise to a right to appeal under section 103;

"excluded day" means a Saturday, a Sunday, a bank holiday, Christmas Day or Good Friday;

"member of the adjudicators' staff" means a person appointed by the Secretary of State under paragraph 5(1) of Schedule 10 to the Act;

"notice of appeal" has the meaning given to it by rule 3(1); and

"party" includes the appellant and the Secretary of State.

(2)   Any reference in these Rules:

(a)   to an adjudicator, in relation to the sending, giving or receiving of notices or other documents, whether by an adjudicator or a party to the appeal, includes a reference to a member of the adjudicators' staff;

(b)   to an adjudicator, in relation to the receiving of a notice of appeal by him, includes a reference to the offices occupied by the adjudicators;

(c)   to the appellant, in relation to the sending or giving of notices or other documents by the adjudicator or the Secretary of State, is also a reference to his representative, if he has one; and

(d)   to a representative is to be construed in accordance with rule 15.

(3)   For the purposes of these Rules, an appeal is determined when an adjudicator gives his adjudication.

NOTES

Initial Commencement
Specified date
Specified date: 3 April 2000: see r 1.

Procedure before determination of appeal

3 Notice of appeal

(1)   A person who wishes to appeal under section 103 of the Act must give notice to an adjudicator by completing in full, and in English, the form for the time being issued by the Secretary of State for the purpose ("notice of appeal"); and any form so issued is to be in the form shown in the Schedule to these Rules or a form to like effect.

(2)   The notice of appeal must be signed by the appellant or his representative.

(3)   Subject to paragraph (4), the notice of appeal must be received by the adjudicator not later than 2 days after the day on which the appellant received the decision letter.

(4)   The adjudicator may extend the time limit for receiving the notice of appeal (either before or after its expiry) if:

(a)   he considers that it is in the interests of justice to do so; and
(b)   he is satisfied that:
   (i)   the appellant; or
   (ii)   his representative (if he has one);
       was prevented from complying with the time limit by circumstances beyond his control.

NOTES

Initial Commencement
Specified date
Specified date: 3 April 2000: see r 1.

4 Procedure after receiving notice of appeal

(1)   On the day that the adjudicator receives notice of appeal or, if not reasonably practicable, as soon as possible on the following day, he must send a copy of the notice of appeal, and any supporting documents, to the Secretary of State by fax.

(2)   On the day after the day on which the adjudicator receives notice of appeal, the Secretary of State must send the appeal bundle to the adjudicator by fax or by hand and to the appellant by first class post or by fax.

(3)   On consideration day, the adjudicator must:

(a)   decide in accordance with rule 5 whether there should be an oral hearing;
(b)   set the date for determining the appeal in accordance with rule 6;
(c)   if there is to be an oral hearing, give notice to the Secretary of State and the appellant, in accordance with rule 7, of the date on which it is to be held.

(4)   "Consideration day" means the day after the day on which the Secretary of State sends the appeal bundle to the adjudicator in accordance with paragraph (2).

NOTES

Initial Commencement
Specified date
Specified date: 3 April 2000: see r 1.

5 Whether there should be an oral hearing

(1)   The adjudicator must decide to hold an oral hearing:

(a)   where the appellant has requested an oral hearing in his notice of appeal; or
(b)   if the adjudicator considers that it is necessary for the appeal to be disposed of justly.

(2)   In all other cases, the appeal may be determined without an oral hearing.

NOTES

Initial Commencement
Specified date
Specified date: 3 April 2000: see r 1.

6 Date for determination of appeal

(1)   If there is to be an oral hearing, the hearing must be held and the appeal determined 4 days after consideration day.

(2)   In all other cases, the appeal must be determined on consideration day, or as soon as possible thereafter, but in any event not later than 4 days after consideration day.

NOTES

Initial Commencement
Specified date
Specified date: 3 April 2000: see r 1.

7 Notification of date of oral hearing

If there is to be an oral hearing, the adjudicator must send a notice to the appellant and to the Secretary of State informing them of the date, time and place of the hearing.

NOTES

Initial Commencement
Specified date
Specified date: 3 April 2000: see r 1.

8 Further evidence provided before the determination of the appeal

(1)   Where the appellant sends to the adjudicator evidence to which this paragraph applies, the appellant must at the same time send a copy of such evidence to the Secretary of State.

(2)   Paragraph (1) applies to evidence which is sent after the appellant has sent notice of appeal to the adjudicator but before the appeal has been determined.

(3)   Where the Secretary of State sends to the adjudicator evidence to which this paragraph applies, the Secretary of State must at the same time send a copy of such evidence to the appellant.

(4)   Paragraph (3) applies to evidence which is sent after the Secretary of State has sent the appeal bundle to the adjudicator but before the appeal has been determined.

NOTES

Initial Commencement
Specified date
Specified date: 3 April 2000: see r 1.

Determination of appeal

9 Hearing of appeal in absence of either party

(1)   If an appellant has indicated in his notice of appeal that he does not want to attend, or be represented at, an oral hearing, the hearing may proceed in his absence.

(2)   Where:

(a)   an appellant has indicated in his notice of appeal that he wants to attend, or be represented at, an oral hearing;

(b)   he has been notified of the date, time and place of the hearing in accordance with rule 7; and

(c)   neither he nor his representative (if he has one) attends the hearing;

the hearing may proceed in his absence.

(3)   Where neither the Secretary of State nor his representative (if he has one) attends the hearing, it may proceed in his absence.

NOTES

Initial Commencement
Specified date
Specified date: 3 April 2000: see r 1.

10 Evidence

(1)   Paragraph (2) applies to all appeals.

(2)   The adjudicator may take into account any matters which he considers to be relevant to the appeal (including matters arising after the date on which the decision appealed against was taken).

(3)   Paragraphs (4) to (6) apply to oral hearings only.

(4)   No person may be compelled to give any evidence or produce any document which he could not be compelled to give or produce on the trial of an action.

(5)   The adjudicator may require any witness to give evidence on oath or affirmation, and for that purpose an oath or affirmation in due form may be administered.

(6)   When the adjudicator takes into consideration documentary evidence at an oral hearing, a party present at the hearing is to be given an opportunity of inspecting and considering that evidence and taking copies if copies have not been provided previously to that party in accordance with these Rules.

NOTES

Initial Commencement
Specified date
Specified date: 3 April 2000: see r 1.

11 Record of proceedings

A record of the proceedings at an oral hearing before the adjudicator is to be made.

NOTES

Initial Commencement
Specified date
Specified date: 3 April 2000: see r 1.

12 Exclusion of public

(1)   Subject to the provisions of this rule, oral hearings are to take place in public.

(2)   Subject to the provisions of paragraph (3), the adjudicator may exclude a member of the public or members of the public generally from a hearing or from part of a hearing if, and to the extent that, he considers it necessary to do so in the public interest.

(3)   But nothing in this rule is to prevent a member of the Council on Tribunals, a member of the Scottish Committee of that Council, the Chief Asylum Support Adjudicator or the Deputy Chief Asylum Support Adjudicator, in their capacity as such, from attending an oral hearing.

NOTES

Initial Commencement
Specified date
Specified date: 3 April 2000: see r 1.

13 Adjudication

(1)   Where an oral hearing is held:

- (a)   the adjudicator must inform all persons present of his adjudication at the conclusion of the hearing;
- (b)   if neither the appellant nor his representative (if he has one) is present at the conclusion of the hearing, the adjudicator must send notice of his adjudication on the same day to the appellant;
- (c)   if the Secretary of State is not present at the conclusion of the hearing, the adjudicator must send notice of his adjudication on the same day to the Secretary of State; and
- (d)   not later than 2 days after the day on which the appeal is determined, the adjudicator must send a reasons statement to the appellant and the Secretary of State.

(2)   Where there is no oral hearing, the adjudicator must on the day that the appeal is determined:

- (a)   send notice of his adjudication to the appellant and the Secretary of State; and
- (b)   send a reasons statement to them.

(3)   An adjudication takes effect from the day on which it is made.

(4)   A "reasons statement" is a written statement giving reasons for the adjudication.

NOTES

Initial Commencement
Specified date
Specified date: 3 April 2000: see r 1.

Miscellaneous

14 Directions

The adjudicator may give directions on any matter arising in connection with an appeal if he considers it necessary or desirable to do so in the interests of justice.

NOTES

Initial Commencement
Specified date
Specified date: 3 April 2000: see r 1.

15 Representation

A party to the appeal may be represented by any other person.

NOTES

Initial Commencement
Specified date
Specified date: 3 April 2000: see r 1.

16 Withdrawal of decision

(1)   Where the Secretary of State withdraws the decision which is appealed against, he must give notice to the adjudicator and the appellant forthwith.

(2)   Where the appellant withdraws his appeal, he must give notice to the adjudicator and the Secretary of State forthwith.

(3)   Where paragraph (1) or (2) applies, the appeal is to be treated for all purposes as at an end.

NOTES

Initial Commencement
Specified date
Specified date: 3 April 2000: see r 1.

17 Notices

In the absence of express provision, any notice or other document required or authorised by these Rules to be sent or given by any party may be sent by first class post, by fax or by hand.

NOTES

Initial Commencement
Specified date
Specified date: 3 April 2000: see r 1.

18 Time

(1)   Subject to paragraph (2), for the purposes of these Rules, a notice or other document is to be taken to have been received on the day on which it was in fact received.

(2)   Where a notice or other document is sent by first class post by the Secretary of State or by the adjudicator, it is to be taken to have been received 2 days after the day on which it was sent, unless the contrary is proven.

(3)   Where reference is made in these Rules to a specified number of days after an event, the number of days is to be calculated from the expiry of the day on which the event occurred.

(4)   Where these Rules provide that an act is to be done or to be taken to have been done:

    (a)   not later than a specified number of days after an event; or
    (b)   a specified number of days after an event;
and that number of days:

    (c)   expires on an excluded day, the act is to be taken to have been done as required if done on the next working day;
    (d)   includes an excluded day, that day is to be discounted.

(5)   Where these Rules provide that an act is to be done or to be taken to have been done on a certain day and that day is an excluded day, the act is to be taken to have been done as required if done on the next working day.

NOTES

Initial Commencement
Specified date
Specified date: 3 April 2000: see r 1.

19 Irregularities

(1) Any irregularity resulting from failure to comply with these Rules before the adjudicator has determined the appeal is not by itself to render the proceedings void.

(2) But the adjudicator must, if he considers that either party may have been prejudiced, take such steps as he thinks fit to remove or reduce the prejudice.

NOTES

Initial Commencement
Specified date
Specified date: 3 April 2000: see r 1.

Barbara Roche
Minister of State
Home Office
2nd March 2000

SCHEDULE
Notice of Appeal

Rule 3(1)

ASYLUM SUPPORT ADJUDICATORS
NOTICE OF APPEAL

Section one

Give your personal details

Full Name: . . . .

Date of Birth: . . . . Nationality: . . . .

Your NASS reference number: . . . .

Section two

Give an address in the United Kingdom
where we can contact you: . . . .

. . . .

. . . .

. . . .

Give a daytime fax or telephone number in the UK
where we can contact you (if you have one): . . . .

Section three

Give the date of the decision letter against which
you are appealing: . . . .

Section four

Do you want an oral hearing of your appeal?   Yes/No

Do you want to attend any oral hearing of your appeal?   Yes/No

If you want to attend the hearing, will you need an interpreter?   Yes/No

If so, in what language?   .. ..

Are you to be represented in this appeal?   Yes/No

If so you must give full details of your representative: name and address, and telephone and fax numbers if available, together with any reference number the representative has given your case. .. ..
.. ..

Will your representative attend any oral hearing of your appeal?   Yes/No

Section five

What are the grounds of your appeal?

What matters in the decision letter do you dispute?

Signed: . . . . Date: . . . .

[Appellant/Representative]

If you have further information which you would like the Adjudicator to take into account when making a decision about your appeal, you should send copies of any documents with this form.

Return this form to:

Asylum Support Adjudicator
Christopher Wren House
113 High Street
Croydon CR0 1GQ

NOTES

Initial Commencement
Specified date
Specified date: 3 April 2000: see r 1.

SOCIAL SECURITY (IMMIGRATION AND ASYLUM) CONSEQUENTIAL AMENDMENTS REGULATIONS 2000

2000 No 636

Made - - - 7th March 2000

Laid before Parliament - - - 13th March 2000

Coming into force - - - 3rd April 2000

The Secretary of State for Social Security, in exercise of the powers conferred upon him by sections 115(3), (4) and (7), 123(5) and (6), 166(3) and 167 of the Immigration and Asylum Act 1999, sections 64(1), 68(4), 70(4), 71(6), 123(1)(a), (d) and (e), 135(1), 136(3) and (4), 137(1) and (2)(i), and 175(1), (3) and (4) of the Social Security Contributions and Benefits Act 1992, section 5(1)(a) and (b), 189(1) and (4) and 191 of the Social Security Administration Act 1992, sections 12(1) and (2), 35(1) and 36(2) and (4) of the Jobseekers Act 1995 and of all other powers enabling him in that behalf, by this Instrument, which contains only regulations made by virtue of, or consequential upon, the Immigration and Asylum Act 1999 and which is made before the end of the period of six months beginning with the coming into force of that Act and, in so far as they relate to housing benefit and council tax benefit, with the agreement of such organisations appearing to him to be representative of the authorities concerned that consultation should not be undertaken hereby make the following Regulations:

1 Citation, commencement and interpretation

(1)   These Regulations may be cited as the Social Security (Immigration and Asylum) Consequential Amendments Regulations 2000.

(2)   These Regulations shall come into force on 3rd April 2000.

(3)   In these Regulations—

> "the Act" means the Immigration and Asylum Act 1999;
> "the Attendance Allowance Regulations" means the Social Security (Attendance Allowance) Regulations 1991;
> "the Claims and Payments Regulations" means the Social Security (Claims and Payments) Regulations 1987;
> "the Contributions and Benefits Act" means the Social Security Contributions and Benefits Act 1992;
> "the Council Tax Benefit Regulations" means the Council Tax Benefit (General) Regulations 1992;
> "the Disability Living Allowance Regulations" means the Social Security (Disability Living Allowance) Regulations 1991;
> "the Housing Benefit Regulations" means the Housing Benefit (General) Regulations 1987;
> "the Income Support Regulations" means the Income Support (General) Regulations 1987;
> "the Invalid Care Allowance Regulations" means the Social Security (Invalid Care Allowance) Regulations 1976;
> "the Jobseeker's Allowance Regulations" means the Jobseeker's Allowance Regulations 1996;
> "the Persons from Abroad Regulations" means the Social Security (Persons from Abroad) Miscellaneous Amendments Regulations 1996;
> "the Severe Disablement Allowance Regulations" means the Social Security (Severe Disablement Allowance) Regulations 1984.

(4)   In these Regulations, unless the context otherwise requires, a reference—

    (a)   to a numbered regulation or Schedule is to the regulation in, or the Schedule to, these Regulations bearing that number;

    (b)   in a regulation or Schedule to a numbered paragraph is to the paragraph in that regulation or Schedule bearing that number.

NOTES

Initial Commencement
Specified date
Specified date: 3 April 2000: see para (2) above.

2 Persons not excluded from specified benefits under section 115 of the Immigration and Asylum Act 1999

(1)   For the purposes of entitlement to income-based jobseeker's allowance, income support, a social fund payment, housing benefit or council tax benefit under the Contributions and Benefits Act, as the case may be, a person falling within a category or description of persons specified in Part I of the Schedule is a person to whom section 115 of the Act does not apply.

(2)   For the purposes of entitlement to attendance allowance, severe disablement allowance, invalid care allowance, disability living allowance, a social fund payment or child benefit under the Contributions and Benefits Act, as the case may be, a person falling within a category or description of persons specified in Part II of the Schedule is a person to whom section 115 of the Act does not apply.

(3)   For the purposes of entitlement to child benefit, attendance allowance or disability living allowance under the Contributions and Benefits Act, as the case may be, a person in respect of whom there is an Order in Council made under section 179 of the Social Security Administration Act 1992 giving effect to a reciprocal agreement in respect of one of those benefits, as the case may be, is a person to whom section 115 of the Act does not apply.

(4)   For the purposes of entitlement to—

    (a)   income support, a social fund payment, housing benefit or council tax benefit under the Contributions and Benefits Act, as the case may be, a person who is entitled to or is receiving benefit by virtue of paragraph (1) or (2) of regulation 12 of the Persons from Abroad Regulations is a person to whom section 115 of the Act does not apply;

    (b)   attendance allowance, disability living allowance, invalid care allowance, severe disablement allowance, a social fund payment or child benefit under the Contributions and Benefits Act, as the case may be, a person who is entitled to or is receiving benefit by virtue of paragraph (10) of regulation 12 is a person to whom section 115 of the Act does not apply.

(5)   For the purposes of entitlement to income support by virtue of regulation 70 of the Income Support Regulations (urgent cases), to jobseeker's allowance by virtue of regulation 147 of the Jobseeker's Allowance Regulations (urgent cases) or to a social fund payment under the Contributions and Benefits Act, as the case may be, a person to whom regulation 12(3) applies is a person to whom section 115 of the Act does not apply.

(6)   For the purposes of entitlement to housing benefit, council tax benefit or a social fund payment under the Contributions and Benefits Act, as the case may be, a person to whom regulation 12(6) applies is a person to whom section 115 of the Act does not apply.

NOTES

Initial Commencement
Specified date
Specified date: 3 April 2000: see reg 1(2).

3 Amendment of the Income Support Regulations

(1)   The Income Support Regulations shall be amended in accordance with the following provisions of this regulation.

(2)   In regulation 2(1) (interpretation)—

(a)   after the definition of "housing benefit expenditure" there shall be inserted the following definition—

""Immigration and Asylum Act" means the Immigration and Asylum Act 1999;" and

(b)   the definition of "immigration authorities" shall be omitted.

(3)   In paragraph (3)(a) of regulation 4ZA, for the words "regulation 70(3)(a)" there shall be substituted the words "paragraph 1 of Part I of the Schedule to the Social Security (Immigration and Asylum) Consequential Amendments Regulations 2000".

(4)   In regulation 21 (special cases)—

(a)   in paragraph (1) for the words "regulation 21ZA" there shall be substituted the words "regulation 21ZB";
(b)   in paragraph (3) the first definition of "person from abroad" shall be omitted;
(c)   in paragraph (3), after the opening words, there shall be inserted the following definition—
""partner of a person subject to immigration control" means a person—
  (i)   who is not subject to immigration control within the meaning of section 115(9) of the Immigration and Asylum Act; or
  (ii)   to whom section 115 of that Act does not apply by virtue of regulation 2 of the Social Security (Immigration and Asylum) Consequential Amendments Regulations 2000; and
  (iii)   who is a member of a couple and his partner is subject to immigration control within the meaning of section 115(9) of that Act and section 115 of that Act applies to her for the purposes of exclusion from entitlement to income support;"; and
(d)   in paragraph (3) in the second definition of "person from abroad" the word "also" shall be omitted.

(5)   For regulation 21ZA (treatment of refugees) after the heading there shall be substituted the following regulation—

"21ZB

(1)   This paragraph applies to a person who has submitted a claim for asylum on or after 3rd April 2000 and who is notified that he has been recorded by the Secretary of State as a refugee within the definition in Article 1 of the Convention relating to the Status of Refugees done at Geneva on 28th July 1951 as extended by Article 1(2) of the Protocol relating to the Status of Refugees done at New York on 31st January 1967.

(2)   Subject to paragraph (3), a person to whom paragraph (1) applies, who claims income support within 28 days of receiving the notification referred to in paragraph (1), shall have his claim for income support determined as if he had been recorded as a refugee on the date when he submitted his claim for asylum.

(3)   The amount of support provided under section 95 or 98 of the Immigration and Asylum Act, including support provided by virtue of regulations made under Schedule 9 to that Act, by the Secretary of State in respect of essential living needs of the claimant and his dependants (if any) as specified in regulations made under paragraph 3 of Schedule 8 to the Immigration and Asylum Act shall be deducted from any award of income support due to the claimant by virtue of paragraph (2).".

(6)   In regulation 40 (calculation of income other than earnings)—

  (a)   at the beginning of paragraph (4) there shall be inserted the words "Subject to paragraph (5)";

  (b)   in paragraph (4) for the words following "paragraph (1)" there shall be substituted the following sub-paragraphs—

  "(a)   any payment to which regulation 35(2)(a) or 37(2) (payments not earnings) applies; or

  (b)   in the case of a claimant who is receiving support provided under section 95 or 98 of the Immigration and Asylum Act including support provided by virtue of regulations made under Schedule 9 to that Act, the amount of such support provided in respect of essential living needs of the claimant and his dependants (if any) as is specified in regulations made under paragraph 3 of Schedule 8 to the Immigration and Asylum Act;";

  (c)   after paragraph (4) there shall be added the following paragraph—

"(5) In the case of a claimant who is the partner of a person subject to immigration control and whose partner is receiving support provided under section 95 or 98 of the Immigration and Asylum Act including support provided by virtue of regulations made under Schedule 9 to that Act, there shall not be included as income to be taken into account under paragraph (1) the amount of support provided in respect of essential living needs of the partner of the claimant and his dependants (if any) as is specified in regulations made under paragraph 3 of Schedule 8 to the Immigration and Asylum Act.".

(7)   In regulation 70 (urgent cases)—

  (a)   in paragraph (2) for sub-paragraph (a) there shall be substituted the following sub-paragraph—

  "(a)   a claimant to whom paragraph (2A) applies (persons not excluded from income support under section 115 of the Immigration and Asylum Act);";

  (b)   after paragraph (2) there shall be inserted the following paragraph—

"(2A)   This paragraph applies to a person not excluded from entitlement to income support under section 115 of the Immigration and Asylum Act by virtue of regulation 2 of the Social Security (Immigration and Asylum) Consequential Amendments Regulations 2000 except for a person to whom paragraphs 3 and 4 of Part I of the Schedule to those Regulations applies."; and

  (c)   paragraphs (3), (3A) and (3B) shall be omitted.

(8)   In regulation 71 (applicable amounts in urgent cases)—

  (a)   in paragraph (1)(d), for the words "paragraph 17" there shall be substituted the words "paragraph 16A"; and

  (b)   in paragraph (2), for the words "paragraph (3)" in each place where they occur, there shall be substituted the words "paragraph 2A".

(9)   In Schedule 1B (prescribed categories of person)—

  (a)   after paragraph 18, there shall be inserted the following paragraph—

"18A

A person to whom regulation 21ZB (treatment of refugees) applies by virtue of regulation 21ZB(2) from the date his claim for asylum is made until the date the Secretary of State makes a decision on that claim.";

    (b)   in paragraph 21, for the words "regulation 70(3)" there shall be substituted the words "regulation 70(2A)".

(10) After paragraph 16 of Schedule 7 (applicable amounts in special cases)—

    (a)   in column (1) there shall be inserted the following paragraph—

"Partner of a person subject to immigration control

16A

    (a)   A claimant who is the partner of a person subject to immigration control.
    (b)   Where regulation 18 (polygamous marriages) applies and the claimant is a person—
        (i)   who is not subject to immigration control within the meaning of section 115(9) of the Immigration and Asylum Act; or
        (ii)   to whom section 115 of that Act does not apply by virtue of regulation 2 of the Social Security (Immigration and Asylum) Consequential Amendments Regulations 2000; and
        (iii)   who is a member of a couple and one or more of his partners is subject to immigration control within the meaning of section 115(9) of that Act and section 115 of that Act applies to her for the purposes of exclusion from entitlement to income support.";
    (b)   in column (2) there shall be inserted the following paragraph—

"16A

    (a)   The amount applicable in respect of the claimant only under regulation 17(1)(a) plus that in respect of any child or young person who is a member of his family and who is not a person subject to immigration control within the meaning of section 115(9) of the Immigration and Asylum Act, and to whom section 115 of that Act does not apply for the purposes of exclusion from entitlement to income support, any amounts which may be applicable to him under regulation 17(1)(b), (c) or (d) plus the amount applicable to him under regulation 17(1)(e), (f) and (g) or, as the case may be, regulation 19 or 21.
    (b)   The amount determined in accordance with that regulation or regulation 19 or 21 in respect of the claimant and any partners of his and any child or young person for whom he or his partner is treated as responsible, who are not subject to immigration control within the meaning of section 115(9) of the Immigration and Asylum Act and to whom section 115 of that Act does not apply for the purposes of exclusion from entitlement to income support.".

(11) In paragraph 17 of Schedule 7 (applicable amounts in special cases) for the words in column (1) there shall be substituted the words "person from abroad" and for the words in column (2) there shall be substituted the word "nil".

(12) In paragraph 21 of Schedule 9 (treatment of income in kind)—

    (a)   in sub-paragraph (1) for the words "Subject to sub-paragraph (2)" there shall be substituted the words "Subject to sub-paragraphs (2) and (3)";
    (b)   in sub-paragraph (1) after the words "except where" there shall be added the following words—

"regulation 40(4)(b) (provision of support under section 95 or 98 of the Immigration and Asylum Act including support provided by virtue of regulations made under Schedule 9 to that Act in the calculation of income other than earnings) or";

(c)   after sub-paragraph (2) there shall be added the following sub-paragraph—

"(3) The first exception under sub-paragraph (1) shall not apply where the claimant is the partner of a person subject to immigration control and whose partner is receiving support provided under section 95 or 98 of the Immigration and Asylum Act including support provided by virtue of regulations made under Schedule 9 to that Act and the income in kind is support provided in respect of essential living needs of the partner of the claimant and his dependants (if any) as is specified in regulations made under paragraph 3 of Schedule 8 to the Immigration and Asylum Act.".

(13) In paragraph 57 of Schedule 9 (disregards in the calculation of income other than earnings) and paragraph 49 of Schedule 10 (capital to be disregarded) for the words "regulation 21ZA" there shall be substituted the words "regulation 21ZB".

NOTES

Initial Commencement
Specified date
Specified date: 3 April 2000: see reg 1(2).

4 Amendment of the Jobseeker's Allowance Regulations

(1)   The Jobseeker's Allowance Regulations shall be amended in accordance with the following provisions of this regulation.

(2)   In regulation 1(3) (interpretation) after the definition of "housing benefit expenditure" there shall be inserted the following definition—

""Immigration and Asylum Act" means the Immigration and Asylum Act 1999;".

(3)   In regulation 85(4) (special cases)—

(a)   the first definition of "person from abroad" shall be omitted;
(b)   in the second definition of "person from abroad" the word "also" shall be omitted; and
(c)   at the beginning of paragraph (4), after the opening words, there shall be inserted the following definition—
""partner of a person subject to immigration control" means a person—
(i)   who is not subject to immigration control within the meaning of section 115(9) of the Immigration and Asylum Act; or
(ii)   to whom section 115 of that Act does not apply by virtue of regulation 2 of the Social Security (Immigration and Asylum) Consequential Amendments Regulations 2000; and
(iii)   who is a member of a couple and his partner is subject to immigration control within the meaning of section 115(9) of that Act and section 115 of that Act applies to her for the purposes of exclusion from entitlement to jobseeker's allowance;".

(4)   In regulation 103(6) (calculation of income other than earnings) for the words following "paragraph (1)" there shall be substituted the following sub-paragraphs—

"(a) any payment to which regulation 98(2)(a) to (e) or 100(2) (payments not earnings) applies; or
(b) in the case of a claimant who is receiving support under section 95 or 98 of the Immigration and Asylum Act including support provided by virtue of regulations made under Schedule 9 to that Act, the amount of such support provided in respect of essential living needs of the claimant and his dependants

(if any) as is specified in regulations made under paragraph 3 of Schedule 8 to the Immigration and Asylum Act.".

(5)   In regulation 147 (urgent cases)—

    (a)   in paragraph (2) for sub-paragraph (a) there shall be substituted the following sub-paragraph—

"(a)   a claimant to whom paragraph (2A) applies (persons not excluded from income-based jobseeker's allowance under section 115 of the Immigration and Asylum Act);";

    (b)   after paragraph (2) there shall be inserted the following paragraph—

"(2A)   This paragraph applies to a person not excluded from entitlement to income-based jobseeker's allowance under section 115 of the Immigration and Asylum Act by virtue of regulation 2 of the Social Security (Immigration and Asylum) Consequential Amendments Regulations 2000 except for a person to whom paragraphs 3 and 4 of Part I to the Schedule to those Regulations applies."; and

    (c)   paragraph (3), (4) and (5) shall be omitted.

(6)   In regulation 148(1)(d) (applicable amount in urgent cases) for the words "paragraph 14" there shall be substituted the words "paragraph 13A".

(7)   After paragraph 13 of Schedule 5 (applicable amounts in special cases)—

    (a)   in column (1) there shall be inserted the following paragraph—

"Partner of a person subject to immigration control

13A

    (a)   A claimant who is the partner of a person subject to immigration control.

    (b)   Where regulation 84 (polygamous marriages) applies and the claimant is a person—

        (i)   who is not subject to immigration control within the meaning of section 115(9) of the Immigration and Asylum Act; or

        (ii)   to whom section 115 of that Act does not apply by virtue of regulation 2 of the Social Security (Immigration and Asylum) Consequential Amendments Regulations 2000; and

        (iii) who is a member of a couple and one or more of his partners is subject to immigration control within the meaning of section 115(9) of that Act and section 115 of that Act applies to her for the purposes of exclusion from entitlement to income-based jobseeker's allowance.";

    (b)   in column (2) there shall be inserted the following paragraph—

"13A

    (a)   The amount applicable in respect of the claimant only under regulation 83(a) plus that in respect of any child or young person who is a member of his family and who is not a person subject to immigration control within the meaning of section 115(9) of the Immigration and Asylum Act and to whom section 115 of that Act does not apply for the purposes of exclusion from entitlement to jobseeker's allowance, any amounts which may be applicable to him under regulation 83(b), (d) or (e) plus the amount applicable to him under regulation 87(2) or (3) or, as the case may be, regulation 85 or 86.

    (b)   The amount determined in accordance with that regulation or regulation 85 or 86 in respect of the claimant and any partners of his and any child or young person for whom he or his partner is treated as responsible, who are not subject to immigration control within the meaning of section 115(9) of the Immigration and Asylum Act and to whom section 115 of that Act does not apply for the purposes of exclusion from entitlement to jobseeker's allowance.".

(8)   In paragraph 14 of Schedule 5, for the words in column (1) there shall be substituted the words "person from abroad" and for the words in column (2) there shall be substituted the word "nil".

(9)   In paragraph 22 of Schedule 7 (treatment of income in kind)—

(a)   in sub-paragraph (1) for the words "Subject to sub-paragraph (2)" there shall be substituted the words "Subject to sub-paragraphs (2) and (3)";

(b)   in sub-paragraph (1) after the words "except where" there shall be added the following words—

"regulation 103(6)(b) (provision of support under section 95 or 98 of the Immigration and Asylum Act including support provided by virtue of regulations made under Schedule 9 to that Act in the calculation of income other than earnings) or"; and

(c)   after sub-paragraph (2) there shall be added the following sub-paragraph—

"(3) The first exception under sub-paragraph (1) shall not apply where the claimant is the partner of a person subject to immigration control and whose partner is receiving support provided under section 95 or 98 of the Immigration and Asylum Act including support provided by virtue of regulations made under Schedule 9 to that Act and the income in kind is support provided in respect of essential living needs of the partner of the claimant and his dependants (if any) as is specified in regulations made under paragraph 3 of Schedule 8 to the Immigration and Asylum Act.".

NOTES

Initial Commencement
Specified date
Specified date: 3 April 2000: see reg 1(2).

5 Amendment of the Claims and Payments Regulations

(1)   The Claims and Payments Regulations shall be amended in accordance with the following provisions of this regulation.

(2)   In paragraph (3C) of regulation 4 (making a claim for benefit) for the words "regulation 21ZA(2)" there shall be substituted the words "regulation 21ZB(2)".

(3)   In paragraph (4D) of regulation 6 (date of claim) for sub-paragraphs (a) and (b) there shall be substituted the following words—

"on the date on which his claim for asylum was recorded by the Secretary of State as having been made.".

(4)   In paragraph (8) of regulation 19 (time for claiming benefit) for the words "regulation 21ZA(2)" there shall be substituted the words "regulation 21ZB".

NOTES

Initial Commencement
Specified date
Specified date: 3 April 2000: see reg 1(2).

6 Amendment of the Housing Benefit Regulations

(1)   The Housing Benefit Regulations shall be amended in accordance with the following provisions of this regulation.

(2)   In regulation 2(1) (interpretation) after the definition of "housing association" there shall be inserted the following definition—

""Immigration and Asylum Act" means the Immigration and Asylum Act 1999;".

(3)   In regulation 7A (persons from abroad)—

    (a)   paragraphs (2), (3), (4)(a), (b), (c), (d), (e)(iv), (v) and (vi), (f) and (g), (4A), (5)(a), (b) and (c) and (5A) shall be omitted;

    (b)   in paragraph (6) the words "Paragraphs (3)(b) and (4A)" shall be substituted by the words "Paragraph 1 of Part I of the Schedule to, and regulation 2 as it applies to that paragraph of, the Social Security (Immigration and Asylum) Consequential Amendments Regulations 2000."; and

    (c)   in paragraph (7) the definitions of the "Common Travel Area" and the "Convention relating to the Status of Refugees" shall be omitted.

(4)   In paragraph (4) of regulation 33 (calculation of income other than earnings) for the words following "paragraph (1)" there shall be substituted the following sub-paragraphs—

    "(a)   any payment to which regulation 28(2) (payments not earnings) applies; or

    (b)   in the case of a claimant who is receiving support under section 95 or 98 of the Immigration and Asylum Act including support provided by virtue of regulations made under Schedule 9 to that Act, the amount of such support provided in respect of essential living needs of the claimant and his dependants (if any) as is specified in regulations made under paragraph 3 of Schedule 8 to the Immigration and Asylum Act.".

(5)   In Schedule A1 (treatment of claims for housing benefit by refugees)—

    (a)   in paragraph 1(1)(b) for the words following paragraph (ii) there shall be substituted the following words "his claim for housing benefit shall be treated as having been made on the date specified in sub-paragraph (2)";

    (b)   in paragraph 1(2) for heads (a) and (b), there shall be substituted the following words—

"on the date on which his claim for asylum was recorded by the Secretary of State as having been made.";

    (c)   after paragraph 1 there shall be inserted the following paragraph—

"Appropriate authority to whom a claim for housing benefit by a refugee shall be made and time for making a claim

2A

(1)   A claim for housing benefit made by a refugee on or after 3rd April 2000 for the relevant period may be made to the appropriate authority for the area in which the dwelling which the claimant occupied as his home was situate and in respect of which he was liable to make payments.

(2)   Where the claimant has occupied more than one dwelling as his home in the relevant period, only one claim for housing benefit shall be made in respect of that period and such a claim shall be made to the authority for the area in which the dwelling occupied by the refugee is situate and in respect of which he was liable to make payments when, after he is notified that he has been recorded by the Secretary of State as a refugee, he makes a claim for housing benefit.

(3)   The appropriate authority to which a claim for housing benefit is made in accordance with this paragraph, shall determine the claimant's entitlement to that benefit for the whole of the relevant period.

(4)   A claim for housing benefit to which this paragraph refers, shall be made within 28 days of a claimant receiving notification from the Secretary of State that he has been recorded as a refugee.

(5)   Regulation 72(15) of these Regulations (backdating of claims) shall not have effect with respect to claims to which this Schedule applies.”; and

    (d)   paragraph 2 shall be omitted.

(6)   In paragraph 21 of Schedule 4 (treatment of income in kind) after the words “income in kind” there shall be added the following words—

“except where regulation 33(4)(b) (provision of support under section 95 or 98 of the Immigration and Asylum Act in the calculation of income other than earnings) applies”.

(7)   In paragraph 62 of Schedule 4 and paragraph 51 of Schedule 5 for the words “regulation 21ZA” there shall be substituted the words “regulation 21ZB”.

NOTES

Initial Commencement
Specified date
Specified date: 3 April 2000: see reg 1(2).

7 Amendment of the Council Tax Benefit Regulations

(1)   The Council Tax Benefit Regulations shall be amended in accordance with the following provisions of this regulation.

(2)   In regulation 2(1) (interpretation) after the definition of “housing benefit” there shall be inserted the following definition—

““Immigration and Asylum Act” means the Immigration and Asylum Act 1999;”.

(3)   In regulation 4A—

    (a)   paragraphs (2), (3), (4)(a), (b), (c), (d), (e)(iv), (v) and (vi), (f) and (g), (4A), (5)(a), (b) and (c) and (5A) shall be omitted;
    (b)   in paragraph (6) the words “paragraphs (3)(b) and (4A)” shall be substituted by the words “Paragraph 1 of Part I of the Schedule to, and regulation 2 as it applies to that paragraph of, the Social Security (Immigration and Asylum) Consequential Amendments Regulations 2000.”; and
    (c)   in paragraph (7) the definitions of the “Common Travel Area” and the “Convention relating to the Status of Refugees” shall be omitted.

(4)   In paragraph (5) of regulation 24 (calculation of income other than earnings) for the words following “paragraph (1)” there shall be substituted the following sub-paragraphs—

    “(a)   any payment to which regulation 19(2) (payments not earnings) applies; or
    (b)   in the case of a claimant who is receiving support under section 95 or 98 of the Immigration and Asylum Act including support provided by virtue of regulations made under Schedule 9 to that Act, the amount of such support provided in respect of essential living needs of the claimant and his dependants (if any) as is specified in regulations made under paragraph 3 of Schedule 8 to the Immigration and Asylum Act.”.

(5)   In Schedule A1 (treatment of claims for council tax benefit by refugees)—

    (a)   in paragraph 1(1)(b) for the words following head (ii) there shall be substituted the following words “his claim for council tax benefit shall be treated as having been made on the date specified in sub-paragraph (2)”;
    (b)   in paragraph 1(2) for sub-paragraphs (a) and (b), there shall be substituted the following words—
    “on the date on which his claim for asylum was recorded by the Secretary of State as having been made.”;

(c)   after paragraph 1 there shall be inserted the following paragraph—

"Appropriate authority to whom a claim for council tax benefit by a refugee shall be made and time for making a claim

2A

(1)   A claim for council tax benefit made by a refugee on or after 3rd April 2000 for the relevant period may be made to the appropriate authority for the area in which the dwelling which the claimant occupied as his home was situate and in respect of which he was liable for council tax.

(2)   Where the claimant has occupied more than one dwelling as his home in the relevant period, only one claim for council tax benefit shall be made in respect of that period and such a claim shall be made to the authority for the area in which the dwelling occupied by the refugee is situate and in respect of which he was liable to make payments when, after he is notified that he has been recorded by the Secretary of State as a refugee, he makes a claim for council tax benefit.

(3)   The appropriate authority to which a claim for council tax benefit is made in accordance with this paragraph, shall determine the claimant's entitlement to that benefit for the whole of the relevant period.

(4)   A claim for council tax benefit to which this paragraph refers, shall be made within 28 days of a claimant receiving notification from the Secretary of State that he has been recorded as a refugee.

(5)   Regulation 72(15) of these Regulations (backdating of claims) shall not have effect with respect to claims to which this Schedule applies."; and

(d)   paragraph 2 shall be omitted.

(6)   In paragraph 22 of Schedule 4 (treatment of income in kind) after the words "income in kind" there shall be added the following words—

"except where regulation 24(5) (provision of support under section 95 or 98 of the Immigration and Asylum Act in the calculation of income other than earnings) applies".

(7)   In paragraph 62 of Schedule 4 and paragraph 51 of Schedule 5 for the words "regulation 21ZA" there shall be substituted the words "regulation 21ZB".

NOTES

Initial Commencement
Specified date
Specified date: 3 April 2000: see reg 1(2).

8 Amendment of the Invalid Care Allowance Regulations

(1)   The Invalid Care Allowance Regulations shall be amended in accordance with the following provisions of this regulation.

(2)   In regulation 9(1) for sub-paragraph (aa) there shall be substituted the following sub-paragraph—

"(ia) he is not a person subject to immigration control within the meaning of section 115(9) of the Immigration and Asylum Act 1999 or section 115 of that Act does not apply to him for the purposes of entitlement to invalid care allowance by virtue of regulation 2 of the Social Security (Immigration and Asylum) Consequential Amendments Regulations 2000, and".

(3)   Paragraph (1A) of regulation 9 shall be omitted.

NOTES

Initial Commencement
Specified date
Specified date: 3 April 2000: see reg 1(2).

9 Amendment of the Severe Disablement Allowance Regulations

(1)   The Severe Disablement Allowance Regulations shall be amended in accordance with the following provisions of this regulation.

(2)   In regulation 3(1) for head (ia) of sub-paragraph (a) there shall be substituted the following head—

> "(ib) he is not a person subject to immigration control within the meaning of section 115(9) of the Immigration and Asylum Act 1999 or section 115 of that Act does not apply to him for the purposes of entitlement to severe disablement allowance by virtue of regulation 2 of the Social Security (Immigration and Asylum) Consequential Amendments Regulations 2000, and".

(3)   Paragraph (1B) of regulation 3 shall be omitted.

NOTES

Initial Commencement
Specified date
Specified date: 3 April 2000: see reg 1(2).

10 Amendment of the Attendance Allowance Regulations

(1)   The Attendance Allowance Regulations shall be amended in accordance with the following provisions of this regulation.

(2)   In regulation 2(1) for head (ia) of sub-paragraph (a) there shall be substituted the following head—

> "(ib) he is not a person subject to immigration control within the meaning of section 115(9) of the Immigration and Asylum Act 1999 or section 115 of that Act does not apply to him for the purposes of entitlement to attendance allowance by virtue of regulation 2 of the Social Security (Immigration and Asylum) Consequential Amendments Regulations 2000, and".

(3)   Paragraph (1A) of regulation 2 shall be omitted.

NOTES

Initial Commencement
Specified date
Specified date: 3 April 2000: see reg 1(2).

11 Amendment of the Disability Living Allowance Regulations

(1)   The Disability Living Allowance Regulations shall be amended in accordance with the following provisions of this regulation.

(2)   In regulation 2(1) for head (ia) of sub-paragraph (a) there shall be substituted the following head—

> "(ib) he is not a person subject to immigration control within the meaning of section 115(9) of the Immigration and Asylum Act 1999 or section 115 of

that Act does not apply to him for the purposes of entitlement to disability living allowance by virtue of regulation 2 of the Social Security (Immigration and Asylum) Consequential Amendments Regulations 2000, and".

(3) Paragraph (1A) of regulation 2 shall be omitted.

NOTES

Initial Commencement
Specified date
Specified date: 3 April 2000: see reg 1(2).

12 Transitional arrangements and savings

(1) Paragraph (2) shall apply where, in relation to a claim for income support, a social fund payment, housing benefit or council tax benefit, as the case may be, a person has submitted a claim for asylum on or before 2nd April 2000 and is notified that he has been recorded by the Secretary of State as a refugee within the definition in Article 1 of the Convention relating to the Status of Refugees done at Geneva on 28th July 1951 as extended by Article 1(2) of the Protocol relating to the Status of Refugees done at New York on 31st January 1967.

(2) Where this paragraph applies—

(a) regulation 21ZA of the Income Support Regulations (treatment of refugees) shall continue to have effect as if regulation 3(4)(a), (5) and (9) had not been made;

(b) regulations 4(3C), 6(4D) and 19(8) of the Claims and Payments Regulations shall continue to have effect as if regulation 5 had not been made;

(c) paragraphs 1 and 2 of Schedule A1, paragraph 62 of Schedule 4 and paragraph 51 of Schedule 5 to the Housing Benefit Regulations (treatment of claims for housing benefit by refugees) shall continue to have effect as if regulation 6(5) and (7) had not been made; and

(d) paragraphs 1 and 2 of Schedule A1, paragraph 62 of Schedule 4 and paragraph 51 of Schedule 5 to the Council Tax Benefit Regulations (treatment of claims for council tax benefit by refugees) shall continue to have effect as if regulation 7(5) and (7) had not been made.

(3) Regulation 70 of the Income Support Regulations and regulation 147 of the Jobseeker's Allowance Regulations, as the case may be, shall apply to a person who is an asylum seeker within the meaning of paragraph (4) who has not ceased to be an asylum seeker by virtue of paragraph (5).

(4) An asylum seeker within the meaning of this paragraph is a person who—

(a) submits on his arrival (other than on his re-entry) in the United Kingdom from a country outside the Common Travel Area a claim for asylum on or before 2nd April 2000 to the Secretary of State that it would be contrary to the United Kingdom's obligations under the Convention for him to be removed or required to leave, the United Kingdom and that claim is recorded by the Secretary of State as having been made before that date; or

(b) on or before 2nd April 2000 becomes, while present in Great Britain, an asylum seeker when—

(i) the Secretary of State makes a declaration to the effect that the country of which he is a national is subject to such a fundamental change of circumstances that he would not normally order the return of a person to that country; and

(ii) he submits, within a period of three months from the date that declaration was made, a claim for asylum to the Secretary of State under the Convention relating to the Status of Refugees, and

      (iii) his claim for asylum under that Convention is recorded by the Secretary of State as having been made; and

  (c) in the case of a claim for jobseeker's allowance, holds a work permit or has written authorisation from the Secretary of State permitting him to work in the United Kingdom.

(5) A person ceases to be an asylum seeker for the purposes of this paragraph when his claim for asylum is recorded by the Secretary of State as having been decided (other than on appeal) or abandoned.

(6) For the purposes of regulation 7A of the Housing Benefit Regulations and regulation 4A of the Council Tax Benefit Regulations, a person who is an asylum seeker within the meaning of paragraph (7) who has not ceased to be an asylum seeker by virtue of paragraph (8), is not a person from abroad within the meaning of paragraph (1) of those regulations.

(7) An asylum seeker within the meaning of this paragraph is a person who—

  (a) submits on his arrival (other than on his re-entry) in the United Kingdom from a country outside the Common Travel Area a claim for asylum on or before 2nd April 2000 to the Secretary of State that it would be contrary to the United Kingdom's obligations under the Convention for him to be removed or required to leave, the United Kingdom and that claim is recorded by the Secretary of State as having been made before that date, or

  (b) on or before 2nd April 2000 becomes, while present in Great Britain, an asylum seeker when—

      (i) the Secretary of State makes a declaration to the effect that the country of which he is a national is subject to such a fundamental change of circumstances that he would not normally order the return of a person to that country; and

      (ii) he submits, within a period of three months from the date that declaration was made, a claim for asylum to the Secretary of State under the Convention relating to the Status of Refugees; and

      (iii) his claim for asylum under that Convention is recorded by the Secretary of State as having been made.

(8) A person ceases to be an asylum seeker for the purposes of this paragraph when his claim for asylum is recorded by the Secretary of State as having been decided (other than on appeal) or abandoned.

(9) In paragraphs (4) and (7) "the Common Travel Area" means the United Kingdom, the Channel Islands, the Isle of Man and the Republic of Ireland collectively and "the Convention" means the Convention relating to the Status of Refugees done at Geneva on 28th July 1951 as extended by Article 2(1) of the Protocol relating to the Status of Refugees done at New York on 31st January 1967.

(10) Where, before the coming into force of these Regulations, a person has claimed benefit to which he is entitled or is receiving benefit by virtue of regulation 12(3) of the Persons from Abroad Regulations or regulation 14B(g) of the Child Benefit (General) Regulations 1976, as the case may be, those provisions shall continue to have effect, for the purposes of entitlement to attendance allowance, disability living allowance, invalid care allowance, severe disablement allowance or child benefit, as the case may be, until such time as—

  (a) his claim for asylum (if any) is recorded by the Secretary of State as having been decided or abandoned; or

  (b) his entitlement to that benefit is revised or superseded under section 9 or 10 of the Social Security Act 1998, if earlier,

as if regulations 8, 9, 10 and 11 and paragraph (2) or paragraph (3), as the case may be, of regulation 13, had not been made.

(11) In the Persons from Abroad Regulations—

    (a)   in paragraph (1) of regulation 12, after the words "shall continue to have effect" there shall be inserted the words "(both as regards him and as regards persons who are members of his family at the coming into force of these Regulations)"; and

    (b)   notwithstanding the amendments and revocations in regulations 3, 6 and 7, regulations 12(1) and (2) of the Persons from Abroad Regulations shall continue to have effect as they had effect before those amendments and revocations came into force.

NOTES

Initial Commencement
Specified date
Specified date: 3 April 2000: see reg 1(2).

13 Revocations

(1)   The provisions specified in the following paragraphs of this regulation are revoked.

(2)   Regulation 12(3) of the Persons from Abroad Regulations.

(3)   Regulation 14B of the Child Benefit (General) Regulations 1976.

NOTES

Initial Commencement
Specified date
Specified date: 3 April 2000: see reg 1(2).

Signed by authority of the Secretary of State for Social Security.

Hugh Bayley

Parliamentary Under-Secretary of State,

Department of Social Security

7th March 2000

SCHEDULE
Persons not Excluded from Certain Benefits Under Section 115 of the Immigration and Asylum Act 1999

Regulation 2

Part I
Persons not Excluded Under Section 115 of the Immigration and Asylum Act from Entitlement to Income-Based Jobseeker's Allowance, Income Support, a Social Fund Payment, Housing Benefit or Council Tax Benefit

1   A person who—

    (a)   has limited leave (as defined in section 33(1) of the Immigration Act 1971) to enter or remain in the United Kingdom which was given in accordance with the immigration rules (as defined in that section) relating to—
        (i)   there being or there needing to be, no recourse to public funds, or
        (ii) there being no charge on public funds,
           during that period of limited leave; and

    (b)   having, during any one period of limited leave (including any such period as extended), supported himself without recourse to public funds, other than any such recourse by reason of the previous application of this sub-paragraph, is temporarily without funds during that period of leave because remittances to him from abroad have been disrupted, provided there is a reasonable expectation that his supply of funds will be resumed.

2   A person who has been given leave to enter or remain in, the United Kingdom by the Secretary of State upon an undertaking by another person or persons pursuant to the immigration rules within the meaning of the Immigration Act 1971, to be responsible for his maintenance and accommodation and who has not been resident in the United Kingdom for a period of at least five years beginning on the date of entry or the date on which the undertaking was given in respect of him, whichever date is the later and the person or persons who gave the undertaking to provide for his maintenance and accommodation has, or as the case may be, have died.

3   A person who—

    (a)   has been given leave to enter or remain in, the United Kingdom by the Secretary of State upon an undertaking by another person or persons pursuant to the immigration rules within the meaning of the Immigration Act 1971, to be responsible for his maintenance and accommodation; and

    (b)   has been resident in the United Kingdom for a period of at least five years beginning on the date of entry or the date on which the undertaking was given in respect of him, whichever date is the later.

4   A person who is a national of a state which has ratified the European Convention on Social and Medical Assistance (done in Paris on 11th December 1953) or a state which has ratified the Council of Europe Social Charter (signed in Turin on 18th October 1961) and who is lawfully present in the United Kingdom.

NOTES

Initial Commencement
Specified date
Specified date: 3 April 2000: see reg 1(2).

PART II
PERSONS NOT EXCLUDED UNDER SECTION 115 OF THE IMMIGRATION AND ASYLUM ACT FROM
ENTITLEMENT TO ATTENDANCE ALLOWANCE, SEVERE DISABLEMENT ALLOWANCE, INVALID CARE
ALLOWANCE, DISABILITY LIVING ALLOWANCE, A SOCIAL FUND PAYMENT OR CHILD BENEFIT

1   A member of a family of a national of a State contracting party to the Agreement on the European Economic Area signed at Oporto on 2nd May 1992 as adjusted by the Protocol signed at Brussels on 17th March 1993.

2   A person who is lawfully working in Great Britain and is a national of a State with which the Community has concluded an agreement under Article 310 of the Treaty of Amsterdam amending the Treaty on European Union, the Treaties establishing the European Communities and certain related Acts providing, in the field of social security, for the equal treatment of workers who are nationals of the signatory State and their families.

3   A person who is a member of a family of, and living with, a person specified in paragraph 2.

4   A person who has been given leave to enter, or remain in, the United Kingdom by the Secretary of State upon an undertaking by another person or persons pursuant to the immigration rules within the meaning of the Immigration Act 1971, to be responsible for his maintenance and accommodation.

NOTES

Initial Commencement
Specified date
Specified date: 3 April 2000: see reg 1(2).

CARRIERS' LIABILITY (CLANDESTINE ENTRANTS) (CODE OF PRACTICE) ORDER 2000

2000 No 684

Made - - - 8th March 2000

Laid before Parliament - - - 10th March 2000

Coming into force - - - 3rd April 2000

Whereas—

(1) in pursuance of section 33 of the Immigration and Asylum Act 1999 ("the 1999 Act") the Secretary of State is required to issue a code of practice to be followed by any person operating a system for preventing the carriage of clandestine entrants;

(2) sections 32 and 34 to 37 of the 1999 Act are commenced (so far as not yet already in force) on 3rd April 2000 by the Immigration and Asylum Act 1999 (Commencement No 3) Order 2000 for the purposes of clandestine entrants concealed in vehicles but not in ships or aircraft;

(3) the Secretary of State has prepared the draft of such a code in relation to prevention of the carriage of clandestine entrants concealed in vehicles;

(4) the Secretary of State has consulted such persons as he considers appropriate about the code, both before and after the passing of the 1999 Act, in satisfaction of the requirements of section 33(2) of that Act; and

(5) in pursuance of section 33(2) of the 1999 Act the Secretary of State has laid a draft of the code of practice before each House of Parliament;

Now, therefore, the Secretary of State, in exercise of the powers conferred upon him by sections 33 and 166(3) of the Immigration and Asylum Act 1999, hereby orders as follows:

1 This Order may be cited as the Carriers' Liability (Clandestine Entrants) (Code of Practice) Order 2000 and shall come into force on 3rd April 2000.

NOTES

Initial Commencement
Specified date
Specified date: 3 April 2000: see above.

2 The code of practice entitled "Immigration and Asylum Act 1999: Civil Penalty: Code of Practice for Vehicles", laid in draft before each House of Parliament on 3rd March 2000 and which concerns the practice to be followed by any person operating a system for preventing the carriage of clandestine entrants concealed in vehicles, shall come into operation on 3rd April 2000.

NOTES

Initial Commencement
Specified date
Specified date: 3 April 2000: see art 1.

Barbara Roche
Minister of State
Home Office
8th March 2000

CARRIERS' LIABILITY (CLANDESTINE ENTRANTS AND SALE OF TRANSPORTERS) REGULATIONS 2000

2000 No 685

Made - - - 8th March 2000

Laid before Parliament - - - 10th March 2000

Coming into force - - - 3rd April 2000

The Secretary of State, in exercise of his powers under sections 32(2), (3) and (10), 35(7) to (9), 36(2), 166(3) and 167 of, and paragraphs 2 and 5 of Schedule 1 to, the Immigration and Asylum Act 1999, hereby makes the following Regulations:

Citation and commencement

1   These Regulations may be cited as the Carriers' Liability (Clandestine Entrants and Sale of Transporters) Regulations 2000 and shall come into force on 3rd April 2000.

NOTES

Initial Commencement
Specified date
Specified date: 3 April 2000: see above.

Interpretation

2   In these Regulations—

"the Act" means the Immigration and Asylum Act 1999;
"clandestine entrant" has the meaning given by section 32(1) of the Act;
"penalty notice" has the meaning given by section 35(2) of the Act;
"notice of objection" has the meaning given by section 35(7) of the Act; and
"responsible person" means a person responsible for a clandestine entrant under section 32 of the Act.

NOTES

Initial Commencement
Specified date
Specified date: 3 April 2000: see reg 1.

[Application to rail freight]

NOTES

Amendment
Inserted by SI 2001/311, reg 2(1), (2).
Date in force: 1 March 2001: see SI 2001/311, reg 1(1).

[2A]

[(1) In this regulation, "the rail freight Regulations" means the Carriers' Liability (Clandestine Entrants) (Application to Rail Freight) Regulations 2001.

(2) To the extent (and with the modification) set out in the Schedule to these Regulations, these Regulations apply in relation to a penalty imposed under section 32 of the Act as applied by regulations 3 and 4 of the rail freight Regulations.

(3) Where these Regulations apply in accordance with paragraph (2), any reference in these Regulations to a provision of the Act is to that provision as applied (with or without modification) by the rail freight Regulations.]

NOTES

Amendment
Inserted by SI 2001/311, reg 2(1), (2).
Date in force: 1 March 2001: see SI 2001/311, reg 1(1).

Clandestine Entrants: Penalty payable in respect of each clandestine entrant

3 The amount prescribed for the purposes of section 32(2) of the Act (the penalty payable in respect of a clandestine entrant or person concealed with him) is £2000.

NOTES

Initial Commencement
Specified date
Specified date: 3 April 2000: see reg 1.

Clandestine Entrants: Period of time within which a penalty must be paid

4 (1) The period prescribed for the purposes of sections 32(3) and 36(2) of the Act (the period within which a penalty imposed under section 32 must be paid) is 60 days from the date the responsible person was served with the penalty notice in respect of the penalty concerned or, if there is more than one responsible person, 60 days from the date the first such person was so served.

(2) In calculating this period of 60 days, no account shall be taken of any period during which the Secretary of State is in receipt of a notice of objection in connection with the penalty concerned but has not notified the person giving it of his determination under section 35(8) of the Act in respect of the penalty.

NOTES

Initial Commencement
Specified date
Specified date: 3 April 2000: see reg 1.

Clandestine Entrants: Prescribed control zone

5 (1) For the purposes of section 32(10) of the Act, that part of the territory of France situated at Coquelles which is a control zone for the purposes of the International Articles or the Tripartite Articles is a prescribed control zone.

(2) In paragraph (1), "the International Articles" has the same meaning as in the Channel Tunnel (International Arrangements) Order 1993 and "the Tripartite Articles" has the same meaning as in the Channel Tunnel (Miscellaneous Provisions) Order 1994.

NOTES

Initial Commencement
Specified date
Specified date: 3 April 2000: see reg 1.

Clandestine Entrants: Period of time within which a notice of objection must be given

6 The period prescribed for the purposes of section 35(7) and (8) of the Act (the period of time within which a notice of objection to a penalty must be given) is 30 days from the date the responsible person was served with the penalty notice in respect of the penalty concerned or, if there is more than one responsible person, 30 days from the date the first such person was so served.

NOTES

Initial Commencement
Specified date
Specified date: 3 April 2000: see reg 1.

Clandestine Entrants: Service of a penalty notice in relation to detached trailers

7 In relation to a detached trailer, a penalty notice served by affixing it to a conspicuous part of the trailer shall have effect as a penalty notice properly served, on the responsible person or persons concerned, under section 35 of the Act.

NOTES

Initial Commencement
Specified date
Specified date: 3 April 2000: see reg 1.

Sale of transporters: notice of proposed sale

8 (1)   Before applying to the court under Schedule 1 to the Act for leave to sell a transporter, the Secretary of State shall take the following steps for bringing the proposed application to the notice of persons whose interests may be affected by a decision of the court to give leave and for affording to any such person an opportunity of becoming a party to the proceedings if the Secretary of State applies for leave:

    (a)   at least 21 days before applying to the court, the Secretary of State shall publish:
        (i)   in the London Gazette and, if the transporter is detained in Scotland, also in the Edinburgh Gazette and if the transporter is detained in Northern Ireland, also in the Belfast Gazette; and
        (ii)   in one or more local newspapers circulating in the locality in which the transporter is detained,
        a notice which complies with the requirements of regulation 9(1); and
    (b)   at least 21 days before applying to the court the Secretary of State shall, unless it is impracticable to do so, serve a notice which complies with the requirements of regulation 9(1):
        (i)   where the proposed sale is to be under section 37(4) of the Act, on any person to whom any relevant penalty notice was addressed;

(ii)　where the proposed sale is to be under section 42(4) of the Act, on those persons on whom he has made a relevant demand for payment under section 40(3) of the Act.

(2)　In paragraph (1):

(a)　"relevant penalty notice" means a penalty notice on the authority of which the transporter concerned is, under section 36(1) of the Act, detained, together with any other penalty notice actually served in respect of the same carriage of clandestine entrants; and

(b)　"relevant demand for payment" means a demand for payment of any charges or expenses in respect of which the transporter concerned is detained under section 42.

NOTES

Initial Commencement
Specified date
Specified date: 3 April 2000: see reg 1.

9　(1)　A notice for the purposes of regulation 8(1) shall:

(a)　(where reasonably possible) state the country of registration and registration number of the transporter;

(b)　state the type of transporter and give any distinguishing features or markings that may serve to identify it;

(c)　state that, on a date specified in the notice, the transporter was detained under (as the case may be):
　　(i)　section 36 of the Act as security for the payment of one or more penalties due under section 32 of the Act; or
　　(ii)　section 42 of the Act as security for the payment of one or more charges due under section 40 of the Act,
　　and, that, unless payment of the sum due and any connected expenses is made within 21 days of the date of publication or (as the case may be) service of the notice, the Secretary of State may, without further notice, apply to the court for leave, under Schedule 1 to the Act, to sell the transporter; and

(d)　invite:
　　(i)　where the notice is published in a Gazette or newspaper, any person who considers his interests may be affected by any sale of the transporter; or
　　(ii)　where the notice is served on a person, that person,
　　to inform the Secretary of State in writing within 21 days of the date of publication or (as the case may be) service of the notice if he wishes to become a party to the proceedings on the application.

(2)　A notice may be served on a person under regulation 8(1)(b) by:

(a)　delivering it to that person;

(b)　leaving it at his proper address;

(c)　sending it to his proper address by first class post in a prepaid registered envelope or by the recorded delivery service;

(d)　facsimile, sent to his usual or last known business facsimile number;

(e)　electronic mail, sent to his usual or last known business electronic mail address.

(3)　Any notice required to be served on any body corporate or unincorporated association under regulation 8(1)(b), other than a partnership, maybe served on the secretary or clerk or other similar officer of that body.

(4)   Any notice required to be served on any partnership under regulation 8(1)(b) may be served on a partner or a person having control or management of the partnership business.

(5)   For the purpose of this regulation, the proper address of any person on whom or to whom any such notice is to be served, shall be his last known place of business or abode, except that such address shall be:

(i)   in the case of a body corporate or its secretary or clerk, the address of the registered office or principal office of the body corporate;

(ii)   in the case of an unincorporated association (other than a partnership) or its secretary or clerk, the address of the principal office of the association; and

(iii)   in the case of a partnership or a partner or person having control or management of the partnership business, the address of the principal office of the partnership,

and for the purposes of this regulation the principal office of a company registered outside the United Kingdom, or of an unincorporated association or partnership carrying on business outside the United Kingdom, shall be, if it has an office within the United Kingdom, its sole or principal office here.

(6)   Any notice which is sent by post in accordance with this regulation to a place outside the United Kingdom shall be sent by airmail or by some other equally expeditious means.

NOTES

Initial Commencement
Specified date
Specified date: 3 April 2000: see reg 1.

Sale of transporters: Application of proceeds of sale

10   The proceeds of any sale under section 37 or 42 of the Act shall be applied as follows, and in the following order:

(a)   in payment of any expenses reasonably incurred by the Secretary of State in connection with the detention and sale of the transporter, including the Secretary of State's expenses in connection with the application to court;

(b)   in payment of the penalties or (as the case may be) charges which the court has found to be due;

(c)   in payment of any duty (whether of customs or excise) chargeable on imported goods or value added tax which is due in consequence of the transporter having been brought into the United Kingdom;

(d)   where the transporter is an aircraft, in payment of any charge in respect of the aircraft which is due by virtue of regulations under section 73 of the Civil Aviation Act 1982;

and the surplus, if any, shall be paid to or among the person or persons whose interests in the transporter have, to the knowledge of the Secretary of State, been divested by reason of the sale.

NOTES

Initial Commencement
Specified date
Specified date: 3 April 2000: see reg 1.

Service of documents

11   For the purposes of these Regulations:

(a)   where a notice is sent by first class post in a prepaid registered envelope or by the recorded delivery service, addressed to the person to whom the notice is required to be served, it is to be taken to have been received by (and served on) that person on the second day after the day on which it was sent;

(b) where a notice is sent by facsimile, to the last known business facsimile number of the person to whom notice is required to be served, it is to be taken to have been received by (and served on) that person on the day on which it was sent;

(c) where a notice is sent by electronic mail, to the last known business electronic mail address of the person to whom notice is required to be served, it is taken to have been received by (and served on) that person on the day on which it was sent; and

(d) where a notice is sent in accordance with regulation 9(6), addressed to the person to whom notice is required to be served, it is to be taken to have been received by (and served on) that person on the second day after the day on which it was sent.

NOTES

Initial Commencement
Specified date
Specified date: 3 April 2000: see reg 1.

Barbara Roche
Minister of State
Home Office
8th March 2000

[SCHEDULE
Application to Rail Freight]

NOTES

Amendment
Inserted by SI 2001/311, reg 2(1), (3).
Date in force: 1 March 2001: see SI 2001/311, reg 1(1).

[regulation 2A]

NOTES

Amendment
Inserted by SI 2001/311, reg 2(1), (3).
Date in force: 1 March 2001: see SI 2001/311, reg 1(1).

[1 Subject to the modification set out in paragraph 2 below, the following provisions of these Regulations apply—

regulation 2;
regulation 3;
regulation 4;
regulation 6;
regulation 8 (except paragraphs (1)(b)(ii) and (2)(b));
regulation 9 (except paragraph (1)(c)(ii));
regulation 10 (except paragraph (d));
regulation 11.

2 In regulation 2, replace "section 32(1)" by "section 39(1)".]

NOTES

Amendment
Inserted by SI 2001/311, reg 2(1), (3).
Date in force: 1 March 2001: see SI 2001/311, reg 1(1).

ASYLUM SUPPORT REGULATIONS 2000

2000 No 704

Made - - - 6th March 2000

Laid before Parliament - - - 13th March 2000

Coming into force - - - 3rd April 2000

The Secretary of State, in exercise of the powers conferred on him by sections 94, 95, 97, 114, 166 and 167 of and Schedule 8 to the Immigration and Asylum Act 1999, hereby makes the following Regulations:

General

1 Citation and commencement

These Regulations may be cited as the Asylum Support Regulations 2000 and shall come into force on 3rd April 2000.

NOTES

Initial Commencement
Specified date
Specified date: 3 April 2000: see above.

2 Interpretation

(1)   In these Regulations—

"the Act" means the Immigration and Asylum Act 1999;
"asylum support" means support provided under section 95 of the Act;
"dependant" has the meaning given by paragraphs (4) and (5);
"the interim Regulations" means the Asylum Support (Interim Provisions) Regulations 1999;
"married couple" means a man and woman who are married to each other and are members of the same household; and
"unmarried couple" means a man and woman who, though not married to each other, are living together as if married.

(2)   The period of 14 days is prescribed for the purposes of section 94(3) of the Act (day on which a claim for asylum is determined).

(3)   Paragraph (2) does not apply in relation to a case to which the interim Regulations apply (for which case, provision corresponding to paragraph (2) is made by regulation 2(6) of those Regulations).

(4)   In these Regulations "dependant", in relation to an asylum-seeker, a supported person or an applicant for asylum support, means, subject to paragraph (5), a person in the United Kingdom ("the relevant person") who—

(a)   is his spouse;
(b)   is a child of his or of his spouse, is dependent on him and is, or was at the relevant time, under 18;
(c)   is a member of his or his spouse's close family and is, or was at the relevant time, under 18;
(d)   had been living as part of his household—

      (i)   for at least six of the twelve months before the relevant time, or
      (ii)   since birth,
           and is, or was at the relevant time, under 18;

  (e)   is in need of care and attention from him or a member of his household by reason of a disability and would fall within sub-paragraph (c) or (d) but for the fact that he is not, and was not at the relevant time, under 18;

  (f)   had been living with him as a member of an unmarried couple for at least two of the three years before the relevant time;

  (g)   is living as part of his household and was, immediately before 6th December 1999 (the date when the interim Regulations came into force), receiving assistance from a local authority under section 17 of the Children Act 1989;

  (h)   is living as part of his household and was, immediately before the coming into force of these Regulations, receiving assistance from a local authority under—
      (i)   section 22 of the Children (Scotland) Act 1995; or
      (ii)   Article 18 of the Children (Northern Ireland) Order 1995; or

  (i)   has made a claim for leave to enter or remain in the United Kingdom, or for variation of any such leave, which is being considered on the basis that he is dependant on the asylum-seeker;

and in relation to a supported person, or an applicant for asylum support, who is himself a dependent of an asylum-seeker, also includes the asylum-seeker if in the United Kingdom.

(5) Where a supported person or applicant for asylum support is himself a dependant of an asylum-seeker, a person who would otherwise be a dependant of the supported person, or of the applicant, for the purposes of these Regulations is not such a dependant unless he is also a dependant of the asylum-seeker or is the asylum-seeker.

(6) In paragraph (4), "the relevant time", in relation to the relevant person, means—

  (a)   the time when an application for asylum support for him was made in accordance with regulation 3(3); or

  (b)   if he has joined a person who is already a supported person in the United Kingdom and sub-paragraph (a) does not apply, the time when he joined that person in the United Kingdom.

(7) Where a person, by falling within a particular category in relation to an asylum-seeker or supported person, is by virtue of this regulation a dependant of the asylum-seeker or supported person for the purposes of these Regulations, that category is also a prescribed category for the purposes of paragraph (c) of the definition of "dependant" in section 94(1) of the Act and, accordingly, the person is a dependant of the asylum-seeker or supported person for the purposes of Part VI of the Act.

(8) Paragraph (7) does not apply to a person who is already a dependant of the asylum-seeker or supported person for the purposes of Part VI of the Act because he falls within either of the categories mentioned in paragraphs (a) and (b) of the definition of "dependant" in section 94(1) of the Act.

(9) Paragraph (7) does not apply for the purposes of any reference to a "dependant" in Schedule 9 to the Act.

NOTES

Initial Commencement
Specified date
Specified date: 3 April 2000: see reg 1.

3 Initial application for support: individual and group applications

(1)   Either of the following—

    (a)   an asylum-seeker, or
    (b)   a dependant of an asylum-seeker,
may apply to the Secretary of State for asylum support.

(2)   An application under this regulation may be—

    (a)   for asylum support for the applicant alone; or
    (b)   for asylum support for the applicant and one or more dependants of his.

(3)   The application must be made by completing in full and in English the form for the time being issued by the Secretary of State for the purpose; and any form so issued shall be the form shown in the Schedule to these Regulations or a form to the like effect.

(4)   The application may not be entertained by the Secretary of State unless it is made in accordance with paragraph (3).

(5)   The Secretary of State may make further enquiries of the applicant about any matter connected with the application.

(6)   Paragraphs (3) and (4) do not apply where a person is already a supported person and asylum support is sought for a dependant of his for whom such support is not already provided (for which case, provision is made by regulation 15).

NOTES

Initial Commencement
Specified date
Specified date: 3 April 2000: see reg 1.

4 Persons excluded from support

(1)   The following circumstances are prescribed for the purposes of subsection (2) of section 95 of the Act as circumstances where a person who would otherwise fall within subsection (1) of that section is excluded from that subsection (and, accordingly, may not be provided with asylum support).

(2)   A person is so excluded if he is applying for asylum support for himself alone and he falls within paragraph (4) by virtue of any sub-paragraph of that paragraph.

(3)   A person is so excluded if—

    (a)   he is applying for asylum support for himself and other persons, or he is included in an application for asylum support made by a person other than himself;
    (b)   he falls within paragraph (4) (by virtue of any sub-paragraph of that paragraph); and
    (c)   each of the other persons to whom the application relates also falls within paragraph (4) (by virtue of any sub-paragraph of that paragraph).

(4)   A person falls within this paragraph if at the time when the application is determined—

    (a)   he is a person to whom interim support applies; or
    (b)   he is a person to whom social security benefits apply; or

(c)   he has not made a claim for leave to enter or remain in the United Kingdom, or for variation of any such leave, which is being considered on the basis that he is an asylum-seeker or dependent on an asylum-seeker.

(5)   For the purposes of paragraph (4), interim support applies to a person if—

(a)   at the time when the application is determined, he is a person to whom, under the interim Regulations, support under regulation 3 of those Regulations must be provided by a local authority;

(b)   sub-paragraph (a) does not apply, but would do so if the person had been determined by the local authority concerned to be an eligible person; or

(c)   sub-paragraph (a) does not apply, but would do so but for the fact that the person's support under those Regulations was (otherwise than by virtue of regulation 7(1)(d) of those Regulations) refused under regulation 7, or suspended or discontinued under regulation 8, of those Regulations;

and in this paragraph "local authority", "local authority concerned" and "eligible person" have the same meanings as in the interim Regulations.

(6)   For the purposes of paragraph (4), a person is a person to whom social security benefits apply if he is—

(a)   a person who by virtue of regulation 2 of the Social Security (Immigration and Asylum) Consequential Amendments Regulations 2000 is not excluded by section 115(1) of the Act from entitlement to—

(i)   income-based jobseeker's allowance under the Jobseekers Act 1995; or

(ii)   income support, housing benefit or council tax benefit under the Social Security Contributions and Benefits Act 1992;

(b)   a person who, by virtue of regulation 2 of the Social Security (Immigration and Asylum) Consequential Amendments Regulations (Northern Ireland) 2000 is not excluded by section 115(2) of the Act from entitlement to—

(i)   income-based jobseeker's allowance under the Jobseekers (Northern Ireland) Order 1995; or

(ii)   income support or housing benefit under the Social Security Contributions and Benefits (Northern Ireland) Act 1992;

(7)   A person is not to be regarded as falling within paragraph (2) or (3) if, when asylum support is sought for him, he is a dependant of a person who is already a supported person.

(8)   The circumstances prescribed by paragraphs (2) and (3) are also prescribed for the purposes of section 95(2), as applied by section 98(3), of the Act as circumstances where a person who would otherwise fall within subsection (1) of section 98 is excluded from that subsection (and, accordingly, may not be provided with temporary support under section 98).

(9)   For the purposes of paragraph (8), paragraphs (2) and (3) shall apply as if any reference to an application for asylum support were a reference to an application for support under section 98 of the Act.

NOTES

Initial Commencement
Specified date
Specified date: 3 April 2000: see reg 1.

Determining whether persons are destitute

5 Determination where application relates to more than one person, etc

(1)   Subject to paragraph (2), where an application in accordance with regulation 3(3) is for asylum support for the applicant and one or more dependants of his, in applying section 95(1) of the Act the Secretary of State must decide whether the applicant and all those dependants, taken together, are destitute or likely to become destitute within the period prescribed by regulation 7.

(2)   Where a person is a supported person, and the question falls to be determined whether asylum support should in future be provided for him and one or more other persons who are his dependants and are—

(a)   persons for whom asylum support is also being provided when that question falls to be determined; or

(b)   persons for whom the Secretary of State is then considering whether asylum support should be provided,

in applying section 95(1) of the Act the Secretary of State must decide whether the supported person and all those dependants, taken together, are destitute or likely to become destitute within the period prescribed by regulation 7.

NOTES

Initial Commencement
Specified date
Specified date: 3 April 2000: see reg 1.

6 Income and assets to be taken into account

(1)   This regulation applies where it falls to the Secretary of State to determine for the purposes of section 95(1) of the Act whether—

(a)   a person applying for asylum support, or such an applicant and any dependants of his, or

(b)   a supported person, or such a person and any dependants of his,

is or are destitute or likely to become so within the period prescribed by regulation 7.

(2)   In this regulation "the principal" means the applicant for asylum support (where paragraph (1)(a) applies) or the supported person (where paragraph (1)(b) applies).

(3)   The Secretary of State must ignore—

(a)   any asylum support, and

(b)   any support under section 98 of the Act,

which the principal or any dependant of his is provided with or, where the question is whether destitution is likely within a particular period, might be provided with in that period.

(4)   But he must take into account—

(a)   any other income which the principal, or any dependant of his, has or might reasonably be expected to have in that period;

(b)   any other support which is available to the principal or any dependant of his, or might reasonably be expected to be so available in that period; and

(c)   any assets mentioned in paragraph (5) (whether held in the United Kingdom or elsewhere) which are available to the principal or any dependant of his otherwise than by way of asylum support or support under section 98, or might reasonably be expected to be so available in that period.

(5)   Those assets are—

(a) cash;
(b) savings;
(c) investments;
(d) land;
(e) cars or other vehicles; and
(f) goods held for the purpose of a trade or other business.

(6) The Secretary of State must ignore any assets not mentioned in paragraph (5).

NOTES

Initial Commencement
Specified date
Specified date: 3 April 2000: see reg 1.

7 Period within which applicant must be likely to become destitute

The period prescribed for the purposes of section 95(1) of the Act is—

(a) where the question whether a person or persons is or are destitute or likely to become so falls to be determined in relation to an application for asylum support and sub-paragraph (b) does not apply, 14 days beginning with the day on which that question falls to be determined;
(b) where that question falls to be determined in relation to a supported person, or in relation to persons including a supported person, 56 days beginning with the day on which that question falls to be determined.

NOTES

Initial Commencement
Specified date
Specified date: 3 April 2000: see reg 1.

8 Adequacy of existing accommodation

(1) Subject to paragraph (2), the matters mentioned in paragraph (3) are prescribed for the purposes of subsection (5)(a) of section 95 of the Act as matters to which the Secretary of State must have regard in determining for the purposes of that section whether the accommodation of—

(a) a person applying for asylum support, or
(b) a supported person for whom accommodation is not for the time being provided by way of asylum support,
is adequate.

(2) The matters mentioned in paragraph (3)(a) and (d) to (g) are not so prescribed for the purposes of a case where the person indicates to the Secretary of State that he wishes to remain in the accommodation.

(3) The matters referred to in paragraph (1) are—

(a) whether it would be reasonable for the person to continue to occupy the accommodation;
(b) whether the accommodation is affordable for him;
(c) whether the accommodation is provided under section 98 of the Act, or otherwise on an emergency basis, only while the claim for asylum support is being determined;
(d) whether the person can secure entry to the accommodation;
(e) where the accommodation consists of a moveable structure, vehicle or vessel designed or adapted for human habitation, whether there is a place where the person is entitled or permitted both to place it and reside in it;

> (f) whether the accommodation is available for occupation by the person's dependants together with him;
>
> (g) whether it is probable that the person's continued occupation of the accommodation will lead to domestic violence against him or any of his dependants.

(4) In determining whether it would be reasonable for a person to continue to occupy accommodation, regard may be had to the general circumstances prevailing in relation to housing in the district of the local housing authority where the accommodation is.

(5) In determining whether a person's accommodation is affordable for him, the Secretary of State must have regard to—

> (a) any income, or any assets mentioned in regulation 6(5) (whether held in the United Kingdom or elsewhere), which is or are available to him or any dependant of his otherwise than by way of asylum support or support under section 98 of the Act, or might reasonably be expected to be so available;
>
> (b) the costs in respect of the accommodation; and
>
> (c) the person's other reasonable living expenses.

(6) In this regulation—

> (a) "domestic violence" means violence from a person who is or has been a close family member, or threats of violence from such a person which are likely to be carried out; and
>
> (b) "district of the local housing authority" has the meaning given by section 217(3) of the Housing Act 1996.

(7) The reference in paragraph (1) to subsection (5)(a) of section 95 of the Act does not include a reference to that provision as applied by section 98(3) of the Act.

NOTES

Initial Commencement
Specified date
Specified date: 3 April 2000: see reg 1.

9 Essential living needs

(1) The matter mentioned in paragraph (2) is prescribed for the purposes of subsection (7)(b) of section 95 of the Act as a matter to which the Secretary of State may not have regard in determining for the purposes of that section whether a person's essential living needs (other than accommodation) are met.

(2) That matter is his personal preference as to clothing (but this shall not be taken to prevent the Secretary of State from taking into account his individual circumstances as regards clothing).

(3) None of the items and expenses mentioned in paragraph (4) is to be treated as being an essential living need of a person for the purposes of Part VI of the Act.

(4) Those items and expenses are—

> (a) the cost of faxes;
> (b) computers and the cost of computer facilities;
> (c) the cost of photocopying;
> (d) travel expenses, except the expense mentioned in paragraph (5);
> (e) toys and other recreational items;
> (f) entertainment expenses.

(5) The expense excepted from paragraph (4)(d) is the expense of an initial journey from a place in the United Kingdom to accommodation provided by way of asylum

support or (where accommodation is not so provided) to an address in the United Kingdom which has been notified to the Secretary of State as the address where the person intends to live.

(6) Paragraph (3) shall not be taken to affect the question whether any item or expense not mentioned in paragraph (4) or (5) is, or is not, an essential living need.

(7) The reference in paragraph (1) to subsection (7)(b) of section 95 of the Act includes a reference to that provision as applied by section 98(3) of the Act and, accordingly, the reference in paragraph (1) to "that section" includes a reference to section 98.

NOTES

Initial Commencement
Specified date
Specified date: 3 April 2000: see reg 1.

Provision of support

10 Kind and levels of support for essential living needs

(1) This regulation applies where the Secretary of State has decided that asylum support should be provided in respect of the essential living needs of a person.

(2) As a general rule, asylum support in respect of the essential living needs of that person may be expected to be provided weekly in the form of vouchers redeemable for goods, services and cash whose total redemption value, for any week, equals the amount shown in the second column of the following Table opposite the entry in the first column which for the time being describes that person.

TABLE

Qualifying couple	£57.37
Lone parent aged 18 or over	£36.54
Single person aged 25 or over	£36.54
Single person aged at least 18 but under 25	£28.95
Person aged at least 16 but under 18 (except a member of a qualifying couple)	£31.75
Person aged under 16	[£30.95]

(3) In paragraph (1) and the provisions of paragraph (2) preceding the Table, "person" includes "couple".

(4) In this regulation—

    (a) "qualifying couple" means a married or unmarried couple at least one of whom is aged 18 or over and neither of whom is aged under 16;

    (b) "lone parent" means a parent who is not a member of a married or unmarried couple;

    (c) "single person" means a person who is not a parent or a member of a qualifying couple; and

    (d) "parent" means a parent of a relevant child, that is to say a child who is aged under 18 and for whom asylum support is provided.

(5) Where the Secretary of State has decided that accommodation should be provided for a person (or couple) by way of asylum support, and the accommodation is provided in a form which also meets other essential living needs (such as bed and breakfast, or half or full board), the amounts shown in the Table in paragraph (2) shall be treated as reduced accordingly.

(6)   The redemption value of the vouchers redeemable for cash which the Secretary of State may be expected to include in the asylum support provided for any week in accordance with paragraph (2) may, as a general rule, be expected not to exceed £10 per person (or, as the case may be, £20 per qualifying couple).

NOTES

Initial Commencement
Specified date
Specified date: 3 April 2000: see reg 1.

Amendment
Para (2): in the table in column (2) in entry relating to a "Person aged under 16" sum "£30.95" in square brackets substituted by SI 2000/3053, reg 2.
Date in force: 4 December 2000: see SI 2000/3053, reg 1.

11 Additional single payments in respect of essential living needs

(1)   At the end of each qualifying period, the Secretary of State may as a general rule be expected to provide, or arrange for the provision of, additional support for an eligible person (in respect of his essential living needs) in the form of a single issue of vouchers redeemable for cash whose total redemption value equals £50.

(2)   In paragraph (1) "eligible person" means a person for whom asylum support has been provided for the whole of the qualifying period.

(3)   Each of the following is a qualifying period—

(a)   the period of six months beginning with the day on which asylum support was first provided for the person; and
(b)   each period of six months beginning with a re-start day.

(4)   Each of the following is a re-start day—

(a)   the day after the day on which the period mentioned in paragraph (3)(a) ends; and
(b)   the day after the day on which a period mentioned in paragraph (3)(b) ends.

(5)   Paragraph (1) applies only if an application for the additional support is made to the Secretary of State by or on behalf of the eligible person.

(6)   Where a person is, in the opinion of the Secretary of State, responsible without reasonable excuse for a delay in the determination of his claim for asylum, the Secretary of State may treat any qualifying period as extended by the period of delay.

NOTES

Initial Commencement
Specified date
Specified date: 3 April 2000: see reg 1.

12 Income and assets to be taken into account in providing support

(1)   This regulation applies where it falls to the Secretary of State to decide the level or kind of asylum support to be provided for—

(a)   a person applying for asylum support, or such an applicant and any dependants of his; or
(b)   a supported person, or such a person and any dependants of his.

(2)   In this regulation "the principal" means the applicant for asylum support (where paragraph (1)(a) applies) or the supported person (where paragraph (1)(b) applies).

(3)   The Secretary of State must take into account—

  (a)   any income which the principal or any dependant of his has or might reasonably be expected to have,

  (b)   support which is or might reasonably be expected to be available to the principal or any dependant of his, and

  (c)   any assets mentioned in regulation 6(5) (whether held in the United Kingdom or elsewhere) which are or might reasonably be expected to be available to the principal or any dependant of his,

otherwise than by way of asylum support.

NOTES

Initial Commencement
Specified date
Specified date: 3 April 2000: see reg 1.

13 Accommodation

(1)   The matters mentioned in paragraph (2) are prescribed for the purposes of subsection (2)(b) of section 97 of the Act as matters to which regard may not be had when exercising the power under section 95 of the Act to provide accommodation for a person.

(2)   Those matters are—

  (a)   his personal preference as to the nature of the accommodation to be provided; and

  (b)   his personal preference as to the nature and standard of fixtures and fittings;

but this shall not be taken to prevent the person's individual circumstances, as they relate to his accommodation needs, being taken into account.

NOTES

Initial Commencement
Specified date
Specified date: 3 April 2000: see reg 1.

14 Services

(1)   The services mentioned in paragraph (2) may be provided or made available by way of asylum support to persons who are otherwise receiving such support, but may be so provided only for the purpose of maintaining good order among such persons.

(2)   Those services are—

  (a)   education, including English language lessons,

  (b)   sporting or other developmental activities.

NOTES

Initial Commencement
Specified date
Specified date: 3 April 2000: see reg 1.

Change of circumstances

15 Change of circumstances

(1)   If a relevant change of circumstances occurs, the supported person concerned or a dependant of his must, without delay, notify the Secretary of State of that change of circumstances.

(2)   A relevant change of circumstances occurs where a supported person or a dependant of his—

 (a) is joined in the United Kingdom by a dependant or, as the case may be, another dependant, of the supported person;

 (b) receives or gains access to any money, or other asset mentioned in regulation 6(5), that has not previously been declared to the Secretary of State;

 (c) becomes employed;

 (d) becomes unemployed;

 (e) changes his name;

 (f) gets married;

 (g) starts living with a person as if married to that person;

 (h) gets divorced;

 (i) separates from a spouse, or from a person with whom he has been living as if married to that person;

 (j) becomes pregnant;

 (k) has a child;

 (l) leaves school;

 (m) starts to share his accommodation with another person;

 (n) moves to a different address, or otherwise leaves his accommodation;

 (o) goes into hospital;

 (p) goes to prison or is otherwise held in custody;

 (q) leaves the United Kingdom; or

 (r) dies.

(3)   If, on being notified of a change of circumstances, the Secretary of State considers that the change may be one—

 (a) as a result of which asylum support should be provided for a person for whom it was not provided before, or

 (b) as a result of which asylum support should no longer be provided for a person, or

 (c) which may otherwise affect the asylum support which should be provided for a person,

he may make further enquiries of the supported person or dependant who gave the notification.

(4)   The Secretary of State may, in particular, require that person to provide him with such information as he considers necessary to determine whether, and if so, what, asylum support should be provided for any person.

NOTES

Initial Commencement
Specified date
Specified date: 3 April 2000: see reg 1.

Contributions

16 Contributions

(1)   This regulation applies where, in deciding the level of asylum support to be provided for a person who is or will be a supported person, the Secretary of State is required to take into account income, support or assets as mentioned in regulation 12(3).

(2)   The Secretary of State may—

 (a) set the asylum support for that person at a level which does not reflect the income, support or assets; and

(b) require from that person payments by way of contributions towards the cost of the provision for him of asylum support.

(3) A supported person must make to the Secretary of State such payments by way of contributions as the Secretary of State may require under paragraph (2).

(4) Prompt payment of such contributions may be made a condition (under section 95(9) of the Act) subject to which asylum support for that person is provided.

NOTES

Initial Commencement
Specified date
Specified date: 3 April 2000: see reg 1.

Recovery of sums by Secretary of State

17 Recovery where assets become realisable

(1) This regulation applies where it appears to the Secretary of State at any time (the relevant time)—

(a) that a supported person had, at the time when he applied for asylum support, assets of any kind in the United Kingdom or elsewhere which were not capable of being realised; but

(b) that those assets have subsequently become, and remain, capable of being realised.

(2) The Secretary of State may recover from that person a sum not exceeding the recoverable sum.

(3) Subject to paragraph (5), the recoverable sum is a sum equal to whichever is the less of—

(a) the monetary value of all the asylum support provided to the person up to the relevant time; and

(b) the monetary value of the assets concerned.

(4) As well as being recoverable as mentioned in paragraph 11(2)(a) of Schedule 8 to the Act, an amount recoverable under this regulation may be recovered by deduction from asylum support.

(5) The recoverable sum shall be treated as reduced by any amount which the Secretary of State has by virtue of this regulation already recovered from the person concerned (whether by deduction or otherwise) with regard to the assets concerned.

NOTES

Initial Commencement
Specified date
Specified date: 3 April 2000: see reg 1.

18 Overpayments: method of recovery

As well as being recoverable as mentioned in subsection (3) of section 114 of the Act, an amount recoverable under subsection (2) of that section may be recovered by deduction from asylum support.

NOTES

Initial Commencement
Specified date
Specified date: 3 April 2000: see reg 1.

Breach of conditions and suspension and discontinuation of support

19 Breach of conditions: decision whether to provide support

(1)   When deciding—

(a)   whether to provide, or to continue to provide, asylum support for any person or persons, or

(b)   the level or kind of support to be provided for any person or persons,

the Secretary of State may take into account the extent to which any relevant condition has been complied with.

(2)   A relevant condition is a condition subject to which asylum support for that person or any of those persons is being, or has previously been, provided.

NOTES

Initial Commencement
Specified date
Specified date: 3 April 2000: see reg 1.

20 Suspension or discontinuation of support

(1)   Asylum support for a supported person and his dependants (if any), or for one or more dependants of a supported person, may be suspended or discontinued if—

(a)   the Secretary of State has reasonable grounds to suspect that the supported person or any dependant of his has failed without reasonable excuse to comply with any condition subject to which the asylum support is provided;

(b)   the Secretary of State has reasonable grounds to suspect that the supported person or any dependant of his has committed an offence under Part VI of the Act;

(c)   the Secretary of State has reasonable grounds to suspect that the supported person has intentionally made himself and his dependants (if any) destitute;

(d)   the supported person or any dependant of his for whom asylum support is being provided ceases to reside at the authorised address; or

(e)   the supported person or any dependant of his for whom asylum support is being provided is absent from the authorised address—

(i)   for more than seven consecutive days and nights, or

(ii)   for a total of more than 14 days and nights in any six month period,

without the permission of the Secretary of State.

(2)   For the purposes of this regulation, a person has intentionally made himself destitute if he appears to be, or to be likely to become within the period prescribed by regulation 7, destitute as a result of an act or omission deliberately done or made by him or any dependant of his without reasonable excuse while in the United Kingdom.

(3)   For the purposes of this regulation, the authorised address is—

(a)   the accommodation provided for the supported person and his dependants (if any) by way of asylum support; or

(b)   if no accommodation is so provided, the address notified by the supported person to the Secretary of State in his application for asylum support or, where a change of his address has been notified to the Secretary of State under regulation 15, the address for the time being so notified.

NOTES

Initial Commencement
Specified date
Specified date: 3 April 2000: see reg 1.

21 Effect of previous suspension or discontinuation

(1) Where—

(a)   an application for asylum support is made,
(b)   the applicant or any other person to whom the application relates has previously had his asylum support suspended or discontinued under regulation 20, and
(c)   there has been no material change of circumstances since the suspension or discontinuation,

the application need not be entertained unless the Secretary of State considers that there are exceptional circumstances which justify its being entertained.

(2)   A material change of circumstances is one which, if the applicant were a supported person, would have to be notified to the Secretary of State under regulation 15.

(3)   This regulation is without prejudice to the power of the Secretary of State to refuse the application even if he has entertained it.

NOTES

Initial Commencement
Specified date
Specified date: 3 April 2000: see reg 1.

Notice to quit

22 Notice to quit

(1) If—

(a)   as a result of asylum support, a person has a tenancy or licence to occupy accommodation,
(b)   one or more of the conditions mentioned in paragraph (2) is satisfied, and
(c)   he is given notice to quit in accordance with paragraph (3) or (4),

his tenancy or licence is to be treated as ending with the period specified in that notice, regardless of when it could otherwise be brought to an end.

(2)   The conditions are that—

(a)   the asylum support is suspended or discontinued as a result of any provision of regulation 20;
(b)   the relevant claim for asylum has been determined;
(c)   the supported person has ceased to be destitute; or
(d)   he is to be moved to other accommodation.

(3)   A notice to quit is in accordance with this paragraph if it is in writing and—

(a)   in a case where sub-paragraph (a), (c) or (d) of paragraph (2) applies, specifies as the notice period a period of not less than seven days; or
(b)   in a case where the Secretary of State has notified his decision on the relevant claim for asylum to the claimant, specifies as the notice period a period at least as long as whichever is the greater of—
(i)   seven days; or
(ii)   the period beginning with the date of service of the notice to quit and ending with the date of determination of the relevant claim for asylum (found in accordance with section 94(3) of the Act).

(4)   A notice to quit is in accordance with this paragraph if—

(a)   it is in writing;
(b)   it specifies as the notice period a period of less than seven days; and
(c)   the circumstances of the case are such that that notice period is justified.

NOTES

Initial Commencement
Specified date
Specified date: 3 April 2000: see reg 1.

Meaning of "destitute" for certain other purposes

23 Meaning of "destitute" for certain other purposes

(1)   In this regulation "the relevant enactments" means—

(a)   section 21(1A) of the National Assistance Act 1948;
(b)   section 45(4A) of the Health Services and Public Health Act 1968;
(c)   paragraph 2(2A) of Schedule 8 to the National Health Service Act 1977;
(d)   sections 12(2A), 13A(4) and 13B(3) of the Social Work (Scotland) Act 1968;
(e)   sections 7(3) and 8(4) of the Mental Health (Scotland) Act 1984; and
(f)   Articles 7(3) and 15(6) of the Health and Personal Social Services (Northern Ireland) Order 1972.

(2)   The following provisions of this regulation apply where it falls to an authority, or the Department, to determine for the purposes of any of the relevant enactments whether a person is destitute.

(3)   Paragraphs (3) to (6) of regulation 6 apply as they apply in the case mentioned in paragraph (1) of that regulation, but as if references to the principal were references to the person whose destitution or otherwise is being determined and references to the Secretary of State were references to the authority or (as the case may be) Department.

(4)   The matters mentioned in paragraph (3) of regulation 8 (read with paragraphs (4) to (6) of that regulation) are prescribed for the purposes of subsection (5)(a) of section 95 of the Act, as applied for the purposes of any of the relevant enactments, as matters to which regard must be had in determining for the purposes of any of the relevant enactments whether a person's accommodation is adequate.

(5)   The matter mentioned in paragraph (2) of regulation 9 is prescribed for the purposes of subsection (7)(b) of section 95 of the Act, as applied for the purposes of any of the relevant enactments, as a matter to which regard may not be had in determining for the purposes of any of the relevant enactments whether a person's essential living needs (other than accommodation) are met.

(6)   Paragraphs (3) to (6) of regulation 9 shall apply as if the reference in paragraph (3) to Part VI of the Act included a reference to the relevant enactments.

(7)   The references in regulations 8(5) and 9(2) to the Secretary of State shall be construed, for the purposes of this regulation, as references to the authority or (as the case may be) Department.

NOTES

Initial Commencement
Specified date
Specified date: 3 April 2000: see reg 1.

Barbara Roche
Minister of State
Home Office
6th March 2000

SCHEDULE
Application Form and Notes

Regulation 3(3)

(The full text of this form is currently unavailable.)

IMMIGRATION (ELIGIBILITY FOR ASSISTANCE) (SCOTLAND AND NORTHERN IRELAND) REGULATIONS 2000

2000 No 705

Made - - - 6th March 2000

Laid before Parliament - - - 13th March 2000

Coming into force - - - 3rd April 2000

In exercise of the powers conferred on him by sections 115(3) and (4), 122(11), 166 and 167 of the Immigration and Asylum Act 1999, the Secretary of State hereby makes the following Regulations:

1 Citation, commencement, interpretation and extent

(1) These Regulations may be cited as the Immigration (Eligibility for Assistance) (Scotland and Northern Ireland) Regulations 2000 and shall come into force on 3rd April 2000.

(2) In these Regulations, "the 1999 Act" means the Immigration and Asylum Act 1999.

(3) Regulation 3 does not extend to Northern Ireland.

(4) Regulation 4 does not extend to Scotland.

NOTES

Initial Commencement
Specified date
Specified date: 3 April 2000: see para (1) above.

2 Eligibility for social assistance—Scotland and Northern Ireland

(1) Subject to paragraphs (2) and (3), any asylum-seeker who made a claim for asylum before 3rd April 2000 and any dependant of such an asylum-seeker shall be treated—

    (a)   in Scotland, for the purposes prescribed by regulation 3 only;
    (b)   in Northern Ireland, for the purposes prescribed by regulation 4 only;

as not being a person to whom section 115 of the 1999 Act (exclusion from benefits of persons subject to immigration control) applies.

(2)   Paragraph (1)(a) does not apply where the person who made the claim for asylum is a person who, by virtue of regulation 2 of the Social Security (Immigration and Asylum) Consequential Amendments Regulations 2000 is not excluded by section 115(1) of the 1999 Act from entitlement to—

    (a)   income-based jobseeker's allowance under the Jobseekers Act 1995; or

    (b)   income support, housing benefit or council tax benefit under the Social Security Contributions and Benefits Act 1992.

(3)   Paragraph (1)(b) does not apply where the person who made the claim for asylum is a person, who by virtue of regulation 2 of the Social Security (Immigration and Asylum) Consequential Amendments Regulations (Northern Ireland) 2000 is not excluded by section 115(2) of the 1999 Act from entitlement to—

    (a)   income-based jobseeker's allowance under the Jobseekers (Northern Ireland) Order 1995; or

    (b)   income support or housing benefit under the Social Security Contributions and Benefits (Northern Ireland) Act 1992.

NOTES

Initial Commencement
Specified date
Specified date: 3 April 2000: see reg 1(1).

3 Eligibility for social assistance—Scottish provisions

Regulation 2(1)(a) applies only for the purposes of the following provisions—

    (a)   sections 12, 13A and 13B of the Social Work (Scotland) Act 1968;

    (b)   sections 7 and 8 of the Mental Health (Scotland) Act 1984.

NOTES

Initial Commencement
Specified date
Specified date: 3 April 2000: see reg 1(1).

Extent
This provision does not extend to Northern Ireland: see reg 1(3).

4 Eligibility for social assistance—Northern Ireland provisions

Regulation 2(1)(b) applies only for the purposes of Articles 7 and 15 of the Health and Personal Social Services (Northern Ireland) Order 1972.

NOTES

Initial Commencement
Specified date
Specified date: 3 April 2000: see reg 1(1).

Extent
This provision does not extend to Scotland: see reg 1(4).

5 Eligibility for support for children—Scotland and Northern Ireland

Subsection (5) of section 122 of the 1999 Act (support for children) does not apply in relation to any person or family in respect of whom or which a relevant authority was, immediately before 3rd April 2000, providing assistance under—

    (a)   section 22 of the Children (Scotland) Act 1995 (local authority support in Scotland for children and their families); or

    (b)   Article 18 of the Children (Northern Ireland) Order 1995 (equivalent provision for Northern Ireland).

NOTES

Initial Commencement
Specified date
Specified date: 3 April 2000: see reg 1(1).

Barbara Roche
Minister of State
Home Office
6th March 2000

PERSONS SUBJECT TO IMMIGRATION CONTROL (HOUSING AUTHORITY ACCOMMODATION AND HOMELESSNESS) ORDER 2000

2000 No 706

Made - - - 7th March 2000

Laid before Parliament - - - 13th March 2000

Coming into force - - - 3rd April 2000

In exercise of the powers conferred on him by sections 118, 119 and 166(3) of the Immigration and Asylum Act 1999, the Secretary of State hereby makes the following Order:

1 Citation, commencement and extent

(1)   This Order may be cited as the Persons subject to Immigration Control (Housing Authority Accommodation and Homelessness) Order 2000 and shall come into force on 3rd April 2000.

(2)   This Order does not extend to Wales.

(3)   Article 4 extends to England only.

(4)   Articles 5 and 8 extend to Northern Ireland only.

(5)   Articles 6 and 9 extend to Scotland only.

(6)   Article 7 extends to Scotland and Northern Ireland only.

NOTES

Initial Commencement
Specified date
Specified date: 3 April 2000: see para (1) above.

Extent
This Order does not extend to Wales: see para (2) above.

2 Interpretation

In this Order—

"the 1971 Act" means the Immigration Act 1971;

"the 1985 Act" means the Housing Act 1985;

"the 1995 Act" means the Jobseekers Act 1995;

"the 1999 Act" means the Immigration and Asylum Act 1999;

"asylum-seeker" means a person who is not under 18 and who made a claim for asylum which is recorded by the Secretary of State as having been made on or before 2nd April 2000 but which has not been determined;

"child in need" means a child—

(a) who is unlikely to achieve or maintain, or to have the opportunity of achieving or maintaining, a reasonable standard of health or development without the provision for him of services by a local authority under Part III of the Children Act 1989 (local authority support for children and families);

(b) whose health or development is likely to be significantly impaired, or further impaired, without the provision for him of such services; or

(c) who is blind, deaf or dumb or suffers from mental disorder of any kind or is substantially and permanently handicapped by illness, injury or congenital deformity or such other disability as may be prescribed by regulations made under section 17 of the Children Act 1989 (provision of services for children in need, their families and others);

"claim for asylum" means a claim that it would be contrary to the United Kingdom's obligations under the Refugee Convention for the claimant to be removed from, or required to leave, the United Kingdom;

"Common Travel Area" means the United Kingdom, the Channel Islands, the Isle of Man and the Republic of Ireland collectively;

"designated course" means a course of any kind designated by regulations made by the Secretary of State for the purposes of paragraph 10 of Schedule 1 to the 1985 Act (student lettings which are not secure tenancies);

"development" means physical, intellectual, emotional, social or behavioural development;

"educational establishment" means a university or institution which provides further education or higher education (or both); and for the purposes of this definition "further education" has the same meaning as in section 2 of the Education Act 1996 (definition of further education) and "higher education" means education provided by means of a course of any description mentioned in Schedule 6 to the Education Reform Act 1988 (courses of higher education);

"family", in relation to a child in need, includes any person who has parental responsibility for the child and any other person with whom he has been living;

"full-time course" means a course normally involving not less than 15 hours attendance a week in term time for the organised day-time study of a single subject or related subjects;

"health" means physical or mental health;

"the immigration rules" means the rules laid down as mentioned in section 3(2) of the 1971 Act (general provisions for regulation and control);

"limited leave" means leave under the 1971 Act to enter or remain in the United Kingdom which is limited as to duration;

"the Refugee Convention" means the Convention relating to the Status of Refugees done at Geneva on 28th July 1951 as extended by Article 1(2) of the Protocol relating to the Status of Refugees done at New York on 31st January 1967;

"specified education institution" means—

(a) a university or other institution within the higher education sector within the meaning of section 91(5) of the Further and Higher Education Act 1992 (interpretation of Education Acts), in respect of a university or other institution in England, or section 56(2) of the Further and Higher Education (Scotland) Act 1992 (interpretation of Part II), in respect of a university or other institution in Scotland;

(b) an institution in England within the further education sector within the meaning of section 91(3) of the Further and Higher Education Act 1992;

(c) a college of further education in Scotland which is under the management of an education authority or which is managed by a board of management in terms of Part I of the Further and Higher Education (Scotland) Act 1992 (further education in Scotland);

(d) a central institution in Scotland within the meaning of section 135(1) of the Education (Scotland) Act 1980 (interpretation);

(e) an institution in England which provides a course qualifying for funding under Part I of the Education Act 1994 (teaching training);

(f) a higher education institution in Northern Ireland within the meaning of Article 30(3) of the Education and Libraries (Northern Ireland) Order 1993 (funding by Department of higher education); or

(g) an institution of further education in Northern Ireland within the meaning of Article 3 of the Further Education (Northern Ireland) Order 1997 (definition of "further education").

NOTES

Initial Commencement
Specified date
Specified date: 3 April 2000: see art 1(1).

Extent
This Order does not extend to Wales: see art 1(2).

3 Housing authority accommodation—England, Scotland and Northern Ireland

The following are classes of persons specified for the purposes of section 118(1) of the 1999 Act (housing authority accommodation) in respect of England, Scotland and Northern Ireland—

(a) Class A—a person recorded by the Secretary of State as a refugee within the definition in Article 1 of the Refugee Convention;

(b) Class B—a person—
   (i) who has been granted by the Secretary of State exceptional leave to enter or remain in the United Kingdom outside the provisions of the immigration rules; and
   (ii) whose leave is not subject to a condition requiring him to maintain and accommodate himself, and any person who is dependent on him, without recourse to public funds;

(c) Class C—a person who has current leave to enter or remain in the United Kingdom which is not subject to any limitation or condition and who is habitually resident in the Common Travel Area other than a person—
   (i) who has been given leave to enter or remain in the United Kingdom upon an undertaking given by another person (his "sponsor") in writing in pursuance of the immigration rules to be responsible for his maintenance and accommodation;
   (ii) who has been resident in the United Kingdom for less than five years beginning on the date of entry or the date on which the undertaking was given in respect of him, whichever date is the later; and
   (iii) whose sponsor or, where there is more than one sponsor, at least one of whose sponsors, is still alive;

(d) Class D—a person who left the territory of Montserrat after 1st November 1995 because of the effect on that territory of a volcanic eruption;

  (e)   Class E—a person who is—
     (i)   a national of a state which has ratified the European Convention on Social and Medical Assistance done at Paris on 11th December 1953 or a state which has ratified the European Social Charter done at Turin on 18th October 1961;
     (ii) lawfully present in the United Kingdom; and
     (iii) habitually resident in the Common Travel Area;

  (f)   Class F—a person who is attending a full-time course at a specified education institution in a case where the housing accommodation which is or may be provided to him—
     (i)   is let by a housing authority to that specified education institution for the purposes of enabling that institution to provide accommodation for students attending a full-time course at that institution; and
     (ii) would otherwise be difficult for that housing authority to let on terms which, in the opinion of the housing authority, are satisfactory.

NOTES

Initial Commencement
Specified date
Specified date: 3 April 2000: see art 1(1).

4 Housing authority accommodation—England

(1)   The following are classes of persons specified for the purposes of section 118(1) of the 1999 Act in respect of England—

  (a)   Class G—a person who is owed a duty under section 21 of the National Assistance Act 1948 (duty of local authorities to provide accommodation);

  (b)   Class H—a person who is either a child in need or a member of the family of a child in need;

  (c)   Class I—a person—
     (i)   who is owed a duty under section 63(1) (interim duty to accommodate in case of apparent priority need), 65(2) or (3) (duties to persons found to be homeless) or 68(1) or (2) (duties to persons whose applications are referred) of the 1985 Act;
     (ii) who is owed a duty under section 188(1) (interim duty to accommodate in case of apparent priority need), 190(2) (duties to persons becoming homeless intentionally), 193(2) (duty to persons with priority need who are not homeless intentionally), 195(2) (duties in case of threatened homelessness) or 200(1), (3) or (4) (duties to applicant whose case is considered for referral or referred) of the Housing Act 1996; or
     (iii) in respect of whom a local housing authority are exercising their power under section 194(1) (power exercisable after minimum period of duty under section 193) of the Housing Act 1996;

  (d)   Class J—an asylum-seeker to whom, or a dependant of an asylum-seeker to whom, a local authority is required to provide support in accordance with regulations made under Schedule 9 to the 1999 Act (asylum support: interim provisions);

  (e)   Class K—a person who is attending a designated course, which is a full-time course, at an educational establishment in a case where the housing accommodation which is or may be provided to him by a local housing authority—
     (i)   is not and will not be let to him as a secure tenancy by virtue of paragraph 10 of Schedule 1 to the 1985 Act (student lettings which are not secure tenancies); and

     (ii)   would otherwise be difficult for that local housing authority to let on terms which, in the opinion of the local housing authority, are satisfactory;

  (f)   Class L—a person who has a secure tenancy within the meaning of section 79 of the 1985 Act (secure tenancies).

(2) "Dependant", in relation to an asylum-seeker within paragraph (1)(d) (Class J), means a person in the United Kingdom who—

  (a)   is his spouse;

  (b)   is a child of his, or of his spouse, who is under 18 and dependent on him; or

  (c)   falls within such additional category as may be prescribed under section 94(1) of the 1999 Act (interpretation of Part VI—support for asylum-seekers), for the purposes of regulations made under Schedule 9 to the 1999 Act (asylum support: interim provisions), in relation to an asylum-seeker.

NOTES

Initial Commencement
Specified date
Specified date: 3 April 2000: see art 1(1).

5 Housing authority accommodation—Northern Ireland

The following are classes of persons specified for the purposes of section 118(1) of the 1999 Act in respect of Northern Ireland—

  (a)   Class M—a person who is a secure tenant of the Northern Ireland Housing Executive or a registered housing association within the meaning of Article 25 of the Housing (Northern Ireland) Order 1983 (secure tenancies);

  (b)   Class N—a person who is owed a duty under Article 8 (interim duty to accommodate in case of apparent priority need), 10(2) or (3) (duties to persons found to be homeless) or 11(2) (duties to persons found to be threatened with homelessness) of the Housing (Northern Ireland) Order 1988.

NOTES

Initial Commencement
Specified date
Specified date: 3 April 2000: see art 1(1).

6 Housing authority accommodation—Scotland

The following are classes of persons specified for the purposes of section 118(1) of the 1999 Act in respect of Scotland—

  (a)   Class O—a person who is a secure tenant within the meaning of Part III of the Housing (Scotland) Act 1987 (rights of public sector tenants);

  (b)   Class P—a person who is owed a duty under section 29 (interim duty to accommodate in case of apparent priority need), 31 (duties to persons found to be homeless), 32 (duties to persons found to be threatened with homelessness) or 34 (duties to persons whose applications are referred to another local authority) of the Housing (Scotland) Act 1987.

NOTES

Initial Commencement
Specified date
Specified date: 3 April 2000: see art 1(1).

7 Homelessness—Scotland and Northern Ireland

(1)   The following are classes of persons specified for the purposes of section 119(1) of the 1999 Act (homelessness: Scotland and Northern Ireland) in respect of Scotland and Northern Ireland—

   (a)   the classes specified in article 3(a) to (e) (Class A, Class B, Class C, Class D and Class E);
   (b)   Class Q—a person who is an asylum-seeker and who made a claim for asylum—
      (i)   which is recorded by the Secretary of State as having been made on his arrival (other than on re-entry) in the United Kingdom from a country outside the Common Travel Area; and
      (ii)   which has not been recorded by the Secretary of State as having been either decided (other than on appeal) or abandoned;
   (c)   Class R—a person who is an asylum-seeker and—
      (i)   who made a relevant claim for asylum on or before 4th February 1996; and
      (ii)   who was, on 4th February 1996, entitled to benefit under regulation 7A of the Housing Benefit (General) Regulations 1987 (persons from abroad) or regulation 7A of the Housing Benefit (General) Regulations (Northern Ireland) 1987 (persons from abroad).

(2)   In paragraph (1)(c)(i), a relevant claim for asylum is a claim for asylum which—

   (a)   has not been recorded by the Secretary of State as having been either decided (other than on appeal) or abandoned; or
   (b)   has been recorded as having been decided (other than on appeal) on or before 4th February 1996 and in respect of which an appeal is pending which—
      (i)   was pending on 5th February 1996; or
      (ii)   was made within the time limits specified in the rules of procedure made under section 22 of the 1971 Act (procedure).

NOTES

Initial Commencement
Specified date
Specified date: 3 April 2000: see art 1(1).

8 Homelessness—Northern Ireland

(1)   The following are classes of persons specified for the purposes of section 119(1) of the 1999 Act in respect of Northern Ireland—

   (a)   Class S—a person who is on an income-based jobseeker's allowance or in receipt of income support and is eligible for that benefit other than because—
      (i)   he has limited leave to enter or remain in the United Kingdom which was given in accordance with the relevant immigration rules; and
      (ii)   he is temporarily without funds because remittances to him from abroad have been disrupted;
   (b)   Class T—a person who is an asylum-seeker and—
      (i)   who was in Northern Ireland when the Secretary of State made a declaration to the effect that the country of which that person is a national is subject to such a fundamental change in circumstances that he would not normally order the return of a person to that country;
      (ii)   who made a claim for asylum which is recorded by the Secretary of State as having been made within a period of three months from the day on which that declaration was made; and
      (iii)   whose claim for asylum has not been recorded by the Secretary of State as having been either decided (other than on appeal) or abandoned.

(2)   For the purposes of paragraph (1)(a) (Class S)—

(a)   "an income-based jobseeker's allowance" means a jobseeker's allowance which is payable under the Jobseekers (Northern Ireland) Order 1995 and entitlement to which is based on the claimant satisfying conditions which include those set out in Article 5 of that Order (the income-based conditions);

(b)   "income support" has the same meaning as in section 123 of the Social Security Contributions and Benefits (Northern Ireland) Act 1992 (income support);

(c)   "relevant immigration rules" means the immigration rules relating to—
(i)   there being or there needing to be no recourse to public funds; or
(ii)   there being no charge on public funds; and

(d)   a person is on an income-based jobseeker's allowance on any day in respect of which an income-based jobseeker's allowance is payable to him and on any day—
(i)   in respect of which he satisfies the conditions for entitlement to an income-based jobseeker's allowance but where the allowance is not paid in accordance with Article 21 of the Jobseekers (Northern Ireland) Order 1995 (circumstances in which a jobseeker's allowance is not payable); or
(ii)   which is a waiting day for the purposes of paragraph 4 of Schedule 1 to that Order (waiting days) and which falls immediately before a day in respect of which an income-based jobseeker's allowance is payable to him or would be payable to him but for Article 21 of that Order.

NOTES

Initial Commencement
Specified date
Specified date: 3 April 2000: see art 1(1).

9 Homelessness—Scotland

(1)   The following are classes of persons specified for the purposes of section 119(1) of the 1999 Act in respect of Scotland—

(a)   Class U—a person who is on an income-based jobseeker's allowance or in receipt of income support and is eligible for that benefit other than because—
(i)   he has limited leave to enter or remain in the United Kingdom which was given in accordance with the relevant immigration rules; and
(ii)   he is temporarily without funds because remittances to him from abroad have been disrupted;

(b)   Class V—a person who is an asylum-seeker and—
(i)   who was in Great Britain when the Secretary of State made a declaration to the effect that the country of which that person is a national is subject to such a fundamental change in circumstances that he would not normally order the return of a person to that country;
(ii)   who made a claim for asylum which is recorded by the Secretary of State as having been made within a period of three months from the day on which that declaration was made; and
(iii)   whose claim for asylum has not been recorded by the Secretary of State as having been either decided (other than on appeal) or abandoned.

(2)   For the purposes of paragraph (1)(a) (Class U)—

(a)   "an income-based jobseeker's allowance" means a jobseeker's allowance which is payable under the 1995 Act and entitlement to which is based on the claimant satisfying conditions which include those set out in section 3 of the 1995 Act (the income-based conditions);

(b) "income support" has the same meaning as in section 124 of the Social Security Contributions and Benefits Act 1992 (income support);

(c) "relevant immigration rules" means the immigration rules relating to—

(i) there being or there needing to be no recourse to public funds; or

(ii) there being no charge on public funds; and

(d) a person is on an income-based jobseeker's allowance on any day in respect of which an income-based jobseeker's allowance is payable to him and on any day—

(i) in respect of which he satisfies the conditions for entitlement to an income-based jobseeker's allowance but where the allowance is not paid in accordance with section 19 of the 1995 Act (circumstances in which jobseeker's allowance is not payable); or

(ii) which is a waiting day for the purposes of paragraph 4 of Schedule 1 to the 1995 Act (waiting days) and which falls immediately before a day in respect of which an income-based jobseeker's allowance is payable to him or would be payable to him but for section 19 of the 1995 Act.

NOTES

Initial Commencement
Specified date
Specified date: 3 April 2000: see art 1(1).

10 Revocation

The following Orders are revoked—

(a) the Housing Accommodation and Homelessness (Persons subject to Immigration Control) Order 1996, in so far as it extends to England and Scotland;

(b) the Homelessness (Persons subject to Immigration Control) (Amendment) Order 1997, in so far as it extends to England and Scotland;

(c) the Housing Accommodation and Homelessness (Persons subject to Immigration Control) (Amendment) Order 1998, in so far as it extends to England;

(d) the Housing Accommodation and Homelessness (Persons subject to Immigration Control) (Northern Ireland) Order 1998;

(e) the Housing Accommodation and Homelessness (Persons subject to Immigration Control) (Amendment) (Scotland) Order 1999; and

(f) the Housing Accommodation (Persons subject to Immigration Control) (Amendment) (England) Order 1999.

NOTES

Initial Commencement
Specified date
Specified date: 3 April 2000: see art 1(1).

Extent
This Order does not extend to Wales: see art 1(2).

Barbara Roche
Minister of State
Home Office
7th March 2000

IMMIGRATION (PASSENGER INFORMATION) ORDER 2000

2000 No 912

Made - - - 29th March 2000

Laid before Parliament - - - 6th April 2000

Coming into force - - - 28th April 2000

The Secretary of State, in exercise of the powers conferred upon him by paragraph 27B(9) and (10) of Schedule 2 to the Immigration Act 1971, hereby makes the following Order:

1 This Order may be cited as the Immigration (Passenger Information) Order 2000 and shall come into force on 28th April 2000.

NOTES

Initial Commencement
Specified date
Specified date: 28 April 2000: see above.

2 (1) Subject to paragraph (2), the information listed in the Schedule to this Order is specified for the purposes of paragraph 27B(9) of Schedule 2 to the Immigration Act 1971 (definition of "passenger information").

(2) The information listed in Part II of the Schedule to this Order is so specified only to the extent that it is known to the carrier.

NOTES

Initial Commencement
Specified date
Specified date: 28 April 2000: see art 1.

Barbara Roche
Minister of State
Home Office
29th March 2000

SCHEDULE
Passenger Information

Article 2

Part I
Information Relating to a Passenger as Given on or Shown by the Passenger's Passport or Other Travel Document

Full name.
Gender.
Date of birth.
Nationality.
The type of travel document held by the passenger and its number.
If the passenger has a United Kingdom visa or other form of United Kingdom entry clearance, its expiry date.

NOTES

Initial Commencement
Specified date
Specified date: 28 April 2000: see art 1.

PART II
OTHER INFORMATION RELATING TO A PASSENGER

Name as it appears on the passenger's reservation.

Ticket number.

Date and place of issue of the ticket.

If not the carrier, the identity of the person who made the passenger's reservation on behalf of the carrier.

Method of payment for the ticket.

Travel itinerary.

Names of all other passengers appearing on the passenger's reservation.

If the passenger is travelling with a car or other vehicle, the vehicle registration number and, if the vehicle has a trailer, the trailer registration number (if different to the vehicle registration number).

NOTES

Initial Commencement
Specified date
Specified date: 28 April 2000: see art 1.

PERSONS SUBJECT TO IMMIGRATION CONTROL (HOUSING AUTHORITY ACCOMMODATION) (WALES) ORDER 2000

2000 No 1036

Made - - - 30th March 2000

Coming into force - - - 1st April 2000

The National Assembly for Wales makes the following Order in exercise of the powers conferred on the Secretary of State by sections 118 and 166(3) of the Immigration and Asylum Act 1999 which are vested in the National Assembly for Wales so far as exercisable in Wales.

1 Citation, commencement and application

(1)   This Order may be cited as the Persons Subject to Immigration Control (Housing Authority Accommodation) (Wales) Order 2000 and shall come into force on 1st April 2000.

(2)   This Order applies to Wales only.

NOTES

Initial Commencement
Specified date
Specified date: 1 April 2000: see para (1) above.

2 Housing authority accommodation

The classes of persons specified in Articles 3 and 4 of the Persons subject to Immigration Control (Housing Authority Accommodation and Homelessness) Order 2000 are specified for the purposes of Section 118(1) of the Immigration and Asylum Act 1999 in relation to Wales and expressions used in those Articles have the meaning given to them by Article 2 of that Order.

NOTES

Initial Commencement
Specified date
Specified date: 1 April 2000: see art 1(1).

3 Revocation

The Housing Accommodation (Persons Subject to Immigration Control) (Amendment) (Wales) Order 1999 is revoked and the orders specified in paragraphs (a), (b) and (c) of Article 10 of the Persons Subject to Immigration Control (Housing Authority Accommodation and Homelessness) Order 2000 are revoked in relation to Wales.

NOTES

Initial Commencement
Specified date
Specified date: 1 April 2000: see art 1(1).

Signed on behalf of the National Assembly for Wales under section 66(1) of the Government of Wales Act 1998.
D Elis Thomas
The Presiding Officer of the National Assembly
30th March 2000

IMMIGRATION (LEAVE TO ENTER AND REMAIN) ORDER 2000

2000 No 1161

Made - - - 19th April 2000

Coming into force - - - Articles 1 to 12, 14 and 15(1) in accordance with article 1(2) Articles 13 and 15(2) 30th July 2000

Whereas a draft of this Order has been laid before Parliament and approved by a resolution of each House in accordance with sections 3A(13) and 3B(6) of the Immigration Act 1971;

Now, therefore, the Secretary of State, in exercise of the powers conferred upon him by sections 3A(1), (2), (3), (4), (6) and (10) and 3B(2)(a) and (c) and (3)(a) of the Immigration Act 1971, hereby makes the following Order:

PART I
GENERAL

Citation, commencement and interpretation

1 (1) This Order may be cited as the Immigration (Leave to Enter and Remain) Order 2000.

(2)   Articles 1 to 12, 14 and 15(1) of this Order shall come into force on 28th April 2000 or, if later, on the day after the day on which it is made and articles 13 and 15(2) shall come into force on 30th July 2000.

(3)   In this Order—

> "the Act" means the Immigration Act 1971;
> "control port" means a port in which a control area is designated under paragraph 26(3) of Schedule 2 to the Act;
> "the Immigration Acts" means:
> (a)   the Act;
> (b)   the Immigration Act 1988;
> (c)   the Asylum and Immigration Appeals Act 1993;
> (d)   the Asylum and Immigration Act 1996; and
> (e)   the Immigration and Asylum Act 1999;
> "responsible third party" means a person appearing to an immigration officer to be:
> (a)   in charge of a group of people arriving in the United Kingdom together or intending to arrive in the United Kingdom together;
> (b)   a tour operator;
> (c)   the owner or agent of a ship, aircraft, train, hydrofoil or hovercraft;
> (d)   the person responsible for the management of a control port or his agent; or
> (e)   an official at a British Diplomatic Mission or at a British Consular Post or at the office of any person outside the United Kingdom and Islands who has been authorised by the Secretary of State to accept applications for entry clearance;
> "tour operator" means a person who, otherwise than occasionally, organises and provides holidays to the public or a section of it; and
> "visit visa" means an entry clearance granted for the purpose of entry to the United Kingdom as a visitor under the immigration rules.

NOTES

Initial Commencement
Specified date
Specified date: 28 April 2000: see para (2) above.

PART II
ENTRY CLEARANCE AS LEAVE TO ENTER

Entry clearance as Leave to Enter

2   Subject to article 6(3), an entry clearance which complies with the requirements of article 3 shall have effect as leave to enter the United Kingdom to the extent specified in article 4, but subject to the conditions referred to in article 5.

NOTES

Initial Commencement
Specified date
Specified date: 28 April 2000: see art 1(2).

Requirements

3   (1)   An entry clearance shall not have effect as leave to enter unless it complies with the requirements of this article.

(2)   The entry clearance must specify the purpose for which the holder wishes to enter the United Kingdom.

(3)   The entry clearance must be endorsed with:

(a)   the conditions to which it is subject; or

(b)   a statement that it is to have effect as indefinite leave to enter the United Kingdom.

NOTES

Initial Commencement
Specified date
Specified date: 28 April 2000: see art 1(2).

Extent to which Entry Clearance is to be Leave to Enter

4   (1)   A visit visa, during its period of validity, shall have effect as leave to enter the United Kingdom on an unlimited number of occasions, in accordance with paragraph (2).

(2)   On each occasion the holder arrives in the United Kingdom, he shall be treated for the purposes of the Immigration Acts as having been granted, before arrival, leave to enter the United Kingdom for a limited period beginning on the date of arrival, being:

(a)   six months if six months or more remain of the visa's period of validity; or

(b)   the visa's remaining period of validity, if less than six months.

(3)   In the case of any other form of entry clearance, it shall have effect as leave to enter the United Kingdom on one occasion during its period of validity; and, on arrival in the United Kingdom, the holder shall be treated for the purposes of the Immigration Acts as having been granted, before arrival, leave to enter the United Kingdom:

(a)   in the case of an entry clearance which is endorsed with a statement that it is to have effect as indefinite leave to enter the United Kingdom, for an indefinite period; or

(b)   in the case of an entry clearance which is endorsed with conditions, for a limited period, being the period beginning on the date on which the holder arrives in the United Kingdom and ending on the date of expiry of the entry clearance.

(4)   In this article "period of validity" means the period beginning on the day on which the entry clearance becomes effective and ending on the day on which it expires.

NOTES

Initial Commencement
Specified date
Specified date: 28 April 2000: see art 1(2).

Conditions

5   An entry clearance shall have effect as leave to enter subject to any conditions, being conditions of a kind that may be imposed on leave to enter given under section 3 of the Act, to which the entry clearance is subject and which are endorsed on it.

NOTES

Initial Commencement
Specified date
Specified date: 28 April 2000: see art 1(2).

Incidental, supplementary and consequential provisions

6   (1)   Where an immigration officer exercises his power to cancel leave to enter under paragraph 2A(8) of Schedule 2 to the Act or article 13(7) below in respect of an

entry clearance which has effect as leave to enter, the entry clearance shall cease to have effect.

(2)   If the holder of an entry clearance—

- (a)   arrives in the United Kingdom before the day on which it becomes effective; or
- (b)   seeks to enter the United Kingdom for a purpose other than the purpose specified in the entry clearance,

an immigration officer may cancel the entry clearance.

(3)   If the holder of an entry clearance which does not, at the time, have effect as leave to enter the United Kingdom seeks leave to enter the United Kingdom at any time before his departure for, or in the course of his journey to, the United Kingdom and is refused leave to enter under article 7, the entry clearance shall not have effect as leave to enter.

NOTES

Initial Commencement
Specified date
Specified date: 28 April 2000: see art 1(2).

Part III

Form and Manner of Giving and Refusing Leave to Enter

Grant and refusal of leave to enter before arrival in the United Kingdom

7   (1)   An immigration officer, whether or not in the United Kingdom, may give or refuse a person leave to enter the United Kingdom at any time before his departure for, or in the course of his journey to, the United Kingdom.

(2)   In order to determine whether or not to give leave to enter under this article (and, if so, for what period and subject to what conditions), an immigration officer may seek such information, and the production of such documents or copy documents, as an immigration officer would be entitled to obtain in an examination under paragraph 2 or 2A of Schedule 2 to the Act.

(3)   An immigration officer may also require the person seeking leave to supply an up to date medical report.

(4)   Failure by a person seeking leave to supply any information, documents, copy documents or medical report requested by an immigration officer under this article shall be a ground, in itself, for refusal of leave.

NOTES

Initial Commencement
Specified date
Specified date: 28 April 2000: see art 1(2).

Grant or refusal of leave otherwise than by notice in writing

8   (1)   A notice giving or refusing leave to enter may, instead of being given in writing as required by section 4(1) of the Act, be given as follows.

(2)   The notice may be given by facsimile or electronic mail.

(3)   In the case of a notice giving or refusing leave to enter the United Kingdom as a visitor, it may be given orally, including by means of a telecommunications system.

(4)   In paragraph (3), "leave to enter the United Kingdom as a visitor" means leave to enter as a visitor under the immigration rules for a period not exceeding six months,

subject to conditions prohibiting employment and recourse to public funds (within the meaning of the immigration rules).

NOTES

Initial Commencement
Specified date
Specified date: 28 April 2000: see art 1(2).

Grant or refusal of leave by notice to a responsible third party

9 (1)   Leave to enter may be given or refused to a person by means of a notice given (in such form and manner as permitted by the Act or this Order for a notice giving or refusing leave to enter) to a responsible third party acting on his behalf.

(2)   A notice under paragraph (1) may refer to a person to whom leave is being granted or refused either by name or by reference to a description or category of persons which includes him.

NOTES

Initial Commencement
Specified date
Specified date: 28 April 2000: see art 1(2).

Notice of refusal of leave

10 (1)   Where a notice refusing leave to enter to a person is given under article 8(3) or 9, an immigration officer shall as soon as practicable give to him a notice in writing stating that he has been refused leave to enter the United Kingdom and stating the reasons for the refusal.

(2)   Where an immigration officer serves a notice under the Immigration (Appeals) Notices Regulations 1984 or under regulations made under paragraph 1 of Schedule 4 to the Immigration and Asylum Act 1999 in respect of the refusal, he shall not be required to serve a notice under paragraph (1).

(3)   Any notice required by paragraph (1) to be given to any person may be delivered, or sent by post to—

   (a)   that person's last known or usual place of abode; or
   (b)   any address provided by him for receipt of the notice.

NOTES

Initial Commencement
Specified date
Specified date: 28 April 2000: see art 1(2).

Burden of proof

11   Where any question arises under the Immigration Acts as to whether a person has leave to enter the United Kingdom and he alleges that he has such leave by virtue of a notice given under article 8(3) or 9, the onus shall lie upon him to show the manner and date of his entry into the United Kingdom.

NOTES

Initial Commencement
Specified date
Specified date: 28 April 2000: see art 1(2).

12   (1)   This article applies where—

   (a)   an immigration officer has commenced examination of a person ("the applicant") under paragraph 2(1)(c) of Schedule 2 to the Act (examination to determine whether or not leave to enter should be given);

   (b)   that examination has been adjourned, or the applicant has been required (under paragraph 2(3) of Schedule 2 to the Act) to submit to a further examination, whilst further inquiries are made (including, where the applicant has made an asylum claim, as to the Secretary of State's decision on that claim); and

   (c)   upon the completion of those inquiries, an immigration officer considers he is in a position to decide whether or not to give or refuse leave to enter without interviewing the applicant further.

(2)   Where this article applies, any notice giving or refusing leave to enter which is on any date thereafter sent by post to the applicant (or is communicated to him in such form or manner as is permitted by this Order) shall be regarded, for the purposes of the Act, as having been given within the period of 24 hours specified in paragraph 6(1) of Schedule 2 to the Act (period within which notice giving or refusing leave to enter must be given after completion of examination).

NOTES

Initial Commencement
Specified date
Specified date: 28 April 2000: see art 1(2).

PART IV
LEAVE WHICH DOES NOT LAPSE ON TRAVEL OUTSIDE COMMON TRAVEL AREA

13   (1)   In this article "leave" means—

   (a)   leave to enter the United Kingdom (including leave to enter conferred by means of an entry clearance under article 2); and

   (b)   leave to remain in the United Kingdom.

(2)   Subject to paragraph (3), where a person has leave which is in force and which was:

   (a)   conferred by means of an entry clearance (other than a visit visa) under article 2; or

   (b)   given by an immigration officer or the Secretary of State for a period exceeding six months,

such leave shall not lapse on his going to a country or territory outside the common travel area.

(3)   Paragraph (2) shall not apply:

   (a)   where a limited leave has been varied by the Secretary of State; and

   (b)   following the variation the period of leave remaining is six months or less.

(4)   Leave which does not lapse under paragraph (2) shall remain in force either indefinitely (if it is unlimited) or until the date on which it would otherwise have expired (if limited), but—

   (a)   where the holder has stayed outside the United Kingdom for a continuous period of more than two years, the leave (where the leave is unlimited) or any leave then remaining (where the leave is limited) shall thereupon lapse; and

   (b)   any conditions to which the leave is subject shall be suspended for such time as the holder is outside the United Kingdom.

(5)   For the purposes of paragraphs 2 and 2A of Schedule 2 to the Act (examination by immigration officers, and medical examination), leave to remain which remains in force under this article shall be treated, upon the holder's arrival in the United Kingdom, as leave to enter which has been granted to the holder before his arrival.

(6)   Without prejudice to the provisions of section 4(1) of the Act, where the holder of leave which remains in force under this article is outside the United Kingdom, the Secretary of State may vary that leave (including any conditions to which it is subject) in such form and manner as permitted by the Act or this Order for the giving of leave to enter.

(7)   Where a person is outside the United Kingdom and has leave which is in force by virtue of this article, that leave may be cancelled:

(a)   in the case of leave to enter, by an immigration officer; or

(b)   in the case of leave to remain, by the Secretary of State.

(8)   In order to determine whether or not to vary (and, if so, in what manner) or cancel leave which remains in force under this article and which is held by a person who is outside the United Kingdom, an immigration officer or, as the case may be, the Secretary of State may seek such information, and the production of such documents or copy documents, as an immigration officer would be entitled to obtain in an examination under paragraph 2 or 2A of Schedule 2 to the Act and may also require the holder of the leave to supply an up to date medical report.

(9)   Failure to supply any information, documents, copy documents or medical report requested by an immigration officer or, as the case may be, the Secretary of State under this article shall be a ground, in itself, for cancellation of leave.

(10) Section 3(4) of the Act (lapsing of leave upon travelling outside the common travel area) shall have effect subject to this article.

NOTES

Initial Commencement
Specified date
Specified date: 30 July 2000: see art 1(2).

PART V
CONSEQUENTIAL AND TRANSITIONAL PROVISIONS

14   Section 9(2) of the Act (further provisions as to common travel area: conditions applicable to certain arrivals on a local journey) shall have effect as if, after the words "British Citizens", there were inserted "and do not hold leave to enter or remain granted to them before their arrival".

NOTES

Initial Commencement
Specified date
Specified date: 28 April 2000: see art 1(2).

15   (1) Article 12 shall apply where an applicant's examination has begun before the date that article comes into force, as well as where it begins on or after that date.

(2)   Article 13 shall apply with respect to leave to enter or remain in the United Kingdom which is in force on the date that article comes into force, as well as to such leave given after that date.

NOTES

Initial Commencement
Specified date
Para (1): Specified date: 28 April 2000: see art 1(2).
Para (2): Specified date: 30 July 2000: see art 1(2).

Jack Straw
One of Her Majesty's Principal Secretaries of State
Home Office
19th April 2000

IMMIGRATION AND ASYLUM ACT 1999 (COMMENCEMENT NO 5 AND TRANSITIONAL PROVISIONS) ORDER 2000

2000 No 1985

Made - - - 22nd July 2000

In exercise of the powers conferred upon him by sections 166(3) and 170(4) and (5) of the Immigration and Asylum Act 1999, the Secretary of State hereby makes the following Order:

1 Citation and interpretation

(1) This Order may be cited as the Immigration and Asylum Act 1999 (Commencement No 5 and Transitional Provisions) Order 2000.

(2) In this Order "the Act" means the Immigration and Asylum Act 1999.

NOTES

Initial Commencement
Date Made
Date made: 22 July 2000: (no specific commencement provision).

2 Commencement of provisions

The provisions of the Act specified in column 1 of the Schedule to this Order shall come into force on the date specified in column 2 of that Schedule, but where a particular purpose is specified in relation to any such provision in column 3 of that Schedule, the provision concerned shall come into force on that date only for that purpose.

NOTES

Initial Commencement
Date Made
Date made: 22 July 2000: (no specific commencement provision).

3 Transitional provisions relating to Part IV of the Act

(1) The new appeals provisions shall have effect from the relevant date as if:

    (a) any reference in them to Part IV of the Act (however expressed) included a reference to the existing appeals provisions;

    (b) the reference in paragraph 1(2) of Schedule 4 to the Act to "the regulations " included a reference to regulations made under section 18 of the 1971 Act.

(2) Paragraph 6 of Schedule 2 to the 1997 Act (as substituted by paragraph 129 of Schedule 14 to the Act) shall have effect from the relevant date as if the reference in it to section 2 of the 1997 Act included a reference to that section as it had effect immediately before the amendment made to it by paragraphs 119 and 120 of Schedule 14 to the Act came into force.

(3) In this article:

"the 1971 Act" means the Immigration Act 1971;
"the 1997 Act" means the Special Immigration Appeals Commission Act 1997;
"the existing appeals provisions" means Part II of the 1971 Act, section 8 of, and Schedule 2 to, the Asylum and Immigration Act 1993 and section 3 of the Asylum and Immigration Act 1996;
"the new appeals provisions" means paragraphs 1, 3 and 4 of Schedule 4 to the Act, together with section 58(2) of the Act so far as it relates to those paragraphs; and
"the relevant date" means 1st August 2000.

NOTES

Initial Commencement
Date Made
Date made: 22 July 2000: (no specific commencement provision).

Jack Straw
Home Office
One of Her Majesty's Principal Secretaries of State
22nd July 2000

THE SCHEDULE

Article 2

Column 1	*Column 2*	*Column 3*
Section 83(4) and (5) (The Commissioner) (so far as not already in force)	30th October 2000	
Section 84(2)(a) and (b), (4)(a) and (d), (5) and (7) (Provision of immigration services)	30th October 2000	Paragraphs (a) and (b) of section 84(2) are commenced in so far as they relate to the provisions of section 85 of the Act commenced by this Order; section 84(4)(a) is commenced in so far as to enable the Commissioner to certify a person as exempt under it; section 84(4)(d) is commenced for the purposes of making subordinate legislation under it.
Section 85(3) (Schedule 6)	1st August 2000	Commenced for the purposes of the provisions of Schedule 6 commenced by this Order on this date.

Appendix 1   UK and EC Legislation

Column 1	Column 2	Column 3
Section 85 (Registration and exemption by the Commissioner) (so far as not already in force)	30th October 2000	
Section 86(10) to (12) (Designated professional bodies)	30th October 2000	For the purpose of making subordinate legislation under them.
Section 87(5) (The Tribunal)	1st August 2000	In so far as it relates to the provisions of Schedule 7 commenced by this Order on this date.
Section 87 (The Tribunal) (so far as not already in force)	30th October 2000	
Section 88 (Appeal upheld by the Tribunal)	30th October 2000	
Section 89 (Disciplinary charge upheld by the Tribunal)	30th October 2000	
Section 90 (Orders by disciplinary bodies)	1st August 2000	For the purposes of enabling subordinate legislation to be made under it.
Section 147 (Interpretation of Part VIII)	1st August 2000	
Section 148(3) (Management of detention centres)	1st August 2000	For the purposes of enabling subordinate legislation to be made under it.
Section 149(1), (3), (6)(a) and (9) (Detention centres: Contracting out)	1st August 2000	
Section 152(2) and (3) (Visiting Committees: Functions)	1st August 2000	For the purposes of enabling subordinate legislation to be made under them.
Section 153 (Detention centre rules)	1st August 2000	For the purposes of enabling subordinate legislation to be made under it.
Section 154(7) (Schedule 11)	1st August 2000	Commenced for the purposes of the provisions of Schedule 11 commenced by this Order.
Section 155(2) (Schedule 12)	1st August 2000	Commenced for the purposes of the provisions of Schedule 12 commenced by this Order.
Section 156(5) (Schedule 13)	1st August 2000	Commenced for the purposes of the provisions of Schedule 13 commenced by this Order.
Section 157 (Short-term holding facilities)	1st August 2000	For the purposes of enabling subordinate legislation to be made under it.

Column 1	Column 2	Column 3
Section 169(1) (Schedule 14)	1st August 2000	Commenced for the purposes of the provisions of Schedule 14 commenced by this Order.
Schedule 5 (Regulatory Functions) (so far as not already in force)	30th October 2000	
In Schedule 6, paragraph 5(1) (Immigration Services Commissioner: Registration: Fees)	1st August 2000	For the purposes of enabling subordinate legislation to be made under it.
Schedule 6 (so far as not already in force)	30th October 2000	
In Schedule 7, paragraphs 7 and 8(3)	1st August 2000	
Schedule 7 (so far as not already in force)	30th October 2000	
In Schedule 11, paragraphs 2(1)(a) and 7(2) and (3) (Detainee custody officers)	1st August 2000	For the purposes of enabling subordinate legislation to be made under them.
In Schedule 12, paragraphs 1, 2 and 3(7) (Discipline etc at detention centres)	1st August 2000	For the purposes of enabling subordinate legislation to be made under them.
In Schedule 13, paragraph 2(1)(a) and (4) (Escort arrangements)	1st August 2000	For the purposes of enabling subordinate legislation to be made under them.
In Schedule 14, paragraphs 118 and 129 (Notices of decisions which are appealable under the Special Immigration Appeals Commission Act 1997)	1st August 2000	Paragraph 118 commenced to the extent that it refers to paragraph 129 of Schedule 14.

NOTES

Initial Commencement
Date Made
Date made: 22 July 2000: (no specific commencement provision).

IMMIGRATION (REMOVAL DIRECTIONS) REGULATIONS 2000

2000 No 2243

Made - - - 16th August 2000

Laid before Parliament - - - 24th August 2000

Coming into force - - - 2nd October 2000

The Secretary of State, in exercise of the powers conferred upon him by sections 10, 166(3) and 167 of the Immigration and Asylum Act 1999, hereby makes the following Regulations:

1 Citation and commencement

These Regulations may be cited as the Immigration (Removal Directions) Regulations 2000 and shall come into force on 2nd October 2000.

NOTES

Initial Commencement
Specified date
Specified date: 2 October 2000: see above.

2 Interpretation

(1)   In these Regulations—

"the Act" means the Immigration and Asylum Act 1999;
"aircraft" includes hovercraft;
"captain" means master (of a ship) or commander (of an aircraft);
"international service" has the meaning given by section 13(6) of the Channel Tunnel Act 1987;
"ship" includes every description of vessel used in navigation; and
"the tunnel system" has the meaning given by section 1(7) of the Channel Tunnel Act 1987.

(2)   In these Regulations, a reference to a section number is a reference to a section of the Act.

NOTES

Initial Commencement
Specified date
Specified date: 2 October 2000: see reg 1.

3 Persons to whom directions may be given

For the purposes of section 10(6)(a) (classes of person to whom directions may be given), the following classes of person are prescribed—

(a)   owners of ships;
(b)   owners of aircraft;
(c)   agents of ships;
(d)   agents of aircraft;
(e)   captains of ships about to leave the United Kingdom;
(f)   captains of aircraft about to leave the United Kingdom; and
(g)   persons operating an international service.

NOTES

Initial Commencement
Specified date
Specified date: 2 October 2000: see reg 1.

4 Requirements that may be imposed by directions

(1) For the purposes of section 10(6)(b) (requirements that may be imposed by directions), the following kinds of requirements are prescribed—

  (a) in the case where directions are given to a captain of a ship or aircraft about to leave the United Kingdom, a requirement to remove the relevant person from the United Kingdom in that ship or aircraft;

  (b) in the case where directions are given to a person operating an international service, a requirement to make arrangements for the removal of the relevant person through the tunnel system;

  (c) in the case where directions are given to any other person who falls within a class prescribed in regulation 3, a requirement to make arrangements for the removal of the relevant person in a ship or aircraft specified or indicated in the directions; and

  (d) in all cases, a requirement to remove the relevant person in accordance with arrangements to be made by an immigration officer.

(2) Paragraph (1) only applies if the directions specify that the relevant person is to be removed to a country or territory being—

  (i) a country of which he is a national or citizen; or

  (ii) a country or territory to which there is reason to believe that he will be admitted.

(3) Paragraph (1)(b) only applies if the relevant person arrived in the United Kingdom through the tunnel system.

(4) "Relevant person" means a person who may be removed from the United Kingdom in accordance with section 10(1).

NOTES

Initial Commencement
Specified date
Specified date: 2 October 2000: see reg 1.

Steve Bassam
Parliamentary Under-Secretary of State
Home Office
16th August 2000

IMMIGRATION AND ASYLUM APPEALS (ONE-STOP PROCEDURE) REGULATIONS 2000

2000 No 2244

Made - - - 16th August 2000

Laid before Parliament - - - 24th August 2000

Coming into force - - - 2nd October 2000

The Secretary of State, in exercise of the powers conferred upon him by sections 74, 75, 76, 166 and 167 of the Immigration and Asylum Act 1999, hereby makes the following Regulations:

1 Citation and commencement

These Regulations may be cited as the Immigration and Asylum Appeals (One-Stop Procedure) Regulations 2000 and shall come into force on 2nd October 2000.

NOTES

Initial Commencement
Specified date
Specified date: 2 October 2000: see above.

2 Interpretation

(1)   In these Regulations—

"the Act" means the Immigration and Asylum Act 1999;
"the 1997 Act" means the Special Immigration Appeals Commission Act 1997;
"claim" means a claim to which section 75 applies;
"decision-taker" means the Secretary of State or an immigration officer, as the case may be;
"notice" means a section 74 or section 75 notice, as the case may be;
"representative" means a person who appears to the decision-taker—
(a)   to be the representative of a requisite person; and
(b)   not to be prohibited from acting as a representative by section 84 of the Act;
"requisite person" means the person on whom the notice is required to be served;
"section 74 notice" means a notice which is required to be served under section 74(4);
"section 75 notice" means a notice which is required to be served under section 75(2);
"statement" means the statement specifying additional grounds which the requisite person has or may have for wishing to enter or remain in the United Kingdom; and
"statement form" means the form shown in Part III of the Schedule to these Regulations.

(2)   Where reference is made in these Regulations to a form shown in the Schedule to these Regulations, that form, or a form to like effect, may be used with such variations as the circumstances may require.

(3)   In these Regulations, a section referred to by number alone is a reference to a section of the Act.

NOTES

Initial Commencement
Specified date
Specified date: 2 October 2000: see reg 1.

One-stop procedure

3 The notice

(1)   A section 74 notice is to be in the form shown in Part I of the Schedule to these Regulations.

(2)   A section 75 notice is to be in the form shown in Part II of the Schedule to these Regulations.

(3)   The notice is to—

(a)   provide a postal address to which the statement may be returned by post;
(b)   provide an address to which the statement may be returned by hand;
(c)   provide a fax number which may be used to return the statement by fax; and
(d)   be accompanied by a copy of the statement form.

(4)   The notice may be served—

(a)   by hand;
(b)   by fax; or
(c)   by sending it by postal service in which delivery or receipt is recorded to—
(i)   the last known or usual place of abode of the requisite person or his representative; or
(ii)   an address provided by him or his representative for correspondence.

(5)   The notice may be served on the requisite person by serving it on his representative.

(6)   If the notice is served by post, addressed to the requisite person, it is to be taken to have been received by the requisite person on the second day after the day on which it was posted, unless the contrary is proved.

NOTES

Initial Commencement
Specified date
Specified date: 2 October 2000: see reg 1.

4 The statement

(1)   The statement is to be made by completing in full, and in English, a statement form.

(2)   The statement form must be signed by the requisite person or his representative.

(3)   For the purposes of section 74(6)(b) (the period before the end of which a statement must be served in response to a section 74 notice)—

(a)   the period of ten days is prescribed, where the applicant is entitled to appeal under the Act;
(b)   the period of five days is prescribed, where the applicant is entitled to appeal under the 1997 Act.

(4)   For the purposes of section 75(3)(b) (the period before the end of which the statement must be served in response to a section 75 notice), the period of ten days is prescribed.

(5)   For the purposes of paragraphs (3) and (4)—

(a)   the prescribed period is to be calculated from the expiry of the day on which the notice was received by the requisite person or his representative; and

(b)   where the prescribed period—

(i)   expires on an excluded day, the statement is to be taken to have been served as required if served on the next day that is not an excluded day;

(ii)   includes an excluded day, that day is to be discounted.

(6)   The statement may be served—

(a)   by hand;
(b)   by post; or
(c)   by fax;

using the address or fax number specified in the notice.

(7)   The statement is to be taken to have been served as required on the day on which it is received at the address or fax number specified in the notice.

(8)   Unless paragraph (9) applies, where the requisite person is in custody, the statement may also be served by giving it to the person who has custody of the requisite person.

(9)   This paragraph applies where a section 74 notice has been served and the requisite person is entitled to appeal under the 1997 Act.

(10)   "Bank holiday" means a day that is specified in, or appointed under, the Banking and Financial Dealings Act 1971.

(11)   "Excluded day" means a Saturday, a Sunday, a bank holiday, Christmas Day, 27th to 31st December or Good Friday.

NOTES

Initial Commencement
Specified date
Specified date: 2 October 2000: see reg 1.

Applications of sections 73, 76 and 77 to section 75 notices

5 Application of sections 73, 76 and 77 to section 75 notices

(1)   Subject to paragraph (2), this regulation applies if a claim is determined against a person on whom a section 75 notice has been served and that person appeals against the determination.

(2)   With the exception of the modification to section 77(5), this regulation does not apply if the claim is determined before the expiry of the period prescribed in regulation 4(4).

(3)   Section 73 applies to the appeal subject to the following modification.

(4)   In subsections (2)(a)(i) and (4) of section 73, the references to "section 74" are to be read as references to "section 75".

(5)   Section 76 applies to the appeal subject to the following modifications—

(a)   in subsection (1)—

(i)   the reference to "section 74(4)" is to be read as a reference to "section 75(2)"; and

(ii)   the reference to "the Secretary of State" is to be read as a reference to "the person who is responsible for the determination of the claim";

(b) in subsection (5)—
  (i) the reference to "section 74(6)(b)" is to be read as a reference to "section 75(3)(b)"; and
  (ii) the reference to "the Secretary of State" is to be read as a reference to "the Secretary of State or an immigration officer".

(6) Section 77 applies to the appeal subject to the following modifications—

  (a) in subsection (2)(b), the reference to "any provision of section 76" is to be read as a reference to "any provision of section 76 as applied and modified by regulations made under section 75(6)";
  (b) in subsection (5)—
    (i) the reference to "the Secretary of State" is to be read as a reference to "the person who is responsible for the determination of the claim"; and
    (ii) the reference to "section 74(4)" is to be read as a reference to "section 75(2)".

NOTES

Initial Commencement
Specified date
Specified date: 2 October 2000: see reg 1.

Family member definitions

6 Relevant member of the applicant's family: section 74

For the purposes of section 74(8), a relevant member of an applicant's family is a person—

  (a) who is the subject of a decision mentioned in subsection (1)(a), (2)(a) or 3(a) of section 74, but is not himself an applicant for the purposes of section 74(4); and
  (b) who appears to the decision-taker to be—
    (i) his spouse;
    (ii) a child of his or of his spouse;
    (iii) a person who has been living with him as a member of an unmarried couple for at least two of the three years before the day on which the decision was made;
    (iv) a person who is dependent on him; or
    (v) a person on whom he is dependent.

NOTES

Initial Commencement
Specified date
Specified date: 2 October 2000: see reg 1.

7 Relevant member of the claimant's family: section 75

For the purposes of section 75(5), a relevant member of a claimant's family is a person—

  (a) who has made an application for leave to enter or remain in the United Kingdom, but is not himself a claimant for the purposes of section 75(2); and
  (b) who appears to the decision-taker to be—
    (i) his spouse;
    (ii) a child of his or of his spouse;

    (iii) a person who has been living with him as a member of an unmarried couple for at least two of the three years before the day on which the claim was made;

    (iv) a person who is dependent on him; or

    (v) a person on whom he is dependent.

NOTES

Initial Commencement
Specified date
Specified date: 2 October 2000: see reg 1.

8 Member of the family: section 76

(1)   For the purposes of section 76(6), "member of the family" means—

    (a) a person on whom the applicant is dependent; or

    (b) a person who, in relation to the applicant—

        (i)   is his spouse;

        (ii) is a child of his or of his spouse;

        (iii) has been living with him as a member of an unmarried couple for at least two of the three years before the day on which the applicant claimed asylum; or

        (iv) is dependent on him.

NOTES

Initial Commencement
Specified date
Specified date: 2 October 2000: see reg 1.

Steve Bassam
Parliamentary Under-Secretary of State
Home Office
16th August 2000

SCHEDULE

Part I

Regulation 3(1)

ONE-STOP NOTICE

Section 74, Immigration and Asylum Act 1999
  To:
  You have been given a notice of decision; you have, or a member of your family has, a right to appeal that decision to an adjudicator. Under section 74 of the Immigration and Asylum Act 1999 I must also give you this one-stop notice. It requires you to state any additional grounds which you have or may have for wishing to enter or remain in the United Kingdom.

<u>If you have not yet taken advice on your position, I strongly advise you to do so now.</u>

The STATEMENT OF ADDITIONAL GROUNDS should be completed and returned to arrive within 10 working days of receipt by you or your representative *

*If your right of appeal is to the Special Immigration Appeals Commission the period is only **5 working days.**

Additional grounds

The **notice of decision** takes into account the reasons you gave for wishing to enter or remain in the United Kingdom. *You are now required to state any reasons you think you have or may have for staying in the United Kingdom which you have not previously disclosed: these will be your "additional grounds".* The decision will be reviewed in the light of what you say. It is in your own interest to now disclose all your grounds for staying in the United Kingdom. But you should not make false claims: do not, for example, apply for asylum unless you have genuine reasons for believing that you qualify in the terms of the 1951 Convention.

Section 74(7) of the Immigration and Asylum Act 1999 says that, if you wish to claim asylum, you must do so in your statement. And if you wish to claim that in taking a decision your human rights have been breached, you must give notice of your claim in your statement.

Your statement

You must use the form **STATEMENT OF ADDITIONAL GROUNDS** which accompanies this notice.

The form must be:

— completed in English
— completed in full
— signed by yourself or your representative if you have one
— returned as instructed below so as to arrive within 10 working days of when you or your representative received it. Saturdays, Sundays, bank and public holidays are not included when counting the 10 days.*

*If your right of appeal is to the Special Immigration Appeals Commission the period is only **5 working days.**

Consequences of failure to disclose additional grounds

The purpose of this procedure is to make sure that there is no unnecessary delay in dealing with your case. Where you have a right of appeal already, it is important that the adjudicator should be able to deal with all the aspects of your case which he is entitled to consider on one single occasion. If you believe you qualify to stay in the United Kingdom, then it is clearly of benefit to you to have a final and comprehensive decision as quickly as possible.

If you raise additional grounds after the period allowed, you may lose the chance to have any decision on them reviewed by an independent adjudicator. It may be concluded that they were put forward late to delay your removal from the United Kingdom or the removal of a member of your family. Even if you still have an opportunity to appeal, the appeal may be limited and the fact that you had not disclosed your grounds when required to do so would not be in your favour.

There are safeguards for exceptional circumstances: for example if you only become aware of a reason for staying in the United Kingdom when it is too late or if you can give a reasonable excuse for not mentioning additional grounds when asked to do so.

The consequences of raising additional grounds late may be serious: you should always disclose your reasons for wishing to stay here and any change of circumstances without delay.

Your right to appeal the decision

If you do not now have a right of appeal this paragraph does not apply to you. The **notice of decision** tells you if you can appeal the decision. If you do have a right of appeal, a **notice of appeal** form will be attached to the **statement of additional grounds**.

1509

— If you do not agree with the reasons given for my decision in the **notice of decision,** then you should explain why in your **notice of appeal.** What you say there is your **"grounds of appeal".** The **statement of additional grounds** is for matters unrelated to those which have already been considered.

— If you make a valid **appeal** and if the **decision** is maintained in the light of your **additional grounds,** those grounds will form part of your appeal so long as they could have done so if you had disclosed them earlier. In that case you will be told why your additional grounds were not acceptable and given the chance to add to your **grounds of appeal** before your papers are sent to the adjudicator. Please do not separate the **statement of additional grounds** form and the **notice of appeal** form. There is also a copy of the **notice of decision** attached to the appeal form: this is for the use of the adjudicator if you appeal, and appeal procedures require you to return it with the appeal form. If you make a photocopy of these papers, or send them by fax, please ensure that all the pages are kept together and in the correct order.

— You may, if you wish, put forward additional grounds without making an appeal. Likewise you should not put forward additional ground with your appeal if you genuinely have none to suggest. But in either case, please return both forms together. If you submit neither an appeal nor additional grounds then you should comply with any instructions to leave the United Kingdom which you have been given.

Service of statement of additional grounds

The statement may be returned by post to the following address:

[to be inserted by signatory]
The statement may be returned by hand to the following address:
[to be inserted by signatory]
The statement may be sent by fax to the following fax number:
[to be inserted by signatory]
   If you are **detained** the statement may be served by giving it to the person who has custody of you.*

*This does not apply if your right of appeal is to the Special Immigration Appeals Commission. The statement should be returned by fax or post.

   Please remember:
— keep any evidence of posting or receipt which you are given
— use a reliable postal service which offers speedy delivery if you can
— if you have been given a **notice of appeal** make sure it is attached to your **statement of additional grounds**
— keep this notice with your copy of the notice of refusal

Family applications

If you have received this notice in a package of notices and forms relating to yourself and other members of your family, please return all the statements and appeals forms together if possible. An envelope was enclosed with the package.

[Signature]

[Immigration Officer/On behalf of the Secretary of State]

[Date]

If you have not seen, or need a further copy of the guidance on how to obtain help ("Getting Advice on Immigration Matters") your nearest Citizen's Advice Bureau can assist. The leaflet is also available at the Immigration and Nationality Directorate's website:

http://www.homeoffice.gov.uk/ind/hpg.htm.

NOTES

Initial Commencement
Specified date
Specified date: 2 October 2000: see reg 1.

PART II

Regulation 3(2)

ONE-STOP NOTICE

Section 75, Immigration and Asylum Act 1999
To:
You have made a claim for asylum, or a claim that it would be in breach of your human rights for you to be removed from, or required to leave, the United Kingdom.
You are also one of the following:

— an illegal entrant, **or**
— a person who is liable to be removed as an overstayer under section 10 of the Immigration and Asylum Act 1999, **or**
— a person who has arrived in the United Kingdom without leave to enter, an entry clearance, or a current work permit in which you are named.

Alternatively you have applied for leave to enter or remain in the United Kingdom as the spouse or dependant of such a person, or because such a person is dependent on you.
Under section 75 of the Immigration and Asylum Act 1999 I must give you this **one-stop notice**. It requires you to state any **additional** grounds which you have or may have for wishing to enter or remain in the United Kingdom.

If you have not yet taken advice on your position, I strongly advise you to do so now.

The STATEMENT OF ADDITIONAL GROUNDS should be completed and returned to arrive within 10 working days of receipt by you or your representative.

Additional grounds

You are now required to state any reasons you think you have or may have for staying in the United Kingdom which you have not previously disclosed when making your application: these will be your "additional grounds". They will be considered together with the application which you have already made.
If you are claiming asylum personally you should now put forward any human rights arguments you may have. If you have made a claim based on your own human rights, you should now put forward any reasons you have for thinking that you qualify for asylum. If your overall claim is refused, you will have the opportunity to appeal that decision to an adjudicator. Your appeal would address both issues at once. You should also mention any other reasons you have for wishing to stay here, but you may not be entitled to raise them at an appeal.
If you are not the person who has made an asylum or human rights claim and their application is refused, your application will also be refused. If you have any reason to think that you have grounds to make an asylum or human rights claim in your own individual right, you should give them now. If your claim is refused, you will have the chance to appeal to an independent adjudicator. You should also mention any other reasons you have for wishing to stay here, but you may not be entitled to raise them at an appeal.

Your statement

You must use the form **STATEMENT OF ADDITIONAL GROUNDS** which accompanies this notice.

The form must be:
— completed in English
— completed in full
— signed by yourself or your representative if you have one
— returned as instructed below so as to arrive within 10 working days of when you or your representative received it. Saturdays, Sundays, bank and public holidays are not included when counting the 10 days.

Consequences of failure to disclose additional grounds

The purpose of this procedure is to make sure that there is no unnecessary delay in dealing with your case. Where you have a right of appeal, it is important that the adjudicator should be able to deal with all the aspects of your case which he is entitled to consider on one single occasion. If you believe you qualify to stay in the United Kingdom, then it is clearly of benefit to you to have a final and comprehensive decision as quickly as possible.

If you raise additional grounds after the period allowed, you may lose the chance to have any decision on them reviewed by an independent adjudicator. It may be concluded that they were put forward late to delay your removal from the United Kingdom or the removal of a member of your family. Even if you still have an opportunity to appeal, the appeal may be limited and the fact that you had not disclosed your grounds when required to do so would not be in your favour.

There are safeguards for exceptional circumstances: for example if you only become aware of a reason for staying in the United Kingdom when it is too late or you can give a reasonable excuse for not mentioning additional grounds when asked to do so.

The consequences of raising additional grounds late may be serious: you should always disclose your reasons for wishing to stay here and any change of circumstances without delay.

Service of statement of additional grounds

The statement may be returned by post to the following address:

[to be inserted by signatory]
The statement may be returned by hand to the following address:
[to be inserted by signatory]
The statement may be sent by fax to the following fax number:
[to be inserted by signatory]
If you are detained the statement may be served by giving it to the person who has custody of you.
Please remember:
— keep any evidence of posting or receipt which you are given
— use a reliable postal service which offers speedy delivery if you can
— keep this notice

Family applications

If you have received this notice in a package of notices and forms relating to yourself and other members of your family, please return all the statements and appeals forms together if possible. An envelope was enclosed with the package.

[Signature]

[Immigration Officer/On behalf of the Secretary of State]

[Date]

If you have not seen, or need a further copy of the guidance on how to obtain help ("Getting Advice on Immigration Matters") your nearest Citizen's Advice Bureau can assist. The leaflet is also available at the Immigration and Nationality Directorate's website:

http://www.homeoffice.gov.uk/ind/hpg.htm.

NOTES

Initial Commencement
Specified date
Specified date: 2 October 2000: see reg 1.

PART III

Regulation 2(1)

STATEMENT OF ADDITIONAL GROUNDS

Section 74 or 75, Immigration and Asylum Act 1999

You should fully complete this form in English and return it as explained in the **ONE-STOP NOTICE.**

[If the following details have already been printed on the form for you, please amend them if they are wrong]

Your reference number:
(as given in the **notice of decision**)

Your family name:

Your other names:

Your date of birth:

Your nationality:

— Please state clearly any reasons which you have or may have for wishing to enter or remain in the United Kingdom and which you have not previously disclosed.
— Continue on the reverse of this page or a separate sheet of paper if necessary.
— Attach any documentary evidence you have which supports your grounds. If you need more time to obtain evidence, please say what it is, and how long it is likely to take.

You **or** your representative if you have one must now make a declaration. If you are not capable of making the declaration, for example if you are too young, someone may make it on your behalf, using the box marked "APPLICANT".

APPLICANT

I declare that the information I have given is **true** and **complete** to the best of my knowledge and belief.

Signature: Date:

If signed on behalf of the applicant please give your full name, relationship to the applicant and address if it is different.

Applicant's address for correspondence if this has changed:

REPRESENTATIVE

I declare that the information I have given is **true** and **complete** to the best of my knowledge and belief; and that the contents of this statement have been explained to and agreed by the applicant.

Signature: Date:

Organisation:

Please give your full name, address and telephone number if you have not previously notified us that you are acting in this case:

NOTES

Initial Commencement
Specified date
Specified date: 2 October 2000: see reg 1.

ASYLUM (DESIGNATED SAFE THIRD COUNTRIES) ORDER 2000

2000 No 2245

Made - - - 16th August 2000

Laid before Parliament - - - 24th August 2000

Coming into force - - - 2nd October 2000

The Secretary of State, in exercise of the powers conferred upon him by section 12(1)(b) of the Immigration and Asylum Act 1999, hereby makes the following Order:

1   This Order may be cited as the Asylum (Designated Safe Third Countries) Order 2000 and shall come into force on 2nd October 2000.

NOTES

Initial Commencement
Specified date
Specified date: 2 October 2000: see above.

2   The Asylum (Designated Countries of Destination and Designated Safe Third Countries) Order 1996 is hereby revoked.

NOTES

Initial Commencement
Specified date
Specified date: 2 October 2000: see art 1.

3   The following countries are designated for the purposes of section 12(1)(b) of the Immigration and Asylum Act 1999 (designation of countries other than EU Member States for the purposes of appeal rights):—

Canada
Norway
Switzerland
United States of America.

NOTES

Initial Commencement
Specified date
Specified date: 2 October 2000: see art 1.

Steve Bassam
Parliamentary Under-Secretary of State
Home Office
16th August 2000

IMMIGRATION AND ASYLUM APPEALS (NOTICES) REGULATIONS 2000

2000 No 2246

Made - - - 16th August 2000

Laid before Parliament - - - 24th August 2000

Coming into force - - - 2nd October 2000

The Secretary of State, in exercise of the powers conferred upon him by section 166(3) of the Immigration and Asylum Act 1999, and by paragraph 1 of Schedule 4 to that Act, hereby makes the following Regulations:

1 Citation and commencement

(1) These Regulations may be cited as the Immigration and Asylum Appeals (Notices) Regulations 2000 and shall come into force on 2nd October 2000.

(2) The Immigration Appeals (Notices) Regulations 1984 are hereby revoked.

NOTES

Initial Commencement
Specified date
Specified date: 2 October 2000: see para (1) above.

2 Interpretation

In these Regulations—

"the 1971 Act" means the Immigration Act 1971;
"the 1997 Act" means the Special Immigration Appeals Commission Act 1997;
"the 1999 Act" means the Immigration and Asylum Act 1999;
"appeal" means an appeal under—
(a) Part IV of the 1999 Act (including any regulations made under section 80 of the 1999 Act, whether or not such regulations are also made under section 2(2) of the European Communities Act 1972);
(b) the 1997 Act;
and "appealable" is to be construed accordingly, unless the context otherwise requires;
"decision-maker" means—
(a) the Secretary of State;
(b) an immigration officer;

(c)   an entry clearance officer;

"entry clearance officer" means a person responsible for the grant or refusal of entry clearance;

"representative" means a person who appears to the decision-maker—

(a)   to be the representative of a requisite person; and

(b)   not to be prohibited from acting as a representative by section 84 of the 1999 Act;

"requisite person" has the meaning given to it by regulation 4(1).

NOTES

Initial Commencement
Specified date
Specified date: 2 October 2000: see reg 1(1).

3 Transitional provision

These Regulations apply to a decision to make a deportation order which, by virtue of paragraph 12 of Schedule 15 to the 1999 Act,—

(a)   is appealable under section 15 of the 1971 Act (appeals in respect of deportation orders);

(b)   would be appealable under section 15 of the 1971 Act, but for section 15(3) (deportation conducive to public good), and is appealable under section 2(1)(c) of the 1997 Act (appeal to Special Immigration Appeals Commission against a decision to make a deportation order).

NOTES

Initial Commencement
Specified date
Specified date: 2 October 2000: see reg 1(1).

4 Notice of appealable decisions and actions

(1)   Subject to the provisions of this regulation and to regulation 6, the decision-maker must give written notice to a person (the "requisite person") of any decision or action taken in respect of him which is appealable.

(2)   If the notice is given to the representative of the requisite person, it is to be taken to have been given to the requisite person.

(3)   Where the notice is given as required by paragraph (1) of a decision to refuse leave to a person to enter the United Kingdom, it is not necessary in addition for notice to be given of the decision that he requires leave unless he claims or has claimed that leave is not required.

(4)   No notice of decision is required to be given under paragraph (1) by reason only of the fact that the decision could be appealed under section 65 of the 1999 Act or section 2A of the 1997 Act if the person in question were to make an allegation that an authority had acted in breach of his human rights [or racially discriminated against him] in taking it; but such notice must be given upon such allegation being made.

(5)   In paragraph (4), "authority" has the meaning given to it by section 65(7) of the 1999 Act.

NOTES

Initial Commencement
Specified date
Specified date: 2 October 2000: see reg 1(1).
Words in square brackets added by the Immigration (European Economic Area) (Amendment) Regulations 2001, SI 2001/868.

5 Contents of notice

(1) A notice given under regulation 4 is to—

    (a) include a statement of the reasons for the decision or action to which it relates; and

    (b) if it relates to the giving of directions for the removal of the person from the United Kingdom, include a statement of the country to which he is to be removed.

(2) The notice is also to include, or to be accompanied by, a statement informing the requisite person of—

    (a) his right of appeal and the statutory provision on which his right of appeal is based;

    (b) the manner in which the appeal is to be brought;

    (c) a postal address to which a notice of appeal may be returned by post;

    (d) an address to which a notice of appeal may be returned by hand;

    (e) a fax number which may be used to return a notice of appeal by fax;

    (f) the time within which an appeal is to be brought; and

    (g) the facilities available for advice and assistance in connection with the appeal.

NOTES

Initial Commencement
Specified date
Specified date: 2 October 2000: see reg 1(1).

6 Certain notices under the 1971 Act deemed to comply with Regulations

(1) This regulation applies where the power to—

    (a) refuse leave to enter; or

    (b) vary leave to enter or remain in the United Kingdom;

is exercised by notice in writing under section 4 of, or paragraph 6(2) of Schedule 2 to, the 1971 Act (notice of decisions as to leave to enter or remain).

(2) If—

    (a) the statements required by regulation 5 are included in or accompany that notice; and

    (b) the notice is given in accordance with the provisions of regulation 7;

the notice is to be taken to have been given under regulation 4(1) for the purposes of these Regulations, and for the purposes of paragraph 2 of Schedule 4 to the 1999 Act.

NOTES

Initial Commencement
Specified date
Specified date: 2 October 2000: see reg 1(1).

7 Service of notice

A notice required to be given by regulation 4 may be—

    (a) given by hand;

    (b) sent by fax;

    (c) sent by postal service in which delivery or receipt is recorded to—

        (i) the last known or usual place of abode of the requisite person or his representative; or

        (ii) an address provided by him or his representative for correspondence.

NOTES

Initial Commencement
Specified date
Specified date: 2 October 2000: see reg 1(1).

[8

Where a notice required to be given by regulation 4 is sent by postal service under regulation 7(1) to a place outside the UK, it shall, unless the contrary is proved, be deemed to have been received on the 28th day after the day on which it was posted.]

NOTES

Regulation 8 added by SI 2001/868.

Steve Bassam
Parliamentary Under-Secretary of State
Home Office
16th August 2000

IMMIGRATION (EUROPEAN ECONOMIC AREA) REGULATIONS 2000

2000 No 2326

Made - - - 30th August 2000

Laid before Parliament - - - 1st September 2000

Coming into force - - - 2nd October 2000

The Secretary of State, being a Minister designated for the purposes of section 2(2) of the European Communities Act 1972 in relation to measures relating to rights of entry into, and residence in, the United Kingdom, in exercise of the powers conferred on him by the said section 2(2), and of the powers conferred on him by section 80 of the Immigration and Asylum Act 1999, hereby makes the following Regulations:

PART I
INTERPRETATION ETC

1 Citation, commencement and revocation

(1)   These Regulations may be cited as the Immigration (European Economic Area) Regulations 2000 and shall come into force on 2nd October 2000.

(2)   Subject to paragraph (3), the Immigration (European Economic Area) Order 1994 is hereby revoked.

(3)   Article 19 of the Order continues to have effect until the commencement of the repeal by the 1999 Act of the Immigration (Carriers' Liability) Act 1987.

NOTES

Initial Commencement
Specified date
Specified date: 2 October 2000: see para (1) above.

Interpretation of Regulations

2 General

(1) In these Regulations—

"the 1971 Act" means the Immigration Act 1971;

"the 1999 Act" means the Immigration and Asylum Act 1999;

"decision-maker" means the Secretary of State, an immigration officer or an entry clearance officer (as the case may be);

"EEA family permit" means a document issued to a person, in accordance with regulation 10 or 13, in connection with his admission to the United Kingdom;

"EEA national" means a national of an EEA State;

"EEA State" means a State, other than the United Kingdom, which is a Contracting Party to the Agreement on the European Economic Area signed at Oporto on 2nd May 1992 as adjusted by the Protocol signed at Brussels on 17th March 1993;

"economic activity" means activity as a worker or self-employed person, or as a provider or recipient of services;

"entry clearance officer" means a person responsible for the grant or refusal of entry clearances;

"military service" means service in the armed forces of an EEA State;

"Regulation 1251/70" means Commission Regulation (EEC) No 1251/70 on the right of workers to remain in the territory of a Member State after having been employed in that State;

"residence document" means a document issued to a person who is not an EEA national, in accordance with regulation 10 or 15, as proof of the holder's right of residence in the United Kingdom; .

"residence permit" means a permit issued to an EEA national, in accordance with regulation 10 or 15, as proof of the holder's right of residence in the United Kingdom;

"spouse" does not include a party to a marriage of convenience;

"United Kingdom national" means a person who falls to be treated as a national of the United Kingdom for the purposes of the Community Treaties;

"visa national" means a person who requires a visa for the United Kingdom because he is a national or citizen of one of the countries or territorial entities for the time being specified in the immigration rules.

(2) In these Regulations unless the context otherwise requires a reference to a regulation is a reference to a regulation of these Regulations; and within a regulation a reference to a paragraph is to a paragraph of that regulation.

NOTES

Initial Commencement
Specified date
Specified date: 2 October 2000: see reg 1(1).

3 "Worker", "self-employed person", "provider" and "recipient" of services, "self-sufficient person", "retired person" and "student"

(1) In these Regulations—

(a) "worker" means a worker within the meaning of Article 39 of the EC Treaty;

(b) "self-employed person" means a person who establishes himself in order to pursue activity as a self-employed person in accordance with Article 43 of the EC Treaty, or who seeks to do so;

(c) "provider of services" means a person who provides, or seeks to provide, services within the meaning of Article 50 of the EC Treaty;

(d) "recipient of services" means a person who receives, or seeks to receive, services within the meaning of Article 50 of the EC Treaty;

(e) "self-sufficient person" means a person who—
- (i) has sufficient resources to avoid his becoming a burden on the social assistance system of the United Kingdom; and
- (ii) is covered by sickness insurance in respect of all risks in the United Kingdom;

(f) "retired person" means a person who—
- (i) has pursued an activity as an employed or self-employed person;
- (ii) is in receipt of—
  - (aa) an invalidity or early retirement pension;
  - (bb) old age benefits;
  - (cc) survivor's benefits; or
  - (dd) a pension in respect of an industrial accident or disease;
      sufficient to avoid his becoming a burden on the social security system of the United Kingdom; and
- (iii) is covered by sickness insurance in respect of all risks in the United Kingdom;

(g) "student" means a person who—
- (i) is enrolled at a recognised educational establishment in the United Kingdom for the principal purpose of following a vocational training course;
- (ii) assures the Secretary of State by means of a declaration, or by such alternative means as he may choose that are at least equivalent, that he has sufficient resources to avoid him becoming a burden on the social assistance system of the United Kingdom; and
- (iii) is covered by sickness insurance in respect of all risks in the United Kingdom.

(2) For the purposes of paragraph (1)(e) and (f), resources or income are to be regarded as sufficient if they exceed the level in respect of which the recipient would qualify for social assistance.

NOTES

Initial Commencement
Specified date
Specified date: 2 October 2000: see reg 1(1).

4 "Self-employed person who has ceased activity"

(1) In these Regulations, "self-employed person who has ceased activity" means—

(a) a person who—
- (i) on the day on which he terminates his activity as a self-employed person has reached the age at which he is entitled to a state pension;
- (ii) has pursued such activity in the United Kingdom for at least the twelve months prior to its termination; and
- (iii) has resided continuously in the United Kingdom for more than three years;

(b) a person who—
- (i) has resided continuously in the United Kingdom for more than two years; and
- (ii) has terminated his activity [there] as a self-employed person as a result of a permanent incapacity to work;

(c) a person who—
- (i) has resided and pursued activity as a self-employed person in the United Kingdom;

    (ii)   has terminated that activity as a result of a permanent incapacity to work; and

    (iii) such incapacity is the result of an accident at work or an occupational illness which entitles him to a pension payable in whole or in part by the state;

(d)   a person who—

    (i)   has been continuously resident and continuously active as a self-employed person in the United Kingdom for three years; and

    (ii) is active as a self-employed person in the territory of an EEA State but resides in the United Kingdom and returns to his residence at least once a week.

(2)   But, if the person is the spouse of a United Kingdom national—

(a)   the conditions as to length of residence and activity in paragraph (1)(a) do not apply; and

(b)   the condition as to length of residence in paragraph (1)(b) does not apply.

(3)   For the purposes of paragraph [(1)(a), (b) and (c)] periods of activity completed in an EEA State by a person to whom paragraph (1)(d)(ii) applies are to be considered as having been completed in the United Kingdom.

(4)   For the purposes of paragraph (1)—

(a)   periods of absence from the United Kingdom which do not exceed three months in any year or periods of absence from the United Kingdom on military service are not to be taken into account; and

(b)   periods of inactivity caused by circumstances outside the control of the self-employed person and periods of inactivity caused by illness or accident are to be treated as periods of activity as a self-employed person.

NOTES

Initial Commencement
Specified date
Specified date: 2 October 2000: see reg 1(1).
Words in square brackets added by Immigration (European Economic Area) (Amendment) Regulations 2001, SI 2001/865.

5 "Qualified person"

(1)   In these Regulations, "qualified person" means a person who is an EEA national and in the United Kingdom as—

(a)   a worker;

(b)   a self-employed person;

(c)   a provider of services;

(d)   a recipient of services;

(e)   a self-sufficient person;

(f)   a retired person;

(g)   a student; or

(h)   a self-employed person who has ceased activity;

or who is a person to whom paragraph (4) applies.

(2)   A worker does not cease to be a qualified person solely because—

(a)   he is temporarily incapable of work as a result of illness or accident; or

(b)   he is involuntarily unemployed, if that fact is duly recorded by the relevant employment office.

(3)   A self-employed person does not cease to be a qualified person solely because he is temporarily incapable of work as a result of illness or accident.

(4)   This paragraph applies to—

    (a)   the family member of a qualified person referred to in paragraph (1)(h), if—
        (i)   the qualified person has died; and
        (ii)   the family member was residing with him in the United Kingdom immediately before his death;

    (b)   the family member of a qualified person referred to in paragraph 1(b) where—
        (i)   the qualified person has died;
        (ii)   the family member resided with him immediately before his death; and
        (iii)   either—
            (aa)   the qualified person had resided continuously in the United Kingdom for at least the two years immediately before his death; or
            (bb)   the death was the result of an accident at work or an occupational disease; or
            (cc)   his surviving spouse is a United Kingdom national.

(5)   For the purposes of paragraph (4)(b), periods of absence from the United Kingdom which do not exceed three months in any year or periods of absence from the United Kingdom on military service are not to be taken into account.

NOTES

Initial Commencement
Specified date
Specified date: 2 October 2000: see reg 1(1).

6 "Family member"

(1)   In these Regulations, paragraphs (2) to (4) apply in order to determine the persons who are family members of another person.

(2)   If the other person is a student, the persons are—

    (a)   his spouse; and
    (b)   his dependent children.

(3)   . . .

(4)   In any other case, the persons are—

    (a)   his spouse;
    (b)   descendants of his or of his spouse who are under 21 or are their dependants;
    (c)   dependent relatives in his ascending line or that of his spouse.

NOTES

Initial Commencement
Specified date
Specified date: 2 October 2000: see reg 1(1).
Paragraph 3 omitted by Immigration (European Economic Area) (Amendment) Regulations 2001, SI 2001/865.

Interpretation of other legislation

7 Carriers' liability

For the purposes of satisfying a requirement to produce a visa under section 40(1)(b) of the 1999 Act (charges to carriers in respect of passengers without proper documents), a "valid visa of the required kind" includes a family permit or residence document required for admission as a visa national under regulation 12.

NOTES

Initial Commencement
Specified date
Specified date: 2 October 2000: see reg 1(1).

8 Persons not subject to restriction on the period for which they may remain

(1)   For the purposes of the 1971 Act and the British Nationality Act 1981, the following are to be regarded as persons who are in the United Kingdom without being subject under the immigration laws to any restriction on the period for which they may remain—

(a)   a self-employed person who has ceased activity;

(b)   the family member of such a person who was residing with that person in the United Kingdom immediately before that person ceased his activity in the United Kingdom;

(c)   a family member to whom regulation 5(4) applies;

(d)   a person who has rights under Regulation 1251/70;

(e)   a person who has been granted permission to remain in the United Kingdom indefinitely.

(2)   However, a qualified person or family member who is not mentioned in paragraph (1) is not, by virtue of his status as a qualified person or the family member of a qualified person, to be so regarded for those purposes.

NOTES

Initial Commencement
Specified date
Specified date: 2 October 2000: see reg 1(1).

PART II
SCOPE OF REGULATIONS

9 General

Subject to regulations 10 and 11 (and to regulations 24(1), 25(1), 26(1) and 28) these Regulations apply solely to EEA nationals and their family members.

NOTES

Initial Commencement
Specified date
Specified date: 2 October 2000: see reg 1(1).

10 Dependants and members of the household of EEA nationals

(1)   If a person satisfies any of the conditions in paragraph (4), and if in all the circumstances it appears to the decision-maker appropriate to do so, the decision-maker may issue to that person an EEA family permit, a residence permit or a residence document (as the case may be).

(2)   Where a permit or document has been issued under paragraph (1), these Regulations apply to the holder of the permit or document as if he were the family member of an EEA national and the permit or document had been issued to him under regulation 13 or 15.

(3)   Without prejudice to regulation 22, a decision-maker may revoke (or refuse to renew) a permit or document issued under paragraph (1) if he decides that the holder no longer satisfies any of the conditions in paragraph (4).

(4)   The conditions are that the person [is a relative of an EEA national or his spouse and]—

    (a)   is dependent on the EEA national or his spouse;

    (b)   is living as part of the EEA national's household outside the United Kingdom; or

    (c)   was living as part of the EEA national's household before the EEA national came to the United Kingdom.

(5)   However, for those purposes "EEA national" does not include—

    (a)   an EEA national who is in the United Kingdom as a self-sufficient person, a retired person or a student;

    (b)   an EEA national who, when he is in the United Kingdom, will be a person referred to in sub-paragraph (a).

NOTES

Initial Commencement
Specified date
Specified date: 2 October 2000: see reg 1(1).
Words in square brackets inserted by Immigration (European Economic Area) (Amendment) Regulations 2001, SI 2001/865.

11 Family members of United Kingdom nationals

(1)   If the conditions in paragraph (2) are satisfied, these Regulations apply to a person who is the family member of a United Kingdom national returning to the United Kingdom as if that person were the family member of an EEA national.

(2)   The conditions are that—

    (a)   after leaving the United Kingdom, the United Kingdom national resided in an EEA State and—
        (i)   was employed there (other than on a transient or casual basis); or
        (ii) established himself there as a self-employed person;

    (b)   the United Kingdom national did not leave the United Kingdom in order to enable his family member to acquire rights under these Regulations and thereby to evade the application of United Kingdom immigration law;

    (c)   on his return to the United Kingdom, the United Kingdom national would, if he were an EEA national, be a qualified person; and

    (d)   if the family member of the United Kingdom national is his spouse, the marriage took place, and the parties lived together in an EEA State, before the United Kingdom national returned to the United Kingdom.

NOTES

Initial Commencement
Specified date
Specified date: 2 October 2000: see reg 1(1).

PART III
EEA RIGHTS

12 Right of admission to the United Kingdom

(1)   Subject to regulation 21(1), an EEA national must be admitted to the United Kingdom if he produces, on arrival, a valid national identity card or passport issued by an EEA State.

(2)   Subject to regulation 21(1) and (2), a family member of an EEA national who is not himself an EEA national must be admitted to the United Kingdom if he produces, on arrival—

   (a)   a valid national identity card issued by an EEA State, or a valid passport; and
   (b)   either—
      (i)   where the family member is a visa national or a person who seeks to be admitted to instal himself with a qualified person, a valid EEA family permit or residence document; or
      (ii)   in all other cases (but only where required by an immigration officer) a document proving that he is a family member of a qualified person.

NOTES

Initial Commencement
Specified date
Specified date: 2 October 2000: see reg 1(1).

13 Issue of EEA family permit

(1)   An entry clearance officer must issue an EEA family permit, free of charge, to a person who applies for one if he is a family member of—

   (a)   a qualified person; or
   (b)   a person who is not a qualified person, where that person—
      (i)   will be travelling to the United Kingdom with the person who has made the application within a year of the date of the application; and
      (ii)   will be a qualified person on arrival in the United Kingdom.

(2)   But paragraph (1) does not apply if—

   (a)   the applicant; or
   (b)   the person whose family member he is
falls to be excluded from the United Kingdom on grounds of public policy, public security or public health.

NOTES

Initial Commencement
Specified date
Specified date: 2 October 2000: see reg 1(1).

14 Right of residence

(1)   A qualified person is entitled to reside in the United Kingdom, without the requirement for leave to remain under the 1971 Act, for as long as he remains a qualified person.

(2)   A family member of a qualified person is entitled to reside in the United Kingdom, without the requirement for such leave, for as long as he remains the family member of a qualified person.

(3)   A qualified person and the family member of such a person may reside and pursue economic activity in the United Kingdom notwithstanding that his application for a residence permit or residence document (as the case may be) has not been determined by the Secretary of State.

(4)   However, this regulation is subject to regulation 21(3)(b).

NOTES

Initial Commencement
Specified date
Specified date: 2 October 2000: see reg 1(1).

PART IV
RESIDENCE PERMITS AND DOCUMENTS

15 Issue of residence permits and residence documents

(1)   Subject to regulations 16 and 22(1), the Secretary of State must issue a residence permit to a qualified person on application and production of—

(a)   a valid identity card or passport issued by an EEA State; and
(b)   the proof that he is a qualified person.

(2)   Subject to regulation 22(1), the Secretary of State must issue a residence permit to a family member of a qualified person (or, where the family member is not an EEA national, a residence document) on application and production of—

(a)   a valid identity card issued by an EEA State or a valid passport;
(b)   in the case of a family member who required an EEA family permit for admission to the United Kingdom, such a permit; and
(c)   in the case of a person not falling within sub-paragraph (b), proof that he is a family member of a qualified person.

(3)   In the case of a worker, confirmation of the worker's engagement from his employer or a certificate of employment is sufficient proof for the purposes of paragraph (1)(b).

NOTES

Initial Commencement
Specified date
Specified date: 2 October 2000: see reg 1(1).

16 Where no requirement to issue residence permit

(1)   The Secretary of State is not required to grant a residence permit to—

(a)   a worker whose employment in the United Kingdom is limited to three months and who holds a document from his employer certifying that his employment is so limited;
(b)   a worker who is employed in the United Kingdom but who resides in the territory of an EEA State and who returns to his residence at least once a week;
(c)   a seasonal worker whose contract of employment has been approved by the Department for Education and Employment; or
(d)   a provider or recipient of services if the services are to be provided for no more than three months.

(2)   The requirement in paragraph (1)(a) to hold a document does not apply to workers coming within the provisions of Council Directive 64/224/EEC of 25 February 1964 concerning the attainment of freedom of establishment and freedom to provide services in respect of activities of intermediaries in commerce, industry and small craft industries.

NOTES

Initial Commencement
Specified date
Specified date: 2 October 2000: see reg 1(1).

17 Form of residence permit and residence document

(1)   The residence permit issued to a worker or a worker's family member who is an EEA national must be in the following form:

> "Residence Permit for a National of an EEA State
>   This permit is issued pursuant to Regulation (EEC) No 1612/68 of the Council of the European Communities of 15 October 1968 and to the measures taken in implementation of the Council Directive of 15 October 1968.
>   In accordance with the provisions of the above-mentioned Regulation, the holder of this permit has the right to take up and pursue an activity as an employed person in the territory of the United Kingdom under the same conditions as United Kingdom national workers.".

(2)   A residence document issued to a family member who is not an EEA national may take the form of a stamp in that person's passport.

NOTES

Initial Commencement
Specified date
Specified date: 2 October 2000: see reg 1(1).

18 Duration of residence permit

(1)   Subject to the following paragraphs and to regulations 20 and 22(2), a residence permit must be valid for at least five years from the date of issue.

(2)   In the case of a worker who is to be employed in the United Kingdom for less than twelve but more than three months, the validity of the residence permit may be limited to the duration of the employment.

(3)   In the case of a seasonal worker who is to be employed for more than three months, the validity of the residence permit may be limited to the duration of the employment if the duration is indicated in the document confirming the worker's engagement or in a certificate of employment.

(4)   In the case of a provider or recipient of services, the validity of the residence permit may be limited to the period during which the services are to be provided.

(5)   In the case of a student, the residence permit is to be valid for a period which does not exceed the duration of the course of study; but where the course lasts for more than one year the validity of the residence permit may be limited to one year.

(6)   In the case of a retired person or a self-sufficient person, the Secretary of State may, if he deems it necessary, require the revalidation of the residence permit at the end of the first two years of residence.

(7)   The validity of a residence permit is not to be affected by absence from the United Kingdom for periods of no more than six consecutive months or absence from the United Kingdom on military service.

NOTES

Initial Commencement
Specified date
Specified date: 2 October 2000: see reg 1(1).

19 Renewal of residence permit

(1)   Subject to paragraphs (2) and (3) and to regulations 20 and 22(2), a residence permit must be renewed on application.

(2)   On the occasion of the first renewal of a worker's residence permit the validity may be limited to one year if the worker has been involuntarily unemployed in the United Kingdom for more than one year.

(3)   In the case of a student whose first residence permit is limited to one year by virtue of regulation 18(5), renewal may be for periods limited to one year.

NOTES

Initial Commencement
Specified date
Specified date: 2 October 2000: see reg 1(1).

20 Duration and renewal of residence permit or residence document granted to a family member

The family member of an EEA national is entitled to a residence permit or residence document of the same duration as the residence permit granted to the qualified person of whose family he is a member; and the family member's residence permit or residence document is subject to the same terms as to renewal.

NOTES

Initial Commencement
Specified date
Specified date: 2 October 2000: see reg 1(1).

PART V
WITHDRAWAL OF EEA RIGHTS

21 Exclusion and removal from the United Kingdom

(1)   A person is not entitled to be admitted to the United Kingdom by virtue of regulation 12 if his exclusion is justified on grounds of public policy, public security or public health.

(2)   A person is not entitled to be admitted to the United Kingdom by virtue of regulation 12(2) if, at the time of his arrival, he is not the family member of a qualified person.

(3)   A person may be removed from the United Kingdom—

    (a)   if he is not, or has ceased to be—
        (i)   a qualified person; or
        (ii)   the family member of a qualified person;
    (b)   if he is a qualified person or the family member of such a person, but the Secretary of State has decided that his removal is justified on the grounds of public policy, public security or public health.

NOTES

Initial Commencement
Specified date
Specified date: 2 October 2000: see reg 1(1).

22 Refusal to issue or renew residence permit or residence document, and revocation of residence permit, residence document or EEA family permit

(1)   The Secretary of State may refuse to issue a residence permit or residence document (as the case may be) if the refusal is justified on grounds of public policy, public security or public health.

(2)   The Secretary of State may revoke, or refuse to renew, a residence permit or residence document if—

(a)   the revocation or refusal is justified on grounds of public policy, public security or public health; or

(b)   the person to whom the residence permit or residence document was issued—

(i)   is not, or has ceased to be, a qualified person;

(ii)   is not, or has ceased to be, the family member of a qualified person.

(3)   An immigration officer may, at the time of the arrival in the United Kingdom of a person who is not an EEA national, revoke that person's residence document if he is not at that time the family member of a qualified person.

(4)   An immigration officer may, at the time of a person's arrival in the United Kingdom, revoke that person's EEA family permit if—

(a)   the revocation is justified on grounds of public policy, public security or public health; or

(b)   the person is not at that time the family member of a qualified person.

NOTES

Initial Commencement
Specified date
Specified date: 2 October 2000: see reg 1(1).

23 Public policy, public security and public health

Decisions taken on grounds of public policy, public security or public health ("the relevant grounds") must be taken in accordance with the following principles—

(a)   the relevant grounds must not be invoked to secure economic ends;

(b)   a decision taken on one or more of the relevant grounds must be based exclusively on the personal conduct of the individual in respect of whom the decision is taken;

(c)   a person's previous criminal convictions do not, in themselves, justify a decision on grounds of public policy or public security;

(d)   a decision to refuse admission to the United Kingdom, or to refuse to grant the first residence permit or residence document, to a person on the grounds that he has a disease or disability may be justified only if the disease or disability is of a type specified in Schedule 1 to these Regulations;

(e)   a disease or disability contracted after a person has been granted a first residence permit or first residence document does not justify a decision to refuse to renew the permit or document or a decision to remove him;

(f)   a person is to be informed of the grounds of public policy, public security or public health upon which the decision taken in his case is based unless it would be contrary to the interests of national security to do so.

NOTES

Initial Commencement
Specified date
Specified date: 2 October 2000: see reg 1(1).

PART VI
APPLICATION OF THE 1971 ACT AND THE 1999 ACT

24 Persons claiming right of admission

(1)   This regulation applies to a person who claims a right of admission to the United Kingdom under regulation 12 as—

(a) the family member of an EEA national, where he is not himself an EEA national; or

(b) an EEA national, where there is reason to believe that he may fall to be excluded from the United Kingdom on grounds of public policy, public security or public health.

(2)   A person to whom this regulation applies is to be treated as if he were a person seeking leave to enter the United Kingdom under the 1971 Act and paragraphs 2 to 4, 7, 16 to 18 and 21 to 24 of Schedule 2 to the 1971 Act (administrative provisions as to control on entry etc) apply accordingly, except that—

(a) the reference in paragraph 2(1) to the purpose for which the immigration officer may examine any persons who have arrived in the United Kingdom is to be read as a reference to the purpose of determining whether he is a person who is to be granted admission under these Regulations; and

(b) the references in paragraph 4(2A) and in paragraph 7 to a person who is, or may be, given leave to enter are to be read as references to a person who is, or may be, granted admission under these Regulations.

(3)   For so long as a person to whom this regulation applies is detained, or temporarily admitted or released while liable to detention, under the powers conferred by Schedule 2 to the 1971 Act, he is deemed not to have been admitted to the United Kingdom.

NOTES

Initial Commencement
Specified date
Specified date: 2 October 2000: see reg 1(1).

25 Persons refused admission

(1)   This regulation applies to a person who is in the United Kingdom and has been refused admission to the United Kingdom—

(a) because he does not meet the requirements of regulation 12 (including where he does not meet those requirements because his residence document or EEA family permit has been revoked by an immigration officer in accordance with regulation 22); or

(b) in accordance with regulation 21(1) or (2).

(2)   A person to whom this regulation applies is to be treated as if he were a person refused leave to enter under the 1971 Act, and the provisions set out in paragraph (3) apply accordingly.

(3)   Those provisions are—

(a) paragraphs 8, 10, 11, 16 to 18 and 21 to 24 of Schedule 2 to the 1971 Act;

(b) paragraph 19 of Schedule 2 to the 1971 Act, except that the reference in that paragraph to a certificate of entitlement, entry clearance or work permit is to be read as a reference to an EEA family permit or residence document; and

(c) sections 67 and 68 of the 1999 Act (appeal concerning objection to removal destination), except that the reference in section 68(1)(b) to a person who held a current entry clearance or was a person named in a current work permit is to be read as a reference to a person who held an EEA family permit or residence document.

NOTES

Initial Commencement
Specified date
Specified date: 2 October 2000: see reg 1(1).

26 Persons subject to removal

(1)   This regulation applies to a person whom it has been decided to remove from the United Kingdom in accordance with regulation 21(3).

(2)   Where the decision is under sub-paragraph (a) of regulation 21(3), the person is to be treated as if he were a person to whom section 10(1)(a) of the 1999 Act applied, and section 10 of that Act (removal of certain persons unlawfully in the United Kingdom) is to apply accordingly.

(3)   Where the decision is under sub-paragraph (b) of regulation 21(3), the person is to be treated as if he were a person to whom section 3(5)(a) of the 1971 Act (liability to deportation) applied, and section 5 of that Act (procedure for deportation) and Schedule 3 to that Act (supplementary provisions as to deportation) are to apply accordingly.

NOTES

Initial Commencement
Specified date
Specified date: 2 October 2000: see reg 1(1).

PART VII
APPEALS

27 Interpretation of Part VII

(1)   In this Part—

"the 1997 Act" means the Special Immigration Appeals Commission Act 1997;
"adjudicator" and "Commission" have the same meaning as in the 1999 Act;
"Refugee Convention" has the same meaning as in the 1999 Act.

(2)   In this Part, "EEA decision" means a decision under these Regulations, or under Regulation 1251/70, which concerns a person's—

(a)   removal from the United Kingdom;
(b)   entitlement to be admitted to the United Kingdom; or
(c)   entitlement to be issued with or to have renewed, or not to have revoked, a residence permit or residence document.

(3)   For the purposes of this Part, [(a) a decision-maker racially discriminates against a person if he acts, or fails to act, in relation to that other person in a way which is unlawful by virtue of s 19B of the RRA 1976 and (b)] a decision-maker acts in breach of a person's human rights if he acts, or fails to act, in relation to that other person in a way which is made unlawful by section 6(1) of the Human Rights Act 1998.

NOTES

Initial Commencement
Specified date
Specified date: 2 October 2000: see reg 1(1).
Words in square brackets inserted by Immigration (European Economic Area) (Amendment) Regulations 2001, SI 2001/865.

28 Scope of Part VII

This Part applies to persons who have, or who claim to have, rights under these Regulations or under Regulation 1251/70.

NOTES

Initial Commencement
Specified date
Specified date: 2 October 2000: see reg 1(1).

29 Appeal rights

(1) Subject to section 80(12) of the 1999 Act (requirement to produce a valid national identity card or passport), and to regulation 33, a person may appeal under these Regulations against an EEA decision.

(2) Such an appeal may in particular be made on the ground that, in taking the decision, the decision-maker acted in breach of that person's human rights or racially discriminated against that person .

(3) Except where an appeal lies to the Commission as a result of regulation 31, an appeal under these Regulations lies to an adjudicator.

(4) Schedule 4 to the 1999 Act (appeals), to the extent (and with the modifications) set out in Schedule 2 to these Regulations, has effect in relation to appeals to the adjudicator under these Regulations.

NOTES

Initial Commencement
Specified date
Specified date: 2 October 2000: see reg 1(1).

30 Out-of-country appeals

(1) Regulation 29 does not entitle a person to appeal while he is in the United Kingdom against an EEA decision—

  (a) to refuse to admit him to the United Kingdom;
  (b) to refuse to revoke a deportation order made against him;
  (c) to refuse to issue him with an EEA family permit.

(2) Paragraph (1) also applies to a decision to remove someone from the United Kingdom which is consequent upon a refusal to admit him.

(3) But paragraphs (1)(a) and (2) do not apply—

  (a) where the right of appeal is to the Commission;
  (b) where a ground of the appeal is that, in taking the decision, the decision-maker acted in breach of the appellant's human rights; or
  (c) where the person held an EEA family permit, or a residence permit or residence document, on his arrival in the United Kingdom.

NOTES

Initial Commencement
Specified date
Specified date: 2 October 2000: see reg 1(1).

31 Appeals to the Commission

(1) An appeal in respect of an EEA decision mentioned in regulation 27(2)(a) lies to the Commission where paragraph (2) applies.

(2) This paragraph applies if the ground of the decision to remove the person concerned was that his removal is conducive to the public good as being in the interests of national

security or of the relations between the United Kingdom and any other country or for other reasons of a political nature.

(3)   An appeal in respect of an EEA decision mentioned in regulation 27(2)(b) lies to the Commission where paragraph (4) applies.

(4)   This paragraph applies if—

   (a)   the Secretary of State certifies that directions have been given by the Secretary of State (and not by a person acting under his authority) for the person concerned not to be admitted to the United Kingdom on the ground that his exclusion is conducive to the public good; or
   (b)   admission was refused in compliance with any such directions.

(5)   An appeal in respect of an EEA decision mentioned in regulation 27(2)(c) lies to the Commission where paragraph (6) applies.

(6)   This paragraph applies where the decision was taken in connection with an EEA decision mentioned in regulation 27(2)(a) or (b) in respect of which an appeal lies to the Commission in accordance with this regulation.

NOTES

Initial Commencement
Specified date
Specified date: 2 October 2000: see reg 1(1).

32 Amendments to the 1997 Act

(1)   The 1997 Act is amended as follows.

(2)   In section 2 (appellate jurisdiction of the Commission), for subsection (1) substitute—

"(1) A person may appeal to the Special Immigration Appeals Commission against a decision which he would be entitled to appeal against under Part IV of the Immigration and Asylum Act 1999 ("the 1999 Act") but for a public interest provision.

(1A) Subsection (1) does not apply to an appeal under section 59(2) of the 1999 Act.

(1B) "Public interest provision" means any of sections 60(9), 62(4), 64(1) or (2) or 70(1) to (6) of the 1999 Act.

(1C) A reference in this Act to an appeal under this section includes a reference to an appeal under regulation 29(1) of the Immigration (European Economic Area) Regulations 2000 (other than on the ground mentioned in paragraph (2) of that regulation) which lies to the Commission as a result of regulation 31 of those Regulations.".

(3)   In section 2A (jurisdiction: human rights), after subsection (6) insert—

"(7) "Appealable decision" means a decision against which a person would be entitled to appeal under Part IV of the 1999 Act but for a public interest provision.

(8)   "The 1999 Act" and "public interest provision" have the same meaning as in section 2.

(9)   A reference in this Act to an appeal under this section includes a reference to an appeal under regulation 29(1) of the Immigration (European Economic Area) Regulations 2000, on the ground mentioned in paragraph (2) of that regulation, which lies to the Commission as a result of regulation 31 of those Regulations.".

(4)   Schedule 14 to the 1999 Act (consequential amendments) is amended as follows—

(a) paragraph 119 is repealed;

(b) paragraph 121 is repealed in so far as it relates to the insertion of subsections (7) and (8) of section 2A in the 1997 Act.

NOTES

Initial Commencement
Specified date
Specified date: 2 October 2000: see reg 1(1).

33 Proof of family membership

Where for the purposes of an appeal under these Regulations a person claims to be the family member of another person, he must produce—

(a) an EEA family permit; or

(b) other proof that he is related as claimed to that other person.

NOTES

Initial Commencement
Specified date
Specified date: 2 October 2000: see reg 1(1).

34 Effects of appeals to the adjudicator

(1) If a person in the United Kingdom appeals under regulation 29 against an EEA decision to refuse to admit him to the United Kingdom, any directions previously given by virtue of the refusal for his removal from the United Kingdom cease to have effect, except in so far as they have already been carried out, and no directions may be so given while the appeal is pending.

(2) If a person appeals under regulation 29 against an EEA decision to remove him from the United Kingdom, any directions given under section 10 of the 1999 Act or Schedule 3 of the 1971 Act for his removal from the United kingdom are to have no effect, except in so far as they have already been carried out, while the appeal is pending.

(3) But the provisions of Part I of Schedule 2, or as the case may be, Schedule 3 to the 1971 Act with respect to detention and persons liable to detention apply to a person appealing under regulation 29 against a refusal to admit him or a decision to remove him as if there were in force directions for his removal from the United Kingdom, except that he may not be detained on board a ship or aircraft so as to compel him to leave the United Kingdom while the appeal is pending.

(4) In calculating the period of two months limited by paragraph 8(2) of Schedule 2 to the 1971 Act for—

(a) the giving of directions under that paragraph for the removal of a person from the United Kingdom, and

(b) the giving of a notice of intention to give such directions,

any period during which there is pending an appeal by him under regulation 29 is to be disregarded.

(5) If a person appeals under regulation 29 against an EEA decision to remove him from the United Kingdom, a deportation order is not to be made against him under section 5 of the 1971 Act while the appeal is pending.

(6) Paragraph 29 of Schedule 2 to the 1971 Act (grant of bail pending appeal) applies to a person who has an appeal pending under regulation 29 as it applies to a person who has an appeal pending under section 59, 65, 66, 67, 69(1) or (5) or 71 of the 1999 Act.

(7)   For the purposes of this regulation, and subject to paragraphs (8) and (9), an appeal is to be treated as pending during the period beginning when notice of appeal is given and ending when the appeal is finally determined, withdrawn or abandoned.

(8)   An appeal is not to be treated as finally determined while a further appeal may be brought; and, if such a further appeal is brought, the original appeal is not to be treated as finally determined until the further appeal is determined, withdrawn or abandoned.

(9)   A pending appeal is not to be treated as abandoned solely because the appellant leaves the United Kingdom.

(10) This regulation does not apply to an appeal which lies to the Commission as a result of regulation 31.

NOTES

Initial Commencement
Specified date
Specified date: 2 October 2000: see reg 1(1).

35 Transitional provisions (EEA decisions)

(1)   Regulation 29 does not have effect in relation to an EEA decision made before 2nd October 2000.

(2)   Notwithstanding the revocation of the Immigration (European Economic Area) Order 1994 by regulation 1(2)—

    (a)   articles 15(1) and 20(2)(b) of the Order continue to have effect where the decision to exclude a person from the United Kingdom was made before 2nd October 2000;

    (b)   articles 15(2) and 20(2)(d) continue to have effect where the decision to remove a person from the United Kingdom was made before 2nd October 2000;

    (c)   articles 18 and 20(2)(c) continue to have effect where the decision to refuse or withdraw a residence permit or residence document was made before 2nd October 2000.

NOTES

Initial Commencement
Specified date
Specified date: 2 October 2000: see reg 1(1).

36 Transitional provisions (the 1997 Act)

(1)   Regulation 32 does not have effect in relation to any decision made before 2nd October 2000.

(2)   In relation to such decisions, section 2(1) of the 1997 Act continues to have effect without the amendments made by regulation 32.

(3)   Section 2(1)(c) of the 1997 Act (appeals against a decision to make a deportation order) continues to have effect without the amendments made by regulation 32 in relation to any person—

    (a)   who applied during the regularisation period fixed by section 9 of the 1999 Act, in accordance with the Immigration (Regularisation Period for Overstayers) Regulations 2000, for leave to remain in the United Kingdom; and

    (b)   on whom the Secretary of State has since served a notice of his decision to make a deportation order.

(4)   In the case of an appeal in respect of which section 2(1)(b) of the 1997 Act (appeals against variation of limited leave or refusal to vary it) continues to have effect in

accordance with paragraph (2), section 7A(7) of the 1997 Act (pending appeals) applies as if the reference to section 62(3) of the 1999 Act were a reference to section 14(3) of the 1971 Act.

(5)   In the case of an appeal in respect of which section 2(1) of the 1997 Act continues to have effect in accordance with paragraph (2) or (3), Schedule 2 of the 1997 Act (supplementary provisions as to appeals) has effect without the amendments made by the 1999 Act.

NOTES

Initial Commencement
Specified date
Specified date: 2 October 2000: see reg 1(1).

Mike O'Brien
Parliamentary Under-Secretary of State
Home Office
30th August 2000

SCHEDULE 1
Specified Diseases and Disabilities

Regulation 23(d)

1   The following diseases may justify a decision taken on grounds of public health—

   (a)   diseases subject to quarantine listed in International Health Regulation No 2 of the World Health Organisation of 25th May 1951;

   (b)   tuberculosis of the respiratory system in an active state or showing a tendency to develop;

   (c)   syphilis;

   (d)   other infectious diseases or contagious parasitic diseases, if they are the subject of provisions for the protection of public health in the United Kingdom.

2   The following diseases or disabilities may justify a decision taken on grounds of public policy or public security—

   (a)   drug addiction;

   (b)   profound mental disturbance; manifest conditions of psychotic disturbance with agitation, delirium, hallucinations or confusion.

NOTES

Initial Commencement
Specified date
Specified date: 2 October 2000: see reg 1(1).

SCHEDULE 2
Appeals to the Adjudicator

Regulation 29(4)

1   In this Schedule, unless the context otherwise requires, a reference to a paragraph is a reference to a paragraph of Schedule 4 to the 1999 Act.

2   Subject to paragraph 3 of this Schedule—

paragraphs 1 to 9[A];
paragraphs 21 to 23; and
paragraph 24(2)
have effect in relation to appeals to the adjudicator under these Regulations.

3 (1)   In paragraph 6(1)(a), for the words "certificate of entitlement, entry clearance or work permit" substitute "EEA family permit, residence document or residence permit".

(2)   For paragraph 7, substitute—

"7   If, under the rules, leave to appeal to the Tribunal is required in cases in which an adjudicator dismisses an appeal in respect of an EEA decision which concerns a person's entitlement to be admitted to the United Kingdom, the authority having power to grant leave must grant it if the authority is satisfied that, at the time of the decision, the appellant held an EEA family permit.".

(3)   Paragraph 9 has effect only to the extent that it relates to a claim under the Human Rights Convention.

(4)   In paragraph 24(2), for the words "entry clearance" substitute "EEA family permit", and after the words "deportation order" insert "made on grounds of public policy, public security or public health".

NOTES

Initial Commencement
Specified date
Specified date: 2 October 2000: see reg 1(1).
Words in square brackets inserted by Immigration (European Economic Area) (Amendment) Regulations 2001, SI 2001/865.

IMMIGRATION AND ASYLUM APPEALS (PROCEDURE) RULES 2000

2000 No 2333

Made - - - 24th August 2000

Laid before Parliament - - - 1st September 2000

Coming into force - - - 2nd October 2000

The Lord Chancellor, in exercise of the powers conferred by sections 58(2) and 166(3) of, and paragraphs 3 and 4 of Schedule 4 to, the Immigration and Asylum Act 1999 and section 22 of the Immigration Act 1971 so far as paragraph 25 of Schedule 2 to that Act relates to section 22, and of all other powers enabling him in that behalf, after consultation with the Council on Tribunals in accordance with section 8 of the Tribunals and Inquiries Act 1992, makes the following Rules—

PART I
INTRODUCTION

1 Citation, commencement and revocation

(1)   These Rules may be cited as the Immigration and Asylum Appeals (Procedure) Rules 2000 and shall come into force on 2nd October 2000.

(2)   Subject to rule 4, the following Rules—

(a)   the Immigration Appeals (Procedure) Rules 1984;
(b)   the Immigration Appeals (Procedure) (Amendment) Rules 1991;

(c)   the Immigration Appeals (Procedure) (Amendment) Rules 1993; and
(d)   the Asylum Appeals (Procedure) Rules 1996;
shall be revoked.

NOTES

Initial Commencement
Specified date
Specified date: 2 October 2000: see para (1) above.

2 Interpretation

(1)   In these Rules—

"the 1971 Act" means the Immigration Act 1971;
"the 1993 Act" means the Asylum and Immigration Appeals Act 1993;
"the 1996 Act" means the Asylum and Immigration Act 1996;
"the 1999 Act" means the Immigration and Asylum Act 1999;
"appellate authority" means the adjudicator or the Tribunal, as the case may be;
"appeal" means, subject to rule 4, any appeal under Part IV of the 1999 Act;
"appellant" has the meaning given in Parts II and III of these Rules and includes an applicant for bail;
"appropriate prescribed form" means the appropriate form in the Schedule to these Rules and those forms, or similar forms, may be used with any variations that the circumstances may require;
"authorised advocate"—
(a)   in relation to England and Wales, has the meaning given in section 119(1) of the Courts and Legal Services Act 1990;
(b)   in relation to Scotland, means a solicitor or advocate; and
(c)   in relation to Northern Ireland, means a solicitor or barrister;
"Chief Adjudicator" includes an adjudicator nominated by the Chief Adjudicator under paragraph 6(2)(a) of Schedule 3 to the 1999 Act;
"determination" means the decision of the appellate authority to allow or dismiss an appeal and the reasons for that decision;
"entry clearance officer" means a person having authority to grant an entry clearance on behalf of the Government of the United Kingdom;
"family visitor appeal" means an appeal made under section 59 by a person who is a family visitor as defined by regulations made under section 60;
"member" means a member of the Tribunal;
"officer" means an immigration officer or an entry clearance officer;
"party" has the meaning given in rule 29;
"President" means the President of the Tribunal;
"previous appeals provisions" means Part II of the 1971 Act, section 8 of the 1993 Act or section 3 of the 1996 Act;
"supplementary grounds of refusal" means the reasons given for maintaining the decision being appealed against after consideration of the additional grounds required under section 74(4); and
"Tribunal" means the Immigration Appeal Tribunal.

(2)   In these Rules, a section referred to by number alone is a reference to a section of the 1999 Act.

NOTES

Initial Commencement
Specified date
Specified date: 2 October 2000: see r 1(1).

3 Application of Rules

Subject to rule 4, these Rules shall apply to—

    (a)   appeals to an adjudicator;

    (b)   applications to the Tribunal for leave to appeal to the Tribunal and appeals to the Tribunal;

    (c)   applications for bail; and

    (d)   applications to the Tribunal for leave to appeal to the Court of Appeal or in Scotland, to the Court of Session.

NOTES

Initial Commencement
Specified date
Specified date: 2 October 2000: see r 1(1).

4 Transitional provisions

(1)   Subject to paragraphs (3) to (9), these Rules shall apply, with appropriate modifications, to any appeal made under the previous appeals provisions pending on 2nd October 2000 or made on or after that date.

(2)   Anything done or any direction given under the Immigration Appeals (Procedure) Rules 1984 ("the 1984 Rules") or the Asylum Appeals (Procedure) Rules 1996 ("the 1996 Rules") in relation to an appeal made under the previous appeals provisions pending on 2nd October 2000 or made on or after that date, shall be treated as if done or given under these Rules.

(3)   Where an appeal is made under Part II of the 1971 Act, the time limits for giving notice of appeal shall be those in rule 4 of the 1984 Rules and the reference to rule 6 in paragraphs (1)(b), (5) and (6) of rule 12 of these Rules shall be read as a reference to rule 4 of the 1984 Rules.

(4)   Where an appeal is made under section 8 of the 1993 Act or section 3 of the 1996 Act, the time limits for giving notice of appeal shall be those in rule 5 of the 1996 Rules and the reference to rule 6 in paragraphs (1)(b), (5) and (6) of rule 12 of these Rules shall be read as a reference to rule 5 of the 1996 Rules.

(5)   Where an appeal made under Part II of the 1971 Act has been determined by an adjudicator before 2nd October 2000, the time limits for making an application to the Tribunal for leave to appeal shall be those in paragraphs (2) to (4) of rule 15 of the 1984 Rules.

(6)   Where an appeal is made under section 8 of the 1993 Act, the reference in rule 11(3) of these Rules to section 69 of the 1999 Act shall be read as a reference to section 8 of the 1993 Act.

(7)   Where an appeal is made under the previous appeals provisions, the reference in rule 12(1)(a)(i) of these Rules to a provision of the 1999 Act shall be read as a reference to a provision of the 1971 Act, the 1993 Act or the 1996 Act specified by the respondent.

(8)   Where an appeal is made to the Tribunal at first instance under section 15(7) of the 1971 Act as provided by rule 3 of the 1984 Rules, Part II of these Rules shall apply as if the appeal had been made to an adjudicator at first instance.

(9)   Rule 41 of the 1984 Rules shall continue to apply to a reference made by the Secretary of State under section 21 of the 1971 Act.

(10) In rule 35(1)(a) of these Rules, before the coming into force of section 84, a person appealing against an immigration decision may be represented by—

(a) a solicitor, barrister, advocate or a person who is a Fellow of the Institute of Legal Executives;

(b) a person appointed by a voluntary organisation in receipt of a grant under section 23 of the 1971 Act or section 81 of the 1999 Act; or

(c) with the leave of the appellate authority, any other person.

NOTES

Initial Commencement
Specified date
Specified date: 2 October 2000: see r 1(1).

PART II
APPEALS TO ADJUDICATORS

5 Application of Part II

(1) This Part applies to appeals to an adjudicator.

(2) In this Part, "appellant" means a person appealing against an immigration decision.

NOTES

Initial Commencement
Specified date
Specified date: 2 October 2000: see r 1(1).

6 Time limit for giving notice of appeal

(1) Where an appellant makes an appeal within the United Kingdom, notice of appeal shall be given not later than 10 days after the notice of the decision was received.

(2) Where the appellant makes an appeal outside the United Kingdom, notice of appeal shall be given—

(a) in a case where the appellant is in the United Kingdom when the decision is made, not later than 28 days after his departure from the United Kingdom; or

(b) in a case where the appellant is not in the United Kingdom when the decision is made, not later than 28 days after the notice of the decision was received.

(3) In this rule, "decision" means the decision against which the appellant is appealing.

NOTES

Initial Commencement
Specified date
Specified date: 2 October 2000: see r 1(1).

7 Late notice of appeal

(1) Where any notice of appeal is not given within the appropriate time limit, it shall nevertheless be treated for all purposes as having been given within that time limit if the person to whom it was given is satisfied that, because of special circumstances, it is just for the notice to be treated in that way.

(2) An adjudicator shall not extend the time limit for giving notice of appeal unless he is satisfied that because of special circumstances, it is just for the notice to be treated in that way.

NOTES

Initial Commencement
Specified date
Specified date: 2 October 2000: see r 1(1).

8 Method of giving notice of appeal

(1)   Subject to paragraph (2), an appeal to an adjudicator shall be made by sending to the person, and at the address, specified in the notice of the decision which is the subject of the appeal, a notice of appeal in the appropriate prescribed form.

(2)   In any case where an appellant is in custody, service under paragraph (1) may be upon the person having custody of him.

(3)   The notice of appeal shall set out the grounds for the appeal.

(4)   Where the appeal is made under section 59, in relation to a family visitor appeal, the appellant shall specify in, or attach to, the notice of appeal all matters he wishes to be considered for the purposes of the appeal.

(5)   The notice of appeal shall state the name and address of the appellant and the name and address of his representative (if he has one).

(6)   The appellant or his representative (if he has one) shall sign the notice of appeal.

(7)   The appellant shall attach to the notice of appeal—

   (a)   a copy of any document which informed him of the decision against which he is appealing and any reasons for that decision; and
   (b)   where a notice has been served on the appellant under section 74(4), a statement form, on which additional grounds which he has or may have for wishing to enter or remain in the United Kingdom may be stated, whether or not that form has been completed.

NOTES

Initial Commencement
Specified date
Specified date: 2 October 2000: see r 1(1).

9 Additional grounds for appealing

Where the appellant is treated as appealing on additional grounds by virtue of section 77(2), he shall serve on the person, and at the address, specified in the supplementary grounds of refusal, any variation of his grounds of appeal not later than 5 days after he received the supplementary grounds of refusal.

NOTES

Initial Commencement
Specified date
Specified date: 2 October 2000: see r 1(1).

10 Despatch of documents to adjudicator

(1)   Whether or not the notice of appeal was given within the time limit specified, the respondent shall send to an adjudicator, the appellant and the appellant's representative—

   (a)   the notice of appeal, together with any documents attached to it under rule 8;
   (b)   any supplementary grounds of refusal;
   (c)   any variation of the grounds of appeal;

(d)   any notes of an asylum interview; and

(e)   any other document (except statutory or public materials) referred to in the decision which is the subject of appeal.

(2)   In this rule, "statutory or public materials" means an enactment or a provision made under an enactment, a convention or other provisions of a similar nature or other documents which are published or publicly available.

NOTES

Initial Commencement
Specified date
Specified date: 2 October 2000: see r 1(1).

11 Variation of notice of appeal

(1)   This rule applies where the documents have been sent to the adjudicator in accordance with rule 10.

(2)   The grounds of the appeal may be varied by the appellant with the leave of the adjudicator.

(3)   Except in the case of an appeal under section 65 or 69, the adjudicator shall not give leave to vary the grounds of appeal unless he is satisfied that because of special circumstances, it is just to allow the variation.

NOTES

Initial Commencement
Specified date
Specified date: 2 October 2000: see r 1(1).

12 Preliminary issues

(1)   When the respondent alleges that—

  (a)   the appellant is not entitled to appeal—
      (i)   by virtue of a provision of the 1999 Act specified by the respondent;
      (ii)   by virtue of a provision of Regulations made under section 2(2) of the European Communities Act 1972 and section 80 of the 1999 Act specified by the respondent;
      (iii)   by reason that a passport or other travel document, certificate of entitlement, entry clearance or work permit on which the appellant relies is a forgery or was issued to, and relates to, another person; or
      (iv)   by reason that notice of appeal has not been signed by the appellant or by his representative (if he has one) or, in the case of an appellant who is a minor or who is for any reason incapable of acting, by any person acting on his behalf; or
  (b)   the notice of appeal was not given within the period specified by rule 6; the respondent shall send to the adjudicator with the documents required under rule 10, and to the appellant and his representative (if he has one), a written statement setting out the allegation, the reasons for it and any relevant facts relating to it.

(2)   The appellant may send a written statement in reply to the respondent's statement given in accordance with paragraph (1) to the adjudicator and the respondent.

(3)   Where a written statement has been given in accordance with paragraph (1), the adjudicator may, and at the request of the respondent shall, determine the validity of the allegation as a preliminary issue.

(4)   At a hearing before the adjudicator in accordance with paragraph (3)—

    (a)   the respondent shall be given an opportunity to explain the allegation contained in his statement and any matters relating to it; and

    (b)   the appellant shall be given an opportunity to respond to the matters raised under sub-paragraph (a).

(5)   Where the adjudicator determines as a preliminary issue that the notice of appeal was not given within the period specified by rule 6, then, except where a deportation order is in force in respect of the appellant, the adjudicator may allow the appeal to proceed if he is satisfied that by reason of special circumstances, it is just to do so.

(6)   Where the adjudicator allows the appeal to proceed in accordance with paragraph (5), the notice of appeal shall be treated for all purposes as if it had been given in accordance with rule 6.

NOTES

Initial Commencement
Specified date
Specified date: 2 October 2000: see r 1(1).

13 Notification of hearing

Notice of the date, time and place fixed for the hearing and any directions given under rule 30 shall be served on the appellant or his representative (if he has one) and any other party.

NOTES

Initial Commencement
Specified date
Specified date: 2 October 2000: see r 1(1).

14 Determining an appeal

(1)   Except where rule 43 or 44 applies, a hearing shall be conducted to determine the appeal.

(2)   A hearing may be conducted or evidence given or representations made by video link or by other electronic means.

NOTES

Initial Commencement
Specified date
Specified date: 2 October 2000: see r 1(1).

15 Giving of determination

Written notice of the adjudicator's determination shall be sent to every party and the appellant's representative (if he has one).

NOTES

Initial Commencement
Specified date
Specified date: 2 October 2000: see r 1(1).

16 Adjudicator's review of determination

(1)   Where a party receives written notice of a determination to which there is no right of appeal to the Tribunal, he may apply to the Chief Adjudicator to review that

determination on the ground that it was wrongly made as a result of an administrative or procedural error by the adjudicator.

(2)   An application under paragraph (1) shall—

(a)   be made not later than 10 days after written notice of the determination was received by the party;
(b)   be in writing;
(c)   identify all matters relied on; and
(d)   be accompanied by copies of all relevant documents.

(3)   In addition to his power to review a determination on an application made under paragraph (1), the Chief Adjudicator may, of his own motion, if satisfied that the interests of justice so require, not later than 10 days after written notice of the determination has been sent to the parties, review that determination on the ground that it was wrongly made as a result of an administrative or procedural error by the adjudicator.

(4)   Where the Chief Adjudicator reviews the determination, he may—

(a)   confirm it; or
(b)   set it aside and direct a re-hearing of the appeal.

(5)   Where the Chief Adjudicator confirms the determination, written notice shall be sent to the parties.

(6)   Where the Chief Adjudicator sets aside the determination, written notice shall be sent to the parties, together with the date, time and place, and any directions, for the re-hearing of the appeal.

(7)   Any notice given under paragraphs (5) and (6) shall contain, in summary form, the reasons for the decision.

NOTES

Initial Commencement
Specified date
Specified date: 2 October 2000: see r 1(1).

PART III
APPEALS TO TRIBUNAL FROM ADJUDICATOR

17 Application of Part III

(1)   This Part applies to—

(a)   applications to the Tribunal for leave to appeal to the Tribunal; and
(b)   appeals to the Tribunal from the determination of an adjudicator.

(2)   In this Part, "appellant" means a party appealing against an adjudicator's determination and includes an applicant for leave to appeal under rule 18 and an applicant for a review under rule 19.

NOTES

Initial Commencement
Specified date
Specified date: 2 October 2000: see r 1(1).

18 Leave to appeal

(1)   An appeal from the determination of an adjudicator may be made only with the leave of the Tribunal.

(2)   An application for leave to appeal shall be made not later than 10 days, or in the case of an application made from outside the United Kingdom, 28 days, after the appellant has received written notice of the determination against which he wishes to appeal.

(3)   A time limit set out in paragraph (2) may be extended by the Tribunal where it is satisfied that because of special circumstances, it is just for the time limit to be extended.

(4)   An application for leave to appeal shall be made by serving upon the Tribunal the appropriate prescribed form, which shall—

(a)   be signed by the appellant or his representative (if he has one);
(b)   be accompanied by the adjudicator's determination;
(c)   identify the alleged errors of fact or law in the adjudicator's determination which would have made a material difference to the outcome, together with all the grounds relied on for the appeal; and
(d)   state whether a hearing of the appeal is desired.

(5)   When an application for leave to appeal has been made, the Tribunal shall notify the other parties.

(6)   The Tribunal shall not be required to consider any grounds other than those included in that application.

(7)   Leave to appeal shall be granted only where—

(a)   the Tribunal is satisfied that the appeal would have a real prospect of success; or
(b)   there is some other compelling reason why the appeal should be heard.

(8)   An application for leave to appeal shall be decided by a legally qualified member without a hearing.

(9)   When an application for leave to appeal has been decided, written notice of the Tribunal's decision on the application shall be sent to the parties and, if granted, the grounds upon which the appellant may appeal.

(10) Where the application for leave to appeal is refused, the notice referred to in paragraph (9) shall include, in summary form, the reasons for the refusal.

(11) Subject to section 77, where evidence which was not submitted to the adjudicator is relied upon in an application for leave to appeal, the Tribunal shall not be required to consider that evidence in deciding whether to grant leave to appeal, unless it is satisfied that there were good reasons why it was not submitted to the adjudicator.

NOTES

Initial Commencement
Specified date
Specified date: 2 October 2000: see r 1(1).

19 Tribunal's review of decision to refuse leave to appeal

(1)   Where the Tribunal has refused an application for leave to appeal, the appellant may apply to the Tribunal to review its decision on the ground that it was wrongly made as a result of an administrative or procedural error by the Tribunal.

(2)   An application under paragraph (1) shall—

(a)   be made not later than 10 days after written notice of the decision refusing leave to appeal was received by the appellant;
(b)   be in writing;
(c)   identify all matters relied on; and
(d)   be accompanied by copies of all relevant documents.

(3) In addition to its power to review a decision on an application made under paragraph (1), the Tribunal may, of its own motion, if satisfied that the interests of justice so require, not later than 10 days after sending to the appellant the notice of its decision, review its decision on the ground that it was wrongly made as a result of an administrative or procedural error by the Tribunal.

(4) A review under this rule shall be conducted by a legally qualified member without a hearing.

(5) Where the Tribunal reviews the decision, it may—

    (a) confirm it; or
    (b) set it aside and re-consider the decision.

(6) Written notice of the Tribunal's decision shall be sent to the parties and shall contain, in summary form, the reasons for the decision.

NOTES

Initial Commencement
Specified date
Specified date: 2 October 2000: see r 1(1).

20 Notice of appeal

(1) Where an application for leave to appeal is granted, it shall be deemed to be the notice of appeal.

(2) Where leave to appeal is granted, written notice of the date, time and place fixed for any hearing shall be sent to—

    (a) every party; and
    (b) every party's representative, except where the representative is acting for the Secretary of State, an officer or the United Kingdom Representative of the United Nations High Commissioner for Refugees.

NOTES

Initial Commencement
Specified date
Specified date: 2 October 2000: see r 1(1).

21 Variation of notice of appeal

The grounds of appeal may be varied by the appellant with the leave of the Tribunal.

NOTES

Initial Commencement
Specified date
Specified date: 2 October 2000: see r 1(1).

22 Evidence

(1) The Tribunal may consider as evidence any note or record made by the adjudicator of any proceedings before him in connection with the appeal.

(2) Subject to paragraph (3), the Tribunal may, of its own motion or on the application of any party, consider evidence further to that which was submitted to the adjudicator.

(3) The Tribunal shall not consider any evidence which is not served in accordance with time limits set out in these Rules or directions given under rule 30, unless the Tribunal is satisfied that there are good reasons to do so.

(4)   Subject to rule 38, the Tribunal shall not in its determination rely on any evidence which was not disclosed to all the parties.

(5)   Where any party wishes to adduce further evidence before the Tribunal in accordance with paragraph (2), he shall give written notice to that effect to the Tribunal indicating the nature of the evidence.

(6)   The notice referred to in paragraph (5) shall be given as soon as practicable after the parties have been notified that leave to appeal has been granted.

(7)   Where the Tribunal decides to admit any evidence under this rule, it may direct that it be given, either—

(a)   orally, in which case the Tribunal may take the evidence itself or remit the appeal to the same or another adjudicator for the taking of that evidence; or

(b)   in writing, in which case it shall be given in any manner and at any time that the Tribunal may direct.

NOTES

Initial Commencement
Specified date
Specified date: 2 October 2000: see r 1(1).

23 Appeals remitted by Tribunal to adjudicator

Unless it considers—

(a)   that it is necessary in the interests of justice, and

(b)   that it would save time and avoid expense

to remit the case to the same or another adjudicator for determination by him in accordance with any directions given to him by the Tribunal, the Tribunal shall determine the appeal itself.

NOTES

Initial Commencement
Specified date
Specified date: 2 October 2000: see r 1(1).

24 Determining an appeal

(1)   Except where rule 43 or 44 applies, a hearing shall be conducted to determine an appeal.

(2)   A hearing may be conducted or evidence given or representations made by video link or by other electronic means.

NOTES

Initial Commencement
Specified date
Specified date: 2 October 2000: see r 1(1).

25 Giving of determination

(1)   Written notice of the Tribunal's determination shall be sent to—

(a)   every party; and

(b)   every party's representative, except where the representative is acting for the Secretary of State, an officer or the United Kingdom Representative of the United Nations High Commissioner for Refugees.

(2)   Where an appeal is determined by a panel of more than one member, the determination may be given by a legally qualified member of that panel or, if the panel contains no legally qualified member, by such member as the President may direct.

NOTES

Initial Commencement
Specified date
Specified date: 2 October 2000: see r 1(1).

Part IV

Appeals from Tribunal

26 Application of Part IV

This Part applies to applications to the Tribunal for leave to appeal, on a question of law, to the Court of Appeal or, in Scotland, to the Court of Session, from a final determination of an appeal by the Tribunal.

NOTES

Initial Commencement
Specified date
Specified date: 2 October 2000: see r 1(1).

27 Leave to appeal

(1)   An application to the Tribunal for leave to appeal shall be made not later than 10 days after the party seeking to appeal has received written notice of the determination.

(2)   An application for leave to appeal shall be made by serving upon the Tribunal and any other party a notice of application for leave to appeal on the appropriate prescribed form and shall include the grounds of appeal.

(3)   The appropriate prescribed form shall be signed by the party seeking leave to appeal or his representative (if he has one).

(4)   An application for leave to appeal shall be decided by a legally qualified member without a hearing.

(5)   Where the Tribunal intends to grant leave to appeal, it may, having given every party an opportunity to make representations, instead, set aside the determination appealed against and direct that the appeal to the Tribunal be re-heard.

(6)   Written notice of the Tribunal's decision shall be sent to the parties.

(7)   Any notice given under paragraph (6) shall contain, in summary form, the reasons for the decision.

NOTES

Initial Commencement
Specified date
Specified date: 2 October 2000: see r 1(1).

Part V

General Provisions

28 Application of Part V

This Part applies to—

(a) proceedings to which Part II applies (appeals to adjudicator);

(b) proceedings to which Part III applies (appeals to the Tribunal from adjudicator);

(c) proceedings to which Part IV applies (applications to the Tribunal for leave to appeal from the Tribunal); and

(d) applications for bail.

NOTES

Initial Commencement
Specified date
Specified date: 2 October 2000: see r 1(1).

29 Parties

(1) Subject to paragraph (2), the parties to the appeal shall be the appellant and the respondent.

(2) Where, in the case of a claim for asylum, the United Kingdom Representative of the United Nations High Commissioner for Refugees gives written notice to the appellate authority at any time during the course of an appeal that he wishes to be treated as a party, he shall be so treated from the date of the notice.

NOTES

Initial Commencement
Specified date
Specified date: 2 October 2000: see r 1(1).

30 Conduct of appeals

(1) The appellate authority may, subject to the provisions of these Rules, regulate the procedure to be followed in relation to the conduct of any appeal.

(2) The overriding objective shall be to secure the just, timely and effective disposal of appeals and, in order to further that objective, the appellate authority may give directions which control the conduct of any appeal.

(3) The appellate authority may give directions under this rule orally or in writing and notice of any written directions given shall be served on the appellant or his representative (if he has one) and any other party.

(4) Directions given under this rule may, in particular,—

(a) relate to any matter concerning the preparation for a hearing and may specify the length of time allowed for anything to be done;

(b) specify the place at which the appeal shall be heard;

(c) provide for—
   (i) a particular matter to be dealt with as a preliminary issue;
   (ii) a pre-hearing review to be held;
   (iii) the furnishing of any particulars which appear to be requisite for the determination of the appeal;
   (iv) whether there should be a hearing of the appeal;
   (v) the witnesses, if any, to be heard;
   (vi) the manner in which any evidence may be given; and
   (vii) in the case of the Tribunal, times to be prescribed within which leave must be sought to submit any evidence or call any witnesses;

(d) require any party to file—
   (i) statements of the evidence which will be called at the hearing specifying in what respect the services of an interpreter will be required;
   (ii) a paginated and indexed bundle of all the documents which will be relied on at the hearing;

> (iii) a skeleton argument which summarises succinctly the submissions which will be made at the hearing and cites all the authorities which will be relied on, identifying any particular passages to be relied on;
> (iv) an estimate of the time which will be needed for the hearing of the appeal;
> (v) a list of the witnesses whom any party wishes to call to give evidence; and
> (vi) a chronology of events;
>
> (e) limit—
> (i) the number or length of documents produced by, for example, requiring a party to specify to another party the passage or part of any document on which he will rely, especially if the document has to be translated into English for the hearing;
> (ii) the length of oral submissions;
> (iii) the time allowed for the examination and cross examination of witnesses by, for example, allowing a witness statement to stand as evidence in chief; and
> (iv) the issues which will be addressed at the hearing;
> (f) facilitate the holding of combined hearings under rule 42.

(5)   A party shall provide to every other party a copy of any document which he is directed to file under paragraph (4).

(6)   In an appeal in which a party is unrepresented, the appellate authority may not give directions under this rule where it is necessary for the party to comply, unless it is satisfied that he is able to comply with those directions.

NOTES

Initial Commencement
Specified date
Specified date: 2 October 2000: see r 1(1).

31 Adjournment of hearings

(1)   Where an adjournment of the appeal is requested, the appellate authority shall not adjourn the hearing unless it is satisfied that refusing the adjournment would prevent the just disposal of the appeal.

(2)   Where a party applies for an adjournment of a hearing, he shall, where practicable, notify all other parties of the application and—

(a)   show good reason why an adjournment is necessary;
(b)   establish any fact or matter relied on in support of the application; and
(c)   offer a new date for the hearing.

(3)   Where a hearing is adjourned, the appellate authority shall give any further directions which it considers to be necessary for the future conduct of the appeal.

(4)   Written notice of the date, time and place of the adjourned hearing shall be sent to—

(a)   every party; and
(b)   every party's representative, except where the representative is acting for the Secretary of State, an officer or the United Kingdom Representative of the United Nations High Commissioner for Refugees.

NOTES

Initial Commencement
Specified date
Specified date: 2 October 2000: see r 1(1).

32 Abandoned appeals

(1) Where a party has, without a satisfactory explanation, failed—

(a) to comply with a direction given under these Rules;
(b) to comply with a provision of these Rules; or
(c) to appear at a hearing of which he had notice in accordance with these Rules;
and the appellate authority is satisfied in all the circumstances, including the extent of the failure and any reasons for it, that the party is not pursuing his appeal, the appellate authority may treat the appeal as abandoned.

(2) Where the appellate authority treats an appeal as abandoned, it shall send a notice to the parties which shall—

(a) inform the parties that the appeal is being treated as abandoned; and
(b) include the reasons.

NOTES

Initial Commencement
Specified date
Specified date: 2 October 2000: see r 1(1).

33 Failure to comply with these Rules

(1) Where a party has failed—

(a) to comply with a direction given under these Rules; or
(b) to comply with a provision of these Rules;
and the appellate authority is satisfied in all the circumstances, including the extent of the failure and any reasons for it, that it is necessary to have regard to the overriding objective in rule 30(2), the appellate authority may dispose of the appeal in accordance with paragraph (2).

(2) The appellate authority may—

(a) in the case of a failure by the appellant, dismiss the appeal or, in the case of a failure by the respondent, allow the appeal, without considering its merits;
(b) determine the appeal without a hearing in accordance with rule 43; or
(c) in the case of a failure by a party to send any document, evidence or statement of any witness, prohibit that party from relying on that document, evidence or statement at the hearing.

NOTES

Initial Commencement
Specified date
Specified date: 2 October 2000: see r 1(1).

34 Bail

(1) An application to be released on bail may be made orally or in writing to an immigration officer, a police officer or the appellate authority.

(2) In an application for bail, an applicant may be represented by any person listed in rule 35(1)(a).

(3) A written application made in accordance with paragraph (1) shall contain the following particulars—

(a) the full name of the applicant and his date of birth;
(b) the address of the place where the applicant is detained at the time when the application is made;

(c)   whether an appeal is pending at the time when the application is made;

(d)   the address where the applicant would reside if his application for bail were to be granted;

(e)   the amount of the recognizance in which he would agree to be bound;

(f)   the full names, addresses and occupations of two persons who might act as sureties for the applicant if his application for bail were to be granted, and the amounts of the recognizance in which those persons might agree to be bound; and

(g)   the grounds on which the application is made and, where a previous application has been refused, full particulars of any change in circumstances which has occurred since the refusal.

(4)   A written application made in accordance with paragraph (1) shall be signed by the applicant or by a person authorised by him to act or, in the case of an applicant who is a minor or who is for any reason incapable of acting, by a person acting on his behalf.

(5)   The recognizance of an applicant and that of a surety shall be on the appropriate prescribed forms.

(6)   Where the appellate authority directs the release of an applicant on bail and the taking of the recognizance is postponed, it shall certify in writing that bail has been granted in respect of the applicant, and shall include in the certificate particulars of the conditions to be endorsed on the recognizance with a view to the recognizance being taken subsequently, the amounts in which the applicant and any sureties are to be bound and the date of issue of the certificate.

(7)   The person having custody of an applicant shall—

(a)   on receipt of a certificate signed by or on behalf of the appellate authority stating that the recognizances of any sureties required have been taken, or on being otherwise satisfied that all such recognizances have been taken; and

(b)   on being satisfied that the applicant has entered into his recognizance;
release the applicant.

(8)   Where the appellate authority directs the release of an applicant on bail and does not require the taking of a recognizance from the applicant or a surety, the person having custody of the applicant shall release him.

(9)   Paragraphs (5) and (6) shall not apply to Scotland, and in its application to Scotland, this rule shall have effect as if—

(a)   for paragraph (3)(e) and (f), there were substituted—
"(e)   the amount, if any, to be deposited if bail is granted;
(f)   the full names, addresses and occupations of such persons, if any, who offer to act as cautioners if the application for bail were to be granted;"; and
(b)   for paragraph (7), there were substituted—

"(7) The person having custody of an applicant shall, on receipt of a certified copy of the decision to grant bail and on being satisfied that the amount, if any, to be deposited has been deposited, release the applicant.".

NOTES

Initial Commencement
Specified date
Specified date: 2 October 2000: see r 1(1).

35 Representation

(1)   In any proceedings in an appeal, a party may act in person or be represented—

(a) in the case of a person appealing against an immigration decision, by any person not prohibited by section 84;

(b) in the case of the Secretary of State or any officer, by an authorised advocate or any officer of the Secretary of State; and

(c) in the case of the United Kingdom Representative of the United Nations High Commissioner for Refugees in an asylum appeal, by a person appointed by him.

(2) A person representing a party may do anything relating to the proceedings that the person whom he represents is by these Rules required or authorised to do.

(3) Each party shall have a duty to maintain contact with his representative (if he has one) until the appeal is finally determined and notify the representative of any change of address.

(4) Where a representative referred to in paragraph (1)(a) ("the first representative") ceases to act, he and the party he was representing, shall forthwith notify the appellate authority and any other party of that fact and of the name and address of any new representative (if known).

(5) Until the appellate authority is notified that the first representative has ceased to act by either the first representative or the party he was representing, any document served on the first representative shall be deemed to be properly served on the party he was representing.

(6) Where a representative begins acting for a party to which these Rules apply, he shall forthwith notify the appellate authority of that fact.

NOTES

Initial Commencement
Specified date
Specified date: 2 October 2000: see r 1(1).

36 Summoning of witnesses

(1) Subject to paragraph (2), the appellate authority may, for the purposes of any appeal, by summons on the appropriate prescribed form, require any person in the United Kingdom to attend as a witness at a hearing of the appeal at the time and place specified in the form and, subject to the provisions of rule 37(2), at the hearing to answer any questions or produce any documents in his custody or under his control which relate to any matter in question in the appeal.

(2) A person shall not be required, in obedience to a summons referred to in paragraph (1), to travel unless the necessary expenses of his attendance are paid or tendered to him, and when the summons is issued at the request of a party, those expenses are paid or tendered by that party.

NOTES

Initial Commencement
Specified date
Specified date: 2 October 2000: see r 1(1).

37 Mode of giving evidence

(1) The appellate authority may receive oral, documentary or other evidence of any fact which appears to that authority to be relevant to the appeal, even though that evidence would be inadmissible in a court of law.

(2) In any proceedings before the appellate authority, a person shall not be compelled to give any evidence or produce any document which he could not be compelled to give

or produce on the trial of an action in that part of the United Kingdom in which the proceedings are conducted.

(3)   The appellate authority may require any witness to give evidence on oath or affirmation or without either, and for that purpose, in a case where an oath or affirmation is required, an oath or affirmation in due form may be administered.

NOTES

Initial Commencement
Specified date
Specified date: 2 October 2000: see r 1(1).

38 Inspection of documentary evidence

Subject to paragraph 6 of Schedule 4 to the 1999 Act, when the appellate authority takes into consideration documentary evidence, every party shall be given an opportunity of inspecting that evidence and taking copies if copies have not been provided pursuant to rule 30.

NOTES

Initial Commencement
Specified date
Specified date: 2 October 2000: see r 1(1).

39 Burden of proof

(1)   If in any proceedings before the appellate authority a party asserts that a decision or action taken against him under any statutory provision ought not to have been taken on the grounds that he is not a person to whom the provision applies, it shall lie on him to prove that he is not such a person.

(2)   If in any proceedings before the appellate authority a party asserts any fact of a kind that, if the assertion were made to the Secretary of State or any officer for the purposes of any statutory provisions or any immigration rules, it would by virtue of those provisions or rules be for him to satisfy the Secretary of State or officer of the truth thereof, it shall lie on that party to prove that the assertion is true.

(3)   In this rule, "immigration rules" means the rules referred to in section 3(2) of the 1971 Act and a reference to "statutory provisions" includes a reference to any provision made under an enactment.

NOTES

Initial Commencement
Specified date
Specified date: 2 October 2000: see r 1(1).

40 Exclusion of public

(1)   Subject to the provisions of this rule, any hearing by the appellate authority shall take place in public.

(2)   Where the appellate authority is considering an allegation referred to in paragraph 6(1) of Schedule 4 to the 1999 Act in accordance with paragraph 6(2) of that Schedule, all members of the public shall be excluded from that hearing.

(3)   Subject to paragraph (4), the appellate authority may exclude any member of the public or members of the public generally from any hearing or from any part of a hearing where—

(a) in the opinion of that authority, it is necessary in the interests of morals, public order or national security;

(b) in the opinion of that authority, the interests of minors or the protection of the private life of the parties so require; or

(c) in special circumstances publicity would prejudice the interests of justice, but only to the extent strictly necessary in the opinion of that authority.

(4) Nothing in this rule shall prevent a member of the Council on Tribunals or of its Scottish Committee from attending a hearing in that capacity.

NOTES

Initial Commencement
Specified date
Specified date: 2 October 2000: see r 1(1).

41 Hearing of appeal in absence of a party

(1) The appellate authority may, where in the circumstances of the case it appears just so to do, hear an appeal in the absence of a party if satisfied that—

(a) he is not in the United Kingdom;

(b) he is suffering from a communicable disease or from a mental disorder;

(c) by reason of illness or accident he cannot attend the hearing;

(d) it is impracticable to give him notice of the hearing and that no person is authorised to represent him at the hearing; or

(e) he has notified the appellate authority that he does not wish to attend the hearing.

(2) Without prejudice to paragraph (1) but subject to paragraph (3), the appellate authority may proceed with the hearing of an appeal in the absence of a party if satisfied that, in the case of that party, notice of the date, time and place of the hearing, or of the adjourned hearing, has been given in accordance with these Rules.

(3) Where the absent party has not furnished the appellate authority with a satisfactory explanation of his absence, it shall proceed with the hearing in pursuance of paragraph (2).

(4) Where in pursuance of this rule the appellate authority hears an appeal or proceeds with a hearing in the absence of a party, it shall determine the appeal on the evidence which has been received.

(5) Any reference to a party in paragraphs (2) to (4) includes a reference to his representative.

NOTES

Initial Commencement
Specified date
Specified date: 2 October 2000: see r 1(1).

42 Combined hearings

Where in the case of two or more appeals it appears to the appellate authority that—

(a) some common question of law or fact arises in both or all of them;

(b) they relate to decisions or action taken in respect of persons who are members of the same family; or

(c) for some other reason it is desirable to proceed with the appeals under this rule,

the appellate authority may, after giving all the parties an opportunity of being heard, decide that the appeals should be heard together.

NOTES

Initial Commencement
Specified date
Specified date: 2 October 2000: see r 1(1).

43 Determination without hearing

(1)   An appeal may be determined without a hearing under this rule if—

   (a)   the appellate authority has decided, after giving every other party an opportunity of replying to any representations submitted in writing by or on behalf of the appellant, to allow the appeal;

   (b)   the appellate authority is satisfied that the appellant, except where the appellant is the Secretary of State or an officer, is outside the United Kingdom or that it is impracticable to give him notice of a hearing and, in either case, that no person is authorised to represent him at a hearing;

   (c)   a preliminary issue has arisen under rule 12 and, the appellant having been given an opportunity to submit a written statement rebutting the respondent's allegation—
     (i)   the appellant has not submitted such a statement, or
     (ii)   the appellate authority is of the opinion that matters put forward by the appellant in such a statement do not warrant a hearing;

   (d)   the appellate authority is satisfied, having given every party an opportunity to make representations and having regard to—
     (i)   the material before it; and
     (ii)   the nature of the issues raised;
       that the appeal could be so disposed of justly;

   (e)   no party has requested a hearing; or

   (f)   the appellate authority is proceeding in accordance with rule 33(2)(b).

(2)   Where, in a family visitor appeal, the appellant has not paid the fee for a hearing at the time he made the appeal, the appellate authority shall determine the appeal without a hearing.

(3)   The appellate authority shall send written notice of the determination to—

   (a)   every party; and

   (b)   every party's representative, except where the representative is acting for the Secretary of State, an officer or the United Kingdom Representative of the United Nations High Commissioner for Refugees.

NOTES

Initial Commencement
Specified date
Specified date: 2 October 2000: see r 1(1).

44 Summary determination of appeals

(1)   Subject to paragraph (2), where it appears to the appellate authority that the issues raised in an appeal have been determined—

   (a)   in the case of an appeal before an adjudicator, by the same or another adjudicator or by the Tribunal, or

   (b)   in the case of an appeal before the Tribunal, by the Tribunal,
in previous proceedings to which the appellant, or a family member, was a party, on the basis of facts which did not materially differ from those to which the appeal relates, the appellate authority may determine the appeal summarily without a hearing.

(2)   Before the appellate authority determines an appeal summarily in accordance with paragraph (1), it shall give the parties an opportunity of making representations to the effect that the appeal ought not to be determined in that way.

(3)   Where an appeal is determined summarily in accordance with paragraph (1), the appellate authority shall send to the parties written notice of that fact, and that notice shall—

    (a)   contain a statement of the issues raised in the appeal; and
    (b)   specify the previous proceedings in which those issues were determined.

(4)   In this rule, "family member" means a person on whom a notice was served under section 74(4) at the same time in relation to the previous proceedings referred to in paragraph (1) that such a notice was served on the appellant.

NOTES

Initial Commencement
Specified date
Specified date: 2 October 2000: see r 1(1).

45 Transfer of proceedings

(1)   Where any proceedings before an adjudicator have not been disposed of by him and the Chief Adjudicator, or any person for the time being carrying out the functions of the Chief Adjudicator, is of the opinion that—

    (a)   it is not practicable without undue delay for the proceedings to be completed by that adjudicator, or
    (b)   for some other good reason the proceedings cannot be completed justly by that adjudicator,

he shall make arrangements for the appeal to be heard by another adjudicator.

(2)   Where any proceedings are transferred to another adjudicator in accordance with paragraph (1)—

    (a)   any notice or other document which is sent or given to or by the adjudicator from whom the proceedings were transferred shall be deemed to have been sent or given to or by the adjudicator to whom the appeal is transferred; and
    (b)   any adjudicator to whom an appeal is transferred shall have power to deal with it as if it had been commenced before him.

(3)   The powers of the Chief Adjudicator under this rule shall, with the appropriate modifications, also apply to the President in relation to proceedings before the Tribunal.

(4)   Where the Secretary of State notifies the Chief Adjudicator or the President, as the case may be, that section 78 applies, the Chief Adjudicator or the President shall transfer the proceedings to the Special Immigration Appeals Commission and shall notify the parties and their representatives (if any) of the transfer.

NOTES

Initial Commencement
Specified date
Specified date: 2 October 2000: see r 1(1).

46 Notices etc

(1)   Any notice or other document required or authorised by these Rules to be sent or given to any person or authority may be delivered or sent by post to an address, or sent by fax to a fax number, specified by the person or authority to whom the notice or document is directed.

(2)   If any notice or other document is sent or given to a person appearing to the authority or person sending it to represent that party, it shall be deemed to have been sent or given to that party.

NOTES

Initial Commencement
Specified date
Specified date: 2 October 2000: see r 1(1).

47 Notification of address

(1)   A party shall inform the appellate authority of the address at which documents may be served on him ("his address for service") and of any changes to that address.

(2)   Until a party gives notice to the appellate authority that his address for service has changed, any document served on him at the most recent address he has given to the appellate authority shall be deemed to have been properly served on him.

(3)   A person representing a party shall inform the appellate authority of his address for service and of any changes to that address.

(4)   Until a person representing a party gives notice to the appellate authority that his address for service has changed, any document served on him at the most recent address he has given to the appellate authority shall be deemed to have been properly served on him.

NOTES

Initial Commencement
Specified date
Specified date: 2 October 2000: see r 1(1).

48 Calculation of time

(1)   This rule applies to any notice or other document sent, served or given under these Rules.

(2)   Subject to paragraphs (3) and (4), any notice or other document that is sent shall, unless the contrary is proved, be deemed to have been received—

(a)   where the notice or other document is sent by post to a place within the United Kingdom, on the second day after it was sent;
(b)   where the notice or other document is sent by post to a place outside the United Kingdom, on the twenty-eighth day after it was sent; and
(c)   in any other case, on the day on which the notice or other document was sent.

(3)   Where a notice or other document is sent by post to the appellate authority, it shall be deemed to have been received on the day on which it was received by that authority.

(4)   Where a notice of appeal is sent by post or by fax to the address or fax number specified in the notice of decision, it shall be deemed to have been given on the day on which it was received at that address or fax number.

(5)   A notice or other document is received by the appellate authority when it is received by any person employed as a clerk to that authority.

(6)   Where an act is to be done not later than a specified period after any event, the period shall be calculated from the end of the day on which the event occurred.

(7)   Where the time provided by these Rules by which any act must be completed ends on a Saturday, a Sunday, a bank holiday, Christmas Day, 27th to 31st December or Good

Friday, the act shall be completed in time if completed on the next day which is not excluded under this paragraph.

(8)   Where, apart from this paragraph, the period in question, being a period of 10 days or less, would include a Saturday, a Sunday, a bank holiday, Christmas Day, 27th to 31st December or Good Friday, that day shall be excluded.

(9)   In this rule, "bank holiday" means a day that is specified in, or appointed under, the Banking and Financial Dealings Act 1971 as a bank holiday.

NOTES

Initial Commencement
Specified date
Specified date: 2 October 2000: see r 1(1).

49 Irregularities

(1)   Any irregularity resulting from failure to comply with these Rules before the appellate authority has reached a decision shall not by itself render the proceedings void.

(2)   Where the appellate authority considers that any person may have been prejudiced by that irregularity, it shall take any steps that it considers necessary to cure it, whether by the amendment of any document, the giving of any notice or otherwise.

NOTES

Initial Commencement
Specified date
Specified date: 2 October 2000: see r 1(1).

50 Correction of accidental errors

(1)   Clerical mistakes in any determination or notice of determination, or errors arising therein from any accidental slip or omission, may at any time be corrected and any correction made to, or to a record of, a determination shall be deemed to be part of that determination or record and written notice of it shall be given as soon as practicable to every party.

(2)   The Tribunal may, after consulting the adjudicator concerned, correct errors in a determination given by an adjudicator and any correction made to, or to a record of, a determination shall be deemed to be part of that determination or record and written notice of it shall be given as soon as practicable to every party and to the adjudicator.

NOTES

Initial Commencement
Specified date
Specified date: 2 October 2000: see r 1(1).

Irvine of Lairg, C

Dated 24th August 2000

SCHEDULE

Form 1
Notice of appeal (United Kingdom)

(The full text of this form is currently unavailable.)

Appendix 1   UK and EC Legislation

NOTES

Initial Commencement
Specified date
Specified date: 2 October 2000: see r 1(1).

FORM 1A (TRIBUNAL)
APPLICATION TO THE IMMIGRATION APPEAL TRIBUNAL FOR LEAVE TO APPEAL (UNITED KINGDOM)

(The full text of this form is currently unavailable.)

NOTES

Initial Commencement
Specified date
Specified date: 2 October 2000: see r 1(1).

FORM 2
NOTICE OF APPEAL (OVERSEAS)

(The full text of this form is currently unavailable.)

NOTES

Initial Commencement
Specified date
Specified date: 2 October 2000: see r 1(1).

FORM 2A (TRIBUNAL)
APPLICATION TO THE IMMIGRATION APPEAL TRIBUNAL FOR LEAVE TO APPEAL (OVERSEAS)

(The full text of this form is currently unavailable.)

NOTES

Initial Commencement
Specified date
Specified date: 2 October 2000: see r 1(1).

FORM 3
NOTICE OF APPEAL (FAMILY VISITOR)

(The full text of this form is currently unavailable.)

NOTES

Initial Commencement
Specified date
Specified date: 2 October 2000: see r 1(1).

FORM 3A (TRIBUNAL)
APPLICATION TO THE IMMIGRATION APPEAL TRIBUNAL FOR LEAVE TO APPEAL (FAMILY VISITOR)

(The full text of this form is currently unavailable.)

NOTES

Initial Commencement
Specified date
Specified date: 2 October 2000: see r 1(1).

FORM 4

RECOGNIZANCE OF APPLICANT

(The full text of this form is currently unavailable.)

NOTES

Initial Commencement
Specified date
Specified date: 2 October 2000: see r 1(1).

FORM 5

RECOGNIZANCE OF APPLICANT'S SURETY

(The full text of this form is currently unavailable.)

NOTES

Initial Commencement
Specified date
Specified date: 2 October 2000: see r 1(1).

FORM 6

WITNESS SUMMONS

(The full text of this form is currently unavailable.)

NOTES

Initial Commencement
Specified date
Specified date: 2 October 2000: see r 1(1).

IMMIGRATION AND ASYLUM ACT 1999 (COMMENCEMENT NO 6, TRANSITIONAL AND CONSEQUENTIAL PROVISIONS) ORDER 2000

2000 No 2444

Made - - - 11th September 2000

In exercise of the powers conferred upon him by sections 166(3) and 170(4) and (5) of the Immigration and Asylum Act 1999, the Secretary of State hereby makes the following Order:

1 Citation and interpretation

(1) This Order may be cited as the Immigration and Asylum Act 1999 (Commencement No 6, Transitional and Consequential Provisions) Order 2000.

(2) In this Order—

> "the 1971 Act" means the Immigration Act 1971;
> "the 1993 Act" means the Asylum and Immigration Appeals Act 1993;

"the 1996 Act" means the Asylum and Immigration Act 1996;
"the 1997 Act" means the Special Immigration Appeals Commission Act 1997;
"the 1999 Act" means the Immigration and Asylum Act 1999.

NOTES

Initial Commencement
Date Made
Date made: 11 September 2000: (no specific commencement provision).

2 Commencement

The provisions of the 1999 Act specified in column 1 of Schedule 1 to this Order shall come into force on the date specified in column 2 of that Schedule, subject to the transitional provisions contained in this Order, but where a particular purpose is specified in relation to any such provision in column 3 of that Schedule, the provision concerned shall come into force on that date only for that purpose.

NOTES

Initial Commencement
Date Made
Date made: 11 September 2000: (no specific commencement provision).

3 Transitional provisions

(1)   Subject to Schedule 2—

   (a)   the new appeals provisions are not to have effect in relation to events which took place before 2nd October 2000 and, notwithstanding their repeal by the provisions of the 1999 Act commenced by this Order, the old appeals provisions are to continue to have effect in relation to such events;
   (b)   the new procedural provisions are to apply to appeals under the old appeals provisions as well as the new appeals provisions; and
   (c)   references in the new procedural provisions to the new appeal rights (however expressed) are to be construed as including a reference to the equivalent provision of the old appeal rights.

(2)   Schedule 2, which makes further transitional provision in respect of the 1999 Act, has effect.

NOTES

Initial Commencement
Date Made
Date made: 11 September 2000: (no specific commencement provision).

4 Definitions for transitional provisions

(1)   In article 3—
   (a)   "the new appeals provisions" means sections 59, 61, 63, 65, 66, 67 and 69 of the 1999 Act; together with any provision (including subordinate legislation) of—
      (i)   the 1999 Act; and
      (ii)   the 1971 and 1993 Acts (as amended by the 1999 Act);
         which refers to those provisions;
   (b)   "the old appeals provisions" means—
      (i)   sections 13 (but not subsections (3AA) and (3AB)), 14, 15, 16, 17 of the 1971 Act;

    (ii)   subsections (1) to (4) of section 8 of the 1993 Act; and

    (iii) subsections (1) and (2) of section 3 of the 1996 Act;
         together with—

    (iv) any subordinate legislation which applies to those provisions; and

    (v)   any provision of the old Immigration Acts (including subordinate legislation) which refers to those provisions;

  (c)   "the new procedural provisions" means—

    (i)   subsections (5) to (10) of section 58 of the 1999 Act; and

    (ii)   paragraphs 6 to 8 and 21 to 24 of Schedule 4 to the 1999 Act.

(2) For the purposes of article 3, an event takes place when—

  (a)   a notice is served;

  (b)   a decision is made or taken;

  (c)   directions are given; and

  (d)   a certificate is issued.

(3) For the purposes of article 3 and Schedule 2—

  (a)   a notice is served;

  (b)   a decision is made or taken;

  (c)   directions are given; and

  (d)   a certificate is issued;

on the day on which it is or they are sent to the person concerned, if sent by post or by fax, or delivered to that person, if delivered by hand.

(4) In this article—

  (a)   "the old Immigration Acts" means the 1971 Act, the 1993 Act and the 1996 Act, all without the amendments made by the 1999 Act;

  (b)   "the person concerned" means the person who is the subject of the notice, decision, directions or certificate or the person who appears to be his representative; and

  (c)   a reference to the issue of a certificate is a reference to the issue of a certificate in relation to the removal of asylum claimants to safe third countries.

NOTES

Initial Commencement
Date Made
Date made: 11 September 2000: (no specific commencement provision).

5 Consequential provision

The reference in section 46(3)(a) of the Criminal Justice Act 1991 to a person who is liable to deportation under section 3(5) of the 1971 Act is to be read, from 2nd October 2000, as including a reference to a person who may be removed from the United Kingdom in accordance with section 10 of the 1999 Act.

NOTES

Initial Commencement
Date Made
Date made: 11 September 2000: (no specific commencement provision).

Barbara Roche
Minister of State
Home Office
11th September 2000

SCHEDULE 1

Article 2

Column 1	*Column 2*	*Column 3*
Section 3 (Continuing of leave pending decision).	2nd October 2000	
Section 10 (Removal of certain persons unlawfully in the United Kingdom) (so far as not already in force).	2nd October 2000	
Section 11 (Removal of asylum claimants under standing arrangements with member States).	2nd October 2000	
Section 12 (Removal of asylum claimants other than under standing arrangements with member States) (so far as not already in force).	2nd October 2000	
Section 23 (Monitoring refusals of entry clearance).	2nd October 2000	
Section 29 (Facilitation of entry) (so far as not already in force).	2nd October 2000	
Sections 32 and 34 to 37 (Clandestines) (so far as not already in force).	18th September 2000	Commenced for the purposes of section 39 (Rail freight) and any regulations made under it (in addition to the purposes specified in relation to these provisions in the Immigration and Asylum Act 1999 (Commencement No 3) Order 2000).
Part IV (appeals) (including Schedules 2, 3 and 4) (except for section 79 and so far as not already in force).	2nd October 2000	
Section 169 (Schedules 14 to 16).	2nd October 2000	Commenced for the purposes of the provisions of Schedules 14 to 16 commenced by this Order.
In Schedule 14 (Consequential amendments), paragraphs 43, 44(2), 46, 49 (except for section 22 of the 1971 Act, so far as that section has effect for the purposes of paragraph 25 of Schedule 2 to that Act, and so far as not already in force), 52 (so far as not already in force), 55, 65, 66, 69, 70, 83, 84, 99, 103 to 106, 108, 114, 115, 118, 120, 121 (so far as it relates to subsections (1) to (6) of section 2A of the 1997 Act), 122 to 128, 129 (so far as not already in force).	2nd October 2000	Paragraph 43 is commenced so far as it relates to paragraphs 44(2), 46, 49, 52, 55, 65, 66, 69 and 70 of the Schedule; paragraph 83 is commenced so far as it relates to paragraph 84 of the Schedule; paragraph 99 is commenced so far as it relates to paragraphs 103 to 106 of the Schedule; paragraph 108 is commenced so far as it relates to paragraphs 114 and 115; paragraph 118 is commenced so far as it relates to paragraphs 120 to 129 of the Schedule.

Column 1	Column 2	Column 3
In Schedule 15 (Transitional provisions and savings), paragraphs 11 and 12.	2nd October 2000	
In Schedule 16 (Repeals), the entries relating to Part II and Schedules 2 and 3 of the 1971 Act (except for section 22 of the 1971 Act, so far as that section has effect for the purposes of paragraph 25 of Schedule 2 to the 1971 Act, and so far as not already in force); the entry relating to section 5 of the Immigration Act 1988; the entries relating to sections 7, 8, 9, 10 and 11 of, and Schedule 2 to, the 1993 Act; the entries relating to sections 1, 2 and 3 of, and Schedules 2 and 3 to, the 1996 Act; the entries relating to section 7(4) of, and paragraph 5 of Schedule 2 to, the 1997 Act.	2nd October 2000	

NOTES
Initial Commencement
Date Made
Date made: 11 September 2000: (no specific commencement provision).

SCHEDULE 2

Article 3

Transitional provisions relating to the 1999 Act

1 (1) In this paragraph, a reference to a section or to a Schedule is to be read as a reference to a section of, or to a Schedule to, the 1999 Act, unless otherwise specified.

(2) Section 10 (removal of certain persons unlawfully in the United Kingdom) is not to have effect in relation to—

(a) any person on whom the Secretary of State has, before 2nd October 2000, served a notice of his intention to make a deportation order; and

(b) any person—
   (i) who applied during the regularisation period fixed by section 9 of the 1999 Act, in accordance with the Immigration (Regularisation Period for Overstayers) Regulations 2000, for leave to remain in the United Kingdom; and
   (ii) on whom the Secretary of State has since served a notice of his decision to make a deportation order.

(3) Subsections (5) to (10) of section 58 (pending appeals) are to apply to appeals under Part II of the 1971 Act, section 8 of the 1993 Act and section 3 of the 1996 Act as they do to appeals under Part IV and—

(a) references to "this Part" are to be construed accordingly; and

(b) when an appeal is made under section 14 of the 1971 Act, the reference to section 61 in subsection (10) of section 58 is to include a reference to section 14 of the 1971 Act.

(4)   Section 59 (appeals against exclusion from the United Kingdom) is not to have effect where the decision to refuse leave to enter the United Kingdom, or to refuse a certificate of entitlement or an entry clearance, was made before 2nd October 2000.

(5)   Section 61 (appeals against decisions about variation of limited leave) is not to have effect where the decision to vary, or to refuse to vary, the limited leave to enter or remain was made before 2nd October 2000.

(6)   Section 63 (appeals in respect of deportation orders) is not to have effect where the decision to make a deportation order, or the decision to refuse to revoke a deportation order, was made before 2nd October 2000.

(7)   Section 65 (human rights appeals) is not to have effect where the decision under the Immigration Acts was taken before 2nd October 2000.

(8)   Section 66 (appeals concerning the validity of directions for removal) is not to have effect where the directions for a person's removal from the United Kingdom were given before 2nd October 2000.

(9)   Section 67 (appeals objecting to the destination specified in removal directions) is not to have effect where the directions for a person's removal from the United Kingdom were given before 2nd October 2000.

(10) If a person has appealed under section 13(1) or section 15 of the 1971 Act, the reference in section 68(2) to an appeal under section 59 or 63 is to include a reference to an appeal under subsection (2) or subsection (3) of section 17 of the 1971 Act.

(11) In section 69 (asylum appeals)—

    (a)   subsection (1) is not to have effect where the decision to refuse leave to enter the United Kingdom was made before 2nd October 2000;

    (b)   subsection (2) is not to have effect where the decision to vary, or to refuse to vary, the limited leave to enter or remain was made before 2nd October 2000;

    (c)   subsection (3) is not to have effect where the decision to refuse leave to enter or remain in the United Kingdom was made before 2nd October 2000;

    (d)   subsection (4) is not to have effect where the decision to make a deportation order, or the decision to refuse to revoke a deportation order, was made before 2nd October 2000; and

    (e)   subsection (5) is not to have effect where the directions for a person's removal from the United Kingdom were given before 2nd October 2000.

(12) If a person has had the right to appeal under section 8(3)(a) of the 1993 Act, the reference in section 70(8) to the right to appeal under section 69(4)(a) is to include a reference to the right to appeal under section 8(3)(a) of the 1993 Act.

(13) The following paragraphs of Schedule 4 are to apply to appeals under Part II of the 1971 Act, section 8 of the 1993 Act and section 3 of the 1996 Act as they do to appeals under Part IV—

    (a)   paragraph 6 (hearings in private);
    (b)   paragraph 7 (leave to appeal);
    (c)   paragraph 8 (offences);
    (d)   paragraph 21 (determination of appeals);
    (e)   paragraph 22 (appeals to Immigration Appeal Tribunal);
    (f)   paragraph 23 (appeals from Immigration Appeal Tribunal); and
    (g)   paragraph 24 (appeals which must be dismissed);

and references in these paragraphs to appeals under Part IV are to include references to appeals under Part II of the 1971 Act, section 8 of the 1993 Act and section 3 of the 1996 Act.

(14) Where an appeal is made under section 13 of the 1971 Act (appeals against exclusion from the United Kingdom), and the adjudicator dismisses that appeal, the reference in paragraph 7 of Schedule 4 (leave to appeal) to an appeal under section 59 (appeals against exclusion from the United Kingdom) is to include a reference to an appeal under section 13 of the 1971 Act.

(15) Where an appeal is made to the Immigration Appeal Tribunal in the first instance, in accordance with section 15 of the 1971 Act (appeals in respect of deportation orders), the references in paragraph 21 of Schedule 4 (determination of appeals) to an adjudicator are to include references to the Immigration Appeal Tribunal.

(16) Where an appeal is made under the 1996 Act, the reference in paragraph 22 of Schedule 4 (appeals to the Immigration Appeal Tribunal) to section 71 (removal to safe countries) is to include a reference to section 3(1)(a) of the 1996 Act (appeals against certificates).

(17) Where an appeal has been determined before 2nd October 2000 on the grounds that it has been abandoned, it is to continue to be treated as determined for the purposes of paragraphs 22 and 23 of Schedule 4 (appeals to and from the Immigration Appeal Tribunal).

(18) Where an appeal is made under section 16 of the 1971 Act (appeals against the validity of removal directions), the reference in paragraph 24(3) of Schedule 4 (appeals which must be dismissed) to section 66(1)(c) is to include a reference to section 16(1)(b) of the 1971 Act.

Transitional provisions relating to the appeals provisions of the 1971 Act

2 (1) In this paragraph, a reference to a section or to a Schedule is to be read as a reference to a section of, or a Schedule to, the 1971 Act, unless otherwise specified.

(2) Section 3C (continuation of leave pending decision), as inserted by section 3 of the 1999 Act, is to apply in relation to an application mentioned in section 3C(1)(a)—

    (a)   which is made before 2nd October 2000; and
    (b)   in respect of which no decision has been made before 2nd October 2000;

as it applies in relation to such an application made on or after 2nd October 2000.

(3) Section 5 (procedure for, and further provisions as to, deportation) is to continue to have effect in relation to—

    (a)   any person on whom the Secretary of State has, before 2nd October 2000, served a notice of his decision to make a deportation order; and
    (b)   any person—
        (i)   who applied during the regularisation period fixed by section 9 of the 1999 Act, in accordance with the Immigration (Regularisation Period for Overstayers) Regulations 2000, for leave to remain in the United Kingdom; and
        (ii) on whom the Secretary of State has since served a notice of his decision to make a deportation order;

and, for the purposes of section 5, such a person is to be taken to be a person who is liable to deportation under section 3(5).

(4) Section 13 (appeals against exclusion from the United Kingdom) is to continue to have effect where the decision to refuse leave to enter the United Kingdom, or to refuse a certificate of entitlement or an entry clearance, was made before 2nd October 2000.

(5) Section 14 (appeals against conditions) is to continue to have effect where the decision to vary, or the refuse to vary, the limited leave to enter or remain was made before 2nd October 2000.

(6)   Section 15 (appeals in respect of deportation orders) is to continue to have effect where the decision to refuse to revoke a deportation order was made before 2nd October 2000.

(7)   Section 16 (appeals against validity of directions for removal) is to continue to have effect where the directions for a person's removal from the United Kingdom were given before 2nd October 2000.

(8)   Section 17 (appeals against removal on objection to destination) is to continue to have effect—

(a)   where the directions for a person's removal from the United Kingdom were given, or the notice specifying the destination of his removal was served, before 2nd October 2000; and

(b)   in relation to any person—
   (i)   who applied during the regularisation period fixed by section 9 of the 1999 Act, in accordance with the Immigration (Regularisation Period for Overstayers) Regulations 2000, for leave to remain in the United Kingdom; and
   (ii)   on whom the Secretary of State has since served a notice of his decision to make a deportation order.

(9)   Section 21 (references of cases by Secretary of State for further consideration) (including that section as applied by paragraph 4 of Schedule 2 to the 1993 Act and by section 3 of the 1996 Act) is to continue to have effect where the Secretary of State has referred a matter for consideration under that section before 2nd October 2000.

(10)   Where an appeal is made under Part II (including that Part as it applies by virtue of Schedule 2 to the 1993 Act and by virtue of section 3 of the 1996 Act)—

(a)   paragraph 28 of Schedule 2 (stay on directions for removal) (including that paragraph as applied by paragraph 9 of Schedule 2 to the 1993 Act) is to continue to have effect;

(b)   the following provisions are not to have effect—
   (i)   paragraph 29(1) of Schedule 2 (grant of bail pending appeal) (including that paragraph as applied by paragraph 9 of Schedule 2 to the 1993 Act and by section 3(6) of the 1996 Act), as amended by paragraph 66 of Schedule 14 to the 1999 Act;
   (ii)   paragraph 3 of Schedule 3 (effect of appeals) (including that paragraph as applied by paragraph 9 of Schedule 2 to the 1993 Act), as amended by paragraph 69 of Schedule 14 to the 1999 Act.

Transitional provisions relating to the appeals provisions of the 1993 Act

3   (1)   In this paragraph, a reference to a section or to a Schedule is to be read as a reference to a section of, or a Schedule to, the 1993 Act, unless otherwise specified.

(2)   In section 8 (asylum appeals)—

(a)   subsection (1) is to continue to have effect where the decision to refuse leave to enter was made before 2nd October 2000;

(b)   subsection (2) is to continue to have effect where the decision to vary, or to refuse to vary, the limited leave to enter or remain was made before 2nd October 2000;

(c)   subsection (3) is to continue to have effect where the decision to make a deportation order, or the decision to refuse to revoke a deportation order, was made before 2nd October 2000;

(d)   subsection (4) is to continue to have effect where the directions for a person's removal from the United Kingdom were given before 2nd October 2000.

(3)   Where an appeal is made under Part II of the 1971 Act (including that Part as it applies by virtue of Schedule 2)—

- (a)   section 9A (bail pending appeal from Immigration Appeal Tribunal), as amended by paragraphs 105 and 106 of Schedule 14 to the 1999 Act, is not to have effect;
- (b)   the reference in section 9A (without the amendments made by the 1999 Act) to section 9 (appeals from Immigration Appeal Tribunal) is to include a reference to paragraph 23 of Schedule 4 to the 1999 Act (appeals from Immigration Appeal Tribunal).

(4)   Where an appeal is made under section 8, the section 8 appeals provisions are to continue to have effect.

(5)   In this paragraph "the section 8 appeals provisions" means—

- (a)   paragraph 1 of Schedule 2 (asylum appeal rights to replace rights under the 1971 Act);
- (b)   paragraph 2 of Schedule 2 (scope of asylum right of appeal);
- (c)   paragraph 3 of Schedule 2 (other grounds for appeal);
- (d)   paragraph 5 of Schedule 2 (special appeals procedures for claims without foundation);
- (e)   paragraph 6 of Schedule 2 (exception for national security);
- (f)   paragraph 7 of Schedule 2 (suspension of variation of limited leave pending appeal);
- (g)   paragraph 8 of Schedule 2 (deportation order not to be made while appeal pending);
- (h)   paragraph 9 of Schedule 2 (stay of removal directions pending appeal and bail).

(6)   Where an appeal is made under section 8, the reference in paragraph 5 of Schedule 2 to section 20(1) of the 1971 Act (appeals to the Immigration Appeal Tribunal) is to include a reference to paragraph 22(1) of Schedule 4 to the 1999 Act (appeals to the Immigration Appeal Tribunal).

Transitional provisions relating to the appeals provisions of the 1996 Act

4   (1)   Sections 2 (removal etc of asylum claimants to safe third countries) and 3 (appeals against certificates under section 2) of the 1996 Act are to continue to have effect where a certificate under section 2(1) of that Act has been issued before 2nd October 2000.

(2)   Where an appeal is made under section 3(1) of the 1996 Act, section 3(6) of that Act (grant of bail pending appeal) is to continue to have effect.

Transitional provisions relating to the 1997 Act

5   (1)   Section 2(2) of the 1997 Act (appeals to the Commission), as amended by paragraph 120 of Schedule 14 to the 1999 Act, is not to have effect where the refusal of entry clearance was made before 2nd October 2000.

(2)   Subsections (1) to (6) of section 2A of the 1997 Act (jurisdiction: human rights), as inserted by paragraph 121 of Schedule 14 to the 1999 Act, are not to have effect where the appealable decision was taken before 2nd October 2000.

NOTES

Initial Commencement
Date Made
Date made: 11 September 2000: (no specific commencement provision).

IMMIGRATION APPEALS (FAMILY VISITOR) (NO 2) REGULATIONS 2000

2000 No 2446

Made - - - 11th September 2000

Laid before Parliament - - - 13th September 2000

Coming into force - - - 2nd October 2000

The Secretary of State, in exercise of the powers conferred on him by sections 60(6) and (10), 166(3) and 167 of the Immigration and Asylum Act 1999, hereby makes the following Regulations:

1 Citation, commencement and revocation

(1)   These Regulations may be cited as the Immigration Appeals (Family Visitor) (No 2) Regulations 2000 and shall come into force on 2nd October 2000.

(2)   The Immigration Appeals (Family Visitor) Regulations 2000 are hereby revoked.

2 Interpretation

(1)   In these Regulations—

"the Act" means the Immigration and Asylum Act 1999;
"entry clearance officer" means a person responsible for the grant or refusal of entry clearance;
"fee" means the fee required to be paid in accordance with regulation 3(1);
"first cousin" means, in relation to a person, the son or daughter of his uncle or aunt;
"repayment" means any repayment required to be made in accordance with regulation 3(3).

(2)   For the purposes of section 60(10) of the Act, a "family visitor" is a person who applies for entry clearance to enter the United Kingdom as a visitor, in order to visit—

(a)   his spouse, father, mother, son, daughter, grandfather, grandmother, grandson, granddaughter, brother, sister, uncle, aunt, nephew, niece or first cousin;
(b)   the father, mother, brother or sister of his spouse;
(c)   the spouse of his son or daughter;
(d)   his stepfather, stepmother, stepson, stepdaughter, stepbrother or stepsister; or
(e)   a person with whom he lived as a member of an unmarried couple for at least two of the three years before the day on which his application for entry clearance was made.

3 Fees

(1)   A family visitor who appeals under section 59 of the Act ("the appellant") must pay to an entry clearance officer at the place where his application for entry clearance was made—

(a)   [£125], if he elects a hearing;
(b)   [£50], in all other cases.

(2)   The appeal is not to be entertained unless the fee has been paid by the appellant.

(3)   If the appeal is successful, the fee is to be repaid to the appellant by an entry clearance officer.

NOTES

Amendment
Para (1): in sub-para (a) sum "£125" in square brackets substituted by SI 2001/52, reg 2(a).
Date in force: 12 January 2001: see SI 2001/52, reg 1.
Para (1): in sub-para (b) sum "£50" in square brackets substituted by SI 2001/52, reg 2(b).
Date in force: 12 January 2001: see SI 2001/52, reg 1.

4 Method of payment

(1)   The fee is to be paid, and the repayment made, in currency circulating at the place of payment.

(2)   The rate of exchange to be used for calculating the equivalent of the fee or repayment in foreign currency is to be based on the rate of exchange which is generally prevailing on the date, and at the place, of payment of the fee.

Barbara Roche
Minister of State
Home Office
11th September 2000

IMMIGRATION (DESIGNATION OF TRAVEL BANS) ORDER 2000

2000 No 2724

Made - - - 3rd October 2000

Laid before Parliament - - - 9th October 2000

Coming into force - - - 10th October 2000

The Secretary of State, in exercise of the powers conferred upon him by section 8B(5) and (6) of the Immigration Act 1971, hereby makes the following Order:

1 This Order may be cited as the Immigration (Designation of Travel Bans) Order 2000 and shall come into force on 10th October 2000.

NOTES

Initial Commencement

Specified date
Specified date: 10 October 2000: see above.

2 The instruments listed in the Schedule to this Order are designated for the purposes of section 8B(4) and (5) of the Immigration Act 1971.

NOTES

Initial Commencement

Specified date
Specified date: 10 October 2000: see art 1.

3 Section 8B(1), (2) and (3) of the Immigration Act 1971 shall not apply in any case where:

(a)   failure to apply these provisions would not be contrary to the United Kingdom's obligations under any of the instruments designated by article 2 of this Order,

(b)   to apply these provisions would be contrary to the United Kingdom's obligations under the Convention for the Protection of Human Rights and Fundamental Freedoms, agreed by the Council of Europe at Rome on 4th November 1950, or

(c)   to apply these provisions would be contrary to the United Kingdom's obligations under the Convention relating to the Status of Refugees done at Geneva on 28th July 1951 and the Protocol to that Convention.

NOTES

Initial Commencement

Specified date
Specified date: 10 October 2000: see art 1.

Barbara Roche
Minister of State
Home Office
3rd October 2000

[SCHEDULE
Designated Instruments]

NOTES

Amendment

Substituted by SI 2000/3338, art 2, Schedule.
Date in force: 21 December 2000: see SI 2000/3338, art 1.

[Article 2]

NOTES

Amendment

Substituted by SI 2000/3338, art 2, Schedule.
Date in force: 21 December 2000: see SI 2000/3338, art 1.

[PART 1
RESOLUTIONS OF THE SECURITY COUNCIL OF THE UNITED NATIONS]

NOTES

Amendment

Substituted by SI 2000/3338, art 2, Schedule.
Date in force: 21 December 2000: see SI 2000/3338, art 1.

[Resolution 1127 (1997) of 28th August 1997 (Angola).

Resolution 1171 (1998) of 5th June 1998 (Sierra Leone).]

NOTES

Amendment

Substituted by SI 2000/3338, art 2, Schedule.
Date in force: 21 December 2000: see SI 2000/3338, art 1.

[PART 2
INSTRUMENTS MADE BY THE COUNCIL OF THE EUROPEAN UNION]

NOTES

Amendment

Substituted by SI 2000/3338, art 2, Schedule.
Date in force: 21 December 2000: see SI 2000/3338, art 1.
[Common Position 97/759/CFSP of 30th October 1997 (Angola).
Common Position 96/635/CFSP of 28th October 1996 (Burma).
Common Position 2000/346/CFSP of 26th April 2000 (Burma).
Common Position 98/240/CFSP of 19th March 1998 (Federal Republic of Yugoslavia).
Common Position 98/725/CFSP of 14th December 1998 (Federal Republic of Yugoslavia).
Common Position 99/318/CFSP of 10th May 1999 (Federal Republic of Yugoslavia).
Common Position 2000/56/CFSP of 24th January 2000 (Federal Republic of Yugoslavia).
Common Position 2000/696/CFSP of 10th November 2000 (Federal Republic of Yugoslavia).
Common Position 98/409/CFSP of 29th June 1998 (Sierra Leone).]

NOTES

Amendment

Substituted by SI 2000/3338, art 2, Schedule.
Date in force: 21 December 2000: see SI 2000/3338, art 1.

IMMIGRATION SERVICES COMMISSIONER (REGISTRATION FEE) ORDER 2000

2000 No 2735

Made - - - 5th October 2000

Laid before Parliament - - - 9th October 2000

Coming into force - - - 30th October 2000

The Secretary of State, in exercise of the powers conferred upon him by sections 85(3) and 166(3) of and paragraph 5(1) of Schedule 6 to the Immigration and Asylum Act 1999 hereby makes the following Order:

Citation and commencement

1 This Order may be cited as the Immigration Services Commissioner (Registration Fee) Order 2000 and shall come into force on 30th October 2000.

NOTES

Initial Commencement
Specified date
Specified date: 30 October 2000: see above.

Interpretation

2   In this Order—

"the Act" means the Immigration and Asylum Act 1999;

"registration" means registration or (as the case may be) continued registration, under section 84(2)(a) or (b) of the Act;

"relevant advisers" means, in respect of—

(a)   an individual, that individual together with—

   (i)   the number of employees of that individual who provide immigration advice or immigration services, excluding such employees who are qualified persons under sections 84(2)(c) to (f) of the Act, or who are persons to whom section 84(4) of the Act applies; and

   (ii)   the number of persons who provide immigration advice or immigration services who work under the supervision of that individual and his employees, excluding such persons who are qualified persons under sections 84(2)(c) to (f) of the Act, or who are persons to whom section 84(4) of the Act applies;

(b)   a body corporate or unincorporate—

   (i)   the number of members and employees of that body who provide immigration advice or immigration services, excluding such members and employees who are qualified persons under sections 84(2)(c) to (f) of the Act, or who are persons to whom section 84(4) of the Act applies; and

   (ii)   the number of persons who provide immigration advice or immigration services who work under the supervision of such members and employees, excluding such persons who are qualified persons under sections 84(2)(c) to (f) of the Act, or who are persons to whom section 84(4) of the Act applies;

"sole immigration adviser" means an individual who does not employ any other person to provide immigration advice or immigration services and who does not have any person who works under his supervision or the supervision of any of his employees who provides immigration advice or immigration services.

NOTES

Initial Commencement
Specified date
Specified date: 30 October 2000: see art 1.

Fee for registration

3   The fee payable by a sole immigration adviser for registration shall be £1,800.

NOTES

Initial Commencement
Specified date
Specified date: 30 October 2000: see art 1.

4   The fee payable by any other person for registration shall be determined by the number of relevant advisers in respect of that person at the date of his application for registration, and shall be the sum specified for such number of relevant advisers in the Schedule to this Order.

NOTES

Initial Commencement
Specified date
Specified date: 30 October 2000: see art 1.

Barbara Roche
Minister of State
Home Office
5th October 2000

SCHEDULE

Article 4

Number of relevant advisers	Fee payable for registration
1	*£1,800*
2 to 4	*£2,675*
5 to 9	*£3,475*
10 to 19	*£4,275*
20 or over	*£6,000*

NOTES

Initial Commencement
Specified date
Specified date: 30 October 2000: see art 1.

IMMIGRATION SERVICES TRIBUNAL RULES 2000

2000 No 2739

Made - - - 4th October 2000

Laid before Parliament - - - 9th October 2000

Coming into force - - - 30th October 2000

The Lord Chancellor, in exercise of the powers conferred upon him by paragraphs 7 and 8(3) of Schedule 7 to the Immigration and Asylum Act 1999 and after consulting the Scottish Ministers and the Council on Tribunals, makes the following Rules:

1 Citation and commencement

These Rules may be cited as the Immigration Services Tribunal Rules 2000 and shall come into force on 30th October 2000.

NOTES

Initial Commencement
Specified date
Specified date: 30 October 2000: see above.

2 Interpretation

In these Rules:—

"appeal" means an appeal under section 87(2) against a decision of the Commissioner, and "appellant" shall be construed accordingly;

"charge" means a disciplinary charge laid by the Commissioner under paragraph 9(1)(e) of Schedule 5 and "person charged" shall be construed accordingly;

"procedural direction" means a direction relating to any of the following matters:—

(a) the suspension of the effect of the decision appealed against pending determination of the appeal (rule 10);

(b) the cancellation or variation of a direction suspending the effect of a decision (rule 11);

(c) restrictions on or prohibition of the provision of immigration advice or immigration services pending determination of a charge (rule 15);

(d) the consolidation of the proceedings with any other proceedings before the Tribunal, whether involving the same or different parties (rule 16(2)(a));

(e) the hearing of any two or more sets of proceedings together (rule 16(2)(b));

(f) the extension of the time limited by these Rules for any step in the proceedings (rule 16(2)(c));

(g) what witnesses are to be heard at the full hearing of an appeal or charge (rule 17);

(h) the provision of information, or disclosure of documents, by any party to the proceedings to any other party or to the Tribunal (rule 18);

(i) the date for the full hearing of an appeal or charge (rule 19);

(j) who may represent any party to an appeal or charge (rule 21(d));

(k) the setting aside of a decision made in the absence of a party and the re-listing of the proceedings for hearing (rule 25);

(l) any other arrangement which, in the opinion of the Tribunal, may facilitate the determination of the appeal or charge (rule 16(2)(d));

a section or Schedule cited by number alone means the section or Schedule so numbered in the Immigration and Asylum Act 1999;

all words and expressions defined in section 82 shall have the same meaning in these Rules.

NOTES

Initial Commencement
Specified date
Specified date: 30 October 2000: see r 1.

3 Composition of the Tribunal

(1) At the hearing of an appeal or charge, the Tribunal shall consist of a legally qualified member and two other members.

(2) The Tribunal shall consist of a legally qualified member alone when considering or deciding, at a hearing or otherwise, whether—

(a) to give a person permission to appeal out of time;

(b) to make, cancel or vary a direction under paragraph 8 of Schedule 7 (suspending the effect of a relevant decision);

(c) to make a direction under paragraph 9(3) of Schedule 5 (restricting or prohibiting the provision of immigration advice or immigration services while the Tribunal deals with a charge);

(d)   to make any other procedural direction; or

(e)   to give effect to a draft order settling proceedings by consent.

(3)   At a preliminary hearing, the Tribunal shall consist of a legally qualified member sitting alone if the hearing relates solely to procedural directions, and of a legally qualified member and two other members otherwise.

(4)   Subject to the preceding paragraphs of this rule and to rule 4, every function of the Tribunal may be exercised by such member of the Tribunal or of its staff as the President shall direct, either generally or in relation to a specified case or description of cases.

NOTES

Initial Commencement
Specified date
Specified date: 30 October 2000: see r 1.

4 The Register

(1)   There shall be a Register of proceedings pending or concluded before the Tribunal.

(2)   That Register shall record:—

(a)   every appeal commenced and every charge laid before the Tribunal, together with the number allotted to it;

(b)   a brief statement of the way in which each appeal or charge was determined.

(3)   That Register shall be open to inspection by the public during normal office hours.

NOTES

Initial Commencement
Specified date
Specified date: 30 October 2000: see r 1.

5 Notice of appeal

(1)   An appeal shall be commenced by sending to the Tribunal written notice of appeal, together with a copy of the decision against which the appeal is brought.

(2)   Every notice of appeal shall be signed and dated, and contain the following information:—

(a)   the name and address of the appellant;

(b)   the name and address of any person representing the appellant;

(c)   the nature and date of the decision against which the appeal is brought;

(d)   the grounds of the appeal; and

(e)   where the appeal is out of time, the reason for the delay.

NOTES

Initial Commencement
Specified date
Specified date: 30 October 2000: see r 1.

6 Acknowledgment of appeal

As soon as practicable after receiving the notice of appeal, the Tribunal shall—

(a)   allot a number to the appeal and enter it in the Register mentioned in rule 4; and

(b)   send an acknowledgment to the appellant and a copy of the notice of appeal to the Commissioner.

NOTES

Initial Commencement
Specified date
Specified date: 30 October 2000: see r 1.

7 Reply to notice of appeal

(1)   Within the period specified in paragraph (2) below, the Commissioner may send to the appellant and the Tribunal a notice in reply, containing the Commissioner's reasons for opposing the appeal.

(2)   The notice in reply may be sent at any time within 28 days from—

    (a)   where the appeal is out of time, the Tribunal's decision to permit the appellant to appeal out of time;

    (b)   otherwise, the sending to the Commissioner of the copy of the notice of appeal.

NOTES

Initial Commencement
Specified date
Specified date: 30 October 2000: see r 1.

8 Time for appealing

The period within which an appeal against any relevant decision of the Commissioner as defined in section 87(3) can be brought is 28 days after the decision is notified to the person aggrieved; and where the decision is notified in writing, the decision shall be deemed to be notified as soon as written notice of it is sent.

NOTES

Initial Commencement
Specified date
Specified date: 30 October 2000: see r 1.

9 Permission to appeal out of time

(1)   A person aggrieved by a decision of the Commissioner may appeal against it after the expiry of the period limited by rule 8 with the permission of the Tribunal.

(2)   An application for permission under this rule shall be made in the notice of appeal, and this notice shall be acknowledged, and a copy sent to the Commissioner, in accordance with rule 6; but no further steps in the appeal shall be taken until the application for permission has been granted.

(3)   The Commissioner may, within 14 days after the sending to him of a copy of a notice of appeal containing an application for permission under paragraph (2) above, send the Tribunal a written statement consenting or objecting to the grant of permission; and whether or not he sends such a statement the Tribunal shall decide on the application as soon as practicable after the expiry of those 14 days.

(4)   Where the Tribunal gives permission to appeal out of time, it may concurrently make an interim direction suspending the effect of the decision appealed against.

(5)   The Tribunal may decide on an application under this rule either—

    (a)   without a hearing, by consideration of the written application for permission, together with the notice from the Commissioner under paragraph (3) if any, or

    (b)   at a hearing at which the applicant and the Commissioner are given the opportunity to be heard.

NOTES

Initial Commencement
Specified date
Specified date: 30 October 2000: see r 1.

10 Applications for suspension of effect of decision

(1)   An application for a direction under paragraph 8 of Schedule 7 (suspending the effect of a relevant decision) shall be made by sending to the Tribunal written notice of the application; and this written notice may—

   (a)   be combined with the written notice of appeal against the decision to which the direction sought relates, or
   (b)   be sent after the notice of appeal and refer to that notice

and in either case shall state the grounds of the application.

(2)   As soon as practicable after receiving a notice of application under paragraph (1), the Tribunal shall send an acknowledgement to the applicant and a copy of the notice of application to the Commissioner.

(3)   Before deciding any application under this rule, the Tribunal may if it sees fit invite representations in writing from the Commissioner or hold a hearing.

(4)   Where a direction is made other than at a hearing at which both parties were present or represented, the Tribunal shall as soon as practicable notify both parties in writing of the terms of the direction.

NOTES

Initial Commencement
Specified date
Specified date: 30 October 2000: see r 1.

11 Cancellation or variation of direction for suspension

(1)   An application by the Commissioner for the cancellation or variation of a direction given under paragraph 8(2) of Schedule 7 shall be made by sending to the Tribunal written notice of the application, which shall state the grounds of the application.

(2)   As soon as practicable after receiving a notice of application under paragraph (1), the Tribunal shall send an acknowledgement to the Commissioner and a copy of the notice of application to the appellant.

(3)   Before deciding any application under this rule, the Tribunal shall either invite representations in writing from the appellant or hold a hearing at which both parties may be heard.

(4)   Where a decision on an application under this rule is made other than at a hearing at which both parties were present or represented, the Tribunal shall as soon as practicable notify both parties in writing of the decision.

NOTES

Initial Commencement
Specified date
Specified date: 30 October 2000: see r 1.

12 Notice of charge

(1)   A charge shall be laid by sending a written notice of charge to the Tribunal.

(2)   Every notice of charge shall contain the following information:—

    (a)   the name and address for service of the person charged;
    (b)   the nature of the complaint giving rise to the charge;
    (c)   the directions under section 89 which, in the Commissioner's opinion, the Tribunal ought to make in relation to the person charged

and shall be accompanied by a copy of the written statement of the Commissioner's decision on the complaint given under paragraph 8 of Schedule 5.

NOTES

Initial Commencement
Specified date
Specified date: 30 October 2000: see r 1.

13 Acknowledgement of notice of charge

As soon as practicable after receiving the notice of charge, the Tribunal shall—

    (a)   allot a number to the charge and enter it in the Register mentioned in rule 4; and
    (b)   send an acknowledgment to the Commissioner and a copy of the notice to the person charged.

NOTES

Initial Commencement
Specified date
Specified date: 30 October 2000: see r 1.

14 Reply to notice of charge

Within 28 days after the sending to him of his copy of the notice of charge, the person charged may send to the Tribunal and the Commissioner a notice in reply, containing his answer to the complaint giving rise to the charge and any representations about the directions sought by the Commissioner.

NOTES

Initial Commencement
Specified date
Specified date: 30 October 2000: see r 1.

15 Interim directions restricting or prohibiting provision of immigration advice or immigration services

(1)   The Commissioner may apply for a direction under paragraph 9(3) of Schedule 5 (restricting or prohibiting the provision of immigration advice or immigration services while the Tribunal deals with a charge) by sending to the Tribunal written notice of the application; and this written notice may—

    (a)   be combined with the written notice of charge to which the direction sought relates, or
    (b)   be sent after the notice of charge and refer to that notice

and in either case shall state the grounds of the application.

(2)   As soon as practicable after receiving a notice of application under paragraph (1), the Tribunal shall send an acknowledgement to the Commissioner and a copy of the notice of application to the person charged.

(3)   Before deciding any application under this rule, the Tribunal shall either invite representations in writing from the person charged or hold a hearing at which all parties may be heard.

NOTES

Initial Commencement
Specified date
Specified date: 30 October 2000: see r 1.

16 Procedural directions in general

(1) Any procedural direction provided for by these Rules may be made by the Tribunal either of its own motion or on the application of either party to the proceedings.

(2) In addition to every other power to make directions conferred by these Rules, the Tribunal may at any time make directions providing for—

    (a)   the consolidation of the proceedings with any other proceedings before the Tribunal, whether involving the same or different parties;

    (b)   two or more sets of proceedings to be heard together;

    (c)   the extension of the time limited by these Rules for any step in the proceedings; or

    (d)   any other arrangement which, in the opinion of the Tribunal, may facilitate the determination of the appeal or charge.

(3) Before making any procedural directions, the Tribunal may invite representations in writing or hold a hearing.

NOTES

Initial Commencement
Specified date
Specified date: 30 October 2000: see r 1.

17 Witnesses

(1) Within 42 days after the Tribunal has sent an acknowledgement under rule 6(b) or 13(b), each party shall notify the Tribunal in writing of the names of all witnesses whom he proposes to call in the proceedings.

(2) The Tribunal may invite any person to appear as a witness at the hearing of an appeal or charge.

(3) At or before the time when it makes arrangements for the hearing, the Tribunal shall notify all parties to the proceedings of the names of all witnesses who are due to appear at the hearing.

NOTES

Initial Commencement
Specified date
Specified date: 30 October 2000: see r 1.

18 Documents

(1) Within 42 days after the Tribunal has sent an acknowledgement under rule 6(b) or 13(b), each party shall—

    (a)   send to the Tribunal copies of all documents on which he proposes to rely in the proceedings; and

    (b)   send to the Tribunal a list of all other documents in his possession or control which may be relevant to issues in the proceedings, stating which he is willing to produce and which he objects to producing, with the ground of any objection.

(2)   The Tribunal, upon receiving the information and documents referred to in paragraph (1) above from any party to the proceedings, shall send copies to all other parties.

(3)   The Tribunal may at any time direct a party to the proceedings to disclose a specified document or documents of a specified description to the other party or parties and to the Tribunal.

(4)   At or before the time when he makes arrangements for the hearing, the Tribunal shall send to each party to the proceedings copies of such of the following documents as are not already in that party's possession:—

(a)   all documents furnished to the Tribunal by any party in response to procedural directions;

(b)   in the case of an appeal, the decision appealed against;

(c)   in the case of a charge, the Commissioner's statement of his decision on the complaint underlying the charge; and

(d)   any other documents in the Tribunal's possession which it considers relevant.

NOTES

Initial Commencement
Specified date
Specified date: 30 October 2000: see r 1.

19 Arrangements for the hearing

(1)   The Tribunal shall make arrangements for the hearing of an appeal or charge as soon as it is satisfied that—

(a)   all outstanding procedural directions have been complied with and there is sufficient information to allow a fair determination of the issues; or

(b)   a party has failed to comply with any reasonable directions as to the conduct of the proceedings and it is expedient for the proceedings to be determined.

(2)   In selecting a date for the hearing, the Tribunal shall consult each party to the proceedings, except that if the circumstance set out in paragraph (1)(b) obtains, the hearing may be arranged so as to take place in the absence of the party in default.

(3)   The President may direct that there shall be one or more preliminary hearings, either on a question of law or for any other purpose.

NOTES

Initial Commencement
Specified date
Specified date: 30 October 2000: see r 1.

20 The hearing

(1)   Every hearing of an appeal or charge shall be open to the public unless the Tribunal directs otherwise.

(2)   A hearing may be held in the absence of a party either—

(a)   in the circumstance set out in rule 19(1)(b), or

(b)   if the party has been notified of the date of the hearing but has failed, without reasonable excuse, to appear before the Tribunal.

(3)   At any time in the course of the hearing the Tribunal may make procedural directions, including a direction that the hearing be adjourned.

(4)   At the conclusion of a hearing, the members of the Tribunal shall retire to consider their determination.

(5)   Any member or representative of the Council on Tribunals shall be allowed to be present at the hearing, including any part of the hearing from which the public is excluded.

(6)   If the members considering an appeal or charge disagree, they shall decide by a majority.

NOTES

Initial Commencement
Specified date
Specified date: 30 October 2000: see r 1.

21 Representation

At the hearing of an appeal or charge, the appellant or person charged may appear in person or be represented by—

    (a)   a person with a general qualification within the meaning of section 71 of the Courts and Legal Services Act 1990;

    (b)   an advocate or solicitor in Scotland;

    (c)   a member of the Bar of Northern Ireland or solicitor of the Supreme Court of Northern Ireland; or

    (d)   with the permission of the Tribunal, any other person.

NOTES

Initial Commencement
Specified date
Specified date: 30 October 2000: see r 1.

22 Evidence

(1)   Oral evidence may be given either on oath or affirmation or unsworn, as the Tribunal may decide.

(2)   Subject to paragraph (3) below, the appellant in appeal proceedings, and the Commissioner in charge proceedings, shall have the burden of proving the facts on which he relies; and in either case proof shall be on a balance of probabilities and the strict rules of evidence shall not apply.

(3)   The burden of proving that any person has been guilty of criminal or fraudulent conduct shall be on the party so alleging, and proof shall be beyond reasonable doubt; but the fact that a person has been convicted of an offence shall be sufficient evidence that he committed it.

NOTES

Initial Commencement
Specified date
Specified date: 30 October 2000: see r 1.

23 Withdrawal of proceedings

(1)   An appellant may withdraw his appeal, or the Commissioner may withdraw a charge, by sending written notice to that effect to the Tribunal at any time between the sending of the notice of appeal or charge and the date of the main hearing.

(2)   The Tribunal shall send a copy of a notice under paragraph (1) to every other party to the proceedings.

(3)   The parties to any proceedings may at any time apply to settle them by sending an agreed draft order to the Tribunal.

(4)   On receiving an agreed draft order, the Tribunal shall either—

  (a)   make an order in the terms of that draft, or
  (b)   state its reasons for not making an order in those terms;
and the Tribunal shall send the order, or as the case may be a letter recording its reasons for not making an order, to the parties.

NOTES

Initial Commencement
Specified date
Specified date: 30 October 2000: see r 1.

24 Determination of the appeal or charge

(1)   The Tribunal may either announce its decision on any appeal or charge at the conclusion of the main hearing or reserve its decision.

(2)   In either case, as soon as possible after the decision the Tribunal shall draw up a formal order, stating:—

  (a)   whether the appeal or charge is upheld or dismissed; and
  (b)   any direction made by the Tribunal under section 88 or 89.

(3)   The order shall be sent to all parties to the proceedings and shall be accompanied by a statement of the reasons for the Tribunal's decision, and both the order and the statement of reasons shall be signed by the member presiding at the hearing (or if he is unavailable, by another member who was present at the hearing).

NOTES

Initial Commencement
Specified date
Specified date: 30 October 2000: see r 1.

25 Reopening of determination made in absence of party

(1)   Where a decision is made following a hearing in the absence of one of the parties, that party may apply to the Tribunal to set aside its decision and re-list the proceedings for hearing.

(2)   An application under paragraph (1) above shall not be granted unless the applicant satisfies the Tribunal that he had a reasonable excuse for failing to comply with the direction, or to attend the hearing, as the case may be.

NOTES

Initial Commencement
Specified date
Specified date: 30 October 2000: see r 1.

26 Irregularities

(1)   Any irregularity resulting from failure to comply with any provision of these Rules before the Tribunal has reached its decision shall not of itself render the proceedings void.

(2)   In any such case the Tribunal shall, if it considers that any person may have been prejudiced, take such steps as it thinks fit to cure the irregularity before reaching its decision.

(3)   Clerical mistakes in any document recording a decision of the Tribunal, or errors arising in such a document from an accidental slip or omission, may be corrected by a legally qualified member.

NOTES

Initial Commencement
Specified date
Specified date: 30 October 2000: see r 1.

27 Notices etc

(1)   Any notice or other document required or authorised by these Rules to be sent or given to any person or authority may be delivered or sent by post to an address, or sent by fax to a fax number, specified by the person or authority to whom the notice or document is directed.

(2)   If any notice or other document is sent or given to a person appearing to the authority or person sending it to represent that party, it shall be deemed to have been sent or given to that party.

NOTES

Initial Commencement
Specified date
Specified date: 30 October 2000: see r 1.

28 Time

Where the time limited by these Rules for doing any thing expires on a Saturday, Sunday, Christmas day, Good Friday or bank holiday, the time limit shall be deemed to have been complied with if that thing is done on the next succeeding working day.

NOTES

Initial Commencement
Specified date
Specified date: 30 October 2000: see r 1.

Signed by authority of the Lord Chancellor
Jane Kennedy
Parliamentary Secretary
Lord Chancellor's Department
Dated 4th October 2000

EUROPEAN LEGISLATION

CONSOLIDATED VERSION OF THE TREATY ON EUROPEAN UNION

(as amended by the Treaty of Amsterdam) signed in Maastricht on 7 February 1992, OJ C191, 29 June 1992

Note   Only provisions relevant to this work are printed below.

(92/C 191/01)

TITLE I   COMMON PROVISIONS

Article 2 *(ex Article B)*

The Union shall set itself the following objectives:

— to promote economic and social progress and a high level of employment and to achieve balanced and sustainable development, in particular through the creation of an area without internal frontiers, through the strengthening of economic and social cohesion and through the establishment of economic and monetary union, ultimately including a single currency in accordance with the provisions of this Treaty;

— to assert its identity on the international scene, in particular through the implementation of a common foreign and security policy including the progressive framing of a common defence policy, which might lead to a common defence, in accordance with the provisions of Article 17;

— to strengthen the protection of the rights and interests of the nationals of its Member States through the introduction of a citizenship of the Union;

— to maintain and develop the Union as an area of freedom, security and justice, in which the free movement of persons is assured in conjunction with appropriate measures with respect to external border controls, asylum, immigration and the prevention and combating of crime;

— to maintain in full the acquis communautaire and build on it with a view to considering to what extent the policies and forms of cooperation introduced by this Treaty may need to be revised with the aim of ensuring the effectiveness of the mechanisms and the institutions of the Community.

The objectives of the Union shall be achieved as provided in this Treaty and in accordance with the conditions and the timetable set out therein while respecting the principle of subsidiarity as defined in Article 5 of the Treaty establishing the European Community.

Article 6 *(ex Article F)*

1.   The Union is founded on the principles of liberty, democracy, respect for human rights and fundamental freedoms, and the rule of law, principles which are common to the Member States.

2.   The Union shall respect fundamental rights, as guaranteed by the European Convention for the Protection of Human Rights and Fundamental Freedoms signed in Rome on 4 November 1950 and as they result from the constitutional traditions common to the Member States, as general principles of Community law.

3.   The Union shall respect the national identities of its Member States.

4.   The Union shall provide itself with the means necessary to attain its objectives and carry through its policies.

Title VI   Provisions on Co-operation in the fields of Justice and Home Affairs

Article 29 *(ex Article K1)*

For the purposes of achieving the objectives of the Union, in particular the free movement of persons, and without prejudice to the powers of the European Community, Member States shall regard the following areas as matters of common interest:

— asylum policy;
— rules governing the crossing by persons of the external borders of the Member States and the exercise of controls thereon;
— immigration policy and policy regarding nationals of third countries;
  (a) conditions of entry and movement by nationals of third countries on the territory of Member States;
  (b) conditions of residence by nationals of third countries on the territory of Member States, including family reunion and access to employment;
  (c) combatting unauthorized immigration, residence and work by nationals of third countries on the territory of Member States;
— combating drug addiction in so far as this is not covered by 7 to 9;
— combating fraud on an international scale in so far as this is not covered by 7 to 9;
— judicial cooperation in civil matters;
— judicial cooperation in criminal matters;
— customs cooperation;
— police cooperation for the purposes of preventing and combating terrorism, unlawful drug trafficking and other serious forms of international crime, including if necessary certain aspects of customs cooperation, in connection with the organization of a Union-wide system for exchanging information within a European Police Office (Europol).

CONSOLIDATED VERSION OF THE TREATY ESTABLISHING THE EUROPEAN COMMUNITY

(as amended by the Treaty on European Union and the Treaty of Amsterdam) signed in Rome on 25 March 1957, OJ C340, 10 November 1997

NOTE
Title as amended by Article G(1) of the Treaty on European Union (hereinafter referred to as 'TEU'). The reader will find in the following pages an amended version of the Treaty establishing the European Economic Community as amended by the Treaty of Amsterdam and the Treaty on European Union. Only provisions relevant to this work are printed below.

Part one   Principles

Article 3 *(ex Article 3)*

1.   For the purposes set out in Article 2, the activities of the Community shall include, as provided in this Treaty and in accordance with the timetable set out therein:

  (*a*) the prohibition, as between Member States, of customs duties and quantitative restrictions on the import and export of goods, and of all other measures having equivalent effect;

(*b*) a common commercial policy;

(*c*) an internal market characterised by the abolition, as between Member States, of obstacles to the free movement of goods, persons, services and capital;

(*d*) measures concerning the entry and movement of persons as provided for in Title IV;

(*e*) a common policy in the sphere of agriculture and fisheries;

(*f*) a common policy in the sphere of transport;

(*g*) a system ensuring that competition in the internal market is not distorted;

(*h*) the approximation of the laws of Member States to the extent required for the functioning of the common market;

(*i*) the promotion of coordination between employment policies of the Member States with a view to enhancing their effectiveness by developing a coordinated strategy for employment;

(*j*) a policy in the social sphere comprising a European Social Fund;

(*k*) the strengthening of economic and social cohesion;

(*l*) a policy in the sphere of the environment;

(*m*) the strengthening of the competitiveness of Community industry;

(*n*) the promotion of research and technological development;

(*o*) encouragement for the establishment and development of trans-European networks;

(*p*) a contribution to the attainment of a high level of health protection;

(*q*) a contribution to education and training of quality and to the flowering of the cultures of the Member States;

(*r*) a policy in the sphere of development cooperation;

(*s*) the association of the overseas countries and territories in order to increase trade and promote jointly economic and social development;

(*t*) a contribution to the strengthening of consumer protection;

(*u*) measures in the spheres of energy, civil protection and tourism.

2.   In all the activities referred to in this Article, the Community shall aim to eliminate inequalities, and to promote equality, between men and women.

Article 5 *(ex Article 3b)*

The Community shall act within the limits of the powers conferred upon it by this Treaty and of the objectives assigned to it therein.

In areas which do not fall within its exclusive competence, the Community shall take action, in accordance with the principle of subsidiarity, only if and insofar as the objectives of the proposed action cannot be sufficiently achieved by the Member States and can therefore, by reason of the scale or effects of the proposed action, be better achieved by the Community.

Any action by the Community shall not go beyond what is necessary to achieve the objectives of this Treaty.

Article 12 *(ex Article 6)*

Within the scope of application of this Treaty, and without prejudice to any special provisions contained therein, any discrimination on grounds of nationality shall be prohibited.

The Council, acting in accordance with the procedure referred to in Article 251, may adopt rules designed to prohibit such discrimination.

Article 13 *(ex Article 6a)*

Without prejudice to the other provisions of this Treaty and within the limits of the powers conferred by it upon the Community, the Council, acting unanimously on a proposal from the Commission and after consulting the European Parliament, may take appropriate action to combat discrimination based on sex, racial or ethnic origin, religion or belief, disability, age or sexual orientation.

Article 14 *(ex Article 7a)*

1.   The Community shall adopt measures with the aim of progressively establishing the internal market over a period expiring on 31 December 1992, in accordance with the provisions of this Article and of Articles 15, 26, 47(2), 49, 80, 93 and 95 and without prejudice to the other provisions of this Treaty.

2.   The internal market shall comprise an area without internal frontiers in which the free movement of goods, persons, services and capital is ensured in accordance with the provisions of this Treaty.

3.   The Council, acting by a qualified majority on a proposal from the Commission, shall determine the guidelines and conditions necessary to ensure balanced progress in all the sectors concerned.

PART TWO   CITIZENSHIP OF THE UNION

Article 17 *(ex Article 8)*

1.   Citizenship of the Union is hereby established. Every person holding the nationality of a Member State shall be a citizen of the Union. Citizenship of the Union shall complement and not replace national citizenship.

2.   Citizens of the Union shall enjoy the rights conferred by this Treaty and shall be subject to the duties imposed thereby.

Article 18 *(ex Article 8a)*

1.   Every citizen of the Union shall have the right to move and reside freely within the territory of the Member States, subject to the limitations and conditions laid down in this Treaty and by the measures adopted to give it effect.

2.   The Council may adopt provisions with a view to facilitating the exercise of the rights referred to in paragraph 1; save as otherwise provided in this Treaty, the Council shall act in accordance with the procedure referred to in Article 251. The Council shall act unanimously throughout this procedure.

TITLE III   FREE MOVEMENT OF PERSONS, SERVICES AND CAPITAL

CHAPTER 1   WORKERS

Article 39 *(ex Article 48)*

1.   Freedom of movement for workers shall be secured within the Community.

2.   Such freedom of movement shall entail the abolition of any discrimination based on nationality between workers of the Member States as regards employment, remuneration and other conditions of work and employment.

3.   It shall entail the right, subject to limitations justified on grounds of public policy, public security or public health:

    (*a*)   to accept offers of employment actually made;
    (*b*)   to move freely within the territory of Member States for this purpose;

(c) to stay in a Member State for the purpose of employment in accordance with the provisions governing the employment of nationals of that State laid down by law, regulation or administrative action;

(d) to remain in the territory of a Member State after having been employed in that State, subject to conditions which shall be embodied in implementing regulations to be drawn up by the Commission.

4.   The provisions of this Article shall not apply to employment in the public service.

Article 40 *(ex Article 49)*

The Council shall, acting in accordance with the procedure referred to in Article 251 and after consulting the Economic and Social Committee, issue directives or make regulations setting out the measures required to bring about freedom of movement for workers, as defined in Article 39, in particular:

(a) by ensuring close cooperation between national employment services;

(b) by abolishing those administrative procedures and practices and those qualifying periods in respect of eligibility for available employment, whether resulting from national legislation or from agreements previously concluded between Member States, the maintenance of which would form an obstacle to liberalisation of the movement of workers;

(c) by abolishing all such qualifying periods and other restrictions provided for either under national legislation or under agreements previously concluded between Member States as imposed on workers of other Member States conditions regarding the free choice of employment other than those imposed on workers of the State concerned;

(d) by setting up appropriate machinery to bring offers of employment into touch with applications for employment and to facilitate the achievement of a balance between supply and demand in the employment market in such a way as to avoid serious threats to the standard of living and level of employment in the various regions and industries.

Article 41 *(ex Article 50)*

Member States shall, within the framework of a joint programme, encourage the exchange of young workers.

Article 42 *(ex Article 51)*

The Council shall, acting in accordance with the procedure referred to in Article 251, adopt such measures in the field of social security as are necessary to provide freedom of movement for workers; to this end, it shall make arrangements to secure for migrant workers and their dependants:

(a) aggregation, for the purpose of acquiring and retaining the right to benefit and of calculating the amount of benefit, of all periods taken into account under the laws of the several countries;

(b) payment of benefits to persons resident in the territories of Member States.

The Council shall act unanimously throughout the procedure referred to in Article 251.

CHAPTER 2   RIGHT OF ESTABLISHMENT

Article 43 *(ex Article 52)*

Within the framework of the provisions set out below, restrictions on the freedom of establishment of nationals of a Member State in the territory of another Member State shall be prohibited. Such prohibition shall also apply to restrictions on the setting-up of agencies, branches or subsidiaries by nationals of any Member State established in the territory of any Member State.

Freedom of establishment shall include the right to take up and pursue activities as self-employed persons and to set up and manage undertakings, in particular companies or firms within the meaning of the second paragraph of Article 48, under the conditions laid down for its own nationals by the law of the country where such establishment is effected, subject to the provisions of the Chapter relating to capital.

Article 44 *(ex Article 54)*

1.   In order to attain freedom of establishment as regards a particular activity, the Council, acting in accordance with the procedure referred to in Article 251 and after consulting the Economic and Social Committee, shall act by means of directives.

2.   The Council and the Commission shall carry out the duties devolving upon them under the preceding provisions, in particular:

  (*a*) by according, as a general rule, priority treatment to activities where freedom of establishment makes a particularly valuable contribution to the development of production and trade;

  (*b*) by ensuring close cooperation between the competent authorities in the Member States in order to ascertain the particular situation within the Community of the various activities concerned;

  (*c*) by abolishing those administrative procedures and practices, whether resulting from national legislation or from agreements previously concluded between Member States, the maintenance of which would form an obstacle to freedom of establishment;

  (*d*) by ensuring that workers of one Member State employed in the territory of another Member State may remain in that territory for the purpose of taking up activities therein as self-employed persons, where they satisfy the conditions which they would be required to satisfy if they were entering that State at the time when they intended to take up such activities;

  (*e*) by enabling a national of one Member State to acquire and use land and buildings situated in the territory of another Member State, insofar as this does not conflict with the principles laid down in Article 33(2);

  (*f*) by effecting the progressive abolition of restrictions on freedom of establishment in every branch of activity under consideration, both as regards the conditions for setting up agencies, branches or subsidiaries in the territory of a Member State and as regards the subsidiaries in the territory of a Member State and as regards the conditions governing the entry of personnel belonging to the main establishment into managerial or supervisory posts in such agencies, branches or subsidiaries;

  (*g*) by coordinating to the necessary extent the safeguards which, for the protection of the interests of members and other, are required by Member States of companies or firms within the meaning of the second paragraph of Article 48 with a view to making such safeguards equivalent throughout the Community;

  (*h*) by satisfying themselves that the conditions of establishment are not distorted by aids granted by Member States.

Article 45 *(ex Article 55)*

The provisions of this Chapter shall not apply, so far as any given Member State is concerned, to activities which in that State are connected, even occasionally, with the exercise of official authority.

The Council may, acting by a qualified majority on a proposal from the Commission, rule that the provisions of this Chapter shall not apply to certain activities.

Article 46 *(ex Article 56)*

1.   The provisions of this Chapter and measures taken in pursuance thereof shall not prejudice the applicability of provisions laid down by law, regulation or administrative action providing for special treatment for foreign nationals on grounds of public policy, public security or public health.

2.   The Council shall, acting in accordance with the procedure referred to in Article 251, issue directives for the coordination of the abovementioned provisions.

Article 47 *(ex Article 57)*

1.   In order to make it easier for persons to take up and pursue activities as self-employed persons, the Council shall, acting in accordance with the procedure referred to in Article 251, issue directives for the mutual recognition of diplomas, certificates and other evidence of formal qualifications.

2.   For the same purpose, the Council shall, acting in accordance with the procedure referred to in Article 251, issue directives for the coordination of the provisions laid down by law, regulation or administrative action in Member States concerning the taking-up and pursuit of activities as self-employed persons. The Council, acting unanimously throughout the procedure referred to in Article 251, shall decide on directives the implementation of which involves in at least one Member State amendment of the existing principles laid down by law governing the professions with respect to training and conditions of access for natural persons. In other cases the Council shall act by qualified majority.

3.   In the case of the medical and allied and pharmaceutical professions, the progressive abolition of restrictions shall be dependent upon coordination of the conditions for their exercise in the various Member States.

Article 48 *(ex Article 58)*

Companies or firms formed in accordance with the law of a Member State and having their registered office, central administration or principal place of business within the Community shall, for the purposes of this Chapter, be treated in the same way as natural persons who are nationals of Member States.

   'Companies or firms' means companies or firms constituted under civil or commercial law, including cooperative societies, and other legal persons governed by public or private law, save for those which are non-profit-making.

CHAPTER 3   SERVICES

Article 49 *(ex Article 59)*

Within the framework of the provisions set out below, restrictions on freedom to provide services within the Community shall be prohibited in respect of nationals of Member States who are established in a State of the Community other than that of the person for whom the services are intended.

   The Council may, acting by a qualified majority on a proposal from the Commission, extend the provisions of the Chapter to nationals of a third country who provide services and who are established within the Community.

Article 50 *(ex Article 60)*

Services shall be considered to be 'services' within the meaning of this Treaty where they are normally provided for remuneration, insofar as they are not governed by the provisions relating to freedom of movement for goods, capital and persons.

'Services' shall in particular include:

- (*a*) activities of an industrial character;
- (*b*) activities of a commercial character;
- (*c*) activities of craftsmen;
- (*d*) activities of the professions.

Without prejudice to the provisions of the Chapter relating to the right of establishment, the person providing a service may, in order to do so, temporarily pursue his activity in the State where the service is provided, under the same conditions as are imposed by that State on its own nationals.

Article 51 *(ex Article 61)*

1.   Freedom to provide services in the field of transport shall be governed by the provisions of the Title relating to transport.

2.   The liberalisation of banking and insurance services connected with movements of capital shall be effected in step with the liberalisation of movement of capital.

Article 52 *(ex Article 63)*

1.   In order to achieve the liberalisation of a specific service, the Council shall, on a proposal from the Commission and after consulting the Economic and Social Committee and the European Parliament, issue directives acting by a qualified majority.

2.   As regards the directives referred to in paragraph 1, priority shall as a general rule be given to those services which directly affect production costs or the liberalisation of which helps to promote trade in goods.

Article 53 (ex Article 64)

The Member States declare their readiness to undertake the liberalisation of services beyond the extent required by the directives issued pursuant to Article 52(1), if their general economic situation and the situation of the economic sector concerned so permit.

To this end, the Commission shall make recommendations to the Member States concerned.

Article 54 *(ex Article 65)*

As long as restrictions on freedom to provide services have not been abolished, each Member State shall apply such restrictions without distinction on grounds of nationality or residence to all persons providing services within the meaning of the first paragraph of Article 49.

Article 55 *(ex Article 66)*

The provisions of Articles 45 to 48 shall apply to the matters covered by this Chapter.

Article 61 *(ex Article 73i)*

In order to establish progressively an area of freedom, security and justice, the Council shall adopt:

(*a*) within a period of five years after the entry into force of the Treaty of Amsterdam, measures aimed at ensuring the free movement of persons in accordance with Article 14, in conjunction with directly related flanking measures with respect to external border controls, asylum and immigration, in accordance with the provisions of Article 62(2) and (3) and Article 63(1)(*a*) and (2)(*a*), and measures to prevent and combat crime in accordance with the provisions of Article 31(*e*) of the Treaty on European Union;

(*b*) other measures in the fields of asylum, immigration and safeguarding the rights of nationals of third countries, in accordance with the provisions of Article 63;

(*c*) measures in the field of judicial cooperation in civil matters as provided for in Article 65;

(*d*) appropriate measures to encourage and strengthen administrative cooperation, as provided for in Article 66;

(*e*) measures in the field of police and judicial cooperation in criminal matters aimed at a high level of security by preventing and combating crime within the Union in accordance with the provisions of the Treaty on European Union.

Article 62 *(ex Article 73j)*

The Council, acting in accordance with the procedure referred to in Article 67, shall, within a period of five years after the entry into force of the Treaty of Amsterdam, adopt:

(1) measures with a view to ensuring, in compliance with Article 14, the absence of any controls on persons, be they citizens of the Union or nationals of third countries, when crossing internal borders;

(2) measures on the crossing of the external borders of the Member States which shall establish:

(*a*) standards and procedures to be followed by Member States in carrying out checks on persons at such borders;

(*b*) rules on visas for intended stays of no more than three months, including:

(i) the list of third countries whose nationals must be in possession of visas when crossing the external borders and those whose nationals are exempt from that requirement;

(ii) the procedures and conditions for issuing visas by Member States;

(iii) a uniform format for visas;

(iv) rules on a uniform visa;

(3) measures setting out the conditions under which nationals of third countries shall have the freedom to travel within the territory of the Member States during a period of no more than three months.

Article 63 *(ex Article 73k)*

The Council, acting in accordance with the procedure referred to in Article 67, shall, within a period of five years after the entry into force of the Treaty of Amsterdam, adopt:

(1) measures on asylum, in accordance with the Geneva Convention of 28 July 1951 and the Protocol of 31 January 1967 relating to the status of refugees and other relevant treaties, within the following areas:

    (*a*) criteria and mechanisms for determining which Member State is responsible for considering an application for asylum submitted by a national of a third country in one of the Member States,

    (*b*) minimum standards on the reception of asylum seekers in Member States,

    (*c*) minimum standards with respect to the qualification of nationals of third countries as refugees,

    (*d*) minimum standards on procedures in Member States for granting or withdrawing refugee status;

(2) measures on refugees and displaced persons within the following areas:

    (*a*) minimum standards for giving temporary protection to displaced persons from third countries who cannot return to their country of origin and for persons who otherwise need international protection,

    (*b*) promoting a balance of effort between Member States in receiving and bearing the consequences of receiving refugees and displaced persons;

(3) measures on immigration policy within the following areas:

    (*a*) conditions of entry and residence, and standards on procedures for the issue by Member States of long term visas and residence permits, including those for the purpose of family reunion,

    (*b*) illegal immigration and illegal residence, including repatriation of illegal residents;

(4) measures defining the rights and conditions under which nationals of third countries who are legally resident in a Member State may reside in other Member States.

Measures adopted by the Council pursuant to points 3 and 4 shall not prevent any Member State from maintaining or introducing in the areas concerned national provisions which are compatible with this Treaty and with international agreements.

    Measures to be adopted pursuant to points 2(*b*), 3(*a*) and 4 shall not be subject to the five year period referred to above.

Article 64 *(ex Article 73l)*

1. This Title shall not affect the exercise of the responsibilities incumbent upon Member States with regard to the maintenance of law and order and the safeguarding of internal security.

2. In the event of one or more Member States being confronted with an emergency situation characterised by a sudden inflow of nationals of third countries and without prejudice to paragraph 1, the Council may, acting by qualified majority on a proposal from the Commission, adopt provisional measures of a duration not exceeding six months for the benefit of the Member States concerned.

Article 65 *(ex Article 73m)*

Measures in the field of judicial cooperation in civil matters having cross-border implications, to be taken in accordance with Article 67 and insofar as necessary for the proper functioning of the internal market, shall include:

    (*a*) improving and simplifying:
       — the system for cross-border service of judicial and extrajudicial documents;
       — cooperation in the taking of evidence;
       — the recognition and enforcement of decisions in civil and commercial cases, including decisions in extrajudicial cases;

    (*b*) promoting the compatibility of the rules applicable in the Member States concerning the conflict of laws and of jurisdiction;

    (*c*) eliminating obstacles to the good functioning of civil proceedings, if necessary by promoting the compatibility of the rules on civil procedure applicable in the Member States.

Article 66 *(ex Article 73n)*

The Council, acting in accordance with the procedure referred to in Article 67, shall take measures to ensure cooperation between the relevant departments of the administrations of the Member States in the areas covered by this Title, as well as between those departments and the Commission.

Article 67 *(ex Article 73o)*

1.   During a transitional period of five years following the entry into force of the Treaty of Amsterdam, the Council shall act unanimously on a proposal from the Commission or on the initiative of a Member State and after consulting the European Parliament.

2.   After this period of five years:

— the Council shall act on proposals from the Commission; the Commission shall examine any request made by a Member State that it submit a proposal to the Council;
— the Council, acting unanimously after consulting the European Parliament, shall take a decision with a view to providing for all or parts of the areas covered by this Title to be governed by the procedure referred to in Article 251 and adapting the provisions relating to the powers of the Court of Justice.

3.   By derogation from paragraphs 1 and 2, measures referred to in Article 62(2)(*b*) (i) and (iii) shall, from the entry into force of the Treaty of Amsterdam, be adopted by the Council acting by a qualified majority on a proposal from the Commission and after consulting the European Parliament.

4.   By derogation from paragraph 2, measures referred to in Article 62(2)(*b*) (ii) and (iv) shall, after a period of five years following the entry into force of the Treaty of Amsterdam, be adopted by the Council acting in accordance with the procedure referred to in Article 251.

Article 68 *(ex Article 73p)*

1.   Article 234 shall apply to this Title under the following circumstances and conditions: where a question on the interpretation of this Title or on the validity or interpretation of acts of the institutions of the Community based on this Title is raised in a case pending before a court or a tribunal of a Member State against whose decisions there is no judicial remedy under national law, that court or tribunal shall, if it considers that a decision on the question is necessary to enable it to give judgment, request the Court of Justice to give a ruling thereon.

2.   In any event, the Court of Justice shall not have jurisdiction to rule on any measure or decision taken pursuant to Article 62(1) relating to the maintenance of law and order and the safeguarding of internal security.

3.   The Council, the Commission or a Member State may request the Court of Justice to give a ruling on a question of interpretation of this Title or of acts of the institutions of the Community based on this Title. The ruling given by the Court of Justice in response to such a request shall not apply to judgments of courts or tribunals of the Member States which have become res judicata.

Article 69 *(ex Article 73q)*

The application of this Title shall be subject to the provisions of the Protocol on the position of the United Kingdom and Ireland and to the Protocol on the position of Denmark and without prejudice to the Protocol on the application of certain aspects of Article 14 of the Treaty establishing the European Community to the United Kingdom and to Ireland.

COUNCIL DIRECTIVE (64/221/EEC)

of 25 February 1964 on the co-ordination of special measures concerning the movement and residence of foreign nationals which are justified on grounds of public policy, public security or public health

The Council of The European Economic Community,

Having regard to the Treaty establishing the European Economic Community, and in particular Article 56(2) thereof;

Having regard to Council Regulation of 16 August 1961[1] on initial measures to bring about free movement of workers within the Community, and in particular Article 47 thereof;

Having regard to Council Directive of 16 August 1961[2] on administrative procedures and practices governing the entry into and employment and residence in a member state of workers and their families from other member states of the Community;

Having regard to the General Programme[3] for the abolition of restrictions on freedom of establishment and on freedom to provide services, and in particular Title II of each such programme;

Having regard to the Council Directive of 25 February 1964[4] on the abolition of restrictions on movement and residence within the Community for nationals of member states with regard to establishment and the provision of services;

Having regard to the proposal from the Commission;

Having regard to the Opinion of the European Parliament[5];

Having regard to the Opinion of the Economic and Social Committee[6];

Whereas co-ordination of provisions laid down by law, regulation or administrative action which provide for special treatment for foreign nationals on grounds of public policy, public security or public health should in the first place deal with the conditions for entry and residence of nationals of member states moving within the Community either in order to pursue activities as employed or self-employed persons, or as recipients of services;

Whereas such co-ordination presupposes in particular an approximation of the procedures followed in each member state when invoking grounds of public policy, public security or public health in matters connected with the movement or residence of foreign nationals;

Whereas in each member state, nationals of other member states should have adequate legal remedies available to them in respect of the decisions of the administration in such matters;

Whereas it would be of little practical use to compile a list of diseases and disabilities which might endanger public health, public policy or public security and it would be difficult to make such a list exhaustive; whereas it is sufficient to classify such diseases and disabilities in groups;

NOTES
1 OJ No 57, 26.8.1961, p 1073/61.
2 OJ No 80, 13.12.1961, p 1513/61.
3 OJ No 2, 15.1.1962, pp 32/62 and 36/62.
4 OJ No 56, 4.4.1964, p 845/64.
5 OJ No 134, 14.12.1967, p2861/62.
6 OJ No 56, 4.4.1964, p 856/64.

Has adopted this Directive:

Article 1

1   The provisions of this Directive shall apply to any national of a member state who resides in or travels to another member state of the Community, either in order to pursue an activity as an employed or self-employed person, or as a recipient of services.

2   These provisions shall apply also to the spouse and to members of the family who come within the provisions of the regulations and directives adopted in this field in pursuance of the Treaty.

Article 2

1   This Directive relates to all measures concerning entry into their territory, issue or renewal of residence permits, or expulsion from their territory, taken by member states on grounds of public policy, public security or public health.

2   Such grounds shall not be invoked to service economic ends.

Article 3

1   Measures taken on grounds of public policy or of public security shall be based exclusively on the personal conduct of the individual concerned.

2   Previous criminal convictions shall not in themselves constitute grounds for the taking of such measures.

3   Expiry of the identity card or passport used by the person concerned to enter the host country and to obtain a residence permit shall not justify expulsion from the territory.

4   The state which issued the identity card or passport shall allow the holder of such document to re-enter its territory without any formality even if the document is no longer valid or the nationality of the holder is in dispute.

Article 4

1   The only diseases or disabilities justifying refusal of entry into a territory or refusal to issue a first residence permit shall be those listed in the Annex to this Directive.

2   Diseases or disabilities occurring after a first residence permit has been issued shall not justify refusal to renew the residence permit or expulsion from the territory.

3   Member states shall not introduce new provisions or practices which are more restrictive than those in force at the date of notification of this Directive.

Article 5

1   A decision to grant or to refuse a first residence permit shall be taken as soon as possible and in any event not later than six months from the date of application for the permit.

The person concerned shall be allowed to remain temporarily in the territory pending a decision either to grant or to refuse a residence permit.

2   The host country may, in cases where this is considered essential, request the member state of origin of the applicant, and if need be other member states, to provide information concerning any previous police record. Such enquiries shall not be made as a matter of routine. The member state consulted shall give its reply within two months.

Article 6

The person concerned shall be informed of the grounds of public policy, public security, or public health upon which the decision taken in his case is based, unless this is contrary to the interests of the security of the state involved.

Article 7

The person concerned shall be officially notified of any decision to refuse the issue or renewal of a residence permit or to expel him from the territory. The period allowed for leaving the territory shall be stated in this notification. Save in cases of urgency, this period shall be not less than fifteen days if the person concerned has not yet been granted a residence permit and not less than one month in all other cases.

Article 8

The person concerned shall have the same legal remedies in respect of any decision concerning entry, or refusing the issue or renewal of a residence permit, or ordering expulsion from the territory, as are available to nationals of the state concerned in respect of acts of the administration.

Article 9

1   Where there is no right of appeal to a court of law, or where such appeal may be only in respect of the legal validity of the decision, or where the appeal cannot have suspensory effect, a decision refusing renewal of a residence permit or ordering the expulsion of the holder of a residence permit from the territory shall not be taken by the administrative authority, save in cases of urgency, until an opinion has been obtained from a competent authority of the host country before which the person concerned enjoys such rights of defence and of assistance or representation as the domestic law of that country provides for.

This authority shall not be the same as that empowered to take the decision refusing renewal of the residence permit or ordering expulsion.

2   Any decision refusing the issue of a first residence permit or ordering expulsion of the person concerned before the issue of the permit shall, where that person so requests, be referred for consideration to the authority whose prior opinion is required under paragraph 1. The person concerned shall then be entitled to submit his defence in person, except where this would be contrary to the interests of national security.

Article 10

1   Member states shall within six months of notification of this Directive put into force the measures necessary to comply with its provisions and shall forthwith inform the Commission thereof.

2   Member states shall ensure that the texts of the main provisions of national law which they adopt in the field governed by this Directive are communicated to the Commission.

Article 11

This Directive is addressed to the member states.

Done at Brussels, 25 February 1964.

Annex

A   Diseases which might endanger public health:

1   Diseases subject to quarantine listed in International Health Regulation No 2 of the World Health Organisation of 25 May 1951;
2   Tuberculosis of the respiratory system in an active state or showing a tendency to develop;
3   Syphilis;

4   Other infectious diseases or contagious parasitic diseases if they are the subject of provisions for the protection of nationals of the host country.

B   *Diseases and disabilities which might threaten public policy or public security:*

1   Drug addiction;
2   Profound mental disturbance; manifest conditions of psychotic disturbance with agitation, delirium, hallucinations or confusion.

REGULATION (EEC) 1612/68 OF THE COUNCIL

of 15 October 1968 on freedom of movement for workers within the Community

The Council of The European Communities,

Having regard to the Treaty establishing the European Economic Community, and in particular Article 49 thereof;

Having regard to the proposal from the Commission;

Having regard to the Opinion of the European Parliament[1];

Having regard to the Opinion of the Economic and Social Committee[2];

Whereas freedom of movement for workers should be secured within the Community by the end of the transitional period at the latest; whereas the attainment of this objective entails the abolition of any discrimination based on nationality between workers of the member states as regards employment, remuneration and other conditions of work and employment, as well as the right of such workers to move freely within the Community in order to pursue activities as employed persons subject to any limitations justified on grounds of public policy, public security or public health;

Whereas by reason in particular of the early establishment of the customs union and in order to ensure the simultaneous completion of the principal foundations of the Community, provisions should be adopted to enable the objectives laid down in Articles 48 and 49 of the Treaty in the field of freedom of movement to be achieved and to perfect measures adopted successively under Regulation No 15[3] on the first steps for attainment of freedom of movement and under Council Regulation No 38/EEC[4] of 25 March 1964 on freedom of movement for workers within the Community;

Whereas freedom of movement constitutes a fundamental right of workers and their families; whereas mobility of labour within the Community must be one of the means by which the worker is guaranteed the possibility of improving his living and working conditions and promoting his social advancement, while helping to satisfy the requirements of the economies of the member states; whereas the right of all workers in the member states to pursue the activity of their choice within the Community should be affirmed;

Whereas such right must be enjoyed without discrimination by permanent, seasonal and frontier workers and by those who pursue their activities for the purpose of providing services;

Whereas the right of freedom of movement, in order that it may be exercised, by objective standards, in freedom and dignity, requires that equality of treatment shall be ensured in fact and in law in respect of all matters relating to the actual pursuit of activities as employed persons and to eligibility for housing, and also that obstacles to the mobility of workers shall be eliminated, in particular as regards the worker's right to be joined by his family and the conditions for the integration of that family into the host country;

Whereas the principle of non-discrimination between Community workers entails that all nationals of member states have the same priority as regards employment as is enjoyed by national workers;

Whereas it is necessary to strengthen the machinery for vacancy clearance, in particular by developing direct co-operation between the central employment services and also between the regional services, as well as by increasing and co-ordinating the exchange of information in order to ensure in a general way a clearer picture of the labour market; whereas workers wishing to move should also be regularly informed of living and working conditions; whereas, furthermore, measures should be provided for the case where a member state undergoes or foresees disturbances on its labour market which may seriously threaten the standard of living and level of employment in a region or an industry; whereas for this purpose the exchange of information, aimed at discouraging workers from moving to such a region or industry, constitutes the method to be applied in the first place but, where necessary, it should be possible to strengthen the results of such exchange of information by temporarily suspending the abovementioned machinery, any such decision to be taken at Community level;

Whereas close links exist between freedom of movement for workers, employment and vocational training, particularly where the latter aims at putting workers in a position to take up offers of employment from other regions of the Community; whereas such links make it necessary that the problems arising in this connection should no longer be studied in isolation but viewed as inter-dependent, account also being taken of the problems of employment at the regional level; and whereas it is therefore necessary to direct the efforts of member states toward coordinating their employment policies at Community level;

Whereas the Council, by its Decision of 15 October 1968[5] made Article 48 and 49 of the Treaty and also the measures taken in implementation thereof applicable to the French overseas departments;

NOTES
1 OJNo 268, 6.11.1967, p 9.
2 ONNo 298, 7.12.1967, p 10.
3 OJNo 57, 26.8.1961, p 1073/61.
4 OJNo 62, 17.4.1964, p 965/64.
5 OJNo 257, 19.10.1968, p 1.

Has adopted this Regulation:

PART I   EMPLOYMENT AND WORKERS' FAMILIES

TITLE I   ELIGIBILITY FOR EMPLOYMENT

Article 1

1   Any national of a member state, shall, irrespective of his place of residence, have the right to take up an activity as an employed person, and to pursue such activity, within the territory of another member state in accordance with the provisions laid down by law, regulation or administrative action governing the employment of nationals of that state.

2   He shall, in particular, have the right to take up available employment in the territory of another member state with the same priority as nationals of that state.

Article 2

Any national of a member state and any employer pursuing an activity in the territory of a member state may exchange their applications for and offers of employment, and may conclude and perform contracts of employment in accordance with the provisions in force laid down by law, regulation or administrative action, without any discrimination resulting therefrom.

Article 3

1   Under this Regulation, provisions laid down by law, regulation or administrative action or administrative practices of a member state shall not apply:

— where they limit application for and offers of employment, or the right of foreign nationals to take up and pursue employment or subject these to conditions not applicable in respect of their own nationals; or

— where, though applicable irrespective of nationality, their exclusive or principal aim or effect is to keep nationals of other member states away from the employment offered.

This provision shall not apply to conditions relating to linguistic knowledge required by reason of the nature of the post to be filled.

2   There shall be included in particular among the provisions or practices of a member state referred to in the first subparagraph of paragraph 1 those which:

(*a*)   prescribe a special recruitment procedure for foreign nationals;

(*b*)   limit or restrict the advertising of vacancies in the press or through any other medium or subject it to conditions other than those applicable in respect of employers pursuing their activities in the territory of that member state;

(*c*)   subject eligibility for employment to conditions of registration with employment offices or impede recruitment of individual workers, where persons who do not reside in the territory of that state are concerned.

Article 4

1   Provisions laid down by law, regulation or administrative action of the member states which restrict by number or percentage the employment of foreign nationals in any undertaking, branch of activity or region, or at a national level, shall not apply to nationals of the other member states.2   When in a member state the granting of any benefit to undertakings is subject to a minimum percentage of national workers being employed, nationals of the other member states shall be counted as national workers, subject to the provisions of the Council Directive of 15 October 1963.[1]

NOTE
1 OJNo 159, 2.11.63, p 2661/63.

Article 5

A national of a member state who seeks employment in the territory of another member state shall receive the same assistance there as that afforded by the employment offices in that state to their own nationals seeking employment.

Article 6

1   The engagement and recruitment of a national of one member state for a post in another member state shall not depend on medical, vocational or other criteria which are discriminatory on grounds of nationality by comparison with those applied to nationals of the other member state who wish to pursue the same activity.

2   Nevertheless, a national who holds an offer in his name from an employer in a member state other than that of which he is a national may have to undergo a vocational test, if the employer expressly requests this when making his offer of employment.

TITLE II   EMPLOYMENT AND EQUALITY OF TREATMENT

Article 7

1   A worker who is a national of a member state may not, in the territory of another member state, be treated differently from national workers by reason of his nationality in respect of any conditions of employment and work, in particular as regards remuneration, dismissal, and should he become unemployed, reinstatement or re-employment;

2   He shall enjoy the same social and tax advantages as national workers.

3   He shall also, by virtue of the same right and under the same conditions as national workers, have access to training in vocational schools and retraining centres.

4   Any clause of a collective or individual agreement or of any other collective regulation concerning eligibility for employment, employment remuneration and other conditions of work or dismissal shall be null and void in so far as it lays down or authorises discriminatory conditions in respect of workers who are nationals of the other member states.

Article 8

1   A worker who is a national of a member state and who is employed in the territory of another member state shall enjoy equality of treatment as regards membership of trade unions and the exercise of rights attaching thereto, including the right to vote [and to be eligible for the administration or management posts of a trade union]1; he may be excluded from taking part in the management of bodies governed by public law and from holding an office governed by public law. Furthermore, he shall have the right of eligibility for workers' representative bodies in the undertaking. The provisions of this Article shall not affect law or regulations in certain member states which grant more extensive rights to workers coming from the other member states.

NOTE
1   Paragraph deleted by Council Regulation (EEC) 312/76 OJL39 14.2.76, p 2.

Article 9

1   A worker who is a national of a member state and who is employed in the territory of another member state shall enjoy all the rights and benefits accorded to national workers in matters of housing, including ownership of the housing he needs.

2   Such a worker may, with the same right as nationals, put his name down on the housing lists in the region in which he is employed, where such lists exist; he shall enjoy the resultant benefits and priorities.

If his family has remained in the country whence he came, they shall be considered for this purpose as residing in the said region, where national workers benefit from a similar presumption.

TITLE III   WORKERS' FAMILIES

Article 10

1   The following shall, irrespective of their nationality, have the right to install

themselves with a worker who is a national of one member state and who is employed in the territory of another member state.

    (*a*)   his spouse and their descendants who are under the age of 21 years or are dependants;

    (*b*)   dependent relatives in the ascending line of the worker and his spouse.

2   Member states shall facilitate the admission of any member of the family not coming within the provisions of paragraph 1 if dependent on the worker referred to above or living under his roof in the country whence he comes.

3   For the purposes of paragraphs 1 and 2, the worker must have available for his family housing considered as normal for national workers in the region where he is employed; this provision, however must not give rise to discrimination between national workers and workers from the other member states.

Article 11

Where a national of a member state is pursuing an activity as an employed or self-employed person in the territory of another member state, his spouse and those of the children who are under the age of 21 years or dependent on him shall have the right to take up any activity as an employed person throughout the territory of that same state, even if they are not nationals of any member state.

Article 12

The children of a national of a member state who is or has been employed in the territory of another member state shall be admitted to that state's general educational, apprenticeship and vocational training courses under the same conditions as the nationals of that state, if such children are residing in its territory.

Member states shall encourage all efforts to enable such children to attend these courses under the best possible conditions.

PART II   CLEARANCE OF VACANCIES AND APPLICATIONS FOR EMPLOYMENT

TITLE I   CO-OPERATION BETWEEN THE MEMBER STATES AND WITH
THE COMMISSION

Article 13

1   The member states or the Commission shall instigate or together undertake any study of employment or unemployment which they consider necessary for securing freedom of movement for workers within the Community.

The central employment services of the member states shall co-operate closely with each other and with the Commission with a view to acting jointly as regards the clearing of vacancies and applications for employment within the Community and the resultant placing of workers in employment.

2   To this end the member states shall designate specialist services which shall be entrusted with organising work in the fields referred to above and co-operating with each other and with the departments of the Commission.

The member states shall notify the Commission of any change in the designation of such services; the Commission shall publish details thereof for information in the *Official Journal of the European Communities*.

Article 14

1   The member states shall send to the Commission information on problems arising in connection with the freedom of movement and employment of workers and particulars of the state and development of employment.   . .[1].

2   [The Commission, taking the utmost account of the opinion of the Technical Committee, shall determine the manner in which the information referred to in paragraph 1 is to be drawn up][2].

3   In accordance with the procedure laid down by the Commission [taking the utmost account of the opinion of the Technical Committee][3], the specialist service of each member state shall send to the specialist services of the other member states and to the European Co-ordination Office such information concerning living and working conditions and the state of the labour market as is likely to be of guidance to workers from the other member states. Such information shall be brought up to date regularly.

The specialist services of the other member states shall ensure that wide publicity is given to such information, in particular by circulating it among the appropriate employment services and by all suitable means of communication for informing the workers concerned.

NOTES
1 Some words deleted in para 1 by Council Regulation (EEC) 2434 OJL245 26.8.92 p 1.
2 Amended by Council Regulation (EEC) 2434 OJL245 26.8.92 p 1.
3 Amended by Council Regulation (EEC) 2434 OJL245 26.8.92 p 1.

TITLE II   MACHINERY FOR VACANCY CLEARANCE

Article 15

1   [The specialist service of each member state shall regularly send to the specialist services of the other member states and to the European Co-ordination Office:

(*a*)   details of vacancies which could be filled by nationals of other member states;
(*b*)   details of vacancies addressed to non-member states;
(*c*)   details of applications for employment by those who have formally expressed a wish to work in another member state;
(*d*)   information, by region and by branch of activity, on applicants who have declared themselves actually willing to accept employment in another country.

The specialist service of each member state shall forward this information to the appropriate employment services and agencies as soon as possible.

2   The details of vacancies and applications referred to in paragraph 1 shall be circulated according to a uniform system to be established by the European Coordination Office in collaboration with the Technical Committee.

If necessary, the European Co-ordination Office may adapt this system in collaboration with the Technical Committee][1].

NOTE
1 Amended by Council Regulation (EEC) 2434 OJL245 26.8.92 p 1 and p 2.

Article 16

1   [Any vacancy within the meaning of Article 15 communicated to the employment services of a member state shall be notified to and processed by the competent employment services of the other member states concerned.

Such services shall forward to the services of the first member state the details of suitable applications.

2   The applications for employment referred to in Article 15(1)(c) shall be responded to by the relevant services of the member states within a reasonable period, not exceeding one month.

3   The employment services shall grant workers who are nationals of the member states the same priority as the relevant measures grant to nationals *vis-à-vis* workers from non-member states.][1]

NOTE
1 Amended by Council Regulation (EEC) 2434 OJL245 26.8.92 p 2.

Article 17

1   The provisions of Article 16 shall be implemented by the specialist services. However, in so far as they have been authorised by the central services and in so far as the organisation of the employment services of a member state and the placing techniques employed make it possible:

   (*a*)   the regional employment services of the member states shall:
      (i)   on the basis of the [details][1] referred to in Article 15, on which appropriate action will be taken, directly bring together and clear vacancies and applications for employment;
      (ii) establish direct relations for clearance:
         — of vacancies offered to a named worker;
         — of individual applications for employment sent either to a specific employment service or to an employer pursuing his activity within the area covered by such a service;
         — where the clearing operations concern seasonal workers who must be recruited as quickly as possible;
   (*b*)   [the services territorially responsible for the border regions of two or more member states shall regularly exchange data relating to vacancies and applications for employment in their area and, acting in accordance with their arrangements with the other employment services of their countries, shall directly bring together and clear vacancies and applications for employment.
      If necessary, the services territorially responsible for border regions shall also set up co-operation and service structures to provide:
         — users with as much practical information as possible on the various aspects of mobility; and
         — management and labour, social services (in particular public, private or those of public interest) and all institutions concerned, with a framework of coordinated measures relating to mobility];[2]
   (*c*)   official employment services which specialise in certain occupations or specific categories of persons shall co-operate directly with each other.

2   The member states concerned shall forward to the Commission the list, drawn up by common accord, of services referred to in paragraph 1; the Commission shall publish such list, and any amendment thereto, in the *Official Journal of the European Communities*.

NOTES
1 Amended by Council Regulation (EEC) 2434 OJL245 26.8.92 p 2.
2 Para 1(*b*) as amended by Council Regulations (EEC) 2434 OJL245 26.8.92 p 2.

Article 18

Adoption of recruiting procedures as applied by the implementing bodies provided for under agreements concluded between two or more member states shall not be obligatory.

TITLE III   MEASURES FOR CONTROLLING THE BALANCE OF THE
LABOUR MARKET

Article 19

[1   On the basis of a report from the Commission drawn up from information supplied by the member states, the latter and the Commission shall at least once a year analyse jointly the results of Community arrangements regarding vacancies and applications.]¹

2   The member states shall examine with the Commission all the possibilities of giving priority to nationals of member states when filing employment vacancies in order to achieve a balance between vacancies and applications for employment within the Community. They shall adopt all measures necessary for this purpose.

[3   Every two years the Commission shall submit a report to the European Parliament, the Council and the Economic and Social Committee on the implementation of Part II of this Regulation, summarising the information required and the data obtained from the studies and research carried out and highlighting any useful points with regard to developments on the Community's labour market.]²

NOTES
1 Amended by Council Regulation (EEC) 2434 OJL245 26.8.92 p 2.
2 Added by Council Regulation (EEC) 2434 OJL245 26.8.92 p 2.

Article 20

Article 20 deleted by Council Regulation (EEC) 2434 OJ245 26.8.92 p 2.

TITLE IV   EUROPEAN CO-ORDINATION OFFICE

Article 21

The European Office for Co-ordinating the Clearance of Vacancies and Applications for Employment, established within the Commission (called in this Regulation the 'European Co-ordination Office', shall have the general task of promoting vacancy clearance at Community level. It shall be responsible in particular for all the technical duties in this field which, under the provisions of this Regulation, are assigned to the Commission, and especially for assisting the national employment services.

It shall summarise the information referred to in Articles 14 and 15 and the data arising out of the studies and research carried out pursuant to Article 13, so as to bring to light any useful facts about foreseeable developments on the Community labour market; such facts shall be communicated to the specialist services of the member states and to the Advisory and Technical Committees.

Article 22

1   The European Co-ordination Office shall be responsible, in particular, for:

   (a)   co-ordinating the practical measures necessary for vacancy clearance at Community level and for analysing the resulting movements of workers;
   (b)   contributing to such objectives by implementing, in co-operation with the Technical Committee, joint methods of action at administrative and technical levels;
   (c)   carrying out, where a special need arises, and in agreement with the specialist services, the bringing together of vacancies and applications for employment for clearance by these specialist services.

2   It shall communicate to the specialist services vacancies and applications for employment sent directly to the Commission, and shall be informed of the action taken thereon.

Article 23

The Commission may, in agreement with the competent authority of each member state, and in accordance with the conditions and procedures which it shall determine on the basis of the Opinion of the Technical Committee, organise visits and assignments for officials of other member states, and also advanced programmes for specialist personnel.

PART III   COMMITTEES FOR ENSURING CLOSE CO-OPERATION BETWEEN THE MEMBER STATES IN MATTERS CONCERNING THE FREEDOM OF MOVEMENT OF WORKERS AND THEIR EMPLOYMENT

TITLE I   THE ADVISORY COMMITTEE

Article 24

The Advisory Committee shall be responsible for assisting the Commission in the examination of any questions arising from the application of the Treaty and measures taken in pursuance thereof, in matters concerning the freedom of movement of workers and their employment.

Article 25

The Advisory Committee shall be responsible in particular for:

(a) examining problems concerning freedom of movement and employment within the framework of national manpower policies, with a view to co-ordinating the employment policies of the member states at Community level, thus contributing to the development of the economies and to an improved balance of the labour market;

(b) making a general study of the effects of implementing this Regulation and any supplementary measures;

(c) submitting to the Commission any reasoned proposals for revising this Regulation;

(d) delivering, either at the request of the Commission or on its own initiative, reasoned opinions on general questions or on questions of principle, in particular on exchange of information concerning developments in the labour market, on the movement of workers between member states, on programmes or measures to develop vocational guidance and vocational training which are likely to increase the possibilities of freedom of movement and employment, and on all forms of assistance to workers and their families, including social assistance and the housing of workers.

Article 26

1   The Advisory Committee shall be composed of six members for each member state, two of whom shall represent the government, two the trade unions and two the employers' associations.

2   For each of the categories referred to in paragraph 1, one alternate member shall be appointed by each member state.

3   The term of office of the members and their alternates shall be two years. Their appointments shall be renewable.

On expiry of their term of office, the members and their alternates shall remain in office until replaced or until their appointments are renewed.

Article 27

The members of the Advisory Committee and their alternates shall be appointed by the Council which shall endeavour, when selecting representatives of trade unions and employers' associations, to achieve adequate representation on the Committee of the various economic sectors concerned.

The list of members and their alternates shall be published by the Council for information in the *Official Journal of the European Communities*.

Article 28

The Advisory Committee shall be chaired by a member of the Commission or his alternate. The Chairman shall not vote. The Committee shall meet at least twice a year. It shall be convened by its Chairman, either on his own initiative, or at the request of at least one third of the members. Secretarial services shall be provided for the Committee by the Commission.

Article 29

The chairman may invite individuals or representatives of bodies with wide experience in the field of employment or movement of workers to take part in meetings as observers or as experts. The Chairman may be assisted by expert advisers.

Article 30

1   An opinion delivered by the Committee shall not be valid unless two-thirds of the members are present.

2   Opinions shall state the reasons on which they are based; they shall be delivered by an absolute majority of the votes validly cast; they shall be accompanied by a written statement of the views expressed by the minority, when the latter so requests.

Article 31

The Advisory Committee shall establish its working methods by rules of procedure which shall enter into force after the Council, having received an opinion from the Commission, has given its approval. The entry into force of any amendment that the Committee decides to make thereto shall be subject to the same procedure.

TITLE II   THE TECHNICAL COMMITTEE

Article 32

The Technical Committee shall be responsible for assisting the Commission to prepare, promote and follow up all technical work and measures for giving effect to this Regulation and any supplementary measures.

Article 33

The Technical Committee shall be responsible in particular for:

(a)   promoting and advancing co-operation between the public authorities concerned in the member states on all technical questions relating to freedom of movement of workers and their employment;

(b)   formulating procedures for the organisation of the joint activities of the public authorities concerned;

(c)   facilitating the gathering of information likely to be of use to the Commission and for the studies and research provided for in this Regulation, and encouraging exchange of information and experience between the administrative bodies concerned;

(d)   investigating at a technical level the harmonisation of the criteria by which member states assess the state of their labour markets.

Article 34

1   The Technical Committee shall be composed of representatives of the Governments of the member states. Each Government shall appoint as member of the Technical Committee one of the members who represent it on the Advisory Committee.

2   Each government shall appoint an alternate from among its other representatives—members or alternates—on the Advisory Committee.

Article 35

The Technical Committee shall be chaired by a member of the Commission or his representative. The Chairman shall not vote. The Chairman and the members of the Committee may be assisted by expert advisers.

Secretarial services shall be provided for the Committee by the Commission.

Article 36

The proposals and opinions formulated by the Technical Committee shall be submitted to the Commission, and the Advisory Committee shall be informed thereof. Any such proposals and opinions shall be accompanied by a written statement of the views expressed by the various members of the Technical Committee, when the latter so request.

Article 37

The Technical Committee shall establish its working methods by rules of procedure which shall enter into force after the Council, having received an opinion from the Commission, has given its approval. The entry into force of any amendment which the Committee decides to make thereto shall be subject to the same procedure.

PART IV   TRANSITIONAL AND FINAL PROVISIONS

TITLE I   TRANSITIONAL PROVISIONS

Article 38

Until the adoption by the Commission of the uniform system referred to in Article 15(2), the European Co-ordination Office shall propose any measures likely to be of use in drawing up and circulating the returns referred to in Article 15(1).

Article 39

The rules of procedure of the Advisory Committee and the Technical Committee in force at the time of entry into force of this Regulation shall continue to apply.

Article 40

Until the entry into force of the measures to be taken by member states in pursuance of the Council Directive of 15 October 1968[1] and where, under the measures taken by the member states in pursuance of the Council Directive of 25 March 1964[2] the work permit provided for in Article 22 of Regulation No 38/64/EEC is necessary to determine the period of validity and extension of the residence permit, written confirmation of engagement from the employer or a certificate of employment stating the period of employment may be substituted for such work permit. Any written confirmation by the employer or certificate of employment showing that the worker has been engaged for an indefinite period shall have the same effect as that of a permanent work permit.

NOTES
1 OJNo 257 19.10.1968, p 13.
2 OJNo 62, 17.4.1964, p 981/64.

Article 41

If, by reason of the abolition of the work permit, a member state can no longer compile certain statistics on the employment of foreign nationals such member state may, for statistical purposes, retain the work permit in respect of nationals of the other member states until new statistical methods are introduced, but no later than 31 December 1969. The work permit must be issued automatically and must be valid until the actual abolition of work permit in such member state.

TITLE II   FINAL PROVISIONS

Article 42

1   This Regulation shall not affect the provisions of the Treaty establishing the European Coal and Steel Community which relate to workers with recognised qualifications in coalmining or steelmaking, nor those of the Treaty establishing the European Atomic Energy Community which deal with eligibility for skilled employment in the field of nuclear energy, nor any measures taken in pursuance of those Treaties.

Nevertheless, this Regulation shall apply to categories of workers referred to in the first subparagraph and to members of their families in so far as their legal position is not governed by the above-mentioned Treaties or measures.

2   This Regulation shall not affect measures taken in accordance with Article 51 of the Treaty.

3   This Regulation shall not affect the obligations of member states arising out of:

— special relations or future agreements with certain non-European countries or territories, based on institutional ties existing at the time of the entry into force of this Regulation; or
— agreements in existence at the time of the entry into force of this Regulation with certain non-European countries or territories, based on institutional ties between them.

Workers from such countries or territories who, in accordance with this provision, are pursuing activities as employed persons in the territory of one of those member states may not invoke the benefit of the provisions of this Regulation in the territory of the other member states.

Article 43

Member states shall, for information purposes, communicate to the Commission the texts of agreements, conventions or arrangements concluded between them in the manpower field between the date of their being signed and that of their entry into force.

Article 44

The Commission shall adopt measures pursuant to this Regulation for its implementation. To this end it shall act in close co-operation with the central public authorities of the member states.

1614

Article 45

The Commission shall submit to the Council proposals aimed at abolishing, in accordance with the conditions of the Treaty, restrictions on eligibility for employment of workers who are nationals of member states, where the absence of mutual recognition of diplomas, certificates or other evidence of formal qualifications may prevent freedom of movement for workers.

Article 46

The administrative expenditure of the Committees referred to in Part III shall be included in the budget of the European Communities in the section relating to the Commission.

Article 47

This Regulation shall apply to the territories of the member states and to their nationals, without prejudice to Articles 2, 3, 10 and 11.

Article 48

Regulation No 38/64/EEC shall cease to have effect when this Regulation enters into force.

This Regulation shall be binding in its entirety and directly applicable in all member states.

Done at Luxembourg, 15 October 1968.

Annex

[Annex deleted by Council Regulation (EEC) 2434 OJL245 36.8.92 p 2.]

COUNCIL DIRECTIVE (68/360/EEC)

on the abolition of restrictions on movement and residence within the Community for workers of member states and their families

The Council of The European Communities,

Having regard to the Treaty establishing the European Economic Community, and in particular Article 49 thereof;

Having regard to the proposal from the Commission;

Having regard to the Opinion of the European Parliament;

Having regard to the Opinion of the Economic and Social Committee;

Whereas Council Regulation (EEC) No 1612/68 fixed the provisions governing freedom of movement for workers within the Community; whereas, consequently, measures should be adopted for the abolition of restrictions which still exist concerning movement and residence within the Community, which conform to the rights and privileges accorded by the said Regulation to nationals of any member state who move in order to pursue activities as employed persons and to members of their families;

Whereas the rules applicable to residence should, as far as possible, bring the position of workers from other member states and members of their families into line with that of nationals;

Whereas the co-ordination of special measures relating to the movement and residence of foreign nationals, justified on grounds of public policy, public security or public health, is the subject of the Council Directive of 25 February 1964 adopted in application of Article 56(2) of the Treaty;

Has adopted this Directive:

Article 1

Member states shall, acting as provided in this Directive, abolish restrictions on the movement and residence of nationals of the said states and of members of their families to whom Regulation (EEC) No 1612/68 applies.

Article 2

1   Member states shall grant the nationals referred to in Article 1 the right to leave their territory in order to take up activities as employed persons and to pursue such activities in the territory of another member state. Such right shall be exercised simply on production of a valid identity card or passport. Members of the family shall enjoy the same right as the national on whom they are dependent.

2   Member states shall, acting in accordance with their laws, issue to such nationals, or renew, an identity card or passport, which shall state in particular the holder's nationality.

3   The passport must be valid at least for all member states and for countries through which the holder must pass when travelling between member states. Where a passport is the only document on which the holder may lawfully leave the country, its period of validity shall be not less than five years.

4   Member states may not demand from the nationals referred to in Article 1 any exit visa or any equivalent document.

Article 3

1   Member states shall allow the persons referred to in Article 1 to enter their territory simply on production of a valid identity card or passport.

2   No entry visa or equivalent document may be demanded save from members of the family who are not nationals of a member state. Member states shall accord to such persons every facility for obtaining any necessary visas.

Article 4

1   Member states shall grant the right of residence in their territory to the persons referred to in Article 1 who are able to produce the documents listed in paragraph 3.

2   As proof of the right of residence, a document entitled 'Residence permit for a national of a member state of the EEC' shall be issued. This document must include a statement that it has been issued pursuant to Regulation (EEC) No 1612/68 and to the measures taken by the member states for the implementation of the present Directive. The text of such statement is given in the Annex to this Directive.

3   For the issue of a residence permit for a national of a member state of the EEC, member states may require only the production of the following documents;

 — by the worker:
  (*a*) the document with which he entered their territory;
  (*b*) a confirmation of engagement from the employer or a certificate of employment;
 — by the members of the worker's family:

    (*c*)   the document with which they entered the territory;

    (*d*)   a document issued by the competent authority of the state of origin or the state whence they came, proving their relationship;

    (*e*)   in the cases referred to in Article 10(1) and (2) of Regulation (EEC) No 1612/68, a document issued by the competent authority of the state of origin or the state whence they came, testifying that they are dependent on the worker or that they live under his roof in such country.

4 A member of the family who is not a national of a member state shall be issued with a residence document which shall have the same validity as that issued to the worker on whom he is dependent.

Article 5

Completion of the formalities for obtaining a residence permit shall not hinder the immediate beginning of employment under a contract concluded by the applicants.

Article 6

1 The residence permit:

    (*a*)   must be valid throughout the territory of the member state which issued it;

    (*b*)   must be valid for at least five years from the date of issue and be automatically renewable.

2 Breaks in residence not exceeding six consecutive months and absence on military service shall not affect the validity of a residence permit.

3 Where a worker is employed for a period exceeding three months but not exceeding a year in the service of an employer in the host state or in the employ of a person providing services, the host member state shall issue him a temporary residence permit, the validity of which may be limited to the expected period of the employment.

Subject to the provisions of Article 8(1)(*c*), a temporary residence permit shall be issued also to a seasonal worker employed for a period of more than three months. The period of employment must be shown in the documents referred to in paragraph 4(3)(*b*).

Article 7

1 A valid residence permit may not be withdrawn from a worker solely on the grounds that he is no longer in employment, either because he is temporarily incapable of work as a result of illness or accident, or because he is involuntarily unemployed, this being duly confirmed by the competent employment office.

2 When the residence permit is renewed for the first time, the period of residence may be restricted, but not to less than twelve months, where the worker has been involuntarily unemployed in the member state for more than twelve consecutive months.

Article 8

1 Member states shall, without issuing a residence permit, recognise the right of residence in their territory of:

    (*a*)   a worker pursuing an activity as an employed person, where the activity is not expected to last for more than three months. The document with which the person concerned entered the territory and a statement by the employer on the expected duration of the employment shall be sufficient to cover his stay; a statement by the employer shall not, however, be required in the case of workers coming within the provisions of the Council Directive of 25 February 1964 on the attainment of freedom of establishment and freedom to provide services in respect of the activities of intermediaries in commerce, industry and small craft industries.

(*b*) a worker who, while having his residence in the territory of a member state to which he returns as a rule, each day or at least once a week, is employed in the territory of another member state. The competent authority of the state where he is employed may issue such worker with a special permit valid for five years and automatically renewable;

(*c*) a seasonal worker who holds a contract of employment stamped by the competent authority of the member state on whose territory he has come to pursue his activity.

2   In all cases referred to in paragraph 1, the competent authorities of the host member state may require the worker to report his presence in the territory.

Article 9

1   The residence documents granted to nationals of a member state of the EEC referred to in this Directive shall be issued and renewed free of charge or on payment of an amount not exceeding the dues and taxes charged for the issue of identity cards to nationals.

2   The visa referred to in Article 3(2) and the stamp referred to in Article 8(1)(*c*) shall be free of charge.

3   Member states shall take the necessary steps to simplify as much as possible the formalities and procedure for obtaining the documents mentioned in paragraph 1.

Article 10

Member states shall not derogate from the provisions of this Directive save on grounds of public policy, public security or public health.

Article 11

1   This Directive shall not affect the provisions of the Treaty establishing the European Coal and Steel Community which relate to workers with recognised skills in coal mining and steel making, or the provisions of the Treaty establishing the European Atomic Energy Community which deal with the right to take up skilled employment in the field of nuclear energy, or any measures taken in implementation of those Treaties.

2   Nevertheless, this Directive shall apply to the categories of workers referred to in paragraph 1, and to members of their families, in so far as their legal position is not governed by the abovementioned Treaties or measures.

Article 12

1   Member states shall, within nine months of notification of this Directive, bring into force the measures necessary to comply with its provisions and shall forthwith inform the Commission thereof.

2   They shall notify the Commission of amendments made to provisions imposed by law, regulation or administrative action for the simplification of the formalities and procedure for issuing such documents as are still necessary for the entry, exit and residence of workers and members of their families.

Article 13

1   The Council Directive of 25 March 1964 on the abolition of restrictions on movement and on residence within the Community of workers and their families shall continue to have effect until this Directive is implemented by the member states.

2   Residence permits issued pursuant to the Directive referred to in paragraph 1 shall remain valid until the date on which they next expire.

Article 14

This Directive is addressed to the member states

Done at Luxembourg, 15 October 1968.

Annex

Text of the statement referred to in Article 4(2):

'This permit is issued pursuant to Regulation (EEC) No 1612/68 of the Council of the European Communities of 15 October 1968 and to the measures taken in implementation of the Council Directive of 15 October 1968.

In accordance with the provisions of the above-mentioned Regulation, the holder of this permit has the right to take up and pursue an activity as an employed person in .... territory under the same conditions as . . .* workers.'

* Belgian, Danish, German, Greek, Spanish, French, Irish, Italian, Luxembourg, Dutch, Portuguese, United Kingdom, depending on which country issues the card.

REGULATION (EEC) 1251/70 OF THE COMMISSION

of 29 June 1970 on the right of workers to remain in the territory of a member state after having been employed in that state

The Commission of The European Communities,

Having regard to the Treaty establishing the European Economic Community, and in particular Article 48(3)(*d*) thereof, and Article 2 of the Protocol on the Grand Duchy of Luxembourg;

Having regard to the Opinion of the European Parliament[1];

Whereas Council Regulation (EEC) No 1612/68[2] of 15 October 1968 and Council Directive No 68/360/EEC of 15 October 1968[3] enabled freedom of movement for workers to be secured at the end of a series of measures to be achieved progressively; whereas the right of residence acquired by workers in active employment has as a corollary the right, granted by the Treaty to such workers, to remain in the territory of a member state after having been employed in that state; whereas it is important to lay down the conditions for the exercise of such right;

Whereas the said Council Regulation and Council Directive contain the appropriate provisions concerning the right of workers to reside in the territory of a member state for the purposes of employment; whereas the right to remain, referred to in Article 48(3)(*d*) of the Treaty is interpreted therefore as the right of the worker to maintain his residence in the territory of a member state when he ceases to be employed there;

Whereas the mobility of labour in the Community requires that workers may be employed successively in several member states without thereby being placed at a disadvantage;

Whereas it is important, in the first place, to guarantee to the worker residing in the territory of a member state the right to remain in that territory when he ceases to be employed in that state because he has reached retirement age or by reason of permanent incapacity to work; whereas, however, it is equally important to ensure that right for the worker who, after a period of employment and residence in the territory of a member state, works as an employed person in the territory of another member state, while still retaining his residence in the territory of the first state;

Whereas, to determine the conditions under which the right to remain arises, account should be taken of the reasons which have led to the termination of employment in the territory of the member state concerned and, in particular, of the difference between retirement, the normal and foreseeable end of working life, and incapacity to work which leads to a premature and unforeseeable termination of activity; whereas special conditions must be laid down where termination of activity is the result of an accident at work or occupational disease, or where the worker's spouse is or was a national of the member state concerned;

Whereas the worker who has reached the end of his working life should have sufficient time in which to decide where he wishes to establish his final residence;

Whereas the exercise by the worker of the right to remain entails that such right shall be extended to members of his family; whereas in the case of the death of the worker during his working life, maintenance of the right of residence of the members of his family must also be recognised and be the subject of special conditions;

Whereas persons to whom the right to remain applies must enjoy equality of treatment with national workers who have ceased their working lives;

NOTES
1 OJNo C65, 5.6.1970, p 16.
2 OJNo L 257, 19.10.1968, p 2.
3 OJNo L 257, 19.10.1968, p 13.

Has adopted this Regulation:

Article 1

The provisions of this Regulation shall apply to nationals of a member state who have worked as employed persons in the territory of another member state and to members of their families, as defined in Article 10 of Council Regulation (EEC)No 1612/68 on freedom of movement for workers within the Community.

Article 2

1   The following shall have the right to remain permanently in the territory of a member state:

(*a*)   a worker who, at the time of termination of his activity, has reached the age laid down by the law of that member state for entitlement to an old-age pension and who has been employed in that state for at least the last twelve months and has resided there continuously for more than three years;

(*b*)   a worker who, having resided continuously in the territory of that state for more than two years, ceases to work there as an employed person as a result of permanent incapacity to work. If such incapacity is the result of an accident at work or an occupational disease entitling him to a pension for which an institution of that state is entirely or partially responsible, no condition shall be imposed as to length of residence;

(*c*)   a worker who, after three years' continuous employment and residence in the territory of that state, works as an employed person in the territory of another member state, while retaining his residence in the territory of the first state, to which he returns, as a rule, each day or at least once a week.

Periods of employment completed in this way in the territory of the other member state shall, for the purposes of entitlement to the rights referred to in subparagraphs (*a*) and (*b*), be considered as having been completed in the territory of the state of residence.

2   The conditions as to length of residence and employment laid down in paragraph 1(*a*) and the conditions as to length of residence laid down in paragraph 1(*b*) shall not apply if the worker's spouse is a national of the member state concerned or has lost the nationality of that state by marriage to that worker.

Article 3

1   The members of a worker's family referred to in Article 1 of this Regulation who are residing with him in the territory of a member state shall be entitled to remain there permanently if the worker has acquired the right to remain in the territory of that state in accordance with Article 2, and to do so even after his death.

2   If, however, the worker dies during his working life and before having acquired the right to remain in the territory of the state concerned, members of his family shall be entitled to remain there permanently on condition that:

—   the worker, on the date of his decease, had resided continuously in the territory of that member state for at least 2 years; or
—   his death resulted from an accident at work or an occupational disease; or
—   the surviving spouse is a national of the state of residence or lost the nationality of that state by marriage to that worker.

Article 4

1   Continuity of residence as provided for in Articles 2(1)and 3(2) may be attested by any means of proof in use in the country of residence. It shall not be affected by temporary absences not exceeding a total of three months per year, nor by longer absences due to compliance with the obligations of military service.

2   Periods of involuntary unemployment, duly recorded by the competent employment office, and absences due to illness or accident shall be considered as periods of employment within the meaning of Article 2(1).

Article 5

1   The person entitled to the right to remain shall be allowed to exercise it within two years from the time of becoming entitled to such right pursuant to Article 2(1)(*a*) and (*b*) and Article 3. During such period he may leave the territory of the member state without adversely affecting such right.

2   No formality shall be required on the part of the person concerned in respect of the exercise of the right to remain.

Article 6

1   Persons coming under the provisions of this Regulation shall be entitled to a residence permit which:

(a)   shall be issued and renewed free of charge or on payment of a sum not exceeding the dues and taxes payable by nationals for the issue or renewal identity documents;
(b)   must be valid throughout the territory of the Member State issuing it;
(c)   must be valid for at least five years and be renewable automatically.

2   Periods of non-residence not exceeding six consecutive months shall not affect the validity of the residence permit.

Article 7

The right to equality of treatment, established by Council Regulation (EEC) No 1612/68, shall apply also to persons coming under the provisions of this Regulation.

Article 8

1   This Regulation shall not affect any provisions laid down by law, regulation or administrative action of one Member State which would be more favourable to nationals of other Member States.

2   Member States shall facilitate re-admission to their territories of workers who have left those territories after having resided there permanently for a long period and having been employed there and who wish to return there when they have reached retirement age or are permanently incapacitated for work.

Article 9

1   The Commission may, taking account of developments in the demographic situation of the Grand Duchy of Luxembourg, lay down, at the request of that State, different conditions from those provided for in this Regulation, in respect of the exercise of the right to remain in Luxembourg territory.

2   Within two months after the request supplying all appropriate details has been put before it, the Commission shall take a decision, stating the reasons on which it is based.

It shall notify the Grand Duchy of Luxembourg of such decision and inform the other Member States thereof;

This Regulation shall be binding in its entirety and directly applicable in all Member States.

Done at Brussels, 29 June 1970.

COUNCIL DIRECTIVE (72/194/EEC)

of 18 May 1972 extending to workers exercising the right to remain in the territory of a member state after having been employed in that state the scope of the Directive of 25 February 1964 on co-ordination of special measures concerning the movement and residence of foreign nationals which are justified on grounds of public policy, public security or public health

The Council of The European Communities,

Having regard to the Treaty establishing the European Economic Community, and in particular Articles 49 and 56(2) thereof;

Having regard to the proposal from the Commission;

Having regard to the Opinion of the European Parliament;

Having regard to the Opinion of the Economic and Social Committee;

Whereas the Council Directive of 25 February 1964[1] co-ordinated special measures concerning the movement and residence of foreign nationals which are justified on grounds of public policy, public security or public health and whereas Commission Regulation (EEC) No 1251/70[2] of 29 June 1970 on the right of workers to remain in the territory of a member state after having been employed in that state laid down conditions for the exercise of such right;

Whereas the Directive of 25 February 1964 should continue to apply to persons to whom that Regulation applies;

NOTES
1 OJNo 56, 4.4.1964, p 850/64.
2 OJNo 142, 30.6.1970, p 24.

Has adopted the following Directive:

Article 1

The Council Directive of 25 February 1964 on co-ordination of special measures concerning the movement and residence of foreign nationals which are justified on grounds of public policy, public security or public health shall apply to nationals of member states and members of their families who, pursuant to Regulation (EEC) No 1251/70, exercise the right to remain in the territory of a member state.

Article 2

Member states shall put into force the measures needed to comply with this Directive within six months of its notification and shall forthwith inform the Commission thereof.

Article 3

This Directive is addressed to the member states.

Done at Brussels, 18 May 1972.

COUNCIL DIRECTIVE (73/148/EEC)

of 21 May 1973 on the abolition of restrictions on movements and residence within the Community for nationals of member states with regard to establishment and the provision of services

The Council of The European Economic Community,

Having regard to the Treaty establishing the European Economic Community, and in particular Articles 54(2) and 63(2) thereof;

Having regard to the General Programmes for the abolition of restrictions on freedom of establishment and freedom to provide services1, and in particular Title II thereof;

Having regard to the proposal from the commission;

Having regard to the Opinion of the European Parliament[2];

Having regard to the Opinion of the Economic and Social Committee[3];

Whereas freedom of movement of persons as provided for in the Treaty and the General Programmes for the abolition of restrictions on freedom of establishment and on freedom to provide services entails the abolition of restrictions on movement and residence within the Community for nationals of member states wishing to establish themselves or to provide services within the territory of another member state;

Whereas freedom of establishment can be fully attained only if a right of permanent residence is granted to the persons who are to enjoy freedom of establishment; whereas freedom to provide services entails that persons providing and receiving services should have the right of residence for the time during which the services are being provided;

Whereas this Directive does not affect measures justified on grounds of public policy, public security or public health; whereas, in pursuance of Article 56(2) of the Treaty, co-ordination of such measures is to be dealt with in a separate Directive;

Whereas Council Directive of 25 February 1964[4] on the abolition of restrictions on movement and residence within the Community for nationals of member states with regard to establishment and the provision of services laid down the rules applicable in this area to activities as self-employed persons;

Whereas Council Directive of 15 October 1968[5] on the abolition of restrictions on movement and residence within the Community for workers of member states and their families, which replaced the Directive of 25 March 1964[6] bearing the same title, has in the meantime amended the rules applicable to employed persons;

Whereas the provisions concerning movement and residence within the Community of self-employed persons and their families should likewise be improved;

Whereas the co-ordination of special measures concerning the movement and residence of foreign nationals, justified on grounds of public policy, public security or public health, is already the subject of the Council Directive of 25 February 1964[7];

NOTES
1 OJNo 2, 15.1.1962, pp 32/62 and 36/62.
2 OJNo 19, 28.2.1972, p 5.
3 OJNo C 67, 24.6.1972, p 7.
4 OJNo 56, 4.4.1964, p 845/64.
5 OJNo L 257, 19.10.1968, p 13.
6 OJNo 62, 17.4.1964, p 981/64.
7 OJNo 56, 4.4.1964, p 850/64.

Has adopted this directive:

Article 1

1   Member states shall, acting as provided in this Directive, abolish restrictions on the movement and residence of:

    (*a*)   nationals of a member state who are established or who wish to establish themselves in another member state in order to pursue activities as self-employed persons, or who wish to provide services in that state;

    (*b*)   nationals of member states wishing to go to another member state as recipients of services;

    (*c*)   the spouse and the children under twenty-one years of age of such nationals, irrespective of their nationality;

    (*d*)   the relatives in the ascending and descending lines of such nationals and of the spouse of such nationals, whose relatives are dependent on them, irrespective of their nationality.

2   Member states shall favour the admission of any other member of the family of a national referred to in paragraph 1(*a*) or (*b*) or of the spouse of that national, which member is dependent on that national or who in the country of origin was living under the same roof.

Article 2

1 Member states shall grant the persons referred to in Article 1 the right to leave their territory. Such right shall be exercised simply on production of a valid identity card or passport. Members of the family shall enjoy the same right as the national on whom they are dependent.

2 Member states shall, acting in accordance with their laws, issue to their nationals, or renew, an identity card or passport, which shall state in particular the holder's nationality.

3 The passport must be valid at least for all member states and for countries through which the holder must pass when travelling between member states. Where a passport is the only document on which the holder may lawfully leave the country, its period of validity shall not be less than five years.

4 Member states may not demand from the persons referred to in Article 1 any exit visa or any equivalent requirement.

Article 3

1 Member states shall grant to the persons referred to in Article 1 right to enter their territory merely on production of a valid identity card or passport.

2 No entry visa or equivalent requirement may be demanded save in respect of members of the family who do have the nationality of a member state. Member states shall afford to such persons every facility for obtaining any necessary visas.

Article 4

1 Each member state shall grant the right of permanent residence to nationals of other member states who establish themselves within its territory in order to pursue activities as self-employed persons, when the restrictions on these activities have been abolished pursuant to the Treaty.
  As proof of the right of residence, a document entitled 'Residence Permit for a national of a member state of the European Communities' shall be issued. This document shall be valid for not less than five years from the date of issue and shall be automatically renewable.
  Breaks in residence not exceeding six consecutive months and absence on military service shall not affect the validity of a residence permit.
  A valid residence permit may not be withdrawn from a national referred to in Article 1(1)(*a*) solely on the grounds that he is no longer in employment because he is temporarily incapable of work as a result of illness or accident.
  Any national of a member state who is not specified in the first subparagraph but who is authorised under the laws of another member state to pursue an activity within its territory shall be granted a right of abode for a period not less than that of the authorisation granted for the pursuit of the activity in question.
  However, any national referred to in subparagraph 1 and to whom the provisions of the preceding subparagraph apply as a result of a change of employment shall retain his residence permit until the date on which it expires.

2 The right of residence for persons providing and receiving services shall be of equal duration with the period during which the services are provided.
  Where such period exceeds three months, the member state in the territory of which the services are performed shall issue a right of abode as proof of the right of residence.
  Where the period does not exceed three months, the identity card or passport with which the person concerned entered the territory shall be sufficient to cover his stay. The member state may, however, require the person concerned to report his presence in the territory.

3   A member of the family who is not a national of a member state shall be issued with a residence document which shall have the same validity as that issued to the national on whom he is dependent.

Article 5

The right of residence shall be effective throughout the territory of the member state concerned.

Article 6

An applicant for a residence permit or right of abode shall not be required by a member state to produce anything other than the following, namely:

(*a*)   the identity card or passport with which he or she entered its territory;
(*b*)   proof that he or she comes within one of the classes of person referred to in Articles 1 and 4.

Article 7

1   The residence documents granted to nationals of a member state shall be issued and renewed free of charge or on payment of an amount not exceeding the dues and taxes charged for the issue of identity cards to nationals. These provisions shall also apply to documents and certificates required for the issue and renewal of such residence documents.

2   The visas referred to in Article 3(2) shall be free of charge.

3   Member states shall take the necessary steps to simplify as much as possible the formalities and the procedure for obtaining the documents mentioned in paragraph 1.

Article 8

Member states shall not derogate from the provisions of this Directive save on grounds of public security or public health.

Article 9

1   Member states shall within six months of notification of this Directive bring into force the measures necessary to comply with its provisions and shall forthwith inform the Commission thereof.

2   They shall notify the Commission of amendments made to provisions imposed by law, regulation or administrative action for the simplification with regard to establishment and the provision of services of the formalities and procedure for issuing such documents as are still necessary for the movement and residence of persons referred to in Article 1.

Article 10

1   The Council Directive of 25 February 1964 on the abolition of restrictions on movement and residence within the Community for nationals of member states with regard to establishment and the provision of services shall remain applicable until this Directive is implemented by the member states.

2   Residence documents issued pursuant to the Directive referred to in paragraph 1 shall remain valid until the date on which they next expire.

Article 11

This Directive is addressed to the member states.

Done at Brussels, 21 May 1973.

COUNCIL DIRECTIVE (75/34/EEC)

of 17 December 1974 concerning the right of nationals of a member state to remain in the territory of another member state after having pursued therein an activity in a self-employed capacity

The Council of The European Communities,

Having regard to the Treaty establishing the European Economic Community, and in particular Article 235 thereof;

Having regard to the General Programme for the abolition of restrictions on freedom of establishment[1], and in particular Title II thereof;

Having regard to the proposal from the Commission;

Having regard to the Opinion of the European Parliament[2];

Having regard to the Opinion of the Economic and Social Committee[3];

Whereas pursuant to Council Directive No 73/148/EEC[4] of 21 May 1973 on the abolition of restrictions on movement and residence within the Community for nationals of member states with regard to establishment and the provision of services, each member state grants the right of permanent residence to nationals of other member states who establish themselves within its territory in order to pursue activities as self-employed persons, when the restrictions on these activities have been abolished pursuant to the Treaty;

Whereas it is normal for a person to prolong a period of permanent residence in the territory of a member state by remaining there after having pursued an activity there; whereas the absence of a right so to remain in such circumstances is an obstacle to the attainment of freedom of establishment; whereas, as regards employed persons, the conditions under which such a right may be exercised have already been laid down by Regulation (EEC) No 1251/70[5];

Whereas Article 48(3)(*d*) of the Treaty recognises the right of workers to remain in the territory of a member state after having been employed in that state; whereas Article 54(2) does not expressly provide a similar right for self-employed persons; whereas, nevertheless, the nature of establishment, together with attachments formed to the countries in which they have pursued their activities, means that such persons have a definite interest in enjoying the same right to remain as that granted to workers; whereas in justification of this measure reference should be made to the Treaty provision enabling it to be taken;

Whereas freedom of establishment within the Community requires that nationals of member states may pursue self-employed activities in several member states in succession without thereby being placed at a disadvantage;

Whereas a national of a member state residing in the territory of another member state should be guaranteed the right to remain in that territory when he ceases to pursue an activity as a self-employed person in that state because he has reached retirement age or by reason of permanent incapacity to work; whereas such a right should also be guaranteed to the national of a member state who, after a period of activity in a self-employed capacity and residence in the territory of a second member state, while still retaining his residence in the territory of the second state;

Whereas, to determine the conditions under which the right to remain arises, account should be taken of the reasons which have led to the termination of activity in the territory of the member state concerned and, in particular, of the difference between retirement, the normal and foreseeable end of working life, and permanent incapacity to work which leads to a premature and unforeseeable termination of activity; whereas special conditions must be laid down where the spouse is or was a national of the member state concerned, or where termination of activity is the result of an accident at work or occupational illness;

Whereas a national of a member state who has reached the end of his working life, after working in self-employed capacity in the territory of another member state, should have sufficient time in which to decide where he wishes to establish his final residence;

Whereas the exercise of the right to remain by a national of a member state working in a self-employed capacity entails extension of such right to the members of his family; whereas in the case of the death of a national of a member state working in a self-employed capacity during his working life the right of residence of the members of his family must also be recognised and be the subject of special conditions;

Whereas persons to whom the right to remain applies must enjoy equality of treatment with nationals of the state concerned who have reached the end of their working lives;

NOTES
1 OJNo 2, 15.1.1962, p 36/62.
2 OJNo C 14, 27.3.1973, p 20.
3 OJNo C 142, 31.12.1972, p 12.
4 OJNo L 172, 28.6.1973, p 14.
5 OJNo L 142, 30.6.1970, p 24.

Has adopted this Directive:

Article 1

Member states shall, under the conditions laid down in this Directive, abolish restrictions on the right to remain in their territory in favour of nationals of another member state who have pursued activities as self-employed persons in their territory, and members of their families, as defined in Article 1 of Directive No 73/148/EEC.

Article 2

1   Each member state shall recognise the right to remain permanently in its territory of:

(a)   any person who, at the time of termination of his activity, has reached the age laid down by the law of that state for entitlement to an old-age pension and who has pursued his activity in that state for at least the previous twelve months and has resided there continuously for more than three years.
   Where the law of that member state does not grant the right to an old-age pension to certain categories of self-employed workers, the age requirement shall be considered as satisfied when the beneficiary reaches 65 years of age;
(b)   any person who, having resided continuously in the territory of that state for more than two years, ceases to pursue his activity there as a result of permanent incapacity to work.
   If such incapacity is the result of an accident at work or an occupational illness entitling him to a pension which is payable in whole or in part by an institution of that state no condition shall be imposed as to length of residence;
(c)   any person who, after three years' continuous activity and residence in the territory of that state, pursues his activity in the territory of another member state, while retaining his residence in the territory of the first state, to which he returns, as a rule, each day or at least once a week.

Periods of activity so completed in the territory of the other member state shall, for the purposes of entitlement to the rights referred to in (*a*) and (*b*), be considered as having been completed in the territory of the state of residence.

2 The conditions as to length of residence and activity laid down in paragraph 1(*a*) and the condition as to length of residence laid down in paragraph 1(*b*) shall not apply if the spouse of the self-employed person is a national of the member state concerned or has lost the nationality of that state by marriage to that person.

Article 3

1 Each member state shall recognise the right of the members of the self-employed person's family referred to in Article 1 who are residing with him in the territory of that state to remain there permanently, if the person concerned has acquired the right to remain in the territory of that state in accordance with Article 2. This provision shall continue to apply even after the death of the person concerned.

2 If, however, the self-employed person dies during his working life and before having acquired the right to remain in the territory of the state concerned, that state shall recognise the right of the members of his family to remain there permanently on condition that:

— the person concerned, on the date of his decease, had resided continuously in its territory for at least two years; or
— his death resulted from an accident at work or an occupational illness; or
— the surviving spouse is a national of that state or lost such nationality by marriage to the person concerned.

Article 4

1 Continuity of residence as provided for in Articles 2(1) and 3(2) may be attested by any means of proof in use in the country of residence. It may not be affected by temporary absences not exceeding a total of three months per year, nor by longer absences due to compliance with the obligations of military service.

2 Periods of inactivity due to circumstances outside the control of the person concerned or of inactivity owing to illness or accident must be considered as periods of activity within the meaning of Article 2(1).

Article 5

1 Member states shall allow the person entitled to the right to remain to exercise such right within two years from the time of becoming entitled thereto pursuant to Article 2(1)(*a*) and (*b*) and Article 3. During this period the beneficiary must be able to leave the territory of the member state without adversely affecting such right.

2 Member states shall not require the person concerned to comply with any particular formality in order to exercise the right to remain.

Article 6

1 Member states shall recognise the right of persons having the right to remain in their territory to a residence permit, which must:

(*a*) be issued and renewed free of charge or on payment of a sum not exceeding the dues and taxes payable by nationals for the issue or renewal of identity cards;
(*b*) be valid throughout the territory of the member state issuing it;
(*c*) be valid for five years and renewable automatically.

2   Periods of non-residence not exceeding six consecutive months and longer absences due to compliance with the obligations of military service may not affect the validity of a residence permit.

Article 7

Member states shall apply to persons having the right to remain in their territory the right of equality of treatment recognised by the Council Directives on the abolition of restrictions on freedom of establishment pursuant to Title III of the General Programme which provides for such abolition.

Article 8

1   This Directive shall not affect any provisions laid down by law, regulation or administrative action of any member state which would be more favourable to nationals of other member states.

2   Member states shall facilitate re-admission to their territories of self-employed persons who left those territories after having resided there permanently for a long period while pursuing an activity there and who wish to return when they have reached retirement age as defined in Article 2(1)(*a*) or are permanently incapacitated for work.

Article 9

Member states may not derogate from the provisions of this Directive save on grounds of public policy, public security or public health.

Article 10

1   Member states shall, within twelve months of notification of this Directive, bring into force the measures necessary to comply with its provisions and shall forthwith inform the Commission thereof.

2   Following notification of this Directive, member states shall further ensure that the Commission is informed, in sufficient time for it to submit its comments, of all proposed laws, regulations or adminsitrative provisions which they intend to adopt in the field covered by this Directive.

Article 11

This Directive is addressed to the member states.

Done at Brussels, 17 December 1974.

COUNCIL DIRECTIVE (75/35/EEC)

of 17 December 1974 extending the scope of Directive No 64/221/EEC on the co-ordination of special measures concerning the movement and residence of foreign nationals which are justified on grounds of public policy, public security or public health to include nationals of a member state who exercise the right to remain in the territory of another member state after having pursued therein an activity in a self-employed capacity

The Council of The European Communities,

Having regard to the Treaty establishing the European Economic Community, and in particular Article 56(2) and Article 235 thereof;

Having regard to the proposal from the Commission;

Having regard to the Opinion of the European Parliament[1];

Having regard to the Opinion of the Economic and Social Committee[2];

Whereas Directive No 64/221/EEC[3] co-ordinated special measures concerning the movement and residence of foreign nationals which are justified on grounds of public policy, public security or public health and whereas Directive No 75/34/EEC[4] laid down conditions for the exercise of the right of nationals of a member state to remain in the territory of another member state after having pursued therein an activity in a self-employed capacity;

Whereas Directive No 64/221/EEC should therefore apply to persons to whom Directive No 75/34/EEC applies;

NOTES
1 OJNo C 14, 27.3.1973, p 21.
2 OJNo C 142, 31.12.1972, p 10.
3 OJNo 56, 4.4.1964, p 850/64.
4 See p 10 of this Official Journal.

Has adopted this Directive:

Article 1

Directive No 64/221/EEC shall apply to nationals of member states and members of their families who have the right to remain in the territory of a member state pursuant to Directive No 75/34/EEC.

Article 2

Member states shall, within twelve months of notification of this Directive, bring into force the measures necessary to comply with its provisions and shall forthwith inform the Commission thereof.

Article 3

This Directive is addressed to the member states.

Done at Brussels, 17 December 1974.

COUNCIL DIRECTIVE (77/486/EEC)

of 25 July 1977 on the education of the children of migrant workers

The Council of the European Communities,

Having regard to the Treaty establishing the European Economic Community, and in particular Article 49 thereof,

Having regard to the proposal from the Commission,

Having regard to the opinion of the European Parliament1,

Having regard to the opinion of the Economic and Social Committee2,

Whereas in its resolution of 21 January 1974 concerning a social action programme3, the Council included in its priority actions those designed to improve the conditions of freedom of movement for workers relating in particular to reception and to the education of their children;

Whereas in order to permit the integration of such children into the educational environment and the school system of the host State, they should be able to receive suitable tuition including teaching of the language of the host State;

Whereas host Member States should also take, in conjunction with the Member States of origin, appropriate measures to promote the teaching of the mother tongue and of the culture of the country of origin of the abovementioned children, with a view principally to facilitating their possible reintegration into the Member State of origin,

NOTES
1 OJ No C 280, 8.12.1975, p 48.
2 OJ No C 45, 27.2.1976, p 6.
3 OJ No C 13, 12.2.1974, p 1.

Has adopted this directive:

Article 1

This Directive shall apply to children for whom school attendance is compulsory under the laws of the host State, who are dependants of any worker who is a national of another Member State, where such children are resident in the territory of the Member State in which that national carries on or has carried on an activity as an employed person.

Article 2

Member States shall, in accordance with their national circumstances and legal systems, take appropriate measures to ensure that free tuition to facilitate initial reception is offered in their territory to the children referred to in Article 1, including, in particular, the teaching – adapted to the specific needs of such children – of the official language or one of the official languages of the host State.

Member States shall take the measures necessary for the training and further training of the teachers who are to provide this tuition.

Article 3

Member States shall, in accordance with their national circumstances and legal systems, and in cooperation with States of origin, take appropriate measures to promote, in coordination with normal education, teaching of the mother tongue and culture of the country of origin for the children referred to in Article 1.

Article 4

The Member States shall take the necessary measures to comply with this Directive within four years of its notification and shall forthwith inform the Commission thereof.

The Member States shall also inform the Commission of all laws, regulations and administrative or other provisions which they adopt in the field governed by this Directive.

Article 5

The Member States shall forward to the Commission within five years of the notification of this Directive, and subsequently at regular intervals at the request of the Commission, all relevant information to enable the Commission to report to the Council on the application of this Directive.

Article 6

This Directive is addressed to the Member States.

Done at Brussels, 25 July 1977.

COUNCIL DIRECTIVE (90/364/EEC)

of 28 June 1990 on the right of residence

The Council of The European Communities,

Having regard to the Treaty establishing the European Economic Community, and in particular Article 235 thereof;

Having regard to the proposal from the Commission[1];

Having regard to the Opinion of the European Parliament[2];

Having regard to the Opinion of the Economic and Social Committee[3];

Whereas Article 3(*c*) of the Treaty provides that the activities of the Community shall include, as provided in the Treaty, the abolition, as between member states, of obstacles to freedom of movement for persons;

Whereas Article 8(*a*) of the Treaty provides that the internal market must be established by 31 December 1992; whereas the internal market comprises an area without internal frontiers in which the free movement of goods, persons, services and capital is ensured in accordance with the provisions of the Treaty;

Whereas national provisions on the right of nationals of the member states to reside in a member state other than their own must be harmonised to ensure such freedom of movement;

Whereas beneficiaries of the right of residence must not become an unreasonable burden on the public finances of the host member state;

Whereas this right can only be genuinely exercised if it is also granted to members of the family;

Whereas the beneficiaries of this Directive should be covered by administrative arrangements similar to those laid down in particular in Directive 68/360/EEC[4] and Directive 64/221/EEC[5];

Whereas the Treaty does not provide, for the action concerned, powers other than those of Article 235;

NOTES
1 OJNo C 191, 28.7.1989, p 5; and OJNo C 26, 3.2.1990, p 22.
2 Opinion delivered on 13 June 1990 (not yet published in official Journal).
3 OJNo C 329, 30.12.1989, p 25.
4 OJNo L257, 19.10.1968, p 13.
5 OJNo 56, 4.4.1964, p 850/40.

Has adopted this Directive:

Article 1

1 Member states shall grant the right of residence to nationals of member states who do not enjoy this right under other provisions of Community law and to members of their families as defined in paragraph 2, provided that they themselves and the members

of their families are covered by sickness insurance in respect of all risks in the host member state and have sufficient resources to avoid becoming a burden on the social assistance system of the host member state during their period of residence.

The resources referred to in the first subparagraph shall be deemed sufficient where they are higher than the level of resources below which the host member state may grant social assistance to its nationals, taking into account the personal circumstances of the applicant and, where appropriate, the personal circumstances of persons admitted pursuant to paragraph 2.

Where the second subparagraph cannot be applied in a member state, the resources of the applicant shall be deemed sufficient if they are higher than the level of the minimum social security pension paid by the host member state.

2   The following shall, irrespective of their nationality, have the right to install themselves in another member state with the holder of the right of residence:

- (*a*)   his or her spouse and their descendants who are dependents;
- (*b*)   dependent relatives in the ascending line of the holder of the right of residence and his or her spouse.

Article 2

1   Exercise of the right of residence shall be evidenced by means of the issue of a document known as a 'Residence permit for a national of a member state of the EEC', the validity of which may be limited to five years on a renewable basis. However, the member states may, when they deem it to be necessary, require revalidation of the permit at the end of the first two years of residence. Where a member of the family does not hold the nationality of a member state, he or she shall be issued with a residence document of the same validity as that issued to the national on whom he or she depends.

For the purpose of issuing the residence permit or document, the member state may require only that the applicant present a valid identity card or passport and provide proof that he or she meets the conditions laid down in Article 1.

2   Articles 2, 3, 6(1)(*a*) and (2) and Article 9 of Directive 68/360/EEC shall apply *mutatis mutandis* to the beneficiaries of this Directive.

The spouse and the dependent children of a national of a member state entitled to the right of residence within the territory of a member state shall be entitled to take up any employed or self-employed activity anywhere within the territory of that member state, even if they are not nationals of a member state.

Member states shall not derogate from the provisions of this Directive save on grounds of public policy, public security or public health. In that event, Directive 64/221/EEC shall apply.

3   This Directive shall not affect existing law on the acquisition of second homes.

Article 3

The right of residence shall remain for as long as beneficiaries of that right fulfil the conditions laid down in Article 1.

Article 4

The Commission shall, not more than three years after the date of implementation of this Directive, and at three-yearly intervals thereafter, draw up a report on the application of this Directive and submit it to the European Parliament and the Council.

Article 5

Member states shall bring into force the laws, regulations and administrative provisions necessary to comply with this Directive not later than 30 June 1992. They shall forthwith inform the Commission thereof.

Article 6

This Directive is addressed to the member states.

Done at Luxembourg, 28 June 1990.

COUNCIL DIRECTIVE (90/365/EEC)

of 28 June 1990 on the right of residence for employees and self-employed persons who have ceased their occupational activity

The Council of The European Communities,

Having regard to the Treaty establishing the European Economic Community, and in particular Article 235 thereof;

Having regard to the proposal from the Commission[1];

Having regard to the opinion of the European Parliament[2];

Having regard to the opinion of the Economic and Social Committee[3];

Whereas Article 3(c) of the Treaty provides that the activities of the Community shall include, as provided in the Treaty, the abolition, as between member states, of obstacles to freedom of movement for persons;

Whereas Article 8(a) of the Treaty provides that the internal market must be established by 31 December 1992; whereas the internal market comprises an area without internal frontiers in which the free movement of goods, persons, services and capital is ensured, in accordance with the provisions of the Treaty;

Whereas Articles 48 and 52 of the Treaty provide for freedom of movement for workers and self-employed persons, which entails the right of residence in the member states in which they pursue their occupational activity; whereas it is desirable that this right of residence also be granted to persons who have ceased their occupational activity even if they have not exercised their right to freedom of movement during their working life;

Whereas beneficiaries of the right of residence must not become an unreasonable burden on the public finances of the host member state;

Whereas under Article 10 of Regulation (EEC) No 1408/71[4], as amended by Regulation (EEC) No 1390/81[5], recipients of invalidity or old age cash benefits or pensions for accidents at work or occupational diseases are entitled to continue to receive these benefits and pensions even if they reside in the territory of a member state other than that in which the institution responsible for payment is situated;

Whereas this right can only be genuinely exercised if it is also granted to members of the family;

Whereas the beneficiaries of this Directive should be covered by administrative arrangements similar to those laid down in particular in Directive 68/630/EEC[6] and Directive 64/221/EEC[7];

Whereas the Treaty does not provide, for the action concerned, powers other than those of Article 235;

NOTES
1 OJNo C 191, 28.7.1989, p 3; and OJNo C 26, 3.2.1990, p 19.
2 Opinion delivered on 13 June 1990 (not yet published in Official Journal).
3 OJNo C 329, 30.12.1989, p 25.

4 OJNo L 149, 5.7.1971, p 2.
5 OJNo L 143, 29.5.1981, p 1.
6 OJNo L257, 19.10.1968, p 13.
7 OJNo 56, 4.4.1964, p 850/64.

Has adopted this Directive:

Article 1

1   Member states shall grant the right of residence to nationals of member states who have pursued an activity as an employee or self-employed person and to members of their families as defined in paragraph 2, provided that they are recipients of an invalidity or early retirement pension, or old age benefits, or of a pension in respect of an industrial accident or disease of an amount sufficient to avoid becoming a burden on the social security system of the host member state during their period of residence and provided they are covered by sickness insurance in respect of all risks in the host member state.

The resources of the applicant shall be deemed sufficient where they are higher than the level of resources below which the host member state may grant social assistance to its nationals, taking into account the personal circumstances of persons admitted pursuant to paragraph 2.

Where the second subparagraph cannot be applied in a member state, the resources of the applicant shall be deemed sufficient if they are higher than the level of the minimum social security pension paid by the host member state.

2   The following shall, irrespective of their nationality, have the right to install themselves in another member state with the holder of the right of residence:

(*a*)   his or her spouse and their descendants who are dependents;
(*b*)   dependent relatives in the ascending line of the holder of the right of residence and his or her spouse.

Article 2

1   Exercise of the right of residence shall be evidenced by means of the issue of a document known as a 'Residence permit for a national of a member state of the EEC', whose validity may be limited to five years on a renewable basis. However, the member states may, when they deem it to be necessary, require revalidation of the permit at the end of the first two years of residence. Where a member of the family does not hold the nationality of a member state, he or she shall be issued with a residence document of the same validity as that issued to the national on whom he or she depends.

For the purposes of issuing the residence permit or document, the member state may require only that the applicant present a valid identity card or passport and provide proof that he or she meets the conditions laid down in Article 1.

2   Articles 2, 3, 6(1)(*a*) and (2) and Article 9 of Directive 68/360/EEC shall apply *mutatis mutandis* to the beneficiaries of this Directive.

The spouse and the dependent children of a national of a member state entitled to the right of residence within the territory of a member state shall be entitled to take up any employed or self-employed activity anywhere within the territory of that member state, even if they are not nationals of a member state.

Member states shall not derogate from the provisions of this Directive save on grounds of public policy, public security or public health. In that event, Directive 64/221/EEC shall apply.

3   This Directive shall not affect existing law on the acquisition of second homes.

Article 3

The right of residence shall remain for as long as beneficiaries of that right fulfil the conditions laid down in Article 1.

Article 4

The Commission shall, not more than three years after the date of implementation of this Directive, and at three-yearly intervals thereafter, draw up a report on the application of this Directive and submit it to the European Parliament and the Council.

Article 5

Member states shall bring into force the laws, regulations and administrative provisions necessary to comply with this Directive not later than 30 June 1992. They shall forthwith inform the Commission thereof.

Article 6

This Directive is addressed to the member states.

Done at Luxembourg, 28 June 1990.

COUNCIL DIRECTIVE (93/96/EEC)

of 29 October 1993 on the right of residence for students

The Council of the European Communities,

Having regard to the Treaty establishing the European Economic Community, and in particular the second paragraph of Article 7 thereof;

Having regard to the proposal from the Commission[1];

In cooperation with the European Parliament[2];

Having regard to the opinion of the Economic and Social Committee[3];

Whereas Article 3(*c*) of the Treaty provides that the activities of the Community shall include, as provided in the Treaty, the abolition, as between member states, of obstacles to freedom of movement for persons;

Whereas Article 8(*a*) of the Treaty provides that the internal market must be established by 31 December 1992; whereas the internal market comprises an area without internal frontiers in which the free movement of goods, persons, services and capital is ensured in accordance with the provisions of the Treaty;

Whereas, as the Court of Justice has held, Articles 128 and 7 of the Treaty prohibit any discrimination between nationals of the member states as regards access to vocational training in the Community; whereas access by a national of one member state to vocational training in another member state implies, for that national, a right of residence in that other member state;

Whereas, accordingly, in order to guarantee access to vocational training, the conditions likely to facilitate the effective exercise of that right of residence should be laid down;

Whereas the right of residence for students forms part of a set of related measures designed to promote vocational training;

Whereas beneficiaries of the right of residence must not become an unreasonable burden on the public finances of the host member state;

Whereas, in the present state of Community law, as established by the case law of the Court of Justice, assistance granted to students, does not fall within the scope of the Treaty within the meaning of Article 7 thereof;

Whereas the right of residence can only be genuinely exercised if it is also granted to the spouse and their dependent children;

Whereas the beneficiaries of this Directive should be covered by administrative arrangements similar to those laid down in particular in Council Directive 68/360/EEC of 15 October 1968 on the abolition of restrictions on movement and residence within the Community for workers of member states and their families[4] and Council Directive 64/221/EEC of 25 February 1964 on the co-ordination of special measures concerning the movement and residence of foreign nationals which are justified on grounds of public policy, public security or public health[5];

Whereas this Directive does not apply to students who enjoy the right of residence by virtue of the fact that they are or have been effectively engaged in economic activities or are members of the family of a migrant worker;

Whereas, by its judgment of 7 July 1992 in Case C–295/90, the Court of Justice annulled Council Directive 90/366/EEC of 28 June 1990 on the right of residence for students 'while maintaining the effects of the annulled Directive until the entry into force of a Directive adopted on the appropriate legal basis';

Whereas the effects of Directive 90/366/EEC should be maintained during the period up to 31 December 1993, the date by which member states are to have adopted the laws, regulations and administrative provisions necessary to comply with this Directive;

NOTES
1 OJ No C166, 17.6.1993, p 16.
2 OJ No C255, 20.9.1993, p 70 and OJNo C315, 22.1.1993.
3 OJ No C304, 10.11.1993, p 1.
4 OJNo L257, 19.10.1968, p 13. Directive as last amended by the Act of Accession of 1985.
5 OJNo 56, 4.4.1964, p 850/64.
6 OJ No L180, 13.7.1990, p 30.

Has adopted this directive:

Article 1

In order to lay down conditions to facilitate the exercise of the right of residence and with a view to guaranteeing access to vocational training in a non-discriminatory manner for a national of a member state who has been accepted to attend a vocational training course in another member state, the member states shall recognise the right of residence for any student who is a national of a member state and who does not enjoy that right under other provisions of Community law, and for the student's spouse and their dependent children, where the student assures the relevant national authority, by means of a declaration or by such alternative means as the student may choose that are at least equivalent, that he has sufficient resources to avoid becoming a burden on the social assistance system of the host member state during their period of residence, provided that the student is enrolled in a recognised educational establishment for the principal purpose of following a vocational training course there and that he is covered by sickness insurance in respect of all risks in the host member state.

Article 2

1   The right of residence shall be restricted to the duration of the course of studies in question.
   The right of residence shall be evidenced by means of the issue of a document known as a 'residence permit for a national of a member state of the Community', the validity of which may be limited to the duration of the course of studies or to one year where the course lasts longer; in the latter event it shall be renewable annually. Where a member of the family does not hold the nationality of a member state, he or she shall

be issued with a residence document of the same validity as that issued to the national on whom he or she depends.

For the purpose of issuing the residence permit or document, the member state may require only that the applicant present a valid identity card or passport and provide proof that he or she meets the conditions laid down in Article 1.

2   Articles 2, 3 and 9 of Directive 68/360/EEC shall apply *mutatis mutandis* to the beneficiaries of this Directive.

The spouse and dependent children of a national of a member state entitled to the right of residence within the territory of a member state shall be entitled to take up any employed or self-employed activity anywhere within the territory of that member state, even if they are not nationals of a member state.

Member states shall not derogate from the provisions of this Directive save on grounds of public policy, public security or public health; in that event, Articles 2 to 9 of Directive 64/221/EEC shall apply.

Article 3

This Directive shall not establish any entitlement to the payment of maintenance grants by the host member state on the part of students benefiting from the right of residence.

Article 4

The right of residence shall remain for as long as beneficiaries of that right fulfil the conditions laid down in Article 1.

Article 5

The Commission shall, not more than three years after the date of implementation of this Directive, and at three-yearly intervals thereafter, draw up a report on the application of this Directive and submit it to the European Parliament and the Council.

The Commission shall pay particular attention to any difficulties which the implementation of Article 1 might give rise in the member states; it shall, if appropriate, submit proposals to the Council with the aim of remedying such difficulties.

Article 6

Member states shall bring into force the laws, regulations and administrative provisions necessary to comply with this Directive not later than 31 December 1993. They shall forthwith inform the Commission thereof.

For the period preceding that date, the effects of Directive 90/366/EEC shall be maintained.

When member states adopt those measures, they shall contain a reference to this Directive or shall be accompanied by such a reference on the occasion of their official publication. The methods of making such references shall be laid down by the member states.

Article 7

This Directive is addressed to the member states.

Done at Brussels, 29 October 1993.

COUNCIL REGULATION (EC) 574/99

of 12 March 1999 determining the third countries whose nationals must be in
possession of visas when crossing the external borders of the Member States

The Council of the European Union,

Having regard to the Treaty establishing the European Community, and in particular
Article 100c thereof,

Having regard to the proposal from the Commission,[1]

Having regard to the opinion of the European Parliament,[2]

(1) Whereas Article 100c of the Treaty requires the Council to determine the third
countries whose nationals must be in possession of a visa when crossing the external
borders of the Member States;

(2) Whereas the drawing up of the common list annexed to this Regulation represents
an important step towards the harmonisation of visa policy; whereas the second
subparagraph of Article 7a of the Treaty stipulates in particular that the internal market
shall comprise an area without internal frontiers in which the free movement of, inter
alia, persons is ensured in accordance with the Treaty; whereas other aspects of the
harmonisation of visa policy, including the conditions for the issue of visas, are matters
to be determined within the appropriate framework;

(3) Whereas risks relating to security and illegal immigration should be given priority
consideration when the said common list is drawn up; whereas, in addition, Member
States' international relations with third countries also play a role;

(4) Whereas the principle that a Member State may not require a visa from a person
wishing to cross its external borders if that person holds a visa issued by another
Member State which meets the harmonised conditions governing the issue of visas and
is valid throughout the Community or if that person holds an appropriate permit issued
by a Member State is a matter that should be determined within the appropriate
framework;

(5) Whereas this Regulation should not prevent a Member State from deciding under
what conditions nationals of third countries lawfully resident within its territory may
re-enter it after having left the territory of the Member States of the Union during the
period of validity of their permits;

(6) Whereas, in special cases justifying an exemption where visa requirements would in
principle exist, Member States may exempt certain categories of person in keeping
with international law or custom;

(7) Whereas, since national rules differ on stateless persons, recognised refugees and
persons who produce passports or travel documents issued by a territorial entity or
authority which is not recognised as a State by all Member States, Member States may
decide on visa requirements for that group of persons, where that territorial entity or
authority is not on the said common list;

(8) Whereas it is necessary, when new entities are added to the list, to take account of
diplomatic implications and guidelines adopted on the matter by the European Union;
whereas, at all events, the inclusion of a third country on the common list is entirely
without prejudice to its international status;

(9) Whereas the determination of third countries whose nationals must be in possession
of visas when crossing the external borders of the Member States should be achieved
gradually; whereas Member States will constantly endeavour to harmonise their visa
policies with regard to third countries not on the common list; whereas the present

provisions must not prejudice the achievement of free movement of persons as provided for in Article 7a of the Treaty; whereas the Commission should draw up a progress report on harmonisation in the first half of the year 2001;

(10) Whereas, with a view to ensuring that the system is administered openly and that the persons concerned are informed, Member States should communicate to the other Member States and to the Commission the measures which they take pursuant to this Regulation; whereas for the same reasons that information must also be published in the Official Journal of the European Communities,

NOTES

1 OJ C 11, 15. 1. 1994, p. 15.
2 OJ C 128, 9. 5. 1994, p. 350. Opinion of the European Parliament of 10 February 1999.

Has adopted this Regulation:

Article 1

1 Nationals of third countries on the common list in the Annex shall be required to be in possession of visas when crossing the external borders of the Member States.

2 Nationals of countries formerly part of countries on the common list shall be subject to the requirements of paragraph 1 unless and until the Council decides otherwise under the procedure laid down in the relevant provision of the Treaty.

Article 2

1 Member States shall determine the visa requirements for nationals of third countries not on the common list.

2 Member States shall determine the visa requirements for stateless persons and recognised refugees.

3 Member States shall determine the visa requirements for persons who produce passports or travel documents issued by a territorial entity or authority which is not recognised as a State by all Member States if that territorial entity or authority is not on the common list.

4 Within 10 working days of the entry into force of this Regulation, Member States shall communicate to the other Member States and the Commission the measures they have taken pursuant to paragraphs 1, 2 and 3. Any further measures taken pursuant to paragraph 1 shall be similarly communicated within five working days.

The Commission shall publish the measures communicated pursuant to this paragraph and updates thereof in the Official Journal of the European Communities for information.

Article 3

During the first half of 2001 the Commission shall draw up a progress report on the harmonisation of Member States' visa policies with regard to third countries not on the common list and, if necessary, submit to the Council proposals for further measures required to achieve the objective of harmonisation laid down in the Treaty.

Article 4

1 A Member State may exempt nationals of third countries subject to visa requirements under Article 1(1) and (2) from such requirements. This shall apply in particular to civilian air and sea crew, flight crew and attendants on emergency or rescue flights and

other helpers in the event of disaster or accident and holders of diplomatic passports, official duty passports and other official passports.

2 Article 2(4) shall apply mutatis mutandis.

Article 5

For the purposes of this Regulation, 'visa' shall mean an authorisation given or a decision taken by a Member State which is required for entry into its territory with a view to:

— an intended stay in that Member State or in several Member States of no more than three months in all,
— transit through the territory of that Member State or several Member States, except for transit through the international zones of airports and transfers between airports in a Member State.

Article 6

This Regulation shall be without prejudice to any further harmonisation between individual Member States, going beyond the common list, determining the third countries whose nationals must be in possession of a visa when crossing their external borders.

Article 7

This Regulation shall enter into force on the day following that of its publication in the Official Journal of the European Communities.

This Regulation shall be binding in its entirety and directly applicable in all Member States.

Done at Brussels, 12 March 1999.

ANNEX

COMMON LIST REFERRED TO IN ARTICLE 1

I. STATES

Afghanistan
Albania
Algeria
Angola
Armenia
Azerbaijan
Bahrain
Bangladesh
Belarus
Benin
Bhutan
Bulgaria
Burkina Faso
Burma/Myanmar
Burundi
Cambodia
Cameroon
Cape Verde
Central African Republic
Chad

China (*)
Comoros
Congo
Côte d'Ivoire
Cuba
Democratic Republic of the Congo
Djibouti
Dominican Republic
Egypt
Equatorial Guinea
Eritrea
Ethiopia
Federal Republic of Yugoslavia (Serbia and Montenegro)
Fiji
Former Yugoslav Republic of Macedonia
Gabon
The Gambia
Georgia

Ghana	Pakistan
Guinea	Papua New Guinea
Guinea-Bissau	Peru
Guyana	Philippines
Haiti	Qatar
India	Romania
Indonesia	Russia
Iran	Rwanda
Iraq	Sao Tomé and Principe
Jordan	Saudi Arabia
Kazakhstan	Senegal
Kyrgyzstan	Sierra Leone
Kuwait	Somalia
Laos	Sri Lanka
Lebanon	Sudan
Liberia	Suriname
Libya	Syria
Madagascar	Tajikistan
Maldives	Tanzania
Mali	Thailand
Mauritania	Togo
Mauritius	Tunisia
Moldavia	Turkey
Mongolia	Turkmenistan
Morocco	Uganda
Mozambique	Ukraine
Nepal	United Arab Emirates
Niger	Uzbekistan
Nigeria	Vietnam
North Korea	Yemen
Oman	Zambia

II. TERRITORIAL ENTITIES AND AUTHORITIES NOT RECOGNISED AS STATES BY ALL THE MEMBER STATES

Taiwan

(*) In respect of China, this does not include holders of the Hong Kong Special Administrative Region passport. Article 2 applies: Member States may decide whether to maintain or review their visa requirements in respect of such persons.

THE DUBLIN CONVENTION

**Convention determining the state responsible for examining applications for asylum
lodged in one of the member states of the european communities**

Signed in Dublin on 15 June 1990
Ratified by the United Kingdom and all other member states

Having regard to the objective, fixed by the European Council meeting in Strasbourg
on 8 and 9 December 1989, of the harmonisation of their asylum policies;

Determined, in keeping with their common humanitarian tradition, to guarantee
adequate protection to refugees in accordance with the terms of the Geneva Convention
of 28 July 1951, as amended by the New York Protocol of 31 January 1967 relating to
the Status of Refugees, hereinafter referred to as the 'Geneva Convention' and the
'New York Protocol' respectively;

Considering the joint objective of an area without internal frontiers in which the free
movement of persons shall, in particular, be ensured, in accordance with the provisions
of the Treaty establishing the European Economic Community, as amended by the
Single European Act;

Aware of the need, in pursuit of this objective, to take measures to avoid any situations
arising, with the result that applicants for asylum are left in doubt for too long as
regards the likely outcome of their applications and concerned to provide all applicants
for asylum with a guarantee that their applications will be examined by one of the
member states and to ensure that applicants for asylum are not referred successively
from one member state to another without any of these states acknowledging itself to
be competent to examine the application for asylum;

Desiring to continue the dialogue with the United Nations High Commissioner for
Refugees in order to achieve the above objectives;

Determined to co-operate closely in the application of this Convention through various
means, including exchanges of information.

[The representatives of the member states of the EEC]...

Have agreed* as follows:

* Denmark has not yet acceded to the Convention.

Article 1

1 For the purposes of this Convention:

  (a) Alien means: any person other than a national of a member state;
  (b) Application for asylum means: a request whereby an alien seeks from a member
       state protection under the Geneva Convention by claiming refugee status within
       the meaning of Article 1 of the Geneva Convention, as amended by the New
       York Protocol;
  (c) Applicant for asylum means: an alien who has made an application for asylum
       in respect of which a final decision has not yet been taken;
  (d) Examination of an application for asylum means: all the measures for
       examination, decisions or rulings given by the competent authorities on an
       application for asylum, except for procedures to determine the state responsible
       for examining the application for asylum pursuant to this Convention;
  (e) Residence permit means: any authorization issued by the authorities of a
       member state authorizing an alien to stay in its territory, with the exception of

visas and 'stay permits' issued during examination of an application for a residence permit or for asylum.

(f) Entry visa means: authorization or decision by a member state to enable an alien to enter its territory, subject to the other entry conditions being fulfilled;

(g) Transit visa means: authorization or decision by a member state to enable an alien to transit through its territory or pass through the transit zone of a port or airport, subject to the other transit conditions being fulfilled.

2 The nature of the visa shall be assessed in the light of the definitions set out in paragraph 1, points (f) and (g).

Article 2

The member states reaffirm their obligations under the Geneva Convention, as amended by the New York Protocol, with no geographic restriction of the scope of these instruments, and their commitment to co-operating with the services of the United Nations High Commissioner for Refugees in applying these instruments.

Article 3

1 Member states undertake to examine the application of any alien who applies at the border or in their territory to any one of them for asylum.

2 That application shall be examined by a single member state, which shall be determined in accordance with the criteria defined in this Convention. The criteria set out in Articles 4 to 8 shall apply in the order in which they appear.

3 That application shall be examined by that state in accordance with its national laws and its international obligations.

4 Each member state shall have the right to examine an application for asylum submitted to it by an alien, even if such examination is not its responsibility under the criteria defined in this Convention, provided that the applicant for asylum agrees thereto.

The member state responsible under the above criteria is then relieved of its obligations, which are transferred to the member state which expressed the wish to examine the application. The latter state shall inform the member state responsible under the said criteria if the application has been referred to it.

5 Any member state shall retain the right, pursuant to its national laws, to send an applicant for asylum to a third state, in compliance with the provisions of the Geneva Convention, as amended by the New York Protocol.

6 The process of determining the member state responsible for examining the application for asylum under this Convention shall start as soon as an application for asylum is first lodged with a member state.

7 An applicant for asylum who is present in another member state and there lodges an application for asylum after withdrawing his or her application during the process of determining the state responsible shall be taken back, under the conditions laid down in Article 13, by the member state with which that application for asylum was lodged, with a view to completing the process of determining the state responsible for examining the application for asylum.

This obligation shall cease to apply if the applicant for asylum has since left the territory of the member states for a period of at least three months or has obtained from a member state a residence permit valid for more than three months.

Article 4

Where the applicant for asylum has a member of his family who has been recognized as having refugee status within the meaning of the Geneva Convention, as amended by the New York Protocol, in a member state and is legally resident there, that state shall be responsible for examining the application, provided that the persons concerned so desire.

The family member in question may not be other than the spouse of the applicant for asylum or his or her unmarried child who is a minor of under eighteen years, or his or her father or mother where the applicant for asylum is himself or herself an unmarried child who is a minor of under eighteen years.

Article 5

1 Where the applicant for asylum is in possession of a valid residence permit, the member state which issued the permit shall be responsible for examining the application for asylum.

2 Where the applicant for asylum is in possession of a valid visa, the member state which issued the visa shall be responsible for examining the application for asylum, except in the following situations:

(a) if the visa was issued on the written authorization of another member state, that state shall be responsible for examining the application for asylum. Where a member state first consults the central authority of another member state, inter alia for security reasons, the agreement of the latter shall not constitute written authorization within the meaning of this provision.

(b) where the applicant for asylum is in possession of a transit visa and lodges his application in another member state in which he is not subject to a visa requirement, that state shall be responsible for examining the application for asylum.

(c) where the applicant for asylum is in possession of a transit visa and lodges his application in the state which issued him or her with the visa and which has received written confirmation from the diplomatic or consular authorities of the member state of destination that the alien for whom the visa requirement was waived fulfilled the conditions for entry into that state, the latter shall be responsible for examining the application for asylum.

3 Where the applicant for asylum is in possession of more than one valid residence permit or visa issued by different member states, the responsibility for examining the application for asylum shall be assumed by the member states in the following order:

(a) the state which issued the residence permit conferring the right to the longest period of residency or, where the periods of validity of all the permits are identical, the state which issued the residence permit having the latest expiry date;

(b) the state which issued the visa having the latest expiry date where the various visas are of the same type;

(c) where visas are of different kinds, the state which issued the visa having the longest period of validity, or where the periods of validity are identical, the state which issued the visa having the latest expiry date. This provision shall not apply where the applicant is in possession of one or more transit visas, issued on presentation of an entry visa for another member state. In that case, that member state shall be responsible.

4 Where the applicant for asylum is in possession only of one or more residence permits which have expired less than two years previously or one or more visas which have expired less than six months previously and enabled him or her actually to enter the territory of a member state, the provisions of paragraphs 1, 2 and 3 of this Article shall apply for such time as the alien has not left the territory of the member states.

Where the applicant for asylum is in possession of one or more residence permits which have expired more than two years previously or one or more visas which have expired more than six months previously and enabled him or her to enter the territory of a member state and where an alien has not left Community territory, the member state in which the application is lodged shall be responsible.

Article 6

When it can be proved that an applicant for asylum has irregularly crossed the border into a member state by land, sea or air, having come from a non-member state of the European Communities, the member state thus entered shall be responsible for examining the application for asylum.

That state shall cease to be responsible, however, if it is proved that the applicant has been living in the member state where the application for asylum was made at least six months before making this application for asylum. In that case it is the latter member state which is responsible for examining the application for asylum.

Article 7

1 The responsibility for examining an application for asylum shall be incumbent upon the member state responsible for controlling the entry of the alien into the territory of the member states, except where, after legally entering a member state in which the need for him or her to have a visa is waived, the alien lodges his or her application for asylum in another member state in which the need for him or her to have a visa for entry into the territory is also waived. In this case, the latter state shall be responsible for examining the application for asylum.

2 Pending the entry into force of an agreement between member states on arrangements for crossing external borders, the member state which authorizes transit without a visa through the transit zone of its airports shall not be regarded as responsible for control on entry, in respect of travellers who do not leave the transit zone.

3 Where the application for asylum is made in transit in an airport of a member state, that state shall be responsible for examination.

Article 8

Where no member state responsible for examining the application for asylum can be designated on the basis of the other criteria listed in this Convention, the first member state with which the application for asylum is lodged shall be responsible for examining it.

Article 9

Any member state, even when it is not responsible under the criteria laid out in this Convention, may, for humanitarian reasons, based in particular on family or cultural grounds, examine an application for asylum at the request of another member state, provided that the applicant so desires.

If the member state thus approached accedes to the request, responsibility for examining the application shall be transferred to it.

Article 10

1 The member state responsible for examining an application for asylum according to the criteria set out in this Convention shall be obliged to:

   (a)   Take charge under the conditions laid down in Article 11 of an applicant who has lodged an application for asylum in a different member state.
   (b)   Complete the examination of the application for asylum.
   (c)   Re-admit or take back under the conditions laid down in Article 13 an applicant whose application is under examination and who is irregularly in another member state.

(d) Take back, under the conditions laid down in Article 13, an applicant who has withdrawn the application under examination and lodged an application in another member state.

(e) Take back, under the conditions laid down in Article 13, an alien whose application it has rejected and who is illegally in another member state.

2 If a member state issues to the applicant a residence permit valid for more than three months, the obligations specified in paragraph 1, points (a) to (e) shall be transferred to that member state.

3 The obligations specified in paragraph 1, points (a) to (d) shall cease to apply if the alien concerned has left the territory of the member states for a period of at least three months.

4 The obligations specified in paragraph 1, points (d) and (e) shall cease to apply if the state responsible for examining the application for asylum, following the withdrawal or rejection of the application, takes and enforces the necessary measures for the alien to return to his country of origin or to another country which he may lawfully enter.

Article 11

1 If a member state with which an application for asylum has been lodged considers that another member state is responsible for examining the application, it may, as quickly as possible and in any case within the six months following the date on which the application was lodged, call upon the other member state to take charge of the applicant.

If the request that charge be taken is not made within the six-month time limit, responsibility for examining the application for asylum shall rest with the state in which the application was lodged.

2 The request that charge be taken shall contain indications enabling the authorities of that other state to ascertain whether it is responsible on the basis of the criteria laid down in this Convention.

3 The state responsible in accordance with those criteria shall be determined on the basis of the situation obtaining when the applicant for asylum first lodged his application with a member state.

4 The member state shall pronounce judgment on the request within three months of receipt of the claim. Failure to act within that period shall be tantamount to accepting the claim.

5 Transfer of the applicant for asylum from the member state where the application was lodged to the member state responsible must take place not later than one month after acceptance of the request to take charge or one month after the conclusion of any proceedings initiated by the alien challenging the transfer decision if the proceedings are suspensory.

6 Measures taken under Article 18 may subsequently determine the details of the process by which applicants shall be taken in charge.

Article 12

Where an application for asylum is lodged with the competent authorities of a member state by an applicant who is on the territory of another member state, the determination of the member state responsible for examining the application for asylum shall be made by the member state on whose territory the applicant is. The latter member state shall be informed without delay by the member state which received the application and shall then, for the purpose of applying this Convention, be regarded as the member state with which the application for asylum was lodged.

Article 13

1 An applicant for asylum shall be taken back in the cases provided for in Article 3(7) and in Article 10 as follows:

    (a)   the request for the applicant to be taken back must provide indications enabling the state with which the request is lodged to ascertain that it is responsible in accordance with Article 3(7) and with Article 10;

    (b)   the state called upon to take back the applicant shall give an answer to the request within eight days of the matter being referred to it. Should it acknowledge responsibility, it shall then take back the applicant for asylum as quickly as possible and at the latest one month after it agrees to do so.

2 Measures taken under Article 18 may at a later date set out the details of the procedure for taking the applicant back.

Article 14

1 Member states shall conduct mutual exchanges with regard to:

— national legislative or regulatory measures or practices applicable in the field of asylum;

— statistical data on monthly arrivals of applicants for asylum, and their breakdown by nationality. Such information shall be forwarded quarterly through the General Secretariat of the Council of the European Communities, which shall see that it is circulated to the member states and the Commission of the European Communities and to the United Nations High Commissioner for Refugees.

2 The member states may conduct mutual exchanges with regard to:

— general information on new trends in applications for asylum;

— general information on the situation in the countries of origin or of provenance of applicants for asylum.

3 If the member state providing the information referred to in paragraph 2 wants it to be kept confidential, the other member states shall comply with this wish.

Article 15

1 Each member state shall communicate to any member state that so requests such information on individual cases as is necessary for:

— determining the member state which is responsible for examining the application for asylum;

— examining the application for asylum;

— implementing any obligation arising under this Convention.

2 This information may only cover:

— personal details of the applicant, and, where appropriate, the members of his family (full name—where appropriate, former name—, nicknames or pseudonyms, nationality—present and former—, date and place of birth);

— identity and travel papers (references, validity, date of issue, issuing authority, place of issue, etc);

— other information necessary for establishing the identity of the applicant;

— places of residence and routes travelled;

— residence permits or visas issued by a member state;

— the place where the application was lodged;

— the date any previous application for asylum was lodged, the date the present application was lodged, the stage reached in the proceedings and the decision taken, if any.

3 Furthermore, one member state may request another member state to let it know on what grounds the applicant for asylum bases his or her application and, where applicable, the grounds for any decisions taken concerning the applicant. It is for the member state from which the information is requested to decide whether or not to impart it. In any event, communication of the information requested shall be subject to the approval of the applicant for asylum.

4 This exchange of information shall be effected at the request of a member state and may only take place between authorities the designation of which by each member state has been communicated to the Committee provided for under Article 18.

5 The information exchanged may only be used for the purposes set out in paragraph 1. In each member state such information may only be communicated to the authorities and courts and tribunals entrusted with:

—   determining the member state which is responsible for examining the application for asylum;
—   examining the application for asylum;
—   implementing any obligation arising under this Convention.

6 The member state that forwards the information shall ensure that it is accurate and up-to-date.

If it appears that this member state has supplied information which is inaccurate or which should not have been forwarded, the recipient member state, shall be immediately informed thereof. They shall be obliged to correct such information or to have it erased.

7 An applicant for asylum shall have the right to receive, on request, the information exchanged concerning him or her, for such time as it remains available.

If he or she establishes that such information is inaccurate or should not have been forwarded, he or she shall have the right to have it corrected or erased. This right shall be exercised in accordance with the conditions laid down in paragraph 6.

8 In each Member State concerned, the forwarding and receipt of exchanged information shall be recorded.

9 Such information shall be kept for a period not exceeding that necessary for the ends for which it was exchanged. The need to keep it shall be examined at the appropriate moment by the Member State concerned.

10 In any event, the information thus communicated shall enjoy at least the same protection as is given to similar information in the Member State which receives it.

11 If data are not processed automatically but are handled in some other form, every Member State shall take the appropriate measures to ensure compliance with this Article by means of effective controls. If a Member State has a monitoring body of the type mentioned in paragraph 12, it may assign the control task to it.

12 If one or more Member States wish to computerise all or part of the information mentioned in paragraphs 2 and 3, such computerisation is only possible if the countries concerned have adopted laws applicable to such processing which implement the principles of the Strasbourg Convention of 28 February 1981 for the Protection of Individuals, with regard to Automatic Processing of Personal Data and if they have entrusted an appropriate national body with the independent monitoring of the processing and use of data forwarded to the Convention.

Article 16

1 Any member state may submit to the Committee referred to in Article 18 proposals for revision of this Convention in order to eliminate difficulties in the application thereof.

2 If it proves necessary to revise or amend this Convention pursuant to the achievement of the objectives set out in Article 8a of the Treaty establishing the European Economic Community, such achievement being linked in particular to the establishment of a harmonised asylum and a common visa policy, the member state holding the Presidency of the Council of the European Communities shall organize a meeting of the Committee referred to in Article 18.

3 Any revision of this Convention or amendment hereto shall be adopted by the Committee referred to in Article 18. They shall enter into force in accordance with the provisions of Article 22.

Article 17

1 If a member state experiences major difficulties as a result of a substantial change in the circumstances obtaining on conclusion of this Convention, the state in question may bring the matter before the Committee referred to in Article 18 so that the latter may put to the member states measured to deal with the situation or adopt such revisions or amendments to this Convention as appear necessary, which shall enter into force as provided for in Article 16(3).

2 If, after six months, the situation mentioned in paragraph 1 still obtains, the Committee, acting in accordance with Article 18(2), may authorize the member state affected by that change to suspend temporarily the application of the provisions of this Convention, without such suspension being allowed to impede the achievement of the objectives mentioned in Article 8a of the Treaty establishing the European Economic Treaty or contravene other international obligations of the member states.

3 During the period of suspension, the Committee shall continue its discussions with a view to revising the provisions of this Convention, unless it has already reached an agreement.

Article 18

1 A Committee shall be set up comprising one representative of the Government of each member state.

The Committee shall be chaired by the member state holding the Presidency of the Council of the European Communities.

The Commission of the European Communities may participate in the discussions of the Committee and the working parties referred to in paragraph 4.

2 The Committee shall examine, at the request of one or more member states, any question of a general nature concerning the application or interpretation of this Convention.

The Committee shall determine the measures referred to in Article 11(6) and Article 13(2) and shall give the authorization referred to in Article 17(2).

The Committee shall adopt decisions revising or amending the Convention pursuant to Articles 16 and 17.

3 The Committee shall take its decisions unanimously, except where it is acting pursuant to Article 17(2), in which case it shall take its decisions by a majority of two-thirds of the votes of its members.

4 The Committee shall determine its rules of procedure and may set up working parties.

The Secretariat of the Committee and of the working parties shall be provided by the General Secretariat of the Council of the European Communities.

Article 19

As regards the Kingdom of Denmark, the provisions of this Convention shall not apply to the Faroe Islands nor to Greenland unless a declaration to the contrary is made by the Kingdom of Denmark. Such a declaration may be made at any time by a communication to the Government of Ireland which shall inform the Governments of the other member states thereof.

As regards the French Republic, the provisions of this Convention shall apply only to the European territory of the French Republic.

As regards the Kingdom of the Netherlands, the provisions of this Convention shall apply only to the territory of the Kingdom of the Netherlands in Europe.

As regards the United Kingdom the provisions of this Convention shall apply only to the United Kingdom of Great Britain and Northern Ireland. They shall not apply to the European territories for whose external relations the United Kingdom is responsible unless a declaration to the contrary is made by the United Kingdom. Such a declaration may be made at any time by a communication to the Government of Ireland, which shall inform the Governments of the other Member States thereof.

Article 20

This Convention shall not be the subject of any reservations.

Article 21

1 This Convention shall be open for the accession of any State which becomes a member of the European Convention. The instruments of accession will be deposited with the Government of Ireland.

2 It shall enter into force in respect of any State which accedes thereto on the first day of the third month following the deposit of its instrument of accession.

Article 22

1 This Convention shall be subject to ratification, acceptance or approval. The instruments of ratification, acceptance or approval shall be deposited with the Government of Ireland.

2 The Government of Ireland shall notify the Governments of the other member states of the deposit of the instruments of ratification, acceptance or approval.

3 This Convention shall enter into force on the first day of the third month following the deposit of the instrument of ratification, acceptance or approval by the last signatory state to take this step.

The state with which the instruments of ratification, acceptance or approval are deposited shall notify the member states of the date of entry into force of this Convention.

INTERNATIONAL MATERIALS

CONVENTION RELATING TO THE STATUS OF REFUGEES

Done at Geneva on 28 July 1951

Entry into force *22 April 1954, in accordance with Article 43*

Text *United Nations Treaty Series No 2545, Vol 189, p 137*

PREAMBLE

The High Contracting Parties

Considering that the Charter of the United Nations and the Universal Declaration of Human Rights approved on 10 December 1948 by the General Assembly have affirmed the principle that human beings shall enjoy fundamental rights and freedoms without discrimination,

Considering that the United Nations has, on various occasions, manifested its profound concern for refugees and endeavoured to assure refugees the widest possible exercise of these fundamental rights and freedoms,

Considering that it is desirable to revise and consolidate previous international agreements relating to the status of refugees and to extend the scope of and the protection accorded by such instruments by means of a new agreement.

Considering that the grant of asylum may place unduly heavy burdens on certain countries, and that a satisfactory solution of a problem of which the United Nations has recognised the international scope and nature cannot therefore be achieved without international co-operation,

Expressing the wish that all states, recognizing the social and humanitarian nature of the problem of refugees, will do everything within their power to prevent this problem from becoming a cause of tension between states,

Noting that the United Nations High Commissioner for Refugees is charged with the task of supervising international conventions providing for the protection of refugees, and recognising that the effective co-ordination of measures taken to deal with this problem will depend upon the co-operation of states with the High Commissioner,

Have agreed as follows:

NOTES

The Convention was adopted by the United Nations Conference of Plenipotentiaries on the Status of Refugees and Stateless Persons, held at Geneva from 2 to 25 July 1951. The Conference was convened pursuant to resolution 429(V), adopted by the General Assembly of the United Nations on 14 December 1950. For the text of this resolution, see Official Records of the General Assembly, Fifth Session, Supplement No 20(A/1775), p 48, The Text of the Final Act of the Conference is reproduced in the Appendix.

CHAPTER 1 GENERAL PROVISIONS

Article 1 Definition of the term 'Refugee'

A For the purposes of the present Convention, the term 'refugee' shall apply to any person who:

(1) Has been considered a refugee under the Arrangements of 12 May 1926 and 30 June 1928 or under the Conventions of 28 October 1933 and 10 February 1938, the Protocol of 14 September 1939 or the Constitution of the International Refugee Organization;

Decisions of non-eligibility taken by the International Refugee Organization during the period of its activities shall not prevent the status of refugee being accorded to persons who fulfil the conditions of paragraph 2 of this section;

(2) As a result of events occurring before 1 January 1951 and owing to well-founded fear of being persecuted for reasons of race, religion, nationality, membership of a particular social group or political opinion, is outside the country of his nationality and is unable or, owing to such fear, is unwilling to avail himself of the protection of that country; or who, not having a nationality and being outside the country of his former habitual residence as a result of such events, is unable or, owing to such fear, is unwilling to return to it.

In the case of a person who has more than one nationality, the term 'the country of his nationality' shall mean each of the countries of which he is a national, and a person shall not be deemed to be lacking the protection of the country of his nationality if, without any valid reason based on well-founded fear, he has not availed himself of the protection of one of the countries of which he is a national.

B (1) For the purposes of this Convention, the words 'events occurring before 1 January 1951' in Article 1, Section A, shall be understood to mean either

   (*a*) 'events occurring in Europe before 1 January 1951'; or
   (*b*) 'events occurring in Europe or elsewhere before 1 January 1951', and each contracting state shall make a declaration at the time of signature, ratification or accession, specifying which of these meanings it applies for the purpose of its obligations under this Convention.

(2) Any contracting state which has adopted alternative (*a*) may at any time extend its obligations by adopting alternative (*b*) by means of a notification addressed to the Secretary-General of the United Nations.

C This Convention shall cease to apply to any person falling under the terms of section A if:

(1) He has voluntarily re-availed himself of the protection of the country of his nationality; or

(2) Having lost his nationality, he has voluntarily re-acquired it, or

(3) He has acquired a new nationality, and enjoys the protection of the country of his new nationality; or

(4) He has voluntarily re-established himself in the country which he left or outside which he remained owing to fear of persecution; or

(5) He can no longer, because the circumstances in connection with which he has been recognized as a refugee have ceased to exist, continue to refuse to avail himself of the protection of the country of his nationality;

Provided that this paragraph shall not apply to a refugee falling under section A(1) of this Article who is able to invoke compelling reasons arising out of previous persecution for refusing to avail himself of the protection of the country of nationality;

(6) Being a person who has no nationality he is, because the circumstances in connection with which he has been recognized as a refugee have ceased to exist, able to return to the country of his former habitual residence;

Provided that this paragraph shall not apply to a refugee falling under section A(1) of this Article who is able to invoke compelling reasons arising out of previous persecution for refusing to return to the country of his former habitual residence.

D This Convention shall not apply to persons who are at present receiving from organs or agencies of the United Nations other than the United Nations High Commissioner for Refugees protection or assistance.

When such protection or assistance has ceased for any reason, without the position of such persons being definitely settled in accordance with the relevant resolutions adopted by the General Assembly of the United Nations, these persons shall *ipso facto* be entitled to the benefits of this Convention.

E This Convention shall not apply to a person who is recognized by the competent authorities of the country in which he has taken residence as having the rights and obligations which are attached to the possession of the nationality of that country.

F The provisions of this Convention shall not apply to any person with respect to whom there are serious reasons for considering that:

(*a*) he has committed a crime against peace, a war crime, or a crime against humanity, as defined in the international instruments drawn up to make provision in respect of such crimes;

(*b*) he has committed a serious non-political crime outside the country of refuge prior to his admission to that country as a refugee;

(*c*) he has been guilty of acts contrary to the purposes and principles of the United Nations.

Article 2 General obligations

Every refugee has duties to the country in which he finds himself, which require in particular that he conform to its laws and regulations as well as to measures taken for the maintenance of public order.

Article 3 Non-discrimination

The contracting states shall apply the provisions of this Convention to refugees without discrimination as to race, religion or country of origin.

Article 4 Religion

The contracting states shall accord to refugees within their territories treatment at least as favourable as that accorded to their nationals with respect to freedom to practise their religion and freedom as regards the religious education of their children.

Article 5 Rights granted apart from this Convention

Nothing in this Convention shall be deemed to impair any rights and benefits granted by a contracting state to refugees apart from this Convention.

Article 6 The term 'in the same circumstances'

For the purpose of this Convention, the term 'in the same circumstances' implies that any requirements (including requirements as to length and conditions of sojourn or residence) which the particular individual would have to fulfil for the enjoyment of the right in question, if he were not a refugee, must be fulfilled by him, with the exception of requirements which by their nature a refugee is incapable of fulfilling.

Article 7 Exemption from reciprocity

1 Except where this Convention contains more favourable provisions, a contracting state shall accord to refugees the same treatment as is accorded to aliens generally.

2 After a period of three years' residence, all refugees shall enjoy exemption from legislative reciprocity in the territory of the contracting states.

3 Each contracting state shall continue to accord to refugees the rights and benefits to which they were already entitled, in the absence of reciprocity, at the date of entry into force of this Convention for that state.

4 The contracting states shall consider favourably the possibility of according to refugees, in the absence of reciprocity, rights and benefits beyond those to which they are entitled according to paragraphs 2 and 3, and to extending exemption from reciprocity to refugees who do not fulfil the conditions provided for in paragraphs 2 and 3.

5 The provisions of paragraphs 2 and 3 apply both to the rights and benefits referred to in Articles 13, 18, 19, 21 and 22 of this Convention and to rights and benefits for which this Convention does not provide.

Article 8 Exemption from exceptional measures

With regard to exceptional measures which may be taken against the person, property or interests of nationals of a foreign state, the contracting states shall not apply such measures to a refugee who is formally a national of the said state solely on account of such nationality. Contracting states which, under their legislation, are prevented from applying the general principle expressed in this Article, shall, in appropriate cases, grant exemptions in favour of such refugees.

Article 9 Provisional measures

Nothing in this Convention shall prevent a contracting state, in time of war or other grave and exceptional circumstances, from taking provisionally measures which it considers to be essential to the national security in the case of a particular person, pending a determination by the contracting state that that person is in fact a refugee and that the continuance of such measures is necessary in his case in the interests of national security.

Article 10 Continuity of residence

1 Where a refugee has been forcibly displaced during the Second World War and removed to the territory of a contracting state, and is resident there, the period of such enforced sojourn shall be considered to have been lawful residence within that territory.

2 Where a refugee has been forcibly displaced during the Second World War from the territory of a contracting state and has, prior to the date of entry into force of this Convention, returned there for the purpose of taking up residence, the period of residence before and after such enforced displacement shall be regarded as one uninterrupted period for any purposes for which uninterrupted residence is required.

Article 11 Refugee seamen

In the case of refugees regularly serving as crew members on board a ship flying the flag of a contracting state, that state shall give sympathetic consideration to their establishment on its territory and the issue of travel documents to them or their temporary admission to its territory particularly with a view to facilitating their establishment in another country.

CHAPTER II JURIDICAL STATUS

Article 12 Personal status

1 The personal status of a refugee shall be governed by the law of the country of his domicile or, if he has no domicile, by the law of the country of his residence.

2 Rights previously acquired by a refugee and dependent on personal status, more particularly rights attaching to marriage, shall be respected by a contracting state, subject to compliance, if this be necessary, with the formalities required by the law of that state, provided that the right in question is one which would have been recognized by the law of that state had he not become a refugee.

Article 13 Movable and immovable property

The contracting states shall accord to a refugee treatment as favourable as possible and, in any event, not less favourable than that accorded to aliens generally in the same circumstances, as regards the acquisition of movable and immovable property and other rights pertaining thereto, and to leases and other contracts relating to movable and immovable property.

Article 14 Artistic rights and industrial property

In respect of the protection of industrial property, such as inventions, designs or models, trade marks, trade names, and of rights in literary, artistic and scientific works, a refugee shall be accorded in the country in which he has his habitual residence the same protection as is accorded to nationals of that country. In the territory of any other contracting state, he shall be accorded the same protection as is accorded in that territory to nationals of the country in which he has his habitual residence.

Article 15 Right of association

As regards non-political and non-profit-making associations and trade unions the contracting states shall accord to refugees lawfully staying in their territory the most favourable treatment accorded to nationals of a foreign country, in the same circumstances.

Article 16 Access to courts

1 A refugee shall have free access to the courts of law on the territory of all contracting states.

2 A refugee shall enjoy in the contracting state in which he has his habitual residence the same treatment as a national in matters pertaining to access to the Courts, including legal assistance and exemption from *cautio judicatum solvi*.

3 A refugee shall be accorded in the matters referred to in paragraph 2 in countries other than that in which he has his habitual residence the treatment granted to a national of the country of his habitual residence.

CHAPTER III GAINFUL EMPLOYMENT

Article 17 Wage-earning employment

1 The contracting state shall accord to refugees lawfully staying in their territory the most favourable treatment accorded to nationals of a foreign country in the same circumstances, as regards the right to engage in wage-earning employment.

2 In any case, restrictive measures imposed on aliens or the employment of aliens for the protection of the national labour market shall not be applied to a refugee who was already exempt from them at the date of entry into force of this Convention for the contracting state concerned, or who fulfils one of the following conditions:

(*a*)   He has completed three years' residence in the country,

(*b*)   He has a spouse possessing the nationality of the country of residence. A refugee may not invoke the benefits of this provision if he has abandoned his spouse,

(*c*)   He has one or more children possessing the nationality of the country of residence.

3 The contracting states shall give sympathetic consideration to assimilating the rights of all refugees with regard to wage-earning employment to those of nationals, and in particular of those refugees who have entered their territory pursuant to programmes of labour recruitment or under immigration schemes.

Article 18 Self-employment

The contracting states shall accord to a refugee lawfully in their territory treatment as favourable as possible and, in any event, not less favourable than that accorded to aliens generally in the same circumstances, as regards the right to engage on his own account in agriculture, industry, handicrafts and commerce and to establish commercial and industrial companies.

Article 19 Liberal professions

1 Each contracting state shall accord to refugees lawfully staying in their territory who hold diplomas recognized by the competent authorities of that state, and who are desirous of practising a liberal profession, treatment as favourable as possible and, in any event, not less favourable than that accorded to aliens generally in the same circumstances.

2 The contracting states shall use their best endeavours consistently with their laws and constitutions to secure the settlement of such refugees in the territories, other than the metropolitan territory, for whose international relations they are responsible.

CHAPTER IV WELFARE

Article 20 Rationing

Where a rationing system exists, which applies to the population at large and regulates the general distribution of products in short supply, refugees shall be accorded the same treatment as nationals.

Article 21 Housing

As regards housing, the contracting states, in so far as the matter is regulated by laws or regulations or is subject to the control of public authorities, shall accord to refugees lawfully staying in their territory treatment as favourable as possible and, in any event, not less favourable than that accorded to aliens generally in the same circumstances.

Article 22 Public education

1 The contracting states shall accord to refugees the same treatment as is accorded to nationals with respect to elementary education.

2 The contracting states shall accord to refugees treatment as favourable as possible, and, in any event, not less favourable than that accorded to aliens generally in the same

circumstances, with respect to education other than elementary education and, in particular, as regards access to studies, the recognition of foreign school certificates, diplomas and degrees, the remission of fees and charges and the award of scholarships.

Article 23 Public relief

The contracting states shall accord to refugees lawfully staying in their territory the same treatment with respect to public relief and assistance as is accorded to their nationals.

Article 24 Labour legislation and social security

1 The contracting states shall accord to refugees lawfully staying in their territory the same treatment as is accorded to nationals in respect of the following matters:

(*a*) In so far as such matters are governed by laws or regulations or are subject to the control of administrative authorities: remuneration, including family allowances where these form part of remuneration, hours of work, overtime arrangements, holidays with pay, restrictions on home work, minimum age of employment, apprenticeship and training, women's work and the work of young persons, and the enjoyment of the benefits of collective bargaining;

(*b*) Social security (legal provisions in respect of employment injury, occupational diseases, maternity, sickness, disability, old age, death, unemployment, family responsibilities and any other contingency which, according to national laws or regulations, is covered by a social security scheme), subject to the following limitations:

   (i) There may be appropriate arrangements for the maintenance of acquired rights and rights in course of acquisition;

   (ii) National laws or regulations of the country of residence may prescribe special arrangements concerning benefits or portions of benefits which are payable wholly out of public funds, and concerning allowances paid to persons who do not fulfil the contribution conditions prescribed for the award of a normal pension.

2 The right to compensation for the death of a refugee resulting from employment injury or from occupational disease shall not be affected by the fact that the residence of the beneficiary is outside the territory of the contracting state.

3 The contracting states shall extend to refugees the benefits of agreements concluded between them, or which may be concluded between them in the future, concerning the maintenance of acquired rights and rights in the process of acquisition in regard to social security, subject only to the conditions which apply to nationals of the states signatory to the agreements in question.

4 The contracting states will give sympathetic consideration to extending to refugees so far as possible the benefits of similar agreements which may at any time be in force between such contracting states and non-contracting states.

CHAPTER V ADMINISTRATIVE MEASURES

Article 25 Administrative assistance

1 When the exercise of a right by a refugee would normally require the assistance of authorities of a foreign country to whom he cannot have recourse, the contracting states in whose territory he is residing shall arrange that such assistance be afforded to him by their own authorities or by an international authority.

2 The authority or authorities mentioned in paragraph 1 shall deliver or cause to be delivered under their supervision to refugees such documents or certifications as would normally be delivered to aliens by or through their national authorities.

3 Documents or certifications so delivered shall stand in the stead or the official instruments delivered to aliens by or through their national authorities, and shall be given credence in the absence of proof to the contrary.

4 Subject to such exceptional treatment as may be granted to indigent persons, fees may be charged for the services mentioned herein, but such fees shall be moderate and commensurate with those charged to nationals for similar services.

5 The provisions of this Article shall be without prejudice to Articles 27 and 28.

Article 26 Freedom of movement

Each contracting state shall accord to refugees lawfully in its territory the right to choose their place of residence and to move freely within its territory, subject to any regulations applicable to aliens generally in the same circumstances.

Article 27 Identity papers

The contracting states shall issue identity papers to any refugee in their territory who does not possess a valid travel document.

Article 28 Travel documents

1 The contracting states shall issue to refugees lawfully staying in their territory travel documents for the purpose of travel outside their territory unless compelling reasons of national security or public order otherwise require, and the provisions of the Schedule to this Convention shall apply with respect to such documents. The contracting states may issue such a travel document to any other refugee in their territory, they shall in particular give sympathetic consideration to the issue of such a travel document to refugees in their territory who are unable to obtain a travel document from the country of their lawful residence.

2 Travel documents issued to refugees under previous international agreements by parties thereto shall be recognized and treated by the contracting states in the same way as if they had been issued pursuant to this article.

Article 29 Fiscal charges

1 The contracting states shall not impose upon refugees duties, charges or taxes, of any description whatsoever, other or higher than those which are or may be levied on their nationals in similar situations.

2 Nothing in the above paragraph shall prevent the application to refugees of the laws and regulations concerning charges in respect of the issue to aliens of administrative documents including identity papers.

Article 30 Transfer of assets

1 A contracting state shall, in conformity with its laws and regulations, permit refugees to transfer assets which they have brought into its territory, to another country where they have been admitted for the purposes of resettlement.

2 A contracting state shall give sympathetic consideration to the application of refugees for permission to transfer assets wherever they may be and which are necessary for their resettlement in another country to which they have been admitted.

Article 31 Refugees unlawfully in the country of refuge

1 The contracting states shall not impose penalties, on account of their illegal entry or presence, on refugees who, coming directly from a territory where their life or freedom was threatened in the sense of Article 1, enter or are present in their territory without authorisation, provided they present themselves without delay to the authorities and show good cause for their illegal entry or presence.

2 The contracting states shall not apply to the movements of such refugees restrictions other than those which are necessary and such restrictions shall only be applied until their status in the country is regularised or they obtain admission into another country. The contracting states shall allow such refugees a reasonable period and all the necessary facilities to obtain admission into another country.

Article 32 Expulsion

1 The contracting states shall not expel a refugee lawfully in their territory save on grounds of national security or public order.

2 The expulsion of such a refugee shall be only in pursuance of a decision reached in accordance with due process of law. Except where compelling reasons of national security otherwise require, the refugee shall be allowed to submit evidence to clear himself, and to appeal to and be represented for the purpose before competent authority or a person or persons specially designated by the competent authority.

3 The contracting states shall allow such a refugee a reasonable period within which to seek legal admission into another country. The contracting states reserve the right to apply during that period such internal measures as they may deem necessary.

Article 33 Prohibition of expulsion or return ('refoulement')

1 No contracting state shall expel or return ('refouler') a refugee in any manner whatsoever to the frontiers of territories where his life or freedom would be threatened on account of his race, religion, nationality, membership of a particular social group or political opinion.

2 The benefit of the present provision may not, however, be claimed by a refugee whom there are reasonable grounds for regarding as a danger to the security of the country in which he is, or who, having been convicted by a final judgment of a particularly serious crime, constitutes a danger to the community of that country.

Article 34 Naturalisation

The contracting states shall as far as possible facilitate the assimilation and naturalisation of refugees. They shall in particular make every effort to expedite naturalisation proceedings and to reduce as far as possible the charges and costs of such proceedings.

CHATER VI EXECUTORY AND TRANSITORY PROVISIONS

Article 35 Co-operation of the national authorities with the United Nations

1 The contracting states undertake to co-operate with the Office of the United Nations High Commissioner for Refugees, or any other agency of the United Nations which may succeed it, in the exercise of its functions, and shall in particular facilitate its duty of supervising the application of the provisions of this Convention.

2 In order to enable the Office of the High Commissioner or any other agency of the United Nations which may succeed it, to make reports to the competent organs of the

United Nations, the contracting states undertake to provide them in the appropriate form with information and statistical data requested concerning:

(a) the condition of refugees,
(b) the implementation of this Convention, and
(c) laws, regulations and decrees which are, or may hereafter be, in force relating to refugees.

Article 36 Information on national legislation

The contracting states shall communicate to the Secretary-General of the United Nations the laws and regulations which they may adopt to ensure the application of this Convention.

Article 37 Relation to previous Conventions

Without prejudice to Article 28, paragraph 2, of this Convention, this Convention replaces, as between parties to it, the Arrangements of 5 July 1922, 31 May 1924, 12 May 1926, 30 June 1928 and 30 July 1935, the Conventions of 28 October 1933 and 10 February 1938, the Protocol of 14 September 1939 and the Agreement of 15 October 1946.

CHAPTER VII FINAL CLAUSES

Article 38 Settlement of disputes

Any dispute between parties to this Convention relating to its interpretation or application, which cannot be settled by other means, shall be referred to the International Court of Justice at the request of any one of the parties to the dispute.

Article 39 Signature, ratification and accession

1 This Convention shall be opened for signature at Geneva on 28 July 1951 and shall thereafter be deposited with the Secretary-General of the United Nations. It shall be open for signature at the European Office of the United Nations from 28 July to 31 August 1951 and shall be re-opened for signature at the Headquarters of the United Nations from 17 September 1951 to 31 December 1952.

2 This Convention shall be open for signature on behalf of all states members of the United Nations, and also on behalf of any other state invited to attend the Conference of Plenipotentiaries on the Status of Refugees and Stateless Persons or to which an invitation to sign will have been addressed by the General Assembly. It shall be ratified and the instruments of ratification shall be deposited with the Secretary-General of the United Nations.

3 This Convention shall be open from 28 July 1951 for accession by the states referred to in paragraph 2 of this Article. Accession shall be effected by the deposit of an instrument of accession with the Secretary-General of the United Nations.

Article 40 Territorial application clause

1 Any state may, at the time of signature, ratification or accession, declare that this Convention shall extend to all or any of the territories for the international relations of which it is responsible. Such a declaration shall take effect when the Convention enters into force for the state concerned.

2 At any time thereafter any such extension shall be made by notification addressed to the Secretary-General of the United Nations and shall take effect as from the ninetieth

day after the day of receipt by the Secretary-General of the United Nations of this notification, or as from the date of entry into force of the Convention for the state concerned, whichever is the later.

3 With respect to those territories to which this Convention is not extended at the time of signature, ratification or accession, each state concerned shall consider the possibility of taking the necessary steps in order to extend the application of this Convention to such territories, subject, where necessary for constitutional reasons, to the consent of the governments of such territories.

Article 41 Federal clause

In the case of a federal or non-unitary state, the following provisions shall apply:

(*a*) With respect to those Articles of this Convention that come within the legislative jurisdiction of the federal legislative authority, the obligations of the Federal Government shall to this extent be the same as those of Parties which are not federal states,

(*b*) With respect to those Articles of this Convention that come within the legislative jurisdiction of constituent states, provinces or cantons which are not, under the constitutional system of the federation, bound to take legislative action, the Federal Government shall bring such Articles with a favourable recommendation to the notice of the appropriate authorities of states, provinces or cantons at the earliest possible moment.

(*c*) A federal state party to this Convention shall, at the request of any other contracting state transmitted through the Secretary-General of the United Nations, supply a statement of the law and practice of the Federation and its constituent units in regard to any particular provision of the Convention showing the extent to which effect has been given to that provision by legislative or other action.

Article 42 Reservations

1 At the time of signature, ratification or accession, any state may make reservations to articles of the Convention other than to Articles 1, 3, 4, 16(1), 33, 36–46 inclusive.

2 Any state making a reservation in accordance with paragraph 1 of this article may at any time withdraw the reservation by a communication to that effect addressed to the Secretary-General of the United Nations.

Article 43 Entry into force

1 This Convention shall come into force on the ninetieth day following the day of deposit of the sixth instrument of ratification or accession.

2 For each state ratifying or acceding to the Convention after the deposit of the sixth instrument of ratification or accession, the Convention shall enter into force on the ninetieth day following the date of deposit by such state of its instrument of ratification or accession.

Article 44 Denunciation

1 Any contracting state may denounce this Convention at any time by a notification addressed to the Secretary-General of the United Nations.

2 Such denunciation shall take effect for the contracting state concerned one year from the date upon which it is received by the Secretary-General of the United Nations.

3 Any state which has made a declaration or notification under Article 40 may, at any time thereafter, by a notification to the Secretary-General of the United Nations, declare

that the Convention shall cease to extend to such territory one year after the date of receipt of the notification by the Secretary-General.

Article 45 Revision

1 Any contracting state may request revision of this Convention at any time by a notification addressed to the Secretary-General of the United Nations.

2 The General Assembly of the United Nations shall recommend the steps, if any, to be taken in respect of such request.

Article 46 Notifications by the Secretary-General of the United Nations

The Secretary-General of the United Nations shall inform all Members of the United Nations and non-member states referred to in Article 39:

- (*a*) of declarations and notifications in accordance with Section B of Article 1;
- (*b*) of signatures, ratifications and accessions in accordance with Article 39;
- (*c*) of declarations and notifications in accordance with Article 40;
- (*d*) of reservations and withdrawals in accordance with Article 42;
- (*e*) of the date on which this Convention will come into force in accordance with Article 43;
- (*f*) of denunciations and notifications in accordance with Article 44;
- (*g*) of requests for revision in accordance with Article 45.

In Faith Whereof the undersigned, duly authorized, have signed this Convention on behalf of their respective Governments,

DONE at Geneva, this twenty-eighth day of July, one thousand nine hundred and fifty-one, in a single copy, of which the English and French texts are equally authentic and which shall remain deposited in the archives of the United Nations, and certified true copies of which shall be delivered to all Members of the United Nations and to the non-member states referred to in Article 39.

SCHEDULE

Paragraph 1

1 The travel document referred to in Article 28 of this Convention shall be similar to the specimen annexed hereto.

2 The document shall be made out in at least two languages, one of which shall be English or French.

Paragraph 2

Subject to the regulations obtaining in the country of issue, children may be included in the travel document of a parent or, in exceptional circumstances, of another adult refugee.

Paragraph 3

The fees charged for issue of the document shall not exceed the lowest scale of charges for national passports.

Paragraph 4

Save in special or exceptional cases, the document shall be made valid for the largest possible number of countries.

Paragraph 5

The document shall have a validity of either one or two years, at the discretion of the issuing authority.

Paragraph 6

1 The renewal or extension of the validity of the document is a matter for the authority which issued it, so long as the holder has not established lawful residence in another territory and resides lawfully in the territory of the said authority. The issue of a new document is, under the same conditions, a matter for the authority which issued the former document.

2 Diplomatic or consular authorities, specially authorised for the purpose, shall be empowered to extend, for a period not exceeding six months, the validity of travel documents issued by their Governments.

3 The contracting states shall give sympathetic consideration to renewing or extending the validity of travel documents or issuing new documents to refugees no longer lawfully resident in their territory who are unable to obtain a travel document from the country of their lawful residence.

Paragraph 7

The contracting states shall recognise the validity of the documents issued in accordance with the provisions of Article 28 of this Convention.

Paragraph 8

The competent authorities of the country to which the refugee desires to proceed shall, if they are prepared to admit him and if a visa is required, affix a visa on the document of which he is the holder.

Paragraph 9

1 The contracting states undertake to issue transit visas to refugees who have obtained visas for a territory of final destination.

2 The issue of such visas may be refused on grounds which would justify refusal of a visa to any alien.

Paragraph 10

The fees for the issue of exit, entry or transit visas shall not exceed the lowest scale of charges for visas on foreign passports.

Paragraph 11

When a refugee has lawfully taken up residence in the territory of another contracting state, the responsibility for the issue of a new document, under the terms and conditions of Article 28, shall be that of the competent authority of that territory, to which the refugee shall be entitled to apply.

Paragraph 12

The authority issuing a new document shall withdraw the old document and shall return it to the country of issue, if it is stated in the document that it should be so returned; otherwise it shall withdraw and cancel the document.

Paragraph 13

1 Each contracting state undertakes that the holder of a travel document issued by it in accordance with Article 28 of this Convention shall be re-admitted to its territory at any time during the period of its validity.

2 Subject to the provisions of the preceding sub-paragraph, a contracting state may require the holder of the document to comply with such formalities as may be prescribed in regard to exit from or return to its territory.

3 The contracting states reserve the right, in exceptional cases, or in cases where the refugee's stay is authorised for a specific period, when issuing the document, to limit the period during which the refugee may return to a period of not less than three months.

Paragraph 14

Subject only to the terms of paragraph 13, the provisions of this Schedule in no way affect the laws and regulations governing the conditions of admission to, transit through, residence and establishment in, and departure from, the territories of the contracting states.

Paragraph 15

Neither the issue of the document nor the entries made thereon determine or affect the status of the holder, particularly as regards nationality.

Paragraph 16

The issue of the document does not in any way entitle the holder to the protection of the diplomatic or consular authorities of the country of issue, and does not confer on these authorities a right of protection.

ANNEX

Specimen Travel Document

The document will be in booklet form (approximately 15 x 10 centimetres).

It is recommended that it be so printed that any erasure or alteration by chemical or other means can be readily detected, and that the words 'Convention of 28 July 1951' be printed in continuous repetition on each page, in the language of the issuing country.

(Cover of booklet)
TRAVEL DOCUMENT
(Convention of 28 July 1951)

No. ....

(1)
TRAVEL DOCUMENT
(Convention of 28 July 1951)

This document expires on ....
unless its validity is extended or renewed.
Name ....
Forename(s) ....
Accompanied by .... child (children)

1. This document is issued solely with a view to providing the holder with a travel document which can serve in lieu of a national passport. It is without prejudice to and in no way affects the holder's nationality.

2. The holder is authorized to return to ....
.... [state here the country whose authorities are issuing the document] on or before... unless some later date is hereafter specified.
[The period during which the holder is allowed to return must not be less than three months]

3. Should the holder take up residence in a country other than that which issued the present document, he must, if he wishes to travel again, apply to the competent authorities of his country of residence for a new document. [The old travel document shall be withdrawn by the authority issuing the new document and returned to the authority which issued it.][1]

(This document contains . . . . pages, exclusive of cover.)

[1] The sentence in brackets to be inserted by Governments which so desire.

(2)

Place and date of birth ....
Occupation ....
Present residence ....
*Maiden name and forename(s) of wife ....
....
*Name of forename(s) of husband ....
....

Description

Height ....
Hair ....
Colour of eyes ....
Nose ....
Shape of face...
Complexion ....
Special peculiarities...

Children accompanying holder

Name	Forename(s)	Place and date of birth	Sex
....	....	....	....
....	....	....	....
....	....	....	....
....	....	....	....

*Strike out whichever does not apply.

(This document contains . . . . . . pages, exclusive of cover.)

(3)

Photograph of holder and stamp of issuing authority
Finger-prints of holder (if required)

Signature of holder ....

(This document contains . . . . . . pages, exclusive of cover.)

(4)

1. This document is valid for the following countries:

....

....

....

....

2. Document or documents on the basis of which the present document is issued:

....

....

....

....

Issued at ....
Date ....

Signature and stamp of authority
issuing the document

Fee paid:

(This document contains . . . . . . pages, exclusive of cover.)

(5)

Extension or renewal of validity

Fee paid: From ....
                                                     To ....
Done at   Date ....

Signature and stamp of authority
extending or renewing the validity
of the document:

Extension or renewal of validity

Fee paid: From ....
                                                     To ....
Done at   Date ....

Signature and stamp of authority
extending or renewing the validity
of the document:

(This document contains . . . . . . pages, exclusive of cover.)

(6)

Extension or renewal of validity

Fee paid: From ....
                                                     To ....
Done at   Date ....

Signature and stamp of authority
extending or renewing the validity
of the document:

Extension or renewal of validity

Fee paid:

Done at

From ....
To ....
Date ....

Signature and stamp of authority
extending or renewing the validity
of the document:

(This document contains . . . . . . pages, exclusive of cover.)

(7–32)

Visas

The name of the holder of the document must be repeated in each visa.

(This document contains . . . . . . pages, exclusive of cover.)

APPENDIX FINAL ACT OF THE 1951 UNITED NATIONS CONFERENCE OF PLENIPOTENTIARIES ON THE STATUS OF REFUGEES AND STATELESS PERSONS

1 The General Assembly of the United Nations, by Resolution 429(V) of 14 December 1950, decided to convene in Geneva a Conference of Plenipotentiaries to complete the drafting of, and to sign, a Convention relating to the Status of Refugees and a Protocol relating to the Status of Stateless Persons.

The Conference met at the European Office of the United Nations in Geneva from 2 to 25 July 1951.

The Governments of the following twenty-six states were represented by delegates who all submitted satisfactory credentials or other communications of appointment authorizing them to participate in the Conference:

Australia	Italy
Austria	Luxembourg
Belgium	Monaco
Brazil	Netherlands
Canada	Norway
Colombia	Sweden
Denmark	Switzerland (the Swiss delegation
Egypt	also represented Liechtenstein)
France	Turkey
Germany, Federal Republic of	United Kingdom of Great Britain
Greece	and Northern Ireland
Holy See	United States of America
Iraq	Venezuela
Israel	Yugoslavia

The Governments of the following two states were represented by observers

Cuba
Iran

Pursuant to the request of the General Assembly, the United Nations High Commissioner for Refugees participated, without the right to vote, in the deliberations of the Conference.

The International Labour Organisation and the International Refugee Organization were represented at the Conference without the right to vote.

The Conference invited a representative of the Council of Europe to be represented at the Conference without the right to vote.

Representatives of the following Non-Governmental Organizations in consultative relationship with the Economic and Social Council were also present as observers:

Category A
International Confederation of Free Trade Unions
International Federation of Christian Trade Unions
Inter-Parliamentary Union

Category B
Agudas Israel World Organization
Caritas Internationalis
Catholic International Union for Social Service
Commission of the Churches on International Affairs
Consultative Council of Jewish Organizations
Co-ordinating Board of Jewish Organizations
Friends' World Committee for Consultation
International Association of Penal Law
International Bureau for the Unification of Penal Law
International Committee of the Red Cross
International Council of Women
International Federation of Friends of Young Women
International League for the Rights of Man
International Social Service
International Union for Child Welfare
International Union of Catholic Women's Leagues
Pax Romana
Women's International League for Peace and Freedom
World Jewish Congress
World Union for Progressive Judaism
World Young Women's Christian Association

Register
International Relief Committee for Intellectual Workers
League of Red Cross Societies
Standing Conference of Voluntary Agencies
World Association of Girl Guides and Girl Scouts
World University Service

Representatives of Non-Governmental Organizations which have been granted consultative status by the Economic and Social Council as well as those entered by the Secretary-General on the Register referred to in Resolution 288 B(X) of the Economic and Social Council, paragraph 17, had under the rules of procedure adopted by the Conference the right to submit written or oral statements to the Conference.

The Conference elected Mr. Knud Larsen, of Denmark, as President, and Mr A Herment, of Belgium, and Mr Talat Miras, of Turkey, as Vice-Presidents.

At its second meeting, the Conference, acting on a proposal of the representative of Egypt, unanimously decided to address an invitation to the Holy See to designate a plenipotentiary representative to participate in its work. A representative of the Holy See took his place at the Conference on 10 July 1951.

The Conference adopted as its agenda the Provisional Agenda drawn up by the Secretary-General (A/CONF 2/2/Rev 1). It also adopted the Provisional Rules of Procedure drawn up by the Secretary-General, with the addition of a provision which authorized a representative of the Council of Europe to be present at the Conference without the right to vote and to submit proposals (A/CONF 2/3/Rev 1).

In accordance with the Rules of Procedure of the Conference, the President and Vice-Presidents examined the credentials of representatives and on 17 July 1951 reported to the Conference the results of such examination, the Conference adopting the report.

The Conference used as the basis of its discussions the draft Convention relating to the Status of Refugees and the draft Protocol relating to the Status of Stateless Persons prepared by the *ad hoc* Committee on Refugees and Stateless Persons at its second session held in Geneva from 14 to 25 August 1950, with the exception of the preamble and Article 1 (Definition of the term 'refugee') of the draft Convention. The text of the preamble before the Conference was that which was adopted by the Economic and Social Council on 11 August 1950 in Resolution 319 B II(XI). The text of Article 1 before the Conference was that recommended by the General Assembly on 14 December 1950 and contained in the Annex to Resolution 429(V). The latter was a modification of the text as it had been adopted by the Economic and Social Council in Resolution 319 B II(XI)[1].

The Conference adopted the Convention relating to the Status of Refugees in two readings. Prior to its second reading it established a Style Committee composed of the President and the representatives of Belgium, France, Israel, Italy, the United Kingdom of Great Britain and Northern Ireland and the United States of America, together with the High Commissioner for Refugees, which elected as its Chairman Mr. G. Warren, of the United States of America. The Style Committee re-drafted the text which had been adopted by the Conference on first reading, particularly from the point of view of language and of concordance between the English and French texts.

The Convention was adopted on 25 July by 24 votes to none with no abstentions and opened for signature at the European Office of the United Nations from 28 July to 31 August 1951. It will be re-opened for signature at the permanent headquarters of the United Nations in New York from 17 September 1951 to 31 December 1952.

The English and French texts of the Convention, which are equally authentic, are appended to this Final Act.

NOTES

1 The texts referred to in the paragraph above are contained in document A/CONF 2/1.

II The Conference decided, by 17 votes to 3 with 3 abstentions, that the titles of the chapters and of the articles of the Convention are included for practical purposes and do not constitute an element of interpretation.

III With respect to the draft Protocol relating to the Status of Stateless Persons, the Conference adopted the following resolution:

The Conference,

Having considered the draft Protocol relating to the Status of Stateless Persons,

Considering that the subject still requires more detailed study,

Decides not to take a decision on the subject at the present Conference and refers the draft Protocol back to the appropriate organs of the United Nations for further study.

IV The Conference adopted unanimously the following recommendations:

A
(Facilitation of refugee travels)[1]

The Conference,

Considering that the issue and recognition of travel documents is necessary to facilitate the movement of refugees, and in particular their resettlement,

Urges Governments which are parties to the Inter-Governmental Agreement on Refugee Travel Documents signed in London on 15 October 1946, or which recognize travel documents issued in accordance with the Agreement, to continue to issue or to recognize such travel documents, and to extend the issue of such documents to refugees as defined in Article 1 of the Convention relating to the Status of Refugees or to recognize the travel documents so issued to such persons, until they shall have undertaken obligations under Article 28 of the said Convention.

NOTES

1 Headline added.

B
(Principle of unity of the family)[1]

The Conference,

Considering that the unity of the family, the natural and fundamental group unit of society, is an essential right of the refugee, and that such unity is constantly threatened, and

Noting with satisfaction that, according to the official commentary of the *ad hoc* Committee on Statelessness and Related Problems (E/1618, p. 40) the rights granted to a refugee are extended to members of his family,

Recommends Governments to take the necessary measures for the protection of the refugee's family, especially with a view to:

(1) Ensuring that the unity of the refugee's family is maintained particularly in cases where the head of the family has fulfilled the necessary conditions for admission to a particular country,
(2) The protection of refugees who are minors, in particular unaccompanied children and girls, with special reference to guardianship and adoption.

NOTES

1 Headline added.

C
(Welfare services)[1]

The Conference,

Considering that, in the moral, legal and material spheres, refugees need the help of suitable welfare services, especially that of appropriate non-governmental organizations,

Recommends Governments and inter-governmental bodies to facilitate, encourage and sustain the efforts of properly qualified organizations.

NOTES

1 Headline added.

D

(International co-operation in the field of asylum and resettlement)

The Conference,

Considering that many persons still leave their country of origin for reasons of persecution and are entitled to special protection on account of their position,

Recommends that Governments continue to receive refugees in their territories and that they act in concert in a true spirit of international co-operation in order that these refugees may find asylum and the possibility of resettlement.

E

(Extension of treatment provided by the Convention)

The Conference,

Expresses the hope that the Convention relating to the Status of Refugees will have value as an example exceeding its contractual scope and that all nations will be guided by it in granting so far as possible to persons in their territory as refugees and who would not be covered by the terms of the Convention, the treatment for which it provides.

In Witness Whereof the President, Vice-Presidents and the Executive Secretary of the Conference have signed this Final Act.

Done at Geneva this twenty-eighth day of July one thousand nine hundred and fifty-one in a single copy in the English and French languages, each text being equally authentic. Translations of this Final Act into Chinese, Russian and Spanish will be prepared by the Secretary-General of the United Nations, who will, on request, send copies thereof to each of the Governments invited to attend the Conference.

The President of the Conference:	Knud Larsen
The Vice-Presidents of the Conference:	A Herment
	Talat Miras
The Executive Secretary of the Conference:	John P Humphrey

PROTOCOL RELATING TO THE STATUS OF REFUGEES OF 31 JANUARY 1967

Entry into force 4 *October 1967, in accordance with Article VIII*

Text United Nations Treaty Series No 8791, Vol 606, p 267

The States Parties to the present Protocol,

Considering that the Convention relating to the Status of Refugees done at Geneva on 28 July 1951 (hereinafter referred to as the Convention) covers only those persons who have become refugees as a result of events occurring before 1 January, 1951,

Considering that new refugee situations have arisen since the Convention was adopted and that the refugees concerned may therefore not fall within the scope of the Convention,

Considering that it is desirable that equal status should be enjoyed by all refugees covered by the definition in the Convention irrespective of the dateline 1 January 1951,

Have agreed as follows:

Article I General provision

1 The states parties to the present Protocol undertake to apply Articles 2 to 34 inclusive of the Convention to refugees as hereinafter defined.

2 For the purpose of the present Protocol, the term 'refugee' shall, except as regards the application of paragraph 3 of this Article, mean any person within the definition of Article 1 of the Convention as if the words 'As a result of events occurring before 1 January 1951 and ...' and the words '... as a result of such events', in Article 1 A (2) were omitted.

3 The present Protocol shall be applied by the states parties hereto without any geographic limitation, save that existing declarations made by states already Parties to the Convention in accordance with Article 1 B (1)(*a*) of the Convention, shall, unless extended under Article 1 B (2) thereof, apply also under the present Protocol.

NOTES

1 The Protocol was signed by the President of the General Assembly and by the Secretary-General on 31 January 1967. The text of the General Assembly Resolution 2198 (XXI) of 16 December 1966 concerning the accession to the 1967 Protocol relating to the Status of Refugees is reproduced in Appendix.

Article II Co-operation of the national authorities with the United Nations

1 The states parties to the present Protocol undertake to co-operate with the Office of the United Nations High Commissioner for Refugees, or any other agency of the United Nations which may succeed it, in the exercise of its functions, and shall in particular facilitate its duty of supervising the application of the provisions of the present Protocol.

2 In order to enable the Office of the High Commissioner, or any other agency of the United Nations which may succeed it, to make reports to the competent organs of the United Nations, the states parties to the present Protocol undertake to provide them with the information and statistical data requested, in the appropriate form, concerning:

- (*a*) The condition of refugees;
- (*b*) The implementation of the present Protocol;
- (*c*) Laws, regulations and decrees which are, or may hereafter be, in force relating to refugees.

Article III Information on national legislation

The states parties to the present Protocol shall communicate to the Secretary-General of the United Nations the laws and regulations which they may adopt to ensure the application of the present Protocol.

Article IV Settlement of disputes

Any dispute between states parties to the present Protocol which relates to its interpretation or application and which cannot be settled by other means shall be referred to the International Court of Justice at the request of any one of the parties to the dispute.

Article V Accession

The present Protocol shall be open for accession on behalf of all states parties to the Convention and of any other State Member of the United Nations or member of any of the specialized agencies or to which an invitation to accede may have been addressed by the General Assembly of the United Nations. Accession shall be effected by the deposit of an instrument of accession with the Secretary-General of the United Nations.

Article VI Federal clause

In the case of a federal or non-unitary state, the following provisions shall apply:

(a) With respect to those articles of the Convention to be applied in accordance with Article 1, paragraph 1, of the present Protocol that come within the legislative jurisdiction of the federal legislative authority, the obligations of the Federal Government shall to this extent be the same as those of states parties which are not federal states;

(b) With respect to those articles of the Convention to be applied in accordance with Article I, paragraph 1, of the present Protocol that come within the legislative jurisdiction of constituent states, provinces or cantons which are not, under the constitutional system of the federation, bound to take legislative action, the Federal Government shall bring such articles with a favourable recommendation to the notice of the appropriate authorities of states, provinces or cantons at the earliest possible moment;

(c) A Federal State Party to the present Protocol shall, at the request of any other state party hereto transmitted through the Secretary-General of the United Nations, supply a statement of the law and practice of the Federation and its constituent units in regard to any particular provision of the Convention to be applied in accordance with Article I, paragraph 1, of the present Protocol, showing the extent to which effect has been given to that provision by legislative or other action.

Article VII Reservations and declarations

1 At the time of accession, any state may make reservations in respect of Article IV of the present Protocol and in respect of the application in accordance with Article I of the present Protocol of any provisions of the Convention other than those contained in Articles 1, 3, 4, 16(1) and 33 thereof, provided that in the case of a state party to the Convention reservations made under this Article shall not extend to refugees in respect of whom the Convention applies.

2 Reservations made by states parties to the Convention in accordance with Article 42 thereof shall, unless withdrawn, be applicable in relation to their obligations under the present Protocol.

3 Any state making a reservation in accordance with paragraph 1 of this Article may at any time withdraw such reservation by a communication to that effect addressed to the Secretary-General of the United Nations.

4 Declarations made under Article 40, paragraphs 1 and 2, of the Convention by a state party thereto which accedes to the present Protocol shall be deemed to apply in respect of the present Protocol, unless upon accession a notification to the contrary is addressed by the state party concerned to the Secretary-General of the United Nations. The provisions of Article 40, paragraphs 2 and 3, and of Article 44, paragraph 3, of the Convention shall be deemed to apply *mutatis mutandis* to the present Protocol.

Article VIII Entry into force

1 The present Protocol shall come into force on the day of deposit of the sixth instrument of accession.

2 For each state acceding to the Protocol after the deposit of the sixth instrument of accession, the Protocol shall come into force on the date of deposit by such state of its instrument of accession.

Article IX   Denunciation

1 Any state party hereto may denounce this Protocol at any time by a notification addressed to the Secretary-General of the United Nations.

2 Such denunciation shall take effect for the state party concerned one year from the date on which it is received by the Secretary-General of the United Nations.

Article X   Notifications by the Secretary-General of the United Nations

The Secretary-General of the United Nations shall inform the states referred to in Article V above of the date of entry into force, accessions, reservations and withdrawals of reservations to and denunciations of the present Protocol, and of declarations and notifications relating hereto.

Article XI   Deposit in the archives of the Secretariat of the United Nations

A copy of the present Protocol, of which the Chinese, English, French, Russian and Spanish texts are equally authentic, signed by the President of the General Assembly and by the Secretary-General of the United Nations, shall be deposited in the archives of the Secretariat of the United Nations. The Secretary-General will transmit certified copies thereof to all states members of the United Nations and to the other states referred to in Article V above.

APPENDIX GENERAL ASSEMBLY RESOLUTION 2198 (XXI)

Protocol relating to the Status of Refugees

The General Assembly,

Considering that the Convention relating to the Status of Refugees, signed at Geneva on 28 July 1951[1], covers only those persons who have become refugees as a result of events occurring before 1 January 1951,

Considering that new refugee situations have arisen since the Convention was adopted and that the refugees concerned may therefore not fall within the scope of the Convention,

Considering that it is desirable that equal status should be enjoyed by all refugees covered by the definition in the Convention, irrespective of the date-line of 1 January 1951,

Taking note of the recommendation of the Executive Committee of the Programme of the United Nations High Commissioner for Refugees[2] that the draft Protocol relating to the Status of Refugees should be submitted to the General Assembly after consideration by the Economic and Social Council, in order that the Secretary-General might be authorised to open the Protocol for accession by Governments within the shortest possible time,

Considering that the Economic and Social Council, in its resolution 1186 (XLI) of 18 November 1966, took note with approval of the draft Protocol contained in the addendum to the report of the United Nations High Commissioner for Refugees and concerning measures to extend the personal scope of the Convention[3] and transmitted the addendum to the General Assembly,

1 *Takes note* of the Protocol relating to the Status of Refugees, the text of which is contained in the addendum to the report of the United Nations High Commissioner for Refugees;

2 *Requests* the Secretary-General to transmit the text of the Protocol to the States mentioned in article V thereof, with a view to enabling them to accede to the Protocol[4].

1495th plenary meeting,

16 December 1966.

NOTES

1 United Nations, *Treaty Series*, vol 189 (1954), No 2545.
2 See A/6311/Rev 1/Add 1, part two, para 38.
3 *Ibid*, part one, para 2.
4 The Protocol was signed by the President of the General Assembly and by the Secretary-General on 31 January 1967.

Convention relating to the status of refugees, 28 July 1951 (UNTS, vol 189, p 137); entry into force: 22 April 1954.

UK GOVERNMENT RESERVATION TO THE 1951 CONVENTION RELATING TO THE STATUS OF REFUGEES

(i)   The Government of the United Kingdom of Great Britain and Northern Ireland understand articles 8 and 9 as not preventing them from taking in time of war or other grave and exceptional circumstances measures in the interests of national security in the case of a refugee on the ground of his nationality. The provision of article 8 shall not prevent the Government of the United Kingdom of Great Britain and Northern Ireland from exercising any rights over property or interests which they may acquire or have acquired as an Allied or Associated Power under a Treaty of Peace or other agreement or arrangement for the restoration of peace which has been or may be completed as a result of the Second World War. Furthermore, the provision of article 8 shall not affect the treatment to be accorded to any property or interests which, at the date of entry into force of this Convention for the United Kingdom of Great Britain and Northern Ireland, are under the control of the Government of the United Kingdom of Great Britain and Northern Ireland by reason of a state of war which exists or existed between them and any other state.

(ii) The Government of the United Kingdom of Great Britain and Northern Ireland accept article 17, paragraph 2, with the substitution of 'four years' for 'three years' in subparagraph (*a*) and with the omission of subparagraph (*c*).

(iii) The Government of the United Kingdom of Great Britain and Northern Ireland cannot undertake to give effect to the obligations contained in article 25, paragraphs 1 and 2, and can only undertake to apply the provision of paragraph 3 so far as the law allows.

UK GOVERNMENT COMMENTARY:

In connection with article 24, paragraph 1, subparagraph (*b*) relating to certain matters within the scope of the National Health Service, the National Health Service (Amendment) Act, 1949, contains powers for charges to be made to persons not ordinarily resident in Great Britain (which category would include refugees) who receive treatment under the Service. While these powers have not yet been exercised it is possible that this might have to be done at some future date. In Northern Ireland the Health Services are restricted to persons ordinarily resident in the country except where regulations are made to extend the Service to others. It is for these reasons that the Government of the United Kingdom while they are prepared in the future, as in the past, to give the most sympathetic consideration to the situation of refugees, find it necessary to make a reservation to article 24, paragraph 1, subparagraph (*b*), of the Convention.

The scheme of Industrial Injuries Insurance in Great Britain does not meet the requirements of article 24, paragraph 2, of the Convention. Where an insured person has died as the result of an industrial accident or a disease due to the nature of his employment, benefit cannot generally be paid to his dependants who are abroad unless they are in any part of the British Commonwealth, in the Irish Republic or in a country with which the United Kingdom has made a reciprocal agreement concerning the payment of industrial injury benefits. There is an exception to this rule in favour of the dependants of certain seamen who die as a result of industrial accidents happening to them while they are in the service of British ships. In this matter refugees are treated in the same way as citizens of the United Kingdom and Colonies and by reason of article 24, paragraphs 3 and 4, of the Convention, the dependants of refugees will be able to take advantage of reciprocal agreements which provide for the payment of United Kingdom industrial injury benefits in other countries. By reason of article 24, paragraphs 3 and 4, refugees will enjoy under the scheme of National Insurance and Industrial Injuries Insurance certain rights which are withheld from British subjects who are not citizens of the United Kingdom and Colonies.

No arrangements exist in the United Kingdom for the administrative assistance for which provision is made in article 25 nor have any such arrangements been found necessary in the case of refugees. Any need for the documents or certifications mentioned in paragraph 2 of that article would be met by affidavits.

CONVENTION RELATING TO THE STATUS OF STATELESS PERSONS

Adopted on 28 September 1954

Entry into force 6 June 1960, in accordance with article 39

PREAMBLE

The High Contracting Parties,

Considering that the Charter of the United Nations and the Universal Declaration of Human Rights approved on 10 December 1948 by the General Assembly of the United Nations have affirmed the principle that human beings shall enjoy fundamental rights and freedoms without discrimination,

Considering that the United Nations has, on various occasions, manifested its profound concern for stateless persons and endeavoured to assure stateless persons the widest possible exercise of these fundamental rights and freedoms,

Considering that only those stateless persons who are also refugees are covered by the Convention relating to the Status of Refugees of 28 July 1951, and that there are many stateless persons who are not covered by that Convention,

Considering that it is desirable to regulate and improve the status of stateless persons by an international agreement,

Have agreed as follows:

CHAPTER I GENERAL PROVISIONS

Article 1 Definition of the term 'Stateless Person'

1 For the purpose of this Convention, the term 'stateless person' means a person who is not considered as a national by any State under the operation of its law.

2 This Convention shall not apply:

   (i)   To persons who are at present receiving from organs or agencies of the United Nations other than the United Nations High Commissioner for Refugees protection or assistance so long as they are receiving such protection or assistance;

   (ii)   To persons who are recognized by the competent authorities of the country in which they have taken residence as having the rights and obligations which are attached to the possession of the nationality of that country;

   (iii)   To persons with respect to whom there are serious reasons for considering that:

      (a)   They have committed a crime against peace, a war crime, or a crime against humanity, as defined in the international instruments drawn up to make provisions in respect of such crimes;

      (b)   They have committed a serious non-political crime outside the country of their residence prior to their admission to that country;

      (c)   They have been guilty of acts contrary to the purposes and principles of the United Nations.

Article 2 General obligations

Every stateless person has duties to the country in which he finds himself, which require in particular that he conform to its laws and regulations as well as to measures taken for the maintenance of public order.

Article 3 Non-discrimination

The Contracting States shall apply the provisions of this Convention to stateless persons without discrimination as to race, religion or country of origin.

Article 4 Religion

The Contracting States shall accord to stateless persons within their territories treatment at least as favourable as that accorded to their nationals with respect to freedom to practise their religion and freedom as regards the religious education of their children.

Article 5 Rights granted apart from this Convention

Nothing in this Convention shall be deemed to impair any rights and benefits granted by a Contracting State to stateless persons apart from this Convention.

Article 6 The term 'in the same circumstances'

For the purpose of this Convention, the term 'in the same circumstances' implies that any requirements (including requirements as to length and conditions of sojourn or residence) which the particular individual would have to fulfil for the enjoyment of the right in question, if he were not a stateless person, must be fulfilled by him, with the exception of requirements which by their nature a stateless person is incapable of fulfilling.

Article 7 Exemption from reciprocity

1 Except where this Convention contains more favourable provisions, a Contracting State shall accord to stateless persons the same treatment as is accorded to aliens generally.

2 After a period of three years' residence, all stateless persons shall enjoy exemption from legislative reciprocity in the territory of the Contracting States.

3 Each Contracting State shall continue to accord to stateless persons the rights and benefits to which they were already entitled, in the absence of reciprocity, at the date of entry into force of this Convention for that State.

4 The Contracting States shall consider favourably the possibility of according to stateless persons, in the absence of reciprocity, rights and benefits beyond those to which they are entitled according to paragraphs 2 and 3, and to extending exemption from reciprocity to stateless persons who do not fulfil the conditions provided for in paragraphs 2 and 3.

5 The provisions of paragraphs 2 and 3 apply both to the rights and benefits referred to in articles 13, 18, 19, 21 and 22 of this Convention and to rights and benefits for which this Convention does not provide.

Article 8 Exemption from exceptional measures

With regard to exceptional measures which may be taken against the person, property or interests of nationals or former nationals of a foreign State, the Contracting States shall not apply such measures to a stateless person solely on account of his having previously possessed the nationality of the foreign State in question. Contracting States which, under their legislation, are prevented from applying the general principle expressed in this article shall, in appropriate cases, grant exemptions in favour of such stateless persons.

Article 9 Provisional measures

Nothing in this Convention shall prevent a Contracting State, in time of war or other grave and exceptional circumstances, from taking provisionally measures which it considers to be essential to the national security in the case of a particular person, pending a determination by the Contracting State that that person is in fact a stateless person and that the continuance of such measures is necessary in his case in the interests of national security.

Article 10 Continuity of residence

1 Where a stateless person has been forcibly displaced during the Second World War and removed to the territory of a Contracting State, and is resident there, the period of such enforced sojourn shall be considered to have been lawful residence within that territory.

2 Where a stateless person has been forcibly displaced during the Second World War from the territory of a Contracting State and has, prior to the date of entry into force of this Convention, returned there for the purpose of taking up residence, the period of residence before and after such enforced displacement shall be regarded as one uninterrupted period for any purposes for which uninterrupted residence is required.

Article 11 Stateless seamen

In the case of stateless persons regularly serving as crew members on board a ship flying the flag of a Contracting State, that State shall give sympathetic consideration to their establishment on its territory and the issue of travel documents to them or their temporary admission to its territory particularly with a view to facilitating their establishment in another country.

CHAPTER II JURIDICAL STATUS

Article 12 Personal status

1 The personal status of a stateless person shall be governed by the law of the country of his domicile or, if he has no domicile, by the law of the country of his residence.

2 Rights previously acquired by a stateless person and dependent on personal status, more particularly rights attaching to marriage, shall be respected by a Contracting State, subject to compliance, if this be necessary, with the formalities required by the law of that State, provided that the right in question is one which would have been recognized by the law of that State had he not become stateless.

Article 13 Movable and immovable property

The Contracting States shall accord to a stateless person treatment as favourable as possible and, in any event, not less favourable than that accorded to aliens generally in the same circumstances, as regards the acquisition of movable and immovable property and other rights pertaining thereto, and to leases and other contracts relating to movable and immovable property.

Article 14 Artistic rights and industrial property

In respect of the protection of industrial property, such as inventions, designs or models, trade marks, trade names, and of rights in literary, artistic and scientific works, a stateless person shall be accorded in the country in which he has his habitual residence the same protection as is accorded to nationals of that country. In the territory of any other Contracting State, he shall be accorded the same protection as is accorded in that territory to nationals of the country in which he has his habitual residence.

Article 15 Right of association

As regards non-political and non-profit-making associations and trade unions the Contracting States shall accord to stateless persons lawfully staying in their territory treatment as favourable as possible, and in any event, not less favourable than that accorded to aliens generally in the same circumstances.

Article 16 Access to courts

1 A stateless person shall have free access to the courts of law on the territory of all Contracting States.

2 A stateless person shall enjoy in the Contracting State in which he has his habitual residence the same treatment as a national in matters pertaining to access to the courts, including legal assistance and exemption from cautio judicatum solvi.

3 A stateless person shall be accorded in the matters referred to in paragraph 2 in countries other than that in which he has his habitual residence the treatment granted to a national of the country of his habitual residence.

CHAPTER III GAINFUL EMPLOYMENT

Article 17 Wage-earning employment

1 The Contracting States shall accord to stateless persons lawfully staying in their territory treatment as favourable as possible and, in any event, not less favourable that that accorded to aliens generally in the same circumstances, as regards the right to engage in wage-earning employment.

2 The Contracting States shall give sympathetic consideration to assimilating the rights of all stateless persons with regard to wage-earning employment to those of nationals, and in particular of those stateless persons who have entered their territory pursuant to programmes of labour recruitment or under immigration schemes.

Article 18 Self-employment

The Contracting States shall accord to a stateless person lawfully in their territory treatment as favourable as possible and, in any event, not less favourable than that accorded to aliens generally in the same circumstances, as regards the right to engage on his own account in agriculture, industry, handicrafts and commerce and to establish commercial and industrial companies.

Article 19 Liberal professions

Each Contracting State shall accord to stateless persons lawfully staying in their territory who hold diplomas recognized by the competent authorities of that State, and who are desirous of practising a liberal profession, treatment as favourable as possible and, in any event, not less favourable than that accorded to aliens generally in the same circumstances.

CHAPTER IV WELFARE

Article 20 Rationing

Where a rationing system exists, which applies to the population at large and regulates the general distribution of products in short supply, stateless persons shall be accorded the same treatment as nationals.

Article 21 Housing

As regards housing, the Contracting States, in so far as the matter is regulated by laws or regulations or is subject to the control of public authorities, shall accord to stateless persons lawfully staying in their territory treatment as favourable as possible and, in any event, not less favourable than that accorded to aliens generally in the same circumstances.

Article 22 Public education

1 The Contracting States shall accord to stateless persons the same treatment as is accorded to nationals with respect to elementary education.

2 The Contracting States shall accord to stateless persons treatment as favourable as possible and, in any event, not less favourable than that accorded to aliens generally in the same circumstances, with respect to education other than elementary education and, in particular, as regards access to studies, the recognition of foreign school certificates, diplomas and degrees, the remission of fees and charges and the award of scholarships.

Article 23 Public relief

The Contracting States shall accord to stateless persons lawfully staying in their territory the same treatment with respect to public relief and assistance as is accorded to their nationals.

Article 24 Labour legislation and social security

1 The Contracting States shall accord to stateless persons lawfully staying in their territory the same treatment as is accorded to nationals in respect of the following matters:

(a) In so far as such matters are governed by laws or regulations or are subject to the control of administrative authorities; remuneration, including family allowances where these form part of remuneration, hours of work, overtime arrangements, holidays with pay, restrictions on home work, minimum age of employment, apprenticeship and training, women's work and the work of young persons, and the enjoyment of the benefits of collective bargaining;

(b) Social security (legal provisions in respect of employment injury, occupational diseases, maternity, sickness, disability, old age, death, unemployment, family responsibilities and any other contingency which, according to national laws or regulations, is covered by a social security scheme), subject to the following limitations:

(i) There may be appropriate arrangements for the maintenance of acquired rights and rights in course of acquisition;

(ii) National laws or regulations of the country of residence may prescribe special arrangements concerning benefits or portions of benefits which are payable wholly out of public funds, and concerning allowances paid to persons who do not fulfil the contribution conditions prescribed for the award of a normal pension.

2 The right to compensation for the death of a stateless person resulting from employment injury or from occupational disease shall not be affected by the fact that the residence of the beneficiary is outside the territory of the Contracting State.

3 The Contracting States shall extend to stateless persons the benefits of agreements concluded between them, or which may be concluded between them in the future, concerning the maintenance of acquired rights and rights in the process of acquisition in regard to social security, subject only to the conditions which apply to nationals of the States signatory to the agreements in question.

4 The Contracting States will give sympathetic consideration to extending to stateless persons so far as possible the benefits of similar agreements which may at any time be in force between such Contracting States and non-contracting States.

CHAPTER V ADMINISTRATIVE MEASURES

Article 25 Administrative assistance

1 When the exercise of a right by a stateless person would normally require the assistance of authorities of a foreign country to whom he cannot have recourse, the Contracting State in whose territory he is residing shall arrange that such assistance be afforded to him by their own authorities.

2 The authority or authorities mentioned in paragraph I shall deliver or cause to be delivered under their supervision to stateless persons such documents or certifications as would normally be delivered to aliens by or through their national authorities.

3 Documents or certifications so delivered shall stand in the stead of the official instruments delivered to aliens by or through their national authorities and shall be given credence in the absence of proof to the contrary.

4 Subject to such exceptional treatment as may be granted to indigent persons, fees may be charged for the services mentioned herein, but such fees shall be moderate and commensurate with those charged to nationals for similar services.

5 The provisions of this article shall be without prejudice to articles 27 and 28.

Article 26 Freedom of movement

Each Contracting State shall accord to stateless persons lawfully in its territory the right to choose their place of residence and to move freely within its territory, subject to any regulations applicable to aliens generally in the same circumstances.

Article 27 Identity papers

The Contracting States shall issue identity papers to any stateless person in their territory who does not possess a valid travel document.

Article 28 Travel documents

The Contracting States shall issue to stateless persons lawfully staying in their territory travel documents for the purpose of travel outside their territory, unless compelling reasons of national security or public order otherwise require, and the provisions of the schedule to this Convention shall apply with respect to such documents. The Contracting States may issue such a travel document to any other stateless person in their territory; they shall in particular give sympathetic consideration to the issue of such a travel document to stateless persons in their territory who are unable to obtain a travel document from the country of their lawful residence.

Article 29 Fiscal charges

1 The Contracting States shall not impose upon stateless persons duties, charges or taxes, of any description whatsoever, other or higher than those which are or may be levied on their nationals in similar situations.

2 Nothing in the above paragraph shall prevent the application to stateless persons of the laws and regulations concerning charges in respect of the issue to aliens of administrative documents including identity papers.

Article 30 Transfer of assets

1 A Contracting State shall, in conformity with its laws and regulations, permit stateless persons to transfer assets which they have brought into its territory, to another country where they have been admitted for the purposes of resettlement.

2 A Contracting State shall give sympathetic consideration to the application of stateless persons for permission to transfer assets wherever they may be and which are necessary for their resettlement in another country to which they have been admitted.

Article 31 Expulsion

1 The Contracting States shall not expel a stateless person lawfully in their territory save on grounds of national security or public order.

2 The expulsion of such a stateless person shall be only in pursuance of a decision reached in accordance with due process of law. Except where compelling reasons of national security otherwise require, the stateless person shall be allowed to submit evidence to clear himself, and to appeal to and be represented for the purpose before competent authority or a person or persons specially designated by the competent authority.

3 The Contracting States shall allow such a stateless person a reasonable period within which to seek legal admission into another country. The Contracting States reserve the right to apply during that period such internal measures as they may deem necessary.

Article 32 Naturalization

The Contracting States shall as far as possible facilitate the assimilation and naturalization of stateless persons. They shall in particular make every effort to expedite naturalization proceedings and to reduce as far as possible the charges and costs of such proceedings.

CHAPTER VI FINAL CLAUSES

Article 33 Information on national legislation

The Contracting States shall communicate to the Secretary-General of the United Nations the laws and regulations which they may adopt to ensure the application of this Convention.

Article 34 Settlement of disputes

Any dispute between Parties to this Convention relating to its interpretation or application, which cannot be settled by other means, shall be referred to the International Court of Justice at the request of any one of the parties to the dispute.

Article 35 Signature, ratification and accession

1 This Convention shall be open for signature at the Headquarters of the United Nations until 31 December 1955.

2 It shall be open for signature on behalf of:

(a) Any State Member of the United Nations;
(b) Any other State invited to attend the United Nations Conference on the Status of Stateless Persons; and
(c) Any State to which an invitation to sign or to accede may be addressed by the General Assembly of the United Nations.

3 It shall be ratified and the instruments of ratification shall be deposited with the Secretary-General of the United Nations.

4 It shall be open for accession by the States referred to in paragraph 2 of this article. Accession shall be effected by the deposit of an instrument of accession with the Secretary-General of the United Nations.

Article 36 Territorial application clause

1 Any State may, at the time of signature, ratification or accession, declare that this Convention shall extend to all or any of the territories for the international relations of which it is responsible. Such a declaration shall take effect when the Convention enters into force for the State concerned.

2 At any time thereafter any such extension shall be made by notification addressed to the Secretary-General of the United Nations and shall take effect as from the ninetieth day after the day of receipt by the Secretary-General of the United Nations of this notification, or as from the date of entry into force of the Convention for the State concerned, whichever is the later.

3 With respect to those territories to which this Convention is not extended at the time of signature, ratification or accession, each State concerned shall consider the possibility of taking the necessary steps in order to extend the application of this Convention to such territories, subject, where necessary for constitutional reasons, to the consent of the Governments of such territories.

Article 37 Federal clause

In the case of a Federal or non-unitary State, the following provisions shall apply

(a) With respect to those articles of this Convention that come within the legislative jurisdiction of the federal legislative authority, the obligations of the Federal Government shall to this extent be the same as those of Parties which are not Federal States;

(b) With respect to those articles of this Convention that come within the legislative jurisdiction of constituent States, provinces or cantons which are not, under the constitutional system of the Federation, bound to take legislative action, the Federal Government shall bring such articles with a favourable recommendation to the notice of the appropriate authorities of States, provinces or cantons at the earliest possible moment;

(c) A Federal State Party to this Convention shall, at the request of any other Contracting State transmitted through the Secretary-General of the United Nations, supply a statement of the law and practice of the Federation and its constituent units in regard to any particular provision of the Convention showing the extent to which effect has been given to that provision by legislative or other action.

Article 38 Reservations

1 At the time of signature, ratification or accession, any State may make reservations to articles of the Convention other than to articles 1, 3, 4, 16 (1) and 33 to 42 inclusive.

2 Any State making a reservation in accordance with paragraph I of this article may at any time withdraw the reservation by a communication to that effect addressed to the Secretary-General of the United Nations.

Article 39 Entry into force

1 This Convention shall come into force on the ninetieth day following the day of deposit of the sixth instrument of ratification or accession.

2 For each State ratifying or acceding to the Convention after the deposit of the sixth instrument of ratification or accession, the Convention shall enter into force on the ninetieth day following the date of deposit by such State of its instrument of ratification or accession.

Article 40 Denunciation

1 Any Contracting State may denounce this Convention at any time by a notification addressed to the Secretary-General of the United Nations.

2 Such denunciation shall take effect for the Contracting State concerned one year from the date upon which it is received by the Secretary-General of the United Nations.

3 Any State which has made a declaration or notification under article 36 may, at any time thereafter, by a notification to the Secretary- General of the United Nations, declare that the Convention shall cease to extend to such territory one year after the date of receipt of the notification by the Secretary-General.

Article 41 Revision

1 Any Contracting State may request revision of this Convention at any time by a notification addressed to the Secretary-General of the United Nations.

2 The General Assembly of the United Nations shall recommend the steps, if any, to be taken in respect of such request.

Article 42 Notifications by the Secretary-General of the United Nations

The Secretary-General of the United Nations shall inform all Members of the United Nations and non-member States referred to in article 35:

(a)   Of signatures, ratifications and accessions in accordance with article 35;

(b)   Of declarations and notifications in accordance with article 36;

(c)   Of reservations and withdrawals in accordance with article 38;

(d)   Of the date on which this Convention will come into force in accordance with article 39;

(e)   Of denunciations and notifications in accordance with article 40;

(f)   Of request for revision in accordance with article 41.

USEFUL ADDRESSES, TELEPHONE NUMBERS AND WEBSITES

This list has been compiled with the assistance of the JCWI website, which in addition gives the addresses of the principal British embassies and consulates abroad.

HOME OFFICE

Immigration and Nationality Directorate
Block C, Whitgift Centre
Wellesley Road
Croydon
CR9 1AT W

tel 0870 2410645
  (application forms)
tel 0870 6081592 (individual cases)
tel 0870 6067766/ fax 0870 7603017 (general enquiries)
website:
  www.ind.homeoffice.gov.uk

Nationality Directorate
3rd floor, India Buildings
Water Street
Liverpool
L2 0QN

tel 0151 237 5200
tel 0151 237 0143/0163
  (application forms)
fax 0151 237 5385

National Asylum Support Service

tel 020 8760 3500
  (voucher enquiries)
tel 0845 602 1739
  (all other enquiries)
fax 0845 601 1143

Work Permits (UK)
Level 5
Moorfoot
Sheffield
S1 4PQ

tel 0114 259 3287 (general enquiries)
fax 0114 259 3776
website: www.workpermits.gov.uk

HOME OFFICE REGIONAL PUBLIC ENQUIRY OFFICES

Belfast Public Enquiry Office
Belfast Immigration Office
Olive Tree House
Fountain Street
Belfast
BT1 5EA

tel 02890 322547

Birmingham Public Enquiry Office
Dominion Court
41 Station Road
Solihull
B91 3RT

tel 0121 606 7345

Glasgow Public Enquiry Office
Dumbarton Court
Argyll Avenue
Glasgow Airport
Paisley
PA3 2TD

tel 0141 887 2255

Liverpool Public Enquiry Office
Graeme House
Derby Square
Liverpool
L2 7SF

tel 0151 236 4909
fax 0151 236 4656

Immigration Service Offices
Becket House
66-68 St Thomas' Street
London
SE1 3QU

tel 020 7238 1300
tel 020 7238 1331/2 (asylum)
fax 020 7378 9107 (duty officer)
fax 020 7378 9110 (casework)

Status Park Enforcement Section
Status Park
Nobel Drive
Harlington
Middlesex
UB3 5EY

tel 020 8745 2400/2462
fax 020 8745 2474/2407

PORTS

London Heathrow Terminal 1
tel 020 8745 6809 (casework)
tel 020 8745 6800/4
  (arrivals control)
fax 020 8745 6814 (asylum/non-
  asylum cases/temporary
  admission/bail cases)
fax 020 8745 2514 (detained cases/
  new arrivals)
fax 020 8745 6828 (general)

London Heathrow Terminal 2
tel 020 8745 6850 (general)
tel 020 8745 6860 (casework)
tel 020 8745 6870/73 (asylum desk)
fax 020 8745 6867/77

London Heathrow Terminal 3
tel 020 8745 6900 (general)
tel 020 8745 6932 (casework)
fax 020 8745 6943

London Heathrow Terminal 4
tel 020 8745 4700 (switchboard)
tel 020 8745 4724 (casework)
tel 020 8745 4722 (asylum)
fax 020 8745 4705

Belfast International Airport
tel 02894 422500

Dover East Immigration
tel 01304 244900
fax 01304 213594

Dover Harbour Police Station
tel 01304 216084
fax 01304 204316

South-East Ports Surveillance Team
tel 01304 200400
Edinburgh
tel 0131 344 3330
fax 0131 335 3197

Gatwick South Terminal
tel 01293 502019 (switchboard)
tel 01293 502627/502508
  (casework)
fax 01293 553643/507097

Gatwick North Terminal
tel 01293 567282 (switchboard)
tel 01293 892524 (casework)
tel 01293 502622 (asylum)
fax 01293 568679

Glasgow Airport
tel 0141 847 5300
fax 0141 887 1566

Gravesend
tel 01474 352308
fax 01474 534731

Harwich Immigration
tel 01255 509700
fax 01255 509718

Hull
tel 01482 593980
fax 01482 219034

Leeds City (also serving airport)
tel 0113 386533
fax 0113 3865756

Liverpool
tel 0151 236 8974
fax 0151 236 4656

Luton
tel 01582 439030
fax 01582 405215

Manchester Airport Terminal 1
tel 0161 489 2657 (casework)
fax 0161 489 2069
tel 0161 489 2367/2369
   (enforcement)
fax 0161 489 2370
tel 0161 437 5700 (detention)
fax 0161 489 5701

Newcastle
tel 0191 214 2700
fax 0191 214 2707

Stansted Airport
tel 01279 680118
tel 01279 680691 (enforcement)
fax 01279 680145

Waterloo International Terminal
tel 020 7919 5910
fax 020 7919 5918

DETENTION CENTRES

Campsfield House
Langford Lane,
Kiddlington
Oxford
OX5 1RE

tel 01865 845700 (switchboard)
tel 01865 377712 (detainees)
fax 01865 377723

Harmondsworth Detention Centre
Building DA, Crown Site
Colme Brook Bypass
Harmondsworth
Middlesex
UB7 ODF

tel 020 8897 8040 (switchboard)
fax 020 8261 1221

Haslar Holding Centre
2 Dolphin Way
Gosport
Hants
PO12 2AW

tel 02392 580 381 (switchboard)
fax 02392 528 631 (immigration
   officers)
fax 02392 510 266 (prison admin)

Rochester Detention Centre
HMP Rochester
1 Fort Road
Rochester
Kent
ME1 3SQ

tel 01634 838100 (switchboard)
fax 01634 838101

Tinsley House Detention Centre
Perimeter Road South
Gatwick Airport
West Sussex
RH6 OPQ

tel 01293 434800 (switchboard)
fax 01293 423221 (for legal
   visits)
fax 01293 434825 (for detainees

Winson Green
HMP Birmingham
Winson Green Road
Birmingham
B18 4AS

tel 0121 554 3838
fax 0121 554 7990

1693

RECEPTION CENTRES

Oakington Reception Centre
Rampton Road
Longstanton
Cambridge
CB4 4EJ

tel 01954 783 300
fax 01954 789 505

HOME OFFICE PRESENTING
  OFFICERS' UNITS

2nd floor, Building 1
Angel Square
1 Torrens Street
London
EC1V 1SX

tel 020 7239 1701
fax 020 7239 1770

10th Floor
Eagle Building
215 Bothwell Street
Glasgow
G2

tel 0141 221 4218
fax 0141 204 5987

Hanover House
Plane Tree Crescent
Feltham
Middlesex
TW13 7JJ

tel 020 8917 2039
fax 020 8890 6489

2nd Floor Springfield House
76 Wellington Street
Leeds
LS1 2AY

tel 0113 244 4205
fax 0113 245 3472

15th Floor West Point
501 Chester Road
Old Trafford
Manchester
M15 9HU

tel 0161 877 6322
fax 0161 877 5955

2nd floor front suite
Virginia House
56 Warwick Road
Olton
Birmingham
B92 7HX

tel 0121 706 9741
fax 0121 706 4495

IMMIGRATION APPELLATE
  AUTHORITY

Taylor House
88 Rosebery Avenue
London
EC1R 4QU

tel 020 7862 4200
fax 020 7862 4211

2nd floor, Sheldon Court
1 Wagon Lane
Birmingham
B26 3DU

tel 0121 685 3300
fax 0121 742 4142

York House
Duke's Green Avenue
Faggs Road
Feltham
Middlesex
TW14 0LS

tel 020 8831 3100

Cardiff Civil Court Centre
2 Park Street
Cardiff
CF1 1ET
(queries to Birmingham office)

7th floor, Lancashire House
5 Linenhall Street
Belfast
BT2 8AA
(queries to Glasgow office)

4th floor, Coronet House
Queen Street
Leeds
LS1 4PW

tel 0113 244 9898
fax 0113 244 6260

5th floor, Eagle Building
215 Bothwell Street
Glasgow
G2 7EZ

tel 0141 221 3489
fax 0141 221 3532

COURTS

Royal Courts of Justice
Strand
London
WC2A 2LL

tel 020 7947 6000

Administrative Court Office
tel 020 7947 6205 (general)
tel 020 7947 6013/7366/6297/6513
 (listing)
fax 020 7947 6802 (general)
fax 020 7947 6802 (list office)

Civil Appeals general office
tel 020 7947 6409

Court of Sessions
tel 0131 225 2595

LEGAL AID

England and Wales:
Legal Services Commission
85 Grays Inn Road
London
WC1X 8TX
tel 020 7759 0000

Community Legal Services Directory
tel 0845 608 1122
website:
 www.legalservices.gov.uk/

Scotland:
Scottish Legal Aid Board
44 Drumsheugh Gardens
Edinburgh
EH3 7SW

tel 0131 226 7061

MEMBERS OF PARLIAMENT/
 PEERS

Houses of Parliament
(Commons and Lords)
London
SW1A 2PW

tel 020 7219 3000

OTHER GOVERNMENT
 DEPARTMENTS

Commission for Racial Equality
Elliot House
10-12 Allington Street
London
SW1E 5EH

tel 020 7828 7022
fax 020 7630 7605
website: www.cre.gov.uk

Department of Social Security
Benefits Agency Overseas Branch
Tyneview Park
Whitley Road
Benton
Newcastle-upon-Tyne
NE98 1BA

tel 0191 218 7777
website: www.dss.gov.uk

Joint Entry Clearance Unit
89 Albert Embankment
Vauxhall
London
SW1

tel 020 7238 3838 (public enquiry
  line)
tel 020 7238 3858 (for application
  forms)
fax 020 7238 3759/3761
email:
  visas.foruk@jecu.mail.fco.gov.uk
website: www.fco.gov.uk

**Home Office (minister's private
  office)**
Queen Anne's Gate
London
SW1H 9AT

tel 020 7273 4604
fax 020 7273 2043

Treasury Solicitor
Queen Anne's Chambers
28 Broadway
London
SW1 9JS

tel 020 7210 3000
fax 020 7222 6006

OTHER ORGANISATIONS

**AIRE Centre (Advice on Individual
  Rights in Europe)**
74 Eurolink Business Centre
49 Effra Road
London
SW2 1BZ

tel 020 7924 0927 (Mon-Thurs 2pm-
  5pm)
fax 020 7733 6786
email: aire@btinternet.com

Amnesty International UK
99-119 Rosebery Avenue
London
EC1R 4RE
tel 020 7814 6200

fax 020 7833 1510
email: information@amnesty.org.uk

Asylum Aid
28 Commercial Street
London
E1 6LS

tel 020 7377 5123
fax 020 7247 7789
email: info@asylumaid.org.uk
website: www.asylumaid.org.uk

**Bail for Immigration Detainees
  (BID)**
28 Commercial Street
London
E1 6LS

tel 020 7247 3590
fax 020 7247 3550
email: bailforimmigrationdetainees
  @yahoo.co.uk

Cellmark Diagnostics
P O Box 265
Abingdon
Oxon
OX14 1YX

tel 01235 528609
fax 01235 528141
website: www.cellmark.co.uk

Children's Legal Centre
University of Essex
Wivenhoe Park
Colchester
Essex
CO4 3SQ

tel 01206 873820 (advice)
tel 01206 872466 (admin)
fax 01206 874206
website: www2.essex.ac.uk/clc

Detention Advice Service
308 Seven Sisters Road
London
N4 2AG

tel 020 8802 3422
fax 020 8802 0684

**Educational Grants Advisory
  Service**
501 Kingsland Road
London
E8 2DY

tel 020 7254 6251
fax 020 7249 5443

Electronic Immigration Network
The Progress Centre
Charlton Place
Ardwick Green
Manchester
M12 6HS

tel 0161 273 7515
fax 0161 274 3159
email: info@ein.org.uk
website: www.ein.org.uk

European Commission
London Office
8 Storey's Gate
London
SW1P 3AT

tel 020 7973 1992
fax 020 7973 1900
website: www.europe.org.uk

European Court of Human Rights
Maison de l'Europe
BP 431 R6 67006
Strasbourg Cedex
France

tel 00 33 8861 4961
fax 00 33 8837 3265

**Foundation for Public Service
  Interpreting**
1 Clements Court
London
EC4N 7HB

tel 020 7626 0220
fax 020 7283 3678
website: www.nisuk.co.uk

Free Representation Unit
Peer House
8-14 Verulam Street
London
WC1X 8LZ

tel 020 7831 0692
fax 020 7831 2398

**Greater Manchester Immigration Aid
  Unit**
400 Cheetham Hill Road
Manchester
M8 9LE

tel 0161 740 7722
fax 0161 740 5172
email: gmiau@ein.org.uk

Human Rights International Project
Fenner Brockway House
37-39 Great Guilford St
London
SE1 0ES

email: hhrr_project@hotmail.com

Human Rights Watch
2nd floor
33 Islington High Street
London
N1 9LH

tel 020 7713 1995
fax 020 7713 1800
website: www.hrw.org

Immigration Advisory Service
County House
190 Great Dover Street,
London
SE1 4YB

tel 020 7357 6917 (advice)
tel 020 7357 7511 (administration)
tel 020 7378 9191 (24 hour helpline)
tel 0800 435 427 (Free support for
    immigrants in detention)
email: advice@ias.org
website: www.iasuk.org

Immigration Law Practitioners'
    Association
Lindsey House
40/42 Charterhouse Street
London
EC1M 6JN

tel 020 7251 8383
fax 020 7251 8384
email: info@ilpa.org.uk

Institute of Race Relations
2-6 Leeke Street
London
WC1X 9HS

tel 020 7837 0041
fax 020 7278 0623
website: www.irr.org.uk

Interights
Lancaster House
33 Islington High Street
London
N1 9LH

tel 020 7278 3230
fax 020 7278 4334

International Social Service of
    Great Britain
Cranmer House
39 Brixton Road
London
SW9 6DD

tel 020 7735 8941
fax 020 7582 0696
email: issuk@charity.vfree.com

Joint Council for the Welfare of
    Immigrants
115 Old Street
London
EC1V 9JR

tel 020 7251 8706
fax 020 7251 5110
website: www.jcwi.org.uk

Justice
59 Carter Lane
London
EC4V 5AQ

tel 020 7329 5100
fax 020 7329 5055
website: www.justice.org.uk

Kalayaan
St Francis Centre
Pottery Lane
London W11 4NQ

tel 020 7243 2942
fax 020 7792 3060

Law Centres Federation
Duchess House
18-19 Warren Street
London
W1P 5DB

tel 020 7387 8570
fax 020 7387 8368

Legal Action Group
242 Pentonville Road
London
N1 9UN

tel 020 7833 2931
fax 020 7837 6094
email: lag@lag.org.uk

Liberty
21 Tabard Street
London
SE1 4LA

tel 7403 3888;
fax 7497 5354;
email: info@liberty-human-
    rights.org.uk
website: www.liberty-
    humanrights.org.uk

**Medical Foundation for the Care of
   Victims of Torture**
96-98 Grafton Road
London NW5 3EJ

tel 020 7813 7777
fax 020 7813 0011
website: www.torturecare.org.uk

Minority Rights Group
379 Brixton Road
London
SW9 7DE

tel 020 7978 9498
fax 020 7738 6265
website: www.minorityrights.org

**National Association of Citizens'
   Advice Bureaux**
Myddleton House
115-123 Pentonville Road
London
N1 9LZ

tel 020 7833 2181
fax 020 7833 4371
website: www.nacab.org.uk

National Union of Students
461 Holloway Road
London
N7 6LJ

tel 020 7272 8900
fax 020 7263 5713

North of England Refugee Service
1st floor, 19 Bigg Market
Newcastle-upon-Tyne
NE1 1UN

tel 0191 222 0406
fax 0191 222 0239

**Panel of Advisors for
   Unaccompanied Refugee Children**
Refugee Council

tel 020 7582 4947

Praxis
1 Pott Street
London
E2 0EF

tel 020 7729 7985
fax 020 7729 0134

Refugee Arrivals Project
41b Crosslances Rd
Hounslow
Middlesex
TW3 2AD

tel 020 8607 6888/6900
fax 020 8607 6851

Refugee Council
3 Bondway
London
SW8 1SJ

tel 020 7820 3000 (switchboard)
fax 020 7582 9929
email:
   info@refugeecouncil.demon.co.uk
website: www.refugeecouncil.org.uk

Refugee Legal Centre
Sussex House
39-45 Bermondsey Street
London
SE1 3XF

tel 020 7827 9090 (administration)
tel 020 7378 6242 (advice)
tel 0831 598057 (emergencies)
tel 0800 592398 (detention)
fax 020 7378 1979

**Royal College of Nursing
   Immigration Advisory Service**
Immigration Dept
20 Cavendish Square
London
W1M 0AB

tel 020 7647 3874
website: www.rcn.org.uk

Runnymede Trust
133 Aldersgate Street
London
EC1A 4JA

tel 020 7600 9666
fax 020 7600 8529
website: www.runnymedetrust.org

Scottish Refugee Council

Edinburgh Office
1st floor, Wellgate House
200 Cowgate Street
Edinburgh
EH1 1NQ

tel 0131 225 9994
fax 0131 225 9997

Glasgow Office
98 West George Street
Glasgow
G2 1PG

tel 0141 333 1850
fax 0141 333 1860

Statewatch
PO Box 1516
London
N16 0EW

tel 8802 1882
fax 8880 1727
email: office@statewatch.org
website: www.statewatch.org

**Stonewall Immigration
   Group**
37 Wharfdale Road
Islington
London
N1 9SE

tel 020 7713 0620
fax/admin 020 7713 8864
email: info@stonewall-
   immigration.org.uk

**UKCOSA, The Council for
   International Education**
9-17 St Alban's Place
London
N1 0NX

tel 020 7226 3762
fax 020 7226 3373
website: www.ukcosa.org.uk

**United Nations High Commission
   for Refugees**
21st floor, Millbank Tower
21-24 Millbank
London
SW1P 1QP

tel 020 7828 9191
fax 020 7630 5349
email: gbrlo@unhcr.ch

University Diagnostics Ltd
LGC Building
Queens Road
Teddington
Middlesex
TW11 0NJ

tel 020 8943 8400
fax 020 8943 8401
website: www.udlgenetics.com

World University Service
14 Dufferin Street
London
EC1Y 8PD

tel 020 7426 5800
fax 020 7251 1314

WEBSITES

Home Office Immigration and
   Nationality Department:
   www.ind.homeoffice.gov.uk

Work permits:
   www.workpermits.gov.uk

Foreign and Commonwealth Office:
   www.fco.gov.uk

Electronic Immigration Network:
www.ein.org

Acts of Parliament:
www.hmso.gov.uk/acts/htm

Statutory instruments:
www.hmso.gov.uk/stat/htm

Parliament:
www.publications.parliament/uk/
pa

Official documents: www.official-
documents.co.uk

Court Service:
www.courtservice.gov.uk

Privy Council:
www.privy.council.org.uk/
judicial-committee/

British and Irish Legal Information
Institute: www.bailii.org/

Scottish courts:
www.scotcourts.gov.uk/

European Court of Human Rights:
www.echr.coe.int/

European Court of Justice:
www.curia.eu.int/

European Commission: Justice and
Home Affairs: www.europa.eu.int/
comm/justice_home

United Nations: www.un.org

UN Human Rights Commission:
www.unhchr.ch/

Amnesty International:
www.amnesty.org

UNHCR: www.unhcr.ch/

US State Dept reports:
www.state.gov/g/drl/rls/hrrpt/

Canadian Immigration and Refugee
Board: www.irb.gc.ca/

Australian courts:
www.austlii.edu.au/databases.html

New Zealand refugee law:
www.refugee.org.nz/hc.htm

Canada courts:
www.lexum.unmontreal.ca/

INDEX

All references are to paragraph numbers

Index

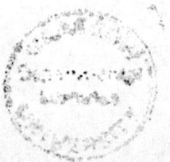